"The Flight of the Soul" from Boethius's De consolationae philosophiae.
(© Gianni Dagli Orti/CORBIS)

NEW
CATHOLIC
ENCYCLOPEDIA

NEW CATHOLIC ENCYCLOPEDIA

SECOND EDITION

15
Index

GALE®

THOMSON
GALE

Detroit • New York • San Diego • San Francisco • Cleveland • New Haven, Conn. • Waterville, Maine • London • Munich

in association with
THE CATHOLIC UNIVERSITY OF AMERICA • WASHINGTON, D.C.

The New Catholic Encyclopedia, Second Edition

Project Editors
Thomas Carson, Joann Cerrito

Editorial
Erin Bealmear, Jim Craddock, Stephen Cusack, Miranda Ferrara, Kristin Hart, Melissa Hill, Margaret Mazurkiewicz, Carol Schwartz, Christine Tomassini, Michael J. Tyrkus

Permissions
Edna Hedblad, Shalice Shah-Caldwell

Imaging and Multimedia
Randy Bassett, Dean Dauphinais, Robert Duncan, Leitha Etheridge-Sims, Mary K. Grimes, Lezlie Light, Dan Newell, David G. Oblender, Christine O'Bryan, Luke Rademacher, Pamela Reed

Product Design
Michelle DiMercurio

Data Capture
Civie Green

Manufacturing
Rhonda Williams

Indexing
Victoria Agee, Victoria Baker, Sylvia Coates, Francine Cronshaw, Lynne Maday, Do Mi Stauber, Amy Suchowski

While every effort has been made to ensure the reliability of the information presented in this publication, The Gale Group, Inc. does not guarantee the accuracy of the data contained herein. The Gale Group, Inc. accepts no payment for listing; and inclusion in the publication of any organization, agency, institution, publication, service, or individual does not imply endorsement of the editors or publisher. Errors brought to the attention of the publisher and verified to the satisfaction of the publisher will be corrected in future editions.

LIBRARY OF CONGRESS CATALOGING-IN-PUBLICATION DATA

New Catholic encyclopedia.—2nd ed.
    p. cm.
        Includes bibliographical references and indexes.
        ISBN 0-7876-4004-2
        1. Catholic Church—Encyclopedias. I. Catholic University of America.
BX841 .N44 2002
282' .03—dc21
2002000924

ISBN: 0-7876-4004-2 (set)
0-7876-4005-0 (v. 1)
0-7876-4006-9 (v. 2)
0-7876-4007-7 (v. 3)
0-7876-4008-5 (v. 4)

0-7876-4009-3 (v. 5)
0-7876-4010-7 (v. 6)
0-7876-4011-5 (v. 7)
0-7876-4012-3 (v. 8)
0-7876-4013-1 (v. 9)

0-7876-4014-x (v. 10)
0-7876-4015-8 (v. 11)
0-7876-4016-6 (v. 12)
0-7876-4017-4 (v. 13)
0-7876-4018-2 (v. 14)
0-7876-4019-0 (v. 15)

Printed in the United States of America
10 9 8 7 6 5 4 3 2 1

Table of Contents

Staff Listings, Second Edition   vii

Staff Listings, Jubilee Volume [2001]   ix

Staff Listings, Volume 19: Supplement 1989–1995   xi

Staff Listings, Volume 18: Supplement 1978–1988 . . .   xiii

Staff Listings, Volume 17: Supplement 1974–1978   xv

Staff Listings, Volume 16: Supplement 1967–1974 . . .   xvii

Staff Listings, First Edition [1967]   xix

Contributors   1

Index   145

For The Catholic University of America Press

EDITORIAL STAFF

Executive Editor
Berard L. Marthaler, O.F.M.Conv., S.T.D., Ph.D.

Associate Editor
Gregory F. LaNave, Ph.D.

Assistant Editors
Jonathan Y. Tan, Ph.D.
Richard E. McCarron, Ph.D.

**Director of The Catholic University of
America Press**
David J. McGonagle, Ph.D.

EDITORIAL ADVISORY BOARD

CONTRIBUTING EDITORS

John Borelli, Ph.D., Associate Director of Secretariat for Ecumenical and Interreligious Affairs, United States Conference of Catholic Bishops, Washington, D.C.

Drew Christiansen, S.J., Ph.D., Senior Fellow, Woodstock Theological Center, Washington, D.C.

Anne M. Clifford, C.S.J., Ph.D., Associate Professor of Theology, Duquesne University, Pittsburgh, Pennsylvania

Raymond F. Collins, M.A., S.T.D., Professor of New Testament, The Catholic University of America, Washington, D.C.

Cyprian Davis, O.S.B., S.T.L., Ph.D., Professor of Church History, Saint Meinrad School of Theology, Saint Meinrad, Indiana

Dennis M. Doyle, Ph.D., Associate Professor of Religious Studies, University of Dayton, Dayton, Ohio

Angelyn Dries, O.S.F., Ph.D., Associate Professor of Religious Studies, Cardinal Stritch University, Milwaukee, Wisconsin

Arthur Espelage, O.F.M., J.C.D., Executive Coordinator, Canon Law Society of America, Washington, D.C.

Eugene J. Fisher, Ph.D., Associate Director of Secretariat for Ecumenical and Interreligious Affairs, United States Conference of Catholic Bishops, Washington, D.C.

Edward J. Furton, Ph.D., Editor-in-Chief, The National Catholic Bioethics Quarterly, Brighton, Massachusetts

James F. Garneau, Ph.D., Academic Dean, The Pontifical College Josephinum, Columbus, Ohio

J. A. Wayne Hellmann, O.F.M.Conv., Dr. Theol., Professor of Theological Studies, St. Louis University, St. Louis, Missouri

Joseph T. Kelley, Ph.D., D.Min., Director of the Center for Augustinian Study, Merrimack College, North Andover, Massachusetts

Judith M. Kubicki, C.S.S.F., Ph.D., Assistant Professor of Theology, Fordham University, Bronx, New York

William P. Loewe, Ph.D., Associate Professor of Religion and Religious Education, The Catholic University of America, Washington, D.C.

Rose M. McDermott, S.S.J., J.C.D., Associate Professor of Canon Law, The Catholic University of America, Washington, D.C.

R. Bruce Miller, M.S.L.S., Head, Theology/Philosophy, Canon Law Libraries, The Catholic University of America, Washington, D.C.

Francis J. Moloney, S.D.B., S.T.L., S.S.L., D.Phil., Professor of Biblical Studies, The Catholic University of America, Washington, D.C.

Katherine I. Rabenstein, BSFS, Sr. Credentialing Specialist, American Nurses Association, Washington, D.C.

Joel Rippinger, O.S.B., M.A., S.T.L., Subprior, Marmion Abbey, Aurora, Illinois

For the Jubilee Volume: The Wojtyła Years

EDITORIAL STAFF

For Volume 19: Supplement 1989–1995

EDITORIAL STAFF

Executive Editor
Berard L. Marthaler, OFMConv, Ph.D., S.T.D.

Assistant Editors
Richard E. McCarron, M.A.
Morris Pelzel, Ph.D.

Photograph Editor
Sarah Davis

EDITORIAL ADVISORY BOARD

For Volume 18: Supplement 1978–1988

EDITORIAL STAFF

For Volume 17: Supplement 1974–1978

EDITORIAL STAFF

EDITORIAL BOARD

For Volume 16: Supplement 1967–1974

EDITORIAL STAFF

EDITORIAL BOARD

SUBJECT AREA PLANNERS

Canon and Civil Law
William W. Bassett
Professor of Law
University of San Francisco

Education
Harold A. Buetow, Ph.D.
Professor of Education
The Catholic University of America

Music
Anthony Doherty, B.Mus.
Merritt Island, Florida

Catechetics
Berard L. Marthaler, OFMConv.
Professor of Religion and Religious Education
The Catholic University of America

History
Francis J. Murphy, Ph.D.
Professor of Modern European History
St. John's Seminary

Religion, Theology
Thomas C. O'Brien, Ph.D., S.T.D.
Professor of Catholic Studies
Hartford Seminary Foundation

Liturgy
John E. Rotelle, O.S.A., S.T.L.
International Commission on English in the Liturgy
Washington, DC

Sacred Scripture
Patrick W. Skehan, S.T.D., LL.D.
Professor of Semitic and Egyptian Language and Literature
The Catholic University of America

Philosophy, Science
William A. Wallace, OP, S.T.D., Ph.D., D.Sc., D.Litt.
Professor of the History and Philosophy of Science
The Catholic University of America

SUBJECT AREA EDITORS

Education
Harold A. Buetow, Ph.D.
Professor of Education
The Catholic University of America

History
Margaret Carthy, Ph.D.
Dean, Undergraduate Studies
University of Maryland

Liturgy
Regis Duffy, OFM, S.T.D.
Provincial Lecturer in Theology
Holy Name College

Canon and Civil Law
John E. Lynch, C.S.P., Ph.D.
Associate Professor of the History of Canon Law
The Catholic University of America

Religion, Theology
Thomas M. McFadden, S.T.D.
Associate Professor of Theology
St. Joseph's College

Catechetics
Berard L. Marthaler, OFMConv., Ph.D.
Professor of Religion and Religious Education
The Catholic University of America

Philosophy, Science
William E. May, Ph.D.
Associate Professor of Religion and Religious Education
The Catholic University of America

Social and Behavioral Sciences
Raymond H. Potvin, Ph.D.
Professor of Sociology
The Catholic University of America

Arts, Humanities
Sister Helen Sheehan, S.N.D., B.A., B.S. in L.S.
Librarian
Trinity College

Sacred Scripture
Patrick W. Skehan, S.T.D., LL.D.
Professor of Semitic and Egyptian Language and Literature
The Catholic University of America

Music
Sister M. Regina Therese Unsinn, IHM, Ph.D.
Associate Professor of Music
Immaculata College

For The New Catholic Encyclopedia, First Edition, 1967

In the fall of 1959 an agreement was made between the McGraw-Hill Book Company, Inc., and The Catholic University of America to undertake the editorial development and publication of the *New Catholic Encyclopedia*. Between that time and the fall of 1966 the text and index were completed. The editors responsible for the final form of the *Encyclopedia* are listed below as the editorial staff from 1962 to 1966. Before 1962 much preliminary work had been done; those who collaborated in this work before the formation of a permanent staff are listed below as the editorial staff from 1959 to 1962.

EDITORIAL STAFF, 1962 TO 1966

Editor in Chief

Most Rev. William J. McDonald, D.D., Ph.D., LL.D., Rector, The Catholic University of America, Washington, DC; Auxiliary Bishop of Washington, DC; Chairman ex officio, NCE Executive Committee.

Associate Editor in Chief

Rt. Rev. James A. Magner, S.T.D., Ph.D., Vice Rector for Business and Finance and Assistant Treasurer, The Catholic University of America, Washington, DC; Director, The Catholic University of America Press; member, NCE Executive Committee.

Senior Editor

Martin R. P. McGuire, Ph.D., L.H.D., Professor of Greek and Latin and of Ancient History, The Catholic University of America, Washington, DC; Associate Editor, *Catholic Historical Review*; Chairman, Executive Committee of *Medieval and Renaissance Latin Translations and Commentaries*; member, NCE Executive Committee.

Managing Editor

Rev. John P. Whalen, M.A., S.T.D., Associate Professor of Theology, School of Sacred Theology, The Catholic University of America, Washington, DC; Executive Secretary, NCE Executive Committee

STAFF EDITORS

Dogmatic Theology
Editor: Earl A. Weis, SJ, M.A., Ph.L., S.T.D., Professor of Dogmatic Theology, Bellarmine School of Theology, North Aurora, IL.

Moral Theology
Editor: Paul K. Meagher, OP, S.T.L., S.T.M., Blackfriars, Cambridge, England; Coeditor in Chief, McGraw-Hill translation of St. Thomas Aquinas's *Summa theologiae*.
Assistant Editor: John Fearon, OP, S.T.Lr., S.T.L., S.T., Praes., Assistant Professor of Theology, Seattle University, Seattle, WA.

Liturgy
Editor: John H. Miller, CSC, Ph.B., S.T.D., Associate Professor of Theology, University of Notre Dame, Notre Dame, IN; member, Board of Directors, North American Liturgical Conference.

Sacred Scripture
Editor: Louis F. Hartman, CSSR, S.S.L., Ling.Orient., Lic., Professor of Semitic Languages and Literatures, The Catholic University of America, Washington, DC; Executive Secretary, Catholic Biblical Association of America; Chairman, Editorial Board for the CCD Version of the Old Testament.

Assistant Editors: Joseph E. Fallon, OP, S.T.L., S.T.Lr., S.S.L., Professor of Scripture, Dominican House of Studies, Washington, DC.

Joseph N. Jensen, OSB, S.T.L., Professor of Sacred Scripture, St. Anselm's Abbey, Washington, DC; Instructor in Sacred Scripture, Department of Religious Education, The Catholic University of America, Washington, DC.

Charles H. Pickar, OSA, S.T.L., S.S.L., Assistant General, Generalate of the Augustinian Friars, Rome, Italy.

Robert G. Vincent, OMI, S.T.L., S.S.L., Professor of Sacred Scripture, Oblate College, Washington, DC.

Non-Christian Religions
Editor: Martin R. P. McGuire, Ph.D., L.H.D.

Philosophy and Psychology
Editor: Wiliam A. Wallace, OP, B.E.E., M.Sc., S.T.L., Ph.D., S.T.D., S.T.Praes., Professor of Philosophy, St. Stephen's College, Dover, MA; Associate Editor, *The Thomist*; Director, Institute of Interdisciplinary Studies of the St. Thomas Aquinas Foundation.

Assistant Editor: James A. Weisheipl, OP, Ph.Lic., S.T.Lr., Ph.D., D.Phil (Oxon.), Associate Professor of History of Medieval Science, Pontifical Institute of Medieval Studies, Toronto, Canada; Director, Leonine Commission, American Section.

Early Church and Byzantine History
Editor: Francis X. Murphy, CSSR, Ph.D., Professor of Patristic Moral Theology, Accademia Alfonsiana, Rome, Italy.

Assistant Editor: George A. Maloney, SJ, B.A., Ph.L., S.T.L., S.E.O.D., Scriptor, John XXIII Center for Oriental Studies, and Professor of Oriental Theology, Fordham University, New York, NY.

Medieval Church History
Editor: Owen J. Blum, OFM, Ph.D., Professor of History, Quincy College, Quincy, IL.

Associate Editor: Mary Jane Hamilton, Ph.D., Assistant Professor of History, Sacramento State College, Sacramento, CA.

Assistant Editor: Sister Consuelo Maria Aherne, SSJ, Ph.D., Professor of History and Chairman of the Department, Chestnut Hill College, Philadelphia, PA.

Early Modern Church History
Editor: Edward D. McShane, SJ, S.T.L., Hist.Eccl.D., Professor of Church History, Alma College, Los Gatos, CA; Pontifical Faculty and School of Sacred Theology, University of Santa Clara, CA; and Graduate Theological Union, Berkeley, CA.

Assistant Editors: Jean Carolyn Willke, Ph.D., Associate Professor of History, Trinity College, Washington, DC.

Patrick S. McGarry, FSC, Ph.D., Professor of History and Head of the Department, Manhattan College, New York, NY.

Late Modern Church History
Editor: John F. Broderick, SJ, S.T.L., Hist.Eccl.D., Professor of Ecclesiastical History, Weston College, Weston, MA.

Assistant Editors: Thomas P. Joyce, CMF, Hist.Eccl.D., Rector and Superior, Claretian House of Studies, Washington, DC.

Damien P. McElrath, OFM, B.A., S.T.Lect., Hist.Eccl.D., Professor of Theology, Holy Name College, Washington, DC.

American Church History
Editor: Sister Mary Peter Carthy, OSU, Ph.D., M.A. (Theology), Professor of History, College of New Rochelle, NY.

Assistant Editors: Arthur J. Ennis, OSA, Hist.Eccl.D., Prior and Professor of Church History, Augustinian College, Washington, DC.

John L. Morrison, Ph.D., Professor of History and Chairman of the Department, Mount St. Mary's College, Emmitsburg, MD.

Latin American Church History
Editors: Jane Herrick, Ph.D., Professor of History, State College, Bridgewater, MA.

Antonine S. Tibesar, OFM, Ph.D., Professor of History, The Catholic University of America, Washington, DC; Director, Academy of American Franciscan History, Bethesda, MD.

Assistant Editor: Barbara Chellis, Ph.D., Associate Professor of English, State College, Bridgewater, MA.

General Church History; Cartography
Editor: Edward P. Colbert, Ph.D., Associate Professor of History, St. John's University, Jamaica, NY.

Associate Editor: Bernard J. Comaskey, Ph.D., Assistant Professor of History, Armstrong State College, Savannah, GA.

Canon and Civil Law
Editor: John J. McGrath, A.B., LL.B., J.C.D., Associate Professor of Comparative Law, The Catholic University of America, Washington, DC.

Assistant Editors: Leonard E. Boyle, OP, S.T.L., D.Phil. (Oxon.), Professor of Palaeography and Medieval History, Angelicum, Rome; Professor of History, Jesus Magister Institute, Lateran University, Rome; Professor of Palaeography, Institute of Mediaeval Studies, Toronto, Canada; Professor of Diplomatics, Toronto University Mediaeval Centre, Toronto, Canada.

John M. Buckley, OSA, M.A., J.C.D., Professor of Canon Law, Augustinian College, Washington, DC.

EDITORIAL STAFF, 1959 TO 1962

Editor in Chief
Most Rev. William J. McDonald, D.D., Ph.D., LL.D., Rector, The Catholic University of America, Washington, DC; Chairman, Executive Committee of the Editorial Committee.

Managing Editor
Rt. Rev. John H. Harrington, P.A., D.L.S., Editor in Chief, *Catholic Encyclopedia for School and Home*; Pastor, St Theresa's Church, Briarcliff Manor, NY.

Secretary
Martin R. P. McGuire, Ph.D., L.H.D., Professor of Greek and Latin and of Ancient History, The Catholic University of America, Washington, DC; Associate Editor, *Catholic Historical Review*; Chairman, Executive Committee of *Medieval and Renaissance Latin Translations and Commentaries*; member, Executive Committee of the Editorial Committee.

EDITORIAL COMMITTEE MEMBERS

Very Rev. Edmond D. Benard, M.A., S.T.D., Ph.D., Associate Professor of Theology and Dean of the School of Sacred Theology, The Catholic University of America, Washington, DC; member, Executive Committee of the Editorial Committee (deceased Feb. 4, 1961).

Thomas V. Cahill, CM, S.T.D., Professor of Theology, St. Thomas Theological Seminary, Denver, CO.

Rt. Rev. Paul Hanly Furfey, Ph.D., LL.D., Professor of Sociology and Director of the Bureau of Social Research, The Catholic University of America Washington, DC; member, Executive Committee of the Editorial Committee.

Very Rev. Theodore M. Hesburgh, CSC, Ph.B., S.T.D., President, University of Notre Dame, Notre Dame, IN.

Stephan Kuttner, J.U.D., S.J.D. (h.c. Bologna), J.C.D., (h.c. Louvain), LL.D., Director, Institute of Research and Study in Mediaeval Canon Law, Yale University, New Haven, CN; member, Executive Committee of the Editorial Committee.

Rt. Rev. John K. Ryan, S.T.B., Ph.D., LL.D., Professor of Philosophy and Dean of the School, The Catholic University of America, Washington, DC; member, Executive Committee of the Editorial Committee.

Very Rev. Walter J. Schmitz, SS, M.A., S.T.D., Professor of Theology and Dean of the School of Sacred Theology, The Catholic University of America Washington, DC.

Rt. Rev. Patrick W. Skehan, S.T.D., LL.D., Professor of Semitic and Egyptian Languages and Literatures and Head of the Department, The Catholic University of America, Washington, DC; member, Executive Committee of the Editorial Committee.

Very Rev. Robert Slavin, OP, Ph.D., President, Providence College, Providence, RI (deceased March 24, 1961).

Very Rev. Antonine S. Tibesar, OFM, Ph.D., Professor of History, The Catholic University of America, Washington, DC; Director, Academy of American Franciscan History, Bethesda, MD.

Helen C. White, Ph.D., LL.D., Litt.D., L.H.D., O.B.E., Professor of English and Chairman of the Department, University of Wisconsin, Madison, WI.

Patrick H. Yancey, SJ, Ph.D., Professor of Biology and Chairman of the Department, Spring Hill College, Mobile, AL.

Rt. Rev. Aloysius K. Ziegler, M.A., S.T.D., Archiviste-paléographe, L.H.D., Professor of Mediaeval Latin Literature and Mediaeval History, The Catholic University of America, Washington, DC; member, Executive Committee of the Editorial Committee.

EDITORIAL PERSONNEL

Assistant to Editor in Chief
Rev. Francis A. Marks, Ph.D.

Senior Staff Editor
Rev. Harold A. Buetow, Ph.D.

Theology and Canon Law
Rev. John P. Whalen, M.A., S.T.D.

Physical and Biological Sciences
Rev. John A Feeley, M.A.

Staff Editors
Sister Mary Julian Baird, RSM, M.A.
Sister Mary Claire Doran, OFM, Ph,D.
Sister Dorothy Marie Hill, DC, Ph.D.
Mother Mary Benedict Murphy, RSHM, Ph.D.
Sister Mary Theophane Power, CCVI, Ph.D.
Sister Leonard Marie Reis, OP, Ph.D.

Art Editor
Sister Judith Stoughton, SSJ, M.F.A.

Bibliography Editor
William Joseph Fitzgerald, B.A., M.A.

CONSULTANTS

Abbo, John A., Rt. Rev., STL, J.C.D., Auditor of the Sacred Roman Rota; formerly professor of Canon Law, School of Sacred Theology, The Catholic University of America, Washington, DC.

Albright, William F., Ph.D., Professor Emeritus of Semitics, Johns Hopkins University, Baltimore, MD.

Allers, Rudolf, M.D., Ph.D., Professor, Edmund A. Walsh School of Foreign Service, Georgetown University, Washington, DC (deceased Dec. 18, 1963).

Arbez, Edward P., SS, S.T.D., Professor Emeritus of Scripture and Semitics, The Catholic University of America, Washington, DC.

Ashley, Benedict M., OP, Ph.D., (Political Science), S.T.Lr., Ph.D. (Philosophy), S.T.Praes., President and Professor of Philosphy, Aquinas Institute of Philosophy and Theology, River Forest, IL.

Baldwin, Marshall W., Ph.D., Professor of History, New York University, New York, NY.

Bastnagel, Clement V., Rt. Rev., J.U.D., Professor of Canon Law and Dean of the School, The Catholic University of America, Washington, DC.

Beck, Henry G. J., Very Rev., S.T.L., Hist.Eccl.D., Professor of Church History, Immaculate Conception Seminary, Darlington, NJ.

Benard, Edmond D., Very Rev., M.A., S.T.D., Ph.D., Associate Professor of Theology and Dean of the School of Sacred Theology, The Catholic University of America, Washington, DC (deceased Feb. 4, 1961).

Bertrand, Kenneth J., Ph.D., Associate Professor of Geography and Head of the Department, The Catholic University of America, Washington, DC.

Bier, William C., SJ, S.T.L., Ph.D., Professor of Psychology and Chairman of the Department, Fordham University, New York, NY; Editor, *ACPA Newsletter*; Editor, Pastoral Psychology Series, Institute for the Clergy on Problems in Pastoral Psychology, New York, NY.

Bouscaren, Timothy L., SJ, M.A., LL.B., S.T.D., Professor Emeritus of Canon Law, Scriptor, Bellarmine School of Theology, North Aurora, IL.

Bouyer, Louis, CongOrat, formerly Professor of Spiritual Theology, Institut Catholique, Paris, France; Professor of Theology, University of Notre Dame, Notre Dame, IN.

Boyle, Robert R., SJ, Ph.L., M.A., Th.L., Ph.D., Professor of English, Regis College, Denver, CO.

Braceland, Francis J., M.D., Sc.D., Psychiatrist in Chief, The Institute of Living, Hartford, CN; Clinical Professor of Psychiatry, Yale University, New Haven, CN; Lecturer on Psychiatry, Harvard University, Cambridge, MA.

Brady, Ignatius C., OFM, Lic.Med.St., Ph.D., Lect.Gen., Lector Jubilatus OFM, Prefect of the Theological Commission, College of St. Bonaventure, Quaracchi (Florence), Italy.

Brady, Leo, M.A., Professor of Drama, The Catholic University of America, Washington, DC.

Brennan, Robert E., OP, B.A., S.T.L., S.T.M., Ph.D., formerly Professor of Psychology, Providence College, Providence, RI; Scriptor, St. Joseph's Priory, Somerset, Ohio.

Briefs, Goetz A., Ph.D., Professor Emeritus of Economics, Georgetown University, Washington, DC.

Brown, Raphael, Senior Reference Librarian, Library of Congress, Washington, DC.

Burghardt, Walter J., SJ, M.A., Ph.L., S.T.D., Professor of Patrology and Patristic Theology, Woodstock College, Woodstock, MD; Managing Editor, *Theological Studies*; Coeditor, *Woodstock Papers*; Coeditor, *Ancient Christian Writers*.

Burke, Eugene M., CSP, S.T.L., Assistant Professor of Theology, School of Sacred Theology, The Catholic University of America, Washington, DC.

Cahill, Thomas V., CM, S.T.D., Professor of Theology, St. Thomas Theological Seminary, Denver, CO.

Cain, Henry E., Ph.D., Professor of English and Head of the Department, The Catholic University of Ameica, Washington, DC.

Campbell, James M., Rt. Rev., Ph.D., LL.D., Litt.D., Dean of the College of Arts and Sciences and Professor of Greek and Latin, The Catholic University of America, Washington, DC; Director, Pacific Coast Branch, The Catholic University of America Summer Session, Dominican College, San Rafael, CA.

Carrièe, Gaston J., OMI, Ph.L., Th.L., Professor of History, University of Ottawa, Ontario, Canada; Editor, *Revue de l'Université d'Ottawa*; Historian of the Oblates of Mary Immaculate in Canada.

Carroll, Eamon R., OCarm, Ph.B., S.T.D., Associate Professor of Theology, School of Sacred Theology, and Director of the Summer Program in Mariology, The Catholic University of America, Washington, DC.

Carroll, John F., Director, American Peoples Library and Educational Division, Grolier Educational Corporation, New York, NY.

Cartwright, John K., Rt. Rev., P.A., Officialis, Diocesan Consultor, Prosynodal Examiner, Archdiocese of Washington; Rector, St. Matthew's Cathedral, Washington, DC.

Cavanagh, John R., M.D., Editor, *Bulletin of the Guild of Catholic Psychiatrists*; Lecturer in Pastoral Psychology, School of Sacred Theology, The Catholic University of America, Washington, DC.

Chase, Frederic H., A.B., S.B., S.T.L., S.E.O.D., Professor of Theology, St. John's Seminary, Brighton, MA (deceased Oct. 15, 1962).

Clark, Aubert J., OFMConv, S.T.L., Dip.Ed. (Oxford), Ph.D., Assistant Dean, Graduate School of Arts and Sciences, and Assistant Professor, School of Education, The Catholic University of America, Washington, DC.

Clark, Colin G., M.A. (Oxon.), M.A. (Cantab.), Sc.D. (h.c.), D.Econ. (h.c.), Director, Institute for Research in Agricultural Economics, Oxford, England.

Coerver, Robert F., CM, S.T.D., Rector, Kenrick Seminary, St. Louis, MO.

Collins, James D., Ph.D., L.H.D., Professor of Philosophy, St. Louis University, St. Louis, MO.

Connell, Francis J., CSSR, S.T.D., LL.D., L.H.D., Dean for Religious Communities and Professor Emeritus of Moral Theology, The Catholic University of America, Washington, DC.

Cook, Sister Genevieve Marie, RSM, Ph.D., Professor of Latin, Xavier College, Chicago, IL.

Cox, Ronald J., J.C.L., Professor of Canon Law, St. John Vianney Seminary, Bloomingdale, Ohio.

Crisafulli, Alessandro S., Ph.D., Professor of Romance Languages and Head of the Department of Modern Languages, The Catholic University of America, Washington, DC.

Cronin, John F., SS, Ph.D., Assistant Director, Social Action Department, National Catholic Welfare Conference, Washington, DC.

DeFerrari, Roy J., Ph.D., LL.D., L.H.D., D.Litt., Ed.D., Professor Emeritus of Greek and Latin, The Catholic University of America, Washington, DC.

De Rosen, John H., L.H.D., formerly Art Consultant on the National Shrine of the Immaculate Conception, and Head of the Shrine Iconography Committee, Washington, DC.

Deutsch, Bernard F., J.C.D., I.C.D., I.R.P.D., Assistant Professor of Roman Law, School of Canon Law, The Catholic University of America, Washington, DC.

Diekmann, Godfrey L., OSB, S.T.D., Professor of Patrology and Theology, St. John's University, Collegeville, MN.

Donnelly, Philip J., SJ, S.T.D., Professor of Theology, Weston College, Weston, MA.

Doronzo, Emmanuel C., OMI, S.T.D., Ph.D., J.C.B., Professor of Theology, School of Sacred Theology, The Catholic University of America, Washington, DC.

Dougherty, George V., Ph.D., Professor of Philosophy, St. Charles Borromeo Seminary, Overbrook, Philadelphia, PA.

Downey, Glanville, Ph.D., Professor of History, Indiana University, Bloomington, IN; Associate of the Section of History and Literature, Royal Belgian Academy.

Droessler, Earl G., A.B., D.Sc. (h.c.), Director, Atmospheric Sciences Program, National Science Foundation, Washington, DC.

Duhamel, Albert P., Ph.D., Professor of English and Director of the Office of Special Programs, Boston College, Chestnut Hill, MA.

Dulles, Avery, SJ, Ph.L., S.T.D., Professor of Fundamental Theology, Woodstock College, Woodstock, MD.

Dvornik, Francis, Very Rev., D.D., Docteur ès Lettres (Sorbonne), D.Litt. (h.c. London), Professor Emeritus of Byzantine History, Harvard University, Dumbarton Oaks Library and Research Center, Washington, DC.

Ellis, John T., Rt. Rev., Ph.D., L.H.D., LL.D., Litt.D., Professor of Church History, University of San Francisco, San Francisco, CA; Associate Editor, *Catholic Historical Review.*

Engel-Janosi, Friedrich, Ph.D., Professor, Historisches Institut, University of Vienna, Vienna, Austria.

Engelbert, Clement C., CSSR, Ph.D., S.E.O.L., Assistant Professor of Scripture and Theology, Fordham University, Bronx, NY.

Fenton, Joseph C., Rt. Rev., P.A., S.T.D., formerly Professor of Theology, School of Sacred Theology, The Catholic University of America, Washington, DC; Pastor, St. Patrick's Church, Chicopee Falls, MA.

Foudy, John T., Rt. Rev., Ph.D., Superintendent of Schools and Director of Confraternity of Christian Doctrine, Archdiocese of San Francisco; Pastor, St. Agnes Church, San Francisco, CA.

Frank, Sister Charles Marie, CCVI, R.N., M.S.N.E., formerly Dean, School of Nursing, The Catholic University of America, Washington, DC; Superior, Convento del Verbo Encarnado, Chimbote, Peru.

Furfey, Paul H., Rt. Rev., Ph.D., LL.D., Professor Emeritus of Sociology and Director of the Bureau of Social Research, The Catholic University of America, Washington, DC.

Furth, Hans G., Ph.D., Associate Professor of Psychology, The Catholic University of America, Washington, DC.

Gabriel, Astrik L., OPraem, Ph.D., Director, Medieval Institute, University of Notre Dame, Notre Dame, IN.

Gallagher, Raymond J., Most Rev., M.S.W., formerly Secretary, National Conference of Catholic Charities; Bishop of the Diocese of Lafayette, IN.

Garvey, John L., B.A., LL.M., Associate Professor of Law and Associate Dean of the Columbus School of Law, The Catholic University of America, Washington, DC.

Geiling, Eugene M. K., M.D., Ph.D., Professor Emeritus of Pharmacology, University of Chicago, Chicago, IL.

Gilchrist, John T,, Ph.D., Senior Lecturer in History, University of Adelaide, Adelaide, Australia.

Gorham, Joseph A., Rt. Rev., M.A., S.T.L., formerly Assistant Professor of Education, The Catholic University of America, Washington, DC; Director, Commission on American Citizenship; Editor, *Catholic Educational Review* (deceased July 7, 1966).

Gowan, Sister Olivia, OSB, R.N., M.A., formerly Dean, School of Nursing, The Catholic University of America, Washington, DC; Saint Mary's Hospital, Duluth, MN.

Hardon, John A., SJ, S.T.D., Professor of Dogmatic Theology, Bellarmine School of Theology, North Aurora, IL; Associate Professor of Comparative

Religion, Western Michigan University, Kalamazoo, MI.

Harte, Thomas J., CSSR, Ph.D., Associate Professor of Sociology, The Catholic University of America, Washington, DC.

Hatzfeld, Helmut A., Ph.D., Professor Emeritus of Romance Languages and Literatures, The Catholic University of America, Washington, DC.

Hayes, Carleton, J. H., Ph.D., Professor of History, Columbia University, New York, NY (deceased Sept. 3, 1964).

Healy, Martin J., S.T.D., formerly Professor of Theology, Immaculate Conception Seminary, Huntington, NY; Pastor, St. Patrick's Church, Glen Cove, NY.

Herzfeld, Regina F., Ph.D., Professor of Anthropology, The Catholic University of America, Washington, DC.

Herzfeld, Karl F., Ph.D., Sc.D. (h.c.), Professor of Physics, The Catholic University of America, Washington, DC.

Hesburgh, Theodore M., Very Rev., CSC, Ph.B., S.T.D., President, University of Notre Dame, Notre Dame, IN.

Higgins, Martin J., Rt. Rev., Ph.D., Professor of Byzantine History, The Catholic University of America, Washington, DC.

Hochwalt, Frederick G., Rt. Rev., Ph.D., Director, Department of Education, National Catholic Welfare Conference, Washington, DC; Secretary-General, National Catholic Educational Association (deceased Sept. 5, 1966).

Hoffman, Ronan R., OFMConv, D.Miss., Associate Professor of Missiology, School of Sacred Theology, The Catholic University of America, Washington, DC.

Hughes, Philip, Rt. Rev., Licencié en Sciences Morales, Dr. Phil. and Lett. (h.c.), D.Litt. (h.c.), LL.D., L.H.D., Professor of History, University of Notre Dame, Notre Dame, IN.

Kerwin, Jerome G., Ph.D., LL.D., Litt.D., Professor Emeritus of Political Science, University of Chicago; Professor of Political Science and Director of the Honors Division, University of Santa Clara, CA.

Kiemen, Mathias C., OFM, Ph.D., Director, Academy of American Franciscan History, Bethesda, MD.

Koren, Henry J., CSSp, S.T.D., Ph.D., Chairman, Department of Philosophy and Department of Theology, Duquesne University, Pittsburgh, PA.

Kritzeck, James, Ph.D., Professor of Oriental Languages and History and Director of the Institute for Higher Religious Studies, University of Notre Dame, IN.

Kuttner, Stephan G., J.U.D., S.J.D. (h.c. Bologna), J.C.D. (h.c. Louvain), LL.D., Lawrison Riggs Professor of Religious Studies and Director of the Institute of Research and Study in Medieval Canon Law, Yale University, New Haven, CN; Coeditor, *Traditio.*

Larkin, Ernest E., OCarm, S.T.D., Assistant Professor of Theology, School of Sacred Theology, The Catholic University of America, Washington, DC.

Lavanoux, Maurice E., Secretary, Liturgical Arts Society, Inc., New York, NY; Editor, *Liturgical Arts.*

Lemaitre, Georges E., Rt. Rev., Professor Emeritus of Theoretical Physics, University of Louvain, Louvain, Belgium.

Lima, Alceu Amorosa, LL.B., LL.D., Professor, Faculty of Philosophy, University of Brazil, Rio de Janeiro; Professor of Literature, Pontifical Catholic University of Rio de Janeiro; member, Brazilian Academy.

Lucas, Henry S., Ph.D., Professor of History, University of Washington, Seattle (deceased Dec. 29, 1961).

Maurer, Armand A., CSB, M.A., L.S.M., Ph.D., Professor of Philosophy, Pontifical Institute of Mediaeval Studies, Toronto, and University of Toronto, Ontario, Canada.

McAllister, Robert J., Ph.D., M.D., Consultant for the Child Center and Lecturer at the National Catholic School of Social Service, The Catholic University of America, Washington, DC; Director, Psychiatric Clinic, Providence Hospital, Washington, DC; Psychiatric Consultant, Fort George G. Meade, MD.

McCall, Raymond J., Ph.D., Professor of Psychology and Director of Clinical Training, Marquette University, Milwaukee, WI.

McClancy, George M., Jr., M.A. (Art History), M.A. (Philosophy), Assistant Professor of Philosophy, La Salle College, Philadelphia, PA; Lecturer in Philosophy, Rosemont College, Rosemont, PA.

McCoy, Charles N. R., Ph.D. (Political Science), Ph.D. (Philosophy), Professor of Political Science, Santa Clara University, Santa Clara, CA; Visiting Lecturer, Stanford University , Stanford, CA.

McDougall, Donald J., B.A. and M.A. (Oxon.), D.Litt., Professor Emeritus of History, University of Toronto, Ontario, Canada.

McGinley, Laurence J., SJ, M.A., S.T.D., LL.D., Litt.D., L.H.D., Academic Vice President, St. Peter's College, Jersey City, NJ.

McKeever, Paul E., S.T.D., Professor of Theology, Immaculate Conception Seminary, Huntington, NY.

MacKenzie, Roderick A. F., SJ, M. A., S.T.L., S.S.L., Rector, Pontifical Biblical Institute, Rome, Italy.

McKeough, Michael J., OPraem, Ph.D., Dean and Professor of Philosophy, St. Norbert College, West De Pere, WI.

McLaughlin, Patrick J. I., B.Sc., B.D., B.C.L., M.Sc., Docteur ès Sciences, formerly Vice President and Professor of Physics, St. Patrick's College, Maynooth, Ireland; Pastor, St. John's Parish, Carrigart, County Donegal, Ireland.

McLean, George F., OMI, Ph.B., Ph.L., S.T.L., Ph.D., Associate Professor of Philosophy, The Catholic University of America, Washington, DC; Professor of Philosophy, Oblate College, Washington, DC.

McNaspy, Clement J., SJ, M.A., Ph.L., S.T.L., Mus.D., Associate Editor, *America and the Catholic Mind.*

Miner, Dorothy E., B.A., LL.D., Curator, Walters Art Gallery, Baltimore, MD.

Mongan, Agnes, A.M., L.H.D., Litt.D., Associate Director, William Hays Fogg Art Museum, Harvard University, Cambridge, MA.

Mongan, Elizabeth, A.B., Formerly Curator of Graphic Arts, National Gallery of Art, Washington, DC.

Moody, Joseph N., Rt. Rev., Ph.D., Associate Professor of European History, The Catholic University of America, Washington, DC; Associate Editor, *Catholic Historical Review.*

Moore, Thomas Verner [Dom Pablo Maria, Ocart], M.D., Ph.D., Cartuja de Santa Maria de Miraflores, Burgos, Spain; Founder of the Child Center and formerly Head of the Department of Psychology and Psychiatry, The Catholic University of America, Washington, DC.

Morse, Harold Marston, Ph.D., Sc.D. (h.c.). LL.D., Litt.D., Professor of Mathematics, Institute for Advanced Study, Princeton, NJ.

Neill, James Kerby, Ph.D., Professor of English Language and Literature and Head of the Department, The Catholic University of America, Washington, DC.

O'Brien, Kenneth R., Very Rev., J.C.D., Synodal Judge, Archdiocese of Los Angeles; Pastor, St. Peter's Church, Los Angeles, CA.

O'Connor, William R., Rt. Rev., S.T.L., Ph.D., P.R.P.A., formerly Professor of Theology, St. Joseph's Seminary, Yonkers, NY; Pastor, St. John the Evangelist Church, New York, NY.

Oesterle, John A., Ph.D., Associate Professor of Philosophy, University of Notre Dame, Notre Dame, IN.

Oesterreicher, John M., Very Rev., S.T.L., Director, Institute for Judaeo-Christian Studies, Seton Hall University, Newark, NJ.

O'Grady, John, Rt. Rev., Ph.D., Dean of the National Catholic School of Social Service and Professor Emeritus of Sociology, The Catholic University of America, Washington, DC; Editor, *Catholic Charities Review*; Secretary, National Conference of Catholic Charities (deceased Jan. 2, 1966).

O'Leary, Timothy F., Rt. Rev., Ph.D., Ed.D., LL.D., formerly Superintendent of Schools, Archdiocese of Boston, MA; Pastor, St. James Church, Salem, MA.

Owens, Joseph, CSSR, M.S.D., F.R.S.C., Professor, Pontifical Institute of Mediaeval Studies, Toronto, Canada; member, Editorial Board, *The Monist.*

Pelikan, Jaroslav, B.D., Ph.D., D.D., Litt.D., M.A. (h.c.), Titus Street Professor of Ecclesiastical History, Yale University, New Haven, CN.

Petersen, Theodore C., CSP, Ph.D., S.T.L., Professor Emeritus of Semitic and Egyptian Languages, The Catholic University of America, Washington, DC (deceased March 14, 1966).

Quasten, Johannes J., Dr. Theol., Kelly Professor of Ecclesiastical History, The Catholic University of America, Washington, DC; Founder and Editor, *Studies in Christian Antiquity*; Founder and Coeditor, *Ancient Christian Writers*; Coeditor, *Stromata Patristica*; Coeditor, *Liturgiewissenschaftliche Quellen und Forschungen.*

Quigley, Joseph A., Rt. Rev., J.C.D., M.S., M.A., Professor of Moral and Fundamental Theology, St.

Charles Borromeo Seminary, Overbrook, Philadelphia, PA.

Reith, Herman R., CSC, S.T.B., Ph.D., Professor of Philosophy and Head of the Department, University of Notre Dame, Notre Dame, IN.

Riley, Lawrence J., Rt. Rev., S.T.D., LL.D., formerly Acting Rector, St. John's Seminary, Brighton, MA; Pastor, Most Precious Blood Church, Hyde Park, MA.

Rommen, Heinrich A., Dr.Rer.Pol., J.U.D., Professor of Government, Georgetown University, Washington, DC.

Rooney, Miriam T., Ph.D., LL.B., Research Professor of Law, Seton Hall University School of Law, South Orange, NJ.

Rush, Alfred C., CSSR, M.A., S.T.D., Professor of Ecclesiastical History, The Catholic University of America, Washington, DC.

Ryan, John J., Rt. Rev., S.T.L., Hist.Eccl.Lic., M.S.L., Lecturer, Boston College Graduate School of Arts and Sciences, Chestnut Hill, MA; member, Board of Directors, Institute of Research and Study in Medieval Canon Law.

Ryan, John K., Rt. Rev., S.T.B., Ph.D., LL.D., Professor of Philosophy and Dean of the School, The Catholic University of America, Washington, DC.

Schiller, A. Arthur, Ph.D., Professor of Roman Law, Columbia University Law School, New York, NY.

Schmitz, Walter J., Very Rev., SS, M.A., S.T.D., Professor of Theology and Dean of the School of Sacred Theology, The Catholic University of America, Washington, DC.

Schneider, Marius G., OFM, M.A., Ph.D., Lect.Gen., Diplompsychologe (Munich), Associate Professor of Philosophy, The Catholic University of America, Washington, DC.

Shannon, James A., M.D., Ph.D., D.Sc. (h.c.), LL.D., Director, National Institutes of Health, Bethesda, MD.

Sherwood, Polycarp R., OSB, S.T.D., Professor of Theology, St. Meinrad Archabbey, St. Meinrad, IN.

Siegman, Edward F., CPPS, S.T.D., S.S.L., Professor of Sacred Scripture, St. Charles Seminary, Carthagena, OH.

Skehan, Patrick W., Rt. Rev., S.T.D., LL.D., Professor of Semitic and Egyptian Languages and Literatures, The

Catholic University of America, Washington, DC; Vice Chairman, Editorial Board for the CCD Version of the Old Testament.

Slavin, Robert, Very Rev., OP, Ph.D., President, Providence College, Providence, RI (deceased March 24, 1961).

Sloyan, Gerard S., S.T.L., Ph.D., Professor of Religious Education and Head of the Department, The Catholic University of America, Washington, DC; founding member, *Societas Liturgica*.

Smith, Vincent E., Ph.D., Professor of Philosophy, St. John's University, Jamaica, NY.

Snee, Joseph M., SJ, B.A., Ph.L., M.A., S.T.L., LL.B., S.J.D., Professor of Law, Georgetown University Law Center, Washington, DC.

Steiner, Ruth, Ph.D., Lecturer in Music, The Catholic University of America, Washington, DC.

Stevenson, Robert M., M.Mus., B.Litt., Ph.D., Professor of Music, University of California at Los Angeles, CA.

Stock, Michael E., OP, B.S., S.T.L., S.T.Lr., Ph.D., President and Professor of Psychology, St. Stephen's College, Dover, MA.

Thomas, John L., SJ, M.A. (English), M.A., (French), S.T.L., Ph.D., Cambridge Center for Social Studies, Cambridge, MA.

Toumanoff, Cyril L. H., Ph.D., Professor of History and Director of Russian Area Studies, Georgetown University, Washington, DC.

Trisco, Robert F., S.T.L., Eccl.Hist.D., Assistant Professor of Church History, The Catholic University of America, Washington, DC; Managing Editor, *Catholic Historical Review*.

Undreiner, George J., Rt. Rev., Ph.D., Professor of History and of Church History, Josephinum Pontifical College, Worthington, OH.

Vann, Gerald, OP, S.T.L., M.A. (Oxon.), formerly Headmaster, Laxton School, Northampton, England; Lecturer, Department of Religious Education, The Catholic University of America, Washington, DC; Lecturer, University of Newcastle-upon-Tyne, England (deceased July 14, 1963).

Vawter, F. Bruce, CM, B.A., S.T.L., S.S.D., Professor of Sacred Scripture, Kenrick Seminary, St. Louis, MO.

Walker, John, A.B., A.F.D., Director, National Gallery of Art, Washington, DC.

White, Helen C., Ph.D., LL.D., Litt.D., L.H.D., O.B.E., Professor of English and Chairman of the Department, University of Wisconsin, Madison.

Witty, Francis, M.S. in L.S., Ph.D., Assistant Professor of Library Science, The Catholic University of America, Washington, DC.

Wojnar, Meletius Michael, OSBM, S.T.L., J.C.D., Associate Professor, School of Canon Law, The Catholic University of America, Washington, DC.

Yancey, Patrick H., SJ, Ph.D., Professor of Biology and Chairman of the Department, Spring Hill College, Mobile, AL; Executive Secretary-Treasurer, Albertus Magnus Guild.

Ziegler, Aloysius K., Rt. Rev., M.A., S.T.D., Archiviste-paléographe, L.H.D., Professor of Mediaeval Latin Literature and Mediaeval History, The Catholic University of America, Washington, DC.

Contributors

An asterisk before a contributor's name indicates that the contribution appeared originally in an earlier volume of the encyclopedia. In such cases, contributors are identified by the position they held at the time and may be listed more than once if contributions were made to multiple volumes at different times.

ABBAS, JOBE, OFM Conv., LL.B., M.Div., J.C.D., Professor of Canon Law, the Pontifical Oriental Institute, Rome. **Article:** Code of Canons for the Eastern Churches.

*ABBO, JOHN A., Rt. Rev., S.T.L., J.C.D., Auditor, Sacred Roman Rota; formerly Professor of Canon Law, School of Sacred Theology, The Catholic University of America, Washington, D.C. **Articles:** Legates, Papal; Pallium; Sacristy; Sacristan.

*ABBONDANZA, ROBERTO, Director, State Archives, Perugia, Italy. **Article:** Alberic of Rosate.

*ABEL, THEODORE, Ph.D., Professor of Sociology and Chairman of the Department, Hunter College, New York, N.Y. **Article:** Weber, Max.

*ABERCROMBIE, NIGEL JAMES, D.Phil., M.A. (Oxon.), Secretary-General, Arts Council of Great Britain, London, England. **Article:** Bishop, Edmund.

*ABETTI, GIORGIO, Ph.D.; Professor Emeritus of Astronomy, University of Florence, Italy; formerly Director, Astrophysical Laboratory of Arcetri-Florence, Italy. **Article:** Sarpi, Paolo.

*ABOU MOUSSA, RICHARD, M.B.A., Maronite Archdiocese of Antelias, Lebanon. **Article:** Rafqa de Himlaya, St.

*ABRAHAM, CHEERAKATHOTTAN ADAI, M.A., B.D., B.Litt. (Oxon.), Vice Principal and Professor of English, Mar Ivanios College, Trivandrum, India; Editor, *Christava Kahalam.* **Article:** Syro-Malankara Church.

*ABRECHT, PAUL ROBERT, A.B., B.D., Executive Secretary, Department on Church and Society (Division of Studies), World Council of Churches, New York, N.Y. **Article:** Life and Work.

*ABRUZZESE, MSGR. JOHN, *Minutante,* Special Council for Europe, General Secretariat of the Synod of Bishops, Vatican City. **Article:** Synod of Bishops.

*ACHA DUARTE, ANGEL NICOLÁS, Ph.M., S.T.L., Diplôme, Institut des Recherches et Formation en Vue du Développement Intégral Harmonisé (Paris), Administrator General of the Archbishopric of Asunción, Paraguay. **Articles:** Bogarin, Juan Sinforiano; Palacios, Manuel Antonio.

*ACHUTEGUI, PEDRO SANTIAGO DE, SJ, M.A., S.T.D., Professor of Dogmatic Theology, Bellarmine College, Shanghai, China, and Bellarmine College, Baguio City, Philippine Islands. **Article:** Philippine Independent Church.

*ADAMS, ELEANOR BURNHAM, A.B., Research Associate in History, University of New Mexico, Albuquerque, N. Mex.; Editor, *New Mexico Historical Review.* **Article:** Cogolludo, Diego Lopez de.

*ADAMS, JEREMY YVON DU QUESNAY, M.A., Teaching Fellow, Department of History and Literature, Harvard University, Cambridge, Mass. **Articles:** Audi Benigne Conditor; Aurora Iam Spargit Polum; Aurora Lucis Rutilat.

*ADAMS, SISTER MARY BONIFACE, SSF, M.A., Dean, De Lisle Junior College, New Orleans, La. **Article:** Holy Family, Congregation of Sisters of the.

*AHERN, BARNABAS, CP, Consultor, Congregation for the Doctrine of the Faith. **Article:** International Theological Commission.

*AHERN, PATRICK HENRY, Ph.D. (deceased Feb. 1, 1965). **Articles:** Keane, John Joseph; Ravoux, Augustin.

*AHERNE, SISTER CONSUELO MARIA, SSJ, Ph.D., Professor of History and Chairman of the Department, Chestnut Hill College, Philadelphia, Pa.; Assistant Staff Editor for Medieval Church History, *New Catholic Encyclopedia,* The Catholic University of America, Washington, D.C. **Articles:** Adeodatus (Deusdedit) II, Pope; Ado of Vienne, St.; Agapetus II, Pope; Agatho, Pope, St.; Boniface, St.; Carloman; Carolingian Renaissance; Carthage, Councils of; Chi-Rho; Dacia; Dark Ages; Donus, Pope; Eck, Johann; Elipandus of Toledo; Eugene I, Pope, St.; Fournier, St. John, Mother; Grace, Controversies on; Joan Popess, Fable of; Leidradus of Lyons; Mary de Cervello, St.; Orange, Councils of; Paul the Deacon; Peter Orseolo, St.; Peter of Pisa; Ripoll, Abbey of; Scheeben, Matthias Joseph; Sergius I, Pope, St.; Sergius II, Pope; Sergius III, Pope; Stilla, Bl.; Tetzel, Johann; Theodore II, Pope; Valerio of Bierzo; Vigilius of Auxerre, St.; Vindicianus of Cambrai-Arras, St.; Vitalian, Pope, St.

*AHMED, SAMI SAID, History Department, College of Arts, Baghdad, Iraq. **Article:** Yezidi Religion.

*AIKINS, HAROLD EDMUND, Ph.D., Professor of European History, Northern Illinois University, De Kalb, Ill. **Articles:** Ceolfrid of Wearmouth, St.; Frideswide of Oxford, St.; Hedda, St.; Hildelide, St.; Waldetrudis (Waudru), St.; Wikterp, St.; Winwaloe, St.

*ALAND, KURT, Lic.theol., D.theol. (h.c. Göttingen), D.D. (h.c. St. Andrews), Professor of Church History and Introduction to the New Testament, University of Münster, Münster in Westfalen, Germany. **Article:** Lietzmann, Hans.

*ALBERTS, WYBE JAPPE, J.D., Professor of Medieval History, University of Utrecht, Netherlands. **Articles:** Brethren of the Common Life; Imitation of Christ; Peter of Dieburg.

*ALBION, GORDON HENRY J., Docteur en sciences historiques, parish priest, St. Edward's, Sutton Park, Guildford, England; formerly Professor of Church History, Wonersh Seminary, Wonersh, England. **Articles:** Andrewes, Lancelot; Biddle, John; Browne, Robert; Caroline Divines; Con, George; Godden, Thomas (Tylden); Mary Stuart, Queen of Scots; Panzani, Gregorio; Rossetti, Carlo; Smyth, John (Smith); Society for Promoting Christian Knowledge; Tyrie, James.

*ALBRECHT, SISTER MARY DE RICCI, OP, Ph.D., Professor of English, St. Mary's Dominican College, New Orleans, La. **Article:** Dominican Sisters—Congregation of St. Mary (New Orleans, La.).

*ALBRIGHT, CHARLES W., CSP, A.B., Co-ordinating Secretary, National Newman Apostolate, Washington, D.C. **Articles:** Keogh, John; Newman Apostolate.

*ALETTI, JEAN-NOËL, SJ, Pontifical Biblical Institute, Rome. **Article:** Lyonnet, Stanislaus.

*ALEXANDER, SISTER MARY CONCEPTA, FIHM, B.S., Teacher of English, Cathedral High School, New York, N.Y., and Handmaids of Mary Novitiate, Staten Island, N.Y. **Article:** Franciscan Sisters—Franciscan Handmaids of the Most Pure Heart of Mary (FHM).

*ALLEN, ELLIOTT BERNARD, CSB, Ph.D., M.S.L., Associate Professor of Theology, Faculty of Theology (Graduate Division), and Chairman of the Faculty of Theology (Professional Division), University of St. Michael's College, Toronto, Canada. **Article:** Harvey Nedellec (Hervaeus Natalis).

*ALLEN, HORACE, M.Div., M.Phil., Union Theological Seminary; Member ICET and Consultation on Common Texts. **Article:** Consultation on Common Texts.

*ALLEN, THOMAS JOHN, OSB, M.A., S.T.L., Professor, St. John's Seminary, Elkhorn, Nebr. **Articles:** Animals, Symbolism of; Colosseum.

*ALLGÄUER, ROBERT, Librarian and Archivist, Head of the Public Library of Liechtenstein, and Head of the Government Archives, Liechtenstein. **Article:** Liechtenstein, The Catholic Church in.

*ALLISON, ANTHONY FRANCIS, B.A. (Lond.), Assistant Keeper, Department of Printed Books, British Museum, London, England; Joint Editor, *Recusant History: A Journal of Research in Post-Reformation Catholic History in the British Isles;* General Editor, Publications of the Catholic Record Society. **Articles:** Anderton, Roger and Lawrence; Barlow, William Rudesind; Bishop, William; Coffin, Edward; Floyd, John; Old Chapter; Smith, Richard (1569–1655); Smith, Richard (1500–1563); Wright, William.

*ALLUNTIS, FELIX, OFM, Ph.D., Lect.Gen., Professor of Philosophy, The Catholic University of America, Washington, D.C. **Articles:** Ortega y Gasset, Jose; Tyrannicide.

*ALONSO SCHÖKEL, LUIS, SJ, Ph.L., S.T.L., S.S.D., Professor of Scripture, Pontifical Biblical Institute, Rome, Italy. **Article:** Form Criticism, Biblical.

*ALSZEGHY, ZOLTÁN, SJ, S.T.D., Professor, Gregorian University, Rome, Italy. **Articles:** Galtier, Paul; Optimism (Theological Aspect); Weltanschauung.

ALVARE, HELEN M., M.A., J.D., Associate Professor of Law, Columbus School of Law, The Catholic University of America, Washington, D.C., **Article:** Abortion (U.S. Law).

ALWAN, KHALIL, Secretary of the Patriarch of Antioch and all the East for the Maronites, and Secretary General of the Council of Catholic Patriarchs of the Orient. **Article:** Council of Catholic Patriarchs of the Orient.

*AMADIO, ANSELM HENRY, OSB, Ph.D., S.T.D., Lector in Dogmatic Theology, Mount St. Scholastica College, Atchison, Kans. **Article:** Branch Theory of the Church.

*AMBROZIC, ALOYSIUS MATTHEW, S.T.L., S.S.L., Professor of Scripture, St. Augustine's Seminary, Scarborough, Ontario, Canada. **Articles:** Providentissimus Deus; Spiritus Paraclitus.

*ANDERSON, CARL, Dean, John Paul II Institute for Studies on Marriage and Family. **Article:** John Paul II Institute on Marriage and Family.

*ANDERSON, FULTON HENRY, Ph.D., LL.D., Litt.D., F.R.S.C., Special Lecturer in Philosophy, University of Toronto, Canada; Special Lecturer in Ethics, University College; Professor Emeritus, Department of Philosophy, Professor Emeritus, Department of Ethics, University College, University of Toronto, Canada. **Article:** Bacon, Francis.

*ANDERSON, JAMES FRANCIS, Ph.D., Professor of Philosophy, Villanova University, Villanova, Pa. **Article:** Existential Metaphysics.

*ANDERSON, LILIAN ARMSTRONG, M.A., Instructor in Art History, Wellesley College, Wellesley, Mass. **Article:** Bellini.

*ANDERSON, TYSON, Ph.D., Professor of Religious Studies and Philosophy, Saint Leo College, Saint Leo, Florida. **Article:** Transcendental Meditation.

*ANDREINI, DONALD, M.A., Graduate School, Brandeis University, Waltham, Mass. **Articles:** Benno II of Osnabruck, Bl.; Berthold of Garsten, Bl.; Bruno of Wurzburg, St.; Eberhard of Tuntenhausen, St.; Gundecar, Bl.; Henry of Bonn, Bl.; Jutta of Sangerhausen, St.; Jutta of Fuchsstadt, Bl.; Kremsmunster, Abbey of; Kuno of Trier, St.; Lindau, Convent of; Magnus of Fussen, St.; Notburga, St.; Quedlinburg, Convent of; Roger le Fort, Bl.; Sibert of Beka; Sturmi, St.; Werner of Oberwesel, St.; Willebold, Bl.; William of Toulouse, St.

*ANDREOLI, SISTER MARY OF ST. VICTORIA, RGS, Ph.D., Psychologist, Provincial Convent of the Good Shepherd, Mount St. Florence, Peekskill, N.Y. **Articles:** Good Shepherd, Sisters of Our Lady of Charity of the; Pelletier, Maria Euphrasia, St.

*ANDREOTTA, STANISLAO, OSB, S.T.D., Monastery of St. Scholastica, Subiaco, Italy. **Article:** Subiaco, Monasteries of.

*ANDREU, FRANCESCO, Very Rev., CR, Ph.D., S.T.L., Professor of Philosophy and Theology, Vicar-General of the Clerics Regular (Theatines), Rome, Italy. **Article:** Ventura di Raulica, Gioacchino.

ANDREWS, FRANCES E., B.A. Hons, Ph.D. (both London University), Lecturer in Medieval History, Department of Medieval History, University of St Andrews, St. Andrews, Scotland. **Article:** Lucius III, Pope.

ANDRIACCO, DANIEL M., D.Min., Director, Office of Communications, Archdiocese of Cincinnati, Ohio. **Article:** Cincinnati, Archdiocese of.

*ANSON, PETER FREDERICK, writer and artist; founder, Society of Marine Artists, London, England. **Article:** Religious Orders, Anglican-Episcopalian.

*ANTL, LOUIS BERTRAND, OFM, S.T.D., Instructor, Sister Formation Program, Joliet, Ill. **Article:** Stephen Langton.

ANTONOPOULOU, THEODORA, M.Phil. (Oxon.), D. Phil. (Oxon.) Dumbarton Oaks Fellow in Byzantine Studies (Trustees for Harvard University) 1995–96; Assistant Professor of Byzantine Literature, Department of Philology, Faculty of Humanities and Social Sciences, University of Patras, Patras, Greece. **Articles:** Leo VI, Byzantine Emperor; Theodora, Byzantine Empress (1).

ANTRY, THEODORE, J., OPraem, Ph.D., Archivist, Daylesford Abbey, Paoli, Pa.; Secretary, Premonstratensian Commission on Canonical Life and Spirit of the Order; Socius, Premonstratensian Historical Commission. **Articles:** Norbert of Xanten, St.; Premonstratensians.

*APOSTOLOS-CAPPADONA, DIANE, Ph.D., Takoma Park, MD. **Article:** Dali, Salvador.

*APPLEGATE, BENNETT, Vicar for Education, Columbus, Oh. **Article:** Elwell, Clarence.

*ARANEDA BRAVO, FIDEL, parish priest, Dean of *Portales*, Santiago, Chile. **Article:** Canas y Calvo, Blas.

*ARB, RENÉE MARIE, Ph.D., Assistant Professor of Art, University of Massachusetts at Boston, Mass. **Article:** Bernini, Giovanni Lorenzo.

*ARBESMANN, RUDOLPH EUGEN, OSA, Ph.D., Professor of Classics, Fordham University, New York, N.Y. **Articles:** Asceticism; Daimon; Henry of Friemar; Prayer; Purification.

*ARCE, FRANCISCO XAVIER GONZÁLEZ, SJ, S.T.L., S.S.L., Professor of Scripture, Montezuma Seminary, Montezuma, N.Mex., and Instituto Libre de Filosofía, Mexico City, Mexico. **Article:** Polyglot Bibles.

ARIENS, MICHAEL S., J.D., LL.M., Professor of Law, St. Mary's University of San Antonio, San Antonio, Tex. **Article:** Church and State in the U.S. (Legal History), 4. Search for Solution (1900-2001).

ARMSTRONG, REGIS J., OFMCap., M.S.Ed., Ph.D., Lecturer and Governor, Fran-

ciscan International Study Centre, Canterbury, Kent, England. **Articles:** Brady, Ignatius Charles; Casey, Solanus; Francis of Assisi, St.; Sheehan, Luke Francis. The articles on Solanus Casey and Luke Sheehan previously appeared in the *Encyclopedia of the Irish in America*, published in 1999 by the University of Notre Dame Press.

*ARNALDEZ, R., Professor, Université de Lyon, Lyon, France. **Article:** Philo Judaeus.

*ARNAUT, SALVADOR DIAS, Licentiate in Medicine, Doctor in History, Assistant Professor, Faculty of Letters, University of Coimbra, Portugal. **Article:** Coimbra, University of.

*ARNOLD, MAGDA B., Professor of Psychology and Director of the Behavior Laboratory, Loyola University, Chicago, Ill. **Article:** Imagination.

*ARNS, EVARISTO PAULO, OFM, Doctorate (Sorbonne), Professor, Catholic University of Petrópolis, Estado do Rio, Brazil; Editor, *Sponsa Christi*. **Article:** Book, The Ancient.

*ARROU, PIERRE, Bach. ès lettres, Secretary, Editorial Board, *Bâtir*, Paris, France. **Article:** Bloy, Léon Henri Marc.

*ASCHMANN, MOTHER MARY FRANCIS, PCC, Abbess, Poor Clares Monastery of Our Lady of Guadalupe, Roswell, N.Mex.; playwright. **Article:** Poor Clares.

ASHKAR, CHORBISHOP DOMINIC F., Ph.D., Pastor, Our Lady of Lebanon, Washington, D.C. **Article:** Sharbel Makhlouf, St.

*ASHLEY, BENEDICT M., OP, Ph.D. (Political Science), S.T.Lr., Ph.D. (Philosophy), S.T.Praes., President and Professor of Philosophy, Aquinas Institute of Philosophy and Theology, River Forest, Ill. **Articles:** Education, Philosophy of, 1. Historical Development; Final Causality; Liberal Arts.

*ASHWORTH, HENRY, OSB, Abbey of Quarr, Ryde, Isle of Wight, England. **Articles:** Gelasian Sacramentary; Gregorian Sacramentary; Leonine Sacramentary; Libelli Missarum; Sacramentaries, I: Historical; Stowe Missal.

*ASPELL, PATRICK JOSEPH, OMI, S.T.L., Ph.D., Professor of Philosophy, Oblate College, Washington, D.C. **Articles:** Anaxagoras; Plato.

*ASSELIN, JEAN PIERRE, CSSR, Diploma in Archival Science (Vatican School),

Hist.Eccl.Lic., Provincial Archivist, Sainte-Anne de Beaupré, Canada. **Article:** Anne and Joachim, SS.

*ATTRIDGE, HAROLD W., Department of Theology, University of Notre Dame, Notre Dame, Ind. **Article:** Hebrews, Epistle to the.

*ATTWATER, DONALD A., writer, translator, and editor, London, England. **Article:** Palmer, William.

*ATZERT, EDWARD PETER, SS, S.T.B., M.A., Professor of Speech and Homiletics, St. John's Provincial Seminary, Plymouth, Mich. **Article:** Lefevere, Peter Paul.

*AUBERT, ROGER FRANÇOIS, Docteur en histoire, Docteur et Maître en théologie, Dr. (h.c.), Professor, University of Louvain, Belgium. **Articles:** Antonelli, Giacomo; Dupanloup, Felix Antoine Philibert; Ferretti, Gabriele; Pius IX, Pope.

*AUMANN, JORDAN, OP, M.A., S.T.Lr., S.T.D., Ph.L., Director, Institute of Spiritual Theology, River Forest, Ill.; Literary Editor, Cross and Crown Series of Spirituality. **Articles:** Arintero, Juan Gonzalez; Bilocation, Mystical; Clairvoyance, Spiritual; Consolations, Spiritual; Contemplation; Ecstasy (in Christian Mysticism); Levitation; Locutions; Louis of Granada; Mystical Phenomena; Recollection; Visions.

*AUMANN, JORDAN, OP, S.T.D., Professor Emeritus at Pontifical University of St. Thomas Aquinas, Rome; Consultor to the Sacred Congregation for the Clergy and Catechetics and to the Sacred Congregation for the Evangelization of Peoples. **Article:** Felici, Pericle.

*AUSTIN, GERARD, Assistant Professor of Liturgy, Catholic University of America, Washington, D.C. **Article:** Liturgy.

*AUVRAY, PAUL FRANÇOIS, COr, Licencié ès lettres, S.T.D., S.S.L., Professor of Sacred Scripture, Scholasticate of the Oratory, Montsoult (Seine-et-Oise), France. **Articles:** Morin, Jean; Simon, Richard; Thomassin (Louis d'Eynac).

*AVATO, ROSE M., Associate Editor, *Catholic Almanac*, Clifton, N.J. **Article:** Catholic Almanac.

*AVELING, HUGH, OSB, B.A. (Cantab.), Headlands, Melbourn-near-Lincoln, England. **Articles:** Belasyse, John; Constable, Cuthbert; Cromwell, Oliver; Gifford, William; John of Feckenham.

AVELLA, STEVEN M., Ph.D., Associate Professor of History, Marquette University, Milwaukee, Wis. **Article:** California, Catholic Church in.

*AVELLAR, GILBERT RALPH, SJ, B.S., M.A., Alma College, Los Gatos, Calif. **Article:** Silveira, Gonçalo da, Ven.

*BAARS, CONRAD W., M.D., psychiatrist, Rochester, Minn. **Article:** Compulsion.

*BACCETTI, ENRICO, OSB, S.T.D., Vicar-General of the Vallombrosian Congregation, Vallombrosa, Italy. **Article:** Vallombrosans.

*BACH, MARGARET MARY, RSHM., M.A., Chairman, Department of Philosophy, Marymount College, Tarrytown, N.Y. **Articles:** Sense Knowledge; Sensibles; Sensism.

*BACIGALUPO, LEONARD F., OFM, M.Ed., Lect.Gen., St. Anthony Friary, Catskill, N.Y. Diploma in Library Science and in Archival Science (Vatican School), President, Immaculate Conception Seminary, College of Philosophy, Troy, N.Y. **Article:** Activism.

*BACKMUND, NORBERT, OPraem, Lector in Ecclesiastical History, Abbey of Windberg, Bavaria, Germany. **Articles:** Airvault, Monastery of; Ardenne, Monastery of; Chur, Monastery of; Floreffe, Monastery of; Frigolet, Monastery of; Gorres-Gesellschaft; Heeswijk, Monastery of; Hildegunde of Meer, Bl.; Hugh of Fosse, Bl.; Kasper, Katharina, Bl.; Mallinckrodt, Pauline von, Bl.; Marienberg, Abbey of; Mont-Cornillon, Monastery of; Nonnberg, Abbey of; Park (Le Parc), Monastery of; Sankt Florian, Monastery of; Tongerloo, Abbey of; Wessobrunn, Abbey of.

*BAGATTI, BELLARMINO, OFM, Arch.Christ.Dr., Professor of Christian Archeology, Franciscan Biblical Institute, Jerusalem, Jordan. **Article:** Palestine, 7. Holy Places.

*BAGLEY, CHARLOTTE HARTWELL, B.A., Vienna, Va. **Article:** Litany of Loreto.

BAILEY, C., **Article:** Pittsburgh, Diocese of.

*BAILEY, JAMES HENRY, Ph.D., historian and editor, Petersburg, Va. **Article:** Van de Vyver, Augustine.

*BAILLARGEON, ANATOLE OMER, OMI, Professor of Speech and Homiletics, Oblate Seminary, South Natick, Mass.; Editor, English edition, *Catholic Homiletic Service,* Catholic Centre, University of Ottawa, Canada. **Article:** Assumption, Sisters of the.

*BAIOCCHI, STEFANO, OSB, Bursar, Guestmaster, and Historian, Abbey of St. Paul, Rome, Italy. **Articles:** Farfa, Abbey of; Saint Paul-outside-the-Walls, Abbey of; San Salvatore (Maggiore), Abbey of; Thomas of Farfa, St.

*BAKER, DUDLEY LOUIS, A.C.S.W., M.S.W., Executive Secretary, Superior Council of the U.S., Society of St. Vincent de Paul, St. Louis, Mo. **Articles:** Mulry, Thomas Maurice; St. Vincent de Paul, Society of.

*BAKER, JOSEPH W., Msgr., Archdiocese of St. Louis, St. Louis, Mo. **Article:** Ritter, Joseph.

*BAKER-SMITH, MALCOLM P. DOMINIC, B.A. and M.A. (Cantab.), Lecturer in English, St. Thomas More College, University of Saskatchewan, Saskatoon, Canada. **Article:** Volusenus, Florientius.

*BALAS, DAVID L., OCis, Chairman, Department of Theology, University of Dallas, Irving, Tx. **Articles:** Apologetics (History of) [part 2].

*BALCH, ROSCOE ARTHUR, Ph.D., Associate Professor, Marist College, Poughkeepsie, N.Y. **Articles:** Alberic of Utrecht, St.; Ansfrid, Bl.; Bernulf, St.; Gregory of Utrecht, St.; Hubert of Maastricht, St.; Jeron (Hieron), St.; Leonius, Bl.; Radbod of Utrecht, St.; Trudo of Brabant (Trond), St.

BALDE, SISTER EVANGELA, OP, B.A., Archivist, Dominican Sisters of Mission San Jose, Fremont, Calif. **Article:** Dominican Sisters—Congregation of the Queen of the Holy Rosary (Mission San Jose, Calif).

*BALDI, DONATUS SANTE, S.T.D., formerly Professor and Rector, Franciscan Biblical Institute, Jerusalem, Jordan (deceased Feb. 15, 1965). **Article:** Jerusalem.

*BALDOVIN, JOHN F., SJ, Associate Professor of Historical and Liturgical Theology, Jesuit School of Theology, Berkeley, Calif. **Article:** Liturgics.

BALDWIN, LOUIS, Staff Writer, *The Catholic Standard & Times,* Pittsburgh, Penn. **Article:** Philadelphia, Archdiocese of.

*BALDWIN, MARSHALL W., Ph.D., Professor of History, New York University, N.Y. **Articles:** Baldwin, King of Jerusalem; Bulla Cruciata; Celestine II, Pope; Godfrey of Bouillon; John of Monte Corvino; Lucius II, Pope; William of Ruisbroek (Ruysbroeck).

*BALIC, CHARLES LAWRENCE, S.T.D., Doctor (h.c.), Professor of Dogmatic and Marian Theology and Scholastic Literature, Antonianum, Rome, Italy; Professor of Marian Theology, University of the Lateran, Rome, Italy; *Peritus,* Vatican Council II. **Articles:** Duns Scotus, John; Henry of Harclay; Scotism.

*BALKAN, PASCHAL JOSEPH, OCSO, St. Joseph's Abbey, Spencer, Mass. **Article:** Precept.

*BALLMANN, EVERETT A., S.T.L., S.S.L., Little Rock, Ark. **Articles:** Cyrus, King of Persia; Darius I, King of Persia; Esther, Book of.

*BANGERT, WILLIAM VALENTINE, SJ, M.A., S.T.L., Professor of History, St. Andrew-on-Hudson, Poughkeepsie, N.Y. **Articles:** Aloysius Gonzaga, St.; Avellino, Andrew St.; Faber, Peter (Favre, Lefevre), Bl.; Kostka, Stanislaus, St.

*BANICK, REV. MONSIGNOR THOMAS V., S.T.D., Pastor, St. Mary's Church, Wilkes-Barre, Pa. **Article:** O'Connor, Martin.

*BANKS, ROBERT JOSEPH, S.T.L., J.C.D., Professor of Canon Law, St. John's Seminary, Brighton, Mass. **Article:** Ceremonies, Congregation of.

*BANNAN, ALFRED JOHN, M.A., Department of History, University of Dayton, Dayton, Ohio. **Articles:** Butler, Charles; Milner, John.

*BANNON, JOHN FRANCIS, SJ, S.T.L., Ph.D., Professor of History and Director of the Department, St. Louis University, St. Louis, Mo. **Articles:** Astrain, Antonio; Lafitau, Joseph Francois; Salvatierra, Juan Maria; Segesser, Philipp.

*BARAUT OBIOLS, CEBRIÀ, OSB, Hist.Eccl.D., paleographer; monk and Archivist, Abbey of Montserrat, Barcelona, Spain. **Articles:** Andorra; Montserrat, Abbey of.

*BARBARITO, LUIGI, Rt. Rev., J.C.D., Auditor of First Class, Sacred Congregation of Foreign Ecclesiastical Affairs; Member of Section I, Foreign Affairs, Papal Secretariate of State, Vatican City, Italy. **Article:** Vatican City, State of.

BARBERO, MARIO, IMC, Ph.D., Rector, Consolata Fathers, Washington, D.C. **Articles:** Allamano, Giuseppe, Bl.; Prisca (Priscilla) and Aquila.

*BARBIERI, AMEDEO LUIGI, PIME, S.T.L., S.S.L., Professor of Scripture, Mary-glade Seminary, Memphis, Mich. **Article:** Nazirites.

*BARBIERI, WILLIAM A., Ph.D., Assistant Professor of Religion and Religious Education, The Catholic University of America, Washington, D.C. **Article:** Animal Rights; Sollicitudo rei socialis.

BARLOW, JONATHAN H., M.Div., Ph.D. Student, Saint Louis University, St. Louis, Missouri. **Article:** John de Sacrobosco.

*BARNES, ANNIE MADELEINE, Dr.Phil. (Berne), Ph.D. (Oxon.), M.A. (Oxon.), Fellow and Tutor in French, St. Anne's College, Oxford, England; University Lecturer in French Literature, University of Oxford, England. **Article:** Duvergier de Hauranne, Jean.

*BARNES, CARL F., JR., Ph.D., Assistant Professor of Art History, The Pennsylvania State University, University Park, Pa. **Articles:** Church Architecture, History of, 5: Gothic; Cluniac Art and Architecture.

*BARNES, MICHAEL H., Ph.D., Department of Religious Studies, University of Dayton. **Article:** Creationism.

*BARNETT, WILLIAM FRANCIS, S.T.L., S.S.L., Associate Editor, *Catholic Star Herald,* Camden, N.J. **Articles:** Booths (Tabernacles), Feast of; Satan.

*BARNOLA, PEDRO PABLO, SJ, S.T.L., Doctor of Philosophy and Letters, Caracas, Venezuela. **Articles:** Coll y Prat, Narciso; Guevara y Lira, Silvestre; Mendez, Ramon Ignacio.

*BARQUIN Y RUIZ, ANDRÉS, Licentiate in Law, Docteur en sciences historiques (Louvain), historian and journalist; Director, Círculo de Estudios Cívicos "San Pío X," and Círculo de Historia "Toribio Esquivel Obregón" en Integrismo Nacional, Mexico City, Mexico. **Article:** Manriquez y Zarate, Jose de Jesus.

*BARRERA, ISSAAC QUIRÓS, Professor of Spanish Literature, Quito, Ecuador. **Article:** González Suárez, Federico.

*BARRETT, SISTER MARY MATILDA, SL, M.A., Archivist, Loretto Motherhouse, Nerinx, Ky. **Articles:** Howlett, William Joseph; Loretto, Sisters of.

*BARRETT, ROBERT PAUL, SMA, Professor of Sacred Scripture, St. Peter's Regional Seminary, Cape Coast, Ghana, Africa. **Articles:** Benjamin; Ephraim; Judah.

*BARRON, WILLIAM STANTON, Ph.D., Assistant Professor of History, Regis College, Weston, Mass. **Articles:** Church, History of, III (Early Modern: 1500–1789); Jacobazzi, Domenico; Reformation, Protestant (on the Continent).

*BARROSSE, THOMAS OAKLEY, CSC, S.T.L., S.S.L., Professor of Sacred Scripture and Dean of Studies, Holy Cross College, Washington, D.C. **Article:** Love (in the Bible).

*BARRY, COLMAN JAMES, OSB, Ph.D., Professor of History and President, St. John's University, Collegeville, Minn. **Articles:** Cahensly, Peter Paul; O'Connell, Denis Joseph; O'Gorman, Thomas; St. John's Abbey and University.

*BARRY, DONALD MATTHEW, SJ, M.A. (Philosophy), M.A. (History), Weston, Mass. **Article:** Arias, Francis; Drexel, Jeremias.

*BARRY, JOHN GERARD, Ph.D., Lecturer in Medieval History, University College, Galway, Ireland. **Articles:** Dowdall, James; Eustace, Maurice; Kenraghty, Maurice; Talbot, Peter and Richard.

*BARRY, SISTER M. JUSTIN, OP, M.A., Mother General of the Sisters of St. Dominic, Congregation of the Most Holy Name, San Rafael, Calif. **Articles:** Anima Christi; Aspilcueta, Martin (Doctor Navarrus); Autpert, Ambrose; Berthier, Jean Baptiste; Carriere, Joseph; Chaumont, Henri; Chautard, Jean Baptiste; Cibot, Pierre Martial; Condren, Charles de; Gay, Charles Louis; Mary of Oignies, Bl.; Poulain, Augustin.

*BARRY, SISTER MARY DAVID, OP, Dominican College of San Rafael, San Rafael, Calif. **Articles:** Hildegard of Bingen, St.; Pontas, Jean.

*BARRY, SISTER MARY MARTIN, OP, Ph.D., Professor of English and Dean of the Graduate School, Dominican College of San Rafael, San Rafael, Calif. **Articles:** Ancrene Riwle; Bruyere, Jeanne Henriette Cecile; Devine, Arthur; Esch, Nicholas van; Fleury, Claude; Hortulus Animae; Marchant, Jacques.

*BARTH, LOUIS ALBERT, SJ, Ph.D., Associate Professor of Philosophy, St. Louis University, St. Louis, Mo. **Articles:** Cynics; Cyrenaics; Pyrrhonism; Sophists.

*BARTMAN, ROGER JOHN, OFM, Ph.D., Associate Professor of History, Bellarmine College and Ursuline College, Louisville, Ky. **Article:** Butler, Alban; Callahan, Patrick Henry; Fabri, Filippo (Faber); Joseph of Cupertino, St.; Leopold of Gaiche, Bl.; Murner, Thomas.

*BARTOCCETTI, VITTORIO, Rt. Rev., Prot.Apost., S.T.D., J.C.D., Jurisp.D., Litt.D., Priest Secretary, Supremo Tribunale della Segnatura Apostolica; Archpriest, Capitolo del Pantheon, Rome, Italy; founder and Director, *Studia Picena,* Fano, Italy. **Article:** Rules of Law (Regulae iuris).

BARTONE, SISTER CARLOTTA, SHCT, M.A., J.C.L., Tribunal Judge, Archdiocese of Philadelphia; Canonical Consultant, Religious Law, Religious Communities, Rosemont, Pa. **Articles:** Abbess; Nun; Religious Habit.

*BARTRA, ENRIQUE TOMÁS, Ph.L., S.T.L., Hist.Eccl.L., Professor, Faculties of Theology and Law, Pontifical Catholic University, Lima, Peru. **Articles:** Chaves de la Rosa, Pedro José; Goyeneche y Barreda, José Sebastián de; Martínez Compañón y Bujanda, Baltasar Jaime; San Martín, Tomás de.

*BARZUN, JACQUES, Ph.D., Seth Low Professor of History and Dean of Faculties and Provost, Columbia University, New York, N.Y. **Article:** Berlioz, Louis Hector.

*BASCOUR, HILDEBRAND, OSB, Ph.D., monk of the Abbey of Mont César, Louvain, Belgium; Director, *Recherches de Théologie ancienne et médiévale,* and *Bulletin de Théologie ancienne et médiévale.* **Article:** John Buridan.

*BASTARRIKA, IÑAKI, OFM, M.A., co-founder, *Jakin;* St. Patrick's Home, Bronx, New York, N.Y. **Articles:** Desmaisières, María Miguela of the Blessed Sacrament, St.; Diego of Cádiz, Bl.; Jornet e Ibars, Teresa, Bl.; López y Vicuña, Vicenta María, St.; Porras y Ayllón, Rafaela, Bl.; Segura y Sáenz, Pedro; Torres Acosta, María Soledad, St.; Vedruna, Joaquina de, St.

*BASTIAN, RALPH JOHN, SJ, M.A., S.T.D., Assistant Professor of Theology and Philosophy, Loyola University, Chicago, Ill. **Articles:** Light of Glory; Poor Souls; Purgatory [part 2].

*BATLLORI, MIQUEL, SJ, M.A., Lic. in Law, S.T.L., Ph.D., Editor, *Archivum historicum Societatis Iesu;* Professor of Church History, Gregorian University, Rome, Italy. **Articles:** Borgia (Borja); Callistus III, Pope.

*BATTERSBY, WILLIAM JOHN, CSC, B.A. (English), B.Sc. (Econ.), B.A. (History), Ph.D., D.H.L. (h.c.), Senior History Master, St. Joseph's College, Beulah Hill, London, England. **Articles:** Benilde, Bl.; Christian Schools of Mercy, Sisters of the; De La Salle, St. John Baptist; Paris, Martyrs of; Postel, Marie Madeleine, St.; Viel, Placida, Bl.

BATTS, PETER M., OP, Ph.D., D.Th., Associate Pastor, St. Dominic Church, Washington, D.C. **Article:** Lacordaire, Jean Baptiste Henri.

*BAUDOIN, LOUIS FRANÇOIS AUGUSTE, Canon, Chancellor of the Diocese of Monaco; Archdeacon of the Cathedral Chapter of Monaco. **Article:** Monaco.

*BAUM, GREGORY G., D.Th., Professor, Faculty of Religious Studies, McGill University, Montreal, Canada. **Article:** Social Sin.

*BAUM, GREGORY G., D.Th., Professor Emeritus, Faculty of Religious Studies, McGill University, Montreal, Canada. **Article:** Laborem exercens.

*BAUM, WILLIAM W., S.T.L., S.T.D., Executive Director, Bishops' Commission for Ecumenical Affairs, Washington, D.C. **Article:** Hogan, John Joseph.

*BAUMANN, EDWARD JOSEPH, M.A., Director, Evening and Saturday Division and Summer Division of Villa Madonna College, Covington, Ky.; Director, Covington Diocesan Federation of Sodalities; Moderator, Catholic Action Center, Covington; President, Council of Directors and Moderators in the National Federation of Sodalities. **Article:** Maes, Camillus Paul.

BAUMBACH, GERARD F., Ph.D., Executive Vice President and Publisher, William H. Sadlier, Inc., New York, N.Y. **Article:** Sadlier.

*BAUMER, REMIGIUS, Dr.Theol., Editor in Chief, *Lexikon für Theologie und Kirche*, Freiburg im Breisgau, Germany. **Article:** Pigge, Albert (Pighius).

*BAUMGAERTNER, MSGR. WILLIAM B., Ph.D., Associate Director, Association of Theological Schools, Vandalia, Ohio. **Article:** Seminary Education, Catholic.

*BAUMGAERTNER, WILLIAM LOUIS, Ph.D., Professor of Philosophy, St. Paul Seminary, St. Paul, Minn. **Articles:** Genus; Porphyrian Tree; Predicables; Property (Logic); Species.

*BAUMGAERTNER, WILLIAM LOUIS, Ph.D., Professor Emeritus, St. Paul Seminary,

St. Paul, Minn.; Former Associate Director, Association of Theological Schools (1984–90). **Article:** Association of Theological Schools.

*BAUR, JOHANNES, Dr. Phil., Dr.Theol., Professor of Pastoral Theology, Bressanone (Brixen), Italy. **Article:** Schmid, Franz.

*BAXTER, JAMES HOUSTON, M.A., B.D., D.Litt., D.D. (h.c. Glasgow), Dr. (h.c. Louvain), Regius Professor of Ecclesiastical History, University of St. Andrews, Scotland. **Articles:** Gerard of York; Henry Murdac; Henry of Newark; John de Offord; Melrose, Abbey of.

*BAYNE, WILLIAM WILFRID, OSB, Priory of St. Gregory the Great, Portsmouth, R.I. **Articles:** Benedictines, English; Liturgical Art, History of, 9: Episcopal and Abbatial.

*BEACH, SISTER FRANCIS MARY, SND, M.S. in L.S., M.A., Assistant Librarian, Trinity College, Washington, D.C. **Articles:** Eugenia, St.; Herrad of Landsberg; Ida, Bl.; Mont Sainte-Odile, Convent of.

*BEAL, JOHN P., J.C.D., Assistant Professor of Canon Law, The Catholic University of America, Washington, D.C. **Article:** Abortion, Canonical Legislation.

BEAL, JOHN P., J.C.D., Associate Professor, School of Canon Law, The Catholic University of America, Washington, D.C. **Article:** Provost, James H.

*BEAL, TARCÍSIO, OFM, M.A., Academy of American Franciscan History, Washington, D.C. **Articles:** Barbosa, Januário da Cunha; Lima, Manuel de Oliveira; Malagrida, Gabriel; Pimenta, Silvério Gomes; Salvador, Vicente do; Sardinha, Pedro Fernandes.

*BEARDSLEY, MONROE CURTIS, Ph.D., Professor of Philosophy, Swarthmore College, Swarthmore, Pa. **Article:** Aesthetics.

*BEAUDRY, JACQUES OVILA, CSV, S.T.L., Professor of Moral Theology, Scolasticat Saint-Charles, Joliette, P.Q., Canada. **Articles:** Domnus of Antioch; Le Quien, Michel; Neophyte; Orans; Orphan (in the Early Church); Smedt, Charles de.

*BEAUFILS, MARCEL, Docteur ès lettres, Professor, Conservatoire National (Classe d'Esthétique générale), and author, Neuilly-sur-Seine, Seine (Paris), France. **Articles:** Villa-Lobos, Heitor; Wagner, Richard.

*BEAUREGARD, ERVING EDWARD, M.A. Associate Professor of History, University of Dayton, Dayton, Ohio. **Articles:** Booth, William; Fry, Elizabeth; Irving, Edward; Liberal Catholic Church.

*BECAMEL, MARCEL, Canon, S.T.D., Professor of Fundamental Theology and Church History, Grand-Seminaire d'Albi, Tarn, France. **Article:** Riviere, Jean.

*BECERRA LÓPEZ, RICARDO, OFM, Licentiate in Pedagogy, Licentiate in Archival Science, Teacher, Universidad Nacional Autónoma, Mexico City, Mexico. **Article:** Borda, Andrés de.

*BECK, HENRY G. J., Very Rev., S.T.L., Hist.Eccl.D., Professor of Church History, Immaculate Conception Seminary, Darlington, N.J. **Articles:** Amandus, St.; Antipope; Arles; Arras, Councils of; Auxerre; Benedict II, Pope, St.; Caesarius of Arles, St.; Constantine, Pope; Eugene II, Pope; Gregory IV, Pope; Gregory of Tours, St.; Grenoble; Hilary of Arles, St.; Hincmar of Reims; Honoratus of Arles, St.; Honorius I, Pope; John IV, Pope; John V, Pope; John VI, Pope; John VII, Pope; Leo II, Pope, St.; Martin of Tours, St.; Merovingians; Narbonne; Nicholas I, Pope, St.; Salvian of Marseilles; Vincent of Lérins, St.

*BECK, LESLIE JOHN, M.A., Ph.D., Licentiate ès lettres, Diplôme des Hautes Études, formerly Lecturer in Philosophy, Merton College, Oxford, England. **Articles:** Cartesianism; Descartes, René.

*BECKER, SISTER JOHANNA, OSB, B.F.A., Associate Professor in Art, College of St. Benedict, and designer, Vestment Department, Convent of St. Benedict, St. Joseph, Minn. **Articles:** Liturgical Art, History of, 8: Liturgical Vestments; St. Anselm Priory (Tokyo).

*BECKMAN, PETER PAUL, OSB, Ph.D., Professor of History, St. Benedict's College, Atchison, Kans. **Articles:** Fink, Louis Mary (Michael); Hersfeld, Abbey of; Hirsau, Abbey of; Prum, Abbey of; St. Benedict's Abbey.

*BECKMANN, MARTIN ALVIN, OSB, S.T.L., St. John Vianney Minor Seminary, Elkhorn, Nebr. **Articles:** Ampullae; Anchor.

*BECQUÉ, MAURICE, CSSR, S.T.D., Rector, Redemptorist House of St. Joseph, Brussels, Belgium. **Article:** Dechamps, Victor Auguste.

*BEECH, GEORGE THOMAS, Ph.D., Associate Professor of History, Western Michigan University, Kalamazoo, Mich. **Articles:** Saint-Jouin-de-Marnes, Abbey of; Saint-Maixent, Abbey of.

*BEGG, CHRISTOPHER, S.T.D., Associate Professor of Theology, The Catholic University of America, Washington, D.C. **Article:** Pentateuchal Studies.

BEGG, CHRISTOPHER, Ph.D., S.T.D., Professor of Old Testament, Department of Theology, The Catholic University of America, Washington, D.C. **Article:** Josephus, Flavius.

*BEGGIANI, SEELY JOSEPH, S.T.D., Instructor in Theology and Philosophy, St. John College of Cleveland, Ohio. **Article:** Catholicos.

*BEGGIANI, SEELY JOSEPH, S.T.D., Chorbishop, Rector of Maronite Seminary, Washington, D.C. **Articles:** Maronite Church (U.S.); Lebanon, Christianity in.

BEGGIANI, SEELY JOSEPH, S.T.D., Adjunct Associate Professor, Department of Religion and Religious Education, The Catholic University of America, Washington, D.C. **Articles:** Maronite Church; Maronite Liturgy.

BEHA, SISTER MARIE, OSC, Ph.D, Monastery of St. Clare, Greenville, South Carolina. **Article:** Franciscans, Second Order.

*BEHRENDS, FREDERICK OTTEN, Ph.D., Assistant Professor of History, University of North Carolina, Chapel Hill, N.C. **Articles:** Benno of Metz; Fulbert of Chartres; Gerald of Aurillac, St.; Hoger of Bremen-Hamburg, St.

*BEICHNER, PAUL EDWARD, CSC, Ph.D., Professor of English and Dean of the Graduate School, University of Notre Dame, Notre Dame, Ind. **Article:** Gower, John.

*BEIKMAN, DONALD R., Ph.D., Assistant Professor of Music, Duquesne University, Pittsburgh, Pa.; organist. **Articles:** Daquin, Louis Claude; Fischer, Johann Kaspar Ferdinand; Froberger, Johann Jakob.

*BEISSEL, ROBERT MANNES, OP, M.A., S.T.L., S.T.Lr., Dominican House of Studies, Washington, D.C. **Articles:** Jacobina of Pisa, Bl.; Lawrence of Ripafratta, Bl.; Meynard, Andre; Piny, Alexander.

*BEITZINGER, ALFONS JOSEPH, Ph.D., Associate Professor of Politics, The Catholic University of America, Washington, D.C. **Articles:** Anarchism; Social Contract.

*BEKKER-NIELSEN, HANS, Cand.Mag., Teaching Fellow, University of Copenhagen, Denmark; Assistant Editor, *The Arnamagnean Dictionary of Old Norse.* **Articles:** Grundtvig, Nikolai Frederik Severin; Hallvard Vebjornsson, St.; Helen of Skovde, St.; Herrisvad, Abbey of; Nicholas of Aarhus, Bl.; Nicholas Hermansson, St.; Olaf I Tryggvesson, King of Norway; Olaf II, King of Norway, St.; Olsson, Erik (Olai); Thorlak Thorhallsson, St.; William of Aebelholt, St.

*BELL, JAMES ERNEST, SM, Assistant General, Office of the Society of Mary, Rome, Italy. **Articles:** Bataillon, Pierre Marie; Chanel, Peter, St.; Oceania, The Catholic Church in.

*BELL, JOHN ALBERT, Ph.L., Director, African Research and Information Center, Washington, D.C. **Articles:** Equatorial Guinea, The Catholic Church in; Kolbe, Frederick Charles; Sudan, The Catholic Church in; Welch, Sidney; Western Sahara.

*BELLANTONIO, ALFREDO, OM, S.T.L., J.C.D., Church of S. Andrea delle Fratte, Rome, Italy. **Articles:** Barré, Nicholas, Bl.; Francis of Paola, St.; Minims.

*BELLET, PAULINUS, OSB, S.T.D., S.S.L., monk of the Abbey of Montserrat, Barcelona, Spain; Associate Professor of Semitics, The Catholic University of America, Washington, D.C. **Articles:** Agobard of Lyons, St.; Claudius of Turin; Florus of Lyons; Severus ibn al-Mukaffa.

*BELVEDERI, RAFFAELE, Doctor of Letters, Lecturer in Modern History, Faculty of Letters, University of Bologna, Italy. **Article:** Passionei, Domenico.

*BENEDETTO, ARNOLD JOSEPH, SJ, S.T.L., Ph.D., Professor of Philosophy, Jesuit House of Studies and Spring Hill College, Mobile, Ala. **Articles:** Concurrence, Divine; Conservation, Divine; Fonseca, Peter da; Maurus, Sylvester; Suarezianism.

*BENNETT, ROLAND L., OMI, Ph.B., Member, Promoting Group, Movement for a Better World, Oblate College, Washington, D.C. **Article:** Movement for a Better World.

*BENTIVEGNA, JOSEPH, SJ, Doctor of Classical Letters, S.T.D., Professor of Theology in the Scholasticate, Ignatianum

Collegium Maximum, Messina, Italy. **Articles:** Apollinaris of Laodicea; Euthymius the Great, St.; Eutychius, Patriarch of Constantinople; Julian of Eclanum; Nepos of Arsinoe.

*BERG, PAUL CLEMENT, Ph.D., Associate Professor of Philosophy, Sacred Heart Seminary, and Instructor of Theology, Mercy College, Detroit, Mich. **Article:** Time (in the Old Testament).

BERGANT, DIANNE, CSA, Ph.D., Professor of Old Testament Studies, Catholic Theological Union, Chicago, Ill. **Article:** Women in the Bible [part 1: Old Testament].

*BERGEN, FRANKLYN JOSEPH, SJ, A.B., Ph.L., S.T.L., Professor of Theology, Loyola University, Chicago, Ill. **Articles:** Judde, Claude; Plus, Raoul.

*BERGMANN, ROSEMARIE LOUISE, Ph.D., Lecturer in Fine Arts, McGill University, Montreal, Canada. **Article:** Pieta.

*BERMEJO, ALOYSIUS MARIA, SJ, Professor of Dogmatic Theology, De Nobili College, and Prefect of Studies, Pontifical Athenaeum, Poona, India. **Articles:** Circumincession; Person, Divine; Properties, Divine Personal.

*BERNAD, MIGUEL ANSELMO, SJ, Ph.D., S.T.L., Professor of Literature, Ateneo de Manila, Philippine Islands. **Article:** Philippine Independent Church.

*BERNARD, LOUIS LEON, Ph.D., Associate Professor of Modern European History, University of Notre Dame, Notre Dame, Ind. **Articles:** Caulet, Francois Etienne; Declaration of the French Clergy; Le Camus, Etienne; Louis XIV, King of France.

*BERNAS, CASIMIR, OCSO, S.T.L., S.S.L., Professor of Sacred Scripture and Christian Archeology and Prefect of Studies, Holy Trinity Abbey, Huntsville, Utah. **Articles:** Agape; Bartolocci, Giulio; Breaking of Bread; Lord's Supper, The; Mammon; Sin Against the Holy Spirit.

*BERNDT, RONALD MURRAY, Ph.D., Professor of Anthropology and Head of the Department, University of Western Australia, Nedlands, Western Australia. **Article:** Totemism.

BERNHARDT, JOHN W., Ph.D. Professor of History, San Jose State University, San Jose, California. **Article:** Henry II, Roman Emperor, St.

*BERRETTI, SISTER MARY CECILY, RCD, B.A., Catechist, Parish Visitor, Span-

ish Apostolate, New York, N.Y. **Article:** Christian Doctrine, Sisters of Our Lady of.

*BERRY, SISTER MARY ST. VIRGINIA, BVM, Xavier High School, St. Louis, Mo. **Article:** Clarke, Mary Frances, Mother.

*BERRYMAN, PHILLIP, Writer and translator, Philadelphia, Pa. **Articles:** Central America, Catholic Church in; Liberation Theology, Latin America.

*BERSCHNEIDER, CLIFFORD JOSEPH, M.A., Assistant Professor of History and Chairman of the Social Science Division, Colby College, Waterville, Maine. **Articles:** Calov, Abraham; Gerhard, Johann; Hollaz, David; Quenstedt, Johann Andreas; Turrettini.

*BERTAUD, EMILE, OSB, monk of the Abbey of Saint-Wandrille (Seine-Maritime), France. **Article:** Reading, Spiritual.

*BERTHELOT DU CHESNAY, CHARLES, CJM, Ph.L., S.T.L., Licencié ès lettres, Archivist, Congrégation de Jésus et Marie (Eudistes), Paris, France; Chargé de cours d'histoire moderne, Catholic University of Angers, France. **Articles:** Anticlericalism; Appeal to a Future Council; Clericalism; Eudes, John, St.; Gallicanism; Laicism.

*BERTIN, GIORGIO, OFM, Nairobi, Kenya. **Article:** Somalia, the Church in.

*BERTOCCI, PETER ANTHONY, Ph.D., Borden Parker Bowne Professor of Philosophy, Boston University, Boston, Mass. **Article:** Brightman, Edgar Sheffield.

*BETANCOURT, ANA MARTA, Maestro de Historia, Research Scholar, Instituto Nacional de Antropología, e Historia, Mexico City, Mexico **Article:** Vetancurt, Agustin de.

*BETHELL, DENIS LESLIE, B.A., M.A., B.Litt., Lecturer, University of Reading, England. **Articles:** Corbeil, William of; Lexinton, Stephen de.

*BETTS, JOHN RICKARDS, Ph.D., Associate Professor of History, Boston College, Chestnut Hill, Mass. **Articles:** Onahan, William James; Orton, William Aylott.

*BEUKEN, W. H., Dr. of Dutch Literature, formerly Headmaster, Roman Catholic Lyceum, Helmond, Netherlands **Article:** Coornhert, Dirck Volkertszoon.

*BEUMER, JOHANNES, SJ, Dr.Theol., Professor of Fundamental Theology,

Hochschule St. Georgen, Frankfurt am Main, Germany. **Articles:** Denzinger, Heinrich Joseph; Lercher, Ludwig.

*BÉVENOT, MAURICE, SJ, M.A. (Oxon.), Mag.Aggreg.Fac.Theol. (Gregorian University), Professor of Fundamental Theology and Lecturer in Patristics, Heythrop College, Oxfordshire, England; Consultor, Secretariate for Promoting Christian Unity, Vatican Council II. **Articles:** Cyprian, St.; Firmilian of Caesarea.

*BEYENKA, SISTER M. MELCHIOR, OP, Ph.D., Professor of Classics and Dean of Studies, Edgewood College, Madison, Wis. **Articles:** Ad Regias Agni Dapes; Adeste Fideles; Consors Paterni Luminis; Creator Alme Siderum; Custodes Hominum Psallimus Angelos; Deus, Tuorum Militum; Ecce Iam Noctis Tenuatur Embra; En Clara Vox Redarguit; En Ut Superba Criminum; Ex More Docti Mystico.

*BEZOU, HENRY CHARLES, M.A., Litt.D., Archdiocesan Superintendent of Schools, New Orleans, La. **Articles:** Baton Rouge, Diocese of; Blanc, Anthony; Chapelle, Placide Louis; De la Croix, Charles; Louisiana, Catholic Church in; New Orleans, Archdiocese of; Odin, John Mary; Penalver y Cardenas, Luis Ignacio; Rummel, Joseph Francis.

*BIALAS, ANDREW ANTHONY, CSV, M.A., S.T.D., Professor of Dogma, Viatorian Seminary, Washington, D.C. **Articles:** Angelology; Angels, 3. Devotion to; Mystical Marriage; Sacra Virginitas.

*BIANCHI, SISTER MARY CLARA, Dr. of Letters, Historiographer, Istituto delle Suore di Carita delle Sante, Milan, Italy; collaborator, *Ascendere.* **Articles:** Capitanio, Bartolomea, St.; Gerosa, Vincenza, St.

*BIANCHINI, PIO, CRS, Dr. of Classical Literature, University of the Sacred Heart, Milan, Italy. **Articles:** Emiliani, Jerome, St.; Somascan Fathers.

*BICHSEL, MARCEL ALFREAD, B.D., M.S.M., Docteur ès lettres, Professor of Church Music and Chairman of the Department, Eastman School of Music, University of Rochester, and Professor of Music, Colgate Rochester Divinity School, Rochester, N.Y. **Articles:** Hymns and Hymnals, I: Historical Developments.

*BIECHLER, JAMES E., Associate Professor of Religion, La Salle College, Philadelphia, Pa. **Article:** Mysticism.

*BIECHLER, JAMES EUGENE, M.A., J.C.L., Secretary to Diocesan Tribunal, Defender of the Bond, La Crosse, Wis. **Article:** La Crosse, Diocese of.

*BIELER, LUDWIG, Ph.D., Professor of Palaeography and Late Latin, University College, Dublin, Ireland. **Articles:** Hibernensis Collectio; Patrick, St.; Penitentials.

*BIERMANN, BENNO M. THEOBALD, OP, Dr. Theol., Lecturer in Missiology, Dominican Studium, Walberberg, Germany. **Articles:** Capillas, Francis de, Bl.; Cruz, Gaspar da; Labat, Jean Baptiste; Morales, Juan Bautista; Ricci, Vittorio; Salazar, Domingo de; Santos, João dos.

*BIEZAIS, HARALDS, Dr.Theol., Dr.Phil., Associate Professor of the History of Religions, University of Uppsala, Sweden. **Article:** Baltic Religion.

*BIGELOW, ARTHUR LYNDS, Ph.L., Professor of Graphics and Bellmaster, Princeton University, Princeton, N.J.; consultant on the design of towers, chimes, and carillons. **Article:** Bells.

*BIGGANE, EDWARD JOSEPH, SMA, S.T.L., M.A. (Social Science), M.A. (History), Professor of History, Queen of Apostles College and Seminary, Dedham, Mass. **Article:** African Missions, Society of.

*BIGGS, ANSELM GORDON, OSB, Ph.D., Chairman of the Department of History, Executive Vice President, Academic Dean, and Admissions Officer, Belmont Abbey College, Belmont, N.C. **Articles:** Anselm of Nonantola, St.; Benedictines; Bernard Tolomei, Bl.; Domingo de la Calzada, St.; Felix of Valois, St.; Gerald of Braga, St.; Haid, Leo Michael; John of Matha, St.; Santiago de Compostela; Thierry of Fleury.

*BIHN, SISTER MARY TERESITA, SHF, M.A., Principal of Holy Ghost School of Religion, Fremont, Calif.; Vocation Directress, Holy Family Motherhouse, Mission San Jose, Calif. **Article:** Holy Family, Sisters of the.

*BILANIUK, PETRO BORYS TERESZKOWYCZ, S.T.D., Assistant Professor of Theology, St. Michael's College, University of Toronto, Canada. **Articles:** Anima Naturaliter Christiana; Soul, Human, 5. Theology; Traducianism.

*BILTON, WILLIAM, CJM, Executive Secretary, National Assembly of Religious Brothers, Buffalo, N.Y. **Article:** National Assembly of Religious Brothers.

*BIRRELL, THOMAS ANTHONY, M.A. (Cantab.), Professor of English and American Literature, Catholic University of Nijmegen, Netherlands. **Articles:** Austin, John; Corker, James Maurus; Oates Plot; Sabran, Louis de; Sergeant, John.

BIRZER, BRAD, Ph.D., Assistant Professor of History, Hillsdale College, Hillsdale, Mich. **Article:** North Dakota, Catholic Church in.

*BISCHOFF, JOHN GREVEN, SJ, A.B., Alma College, Los Gatos, Calif. **Articles:** Frins, Victor; Raynaud, Théophile; Regis, John Francis, St.

*BISCHOFF, WILLIAM NORBERT, SJ, S.T.B., Ph.D., Chairman, Department of History, Gonzaga University, Spokane, Wash. **Articles:** Cataldo, Joseph Mary; Palladino, Lawrence Benedict.

*BISSON, THOMAS NOEL, Ph.D., Assistant Professor of History, Brown University, Providence, R.I. **Article:** Saint-Guilhem-du-Désert, Abbey of.

*BISSONNETTE, TOMÁS G., M.A., Cert., Instituto Pastoral Latinoamericano, Quito; Hispanic Ministry, Mundelein College; Teacher, Midwest Hispanic Center, Chicago, Ill. **Article:** Basic Christian Communities.

*BLACHERE, MOTHER MARIE-DENYSE DU ST. SACREMENT, Superior General, Institut de l'Assomption, Paris, France. **Article:** Assumption, Religious of the.

*BLACKLEY, FRANK DONALD, Ph.D., Professor of History, University of Alberta, Edmonton, Canada. **Articles:** John of Langton; John of Appleby; Ralph Strode; Ralph Higden; Robert Waldby of York; Roger of Swynesheed; Taylor, William; Uthred of Bolden; Wykeham, William of.

*BLACKWELL, RICHARD JOSEPH, Ph.D., Associate Professor of Philosophy, St. Louis University, St. Louis, Mo. **Articles:** Democritus; Empedocles; Pythagoras and the Pythagorean; Wolff, Christian; Zeno of Elea.

*BLAIN, LIONEL ALBERT, S.T.L., Ph.D., Professor of Philosophy, Our Lady of Providence Seminary, Warwick, R.I. **Article:** Jaspers, Karl.

*BLAKELEY, THOMAS JOHN, Ph.D., First Assistant, Institute of East-European Studies, University of Fribourg, Switzerland; Managing Editor, *Studies in Soviet Thought.* **Article:** Materialism, Dialectical and Historical.

BLANCHETTE, OLIVA, Ph.D., Professor of Philosophy, Boston College, Chestnut Hill, Mass. **Article:** Blondel, Maurice.

*BLAND, SISTER JOAN, SND, M.A., Ph.D., Professor of History, Trinity College, Washington, D.C.; Director of Provincial Development, Sisters of Notre Dame de Namur. **Articles:** Billiart, Marie Rose Julie, St.; McGroarty, Julia, Sister; Notre Dame de Namur, Sisters of; Secret Societies, Church Policy on; Van der Schrieck, Louise, Sister.

*BLANKINSHIP, KHALID YAHYAH, Ph.D., Department of Religion, Temple University, Philadelphia, PA. **Article:** Sunnites.

BLANTZ, THOMAS E., CSC, Ph.D., Professor of History, University of Notre Dame, Notre Dame, Ind. **Article:** Notre Dame du Lac, University of.

*BLECKER, PAULIN MICHAEL, OSB, Ph.D., Professor of History, St. John's University, Collegeville, Minn. **Articles:** Austreberta, St.; Bertha of Blangy, St.; Bertulf of Renty, St.; Bonitus of Clermont, St.; Claudius of Condat, St.; Ermin, St.; Eusebia of Saint-Cyr, St.; Évroul (Ebrulf), St.; Reginald of Canterbury; Ursmar, St.

*BLENKINSOPP, JOSEPH, SDB, S.T.L., S.S.L., Professor of Sacred Scripture, Melchet Court, Hampshire, England. **Article:** Type and Antitype.

*BLET, PIERRE EMILE-MARIE, SJ, Ph.L., S.T.L., Doctorat ès lettres, Professor of Church History, Gregorian University, Rome, Italy. **Articles:** La Chaize, Francois de; Le Clerc Du Tremblay, Francois; Mazarin, Jules; Richelieu, Armand Jean du Plessis de.

*BLIED, BENJAMIN JOSEPH, M.A., S.T.B., Ph.D., Professor of History, Marian College, Fond du Lac, Wis. **Articles:** Heiss, Michael; Katzer, Frederick Francis Xavier; Leopoldinen Stiftung (Leopoldine Society); Ludwig Missionsverein (Ludwig Mission Society); Verwyst, Chrysostom Adrian.

*BLIGNY, BERNARD, Doctorat ès lettres, Professor of Medieval History, University of Grenoble, France. **Article:** Bruno the Carthusian, St.

*BLISS, SISTER MARY BERNADETTE, FC, B.A. Hons., Motherhouse, Filles de la Croix, Liège, Belgium. **Articles:** Daughters of the Cross of Liege; Haze, Marie Thérèse, Bl.

*BLOCH, HERBERT, Professor of Greek and Latin, Harvard University, Cambridge,

Mass., and Senior Fellow of the Society of Fellows; Member of the Board of Syndics, Harvard University Press. **Articles:** Gelasius II, Pope; Monte-Cassino, Archabbey of; Peter the Deacon of Monte Cassino; Pierleoni.

*BLOCKER, HYACINTH FRED, OFM, M.A., Chaplain, Mt. Alverno School, Cincinnati, Ohio. **Article:** St. Francis, Brothers of the Poor of.

*BLUM, OWEN J., OFM, Ph.D., Professor of History, Quincy College, Quincy, Ill.; Staff Editor for Medieval Church History, *New Catholic Encyclopedia,* The Catholic University of America, Washington, D.C. **Articles:** Ad Perennis Vitae Fontem; Alberic of Ostia; Arnulf of Metz, St.; Bernold of Ottobeuren, Bl.; Conrad of Ottobeuren, Bl.; Constantine the African; Frutolf of Michelsberg; Gerard of Villamagna, Bl.; Gregory VI, Pope; Guido of Pomposa, St.; Herman the German, Bl.; Leo VII, Pope; Leo VI, Pope; Leo V, Pope; Leo VIII, Pope; Leo IX, Pope, St.; Miter; Oliger, Livarius; Pacificus of Novara, Bl.; Peter Damian, St.; Peter the Deacon of Rome, Bl.; Pontius of Balmey, Bl.; Raymond Nonnatus, St.; Robert of Torigny; Saint-Leonard-le-Noblat, Monastery of; Sant' Antimo, Abbey of; Thangmar of Hildesheim; Thietmar (Dietmar) of Merseburg; Thiofrid of Echternach; Thomas II of York; Vacarius; Veremundus, St.; Wandrille (Wandregisilus), St.

BLUMENTHAL, UTA-RENATE, Ph.D., Ordinary Professor of History, The Catholic University of America, Washington, D.C. **Articles:** Clement III, Pope; Clement II, Pope; Nicholas II, Pope; Stephen IX (X), Pope; Victor III, Pope, Bl.

*BOBERG, JOHN T., SVD, Secretary-Treasurer, Association of Professors of Missions, Catholic Theological Union, Chicago, Ill. **Article:** Association of Professors of Missions.

*BOBIK, JOSEPH, Ph.D., Associate Professor of Philosophy, University of Notre Dame, Notre Dame, Ind. **Articles:** Entelechy; Faculties of the Soul; Soul; Soul, Human, 4. Philosophical Analysis.

*BOENKI, OTTO ALOYSIUS, SAC, M.A., Spiritual Director, Pallotti College, W. Hyattsville, Md. **Articles:** Blessed; St. Raphael's Society.

*BOKENKOTTER, THOMAS STEPHEN, S.T.L., Docteur ès sciences hi-

storiques, Assistant Professor of Church History, Mt. St. Mary of the West, Norwood, Ohio. **Articles:** Froude, Richard Hurrell; Halifax, Charles Lindley Wood; Keble, John; Oxford Movement; Pusey, Edward Bouverie; Schmalkaldic League; Staupitz, Johann von; Tractarianism; Ursinus, Zacharias; Whately, Richard.

*BOLAND, DANIEL ANTHONY, Very Rev., SSC, M.A., Director, The Columban Fathers, St. Columbans, Nebr. **Article:** Columban Fathers.

*BOLAND, FRANK JOHN, CSB, Ph.D., University of Windsor, Ontario, Canada. **Article:** La Salle, Robert Cavelier de.

*BOLDRICK, CHARLES CARTER, Rt. Rev., S.T.D., Ph.D., Pastor, Holy Trinity Church, Louisville, Ky. **Article:** McCloskey, William George.

*BOLL, SISTER MARY HENRICA, PHJC, Ph.B., M.A., Teacher of Rhetoric and Literary Types, Ancilla Domini Junior College, Donaldson, Ind. **Article:** Poor Handmaids of Jesus Christ.

*BOLLE, KEES WILLEM, Ph.D., Assistant Professor for History of Religions and Sanskrit, Brown University, Providence, R.I. **Articles:** Expiation; Sin (Phenomenology of); Temples; Votive Offerings [part 1].

BOLTON, BRENDA M., M.A. F.S.A. (Fellow of the Society of Antiquaries of London), Senior Lecturer in History (Emerita), University of London, London, United Kingdom. **Articles:** Adrian IV, Pope; Alexander III, Pope; Celestine III, Pope.

*BONANSEA, BERNARDINE M., OFM, Ph.D., Lect.Gen., Professor of Philosophy, The Catholic University of America, Washington, D.C. **Articles:** Campanella, Tommaso; God in Philosophy, 2. Existence; Hylozoism; Panpsychism; Telesio, Bernardino; William of Champeaux.

*BONDI, EUGENE, OP, S.T.L., S.T.Lr., Ph.L., Ph.D., Professor of Logic and Dean of Studies, Dominican Studium at St. Stephen's Priory, Dover, Mass. **Articles:** Argumentation; Definition; Sign; Syllogism.

*BONÉ, EDOUARD LOUIS, SJ, Ph.L., Lic.Sc.Zool., S.T.L., Ph.D., Professor of Biology and Anthropology, Facultés Philosophie et Theologie S.J., Louvain, Belgium; Head of the Department of Vertebrate Paleontology, and Lecturer in Paleontology and Anthro-

pology, University of Louvain, Belgium. **Article:** Teilhard de Chardin, Pierre.

*BONNER, DISMAS W., OFM, J.C.D., Professor of Canon Law, St. Joseph Seminary, Teutopolis, Ill. **Articles:** Dimissorial Letters; Reiffenstuel, Anacletus (Johann Georg); Schmalzgrueber, Franz.

BONNER, GERALD, Ph.D., Professor Emeritus, University of Durham, Durham, England. **Article:** Augustine, Rule of St.

*BONNEVILLE, SISTER ST. REGINALD, SM, Director of Vocations, Sisters' Vocation Council in the Archdiocese of New York, Misericordia Hospital, Bronx, N.Y. **Article:** Misericordia Sisters.

*BONNICI, ARTHUR, Very Rev., B.A., J.C.B., D.D., Hist. Eccl.Lic., Professor of Church History and Christian Archeology, Royal Malta University; Secretary-General of the Archdiocese of Malta. **Article:** Malta, The Catholic Church in.

*BONNIWELL, WILLIAM RAYMOND, OP, M.A., Research Scholar in Medieval History and History of Dominican Rite, St. Vincent's Priory, New York, N.Y. **Articles:** Innocent VII, Pope; Innocent VI, Pope; Innocent VIII, Pope; Margaret of Metola, Bl.

*BOOS, JACQUES THOMAS, OSB, monk of the Solesmes Congregation, Quarr Abbey, Ryde, Isle of Wight, England. **Article:** Nicholas of Flue, St.

*BORAN, MOTHER FRANCIS DE SALES, RSHM, Ph.D., Professor of History, Marymount Junior College, Arlington, Va. **Articles:** Aubenas, Martyrs of; Aubigne, Jean Henri Merle d'; Butler, Marie Joseph, Mother; Fidelis of Sigmaringen, St.; Gorkum, Martyrs of; Phelan, Gerard, Mother; Sacred Heart of Mary, Religious of the; Wagner, Liborius, Bl.

*BORCHERS, CLEMENT FRANK, Very Rev., Superior General, The Glenmary Home Missioner Society, Glendale, Ohio. **Article:** Bishop, William Howard.

BORELLI, JOHN, Ph.D., Associate Director of Secretariat for Ecumenical and Interreligious Affairs, United States Conference of Catholic Bishops, Washington, D.C. **Articles:** Anglican/Roman Catholic Consultation in the United States (ARC-USA); Angli-

can/Roman Catholic International Commission (ARCIC); Hotchkin, John F.

*BORER, ANTON JOSEPH, Very Rev., SMB, S.T.B., Assistant, Church of the Most Blessed Sacrament, Denver, Colo.; Regional Superior, Bethlehem Fathers. **Articles:** Bethlehem Fathers; Bondolfi, Pietro.

*BORROFF, EDITH, Ph.D., Associate Professor of Music, University of Wisconsin, Madison, Wis. **Articles:** Charpentier, Marc Antoine; Couperin, François; Gossec, François Joseph; Gretry, Andre Ernest Modeste; Lully, Jean Baptiste; Rameau, Jean Philippe.

*BOTTE, BERNARD, OSB, monk of the Abbey of Mont César, Professor of Liturgy, University of Louvain, Belgium; Director, Institut Supérieur de Liturgie, Paris, France. **Article:** Saturnalia.

*BOUCHAUD, JOSEPH, CSSp, B.A, Secretary, Institut de Presse Missionnaire, and Director, Centre de, Documentation et d'Information CSSp, Paris, France. **Articles:** Benin, The Catholic Church in; Cameroon, The Catholic Church in; Chad, The Catholic Church in; Comoros, The Catholic Church in; Congo, Republic of, The Catholic Church in; Gambia, The Catholic Church in; Guinea, The Catholic Church in; Madagascar, The Catholic Church in; Mauritania, The Catholic Church in; Mauritius, The Catholic Church in; Niger, The Catholic Church in; Nigeria, The Catholic Church in; Senegal, The Catholic Church in; Seychelles, The Catholic Church in; Sierra Leone, The Catholic Church in.

BOUCHER, ANNE-MARIE, Regional Provincial, Little Sisters of Jesus, Baltimore, Md. **Article:** Little Sisters of Jesus.

*BOUCHER, ROBERT GEORGE, CSSR, S.T.L., S.S.L., Professor, Immaculate Conception Seminary, Oconomowoc, Wis. **Articles:** Apollos; Timothy, St.; Titus, St.

*BOUDENS, ROBRECHT MAURITS, OMI, Hist.Eccl.D., Professor of Church History and Patrology, OMI Scholasticate, Gijzegem, Belgium. **Articles:** Lamennais, Hugues Felicite Robert de; Sri Lanka, the Catholic Church in.

*BOURKE, MYLES MATTHEW, Rt. Rev., S.T.D., S.S.L., Dean of Studies, St. Joseph's Seminary, Dunwoodie, Yonkers, New York, N.Y.; Adjunct Professor of Sacred Scripture, Fordham University, New York; Chairman,

Committee of the CCD Translation of the New Testament from the Original Greek. **Articles:** Driscoll, James F.; Gigot, Francis Ernest; Infancy Narratives.

*BOURKE, SIMON JOHN, SM, Assistant General, Marist Fathers, Rome, Italy. **Article:** Oceania, The Catholic Church in.

*BOURKE, VERNON JOSEPH, Ph.D., Professor of Philosophy, St. Louis University, St. Louis, Mo.; Adviser and Editor, *Speculum, The Modern Schoolman, Natural Law Forum.* **Articles:** Ethics; Will.

*BOUSCAREN, TIMOTHY LINCOLN, SJ, M.A., LL.B., S.T.D., Professor Emeritus of Canon Law, Scriptor, and Censor Librorum, West Baden College, West Baden Springs, Ind. **Article:** Apostolic Camera.

*BOUTON, JEAN DE LA CROIX, OCSO, Abbaye Notre Dame d'Aiguebelle, Grignan (Drome), France. **Articles:** Saint-Gildas-de-Rhuys, Abbey of; Saint-Maur-sur-Loire, Abbey of; Saint-Robert-de-Cornillon, Priory of; Solignac, Abbey of; Souillac, Abbey of; Vendome (Sainte-Trinite), Abbey of.

*BOWMAN, DAVID JOSEPH, SJ, M.A., Ph.Lic., S.T.D., Assistant Director, Faith and Order Department, National Council of Churches, New York, N.Y. **Articles:** Mott, John Raleigh; New Jerusalem Church; Temple, William.

*BOWMAN, DAVID JOSEPH, SJ, Director, Ireland Program and Associate Director for Europe, National Council of the Churches of Christ in the U.S.A., New York, N.Y. **Articles:** National Council of Churches of Christ in the U.S.A.; Northern Ireland.

*BOWSKY, WILLIAM MARVIN, Ph.D., Associate Professor of History, University of Nebraska, Lincoln, Nebr. **Articles:** Henry VII, Holy Roman Emperor; Lombard League.

*BOYD, CATHERINE EVANGELINE, Ph.D., Professor of History, Carleton College, Northfield, Minn. **Articles:** Beatrice of Tuscany; Lambert of Spoleto, German Emperor; Italy, The Catholic Church in, 1. To 1500; Leo of Vercelli; Matilda of Tuscany.

*BOYD, ELIZABETH, Curator of Spanish Colonial Department, Museum of New Mexico, Santa Fe, N.Mex. **Articles:** Chimayo, Santuario de; Santo.

*BOYD, THEOPHANE, OCSO, Novicemaster and Professor of Liturgy, St. Benedict's Monastery, Snowmass, Colo. **Articles:** Bona, Giovanni; Cistercian Rite.

*BOYEA, EARL, S.T.L., Ph.D., Dean of Studies, Sacred Heart Major Seminary, Detroit, MI. **Article:** Dearden, John Francis.

BOYEA, EARL, Most Reverend, S.T.L., Ph.D., Auxiliary Bishop of Detroit, MI. **Articles:** Detroit, Archdiocese of; Michigan, Catholic Church in; Wisconsin, Catholic Church in.

*BOYER, MARJORIE NICE, Ph.D., Lecturer in the School of General Studies, Brooklyn College, Brooklyn, NY. **Article:** Benezet, St.

*BOYLE, LEONARD EUGENE, OP, S.T.L., D.Phil (Oxon.), Professor of Palaeography and Medieval History, Angelicum, and Professor of History in Jesus Magister Institute for Brothers, Lateran University, Rome, Italy; Professor of Palaeography, Institute of Mediaeval Studies, Toronto, Ontario, Canada; Professor of Diplomatics, Toronto University Medieval Centre. **Articles:** Alanus Anglicus; Ausculta Fili; Bernard of Compostella, the Younger; Bulla; Canon Law, History of, 4. Classical Period; Chabham, Thomas; Chronology, Medieval, 2. The West in the Middle Ages; Clementinae; Collatio; Compurgation; Computus; Corpus Iuris Canonici; Decretalists; Decretists; Devolution, Right of; Dominical Letter; Extravagantes; Gilbertus Anglicus; Gravamina; Gregory IX, Decretals of; Guelfs and Ghibellines; John of Acton; John of Wales; Liber Sextus; Liturgical Calendars, I: Catholic; Lyndwood, William; Mendicant Orders; Nepotism; Oblate; Ordeal [part 3]; Peace of God; Pisa, Council of; Provision; Regalia; Rufinus; Sicardus of Cremona; Thionville (Diedenhofen), Councils of; William of Pagula (Poul).

*BOYLE, PAUL, CP, Passionist Retreat House, Fukuoka, Japan. **Article:** Leadership Conference of Women Religious.

*BOYLE, SISTER RITA, OSF, R.N., B.S. in Nursing Education, Novice Mistress, Our Lady of the Lake Hospital, Baton Rouge, La. **Article:** Franciscan Sisters—Franciscan Missionaries of Our Lady (OSF).

*BOYLE, ROBERT RICHARD, SJ, Ph.L., M.A., Th.L., Ph.D., Professor of En-

glish, Regis College, Denver, Colo. **Article:** Sonnet, Religious Use of.

*BRADLEY, ROBERT IGNATIUS, SJ, M.A., S.T.L., Ph.D., Professor of History and Chairman of the Department, Seattle University, Seattle, Wash. **Articles:** Abington, Thomas (Habington); Coleman, Edward, Bl.; Gerard, Richard; Phillip, Robert; Presbyterianism; Russell, Richard; Westminster Confession; White, Thomas.

BRADLEY, ROBERT I., SJ, Ph.D., S.T.D., Adjunct Professor of Theology and Catechetics, Institute of Pastoral Theology, Ave Maria University, Ypsilanti, Mich. **Article:** Catechism of the Council of Trent.

*BRADY, CHARLES ANDREW, M.A., L.H.D., Professor of English, Canisius College, Buffalo, N.Y. **Article:** Hemingway, Ernest Miller.

*BRADY, IGNATIUS CHARLES, OFM, Lic.Med.St., Ph.D., Lect. Gen., Lector Jubilatus OFM, Prefect of the Theological Commission, College of St. Bonaventure, Quaracchi (Florence), Italy. **Articles:** Adam Wodham; Costa ben Luca; Immortality, 1. History of Problem; Isaac of Stella; John of La Rochelle (de Rupella); John of Rodington; Nemesius of Emesa; Peter Lombard; Peter Thomae; Philosophy, History of, 2. Ancient; Philosophy, History of, 3. Medieval; Quaracchi; Robert of Courcon; Robert Pullen; Scholasticism, 1. Medieval; Soul, Human, 1. Oriental and Greek Conceptions; Soul, Human, 2. Patristic and Medieval Writers; Walter of Chatton; William of Vaurouillon; William of Alnwick.

*BRADY, JOHN EUGENE, OMI, parish priest, St. Therese, Edenvale, Transvaal, South Africa. **Articles:** Botswana, The Catholic Church in; Griffith, Patrick Raymond; Lesotho, The Catholic Church in; Namibia, The Catholic Church in; Pfanner, Franz; South Africa, The Catholic Church in; Swaziland, The Catholic Church in.

*BRADY, JOSEPH H., Rt. Rev., Ph.D., Immaculate Conception Seminary, Darlington, N.J. (deceased July 3, 1961). **Article:** New Jersey.

*BRADY, JULES MALACHY, SJ, Ph.D., Professor of Philosophy, Rockhurst College, Kansas City, Mo. **Article:** Seminal Reasons.

*BRADY, SISTER MARY TERESA, RDC, Ph.D., Chairman of the Department of

English, Good Counsel College, White Plains, N.Y. **Article:** Divine Compassion, Sisters of the.

*BRADY, THOMAS ALLAN, Ph.D., formerly Professor of Ancient History, University of Missouri, Columbia, Mo. (deceased June 10, 1964). **Articles:** Aesculapius, Cult of; Augury; Battle Standards, Cult of; Chaldeans; Cybele; Delphi, Oracle of; Etruscan Religion; Incantation; Isis and Osiris; Necromancy.

*BRAKKEE, CORNELIS FRANCISCUS JORDANNUS, OP, S.T.Lr., Catholic University of Nijmegen, Netherlands. **Article:** Alan de la Roche.

*BRANCA, VITTORE, Doctor of Letters, Professor of Italian Literature, University of Padua, Italy; Secretary-General, Fondazione G. Cini. **Article:** Boccaccio, Giovanni.

BRAND, CHARLES M., Ph.D., Professor Emeritus of History, Bryn Mawr College, Bryn Mawr, Pennsylvania. **Articles:** Alexius I Comnenus, Byzantine Emperor; Latin Empire of Constantinople.

*BRANDL, GARY, General Manager, New City Press, Hyde Park, New York. **Article:** Focolare Movement.

BRANDT, PATRICIA, B.S., M.Mus.Ed., M.A.L.S., retired professor (reference librarian), Oregon State University, Corvalis, Ore. **Articles:** Baker, Diocese of; Oregon, Catholic Church in; Portland, Archdiocese of [Ore.].

*BRAUCH, SISTER MARIE SUZANNE, CDP, M.A., B.S. in L.S., Mistress of Novices, St. Anne Convent, Melbourne, Ky. **Article:** Sisters of Divine Providence of Kentucky.

*BRAUNLICH, HELMUT KARL, Artist's Diploma, Mozarteum, Salzburg, Austria, B.M., M.M., Teacher of Violin and Music Theory, The Catholic University of America, Washington, D.C. **Articles:** Hindemith, Paul; Respighi, Ottorino.

BRECHENMACHER, THOMAS, Dr.phil., Wissenschaftlicher Assistent, Bundeswehruniversität, Munich. Munich, Germany. **Article:** Pius XI, Pope.

*BREDIGER, LAWRENCE, MSSST (deceased Feb. 9, 1962). **Article:** Judge, Thomas Augustine.

*BREEN, QUIRINUS, Ph.D., Professor Emeritus of History, University of Oregon, Eugene, Ore.; Resident Scholar, Institute for Advanced Study, Princeton, N.J. **Articles:** Calixtus, Georg; Crypto-Calvinism; Gnesiolutheranism; Major, Georg (Maier); Majoristic Controversy; Philippism.

*BRENTANO, ROBERT, D.Phil., Associate Professor in History, University of California at Berkeley, Calif. **Articles:** Walter Giffard; Walter de Gray (Grey); William Wickwane.

*BRESLIN, SISTER MARY THOMAS, UTSV, M.A., Teacher of French and Religion, Notre Dame School, New York, N.Y.; Directress, Studies for the Religious. **Articles:** St. Ursula, Society of; Xainctonge, Anne de, Ven.

*BRESNAHAN, JOHN EDWARD, OSA, Ph.D., Professor of Apologetics and Patrology, Augustinian College, Washington, D.C. **Articles:** Angelus de Scarpetis, Bl.; Anthony Pavonius, Bl.; Brictinians; Cherubin of Avigliana, Bl.; Galdinus, St.; Helen of Udine, Bl.; Herman of Schildesche; Magdalen Albrici, Bl.; William of Cremona.

*BRINKMAN, GABRIEL, OFM, Ph.D., Vice President and Associate Professor of Sociology, Quincy College, Quincy, Ill. **Article:** Lugo, Juan de.

*BRINKMAN, JOHN ANTHONY, Ph.D., Assistant Professor of Assyriology and Ancient History, Oriental Institute, University of Chicago, Chicago, Ill. **Articles:** Alma; Enuma Elish; Gilgamesh Epic; Panbabylonism; Pohl, Alfred.

*BRITTON, SISTER M. ANGELENA, OSF, M.A., English Teacher, St. Francis Woods, Mokena, Ill. **Article:** Franciscan Sisters—Franciscan Sisters of the Sacred Heart (OSF).

*BROADBENT, JOHN, Wellington, New Zealand. **Article:** New Zealand, the Church in.

*BROCK, PETER DE BEAUVOIR, B.A. and M.A. (Oxon.), Ph.D., D.Phil., Associate Professor of History and Staff Member of the Program on East Central Europe, Columbia University, New York, N.Y. **Articles:** Bohemian Brethren; Lukas of Prague.

*BROCKMAN, JAMES R., SJ, M.A., Ph.L., S.T.B., St. Ignatius Parish, Chicago. **Article:** Romero, Oscar A.

*BRODERICK, FRANCIS LYONS, Ph.D., Director, United States Peace Corps, Ghana, Africa. **Articles:** New Hampshire; Ryan, John Augustine.

*BRODERICK, JOHN FRANCIS, SJ, S.T.L., Hist.Eccl.D., Professor of Ecclesiastical History, Weston College, Weston, Mass.; Staff Editor for Modern Church History, *New Catholic Encyclopedia*, The Catholic University of America, Washington D.C. **Articles:** Jesuits; Paccanarists; Papacy, 4. Modern Period (1789–1958); Sacred Heart of Jesus, Society of the; Servants of Mary, Sisters; St. Thomas of Villanova, Sisters of; St. Teresa of Jesus, Society of; Tournely, Eleonor Francois de.

*BRODERICK, JOSEPH ALBERT, OP, Professor of Law, North Carolina Central University, Durham, N.C. **Article:** Civil Disobedience.

*BROEDERS, PETRUS NOLASCUS, Brother of the Congregation of Our Lady Mother of Mercy, Master of English, St. Stanislaus' College, Tilburg, Netherlands. **Article:** Our Lady Mother of Mercy, Brothers of.

*BROGAN, SISTER MARY MAGDALEN OF JESUS, OSS, A.B., Blessed Sacrament Monastery, Yonkers, N.Y. **Article:** Sacramentine Nuns.

*BROOKE, ROSALIND BECKFORD, B.A. (Cantab.), M.A., Ph.D., author, Willaston, Wirral Cheshire, England. **Articles:** Haymo of Faversham; Hugh of Digne; John Parenti; Thomas of Eccleston; Ubertino of Casale.

*BROOKS, CATHERINE VIRGINIA, Ph.D., Librarian, Cliffside Park, N.J. **Articles:** Binchois, Gilles; Busnois, Antoine; Dufay, Guillaume.

*BROOKS, CLEANTH, B.A., M.A., B.A. (Oxford), B.Litt. (Oxford), Gray Professor of Rhetoric, Yale University, New Haven, Conn.; Cultural Attaché, American Embassy, London, England. **Article:** Yeats, William Butler.

*BROUETTE, ÉMILE PAUL, Ph.L., Docteur en Histoire, Bach. en Histoire de l'Art, Professor of History and History of Civilization, Athénée royal d'Ixelles-Bruxelles, Belgium; Director, *Revue beige de Numismatique*. **Articles:** Anstrudis, St.; Anthelm of Chignin, St.; Bathildis, St.; Begga, St.; Bernard of Tiron, St.; Bertilla of Chelles, St.; Emebert of Cambrai, St.; Eucherius of Orléans, St.; Evrard of Béthune; Gangolf, St.; Gertrude of Nivelles, St.; Glodesindis, St.; Haimar of Auxerre, St.; Ida of Boulogne, Bl.; Iduberga, St.; Ivo Hélory, St.; Jacques de Molay; Landry (Landrich), SS; Leutfred (Leufroy), St.; Odo of Châteauroux; Peter of Vaux-de-Cernay; Sigebert of Austrasia, St.; Victor of Plancy, St.; Walarich (Valéry), St.; William of Neuchâtel; William of Notre Dame de l'Olive, St.; William of Puylaurens; Wulmar, St.; Ysarnus, St.

*BROUTIN, PAUL, SJ, Lille (Nord), France. **Articles:** Duprat, Guillaume; Lallemant, Jacques Philippe; Zola, Giuseppe.

*BROWN, BONAVENTURE ANTHONY, OFM, S.T.D., Professor of Moral Theology and Regional Commissary Provincial of the Third Order of St. Francis, Western New York and Eastern Pennsylvania, Buffalo, N.Y. **Article:** Stations of the Cross.

*BROWN, BRENDAN FRANCIS, A.B., LL.B., LL.M., J.U.D., D.Phil. (in law), Professor of Law, Loyola University School of Law, New Orleans, La. **Article:** Natural Law [part 1].

*BROWN, DONALD FOWLER, Ph.D., Professor of Modern Languages, Villanova University, Villanova, Pa. **Article:** Unamuno y Jugo, Miguel de.

*BROWN, LEN, C.M.F., Provincial Superior, Claretian Missionaries, Oak Park, Illinois. **Article:** Barbastro, Martyrs of, Bl.

*BROWN, LEO CYRIL, SJ, S.T.L., Ph.D., Professor of Economics, St. Louis University, St. Louis, Mo.; Research Associate, Cambridge Center for Social Studies, Cambridge, Mass.; labor arbitrator and mediator; Member, Atomic Energy Labor-Management Relations Panel; Staff Editor for Social Sciences, *New Catholic Encyclopedia,* The Catholic University of America, Washington, D.C. **Article:** Automation.

*BROWN, PETER SCHUYLER, SJ, A.B., Ph.L., Th.L., Woodstock College, Woodstock, Md. **Article:** Anglo-Catholics.

*BROWN, RAPHAEL, Senior Reference Librarian, Library of Congress, Washington, D.C. **Articles:** Anthony of Stroncone, Bl.; Assisi; Charles of Sezze, St.; Conrad of Offida, Bl.; Fioretti, The; Guido of Cortona, Bl.; Hutterites; John of La Verna, Bl.; Leprosy (in the Bible); Luchesius of Poggibonsi, Bl.; Portiuncula; Sabatier, Paul.

*BROWN, RAYMOND E., SS, M.A., S.T.D., Ph.D., S.S.L., Professor of New Testament, St. Mary's Seminary, Baltimore, Md. **Articles:** Essenes; Johannine Writings; John, Apostle, St.; John, Gospel according to; Mystery (in the Bible); Parables of Jesus.

*BROWN, RAYMOND E., SS, S.T.D., Ph.D., S.S.L., Auburn Distinguished Professor of Biblical Studies, Union Theological Seminary, New York. **Article:** Johannine Writings.

*BROWN, SISTER RITA MARIE, OP, M.A., Secretary-General, Dominican Sisters of Mission San Jose, Calif. **Article:** Dominicans—Sisters, Dominican Sisters of Mission San Jose, Calif.

*BROWNE, JOSEPH PETER, CSC, A.B., S.T.D., M.S. in L.S., Professor of Moral Theology, Holy Cross College, Washington, D.C. **Articles:** Grace, The State of; Smuggling.

*BROWNING, COLUMBAN, CP, S.T.B., Rector, St. Gabriel Monastery, Des Moines, Iowa. **Articles:** Friendship, Particular; Friendship, Spiritual.

*BROWNING, ROBERT, M.A. (Glasgow), M.A. (Oxon.), Reader in Greek and Latin, University of London, England. **Articles:** Aurelius of Armenia, St.; Clement the Bulgarian, St.; George Hamartolus; John Malalas; Michael I, the Syrian, Patriarch of Antioch; Zonaras, John.

*BRUCE-MITFORD, RUPERT LEO SCOTT, M.A. (Oxon.), Keeper of British and Medieval Antiquities in the British Museum, London, England. **Articles:** Durrow, Book of; Irish Crosses; Kells, Book of; Lindisfarne Gospels.

*BRÜCKMANN, J., Ph.D., L.M.S., Assistant Professor of Medieval History, Department of History, York University in the University of Toronto, Canada. **Articles:** Arcadius, Roman Emperor; Battle, Abbey of; Botulph of Icanhoe, St.; Emygdius of Ancona, St.; Gervase and Protase, SS.; Gordian and Epimachus, SS.; Gorgonia, St.; Hexham, Monastery of; John, King of England; John de Grey (Gray); Kirkstall, Abbey of; Lawrence, St.; Wearmouth, Abbey of; Wulfstan of Worcester, St.

*BRUCKNER, ALBERT, Dr.Phil., Professor of History, University of Basel, Switzerland; Director of the Public Archives, Basel, Switzerland. **Articles:** Book, The Medieval; Roll and Codex; Scriptorium.

*BRUNDAGE, JAMES ARTHUR, Ph.D., Associate Professor of History, University of Wisconsin, Milwaukee, Wis. **Articles:** Alexander IV, Pope; Arnold of Brescia; Brehier, Louis; Fulcher of Chartres; Holy Lance; Hospitallers of St. Lazarus of Jerusalem; Hugh of Die; Mortmain; Pastoureaux, Crusade of

the; Peter the Hermit; Peter of Anagni, St.; Raymond of Toulouse, St.; Raymond of Toulouse; Widukind of Corvey.

*BRUNI, JOHN PIUS, MSC, M.A., Instructor in Speech, Homiletics, and Catechetics, Sacred Heart Seminary, Shelby, Ohio. **Articles:** Sacred Humanity, Devotion to the; Wounds of Our Lord, Devotion to.

*BRUNNER, FRANCIS ADAM, CSSR, M.A., St. Alphonsus Church, Chicago, Ill. **Articles:** Anamnesis; Embolism; Introit; Leonine Prayers; Roman Rite.

*BRUNOT, AMÉDÉE, SCJ, S.T.L., Docteur ès sciences bibliques, Superior, Grand Séminaire des Prêtres du Sacré-Coeur de Jésus, Floirac (Gironde), France. **Articles:** Abrabanel, Isaac (Abravanel); Albo, Joseph; Duran, Profiat (Ephodi); Ibn Ezra, Abraham Ben Meir; Jashar (Yashar), Book of; Levi ben Gerson; Rashi (Rabbi Shelomoh ben Yishaq); Yesirah, Book of.

*BRUNS, JAMES EDGAR, M.A., S.T.D., S.S.L., Associate Professor of Theology and Scripture, St. Michael's College, University of Toronto, Ontario, Canada. **Articles:** Genealogy of Jesus; Judith, Book of; Judith, Canticle of.

*BRUSHER, JOSEPH STANISLAUS, SJ, S.T.L., Ph.D., Professor of History, University of Santa Clara, Santa Clara, Calif. **Articles:** Benedict XIII, Pope; Clement XII, Pope; Clement IX, Pope; Innocent X, Pope; Innocent XIII, Pope.

*BRYAN, ROBERT JOHN, CSSR, B.A., M.R.E., S.T.L., Philosophisch-theologische Hochschule, Trier, Germany. **Articles:** Depositio Martyrum; Martyrology of St. Jerome.

*BSTEH, PETRUS, Director, Kontaktstelle für Weltreligionen, Vienna, Austria. **Article:** König, Franz Borgia.

*BUCHER, OTTO NORMAN, OFMCap, A.B., S.T.L., Capuchin Seminary of Saint Anthony, Marathon, Wis. **Article:** Levites.

*BUCK, FIDELIS, SJ, S.T.L., S.S.D., Professor of Old Testament, Regis College, Willowdale, Ontario, Canada. **Articles:** David; Nathan.

*BUCKLEY, FRANCIS JOSEPH, SJ, S.T.D., Assistant Professor of Theology, University of San Francisco, Calif. **Articles:** Felix, Marcus Antonius; Festus, Porcius; Gregory of Elvira, St.; Pilate, Pontius.

*BUCKLEY, FRANCIS JOSEPH, SJ, S.T.D., Professor of Systematic and Pastoral

Theology, University of San Francisco. **Article:** Hofinger, Johannes.

*BUCKLEY, GERALD ALBERT, OP, S.T.L., S.T.Lr., Professor of Theology and Sacred Scripture, Dominican College of San Rafael, San Rafael, Calif. **Articles:** Blasphemy; Heresy, Sin of.

*BUCKLEY, JAMES CLEMENT, CSC, Ph.B., S.T.L., M.A., Instructor in Philosophy, University of Notre Dame, Notre Dame, Ind. **Articles:** Frohschammer, Jakob; Lipsius, Justus.

*BUCKLEY, JOHN MAURICE, OSA, M.A., J.C.D., Professor of Canon Law, Augustinian College, Washington, D.C.; Assistant Staff Editor for Canon Law, *New Catholic Encyclopedia,* The Catholic University of America, Washington, D.C. **Articles:** Barbosa, Agostino; Bartolo of Sassoferrato; Bernard of Parma; Burchard of Worms; Cabassut, Jean; Concubinage; Glossa Ordinaria; Laborans; Nerses Gratiosus (Snorhali); Nomocanon; Omnibonus (Omnebene); Potthast, August; Praepositus (Joannes de San Georgio); Quesnelliana Collectio.

*BUCKLEY, THOMAS WILLIAM, M.A., S.S.L., S.T.D., Associate Chaplain to the Roman Catholics, Harvard University and Radcliffe College, Cambridge, Mass.; Lecturer in Old Testament History, St. John's Seminary, Brighton, Mass. **Article:** Steuernagel, Carl.

*BUCZEK, DANIEL STEPHEN, Ph.D., Associate Professor of History, Fairfield University, Fairfield, Conn. **Articles:** Lietbert of Cambrai-Arras, St.; Louis d'Aleman, Bl.; Matthew of Albano; Palomar, John of; Poppo of Stavelot, St.; Theobald of Provins, St.; Ursulina Venerii, Bl.; Wazo of Liege.

*BUEHRLE, MARIE CECILIA, M.A., Chicago, Ill. **Articles:** Goretti, Maria, St.; Smet, Eugenie de, Bl.

*BUESCHER, GABRIEL NORBERT, OFM, S.T.D., Professor of Dogmatic Theology, St. Leonard College, Dayton, Ohio. **Article:** Faith, Beginning of.

*BUETOW, HAROLD ANDREW, Ph.D., Instructor in Education, The Catholic University of America, Washington, D.C. **Articles:** Lowell Plan; Poughkeepsie Plan.

*BUETOW, HAROLD ANDREW, School of Education, Catholic University of America, Washington, D.C. **Article:** Catholic Education Review.

*BUGARIN, G. MICHAEL, Director, Pope John Paul II Cultural Center, Washing-
ton, D.C. **Articles:** Pope John Paul II Cultural Center.

*BUGNINI, ANNIBALE, CM, S.T.D., Arch.Christ.Lic., Professor of Liturgy, Pontifical Urban University, Pontifical Institute of Sacred Music, Rome, Italy; Director, *Ephemerides Liturgicae;* Consultor, Sacred Congregation of Rites and Congregation for the Propagation of the Faith. **Article:** Tommasi, Giuseppe (Thomasius), Bl.

*BUI, THU, Ph.D. Vienna, Virgina. **Article:** Vietnam, Martyrs of, SS.

*BUKOVSKY, JOHN JAMES, SVD, S.T.L., S.S.L., Professor of Scripture, Divine Word Seminary, Techny, Ill. **Articles:** Patience (in the Bible); Suffering [part 1].

*BULL, GEORGE ANTHONY, M.A., OBE, FRSL, Director, Anglo-Japanese Economic Institute; Editor, *International Minds.* London, England. **Article:** Sistine Chapel, Restoration of.

*BULLOUGH, SEBASTIAN, OP, M.A., S.T.L., S.T.Lr., Teacher of Hebrew and Old Testament, Faculties of Divinity and Oriental Studies, University of Cambridge, England. **Articles:** Buckler, Reginald; Jarrett, Bede; McNabb, Vincent; Wilberforce, Bertrand.

*BULLOUGH, VERN L., Ph.D., Associate Professor of History, San Fernando Valley State College, Northridge, Calif. **Articles:** Adjutor, St.; Albert of Jerusalem, St.; Aubusson, Pierre d'; Baudrillart, Henri Marie Alfred; Fulk of Neuilly, Bl.; Guibert of Nogent; Haymarus Monachus; Morosini.

*BULTEAU, MARIE-GEORGES, M.A., S.T.L., S.S.L., Professor of Holy Scripture and Fundamental Dogmatic Theology, Major Seminary, Montreal, P.Q., Canada. **Article:** Poidebard, Antoine.

*BUNTER, ADELHELM, OFMCap, Dr.Phil., Teacher of Philosophy, College St. Fidelis, Stans (Diocese of Chur), Switzerland. **Article:** Florentini, Theodosius.

*BURBACH, MAUR RALPH, Very Rev., OSB, M.A., Ph.D., M.S.L., Professor of Philosophy and Rector of Immaculate Conception Seminary, Conception, Mo. **Article:** Benediction of the Blessed Sacrament.

*BURCH, FRANCIS FLOYD, SJ, Ph.L., M.A., S.T.L., Woodstock College, Woodstock, Md. **Article:** Old Deluder Satan Act.

*BURCH, MEINRAD, jeweller, artist, and art historian, Zurich, Switzerland. **Article:** Liturgical Art, History of, Pt 7: Liturgical Vessels.

*BURGHARDT, WALTER JOHN, SJ, M.A., Ph.L., S.T.D., Professor of Patrology and Patristic Theology, Woodstock College, Woodstock, Md.; Managing Editor, *Theological Studies;* Coeditor, *Woodstock Papers;* Coeditor, *Ancient Christian Writers;* President, The Patristic Academy of America. **Articles:** Cyril of Alexandria, St.; Fathers of the Church; Najran, Martyrs of; Patristic Studies; Weigel, Gustave.

*BURKE, DENNIS MAURICE, OPraem, S.T.D., J.C.D., President, St. Norbert College, West De Père, Wis. **Article:** Precepts, Canonical.

*BURKE, EDMUND, CP, St. Paul's Retreat, Mount Argus, Dublin, Ireland. **Article:** Possenti, Gabriel, St.

*BURKE, EUGENE M., CSP, S.T.L., Assistant Professor of Dogmatic Theology, School of Sacred Theology, The Catholic University of America, Washington, D.C. **Articles:** Dogmatic Theology; Grace (Theology of); Natural Order; Omniscience; Pure Nature, State of.

*BURKE, JOHN DE SALES, FPM, B.A. Hons., Higher Diploma in Education, Headmaster in Coláiste Chríost Rí, Cork, Ireland. **Article:** Presentation Brothers.

*BURKE, REDMOND A., Ph.D., School of Library Science, University of Wisconsin-Oshkosh, Oshkosh, Wis. **Article:** Archives, Ecclesiastical.

BURKHARD, JOHN J., OFMConv, S.T.L., Dr. Sc. Rel., Associate Professor of Systematic Theology, Washington Theological Union, Washington, D.C. **Articles:** Apostolicity; Sensus Fidelium; Subsidiarity in the Church.

*BURKLEY, FRANCIS JOSEPH, A.B., St. Mary's Church, Greenwich, Conn.; musicologist. **Articles:** Brahms, Johannes; Liturgical Music, History of, 8: Post-Romanticism; Mendelssohn-Bartholdy, Felix; Schoenberg, Arnold; Smetana, Bedrich.

*BURNETT, EUGENE DAVID, OFM, M.A., Teacher of History, Serra Catholic High School, Salem, Ore. **Articles:** Deyman, Clementine; Palou, Francisco; Pious Fund.

BURNETT, JOHN T., Ph.D., Adjunct Professor, Department of Religion and Religious Education, The Catholic University of America, Washington, D.C. **Article:** Barth, Karl.

*BURNS, JOHN VINCENT, CM, Ph.D., Professor of Philosophy, Niagara University, Niagara University, N.Y. **Article:** Cosmology.

*BURNS, ROBERT IGNATIUS, SJ, M.A. (Phil.), M.A. (Hist.), Ph.D., D. ès Sc.Hist. (Fribourg), Ph.L., S.T.L., Associate Professor of History, University of San Francisco, Calif. **Articles:** James II, King of Aragon; Oldegar, St.; Peter Nolasco, St.; Peter Gonzalez, St.; Sahagun, John of, St.

*BURNS, VINCENT MORTIMER, SJ, M.A., Ph.L., S.T.D., Professor of Moral and Pastoral Theology, Weston College, Weston, Mass. **Article:** Deus Scientiarum Dominus.

*BURRELL, DAVID B., CSC, Chairman, Department of Theology, University of Notre Dame. **Article:** Conservatism and Liberalism, Theological.

*BURRELL, SIDNEY ALEXANDER, Ph.D., Associate Professor of History, Barnard College, Columbia University, New York, N.Y. **Articles:** Cameron, John; Society for the Propagation of the Gospel.

*BURROUGHS, JOSEPH ALVIN, CM, Ph.D., Professor of Philosophy and Vice Rector, Cardinal Glennon College, St. Louis, Mo. **Articles:** Character; Indifferent Acts; Omission; Will Power.

BURROWS, WILLIAM R., Ph.D., Managing Editor of Orbis Books, Maryknoll, N.Y. **Articles:** Evangelii Nuntiandi; Evangelization of Peoples, Congregation for the; Zago, Marcello.

*BURRUS, ERNEST JOSEPH, SJ, M.A. (Philosophy), M.A. (Classics), Litt.D., Staff Historian, Jesuit Historical Institute, Rome, Italy; Vice Director, American Division, Jesuit Historical Institute, St. Louis University, St. Louis, Mo. **Article:** Marquette, Jacques.

*BURTCHAELL, JAMES TUNSTEAD, CSC, A.B., S.T.L., S.S.L., Ph.D., Professor of Theology, University of Notre Dame, Notre Dame, Ind. **Articles:** Anonymity and Pseudonymity; Glory (in the Bible); Shekinah; Theophany.

*BURTON, KATHERINE, Litt.D., Writer, Women's Editor, *The Sign*, and lecturer, Bronxville, N.Y. **Articles:** Carmelite Sisters—Carmelite Sisters Of Corpus Christi (OCarm); Daughters of Our Lady of Mercy; Drexel, Katharine Marie, St.

*BUSCHIAZZO, MARIO JOSÉ, Architect, Facultad de Arquitectura y Urbanismo, Buenos Aires, Argentina. **Article:** Muñoz, Vicente.

*BUSCHMILLER, ROBERT JOSEPH, Ph.L., S.T.D., Professor of Dogmatic Theology and Philosophy, Mt. St. Mary's of the West Seminary, Cincinnati, Ohio. **Article:** God, 2. In Christian Tradition.

*BUSH, JOHN WILLIAM, SJ, Ph.D., Associate Professor of History and Chairman of the Department of History and Political Science, Le Moyne College, Syracuse, N.Y. **Articles:** Boulay, César Égasse Du (Bulaeus); Marca, Pierre de; Retz, Jean François Paul de Gondi de.

*BUSHINSKI, LEONARD ANTHONY, CSSp, B.A., S.T.L., S.S.L., Associate Professor, Duquesne University, Pittsburgh, Pa. **Articles:** Dibelius, Martin; Gunkel, Hermann; Kittel, Gerhard; Loisy, Alfred; Nineveh; Spirit of God; Spirit (in the Bible).

BUTKOVICH, SISTER M. VIRGINIA, OSF, Ph.D., Archivist & Liturgist, Immaculate Conception Convent, West Peoria, Ill. **Article:** Franciscan Sisters—Sisters of St. Francis of the Immaculate Conception (OSF).

BUTLER, ANNE M., Ph.D., Editor, *Western Historical Quarterly*; Trustee Professor of History, Utah State University, Logan, Utah. **Article:** Utah, Catholic Church in.

*BUTLER, FRANCIS J., Ph.D., Associate Secretary for Domestic Social Development, USCC. **Article:** Call to Action Conference.

BUTLER, FRANCIS J., Executive Director, FADICA, Washington, D.C. **Article:** FADICA.

*BUTLER, LIONEL HARRY, M.A., D.Phil., Professor of Mediaeval History and Head of the Department, University of St. Andrews, Scotland. **Article:** Hospitallers and Hospital Sisters.

*BUTLER, RICHARD EDMUND, OP, A.B., Ph.L., S.T.Lr., Ph.D., Provincial Director of the Newman Apostolate for the Dominican Province of St. Albert the Great, St. Pius Priory, Chicago, Ill. **Article:** Santayana, George.

*BYERLY, BENJAMIN FRANKLIN, Ph.D., Assistant Professor of History, Colorado State College, Greeley, Colo. **Articles:** Alban, St.; Crumpe, Henry; Gildas, St.; John Le Romeyn.

*BYERLY, CATHERINE RIDDER, M.A., Colorado State College, Greeley, Colo. **Articles:** Bertrand of Aquileia, St.; Folcwin, St.; Honoratus of Amiens, St.; Irmgardis of Cologne, St.; Joan of Signa, Bl.; John of Bastone, Bl.; Justina of Arezzo, Bl.; Macarius Scottus, Bl.; Nauclerus, John.

*BYRNE, AIDEN, OSCO, Caldey Island Abbey, Tenby (Pens), England. **Article:** Caldey, Abbey of.

*BYRNES, ROBERT F., Ph.D., Professor of History, Indiana University, Bloomington, Ind. **Articles:** Alexander I, Emperor of Russia; Nicholas I, Emperor of Russia; Pobedonostev, Konstantin Petrovich.

*BYRON, JOSEPH FRANCIS, B.A., J.C.B., Catholic Chaplain, American University, Washington, D.C. **Article:** Cursillo Movement.

*CABANELAS RODRIGUEZ, DARÍO, OFM, Dr.Phil. and Letters, Professor of Arabic, University of Granada, Spain. **Articles:** John of Spain (Hispanus); Raymond of Sabunde.

*CABANISS, JAMES ALLEN, B.A., B.D., Ph.D., Presbyterian minister, Professor of History, University of Mississippi, University, Miss. **Articles:** Dance of Death; Hemma, Bl.; Irmengard, Bl.

*CADBURY, HENRY JOEL, Ph.D., Litt.D., D.D. (Hon.), L.H.D., Professor Emeritus of Divinity, Harvard University, Cambridge, Mass.; Lecturer at Pendle Hill and at various universities; Honorary Chairman, American Friends Service Committee. **Articles:** Friends, Religious Society of; Penn, William.

*CADORETTE, CURT, MM, Ph.D., John Henry Newman Associate Professor of Roman Catholic Studies, University of Rochester, New York. **Article:** Peru, the Catholic Church in.

*CAGGIANO, ANTONIO, His Eminence Cardinal Archbishop of Buenos Aires, Argentina. **Article:** Solano, Francis, St.

*CAHILL, JOHN MICHAEL, OP, S.T.D., Professor of Dogmatic Theology, Irish Dominican *Studium Generale,* St. Mary's, Tallaght, County Dublin, Ireland. **Article:** Emotion (Moral Aspect).

*CAHILL, PETER JOSEPH, SJ, M.A., Ph.L., S.T.D., Assistant Professor of Theology, West Baden Springs, Ind. **Articles:** Apologetics (History of) [part 1]; Demythologizing; Fundamental Theology.

*CAIMANO, SISTER ROSE AQUIN, OP, M.A., Teacher of French and Spanish, Dominican College of Blauvelt, Blauvelt, N.Y. **Article:** Dominican Sisters—Congregation of St Dominic (Blauvelt, NY).

*CALBRECHT, JOSEPH LEO, CICM, Doctor in Moral and Historical Sciences, Professor of Church History, Louvain, Belgium. **Article:** De Meester, Marie Louise, Mother.

*CALDECOTT, STRATFORD, Director, Centre for Faith & Culture, Plater College, Oxford, United Kingdom. **Article:** Centesimus Annus.

*CALDERONE, PHILIP JOSEPH, SJ, M.A., S.T.L., S.S.D., Professor of Scripture, San Jose Seminary and Jesuit Scholasticate, Manila, Philippine Islands. **Articles:** Fernandez Truyols, Andres; Ruth, Book of.

*CALDWELL, ROBERT A., Ph.D., Professor of English, University of North Dakota, Grand Forks, N.Dak. **Article:** Geoffrey of Monmouth.

*CALDWELL, THOMAS AUGUSTINE, SJ, Ph.L., S.T.L., S.S.L., University of Vienna, Austria. **Article:** Samaritans.

*CALHOUN, JOHN CHARLES, A.B., S.T.B., J.C.L., Assistant Chancellor, Diocese of Brooklyn, N.Y. **Article:** Censorship of Books (Canon Law).

*CALICCHIO, ISAAC JOGUES, OFM, M.A. Mount Alvernia Seminary, Wappingers Falls, N.Y. **Articles:** Innocent XII, Pope; Monarchia Sicula; Polignac, Melchior de.

CALIMAN, ARTHUR, CFX. **Article:** Xaverian Brothers.

*CALLAHAN, EDWARD REYNOLDS, SJ, M.A., Ph.L., S.T.D., Professor of Sacramental Theology, Weston College, Weston, Mass. **Article:** Conscience, 2. In the Bible.

*CALLAHAN, SISTER MARY GENEROSA, CDP, Ph.D., Professor of English and Chairman of the Department, Our Lady of the Lake College, San Antonio, Tex. **Articles:** Domenech, Emmanuel; Sisters of Divine Providence of Texas.

*CALLAHAN, NELSON JAMES, Notary in the Marriage Tribunal, Diocese of Cleveland; Teacher of Theology, St. John College of Cleveland, Cleveland, Ohio. **Article:** Houck, George Francis.

*CALLAHAN, ROBERT THOMAS, SS, M.A., S.T.L., Professor of Dogma, Liturgy, and Rubrics, St. John's Provincial Seminary, Plymouth, Mich. **Articles:** Andrieu, Michel; Breviary, Roman; Ceremonial of Bishops; Ordinals, Roman; Ordo, Roman.

*CALLAHAN, WILLIAM REED, SJ, M.A., Ph.D. **Article:** Gonzalez de Santalla, Tirso.

*CALLAN, MOTHER LOUISE, RSCJ, Ph.D., Professor of History and Sacred Doctrine, Maryville College of the Sacred Heart, St. Louis, Mo. **Articles:** Duchesne, Rose Philippine, St.; Galitzin, Elizabeth.

*CALLUS, DANIEL ANGELO, OP, Blackfriars, St. Giles, Oxford, England (deceased May 26, 1965). **Articles:** Adam of Buckfield; Correctoria; Forms, Unicity and Plurality of; Grosseteste, Pseudo-; John Blund; Richard Knapwell (Clapwell); Richard Fishacre; William de la Mare.

*CALVET, JEAN, Rt. Rev. (deceased Jan. 26, 1965). **Article:** Bremond, Henri.

*CALVEZ, JEAN-YVES, SJ, Editor, *Revue de l'Action Populoire;* Professor, Institut d'Études Politiques, and Director, Institut d'Études Sociales, Institut Catholique, Paris, France. **Article:** Social Justice.

*CAMACHO, ANGELO HENRY, OP, A.B., S.T.B., S.T.L., Los Padres Dominocos, Chimbote, Peru. **Articles:** Alvarez of Cordoba, Bl.; Andrew Abellon, Bl.; Giles of Santarem, Bl.; John of Salerno, Bl.

*CAMACHO, LUIS, Department of Philosophy, University of Costa Rica, Costa Rica. **Article:** Induction.

*CAMBELL, JACQUES, OFM, member, Liturgical Commission OFM, Pontificium Athenaeum Antonianum, Rome, Italy. **Articles:** Angelus Clarenus; Anthony Bonfadini, Bl.; Aubrac, Order of; Benvenutus Scotivoli, St.; Berard of Caribo and Companions, SS.; Bernard of Besse; Cheffontaines, Christophe de; Christopher Maccassoli, Bl.; Clareni; Guibert of Tournai; Humiliana de Circulis, Bl.; John Capistran, St.; John Lobedau, Bl.; Julian of Le Mans, St.; Leodegar of Autun, St.; Margaret Colonna, Bl.; Michael of Cesena; Mombritius, Boninus; Peter of Mogliano, Bl.; Philippa Mareri, Bl.; Ravaschieri, Balthasar, Bl.; Roch, St.; Salimbene; Thomas of Pavia; Vivald (Ubald), Bl.; Zierikzee, Cornelius of.

*CAMELI, LOUIS J., Director of Ongoing Formation of Priests, Archdiocese of Chicago, Chicago, Illinois. **Article:** Chicago, Archdiocese of.

*CAMELOT, PIERRE THOMAS, OP, Licencié ès lettres, S.T.D., S.T.M., Professor, Faculté Dominicaine de Théologie, Le Saulchoir, Etiolles (Oise-et-Seine), France. **Articles:** Anatolius of Constantinople; Chalcedon; Chalcedon, Council of; Ephesus, Council of; Ephesus, Robber Council of; Eutyches; Flavian, Patriarch of Constantinople, St.; Innocent I, Pope, St.; Liberius, Pope; Nestorianism; Nestorius; Siricius, Pope, St.; Theodotus of Ancyra; Virginity.

CAMERON-MOWAT, ANDREW, S.J. M.Div., S.T.L., Ph.D., Lecturer in Liturgy, Heythrop College, University of London, London, England **Article:** Liturgical History, III: Reformation to Vatican II.

*CAMPANA, JOSEPH HECTOR, SJ, A.B., M.S., Alma College, Los Gates, Calif. **Articles:** Castner, Gaspar; Genicot, Edouard; Grueber, Johannes; Gury, Jean Pierre; Hallerstein, Augustin von; Ravignan, Gustave Francois Xavier de; Rougemont, Francois; Tamburini, Michelangelo.

*CAMPBELL, DONALD ROBERT, Ph.D., Chairman, Department of History, University of San Francisco, San Francisco, Calif. **Articles:** Apostolici Regiminis; Carvajal; Carvajal, Gaspar de; Della Rovere; Gregory XIII, Pope; Julius II, Pope; Le Tellier, Charles Maurice; Le Tellier, Michel; Noailles, Louis Antoine de; Pius III, Pope; Schiner, Matthaus; Second Sophistic; Sixtus V, Pope; Vigerio, Marco.

*CAMPBELL, FRANCIS MICHAEL, M.A., Principal, Regis High School, Stayton, Ore. **Article:** Oregon, Catholic Church in.

*CAMPBELL, JAMES DOWNEY, OP, A.B., S.T.B., S.T.L., Professor of Philosophy and Theology, Marist College, Poughkeepsie, N.Y. **Articles:** Andrew of Longjumeau; James de Benefactis, Bl.

*CAMPBELL, JOHN LORNE, B.A., Diploma in Rural Economy, M.A., LL.D., D.Litt., folklorist and editor, Canna House, Isle of Canna, Scotland. **Articles:** MacDonald, Alexander; MacEachen, Evan.

*CAMPION, DONALD R., SJ, Editor-in-Chief, *America*, New York, N.Y. **Article:** Gardiner, Harold Charles.

*CAMPION, DONALD RICHARD, SJ, A.B., S.T.L., Ph.L., A.M., Ph.D., Executive Director, Fordham-Nativity Community Action and Research Project, New York, N.Y. **Article:** Capital Punishment.

CAMPION, MSGR. OWEN, Associate Publisher, *Our Sunday Visitor,* Huntington, Ind. **Article:** Tennessee, Catholic Church in.

*CAMPOS, LEOPOLDO JOSE, OFM, S.T.D., Cronista y Archivista, Provincia de S. Pedro y S. Pablo, Celaya, Mexico. **Article:** Gante, Pedro de.

*CANART, PAUL, Bach. en philosophie thomiste, S.T.B., Lic. phil. et lettres, Scriptor, Vatican Library, Vatican City, Italy. **Article:** Zigabenus, Euthymius.

*CANAVAN, FRANCIS, SJ, B.S., Ph.L., S.T.L., Ph.D., Associate Editor, *America,* New York, N.Y. **Article:** Burke, Edmund.

*CANEDO, LINO GÓMEZ, OFM, Hist.Eccl.D., Paleographer-Archivist (Rome), Research Scholar, Academy of American Franciscan History, Washington, D.C. **Articles:** Arricivita, Juan Domingo; Bolanos, Luis de; Cardenas, Bernardino de; Civezza, Marcellino da; Cordova y Salinas, Diego de; Espinar, Alonso de; Espinosa, Isidro Felix de; Marti, Mariano; Morales, Francisco de; Parras, Pedro Jose; Salinas y Cordova, Buenventura de; Torrubia, Jose.

*CANFIELD, FRANCIS XAVIER, Rt. Rev., M.A. (English), M.A. (Library Science), Ph.D., Rector and President, Sacred Heart Seminary, Detroit, Mich. **Articles:** Borgess, Gaspar Henry; Detroit, Archdiocese of; Michigan, Catholic Church in; Mooney, Edward Francis.

*CANGELOSI, PIUS RAYMOND, OP, B.A., Dominican House of Studies, Washington, D.C. **Article:** Gardeil, Ambroise.

*CANHAM, ERWIN DAIN, B.A., M.A., Editor in Chief, *The Christian Science Monitor,* Boston, Mass. **Article:** Christian Science (Church of Christ, Scientist).

*CANIVET, PIERRE, SJ, Docteur ès lettres Maître de Conférences (Patristique grecque), Institut Catholique, Paris, France. **Articles:** Epiphanius of Salamis, St.; Meletian Schism; Synesius of Cyrene; Theodoret of Cyr; Titus of Bostra.

*CANTLEY, MICHAEL JOSEPH, B.A., S.T.D., Assistant Professor of Theology, St.

Joseph's College for Women, Brooklyn, N.Y. **Articles:** Emmanuel; Messiah; Messianism.

*CANTWELL, DANIEL MICHAEL, M.A., chaplain to Catholic lay action organizations, Archdiocese of Chicago, Ill. **Article:** Friendship House.

*CAPLAN, HARRY, Ph.D., Goldwin Smith Professor of Classics, Cornell University, Ithaca, N.Y. **Article:** Ars Praedicandi.

*CAPLICE, RICHARD IGNATIUS, SJ, Ph.D., Woodstock College, Woodstock, Md. **Articles:** Assyria; Babylonia; Berossus; Mesopotamia, Ancient, 1. Geography; Nebo (Nabu); Philo of Byblos.

*CAPONIGRI, ALOYSIUS ROBERT, Ph.D., Professor of Philosophy, University of Notre Dame, Notre Dame, Ind. **Articles:** Bauch, Bruno; Brunschvicg, Leon; Croce, Benedetto; Gentile, Giovanni; Neo-Kantianism; Romanticism, Philosophical; Schelling, Friedrich Wilhelm Joseph von; Vico, Giambattista.

*CARAMAN, PHILIP, SJ, M.A. (Oxon.), F.R.S.L., Promoter of the Cause of the English and Welsh Martyrs, London, England. **Articles:** Campion, Edmund, St.; England, Scotland, and Wales, Martyrs of; Gerard, John; Southwell, Robert, St.; Thurston, Herbert; Weston, William.

*CARBINE, FRANCIS A., Assistant Professor English, Saint Charles Seminary, Overbrook, Philadelphia, Pa. **Article:** Brennan, Francis.

*CARDINAL, EDWARD VICTOR, CSV, Ph.D., St. Viator Parish, Chicago, Ill. **Articles:** Campeggio, Lorenzo; O'Neill, Sara Benedicta; Viatorians.

*CARGAS, HARRY J., Webster College, St. Louis, Mo. **Articles:** Mauriac, Francois; Tolkien, J. R. R.

CARIE, GILES G., OFMConv., STL, Associate Judge, Marriage Tribunal, Diocese of El Paso, El Paso, TX **Articles:** Age (Canon Law); Apostolic See; El Paso, Diocese of; Texas, Catholic Church in; Vicar Forane.

*CARILLO, JANUARIUS M., FSCJ, S.T.L., Professor and missionary, Yorkville, Ill. **Articles:** Comboni, Daniele, Bl.; Comboni Missionaries of the Heart of Jesus.

*CARLEN, SISTER M. CLAUDIA, IHM, A.M.L.S., Librarian, Marygrove College, Detroit, Mich.; Associate Editor,

The Pope Speaks; President, Catholic Library Association; Index Editor, *New Catholic Encyclopedia,* The Catholic University of America, Washington, D.C. **Article:** Encyclopedias and Dictionaries, Catholic.

*CARLEY, EDWARD BERNARD, S.T.L., Vice Officialis, Diocesan Tribunal, and Assistant Rector, St. Peter's Cathedral, Wilmington, Del. **Articles:** Becker, Thomas Andrew; Curtis, Alfred Allen; Delaware, Catholic Church in; Wilmington, Diocese of.

*CARLO, WILLIAM E., M.D., L.S.M., Ph.D., Associate Professor of Philosophy, Boston College, Chestnut Hill, Mass. **Article:** Possibility [part 1].

*CARMODY, CHARLES JOSEPH, M.A. (History), M.A. (Education), Assistant Professor of Theology, Loyola University, Chicago, Ill. **Articles:** Mrak, Ignatius; Vertin, John.

*CARMODY, FRANCIS JAMES, Ph.D., Professor of French, University of California at Berkeley, Calif. **Articles:** Bestiary; Physiologus.

*CARMODY, JAMES M., SJ, M.A., S.T.L., Gregorian University, Rome, Italy. **Articles:** Apotheosis; Homoousios; Hypostasis; Kenosis; Prone; Ransom; Theotokos.

*CARNEY, EDWARD JOHN, OSFS, M.A., S.T.D., Superior, House of Studies, De Sales Hall, Hyattsville, Md. **Articles:** Brisson, Louis Alexandre; Chantal, Jane Frances de, St.; Chappuis, Maria Salesia, Ven.; Free Will and Providence; Providence of God (Theology of).

*CAROL, JUNIPER BENJAMIN, OFM, S.T.D., Professor of Dogmatic Theology, Tombrock College, Paterson, N.J.; member, Pontifical International Mariology Commission; member, Pontifical Academy of Immaculate Conception. **Article:** Immaculate Conception, Missionary Sisters of the; Mary, Blessed Virgin, II (in Theology) [Mediatrix of All Graces].

*CARON, ARTHUR JAMES, OMI, Ph.D., S.T.D., D.C.L., LL.D., Professor of Canon Law and Vice Rector, University of Ottawa, Ontario, Canada. **Article:** Latin Rite.

*CARON, SISTER JACQUES DE COMPOSTELLE, WS, Editor, *Africa* (U.S.), *Soeurs Blanches* (Canada), *White Sisters* (England), *Hermanas Blancas* (Spain); Associate Editor, *Vivante Afrique*

(France and Belgium); Missionary Sisters of Our Lady of Africa, Rome, Italy. **Article:** Missionary Sisters of Our Lady of Africa.

*CARON, JEANNE, Licenciée ès lettres et Diplomée d'Études Supérieures d'Histoire, Professor of History, Sainte-Marie de Neuilly, and Université libre, Neuilly, France. **Articles:** Harmel, Leon; Sangnier, Marc.

*CARRIER, HERVÉ, S.J., S.T.L. Professor Emeritus of Sociology of Religion and Culture, Gregorian University, Rome. **Article:** Dezza, Paolo.

*CARRIERE, GASTON JOSEPH, OMI, Ph.L., Th.L., Professor, University of Ottawa, Ontario, Canada; Editor, *Revue de l'Université d'Ottawa;* historian of the Oblates in Canada. **Articles:** Canada, The Catholic Church in; Chiniquy, Charles Pascal; Grandin, Vital; Lacombe, Albert; Lauzon, Pierre de; LeLoutre, Jean Louis; Oblates of Mary Immaculate.

*CARRILLO, ELISA ANNA, Ph.D., Professor of History and Chairman of the Department, Marymount College, Tarrytown, N.Y.; Secretary, New York State Association of European Historians. **Articles:** Bonomelli, Geremia; Carnesecchi, Pietro; Figliucci Felix, (Filliucius); Garibaldi, Giuseppe; Gasperi, Alcide de; Toniolo, Giuseppe.

*CARROLL, MOTHER CATHERINE AGNES, RSCJ, B.Mus., B.S.M., M.M., Ph.D., AAGO, Professor of Music and Chairman of the Department, Manhattanville College of the Sacred Heart, Purchase, N.Y. **Articles:** Vierne, Louis Victor; Widor, Charles Marie.

*CARROLL, CATHERINE AGNES, RSC, Ph.D., A.A.G., Professor of Music, Manhattanville College, Purchase, N.Y. **Article:** Ward, Justine Bayard Cutting.

*CARROLL, EAMON RICHARD, OCarm, Ph.B., S.T.D., Associate Professor of Theology, and Director of the Summer Program in Mariology, The Catholic University of America, Washington, D.C. **Articles:** Albert of Trapani, St.; Aloysius Rabata, Bl.; Baptist of Mantua (Spagnoli), Bl.; Frances d'Amboise, Bl.; Franco Lippi, Bl.; Mary, Blessed Virgin, Queenship of; Mary, Blessed Virgin, Devotion to; Recapitulation in Christ; Soreth, John, Bl.

*CARROLL, EAMON RICHARD, Whitefriars Hall, Washington, D.C. **Article:** Mariology.

*CARROLL, JOHN FRANCIS, Lt. Col., U.S.A.R., M.A., Director, American Peoples Library and Educational Division, Grolier Educational Corporation, New York, N.Y. **Article:** Collier, Peter Fenelon.

*CARROLL, SISTER M. THOMAS AQUINAS, RSM, Ph.D., L.H.D., Mother General of the Congregation, Pittsburgh Sisters of Mercy, Diocese of Pittsburgh; President, Mount Mercy College, Pittsburgh, Pa. **Articles:** Anselm of Liège; Hadrian of Canterbury, St.; Warde, Mary Francis Xavier, Mother.

*CARROLL, THOMAS PATRICK, B.A., Assistant Pastor, Mary Queen of the Universe Parish, St. Louis, Mo. **Article:** Legion of Mary.

*CARSON, ROBERT E., OPraem, M.A., Teacher of Social Studies, Abbot Pennings High School, De Pere, Wis.; retreat master. **Articles:** Dutton, Joseph, Brother; Veuster, Joseph de (Fr. Damien), Bl.

CARSON, THOMAS EDWARD, Ph.D. Editor, Gale Publishing. Lecturer in History and Humanities, Wayne State University, Detroit, Michigan. **Articles:** Frederick I Barbarossa, Roman Emperor; Henry III, Roman Emperor; Mediaeval Academy of America; Popes, List of.

*CARTER, REV. MOTHER CELINE TERESA, CST, Superior General, Villa Teresa, Oklahoma City, Okla. **Article:** Carmelite Sisters—Carmelite Sisters of St. Therese of the Infant Jesus.

*CARTER, ELLEN DALE, A.B., Editorial Assistant to Staff Editor for Early Church History, *New Catholic Encyclopedia,* The Catholic University of America, Washington, D.C. **Articles:** Euphrasia, St.; Fabiola, St.; Innocent, St.; Mary of Egypt, St.; Maximillian, SS.; Moses the Black, St.; Paulicians.

*CARTHY, MOTHER MARY PETER, OSU, Ph.D., M.A. (Theology), Staff Editor for American Church History, *New Catholic Encyclopedia,* The Catholic University of America, Washington, D.C.; Professor of History, College of New Rochelle, New Rochelle, N.Y. **Articles:** Anchorage, Archdiocese of; New York, Catholic Church in; Purcell, John Baptist.

CARTY, THOMAS J., Ph.D., Assistant Professor, Springfield College, Springfield, Mass. **Article:** Connecticut, Catholic Church in.

*CARVER, JAMES EDWARD, Ph.D., Professor of English and Chairman of the Division of Languages and Literature, St. Andrews College, Laurinburg, N.C. **Article:** Preaching (Medieval English).

*CASALANDRA, SISTER M. ESTELLE, OP, M.A., Professor of English, Albertus Magnus College, New Haven, Conn. **Article:** Margaret of Savoy, Bl.

*CASEY, THOMAS FRANCIS, Eccl.Hist.D., Professor of Church History, St. John's Seminary, Brighton, Mass.; Chaplain, Catholic Graduates Club of Greater Boston. **Articles:** Boston, Archdiocese of; Couderc, Marie Victoire Therese, Bl.; Cowley Fathers; Della Somaglia, Giulio Maria; Fenwick, Benedict Joseph; Garin, Andre; Jugan, Jeanne, Bl.; Leo XI, Pope; Leo XII, Pope; Little Missionary Sisters of Charity; Lourdes; Matignon, Francis Anthony; O'Callaghan, Jeremiah; Orione, Luigi, Bl; Paul V, Pope; Pius VIII, Pope; Soubirous, Bernadette, St.; Thayer, John; Vianney, Jean Baptiste Marie, St.

*CASEY, WILLIAM VAN ETTEN, SJ, M.A., S.T.L., Professor of Theology, Holy Cross College, Worcester, Mass. **Article:** Megiddo.

*CASPER, HENRY WEBER, SJ, S.T.L., Ph.D., Professor of History, Marquette University, Milwaukee, Wis. **Articles:** Creighton; Flanagan, Edward Joseph; Omaha, Archdiocese of.

*CASSESE, JOHN-MARIE, OFM, M.A., Provincial Curia, Franciscan Province of the Immaculate Conception, New York, N.Y. **Article:** Ruiz Blanco, Matias.

*CASSIDY, SISTER MARY BRIGH, OSF, M.S.N.Ed., M.B.A., Administrator, St. Marys Hospital, Rochester, Minn.; Part-time Instructor, St. Marys School of Nursing, Rochester, and College of St. Teresa, Winona, Minn. **Article:** Dempsey, Mary Joseph, Sister.

*CASTANHO DE ALMEIDA, LOUIZ, Rt. Rev., Sorocaba, Sãamo Paulo, Brazil. **Article:** Feijo, Diogo Antonio.

*CASTELOT, JOHN JOSEPH, SS, M.A., S.S.L., S.T.D., Professor of Sacred Scripture and Sacred Music, St. John's Provincial Seminary, Plymouth, Mich. **Articles:** Gentiles; Peter, Apostle, St.; Van Noort, Gerard.

*CASTILLERO, ERNESTO DE JESUS, Professor Emeritus of History, one-time Director General of Education, and Director of the National Library, Panama, Republic of Panama. **Articles:** Lasso de la Vega, Rafael; Panama, The Catholic Church in; Quevedo, Juan de.

CATALDO, PETER J., Ph.D., Director of Research, The National Catholic Bioethics Center, Boston, Mass. **Article:** Anovulants (Moral Aspect).

*CATTA, ETIENNE RENÉ, Docteur ès lettres, Honorary Canon of Nantes; Professor, Catholic University of Angers, France. **Article:** Angers.

*CATURELLI, ALBERTO, Ph.D., Professor of Medieval Philosophy and Philosophy of History, University of Córdoba, Argentina. **Article:** Esquiu, Mamerto.

*CAUCHY, VENANT, D.Phil., Professor of Philosophy and Secretary of the Faculty of Philosophy, University of Montreal, Canada; Editor, *Dialogue*. **Articles:** Epicureanism; Epicurus; Skepticism; Stoicism [part 1].

*CAVANAUGH, BRENDAN R., B.A., Washington, D.C. **Articles:** Agnelli, Giuseppe; Alfonso de Castro; Amelry, Francis; Anthony of the Holy Ghost; Cerbonius, St.; Constantius of Fabriano, Bl.; Deodatus of Blois, St.; Eparchius, St.; Eptadius, St.; Florinus, St.; Gerold, St.; Gerulf, St.; Gislenus, St.; Gregory of Einsiedeln, Bl.; Gudwal, St.; James Salomonius, Bl.; James of Bevagna, Bl.; Nicholas Paglia, Bl.; Orozco y Jimenez, Francisco; Orozco, Alfonso de, Bl.; Peter of Tiferno (Capucci), Bl.; Saint-Maximin, Abbey of; Venturino of Bergamo; William de Hothum; Wirt, Wigand.

*CAVERT, SAMUEL MCCREA, Bronxville, N.Y. **Article:** National Council of the Churches of Christ in the U.S.A.

*CAYER, SISTER LOUIS-RICHARD, SGC, B.A., Business Manager, St. Joseph's Hospital, Lowell, Mass. **Article:** Grey Nuns.

*CAZEAUX, ISABELLE ANNE-MARIE, M.A., M.S. in Library Service, Ph.D. in Musicology, Professor of Music History and Musicology, Bryn Mawr College, Bryn Mawr, Pa. **Articles:** Compére, Loyset; Gombert, Nicolas; Goudimel, Claude; Janequin, Clement; Sermisy, Claude de.

*CENKNER, WILLIAM, OP, S.T.L., Ph.D., Dean, School of Religious Studies, The Catholic University of America, Washington, D.C. **Article:** Eliade, Mircea.

*CENTURION, CARLOS ROBERTO, writer; formerly Professor of Philosophy of

Law, Sociology, and Public International Law, Asunción, Paraguay. **Article:** Paraguay, The Catholic Church in.

*CEROKE, CHRISTIAN PAUL, OCarm, S.T.D., Associate Professor, Department of Religious Education, The Catholic University of America, Washington, D.C. **Articles:** Mark, Evangelist, St.; Mary, Blessed Virgin, I (in the Bible); Parousia, 1. In the Bible.

*CEROKE, CHRISTIAN PAUL, OCarm., S.T.D. Professor, Dept. of Religion and Religious Education, The Catholic University of America, Washington, D.C. **Articles:** Biblical Theology; Resurrection of Christ, 1. In the New Testament.

*CERULLI, ENRICO, LL.D., Ph.D. (h.c.), Ambassador of Italy, Counselor of State, Rome, Italy. **Article:** Frumentius, St.

*CERVANTES, LUCIUS FERDINAND, SJ, Ph.D., Associate Professor of Sociology and Anthropology, St. Louis University, St. Louis, Mo.; member, Executive Council, American Catholic Sociological Society, and Advisory Board, Family Life Bureau, NCWC. **Article:** Woman.

CESSARIO, ROMANUS, OP, S.T.D., Professor of Theology, St. John's Seminary, Brighton, Mass. **Articles:** Casuistry; Consequentialism.

*CEVETELLO, JOSEPH F. X., B.A., Chaplain and Instructor in Theology, Villa Walsh, Morristown, N.J. **Article:** Purgatory [part 1].

*CEYSSENS, LUCIEN, OFM, Hist.Eccl.D., Professor of Ecclesiastical History, Brussels, Belgium. **Articles:** Boonen, Jacques; Calenus, Henri; Chigi; Du Pac de Bellegarde, Gabriel; Gerberon, Gabriel; Sinnich, John; Triest, Antoine.

*CHADWICK, HENRY, M.A., D.D., Hon. D.D., Canon of Christ Church and Regius Professor of Divinity, University of Oxford, England. **Articles:** Justin Martyr, St.; Sextus, Sentences of.

*CHADWICK, WILLIAM OWEN, D.D., Hon. D.D., Professor of Church History, University of Cambridge, England. **Articles:** Bucer, Martin (Butzer); Poissy, Conference of.

*CHALLENOR, JOHN, M.A., B.D., priest of the Birmingham Oratory; Head, Department of Religion, St. Philip's

Grammar School, Birmingham, England. **Articles:** Almici, Camillo; Grassi, Anthony, Bl.; Neri, Philip, St.; Valfre, Sebastian, Bl.; Vignier, Jerome.

*CHAMPAGNE, ANTOINE J. L., CRIC, S.T.D., historian, Tache Hospital, St. Boniface, Mantioba, Canada. **Articles:** Provencher, Joseph Norbert; Tache, Alexandre Antonin.

*CHAN, ALBERT, SJ, Ph.D., Wah Yan College, Hong Kong, China. **Article:** Wu Li.

*CHANEY, WILLIAM A., Ph.D., George McKendree Steele Associate Professor of History, Lawrence University, Appleton, Wis. **Articles:** Aelfric Grammaticus; Aelfric of Canterbury, St.; Alphege of Winchester, St.; Ealdred (Aldred) of York; Ethelhard (Aethelheard) of Canterbury; Ethelnoth (Aethelnoth) of Canterbury, St.; Ethelwold of Winchester, St.; Grimbald, St.; Oswald of York, St.; Plegmund of Canterbury; Whitby, Abbey of.

*CHANTRAINE, GEORGES, SJ, Professor of Church History and Dogmatic Theology, Faculté SJ de Théologie, Belgium. **Articles:** Balthasar, Hans Urs von; Lubac, Henri de.

*CHAPIN, JOHN, M.A; literary agent, New York, N.Y. **Articles:** Agapetus I, Pope, St.; Benedict I, Pope; Boniface I, Pope, St.; Callistus I, Pope, St.; Cornelius, Pope, St.; Dioscorus, Antipope; Felix IV, Pope, St.; Felix III, Pope, St.; Gelasius I, Pope, St.; Hilary, Pope, St.; Hormisdas, Pope, St.; John I, Pope, St.; John III, Pope; John II, Pope; Julius I, Pope, St.; Mark, Pope, St.; Miltiades, Pope, St.; Pelagius II, Pope; Silverius, Pope, St.; Simplicius, Pope, St.; Sixtus III, Pope, St.; Sylvester I, Pope, St.; Symmachus, Pope, St.; Zosimus, Pope, St.

CHAPPELL, PATRICIA, SNDdeN, President, National Black Sisters' Conference, Washington, D.C. **Article:** National Black Sisters' Conference.

*CHARANIS, PETER, Ph.D., Voorhees Professor of History and Chairman of the Department, Rutgers University, New Brunswick, N.J. **Articles:** Constans II Pogonatus, Byzantine Emperor; Constantine IV, Byzantine Emperor; Constantine V, Byzantine Emperor; George Syncellus; Leo III, Byzantine Emperor; Procopius of Caesarea; Theophanes the Confessor, St.

*CHATHAM, JOSIAH GEORGE, Rt. Rev., Ph.B., J.C.D., Pastor, St. Richard's

Parish, Jackson, Miss. **Article:** Force and Fear (Canon Law).

*CHATILLON, JEAN, Docteur en théologie, Ph.L., Licencié ès lettres (Philosophie), Professor, Grand Séminaire, Metz, France; Professor and Dean of the Faculty of Philosophy, Institut Catholique, Paris, France. **Article:** Achard of Saint-Victor.

*CHAUVET, FIDEL DE JESÚS, OFM, Ph.D., Professor of Philosophy and Theology; President, Comisión Mariana Franciscana de México, Mexico City, Mexico. **Articles:** Aparicio, Sebastian de, Bl.; Zumarraga, Juan de.

*CHAUVIN, SISTER MARY JOHN OF CARMEL, SSA, Ph.D., Dean of Students and Head of English Department, Anna Maria College, Paxton, Mass. **Article:** St. Anne, Sisters of.

*CHAVEZ, ANGELICO, OFM, B.A., M.A. (h.c.), St. Joseph Church, Cerillos, N.Mex. **Articles:** Lamy, John Baptist; Santa Fe, Archdiocese of.

*CHENEY, BRAINARD, free-lance writer, Smyrna, Tenn. **Article:** O'Connor, Mary Flannery.

*CHERESO, CAJETAN JAMES, OP, Ph.L., S.T.D., Assistant Professor of Theology, College of St. Thomas, St. Paul, Minn. **Articles:** Exemplarity of God; Image of God.

*CHEVALLIER, PIERRE, Diplôme d'Études Supérieures d'Histoire, Docteur ès lettres, Professeur agregé d'histoire, Lycée de Troyes, France. **Article:** Commission of Regulars.

CHIA, EDMUND, FSC, M.A., Executive Secretary, Office of Ecumenism and Interreligious Affairs, Federation of Asian Bishops' Conferences. **Article:** Malaysia, the Catholic Church in.

*CHIASSON, ELIAS JOSEPH, Ph.D., Associate Professor of English, St. Louis University, St. Louis, Mo. **Article:** Swift, Jonathan.

*CHIBNALL, MARJORIE MCCALLUM, D.Phil. (Oxford), Ph.D. (Cantab.), Fellow, Lecturer, and Director of Studies in History, Girton College, Cambridge, England. **Articles:** Florence of Worcester; Haimo of Landecop, Bl.; Henry of Blois; John Gilbert; Ralph of Diceto; Richard of Canterbury; Theobald of Etampes; William of Newburgh; William de Montibus.

*CHINEWORTH, SISTER MARY ALICE, OSP, M.A., Registrar and Instructor in Psy-

chology, Mount Providence Junior College, Baltimore, Md. **Article:** Oblate Sisters of Providence.

*CHINI, SILVIO JOSEPH, OSJ, Litt.D., Catholic Journalist, Pittston, Pa. **Article:** Oblates of St. Joseph.

CHINNICI, JOSEPH PATRICK, O.F.M., D.Phil.Oxon., Professor of Church History, Franciscan School of Theology, Graduate Theological Union, Berkeley, Calif. **Article:** Bentivoglio, Maria Maddalena.

*CHIOVARO, FRANCESCO PAOLO, CSSR, Eccl.Hist.D., Lic. Sci.Soc., Palaeographer and Archivist; Professor of Ecclesiastical History, Pontifical University of St. Thomas, Rome, Italy. **Articles:** Apollinarianism; Athanasius I, Patriarch of Constantinople; Caesarius of Nazianzus, St.; Cassian, John (Johannes Cassianus); Elias of Thessalonika, St.; Glycas, Michael; Gregory II Cyprius, Patriarch of Constantinople; John the Almsgiver, St.; John XIV Calecas, Patriarch of Constantinople; Joseph I, Patriarch of Constantinople; Macarius of Pelecete, St.; Metochites, George; Metrophanes Critopoulos; Michael III, Patriarch of Constantinople; Paul IV, Patriarch of Constantinople, St.; Paulus Euergetinos; Peter Grossolano; Philotheus Coccinus, Patriarch of Constantinople; Planudes, Maximus; Plethon, Gemistos; Presbyter [part 2]; Proterius, Patriarch of Alexandria, St.; Relics; Sozomen; Theodore of Rhaithu; Timothy Aelurus, Monophysite Patriarch; Waal, Anton Maria de.

*CHIRAT, HENRI, Dr.Theol., Dr. ès sciences ecclésiastiques orientales, Maître de conférence, Faculté de Théologie Catholique, University of Strasbourg, France. **Articles:** Acacian Schism; Cross, Finding of the Holy; Cyril of Scythopolis; Leo V, Byzantine Emperor; Leo I, Byzantine Emperor; Marcian, Byzantine Emperor; Theonas of Alexandria, St.

*CHIRICO, PETER FRANCIS, SS, B.A., S.T.D., Professor of Fundamental Theology, St. Thomas Seminary, Kenmore, Wash. **Articles:** Article of Faith; Deposit of Faith; Holiness of the Church; Robert, Andre; Triumphalism; Unicity of the Church; Unity of Faith; Vigouroux, Fulcran Gregoire; Visibility of the Church.

*CHOUX, JACQUES, priest of the Diocese of Nancy; Diplomé de l'École pratique des Hautes Études, Paris; Conservateur

du Musée Historique Lorrain, and Conservatur des Antiquités et objets d'art de Meurthe-et-Moselle, Nancy, France. **Articles:** Aper (Evre) of Toul, St.; Flavigny-sur-Moselle, Abbey of; Gauzelin of Toul, St.; Gerard of Toul, St.; Ludanus, St.; Murbach, Abbey of; Niedermunster (Alsace), Convent of; Remiremont, Abbey of; Saint-Mihiel, Abbey of; Verdun-Sur-Meuse, Abbey of.

*CHRISTENSEN, ALICE MARGARET, Ph.D., Professor of History, Our Lady of the Lake College, San Antonio, Tex. **Articles:** Castro, Mateo de; Eckart, Anselm von; Rinaldi, Odorico (Raynaldus).

CHRISTIANSEN, DREW, SJ, Ph.D., Counselor for International Affairs, United States Conference of Catholic Bishops; Senior Fellow, Woodstock Theological Center, Georgetown University, Washington, D.C. **Article:** War, Morality of.

*"CHRISTOPHERS, THE", New York, N.Y. **Article:** Keller, James G.

*CHRYSOSTOMUS BLASCHKEWITZ, JOHANNES, OSB, S.T.D., monk of the Monastery of Nieder-Altaich, Lower Bavaria, Germany; Ökumenisches Institut, Lower Bavaria, Germany. **Article:** Russia, The Catholic Church in.

*CHUDOBA, BOHDAN, Ph.D., Ph. et Lit.D., Professor of History, Iona College, New Rochelle, N.Y. **Articles:** Amalric of Bene; Amalricians; Brothers and Sisters of the Free Spirit; Heresy, History of, 2. Medieval Period; Picards.

CHUMSRIPHAN, SURACHAI, STD, Professor of Church History, Lux Mundi College, Major Seminary, Bangkok, Thailand. **Article:** Thailand, the Catholic Church in.

CHWALEK, ADELE R., M.S.L.S., Director of Libraries, The Catholic University of America, Washington, D.C. **Article:** Catholic Library Association.

CIFERNI, ANDREW D., O.Praem., S.T.L., Ph.D., *Praeses* of the Premonstratensian Commission on Canonical Life and Spirit of the Order; Liturgy Director and Rector, Daylesford Abbey Church, Paoli, Pa.; Executive Committee of the Catholic Academy of Liturgy. **Articles:** Premonstratensian Rite; Premontre, Monastery of.

*CIUBA, EDWARD JOSEPH, S.T.L., S.S.L., Professor of Sacred Scripture, Immaculate Conception Seminary, Darlington, N.J. **Articles:** Blood Vengeance; Kingship in the Ancient Near East; Ordeal [part 2].

*CIUBA, GARRY M., Ph.D., Associate Professor of English at Kent State University, Warren, OH. **Article:** Percy, Walker.

*CLANCY, PATRICK MICHAEL JAMES, OP, A.B., S.T.Lr., J.C.D., S.T.M., Associate Professor of Philosophy, Loras College, Dubuque, Iowa. **Article:** Fast and Abstinence.

*CLANCY, THOMAS HANLEY, SJ, M.A., S.T.L., Ph.D., Professor of Political Science, Loyola University, New Orleans, La. **Articles:** Douai (Douay); Martiall (Marshall), John; Preston, Thomas (Roger Widdrington); St. Omer, College of; Worthington, Thomas.

CLARAHAN, MARY ANN, RSHM, M.A., Annunciation Convent, Gwynedd Valley, Pa. **Article:** Litany.

*CLARE, MARY, St. Benedict Center, Still River, Mass. **Article:** Feeney, Leonard.

*CLARK, AUBERT JACQUES, OFMConv, S.T.L., Dip.Ed. (Oxford), Ph.D., Assistant Dean, Graduate School of Arts and Sciences, The Catholic University of America, Washington, D.C. **Articles:** Abraham of Sancta Clara; Bernieres-Louvigny, Jean de; Elbel, Benjamin; Herincx, William; Hess, Bede Frederick; Lejeune, Jean; Willmann, Otto.

*CLARK, DOUGLAS K., S.T.L., Editor, *The Southern Cross*, Savannah, Georgia. **Article:** Evangelium vitae.

CLARK, DOUGLAS K., S.T.L., Editor, *The Southern Cross*, Savannah, Ga. **Articles:** Atlanta, Archdiocese of; Beasley, Mother Mathilda; Georgia, Catholic Church in; Savannah, Diocese of.

*CLARK, EUGENE VINCENT, Ph.D., Teacher, Cardinal Spellman High School, New York, N.Y. **Article:** Taylor, Jeremy.

*CLARK, JOSEPH THOMAS, SJ, Ph.L., S.T.L., Ph.D., Associate Professor of Philosophy, Canisius College, Buffalo, N.Y. **Article:** Gassendi, Pierre.

*CLARK, PHILIP KNOWLTON, SJ, M.A., Alma College, Los Gatos, Calif. **Articles:** Sa, Manoel; Saint-Jure, Jean Baptiste; Viva, Domenico.

*CLARKE, THOMAS EMMET, SJ, Ph.L., S.T.D., Professor of Dogmatic Theology, Woodstock College, Woodstock, Md. **Articles:** Consubstantiality; Created Actuation by Uncreated Act; Hypostatic Union, Grace of; Incommunicability; Subsistence (in Christology).

*CLASEN, SOPHRONIUS ANTON, OFM, Dr.Theol., Dr.Phil., Lector in Church History, History of the Franciscan Order and Patrology, Johannes-Duns-Skotus-Akaademie, München-Gladbach, Germany. **Articles:** Anthony of Padua, St.; Poverty Controversy; Poverty Movement.

*CLAYTON, CHARLES MURRAY, priest of the Diocese of Alexandria, La.; Editor, *North-Central Louisiana Register*, and Director of the Information Bureau. **Article:** Alexandria, Diocese of.

*CLEARY, DENIS ANTHONY, IC, S.T.L., Ph.D., Director of Studies, English Province Theologate, Institute of Charity, St. Mary's, Derrys Wood, Wonersh, Guildford, Surrey, England. **Article:** Ontologism.

CLEARY, DENIS ANTHONY, S.T.L., Ph.D., Director, Rosmini House, Durham, United Kingdom. **Article:** Rosmini-Serbati, Antonio.

*CLEARY, JOHN MARTIN, B.A. Headmaster, St. Joseph's Secondary School, Wrexham, Wales. **Article:** Clenock, Maurice (Clynnog).

CLEMENT, CAROL DORR, Ph.D., Lecturer, Washington Theological Union, Washington, D.C. **Articles:** Catholic Daughters of the Americas; Duffy, Mary C.; Marks, Miriam.

*CLERCX-LEJEUNE, SUZANNE, Docteur en Histoire de l'Art et Philologie, Professor, University of Liège, Belgium. **Article:** Ciconia, Johannes.

CLIFFORD, ANNE, CSJ, Ph.D., Associate Professor of Theology, Duquesne University, Pittsburgh, Pa. **Articles:** Ecofeminism and Ecofeminist Theology; Feminism; Feminist Hermeneutic.

*CLIFFORD, SISTER ELIZABETH ANN, OLVM, M.A. (Liturgy), member, General Council, Our Lady of Victory Missionary Sisters, Huntington, Ind.; Instructor in Liturgy, Victory Noll Junior College. **Article:** Our Lady of Victory Missionary Sisters.

*CLIFFORD, SISTER MARY DORITA, BVM, Ph.D., Chairman, Department of History, and Director of Non-Western Studies, Clarke College, Dubuque, Iowa. **Article:** Harty, Jeremiah James.

*CLINCH, THOMAS ANTHONY, Ph.D., Associate Professor of History and Head of the Department, Carroll College, Helena, Mont. **Articles:** Carroll, John Patrick; Montana, Catholic Church in.

*CLOONEY, DAVID, Rector, St. Josaphat Ukrainian Catholic Seminary, Washington, D.C. **Article:** Slavorum apostoli.

*CLOSS, ALOIS, Dr.Phil. University Professor with special emphasis on Comparative Religion, University of Graz, Austria. **Articles:** Ancestor Worship; Blood, Religious Significance of; Dead, Worship of the; Nudity; Reitzenstein, Richard; Sacrifice, I (Human).

*CLUNE, JOSEPH THOMAS, Rt. Rev., Ph.D. (Louvain), Lecturer, Good Counsel College, White Plains, N.Y.; Director, Westchester Catholic Hour, New York (deceased May 27, 1964). **Article:** Dominican Sisters—Congregation of St Rose of Lima (The Servants of Relief for Incurable Cancer in the US, Hawthorne, NY).

CO, S. MARIA ANICIA BATION, RVM, M.A., S.T.D. Lecturer at Maryhill School of Theology, Loyola School of Theology, San Carlos Seminary, Institute of Formation and Religious Studies, Philippines. **Article:** Acts of the Apostles.

*CODE, JOSEPH BERNARD, Rt. Rev., Docteur en sciences historiques, Keokuk, Iowa. **Article:** Lalor, Teresa, Mother.

*CODY, AELRED, OSB, Collegio di Sant' Anselmo, Rome, Italy. **Article:** Tappouni, Ignatius Gabriel.

*CODY, AELRED, OSB, S.T.D., S.S.D., St. Meinrad Archabbey, St. Meinrad, Ind. **Article:** Worship (in the Bible).

CODY, MSGR. JOHN K., J.C.L., Judge, Tribunal of the Diocese of Columbus; Columbus, Ohio. **Article:** Clerical Dress (Canon Law).

*CODY, SISTER PATRICIA, MMB, B.A., M.A., Mission Directress for Elementary Schools, Diocese of Kansas City—St. Joseph, Kansas City, Mo. **Article:** Mercedarian Missionaries of Berriz.

*COFFEY, JAMES REGINALD, OP, Dominican House of Studies, Washington, D.C. **Articles:** Callan, Charles Jerome; Monsabre, Jacques Marie.

*COFFEY, SISTER LOYOLA MARIA, SSJ, Ph.D., Professor of Theology and French and Academic Dean, Chestnut Hill College, Chestnut Hill, Pa. **Articles:** Amabilis, St.; Desiderius of Langres, St.; Perpetuus of Tours, St.; Victurius of Le Mans, St.; Volusianus of Tours, St.

*COGAN, PATRICK, SA, S.T.L., Ph.D., J.C.D., Executive Coordinator, Canon Law Society of America, Washington, D.C. **Article:** Horgan, Thaddeus Daniel.

*COGNET, LOUIS JEAN, S.T.D., Professor, Institut Catholique, Paris, France. **Articles:** Acceptants; Ad Sanctam Beati Petri Sedem; Appellants; Auctorem fidei; Augustinus; Comma Pianum; Cum Occasione; Ex Omnibus Afflictionibus; Jansen, Cornelius Otto (Jansenius); Port-Royal; Quesnel, Pasquier (Paschase); Regiminis apostolici; Richer, Edmond; Unigenitus.

*COHALAN, FLORENCE DERMOT, Very Rev., M.A., Professor of History, Cathedral College, New York, N.Y. **Articles:** Brann, Henry Athanasius; Connolly, John; Cummings, Jeremiah Williams; Delany, Selden Peabody; Duffy, Francis Patrick; Farley, John Murphy; Hayes, Patrick Joseph; Hughes, John Joseph; Lavelle, Michael Joseph; Moore, Edward Roberts; Power, John; Preston, Thomas Scott; Smith, John Talbot.

*COHEN, NOAH JUDAH, Ph.D., consultant in linguistics, U.S. Government, Washington, D.C. **Articles:** Acosta, Gabriel (Uriel); Crescas, Hasdai ben Abraham; Gikatilla, Joseph ben Abraham; Isaac ben Abraham; Luria, Isaac.

*COLBERT, EDWARD PAUL, Ph.D., Staff Editor for General Church History and Cartography, *New Catholic Encyclopedia,* The Catholic University of America, Washington, D.C.; Assistant Professor of History, St. John's University, New York, N.Y. **Articles:** Adelelm of Burgos, St.; Albornoz, Gil Alvarez Carrillo de; Alvaro Pelayo; Argimir, St.; Attilanus, St.; Aurea of Cordoba, St.; Aurelius and Sabigotona, SS.; Beauvais; Biondo, Flavio; Cabrol, Fernand; Carthage; Chartres [History]; Columba and Pomposa, SS.; Constance, Council of [part 1]; Didacus of Alcala, St.; Dominic of Silos, St.; Este; Florentina, St.; Florez, Enrique; Froilan, St.; Fulgentius of Ecija, St.; Gaetani (Caetani); Gams, Pius; Garcia of Toledo; Garcia Villada, Zacarias; Gennadius of Astorga, St.; Herrera y Tordesillas, Antonio de; Hydatius; Irene of Portugal, St.; John of Biclaro; Julian of Cuenca, St.; Justus of Urgel, St.; Martin of Leon, St.; Maximus of Sara-

gossa, St.; Merida; Morocco, The Catholic Church in; Peter Pascual, St.; Peter Armengol, Bl.; Pistoia; Quarr Abbey; Spain, 2. Medieval; Theresia, Bl.; Thomar (Tomar), Monastery of; Valentinian III, Roman Emperor; Victor of Tunnuna.

*COLBORN, FRANCIS, St. Johns Seminary, Camarillo, Ca. **Article:** Grace (Theology of).

*COLE, RUSSAN LAWRENCE, OFMConv, S.T.L., M.A., Professor of, and Lecturer on, Moral Theology, Assumption Seminary, Chaska, College of St. Catherine, and College of St. Thomas, St. Paul, Minn. **Article:** Zeal.

*COLE, WILLIAM JOSEPH, SM, S.T.D., Associate Professor of Theology, University of Dayton, Dayton, Ohio. **Article:** Mary, Blessed Virgin, II (in Theology) [Spiritual Maternity of Mary].

*COLEMAN, JAMES WALTER, Ph.D., Rust College, Holly Springs, Miss. **Articles:** Garesche, Julius Peter; Knights of Labor.

*COLEMAN, JOHN A., SJ, Jesuit School of Theology at Berkeley, Berkeley, Cal. **Article:** Theology and Sociology.

*COLEMAN, WILLIAM JACKSON, MM, Ph.D., Instructor in History, Maryknoll College, Glen Ellyn, Ill. **Articles:** Byrne, Patrick James; Ford, Francis Xavier; Muzi, Giovanni.

*COLERIDGE, MSGR. MARK, S.S.D., Official of the First Section (General Affairs), Secretariat of State, Vatican City. **Article:** Domus Sanctae Marthae.

*COLESS, GABRIEL M., OSB, St. Mary's Abbey, Norristown, N.J. **Article:** Liturgical History, IV: Vatican II's Program of Liturgical Reform.

*COLGRAVE, BERTRAM, M.A., D.Litt., Emeritus Reader in English, University of Durham, England. **Articles:** Aidan of Lindisfarne, St.; Benedict Biscop, St.; Cedd (Cedda), St.; Chad (Ceadda), St.; Cuthbert of Canterbury; Cuthbert of Wearmouth; Cuthbert of Lindisfarne, St.; Guthlac, St.; Hilda of Whitby, St.; John of Beverley, St.; Oswald, King of Northumbria, St.; Theodore of Canterbury, St.; Wilfrid of York, St.; Willibald of Eichstatt, St.; Winnebald, St.

*COLLEDGE, EDMUND, OSA, St. Patrick's, Rome, Italy. **Articles:** Mystics, English; Rolle de Hampole, Richard; Ruysbroeck, Jan van, Bl.; Tauler, Johannes.

*COLLERAN, JOSEPH MOYLAN, CSSR, Ph.D., Professor of Philosophy, St. Alphonsus College, Suffield, Conn. **Article:** Desurmont, Achille.

*COLLINGE, WILLIAM J., Ph.D., Father James M. Forker Professorship in Catholic Social Teaching, Theology and Philosophy, Mount Saint Mary's College, Emmitsburg, Md. **Article:** Fides et ratio.

COLLINGE, WILLIAM J., Ph.D., Professor of Theology and Philosophy and Forker Professor of Catholic Social Teaching, Mount Saint Mary's College, Emmitsburg, Md. **Article:** Mount St. Mary's College and Seminary.

*COLLINGWOOD, FRANCIS JOSEPH, Ph.D., Associate Professor of Philosophy, Marquette University, Milwaukee, Wis. **Articles:** Dynamism; Form [Systematic Analysis].

*COLLINS, JAMES DANIEL, Ph.D., L.H.D., Professor Philosophy, St. Louis University, St. Louis, Mo. **Articles:** Philosophy, History of, 4. Modern; Philosophy, History of, 5. Twentieth Century.

COLLINS, JOHN F., Ph.D., Adjunct Professor of Classics, Brooklyn College, Brooklyn, N.Y. **Article:** Latin (in the Church).

*COLLINS, JOSEPH BURNS, SS, Theological College, Washington, D.C. **Article:** Bandas, Rudolph G.

*COLLINS, JOSEPH BURNS, SS, Ph.D., Professor of Catechetics, The Catholic University of America, Washington, D.C. **Article:** Munich Method in Catechetics.

*COLLINS, SISTER M. EMMANUEL, OSF, Ph.D., D.Litt., Vice President and Dean, College of St. Teresa, Winona, Minn.; Council Member, Sisters of St. Francis of the Congregation of Our Lady of Lourdes, Rochester, Minn. **Articles:** Elfleda, St.; Lebuinus (Lebwin), St.; Molloy, Aloysius, Sister; Morality Plays; Werburga, St.; Witta, St.

*COLLINS, MARY, OSB, Ph.D., Associate Professor of Religion and Religious Education, The Catholic University of America, Washington, D.C. **Article:** Eucharistic Fast.

*COLLINS, RAYMOND F., S.T.D., Professor of NT Studies, Catholic University of Louvain, Belgium. **Article:** Cerfaux, Lucien.

*COLLINS, RAYMOND F., S.T.D. Dean, School of Religious Studies, The Catholic University of America, Washington, D.C. **Article:** Janssens, Louis.

COLLINS, RAYMOND F., M.A., S.T.D., Professor New Testament, Department of Theology, The Catholic University of America, Washington, D.C. **Articles:** Adultery (in the Bible); Corinthians, Epistles to the; Epistles, New Testament; Fornication (in the Bible); Louvain, American College at; Luke, Gospel according to; Miracles (in the Bible); New Testament Scholarship; Pastoral Epistles; Sex (in the Bible); Thessalonians, Epistles to the.

*COLLINS, THOMAS AQUINAS, OP, S.T.D., S.T.Lr., S.S.B, Professor of Sacred Scripture and Theology, Providence College, Providence, R.I. **Article:** Fundamentalism, Biblical.

*COLOMBO, JOSEPH A., Ph.D., Assistant Professor, Department of Theological and Religious Studies, University of San Diego. **Article:** Revisionist Theology.

*COMASKEY, BERNARD JOHN, M.A., Ph.D., Associate Staff Editor for Medieval Church History, General Church History, and Cartography, *New Catholic Encyclopedia,* The Catholic University of America, Washington, D.C.; Assistant Professor of History, Armstrong State College, Savannah, Ga. **Articles:** Adalar, St.; Adrian V, Pope; Agil, St.; Andrew of Strumi, Bl.; Ave Maris Stella; Avitus, St.; Bavo (Allowin), St.; Bernard of Cluny; Bernardino of Feltre, Bl.; Bobbio, Abbey of; Bracton, Henry de; Cathedral; Claritus, Bl.; Daniel Palomnik; Demetrian of Khytri, St.; Eckbert of Schonau; Engelbert of Admont; Estonia, The Catholic Church in; Eustace of Luxeuil, St.; Gezelinus, Bl.; Gilbert of Sempringham, St.; Gilbertines; Innocent of Le Mans, St.; John Benincasa, Bl.; John de Saint-Pol; Lucius, St.; Magistri Comacini; Nilus of Rossano, St.; Notker Labeo; Olga, St.; Ortolana (Hortulana), Bl.; Peter the Painter; Peter Petroni, Bl.; Pontius of Faucigny, Bl.

*COMBE, PIERRE, OSB, member, *Paléographie Musicale,* Abbey of Solesmes, France. **Article:** Mocquereau, Andre.

*COMHAIR-SYVAIN, SUZANNE, Ph.D., Paris, France. **Article:** Voodoo.

*COMMINS, WILLIAM DOLLARD, Ph.D., Professor of Psychology, The Catholic University of America, Washington, D.C. **Article:** Measurement [Psychological Measurements].

*COMTOIS, MOTHER CECILE DE LA PROVIDENCE, FSE, Ph.D., Regional Superior of the Congregation's Missions, Antofagasta, Chile. **Article:** Holy Spirit, Daughters of the.

*CONCANNON, SISTER M. JOSEPHINA, CSJ, D.Ed., Boston College School of Education, Chestnut Hill, Mass. **Article:** Montessori, Maria.

*CONDIT, ANN, Ph.D., Professor of Latin and Greek, St. Mary's College, Graduate School of Sacred Theology, Notre Dame, Ind. **Articles:** Anse, Councils of; Attigny, Councils of; Autun, Councils of; Avranches, Council of; Chalon-sur-Saone, Councils of; Guastalla, Council of; Maurice of Carnoet, St.; Nicholas of Basel; Telesphorus of Cosenza.

*CONDON, SISTER M. FRANCIS OF THE STIGMATA, FMM, M.H.A., Director of Public Relations, U.S. Province of St. Francis, Franciscan Missionaries of Mary; Editor, *Far Away Missions,* North Providence, R.I. **Articles:** Chappotin de Neuville, Helene de, Ven.; Pallotta, Maria Assunta, Bl.

*CONLAN, SISTER MARY SAMUEL, OP, Ph.D., Assistant Professor of English and Humanities, Dominican College of San Rafael, San Rafael, Calif. **Articles:** Bellinzaga, Isabella Cristina (Lomazzi); Bridget of Sweden, St.; Busaeus (de Buys) [part 1]; Castellino da Castelli; Farges, Albert; Florentius Radewijns; Mausbach, Joseph; Our Lady of the Snow.

*CONLEY, ARTHUR JEROME, M.B.A., Assistant to the Executive Vice President, Hussmann Refrigeration, Inc., St. Louis, Mo. **Article:** Sodalities of Our Lady, National Federation of.

*CONLEY, KIERAN, OSB, S.T.D., Professor of Doctrinal Theology, St. Meinrad Seminary, St. Meinrad, Ind. (deceased Jan. 17, 1966). **Article:** Wisdom.

*CONLEY, PETER V., S.T.L., Pope John XXIII National Seminary, Weston, Mass. **Article:** Medeiros, Humberto.

CONLEY, RORY. T., Ph.D., Pastor, St. Aloysius Church, Leonardtown, Md. **Articles:** Baltimore, Archdiocese of; Maryland, Catholic Church in; Washington, D.C., Archdiocese of.

*CONLON, SISTER M. RAPHAEL, OSF, M.A., Instructor in English, Ladycliff College, Highland Falls, N.Y. **Article:** Franciscan Sisters—Missionary Sisters of the Third Order of St. Francis (FMSC).

*CONNELL, FRANCIS JEREMIAH, CSSR, S.T.D., LL.D., L.H.D., Professor Emeritus of Moral Theology and Dean for Religious Communities, The Catholic University of America, Washington, D.C. **Articles:** Compensationism; Correction, Fraternal; Double Effect, Principle of; Doubt, Moral; Equiprobabilism; Laxism; Morality, Systems of; Probabiliorism; Probabilism; Reflex Principles; Rigorism; Tutiorism.

CONNELL, MARTIN F., Ph.D., Assistant Professor, School of Theology, Saint John's University, Collegeville, Minn. **Articles:** Candlemas; Corpus et Sanguinis Christi, Solemnity of; Epiphany, Solemnity of.

*CONNELLY, JAMES FRANCIS, S.T.L., Hist.Eccl.D., M.A. (h.c.), Professor of History, St. Charles Seminary, Philadelphia, Pa.; Secretary to the Archbishop of Philadelphia. **Articles:** Bedini, Gaetano; Dougherty, Dennis; Egan, Michael; Philadelphia, Archdiocese of.

*CONNELLY, JAMES T., CSC, Archivist, Priests of the Holy Cross, Indiana Province. **Article:** Cavanaugh, John Joseph.

CONNELLY, JAMES T., CSC, Ph.D., Associate Professor of History, University of Portland, Portland, Ore. **Article:** Holy Cross, Congregation of.

*CONNELLY, JOHN JOSEPH, S.T.D., Professor of Dogmatic Theology, St. John's Seminary, Brighton, Mass. **Article:** Perseverance, Final.

CONNELLY, THOMAS J., LL.M., Vice Chancellor, The Archdiocese for the Military Services, Washington, D.C. **Article:** Military Services, USA, Archdiocese for.

*CONNELLY, FRANCIS XAVIER, Ph.D., Professor of English, Fordham University, New York, N.Y. (deceased Nov. 17, 1965). **Article:** Newman, John Henry [part 2].

*CONNELLY, JAMES LOUIS, Most Rev., Ph.D., D.D., Bishop of Fall, River, Mass. **Article:** Fall River, Diocese of.

*CONNELLY, JAMES MICHAEL, M.A., Chairman of the Department of Religion and Librarian, Bishop Dubois High School, New York, N.Y.; President, Religion Teachers Council of Archdiocese of New York; Editor, *The Promise.* **Article:** Humani generis.

*CONNELLY, MATTHEW FRANCIS, Rt. Rev., B.A., Director, Apostleship of the Sea, San Francisco, Calif. **Article:** Apostleship of the Sea.

*CONNOLLY, SISTER REGINALD MARIE, OP, Ph.D., Assistant to the Supervisor of Schools, Brooklyn, N.Y. **Article:** Dominican Sisters—Congregation of the Holy Cross (Amityville, NY).

*CONNOLLY, THOMAS KEVIN, OP, S.T.Lr., S.T.D., Dominican House of Studies, Washington, D.C. **Articles:** Alumbrados (Illuminati); Molinos, Miguel de; Motive; Quietism.

*CONNOR, JAMES L., SJ, S.T.D., Director, Woodstock Theological Center, Washington, D.C. **Article:** Woodstock Theological Center.

*CONNORS, JOSEPH MICHAEL, SVD, Ph.D., Provincial Superior of the Northern Province of Divine Word Missionaries, U.S.A., Techny, Ill. **Articles:** Homiletics; Preaching, II (Homiletic Theory), 1. Patristic Times; Preaching, II (Homiletic Theory), 3. Modern Times; Preaching, II (Homiletic Theory), 2. Medieval Times.

*CONSIDINE, JOSEPH SYLVESTER, Very Rev., OP, S.T.Lr., S.T.M., St. Thomas Aquinas Priory, Dominican House of Studies, River Forest, Ill. **Article:** Babylon, City of.

*CONWAY, SISTER GEORGE EDWARD, SSJ, Ph.D., Instructor in Classics, Chestnut Hill College, Chestnut Hill, Pa. **Articles:** Amatus of Remiremont, St.; Exuperius of Toulouse, St.; Jura, Fathers of; Leontius of Frejus, St.; O Filii Et Filiae; O Deus Ego Amo Te; Omni Die Dic Mariae; Sacra Iam Splendent; Salve Mundi Salutare; Salvete Christi Vulnera; Sanctorum Meritis; Urbs Beata Jerusalem Dicta Pacis Visio; Ut In Omnibus Glorificetur Deus; Venantius of Tours, St.; Virginis Proles Opifexque Matris.

*CONWAY, JOSEPH PATRICK, M.A., Vice Chancellor, Diocese of Albany, N.Y. **Article:** Cusack, Thomas Francis.

*CONWAY, PIERRE HYACINTH, OP, S.T.Lr., Ph.D., St. Stephen's Priory, Dover, Mass.; Teacher of Philosophy, Xaverian Brothers Novitiate, Newton Highlands, Mass. **Articles:** Possibility [part 2]; Reality.

*CONWELL, JOSEPH FRANCIS, SJ, S.T.D., Chairman of the Department of Theology and Dean of the Graduate School, Gonzaga University, Spokane, Wash. **Articles:** Active Life, Spiritual; Contemplative Life; Nadal, Geronimo.

*CONZEMIUS, VICTOR JOHN, Dr.Phil., priest of the Diocese of Luxembourg, and research scholar in Church history, Grenchen (Solothurn), Switzerland. **Articles:** Bruck, Heinrich; Clemens Wenzeslaus; Czerski, Johann; Freppel, Charles Emile; Germany, The Catholic Church in [1500 to 1789, Since 1789]; Ginoulhiac, Jacques Marie Archille; Granderath, Theodor; Hefele, Carl Joseph von; Hergenrother, Joseph; Loyson, Charles; Luxembourg, The Catholic Church in; Maret, Henri Louis Charles; Reisach, Karl August von; Reusch, Franz Heinrich; Ronge, Johann; Schneemann, Gerhard; Senestrey, Ignaz von; Trier; Turmel, Joseph; Wessenberg, Ignaz Heinrich von.

*COOK, SISTER GENEVIEVE MARIE, RSM, Ph.D., Professor of Latin, Xavier College, Chicago, Ill. **Articles:** Apollinaris of Valence, St.; Avitus of Vienne, St.; Cyprian of Toulon, St.; Eleutherius of Tournai, St.; Epiphanius of Pavia, St.; Eugendus of Condat, St.; Ferreolus of Uzes, St.; Gall of Clermont, St.; Hilarus of Mende, St.; Philip of Greve; Praetextatus of Rouen, St.; Quinctian of Clermont, St.; Sulpicius of Bourges, SS.; Vedast (Vaast) of Arras, St.; Venantius of Viviers, St.; Vitonus (Vanne), St.

*COOKE, BERNARD JOHN, SJ, S.T.D., Professor of Theology and Chairman of the Department, Marquette University, Milwaukee, Wis. **Article:** Sacrifice, IV (in Christian Theology).

*COOKE, LESLIE EDWARD, D.D. (h.c.), LL.D., Associate General Secretary of the World Council of Churches, and Director of the Division of Inter-Church Aid, Refugee and World Service, New York, N.Y. **Article:** World Council of Churches.

*COOLEN, GEORGES, Licencié ès lettres, Librarian-Archivist, Saint-Omer, France; Secretary, Société académique des Antiquaires de la Morinie. **Articles:** Bertinus, St.; Erkembodo, St.; Guntbert of Saint-Bertin; Omer of Therouanne, St.; Saint-Bertin, Abbey of.

*COONEN, LESTER PETER, Ph.D., Professor of Biology, University of Detroit, Detroit, Mich. **Articles:** Darwin, Charles Robert; Wasmann, Erich.

*COONEY, JOSEPH RAYMOND, OP, S.T.B., Dominican House of Studies, Washington, D.C. **Articles:** Ambrosius Catharinus (Lancelot Politi); Bartholomew of San Concordio (of Pisa).

*COONEY, SISTER MARY LOYOLA, PVMI, B.S., Editor, *The Parish Visitor*, Mary-

crest Convent, Parish Visitors of Mary Immaculate, Monroe, N.Y. **Article:** Parish Visitors of Mary Immaculate.

*COONEY, PATRICK R., Director, Department of Christian Worship, Archdiocese of Detroit, Detroit, Mich. **Article:** Sunday.

COOPER, SR. ANTONIA, OSF, Local Minister, Portiuncula Convent, North Plainfield, N.J. **Article:** Franciscan Sisters—Congregation of the Servants of the Holy Child Jesus of the Third Order Regular of St. Francis (OSF).

COPELAND, M. SHAWN, Ph.D., Director of Graduate Studies and Associate Professor of Theology, Marquette University, Milwaukee, Wis. **Article:** Womanist Theology.

*COPELAND, RAYMOND FRANCIS, SJ, S.T.L., Ph.D., Professor of History and Superior of the Jesuit Community, University of Santa Clara, Santa Clara, Calif. **Articles:** Acciaioli; Pignatelli, Joseph Mary, St.; Ricci, Lorenzo; Tanucci, Bernardo.

COPPA, FRANK JOHN, Ph.D. Professor of History, St. John's University, Jamaica, New York. **Articles:** Alexander VIII, Pope; Alexander VI, Pope; Alexander VII, Pope; Church, History of, IV (Late Modern: 1789–1965); Church, History of, 5. Contemporary; Papacy, 5. Contemporary (1958–2001); States of the Church [part 2].

*COPPENS, JOSEPH-CONSTANT, Rt. Rev., Dr. and Mag.Theol., Professor and Dean of the Faculty of Theology, University of Louvain; President, College of Pope Adrian VI, Louvain, Belgium; Honorary Canon of Ghent. **Articles:** Imposition of Hands; Martin, Raymond Joseph.

*CORBETT, JAMES A., A.B., Archiviste-Paléographe, Professor of Medieval History, University of Notre Dame, Notre Dame, Ind. **Articles:** Firmin of Amiens, St.; Giraldus Cambrensis; Hughes, Phillip; Maurice of Sully; Stephen of Salagnac; Stephen of Narbonne, St.; Stephen of Die, St.

*CORBETT, PHILIP B., M.A. Latin and French, B.A. Greek (1st Class Hons.), Docteur en philosophie et lettres, Lecturer in Humanity, University of Aberdeen, Scotland. **Articles:** Hugh of Amiens; Lambert of Saint-Omer; Lambert of Saint-Bertin; Regula Magistri; Remigius of Rouen, St.

*CORBETT, SISTER THOMAS ALBERT, OP, Ph.D., Director of Institutional Research, College of St. Mary of the Springs, Columbus, Ohio. **Article:** Masses.

*CORBIN, SOLANGE, Docteur ès lettres, Professor, Faculty of Letters, University of Poitiers, Directeur d'Études, École Pratique des Hautes Études, The Sorbonne, Paris, France. **Articles:** Fetis, Francois Joseph; Rimed Office.

*CORBISHLEY, THOMAS, SJ, M.A., Superior of Farm Street Church, London, England; author; formerly Master of Campion Hall, Oxford, England. **Articles:** Davis, Henry; Mysticism; Sayers, Dorothy Leigh.

*CORCORAN, CHARLES JOSEPH, CSC, Ph.D., S.T.D., Professor of Theology, University of Notre Dame, Notre Dame, Ind. **Articles:** Agility; Glorified Body; Halo.

*CORCORAN, SISTER MARY LOUISE, SSMN, M.S., Mount St. Mary Teacher Training School, Kenmore, N.Y. **Article:** St. Mary of Namur, Sisters of.

*CORDOVANA, MICHAEL DOMINIC, M.M., Ph.D., Assistant Professor of Music and Administrative Assistant to the Head of the Music Department, The Catholic University of America, Washington, D.C. **Articles:** Caldara, Antonio; Jommelli, Niccolo.

*CORETH, EMERICH, SJ, Ph.L., Dr.Theol., Dr.Phil., Professor of Philosophy, University of Innsbruck, and Rector of the Jesuit College, Innsbruck, Austria. **Article:** Hegel, Georg Wilhelm Friedrich.

*CORIDEN, JAMES A., J.C.D., J.D., Academic Dean, Washington Theological Union, Silver Spring, Md. **Articles:** Censorship of Books (Canon Law); Nihil Obstat; Washington Theological Union.

*CORISH, PATRICK JOSEPH, M.A., Professor of Ecclesiastical History, St. Patrick's College, Maynooth, Ireland. **Articles:** Furlong, Thomas; Lanigan, John; Rinuccini, Giovanni Battista; Scarampi, Pier Francesco; St. John of God, Sisters of.

CORISH, MSGR. PATRICK JOSEPH, M.A., D.D., M.R.I.A., Honorary Archivist, Maynooth College, County Kildare, Ireland. **Article:** Maynooth, St. Patrick's College.

*CORLEY, FRANCIS JOSEPH, SJ, Ph.L., S.T.L., M.A., Assistant Professor of Religion, St. Louis University, St. Louis, Mo. **Article:** Man, 3. In Theology.

*CORNELL, ROBERT J., OPraem, St. Norbert College, West De Pere, Wis. **Articles:** Pennings, Bernard Henry; Premonstratensians.

*CORNIDES, AUGUSTINE W., OSB, Monasterio San Antonio Abad, Humacao, Puerto Rico. **Articles:** All Souls' Day; Catafalque; Concelebration; Requiem Mass.

*CORREA, EDUARDO J., Mexico City, Mexico (deceased June 2, 1964). **Article:** Guizar, Rafael Valencia, Bl.

*CORRIGAN, DAME FELICITAS, OSB, Stanbrook Abbey, Callow End, Worcester, England. **Articles:** Barking Abbey; Folkstone, Abbey of; Stanbrook Abbey; Wilton Abbey; Wimborne Abbey.

*CORVEZ, MAURICE, OP, S.T.Lr., Lecteur présenté, Provincial, Dominican Province of Lyons, France. **Articles:** Essence; Individuality.

*COSENTINI, JOHN WALTER, Ph.D., Professor of French, St. John's University, New York, N.Y. **Article:** Fenelon, Francois de Salignac de la Mothe.

*COSS, JOHN, Framingham, Mass. **Article:** Sons of Mary Health of the Sick.

*COSTA, FRANCIS DORILA, Very Rev., SSS, S.T.D., Provincial Superior, SSS, U.S.A., New York, N.Y. **Article:** Holy Hour.

*COSTELLOE, MARTIN JOSEPH, SJ, M.A., Ph.L., S.T.L., Ph.D., Professor of Classical Languages and Chairman of the Department, Creighton University, Omaha, Nebr. **Articles:** Abdias of Babylon, St.; Abundis of Como, St.; Acts of the Martyrs; Agnes, St.; Alexander of Comana, St.; Apollonia of Alexandria, St.; Assyrian Church of the East; Barbara, St.; Basilides, St.; Blaise of Sebaste, St.; Blandina of Lyons, St.; Catherine of Alexandria, St.; Cecilia, St.; Chrysanthus and Daria, SS.; Chrysogonus, St.; Claudius and Companions, SS.; Decius, Roman Emperor; Domitian, Roman Emperor; Galerius, Roman Emperor; Gallienus, Roman Emperor; Hadrian, Roman Emperor; Marcus Aurelius, Roman Emperor; Nero, Roman Emperor; Pontifical Universities, Roman; Tiberius, Roman Emperor; Trajan, Roman Emperor; Valerian, Roman Emperor.

*COTE, LÉON, Very Rev., Docteur ès lettres, Professor of Literature, and Archpriest of Vichy, until retirement (1963), Vichy, France. **Article:** Souvigny, Abbey of.

*COTTER, SISTER MARIE CHANTAL, DMJ, M.A., Directress of Study for the Congregation, and Teacher of English in summer at Marist Brothers' Normal Teachers' College, Guadalajara, Mexico. **Article:** Daughters of Mary and Joseph.

*COTTER, MOTHER ST. VIRGINIA MARIE, CND, M.S., Ph.D., Professor of Biology, Notre Dame College of Staten Island, Grymes Hill, N.Y. **Article:** Bourgeoys, Marguerite, St.

*COUCH, MARY KATHLEEN, Public Relations, Little Company of Mary Hospital, Evergreen Park, Ill. **Article:** Potter, Mary.

*COULON, GEORGE LEO, CSC, S.T.L., Professor of Dogmatic Theology, Holy Cross College, Washington, D.C. **Article:** Symbolism, Theological.

*COUREL, FRANÇOIS, SJ, Licence ès lettres, Ph.L., S.T.L., Editor and Assistant Manager, *Christus*, Paris, France; Master of Novices, Society of Jesus. **Articles:** Lallemant, Louis; Surin, Jean Joseph.

*COURTNEY, FRANCIS JOSEPH ANTHONY, SJ, B.A., S.T.D., Professor of Dogmatic Theology, and Librarian, Heythrop College, Oxfordshire, England. **Articles:** Cano, Melchior; Caputiati; Ekkehard of Sankt Gallen; Flagellation; Manegold of Lautenbach; Micrologus; Peter of Onesti; Ribadeneyra, Pedro de; Rolevinck, Werner; Roscelin of Compiegne; Savaric of Bath; Stevenson, Joseph; Torquemada, Juan de (1388–1468).

*COUSIN, PATRICK, OSB, Licencié ès lettres classiques, monk of the Abbey of La Pierre-qui-Vire, French Province of the Subiaco Congregation, Avallon, France. **Articles:** Aldric of Sens, St.; Anchin, Abbey of; Aniane, Abbey of; Ansegis, St.; Aunarius (Aunacharius) of Auxerre, St.; Bec (Le Bec-Hellouin), Abbey of; Bernay, Abbey of; Deodatus (Die) of Nevers, St.; Ebbo of Sens, St.; Faremoutiers, Abbey of; Fecamp, Abbey of; Frodobert, St.; Gumbert of Ansbach, St.; Jumieges, Abbey of; Lupus of Sens, St.; Saint-Remi, Abbey of; Saint-Vaast (Arras), Abbey of; Wulfram of Sens, St.

*COUTURE, ROGER AIMÉ, OMI, S.T.D., Professor of Moral Theology, Oblate College and Seminary, Natick, Mass. **Articles:** Azor, Juan; Cordoba, Antonio de; Diana, Antonino; Reginald, Valerius; Salmanticenses.

*COUTURIER, GUY PIERRE, CSC, M.A., S.T.L., S.S.L, Seminary of the Fathers of the Holy Cross, Montreal, Canada. **Articles:** Jeremiah; Jeremiah, Book of.

*COVERT, JAMES THAYNE, M.A., Ph.D., Assistant Professor of History, University of Portland, Portland, Ore. **Articles:** Challoner, Richard; Creighton, Mandell; Pastor, Ludwig von; Pfefferkorn, Johannes.

COWDREY, H. E. J., D.D., F.B.A. (Fellow of the British Academy) Emeritus Fellow of St Edmund Hall, University of Oxford, Oxford, United Kingdom. **Article:** Gregory VII, Pope, St.

*COYLE, SISTER PATRICIA MARIA, SNJM, M.A., Teacher of Dogma and Biblical Science, Novitiate at Marylhurst, Ore.; consultant for the teaching of religion in the high schools directed by the Community. **Article:** Life, Concept of (in the Bible).

*COYNE, SISTER ST. CLAIRE, CSJ, M.A., Assistant Professor of History and Chairman of the Department, Mount St. Mary's College, Los Angeles, Calif. **Article:** Pommerel, Celestine, Mother.

*CRAIG, MAURICE, OFMCap, B.A., St. Anthony Friary, Marathon, Wis. **Article:** Cassiano da Macerata.

*CRANE, THOMAS EUGENE, S.T.L., S.S.L, Professor of Sacred Scripture, St. John Vianney Seminary, East Aurora, N.Y. **Articles:** Temptation (in the Bible); Trial of Jesus.

*CRANNY, TITUS FRANCIS, SA, S.T.D., Director, Chair of Unity Apostolate, Graymoor, Garrison, N.Y. **Articles:** Bribery; Franciscan Friars of the Atonement; Graft; Irenicism; Mortalium animos.

*CREACH, MOTHER MARIE GERTRUDE, SSCC, Regina Pacis Provincial House of Studies, Honolulu, Hawaii. **Article:** Sacred Hearts, Sisters of the.

*CREAMER, SISTER JOHN ELIZABETH, SVSC, M.A., Principal, New Regional Girls High School, Taunton, Mass. **Article:** Holy Union Sisters.

*CREHAN, JOSEPH HUGH, SJ, M.A. (Oxon.), Editor, *Catholic Dictionary of Theology*, Farm Street Church, London, England. **Articles:** Ambrosiaster; Apologists, Greek; Athenagoras.

CREWS, CLYDE F., OFMConv, Ph.D., Professor of Theology, Bellarmine University, Louisville, Ky. **Articles:** Kentucky, Catholic Church in; Lexington, Diocese of; Louisville, Archdiocese of; Owensboro, Diocese of; Petre, Maude Dominica.

*CRILLY, WILLIAM HUMBERT, OP, Ph.L., S.T.Lr., S.T.L., Ph.D., Professor of the History of Modern and Contemporary Philosophy, Aquinas Institute of Philosophy, River Forest, Ill. **Article:** Scholastic Philosophy.

*CRONIN, BERNARD CORNELIUS, Ph.D., Pastor, St. Matthew's Church, San Mateo, Calif. **Article:** Yorke, Peter Christopher.

*CRONIN, GROVER JEREMIAH, Jr., Ph.D., Professor of English and Chairman of the Department, Fordham University, New York, N.Y. **Article:** Pope, Alexander.

*CRONIN, VINCENT, B.A. (Hons.), writer and editor, London, England. **Articles:** Indian Rites Controversy; Nobili, Roberto de.

CRONIN-MARTHALER, MAUREEN, R.N., M.S., Assistant Professor of Nursing, Purdue University Calumet, Hammond, Ind. **Article:** Hospice Movement.

*CROOKER, ROBERT WILLIAM, CSB, M.A., J.C.D., Associate Professor of Canon Law, St. Basil's Seminary, and Registrar, Pontifical Institute of Mediaeval Studies, Toronto, Canada. **Article:** Exemption, History of.

*CROSBY, JEREMIAH MICHAEL, OFMCap, B.A., Capuchin Seminary of St. Anthony, Marathon, Wis. **Article:** Giuliani, Veronica, St.

*CROSBY, MICHAEL H., OFMCap, Justice and Peace Center, Milwaukee, Wis. **Article:** National Catholic Coalition for Responsible Investment.

*CROSBY, SUMNER MCKNIGHT, Ph.D., Professor of the History of Art and Chairman of the Department, Yale University, New Haven, Conn.; Curator of Medieval Art, Yale Gallery. **Article:** Suger of Saint-Denis.

CROSS, J., **Article:** Sons of Divine Providence.

*CROSSAN, DOMINIC M., OSM, S.T.D., S.S.L., Professor of Sacred Scripture, St. Norbert's Abbey, De Pere, Wis. **Articles:** Barabbas; Justice of Men [part 1]; Justice of God [part 1]; Justification; Logos, 1. In the Bible; Paraclete.

*CROSSON, FREDERICK JAMES, Ph.D., Director, General Program of Liberal Studies, University of Notre Dame, Ind. **Articles:** Consciousness [part 2]; Objectivity; Phenomenology.

CROUCH, JACE T., Ph.D., Special Instructor, Department of History, Oakland University, Rochester, Mich. **Article:** Isidore of Seville, St.

*CROUZEL, HENRI MARIE, SJ, Docteur ès lettres, Professor of Moral Theology, Institut Catholique, Toulouse, France; Lecturer, Gregorian University, Rome, Italy. **Articles:** Caesarea, School of; Gregory Thaumaturgus, St.; Origen and Origenism; Pamphilus, St.

*CROWE, FREDERICK ERNEST, SJ, S.T.D., Ph.L., Professor of Theology, Regis College, Toronto, Canada. **Articles:** Insight; Intuition; Theological Terminology; Understanding (Intellectus).

*CROWE, MICHAEL BERTRAM, M.A., B.D., Ph.D., Lecturer in Philosophy, University College, Dublin, Ireland. **Articles:** Peter of Ireland; Richard Fitzralph.

*CROWLEY, DANIEL J., Ph.D., Associate Professor of Anthropology and Art, University of California at Davis, Calif. **Article:** Shaman and Medicine Man.

*CROWLEY, EDWARD JOHN, CSSR, S.T.L., S.S.L, Professor of Sacred Scripture, Holy Redeemer College and University of Windsor, Ontario, Canada; Lecturer, Marygrove College, Detroit, Mich. **Article:** Ark of the Covenant.

*CROWLEY, PATRICK F., A.B., J.D., Executive Secretary, Christian Family Movement, Chicago, Ill.; member, Papal Commission on Family, Population, and Birth. **Article:** Christian Family Movement.

*CROWLEY, THEODORE CORNELIUS, OFM, Ph.D., Sc.Hist.Lic., Department of Scholastic Philosophy, The Queen's University of Belfast, North Ireland. **Articles:** Andrew de Comitibus, Bl.; Andrew Caccioli, Bl.; Barnard of Vienne, St.; Bernard of Parma, St.; Caccioli, Andrew, Bl.; Christopher of Romandiola, Bl.; Daniel of Belvedere, St.; Eva of Liege, Bl.; Gabriel Ferretti, Bl.; Gandolf of Binasco, Bl.; John de Seccheville (Secheville); Plummer, Alfred; Richard of Conington; Scholasticus; Simon de Ghent; Tewkesbury, Abbey of; Thomas of Bungey; Zamometic, Andrea.

*CRUSZ, ROBERT, Tulana Research Centre, Sri Lanka. **Article:** Sri Lanka, the Catholic Church in.

CRUZAT, SR. HELOISE, OP, M.A., Prioress, Dominican Sisters of Houston, Tex. **Article:** Dominican Sisters—Dominican Sisters of Houston, Texas (Congregation of the Sacred Heart).

CRYSDALE, CYNTHIA S. W., Ph.D., Associate Professor, Department of Religion and Religious Education, The Catholic University of America, Washington, D.C. **Article:** Human Genome.

*CSAKY, MÓRIC, Hist.Eccl.L., Dr.Phil., Assistant, Institut für Kirchliche Zeitgeschichte (IFZ), Salzburg, Austria. **Articles:** Drey, Johann Sebastian von; Egres, Abbey of; Hadalinus, St.; Hadeloga, St.; Hildigrim, St.; Hunegundis, St.; Irmhart, Oser; Isaac the Good of Langres, St.; Jordan Forzate, Bl.; Maglorius, St.; Medard of Noyon, St.; Peter Acontato, Bl.; Rolendis, St.; Roseline, St.

*CUDAHY, BRIAN JAMES, Ph.D., Assistant Professor of Philosophy, Boston College, Chestnut Hill, Mass. **Article:** Hobbes, Thomas.

*CUFFE, EDWIN D., SJ, America House, New York, N.Y. **Article:** Ward, Maisie.

*CUK, ALPHONSE MARIA, S.T.D., Ph.D., Associate Professor of Psychology and Chairman of the Department, St. Vincent College, Latrobe, Pa. **Article:** Dream.

*CULKIN, GERARD, formerly Lecturer in Ecclesiastical History, Ushaw College, Durham, England (deceased Feb. 12, 1965). **Articles:** England, The Catholic Church in; Lingard, John.

*CULLEN, JOHN HUGH, Rt. Rev., B.A., Vicar-General, Archdiocese of Hobart, Tasmania, Australia. **Article:** Willson, Robert William.

*CULLEN, TREVOR, SMM, S.T.B., M.A., Vatican Radio, Vatican City, Europe. **Article:** Malawi, The Catholic Church in.

*CULLEY, THOMAS D., SJ, M.A. (Music), Weston College, Weston, Mass. **Articles:** Carissimi, Giacomo; Cavalli, Francesco; Corelli, Arcangelo; Marcello, Benedetto.

*CUMMINGS, JOHN THOMAS, Ph.D., Instructor in Classics, Middlebury College, Middlebury, Vt. **Article:** Gregory of Nazianzus, St.

*CUNLIFFE, CHARLES RICHARD ANTHONY, M.A. (Logic and Methodology), B.A. (Philosophy and Theology), Lecturer, Institute of Education, University of London, England; Senior Lecturer in the Philosophy of Education, Digby Stuart College of the Sacred Heart, Roehampton (London), England. **Article:** Liturgical Languages.

*CUNNINGHAM, JOSEPH L., Executive Secretary, Liturgy, Music, Art and Architecture, Diocese of Brooklyn, Brooklyn, N.Y. **Article:** Federation of Diocesan Liturgical Commissions (FDLC).

*CUNNINGHAM, LAWRENCE S., Department of Religion, Florida State University, Tallahassee, Florida. **Article:** Marks of the Church.

*CUNNINGHAM, LAWRENCE S., Ph.D., Professor of Theology, Department of Theology, University of Notre Dame, Notre Dame, Indiana. **Article:** Martyrdom, Theology of.

CUNNINGHAM, BROTHER MATTHEW, FSR, MEd., Chancellor, Diocese of Reno, Reno, Nev. **Articles:** Las Vegas, Diocese of; Nevada, Catholic Church in.

*CUNNINGHAM, MAURICE PATRICK, Ph.D., Jones Professor of Classics, Lawrence University, Appleton, Wis. **Articles:** Ovid in Christian Culture; Paulinus of Nola, St.; Prudentius.

*CUNNINGHAM, RAYMOND JOSEPH, Ph.D., Assistant Professor of History, Fordham University, New York, N.Y. **Articles:** Bentham, Jeremy; Hedonism; Mill, James; Mill, John Stuart; Positivism; Relativism; White, Charles Ignatius.

*CUOQ, JOSEPH MARIE, WF, Consultor to the Congregation for the Oriental Churches and to the Congregation for the Propagation of the Faith, Rome, Italy. **Articles:** Algeria, The Catholic Church in; Libya, The Catholic Church in; Morocco, The Catholic Church in; Tunisia, The Catholic Church in.

CURLEY, AUGUSTINE, OSB, Ph.D. Newark Abbey, Newark, N.J. **Article:** New Jersey, Catholic Church in.

*CURLEY, MICHAEL JOSEPH, CSSR, Ph.D., specialist in Redemptorist history, engaged in historical research for the cause of Francis X. Seelos, CSSR, Church of Our Lady of Perpetual Help, Brooklyn, N.Y. **Articles:** Currier, Charles Warren; Majella, Gerard, St.; Neumann, John Nepomucene, St.; Putzer, Joseph; Redemptorists; Seelos, Francis Xavier, Bl.; Sportelli, Caesar, Ven.

*CURRAN, CHARLES EDWARD, S.T.L., S.T.D., Professor of Moral Theology, St. Bernard's Seminary, Rochester, N.Y. **Articles:** Epikeia; Taxation and Moral Obligation.

*CURRAN, CHARLES EDWARD, S.T.D., Scurlock Professor of Human Values, Perkins School of Theology, Southern Methodist University, Dallas, Texas. **Article:** McCormick, Richard A.

*CURRAN, FRANCIS XAVIER, SJ, A.B., Ph.L., S.T.L., Ph.D., Associate Professor of History, Fordham University, New York, N.Y.; Historian of the New York Province, Society of Jesus. **Articles:** Farmer, Ferdinand; LeBuffe, Francis Peter; Weninger, Francis Xavier.

*CURRAN, JOHN WILLIAM, OP, S.T.D., formerly Professor of Theology, Loyola University, Chicago, Ill. (deceased Feb. 25, 1965). **Article:** Devotion.

*CURRAN, PETER CARROL, OP, S.T.D., Professor of Theology, Mount St. Mary's College, Los Angeles, Calif. **Articles:** Joy; Peace; Tempting God.

*CURRY, SISTER MARY WILLIAM, OSU, M.A., Directress of Education, Ursuline Nuns of Cleveland, Ohio, and Teacher of History, Ursuline College, East Campus, Cleveland, Ohio. **Article:** Ursulines.

*CURTIS, MARY MARGARET, Ph.D., Senior Tutor and Lecturer in English, St. Mary's College, University of Durham, England. **Articles:** Clerk, John; Kedermyster, Richard.

CUSATO, MICHAEL F., OFM, Ph.D., Associate Professor, The Franciscan Institute, St. Bonaventure University, St. Bonaventure, N.Y. **Articles:** John of Parma, Bl.; Quaracchi.

*CUTLER, ANTHONY, Ph.D., Assistant Professor of Art History, Emory University, Atlanta, Ga. **Article:** Saint Mark's (Venice).

*CUTOLO, VICENTE OSVALDO, lawyer, Professor of History, Instituciones Juridicas Argentinas, Facultad de Derecho y Ciencias Sociales, Buenos Aires; Professor, Introducción al Derecho, Facultad de Derecho de Olivos (Province of B.A.), Historia Económica Argentina y Americana, Facultad de Ciencias Económicas de Olivos, and Introducción al Derecho, Facultad de Derecho de Morón (Province of B.A.); Abogado Jefe Asesor del Ministerio de Economia de la Nación; Miembro del cuerpo editor de la Biblioteca Mayo, del Senado de la Nación; Professor, Historia e Instrucción Cívica, Escuela Normal de Maestras "Julio A. Roca," Buenos Aires, Argentina. **Articles:** Fagnano, Jose; Gomez, Jose Valentin; Grote, Federico; Medrano, Mariano.

*CUTTER, PAUL F., Associate Professor, Texas Tech University, Lubbock, Tx. **Article:** Old Roman Chant.

*CUYLER, CORNELIUS MOHLER, SS, S.T.B., Ph.D., St. Charles College, Catonsville, Md. **Articles:** Fenlon, John F.; Hogan, John Baptist; Magnien, Alphonse; Marechal, Ambrose; Vieban, Anthony.

*CUYLER, LOUISE ELVIRA, Ph.D., Professor of Music and Chairman of the Department of Musicology, University of Michigan, Ann Arbor, Mich. **Articles:** Isaak, Heinrich; Stabat Mater.

*CYPRIANO, JOSEPH L., M.A., Professor of Moral and Dogmatic Theology, Diocesan Sisters College, Hartford, Conn. **Article:** Transfiguration.

*DABASH, ADRIAN GEORGE, OP, M.A., Dominican House of Studies, Washington, D.C. **Articles:** John of Bromyard; Peter of Ruffia, Bl.; Peter Geremia, Bl.; Raymond of Capua, Bl.; Thomas Jorz.

*DAHLSTROM, DANIEL O., Ph.D., Associate Professor, School of Philosophy, The Catholic University of America, Washington, D.C. **Article:** Ontology.

*DAHMUS, JOSEPH HENRY, Ph.D., Professor of Medieval History, Pennsylvania State University, University Park, Pa. **Articles:** Courtenay, Peter; Courtenay, William; Courtenay, Richard; Wyclif, John.

*DAHOOD, MITCHELL JOSEPH, SJ, S.T.L., Ph.D., Professor of Ugaritic Language and Literature, Pontifical Biblical Institute, Rome, Italy. **Articles:** Canaan and Canaanites; Hebrew Language; Hebrew Studies (in the Christian Church); Mesha Inscription; Siloam Inscription; Ugarit; Ugaritic-Canaanite Religion.

*DAILY, SISTER MARIA RENATA, CSC, Ph.D., President, St. Mary's College, Notre Dame, Ind. **Articles:** Gillespie, Angela, Mother; Holy Cross, Congregation of Sisters of the.

*DALCOURT, GERARD JOSEPH, M.A., M.S. in L.S., Ph.D., Assistant Professor of Philosophy, Seton Hall University, South Orange, N.J. **Articles:** Egoism; Ethical Formalism; Ethics, History of.

*DALCOURT, GERARD JOSEPH, Ph.D., Professor of Philosophy, Seton Hall University, South Orange, N.J. **Articles:** Conscience, Freedom of; Tolerance.

*DALEY, JOHN MICHAEL, SJ, Ph.L., M.A., S.T.L., Ph.D., Provincial, Maryland Province, Society of Jesus, Baltimore, Md. **Articles:** Bohemia Manor; Molyneux, Robert; Neale, Leonard; Newton Manor School.

*DALLEN, JAMES, S.T.D., Professor of Theology, Rosemont College, Rosemont, Pa. **Articles:** Chrism Mass; Exorcism [part 3].

DALLEN, JAMES, S.T.D., Professor of Religious Studies, Gonzaga University, Spokane, WA. **Articles:** Communion Service; Penance, Sacrament of.

*DALMAIS, HENRY IRENÉE, OP, Lic. Philos. scholast., S.T.L., S.T.Lr., Diplôme Écoles des Hautes Études Religieuses, Professor of Eastern Liturgies, Institut Supérieur de Liturgie, Paris, France. **Articles:** Callistus I, Patriarch of Constantinople; Mystery Theology; Nicephorus Blemmydes; Nicholas III, Patriarch of Constantinople; Nicholas, Studite Abbot, St.; Zacharias, Patriarch of Jerusalem.

*DALMAU, JOSÉ MARÍA, SJ, Lic. in Phil. and Letters, Doctor en Filosofía y Teología S.I., Professor of Eastern Theology and History of Dogma, Colegio Máximo de San Cugat, Barcelona, Spain. **Articles:** Cienfuegos, Alvaro; Lainez, Diego; Suarez, Francisco; Vazquez, Gabriel.

*D'ALVERNY, MARIE-THÉRÈSE, Archiviste-Paléographe, Licence és lettres; Diplôme de l'École des Hautes Études, Doctorat (Sorbonne), Conservateur aux Manuscrits, Bibliothèque nationale, Paris; Maître de Recherche au Centre national de la Recherche scientifique; Professeur au Centre d'Études supérieures de Civilisation Médiévale, University of Poitiers, France. **Article:** Dominic Gundisalvi (Gundissalinus).

*DALY, JOHN EMMANUEL, FSCH, Ph.D., Associate Professor of Philosophy, Iona College, New Rochelle, N.Y. **Article:** Transcendentalism.

*DALY, SISTER MARY JULIA, SSJ, A.B., Assistant Professor of Art, Chestnut Hill College, Chestnut Hill, Pa. **Article:** Beatus of Liebana.

*D'AMATO, ALFONSO, OP, Litt.D., Ph.D., Th.Lr., Diploma in Paleography and Archival Science (Vatican School),

Professor of Philosophy, Provincia Domenicana "Utriusque Lombardiae," Bologna, Italy. **Article:** Roland of Cremona.

*D'AMOUR, O'NEIL CHARLES, Rt. Rev., M.A., Associate Secretary, Department of School Superintendents, National Catholic Educational Association, Washington, D.C. **Article:** Faribault Plan.

*DANET, AMAND MARIE, S.T.L., Professor of Theology, Faculté de Théologie Catholique, Paris, France. **Articles:** Brice of Tours, St.; Brieuc, St.; Severin, SS.

*DANIEL, CATHERINE MEGAN, B.A., author of articles in Welsh and English on religious, sociopolitical, and literary topics; contributor to television and radio, Rhos Mari, Menai Bridge, Anglesey, Wales. **Articles:** Emrys Ap Iwan; Wales, The Catholic Church in; Williams, William.

*DANSETTE, ADRIEN, Docteur en Droit, Diplôme de l'École des Sciences Politiques, writer; Académie des Sciences Morales et Politiques, Institut de France, Paris, France. **Articles:** Action Française; Daudet, Leon; France, The Catholic Church in [1789–1965]; Maurras, Charles; Ralliement.

*DAOUST, JOSEPH, Docteur ès lettres, Professor, Université Catholique de Lille, France. **Articles:** Abondance, Monastery of; Aldric of Le Mans, Bl.; Aurelian of Arles, St.; Bernard of Fontcaude; Brogne, Abbey of; Busaeus (de Buys) [part 2]; Cuxa, Abbey of; Douceline of the Midi, St.; Ebbo (Ebo) of Reims; Eon of Stella; Ferotin, Marius; Geoffrey of Clairvaux; Gerard of Brogne, St.; Giry, Francois; Guy de Montpellier; Hotel-Dieu de Paris; Malmedy, Abbey of; Mignot, Eudoxe Irenee; Nicolas, Jean Jacques Auguste; Noailles, Pierre Bienvenu; Petit, Louis; Quimperle, Abbey of; Ruinart, Thierry; Saint-Quentin, Monastery of; Saint-Trond, Abbey of; Segur, Louis Gaston de; Simon of Saint-Quentin; Taine, Hippolyte; Veranus of Cavaillon, St.; Villeneuve-les-Avignon, Abbey of; Vincent Madelgarius, St.; Winnoc, St.

DARCY, SISTER CATHERINE, RSM, J.C.D., Ph.D., Chancellor, Diocese of Las Cruces, N.M. **Article:** Sisters of Mercy.

*D'ARCY, ERIC, M.A., Ph.D., D.Phil. (Oxon.), Pastor, St. Carthage's, Melbourne, Australia; Senior Lecturer in

Professor of Composition, Royal Academy of Music, London, England; composer, author, broadcaster, lecturer, examiner, adjudicator. **Articles:** Franck, César Auguste; Gounod, Charles François.

*DENHOLM-YOUNG, NOËL, D.Litt., F.R.H.S., formerly Senior Lecturer in Medieval History, University College of Northern Wales, Bangor, Wales. **Articles:** Cursus; Exeter, Ancient See of; Saint Asaph, Ancient See of; Saint Davids, Ancient See of; Walter de Stapledon.

*DENIS, VALENTIN, Docteur en histoire de l'art et archéologie, Professor of the History of Art, Archeology, and Musicology, University of Louvain, Belgium. **Articles:** Last Supper, Iconography of; Louvain, American College at.

*DENNIS, GEORGE THOMAS, SJ, S.T.L., Sc.Eccl.Or.D., Assistant Professor of History and Theology, Loyola University of Los Angeles, Calif. **Articles:** Elias of Reggio, St.; Epiphanius, Patriarch of Constantinople; Gauderich of Velletri; John Italus; John of Otzun; John III Ducas Vatatzes, Byzantine Emperor; John the Deacon of Naples; John of Egypt, St.; John VII Grammaticus, Patriarch of Constantinople; Leo Luke, St.; Manuel II, Patriarch of Constantinople; Manuel II Palaeologus, Byzantine Emperor; Nisibis; Nisibis, School of; Oxyrhynchus; Pachymeres, George; Philoxenus of Mabbugh; Pulcheria, Byzantine Empress, St.; Simeon of Syracuse, St.; Tarasius, Patriarch of Constantinople, St.; Turkey, The Catholic Church in.

*DENOMME, ROBERT THOMAS, Ph.D., Assistant Professor of French, University of Chicago, Chicago, Ill. **Article:** France, Anatole.

*DE PAEPE, NORBERT, Docteur en philosophie et lettres, Chargé de Recherche du Fond National de Recherches scientifiques, University of Louvain, Belgium. **Article:** Hadewijch, Bl.

*DE PICCOLI, IGNAZIO, OSB, S.T.L., San Paolo fuori le Mure, Rome, Italy. **Articles:** Fruttuaria, Abbey of; La Cava (SS. Trinita), Abbey of; Leo of Cava; Piona, Abbey of; Sagra Di San Michele, Abbey of; San Benedetto di Polirone, Abbey of; San Vincenzo al Volturno, Abbey of; San Pietro in Breme, Abbey of; Sant' Eutizio di Norcia, Abbey of; Santa Maria di Polsi, Abbey of; Sesto al Reghena,

Abbey of; Settimo, Abbey of; Sora (Sor), Abbey of.

*DE POBLADURA, RAFAEL TURRADO MELCHIOR, OFMCap, Director of the Istituto Histórico OFMCap, and Professor of Church History at the Pontifical Institute, Regina Mundi, Rome, Italy. **Articles:** Abbeville, Claude d'; Basile of Soissons; Knoll, Albert.

*DE SA, FIDELIS LOUIS, CSSR, B.A., Hist.Eccl.L., Gregorian University, Rome, Italy. **Articles:** Anastasius Sinaita, St.; Anastasius, Patriarchs of Antioch, SS.; Anastasius, Patriarch of Constantinople; Bihlmeyer, Karl; Cosmas the Melodian; Eckhel, Joseph Hilarius von; Elias, Patriarch of Jerusalem, St.; Eulogius, Patriarch of Alexandria, St.; Germanus I, Patriarch of Constantinople, St.; Gregory Sinaites.

*DE SANTIS, VINCENT PAUL, Ph.D., Professor of History and Head of the Department, University of Notre Dame, Notre Dame, Ind. **Article:** Kenna, John Edward.

*DESAUTELS, ALFRED ROGER, SJ, M.A., Docteur de l'Université de Paris, Associate Professor of French Literature, Holy Cross College, Worcester, Mass. **Article:** Bergier, Nicolas Sylvestre.

DESIANO, FRANK P., C.S.P., D. Min. Pastor, Old St. Mary's Church, Chicago, Ill. **Article:** Converts and Conversion.

*DE SOUSA COSTA, ANTONIO DOMINGUES, OFM, J.C.D., Extraordinary Professor of Canon Law, Faculty of Theology, and Professor of Ius Publicum Ecclesiasticum and Ius Concordatarium, Faculty of Canon Law, Antonianum, Rome, Italy; Defender of the Bond in Sacra Congregatione Discipl. Sacramentorum. **Articles:** Canon Law, History of, 5. The Corpus Iuris Canonici to the Council of Trent; Joannes de Deo.

*DES PLACES, EDOUARD, SJ, Docteur ès lettres, Élève diplôme de l'École des Hautes Études, Professor, Pontifical Biblical Institute, Rome, Italy. **Articles:** Anthropomorphism; Diadochus of Photice; Ephrem the Syrian, St.; Epithets, Divine; Eusebius of Emesa; Golden Age; Greek Religion; Sacrifice, II (Greco-Roman); Sibylline Oracles.

*DESTRO, ROBERT A., J.D., Associate Professor, Columbus School of Law, The Catholic University of America, Washington, D.C. **Article:** Nuncio, Apostolic.

*DE VAULX, JULES AIMÉ MARIE VICTOR, Licencié es lettres, S.T.L., S.S.L., Élève de l'École Biblique de Jérusalem, Professor of Sacred Scripture and Librarian, Grand Séminaire, Nancy, France. **Article:** Vacant, Alfred.

*DEVENNEY, JOSEPH AUSTIN, SJ, S.T.L., Ph.D., Professor of Philosophy and Dean of the Graduate School of Arts and Sciences, Boston College, Chestnut Hill, Mass. **Articles:** Abū 'L-Barakāt; Arabia, 5. Christianity in Arabia; Babylon of the Chaldeans, Patriarchate of; Bukhtishu; Cilicia of the Armenians, Patriarchate of; Iraq, The Catholic Church in; Kindīi, 'Abd Al-Masih Al-; Saudi Arabia, The Catholic Church in; Theōdūrus Abū Qurra.

*DEVINE, JAMES FRANCIS, SJ, M.A., S.T.L., Assistant Professor of Biblical Theology and Greek, Boston College, Chestnut Hill, Mass. **Article:** Antiochus IV Epiphanes.

*DE VOOGHT, PAUL, OSB, St.-Germain-en-Laye, Seine-et-Oise, France. **Articles:** Hus, John; Hussites.

*DEVOS, PAUL, SJ, Bollandist, Brussels, Belgium. **Articles:** Anastasius the Librarian; Cyril (Constantine) and Methodius, SS.

*DE WALD, ERNEST THEODORE, Ph.D., L.H.D., Professor Emeritus, Department of Art and Archaeology, and Director Emeritus, Art Museum, Princeton University, Princeton, N.J. **Articles:** Assisi; Fiesole, Guido da (Fra Angelico), Bl.; Giotto di Bondone; Sistine Chapel.

DEWAN, LAWRENCE, O.P., Ph.D., Professor, Dept. of Philosophy, Dominican College of Philosophy and Theology, Ottawa, Canada. **Article:** Tillard, Jean-Marie Roger.

*DEWAN, WILFRID FRANCIS, CSP, S.T.L., S.T.D., Professor of Dogmatic Theology, St. Paul's College, Washington, D.C. **Articles:** Confessions of Faith, I: New Testament to Middle Ages; Profession of Faith; Witness, Christian.

*DE WOLF, L. HAROLD, S.T.B., Ph.D., S.T.D. (h.c.), Professor of Systematic Theology, Boston University, Boston, Mass. **Article:** Knudson, Albert Cornelius.

*D'HAENENS, ALBERT, Docteur en Philosophie et Lettres, Membre de l'Institut historique belge de Rome; Conservateur du Departement des Archives et Manuscrits de la Bibliothèque Centrale

de l'Université de Louvain; Archiviste-adjoint de la Cathédrale St. Michel de Bruxelles; Directeur des Archives du château d'Arenberg, Brussels, Belgium. **Article:** Saint-Martin of Tournai, Abbey of.

*DHAVAMONY, MARIASUSAI, SJ, S.T.L., Ph.D., Professor of Philosophy, Jesuit Scholasticate, Sacred Heart College, Shembaganur, South India. **Article:** Indian Philosophy.

*DI AGRESTI, GUGLIELMO M., OP, S.T.D., Professor of the History of Dogma, Studium Generale S. Thomae (Pistoia), Florence, Italy; Director, *Collana Ricciana* (*Studi su S. Caterina de'icci*). **Article:** Lawrence Justinian, St.

*DIAMOND, RAPHAEL, OCart, Prior, Charterhouse of the Transfiguration, Arlington, Vt. **Article:** Moore, Thomas Verner.

*DIAMOND, STANLEY, Ph.D., Professor of Anthropology, Maxwell Graduate School, Syracuse University, Syracuse, N.Y. **Article:** Afterlife, 1. In Primitive Culture.

*DI CESARE, MARIO ANTHONY, Ph.D., Assistant Professor of English, Harpur College, State University of New York, Binghamton, N.Y. **Article:** Vida, Marco Girolamo.

*DICHARRY, WARREN FLORIAN, CM, B.A., S.T.L., S.S.L., Dean, Registrar, and Professor of Scripture, Theology, and Greek, St. Mary's Seminary, Houston, Tex. **Articles:** Charism [part 1]; Christian (the Term); Hellenist; Lord's Day, The; Martyr.

*DICK, JOHN A., Ph.D., S.T.D., Coordinator of International Research and Programming, European Centre for Ethics, Catholic University of Leuven, Belgium. **Article:** Hamer, Jean Jérome.

DICK, JOHN A., Ph.D, Professor, European Centre for Ethics, Catholic University of Leuven, Leuven, Belgium; Managing Editor, Ethical Perspectives; Head, LIBISMA—Library for the Interdisciplinary Study of Marriage, Sint Genesius Rode, Belgium. **Article:** Louvain, Catholic University of.

*DICKINSON, J. C., University of Birmingham, England. **Articles:** Canons Regular of St. Augustine; Fontevrault, Convent of; Grandmont, Abbey and Order of; Stephen of Muret, St.; Walsingham, Monastery of; Winchester, Ancient See of.

*DIDIER, JEAN CHARLES, Very Rev., Canon, Docteur en théologie, formerly Professor and Dean of the Faculty of Theology, Lille, France; Professor of Theology, Faculty of Theology, Montreal, Canada. **Articles:** Garnerius of Rochefort; Val-des-Ecoliers, Monastery.

*DIEDERICH, EVERETT ALOYSIUS, SJ, S.T.D., Professor of Dogmatic Theology, St. Mary's College, St. Marys, Kans. **Article:** Ellard, Gerald.

*DIERICKX, MICHEL LEOPOLD, SJ, Ph.L., S.T.L., Eccl. Hist.D., Professor of Church History and Christian Archeology, Jesuit Faculty of Theology, Louvain-Heverlee, Belgium; Editor for history, *Streven;* Director of two series of historical textbooks, *Historia.* **Articles:** Antwerp; Backer, Augustin de; Belgium, The Catholic Church in [part 1]; Carayon, Auguste; Liège.

*DIETLEIN, DAMIAN LEO, OSB, S.T.L., S.S.L., Assumption Abbey, Richardton, N.Dak. **Articles:** Showbread; Tithes.

*DILELLA, ALEXANDER ANTHONY, OFM, S.T.L., Ph.D., S.S.L., Professor of Old Testament, Holy Name College, Washington, D.C.; Visiting Lecturer in Semitic Languages and Literatures, The Catholic University of America, Washington, D.C. **Articles:** Jordan, The Catholic Church in; Phoenicians.

DILELLA, ALEXANDER ANTHONY, O.F.M., S.T.L., S.S.L., Ph.D., Professor of Biblical Studies, The Catholic University of America, Washington, D.C. **Articles:** Daniel, Book of; Ecclesiasticus; Sirach, Book of; Wisdom of Ben Sira.

*DILL, EDWIN, ST, Mission Procurator, Missionary Servants of the Holy Trinity, Trinity Missions, Silver Spring, Md. **Article:** National Catholic Development Conference.

*DILLON, EDWARD J., Ph.D., Philadelphia, Pa. **Articles:** Capital Punishment; Hildebrand, Dietrich von; Lunn, Arnold; Medellín Documents; Shuster, George N.

*DIMIER, M.-ANSELME, OC, Abbaye Notre-Dame de Scourtmont, Forges-les-Chimay, Par Bourlers, Belgium. **Articles:** Cistercians, Art and Architecture of; Cîteaux, Abbey of; Clairvaux, Abbey of; Hugh Bonnevaux, St.; La Trappe, Abbey of; La Ferté, Abbey of; Le Thoronet, Abbey of; Les Dunes, Abbey of; Morimond, Abbey of; Pontigny, Abbey of; Sept-Fons (-Fonds), Abbey of.

DIMOCK, GILES, OP, S.T.D., Dean, Dominican House of Studies, Washington, D.C. **Article:** Dominican Rite.

*DINGES, WILLIAM, Ph.D., Associate Professor of Religion and Religious Education, The Catholic University of America, Washington, D.C. **Articles:** Catholic Traditionalism; Cults; Lefebvre, Marcel; New Age Movement; New Religious Movements; Sect.

*DINOIA, J. A., OP, Ph.D., Executive Director, Secretariat for Doctrine and Pastoral Practices, National Conference of Catholic Bishops, Washington, DC. **Article:** Neocatechumenal Way.

DIRKX, DOROTHY ANN, SSM, Provincial, Sisters of the Sorrowful Mother, Broken Arrow, Oklahoma. **Article:** Franciscan Sisters—Franciscan Sisters of the Sorrowful Mother (SSM).

*DIRVIN, JOSEPH IGNATIUS, CM, M.A., Assistant Director, Central Association of the Miraculous Medal, Germantown, Pa.; Editor, *Miraculous Medal.* **Articles:** Labouré, Catherine, St.; Miraculous Medal.

DITEWIG, WILLIAM T., Ph.D. cand., Executive Director, Secretariat for the Diaconate, United States Conference of Catholic Bishops, Washington, DC; Governing Board, International Diaconate Centre, Rottenburg, Germany. **Article:** Deacon.

*DIVINE, THOMAS FRANCIS, SJ, Ph.D., Marquette University, Milwaukee, Wis. **Article:** Usury.

*DLOUHY, MAUR JOHN, OSB, J.C.D., St. Procopius Abbey, Lisle, Ill. **Article:** Abbot (Canon Law).

*DOBSON, MOTHER M. VERONICA, CSB, United States Regional Superior, Brigidine Convent, San Antonio, Tex. **Article:** Brigidines.

*DOHENY, MOTHER MARY OF THE ANGELS, SSCM, M.S.N., Mistress of Novices, Holy Heart of Mary Novitiate, Batavia, Ill. **Article:** Holy Heart of Mary, Servants of the.

*DOHERTY, ANTHONY, B.Mus., Princeton University, Princeton, N.J. **Article:** Cabezón, Antonio de.

*DOHERTY, ANTHONY, Merritt Island, Fl. **Articles:** Beneventan Chant; Stravinsky, Igor Feodorovich.

*DOHERTY, REGINALD GEORGE, OP, M.A., S.T.D., Professor of Moral Theology, Aquinas Institute of Theology and Mt.

St. Bernard Seminary, Dubuque, Iowa; Associate Editor, *Cross and Crown*. **Articles:** Long-Suffering; Magnanimity; Magnificence; Patience; Perseverance; Pusillanimity.

*DOLAN, GERALD M., OFM, S.T.D., St. Anthony Shrine, Boston, MA. **Article:** Lyke, James Patterson.

*DOLAN, JOHN PATRICK, CSC, Ph.D., Professor of History, University of Notre Dame, Notre Dame, Ind. **Articles:** Karlstadt, Andreas Rudolf Bodenstein von; Luther, Martin; Millenarianism [part 2]; Miltitz, Karl von; Witzel, Georg (Wicelius).

*DOLAN, SISTER MARIAN, NDS, M.A., Mistress of Novices, Sisters of Sion, Saskatoon, Saskatchewan, Canada. **Article:** Notre Dame De Sion, Congregation of.

*DOMARADZKI, THEODORE FELIX, Ph.M. (History), Doctor of Letters in Slavistics, Professor of Polish Literature and Slavic Civilization, Director of the Center of Polish Documentation and Research, Faculty of Letters, University of Montreal, Canada. **Article:** Skarga, Piotr.

*DOMER, JOAN GILBERT, B.Mus., Bibliographer, *New Catholic Encyclopedia,* The Catholic University of America, Washington, D.C. **Article:** Viadana, Lodovico da.

*DONADONI, DINO TOMASO, writer, translator, contributor to Catholic papers and reviews, Bergamo, Italy. **Articles:** Sacred Heart (Bergamo), Daughters of the; Verzeri, Teresa Eustochio, St.

*DONAHUE, AMBROSE, OSB, M.A., monk of St. Anselm's Abbey, Washington, D.C. **Articles:** Anchorites; Cenobites; Chapter of Faults; Cowl; Hermits; Monk; Prior; Prioress; Priory.

*DONAHUE, CHARLES, Ph.D., LL.D., Professor of English, Fordham University, New York, N.Y.; member of the Editorial Board, *Thought* and *Religious Education*. **Articles:** Bede, St.; Caedmon, St.; Cynewulf.

*DONAHUE, JOHN R., SJ, S.T.L., Ph.D., Professor of New Testament, Jesuit School of Theology and the Graduate Theological Union, Berkeley, Calif. **Article:** Parables of Jesus.

*DONAHUE, MOTHER SAINT RITA MARIE, Ph.D., President, Notre Dame College of Staten Island, N.Y. **Article:** Notre Dame, Sisters of the Congregation De.

*DONCEEL, JOSEPH FLORENT, SJ, Ph.D., Professor of Philosophy, Fordham University, New York, N.Y. **Articles:** Intellect; Knowledge, Process of; Marechal, Joseph; Sensation.

DONDERS, J.G., MAfr., Ph.D., Adjunct Professor of Mission and Cross-Cultural Studies, Washington Theological Union, Washington, D.C. **Article:** Missionaries of Africa.

*DONLAN, THOMAS CAJETAN, OP, S.T.Lr., S.T.L., S.T.D., President, The Priory Press, Dubuque, Iowa; Provincial Director of Education, Dominican Province of St. Albert the Great, Chicago, Ill. **Articles:** Farrell, Walter; Will of God.

DONLEY, ROSEMARY, SC, RN, Ph.D., C-ANP, Ordinary Professor of Nursing and Director of the Care of Vulnerable People Graduate Program, The Catholic University of America, Washington, D.C. **Article:** Hospitals, History of, 3. Catholic Hospitals.

*DONLON, STEPHEN EDWARD, SJ, M.A., S.T.D., Professor of Fundamental Theology, St. Mary of the Lake Seminary, Mundelein, Ill. **Articles:** Archbishop; Archdiocese; Authority, Ecclesiastical; Freedom of Speech (in Church Teaching); Gelasian Letter; Miracle, Moral (the Church); Miracle, Moral; Monarchical Episcopate; Office, Ecclesiastical [part 1]; Pontiff.

*DONNELLY, SISTER GERTRUDE JOSEPH, CSJO, Ph.D., Chairman, Department of Classics, St. Joseph College, Orange, Calif. **Articles:** Aubert of Avranches, St.; Chlodulf (Cloud) of Metz, St.; Dalberg; Echter von Mespelbrunn, Julius; Giles, St.; Gondulphus of Metz, St.; Hunfried, St.; Ida of Herzfeld, St.; Latomus, Jacobus; Latomus, Bartholomaeus (Steinmetz); Liutwin of Trier, St.; Staphylus, Friedrich; Sterzinger, Ferdinand; Theodard of Narbonne, St.; Vincentian (Viance), St.; Wala, St.; Warin, Bl.

*DONNELLY, JAMES BERNHARD, SJ, M.A., Woodstock College, Woodstock, Md. **Article:** Berruyer, Isaac Joseph.

*DONNELLY, JOSEPH PETER, SJ, S.T.D., Ph.D., Professor of History, Marquette University, Milwaukee, Wis. **Article:** Gibaut, Pierre.

*DONNELLY, MALACHI JAMES, S.T.D., Associate Professor of Systematic Theology, St. Mary's College, St. Marys, Kans. **Article:** God (Holy Spirit).

*DONNELLY, PHILIP JOHN, SJ, S.T.D., Professor of Dogma, Weston College, Weston, Mass. **Article:** Baius and Baianism.

*DONOGHUE, MOST REVEREND JOHN F., D.D., Bishop of Charlotte, Charlotte, N.C. **Article:** O'Boyle, Patrick.

DONOHUE, JAMES MICHAEL, C.R., Ph.D., Assistant Professor, Department of Theology, Mount Saint Mary's College, Emmitsburg, Md. **Articles:** Anointing of the Sick, I (Theology of); Anointing of the Sick, II (Liturgy of); Commendation of the Dying; Viaticum.

*DONOHUE, JOHN AUGUSTINE, SJ, S.T.L, Ph.D., Associate Professor of History, Loyola University of Los Angeles, Los Angeles, Calif. **Article:** Kino, Eusebio Francisco.

*DONOHUE, JOHN JOSEPH, SJ, MA., S.T.L., Harvard University, Cambridge, Mass. **Articles:** Islamic Traditions (Hadīth); Sunnites.

*DONOHUE, JOHN WALDRON, SJ, S.T.L., Ph.D., Associate Professor of the History and Philosophy of Education, School of Education, Fordham University, New York, N.Y. **Article:** Ratio Studiorum.

DONOVAN, SR. GERALDINE, OSF, Ph.D., Congregation Historian, Franciscan Sisters of Allegany, New York, St. Elizabeth Motherhouse, Allegany, N. Y. **Article:** Franciscan Sisters—Franciscan Sisters of Allegany (OSF).

*DONOVAN, MOTHER M. LORETO, SP, R.N., Superior General, Sisters of Providence, Holyoke, Mass. **Article:** Sisters of Providence.

*DONOVAN, PAUL M., OSST, Principal, De Matha Catholic High School, Hyattsville, Md. **Article:** John Baptist of the Conception, St.

*DONOVAN, S. M., **Article:** Bell, Arthur, Bl.

*DONOVAN, THOMAS FRANCIS, B.A., J.C.L., The Catholic University of America, Washington, D.C. **Articles:** Assemani, Joseph Aloysius; Barbatia, Andreas de (Andreas Siculus); Laymann, Paulus.

*DONOVAN, WILLIAM JOSEPH, Rt. Rev., M.A. in Ed., Pastor, Holy Cross Church, Batavia, Ill. **Article:** Heart of Mary, Daughters of the.

*DOOLAN, AEGIDIUS JOHN, OP, S.T.L., St. Saviour's Priory, Dublin, Ireland. **Articles:** Consent, Moral; Pleasure; Restitution; Theft.

DOOLEY, CATHERINE A., O.P., Ph.D., Associate Professor, Department of Religion and Religious Education, The Catholic University of America, Washington, D.C. **Articles:** Catechist; First Communion; Lectionary for Masses with Children; Liturgical Catechesis.

*DORAN, SISTER MARY CLAIRE, OSF, B.S., M.A., writing and editorial work, Duns Scotus House of Studies, Washington, D.C. **Article:** Franciscan Sisters—Sisters of the Third Franciscan Order (OSF).

*DORCEY, SISTER MARY JEAN, OP, M.F.A., Teacher, commercial artist and writer, Convent of the Assumption, San Leandro, Calif. **Articles:** Catherine Thomas, St.; Chézard de Matel, Jeanne Marie; Joan of France (Valois), St.; Michael de Sanctis, St.

*DORENKEMPER, MARK JOSEPH, CPPS, S.T.D., M.A. in Phil., Professor of Dogmatic Theology, St. Charles Seminary, Carthagena, Ohio; Part-time Professor, St. Joseph College, and University of Dayton, Dayton, Ohio. **Articles:** Nature (In Theology); Person (In Theology).

*DORSEY, SISTER MARY LOURDES, MSC, M.A., Teacher of English, Academy of Holy Angels, New Orleans, La. **Article:** Marianites of the Holy Cross.

*DOSHNER, JOSEPH ALBERT, OP, M.A., S.T.B., Dominican House of Studies, Washington, D.C. **Articles:** Alexandre, Noel; Cecilia Romana, Bl.; Maria-Modingen, Convent of.

*DOSSAT, YVES, Agrégé d'histoire et géographie, Docteur ès lettres, Chargé de Recherche au Centre National de la Recherche Scientifique, Paris, France. **Articles:** Cathari; Guiraud, Jean; Waldenses.

*DOUGHERTY, CHARLES THOMAS, Ph.D., Associate Professor of English, St. Louis University, St. Louis, Mo. **Articles:** Ruskin, John; Thompson, Francis.

*DOUGHERTY, JOHN JOSEPH, Most Rev., D.D., S.S.D., L.H.D., LL.D., President, Seton Hall University, South Orange, N.J.; Auxiliary Bishop of Newark, N.J. **Articles:** Akiba ben Joseph; B'nai B'rith; Gamaliel.

*DOUGHERTY, JOHN MICHAEL, SS, S.T.D., Professor of Sacred Scripture and Latin, St. Thomas' Seminary, and of Greek, St. Edward's Seminary, Kenmore, Wash. **Articles:** Herodians; Publicans; Therapeutae; Zealots.

*DOUGHERTY, JUDE PATRICK, Ph.D., Associate Professor of Philosophy, Bellarmine College, Louisville, Ky. **Articles:** Idealism [part 3]; Naturalism.

*DOUGHERTY, JUDE PATRICK, Ph.D., Dean of the School of Philosophy, The Catholic University of America, Washington, DC. **Article:** Kirk, Russell.

*DOUGHERTY, KENNETH FRANCIS, S.T.D., Ph.D., Lector in Metaphysics, St. Pius X College, Graymoor, Garrison, N.Y.; Professor of Ethics, Marist College, Poughkeepsie, N.Y. **Article:** Atonement.

*DOUGHERTY, THOMAS DAVID, J.C.B., Assistant Chancellor and Notary, Diocese of Brooklyn, N.Y.; The Catholic University of America, Washington, D.C. **Articles:** Ferraris, Lucio; Irnerius; Pichler, Vitus.

*DOUGLAS, RICHARD MATEER, Ph.D., Professor of History and Chairman of the Department of Humanities, Massachusetts Institute of Technology, Cambridge, Mass. **Article:** Sadoleto, Jacopo.

*DOUIE, DECIMA LANGWORTHY, Ph.D., Oxford, England. **Articles:** Franciscan Spirituals; Fraticelli; Little, Andrew George.

*DOWNEY, BERCHMANS, SC, M.A., M.L.S., Librarian, St. Joseph's High School, Metuchen, N.J. **Article:** Sacred Heart Brothers.

*DOWNEY, GLANVILLE, Ph.D., Professor of History, Indiana University, Bloomington, Ind.; Associate of the Section of History and Literature, Royal Belgian Academy. **Articles:** Alexandria; Antioch; Constantinople (Byzantium, Istanbul); John Climacus, St.

DOWNS, PATRICK, editor, Hawaii Catholic Herald, Honolulu, Hawaii **Article:** Hawai'i, Catholic Church in.

*DOYÈRE, PIERRE, OSB, Prior, Abbey of Saint-Paul de Wisques, Wizernes (Pas de Calais), France. **Article:** Gertrude (the Great), St.

DOYLE, BRIAN M., Ph.D. cand., Assistant Professor of Theology, Marymount University, Arlington, Va. **Article:** Synod of Bishops (Assemblies).

*DOYLE, DENNIS M., Ph.D., Assistant Professor of Religious Studies, University of Dayton, Dayton, Ohio. **Articles:** Beliefs; Utopia and Utopianism.

DOYLE, DENNIS M., Ph.D., Professor, Religious Studies Department, University of Dayton, Dayton, Ohio. **Articles:** Abiding in Christ; Church, II (Theology of); Ecclesiology [History]; Ecclesiology [Developments and Issues]; Incorporation in Christ; Journet, Charles; Mystical Body of Christ; Mystici Corporis; Society (Church as); Votum.

*DOYLE, JOHN JOSEPH, Rt. Rev., Ph.D., Officialis, Consultor, Synodal Examiner, and Chairman of the School Board of the Archdiocese of Indianapolis; Chaplain and Chairman of Department of Philosophy, Marian College, Indianapolis, Ind. **Articles:** Opposition; Predication; Proposition.

*DOYLE, SISTER MARY VÉNARD, B.A., Higher Diploma in Education, University College (Dublin), Assistant Mistress of Novices, St. Columban's Novitiate, Hyde Park, Mass. **Article:** St. Columban, Missionary Sisters of.

*DOYLE, STEPHEN CLARE, OFM, S.T.L., Professor of Old Testament and Biblical Greek, St. John Vianney Seminary, Buffalo, N.Y. **Articles:** Census (in the Bible); Genealogies, Biblical.

*DOYLE, SISTER TERESA ANN, OSB, Ph.D., Professor of English and Head of the Department, Mount St. Scholastica College, Atchison, Kans.; Visiting Professor, St. John's University, Collegeville, Minn. **Article:** Benedictine Nuns and Sisters.

*DOYLE, THOMAS PATRICK, CPM, B.A., Cold Spring on Hudson, N.Y. **Article:** Mercy, Fathers of.

*DOYON, BERNARD, OMI, Eccl.Hist.D., Professor of Philosophy, History, and Liturgical Music, Oblate College of the Southwest, San Antonio, Tex. **Article:** San Antonio, Archdiocese of.

*DOZOIS, CAMILLE JOSEPH, S.T.D., Professor and Librarian, St. Joseph's Seminary, Edmonton, Canada. **Article:** O'Leary, Henry Joseph.

*DRAGUET, RENÉ HENRI, Very Rev. Canon, Master in Theology, Professor, University of Louvain, Belgium; Editor, *Corpus Scriptorum Christianorum Orientalium.* **Article:** Syriac Language and Literature.

*DRAINA, CYRIL, MSSST, S.T.L., Professor of Sacred Scripture and Sacred Liturgy, Holy Trinity Mission Seminary, Winchester, Va. **Articles:** Johannine Comma; Trinity, Holy (in the Bible).

*DRENNEN, DONALD ARTHUR, Ph.D., Visiting Professor of Philosophy, Marist

College, Poughkeepsie, N.Y.; General Editor, *Free Press Texts in Christian Philosophy* (Macmillan). **Article:** Berdiaev, Nikola˘i Aleksandrovich.

*DRESSLER, FRIDOLIN, Dr. Phil., Head, Public Library, Bamberg, Germany. **Articles:** Dominic Loricatus, St.; Gregory V, Pope; John of Lodi, St.; Kunigunde, German Empress, St.; Otto of Bamberg, St.

*DRESSLER, HERMIGILD, OFM, A.M., L.G., Ph.D., Professor of Greek and Latin, The Catholic University of America, Washington, D.C. **Articles:** Adalbero of Augsburg, Bl.; Aeterna Christi Munera; Aeterna Caeli Gloria; Aeterne Rex Altissime; Aeterne Rerum Conditor; Aldegundis, St.; Aldetrude, St.; Alto, St.; Amandus of Worms, St.; Ansbald, St.; Asia Minor, Early Church in; Aunemund of Lyons, St.; Austregisilus (Outril), St.; Baghdad; Bardo of Oppershofen, St.; Beatus of Trier, St.; Bertram of Le Mans, St.; Caesarea in Palestine; Clement I, Pope, St.; Drogo of Metz; Emesa (Homs); Erhard, St.; Évroul (Ebrulf) of Saint-Fuscien-au-Bois, St.; Ewald, SS.; Gansfort, Johannes Wessel; Gervase of Reims; Géry of Cambrai, St.; Goar of Trier, St.; Gottschalk of Limburg; Greece, The Catholic Church in [part 1]; Greek Language, Early Christian and Byzantine; Hadoindus, St.; Hadrumetum; Haimo of Auxerre; Hegemonius; Hegesippus; Irenaeus, St.; John of Gorze, Bl.; Judicaël of Quimper, St.; Landulf of Evreux, St.; Laodicea; Licinius of Angers, St.; Magnobod of Angers, St.; Marozia; Neocaesarea; Odilia, St.; Poggio Bracciolini, Giovanni Francesco; Preaching, I (History of) [part 1]; Pseudo-Clementines; Salmasius, Claudius; Socrates, Byzantine Historian.

*DREW, KATHERINE FISCHER, Ph.D., Professor of History and Associate Chairman, Department of History and Political Science, Rice University, Houston, Tex. **Articles:** Desiderius, King of the Lombards; Lombards.

DRIES, ANGELYN, OSF, Ph.D., Associate Professor and Chair, Religious Studies Dept., Cardinal Stritch University, Milwaukee. **Articles:** Catholic Students Mission Crusade; Cope, Marianne; Manna, Paolo; Mulherin, Mary Gabriella; Neill, Stephen Charles.

DRISCOLL, MICHAEL S., Ph.D., S.T.D., Tisch Family Associate Professor, Coordinator of Liturgical Studies, Department of Theology, University of Notre Dame, Ind. **Articles:** Evangelary (Book of Gospels); Lectionaries, I: Historical; Lectionaries, II: Contemporary Roman Catholic.

*DROUIN, EDMOND GABRIEL, FIC, M.S.L.S., Librarian, Walsh College, Canton, Ohio. **Articles:** Brothers of Christian Instruction of Ploërmel; Brothers of Christian Instruction of St. Gabriel; Deshayes, Gabriel; Forbin-Janson, Charles deLa Mennais, Jean Marie Robert de, Ven.

*DRURY, GEORGE FRANCIS, A.B., S.T.B., Ph.D., Associate Professor of Social Science and Humanities, Monteith College, Wayne State University, Detroit, Mich. **Article:** Rhetoric.

*DRUSE, JOSEPH LAWRENCE, Ph.D., Associate Professor of Humanities, Michigan State University, East Lansing, Mich. **Articles:** Eoban, St.; Erconwald of London, St.; Ermenburga, St.; Erminfrid, St.; Ethelbert, King of Kent, St.; Ethelburga, SS.; Ethelreda, Queen of Northumbria, St.; Lioba, St.; Swithbert (Suitbert), St.; Werenfrid, St.; Wigbert of Hersfeld, St.; Wilgis, St.; Willaik, St.; Willibrord of Utrecht, St.

*DUBAY, THOMAS, SM, Marist Administration Center, Washington, D.C. **Articles:** Holiness, Universal Call to; Holiness of the Church.

*DUBÉ, ARTHUR JOSEPH, J.C.D., Pastor, Notre Dame de Lourdes Church, Saco, Maine, and Vice Officialis, Diocese of Portland (deceased Oct. 26, 1964). **Article:** Time (In Canon Law).

*DU BOURGUET, PIERRE, SJ, Licencie ès lettres, Diplôme de l'École des Hautes Études Philologiques, Historiques et Religieuses, Sorbonne, Paris, France; Professor of Ancient Egyptian and of Coptic, Institut Catholique, Paris; Conservateur, Musée du Louvre et Professor of Christian Archeology, École du Louvre. **Article:** Art, Early Christian.

*DUBRAY, CHARLES ALBERT, SM, S.T.B., Ph.D. (deceased Nov. 5, 1962). **Article:** Emanationism.

*DUCEY, WILLIAM MICHAEL, OSB, St. Benedict's Abbey, Benet Lake, Wis. **Articles:** Guéranger, Prosper; Mass, Dry.

*DUCHENSE-GUILLEMIN, JACQUES, Docteur en philosophie et lettres, Diplôme de l'École des Hautes Études; Certificat d'études indiennes; Diplôme de l'Institut de linguistique, Institut catholique de Paris; Diplôme d'arménien classique, Professor, University of Liège, Belgium. **Articles:** Ahura Mazda (Ohrmazd) and Ahriman; Amesha Spenta; Avesta; Daēvas; Fravashi; G&amcr;th&amcr;s; Haoma; Magi; Mithras and Mithraism; Parsees; Sūtras; Upanishads; Zervanism; Zoroaster (Zarathushtra).

*DUERR, CHARLES JOSEPH, J.C.D., Pastor, Church of Saints Mary and Hubert, Luxemburg, Wis. **Article:** Notary (Canon Law).

*DUFF, EDWARD JOSEPH, SJ, M.A., D. ès Sc.Pol., Ph.L., Th.L., Professor of Political Science, Holy Cross College, Worcester, Mass. **Articles:** Ecumenical Movement; Rauschenbusch, Walter; Social Gospel.

*DUFFEY, SISTER MARY OF THE IMMACULATE CONCEPTION, SND, Ph.D., Professor of History, Emmanuel College, Boston, Mass. **Articles:** Adrian of Castello (de Corneto); Pirkheimer, Willibald; Pirkheimer, Charitas.

*DUFFY, STEPHEN JOSEPH, SM, S.T.L., Professor of Dogmatic Theology, Notre Dame Seminary, New Orleans, La. **Article:** Parousia, 2. In Theology.

*DUFFY, WALTER MARY, OFMConv, S.T.D., Auxiliary Chaplain, Villa Maria, Plainfield, N.J. **Articles:** Edomites; Moabites.

*DUGGAN, CHARLES, B.A. (Lond.), Ph.D. (Cantab.), F.R.H.S., Reader in History, Warden of King's College Hall, Deputy Warden of Commonwealth Hall, University of London, England. **Articles:** Baldwin of Canterbury; Bartholomew of Exeter; Bath and Wells, Ancient See of; De Heretico Comburendo; Decretals (Epistolae Decretales, Litterae Decretales); Decretals, Collections of; Golden Rose; John of Oxford; Lateran Councils; Peter des Roches; Quinque compilationes antiquae; Roger of Worcester; William I, King of England.

*DUGMORE, CLIFFORD WILLIAM, M.A., B.D., D.D., priest of the Church of England, Professor of Ecclesiastical History, University of London, England. **Article:** Cranmer, Thomas.

*DUIN, JOHANNES LOSER, Ph.B., S.T.D., parish priest, Hamar, Norway. **Article:** Norway, The Catholic Church in.

*DU LAC, HENRI JOSEPH, S.T.L., Ph.D., Professor of Philosophy and Chairman of the Department, College of St. Thomas, St. Paul, Minn. **Articles:** Excluded Middle, Principle of the; Wonder.

DULLES, AVERY, CARDINAL, S.J., Ph.L., S.T.D., Laurence J. McGinley Professor of Religion and Society, Fordham University, Bronx, N.Y. **Articles:** Evangelization, New; Fundamentalism; Lima Text; Mystery (in Theology); Revelation, Fonts of; Revelation, Theology of; Symbol in Revelation.

*DUMM, DEMETRIUS ROBERT, OSB, B.A., S.T.D., S.S.L., St. Vincent Archabbey, Latrobe, Pa. **Articles:** Ahikar (Achoir); Tobit (Tobias), Book of.

*DUMORTIER, JEAN, Honorary Canon of Lille, Professor of Greek Language and Literature and Dean of the Faculty of Letters and Human Sciences, Catholic University of Lille, France. **Article:** Cretan-Mycenaean Religion.

*DUMOULIN, HEINRICH, SJ, Dr. Phil., S.T.L., Doctorate in the History of Religions, University of Tokyo, Japan; Professor of Philosophy and History of Religion, Sophia University, Tokyo, Japan. **Article:** Zen.

*DU MOUSTIER, BENOÎT (pseudonym of Dom Benedict M. Lambres, OCart), Chartreuse de la Valsainte, Fribourg, Switzerland. **Articles:** Denis the Carthusian; Dominic of Prussia; Dorland, Peter (Dorlandus); Guigo II; Guigo I; Guigo de Ponte; Hugh of Balma; Lanspergius, Johannes Justus; Le Masson, Innocent; Ludolph of Saxony; Pollien, François de Sales; Surius, Lawrence.

DUNCAN, JASON K., Ph.D., Assistant Professor, Department of History, Aquinas College, Grand Rapids, Mich. **Article:** Iowa, Catholic Church in.

*DUNKERLEY, MOTHER DOROTHEA, OSU, Ph.D., L.H.D., Professor of Psychology, College of New Rochelle, New Rochelle, N.Y. **Article:** Ursulines.

*DUNN, ELLEN CATHERINE, Ph.D., Professor of English, The Catholic University of America, Washington, D.C. **Articles:** Drama, Medieval; Everyman; Exemplum; Gesta Romanorum; Passion Plays.

*DUNN, JAMES, SSP, Brookline, Mass. **Article:** Pauline Fathers and Brothers.

*DUNN, JOHN FRANCIS, M.A., Doctorat d'université (Laval), Associate Professor of French and Chairman of the Department of Modern Languages, St. Peter's College, Jersey City, N.J. **Article:** Montaigne, Michel Eyquem de.

*DUNN, SISTER M. LORETTA CLAIRE, OP, M.A., Professor of History and Assistant to the President, Caldwell College, Caldwell, N.J. **Article:** Lathrop, Alphonsa, Mother.

*DUNN, SISTER REGINA, FMA, M.S., New York, N.Y. **Article:** Salesian Sisters.

*DUNN, WILLIAM KAILER, A.B., M.A., Baltimore, Md. (deceased May 28, 1964). **Articles:** Fay, Cyril Sigourney Webster; McMahon, Thomas John; Pise, Charles Constantine.

*DUNNE, EDWARD JAMES, SJ, Ph.D., Associate Professor of History, St. Peter's College, Jersey City, N.J. **Article:** Reformkatholizismus.

*DUNNE, GEORGE HAROLD, SJ, Ph.D., Assistant to the President of Georgetown University for International Programs; author and playwright, Georgetown University, Washington, D.C. **Article:** Schall von Bell, Johann Adam.

*DUNNING, JAMES B., Ph.D., President, The National Organization for Continuing Education of Roman Catholic Clergy, Oakland, Cal. **Article:** National Organization for Continuing Education of Roman Catholic Clergy (NOCERCC).

*DUNNING, THOMAS PATRICK, CM, Ph.D., Diploma in Education (London), Professor of Old and Middle English Language and Literature, University College, Dublin, Ireland. **Articles:** John of Bridlington, St.; Richard of Kilvington; Ullerston, Richard.

*DÜNNINGER, JOSEF, Dr. Phil., Professor of Germanic Philology and Folklore, University of Würzburg, Germany. **Article:** Fourteen Holy Helpers.

*DUPONT, REV. GERALD E., SSE, M.A., Licentiate in Medieval Studies, Ph.D., President, St. Michael's College, Winooski, Vt. **Articles:** Goesbriand, Louis de; Muard, Marie Jean Baptiste; St. Edmund, Society of.

*DUPRÉ, LOUIS KAREL, Docteur en philosophie, Th.L., Associate Professor of Philosophy, Georgetown University, Washington, D.C. **Articles:** Feuerbach, Ludwig Andreas; Hegelianism and Neo-Hegelianism; Kierkegaard, Søren Aabye.

*DUPRÉ, WILHELM, studies in Theology, Philosophy, Ethnology, and Relig. Sciences, St. Gabriel-Mödling (Vienna); Ph.D., Assistant, Institute of Philosophy, University of Vienna, Austria; Visiting Professor, De Paul University, Chicago, Ill. **Articles:** Conscience, 1. General Concept; Curse; Henotheism; Magic; Myth and Reflective Thought; Sky and Sky Gods; Sun Worship.

*DUPUIS, ADRIAN MAURICE, Ph.D., Associate Professor of History and Philosophy of Education, Marquette University, Milwaukee, Wis. **Article:** Functionalism.

*DURATSCHEK, SISTER CLAUDIA MARY, OSB, Ph.D., Head of the Department of History, Mount Marty College, Yankton, S.Dak. **Articles:** Marty, Martin; South Dakota, Catholic Church in.

*DURBIN, PAUL REGINALD, OP, S.T.Lr., S.T.L., M.A., Professor of Natural Philosophy and Philosophy of Science, St. Stephen's House of Studies, Dover, Mass. **Articles:** Action and Passion; Agent; Bilocation; Location (Ubi); Place; Randomness; Situation (Situs).

*DURBIN, PAUL T., Professor, Philosophy Department, University of Delaware, Newark, De. **Article:** Technology, Philosophy of.

*DURKAN, JOHN, *Innes Review,* Glasgow, Scotland. **Article:** Scotland, Church of.

*DURKIN, JOSEPH THOMAS, SJ, Ph.D., Professor of American History, Georgetown University, Washington, D.C. **Article:** Ryan, Patrick John.

*DUROZOY, MARIE-FRANCE JEANNE, B.A., Licenciée ès lettres (histoire), Diplôme Supérieur de Bibliothécaire, Librarian, University of Paris, France. **Article:** David, Armand.

*DURRWELL, FRANÇOIS XAVIER, CSSR, S.T.L., S.S.L., Superior, Redemptorist's Seminary, Echternach, Luxembourg; Professor, International Institute, *Lumen Vitae,* Brussels, Belgium. **Articles:** Lamb of God [part 1]; Resurrection of Christ, 2. Theology of.

*DURST, LUANNE, OSF, Administrative Assistant, Bishops' Committee on Liturgy, Washington. D.C. **Article:** Sequence.

*DUSICK, ROLAND JEROME, OFMCap, Member, Capuchin Mission Band, Milwaukee, Wis. **Article:** Roemer, Theodore.

*DUVAL, ANDRÉ, OP, Docteur en théologie, Professor of Ecclesiastical and Dominican History and Rector of the Facultés dominicaines du Saulchoir, Saulchoir, France. **Articles:** Álvarez, Diego; Campeggi, Camillo; Hugon, Edouard; Touron, Antoine.

*DUVIGNAU, PIERRE, SCJ, S.T.D., Assistant General, Congregation of Bétharram Fathers, Lestelle-Bétharram (Basses-Pyrénées), France. **Articles:** Bétharram Fathers; Garicoïts, Michael, St.

*DVORNIK, FRANCIS, Very Rev., D.D., Docteur ès lettres (Sorbonne), D.Litt. (h.c. London), Professor Emeritus of Byzantine History, Harvard University, Dumbarton Oaks Center for Byzantine Studies, Washington, D.C. **Articles:** Councils, General (Ecumenical), History of; Ignatius, Patriarch of Constantinople, St.; Methodius I, Patriarch of Constantinople, St.; Metrophanes of Smyrna; Nicetas David; Photius, Patriarch of Constantinople; Stylianos of Neocaesarea; Theodora, Byzantine Empress (2).

*DWYER, JOSEPH G., Ph.D., Professor of History and Chairman of the Division of Arts, Iona College, New Rochelle, N.Y. **Articles:** Aske, Robert; Beaton, James (Bethune) [1473–1539]; Beaton, James (Bethune) [1517–1603]; Bedyll, Thomas; Longland, John; Pole, Reginald; Pole, Margaret Plantagenet, Bl.

*DYER, GEORGE JOHN, S.T.D., Professor of Patrology and Librarian, St. Mary of the Lake Seminary, Mundelein, Ill.; Editor, *Chicago Studies*. **Articles:** Antichrist [part 2]; Chiliasm; Elijah (Second Coming of).

*EADS, JOAN, Zone Coordinator, L'Arche U.S.A. **Article:** Arche International, L'.

*EAGAN, JAMES MICHAEL, Ph.D., Vice President, National Conference of Christians and Jews, and Director, Parent-Centered Programs on Rearing Children of Good Will, New York, N.Y. **Article:** National Conference for Community and Justice.

*EARLY, TRACY, New York, N.Y. **Articles:** Agagianian, Gregory Peter XV; Assemblies of God; Athenagoras I; Cicognani, Amleto Giovanni; Conway, William; Dodd, Charles Harold; Haec Sancta; Horton, Douglas; Knutsen, Kent Sigvart; Kodaly, Zoltan; Marcel, Gabriel; Rahner, Hugo; Soka Gakkai; World Council of Churches.

*EASTERLY, FREDERICK JOHN, CM, Ph.D., Vice President for Student Personnel Services, St. John's University, Jamaica, N.Y. **Article:** Rosati, Joseph.

*EASTON, JOY BROMBERG, M.S., Instructor in Mathematics, West Virginia University, Morgantown, W.Va. **Article:** Clavius, Christopher.

*EATON, LEONARD KIMBALL, Ph.D., Professor of Architecture, University of Michigan, Ann Arbor, Mich. **Article:** Stave Churches.

*EATON, MOTHER MARY BERNARDINO, SSL, Louisville Convent, Woodland Hills, Calif. **Article:** St. Louis, Sisters of.

*EATON, SISTER MARY ELEANOR, SND, Ph.D., Professor of English, College of Notre Dame, Belmont, Calif. **Article:** Cloud of Unknowing, The.

*EBERHARDT, NEWMAN CHARLES, CM, M.A., S.T.L., St. John's Seminary, Camarillo, Calif. **Articles:** Amat, Thaddeus; Cantwell, John Joseph; Vincentians.

ECKERMANN, WILLIGIS, OSA, University of Würzburg, Würzburg, Germany. **Articles:** Hugolino of Orvieto; Simon Fidati of Cascia, Bl.

*EDELBY, NEOPHYTOS, Archeveche Grec Melkite Catholique, Alep, Syria. **Article:** Maximos IV Sayegh.

*EDWARDS, FRANCIS OBORN, SJ, B.A. (Hons.), S.T.L., Archivist (Historical Section), English Province of the Society of Jesus, London, England. **Articles:** Alford, Michael; Bagshaw, Christopher; Bawden, William (Baldwin).

*EDWARDS, OWEN DUDLEY, B.A., Visiting Lecturer, Department of History, University of Oregon, Eugene, Ore. **Article:** Nativism, American.

*EDWARDS, PHILIP, OSB, B.A., B.S., B.Th., monk of St. Andrew's Priory, Vallermo, Calif. **Articles:** Amadeus of Lausanne, St.; Cisneros, Garcia de; Gilbert of Holland (Hoyland); Peter of Celle; Peter the Venerable, Bl.Thomas Gallus of Vercelli.

*EDWARDS, ROBERT DUDLEY, Ph.D., D.Litt., Professor of Modern Irish History, University College, Dublin, Ireland. **Articles:** Act of Settlement, Irish; Brady, William Maziere; Brown, George; D'Alton, Edward Alfred; Emancipation, Catholic; Ireland, The Catholic Church in; Ireland, Church of; Northern Ireland, the Catholic Church in; O'Connell, Daniel.

*EDWARDS, SUZANNE CLARE, Ph.D., Assistant Professor of Art, University of California at Santa Barbara, Calif. **Articles:** Church Architecture, History of, 04: Romanesque.

*EFROYMSON, DAVID P., Ph.D., Professor, Department of Religion, La Salle College, Philadelphia, Pa. **Article:** Patristic Studies.

*EGAN, BARTHOLOMEW, OFM, M.A., Ph.D., Diploma in Library Science (Vatican School), Guardian Irish Franciscan College, Louvain, Belgium. **Articles:** Bar, Catherine de; Benard, Laurent; Cajetan, Constantino; Gasquet, Francis Neil Aidan; Molloy, Francis.

*EGAN, EDWARD ARTHUR, labor executive in government and industry, Chicago, Ill. **Article:** Ryan, Abram Joseph.

*EGAN, KEITH JAMES, OCarm, Ph.D., Associate Professor of History, Mt. Carmel College, Niagara Falls, Ontario, Canada. **Articles:** Bostius, Arnold; Cyril of Constantinople, St.; Fuente, Michael de la; Henry of St. Ignatius; Hunt, Walter; James of Certaldo, Bl.; John Kynyngham; Lezana, Juan Bautista de; Mark of the Nativity; William of Sandwich, Chronicle of.

*EGAN, KEITH JAMES, Associate Professor, Department of Theology, Marquette University, Milwaukee, Wis. **Article:** Knowles, David.

EGAN, MARIE, IHM, M.A., S.T.D., Professor Emeritus, Mount St. Mary's College, Los Angeles, Calif. **Article:** Immaculate Heart of the Blessed Virgin Mary, Sisters of.

*EGAN, PATRICK KEVIN, CC, B.A., Ph.D., Editor, *Journal of Galway Archaeological and Historical Society*, Ballinasloe, County Galway, Ireland. **Article:** MacHale, John.

*EGENDER, NICOLAS, OSB, S.T.L., Prior, Priory Sainte-Croix d'Amay, Chevetogne, Belgium. **Article:** Chevetogne, Monastery of.

*EGRES, ODO JOSEPH, SOCist, Ph.D., Associate Professor of German and Chairman of the Language Department, University of Dallas, Dallas, Tex. **Articles:** Balassa, Balint; Pazmany, Peter.

*EGUILUZ, ANTONIO ANGOITIA, OFM, S.T.L., Professor of Theology, Nuestra Senora de Regla, Chipiona (Cadiz), Spain. **Articles:** Alva y Astorga, Pedro de; Focher, Juan; Tenorio, Gonzalo.

*EHR, DONALD JOHN, SVD, S.T.D., St. Mary's Seminary, Techny, Ill. **Articles:** Creation, 2. Theology of; Glory of God (End of Creation).

*EIZENHOFER, LEO, OSB, Dr. Phil., monk of the Abbey of Neuburg (near Heidelberg), Germany. **Article:** Siffrin, Peter.

*EL HAYAK, ELIAS YOUSSEF, S.T.L., J.U.D., Rector, Our Lady of Lebanon Marionite Seminary, Washington D.C. **Articles:** Abraham Ecchellensis; Antonines (Antonians); Gregory; Jacobites (Syrian); Maronite Church; Mechitar; Mechitarists; Theophanes.

*ELDAROV, GIORGIO, OFMConv, S.T.D., Ordinary Professor of Ecclesiology, Seraphicum, Rome, Italy. **Articles:** Communion and Liberation; Florovsky, George; Slipyj, Josyf.

*ELDAROV, GIORGIO, OFMConv, S.T.D., S.E.O.D., Director of ABAGAR (*Archivio cattolico bulgaro di Roma*) Rome, Italy. **Articles:** Bossilkov, Evgenij, Bl.; Bulgaria, The Catholic Church in [part 2].

*ELDAROV, GIORGIO, OFMConv., S.T.D., S.E.O.D., Director of AGABAR (*Archivio cattolico bulgaro di Roma*), Professor Emeritus of Ecclesiology, Seraphicum, Rome. **Article:** Casaroli, Agostino.

ELLARD, PETER, Ph.D., Visiting Professor of Religious Studies, Siena College, Loudonville, New York. **Articles:** Alan of Lille; Bernard Silvestris (of Tours); Bernard of Chartres; John of Salisbury; Thierry of Chartres; William of Conches.

*ELLENBRACHT, MARY P., CPPS, St. Mary's Institute, Inc., O'Fallen, Mo. **Article:** Liturgical Gestures.

*ELLINGER, ILONA ELIZABETH, M.F.A., Ph.D., Professor of Art and Chairman of the Department, Trinity College, Washington, D.C. **Article:** Egypt, Ancient, 2. Architecture and Art.

*ELLINWOOD, LEONARD WEBSTER, M.Mus., Ph.D., Deacon, Assistant at Washington Cathedral and Instructor, College of Church Musicians; Senior Subject Cataloger in the Humanities, Library of Congress, Washington, D.C. **Articles:** Frere, Rudolph Walter Howard; Landini, Francesco; Sarum Use.

*ELLIS, FRANK RICHARD, Ph.D., Associate Professor of Philosophy, St. Mary's College of California, St. Mary's, Calif. **Article:** Knowledge, Theories of [part 1].

*ELLIS, JOHN TRACY, Rt. Rev., Ph.D., L.H.D., LL.D., Litt. D., Professor of Church History, University of San Francisco, San Francisco, Calif.; Associate Editor, *Catholic Historical Review*. **Articles:** Catholic University of America, The; Gibbons, James; Guilday, Peter; Hallinan, Paul J.; Maguire, John William Rochfort; Sheen, Fulton J.; Washington, D.C., Archdiocese of.

ELLIS, KAIL, OSA, Ph.D., Dean of Arts and Sciences, Villanova University, Villanova, Pa. **Articles:** Mendel, Gregor Johann; Villanova University.

*ELLIS, PETER FRANCIS, CSSR, S.T.L., S.S.L., Professor of Sacred Scripture, Mt. St. Alphonsus, Esopus, N.Y. **Articles:** Hasidaeans; Maccabees, History of the; Maccabees, Books of the.

*ELLISON, FRED PITTMAN, Ph.D., Professor of Romance Languages, University of Texas, Austin, Tex. **Article:** Vieira, Antonio.

*ELMER, LAWRENCE JOHN, CSB, S.T.D., Professor of Theology, St. Michael's College, University of Toronto, Canada. **Articles:** Demon (Theology of); Diabolical Possession (Theology of); Diabolical Obsession; Exorcism [part 2].

ELTON, HUGH, D.Phil., Literae Humaniores, Oxford. Director, British Institute of Archaeology at Ankara, Ankara, Turkey. **Articles:** Anastasius I, Byzantine Emperor; Basiliscus, Byzantine Emperor; Zeno, Byzantine Emperor.

*ELZE, MARTIN, Dr. Theol., Privatdocent for Church History, Evangelical Theological Faculty, University of Tübingen, Germany. **Article:** Tubingen, University of.

*EMERY, ANDREE, M.A., Professor of Sociology, Mary Mount College, Los Angeles, Calif; family counselor and psychiatric therapist. **Article:** Our Lady of the Way, Society of.

*EMERY, RICHARD W., Ph.D., Professor of History, Queens College of the City University of New York, N.Y. **Articles:** Bethlehemites; Crutched Friars (Friars of the Cross); Sack, Friars of the.

*EMINYAN, MAURICE, SJ., Ph.L., Th.L., S.T.D., Professor of Dogmatic Theology, Pontifical Faculty of the Royal University of Malta, Valletta, Malta. **Articles:** Necessity of Means; Necessity of Precept; Salvation, Necessity of the Church for.

*EMMEN, AQUILINUS, OFM, S.T.D., Research Scholar in the Theological Section, Collegio S. Bonaventura, Quaracchi-Florence, Italy. **Articles:** Alexander Neckham; Alexander of Hales; Anfredus Gonteri; Bartholomaeus Anglicus; Caracciolo, Landolf; Henry of Herp (Harphius van Erp); Hugh of Newcastle (Novocastro); John Peckham (Pecham); Maes, Boniface; Peter of Ailly (Alliaco); Roger Marston; William of Ware.

*ENCK, MOTHER M. ALOYSIA, CarmelDCJ, La Mesa, Calif. **Article:** Carmelite Sisters—Carmelite Sisters of the Divine Heart of Jesus.

*ENDRES, JOHN BENEDICT, OP, Ph.L., S.T.Lr., S.T.D., Professor of Theology, Aquinas Institute School of Theology and Mount St. Bernard Seminary, Dubuque, Iowa. **Article:** Appropriation.

ENGEL, LAWRENCE JOHN, Ph.D. Director of the Center for Democracy in Action, Edgewood College, Madison, Wis. **Article:** Alinsky, Saul.

*ENGELBREGT, JACOBUS HENDRICUS ANTONIUS, OFM, Doctor artis historiae, Lect.S.Theol., Assistant Professor of Early Christian and Medieval Art and Iconography, University of Utrecht, Netherlands; Editor in Chief, *De Katholieke Encyclopedie* (Amsterdam 1949–1955). **Article:** Iconology and Iconography.

*ENGELMANN-BEURON, URSMAR, OSB, Dr.Phil., Prior and Librarian and Lecturer in Church History, History of Art, and Patrology, Archabbey of Beuron, Hohenzollern, Germany. **Articles:** Beuron, Abbey of; Beuronese Art; Lenz, Desiderius.

*ENNIS, ARTHUR JOHN, Very Rev., OSA, Hist.Eccl.D., Prior and Professor of Church History, Augustinian College, Washington, D.C. **Articles:** Adrian III, Pope, St.; Adrian II, Pope; Amalric Augerius; Andre, Bernard (Andreas); Augustine Novellus, Bl.; Basalenque, Diego; Boniface VI, Pope; Brigittine Sisters; Calancha, Antonio de la; Carr, Thomas Matthew; Christian Doctrine (Nancy), Sisters of; Galberry, Thomas; Grijalva, Juan de; Handmaids of the Sacred Heart of Jesus; Handmaids of the Blessed Sacrament and of Charity, Sisters Adorers; Hickey, Joseph Aloysius; Holy Family of Villefranche, Sisters of the; Hurley, Michael; Jones, William Ambrose; Little Sisters of the Holy Family; Moriarty, Patrick Eugene; Noris, Henry; Oblate Sisters of the Most Holy Redeemer; Our Lady of Good Counsel; Padilla, Diego Francisco; Ste. Chretienne, Sisters of; Vazquez, Francisco Javier; Villarroel, Gaspar de; Zapata y Sandoval, Juan.

*ENO, ROBERT B., SS, S.T.D., Associate Professor of Church History, The Catholic University of America, Washington, D.C. **Article:** Quasten, Johannes.

*ENTRAIGAS, RAUL AGUSTIN, SDB, S.T.D., engaged in historical research and publication, Buenos Aires, Argentina. **Article:** Cagliero, Juan.

*ERDMAN, DAVID V., Ph.D., Editor of Publications, New York Public Library, New York, N.Y. **Article:** Blake, William.

*ERIKSON, JOHN H., M. Phil., M.Th., Associate Professor of Canon Law and Church History and Associate Dean for Academic Affairs, St. Vladimir's Orthodox Theological Seminary, Crestwood, N.Y. **Article:** Meyendorff, John.

*ERMATINGER, CHARLES J., Librarian, Knights of Columbus Foundation, St. Louis, Mo. **Article:** Wolfhelm, Bl.

*ERNEST, WELDEN ARENAS, Ph.D., Assistant Professor of History, University of Hawaii, Honolulu, Hawaii. **Articles:** Lupold of Bebenburg; Trudpert, St.

*ESCRIBANO ALBERCA, IGNACIO, Ph.L., Theol.D., Privatdocent, Theological Faculty, University of Munich, Germany. **Article:** Toledo, Councils of.

*ESCUDERO, ALFONSO MARÍA, OESA, Professor, Liceo San Agustín de Santiago and Universidad Católica de Chile, Santiago, Chile. **Articles:** Balmaceda, Francisco; Donoso, Justo; Lizarraga, Reginaldo de; Valdivieso, Rafael Valentin; Vicuna Larrain, Manuel.

*ESLICK, LEONARD JAMES, Ph.D., Professor of Philosophy, St. Louis University, St. Louis, Mo. **Articles:** Bradley, Francis Herbert; Idealism [parts 1 and 2]; Royce, Josiah.

ESPELAGE, ARTHUR J., O.F.M., Executive Secretary, Canon Law Society of America, Washington, D.C. **Articles:** Camerlengo; Canon Law Society of America; Convent; Episcopal Conferences; Gallup, Diocese of; Laicization (Loss of Clerical State); Mission and Evangelization in Canon Law.

*ESTANG, LUC, Member, Directorial Committee for Editions du Seuil; Literary Critic of Novels for *Figaro littéraire;* collaborator in literary broadcasts, Paris, France. **Articles:** Bernanos, Georges; Claudel, Paul Louis Charles Marie.

*ESTIENNE, JEAN, Archiviste-paléographe, Directeur des Services d'archives, Département de la Somme, Amiens, Somme, France. **Article:** Amiens.

*ETTELDORF, RAYMOND P., B.A., J.C.L., Secretary-General, Superior Council of the Society for the Propagation of the Faith, Rome, Italy. **Article:** Eastern Churches, Congregation for the.

*ETZKORN, FERDINAND GIRARD, OFM, Ph.D., Professor of Philosophy and Master of Clerics, Our Lady of Angels Seminary, Quincy, Ill. **Articles:** James of the Marches, St.; Jeanne Marie de Maille, Bl.

*EVANS, DAVID BEECHER, B.A., B.D., Minister of the United Church of Christ, Washington, D.C.; Junior Fellow, Harvard University, Dumbarton Oaks Center for Byzantine Studies, Washington, D.C. **Articles:** Hypatius of Ephesus; John of Scythopolis; Leontius of Byzantium; Leontius of Jerusalem; Sergius of Resaina; Stephen bar-Sudhaile; Theodore Ascidas.

*EVANS, ILLTUD, OP, Editor, *Blackfriars,* London, England. **Articles:** Illtud, St.; Martindale, Cyril Charles; Punishment.

EVANS, JAMES ALLAN, Ph.D. (Yale), FRSC (Fellow of the Royal Society of Canada), Professor Emeritus of History, University of British Columbia, Vancouver, British Columbia. **Articles:** Justin I, Byzantine Emperor; Justin II, Byzantine Emperor; Justinian I, Byzantine Emperor; Roman Empire.

*EVANS, JOHN WHITNEY, M.A. (Church History), M.A. (Education), Chaplain of Catholic Students, University of Minnesota at Duluth, Minn. **Article:** Shields, Thomas Edward.

EVANS, JOHN WHITNEY, Ph.D., Associate Professor, Religious Studies Dept., College of St. Scholastica, Duluth, Minn. **Article:** Newman Apostolate.

*EVANS, JOSEPH W., Director, Jacques Maritain Center, University of Notre Dame, Notre Dame, In. **Article:** Maritain, Jacques.

*EVANS, MARY ELLEN, M.A., Associate Editor for Music, *New Catholic Encyclopedia,* The Catholic University of America, Washington, D.C.; Editor, P. J. Kenedy & Sons, New York, N.Y.;

researcher, writer. **Articles:** Boccherini, Luigi; Catherine de Ricci, St.; Chopin, Frederic François; Purcell, Henry; Vaughan Williams, Ralph; Wagner, Richard; Weber, Carl Maria von.

*EVANS, RICHARD ISADORE, M.S., Ph.D., Professor of Psychology, University of Houston, Houston, Tex. **Article:** Jung, Carl Gustav.

*EYZAGUIRRE, JAIME, Licentiate in Juridical and Social Sciences, Professor of Constitutional History and History of Law, University of Chile and Catholic University of Chile, and Director, Institute of History, Catholic University of Chile, Santiago, Chile. **Article:** Eyzaguirre, Jose Alejo; Eyzaguirre, Jose Ignacio Victor.

*FABRO, CORNELIO REMIGIO, Ph.D., Professor of Philosophy, University of Perugia, Italy; Director, Institute of History of Atheism, Pontifical Urban University, Rome, Italy. **Articles:** Existence; Fichte, Johann Gottlieb; Participation.

*FADNER, FRANK LESLIE, SJ, Ph.L., Ph.D., Th.L., Regent of the Institute of Languages and Linguistics, Head of the Division of Russian Language, and Professor of Russian History, Georgetown University, Washington, D.C. **Articles:** Nikon, Patriarch of Moscow; Raskolniks; Slavophilism.

*FAGGIN, GIUSEPPE, Doctorate in Philosophy, Professor of the History of Philosophy, Liceo Classico ''Pigafetta'' di Vicenza; Docent in the History of Philosophy; in charge of the course in aesthetics, University of Padua, Italy. **Article:** Fate and Fatalism.

*FAHEY, JOHN FRANCIS, S.T.D., M.A., Prefect of Studies, Quigley Preparatory Seminary, South Chicago, Ill. **Articles:** Adalbert the Deacon, St.; Adaldag, St.; Agnes of Poitiers, St.; Albinus (Aubin) of Angers, St.; Amalberga, SS.; Arbogast of Strasbourg, St.; Eberhard of Einsiedeln, Bl.; Remigius of Lyons, St.

*FAHEY, MICHAEL ANDREW, SJ, A.B., Ph.L., M.A., Managing Editor, *New Testament Abstracts,* Weston, Mass. **Articles:** Crasset, Jean; Gagliardi, Achille.

*FAIR, BARTHOLOMEW FRANCIS, M.A., S.T.L., J.C.D., Professor and Librarian, St. Charles Seminary, Overbrook, Philadelphia, Pa. **Article:** Wolff, George Dering.

*FAIRBANKS, MATTHEW JEROME, Ph.D., Assistant Professor of Philosophy and Chairman of the Honors Program, University of Scranton, Scranton, Pa. **Article:** Organicism.

*FALARDEAU, ERNEST RENÉ, SSS, S.T.D., M.S.L.S., St. Joseph Seminary, Cleveland, Ohio. **Article:** Religion, Virtue of.

*FALEY, ROLAND JAMES, TOR, S.T.L., S.S.L., S.T.D., Professor of Sacred Scripture, Our Lady of Loretto Seminary, Loretto, Pa. **Articles:** Book of the Covenant; Holiness, Law of; Leviticus, Book of; Scapegoat.

*FALK, CONRAD RICHARD, OSB, B.A., Ph.L., monk of Conception Abbey and Rector of Immaculate Conception Seminary, Conception, Mo. **Articles:** Abdinghof, Abbey of; Annecy, Monastery of; Argenteuil, Abbey of; Groenendael, Abbey of; Lerins, Abbey of; Liesborn, Abbey of; Lobbes, Abbey of; Tegernsee, Abbey of.

*FALLON, JOHN ANTONINUS, OP, S.T.L., S.T.Lr., Mount St. Mary College, Newburgh, N.Y. **Articles:** Anger (in the Bible); Blasphemy (in the Bible); Theft (in the Bible).

*FALLON, JOSEPH EDWARD, OP, S.T.L., S.T.Lr., S.S.L., Professor of Scripture, Dominican House of Studies, Washington, D.C.; Assistant Staff Editor for Scripture, *New Catholic Encyclopedia*, The Catholic University of America, Washington, D.C. **Articles:** Enmity (in the Bible); Hope of Salvation (in the Bible); Hope (in the Bible); Israel, 3. History of Israel; Mary Magdalene, St.; Retribution; Salvation History (Heilsgeschichte) [part 3].

*FALLON, THOMAS LEONARD, OP, S.T.L., S.T.Lr., M.A., Professor of Sacred Scripture and Theology, Providence College, Providence, R.I. **Articles:** Angel of the Lord; Angels, Guardian (in the Bible); Angels, 1. In the Bible; Cherubim; Gabriel, Archangel; Michael, Archangel; Raphael, Archangel; Seraphim; Uriel.

*FANG, MARK, SJ, S.S.D., Dean of the Graduate Schhool of Religious Sciences, Fujen Catholic University, Taipei-Hsien, Taiwan. **Article:** Taiwan, the Catholic Church in.

*FANK, ANTON PIUS, CRSA, Librarian and Archivist, Augustiner Chorherrenstift, Vorau, Austria. **Article:** Vorau, Monastery of.

*FARDELLONE, EMIL FRANCIS, SDB, M.A., Superintendent of Schools, Eastern Province of the Congregation, Office 67 of the Provincial, Salesians of Don Bosco, New Rochelle, N.Y. **Articles:** Bosco, John, St.; Savio, Dominic, St.

*FARLEY, MARGARET A., RSM, The Divinity School, Yale University, New Haven, Conn. **Article:** Sexism.

*FARMER, DAVID HUGH, OSB, monk of Quarr Abbey, England; Redrice School, Andover, Hants, England. **Articles:** Aldhelm, St.; Augustine of Canterbury, St.; Canterbury, Ancient See of; Dunstan of Canterbury, St.; Edward the Confessor, King of England, St.; Farne; Hugh of Lincoln, St. (d. 1225); Hugh of Lincoln, St. (1140–1200); Lincoln, Ancient See of; London Charterhouse; Matthew Paris; Monk of Farne; William of Malmesbury; Witham Charterhouse.

FARMER, MICHAEL L., Chancellor, Archdiocese of Mobile, Ala. **Article:** Alabama, Catholic Church in.

*FARNIK, JOHN METHODIUS, CSSR, S.T.L., Accademia Alfonsiana, Rome, Italy. **Article:** Reliquaries.

*FARRAHER, JOSEPH JAMES, SJ, Jesuit Community, University of Santa Clara, Santa Clara, Calif. **Article:** Morality.

*FARRAHER, JOSEPH JAMES, SJ, M.A., S.T.D., Professor of Moral and Pastoral Theology and Rector of Alma College, Los Gatos, Calif.; Advocate, Archdiocesan Tribunal of San Francisco. **Articles:** Fault; Masturbation; Moral Theology, History of (20th-Century Developments).

*FARRE, GEORGE L., Ph.D., Associate Professor of Logic and the Philosophy of Science, Georgetown University, Washington, D.C. **Article:** De Morgan, Augustus.

*FARRELL, JOHN THOMAS, Ph.D., Professor of American History, The Catholic University of America, Washington, D.C. **Article:** Riggs, Thomas Lawrason.

*FARRELLY, M. JOHN, OSB, M.A., S.T.D., Professor of Dogmatic Theology, St. Anselm's Abbey, Washington, D.C. **Article:** Walsh, Francis Augustine.

*FARREN, JOHN AQUINAS, OP, M.A., S.T.B., Dominican House of Studies, Washington, D.C. **Article:** Candido, Vincenzo.

*FASANELLO, SISTER MARY ANDREW, FMDC, Regina Coeli Acres, Williams-ville, N.Y. **Article:** Franciscan Sisters—Franciscan Missionary Sisters of the Divine Child (FMDS).

*FASCHING, DARRELL J., Ph.D., Professor of Religion, Ethics, and Public Policy, University of South Florida, Tampa. **Article:** Ellul, Jacques.

*FASOLA, UMBERTO MARIA, CRSP, Doctorate in Letters, S.T.L., Doctorate in Christian Archeology, Postulator General of the Barnabite Order; Vice Secretary, Pontifical Commission of Sacred Archeology; Docent, Pontifical Institute of Christian Archeology, Rome, Italy. **Articles:** Barnabites; Bianchi, Francesco Saverio Maria, St.; Carpani, Melchiorre; Ferrari, Bartolomeo, Ven.; Sauli, Alexander, St.; Zaccaria, Anthony Mary, St.

FASTIGGI, ROBERT, Ph.D., Associate Professor of Systematic Theology, Sacred Heart Seminary, Detroit, Mich. **Articles:** Denzinger; Pius X, Pope, St.; Swiss Guards; Yves de Paris.

*FAUL, DENIS O'BEIRNE, B.A., B.D., S.T.L., Teacher, St. Patrick's Academy, Dunganon, North Ireland. **Articles:** Donatism; Donatus.

*FAUPEL, JOHN FRANCIS, MHM, M.A., Chaplain, Uganda Technical College, Kampala, Uganda, Africa. **Articles:** Lwanga, Charles, St.; Uganda, The Catholic Church in; Uganda, Martyrs of.

*FEARNS, JAMES VINCENT, Ph.D., Assistant, Department of Medieval History, University College, Dublin, Ireland. **Article:** Lea, Henry Charles.

*FEARON, JOHN D., OP, S.T.Lr., S.T.L., S.T.Praes., Assistant Professor of Theology, Seattle University, Seattle, Wash. **Articles:** Accusation; Anger; Cheating; Holiness; Meekness; Onanism; Purpose of Amendment; Superstition; Vice.

*FECHER, VINCENT JOHN, SVD, M.A., Hist.Eccl.D., Christ the King Seminary, Manila, Philippines. **Articles:** Divine Word, Society of the; Janssen, Arnold, Bl.; Perpetual Adoration, Sister Servants of the Holy Spirit of.

FEELEY, ALICE V., RDC, M.A., President of the Sisters of the Divine Compassion, White Plains, N.Y. **Article:** Divine Compassion, Sisters of the.

*FEELY, THOMAS FRANCIS, CM, M.A., Teacher, St. Thomas Seminary, Denver, Colo. **Article:** Denver, Archdiocese of.

FEENEY, JOSEPH J., SJ, Ph.L., S.T.L., Ph.D., Professor of English, Saint Joseph's University, Philadelphia, Pa. **Article:** Hopkins, Gerard Manley.

*FEHLNER, PETER DAMIAN, OFMConv, S.T.D., Lecturer in Theology, Pontifical Theological Faculty of St. Bonaventure, Rome, Italy. **Articles:** Adragna, Antonio Maria; Brancati, Lorenzo; Delfini, John Anthony; Musso, Cornelius; O'Fihely, Maurice; Saraceni, Maurus; Sgambati, Andreas.

FEHRING, RICHARD J., DNSc, RN, Associate Professor and Director Marquette University College of Nursing Institute for Natural Family Planning and Editor of Current Medical Research a supplement of NFP Forum (Diocesan Activity Report), Milwaukee, Wis. **Article:** Natural Family Planning.

*FEIERTAG, SISTER LORETTA CLARE, SC, Ph.D., Professor of History, Department of History and Political Science, College of Mount St. Joseph, Mount St. Joseph, Ohio. **Article:** O'Connell, Anthony, Sister.

*FELHOELTER, SISTER MARY CLARITA, OSU, Ph.D., Teacher, Ursuline College, Louisville, Ky. **Article:** Ursulines.

FELICES, FERNANDO B., J.D. Juris Doctor in Law, Harvard University, M.Theol., St. John's Seminary in Massachusetts. Chancellor of the Archdiocese of San Juan, San Juan, Puerto Rico. **Article:** Caribbean, The Catholic Church in.

*FELICIJAN, JOSEPH, Ph.D., Associate Professor, St. John College of Cleveland, Cleveland, Ohio. **Article:** Klesl, Melchior.

*FELIKS, JEHUDA, Ph.D., Associate Professor, Department of Botany, Bar Ilan University, Ramath Gan, Israel. **Article:** Palestine, 4. Natural History.

*FELL, SISTER MARIE LÉONORE, SC, Ph.D., Professor of History and Sociology and Chairman of the Department of History, College of Mount St. Vincent, New York, N.Y. **Articles:** Erastianism; Fitzgibbon, Mary Irene, Sister; Hughes, Angela, Mother; Know-Nothingism.

*FELLER, JOHN QUENTIN, JR., M.A., Assistant Archivist, Archdiocese of Baltimore, Md. **Articles:** Channing, William Ellery; Dooley, Thomas Anthony; Lasance, Francis Xavier; Lay Congresses, American Catholic; Matthews, William; Mission in Colonial

America III (French Missions); Rey, Anthony; Richard, Gabriel; Taylor, Myron Charles.

*FELLERER, KARL GUSTAV, Dr.Phil., Dr. (h.c.), Professor of Musicology, University of Cologne, Germany. **Articles:** Albrechtsberger, Johann Georg; Martini, Giovanni Battista; Richter, Franz Xaver; Vicentino, Nicola.

*FENTON, NORMAN E., OP, Associate Professor of Philosophy and Associate Editor of *The Thomist,* Dominican House of Studies, Washington, D.C. **Article:** Weisheipl, James A.

*FERNANDEZ, JOHNSON, Catholic News Office, Archdiocese of Singapore. **Article:** Singapore, Catholic Church in.

*FERNANDEZ-ALONSO, JUSTO, Hist.Eccl. D., Director, Instituto español de Historia eclesiástica; Consultor, Sacred Congregation of Rites; Associate, Instituto Flórez de Historia ecclesiástica, Madrid, Spain. **Article:** Spain, the Catholic Church in.

*FERRAIRONI AMABILE, SISTER MARY FRANCIS, Archivist, Casa Generalizia, Istituto Figlie Maria SS. dell' Orto; Directress, *Lungo la via del Gianelli,* Rome, Italy. **Articles:** Gianelli, Anthony, St.; Our Lady of the Garden, Sisters of.

*FERRARI, GIACOMO, CSSR, Hist.Eccl.D., Professor of Church History, Redemptorist House of Studies, Collegio PP. Redentoristi, Cortona (Arezzo), Italy. **Article:** Secret, Discipline of the.

FESUH, TESFAYE W., Pastor, Our Lady of Perpetual Help Ge'ez Catholic Church, Washington, D.C. **Article:** Falashas.

*FIALA, MILOSLAV, Spokesman of the Czech Episcopal Conference, Praha, Czech Republic. **Articles:** Czech Republic, The Catholic Church in [part 2]; Slovakia, The Catholic Church in.

*FIALA, VIRGIL ERNST, OSB, Dr.Phil., monk of the Archabbey of Beuron, Lector in Liturgy, Theologische Hochschule, Beuron, Germany. **Articles:** Dold, Alban; Schott, Anselm; Wolter, Maurus.

*FICHTER, JOSEPH H., SJ, Department of Sociology, Loyola University, New Orleans, La. **Article:** Unification Church.

*FICHTNER, JOSEPH, OSC, S.T.D., Department of Theology, Mt. St. Mary's College, Emmitsburg, Md. **Articles:** Faith, Act of; Tradition (in Theology).

*FIELD, COLIN WALTER, Local Government Officer, The Twenty-Sixth

House, Robertsbridge, Sussex, England. **Articles:** Bridgewater, John; Marian Priests.

*FILAS, FRANCIS LAD, SJ, S.T.D., Chairman, Department of Theology, Loyola University, Chicago, Ill. **Articles:** Joseph, St.; Joseph, St., Devotion to.

*FILTEAU, JEROME, Catholic News Service, Washington, D.C. **Article:** Reno, Diocese of.

FINDIKYAN, MICHAEL DANIEL, M.Div., M.A., S.E.O.D., Archbishop Tiran Nersoyan Professor of Liturgy, St. Nersess Armenian Seminary, New Rochelle, N.Y. **Article:** Armenian Liturgy.

*FINEGAN, FRANCIS JOSEPH, SJ, Curator, Irish Jesuit Historical Archives and Sub-editor, *Studies,* Dublin, Ireland. **Articles:** Collins, Dominic, Bl.; Fitzsimon, Henry; Holywood, Christopher; Irish Colleges on the Continent; Irish Confessors and Martyrs; O'Donnell, Edmund.

*FINK, KARL AUGUST, Dr.Theol., Professor of Medieval and Modern History, University of Tübingen, Germany. **Articles:** Archives, Ecclesiastical; Martin V, Pope; Mercati, Angelo.

*FINK, PETER E., SJ, Ph.D., Professor of Sacramental and Liturgical Theology, Weston School of Theology, Cambridge, Mass. **Article:** Liturgical Theology.

*FINK, WILHELM, OSB, Professor Emeritus, Gymnasium Metten, Abtei Metten, bei Deggendorf, Niederbayern, Germany (deceased Feb. 13, 1965). **Articles:** Andechs, Abbey of; Metten, Abbey of; Sankt Paul, Abbey of (Carinthia); Sankt Lambrecht, Abbey of.

*FINLAY, JAMES CHARLES, SJ, S.T.L., Ph.D., Assistant Professor and Chairman of Department of Political Philosophy and Government, Fordham University, New York, N.Y. **Article:** Montalembert, Charles Forbes Rene de.

*FINN, EDWARD ERNEST, SJ, M.A., Ph.L., S.T.L., Member, Department of Theology, Marquette University, Milwaukee, Wis. **Articles:** Alexandrian Liturgy; Antiochene Liturgy; Coptic Liturgy; Ethiopian (Ge'ez) Liturgy.

*FINN, JAMES, Editor *Worldview,* New York, N.Y. **Article:** Torres, Camilo.

*FINNEGAN, JAMES MICHAEL, SJ, S.T.L., Professor of Philosophy, Oriental

Seminary, St. Joseph's University, Beirut, Lebanon. **Articles:** Alfarabi (Farabi, al-); Algazel (Ghazzali, al-).

*FINNEGAN, SISTER MARY JEREMY, OP, Ph.D., Chairman, Department of English, Rosary College, River Forest, Ill. **Articles:** Agnes of Montepulciano, St.; Alfonsus Bonihominis; Augustine Kazotic, Bl.; Catherine of Sweden, St.; Christina of Stommeln, Bl.; Columba of Rieti, Bl.; Damian of Finario, Bl.; Guala of Bergamo, Bl.; Hyacinth, St.; Ilga, Bl.; Joan of Orvieto, Bl.; Joan of Aza, Bl.; John of Falkenberg; Lambertini, Imelda, Bl.; Sibyllina Biscossi, Bl.

FIORELLI, S. LEWIS, OSFS, STD, Superior General of the Oblates of St. Francis de Sales, Washington, D.C. **Article:** Oblates of St. Francis de Sales.

*FIORENZA, FRANCIS P. SCHÜSSLER, Ph.D., Department of Theology, Villanova University, Villanova, Pa. **Articles:** Liberation Theology; Political Theology.

FIORENZA, FRANCIS P. SCHÜSSLER, Dr. Theol. Stillman Professor of Roman Catholic Theological Studies, Harvard Divinity School, Cambridge, Mass. **Article:** Foundational Theology.

*FIRTH, FRANCIS, CSB, M.A., L.M.S., Lecturer in Religious Studies and in Philosophy, University of British Columbia, Vancouver, British Columbia, Canada. **Article:** Robert of Flamborough.

*FISCHER, BALTHASAR, DD, Professor of Liturgy and Homiletics, Theologische Fakultät, Trier, Germany. **Articles:** Meurers, Heinrich von; Stohr, Albert.

*FISCHER, HEINRICH, Very Rev., Generalpräses des Kolping-werkes, Köln, Germany. **Article:** Kolping, Adolf, Bl.

*FISCHER, JOSEPH ANTON, Dr.Theol., Professor of Church History and Patrology, Philosophisch-theologische Hochschule, Freising, Bavaria, Germany. **Articles:** Apostolic Fathers; Dura-Europos; Washing of the Feet.

*FISCHER, ROBERT HARLEY, Ph.D., Professor of Historical Theology, Lutheran School of Theology, Chicago, Ill. **Articles:** Arnold, Gottfried; Berquin, Louis de; Bugenhagen, Johann; Carpzov.

*FISHER, ALDEN LOWELL, M.A., Docteur en psychologie, Associate Professor of Philosophy, St. Louis University, St. Louis, Mo. **Article:** Merleau-Ponty, Maurice.

*FISHER, BERNARD CHARLES, Archivist, Westminster Archives; Chaplain, London Newman Circle, Cardinal Vaughan School, London, England. **Articles:** Bodey, John, Bl.; Cottan, Thomas, Bl.; Felton, John, Bl.; Fortescue, Adrian, Bl.

*FISHER, EUGENE J., Executive Secretary, Secretariat for Catholic-Jewish Relations, National Conference of Catholic Bishops, Washington, D.C. **Article:** Hebrew Scriptures.

FISHER, EUGENE J., Ph.D., Associate Director of Secretariat for Ecumenical and Interreligious Affairs, United States Conference of Catholic Bishops, Washington, D.C. **Articles:** Holocaust (Shoah); Oesterreicher, John.

*FITTS, SISTER MARY PAULINE, GNSH, Ph.D., Chairman of Department of Philosophy, D'Youville College, Buffalo, N.Y. **Article:** Grey Nuns.

*FITZGERALD, ALLAN D., OSA, Department of Theology, Catholic University of America, Washington, D.C. **Articles:** Chasuble; Liturgical Vessels; Liturgical Vestments.

*FITZGERALD, DESMOND JAMES, Ph.D., Professor of Philosophy, University of San Francisco, San Francisco, Calif. **Article:** Renaissance Philosophy.

*FITZGERALD, GERALD OF THE HOLY SPIRIT, SP, Founder, Servants of the Holy Paraclete and Handmaids of the Precious Blood, Via Coeli, Jemez Springs, N.Mex. **Article:** Paraclete, Servants of the.

*FITZGERALD, SISTER MARY PAUL, SCL, Ph.D., formerly Chairman, Department of History, St. Mary College, Xavier, Kans. (deceased April 16, 1962). **Article:** Miège, John Baptist.

*FITZGERALD, PAUL RICHARD, OCSO, B.S., Our Lady of the Holy Cross Abbey, Berryville, Va. **Article:** Idleness, Moral Aspects of.

*FITZGIBBON, MARJORIE MARY, M.A., Editorial Assistant to Index Editor, *New Catholic Encyclopedia,* The Catholic University of America, Washington, D.C. **Articles:** Kreisler, Fritz; Stuart, Janet Erskine.

*FITZHERBERT, MARGARET EVELYN [MRS. G.], author; research assistant to Philip Caraman, SJ, Catholic Truth Society, London, England. **Articles:** Almond, John, St.; Arrowsmith, Edmund, St.; Barlow, Ambrose (Edward), St.; Briant, Alexander, St.; Clitherow, Margaret, Bl.; Evans, Philip, St.; Garnet, Thomas, St.; Gennings, Edmund, Bl.; Gwyn, Richard (White), Bl.; Howard, Philip, St.; Jones, John, St.; Kemble, John, St.; Kirby, Luke, St.; Lewis, David, St. (Charles Baker); Line, Anne, St.; Lloyd, John, St.; Mayne, Cuthbert, St.; Owen, Nicholas, St.; Paine, John, St.; Plessington, John (William), St.; Reynolds, Richard, St.; Rigby, John, St.; Roberts, John, St.; Roe, Alban (Bartholomew), St.; Sherwin, Ralph, St.; Southworth, John, St.; Stone, John, St.; Wall, John, St.; Walpole, Henry, St.; Ward, Margaret, St.

FITZMYER, JOSEPH A., S.J., S.S.L., Ph.D. Professor Emeritus of Biblical Studies, The Catholic University of America, Washington, D.C. **Articles:** Aramaeans; Aramaic Language, 1. Ancient; Bar Kokhba, Simon (Bar Cocheba); Brown, Raymond Edward; Dead Sea Scrolls; Qumran Community; Romans, Epistle to the.

*FITZPATRICK, FRANKLIN EUGENE, M.A., Principal, Bishop McDonnell Memorial High School, Brooklyn, N.Y. **Article:** Malone, Sylvester.

*FITZSIMONS, JOHN EDWARD, Dip. of Political and Social Science, M.A. (Oxon.), Pastor of St. Timothy, Liverpool, England. **Article:** Sword of the Spirit.

*FLANAGAN, JOHN JOSEPH, SJ, LLB., M.A., Executive Director, Catholic Hospital Association, and Executive Editor, *Hospital Progress,* St. Louis, Mo. **Articles:** Hospitals, History of, 2. 1500 to Present; Hospitals, History of, 3. Catholic Hospitals.

*FLANAGAN, NEAL M., OSM, S.T.D., S.S.L., Eleve Titulaire de l'École Biblique, Professor of Scripture, Our Lady of Benburb Priory, Benburb, County Tyrone, Ireland. **Articles:** Jerusalem, Council of; Judas Iscariot.

*FLANAGAN, RAYMOND, OCSO, M.A., S.T.L., Our Lady of Gethsemani Seminary, Ky. **Articles:** Dunne, M. Frederic; Obrecht, M. Edmond; Trappists.

FLANIGAN, M. F., **Article:** Franciscan Sisters—Franciscan Sisters of the Atonement (SA).

*FLANIGAN, SISTER MARY KENNETH, HHM, B.S.E., Principal, St. Martha Elementary School, Akron, Ohio. **Article:** Humility of Mary, Sisters of the.

*FLANNERY, EDWARD H., A.B., Editor, *The Providence Visitor,* Providence, R.I. **Articles:** Marranos; Mortara Case.

FLANNERY, MARY ELLEN, OSF, Major Superior, Sisters of the Third Order of St. Francis, East Peoria, Ill. **Article:** Franciscan Sisters—Sisters of the Third Order of St. Francis (OSF).

*FLANNERY, REGINA, Ph.D., Professor of Anthropology and Head of Department, The Catholic University of America, Washington, D.C.; Editor, *Catholic University of America Anthropological Series.* **Article:** Cooper, John Montgomery.

*FLEECE, URBAN H., Ph.D., Professor of Education and Associate Vice President, De Paul University, Chicago, Ill. **Article:** Attitudes.

*FLEISCHNER, EVA, Montclair State College, N.J. **Article:** Holocaust (Shoah).

*FLINT, VALERIE IRENE JANE, B.A. (Hons.), B.Phil., Assistant, Department of Medieval History, University College, Dublin, Ireland. **Articles:** Anastasius, St.; Bercharius, St.; Boniface of Savoy, Bl.; Carileffus, St.; Charles of Blois, Bl.; Chester, Ancient See of; Desideratus of Bourges, St.; Desiderius Rhodonensis, St.; Ebba, SS.; Egbert (Ecgbert) of York; Eligius of Noyon, St.; Erdington, Abbey of; Ethelbert of York; Goswin, St.; Laudus (Lo), St.; Philibert of Rebais, St.; Sheen Charterhouse; Wallingford, William.

*FLUSCHE, ERNEST A.; Ph.D., Principal, Bishop McGuiness High School, and Superintendent, Catholic Schools of Oklahoma, Oklahoma City, Okla. **Article:** Kelley, Francis Clement.

*FLYNN, JEROME TERENCE, OCD, Professor of Ecclesiastical History, College of Our Lady of Mt. Carmel, Washington, D.C. **Articles:** Cameron, John (1826–1910); Charbonneau, Joseph; Coady, Moses Michael; Connolly, Thomas Louis; Emard, Joseph Medard; Fallon, Michael Francis; Lynch, John Joseph; MacDonell, Alexander; McNeil, Neil; Walsh, John.

*FLYNN, JOHN LEO, SJ, M.A., Alma College, Los Gatos, Calif. **Articles:** D'Elia, Pasquale; Dahlmann, Joseph; Huonder, Anton; Mazzella, Camillo; Palmieri, Domenico.

*FLYNN, JOSEPH PATRICK, CSP, M.A., Rector, St. Paul's College, Washington, D.C. **Articles:** Hewitt, Augustine Francis; Walworth, Clarence Augustus.

*FLYNN, RICHARD JOSEPH, CM, B.A., Mary Immaculate Seminary, Northampton, Pa. **Articles:** Corban; Votive Offerings [part 2].

*FOERSTER, HANS, Professor, University of Fribourg, Switzerland. **Article:** Liber Diurnus Romanorum Pontificum.

FOGARTY, GERALD P., SJ, Ph.D., William R. Kenon, Jr., Professor of Religious Studies and History, University of Virginia, Charlottesville, Va. **Article:** Virginia, Catholic Church in.

*FOGARTY, WILLIAM EDWARD, MTC, S.T.L., Assistant Novice Master, Marian Fathers Scholasticate, Washington, D.C. **Article:** Matulaitis, Jurgis, Bl.

*FOLEY, ALBERT SIDNEY, SJ, Ph.D., Professor of Sociology and Chairman of the Department of Sociology and Psychology, Spring Hill College, Mobile, Ala.; Director, Executive Development Programs, Human Relations Institutes and Workshops. **Articles:** Healy, James Augustine; Propaganda.

*FOLEY, GERTRUDE, SC, Sisters of Charity of Seton Hill, Greensburg, Pa. **Article:** Charisms in Religious Life.

*FOLEY, IGNATIUS LOYOLA, CM, S.T.L., Professor of Canon Law and Moral Theology, Kenrick Seminary, St. Louis, Mo.; Director, Daughters of Charity in Japan. **Article:** Titular See.

*FOLEY, LEO ALBERT, SM, Ph.D., Professor of Philosophy, The Catholic University of America, Washington, D.C. **Articles:** Postulate; Theory.

FOLEY, PATRICK, Ph.D., Editor, *Catholic Southwest: A Journal of History and Culture,* Azle, Tex. **Articles:** Arizona, Catholic Church in; Missouri, Catholic Church in.

*FOLEY, RICHARD LONERGAN, M.A., S.T.L., Assistant Pastor, St. Thomas the Apostle Church, and Lecturer in Theology, St. Joseph College, West Hartford, Conn. **Articles:** Bentivoglio; Circumcision; Delfino; Grassi (De Grassis); Gregory XIV, Pope; Innocent IX, Pope; Nativity of Christ; Sfondrati.

*FORBES, CLARENCE ALLEN, Ph.D., Professor of Classical Languages, Ohio State University, Columbus, Ohio. **Article:** Firmicus Maternus, Julius.

*FORBES, DALSTON JOSEPH, OMI, Ph.L., S.T.D., Lecturer in Dogmatic Theology and Dean of Studies, Our Lady of Lanka Seminary, Kandy, Ceylon. **Article:** Humanism, Christian.

*FORBES, EUGENE ANTHONY, Rt. Rev., S.T.L., J.C.D., Vicar-General, Diocese of Saginaw, Mich. **Article:** Chancellor, Diocesan (Eparchial).

*FORD, J. MASSYNGBERDE, Associate Professor, Department of Theology, University of Notre Dame, Notre Dame, In. **Articles:** Deaconess; Glossolalia.

*FORD, JOHN T., CSC, Associate Professor of Theology, Catholic University of America, Washington, D.C. **Articles:** Consultation on Church Union; Ecumenical Movement; Hierarchy of Truths; Infallibility.

*FORD, JOHN THOMAS, CSC, M.A., S.T.D., Professor of Ecclesiastical History, Holy Cross College, Washington, D.C. **Articles:** Easter Controversy; Quartodecimans.

FORD, LEWIS S., Ph.D., Louis I. Jaffe Professor of Philosophy Emeritus, Old Dominion University, Norfolk, Va. **Articles:** Process Philosophy; Process Theology.

*FORELL, GEORGE WOLFGANG, Th.D., Professor of Protestant Theology, School of Religion, State University of Iowa, Iowa City, Iowa. **Articles:** Grebel, Conrad; Hoffman, Melchior; Hubmaier, Balthasar; Hutter, Jakob; Joris, David; Munzer, Thomas.

*FORESTELL, JAMES TERENCE, CSB, S.T.L., S.S.L., Professor of Sacred Scripture, St. Basil's Seminary and the University of St. Michael's College, Toronto, Canada. **Articles:** Inerrancy, Biblical; Inspiration, Biblical.

*FOREVILLE, RAYMONDE GERMAINE, Licence ès lettres, Diplôme d'Études Supérieures et Agrégation d'Histoire, Doctorate d'État (Paris), Diplôme de L'École pratique des Hautes Études (Sciences religieuses), Professor of Medieval History, University of Rennes, France. **Article:** Normans.

*FORGAC, JAMES ALBERT, OSB, M.A., S.T.D., Teacher, Benedictine High School, Cleveland, Ohio; Visiting Lecturer, Graduate Department of Religion, University of Ottawa, Canada. **Article:** Apostolic Constitution.

*FORGET, SUZANNE, S.G.M., Sisters of Charity of Montreal, "Grey Nuns," St. Joseph Province, Provincial Administration, Lexington, Mass. **Article:** Youville, Marie Marguerite d', St.

*FORREST, SISTER MARY PATRICIA, OSF, Ph.D., Teacher of English, Alverno College, Milwaukee, Wis. **Article:** Franciscan Sisters—Sisters of St. Francis of the Immaculate Heart of Mary (OSF).

*FORSHAW, BERNARD, S.T.L., D.D., Senior Professor of Dogmatic Theology,

Upholland College, Wigan, Lancashire, England. **Articles:** Accessus; Apostolic Blessing; Archdeacon; Archpriest; Benedictus Deus; Chair of Peter; Conclave; Doctor of the Church; Father (Religious Title); Fides Quaerens Intellectum; Fisherman's Ring; Heaven (Theology of); Holiness (Papal Title); Holy See; Prescription, Theological Use of.

*FORSTER, ANN MARY CECILIA, M.D., M.A. (Oxon.), Burradon, Thropton, Morpeth, Northumberland, England. **Articles:** Boste, John, St.; Morse, Henry, St.; Plasden, Polydore, St.; Wells, Swithun, St.; White, Eustace, St.

*FORSYTH, BRENDAN FRANCIS, OSB, M.A., J.C.L., monk of St. John's Abbey, Collegeville, Minn.; Chancellor and Officialis, Diocese of Nassau, Bahamas; Rector, St. Francis Xavier's Cathedral, and Superintendent of Catholic Schools, Nassau, Bahamas. **Article:** Bahamas, The Catholic Church in.

*FORTE, STEPHEN LAWRENCE, OP, S.T.Lr., B.Litt., Socius Instituti Historici, S. Sabina, Rome, Italy. **Articles:** Bernard Gui; Dominici, John, Bl.; John of Vercelli, Bl.

*FORTMAN, EDMUND J., SJ, Professor of Dogmatic Theology, Bellarmine School of Theology, North Aurora, Ill. **Articles:** Censure, Theological; Error, Theological; Notes, Theological.

*FORTMANN, HERMAN M. M., Professor of Psychology of Culture and Religion, Catholic University of Nijmegen, Netherlands. **Article:** Leeuw, Gerardus van der.

*FOSSATI, LUIGI, S.T.L., Doctorate in Social Sciences, Professor of History, Seminary, Brescia; Provost and Canon, Cathedral of Brescia, Italy. **Articles:** Di Rosa, Maria Crocifissa, St.; Handmaids of Charity.

*FOSTER, KENELM FRANCIS, OP, M.A., Ph.D., Lecturer, Department of Italian, University of Cambridge, England. **Articles:** Casa, Giovanni della; Catherine of Siena, St.; Colonna, Vittoria; Savonarola, Girolamo.

*FOTHERGILL, BRIAN, Associate of King's College and author, London, England. **Articles:** Acton, Charles Januarius; Stuart, Henry Benedict Maria Clement; Weld, Thomas; Wiseman, Nicholas Patrick.

*FOTITCH, TATIANA, Ph.D., Professor of Romance Languages and Literatures,

The Catholic University of America, Washington, D.C. **Articles:** Bistrita, Abbey of; Hurezi (Horezi), Abbey of; Moldovita (Vatra Moldovitei), Abbey of.

*FOUDY, JOHN THOMAS, Rt. Rev., Ph.D., Superintendent of Schools, Archdiocese of San Francisco; Director, Confraternity of Christian Doctrine; Archdiocesan Consultor; Pastor of St. Agnes Church, San Francisco, Calif. **Article:** San Francisco, Archdiocese of.

*FOX, HENRY FREDERICK, SJ, Th.B., Ph.D., Chairman, Department of Education, Graduate School of Arts and Sciences, Ateneo de Manila, Philippine Islands. **Article:** Dietz, Peter Ernest.

*FOX, JEAN ANN, M.A., Administrative Assistant in Public Information, Manhattanville College of the Sacred Heart, Purchase, N.Y. **Article:** Pius X School of Liturgical Music.

*FOX, JOSEPH E., OP, University of St. Thomas Aquinas, Rome. **Article:** Ottaviani, Alfredo.

*FOYE, BARBARA EUGENIA, B.A., Assistant Style Editor, *New Catholic Encyclopedia,* The Catholic University of America, Washington, D.C. **Article:** Foy, St.

FOYSTER, G., **Article:** Franciscan Sisters—Missionary Franciscan Sisters of the Immaculate Conception (MFIC).

*FRAILE, GUILLERMO MARTIN, OP, S.T.D., S.T.M., Professor of the History of Philosophy, Pontifical University of Salamanca; Professor of Religious Training, State University of Salamanca, Spain. **Articles:** Balmes, Jaime Luciano; Gonzalez y Diaz Tunon, Ceferino; Philosophy, History of, 1. General Notions.

*FRANCO, HILARY CARMINE, M.A., S.T.D., National Office of the Propagation of the Faith, New York, N.Y. **Article:** Slavery (in the Bible).

*FRANÇOIS, MICHEL, Archiviste-paléographe, Docteur ès lettres, Professor of History of Institutions, École des Chartes; Chargé de cours, Sorbonne (Initiation à la recherche historique); Dean and Professor of Medieval History, Institut Catholique, Paris, France. **Articles:** Paul II, Pope; Vienne, Council of.

*FRANK, RICHARD MACDONOUGH, Ph.D., Professor of Semitics, The Catholic

University of America, Washington, D.C. **Articles:** Ḥajj; Hijra; Mecca; Medina; Mosque; Qur'ān; Ramadan.

*FRANZ, EDWARD QUINLISK, Ph.D., Professor of Philosophy, Gannon College, Erie, Pa., and St. Mary of the Plains, Dodge City, Kans. **Articles:** Logicism; Scientism.

*FRANZEN, AUGUST, S.T.D., J.C.L., Diploma of Archivist and Palaeographer (Vatican School of Palaeography), Professor of Ecclesiastical History, Faculty of Theology, University of Freiburg, Germany. **Article:** Billick, Eberhard.

*FRATTIN, PIERO LUIGI, J.C.D., J.C.C.D., Professor of Canon Law, Viatorian Seminary, Washington, D.C.; Lecturer in Canon Law, St. John's University, New York, N.Y. **Article:** Syntagma Canonum Antiochenum.

*FRAWLEY, MARY ALPHONSE, Ph.D., Professor of History and Chairman of the Department, Regis Sister M. Alphonsine, CSJ College, Weston, Mass. **Articles:** Bingham, Joseph; Brownson, Josephine Van Dyke; Butler, Joseph; Jewel, John.

FRAZER, EDWARD J., SS, M.A., S.T.L., Theological College, Washington, D.C. **Article:** Sulpicians.

*FREEDMAN, DAVID NOEL, Th.B., Ph.D., Professor of Hebrew and Old Testament Literature, San Francisco Theological Seminary, San Anselmo, Calif., and Graduate Theological Union, Berkeley, Calif. **Article:** Albright, William Foxwell.

*FREEMAN, ANN, Ph.D., Associate Professor of History, Chatham College, Pittsburgh, Pa. **Articles:** Libri Carolini; Theodulf of Orleans.

*FREEMAN, HILARY JUSTIN, OP, Ph.L., Assistant Professor of Philosophy, College of St. Catherine, St. Paul, Minn. **Article:** Luck.

*FREEMAN, LAURENCE, OSB, M.A. (oxon.), Monastery of Christ the King, London; Director, World Community for Christian Meditation. **Article:** Griffiths, Bede.

FREI, CAROLYN J.; M.A.T., Retired Educator, Grangeville, Idaho Schools. **Article:** Idaho, Catholic Church in.

*FRENCH, HOWARD, S.T.D., Director, Catholic Education, Fort Knox, Ky. **Article:** Presentation of Mary.

*FREUDENTHAL, HANS W. L., Ph.D., Professor of European History, College of St.

Teresa, Winona, Minn. **Articles:** Faulhaber, Andreas; Frederick II (the Great), King of Prussia; Kulturkampf.

*FREUND, JOHN BERNARD, CM, B.A., Mary Immaculate Seminary, Northampton, Pa. **Articles:** Peace Offering (in the Bible); Holocaust.

*FRIDAY, ROBERT M., S.T.D., Assistant Professor of Religion and Religious Education; Associate Dean, School of Religious Studies, The Catholic University of America, Washington, D.C. **Article:** Triage.

FRIDAY, ROBERT M., S.T.D., Assistant Professor of Religion and Religious Education, The Catholic University of America, Washington, D.C. **Article:** Euthanasia.

*FRIEDMAN, MAURICE STANLEY, Ph.D., LL.D., Professor of Philosophy, Manhattanville College of the Sacred Heart, Purchase, N.Y.; Member of the Faculty, New School for Social Research, New York, N.Y.; lecturer, writer, editor, translator. **Article:** Buber, Martin.

FRIEDRICHSEN, TIMOTHY, Ph.D., Assistant Professor, Department of Religion and Religious Education, The Catholic University of America, Washington, D.C. **Articles:** Disciples; Masturbation; Time (in the New Testament).

*FRISKE, JOSEPH PETER, M.A., Assistant Pastor, St. Bernard's Parish, Alpena, Mich. **Article:** Bellarmine, Robert, St.

FROHLICH, MARY, Ph.D., Associate Professor of Spirituality, Catholic Theological Union, Chicago, Ill. **Articles:** Ecstasy; Ecstasy (in the Bible); Rapture.

*FRYE, RICHARD NELSON, Ph.D., Aga Khan Professor of Iranian, Harvard University, Cambridge, Mass. **Articles:** Medes; Persia.

*FUHRMANN, HORST GERHARD, Dr.Phil., Professor of Medieval and Modern History, University of Tübingen, Germany. **Articles:** Canon Law, History of, 2. Carolingian Era; False Decretals (Pseudo-Isidorian Forgeries).

*FULCO, WILLIAM JAMES, SJ, M.A., Alma College, Los Gatos, Calif. **Articles:** Druzbicki, Gaspar; Santarelli, Anton; Segneri, Paolo, the Younger; Segneri, Paolo; Taparelli d'Azeglio, Luigi.

FUNK, VIRGIL C., President and CEO, National Association of Pastoral Musicians, Washington, D.C. **Articles:**

Liturgical Music, Theology and Practice of; National Association of Pastoral Musicians (NPM).

*FURER, IVO, Bishop of St. Gall, Switzerland; Former General Secretary, Consilium Conferentiarum Episcoporum Europae. **Article:** Council of European Bishops' Conferences (CCEE).

*FURFEY, PAUL HANLY, Rt. Rev., Ph.D., LL.D., Professor of Sociology and Director of the Bureau of Social Research, The Catholic University of America, Washington, D.C. **Article:** Kerby, William Joseph.

*FURLAN, WILLIAM P., St. Charles Church, Herman, Minn. **Article:** Pierz, Francis Xavier.

*FURLONG, GUILLERMO CARDIFF, SJ, Ph.D., S.T.L., Doctor in History (h.c.), Professor, Counselor, and Head of the University Library, Salvador University, Buenos Aires, Argentina. **Articles:** Aneiros, Leon Federico; Argentina, The Catholic Church in; Castaneda, Francisco de Paula; Clara, Jeronimo Emiliano; De Andrea, Miguel; Franceschi, Gustavo Juan; Muriel, Domingo; Primoli, Juan Bautista; Trejo y Sanabria, Fernando de.

*FURTH, HANS G., Ph.D., Associate Professor of Psychology, The Catholic University of America, Washington, D.C. **Article:** Piaget, Jean.

*FURTON, EDWARD J., M.A., Assistant Editor, *The New Catholic Encyclopedia,* The Catholic University of America, Washington, D.C. **Article:** Scientology.

FURTON, EDWARD J., Ph.D., Editor-in-Chief, The National Catholic Bioethics Quarterly, Brighton, Mass. **Article:** Soul, Human, Origin of.

*FUS, EDWARD ANTHONY, J.C.D., Curia, Diocese of Brooklyn; Defender of the Marriage Bond, Diocesan Tribunal of Brooklyn, N.Y. **Article:** Mixed Marriages, Prohibition of.

*GAFFNEY, JOHN PATRICK, SMM, S.T.D., Superior, St. Louis de Montfort Seminary, Litchfield, Conn. **Articles:** Grignion de Montfort, Louis Marie, St.; Montfort Fathers; Purification of Mary.

GAGGAWALA, PAUL O., AJ, M.A., U.S. Coordinator of the Apostles of Jesus, Shenandoah, Pa. **Article:** Apostles of Jesus.

*GAGNÉ, LUCIEN ERNEST, CSSR, B.A., Licence en Pédagogie, Ph.D. (History),

Professor of Pedagogy, University of Laval, and Dean of Studies, Séminaire St. Alphonse, Ste.-Anne-de-Beaupré, Quebec, Canada. **Article:** Sainte Anne de Beaupré, Shrine of.

*GAILLARD, LOUIS, OSB, Licencié en Histoire et Géographie, Diplôme d'études supérieures de Géographie, monk of the Congregation of Solesmes, France; Librarian, Facultés Catholiques, Lille, France. **Articles:** Ainay, Abbey of; Aurillac, Abbey of; Conques, Abbey of; Ferrieres-en-Gatinais, Abbey of; Flavigny-sur-Ozerain, Abbey of; Moissac, Abbey of; Montmajour, Abbey of.

*GÁL, GEDEON LADISLAUS, OFM, Ph.D., Associate Editor, *Franciscan Studies* and associate editor of the philosophical and theological works of William of Ockham, Franciscan Institute, St. Bonaventure University, St. Bonaventure, N.Y. **Articles:** Arbiol y Diez, Antonio; Gonsalvus Hispanus; Gregory of Rimini; Louis of Besse; Matthew of Aquasparta; Peter John Olivi; Richard Rufus of Cornwall; Richard of Middleton (Mediavilla); Sporer, Patritius; William of Ockham; William of Auxerre; William of Melitona (Middleton).

*GALANTIĆ, Ivan, M.F.A., M.A., Senior Fellow, The Warburg Institute, University of London, England. **Article:** Siena [Art].

*GALAVARIS, GEORGE P., B.A., M.F.A., Ph.D., Associate Professor of Fine Arts, McGill University, Montreal, Canada. **Articles:** Doors, Church; Grunewald, Matthias (Mathis Gothart Nithart).

*GALLAGHER, DONALD A., Boston College, Chestnut Hill, Mass. **Article:** Maritain, Jacques.

*GALLAGHER, EUGENE V., M.A., Lecturer, Religious Studies, Indiana University at Indianapolis, Indianapolis, Ind. **Article:** Religions, Comparative Study of.

*GALLAGHER, IDELLA JANE, Ph.D., Assistant Professor of Philosophy, Boston College, Chestnut Hill, Mass. **Articles:** Bergson, Henri Louis; Maritain, Raissa Oumansoff.

*GALLAGHER, JOHN FRANCIS, Rt. Rev., J.C.D., San Diego, Calif. **Article:** Public Propriety (Impediment to Marriage).

*GALLAGHER, JOHN G., Ph.D., Associate Professor of History, Southern Illinois

University, Edwardsville, Ill. **Articles:** Accolti, Pietro and Benedetto; Albrecht of Brandenburg; Arcimboldi, Giovannangelo; George (the Bearded) of Saxony; Joachim of Brandenburg; Leo X, Pope; William IV of Bavaria.

*GALLAGHER, JOHN JOSEPH, B.A., Archdiocesan Archivist, Consulting and Executive Editor, *Baltimore Catholic Review,* Director of Radio, TV, Bureau of Information, and Chaplain of Mission Helpers Motherhouse, Archdiocese of Baltimore, Md. **Articles:** Baltimore, Archdiocese of; Curley, Michael Joseph; Keough, Francis Patrick.

*GALLAGHER, KENNETH THOMAS, Ph.D., Associate Professor of Philosophy, Fordham University, New York, N.Y. **Article:** Marcel, Gabriel.

*GALLAGHER, LOUIS JOSEPH, SJ, A.M., S.T.D., LL.D., Scriptor, Georgetown University, Washington, D.C. **Articles:** Bobola, Andrew, St.; Walsh, Edmund Aloysius.

*GALLAGHER, MICHAEL PAUL, SJ, M. Litt., Ph.D., Former Lecturer in literature, University College, Dublin, Ireland; staff member, Pontifical Council for Culture. **Article:** Pontifical Council for Culture.

GALLARO, GEORGE DIMITRI, Ph.B., S.T.L., J.C.O.D., Professor of Eastern Canon Law and Ecumenical Theology, Saints Cyril and Methodius Seminary, Pittsburgh, Pa. **Article:** Melkite Greek Catholic Church.

*GALLEGOS, JOSÉ IGNACIO, Professor of History of Durango and Mexico, Juárez University of Durango, Mexico. **Articles:** Espinareda, Pedro de; Hermosillo, Archdiocese of; Tamaron y Romaral, Pedro.

*GALLÉN, JARL WILHELM ERIK, D.Ph., Professor of History, University of Helsinki, Finland. **Articles:** Finland, The Catholic Church in; Valamo, Abbey of.

*GALLIN, MOTHER MARY ALICE, OSU, Ph.D., Associate Professor of History and Chairman of the Department, and Director of Public Relations, College of New Rochelle, New Rochelle, N.Y. **Articles:** Faulhaber, Michael von; Galen, Clemens Augustinus von; Kaas, Ludwig; Merici, Angela, St.

*GALLO, SISTER ADOLFA, CSJB, M.A., Retreat Coordinator, St. Joseph's Villa House of Retreats, Peapack, N.J. **Article:** St. John the Baptist, Sisters of.

*GALOT, JEAN, SJ, Doctor in Law, S.T.D., Professor of Dogmatic Theology, Collège S. Albert S.J., Louvain, Belgium. **Article:** Billot, Louis.

*GALVIN, JOHN P., Dr. Theol., Associate Professor of Theology, The Catholic University of America, Washington, D.C. **Article:** Schoonenberg, Piet.

*GAMBASIN, ANGELO, Hist.Eccl.D., Professor of Contemporary History, Faculty of Political Science, University of Padua, Italy. **Article:** Italy, The Catholic Church in, 3. 1789 to the Present.

*GANNON, DAVID FRANCIS, SA, writer, Graymoor, Garrison, N.Y. **Article:** Wattson, Paul James Francis.

GANNON, MARGARET, IHM, Ph.D., C.M.F.C., Professor of History, Marywood University, Scranton, Pa. **Articles:** Duchemin, M. Theresa Maxis, Mother; Immaculate Heart of Mary, Sisters, Servants of the.

*GANNON, TIMOTHY JOSEPH, Rt. Rev., S.T.D., Ph.D., Founder, Professor, and Chairman, Department of Psychology, and Chairman, Committee on Guidance and Counseling, Loras College, Dubuque, Iowa. **Article:** Personality.

*GARCÍA, ANTONIO, OFM, J.C.D., Professor of the History of Law, Pontifical University of Salamanca, Spain. **Articles:** Damasus; Lawrence of Spain; Vincent of Spain.

*GARCIA, J., LC, Prefect, Center of Higher Studies of Legionaries of Christ, Rome. **Article:** Legionaries of Christ.

*GARCÍA-VILLOSLADA, RICARDO, SJ, S.T.D., Eccl.Hist.D., Professor of Modern Ecclesiastical History, Gregorian University, Rome, Italy. **Article:** Devotio Moderna.

*GARDET, LOUIS, Codirector of the Series, *Études musulmanes,* Professor, Collège Philosophique et Théologique, Toulouse, France. **Articles:** Avicenna (Ibn Sina, abu Ali al-Husayn); Sufism.

*GARDINER, HAROLD CHARLES, SJ, S.T.L., Ph.D., Staff Editor for Literature, *New Catholic Encyclopedia,* The Catholic University of America, Washington, D.C.; Literary Editor, *America* (1940-62); author and lecturer. **Articles:** Erotic Literature; Holy Grail, The; Humanism, Devout; Mysticism in Literature; Speech, Indecent and Vulgar; Talbot, Francis Xavier; Whitford, Richard.

*GARDINER, LYNDSAY, M.A., University Tutor, University of Melbourne, Aus-

tralia. **Article:** Chisholm, Caroline (Jones).

*GARDINIER, MEG E., Executive Director, International Catholic Child Bureau, Inc., New York, N.Y. **Article:** Bureau International Catholique de l'Enfance (BICE).

*GARGAN, EDWARD T., Ph.D., Professor of History, Wesleyan University, Middletown, Conn. **Articles:** Buchez, Philippe Joseph Benjamin; Coux, Charles de; Gerbet, Olympe Philippe; Melun, Armand de; Perin, Henri Charles Xavier.

*GARIBAY KINTANA, ANGEL MARIA, S.T.D., Doctor of Philosophy and Letters, Académico de la Lengua y Academico de la Historia, Canon of the Chapter of Guadalupe, Mexico City, Mexico. **Article:** Guadalupe, Our Lady of.

GARNEAU, REV. JAMES F., Ph.D., Interim Rector-President, Academic Dean, The Pontifical College Josephinum, Columbus, Ohio. **Articles:** Charlotte, Diocese of; Josephinum, Pontifical College; Missionary Society of St. James the Apostle; North Carolina, Catholic Church in; Papal Volunteers for Latin America (PAVLA); Raleigh, Diocese of.

*GARRETT, ALLEN MCCAIN, Ph.D., Associate Professor of Musicology, The Catholic University of America, Washington, D.C. **Articles:** Bay Psalm Book; Gospel Song; Psalters, Metrical.

*GARRIGAN, OWEN WALTER, S.T.L., Ph.D., Associate Professor, Department of Chemistry, Seton Hall University, South Orange, N.J. **Article:** Evolution [part 2: Catholic Teaching].

*GARSIDE, CHARLES, JR., Ph.D., Associate Professor of History, Yale University, New Haven, Conn. **Articles:** Capito, Wolfgang; Myconius, Oswald; Oecolampadius, Johannes; Zwingli, Huldrych.

*GARTHOEFFNER, WILLIAM CHARLES, S.T.L., J.C.D., Chancery Office, Oklahoma City, Okla. **Articles:** Oklahoma, Catholic Church in; Oklahoma City, Archdiocese of.

*GARVIN, JOSEPH NORBERT, CSC, Ph.D., Professor of Greek and Latin, Classics Department and Mediaeval Institute, University of Notre Dame, Notre Dame, Ind. **Articles:** Gerard of Cambrai; Johannes Cornubiensis; Merida, Fathers of; Peter Comestor; Praepositinus of Cremona; Ratherius of Verona; Simon of Tournai; Udo.

*GASPAR, JOSEPH WENZEL, MSC, S.T.D., Provincial Missionaries of the Sacred Heart, Sacred Heart Monastery, Hyde Park, Reading, Pa. **Article:** Missionary Sisters of the Most Sacred Heart of Jesus of Hiltrup.

*GAUDEMET, JEAN, Licencié ès lettres, Docteur en Droit, Diplôme de l'École des Hautes Études (Sciences religieuses), Professor, Faculty of Law, Paris, and at the Institute of Canon Law, University of Strasbourg, France. **Articles:** Anointing [part 2]; Avellana Collectio; Gregorian Reform; Investiture; Investiture Struggle; Paris, University of; Property, Early Church.

*GAVIGAN, JOHN JOSEPH, OSA, Ph.D., Hist.Eccl.D., Professor of Church History, Collegium Internationale Augustinianum, Rome, Italy; Editor, *Augustinianum.* **Articles:** Beata Nobis Gaudia; Caelestis Urbs Jerusalem; Caelestis Aulae Nuntius; Caelestis Agni Nuptias; Caeli Deus Sanctissime; Caelitum Joseph Decus; Holy Year; Madaura, Martyrs of; North Africa, Early Church in; Palestine, Early Church in; Syrian Christianity, I: Early History; Te Lucis Ante Terminum.

*GAVIN, DONALD PHILIP, M.A., Professor of History and Director of the Department, John Carroll University, Cleveland, Ohio. **Article:** Catholic Charities USA.

*GAVIN, SISTER HELEN, CSJ, Ph.D., Assistant Professor of Psychology, College of St. Catherine, St. Paul, Minn. **Article:** Fear.

*GEANAKOPLOS, DENO JOHN, Ph.D., Professor of Medieval and Byzantine History, University of Illinois, Urbana, Ill. **Articles:** Argyropoulos, John; Michael VIII Palaeologus, Byzantine Emperor.

*GEANEY, DENNIS JOSEPH, OSA, Director of Field Education, Catholic Theological Union, Chicago, Ill. **Article:** Catholic Action.

*GECYS, CASIMIR C., Th.D., Ph.D., Assistant Professor, Fordham University, New York, N.Y. **Article:** Nihilism.

*GEDDES, LEONARD WILLIAM, SJ, formerly Professor of Philosophy, St. Beuno's College, St. Asaph, Flintshire, England; author (deceased March 15, 1965). **Article:** Person (in Philosophy).

*GEIGER, JAMES HOWARD, CSSR, M.A., St. Alphonsus College, Suffield, Conn. **Articles:** Andronicus II Palaeologus,

Byzantine Emperor; Andronicus III Palaeologus, Byzantine Emperor; Helena, St.; Monica, St.

*GEIGER, LOUIS-BERTRAND, OP, S.T.Lr., Licence ès lettres, Doctorat en philosophie, S.T.M., Professor of Philosophy, Saulchoir, Paris, France, and University of Montreal, Canada. **Article:** Christian Philosophy.

*GEIGER, SISTER M. VIRGINIA, SSND, Ph.D., Chairman, Department of Philosophy, College of Notre Dame of Maryland, Baltimore, Md. **Articles:** Carroll, Daniel; Fourier, Peter St.; Matthews, Mary Bernardina, Mother-School Sisters of Notre Dame.

*GEIGER, MAYNARD JOSEPH, OFM, Ph.D., Archivisit of Mission Santa Barbara and Historian for the Franciscan Fathers of St. Barbara Province of the Pacific Coast, Santa Barbara, Calif. **Articles:** California, Catholic Church in; Engelhardt, Zephyrin; Lasuen, Fermin Francisco de; Pareja, Francisco de; Serra, Junípero Xavier, Bl.

*GEIGER, RICHARD ELMER, M.A., Assistant Professor of History, St. Ambrose College, Davenport, Iowa. **Articles:** Barbatus, St.; Cataldus of Rachau, St.; Gregory of Ostia, St.; Rainald of Ravenna, Bl.

*GEISELMANN, JOSEF RUPERT, Theol.Dr., Professor Emeritus of Fundamental Theology and Dogma, Rottenberg, Germany. **Articles:** Kuhn, Johannes; Schanz, Paul.

*GÉLINAS, ANDRÉ, SJ, M.A., Director, a student center for Vietnamese youth, Saigon, South Vietnam. **Article:** Vénard, Jean Théophane, Bl.

GELL, MADA-ANNE, VHM, Ed.D. Archivist, Georgetown Visitation, Washington, D.C. **Articles:** Georgetown Visitation; Visitation Sisters, Martyrs of, BB.

*GELLHAUS, VICTOR JOSEPH, OSB, Ph.D., monk of St. Benedict's Abbey, and Professor of History, St. Benedict's College, Atchison, Kans. **Articles:** Angilbert, St.; Benedict VIII, Pope; Benedict IX, Pope; Damasus II, Pope; Hermits of St. Paul; Leo Marsicanus; Marinus I, Pope; Maurus of Subiaco, St.; Monasticism, 2. Medieval (600–1500); Peter of Jully, Bl.; Robert of Soleto, Bl.

*GELPI, DONALD L., SJ, Shalom House, Berkeley, Ca. **Article:** Pentecostalism.

*GENDERNALIK, LEONARD, Sch.P., Provincial Office, Piarist Fathers, USA Prov-

ince, Washington, D.C. **Articles:** Agramunt Riera, Juan, Bl.; Canadell Quintana, Enrique, Bl.; Carceller Galindo, Francisco, Bl.; Cardona Meseguer, Matias, Bl.; Casanovas Perramon, Ignacio, Bl.; Ferrer Esteve, Jose, Bl.; Maranon, David, Bl.; Navarro Miguel, Carlo, Bl.; Naya, Florentino, Bl.; Oteiza Segura, Faustino, Bl.; Pamplona, Dionisio and Companions, BB.; Parte Saiz, Alfredo, Bl.; Segura Lopez, Manuel, Bl.

*GENDREAU, BERNARD ALPHONSE, L.Ph., Ph.D., M.M.S., Professor of Philosophy, Xavier University, Cincinnati, Ohio. **Articles:** Immanence; Object; Subject; Transcendence.

*GENOSKY, LANDRY, OFM, Quincy College, Quincy, Ill. **Article:** Illinois, Catholic Church in.

GENTRUP, C., **Article:** Franciscan Sisters—Sisters of St. Francis of Perpetual Adoration (OSF).

*GEORGE, A. RAYMOND, Tutor, Wesley College, Bristol, England. **Article:** International Consultation on English Texts (ICET).

GEORGE, MARIE I., Ph.D., Associate Professor of Philosophy, St. John's University, Jamaica, N.Y. **Articles:** Biology, II (Current Status); Life, Origin of.

*GERHARDT, BERNARD CONNOR, S.T.L., J.C.D., Officialis, The Tribunal, Washington, D.C. **Articles:** Monsignor; Rescripts; Woywod, Stanislaus.

*GERHART, MARY, Assistant Professor of Religious Studies, Hobart and William Smith Colleges, Geneva N.Y. **Article:** Transcendental Method.

*GERKEN, JOHN DIEDRICH, SJ, M.A., Ph.L., S.T.D., Assistant Professor of Theology and Director of the Department, John Carroll University, Cleveland, Ohio. **Article:** Counsels, Evangelical.

*GEROW, RICHARD OLIVER, Most Rev., D.D., S.T.D., LL.D., Bishop of the Diocese of Natchez-Jackson, Miss. **Articles:** Jackson, Diocese of; Mississippi, Catholic Church in.

*GERRITY, FRANK XAVIER, Ph.D., Professor of History; Chairman, Division of Social Sciences; and Director, Honors Program, St. Joseph's College, Philadelphia, Pa. **Articles:** Chandler, Joseph Ripley; Griffin, Martin Ignatius Joseph; Pallen, Condé Benoist.

GERSBACH, KARL, OSA, Ph.D., Augustinian Historical Institute, Villanova University, Villanova, Pa. **Articles:** Augustinian Nuns and Sisters; Augustinians; Clare of Montefalco, St.; Nicholas of Tolentino, St.; Panvinio, Onofrio.

*GERSTINGER, HANS JOHANN, Dr.Phil., Librarian Director of the Manuscript and Papyrus Collection, National Library, Vienna, Austria; Professor Emeritus of Classical Philology, University of Graz. **Article:** Papyrology.

*GERVAIS, MARCEL ANDRÉ, B.A., S.T.B., S.S.B., S.S.L., St. Peter's Seminary, London, Ontario, Canada. **Article:** Suffering Servant, Songs of the.

*GETLEIN, FRANK JOSEPH, M.A., Political Columnist and Art Critic, Washington *Evening Star,* Washington, D.C.; Art Critic, *The New Republic.* **Article:** La-Farge [John (1835–1910)].

*GIABBANI, VICTOR ANSELM, OSB, monk of the Camaldolese Congregation, Ph.D., and Procurator General, Camaldolese Congregation, Camaldoli (Arezzo), Italy. **Article:** Camaldolese.

*GIACCHI, MARIO JOHN, Company of St. Paul, M.A., S.T.B., Washington, D.C. (deceased Sept. 11, 1965). **Article:** Epictetus.

*GIANNINI, JOHN MARTIN, OP, B.S., M.B.A., B.A. (Philosophy), S.T.Lr., Assistant Pastor, St. Peter Martyr Church, Pittsburgh, Calif. **Article:** Hatred.

*GIBBONS, JAMES P., CSC, Moreau Seminary, Notre Dame, Ind. **Article:** Foik, Paul Joseph.

*GIBBONS, ROBERT J., Ph.D., Director, Administrative Research and Development, American Institute for Property and Liability Underwriters, Malvern, Pa. **Article:** Mindszenty, József.

*GIBBONS, WILLIAM J., SJ, S.T.L., B.S., Ph.D., Associate Professor of Sociology and Office of the Director, Scientific Manpower Survey, Fordham University, New York, N.Y. **Article:** Population.

*GIBLIN, CATHALDUS, OFM, B.A., D.D., Member, research group at work on Irish history and Celtic Studies, The Franciscan House of Studies, Dún Mhuire, Killiney, County Dublin, Ireland. **Articles:** Colgan, John; Hickey, Antony; Porter, Francis; Ward, Hugh; Ward, Cornelius.

*GIBSON, ARTHUR, S.T.D., The Catholic University of America, Washington,

D.C. **Articles:** Amphilochius of Iconium, St.; Britain, Early Church in; Diptychs, liturgical use of; Labarum; Lamps and Lighting, Early Christian; Nicholas of Myra, St.; Shenoute of Atripe; Troitskaya Laura (Zagorsk Monastery); Widow (in the Early Church).

*GIBSON, DAVID E., Catholic News Service, Washington, D.C. **Article:** Christifideles laici.

*GIBSON, SISTER LAURITA, SCN, Ph.D., Professor of History and Social Sciences, Catherine Spalding College, Louisville, Ky. **Article:** Allen, Frances Margaret, Sister.

*GIEBEN, SERVUS H. J., OFMCap, Ph.D., Member, *Istituto Storico dei Frati Minori Cappuccini,* Rome, Italy; Director, *Bibliographia Franciscana;* Vice Director, *Collectanea Franciscana.* **Article:** John Lutterell.

*GIGANTE, SISTER JOAN ANTIDA, SCSJA, M.Ed., Teacher, St. Joan Antida High School, Milwaukee, Wis. **Article:** Thouret, Joan Antida, St.

GIGNAC, FRANCIS T., SJ, M.A., S.T.L., D.Phil., Chair and Professor of Biblical Studies, The Catholic University of America, Washington, D.C. **Articles:** Greek Language, Biblical; Greek Language, Early Christian and Byzantine; McKenzie, John Lawrence; New American Bible.

*GILBY, THOMAS, OP, S.T.Lr., Ph.D., General Editor, new edition of the *Summa* of St. Thomas, with English translation, Blackfriars, Cambridge, England. **Articles:** Ambition; Charity; Honor; Martyrdom, Theology of; Prudence; Temperance, Virtue of.

*GILCHRIST, JOHN THOMAS, Ph.D., Senior Lecturer in History, University of Adelaide, Australia. **Articles:** Anonymous of York; Anselm II of Lucca, St.; Commendation; Humbert of Silva Candida; Laity in the Middle Ages; Lateran; Liber Censuum; Papal Registers; Paschal II, Pope; Proprietary Churches; Rainald of Dassel; Reordination; Seventy-four Titles, Collection of; Simony; Stephen IX (X), Pope.

*GILHOOLEY, LEONARD, CFX, M.Ed., M.A., Ph.D., Assistant Staff Editor for Literature, *New Catholic Encyclopedia,* The Catholic University of America, Washington, D.C.; Dean, Xaverian College, Silver Spring, Md.; Member, Provincial Educational Council (Xave-

rian Brothers); Member, Commission on English, National Catholic Educational Association. **Article:** Ridder, Charles H.

*GILL, JOSEPH, SJ, Ph.D. (Greg.), B.A. (London), S.T.L., Ph.D. (London), Rector, Pontifical Oriental Institute, Rome, Italy; Professor of Byzantine Greek Language and of Byzantine History, Pontifical Oriental Institute, and of Anglican Theology, Pontifical Gregorian University, Rome. **Articles:** Basel, Council of; Chrysoberges, Andrew; Constantine XI Palaeologus, Byzantine Emperor; Eugene IV, Pope; Eugenicus, Mark, Metropolitan of Ephesus; Filioque; Florence, Council of; Gennadius II Scholarius, Patriarch of Constantinople; Isidore of Kiev; Joseph of Methone; Nicholas V, Pope; Syropoulos, Sylvester.

*GILLEMAN, GÉRARD AUGUSTE, SJ, S.T.D., St. Mary's Theological College, S.J., and Professor of Dogmatic Theology, Spiritual Director of the Theologians, Kurseong, India. **Articles:** Contritionism; Exomologesis; Humility; Law in Christian Life.

*GILLETT, HENRY MARTIN, B.A., research scholar, London, England. **Articles:** Fátima; La Salette; Shrines.

*GILLGANNON, SISTER MARY MCAULEY, RSM, Ph.D., Assistant Professor of History and Chairman of the Department, College of St. Mary, Omaha, Nebr.; CCD Coordinator, Sisters of Mercy, Province of Omaha. **Article:** Sisters of Mercy.

*GILLGANNON, MICHAEL J., Director of Campus Ministry, Archdiocese of La Paz, Bolivia. **Article:** Bolivia, The Catholic Church in.

*GILLIS, JAMES RAPHAEL, OP, A.B., S.T.D., Prior, Blessed Sacrament Priory, Madison, Wis. **Articles:** God, 2. In Christian Tradition; Jesus Christ (in Theology) 3. Special Questions; 7. Will.

GILLMAN, FLORENCE MORGAN, Ph.D., S.T.D., Department of Theology and Religious Studies, University of San Diego, San Diego, Calif. **Articles:** Parenesis; Paul, Missionary Journeys; Abba.

*GILLMAN, JOHN L., Ph.D., Lecturer, Department of Religious Studies, San Diego State University, San Diego, Calif. **Article:** Peace (in the Bible).

*GILMORE, MYRON PIPER, Ph.D., L.H.D., Director, Villa I Tatti, The Harvard

University Center for Italian Renaissance Studies, Florence, Italy; Professor of History, Harvard University, Cambridge, Mass. **Article:** Erasmus, Desiderius.

*GINGRAS, GEORGE EDWARD, Ph.D., Assistant Professor of Modern Languages, The Catholic University of America, Washington, D.C. **Articles:** Celles-sur-Belle, Monastery of; Micy, Abbey of; Montreuil, Abbey of; Redon, Abbey of; Rolduc, Monastery of; Romainmôtier, Abbey of; Rougemont, Abbey of; Saint-Antoine-de-Viennois, Abbey of; Saint-Calais, Abbey of; Saint-Claude, Abbey of; Saint-Florent-le-Vieil, Abbey of; Saint-Savin-sur-Gartempe, Abbey of; Saint-Sever-de-Rustan, Abbey of.

GINGRAS, GEORGE EDWARD, Ph.D., Professor Emeritus of Modern Languages, The Catholic University of America, Washington, D.C. **Article:** Egeria, Itinerarium of.

*GIORDANI, IGINO, Doctorate in Letters, Director, *Città Nuova;* Rector, International Institute *Mystici Corporis* for Formation of Lay Apostles; Bibliotheca Vaticana, Vatican City, Italy. **Article:** Social Thought, Catholic, 2. In the Bible.

*GIORDANO, CHARLES BASIL, Ph.D., Interim Assistant Professor of Modern Languages, The Catholic University of America, Washington, D.C. **Article:** Grillparzer, Franz.

*GIRBAL, FRANÇOIS, Licence ès lettres, Diplôme d'Études Supérieures, Doctorat en Sciences des Religions, Professor of Literature and Philosophy, Oratorian College of Guilly, Seine et Marne, France. **Article:** Lamy, Bernard.

*GISBERT, TERESA DE MESA, Professor of the History of Arts and Professor of Bolivian Civilization, Universidad Mayor de San Andrés, La Paz, Bolivia. **Article:** Bitti, Bernardo.

GITTINS, ANTHONY J., CSSp, Ph.D., Bishop F.X. Ford M.M. Professor of Missiology, Catholic Theological Union, Chicago, Ill. **Article:** Le Roy, Alexander.

*GLANVILLE, JOHN JOSEPH, Ph.D., Associate, Faculty Seminar on Interpretations, Columbia University, New York, N.Y. **Articles:** Aristotelianism; Distinction, Kinds of; Division (Logic); Quiddity; Zabarella, Jacopo.

*GLAZEBROOK, PETER ROWLAND, B.A., M.A. (Oxon.), Lecturer in Law, University of Exeter, England. **Article:** Oaths, English Post-Reformation.

*GLAZIK, JOSEPH, MSC, Dr.Theol., Professor, Institut für Misionswissenschaft, University of Münster, Germany. **Articles:** Mission History, II: Orthodox; Oceania, The Catholic Church in.

*GLEASON, SISTER ANGÈLE, CSJ, College of St. Catherine, St. Paul, Minn. (deceased Dec. 20, 1962). **Articles:** Ireland, Seraphine, Mother; McHugh, Antonia, Sister.

*GLEASON, ELISABETH GREGORICH, Ph.D., Assistant Professor of History, San Francisco State College, San Francisco, Calif. **Articles:** Piccolomini; Sforza; Sixtus IV, Pope; Villani, Giovanni.

GLENN, JASON, Ph.D., Assistant Professor of History, University of Southern California, Los Angeles, California. **Article:** Sylvester II, Pope.

GLINECKIS, SR. EUGENIA, CJC, Brockton, Mass. **Article:** Poor Sisters of Jesus Crucified and the Sorrowful Mother.

*GLORIEUX, PALÉMON JEAN, Rt. Rev., P.A., Ph.D., S.T.D., Honorary Rector, Catholic University of Lille, France; Secretary of Cardinal Liénart. **Articles:** Adam Pulchrae Mulieris; Adenulf of Anagni; Bernard Lombardi; Bernard of Auvergne (Alvernia); Bombolognus of Bologna; Gerard of Cremona; Gerson, Jean; Hannibaldus de Hannibaldis; Henry of Lausanne; Heriger of Lobbes; Hilduin of Saint-Denis; James of Viterbo; John of Naples; Nicholas of Clamanges; Rambert of Bologna; Remigio de' Girolami; Romano of Rome; Sentences and Summae; Sorbon, Robert de; William of Peter of Godin.

*GLUTZ, MELVIN ALBERT, CP, Ph.D., Professor of Philosophy, Passionist Seminary, Louisville, Ky. **Articles:** Becoming; Demonstration; Motion [part 1]; Proof; Rest.

*GODA, PAUL JOSEPH, SJ, B.S., A.B., Ph.L., LL.B., Alma College, Los Gatos, Calif. **Article:** Vitelleschi, Mutius.

GODFREY, KEVIN, OFM, Ph.D., Assistant Professor of Theology, Alvernia College, Reading, Pa. **Articles:** Ecclesiam Suam; Mysterium Fidei; Populorum Progressio.

*GODSEY, JOHN D., Professor of Systematic Theology, Wesley Theological Seminary, Washington, D.C. **Article:** Barth, Karl.

GODZIEBA, ANTHONY J., Ph.D., Associate Professor, Department of Theology and Religious Studies, Villanova University, Villanova, Pa. **Article:** Hermeneutics.

*GOEDICKE, HANS, Ph.D., Assistant Professor in the Oriental Seminary, Johns Hopkins University, Baltimore, Md. **Article:** Egypt.

GOERDT, STEPHEN, M.A., Writer, Sinsinawa Dominicans, Sinsinawa, Wis. **Article:** Dominican Sisters—Sinsinawa Dominican Congregation of the Most Holy Rosary (Sinsinawa, Wis).

*GOETTELMANN, PAUL AUGUSTE, M.A., Arch.D., Diploma, Beaux-Arts Institute of Design, Fontainebleau School of Fine Arts, Professor of Architecture and Head of the Department, and Assistant Dean for Architecture, School of Engineering and Architecture, The Catholic University of America, Washington, D.C. **Articles:** Keely, Patrick Charles; LaFarge [Christopher Grant].

*GOETZ, JOSEPH, SJ, Ph.L., Lic.Litt., S.T.L., Professor of Religious Ethnology, Gregorian University, Rome, Italy; Professor of History of Religions, Catholic University of Lyons, France. **Articles:** Religion; Religion and Morality.

*GOFFART, WALTER ANDRÉ, Ph.D., Assistant Professor of History, University of Toronto, Canada. **Articles:** Cloud, St.; Dagobert II, King of Austrasia, St.; Fredergarius; Hermenegild, St.; Ouen of Rouen, St.; Radegunda, Queen of the Franks, St.

GOMEZ, RAUL R., SDS, M.Div., M.P.A., Ph.D., Vice Rector, Sacred Heart School of Theology, Hales Corners, Wis. **Articles:** Mozarabic Rite, Visigoths.

*GOMEZ HOYOS, RAFAEL, Very Rev., J.C.D., Canon, Vice Officialis, Tribunal Eclesiástico de la Curia Primada de Bogotá y Delegado Arzobispal paras Partidas, Professor of Philosophy of Law, Universidad de la Gran Colombia, Bogotá, Colombia. **Articles:** Baluffi, Gaetano; Luque, Cristano.

*GÓMEZ TAGLE, ERNESTO, Very Rev., J.C.L., Penitentiary Canon of the Basilica of Our Lady of Guadalupe, Mexico City, Mexico. **Articles:** Aduarte, Diego Francisco; Arlegui, Jose; Burgoa, Francisco de; Casas Martinez, Felipe de Jesus, St.; Castorena y Ursua,

Juan Ignacio de; Coronel, Juan; Davila y Padilla, Agustin; Diez Laurel, Bartolome, Bl.; Morfi, Juan Agustin de; Pareja, Francisco; Ponce, Alonso; Rea, Alonso de la; Tello, Antonio; Valverde Tellez, Emeterio.

*GONDA, EUGENE FRANK, Ph.D., Associate Professor of History and Political Science, Catonsville Community College, Catonsville, Md. **Article:** Harlay; La Rochefoucauld.

*GÓNGORA, MARIO, Professor, Universidad de Chile, Santiago de Chile. **Articles:** Cienfuegos, Jose Ignacio; Martinez de Aldunate, Jose Antonio; San Alberto, Jose Antonio de.

*GONSALVES DE MELLO, JOSÉ ANTONIO, Bachelor in Juridical and Social Sciences, Professor of History, Institute of Sciences, University of Recife, Pernambuco, Brazil. **Article:** Batista, Cicero Romao.

*GONZÁLEZ, ARIOSTO DOMINGO, Director of Economic Division, Ministry of Foreign Relations, Montevideo, Uruguay. **Articles:** Gomensoro, Tomas Xavier de; Soler, Mariano; Vera, Jacinto.

GONZALEZ, R. C., **Article:** Franciscan Sisters—Missionary Sisters of the Immaculate Conception of the Mother of God (SMIC).

GOODING, SISTER BARBARA ANNE, RSM, Ph.D., Council Coordinator, Council of Major Superiors of Women Religious in the United States, Washington, D.C. **Article:** Council of Major Superiors of Women Religious (CMSWR).

*GOODMAN, EDWARD J., Ph.D., Professor of History, Xavier University, Cincinnati, Ohio. **Articles:** Garabito, Juan de Santiago y Leon; Garces, Julian; Mota y Escobar, Alonso de la.

*GOODROW, SISTER ESTHER MARIE, SL, Ph.D., Professor of History and Chairman of the Department, Loretto Heights College, Loretto, Colo. **Article:** Colorado, Catholic Church in.

*GOOLEY, LAURENCE LEO, SJ, B.E., A.B., Ph.L., S.T.L., Alma College, Los Gatos, Calif. **Articles:** Sanchez, Thomas; Zaccaria, Francesco Antonio.

*GORDINI, GIAN DOMENICO, Hist.Eccl.D., Ph.D., Diploma in Library Science (Vatican Library School), Teacher of Ecclesiastical History in the Seminary of Faenza, Professor of Ecclesiastical

History and Patrology in the Pontifical Regional Seminary, Bologna, Italy; Honorary Canon of the Cathedral Basilica of Faenza. **Article:** Ravenna [History].

*GORMAN, JOHN CHANDLER, S.T.D., J.U.D., Associate Professor of Sacred Doctrine, St. Mary's University, San Antonio, Tex. **Article:** Sorrows of Mary.

*GORMAN, MARGARET, RSCJ, Ph.D., Professor of Psychology, Newton College of the Sacred Heart, Newton, Mass.; Lecturer, Personnel Management for Executives of the U.S. Army, Boston, Mass. **Articles:** Self, The; Semantics; Soul, Human, 3. Modern and Contemporary Thought.

*GORMAN, SISTER MARY ADELE FRANCIS, OSF, Ph.D., Our Lady of Angels College, Glen Riddle, Pa. **Article:** American Federation of Catholic Societies.

*GORMAN, ROBERT, St. Mary-of-the-Woods College, St. Mary-of-the-Woods, Ind. **Articles:** Chatard, Francis Silas; Indiana, Catholic Church in; Indianapolis, Archdiocese of.

*GORSKI, ISIDORE HENRY, L.S.S., S.T.L., Professor of Sacred Scripture, Regina Cleri Seminary, Regina, Saskatchewan, Canada. **Articles:** Gehenna; Hades; Hell (in the Bible).

*GOUBERT, PAUL LOUIS MARIE JOSEPH, SJ, Docteur ès lettres, Professor of Archeology and of Byzantine History, Pontifical Oriental Institute, Rome, Italy. **Article:** Herbigny, Michael d'.

*GOUILLARD, JEAN MAURICE, Docteur ès lettres, Maître de recherche (Histoire médiévale), Centre National de la Recherche Scientifique, Paris, France. **Article:** Iconoclasm.

*GOULD, PHILIP, Docteur de l'Université (Paris), Professor of Art History, Sarah Lawrence College, Bronxville, N.Y. **Article:** Mâle, Émile.

*GOURHAND, J., Diplôme d'archiviste-paléographe, Conservateur, Archives du Calvados, Caen, France. **Article:** Bayeux.

*GRABAR, OLEG, Ph.D., Professor of Near Eastern Art, Univeristy of Michigan, Ann Arbor, Mich. **Article:** Islamic Art.

*GRABIAK, SISTER MARY OF ST. AUGUSTINE, OLCR, B.S. in Commerce, Green Bay, Wis. **Article:** Our Lady of Charity, North American Union Sisters of.

*GRABKA, GREGORY MARIA, Very Rev., OFMConv, S.T.D., S.T.M., St. Anthony's Convent, Buffalo, N.Y. **Articles:** Almain, Jacques; Collius, Francesco (Collio); Hosius, Stanislaus; Peter Cantor; Vulpes, Angelo.

*GRABNER, DONALD RAYMOND, OSB, S.T.D., Prior, Conception Abbey; Dean, School of Theology, Conception Seminary, and Professor of Dogmatic Theology and Liturgy, Conception, Mo. **Articles:** Jesus Christ (in Theology) 3. Special Questions; 5. Natural Defects; Jesus Christ (in Theology) 3. Special Questions; 11. Prophet, Priest, and King; Preface; Propassions of Christ.

*GRADY, SISTER MARY DOLOROSA, OP, B.S., M.T. (ASCP), Secretary General of Congregation, Supervisor of Laboratories, St. Catherine's Hospital, Kenosha, Wis. **Article:** Dominican Sisters—Congregation of the Dominican Sisters of St Catherine of Siena of Kenosha (Kenosha, Wis).

*GRADY, THOMAS JOSEPH, Rt. Rev., M.A., Director, National Shrine of the Immaculate Conception, Washington, D.C. **Article:** National Shrine of the Immaculate Conception.

*GRAEF, HILDA, Oxford, England. **Articles:** Emmerich, Anne Catherine; Lateau, Louise; Taigi, Anna Maria, Bl.

GRAFFIUS, PEREGRINE M., OSM, Assistant Provincial, Order of Friar Servants of Mary, USA Province, Chicago, Ill. **Article:** Servites.

*GRAHAM, JOHN THOMAS, Ph.D., Assistant Professor of History, Gonzaga University, Spokane, Wash. **Articles:** Arnoldi, Bartholomaeus; Brask, Hans; Cochlaeus, Johannes (Johann Dobeneck); Donoso Cortes, Juan Francisco Maria de la Salud; Faber, Johannes.

*GRAHAM, ROBERT, La Civilta Cattolica, Rome, Italy. **Article:** Gundlach, Gustav.

*GRAJEWSKI, MAURICE JOHN, Ph.D., J.C.D., General Definitor for English-speaking countries of Order of Friars Minor, Rome, Italy. **Articles:** Antonius Andreas; Vital du Four; Walter of Bruges.

*GRANDPRÉ, SISTER SAINTE LUCILLE, M.A., Teacher, Sacred Heart Novitiate, Littleton, N.H. **Article:** Sacred Heart of Jesus, Daughters of the Charity of the.

GRANFIELD, PATRICK, OSB, Ph.D., S.T.D., Professor of Systematic Theology, Department of Theology, The Catholic University of America, Washington, D.C. **Articles:** Ecclesiology [Developments and Issues]; Fenton, Joseph Clifford; Paul VI, Pope.

*GRANNELL, THOMAS FRANCIS, SSCC, S.T.L., Licentiate in Mission Science, Secretary, Missions of the Congregation of the Sacred Hearts, Convento dei SS. Cuori, Rome, Italy. **Article:** Oceania, The Catholic Church in.

*GRANT, EDWARD, Ph.D., Professor of the History of Science, Department of History and Philosophy of Science, Indiana University, Bloomington, Ind. **Article:** Science (in the Middle Ages).

*GRANT, FREDERICK CLIFTON, Th.D.; Honorary D.D., D.S. Litt., D.C.L., L.H.D., Litt.D., S.T.D., D.H.L., Professor Emeritus of Biblical Theology, Union Theological Seminary, New York, N.Y.; observer for Anglican Communion, Vatican Council II. **Article:** Astral Religion.

*GRANT, JOHN JOSEPH, M.A., Editor, *The Pilot,* Archdiocese of Boston, Mass. **Article:** Medical Missionaries of Mary.

*GRAPE, WOLFGANG, Kunsthistorisches Institut der Universität Wien, Vienna, Austria. **Articles:** Reichenau, Abbey of; Sankt Gallen, Abbey of.

*GRASSI, JOHN LOUIS, MM, D. Phil., Senior Lecturer in History, St. Mary's College, Strawberry Hill, Twickenham, England. **Articles:** Adalgott, SS.; Adam of Ebrach, Bl.; Adelhelm I, Bl.; Alexander of Jerusalem, St.; Amatus of Nusco, St.; Arnold of Hiltensweiler, Bl.; Beatus, St.; Benedict of Benevento, St.; Christiana of Lucca, Bl.; Conrad Bosinlother, Bl.; Salisbury, Ancient See of; Sherborne, Abbey of; Thomas of Corbridge; Thomas of Cobham.

*GRASSI, JOSEPH A., MM, S.T.L., S.S.L., Instructor in Sacred Scripture, Maryknoll Seminary, Maryknoll, N.Y. **Articles:** Agabus, St.; Beatitudes (in the Bible); Lord's Prayer, The; Simon Magus.

*GRATSCH, EDWARD JOSEPH, S.T.D., Professor of Fundamental Theology, Mt. St. Mary's Seminary, Cincinnati, Ohio. **Articles:** Apologies, Liturgical; Asperges; Bread, Liturgical Use of; Doxology, Liturgical; Exorcism [part 1]; Gunther, Anton; Hermesianism; Holy Oils; Improperia; Oremus; Sanctus; Semirationalism; Trisagion; Water, Liturgical Use Of.

*GRATTAN, WILLIAM JOSEPH, Ph.D., Professor, Department of History and Political Science, College of the Holy Cross, Worcester, Mass. **Article:** Blenkinsop.

*GRAY, ANDREW, OCart, Monk of Parkminster (St. Hugh's Charterhouse) Partridge Green, Horsham, Sussex, England. **Article:** Parkminster (Charterhouse).

*GRAY, SISTER GERTRUDE MARY, SNJM, Ph.D., Professor of History and Chairman of the Department of Social Sciences, College of the Holy Names, Oakland, Calif. **Articles:** Duglioli, Helena, Bl.; Fornari-Strata, Maria Victoria, Bl.; Galantini, Hippolytus, Bl.; Moye, John Martin, Bl.; Spadafora, Dominic, Bl.; Valliscaulian Order.

*GREEN, AUSTIN EDWARD, OP, Ph.L., S.T.L., S.T.Lr., Novice Master for Laybrothers, and Professor of Church History, Aquinas Institute, River Forest, Ill. **Articles:** Beatification; Dogmatic Fact; Faith and Morals; Revelation, Virtual; Venerable.

*GREEN, MOTHER MARGUERITE MARY, RSCJ, Ph.D., Professor of History and Political Science, Barat College of the Sacred Heart, Lake Forest, Ill. **Article:** Hardey, Mary Aloysia, Mother.

*GREEN, RICHARD HAMILTON, Ph.D., Associate Professor of English, Johns Hopkins University, Baltimore, Md.; Member, Editorial Board, *English Literary History*. **Article:** Courtly Love.

*GREEN, THOMAS J., S.T.D., Associate Professor of Canon Law, The Catholic University of America, Washington, D.C. **Article:** Excommunication [part 2: Canon Law].

*GREENEWALD, GERARD MARIA, OFM-Cap, S.T.B., Ph.D., Seminary Professor, Retreat Master for Religious, St. Mary's Monastery, Herman, Pa. **Articles:** Divinum illud munus; Missions, Divine; Spiration.

*GREENFIELD, ROBERT HARVIE, B.A., B.Litt., D.Phil., Chaplain, St. Helena's Hall (Episcopal), Portland, Ore. **Articles:** Hooker, Richard; Whitgift, John.

*GRÉGOIRE, RÉGINALD, OSB, S.T.D., monk of the Abbey of Clervaux, Luxembourg; Member, Pontifical Abbey of St. Jerome for the Revision of the Vulgate. **Articles:** Alferius, St.; Aymard, Bl.; Berno, Bl.; Bruno of Segni, St.; Charite-sur-Loire, Abbey of; Cluniac Reform; Cluny, Abbey of;

Guitmond of Aversa; Hugh of Cluny, St.; Odilo of Cluny, St.; Odo of Cluny, St.

*GREGORICH, JOSEPH, Chicago, Ill.; Historian for the cause of Bishop Baraga. **Article:** Baraga, Frederic.

*GREGORY, TULLIO, Ph.D., Professor of the History of Medieval Philosophy, University of Rome, Italy. **Article:** World Soul (Anima Mundi).

*GRENNEN, JOSEPH EDWARD, Ph.D., Assistant Professor of English, Graduate School of Arts and Sciences, Fordham University, New York, N.Y. **Article:** Alchemy.

*GRES-GAYER, JACQUES M., Dr.Theol., Dr.Hist., Professor of Church History, The Catholic University of America, Washington, D.C. **Article:** France, the Catholic Church in [1965–].

GRES-GAYER, JACQUES M., S.T.D., Ph.D., Professor of Church History, The Catholic University of America, Washington, D.C. **Articles:** Alexandre, Noel; Arnauld; Auctorem fidei; Augustinus; Bossuet, Jacques Benigne; Boulay, Cesar Egasse Du (Bulaeus); Dupin, Louis Ellies; Gallicanism; Habert, Isaac; Jansenism; Jansenistic Piety; Launoy, Jean de; Noailles, Louis Antoine de; Pistoia, Synod of; Port-Royal; Quesnel, Pasquier (Paschase); Tournely, Honore de; Ultramontanism; Ysambert, Nicolas.

*GRETSCH, HERBERT F., Gonzaga University, Spokane, Wash. **Articles:** Atkinson, Matthew (Paul of St. Francis); Bedingfeld, Frances; Cordell, Charles; Eyre, Thomas; Eyston, Charles; Maxwell, Winifred.

*GREYTAK, WILLIAM J., Carroll College, Helena, Mont. **Article:** Brondel, John Baptist.

GREYTAK, WILLIAM J., Ph.D., Professor of Modern European History, Carroll College, Helena, Mont. **Article:** Montana, Catholic Church in.

GRIBBLE, RICHARD, CSC, Ph.D., Assistant Profesor of Religious Studies, Stonehill College, North Easton, Mass. **Article:** Hanna, Edward Joseph.

*GRIBOMONT, JEAN, OSB, Docteur en philologie et histoire orientales, Prior, Pontifical Abbey of St. Jerome, Rome, Italy. **Articles:** Basil, St.; Basilian Monasticism; Caesarea in Cappadocia; Cenobitism; Monastery, Double; Monasticism, 1. Early Christian (to 600); Monasticism, 5. Eastern, a. (To 1453).

*GRIESBACH, MARC F., Ph.B., Lic. Med.Stud., M.A., Ph.D., Assistant Professor of Philosophy, Marquette University, Milwaukee, Wis. **Article:** Logical Positivism.

*GRIFFIN, MICHAEL DENNIS, Very Rev., OCD, S.T.B., Carmelite Monastery, Washington, D.C. **Articles:** Demonology; Devil Worship; Fire of Judgment; Satanism; Spiritism.

*GRIFFITHS, ALAN BEDE, OSB, B.A., Founder and Subprior, Kurisumala Ashram, Monastery of Syrian Rite in South India, Peermade Kerala, South India. **Articles:** Brahman; Caste System, Indian; Hinduism; Jainism; Kali; Karma; Mantra; Reincarnation; Siva; Tantrism; Vaishnavism; Vedanta; Vedas; Vishnu; Yoga.

*GRIM, JOHN, Professor of Comparative Religion, Sarah Lawrence College, New York, N.Y. **Article:** Campbell, Joseph.

*GRISEZ, GERMAIN GABRIEL, M.A., Ph.L., Ph.D., Associate Professor of Philosophy, Georgetown University, Washington, D.C. **Articles:** Good, The Supreme; Man, Natural End of.

*GRISPINO, JOSEPH ALOYSIUS, SM, S.T.L., S.S.L., M.Ed., Professor of Old Testament, Marist College, Washington, D.C. **Article:** Butin, Romanus.

*GRONER, JOSEPH FULKO, OP, Dr. Theol., Professor of Moral Theology, University of Fribourg, Switzerland. **Articles:** Geiler von Kaysersberg, Johannes; Sailer, Johann Michael.

GROS, BROTHER JEFFREY, FSC, Ph.D., Associate Director of Ecumenical and Interreligious Affairs, US Conference of Catholic Bishops, Washington, D.C. **Articles:** Faith and Order Commission; Ut unum sint.

*GROSSCHMID-ZSOGOD, GEZA, J.U.D., Professor of Economics, Director, Institute of African Affairs and African Language and Area Center, Duquesne University, Pittsburgh, Pa. **Articles:** Knights of Dobrin; Knights of the Sword; Order of the Swan; Templars.

*GROSSI, ISNARDO PIO, OP, S.T.L., S.T.Lr., National Promoter, Third Order, and Archivist, Roman Province of the Dominicans, Rome, Italy. **Article:** Zigliara, Tommaso.

*GROUCHY, MOTHER MARY MARGARET, OP, M.S. in L.S., Librarian, Regina Coeli Junior College at Eucharistic Novitiate Regina Coeli, Covington, La. **Article:** Dominican Sisters—Eucharistic Missionaries of St. Dominic.

*GRUBER, JACOB WILLIAM, Ph.D., Associate Professor of Anthropology and Chairman of the Department, Temple University, Philadelphia, Pa. **Article:** Mivart, St. George Jackson.

*GRUENBERG, GLADYS WALLEMAN, Ph.D., private researcher and writer, teacher of labor economics, St. Louis, Mo. **Articles:** Engels, Friedrich; Marx, Karl.

*GRUMEL, VENANCE, AA, Ph.L., S.T.D., Member and Secretary, Institut d'Études Byzantines, Paris, France. **Articles:** Chronology, Medieval, 1. The Christian East; Eras, Historical; Indiction.

*GUENNOU, JEAN, MEP, Ph.L., Diplôme de l'École Pratique des Hautes Études, Archivist, Société des Missions Étrangères de Paris, France. **Articles:** Burma/Myanmar, The Catholic Church in; Cambodia, The Catholic Church in; Laos, The Catholic Church in; Moine, Claudine; Paris Foreign Mission Society.

*GUENTNER, FRANCIS JOSEPH, SJ, M.A., M.Mus., Associate Professor, St. Louis University, St. Louis, Mo. **Articles:** Allegri, Gregorio; Congregational Singing; Festa, Costanzo; Stradella, Alessandro; Stradivari, Antonio; Tartini, Giuseppe.

*GUGGENBERGER, ALOIS, CSSR, Dr.Phil., Dr.Theol., Professor of Philosophy (Metaphysics and History of Modern Philosophy), Gars am Inn, Upper Bavaria, Germany. **Article:** Hartmann, Nicolai.

*GUGUMUS, JOHANNES EMIL, Rt. Rev., Ph.D., Rector, Collegio Teutonico del Campo Santo, Rome, Italy. **Article:** Campo Santo Teutonico.

GUIDER, MARGARET ELETTA, OSF, Th.D., Associate Professor of Missiology, Weston Jesuit School of Theology, Cambridge, Mass. **Article:** Mission Theology.

GUIDRY, MITCHELL G., M.A., Pastor, Sacred Heart Church, Baldwin, La. **Articles:** Alexandria, Diocese of; Baton Rouge, Diocese of; Lafayette, Diocese of, Louisiana, Catholic Church in.

*GUILFOYLE, GEORGE HENRY, Most Rev., D.D., LL.D., LL.B., LL.M., Auxiliary Bishop of New York and Executive Director, Catholic Charities, Archdiocese of New York, N.Y. **Article:** Garcia Diego y Moreno, Francisco.

*GUINAN, MICHAEL D., OFM, Franciscan Brothers Graduate Theological Union, Berkeley, Calif. **Article:** Jacob of Sarug (Serugh).

*GUISA Y AZEVEDO, JESÚS, Dr.Phil. (Louvain), writer and editor, Director, *Lectura*, Mexico City, Mexico. **Articles:** Elguero, Francisco; Martinez, Luis Maria.

*GUIZAR DIAZ, RICARDO, Ph.L., S.T.L., Professor of Philosophy and Spiritual Director, major seminary, Archdiocese of Puebla de Los Angeles, Pueblo, Mexico. **Article:** Ibarra y Gonzalez, Ramon.

*GUMBLEY, GEORGE WALTER, OP, F.R.H.S., Preacher General and Provincial Archivist, Blackfriars, Oxford, England. **Article:** Pope, Hugh.

*GUNDERSON, DORA JOSEPHINE, Ph.D., Professor of History, Mercy College of Detroit, Detroit, MI. **Articles:** Latimer, Hugh; Ridley, Nicholas.

*GURR, JOHN EDWIN, SJ, M.A., S.T.L., Ph.D., Superintendent of Schools, Diocese of Fairbanks, Alaska. **Articles:** Rationalism; Scholasticism, 2. Modern.

*GURRIERI, JOHN A., Associate Director, NCCB Committee on the Liturgy, Washington, D.C. **Articles:** Acolyte; Lector; Liturgy of the Hours.

*GUSINDE, MARTIN, SVD, Ph.D., St. Gabriel, Mödling bei Wien, Austria. **Article:** Schmidt, Wilhelm.

*GUSMER, CHARLES W., S.T.D., Professor of Liturgy and Sacramental Theology, Darlington Seminary, Mahwah, N.J. **Article:** Liturgical Year in the Roman Rite.

*GUTHRIE, FREDERICK L., M.Ed., Associate Director of Resource Community, Worldwide Marriage Encounter, Washington, D.C. **Article:** Worldwide Marriage Encounter.

*GUTIERREZ, ERNESTO, civil engineer, with higher studies in hydrology in Brazil and France, Professor of Hydrology, Universidad Nacional de Nicaragua, León, Nicaragua, and Universidad Centroamerica, Managua, Nicaragua. **Article:** Nicaragua, the Catholic Church in.

*GUTMAN, SISTER MARY OCTAVIA, CPPS, M.A., General Councilor and Secretary-General, Congregation of the Sisters of the Precious Blood, Dayton, Ohio. **Article:** Precious Blood Sisters—Sisters of the Precious Blood.

*GUYOT, GILMORE HENRY, CM, S.T.L., S.S.B., Professor of Sacred Scripture and Theology, St. Mary's Seminary, Perryville, Mo. **Articles:** Brothers and Sisters of Jesus; Temptations of Jesus; Transfiguration.

*HAAS, WILLIAM PAUL, Very Rev., OP, S.T.L., S.T.Lr., Ph.D., President, Providence College, Providence, R.I. **Articles:** Humanism, Secular; Peirce, Charles Sanders.

*HABERL, FERDINAND, Very Rev., Comps.S.D., Dr.Theol., Director, Kirchenmusikschule, and Lector for Choral Music and History of Church Music, Philosophisch-Theologische Hochschule, Regensburg, Germany. **Article:** Fux, Johann Joseph.

*HABERSPERGER, GUSTAVO, SSCC, Professor and Spiritual Director in Institutions of his Congregation in Los Perales, Chile, and Lima, Peru. **Article:** Dintilhac, Jorge.

*HABIG, MARION ALPHONSE, OFM, M.A., L.G., Guardian of St. Augustine Friary, Chicago, Ill.; Editor, *Marian Era* (Chicago); Associate Editor, *Franciscan Herald and Forum* (Chicago); Member of Board of Editors, *Worldmission* (New York). **Articles:** John of Montfort, Bl.; Jolenta of Hungary, Bl.; Odoric of Pordenone, Bl.; Silvester Guzzolini, St.; William of Maleval, St.; William of Vercelli, St.; Williamites.

HACKETT, BENEDICT, O.S.A., Ph.D., St. Mary's Priory, Birmingham, England. **Article:** Flete, William.

*HACKETT, JOHN HENRY, J.C.D., Vice Chancellor, Defender of the Bond, Diocesan Tribunal, Diocese of Fall River, Mass. **Article:** Public Order (Canon Law).

*HACKETT, MICHAEL BENEDICT, OSA, B.A., H.Dip.Ed., Ph.D., Lect.Phil., Master of Novices and Subprior, Augustinian Novitiate, Clare Priory, Suffolk, England. **Article:** Tirry, William.

*HADOT, PIERRE, Lic.Ph., Diplôme de l'École Pratique des Hautes Études (Sciences religieuses), Paris; Director of Studies, École pratique des Hautes Études (Sciences religieuses); and Chargé de recherches, Centre National de la Recherche Scientifique, Paris, France. **Articles:** Marius Victorinus; Neoplatonism; Porphyry.

*HAENNI, GÉRARD, OSB, theological studies at the Abbey of St. Benoît de Port-Valais, at the Abbey in Einsiedeln, and at the University of Fribourg, Professor of Theology, Abbey of St. Benoît de Port-Valais, Le Bouveret (Valais), Switzerland. **Article:** Dacheriana Collectio.

*HAGEMANN, EDWARD HUGO, SJ, M.A., Spiritual Counselor, Alma College, Los Gatos, Calif. **Articles:** Gerbillon, Jean Francois; Pereira, Tomas.

HAGSTROM, AURELIE A., Ph.D., Chair, Department of Theology/Philosophy; University of St. Francis, Joliet, Ill. **Article:** Laity, Theology of.

*HAHN, CORNELIUS JAMES, OP, A.B., Dominican House of Studies, Washington, D.C. **Articles:** Chardon, Louis; Stagel, Elsbeth (Elbethe).

*HALADUS, JEROME JOACHIM, OP, B.A., S.T.B., Dominican House of Studies, Washington, D.C. **Articles:** Burke, Thomas; Massoulie, Antonin.

*HALKIN, FRANÇOIS, SJ, S.T.D., Bollandist, Brussels, Belgium. **Article:** Hagiography.

*HALL, SISTER THELMA, RC, Convent of Our Lady of the Retreat in the Cenacle, Mount Kisco, N.Y. **Article:** Cenacle, Religious of the.

*HALLER, ROBERT B., OP, Providence College, Providence, R.I. **Articles:** Congregational Singing; Hymnology.

*HALLIE, PHILIP PAUL, Ph.D., B.Litt., M.A., Professor of Philosophy and Humanities, Wesleyan University, Middletown, Conn. **Article:** Maine de Biran.

*HALLIGAN, NICHOLAS, OP, S.T.D., S.T.M., Professor of Fundamental Theology, St. Stephen's Priory, Dover, Mass. **Article:** Holy Orders.

*HALLIGAN, NICHOLAS, OP, S.T.M., S.T.D., Judicial Vicar, Archdiocese for the Military Services, Silver Spring, Md. **Articles:** Military Services, USA, Archdiocese for; Vagnozzi, Egidio.

*HALLINAN, PAUL JOHN, Most Rev., D.D., Ph.D., LL.D., Archbishop of Atlanta, Ga. **Article:** Gilmour, Richard.

*HALPHEN, MARSHALL JOSEPH, OSA, M.A., Instructor in Theology, Villanova University, Villanova, Pa. **Article:** Bellesini, Stefano, Bl.

*HALTON, THOMAS PATRICK, B.A., S.T.B., H.Dip.Educ., Ph.D., Professor of

Greek and Latin, The Catholic University of America, Washington, D.C. **Articles:** Aeonius of Arles, St.; Dungal; Henricus Aristippus; John of Ravenna; John of Reome, St.; Paideia, Christian; Pyrrhus I, Patriarch of Constantinople; Patristic Studies.

*HAMBYE, EDWARD RENÉ, SJ, Ph.L., S.T.L., Doctorate in Philosophy and Letters (History), Professor of Church History, Missions History, Oriental Questions, and Syriac, St. Mary's Theological College, Kurseong, India, and Papal Seminary, Poona, India. **Articles:** Bhutan, The Catholic Church in; Hartmann, Anastasius, Ven.; Ivanios, Mar (Givergis Thomas Panikervirtis); Tibet, The Catholic Church in.

*HAMEL, EDWARD, SJ, Ph.L., S.T.D., Professor of Moral Theology, Gregorian University, Rome, Italy. **Article:** Casuistry.

*HAMELIN, MOTHER MARIE DU BEL AMOUR, RJM, Ph.D., Provincial Councilor, Provincial Directress of Studies, President of Thevenet Institute, and Community Supervisor of Schools, Convent of Jesus and Mary, Hyattsville, Md. **Article:** Religious of Jesus and Mary.

*HAMELL, PATRICK JOSEPH, M.A. (Honors), S.T.D., Vice President and Professor of Dogmatic Theology, St. Patrick's College, Maynooth, Ireland. **Articles:** Modalism; Monarchianism; Subordinationism; Trinity, Holy, Controversies on.

*HAMILL, HUGH MAXWELL, JR., Ph.D., Associate Professor of History, University of Connecticut, Storrs, Conn. **Article:** Pradt, El Abate de.

*HAMILTON, BERNARD, Ph.D., Lecturer in History, University of Nottingham, England. **Articles:** Constantine IX Monomachus, Byzantine Emperor; Crescentii; John Gualbert, St.; Lewes, Priory of; Majolus of Cluny, St.; Mont-Saint-Michel, Abbey of; Robert of Arbrissel, Bl.; Romuald, St.; William of Hirsau, Bl.; William of Aquitaine, St.; William of Saint-Benigne of Dijon, St.

*HAMILTON, MARY JANE, Ph.D., Associate Staff Editor for Medieval Church History, *New Catholic Encyclopedia*, The Catholic University of America, Washington, D.C.; Assistant Professor of History, Sacramento State College, Sacramento, Calif. **Articles:** Benedict of Peterborough; Bona, St.; Chichester, Ancient See of; Coventry and Lichfield, Ancient See of; Dryburgh, Monastery of; Gervase of Tilbury; Herman Joseph of Steinfeld, St.; John of Hoveden; Peter's Pence; Peterborough, Abbey of; Richard of Gravesend (?–1303); Robert Cowton; Saint Albans, Abbey of; Shepey, John de; Walter of Coincy.

*HAMILTON, RAPHAEL NOTEWARE, SJ, Ph.D., Professor Emeritus of American History and University Archivist, Marquette University, Milwaukee, Wis. **Articles:** Charlevoix, Pierre Francois Xavier de; Meurin, Sebastien Louis.

HAMMOND, M. JAY, Ph.D., Assistant Professor of Historical Theology and Director, Center for Franciscan Thought, Quincy University, Quincy, Ill.; Associate Director, Sacratech Foundation, St. Louis, Mo. **Articles:** Bonaventure, St.; Franciscan Spirituality.

*HAMP, VINZENZ, Dr.Theol., Professor of Old Testament Exegesis and Oriental Biblical Languages, University of Munich, Germany. **Article:** Kittel, Rudolf.

*HAMROGUE, JOHN MICHAEL, CSSR, M.A., Teacher of History, St. Alphonsus College, Suffield, Conn. **Articles:** Eusebius of Samosata, St.; Evodius of Antioch, St.; Itineraria.

*HANDSPICKER, MEREDITH BROOK, A.B., B.D., M.A., Clergyman of the United Church of Christ, Assistant Secretary, Commission on Faith and Order, World Council of Churches, Geneva, Switzerland. **Article:** Faith and Order Commission.

*HANISCH, WALTER ESPINDOLA, SJ, S.T.L., Professor of History and Philosophy, Colegio de San Ignacio; Professor of Church History, Catholic University of Chile; and Professor of American Church History, Instituto Catequístico Latino Americano, Santiago, Chile. **Articles:** Caro Rodríguez, Jose Maria; Rodríguez Zorrilla, Jose Santiago.

*HANLEY, PHILIP LOUIS, OP, S.T.Lr., M.A., Associate Professor of Theology, University of Notre Dame, Notre Dame, Ind. **Articles:** Ex Opere Operantis; Reviviscence, Sacramental; Sacraments, Conditional Administration of.

*HANLEY, THOMAS O'BRIEN, SJ, Ph.D., Assistant Professor of History, Marquette University, and Director of the American Historical Collection and

Studies, Milwaukee, Wis. **Articles:** Brouillet, John; Calvert; Church and State in the U.S. (Legal History), 1. Colonial Period (1607–1776); Ewing, Thomas and Charles; Grassel, Lorenz; Kohlmann, Anthony; Mission in Colonial America IV (English Missions); Toleration Acts of 1639 and 1649, Maryland; Van den Broek, Theodore.

*HANLON, SISTER JOSEPH DAMIEN, CSJ, Ph.D., Associate Professor of History and Director of Public Relations, St. Joseph's College for Women, Brooklyn, N.Y. **Articles:** Abercromby, Robert; Anne of Denmark; Bourne, Gilbert; Cole, Henry; Goodman, Godfrey; Heath, Nicholas; Percy, Thomas, Bl.; Whiting, Richard, Bl.

*HANNAH, WILLIAM WALTON THOMSON, M.A. (Hons. English), Member, Catholic Inquiry Forum, Montreal, Canada; Book Review Editor, *Canadian Register;* Lecturer, Marianopolis College, University of Montreal, Canada. **Articles:** British Council of Churches; Davidson, Randall Thomas; Free Churches; Gore, Charles; Kirk, Kenneth Escott; Lambeth Conference; Lidgett, John Scott; Lux Mundi; Martineau, James; Maurice, Frederick Denison; Milman, Henry Hart; Spurgeon, Charles Haddon.

*HANRAHAN, NOEL, SMSJ, S.T.L., Professor of Fundamental Theology, St. Joseph's College, Mill Hill, London, England. **Article:** Mill Hill Missionaries.

HANSEN, JAMES, B., Mus.Ed., M.A. Ed., Director of Spiritual Development Services, Diocese of Marquette, Mich. **Article:** Cantor in Christian Liturgy.

*HAPPEL, STEPHEN, Ph.D., S.T.D., Associate Professor of Religion and Religious Education, The Catholic University of America, Washington, D.C. **Article:** Deconstructionism.

*HARDICK, LOTHAR, OFM, Dr.Theol., Lector for History of the Franciscan Order, Franciscan Hochschule, Münster in Westfalen, Germany; Editor, *Franziskanische Studien* and *Franziskanische Quellenschriften.* **Articles:** Agnellus of Pisa, Bl.; Elzear of Sabran, St.; Jordan of Giano.

*HARDON, JOHN ANTHONY, SJ, S.T.D., Professor of Dogmatic Theology, Bellarmine School of Theology, North Aurora, Ill., and Associate Professor of Comparative Religion, Western Michigan University, Kalamazoo, Mich. **Ar-**

ticles: Anthroposophy; Christian Church (Disciples of Christ); Community Churches; Holiness Churches; National Council of the Churches of Christ in the U.S.A.; New Thought; Pilgrim Holiness Church; Reformed Churches, II: North America; Steiner, Rudolf.

*HARDWICK, EDGAR GEORGE, Doctorate in Scholastic Philosophy (Valladolid), Coldham Cottage, Lawshall, near Bury-St.-Edmunds, England. **Articles:** Damnation; Definition, Dogmatic; Ex Cathedra; Hell (Theology of); Hellfire; Matter, Theology of; Son of God [part 2].

*HARE, PETER H., Professor and Chairman, Department of Philosophy, State University of New York, Buffalo, N.Y. **Article:** Ducasse, Curt John.

*HARGROVE, MOTHER KATHARINE, RSCJ, M.A., M.A.R.E., Associate Professor of Religion, Manhattanville College of the Sacred Heart, Purchase, N.Y. **Articles:** Cologne, School of; Congruism; Synergism.

*HÄRING, BERNARD, CSSR, Dr.Theol., LL.D., Professor of Moral Theology, Accademia Alfonsiana, and Professor of Pastoral Sociology, Pastoral Institute of the Lateran University, Rome, Italy. **Articles:** Asceticism (Theological Aspect); Commandments, Ten [part 2]; Freedom, Spiritual; Justice.

*HARING, NICHOLAS MARTIN, SAC, S.T.D., D.Med.St., Professor of the History of Patristic and Pre-Scholastic Theology, Pontifical Institute of Medieval Studies, and Professor of Religious Knowledge, St. Michael's College, Toronto, Canada. **Articles:** Alger of Liège (Alger of Cluny, Algerus Magister); Boethius; Clarenbaud of Arras; Everard of Ypres; Gilbert de la Porree; Hugh of Honau; Paschasius Radbertus, St.; Peter of Vienna.

*HARKINS, PAUL WILLIAM, Ph.D., LL.D., Professor of Classical Languages, Xavier University, Cincinnati, Ohio. **Articles:** Gennadius I, Patriarch of Constantinople, St.; Gerasimus, St.; John Chrysostom, St.; Lucian of Antioch, St.; Mark the Hermit; Nilus of Ancyra, St.; Oak, Synod of the; Olympias, St.; Porphyry of Gaza, St.; Tall Brothers.

*HARNEY, CYRIL JAMES, OP, M.A., S.T.L., Fenwick High School, Chicago, Ill. **Article:** Scrupulosity.

*HARNEY, MARTIN PATRICK, SJ, M.A., Professor of History, Boston College,

Chestnut Hill, Mass. **Article:** Maunoir, Julien, Bl.

*HARNEY, ROBERT FOREST, Ph.D., Lecturer in History, University of Toronto, Canada. **Article:** Rossi, Pellegrino.

HARPER, MARY, SA, M.A., Archivist, St. Francis Convent, Graymoor, Garrison, N.Y. **Article:** Franciscan Sisters— Franciscan Sisters of the Atonement (SA).

HARRELL, JOY P., Ph.D. cand., Department of Theology, The Catholic University of America, Washington, D.C. **Article:** Gutenberg Bible.

HARRINGTON, LINDA S., Ph.D. cand., School of Religious Studies, The Catholic University of America, Washington D.C.; Adjunct Professor of Theology, Briar Cliff University, Sioux City, Iowa. **Articles:** Allegory; Sexism; Wicca; Woman.

*HARRISON, GEORGE BAGSHAWE, B.A., M.A. (Cantab.), Ph.D., Litt.D., LL.D., Professor of English, University of Michigan, Ann Arbor, Mich. **Article:** Shakespeare, William.

HARRISON, SISTER MARGARET, OP, M.A., Archivist, Dominican Congregation of Our Lady of the Rosary, Sparkhill, N.Y. **Articles:** Dominican Sisters— Congregation of Our Lady of the Rosary (Sparkhill, N.Y.).

HARSHMAN, R. D., **Article:** Rose of Viterbo, St.

*HART, SISTER MARY ADORITA, BVM, Ph.D., Professor of English and Chairman of the Department, Clarke College, Dubuque, Iowa. **Article:** Belloc, Joseph Hilaire Pierre.

*HARTDEGEN, STEPHEN JOSEPH, OFM, S.T.B., S.S.L., Professor of Sacred Scripture, Holy Name College, and Professor of Biblical Greek, The Catholic University of America, Washington, D.C.; Secretary, Final Board of Editors of the Old Testament from the Original Languages (Confraternity Version); Originator in U.S.A. of the Secular Institutes of Missionaries. **Articles:** Missionaries of the Kingship of Christ; New American Bible; Stephen Protomartyr, St.

*HARTE, THOMAS JOSEPH, CSSR, Ph.D., Associate Professor of Sociology, The Catholic University of America, Washington, D.C. **Articles:** Federated Colored Catholics; Mater et Magistra; Social Thought, Catholic, 1. Introduction; Social Thought, Papal, 1. History; Summi Pontificatus.

*HARTIGAN, PATRICIA M., OP, National Coordinator, Movement for a Better World, Silver Spring, Md. **Article:** Movement for a Better World.

*HARTMAN, LOUIS FRANCIS, CSSR, S.S.L., Ling.Orient.Lic., Professor of Semitic Languages and Literatures, The Catholic University of America, Washington, D.C.; Executive Secretary, Catholic Biblical Association of America; Chairman of the Editorial Board for the CCD Version of the Old Testament; Staff Editor for Sacred Scripture, *New Catholic Encyclopedia*, The Catholic University of America, Washington, D.C. **Articles:** Azevedo, Luiz de; Bedjan, Paul; Bible; Biblical Languages; Bonfrere, Jacques; Canticles, Biblical; Christ; Cosmogony (in the Bible); Demon (in the Bible); Devil; Etiology (in the Bible); Exegesis, Biblical, 2 Exegesis of the Old Testament in the New Testament; Exegesis, Biblical, 3 Jewish Exegesis; Exegesis, Biblical, 10 New Testament Exegesis in the 19th and 20th Centuries; Exegesis, Biblical, 1 Introductory; Exegesis, Biblical, 8 From the Medieval to the 19th Century; Exegesis, Biblical, 9 Old Testament Exegesis in the 19th and 20th Centuries; Exegesis, Biblical, 4 Patristic Exegesis; Galatia; Genebrard, Gilbert; Gospel; Israel, 3. History of Israel; Jesus (the Name); Jonah ben Jishaq, Jehudah; Leviathan; Malvenda, Tomas; Martin, Gregory; Mesopotamia, Ancient (Introduction); Minor Prophets; Mishnah; Myth and Mythology (in the Bible); Paul of Burgos; Pellicanus, Konrad (Kurschner); Pineda, Juan de; Precious Stones (in the Bible); Prophetic Books of the Old Testament; Qatar, The Catholic Church in; Reimarus, Hermann Samuel; Sabatier, Pierre; Salmeron, Alfonso; Sirleto, Guglielmo; Vulgate.

*HARTMANN, ARNULF CHARLES, Very Rev., OSA, Prior of the Augustinian Priory at Marylake, King City, Ontario, Canada. **Article:** Gutierrez Rodriguez, Bartolome, Bl.

*HARTNETT, ROBERT CLINTON, SJ, S.T.L., Ph.D., Professor of Political Science, Loyola University, and Lecturer in the Philosophy of Law and Government, Loyola University School of Law, Chicago, Ill. **Article:** Siedenburg, Frederic.

*HARTT, FREDERICK, Ph.D., Professor of the History of Art and Chairman of the Department of Art, University of Pennsylvania, Philadelphia, Pa. **Article:** Michelangelo Buonarroti.

*HARTZEL, THOMAS V., St. Joseph's College, Philadelphia, Pa. **Article:** Gallitzin, Demetrius Augustine.

*HARVANEK, ROBERT FRANCIS, SJ, Ph.D., Professor of Philosophy, Bellarmine School of Theology, North Aurora, Ill. **Articles:** Gregory of Nyssa, St.; Patristic Philosophy; Pluralism, Philosophical.

*HARVEY, JULIEN, SJ, B.A., Ph.L., S.T.L., M.A., S.S.D., Professor of Old Testament Scripture, Facultés S.J. de Montréal (Scolasticat de l'Immaculée-Conception), Montreal, Canada. **Article:** Inheritance (in the Bible).

*HASTING, MARTIN FRANKLIN, SJ, S.T.L., Ph.D., Associate Professor and Director of the doctoral program in American Studies, St. Louis University, St. Louis, Mo. **Articles:** Phelan, David Samuel; Verhaegen, Peter J.

*HATHAWAY, RONALD FREDERICK, Ph.D., Junior Fellow, Dumbarton Oaks Research Library and Collection, Harvard University, Washington, D.C. **Article:** Athens, Schools of.

*HATZFELD, HELMUT ANTHONY, Ph.D., Professor Emeritus of Romance Languages and Literatures, The Catholic University of America, Washington, D.C. **Article:** Baroque, The.

HAUGHT, JOHN F., Ph.D., Professor of Theology, Georgetown University, Washington, D.C. **Article:** Ecology.

*HAUSER, FRANZ, CSSR, S.T.L., Accademia Alfonsiana, Rome, Italy. **Articles:** Lapsi; Libellatici; Pneumatomachians; Psychics.

*HAVRAN, MARTIN JOSEPH, Ph.D., Assistant Professor of English History, Kent State University, Kent, Ohio. **Articles:** Baxter, Richard; Cartwright, Thomas; Church and State [part 3]; Coverdale, Miles; Puritans; Sabbatarianism; Seekers.

*HAWKINS, DENIS JOHN BERNARD, Canon, D.D., Ph.D., Archdiocese of Southwark, England (deceased Jan. 16, 1965). **Article:** Sufficient Reason, Principle of.

*HAY, DENYS, B.A. (Oxon.), Professor of Medieval History, University of Edinburgh, Scotland. **Article:** Vergil, Polydore.

*HAYBURN, ROBERT FRANCIS, Mus.D., Assistant Superintendent of Schools and Archdiocesan Director of Music, San Francisco, Calif. **Articles:** Chant

Books, Printed Editions of; Liturgical Music, History of, 10: Pre-Vatican II Legislation.

*HAYDEN, JAMES MICHAEL, Ph.D., Assistant Professor of History, University of Detroit, Detroit, Mich. **Articles:** France [1515–1789]; Thou, Nicolas and Jacques Auguste de.

HAYES, PATRICK J., Ph.D. cand., Department of Religion and Religious Education, The Catholic University of America; Adjunct Professor of Religious Studies and Theology, Fordham University, Fairfield University, Sacred Heart University, and Iona College. **Articles:** Bureau International Catholique de l'Enfance (BICE); Catholic Charities USA; Catholic Medical Association; Catholic Commission on Intellectual and Cultural Affairs; Conference for Pastoral Planning and Council Development; De Mello, Anthony; International Catholic Deaf Association; International Catholic Stewardship Council; International Catholic Migration Commission; Liberal Catholic Church; National Catholic Development Conference; National Catholic Student Coalition (NCSC); National Apostolate for Inclusion Ministry (NafIM); National Catholic Pharmacists Guild of the U.S.; National Council of Catholic Women (NCCW); National Catholic Conference for Interracial Justice; National Organization for Continuing Education of Roman Catholic Clergy (NOCERCC); National Catholic Coalition for Responsible Investment; National Conference for Community and Justice; Office for Film and Broadcasting; Pontifical Universities, Roman; Pontifical Academies; Pontifical Council for Interreligious Dialogue; Pontifical Councils; Ross, John Elliot; Two Ways.

*HAYES, THOMAS JAMES, OP, B.A., S.T.Lr., Chaplain, St. Mary's College of California, St. Mary's, Calif. **Articles:** Assault; Continence.

*HAYES, WILLIAM, OP, Assistant Professor of Social Ethics, Catholic University of America, Washington, D.C. **Article:** Niebuhr, Reinhold.

HAYES, ZACHARY, O.F.M., Dr.Theol., Duns Scotus Professor of Spirituality, Catholic Theological Union, Chicago, Ill. **Article:** Hexaemeron.

*HAYS, RHŶS WILLIAMS, Ph.D., Associate Professor of History, Wisconsin State University, Stevens Point, Wis. **Articles:** Adam of Orleton; Ball, John;

Bury-St.-Edmunds, Abbey of; Ivo, St.; Pembroke, Priory of; Richard of Gravesend (?–1279); Scrope, Richard; Stephen of Gravesend; Walter Map.

*HEALEY, JOHN EDWARD, SJ, M.A., S.T.L., Dean of Studies and Professor of History, St. Mary's University, Halifax, Nova Scotia, Canada. **Articles:** Hereford, Nicholas; Payne, Peter; Purvey, John; Repington, Philip (Repyngdon); Rygge, Robert; William Woodford.

*HEALEY, JOHN WILLIAM, SJ, M.A., Ph.L., S.T.D., Professor of Dogmatic Theology, Woodstock College, Woodstock, Md. **Article:** Hermes, Georg.

*HEALY, KILIAN JOHN, OCarm, S.T.D., Prior General of the Carmelite Order, Rome, Italy. **Articles:** Prayer (Theology of); Presence of God, Practice of.

*HEALY, VALENTINE JOHN, Very Rev., OFM, Ph.D., President, San Luis Roy College, San Luis Rey, Calif. **Articles:** Belsunce de Castelmoran, Henri Francois Xavier de; Tencin, Pierre Guerin de.

*HEANEY, JOHN JOSEPH, SJ, M.A., S.T.D., Teacher, St. Andrew-on-Hudson, Poughkeepsie, N.Y. **Articles:** Hebert, Marcel; Houtin, Albert; Lamentabili; Modernism; Modernism, Oath Against; Pascendi.

*HEARON, SISTER MICHAEL FRANCIS, OSU, M.A., Professor of English, Ursuline College for Women, Cleveland, Ohio. **Article:** Kazel, Dorothy.

*HEATH, MARK, OP, Regent of Studies of the Eastern Province of the Dominicans and Professor of Pastoral Studies, Dominican House of Studies, Washington, D.C. **Article:** Signs of the Times.

*HEATH, THOMAS, OP, Dominican House of Studies, Washington, D.C. **Article:** Conscientious Objection.

*HEATH, THOMAS RICHARD, OP, Ph.D., S.T.Lr., Professor of Theology, St. Mary's College, Notre Dame, Ind. **Articles:** Adam; Eve [part 1].

*HEBBLETHWAITE, PETER, journalist, Oxford, England. **Articles:** Benelli, Giovanni; Mayer, Rupert, Bl.; Villot, Jean.

*HÉBERT, GÉRARD J., SJ, Ph.L., S.T.L., Ph.D., Editor, *Relations*, and part-time Lecturer, Industrial Relations, McGill University, Montreal, Canada. **Article:** Jehovah's Witnesses.

*HEBGA, MEINRAD P., SJ, Ph.D., Professor of Philosophy, University of Yaoundé,

Cameroon. **Article:** Cameroon, The Catholic Church in.

*HECTOR, LEONARD CHARLES, M.A., Principal Assistant Keeper, Public Record Office, London, England. **Articles:** Names, Medieval; Sigillography.

*HEFFERMAN, ANNE EILEEN, FSP, M.A., Provincial Councillor, Pious Society of the Daughters of St. Paul. **Article:** St. Paul, Pious Society Daughters of.

HEFFERRNAN, J. B., **Articles:** Alexandrine Bulls; Columbus, Christopher; Lepanto, Battle of.

*HEFT, JAMES L., SM, Ph.D., Chair, Department of Religious Studies, University of Dayton. **Article:** Infallibility.

HEFT, JAMES L., SM, Ph.D., University Professor of Faith and Culture and Chancellor of the University of Dayton, Dayton, Ohio; Chairman of the Board of Directors of the Institute for Advanced Catholic Studies. **Articles:** Academic Freedom; Dayton, University of.

*HEGARTY, SISTER M. LOYOLA, CCVI, Villa de Matel, Houston, Tex. **Article:** Incarnate Word, Sisters of Charity of the.

*HEGEL, EDUARD, Ph.D., Dr.Theol., Professor of Medieval and Modern Church History, University of Münster, Münster in Westfalen, Germany. **Article:** Enlightenment.

*HEIDERSCHEIT, D., **Article:** Franciscan Sisters—Sisters of St. Francis of the Holy Family (OSF).

*HEIDT, WILLIAM GEORGE, OSB, M.A., S.T.D., Professor of Biblical Languages and Sacred Scripture, St. John's Seminary, Collegeville, Minn. **Articles:** Ecclesiastes, Book of; Proverbs, Book of.

*HEIMAN, AMBROSE JOSEPH, CPPS, M.S.L., Ph.D., Professor of Philosophy and Vice Rector, St. Charles Seminary, Carthagena, Ohio. **Articles:** David of Dinant; Gerard of Abbeville; John (Quidort) of Paris; William of Saint-Amour.

*HEINRICH, WALTER, Dr.rer.pol., Professor of Economics, Institute of Commerce (Hochschule für Welthandel), Vienna, Austria. **Article:** Spann, Othmar.

HEISER, BASIL, OFMConv., S.T.D., Ph.D., Curia Generalizzia O.F.M.Conv., Rome, Italy. **Article:** Penitentiary, Apostolic.

*HELD, SISTER MARY LEONTINE, SSND, Ph.D., Vice President and Teacher of

Scripture, Notre Dame College, St. Louis, Mo. **Articles:** Apostle; Twelve, The; Widow (in the Bible).

*HELDE, THOMAS TOLMAN, Ph.D., Associate Professor of History, Georgetown University, Washington, D.C. **Articles:** Lamormaini, Wilhelm; Wartenberg, Franz Wilhelm von.

*HELLMAN, C. DORIS, Ph.D., Professorial Lecturer, Pratt Institute, and Adjunct Professor of the History of Science, New York University, N.Y.; Associate, Columbia University Seminar on the Renaissance. **Article:** Kepler, Johann.

*HELLMAN, JOHN, Professor, Department of History, McGill University, Montreal, Canada. **Article:** Dawson, Christopher.

HELLMANN, J. A. WAYNE, OFM. Conv., Dr.Theol., Director of Graduate Studies, Department of Theological Studies, Saint Louis University, Saint Louis, Mo. **Articles:** Elias of Cortona; Franciscan Spirituality; Julian of Speyer; Thomas of Celano.

*HELLMANN, MANFRED, Dr.Phil., Professor of Eastern European History, University of Münster, Münster in Westfalen, Germany. **Articles:** Herman of Salza; Teutonic Knights.

*HELM, ROBERT MEREDITH, Ph.D., Professor of Philosophy, Wake Forest College, Winston-Salem, N.C. **Article:** Inge, William Ralph.

*HENGEL, JOHN VAN DEN, SCJ, Professor of Systematic Theology, St. Paul University, Ottawa, Canada. **Article:** Ricoeur, Paul.

*HENKEY, CHARLES HOENIG, Ph.D., S.T.L., J.C.B., S.T.D., Associate Professor of Theology, Loyola College, Montreal, Canada. **Articles:** Apocrypha, 2. Apocrypha of the New Testament; Drascovic, Georg de Trakoscan; Jesus Christ, Biographical Studies of.

*HENNELLY, ALFRED T., SJ, Ph.D., Professor of Theology, Fordham University, Bronx, New York. **Article:** Santo Domingo (1992).

*HENNESEY, JAMES JOHN, SJ, B.A. (Classics), Ph.L., S.T.L., M.A., Ph.D., Assistant Professor of History, Fordham University Graduate School and Loyola Seminary, N.Y.; Adjunct Professor of American Church History, Gregorian University, Rome, Italy. **Articles:** Baltimore, Councils of; Corcoran, James Andrew; Holaind, Rene; Keogh, James; O'Connor, Michael; Sabetti, Luigi; Vatican Council I.

*HENNESSEY, ROBERT JUSTIN, OP, B.S., A.B., S.T.Lr., S.T.D., Visiting Professor of Systematic Theology, Aquinas Institute, Dubuque, Iowa. **Articles:** Contumely; Cowardice; Derision; Extrinsicism; Foolhardiness; Good Works; Human Respect; Indifferent Acts; Insult; Kollin, Conrad; Salutary Acts; Supererogation, Works of; Vainglory.

*HENNESSY, AUGUSTINE PAUL, CP, S.T.D., Master of Novices, Province of St. Paul of the Cross, St. Paul's Monastery, Pittsburgh, Pa. **Articles:** Sacrifice of the Cross; Satisfaction of Christ.

*HENRIOT, PETER J., SJ, Director, Jesuit Centre for Theological Reflection, Lusaka, Zambia. **Article:** Zambia, The Catholic Church in.

*HENRY, CHARLES WILLIAM, OSB, B.A., S.T.L., J.C.D., Rector, School of Theology, and Professor of Canon Law and Moral Theology, St. Maur's Priory, South Union, Ky. **Article:** Affinity.

*HENRY, EDWARD LEROY, M.A., M.B.A., Ph.D., Professor of Government and Chairman of the Department, St. John's University, Collegeville, Minn.; Mayor of St. Cloud, Minn. **Article:** Government.

*HENZE, CLEMENS MARY, CSSR, J.C.D., editor and writer, Sant' Alfonso, Rome, Italy. **Article:** Our Lady of Perpetual Help (Succour).

*HERAN, PATRICK JOHN, SSCC, Sacred Hearts Novitiate, Cootehill, County Cavan, Ireland. **Articles:** Aymer de la Chevalerie, Henriette; Coudrin, Pierre Marie Joseph.

*HERBERMANN, HENRY FREDERICK, A.B., LL.B., lawyer, New York, N.Y. **Article:** Herbermann, Charles George.

*HERBOLD, ANTHONY EVERETT, Ph.D., Instructor in English Literature, Dartmouth College, Hanover, N.H. **Article:** Chesterton, Gilbert Keith.

*HERBST, CLARENCE ANTHONY, SJ, A.B., S.T.L., M.A., Ph.D., Professor of History, Sogang Jesuit College, Seoul, Korea. **Articles:** Korea, Martyrs of, SS.; Korea, the Catholic Church in.

*HERBST, WINFRID JOHN, SDS, editor, author, retreat master, home missionary, columnist, and free-lance writer, Jordan Seminary, Menominee, Mich. **Ar-**

ticles: Becker, Christopher Edmund; Clemency; Courtesy; Envy; Eutrapelia; Jealousy; Kindness; Respect; Reverence (Observantia).

HERDE, PETER, emeritierter Universitaetsprofessor fuer Geschichte, insbesondere mittlere Geschichte, Landesgeschichte und historische Hilfswissenschaften an der Philosophischen Fakultaet II der Universitaet Wuerzburg. Bayerische-Julius-Maximilians-Universität Würzburg (University of Würzburg) Würzburg, Germany. **Article:** Celestine V, Pope, St.

*HERLIHY, DAVID JOSEPH, Ph.D., Professor of History, University of Wisconsin, Madison, Wis. **Articles:** Church and State [part 2]; Church Property; Secularization of Church Property; Social Thought, Catholic, 3. Patristic and Medieval.

*HERMANIUK, MAXIM, Most Rev., CSSR, S.T.D., Auxiliary Bishop of Winnipeg, Manitoba, Canada; Archbishop Metropolitan of Winnipeg for the Ukrainians. **Article:** Maximus the Confessor, St.

*HERRICK, JANE, Ph.D., Professor of History, State College, Bridgewater, Mass.; Staff Editor for Latin American Church History, *New Catholic Encyclopedia,* The Catholic University of America, Washington, D.C. **Articles:** Buyl, Bernal (Boyl); Conquistadores; Duran, Diego; Guyana, The Catholic Church in; Honduras, The Catholic Church in; Moreno, Juan Ignacio; Remesal, Antonio de; Suriname, The Catholic Church in.

*HERRON, MATTHEW CARROLL, TOR, S.T.D., Head, Department of Theology, St. Francis College, Loretto, Pa. **Articles:** Oaths; Perjury; Sacrilege; Sunday and Holyday Observance.

*HESS, HAMILTON, M.A., D.Phil., Lecturer in Theology, Marquette University, and Associate Editor, Hi-Time Publications, Inc., Milwaukee, Wis. **Article:** Theodosius the Deacon, Collection of.

HESTER, KEVIN L., Ph.D., Research Fellow and Adjunct Professor in the Department of Theological Studies, Saint Louis University, St. Louis, Mo. **Articles:** Gelasius I, Pope, St.; Gregory I (the Great), Pope, St.

*HESTON, EDWARD LOUIS, Very Rev., CSC, Ph.D., S.T.D., J.C.D., Procurator and Postulator General, Congregation of Holy Cross, Rome, Italy; Consultor, Sacred Congregation of Religious; Commission Member, Sacred Congregation of the Sacraments for Nonconsummation Marriage Cases; *Peritus*, Vatican Council II. **Articles:** Holy Cross, Congregation of; Moreau, Basil Anthony.

*HEUFELDER, EMMANUEL MARIA, OSB, Abbot, Abbey of Niederaltaich, Lower Bavaria, Germany. **Article:** Niederaltaich, Abbey of.

*HEYMANN, FREDERICK G., Ph.D., Professor of History and Head of the Department, University of Alberta, Calgary, Canada. **Article:** Zinzendorf, Nikolaus Ludwig von.

*HEYNCK, VALENS BERNHARD, OFM, Dr.Theol., Lector in Moral Theology, Franciscan Hochschule, Paderborn, Germany. **Article:** Biel, Gabriel.

*HICKEY, DANIEL FRANCIS, CSSR, S.T.L., Assistant Editor, *Perpetual Help Magazine*, Mt. St. Alphonsus, Esopus, N.Y. **Article:** Dormition of the Virgin.

HICKEY, MARGARET, ND, President, American Province, Notre Dame Sisters, Omaha, Neb. **Article:** Notre Dame Sisters.

*HICKS, LEO JOHN, SJ, Corpus Christi, Boscombe, Hants, England. **Articles:** Garnet, Henry; Persons, Robert.

*HIEGEL, LOUIS JOHN, SJ, S.T.L., J.C.D., LL.B., Associate Professor of Law, Loyola University, New Orleans, La.; Procurator-Advocate and Defender of the Bond for local Ecclesiastical Tribunal. **Article:** Red Mass.

*HIGGINS, GEORGE G., Rt. Rev., Ph.D., Director, Social Action Department, National Catholic Welfare Conference, Washington, D.C.; *Peritus*, Vatican Council II. **Article:** Haas, Francis Joseph.

*HIGGINS, MARTIN JOSEPH, Rt. Rev., Ph.D., Professor of Byzantine History, The Catholic University of America, Washington, D.C. **Articles:** Constantine VII Porphyrogenitus, Byzantine Emperor; Euthymius I, Patriarch of Constantinople; Evagrius Scholasticus; John III Scholasticus, Patriarch of Constantinople; John IV the Faster, Patriarch of Constantinople; Maurice, Byzantine Emperor; Michael Cerularius, Patriarch of Constantinople; Moechian Controversy; Nicephorus I, Patriarch of Constantinople, St.; Nicetas Stethatos; Nicholas I, Patriarch

of Constantinople; Patriarchate, II: Ecumenical Patriarchate of Constantinople; Romanus I Lecapenus, Byzantine Emperor.

*HIGGINS, MICHAEL W., Associate Director and Chair, Department of Religious Studies, University of St. Jerome's College, University of Waterloo, Waterloo, Ontario. **Articles:** Canada, The Catholic Church in; Roy, Maurice.

*HIGGINS, MICHAEL W., Ph.D., Associate Professor of English and Religious Studies, Academic Dean, University of St. Jerome's College, University of Waterloo, Ontario, Canada. **Article:** Léger, Paul-Emile.

*HIGGINS, THOMAS JOSEPH, SJ, Ph.D., Professor of Ethics, Loyola College, Baltimore, Md. **Articles:** Deontologism; Good [part 2]; Morality.

*HILFERTY, MARY CECILIA, RSM, M.A., The Catholic University of America, Washington, D.C. **Articles:** Arcosolium; Basilica; Egypt, Early Church in; Gaul, Early Church in; Ichthus; Justinianus, St.; Leo Thaumaturgus, St.; Manuel Calecas; Michael of Maleinos, St.; Nicetas Choniates.

HILKERT, MARY CATHERINE, OP, Ph.D., Associate Professor of Theology, University of Notre Dame, Notre Dame, Ind. **Articles:** Hill, William Joseph; Preaching, III (Theology of).

*HILL, BENNETT DAVID, Ph.D., Assistant Professor of History, University of Illinois, Urbana, Ill. **Articles:** Alphanus of Salerno, St.; Bertharius, St.; Charles of Villers, Bl.; Lorsch, Abbey of; Lull of Mainz, St.; Marius of Avenches, St.; Meinrad of Einsiedeln, St.; Merbot, Bl.; Oderisius, Bl.; Othmar, St.; Peter Pappacarbone, St.

*HILL, JEANNE, OP, Retreat Director, Benedictine Abbey, Pecos, N.M. **Article:** Healing, Christian.

*HILL, PAUL JAMES, MSC, S.T.D., Professor of Theology, Dean of Studies, and Spiritual Prefect of Scholastics, Sacred Heart Seminary, Shelby, Ohio. **Article:** Limbo.

*HILL, THOMAS, OFMCap, Executive Secretary Team, National Marriage Encounter, St. Paul, Minn. **Article:** Marriage Encounter.

*HILL, WILLIAM FRANCIS, SS, M.A., S.T.D., Professor of Sacred Scripture, St. Mary's Seminary and University, Baltimore, Md. **Articles:** Isaiah; Isaiah, Book of.

*HILL, WILLIAM JOSEPH, OP, S.T.L., S.T.Lr., S.T.Praes., Professor of Dogmatic Theology, Dominican House of Studies, Washington, D.C. **Articles:** Báñez and Bañezianism; Experience, Religious; History, Theology of; Perfection, Ontological; Simplicity of God; Unicity of God.

*HILL, WILLIAM JOSEPH, OP, Catholic University of America, Washington, D.C. **Articles:** God in Philosophy, 1. Place; God in Philosophy, 3. Nature; Thomism, Transcendental.

*HILL, WILLIAM JOSEPH, OP, Associate Professor of Systematic Theology, Catholic University of America. Washington, D.C. **Article:** Theology, History of.

*HILL, WILLIAM JOSEPH, OP, S.T.D., Emeritus Professor of Theology, The Catholic University of America, Washington, D.C. **Article:** Trinity, Holy.

*HILLGARTH, JOCELYN NIGEL, Ph.D., Visiting Lecturer, University of Texas, Austin, Tex. **Articles:** Elvira, Council of; Julian of Toledo, St.; Priscillian; Priscillianism; Spain, 1. Early.

*HILPISCH, STEPHAN, OSB, Dr.Phil., Lecturer in Church History, monk of the Abbey of Maria Laach, near Koblenz, Germany; member of the Abbot Herwegen-Institute, Koblenz, Germany, of the Bavarian Benedictine Academy, and of the Historical Commission for Hessen and Waldeck. **Articles:** Benedict of Aniane, St.; Boniface, St.

*HINNEBUSCH, JOHN FREDERICK, OP, M.A., Professor of History and Assistant Librarian, Providence College, Providence, R.I. **Articles:** Bartholomew of Vicenza, Bl.; Bernard of Trille; Crockaert, Peter; Dominic of Flanders; John of Ragusa; John of Lichtenberg; Nicholas of Strassburg; Peter Martyr, St.; Peter of Bergamo; Peter Nigri (Schwarz); Quetif, Jacques; Robert Bacon; Robert of Orford (de Colletorto); Simon Hinton; Ulric of Strassburg; William of Tripoli.

HINNEBUSCH, JOHN FREDERICK, OP, S.T.L., Ph.D., Director, Leonine Commission, Dominican House of Studies, Washington, D.C. **Article:** Leonine Commission.

*HINNEBUSCH, WILLIAM A., OP, S.T.Lr., Ph.D., Professor of Ecclesiastical History, Pontifical Faculty of Theology of the Immaculate Conception, Dominican House of Studies, Washington, D.C. **Articles:** Andrew Franchi, Bl.; Ascellino; Dominican Spirituality; Dominicans; Friends of God; Henry Suso, Bl.; Isnard of Chiampo, Bl.; John of Freiburg (Rumsik); O'Brien, William Vincent; O'Daniel, Victor Francis; Rosary; Spirituality of the Low Countries; Spirituality, Rhenish.

*HINRICHSEN, CARL DERIVAUX, S.T.L., Ph.D., Professor of Church History, Immaculate Conception Seminary, Darlington, N.J. **Articles:** Corrigan, Patrick; De Concilio, Januarius Vincent; Doane, George Hobart; Seton, Robert; Wigger, Winand Michael.

*HINTON, NORMAN D., Associate Professor of English, St. Louis University, St. Louis, Mo. **Articles:** Owl and the Nightingale, The; Pearl, The; Sawles Ward.

*HIRSCHBERGER, JOHANNES, Very Rev., Dr.Phil., Professor of the Catholic Philosophy of Religion, University of Frankfurt, Frankfurt am Main, Germany. **Articles:** Enlightenment, Philosophy of [part 2]; Hamann, Johann Georg; Jacobi, Friedrich Heinrich; Leibniz, Gottfried Wilhelm von; Monad.

HITCHCOCK, JAMES, Ph.D. (Princeton), Professor of History, St. Louis University, St. Louis, Mo. **Articles:** Baroque, The; Benedict XV, Pope.

*HITTI, PHILIP K., Ph.D., Professor Emeritus of Semitic Literature, Princeton University, Princeton, N.J. **Articles:** Babism; Dervishes; Druzes; Islamic Confraternities; Kindi, abu Yusuf Ya'qub ibn-Ishaq al-; Lebanon, The Catholic Church in; Mahdi, al-; Wahhabis.

*HITTINGER, F. RUSSELL, Ph.D., Warren Professor of Catholic Studies and Research Professor of Law, University of Tulsa, Tulsa, Oklahoma. **Article:** Solidarity.

*HOADE, EUGENE, OFM, D.D., B.C.L., Penitentiary in the Lateran Basilica, Rome, Italy. **Articles:** George, St.; Perpetua and Felicity, SS.; Priscilla, St.; Protus and Hyacinth, SS.; Pudens, Pudentiana, and Praxedes, SS.; Sabas, SS.; Sabina of Rome, St.; Sebastian, St.; Susanna, St.Vitus, Modestus, and Crescentia, SS.

*HOAGLAND, VICTOR, C.P., St. Michael Residence, Union City, New Jersey. **Article:** Daimiel, The Martyrs of, BB.

*HOCKEY, STANLEY FREDERICK, OSB, monk of the Solesmes Congregation,

B.A., Quarr Abbey, Ryde, Isle of Wight, England. **Article:** Waverley, Abbey of.

HOEGERL, CARL, CSsR, M.A., Historian, Baltimore Province, Redemptorist Fathers, Brooklyn, N.Y. **Article:** Redemptorists.

*HOELLE, PHILIP CHARLES, SM, S.T.L., Ph.D.; Associate Professor of Theology, Director of the Marian Library, University of Dayton, Dayton, Ohio; Director of Chaminade Auxiliaries from North America (Cana Lay Missioners); Chairman of the Board, *Mary Today*. **Article:** Mother of God.

*HOFER, MAURICE ALOYSIUS, Rt. Rev., B.A., S.S.L., Professor of General Introduction to the Bible, Exegesis of the Old Testament, Biblical Hebrew, and Greek, Pontifical College Josephinum, Columbus, Ohio. **Articles:** Burial, I (in the Bible); Ossuaries.

*HOFFMAN, JOHN CHARLES, Ph.D., Th.D., Minister, United Church of Canada; Assistant Professor of Theology, University of Windsor; and Principal, Iona College, Windsor, Ontario, Canada. **Article:** Pietism.

*HOFFMAN, LOUIS JOSEPH, SF, Superior, Holy Family Seminary, Silver Spring, Md. **Article:** Holy Family, Sons of the.

*HOFFMAN, RONAN RICHARD, OFMConv, M.A., S.T.L., D.Miss., Associate Professor of Missiology, School of Sacred Theology, The Catholic University of America, Washington, D.C. **Articles:** Propagation of the Faith, Congregation for the; Vendville, Jean.

*HOFFMANN, FRITZ L., Ph.D., Professor of Latin American History and Chairman of the Department of History, University of Colorado, Boulder, Colo. **Article:** Beltran, Luis.

*HOFINGER, JOHANNES, SJ, Associate Director in Charge of Adult Education, Archdiocese of New Orleans, New Orleans, La.; Member, East Asian Pastoral Institute, Manila, Phillipines. **Article:** Jungmann, Josef Andreas.

*HOFSTETTER, SISTER ADRIAN MARIE, OP, M.S., Ph.D., Chairman of the Department of Biology, Siena College, Memphis, Tenn. **Articles:** Life, Origin of; Spontaneous Generation.

*HOGAN, JOHN P., Ph.D., Associate Director of the Peace Corps, former Director of Catholic Relief Services in Haiti. **Articles:** Haiti, The Catholic Church in; Puebla.

HOGAN, JOHN P., Ph.D., Associate Director (retired) of International Operations, Peace Corps, Washington, D.C. **Article:** Liberation Theology, Latin America.

*HOGAN, MICHAEL PATRICK, OSA, M.A., M.Ed., Instructor, Senior Counselor, and Director of Public Relations, St. Rita High School, Chicago, Ill. **Article:** Middleton, Thomas Cooke.

*HOGAN, PETER EDWARD, SSJ, M.A., Certificate in Archival Administration, Archivist of the Josephite Fathers, Baltimore, Md. **Articles:** Conaty, Thomas James; Spalding, Martin John.

*HOGAN, WILLIAM FRANCIS, CSC, J.C.D., Chairman, Department of Theology, Stonehill College, North Easton, Mass. **Articles:** Aeterni Patris; Armenians, Decree for; Dum Acerbissimas; Quanta cura; Syllabus of Errors; Testem benevolentiae.

*HOGUE, ARTHUR REED, Ph.D., Associate Professor of History, Indiana University, Bloomington, Ind. **Articles:** Ely, Ancient See and Abbey of; Godfrey Giffard; Gray, William; Jocelin of Brakelond; William of Turbeville.

*HOHL, CLARENCE LEONARD, JR., Ph.D., Professor of History and Chairman of the Department, Manhattanville College of the Sacred Heart, Purchase, N.Y. **Articles:** Agustin, Antonio; Albrecht of Brandenburg-Ansbach; Beatrice d'Este, Bl.; Celestines; Centuriators of Magdeburg; Flacius Illyricus, Matthias; Paul III, Pope; Annius, John (Nanni).

*HOLDEN, VINCENT FRANCIS, CSP, Ph.D., Archivist and Historian of the Paulist Fathers, Mount Paul, Oak Ridge, N.J. **Articles:** Baker, Francis Asbury; Deshon, George; Elliott, Walter; Hecker, Isaac Thomas; Wadhams, Edgar Philip.

*HOLL, ADOLF, Dr.Theol., Dr.Phil., Lecturer in the Science of Religion (*Religionswissenschaft*), Catholic Theological Faculty, University of Vienna, Austria. **Articles:** Otto, Rudolf; Wach, Joachim.

*HOLLAND, CAROLINE CELESTE, Ph.B., B.Mus., Translator for Findlay Galleries, Inc., and Personal Secretary to Head of the Galleries, Chicago, Ill. **Article:** Porres, Martin de, St.

HOLLAND, SHARON L., IHM, J.C.D., Office Head, Congregation for Institutes of Consecrated Life and Societies of Apostolic Life; Professor of Canon Law, Regina Mundi Institute, Rome, Italy. **Article:** Secular Institutes.

*HOLLENBACH, SISTER MARY WILLIAM, SSND, Ph.D., Professor of Philosophy and Chairman of the Department, Notre Dame College, St. Louis, Mo. **Articles:** Courage; Dogmatism; Illuminism; Sadness; Synderesis.

*HOLLIS, MAURICE CHRISTOPHER, B.A., free-lance journalist and author, Little Claveys, Mells, near Frome, Somerset, England. **Articles:** Knox, Ronald Arbuthnott; Noyes, Alfred.

*HOLLOHAN, JOHN JOSEPH, SJ, A.B., Ph.L., Weston College, Weston, Mass. **Article:** Stocklein, Joseph.

*HOLLOWAY, MAURICE REDMOND, SJ, Ph.D., Associate Professor of Philosophy, Rockhurst College, Kansas City, Mo. **Articles:** Agnosticism; Occasionalism.

*HOLMES, CATHERINE ELEANOR, M.A., Docteur de l'Université (Paris), York University, Toronto, Canada. **Articles:** Labbe, Philippe; Pseaume, Nicolas.

*HOLMES, WILLIAM CARL, Ph.D., Assistant Professor of Music, Cornell University, Ithaca, N.Y. **Articles:** Biber, Heinrich Johann Franz von; Buxtehude, Dietrich; Campra, André; Hasse, Johann Adolph; Paisiello, Giovanni; Porpora, Nicolo Antonio; Praetorius, Michael; Rossi, Luigi; Scarlatti, Domenico; Scarlatti, Alessandro; Spontini, Gaspare; Valentini, Pier Francesco.

*HOMLISH, JOHN STEPHEN, CM, B.A., Niagara University, Niagara University, N.Y. **Article:** Sacrifice, III (in Israel).

*HONSELMANN, KLEMENS, Dr.Theol., Director of the Archiepiscopal Academy Library and Professor of Ecclesiastical History and Patrology, Philosophisch-Theologische Akademie, Paderborn, Germany. **Article:** Martin, Konrad.

*HOOFT, W. A. VISSER'T, Th.Dr., L.H.D., General Secretary, World Council of Churches, Geneva, Switzerland. **Article:** World Council of Churches.

HOONHOUT, MICHAEL A., Ph.D., Assistant Professor of Systematic Theology, Department of Theology, The Catholic University of America, Washington, D.C. **Articles:** God, 1. In Revelation; God, 2. In Christian Tradition.

HOPHAN, SISTER RONALDA, M.A., Executive Congregational Secretary, St.

Rose Convent, La Crosse, Wis. **Article:** Franciscan Sisters—Congregation of the Sisters of the Third Order of St. Francis of Perpetual Adoration (FSPA).

*HOPKINS, MARTIN, K., OP, M.A., S.T.L., S.S.L., St Thomas Aquinas Priory, River Forest, Ill. **Article:** People of God.

*HOPKINS, MARTIN KEITH, OP, Ph.L., S.T.Lr., Professor of Theology and Scripture, St. Mary's College, Winona, Minn. **Articles:** Eschatologism; Manna; People of God.

*HOPKINS, VINCENT C., SJ, S.T.L., Ph.D., formerly Editor, *Catholic Encyclopedia Supplements,* and Editorial Adviser to *Thought* (deceased April 3, 1964). **Articles:** Campbell, Thomas Joseph; Larkin, John; Thebaud, Augustus.

*HOPPE, LESLIE, OFM, Ph.D., Associate Professor of Old Testament, Catholic Theological Union, Chicago. **Article:** Biblical Archeology.

*HORGAN, MAURYA, Ph.D., The Scriptorium, Denver, Colo., Adjunct Faculty, The Iliff School of Theology, Denver, Colo. **Articles:** Colossians, Epistle to the; Deutero-Pauline Literature; Ephesians, Epistle to the.

*HORGAN, THADDEUS FRANCIS, SA, A.B., S.T.L., St. Paul's Friary, Graymoor, Garrison, N.Y. **Articles:** Amana Society; Christian Endeavor Society; Mercersburg Theology; Moravian Church; New Haven Theology; Polish National Catholic Church; Strachan, John; Sunday, William Ashley (Billy).

*HORVATH, PETER, Ph.D., Associate Professor of Economics, Marymount College, Tarrytown, N.Y. **Articles:** Caesarea Philippi; Tabor, Mount.

*HORVATH, TIBOR, SJ, Professor of Systematic Theology, Regis College, Toronto, Canada. **Article:** Preambles of Faith.

*HOSIE, STANLEY WILLIAM, SM, S.T.L., M.A., General House of Marist Fathers, Rome, Italy. **Articles:** Colin, Jean Claude Marie, Ven.; Marist Sisters.

*HOSTE, ANSELM, OSB, monk of St. Peter's Abbey, Steenbrugge, Belgium. **Article:** Aelred (Ailred), St.

*HOTCHKIN, JOHN F., Director, Bishops' Committee for Ecumenical and Interreligious Affairs, National Conference of Catholic Bishops, Washington, D.C.

Articles: Faith and Order Commission; Secretariat for Non-Believers; Secretariat for Non-Christians.

*HOTCHKIN, JOHN F., S.T.D., Director, Committee for Ecumenical and Interreligious Affairs, National Conference of Catholic Bishops, Washington, D.C. **Article:** Ecumenical Dialogues.

*HOTCHKIN, JOHN F., S.T.D., Executive Director, Secretariat for Ecumenical and Interreligious Affairs, National Conference of Catholic Bishops, Washington, D.C. **Article:** Ecumenical Directory.

*HOUDE, ROLAND, Professor, Faculté de Philosophies, University of Montreal, Canada. **Articles:** Deduction; Induction.

*HOURDIN, GEORGES FRÉDÉRIC, Licencié en Droit, Diplôme supérieur d'Économie Politique, Diplôme supérieur de Droit Public, Director, *La Vie Catholique Illustrée,* and Director, *Informations Catholiques Internationales, Telerama, Croissance des Jeunes Nations,* and *Cri,* Paris, France. **Articles:** Bailly, Vincent de Paul; Bernadot, Marie Vincent.

*HOVDA, ROBERT W., Editorial Director, The Liturgical Conference, Washington, D.C. **Article:** Liturgical Conference.

HOVEY, MICHAEL W., M.A., Coordinator, Peace and Justice Education, Iona College, New Rochelle, N.Y. **Article:** Conscientious Objection.

*HOVEY, WALTER READ, M.A., Henry Clay Frick Fine Arts Professor, University of Pittsburgh, Pittsburgh, Pa. **Article:** Carolingian Art.

*HOWARD, BRICE JOHN, OSB, M.A., Associate Professor of Philosophy, St. John's University, Collegeville, Minn. **Article:** Kevenhoerster, John Bernard.

*HOWELL, CLIFFORD WALTER, SJ, M.Sc., A.R.C.Sc., D.I.C., writer, preacher, and lecturer on liturgy, Harborne, Birmingham, England. **Articles:** Burse; Chalice, Paten, and Veil; Ciborium; Dix, Gregory; Gosling, Samuel; Liturgical Vessels; Monstrance; Pyx.

*HOYT, ROBERT STUART, Ph.D., Professor of Medieval History, University of Minnesota, Minneapolis, Minn. **Articles:** Chartulary; Hereford, Ancient See of; Hertford, Council of; Roger de Pont l'Eveque; Thomas of Cantelupe, St.; Thomas of Bayeux; Worcester, Ancient See of.

*HOYT, WILLIAM DANA, JR., Ph.D., engaged in editing the John Carroll Papers, Rockport, Mass. **Article:** Cambridge Platform.

*HRUBY, KURT, Chargé de cours (Rabbinic Hebrew), Institut Catholique, Paris, France; Maître de Conférences and Professor, Institut Supérieur de Liturgie; and Director, Études du Centre d'Études des Cahiers Sioniens, Paris, France. **Articles:** Falashas; Jews, Post-Biblical History of the; Khazars; Sa'adia ben Joseph, Gaon; Zohar.

*HUBBARD, ANNE M., MMM, Regional Superior, Medical Missionaries of Mary, Bronx, N.Y. **Article:** Martin, Mother Mary.

*HUCHET, JOSEPH AUGUSTE MARIE, M.A.L., Sanatorium des Missions Africaines, La Croix Valmer (Var), France. **Article:** Ivory Coast, The Catholic Church in.

*HUCK, GABE, M.A., Director, Liturgy Training Publications, Chicago, Ill. **Article:** Hovda, Robert.

*HUCK, GABRIEL DONALD, OSB, B.A., St. John Vianney Seminary, Mt. Michael Abbey, Elkhorn, Nebr. **Article:** Flowers, Symbolism of.

*HUCKE, HELMUT, Dr.Phil., Assistant, Musikwissenschaftliches Institut, University of Frankfurt, Frankfurt am Main, Germany. **Articles:** Creed in Eucharistic Liturgy; Pergolesi, Giovanni Battista; Sanctus; Schola Cantorum.

HUEBSCH, BILL, MTS, Catholic Theological Union, Chicago, Ill. **Article:** New Ulm, Diocese of.

*HUELLER, SISTER M. MAURELIA, OSF, M.M., Associate Professor of Music, Alverno College, Milwaukee, Wis. **Article:** Hymns and Hymnals, I: Historical Developments.

HUELS, JOHN M., OSM, J.C.D., M.A., M.Div., Professor of Canon Law, Saint Paul University, Ottawa, Ontario, Canada. **Articles:** Liturgical Laws, Authority of; Religious, Exemption of.

*HUESMAN, JOHN EDWARD, SJ, S.T.L., Ph.D., S.S.L., Professor of Old Testament and Hebrew, Alma College, Los Gatos, Calif. **Articles:** Exodus, Book of; Hammurabi (Hammurapi), King of Babylon; Hittites.

*HUG, JAMES E., SJ, Ph.D., Executive Director, Center of Concern, Washington, D.C. **Article:** Land, Phillip S.

*HUG, PACIFIC LAWRENCE, OFM, Ph.D., Lect.Gen., Chairman, Department of Philosophy and Psychology, Quincy College, Quincy, Ill. **Articles:** Angilramnus of Metz; Athanasius of Naples, St.; Bartholomew of Simeri, St.; Burchard of Wurzburg, St.; Catherine of Genoa, St.; Dilthey, Wilhelm; History, Theology of; Holy Spirit, Order of the; John Vicentius, St.; Spengler, Oswald.

*HUGHES, GERALD P., Executive Director, Cursillo Movement, National Center, Dallas, Tex. **Article:** Cursillo Movement.

*HUGHES, GERARD J., SJ, M.A., Ph.D., Head of the Department of Philosophy, Heythrop College, University of London. **Article:** Copleston, Frederick C.

HUGHES, JOHN J., Dr.theol., Peritus, Archdiocese of St. Louis, St. Louis, Mo. **Article:** Pius XI, Pope.

*HUGHES, KATHLEEN, RSCJ, Ph.D., Vice President and Academic Dean, Catholic Theological Union, Chicago, Ill. **Articles:** Catholic Theological Union (Chicago); Diekmann, Godfrey.

*HUGHES, PAUL L., Ph.D., Professor of European History, De Paul University, Chicago, Ill. **Articles:** Peasants' War (1524–25); Philip of Hesse; Spalatin, Georg.

*HUGHES, WALTER DOMINIC, OP, S.T.Lr., S.T.D., M.A., Professor, Pontifical Institute of Mediaeval Studies, Toronto, Canada; Professor, St. Michael's College, Graduate Theological Division, Toronto, Canada. **Articles:** John of St. Thomas; Lemos, Tomas de; Lying; Mental Reservation; Nacchianti, Giacomo (Naclantus); Pegues, Thomas; Truthfulness (Veracity).

*HUGLO, MICHEL RENÉ, Chargé de Recherche, Centre National de la Recherche Scientifique (Section Linguistique), Paris, France. **Articles:** Communion Antiphon; Gradual; O Antiphons; Te Deum; Tract.

*HUMBERT, ALPHONSE, CSSR, Sant' Alfonso, Rome, Italy. **Article:** Docetism.

*HUNGER, HERBERT, Dr.Phil., Professor of Byzantine Studies, University of Vienna, Austria. **Article:** Paleography, Greek.

*HUNGERMAN, SISTER MARIE GABRIEL, IHM, Ph.D., Head of the Department of Philosophy, Marygrove College, Detroit, Mich. **Article:** Eudaemonism.

*HUNNEFELD, FREDERICK JOSEPH, CPPS, S.T.D., Professor of Moral Theology, St. Charles Seminary, Carthagena, Ohio. **Article:** Deliberation and Morality.

*HUNT, IGNATIUS JOSEPH, OSB, S.T.D., S.S.B., Professor of Sacred Scripture, Conception Seminary, Conception, Mo. **Articles:** Eden, Garden of; Original Sin [part 1]; Paradise; Serpent (as Symbol); Tree of Knowledge.

*HUNT, MARK JARLATH, FSCH, M.A. in Rel. Ed., Professor of Theology and Chairman of the Department, Iona College, New Rochelle, N.Y. **Articles:** Evangelist; Magic (in the Bible); Red Sea.

*HUNTER, DANIEL HONORIUS, OP, M.A., S.T.Lr., Professor of Theology and Homiletics, Mt. St. Bernard Seminary, and Aquinas Institute School of Theology, Dubuque, Iowa; Director, Theological Institute, St. Xavier College, Chicago, Ill. **Articles:** Barlaam of Calabria; Blastares, Matthew; Cabasilas, Nilus; Cabasilas, Nicolas; Callistus II Xanthopulus, Patriarch of Constantinople; Gregorius Akindynos; Palamas, Gregory.

HURKES, CHARLES F., OMI, M.A., Director, Communications Office, Missionary Oblates of Mary Immaculate, Washington, D.C. **Article:** Oblates of Mary Immaculate.

*HURLEY, JOSEPH MICHAEL, SJ, B.A., Editor, *Timire an Chroí Naofa* (Irish organ of the Apostleship of Prayer), Belvedere College, Dublin, Ireland. **Articles:** Dowdall, George; O'Donnell, Hugh Roe; O'Hurley, Dermot, Bl.

*HURLEY, JOSEPH P., Most R., D.D., Bishop of the Diocese of St. Augustine, Fla. **Article:** Lopez de Mendoza Grajales, Francisco.

*HURLEY, MARK J., Rt. Rev., Ph.D., J.C.B., Chancellor, Diocese of Stockton, Calif.; *Peritus,* Vatican Council II. **Articles:** Gallagher, Hugh Patrick; Riordan, Patrick William.

*HURLEY, SISTER MARY RITA, OP, Yakima, Wash. **Article:** Dominican Sisters—Congregation of St Thomas Aquinas (Tacoma, Wash).

*HURLEY, PHILIP STEPHEN, SJ, M.A., S.T.L., Assistant Professor of Theology, Fordham College, New York, N.Y. **Article:** LaFarge [John (1880–1963)].

*HURST, HENRY DAVID, OSB, M.A., Teacher of Classics, Portsmouth Priory School, Portsmouth, R.I. **Article:** Compunction.

*HUSSEY, JOAN M., Professor, Royal Holloway College, Englefield Green, Surrey, England. **Articles:** Constantine III, Leichudes, Patriarch of Constantinople; Symeon the New Theologian, Monk of the Studion; Theodosius I Boradiotes, Patriarch of Constantinople.

*HUYGHEBAERT, NICHOLAS, OSB, Licencié en philosophie et lettres, Centre National (belge) de Recherches d'histoire religieuse, Brussels, Belgium. **Articles:** Affligem, Abbey of; Beauduin, Lambert; Callewaert, Camille; Capelle, Bernard; Cassander, George; Egmond (Egmont), Abbey of; Leroquais, Victor Martial; Puniet de Parry, Pierre de; Saint-Andre-lez-Bruges, Abbey of; Van Caloen, Gerard.

*HYMAN, ARTHUR, Rabbi, Ph.D., M.H.L., Associate Professor of Philosophy, Yeshiva University, New York, N.Y.; Chairman, Executive Committee, Conference on Jewish Philosophy; Member of the Editorial Board, *Judaism Magazine.* **Article:** Jewish Philosophy.

*HYNES, RICHARD P., President, National Federation of Priests' Councils, Chicago. **Article:** Presbyteral Councils.

*HYODO, MASANOSUKE, B.A., Professor at Kanto Gakuin Junior College and Lecturer at Kanto Gakuin University, Yokohama, Japan. **Article:** Shimazaki, Toson.

*HYRTEK, SISTER MARY THEOPHANE, OSF, F.A.G.O., Ph.D., Director, Department of Music, Alverno College, Milwaukee, Wis. **Articles:** Cavazzoni, Girolamo; Merulo, Claudio.

*IMBERT, JEAN, Diplôme de l'École des Hautes Études, Professor, Faculty of Law, University of Paris, France. **Article:** Palace Schools.

INWOOD, PAUL, Head, Department for Liturgical Formation and Diocesan Director of Music, Roman Catholic Diocese of Portsmouth, England. **Article:** Universa Laus.

*IONE, JEAN [O'REILLY], New York, N.Y. **Article:** Little Sisters of the Assumption.

*IPARRAGUIRRE, I IGNACIO, SJ, Ph.L., S.T.L., Eccl.Hist.D., Member, Institutum Historicum, and Professor of Spiritual Theology, Gregorian University, Rome, Italy; *Peritus,* Vatican Council II. **Articles:** Alvarez, Baltasar; Alvarez de Paz, Diego; Bobadilla, Nicolas Alfonso de; La Puente, Luis de, Ven.; Rodriguez, Alfonso.

*IRANYI, LADISLAUS ANTHONY, SP, Ph.D., S.T.D., Superior, Washington House of Studies, Washington, D.C.; Professor of Dogmatic Theology, Mt. St. Mary's Seminary, Emmitsburg, Md. **Articles:** Baruch, Book of; Baruch; Jeremiah, Letter of; Joseph Calasanctius, St.; Pirrotti, Pompilius, St.

IRWIN, KEVIN W., M.A., S.T.D., Professor of Liturgical and Sacramental Theology, Department of Theology, The Catholic University of America, Washington, D.C. **Article:** Sacramental Theology.

*IRWIN, MARY ELIZABETH, Editor, *National Catholic Educational Bulletin* of the National Catholic Educational Association, Washington, D.C. **Article:** National Catholic Educational Association.

*ISERLOH, E ERWIN, Dr.Theol., Diploma, Vatican School of Palaeography, Professor of Medieval and Modern Church History, Theologische Fakultät, Trier, Germany. **Articles:** Nausea, Friedrich (Grau); Paulus, Nikolaus; Wimpina, Konrad Koch.

*ISWOLSKY, H HELENE, B.A., Assistant Professor and Chairman of the Department of Russian Language and Literature, Seton Hill College, Greensburg, Pa. **Article:** Dostoevskii, Fedor Mikhailovich.

IVORY, MSGR. THOMAS PETER, S.T.D., Pastor, Church of the Presentation, Upper Saddle River, N.J. **Article:** Newark, Archdiocese of.

*IWELE, GODÉ, OMI, S.T.L., D.E.S., African Institute of Mission Studies, Kinshasha, Zaire. **Articles:** Congo, Democratic Republic of (Kinshasa), The Catholic Church in; Missal for the Dioceses of Zaire.

*JACOB, ERNEST FRASER, D.Phil., D.Litt.(hon.), Fellow and Librarian of All Souls College, Emeritus Chichele Professor of Modern History, University of Oxford, England. **Articles:** Brouns, Thomas; Bubwith, Nicholas; Pecock, Reginald; Stafford, John; Walsingham, Thomas.

*JACOBSEN, JEROME VINCENT, SJ, Ph.D., Professor of History, Loyola University, Chicago, Ill.; Editor, *Mid-America* (Chicago). **Article:** Garraghan, Gilbert Joseph.

JACOBSON, PAUL A., Ph. D., Director of Advancement, The Holton-Arms School, Bethesda, Md. **Article:** Amalarius; Liturgical History, II: Medieval.

*JACOPIN, ARMAND JOHN, M.A., Assistant Professor of Art, College of Notre Dame of Maryland, Baltimore, Md. **Article:** Ravenna [Art of].

*JADAA, JOHN, Very Rev., B.S., S.T.L., Rector, St. Basil's Seminary, Methuen, Mass. **Article:** Maximos III Mazlum.

*JADIN, LOUIS, Very Rev., Canon, Docteur en philosophie (History), S.T.D., Professor and Maître de conférence, Universities of Louvain, Belgium, and Lovanianum, Léopoldville, Republic of the Congo, Africa. **Article:** Congo, Democratic Republic of (Kinshasa), The Catholic Church in.

*JAKOBSSON, MARTEINN PÈTUR, SMM, Apostolic Vicariate of Iceland, engaged in the study of Old Icelandic-Norse history and literature, Iceland. **Article:** Iceland, The Catholic Church in.

*JALABERT, HENRI, SJ, Licence ès lettres (Histoire et Géographie), Professor, Institut de Lettres Orientales, Université Saint-Joseph, Beirut, Lebanon. **Article:** Damascus, Martyrs of.

*JAMES, JAMES THOMAS LAWRENCE, B.A., L.Th., S.T.B., Anglican Chaplain and Lecturer in Theology, University of Windsor, Ontario, Canada. **Article:** Underhill, Evelyn.

*JAMES, SISTER MARY CATHERINE ANN, OSF, B.S. in N.E., Medical Record Librarian, St. Francis Hospital, Peoria, Ill. **Article:** Franciscan Sisters—Sisters of the Third Order of St. Francis (OSF).

JAMESON, R., **Article:** Franciscan Sisters—Bernardine Sisters of the Third Order of St. Francis (OSF).

*JAMME, ALBERT JOSEPH, WF, S.T.D., D.Or., S.S.L., Research Professor in South Arabic Studies, The Catholic University of America, Washington, D.C. **Articles:** Arabia, 4. Paganism in South Arabia; Arabia, 2. Arabia in the Bible; Bahrain, The Catholic Church in; Kuwait,The Catholic Church in; Oman, The Catholic Church in; Saba (Sheba); Yemen, The Catholic Church in.

*JAN, JEAN-MARIE, Most Rev., S.T.D., Ph.D., formerly Bishop of Cap Haitien, Haiti, and Titular Bishop of Edistiana. **Article:** Kersuzan, Francois Marie.

*JANOTA, SISTER MARY ILLUMINATA, OSF, M.A., Associate Professor of English, Marillac College, Normandy,

Mo.; Directress of Studies, Franciscan Sisters of Our Lady of Perpetual Help, Ferguson, Mo.; Moderator, *Marillac Magazine*. **Article:** Franciscan Sisters—Franciscan Sisters of Our Lady of Perpetual Help (OSF).

*JANSSEN, PETER WILHELMUS; OCarm, Ph.D., Titus-Brandsmacollege, Dordrecht, Netherlands. **Articles:** John of Saint-Samson; Touraine Reform.

*JANTO, STEPHEN ANTHONY, OFM, Ph.D., Professor of History, Siena College, Loudonville, N.Y. **Article:** Oriol, Joseph, St.

*JARLOT, GEORGES M., SJ, Professor, Institute of Social Sciences, Gregorian University, Rome, Italy. **Article:** Bureau, Paul.

*JARRY, EUGÈNE, Very Rev., Canon, Licencié ès lettres, Professor, Faculté des Lettres, and Faculté de Théologic, Institut Cathotique, Paris, France; Editor, *Histoire de l'Église* (Fliche-Martin). **Articles:** Aix, Archdiocese of; Albi, Archdiocese of; Avignon; Cambrai, Archdiocese of; Daniel-Rops, Henri; Marseilles; Martin, Victor; Mourret, Fernand; Paris, Institut Catholique de; Reims; Saint-Gilles; States of the Church [part 2]; Tours, Archdiocese of; Zouaves, Papal.

JASKEL, SISTER MARY, OSF, M.Ed., Congregation Archivist, Sisters of St. Francis of the Providence of God, Pittsburgh, Pa. **Article:** Franciscan Sisters—Sisters of St. Francis of the Providence of God (OSF).

*JASKIEVICZ, WALTER CHARLES, SJ, S.T.L., Ph.D., Associate Professor of Slavic Languages and Linguistics, Director, Institute of Contemporary Russian Studies, and Electronic Learning Laboratory, Fordham University, New York, N.Y. **Articles:** Catherine II (the Great), Empress of Russia; Peter I (the Great), Emperor of Russia.

*JEDIN, HUBERT, Dr. Theol. (h.c.), Dr. Phil. (h.c.), Professor of Church History, University of Bonn, Germany; Editor, *Handbuch der Kirchengeschichte; Peritus,* Vatican Council II. **Articles:** Historiography, Ecclesiastical; Seripando, Girolamo; Trent, Council of.

JEFFREYS, ELIZABETH M., M.A. (Cantab.), B.Litt. (Oxon.), Bywater and Sotheby Professor of Byzantine and Modern Greek Language and Literature, University of Oxford, Oxford, United Kingdom. **Article:** Byzantine Literature.

*JEGEN, SISTER MARY EVELYN, SND, A.B., Southwark, London, England. **Articles:** Catechesis, II (Medieval); Catechesis, III (Reformation).

*JELLY, FREDERICK M., OP, Dominican House of Studies, Washington, D.C. **Articles:** Mariology; Mary, Redemptoris Mater; Secularity.

*JELLY, FREDERICK M., OP. Academic Dean, School of Theology, Pontifical College, Josephinum, Worthington, Ohio. **Articles:** Mary, Blessed Virgin, II (in Theology) [Mary and the Church] Virgin Birth.

*JENSEN, JOSEPH B., OSB, S.S.L., S.T.D., Executive Secretary, Catholic Biblical Association; Associate Professor, Department of Religion and Religious Education, The Catholic University of America, Washington, D.C. **Articles:** Ahern, Barnabas Mary; Prophetism (in the Bible); Skehan, Patrick.

JENSEN, JOSEPH B., OSB, S.S.L., S.T.D., Executive Secretary, Catholic Biblical Association; Associate Professor, Department of Religion and Religious Education, The Catholic University of America, Washington, D.C. **Articles:** Diabolical Possession (in the Bible); Redemption (in the Bible); Revelation, Concept of (in the Bible); Son of Man; Tradition (in the Bible).

JENSEN, JOSEPH E., Ph.D. Cand., School of Religious Studies, The Catholic University of America, Washington, D.C. **Articles:** Flood; Noah.

*JENSEN, JOSEPH N., OSB, Professor, St. Anselm's Abbey, Washington, D.C. **Article:** Cummins, Patrick.

*JOANNOU, PÉRICLÈS-PETROS, Dr.Phil. (Munich), Licencié ès lettres (Sorbonne), Professor of Classical Philology and Byzantine Studies, University of Munich, Germany. **Articles:** Ambarach, Peter (Mubarach, Benedictus); Ancyra; Anthony, Patriarchs of Constantinople (I-IV); Atticus of Constantinople, St.; Chorbishop; Cydones, Prochorus; Cydones, Demetrius; Germanus II, Patriarch of Constantinople; Schwartz, Eduard; Sirmium; Synods, Early Church.

*JOHANN, ROBERT OLIVER, SJ, Ph.D., S.T.L., Associate Professor of Philosophy, College of Philosophy and Letters, Fordham University (Shrub Oak), N.Y.; Adjunct Professor of Christian Ethics, Department of Theology, Fordham University, New York, N.Y. **Article:** Love.

*JOHN, ERIC, M.A., University Lecturer in History, University of Manchester, England. **Articles:** Aelfryth of Crowland, St.; Bath, Abbey of; Bega (Bee), St.; Birinus, St.; Cuthburga, St.; Domesday Book; Fountains Abbey; Honorius of Canterbury, St.; Ine, King of Wessex; Magna Carta; Saint Augustine, Abbey of; Tatwine of Canterbury, St.; Withburga (Witburh), St.

JOHN, JAMES J., D.M.S., Professor of Paleography and Medieval History Emeritus, Cornell University, Ithaca, N.Y. **Article:** Paleography, Latin.

*JOHN, JAMES JOSEPH, D.M.S., University of Wisconsin, Madison, Wis. **Articles:** Dodo of Asch, Bl.; Isfried, St.

*JOHNSON, EARL JAMES, OSB, S.T.D., University of Notre Dame, Notre Dame, Ind. **Articles:** Ashes, Liturgical Use of; Easter and its Cycle.

JOHNSON, ELIZABETH A., CSJ, Ph.D., Distinguished Professor of Theology, Fordham University, New York, N.Y. **Article:** Mary (in Catholic-Protestant Dialogue).

*JOHNSON, JAMES ROSSER, Ph.D., Associate Curator of Education, The Cleveland Museum of Art, Cleveland, Ohio. **Articles:** Chartres [Cathedral]; Tree of Jesse.

*JOHNSON, JOHN G., M.A., J.C.L., Diocese of Columbus, Columbus, Ohio. **Article:** Legates, Papal.

JOHNSON, JOSEPH, B.A., S.T.L., S.T.D.(candidate), diocesan priest of the Archdiocese of Saint Paul and Minneapolis. **Article:** Rome.

*JOHNSON, LAWRENCE, Executive Director, Office for Divine Worship, Diocese of Wilmington, Wilmington, Del. **Article:** Blessings, Liturgical.

*JOHNSON, MARK F., Ph.D., Assistant Professor of Theology, Marquette University, Milwaukee, Wis. **Article:** Moral Theology, Methodology of; Thomas Aquinas, St. [part 1]; Thomas Aquinas, St. [part 2].

*JOHNSON, PETER LEO, Rt. Rev., S.T.D., Litt. D., Professor of History, St. Francis Seminary, Milwaukee, Wis.; Editor, *Salesianum*. **Articles:** Abbelen, Peter; Henni, John Martin; Kundig, Martin; Messmer, Sebastian Gebhard; Milwaukee, Archdiocese of; Salzmann, Joseph; Wisconsin, Catholic Church in.

JOHNSON, TIMOTHY JOHN, S.T.D., Chairman, Department of Liberal Studies,

Flagler College, St. Augustine, Fla. **Article:** Franciscan Theological Tradition.

*JOHNSTON, FRANCIS RAYMUND, M.A., Dip.Ed., A.R.Hist. S., Head of Arts Department, St. Patrick Lee School, Eccles, Manchester, England. **Article:** Athelney, Abbey of; Crowland, Abbey of; Gloucester, Abbey of; Hyde, Abbey of; Malvern, Abbey of; Norwich, Ancient See of; Ramsey, Abbey of; Syon, Abbey of; Thorney, Abbey of; Waltham, Monastery of; Wenlock, Abbey of.

*JOHNSTONE, BRIAN V., CSSR, S.T.D., Professor of Moral Theology, Accademia Alfonsiana, Rome. **Article:** Häring, Bernard.

*JOLIVET, REGIS VICTOR, Rt. Rev., Docteur en Philosophie, Docteur ès lettres, Docteur honoris causa (Louvain), Doyen honoraire and Professor, Faculté de philosophie de l'Université Catholique de Lyon, France. **Articles:** Cousin, Victor; Evil; Gratry, Auguste Joseph Alphonse; Olle-Laprune, Leon.

*JOLLEY, JOHN FRANKLIN, University of Nebraska, Lincoln, Nebr. **Articles:** Fillastre, Guillaume; Gonfalonieri; Hallum, Robert.

*JONES, ARTHUR, Editor and Publisher, *National Catholic Reporter,* Kansas City, Mo. **Article:** Thorman, Donald Joseph.

JONES, CHARLES B., Ph.D., Associate Professor of Religion and Religious Education, The Catholic University of America, Washington, D.C. **Articles:** Animism; Bodhisattva; Buddhism; Chinese Philosophy; Dharma; Hinayana; Mahayana.

JONES, LYNN, Ph.D., Mellon Fellow in Art History, Cornell University, Ithaca, N.Y. **Articles:** Byzantine Art; Hagia Sophia; Icon; Mosaics; Ravenna [Art of].

*JONES, WILLIAM HUBERT, Very Rev., Ph.D., Superintendent of Schools, Archdiocese of Denver, Colo. **Article:** Machebeuf, Joseph Projectus.

*JONSEN, ALBERT RUPERT, SJ, M.A., S.T.M., Yale University, New Haven, Conn. **Article:** Faith, 2. Patristic Tradition and Teaching of the Church.

JORDAN, PATRICK, Managing Editor, *Commonweal,* New York, N.Y. **Article:** Commonweal; Skillin, Edward Simeon.

JOSEPH, M. VINCENTIA, SFCC, DSW, Professor Emeritus, The National Catholic School of Social Service, The Catholic University of America, Washington, D.C. **Article:** Sisters for Christian Community.

*JOYCE, EDWARD JOHN, CPPS, A.B., Assistant Professor of Theology, St. Joseph's College, Collegeville, Ind. **Articles:** Innocents, Holy; Magi.

*JOYCE, THOMAS JOSEPH, SJ, M.A., Weston College, Weston, Mass. **Article:** Brou, Alexandre.

*JOYCE, THOMAS PATRICK, CMF, Hist.Eccl.D., Assistant Editor for Modern Church History, New *Catholic Encyclopedia,* The Catholic University of America, Washington, D.C.; Claretian House of Studies, Washington, D.C. **Articles:** Benigni, Umberto; Bichier des Ages, Jeanne Elisabeth, St.; Chalmers, Thomas; Claret, Anthony Mary, St.; Claretians; Fournet, Andre Hubert, St.; Ghebremichael, Bl.; Iran, The Catholic Church in; Jacobis, Giustino de, St.; Mazzarello, Maria Domenica, St.; Soubiran, Marie Therese de, Bl.; Walsh, William Joseph.

JUDD, STEPHEN P., MM, Ph.D., Director of Campus Ministry Program, Puno, Peru. **Article:** Mission in Postcolonial Latin America.

*JUDGE, SISTER MAURA, CSJ, Ph.D., Teacher of Scripture and Theology, St. Joseph College, Orange, Calif. **Article:** Passion of Christ, I (in the Bible).

*JUHASZ, WILLIAM PATRICK, Ph.D., Lecturer in Hungarian Literature and Cultural History, Columbia University, New York, N.Y.; Plan Adviser, Free Europe Committee and International Advisory Council, N.Y. **Article:** Hungary, The Catholic Church in.

*JUNCO, ALFONSO, formerly active in the business world, now engaged in writing and journalism, Mexico City, Mexico. **Articles:** San Juan, Catarina de; Silva, Atenogenes.

*JUNGMANN, JOSEPH ANDREAS, SJ, Dr.Theol., Professor Emeritus of History of Liturgy, University of Innsbruck, Austria. **Article:** Baptism, Sacrament of.

*JURGENS, WILLIAM ANTHONY, Eccl.Hist.D., Professor of History and Patrology and Instructor in Sacred Music, St. Mary Seminary, Cleveland, Ohio; Instructor in Sacred and Profane Music, Borromeo Seminary, Wickliffe, Ohio; Diocesan Director of Sacred Music and Chairman of the Diocesan Commission for Sacred Music. **Articles:** Amator, SS.; Auctor of Metz, St.; Auraeus, St.; Evergislus, St.; Ingenuin, St.; Isaac of Monte Luco, St.; John Bonus of Milan, St.; Livarius of Metz, St.; Magnericus of Trier, St.; Schrembs, Joseph; Ursicinus of Ravenna, St.

*JÚSSEN, KLAUDIUS, Dr.Theol., Professor of Theology, University of Freiburg im Breisgau, Germany. **Article:** Diekamp, Franz.

*KAEGI, WALTER EMIL, JR., Ph.D., Assistant Professor of Byzantine and Roman History, University of Chicago, Chicago, Ill. **Articles:** Heraclius, Byzantine Emperor; Severian of Gabala; Theodore of Sykeon, St.; Theodore Lector; Theodosius of Palestine, St.; Theodosius, Monophysite Patriarch of Alexandria; Timotheus I, Patriarch of Constantinople; Wilpert, Joseph.

KAEGI, WALTER EMIL, JR., Ph.D. Professor of History, Permanent Voting Member, the Oriental Institute, University of Chicago. **Articles:** Byzantine Civilization; Byzantine Empire.

*KAFTANDJIAN, JOSEPH, Ph.D., S.T.D., Rome, Italy. **Articles:** Armenian Christianity, I: Armenian Apostolic Church; Armenian Christianity, II: Armenian Catholic Church.

*KAISER, EDWIN GEORGE, CPPS, S.T.D., St. Joseph's College, Rensselaer, Ind. **Articles:** Perichoresis, Christological; Precious Blood, II (Theology of).

*KAISER, OTTO, Dr.Theol., Professor of Old Testament, University of Marburg, Marburg-Lahn, Germany. **Article:** Bousset, Wilhelm.

KAISING, MOST REVEREND JOHN J., DD, Auxiliary Bishop and Vicar for Priests, Archdiocese for the Military Services USA, Washington, D.C.; Deeper Team Priest, World Wide Marriage Encounter. **Articles:** Marriage Encounter; Worldwide Marriage Encounter.

*KANE, SISTER MARGUERITE CATHERINE, DW, M.S., Assistant Principal, Maryhaven School for Exceptional Children, Port Jefferson, Long Island, N.Y. **Article:** Wisdom, Daughters of.

*KANE, THOMAS CORNELIUS, OP, S.T.D., Assistant Professor of Theology, The Catholic University of America, Washington, D.C.; Associate Editor, *Thomist.* **Articles:** Curiosity; Fortitude, Virtue of; Studiousness, Virtue of; Suicide.

*KANE, WILLIAM HUMBERT, OP, Ph.D., S.T.M., Professor of Philosophy, St. Rose Priory, Dubuque, Iowa. **Articles:** Aporia; Criterion (Criteriology); Element; Immateriality; Motion, First Cause of; Necessity; Part; Principle; Whole.

*KAPSNER, OLIVER LEONARD, OSB, Ph.L., S.T.B., L.H.D., St. John's Abbey, Collegeville, Minn. **Articles:** Blarer; Bova, St.; Domnolus of Le Mans, St.; Faro of Meaux, St.; Fridolin of Sackingen, St.; Germerius, St.; Godo, St.; Hohenbaum van der Meer, Moritz; Jonatus, St.; Leobard, SS.; Mezger; Wenailus, St.; Wendelin, St.; Wimmer, Boniface.

*KARDONG, TERRENCE GERALD, OSB, B.A., High School Latin Instructor, Assumption Abbey, Richardton, N.Dak. **Article:** Bethel.

*KARDOS, SYLVESTER MARY, OFMConv, Lector of Moral and Spiritual Theology, St. Anthony-on-Hudson, Rensselaer, N.Y. **Articles:** Arcanum; Casti Connubii.

KASHUBA, MARY HELEN, SSJ, D.M.L., Professor of French and Russian, Chestnut Hill College, Philadelphia Pa. **Articles:** Fontbonne, Mother Saint John; St. Joseph, Sisters of.

KASLYN, ROBERT J., SJ, J.C.D., Associate Professor of Canon Law, The Catholic University of America, Washington, D.C. **Articles:** Exemption, History of; Governance, Power of; Office, Ecclesiastical [part 2]; Rules of Law (Regulae iuris).

*KATTSOFF, LOUIS O., Ph.D., Professor of Mathematics and Logic, Boston College, Chestnut Hill, Mass. **Article:** Measurement [Mathematical Aspects].

KAUFFMAN, CHRISTOPHER J., Ph.D., Catholic Daughters of the Americas Professor of American Church History, The Catholic University of America, Washington, D.C. **Articles:** Barry, Colman; Knights of Columbus; Marianists.

*KAVANAUGH, JOSEPH WILLIAM, Pastor, Transfiguration Church, Philadelphia, Pa. **Article:** Master of Ceremonies.

*KAVANAUGH, KIERAN, OCD, S.T.L., Professor of Spiritual Theology, College of Our Lady of Mt. Carmel, Washington, D.C. **Articles:** Abandonment, Spiritual; Aridity, Spiritual; Dark Night of the Soul; John of the Cross, St.; Purification, Spiritual; Self-Abandonment, Spiritual; Spirituality, Christian (History of).

*KAY, HUGH, Jesuit Information Officer, London, England. **Articles:** Corbishley, Thomas; D'Arcy, Martin Cyril.

*KAY, RICHARD LORIN, Ph.D., Assistant Professor of History, University of Kentucky, Lexington, Ky. **Articles:** Adalbert of Bremen; Bonizo of Sutri; Langres, Councils of; Lombers, Council of; Melfi, Councils of; Quiercy (Quierzy), Councils of; Sutri, Councils of; Toul, Councils of; Valence, Councils of; Worms, Concordat of; Worms, Council of.

*KEALEY, EDWARD J., Ph.D., Assistant Professor of History and Adviser for Graduate Studies, College of the Holy Cross, Worcester, Mass. **Articles:** Alphege of Canterbury, St.; Bertrand of Comminges, St.; Constabilis, St.; Gaucherius, St.; Gervin of Oudenburg, St.; Giraldus of Salles, Bl.; Girard of Angers, St.; Godfrey of Amiens, St.; John of Chatillon, St.; John of Matera, St.; Roger of Salisbury; Vitalis of Savigny, St.; William of Norwich, St.; Wulphilda, St.

*KEALY, THOMAS M., J.C.D., Rt. Rov., Vicar-General, Diocese of Lincoln, Nebr. **Article:** Dowry.

*KEARNEY, JAMES EDWARD, Most Rev., S.T.B., J.C.B., LL.D., Bishop of Rochester, N.Y. **Article:** Hunt, Duane Garrison.

*KEARNEY, PETER JOSEPH, B.A., S.T.L., S.S.L., Teacher of Religion and English and Guidance Counselor, Our Lady of Lourdes High School, Poughkeepsie, N.Y. **Articles:** Altar, 2. In the Bible; Shechem.

*KEATING, JOHN RAYMOND, SJ, Ph.L., M.A., S.T.L., S.S.L., Pontifical Biblical Institute, Rome, Italy. **Article:** Prat, Ferdinand.

*KEATING, JOHN RICHARD, B.A., S.T.L., J.C.D., Assistant Chancellor, Archdiocese of Chicago, Ill. **Article:** Administrator, Apostolic.

*KEATING, TIMOTHY PETER, Founder and first President, National Catholic Pharmacists Guild of the U.S.; Editor, *National Catholic Pharmacists Guide Newsletter,* New Bedford, Mass. **Article:** National Catholic Pharmacists Guild of the U.S.

*KECKEISSEN, SISTER MARY GERTRUDE, SC, Ph.D., Associate Professor of Psychology, College of Mount St. Vincent, New York, N.Y. **Article:** Ebbinghaus, Hermann.

KEEFE, JEFFREY, O.F.M.Conv., Ph.D., S.T.L. Province psychologist, Friars Minor Conventual; Consultant to several dioceses and religious orders. **Article:** Homosexuality.

KEEGAN, TERENCE J., OP, S.T.D., Professor, Department of Theology and Executive Vice President, Providence College, Providence, RI. **Article:** Collins, Thomas Aquinas.

*KEENE, MICHAEL J., OSB, J.C.D., Huaroz, Peru. **Article:** Ordinaries, Ecclesiastical.

*KEEVEN, SISTER MARY MAURICE, OSF, M.A., Principal, Transfiguration School, Wauconda, Ill. **Article:** Franciscan Sisters—Franciscan Sisters, Daughters of the Sacred Hearts of Jesus and Mary (OSF).

*KEKUMANO, CHARLES ALVIN, Very Rev., J.C.D., Chancellor-Secretary, Diocese of Honolulu, Hawaii. **Article:** Archives, Ecclesiastical.

*KELLEHER, DENNIS P., CSSR, B&A., S.T.L., Teacher, Holy Redeemer College, Oakland, Calif. **Articles:** Autun; Chi-Rho; Dionysius of Corinth, St.; Genevieve, St.; Germain, St.

*KELLEHER, JEREMIAH T., OP, Dominican House of Studies, Washington, D.C. **Articles:** Bauny, Etienne; Becanus, Martin; Binet, Etienne; Bourgoing, Francois.

*KELLEHER, MARGARET M., OSU, Ph.D., Assistant Professor, Department of Religion and Religious Education, The Catholic University of America, Washington, D.C. **Article:** Ritual Studies.

*KELLER, JAMES GREGORY, MM, M.A., Founder and Director, The Christophers, New York, N.Y.; writer. **Article:** Christophers, The.

*KELLER, JOSEPH BRUNO, Zürich, Switzerland. **Articles:** Lavater, Johann Kasper; Pestalozzi, Johann Heinrich.

*KELLER, WILLIAM, A.B., S.T.L., A.M., Associate Professor of History and Political Science, Seton Hall University, South Orange, N.J.; Director, Graduate Scholarship Office, Codirector, Humanities Honor Program; member of the Editorial Board, *Advocate* (Newark). **Article:** Granvelle, Antoine Perrenot de.

*KELLEY, FRANCIS MATTHEW, OP, S.T.L., S.T.Lr., Dominican House of Studies, Washington, D.C. **Articles:** Holy Name, Devotion to the; Sylvius, Francis (Du Bois).

*KELLEY, JOSEPH T., OSA, Professor in Religious Studies, Merrimack College, North Andover, Mass. **Article:** Masses, Votive.

*KELLEY, SISTER M. CHAMINADE, OSF, M.S.N., Assistant Novice Mistress, St. Francis Convent, Springfield, Ill. **Article:** Franciscan Sisters—Hospital Sisters of the Third Order of St. Francis (OSF).

*KELLEY, WILLIAM FRANCIS, SDB, Secretary to the Provincial, New Rochelle, N.Y. **Article:** Salesians.

*KELLOGG, ALFRED LATIMER, Ph.D., Professor of English, Rutgers University, New Brunswick, N.J. **Article:** Chaucer, Geoffrey.

*KELLY, COLUMBA, OSB, S.T.L., D.Musicae Sacrae, Choirmaster, Music Instructor, St. Meinrad College and School of Theology, St. Meinrad, Ind. **Articles:** Agnus Dei; Benedicamus Domino; Gloria; Ite Missa Est; Kyrie Eleison.

*KELLY, GEORGE ANTHONY, Very Rev., Ph.D., Director, Family Life Bureau, Archdiocese of New York, N.Y.; Member, NCWC Advisory Board. **Articles:** Drumgoole, John Christopher; Keegan, Robert Fulton; Monaghan, John Patrick.

*KELLY, JAMES RONALD, SJ, M.A., Ph.L., Cambridge, Mass. **Article:** Leisure.

KELLY, JOSEPH F., Ph.D. President of the North American Patristic Society, 1994–1996, Professor of Church History, John Carroll University, Cleveland, Ohio. **Articles:** Anacletus (Cletus), Pope, St.; Anastasius II, Pope; Anastasius I, Pope, St.; Anicetus, Pope, St.; Anterus, Pope, St.; Celestine I, Pope, St.; Eulalius, Antipope; Felix II, Antipope; Heraclius, Antipope; Lawrence, Antipope; Pelagius I, Pope; Stephen I, Pope, St.; Ursinus, Antipope.

*KELLY, SISTER MARY GILBERT, OP, Ph.D., Professor of History, Rosary College, River Forest, Ill. **Articles:** Coughlin, Mary Samuel, Mother; Irish Catholic Colonization Association of U.S.; Trecy, Jeremiah.

*KELLY, SISTER MARY ROSALITA, IHM, Ph.D., formerly Professor of History, Marygrove College, Detroit, Mich. (deceased Jan. 16, 1964). **Article:** Michigan, Catholic Church in.

*KELLY, PATRICK J., OP, St. Peter Martyr Priory, Los Angeles, Calif. **Article:** Meagher, Paul Kevin.

*KELLY, PATRICK JOHN, OP, S.T.Lr., S.T.D., S.T.M., Chairman, Department of Theology, Mt. St. Mary's College, Los Angeles, Calif. **Articles:** Death, Preparation for; Gratitude; Impeccability; Mathew, Theobald; Talbot, Matt.

KELLY, PHIL, OFMConv., M.A., C.P.E., St. Francis Friary, Syracuse, N.Y. **Article:** Alcoholics Anonymous.

*KELLY, MOST REVEREND THOMAS C., O.P., D.D., J.C.D., Archbishop of Louisville, Kentucky. **Article:** Ad limina visit.

*KEMP, BRIAN RICHARD, B.A. (Hons.), Researcher, Department of History, University of Reading, England. **Article:** Reading, Abbey of.

KENDALL, KATHERINE, musician, lecturer, and writer, Convent of the Cenacle, Grayshott, Hindhead, Surrey, England. **Article:** Steuart, Robert Henry.

*KENDRICK, THOMAS DOWNING, Sir, M.A., D.Litt., formerly Director and Principal Librarian, British Museum, Poole, Dorset, England. **Article:** Anglo-Saxon Art.

*KENEALY, WILLIAM JAMES, SJ, Ph.D., S.T.L., LL.B., Professor of Law, Boston College Law School, Chestnut Hill, Mass. **Article:** Natural Law and Jurisprudence.

*KENEL, SALLY A., Ph.D., Associate Professor, Department of Theology, St. John's University, Staten Island, N.Y. **Article:** Deadly Sins; Grace (Theology of).

*KENNEALLY, FINBAR, OFM, B.A., H.Dip.Ed., Ed.D., member, Academy of American Franciscan History, Washington, D.C. **Article:** Verger, Rafael.

KENNEDY, CAMILLA, MM, Ph.D., Congregational Historian, Maryknoll Sisters, Maryknoll, N.Y. **Articles:** Maryknoll Sisters; Rogers, Mary Joseph, Mother.

*KENNEDY, DIANE, OP, Executive Director, PARABLE, Minneapolis, Minn. **Article:** Prayer, Centering.

KENNEDY, SISTER FRANCIS ASSISI, OSF, Archivist, Sisters of St. Francis, Oldenburg, Ind. **Article:** Franciscan Sisters—Franciscan Sisters of Oldenburg (OSF).

*KENNEDY, GERALD THOMAS, OMI, B.S.L.S., M.A., S.T.D., Professor of Sacred Scripture, Oblate College, Washington, D.C. **Articles:** Anointing [part 1]; Fast and Abstinence; Flagellation (in the Bible).

*KENNEDY, JOHN HAROLD, OMI, Ph.D., Professor of Church History and Theology, Oblate College, Washington, D.C. **Article:** McGrath, James.

*KENNEDY, SISTER MARIE ENDA, OP, Ed.D., Dean, St. Thomas Aquinas College, Sparkill, N.Y. **Article:** Miami, Archdiocese of.

*KENNEDY, MARY LOUISE MAYTAG, writer, philanthropist, and promoter of liturgical art, Pittsburgh, Pa. **Article:** Escrivá de Balaguer y Albas, Josemaria, Bl.

KENNEDY, ROBERT P., Ph.D., Assistant Professor of Religious Studies, St. Francis Xavier University, Antigonish, Nova Scotia, Canada. **Articles:** Anscombe, Gertrude Elizabeth Margaret; British Moralists.

KENNEDY, ROBERT T., J.D., J.U.D., Associate Professor of Canon Law, The Catholic University of America, Washington, D.C. **Article:** Church and State (Canon Law).

*KENNER, WILLIAM HUGH, Ph.D., Professor of English, University of California at Santa Barbara, Calif. **Article:** Eliot, Thomas Stearns.

*KENNET-DAWSON, MOTHER M. ST. JOHN, OSF, B.A., Superior, Convent of Our Lady and St. Francis; Principal, St. Francis School for Special Education, Baltimore, Md. **Article:** Franciscan Sisters—Franciscan Sisters of Baltimore (OSF).

*KENNEY, SYLVIA WISDOM, Ph.D., Associate Professor of Music, Bryn Mawr College, Bryn Mawr, Pa.; Visiting Associate Professor of Music, Yale University, New Haven, Conn. **Articles:** Fayrfax, Robert; Tallis, Thomas; Taverner, John; Tye, Christopher.

*KENNY, JOHN PETER, SJ, S.T.L., Professor of Dogmatic Theology and Liturgy, Canisius College, Pymble, Australia. **Articles:** Concupiscence; Elevation of Man; Supernatural Order; Supernatural; Supernatural Existential.

*KENTON, EGON FRANCIS X., M.A., formerly Professor of Music, University of Connecticut, Storrs, Conn.; Librarian, Mannes College of Music, New York, N.Y. **Articles:** Gabrieli, Andrea; Gabrieli, Giovanni.

*KERBY, SISTER MARY AUGUSTINE, SMSM, Founder and Editor, *Marist,* Director of Public Relations, Marist Mission Center, Waltham, Mass. **Article:** Marist Missionary Sisters.

*KERIN, CHARLES AUGUSTINE, SS, S.T.B., J.C.D., Vice Rector and Professor of

Canon Law, St. Thomas Seminary, Kenmore, Wash. **Article:** Funerals (Canon Law).

*KERKHOFS, JAN, SJ, Emeritus Professor of Pastoral Theology, Faculty of Theology and Faculty of Social Sciences, Katholieke Universiteit Leuven, Belgium. **Articles:** Belgium, The Catholic Church in [part 2]; Pro Mundi Vita.

*KERR, FERGUS, OP, Honorary Fellow of the Faculty of Divinity, The University of Edinburgh, Scotland. **Article:** Chenu, Marie-Dominique.

*KERSHNER, JOSEPH JOHN, SP, A.B., S.T.B., Assistant Director of Vocations, American Province of the Piarist Fathers, Devon Preparatory School, Devon, Pa. **Article:** Piarists.

*KERWIN, JEROME GREGORY, Ph.D., LL.D., Litt.D., Professor of Political Science and Director of the Honors Division, University of Santa Clara, Santa Clara, Calif.; Professor Emeritus of Political Science, University of Chicago. **Article:** Democracy.

KESSLER, SISTER ANN, OSB, Ph.D., Professor Emerita of History, Mount Marty College, Yankton, S.D.; Oblate Director, Benedictine Monastery, Yankton, S.D. **Articles:** Rapid City, Diocese of; Sioux Falls, Diocese of; South Dakota, Catholic Church in.

KESSLER, SISTER DONNA MARIE, OSF, M.A., Archivist, Holy Family Convent, Manitowoc, Wis. **Article:** Franciscan Sisters—Franciscan Sisters of Christian Charity (OSF).

*KEVANE, EUGENE, Rt. Rev., M.A., Ph.L., Ph.D., Professor of Education, The Catholic University of America, Washington, D.C. **Articles:** Fitzpatrick, Edward Augustus; Johnson, George; Jordan, Edward Benedict.

*KHOURI-SARKIS, GABRIEL EPHREM, Most Rev., Chorbishop, Patriarchal Vicar for the Syrians in France, Bernon, Eure, France; Founder, Director, and Editor, *L'Orient Syrien;* restorer of the Ancient Syrian Liturgy. **Articles:** Syrian Christianity, II: Syrian Orthodox Church (Oriental Orthodox); Syrian Christianity, III: Syrian Catholic Church (Eastern Catholic).

*KIBRE, PEARL, Ph.D., Professor of History, Hunter College, New York, N.Y.; Fellow of the Mediaeval Academy of America. **Articles:** Heloise; Paris, University of; Richard of Wallingford; Saint-Denis-en-France, Abbey of; Tempier, Etienne; Turpin of Reims.

*KIEMEN, MATHIAS CHARLES, OFM, Ph.D., Director, Academy of American Franciscan History, Washington, D.C. **Articles:** Aldeiamento System in Brazil; Brazil, The Catholic Church in; Lisboa, Cristovao de; Monteiro da Vide, Sebastiao; Seixas, Romualdo Antonio de.

*KILEY, MARK, Ph.D., Assistant Professor of Biblical Studies, St. Jerome College, Waterloo, Ontario. **Articles:** Catholic Epistles; Peter, Epistles of.

*KILMARTIN, EDWARD J., SJ, S.T.D., Pontifical Oriental Institute, Rome, Italy. **Articles:** Epiclesis; Ex Opere Operato.

*KINES, LOUIS BERKELEY, SJ, M.A. (Phil.), M.A. (Am. Hist.), Professor of History, St. Joseph's College, Philadelphia, Pa. **Article:** McElroy, John.

*KING, ARCHDALE ARTHUR, B.A. (Hons.), author, Weston Manor, Totland Bay, Isle of Wight, England. **Articles:** Aquileian Rite; Beneventan Rite.

*KING, HEINZ PETER, B.A. (Hons.), M.A., College Lecturer in History, University College, Dublin, Ireland. **Article:** Evesham, Abbey of.

*KING, JAMES DESMOND, OSA, J.C.D., Professor of Canon Law, Augustinian College, Washington, D.C. **Article:** Proxy (Canon Law).

*KINGDON, ROBERT MCCUNE, Ph.D., Professor of History, State University of Iowa, Iowa City, Iowa. **Articles:** Beza, Theodore; Camisards; Daille, Jean; Servetus, Michael.

*KINIERY, PAUL, Ph.D., Professor of History and Assistant Dean of the Graduate School, Loyola University, Chicago, Ill. **Article:** Lewis, Frank J.

*KINNIREY, SISTER ANN JULIA, SND, M.A., Ph.D., Professor of Philosophy, Trinity College, Washington, D.C. **Articles:** Rector Potens, Verax Deus; Rerum Deus Tenax Vigor; Rex Sempiterne Caelitum; Rex Gloriose Martyrum; Veni Sancte Spiritus.

*KINSEL, PASCHAL, OFM, S.T.B., J.C.B., Director of Holy Land Crusade Work, and Editor, *Crusader's Almanac.* **Article:** Commissariat of the Holy Land.

*KIRK, PAMELA J., Dr. Theol., Assistant Professor, St. Anselm College, Manchester, N.H. **Article:** Speyr, Adrienne von.

KIROV, DIMITAR POP-MARINOV, Ph.D., Senior Assistant Professor and Vice Dean, Faculty of Theology, University of Ternovo, Ternovo, Bulgaria. **Article:** Orthodox Church of Bulgaria.

*KIRWIN, DANIEL, Rt. Rev., Vienna, W.Va. **Article:** Swint, John Joseph.

*KIRWIN, GEORGE FRANCIS, OMI, Ph.L., S.T.L., Professor of Theology, Oblate College, Washington, D.C. **Article:** Conversion and Grace, Controversies on.

*KISHPAUGH, SISTER MARY JEROME, OP, Ph.D., Dominican High School, Detroit, Mich. **Articles:** Heimo of Michelsberg; Walfrid, St.

*KISTNER, HILARION HENRY, OFM, S.T.D., S.S.L., Professor of Sacred Scripture, St. Leonard College, Dayton, Ohio. **Articles:** Salvation History (Heilsgeschichte) [part 1]; Savior [part 1].

*KLAIBER, JEFFREY LOCKWOOD, SJ, Ph.D., Ordinary Professor of History, Pontificia Universidad Católica del Perú, Lima, Peru. **Articles:** Mission in Colonial America I (Spanish Missions); Mission in Colonial America II (Portuguese Missions); Reductions of Paraguay.

*KLAUS, ERMIN, OFM, Ph.D., Associate Professor of History, St. Bonaventure University, St. Bonaventure, N.Y. **Article:** Faust, Mathias.

*KLINE, ROBERT REEVES, Rt. Rev., Ph.D., President, Mt. St. Mary's College and Seminary, Emmitsburg, Md. **Articles:** Axiology; Value Judgment.

*KLINEFELTER, RALPH ALBERT, Ph.D., Public Relations Consultant, Pittsburgh, Pa. **Article:** Knights of St. George.

KLINGSHIRN, WILLIAM, Ph.D., Associate Professor, Department of Greek and Latin, Associate Director, Center for the Study of Early Christianity, The Catholic University of America; Washington, D.C. **Articles:** Caesaria, SS.; Caesarius of Arles, St.

*KLINKENBERG, HANS MARTIN, Dr.Phil., Director, Historisches Institut, Rhein.-Westfalische Technische Hochschule, Aachen, Germany. **Article:** Liutprand of Cremona.

*KLINKHAMER, SISTER MARIE CAROLYN, OP, Ph.D., Professor of History, Barry College, Miami, Fla. **Article:** Blaine Amendment.

*KLOCKER, HARRY ROBERT, SJ, S.T.L., Ph.D., Associate Professor of Philosophy and Head of the Department, Regis College, Denver, Colo. **Articles:** Empiricism; Locke, John; Ockhamism.

*KLOPPENBURG, BONAVENTURE, OFM, S.T.D., Editor in Chief, *Revista Eclesiastica Brasileira;* Professor of Dogmatic Theology, Petrópolis, Brazil; *Peritus,* Vatican Council II. **Articles:** Brazil, The Catholic Church in; Kardec, Allan.

*KLOSTERMANN, FERDINAND, Dr.Theol., University Professor of Pastoral Theology, University of Vienna, Austria. **Articles:** Apostle; Apostolate and Spiritual Life; Apostolic.

*KLUBERTANZ, GEORGE PETER, SJ, Ph.L., S.T.L., Ph.D., Professor of Philosophy and Dean of the College of Philosophy and Letters, St. Louis University, St. Louis, Mo. **Articles:** Analogy; Cogitative Power; Discursive Power; Estimative Power.

*KLUEG, FREDERICK EUGENE, OP, M.A., S.T.Lr., S.T.D., S.T.Praes., Professor, Mt. St. Bernard Seminary and Aquinas Institute, School of Theology, Dubuque, Iowa. **Articles:** Sin, Occasions of; Sin, Cooperation in; Sinner, Habitual.

*KNAPKE, PAUL JUSTIN, CPPS, S.T.D., Rector and Professor of Church History, St. Charles Seminary, Carthagena, Ohio. **Articles:** Brunner, Francis de Sales; Dwenger, Joseph Gerhard.

*KNOWLES, MICHAEL DAVID, OSB, Litt.D., Hon.D.Litt., Hon.Litt.D., formerly Regius Professor of Modern History, University of Cambridge, Fellow of the British Academy, Corresponding Fellow of the Medieval Academy of America, Wimbledon, London, England. **Articles:** Becket, Thomas St.; Benedictine Rule; Butler, Edward Cuthbert; Church, History of, II (Medieval); Clarendon, Constitutions of; England, The Catholic Church in; Foliot, Gilbert.

*KOCH, JOSEF CARL, Rt. Rev., Dr.Phil., Dr.Theol., Professor Emeritus, University of Cologne, Germany. **Article:** Nicholas of Cusa.

*KOCOUREK, ROMAN A., Ph.D., Chairman of the Department of Philosophy, University of San Diego, San Diego College for Women, San Diego, Calif. **Articles:** Chance; Fortune; Quantity.

*KOEHLER, JOHN EDWARD, SJ, Ph.D., Alma College, Los Gatos, Calif. **Articles:** Deharbe, Joseph; Hurtado, Caspar; Ripalda, Juan Martinez de.

*KOENIG, HARRY CORCORAN, S.T.D., Pastor, St. Joseph Church, Libertyville, Ill.

Articles: Chicago, Archdiocese of; Feehan, Patrick Augustine; Mundelein, George William; Quarter, William.

*KOHLER, SISTER MARY HORTENSE, OP, M.A., Professor of Social Science, Dominican College, Racine, Wis. **Article:** Dominican Sisters—Congregation of St Catherine of Siena (Racine, Wis).

*KOHLS, GERALD VICTOR, SJ, M.S., Alma College, Los Gatos, Calif. **Articles:** Lugo, Francisco de; Pesch, Christian; Tamburini, Tommaso.

*KOLLER, SISTER MARY CARMELINE, SSM, M.Mus., Teacher in the Motherhouse of the Community and in charge of the Music Department, Mater Dolorosa College; member of Curriculum Committee—Music, Archdiocesan Office of Education, Milwaukee, Wis. **Articles:** Franciscan Sisters—Sisters of the Sorrowful Mother of the Third Order of St. Francis (SSM).

*KOMONCHAK, JOSEPH A., S.T.L., Ph.D., Professor of Religion and Religious Education, The Catholic University of America, Washington, D.C. **Articles:** Congar, Yves Marie-Joseph; Ex corde Ecclesiae; Society (Theology of).

KOMONCHAK, JOSEPH A., S.T.L., Ph.D., Professor of Religion and Religious Education, The Catholic University of America, Washington, D.C. **Articles:** Murray, John Courtney; Vatican Council II.

*KONDOLEON, THEODORE JOSEPH, Assistant Professor of Philosophy, Loyola University, Chicago, Ill. **Articles:** Exemplarism; Exemplary Causality.

*KONERMAN, EDWARD H., SJ, Secretary, Catholic Theological Society of America; Professor, St. Mary of the Lake Seminary, Mundelein, Ill. **Article:** Catholic Theological Society of America.

*KONSTANT, RIGHT REVEREND DAVID EVERY, Bishop of Leeds, Great Britain. **Article:** Hume, George Basil.

*KOOB, C. ALBERT, OPraem, President, National Catholic Educational Association, Washington, D.C. **Article:** National Catholic Educational Association.

*KOPERSKI, VERONICA, SFCC, Ph.D., S.T.D., Professor of Theology, Barry University, Miami Shores, Fla. **Articles:** Captivity Epistles; Philemon, Epistle to; Philippians, Epistle to the.

*KOREN, HENRY JOSEPH, CSSp, Ph.D., S.T.D., Chairman, Department of Phi-

losophy, and Department of Theology, Duquesne University, Pittsburgh, Pa. **Articles:** Holy Ghost Fathers; Leen, Edward; Poullart des Places, Claude Francois.

*KORFMACHER, WILLIAM CHARLES, Ph.D., F.I.A.L., Professor and Director of the Department of Classical Languages, St. Louis University, St. Louis, Mo. **Articles:** Atto of Vercelli; Hermannus Contractus; Lauda Sion Salvatorem; Remigius of Reims, St.; Walter of Chatillon.

*KORNFELD, WALTER JOHANN, D.D., S.S.L., Professor of History of Religions, University of Vienna, Austria. **Article:** Sacred and Profane [part 1].

*KORTENDICK, JAMES JOSEPH, SS, S.T.B., B.S. in L.S., Ph.D., Associate Professor of Library Science and Head of the Department, The Catholic University of America, Washington, D.C. **Article:** Serra International.

KOS, FR. DONALD, OFMConv., STD, JCD, Diploma Rotal Lawyer, Official of the Apostolic Penitentiary, Judge of the Vatican Tribunal of the First Instance, Invited Professor at the Urbaniana University. **Article:** Penitentiary, Apostolic.

KOSANKE, CHARLES, Rev., B.A. philosophy, M.T.S. and M.Div., S.T.L., S.T.D., Pontifical Gregorian University in Rome, Director of Undergraduate Seminarians, Associate Professor of Theology, Sacred Heart Major Seminary, Detroit, Michigan. **Articles:** Lateran; Vatican Archives; Vatican; Vatican Library.

*KOSTER, HENRY PETER, SVD, S.T.L., S.S.L., Professor of Sacred Scripture and Associate Dean of Studies, Divine Word Seminary, Techny, Ill. **Articles:** Afterlife, 2. In the Bible; Death (in the Bible); Sheol.

*KOTTER, BONIFATIUS BALTHASAR, OSB, Dr.Phil., Director, Byzantinisches Institut, Abtei Scheyern, Scheyern, Bavaria, Germany. **Article:** John Damascene, St.

*KOVACH, FRANCIS J., Ph.D., Skogsberg Associate Professor of Philosophy, University of Oklahoma, Norman, Okla. **Article:** Beauty [Beauty as a Transcendental].

*KOZLOWSKI, LAWRENCE RICHARD, OCD, J.C.L., Washington, D.C. **Articles:** Bar-Cursus (Johannes Tellensis); Coussa, Acacius; Coustant, Pierre; Demetrius Chomatianus; Leuren, Peter; Passerini Pietro Maria; Roskovanyi, Augustus.

*KRAABEL, ALF THOMAS, Associate Professor, Classics Department and Chairman, Religious Studies, University of Minnesota, Minneapolis, Minn. **Article:** Synagogues, Ancient.

*KRABBE, SISTER M. KATHRYN CLARE, CSC, Ph.D., Chairman of the Department of Classical Languages, Saint Mary's College, Notre Dame, Ind. **Article:** Demetrias, St.

*KRAHL, JOSEPH, SJ, S.T.L., Eccl.Hist.D., Professor of Ecclesiastical History, Bellarmine College, Baguio, Philippine Islands, and Pontifical Seminary, Dalat, Vietnam. **Articles:** Favier, Alphonse; Grassi, Gregorio, St.; Lantrua, Giovanni of Triora, St.; Perboyre, Jean-Gabriel, St.; Taiwan, the Catholic Church in.

*KRAHN, CORNELIUS, Th.D., M.A., Professor of Church History, Bethel College, North Newton, Kans.; Director, Bethel College Historical Library. **Articles:** Marbeck, Pilgram; Mennonite Churches; Niclaes, Hendrik; Schwenckfelder Church.

*KRAJCAR, JOHN, SJ, Ph.L., S.T.L., Hist.Eccl.D., Professor, Pontifical Oriental Institute, Rome, Italy. **Articles:** Czech Republic, The Catholic Church in [part 1]; Papadopoulos, Chrysostomos.

*KRAMER, THOMAS E., Cathedral of the Holy Spirit, Bismarck, N.D. **Article:** Collins, Joseph Burns.

KRAMER, REV. THOMAS E., M.A., S.T.L., Pastor, Cathedral of the Holy Spirit, Bismarck, N.D., Vicar General, Diocese of Bismarck. **Article:** Bismarck, Diocese of.

KRANTZ, SISTER MARGARET, SMDC, M.Ed., former Minister General, Franciscan Missionary Sisters of the Divine Child, Williamsville, N.Y. **Article:** Franciscan Sisters—Franciscan Missionary Sisters of the Divine Child (FMDS).

*KRASENBRINK, JOSEF, OMI, S.T.L., Assistant, Seminary for Church History, Catholic Theological Faculty, University of Bonn, Germany. **Articles:** Scioppius, Kaspar; Spanheim, Ezechiel and Friedrich.

*KRASTEL, JOSEPH F., CSSR, Holy Redeemer College, Washington, D.C. **Articles:** John of Antioch; John of Ephesus.

*KRAUS, JAMES EDWARD, S.T.D., Diocesan Director of Confraternity of Christian Doctrine; Professor of Religious Education, St. Charles Seminary, Columbus, Ohio. **Article:** Confraternity of Christian Doctrine.

*KRAUSE, ADALBERT ALFRED, OSB, Dr.Theol., Dr. Phil., monk of Admont Abbey, Diocese of Seckau, Austria. **Articles:** Admont, Abbey of; Rupert of Salzburg, St.; Ulric of Augsburg, St.

*KRAUSE, FRED, OFMCap, Washington Theological Coalition, Washington, D.C. **Article:** Altar in Christian Liturgy.

KREBS, SR. CAROLYN A., OP, M.A., President, Congregation of St. Catherine de Ricci, Elkins Park, Pa. **Article:** Dominican Sisters—Congregation of St. Catherine de Ricci (Elkins Park, Pa.).

*KREILKAMP, HERMES DONALD, OFMCap, Ph.D., Lector, Capuchin Seminary of St. Mary, Crown Point, Ind. **Article:** Constantinople I, Council of.

*KREMER, EVA MARIA, CPS, Oxford Certificate of Education, Theologische Laienbildung (Wien), Special Studies in Journalism; writer, Provincial House Neuenbeken bei Paderborn, Germany. **Article:** Missionary Sisters of the Precious Blood.

*KRESS, ROBERT, M.A., Ph.D., S.T.L., Professor, Department of Philosophy and Religion, University of Evansville, Evansville, Ind. **Articles:** Catholicity; Collegiality, Episcopal; Communio; Frankfurt School; Jaeger, Lorenz; Journet, Charles.

*KRESS, ROBERT, S.T.L., Ph.D., Associate Professor and Head of Theological and Religious Studies Department, University of San Diego. **Article:** Fransen, Pieter Frans.

*KREUZER, ILDEFONS GABRIEL, OSB, monk of the Abbey of Scheyern, Bavaria, Germany. **Article:** Scheyern, Abbey of.

*KREWITT, HELWICK ALBERT, OFM, monthly contributor to the *Kolping Banner*, National President of the Catholic Kolping Society of America, St. Louis, Mo. **Article:** Kolping Society, Catholic.

*KREYCHE, GERALD FRANCIS, Ph.D., Associate Professor of Philosophy and Chairman of the Department, De Paul University, Chicago, Ill. **Articles:** Causality; Causality, Principle of; Condition; Finality, Principle of; Metaphysics, Validity of; Occasion.

*KRIEG, ROBERT A., CSC, Ph.D., Associate Professor, Department of Theology, University of Notre Dame, South Bend, Ind. **Article:** Peyton, Patrick Joseph.

*KRINSKY, RAYMOND, Rabbi, Ph.D., Director of the B'nai B'rith Hillel Foundation, University of Virginia, Charlottesville, Va. **Articles:** Caro, Joseph ben Ephraim; Dositheus of Samaria; Frank, Jacob; Gemarah; Ghetto; Haggadah; Halakah; Ibn Tibbon; Justus of Tiberias; Rabbinical Bibles.

*KRITZECK, JAMES, Ph.D., Professor of Oriental Languages and History and Director of the Institute for Higher Religious Studies, University of Notre Dame, Notre Dame, Ind. **Articles:** Ahmadiyyah; Arabia, 1. History; Baha'ism; Bahira Legend; Islam; Ismailis; Muḥammad; Safavids; Merton, Thomas.

KROEGER, JAMES H., MM, D.Miss., Professor of Systematic Theology, Mission Studies and Islamics, Loyola School of Theology, Ateneo de Manila University, Manila, Philippines. **Article:** Philippines, the Catholic Church in the; Redemptoris Missio.

*KRONZER, COLMAN L., OFMCap, B.A., Capuchin Seminary of St. Anthony, Marathon, Wis. **Article:** Angelo of Acri, Bl.

*KROSNICKI, THOMAS A., SVD, Associate Director, Bishops' Committee on the Liturgy, Washington, D.C. **Articles:** Easter and its Cycle; Lent; Marian Feasts; Sanctoral Cycle.

*KROUSE, DENNIS W., S.T.D., Director, Center for Liturgy and Prayer, Diocese of San Diego: Assistant Professor of Religious Studies, University of San Diego, San Diego, Calif. **Article:** Liturgy.

*KRYSA, CZESŁAW MICHAL, PhD., Professor of Liturgy and Liturgical Moderator, Graduate School of Theology, SS. Cyril & Methodius Seminary, Orchard Lake, Michigan. **Articles:** Popular Piety, Polish; Shrove Tuesday.

*KRZYZANOWSKI, CASIMIR JOHN, MIC, S.T.D., Assistant of the Postulator General, Congregation of the Marian Fathers, Rome, Italy. **Article:** Wyszynski, Casimir, Ven.

KUBICKI, JUDITH M., CSSF, M.L.M., Ph.D. Assistant Professor of Theology, Fordham University, Bronx, N.Y. **Articles:** Berthier, Jacques; Hymns and Hymnals, II: Vatican II and Beyond; Liturgical Acclamations; Taize, Music of.

*KUBLER, GEORGE ALEXANDER, Ph.D., Robert Lehman Professor of the History of Art, Yale University, New Haven, Conn. **Article:** Escorial; Herrera, Juan de.

*KUEHNER, RALPH JOSEPH, Very Rev., S.T.L., S.S.L., Professor of New Testament, Pontifical College Josephinum, Worthington, Ohio. **Article:** Millenarianism [part 1].

*KUEN, BENEDIKT, OSB, S.T.L., University of Munich, Germany. **Article:** Ottobeuren, Abbey of.

*KUGELMAN, RICHARD FRANCIS, CP, S.T.L., S.S.L., Professor of New Testament Exegesis in Passionist Theologate, St. Michael's Monastery, Union City, N.J.; Professorial Lecturer in Sacred Scripture, Theology Department, St. John's University, New York, N.Y. **Articles:** Maranatha; Pauline Privilege; Virgines Subintroductae [part 1].

*KUJAWA, ROBERT JOHN, CM, Mary Immaculate Seminary, Northampton, Pa. **Article:** Sin Offering (in the Bible).

*KUJOORY, PARVIN, MA, The Catholic University of America, Washington, D.C. **Article:** Kismet.

*KULACZ, SISTER EILEEN VALERIE, OSF, BS, Congregational Secretary, Our Lady of Angels Convent, Aston, Pa. **Article:** Franciscan Sisters—Sisters of St. Francis of Philadelphia (OSF).

*KUMMER, EDMUND, OSB, Ph.D., Stiftsgymnasium Melk, Austria. **Article:** Melk, Abbey of.

*KUNG, GUIDO, Ph.D., Assistant Professor of philosophy, University of Notre Dame, Notre Dame, Ind. **Article:** Nominalism.

*KUNG, HANS, S.T.D., Professor of Fundamental Theology, Catholic Theological Faculty, University of Bonn, Germany; *Peritus,* Vatican Council II; Coeditor, *Theologische Quartalschrift;* Associate Editor, *Journal of Ecumenical Studies;* Coeditor, *Revue Internationale de Théologie, Concilium.* **Article:** Freedom, Intellectual.

*KUNTZ, PAUL G., Professor, Grinnell College, Grinnell, Iowa. **Article:** Order.

*KUNZ, ADRIAN, OFMCap, Lector emer. S. Theol., Vice-postulator for the Beatification of Bishop Anastasius Hartmann, Stans, Switzerland. **Article:** Scherer, Maria Theresia, Bl.

*KUNZ, GERMAIN BENEDICT, M.A., Pastor, Church of the Holy Rosary, Graceville, Minn. **Article:** New Ulm, Diocese of.

KUPKE, MSGR. RAYMOND J., Instructor, Historical Studies, Immaculate Conception Seminary, Seton Hall University, South Orange, N.J.; Archivist, Diocese of Paterson, N.J. **Article:** New Mexico, Catholic Church in.

*KURRAS, LOTTE, Dr.Phil., Cataloger of Manuscripts, Württembergische Landesbibliothek, Stuttgart, Germany. **Articles:** Bernold of Constance; Erminold of Prufening, Bl.; Gottschalk, St.; Guido of Anderlecht, St.; Ulric of Zell, St.; Weissenau, Monastery of; Willehad of Bremen, St.

*KURTH, SISTER MARY BEDE, CMP, M.A., Personnel Director, St. Mary's Hospital, Huntington, W.Va. **Article:** Pallottine Missionary Sisters.

*KURZ, WILLIAM S., SJ, Ph.L., S.T.L., Ph.D., Associate Professor of New Testament, Marquette University, Milwaukee, Wis. **Article:** Luke-Acts.

*KURZWERNHART, ALBERT, OSB, Abbot, Benedictine Monastery Seitenstetten, Lower Austria. **Article:** Seitenstetten, Abbey of.

*KUSIELEWICZ, EUGENE FRANCIS, Ph.D., Associate Professor of History, St. John's University, Brooklyn, N.Y.; Vice President of the Kosciuszko Foundation; Assistant Editor, *Polish American Studies.* **Articles:** John III Sobieski, King of Poland; Josaphat Kuncevyc, St.; Laski, Jan and Jan (Lasco).

*KUTTNER, STEPHAN G., J.U.D., S.J.D. (h.c. Bologna), J.C.D. (h.c. Louvain), Honorary Doctorate (University of Paris), LL.D., Lawrison Riggs Professor of Religious Studies and Director of the Institute of Medieval Canon Law, Yale University, New Haven, Conn. **Articles:** Bernard of Compostella, the Elder; Duranti, William, the Elder; Honorius Magister; Rainerius of Pomposa; Richard de Mores (Ricardus Anglicus).

*KUTYS, DANIEL, M. Div., Executive Director, Office for the Catechism, National Conference of Catholic Bishops, Washington, D.C. **Article:** Catechism of the Catholic Church.

*KWIATKOWSKI, MOTHER MARY EWALDINE, M.A., Mother General, Congregation of the Sisters of the Holy Ghost, Diocese of Pittsburgh, Pa. **Article:** Holy Spirit, Sisters of the.

*KWITCHEN, SISTER MARY AUGUSTINE, OSF, Ph.D., Librarian and Instructor, College of Regina Mundi, Lima, Peru. **Article:** McMaster, James Alphonsus.

*LABANDE, EDMOND RENÉ, Docteur ès lettres, Professor of Medieval History, Faculty of Letters, University of Poitiers; Associate Director, Centre d'Études Supérieures de Civilisation médiévale, and Editor in Chief, *Cahiers de civilisation médiévale,* Poitiers, France. **Articles:** Gregory XI, Pope; Pilgrimages, 3. Medieval and Modern.

*LABOURDETTE, MARIE-MICHEL, OP, S.T.D., S.T.M., Studium de Toulouse, Haute Garonne, France. **Article:** Moral Theology, Methodology of.

LACHANCE, PAUL, OFM. Adjunct Professor, Catholic Theological Union, Chicago, Ill. **Articles:** Giles of Assisi, Bl.; Jacopone da Todi; Margaret of Cortona, St.; Angela of Foligno, Bl.

*LACHOWSKI, JOSEPH MICHAEL, CM, S.T.D., Director of Students, Teacher of Religion, Science, and Music, St. John Kanty Prep, Erie, Pa. **Articles:** Ascetisicm (in the New Testament); Forgiveness of Sins (in the Bible); Guilt (in the Bible); Holiness (in the Bible); Pure and Impure; Sacred and Profane [part 2]; Sin (in the Bible).

LA CIVITA, MICHAEL, Director of Communications, Catholic Near East Welfare Association, New York, N.Y. **Articles:** Catholic Near East Welfare Association; Pontifical Mission for Palestine.

*LACKO, MICHAEL, SJ, S.T.L., Eccl.Hist.D., Ph.D., Professor, Pontifical Oriental Institute, Rome, Italy. **Articles:** Albania, The Catholic Church in [part 1]; Bulgaria, The Catholic Church in [part 1]; Romania, The Catholic Church in; Slovakia, The Catholic Church in.

*LACOMBE, AMÉRICO JACOBINA, Bacharel em Direito, Professor, Pontifical Catholic University, and Director, Casa de Rui Barbosa, Rio de Janeiro, Brazil; Director of the Collection *Brasiliana.* **Articles:** Joana Angelica de Jesus; Nobrega, Manuel da.

*LACROIX, BENOÎT, OP, S.T.L., M.S.D. (Toronto), Ordinary Professor and Director, Institut d'Études Médiévales, Faculté de Philosophie, University of Montreal, Canada. **Articles:** Flodoard (Frodoard) of Reims; Hugh of Fleury; Ordericus Vitalis; William of Tyre.

*LADOWICZ, FRANCIS JOHN, Ph.D., Teacher of Polish and German, Loyola University, Chicago, Ill. **Articles:** Angelina, St.; Brest, Union of; Karnkowski, Stanislaw; Kromer, Martin (Cromer); Lucaris, Cyril; Sarkander, Jan, St.

*LADRIÈRE, JEAN ALFRED, Licencié en sciences mathématiques, Professor of Philosophy, University of Louvain, Belgium. **Articles:** Axiomatic System; DeRaeymaeker, Louis; Reasoning; Verification.

*LAFONTAINE, CHARLES, V., SA, Co-Director, Graymoor Ecumenical Institute, Graymoor/Garrison, N.Y., Editor, *Ecumenical Trends*. **Article:** Ecumenical Movement.

*LAFONTAINE-DOSOGNE, JACQUELINE LUCIE, Lic. in Class.Phil., Lic. Art and Arch., Docteur en Philosophie et Lettres, Chargé de Recherches, Fonds National de la Recherche Scientifique, Brussels, Belgium. **Article:** Mary, Blessed Virgin, Iconography of.

*LAGHI, MOST REVEREND PIO, S.T.D., J.C.D., Apostolic Pro-Nuncio to the United States of America, Washington, D.C. **Article:** Lateran Pacts 1985.

*LA GUARDIA, DACIAN JOSEPH, OFMCap, B.A., M.A., Capuchin College, Washington, D.C. **Article:** Ubald d'Alencon.

*LAHIFF, BARTHOLOMEW PATRICK, SJ, M.A., S.T.L., Georgetown University, Washington, D.C. **Articles:** Amiot, Jean Joseph Marie; Avril, Philippe; Buglio, Ludovico; Filippucci, Alessandro Francesco Saverio; Hinderer, Roman; Intorcetta, Prospero.

*LALLY, FRANCIS J., Rt. Rev., Sacred Heart Rectory, Roslindale, Ma. **Article:** Cushing, Richard.

*LAMADRID, LÁZARO I., OFM, Lic. Philosophy and Letters (Madrid), Historical Advisor for the Cause of Beatification of the Venerable Pedro de San José Betancur, and Historical Advisor for the Restoration of the Church of Saint Francis in Antigua, Guatemala; Iglesia de la Recolección, Padres Franciscanos, Guatemala City, Guatemala. **Articles:** Betancur (Bethancourt), Pedro de San Jose (Peter of St. Joseph), Bl.; El Salvador, The Catholic Church in; Garcia Xerez, Nicholas; Marroquin, Francisco; Pereira y Castellon, Simeon; Rojas, Jose Ramon; Thiel, Bernardo Augusto; Vazquez de Herrera, Francisco.

*LAMBERT, JAMES HENRY, SM, S.T.L., S.S.L., Assistant General and Secretary-General of the Marist Fathers, Rome, Italy. **Article:** Venerini Sisters.

LAMBRECHT, JAN, SJ, Doctor S.S., Professor Emeritus, Catholic University of Leuven (Louvain), Belgium. **Articles:** Galatians, Epistle to the; Pontifical Biblical Commission.

*LAMPE, ELMER LEWIS, JR., M.A., Instructor in History, The Catholic University of America, Washington, D.C. **Article:** Counter Reformation.

LANAVE, GREGORY F., Ph.D., Associate Editor, *New Catholic Encyclopedia*, second edition; Managing Editor, The *Thomist,* Washington, D.C.; Acquisitions Editor, The Catholic University of America Press, Washington, D.C. **Articles:** Church, Articles on; Creation, Articles on; Dogmatic Theology, Articles on; Eschatology, Articles on; God, Articles on; Grace, Articles on; Jesus Christ, Articles on; Man, Articles on; Mary, Blessed Virgin, Articles on; Theology, Articles on; Trinity, Holy, Articles on; Veritatis splendor.

*LANDRY, MADELEINE, Provincial House of the Presentation of Mary, Methuen, Mass. **Article:** Presentation of Mary, Sisters of the.

*LANE, DERMOT A., S.T.D., Mater Dei Institute of Education, Dublin, Ireland. **Article:** Praxis.

LANE, DERMOT A., S.T.D., President of Mater Dei Institute of Education, A College of Dublin City University, Pastor of Balally Parish in Dublin, Ireland. **Article:** Eschatology (in Theology) 2. Contemporary Catholic Theology.

LANE, MSGR. FRANK P., Ph.D., The Pontifical College Josephinum, Columbus, Ohio. **Article:** Ohio, Catholic Church in.

*LANE, SISTER JOHN MARY, SNJM, M.A., Professor of Biblical Science and Chairman of the Division of Biblical Science and Theology, Marylhurst College, Marylhurst, Ore.; member, Archdiocesan Commission for Religious Unity, Archdiocese of Portland, Ore. **Articles:** Jonah, Sign of; Jonah, Book of.

*LANE, RALPH, JR., Ph.D., Associate Professor of Sociology and Chairman of Department, University of San Francisco, San Francisco, Calif. **Article:** Beccaria, Cesare Bonesana.

LANE, RONALD E., Ph.D., retired Professor of Philosophy, College of St. Benedict, St. Joseph, Minn. **Article:** Leisure.

*LANG, GOTTFRIED O., Ph.D., Professor of Anthropology, The Catholic Universi-

ty of America, Washington, D.C. **Article:** Culture.

LANG, SISTER MARLA, M.S., President, St. Rose Convent, La Crosse, Wis. **Articles:** Franciscan Sisters—Congregation of the Sisters of the Third Order of St. Francis of Perpetual Adoration (FSPA).

*LANGFORD, JEROME JAMES, OP, Ph.L., M.A., S.T.Lr., Aquinas Institute School of Theology, Dubuque, Iowa. **Article:** Galilei, Galileo.

*LANGIS, JEAN JOSEPH, SS, S.T.L., Secrétaire provincial, Chaplain, Notre-Dame-de-Bonsecours, Montreal, Canada. **Articles:** Belmont, Francois Vachon de; Colin, Frederic Louis.

*LANGLEY, HAROLD DAVID, Ph.D., Associate Professor of History, The Catholic University of America, Washington, D.C. **Articles:** Penn's Charter of Liberties; Temperance Movements.

*LANGLEY, WENDELL E., SJ, Ph.D., Professor of Church History, Creighton University, Omaha, Nebr. **Articles:** Baluze, Etienne; Belloy, Jean Baptiste de; Bonal, Francois de; Burigny, Jean Levesque de; Dubois, Guillaume; Fleury, Andre Hercule de; Labre, Benedict Joseph, St.; Lomenie de Brienne, Etienne Charles de; Louis XV, King of France; Louise of France (Therese de St. Augustin), Ven.

*LANGLINAIS, JOSEPH WILLIS, SM, B.S. in Ed., S.T.D., Professor of Dogmatic Theology, St. Mary's University, San Antonio, Tex. **Articles:** Assumption of Mary; Munificentissimus Deus.

*LANGLOIS, PIERRE, Licence ès lettres, Agrégé de l'Université, Elève titulaire de l'École pratique des Hautes Études, Professor, University of Caen, France. **Article:** Greek Philosophy (Religious Aspects).

*LANNIE, VINCENT PETER, M.A., Ed.D., Assistant Professor of Education, Western Reserve University, Cleveland, Ohio. **Article:** Education, Philosophy of, 2. Modern Theories.

*LAPOINTE, SISTER MARIE WILLIAM, OP, Provincial Council of the Dominican Sisters of the Presentation in the U.S.; Administrator, Rosary House of Studies, Washington, D.C. **Article:** Poussepin, Marie, Bl.

LAPOINTE, SISTER MARIE WILLIAM, OP, B.A., director, Rosary House of

Studies, Washington, D.C. **Article:** Dominican Sisters—Dominican Sisters of Charity of the Presentation of the Blessed Virgin Mary (Dighton, Mass).

*LAPOMARDA, VINCENT ANTHONY, SJ, Ph.L., A.M., Weston College, Weston, Mass. **Articles:** Cerioli, Costanza, Bl.; Guanella, Luigi, Bl.; Le Gaudier, Anthony; Riccardi, Placido, Bl.; Rodat, Emilie de, St.; Rossello, Maria Giuseppa, St.; Vialar, Emilie de, St.

LAPOMARDA, VINCENT ANTHONY, SJ, Ph.D., Coordinator, Holocaust Collection, Department of History, College of the Holy Cross, Worcester, Mass. **Articles:** Alhambra, International Order of; Jesuits; Portland, Diocese of [Maine]; Vermont, Catholic Church in.

*LAPORTE, JEAN MARIE-CALIXTE, OSB, Monk of the Abbey of St. Wandrille, Normandy, France; historian. **Articles:** Carmelite Sisters—Carmelite Sisters for the Aged and Infirm (Ocarm); Chezal-Benoit, Abbey of; Fontenelle (Saint-Wandrille), Abbey of; Tiron, Abbey of.

*LARKIN, ERNEST ELDON, OCarm, S.T.D., Assistant Professor of Theology, The Catholic University of America, Washington, D.C. **Articles:** Mysticism in Literature; Pazzi, Mary Magdalene de', St.; Spirituality, Christian; Three Ways, The.

*LARKIN, FRANCIS, SSCC, M.A., National Director of the Enthronement of the Sacred Heart and Night Adoration in the Home, Washington, D.C. **Articles:** Crawley-Boevey, Mateo; Sacred Heart, Enthronement of the; Sacred Hearts of Jesus and Mary, Congregation of the.

*LARNEN, JOHN BRENDAN, OP, M.A., Editor, *Holy Name Journal*, New York, N.Y. **Article:** Nagle, Urban.

*LARROQUE, HENRI ALEXANDRE, J.C.L., The Catholic University of America, Washington, D.C. **Articles:** Antonius de Butrio; Decius, Philippus (Philippe de Dexio); Dumoulin, Jean (Johannes Molinaeus); Ibn al-Assal; Joannes Lapus Castilioneus; Lancelotti, Giovanni Paolo; Le Plat, Jodocus; Turner, Cuthbert Hamilton.

LARSON-MILLER, LIZETTE, Ph.D., Associate Professor of Liturgy, The Church Divinity School of the Pacific, Berkeley, Calif. **Article:** Liturgical History, I: Early.

*LATKO, ERNEST FRANCIS, OFM, S.T.D., Lect.Gen., Professor of Dogmatic The-

ology and of Applied Psychology, Christ the King Seminary, West Chicago, Ill.; Professor of Ethics and Religion, College of St. Francis, Joliet, Ill. **Article:** Confession, Auricular.

*LATKOVSKI, LEONARD, Magister Philologiae, Professor of Greek, Latin, German, French, Spanish, and Russian, Bellarmine College, Louisville, Ky. **Article:** Latvia, The Catholic Church in.

*LATOURETTE, KENNETH SCOTT, D.D., Ph.D., LL.D., S.T.D., L.H.D., D.Sc. of Rel., Sterling Professor Emeritus of Missions and Oriental History, Yale University, New Haven, Conn. **Articles:** Carey, William; Great Awakening; Half-Way Covenant; Mission History, III: Protestant; Student Volunteer Movement.

*LATREILLE, ANDRÉ, Docteur ès lettres, Dr. (h.c.), Professor and Dean Emeritus, Faculté des Lettres de Lyon, Facultés Catholiques de Lyon, Lyons, France; Correspondant de l'Institut. **Articles:** Catechism, Imperial; Civil Constitution of the Clergy; Fesch, Joseph; French Revolution; Maury, Jean Siffrein; Pius VI, Pope.

*LATRÉMOUILLE, RENÉ, OMI, D.Ph., D.D.C., LL.D., Professor of Canon Law and Vice-Dean, Faculty of Canon Law, University of Ottawa, Ontario, Canada. René, OMI, D.Ph., D.D.C., LL.D., Professor of Canon Law and Vice-Dean, Faculty of Canon Law, University of Ottawa, Ontario, Canada. **Article:** Canons, Chapter of.

*LAUBACHER, JAMES AUSEON, SS, S.T.D., Professor of Dogmatic and Ascetical Theology, St. Mary's Seminary, Baltimore, Md. **Articles:** Tanquerey, Adolphe Alfred; Tronson, Louis.

*LAUBENTHAL, ALLAN, St. Mary Seminary, Cleveland, Ohio. **Article:** Unicity of the Church.

*LAUER, ROSEMARY ZITA, Ph.D., Associate Professor of Philosophy, St. John's University, New York, N.Y. **Articles:** Deism; Encyclopedists; Enlightenment, Philosophy of [part 1]; Freethinkers; Holbach, Paul Heinrich Dietrich; Theism.

*LAUGHLIN, SISTER M. FRANCES LEA, SMIC, Ph.D., Professor of Philosophy and Art, Tombrock College of Sister Formation, Paterson, N.J. **Articles:** Abbess; Agnes of Assisi, St.; Calafato, Eustochia, St.; Catherine of Bologna, St.; Charnel House; Chorisantes; Clare

of Rimini, Bl.; Colette, St.; Constantine of Barbanson; Crown, Franciscan; David of Augsburg; Delphina of Signe, Bl.; Diego of Estella; Elizabeth of Schonau, St.; Elizabeth of Portugal, St.; Holy Spirit, Devotion to; Homines Intelligentiae; Humiliati; Joachim of Fiore; Juan de los Angeles; Kalands Brethren; Kinga, St.; Leo of Assisi (Brother Leo); Luke Belludi, Bl.; Mechtild of Magdeburg; Mechtild of Hackeborn, St.; Overberg, Bernard; Strepa, James, Bl.

*LAURAS, ANTOINE, SJ, Licence ès lettres, Licence en Philosophie scolastique, S.T.L., Prefect of Studies of the French Juniorate of the Society of Jesus, Adjunct Professor, Institut Catholique, and Professor, École de Bibliothécaires, Paris, France. **Article:** Cumont, Franz.

*LAURENT, VITALIEN, AA, Director, Institut français d'Études Byzantines, Paris, France. **Articles:** Constantinople III, Council of; Constantinople IV, Council of; Nicaea II, Council of; Xanthopulus, Nicephorus Callistus.

*LAUSBERG, HEINRICH, Dr.Phil., Professor of Romance Philology, Director of the Institute of Romance Philology and Institutum Erasmianum, University of Münster, Münster in Westfalen, Germany. **Article:** Memory in Ancient and Medieval Thought.

*LAUWERS, JOZEF KAREL, MSC, Licencié en philologie classique et histoire, Archiviste Général de la Congrégation, Rome, Italy. **Article:** Couppe, Louis.

*LAVANOUX, MAURICE EMILE, Secretary of the Liturgical Arts Society, Inc., New York, N.Y.; Editor, *Liturgical Arts*. **Article:** Liturgical Arts Society.

*LAVERY, EMMET GODFREY, LL.B., writer for stage and screen, Co-founder, Catholic Theater Conference, Los Angeles, Calif. **Article:** Connolly, Myles.

*LAVIN, MOTHER MARY OF OUR LADY OF SORROWS, SMR, M.A., Superior Convent of Mary Reparatrix, New York, N.Y. **Article:** Mary Reparatrix, Society of.

*LAVRIN, JANKO MATTHEW, M.A., Professor Emeritus, Nottingham University, Nottingham, England; Honorary Vice-President, London Institute of Linguistics; Corresponding Member, Slovene Academy of Arts and Sciences. **Article:** Slomšek, Anton Martin, Bl.

*LAWLER, PETER, Lecturer, Oscott College, Sutton Coldfield, Warwickshire,

England. **Articles:** Julius Africanus, Sextus; Minucius Felix; Victorinus of Pettau, St.

*LAWLER, THOMAS COMERFORD, Coeditor, *Ancient Christian Writers,* Alexandria, Va. **Articles:** Eustochium, St.; Marcella, St.; Pammachius.

*LAWLOR, FRANCIS XAVIER, SJ, M.A., Ph.L., S.T.D., Professor of Dogmatic Theology, Weston College, Weston, Mass. **Articles:** Abiding in Christ; Apostasy; Brother in Christ; Church, II (Theology of); Communion of Saints; Excommunication [part 1: History]; Heresy; Incorporation in Christ; Infallibility; Mystical Body of Christ; Mystici Corporis; Schism; Society (Church as); Soul of the Church; Votum.

*LAWLOR, SISTER MARY, SND, Ph.D., Professor of History and Chairman of the Department, Trinity College Washington, D.C. **Articles:** Arras, Martyrs of; Compiègne, Martyrs of; Decadi, Cult of; Laval, Martyrs of; Orange, Martyrs of; Pinot, Noel, Bl.; Reason, Cult of Goddess of; Rogue, Pierre Rene, Bl.; Supreme Being, Cult of the; Theophilanthropy; Valenciennes, Martyrs of.

*LAWRENCE, CLIFFORD HUGH, D.Phil., Reader in History, University of London, England. **Articles:** Abingdon, Abbey of; Edmund of Abingdon, St.; Richard Grant of Canterbury; William de Gaynesburgh.

*LAWRENCE, FREDERICK G., Associate Professor of Theology, Boston College, Chestnut Hill, Mass. **Articles:** Gadamer, Hans-Georg; Lonergan, Bernard.

*LAWRENCE, SISTER MARY CONCORDIA, B.A., Instructor of Moral Guidance and Social Studies, Madonna High School, Chicago, Ill. **Article:** Franciscan Sisters—Franciscan Sisters of Chicago (OSF).

LAWRENCE, RICHARD T., Ph.D., Pastor of St. Vincent de Paul Church, Baltimore, Md. **Articles:** Conversion, II (Theology of); Conversion, III (Psychology of).

LAZCANO, RAFAEL, OSA, S.T.D., Director, Colegio Mayor Universitario San Agustin, Madrid, Spain. **Article:** Leon, Luis de.

*LAZENBY, FRANCIS DU PONT, Ph.D., A.M.L.S., Assistant Director of Libraries, Humanities Division, and Associate Professor of Classics, University of Notre Dame, Notre Dame, Ind. **Articles:** Simeon of Polirone, St.; Simon of Cramaud; Simon of Trent; Sperandea, St.; Thomas Bellaci, Bl.; Thomas Helye, Bl.; Thomas of Tolentino, Bl.; Thomas Corsini, Bl.; Uguzo, St.; William of Saint-Brieuc, St.; William of Bourges, St.; Wirnt, Bl.; Wiwina, St.

*LAZOR, BERNARD ALOYSIUS, OSA, B.A., S.T.L., S.S.L., Regent of Studies and Professor of Sacred Scripture, Hebrew, and Liturgy, Augustinian College, Washington, D.C. **Articles:** Ciasca, Agostino; New Testament Books; Theocentrism.

*LAZUR, JOSEPH EDWARD, CPPS, B.A., S.T.L., Assistant Professor of Theology and Director of the Annual Bible Worship for Sisters, St. Joseph's College, Rensselaer, Ind. **Article:** Strauss, David Friedrich.

*LEAHY, EUGENE JOSEPH, A.B., M.Mus., DFA, Associate Professor of Music, University of Notre Dame, Notre Dame, Ind. **Articles:** Sequence; Trope.

*LEAHY, JOHN AUSTIN, M.A., Professor of Church History, Dean of History and Social Sciences, and Registrar, Borromeo Seminary of Ohio, Wickliffe, Ohio. **Article:** Reformed Churches, I: Europe.

*LEAHY, THOMAS WILLIAM, SJ, S.T.L., Ph.D., S.S.L., Professor of New Testament and Secretary of the Faculty, Alma College, Los Gatos, Calif. **Articles:** Jude, Epistle of; Peter, Epistles of.

*LEAHY, WILLIAM KYRAN, S.T.D., S.S.L., Holy Saviour Rectory, Lindwood, Pa. **Article:** Praetorium.

*LEBEAU, PAUL, SJ, Ph.L., Licencié en Philosophie et Lettres, S.T.D., Collège St. Albert, Egenhoven-Louvain, Belgium. **Articles:** Paul of Samosata; Sabellianism; Patripassianiam.

*LEBEAU, PAUL, SJ, President, Institut d'Etudes Théologiques, Brussels. **Article:** Suenens, Leon-Joseph.

*LE BRAZ, JACQUELINE TRÉMENBERT, Diplôme d'archiviste-paléographe, Chef de la Section de Diplomatique, Institut de Recherche et d'Histoire des Textes (C.N.R.S.), Paris, France. **Articles:** Saint-Savin-de-Bigorre, Abbey of; Saint-Sever, Abbeys of.

*LE BRETON, DAGMAR RENSHAW, M.A., Professor Emeritus of French, Newcomb College, Tulane University, New Orleans, La. **Article:** Rouquette, Adrien Emmanuel.

*LE BRUN, JEAN PIERRE MARIE, CSSR, Élève titulaire de l'École pratique des Hautes Études de Paris, Professor of Biblical Exegesis, Redemptorist Scholasticate, Dreux, France. **Articles:** Martyrologies; Martyrology, Roman; Saints, Legends of the.

*LECHNER, ROBERT FIRMAN, CPPS, Ph.D., Professor of Philosophy, St. Charles Seminary, Carthagena, Ohio; Editor, *Philosophy Today.* **Article:** Bragan Rite.

*LECKEY, DOLORES R., Executive Director, NCCB Secretariat for the Laity, Washington, D.C. **Article:** Powers, Jessica.

*LECLERCQ, JEAN, OSB, S.T.D., Doctor Philologiae (h.c.), monk of the Abbey of Clervaux, Luxembourg, Professor, Pontifical Institute of St. Anselm, Rome, Italy. **Articles:** Benedictine Spirituality; Gilbert Crispin; Ivo of Chartres, St.; Monastic Schools; Theology and Prayer.

*LEDERER, LAURA, Program on Studies in Religion, University of Michigan, Ann Arbor, Mich. **Article:** Albright, William Foxwell.

*LE DIEU, MOTHER SALESIA, MSC, M.A., Mother Cabrini High School, New York, N.Y. **Article:** Missionary Sisters of the Sacred Heart.

*LEDLEY, ROBERT STEVEN, M.A., President and Research Director, National Biomedical Research Foundation, Inc., Silver Spring, Md. **Article:** Cybernetics.

*LEDRÉ, CHARLES, Ph.L., Docteur ès lettres, Professeur d'Enseignement supérieur privé, Taverny, Seine et Oise, France. **Articles:** Bonnechose, Henri Marie Gaston de; Edgeworth de Firmont, Henry Essex; Merry del Val, Rafael; Pius X, Pope, St.

*LEDRUS, MICHEL, SJ, B.Litt., Ph.D., D.D., College of St. Robert Bellarmine, Rome, Italy. **Article:** Antolinez, Augustin.

*LEE, ANTHONY DAMIAN, OP, B.A., S.T.L., S.T.Lr., Managing Editor, *Thomist,* Washington, D.C. **Articles:** Cognition, Speculative-Practical; Images, Veneration of.

*LEE, BASIL LEO, FSC, Ph.D., Associate Professor of History, Manhattan College, New York, N.Y. **Article:** Meehan, Thomas Francis.

*LEE LOPEZ, ALBERTO, OFM, S.T.L., Hist.Eccl.D., Professor of Ecclesiastical History, History of the Franciscan Order, and History of Art and Methodology, Colegio Mayor de San Buenaventura, Bogotá, Colombia. **Article:** Zapata de Cardenas, Luis.

*LEEMING, BERNARD, SJ, Ph.D., S.T.D., LL.D., Magister Aggregatus Universitatis Gregorianae, Professor Emeritus, Heythrop College, Oxfordshire, England. **Article:** Lambeth Quadrilateral.

*LEETHAM, CLAUDE RICHARD, Very Rev., IC (Rosminian), B.A. (hons.), M.A., Catholic Education Council, Schools Adviser to *Sword of the Spirit;* Ratcliffe College, Leicester, England; *Peritus,* Vatican Council II. **Article:** Rosminians.

*LEFEBVRE, CHARLES, Docteur en droit civil, Docteur en philosophie scolastique, S.T.D., J.C.D., Professor, Faculté de droit canonique, Institut Catholique, Paris, France; Auditor, Sacred Roman Rota, Rome, Italy. **Article:** Hostiensis (Henry of Segusio).

*LEFLON, JEAN ADOLPHE MARIE, Rt. Rev., Professor emeritus, Institut Catholique, Paris, France. **Articles:** Bernier, Etienne Alexandre; Caprara, Giovanni Battista; Casoni, Filippo; Concordat of Fontainebleau; Concordat of 1801 (France); Emery, Jacques Andre; Gobel, Jean Baptiste Joseph; Gregoire, Henri Baptiste; Mazenod, Charles Joseph Eugéne de, St.; Napoleon I; Pacca, Bartolomeo; Pius VII, Pope; Spina, Giuseppe.

*LEFRANÇOIS, JOSEPH ANDRÉ, MS, S.T.L., Professor of Sacred Scripture and Liturgy, La Salette Seminary, Ipswich, Mass.; Professor of Sacred Scripture, Maryknoll Sisters' Novitiate, Topsfield, Mass. **Article:** Matthew, Apostle, St.

*LE GALL, J. P., CSSp, Editor, *La Semaine Africaine,* Brazzaville, Congo, Africa. **Articles:** Central African Republic, The Catholic Church in; Gabon, The Catholic Church in.

*LEGENDRE, PIERRE, Professor, Université de Lille, France. **Articles:** Bernard of Montmirat; Bertrand, Pierre; Fredol, Berenger (Berengarius Fredoli); John Le Moine.

*LE GRAND, MÈRE JEANNE, SHIS, Licenciée ès sciences, Motherhouse, Religieuses de Saint Maur, Paris, France. **Article:** Holy Infant Jesus, Sisters of the.

*LEGRAND, WILLIAM MARIE HENRI, Docteur en philosophie et lettres (Phil.Class.), Professor Emeritus of Latin Rhetoric, Athenée royal de Stavelot, Belgium; Collaborator, *Biographie nationale.* **Article:** Stavelot, Abbey of.

*LEHNER, FREDERIC K., Ph.D., Assistant Professor of Anthropology and Linguistics, University of Illinois, Urbana, Ill. **Articles:** Amico, Francesco; Bouvier, Jean Baptiste; Cardenas, Juan de; Coninck, Giles de; Du Hamel, Jean Baptiste (Duhamel); Gatterer, Michael; Henriquez, Enrique; Henry of Kalkar; Hirscher, Johann; Marchant, Pierre; Mazzolini, Sylvester; Mey, Gustav; Molina, Anthony de; Music (Philosophy); Schmid, Christoph von.

*LE HOULLIER, ALBAN, OMI, Ph.D., S.T.D., Professor, Oblate College and Seminary, Natick, Mass. **Articles:** Ephpheta; Nunc Dimittis (Canticle of Simeon).

LEHTOLA, LORI A., M.A., Ph.D. Cand. (University of Houston). Adjunct Professor of History, Department of History, University of St. Thomas, Houston, Tex. **Articles:** Aethelflaed, Lady of the Mercians; Alfred the Great, King of England; Athelstan, King of England; Malmesbury, Abbey of.

*LEIBER, ROBERT, SJ, S.T.D., Professor of Church History, Gregorian University, Rome, Italy; confidant of Pope Pius XII. **Articles:** Maglione, Luigi; Pius XII, Pope; Tardini, Domenico.

*LEIBRECHT, JOHN JOSEPH, Ph.D., Assistant Superintendent of Schools, Archdiocese of St. Louis, Mo. **Articles:** Holweck, Frederick G.; Kenrick, Peter Richard.

*LEISCHING, PETER, Dr.Iur., University Docent for the History of Canon Law, Juridical Faculty, University of Vienna, Austria. **Article:** Canon Law, History of, 6. The Council of Trent to the Code of Canon Law.

LEISING, SISTER BEATRICE, OSF, B. A., Assistant General Minister, Sisters of St. Francis of the Third Order Regular of Buffalo, Williamsville, N.Y. **Article:** Franciscan Sisters—Sisters of St. Francis of the Third Order Regular Williamsville, New York (OSF).

*LEITE, LAURENCE A., Ph.D., Associate Professor of Art History, George Washington University, Washington, D.C. **Article:** Jesus Christ, Iconography of.

*LEKAI, LOUIS JULIUS, SOCist, Ph.D., Professor of History, University of Dallas, Dallas, Tex. **Articles:** Adam of Perseigne; Alcobaca, Abbey of; Barbeaux, Abbey of; Barriere, Jean de la; Cadouin, Abbey of; Caulites; Cistercian Nuns; Cistercians; Emmanuel, Bl.; Eskil of Lund; Fastred, Bl.; Feuillants; Florians (Floriacenses); Fontfroide, Abbey of; Fossanova, Abbey of; Gervaise, Francois Armand; Hanthaler, Chrysostomus (Johannes Adam); Hautecombe, Abbey of; Heilsbronn, Abbey of; Heisterbach, Abbey of; Jouarre-en-Brie, Abbey of; Martinuzzi, Gyorgy (Juraj Utjesenovic); Maubuisson, Abbey of; Molesme, Abbey of; Montreuil-les-Dames, Abbey of; Nivard, Bl.; Nonantola, Abbey of; Obazine (Aubazine), Abbey of; Pannonhalma, Abbey of; Peter of Tarentaise, St.; Peter Monoculus, Bl.; Pforta, Abbey of; Rance, Armand Jean Le Bouthillier de; Robert of Newminster, St.; Saint Laumer of Blois, Abbey of; Sancia, St.; Sauvecanne (Silvacane), Abbey of; Savigny, Abbey of; Simon of Aulne, Bl.; Stephen of Obazine, Bl.; Vaux-de-Cernay, Abbey of; Villers, Abbey of; Visch, Charles de; Zirc, Abbey of.

*LELEU, MICHÈLE, Licence ès lettres, Diplôme d'Études Supérieures de Philosophie, Professor of Contemporary French Literature, École Normale Libre de Neuilly, Neuilly sur Seine, France. **Article:** Du Bos, Charles.

*LENAERTS, RENÉ BERNARD, Ph.D., Canon, Diocese of Antwerp, Ordinary Professor of Musicology, University of Louvain, Belgium; Extraordinary Professor, University of Utrecht, Netherlands. **Article:** Monte, Philippe de.

*LENCYK, WASYL, S.T.L., Ph.D., Associate Professor of Social Science, St. Basil's College, Stamford, Conn., and Seton Hall University, South Orange, N.J. **Article:** Antonii (Aleksei Pavlovich Khrapovitskii).

*LENGELING, EMIL J., Ph.L., S.T.D., University Professor of Liturgical Science, Catholic Theological Faculty, University of Münster, Münster in Westfalen, Germany. **Article:** Pericopes.

*LENHART, LUDWIG, Rt. Rev., Dr.Theol., University Professor for Church History, Patrology, Homiletics, and Catechetics, University of Mainz, Germany. **Articles:** Dalberg [Karl Theodore von]; Ketteler, Wilhelm Emmanuel von.

*LENTINI, ANSELMO, OSB, Ph.D., S.T.D., Doctorate in Literature, monk of the

Abbey of Montecassino, Italy. **Articles:** Aldemar, St.; Apollinaris of Monte Cassino, St.; Deusdedit of Monte Cassino, St.; Dominic of Sora, St.; John of Monte Marano, St.

*LEONARD, EDWARD FRANCIS, M.A., Assistant Professor of History, Department of History and Political Science, Iona College, New Rochelle, N.Y. **Article:** Ives, Levi Silliman.

*LEONARD, SISTER JOAN DE LOURDES, CSJ (Brentwood, N.Y.), Ph.D., Professor of History and Dean of Students, St. Joseph's College for Women, Brooklyn, N.Y. **Articles:** Brent, Margaret; Tekakwitha, Kateri, Bl.

*LEONARD, WILLIAM J., SJ, Professor Emeritus, Department of Social Sciences, Boston College; Superior, America House, New York, N.Y. **Article:** Reinhold, Hans A.

*LERCH, JOSEPH ROBINSON, SJ, A.B., M.A., Ph.L., S.T.L., Professor of Fundamental Theology, St. Mary's College, Kurseong, India. **Article:** Ecclesiology [History].

*LERCH, JOSEPH ROBINSON, SJ, M.A., S.T.L., Professor of Systematic Theology, Jamshedpur, Bihar, India. **Article:** Teaching Authority of the Church (Magisterium).

*LERHINAN, JOHN PATRICK, CSSR, Ph.D., Rector, Holy Redeemer College, Washington, D.C. **Article:** Divini Redemptoris.

*LERNER, EDWARD ROBERT, Ph.D., Associate Professor of Music, Queens College, New York, N.Y. **Articles:** Arcadelt, Jakob; Petrus de Cruce; Tinctoris, Johannes; Willaert, Adrian; Zarlino, Gioseffo.

*LEROY, FRANÇOIS JOSEPH, SJ, Ph.L., S.T.B., Doctorat en Philosophie et Lettres, Instructor in Classics and Librarian in Chief, Université Officielle, Bujumbura, Burundi, East Central Africa. **Article:** Proclus, St.

*LE SAINT, WILLIAM, SJ, M.A., S.T.D., Professor of Dogmatic Theology and Patrology, Bellarmine School of Theology, North Aurora, Ill.; Prefect of Studies and Dean of the Theologate. **Articles:** Montanism; Tertullian.

*LE TROCQUER, RENÉ, SS, Dean, Faculty of Philosophy, Facultés catholiques de Lyon, Lyon, France. **Article:** God in Philosophy, 3. Nature.

*LEUTENEGGER, BENEDICT, OFM, St. Peter's Church, Chicago, Ill. **Article:** Margil, Antonio, Ven.

*LEVIE, JEAN, SJ, Collège St-Albert, Louvain, Belgium. **Articles:** Hocedez, Edgar; Mersch, Emile.

*LEVINE, PHYLLIS M., Researcher, Medieval Church History, Catholic University of America, Washington, D.C. **Articles:** Erlembald, St.; Landulf.

*LEWIS, EUGENE JAMES, OP, B.A., M.A., Dominican House of Studies, Washington, D.C. **Articles:** Felbiger, Johann Ignaz von; Hollweck, Josef; Jocham, Magnus; Pichler, Johann and Wilhelm.

*LEWIS, JACQUES BRUNO, SJ, Ph.L., S.T.D., Professor of Dogmatic and Ascetical Theology, College of the Immaculate Conception, Montreal, Canada. **Articles:** Ignatian Spirituality; Spiritual Exercises.

*LEWIS, VIRGINIA ELNORA, A.M., Professor of the History of Art and Assistant Director and Curator of the Henry Clay Frick Fine Arts Building and Museum, University of Pittsburgh, Pittsburgh, Pa. **Article:** Book, The Printed.

*LIEGEY, GABRIEL MICHAEL, M.A., LL.B., Ph.D., Professor of English, Fordham University, New York, N.Y. **Article:** Vision (Dream) Literature.

*LILL, RUDOLF, Dr.Phil., Wissenschaftlicher Assistent, Deutsches Historisches Institut, Rome, Italy. **Articles:** Cologne; Cologne, Mixed Marriage Dispute in; Droste zu Vischering, Clemens August von; Dunin, Martin von; Geissel, Johannes von; Melchers, Paulus; Spiegel, Ferdinand August.

*LIMOUZIN-LAMOTHE, RAYMOND, Docteur ès lettres, Professor Emeritus (Paris), Director, *Dictionnaire de Biographie française;* member, Editorial Committee, *Revue d'Histoire de l'Église de France,* Paris, France. **Articles:** Amette, Leon Adolphe; Clermont-Tonnerre, Anne Antoine Jules de; Dubois, Louis Ernest; Mathieu, Francois Desire; Pie, Louis Francois Desire; Quelen, Hyacinthe Louis de; Richard de la Vergne, François Marie; Suhard, Emmanuel Celestin; Veuillot, Lous Francois.

LINCK, JOSEPH C., Ph.D., Instructor, Permanent Diaconate Formation Program, Diocese of Bridgeport, Conn. **Articles:** Maine, Catholic Church in; Pennsylvania, Catholic Church in.

*LINDEMANS, STEPHEN PETER CONSTANT, CICM, S.T.B., Hist.Eccl.D., Professor of Church History and Patrology and Student Counselor, Missiën van Scheut, Louvain. **Articles:** Auxilius of Naples; Eugenius Vulgarius.

LINDER, H., OSF, archivist, Sisters of St. Francis, Tiffin, Ohio. **Articles:** Franciscan Sisters—Franciscan Sisters of Penance and Charity of Tiffin, Ohio (OSF).

*LINES, JORGE AGUSTÍN, Professor Emeritus, University of Costa Rica, San José Costa Rica. **Article:** Costa Rica, The Catholic Church in.

*LINGLEY, ANNE, Editorial Director, *Living City Magazine,* Hyde Park, New York. **Article:** Focolare Movement.

*LINSCOTT, MARY, SNDdeN, President, International Union of Superiors General (UISG), Rome, Italy. **Article:** International Union of Superiors General (Women).

*LINZ, WERNER M., Treasurer, Herder and Herder, New York, N.Y. **Article:** Herder.

*LIPSCOMB, OSCAR HUGH, Ph.B., S.T.L., Ph.D., Vice Chancellor, Diocese of Mobile-Birmingham; Archivist; Diocesan Director of Vocations, Mobile, Ala. **Articles:** Allen, Edward Patrick; Portier, Michael.

*LIPSCOMB, REV. MSGR. OSCAR HUGH, Chancellor, The Chancery, Diocese of Mobile, Ala. **Article:** Toolen, Thomas Joseph.

LIPSCOMB, MOST REVEREND OSCAR HUGH, Ph.B., S.T.L., Ph.D., Archbishop of Mobile, Ala. **Article:** Mobile, Archdiocese of.

*LIPTAK, DAVID QUENTIN, Associate Editor, *Catholic Transcript,* Hartford, Conn. **Article:** McFarland, Francis Patrick.

*LIRETTE, SISTER MARY GERARDA, SCIM, M.A., Good Shepherd Convent, Lawrence, Mass. **Article:** Good Shepherd Sisters of Quebec.

*LITZ, FRANCIS EDWARDS, Ph.D., Professor Emeritus of English Language and Literature, The Catholic University of America, Washington, D.C. **Article:** Tabb, John Banister.

*LIUIMA, ANTANAS JUOZAS, SJ, Ph.L., S.T.L., Professor, History of Spirituality, Gregorian University, Rome, Italy; President, Académie Lituanienne Catholique des Sciences; Editor, *Actes des Congrès de l'Académie Lituanienne des Sciences.* **Article:** Berulle, Pierre de.

*LLOYD, JAMES B., CSP, B.A., Director, Paulist Information Center, New York, N.Y. **Article:** Goldstein, David.

LOCH, BRO. EDWARD J., SM, M.A, Archivist, Archdiocese of San Antonio, San Antonio, Tex. **Article:** San Antonio, Archdiocese of.

LOCKE, JOHN K., SJ, Executive Secretary, Office of Theological Concerns, Federation of Asian Bishops' Conferences. **Article:** Nepal, Catholic Church in.

LOEWE, WILLIAM P., Ph.D., Associate Professor, Department of Religion and Religious Education, The Catholic University of America, Washington, D.C. **Articles:** Christology; Historical Jesus; Jesus Christ (in Theology) 1. Formation of Classical Dogma; Jesus Christ (in Theology) 3. Special Questions; 16. Jesus Christ and World Religions; Jesus Christ (in Theology) 2. Scholasticism, Medieval and Modern; Jesus Christ (in Theology) 3. Special Questions; 14. Christ and Theologies of Liberation; Jesus Christ (in Theology) 3. Special Questions; 15. Feminist Christologies; Jesus Christ (in Theology) 3. Special Questions; 13. The Historical Jesus.

*LOGAN, FRANCIS DONALD, M.A., M.S.L., M.S.D., Assistant Professor of History, Emmanuel College, Boston, Mass. **Articles:** Bek, Anthony; Ordines Judiciarii; Simon Islip; Walter Reynolds; William de Grenefield; William la Zouche; William de Melton; William of Drogheda.

*LOGAN, JAMES C., Professor of Systematic Theology, Wesley Theological Seminary, Washington, D.C. **Article:** Ecology; United Methodist Church.

*LOGAN, SISTER MARY AQUINAS, OP, M.A., Vicaress-general of the Congregation of the Holy Cross, Instructor, Seattle University College of Sister Formation, Edmonds Campus, Seattle, Wash. **Article:** Dominican Sisters— Dominican Sisters Congregation of Holy Cross (Edmonds, Wash.).

*LOHKAMP, NICHOLAS LAWRENCE, OFM, S.T.D., Professor of Moral Theology, and of Spiritual Theology, Master of Clerics, and Dean of Studies, St. Leonard College, Dayton, Ohio. **Articles:** Consecration, Personal; Custody of the Senses; Mystical Union.

*LOHMANN VILLENA, GUILLERMO, Doctor en Historia, Chief, Departamento de Fronteras (Ministerio de Relaciones Exteriores); Professor of the History of Peru, University of Lima, Professor of Institutions, Pontifical Catholic University of Peru, and Professor of Criticism, National University of San Marcos, Lima, Peru. **Articles:** Briceno, Alonso; Olavide y Jauregui, Pablo de; Peru, the Catholic Church in.

*LOHR, BENEDICT, OCSO, B.S.; Ph.L., monk of the Monastery, Hundred Acres, New Boston, N.H. **Article:** William of Saint-Thierry.

*LOMASNEY, DENIS JAMES, FSP, B.A., H.D.E., Master of Novices, Our Lady of Lourdes Novitiate, Ballon, County Carlow, Ireland. **Article:** Patrician Brothers.

*LOMAX, DEREK WILLIAM, M.A., D.Phil., Lecturer in School of Hispanic Studies, University of Liverpool, England. **Articles:** Escorial; Huelgas de Burgos, Abbey of; Isabella I, Queen of Castile; Mendoza, Pedro Gonzalez de; Peter Arbues, St.; Segovia, John of; Torquemada, Tomas de; Ximenez de Rada, Rodrigo.

*LONG, HERBERT STRAINGE, Ph.D., Edward North Professor of Greek, Hamilton College, Clinton, N.Y. **Articles:** Astrology; Dionysus, Cult of; Euhemerus; Horoscopes; Neo-Pythagoreanism; Resurrection, Greco-Oriental; Taurobolium; Transmigration of Souls.

LONG, STEVEN A., Ph.D., Assistant Professor of Philosophy, University of Saint Thomas, St. Paul, Minn. **Articles:** Natural Law [part 1]; Natural Law [part 2]; Natural Law [part 3].

*LONGYEAR, REY MORGAN, Ph.D., Associate Professor of Music, University of Tennessee, Knoxville, Tenn.; solo timpanist, Knoxville Symphony Orchestra. **Articles:** Dvorak, Antonin; Elgar, Sir Edward; Hummel, Johann Nepomuk; Indy, Vincent d'; Liturgical Music, History of, 7: Romanticism and its aftermath; Massenet, Jules; Puccini, Giacomo; Rossini, Gioacchino; Saint-Saens, Camille; Spohr, Louis (Ludwig).

*LOOR, WILFRIDO, J.D., lawyer, writer, and publicist, Quito, Ecuador. **Article:** Checa y Barba, Jose Ignacio.

*LOSCHIAVO, LUIGI, CRL, Teacher of the History of the Order, and writer, Curia Generalizia, CRL, Rome, Italy. **Article:** Trombelli, John Chrysostom.

*LOTZ, JOHANNES BAPTIST, SJ, Dr.Phil., Professor of Philosophy, Berchmanskolleg, Pullach bei München, Germany, and Gregorian University, Rome, Italy. **Articles:** Kant, Immanuel; Kantianism; Noumena; Phenomena; Transcendental (Kantian); Transcendentals.

*LOUGHRAN, CHARLES P., SJ, M.A., Professor of History, Fordham University, New York, N.Y. **Articles:** Aldebert and Clement; Anglo-Saxons; Anianus and Marinus, SS.; Bertulf of Bobbio, St.; Domitian of Maastricht, St.; Ermelinde, St.; Landoald, St.

*LOVATT, ROGER WALFORD, M.A., Fellow of Peterhouse, University of Cambridge, England. **Article:** Blackman, John.

*LOVELEY, EDWARD MCLEAN, SJ, S.T.D., Associate Professor of Theology, University of Detroit, Detroit, Mich. **Article:** Creation, 1. In the Bible; Election, Divine.

*LOWE, ELIAS AVERY, Ph.D., D.Litt., LL.D., Professor of Palaeography, Institute for Advanced Study, Princeton, N.J.; Fellow of Mediaeval Academy of America; Corresponding Fellow of the British Academy. **Article:** Traube, Ludwig.

*LOWE, ROBERT WILLIAM, M.A., Docteur de l'Université (Paris), Professor of French and History of Music, Georgetown University, Washington, D.C. **Articles:** Bellini, Vincenzo; Cimarosa, Domenico; Donizetti, Gaetano; Gluck, Christophe Willibald.

*LOWERY, DANIEL LORNE, CSSR, M.A., S.T.L., Diploma, Moral Theology, Academia Alphonsiana, Rome, Italy; *Liguorian,* Redemptorist Fathers, Liguori, Mo. **Articles:** Immortale Dei; Libertas; Just Price.

*LOZIER, DONALD CHRISTOPHER, OP, M.A., S.T.B., Dominican House of Studies, Washington, D.C. **Articles:** Contenson, Guillaume Vincent de; Humbert of Romans; Merkelbach, Benoit Henri; Prummer, Dominikus; Thomas Agni.

*LUBY, SYLVESTER DANIEL, Rt. Rev., M.A., S.T.B., Pastor, St. Anthony's Church, Dubuque, Iowa. **Article:** Dubuque, Archdiocese of.

*LUCAL, JOHN A., SJ, General Secretary, SODEPAX, Geneva, Switzerland. **Article:** Sodepax.

*LUCATELLO, ENRICO, Ph.D., Journalist, Head and Secretary, Agenzia Nazionale Stampa Associata (ANSA), and in charge of Religious Information Service, Rome, Italy. **Articles:** Albertario, Davide; Crispolti, Filippo; Grosoli, Giovanni; Margotti, Giacomo.

*LUCEY, BEATUS TIMOTHY, OSB, M.F.A., Chairman of the Department of Art, Dean of Lower School, Housemaster, and Instructor in Art and English, Delbarton School, Morristown, N.J. **Article:** Liturgical Art, History of, Pt 4: Renewal Societies; St. Patrick's Missionary Society.

*LUCEY, WILLIAM LEO, SJ, S.T.L., Ph.D., Professor of American History and Librarian of Dinand Library, Holy Cross College, Worcester, Mass. **Articles:** Bacon, David William; Bapst, John; Fitton, James; Massachusetts, Catholic Church in; Rale, Sebastian; Springfield in Massachusetts, Diocese of; Worcester, Diocese of.

*LUCIANI, VINCENT JEROME, Ph.D., Professor Emeritus, City College of New York, N.Y. **Articles:** Dominis, Marcantonio de; Guicciardini, Francesco.

*LUKKENAER, PETRUS, Director, Sint Chrysostomus College, Boxmeer, Netherlands. **Article:** Bosboom-Toussaint, Anna Louisa Geertruida.

LUNZ, SISTER MARCIA, OSF, M.A., Director of the Congregation Sisters of St. Francis of Assisi, St. Francis Convent, St. Francis Wis. **Article:** Franciscan Sisters—Sisters of St. Francis of Assisi (OSF).

*LUOMA, JOHN K., Hartford Seminary Foundation, Hartford, Conn. **Articles:** Dibelius, Otto; Jaspers, Karl; Latourette, Kenneth Scott; Lutheran Churches in North America.

*LUSSIER, JOSEPH ERNEST, SSS, S.T.L., S.S.L., Professor of Scripture, Biblical Languages, and Christian Archeology, St. Joseph Seminary, Cleveland, Ohio. **Articles:** Bethlehem; Cenacle; Jericho; Palestine, 1. The Name; Palestine, 2. Physical Geography; Sepulcher, Holy.

*LUTZ, HEINRICH, Dr.Phil., Professor of Modern History, Universität des Saarlandes, and Director, Historisches Institut, Saarbrücken, Germany. **Articles:** Camaiani, Pietro; Commendone, Giovanni Francesco; Morone, Giovanni.

*LUYTEN, ALFONS NORBERT, OP, S.T.Lr., Dr.Phil., Professor of Natural Philosophy and Philosophical Psychology, University of Fribourg, Switzerland; Vice Dean, Philosophical Faculty. **Article:** Man, 2. In Philosophy; Soul-Body Relationship.

*LUZNYCKY, GREGORY NICHOLAS, Ph.D., Lecturer, Slavic Department, Universi-

ty of Pennsylvania, Philadelphia, Pa. **Articles:** Alexius the Studite, Patriarch of Constantinople; Argyros, Isaac; Cyril of Turiv; Dishypatos, David; Doxopatres, Neilos; Elias Ekdikos; Nicomedia.

*LYNCH, SISTER CLAIRE, OSB, Ph.D., Principal, Archbishop Murray Memorial High School, St. Paul, Minn. **Articles:** Bartholomites; Benedict the Moor, St.; Germaine of Pibrac, St.; Holzhauser, Bartholomew; John Joseph of the Cross, St.; Ranfaing, Elizabeth of, Ven.

*LYNCH, CYPRIAN J., OFM, M.A., Professor of History and Vice Rector, St. Joseph's Seminary, Callicoon, N.Y. **Articles:** Egidio Maria of St. Joseph, St.; Gubernatis, Domenico de; Lawrence of Villamagna, Bl.; Margaret of Lorraine, Bl.; Pacifico of San Severino, St.; Paschal Baylon, St.; Pontillo, Egidio Maria di San Guiseppe, St.

*LYNCH, JOHN, Ph.D., Leverhulme Lecturer in Hispanic and Latin American History, University College, University of London, England. **Article:** Philip II, King of Spain.

*LYNCH, JOHN EDWARD, CSP, M.A., M.S.L., Ph.D., Professor of History and Patrology, St. Paul's College, Washington, D.C. **Articles:** Adalgis of Novara, St.; Alexander of Fiesole, St.; Ambrose of Cahors, St.; Athala of Bobbio, St.; Barontus, St.; Damian of Pavia, St.; Eldrad, St.; Gudula, St.; Gummar, St.; Lambert of Maastricht, St.

*LYNCH, JOHN EDWARD, CSP, Ph.D., Professor of Canon Law and Medieval History, The Catholic University of America, Washington, D.C. **Article:** Fast and Abstinence.

*LYNCH, JOHN EDWARD, CSP, Associate Professor, Catholic University of America, Washington, D.C. **Article:** Kuttner, Stephan George.

LYNCH, JOHN EDWARD, CSP, M.S.L., Ph.D., Professor of Canon Law, The Catholic University of America, Washington, D.C. **Articles:** Canon Law, History of, 7. The 1917 Code of Canon Law; Canon Law, History of, 8. The 1983 Code of Canon Law to the Present.

*LYNCH, JOHN JAMES, SJ, M.A., S.T.D., Professor of Moral and Pastoral Theology, Weston College, Weston, Mass.; Moral Consultant to Catholic Hospital

Association and to Federation of Catholic Physicians' Guilds; Associate Editor, *Linacre Quarterly*. **Article:** Experimentation, Medical [part 1: Principles].

*LYNCH, KILLIAN, OFM, St. Bonaventure University, St. Bonaventure, N.Y. **Article:** Odo Rigaldus.

*LYNCH, LAWRENCE EDWARD, M.A., L.M.S., Ph.D., Professor of Philosophy and Head of the Department, St. Michael's College, University of Toronto, Canada. **Articles:** Heiric of Auxerre; John Scotus Eriugena; Remigius of Auxerre.

*LYNCH, WILLIAM A., M.D., President, National Federation of Catholic Physicians Guilds, Milton, Mass. **Article:** Catholic Medical Association.

*LYNCH, WILLIAM EDWARD, CM, S.T.L., S.S.L., Professor of Scripture, Assumption Seminary, San Antonio, Tex. **Articles:** Heart (in the Bible); Man, 1. In the Bible; Soul (in the Bible).

*LYNCH, WILLIAM FRANCIS, SJ, Ph.D., Writer in Residence, St. Peter's College, Jersey City, N.J. **Article:** Ugliness.

*LYNN, SISTER MARY LOYOLA, VHM, B.S., Monastery of the Visitation, Wilmington, Del. **Articles:** Alacoque, Margaret Mary, St.; Paray-le-Monial; Visitation Nuns.

*LYON, BRYCE DALE, Ph.D., Professor of Medieval History, University of California at Berkeley, Calif. **Article:** Normandy.

*LYONS, SISTER JEANNE MARIE, Ph.D., President, Mary Rogers College, Maryknoll, N.Y. **Articles:** Maryknoll Sisters; Rogers, Mary Joseph, Mother.

*LYONS, SISTER LETITIA MARY, SNJM, Ph.D. Professor of Social Science, Fort Wright College of the Holy Names, Spokane, Wash. **Articles:** Blanchet, Francis Norbert; Holy Names of Jesus and Mary, Sisters of the.

*MAAS, ROBIN, Ph.D., Assistant Professor of Christian Education, Wesley Theological Seminary, Washington, D.C. **Article:** Narrative Theology.

*MAASS, FERDINAND, SJ, Dr. Phil., Professor of Church History, Theological Faculty, University of Innsbruck, Austria. **Articles:** Colloredo, Hieronymus; Ems, Congress of; Erthal, Friedrich Karl Joseph and Franz Ludwig von; Espen, Zeger Bernhard van;

Frankenberg, Johann Heinrich; Gasser, Vinzenz Ferrer; Haynald, Ludwig; Hontheim, Johann Nikolaus von; Joseph II, Holy Roman Emperor; Josephinism; Maria Theresa of Austria; Migazzi, Christoph Anton; Rauscher, Joseph Othmar von; Rautenstrauch, Franz Stephan; Simor, Janos.

*MACCURTAIN, M. B., (Sister Benvenuta) OP, Ph.D., Sion Hill Dominican Secondary School, County Blackrock, Dublin, Ireland; Tutor in History; National University, Dublin, Ireland. **Articles:** O'Daly, Daniel; Walsh, William.

*MACDONALD, SEBASTIAN KILLORAN, CP, S.T.D., Professor of Moral Theology, Passionist and Benedictine Theologates, St. Meinrad, Ind. **Article:** Messiah.

*MACDOUGALL, HUGH ANDREW, OMI, Ph.D., Dean of the Faculty of Arts, St. Patrick's College of the University of Ottawa, Ontario, Canada. **Article:** Acton, John Emerich Edward Dalberg.

*MACEOIN, GEARÓID SÉAMAS, D.Phil., Assistant Professor, Dublin Institute for Advanced Studies, Dublin, Ireland. **Article:** O'Clery, Michael.

*MACFARLANE, LESLIE, JOHN, Ph.D., Lecturer in Medieval History, University of Aberdeen, Scotland; Visiting Professor in History, Macalester College, St. Paul, Minn. **Articles:** Adam Easton; Arbroath, Abbey of; Ardchattan, Priory of; Balmerino, Abbey of; Carlisle, Ancient See of; David I, King of Scotland; Deer, Abbey of; Dundrennan, Abbey of; Dunfermline, Abbey of; Durham, Ancient See of; Elphinstone, William; Fort Augustus, Abbey of; Holy Rood, Abbey of; Jedburgh, Monastery of; Kentigern (Mungo), St.; Kilwinning, Abbey of; Kinloss, Abbey of; Lindores, Abbey of; Lollards; Margaret of Scotland, St.; New Abbey (Sweetheart); Newbattle (Newbottle), Abbey of; Nunraw, Abbey of; Pluscarden Priory; Sodor and Man, Ancient See of; Wardlaw, Henry de; Whithorn, Priory of; Scotland, the Catholic Church in [part 1].

*MACIVER, MOTHER M. EMMANUEL, OSU, Ph.D., Assistant Professor of Theology, College of New Rochelle, N.Y. **Article:** John the Baptist, St.

MACKENZIE, ROSS, Ph.D., Historian, The Chautauqua Institution, Chautauqua, N.Y. **Article:** Chautauqua Movement.

*MACKINNON, HUGH, Ph.L., S.T.L., D.Phil., Professor of History, University of Waterloo, Ontario Canada. **Articles:** Arnulf of Soissons, St.; Gunther of Pairis; Herluka of Bernried, Bl.; Hildebert of Lavardin; Hugh of Grenoble, St.; Walter of Pontoise, St.

*MACKRELL, JOHN QUENTIN COLBORNE, M.A. (Oxon.), Ph.D. (London), Lecturer in History, University of Glasgow, Scotland. **Articles:** Arnauld; Choiseul du Plessis Praslin, Gilbert de; Le Maistre, Antoine and Isaac; Rapin, Rene.

*MACMASTER, RICHARD KERWIN, M.A., Teaching Fellow, Department of History, Georgetown University, Washington, D.C. **Articles:** Abbott, Lyman; Albright, Jacob; Alexander, Archibald; Asbury, Francis; Assemblies of God; Boehm, John Philip; Boehm, Martin; Brethren; Briggs, Charles Augustus; Brooks, Phillips; Campbell, Alexander; Church of the Nazarene; Edwards, Jonathan; Embury, Philip; Emmons, Nathanael; Evangelical Alliance; Evangelicalism; Finney, Charles Grandison; Foursquare Gospel, International Church of the; Frelinghuysen, Theodore Jacobus; Hodge, Charles; Judson, Adoniram; Mills, Samuel J.; Moody, Dwight Lyman; Nevin, John Williamson; Otterbein, Philip William; Paine, Thomas; Parker, Theodore; Rapp, Johann Georg; Rice, Luther; Rosicrucians; Schaff, Philip; Schlatter, Michael; Seabury, Samuel; Spangenberg, Augustus Gottlieb; Taylor, Nathaniel William; Theosophy; Walther, Carl Ferdinand William; Warfield, Benjamin Breckinridge; Whitefield, George; Williams, Roger; Witherspoon, John; Woolman, John.

*MACMILLAN, FRANCIS GERARD, M.A. (Hons.), Principal and Teacher of Modern Languages; Holyrood Senior Secondary School, Glasgow, Scotland. **Article:** Ozanam, Antoine Frédéric, Bl.

*MACRAE, GEORGE WINSOR, SJ, Ph.L., M.A., S.T.L., doctoral research in Scripture and Early Christian History, Christ's College, University of Cambridge, England. **Articles:** Alexander of Abonoteichos; Atonement, Day of (Yom Kippur); Bardesanes (Bar Daisan); Basilides; Carpocrates; Dedication of the Temple, Feast of; Feasts, Religious; Gnosis; Gnosticism; Heracleon; Hermetic Literature; Mandaean Religion; New-Moon Feast, Hebrew; Passover, Feast of; Purim, Feast of; Theodotus; Valentinus.

*MACRAE, GEORGE WINSOR, SJ, Stillman Professor, Harvard Divinity School, Institute Antiquity Christianity, Claremont Graduate School, Claremont, Ca. **Article:** Chenoboskion, Gnostic Texts of.

MACRIDES, RUTH, Ph.D., Lecturer in Byzantine Studies, The Centre for Byzantine, Ottoman, and Modern Greek Studies, The University of Birmingham, United Kingdom. **Article:** Arsenius Authorianus, Patriarch of Constantinople.

*MACSUIBHNE, PEADAR, PP, B.A., M.A., Kildare, County Kildare, Ireland. **Article:** Cullen, Paul.

*MACVICAR, THADDEUS, OFMCap, Eccl.Hist.D., Lector in Church History, Franciscan History, and Liturgy, Mary Immaculate Friary, Glenclyffe, Garrison, N.Y. **Articles:** Bernard of Corleone, St.; Conrad of Parzham, St.; Dionigi da Piacenza; Felix of Cantalice, St.; Felix of Nicosia, Bl.; Francesco Maria of Camporosso, St.; Ignatius of Laconi, St.; Innocenzo of Berzo, Bl.; Lawrence of Brindisi, St.; Massaja, Guglielmo.

*MADAJ, MENCESLAUS JOHN, Ph.D., Professor of Social Studies and Religion, Quigley Preparatory Seminary, Chicago, Ill. **Articles:** Gilbert of Neuffontaines, St.; Ludolf of Ratzeburg, St.

*MADAJ, MENCESLAUS JOHN, Archivist of the Archdiocese of Chicago, Research Professor of Church History at St. Mary of the Lake Seminary, Mundelein, Il.; Executive Secretary of the Polish American Historical Association. **Article:** Sheil, Bernard J.

MADDEN, MARY RODGER, SP, M.A., Pilgrimage Coordinator, Sisters of Providence, Saint-Mary-of-the-Woods, Ind. **Articles:** Bradley, Ritamary; Guerin, Mother Théodore, Bl.; Sister Formation Movement; Sisters of Providence of St. Mary-of-the-Woods.

*MADDEN, RICHARD CAIN, Rt. Rev., M.A., Pastor, St. Andrew's Church, Myrtle Beach, S.C. **Articles:** Barry, John (1799–1859); Cloriviere, Joseph Pierre Picot de; England, John; Gallagher, Simon Felix; Lynch, Patrick Nelson; Lynch, Baptista, Mother; Russell, William Thomas.

*MADIGAN, MOTHER M. FELICITAS, IBVM, St. Adrian Convent, Chicago, Ill. **Articles:** Dease, Mary Teresa, Mother; Loretto Sisters (Institute of the Blessed Virgin Mary).

*MAESTRINI, NICHOLAS, PIME, S.T.B., President, Mary-glade College, Memphis, Mich.; Provincial Superior of United States Province, PIME. **Article:** Pontifical Institute for Foreign Missions.

*MAGARET, HELENE, Ph.D., Chairman, Department of English, Marymount College, Tarrytown, N.Y. **Article:** Gailhac, Pierre Jean Antoine.

*MAGILL, GERARD, S.T.L., Ph.D., Associate Professor of Historical and Moral Theology, Saint Louis University, St. Louis, Mo. **Article:** Scotland, the Catholic Church in [part 2].

*MAGNER, JAMES ALOYSIUS, Rt. Rev., S.T.D., Ph.D., Vice Rector for Business and Finance and Assistant Treasurer, The Catholic University of America; Director, The Catholic University of America Press; and Associate Editor in Chief, *New Catholic Encyclopedia*, The Catholic University of America, Washington, D.C. **Articles:** Becerra Tanco, Luis; Gonzalez Flores, Anacleto; Munguia, Clemente de Jesus.

*MAGNETTI, DONALD LOUIS, SJ, Ph.L., Ph.D., Baltimore, Md. **Article:** Nebuchadnezzar, King of Babylon.

MAGRO, EMANUEL P., Ph.D., M.S.L.S., Headmaster, Sacred Heart Minor Seminary, Victoria, Malta. **Articles:** Falzon, Ignatius, Bl.; Pisani, Mary Adeodata, Bl.; Preca, George, Bl.

*MAGUIRE, ALBAN ANTHONY, OFM, S.T.D., Guardian and Rector of Holy Name College, Franciscan House of Studies, Washington, D.C. **Article:** Reparation.

*MAGUIRE, CATHERINE ELIZABETH, RSCJ, Ph.D., Professor of English, Newton College of the Sacred Heart, Newton, Mass. **Articles:** Barat, Madeleine Sophie, St.; Javouhey, Anne Marie, Bl.; Varin d'Ainville, Joseph Desire.

*MAHONEY, SISTER DENIS, OSU, Ph.D., Associate Professor of English, College of New Rochelle, New Rochelle, N.Y. **Article:** Marie de l'Incarnation Martin, Bl.

MAHONEY, EDWARD P., Ph.D., Professor of Philosophy, Duke University, Durham, N.C. **Article:** Nifo, Agostino.

*MAHONEY, JOHN F., Ph.D., Professor of English and Comparative Literature, University of Detroit, Detroit, Mich. **Article:** Ubald of Gubbio, St.

*MAHONEY, JOHN JOSEPH, OP, S.T.B., Ph.D., Professor, Department of Political Science and Government, Providence College, Providence, R.I. **Articles:** Christian of Stablo; Estius, Gulielmus; Jansen, Cornelius (the Elder).

*MAHONEY, LEONARD PAUL, SJ, A.M., Ph.L., S.T.L., Ph.D., Assistant Professor of History and International Relations, Boston College, Chestnut Hill, Mass. **Articles:** Baudouin, Louis Marie, Ven.; Chatel, Ferdinand Toussaint; Frayssinous, Denis; Petite Eglise.

*MAHONEY, MARGARET H., Ph.D., Professor and Chair, Department of History, Bellarmine College, Louisville, Ky. **Articles:** Sheed, Francis Joseph; Ward, Barbara (Jackson).

*MAHONEY, PAUL JOHN, OP, Ph.L., S.T.Lr., Professor of Theology, De Paul University, Chicago, Ill. **Article:** Intercession; Mary, Blessed Virgin, II (in Theology) [Knowledge of Mary].

*MAHONEY, WILLIAM BERTRAND, OP, S.T.Lr., Ph.D., Dean of School of Philosophy and Professor of Natural Philosophy, *Magister Studiorum*, Pontifical Philosophical Faculty, Aquinas Institute of Philosophy and Theology, River Forest, Ill. **Articles:** Impenetrability; Privation (Philosophy).

MAIER, CHRISTOPH T., Dr. phil., Historisches Seminar, Universität Zürich, Zürich, Switzerland. **Articles:** Crusades; Gregory VIII, Pope.

MAILHIOT, GILLES-DOMINIQUE, OP, Master of Sacred Theology, S.S.L., Emeritus Professor of Holy Scripture, Dominican College of Philosophy and Theology, Ottawa, Canada. **Article:** Tillard, Jean-Marie Roger.

*MAILLEUX, PAUL ANTONY, SJ, priest of Byzantine Rite, Ph.D., S.T.L., Superior, John XXIII Center for Eastern Christian Studies, Fordham University, New York, N.Y. **Articles:** Bulgakov, Macarius; Feodorov, Leonid; Moghila, Petrus; Svetlov, Pavel Iakovlevich.

*MAISSEN, AUGUSTIN, M.A., Ph.D., Associate Professor of Romance Languages, Utica College, Syracuse University, Syracuse, N.Y.; Coeditor, *Revista Retorromancha*. **Articles:** Disentis, Abbey of; Einsiedeln, Abbey of; Great Saint Bernard Hospice; Hauterive, Abbey of; Muri, Abbey of; Pfafers, Abbey of; Rheinau, Abbey of; Saint-Maurice, Abbey of.

*MAKAREWICZ, SYLVESTER EDWARD, OFM, S.T.L., S.S.L., S.S.Lect.Gen., Rector and Professor of Sacred Scripture and Hebrew, Christ the King Theological Seminary, West Chicago, Ill. **Articles:** Epikeia (in the Bible); Seven Last Words.

*MAKDISI, GEORGE, Docteur ès lettres, M.A.(hon.), Professor of Arabic, Harvard University, Cambridge, Mass. **Articles:** Caliph; Dhimmi; Imam; Islamic Law; Rhazes (Razes, al-Razi).

*MALAGON BARCELÓ, JAVIER, Doctorate in Law, Technical Secretary, OSA Fellowship and Professorship Program, Organization of American States, and Visiting Professor of History, The Catholic University of America, Washington, D.C. **Article:** Cordoba, Pedro de.

*MALAINA Y GONZÁLEZ, SANTIAGO, SJ, Iglesia de San Jose, San Salvador, El Salvador. **Article:** Aguilar, Nicolas.

*MALANCZUK, VLADIMIR, CSSR, S.T.L., D.Phil., Bishop Exarch for Ukrainians in France, Paris, France. **Articles:** Byzantine Theology; Vyshensky, Ivan.

*MALANOWSKI, GREGORY, OFMConv, S.T.D., Assistant Professor of Theology, The Catholic University of America, Washington, D.C. **Article:** Communio.

*MALDONADO, FRANCISCO ARMANDO, Rt. Rev., S.T.L., C.J.B., Coordinator, Permanent Secretariate of the Venezuelan Episcopate, Palacio Arzobispal, Caracas, Venezuela. **Article:** Venezuela, the Catholic Church in.

*MALDOON, DOROTHY AND RAYMOND, Executive Directing Couple, Christian Family Movement, Calumet College Center, Whiting, Ind. **Article:** Christian Family Movement.

MALLOY, CHRISTOPHER J., Ph.D., Assistant Professor of Theology, University of Dallas, Irving, Tex. **Article:** Justice, Double.

*MALO, ADRIEN MARIE, OFM, S.S.Lect.Gen., L.Jub., S.T.D. (h.c.), Professor of Exegesis, University of Montreal, and Chairman, Canadian Society of Mariology, Montreal, Canada. **Articles:** Astruc, Jean; Castellio, Sebastian (Chateillon); Renan, Joseph Ernest.

*MALONE, EDWARD EUGENE, OSB, S.T.D., Rector, St. John Vianney Seminary, Elkhorn, Nebr. **Articles:** Aureole (Nimbus); Loculus.

*MALONE, EDWARD FRANCIS, MM, B.A., M.R.E., S.T.D., Professor of Dogmatic Theology and Dean, Maryknoll Seminary, Maryknoll, N.Y. **Articles:** Kerygma; Kerygmatic Theology.

*MALONE, MOTHER MARY AUGUSTA, OSU, M.A., Assistant Professor of Latin, College of New Rochelle, New Rochelle, N.Y. **Articles:** Iste Confessor Domini Colentes; Jesu, Corona Virginium; Jesu, Redemptor Omnium; Quem Terra, Pontus, Sidera; Quicumque Christum Quaeritis.

*MALONEY, CORNELIUS F., B.A., Executive Editor, *Waterbury Republican, Waterbury American,* and *Waterbury Sunday Republican,* Waterbury, Conn. **Article:** McGivney, Michael Joseph.

*MALONEY, GEORGE A., Contemplative Ministries, Seal Beach, Calif. **Article:** Apophatic Theology.

*MALONEY, GEORGE ANTHONY, SJ, B.A., Ph.L., S.T.L., S.E.O.D., Scriptor, John XXIII Center for Eastern Christian Studies, and Professor of Oriental Theology, Graduate School and College of Arts and Sciences, Fordham University, New York, N.Y. **Articles:** Alexandria, Patriarchate of; Antioch, Patriarchate of; Athanasius the Athonite, St.; Byzantine Liturgy; Byzantine Christianity, II: Byzantine Catholic Churches; Byzantine Christianity, I: Orthodox Churches; Constantinople, Ecumenical Patriarchate of; Eastern Churches; Epiclesis; Greek Theology; Greek Catholic Church (Eastern Catholic); Jerusalem, Patriarchate of; Julianists (Aphthartodocetism); Mount Athos, Monastic Republic of; Nicodemus the Hagiorite; Orthodox Church of Greece; Orthodox Church of Cyprus; Orthodox and Oriental Orthodox Churches; Palmieri, Aurelio; Rasputin, Grigorii Efimovich; Rome, Patriarchate of; Russian Liturgy; Russian Chant; Sergius, Patriarch of Moscow; Studion (Studiu); Syrian Liturgy; Theoleptus, Metropolitan of Philadelphia; Theophylactus of Ochryda; Tikhon, Patriarch of Moscow; Toth, Alexis; Velitchkovsky, Paissy; Zatvornik, Theophan.

*MALOUF, LUCIEN, B.S., S.T.L., Licencié ès lettres, Pastor, Our Lady of the Annunciation Church, Boston, Mass.; Secretary of the Basilian Salvatorian Order and Director-Assistant to the Regional Superior. **Articles:** Abdallah Zahir; Agapios of Hierapolis; Ain-Traz, Synods of; Bacha, Constantine; Eutychios of Alexandria; Saifi, Euthymois.

*MALTMAN, SISTER M. NICHOLAS, OP, Ph.D., Chairman, Department of English, Dominican College of San Rafael, San Rafael, Calif. **Articles:** Boy Bishop; Feast of Fools; Feast of Asses; Kempe, Margery.

*MALY, EUGENE HARRY, S.T.D., S.S.D., Professor of Sacred Scripture, Mt. St. Mary's of the West Seminary, Norwood, Ohio. **Articles:** Colossae; Colossians, Epistle to the; Deuteronomists; Elohist; Ephesians, Epistle to the; Genesis, Book of; Hexateuch; Pentateuchal Studies, I: Origins until 1965; Priestly Writers, Pentateuchal; Yahwist.

*MANDIOLA, ANNA, Boston, Mass. **Article:** Teresian Institute.

*MANGINI, SISTER ROSE MATTHEW, IHM, Ph.D., Archdiocesan Consultant on Social Studies and Director of the Graduate Program, Marygrove College, Detroit, Mich. **Article:** St. Mary's School (Philadelphia, Pa.).

*MANIER, AUGUST EDWARD, Ph.D., Assistant Professor of Philosophy, University of Notre Dame, Notre Dame, Ind. **Articles:** Instinct; Mechanism, Biological; Plant Life (Philosophical Aspects).

MANISCALCO, MSGR. FRANCIS JOHN, Ph.D., Director of Communications, U.S. Conference of Catholic Bishops, Washington, D.C. **Article:** United States Conference of Catholic Bishops.

*MANKEL, F. XAVIER, V.G., Chancellor, Diocese of Knoxville, Tenn. **Article:** Knoxville, Diocese of.

*MANN, JESSE ALOYSIUS, Ph.D., Associate Professor of Philosophy and Chairman of the Department, Georgetown University, Washington, D.C. **Article:** Instrumentalism; Personalism.

*MANNING, TIMOTHY, Most Rev., D.D., J.C.D., Auxiliary Bishop of Los Angeles, Calif. **Article:** Los Angeles, Archdiocese of.

*MANNION, JOHN BERNARD, Executive Secretary, The Liturgical Conference, Washington, D.C. **Article:** Liturgical Conference.

*MANTE, GABRIEL AKWASI ABABIO, S.T.L., Bishop of Jasikan, Ghana; Former professor in Systematic Theology at St. Peter's Regional Seminary, Cape Coast, Pedu, Ghana. **Article:** Ghana, The Catholic Church in.

*MANVEL, ALEXANDER, graduate of the University of Tiflis (Tiblisi), Georgia, editor and historian, West Hyattsville, Md. **Articles:** Georgian Byzantine Catholics; Orthodox Church of Georgia.

*MARAS, RAYMOND J., Ph.D., Associate Professor, Modern European History, University of Dayton, Dayton, Ohio. **Articles:** Condillac, Etienne Bonnot de; Napoleon III; Robespierre, Maximilien Francois de.

*MARCHEGIANI, SISTER MARIA FRANCISCA, Pious Disciples of the Divine Master (Pie discepule del Divin Maestro); in charge of training in the schools of the Congregation, Rome, Italy. **Article:** Pious Disciples of the Divine Master.

*MARCHIONE, SISTER MARGHERITA FRANCES, MPF, Ph.D., Professor, Villa Walsh College, Morristown, N.J.; Lecturer in Italian, Seton Hall University, South Orange, N.J.; Provincial Secretary, Pontifical Institute of the Religious Teachers Filippini, Villa Walsh, Morristown, N.J. **Articles:** Filippini, Lucy, St.; Religious Teachers Filippini.

*MARCZUK, BOLESLAW, higher education in Poland, Germany, and U.S., writer on archeology and education in *Dzziennik Chicagoski,* Chicago, Ill. **Articles:** Book of the Dead; Egypt, Ancient, 3. Language and Literature.

MARETT-CROSBY, ANTHONY, OSB, D.Phil., monk of Ampleforth Abbey, Ampleforth, York, England. **Article:** Ampleforth, Abbey of.

*MARGIOTTI, FORTUNATO, OFM, Missionol.D., collaborator in the series *Sinica Franciscana,* Collegio Internazionale S. Antonio, Rome, Italy. **Article:** Rist, Valerius.

*MARICHAL, ROBERT PIERRE, Archiviste-paléographe, Professor of Latin Paleography, Paris (Sorbonne); Professor, French Language and Literature of the Middle Ages, Faculté des Lettres, Institut Catholique, Paris, France. **Article:** Paleography, Latin.

*MARING, NORMAN HILL, A.B., Th.B., Ph.D., Professor of Church History, Eastern Baptist Theological Seminary, Philadelphia, Pa. **Article:** Baptists.

*MARION, RAYMOND JOSEPH, Ph.D., Chairman, Department of History, and Chairman, Division of Social Sciences, Assumption College, Worcester, Mass. **Articles:** Anthelmi, Joseph; Godeau, Antoine.

*MARIQUE, JOSEPH M.-F., SJ, S.T.D., Ph.D., Director of the Hellenic Tradition Seminar and Director of *Prosopographia Christiana Hispanica,* College of the Holy Cross, Worcester, Mass. **Article:** Caesarius of Heisterbach.

*MARKHAM, JAMES JOSEPH, A.B., S.T.L., J.C.D., Diocese of Manchester, N.H. **Articles:** Curia, Roman; Peterson, John Bertram.

*MARKOWSKI, MELCHIOR EDWARD, OP, M.A., Pontifical Faculty of Theology of the Immaculate Conception, Dominican House of Studies, Washington, D.C. **Articles:** Ledesma, Pedro de; Reginald of Orleans, Bl.

*MARQUES, LUIZ CARLOS, C.Ss.R., Ph.D., São Paolo, Brazil. **Article:** Camara, Helder Pessoa.

*MARRARO, HOWARD R., Ph.D., Litt.D., Professor Emeritus of Italian, Columbia University, New York, N.Y. **Articles:** Capecelatro, Alfonso; Ferrini, Contardo, Bl.; Mezzofanti, Giuseppe; Moroni, Gaetano; Tosti, Luigi.

*MARROW, STANLEY B., SJ, M.A., Ph.L., S.T.L., Al-Hikma University, Baghdad, Iraq. **Articles:** Biblical Theology; Bonsirven, Joseph; Resurrection of the Dead, 1. In the Bible; Immortality, 3. In the Bible.

*MARSHALL, HUGH JOSEPH, MSSST, Ph.D., Spiritual Director and Professor, Father Judge Mission Seminary, Monroe, Va. **Article:** Missionary Servants of the Most Holy Trinity.

*MARSHALL, WILLOUGHBY MARKS, B.F.A., B.A., architect specializing in church design, Cambridge, Mass. **Article:** Ambo.

MARSTALL, DAVID THOMAS, B.A., Pontifical College Josephinum, Columbus, Ohio. **Articles:** Kansas, Catholic Church in; Wichita, Diocese of.

*MARTENSEN, DANIEL F., Director, Washington Theological Consortium and the affiliated Washington Institute of Ecumenics. **Article:** Visser't Hooft, W. A.

*MARTHALER, BERARD LAWRENCE, OFM-Conv, S.T.D., M.A., Professor of Religious Education, The Catholic University of America, Washington, D.C.; Editor, *Franciscan Educational Conference Report.* **Articles:** Abbo of Metz, St.; Abraham of Clermont, St.; Abraham of Ephesus, St.; Abrunculus of Trier, St.; Acharius of Noyon, St.;

Adalbald of Ostrevand, St.; Aemilian, SS.; Anianus of Orleans, St.; Anianus of Chartres, St.; Binius, Severin; Eisengrein, Marting and Wilhelm; Jonas of Bobbio; Lohelius, Johann (Lochel); Pflug, Julius von.

*MARTHALER, BERARD LAWRENCE, Department of Religion and Religious Education, Catholic University of America, Washington, D.C. **Article:** Catechetical Directories, National.

*MARTHALER, BERARD LAWRENCE, OFM-Conv., Chairman, Department of Religious Studies/Religious Education, Catholic University of America, Washington, D.C. **Article:** Religious Education.

*MARTHALER, BERARD LAWRENCE, OFM-Conv, S.T.D., Ph.D., Professor of Religion and Religious Education, The Catholic University of America, Washington, D.C. **Articles:** Filioque; Missionaries of Charity.

*MARTHALER, BERARD LAWRENCE, OFM-Conv, S.T.D., Ph.D., Warren-Blanding Professor of Religion, The Catholic University of America, Washington, D.C. **Articles:** Ryan, Mary Perkins; Stuhlmueller, Carroll; World Youth Day.

MARTHALER, BERARD LAWRENCE, OFM-Conv., S.T.D., Ph.D., Executive Editor, *New Catholic Encyclopedia,* Professor Emeritus of Religion and Religious Education, The Catholic University of America, Washington, D.C. **Articles:** Commandments, Ten [part 3]; Creed in Eucharistic Liturgy; General Directory for Catechesis; Mother Teresa of Calcutta; Religious Education, Articles on; Tertio millennio adveniente.

*MARTIN, DANIEL WILLIAM, CM, B.A., S.T.L., S.S., Professor of Sacred Scripture, St. Thomas Seminary, Denver, Colo. **Article:** Tischendorf, Konstantin von.

MARTIN, DENNIS D., Ph.D., Associate Professor of Historical Theology, Loyola University, Chicago, Ill. **Article:** Carthusian Spirituality.

*MARTIN, EDWARD JOSEPH, CM, B.A., S.T.L., M.A., Teacher of Latin and Greek, St. Joseph's College, Princeton, N.J. **Articles:** Abraham, Patriarch; Hagar.

*MARTIN, FRANCIS XAVIER, OSA, M.A., B.D., L.Ph., Ph.D. (Cantab.), Professor of Medieval History, University College, Dublin, Ireland. **Articles:** Giles of Viterbo; Nugent, Francis.

*MARTIN, SISTER M. AQUINATA, Ph.D., Professor Emeritus of History, St. Catharine Motherhouse, St. Catharine, Ky. **Article:** Dominican Sisters—Congregation of St Catharine of Siena (St. Catharine, Ky).

*MARTIN, MATTHIAS BENEDICT, SJ, M.A., Dean of Students, St. Louis University, St. Louis, Mo. **Articles:** Andrade, Antonio de; Buffier, Claude; Fridelli, Xaver Ehrenbert (Friedel); Mariana, Juan de.

*MARTIN, SISTER MARY ERNESTINE, MHS, historian of the Community, Sisters of the Most Holy Sacrament, Lafayette, La. **Article:** Sisters of the Most Holy Sacrament.

*MARTIN, NORMAN, Professor, University of Texas, Austin, Tx. **Article:** Carnap, Rudolf.

*MARTIN, NORMAN FRANCIS, SJ, Ph.D., S.T.L., Jesuit Institute of History, Rome, Italy; Department of History, University of Santa Clara, Santa Clara, Calif. **Articles:** Araujo, Antonio de; Boturini Benaduci, Lorenzo; Cuevas, Mariano; Perez de Rivas, Andres.

MARTIN, THOMAS, OSA, Ph.D., Professor, Department of Theology and Religious Studies, Villanova University, Villanova, Pa. **Article:** Augustinian Spirituality.

*MARTIN, THOMAS OWEN, Rt. Rev., Ph.D., S.T.D., J.C.D., LL.M., Professor, St. Joseph's Seminary, Grand Rapids, Mich.; Defender of the Bond and Chairman of the Marriage Advisory Board, Diocese of Grand Rapids. **Article:** Piety, Familial.

*MARTIN, VINCENT M., OP, S.T.Lr., Ph.D., S.T.Praes., S.T.M., Professor of History of Philosophy, St. Stephen's College, Dominican House of Philosophy, Dover, Mass. **Articles:** Absurdity; Eclecticism; Existentialism; Sartre, Jean-Paul; Anxiety.

*MARTIN, WILLIAM OLIVER, Ph.D., Professor of Philosophy and Chairman of the Department, University of Rhode Island, Kingston, R.I. **Article:** Religion, Philosophy of.

*MARTINDALE, ANDREW HENRY ROBERT, M.A. (Oxon.), Lecturer, Courtauld Institute of Art, University of London, England. **Article:** Pucelle, Jean.

MARTINEZ, GERMAN, OSB, S.T.D., Associate Professor of Theology and Liturgy, Fordham University, Bronx, N.Y. **Article:** Matrimony, Sacrament of.

MARTINEZ CUESTA, ANGEL, OAR, President, Instituto Historico OAR, Rome, Italy. **Article:** Augustinian Recollects.

*MARTÍNEZ DIEZ, GONZALO, J.C.D., Licentiate in Spanish Civil Law, S.T.L., Ph.L., Professor of the History of Canon Law, Faculty of Canon Law, Pontifical University of Comillas, Madrid, Spain. **Article:** Hispana Collectio (Isidoriana).

*MARTÍNEZ PAZ, ENRIQUE, Doctor of Law and Social Sciences, Professor of Constitutional and Administrative Law, University of Córdoba, Córdoba, Argentina; Professor, Faculty of Economic Sciences, Catholic University of Córdoba. **Article:** Funes, Dean Gregorio.

*MARTINI, ANGELO, SJ, Ph.L., S.T.L.; Hist.Eccl.D., Editor for History, *Civiltà Cattolica,* Rome, Italy. **Articles:** Bilio, Luigi; Murri, Romolo.

*MARUCA, DOMINIC WILLIAM, SJ, M.A., Ph.L., S.T.D., Master of Novices, Jesuit Novitiate, Wernersville, Pa. **Article:** Meschler, Moritz.

*MARX, PAUL, OSB, St. John's Abbey, Collegeville, Minn. **Article:** Michel, Virgil.

*MARZULLO, SISTER MARIE THERESE, MZSH, M.A., Teacher of English and Head of the Department, Sacred Heart Academy, Hamden, Conn.; lecturer at Mt. Sacred Heart Junior College. **Article:** Sacred Heart of Jesus, Apostles of the.

*MASCARENHAS, LOUIS JOSEPH, OFM, S.T.D., Professor of History, Patrology, and Mission Theology, Regional Seminary of West Pakistan, Karachi, Pakistan; Assistant Director, Institute for Religious and Social Studies, Karachi. **Article:** Afghanistan, The Catholic Church in.

*MASIELLO, RALPH JOHN, Ph.D., Associate Professor of Philosophy, Maryknoll Seminary, Glen Ellyn, Ill. **Articles:** Experience; Species, Intentional.

MASSARO, THOMAS J., SJ, Ph.D., Assistant Professor of Moral Theology, Weston Jesuit School of Theology, Cambridge, Mass. **Articles:** Common Good; Social Justice; Social Thought, Papal, 1. History; Social Thought, Papal, 2. Basic Concepts; Social Thought, Catholic, 4. Modern; Subsidiarity.

*MASSAUT, JEAN-PIERRE JOSEPH CHARLES, Licence en philosophie et lettres, Diplôme de l'École pratique des Hautes Études, University of Liège, Belgium. **Article:** Leo of St. John.

*MAST, SISTER M. DOLORITA, SSND, B.A., engaged in research and writing, School Sisters of Notre Dame, Baltimore, Md. **Article:** Gerhardinger, Karolina Elizabeth Frances, Bl.

*MASTERMAN, SISTER M. ROSE EILEEN, CSC, M.A. (Education), Ph.D., Professor of Theology, Dunbarton College of the Holy Cross, Washington, D.C. **Articles:** Act, First; Amen; Annihilation; Cause, First; Doxology, Biblical; Economy, Divine; Ecstasy (in the Bible); Finis Operantis; Finis Operis; Hosanna; Prayer (in the Bible); Providence of God (in the Bible); Vow (in the Bible).

*MASTERSON, REGINALD, OP, Ph.L., S.T.Lr., S.T.D., Prior, St. Rose Priory, and Professor of Dogmatic Theology and Ascetical Theology, Aquinas Institute School of Theology, Dubuque, Iowa. **Articles:** Instrumental Causality; Perfection, Spiritual.

*MATCZAK, SEBASTIAN ALEXANDER, Mag.Phil., Mag.Hist., S.T.D., Ph.D. (Scholastic Philosophy), Ph.D. (Philosophy), Associate Professor of Philosophy and Theology, St. John's University, Jamaica, N.Y. **Article:** Fideism; Traditionalism.

*MATEO, R. P., Sch.P., Piarist Fathers, Rome. **Article:** Casani, Pietro, Bl.

*MATEOS, FRANCISCO ORTÍN, SJ, S.T.D., Editor, *Razóny Fe* and *Missionalia Hispanica;* Collaborator, Instituto Santo Toribo de Mogrovejo de Misionología; and Consejo Superior de Investigaciones Científicas, Madrid, Spain. **Articles:** Acuna, Christobal de; Anchieta, José (Joseph) de, Bl.; Lacunza y Diaz, Manuel de; Ovalle, Alonso de.

MATERA, FRANK J., M.A., Ph.D., Professor of New Testament, Department of Theology, The Catholic University of America, Washington, D.C. **Article:** Mark, Gospel according to.

*MATHEWS, THOMAS FRANCIS, SJ, M.A., S.T.L., Weston College, Weston, Mass.; Assistant Staff Editor for Art and Architecture, *New Catholic Encyclopedia,* The Catholic University of America, Washington, D.C. **Articles:** Church Architecture, History of, 3: Byzantine; Church Architecture, History of, 2: Early Christian; Diaconicum.

MATOVINA, TIMOTHY, Ph.D., Associate Professor of Theology, Notre Dame University, Ind. **Article:** Popular Piety, Hispanic, in the United States.

*MATTEUCCI, BENVENUTO, Rt. Rev., D.Th., Commentator at Vatican Council II for *Osservatore Romano* and Radio Vaticana; journalist and author; Canon, Pistoia Cathedral, Pistoia, Italy; Lecturer in Liturgical Spirituality, Pontifical Lateran University, Rome, Italy. **Articles:** Pistoia, Synod of; Ricci, Scipione de'.

*MATTHEW, DONALD JAMES ALEXANDER, D.Phil., University Lecturer in Medieval History, University of Liverpool, England. **Articles:** Daventry, Priory of; Louis IX, King of France, St.; Saint-Evroult-d'Ouche, Abbey. of; Saint-Florent-les-Saumur, Abbey of; Saint-Lo, Monastery of; Saint-Ouen, Abbey of; Saint-Pierre-sur-Dives, Abbey of; Troarn, Abbey of.

*MATTINGLY, BASIL MICHAEL, OSB, Ph.D., Professor of Philosophy, Subprior, Senior Brother Instructor, and Head of Religion and Philosophy Division, St. Meinrad Archabbey, St. Meinrad, Ind. **Article:** Similarity; Relation.

*MATTINGLY, JOHN FRANCIS, SS, M.A., S.T.L., S.S.L., Professor of Scripture, St. Patrick's Seminary, Menlo Park, Calif. **Article:** Melchizedec.

*MATTOSO, JOSÉ, OSB, Licentiate in Historical Sciences, Masteiro de Singeverga, Negrelos, Minho, Portugal. **Article:** Portugal, The Catholic Church in [part 1].

*MATZERATH, ROGER EDWIN, B.A., S.T.D., Professor of Moral Theology, Atonement Seminary, Washington, D.C. **Articles:** American Council of Christian Churches; Bushnell, Horace; Calvinism; Episcopal Church, U.S.; Evangelical Church; Infralapsarians (Sublapsarians); National Association of Evangelicals; Pentecostal Churches; Supralapsarians.

*MAURER, ARMAND AUGUSTINE, CSB, M.A., L.S.M., Ph.D., Professor of Philosophy, Pontifical Institute of Mediaeval Studies, and University of Toronto, Toronto, Canada. **Articles:** Averroism, Latin; Boethius of Sweden (Dacia); Gilson, Etienne Henry; John Baconthorp; Marsilius of Inghen; Nicholas Oresme; Phelan, Gerald Bernard; Robert Holcot; Siger of Brabant.

*MAURER, ARMAND AUGUSTINE, CSB, Professor of Philosophy Emeritus, Pontifical Institute of Mediaeval

Studies, Toronto. **Article:** Pegis, Anton Charles.

*MAURI, SISTER MARY, formerly Superior Delegate of the Daughters of St. Mary of Providence (deceased July 24, 1963). **Article:** Daughters of St. Mary of Providence.

*MAURICIO GOMES DOS SANTOS, DOMINGO, SJ, S.T.D., editor, journalist, and historian, Lisbon, Portugal. **Article:** Mission in Colonial America II (Portuguese Missions).

*MAURILIUS OF THE SACRED HEART, CMI [Antony Chacko Kakkanatt], B.S., member, Religious Congregation of the Carmelites of Mary Immaculate of the Chaldean Rite of India, and Vice-Postulator, St. Joseph's Monastery, Mannanam P.O., Kerala, South India. **Article:** Chavara, Kuriackos (Cyriac) Elias, Bl.

*MAY, ERIC EDWARD, OFMCap, S.T.D., S.S.L., Professor of Scripture, Mary Immaculate Friary, Garrison, N.Y. **Article:** Lazarus; Nativity of Mary.

*MAY, GEORG, J.C.D., Professor of Canon Law, Catholic Theological Faculty, University of Mainz, Germany. **Articles:** Benedict the Levite; Polycarpus; Regino of Prum, Collection of.

*MAY, WILLIAM E., Ph.D., Professor of Moral Theology, The Catholic University of America, Washington, D.C. **Article:** Personalist Ethics.

*MAY, WILLIAM E., Ph.D., Michael J. McGivney Professor of Moral Theology, John Paul II Institute for Studies on Marriage and Family, Washington, D.C. **Article:** International Theological Commission.

*MAY, WILLIAM EUGENE, M.A., Ph.D., Book Editor for Bruce Publishing Company, Milwaukee, Wis. **Articles:** Creative Imagination; Knowledge, Connatural.

MAYER, HELENA G., SHCJ, Archivist, Society of the Holy Child Jesus, Sharon Hill, Pa. **Article:** Holy Child Jesus, Society of the.

*MAYER, SUSO FRANZ, OSB, J.C.D., monk of the Archabbey of Beuron, Germany (deceased May 22, 1963). **Article:** Baumer, Suitbert.

*MAYEUR, JEAN-MARIE, Licencié d'Histoire, Agrégé d'Histoire, Centre National de la Recherche Scientifique, Paris, France. **Articles:** Jacobini, Ludovico; Leo XIII, Pope; Nina, Lorenzo; Rampolla del Tindaro, Mariano.

*MAYR-HARTING, HENRY MARIA ROBERT EGMONT, D.Phil. (Oxon.), Lecturer in Medieval History, University of Liverpool, England. **Articles:** Aymer de Lusignan; Boso, Cardinal; Hilary of Chichester; Sewal de Bovill; Theobald of Canterbury; Walter of Cantelupe; William Fitzherbert, St.; William of Kilkenny.

*MAZIARZ, EDWARD A., CPPS, Ph.D., Professor of Philosophy and Mathematics, St. Joseph's College, Rensselaer, Ind. **Articles:** Mathematics, Philosophy of; Philosophy.

*MCALEER, JOHN JOSEPH, Ph.D., Professor of English, Boston College, Chestnut Hill, Mass. **Articles:** Thoreau, Henry David; Transcendentalism, Literary.

*MCAULIFFE, CLARENCE RICHARD, SJ, S.T.D., Professor of Dogmatic Theology, School of Divinity of St. Louis University, St. Marys College, St. Marys, Kans. **Article:** Kelly, Gerald Andrew.

*MCAULIFFE, HAROLD JAMES, SJ, M.A., Associate Professor of Speech and Drama, Creighton University, Omaha, Nebr. **Article:** Dempsey, Timothy.

*MCAVOY, THOMAS T., CSC, Ph.D., Professor of History and Archivist, University of Notre Dame, Notre Dame, Ind. **Articles:** Americanism; Hudson, Daniel Eldred; Indiana, Catholic Church in; Noll, John Francis; O'Hara, Edwin Vincent; O'Hara, John Francis; Sorin, Edward Frederick.

*MCBREARTY, WILLIAM JAMES, SJ, S.T.L., M.A., Instructor in Russian Language and Literature, Institute of Contemporary Russian Studies, Fordham University, New York, N.Y. **Articles:** Khomiakov, Aleksei Stepanovich; Tolstoi, Leo Nikolaevich.

*MCCABE, MARTIN, OFMCap, S.T.D., Associate Professor of Anthropology and Social Science, Catholic University of Puerto Rico, Ponce, P.R. **Article:** Puerto Rico.

*MCCALL, ROBERT EDWARD, SSJ, Ph.D., Professor of Philosophy, St. Joseph's Seminary, Washington, D.C.; Dean of the Catholic Sisters College and Director of the Campus School, The Catholic University of America, Washington, D.C. **Articles:** Accident; Substance.

*MCCANCE, MURRAY ALLEN, M.A., vestment maker, St. Thomas, Ontario, Canada. **Articles:** Alb; Amice; Biretta;

Cassock; Chasuble; Cope and Humeral Veil; Dalmatic; Incense [part 2]; Liturgical Vestments; Liturgical Colors; Maniple; Stole; Surplice.

*MCCANN, JAMES CUTHBERT, OSB, monk of Downside Abbey, teacher, Downside School, Bath, Stratton on the Fosse, Somersetshire, England. **Article:** Downside Abbey.

*MCCARRON, RICHARD E. J., M.A., Department of Religion and Religious Education, The Catholic University of America, Washington, D.C. **Articles:** Hebblethwaite, Peter; Inculturation, Liturgical.

MCCARRON, RICHARD E. J., Ph.D., Assistant Editor, New Catholic Encyclopedia, second edition; Assistant Professor of Liturgy, Catholic Theological Union, Chicago, Ill. **Articles:** Baptism of the Lord [part 2]; Baptism of the Lord [part 1]; Descent of Christ into Hell; East Syrian Liturgy.

MCCARTHY, D., **Articles:** Poverty; Poverty Movement.

*MCCARTHY, DENNIS JOHN, SJ, S.T.D., S.S.L., Professor of Old Testament Languages and Literature, St. Marys College, St. Marys, Kans. **Articles:** Prophecy (in the Bible); Prophet.

MCCARTHY, J., **Article:** Fortescue, Adrian.

*MCCARTHY, JOHN L., Very Rev. Canon, D.D., D.C.L., SS. Peter and Paul, Athlone, Ireland. **Article:** Secrets.

*MCCARTHY, MOTHER MARIA CARITAS, SHCJ, Ph.D., Assistant Professor of History, Rosemont College, Rosemont, Pa. **Articles:** Abraham the Simple, St.; Amantius of Rodez, St.; Ansbert of Rouen, St.; Aredius, St.; Connelly, Cornelia, Mother; Desert Fathers; Holy Child Jesus, Society of the; Laura; Mamertus of Vienne, St.; Noetus of Smyrna; Pachomius, St.; Paphnutius; Phileas of Thmuis, St.; Pilgrimages, 2. Early Christian (to 600); Quo Vadis; Recluse; Tabennisi; Thebaid; Thmuis; Wulflaicus, St.; Zachary, Pope, St.

*MCCARTHY, SISTER MARY FRANCES, SND, Ph.D., Associate Professor and Chairman of the Departments of German and Russian, Trinity College, Washington, D.C. **Articles:** Adelaide of Vilich, St.; Agilulf of Cologne, St.; Altotting, Monastery of; Anno of Cologne, St.; Benno of Meissen, St.; Berno of Reichenau; Bruno of Cologne, St.; Caesaria, SS.; Conrad of

Querfurt; Cunibert of Cologne, St.; Emmeram, St.; Engelbert I of Cologne, St.; Ermenrich of Passau; Gero of Cologne, St.; Heribert of Cologne, St.; Lessing, Gotthold Ephraim; Nicholas of Prussia, Bl.; Notker Balbulus, Bl.; Rabanus Maurus, Bl.; Sacris Solemniis; Walafrid Strabo.

*MCCARTHY, SISTER MARY JOSEPH, RU, B.A., Community Registrar, Directress of Studies, Ursuline Novitiate, Blue Point, Long Island, N.Y. **Article:** Ursulines.

*MCCARTHY, RICHARD JOSEPH, SJ, M.A., Ph.L., S.T.L., D.Phil. (Oxon.), Director of the Institute of Arabic Studies in al-Hikma University of Baghdad, Baghdad, Republic of Iraq. **Articles:** Ash'ari, al- (abu al-Hasan 'Ali); Kalam; Mu'tazilites.

MCCARTHY, SALLYANN LESSNER, B.A., Director of Communications; Sisters of St. Francis, Clinton, Iowa. **Article:** Franciscan Sisters—Sisters of St. Francis, Clinton, Iowa (OSF).

MCCARTHY, WILLIAM DANIEL, MM, M.Div., H.E.L., Senior Researcher, Center of Mission Research and Study at Maryknoll. **Articles:** Charles, Pierre; Maryknoll Fathers and Brothers; Maryknoll Mission Association of the Faithful; Orbis Books; Price, Thomas Frederick; Walsh, James Edward; Walsh, James Anthony.

*MCCLAIN, JOSEPH PATRICK, CM, S.T.D., Mary Immaculate Seminary, Northampton, Pa. **Article:** Anointing of the Sick, I (Theology of).

*MCCLELLAND, VINCENT ALAN, M.A., Lecturer in Education, University of Liverpool, England. **Articles:** Baines, Peter Augustine; De Lisle, Ambrose Lisle March Phillipps; Doyle, James Warren; Gladstone, William Ewart; Manning, Henry Edward; Ullathorne, William Bernard.

*MCCOOL, GERALD, SJ, Department of Philosophy, Fordham University, Bronx, N.Y. **Articles:** Death of God Theology; Radical Theology.

MCCORD, H. RICHARD, Ed.D., Executive Director, Secretariat for Family, Laity, Women and Youth, U.S. Conference of Catholic Bishops, Washington, D.C. **Article:** Laity, Formation and Education of.

*MCCORKLE, JOHN, SS, M.A., B.A. in L.S., Instructor in Church History and Librarian, St. Thomas Seminary, Kenmore, Wash. **Article:** Seattle, Archdiocese of.

*MCCORMICK, JOHN PATRICK, Very Rev., SS, S.T.B., Ph.D., Rector, Theological College, The Catholic University of America, Washington, D.C. **Articles:** Exsultet Orbis Gaudiis; Festivis Resonent Compita Vocibus; Fortem Virili Pectore; Iam Christus Astra Ascenderat; Iam Sol Recedit Igneus; Iam Toto Subitus Vesper; Pourrat, Pierre.

*MCCORMICK, SISTER M. JOHN ALOYSE, CRSM, Ph.D., Registrar and Instructor in Latin and Greek, Gwynedd-Mercy College, Gwynedd Valley, Pa. **Article:** James of Voragine, Bl.

*MCCORMICK, RICHARD ARTHUR, SJ, M.A., S.T.D., Professor of Moral and Pastoral Theology, Bellarmine School of Theology, North Aurora, Ill. **Articles:** Prizefighting; War, Morality of.

*MCCOY, JOSEPH ALOYSIUS, SM, Ph.D., Director, Marianist Mission and Marianist Promotion Service, Mount St. John, Dayton, Ohio. **Articles:** Jaricot, Pauline; Streit, Robert; Streit, Karl.

*MCCUE, JOHN JOSEPH GERALD, Ph.D., Physicist, Lincoln Laboratory, Massachusetts Institute of Technology, Cambridge, Mass. **Article:** Science (in Antiquity).

*MCCURRY, JAMES, O.F.M.Conv., M.A., National Director of the Militia of Mary Immaculate, Granby, Massachusetts. **Articles:** Czestochowa; Kolbe, Maximilian, St.

MCDADE, JOHN, SJ, Ph.D., Principal, Heythrop College, London, England. **Article:** Heythrop College.

*MCDERMOTT, ERIC, SJ, M.A., Associate Professor of History, Georgetown University, Washington, D.C. **Articles:** Aikenhead, Mary; Anglican Communion; Anglicanism; Broad Church; Galvin, Edward J.; Griffin, Bernard William; High Church; Latitudinarianism; Low Church; McAuley, Catherine Elizabeth; Thirty-Nine Articles.

MCDERMOTT, ROSE, SSJ, J.C.D., Associate Professor of Canon Law, The Catholic University of America, Washington, D.C. **Articles:** Cloister, Canonical Rules for; Consecrated Life (Canon Law); Religious, Constitutions of; Woman, Canon Law on.

*MCDONAGH, ENDA, Professor of Moral Theology, Director of Postgraduate Studies in Theology, St. Patrick's College, Maynooth, Ireland. **Articles:** Fundamental Option; Mortal Sin.

*MCDONAGH, FRANCIS, Brazil specialist for the Catholic Institute for International Relations, 1987–1995; Communications Officer for OXFAM, Recife, Brazil. **Article:** Consejo Episcopal Latinoamericano (CELAM).

MCDONAGH, SISTER KATHLEEN, IWBS, M.S., M.A., Director, Charism Office, Incarnate Word Convent, Corpus Christi, Tex.; Director, Office of Consecrated Life, Diocese of Corpus Christi. **Article:** Incarnate Word and Blessed Sacrament, Congregation of the.

MCDONALD, DEDRA S. [BIRZER], Ph.D., Lecturer in History, Hillsdale College, Hillsdale, Mich. **Article:** Colorado, Catholic Church in.

MCDONALD, SISTER GRACE, Ph.D., Historian, St. Rose Convent, La Crosse, Wis. **Article:** Franciscan Sisters—Congregation of the Sisters of the Third Order of St. Francis of Perpetual Adoration (FSPA).

*MCDONALD, JOHN JAMES, OP, S.T.Lr., S.T.D., S.T.M., Professor and Chairman of the Department of Systematic Theology, Aquinas Institute School of Theology, Dubuque, Iowa; Editor, *Cross and Crown*. **Article:** Possessor in Good, Bad, or Dubious Faith.

*MCDONALD, SISTER MARY FRANCIS, OP, Ph.D., Professor of Classics, Mount St. Mary-on-the-Hudson, Newburgh, N.Y. **Article:** Phoenix.

*MCDONNELL, ERNEST WILLIAM, Ph.D., Professor of History, Rutgers University, New Brunswick, N.J. **Articles:** Apocalyptic Movements; Apostolici; Beguines and Beghards; Isabelle of France, Bl.; Jacques de Vitry; Ortlibarii; Peter of Bruys; Petrobrusians.

*MCDONNELL, KILIAN, OSB, S.T.D., President, Institute for Ecumenical and Cultural Research, Collegeville, Minn. **Articles:** Baptism of the Lord [part 1]; Charismatic Renewal, Catholic.

*MCDONNELL, MARIAN E., M.F.A., Brighton, Boston, Mass. **Article:** Marquette League.

*MCDONOUGH, ELIZABETH, OP, J.C.D., Associate Professor of Canon Law, The Catholic University of America, Washington, D.C. **Article:** Curia, Roman.

*MCELENEY, NEIL JOSEPH, CSP, M.A., S.T.L., S.S.L., Professor of Sacred Scripture, St. Paul's College, Washington, D.C. **Articles:** Chronicler, Biblical; Ezra; Ezra, Book of; Nehemiah, Book of; Nehemiah; Paralipomenon (Chronicles), Books of.

*MCELRATH, DAMIAN P., OFM, B.A., S.T.Lect., Hist. Eccl.D., Professor of Theology, Holy Name College, Washington, D.C. **Articles:** Carmelite Sisters—Carmelite Sisters of Charity; Robinson, Paschal; Schaaf, Valentine Theodore.

*MCELWAIN, HUGH M., OSM, S.T.D., Professor of Dogmatic Theology and Director of Studies, Stonebridge Priory, Lake Bluff, Ill. **Article:** Resurrection of the Dead, 2. Theology of.

*MCENIRY, SISTER BLANCHE MARIE, Ph.D., Professor of History and Chairman of the Department, College of St. Elizabeth, Convent, N.J. **Article:** Mehegan, Mary Xavier, Mother.

*MCENTEE, SISTER M. REGINA, OP, Ph.D., Professor of History and Political Science, Caldwell College for Women, Caldwell, N.J. **Article:** Dominican Sisters—Sisters of St. Dominic of the American Congregation of the Sacred Heart of Jesus (Dominican Sisters of Caldwell, NJ).

*MCENTEGART, BRYAN JOSEPH, Most Rev., M.A., LL.D., L.H.D., Bishop of Brooklyn, N.Y. **Article:** Molloy, Thomas Edmund.

*MCEVENUE, SEAN EDWARD, SJ, M.A. (Theology), S.S.L., Professor of Scripture, Regis College, Willowdale, Ontario, Canada. **Article:** Fonck, Leopold.

*MCFADDEN, THOMAS M., Department of Theology, St. Joseph's College, Philadelphia, Pa. **Articles:** Anthropology, Theological; Brunner, Heinrich Emil; College Theology Society; Gogarten, Friederich; Hominisation.

MCFADDEN, WILLIAM C., SJ, S.T.D., Department of Theology, Georgetown University, Washington, D.C. **Article:** Georgetown University.

*MCGANN, SISTER AGNES GERALDINE, SCN, Ph.D., President, Nazareth College of Kentucky, Nazareth, Ky. **Article:** Spalding, Catherine, Mother.

*MCGANN, SISTER MARY ISIDORE, SHG, M.A., Teacher, St. Peter Claver High School, and Treasurer General of the Community, San Antonio, Tex. **Article:** Holy Spirit and Mary Immaculate, Sisters of the.

*MCGARRAGHY, JOHN JOSEPH, M.A., Assistant Director of Education, Archdiocese of Washington, D.C. **Article:** Censer; Incense [part 1].

*MCGARRAGHY, MARY CATHERINE, A.B., Editorial Assistant, *New Catholic Encyclopedia,* The Catholic University of America, Washington, D.C. **Article:** Beelen, Jan Theodoor.

*MCGARRY, DANIEL DOYLE, Ph.D., Professor of History, St. Louis University, St. Louis, Mo.; Acting Chairman for Research and member, National Board of Trustees and National Executive Committee, Citizens for Educational Freedom; Editor, *Educational Freedom.* **Articles:** Callistus II, Pope; Marbod of Rennes; Mennas, Patriarch of Constantinople; Vergerio, Pier Paolo.

*MCGARRY, PATRICK STEPHEN, FSC, Ph.D., Professor of History and Head of the Department, Manhattan College, New York, N.Y.; Assistant Editor for Early Modern History, *New Catholic Encyclopedia,* The Catholic University of America, Washington, D.C. **Articles:** Arden, Edward; Barton, Elizabeth; Gennings, John; Kastl, Abbey of; Lee, Edward; O'Brien, Terence Albert; O'Reilly, Edmund; Olah, Miklos (Olahus); Parkinson, Anthony; Piccolomini, Alessandro; Plowden, Edmund; Plowden, Charles and Francis; Plunket, Oliver, St.; Pombal, Sebastiao Jose de Carvalho e Mello; Restitution, Edict of; Rich, Richard; Simonetta; Stanyhurst, Richard; Thirty Years' War; Tresham; Wallenstein, Albrecht Eusebius Wenzel von; Westphalia, Peace of; Woodhouse, Thomas, Bl.

*MCGINLEY, MONICA, National Public Relations Director, Medical Mission Sisters, Philadelphia, Pa. **Article:** Dengel, Anna.

*MCGLOIN, JOHN BERNARD, SJ, Ph.D.; Professor of History, University of San Francisco, San Francisco, Calif. **Articles:** Accolti, Michael; Alemany, Joseph Sadoc; Bouchard, James; California, Catholic Church in; Dunne, Peter Masten; Nobili, John; Ravalli, Antonio.

*MCGLOIN, JOSEPH THADDEUS, SJ, M.A., writer, retreat master, and teacher, Jesuit Residence, Minneapolis, Minn. **Article:** Lord, Daniel Aloysius.

*MCGLYNN, JAMES VINCENT, SJ, Litt.B., Ph.L., M.A., S.T.L., Ph.D., Dean, Graduate School, University of Detroit, Detroit, Mich. **Article:** Existential Ethics.

*MCGLYNN, THOMAS MATTHEW, OP, B.A., sculptor, Studio Pietrasanta, Pietrasanta, Lucca, Italy. **Article:** Clare Gambacorta, Bl.

*MCGOUGH, COLUMBAN, OCD, S.T.L., Professor of Scripture and Theology, College of Our Lady of Mt. Carmel, Washington, D.C. **Articles:** Carmel, Mount; Horeb, Mount; Lamentations, Book of; Sinai, Mount.

*MCGOVERN, LEO JAMES, SJ, S.T.D., Professor of Sacramental Theology, Weston College, Weston, Mass. **Article:** Filiation.

*MCGRATH, BRENDAN, Very Rev., OSB, M.A., S.T.D., Rector and Professor of Sacred Scripture, St. Procopius Seminary, Lisle, Ill. **Articles:** Elijah; Elisha; Solomon.

*MCGRATH, CUTHBERT, OFM, Ph.D. (N.U.I.), Dublin Institute of Advanced Study, Dublin, Ireland; Lecturer, University College of North Wales, Bangor, Wales. **Articles:** Acca of Hexham, St.; Boyle, Abbey of; Clonmacnois, Monastery of; Culdees; Daig MacCairill, St.; Finan of Lindisfarne, St.; Frigidian of Lucca, St.; Gall, St.; Indrechtach, St.; Iona (Hy), Abbey of; Ita of Killeedy, St.; Jarrow, Abbey of; Kells, Abbey of; Laudabiliter; Lawrence O'Toole, St.; Lismore, Abbey of; Malachy, St.; Marianus Scotus; Petronax of Brescia, St.; Ronan (Rumon), St.; Roscrea, Abbey of; Senan, St.

*MCGRATH, JOHN JOSEPH, A.B., LL.B., J.C.D., Associate Professor of Comparative Law and Staff Editor for Canon and Civil Law, *New Catholic Encyclopedia,* The Catholic University of America, Washington, D.C.; Fulbright Lecturer on Comparative Law, Faculty of Law, University of Chile, Santiago, Chile (1965–66). **Article:** Patriarchate, I: Historical Developments.

*MCGRATH, MOTHER MARY CHARLES, OSU, M.A., Superior of Ursuline Sisters, Paola, Kans. **Article:** Ursulines.

*MCGRATH, PATRICK VINCENT, M.A., Reader in History, University of Bristol, England. **Articles:** Allen, William; Elizabeth I, Queen of England; Tootell, Hugh (Charles Dodd).

*MCGRATH, RICHARD HENRY, S.T.D., Professor of Theology and Head of the Department, Villa Madonna College, Covington, Ky. **Articles:** Concubine (in the Bible); Levirate Marriage (in the Bible).

*MCGUCKIN, DENIS ANTHONY, OFM, M.A., M.L.S., Professor of Homiletics and Librarian, Holy Name College, Franciscan House of Studies, Washington, D.C. **Articles:** Dominicus Germanus; Meistermann, Barnabas; Quaresmio, Francesco.

*MCGUINESS, JOSEPH IGNATIUS, OP, M.A., S.T.D., S.T.Lr., Ph.D., S.T.M., Chairman, Department of Theology, Marymount Manhattan College, New York, N.Y. **Article:** Sin (Theology of).

*MCGUINNESS, BERNARD FRANCIS, M.A., B.Phil., Fellow and Praelector in Philosophy and University Lecturer in Philosophy, Queen's College, Oxford, England. **Articles:** Russell, Bertrand; Wittgenstein, Ludwig.

*MCGUIRE, JAMES DANIEL, OAR, J.C.D., Lector in Canon Law, Provincial Residence, Order of Recollects of St. Augustine, West Orange, N.J. **Article:** Age (Impediment to Marriage).

*MCGUIRE, MARTIN RAWSON PATRICK, Ph.D., L.H.D., Professor of Greek and Latin and of Ancient History and Senior Editor, *New Catholic Encylopedia,* The Catholic University of America, Washington, D.C.; Coeditor, The Catholic University of America Patristic Studies; Coeditor, The Catholic University of America Studies in Mediaeval and Renaissance Latin Language and Literature; Associate Editor, *Catholic Historical Review;* Chairman, Executive Committee, Mediaeval and Renaissance Latin Translations and Commentaries. **Articles:** Abraxas; Acrostic; Ad Bestias; Adrianus; Ambrose, St.; Amidism; Annals and Chronicles; Apollonius of Tyana; Asterius the Sophist; Baths; Bentley, Richard; Bertha of Val d'Or, St.; Bury, John Bagnell; Celsus; Celtic Religion; Chain of Causation; Chelidonia, St.; Chronographer of 354; Church and State [part 1]; Cicero, Marcus Tullius; Cyprus, The Catholic Church in; Damasus I, Pope, St.; Diana (Artemis) of the Ephesians; Divination; Egino, Bl.; Epigraphy, Christian; Ferrandus of Carthage; Fructuosus of Tarragona, St.; Gaudentius of Brescia, St.; Germain of Auxerre, St.; Gratian, Roman Emperor; Henry of Huntingdon; Higher Criticism; History and Historicity (Geschichtlichkeit); Italy, The Catholic Church in, 2. 1500 to 1789; Joan of Santa Lucia, Bl.; John the Grammarian, of Caesarea; Joscio, Bl.; Junilius Africanus; Laetus, St.; Laudomar, St.; Lebreton, Jules; Leobin of Chartres, St.; Lucifer of Cagliari; Marcellus, SS.; Martin of Braga, St.; Maximus of Turin, St.; Morandus, St.; Nicetas of Remesiana; Numerology; Odysseus; Ordeal [part 1]; Pagan; Peli-

can; Phillimore, John S.; Pliny the Younger; Poeta Saxo; Precious Stones; Prostitution (Sacred); Raymond of Roda-Barbastro, St.; Roman Religion; Rosalia, St.; Satyrus of Milan, St.; Sophronius, St.; Sortes Homericae, Vergilianae, Biblicae; Spee, Friedrich von; Stones, Sacred; Symmachus, Quintus Aurelius; Theophilus (Rugerus); Triumph, Roman; Vergil (Publius Vergilius Maro); Vestal Virgins; Viventiolus, St.; Wine, Liturgical Use Of; Wolfhard of Verona, St.; Zabarella, Francesco.

*MCHUGH, SISTER MARY ANGELA, HHS, M.A., Chairman, Committee on Standards for CCD Methods Courses, New York, N.Y.; teacher training in catechetics and writing in the field. **Article:** Helpers of the Holy Souls.

*MCHUGH, SISTER MARY XAVERIA, SSMO, A.B., Instructor in History, English, and Biology, Marylhurst College Extension, Marylhurst, Ore.; Instructor in English, St. Mary of the Valley Academy. **Article:** St. Mary of Oregon, Sisters of.

*MCINERNY, RALPH MATTHEW, M.A., Ph.L., Ph.D., Associate Professor of Philosophy, University of Notre Dame, Notre Dame, Ind. **Articles:** Absolute, The; Being; Categories of Being; De Koninck, Charles; Dualism; Involuntarity; Voluntarity.

MCINERNY, RALPH, Ph.D., Michael J. Grace Professor of Philosophy. Director, Jacques Maritain Institute, University of Notre Dame, Notre Dame, Ind. **Article:** Pius XII, Pope.

MCINTYRE, SHEILA MARIE, OP, Ed.M., Secretary General, St. Mary of the Springs, Columbus, Ohio. **Article:** Dominican Sisters—Dominican Sisters, St. Mary of the Springs (Columbus, Ohio).

*MCIVER, MOTHER M. EMMANUEL, OSU, Ph.D., Assistant Professor of Theology, College of New Rochelle, N.Y. **Articles:** Elizabeth, St.; Magnificat (Canticle of Mary); Visitation of Mary.

*MCKENNA, CHARLES HUGH, OP, M.A., B.Litt., LL.D., Vice President in Charge of Community Affairs, Providence College, Providence, R.I. **Article:** Vitoria, Francisco de.

*MCKENNA, JOSEPH PERRY, B.S., Ph.D., Professor of Economics, Boston College, Chestnut Hill, Mass.; Visiting Professor, Bologna Center, School of Advanced International Studies, Johns

Hopkins University, Baltimore, Md. **Article:** Malthus, Thomas Robert.

*MCKENNA, OWEN PATRICK, SJ, M.A., S.T.L., formerly Associate Professor of History, Holy Cross College, Worcester, Mass. (deceased July 30, 1965). **Article:** Lyons, Councils of.

*MCKENNA, STEPHEN JOSEPH, CSSR, Ph.D., Associate Professor of History, Catholic University of Puerto Rico, Ponce, P.R. **Articles:** Adoptionism; Asterius of Amasea; Bachiarius; Benedict III, Pope; Benedict V, Pope; Benedict VI, Pope; Benedict IV, Pope; Benedict VII, Pope; Ennodius, Magnus Felix; Hilary of Poitiers, St.; Ildefonsus of Toledo, St.; John XIV, Pope; John XII, Pope; John XIII, Pope; John X, Pope; Leander of Seville, St.; Orosius; Pacian of Barcelona, St.; Pelagius and Pelagianism; Semi-Pelagianism.

*MCKENZIE, JOHN LAWRENCE, SJ, M.A., S.T.D., Professor of History, Loyola University, Chicago, Ill. **Article:** Amorrites; Diaspora, Jewish.

*MCKEON, RICHARD PETER, Ph.D., Litt.D., Dr. (h.c. Aix-Marseilles), L.H.D., Distinguished Service Professor of Philosophy and Greek, University of Chicago, Chicago, Ill. **Articles:** Analysis and Synthesis; Methodology (Philosophy); Synthesis.

*MCKEOUGH, SISTER MARY PAUL, OP, M.A., Ph.D., President-Dean, St. Dominic College, St. Charles, Ill. **Articles:** Barry, Gerald, Mother; Dominican Sisters—Congregation of the Most Holy Rosary (Adrian, Mich).

*MCKEOWN, LEO MICHAEL, parish priest, Newtonards, County Down, Northern Ireland. **Article:** O'Devany, Conor, Bl.

*MCLAUGHLIN, MARY MARTIN, Ph.D., Assistant Professor of History, Vassar College, Poughkeepsie, N.Y. **Article:** Gregory of Bergamo.

*MCLAUGHLIN, SISTER MARY RAYMOND, OSB, Ph.D., Certificate, Pontificium Institutum "Regina Mundi," Rome, Italy; Professor, College of St. Scholastica, Duluth, Minn. **Article:** Alain (Emile Auguste Chartier).

*MCLAUGHLIN, TERENCE PATRICK, CSB, J.C.D., Professor of History of Canon and Civil Law, Pontifical Institute of Mediaeval Studies, Toronto, Ontario, Canada. **Articles:** Bazianus; Joannes Faventinus; Paucapalea; Simon of Bisignano; Summa Parisiensis.

*MCLEAN, GEORGE FRANCIS, OMI, Ph.B., Ph.L., S.T.L., Ph.D., Associate Professor of Philosophy, The Catholic University of America, and Professor of Philosophy, Oblate College, Washington, D.C.; Secretary, American Catholic Philosophical Association. **Article:** Metaphysics.

MCMAHON, CHRISTOPHER, M.A., Assistant Professor, Department of Religious Studies, Mount Marty College, Yankton, S.D. **Articles:** Andrew, Apostle, St.; Bartholomew, Apostle, St.; Matthias, Apostle, St.; Thomas, Apostle, St.

MCMAHON, DEIRDRE, Professor of History, Mary Immaculate College, University of Limerick, Ireland. **Article:** McQuaid, John Charles.

MCMAHON, KEVIN, Ph.D., Professor, Department of Theology, Saint Anselm College, Manchester, N.H. **Articles:** Monogenism and Polygenism; Original Sin [part 2].

*MCMAHON, NORBERT, OH, St. John of God's Hospital, Scorton, Richmond, Yorks, England. **Articles:** Hospitallers of St. John of God; Hospitallers of St. John of God, Martyrs of the, BB.

MCMAHON, PATRICK, OCarm, M.T.S., Ph.D., President, Institutum Carmelitanum, Rome, Italy. **Article:** Carmelite Spirituality.

*MCMAHON, THOMAS FRANCIS, CSV, Professor, Socio-Legal Studies Department, Loyola University of Chicago, Chicago, Ill. **Article:** Indifferentism.

*MCMAHON, THOMAS FRANCIS, CSV, S.T.D., Dean of Studies and Professor of Moral Theology, Viatorian Seminary, Washington, D.C. **Article:** Happiness; Secularism.

*MCMANAMIN, FRANCIS GERARD, SJ, Ph.D., Instructor in History, Loyola College, Baltimore, Md. **Articles:** Augustinis, Aemilio de; Muldoon, Peter James; White, Andrew; Williams, John Joseph.

*MCMANUS, FREDERICK R., A.B., J.C.D., Associate Professor of Canon Law, The Catholic University of America, Washington, D.C.; Consultor, Pontifical Preparatory Commission on the Sacred Liturgy for Vatican Council II; *Peritus,* Vatican Council II; Member, Advisory Council, National Liturgical Conference. **Article:** Rites, Congregation of.

*MCMANUS, FREDERICK R., Vice Provost and Dean of Graduate Studies, Catholic University of America, Washington, D.C. **Articles:** Altar in Christian Liturgy; Consilium; Divine Worship and the Discipline of the Sacraments, Congregation for; Tabernacle.

*MCMANUS, MSGR. FREDERICK R., J.C.D., LL.D., Editor, *The Jurist,* Professor of Canon Law, The Catholic University of America, Washington, D.C. **Articles:** Bugnini, Annibale; English Language Liturgical Consultation (ELLC); Sapientia Christiana; Winstone, Harold E.

*MCMANUS, FREDERICK R., J.C.D., LL.D., Professor Emeritus and Professorial Lecturer in Canon Law, The Catholic University of America, Washington, D.C. **Article:** Profession of Faith and Oath of Fidelity.

*MCMANUS, THOMAS J., S.T.L., Adjunct Professor, Saint Charles Borromeo Seminary, Overbrook, Pa. **Article:** Krol, John Joseph.

MCMICHAEL, STEVEN J., OFMConv., S.T.D., Assistant Professor of Theology, University of Saint Thomas, Saint Paul, Minn. **Article:** Alonso da Espina.

*MCMORROW, GEORGE JOSEPH, Ph.D., Professor of Philosophy and Chairman of the Philosophy-Theology Department, Nazareth College, Kalamazoo, Mich. **Articles:** Authority; Simon, Yves Rene Marie.

*MCMULLIN, ERNAN, B.Sc., B.D., L.Ph., Ph.D., Associate Professor of Philosophy, University of Notre Dame, Notre Dame, Ind.; Visiting Lecturer, University of Minnesota, and Research Associate, Minnesota Center for Philosophy of Science, Minneapolis, Minn. **Article:** Matter, Philosophy of.

*MCMURRY, VINCENT DE PAUL, SS, M.A., S.T.L., Prefect of Discipline, St. Thomas Seminary, Louisville, Ky. **Articles:** David, John Baptist Mary; Kentucky, Catholic Church in; Verot, Jean Pierre Augustin Marcellin.

MCNALLY, MICHAEL J., Ph.D., Professor of Church History, St. Charles Borromeo Seminary—Overbrook, Wynnewood, Pa. **Article:** Florida, Catholic Church in.

*MCNALLY, ROBERT EDWIN, SJ, S.T.L., Ph.D., Professor of Church History, Fordham University, New York, N.Y. **Articles:** Ember Days; Exegesis, Biblical, 5 From the Patristic to the Medieval; Exegesis, Biblical, 6 Monastic Exegesis.

*MCNAMARA, ANNE MARIE, Newton College of the Sacred Heart, Newton, Mass. (deceased May 25, 1964). **Article:** Christian Education, Religious of.

*MCNAMARA, MARTIN JOSEPH, MSC, S.T.L., S.S.L., S.S.D., Sacred Heart College, Moyne Park, Ballyglunin, County Galway, Ireland. **Articles:** Bel and the Dragon; Daniel; Daniel, Book of; Seventy Weeks of Years; Susanna; Targums.

*MCNAMARA, ROBERT FRANCIS, A.M., S.T.L., Professor of Church History, Lecturer in History of Christian Art and Instructor in Italian, St. Bernard's Seminary, Rochester, N.Y. **Articles:** Crib, Christmas; Edes, Ella B.; Heortology; Lambert, Louis Aloysius; Macnutt, Francis Augustus; McQuaid, Bernard John; North American College; Schulte, Augustine Joseph; Schuster, Alfredo Ildephonse, Bl.; Stational Church; Trusteeism.

*MCNAMEE, MAURICE BASIL, SJ, S.T.L., Ph.D., Professor of English, St. Louis University, St. Louis, Mo. **Article:** Beowulf.

*MCNASPY, CLEMENT JAMES, SJ, M.A., Ph.L., S.T.L., Mus.D., Associate Editor, *America* and *Catholic Mind,* New York, N.Y. **Articles:** Liturgical Music, History of, 11: Second Vatican Council; Spirituals.

*MCNASPY, CLEMENT JAMES, SJ, University Professor, Loyola University, New Orleans, La. **Articles:** Lavanoux, Maurice Emile; Twomey, Louis J.

*MCNEELY, JOHN HAMILTON, Ph.D., Associate Professor of History, Texas Western College of the University of Texas, El Paso, Tex. **Article:** Perpetual Adoration of the Blessed Sacrament, Nuns of the.

*MCNEELY, SISTER THERESE MARIE, SSpS, M.A., M.R.E., Mistress of Junior Sisters, Motherhouse; Teacher of Ascetical Theology, Holy Ghost College, and of American History, Holy Ghost Academy, Techny, Ill. **Article:** Holy Spirit Missionary Sisters.

MCNEIL, BETTY ANN, DC, MSW, Archivist, Daughters of Charity of Saint Vincent de Paul, Saint Joseph's Provincial House, Emmitsburg, Md. Secretary, Vincentian Studies Institute of the United States, DePaul University, Chicago, Ill. **Articles:** Seton, Elizabeth Ann Bayley, St.; Sisters of Charity, Federation of.

*MCNEIL, SISTER MARY GERMAINE, CSJ, Ph.D., Chairman, Department of Classical Languages, and Assistant to the President, Mt. St. Mary's College, Los Angeles, Calif. **Articles:** Andrew of Peschiera, Bl.; Andrew of Rinn, Bl.; Christina of Hamm, Bl.; Christina of Spoleto, Bl.; Eugene II (III) of Toledo, St.; Giustiniani; Jesuati; John Colombini, Bl.; Lestonnac, Jeanne de, St.; Louise of Savoy, Bl.; Simon Ballachi, Bl.; Zita, St.; Frangipani.

*MCNEILL, JOHN THOMAS, B.A., B.D., Ph.D., D.D., LL.D., Professor Emeritus of Church History, Union Theological Seminary, New York, N.Y. **Articles:** Amyraut, Moise; Gomarus, Franciscus; Olivetan, Pierre Robert; Viret, Pierre.

*MCNICHOLL, AMBROSE JAMES, OP, S.T.Lr., S.T.L., Ph.D., Professor, Faculty of Philosophy, Pontifical University of St. Thomas, Rome, Italy; Pius XII Graduate Institute of Fine Art, Florence, Italy. **Articles:** Art, 2. Art and Christianity; Spirit; Spiritualism.

*MCNICKLE, WILLIAM D'ARCY, Executive Director, American Indian Development, Inc., Boulder, Colo. **Article:** LaFarge [John Louis Bancel (1865–1938)].

*MCPADDEN, AGNES BYRNE, M.SS.W., A.S.W., Associate Editor for Social Sciences, *New Catholic Encyclopedia*, The Catholic University of America, Washington, D.C. **Articles:** Hospitals, History of, 2. 1500 to Present; McGowan, Raymond Augustine; Montes Pietatis.

*MCPOLIN, JAMES CHRISTOPHER, SJ, B.A., Diploma in Education, Ph.L., S.T.L., Pontifical Biblical Institute, Rome, Italy. **Article:** Power, Edmund.

*MCREAVY, LAWRENCE LESLIE, Rt. Rev., M.A., J.C.D., Professor of Fundamental Moral Theology and General Canon Law, Ushaw College, Durham, England; *Peritus*, Vatican Council II. **Article:** Pacifism.

*MCREDMOND, LOUIS, M.A., Barrister-atLaw; Dublin Correspondent of *The Tablet* (London). **Article:** Ireland, The Catholic Church in.

*MCROBERTS, DAVID, Very Rev., S.T.L., Chaplain to St. Charles' Private Hospital, Carstairs, Lanarkshire, England; Editor; *Catholic Directory for the Clergy and Laity in Scotland, Western Catholic Calendar, Saint Andrew Annual, Innes Review.* **Articles:** Barclay, John (1734–1798); Cameronians; Covenanters; Diamond, Charles; Keane,

Augustus Henry; MacPherson, John; Melville, Andrew; Smith, James; Wishart, George.

*MCSHANE, EDWARD DANIEL, SJ, S.T.L., Hist.Eccl.D., Professor of Church History at Alma College, Los Gatos, Calif., at Pontifical Faculty and School of Sacred Theology, University of Santa Clara, Santa Clara, Calif., and at the Graduate Theological Union, Berkeley, Calif.; Staff Editor for Renaissance and Reformation Church History, *New Catholic Encyclopedia*, The Catholic University of America, Washington, D.C. **Articles:** Alberto Castellani; Alegambe, Philippe; Anne of Jesus, Ven.; Anne of St. Bartholomew, Bl.; Benediktbeuren, Abbey of; Bernis, Francois Joachim de Pierre de; Bonne-Esperance, Monastery of; Borghese; Brouwer, Christoph; Bullinger, Heinrich; Calas, Jean; Castel Sant'Angelo; Catrou, Francois; Charles V, Holy Roman Emperor; Clement XIII, Pope; Clement XIV, Pope; Diaz Manuel; Divine Love, Oratory of; Emser, Hieronymus; Faber, Johann Augustanus; Farlati, Daniele; Feneberg, Johann Michael; Gattinara, Mercurino Arborio di; Gembloux, Abbey of; Gretser, Jakob; Hardouin, Jean; Heresy, History of, 3. Modern Period; Hugo, Charles Hyacinthe; Interims; Jeningen, Philipp, Ven.; Julius III, Pope; Madruzzo; Maimbourg, Louis; Malaspina, Germanico; Marcellus II, Pope; Marmoutier, Abbey of; Miraeus, Aubert (Le Mire); Nielsen, Laurentius; Nunes Barreto, Joao; Orval, Abbey of; Rodriguez, Alphonsus, St.; Rubino, Antonio; Schatzgeyer, Kaspar; Swiss Guards; Thyraus, Hermann; Trebnitz, Abbey of; Truchsess von Waldburg, Otto and Gebhard; Urban VII, Pope; Visdelou, Claude de; Zwinglianism.

MCVEY, THOMAS CHRYS, OP, S.T.L., Regent of Studies, Dominican ViceProvince of Pakistan. **Article:** Pakistan, The Catholic Church in.

*MEAD, JUDE, CP, M.A., LL.D., Retreat Master, St. Gabriel's Monastery, Brighton, Mass.; Instructor in Scripture, Mt. St. Joseph College, Wakefield, R.I. **Articles:** Crown of Thorns (Relic); Passion of Christ, II (Devotion to).

*MEADE, JOAQUÍN FELIPE, engaged in historical research, Mexico City, Mexico. **Article:** Olmos, Andres de.

*MEAGHER, JOHN JOSEPH, B.A., assistant parish priest, St. Catherine's Church,

Dublin, Ireland. **Articles:** Alen, John; Byrne, Edmund; Fleming, Thomas; Inge, Hugh; Murphy, John; Nagle, Nano (Honoria); Nary, Cornelius; Tanner, Edmund.

*MEAGHER, SISTER LUANNE, OSB, Ph.D., Associate Professor of Classics, College of St. Catherine, and Juniorate, St. Paul's Priory, St. Paul, Minn. **Articles:** Adela, St.; Gunthildis, SS.; Hildegard of Kempten, Bl.; Irmina, St.; Thecla, St.

*MEAGHER, PAUL KEVIN, OP, S.T.L., S.T.M., Blackfriars, Cambridge, England; Coeditor in Chief, McGraw-Hill translation of St. Thomas Aquinas's *Summa Theologiae;* Staff Editor for Moral Theology, *New Catholic Encyclopedia,* The Catholic University of America, Washington, D.C. **Articles:** Amort, Eusebius; Angelo Carletti di Chivasso, Bl.; Authority, Civil; Avarice; Benavides, Miguel de; Cult (Worship); Drunkenness; Elizalde, Miguel de; Faith, 3. Theology of [part 2]; Fidelity; Gluttony; Idolatry; Injury, Moral; Intention, Purity of; Law, Divine Positive; Laws, Conflict of; Liberality, Virtue of; Motive, Unconscious; Neophyte; Novena; Presumption; Profanity; Promise, Moral Obligation of a; Rash Judgment; Reason, Use of; Reguera, Emmanuel de la; Salas, Juan de; Sanchez, Juan; Sanction; Sasserath, Rainer; Sayer, Robert Gregory (Seare); Scavini, Pietro; Schwane, Joseph; Simplicity, Virtue of; Sin Against the Holy Spirit; Sobriety; Terill, Anthony (Bonville); Theologia Germanica; Tithes; Torres, Luis de; Torture; Tournely, Honore de; Trithemius, Johannes (Tritheim); Vann, Gerald; Vega, Andreas de; Vengeance; Veronica; Vives, Juan Bautista; Ysambert, Nicolas.

*MEAGHER, RICHARD BYRNE, SJ, M.A., S.T.L., missionary in Taiwan (Formosa), Professor of Chemistry, Taiwan Provincial Chung Hsing University, Taichung, Taiwan; Auxiliary Civilian Chaplain, U.S. Navy. **Articles:** Auger, Edmond; Bourdaloue, Louis.

MEAGHER, TIMOTHY J., Ph.D., University Archivist, The Catholic University of America, Washington, D.C. **Article:** Archives, U. S. Catholic.

*MEDINA-ASCENSIO, LUIS, SJ, Eccl.Hist.D., Professor of Church History and History of Mexico and Librarian of Central Library, Montezuma Seminary (Mexican National Semi-

nary), Montezuma, N.Mex. **Articles:** Belaunzaran, Jose Maria de Jesus; Gillow y Zavalza, Eulogio Gregorio; Labastida y Davalos, Pelagio Antonio de.

*MEEHAN, DENIS MOLAISE, OSB, B.D., S.T.L., M.A., St. Andrew's Priory, Valyermo, Calif. **Article:** Macrina, SS.

*MEEHAN, FRANCIS, CSSR, Lector in Church History and Patrology, Mount St. Alphonsus, Esopus, N.Y. **Articles:** Hilarion, St.; Honorius, Roman Emperor.

*MEEHAN, FRANCIS X., S.T.D., Our Lady of Mt. Carmel Church, Doylestown, Pa. **Article:** Pacifism.

*MEEKING, MOST REVEREND BASIL, S.T.D., Bishop Emeritus of Christchurch, New Zealand. **Article:** Willebrands, Johannes Gerardus Maria.

*MEGIVERN, JAMES J., CM, B.A. (Philosophy), S.T.D., Professor of Sacred Scripture, Mary Immaculate Seminary, Northampton, Pa. **Article:** Liturgical Rites.

MEGIVERN, JAMES J., Th.D., S.S.L., Professor Emeritus of Philosophy and Religion, University of North Carolina at Wilmington, Wilmington, N.C. **Article:** Capital Punishment.

*MEIJER, PAUL HERMAN ERNST, Ph.D., Professor of Physics, The Catholic University of America, Washington, D.C. **Article:** Uncertainty Principle.

*MEILACH, MICHAEL DAVID, OFM, A.A., M.A., Editor, *Cord,* St. Bonaventure, N.Y. **Articles:** Jesus Christ (in Theology) 3. Special Questions; 12. Primacy; Quas primas.

*MEINBERG, CLOUD HERMAN, OSB, B.S. in Architecture, B.A., Teacher of Art and Architecture, St. John's University, Collegeville, Minn. **Articles:** Cornerstone, Church; Cross.

*MELLON, KNOX, JR., M.A., Chairman, Department of History, Immaculate Heart College, Los Angeles, Calif. **Article:** Burnett, Peter Hardeman.

*MELVILLE, ANNABELLE M., Ph.D., Commonwealth Professor of History, State College, Bridgewater, Mass. **Articles:** Cabrini, Francis Xavier, St.; Carroll, John; Cheverus, Jean Louis Lefebvre de; Maynard, Theodore; Romagne, James Rene.

MENACHE, SOPHIA, Ph.D., Life Member of Clare Hall, University of Cambridge,

Cambridge, United Kingdom. Professor of Medieval History, University of Haifa, Haifa, Israel. **Articles:** Clement V, Pope; Honorius IV, Pope; John XXII, Pope; Nicholas IV, Pope; Nicholas III, Pope.

*MENARD, EUSÈBE MARIE, Very Rev., OFM, Founder and Superior General, Missionaries of the Holy Apostles, Washington, D.C. **Article:** Missionaries of the Holy Apostles.

*MENATO, MOTHER AGNES, FdeC, B.A. (Hons. English), Diploma of Education, Headmistress, Mater Dei College, Welwyn Garden City, Herts, England. **Article:** Canossa, Maddalena Gabriella, St.

*MENDELS, JUDICA IGNATIA H., Ph.D., Professor of German, Canisius College, Buffalo, N.Y. **Article:** Alberdingk Thijm, Josephus Albertus.

*MENDÍA, SISTER EULOGIA, FSJ, Religious Hijas de San Jose, Gerona, Spain. **Article:** St. Joseph (Gerona), Daughters of.

*MENTAG, JOHN VIRGIL, SJ, Ph.D., Assistant to the President, Loyola University, Chicago, Ill. **Articles:** Aleni, Giulio; Bouvet, Joachim; Herdtrich, Christian Wolfgang; Le Gobien, Charles; Mailla, Joseph Anne Marie Moyria de; Rho, Giacomo.

*MERCIER, SISTER LUCILLE DU SACRE-COEUR, ASV, M.A., M.R.E., Teacher, Anna Maria College, Paxton, Mass. **Article:** Maistre, Joseph Marie de.

*MERCURIO, ROGER JOHN, CP, S.T.L., S.S.L., Rector, Mother of Good Counsel Seminary, Warrenton, Mo. **Articles:** Centurion; Pharisees; Sadducees; Scribes (in the Bible); Tetrarch.

*MERINO, LUIS, Ph.D., Secretary-General and Registrar, San Agustin University, Iloilo, Philippine Islands. **Article:** Urdaneta, Andres de.

*MERKEL, INGRID GERTRUD, M.A., Instructor in German, Institute of Languages and Linguistics, Georgetown University, Washington, D.C. **Article:** Herder, Johann Gottfried von.

*MERTENS, CLÉMENT ROBERT, SJ, Ph.L., S.T.L., Docteur de Pol.Sc. et Soc., Professor of Social Ethics and Economics, Jesuit Philosophical College, Louvain, Belgium; Founder and President, Institute of Social Sciences, Gregorian University, Rome, Italy. **Article:** Fallon, Valere.

*MERTON, THOMAS, (Father Louis, OCSO), M.A., LL.D., Novice Master,

Abbey of Gethsemani, Trappist, Ky.; author. **Article:** Gethsemani, Abbey of.

*MERZBACHER, FRIEDRICH PHILIPP, Dr.iur., Dr.Phil., Würzburg, Germany. **Article:** Witchcraft.

*MESEGUER FERNÁNDEZ, JUAN, OFM, Eccl.Hist.D., Licentiate in Philosophy and Letters, Diploma, Vatican Library School, member, Editorial Board, *Archivo Ibero-Americano,* and Professor of Religion, Colegio de la B.V.M., Madrid, Spain. **Articles:** Quinones, Francisco de; Ximenez de Cisneros, Francisco; Perez, Juan.

*MESKO, LOUIS, Sch.P., Piarist Fathers, Rome. **Article:** Casani, Pietro, Bl.

*MESNARD, JEAN, Agrégation des Lettres, Professor, Faculty of Letters, University of Bordeaux, France. **Article:** Pascal, Blaise.

MESSBARGER, PAUL R., Ph.D., Professor Emeritus, Department of English, Loyola University of Chicago, Chicago, Ill. **Articles:** Meynell, Alice and Wilfrid; Pornography; West, Morris L.

*MESSNER, JOHANNES, Dr.iur., Dr.oec.publ., Dr.Theol. (h.c.), Dr.rer.pol. (h.c.), Professor Emeritus of General, Political, and Social Ethics, University of Vienna, Austria. **Article:** Communication, Philosophy of; Society [part 1].

*METZGER, CHARLES HENRY, SJ, Ph.D., Professor of History, Bellarmine School of Theology, North Aurora, Ill. **Article:** Quebec Act of 1774.

*MEURGEY DE TUPIGNY, JACQUES PIERRE, Archiviste-Paléographe, Lauréat de l'Institut de France, attaché à la conservation du Musée des Arts décoratifs; Conservateur, Archives Nationale de France; and Conservateur en chef emeritus, Paris, France. **Article:** Heraldry.

*MEYER, BEN FRANKLIN, SJ, A.B., S.T.M., S.S.L., S.T.D., Professor of Ecclesiology, Alma College, Los Gatos, Calif. **Articles:** Expiation (In the Bible); Pentecost.

*MEYER, CARL STAMM, Ph.D., D.D., Professor of Historical Theology and Director of the School for Graduate Studies, Concordia Seminary, St. Louis, Mo. **Articles:** Barclay, Robert; Fox, George; Foxe's Book of Martyrs.

*MEYER, CHARLES ROBERT, M.A., S.T.D., B.S.L.S., Prefect of Theologians and

Professor of Church History, Archeology, Catechetics, and Rites, St. Mary of the Lake Seminary, Mundelein, Ill. **Articles:** Campana, Emilio; Cayet, Pierre Victor; Chalmers, William (Camerarius); Chapt de Rastignac, Armand, Bl.; Charles of the Assumption (Charles de Bryas); Faure, Giovanni Battista; Franzelin, Johannes Baptist; Garet, Jean (Garetius); Habert, Isaac; Haller, Leonhard; Heinrich, Johann Baptist; Henry of Gorkum; Kleutgen, Joseph; Lessius, Leonard; Probst, Ferdinand; Schwetz, Johann Baptist Tapper, Ruard.

*MEYER, HANS GERHARD, Dr.Phil., Professor Emeritus of Philosophy, University of Würzburg, Germany. **Articles:** Hartmann, Eduard von; Materialism.

MEYER, JEAN, OP, Archivist, Dominican Sisters of Hope, Newburgh, N.Y. **Article:** Dominican Sisters—Dominican Sisters of Hope.

*MEYER, ROBERT T., Ph.D., Professor of Celtic and Comparative Philology, The Catholic University of America, Washington, D.C.; Lecturer in Celtic, Jesus College, Oxford, 1965; Member, Editorial Board, *Annuale Mediaevale;* Director, Research Project, Celtic Group, Modern Language Association of America. **Articles:** Adamnan of Iona, St.; Adrian, St.; Andrew of Fiesole, St.; Anthony of Egypt, St.; Bible, Irish Versions; Corbinian of Freising, St.; Deicolus of Lure, St.; Disticha Catonis; Egbert of Iona, St.; Four Masters, Annals of the; Fursey (Furseus), St.; Gerald of Mayo, St.; Lausiac History (Palladius); Maclovius, St.; Neot, St.; Palladius of Helenopolis; Philology; Plummer, Charles.

*MEYERS, HERMAN EMERSON, Artist Diploma in Piano, composer, pianist, teacher, conductor; Professor of Music, The Catholic University of America, Washington, D.C. **Articles:** Paderewski, Ignacy Jan; Toscanini, Artruo.

*MEYERS, JOHN F., President, National Catholic Educational Association, Washington, D.C. **Article:** National Catholic Educational Association.

*MEYVAERT, GEOFFREY PAUL, OSB, Monk of the Solesmes Congregation, Quarr Abbey, Ryde, Isle of Wight, Great Britain. **Article:** Erchempert.

*MICEK, ADAM ANDREW, A.B., S.T.D., Professor of Theology, St. John's Seminary, and Diocesan Director of Vocations, Little Rock, Ark. **Article:** Byrne, Andrew.

*MICHAEL, CHESTER P., Msgr., St. Mary's Seminary and University, Baltimore, Md. **Article:** Murray, John Courtney.

*MICHAUD-QUANTIN, PIERRE R., Diplôme d'Études Supérieures philosophie, Doctorat ès lettres, Diplôme d'École pratique des Hautes Études, Ingénieur, Centre National de la Recherche Scientifique (Section Philosophie), Chief of the Service, Glossaire du Latin philosophique médiéval, Faculté des Lettres, Paris, France. **Articles:** Alcher of Clairvaux; Dialectics in the Middle Ages; Godfrey of Saint-Victor; Walter of Saint-Victor.

*MICHELS, SISTER M. MATTHIAS, OP, M.A., Chairman, Division of Fine Arts, Edgewood College of the Sacred Heart, Madison, Wis. **Article:** Nazarenes (Brotherhood of St. Luke).

*MICHL, JOHANN, Dr.Theol., S.S.L., Professor of Theology, Philosophisch-Theologische Hochschule, Freising (Munich), Germany. **Article:** Angels, 2. Theology of.

*MICK, LAWRENCE, Office for Worship, Dayton, Ohio. **Article:** Sponsors.

*MIGUEL I VERGÉS, JOSE MARIA, Mexico City, Mexico. **Article:** Mier, Servando Teresa de.

*MIKLAS, SEBASTIAN F., OFMCap, Capuchin College, Washington, D.C. **Article:** Padre Pio (Francesco Forgione), St.

MIKOLAJEK, LISA V., Communications Specialist, Sisters of the Holy Family of Nazareth, St. Joseph Province, Pittsburgh, Pa. **Articles:** Holy Family of Nazareth, Sisters of the; Siedliska, Franciszka, Bl.

*MILBURN, DAVID, Docteur en Sciences Historiques, Senior History Master, Ushaw College, Durham, England. **Articles:** Barberi, Dominic, Bl.; Bourne, Francis; Godfrey, William; Hallahan, Margaret Mary; Hinsley, Arthur; Poynter, William; Taunton, Ethelred Luke; Vaughan, Herbert Alfred; Vaughan, Bernard John; Ward, Bernard.

*MILLER, DAVID, Department of Philosophy, University of Warwick, Coventry, U.K. **Article:** Popper, Karl.

*MILLER, DEAN ARTHUR, Ph.D., Assistant Professor of History, University of Rochester, Rochester, N.Y. **Articles:** Irene, Byzantine Empress; Paul II, Patriarch of Constantinople; Sergius I, Patriarch of Constantinople.

*MILLER, JOAN M., Pittsburgh, Pa. **Article:** Structuralism.

*MILLER, JOHN HAROLD, CSC, Ph.B., S.T.D., Associate Professor of Theology, University of Notre Dame, Notre Dame, Ind.; Staff Editor for Liturgy, *New Catholic Encyclopedia,* The Catholic University of America, Washington, D.C.; member, Board of Directors, North American Liturgical Conference. **Articles:** Bonnetty, Augustin; Bunderius, Jan (van den Bundere); Coeffeteau, Nicolas; Crucifix; Espence, Claude Togniel de; Goar, Jacques; Illyricus, Thomas; Liturgy; Rogation Days.

*MILLER, LORAN DONALD, OFMCap, Capuchin Seminary of St. Anthony, Marathon, Wis. **Article:** Magni Valeriano.

*MILLER, LOUIS GERARD, CSSR, B.A., Editor, *Liguorian,* Liguori, Mo. **Articles:** Adultery; Fornication; Incest; Scandal.

*MILLER, MOTHER M. GONZAGA, OSF, Ph.D., Mistress of Junior Professed Sisters, Stella Niagara Seminary and Stella Niagara Cadet School, Stella Niagara, N.Y. **Article:** Franciscan Sisters—Sisters of St. Francis of Penance and Christian Charity (OSF).

*MILLER, NORBERT HAROLD, OFMCap, M.A., Professor of Homiletics and Church History, Capuchin College, Washington, D.C. **Articles:** Persico, Ignatius; Whelan, Charles Maurice.

MILLER, R. BRUCE, M.S.L.S., Head, Theology/Philosophy, Canon Law Libraries, The Catholic University of America, Washington, D.C. **Articles:** Annuario Pontificio; Byzantine Christianity, I: Orthodox Churches; Byzantine Christianity, II: Byzantine Catholic Churches; Byzantine Liturgy; Catholic Directory, Official; Encyclopedias and Dictionaries, Catholic; Orthodox Church in America (OCA).

*MILLER, R. H., Ph.D., Professor and Chair, Department of English, University of Louisville, Louisville, Ky. **Article:** Greene, Graham.

*MILLER, RAYMOND JOSEPH, CSSR, J.C.D., Parish Assistant, Holy Redeemer Church, Detroit, Mich. **Article:** Quadragesimo anno.

*MILLER, ROBERT GRACE, CSB, Ph.D., Chairman, Department of Philosophy, St. John Fisher College, Rochester, N.Y. **Article:** Conceptualism; Universals [part 2].

*MILLER, SAMUEL JEFFERSON, Ph.D., Professor of History, Boston College,

Chestnut Hill, Mass. **Articles:** La Valette, Jean Parisot de; Llorente, Juan Antonio; Malines Conversations; Soderblom, Nathan; Spinola, Cristobal Rojas de; Una Sancta.

*MILLER, WILLIAM D., author, Lloyd, Fla. **Article:** Day, Dorothy.

*MILLETT, AUSTIN MATTHEW BENIGNUS, OFM, Eccl.Hist.D., Research Scholar in History, Librarian and Archivist, Dun Mhuire, Killiney, County Dublin, Ireland; General Editor, *Collectanea Hibernica.* **Articles:** Caron, Redmond; Harold, Francis; Meehan, Charles, Bl.; Mihan, Charles, Ven.; Punch, John; Wadding, Luke; Walsh, Peter.

MILLIGAN, MARY, RSHM, Provincial Superior, Western American Province, Religious of the Sacred Heart of Mary, Montebello, Calif. **Articles:** Marymount Colleges and Universities; Sacred Heart of Mary, Religious of the.

*MILLON, HENRY ARMAND, Ph.D., Associate Professor of History of Architecture, Massachusetts Institute of Technology, Cambridge, Mass. **Article:** Church Architecture, History of, 7: Baroque.

*MILNER, ANTHONY FRANCIS DOMINIC, Graduate of Royal College of Music, Senior Lecturer in Music, King's College, University of London, England; composer. **Articles:** Bach, Johann Sebastian; Bach, Johann Christian; Liturgical Music, History of, 5: The Baroque Period; Reger, Max; Schumann, Robert; Verdi, Giuseppe.

*MILONE, GIOVANNI, PSSJ, Doctorate in Letters, Archivist, B.D., General Archivist of the Pious Society of St. Joseph and in charge of its press, Turin, Italy. **Articles:** Murialdo, Leonardo, Bl.; St. Joseph, Congregation of (Turin).

*MINNICH, NELSON H., Ph.D., Associate Professor of Church History, The Catholic University of America, Washington, D.C. **Article:** Ellis, John Tracy.

MINNICH, NELSON H., S.T.B., Ph.D., Professor of History and Church History, The Catholic University of America, Washington, D.C. **Articles:** Lateran Councils; Peter, Carl Joseph.

MIRANDA, SALVADOR, M.A., M.S., Assistant Director for Collection Management, Florida International University Library, Miami, Fla. **Articles:** Cardinal; Popes, Election of; Tomášek, František.

*MIRAVALLE, MARK I., S.T.D., Assistant Professor of Theology, Franciscan University of Steubenville, Steubenville, Ohio. **Article:** Medjugorje.

MIRYAM OF THE TRINITY, BONESKI, SR. JUDITH MIRYAM, OP, B.A., Monastery of Our Lady of the Rosary, Summit, N.J. **Article:** Dominican Nuns (Nuns of the Order of Preachers).

*MISIAK, HENRYK, Ph.D., Associate Professor of Psychology, Fordham University, New York, N.Y. **Article:** Gemelli, Agostino.

*MISNER, PAUL, Professor, Theology Department, Boston College, Chestnut Hill, Ma. **Articles:** Adam, Karl; Guardini, Romano.

*MISNER, PAUL, Ph.D., Everett, Mass. **Article:** Unity of the Church.

*MISONNE, DANIEL BENOIT, OSB, S.T.B., monk of the Monastery of Maredsous, France; Professor of History, Collège St. Benoît de Maredsous; Collaborator, *Revue Bénédictine, Revue d'Histoire Ecclésiastique,* and *Scriptorium;* and Editor, ''Bulletin d'Histoire Bénédictine,'' *Revue Bénédictine.* **Article:** Maredsous, Abbey of.

*MISRAHI, JEAN PAUL, Certificate d'Études superieures de Grammaire comparée des Langues romanes, Ph.D., Professor of French, Fordham University, New York, N.Y.; associate member, Columbia University Seminar on Medieval Studies. **Article:** Holy Grail, The.

*MISTRETTA, SISTER MARY LIGUORI, R.D.C., Ph.D., Professor of Latin and Spanish, Convent of Our Lady of Good Counsel, White Plains, N.Y. **Articles:** Alan of Tewkesbury; Geoffrey of Dunstable; Lawrence of Durham.

*MITCHELL, LEONEL L., Professor of Liturgics, Seabury-Western Theological Seminary, Evanston, Ill. **Article:** Mystagogy.

MITCHELL, NATHAN D., Ph.D., Associate Director for Research in the Institute for Church Life, Professor of Theology, University of Notre Dame, Notre Dame, Ind. **Articles:** Benediction of the Blessed Sacrament; Eucharist, Exposition of the; Eucharist outside Mass, Worship of the; Eucharistic Congresses; Eucharistic Devotion; Forty Hours Devotion.

*MOCK, TIMOTHY, CMM, J.C.D., Pastor of Our Lady of Grace Church, Dearborn Heights, Mich. **Article:** Mariannhill Missionaries, Congregation of.

*MOELL, CARL JOSEPH, SJ, A.B., Ph.L., S.T.D., Professor of Dogmatic and Spiritual Theology and Faculty Editor, *Chicago Studies,* St. Mary of the Lake Seminary, Mundelein, Ill. **Articles:** Gallifet, Joseph Francois de; Sacred Heart, Devotion to; Theandric Acts of Christ.

*MOELLER, DONALD JOSEPH, A.B., S.T.L., S.S.L., Instructor, Department of Theology, Villa Madonna College, Covington, Ky. **Articles:** Habakkuk, Book of; Zephaniah, Book of.

*MOFFAT, RONALD ALLAN, SJ, B.A., Editor, *Month,* London, England. **Article:** Pollen, John Hungerford.

*MOGAVERO, I. FRANK, B.S., Ph.D., Professor of Social Studies and Chairman of the Department, Mt. St. Joseph Teachers College, Buffalo, N.Y. **Articles:** Timon, John; Turner, William.

*MOHAN, ROBERT PAUL, SS, Ph.D., S.T.L., Associate Professor of Philosophy and Director of Summer Session and Workshops, The Catholic University of America, Washington, D.C. **Articles:** Historicism; History, Philosophy of.

*MOHLER, DOROTHY ABTS, Ph.D., Associate Professor, National Catholic School of Social Service, The Catholic University of America, Washington, D.C. **Articles:** Merrick, Mary Virginia; Regan, Agnes Gertrude.

*MOLECK, FRED JEROME, Ph.D., Director of Music and Organist, St. John's Church, Uniontown, Pa. **Articles:** Caecilian Movement; Haydn, Michael; Liturgical Music, History of, 6: The Classical Style.

*MOLINARI, PAUL, SJ, Ph.L., S.T.L., S.T.D., Postulator General of the Society of Jesus; President of the Council of Postulators General SJ; Professor, Pontifical Gregorian University, Rome, Italy; *Peritus,* Vatican Council II; member, Theological Commission of the Council. **Articles:** Canonization of Saints (History and Procedure); Devil's Advocate; Ledochowska, Maria Teresa, Bl.; Ledochowski, Wladimir; Missionary Sisters of St. Peter Claver; Saints, Intercession of.

*MOLITOR, EDOUARD, Doctorat en Philosophe et Lettres, Professor, Lycée de Garçons, Luxembourg. **Article:** Kirsch, Johann Peter.

*MOLLAT, GUILLAUME, Rt. Rev., Docteur ès lettres, Dr. (h.c.), Professor Emeritus of Medieval Institutions, University of Strasbourg, France; member, Académie des Inscriptions et Belles Lettres, Paris, France. **Articles:** Bainvel, Jean Vincent; Benedict XII, Pope; Brevicoxa (Jean Courtecuisse); Caperan, Louis; Clement VI, Pope; Conrad of Gelnhausen; Dolcino, Fra; Duranti, William, the Younger; Estouteville, Guillaume d'; James Gaetani Stefaneschi; Launoy, Jean de; Montcheuil, Yves de; Urban V, Pope, Bl.; Urban VI, Pope.

*MOLLEN, ROY CARLTON, SDS, B.A., Editor, *Catholic Youth* and *Salvatorian,* and Assistant Director, Salvatorian Center, New Holstein, Wis. **Articles:** Jordan, Francis Mary of the Cross; Salvatorians.

MOLONEY, FRANCIS J., S.D.B., S.T.L., S.S.L., Ph.D., Professor of Biblical Studies, The Catholic University of America, Washington, D.C. **Articles:** Conversion, I (in the Bible); International Theological Commission; Johannine Comma; Johannine Writings; John, Epistles of; John, Apostle, St.; John, Gospel according to; Salesians.

*MOLONEY, JOSEPH, OSF, Executive Director, National Apostolate for the Mentally Retarded, Brooklyn, N.Y. **Article:** National Apostolate for Inclusion Ministry (NAfIM).

*MOLS, ROGER, SJ, Docteur en philosophie et lettres, Professor of Church History, Facultés St. Albert, Egenhoven-Louvain, Belgium. **Articles:** Borromeo, Charles, St.; Borromeo, Federigo.

*MONACO, MICHELE, Pol.Sc.Dr., Assistant Professor of History, Pontifical College of S. Maria Assunta, Rome, Italy. **Articles:** Andrew Corsini, St.; Beheim, Lorenz; Cola di Rienzo; Contarini, Giovanni; Frances of Rome, St.; Henry of Bolzano, Bl.

*MONAGHAN, JOHN P., New York, N.Y. (deceased July 26, 1961). **Article:** Chidwick, John Patrick.

*MONAHAN, ARTHUR PATRICK, Ph.D., L.S.M., Associate Professor of Philosophy and Chairman of the Department, St. Mary's University, Halifax, Nova Scotia, Canada. **Article:** Peter of Auvergne (Alvernia).

*MONDIN, GIOVANNI BATTISTA, SX, Ph.D., Professor of Philosophy, Istituto Saveriano, Tavernerio (Como), Italy; *Peritus,* Vatican Council II. **Articles:** Analogy, Theological Use of; Conve-

nientia, Argumentum ex; Theological Conclusion.

*MONDIN, P. GIANBATTISTA, SX, Dean of Philosophy, Pontificia Universitas Urbaniana, Rome; Director, Institute for the Study of Atheism. **Article:** Atheism.

*MONGOVEN, ANNE MARIE, OP, Ph.D., Director, Graduate Program in Catechetics, Santa Clara University, Santa Clara, Calif. **Article:** Schorsch, Dolores.

*MONK OF THE GRANDE CHARTREUSE, A, Isère, France. **Article:** Carthusians.

*MONTAGUE, GEORGE T., SM, S.T.D., Chairman of the Graduate Division of Sacred Doctrine and Professor of Scripture, St. Mary's University, San Antonio, Tex. **Articles:** Edification (in the Bible); Son of God [part 1]; Sons of God.

*MONTAGUE, GEORGE T., SM, Marianist American Seminary, St. Basil's College, Toronto, Canada. **Article:** Charismatic Prayer; Holy Spirit, Baptism in.

MONTAGUE, GEORGE T., SM, S.Th.D., Professor of Theology, St. Mary's University, San Antonio, Tex. **Article:** Hermeneutics, Biblical.

*MONTALBANO, FRANK JOSEPH, OMI, S.T.L., S.S.L., Professor of Sacred Scripture, Homiletics, and Fundamental Dogma, Obate College of Southwest, San Antonio, Tex. **Articles:** Abomination of Desolation; Nudity; War (in the Bible).

*MONTANO, ROCCO, Doctor of Letters and Philosophy, Professor of Comparative Literature, University of Maryland, College Park, Md. **Articles:** Cavalcanti, Guido; Dante Alighieri; Petrarch, Francesco; Valla, Lorenzo.

*MONTEJANO Y AGUINAGA, Rafael, S.T.L., Hist.Eccl. Lic., Certificate in Library Science, Vatican Library School, Studies in Anthropology, Archeology, and History, University of San Luís Potosí, Mexico; historian, librarian, and archivist. **Article:** Vazquez, Pablo.

MONTI, DOMINIC, OFM, Ph.D., Professor of Church History, Department of Theology, St. Bonaventure University, St. Bonaventure, N.Y. **Article:** Franciscans, First Order.

*MOODY, JOSEPH, Department of History, The Catholic University of America, Washington, D.C. **Article:** Cardijn, Joseph.

*MOODY, JOSEPH NESTOR, Rt. Rev., Ph.D., Associate Professor of European History, The Catholic University of America, Washington, D.C.; Associate Editor, *Catholic Historical Review.* **Articles:** Church and State [part 4]; Jocism.

MOORE, BRIAN R., Ph.D., Associate Professor of New Testament, Pontifical College Josephinum, Columbus, Ohio. **Article:** Dodge City, Diocese of.

*MOORE, JOHN CLARE, Ph.D., Assistant Professor of History, Hofstra University, Hempstead, N.Y. **Articles:** Bartholomew of Marmoutier, St.; Bernger, Bl.; Edigna, Bl.; Famian, St.; Ida (Idda) of Toggenburg, Bl.; Jutta, Bl.; Peter of Luxemburg, Bl.; Saint-Hubert, Abbey of; William Firmatus, St.

*MOORE, KENNETH BERNARD, OCarm, A.B., S.T.D., Whitefriars Hall, Washington, D.C. **Articles:** Calumny; Defamation; Detraction; Reputation, Moral Right to; Talebearing.

*MOORE, PHILIP SAMUEL, CSC, Ph.D., LL.D., Archiviste-Paléographe, Academic Assistant to the President, University of Notre Dame, Notre Dame, Ind. **Article:** Peter of Poitiers.

MOORE, R. SCOTT, Ph.D., Assistant Professor, Department of History Indiana University of Pennsylvania, Indiana, Pennsylvania. **Article:** Justinian II, Byzantine Emperor.

*MOR, CARLO GUIDO, Iur.Dr., Professor of the History of Italian Law, University of Padua, Italy. **Article:** Anselmo Dedicata, Collectio.

MORACZEWSKI, ALBERT S., OP, Ph.D., President Emeritus, Distinguished Scholar in Residence, National Catholic Bioethics Center, Boston, Mass. **Articles:** Experimentation, Medical [part 2: Recent Developments]; Medical Ethics.

*MORAGAS, BEDA, OSB, Licentiate in Gregorian Chant, Pontifical Institute of Sacred Music, Rome, Italy; monk of the Abbey of Montserrat, Spain. **Article:** Sunol, Gregorio Maria.

*MORALES, ALFONSO RAMÍREZ, OMERCED, Higher Studies in Social Sciences and Education, formerly Professor, Colegio San Pedro Nolasco, now Rector, Basilica de la Merced, Santiago, Chile. **Article:** Mercedarians.

*MORAN, GABRIEL, FSC, M.A., Instructor in Theology, De La Salle College, Washington, D.C. **Articles:** Intervention, Divine; Revelation, Primitive.

*MORAN, GABRIEL, Ph.D., Director of the Graduate Program of Religious Education, New York University. **Article:** Thanatology.

MORAN, GABRIEL, Ph.D., Professor, Dept. of Humanities and the Social Sciences, New York University, New York. **Articles:** Religious Education Association; Religious Education Movement.

*MORAN, WILLIAM LAMBERT, SJ, Ph.D., S.S.L., Associate Professor of Old Testament and Dean of the Faculty of Oriental Studies, Pontifical Biblical Institute, Rome, Italy. **Articles:** Habiru (Habiri); Hebrews; Mesopotamia, Ancient, 2. History; Mesopotamia, Ancient, 3. Religion; Hittite and Hurrian Religions.

*MOREAU, PIERRE HENRI, Docteur ès lettres, Dean Emeritus, Faculty of Letters, University of Besançon, and Professor at the Sorbonne, Paris, France. **Article:** Chateaubriand, Francoise Rene de.

*MORI, RENATO, J.D., Professor of the History of the Risorgimento, University of Rome, Italy; member, Commissione per la pubblicazione dei documenti diplomatici italiani; Superintendent, Archivio storico del Ministero degli Affari Esteri. **Articles:** Guarantees, Law of; Non expedit; Roman Question; States of the Church [part 2].

*MORIARITY, JOHN JOSEPH, SSC, S.T.L., S.S.L., St. Columbans Major Seminary, Milton, Mass. **Articles:** Gideon; Joel, Book of; Judges, Book of; Judges (in the Bible); Micah, Book of; Nahum, Book of; Obadiah, Book of; Samson; Shibboleth.

*MORIARTY, FREDERICK LEO, SJ, M.A., S.S.L., S.T.D., Professor of Old Testament Studies, Weston College, Weston, Mass., and Gregorian University, Rome, Italy. **Article:** Balaam; Numbers, Book of.

*MORREALE, MARGHERITA, Professor of Spanish Language and Literature, Corso di Lingue, University of Bari, Italy. **Article:** Castiglione, Baldassare.

*MORRIS, JAMES VINCENT, CM, S.T.L., S.S.L., St. Vincent's Seminary, Baynton Beach, Fla. **Articles:** Blessing (in the Bible); Curse; Oaths (in the Bible).

*MORRIS, JOAN URSULA, M.A., member, Secular Institute of the Company of St. Paul, Rome, Italy; Director, Ikonographic Films, Ltd., London, England; artist-producer of liturgical films; and

Producer, Damascene Pictures; lecturer. **Articles:** Holy Name, Iconography of; Pentecost, Iconography of; McLaren, Agnes; Sacred Heart, Iconography of; Saints, Iconography of, 2. Historical Evolution.

*MORRIS, SISTER MARIA BAPTISTA, Ph.D., Associate Professor of History, College of St. Elizabeth, Convent Station, N.J. **Articles:** Andrew Dotti, Bl.; Franca, SS.; John of Caramola, Bl.; Philip Benizi, St.; San Giovanni in Fiore, Abbey of; San Galgano, Abbey of; Santa Maria d'Arabona, Abbey of; Tornielli, Bonaventure, Bl.; Tre Fontane, Abbey of.

*MORRIS, SISTER MARY, SSD, M.A., Teacher, Academy of St. Dorothy, Staten Island, N.Y. **Article:** Dorotheans.

*MORRIS, RUDOLPH E., J.U.D., Professor of Sociology, Marquette University, Milwaukee, Wis. **Article:** Troeltsch, Ernst.

*MORRISEY, FRANCIS G., OMI, Dean, Faculty of Canon Law, Saint Paul University, Ottawa, Canada. **Article:** Popes, Election of.

*MORRISEY, FRANCIS G., OMI, S.T.L., Ph.D., J.C.D., Professor of Canon Law, St. Paul University, Ottawa. **Article:** Canon Law, 1983 Code.

MORRISEY, FRANCIS G., OMI, J.C.D., Ph.D., Titular Professor, Faculty of Canon Law, Saint Paul University, Ottawa, Ontario, Canada. **Articles:** Acta Apostolicae Sedis; Apostolic Exhortation; Encyclical; Pronouncements, Papal and Curial.

*MORRISON, JOHN LEE, Ph.D., Professor of History and Chairman of the Department, Mount St. Mary's College, Emmitsburg, Md. **Articles:** American Protective Association; Bradley, Denis Mary; Ewing, Thomas and Charles; Gillis, James Martin; Hennepin, Louis; Ku Klux Klan; Manogue, Patrick; McKenna, Charles Hyacinth; Mengarini, Gregorio; O'Reilly, Bernard; Oertel, John James Maximilian; Parsons, Wilfrid; Scanlan, Lawrence; Shea, John Dawson Gilmary; Sheeran, James B.; Sherman, Thomas Ewing; Shipman, Andrew Jackson; Spalding, John Lancaster; Ward, Wilfrid Philip; Weber, Anselm.

*MORRISON, KARL FREDERICK, Ph.D., Assistant Professor of History, University of Minnesota, Minneapolis, Minn. **Articles:** Dictatus Papae; Papal Election Decree (1059); Patricius Romanorum.

*MORRISSY, JOHN DAVID, SJ, Ph.L., M.A., Instructor in Economics, Al-Hikma University, Baghdad, Iraq. **Article:** Gobat, George.

*MORRY, MATTHEW FLAVIAN, OP, A.B., B.S., S.T.D., Professor of Philosophy, Providence College, Providence, R.I. **Article:** Omnipresence.

*MOSER, THOMAS COLBURN, Ph.D., Professor of English and Executive Head, Department of English, Stanford University, Stanford, Calif. **Article:** Conrad, Joseph.

*MOST, WILLIAM GEORGE, Ph.D., Professor of Latin and Greek, Loras College, Dubuque, Iowa. **Articles:** Canon, Biblical, 1. Introductory; Grace (in the Bible); Muratorian Canon.

*MOTHERWAY, THOMAS JOHN, SJ, A.M., S.T.D., Professor of Theology, St. Mary of the Lake Seminary, Mundelein, Ill. **Articles:** Desire to See God, Natural; Imputation of Justice and Merit; Justice, Double.

MOTTE, M., **Article:** Franciscan Sisters—Franciscan Missionaries of Mary (FMM).

MOTZEL, JACQUELINE, FSM, M.S., President, Franciscan Sisters of Mary, St. Louis, Mo. **Article:** Franciscan Sisters—Franciscan Sisters of Mary (FSM).

*MOURANT, JOHN ARTHUR, Ph.D., Professor of Philosophy, Pennsylvania State University, University Park, Pa. **Article:** James, William.

*MOURGUE, GÉRARD, Licentiate in Law, Director, Librairies et de Galeries d'Art Moderne, Paris, France; literary critic. **Article:** Peguy, Charles Pierre.

*MROZ, SISTER MARY BONAVENTURE, OSF, Ph.D., Associate Professor of English, University of Detroit, Detroit, Mich. **Article:** Franciscan Sisters—Sisters of St. Francis Congregation of Our Lady of Lourdes (OSF).

*MUDROCH, VACLAV, Iur.Dr., Ph.D., Associate Professor of History, Carleton University, Ottawa, Ontario, Canada. **Articles:** Alexander Neville; Bowet, Henry; Despenser, Henry; John of Thoresby; John de Grandisson; Merks, Thomas; Simon Mepham; Thomas of Buckingham; Walter of Skirlaw; William of Edyndon.

*MUELLER, HERMAN, SVD, S.T.L., S.S.L., M.A., Professor of Scripture, St. Augustine's Seminary, Bay St. Louis,

Miss. **Articles:** Amon; Astarte; Baal; Baptism (in the Bible); Bel; Dagon; Fertility and Vegetation Cults (in the Bible); Marduk; Ra (Re); Tammuz.

*MULCAHY, GEORGE DANIEL, Rt. Rev., B.A., M.A., Mount St. Mary's Seminary, Emmitsburg, Md. **Article:** McCaffrey, John Henry.

*MULCAHY, MAURICE WARWICK, SM, S.T.D., Archivist, Marist Order in New Zealand; National Director, Third Order of Mary; Editor, national Catholic monthly *Marist Messenger,* Wellington, New Zealand. **Articles:** New Zealand, the Catholic Church in; Pompallier, Jean Baptiste Francois.

*MULCAHY, RICHARD E., SJ, University of San Francisco, San Francisco, Calif. **Articles:** Solidarism; Subsidiarity.

*MULDOON, JAMES MICHAEL, Ph.D., Assistant Professor of History, St. Michael's College, Winooski, Vt. **Articles:** Gregory XII, Pope; Honorius II, Pope.

*MULHERN, PHILIP FABIAN, OP, S.T.D., S.T.M., Professor of Sacred Eloquence, Dominican House of Studies, Washington, D.C. **Articles:** Annibale, Guiseppe d'; Bartholomew of Lucca; Beatitudes (in the Christian Life); Caramuel Lobkowitz, Juan; Counsel, Gift of; Discalced Orders; Discipline, The; Expiation (in Theology) [part 2]; Fear of the Lord [part 2]; Fortitude, Gift of; Francis of Geronimo, St.; Hair Shirt; Holy Spirit, Fruits of; Holy Spirit, Gifts of; Knowledge, Gift of; Medals, Religious; Medina, Juan; Months, Special Devotions for; Mortification; Panigarola, Francesco; Penance, Practices of; Piety, Gift of; Pouget, Francois Aime; Raymond Martini; Reparation; Ripa, Matteo; Saudreau, Auguste; Scupoli, Lorenzo; Self-Denial; Self-Oblation; Sermon; Solitude; Spiritual Combat; Thomas a Kempis; Threat; Triduum; Trinity, Holy, Devotion to; Understanding, Gift of; Wisdom, Gift of.

*MULHERN, PHILIP FABIAN, OP, S.T.M., University of St. Thomas Aquinas, Rome. **Articles:** Attwater, Donald; Dopfner, Julius; Hollis, (Maurice) Christopher; Office of the Dead.

*MULHOLLAND, SISTER MARY AMBROSE, BVM, Ph.D., Chairman, Department of History, Clarke College, Dubuque, Iowa. **Articles:** Ambrosians; John XI, Pope; Peter of Castelanu, Bl.; Simeon of Durham; Sisinnius, Pope; Stephen VII (VIII), Pope; Stephen VIII (IX), Pope; Valentine, Pope.

*MULLAHY, BERNARD IGNATIUS, CSC, Ph.L., S.T.L., Ph.D., Holy Cross Novitiate, Bennington, Vt. **Articles:** Kiss of Peace; Light, Liturgical Use of; Liturgical Gestures; Processions, Religious.

*MULLANEY, MATTHEW JAMES, Jr., A.B., LL.B., Assistant Corporation Counsel for the District of Columbia, Washington, D.C. **Article:** Church and State in the U.S. (Legal History), 2. Disestablishment Period (1776–1834).

*MULLANEY, THOMAS URBAN, OP, S.T.D., S.T.M., Professor of Dogmatic Theology, Pontifical Faculty of Theology, Dominican House of Studies, Washington, D.C. **Articles:** Mode; Subsistence.

*MULLAY, SISTER CAMILLA, OP, M.A., Teacher of History, Adrian Dominican House, Washington, D.C. **Article:** Margaret of Hungary, St.

*MULLEN, JAMES ERNEST, CPS, Waterville, N.Y. **Articles:** Bertoni, Gaspare Luigi Dionigi, St.; Stigmatine Fathers.

*MÜLLER, ANSELM WINFRIED, OSB, St. Bonet's Hall, St. Giles, Oxford, England. **Article:** Gredt, Joseph August.

*MULLER, HERMAN JOSEPH, SJ, S.T.L., Ph.D., Chairman, Department of History, University of Detroit, Detroit, Mich. **Articles:** Bohme, Jakob; Labadie, Jean de; Spener, Philipp Jakob.

*MÜLLER, KARL, SVD, Dr.Missiol., Dr.Theol., Secretary for Studies, Generalate, Collegio del Verbo Divino, Rome, Italy. **Article:** Schmidlin, Joseph.

*MÜLLER, WOLFGANG, Dr.Theol., Dr.Phil., University Professor of Regional Church History, University of Freiburg, Germany. **Article:** Vicari, Hermann von.

*MULLIGAN, ROBERT WILLIAM, SJ, Ph.D., Vice President, Loyola University, Chicago, Ill. **Article:** Knowledge, Theories of [part 3].

*MULLIN, JOHN FRANCIS, SJ, M.A., Ph.L., Weston College, Weston, Mass. **Article:** Guibert, Joseph de.

*MULLINS, SISTER PATRICK JEROME, OP, Ph.D., Professor of Theology, Siena Heights College, Adrian, Mich. **Articles:** Abbo of Fleury, St.; Boniface IV, Pope; Boniface V, Pope; Boniface III, Pope; Chapel; Following of Christ (in the Christian Life); Lando, Pope; Romanus, Pope; Sabinian, Pope; Stephen II, Pope; Stephen V (VI), Pope; Stephen VI (VII), Pope; Theodore I, Pope.

*MULLINS, MSGR. WILLIAM A., M.A., *Peritus,* Congregation for Catholic Education, Rome, Italy. **Article:** Knox, James Robert.

MULRYAN, JOHN, John, Ph.D., Distinguished Board of Trustees Professor, English Department, St. Bonaventure University, St. Bonaventure, N.Y. **Article:** St. Bonaventure University.

MUNDADAN, ANTONY MATHIAS, CMI, S.T.L., Hist.Eccl.Lic., Ph.D., Professor Emeritus of Church History and Theology, Dharmaram Vidyakshetram, Bangalore, India. **Articles:** Carmelite Sisters—Congregation of the Mother of Carmel (Syro-Malabar); Carmelites of Mary Immaculate; Sisters of the Adoration of the Blessed Sacrament (Syro-Malabar); Syro-Malabar Liturgy; Syro-Malabar Church.

*MUNIER, CHARLES, Licencié ès lettres, J.C.D., S.T.D., Diploma, Vatican School of Paleography, Vice Officialis, Diocese of Strasbourg, and Chargé de cours, Institute of Canon Law, University of Strasbourg, France. **Articles:** Burchard, Decretum of; Canon Law, History of, 3. False Decretals to Gratian; Ivo of Chartres, Collection of.

*MUNN, THOMAS J., Woodward, Iowa. **Article:** John of God, St.

*MURAWSKI, EDWARD JOSEPH, SJ, M.A., Weston College, Weston, Mass. **Article:** Pinard de la Boullaye, Henri.

*MURPHY, ALFRED WILLIAM CAMILLUS, OP, M.D., S.T.D., St. Dominic's Hospital, Bahawalpur, West Pakistan. **Article:** Hippocratic Oath.

*MURPHY, FRANCIS J., Department of History, Boston College, Chestnut Hill, Ma. **Article:** Lienart, Achille.

*MURPHY, FRANCIS XAVIER, CSSR, Ph.D., Professor of Patristic Moral Theology, Accademia Alfonsiana, Rome, Italy; Staff Editor for Patrology, Early Church History, and Byzantine Church History, *New Catholic Encyclopedia,* The Catholic University of America, Washington, D.C. **Articles:** Abdisho IV (Ebedjesu), Chaldean Patriarch; Abdisho of Kaskar, St.; Abdisho bar Berika; Abgar, Legends of; Addai and Mari, SS.; Ales, Adhemar d'; Alogoi; Alzog, Johann Baptist; Anatolius of Laodicea, St.; Anthemius; Anthimus; Apocrisiarius; Apostles' Creed; Aquileia; Arbela, Chronicle of; Arethas, Archbishop of Caesarea; Aristides; Ballerini, Pietro and Girolamo;

Balsamon, Theodore; Bar-Hebraeus (Gregorius ibn al-Ibri); Bardy, Gustave; Batiffol, Pierre; Bessarion, Cardinal; Bessarion of Egypt, St.; Bryennios, Philotheus; Callistus Angelicudes; Cassiodorus Senator, Flavius Magnus Aurelius Senator; Catacombs; Catechesis, I (Early Christian); Cave, William; Ceillier, Remi; Chapman, John; Christian Way of Life (Early Church); Christology, Controversies on (Patristic); Church, History of, I (Early); Constantine I, the Great, Roman Emperor; Constantinople II, Council of; Creed; Creed in Eucharistic Liturgy; Dexios, Theodore; Diaconia; Dioscorus, Patriarch of Alexandria; Duchesne, Louis; Ebionites; Edessa, School of; Ethiopia, The Catholic Church in; Facundus of Hermiane; Greece, The Catholic Church in [part 2]; Gregory the Illuminator, St.; Grosjean, Paul; Harnack, Adolf von; Hesychasm; Hesychius of Jerusalem; Hurter, Hugo von; Ignatius of Antioch, St.; Isidore of Pelusium, St.; Jerome, St.; Jesus Prayer; Kerygma; Labriolle, Pierre de; Lebon, Joseph; Leclercq, Henri; Leo I, Pope, St.; Liberatus of Carthage; Liberian Catalogue; Macarius Magnes; Mai, Angelo; Marius Mercator; Martyr; Martyrium; Maruthas of Martyropolis; Maruthas of Tagrit; Maurists; Melania the Younger, St.; Melania the Elder; Migne, Jacques Paul; Monophysitism; Montfaucon, Bernard de; Moral Theology, History of (to 700); Morin, Germain; Mowinckel, Sigmund; Names, Christian; Nonnus of Panopolis; Numismatics; Palms, Liturgical Use Of; Papias of Hierapolis; Passio; Patristic Theology; Paula, St.; Penitential Controversy; Petau, Denis (Petavius); Philostorgius; Pierius, St.; Pilgrimages, Roman; Pitra, Jean Baptiste; Polycarp, St.; Prosper of Aquitaine, St.; Pseudo-Dionysius; Quadratus, St.; Quinisext Synod; Refrigerium; Rings, Liturgical Use Of; Rome; Rome, Legends of Christian; Rossi, Giovanni Battista de; Sheptyts'kyi Andrii; Sirmond, Jacques; Symbolism, Early Christian; Synaxary; Theognostos; Theophilus of Alexandria; Three Chapters; Tillemont, Louis Sebastien le Nain de; Tixeront, Joseph; Ulfilas; Vatican; Vigilius, Pope; Virgines Subintroductae [part 2]; Zachary the Rhetor.

*MURPHY, JOHN FRANCIS, S.T.D., St. Francis Seminary, Milwaukee, Wis. **Articles:** Immaculate Heart of Mary; Mary, Blessed Virgin, II (in Theology) [Holiness of Mary].

*MURPHY, JOHN LAWRENCE, M.A., S.T.D., Professor of Dogmatic and Sacramental Theology, St. Francis Seminary, Milwaukee, Wis. **Article:** Analogy of Faith.

*MURPHY, JOSEPH FRANCIS, OSB, Ph.D., Chairman of the Department of History and Dean of Men, St. Gregory's College, and Pastor, St. Benedict's Church, Shawnee, Okla. **Articles:** Oklahoma, Catholic Church in; Robot, Isidore.

*MURPHY, SISTER M. GREGORY, OP, St. Mary's Dominican Convent, Cobra, Dublin, Ireland. **Article:** Dominican Sisters—Dominican Sisters of Our Lady of the Rosary and of St. Catherine of Siena, Cabra.

*MURPHY, MOTHER MARY BENEDICT, RSHM, Ph.D., Fulbright Lecturer, Xavier University, Cagayan de Oro City, Philippine Islands (1966-67); Staff Editor for Education, *New Catholic Encyclopedia,* The Catholic University of America, Washington, D.C.; Dean of Education and Director of Teacher Training, Marymount College Tarrytown, N.Y. **Articles:** Salamanca, University of; San Marcos, Main National University of.

*MURPHY, RICHARD JOHN, OMI, S.T.L., J.C.D., Rector and Professor of Canon Law, Oblate College, Washington, D.C. **Article:** Prelate; Rectors.

*MURPHY, RICHARD THOMAS AQUINAS, OP, S.T.D., S.S.D., Professor of New Testament Exegesis, Aquinas Institute of Theology, St. Rose Priory, Dubuque, Iowa. **Articles:** Adonai; Anthropomorphism (in the Bible); El (God); Elohim; God, Name of; Jehovah; Lagrange, Marie Joseph; Lord, The; Luke, Gospel according to; Luke, Evangelist, St.; Sabaoth; Shaddai; Voste, Jacques Marie; Yahweh.

*MURPHY, ROLAND EDMUND, OCarm, M.A. (Philosophy), M.A. (Semitics), S.T.D., S.S.L., Professor of Sacred Scripture, School of Sacred Theology, The Catholic University of America, Washington, D.C. **Articles:** Alphabetic Psalms; Penitential Psalms; Sapiential Books; Song of Songs; Wisdom (in the Bible).

*MURPHY, ROLAND EDMUND, O. Carm., S.T.D., S.S.L., George Washington Ivey Professor Emeritus, Divinity School, Duke University. **Article:** Canon, Biblical, 4. Canon Criticism.

*MURPHY, T. AUSTIN, Most Rev. D.D., Saint Rose of Lima Church, Baltimore, Md. **Article:** Shehan, Lawrence.

*MURPHY-O'CONNOR, JEROME, OP, S.T.D., S.S.L., Professor of New Testament, École Biblique et Archéologique Française, Jerusalem, Israel. **Article:** Benoit, Pierre.

MURPHY-O'CONNOR, JEROME, OP, S.T.D., S.S.L., Professor of New Testament, École Biblique et Archéologique Française, Jerusalem. **Article:** École Biblique.

*MURRAY, EDMUND JOSEPH, CSC, Ph.D., Assistant Professor of History, University of Notre Dame, Notre Dame, Ind. **Articles:** Fleming, Patrick; O'Hely, Patrick, Bl.; White, Stephen.

*MURRAY, JOHN CLIFFORD, CSB, S.T.D., Assistant Professor of Theology, University of Windsor, Ontario, Canada. **Articles:** Ascension of Jesus Christ [part 2]; Savior [part 2].

*MURRAY, LINDA MARY, Academic Diploma in the History of Art (University of London), Lecturer in the History of Art, Extra-Mural Department, University of London, England. **Article:** Vence, Chapelle du Rosaire.

*MURRAY, PAUL VINCENT, M.A., LL.D., Administrator General, Mexico City Center of Bilingual Studies, Mexico City, Mexico. **Article:** Bustamante, Carlos Maria.

*MURRAY, PETER JOHN, B.A. (hons.), Ph.D., F.S.A., Lecturer, Courtauld Institute of Art, University of London, England. **Articles:** Church Architecture, History of, 6: Renaissance; St. Peter's Basilica.

*MURTAGH, JAMES GEORGE, M.A., Pastor, St. Roch's Church, Glen Iris, Melbourne, Australia. **Articles:** MacKillop, Mary Helen, Bl.; Mannix, Daniel; Moran, Patrick Francis; New Norcia, Abbey of; Polding, John Bede; Therry, John Joseph; Vaughan, Roger William Bede.

*MURTAGH, JOHN M., A.B., LL.B., LL.D., Administrative Judge of the Criminal Court of the City of New York, N.Y. **Article:** Prostitution.

*MURTHA, RONIN JOHN, OSB, Ph.D., St. Vincent Archabbey, Latrobe, Pa. **Articles:** Lemke, Peter Henry; St. Vincent Archabbey.

*MUSHOLT, SILAS ALOIS, OFM, S.T.L., Lect.Gen., Professor of Scripture, St.

Joseph Seminary, Teutopolis, Ill. **Articles:** Calvary; Capernaum; Mount of Olives; Nazareth; Silas (Silvanus); Zion.

*MUSSBACHER, NORBERT FRIEDRICH, SOCist, Editor, *Waldmark,* Lilienfeld, Germany. **Article:** Lilienfeld, Abbey of.

*MUSSET, LUCIEN EMILE, Agrégé d'Histoire et Géographie, École des Hautes Études, Professor of Medieval History, University of Caen, France. **Articles:** Absalon of Lund; Bourgueilen-Vallee, Abbey of; Canute IV, King of Denmark, St.; Canute Lavard, St.; Kjeld, St.; Margaret of Roskilde, St.

*MUSURILLO, HERBERT ANTHONY, SJ, A.B., S.T.L., D.Phil. (Oxon.), Ph.D., Professor of Classical Languages and Head of the Department, Fordham University, New York, N.Y. **Articles:** Barlaam and Joasaph; Basil of Ancyra; Dialogue (Literary Genre); Methodius of Olympus, St.; Peter of Alexandria, St.; Suetonius.

*MUZAS, JOSEPH J., SDB, B.A., J.C.D., Salesian High School, New Rochelle, N.Y. **Articles:** Fliche, Augustin; John the Deacon of Rome (Hymmonides); Vicar of Christ.

*MYERS, DONNA LEE, M.A., National Secretariat, The Grail; Secretary, Grail Ecumenical Committee; and Editor, *Ecumenical Notes,* Loveland, Ohio. **Article:** Grail, The.

*MYERS, EDWARD TIMOTHY, OP, A.B., M.A., S.T.B., Dominican House of Studies, Washington, D.C. **Article:** Drouin, Hyacinthe Rene (Drouven).

*MYERSCOUGH, SISTER ANGELITA, AdPPS, Ph.D., Instructor in Theology, St. Louis University, St. Louis, Mo. **Article:** Precious Blood Sisters—Adorers of the Blood of Christ.

*NABER, SISTER M. VERA, CSA, M.A., Community Supervisor, schools conducted by the Community in Indiana, Convent of St. Agnes, Fond du Lac, Wis. **Article:** St. Agnes, Congregation of Sisters of.

*NABUCO, JOAQUIM, Rt. Rev., A.P., Rector, Church of Saint Teresa, Rio de Janeiro, Brazil; Consultor, Sacred Congregation of Rites and of Ceremonial; *Peritus,* Vatican Council II. **Articles:** Fanon; Papal Ceremony and Vesture; Pontifical, Roman; Rings, Liturgical Use Of; Tiara, Papal.

*NAHSTOLL, MARTIN EDWARD, B.A., Pastor, St. Peter of Alcantara Church,

Stanley, Ky. **Article:** Owensboro, Diocese of.

NAMORATO, MICHAEL V., Ph.D., Professor of History, University of Mississippi, University, Miss. **Articles:** Biloxi, Diocese of; Jackson, Diocese of.

*NASALLI-ROCCA, EMILIO, Iur.D., Diploma in Paleography and Archival Science, Lecturer in the History of Italian Law, Director, Biblioteca Comunale, Piacenza, Italy; Lecturer, Catholic University of Milan, Italy. **Article:** Hospitals, History of, 1. To 1500.

*NASH, PETER WHITWELL, SJ, S.T.L., Ph.D., Rector and Professor of Philosophy and Psychology, Campion College, Regina, Canada. **Articles:** Giles of Rome; Robert of Melun (Hereford).

*NAUERT, CHARLES G. JR., Ph.D., Associate Professor of History, University of Missouri, Columbia, Mo. **Articles:** Crotus Rubianus (Johannes Jager); Epistolae Obscurorum Virorum; Lang, Andreas; Loos, Cornelius; Reuchlin, Johann; Riario; Salat, Hans; Shirwood, John.

*NAUGHTON, E. RUSSELL, Ph.D., Professor of Philosophy and Chairman of the Department, La Salle College, Philadelphia, Pa. **Articles:** Panentheism; Pantheism.

*NEAL, MARIE AUGUSTA, SNdeN., Professor of Sociology, Emmanuel College, Boston, Mass. **Article:** Civil Religion.

*NEALY, FRANCIS DOMINIC, OP, S.T.Lr., Ph.D., St. Joseph's Priory, Somerset, Ohio. **Articles:** Advertence; Ignorance [part 2]; Marin-Sola, Francisco; Soto, Pedro de; Soto, Domingo de.

*NÉDONCELLE, MAURICE, Rt. Rev., Docteur de l'Université de Paris, Docteur ès lettres, S.T.D., Dr. (h.c.), Professor and Dean, Faculty of Catholic Theology, University of Strasbourg, France. **Articles:** Lavelle, Louis; Le Senne, Rene.

*NEILL, THOMAS PATRICK, Ph.D., Professor of History, St. Louis University, St. Louis, Mo. **Article:** Condorcet, Marie Jean Antoine Caritat.

*NEMEC, LUDVIK, S.T.D., Professor of History, Rosemont College, Rosemont, Pa.; Lecturer in History (Summer Sessions), Villanova University, Villanova, Pa.; Visiting Professor of Comparative Religion, Chestnut Hill College, Chestnut Hill, Pa. **Articles:** Archiereus; Autocephaly; Beran, Jo-

seph; Ernest of Pardubice (Pardubitz); Exarch; Infant Jesus of Prague; Sobornost; Strahov, Monastery of; Taborites; Tepl, Monastery of; Utraquists; Zizka, John; Zobor, Abbey of.

NEMER, LAWRENCE, SVD, Ph.D., President, Missionary Institute, London. **Articles:** Mission History, I: Catholic; Mission and Missions.

*NEMETZ, ANTHONY A., Ph.D., L.H.D., Associate Professor of Philosophy, Ohio State University, Columbus, Ohio. **Articles:** Common Good; Ontological Argument.

*NEUNHEUSER, BURKHARD, OSB, Dr.Theol., Professor of Philosophy, Maria Laach Abbey, Germany; Professor of Liturgy, Pontificium Institutum Liturgicum, San Anselmo, Rome, Italy. **Articles:** Baumstark, Anton; Braun, Joseph; Browe, Peter; Casel, Odo; Hittorp, Melchior; Thalhofer, Valentin.

*NEUWIRTH, ADOLF, CSSR, Dr.Theol., St. Alphonsus Church, Rome, Italy. **Articles:** Apamea; Eucherius of Lyons, St.; Faustus of Riez; Fulgentius of Ruspe; Gennadius of Marseilles.

*NEWBOLD, ROBERT CLIFFORD, Ph.D., Vice Rector, Our Lady of Providence Seminary, Warwick, R.I. **Article:** Garakonthie, Daniel.

*NEWLIN, DIKA, Ph.D., Chairman, Department of Music, Drew University, Madison, N.J. **Articles:** Bruckner, Anton; Mahler, Gustav; Webern, Anton von.

*NEWMAN, JEREMIAH JOSEPH, M.A., B.D., D.Ph., Professor of Sociology, St. Patrick's College, Maynooth, Ireland; Editor, *Christus Rex.* **Articles:** Pacem in terris; Rerum novarum; Social Thought, Catholic, 4. Modern.

*NEWSTEAD, HELAINE, Ph.D., Professor of English, and Executive Officer, Ph.D. Program in English and Comparative Literature, Hunter College of the City University of New York, N.Y. **Article:** Arthurian and Carolingian Legends.

NGUYEN, CECILIA THUY, OP, M.A., Dept. of Religion & Religious Education, The Catholic University of America, Washington, D.C. **Article:** Dominican Sisters—Vietnamese Dominican Sisters of St. Catherine of Siena (Mary Immaculate Province, Houston, Texas).

*NICHOLL, DONALD, B.A., Senior Lecturer in History, University of Keele, Staffordshire, England. **Articles:** Beaufort, Henry; Gervase of Canterbury; Hubert Walter; Jocelin of Glasgow; Jocelin of Wells; John Stratford; London, Ancient See of; Morton, John; Netter, Thomas; Richard of Bury; Samson of Bury-St.-Edmunds; Simon Langham; Simon of Sudbury; Thurstan of York; Walter of Merton.

*NICKELS, MARILYN W., Ph.D., Education Specialist, Bureau of the Census, Washington, D.C. **Article:** Turner, Thomas Wyatt.

NICKS, FIONA, MA, D.Phil., Lecturer in Byzantine Language and Literature, Department of Classics/Department of Byzantine and Modern Greek Studies, King's College, London, United Kingdom. **Articles:** Byzantine Church, History of; Constantine VII Porphyrogenitus, Byzantine Emperor; Iconoclasm; Maurice, Byzantine Emperor; Ravenna [History]; Ravenna [Exarchate of]; Sisinnius I, Patriarch of Constantinople.

*NIEHAUS, EARL FRANCIS, SM, Ph.D., Professor of History, Marycrest College, Davenport, Iowa. **Article:** Sedella, Antonio de.

*NIELSEN, HARRY ANDERSEN, Ph.D., Associate Professor of Philosophy, University of Notre Dame, Notre Dame, Ind. **Articles:** Ambiguity; Antinomy; Operationalism; Paradox.

*NIENALTOWSKI, RAPHAEL, OFMCap, Broken Arrow, Okla. **Article:** Mohler, Johann Adam.

*NIESER, ALBERT, OP, Milwaukee, Wis. **Articles:** Anunciacion, Domingo de la; Betanzos, Domingo de; Cepeda, Francisco; Cordova, Matias de; Monroy e Hijar, Antonio; Montesino, Antonio; Sanctis, Dionisio de.

*NISBET, ROBERT A., Ph.D., Professor of Sociology, University of California at Davis, Calif. **Articles:** Comte, Auguste; Durkheim, Emile.

NOBLE, THOMAS F. X., Ph.D., Director of the Medieval Institute, University of Notre Dame, Notre Dame, Ind. **Articles:** Liber Pontificalis; States of the Church [part 1].

*NOETHER, EMILIANA PASCA, Ph.D., Italian Section Editor, *American Historical Review;* Professor of History, Simmons College, Boston, Mass. **Articles:** Risorgimento; Victor Emmanuel II.

*NOGAR, RAYMOND JUDE, OP, S.T.L., Ph.D., Professor of Philosophy and of

Biology and Anthropology, Aquinas Institute, River Forest, Ill. **Articles:** Alexander, Samuel; Cournot, Antoine Augustin; Evolution [part 1: Philosophical Evaluation].

NOLAN, CHARLES E., H.E.D., Archivist, Archdiocese of New Orleans, Adjunct Professor of Pastoral and Historical Theology, Notre Dame Seminary. **Articles:** Mississippi, Catholic Church in; New Orleans, Archdiocese of.

*NOLAN, HUGH JOSEPH, Ph.D., Professor of American Church History, Immaculata College, Immaculata, Pa.; Editor, Records of American Catholic Historical Society. **Articles:** Barbelin, Felix Joseph; Barron, Edward; Conwell, Henry; Domenec, Michael; Harold, William Vincent; Hogan, William; Kenrick, Francis Patrick; Kirlin, Joseph; Loughlin, James F.; Prendergast, Edmond Francis.

*NOLAN, KIERAN PETER, OSB, Dr.Theol., Professor of Moral Theology, St. John's Seminary, Collegeville, Minn. **Articles:** Albert of Pontida, St.; Albert of Sarteano, Bl.; Albertinus of Fonte Avellana, St.; Bononius, St.; James Cinti de Cerqueto, Bl.; Lidanus, St.; Peter Crisci of Foligno, Bl.; Seraphina (Fina), St.; Torello, Bl.

*NOLAN, PAUL, Ph.D., Assistant Professor of Philosophy, The Catholic University of America, Washington, D.C. **Article:** Consciousness [part 1]; Free Will.

*NOONAN, CARROLL JOHN, SS, A.B., S.T.B., Ph.D., St. Mary's Seminary, Roland Park, Baltimore, Md. **Articles:** Nagot, Francis Charles; Olier, Jean Jacques; Reilly, Wendell; Sulpicians; Whitfield, James.

NOONAN, GEORGE M., Chancellor, Diocese of Kansas City-St. Joseph, Kansas City, Mo. **Article:** Kansas City-St. Joseph, Diocese of.

*NOONAN, JOHN T., JR., Ph.D., Professor of Law, Director of Natural Law Institute, and Editor, *Natural Law Forum,* University of Notre Dame, Notre Dame, Ind. **Article:** Contraception.

*NOONAN, RAYMOND C., Evansville, Ind. **Article:** Knights of St. John.

NOONE, TIMOTHY B., Ph.D., Associate Professor of Philosophy, The Catholic University of America, Washington, D.C. **Articles:** Duns Scotus, John; Scotism.

*NORLING, BERNARD PATRICK, Ph.D., Associate Professor of History, Universi-

ty of Notre Dame, Notre Dame, Ind. **Articles:** Law, William; Nonconformists; Nonjurors, English; Parker, Matthew.

*NÖRR, KNUT WOLFGANG, D.Jur., Wissenschaftlicher Assistent, University of Munich, Faculty of Law; Associate, Max-Planck Institut für vergleichende europäische Rechtsgeschichte, Frankfurt am Main, Germany. **Articles:** Glosses, Canon Law; Guido de Baysio; Tudeschis, Nicolaus de.

*NORTH, ARTHUR A., SJ, S.T.L., Ph.D., Associate Professor of Public Law and Government, Fordham University, New York, N.Y. **Article:** Sovereignty.

NORTH, ROBERT, SJ, S.S.D., retired Professor of Exegesis and Archeology, Pontifical Biblical Institute, Rome. **Articles:** Byblos; Jubilee Year; Palmyra; Roothaan, Johann Philipp; Sabbath Year; Sabbath.

*NÔTRE, SISTER MARIE RAFFAELLA DE SION, NDS, M.A., Executive Secretary, Ratisbonne Center, Kansas City, Mo. **Articles:** Fathers of Sion; Ibn Paquda; Ratisbonne.

NOWELL, IRENE, OSB, Ph.D., Adjunct Professor, St. John's University, Collegeville, Minn. **Articles:** Hebrew Poetry; Psalms, Book of.

*NOWLAN, KEVIN BARRY, B.A., M.A., Ph.D., barrister at law, Lecturer in History, University College, Dublin, Ireland. **Article:** Murray, Daniel.

*NUESSE, C. JOSEPH, Ph.D., LL.D., Professor of Sociology, and Staff Editor for Social Sciences, *New Catholic Encyclopedia,* The Catholic University of America, Washington, D.C. **Articles:** Villeneuve-Bargemont, John Paul Alban de; Mermillod, Gaspard.

*NUGENT, JAMES BRENNAN, S.T.L., Ph.D., Professor of Philosophy and Dean of the College Department, St. John Vianney Seminary, Bloomingdale, Ohio. **Articles:** Doubt; Error; Ignorance [part 1].

*NUGENT, SISTER MARGARET LOUISE, CBS, M.S.N., Instructor in Medical-Surgical Nursing, Bon Secours Hospital School of Nursing, Baltimore, Md. **Article:** Bon Secours, Sisters of.

*NUMAZAWA, KIICHI FRANCIS, SVD, S.T.B., Ph.D., Professor of Ethnology, Nanzan University, Nagoya, Japan. **Article:** Shintoism.

*OBERHAUSER, VINCENT MARY, CP, Professor of Liturgy, Passionist Seminary,

Louisville, Ky. **Article:** Lamb of God [part 2].

*O'BRIEN, GERALD JOHN, SJ, B.A., S.T.D., Professor of Theology, Loyola College, Montreal, Quebec, Canada. **Article:** Integralism; Sodalitium Pianum.

*O'BRIEN, JAMES FRANCIS, M.S., M.A., Ph.D., Associate Professor of Philosophy, Villanova University, Villanova, Pa. **Article:** Mechanism.

O'BRIEN, MAUREEN R., Ph.D., Assistant Professor of Theology and Director of Pastoral Ministry, Duquesne University, Pittsburgh, Pa. **Article:** Women and Papal Teaching.

*O'BRIEN, PETER, OP, S.T.M., Ph.D., Professor of Moral Theology, St. Rose Priory, and professor of Moral Theology and Fundamental Theology, Mt. St. Bernard Seminary, Dubuque, Iowa. **Article:** Concina, Daniel.

*O'BRIEN, THOMAS CHRYSOSTOM, OP, S.T.Lr., Ph.D., S.T.D., S.T.Praes., Professor of Theology, Dominican House of Studies, Washington, D.C. **Articles:** Causality, Divine; God in Philosophy, 1. Place; Predetermination; Premotion, Physical; Virtue.

*O'BRIEN, THOMAS CHRYSOSTOM, Executive Editor, *New Catholic Encyclopedia,* Vol. 17, Catholic University of America, Washington, D.C. **Articles:** Gilby, Thomas; John Paul I, Pope; Pontifical, Roman.

*O'BRIEN, THOMAS CHRYSOSTOM, International Commission on English in the Liturgy, Washington, D.C. **Article:** Tridentine Mass.

*O'CALLAGHAN, JOSEPH FRANCIS, Ph.D., Associate Professor of Medieval History, Fordham University, New York, N.Y. **Articles:** Aviz, Order of; Brethren of the Cross; Calatrava, Order of; Chivalry; Hieronymites (Los Jeronimos); Knights of the Holy Sepulcher; Knights of St. James; Knights of Alcantara; Knights of Montesa; Military Orders; Order of Christ; Raymond of Fitero, Bl.

*O'CALLAGHAN, SISTER M. ROSARIA, PBVM, B.S., Teacher of Art and Secretarial Science, Notre Dame Academy, Sioux Falls, S.Dak. **Article:** Presentation of the Blessed Virgin Mary, Sisters of the.

*O'CALLAGHAN, SISTER MARY, RSCJ, Ph.D., Professor of History and Sacred Doctrine, Maryville College of the Sacred Heart, St. Louis, Mo. **Articles:** Barbarigo, Gregory, St.; Febronianism; Gelasian Decree; Marescotti, Hyacintha, St.; Papal Elections, Veto Power in; Secular Arm.

OCHOA, MARINA, Archivist, Archdiocese of Santa Fe, Santa Fe, N.M. **Article:** Santa Fe, Archdiocese of.

*Ó CONBHUÍ, COLMCILLE SÉAMAS, OCSO, monk of Our Lady of Mellifont Abbey, County Louth, Ireland. **Articles:** Melleray, Abbey of; Mellifont, Abbey of; O'Cullenan, Gelasius (Glaisne).

*O'CONNELL, JAMES EDWARD, Rt. Rev., Ph.D., Rector, St. Johns Home Mission Seminary, Little Rock, Ark. **Article:** Fitzgerald, Edward.

*O'CONNELL, JOHN BERTRAM, B.A., B.D., Catholic Church, Builth Wells, Breconshire, Wales. **Articles:** Antependium; Baldachino; Candles; Tabernacle.

*O'CONNELL, KEVIN GEORGE, SJ, A.B., A.M., Ph.L., John La Farge House, Cambridge, Mass. **Article:** Tower of Babel.

*O'CONNELL, MARVIN R., Ph.D., Assistant Professor of History, College of St. Thomas, St. Paul, Minn. **Article:** Reformation, Protestant (in the British Isles).

*O'CONNELL, MATTHEW JOSEPH, SJ, A.B., M.A., Professor of Sacramental Theology, Woodstock College, Woodstock, Md. **Article:** De la Taille, Maurice.

*O'CONNELL, MAURICE RICKARD, Ph.D., Assistant Professor of History, University of Portland, Portland, Ore. **Articles:** Bonner, Edmund; Brookes, James (Brooks); Peyto, William (Peto); Tunstall, Cuthbert.

*O'CONNELL, TIMOTHY E., Ph.D., Associate Professor of Moral Theology, St. Mary of the Lake Seminary, Mundelein, IL. **Article:** Relativism, Moral.

*O'CONNELL, TIMOTHY E., Ph.D., Associate Professor, Director of Pastoral Studies, Loyola University, Chicago. **Article:** Proportionality, Principle of.

*O'CONNELL, TIMOTHY E., S.T.L., Ph.D., Professor of Pastoral Studies, Loyola University, Chicago. **Article:** Fuchs, Josef.

*O'CONNELL, MOTHER ZOE, St. Joseph's Convent, Fitchburg, Mass. **Article:** Sisters, Faithful Companions of Jesus.

O'CONNELL KILLEN, PATRICIA, Ph.D., Professor, Department of Religion, Pacific Lutheran University, Tacoma, Wa. **Article:** Washington, Catholic Church in.

O'CONNOR, CATHERINE, CSJP, Archivist, Congregation of the Sisters of St. Joseph of Peace, Washington, D.C. **Articles:** Cusack, Margaret Anna; St. Joseph of Peace, Sisters of.

*O'CONNOR, EDWARD DENNIS, CSC, A.B., S.T.D., Associate Professor, Department of Theology and the Institute of Mediaeval Studies, University of Notre Dame, and Director of Studies, Moreau Seminary, Notre Dame, Ind. **Article:** Immaculate Conception.

*O'CONNOR, FRANCIS MICHAEL, SJ, M.A., Ph.L., S.T.D., Professor of Dogmatic Theology, Woodstock College, Woodstock, Md. **Articles:** Buonaiuti, Ernesto; Hügel, Friedrich von; Laberthonniere, Lucien; Tyrrell, George.

*O'CONNOR, JOHN JOSEPH, LL.B., Ph.D., Professor of History, Georgetown University; Director, Human Relations Institute, The American University; Lecturer, Adult Education Institute, The Catholic University of America, Washington, D.C. **Articles:** Laud, William; Mary Tudor, Queen of England; Sander, Nicholas (Sanders).

*O'CONNOR, JOHN THOMAS, SCJ, S.T.D., Professor of Moral Theology, Sacred Heart Monastery, Hales Corners, Wis. **Articles:** Dehon, Leon Gustave; Sacred Heart of Jesus, Priests of.

O'CONNOR, M. **Article:** Franciscan Sisters—Hospital Sisters of the Third Order of St. Francis (OSF).

O'CONNOR, THOMAS H., Ph.D., Professor Emeritus of History, Boston College, Chestnut Hill, Mass. **Articles:** Boston, Archdiocese of; Boston College; Massachusetts, Catholic Church in.

*O'DEA, JOSEPH, OCSO, Monte Cistello, Rome, Italy. **Articles:** Jervaulx, Abbey of; Saint Andrews, Priory of.

*O'DEA, THOMAS FRANCIS, Ph.D., Professor of Sociology, Department of Religion, Columbia University, New York, N.Y. **Articles:** Latter-day Saints, Church of Jesus Christ of; Religion, Sociology of; Smith, Joseph; Young, Brigham.

*ODENIUS, OLOPH, Dr.Phil., Stockholm, Sweden. **Articles:** Alvastra, Abbey of; Ås (Asylum), Abbey of; Bridgit, Abbey of.

*ODOARDI, GIOVANNI, OFMConv, S.T.D., Professor of Ecclesiastical History and Secretary of the Pontifical Faculty, S.

Bonaventura OFMConv, Rome, Italy; Collaborator, *Dizionario Biografico degli Italiani,* and *Bibliotheca Sanctorum.* **Article:** Bonet, Nicholas.

O'DONNELL, ANNE M., SND, Ph.D., Professor of English, The Catholic University of America, Washington, DC. **Article:** Tyndale, William.

*O'DONNELL, AUGUSTINE, B.A., S.T.L., Hist.Eccl.L., Professor of Ecclesiastical History, St. Patrick's College, Thurles, County Tipperary, Ireland. **Article:** Croke, Thomas William.

O'DONNELL, GABRIEL B., OP, S.T.D., Professor, University of St. Thomas (Angelicum), Rome, Italy; Postulator for causes of Father Michael J. McGivney & Rose Hawthorne. **Articles:** Canonization of Saints (History and Procedure); McGivney, Michael Joseph.

*O'DONNELL, JAMES REGINALD, CSB, Ph.D., F.R.S.C., Professor of Palaeography and Latin, Pontifical Institute of Mediaeval Studies, Toronto, Canada. **Articles:** Calcidius; Crathorn, John; John of Mirecourt; John of Ripa; John Philoponus; Macrobius; Nicholas of Autrecourt; William of Auvergne (of Paris).

*O'DONNELL, JOSEPH MARTIN, CM, B.A., Professor of Church History, St. Vincent de Paul Seminary, Baynton Beach, Fla. **Articles:** Gottschalk of Orbais; Joannes Parvus; Paulinus of Aquileia, St.; Smaragdus of Saint-Mihiel.

O'DONNELL, ROBERT J., CSP, Ph.D., Pastor, St. Paul the Apostle Church, New York, N.Y. **Articles:** Converts and Conversion; Paulists.

*O'DONNELL, ROBERT PATRICK, M.A., Glenmary Missioner, Chaplain for the Glenmary Sisters, Fayetteville, Ohio, and Teacher of Philosophy and Art; Lecturer in Philosophy, Our Lady of the Fields Seminary, Glendale, Ohio; Editor, *Glenmary's Challenge.* **Article:** Glenmary Home Missioners.

*O'DONNELL, THOMAS JOSEPH, SJ, Ph.L., M.A., S.T.B., Professorial Lecturer in Medical Ethics, Georgetown Medical School, Washington, D.C.; Spiritual Director, Woodstock College, Woodstock, Md. **Articles:** Hysterectomy; Ovariotomy.

*O'DONNELL, THOMAS MICHAEL, A.B., Instructor in Social Sciences, Carroll College, Helena, MT. **Article:** Day, Victor.

*O'DONOGHUE, PATRICK, MM, Ph.D., Editor, *Japan Mission Journal,* Tokyo, Japan. **Articles:** Endo, Shusaku; Japan, The Catholic Church in.

*O'DONOHOE, JAMES A., J.C.D., Professor of Canon Law and Moral Theology, St. John's Seminary, Brighton, Mass. Professor of Contemporary Moral Problems, Boston College, Chestnut Hill, Mass. **Article:** Seminary Education.

*O'DONOHOE, JAMES A., J.C.D., Professor of Theological Ethics, St. John's Seminary, Brighton, Mass. **Article:** Human Act.

*O'DONOHUE, JOHN FRANCIS, WF, M.A., Staff Member, White Fathers' Generalate, Rome, Italy. **Articles:** Malawi, The Catholic Church in; Zambia, The Catholic Church in; Zimbabwe, The Catholic Church in.

*O'DONOVAN, LEO J., SJ, S.T.L., Th.D., Professor, Weston School of Theology, Cambridge, Mass. **Article:** Rahner, Karl.

*OESCH, HANS, Dr.Phil., Privatdocent for Ethnomusicology and Medieval Music, Universities of Zürich and Basel, Switzerland. **Article:** Guido of Arezzo.

*OESTERLE, JOHN ARTHUR, Ph.D., Associate Professor of Philosophy, University of Notre Dame, Notre Dame, Ind. **Articles:** Art (Philosophy); Circumstances, Moral; Fear; Force and Moral Responsibility; Human Act; Poetics (Aristotelian); Supposition (Logic).

*OESTERREICHER, JOHN M., Very Rev., S.T.L., Director, Institute for Judaeo-Christian Studies, Seton Hall University, Newark, N.J.; Consultor, Secretariate for Christian Unity, Rome, Italy. **Articles:** Hasidism; Judaism.

*O'FARRELL, FRANCIS PHILIP, SJ, B.A., S.T.L., Ph.D., Professor of General Metaphysics, Gregorian University, Rome, Italy. **Articles:** Falsity; Intelligibility, Principle of; Truth [part 1]; Truth [part 3].

*Ó FIAICH, TOMÁS, M.A., Lic.Sc.Hist., Professor of Modern History, St. Patrick's College, Maynooth, Ireland. **Articles:** Armagh, Primatial See of; Clement of Ireland, St.; Coloman, St.; Kilian of Wurzburg, St.

*O'GARA, JAMES, Editor, *Commonweal,* New York, N.Y. **Article:** Cogley, John.

*O'GORMAN, EDMUNDO RAFAEL, Degree in Law, M.A., Ph.D., Professor, Faculty

of Philosophy and Letters, and member, Board of Governors, National University of Mexico, Mexico City, Mexico. **Article:** Acosta, Jose de.

*O'GRADY, GERALD LEO, Ph.D., Assistant Professor, Department of English, Rice University, Houston, Tex. **Article:** Piers Plowman.

*O'HARA, ALBERT RICHARD, SJ, M.A., S.T.L., Ph.D., Professor of Sociology and Labor Relations, National Taiwan University, Taiwan; NCWC News Correspondent. **Article:** Lebbe, Frederic Vincent.

*O'HARA, SISTER M. KEVIN, CSJ, Ph.D., Professor of Philosophy, College of St. Catherine, St. Paul, Minn. **Article:** Normality.

*O'HARE, FRANCIS C., A.B., S.T.D., Professor of Moral Theology and of Sacred Eloquence, St. John's Seminary, Brighton, Mass. **Articles:** Gambling; Compensation, Occult.

*O'HARE, JOSEPH A., SJ, AMERICA, New York, N.Y. **Article:** Roberts, Thomas D'Esterre.

*O'KEEFE, CYRIL BLAISE, SJ, Ph.D., Associate Professor of History and Dean of Arts and Science, Loyola College, Montreal, Quebec, Canada. **Articles:** Albani; Bouillon, Emmanuel Theodose de La Tour d'Auvergne; Clement XI, Pope.

*O'KEEFE, VINCENT, SJ, S.T.D, Assistant General of the Society of Jesus, 1965–1982, New York, NY. **Article:** Arrupe, Pedro.

*OLIN, JOHN CHARLES, Ph.D., Assistant Professor, Department of History, Fordham University, New York, N.Y. **Articles:** Calvin, John; Farel, Guillaume; Institutes of Calvin.

*OLIVIERI, SAMUELE, OFM, Professor of Dogmatic Theology and Patrology, Studio Teologico Francescano, Fiesole (Florence), Italy. **Articles:** Camaldoli, Abbey of; John Discalceatus, Bl.; John Pelingotto, Bl.; Orsi, Giuseppe Agostino; Peter Igneus, Bl.; Pomposa, Abbey of; Saint Alexander of Orosh (Oroshi), Abbey of; San Fruttuoso (Capodimonte), Abbey of; San Martino al Monte Cimino, Abbey of; Santa Marie di Finalpia, Abbey of; Strumi, Abbey of; Vallombrosa, Abbey of; Vangadizza, Abbey of.

*OLLIVIER, GRÉGOIRE, OSB, Diplomé d'études supérieures juridiques, Lecturer in Theology and Canon Law, Abbaye Saint-Guénolé, Landévennec (Finistère), France. **Article:** Landévennec, Abbey of.

*OLMEDO, DANIEL THOMAS, SJ, Ph.D., Professor of Dogmatic Theology and Church History, Montezuma Seminary, Montezuma, N.Mex. **Articles:** Díaz y Barreto, Pascual; Mexico (Modern), The Catholic Church in; Mexico (Colonial); Ruíz y Flores, Leopoldo.

*OLPHE-GALLIARD, MICHEL, SJ, Licencié ès lettres, Professor Emeritus, Institut Catholique de Toulouse; former Director, *Revue d' Ascétique et de Mystique;* Coeditor, *Dictionnaire de Spiritualité ascétique et mystique,* Paris, France. **Article:** Caussade, Jean Pierre de.

*OLSEN, THORKIL DAMSGAARD, Ph.D., Associate Editor, Arnamagnean Dictionary of Old Norse; Secretary, Society of Scandinavian Philology, Copenhagen, Denmark. **Articles:** Petrus de Dacia; Swedenborg, Emanuel; Tausen, Hans.

O'MAHONEY, KEVIN, M.Afr., Ph.L., Provincial, Missionaries of Africa. **Article:** Ethiopian (Ge'ez) Catholic Church.

*O'MALLEY, AUSTIN, FSC, Ph.D., Associate Professor of History, Manhattan College, New York, N.Y. **Articles:** Isidore the Farmer, St.; Joan of Portugal, Bl.; John XX, Pope; Santa Cruz (Coimbra), Monastery of; Theotonius, St.

*O'MALLEY, JOHN W., SJ, Professor of History, University of Detroit, Detroit, Mich. **Article:** Historical Theology.

O'MALLEY, KENNETH G., CP, Ph.D., Director, Paul Bechtold Library, Catholic Theological Union, Chicago, Ill. **Article:** Passionists.

*O'MARA, WILLIAM ANTHONY, A.B., J.C.D., Pastor, Holy Cross Church, Scranton, Pa.; Officialis, Diocese of Scranton. **Article:** Abduction (Impediment to Marriage).

*O'MEARA, JOHN JOSEPH, CSSp, B.A., H.Dip.Education, Dip.Education, General Secretary, Kenya Catholic Secretariat and Educational Secretary-General for the Catholic Missions, Nairobi, Kenya, Africa. **Article:** Kenya, The Catholic Church in.

*OÑATIBIA, IGNACIO, S.T.D., Professor of Dogmatic Theology, Liturgy, Patrology, and Christian Archeology, Diocesan Seminary of Vitoria, Spain. **Article:** Torres, Francisco.

*O'NEIL, LEWIS BOYD, SJ, B.S., Ph.L., M.A., Alma College, Los Gatos, Calif. **Articles:** Cathrein, Viktor; Comitoli, Paolo; Harent, Etienne.

*O'NEILL, COLMAN, OP, Albertinum, Fribourg, Switzerland. **Article:** Saints, Devotion to the.

*O'NEILL, JAMES C., Catholic Relief Services, USCC, New York, N.Y. **Article:** Norris, James Joseph.

*O'NEILL, REGINALD F., SJ, Ph.L., S.T.L., Ph.D., Dean, and Professor of Epistemology and History of Modern and Contemporary Philosophy, Boston College School of Philosophy at Weston, Mass. **Articles:** Certitude; Opinion; Quality.

*O'NEILL, THOMAS, SJ, East Asian Pastoral Institute, Manila, Phillipines. **Article:** Sheridan, Terence James.

*O'NEILL, WILLIAM HENRY, M.A. (Lond.), Ph.D., Assistant Professor of Ancient and Mediaeval Philosophy, University of Southern California, Los Angeles, Calif. **Articles:** God in Pagan Thought; Iamblichus; Lucretius; Plotinus; Socrates.

*ONG, WALTER JACKSON, SJ, Ph.L., S.T.L., Ph.D., Professor of English, St. Louis University, St. Louis, Mo. **Articles:** Humanism; Ramus, Peter.

*O'RIORDAN, SEAN IGNATIUS, CSSR, S.T.D., Professor of Moral and Pastoral Theology, Sant' Alfonso, University of the Lateran, Rome, Italy. **Articles:** Chastity; Modesty.

*ORLANDELLI, GIANFRANCO, Doctorate in Letters and Philosophy, Professor of Paleography and Diplomatics and Secretary, Istituto per la Storia, University of Bologna, Italy. **Article:** Bologna, University of.

*ORLANDI, GIUSEPPE, CSSR, Hist.Eccl.L., Diploma, Vatican School of Paleography and Diplomatics, Professor of Church History, Redemptorist House of Studies, Cortona, Italy. **Articles:** Chromatius of Aquileia, St.; Edessa; Sicily.

*ORLETT, RAYMOND FRANCIS, Glenmary Home Missioner, A.B., S.T.L., S.S.L., Professor of Sacred Scripture, Seminary of Our Lady of the Fields, Cincinnati, Ohio. **Article:** Jesus Christ (in the Bible).

*O'ROURKE, JOHN JAMES JOSEPH, M.A., S.T.L., S.S.L., Professor of Sacred Scripture and Biblical Languages, St.

Charles Seminary, Overbrook, Philadelphia, Pa. **Articles:** Bishop (in the Bible); Church, I (in the Bible); Deacon; Presbyter [part 1]; Rosetta Stone.

*O'ROURKE, MATTHEW JOSEPH, SSJ, M.Ed., Director of Education, Josephite Fathers, Baltimore, Md. **Article:** Josephites.

*O'ROURKE, THADDEUS BRYAN, OFMCap, Capuchin Seminary of St. Anthony, Marathon, Wis. **Article:** Crispin of Viterbo, St.

ORSUTO, DONNA LYNN, S.T.D., Professor "Aggiunta," Institute of Spirituality, Gregorian University, Rome, Italy; Director, The Lay Centre at Foyer Unitas. **Article:** Lay Spirituality.

*ÖRSY, LADISLAS M., SJ, Ph.L., S.T.L., J.C.D., B.A. and M.A. (Oxon.), Professor of Canon Law, Gregorian University, Rome, Italy. **Articles:** Conciliarism (Theological Aspect); Councils, General (Ecumenical), Theology of.

*ÖRSY, LADISLAS M., SJ, L.Ph., L.S.T., S.T.L., M.A. (Oxon, Law), J.C.D., Professor of Canon Law, The Catholic University of America, Washington, D.C. **Article:** Marriage Legislation (Canon Law).

*ORTEGA, JOAQUIN L., Dr. Hist., Director, Biblioteca de Autores Cristianos, Madrid, Spain. **Article:** Spain, the Catholic Church in.

*ORTEGAT, PAUL, SJ, Ph.D., S.T.D., Docteur en lettres, en Philosophie, en Theologie, Professor, Facultés universitaires de Namur, Belgium. **Articles:** Intellectualism; Voluntarism.

*ORTIZ DE URBINA, IGNACIO, SJ, S.T.D., Dr.Theol., Professor of Oriental Patrology, Pontifical Oriental Institute and regorian University, Rome, Italy; Director of the series, *Orientalia Christiana Analecta;* Collaborator, Radio Vaticana. **Articles:** Aphraates; Baradai, James; Edessa, Chronicle of; Nicaea I, Council of; Osrhoene; Sardica, Council of.

*OSBORNE, FRANCIS JOSEPH, SJ, B.A., M.A., Member, National Historical Trust Commission of Jamaica, West Indies. **Article:** Jamaica, The Catholic Church in.

*OSBOURN, RAYMOND ALLEN, M.D., Diplomate of the American Board of Dermatology, Clinical Associate Professor of Dermatology, Georgetown

University School of Medicine, Washington, D.C.; member, Active Staff, Providence Hospital and Georgetown University Hospital; Consultant, Glenn Dale Hospital, Walter Reed General Hospital, Mt. Alto Veterans Hospital. **Article:** Hippocrates.

*OSGNIACH, AUGUSTINE JOHN, OSB, Ph.D., Head, Department of Philosophy, St. Martin's College, Olympia, Wash. **Articles:** Aristocracy; Monarchy.

*O'SHEA, WILLIAM JAMES, SS, Litt.B., S.T.D., Assistant Professor of Theology, School of Sacred Theology, The Catholic University of America, Washington, D.C. **Articles:** Advent; Christ the King, Feast of; Easter Vigil; Eucharistic Elevation; Good Friday; Holy Thursday; Holy Week; Homily; Lent; Mediator Dei; Oratio Super Populum; Ordinations in the Roman Rite; Palm Sunday; Washing of the Feet.

OSTFELD, BARBARA J., DSM, Cantor, Temple Beth Am, Williamsville, N.Y. **Article:** Cantor in Jewish Liturgy.

*O'SULLIVAN, JEREMIAH F., Ph.D., Professor of Medieval History, Fordham University, New York, N.Y. **Articles:** Hassard, John Rose Greene; Robert of Molesme, St.

*O'SULLIVAN, KEVIN PATRICK, OFM, D.D., Lect.Gen., S.S.L., Professor of Pastoral Theology, St. Anthony's College, Galway, Ireland. **Articles:** Geddes, Alexander; MacEvilly, John; MacRory, Joseph; Ussher, James.

*O'SULLIVAN, MOTHER M. GERALDINE, SMG, Superior General, Poor Servants of God, Maryfield, Roehampton, London, England. **Articles:** Poor Servants of the Mother of God; Taylor, Frances Margaret.

*O'TOOLE, ROBERT FRANCIS, SJ, M.A., Ph.L., Teacher, St. John's College, Belize. **Article:** Belize, The Catholic Church in.

*OTTERSON, PLACID HARRY, OCarm, S.T.L., M.S.L.S., Librarian and Teacher of Fundamental Theology, Whitefriars Hall, Washington, D.C. **Article:** Carmelite Sisters—Carmelite Nuns, Calced (OCarm).

OTTING, LORAS C., M.A., Director of the Archives and Historical Records, The Archdiocese of Dubuque, Dubuque, Iowa. **Article:** Dubuque, Archdiocese of.

*OTTO, ALFRED JOACHIM, SJ, Dr.Phil., Sct. Knuds Skole, Stenosgade, Copenhagen, Denmark. **Article:** Denmark, The Catholic Church in.

*OUSPENSKY, LEONIDE ALEXANDROVITCH, Icon Painter, Teacher of Icon Painting, and Professor of Iconology, Seminary of the Exarchate of the Moscow Patriarchate in Western Europe, Paris, France. **Article:** Rublëv, Andrĕi.

*OWENS, JOSEPH, CSSR, M.S.D., F.R.S.C., Professor, Pontifical Institute of Mediaeval Studies, Toronto, Ontario, Canada; member, editorial board, *Monist.* **Articles:** Aristotle; Greek Philosophy; Heraclitus; Parmenides.

*OWENS, LOUIS GERARD, CSSR, S.T.D., Professor of Dogmatic Theology, St. Mary's College, Brockville, Ontario, Canada. **Articles:** Athanasian Creed; Eutychianism; Monothelitism; Virgin Birth.

*OZELT, HADMAR HERMANN, SOCist, Librarian and Archivist, Stift Zwettl, and Teacher, Sängerknabenkonvikt, Zwettl, Austria. **Article:** Zwettl, Abbey of.

*PACETTI, DIONISIO TULLIO, OFM, Ph.D., Prefect of the Bernardine Commission, Collegio S. Bonaventura, Quaracchi-Florence, Italy. **Article:** Bernardine of Siena, St.

*PACHECO, JUAN MANUEL, SJ, S.T.L., Professor of Ecclesiastical History, Faculty of Theology, Universidad Javeriana, and Colegio de San Bartolomé, Bogotá, Colombia. **Articles:** Biffi, Eugenio; Gallo, Andres Maria; Jimenez de Enciso, Salvador.

*PADIPURACKAL, JOHN, Ph.D., Dean, St. Mary's Malankara Seminary, Nalanchira, Thiruvananthapuram, India. **Article:** Syro-Malankara Church.

*PAGE, JOHN R., Associate Executive Secretary, International Commission on English in the Liturgy (ICEL), Washington, D.C. **Article:** International Commission on English in the Liturgy (ICEL).

*PAGÉS, SISTER MARY HELENE, OSU, M.Ed., M.L.S., Librarian, Althoff Catholic High School, and Dean, Graduate Students of the Belleville Motherhouse, Belleville, Ill. **Article:** Ursulines.

*PAIKERT, GEZA CHARLES, J.U.D., Professor of History and Political Science, Le Moyne College, Syracuse, N.Y. **Articles:** Bakocz, Tamas; Bathory; Szanto, Istvan (Arator).

*PAINTER, JOHN, Ph.D., Professor of Theology, St Mark's National Theological Centre, Charles Sturt University Canberra Campus, Australia. **Article:** James, Epistle of.

*PALERM, ANGEL, Dr., Pan American Union, Washington, D.C. **Article:** Sahagún, Bernardino de.

*PALLADINO, ALFONSO GUSTAVO, M.A., S.T.D., Professor of Dogmatic Theology, St. John's Seminary, Brighton, Mass. **Articles:** Predestination (in Catholic Theology); Predestination (in Non-Catholic Theology).

*PALMER, PAUL FRANCIS, SJ, M.A., S.T.D., Professor of Theology, Graduate and Undergraduate Department of Sacred Sciences, Fordham University, New York, N.Y. **Articles:** Attrition and Attritionism; Indulgences.

*PALMER, ROBERT BAUER, Ph.D., Professor of Classical Languages and Literature, Scripps College, Claremont, Calif. **Articles:** Geoffrey of Vendome; Hincmar of Laon; Osbern of Gloucester.

*PANELLA, DONALD ANTHONY, M.A., S.T.L., S.S.L., Professor of Old Testament, St. Joseph's Seminary, Dunwoodie, N.Y. **Articles:** Philistines; Proto-Evangelium.

*PANIAGUA, JUAN ANTONIO, M.D., Professor of the History of Medicine, Faculty of Medicine, and Secretary-General of the Catholic University of Navarre, Spain. **Article:** Navarre, University of.

*PANTEGHINI, GABRIELE, OFMConv, Padua, Italy. **Article:** Buonaccorsi, Filippo.

*PAP, MICHAEL STEPHAN, Ph.D., Professor of History and Political Science and Director of the Institute for Soviet Studies, John Carroll University, Cleveland, Ohio. **Article:** Lenin, N.

PAPADAKIS, ARISTEIDES, Ph.D., Professor of History, University of Maryland, Baltimore, Md. **Article:** John X Camateros, Patriarch of Constantinople.

*PAPI, MELLITO, OSB, monk of the Sylvestrine Benedictine Congregation, Rome, Italy. **Article:** Benedictines, Sylvestrine.

*PAPIN, JOSEPH, Ph.D., S.T.D., LL.D., Professor of History, Villanova University, Villanova, Pa. **Articles:** Bulgakov, Sergei Nikolaevich; Cholmogory, Abbey of; Cieplak, Jan; Filaret (Vasilii Mikhailovich Drozdov); Florenskii,

Pavel Aleksandrovich; Gagarin, Ivan Sergeevich; Holy Synod; Jasov, Abbey of; Jerome of Prague; John Milic; Ladislaus, King of Hungary, St.; Ladislaus of Gielniow, Bl.; Losskii, Nikolai Onufrievich; Neamtu, Abbey of; Prokopovich, Feofan; Solov'ev, Vladimir Sergeevich; Stefan (Semen Iavorskii); Wenceslaus IV, King of Bohemia; Wenceslaus, St.; Zoerardus and Benedict, SS.

*PARACHINI, PATRICIA A., SNJM, D.Min., Coordinator, Spiritual Development, Paulist Seminary, Washington, D.C. **Article:** Durocher, Marie Rose, Bl.

*PARADIS, WILFRID HENRY, Very Rev., J.C.D., Ph.D., Vice Chancellor, Diocese of Manchester, N.H.; *Peritus,* Vatican Council II. **Articles:** Brady, Matthew Francis; New Hampshire, Catholic Church in.

*PARADIS, REV. MSGR. WILFRID HENRY, Project Director, National Catechetical Directory, NCCB, Washington, D.C.: Secretary for Education, USCC. **Article:** Catechetical Directories, National.

PARANA, F., **Article:** Franciscan Sisters—School Sisters of the Third Order Regular of St. Francis (OSF).

*PAREDI, ANGELO, S.T.D., Ph.D., Assistant Director, Biblioteca Ambrosiana, Milan, Italy. **Article:** Ambrosian Rite.

*PARENT, NEIL A., M.A., Executive Director, National Conference of Catechetical Leadership, Washington, D.C. **Article:** National Conference of Catechetical Leadership.

*PARK, MUN SU, SJ, Ph.D., Professor of Sociology, Sogang University, Seoul, Korea. **Article:** Korea, the Catholic Church in.

*PARMISANO, STANLEY FABIAN, OP, B.A. (Philosophy), S.T.Lr., M.A. (English), Prior of the Dominican Novitiate, Province of the Holy Name, Hidden Valley (Thousand Oaks), Calif. **Articles:** Deceit; Desire; Dissimulation; Hypocrisy; Pride; Simulation.

*PARMITER, GEOFFREY VINCENT DE CLIFTON, M.A., barrister-at-law and publisher, London, England. **Articles:** Advertisements, Book of; Barlow, William; Uniformity, Acts of.

*PARSONS, SAMUEL RAYMOND, OP, B.A., S.T.Lr., S.S.L., Professor of Scripture, St. Albert's College, Oakland, Calif. **Article:** Rebirth (in the Bible).

*PARTNER, PETER DAVID, B.A., D.Phil., House Master, Winchester College, Winchester, England. **Article:** States of the Church [part 1].

*PASCAL, PIERRE, Docteur ès lettres, Professor Emeritus, École des Langues orientales, and Professor Emeritus, Sorbonne, Paris, France. **Article:** Avvakum.

*PASCHER, JOSEPH, Dr.Phil., Dr.Theol., Professor of Pastoral Theology, University of Münster, Münster in Westfalen, Germany. **Article:** Matins.

*PÁSZTOR, LAJOS, D.Phil., Keeper of Records, Vatican Secret Archives, Vatican City, Italy. **Article:** Lambruschini, Luigi.

*PATER, THOMAS GEORGE, A.B., S.T.D., Ph.D., Librarian, The Catholic University of America, Washington, D.C. **Article:** Miracles (Theology of).

*PATHIL, KUNCHERIA, CMI, Ph.D., Professor of Systematic Theology and Ecumenics, Dharmaram Vidyakshetram, Bangalore, India. **Articles:** Diamper, Synod of; Goa; India, Christianity in.

*PATRICK, ANNE E., SNJM, Ph.D., Professor of Religion, Carleton College, Northfield, Minn. **Article:** Feminist Theology.

*PATRICK, JAMES, Ph.D., Chairman, Department of Theology, University of Dallas, Irving Tex. Member, Disciples of Christ/Roman Catholic Consultation. **Article:** Christian.

*PATTEE, RICHARD, D.Litt., Professor, Faculty of Letters, and Director of the Department of Modern Languages and Hispanic Center, Laval University, Quebec, Canada. **Articles:** Angola, The Catholic Church in; Cape Verde, The Catholic Church in; Guinea-Bissau, The Catholic Church in; Mozambique, The Catholic Church in; Sao Tome and Principe, The Catholic Church in.

*PAUL, HENRY A., OSFS, M.A., Ed.D., Registrar, Allentown College of St. Francis de Sales, Center Valley, Pa. **Article:** Oblate Sisters of St. Francis de Sales.

*PAUL, J. E., Drayton, near Portsmouth, Hants, England. **Articles:** Abell, Thomas, Bl.; Beche, John, Bl.; Bocking, Edward; Catherine of Aragon; Day, George; Hamilton, Patrick.

*PAULUS, JEAN JOSEPH, Ph.D., Professor, University of Liège, Belgium. **Article:** Henry of Ghent.

*PAULUS, MOTHER MARY ROSALIA, OP, B.S.E., M.A., B.S. in L.S., Mother General, Sisters of St. Dominic of Akron, Ohio. **Article:** Dominicans—Sisters, Dominican Sisters of Akron, Ohio.

*PAULY, REINHARD G., Ph.D., Professor of Music, Lewis and Clark College, Portland, Ore. **Articles:** Haydn, Franz Joseph; Mozart, Wolfgang Amadeus.

*PAVAN, PIETRO P., Ph.D., S.T.D., Doctorate in Social-Political Sciences, Professor of Social Economics, University of the Lateran, Rome, Italy. **Article:** Social Thought, Papal, 2. Basic Concepts.

*PAZ PANI CARRAL, MARIA DE LA, Mexico City, Mexico. **Article:** Cavo, Andrés.

*PEACHEY, PAUL, Ph.D., Professor, Department of Sociology, Catholic University of America, Washington, D.C. **Article:** Russia, The Catholic Church in.

*PEACOCK, PETER EVARIST, OFMCap, D.Mus., A.R.C.M., Warden of Franciscan Uuniversity House at Oxford, Lecturer in Music, University of Oxford and Uuniversity of Reading, England. **Article:** Palestrina, Giovanni Pierluigi da.

*PEARSON, SAMUEL C., Dean of Social Sciences, Southern Illinois University at Edwardsville. **Article:** Americans United for the Separation of Church and State.

*PECKLERS, KEITH F., SJ, Professor of Liturgical History, Pontifical Liturgical Institute, Rome, Italy. **Articles:** Liturgical Movement, I: Catholic; Liturgical Movement, III: Ecumenical Convergences; Liturgical History, III: Reformation to Vatican II; Liturgical Movement, II: Anglican and Protestant.

*PEDERSEN, AMY M., Staff Assistant, *The New Catholic Encyclopedia.* **Article:** Worldwide Church of God.

*PEEBLES, BERNARD MANN, Ph.D., Professor of Greek and Latin and Head of the Department, The Catholic University of America, Washington, D.C.; Coeditor, The Catholic University of America Patristic Studies, and Studies in Mediaeval and Renaissance Latin Language and Literature; Coeditor, *Traditio.* **Articles:** Bartholomew of Urbino; Forcellini, Egidio; O Roma Nobilis; Sulpicius Severus; Wilmart, Andre.

*PEEL, HENRY EDWARD, OP, S.T.Lr., M.A., Professor of Church History and

Sacred Eloquence, Dominican House of Studies, Tallaght, County Dublin, Ireland. **Article:** Troy, John Thomas.

*PEERS-SMITH, WILLIAM, SJ, St. Beuno's College, St. Asaph, Flintshire; North Wales. **Article:** Goodier, Alban.

*PEGON, JOSEPH STANISLAS, SJ, Licentiate in Letters, Licentiate in Scholastic Philosophy, S.T.D., Professor of Dogmatic Theology, Lyon-Fourvière, Chantilly, France; Université St. Joseph, Beyrouth, Syria, and Institut Supérieur de Théologie, Tananarive, Malagasy Republic (Madagascar). **Article:** Discernment, Spiritual.

*PEIFER, CLAUDE JOHN, OSB, A.B., S.T.L., S.S.L., Professor of Sacred Scripture, St. Bede Abbey Seminary, Peru, Ill. **Articles:** Bible and Piety; Fear of the Lord [part 1]; New American Bible; Passover Lamb; Unleavened Bread (in the Bible); Works of God.

*PEIFER, JOHN FREDERICK, B.A., S.T.L., Ph.L., Ph.D., Professor of Philosophy and Dean of Senior College, St. Francis Seminary, Milwaukee, Wis. **Articles:** Apprehension, Simple; Concept; Idea; Term (Logic); Word.

*PELIKAN, JAROSLAV, B.D., Ph.D., D.D., Litt.D., M.A. (h.c.), Titus Street Professor of Ecclesiastical History, Yale University; New Haven, Conn. **Article:** Confessions of Faith, II: Protestant Confessions of Faith.

PELLITERO, RAMIRO, S.T.D., Profesor Adjunto de Teología Pastoral, Universidad de Navarra, Spain. **Articles:** Navarre, University of; Opus Dei.

*PELOQUIN, CHARLES ALEXANDER, D.Mus. (h.c.), faculty member, Boston College, Chestnut Hill, Mass., and Salve Regina College, Newport, R.I.; conductor and composer, Providence, R.I. **Articles:** Choir; Poulenc, Francis.

*PELZEL, MORRIS, Ph.D., Associate Professor of Systematic Theology, Saint Meinrad School of Theology, Saint Meinrad, Ind. **Articles:** Christian Anthropology; Dives in misericordia; Dominum et vivificantem; Redemptor hominis.

PELZEL, PAMELA M., Ph.D. cand., Department of Theology, The Catholic University of America, Washington, DC. **Article:** Gremillion, Joseph Benjamin.

PELZER, ANNE-MARIE, Ph.D., Secretary, L'Alliance Internationale Jeanne d'Arc (Section Belge), Liege, Belgium. **Article:** St. Joan's International Alliance.

*PEÑA, BRAULIO, OP, Ph.L., S.T.B., Dominican House of Studies, Washington, D.C. **Article:** William of Macclesfield; Vallgornera, Tomas de.

*PENN, DONALD ROBERT, Ph.D., Professor of History and Chairman of the Department, Georgetown University, Washington, D.C. **Articles:** Amyot, Jacques; Duperron, Jacques Davy; Duplessis-Mornay, Philippe; Henry IV, King of France; Nantes, Edict of.

*PENNA, ANGELO, CRL, S.T.L., S.S.D., Professor of Hebrew and Comparative Semitic Philology, University of Bari, Italy. **Articles:** Severus of Antioch; Simeon Barsabae, St.; Singidunum, Martyrs of; Sisinnius I, Patriarch of Constantinople; Sisinnius II, Patriarch of Constantinople.

PENNINGTON, KENNETH, Ph.D., Kelly-Quinn Professor of Ecclesiastical and Legal History School of Religious Studies, The Catholic University of America. **Articles:** Frederick II, Roman Emperor; Holy Roman Empire; Innocent IV, Pope.

*PENNINGTON, M. BASIL, OCSO, Monk of St. Joseph's Abbey, Spencer, Mass. **Article:** Prayer, Centering; Spirituality, Christian (History of).

*PENNINGTON, M. BASIL, OCSO, S.T.L., J.C.L., Abbot Emeritus, Abbey of Our Lady of Saint Joseph, Spencer, Mass.; Founder-Director, Cistercian Publications, Institute of Cistercian Studies, Western Michigan University; Director, International Thomas Merton Society. **Articles:** Concilium Monasticum Iuris Canonici; Trappists.

*PEPLER, STEPHEN CONRAD, OP, S.T.L., D.D., Warden of Spode House, Hawkesyard Priory, Rugeley, Staffordshire, England. **Article:** Ditchling Guild of St. Joseph and St. Dominic.

*PEPLINSKI, SISTER JOSEPHINE MARIE, SSJ-TOSF, M.A., Historian, St. Joseph Congregational Home, Stevens Point, Wisc. **Article:** Franciscan Sisters—Sisters of St. Joseph of the Third Order of St. Francis (SSJ-TOSF).

*PEREIRA SALAS, EUGENIO, Licentiate in History, Professor of History and Chairman of Department, University of Chile, Santiago, Chile; Director, Centro de Investigaciones de Historia Americana; President, Chilean Academy of History. **Articles:** Guzman y Lecaros, Joseph Javier; Meneses, Juan Francisco.

*PEREÑA DE MALAGÓN, HELENA, Dr. in Law, Licentiate, Escuela de Administracion Publica, Translator, Pan American Health Organization, World Health Organization Regional Office, Washington, D.C. **Articles:** Gonzalez Davilla, Gil; Montemayor, Juan Francisco; Palafox y Mendoza, Juan de.

*PÉREZ-CABRERA, JOSÉ MANUEL, Dr. in Civil Law, Dr. in Philosophy and Letters, Professor Emeritus, Historian, Marianao, La Habana, Cuba. **Articles:** Cuba, The Catholic Church in; Espada y Landa, Juan Jose Diaz de.

*PÉREZ DE URBEL, JUSTO, OSB, Doctorate in Philosophy and Letters, Professor of Medieval History, University of Madrid, Spain. **Articles:** Albelda, Abbey of; Ferdinand, Bl.; Fitero, Abbey of; John Bassandus, Bl.; Maria Laurentia Longo, Ven.; Moreruela, Abbey of; Piedra, Abbey of; Pombeiro, Abbey of; Santas Creus, Abbey of; Silos, Abbey of; Tostado, Alonzo; Veruela, Abbey of.

PERKO, F. MICHAEL, S.J., Ph.D., Professor of Education & History, Loyola University of Chicago, Chicago, Illinois. **Article:** Church Membership (U.S.).

*PERLER, OTHMAR, Rt. Rev., Dr.Theol., Professor of Early Christian Literature and Archeology, Theologoical Faculty, University of Fribourg, Switzerland. **Article:** Hippo Regius.

*PERNOUD, RÉGINE, Licence ès lettres classiques, Diplôme d'archiviste-paléographe, Doctorat ès lettres, Diplôme de muséographie, Conservateur aux Archives Nationales, Paris, France. **Article:** Joan of Arc, St.

*PERRAUDIN, JEAN, WF, S.T.D., Professor, Major Seminary of Bujumbura, Burundi, Africa. **Articles:** Burundi, The Catholic Church in; Rwanda, The Catholic Church in.

*PERREAULT, AIMO M. GEORGES, OP, B.A., S.T.L., D.Ph. (Montreal), Professor of Philosophy, Social Psychology, and Pastoral Psychology, Pontifical University of St. Thomas Aquinas, Rome, Italy; counselor for priests, religious, and nuns; Consultor, Sacred Congregation of Religious. **Articles:** Central Sense; Phantasm; Senses.

*PERRIN, JOSEPH-MARIE, OP, S.T.Lr., founder of the secular institutes Caritas Christi and Caritas Christi Sacerdotalis, Marseilles, France. **Articles:** Alms and Almsgiving (in the Church); Mercy; Mercy, Works of; Weil, Simone.

*PERROTTA, PAUL CHRISTOPHER, OP, M.A., Ph.D., S.T.Lr., Professor of Theology and Philosophy, Caldwell College, Caldwell, N.J.; Lecturer in Lay Theology, St. Vincent Ferrer School, New York, N.Y., and St. Philip's, Clifton, N.J. **Articles:** Equivocation (Logic); Fallacy.

*PERRY, EUGENE BOONE, M.D., Medical Director and Officer in Medical and Hospital Associations, Houston Tex. **Article:** Knights of Peter Claver.

*PERZANOWSKI, SISTER MARY LORETTA, CFM, M.A., Daughters of Mary of the Immaculate Conception, New Britain, Conn. **Article:** Immaculate Conception, Daughters of Mary of the.

*PETER, CARL JOSEPH, Ph.L., S.T.D., Ph.D., Assistant Professor of Dogmatic Theology, The Catholic University of America, Washington, D.C. **Articles:** Generation of the Word; God (Son); Jesus Christ (in Theology) 3. Special Questions; 10. Psychological Unity; Jesus Christ (in Theology) 3. Special Questions; 9. Messianic Consciousness; Logos, 2. Theology of; Original Justice; Original Sin [part 2]; Word, The.

*PETERFY, SISTER IDA, SDSH, Ph.D., Superior General, Society Devoted to the Sacred Heart, Los Angeles, Calif. **Article:** Sacred Heart, Sisters of the Society Devoted to the.

*PETERMAN, EUGENE LEO, CP, S.T.D., Professor of Systematic Theology and Spiritual Theology, St. Meinrad Seminary, St. Meinrad, Ind. **Articles:** Redemption (Theology of); Salvation History (Heilsgeschichte) [part 2]; Soteriology.

PETERMAN, THOMAS J., S.T.L., Ph.D., priest of the Diocese of Wilmington, Del. **Articles:** Delaware, Catholic Church in; Wilmington, Diocese of.

PETERS, EDWARD, Ph.D., Henry Charles Lea Professor of Medieval History, University of Pennsylvania. **Articles:** Feudalism; Inquisition; Middle Ages.

*PETERS, EDWARD HENRY, CSP, A.M., S.T.D., S.S.L., Editorial Consultant, Paulist Press, New York, N.Y. **Articles:** Adam; Eve [part 2].

*PETERS, FRANCIS EDWARD, Ph.D., Assistant Professor, Department of Classics, New York University, New York, N.Y. **Article:** Avicebron (Ibn Gabirol, Solomon ben Judah).

*PETERS, SISTER M. FRIDIAN, OSF, Ph.D., Vice President and Director of Graduate Studies, St. Francis College, Fort Wayne, Ind. **Articles:** Bonzel, Maria Theresia, Mother; Franciscan Sisters—Sisters of St. Francis of Perpetual Adoration (OSF).

*PETERS, SISTER MARY JOAN, M.S.Ed., Novice Mistress, St. Francis Convent, Nevada, Mo. **Article:** Franciscan Sisters—Sisters of St. Francis of the Holy Eucharist of Independence, MO. (OSF).

*PETERS, WALTER HERMAN, S.T.L., S.S.B., M.A., Ph.D., Chairman of the Department of Religion, College of St. Thomas, St. Paul, Minn. **Articles:** Ferrata, Domenico; Gasparri, Pietro; Merode, Frederic Chislain de.

*PETERSEN, THEODORE CHRISTIAN, CSP, Ph.D., S.T.L., Professor Emeritus, Department of Semitic and Egyptian Language, The Catholic University of America, Washington, D.C. (deceased March 14, 1966). **Articles:** Chabot, Jean Baptiste; Hyvernat, Henri.

PETERSON, SISTER INGRID J., OSF, M.S., Ph.D., Adjunct Professor, Franciscan Institute, Saint Bonaventure University, Saint Bonaventure N.Y. **Article:** Clare of Assisi, St.

*PETIT, LEO FRANCIS, MSC, M.A., Teacher of English and Religion and Seminary Librarian, Sacred Heart Mission Seminary, Geneva, Ill. **Articles:** Chevalier, Jules; Our Lady of the Sacred Heart, Daughters of; Sacred Heart Missionaries.

*PETRASEK, MOTHER EMERENTIA MARY, SSCM, M.A., Instructor, Novitiate Teacher Training Institute, Villa Sacred Heart, Danville, Pa. **Article:** SS. Cyril and Methodius, Sisters of.

*PETRICCIONE, VINCENT FRANCIS, TOR, Ph.B., S.T.L., Archivist of the TOR in the Americas, St. Francis College, Loretto, Pa. **Articles:** Bordoni, Francesco; Hoss, Crescentia, Bl.; Lambertenghi of Como, Geremia, Bl.

*PETRU, FRANCIS ANTHONY, SJ, M.A., Ph.L., S.T.L., S.S.L., Teacher of Sacred Scripture, St. Marys College, St. Marys, Kans. **Article:** Gruenthaner, Michael.

*PETTA, MARCO MATTEO, Hieromonk and Librarian of the Basilian Abbey of Grottaferrata, Rome, Italy. **Articles:** Grottaferrata, Monastery of; Italo-Albanian Catholic Church (Eastern Catholic); Luke of Armento, St.; Nicodemus of Mammola, St.; Sabas the Younger, St.; San Salvatore di Messina, Monastery.

*PETTI, ANTHONY GAETANO, B.A., M.A., Lecturer in English Language and Literature, University College, London, England; Choirmaster, University of London Catholic Choir. **Articles:** Digby, Sir Everard; Recusant Literature; Verstegan, Richard (Rowlands).

*PFALLER, LOUIS LAWRENCE, OSB, M.A., Teacher, Assumption Abbey High School and Seminary, Richardton, N.Dak. **Articles:** Bismarck, Diocese of; Wehrle, Vincent de Paul.

*PFNAUSCH, EDWARD, J.C.D., Assistant Professor of Canon Law, The Catholic University of America, Washington, D.C. **Articles:** Directory for the Ministry and Life of Priests (1994); Whealon, John Francis.

PHAM, VAN T., Ph.D., Visiting Professor of Theology, Xavier University, Cincinnati, Ohio. **Articles:** Cao Dai; Congregation of the Mother Co-Redemptrix; Congregation of Mary, Queen; La Vang, Our Lady of; Vietnam, the Catholic Church in.

PHAN, PETER C., S.T.D., Ph.D., D.D., Warren-Blanding Professor of Religion and Culture, The Catholic University of America, Washington, D.C. **Articles:** Processions, Trinitarian; Relations, Trinitarian; Rhodes, Alexandre de; Vietnam, the Catholic Church in.

PHAN, THANH THUY THERESA, LHC, M.A., Director, Office of Asian-Pacific Islander Ministry, Diocese of San Bernardino, Calif. **Article:** Lovers of the Holy Cross.

*PHELAN, JOHN LEDDY, Ph.D., Associate Professor of History, University of Wisconsin, Madison, Wis. **Articles:** Mendieta, Geronimo de; Torquemada, Juan de (1563?–1624).

*PHELPS, JANE L., Ph.D., Assistant Professor of History, College of New Rochelle, New Rochelle, N.Y. **Article:** Organ, Liturgical Use Of.

PHILIBERT, PAUL, OP, S.T.D., Distinguished Visiting Professor of Church and Society, Aquinas Institute, Saint Louis, Mo. **Article:** Dominicans.

*PHILIBERT, PAUL J., OP, Boys Town Center for the Study of Youth Development, Department of Religious Studies/Religious Education, Catholic University of America, Washington, D.C. **Article:** Moral Education.

*PHILIPON, MICHEL, OP, S.T.M., Professor of Theology, Dominican House of

Studies, Toulouse, France; *Peritus,* Vatican Council II. **Article:** Elizabeth of the Trinity, Bl.

*PHILIPS, GERARD, Rt. Rev., S.T.D., Professor of Dogma, University of Louvain, Belgium; *Peritus,* Vatican Council II. **Article:** Janssens, Aloysius.

*PHILLIPS, HUGH JOSEPH, M.A., M.S. in L.S., Library, Mount St. Mary's College and Seminary, Emmitsburg, Md. **Article:** Byrne, William.

PHILLIPS, JONATHAN P., Ph.D., Senior Lecturer in Medieval History, Royal Holloway, University of London, England. **Article:** Crusaders' States.

*PICASSO, GIORGIO, OSBOliv, Ph.D., monk of the Abbey of Seregno (Milan), Diploma in Paleography, Diplomatics, and Archival Science, Assistant Professor of Medieval History, Catholic University of Milan, Italy. **Article:** Benedictines, Olivetan.

*PICHARD, JOSEPH, Editor, *Art Chrétien,* Paris, France. **Articles:** Bellot, Paul; Couturier, Pierre Marie Alain; Liturgical Art, History of, Pt 3: 20th Century Renewal Efforts.

*PICKAR, CHARLES HERMAN, Very Rev., OSA, S.T.L., S.S.L., Assistant General, Generalate of the Augustinian Friars, Rome, Italy. **Articles:** Bomberg, Daniel; Estienne (Etienne); Faith, 1. In the Bible; Idolatry (in the Bible); Images, Biblical Prohibition of; Philip, Apostle, St.; Philip the Deacon.

*PICKER, MARTIN, Ph.D., Assistant Professor of Music, College of Arts and Sciences, Rutgers University, New Brunswick, N.J. **Articles:** Clemens non Papa, Jacobus; Desprez, Josquin; La Rue, Pierre de; Lasso, Orlando di.

*PIEPKORN, ARTHUR CARL, B.D., Ph.D., Minister in the Lutheran Church, Missouri Synod; Graduate Professor of Systematic Theology and Chairman of the Department, Concordia Seminary, St. Louis, Mo. **Articles:** Concord, Formula and Book of; Heidelberg Catechism.

PIERCE, JOANNE M., Ph.D., Associate Professor of Religious Studies, College of the Holy Cross, Worcester, Mass. **Articles:** Missal, Roman; Ritual, Roman; Sacramentaries, I: Historical.

*PIERCE, JUSTIN ANTHONY, SDS, S.T.L., S.S.L., Professor of Biblical Greek and Latin, St. Pius X Seminary, Galt, Calif.

Articles: Israel, 1. Introduction; Jacob, Patriarch; Weights and Measures (in the Bible).

*PIERONI, PIETRO, OMD, Special Studies in Library Science, Vatican Library, Rector of the Religious House, S. Giovanni Leonardi, Rome, Italy; Librarian, central library of the order. **Article:** Clerks Regular of the Mother of God.

*PIKE, FREDERICK BRAUN, Ph.D., Associate Professor of History, University of Notre Dame, Notre Dame, Ind. **Articles:** Arrieta, Francisco Sales de; Errazuriz y Valdiviesco, Crescente.

*PIKE, PACHITA TENNANT, B.A., Lecturer on Latin American Affairs, Latin American Foreign Student Adviser, University of Notre Dame, Notre Dame, Ind. **Articles:** Delgado, José Matís; Morazán, Francisco.

PINEDA-MADRID, NANCY, M.Div., Ph.D. cand., Graduate Theological Union, Berkeley, Calif. **Article:** Latina Theology.

*PINILLA COTE, ALFONSO MARIA, Canon, S.T.D., Professor of Ecclesiastical History and Patrology, Seminario Conciliar, Nueva Pamplona, Colombia. **Article:** Sanchez de Tejada, Ignacio.

*PIROTTO, ARMANDO DIEGO, Dr. in Law and Social Sciences, Professor of Medieval History, Facultad de Humanidades, Montevideo, Uruguay; Professor of Historiography, Instituto de Profesores del Uruguay **Article:** Uruguay, the Catholic Church in.

*PISKULA, BOSCO ROBERT, OFM, A.B., J.C.L., Holy Name College, Washington, D.C. **Articles:** Engel, Hans Ludwig; Gallandi, Andrea; Pirhing, Ehrenreich; Pithou, Pierre; Poltzmacher, Johann; Pontanus Romanus, Lucovicus.

*PITTS, WILLIAM, Ph.D., Professor of Religion, Baylor University, Waco, TX. **Article:** Davidians.

*PIZZORNI, REGINALDO MARIA, OP, S.T.D., Ph.D., Professor, Pontifical University of St. Thomas Aquinas, Pontifical University of the Lateran, and the International University of Social Studies *Pro Deo,* Rome, Italy. **Articles:** Garrigou-Lagrange, Reginald; Liberatore, Matteo; Sanseverino, Gaetano.

*PLAISANCE, ALOYSIUS FREDERICK, OSB, Ph.D., Professor of History and Chairman of the Department, St. Bernard College, Cullman, Ala. **Article:** Bannon, John B.

*PLANGGER, ALBERT B., SMB, M.A., Mambo Press, Zimbabwe. **Article:** Mozambique, The Catholic Church in.

*PLASTARAS, JAMES CONSTANTINE, CM, M.A., S.T.L., S.S.L., Seminary of Our Lady of Angels, Albany, N.Y. **Articles:** Abraham's Bosom; Enoch; Heaven (in the Bible).

*PLATELLE, HENRI, Docteur ès lettres, S.T.L., Professor, Facultés catholique de Lille, and Director, Séminaire Académique de Lille, France. **Articles:** Liessies, Abbey of; Saint-Amand-les-Eaux, Abbey of; Saint-Riquier, Abbey of; Saint-Valery-sur-Somme, Abbey of.

*PLATT, STEWART JOSEPH, Assistant Pastor, St. Edward Church, Youngstown, Ohio; Provincial Director of Novice Masters, U.S. Province, Institute of the Heart of Jesus. **Article:** Heart of Jesus, Institute of the.

*PLÖCHL, WILLIBALD MARIA, Iur.Dr., Professor of Law and Head of the Institute of Canon Law and the Institute of European Law History, University of Vienna, Austria. **Articles:** Diplomatics, Ecclesiastical; John XVIII, Pope; John XVII, Pope; John XV, Pope; Jordan of Quedlingburg; Theodora; Theophylactus; Tusculani.

*POCH, SISTER M. CLEMENTINE, FDC, B.A., Teacher, St. Joseph Hill Academy, Staten Island, New York, N.Y. **Article:** Divine Charity, Daughters of.

*POCHIN MOULD, DAPHNE DESIRÉE CHARLOTTE, B.Sc., Ph.D., Aherla House, Aherla, County Cork, Ireland. **Articles:** Brendan, SS.; Colman, SS.; Finan (Cam), St.; Finnian, SS.; Fintan, SS.; Jon Ogmundsson, St.; Kenneth (Canice) of Derry, St.; Kilian of Aubigny, St.

*POETZEL, RICHARD KARL, CSSR, B.A., Librarian and Professor of Religious Education, Mt. St. Alphonsus, Esopus, N.Y. **Articles:** Alipius, St.; Arnobius the Younger; Arnobius the Elder; Bassianus of Ephesus; Beryllus of Bostra; Domitian of Ancyra; Eusebius, Pope, St.; Felicissimus and Agapitus, SS.; Pelagia, SS.; Possidius, St.

*POLAN, STANLEY MORRIS, SSCC, S.T.L., S.S.L., Professor of Sacred Scripture, Queen of Peace Seminary, Jaffrey Center, N.H. **Articles:** Adoption (in the Bible); Aquinas, Philippus; Circumcision; Commandments, Ten [part 1]; Dietary Laws, Hebrew; Phylacteries; Pilgrimages, 1. In the Bible;

Pratensis, Felix; Purification (in the Bible); Wandering Jew, Legend of the; Zamora, Alfonso de.

*POLKING, JOSEPH C., B.A., LL.B., Assistant to Staff Editor for Canon and Civil Law, *New Catholic Encyclopedia,* The Catholic University of America, Washington, D.C. **Article:** Church and State in the U.S. (Legal History), 3. Period of Conflict (1834–1900).

*POLLACK, ANDREW JOHN, CPPS, A.B., S.T.D., Assistant Professor of History, Patrology, and Oriental Theology, St. Charles Seminary, Carthagena, Ohio. **Articles:** Bufalo, Gaspare del, St.; Mattias, Maria de, Bl.; Merlini, Giovanni.

*POLLARD, JOHN E., S.T.L., Representative for Catechesis and Leadership Development, Department of Education, United States Catholic Conference, Washington, D.C. **Articles:** Catechism of the Catholic Church; International Council for Catechesis (COINCAT).

*POLLOCK, ROBERT CHANNON, B.S., Ph.D., LL.D., Professor of Philosophy, Fordham University; Professor of Philosophy, New School for Social Research; Adjunct Professor of Philosophy, Pace College; and President, Luigi Sturzo Foundation for Sociological Studies, New York, N.Y. **Articles:** Emerson, Ralph Waldo; Sturzo, Luigi.

*POLMAN, PONTIEN A. J. M., OFM, Dr.Theol., Mag.Theol., at Rome, by order of the Dutch government, for editing of historical sources; member, Royal Netherlands Academy of Sciences and Letters, Utrecht, Netherlands. **Articles:** Neercassel, Joannes van; Rovenius, Philippus.

*POND, KATHLEEN ELIZABETH, Honours Degree in Modern Languages (University of London), tutor in modern languages (French and Spanish) to university students; translator and writer, Oxford, England. **Articles:** Agreda, Mary of; Bernardino of Laredo; Francis of Osuna; Peers, Edgar Allison.

*PONKO, VINCENT HARRY, JR., Ph.D., Assistant Professor of History, Villanova University, Villanova, Pa. **Articles:** Atwater, William; Barberini; Chieregati, Francesco; Convocation of the English Clergy; Fitzalan, Henry; Foxe, Richard (Fox); Holden, Henry; Urban VIII, Pope.

*POPKIN, RICHARD H., Ph.D., Professor of Philosophy and Chairman of Department, University of California at San Diego, Calif. **Articles:** Bayle, Pierre; Charron, Pierre; Huet, Pierre Daniel; Sanches, Francisco (Sanchez).

*POPPI, ANTONINO, OFMConv, S.T.D., Ph.D., Assistant Professor of Moral Philosophy, University of Padua, and Professor of Scholastic Philosophy, Istituto S. Antonio Dottore, Padua, Italy. **Articles:** Trombetta, Antonio; Zimara, Marco Antonio.

*PORRAS, WILLIAM MUÑOZ, M.C.L., M.A., J.S.D., J.C.D., Forest Hills, Long Island, N.Y. **Article:** Patronato Real [Patronato of Spain].

*PORTER, THOMAS AQUINAS, OCSO, B.A., J.C.L., Our Lady of the Holy Cross Abbey, Berryville, Va. **Articles:** Forgiveness of Sins; Repentance; Spiritual Theology.

*POSHEK, DONNA M., M.A., The Catholic University of America, Washington, D.C. **Article:** Henana.

*POSPISHIL, VICTOR JOHN, Very Rev., J.C.D., Sc.Eccl. Orient.Lic., Pastor of the Byzantine Rite, Diocese of Krizhevtsi, Pittsburgh, Pa. **Articles:** Exarchy; Orthodox Church of Serbia.

*POTVIN, RAYMOND HERVE, S.T.B., Ph.D., Associate Professor of Sociology, The Catholic University of America, Washington, D.C. **Articles:** Secularization; Society [part 2].

*POULIOT, LÉON JOSEPH, SJ, Ph.D., S.T.D., Eccl.Hist.D., Historical Research, Collège Sainte Marie, Montreal, Canada. **Articles:** Allouez, Claude Jean; Bourget, Ignace; Bruchesi, Louis Joseph Paul Napoleon; Dablon, Claude; Jesuit Relations; Mance, Jeanne; North American Martyrs.

*POUPARD, PAUL JOSEPH, Doctorat en theologie, Docteur en Histoire, Diplome de l'Ecole des Hautes Etudes, attached to the Papal Secretariate of State, Vatican City, Italy. **Article:** Bautain, Louis Eugene Marie.

*POWELL, JAMES, Ph.D., Assistant Professor of History, University of Illinois, Urbana, Ill. **Articles:** Henry III, Roman Emperor; Henry IV, Roman Emperor; Tancred (mid-1070s–1112); Urban III, Pope.

POWELL, JAMES, Ph.D., Professor Emeritus of History, Syracuse University, Syracuse, New York. **Articles:** Albigenses; Gregory IX, Pope; Honorius III, Pope; Innocent II, Pope; Innocent III, Pope.

*POWELL, RALPH AUSTIN, OP, Ph.D., S.T.Lr., Professor of Social Philosophy, Aquinas Institute, School of Philosophy, River Forest, Ill. **Article:** Lachelier, Jules.

*POWER, SISTER ALACOQUE, CCVI, Ph.D., Chairman, English Department, Incarnate Word College, San Antonio, Tex. **Article:** Incarnate Word, Sisters of Charity of the.

*POWER, CORNELIUS MICHAEL, Rt. Rev., J.C.D., Chancellor, Archdiocese of Seattle, and Pastor, Our Lady of the Lake Parish, Seattle, Wash. **Article:** Cemeteries, Canon Law of.

*POWER, DAVID NOEL, OMI, Associate Professor of Systematic Theology, Catholic University of America, Washington, D.C. **Article:** Ministry (Ecclesiology).

POWER, DAVID NOEL, OMI, S.T.D., Professor-Emeritus of Systematic Theology, Department of Theology, The Catholic University of America, Washington, D.C. **Articles:** Eucharist in Contemporary Catholic Theology; Priesthood in Christian Tradition.

*POWER, EDWARD JOHN, Ph.D., Professor of Education, Boston College, Chestnut Hill, Mass. **Article:** Burns, James Aloysius.

POWER, JOSEPH, OSFS, DeSales Resource Center, Stella Niagara, N.Y. **Article:** Francis de Sales, St.

POWERS, DAVID, Sch.P., Devon, Penn. **Article:** Piarists.

*POWERS, RAYMOND JUDE, OP, A.B., Dominican House of Studies, Washington, D.C. **Articles:** Lopez, Ludovico; Martinez, Juan de Prado.

*POWERS, RAYMOND THOMAS, B.A., S.T.L., S.T.D., Professor of Moral Theology and Canon Law, St. Joseph's Seminary, Yonkers, N.Y.; Professor of Theology, College of Mount St. Vincent, New York, N.Y. **Articles:** Conscientious Objection; Military Service.

*PRETE, SERAFINO, Eccl.Hist.D., Diploma in Paleography and Diplomatics (Vatican School), Professor of Ancient Christian Literature, University of Bologna, Italy. **Article:** Mercati, Giovanni.

*PRINCIPE, WALTER HENRY, CSB, M.A., M.S.L., M.S.D., Diplôme de l'École des Hautes Études, Professor of Dogmatic Theology, St. Basil's Seminary, Toronto, Canada. **Articles:** Bus, Cesar de, Bl.; Celestine IV, Pope; Compagnie du Saint-Sacrement; Destiny, Supernatural; Innocent V, Pope, Bl.; Obediential Potency; Orleans-Longueville, Antoinette d'; Preternatural; Spondanus, Henri (de Sponde).

PRIOR, JOHN MANSFORD, SVD, Ph.D., Executive Secretary, Candraditya Research Centre for the Study of Culture and Religion in Maumere, Flores, Indonesia. **Articles:** East Timor, Catholic Church in; Indonesia, Catholic Church in.

*PRIVETT, STEPHEN A., SJ, Ph.D., Assistant Professor, Graduate Program in Catechetics, Pastoral Liturgy and Spirituality, Santa Clara University. **Article:** Lucey, Robert Emmet.

*PROUVOST, HENRY, MEP, Librarian, Missions Étrangères, Paris, France. **Articles:** Brisacier, Jacques Charles de; Lambert de la Motte, Pierre; Pallu, Francois.

*PROVOST, HONORIUS, Ph.L., S.T.L., M.A. (History), Assistant Archivist, Laval University and Seminary, Quebec, Canada. **Articles:** Begin, Louis Nazaire; Briand, Jean Olivier; Esglis, Louis Philippe Mariauchau d'; Hubert, Jean Francois; Laval, François de Montmorency, Bl.; Plessis, Joseph Octave; Rouleau, Felix Raymond Marie; Saint-Vallier, Jean Baptiste de la Croix Chevrieres de; Taschereau, Elzear Alexandre; Villeneuve, Jean Marie Rodrigue.

*PRPIC, GEORGE JURE, Ph.D., Assistant Professor of History and member of the Institute for Soviet and East European Studies, John Carroll University, Cleveland, Ohio. **Articles:** Krizanic, Juraj; Smotryts'kyi, Meletii; Stepinac, Alojzije Viktor, Bl.; Strossmayer, Josip Juraj.

*PRUFER, THOMAS, Ph.D., Associate Professor of Philosophy, The Catholic University of America, Washington, D.C. **Articles:** Heidegger, Martin; Nonbeing.

*PRÜMM, KARL, SJ, Dr.Theol., Dr.Phil., Professor of Early Christianity and the History of Religion, Pontifical Biblical Institute, Rome, Italy. **Articles:** Chthonic Divinities, Worship of; Earth-Mother, Worship of the; Mystery Religions, Greco-Oriental; Oracle; Winds, Worship of the.

PRZEWOZNY, BERNARD J., OFMConv., S.T.D., Professor Emeritus, Pontifical Theological Faculty of St. Bonaven-

ture, Rome, Italy. **Article:** Christocentrism.

*PRZEZDZIECKI, JOSEPH J., S.T.L., L.M.S., Ph.D., Professor of Metaphysics and Ancient and Medieval Philosophy, Immaculate Conception Seminary, Darlington, N.J.; Professor of Ethics, Ladycliff College, Highland Falls, N.Y. **Articles:** Durandus of Aurillac; John of Sterngassen; Peter Aureoli; Thomas Bradwardine; Thomas of Sutton; Thomas of Claxton.

*PUPI, ANGELO, Ph.D., Assistant Professor of the History of Philosophy, Catholic University of the Sacred Heart, Milan, Italy. **Article:** Bruno, Giordano.

*PURCELL, LAWRENCE M., S.T.D., Pastor, St. James Catholic Community, Solana Beach, CA. **Article:** Jadot, Jean.

*PURCELL, MICHAEL, Ph.B., Ph.L., Ph.D., Lecturer in Systematic Theology, University of Edinburgh, Scotland. **Article:** Winning, Thomas Joseph.

PYNE, TRICIA T., Historian and Archivist, Diocese of Wheeling-Charleston, Wheeling, WV. **Article:** West Virginia, Catholic Church in.

*QUAINTANCE, DAVID ALOYSIUS, FSC, M.A., Ed.D., Director of Reading Development, La Salle College, Philadelphia, Pa. **Article:** Hawks, Edward.

*QUASTEN, JOHANNES, Dr. Theol., Kelly Professor of Ecclesiastical History, The Catholic University of America, Washington, D.C.; Founder and Editor, *Studies in Christian Antiquity;* Founder and Coeditor, *Ancient Christian Writers;* Coeditor, *Stromata Patristica;* Coeditor, *Liturgiewissenschaftliche Quellen und Forschungen* **Articles:** Abercius, Epitaph of; Altaner, Berthold; Apostolic Constitutions; Apostolic Church Order; Didascalia Apostolorum; Dolger, Franz Joseph; Ehrhard, Albert; Fish, Symbolism of; Gallican Rites; Good Shepherd; Pectorius, Epitaph of; Plumpe, Joseph Conrad; Serapion of Thmuis, St.

*QUIGLEY, JAMES FERRER, OP, M.A., Pontifical Faculty of Theology of the Immaculate Conception, Dominican House of Studies, Washington, D.C. **Articles:** Cunialati, Fulgenzio; Didacus of Azevedo, Bl.; Nider, Johann.

QUIGNEY, SISTER THERESE ANN, OSF, M.Ed., Vocation Director, Mount Assisi Convent, Lemont, Ill. **Article:** Franciscan Sisters—School Sisters of St. Francis of Christ the King (OSF).

*QUINLAN, JOHN, S.T.L., S.T.D., S.S.L., Professor of New Testament, School of Sacred Theology, The Catholic University of America, Washington, D.C. **Article:** Matthew, Gospel according to.

*QUINLAN, MARY HALL, RSCJ, Ph.D., Professor of History and Dean, Newton College of the Sacred Heart, Newton, Mass. **Articles:** Astros, Paul Therese David d'; Bonald, Louis Gabriel Ambroise de; Deluil-Martiny, Marie of Jesus, Bl.; Goyau, Georges; Rohrbacher, Rene Francois.

QUINN, MOST REV. A. JAMES, J.D., J.C.D. Auxiliary Bishop and Vicar General, Diocese of Cleveland, Ohio. **Articles:** Bishop, Auxiliary; Bishop, Diocesan (Canon Law).

*QUINN, JAMES, SJ, M.A., Vice Postulator, Cause of Bl. John Ogilvie, SJ, St. Mary's, Woodhall House, Juniper Green, Edinburgh, Scotland. **Articles:** Forbes, Alexander Penrose; Hay, George; Ogilvie, John, St.

*QUINN, JEROME DONALD, M.A., S.T.L., S.S.L., Professor of Sacred Scripture, St. Paul Seminary, St. Paul, Minn. **Articles:** Ascension of Jesus Christ [part 1]; Descent of Christ into Hell.

*QUINN, JOHN MICHAEL, OSA, Ph.D., Biscayne College, Miami, Fla. **Articles:** Eternity; Instant; Now; Phenomenalism; Present, The; Time.

*QUINN, JOHN R., Ph.B., S.T.L., Professor of Classical Languages and Theology and President, St. Francis College, Minor Seminary, Diocese of San Diego, El Cajon, Calif. **Articles:** Blessings, Liturgical; Sacramentals.

*QUINN, JOHN STEPHEN, Very Rev., M.A., S.T.B., J.C.D., Officialis, Archdiocese of Chicago, Ill.; *Peritus,* Vatican Council II. **Article:** Judicial Vicar (Officialis).

*QUINN, PATRICK JAMES, B.Arch. (Hons.), Arch.M., Architect and Consultant on Liturgical Arts and Assistant Professor of Architecture, College of Environmental Design, University of California at Berkeley, Calif. **Article:** Church Architecture, History of, 11: United States.

*QUINN, RICHARD MARTIN, Very Rev., M.A., Rector, St. Andrew's Seminary, Rochester, N.Y. **Article:** Hendrick, Thomas Augustine.

*RAAD, VIRGINIA LEE, B.A., Diplôme, École Normale de Musique, Paris,

Docteur de l'Université (Paris), Lecturer, Concert Pianist, Artist-in-Residence, Salem College, Salem, W.Va. **Articles:** Debussy, Achille Claude; Faure, Gabriel Urbain.

*RABBAN, RAPHAEL, Most Rev., Ph.D., S.T.D., Archbishop (Chaldean Rite), Diocese of Kerkuk, Iraq; Consultor, Sacred Oriental Congregation, Rome, Italy. **Article:** Chaldean Catholic Church (Eastern Catholic).

RABENSTEIN, KATHERINE I., B.S.F.S., Senior Credentialing Specialist, American Nurses Association, Washington, D.C. **Articles:** Abad Casasempere, Amalia, and Companions, BB.; Abbot, Henry, Bl.; Adams, John, Bl.; Agnes of Bohemia, St.; Agostini, Zeferino, Bl.; Aguilar Aleman, Rodrigo, St.; Albert, Federico, Bl.; Alcober Figuera, Juan Tomas, St.; Alfield, Thomas, Bl.; Almería, Martyrs of, BB.; Alvarado Cardozo, Laura Elena, Bl.; Alvarez Mendoza, Julio, St.; Amias, John, Bl.; An-Xing, Anna, and Companions, SS.; Anderton, Robert, Bl.; Andlauer, Modeste, St.; Andleby, William, Bl.; Andrew the Catechist, Bl.; Apor, Vilmos, Bl.; Armenia, Martyrs of, BB.; Arnáiz Barón, Rafael, Bl.; Asensio Barroso, Florentino, Bl.; Ashley, Ralph, Bl.; Astorch, María Angela, Bl.; Atkinson, Thomas, Bl.; Aviat, Francesca Salesia, Bl.; Baccilieri, Ferdinando Maria, Bl.; Bakanja, Isidore, Bl.; Bakhita, Giuseppina, St.; Balat, Theodoric, St.; Baldo, Giuseppe, Bl.; Bales, Christopher, Bl.; Bamber, Edward, Bl.; Bandrés y Elósegui, María Antonia, Bl.; Baouardy, Maríam, Bl.; Barbal Cosan, Jaime Hilario, St.; Barbantini, María Domenica Brun, Bl.; Barbieri, Clelia Maria Rachel, St.; Barkworth, Mark, Bl.; Batiz Sainz, Luis, St.; Bauer, Andre, St.; Bays, Marguerite, Bl.; Beesley, George, Bl.; Belanger, Dina, Bl.; Bell, James, Bl.; Bell, Arthur, Bl.; Belson, Thomas, Bl.; Bessette, André, Bl.; Bickerdike, Robert, Bl.; Blake, Alexander, Bl.; Blanes Giner, Marino, Bl.; Blondin, Marie-Anne Sureau, Bl.; Boccardo, Giovanni Maria, Bl.; Bojanowski, Edmund Wojciech Stanislas, Bl.; Bonilli, Pietro, Bl.; Bonino, Giuseppina Gabriella, Bl.; Bosatta, Chiara Dina, Bl.; Bouteiller, Marthe le, Bl.; Bowes, Marmaduke, Bl.; Bracco, Teresa, Bl.; Brandsma, Titus, Bl.; Brazil, Martyrs of, BB.; Bretton, John, Bl.; Brottier, Daniel Jules Alexis, Bl.; Bullaker, Thomas, Bl.; Burden, Edward, Bl.; Burke, Sir John; Burke, Honoria; Butler, María Bernarda, Bl.; Buxton,

Christopher, Bl.; Cadwallador, Roger, Bl.; Caiani, María Margherita del Sacro Cuore, Bl.; Calabria, Giovanni, St.; Callo, Marcel, Bl.; Caloca Cortes, Agustin, St.; Calungsod, Pedro, Bl.; Campidelli, Pius (Pio), Bl.; Campion, Edward, Bl.; Canori-Mora, Elisabetta, Bl.; Caravario, Callisto (Kalikst), St.; Catanoso, Gaetano (Cajetan), Bl.; Catherick, Edmund, Bl.; Centurione Bracelli, Virginia, Bl.; Cevoli, Florida, Bl.; Ch'en, Rose and Teresa, SS.; Chavara, Kuriackos (Cyriac) Elias, Bl.; Chavez Orozco, María Vicenta of Santa Dorothea, Bl.; Chen Ximan, Simon, St.; Chevrier, Antoine Marie, Bl.; Chmielowski, Albert, St.; Chylinski, Rafal Melchoir, Bl.; Cimatti, Maria Raffaella, Bl.; Cipitria y Barriola, Cándida María de Jesús, Bl.; Cirer Carbonel, Francinaina, Bl.; Cittadini, Caterina, Bl.; Cocchetti, Annuciata, Bl.; Coll Guitart, François, Bl.; Colombière, Claude de la, St.; Comboni, Daniele, Bl.; Comensoli, Geltrude Caterina, Bl.; Conforti, Guido Maria, Bl.; Cordier, Jean-Nicolas, Bl.; Cormier, Hyacinthe-Marie, Bl.; Cornelius, John, Bl.; Correa Magallanes, Mateo, St.; Crockett, Ralph, Bl.; Crow, Alexander, Bl.; Cruz Alvarado, Atilano, St.; Cusmano, Giacomo, Bl.; Darowska, Marcelina Kotowicz, Bl.; Davies, William, Bl.; Dean, William, Bl.; Delanoue, Jeanne (Joan), St.; Diaz Gandia, Carlos, Bl.; Diaz del Rincon, Francisco, St.; Dibdale, Robert, Bl.; Dickenson, Roger, Bl.; Dierkx, Anne Catherine, St.; Diez y Bustos de Molina, Vitoria, Bl.; Domingo y Sol, Manuel, Bl.; Dominguito of Saragossa, St.; Dong Bodi, Patrick, St.; Douglas, George, Bl.; Drury, Robert, Bl.; Duke, Edmund, Bl.; Dusmet, Giuseppe Benedetto, Bl.; Ebner, Margaretha, Bl.; Errington, George, Bl.; Esqueda Ramirez, Pedro, St.; Euse Hoyos, Mariano de Jesús, Bl.; Exmew, William, Bl.; Faa di Bruno, Francesco, Bl.; Farina, Giovanni Antonio, Bl.; Faringdon, Hugh, Bl.; Fasani, Francesco Antonio, St.; Fasce, Maria Teresa, Bl.; Faubel Cano, Juan Bautista, Bl.; Febres Cordero Muñoz, Miguel Francisco, St.; Felton, Thomas, Bl.; Feng De, Matthew, St.; Fenn, James, Bl.; Fenwick, John, Bl.; Fernandez Solar, Teresa de los Andes, St.; Ferragud Girbes, Jose Ramon, Bl.; Ferrari, Andreas Carlo, Bl.; Fetherston, Richard, Bl.; Filby, William, Bl.; Filcock, Roger, Bl.; Finch, John, Bl.; Fingley, John, Bl.; Flathers, Matthew, Bl.; Flores Garcia, Margarito, St.; Flores Varela,

Jose Isabel, St.; Flower, Richard, Bl.; Ford, Thomas, Bl.; Forest, John, Bl.; Francia, Annibale Maria di, Bl.; Frassati, Pier Giorgio, Bl.; Frassinello, Benedetta Cambiagio, Bl.; Freeman, William, Bl.; Frelichowski, Stefan Wincenty, Bl.; Friedhofen, Peter, Bl.; Gabriel, Colomba Joanna, Bl.; Galand, Agnes of Jesus, Bl.; Galbis Girones, Vicente, Bl.; Galvan Bermudez, David, St.; Galvão de Franca, Antonio de Sant'Ana, Bl.; Gapp, Jakob, Bl.; Gárate, Francisco, Bl.; Gardiner, German, Bl.; Garlick, Nicholas, Bl.; Gattorno, Rosa Maria Benedetta, Bl.; Gavan, John, Bl.; Gerard, Miles, Bl.; Gérard, Josef Valencia, Bl.; Gervase, George, Bl.; Giaccardo, Timoteo Giuseppe Domenico Vicenzo Antonio, Bl.; Gibson, William, Bl.; Gil Valls, Encarnacion, Bl.; Gimenez Malla, Ceferino Bl.; Giuliani, Marianna, St.; Gonzalez Garcia, Manuel, Bl.; Grande Roman, Juan, St.; Granzotto, Claudio, Bl.; Green, Hugh, Bl.; Grimston, Ralph, Bl.; Grissold, Robert, Bl.; Grivot, Irma, St.; Gross, Nikolaus, Bl.; Guadalajara (Mexico) Martyrs of; Guerrero Gonzalez, Angela de la Cruz, Bl.; Hambley, John, Bl.; Hanse, Everard, Bl.; Harcourt, William, Bl.; Hardesty, Robert, Bl.; Harold of Gloucester, St.; Harrington, William, Bl.; Hart, William, Bl.; Hartley, William, Bl.; Haydock, George, Bl.; Heath, Henry, Bl.; Hedwig of Anjou, St.; Hemerford, Thomas, Bl.; Herst, Richard, Bl.; Hesselblad, Elisabeth, Bl.; Hewett, John, Bl.; Hill, Richard, Bl.; Hodgson, Sydney, Bl.; Hogg, John, Bl.; Holiday, Richard, Bl.; Horner, Nicholas, Bl.; Houben, Charles of Mount Argus, Bl.; Hunt, Thurstan, Bl.; Hunt, Thomas, Bl.; Hurtado Cruchaga, Alberto, Bl.; Imbert, Joseph, Bl.; Ingleby, Francis, Bl.; Ingram, John, Bl.; Ireland, John, Bl.; Isore, Remi, St.; Iturrate Zubero, Domingo, Bl.; Jablonska, Bernardina, Bl.; Jamet, Pierre-François, Bl.; Janssoone, Frederic Cornil, Bl.; Jarrige, Catherine, Bl.; Jeuris, Pauline, St.; John of Dukla, St.; Johnson, Thomas, Bl.; Johnson, Robert, Bl.; Jones, Edward, Bl.; Joubert, Eugénie, Bl.; Jugan, Jeanne, Bl.; Kafka, Maria Restituta, Bl.; Kalinowski, Rafal of St. Jozef, St.; Karlowska, Maria, Bl.; Kassab, Nimatullah al-Hardini Yousef, Bl.; Kazimierczyk, Stanislas, Bl.; Kergun, Jeanne Marie, St.; Kern, Jakob Franz, Bl.; Kinga, St.; Kirkman, Richard, Bl.; Kitbamrung, Nicholas Bunkerd, Bl.; Knight, William, Bl.; Korea, Martyrs of, SS.; Kosice, Martyrs of, SS.; Kostistk, Geremia of Valachia, Bl.; Kowalska, Faustina, St.; Kozal, Michal, Bl.; Kozka, Karolina, Bl.; Kozminski, Honorat, Bl.; Lacey, William, Bl.; Lambton, Joseph, Bl.; Lament, Boleslawa Maria, Bl.; Langhorne, Richard, Bl.; Langley, Richard, Bl.; Lara Puente, Salvator, St.; Larke, John, Bl.; Laval, François de Montmorency, Bl.; Laval, Jacques Désiré, Bl.; Ledóchowska, Urszula (Ursula) Desire, Bl.; Leigh, Richard, Bl.; Leisner, Karl Friedrich Wilhelm Maria, Bl.; Lentini, Domenico, Bl.; Lichtenberg, Bernhard, Bl.; Liu Ziyn, Peter, St.; Lockwood, John, Bl.; Longo, Bartolo, Bl.; Loor, Isidore of St. Joseph de, Bl.; Lowe, John, Bl.; Lucci, Antonio, Bl.; Ludlam, Robert, Bl.; Magallanes Jara, Cristobal (Christopher), St.; Maldonado Lucero, Pedro (Peter) de Jesus, St.; Mandic, Leopold Bogdan, St.; Manetti, Teresa María della Croce, Bl.; Mankidiyan, Mariam Thresia Chiramel, Bl.; Manyanet y Vives, Jose, Bl.; March Mesa, Nazaría Ignacia, Bl.; Marchisio, Clemente, Bl.; Marello, Giuseppe, Bl.; Martillo Morán, Narcisa de Jesus, Bl.; Martin, Richard, Bl.; Maxfield, Thomas, Bl.; Mazzarella, Modestino, Bl.; Mazzucconi, Giovanni Battista, Bl.; Medieval Boy Martyrs; Meinhard of Livonia, St.; Mendez Montoya, Jesus, St.; Menni Figini, Benedetto, St.; Merten, Blandina, Bl.; Mesina, Antonia, Bl.; Michel, Teresa Grillo, Bl.; Middlemore, Humphrey, Bl.; Middleton, Robert, Bl.; Middleton, Antony, Bl.; Míguez, Faustino, Bl.; Milner, Ralph, Bl.; Mogas Fontcuberta, María Ana, Bl.; Molas y Vallvé, María Rosa Doloribus Francisca, St.; Molina, Mercedes de Jesus, Bl.; Molla, Gianna (Joan) Beretta, Bl.; Montaignac de Chauvance, Louisa-Therese de, Bl.; Montal Fornes, Paula, St.; Monte, Bartholomew Maria dal, Bl.; Monteagudo, Ana de los Angeles, Bl.; Mora, Miguel (Michael) de la, St.; Moragas Cantarero, María Sagrario of San Luis Gonzaga Maria dal, Bl.; Morales, Manuel, St.; Morano, Maddalena Caterina, Bl.; More, Hugh, Bl.; Moreau, Louis-Zephyrin, Bl.; Moreau, Anne Francoise, St.; Morello, Brigida di Gesu, Bl.; Moreno y Díaz, Ezequiel, St.; Morosini, Pierina, Bl.; Morton, Robert, Bl.; Moscati, Giuseppe Mario Carolo Alphonse, St.; Motril, Martyrs of, BB.; Muttathupandatu, Alphonsa, Bl.; Nanetti, Clelia, St.; Napper, George, Bl.; Nascimbeni, Giuseppe,

Bl.; Naval Girbes, Josefa, Bl.; Nelson, John, Bl.; Nengapete, Marie-Clementine Anuarite, Bl.; Neururer, Otto, Bl.; Newdigate, Sebastian, Bl.; Nichols, George, Bl.; Nicola da Gésturi, Bl.; Nicolantonio, Mariano da Roccacasale, Bl.; Nieves, Elias del Socorro, Bl.; Nisch, Ulricha Franziska, Bl.; Norton, John, Bl.; Nowogródek, Martyrs of, BB.; Nutter, Robert, Bl.; Oddi, Diego, Bl.; Orona, Justino, St.; Osbaldeston, Edward, Bl.; Ossó y Cervelló, Enrique de, St.; Oultremont, Emilie d', Bl; Page, Anthony, Bl.; Palaser, Thomas, Bl.; Palau y Quer, Francisco, Bl.; Palmentieri, Ludovico da Casoria, Bl.; Pampuri, Riccardo, St.; Paradis, Marie-Leonie, Bl.; Patenson, William, Bl.; Patron Saints; Pelczar, Jozef Sebastian, Bl.; Pérez Florido, Petra de San Jose, Bl.; Peter To Rot, Bl.; Petrilli, Savina, Bl.; Piamarta, Giovanni Battista, Bl.; Pibush, John, Bl.; Pickering, Thomas, Bl.; Pidal y Chico de Gúzman, María Maravillas de Jesus, St.; Pietrantoni, Agostina Livia, St.; Pike, William, Bl.; Pilcher, Thomas, Bl.; Polanco Fontecha, Anselmo, Bl.; Pollo, Secondo, Bl.; Poppe, Edward Johannes Maria, Bl.; Pormort, Thomas, Bl.; Postgate, Nicholas, Bl.; Povedo Castroverde, Pedro, Bl.; Powel, Philip, Bl.; Powell, Edward, Bl.; Prat y Prat, Mercedes, Bl.; Pratulin, Martyrs of, BB.; Pritchard, Humphrey, Bl.; Protman, Regina, Bl; Rafols, María, Bl.; Rasoamanarivo, Victoria, Bl.; Rebuschini, Enrico, Bl.; Rèche, Jules-Nicolas, Bl.; Renzi, Elisabetta, Bl.; Repetto, María, Bl.; Reyes Salazar, Sabas, St.; Richardson, William, Bl.; Richardson, Laurence, Bl.; Rinaldi, Filippo, Bl.; Ripoll Morata, Felipe, Bl.; Rivier, Marie-Anne, Bl.; Robert of Bury Saint Edmunds, St.; Robinson, Christopher, Bl.; Robles Hurtado, Jose Maria, St.; Roccacasale, Mariano da, Bl.; Rochefort Ships, Martyrs of, BB.; Rochester, John, Bl.; Rodriguez Santiago, Carlos Manuel Cecilio, Bl.; Rojas, Simon de, St.; Roland, Nicholas, Bl.; Roldan Lara, David, St.; Romo Gonzalez, Toribio, St.; Rosal Vasquez, María Vicente, Bl.; Rosales, Roman Adame, St.; Rosaz, Edoardo Giuseppe, Bl.; Roscelli, Agostino, St.; Rousseau, Scubilion, Bl.; Rowsham, Stephen, Bl.; Rubatto, Maria Francesca, Bl.; Rubio y Peralta, José María, Bl.; Rugg, John, Bl.; Sagheddu, María Gabriella, Bl.; Saints and Beati; Sala, Maria Anna, Bl.; Salawa, Aniela, Bl.; Sallés y Barangueras, María del Carmen, Bl.; Salvi, Lo-

renzo Maria, Bl.; San Vitores, Diego Luis de, Bl.; Sanchez Delgadillo, Jenaro, St.; Sancho de Guerra, María Josefa del Corazon de Jesus, Bl.; Sandys, John, Bl.; Santamaria, Grimoaldo of the Purification, Bl.; Sanz y Jorda, Pedro Martir, St.; Sarnelli, Gennaro Maria, Bl.; Satellico, Elisabetta Maria, Bl.; Schäffer, Anna, Bl.; Schinina, Maria of the Sacred Heart, Bl.; Schwartz, Anton Maria, Bl.; Scott, Montford, Bl.; Scrosoppi, Luigi, St.; Sergeant, Richard, Bl.; Shelley, Edward, Bl.; Shen Jihe, St.; Shert, John, Bl.; Sherwood, Thomas, Bl.; Silvestrelli, Bernard Maria of Jesus, Bl.; Simon de Longpré, Marie Catherine of St. Augustine, Bl.; Simpson, Richard, Bl.; Slomšek, Anton Martin, Bl.; Smaldone, Filippo Mariano, Bl.; Snow, Peter, Bl.; Southerne, William, Bl.; Speed, John, Bl.; Spenser, William, Bl.; Spinelli, Francesco de, Bl.; Spinola y Maestre, Marcelo, Bl.; Sprott, Thomas, Bl.; Stangassinger, Kaspar, Bl.; Stepinac, Alojzije Viktor, Bl.; Stollenwerk, Helena, Bl.; Story, John, Bl.; Stransham, Edward, Bl.; Sugar, John, Bl.; Sutton, Robert, Bl.; Sykes, Edmund, Bl.; Tadini, Arcangelo, Bl.; Talbot, John, Bl.; Tansi, Cyprian Michael Iwene, Bl.; Taylor, Hugh, Bl.; Tezza, Luigi, Bl.; Thailand, Seven Martyrs of, BB.; Thévenet, Claudine, St.; Thirkeld, Richard, Bl.; Thompson, James, Bl.; Thomson, William, Bl.; Thorp, Robert, Bl.; Thules, John, Bl.; Thwing, Thomas, Bl.; Thwing, Edward, Bl.; Tlaxcala, Martyrs of, BB.; Tommaso da Cori, St.; Tornay, Maurice, Bl.; Torres Lloret, Pascual, Bl.; Torres Moráles, Genoveva, Bl.; Torro Garcia, Manuel, Bl.; Tovini, Giuseppe Antonio, Bl.; Trichet, Marie-Louis of Jesus, Bl.; Troiani, Caterina, Bl.; Truszkowska, Angela Maria, Bl.; Tschiderer zu Gleifheim, Johann Nepomuk, Bl.; Turner, Anthony, Bl.; Turón, Martyrs of, SS.; Ubiarco Robles, Tranquilino, St.; Uribe Velasco, David, St.; Valls Espi, Crescencia, Bl.; Vendramini, Elisabetta, Bl.; Venegas de la Torre, María de Jesus Sacramentado, St.; Versiglia, Luigi, St.; Vicuña, Laura, Bl.; Vietnam, Martyrs of, SS.; Vilar David, Vincente, Bl.; Visintainer, Amabile Lucia, Bl.; Volpicelli, Caterina, Bl.; Wang Yumei, Joseph, St.; Wang Erman, Peter, St.; Wang Rui, John, St.; Wang Li, Mary, St.; Ward, William, Bl.; Waterson, Edward, Bl.; Watkinson, Thomas, Bl.; Way, William, Bl.; Webley, Henry, Bl.; Welbourne, Thomas, Bl.; Wharton, Christopher, Bl.; Whitaker, Thomas, Bl.; Whitbread, Thomas, Bl.; Wiaux, Mutien-Marie, St.; Widmerpool, Robert, Bl.; Wilcox, Robert, Bl.; Woodcock, John, Bl.; Woodfen, Nicholas, Bl.; Wrenno, Roger, Bl.; Wright, Peter, Bl.; Wu Anbang, Peter, St.; Yan Guodong, James, St.; Yaxley, Richard, Bl.; Ybarra de Villalonga, Rafaela, Bl.; Yermo y Parres, José María de, St.; Zdislava of Lemberk, St.; Zhang Rong, Francis, St.; Zhang Huailu, St.; Zhang Banniu, Peter, St.; Zhang He, Therese, St.; Zhang Jingguang, St.; Zhang Huan, John, St.; Zhang Zhihe, Philip, St.; Zhao Quanxin, James, St.; Zhao, Mary, Mary, and Rosa, SS.; Zhao, John Baptist and Peter, SS.; Zhu Wurui, John Baptist, St.; Zhu Wu, Mary, St.; Zhu Rixin, Peter, St.

*RABIKAUSKAS, PAULIUS, SJ, Eccl.Hist.D., Professor of Latin Paleography and Diplomatics, Faculty of Church History, Gregorian University, Rome, Italy. **Articles:** Lithuania, The Catholic Church in; Popes, Names of.

*RACLE, GABRIEL, OCD, Ph.B., S.T.L., Professor of Patrology and Theology, Couvent des Carmes Avon (Seine-et-Marne), France. **Article:** Melito of Sardes.

RADKE, F. C., **Article:** Franciscan Sisters—Franciscan Sisters of Chicago (OSF).

*RADZILOWSKI, PAUL, Ph.D., Assistant Professor of History, Saint Mary's College, Orchard Lake, Michigan. **Articles:** Sapieha, Adam Stefan; Tischner, Jozef Casimir; Wyszynski, Stefan.

RADZILOWSKI, THADDEUS, Ph.D., President, St. Mary's College of Ave Maria University, Orchard Lake, Michigan. **Article:** Orchard Lake.

*RAHALEY, MOTHER MARY OF THE INCARNATE WORD, MSBT, Blessed Trinity Missionary Cenacle, Philadelphia, Pa. (deceased Dec. 21, 1964). **Article:** Missionary Servants of the Most Blessed Trinity.

*RAHILL, PETER JAMES, Ph.D., formerly Editor, The Catholic University of America Press, The Catholic University of America, Washington, D.C.; St. Louis, Mo. **Articles:** Dubourg, Louis William Valentine; Glennon, John Joseph; Missouri, Catholic Church in; St. Louis, Archdiocese of.

*RAKAUSKAS, SISTER ANNA MARIE, SSC, Ph.B., Teacher of Journalism, Music, Drama, Speech, Lithuanian Literature, and Nursing, Villa Joseph Marie High

School, Newton, Pa. **Article:** St. Casimir, Sisters of.

*RAMACKERS, JOHANNES, Dr. Phil., Professor, Pädagogische Hochschule, Aachen, Germany. **Article:** Aachen.

*RAMBAUD-BUHOT, JACQUELINE, Archiviste-paléographe, Licenciée en Droit, Conservateur, Cabinet des Manuscrits de la Bibliothèque Nationale, Chargée de la rédaction du catalogue des manuscrits de Droit canonique, Paris, France. **Articles:** Dionysiana Collectio; Dionysius Exiguus; Gratian, Decretum of; Hadriana Collectio.

RAMBUSCH, VIGGO B., Honorary Chairman and Senior Project Manager, Rambusch Decorating Company, New York, N.Y. **Article:** St. Ansgar's Scandinavian Catholic League.

*RAMBUSCH, VIGGO F. E., M.Arch., President, Rambusch Decorating Company, New York, N.Y. **Article:** St. Ansgar's Scandinavian Catholic League.

*RAMGE, SEBASTIAN VICTOR, OCD, M.A. in Rel.Ed., Editor, *Spiritual Life;* Vice Postulator for the Cause of Pope Bl. Innocent XI; Milwaukee, Wis. **Articles:** Clement X, Pope; Innocent XI, Pope Bl.; Quiet, Prayer of; Teresa Margaret of the Sacred Heart, St.; Teresa of Avila, St. [part 2].

*RAMIREZ, MOTHER MARIA EVA, MCM, Superior General, San Antonio, Tex. **Article:** Cordi-Marian Missionary Sisters.

*RAMIREZ DULANTO, JACOBUS M., OP, S.T.D., S.T.M., Rector, Faculty of Theology, San Esteban of Salamanca, Spain. **Articles:** Hope; Moral Theology.

*RAMÍREZ TORRES, RAFAEL, SJ, Ph.D., Professor of Oratory and Greek, Director, Curso de Cultura Helena, Instituto de Literatura, Puente Grande, Jal, México. **Article:** Pro Juarez, Miguel Augustin, Bl.

*RAMÓN FOLCH, JOSÉ ARMANDO DE, Licentiate in Juridical and Social Sciences, Professor of Historical Research and of American History, Department of History, Catholic University of Chile, Santiago, Chile. **Article:** Chile, The Catholic Church in.

*RAMOS PEREZ, DEMETRIO, Doctorate in Philosophy and Letters, Professor of American History, University of Barcelona, Spain; Collaborator, Instituto Gonzalo Fernandez de Oviedo (under

the Consejo Superior de Investigaciones Cientificas); member, Editorial Board, *Revista de Indias* (Madrid); Editor in Chief, *Boletin Americanista.* **Article:** Aguado, Pedro de.

*RANDALL, ALEC WALTER, B.A., K.C.M.G., retired ambassador, writer, and critic, Oxted, Surrey, England. **Articles:** Bernetti, Tommaso; Castel Gandolfo; Lateran Pacts; Russell, Odo; Satolli, Francesco; Severoli, Antonio Gabriele; Soglia Ceroni, Giovanni.

*RANDOLPH, NORBERT EUGENE, M.A., S.T.B., Pastor, St. Anthony Church, Chicago, Ill. **Article:** O'Connell, John Patrick.

*RANIERI, JOSEPH A., S.T.L., M.A., Teacher of Latin, Cathedral Latin School, Washington, D.C. **Article:** Franciscan Sisters—Sisters of St. Francis of the Mission of the Immaculate Virgin (OSF).

*RANLY, ERNEST WILLIBALD, CPPS, Ph.D., Assistant Professor of Philosophy, St. Joseph's College, Rensselaer, Ind. **Articles:** Husserl, Edmund; Scheler, Max.

RASCHKO, MICHAEL B., Ph.D., Assistant Professor, School of Theology and Ministry at Seattle University, Seattle, Wa. **Articles:** Assumptus-Homo Theology; Subsistence (in Christology).

*RAUH, SISTER MIRIAM JOSEPH, CSC, Ph.D., Professor of English, St. Mary's College, Notre Dame, Ind. **Article:** Madeleva (Wolff), Mary, Sister.

*RAUSCH, JEROME WILLIAM, OSC, S.T.D., Professor of Sacramental Theology and Dean of Studies, Crosier House of Studies, and Professor of Theology, St. Francis College, Fort Wayne, Ind. **Articles:** Crosier Fathers; Dead Sea; Jordan, The.

*REARDON, MAURICE EDWARD, A.B., Litt.D., S.T.D., Professor of English, St. Gregory's Seminary, Cincinnati, Ohio. **Article:** McNicholas, John Timothy.

*RECK, CARLEEN J., SSND, Executive Director, Department of Elementary Schools, NCEA, Washington, D.C. **Article:** Teachers, Ministry of.

*RECKTENWALD, DIONYSIUS, CFX, Ph.D., Instructor in French, Our Lady of Good Counsel High School, Wheaten, Md. **Article:** Webb, Benedict Joseph.

*REDIGONDA, LUIGI ABELE, OP, S.T.D., Diploma in Paleography, Diplomatics, and Archival Science (Vatican School), Professor of Church History and Oriental Theology, Facoltà di S. Tommaso, Bologna, Italy; Director of the Library and Archivist and Chronicler of his Convent and Province. **Articles:** Alberti, Leandro; Allegranza, Joseph; Liccio, John, Bl.; Ninguarda, Feliciano.

*REDLE, SISTER MARY JUDE, SCL, Ph.D., Associate Professor of Theology and Scripture, St. Mary College, Xavier, Kans. **Articles:** Beatific Vision; God, Intuition of; Plagues of Egypt.

*REDLICH, VIRGIL HERBERT, OSB, Dr.Phil., Professor, Universities of Graz and Salzburg, Austria; member, Bayerische Benediktiner Akademie. **Articles:** Gebhard of Salzburg, Bl.; Hartwich of Salzburg, Bl.; Kakubilla, St.; Leopold III of Austria, St.; Seckau, Abbey of; Walburga of Heidenheim, St.

*REDMOND, RICHARD XAVIER, SS, M.A., S.T.D., Professor of Church History, Liturgy, and Sacred Scripture, St. Thomas Seminary, Kenmore, Wash. **Articles:** Altar in Christian Liturgy; Immanence Apologetics; Lyonese Rite; Prophecy (Theology of).

*REED, GEORGE EDWARD, A.B., LL.B., LL.M., Associate Director, Legal Department, National Catholic Welfare Conference, Washington, D.C. **Articles:** Freedom of Religion (in U.S. Constitution); Montavon, William F.; Oregon School Case.

*REED, JOHN FRANCIS, B.A., S.T.L., Diocese of Sault Sainte Marie, Ontario, Canada. **Article:** Black, William; Inglis, Charles.

*REEL, CASSIAN, OFMCap, B.Litt., Lector in Church History, House of Studies, Franciscan Friary, Olton, Solihull, Warwickshire, England. **Articles:** Bascio, Matteo Serafini da; Fitch, William Benedict (Benedict of Canfield); Forbes, John; Joyeuse, Henri, Duc de.

*REESE, GUSTAVE, LL.B., Mus.B., Mus.D. (h.c.), Professor of Music, New York University, New York, N.Y. **Article:** Liturgical Music, History of, 4: Polyphonic Music, 1450s to 1600s.

*REESE, JAMES MILLER, OSFS, M.A., S.T.L., S.S.L., Professor of Sacred Scripture, De Sales Hall, Hyattsville, Md. **Article:** Bible (Texts), 2. Text of the New Testament.

*REFOULÉ, FRANÇOIS, OP, Licencié en droit, S.T.L., Licencié ès lettres, Dominican House of St. Thomas, Lund, Sweden; Editor, *Lumen.* **Article:** Evagrius Ponticus.

*REGAN, AUGUSTINE RICHARD, CSSR, S.T.D., Professor of Systematic Moral Theology, Accademia Alfonsiana, Rome, Italy. **Article:** Lust.

*REGAN, CRONAN, CP, S.T.D., Lector of Dogmatic Theology, St. Ann's Monastery, Scranton, Pa. **Article:** Free Will and Grace; Grace and Nature.

REGAN, JANE E., Ph.D., Associate Professor of Religious Education and Theology, Boston College, Chestnut Hill, Mass. **Article:** Conscience, Examination of.

*REGAN, SISTER M. JEAN MICHAEL, BVM, M.A., Chairman, Department of Philosophy, Mundelein College, Chicago, Ill. **Article:** Cassirer, Ernst.

*REGAN, PATRICK, OSB, St. Joseph's Abbey, St. Benedict, La. **Article:** Liturgy of the Hours.

*REHKOPF, SISTER MARTHES DE PORRES, O.P., Subprioress, Our Lady of the Bayous Convent, Abbeville, La. **Article:** Dominican Sisters—Dominican Rural Missionaries.

*REHWINKEL, CHRISTOPHER AUGUST, OFM, S.T.D., S.S.Lect. Gen., Professor of Scripture, St. Joseph's Seminary, Teutopolis, Ill. **Article:** Wellhausen, Julius.

REICHART, K., **Article:** Franciscan Sisters—Sisters of St. Francis of Savannah, Missouri (OSF).

*REICHERT, ROBERT WALTER, Ph.D., Associate Professor of History, Marquette University, Milwaukee, Wis. **Article:** Darboy, Georges.

REID, BARBARA E., OP, Ph.D., Professor of New Testament Studies, Catholic Theological Union, Chicago, Ill. **Article:** Women in the Bible [part 2: New Testament].

*REID, JOHN PATRICK, OP, Providence College, Providence, R.I. **Article:** Atheism.

*REILLY, CHARLES A., Ph.D., Senior Research Fellow and Adjunct Professor, Georgetown University, Washington, D.C. **Article:** Mexico (Modern), The Catholic Church in.

*REILLY, GEORGE CAJETAN, OP, Ph.D., S.T.M., S.T.Lr., Professor of Philosophy, The Catholic University of America, Washington, D.C. **Articles:** Epistemology; Gnoseology; Knowledge; Solipsism; Truth [part 2].

*REILLY, JAMES P., JR., Ph.D., Department of Philosophy, University of Detroit, Detroit, Mich. **Article:** Thomas of York.

REILLY, M. L., **Article:** Franciscan Sisters—Franciscan Sisters of Our Lady of Lourdes (OSF).

*REINERT, PAUL C., SJ, S.T.L., Ph.D., LL.D., President, St. Louis University, St. Louis, Mo. **Article:** St. Louis University.

*REINHARD, WILLIAM THOMAS, OMI, D. Miss., Coordinator of the Pastoral Housing Commission, Archdiocese of São Paulo, Brazil. **Article:** Brazil, The Catholic Church in.

*REINHARDT, KURT FRANK, Ph.D., Professor Emeritus, Department of Modern European Languages, Stanford University, Stanford, Calif. **Articles:** Nietzsche, Friedrich Wilhelm; Schopenhauer, Arthur; Vera Cruz, Alonso de la.

*REINHOLD, HANS ANSCAR, D.D., D.H.L., retired pastor, Pittsburgh, Pa. **Articles:** Herwegen, Ildefons; Kramp, Joseph.

*REINMUTH, HOWARD STUART, JR., Ph.D., Assistant Professor of History, University of Utah, Salt Lake City, Utah. **Articles:** Alcock, John; Arundel, Thomas; Bainbridge, Christopher; Beauchamp, Richard; Bekynton, Thomas (Beckington); Codrington, Thomas; Coleman, Walter; Howard, Philip Thomas; Jacobites (English); Pounde, Thomas; Rochester, Ancient See of; Southwell, Nathaniel (Bacon); York, Ancient See of.

REISKE, STEVEN R. W., Chancellor, Diocese of Fargo, Fargo, N.D. **Article:** Fargo, Diocese of.

*REITH, HERMAN ROBERT, CSC, S.T.B., Ph.D., Professor of Philosophy and Head of the Department, University of Notre Dame, Notre Dame, Ind. **Article:** Intellectual Life.

*REMEC, PETER PAVEL, Dr.Iur., Dr.Rer.Pol., Ph.D., Diploma, Hague Academy of International Law, Associate Professor of International Relations, Department of Political Philosophy, Fordham University, New York, N.Y. **Article:** Grotius, Hugo.

*RENFRO, SISTER JEAN MARIE, SSS, M.A., Supervisor, Confraternity of Christian Doctrine, Diocese of Kansas City—St. Joseph, Kansas City, Mo. **Article:** Social Service, Sisters of.

*RENNER, SISTER EMMANUAL, OSB, Ph.D., Associate Professor of History and Chairman of the Department, College of St. Benedict, St. Joseph, Minn. **Article:** Magnus, Johannes and Olaus.

RENNER, LOUIS L., S.J., Ph.D., writer in residence, Gonzaga University, Spokane, Wash.; former editor, The Alaskan Shepherd; Professor of German, Emeritus, University of Alaska-Fairbanks. **Article:** Alaska, Catholic Church in.

*RENOLD, PENELOPE, B.A. (Hons.), M.A., Research Historian, Worcester Park, Surrey, England. **Article:** Archpriest Controversy; Blackwell, George.

*RESTREPO POSADA, JOSÉ, Rt. Rev., Canon of the Cathedral of Bogotá and Chancellor of the Archdiocese of Bogotá, Colombia; Former President, Academia de la Historia. **Articles:** Bertrand, Louis, St.; Caballero y Gongora, Antonio; Castillo y Guevara, Francisca Josefa del; Dominguez, Isidoro; Fernandez de Piedrahita, Lucas; Mosquera, Manuel Jose.

*REYLING, AUGUST EDWIN, OFM, M.S. in L.S., Secretary of the Franciscan Province of the Sacred Heart (St. Louis-Chicago), St. Louis, Mo.; Librarian, St. Anthony of Padua Friary, St. Louis, Mo. **Article:** Steck, Francis Borgia.

*REYNOLDS, ERNEST EDWIN, Essenden, Maudlin Lane, Steyming, Sussex, England. **Articles:** Clement, Caesar; Fisher, John, St.; Gordon Riots; Rastell, John and William; Roper, William.

*REYNOLDS, JAMES A., Very Rev., B.A., Ph.D., Professor of History, St. Joseph's Seminary, Dunwoodie, Yonkers, N.Y. **Articles:** Corrigan, Michael Augustine; Dubois, John; McCloskey, John; New York, Archdiocese of; Raffeiner, John Stephen.

RHODES, JAMES N., M.A., Lecturer, Department of Theology, The Catholic University of America. **Articles:** Aristeas, Letter of; Barnabas, St.; Barnabas, Epistle of; Didache.

*RICART, DOMINGO, Lic. in Philosophy and Letters, Diploma, Sorbonne, Professor of Romance Languages, University of Kansas, Lawrence, Kans. **Article:** Valdes, Juan de.

*RICCI, VINCENZO, CSSR, S.T.L., Litt.D., Professor of the History of Ancient Philosophy and Professor of Christian Archeology, History of Art, and Italian Literature, Redemptorist House of Studies, Cortona, Italy. **Articles:** John and Paul, SS.; Sarcophagus; Sator Arepo; Zoilus of Alexandria.

*RICE, EUGENE FRANKLIN, Jr., Ph.D., Professor of History, Columbia University, New York, N.Y. **Article:** Lefevre, Jacques d'Etaples.

*RICE, PATRICK WILLIAM, J.C.D., Pastor, St. Basil's Church, Pittsburgh, Pa.; member, Diocesan Tribunal, Diocese of Pittsburgh. **Article:** Vicar Forane.

*RICHARD, SISTER HELEN MARIE, FSM, B.S. in N.E., Regional Superior, Province of the United States, Daughters of St. Mary of the Presentation, Valley City, N.Dak. **Article:** Presentation, Sisters of Mary of the.

*RICHARD, JEAN, Professor, University of Dijon, Côte-d'Or, France. **Articles:** Jerusalem, Kingdom of; Prester John.

*RICHARD, LUCIEN, OMI, Ph.L., S.T.L., Professor of Dogmatic Theology, Oblate Seminary, Natick, Mass. **Article:** Expiation (in Theology) [part 1].

*RICHARD, ROBERT LEO, SJ, M.A., S.T.D., Professor of Theology, Weston College, Weston, Mass., and Boston College, Chestnut Hill, Mass. **Articles:** Agennetos; Anthropomorphism (in Theology); God (Father); Paternity, Divine; Trinity, Holy.

*RICHÉ, PIERRE RENÉ, Diplôme d'Études Supérieures, Agrégation, Professor, Faculté des Lettres, University of Rennes, France. **Article:** Greco-Roman Schooling.

*RICHSTATTER, THOMAS, OFM, Th.D., Liturgy Teacher, St. Leonard Franciscan Seminary, Dayton, Ohio. **Articles:** General Intercessions; Liturgical Rites.

*RICKS, ROBERT WAYNE, M.A., Assistant Professor of Music, The Catholic University of America, Washington, D.C. **Article:** Dusek, Jan Ladislav.

RIEDE, RANDAL, CFX, Librarian (retired), North American College, Rome, Italy. **Article:** North American College.

*RIEDL, JOHN ORTH, Ph.D., Professor of Philosophy, Marquette University, Milwaukee, Wis. **Article:** Platonism.

*RIEGO, RUTILIO J. DEL, Diocesan Laborer Priests House of Studies, Washington, D.C. **Article:** Ruiz de los Paños y Angel, Pedro, and Eight Companions, BB.

*RIEHLE, SISTER MARY EDITH, MM, Lic.M.S., Ph.D., Professor of History, Mary Rogers College, Maryknoll, N.Y. **Articles:** Aquilinus, St.; Arialdo, St.; Bernard of Aosta, St.; Gregory of Cerchiara, St.; Guarinus of Palestrina, St.; Guido the Lombard, Bl.; Peter of Trevi, St.; Warmund of Ivrea, Bl.

*RIES, JULIEN CAMILLE, S.T.L., Licentiate in Oriental Philosophy and History, S.T.D., Curé-doyen, Messancy, Belgium; Lecturer on Manichaeism, Institut Orientaliste, Louvain, Belgium. **Article:** Manichaeism.

*RIGA, PETER J., M.S. in L.S., S.T.D., St. John Vianney Seminary, East Aurora, N.Y. **Articles:** Baker, Nelson Henry; Suffering [part 2].

*RIGALI, NORBERT J., SJ, S.T.L., Ph.D., Professor, Department of Theological and Religious Studies, University of San Diego. **Article:** Moral Theology, History of (Contemporary Trends); Love, Virtue of.

RIGGS, CHRISTINA JOY, Dphil., Barns and Griffith Research Fellow in Egyptology, The Queen's College, Oxford University, Oxford, United Kingdom. **Article:** Egypt.

*RIGNEY, JAMES FRANCIS, Very Rev., B.A., S.T.D., Secretary to Cardinal Spellman, New York, N.Y. **Articles:** Communication of Idioms; Impenitence.

RILEY, JAMES, Ph.D., Professor of History, The Catholic University of America, Washington, D.C. **Article:** Tibesar, Antonine.

*RILEY, LAWRENCE J., S.T.D., Auxiliary Bishop of Boston, Hyde Park, Ma. **Article:** Connell, Francis J.

*RILEY, SISTER MARY BERNARDINE, DC, M.A., Assistant Superior, Daughters of the Cross, Shreveport, and Head of the English Department, St. Vincent's Academy, Shreveport, La. **Article:** Daughters of the Cross.

*RILEY, THOMAS JOSEPH, Most Rev., A.B., Ph.D., LL.D., Auxiliary Bishop of Boston, Mass. **Articles:** Acolyte; Deacon; Deaconess; Lector; Porter; Subdeacon; Tonsure.

*RILL, GERHARD, Dr.Phil., State Archivist, Haus-, Hof-und Staatsarchiv, Vienna, Austria. **Articles:** Conrad II, Roman Emperor; John XIX, Pope.

RINERE, ELISSA, CP, J.C.D., Associate Professor of Canon Law, The Catholic University of America, Washington, D.C. **Articles:** Ad tuendam fidem; Laity, Canon Law; Passionist Sisters; Passionist Nuns; Preaching, IV (Canon Law of); Team Ministry (Canon Law).

*RIOS, MANUEL, S.T.L., Hist.Eccl.D., Licentiate in Philosophy and Letters, Diploma in Archival Science (Vatican

School of Paleography), Professor of Ecclesiastical History and Patrology, Major Seminary, Santiago, Chile; Assistant Professor, Faculty of Philosophy and Letters; Professor of Religions Training in the University. **Article:** Santiago de Compostela.

RIPPINGER, JOEL, OSB, M.A., S.T.L., Subprior, Marmion Abbey, Aurora, Ill. **Articles:** Benedict, St.; Benedictine Abbeys and Priories in the U.S.; Monasticism, 4. Contemporary (1960–2000); Monasticism, 3. Modern (1500 to 1960).

*RITSCHL VON HARTENBACH, DIETRICH HANS GUSTAV ALBRECHT, Ph.D., Professor of Theology and History of Doctrine, Pittsburgh Theological Seminary, Pittsburgh, Pa.; Minister of the Presbyterian Church in the United States of America; Coeditor, *Journal of Ecumenical Studies*. **Articles:** Erlangen School; Lipsius, Richard Adelbert; Ritschl, Albrecht.

*RIUS FACIUS, ANTONIO, creative writer and journalist, Mexico City, Mexico. **Articles:** Calles, Plutarco Elias; Mora y del Rio, Jose.

*RIVERA, PEDRO, SJ, M.A., S.T.D., Director of the International Department, Universidad Ibero-Americana, Mexico City, Mexico. **Article:** Thinking with the Church, Rules for.

*RIVET, MOTHER MARY CLAIRE, OSU, M.A., Teacher, Community Archivist, New Orleans, La. **Article:** Tranchepain, Marie St. Augustin, Mother.

*ROACH, JOHN PETER CHARLES, Ph.D., Fellow of Corpus Christi College, Lecturer in Education, University of Cambridge, England. **Article:** Cambridge, University of.

*ROBERSON, RONALD G., CSP, M.A., S.E.O.L., S.E.O.D., Associate Director of Formation, St. Paul's College, Washington, D.C. **Articles:** Orthodox Church of Romania; Orthodox Church of Russia; Romania, The Catholic Church in; Romanian Catholic Church (Eastern Catholic); Staniloae, Dumitru.

*ROBERT, JEAN DOMINIQUE, OP, S.T.Lr., Professor of Metaphysics and Noetics, Dominican College of Philosophy and Theology, La Sarte, Huy, Belgium. **Article:** Act.

*ROBERT, JOSEPH DOMINIQUE, OP, Héllemmes-Lille, France. **Article:** Worker Priests.

*ROBERT, LÉON ROMAIN, OSB, Licencié ès sciences biologiques, Professor of Church History, Abbaye Saint-Pierre de Solesmes, Sablé-sur-Sarthe (Sarthe), France. **Article:** Solesmes, Abbey of.

*ROBERTSON, ANDREW, H., Ph.D., Associate Professor of Philosophy, St. John's University, Jamaica, N.Y. **Article:** Cherubini, Luigi.

*ROBERTSON, SISTER MARY CLEMENT, SN, M.A., Teacher, Convent of the Poor Sisters of Nazareth, San Diego, Calif. **Article:** Poor Sisters of Nazereth.

*ROBICHAUD, PAUL G., CSP, Ph.D., Archivist/Historian, Paulist Fathers; Assistant Professor of American History, The Catholic University of America. **Article:** Illig, Alvin Anthony.

*ROBINSON, ANDREW, H., Ph.D., Associate Professor of Philosophy, St. John's University, Jamaica, N.Y. **Articles:** Generation-Corruption; Substantial Change.

*ROBINSON, DELBERT WILLIAM, MM, M.A., Secretary-General, Catholic Secretariat, Tanganyika Episcopal Conference, Dar Es Salaam, Tanganyika. **Article:** Tanzania, the Catholic Church in.

*ROBINSON, RICHARD A. H., M.A., D. Phil. (Oxon.), F.R.Hist.S., Reader in Iberian History, The University of Birmingham, England. **Article:** Portugal, The Catholic Church in [part 2].

*ROBLES, OSWALDO, Ph.D., Psych.D., Sc.Soc.D. (h.c.), Professor Emeritus of Philosophy and of Psychology, Faculty of Philosophy and Letters, Seminar Director and author, Universidad Nacional Autónoma de México, Mexico City, Mexico. **Articles:** Mercado, Tomas de; Rubio, Antonio.

*ROCHAIS, HENRI, OSB, monk of the Abbey of St. Martin of Ligugé, France; Editor, Medieval Latin Religious Texts, Maumont, Juignac de Montmoreau (Charente), France. **Articles:** Florilegia; Liguge, Abbey of.

*ROCHE, MAURICE AUGUSTINE, CM, B.A., S.T.D., Professor of Church History and Liturgy, Seminary of Our Lady of Angels, Albany, N.Y. **Articles:** Argentre, Charles du Plessis d'; Bovillus, Carolus (Charles de Bouelles); Gibieuf, Guillaume; Le Vacher, Jean; Louise de Marillac, St.; Solminihac, Alain de, Bl.; Vincent de Paul, St.

*ROCHE, PIERRE JOSEPH, CSSR, Hist.Eccl.Lic., Dreux, France. **Arti-**

cles: Afra, St.; Agatha, St.; Agricius of Trier, St.; Anthimus of Trebizond; Belisarius; Billy, Jacques de; Bollandists; Bryennios, Joseph; Claudianus Mamertus; Delehaye, Hippolyte; Didymus the Blind; Dorotheus; Franchi de' Cavalieri, Pio; Heresy, History of, 1. In the Early Church; John the Silent, St.; Lazarus the Confessor, St.; Mabillon, Jean; Macarius of Alexandria, St.; Marcellinus, Flavius; Palladius, St.; Paul of Canopus; Peter of Jerusalem; Peter of Apamea; Rabbula; Romanus, SS.; Sergius of Radonezh, St.; Victor, SS.

*ROCHFORD, E. BURKE, JR., Assistant Professor, Department of Sociology and Anthropology, Middlebury College, Middlebury, Vt. **Article:** Hare Krishna.

*ROCK, AUGUSTINE, OP, S.T.Lr., M.A., S.T.D., Religious Superior of Blackfriars (Dominican House of Publications), Chicago, Ill.; Vice President and Treasurer, Priory Press. **Articles:** Berti, Giovanni Lorenzo; Bertieri, Giuseppe; Chardon, Mathias Charles; Dieringer, Franz Xaver; Hettinger, Franz; Le Jay, Claude (Jajus); Murray, Patrick; Nicole, Pierre; Schazler, Konstantin von; Schrader, Klemens; Zimmer, Patrick.

RODDY, ROBERT, OFM Conv., B.A., Bonaventure Friary, Washington, D.C. **Articles:** Franciscan Sisters—Franciscan Missionary Sisters of the Infant Jesus (FMIJ); Franciscan Sisters; Franciscan Sisters—St. Francis Mission Community (OSF); Franciscan Sisters—Franciscan Sisters of Peace (FSP); Franciscan Sisters—Franciscan Hospitaller Sisters of the Immaculate Conception (FHIC).

RODER, RICHARD JAMES, B.A., Freelance Writer, Remsen, Iowa. **Article:** Sioux City, Diocese of.

*RODIS-LEWIS, GENEVIÈVE, Doctorat ès lettres, Professor of the History of Philosophy, Faculté des lettres et sciences humaines, Lyon, France. **Articles:** Lamy, Francois; Malebranche, Nicolas; Regis, Pierre Sylvain.

*RODRÍGUEZ, MAURO, SDB, Prefect of Studies, Instituto Teológico, Salesiano, Mexico City, Mexico; Director, Secretariado Permanente, CIRM (Conferencia de Institutos de la República Mexicana). **Articles:** Alms and Almgiving (in the Bible); Antichrist [part 1]; Responsibility (in the Bible).

*RODRIGUEZ CUESTA, OTILIO, Professor and Lector, College of Our Lady of

Mount Carmel, Washington, D.C. **Articles:** Balthasar of St. Catherine of Siena; Bruno de Jesus Marie; Crisogono de Jesus Sacramentado; Gabriel of St. Mary Magdalen; Gratian, Jerome; John of Jesus Mary (Juan de San Pedro y Ustarroz); Joseph of the Holy Spirit; Lawrence of the Resurrection; Margaret of the Blessed Sacrament, Ven.; Marie de l'Incarnation, Bl.; Mary of St. Joseph Salazar; Philip of the Blessed Trinity (Esprit Julien); Silverio of St. Teresa; Thomas of Jesus (Diaz Sanchez de Avila).

*RODRIGUEZ DEMORIZI, EMILIO, Licentiate in Law, lawyer, historian, and writer; President, Academia Dominicana de la Historia, Santo Domingo, Dominican Republic. **Articles:** Dominican Republic, The Catholic Church in; Geraldini, Alejandro; Padilla y Estrada, Ignacio de.

*ROEGELE, OTTO B., Dr.Phil., M.D., Professor of Journalism, University of Munich, Germany; Editor, *Rheinischer Merkur.* **Article:** Muth, Carl.

*ROENSCH, FREDERICK JAMES, S.T.L., Ph.D., St. Gerard's Church, Milwaukee, Wis.; Instructor in Philosophy, Cardinal Stritch College and Divine Savior Junior College, Milwaukee, Wis. **Articles:** Alamanni, Cosmo; Commer, Ernst; Complutenses; Godoy, Pedro de; Gotti, Vincenzo Lodovico; Goudin, Antoine; Javelli, Giovanni Crisostomo; Lepidi, Alberto; Rickaby, Joseph; Roselli, Salvatore Maria; Rousselot, Pierre.

*ROESSLER, EMMANUEL JAMES, TOR, S.T.L., Teacher, Department of Theology, St. Francis College, Loretto, Pa. **Articles:** Aaron; Moses.

*ROGERS, DAVID MACGREGOR, M.A., D.Phil., Assistant, Bodleian Library, Oxford, England. **Articles:** Brinkley, Stephen; Carter, William, Bl.; Carvajal, Luisa de; Pitts, John.

*ROGERS, EDWIN MANNES, OP, A.B., S.T.B., Business Manager, Thomist Press, Washington, D.C. **Articles:** Alcoholics Anonymous; Ferrariensis (Francesco Silvestri); Jordan of Saxony, Bl.; Medina, Bartolome de.

*ROGERS, FRANCIS MILLET, Ph.D., Litt.D., L.H.D., LL.D., Dr. (h.c.; University of Bahia, Brazil), Professor of Romance Languages and Literatures, and Dean of the Graduate School of Arts and Sciences, Harvard University, Cambridge, Mass. **Articles:** Alvares, Francisco; Gois, Damiao de; Lobo, Jeronimo.

*ROGGI, CLEMENT CELESTINO, OSBCam, Prior, New Camaldoli Hermitage, Big Sur, Calif. **Article:** Fonte Avellana, Monastery of.

*ROHLING, JOSEPH HENRY, CPPS, S.T.D., Chaplain, St. Agnes Convent, Fond du Lac, Wis. **Articles:** Descent of Christ into Hell; Precious Blood, III (Devotion to).

*ROHNER, SISTER M. INGEBORG, OSF, B.S. in Medical Technology, R.N., Laboratory Supervisor, Alton, Ill. **Article:** Franciscan Sisters—Sisters of St. Francis of the Martyr St. George (OSF).

*ROHRBACH, PETER-THOMAS, OCD, Ph.B., M.A., Prior, Discalced Carmelite Monastery, Washington, D.C. **Articles:** Carmelite Sisters—Carmelite Nuns, Discalced; Carmelites, Discalced; Cohen, Hermann (Augustine Mary of the Blessed Sacrament); Dionysius of the Nativity, Bl. (Pierre Berthelot); Guadagni, Bernardo Gaetano; Therese de Lisieux, St.

*ROHRIG, FLORIDUS HELMUT, CRSA, Dr.Phil., Dr.Theol., Librarian and Keeper of the Cartulary and the Museum of the Monastery; Professor of Ecclesiastical History and History of Art, Theological Academy of Klosterneuburg, Austria; Editor, *Jahrbuch des Stiftes Klosterneuburg* and *Klosterneuburger Kunstschätze.* **Article:** Klosterneuburg, Monastery of.

ROLL, BERTIN, OFM, C.A.P., Archconfraternity of Christian Mothers, Pittsburgh, P.A. **Article:** Christian Mothers, Archconfraternity of.

ROLL, SUSAN K., Ph.D., Assistant Professor, Christ the King Seminary, East Aurora, N.Y. **Articles:** Advent; Christmas and Its Cycle.

*ROLLER, DUANE HENRY DUBOSE, Ph.D., McCasland Professor of the History of Science and Curator of the DeGolyer Collection, University of Oklahoma, Norman, Okla. **Articles:** Einstein, Albert [Life and Works]; Gilbert, William.

*ROLLET, HENRI ANTOINE, Diplomé d'études supérieures, Docteur ès lettres, President, International Federation of Catholic Men; Lay Auditor at Vatican Council II; Paris, France. **Articles:** La Tour du Pin, Charles Humbert Rene (Marquis de la Charce); Lemire, Jules.

*ROMAGOSA, SISTER MARY EDWARD, OCarm, Ph.D., Chairman, English De-

partment, Mt. Carmel Junior College and Mt. Carmel Academy, New Orleans, La. **Article:** Carmelite Sisters—Congregation Of Our Lady Of Mt. Carmel (OCarm).

*ROMANINI, ANGIOLA MARIA, Litt.D., Professor of the History of Medieval Art, University of Pavia, Italy. **Article:** Bible Cycles in Art.

*ROMBATUS, JAN EDWARD, Doctorate in Philosophy and Letters, Doctorate in Netherlandic Literature, Professor of Netherlandic (Flemish and Dutch) Literature, Faculty of Philosophy and Letters, University of Louvain, Belgium. **Article:** Poirters, Adriaen.

*ROMERO, MARIO GERMÁN, Rt. Rev., Secretary to the Cardinal Archbishop of Bogatá, Colombia; historian. **Article:** Colombia, The Catholic Church in.

*ROMMEN, HEINRICH ALBERT, Dr.Rer.Pol., J.U.D., Professor of Government (Political Theory), Georgetown University, Washington, D.C. **Article:** State, The.

*RONAN, CHARLES EDWARD, SJ, Ph.D., Associate Professor of Latin American History, Loyola University, Chicago, Ill. **Articles:** Clavigero, Francisco Javier; Lorenzana, Francisco Antonio de; Puerto, Nicolas del.

*RONAN, JAMES LESLIE, S.T.L., S.S.L., St. Francis of Assisi Church, Vineland, N.J.; Member, Diocesan Liturgical Commission. **Articles:** Aeon (in the Bible); Pentecost; World (in the Bible); Worship (in the Bible).

*RONDEAU, MARIE-J., Professor, University of Caen, France; Vice President, Amis du Cardinal Daniélou. **Article:** Daniélou, Jean.

*ROONEY, JOHN WILLIAM, JR., Docteur en Histoire, Assistant Professor of History and Honors Program Director, Spring Hill College, Mobile, Ala. **Articles:** Bolsec Jerome Hermes; Possevino, Antonio.

*ROONEY, SISTER M. NELLIE, OSF, M.A., Instructor in History, College of Our Savior, St. Francis Convent, Amarillo, Tex. **Article:** Franciscan Sisters—Franciscan Sisters of Mary Immaculate (FMI).

*ROONEY, MIRIAM THERESA, Ph.D., LL.B., Research Professor of Law, Seton Hall University, School of Law, South Orange, N.J. **Article:** Law, Philosophy of.

*ROOSE, LODE, Doctorate in Philosophy and Letters, Bachelor of Thomistic

Philosophy, Professor, St. Ignatius Commercial College, Antwerp, Belgium; Lecturer, Catholic University of Louvain, Belgium. **Article:** Bijns, Anna.

*ROOTH, LARS, SJ, S.T.L., Chaplain of Students, writer, in charge of Swedish Broadcasts from Vatican Radio, Uppsala, Sweden. **Article:** Sweden, The Catholic Church in.

*ROPE, HENRY EDWARD GEORGE, M.A., priest of the Diocese of Shrewsbury, creative writer and historian, Pallotti Hall, Macclesfield, Cheshire, England. **Articles:** Bristow, Richard; Dalgairns, John Dobree.

*ROS, LLOPIS, AMPARO, H.D.C., Superior General, Hermanas de la Doctrina Cristiana, Mislata, Valencia, Spain. **Article:** Sisters of Christian Doctrine, Martyrs of, BB.

*ROSEMEYER, SISTER MARY REBECCA, OSF, M.A., Teacher of English and Dean of Girls, Wahlert High School, Dubuque, Iowa. **Article:** Franciscan Sisters—Sisters of St. Francis of the Holy Family (OSF).

*ROSEN, CYPRIAN M., OFMCap, J.C.L., Immaculate Heart of Mary Seminary, Geneva, N.Y. **Articles:** Giles of Foscarari; Joannes Andreae; Joannes de Lignano; Paulus de Liazariis.

*ROSENBERG, JEAN RANDALL, Ph.D., Professor of Philosophy, College of Notre Dame of Maryland; Professorial Lecturer, Loyola College, Baltimore, Md. **Article:** Individuation.

*ROSS, C. D., M.A. and Ph.D. (Oxon.), Reader in Medieval History, University of Bristol, England. **Articles:** Andrewe, Richard; Beaufort, Lady Margaret; Booth, Lawrence; Booth, William [b. 1464]; Bourgchier, Thomas (Bourchier); Gigli, Giovanni; Kemp, Thomas; Russell, John; Stillington, Robert; Waynflete, William.

*ROSS, EVA J., Ph.D., D.Litt., Professor of Sociology and Head of Department, Trinity College, Washington, D.C. **Article:** Spencer, Herbert.

*ROSS, IAN ANTHONY, OP, S.T.L., Chaplain of Catholic Students, University of Edinburgh, Scotland; Extra-Mural Lecturer, Universities of Glasgow and Edinburgh; Chairman of the Scottish Catholic Historical Association. **Article:** Our Lady of the Missions, Sisters of.

ROSSER, JOHN, Ph.D., Associate Professor of History, Department of History,

Boston College. **Article:** Theophilus, Byzantine Emperor.

*ROSSO, ANTONIO SISTO, OFM, Ph.D., Pontificio Ateneo Antoniano, Rome, Italy. **Articles:** Bodhisattva; Brollo, Basilio; Buddhism; Caballero, Antonio; Della Chiesa, Bernardino; Dharma; Elements of Existence; Mozi; Nirvana; Pali Canon; Prado, John of Bl.; Sikhism; Vajrayana (Diamond Vehicle); Weiss, Liberat.

ROTELLE, JOHN E., OSA, Director, Augustinian Heritage Institute, Villanova, Pa. **Articles:** Augustinian Heritage Institute; Thomas of Villanova, St.

*ROTH, ANSELM, OSB, S.T.L., Librarian, Lector in Church History, St. Joseph's Abbey, Gerleve, Westfalen, Germany. **Articles:** Oppenheim, Philipp; Stolz, Anselm.

*ROTH, FRANCIS GEORGE, Very Rev., OSA, New York, N.Y. **Articles:** Calepino, Ambrogio; Canal, Jose de la; Guasto, Andrea del; Hugolino of Gualdo Cattaneo, Bl.; John Klenkok; John of Waldby; Lowe, John; Rita of Cascia, St.; Rocca, Angelo; Veneto, Paolo; William of Hecham; Zachariae, Johann.

ROTHWEIL, SR. AUDREY MARIE, OSF, M.A., Congregational Historian, Our Lady of the Angels, Wheaton, Illinois. **Article:** Franciscan Sisters—Franciscan Sisters, Daughters of the Sacred Hearts of Jesus and Mary (OSF).

*ROUILLARD, PHILIPPE, OSB, S.T.D., Professor of Liturgy, Catholic University of Lille, France. **Articles:** Annunciation; Marian Feasts; Mother of God; Sanctoral Cycle.

*ROULEAU, FRANCIS ALBERT, SJ, Ph.D., Researcher and Writer, Historical Institute of the Society of Jesus, Rome, Italy. **Articles:** Martini, Martino; Mezzabarba, Carlo Ambrogio; Navarrete, Domingo Fernandez; Ricci, Matteo; Tournon, Charles Thomas Maillard de; Trigault, Nicolas.

*ROUSSEAU, SISTER MARY ISAAC JOGUES, SSND, Ph.D., Assistant Professor of Classics, Mount Mary College, Milwaukee, Wis. **Articles:** Adoro Te Devote; Chevalier, Ulysse; Christe Sanctorum Decus Angelorum; Cor Arca Legem Continens; Fulcoius of Beauvais; Hymnary; Memorare; Odo of Cambrai, Bl.; Peter Riga; Veni Creator Spiritus; Vexilla Regis Prodeunt; Victimae Paschali Laudes.

*ROUSSEAU, PIERRE, Abbé, Évreux (Eure), France. **Article:** Anselm of Laon.

ROUTLEDGE, MICHAEL J., Ph.D, Dip.Trans, ILTM. Senior Lecturer in French, Royal Holloway, University of London, London, United Kingdom. **Article:** Crusade Literature.

*ROVER, THOMAS D., OP, Providence College, Providence, R.I. **Article:** Homily; Preaching, I (History of) [part 2].

*ROWE, JOHN GORDON, Ph.D., priest, Anglican Church of Canada, Dean of Arts and Head of the Department of History, Huron College, London, Ontario, Canada; Professor of History, Faculty of Graduate Studies, University of Western Ontario. **Articles:** Albergati, Niccolo, Bl.; Capranica, Domenico and Angelo; Pius II, Pope.

*ROXBURGH, GILBERT JAMES, OP, Ph.L., Professor of Theology, St. Mary's Dominican College, New Orleans, La. **Article:** Omnipotence; Truth, Divine.

*ROY, JOSEPH HENRY, SSS, S.T.L., Hist.Eccl.L., Lecturer in Church History, Blessed Sacrament Seminary and John Carroll University, Cleveland, Ohio. **Articles:** Blessed Sacrament, Servants of the; Blessed Sacrament Fathers; Eymard, Pierre Julien, St.

*ROY, SISTER MARIE DE ST. THÉODORE DE JESUS, Servants of Our Lady Queen of the Clergy, Lac-au-Saumon, Quebec, Canada. **Article:** Servants of Our Lady Queen of the Clergy.

ROY, NEIL J., S.T.L., Ph.D., Assistant Professor of Liturgy and Sacramental Theology, Department of Theology, The Catholic University of America, Washington, D.C. **Article:** Hippolytus of Rome, St.

*ROYCE, JAMES EMMET, SJ, Ph.D., S.T.L., Professor of Psychology, University of Seattle, Seattle, Wash. **Articles:** Immortality, 2. Philosophical Analysis; Metempsychosis; Soul, Human, Origin of.

*ROZARIO, HORACE VICTOR, SJ, B.A., attached to Calcutta Vice Province of Society of Jesus, Calcutta, India; Editor, *Herald,* Catholic weekly, Calcutta. **Articles:** Dandoy, George; Hull, Ernest Reginald.

*ROZARIO, SUNIL DANIEL, Director, Christian Communications Centre, Dhaka, Bangladesh. **Article:** Bangladesh, the Catholic Church in.

*RUBIN, JOAN, Ph.D., Assistant Professor, Department of Sociology and Anthro-

pology, American University, Washington, D.C. **Articles:** Aztec Religion; Chibcha Religion; Inca Religion; Maya Religion.

*RUBIO, JOSE ANTONIO, Director of Ecumenical and Interreligious Affairs, Diocese of San Jose, Santa Clara, California. **Article:** Juan Diego, Bl.

*RUBLE, RONALD ALVIN, Ed.D., Director of Attendance Services, Albuquerque Public Schools, Albuquerque; Lecturer in Education, University of New Mexico, Albuquerque, N.Mex. **Article:** Company of Mary.

*RUEGG, S. DOMINIC, FSC, M.A., Ph.D., Associate Professor of Religion, St. Mary's College, St. Mary's, Calif. **Article:** Benedictus (Canticle of Zechariah).

*RUETZ, ALBERT ANTHONY, CR, M.A., Chaplain, Loretto Motherhouse, Nerinx, Ky. **Article:** Resurrectionists.

*RULAND, VERNON JOSEPH, SJ, West Baden College, West Baden, Ind. **Article:** Covenant Theology.

*RUMMEL, LEONARD LEO, OPraem, Ph.D., Chaplain, St. Mary's Hospital, Madison, Wis. **Articles:** Bronislawa, St.; Elmo, St.; Gerlach, St.; Herman of Scheda; Hroznata, Bl.; St. Elmo's Fire; Tanchelm; Waltman of Antwerp, Bl.

*RUMPLER, HELMUT, Dr.Phil., Hochschulassistent, Historisches Institut, University of Vienna, Austria; Secretary, Kommission für die Geschichte der österreichischungarischen Monarchie an der österr. Akademie der Wissenschaften. **Articles:** Denifle, Heinrich Seuse; Katerkamp, Johann Theodor Hermann; Mansi, Giovanni Domenico; Mittarelli, Giovanni Benedetto; Mone, Franz Joseph; Muratori, Lodovico Antonio; Quentin, Henri; Theiner, Augustin.

*RUPPEL, GEORGE JOSEPH, SM, Ph.D., Associate Professor of History and Assistant Dean of the College of Arts and Sciences, University of Dayton, Dayton, Ohio. **Articles:** Chaminade, Guillaume Joseph, Bl.; Friedel, Francis; Garvin, John E.; Marianist Sisters; Resch, Peter Anthony; Waldron, John A.

*RUSCIN, TERRY, Researcher and Author, San Diego, California. **Article:** Serra, Junípero Xavier, Bl.

*RUSH, ALFRED CLEMENT, CSSR, M.A., S.T.D., Professor of Ecclesiastical History, The Catholic University of America, Washington, D.C. **Articles:** Burial, II (Early Christian); Felix of Nola, St.; Gregory I (the Great), Pope, St.; Victor of Vita; Zeno of Verona, St.

*RUSH, VINCENT EDMUND, M.A., S.T.B., Ph.L., Ph.D., Chairman of the Department of Philosophy and Chairman of the Division of Theology and Philosophy, Mount Senario College, Ladysmith, Wis. **Article:** Koudelka, Joseph Maria.

*RUSK, WILLIAM SEUER, Ph.D., Professor Emeritus of Fine Arts, Wells College, Aurora, N.Y. **Article:** St. Paul's Cathedral (London).

*RUSKOWSKI, LEO F., SS, S.T.B., Ph.D., Professor of Church History and American Constitutional History, St. Patrick's Seminary, Menlo Park, Calif. **Articles:** Arminianism; Arminius, Jacobus; Remonstrants.

*RUSSELL, ROBERT PHILIP, OSA, Ph.D., Chairman, Department of Philosophy, Villanova University, Villanova, Pa. **Articles:** Augustine (Triumphus) of Ancona; Augustinianism, Theological School of; Augustinianism; Thomas of Strassburg.

*RUST, RICHARD JOHN, OP, M.A., S.T.B., Pontifical Faculty of Theology of the Immaculate Conception, Dominican House of Studies, Washington, D.C. **Article:** Baron, Vincent.

RUSTEMEYER, ROSANNE, SSND, Executive Director, United States Catholic Mission Association, Washington, D.C. **Article:** United States Catholic Mission Association.

RUTHERFORD, H. RICHARD, C.S.C., Ph.D., Professor, Department of Theology, University of Portland, Portland, Oregon. **Articles:** Cremation; Funeral Rites.

*RYAN, ALVAN SHERMAN, Ph.D., Professor of English and Head of Department, University of Notre Dame, Notre Dame, Ind. **Article:** Brownson, Orestes Augustus.

*RYAN, EDMUND GRANVILLE, SJ, Ph.L., S.T.L., Ph.D., Educational Consultant to the Provincial of the New York Province; Dean, St. Peter's College, Jersey City, N.J. **Articles:** Agape, SS.; Anastasia, SS.; Bouquillon Controversy; Cathedral and Episcopal Schools; Comenius, John Amos (Komensky); Cosmas and Damian, SS.; Crispina, Crispin, Crispinian, SS.; Demetrius,

SS.; Denis of Paris, St.; Desiderius of Vienne, St.; Diocletian, Roman Emperor; Diocletian, Persecution of; Dionysius of Alexandria, St.; Domitilla, Flavia, St.; Dorothy, St.; Education, Scholastic; Forty Martyrs, SS.; Four Crowned Martyrs; Francke, August Hermann; Furstenberg, Franz von; Januarius, St.; Lucy, St.; Marcellinus and Peter, SS.; Wynne, John Joseph.

*RYAN, EDMUND JOSEPH, CPPS, Ph.D., Associate Professor of Philosophy, St. Louis University, St. Louis, Mo.; Chaplain, Motherhouse of the Sisters Adorers of the Precious Blood, Ruma, Ill. **Article:** Aggression.

*RYAN, EDWARD ANTHONY, SJ, Ph.D., Sacred Heart Retreat House, Auriesville, N.Y. (deceased Nov. 17, 1964). **Article:** Scaramelli, Giovanni Battista.

*RYAN, FRANCIS CELESTINE, OP, M.A., S.T.B., Dominican House of Studies, Washington, D.C. **Articles:** Anthony Neyrot, Bl.; Bartholomew of Trent.

*RYAN, JOHN BARRY, Ph.D., former Director Notre Dame Center for Pastoral Liturgy, University of Notre Dame, Notre Dame, Ind.; Assistant Professor of Religious Studies, Manhattan College, Bronx, N.Y. **Article:** North American Academy of Liturgy.

*RYAN, JOHN JAMES HANLY, B.A., M.A., D.Litt., Professor of Early Irish History, Dublin College, National University of Ireland. **Articles:** Ardbraccan, Abbey of; Bangor, Abbeys of; Bishop, Monastic; Brigid of Ireland, St.; Columba of Iona, St.; Columban, St.; Comgall, St.; Croagh Patrick; Glendalough, Monastery of; Holy Cross, Abbey of; Kevin, St.; Kildare, Abbey of; Lindisfarne, Abbey of; Monasticism, Early Irish; Ninian, St.; Pilgrim of Passau; Purgatory, St. Patrick's; Tallaght, Abbey of; Tuam, Abbey of.

*RYAN, JOHN JOSEPH, Rt. Rev., S.T.L., Hist.Eccl.Lic., M.S.L., M.S.D., Lecturer, Boston College Graduate School of Arts and Sciences, Chestnut Hill, Mass.; Board of Directors, Institute of Research and Study in Medieval Canon Law. **Articles:** Alexander II, Pope; Atto of Milan; Atto, Collection of; Candidus of Fulda (Bruun); Deusdedit, Collection of; Hugh of Remiremont; Ratramnus of Corbie.

*RYAN, JOHN K., Rt. Rev., S.T.B., Ph.D., LL.D., Professor of Philosophy and Dean of the School, The Catholic University of America, Washington, D.C.

Articles: British Moralists; Cambridge Platonists; Pace, Edward Aloysius; Smith, Henry Ignatius.

*RYAN, SISTER MARY BRIDE, OP, Ph.D., Chairman, Department of English, Aquinas College, Grand Rapids, Mich. **Articles:** Adelphus of Metz, St.; Deochar, St.; Eusebia of Hamay, St.; Germanus of Munster-Granfelden, St.; Herkumbert, St.; Liutbirg, St.; Lufthildis, St.

*RYAN, SISTER MARY MICHAEL, RPB, B.A., London, Ontario, Canada. **Article:** Sisters Adorers of the Precious Blood.

*RYAN, SISTER MARY ROSALIE, CSJ, Ph.D., Associate Professor of English and Theology, College of St. Catherine, St. Paul, Minn. **Article:** Beelzebul.

*RYAN, PAUL EDWARD, Rt. Rev., B.A., Pastor, Cathedral Basilica of the Assumption, Covington, Ky. **Articles:** Covington, Diocese of; Howard, Francis William.

*RYAN, THOMAS J., Ph.D., Department of Theology, St. Joseph's College, Philadelphia, Pa. **Articles:** Bultmann, Rudolf Karl; Demythologizing.

*RYAN, THOMAS MCKAY, FSC, A.M. (Greek and Latin), S.T.L., A.M. (Semitics), Instructor in Greek and Theology, De La Salle College Extension of The Catholic University of America, Washington, D.C. **Articles:** Congregatio de Auxiliis; Nicene Creed.

*RYAN, WILLIAM BERTRAND, OP, B.S., S.T.L., S.T.Lr., J.C.D., S.T.M., Master of Studies and Professor of Canon Law and Pastoral Theology, Pontifical Faculty of Theology, Dominican House of Studies, Washington, D.C. **Articles:** Convent; Definitor, Religious; Friars.

*RYSKA, JUSTIN M., OSM, S.T.L., Diploma in Marian Theology, M.A. (Med. History), Hist.Eccl.Lic., Professor of Church History and Liturgy, Stonebridge Priory, Lake Bluff, Ill.; Historian, Our Lady of Sorrows Province, Motherhouse, Chicago, Ill. **Articles:** Lepicier, Alexis; Pucci, Antonio Maria, St.; Servants of Mary; Servites.

*RZESZUTEK, MARTIN PAUL, MIC, S.T.L., Superior, Marian Fathers Scholasticate, Washington, D.C. **Articles:** Marian Fathers; Papczynski, Stanislaus.

*SABATINI, LAWRENCE P., PSSC, Ph.L., S.T.L., J.C.D., Professor of Moral Theology and Canon Law, St. Charles Seminary, Staten Island, New York, N.Y. **Article:** Scalabrini, Giovanni Battista, Bl.

SABELLA, BERNARD, Ph.D., Director, Department of Social Science, Bethlehem University, Bethlehem, Palestinian Autonomous Area. **Article:** Jerusalem.

*SAGRERA, ANTHONY, CR, Ph.D., S.T.B., Plattekill, N.Y. **Articles:** Benincasa, Ursula, Ven.; Cajetan, St. (Gaetano da Thiene); Galano, Clemente; Theatines; Vezzosi, Antonio Francesco.

*SAGUÉS, SISTER MARIE, OP, M.A., Instructor in Music and Humanities, Dominican College of San Rafael, San Rafael, Calif. **Article:** Dominican Sisters—Congregation of the Most Holy Name (San Rafael, Calif).

SAHM, M. L. **Article:** Franciscan Sisters—Franciscan Sisters of the Poor (SFP).

*ST. JOHN, HENRY, OP, M.A., Chaplain, St. Dominic's Priory, Cansbrooke, Isle of Wight, England. **Article:** Cromwell, Thomas.

*SAINT-LU, ANDRÉ, Licentiates in Spanish and Portuguese, Agrégation d'Espagnol, Maître de Conférences, Faculté des Lettres et Sciences humaine, University of Poitiers, France. **Article:** Las Casas, Bartolome de.

*SAIZ, ODORICO, OFM, Professor, Franciscan Seminary, Concepción, Ocopa, Peru. **Articles:** Gual, Pedro; Herrero, Andres; Perez, Esteban; Sobreviela, Manuel.

SAKOWSKI, DEREK, Pontifical College Josephinum, Columbus, Ohio. **Article:** La Crosse, Diocese of.

*SALAZAR ORSA, JOSÉ ABEL, ORSA, J.C.D., Procurator General of his Order, Rome, Italy. **Article:** Gilij, Filippo Salvatore.

*SALEM, GABRIEL, BA (Ordre Basilien Alépin), S.T.L., J.U.D., and Special Diploma in Oriental Laws, Professor of Canon Law and Islamology, Major Seminary of the Melkite Church of St. Anne of Jerusalem, Jordan. **Articles:** Patriarchate, III: Eastern Catholic Churches; Patriarchate, IV: Patriarchates in the Latin Church.

*SALLER, SYLVESTER JOHN, OFM, Lect.Gen.SS., Professor of Biblical Archaeology at the Flagellation, Jerusalem. **Article:** Palestine, 5. Archaeology.

*SALM, C. LUKE, FSC, M.A., S.T.D., Head, Theology Department, Manhattan College, New York, N.Y. **Article:** Catholic Theological Society of America.

SALM, LUKE, FSC, S.T.D., Professor Emeritus of Religious Studies, Manhattan College, Bronx N.Y. **Articles:** Brothers of the Christian Schools; De La Salle, St. John Baptist.

*SALMON, ELIZABETH GENEVIEVE, Docteur en philosophie, Associate Professor, Graduate School of Arts and Sciences, Fordham University, New York, N.Y.; Associate Editor, *The New Scholasticism.* **Articles:** Good [part 1]; Unity.

*SALMON, PIERRE, Most Rev., OSB, Ph.L., Titular Bishop of Jucundiana, President of the Pontifical Commission on the Revision of the Vulgate, Rome, Italy. **Article:** Liturgy of the Hours.

*SAMBURSKY, SAMUEL, Ph.D., Professor and Chairman of the Department of History and Philosophy of Science, The Hebrew University, Jerusalem, Israel. **Article:** Ptolemy (Claudius Ptolemaeus).

*SAMPERS, ANDRÉ MARIE, CSSR, Ph.D. (History), S.T.D., General Archivist of Redemptorists, Professor and Secretary-General, Accademia Alfonsiana, Rome, Italy; Consultor for History, Sacred Congregation of Rites. **Articles:** Aertnys, Jozef; Donders, Peter, Bl.; Konings, Anthony; Low, Joseph.

*SANABRIA FERNANDEZ, HERNANDO, Doctor of Law, Doctor of Letters, Diploma in Education and Social Studies, Professor of History, Colegio Nacional Florida, and Colegio de Santa Ana; Director, Departamento de Extensión Cultural, Universidad Gabriel René Moreno, and Professor of Sociology, Faculty of Law and Social Sciences, Santa Cruz de la Sierra, Bolivia. **Articles:** Armentia, Nicolas; Bolivia, The Catholic Church in; Taborga, Miguel de los Santos.

*SANDERS, GABRIEL MICHEL, Doctorate in Philosophy and Letters (Classical Philology), Associate Professor of Ancient History, Faculty of Philosophy and Letters, University of Ghent, Belgium. **Articles:** Afterlife, 3. In Greco-Roman Religion; Cosmogony; Evil Eye; Fire, Use and Symbolism of; Pettazzoni, Raffaele.

*SANFORD, ARTHUR, CFA, Provincial, Alexian Brothers, Chicago, Ill. **Article:** Alexian Brothers.

*SANKER, SISTER MARY HELEN, OSU, M.A., Treasurer, Ursuline Sisters of

Cincinnati; Juniorate Mistress of Sister Formation, St. Ursula Villa, Cincinnati, Ohio; Teacher of High School English. **Article:** Ursulines.

*SANT, CARMEL, B.A., D.D., S.S.L., Professor of Holy Scripture, Malta Archiepiscopal Seminary, Tarxien, Malta. **Article:** Miracles (in the Bible).

SANTICH, JAN JOSEPH, Ph.D., St. Patrick Church, Wheatland, Wyoming. **Article:** Wyoming, Catholic Church in.

*SARGENT, BENJAMIN FRANCIS, SJ, M.A., Ph.L., S.T.B., St. Ignatius High School, San Francisco, Calif. **Article:** Grandmaison, Leonce de.

SAUER, MICHELLE M., Ph.D., Assistant Professor of English and Linguistics, Minot State University, Minot, ND. **Article:** Dorothea von Montau, St.

*SAUM, SISTER TERESA OF THE INCARNATION, M.A., Professor of History, Saratoga Campus, College of Notre Dame, Belmont, Calif. **Article:** Adrian VI, Pope.

*SAUSE, BERNARD AUSTIN, OSB, Ph.D., J.C.D., Professor of Canon Law and Liturgy, St. Benedict's Abbey Seminary, and Professor of Religion, St. Benedict's College, Atchison, Kans. **Article:** Monastery.

*SAUTER, JOHN D., priest of the Archdiocese of Cincinnati, Ohio. **Articles:** De Neve, John; Fenwick, Edward Dominic; Kindekens, Peter; Peter, Sarah Worthington King.

*SAVAGE, MOTHER ANNE OF JESUS, SHJM, Sacred Heart Convent, Watsonville, Calif. **Article:** Sacred Hearts of Jesus and Mary, Sisters of the.

SAVAGE, PAUL M., Ph.D. Instructor, Judge Memorial Catholic High School, Salt Lake City, Utah. **Articles:** Albert (Adalbert), Antipope; Alexander V, Antipope (Peter of Candia); Anacletus II, Antipope; Benedict X, Antipope; Benedict XIII, Antipope; Boniface VII, Antipope; Callistus III, Antipope; Celestine II, Antipope; Christopher, Antipope; Clement III, Antipope; Clement VIII, Antipope; Constantine II, Antipope; Felix V, Antipope (Amadeus VIII of Savoy); Gregory VI, Antipope; Gregory VIII, Antipope; Honorius II, Antipope; Innocent III, Antipope; John XXIII, Antipope; John XVI, Antipope; John VIII, Antipope; Paschal III, Antipope; Paschal, Antipope; Philip, Antipope; Sylvester IV, Antipope; Theodore, Antipope; Theodoric, Antipope; Victor IV (1159), Antipope; Victor IV (1138), Antipope.

*SAWKINS, SISTER ALPHONSUS MARIE, IHM, M.A., Associate Professor of History, Marygrove College, Detroit, Mich. **Article:** Stapleton, Thomas.

SAYAH, PAUL N., Most Rev., Ph.D., Maronite Archbishop of Haifa and the Holy Land, and Patriarchal Vicar for Jerusalem, Jordan and Palestine. **Article:** Middle East Council of Churches (MECC).

*SAYDON, PAUL PETER, B.Litt., D.D., S.S.L., Hon. D.Litt., Professor of Holy Scripture, Hebrew, and Biblical Greek and Honorary Librarian of the Royal University of Malta. **Articles:** Areopagus; Asia, Roman Province of.

*SCADUTO, MARIO, SJ, S.T.L., Hist.Eccl.D., Editor for Jesuit History, *Enciclopedia Ecclesiastica;* publicist, engaged in research on the medieval history of Sicily and in continuing the work of Tacchi Venturi on the history of Jesuits in Italy, Rome, Italy. **Article:** Charity, Works of.

*SCANDAR, ALEXANDROS HABIB, Bishop Metropolite of Lycopolis (Assiut), Upper Egypt, and Consultor for Liturgy in the Oriental Congregation (deceased Dec. 29, 1964). **Articles:** Coptic Christianity, I—Coptic Orthodox Church; Coptic Christianity, II—Coptic Catholic Church.

*SCANLON, MICHAEL J., OSA, Washington Theological Coalition, Washington, D.C. **Article:** Anonymous Christian.

*SCANNELL, ANTHONY, OFMCap, President, UNDAUSA, Los Angeles, Cal. **Article:** Unda.

*SCARISBRICK, JOHN JOSEPH, B.A., M.A., Ph.D., Lecturer in History, Queen Mary College, University of London, England. **Articles:** Defender of the Faith; Gardiner, Stephen; Henry VIII, King of England; Pilgrimage of Grace; Warham, William; Wolsey, Thomas.

*SCHAAK, HERBERT EWALD, SAC, J.C.D. (deceased Sept. 8, 1964). **Articles:** Pallotti, Vincent, St.; Pallottines.

*SCHACHER, ALOIS A., Ph.D., Assistant Professor, Department of Modern Languages, The Catholic University of America, Washington, D.C. **Articles:** Altmann of Passau, St.; Bernward of Hildesheim, St.; Crucifixion (in Art); Gandersheim, Convent of; Gebhard III of Constance; Gebhard II of Constance, St.; Gorze, Abbey of; Hartmann of Brixen, Bl.; Helfta, Convent of; Sankt Emmeram, Abbey of; Sankt

Blasien, Abbey of; Unterlinden, Convent of; Weissenburg, Abbey of; Werner of Tegernsee; Wolfgang of Regensburg, St.

*SCHAEFER, SISTER M. ROBERTA, OP, M.A., Teacher in the schools conducted by the Sisters of the St. Cecilia Congregation, St. Cecilia Convent, Nashville, Tenn. **Article:** Dominican Sisters—Congregation of St Cecilia (Nashville, Tenn).

*SCHAEFER, MARY M., M.A., Ph.D., Associate Professor of Christian Worship Atlantic School of Theology, Halifax, Nova Scotia, Canada. **Article:** Kilmartin, Edward J.

*SCHAEFER, MARY MARTINA, M.A., Instructor, Bradford Junior College, Bradford, Mass. **Articles:** Della Robbia; Pacher, Michael; Perugino (Pietro Vannucci); Wiligelmo da Modena.

*SCHAEFER, VICTOR ANTHONY, A.B., A.M.L.S., Director of Libraries, University of Notre Dame, Notre Dame, Ind. **Articles:** Arnulf of Lisieux; Arnulf of Milan; Haymo of Halberstadt; John of Mecklenburg, St.; Rembert of Bremen-Hamburg, St.

*SCHALL, JAMES VINCENT, SJ, Ph.D., Alma College, Los Gatos, Calif. **Articles:** Theocracy; Tyranny.

*SCHANEN, SISTER MARY MARISTELL, OSF, Ph.D., President and Instructor in Philosophy, Theology, and Sacred Scripture, St. Clare College, Little Falls, Minn.; Member of the General Council of the Franciscan Sisters of the Immaculate Conception. **Article:** Integrity, Gift of.

*SCHANZ, JOHN PHILIP, Ph.D., Associate Professor of Theology, Gannon College, Erie, Pa. **Article:** Crucifixion,Theological Significance of.

*SCHARDT, JORDAN NORMAN, OFMCap, Capuchin Seminary of St. Anthony, Marathon, Wis. **Article:** Cassian of Nantes, Bl.

*SCHARPER, STEPHEN B., Editor, Twenty-Third Publications, Mystic, Conn. **Article:** Scharper, Philip J.

*SCHAUF, HERIBERT LOTHAR, Rt. Rev., Dr.Phil., Dr.Theol., Professor and Vice Rector, Major Seminary, Aachen, Germany; *Peritus,* Vatican Council II. **Article:** Passaglia, Carlo.

*SCHAUINGER, JOSEPH HERMAN, Ph.D., B.L.S., Professor of History, College of St. Thomas, St. Paul, Minn. **Articles: Badin, Stephen Theodore; Durbin, Elisha John; Elder, George; Flaget, Benedict Joseph; Gaston, William Joseph; Louisville, Archdiocese of; Nerinckx, Charles; Pokagon, Leopold and Simon.

*SCHAUM, KONRAD J., Ph.D., Associate Professor of German, Department of Germanic Languages and Literatures, Princeton University, Princeton, N.J. Articles: Faust Legend; Goethe, Johann Wolfgang von.

*SCHEEL, NIVARD, CFX, Ph.D., Superior, Xaverian Brothers Scholasticate, Xaverian College, Silver Spring, Md.; Staff Editor for Physical and Biological Sciences, New Catholic Encyclopedia, The Catholic University of America, Washington, D.C. Article: Science (in the Renaissance).

*SCHELLMAN, JAMES M., M.A., Associate Executive Secretary, International Commission on English in the Liturgy, Washington, DC. Articles: Lectionaries, III: Ecumenical; Liturgical Books of Roman Rite; O'Brien, Thomas C.

*SCHEPERS, MAURICE BONAVENTURE, OP, S.T.D., Professor, St. Stephen's Priory, Dover, Mass. Articles: Apostolate and Spiritual Life; Barth, Karl; Baur, Ferdinand Christian; Dialectical Theology; Existential Theology; Experience Theology; Liberalism, Theological; Lutheranism; Neo-Orthodoxy; Netherlands Reformed Church; Sabatier, Louis Auguste; Sacramentarians; Schlatter, Adolf; Self-Love; Tubingen School; Ubiquitarianism; Vinet, Alexandre Rodolphe.

*SCHERER, BERNARD F., Ph.D., Chairman, Department of History, St. Vincent College, Latrobe, Pa. Articles: Aigulf of Lerins, St.; Berliere,Ursmer; Clarus, St.; Desiderius of Cahors, St.; Donatus of Besancon, St.; Fara, St.; Haller, Johannes; Humbert of Maroilles, St.; Kehr, Paul Fridolin; Luxeuil, Abbey of; Nazarius of Lerins, St.; Virgilius of Arles, St.

*SCHERZ, GUSTAV FELIX CARL, CSSR, Dr.Phil., Dr.Theol. (h.c.), Dr.Rer.Nat. (h.c.), Stenoniana Catholica, Copenhagen, Denmark. Article: Stensen, Niels, Bl.

*SCHIDEL, GEORGE EDWARD, CSC, M.A. (Liturgy), Teacher of Latin and Liturgy, Sacred Heart Novitiate, Jordan, Minn. Articles: Compline; Lauds; Little Hours; Little Office of the BVM; Mathis, Michael Ambrose; Office of the Dead; Vespers.

*SCHIEL, HUBERT, Dr.Phil., formerly Library Director, Trier, Germany. Article: Kraus, Franz Xaver.

*SCHIER, SISTER LEO MARIE, OP, M.A., Principal and Superior, St. Joan of Arc School, Camden, N.J. Articles: Bertrand de Garriga, Bl.; James Griesinger of Ulm, Bl.

*SCHINDLER, DAVID L., Ph.D., Editor, Communio (North American edition); Gagnon Professor of Fundamental Theology, John Paul II Institute for Studies on Marriage and Family, Washington, D.C. Article: Communio: International Catholic Review.

SCHINELLI, GILES ANTHONY, TOR, Franciscan Friars TOR, Immaculate Conception Province, Hollidaysburg, Pa. Articles: Elizabeth of Hungary (Thuringia), St.; Franciscans, Third Order Regular; Juana de la Cruz.

*SCHLAFLY, JAMES JOSEPH, M.A., Pastor of Guardian Angels Church and Historian of the Diocese of Kansas City, Mo. Article: Kansas City—St. Joseph, Diocese of.

*SCHLAX, SISTER MARY JOHN, General Councilor, Motherhouse, Little Company of Mary Sisters, Rome, Italy. Article: Little Company of Mary.

*SCHLECK, CHARLES A., CSC, S.T.D., Professor of Dogmatic and Spiritual Theology, Holy Cross College, Washington, D.C. Article: Grace, Sacramental.

SCHLEGEL, DONALD, Catholic Record Society, Diocese of Columbus, Columbus, Ohio. Article: Columbus, Diocese of.

*SCHLEICH, ALLAN MARTIN, Ph.D., Associate Professor and Chairman of the Department of History, Creighton University, Omaha, Nebr. Articles: Charles II, King of England; Harris, Howell; James I, King of England.

*SCHMANDT, RAYMOND HENRY, JR., Ph.D., Associate Professor, Department of History, Loyola University, Chicago, Ill. Articles: Adalbero of Metz; Alans; Albert Behaim; Albuin of Saben-Brixen, St.; Avars; Clotilde, St.; Conrad of Constance, St.; Constans I, Roman Emperor; Constantius II, Roman Emperor; Godard of Hildesheim, St.; Goths; Heimerad, St.; Huns; Julian the Apostate; Mann, Horace Kinder; Meinwerk of Paderborn, Bl.; Othlo of Sankt Emmeram; Theodoric the Great; Theodosius II, Byzantine

Emperor; Theodosius I, Roman Emperor; Valens, Roman Emperor; Valentinian I, Roman Emperor; Vicelinus of Oldenburg, St.; Willigis of Mainz, St.

*SCHMAUS, MICHAEL, Very Rev., Ph.D., Dr.Theol., Professor of Dogmatic Theology, University of Munich, Germany; Founder and Head, Dogmatischer Arbeitskreis, in the German Language area; Founder, Grabmann-Institut zur Ersforschung der mittelalterlichen Philosophie und Theologie; Founder, Die Deutsch-Japanische Gesellschaft im Bayern; Editor, Coeditor of, or contributor to, numerous scholarly publications; member, Bavarian Academy of Sciences. Articles: Schell, Hermann; Wirceburgenses.

*SCHMID, JOSEF, Dr.Theol., Dr.Theol. (h.c.), Professor Emeritus of New Testament Exegesis, University of Munich, Germany; Coeditor, Studien zum Alten und Neuen Testament. Articles: Billerbeck, Paul; Glenmary Home Mission Sisters; Holtzmann, Heinrich Julius.

*SCHMID, MICHAEL HEINRICH, CRSA (Austrian Congregation), Professor, Master of Novices, and Secretary General of the Congregation, Klosterneuberg, Austria. Articles: Gottweig, Abbey of; Reichersberg, Monastery of.

*SCHMID, TONI, Dr.Phil., Royal Academy, Uppsala, Sweden. Articles: Botvid, St.; David of Vastmanland, St.; Eric IX Jedvardsson, King of Sweden, St.; Eskil, St.; Hemming, Bl.; Henry of Uppsala, St.; Sigfrid, St.

*SCHMIDT, EMERY GERALD, OFMCap, B.A., Seminary of St. Anthony, Marathon, Wis. Article: Seraphino, St.

*SCHMIDT, PHILIPP, SJ, author and journalist, Cologne, Germany. Articles: Occultism; Swastika.

*SCHMIDT, ROBERT WILLIAM, SJ, M.A., Ph.L., S.T.L., Ph.D., Professor of Philosophy, Xavier University, Cincinnati, Ohio. Articles: Judgment; Reflection.

*SCHMITT, CHARLES BERNARD, Ph.D., Assistant Professor of Philosophy, Graduate School of Arts and Sciences, Fordham University, New York, N.Y. Articles: Ficino, Marsilio; Pico della Mirandola; Pomponazzi, Pietro.

*SCHMITT, FRANCISCUS SALESIUS, OSB, S.T.L., Dr.Theol. (h.c.), Benedictine Abbey, Bad Wimpfen am Neckar, Baden, Germany. Article: Anselm of Canterbury, St.

*SCHMITT, KARL MICHAEL, Ph.D., Associate Professor of Government, University of Texas, Austin, Tex. **Articles:** Fonte, Pedro Jose; Posada y Garduno, Manuel.

*SCHMITZ, EDWIN FRANCIS, SS, S.T.L., M.A., Professor, St. Charles College, Catonsville, Md. **Article:** Eccleston, Samuel.

*SCHMITZ, JOSEPH W., SM, Ph.D., Vice President and Dean of Faculties, St. Mary's University, San Antonio, Tex. **Articles:** Litz, Damian; Texas, Catholic Church in.

*SCHMITZ, KENNETH L., Ph.D., Professor Emeritus of Philosophy and Fellow of Trinity College, University of Toronto, Toronto, Ontario, Canada. **Article:** Man, 2. In Philosophy.

SCHMUGGE, LUDWIG, Dr. phil., Professor of Medieval History, University of Zürich, Zürich, Switzerland. **Articles:** Boniface VIII, Pope; Martin V, Pope; Papal Registers.

*SCHNEIDER, AMBROSIUS, SOCist, Dr.Phil., Editor, *Analecta S.O.Cist.,* Rome, Italy. **Articles:** Achard (Aichardus), Bl.; David of Himmerod, Bl.; Eberbach, Abbey of; Ebrach, Abbey of; Himmerod, Abbey of; Leubus, Abbey of; Loccum, Abbey of; Oliva, Abbey of; Viktring, Abbey of; Walter of Birbeck, Bl.

*SCHNEIDER, BURKHART, SJ, Dr.Theol., Eccl.Hist.D., Professor of Church History, Faculty of Church History, Gregorian University, Rome, Italy. **Articles:** Acquaviva, Claudius; Canisius, Peter, St.; Monita Secreta.

*SCHNELL, HUGO KARL MARIA, Dr.Phil., art historian and publisher, Scheidegg-Allgäu am Blauberg, Bavaria, Germany. **Article:** Church Architecture, History of, 10: 20th century Europe.

*SCHNITZER, MOTHER CONSTANCE, SCSC, M.A. in L.S., Provincial Superior of the Holy Cross Sisters, Merrill, Wis. **Article:** Holy Cross, Sisters of Mercy of the.

*SCHNITZLER, THEODOR, Dr.Phil., Dr.Theol., Pastor, Church of the Holy Apostles, Cologne, and Professor of Liturgy, Major Seminary, Essen, Germany. **Article:** Parsch, Pius.

*SCHOBERG, FERDINAND WILLLIAM, SJ, Ph.D., Regional Director, Apostleship of Prayer, for Maryland Province, Society of Jesus, Philadelphia, Pa. **Article:** Apostleship of Prayer.

*SCHODER, RAYMOND VICTOR, SJ, Ph.D., S.T.L., Professor of Classical Literature and Archeology, Loyola University, Chicago, Ill.; lecturer and writer in classical archeology. **Article:** Decapolis.

*SCHOECK, RICHARD J., Ph.D., Professor of English, St. Michael's College, University of Toronto, Ontario, Canada. **Articles:** Arches, Court of; Colet, John; Gaguin, Robert; Heywood; More, School of; More, Sir Thomas, St. [part 2].

*SCHOENBERG, MARTIN WILLIAM, OSC, S.S.L., S.T.D., Professor of Scripture, Hebrew, and Greek, Crosier House of Studies, Fort Wayne, Ind. **Articles:** Crucifixion; Nails, Holy.

*SCHOETERS, KAREL L., SJ, Apostolische School, Turnhout, Belgium. **Article:** Berchmans, Jan (John), St.

*SCHOLES, FRANCE VINTON, Ph.D., Research Professor Emeritus of History, University of New Mexico, Albuquerque, N.Mex. **Article:** Landa, Diego de.

*SCHOLSKY, MARTIN JOSEPH, M.A., Instructor in Greek and Latin, St. Thomas Seminary, Bloomfield, Conn. **Article:** Hartford, Archdiocese of.

*SCHOLZ, BERNHARD W., Ph.D., Assistant Professor of History, Seton Hall University, South Orange, N.J. **Articles:** Edgar the Peaceful, King of England; Edmund the Martyr, King of East Anglia, St.; Edward the Martyr, King of England, St.; Edwin, King of Northumbria, St.; Ethelbert, King of East Anglia, St.; Lanfranc; Odo (Oda) of Canterbury, St.

*SCHORK, RUDOLPH JOSEPH, JR., D.Phil., Associate Professor of Classics and Chairman of the Department, Georgetown University, Washington, D.C. **Articles:** Callinicus, Patriarch of Constantinople; Julian of Halicarnassus; Procopius of Gaza; Romanus Melodus, St.; Theodore the Studite, St.

*SCHORR, GEORGE FENWICK, Very Rev., J.C.D., College of St. Charles Borromeo, Columbus, Ohio. **Article:** Celebret.

*SCHREINER, SISTER MARY VIRGINIA, SFP, B.A., Assistant to the Mistress of Novices, St. Clare Convent, Cincinnati, Ohio. **Article:** Schervier, Franziska, Bl.

SCHREITER, ROBERT, CPPS, Theology Dr., Bernardin Center Professor of Vatican

II Theology, Catholic Theological Union, Chicago, Ill. **Article:** Precious Blood, Missionaries of the.

*SCHROEDER, FRANCIS JOSEPH, SSJ, S.T.D., S.S.L., Professor of Sacred Scripture, Greek, Spiritual Theology, and Music and Spiritual Director, St. Joseph's Seminary, Washington, D.C. **Articles:** Canon, Biblical, 3. History of New Testament Canon; Paul, Apostle, St.

* SCHROEDER, SISTER MARY CAROL, OSF, Ph.D., Professor of History and Chairman of the Department, Marian College, Indianapolis, Ind. **Articles:** Alerding, Herman Joseph; Bazin, John Stephen; Lambing, Andrew Arnold.

*SCHRÖER, ALOIS, Dr.Phil., Dr. Theol., Honorary Professor, University of Münster, Germany; Director, Institut für religiöse Volkskunde; Editor, *Forschungen zur Geschichte und Kultur.* **Article:** Gallitzin, Amalia.

*SCHUBERT, KURT, Dr.Phil., Professor of Jewish Studies, University of Vienna, Austria; President, Catholic *Akademikerverband* of Austria; President, Coordinating Committee for Christian-Jewish Cooperation in Austria. **Articles:** Cabala; Gnosticism, Jewish; Midrashic Literature; Talmud.

*SCHUIT, WILLIAM N., B.A., S.T.L., S.S.L., Professor of Sacred Scripture, St. Francis Major Seminary, Milwaukee, Wis. **Articles:** Book of Life; Testimonia.

*SCHULLER, SISTER MARY VIATORA, OSF, Ph.D., President, College of St. Joseph on the Rio Grande, Albuquerque, N.Mex. **Articles:** Fürstenberg, Franz and Wilhelm Egon von; Schönborn.

*SCHULTZE, BERNHARD, SJ, Dr.Phil., Dr.Theol., Dr.Sc.Or., Professor of Eastern Theology, Pontifical Oriental Institute and Gregorian University, Rome, Italy. **Articles:** Bulgaris, Eugenius; Glubokovskii, Nikolai Nikanorovich; Orthodox Symbolic Books; Russian Theology.

*SCHULZ, SIEGFRIED A., Ph.D., Associate Professor of German and Comparative Philology, The Catholic University of America, Washington, D.C. **Articles:** Angelus Silesius; Ansgar, St.; Brant, Sebastian (Brandt); Helentrudis, St.; Ludger of Munster, St.; Wiltrude, Bl.

SCHUMACHER, U., **Articles:** Franciscan Sisters—Sisters of St. Francis of the Holy Cross (OSF).

*SCHÜSSLER, HERMANN EVERHARD, Dr.Theol. (Kiel), Research Scholar, Institute of European History, Mainz, Germany. **Article:** Evangelical Church in Germany (EKD).

*SCHUTH, KATARINA, OSF, Director of Planning and Registrar, Weston School of Theology, Cambridge, Mass. **Article:** Seminary Education.

*SCHÜTTE, JOSEF FRANZ, SJ, Hist.Eccl.D., Institutum Historicum SJ, Rome, Italy. **Articles:** Cerqueira, Luis de; Japan, Martyrs of; Rodriguez Tcuzu, Joao; Valignano, Alessandro.

*SCHUTZINGER, CAROLINE EVA, Ph.D., Professor of Philosophy and Chairman of the Department, Mercy College, Detroit, Mich. **Articles:** Illumination; Irrationalism; Light, Metaphysics of; Lotze, Rudolf Hermann.

*SCHWADE, ARCADIO, SJ, Eccl.Hist.D., Assistant Professor of the History of Relations between Japan and Europe, Sophia University, Tokyo, Japan. **Articles:** Kagawa, Toyohiko; Japan, The Catholic Church in.

*SCHWAIGER, GEORG, Dr.Theol., Professor of Bavarian Church History, Catholic Theological Faculty, University of Munich, Germany. **Articles:** Papacy, 3. Renaissance and Early Modern Period; Pius XI, Pope.

*SCHWARTE, KARL-HEINZ, Dr.Phil., Wissenschaftlicher Assistent, Ancient History Seminar, University of Bonn, Germany. **Article:** Holtzmann, Walther.

*SCHWARTZ, JOSEPH, Ph.D., Associate Professor of English and Chairman of the Department, Marquette University, Milwaukee, Wis. **Article:** Adams, Henry Brooks.

*SCHWARZ, JOHN STEPHEN, SJ, M.A., Alma College, Los Gatos, Calif. **Articles:** Parrenin, Dominique; Premare, Joseph Henri de.

*SCHWARZENBERG, KARL, Dr.Phil., Archivist, Schwarzenbergisches Archiv, Murau, Steiermark, Austria. **Articles:** Saint Hubert, Order of; St. George, Orders of.

*SCHWEIGHOFER, GREGOR, Archivist, Librarian, and Architectural Director, Stift Altenburg, Lower Austria. **Article:** Altenburg, Abbey of.

*SCHWIEBERT, ERNEST GEORGE, Ph.D., Command Historian, Air Force Systems Command, Andrews Air Force Base, Washington, D.C. **Articles:** Chemnitz, Martin; Osiander, Andreas; Petri, Olaus; Wittenberg.

*SCIACCA, MICHELE FEDERICO, Ph.D., Professor of Theoretical Philosophy, University of Genoa, Italy. **Articles:** Common Sense; Galluppi, Pasquale; Gioberti, Vincenzo; Machiavelli, Niccolo; Reid, Thomas; Scottish School of Common Sense.

*SCOLLARD, ROBERT JOSEPH, CSB, B.A., A.M. in L.S., Secretary-General, Basilian Fathers, Toronto, Ontario, Canada. **Articles:** Basilians; Carr, Henry; Charbonnel, Armand François Marie de; Kelly, Michael Vincent; Soulerin, Jean Mathieu.

*SCOTT, ROLAND WALDECK, B.A., B.D., M.A., Ph.D., Ordained Minister, Methodist Church; member, Switzerland Annual Conference; Assistant General Secretary, World Council of Churches, Geneva, Switzerland. **Article:** International Missionary Council.

*SCOTT-MONCRIEFF, GEORGE IRVING, author, Newmains, Stenton, Dunbar, East Lothian, Scotland. **Article:** Boswell, James.

SCOTTI, DOM PASCHAL, OSB, J.C.L., Chairman, Christian Doctrine Department, Portsmouth Abbey School, Portsmouth, R.I. **Article:** Rhode Island, Catholic Church in.

SCOURTIS, CONSTANTINA, Ph.D., Assistant Professor of Christianity and Byzantine Theology, University of Notre Dame, Notre Dame, Indiana. **Article:** Eastern Schism.

*SCOZZAFAVA, ETTORE, Hist.Eccl.Lic., S.T.L., Professor of Ancient Church History and Patristics and Librarian, Major Seminary, Florence, Italy. **Articles:** Florence [History]; Siena [The Bishopric and the City].

*SCREECH, MICHAEL ANDREW, B.A., D.Litt., Reader in French Language and Literature, University College, London, England. **Article:** Rabelais, François.

*SCULLY, JOSEPH WILLIAM, B.A., New Haven, Conn. **Article:** Barber.

*SEALY, ROBERT JAMES, SJ, M.A., Ph.L., S.T.L., Docteur de l'Université (Paris), Assistant Professor of French, Director of Junior Year Abroad, and Assistant Director of Honors Program, Fordham College, New York, N.Y. **Articles:** Barruel, Augustin de; Olivaint, Pierre.

*SEARS, LAWRENCE RICHARD, M.S. in L.S., Organist and Choirmaster, Shrine of the Most Blessed Sacrament, Chevy Chase, Md.; Director, Blessed Sacrament Choir School; Lecturer in Gregorian Chant, The Catholic University of America; Conductor, St. Cecilia Choral Society; President, NCMEA; member, Archdiocesan Music Commission, Washington, D.C. **Article:** Frescobaldi, Girolamo.

*SEASOLTZ, ROBERT KEVIN, OSB, B.A., S.T.L., J.C.D., Instructor in Religious Education, The Catholic University of America, Washington, D.C. **Article:** Abbot, Blessing of; Liturgical Art, History of, Pt 2: Legislation before Vatican II.

*SEASOLTZ, ROBERT KEVIN, OSB, J.C.D., Rector, St. John's Seminary, Collegeville, Minn. **Articles:** Sacred Space; Sacred Time.

SEASOLTZ, ROBERT KEVIN, OSB, S.T.L., J.C.D., Professor, School of Theology, St. John's University, Collegeville, Minn. **Articles:** Benedictine Rule; Benedictine Spirituality; Benedictines; Leclercq, Jean; Poverty, Religious.

*SECONDO, LOUIS JOSEPH, TOR, S.T.D., Ph.D., Procurator-General, Third Order Regular of St. Francis, Basilica dei SS. Cosma e Damiano, Rome, Italy. **Article:** Franciscans, Third Order Regular.

*SEIBERT, MARY KEVAN, SND, Chancellor, Diocese of Lexington. **Article:** Lexington, Diocese of.

*SELHORST, EUGENE JOSEPH, Ph.D., Professor of Music Literature, Head of the Department, and Associate Dean for Graduate Studies, Eastman School of Music, Rochester, N.Y. **Article:** Hymns and Hymnals, I: Historical Developments.

*SELMER, CARL, Ph.D., Professor of German, Hunter College, City University of New York, N.Y.; Coeditor, PMLA, and Consultant for PMLA and Modern Language Association. **Article:** Germanic Religion.

*SELVAGGI, FILIPPO, SJ, Ph.L., S.T.L., Ph.D., Professor of Cosmology and the Philosophy of Science and Dean of the Faculty of Philosophy, Gregorian University, Rome, Italy. **Articles:** Physical Laws, Philosophy of; Space; Uniformity.

*SEMMLER, JOSEF, Dr.Phil., Assistent, Deutsches Historisches Institut, Paris, France. **Articles:** Adalard, St.; Fulda, Abbey of.

*SENA, THOMAS J., Executive Aide, Dignity, Inc., Washington, D.C. **Article:** Dignity/USA.

*SEPER, FRANCIS HENRY, MSC, S.T.L., S.S.L., Professor of Sacred Scripture and Dean of Studies, Sacred Heart Seminary, Shelby, Ohio. **Articles:** Palestine, 3. Political Geography; Palestine, 6. Pre-Israelite Ethnology.

*SERMAK, RONALD M., OFMConv, B.A., I.C.L., Immaculate Heart of Mary Friary, Baltimore, Md. **Article:** Religious Habit.

*SERRUYS, HENRY, CICM, Ph.D., Research Scholar in Chinese History and Literature, Convent of Perpetual Adoration, Beallesville, Md. **Article:** Lamaism.

*SESANA, RENATO KIZITO, MCCJ, Ph.D., Professor of Social Communication and Director of New People Media Center, Nairobi. Founder and Editor, *New People Magazine,* Nairobi, Kenya. **Article:** Sudan, The Catholic Church in.

*SETIAN, NERSÈS MICHAËL, S.T.L., J.C.D., Archpriest of the Catholic Armenian Patriarchate, Rector of the Pontifical Armenian College, Rome, Italy. **Articles:** Ani; Armenia, The Catholic Church in; Dwin; Isaac the Great, Armenian Catholicos, St.; Mesrop; Nerses; Tiridates III, Armenian King; Vardan, Mamikonian, St.

*SEVERUS, EMMANUEL VON, OSB, Dr.Phil., Prior, Abbey of Maria Laach, Germany. **Articles:** Maria Laach, Abbey of; Mohlberg, Kunibert.

*SEVILLA, CARLOS ARTHUR, SJ, M.A., Alma College, Los Gatos, Calif. **Articles:** Grisar, Hartmann; Jungmann, Josef.

*SEXTON, VIRGINIA STAUDT, Ph.D., Associate Professor of Psychology, Hunter College of the City University of New York, N.Y.; Certified Psychologist, New York State. **Articles:** Fröbes, Joseph; Marley, Marie Hilda, Sister; Vittorino da Feltre; Vegius, Mapheus.

*SHALLOW, SISTER MARY DOMINICA, OSF, B.A., B.L.S., Librarian, Junior College, OSF Convent, Green Bay, Wis. **Article:** Franciscan Sisters—Sisters of St. Francis of the Holy Cross (OSF).

*SHANAHAN, DANIEL, Very Roy., J.C.D., Chancellor of Brentwood Diocese, Pastor of Hornchurch, Essex, England. **Article:** Petre.

*SHANAHAN, MOTHER MARGARET MARY, IBVM, B.A., H.Dip. in Ed., Teaching Staff, Institute of the Blessed Virgin Mary, Loreto College, Dublin, Ireland. **Article:** Ball, Frances Mary Teresa.

*SHANAHAN, ROBERT JOHN, SJ, Ph.D., Assistant Professor of American History, Creighton University, Omaha, Nebr. **Article:** Catholic Health Association.

*SHANNON, JAMES P., Most Rev., Ph.D., Auxiliary Bishop of St. Paul, Minn. **Articles:** Cretin, Joseph; Dowling, Austin; Ireland, John.

*SHARKEY, NEIL, CP, S.T.D., Lector of Fundamental Theology, The Passionist Monastery, Jamaica, Long Island, N.Y. **Article:** Docta Ignorantia.

*SHARP, JOHN K., Rt. Rev., Pastor, St. Mary's Parish, Manhasset, Long Island, N.Y. **Article:** Loughlin, John.

*SHARPLES, SISTER MARIAN, IHM, Ph.D., Associate Professor of English, Immaculate Heart College, Los Angeles, Calif. **Article:** Immaculate Heart of the Blessed Virgin Mary, Sisters of.

*SHARRATT, MOTHER MARY THÉOPHANE, FMSJ, Third General Councillor and Secretary-General, Congregation of the Franciscan Missionaries of St. Joseph, Franciscan Convent, Broughton Hall, Eccleshall, Staffordshire, England. **Article:** Franciscan Sisters—Franciscan Missionaries of St. Joseph (SMSJ).

*SHARROCK, DAVID JOHN, CSSR, S.T.D., Teacher of Latin and English and Registrar, St. Mary's Minor Seminary, North East, Pa. **Article:** Hofbauer, Clement Mary, St.

*SHAUGHNESSY, JAMES D., University of Notre Dame, Notre Dame, In. **Articles:** Federation of Diocesan Liturgical Commissions (FDLC); Ordinations in the Roman Rite.

*SHAW, RUSSELL, M.A., Director of Public Information of the Knights of Columbus, Washington, DC. **Articles:** McDevitt, John W.; Portillo, Alvaro del.

*SHAY, MARY LUCILLE, Ph.D., Assistant Professor Emerita of History, University of Illinois, Urbana, Ill. **Articles:** Benedict XIV, Pope; Caracciolo; Cavour, Carmillo Benso di; Cesarini; Colonna; Corsini; Falconieri; Farnese; Garampi, Giuseppe; Gonzaga; Gregory XV, Pope; Maffei; Maria Cristina of Savoy, Ven.; Neo-Guelfism; Orsini; Pazzi; Ruffo, Fabrizio; Sanfedists; Savelli; Trivulzio.

*SHEA, ANN MARIE, M.A., Director of Drama, College Misericordia, Dallas, Pa. **Article:** Genesius, SS.

SHEA, PATRICK, OFM, J.D., J.C.L., Defender of the Bond, Tribunal, Diocese of Springfield in Illinois, Springfield, Ill. **Articles:** Religious (Men and Women); Religious, Canon Law of.

*SHEEDY, CHARLES EDMUND, CSC, A.B., LL.B., S.T.D., Professor of Theology and Dean of the College of Arts and Letters, University of Notre Dame, Notre Dame, Ind. **Articles:** Berengarius of Tours; Chrodegang of Metz, St.; Deusdedit I, Pope, St.; Gerhoh of Reichersberg; John VIII, Pope; Jonas of Orléans; Pirmin, St.; Roswitha of Gandersheim.

*SHEEHAN, MICHAEL MCMAHON, CSB, B.A., M.S.D., Professor of Church History, Faculty of Theology, St. Michael's College, and Professor of History, Pontifical Institute of Mediaeval Studies, University of Toronto, Canada. **Articles:** Annates; Asylum, Right of; Necrology.

*SHEEN, FULTON JOHN, Most Rev., J.C.B., Ph.D., S.T.D., LL.D., Litt.D., L.H.D., Auxiliary Bishop of New York; National Director, Society for the Propagation of the Faith, New York, N.Y. **Article:** Propagation of the Faith, Society for the.

*SHEERIN, FRANCIS LOUIS, SJ, M.A., S.T.D., Mag.Aggreg. (Gregorian University, Rome), Professor of Dogmatic Theology and Patrology, Alma College, Los Gatos, Calif. **Articles:** Futurible; Grace, Sufficient; Grace, Created and Uncreated; Grace, Efficacious; Molina, Luis de; Molinism; Predefinition; Reprobation; Reviviscence of Merit; Scientia media.

*SHEERIN, JOHN B., CSP, former editor *Catholic World,* Paulist Fathers, Washington, D.C. **Articles:** Burke, John J.; Civil Disobedience.

*SHELLEY, THOMAS J., Ph.D., St. Joseph's Seminary, Dunwoodie, Yonkers, N.Y. **Article:** Cooke, Terence.

*SHELLEY, MSGR. THOMAS J., Ph.D., Church of St. Thomas More, New York, N.Y. **Article:** O'Connor, John Joseph.

SHELLEY, MSGR. THOMAS J., Ph.D., Associate Professor of Historical Theology, Fordham University, Bronx, N.Y. **Article:** New York, Archdiocese of.

SHELTON, PAMELA, B.A., University of Connecticut, graduate studies at Wayne State University, Detroit, MI, writer and editor, Avon, CT. **Articles:**

Belarus, the Catholic Church in; Bosnia-Herzegovina, the Catholic Church in; Brunei, the Catholic Church in; Croatia, the Catholic Church in; Eritrea, the Catholic Church in; Macedonia, the Catholic Church in; Moldova, the Catholic Church in; Norway, the Catholic Church in; Slovenia, the Catholic Church in; Ukraine, the Catholic Church in; United Arab Emirates, the Catholic Church in.

SHELTRA, FRANCES, International Regent, Daughters of Isabella. **Article:** Daughters of Isabella.

SHENK, WILBERT R., Ph.D., Paul E. Pierson Professor of Mission History and Contemporary Culture, Fuller Theological Seminary, Pasadena, Calif. **Article:** American Society of Missiology.

SHEPHERD, KENNETH R., M.A., Ph.D. Cand. (Wayne State University), Detroit, Michigan. **Article:** Charles I, King of England.

*SHEPHERD, MASSEY HAMILTON, JR., Ph.D., S.T.D., D.D., Priest, Protestant Episcopal Church, Professor of Liturgics, Church Divinity School of the Pacific, Berkeley, Calif. **Articles:** Book of Common Prayer; Liturgical Movement, II: Anglican and Protestant.

SHEPHERD, WILLIAM JOHN, M.A., Associate Archivist, The Catholic University of America, Washington, D.C. **Article:** Archives, U. S. Catholic.

SHEPPARD, JAMES ANDREW, Ph.D., Professor of Philosophy, Southwestern College, Winfield, Kansas. **Articles:** Clement VII, Antipope; Eugene III, Pope, Bl.; Gregory X, Pope, Bl.; John XXI, Pope (Peter of Spain); Nicholas V, Antipope; Sergius IV, Pope; Severinus, Pope; Sylvester III, Pope.

*SHEPPARD, LANCELOT CAPEL, author and translator; General Editor, *Twentieth Century Encyclopedia of Catholicism;* Editor, *Twentieth Century Catholicism,* Capel Cottage, Oakhill, Bath, Somerset, England. **Articles:** Bangor Use; Bridgett, Thomas Edward; Carthusian Rite; Celtic Rite; Hereford Use; Liturgical Books of Roman Rite; York Use.

*SHERBOWITZ-WETZOR, OLGERD P. M. V., M.A., Ph.D., Professor Emeritus of History, Georgetown University, Washington, D.C. **Articles:** Adalbert of Prague, St.; Alexander Nevski; Boris I of Bulgaria; Bruno of Querfurt, St.; Knights of Malta; Ludmilla, St.; Slavic Religion; Vladimir, St.

SHERIDAN, DANIEL P., Ph.D., Provost, St. Joseph's College of Maine, Standish, Maine. **Articles:** Hummel, Maria Innocentia; Index of Prohibited Books; Oberammergau; Pax Christi International.

*SHERIDAN, ROBERT E., M.M., author. **Article:** Considine, John J.

*SHERWOOD, POLYCARP ROBERT, OSB, S.T.D., Professor, St. Meinrad Archabbey of the Swiss-American Congregation, St. Meinrad, Ind. **Article:** Moschus, John.

*SHERZER, WILLIAM JAMES, M.A., S.T.L., Dean of Students and Professor of History, Sacred Heart Seminary, Detroit, Mich.; Chairman of the Liturgical Commission of the Archdiocese of Detroit. **Article:** Sunday.

*SHIELDS, JOSEPH ANTHONY, J.C.D., Registrar, Cardinal Dougherty High School, Philadelphia, Pa.; Advocate, Metropolitan Tribunal. **Article:** Clerical Dress (Canon Law).

*SHIELS, WILLIAM EUGENE, SJ, Ph.D., Professor of History and Chairman of Department, Xavier University, Cincinnati, Ohio. **Articles:** Finn, Francis James; Tapia, Gonzalo de.

SHIVANANDAN, MARY, S.T.D., Professor of Theology, John Paul II Institute for Studies on Marriage and Family at The Catholic University of America, Washington, D.C. **Article:** Sex.

*SHOOK, LAURENCE KENNEDY, CSB, M.A., A.M., Ph.D., President (1961–1973) of the Pontifical Institute of Mediaeval Studies and (1984–1985) of the Medieval Academy of America. **Articles:** Gilson, Etienne Henry; Heliand.

SHORE, PAUL, Ph.D., Associate Professor of Educational Studies, Saint Louis University, St. Louis, MO. **Article:** Reinert, Paul C.

*SHORTER, AYLWARD, M. Afr., Ph.D., President, Missionary Institute London. **Article:** Inculturation, Theology of.

SHORTER, AYLWARD, M.Afr., Ph.D., former President, Missionary Institute of London, England. **Article:** Missiology.

*SHUSTER, GEORGE NAUMAN, Ph.D., LL.D., Litt.D., L.H.D., President Emeritus, Hunter College, New York, N.Y.; Assistant to the President, Notre Dame University, Notre Dame, Ind. **Article:** Williams, Michael.

SIA, SANTIAGO, Ph.D. Professor of Philosophy, Loyola Marymount University, Los Angeles, California. **Articles:** Hartshorne, Charles; Panentheism.

*SIEBENECK, ROBERT T., CPPS, S.T.L., S.S.L., Professor of Sacred Scripture, St. Charles Seminary, Carthagena, Ohio. **Articles:** Blood, Religious Significance of; Precious Blood, I (in the Bible); Wisdom, Book of.

*SIEGMAN, EDWARD FERDINAND, CPPS, S.T.D., S.S.L., Professor of Sacred Scripture, St. Charles Seminary, Carthagena, Ohio. **Articles:** Angels of the Churches; Nicolaites; Revelation, Book of; Woman Clothed with the Sun.

*SIEKANIEC, LADISLAS JOHN, OFM, Ph.D. in Ed., Pastor, St. Francis Church; Superior, St. Francis Friary; Superintendent, Central Catholic School, Humphrey, Nebr. **Articles:** Bogumił of Gniezno, St.; Casimir, St.; Ceslaus of Silesia, Bl.; Długosz, Jan; Gaudentius of Gniezno, St.; Gerard of Csanád, St.; Isaias Boner of Cracow, Bl.; Jadwiga of Poland, St.; Jagiełło (Władysław II); John Cantius, St.; John Prandota of Cracow, Bl.

*SIEVERS, HARRY JOSEPH, SJ, Ph.D., Professor of History, Loyola College and Seminary, Shrub Oak Campus of Fordham University, N.Y. **Article:** Blessed Sacrament, Sisters of the.

*SIGER, LEONARD PAUL, M.A., Ph.D., Professor of English, and Coordinator of the Humanities, Gallaudet College, and Associate Staff Editor for Art and Architecture, *New Catholic Encyclopedia,* The Catholic University of America, Washington, D.C. **Articles:** God the Father, Iconography of; Holy Spirit, Iconography of; Jesus Christ, Iconography of; Manuscript Illumination.

*SIGMUND, PAUL EUGENE, Ph.D., Associate Professor of Politics, Princeton University, Princeton, N.J. **Article:** Natural Law in Political Thought.

*SILLEM, EDWARD AUGUSTINE, Ph.D., Priest of the Archdiocese of Southwark, England (deceased Sept. 15, 1964). **Articles:** Berkeley, George; Clarke, Samuel; Hamilton, Sir William; Hawkins, Denis John Bernard; Herbert of Cherbury, Edward; Hume, David; Paley, William.

*SILVA REGO, ANTONIO DA, Licencié en Sciences Historiques, Professor, Instituto Superior de Ciências Sociais e

Política Ultramarina, University of Lisbon, Portugal; President, Centro de Estudos Históricos Ultramarinos; Director, Filmoteca Ultramarina Portuguesa. **Article:** Patronato Real (Padroado of Portugal).

*SILVEIRA, ILDEFONSO LAUDELINO, OFM, Hist.Eccl.D., Professor, Franciscan Theologate, Petrópolis, Brazil. **Articles:** Arcoverde de Albuquerque Cavalcanti, Joaquim; Conceição, Apolinário da; Leme da Silveira Cintra, Sebastião.

*SIMCOX, CARROLL E., editor, *The Living Church*, Milwaukee, Wi. **Articles:** Anglican Communion; Episcopal Church, U.S.; Lambeth Conference.

*SIMMONS, EDWARD DWYER, S.T.B., Ph.D., Associate Professor of Philosophy, Marquette University, Milwaukee, Wis. **Articles:** Abstraction; Sciences, Classification of.

*SIMON, ALOIS VICTOR, Docteur en philosophie et lettres, formerly Professor, Faculté universitaire St.-Louis, Brussels, Belgium (deceased Dec. 7, 1964). **Articles:** Broglie, Maurice Jean de; Goossens, Pierre Lambert; Gregory XVI, Pope; Liberalism, Religious; Sterckx, Engelbert.

*SIMONETTI, MANLIO, Doctorate in Letters, Professor of Ancient Christian Literature, Faculty of Letters, University of Cagliari, Sardinia, Italy. **Article:** Rufinus of Aquileia.

*SINISHTA, GJON, Editor, *Albanian Catholic Bulletin;* Executive Secretary, Daniel Dajani, S.J. Albanian Catholic Institute, University of San Francisco. **Article:** Albania, The Catholic Church in [part 2].

*SINOR, DENIS, M.A., Professor of Altaic Studies and History, Chairman Uralic and Altaic Program, University of Indiana, Bloomington, Ind. **Articles:** Emeric of Hungary, St.; Gisela, Bl.; John da Pian del Carpine; Mongols; Seljuks; Stephen I, King of Hungary, St.

*SITWELL, FRANCIS GERARD, OSB, B.A., M.A., Master of St. Benet's Hall, Oxford, England. **Articles:** Baker, David Augustine; Blosius, Francis Louis (de Blois).

*SIWEK, PAUL, SJ, Ph.D., S.T.D., Docteur ès lettres, Mag. Aggreg. (Gregorian University), Professor of Philosophy, University of the Lateran, Rome, Italy. **Articles:** Introspection; Neumann,

Theresa; Optimism; Pessimism; Spinoza, Baruch (Benedict); Stigmatization.

*SKEABECK, ANDREW HERMAN, CSSR, M.A., Professor of History, Redemptorist Seminary, Suffield, Conn. **Articles:** Boniface II, Pope; Bulla; Fortunatus, Venantius Honorius Clementianus; Gross, William Hickley.

*SKEHAN, PATRICK WILLIAM, Rt. Rev., S.T.D., LL.D., Professor and Head of the Department of Semitic and Egyptian Languages and Literatures, The Catholic University of America, Washington, D.C.; Vice Chairman, Editorial Board for the Old Testament Translation from the original languages sponsored by the Episcopal Committee of the Confraternity of Christian Doctrine. **Articles:** Arbez, Edward Philip; Bible (Texts), 1. Text of the Old Testament; Hexapla; Enoch Literature; Job, Book of; Renaudot, Eusebe; Septuagint.

*SKVARLA, NORBERT ROBERT, OSB, M.A., Professor of History and Head of the Department, St. Procopius College Academy, Lisle, Ill. **Articles:** Armellini, Mariano; Petit-Didier, Matthieu; Scholliner, Hermann.

*SLATTERY, SISTER MARY FRANCIS, SC, Ph.D., Assistant Professor of English, College of Mt. St. Vincent-on-Hudson, New York, N.Y.; Style Editor, *New Catholic Encyclopedia,* The Catholic University of America, Washington, D.C. **Article:** Beauty [in Aesthetics].

*SLOANE, CHARLES O'CONOR, LL.B., M.A., S.S.L., Pastor, SS. Peter and Paul Church, Mount Vernon, N.Y. **Articles:** Catenae, Biblical; Glosses, Biblical; Scholium.

*SLOK, JOHANNES FRIIS, Ph.D., Professor of the History of Ideas, University of Aarhus, Denmark. **Article:** Myth and Mythology.

*SLOTTMAN, WILLIAM BRADLEY, Ph.D., Assistant Professor of History, University of California at Berkeley, Calif. **Articles:** Ferdinand II, Holy Roman Emperor; Hapsburg (Habsburg), House of; Innitzer, Theodor; Lang, Matthaus; Los-von-Rom Movement; Manharter; Piffl, Friedrich Gustav; Rudigier, Franz Joseph, Ven.

*SLOYAN, GERARD STEPHEN, S.T.L., Ph.D., Professor of Religious Education and Head of the Department, The Catholic University of America, Washington, D.C.; founding member,

Societas Liturgica. **Article:** Catechisms.

SLOYAN, VIRGINIA, The Liturgical Conference. **Article:** Liturgical Conference.

*SMALL, FRANCIS ALOYSIUS, SJ, M.A. (Phil.), M.A. (Hist.), S.T.L., M.S.L.S., Coordinator, Division of Social Sciences, Chairman, Department of History and Government; and Director of Libraries, Fairfield University, Fairfield, Conn. **Articles:** Azevedo, Ignacio de, Bl.; Baldinucci, Antonio, Bl.

*SMALLEY, BERYL, M.A., Ph.D., Vice Principal and History Tutor, St. Hilda's College, Oxford; Ford's Lecturer, University of Oxford, England. **Article:** Callus, Daniel Angelo Philip.

*SMET, JOACHIM FREDERICK, OCarm, B.L.S., Ph.D., Member, Institute for Carmelite Studies, Rome, Italy; Editor, *Carmelus: Commentarii ab Instituto Carmelitano Editi;* Assistant General for the English-speaking provinces of the Carmelite Order. **Article:** Doswald, Hilary Joseph.

SMET, JOACHIM FREDERICK, OCarm, H.E.D., member, Institutum Carmelitanum, Rome, Italy. **Articles:** Carmelites; Carmelite Sisters.

*SMITH, ALAN, OP, A.B., S.T.Lr., S.T.L., Pro L.SS., Professor of Sacred Scripture, Pontifical Faculty of Theology of the Immaculate Conception, Dominican House of Studies, Washington, D.C. **Articles:** Foreiro, Francisco; Hugh of Saint-Cher; Pagnini, Santes; Sixtus of Siena.

*SMITH, BERNARD SIDNEY, B.A., M.A., Ph.D., Assistant Professor of History, University of Delaware, Newark, Del. **Articles:** Michael de Northburgh; Robert of Winchelsea; Rupert of Deutz.

*SMITH, CLAVER WILLIAM, OCarm, B.A., S.T.L., Professor of Dogmatic Theology, International College of St. Albert, Rome, Italy; Professor of Liturgy, Pontifical Institute, Regina Mundi, Rome; member, Liturgical Commission, Order of Carmelites. **Article:** All Saints, Solemnity of.

*SMITH, EDWARD HAROLD, S.T.L., M.A., Pastor of Church of Our Saviour, Bronx, N.Y. **Articles:** Burtsell, Richard Lalor; McGlynn, Edward.

*SMITH, ELLEN HART, Owensboro, Ky. **Article:** Carroll, Charles.

*SMITH, ELWYN ALLEN, Ph.D., B.D., Th.M., Minister of the United Presby-

terian Church in the U.S.A., Pittsburgh Theological Seminary, Pittsburgh, Pa. **Articles:** Makemie, Francis; Presbyterian Churches in the United States; Speer, Robert Elliott.

*SMITH, F. JOSEPH, Ph.D., Associate Professor of Philosophy and Musicology, Department of Music, Duquesne University, Pittsburgh, Pa. **Articles:** Artusi, Giovanni Maria; Rore, Cipriano de.

*SMITH, G. E. KIDDER, M.F.A., architect, author, lecturer, New York, N.Y. **Articles:** Coventry Cathedral; Perret, Auguste; Raincy, Notre-Dame du.

*SMITH, HOWARD SYLVESTER, Ph.B.Jour., Associate Editor, *Industrial Arts and Vocational Education,* Milwaukee, Wis. **Article:** Bruce.

*SMITH, JEREMIAH JACOB, OFMConv, Ph.D., Professor of History and Chairman of the Department, Bellarmine College, Louisville, Ky. **Articles:** Bonal, Raymond; Clement IV, Pope; Eubel, Konrad; John de Ridevall; Juliana of Liège, Bl.; Lorraine, Cardinals of; Papini Tartagni, Niccolò; Paulinus of Venice; Pavillon, Nicolas; Roger of Todi, Bl.; Rubeis, Leonardo de (Rossi); Sbaraglia, Giovanni Giacinto (Sbaralea); Thomas of Celano; Vitalis, St.

*SMITH, MARINER THEODORE, OP, A.B., S.T.Lr., J.C.B., J.C.D., S.T.M., Professor of Canon Law, Pontifical Faculty of Theology of the Immaculate Conception, Dominican House of Studies, Washington, D.C. **Article:** Raccolta.

*SMITH, SISTER MARY MICHELLA, SND, M.S., Provincial Secretary and Archivist of the Sisters of Notre Dame, Province of Christ the King, Cleveland, Ohio. **Article:** Notre Dame, Sisters of (SND).

*SMITH, SISTER PETER DAMIAN, GNSH, M.A., Instructor in History, D'Youville College, Buffalo, N.Y. **Articles:** Casanate, Girolamo; Cornaro, Elena Lucrezia Piscopia; Rossi, John Baptist, St.

SMITH, R. S. **Article:** Franciscan Sisters—Sisters of St. Francis of the Mission of the Immaculate Virgin (OSF).

*SMITH, RAYMOND CARROLL, OP, S.T.Lr., Ph.D., Master of Students, St. Stephen's Priory, Dover, Mass. **Articles:** Docility; God, Proofs for the Existence of; Scholastic Terms and Axioms.

*SMITH, ROBERT S., FSC, St. Mary's College, St. Mary's, Calif. **Article:** Abelard, Peter.

SMITH, ROSEMARY, SC, J.C.D., Adjunct Professor of Canon Law, University of St. Thomas, St. Mary's Seminary, Houston, Tex. **Articles:** Chapters, Religious; Novitiate, Canon Law of.

*SMITH, VINCENT E., Ph.D., Professor of Philosophy, St. John's University, Jamaica, N.Y. **Articles:** Matter and Form; Philosophy of Nature; Philosophy and Science.

*SMITH, WILLIAM CASPER, A.B., Vice President in charge of Liturgical Publications, Benziger Brothers, New York, N.Y. **Article:** Benziger.

*SMITS, BRENDAN KENNETH, OFMCap, B.A., Milwaukee, Wis. **Article:** Bernard of Offida, Bl.

SMOLKO, JOHN F., S.T.L., M.A., Lecturer, The Catholic University of America; Washington D.C. **Article:** Artificial Intelligence.

*SMYTH, EDMOND JOHN, SJ, M.A., S.T.L., Associate Professor of History and Dean of the College of Liberal Arts and Science, University of San Francisco, San Francisco, Calif. **Articles:** Benedict XI, Pope, Bl.; Boniface IX, Pope; Clericis Laicos; Geoffrey of York; Geoffrey Hardeby; Unam Sanctam.

*SNOW, ROBERT J., Ph.D., Department of Music, University of Pittsburgh, Pittsburgh, Pa. **Articles:** Regina Caeli Laetare; Requiem Mass; Salve Regina.

SOERGEL, PHILIP, Ph.D., Associate Professor of History, Department of History, Arizona State University, Tempe, Arizona. **Articles:** Anabaptists; Augsburg Confession; Augsburg, Peace of; Auto-da-fé; Avignon Papacy; Calvinism; Counter Reformation; Knox, John; Mary Stuart, Queen of Scots; Melanchthon, Philipp; Reformation, Protestant (on the Continent); Westminster Confession; Westphalia, Peace of.

*SOFRANOV, IVAN SOFRONIUS, CP, Eccl.Sc.Or.D., Scientific Work and Apostolate among the Bulgarians in Rome, Italy; Consultor, Papal Oriental Commission, Vatican Council II. **Article:** Bulgarian Catholic Church (Eastern Catholic).

*SOLA-SOLE, JOSEP MARIA, Diplomé de l'École Pratique des Hautes Études (Paris), Doctor en Filosofía y Letras, Associate Professor of Spanish and Oriental Languages, The Catholic University of America, Washington, D.C.

Articles: Aramaic Language, 2. Biblical; Burkitt, Francis Crawford; Dhū-Nuwā Masruk; Elias bar Shināyā; Gabriel Sionita; Īshōʿdād of Merv; Timotheus I, Nestorian Patriach.

*SOLARI, JAMES KENNETH, OSB, S.T.L., S.S.L., Professor of Theology and Chairman of Department, Belmont Abbey College, and Rector of the Theological House of Study, Belmont, N.C. **Articles:** Amos, Book of; Hosea, Book of.

*SOLOVIEV, ALEXANDER V., Iur. Dr., Professor of Slavic Languages and Literatures, University of Geneva, Switzerland. **Article:** Bogomils.

*SOLZBACHER, JOSEPH KARL, Rt. Rev., Dr. Theol., Professor, Pädagogische Hochschule, Neuss-Rhein, Germany. **Articles:** Fey, Clara; Poor Child Jesus, Sisters of the.

*SOMERVILLE, JAMES MIDDLETON, SJ, M.A. (Experim. Psych.), S.T.L., Ph.D., Chairman, Department of Philosophy, Fordham University, New York, N.Y. **Articles:** Boutrox, Étienne Émile Marie; Le Roy, Édouard; Life Philosophies; Symbol.

SOMERVILLE, ROBERT EUGENE, Ph.D., Tremaine Professor of Religion, Department of Religion, Columbia University, New York City. **Article:** Urban II, Pope, Bl.

*SOMMERFELDT, JOHN ROBERT, Ph.D., Associate Professor of History and Chairman of the Medieval Studies Program, Western Michigan University, Kalamazoo, Mich. **Articles:** Glastonbury, Abbey of; Henry of Heisterbach, Bl.; Henry of Clairvaux, Bl.; Humbeline, Bl.; Idesbald, Bl.; John of Valence, St.; Norbert of Xanten, St.

SONSKI, PETER, Washington, D.C. **Article:** National Shrine of the Immaculate Conception.

*SORENSON, HOWARD JOSEPH, OMI, B.Ph., S.T.L., S.S.L., Professor, Holy Rosary Scholasticate, Ottawa; and "Sedes Sapientiae" Centre, Ottawa University, Ottawa, Canada. **Articles:** Creation, 1. In the Bible; Numerology (in the Bible).

*SOTTOCORNOLA, FRANCO GIUSEPPE, SX, Ph.D., Vice Rector and Professor of Philosophy, Xaverian Missionary Fathers Major Seminary, Parma, Italy. **Articles:** Boscardin, Maria Bertilla, St.; Conforti, Guido Maria, Bl.; Cottolengo, Giuseppe Benedetto, St.;

Frassinetti, Paola Angela Maria, St.; Galgani, Gemma, St.; Gallo, Maria Francesca of the Five Wounds, St.; Guerra, Elena, Bl.; Lanteri, Pio Brunone; Lapini, Anna Maria; Louis of Casoria, Ven.; Sacramentine Sisters of Bergamo; San Marino, The Catholic Church in; Sulprizio, Nunzio, Bl.; Vannini, Giuseppina, Bl.; Xaverian Missionary Fathers.

*SOUTHERN, RICHARD WILLIAM, M.A. (Oxon.), Hon. D.Litt., Chichele Professor of Modern History and Fellow of All Souls College, University of Oxford, England. **Article:** Eadmer of Canterbury.

*SOWERS, ROBERT WATSON, M.A., stained-glass artist, Brooklyn, N.Y. **Article:** Stained Glass.

*SPAHR, COLUMBAN, OCist, Ph.D., J.C.D., Professor of History and Geography, Abbey Nullius Wettingen-Mehrerau, Bregenz, Austria. **Articles:** Christian of Prussia; Conrad of Bavaria, Bl.; Eberhard of Rohrdorf, Bl.; Gezzelinus, Bl.; Henry of Vitskól, Bl.; Hildegunde of Schönau; Ida, Bl.; Mehrerau, Abbey of; Waldsassen, Abbey of; Wettingen-Mehrerau, Abbey of; Wilhering, Abbey of.

*SPAHR, HERBERT GEBHARD, OSB, Dr.Phil., Head of the Progymnasium of the Abbey of Beuron, and Librarian, of the Abbey of Weingarten, Württemberg, Germany. **Articles:** Adalgar of Bremen, St.; Alpirsbach, Abbey of; Altdorf, Abbey of; Ansuerus, St.; Brauweiler, Abbey of; Corvey, Abbey of; Ellwangen, Abbey of; Ernest of Zwiefalten, St.; Gebizo, St.; Günther of Niederaltaich, Bl.; Henry of Zwiefalten, Bl.; Judith of Neideraltaich, Bl.; Kempten, Abbey of; Lambach, Abbey of; Lantbert of Freising, St.; Ludolf of Corvey, St.; Petershausen, Abbey of; Sankt Ulrich von Augsburg, Abbey of; Unni of Hamburg, St.; Weingarten, Abbey of; Windesheim, Monastery of; Zwiefalten, Abbey of.

*SPAIN, EUGENE T., Ph.D., Assistant Professor of Physics, Immaculate Heart College, Hollywood, Calif. **Articles:** Benoît, Michel; Kircher, Athanasius.

*SPALDING, DAVID, CFX, M.A., Instructor in History, Xaverian College, Silver Spring, Md. **Articles:** Ryken, Frances Xavier, Brother; Xaverian Brothers.

*SPANNEUT, MICHEL, S.T.D., Docteur ès lettres, Professor of Classical Philology, Faculté Libre des Lettres, Lille, and

Assistant to the Dean, Lille, Nord, France. **Articles:** Clement of Alexandria; Eustathius of Antioch, St.; Seneca, Lucius Annaeus; Stoicism [part 2].

SPELLACY, MARIE E., Ph.D., Dayton, Ohio. **Article:** Walsh, Mary Rosalia.

*SPELTZ, GEORGE HENRY, Most Rev., Ph.D., D.D., LL.D., Auxiliary Bishop of Winona and Pastor, Saint Mary's Church, Winona, Minn. **Article:** Winona, Diocese of.

*ŠPIDLÍK, THOMAS, SJ, S.T.L., Sc.Eccl.Or.D., Professor of Eastern Spirituality, Pontifical Oriental Institute, Rome, Italy. **Articles:** Monasticism, 5. Eastern, b. (Since 1453); Stylites.

*SPIKKER, HONORIUS, OCarm, Hist.Eccl.Lic., Master of Students, International College, Rome, Italy. **Articles:** Aiguani, Michele (Anguani, Angriani); Carmelite Rite; Consobrino, João (Sobrinho); Foscarini, Paolo Antonio.

*SPITZ, LEWIS WILLIAM, B.D., Ph.D., Associate Professor of History, Stanford University, Stanford, Calif.; President, American Society for Reformation Research; member, Editorial Board, *Journal of Modern History.* **Articles:** Amerbach, Veit; Amsdorf, Nikolaus von; Anderson, Lars (Laurentius Andreae); Berthold of Chiemsee (Berthold Purstinger); Brenz, Johann; Eberlin, Johannes; Fugger; Gratius, Ortwin (van Graes); Hutten; Jonas, Justus (Jodocus Koch); Malatesta; Medici; Mirror of Princes (Literature); Myconius, Friedrich.

*SPITZIG, JOSEPH ANTHONY, Rt. Rev., B.A., S.T.B., S.T.D., Professor of Dogmatic Theology, St. Mary's Seminary, Cleveland, Ohio; member, Cursillo Commission. **Article:** Lay Confession.

*SPRINGER, ROBERT HILL, SJ, S.T.D., Assistant Professor of Philosophy, Loyola Seminary, Shrub Oak, N.Y. **Articles:** Temptation; Thoughts, Morality of.

*SRINIVASA IYENGAR, KODAGANALLUR RAMASWAMI, M.A., D.Litt., Professor of English and Head of the Department of English Language and Literature, and President, Faculty of Arts, Andhra University, Waltair, India. **Articles:** Beschi, Constanzo Giuseppe; Gandhi, Mohandas Karamchand; Ghose, Aurobindo; Stephens, Thomas; Tagore, Rabindranath.

STAAB, JEFF, J.C.L., The Catholic University of America, Washington, D.C. **Articles:** Administrator, Apostolic; Funerals (Canon Law); Ius Publicum; Proxy (Canon Law).

*STALLINGS, SISTER MARY JORDAN, OSF, Dottore in Lettere, Ph.D., Acting Chairman, Department of Classics, College of St. Teresa, Winona, Minn. **Articles:** Ter Doest, Abbey of; Thiemo, Bl.; Tozzo, St.; Waningus, St.; Wiborada, St.

STAMOOLIS, JAMES JOHN, B.S.I.E., M. Div., Th.M., Th.D.; North American Director of the Caspari Center for Biblical and Jewish Studies, Cross Plains, Tenn. **Article:** Mission History, II: Orthodox.

STAMSCHROR, ROBERT P., M.A., Retired Representative for Religious Education, United States Catholic Conference and Executive Secretary for National Conference of Diocesan Directors of Religious Education-CCD, Winona, Minn. **Article:** Winona, Diocese of.

STANCIL, WILBURN THOMAS, Ph.D., Associate Professor of Theology, Rockhurst University, Kansas City, Mo. **Articles:** Darby, John Nelson; Dispensational Theology; Scofield, C.I.

*STANDAERT, MAUR, OCSO, Docteur en théologie, Abbaye Notre-Dame de Scourmont, Forges-les-Chimay, Par Bourlers, Belgium. **Articles:** Aulne-sur-Sambre, Abbey of; Guarinus (Guérin) of Sion, St.; John of Montmirail, Bl.; Rainald of Bar, Bl.; Robert of Bruges, Bl.

*STANKIEWICZ, WLADYSLAW JOZEF, Ph.D., Professor of Political Science, University of British Columbia, Vancouver, Canada. **Articles:** Catherine de Medicis; Guise; Huguenots; League, The Holy; St. Bartholomew's Day, Massacre of.

*STANLEY, DAVID M., SJ, Regis College, Willowdale, Ontario, Canada. **Article:** Bea, Augustin.

*STANSELL, HAROLD LEROY, SJ, Ph.D., Chairman, Department of History, Regis College, Denver, Colo. **Article:** Boisgelin de Cuce, Jean de Dieu Raymond de.

*STANTON, PHOEBE BAROODY, Ph.D., Assistant Professor of Art History, Johns Hopkins University, Baltimore, Md. **Article:** Pugin, Augustus Welby.

*STARCKY, JEAN, S.T.L.; S.S.L., Paris, France. **Article:** Arabia, 3. Paganism in North Arabia.

*STARING, ADRIAN, OCarm, Eccl.Hist.D., Professor, Collegio S. Alberto, Rome, Italy; Vice Postulator for Cause of Titus Brandsma. **Articles:** Brandsma, Titus, Bl.; Helgesen, Povl (Paulus Heliae); Simon Stock, St.

*STARK, WERNER, Dr.Rer.Pol., Dr.Jur., M.A. (h.c.), Professor of Sociology, Fordham University, New York, N.Y. **Articles:** Montesquieu, Charles de; Saint-Simon, Claude Henri de Rouvroy.

*STARRS, PAUL M., OP, A.B., S.T.B., S.T.Lr., S.T.L., S.T.Praes., Regent of Studies and Professor of Theology and Ecclesiastical History, St. Albert's College, Oakland, Calif.; Professor of Church History, Graduate Theological Union, Berkeley, Calif. **Articles:** Aimeric of Piacenza; Albert II of Riga; Conformity to the Will of God; Guido Marramaldi, Bl.; Ricoldus de Monte Croce; Vilarrasa, Francis Sadoc; Wichmann of Arnstein, Bl.; William Arnaud, Bl.

STASIAK, KURT, OSB, S.T.D., Associate Professor of Sacramental/Liturgical Theology, Saint Meinrad School of Theology, Saint Meinrad, Ind. **Articles:** Baptism, Sacrament of; Baptism of Infants; Limbo.

*STASIEWSKI, BERNHARD CLEMENS, Dr.Phil., Dr.Theol., Professor of Modern and Contemporary Church History and Church History of Eastern Europe, University of Bonn, Germany; Head, Institut für ostdeutsche Kirchen- und Kulturgeschichte. **Articles:** Hlond, Augustyn; Ledóchowski, Mieczysław Halka; Mariavites; Poland, The Catholic Church in.

STAUB, KATHRYN SCHOFIELD, M.A., Director, Diocesan Museum, Manchester, N.H. **Article:** New Hampshire, Catholic Church in.

STAUFFER, S. ANITA, B.A., M.Div. Former Study Secretary for Worship, Lutheran World Federation, Geneva, Switzerland. **Article:** Baptisteries and Baptismal Fonts.

*STECKLER, GERARD GEORGE, SJ, Ph.D., Assistant Professor of History, Seattle University, Seattle, Wash. **Article:** Seghers, Charles John.

*STEELS, PAUL, CSSR, S.T.L., Accademia Alfonsiana, Rome, Italy. **Article:** Funk, Franz Xaver von.

*STEGGINK, OTGER GERHARDUS MARINUS, OCarm, Hist. Eccl.D., S.T.L., Professor of Spiritual Theology, Studium Generale of the Carmelites, Rome, Italy; Director, Titus Brandsma Institute of Spirituality, Nijmegen, Netherlands; Director, Dutch Institute for Carmelite Studies. **Article:** Teresa of Avila, St. [part 1].

*STEICHEN, ALAN J., OSB, Headmaster, St. John's Preparatory School, Collegeville, Minn. **Article:** Homiletics, Teaching of.

*STEINBICKER, CARL RICHARD, A.B., S.T.D., Cincinnati, Ohio. **Article:** Elder, William Henry.

*STEINDL-RAST, DAVID F. K., OSB, Monastery of Mt. Saviour, Pine City, N.Y. **Article:** Counsels, Evangelical.

*STEINER, LUKE JOSEPH, OSB, B.A., S.T.L., S.S.L., Professor of Scripture, St. John's Abbey and Seminary, Collegeville, Minn.; Graduate Program of Sacred Theology, St. John's Abbey. **Article:** Primeval Age in the Bible.

*STEINER, RUTH, Ph.D., Lecturer in Music, The Catholic University of America, Washington, D.C. **Articles:** Alma Redemptoris Mater; Ave Regina Caelorum; Ave Maria (Antiphon); Beethoven, Ludwig van; Galuppi, Baldassare; Leo, Leonardo; Marian Antiphons.

*STEINER, WILFRED JOSEPH, Ph.D., Professor of History and Chairman of the Department, University of Dayton, Dayton, Ohio. **Articles:** Assemblies of French Clergy; Briconnet; Clement VII, Pope; Giberti, Gian Matteo; L'Hôpital, Michel de (L'Hospital); Valdés, Fernando de.

STEINHAUSER, KENNETH B., Dr. Theol., Associate Professor of Theology, Saint Louis University, St. Louis, Mo. **Articles:** Gregory of Nazianzus, St.; Gregory of Nyssa, St.

*STEINHAUSER, MICHAEL G., S.T.L., D.Th., Director for Advanced Degree Studies Programs, Toronto School of Theology, Toronto Ontario. **Article:** Synoptic Gospels.

*STEINMUELLER, JOHN EMIL, Rt. Rev., S.T.D., S.S.L., Pastor, St. Barbara's Church, Brooklyn, N.Y.; Diocesan Dean (V.F.); *Peritus,* Vatican Council II. **Articles:** Asylum, Cities of; Chief Priests; Oracle (in the Bible); Ruffini, Ernesto; Temples (in the Bible); Tent of Meeting; Ur; Urim and Thummim.

*STENGER, ROBERT PIUS, OP, S.T.L., S.T.Lr., S.T.D., Assistant Professor of Theology and Philosophy, and Head of Department, Dominican College, Racine, Wis. **Articles:** Billuart, Charles René Gonet, Jean Baptiste; Raymond of Peñafort, St.

*STÉPHAN, PETER JOHN, OSB, Monk of Buckfast Abbey, Buckfastleigh, Devonshire, England; writer and lecturer, F.R.Hist.S., President of the Devonshire Association. **Articles:** Buckfast, Abbey of; Ealing Abbey; Farnborough Priory; Louismet, Savinien; Prinknash Abbey; Vonier, Anscar.

STEPHENS, ROBERT J., Senior Editor, Catholic Health Association of the United States. **Article:** Catholic Health Association.

*STEPHENSON, ANTHONY ALOYSIUS, SJ, B.A., M.A., S.T.L., Professor, Department of Religion, University College, McMaster University, Hamilton, Ontario, Canada. **Articles:** Cyril of Jerusalem, St.; John of Jerusalem; Macarius of Jerusalem, St.; Macarius the Egyptian, St.; Macedonius, St.; Marcellus Akimetes, St.; Marcion.

STEPHENSON, PAUL, M.St., Ph.D., John W. and Jeanne M. Rowe Professor of Byzantine History, Department of History, University of Wisconsin, Madison, Wisconsin. **Articles:** Romanus I Lecapenus, Byzantine Emperor; Sergius II, Patriarch of Constantinople.

*STERN, SAMUEL MIKLOS, M.A., D.Phil., Fellow of All Souls College, Oxford, England. **Article:** Isaac Israeli.

*STEVENS, DENIS WILLIAM, B.A., M.A. (Oxon.), Department of Music, Columbia University, New York, N.Y. **Articles:** Byrd, William; Dunstable, John; Franco of Cologne; Gesualdo, Carlo; Machaut, Guillaume de; Monteverdi, Claudio; Motet; Obrecht, Jakob; Okeghem, Jan van; Power, Lionel; Schütz, Heinrich; Sweelinck, Jan Pieters; Tenebrae; Vitry, Philippe de; Vivaldi, Antonio.

*STEVENS, HALSEY, M.Mus.,Professor of Music and Chairman of the Department of Composition, School of Music, University of Southern California, Los Angeles, Calif. **Articles:** Bartók, Béla; Janáček, Leoš.

*STEVENS, JOHN EDGAR, Ph.D., Fellow, Tutor, and Precentor of Magdalene College, Cambridge, and University Lecturer in English, University of Cambridge, England. **Article:** Carol.

*STEVENSON, JAMES, B.A., M.A. (Cantab.), A.M., Fellow of Downing College and University Lecturer in Divinity, Cambridge, England. **Articles:** Eusebius of Caesarea; Lactantius.

STEVENSON, MARGARET, Ph.D. cand., Harvard University, Cambridge, Mass. **Articles:** Genealogy of Jesus; Infancy Narratives; Magi; Vulgate.

*STEVENSON, ROBERT MURRELL, M.Mus., B.Litt., Ph.D., Professor of Music, University of California at Los Angeles, Calif. **Articles:** Falla, Manuel de; Gomes, Antonio Carlos; Lobo, Duarte; Morales, Cristóbal de; Ponce, Manuel María; Spirituals; Tomás de Santa María; Victoria, Tomás Luis de.

*STEWART, RICHARD LOUIS, S.T.L., Professor of Fundamental and Dogmatic Theology, St. John's Seminary, Wonersh, Surrey, England. **Articles:** Acts, Notional; Life, Concept of (in Theology).

*STEWART, ZEPH, A.B., A.M. (h.c.), Professor of Greek and Latin and Master of Lowell House, Harvard University, Cambridge, Mass. **Article:** Nock, Arthur Darby.

*STIASSNY, JOSEPH MARIE, N.D.S., S.T.L, Diplôme, École Pratique des Hautes Études, Paris, France; Superior of the Convent and Director of the Ratisbonne Centre of Jewish Studies, Jerusalem, Israel. **Articles:** Cantor in Jewish Liturgy; Geniza; Haskalah; Israel (State of), The Catholic Church in; Johanan ben Zakkai; Judah ha-Nasi; Shabbataiïsm.

*STICKLER, ALFONS MARIA, S.D.B., J.U.D., Professor of Canon Law and History of Canon Law, Faculty of Canon Law, Pontifical Athenaeum Salesianum, Turin and Rome, Italy; Director of *Salesianum;* Member of the Board of Directors, Institute of Research and Study in Medieval Canon Law, Yale University; Consultor of the Sacred Congregation of Seminaries and Universities; *Peritus,* Vatican Council II. **Articles:** Bartholomew of Brescia; Canonical Collections before Gratian; Huguccio (Hugh of Pisa); Joannes Teutonicus (Zemecke); Petrus Collivaccinus (Beneventanus).

*STOCK, MICHAEL EDWARD, OP, B.S., S.T.L., S.T.Lr., Ph.D., Professor of Psychology and President, St. Stephen's College, Dover, Mass. **Articles:** Appetite; Disposition; Habit; Psychology (Classical); Temperament.

*STOEBER, MICHAEL, Ph.D., Assistant Professor of Religion and Religious Education, The Catholic University of America, Washington, D.C. **Article:** World's Parliament of Religions.

STOEBER, MICHAEL, Ph.D., Associate Professor of Spiritual Theology, Regis College, Toronto School of Theology, University of Toronto, Toronto, Canada. **Articles:** Smart, Roderick Ninian; Smith, Wilfrid Cantwell.

*STOKELY, PAUL SCOTT, Ph.D., Professor of Biology and Head of the Department, and Chairman of the Science Division, College of Steubenville, Steubenville, Ohio. **Article:** Biology, I (History of).

*STOKES, WALTER ELLIOTT, SJ, S.T.L., Ph.D., Assistant Professor of Philosophy, Loyola Seminary and Graduate School, Fordham University, New York, N.Y. **Article:** Whitehead, Alfred North.

*STOODY, RALPH WAINMAN, S.T.D., D.D. (h.c.), Litt.D., retired Methodist Pastor, Jackson Heights, New York, N.Y. **Articles:** Lewis, Edwin; Methodist Churches, II: North America.

*STOREY, ROBIN LINDSAY, B.A., M.A., Ph.D., Senior Lecturer in Medieval History, University of Nottingham, England. **Articles:** Chillenden, Thomas; Clifford, Richard; Goldwell, James; Lacy, Edmund; Langdon, John; Morgan, Philip; Polton, Thomas.

*STORNI, HUGO, SJ, Ph.L., S.T.L., member of the Jesuit Historical Institute, responsible for the division, "Paraguay"; Buenos Aires, Argentina. **Articles:** Cardiel, José; Cataldino, José; Dobrizhoffer, Martin; Falker, Tomás; González, Roque, St.; Lozano, Pedro; Paraguay, Jesuit Martyrs of, SS.; Reductions of Paraguay; Ruíz de Montoya, Antonio; Techo, Nicolás del; Torres Bollo, Diego de.

*STRANGE, MARCIAN, OSB, M.A., S.S.L., Professor of Sacred Scripture, St. Meinrad Seminary, St. Meinrad Abbey, St. Meinrad, Ind. **Articles:** Calmet, Augustin (Antoine); Haneberg, Daniel Bonifatius; Historical Books of the Old Testament; Joshua, Son of Nun; Joshua, Book of.

*STRATMAN, SISTER MARY AGATHA, IHM, Ph.D., Laboratory Technologist, St. Mary Desert Valley Hospital, Apple Valley, Calif. **Article:** Linacre, Thomas.

*STRAUSS, FELIX F., Ph.D., Associate Professor of History, Polytechnic Institute of Brooklyn, Brooklyn, N.Y. **Articles:** Contarini, Gasparo; Cortese, Gregorio; Ferreri, Zaccaria.

*STRAYER, JOSEPH REESE, Ph.D., L.L.D., Dayton-Stockton Professor of History, Princeton University, Princeton, N.J. **Articles:** Henry II, King of England; Philip IV, King of France.

*STRITCH, ALFRED G., M.A., Chairman of the Department of History, Head of the Division of Social Sciences, and Chaplain of Our Lady of Cincinnati College, Cincinnati, Ohio. **Article:** Cincinnati, Archdiocese of.

*STRITTMATTER, ANSELM, OSB, M.A., Prior, St. Anselm's Abbey, Washington, D.C. **Article:** Exsultet Iam Angelica Turba.

*STRUGNELL, JOHN, B.A., M.A. (Oxon.), Assistant Professor of Old Testament, Divinity School, Duke University, Durham, N.C. **Articles:** Josephus, Flavius; Josippon.

STRYNKOWSKI, MSGR. JOHN J., S.T.D., Executive Director, Secretariat for Doctrine and Pastoral Practices, United States Conference of Catholic Bishops, Washington, D.C. **Articles:** Mandatum, Academic; Reasoning, Theological.

STUDZINSKI, RAYMOND, OSB, Ph.D., Associate Professor of Religion and Religious Education, The Catholic University of America, Washington, D.C. **Articles:** Discernment, Spiritual; Guilt; Guilt, Theology of; Shame.

*STUHLMUELLER, CARROLL, CP, S.T.L., S.S.L., Professor of Scriptural Exegesis and Hebrew, Passionist Fathers Seminary, Louisville, Ky. **Articles:** Annunciation; Apocalyptic; Apocrypha, 1. Apocrypha of the Old Testament; Haggai, Book of; Malachi, Book of; Zechariah, Book of.

*STUIBER, ALFRED JOHANN, Dr.Theol., Professor, Catholic Theological Faculty, University of Bonn, Germany. **Article:** Optatus of Milevis, St.

*STULZER, AURÉLIO, OFM, Assistant Director of the Publishing House, Editôro Vozes Ltda., Petrópolis, Brazil; Editor, *Vozes* and *Que Hei de Ler.* **Articles:** Figueiredo, Jackson de; Sinzig, Pedro.

*SUBAR, ELI, M.A., Cataloger of Hebrew and Yiddish Literature, Library of Congress, Washington, D.C. **Articles:** Berakhot; Eldad ha-Dani; Kaddish; Mahzor; Pirke Avoth; Responsa, Jewish; Tarphon, Rabbi.

*SUELZER, SISTER ALEXA, SP, Ph.D., Professor of Religion, St. Mary-of-the-Woods College, St. Mary-of-the-Woods, Ind. **Articles:** Judgment, Divine (in the Bible); Stones, Sacred (in the Bible).

*SUELZER, SISTER MARY JOSEPHINE, SP, Ph.D., Academic Dean, St. Mary-of-the-Woods College, St. Mary-of-the-Woods, Ind. **Article:** Pomerius.

*SULLIVAN, C. STEPHEN, FSC, M.A. (Classics), M.A. (Philosophy), S.T.D., Academic Vice President, Manhattan College, New York, N.Y. **Article:** Merit.

*SULLIVAN, EUGENE H., S.T.L., J.C.D., Spiritual Director, Seminary of St. Charles Borromeo, Overbrook, Philadelphia, Pa. **Article:** Sponsors.

SULLIVAN, FRANCIS A., S.J., S.T.D., Professor emeritus, Faculty of Theology, Gregorian University, Rome; Adjunct professor, Department of Theology, Boston College, Chestnut Hill, Mass. **Articles:** Apostolic Succession; Apostolic See; Binding and Loosing; Bishop (in the Church); Diodore of Tarsus; Gates of Hell; Keys, Power of; Mopsuestia; Pope; Primacy of the Pope; Theodore of Mopsuestia.

*SULLIVAN, JAMES, Vice President of Catholics United for the Faith and Editor of *Lay Witness*. **Article:** Stebbins, H. Lyman.

*SULLIVAN, JOHN J., O.C.D., S.T.D., Publisher, Institute of Carmelite Studies, Washington, D.C. **Article:** Stein, Edith (Teresa Benedicta of the Cross), St.

SULLIVAN, JOHN J., OCD, S.T.D., Chairman, Institute of Carmelite Studies, Washington, D.C.; Publisher, ICS Publications. **Articles:** Carmelite Rite; Sacramentaries, II: Contemporary.

*SULLIVAN, JOSEPH DANIEL, B.S., B.L.S., Librarian, St. Michael's College, Winooski, Vt. **Article:** Goesbriand, Louis de.

*SULLIVAN, MOTHER KATHRYN, RSCJ, Ph.D., Litt.D., Professor of Religion, Manhattanville College of the Sacred Heart, Purchase, N.Y. **Articles:** Burnt Offering; Son of David.

SULLIVAN, LESTER, CA, M.A., University Archivist and Head of Special Collections, Xavier University of Louisiana, New Orleans; Adjunct Professor, Department of History, The University of New Orleans, New Orleans, La. **Article:** Xavier University of Louisiana.

SULLIVAN, RICHARD, Ph.D., Professor Emeritus of History, Dean Emeritus of the College of Arts and Letters, Michigan State University, East Lansing, Michigan. **Articles:** Adrian I, Pope; Carolingian Reform; Carolingians; Charlemagne; Clovis I, King of the Franks; Conon, Pope; Einhard; Formosus, Pope; Franks; Gregory III, Pope, St.; Gregory II, Pope, St.; John IX, Pope; Leo III, Pope, St.; Leo IV, Pope, St.; Marinus II, Pope; Martin I, Pope, St.; Merovingians; Nicholas I, Pope, St.; Paschal I, Pope, St.; Paul I, Pope, St.; Stephen II (III), Pope; Stephen IV (V), Pope; Stephen III (IV), Pope; Usuard.

SUNDARARAJAN, K. R., Ph.D., Professor, Department of Theology, St. Bonaventure University, St. Bonaventure, N.Y. **Articles:** Hinduism; Indian Philosophy.

SUNQUIST, SCOTT W., Ph.D., Associate Professor of Mission and Evangelism, Pittsburgh Theological Seminary, Pittsburgh, Pa. **Articles:** Mission History, III: Protestant.

*SURLIS, PAUL, S.T.D., Associate Professor, Moral Theology and Social Ethics, St. John's University, New York. **Article:** Option for the Poor.

SUTERA, JUDITH, OSB, M.A., Mount St. Scholastica, Atchison, Kans.; Co-Editor, Magistra: Journal of Women's Spirituality; Editor, American Monastic Newsletter. **Articles:** Benedictine Nuns and Sisters; More, Gertrude.

*SVOBODA, CYRIL PAUL, SSC, Ph.D., Vice Rector and Professor, St. Columban's College and Seminary, Oconomowoc, Wis. **Articles:** Brentano, Franz; Poltergeist.

*SWAN, DARLIS J., Ph.D., Associate Director, Office for Ecumenical Affairs, The Evangelical Lutheran Church in America, Chicago. **Article:** Evangelical Lutheran Church in America.

*SWANER, JAMES JOSEPH, M.A., Teacher of Latin and Social Studies, Sisters' Chaplain and Guidance Director, Marquette High School, and Assistant Pastor, St. Columba Church, Ottawa, Ill. **Article:** Schlarman, Joseph Henry.

*SWASTEK, JOSEPH VINCENT, M.A., Head of History Department, SS. Cyril and Methodius Seminary, Orchard Lake, Mich. **Articles:** Barzyński, Vincent; Dabrowski, Joseph.

*SWEENEY, CHARLES LEO, SJ, Ph.D., Associate Professor, Department of Phi-

losophy, St. Louis University, St. Louis, Mo. **Articles:** Infinity; Liber de Causis; Proclus.

*SWEENEY, DAVID F., OFM, Professor of History, St. Francis College, Rye Beach, N.H. **Articles:** Caldwell, Mary Gwendoline; Maguire, Charles Bonaventure.

*SWEENEY, FRANCIS W., SJ, M.A., Assistant Professor of English, Boston College, Chestnut Hill, Mass.; author. **Article:** Realino, Bernardine, St.

SWEET, WILLIAM, D.E.A., Ph.D., S.T.B., D.Ph., Editor, *Maritain Studies*; Professor of Philosophy, St. Francis Xavier University, Antigonish, Nova Scotia, Canada. **Article:** Maritain, Jacques.

*SWIDLER, LEONARD JOSEPH, Ph.D., S.T.L., Associate Professor of History and Theology, Duquesne University, Pittsburgh, Pa.; Coeditor, *Journal of Ecumenical Studies*. **Articles:** Bauer, Bruno; Lohe, Johann Konrad Wilhelm; Seeberg, Reinhold.

*SWIFT, ARTHUR, MSSST, J.C.D., Professor of Canon Law and Pastoral Theology, Holy Trinity Mission Seminary, Winchester, Va. **Articles:** Legitimacy of Children (Canon Law); Popes, Election of.

*SWINT, JOHN JOSEPH, B.A., S.T.B., Bishop of Wheeling, W.Va., and Archbishop ad personam (deceased Nov. 22, 1962). **Article:** McDonnell, Thomas John.

*SYLVESTER, RICHARD STANDISH, Ph.D., Associate Professor of English, Yale University, New Haven, Conn.; Executive Editor, Yale Edition of the Works of St. Thomas More. **Article:** More, Sir Thomas, St. [part 1].

*SYNAN, EDWARD ALOYSIUS, S.T.L., L.M.S., Ph.D., Professor of History of Mediaeval Philosophy, Institute, St. Michael's College, and School of Graduate Studies, University of Toronto, Ontario, Canada; Associate Editor, *Bridge*. **Articles:** Adelard of Bath; Honorius of Autun; Knowledge, Theories of [part 2]; Maimonides (Moses ben Maimon); Montefiore, Claude Joseph Goldsmid; Nahmanides (Moses ben Nahman); Richard of Campsall; Universals [part 1]; Walter of Mortagne; Walter Burley.

*SYNON, MARY, B.A., LL.D., author and editor (deceased Oct. 9, 1965). **Article:** Power, Emily, Mother.

*SZCZESNIAK, BOLESLAW BOYM, Dip.M.A., Ph.D., Professor of History, University of Notre Dame, Notre Dame, Ind. **Articles:** John of Nepomuc, St.; Matthew of Cracow; Sigismund, Holy Roman Emperor; Sigismund, St.; Stanislaus of Cracow, St.

*SZÖVÉRFFY, JOSEPH, Ph.D., Professor of Modern Languages, Boston College, Chestnut Hill, Mass. **Articles:** Ave Verum Corpus; Decora Lux Aeternitatis; Dies Irae; Egregie Doctor Paule; Gentis Polonae Gloria; Gloria, Laus, et Honor; Hymnology; Jesu, Dulcis Memoria; Pange Lingua Gloriosi; Ut Queant Laxis Resonare Fibris; Verbum Supernum Prodiens.

*TAHENY, THEODORE THOMAS, SJ, M.A., S.T.D., Professor of Theology, University of San Francisco, San Francisco, Calif. **Articles:** Lapide, Cornelius; Menochio, Giovanni Stefano; Ribera, Francesco de.

*TALBOT, CHARLES HOLWELL, F.R.Hist.S., Research Scholar for History of Medicine, Wellcome Historical Medical Museum, London, England. **Articles:** Buckland, Abbey of; Christina of Markyate; Gerard of Clairvaux, Bl.; Meaux (Melsa), Abbey of; Rievaulx, Abbey of; Roger of Elan, Bl.; Stephen Harding, St.; Theobald of Vaux-de-Cernay, St.; Tintern, Abbey of; Waltheof, St.

*TALLEY, THOMAS J., Th.D., Professor of Liturgics, The General Theological Seminary, New York, N.Y. **Articles:** Liturgical Calendars, II: Ecumenical; Liturgical Movement, III: Ecumenical Convergences.

TAN, JONATHAN YUN-KA, LL.B. (Hons), Ph.D., Assistant Professor of Theology, Xavier University, Cincinnati, Ohio; Assistant Editor, *New Catholic Encyclopedia*, second edition. **Articles:** Cambodia, The Catholic Church in; Catholic Theological Society of America; Chinese Religions; Chinese Philosophy; Confucianism and Neo-Confucianism; Confucius (Kongfuzi); Daoism (Taoism); East Asian Pastoral Institute (EAPI); Federation of Asian Bishops' Conferences; Laozi (Lao-Tzu); Liturgy, Articles on; Malaysia, the Catholic Church in; Mencius (Mengzi); Mission, Articles on; Mission and Evangelization, Papal Writings on; Sacraments, Articles on; Vietnam, the Catholic Church in.

*TANCK, DOROTHY ELIZABETH, M.A., University of California at Berkeley, Calif.

Article: Catechisms in Colonial Spanish America.

*TANNER, PAUL FRANCIS, Most Rev., Titular Bishop of Samasba, Algeria; General Secretary, National Catholic Welfare Conference, Washington, D.C. **Articles:** Carroll, Howard Joseph; Carroll, Walter Sharp.

*TAPIA, RALPH JOHN, Rt. Rev., S.T.D., M.A. (History), Assistant Professor of Theology, Fordham University, New York, N.Y., and Notre Dame College, Staten Island, N.Y. **Articles:** Charism [part 2: In the Church]; Habit (in Theology).

*TAPKE, RAY, Frederick Pustet Company, New York, N.Y. **Article:** Pustet.

*TAPPE, WALTER JOHN, Rt. Rev., Vicar-General, Diocese of Santa Rosa; Pastor, St. Rose Church, Santa Rosa, Calif. **Article:** Mitty, John Joseph.

*TAPPERT, THEODORE GERHARDT, M.A., D.D., Litt.D., Lutheran Minister, Professor of Church History, Lutheran Theological Seminary, Philadelphia, Pa. **Articles:** Esbjorn, Lars Paul; Krauth, Charles Porterfield; Lutheran Churches in North America; Muhlenberg, Henry Melchior; Schmucker, Samuel Simon.

*TARAN, JUDE FRANCIS, SA, A.B., Teacher of Latin and Lecturer on Ecumenism, St. John's Seminary, Montour Falls, N.Y. **Article:** Spiritualists.

*TARDIF, HENRI PIERRE, Honorary Canon and Officialis, Diocese of Meaux, France; member, Commission Diocésaine de Liturgie, and Editor, *Ordo; Theological Adviser, Masses Ouvrières*, Paris, France. **Articles:** Chelles, Convent of; Lagny-sur-Marne, Abbey of; Saint-Maur-des-Fosses, Abbey of.

*TAUTU, LOUIS ALOYS, Rt. Rev., S.T.D., Member, Pontifical Commission of Oriental Canon-Law Codification; Rector, Catholic Church of the Rumanian Rite, SS. Salvatore alle Coppelle, Rome, Italy; Consultor, Sacred Congregation for the Oriental Church. **Articles:** Orthodox Church of Romania; Romanian Catholic Church (Eastern Catholic).

*TAVARD, GEORGE HENRY, AA, S.T.D., Professor of Theology and Chairman of the Department, Mount Mercy College, Pittsburgh, Pa. **Article:** D'Alzon, Emmanuel.

TAVARD, GEORGE HENRY, AA, S.T.D, Professor emeritus of Theology, Method-ist Theological School in Ohio. **Articles:** Anglican Orders; Apostolicae Curae; Assumptionists; Indulgences; Justification; Satis cognitum.

*TAVÉS, ALAIN JEAN, Diplôme, École Spéciale d'Architecture, Paris, Architect Assistant, in the Studio of M. Le Corbusier, La Celle, St. Cloud (Seine et Oise), France. **Article:** Ronchamp, Notre-Dame du Haut.

*TAYLOR, JOSEPH CELESTINE, OP, Ph.L., S.T.Lr., Ph.D., retreat master, Pontifical Faculty of Theology of the Immaculate Conception, Dominican House of Studies, Washington, D.C. **Articles:** Essence and Existence; Potency and Act.

TAYLOR, MICHAEL ALLYN, STD, Executive Director, National Committee for a Human Life Amendment, Washington, D.C. **Article:** Abortion.

*TAYLOR, OVERTON HUME, Ph.D., Professor of Economics, Vanderbilt University, Nashville, Tenn. **Article:** Smith, Adam.

TEGEDER, REV. VINCENT G., OSB, Ph.D., Professor Emeritus, Department of History, Saint John's University, Collegeville, Minn. **Article:** St. John's Abbey and University.

*TEGELS, AELRED HILARY, OSB, B.A., Licentiate in Historical Sciences, Certificate, Paris Institute of Liturgy, Professor of Liturgy, St. John's University, Collegeville, Minn. **Articles:** Chaise-Dieu, Abbey of; Prudentius of Troyes; Saint-Jean-d' Angely, Abbey of.

*TELLECHEA IDÍGORAS, JOSE IGNACIO, S.T.D., Eccl. Hist.L., Professor of Dogmatic Theology and Ecclesiastical History, Seminario de San Sebastián, and Professor of Ecclesiastical History, Seminario Hispano-Americano, Madrid, Spain. **Articles:** Carranza, Bartolome; Maldonatus, Johannes.

*TENNELLY, JOHN BENJAMIN, SS, M.A., S.T.D., Director, Bureau of Catholic Indian Missions, and Secretary, Commission of Catholic Missions for Colored People and Indians, Washington, D.C. **Article:** Ketcham, William Henry.

TENTLER, THOMAS N., Ph.D., Professor Emeritus of History, University of Michigan, Ann Arbor, Michigan; Adjunct Professor of History, Catholic University of America, Washington, D.C. **Article:** Ars Moriendi.

*TERRY, THOMAS DUTTON, SJ, S.T.L., Ph.D., Dean of the College of Arts and Sciences, University of Santa Clara, Santa Clara, Calif. **Article:** Wine, Liturgical Use Of.

TESKE, ROLAND J., SJ, Ph.D., Professor of Philosophy, Marquette University, Milwaukee, Wis. **Article:** Augustine, St.

*TESSAROLO, GIULIVO, PSSC, S.T.D., Superior General, Missionary Fathers of St. Charles, Rome, Italy. **Article:** Scalabrinians.

*TESTORE, CELESTINO, SJ, S.T.D., Ph.D., Member of the Staff, *Civiltà Cattolica,* and Editor in Chief, *Enciclopedia Cattolica,* Rome, Italy. **Articles:** Nilles, Nikolaus; Perrone, Giovanni; Spedalieri, Nicola.

*TETREAU, RICHARD D., Ph.D., Director of Library, St. Peter's College, Jersey City, N.J. **Article:** Focolare Movement.

*THAMAN, SISTER MARY PATRICE, CPPS, Ph.D., Associate Professor of History, Marillac College, Normandy, Mo. **Article:** Precious Blood Sisters—Sisters of the Most Precious Blood.

THAVIS, JOHN M., Rome Bureau Chief, Catholic News Service, Rome, Italy. **Article:** Civilta Cattolica, La.

*THIEME, HANS WILHELM, Dr.Iur., Professor of the History of Law, University of Freiburg, Germany; Coeditor, *Zeitschrift der Savignystiftung für Rechtsgeschichte: Germanistische Abteilung.* **Article:** Leges Romanae Barbarorum.

*THIERRY, SISTER ISABELLE MARIE, LSA, Little Sisters of the Assumption, New York, N.Y. **Article:** Pernet, Etienne Claude.

*THILS, GUSTAVE, S.T.D., S.T.M., Professor of Fundamental Theology, University of Louvain, Belgium. **Articles:** Catholicity; Marks of the Church.

*THOMAS, DAVID M., Ph.D., Professor, School of Theology, St. Meinrad's Seminary, St. Meinrad, Ind. **Article:** Technology, Social Effects of.

*THOMAS, ISAAC, JR., M.F.A., Assistant Professor of Music, The Catholic University of America, Washington, D.C. **Articles:** Akathistos; Byzantine Chant; Octoechos.

*THOMAS, IVO, Very Rev., OP, B.A., M.A., S.T.M., University of Notre Dame, Notre Dame, Ind. **Articles:** Logic, History of; William of Sherwood (Shyreswood).

*THOMAS, JOHN LAWRENCE, SJ, M.A. (English), M.A. (French), S.T.L., Ph.D., Research Associate, Cambridge Center for Social Studies, Cambridge, Mass. **Article:** Natural Family Planning.

*THOMAS, SISTER MARY EVANGELINE, CSJ, Ph.D., Chairman of the Department of History and Director of College Relations, Marymount College, Salina, Kans. **Articles:** Dodge City, Diocese of; Kansas City, Archdiocese of.

THOMAS, YOLANDA, M.A. (Arizona State University). **Articles:** Anastasius III, Pope; Anastasius IV, Pope.

*THOMPSON, JOHN ERIC SIDNEY, LL.D., Litt.H.D., F.B.A., archeologist, Ashdon, Saffron Walden, Essex, England. **Article:** Gage, Thomas.

THOMPSON, NILS F., OFM, Guadalupe Province, Albuquerque, N.M. **Article:** Franciscans, Third Order Secular.

*THOMPSON, WILLIAM G., SJ, S.T.L., Ph.D., S.S.L., Ignatius House, Chicago. **Article:** Matthew, Gospel according to.

*THOMSON, E. JULIANA, Doctorate in Letters and Philosophy, Professor of History and Head of the Department of History and Social Sciences, Mercy College, Detroit, Mich. **Articles:** Acquaviva; Alberoni, Giulio; Barbarigo, Marc' Antonio and Giovanni Francesco; Litta, Alfonso and Lorenzo.

*THORNHILL, JOHN EDWARD, SM, S.T.L., Ph.D., Lecturer in Dogmatic Theology and Sociology, Marist Scholasticate, Toongabbie, New South Wales, Australia. **Articles:** Anthropocentrism; Loci Theologici.

THORNHILL, JOHN EDWARD, SM, S.T.L., Ph.D., Chair, Department of Systematic Theology, Catholic Theological Union, Hunters Hill, N.S.W., Australia. **Article:** Australia, the Catholic Church in.

*THORNTON, SISTER MARY CRESCENTIA, BVM, Ph.D., Professor of Latin American History and Chairman of the Department, Mundelein College, Chicago, Ill. **Articles:** Gonçalves de Oliveira, Vital María; Macedo Costa, Antônio de.

*THURSTON, ETHEL, Ph.D., Associate Professor of Music, St. John's University, New York, N.Y. **Articles:** Léonin; Liturgical Music, History of, 3: Polyphonic Music, Origins to 1450s; Pérotin.

*TIBESAR, ANTONINE SEVERIN, OFM, Ph.D., Professor of History and Staff Editor for Latin American Church History, *New Catholic Encyclopedia,* The Catholic University of America, Washington, D.C.; Director, Franciscan Academy of History, Bethesda, Md. **Articles:** Alternativa; Ecuador, The Catholic Church in; Encomienda-Doctrina System in Spanish America; Herraera, Bartolomé; Mission in Colonial America I (Spanish Missions); Oré; Luis Gerónimo de; San José de la Paz, María Antonia; Vázquez de Espinosa, Antonio; Vigil, Francisco de Paula González; Vizcardó, Juan Pablo.

*TIERNEY, BRIAN, Ph.D., Dr.Theol. (h.c.), Professor of Medieval History, Cornell University, Ithaca, N.Y. **Article:** Boniface VIII, Pope; Capitulations; Conciliarism (History of); Constance, Council of [part 2]; Marsilius of Padua; Praemunire, Statute of; Provisors, Statute of.

*TIERNEY, JOHN J., SJ, St. Thomas Seminary, Louisville, Ky. **Articles:** Bruté de Rémur, Simon William Gabriel; Maryland, Catholic Church in.

*TIFFANY, GEORGE F., St. Joseph's Seminary, Yonkers, N.Y. **Article:** Spellman, Francis.

*TIJAN, PABLO, Ph.D., Madrid, Spain. **Article:** Marulić, Marko.

*TILLARD, JEAN M. R., OP, Faculté Dominicaine de Théologie, Ottawa, Canada. **Articles:** Apostolic Faith; Incorporation Into the Church (Membership).

TILLEY, MAUREEN A., Ph.D., Associate Professor of Religious Studies, University of Dayton, Dayton, Ohio. **Article:** Philomena, St., Legend of.

*TIMMERMAN, SISTER M. FIDES, MHSH, M.A., Instructor in Religious Education and Diocesan Supervisor of CCD Schools of Religion, Diocese of Erie, Pa. **Article:** Mission Helpers of the Sacred Heart.

*TINSLEY, SISTER LUCY, SND, Ph.D., Professor of French and Chairman of the Language Department, College of Notre Dame, Belmont, Calif. **Articles:** Bossuet, Jacques Bénigne; Guyon, Jeanne Marie de la Motte.

TIRONE, P., **Article:** Franciscan Sisters—Franciscan Sisters of St. Joseph of Hamburg, New York (FSSJ).

TISDALE, THOMAS, B.A., J.D., independent writer, Charleston, S.C. **Article:** South Carolina, Catholic Church in.

*TOBAR DONOSO, JULIO, Doctor of Law, LL.D. (h.c.), Judge of the Supreme Court of Justice of Ecuador and Dean of the Faculty of Law, Catholic University of Ecuador, Quito, Ecuador. **Articles:** Cuero y Caicedo, José de; Yerovi, José María.

*TOBIAS, NORMAN, M.A., Adj. Assistant Professor, Rutgers University, New Brunswick, N.J.; and Newark College of Engineering, Newark, N.J. **Article:** Ravenna [Exarchate of].

*TOBIN, RONALD WILLIAM, M.A., Ph.D., Associate Professor of French Literature and Associate Chairman of the Romance Language Department, University of Kansas, Lawrence, Kans. **Article:** Racine, Jean Baptiste.

*TOCKERT, SISTER MARY THEODOSIA, OP, M.S., Teacher, Immaculate Conception High School and Immaculate Conception College; member of the General Council and Secretary-General of the Congregation, Great Bend, Kans. **Article:** Dominican Sisters—Dominican Sisters of Great Bend (Great Bend, Kansas).

*TODD, JOHN MURRAY, B.A., author and publisher; Director, Darton, Longman & Todd Ltd., London, England. **Article:** Marion-Brésillac, Melchior Marie Joseph de.

*TOMKA, PROF. DR. MILKLÓS, Hungarian Religious Research Centre, Budapest. **Article:** Hungary, The Catholic Church in.

*TONDA, AMÉRICO ALFREDO, S.T.D., Professor of Theology, History, and Greek, Seminary of Santa Fe, Argentina; Dean of the Faculty of History, Catholic University of Santa Fe; Canon of the Cathedral of Santa Fe. **Article:** Rivadavia, Bernardino.

*TONGUE, WILLIAM RICHARD F., Ph.D., Professor of Greek and Latin, The Catholic University of America, Washington, D.C. **Articles:** Ammianus Marcellinus; Tacitus.

*TONSOR, STEPHEN JOHN, Ph.D., Associate Professor of History, University of Michigan, Ann Arbor, Mich. **Articles:** Baader, Franz Xaver von; Bunsen, Christian Karl Josias von; Diepenbrock, Melchior von; Döllinger, Johannes Joseph Ignaz von; Friedrich, Johann; Görres, Johann Joseph von; Old Catholics; Phillips, George; Ranke, Leopold von.

*TOPMOELLER, WILLIAM GEORGE, SJ, S.T.D., Professor of Dogmatic Theology and Professor of Ecumenism, St. Mary of the Lake Seminary, Mundelein, Ill.; Summer Session Lecturer in Dogmatic and Moral Theology, Xavier University, Cincinnati, Ohio. **Article:** Salvation.

TORPIS, PATRICIA, M.A., Ph.D. Cand. (University of Houston), Teacher, The Tenney School, Houston, Texas. **Articles:** Aethelred II, King of England; Canute, King of England and Denmark; Harold II, King of England.

TORRES, THERESA, OSB, M.A., Dept. of Religion and Religious Education, The Catholic University of America, Washington, D.C. **Article:** Posadas.

*TOUMANOFF, CYRIL LEO HERACLIUS, Ph.D., Professor of History and Director of Russian Area Studies, Georgetown University Washington, D.C. **Articles:** Cyrion (Kyrion); Georgia, Church in Ancient; Knights of Malta; Michael III, Byzantine Emperor; Mirian (Meribanes); Typos.

*TRACY, ROBERT EMMET, Most Rev., D.D., LL.D., Bishop of Baton Rouge, La. **Article:** Lafayette, Diocese of, Louisiana.

*TRAME, RICHARD HENRY, SJ, Ph.D., S.T.L., Associate Professor of History, Loyola University of Los Angeles, Calif. **Articles:** Arévalo, Rodrigo Sánchez de; Armada, The Spanish; Bartholomew of Rome; Escobar, Andrés de; Ferdinand III, King of Castile, St.

*TRAUTH, SISTER MARY PHILIP, SND, Ph.D., Associate Professor of History, Villa Madonna College, Covington, Ky. **Articles:** Caracciolo, Francis, St.; Carbonari; Le Clerc, Alix, Bl.; Leonardo, John, St.; Obregonians (Poor Infirmarians); Ward, Mary.

*TREANOR, NOËL, S.T.L., Secretary General, Commission des Épiscopats de la Communauté Européene. **Article:** Commission of the Bishops' Conferences of the European Community (COEMECE).

*TRECCO, MARIO, PSSC, S.T.L., S.S.L., Professor of Dogmatic Theology and Sacred Scripture, St. Charles Seminary, Staten Island, N.Y. **Article:** Syria, The Catholic Church in.

*TRÉPANIER, EMMANUEL MARCEL, Ph.D., Professor, Faculty of Philosophy, University of Laval, Quebec, Canada. **Article:** First Principles.

*TRESSERRAS, BUENAVENTURA, FMS, Doctorate in Philosophy and Letters, Professor of Oratory, Liceo Salvadoreño, and Adviser, Academia Filosófico-Literaria *Francisco Gavidia*, San Salvador, El Salvador, Central America. **Article:** Guatemala, The Catholic Church in.

*TRICHET, PIERRE, SMA, Director of the Centre culturel de la cathédrale d'Abidjan; Director of *La Nouvelle*, Abidjan, Ivory Coast. **Article:** Ivory Coast, The Catholic Church in.

*TRIGGER, BRUCE GRAHAM, Ph.D., Assistant Professor, Department of Sociology and Anthropology, McGill University, Montreal, Canada. **Article:** Nubia.

*TRIPOLE, MARTIN R., SJ, Assistant Professor, Theology, St. Joseph's College, Philadelphia, Pa. **Article:** Theology of Hope.

*TRISCO, ROBERT FREDERICK, S.T.L., Eccl.Hist.D., Associate Professor of Church History, The Catholic University of America, Washington, D.C.; Managing Editor, *Catholic Historical Review; Peritus* and Member of the United States Bishops' Press Panel, Vatican Council II. **Articles:** American Board of Catholic Missions; Apostolic Delegation in the U. S.; Chicago, Archdiocese of; John XXIII, Pope, Bl.; Meyer, Albert Gregory; Stritch, Samuel Alphonsus; Vatican Council II.

*TRISCO, ROBERT FREDERICK, S.T.L., Eccl.Hist.D., Professor of Church History, The Catholic University of America; Editor, *The Catholic Historical Review*. **Articles:** Cody, John Patrick; McGuire, Martin R. P.; Melville, Annabelle McConnell.

TRISCO, ROBERT FREDERICK, S.T.L., Eccl.Hist.D., Editor, *The Catholic Historical Review*; Professor emeritus of Church History, The Catholic University of America, Washington, D.C. **Articles:** American Catholic Historical Association; Illinois, Catholic Church in.

*TROCKUR, EMANUEL JOHN, OFM, Navaho Indian Mission, St. Michaels, Ariz. **Article:** Gallup, Diocese of.

TRUAX, JEAN A., Ph.D. (University of Houston), Houston, Tex. **Articles:** Matilda, Empress; Stephen, King of England.

*TRUHLAR, KAREL VLADIMIR, Lic.Phil., Doctor Theol., Professor of Spiritual Theology, Gregorian University, Rome, Italy. **Articles:** Obedience; Virtue, Heroic.

*TRUJILLO MENA, VALENTIN, S.T.L., J.C.D., Professor of Oriental Theology, Facultad de Teología Eclesiastica y Civil; Director, Archiepiscopal Archives, Lima, Peru. **Article:** Rodríguez de Mendoza, Toribio.

*TSEU, AUGUSTINUS ALOYSIUS, S.T.L., Ph.D., Dean of the Graduate School, Pontifical Fu-Jen University, Taipei, Taiwan. **Article:** Zhuangzi (Chuang-Tzu).

*TSUJI, SHIGEBUMI, B.F.A., M.F.A., Department of Art and Archeology, Princeton University, Princeton, N.J. **Articles:** Angels, 4. Iconography of; Apocrypha, Iconography of the; Ecce Homo; Evangelists, Iconography of; John the Baptist, St., Iconography of.

*TÜCHLE, HERMANN, Dr.Theol., Professor of Church History, University of Munich, Germany. **Articles:** Germany, The Catholic Church in [From the Beginnings to the Reformation]; Pragmatic Sanction; Prince-Bishop.

*TUFARI, PAOLO, SJ, M.A. (Philosophy); M.A. (Theology), Ph.D., Professor of Sociology, Gregorian University, Rome, Italy. **Article:** Knowledge, Sociology of.

*TULL, CHARLES J., Ph.D., Professor of History, Indiana University at South Bend. **Article:** Coughlin, Charles Edward.

*TUOHEY, JOHN, Ph.D., Visiting Assistant Professor, Department of Religion and Religious Education, The Catholic University of America, Washington, D.C. **Articles:** AIDS; Teleological Ethics.

TUOHEY, JOHN F., Ph.D., Chair, Applied Health Care Ethics, Providence St. Vincent Medical Center, Portland, Ore. **Article:** Suicide.

TUREK, DORIS MARY, SSND, J.D., Staff Advisor-Multicultural Liturgy, Secretariat for the Liturgy, United States Conference of Catholic Bishops, Washington, D.C. **Article:** School Sisters of Notre Dame.

*TURNER, EDITH, Lecturer, Department of Anthropology, University of Virginia. **Article:** Turner, Victor.

*TURNER, MARY DANIEL, SNDdeN, Superior General, Rome; former Executive Director, Leadership Conference of Women Religious. **Article:** Leadership Conference of Women Religious in the U.S.A. (LCWR).

TURNER, PAUL, S.T.D., Pastor, St. John Francis Regis Catholic Church, Kansas City, Mo. **Article:** Confirmation.

*TURNER, VICTOR WITTER, Ph.D., Professor of Anthropology, Cornell University, Ithaca, N.Y. **Article:** Religion (in Primitive Culture).

*TURNER, WALTER HENRY, Ph.D., L.M.S., Professor of Philosophy and Chairman of the Department, University of Detroit, Detroit, Mich. **Article:** Contingency.

*TURNEY, SISTER ANNA DAVID, CDP, M.A., Instructor in Theology, Our Lady of the Lake College, San Antonio, Tex. **Article:** Apocatastasis.

*TURRO, JAMES C., S.T.L., S.S.L., M.A., Professor of Sacred Scripture, Darlington Seminary, Ramsey, N.J. **Articles:** Bar Mitzvah; Canon, Biblical, 2. History of Old Testament Canon; Menorah; Mezuzah; Rabbi; Synagogue.

*TUTWILER, PAUL, OSCam, Ph.D., Superior, St. Camillus Hospital, Whitinsville, Mass. **Articles:** Camillians; Camillus de Lellis, St.

TWETTEN, DAVID B., Ph.D., Associate Professor of Philosophy, Marquette University, Milwaukee, Wis. **Article:** Theology, Natural.

*UBACHS, WINIFRED, FIC, M.A., Librarian and Archivist, Congregation of the Brothers of Maastricht, Nijmegen, Netherlands. **Article:** Immaculate Conception Brothers.

*UDELL, SISTER MARY GONZAGA, OP, Ph.D., Professor of Philosophy and Chairman of the Department; Director of Graduate Division, Aquinas College, Grand Rapids, Mich. **Article:** Dominican Sisters—Congregation of Our Lady of the Sacred Heart (Grand Rapids, Mich).

*UHLIRZ, MATHILDE, Dr.Phil., Graz, Steiermark, Austria. **Article:** Ottonian Renaissance.

*ULLMAN, BERTHOLD LOUIS, Ph.D., Litt.D., Kenan Professor Emeritus of Classics, University of North Carolina, Chapel Hill, N.C. (deceased June 21, 1965). **Articles:** Corbie, Abbey of; Pecia; Salutati, Coluccio.

*ULLMANN, WALTER, J.U.D., M.A., Litt.D., Professor of Medieval Ecclesiastical Institutions and Fellow of Trinity College, University of Cambridge, England. **Articles:** Caesaropapism; Chichele, Henry; Donation of Constantine; Gregory VII, Pope, St.; Kemp, John (Kempe); Papacy, 2. Medieval Period; Papacy, 1. Early Period; Western Schism.

ULLOA, SR. MARIA, OSF, Superior, Immaculate Conception Convent, Hastings-on-Hudson, N.Y. **Article:** Franciscan Sisters—Franciscan Missionary Sisters of the Immaculate Conception (OSF).

*UNDREINER, GEORGE JOSEPH, Rt. Rev., Ph.D., Professor of History and of Church History, Josephinum Pontifical College, Worthington, Ohio. **Article:** Niza, Marcos de.

*UNTENER, KENNETH E., S.T.D., Rector, St. John's Provincial Seminary, Plymouth, Mich. **Article:** Reconciliation, Ministry of.

*UPTON, JAMES MORGAN, A.M., M.S., S.T.M., Instructor in Mathematics, Honors Program, Seattle University, Seattle, Wash. **Articles:** Arregui, Antonio Maria; Noldin, Hieronymus; Vermeersch, Arthur.

*URDÁNOZ, THEOPHILE, OP, S.T.Lr., S.T.D., S.T.M., Professor of Speculative Moral Theology, University of Fribourg, Switzerland; Consulter, Vatican Council II. **Article:** Faith, 3. Theology of [part 1].

*URRIZA, JUAN, SJ, Dr. en Historia, Professor of the History of Philosophy and Science and Professor of Cultural History, Tudela (Navarre), Spain. **Article:** Alcala, University of.

*VAILLANCOURT, NORMAND LEO, M.S., S.T.L., S.S.L., Professor of Sacred Scripture, La Salette Seminary, Attleboro, Mass. **Article:** Patriarchs, Biblical.

*VALCÁRCEL, CARLOS DANIEL, Dr. en Letras, Dr. en Educación, formerly Professor of History, University of San Marcos, Lima, Peru. **Article:** Avila, Francisco de.

*VAN ACKEREN, GERALD, SJ, M.A. (Classics), Ph.L., M.A., (Philosophy), S.T.L., S.T.D., Dean and Associate Professor of Dogmatic Theology, St. Louis University School of Divinity, St. Marys College, St. Marys, Kans.; Editor, *Theology Digest*. **Articles:** Gregory of Valencia; Methodology (Theology); Theology; Toledo, Francisco de.

*VAN ANTWERP, EUGENE IGNATIUS, SS, A.B., S.T.D., Professor of Dogmatic

Theology and Spiritual Director, St. Patrick's Seminary, Menlo Park, Calif. **Article:** Bruneau, Joseph.

*VAN CAENEGEM, RAOUL CHARLES, Doctor of Law, Doctor of Philosophy and Letters, Professor of Medieval History, University of Ghent, Belgium. **Article:** Capitularies, Imperial and Ecclesiastical.

*VAN DE KAMP, SISTER M. CECILIA, SDS, M.Mus., Instructor, Divine Savior College, Milwaukee, Wis. **Article:** Divine Savior, Sisters of the.

*VANDENBROUCKE, FRANÇOIS, OSB, Bachelier en Philosophie thomiste (Louvain), graduate of Studium Theologicum, Abbaye de Mont César, Director, *Questions Liturgiques et Paroissiales,* Abbaye du Mont César, Louvain, Belgium, and Collaborator, *Bulletin de Théologie ancienne et médiévale.* **Article:** Eckhart, Meister.

*VAN DEN EYNDE, DAMIAN, OFM, S.T.D., S.T.M., Professor of Dogmatic Theology and Rector Magnificus, Athenaeum Antonianum, Rome, Italy; member of several commissions, Vatican Council II. **Article:** Hugh of Saint-Victor.

*VAN DER PLOEG, JOANNES PETRUS MARIA, OP, S.T.D., S.S.D., S.T.M., Professor of Old Testament Exegesis, Hebrew and Syriac, Catholic University of Nijmegen, Netherlands; Chorepiscopus of the Syriac Rite of Antioch. **Articles:** Law, Ancient Near-Eastern; Law, Mosiac.

*VAN DER VELDT, JAMES HERMAN, OFM, Ph.D., Agrégé de Philosophie, Lect.Gen.O.F.M., Litt.D., Professor Emeritus, The Catholic University of America, Washington, D.C. **Articles:** Associationism; Psychologism.

VAN DIJCK, G., A Monk of the Grand Chartreuse. **Article:** Carthusians.

*VAN DIJK, STEPHEN JOSEPH PETER, OFM, D.Phil., F.R. Hist.S., Lecturer, Liberal Studies, Woolwich Polytechnic, London, England. **Articles:** Ambry (Armarium); Biblia Pauperum.

*VAN DOREN, ROMBAUT LOUIS RENÉ, OSB, Docteur en Sciences historiques, monk of the Abbey of Mont César, Louvain, Belgium; Consultor in Sacred Liturgy, Vatican Council II. **Article:** Liturgical Year in the Roman Rite.

*VAN GESTEL, C., OP, Docteur en Theologic, Docteur en Sciences politiques et sociales, S.T.M., Professor, University of Louvain and other institutions of higher learning, Louvain, Belgium. **Article:** Association.

*VAN HECKEN, JOSEPH LEONARD, CICM, M.A., Professor of Missiology and the Chinese Language, Universities of Louvain, Belgium, and Nijmegen, Netherlands. **Article:** Mongolia, The Catholic Church in.

VAN HOVE, BRIAN, SJ, Ph.D., Assistant Professor of Theology, Pontifical College Josephinum, Columbus, Ohio. **Articles:** Danielou, Jean; Jedin, Hubert.

*VAN KAAM, ADRIAN LEO, CSSp, Ph.D., Associate Professor of Psychology and Director of the Institute of Man, Duquesne University, Pittsburgh, Pa.; Editor, *Review of Existential Psychology and Psychiatry.* **Articles:** Existential Psychology; Libermann, François Marie Paul, Ven.

*VAN LAER, HENRY, Very Rev., D.Sc., Professor of Thomistic Philosophy, University of Leiden, Netherlands. **Article:** Void.

*VAN LIERDE, PETER CANISIUS, Most Rev., OESA, S.T.D., S.S.L., Diploma in Organ, Titlular Bishop of Porphyreon, Sacristan and Vicar-General of His Holiness the Pope, Vatican City, Italy. **Articles:** Commissary Apostolic; Consistory; Decorations, Papal; Domestic Prelate; Monsignor.

*VAN OMMEREN, WILLIAM M., J.C.D., Rector, Mater Cleri Seminary; Rector, Bishop White Seminary; and Chancellor, Diocese of Spokane, Wash. **Articles:** Ne temere; Tametsi.

*VAN PAASSEN, JOANNES, MSC, S.T.D., Professor of Moral Theology, Major Seminary of Pineleng (Diocese of Manado), Sulawesi Utarah (North Celebes), Indonesia. **Articles:** Continence; Digamy; Gangra; Henoticon; Hospitality; Julian Sabas, St.; Leonides, St.; Marcian of Cyr, St.; Marinus, SS.; Mark of Arethusa, St.; Maro of Cyr, St.; Martina, St.; Peter Chrysologus, St.; Samosata.

*VAN ROEY, ALBERT, Very Rev., Canon, Dr. Theol., Dr. Oriental Philology and History, Professor of Patrology, Oriental Theology, Dogmatic Theology, and Arabic, University of Louvain, Belgium. **Articles:** Alexandria, School of; Antioch, School of.

VAN SLYKE, DANIEL G., Ph.D., Assistant Professor, Department of Theology and Philosophy, Caldwell College, Caldwell, New Jersey. **Articles:** Geiseric, King of the Vandals; Quodvultdeus; Vandals.

*VANSTEENKISTE, JORIS C., OP, Professor, Athenaeum Angelicum, Rome, Italy. **Articles:** Doctor (Scholastic Title); Giles of Lessines; Thomas of Cantimpre; William of Moerbeke.

*VAN TRUMP, JAMES DENHOLM, M.A., Editor, *Charette* (Pennsylvania journal of architecture); Visiting Critic, Department of Architecture, Carnegie Institute of Technology, Pittsburgh, Pa.; Vice President, Pittsburgh History and Landmarks Foundation; Director, Council of the Alleghenies. **Articles:** Church Architecture, History of, 8: 18th century Europe; Church Architecture, History of, 9: 19th century Europe.

*VARGA, SISTER MARY ALICE, DDR, M.A., Teacher, Divine Redeemer Academy, Elizabeth, Pa. **Articles:** Divine Redeemer, Sisters of the; Eppinger, Elisabeth.

*VARGAS, JOSE MARIA, OP, Professor in the Faculties of Law, Economics, and Pedagogy, Catholic University of Quito, Ecuador. **Articles:** Bedon, Pedro; Masias, Juan, St.; Melendez, Juan de; Paredes y Flores, Mariana de Jesus, St.; Pena Montenegro, Alonso de la; Ricke, Jodoco; Rose of Lima, St.; Valverde, Vincente de.

VASKO, PETER, OFM, KHS (Knight of the Holy Sepulcher), President, The Holy Land Foundation, St. Saviour's Monastery, Jerusalem, Israel. **Articles:** Jerusalem.

*VAUGHAN, JAMES HUBERT, FSCH, M.A., Provincial Consultor, Christian Brothers of Ireland, American Province; Supervisor of Schools, American Province; Director of Council on Education, American Province, New Rochelle, N.Y. **Articles:** Irish Christian Brothers; Rice, Edmund Ignatius, Bl.

*VAUGHAN, RICHARD PATRICK, SJ, S.T.L., Ph.D., Associate Professor of Psychology and Chairman of the Department, University of San Francisco, San Francisco, Calif. **Article:** Antipathy.

VAUGHAN, SALLY, Ph.D., Professor of History, Department of History, University of Houston. **Articles:** Henry I, King of England; Normandy; Normans; William II Rufus, King of England.

*VAWTER, FRANCIS BRUCE, CM, B.A., S.T.L., S.S.D., Professor of Sacred

Scripture, Kenrick Seminary, St. Louis, Mo. **Articles:** Ezekiel; Ezekiel, Book of; Israel, 2. Religion of Ancient Israel.

*VEATCH, HENRY BABCOCK, Ph.D., Professor of Philosophy, Northwestern University, Evanston, Ill. **Article:** Intentionality.

*VEATCH, HENRY BABCOCK, Professor Emeritus, Georgetown University, Washington, D.C. **Article:** Foundationalism.

VEIT, SR. CONSTANCE CAROLYN, LSP, Publications Coordinator, Little Sisters of the Poor, Baltimore, Md. **Article:** Little Sisters of the Poor.

*VENCHI, GIUSEPPE INNOCENZO, OP, S.T.L., Segretario Postulazione Generale OP, Curia Generalizia dell'Ordine dei Frati Predicatori, Rome, Italy. **Article:** Catherine of Racconigi, Bl.

*VERBILLION, JUNE M., Ed.D., Assistant Professor of English, Chicago Teachers College North, Chicago, Ill. **Articles:** Beatrice of Nazareth, Bl.; Claret de la Touche, Louise; Du Houx, Jeanne; Escobar, Marina de, Ven.; Faber, Frederick William; Leseur, Elizabeth; Lucie-Christine; Lutgardis, St.; Menendez, Josefa, Sister; Raclot, Mathilde.

*VERDIER, PHILIPPE MAURICE, Professor agrégé ès lettres, Curator of Sculpture and Decorative Arts, The Walters Art Gallery, Baltimore, Md.; Lecturer in the History of Art, Johns Hopkins University; Consultant, Museum of Art, Carnegie Institute, Pittsburgh, Pa. **Articles:** Apocalypse, Iconography of; Apostles, Iconography of; Bible Moralisee; Sacraments, Iconography of; Trinity, Holy, Iconography of; Virtues and Vices, Iconography of.

*VEREECKE, LOUIS GUSTAVE, CSSR, S.T.D., Diplôme des Langues Orientales (Paris), Professor of the History of Moral Theology, Accademia Alfonsiana, Rome, Italy; Professor of Theology, Centre d'Études, Dreux, France. **Articles:** Alphonsus Liguori, St.; Andrew of Crete, St.; Busenbaum, Hermann; Euphemia, St.; Fructuosus of Braga, St.; Gregory III, Patriarch of Constantinople; John XI Beccus, Patriarch of Constantinople; Moral Theology, History of (700 to Vatican Council I); Schrijvers, Joseph; Sidonius Apollinaris, St.

*VERGANA, MIGUEL ANGEL, Very Rev., Canon and formerly Vicar-General of the Archdiocese of Salta, Argentina; Director, *El Pueblo;* Director, Museo Historico del Notre, Salta; Adviser to Acción Católica. **Articles:** Gorriti, Juan Ignacio de; Ortiz de Zarate, Pedro, Ven.; Zegada, Escolastico.

*VERGOTE, JOZEF, Ph.D., Licentiate in Oriental History and Philology, Professor of Greek, Egyptian Languages, and Papyrology, University of Louvain, Belgium. **Articles:** Akhnaton (Amenhotep IV); Egypt, Ancient, 1. Religion.

*VERLINDEN, JEAN CHARLES, Ph.D., Professor of History, University of Ghent, Belgium; Director, Academia Belgica, Rome, Italy. **Articles:** Bermudez, Joao; Slavery (History of).

*VEROSTKO, BERNARD THOMAS, Washington, D.C. **Articles:** Deuteronomy, Book of; Lightfoot, Joseph Barber; Westcott, Brooke Foss.

*VEROSTKO, ROMAN JOSEPH, OSB, M.F.A., Professor of Art, St. Vincent College, Latrobe, Pa.; Staff Editor for Art and Architecture, *New Catholic Encyclopedia,* The Catholic University of America, Washington, D.C.; artist and lecturer. **Articles:** Assy, Notre-Dame-de-Toute-Grace; Castiglione, Giuseppe; Liturgical Art, History of, Pt 2: Legislation before Vatican II; Liturgical Art, History of, Pt 1: Definition; Liturgical Art, History of, Pt 6: Church Furnishing; Liturgical Art, History of, Pt 5: Impact of Vatican II; Liturgical Art, History of, Pt 3: 20th Century Renewal Efforts; Murillo, Bartolome Esteban; Saints, Iconography of, 1. Classifications.

*VERRET, SISTER MARY CAMILLA, RSM, M.Mus., Instructor in Music and French, Glennon High School, Kansas City, Mo. **Article:** Liturgical Music, History of, 9: United States.

*VERSTRAETE, ARTHUR FREDERICK, CICM, M.A., Editor, *Missionhurst,* Immaculate Heart Missions, Arlington, Va. **Articles:** Immaculate Heart of Mary, Congregation of the (Missionhurst); Verbist, Theophile.

*VESZELOVZKY, ALBIN VLADIMIR, OPraem, S.T.D., Professor of Moral Theology, St. Norbert Abbey, De Pere, Wis. **Article:** Dulia.

*VIAL, FERNAND, Ph.D., Professor of French and Chairman of the Department of Romance Languages, Fordham University, New York, N.Y. **Article:** Rousseau, Jean Jacques; Voltaire.

*VICAIRE, MARIE-HUMBERT, OP, S.T.Lr., Professor of Church History, University of Fribourg, Switzerland. **Articles:** Dominic, St.; Mandonnet, Pierre; Sertillanges, Antonin Gilbert.

*VIGLINO, UGO, IMC, Ph.D., S.T.D., Dean, Faculty of Philosophy, Pontifical Urban University, Rome, Italy; Director, philosophical section of *Enciclopedia Cattolica.* **Articles:** Consolata Missionaries; Contradiction, Principle of; Identity, Principle of.

*VILLASANTE CORTABITARTE, LUIS, OFM, S.T.D., Professor of Theology, Franciscan Theologate at Aránzazn, Diocese of San Sebastián, Spain. **Article:** Sorazu, Angeles.

*VILLELLA, MOTHER MARY SANTINA, OSST, M.S., Provincial Superior, Sisters of the Most Holy Trinity, Euclid, Ohio. **Article:** Trinity, Sisters of the Most Holy.

*VILLIGER, JOHANN BAPTIST, Very Rev., Eccl.Hist.D., Canon of St. Leodegar and Professor of Church History and Patristics, Theological Faculty, Lucerne, Switzerland; Editor, *Schweizerische Kirchenzeitung.* **Articles:** Lachat, Eugene; Switzerland, The Catholic Church in.

*VINCENT, ROBERT GEORGE, OMI, S.T.L., S.S.L., Professor of Sacred Scripture, Oblate College, Washington, D.C. **Article:** American Schools of Oriental Research.

*VINCITORIO, GAETANO LEONARD, Ph.D., Professor of History, Graduate School of Arts and Science, St. John's University, Jamaica, N.Y. **Articles:** Methodist Churches, I: England; Wesley, Charles; Wesley, John.

*VIOLANTE, CINZIO, Doctor of Letters and Philosophy, Professor of Medieval History, Università Cattolica del Sacro Cuore, Milan, Italy. **Article:** Patarines.

*VIVAS SALAS, HILDA, B.A., translator of French and English; Secretary, Palacio de Miraflores-Secretaria General, Caracas, Venezuela. **Article:** Claver, Peter, St.

*VIVES GATELL, JOSÉ, S.T.L., Dr. of Philosophy and Letters, Dr. (h.c., University of Freiburg, Germany), Director, Instituto Enrique Flórez, and Director, Biblioteca Balmes, Barcelona, Spain; Director, *Analecta Sacra Tarraconensia;* Director, *Hispania Sacra.* **Articles:** Cordoba; Santiago de Compostela.

VIVIANO, BENEDICT THOMAS, OP, Ph.D., Professor of New Testament and Rabbinics, University of Fribourg, Switzerland; Editor, Studia Friburgensia. **Article:** Kingdom of God.

VO, PETER DE TA, SVD, Ph.D, Beginning Scholar, Department of Word and Worship, Catholic Theological Union, Chicago, Ill. **Article:** Chinese Rites Controversy.

*VOEGTLE, LEONARD ALPHONSE, FMS, M.A., J.C.D., Teacher, Collegio Internazionale Fratelli Maristi, Rome, Italy. **Articles:** Abbreviators; Champagnat, Marcellin Joseph Benoit, St.; Marist Brothers.

VOELKER, SISTER MARIAN, OSF, M.A., M.A.L.S., Archivist, The Sisters of St. Francis of Mary Immaculate, Joliet, Ill. **Article:** Franciscan Sisters—Congregation of the Third Order of St. Francis of Mary Immaculate (OSF).

*VOGEL, CYRILLE, Licencié è lettres, Docteur en théologie, Diploma in Christian Archeology (Rome), Professor of the History of Religion, Faculty of Catholic Theology, University of Strasbourg, France. **Articles:** Canon Law, History of, 1. Early Church; Hispana Versio; Prisca Versio; Statuta Ecclesiae Antiqua.

*VOLK, PAULUS LEOPOLD, OSB, Dr.Phil., Professor Emeritus of Medieval and Modern History and of the History of the Benedictine Order, Abbey of Maria Laach, Andernach, Germany. **Articles:** Abbot; Benignus of Dijon, St.; Bursfeld, Abbey of; Echternach, Abbey of; Marbach, Abbey of; Nicetius of Trier, St.; Stein-am-Rhein, Abbey of; Tournus, Abbey of; Victricius of Rouen, St.; Werden, Abbey of.

*VOLL, WALTER URBAN, OP, M.A., S.T.L., S.T.D., Professor of Moral Theology, Dominican House of Studies, Washington, D.C. **Articles:** Acedia; Deadly Sins; Lukewarmness; Religion, Teacher of; Society of Catholic College Teachers of Sacred Doctrine.

*VOLLERT, CYRIL, SJ, Ph.D., S.T.D., Professor of Dogmatic Theology, St. Louis University School of Divinity, St. Marys College, St. Marys, Kans. **Articles:** Mary, Blessed Virgin, II (in Theology) [Mary and the Church]; Transubstantiation.

*VOLLMAR, EDWARD ROBERT, SJ, Ph.D., B.S. in L.S., Certificate in Archival Administration, Associate Professor of History and Associate Director of Libraries, St. Louis University, St. Louis, Mo. **Articles:** Cotton, John; Garesche, Edward Francis; O'Connor, Thomas Francis; Revivalism; Shakers; Van Quickenborne, Charles Felix.

*VON HILDEBRAND, DIETRICH, Ph.D., Professor Emeritus of Philosophy, Fordham University, New York, N.Y.; author. **Article:** Sex.

*VOOR, JOSEPH HERMAN, Ph.D., Chairman, Department of Psychology, Bellarmine College, Louisville, Ky. **Article:** Motion [part 2].

*VÖÖRBUS, ARTHUR, Mag.Theol., Dr.Theol., Professor, Lutheran School of Theology, Chicago, Ill. **Articles:** Diatessaron; Peshitta.

*WADDELL, CHRYSOGONUS, OCSO, Diploma, Liturgical Institute of Sant' Anselmo, Rome, S.T.D., organist choirmaster, Professor of Liturgy, Abbey of Gethsemani, Ky. **Articles:** Cassant, Marie Joseph; Guerric of Igny, Bl.; Helinand of Froidmont; Lehodey, Vital.

*WAGNER, LAVERN JOHN, M.Mus., Ph.D., Head, Music Department, Quincy College, Quincy, Ill. **Articles:** A Cappella; Improperia; Magnificat (Canticle of Mary); Marenzio, Luca; Senfl, Ludwig.

*WAHL, EDWARD VINCENT, COr, A.B., J.C.L., The Oratory, Rock Hill, S.C. **Article:** Oratorians.

*WAHL, JOSEPH ANTHONY, COr, A.B., S.T.D., The Oratory, Rock Hill, S.C. **Articles:** Baronius, Caesar, Ven.; Vaz, Joseph, Bl.

*WAHLEN, JOSEPH JOHN, MSF, M.A., Teacher of History, Incarnate Word Academy, and Teacher of Theology, Christopher College, Corpus Christi, Tex. **Article:** Holy Family Missionaries.

*WAINWRIGHT, GEOFFREY, M.A., B.D., Ph.D. in Theology; Methodist Minister; Professor of Systematic Theology, The Queen's College, Birmingham, England. **Article:** Societas Liturgica.

WALDVOGEL, CHRIS, B.J., publications editor, Saint Louis University, St. Louis, Mo. **Article:** St. Louis University.

*WALGRAVE, JAN, OP, Catholique Université de Louvain, Belgium. **Article:** Doctrine, Development of.

*WALKER, JAMES BERNARD, OP, Ph.D., S.T.Lr., Chaplain, Dominican Motherhouse, Sinsinawa, Wis. **Articles:** Antoninus, St.; Dominican Nuns (Nuns of the Order of Preachers); Mazzuchelli, Samuel; O'Brien, Matthew Anthony; Vincent Ferrer, St.

*WALKER, LESLIE JOSEPH, SJ, M.A., Professor of Philosophy, Stonyhurst College, Lancashire, England, and author (deceased Sept. 2, 1958). **Article:** Voluntarism.

*WALL, A. E. P., Former Editor and President of the *Chicago Catholic*. **Articles:** Bernardin, Joseph Louis; Chicago, Archdiocese of.

*WALL, DONALD RAPHAEL, M.Arch., Assistant Professor, Department of Architecture, The Catholic University of America, Washington, D.C. **Article:** Church Architecture, History of, 1: Introduction.

*WALL, EDWARD FLAVIN, JR., M.A., Instructor in History, College of the Holy Cross, Worcester, Mass. **Article:** James II, King of England.

*WALL, JOSEPH B., SJ, Alma College, Los Gatos, Calif. **Article:** Conscience, Examination of; Self-Knowledge.

*WALL, KEVIN ALBERT, OP, S.T.L., S.T.Lr., Ph.D., Professor of Dogmatic Theology and Theory of Knowledge, St. Albert's College, Oakland, Calif.; Vice Regent of Studies; Faculty Member, Graduate Theological Union, Berkeley, Calif. **Articles:** Direction, Spiritual; Identity.

*WALLACE, RUTH A., Ph.D., Professor of Sociology, George Washington University, Washington, D.C. **Article:** Fichter, Joseph H.

*WALLACE, WILLIAM AUGUSTINE, OP, B.E.E., M.Sc., S.T.L., Ph.D., S.T.D., S.T.Praes., Professor of Philosophy, Dominican House of Philosophy, St. Stephen's College, Dover, Mass.; Staff Editor for Philosophy, *New Catholic Encyclopedia,* The Catholic University of America, Washington, D.C.; Associate Editor, *Thomist;* Director, Institute of Interdisciplinary Studies of the St. Thomas Aquinas Foundation. **Articles:** Action at a Distance; Atomism; Choice; Cosmological Argument; Cybernetics; Einstein, Albert [Religion and Philosophy]; Emanationism; Form [History of the Concept]; Friendship; Hylomorphism; Hylosystemism; Logic, Symbolic; Measurement [Measurement in General]; Monism; Passion; Person (in Philosophy); Science (Scientia); Theodoric Borgognoni of

Lucca; Theodoric (Dietrich) of Freiberg; Thing; Thomas Aquinas, St. [part 1]; Uncertainty Principle; Witelo.

*WALLACH, LUITPOLD, Dr.Phil., Ph.D., Professor of Classics, Marquette University, Milwaukee, Wis. **Article:** Alcuin, Bl.

*WALLAIK, WILLIAM HENRY, B.A., S.T.D., Professor of European History, De Sales Preparatory Seminary, Milwaukee, Wis. **Articles:** Archchancellor; Barbaro; Rupert of Ottobeuren, Bl.

*WALSH, AUGUSTINE THOMAS, OSST, S.T.B., M.A., Instructor, Sacred Heart College, Pikesville, Md. **Article:** Trinitarians.

*WALSH, CHAD, Ph.D., D.Litt., Professor of English and Chairman of the Department, Beloit College; assistant priest, St. Paul's Episcopal Church, Beloit, Wis. **Article:** Utopia and Utopianism.

*WALSH, EUGENE ALOYSIUS, SS, M.A., S.T.D., Professor of Education and Director of Music, St. Mary's Seminary, Baltimore, Md. **Article:** Spirituality, French School of.

*WALSH, JAMES IGNATIUS, SJ, M.A., Ph.L., S.T.L., S.T.D., Assistant Editor, *Month;* Founder and Editor, *Way,* London, England; Vice Postulator for the cause of the English and Welsh martyrs and for the cause of Mother Cornelia Connelly. **Articles:** Hilton, Walter; Julian of Norwich.

*WALSH, JAMES PATRICK, SJ, A.B., Ph.L., St. Andrew Bobola House, Boston, Mass. **Articles:** Agrippa I and II; Hasmonaeans; Herod Antipas; Herod the Great; Herodias.

WALSH, JEROME T., S.S.L., Ph.D., Professor, Department of Theology, University of Dallas, Irving, Tex. **Articles:** Kings, Book(s) of; Samuel, Book(s) of; Samuel.

*WALSH, JOHN J., SJ, S.T.D., Professor of Theology, Weston College, Weston, Mass. **Articles:** Christology; Incarnation, Necessity of the; Jesus Christ (in Theology) 2. Scholasticism, Medieval and Modern; Jesus Christ (in Theology) 1. Formation of Classical Dogma.

*WALSH, KILIAN JAMES, OCSO, Teacher at College and Master of Laybrothers, Abbey of Mount Melleray, County Waterford, Ireland. **Article:** Mount Melleray Abbey.

*WALSH, SISTER MARY KATHLEEN, OP, M.A., Teacher, Sacred Heart Academy, Springfield, Ill. **Article:** Dominican Sisters—Dominican Sisters of Springfield in Illinois.

*WALSH, MARY PAULA, Ph.D., Assistant Professor of Church History and Society, Director of Paulssen Center for Church and Society, Lutheran Theological Seminary, Gettysburg, Pa. **Article:** Socialization, Religious.

WALSH, MICHAEL J., MA (Oxon), S.T.L., Formerly Librarian, Heythrop College, University of London, London, England. **Articles:** Dublin Review; Month, The; Tablet, The; Worlock, Derek John Harford.

*WALSH, ROBERT PATRICK, General Secretary, Catholic Social Guild, Oxford, England; Editor, *Christian Democrat.* **Article:** Distributism.

WALTER, C., **Article:** Franciscan Sisters—Sisters of the Third Franciscan Order (OSF).

*WALTERS, LEROY, Director, Center for Bioethics, Kennedy Institute, Georgetown University, Washington, D.C. **Article:** Medical Ethics.

*WALTON, FRANCIS REDDING, Ph.D., Librarian of the Gennadius Library, Athens, Greece. **Article:** Orphism.

*WALZ, ANGELUS MARIA, OP, Diploma, Vatican School of Paleography and Diplomatics, S.T.D., Professor of Church History, Pontifical University of St. Thomas Aquinas (Angelicum), Rome, Italy. **Articles:** Badia, Tommaso; Ehrle, Franz; Grabmann, Martin; Reginald of Piperno; Weiss, Albert Maria.

*WAND, AUGUSTIN C., SJ, Ph.D., Director of Museum and Archivist of the Museum and Archives of Jesuit Activity in Kansas, St. Marys College, St. Marys, Kans. **Articles:** Apophthegmata Patrum; Pallavicino, Pietro Sforza.

*WARD, DENIS, OSC, St. Francis, Notting Hill, London, England. **Article:** Oblates of St. Charles.

*WARDROPPER, BRUCE WEAR, Ph.D., William H. Wanamaker Professor of Romance Languages, Duke University, Durham, N.C. **Article:** Autos Sacramentales.

*WARE, RONALD DEAN, Ph.D., Associate Professor of History, Illinois State University, Normal, Ill. **Articles:** Brithwald of Canterbury, St.; Brithwald of Wilton, St.; Caedwalla, King of Wessex, St.; Cyneburg, St.; Justus of Canterbury, St.; Lawrence of Canterbury, St.; Mellitus of Canterbury, St.; Osmund of Salisbury, St.; Paulinus of York, St.; Ripon, Abbey of; Swithin of Winchester, St.

WARNER, DAVID A., Ph.D., Associate Professor of History, Rhode Island School of Design, Providence, R.I. **Articles:** Lothair II, Frankish King; Lothair I, Medieval Emperor; Otto I, Roman Emperor; Otto II, Roman Emperor; Otto III, Roman Emperor; Victor II, Pope.

WARREN, SISTER ANNE MARIE, OSF, B.S., Superior General, Franciscan Missionary Sisters of Our Lady of Sorrows, Beaverton, Ore. **Article:** Franciscan Sisters—Franciscan Missionary Sisters of Our Lady of Sorrows (OSF).

*WARREN, FINTAN BENEDICT, OFM, Ph.D., Editor, *Americas,* Academy of American Franciscan History, Bethesda, Md. **Articles:** Benavides, Alonso de; Betanzos, Pedro de; Molina, Alonso de; Motolinia, Toribio de Benavente; Padilla, Juan de; Pfefferkorn, Ignaz; Quiroga, Vasco de; Testera, Jacobo de; Valencia, Martin de.

*WARREN, JOHN J., Ph.D., Professor of Philosophy and Chairman of the Department, Merrimack College, North Andover, Mass. **Article:** End.

*WASHINGTON, SYLVIA JUANITA, M.A., Assistant Professor of French, Trinity College, Washington, D.C. **Article:** Massillon, Jean Baptiste.

*WASSMER, THOMAS AQUINAS, SJ, Ph.L., S.T.L., Ph.D., Associate Professor of Philosophy, St. Peter's College, Jersey City, N.J. **Articles:** Categorical Imperative; Criticism, Philosophical; Natural Law [part 3].

*WATERS, EDWARD NEIGHBOR, M.Mus., Assistant Chief, Music Division, Library of Congress, Washington, D.C.; Editor, *Notes of the Music Library Association.* **Article:** Liszt, Franz.

WATKINS, PRISCILLA D., Ph.D. (University of Houston). **Articles:** Louis VI, King of France; Louis VII, King of France; Northmen; Philip I, King of France.

*WATZL, HERMANN NORBERT, OCist, Archivist, Abbey of Heiligenkreuz, Lower Austria. **Article:** Heiligenkreuz, Abbey of.

*WAYMAN, DOROTHY GODFREY, Litt.D., Reference and Research Librarian, St. Bonaventure University, St. Bonaventure, N.Y.; Staff Writer, *Times Herald,* Olean, N.Y. **Article:** O'Connell, William Henry.

*WEAKLAND, REMBERT GEORGE, Rt.Rev., OSB, M.S., D.D., L.H.D., Archabbot, St. Vincent Archabbey, Latrobe, Pa.; Staff Editor for Music, *New Catholic Encyclopedia,* The Catholic University of America, Washington, D.C. **Articles:** Alleluia; Ambrosian Chant; Antiphon; Aurelian of Reome; Choir; Gregorian Chant; Hucbald of Saint-Amand; Liturgical Music, History of, 1: Early Christian Music; Liturgical Music, History of, 2: Monophonic Music to 1200s; Responsorial Psalm.

*WEBER, MSGR. FRANCIS J., Archivist, Archdiocese of Los Angeles. **Article:** McIntyre, James Francis Aloysius; Serra, Junípero Xavier, Bl.

WEBER, MSGR. FRANCIS J., A.C.A., Archivist, Archdiocese of Los Angeles; Director, San Fernando Mission, Mission Hills, Calif. **Article:** Manning, Timothy.

*WEBER, GERALD MICHAEL, M.A., Pastor, Assumption Church, Pembina, N.Dak. **Articles:** Fargo, Diocese of; Muench, Aloisius Joseph.

*WEBER, JEROME F., OSB, M.A., Abbot, St. Peter's Abbey, Muenster, Saskatchewan, Canada. **Articles:** Ott, Michael; St. Peter of Muenster, Abbey of.

*WEBER, NICHOLAS ALOYSIUS, SM, S.T.D., Marist College, Washington, D.C. **Article:** Shaughnessy, Gerald.

*WEBER, RALPH EDWARD, Ph.D., Associate Professor of History, Marquette University, Milwaukee, Wis. **Article:** Zahm, John Augustine.

*WEBER, THOMAS HOWARD, S.T.L., S.S.L., Professor of Sacred Scripture and Vice Rector, St. Mary's Seminary, Cleveland, Ohio; Professor of Sacred Scripture, Borromeo Seminary of Ohio, Wickliffe, Ohio. **Articles:** Ostracon; Palimpsest; Scarab; Scroll; Seal; Stele.

*WECKMANN MUNOZ, LUIS, Doctor en Derecho, Doctor en Historia, Professor, Faculty of Philosophy and Letters, National Autonomous University of Mexico, Mexico City, Mexico; Director General, International Educational Affairs, Secretariate of Public Education and Secretary General, Advisory Council of the Mexican Government for UNESCO. **Article:** Alexandrine Bulls.

WEIDNER, S. ANTHONY, M.A., Omaha, Neb. **Articles:** Nebraska, Catholic Church in; Omaha, Archdiocese of.

*WEIGAND, RUDOLF BRUNO, Dr.Theol., Lic.Iur.Can., Assistant in Canon Law, University of Munich, Germany; Corresponding Member, Institute of Research and Study in Medieval Canon Law, Yale University, New Haven, Conn. **Article:** James of Albenga.

WEIGEL, GEORGE, M.A., Senior Fellow and John M. Olin Chair in Religion and American Democracy, Ethics and Public Policy Center, Washington, D.C. **Article:** John Paul II, Pope.

*WEIHER, CHARLES FREDERICK, CSC, Ph.D., Assistant Professor of Philosophy, University of Notre Dame, Notre Dame, Ind. **Articles:** Continuum; Extension; Indivisible; Multitude.

WEIL, LOUIS, S.T.D., James F. Hodges Professor of Liturgics, the Church Divinity School of the Pacific, Berkeley, Calif. **Article:** Book of Common Prayer.

*WEILER, ANTONIUS GERARDUS, L.Phil., Doctorate in History, Professor of Medieval History and Auxiliary Sciences, Catholic University of Nijmegen, Netherlands; Editorial Secretary, *Christian Centuries;* Adjunct-Director, Section on Church History of *Concilium.* **Articles:** Jong, Johannes de; Netherlands, The Catholic Church in; Utrecht, Schism of; Van Rossum, Willem Marinus.

WEINANDY, THOMAS G., OFMCap, Ph.D., Warden of Greyfriars, Oxford; Tutor and Lecturer in History and Doctrine, University of Oxford, Oxford, England. **Articles:** Eternity of God; Holiness of God; Immutability of God; Impassibility of God; Ineffability of God; Infinity of God; Jealousy of God; Justice of God [part 1]; Justice of God [part 2]; Mercy of God; Will of God.

*WEINHEIMER, SISTER MARY DE SALES, CSA, Mount Augustine, West Richfield, Ohio (deceased Sept. 7, 1962). **Article:** St. Augustine, Sisters of Charity of.

*WEIS, EARL AUGUST, SJ, M.A., Ph.L., S.T.D., Professor of Dogmatic Theology, Bellarmine School of Theology, North Aurora, Ill.; Staff Editor for Dogmatic Theology, *New Catholic Encyclopedia,* The Catholic University of America, Washington, D.C. **Articles:** Hypostatic Union; Impeccability of Christ; Incarnation; Incarnation, Necessity of the.

*WEISENGOFF, JOHN PETER, M.A., S.T.L., S.S.L., S.T.D., Associate Professor of Sacred Scripture, De Paul University, Chicago, Ill. **Article:** Deportation (in the Bible).

*WEISENSEL, LAWRENCE ERHARDT, OSC, M.A., Vice Rector, Our Lady of the Lake Minor Seminary, Wawasee (Syracuse), Ind. **Article:** Firmian.

*WEISHEIPL, JAMES ATHANASIUS, OP, Ph.Lic., S.T.Lr., Ph.D., D.Phil., Associate Professor of History of Mediaeval Science, Pontifical Institute of Mediaeval Studies, Toronto, Canada; Director of Leonine Commission, American Section. **Articles:** Adam Marsh; Albert of Saxony; Albert the Great (Albertus Magnus), St.; Cajetan (Tommaso de Vio); Capreolus, John; Dialectics in the Middle Ages; Durandus of Saint-Pourcain; Education, Scholastic; Eschmann, Ignatius T.; Impetus; James of Metz; John of Wales (d. 1285); John of Jandun; John Welles; John of Wales (1349–1378); John of Dumbleton; Maier, Anneliese; Neoscholasticism and Neothomism; Nicholas Trevet; Oxford, University of; Peter of La Palu (Paludanus); Richard of Swynesbed; Robert Kilwardby; Robert Grosseteste; Roger Bacon; Roger of Notingham; Scholastic Method; Scholasticism, 3. Contemporary; Scotism; Thomas Aquinas, St. [part 2]; Thomas Waleys; Thomas of Wilton; Thomism; Vincent of Beauvais; William of Heytesbury; William of Notingham.

*WEISS, ROBERTO, B.A. (Oxon.), Professor of Italian, University of London, London, England. **Articles:** Moleyns, Adam; Trevisa, John.

*WEISSENBERGER, PAULUS, OSB, Dr.Phil., Prior, Abbey of Neresheim, Würtemburg, Germany. **Article:** Neresheim, Abbey of.

*WEITEKAMP, BONIFACE RAYMOND, FSC, Ph.D., Director, Hillside Hall Scholasticate, Troy, N.Y. **Articles:** De Courcy, Henry; McDonald, Barnabas Edward, Brother; Mullany, Azarias of the Cross, Brother.

*WELCH, ROBERT JOSEPH, M.A., priest of the Diocese of Davenport, Catholic Professor in the School of Religion, State University of Iowa, Iowa City, Iowa. **Articles:** Cosgrove, Henry; Iowa, Catholic Church in.

WELLE, SR. JANICE, OSF, M.A., Little Falls, Minn. **Article:** Franciscan Sisters—Franciscan Sisters of Little Falls, Minnesota (OSF).

*WELLS, NORMAN JOSEPH, Ph.D., Associate Professor of Philosophy, Boston College, Chestnut Hill, Mass. **Articles:** Pesch, Tilmann; Tongiorgi, Salvatore; Urraburu, Juan Jose.

*WELSH, ALOYSIUS J., S.T.D., Executive Director, National Catholic Conference for Interracial Justice, Washington, D.C. **Article:** National Catholic Conference for Interracial Justice.

*WELSH, ROBERT JOSEPH, OSA, A.B., Ph.L., S.T.D., Dean, College of Liberal Arts and Sciences, Villanova University, Villanova, Pa. **Articles:** Flete, William; Thomas of Jesus (de Andrada).

*WELTIN, EDWARD GEORGE, Ph.D., Associate Professor of History, Washington University, St. Louis, Mo. **Articles:** Alexander I, Pope, St.; Dionysius, Pope, St.; Eleutherius, Pope, St.; Eutychian, Pope, St.; Evaristus, Pope, St.; Fabian, Pope, St.; Felix I, Pope, St.; Gaius (Caius), Pope, St.; Hyginus, Pope, St.; Linus, Pope, St.; Lucius I, Pope, St.; Marcellinus, Pope, St.; Marcellus I, Pope, St.; Pius I, Pope, St.; Pontianus, Pope St.; Sixtus I, Pope, St.; Sixtus II, Pope, St.; Soter, Pope, St.; Stephen I, Pope, St.; Telesphorus, Pope, St.; Urban I, Pope, St.; Victor I, Pope, St.; Zephyrinus, Pope, St.

*WESLEY, SISTER ROSEMARY, SCC, M.A., Head of the Department of Religion, Librarian, Administrative Consultant, and Moderator of Activities, Josephinum High School, Chicago, Ill. **Article:** Christian Charity, Sisters of.

WESOLOWSKI, L., **Article:** Franciscan Sisters—Sisters of St. Francis of the Immaculate Virgin Mary Mother of God (OSF).

*WESTFALL, CHARLES WILLIAM, CR, B.A., Teacher of French, North Bay College, North Bay, Ontario, Canada. **Article:** Lafleche, Louis Francois Richer.

*WETHEY, HAROLD EDWIN, Ph.D., Professor, Department of History of Art, University of Michigan, Ann Arbor, Mich. **Article:** Greco, El (Domenico Theotocopuli).

*WEYER, HANS, CSSR, Dr.Phil., Bonn, Germany. **Article:** Novatian (Antipope) and Novatianism.

*WHALEN, JOHN PHILIP, M.A., S.T.D., Associate Professor of Theology, School of Sacred Theology, and Managing Editor, *New Catholic Encyclopedia,* The Catholic University of America, Washington, D.C. **Articles:** Bouquil-

lon, Thomas Joseph; Certitude of Faith; Newman, John Henry [part 1]; Preambles of Faith; Schroeder, Peter Joseph; Temporal Values, Theology of.

*WHALEN, JOSEPH M., S.T.L., Chancery Office, Allentown, Pa. **Article:** Raimondi, Luigi.

*WHALEN, WILLIAM JOSEPH, M.S., University Editor and Assistant Professor of English, Purdue University, West Lafayette, Ind. **Articles:** Adventists; Amish Churches; Catholic Apostolic Church; Christadelphians; Christian Reformed Church; Christian and Missionary Alliance; Church of the Brethren (Dunkers); Darby, John Nelson; Doukhobors; Eddy, Mary Baker; Evangelical and Reformed Church; Evangelical United Brethren; McPherson, Aimee Semple; Miller, William; New Apostolic Church; Plymouth Brethren; Reformed Episcopal Church; River Brethren; Russell, Charles Taze; Rutherford, Joseph Franklin; Seventh-day Adventists; United Brethren.

*WHALLEY, GEORGE, B.A., M.A., Ph.D., F.R.S.C., Professor of English and Head of the Department, Queen's University, Kingston, Ontario, Canada. **Article:** Coleridge, Samuel Taylor.

*WHATMORE, LEONARD ELLIOTT, M.A., parish priest, St. Anselm's, Hindhead, Surrey, England. **Articles:** Houghton, John, St.; Lawrence, Robert, St.; Webster, Augustine, St.

*WHEALON, JOHN FRANCIS, Most Rev., S.T.L., S.S.L., M.A. (Education), LL.D., Titular Bishop of Andrapa and Auxiliary Bishop and Vicar-General of the Diocese of Cleveland Ohio. **Article:** Divino afflante Spiritu.

*WHEATON, JOHN BARRY, CJM, S.T.L., S.S.L., Professor of Sacred Scripture, Holy Heart Seminary, Halifax, N.S., Canada. **Articles:** Chaldeans; Ethiopians (Cushites).

*WHELAN, CECIL BASIL, OSB, B.A., M.A., F.R.H.S., monk of Belmont Abbey, Hereford, England. **Articles:** Berington, Charles; Dicconson, Edward; Ellis, Philip (Michael); Giffard, Bonaventure; Griffiths, Thomas; Huddleston, John; Talbot, James.

*WHIPPLE, SISTER MARY LEONARD, OVSM, M.A., Assistant Superior of the Community, Teacher of Religion, Georgetown Visitation College, Washington, D.C. **Article:** Georgetown Visitation.

*WHITE, HELEN CONSTANCE, Ph.D., LL.D., Litt.D., L.H.D., O.B.E., Professor of English and Chairman of the Department, University of Wisconsin, Madison, Wis. **Article:** Donne, John.

WHITE, JAMES D., Historian, Diocese of Tulsa, Oklahoma. **Articles:** Oklahoma, Catholic Church in; Oklahoma City, Archdiocese of; Tulsa, Diocese of.

*WHITE, JOHN LLOYD, SM, B.S. in L.S., M.A., Professor of Church History, Marist College, Washington, D.C.; Founder and Editor, *Provincial News Letter.* **Article:** Marist Fathers.

*WHITE, MARAGARET, Medical Practitioner, Diplomate of the Royal College of Obstetricians and Gynecologists; Vice-President of the Society for the Protection of Unborn Children; founding member of the World Federation of Doctors Who Respect Human Life. **Article:** Lejeune, Jérôme.

*WHITE, THOMAS ANTHONY, Very Rev., B.Ph., S.T.L., J.C.D., Secretary, Apostolic Delegation, Nairobi, East Africa. **Articles:** Djibouti, The Catholic Church in; Somalia, The Catholic Church in.

WHITNEY, BARRY, Ph.D., Editor, *Process Studies*; Professor, Philosophy of Religion and Culture, University of Windsor, Windsor, Ontario, Canada. **Articles:** Evil; Theodicy; Tillich, Paul.

*WHITSON, ROBLEY, President, The United Institute, Hartford, Ct. **Article:** Community.

*WHITTAKER, MOLLY, M.A., B.Litt., B.D., Senior Lecturer in Classics, University of Nottingham, England. **Articles:** Diognetus, Epistle to; Hermas, Shepherd of; Pantaenus, St.; Tatian; Theophilus of Antioch.

*WICKI, JOSEF, SJ, Eccl.Hist.D., Professor of Church History, Gregorian University, Rome, Italy; Editor, *Monumenta Historica S.J.* **Articles:** Criminali, Antonio, Ven.; Gnecchi Soldo, Organtino; Goa; Hanxleden, Johann Ernst; Henriques, Henrique; John de Britto, St.; Roth, Heinrich; Rudolf Acquaviva and Companions, BB.; Storer, Franz; Strobl, Andreas; Tieffentaller, Joseph; Xavier, Francis, St.

*WICKI, NIKOLAUS, Dr.Theol., Professor of Fundamental Theology, Theological Faculty of Lucerne, Switzerland. **Article:** Philip the Chancellor.

*WICKS, WALTER JARED, SJ, M.A., University of Münster and Ecumenical Institute, Münster, Germany. **Article:** Tanner, Adam.

*WIDDICOMBE, CATHERINE, M. Phil., President of the Grail, 1993–1996, Great Britain. **Article:** Drakestein, Yvonne Bosch van.

*WIERUSZOWSKI, HELENE, Ph.D., Professor Emeritus of History, City College, and Instructor, New School of Social Research, New York, N.Y. **Articles:** Martin IV, Pope; Otto of Freising; Roger of Sicily; Urban IV, Pope.

WIEST, JEAN-PAUL, S.T.L., Ph.D., Senior Researcher, the Center for Mission Research & Study at Maryknoll, and Visiting Scholar at the Centre of Asian Studies of The University of Hong Kong. **Articles:** China, Christianity in; Hong Kong, the Catholic Church in; Macau, Catholic Church in.

*WIEST, WALTER E., Ph.D., Minister, United Presbyterian Church in the U.S.A., Professor of Philosophy of Religion, Pittsburgh Theological Seminary, Pittsburgh, Pa. **Article:** Schleiermacher, Friedrich Daniel Ernst.

*WILBERFORCE, ROBERT, B.A. Oxon., barrister, retired from British Foreign Service, London, England. **Article:** Wilberforce, William.

*WILCOX, JOHN R., Director, Center for Professional Ethics, Associate Professor of Religious Studies, Manhattan College, Bronx, N.Y. **Article:** Professional Ethics.

*WILD, ROBERT, Priest of Madonna House, Combermere, Ontario. **Article:** De Hueck Doherty, Catherine.

WILD, ROBERT ANTHONY, SJ, Ph.D., President and Professor of Theology, Marquette University, Milwaukee, Wis. **Article:** Shroud of Turin.

WILDE, CLARE, The Catholic University of America, Washington, D.C. **Article:** Islam.

*WILFRED, FELIX, Professor, Department of Christian Studies, University of Madras, India. **Article:** Federation of Asian Bishops' Conferences.

*WILHELMSEN, FREDERICK DANIEL, Doctorate in Philosophy and Letters, Professor of Philosophy, Catholic University of Navarre, Spain. **Articles:** Immanentism; Innatism; Realism.

WILKEN, A. P., **Article:** Franciscan Sisters—Franciscan Sisters of Our Lady of Perpetual Help (OSF).

*WILKIE, WILLIAM E., S.T.L., M.A., Member, Department of History, Loras College, Dubuque, Iowa. **Articles:** Bilhild, St.; Druthmar, St.; Durandus of Troarn; Folcwin of Lobbes; Fulcran of Lodeve, St.; Gerard of Sauve-Majeure, St.; Herluin of Bec, Bl.; Hugh of Fouilloy; Imma, Bl.; Loras, Jean Mathias Pierre; Notker of Liege, Bl.; Utto, Bl.; Winthir, St.

*WILKINSON, SISTER MARY MICHAEL, OSSR, Mistress of Novices, Mother of Perpetual Help Monastery, Esopus, N.Y. **Article:** Redemptoristines.

*WILKINSON, WALTER WILFORD, Ph.D., Professor of History, Georgetown University; Washington, D.C. **Article:** Renaissance.

*WILLGING, EUGENE PAUL, A.B., A.B. in L.S., LL.D., Director of Libraries and Library Consultant to the *New Catholic Encyclopedia,* The Catholic University of America, Washington, D.C. (deceased Sept. 20, 1965). **Articles:** Froben, Johann; Lucas, Fielding, Jr.; Manutius; Murphy, John Joseph; Plantin, Christophe; Preuss, Arthur; Sadlier; Sweynheym, Konrad.

*WILLIAMS, AQUINAS BRUCE, OP, M.A., Ph.D., Pontifical Faculty of Theology of the Immaculate Conception, Dominican House of Studies, Washington, D.C. **Article:** Cormier, Hyacinthe-Marie, Bl.; Walter Jorz.

WILLIAMS, BRUCE, OP, Ph.D., S.T.D., Professor "Incaricatus," Faculty of Theology, Pontifical University of St. Thomas (Angelicum), Rome, Italy. **Articles:** Homosexuals, Pastoral Care of; Humanae Vitae.

*WILLIAMS, CORNELIUS WILLIAM, OP, S.T.D., Professor of Moral Theology, Faculty of Theology, University of Fribourg, Switzerland. **Articles:** Conscience, 3. In Theology; Obligation, Moral; Slavery (and the Church).

*WILLIAMS, GEORGE HUNTSTON, Th.D, D.D., LL.D., Minister of the United Church of Christ; Minister of the Unitarian Universalist Association; Hollis Professor of Divinity, Harvard University Divinity School, Cambridge, Mass. **Articles:** Blandrata, Giorgio; David, Franz; Le Clerc, Jean; Lubieniecki, Stanislaw; Ochino, Bernardino; Socinianism.

*WILLIAMS, GLANMOR, B.A., M.A., D.Litt., Professor of History, University College of Swansea, University of Wales, Swansea, Wales. **Articles:** Bangor, Ancient See of; Catrik, John; Caunton, Richard; Deane, Henry; Llandaff, Ancient See of; Llanthony, Monastery of.

*WILLIAMS, JOHN ALDEN, Ph.D., Assistant Professor in Islamic History, Institute of Islamic Studies, McGill University, Montreal, Quebec, Canada. **Articles:** Abbasids; Ali (Ali ibn Abi Talib); Declaration of Rights of 1689; Nizaris; Ottoman Turks; Recusant; Revolution of 1688 (England); Royal Declaration; Saladin; Timur (Tamerlane); Umayyads.

*WILLIAMS, MOTHER MARGARET ANNE, RSCJ, B.A. and M.A. Oxon.), Professor of English, Manhattanville College of the Sacred Heart, Purchase, N.Y. **Articles:** Bunyan, John; Sacred Heart, Society of the.

*WILLIAMS, MICHAEL EDWARD, S.T.D., Professor of Dogmatic Theology, Liturgy, and History of Theology and Vice President of the English College, Lisbon, Portugal. **Articles:** Anathemas of Cyril; Assumptus-Homo Theology; Catholic; Doctrine; Dogma; End of the World; Eschatology (in Theology) 1. Historical Perspectives; God-Man; Immortality, 4. Revelational Data; Indefectibility; Orthodoxy; Roman Catholic; Rule of Faith; Sanction, Divine.

*WILLIAMS, NEVILLE JOHN, M.A. (Oxon.), D.Phil. (Oxon.), Assistant Keeper of the Public Records, Public Records Office, London, England. **Article:** Norfolk.

WILLIAMS, RICHARD B., OP, J.D., Pastor, St. Thomas More University Parish, Tulane University, New Orleans, La. **Article:** Dominicans.

*WILLIAMS, SCHAFER, S.T.B., Ph.D., Professor of Medieval History, University of Massachusetts at Amherst, Mass. **Articles:** Adalbero of Wurzburg, St.; Arnulf of Gap, St.; Benzo of Alba; Henry Heinbuche of Langenstein; Henry V, Roman Emperor; Manasses I of Reims; Papal Arbitration; Sigebert of Gembloux; Walram of Naumberg; Wenrich of Trier; Wibald of Stavelot.

*WILLIS, JOHN R., SJ, Flannery Professor of Religious Studies, Gonzaga University, Spokane, Wash. **Article:** Lewis, Clive Staples.

*WILLIS, JOHN RANDOLPH, SJ, B.A.; B.D., Ph.D., Boston College, Chestnut Hill, Mass. **Articles:** Beecher; Congregational Churches; Dwight, Timothy;

Unitarian Universalist Association; Unitarians; United Church of Christ; Universalists.

*WILLKE, JEAN CAROLYN, Ph.D., Associate Professor of History, Trinity College; Assistant Staff Editor for Renaissance and Reformation Church History, *New Catholic Encyclopedia*, The Catholic University of America, Washington, D.C. **Articles:** Aldobrandini; Antoine, Paul Gabriel; Araujo, Francisco de; Arnold of Bonneval (Marmoutier); Arriaga, Rodrigo de; Aversa, Raphael; Ballerini, Antonio; Bernardes, Manoel; Berse, Gaspar (Barzeo); Berthier, Guillaume Francois; Cacciaguerra, Bonsignore; Cafasso, Joseph, St.; Cattaneo, Lazzaro; Chrysostom of Saint-Lo, John; Clement VIII, Pope; Costantini, Celso; Coton, Pierre; Dueling; Fagnani, Prospero; Frassinetti, Giuseppe; Grou, Jean Nicolas; Huc, Evariste Regis; Jaegen, Jerome; John of Avila, St.; Lacroix, Claude; Malderus, John; Marmion, Joseph Columba, Bl.; Mastrius, Bartholomaeus; Mombaer, John; Pamplona, Francis of; Philip of Harvengt; Quadrupani, Carlo Giuseppe; Rassler, Christoph; Ribet, Jerome.

*WILSON, JOHN, B.D., Archdiocese of Dublin, Ireland. **Article:** Ryan, Dermot.

*WILSON, MOTHER MARY GABRIEL, B.A., H.Dip. in Ed., M.A., Superior General, Missionary Sisters of Our Lady of the Holy Rosary, Killeshandra, County Cavan, Ireland. **Article:** Missionary Sisters of the Holy Rosary.

*WILTGEN, RALPH MICHAEL, SVD, Doctor, of Missiology, Founder and Director, Council News Service, Rome, Italy. **Articles:** Ghana, The Catholic Church in; Liberia, The Catholic Church in; Oceania, The Catholic Church in; Togo, The Catholic Church in.

*WINKLER, JUDE, OFMConv, S.S.L., Instructor of Sacred Scripture at St. Hyacinth College and Seminary, Granby, Mass. **Article:** Revelation, Book of.

*WINSCHEL, SISTER M. ALACOQUE, CDP, B.A., Sisters of Divine Providence, Allison Park, Pa. **Article:** Sisters of Divine Providence.

*WINSLOW, FRANCIS J., MM, S.T.B., J.C.D., Teacher, Maryknoll Seminary, Ossining, N.Y. **Article:** Titular Bishop.

*WINSNES, ANDREAS HOFGAARD, Dr.Phil. Professor Emeritus of the History of Ideas, University of Oslo, Norway. **Article:** Undset, Sigrid.

*WINSTONE, HAROLD, St. Thomas More Centre for Pastoral Theology, London, England. **Article:** Liturgical Languages.

WINTERSGILL, H. G., **Article:** Flathers, Matthew, Bl.

*WINZEN, DAMASUS, OSB, Ph.D., Founder and Prior of Mount Saviour Monastery, Elmira, N.Y. **Article:** Church, Symbols of.

*WIPPEL, JOHN FRANCIS, S.T.L., Ph.D., Instructor, School of Philosophy, The Catholic University of America, Washington, D.C. **Articles:** O'Toole, George Barry; Pohle, Joseph.

*WIPPEL, JOHN FRANCIS, Ph.D., Ordinary Professor of Philosophy, The Catholic University of America, Washington, D.C. **Article:** Van Steenberghen, Fernand.

WIPPEL, MSGR. JOHN FRANCIS, Ph.D., Theodore Basselin Professor of Philosophy, The Catholic University of America, Washington, D.C. **Article:** Godfrey of Fontaines.

*WITHERSPOON, JOSEPH PARKER, A.B., LL.B., S.J.D., Professor of Law, University of Texas School of Law, Austin, Tex. **Article:** Positivism in Jurisprudence.

*WITTY, FRANCIS JOSEPH, M.A., M.S. in L.S., Ph.D., Assistant Professor of Library Science, The Catholic University of America, Washington, D.C. **Article:** Prayer Books.

*WIXTED, WILLIAM GLEESON, Sr., Ph.D., Professor Emeritus, Hunter College, and Lecturer, Marymount College, New York, N.Y. **Articles:** Frobel, Friedrich Wilhelm; Pestalozzi, Johann Heinrich.

*WODKA, JOSEF, Very Rev., Dr.Phil., Dr.Theol., Professor of Ecclesiastical History, Major Seminary, St. Pölten, Austria. **Articles:** Austria,The Catholic Church in; Schwarzenberg, Friedrich Joseph von; Seipel, Ignaz.

*WOJNAR, MELETIUS MICHAEL, OSBM, S.T.L., J.C.D., Associate Professor, School of Canon Law, The Catholic University of America, Washington, D.C. **Articles:** Basilians (Byzantine); Basilians—Sisters of the Order of St Basil the Great (OSBM); Mary Immaculate, Sisters Servants of; Ukrainian Catholic Church (Eastern Catholic).

*WOLF, DONALD JOSEPH, SJ, M.A., Ph.D., St. Robert's Hall, Pomfret Center, Conn. **Articles:** Absolutism; Divine Right of Kings; Mounier, Emmanuel.

*WOLF, NORBERT GEORGE, M.A., Treasurer, Gannon College. **Articles:** Amadeus IX of Savoy, Bl.; Ambrose Traversari, Bl.; Ammanati de' Piccolomini, Jacopo; Angelina of Marsciano, Bl.; Antonia of Florence, Bl.; Archangela Girlani, Bl.; Archangelo of Calatafirmi, Bl.; Eustochia of Padua, Bl.; Seraphina Sforza, Bl.

*WOLFF, KONRAD M., J.U.D., Diplôme d'Études Supérieures de Droit, M.A.Mus., Teacher of Advanced Piano and of Piano Literature, Peabody Institute, Baltimore, Md. **Article:** Schubert, Franz.

*WOLFRAM, HERWIG, Ph.D., Assistent, Institut für österreichische Geschichtsforschung, Vienna, Austria. **Articles:** Albert I of Riga; Aribo of Mainz; Arnaldus Amalrici; Bohm, Hans; Lothair III, Roman Emperor; Martin of Troppau; Nicholas of Dinkelsbuhl; Nieheim (Niem), Dietrich of; Virgilius (Fergal, Feirgil) of Salzburg, St.; Vitalis of Salzburg, St.

WOLKERSTORFER, SISTER JOHN CHRISTINE, CSJ, Ph.D., Professor Emerita of History, The College of St. Catherine, St. Paul, Minn. **Articles:** Minnesota, Catholic Church in; St. Paul and Minneapolis, Archdiocese of.

*WOLTER, ALLAN BERNARD, OFM, Ph.D., Lect.Gen., Professor of Philosophy, The Catholic University of America, Washington, D.C. **Articles:** Boehner, Philotheus Heinrich; Efficient Causality; Knowledge, Infused.

*WOOD, CHARLES TURTLE, Ph.D., Assistant Professor of Medieval History, Dartmouth College, Hanover, N.H. **Article:** Philip II Augustus, King of France.

*WOOD, GEOFFREY FRANCIS, SA, B.A., S.T.D., S.S.L., Professor of Scripture, Atonement Seminary; formerly Instructor, Department of Religious Education, The Catholic University of America, Washington, D.C. **Article:** Zolli, Eugenio.

WOOD, SUSAN K., S.C.L., Ph.D., Professor, School of Theology, St. John's University, Collegeville, Minn. **Articles:** Bishop (in the Church); Bishop (Sacramental Theology of).

*WOOD, SUSAN MERIEL, B.A., M.A. and B.Litt. (Oxon.), Fellow and Tutor in Medieval History, St. Hugh's College,

Oxford, England. **Articles:** Anglessey, Priory of; Dorchester, Abbey of; Thetford, Priory of; Tynemouth, Priory of; Westminster Abbey.

*WOOD, THOMAS OLYS, SS, S.T.L., M.A. (Education), M.A. (History), St. Edward's University, Kenmore, Wash. **Article:** Levadoux, Michael.

*WOODHOUSE, ARTHUR SUTHERLAND PIGOTT, M.A., D.Litt., L.H.D., LL.D., Professor of English and Head of the Department, University of Toronto, Canada (deceased Nov. 2, 1964). **Article:** Milton, John.

*WOODRUFF, JOHN DOUGLAS, M.A., Editor, *Tablet,* London, England. **Articles:** Coleridge, Henry James; Lucas, Frederick; Oldmeadow, Ernest James; Ward, William George; Wilberforce, Henry William.

WOODS, J. M. **Articles:** Arkansas, Catholic Church in; Little Rock, Diocese of.

*WORK, MARTIN HAVERTY, A.B., M.A., D.Litt., Executive Director, National Council of Catholic Men, Washington. **Article:** National Council of Catholic Men (NCCM).

*WORTMAN, ILDEPHONSE JAMES, OSB, M.A., B.A.Mus., Choirmaster at St. Vincent Archabbey and Associate Professor of Music, St. Vincent College, Latrobe, Pa. **Articles:** Gallican Rites, Chants of; Gerbert von Hornau, Martin; Mozarabic Chant; Rheinberger, Josef Gabriel von.

*WOUTERS, ANTHONY JOSEPH, WF, S.T.D., Procurator General, Society of Missionaries of Africa, Rome, Italy; promoter of the canonization of the martyrs of Uganda (deceased Dec. 25, 1965). **Articles:** Foucauld, Charles Eugene de; Little Brothers of Jesus; Little Sisters of Jesus.

*WOYTKO, SISTER MARY GABRIELLE, OP, M.A., Teacher of History, Bishop McCort High School, Johnstown, Pa. **Article:** Dominican Sisters—Congregation of St Rose of Lima (Oxford, Mich).

WREGELSWORTH, JOHN ERIC, Ph.D., Fellowship in the Centre for Mediterranean Studies, University of Exeter, Exeter, United Kingdom. **Articles:** Braulio, St.; Charles Martel; Paulus Albarus; Pepin III, King of the Franks.

*WREN, CAROL, SSJ, M.A., College of Our Lady of the Elms, Chicopee, Mass. **Article:** Commitment.

*WRIGHT, ADDISON GEORGE, SS, M.A., S.T.D., S.S.L., Professor of Sacred Scripture and Hebrew, St. Mary's Seminary, Baltimore, Md. **Articles:** High Priest; Midrash.

*WRIGHT, JOHN HICKEY, SJ, PH.L., M.A., S.T.D., Professor of Theology, Alma College, Los Gatos, Calif. **Articles:** Dead, Prayers for the; Death (Theology of); Judgment, Divine (in Theology); Universe, Order of.

*WRIGHT, JOHN JOSEPH, Most Rev., A.B., S.T.D., Bishop of Pittsburgh, Pa.; Member, Theological Commission, Vatican Council II. **Article:** Patriotism.

*WRIGLEY, JOHN EVELETH, A.M., M.A., Ph.D., Teacher, Roman Catholic High School and La Salle College, Philadelphia, Pa. **Articles:** Bethesda; Cana of Galilee.

*WU, JOHN C. H., LL.B., J.D., LL.D., Litt.D., Professor of Asian Studies, Seton Hall University, South Orange, N.J. **Articles:** Law; Natural Law [part 2].

*WUERL, DONALD W., Most Reverend, S.T.D., D.D., Bishop of Pittsburgh, Pa. **Article:** Wright, John Joseph.

*WUEST, JOHN BERCHMANS, OFM, Lect.Gen., Assistant Chaplain, Mercy Hospital, Hamilton, Ohio. **Articles:** Leonard of Port Maurice, St.; Peter of Alacantara, St.; Salvator of Horta, St.; Theophilus of Corte, St.

*WYDEVEN, VALERIAN DONALD, OFM-Cap, B.A., Capuchin Seminary of St. Anthony, Marathon, Wis. **Article:** Joseph of Leonessa, St.

*WYLLEMAN, ANDRE LOUIS, S.T.B., Ph.D., Professor of Philosophy, University of Louvain, Belgium; Honorary Canon of the Cathedral of Ghent. **Articles:** De Wulf, Maurice; Mercier, Desire Joseph.

*WYSE, ALEXANDER, OFM, M.A., St. Anthony Shrine, Boston, Mass. **Article:** Franciscan Martyrs of Georgia.

*WYSOCKI, JOSEPH, International Commission of English in the Liturgy, Washington, D.C. **Article:** Liturgical Books of Roman Rite.

*YANCEY, PATRICK HENRY, SJ, Ph.D., Chairman, Department of Biology, Spring Hill College, Mobile, Ala.; Executive Secretary-Treasurer, Albertus Magnus Guild. **Article:** Macelwane, James Bernard.

YARNOLD, EDWARD J., Ph.D., Campion Hall, Oxford, England. **Article:** Catechumenate.

*YATES, FRANCES AMELIA, M.A., F.R.L.S., Reader in the History of the Renaissance, Warburg Institute, University of London, England. **Article:** Lull, Raymond, Bl.

*YEAGER, SISTER MARY HILDEGARDE, CSC, Ph.D., Professor of History, Dunbarton College of the Holy Cross, Washington, D.C. **Article:** Bayley, James Roosevelt.

YOCK, PETER, OSB, St. Meinrad Archabbey, Saint Meinrad, Ind. **Article:** St. Meinrad Archabbey.

YOHE, KATHERINE MARI, Ph.D., Visiting Assistant Professor, Department of Religion and Religious Education, The Catholic University of America, Washington, D.C. **Article:** Meditation.

*YONICK, ANACLETE STANLEY, OFM, B.A., S.T.L., Franciscan Biblical Institute, Jerusalem, Jordan. **Articles:** Covenant (in the Bible); Testament (in the Bible).

*YOUNG, WALTER GEORGE, free-lance writer, Williamsville, N.Y. **Article:** Ad Majorem Dei Gloriam (A.M.D.G.); Mercy, Brothers of.

YOUROUKOV, MILKO, Ph.D., Adjunct Lecturer, Department of Religion & Religious Education, The Catholic University of America, Washington, D.C. **Articles:** Orthodox Church in America (OCA); Orthodox Church of Bulgaria; Schmemann, Alexander.

*YUHAUS, C. CASSIAN JOSEPH, CP, M.A., Eccl. Hist. D., Professor of Ecclesiastical History, Christian Archaeology, and Biblical Theology, St. Ann Monastic Seminary, Scranton, Pa. **Articles:** Passionists; Paul of the Cross, St.; Purcell, Harold; Stone, James Kent; Strambi, Vincenzo Maria, St.

*YZERMANS, VINCENT, journalist, editor, author, priest of the Diocese of St. Cloud, Minn. **Articles:** Ligutti, Luigi G.; Rausch, James.

*ZAMMIT, PAUL NATALE, OP, Queen of the Holy Rosary College, Mission San Jose, Calif. **Article:** Scapulars.

*ZEDLER, BEATRICE HOPE, Ph.D., Professor of Philosophy, Marquette University, Milwaukee, Wis. **Articles:** Arabian Philosophy; Avempace (Ibn Bajjah, abu Bakr Muhammad ibn Yahya); Averroes (ibn-Rushd); Double Truth, Theory of; Intellect, Unity of.

*ZEENDER, JOHN KARL, Ph.D., Associate Professor of History, The Catholic

*ZELL, ROBERT LOREN, A.B., B.D., M.A., B.Phil., Assistant Professor of Theology, Marquette University, Milwaukee, Wis. **Articles:** Sanday, William; Smith, William Robertson.

*ZELLER, SISTER MARY CLAUDIA, OSF, Ph.D., Dean, College of St. Francis, Joliet, Ill. **Articles:** Copernicus, Nicolaus; Pacioli, Luca.

*ZERBI, PIERO, Ph.D., Professor of Medieval History, Università Cattolica del Sacro Cuore, Milan, Italy; Canon of the Cathedral of Como. **Article:** Bernard of Clairvaux, St.

*ZIEGLER, ADOLF WILHELM, Rt. Rev., Professor of Church History, University of Munich, Germany. **Article:** Milan, Edict (Agreement) of.

*ZIEGLER, ALOYSIUS KIERAN, Rt. Rev., M.A., S.T.D., École Nationale des Chartes, Archiviste-paléographe, L.H.D., Professor of Mediaeval Latin Literature and Mediaeval History, The Catholic University of America, Washington, D.C.; Editor in Chief, *American Ecclesiastical Review.* **Articles:** Healy, Patrick Joseph; Medieval Latin Literature.

*ZIEGLER, SISTER EUGENIA MARY, CSAC, M.S. in Ed., Ph.D., Teacher of French and Principal, Holy Rosary Academy, Union City, N.J.; Instructor in Education, Queen of Apostles College, Harriman, N.Y. **Article:** Pallottine Sisters of the Catholic Apostolate.

*ZIEGLER, JOHN JAMES, Ph.D., Professor of Philosophy and Chairman of the Department, St. Xavier College, Chicago, Ill. **Article:** Dialectics.

ZIELINSKI, SISTER KAREN, OSF, Director of Communications, Sisters of St. Francis of the Congregation of Our Lady of Lourdes, Sylvania, Ohio **Article:** Franciscan Sisters—Sisters of St. Francis Congregation of Our Lady of Lourdes (OSF).

*ZIELINSKI, REV. ZYGMUNT, Katholic University of Lublin, Poland. **Article:** Poland, The Catholic Church in (1965–2000).

*ZIJL, THEODORE P. VAN, SVD, M.S. in L.S., Ph.D., Professor of European History, Graduate School of Arts and Sciences, University of San Carlos, Cebu City, Cebu Island, Philippine Islands. **Article:** Groote, Gerard.

ZINN, GROVER A., Ph.D., William H. Danforth Professor of Religion and Associate Dean, College of Arts and Sciences, Oberlin College, Oberlin, Ohio. **Articles:** Achard of Saint-Victor; Andrew of Saint-Victor; Hugh of Saint-Victor; Richard of Saint-Victor; Thomas Gallus of Vercelli; Victorine Spirituality.

*ZOEPFL, FRIEDRICH, Dr.Theol., Professor Emeritus of History and the History of Art, Philosophisch-theologische Hochschule, Dillingen, Germany. **Article:** Augsburg.

*ZUBILLAGA, FÉLIX AGUIRRE, SJ, Hist.Eccl.D., Editor, *Monumenta Historica Societatis Iesu;* Professor of the Church History of Spanish America, Gregorian University, Rome, Italy. **Articles:** Alegre, Francisco Javier; Arrillaga, Basilio; Carocci, Horacio; Castro, Agustin Pablo; Velasco, Pedro de.

*ZUKOWSKI, ANGELA ANN, M.H.S.H., M.A., D.Min., Associate Professor, Department of Religious Studies, University of Dayton, Dayton, Ohio. **Article:** Eternal Word Television Network (EWTN).

*ZUMKELLER, ADOLAR, OESA, Dr.Theol., Dr.Phil., Prior, Augustinerkloster, Munich, Germany; Associate Editor, *Cassiciacum, Augustinus der Seelsorger,* and *Sankt Augustinus der Lehrer der Gnade;* Head, Augustinus-Institut der deutschen Augustiner, Würzburg, Germany. **Article:** Klupfel, Engelbert.

*ZYKAN, MARIA MAGDALENA, doctoral candidate in history, the history of art, and archeology, University of Vienna, Austria. **Articles:** Ebendorfer, Thomas; Sankt Peter, Abbey of.

*ZYLLA, PAUL JOSEPH, M.A., S.T.D., Vice Chancellor, Diocese of St. Cloud, Minn. **Articles:** Belcourt, George Anthony; St. Cloud, Diocese of.

About This Index

Locators. Locators give the volume number followed by a colon and page numbers (4:157). Further locators in the same volume do not have repeated volume numbers (4:157, 159, 160). Entries for subjects of encyclopedia articles are indicated by boldface locators: **5:26–28**. Subjects of illustrations are indicated by italic locators (6:*524*).

Arrangement. Entries are in word-by-word order. The order of precedence is:

one word

one word followed by a [space] (

one word followed by ,

one word followed by a [space] number

one word followed by a [space] letter

The following example illustrates these sorting principles. Notice that names followed by numerals are sorted in numerical order.

Charles (Archduke), 3:**422**

Charles (Duke of Mayenne), 3:872

Charles, Josephine, 1:158

Charles, Paul-Jean, 12:276

Charles I (Card. of Lorraine, 1524–1574), 8.787

Charles I (Emperor of Austria), 6.642

Charles II (Card. of Lorraine, 1567-1607), 8.788

Charles II (King of England), 3.433

Charles Emmanuel II (Duke of Savoy), 3.433

Charles Martel, 3:466–473

Charles of Valois, 12:*567*

Articles at the beginning of a title (a, an, the, and their foreign equivalents) are disregarded in order arrangement. In the case of papal documents, however, the article is retained for filing purposes, since it is an integral part of the incipit from which the title is derived. Function words (prepositions and conjunctions) at the beginnings of subheadings are disregarded in order arrangement.

Index

A

A cappella style, **1:1**, 2:842, 3:523, 8:471

A posteriori (from what comes afterward), 12:750

A priori (from what comes before), 12:750

Aachen (Germany), **1:1–2**, 3:697, 8:795, 13:91

Aachen, Synods of
First (802), 3:240
Second (816-817)
Aniane Abbey, 1:453
Canon Law, 3:42
works of charity, 3:410–411

Aachen, Diet of (813), 3:373

Aachen, Treaty of (812), 4:370

Aachen Cathedral (Germany), 1:1, 3:697

Aalto, Alvar, 3:670, 697

Aaron (brother of Moses), **1:2–3**, 8:525, 10:6–7, 7

Ab esse ad posse valet illatio (From actual existence, the possibility of existence is validly inferred), 12:754

Aḃa II (Patriarch), 5:5

Abad Casasempere, Amalia, Bl., **1:4**

Abadie, Paul, 3:709

Abandon à la Providence divine, 3:309–310

Abandonment, spiritual, **1:5**

Abba (Father), **1:5–6**, 13:315, 322

'Abbas I (King of Persia), 11:140

'Abbāsids, **1:6–7**
Agapios of Hierapolis, 1:172
Armenia, 1:700
Bukhtīshū' family, 2:677–678
empire, 1:611
Kalām, 8:110

Abbatia nullius diocesis (papal bull, Pius X), 10:437–438

Abbelen, Peter M., **1:7–8**, 354

Abbesses, **1:8**

Abbeville, Claude d', **1:8**, 2:590

Abbey Press, 12:568

Abbeys. *See* Monasteries; Monasticism; *specific abbeys*

Abbo of Fleury, St., **1:8–9**
Adso of Montier-en-der, 1:130
biographer of Edmund the Martyr, 5:86
Canon Law, 3:44, 60
Ramsey Abbey, 11:905
Saint-Benoît-sur-Loire Abbey, 12:539

Abbo of Metz (Bp.), St., **1:9**

Abbot, George (Abp. of Canterbury), 1:467, 12:271

Abbot, Henry, Bl., **1:12**, 5:233, 8:189

Abbots, **1:9–10**
Benedictine Rule, 1:9–10, 3:334
as bishops, 2:422
monasteries, 9:783

Abbots, blessing for, **1:11–12**

Abbots, Canon Law on, **1:10–11**

Abbott, Lyman, **1:12**, *13*

Abbreviatio decreti (Omnebene), 10:591

Abbreviators, **1:12–13**

L'ABC des Simples Gens (Gerson), 3:232, 241

'Abd-al-Bahā (Muslim leader), 2:12–13

'Abdallāh Zāḥir, **1:13**

Abdias of Babylon (Bp.), St., **1:13–14**

Abdinghof Abbey (Westphalia), **1:14**

'Abdīshô IV (Ebedjesu) (Chaldean Patriarch), **1:14**, 807

Abdisho V Khayyāth (Chaldean Patriarch), 3:369

'Abdisho Bar Berīkā (Metropolitan of Nisibis), **1:14**

Abdisho of Kaskar, St., **1:14–15**

Abduction, as impediment to marriage, **1:15**

Abdullah II (King of Jordan), 7:1030, 1032

'Abdulmassih (Patriarch of Syria), 13:707

Abecedario espiritual (Spiritual Alphabet) (Frances of Osuna), 5:872

Abeel, David, 3:499

Abel (Abp. of Reims), 12:36

Abel, Felix-Marie, 4:385, 5:50

Abel, Henry, 1:915

Abel, Leonard (Abp. of Sidon), 3:367

Abelard, Peter, **1:15–19**, *16*
adoptionism, 1:119
Anselm of Laon, 1:18, 498
Arnold of Brescia, 1:719
Bernard of Clairvaux, St., 1:18, 19, 2:308–309, 5:844
biblical catenae, 3:258
Canon Law, 3:45, 47, 60
Celestine I (Pope), St., 3:318
Celestine III (Pope), 3:319
censorship, 3:336
Clarenbaud of Arras, 3:761
contrition, 4:225
descent of Christ into hell, 4:685
dialectics, 4:726
indifferent acts, 5:212
ethics, 5:394
exegetical works, 5:516–517
faith, 5:597, 13:905
knowledge theories, 8:215
Latin literature, 3:601, 9:452
liberal arts, 8:537
logic, 8:749–750
logicism origins, 8:758
number symbolism, 3:673
Robert of Melun, 12:268
Saint-Gildas-de-Rhuys Abbey, 12:548
universals, 14:323
William of Champeaux, 14:738

Abell, Thomas, Bl., **1:19–20**, 5:226, 700, 800

Abenaki people, 9:55, 11:898

Die Abendstunde eines Einsiedlers
(Pestalozzi), 11:170

Abercius (Bp. of Hierapolis), 7:277,
11:351–352

Abercius (Bp. of Hierapolis), epitaph of,
1:20, 785, 12:351

Abercromby, Robert, **1:20–21**, 21, 467

Aberdeen, University of (Scotland),
5:175

Abgar, legends of, **1:21**, 10:706

Abgar IX (King), 1:21, 5:82, 104

Abiding in Christ, **1:21–22**

Abingdon Abbey (England), **1:22**, 5:387

Abington, Thomas (Habington), **1:22**

Abington School District v. Schempp
(1963), 3:666, 667

Abiogenesis. *See* Spontaneous generation

Abjuration, Oath of (1643-1655), 10:501

Abner (Hebrew general), 2:282

Abolionan, Elias (Abp. of Mosul), 2:198

Abolition Movement
  Asbury, Francis, 1:768
  evangelicalism, 1:444
  U.S., 1:156, 2:199–200
  See also Slavery

Abomination of desolation, **1:22–23**, 529

Abondance Monastery (France), **1:23–24**

Abortion, **1:24–31**
  Casti Connubii, 3:214
  Church teaching, 1:25–29
  double effect principle, 4:881–882
  hominisation, 7:64
  John Paul II (Pope), 7:999
  Lejeune, J., 8:464
  O'Boyle, Patrick, 10:521
  Pius XI (Pope), 11:515
  practice, 1:24–25
  pro-choice activism, 1:27
  pro-life activism, 1:25, 26, 33,
    34–35, 34
  soul's origins, 13:356
  Summer of Mercy (KS), 8:116
  Andorra, 1:401
  Argentina, 1:656
  Austria, 1:917
  Belgium, 2:221
  Bolivia, 2:470
  Brazil, 2:599
  Canada, 3:11
  Germany, 6:187
  Ireland, 7:568
  Italy, 7:674
  Portugal, 11:540
  U.S., 12:575, 14:315

Abortion, Canon Law on, **1:31–32**

Abortion, U.S., **1:32–35**

Abrabanel, Isaac (Abravanel), **1:35–36**,
232

Abraham (Patriarch), **1:36–37**, *37*,
10:948
  Abraham Offering up His Son Isaac
    (engraving), 12:*511*
  altars, 1:319
  Bethel, 1:36, 2:346
  Chaldeans, 3:369
  faith of, 8:166
  covenant, 4:326, 327–328
  era, 5:313
  justification by faith, 8:79
  as Muslim, 8:170
  in the Qur'ān, 11:879–880
  The Sacrifice of Isaac (Mantegna),
    10:*949*
  Shechem, 13:71

Abraham (Roswitha of Gandersheim),
12:390

Abraham I (Armenian catholicos), 4:958

Abraham II (Bp. of Arbela), 1:628

Abraham Ardzivean (Armenian
  Catholicos), 1:706

Abraham bar Ḥiya, 2:832

Abraham ben David, 2:831

Abraham ben Esra, 13:418

Abraham ben Isaac, 2:831

Abraham Ecchellensis, **1:37**, 534

Abraham ibn Daoud (Avendauth), 1:938

Abraham of Clermont, St., **1:37–38**

Abraham of Crete, 4:302

Abraham of Ephesus (Bp.), St., **1:38**

Abraham of Kashkar, 1:806

Abraham of Sancta Clara, **1:38–39**, 913

Abraham the Simple, St., **1:39**

Abraham's bosom, 1:*39*, **39–40**
  Divine judgment, 8:32
  Lazarus the Poor Man, 8:421
  sheol, 13:37, 79

Abramovitz, Max, 3:675, 716, 717

Abraxas, **1:40**

Abrunculus of Trier, St., **1:40**

Absalom (son of King David), 4:537,
8:1

Absalom and Achitophel (Dryden),
10:494

Absalon of Lund (Abp.), **1:40**, 4:665,
8:187

Absence of God. *See* Atheism

The Absolute, **1:40–44**
  atheism, 1:823
  conceived as transcendent, 14:142
  consciousness and nature, 14:146

contradiction, 4:223
  Günther, Anton, 14:204
  Schelling, Friedrich Wilhelm Joseph
    von, 12:733, 734

"Absolute becoming," 13:580

Absolute ego, 4:369

Absolute futures, 9:770

Absolute historicism, 4:372–374

Absolute identity, 6:705–706

Absolute perfection, 11:117

Absolute presence, 13:562

Absolute sovereignty, 6:376

Absolute ubication, 13:562

Absolution, 7:436–437

Absolutism, **1:44**
  democracy, 4:639, 640
  Germany, 6:182
  Louis XIV, 5:851
  Protestant Reformation, 3:637
  totalitarianism, 3:642

Abstinence. *See* Fast and abstinence

Abstraction, **1:44–48**
  Aquinas, 12:820
  Aristotle, 1:45, 683, 13:408
  Berkeley, George, 2:299
  categories of being, 3:257
  causality, 1:46, 3:308
  cogitative power, 3:823
  cybernetics, 4:453
  distinction, 4:779
  form, 5:805–806
  illumination, 7:320
  matter, 9:343–344
  metaphysics, 9:550
  sense knowledge, 8:208

Abstrahentium non est mendacium (The
  work of abstracting is not a lie),
  12:754

Absurdity, **1:48–49**, 4:25, 5:546

Abt-Herwegen Institute, 13:110

Abū ʿAlī al-Jubbāʾī, 1:781

Abu Bishr Matta ibn-Yunus, 1:671–672

Abu Ḥalim. *See* Elias III (Patriarch)

Abū ʾl-Barakāt, **1:49**, 4:254, 255,
  12:809–810

Abū Muslim (Iranian propagandist), 1:6

Abubacer. *See* Ibn-Ṭufail, Abū-Bakr

Abū-Bakr Ibn-Tufail, 1:673, 940

Abundius of Como (Bp.), St., **1:49**

Abyssinia, 3:790

Acacian Schism, **1:49–50**
  Anastasius I (Byzantine Emperor),
    1:50, 386, 387, 3:595, 5:667
  Anastasius II (Pope), 1:50, 387,
    3:595

Dionysius of Corinth, 4:756

diptychs, 4:759

Elias (Patriarch of Jerusalem), 5:155

Ennodius, Magnus Felix, 5:264

Epiphanius (Patriarch of Constantinople), 5:291

Gelasian Letter, 6:119

Justin I, 8:92

Justinian I, 8:96

named for Acacius (Patriarch of Constantinople), 5:23

Acacius (Assyrian Catholicos), 1:806

Acacius (Patriarch of Constantinople)

Basiliscus, 2:149

condemnation, 7:111

Felix III (Pope), St., 4:186

Simplicius (Pope), St., 13:140

See also Acacian Schism

Acacius of Beroea (Bp.), **1:50**, 4:466

Acacius of Caesarea, **1:50–51**

Arianism, 1:663, 12:692

Council of Sardica, 12:692

Cyril of Jerusalem, 4:470, 471

School of Caesarea, 2:846

Academia Pontaniana, 13:17

Academic freedom, 1:51, 51–54, **51–57**, 5:911, 942

Académie Française, 12:239

Academy of American Franciscan History (Washington, DC), 5:648

Academy of Catholic Hispanic Theologians of the United States (ACHTUS), 5:204

Academy of Sacred Liturgy, 12:790

Academy of St. Thomas Aquinas (Italy), 12:671

Acadians

Georgia (U.S.), 6:150

Louisiana, 8:809, 813

Maine resettlement, 9:56

political consciousness, 3:9

Acarie, Barbé. *See* Marie de l'Incarnation, Bl.

Acaxees Jesuit Mission (Mexico), 9:708–709

Acca of Hexham, St., **1:57**

Acceptants, **1:57**

Accessus, **1:57**

Acciaioli, Angelo (Card.), 1:58

Acciaioli, Donato, 1:659

Acciaioli, Filippo, 1:58–59, 3:791

Acciaioli, Niccolò, 1:58, *58*

Acciaioli family, **1:57–59**

Accident, **1:59–65**

abstraction, 1:47

action and passion, 1:61, 77

action at a distance, 1:80

Aristotle, 1:59–60, 61, 63, 682, 683, 9:347

being, 2:206

categories of being, 1:59–60, 3:256

demonstration, 4:652

dialectics, 4:723

Eucharist, 1:60, 64–65

predicability, 11:660

relation, 12:41

substance vs., 13:575–576

Accidental perfection (philosophy), 11:117

Accolti, Benedetto (Card.), **1:66**, 4:401

Accolti, Leonardo, 4:401

Accolti, Michael, **1:65**, 12:646

Accolti, Pietro (Card.), **1:65–66**

The Accord between Religion and Philosophy (Averroës), 1:622

Accuracy in measurement, 9:410

Accusation, **1:66**

Acedia, **1:66–67**, 3:399, 14:473

Acerba animi (encyclical, Pius XI), 12:408

Acerbo nimis (encyclical, Pius X), 4:94, 11:390, 391

Achaemenid Dynasty, 11:135–136

Achard (Aichardus), Bl., **1:67**, 5:29

Achard of Saint-Victor, **1:67–68**

Acharius of Noyon (Bp.), St., **1:68**

Achéry, Jean Luc d', 4:492

Achillini, Alexander, 1:676, 834, 937

Achior (biblical figure), 1:191

Achitopel (biblical figure), 8:15–16

Acisclus (3rd. c. martyr), 4:261

Ackerman, Richard Henry (Bp. of Covington), 4:331

Acolyte (periodical), 10:410

Acolytes, **1:68–69**, 7:37, 10:639

Aconcio, Giacomo, 9:565

Acosta, Gabriel (Uriel), **1:69–70**

Acosta, José de, **1:70**

Acquaderni, Giovanni, 7:673

Acquapendente, Fabrizio d', 3:418

Acquaviva, Claudius, **1:71–72**

congruism, 4:121

Henríquez, Enrique, 6:735

Jesuits, 4:311, 12:401

Persons, Robert, 11:157

prayer, 7:309

preaching, 11:621

Salas, Juan de, 12:612

scholasticism, 12:766

Thomism, 14:49

Acquaviva, Giulio (Card.), 1:70

Acquaviva, Ottavio (the Elder) (Card.), 1:70–71, *71*

Acquaviva, Ottavio (the Younger) (Card.), 1:71

Acquaviva, Rudolf, Bl., 7:406, 784, 12:401

Acquaviva, Trojano (Card.), 1:71

Acquaviva family, **1:70–71**

Acquired Immune Deficiency Syndrome. *See* AIDS

Acre (Palestine), 4:401, 411

Acropolites, Georgius, 2:787, 800, 826

Acrostics, **1:72–73**

alphabetic psalms, 1:305–306

Byzantine influence on hymns, 7:253

fish as eucharistic symbol, 5:747, 7:277

Act, **1:73–75**

Aristotelianism, 1:678, 682

aseity, 1:779

causality, 3:307

created actuation by uncreated act, 4:335–336

Thomistic notion, 10:907

See also Human act

Act, first, **1:75**

Act Against Heresy (MA, 1646), 3:647

Act for Establishing Religious Freedom (VA, 1786), 3:641

Act of 1727 (CT), 3:647

Act of Explanation (England, 1665), 1:76

Act of Settlement (Ireland, 1662), **1:75–77**

Act of Six Articles (England, 1539), 8:445

Act of Succession (England, 1534), 5:249, 749, 7:140, 10:498, 499

Act of Treason (England, 1534), 5:749

Act of Uniformity (England, 1559), 5:224, 245, 12:227

Acta Apostolicae Sedis (periodical), 1:77, **77**, 581, 3:55

Acta Archelai (Hegemonius), 6:713

Acta breviora (Diedo), 12:276

Acta Concilioru Oecumenicorum, 12:793

Acta de los Nublados (Nicaragua, 1821), 6:94

Acta Edessena (Eusebius of Caesarea), 1:21

Acta et Decreta Concilii Vaticani (1890), 6:416

Acta et decreta s. conciliorum recentiorum, 12:745

Acta legationis helveticae ab anno 1723 ad annum 1729 (Passionei), 10:930

Acta primorum martyrum sincera (Ruinart), 12:407

Acta Sanctorum (hagiographic work), 6:615, 876, 7:782, 12:56

Acta Sanctorum Hiberniae (Colgan), 5:833

Acta Sanctorum Hiberniae (O'Clery), 10:537

Acta SS. Fructuosi, Augurii et Eulogii (hagiographic work), 6:16

Actian era, 5:311, 312

Action
    causa finalis, 10:27
    motion as, 10:18
    motive, 10:24–26
    Nemesius of Emesa, 10:232
    omission, 10:590–591
    unconscious motive, 10:26–28

L'Action (Blondel), 2:440–441

L'Action (Ollé-Laprune), 10:586

Action and passion, 1:61, 77, **77–80**, 4:73

Action at a distance, 1:80, **80–81**, 834, 4:960

Action Française (A.F.), **1:81–82**
    Bernanos, Georges, 2:303
    Billot, Louis, 1:82, 2:395
    French Revolution, 3:617
    La Tour du Pin, Charles, 8:371
    Maurras, Charles, 9:373
    Pius XI (Pope), 5:856
    Sodalitium pianum, 13:295

Actiones sunt suppositorum (Actions are of the individual), 12:754

Active life, spiritual, **1:83**

Active potency, 11:556

Activism, ecclesiastical, **1:83–84**, 8:549

Acton, Charles Januarius (Card.), **1:84**, 7:528

Acton, John Emerich Edward Dalberg, **1:84–86**, 85, 678, 4:824, 5:252

Actor et reus, 10:642

Acts, notional, **1:86**

Acts and Monuments of These Latter and Perilous Times (Foxe), 9:293–294

Acts of Andreas, 1:559

Acts of Andrew, 1:403

Acts of Martyrs and Saints of the East (Bedjan), 2:198

Acts of Paul (apocryphon), 1:559, 3:31

Acts of Peter, 11:873–874

Acts of Phileas, 1:93

Acts of SS. Carpus, Papylus, and Agathonice, 1:93

Acts of Supremacy (England), 3:638, 4:244, 5:224, 245, 6:740, 12:279
    See also Henry VIII (King of England)

Acts of the Apostles, **1:87–90**
    agape, 1:170
    apostolic councils, 5:22
    Areopagus speech, 1:646
    Ascension of Christ, 1:770
    baptism, 2:57, 59, 60, 61
    Barabbas' work with Paul, 2:85, 102–103
    Bartholomew, Apostle, St., 2:123
    breaking of bread, 2:599
    canonicity, 3:31, 34
    catechesis, 3:228
    catechumenate, 3:249
    Christian (term), 3:528–529, 530
    Christian healing, 6:678
    Christian law, 8:404
    Christian way of life, 3:546
    the Church, 3:575, 578, 590–591
    Church of Christ, 13:439
    communal unity, 13:238
    Confirmation, 4:85, 86
    conscience, 4:143
    covenant, 4:327–328
    creedal statements, 4:350
    Day of the Lord, 4:548
    deacons, 4:550
    diaconia, 4:719
    dietary laws, 4:743
    disciple as term, 4:768–773
    Divine election, 5:146
    Divine judgment, 8:39
    ecclesiastical authority, 1:922–923
    enmity, 5:264
    Galatia, 6:51–52
    Gamaliel I, 6:84
    gates of hell, 6:107
    Gentiles, 6:140
    glorified body, 6:242
    glossolalia, 3:391, 6:249
    Gnosis, 6:254
    God's spirit, 13:426, 427, 428
    Gospel tradition on Passion, 10:921–922
    Hades, 6:604
    Hebrews, 6:698
    heresy, 6:769–770
    Holy Spirit, 7:45
    hours to prayer, 8:610
    house churches, 2:145
    ignorance, sinful, 13:36
    Jesus, 2:72, 8:781
    John the Baptist, St., 2:58
    justification, 8:78
    kerygma, 8:157
    Kingdom of God, 8:174
    lamps and lighting, 8:314
    lay spirituality, 8:413
    lectionaries, 8:434–435
    ''Lord'' as term, 8:780–781
    Lord's Day, 8:782
    Lord's Supper, 8:785
    Luke, Evangelist, St., 8:855
    Luke's Gospel, 8:861–865
    Magi, 9:34
    magic, 9:39
    Matthias, St., 9:363
    miracles, 9:663–664
    Nazirites, 10:218
    peace, 11:49
    Pentecost, 11:101, 102
    political authority, 13:248
    praetorium, 11:580
    Precious Blood, 11:641
    pre-Gospel Passion narrative, 10:920
    presbyters, 11:672–673
    ransom, 11:909
    redaction, 10:303–304
    resurrection, 12:149–150
    sacred spaces, 12:501
    Samaritans' conversion, 13:130–131
    saving deeds, 13:439
    Seven Last Words, 13:36
    Sicily, 13:103
    Silas (Silvanus), 13:119
    Simon the Apostle, 13:126
    simony, 13:135
    sin, 8:16, 13:147
    social principle, 13:249
    Son of David, 13:310
    Son of Man, 13:317
    soul, 13:336
    spirit, 13:424, 425
    Stephen, Protomartyr, St., 13:509–511
    union with Christ, 13:438
    women, 14:831
    works of charity, 3:401–402

Acts of the Apostles (Tye), 14:252

Acts of the English Martyrs (Pollen), 14:67

Acts of the Martyrs (Eusebius of Caesarea), 12:606

Acts of the Martyrs (official court records), **1:90–94**

Acts of the Scillitan Martyrs (180), 1:93, 8:362

Acts of Thomas, 5:82

Acts of Uniformity (England, 1549-60), 10:418, 11:958, **14:300–301**

    Book of Common Prayer, 2:524

    Convocation, 4:244

    Coverdale, Miles, 4:331

Actu exercito (obliquely), 12:750

Actu signato (directly), 12:750

Actual grace, 6:397–398

Actual idealism, 6:139

Actus Beati Francisci et Sociorum Ejus, 5:736–737

Actus est prior potentia (Act is prior to potency), 12:754

Actus limitatur per potentiam (Act is limited through potency), 12:754

Actus pontificum Cantuariensis ecclesiae (Gervase of Canterbury), 6:193

Acuña, Cristóbal de, **1:94–95**

Ad abolendam (papal decree, Lucius III), 1:231, 3:86–87, 7:488

Ad adolescentes, de legendis libris Gentilium (St. Basil), 2:136

Ad aegrocerotem Emserianum M. Lutheri additio (Luther), 5:200

Ad apostolorum principis (encyclical, Pius XII), 1:823, 3:502

Ad Armenos (St. Germanus I), 6:170

Ad beatissimi Apostolorum (encyclical, Benedict XV), 7:504

Ad bestias, **1:95**

Ad Caeli Reginam (encyclical, Pius XII), 11:399

Ad Catholici sacredotii (encyclical, Pius XI), 11:393

Ad conditorem cartonum (Richard of Conington), 12:232

Ad decorem (papal bull, Benedict XII), 3:68

Ad decorum militantis Ecclesiae (papal bull, Sixtus IV), 14:396, 420

Ad Deum vadit (Gerson), 6:190

Ad Diognetum, 1:587

Ad Duas Lauras Cemetery (Rome), 3:224

Ad Ecclesiam (Salvian of Marseilles), 12:633

Ad Elipandum epistulae (Beatus of Liébana), 2:182

Ad extirpanda (papal decree, Innocent IV), 7:488

Ad extremas orientis plagas (papal letter, Leo XIII), 9:681

Ad gentes (*Decree on Church's Missionary Activity*) (Vatican Council II), 3:252–253, 5:480, 741, 14:309

Ad gentes divinitus (treatise, Paul VI), 9:684–685

Ad hoc usque tempus (*motu proprio,* Paul VI), 3:106

''Ad liberandam'' (Innocent III), 4:409

Ad limina visits, **1:95**

    Counter Reformation, 3:611

    John Paul II (Pope), 7:1005

    medieval origins, 3:603

    Pius XI, 10:848

    Sixtus V (Pope), 13:198

Ad lucem, 8:564

Ad Majorem Dei Gloriam, **1:95–96**

Ad martyres (Tertullian), 4:83

Ad Miltonern responsio (Salmasius), 12:620

Ad Monimum (Fulgentius of Ruspe), 6:24

Ad nostrum qui desideranter (papal decree, Clement V), 2:205

Ad pastoralis dignitatis fastigium (papal brief, Benedict XIV), 1:307, 308

Ad perennis vitae fontem, **1:96–97**

Ad Petri cathedram (encyclical, John XXIII), 7:936

Ad purpuratorum (*motu proprio,* Paul VI), 3:106

Ad reclusos et simplices (Hincmar of Reims), 6:838

Ad regias agni dapes (hymn), **1:97**

Ad sanctam beati petri sedem (papal bull, Alexander VII), **1:97**, 893, 7:717

Ad Theodorum lapsum (St. John Chrysostom), 7:948

Ad Thrasamundum regem (Fulgentius of Ruspe), 6:24

Ad tuendam fidem (To Protect the Faith) (*motu proprio,* John Paul II), **1:97–98**, 3:58

Ad uxorem (Tertullian), 13:836

Ad videndum an sermones Peripateticorum fuerini demonstrativi (Nicholas of Autrecourt), 10:370

Ad Vitellionem (Kepler), 8:155

Adagia (Erasmus), 12:123

Adalar, St., **1:98**

Adalard (Viscount of Flanders), 1:845

Adalard, St., **1:98–99**, 4:280, 6:162

Adalard II (Abbot of Saint-Trond), 12:587

Adalbald of Ostrevand, St., **1:99**, 5:450

Adalbero (Bp. of Laon), 9:450

Adalbero I of Metz (Bp.), 1:99

Adalbero II of Metz (Bp.), 1:100

Adalbero of Augsburg (Bp.), Bl., **1:99**, 8:303

Adalbero of Metz, **1:99–100**

Adalbero of Reims, 1:130

Adalbero of Würzburg (Bp.), St., **1:100**

Adalbert (Antipope). *See* Albert (Adalbert) (Antipope)

Adalbert I of Metz (Bp.), 12:587

Adalbert II de Medell, 4:775

Adalbert of Bremen (Abp.), **1:100**

Adalbert of Prague (Bp.), St., **1:100–102**, *101*

    Anastasius, St., 1:385

    Gaudentius of Gniezno, St., 6:110

    Géza, 7:209

    Otto III, 10:714, 720

    reform, 4:479

Adalbert of Zollern, 1:312

Adalbert the Deacon, St., **1:102**, 5:106

Adaldag, St., **1:102**, 4:663

Adalgar of Bremen, St., **1:102–103**, 10:719, 12:105

Adalgis of Novara, St., **1:103**

Adalgott, SS., **1:103**

Adalgott I, St., 1:103, 4:775

Adalgott II (Bp. of Chur), St., 1:103

Adam (biblical figure), **1:103–107**

    concupiscence, 4:68–69

    Council of Trent, 10:663

    elevation, 5:149, 150

    gifts, 11:687

    iconography, 13:*21, 141*

    infused knowledge, 8:207

    justification, 8:78–79

    Leo I (Pope), St., 8:477

    Manichaeism, 9:112

    original sin, 9:93–94, 10:665–667, 668–669, 670

    parallel with Christ, 10:100

    sins, 8:871, 9:87

    terms for man, 13:316

    theology, 2:20

Adam (disciple of Abelard), 1:19

Adam, Balien. *See* Salimbene (Franciscan chronicler)

Adam, Karl, **1:107**, 5:37, 6:185

Adam, Louis-Armand-Joseph, 12:276

Adam, Master, 3:52

Adam and Eve (Masaccio), 13:*813*

Adam and Eve (Morris), 5:*483*

Adam and Eve in Paradise (13th c. painting), 10:*665*

Adam Bouchermefort. *See* Adam of Buckfield

Adam Easton (Card.), **1:107**

Adam Marsh, **1:107**, 108, 12:233

Adam of Balsham, 8:750

Adam of Bremen, 1:462

Adam of Buckfield, **1:108**, 110, 225, 935, 12:760

Adam of Ebrach, Bl., **1:108**

Adam of Orleton, **1:108–109**

Adam of Perseigne, **1:109**, 3:749, 9:454

Adam of Saint-Victor, **1:109–110**, 3:601, 7:249, 9:459, 13:5

Adam Pulchrae Mulieris, **1:110**

Adam Wodham, **1:110**

Adamnan of Iona, St., **1:110–111**, 7:676, 9:441

Adams, Henry Brooks, 1:*111*, **111–112**, 3:694, 8:276

Adams, John (U.S. president), 7:788, 10:169, 484

Adams, John, Bl. (martyr), **1:112**, 5:229

Adams, William, 7:740

Adamson, Robert, 10:238

Adana, Council of (1316), 1:706, 3:733

Adarnase IV (King of Iberia), 6:153

Al-'Adawīyah, Rābi'ah, 7:620

Addai, Chronicle of, 5:82

Addai and Mari, SS., **1:112**, 3:593, 5:4, 5

Addiction, shame of, 13:68

Ad-Din, Nur, 4:404

Addis Ababa Accord (1972), 13:582–583

Addison, Alexander, 3:181

Addison, Joseph, 1:145

Address to the Christian Nobility of the German Nation (Luther), 12:16

Address to the Roman Catholics of the United States of America (Carroll), 3:179

Adela, St., **1:113**

Adelaide of Vilich, St., **1:113**, 7:927

Adelard of Bath, **1:113–114**, 672, 674, 833, 9:453

Adelard of Verona (Bp.), 1:231

Adelelm of Burgos, St., **1:114**

Adelelme, William II (Bp. of Poitiers), 3:329

Adelfia, 3:100

Adelham, Placid, 5:238

Adelheid (Dowager Empress of Germany), 10:714

Adelhelm I, Bl., **1:114**

Adelinus, St. *See* Hadalinus, St.

Adeloga, St. *See* Hadeloga, St.

Adelperga (Lombard princess), 11:36

Adelphius (4th c. Bp.), 2:621

Adelphus of Metz, St., **1:114**

Adelson e Salvini (Bellini), 2:229

Adenulf of Anagni, **1:114–115**

Adeodatus (Deusdedit) II (Pope), **1:115**, 4:719–720, 12:746

Adeodatus (Pope), St. *See* Deusdedit I (Pope), St.

Adequatio rei et intellectus (adequation of the thing and the intellect), 12:750

Adeste Fideles (hymn), **1:115**, 7:254

Adhémar of Chabannes, 9:451

Adinath Temple (India), 7:697

Adinolfo (Abbot), 12:655

Adjutor, St., **1:115**

Adler, Alfred, 4:905

Adler, Mortimer, 5:92, 94, 9:100

Administrators, apostolic, **1:115–116**, 8:42–43

Admonet nos (papal bull, Pius V), 10:247

Admonitio generalis, 3:42, 156, 425

Admonition controversy, 3:197

Admonition to Peace (Luther), 12:17

The Admonitions (Pazzi), 11:47

Admonitions to Young Men on the Profitable Use of Pagan Literature (St. Basil), 6:431

Admont Abbey (Austria), **1:116–117**, *117*, 909–910, 5:220–221

Adnotationes in Novum Testamentum (Valla), 14:377

Ado of Vienne, St., **1:117–118**

   chronicle, 1:462

   Ferrières-en-Gâtinais Abbey (France), 5:695

   hagiography, 3:161

   Solemnity of All Saints, 1:289

Adolf of Essen, 3:192

Adonai, **1:118**

Adonizedek (King of Jerusalem), 7:765

Adoption, in the Bible, **1:118–119**

Adoptionism, **1:119–120**

   Alcuin, Bl., 1:119, 243

   assumptus homo theology, 1:802

   Beatus of Liébana, 2:181–182

   Carolingian reform, 1:123, 3:156, 425, 561, 599

   Charlemagne, 8:480

   Christmas, 3:551

   Claudius of Turin, 3:769

   Córdoba (Spain), 4:262

   described, 10:252

   Elipandus of Toledo, 5:160–161, 9:446

   Felix of Urgel, 9:446

   hypostasis, 7:263, 265

   Jesus Christ, 7:817

   Leidradus, 8:458

   Logos, 8:763

   Tertullian, 3:560

   See also Christology controversies (patristic era)

Adoration, 11:594, 12:85

Adoration and Worship in Spirit and Truth (Cyril of Alexandria, St.), 5:511

Adoration Maria Virgo (Sister). *See* Stollenwerk, Helena (Sister), Bl.

Adoration of the Magi (carving), 9:*35*

Adoration of the Magi (Fredi), 9:*36*

Adorers of the Blood of Christ, 11:643–644

The Adornment of the Spiritual Marriage (Ruysbroeck), 10:118

Adorno, Theodor, 5:914

Adoro Te Devote, **1:120**

Adosinda (Queen of León), 2:182

Adradas Gonzalo, Juan Jesús, Bl., 7:125

Adragna, Antonio Maria, **1:120**

Adraldus of Chartres (Bp.), 12:655

Adret, Solomon ben, 12:140

Adrian (Patriarch of Moscow), 7:53

Adrian, St., **1:120**, 4:719

Adrian, William L. (Bp. of Nashville, TN), 13:823

Adrian I (Pope), 1:*121*, **121–124**

   adoptionism, 1:119, 5:162

   Canon Law, 3:42, 60, 157

   Charlemagne, 1:121–122, 3:422, 425

   Coventry and Lichfield See, 4:330

   diaconia, 4:719

   filioque, 1:123, 2:752, 821

   iconoclasm, 1:123, 2:751, 752, 7:282

   nepotism, 10:247

   notaries, 4:757

   papacy development, 10:842

   Spanish bishops, 13:378

   works of charity, 3:411

   writings of Pseudo-Dionysius, 11:801

Adrian II (Pope), **1:124–125**, *125*

   Ado of Vienne, St., 1:117

   Byzantine Church, 1:124, 2:754–755

   Constantinople Council IV, 4:194

   False Decretals, 1:433

   Gauderich of Velletri, 6:110

   Ignatius of Constantinople, 7:310

   Photius, 11:312

   prohibited books, 7:390

   Roman primacy, 3:600

   Slavonic liturgy, 4:370, 475

Adrian III (Pope), St., **1:125**

Adrian IV (Pope), **1:125–127**

   Abondance Monastery, 1:23

   Alexandrine bulls, 1:274

Arnold of Brescia, 1:126, 719

Celestine III (Pope), 3:319

first English pope, 12:532

Gerlach, St., 6:167

Ireland, 7:554, 8:379

Lateran Councils, 12:356

Scandinavia, 5:444

Adrian V (Pope), **1:127–129**, 7:85, 12:233

Adrian VI (Pope), 1:*129*, **129–130**

Charles V (Holy Roman Emperor), 1:129, 3:429

Diet of Nuremberg, 3:482, 483

Knights of Alcántara, 8:189

Louvain University, 8:823

mendicant orders, 8:318

papal and ecclesiastical reform, 4:311

Protestant Reformation, 1:129, 3:609

Adrian of Castello (de Corneto) (Card.), **1:130**

Adrian of Utrecht. *See* Adrian VI (Pope)

Adrianus (5th c. exegete), **1:130**, 5:511

Adso of Montier-en-der, **1:130**, 7:247

Aduarte, Diego Francisco, **1:131**

Adulfus (martyr of Córdoba), 4:261

Adultery, **1:131**

Moechian controversy, 9:759

See also Marriage

Adultery, in the Bible, **1:131–133**

divorce, 13:49

Old Testament condemning, 8:871

sin of lust, 8:875

sin of married women, 13:50

sin of unmarried women, 14:544

Advaita (Nonduality), 6:846, 7:408

Advancement of Learning (Bacon), 2:9–10

The Advantages and Privileges of Religious Life (De utilitate et prerogativis religionis) (Hilton), 6:834

Advent, **1:133–135**, 8:642, 719

Advent Christian Church, 1:135

Adventism. *See* Seventh-Day Adventists

Adventists, **1:135**, 4:541–543, 9:637–638

See also Seventh-Day Adventists

Adversus Arianos (Eustathius of Antioch), 5:456

Adversus haereses (St. Irenaeus), 5:509, 6:112, 256, 773, 7:570

Adversus nationes (Arnobius the Elder), 1:717

Adversus nestorianos (Leontius of Jerusalem), 8:503

Adversus Praxean (Tertullian), 13:837

Adversus simoniacos (Humbert), 6:471

Adversus subintroductas (St. John Chrysostom), 7:948

Advertence, **1:135**

Advertisements, Book of. See Book of Advertisements

Æthelflæd (Lady of the Mercians), **1:148**

Aedesius (4th c. apostle), 6:16

Aegidius, St. *See* Giles, St.

Aegidius Cantoris, 7:64

Aelfgyfu (Queen of England), 14:*769*

Aelfric Grammaticus, **1:136**, 11:632–633

Aelfric of Canterbury (Abp.), St., **1:136–137**

Aelfryth of Crowland, St., **1:137**

Aelius Aristides, 12:308–309

Aelred (Ailred) of Rievaulx, St., **1:137–138**

influence, 3:601

medieval Latin literature works, 9:454

mysticism, 3:749

Rieaulx Abbey, 12:244

Aelward (Abbot of Evesham), 5:486

Aemilian (4th c. martyr), St., 1:139

Aemilian (Bp. of Cyzicus), St., 1:139

Aemilian (Bp. of Nantes), St., 1:139

Aemilian, SS., **1:138–139**

Aemilian of Cogolla, St., 1:139

Aemilian of Lagny, St., 1:139

Aeneas (Bp. of Paris), 4:356, 12:566

Aeneid (Vergil), 1:167–168, 12:307, 14:448

Aenesidemus (Schulze), 12:345

Aenigma fidei (William of Saint-Thierry), 14:753

Aenigma theologicum (Cienfuegos), 3:731

Aeonius of Arles, St., **1:140**

Aeons, in the Bible, **1:139–140**

Aertnys, Jozef, **1:140**, 311

Aeschylus (Greek philosopher), 6:453

Aesculapius, cult of, **1:140–141**

Aesthetic humanism, 7:196–197

Aesthetic monism, 9:811

Aesthetic Papers (Peabody), 14:149

Aesthetica (Baumgarten), 3:679

Aesthetics, **1:141–146**

beauty, 2:186–188

creative imagination, 4:347–349

Croce, Benedetto, 7:300

Kantian doctrine, 8:123

See also Architecture; Art

Aeterna Caeli Gloria (hymn), **1:146**

Aeterna Christi Munera (hymn), **1:146**, 7:243

Aeterna Dei (encyclical, John XXIII), 7:937

Aeterne Rerum Conditor (hymn), **1:147**, 7:243

Aeterne Rex Altissime (hymn), **1:147**

Aeterni patris, **1:147**

See also Aeterni patris (1879) (encyclical, Leo XIII)

Aeterni patris (1621) (papal bull, Gregory XV), 3:91, 5:588

Aeterni patris (1879) (encyclical, Leo XIII), 1:74, 147, 592, 678–679, 3:624, 6:287, 7:503, 9:752, 10:244, 440, 11:301, 14:23

fideism, 5:712

first draft, 8:188

speculative theology, 4:813

Thomism, 8:492, 499, 824, 12:774

Aeterni patris (apostolic letter, Pius IX), 1:147

Aethelhelm (Bp. of Wells), 2:152

Aethelred II (King of England), **1:149–150**

Aethelric of Sussex (Bp.), 5:386

Aethelwig (Abbot of Evesham), 5:486–487

Aethelwulf (Bp. of Carlisle), 3:124

Aetheria (4th c. nun), 4:383–384, 11:344

Aethicus Ister. *See* Virgilius of Salzburg, St.

Aëtius (Arian leader), 5:448

Afanasiev, N., 12:436

Affect theory, 13:68

Affection, 6:7

Affective inclination, 8:206

Affective prayer, 11:599

Affinity, **1:150–152**, 12:7

Affirmative propositions, 11:769

Affirmative theology, 7:1011

Affligem Abbey (Belgium), **1:152**, 7:289

Affre, Denis Auguste (Abp. of Paris), 5:854, 10:883

Affusion, baptism, 2:75–76

Al-Afghāni, Jamāal-al-Dī, 7:613

Afghanistan, **1:152–153**, *154*

Afiarta, Paul, 1:121

AFL (American Federation of Labor), 10:171

Afra, St., **1:153–154**, 12:671

Africa

Anglican-Episcopalian Religious Orders, 12:102

early Latin language use, 8:362

Martyrs of Madura, 9:28

Martyrs of Uganda, SS., 14:263–264

patron saints, 10:974

Africa *(continued)*
  slave trade origins, 13:212–215
  Vandals' rule (429-534), 10:431–432, 14:382
  See also African mission; African Missions, Society of (SMA); Ethiopian (Ge'ez) Catholic Church; Missionaries of Africa; North Africa, early Church in; *specific countries*
Africa (Petrarch), 11:215–216, 12:114, 115
Africa, Council of (419), 3:38
African American Catholic Congregation, 1:161
African Americans, **1:154–162**
  Alabama, 1:201
  Arkansas, 1:692, 693, 8:613, 614
  Atlanta Archdiocese (GA), 1:831
  Baltimore Councils, 2:46
  Baptists, 2:80, 81
  Bowman, Thea, 2:573–574
  Burtsell, Richard Lalor, 2:711
  California, 2:870
  Catholic University of America, 1:160, 3:291
  Charleston (SC), 13:365, 367
  Chicago, 3:479
  Civil Rights Movement, 1:160–161
  Civil War, 1:156–157
  colonial period, 1:155
  Columbus Diocese (OH), 3:868
  confraternities, 1:159
  Congregation of the Sisters of the Holy Family, 7:23
  congregational singing, 4:119
  Duchemin, M. Theresa Maxis, 4:925–927
  Federated Colored Catholics, 5:660
  Friendship House, 6:9–10
  Georgia programs, 2:168
  gospel songs, 6:368
  Illinois, 7:317
  Josephites, 7:1047, 13:405
  Kansas settlement, 8:113
  Kentucky, 8:149
  Knights of Peter Claver, 8:195–196
  laity, 1:159–160
  Little Rock Diocese (AR), 8:613, 614
  liturgy, 7:387, 8:646
  Louisiana, 8:808–816
  Lyke, James Patterson (Abp. of Atlanta), 8:903
  Maryland missions, 8:277
  mission work, 13:405
  Mississippi, 2:397
  music, 7:261–262, 8:709, 13:456–457
  Oblate Sisters, 4:926, 8:812
  Perry, Harold R. (Bp.), 8:815
  Philadelphia (PA), 2:93
  priesthood, 1:158–159, 9:739
  religious orders, 1:157–158
  religious women, 10:157–158
  Savannah Archdiocese (GA), 12:710
  Sisters of the Blessed Sacrament, 2:437
  slavery, 1:155–156, 8:815–816
  spirituals, 7:257–258, 13:456–457
  Washington, DC, 8:134
  What We Have Seen and Heard (pastoral letter), 8:903
  womanist theology, 14:822–823
  Xavier University of Louisiana, 14:879–881
African Church. *See* North Africa, early church in
African Independent Churches, 9:700
African Initiated Churches, 9:700
African Methodist Episcopal Church (U.S.), 4:199–200, 9:562
African Methodist Episcopal Zion Church (U.S.), 4:199–200, 9:562
African mission
  Algeria, 1:285
  Angola (Protestant), 1:450
  Benin, 2:280–281
  Botswana, 2:559
  Burkina Faso, 2:704
  Burundi, 2:712
  Cameroon, 2:913
  Cape of Good Hope, 6:529
  catechumenate, 3:252
  Central African Republic, 3:344
  Chad, 3:359–360
  Congo, 2:219, 11:536
  early Latin language use, 8:362
  Ethiopia, 1:952, 5:400, 401, 7:689–690, 8:742
  French West Africa, 2:118
  Gabon, 6:39, 40
  Gambia, 6:85
  Ghana (Protestant), 6:198
  Guinea, 6:574
  Guinea-Bissau, 6:575–576
  Ivory Coast, 7:681
  Jesuits, 7:784
  Kenya, 1:291, 8:150
  Madagascar, 9:26–27
  Malawi, 9:67
  Mali, 9:76
  Morocco, 13:382–383
  Mozambique, 11:536
  Senegal, 12:905
  Sierra Leone, 11:162, 13:110
  South Africa, 9:700, 11:223, 13:360
  Sudan, 4:1, 2, 13:582, 584
  Swaziland, 13:633
  Tanzania, 13:755–756
  20th century, 3:625
  Zambia, 14:907
  Zimbabwe, 14:926
  See also African Missions, Society of (SMA); Missionaries of Africa
African Missions, Society of (SMA), **1:162**, 3:622, 10:393, 14:98
African Orthodox Church, 9:696
Africanus, Sextus Julius, 6:126, 12:320
Afrikaans Apostolate, 13:360
Afro-Asian Institute (Vienna), 8:232
Afterlife, **1:163–168**
  Divine judgment, 8:28
  Ecclesiastes, 5:35
  Egyptian beliefs, 5:128–129
  Etruscan religious beliefs, 5:409
  nether world, 13:79
  Old Testament, 9:87
  Pharisees, 8:6
  See also Hades; Heaven; Hell
Agabus, St., **1:169**
Agagianian XV, Gregory Peter (Card.), 1:*169*, **169**
Against All Heresies (Syntagma) (St. Hippolytus of Rome), 6:859
Against Apion (Josephus), 7:1049–1050
Against Celsus (Origen), 3:329
Against Hierocles (Eusebius of Caesarea), 5:452
Against Marcellus (Eusebius of Caesarea), 5:452
Against Porphyry (Eusebius of Caesarea), 5:452
Against the Fanatics (Luther), 5:427
Against the Galileans (Julian the Apostate), 8:51
Against the Manichees (Titus of Bostra), 14:93
Against the Robbing and Murderous Hordes of the Peasantry (Luther), 11:53, 12:17
Āgamas (Hindu manuals), 6:848
Agape, **1:169–171**, 8:826
Agape (Charity), St., 1:171
Agape (martyr of Antioch), St., 1:171
Agape, SS., **1:171**
Agape of Terni, St., 1:171
Agape of Thessalonika, St., 1:171

Agapetus I (Pope), St., **1:171–172**, 503, 3:596, 4:186

Agapetus II (Pope), **1:172–173**, 4:450

Agapios of Hierapolis (Bp.), **1:173**

Agapitus, St. *See* Felicissimus, and Agapitus, SS.

Agassiz, Louis, 1:111

Agate, alleged magical properties of, 11:646

Agatha, St., **1:173**, 5:*449*, 13:103

Agathias (Byzantine historian), 2:798

Agatho (Pope), St., **1:173–174**, 4:370, 7:81, 8:478, 11:801, 12:355

Agde, Synod of (*c.* 506), 3:409, 724

Age, Canon Law on, **1:174**, 4:88–89, 7:40

Age, marriage and, **1:174–175**

The Age of Reason (Paine), 5:262, 10:757

The Age of the Gods (Dawson), 4:545

Agennèsia, 1:660

See also Arianism

Agennētos, **1:175**

Agent, **1:175–176**

　accident, 1:61

　action and passion, 1:78

　action at a distance, 1:80–81

　Aristotle, 1:682

　causality, 1:175, 3:297, 302

　condition, 4:73

　God as primary cause, 5:99

　immanence, 7:340

Agent intellect, 7:507

Agere sequitur esse (Acting depends on being), 12:754

Aggression, **1:176**

Agha Khans, 10:402

Agil, St., **1:176**, 5:456

Agility, **1:176–177**, 2:397, 6:689, 10:108

Agiltrude (Lombard Princess), 8:305

Agilulf of Cologne, St., **1:177**

Aglipay, Gregorio, 4:886, 11:254

Aglipayans. *See* Philippine Independent Church

Agnelli, Giuseppe, **1:177**

Agnellus of Pisa, Bl., **1:177–178**

Agnellus of Ravena (Bp.), 11:928–929

Agnes (Holy Roman Empress), 2:181

Agnes, J. (Sister), 12:531

Agnes, St., 1:*178*, **178**

Agnès de Langeac. *See* Galand, Agnès of Jesus, Bl.

Agnès de Lauvens (Veuillot), 14:466

Agnes of Assisi, St., **1:178–179**, 3:760

Agnes of Bohemia, St., **1:179**

Agnes of Montepulciano, St., **1:179**

Agnes of Poitiers, St., **1:179–180**

Agnes of Prague. *See* Agnes of Bohemia, St.

Agnosticism, **1:180–184**, 6:312, 318

　Garrigou-Lagrange, Réginald, 6:102

　Scottish School of Common Sense, 12:840–841

　transcendence, 14:143

Agnus Dei, **1:184–186**, *185*

　cross as symbol, 4:379

　lamb iconography, 8:302

　litany in Mass, 8:602

　Sergius I (Pope), St., 12:328

Agobard of Lyons, St., **1:186**, 3:43, 189, 5:783, 8:905

The Agony in the Garden (Bellini), 7:*803*

Agostini, Zeferino, Bl., **1:186–187**

Agramunt Riera, Juan, Bl., **1:187**, 10:816

Agreement of 1639 (NH), 3:647

Agrestius (monk), 1:333, 5:456

Agricius of Trier, St., **1:187–188**

Agricola (Tacitus), 12:308

Agricola, Alexander, 2:717

Agricola, Gregorius, 12:768

Agricola, Johann, 8:889

Agricola, Julius, 12:308

Agricola, Michael Olavi, 5:732

Agricola, Rodolphus (Roelof Huysman)

　Cano, Melchior, 3:20

　methodology, 9:565

　Renaissance philosophy, 7:190, 12:119, 123

Agricultural Christian Youth (JEC), 5:857

Agricultural syndicates, 8:371

Agrippa, Marcus Vipsanius, 12:299, 304

Agrippa I (King of Judea), **1:188**

Agrippa II (King of Judea), **1:188**, 8:103

Agrippinus (Bp. of Carthage), 3:186, 188

Aguado, Pedro de, **1:188–189**

Agudeza y arte de ingenio (Gracián), 2:115

Agüero, Diego de, 4:288

Aguilar, Nicolás, **1:189**

Aguilar Alemán, Rodrigo, St., **1:189**

Aguilar v. Felton (1986), 3:668

Aguillard, Edwards v. (1987), 3:667

Aguirre, Joseph Saenz d', 12:767

Aguirre, Martín de la Ascención, St., 7:732

Agustín, Antonio (Abp. of Tarragona), **1:189–190**, 4:302

Ahab (King of Israel), 7:640

Aharoni, Y., 2:379

Ahaz (King of Judah), 5:192, 7:641, 9:542–543

Ahern, Barnabas Mary, **1:190**, 5:523, 7:528

Ahikar (Achior), **1:190–191**

Aḥmad, Mīrzā Ghulām, 1:191

Aḥmadiyya Movement, **1:191**

Al-Ahsa'i (Muslim leader), 2:3

Ahsa'i, al-Shaykh Ahmad. *See* Al-Ahsa'i (Muslim leader)

Ahura Mazda and Ahriman (Zoroastrianism spirits), **1:191–192**, 11:143

Ahuras, 4:492

Aiazza, Vespasian, 1:23

Aibara, Leo, Bl., 7:734

Aibara, Romanus, Bl., 7:734

Aiblinger, Johann Caspar, 2:841

Aidan of Lindisfarne, St., **1:192**

　Bede, St., 2:196

　Chad, St., 1:192, 3:359

　conversion in England, 3:598, 10:707

　Honorius of Canterbury, 7:89

AIDS, **1:192–194**

　AIDS quilt, 1:*193*

　Argentina, 1:656

　Benin, 2:280

　Botswana, 2:560

　Zimbabwe, 14:928

Aiguani, Michele, **1:194**, 3:133, 141, 142

Aigulf of Lérins, St., **1:194**

Aikenhead, Mary, **1:194**, *195*, 10:68

Ailbert d'Antoing, 12:292

Ailworth, Mr. (16th c. English martyr), 5:237

Aimeric (Card.), 1:370

Aimeric of Angoulême, 9:449

Aimeric of Piacenza, **1:194–195**

Aimery of Lusignan, 7:774

Aimon of Fleury, 9:448

Ainay Abbey (France), **1:195–196**

Ainsworth Psalter, 11:798

Ain-Traz, Synods of (1835, 1909), **1:195**

Aion of Modena, 10:95

Air Force Academy Chapel (Colorado Springs, CO), 3:716–717

Airvault Monastery (France), **1:196**

Ais-Eiridh na Sean Chánoin Albannaich (The Resurrection of the Ancient Scottish Language) (Macdonald), 9:12

Aistulf (King of the Lombards), 3:124, 563, 13:515–516

See also Lombards

Aix Archdiocese (France), **1:196–197**, *197*

Aix-la-Chapelle, Councils of
adoptionism, 1:119
Confirmation, 4:86–97

Aix-la-Chapelle, Treaty of (1748), 7:671

Akahoshi, Thomas, Bl., 7:733

Akathistos (hymn), **1:197–198**, 2:742, 7:242, 12:348

Akhidjan, Andrew (Patriarch of Antioch), 13:706–707

Akhnaton (Amenhotep IV), **1:198–199**, 810, 3:630

Akiba ben Joseph, 1:94, **199–200**, 8:108

Akidgean, Andrew (Syrian Catholic Patriarch of Antioch), 1:526

Akindynos, Gregorius, 2:763, 826, 827

Akkad. *See* Babylonia

Akkad Dynasty (2360-2180 B.C.), 9:528, 534

Akkadians
Ahikar, 1:190–191
cherubim, 3:467
covenant, 4:324, 325

Akron v. Akron Center for Reproductive Health, 1:33

Akvilonov, Eugene P., 12:435

Alabama, **1:200–203**, 295, 8:778

See also specific dioceses and archdioceses

Alabaster, William, 11:960

Alacoque, Margaret Mary, St., **1:203**
Basilica of the Sacred Heart (France), 10:880
Colombière, St. Claude de la, 1:203, 3:853
Holy Hour, 7:30
private revelations, 12:201, 491, 493, 499

Alain (Émile Auguste Chartier), **1:203–204**

Alais, Edict of (1629), 10:145

Alamanni, Cosmo, **1:204**, 12:766, 14:49

Alamanni people, 13:646–647

Alan de la Roche, Bl., **1:204–205**

Alan of Lille, **1:205–206**
attrition and contrition, 1:842, 4:225–226
Catharism, 3:260
courtly love, 4:320
Eucharist, 1:65
Latin literature, 9:457
preaching, 11:619

Alan of Tewkesbury, **1:206**

Aland, Kurt, 2:70, 363, 367

Alans (nomadic people), **1:206**, 7:223

Alanus Anglicus, **1:206–207**, 3:48

Alaric (King of the Visigoths), 1:631, 859

Alaska, **1:207–211**

See also specific dioceses and archdioceses

Alba, Duke of. *See* Álvarez de Toledo, Fernando (Duke of Alba)

Alban, St., **1:212**, 2:620, 13:93

Albanenses, 3:259

Albani, Alessandro (Card.), 1:212

Albani, Annibale (Card.), 1:212

Albani, Giovanni Francesco (1700-21). *See* Clement XI (Pope)

Albani, Giovanni Francesco (Card., 1700-21). *See* Clement XI (Pope)

Albani, Giovanni Francesco (Card., 1727-1803), 1:212

Albani, Giuseppe (Card.), 1:212

Albani family, **1:212**

Albania, **1:212–218**, *214, 215*

Albanian Orthodox Church
Communism, 1:215, 2:746
Eastern Schism, 1:214
ecclesiastical organization, 1:213

Albanians, 7:649, 9:15–16

Albany, Duke of. *See* Steward, John (Duke of Albany)

Albar of Córdoba, 4:262, 7:246

Albaud (Abbot), 12:546

Albee, Edward, 1:48, 5:544, 546

Albelda Abbey (Spain), **1:218**

Albemarle, Duke of. *See* Monck, George (Duke of Albemarle)

Albensis, Petrinus Belli, 3:52

Albera, Paul, 12:614

Alberca, Nicholas, 4:503

Alberdingk Thijm, Josephus Albertus, **1:218–219**, 10:261

Albergati, Niccolò (Card.), Bl., **1:219**, 3:192

Alberic, St., 3:746, 751

Alberic I of Spoleto, 3:213, 562

Alberic II (self-proclaimed Prince of Rome)
Agapetus II (Pope), 1:172–173
John XI (Pope), 7:925
Leo VII (Pope), 8:484
Marinus II (Pope), 9:168
Stephen VIII (IX) (Pope), 13:521

Alberic of Como (Bp.), 12:655

Alberic of Ostia (Card.), **1:219**

Alberic of Rosate, 1:219–220, **219–220**, 3:48

Alberic of Trois-Fontaines, 1:764

Alberic of Utrecht (Bp.), St., **1:220**

Alberione, Giacomo, 11:357, 12:570

Alberoni, Giulio (Card.), **1:220**, 3:790

Albert (Adalbert) (Antipope), **1:220–221**

Albert (Bp. of Liège), 3:319

Albert (Patriarch of Jerusalem), St., 1:222, *222*, 3:125, 140, 141

Albert, Federico, Bl., **1:221**

Albert I of Riga (Bp.), St., **1:221**, 5:376, 8:375

Albert II of Riga (Abp.), **1:221–222**

Albert V (Duke of Bavaria), 3:327

Albert Behaim, **1:222**

Albert de Morisa, 4:600

Albert of Austria (Card.), 2:50

Albert of Brescia, 14:47

Albert of Pontida, St., **1:222–223**

Albert of Sarteano, Bl., **1:223**

Albert of Saxony, **1:223**, 7:363, 8:750, 12:762

Albert of Trapani, St., **1:223**

Albert of Vercelli (Albert of Avogardo), 3:131

Albert the Great, St., **1:224–228**
Adam of Buckfield, 1:108, 225
alchemy, 1:239
analogy, 1:372
Anointing of the Sick, 1:482
Aquinas, 14:15–16
Arabian philosophy, 1:622, 623, 672
atomism, 1:833, 834
beauty, 2:185
biblical theology, 2:382
biology, 2:401, 12:814
Canon Law, 3:50
Christian philosophy, 3:540
cogitative power, 3:823
communion of saints, 4:36
concept of time, 14:78
conformity, 4:92
contemplation, 4:847–848
David of Dinant, 4:541
division, 4:793
essence and existence, 5:364
exegetical works, 5:517
heretics of Swabian district of Ries, 10:702
hylomorphism, 7:238
Latin Averroism, 1:224, 225, 674, 934, 935
Liber de causis, 8:533
liberal arts, 8:537

Maimonides, 1:673
Mariology, 9:170
music, 10:72
nature, 10:209, 13:618
pantheism, 1:225, 2:629
scholasticism, 12:760
soul, 13:344
state, nature of, 13:253
studies at Cologne, 6:177
transcendentals, 14:150
unicity thesis, 5:817
unity of intellect, 7:511
universals, 14:324
University of Paris, 3:603
venial sin, 13:155
will and willing, 14:722
writings, 12:777
Albertario, Davide, **1:228**
Alberti, Leandro, **1:228**
Alberti, Leon Battista
  Malatesta Temple (Rimini, Italy),
    3:692
  number symbolism, 3:674
  Platonism, 3:700–701
  Renaissance painting, 12:115
  St. Peter's Basilica, 12:578
Alberti, Manuel, 1:650
Albertines, 1:221, 7:685
Albertini, Francesco, 2:674
Albertinus of Fonte Avellana, St., **1:228**,
  5:792
Alberto (Card.) (Portuguese Grand
  Inquisitor), 4:111
Alberto Castellani, **1:228–229**, 486
Albertoni, Lodovica, Bl., 2:325
Albertz, M., 5:521, 812
Albi, Synod of (1254), 3:240
Albi Archdiocese (France), **1:229**
Albigensians, **1:229–231**
  Alberic of Ostia, 1:219
  Albi Archdiocese, 1:229
  Anthony of Padua, St., 1:506
  Church property, 3:727
  Crusade, 1:231, 714, 2:688, 4:377,
    400, 413, 5:220
  Didacus of Azevedo, 4:737
  Fourth Lateran Council, 8:353
  Honorius III (Pope), 7:84
  Lombers, Council of, 8:770
  mysticism, 8:877
  papal Antichrist, 1:517
  suppression methods, 8:295
  transubstantiation, 5:424
  works of charity, 3:413

See also Catharism; Manichaeism
Albigensis, 3:40
Albinus (Aubin) of Angers, St.,
  1:231–232, 431
Albinus, Decimus Clodius Septimus,
  12:304–305, 311
Albinus, St. *See* Witta, St.
Albinus of Albano (Card.), 3:776
Albion (Richard of Wallingford), 12:236
Albius, Thomas. *See* White, Thomas
Albizzi, Rinaldo degli, 9:433
Albo, Joseph, **1:232**, 4:361
Albornoz, Gil Álvarez Carrillo de
  (Card.), **1:232–233**
  Alvaro Pelayo, 1:327
  Avignon papacy, 1:943
  Ciconia, Johannes, 3:731
  Rienzo, Cola di, 3:829
  States of the Church, 14:338
Albrecht, Karl, 7:794
Albrecht of Brandenburg (Card.), **1:233**
  benefices and Luther, 8:879
  financing candidacy, 8:487–488, 879
  Fugger family, 6:20
  Indulgence controversy, 12:14, 15
  as Lutheran, 4:309
Albrecht of Brandenburg-Ansbach (Duke
  of Prussia). *See* Prussia, Albrecht of
  Brandenburg-Ansbach, Duke of
Albrechtsberger, Johann Georg, **1:234**
Albright, Jacob, **1:234**, 5:469, 471–472
Albright, William Foxwell, **1:234–235**
  biblical archaeology, 2:379
  on biblical chroniclers, 3:565, 566
  biblical theology, 2:385
Albs, **1:211–212**, 8:632–633, 635–636
Albuin (Saxon prince), 1:840
Albuin, St. *See* Witta, St.
Albuin of Säben-Brixen (Bp.), St.,
  1:235, 910
Alcalá, University of (Spain), **1:236–237**
Alcalá Polyglot Bible, 2:355
Alcalde Alcalde, Juan, Bl., 7:125
Alcalde Negredo, Pedro María, Bl.,
  7:125
Alcfrith (sub-king of Deira), 4:454
Alchemy, **1:237–239**
  Al-Kindī, 8:171
  Arabic development, 12:810
  Daoist, 4:525
  Middle Ages, 12:809
  Rhazes, 12:210
Alcher of Clairvaux, **1:239–240**
Alciati, Andreas, 3:52
Alcibiades, 4:636

Alciphron, or the Minute Philosopher
  (Berkeley), 2:298
Alcobaça Abbey (Portugal), **1:240**,
  3:750, 827
Alcobendas Church (Madrid), 3:713
Alcober, Juan, 4:732
Alcober Figuera, Juan Tomas, St.,
  1:240–241, 3:498
Alcock, John (Bp. of Rochester), **1:241**,
  12:278
Alcoholics Anonymous (AA),
  1:241–242, 13:239
Alcott, Amos Bronson, 7:301, 14:*148*,
  149
Alcuin, Bl., **1:242–244**
  Adalard, St., 1:98
  adoptionism, 1:119, 243, 5:161
  Alberic of Utrecht, St., 1:220
  Amalarius of Metz, 1:329
  Angilbert of Saint-Riquier, St., 1:432
  Anglo-Saxon origins, 1:449
  Augustinianism, 1:877
  biblical catenae, 3:258
  Carolingian reform, 1:243, 3:156,
    425, 599
  Carolingian Renaissance, 1:98, 243,
    3:153, 159, 166–167, 425
  Cassian, John, 3:207
  catechesis, 3:241
  cathedral and episcopal schools,
    3:263–264
  Clement of Ireland, St., 3:799
  Ecce iam noctis tenuatur umbra, 5:33
  as Einhard's teacher, 5:139
  Ethelbert of York, 5:385
  Ferrières-en-Gâtinais Abbey, 5:695
  filioque, 2:822
  hymns, 7:245–246
  hypostatic union, 7:265
  iconoclasm, 2:733
  Latin literature, 9:444
  liberal arts, 8:537, 10:763
  Libri carolini, 8:557
  Ludger of Münster, 8:851
  preaching, 11:619
  prescholasticism, 12:757
  Solemnity of All Saints, 1:289
  Vulgate Bible, 14:594–595
Alcuin Club, 8:673
Alcuin of York, Bl. *See* Alcuin, Bl.
Alcuin's Supplement, 6:474–475
Aldaz, Tomáas Urdanoz, 7:123
Aldebert and Clement (pseudosaints),
  1:244, 2:496
Aldegundis, St., **1:244**, 6:233

Aldeiamento system (Brazil), **1:244–245**, 394, 2:588

Aldemar, St., **1:245**

Aldemaro, St., 12:679

Alderotti, Taddeo, 7:121

Alderspach Abbey (Germany), 1:108

Aldetrude, St., **1:245**

Aldhelm, St., **1:245–246**
  hymns, 7:145
  Latin literature, 9:442
  Malmesbury Abbey, 5:239, 9:79–80
  Sherborne Abbey, 12:616, 13:80

Aldobrandini, Alessandro, 1:248

Aldobrandini, Baccio (Card.), 1:248

Aldobrandini, Camillo (Borghese), 2:535

Aldobrandini, Giacomo, 1:248

Aldobrandini, Gian Francesco, 1:246, 248

Aldobrandini, Ippolito. See Clement VIII (Pope)

Aldobrandini, Pietro (Card.), 1:246

Aldobrandini, Silvestro, 1:246, 247

Aldobrandini family, **1:246–248**

Aldred of York. See Ealdred (Aldred) (Abp. of York)

Aldric of Le Mans, St., **1:248**, 8:48

Aldric of Sens, St., **1:248**, 5:695

Aldrich, Thomas, 2:638

Alegambe, Philippe, **1:249**

Alegre, Francisco Javier, **1:249**, 3:149

Alejandre (Father), 4:288

Aleksii II (Patriarch of Moscow), 12:430

Alemán, Rodrigo Aguilar, St., 6:545

Alemany, Joseph Sadoc (Abp. of San Francisco), **1:249–250**
  Elder, William Henry, 5:144
  Pious Fund, 2:867
  return of mission properties, 8:789
  San Francisco Archdiocese, 12:250, 646–647
  Scanlan, Lawrence, 12:720
  Sisters of Mercy in California, 12:417

Alembert, Jean LeRond d', 11:543
  Enlightenment, 5:255, 261
  religious encyclopedias, 5:207, 208, 209

Alen, John (Abp. of Dublin), **1:250**

Alencastre, Stephen (Bp.), 6:671

Aleni, Giulio, **1:250**

Aleppian Maronite Order of St. Anthony, 1:534

Aleppo Codex, 2:356–357

Alerding, Herman Joseph (Bp. of Fort Wayne), **1:250–251**

Alert Catholic Men, Program and Training, 10:164

Alès, Adhémar d', **1:251**, 5:365

ALESCO (American Library and Education Service Company), 7:316

Alesky II (Patriarch of Moscow), 10:695

Alessandri, Arturo, 3:487

Alessandrino (Card.). See Pius V (Pope), St.

Alet, Pavillon d' (Card.), 3:786

Alethians. See Shakers

Alexander (Collucianite), 1:527

Alexander (Patriarch of Alexandria), St., **1:266–267**
  Arian controversy, 5:454
  Arius, 1:266, 268, 661, 685
  Byzantine literature, 2:792

Alexander, Archibald, **1:251**

Alexander, Eventius, and Theodulus, SS., cemetery of (Rome), 3:224

Alexander, Samuel, **1:251–252**, 10:827

Alexander I (Emperor of Russia), **1:252–253**
  Knights of Malta, 8:194
  relations with Georgia, 6:156
  Russian Church rule, 12:424

Alexander I (King of Georgia), 6:154

Alexander I (Pope), St., **1:253**

Alexander II (Emperor of Russia), 6:156

Alexander II (King of Scotland), 2:32

Alexander II (Pope), **1:253–254**
  Anno of Cologne, St., 1:472
  Arialdo, St., 1:660
  Clement III (Antipope), 3:777
  Councils of Chalon-Sur-Saône, 3:373
  election, 5:912, 7:83
  Henry II, 2:194
  Muslims, 2:688

Alexander III (Emperor of Russia), 11:446

Alexander III (Pope), **1:254–257**, 255
  adoptionism, 1:119
  Adrian IV (Pope), 1:127
  Anointing of the Sick, 1:482
  Anthelm of Chignin, St., 1:502
  Arnulf of Lisieux, 1:720
  Bartholomew of Exeter, 2:125
  Becket affair, 1:255–256, 947
  Boso, Cardinal, 2:548
  Callistus III (Antipope), 1:254, 2:882
  Canon Law, 3:47, 50
  cardinalate, 3:105
  Celestine III (Pope), 3:319
  Clarendon Constitutions, 3:762
  decretals as form, 4:600, 602, 604

election, 5:925
  Frederick I Barbarossa, 7:43
  Gerhoh of Reichersberg, 6:167
  heresy, 7:487
  Hugh Bonnevaux, 7:149
  Humiliati and Waldenses, 7:204, 11:612
  Irish Church, 7:554–555
  League of Verona, 8:767
  marriage, impediments to, 1:151, 11:717
  papal development under, 10:838
  papal elections, 11:499
  Third Lateran Council, 8:352
  Tusculum regained, 14:249
  Victor IV (Antipope), 14:480–481

Alexander IV (Pope), **1:257**
  Albert Behaim, 1:222
  Church-State relations, 3:636
  Hugh of Saint-Cher, 7:156
  Joannes de Deo, 7:883
  Latin Averroism, 1:935
  Maronite Church, 9:196
  mendicant controversy, 2:481
  mendicant privileges, 14:16
  reign, 12:357
  Salamanca University, 12:610–611
  support granted to Aquinas and Bonaventure, 14:16–17

Alexander V (Antipope), **1:257–259**
  Aix University, 1:197
  Benedict XIII (Antipope), 2:246
  Caracciolo, Landolf, 3:96
  cardinalate, 3:107
  Carmelites, 3:142
  Simon of Cramaud, 13:132
  See also Western Schism (1378-1417)

Alexander V (Pope), 11:361, 14:693

Alexander VI (Pope), **1:259–261**, 260
  Annius, John, 1:472
  attempts to restrain Torquemada during Inquisition, 14:114
  Beheim, Lorenz, 2:206
  Callistus III (Pope), 1:259, 2:881
  Castel Sant'Angelo, 1:261, 3:213
  censorship, 3:336
  Chigi, Agostino, 3:483
  confusion over numbering, 11:502
  election, 8:54, 56
  family, 2:536
  mission and evangelization, 9:680–681
  nepotism, 10:247
  papacy development under, 10:841

patronato of Spain, 10:978

Patronato Real, 1:259, 2:862

pre-Reformation spiritual hunger, 3:606, 607

Renaissance humanism, 12:118

Savonarola, Girolamo, 12:714–715

University of Alcalá, 1:236

works of charity, 3:414

See also Alexandrine bulls

Alexander VII (Pope), **1:261–262**

Abraham Ecchellensis, 1:37

Barbarigo, St. Gregory, 2:89

Bollandists, 2:471

Busenbaum, Hermann, 2:716

Caramuel, Juan Lobkowitz, 3:98

Carthusians, 3:195

Charles of Sezze, St., 3:435

China, 3:514

Cistercians, 3:747, 748

Clement IX (Pope), 3:786

Congregation of Our Lady of Charity of the Refuge, 5:440

Dominicans and moral theology, 2:104

family, 3:484

grace controversy, 7:717

Holy Year, 7:57

Index of Prohibited Books, 7:390

Jansenism condemned, 1:97, 262, 843, 3:786, 816, 12:28–29

papacy development under, 10:843

Piarists, 7:1043

Sylvestrine Benedictines, 2:275

Trappists, 14:161

Alexander VIII (Pope), **1:262**

China, 3:497

Declaration of the French Clergy, 6:77

Gallicanism, 1:262, 3:54, 6:78

rigorism condemned, 12:246

Sylvestrine Benedictines, 2:275

Alexander de Nevo, 3:52

Alexander Jannaeus, 6:664

Alexander Neckham, **1:262–263**, 9:456

Alexander Neville (Abp. of York), **1:263**

Alexander Nevski, **1:263–264**

Alexander of Abonoteichos, **1:264**

Alexander of Aphrodisias

Alfarabi, 1:277

analysis and synthesis, 1:381

atomism, 1:833

Herminus, 1:669

Kindī, 'Abd Al-Masīḥ Al-, 1:621

Latin Averroism, 1:676, 677

unity of intellect, 7:510

Alexander of Auersperg, Antony (Count), 1:914

Alexander of Cappadocia (Bp.), 3:797

Alexander of Comana (Bp.), St., **1:264**

Alexander of Cyprus, 4:383

Alexander of Fiesole, St., **1:264–265**

Alexander of Hales, **1:265–266**

Augustinianism, 1:266, 878

Avicebron, 1:939

beauty, 2:185

Bonaventure, St., 1:265, 2:479

cogitative power, 3:823

eternity, 5:381

faith, 5:587

Franciscan theology, 5:899, 12:285

incommunicability, 7:379

John of La Rochelle, 7:972

scholasticism, 12:760

transcendentals, 14:150

University of Paris, 1:265–266, 3:603

Alexander of Jerusalem, St., **1:266**

Alexander of Juliers (Bp. of Liège), 2:625

Alexander of Jumièges Abbey (Abbot), 8:59

Alexander of Lacu, 1:912

Alexander of St. Elpidio, 1:879, 883

Alexander Polyhistor, 2:329

Alexander Severus. *See* Severus Alexander (Roman Emperor)

Alexander the Great

Aristotle, 1:680

Cilicia, 3:732

epitaph, 1:20

era of, 5:311

leprosy, 8:509

Alexandra (Queen of Judea), 6:664

Alexandre, Noël, **1:267–268**

Alexandreis (Walter of Châtillon), 9:458, 14:626

Alexandria (Egypt), **1:268–270**

art, 1:270

Byzantine Empire, 2:783

Church property, 3:724

homoousios, 4:197

Jewish diaspora, 4:730, 731

library, 1:269

liturgical history, 8:651

Nestorianism, 1:268–269, 523

Alexandria, Church of, 5:136

Alexandria, Council of (362), 5:455

Alexandria, Patriarchate of, **1:271–272**, 4:185, 195–196, 252–253, 5:18

See also specific Patriarchs

Alexandria, School of, **1:272–273**, 5:510–511, 642

Alexander of Jerusalem, St., 1:266

Byzantine literature, 2:791

Byzantine theology, 2:820

Clement of Alexandria, 1:268, 269, 272, 3:797

School of Antioch, 1:269, 272, 524, 8:844

School of Caesarea, 2:845

theocentrism, 1:508

See also Clement of Alexandria, St.

Alexandria, Synods of (362-378)

Apollinarianism, 1:559

Arianism, 1:663, 818

Alexandria Diocese (LA), **1:270–271**

Alexandrian art, 1:270

Alexandrian liturgy, 1:271, **273**

Alexandrine bulls, 1:259, 261, **273–274**, 274

mission and evangelization, 9:680–681

Alexandrine era, 5:312, 313

Alexian Brothers (Beghards), 1:2, **275**, 7:120

Alexipharmacon (Jansen), 7:714

Alexis de Menezes (Abp. of Goa), 4:728–729

Alexius I Comnenus (Byzantine Emperor), **1:275–276**

Crusades, 1:275, 2:738, 787, 4:401, 407

John Italus, 1:276, 2:758, 759

Urban II (Pope), Bl., 2:760

Alexius III Angelos (Byzantine Emperor), 2:787

Alexius the Studite (Patriarch of Constantinople), **1:276**

Alfabeto cristiano (Valdés), 14:368, 369

Alfarabi (Fārābī, al-), **1:276–277**

Algazel, 1:277, 281

Aristotelianism, 1:671, 672

Avicenna, 1:940

emanationism, 5:181–182

existence, 5:533

Liber de causis, 8:533

light symbolism, 3:674

overview, 1:621

pantheism, 10:826

Alfāsi, Isaac, 3:148

Alferius, St., **1:277–278**, 8:268

Alfield, Thomas, Bl., **1:278**, 5:228

Alfieri, Pietro, 2:841, 842

Alfonso I (Duke of Ferrara), 5:372

Alfonso I (King of Aragon), 4:412

Alfonso I (King of Portugal), 1:256, 11:534

Alfonso II (Duke of Ferrara), 5:372

Alfonso II (King of Naples), 1:259

Alfonso II (King of Portugal), 11:534, 12:683

Alfonso III (King of Portugal), 11:534, 12:684

Alfonso V (King of Aragon), 2:881, 3:418, 786

Alfonso VIII (King of Castile), 3:744

Alfonso IX (King of León), 12:610

Alfonso X (King of Castile), 8:401, 12:610, 611

Alfonso de Castro, **1:278**

Alfonso of Burgos (Bp.), 12:529

Alfonso of Cartagena, 1:647

Alfonso the Wise, 1:155

Alfonsus, Bonihominis, **1:278**

Alfonsus of Toledo, 1:883

Alford, Michael, **1:278–279**

Alfred of Sarashel, 1:674

Alfred the Great (King of England), 1:*279*, **279–281**

    Aldhelm, St., 1:246

    catechesis, 3:230

    Christianity in England, 5:240

    Latin literature, 9:455

    Neot, St., 10:244

    palace school, 10:763, 764

    Vikings, 1:279–281, 449, 10:445

Algar (Bp.), 12:558

Algazel (Ghazzālī, al-), **1:281–282**

    Adam of Buckfield, 1:108

    Alfarabi, 1:277, 281

    Aristotelianism, 1:672–673

    Avicenna, 1:281, 622, 940

    overview, 1:622

    sūfīsm, 7:612, 13:614

Alger of Cluny (Algerus Magister). *See* Alger of Liége

Alger of Liége, **1:282–283**, 3:45, 47, 60

Algeria, **1:283–286**, *284, 285,* 7:874

Algorismus (John de Sacrobosco), 7:956

Alhambra. *See* International Order of Alhambra

Ali ('Alī Ibn Abī Tālib), **1:287**, 13:83

Alia, 10:45

Aliaga Turó, Miguel (Father), 5:645

Alien and Sedition Acts (U.S., 1798), 10:169

Alien Enemies Act (U.S., 1798), 10:169

Alien Registration Act (U.S., 1940), 10:172

Alienation (philosophy), 6:711

Alinsky, Saul David, **1:287–288**, 2:872, 13:77

Alipius, St., **1:288**, 888

Aliquot, Marie Jeanne, 7:23

Alison, Archibald, 1:145

Alkindus. *See* Al-Kindī, Abū Yūsuf Ya'qūb Ibn-Isḥāq

All for Jesus (Faber), 5:582

All Saints, Margaret Street Church (London), 3:709

All Saints, Solemnity of, **1:288–290**, 8:*810*

All Souls' Day, **1:290–291**, 11:512

Allamano, Giuseppe, Bl., **1:291**, 4:166

All-American Council (1918-19), 10:682

Allard, Francis, 7:34

Allatae sunt (encyclical, Benedict XIV), 3:817

Allatius, Leo, 6:458

Allegiance, Oath of (England). *See* Oath of Allegiance (England)

Allegory, **1:291–293**

    autos sacramentales, 1:925

    Beowulf, 2:289–290

    bestiaries, 2:342–344

    biblical exegesis, 1:292, 337, 6:792

    Greek philosophers, 6:786–787

    Origen, 10:654–655

    St. John Chrysostom, 7:948

Allegranza, Joseph, **1:293**

Allegri, Gregorio, **1:293**

Alleluia, **1:293–295**

    Amalarius on sequence, 13:2

    Ambrosian chant, 1:341

    Easter Vigil Mass, 5:17

    Lent, 8:470

    sequence tradition, 7:247

Alleluia Tuesday. *See* Shrove Tuesday

Allemagne religieuse (Goyau), 6:378

Allen, Board of Education v. (1968), 3:667

Allen, Edward Patrick (Bp. of Mobile, AL), 1:201, **295**, 9:749

Allen, Ethan, 1:295, 4:617

Allen, Frances Margaret (Sister), **1:295**, 14:454

Allen, Mueller v. (1983), 3:668

Allen, William (Card.), **1:295–296**

    archpriest controversy, 1:642

    Bristow, Richard, 2:619

    Elizabeth I, 5:165

    English College (Douai seminary), 4:879, 880, 5:224, 247

    Gifford, William, 6:210

Allende, Salvador, 3:487

Allgeier, Joseph L., 11:625

Allgemeine Dekrete der Römischen Inquisition aus den Jahren (Pastor), 10:938

Allgemeine Moraltheologie (Schwane), 12:793

L'Alliance (periodical), 12:551

Alliance Internationale Jeanne d'Arc, 12:550–551

Alliance Israélite Universelle, 9:904

L'Alliance Sacerdotale, 3:763

Allio, Donato Felice d', 1:913

Allison, William, 5:238

The All-Knowing God (L'omniscienza di Dio) (Pettazzoni), 11:221

''Allocution to Midwives'' (Pius XII), 1:28

Allocutions, papal, 11:748

Allouez, Claude Jean, **1:296–297**, 3:5, 4:491, 7:317, 14:778

Allowin, St. *See* Bavo, St.

Allport, Gordon, 7:197

Alma Adolphina, 4:498

Alma prophecy, **1:297**

Alma Redemptoris Mater (Marian antiphon), **1:297–298**, 9:449, 10:522

Almagest (Ptolemy), 11:807, 12:805

Almain, Jacques, **1:298**

Almato, Pedro, 14:491

Almeida, Luis d' (Brother), 3:416, 7:737

Alméras, René, 13:172

Almería martyrs, SS., **1:298–299**

Almici, Camillo, **1:299**

Almond, John, St., **1:299–300**, 5:235

Alms and almsgiving

    charity, 3:399

    in Islam, 7:609

    liberality, 8:544

    Roman persecution, 3:402–403

    See also Charity, works of

Alms and almsgiving, in the Bible, **1:300**

Alms and almsgiving, in the Church, **1:300–304**

Almsgiving. *See* Alms and almsgiving; Charity, works of

Alogoi, **1:304**

Alois (Prince of Lichtenstein), 1:914

Alonso, J. M., 10:15

Alonso de Espina, **1:304**

Alonso de Tobes (Bp. of Santa Marta), 3:848

Alopen (Nestorian missionary), 3:489

Aloysius Gonzaga, St., **1:304–305**, 3:563

Aloysius of Udine. *See* Scrosoppi, Luigi, St.

Aloysius Rabatá, Bl., **1:305**

Alpha and Omega, 12:704

Alpha et Omega (Hildebert of Lavardin), 9:459

Alphabet numerology, 10:476

Alphabetic psalms, **1:305–306**

Alphabeticum divini amoris (Nider), 10:386

Alphabetum (Gobat), 6:269

Alphanus of Salerno (Abp.), St., **1:306**
  Constantine the African, 4:184
  hymns of, 7:248
  Latin literature, 9:450

Alphege of Canterbury (Abp.), St., **1:306**
  Aelfric Grammaticus, 1:136
  Dunstan of Canterbury, 4:941
  martyrdom, 3:70
  relics, 5:386

Alphege of Winchester, St., **1:306–307**, 5:387

Alphonsa (Sister), Bl., 7:406

Alphonse of Valdes, 3:215

Alphonsian Academy (Rome), 11:486

Alphonsine Nengapete. *See* Nengapete, Marie-Clémentine Anuarite, Bl.

Alphonsus Liguori, St., 1:*307*, **307–312**
  Amort, Eusebius, 1:311, 363
  Angela of Foligno, Bl., 1:412
  bilocation, 2:397
  Busenbaum, Hermann, 1:310, 2:715–716
  Cafasso, St. Joseph, 2:851
  Caramuel, Juan Lobkowitz, 3:99
  casuistry, 3:221
  congruism, 4:121
  Denis the Carthusian, 4:661
  equiprobabilism, 9:864
  eucharistic devotion, 5:435
  moral theology, development, 14:48, 285
  preaching, 11:622
  probabilism, 14:51
  religious freedom in principle, 5:949
  rule, 12:609
  Sarnelli, Gennaro Maria, 12:694
  scholasticism, 12:766
  sin, proximate occasion, 13:157
  tyrannicide, 14:256
  works of charity, 1:302

Alphonsus of Toledo, 3:96

Alpirsbach Abbey (Germany), **1:312–313**

Alsace de Boussu, Thomas Philippe d' (Abp.), 5:358

Alsace-Lorraine (France), 4:63

Alsted, Johann Heinrich, 12:768

Alt, Albrecht, **1:313**, 2:385

Altamirano, Diego Francisco de, **1:313**

Altaner, Berthold, **1:313–314**, 10:963

Altar cloths, 1:318

Altar in Christian liturgy, 1:314–318, 8:627, 657

Altar of holocausts, 1:319–320

Altar of incense, 1:320

Altar servers, 1:68

Altarpiece of the Four Latin Fathers (Pacher), 10:742

Altars, **1:314–320**, *316, 317,* 11:*143*
  altarpieces, 1:*315, 318*
  ambries, 1:348
  antependia, 1:318, 501
  Bible on, 1:319–320
  church architecture, 3:671, 705, 711, 712, 715
  stripping, 7:54

Altdorf Abbey (France), **1:320–321**

Altdorfer, Erhard, 1:545

Altenburg Abbey (Austria), **1:321**

Altensaig, J., 12:764

Alter, Karl J. (Abp. of Cincinnati), 3:736–737, 6:238

Alternation, in socialization, 13:272, 273

Alternativa, **1:321**

Altertumswissenschaft, 11:274

Althoff, John (Father), 1:208

Altieri, Emilio Bonaventura. *See* Clement X (Pope)

Altieri, Laurentius, 12:770

Altizer, Thomas J. J.
  atheism, 1:825
  death of God theology, 4:585
  deconstructionism, 4:594
  radical theology, 11:890

Altmann of Passau, St., **1:322**
  Canons Regular of St. Augustine, 3:67
  Göttweig Abbey, 6:372
  investiture struggle, 1:909
  Sankt Florian Monastery, 12:668

Alto, St., **1:322**

Altomonte, Bartolomeo, 1:117, 8:303

Altomünster Monastery (Germany), 1:322

Altötting Monastery (Germany), **1:322–323**, 4:137

Alumbrados (illuminati), **1:323**, 325, 629, 3:99
  Ignatius of Loyola suspected as, 7:312
  illuminism, 7:320–321

Spanish reform, 13:392

The Alumni, St. Lawrence College (Roemer), 12:283

Alva, Duke of. *See* Álvarez de Toledo, Fernando (Duke of Alba)

Alva y Astorga, Pedro de, **1:323–324**

Alvarado, Atilano Cruz, St., 6:545

Alvarado, Pedro de, 4:130, 5:175

Alvarado Cardozo, Laura Evangelista, Bl., **1:324**

Álvares, Francis, Bl., 1:951

Álvares, Francisco, **1:324–325**

Álvares, Gaspar, Bl., 1:951

Álvares, Manuel, Bl., 1:951

Alvares Guerreiro, Alphonsus, 3:52

Álvarez, Baltasar, **1:325**

Álvarez, Diego (Bp. of Trani), **1:325–326**

Alvarez, Matheus, Bl., 7:734

Álvarez de Paz, Diego, **1:326**, 7:782

Álvarez de Toledo, Fernando (Duke of Alba), 3:266

Álvarez de Toledo, Juan (Card.), 12:684

Alvarez Mendoza, Julio, St., **1:326**

Álvarez of Córdoba, Bl., **1:326–327**

Alvaro Pelayo (Bp. of Silves), **1:327**, 3:727

Alvarotto, Giacomo, 5:702

Alvarus Pelagii, 3:52

Alvastra Abbey (Sweden), **1:327**

Alvisus of Anchin, 1:396

Always Our Children (pastoral letter), 7:69–70

Alwig of Sulz, 1:312

Alzog, Johann Baptist, **1:328**

Amabilis, St., **1:328**

Amadeus IV (King of Savoy), 4:413

Amadeus IX of Savoy, Bl., **1:328**

Amadeus of Lausanne, St., **1:328–329**

Amakusa Shirō, 7:730

Amaladoss, Michael, 7:405

Amalarius (Bp.), **1:329**
  Agobard of Lyons, St., 1:186
  Alleluia verses, 1:293–294, 13:1–2
  ambos, 1:336
  anointing, 7:35
  Apostles' Creed, 1:577
  dispute with Gottschalk of Orbais, 5:783
  hymns, 7:246
  Latin literature, 9:445
  liturgical gestures, 8:647
  significance, 8:656

Amalasuntha (Queen of Ostrogoths), 1:172

Amalberga, SS., **1:329**, 5:188

Amalfi doors, 4:872–873

Amalorpavadass, D. S., 7:405

Amalric Augerius, **1:329**

Amalric of Bène, 1:225, **330**, 2:629, 10:826, 12:267

Amalricians (heretical group), **1:330**, 2:629, 11:572

Amana Society, **1:330–331**

Amandus, St., **1:331**, 12:532
    Acharius of Noyon, St., 1:68
    evangelization of Belgium, 1:538, 2:216
    Landoald, St., 8:322
    Moissac Abbey, 9:764

Amandus of Worms, St., **1:331**

Amann, Émile, 8:282, 10:253

Amantius of Rodez, St., **1:331–332**

Amarna Letters, 1:477–478

Amasia, 5:87

Amat, Thaddeus (Bp. of Monterey), **1:332**, 2:867, 868, 8:790

Amator, St., 1:332

Amator, SS., **1:332**

Amator of Auxerre (Bp.), St., 1:332, 927

Amator of Lucca, St., 1:332

Amatus of Nusco (Bp.), St., **1:333**

Amatus of Remiremont, St., **1:333**

Amaziah (King of Judah), 7:640

Ambarach, Peter (Mubarach, Benedictus), **1:333–334**

Ambiguity, **1:334**, 5:310, 12:890

Ambition, **1:334**, 9:42

Amboise, Jacques d', 5:847, 7:167

Amboise, Louis d' (Bp. of Albi), 1:229, 3:142, 13:326

Ambos, **1:334–336**, *335, 336*

Ambries (Armaria), **1:347–348**

Ambroise (Father). *See* Gardeil, Ambroise

Ambronay Monastery (France), 2:104

Ambrose, St., **1:337–340**
    Agnes, St., 1:178
    Alipius, St., 1:288
    Ambrosian Rite, 1:342, 343, 344, 346
    Arianism, 1:338, 339
    Assumption of Mary, 1:800
    atonement, 1:837
    Augustine, St., 1:857
    baptism, 2:67
    beatific vision, 2:173
    bestiaries, 2:343
    capital punishment, 3:86
    catechesis, 3:228

catechumenate, 3:251

censorship, 3:336

chastity, 3:444

Christmas, 3:553

Church-State relations, 1:338, 339, 922, 3:633

Cicero, Marcus Tullius, 3:730

communion of saints, 4:35

congregational singing, 4:118

consecrated basilica in Florence, 5:766

Consors Paterni Luminis, 4:167

contraception, 4:220

Council of Aquileia, 3:564

on the cross, 4:384, 385

cult of relics, 12:51, 52

exegetical works, 5:512

Fathers of the Church, 5:642

Gervase and Protase, SS., 6:194

God, friendship with, 6:10

hexaemeron, 6:815

Honorius (Roman Emperor), 7:87

hymnody, 7:243, 252–253

hymns, 1:97, 146, 147, 339, 5:16, 201, 7:243–244, 12:136

importance, 3:594

laity and clergy, 8:282

liturgical history, 8:653

morality, 5:393

penance, 4:25

philosophy, 10:958

preaching, 11:610

property, 11:757, 758

prudence, 11:789

religious habit, 12:99

Satyrus of Milan, 12:705

Sixtus V (Pope), 13:198

sorrows of Mary, 13:327

spiritual direction, 4:760

studies about, 8:268

theology of Church, 3:586

virginity, 12:465

works of charity, 1:338, 3:406

writing style, 8:365

Ambrose of Cahors, St., **1:340**

Ambrose Traversari, Bl., **1:340**, 10:6

Ambrosian Chant, **1:340–342**
    Alleluia, 1:294, 341
    Communion antiphon, 4:32
    Credos, 4:357
    Deus, tuorum militum, 4:700
    hymnology, 7:243–244, 252–253
    Latinization of liturgy, 8:365
    See also Liturgical music

Ambrosian Rite, **1:342–346**
    Agnus Dei, 1:185
    authentic week (Holy Week), 7:56
    history, 8:713–714
    readings in liturgy, 8:437
    sacramentaries, 12:483

Ambrosians, **1:346**

Ambrosiaster (commentary author), **1:346–347**
    bishops, 2:417
    commentary on Pauline Epistles, 5:512
    prophecy, 11:761
    slavery, 13:211

Ambrosius Catharinus (Lancelot Politi), **1:347**

Ambrosius Theodosius. *See* Macrobius

L'Âme de tout apostolat (*The Soul of the Apostolate*) (Chautard), 3:458

Amelii, Petrus (Card.), 3:51

Amelry, Francis, **1:348**

Amen, **1:348–349**, 8:617, 10:45, 46

Amerbach, Veit, **1:349**

America (Jesuit weekly), 8:277, 10:158, 342, 904, 14:73

America (Schaaf), 12:726

América española (Elguero), 5:154

La América un tiempo española, considerada por su aspecto religioso, desde su descubrimiento hasta 1843 (Baluffi), 2:47

American Academy of Religion (AAR), **1:349–350**, 12:259

American Association of University Professors (AAUP), 1:52–53, 54, 55

American Baptist Association, 2:80

American Baptist Convention, 2:80, 81, 8:372

American Benedictine Review, 12:552

American Bible Society, 5:473, 9:638

American Bishops, Meeting of (Baltimore, 1810), 2:43

American Board of Catholic Missions (ABCM), **1:350**, 12:642

American Board of Commissioners for Foreign Missions, 8:46

American Cassinese Congregation (Benedictines), 2:254–255

American Catholic Historical Association, **1:350–351**, 6:566, 13:59

American Catholic Historical Society Archives, 1:637, 640

American Catholic Philosophical Association, 12:777

American Catholic Philosophical Quarterly, 12:777

American Catholic Quarterly Review, 4:260, 8:798

American Catholic Social Action Conference, 9:398

American Catholic Tribune (periodical), 10:570

American Catholic Who's Who, 10:341

American Catholicism (Ellis), 5:170

American Celt (periodical), 12:524

American Center for Oriental Research, 2:379

American Civil Liberties Union, County of Allegheny v. (1989), 3:668

American Civil War (1861-65)

  African American Catholics, 1:156–157

  Alabama, 1:201

  Arkansas, 1:691

  chaplains, 8:303

  Cincinnati Archdiocese, 3:735

  Confederate cause, 8:904

  Confederate chaplain, 13:75–76

  Elder, William Henry, 5:144

  Ewing, Charles, 5:498

  Feehan, Patrick Augustine, 5:662–663

  Ireland, John (Father), 12:572

  Kenrick, Francis Patrick (Abp. of Baltimore), 8:145

  Kenrick, Peter Richard (Abp. of St. Louis, MO), 8:146

  Kentucky, 8:149, 13:405

  Lambert, Louis Aloysius, 8:303

  Louisiana, 8:811–812

  Lutheran synods, 8:886

  Massachusetts, 2:555, 9:307

  Ryan, Abram Joseph, 12:443

  Sisters of Providence, 13:189

  Sisters of the Holy Cross, 7:22

  South Carolina, 13:365–366, *365*

  Tennessee, 13:822

  U.S.-Holy See relations, 3:659

  Valle Crucis Convent (GA), 8:903

  Virginia, 14:542

American College of Louvain (Belgium), 8:169, 449, 13:404

American College of Obstetricians and Gynecologists, Thornburgh v., 1:33–34

American Colonization Society, 8:551

American Council of Christian Churches (ACCC), **1:351**, 5:473

The American Crisis (Paine), 10:757

American Ecclesiastical Review, 6:813, 8:156, 10:68, 12:789, 14:246

American Episcopal Conference (1968), 11:166

American Federation of Catholic Societies, **1:351–352**, 10:56

American Federation of Labor (AFL), 10:171

American Indian Movement, 12:575

American Library and Education Service Company (ALESCO), 7:316

American Lutheran Church (ALC), 5:470, 8:227, 887

American Lutheran-Roman Catholic Church, 12:477

American Missionary Association, 4:116

American Notes (Dickens), 14:149

American Oxford Movement, 5:652

American Party. *See* Know-Nothingism

American philosophy, 11:296–297

American Protective Association (APA), **1:352–353**, 2:868, 7:542, 10:170

  California, 8:791, 12:648

  Knights of Columbus, 8:190

"American Protestant Association" (Brownlee), 10:313

American Protestant Vindicatory (Brownlee, ed.), 10:170

American Psychiatric Association (APA), 7:67, 69

American Revolution (1775-83), 3:176–178, 179, 649–652

  Baptist role, 2:79

  Briand, Joseph, 6:204

  Georgian Catholics, 6:150

  New York, 10:322

  Pennsylvanian Catholics, 11:82

"American Scholar Address" (Emerson), 14:147

American Schools of Oriental Research (ASOR), **1:353**, 2:379

American Sisters of Charity, 13:30

American Society for the Promotion of Temperance. *See* American Temperance Society

American Society of Church History, 8:372, 12:726

American Society of Missiology (ASM), **1:353–354**, 794

American Temperance Society, 13:797

American Temperance Union, 13:799

American transcendentalism, 14:146–147

American Unitarian Association, 4:116

American Visitadines, 8:299

Americanism, **1:354–356**, 3:624

  activism, 1:84

  Brownson, Orestes Augustus, 2:640

  Cahensly, Peter Paul, 1:354, 2:852

  European controversy, 8:135

  heresy, 6:779

  Ireland, John, 12:573

  Leo XIII (Pope), 8:493

  Paulist condemnation, 11:41

  religious liberalism, 8:541

  Spalding, John Lancaster (Bp. of Peoria, IL), 13:403

  Testem benevolentiae, 13:838

Americanism versus Romanism (Chapman), 10:168

Americanization Movement, 8:886, 9:656–657

  See also Americanism; Nationalism

Americans United for Separation of Church and State, **1:356–357**

Americans United for Separation of Church and State v. Reagan, 10:486

The Americas: A Quarterly Review of Inter-American Cultural History, 14:70

America's Forgotten Priests (Fichter), 5:709

Ames, William, 3:646, 12:768

Les Âmes confiantes (Schrijvers), 12:787

Amesha Spenta (Persian deity), **1:357**, 11:143

Amethyst, alleged magical properties of, 11:646

Amette, Léon Adolphe (Card.), **1:357**

Amfiteatrov, Antonius, 12:434

Amias (Anne), Robert, Bl., 5:230

Amias, John, Bl., **1:358**, 4:733

Amices, **1:358**, 8:633, 635–636

Amici mei (St. Catherine de' Ricci), 3:267

Amicizia Cattolica, 8:327

Amicizia Cristiana, 8:327

Amico, Francesco, **1:358**

Amidism, **1:358**

Amiens (France), **1:359**

Amiens Cathedral (France), 1:359, 544, 3:601, 696, 697

El Amigo del puebla (weekly), 10:706

Amiot, Jean Joseph Marie, **1:359–360**

Amiran, R., 2:379

Amish churches, 1:*360*, **360–361**, 369, 3:663

Amistad (slave mutiny), 4:116

Amity Foundation (China), 3:504

Ammaestramenti degli antichi (Bartholomew of San Concordio), 2:126

Amman, Jacob, 1:360

Amman, Johan Konrad, 3:418

Ammanati de' Piccolomini, Jacopo (Card.), **1:361**, 11:321

Ammianus, Marcellinus, **1:361–362**, 3:725, 5:293, 7:223, 12:319

Ammon (3rd c. Cenobite), 4:686

Ammonas (Bp. of Oxyrhynchus), 9:788

Ammonius (Nitrian monk), 4:465

Ammonius Hermeae, 1:670

Ammonius of Alexandria, 2:796

Ammonius Saccas, 1:268, 381

Amon (Egyptian deity), **1:362**

Amon (King of Judah), 7:642

El Amor Brujo (Falla), 5:612

Amor de Dios (charity) (Mexico), 3:415

Amor poenitens (Neercassel), 10:230

Amoraim, 13:746

Amoris officio (apostolic letter, Paul VI), 11:481

Amorós Hernández, José María, 2:92

Amorosa visione (Boccaccio), 2:448

Amorrites, **1:362–363**, 13:71

Amort, Eusebius, 1:187, 311, 363, **363**

Amos, Book of, **1:363–365**
  covenant, 4:327
  Day of the Lord, 4:547–548
  eschatology, 5:334
  God's spirit, 13:426
  justice of men, 8:73
  Lord as honorific title, 8:780
  serpent as symbol, 13:19
  sin, 13:143
  slavery, 13:206

Ampère, André Marie, 1:80

Amphibology. See Equivocation (Logic)

Amphilochius of Iconium, St., **1:365**, 11:610

Ampleforth Abbey (England), **1:365–366**

Amplissima collectio (Mansi), 6:876

Ampullae, **1:366**

Amsdorf, Nikolaus von, **1:366**, 5:754, 6:253, 8:889

Amulo, 5:783

Amyot, Jacques (Bp. of Auxerre), **1:366–367**, *367*

Amyraut, Moïse, **1:367**, 4:494

An liceat sacerdotibus inire matrimonium (Ulric of Augsburg), 3:326

An Linghua, Mary, St., 1:367

Anabaptists, **1:368–370**
  anarchism, 1:384
  apocalyptic movements, 1:548
  apostolici, 1:594
  Brethren, 2:606, 3:721
  Brothers and Sisters of the Free Spirit, 2:629
  Capito, Wolfgang, 3:89

Cassander, George, 3:204
  Church-State relations, 3:637
  confessions of faith, 4:80–81
  Grebel, Conrad, 6:426
  heresy, 6:776
  Hubmaier, Balthasar, 7:145
  Hutter, Jakob, 7:233–234
  infant baptism, 2:69
  justification, 8:87
  Low Countries, 10:259
  millenarianism, 9:637
  pacifism, 10:746
  Parousia, 1:135
  Protestant Reformation, 12:16
  Radical Reformation, 3:608
  within Lutheranism, 8:889
  See also Hutterites; Mennonite churches

Anabasis (Xenophon), 12:309

Anacephalaeosis, 14:767–768

Anacletus (Pope), St., **1:370**, 3:103, 318, 7:469

Anacletus II (Antipope), 1:219, **370–371**, 720, 4:300, 604

Anaguta people, 1:163, 164

Anahita (East Anatolian deity), 10:87

Anaïs (Mother), 4:293

Analecta Bollandiana (periodical), 13:230

Analecta hymnica (Dreves), 12:246

Analectes de l'Ordre de Prémontré (periodical), 10:891

Analogues, symbols vs., 13:661

Analogy, **1:371–380**
  anthropomorphism, 1:512
  Aristotle, 9:346–347
  Augustine, St., 1:371–372
  Butler, J., theory, 10:338
  ex convenientia distinguished from, 4:230
  God in philosophy, 6:318–319
  Greek philosophy, 1:371, 376, 377
  identity principle, 7:304
  ontological truth, 14:229–230
  origins of doctrine, 10:960–961
  panentheism, 10:821
  Protestant theology, 1:373, 379
  recent thought, 1:373–374
  relation, 12:44
  scholasticism, 1:372–373, 378–379
  similarity, 13:126
  simple apprehension, 1:605
  speculative theology, 13:899–900
  Thomistic doctrine, 1:372, 374–379, 10:908, 909–910

unity and multiplicity opposition, 10:58

Analogy in theology, **1:377–380**

Analogy of being, 4:24

Analogy of faith, **1:380–381**
  doctrine, 4:807
  positive theology, 4:816–817
  speculative theology, 4:818–819

Analysis and synthesis, **1:381–382**, 4:793, 11:948

Analytical philosophy, 4:808–809, 11:297

Anamnesis, **1:382–383**, 5:422, 426

Anaphora of Addai and Mari, 5:422

Anaphora of Basil, 5:422

Anaphora of John Chrysostom, 5:422

Anaphora of St. Mark, 1:273

Anaphoras
  East Syrian liturgy, 5:4, 5
  Ethiopian liturgy, 5:402, 406
  eucharistic liturgy, 5:421, 422

Anarchism, **1:383–385**
  authority, 1:921
  coercion, 6:377
  economic democracy, 4:643

Añasco, Pedro de, 1:649

Anastasia, SS., **1:385**, *386*, 3:555, 572

Anastasis Rotunda (Jerusalem), 1:576, 3:685, 687

Anastasius (Abbot), 12:673

Anastasius (Abp.), St., **1:385–386**

Anastasius (papal representative), 2:750

Anastasius (Patriarch of Constantinople), **1:388**, 7:281

Anastasius, Hartmann, Ven., 7:406

Anastasius I (Byzantine Emperor), **1:386**
  Acacian Schism, 1:50, 386, 387, 3:595, 5:667
  Elias (Patriarch of Jerusalem), 5:155
  Gelasian Letter, 6:119–120
  Monophysitism, 1:386, 523, 7:111
  reign, 12:322
  Severus of Antioch, 13:43

Anastasius I (Patriarch of Antioch), St., **1:388–389**, 8:52

Anastasius I (Pope), St., **1:386–387**, 5:264

Anastasius II (Byzantine Emperor), 4:178, 6:122

Anastasius II (Patriarch of Antioch), St., **1:388–389**, 8:52

Anastasius II (Pope), 1:50, 387, **387**, 3:595

Anastasius III (Pope), 1:140, **387–388**

Anastasius IV (Pope), 1:126, **388**, 3:319

Anastasius Sinaita, St., **1:389**, 2:793

Anastasius the Disciple, 2:750

Anastasius the Librarian, **1:389–390**
> Adrian II (Pope), 1:124
> Constantinople Council IV, 4:194
> *Liber pontificalis*, 8:535
> Nicholas I (Pope), St., 3:600, 10:364

Anath (deity), 14:270–271

Anathemas, **1:390**, 662, 685

Anathemas of Cyril, **1:390–392**

Anatolia, St. *See* Victoria and Anatolia, SS.

Anatolius (Bp. of Emesa), 5:191

Anatolius of Constantinople (Patriarch), 1:392, *392*, 3:363, 365, 4:196

Anatolius of Laodicea, St., **1:392**, 3:570, 4:46, 5:13

Anatomy, 12:806, 817–818

Anatomy of the Body of Christ (Godfrey of Saint-Victor), 6:328

Anawarite Nengapete. *See* Nengapete, Marie-Clémentine Anuarite, Bl.

Anaxagoras (Greek philosopher), **1:392–393**, 6:441, 11:287
> atomism, 1:831, 832
> causality, 3:297, 302
> creator-gods, 6:306–307
> fatalism, 5:638
> final causality, 5:723
> matter, 9:339–340
> physical sciences, 12:801
> soul, 13:332–333, 338
> trial, 3:630–631

Anaximander (Greek philosopher), 6:440
> causality, 3:297
> hylozoism, 7:239
> infinity, 7:456
> physical sciences, 12:801

Anaximenes (Greek philosopher), 6:440–441
> Anaxagoras, 1:392
> atomism, 1:832, 4:958
> causality, 3:297
> hylozoism, 7:239
> matter, 9:339
> physical sciences, 12:800

Anaya, Jacinto, 2:467

Ancel, Charles-Antoine-Nicolas, 12:276

Ancestor worship, **1:394**
> China, 1:394, 3:497, 500, 507, 513–517
> Confucianism, 4:98, 100–101
> cults of the dead, 12:66–67
> fertility and vegetation cults, 5:697–698
> Korea, 8:238

Shintoism, 13:86

Zaire, 9:675

Anchieta, José de, Bl., **1:394–395**, *395*, 2:588, *594*, 7:785

Anchin Abbey (France), **1:395–396**

Anchor symbolism, **1:396**

Anchorage Archdiocese (AK), **1:396–397**

Anchorites, **1:397**, 9:787, 13:557
> Basil, St., opposition to, 2:140
> Culdees as, 4:423
> Liutbirg, St., 8:736
> *See also* Recluses

Ancienne et nouvelle discipline de l'Église touchant les bénéfices et les bénéficiers (Thomassin) (Louis d'Eynac), 14:40

Ancient books, **2:510–515**

Ancient Mystical Order Rosae Crucis (AMORC), 12:382

Ancient Observance, 3:136, 139

Ancient of Days iconography, 14:207

Ancient sees
> Antioch (Asia Minor), 9:193–194
> Bangor (Wales), 2:54
> Bath and Glastonbury (England), 2:152
> Bath and Wells (England), 2:152–153, 3:262
> Canterbury (England), 1:635, 3:70–73, 14:894
> Carlise (England), 3:123–124
> Chester (England), 3:468–469
> Chichester (England), 3:481–482
> Coventry and Lichfield (England), 4:330
> Durham (England), 3:124, 4:951
> Ely (England), 5:179–180
> Exeter (England), 4:317
> Glasgow (Scotland), 3:124
> Hereford (England), 6:768
> Lincoln (England), 8:592
> Llandaff (Wales), 8:738–739
> London (England), 3:70
> Norwich (England), 4:317
> Rochester (England), 3:70
> Saint Asaph (Wales), 12:535–536
> Saint Davids (Wales), 12:543–544
> Salisbury (England), 12:616–618
> Sherborne (England), 12:616–617
> Sirmium (Yugoslavia), 4:475
> Sodor and Man (Isle of Man), 13:297–298
> Winchester (England), 1:22, 3:481, 14:768
> Worcester (England), 14:835

York (England), 3:70, 72, 124, 14:893–894

Ancilla Domini Sisters. *See* Poor Handmaids of Jesus Christ

Ancillae Sacri Cordis Jesu. *See* Handmaids of the Sacred Heart of Jesus

Ancona, March of, 4:136

Ancoratus (Epiphanius of Salamis), 5:292–293

Ancrene Riwle, **1:397–398**, 10:119, 13:128

Ancyra (Galatia), **1:398**

Ancyra (Phrygia), **1:398**

Ancyra, Synods of (273-375), 1:398, 663
> Canon Law, 3:38
> clerical celibacy and marriage, 3:323, 324

Die Andacht zum Heiligsten Herzen Jesu (Noldin), 10:409

Andechs Abbey (Germany), **1:398–399**

Anderledy, Anton, 7:790

Anderson, Carl, 8:192

Anderson, Lars (Laurentius Andreae), **1:399**

Anderson, Peter Augustine, 2:866, 12:646

Anderson, William. *See* Richardson, William, Bl. (d. 1603)

Anderton, Lawrence, **1:399–400**

Anderton, Robert, Bl., **1:399**, 5:229

Anderton, Roger, **1:399–400**

Andlauer, Modeste, St., **1:400**

Andleby, William, Bl., **1:400**, 5:233

Andorra, **1:400–401**, *402*

Andover Newton (theological school), 12:227

Andrade, Antonio de, **1:401–402**

Andrade, James de, Bl., 1:951

Andradius, 3:463

André, Bernard Andreas, **1:402**

André, Yves Marie, 9:75–76

Andrea, Johann Valentin, 12:382, 14:360

Andrea, Miguel de, 1:652

Andrea de Gagliano, 5:921

Andreae, James, 4:60, 78

Andreas Siculus. *See* Barbatia, Andreas de

Andreas Tartagnus, 3:52

Andreas the Presbyter, 3:258

Andreis, Felix de, 14:*525*, 528

Andrés, Juan, 12:770

Andrés de la Madre de Díos, 12:619

Andres Garcia (Father), 12:685

Andrew (Bp. of Iria), 12:683

Andrew, Apostle, St., **1:402–403**
  attributes, 12:600
  Constantinople Church, 4:185
  Greece, 6:424
  shrine, 13:94
Andrew II (King of Hungary), 5:108, 7:210, 13:841–842
Andrew III (King of Hungary), 7:210
Andrew Abellon, Bl., **1:403**
Andrew Caccioli, Bl., **1:403–404**, **2:840**
Andrew de Comitibus, Bl., **1:404**
Andrew Dotti, Bl., **1:404–405**
Andrew Franchi, Bl., **1:405**
Andrew of Antioch, Bl., 1:470
Andrew of Crete (of Jerusalem), St., **1:405**
  Byzantine chant, 2:742, 803
  Eastern Schism, 2:762
  execution of, 7:281
  kanon, 7:242
  Protoevangelium Jacobi, 1:469
Andrew of Fiesole, St., **1:405–406**
Andrew of Longjumeau, **1:406**
Andrew of Peschiera, Bl., **1:406**
Andrew of Rinn, Bl., **1:406**
Andrew of Saint-Victor, **1:406–407**, 5:516
Andrew of Samosata, 1:391
Andrew of Strumi, Bl., **1:407**
Andrew of Wyntoun, 12:533
Andrew the Catechist, Bl., **1:407–408**
Andrewe, Richard, **1:408**
Andrewes, Lancelot (Bp. of Winchester), **1:408–409**, 444, 3:152
Andrews, University of (Scotland), 14:651
Andrieu, Michel, 1:82, **409**, 10:633
Andronicus I Comnenos (Byzantine Emperor), 2:787
Andronicus II Palaeologus (Byzantine Emperor), **1:409**, 2:787, 788, 826
Andronicus III Palaeologus (Byzantine Emperor), **1:409–410**, 2:826
Andronicus IV (Byzantine Emperor), 9:125–126
Andronicus of Rhodes, 1:669, 684, 5:46, 10:605
Andrzejuk, Jan, 11:583
Aneiros, León Federico (Abp. of Buenos Aires), **1:410**
Anekdota, or Secret History (Procopius of Caesarea), 12:320
Anfredus Gonteri, **1:410–411**
Angadrisma, St., 2:188
Angamaly Padiyola (1787), 7:399–400

Ange de Joyeuse. *See* Joyeuse, Henri, Duc de
The Angel Departing from the Family of Tobias (Rembrandt), 14:*96*
Angel of the Lord, **1:411**, 8:780
Angela Maria Truszkowska, Bl., 8:246
Angela of Foligno, Bl., **1:411–413**, 5:892, 894, 898
Angelelli, Enrique, 1:655
Angelica (Mother) (Rita Frances Rizzo), 5:379–380
Angelicals of St. Paul, 14:902
Angelicum (Pontifica Università di S. Tommaso d'Aquino in Urbe) (Rome), 11:487
Angelina, St., **1:413**
Angelina of Marsciano, Bl., **1:413**, 5:876
Angelis, Jeronymo de, Bl., 7:734
Angell, James, 6:24, 25
Angelo Carletti di Chivasso, Bl., **1:413–414**
Angelo of Acri, Bl., **1:414**
Angelo of Arezzo, 1:675, 937
Angelo of Clareno, 5:896
Angelology, **1:414–415**, 3:467
Angelomus (disciple of St. Ansegis of Fontenelle), 1:494
Angels, 1:*415*, **415–425**, *416*, *426*
  Annunciation, 1:476
  Bible, 1:415–418, 422, 425–427
  cherubim, 3:466–467
  concupiscence, 4:67
  devotion to, 1:423–424
  evidence, 13:423
  iconography, 1:424–425
  intellectual ability, 7:508
  intercession, 7:519–520
  nature of, 10:212
  prayer, 11:596
  serpahim, 13:5–6
  sons of God, 13:321–322
  theology, 1:418–422
Angels, Guardian, 1:422, 423–424, **425–427**, *426*
The Angels' Kitchen (Murillo), 10:66
Angels of the churches, 1:418, **427**
''Angels Welcoming the Saved into Heaven'' (Morris), 6:*683*
Angelus, **1:427–428**, 12:29
Angelus (17th c. Irish martyr), 7:581
Angelus Clarenus, **1:428**, 3:762, 5:897, 921
Angelus de Castro, 3:52
Angelus de Clavasio, 3:52
Angelus de Scarpetis, Bl., **1:428**
Angelus Maria Montursius, 13:28

Angelus Silesius, **1:428–429**, 2:115
Anger, **1:429–430**
Anger, in the Bible, **1:430–431**
Angers (France), 1:*431*, 431–432
Angers, Henri Arnauld d' (Card.), 3:786
Anghern, Benedikt Maria (Abbot), 12:671
Anghiera, Pietro Martire d', 12:118
Angilbert of Saint-Riquier, St., **1:432–433**
  Adalard, St., 1:98
  Carolingian Renaissance, 1:98, 432, 3:160, 12:583
Angilramnus of Metz (Bp.), **1:433**
Anglesey Priory (England), **1:433**
Anglica historia (Vergil), 14:449
Anglican Church. *See* Anglicanism
Anglican Communion, **1:433–434**
  communio, 4:30
  Communion by extension, 4:36
  Ecumenical dialogues, 5:67
  Lambeth Conference, 8:306
  liturgical Movement, 8:677
  low church, 8:836
  See also Episcopal Church (U.S.)
Anglican Consultative Council, 8:306
Anglican orders problem, **1:434–439**, 441, 592–594, 8:492
Anglican Reformation, 1:442–444, 3:782
  Bonner, Edmund, 2:507
  Book of Common Prayer, 3:608–609
  Caribbean area, 3:110
  Douai (Douay) University, 1:295–296
  See also Anglicanism; Henry VIII (King of England), divorce of
Anglican-Catholic dialogue
  Anglican orders problem, 1:438–439
  Anglican/Roman Catholic International Commission, 1:440–442
  Caroline Divines, 3:153
  Malines Conversations, 3:625
  United States, 1:439–440
Anglican-Episcopalian Religious Orders, 12:101–103
Anglicanism, **1:442–446**
  Andrewe, Richard, 1:408–409
  Anglican Communion, 1:433–434
  Anglican orders problem, 1:434–439, 441, 592–594
  archdeacons, 1:634
  architecture, 2:112, 3:707, 714
  Athanasian Creed, 1:817
  branch theory of the Church, 2:582–583

Broad Church, 1:444, 2:624–625, 8:370

Caesaropapism, 3:638

Canada, 3:9

Canterbury, 3:72

Caroline divines, 1:409, 444, 3:152–153, 832

Cave, William, 3:312

Charles I (King of England), 3:432

Chile, 3:486

confessions of faith, 4:80

Confirmation, 4:92

Cowley Fathers, 4:332–333

Cranmer, Thomas, 4:333–334

ecclesiastical organization, 1:445–446

heresy, 6:777

High Church, 1:444, 446–447, 3:432, 8:135

Hooker, Richard, 7:90–92

impact on liturgical reforms, 8:360

Lamb of God, 8:30

Lambeth Conferences, 1:440–441, 442, 445, 577, 2:525, 8:305–306

Lambeth Quadilateral, 8:306

Laud, William (Abp. of Canterbury), 8:377–378

Law, W., 8:402–403

Lightfoot, J. B., 8:585

liturgy, comparative, 8:722

Low Church, 1:444, 8:836

Malines conversations, 9:78

Manning, Henry Edward, 9:120

Methodist Movement, 9:557–558, 559, 14:683–684

Morone, Giovanni, on reunificaiton, 9:900

music, 8:691, 697

Nicene Creed, 8:306

ordination of women, 1:435, 439, 441, 447, 7:203

orthodox, 8:377–378

Parish and People Movement, 8:663

Puritans, 11:836–837

Shakespeare, Wm., 13:65

Society for Promoting Christian Knowledge, 13:288

theology, 13:910, 912

U.S. Church-State relations, 3:645–646, 647, 648, 651, 652

women deacons, 4:554

See also Anglican Reformation; Anglican-Catholic dialogue; Book of Common Prayer; High Church; Lambeth Conferences

Anglican-Roman Catholic Consultation in the United States (ARC-USA), **1:439–440**

Anglican-Roman Catholic International Commission (ARCIC), 1:439, **440–442**, 5:40, 67–68, 11:31

Anglican-Roman Catholic International Consultation (ARCIC-II), 8:91

Anglo-Catholics, 1:444, **446–447**

Lingard, J., 8:595–596

Lunn, A., 8:868–869

Lux Mundi (Gore), 8:896

Sergeant, J., 13:11–12

Anglo-Chinese College (Malacca), 3:499

Anglo-Genevan Psalter, 11:798

Anglo-Israelitism, 14:848

Anglorum chronicon (Langdon), 8:325

Anglo-Saxon art, **1:447–448**

Anglo-Saxons, **1:448–449**

anointing, 1:479

Augustine of Canterbury, St., 1:449, 2:621

baptismal names, 10:140

Birinus, St., 2:408–409

Caedwalla, St., 2:843–844

Cedd, St., 3:316

chorbishops, 3:526

development of surnames, 10:142–143

pilgrims in Rome, 11:353

Wessex royal line, 10:446

William I conquest, 10:427

Anglus, Thomas. See White, Thomas

Angola, **1:449–452**, 451

Angoulême Cathedral (France), 1:575, 3:693

An-Guo, Mary, St., 1:367

Angus, Earl of. See Douglas, Archibald (Earl of Angus)

Angusiola, Lucius, 3:328

Ani (Armenian city), **1:453**

Ani, Synods of (969, 1039), 1:453

Anian (Bp. of Bangor, Wales), 2:54

Aniane Abbey (France), **1:453–454**, 12:549

Anianus (Aignan) of Orléans (Bp.), St., **1:454**

Anianus and Marinus, SS., **1:454–455**

Anianus of Chartres, St., **1:454**

Aniceto Adolfo (Brother), 14:247

Anicetus (Pope), St., **1:455**, 4:50

Anima Christi, **1:455**

L'Anima desolata (Sarnelli), 12:694

L'Anima illuminata (Sarnelli), 12:694

Anima mundi. See World soul

Anima naturaliter christiana, **1:455–456**, 489

Animal Farm (Orwell), 1:292

Animal rights, **1:456–457**

Animal symbolism, **1:457–458**, 574

Animals, in the Bible

Bel and the dragon, 2:210

horses, 6:898

serpents, 11:776

tale of the talking ass, 2:26

Animals, patron saint of, 5:31

Animism, **1:458–459**

anthropomorphism, 1:510

hylozoism compared to, 7:239

Korea, 8:238

Laos, 8:331

Lithuania, 8:603

religious significance of blood, 2:443

Slavic religion, 13:215

An-Jiao, Anna, St., 1:367–368

Anjos Beirao, Raimundo dos, Rev., 5:878

Anna, Canticle of, 3:73

Anna Karenina (Tolstoi), 14:106

Anna Komnene (Comnena), 2:774, 800, 804

Annabring, Joseph J. (Bp. of Superior, WI), 14:783

Annalen der Glaubensverbreitung (periodical), 8:853

Annales (Bartholomew of Lucca), 2:126

Annales (Tacitus), 13:729–730

Annales Altahenses (Herman), 10:387

Annales bénédictines, 12:453

Annales Camaldulenses ordinis S. Benedicti (Mittarelli), 9:745

Annales de la philosophie chrétienne (periodical), 8:265

Annales ecclesiastici (Baronius), 2:105, 3:348, 6:875, 9:84, 10:248

Annales ecclesiastici (Baronius and Rinaldi), 5:754, 12:248

Annales franciscaines (periodical), 14:261

Annales necrologici, 10:229

Annales Ordinis Servorum (Giani), 13:29

Annales Parchenses, 10:891

Annales Patherbrunnenses, 1:14

Annales Plantiniennes depuis la fondation de l'imprimerie jusqu'à la mort de Christophe Plantin (Backer, ed.), 2:9

Annales reformationis (Spalatin), 13:401

Annales sex regum Angliae (Nicholas Trevet), 10:381

ANNALES VETERIS ET NOVI TESTAMENTI (USSHER)

Annales Veteris et Novi Testamenti (Ussher), 14:352

Annali d'Italia (Muratori), 10:63

Annals (Nazm al-Jawhar) (Eutychios of Alexandria), 5:463–464

Annals (Tacitus), 3:529

Annals and chronicles, **1:459–466**
  Anselm of Liège, 1:498
  Byzantine, 2:795–796, 801–802
  Carolingian Dynasty, 5:923
  early Christian, 8:58–59

Annals of Donegal. See Four Masters, Annals of the

Annals of Roscrea, 12:378

The Annals of the Four Masters (O'Clery), 10:537

Annates, 1:267, **466–467**, 3:726

Anne (Queen of England), 4:244

Anne and Joachim, SS., **1:468–470**, 9:275–276, 277

Anne of Denmark (Queen of England), 1:21, 467, **467–468**

Anne of Guise, 5:371

Anne of Jagello, 2:153

Anne of Jesus, Ven., **1:468**, 3:128, 136

Anne of St. Bartholomew, Bl., 1:468, **468**, 3:128, 136

Anne of Savoy, 7:918, 919

Annecy Monastery (France), **1:470**

L'Année Liturgique (Guéranger), 6:557, 8:671

Annegray Abbey (Burgundy), 3:864

Annibaldi, Richard (Card.), 1:886

Annibale, Giuseppe d' (Card.), **1:470**

Annihilation, **1:470–472**, 4:161

Annius, John (Nanni), **1:472**

Anno of Cologne, St., **1:472**, 3:843, 7:83, 8:257

Annuario Pontificio, **1:472–473**

Annum sacrum (encyclical, Leo XIII), 8:491, 12:491, 492, 493

Annunciatae of Lombardy, 1:346

Annunciation, **1:473–477**, *474, 475,* 7:49, 9:278–279

The Annunciation (Fra Lippo Lippi), 1:*475*

Annunciation (Sarto), 9:*170*

Annunciation, Feast of the, 1:197, 476–477

Annunciation Congregation, 2:273

Anointing, **1:477–480**, 7:34–35
  See also Anointing of the Sick, Sacrament of

Anointing of the Sick, Liturgy of, 1:482, **484–487**, 710

Anointing of the Sick, Sacrament of, **1:480–484**, 6:678–680
  conditional administration, 12:484–485
  death, 4:576, 583
  liturgy, 1:482, 710, 4:257
  oils used, 7:34, 35
  reviviscence of sacramental power, 12:206

Anomoeans, 1:663

Añon, Miguel de, 5:875

Anonymity/pseudonymity, **1:487–488**

Anonymous Christian, **1:488–489, 9:678**

Anonymous of York, **1:489**, 7:538

Anovulants, **1:489–491**

Ansano, St., 13:106

Ansbald, St., **1:491**

Ansbert, St., **1:491–492**, 926

Anscombe, Gertrude Elizabeth Margaret, **1:492–493**

Anse, Councils of (994-1300), **1:493**, 3:326

Ansebert (Abbot), 5:793

Ansegis of Fontenelle, St., **1:493–494**, 3:42, 5:793

Ansegisus of Saint-Wandrille, 3:90

Anselm (Abp. of Milan), 3:44

Anselm, School of (Laon), 5:516

Anselm II of Lucca (Bp.), St., **1:494–495**
  Arialdo, St., 1:660
  Canon Law, 1:841, 3:45, 60

Anselm of Bury-St.-Edmunds, 2:713

Anselm of Canterbury (Abp.), St., **1:495–497**, 3:72, 5:140
  absolute, 1:41
  Adam, 1:105
  Alexander of Hales, 1:266
  Alphege of Canterbury, St., 1:306
  ars moriendi, 1:728–729
  aseity, 1:779, 780
  Augustine, St., 1:496, 876, 877
  beauty, 2:184
  as Bec Abbey prior, 2:189, 190
  causality, 3:304
  Christian philosophy, 3:539
  dialectics, 4:726
  Eadmer, biographer of, 5:1
  exegetical works, 5:515, 517
  free will, 5:930
  freedom, 5:937
  Gerard of York, 6:163
  Gilbert Crispin, 6:213
  grace, 6:387

Henry I (King of England), 6:736, 10:916
  Holy Name, 7:31
  Ida of Boulogne, 7:289
  Immaculate Conception, 7:333
  influence, 3:601
  knowledge, 8:215
  Lambert of Saint-Bertin, 8:304
  Latin literature, 3:601, 9:452
  mystery of God, 6:283
  necessity of the Incarnation, 7:375
  ontological argument, 10:600–602
  proof of God's existence, 5:715–716
  rationalism, 11:922
  reparation, 12:129
  satisfaction of Christ, 12:700
  scholasticism, 12:758
  spiritual direction, 4:761

Anselm of Como, 1:937

Anselm of Havelberg, 3:413

Anselm of Laon, 1:18, 498, **498**, 12:758

Anselm of Liège, **1:498**

Anselm of Lucca, St., 12:643

Anselm of Nonantola, St., **1:498–499**

Anselmo Dedicata, Collectio, **1:499**

Ansfrid (Bp. of Utrecht), Bl., **1:499**

Ansgar, St., **1:500**, 4:258
  Corvey Abbey, 4:280
  Denmark, 4:662–663
  Rembert of Bremen-Hamburg, 12:105

Anson, Peter, 1:578

Ansonia Council, 8:190

Anstrudis, St., **1:500–501**

Ansuerus, St., **1:501**

Answer to More (Tyndale), 14:254

L'Anté-christ (Renan), 12:126

Antependia, 1:318, **501**

Anterus (Pope), St., **1:501**, 5:584

Anthelm of Belley, St., 3:192

Anthelm of Chignin, St., **1:501–502**, 3:194

Anthelmi, Joseph, **1:502**

Anthemius (prefect of the Orient), **1:502**

Anthemius of Constantia, **1:502**

Anthemius of Poitiers, St., **1:502**

Anthimus (Abp.) (Bulgaria), **1:503**

Anthimus (Bp. of Nicomedia), St., **1:502–503**

Anthimus, St. (hymnographer), **1:503**

Anthimus, St. (priest and martyr), **1:503**

Anthimus I (Patriarch of Constantinople). *See* Anthimus of Trebizond (Patriarch of Constantinople)

168

NEW CATHOLIC ENCYCLOPEDIA

Anthimus II (Patriarch of Constantinople), **1:503**

Anthimus III (Patriarch of Constantinople), **1:503**

Anthimus IV (Patriarch of Constantinople), **1:503**, 4:355

Anthimus V (Patriarch of Constantinople), **1:503**

Anthimus VI (Patriarch of Constantinople), **1:503**, 6:459, 10:701

Anthimus VII (Patriarch of Constantinople), **1:503**, 4:355, 6:459, 10:701

Anthimus of Trebizond (Patriarch of Constantinople), 1:172, 503, **503–504**, 8:97

Anthimus of Tyana (Bp.), **1:503**, 6:514, 13:43

Anthologia Latina, 9:439

Anthony, Bl. (17th c. Japanese martyr) (d. 1622), 7:733

Anthony, St. (17th c. Japanese martyr) (d. 1597), 7:732

Anthony, Susan B., 13:*797*

Anthony I (Patriarch of Constantinople), **1:504**

Anthony II Cauleas (Patriarch of Constantinople), **1:504**, 2:756

Anthony III (Patriarch of Constantinople), **1:504**

Anthony IV (Patriarch of Constantinople), **1:504**

Anthony Bonfadini, Bl., **1:504–505**

Anthony de S. Francisco, Bl., 7:734

Anthony Neyrot, Bl., **1:505**

Anthony of Egypt, St., 1:*505*, **505–506**, *538*, 10:968
  Antonines, 1:534
  Athanasius, 12:606
  burial, 2:699
  as confessor, 4:83
  contemplative life, 4:210
  following of Christ, 5:788
  monasticism, 9:787–788
  relics, 12:535
  Serapion's friend, 13:7

Anthony of Jesus, 3:144

Anthony of Padua, St., **1:506–507**, *507*
  Andrew Caccioli, Bl., 1:404, 2:840
  bilocation, 2:397
  Divine Office, 8:50
  Franciscan spirituality, 5:894–895
  Franciscan theology, 5:898
  Luke Belludi, 8:865

Anthony of Parma, 1:937

Anthony of Stroncone, Bl., **1:507**

Anthony of Tarsus, 1:527

Anthony of the Holy Ghost, **1:507–508**

Anthony of the Mother of God, 4:44

Anthony Pavonius, Bl., **1:508**

Anthropocentrism, **1:508**, 5:48
  anonymous Christian, 1:489
  models of charity, 8:833–834
  theocentrism vs., 13:865

Anthropogenesis, 8:840

Anthropogonic myths, 10:127

Anthropology
  Cooper, John Montgomery, 4:247–248
  culture-historical method in ethnology, 12:744
  Gnosticism, 6:258
  Schmidt, Wilhelm, 12:744
  Theodore (Bp. of Mopsuestia in Cilicia), 13:875
  theology, 13:916
  See also Culture

Anthropology, theological, **1:508–510**
  eschatology, 5:348–349
  feminism, 5:679
  natural law doctrine, 10:194–195
  naturalism, 10:206
  religion in primitive cultures, 12:64–69
  ritual studies, 12:258–260
  Sahagún, Bernardino de, 12:528–529

Anthropomorphism
  Greek and Roman religion, 1:510, 6:451–452, 12:325

Anthropomorphism, in the Bible, **1:511–512**, 8:3

Anthropomorphism, in theology, **1:512**

Anthropos (periodical), 12:744

Anthropos Institute, 4:789, 12:744

Anthroposophy, **1:512–513**, 9:110, 13:507

Anti-Aristotelian philosophy, 2:9–10

Anti-Catholicism. *See* Anti-Catholicism, England; Anti-Catholicism, U.S.; Anti-Catholicism, worldwide; *specific countries*

Anti-Catholicism, England, 5:*246*
  Bodey, John, Bl., 2:452
  Bourne, Gilbert, 2:569
  Carvajal, Luisa de, 3:198
  Challoner, Richard, 3:371
  Clitherow, Bl. Margaret, 3:805–806
  Coleman, Walter, 3:830
  Cromwell, Oliver, 4:375–376
  Cromwell, Thomas, 4:376–377
  Declaration of Rights (1689), 4:590
  Oates Plot, 3:433, 829, 830, 853

overview, 3:609, 612–613
  Persons, Robert, 1:296, 2:611, 618–619, 921
  Royal Declaration, 12:396–397
  See also Anglican Reformation; Catholic Emancipation; England, Scotland, and Wales, Martyrs of

Anti-Catholicism, U.S.
  American Protective Association, 1:352–353, 2:868
  Arkansas, 1:692–693
  Baltimore Council discussions (1833, 1837), 2:44
  Bedini, Gaetano, 2:197
  California, 2:868
  Connecticut, 4:122–124
  Delaware, 4:624–625
  history, 10:169–172
  Kentucky, 13:404
  Maryland, 9:724–725
  Massachusetts, 2:552–553, 554
  Michigan, 9:607
  Milwaukee (WI), 9:646–647
  Ohio, 7:139
  Oregon Territory, 11:529, 530
  Philadelphia (PA), 7:161
  St. Paul (MN), 9:655–656
  Utah, 7:224
  Virginia, 14:540, 543
  See also Know-Nothingism; Nativism

Anti-Catholicism, worldwide
  Argentina, 4:567
  Czechoslovakia, 4:485–487
  Denmark, 4:665–666
  Germany, 7:26
  Greece, 7:934
  Hungary, 7:219–222
  Mexico, 4:416, 441, 854, 9:579–580
  Spain, 4:441, 739
  See also French Revolution; Mexico; Spain

Antichità estensi (Muratori), 10:63

Antichrist, **1:513–517**, *514*
  apocalyptic movements, 1:547
  Beatus of Liébana, 13:379
  in the Book of Revelation, 12:185
  millenarianism, 9:635–636

Antichrist (St. Hippolytus of Rome), 6:859

Anticlaudianus (Alan of Lille), 1:205

Anticlericalism, **1:517–519**
  Alumbrados, 1:323
  Carbonari, 3:101
  Claretians, 3:764
  clericalism, 3:802

Anticlericalism *(continued)*
  Crotus Rubianus, 4:386
  France, 11:390
  Holy Family Missionaries, 7:23–24
  laicism, 8:283
  Leo XIII (Pope), 8:492–493
  liberalism, 3:619
  papal taxation, 3:727
  Protestant Reformation, 3:607
  See also French Revolution,
    suppression of religious
Anticommunism
  John Paul II (Pope), 8:250
  Knights of Columbus, 8:191
  Ku Klux Klan, 8:252
  Sheil, Bernard J. (Bp.), 13:77
Antidefamation, 8:189–192
Antidialogues (Nicetas Stethatos), 10:357
Antidotum in acta Synodi Tridentinae
  (Calvin), 14:430
Antigonish Movement (Canada),
  3:815–816, 10:56
Antigonus (King of Judea), 6:665
Antigua, 3:120
Antihaeresis (Evrard of Béthune), 5:496
Antiheretical literature, 5:641
Anti-Janus (Hergenröther), 6:780
Antillean Episcopal Conference, 3:121
*Anti-Lucretius sive de Deo et natura
  libri novem* (Polignac), 11:458
Antimachiavel (Frederick the Great),
  5:923
Anti-Masonry, 10:169
Antimonies, **1:519–521**
Antioch, **1:521–524**
  art, 1:524
  Byzantine Empire, 2:783
  Church property, 3:724
  Constantinople, 4:185, 195–196
  Crusaders' states, 4:401–405
  holy lance, 7:31
  homoousios, 4:197
  Jewish diaspora, 4:730, 731
  justification, 8:78
  as liturgical center, 5:4
  See also Edessa
Antioch, Ancient See of (Asia Minor),
  9:193–194, 197
Antioch, Councils of (268-424), 1:661,
  817
  Acacius of Caesarea, 1:50
  Apollinarianism, 1:559
  Arianism, 1:662, 685
  Canon Law, 3:37, 38
  chorbishops, 3:526

Church property, 3:724
  Damasus I (Pope), 4:504
  Eusebius of Caesarea, 5:451
  homoousios, 4:353
  Paul of Samosata, 4:753–754
  Pelagianism, 1:523
  School of Antioch, 1:526
  subdiaconate, 7:37
Antioch, Creed of, 4:352
Antioch, Patriarchate of, 4:295–296,
  5:18
Antioch, School of, **1:526–527**, 5:511,
  642
  Adrianus, 1:130
  anthropocentrism, 1:508
  Byzantine theology, 2:820
  Diodore of Tarsus, 4:750–751
  founding, 12:635
  Lucian of Antioch, 8:844
  nature of Christ and Mary's
    motherhood, 10:14
  School of Alexandria, 1:269, 272,
    524
  Severian influenced, 13:41
Antioch, Synods of. *See* Antioch,
  Councils of
Antioch Patriarchate, **1:525–526**,
  527–528, 3:733
Antiochene liturgy, **1:527–528**, 5:4,
  8:435, 712
Antiochene Orthodox Church, 9:479,
  480
Antiochene theology, 5:83
Antiochus IV Epiphanes (King of Syria),
  1:528–529
  abomination of desolation, 1:22–23,
    529
  altars, 1:319, 320
  Antichrist, 1:515
  apocalyptic style, 1:546
  ars moriendi, 1:728
  Church-State relations, 3:631
  circumcision, 3:741
  Hellenization of Judea, 9:9–10
  Maccabee, Judas, 9:11
  persecution of Jews, 13:40
Antiochus of Ascalon, 1:669, 5:46,
  13:339
Antipathy, **1:529**
Antiphonary of Bangor (liturgical
  manuscript), 2:54
Antiphons, 1:297–298, **529**, 929–931,
  8:655
Antipodes question, **1:529–530**

Antipopes, **1:530**, *531*, 7:43
  See also Popes, list of; *specific
    antipopes*
Anti-Poverty Society, 9:397–398
Anti-Protestantism, 9:403
*Antiquiores consuetudines monasterii
  Cluniacensis* (Ulric of Zell), 14:283
Antiquitates Italicae medii aevi
  (Muratori), 10:63
Antiquitatum variarum volumina
  (Annius), 1:472
Antiquities (Varro), 11:459
Antiquities of the Anglo-Saxon Church
  (Lingard), 6:877–878
Antiquities of the Jews (Josephus),
  12:308, 14:68–69
Antiquorum habet (papal bull, Boniface
  VIII), 7:57
Anti-religion, 14:579
Antirhetikoi (Nichphorus I), 10:355
Antirrhetica (Philotheus Coccinus),
  11:307–308
Antirrheticus adversus Apollinarem (St.
  Gregory of Nyssa), 6:518–519
Anti-Saloon League of America, 13:801
Anti-Semitism
  Argentina, 1:656
  Austria, 1:917
  Byzantine Empire, 7:868
  Catholic Church regret, 3:628
  Chaucer, Geoffrey, 3:454
  Christian Roman Empire, 7:867
  Crusades and Spanish Inquisition,
    7:869–870
  during early 20th century in U.S.,
    10:171, 172
  European expulsions, 7:868, 870
  France, 7:874
  Germany, 7:870–871, 873–874
  John Paul II (Pope), denouncement
    of, 10:853
  Kittel, Gerhard, 8:186
  Pius XI (Pope), 11:395
  U.S., 7:874
  See also Holocaust (Shoah); Jews,
    persecution of
Antisthenes, 4:455, 5:393
Antithesis (Marcion), 5:509, 6:260
Antitranscendentalists, 2:186
Antoine, Paul Gabriel, **1:530**, *532*, 3:309
Antoine, Père. *See* Sedella, Antonio de
Antolínez, Agustín, **1:532**
Antonelli, Giacomo (Card.), **1:532–533**,
  2:535, 596, 12:417
Antonia of Florence, Bl., **1:533**
Antoniano, Silvio (Card.), 5:820

Antonians. *See* Antonines

Antonii (Aleksei Pavlovich Khrapovitskii) (Metropolitan of Kiev), **1:533–534**, 12:435

Antonines, **1:534–536**, 3:412, 7:119–120

Antoninus (Bp. of Fussala), 2:498, 3:317

Antoninus, Marcus Aurelius. *See* Marcus Aurelius (Roman Emperor)

Antoninus, Marcus Aurelius (Caracalla), 3:594

Antoninus, St., 1:*536*, **536–537**, 14:47
    Anthony Neyrot, Bl., 1:505
    Canon Law, 3:52
    chronicle, 1:465
    Constantius of Fabriano, 4:197
    Devotio Moderna, 3:605
    Latin literature, 9:461
    preaching, 11:619

Antoninus Pius (Roman Emperor), 3:592

Antonio (Martyr of Tlaxcala), 14:95

Antonio da Venezia, 12:679

Antonio de Bitonto, 3:52

Antonio de la Anunciación, 3:137

Antonio de la Madre de Díos, 12:618, 619

Antonio de S. Buenaventura, Bl., 7:734

Antonio de S. Domingos, Bl., 7:734

Antonio de San Juan Bautista, 12:619

Antonio del Espíritu Santo, 3:137

Antonius (Eastern Patriarch), 3:634

Antonius Andreas, **1:538**, 12:762

Antonius Corsetus, 3:52

Antonius de Butrio, **1:538**, 3:51

Antonius de Corduba, 1:27

Antonius Pius (Titus Aurelius Flavius Boionius Arius Antoninus) (Roman Emperor), 12:304, 310

Antwerp, **1:538–539**, *539*
    Anne of St. Bartholomew, Bl., 1:468, 3:128
    art, 1:539

Anuarite Nengapete. *See* Nengapete, Marie-Clémentine Anuarite, Bl.

Anunciación, Domingo de la, **1:539–540**

Anwendung, 14:852

Anxiety, **1:540–541**, 5:546

An-Xing, Anna, and Companions, SS., **1:367–368**

Anza, Juan Bautista, 12:644

APA. *See* American Protective Association (APA); American Psychiatric Association (APA)

Apa Menas (Egypt), 1:758

Ápád, 7:209

Apamea (ancient cities), **1:541–542**

Aparicio, Sebastián de, Bl., **1:542**

Aparicio Sanz, José, 5:645, 691

Apathy, will power vs., 14:726

APB. *See* Sisters Adorers of the Precious Blood

Apelles, 5:509

Aper of Toul (Bp.), St., **1:542**

Aphorismes de politique social (La Tour du Pin), 8:371

Aphorismi Confessariorum ex Doctorum sententiis collecti (Sa), 12:449

Aphraates, **1:542–543**, 806, 8:652, 13:124

Aphrodite (Greek goddess), 4:461, 10:87

Aphthartodocetism
    Anastasius I (Patriarch of Antioch), St., 1:388
    Julian of Halicarnassus, 8:48
    Justinian I, 8:99

Apiarian controversy
    Boniface I (Pope), St., 2:498
    Canon Law, 3:40

Apiarius, 3:317

Apocalypse, Book of. *See* Revelation, Book of

Apocalypse, Christian, 9:635–636

Apocalypse, the Book of Revelation (Ellul), 5:172

Apocalypse, iconography of, **1:543–545**, *545*

Apocalypse of Bahira. See Bahira legend

Apocalypse of Isaiah, 7:596–597, 598–599

Apocalypse of Moses, 1:550

Apocalypse of Peter, 1:168, 3:31

Apocalyptic
    Jewish literature, 8:4
    Judith, Book of, 8:45
    Kingdom of God, 8:173–174
    See also Revelation, Book of

Apocalyptic style, **1:545–547**

Apocalyptic theology, **1:547–548**, 2:481, 492–493
    See also Revelation, Book of

Apocalyptism
    Gnosticism, 6:262
    von Speyr, 13:416

Apocatastasis, **1:548**
    Origen's doctrine, 10:658
    refutation, 4:649

Apocrisiarius (Nuncio), **1:548**
    papal legates, 8:450
    patriarchate, 10:947
    Sabinian (Pope), 12:463

Apocriticus (Response) (Macarius Magnes), 9:1

Apocrypha, **1:548–558**
    Acts of John, 5:4
    Acts of Thomas, 5:4
    biblical canon, 3:20, 27
    biblical exegesis, 5:515
    concept of mystery, 10:80
    Day of the Lord, 4:548
    descent of Christ into hell, 4:684
    Gnostic gospels, 6:257
    moral-didactic, 1:554–557
    nativity of Mary in the, 10:175
    New Testament, 1:558
    prophetic-apocalyptic, 1:551–554
    pseudohistorical, 1:549–551
    See also specific books

Apocrypha, iconography of, **1:558–559**

Apodictic law, 4:6

Apokalypsse der deutschen Seele (Balthasar), 2:34

Apollinarianism, **1:559–560**
    Acacius of Beroea, 1:50
    Arcadius, 1:631
    condemnation, 4:185
    Constantinopolitan Creed, 4:354
    Cyril of Alexandria, St., 1:391, 559, 561, 2:792, 4:468
    Damasus, 4:504
    Diodore of Tarsus, 4:750–751
    homoousios, 4:198
    hypostasis, 7:263, 264
    soul's origins, 13:354

Apollinaris of Alexandria, 4:191

Apollinaris of Hierapolis (Bp.), St., **1:560**, 785

Apollinaris of Laodicea (the Younger) (Bp.), 1:559, **560–561**, 4:83, 5:462, 8:328
    School of Alexandria, 1:272
    School of Antioch, 1:527, 5:511
    soul of Christ, 7:812–813
    See also Apollinarianism

Apollinaris of Monte Cassino, St., **1:561**

Apollinaris of Valence (Bp.), St., **1:561**

Apollo (Greek deity), 6:452, 10:618–619

Apollonaris (Bp. of Ravena), 11:928

Apollonia, Bl. (17th c. Japanese martyr), 7:733

Apollonia of Alexandria, St., **1:561–562**, *562*

Apollonius (Christian apologist), 1:567

Apollonius of Tyana, **1:562**, 5:453, 10:243

Apollos (Christian apologist), 1:268, **562–563**

Apologéica historia (Las Casas), 8:341

Apologetics, **1:563–566**, 5:855–856
    foundational theology, 5:827
    Garrigou-Lagrange, Réginald, 6:102
    Hermesianism, 6:798
    modern, 1:565–566, 3:624
    patristic theology, 10:965
    prophecy, 11:761–762
    Russian theology, 12:434–435
    scholasticism, 12:777

Apologeticus (Samson), 9:446, 13:379

Apologeticus major (Nicephorus I), 10:355

Apologeticus minor (Nicephorus I), 10:355

Apologhi (Ochino), 10:535

Apologia (St. Bernard of Clairvaux), 3:750, 12:601

Apologia ad Anastasium papam (Rufinus of Aquileia), 12:405

Apologia compendaria (Fludd), 12:382

Apologia contra hieronymum (Rufinus of Aquileia), 12:404

Apologia de convenientia institutorum Romanae ecclesiae cum evangelica libertate (Ferrariensis), 5:693

Apologia ecclesiae Anglicanae (Jewel), 7:862

Apologia fratrum praedicatorum in provincia hispaniae sacrae theologiae professorum, adversus novas quasdam assertions cuiusdam doctoris Ludovici Molinae nuncupati (Báñez, et al), 2:50

Apologia pauperum contra calumniatorem (St. Bonaventure), 14:20

Apologia pro Galileo (Campanella), 6:61

Apologia pro responsione ad librum Jacobi I (Bellarmine), 10:500

Apologia pro vita sua (Newman), 10:334, 339, 733

Apologia sacri Pisani concilii moderni (Ferreri), 5:694

Apologie de la mission de saint Maur en France (Ruinart), 12:407

Apologie des Christentums (Hettinger), 6:813

Apologie des Christentums (Schanz), 12:729

Apologie des Christentums (Schell), 12:732

Apologie oder Schutzschrift für die vernünftigen Verehrer Gottes (Reimarus), 5:255, 12:35

Apologie pour feu M. l'ábbe de Saint-Cyrian (Le Maistre, A.), 8:464

Apologies, liturgical, **1:566–567**

Apologists, Greek, 1:563–564, **567–568**, 3:592–593, 5:641
    anonymous Christian, 1:489
    Aristides, 1:567, 666–667
    Canon Law, 3:38
    catechesis, 3:228
    Christian philosophy, 3:539
    Christology, 3:559, 560
    Cicero, Marcus Tullius, 3:729–730
    considerations of Christian mysteries, 10:85
    Greek language, 6:439
    moral theology, 9:859
    Quadratus, St., 1:567, 587, 666
    See also Clement of Alexandria, St.; Justin Martyr, St.; Melito of Sardes; Patristic era

Apology (Justin Martyr, St.), 5:509

Apology (Tertullian), 13:835

Apology against Julian (Cyril of Alexandria), 4:467

Apology for Origen (Pamphilus), 10:659–660, 815–816

Apology of the Augsburg Confession, 4:78

Aponte, Pedro Juan, 10:879

Apophatic theology, **1:568**

Apophthegmata patrum, 1:39, **568–569**, 3:594

Apopompaeus (Raynaud), 11:939

Apor, Vilmos (Bp. of Györ), Bl., **1:569**

Aporia, **1:570**, 4:883, 8:514

Apostasy, **1:570**, 8:333

Apostates, denial of Church funeral of, 6:33

The Apostle Bartholomew (Rembrandt), 2:*123*

Apostle Clerics of St. Jerome. *See* Jesuati

"Apostle of Union." *See* Josaphat Kuncevyč, St.

The Apostle Paul (Sabatier), 12:453

The Apostle Simon (Von Landshut), 13:*127*

Apostles, **1:570–573**, *571*, *574*, *575*
    authority, 3:29, 32
    charisms, 3:389
    disciple as term, 4:769–774
    doctrine, 4:802–803
    Dominicanism, 4:847
    hope of salvation, 7:106–107
    ministries, 9:652, 13:777
    as People of God, 11:107
    as teaching authority of the Church, 13:775
    as witnesses of Jesus Christ, 14:802

    See also Apostolicity; *specific apostles*

The Apostles (oratorio by Elgar), 5:153

Apostles, iconography of, **1:573–577**
    Judas Iscariot, 8:14–16
    Last Supper, 8:344, 345
    shrines, 13:94

Apostles' Creed, **1:577**
    catechesis, 3:234, 240
    Catholic Apostolic Church, 3:279
    communion of saints, 4:34–36
    descent of Christ into hell, 4:685
    Divine judgment, 8:39
    eschatology, 5:346–347
    Leo I (Pope), St., 8:477
    marks of the Church, 9:190–191
    Rufinus of Aquileia, 12:405

Apostles of Jesus (AJ), **1:577–578**, 14:250–251

Apostles of the Sacred Heart of Jesus, **12:495**, 718

Apostleship of Prayer, **1:578**, 8:445

Apostleship of the Sea (*Opus Apostolatus Maris*), **1:578**

Apostolate and spiritual life, **1:578–579**

Apostolatus Benedictinorum in Anglia (Baker), 2:22

Apostolatus peragendi (*motu proprio*, Paul VI), 11:481

Apostolic Blessing, **1:580**

Apostolic briefs
    Caritas (Pius VI), 11:377
    Commissum divinitus (Gregory XVI), 6:509
    Compertum exploratumque (Clement XII), 7:412
    definition, 4:758
    Divina (Pius VI), 1:297
    Dominus ac Redemptor (1773), 5:43
    Dominus ac Redemptor (Clement XIV), 3:92, 795–796, 7:787
    Etsi apostolici principatus (Pius VII), 4:62
    Ex iniuncto (Clement XIV), 1:534
    Exponi nobis (Clement XIII), 11:467
    Exponi nobis (Urban VIII), 2:143
    His praecipue (Innocent III), 7:51–52
    Inter plura illa mala (Pius VII), 4:62
    Litteris altero (Pius VIII), 11:382
    Multa praeclare (Gregory XVI), 6:268, 510
    Multum ad movendos animos (Pius IX), 2:842
    Pastoralis officii (Clement XI), 1:600
    Quod aliquantum (Pius VI), 11:377
    Romani Pontificis (Leo XIII), 7:391

Sedula Cura (Paul VI), 11:477

Tam multa (Pius VII), 11:212

Apostolic Camera, **1:580**, 944–945

Apostolic Chancery, 1:12–13

Apostolic Church Order, **1:580–581**

Apostolic Colleges of Propaganda Fide (Franciscans), 9:707

Apostolic Constitution on the Sacrament of the Anointing of the Sick (Paul VI), 1:484

Apostolic constitutions, **1:581**

   Apostolic Constitution on the Sacrament of the Anointing of the Sick (Paul VI), 1:484

   Apostolica sedes (Pius XI), 7:652

   Apostolicae Sedis (Pius IX), 1:470

   Benedictus Deus (Benedict XII), 2:173, 244, 276, 10:900

   Bis saeculari (Pius XII), 13:295

   Caelestis pastor (Innocent XI), 11:866

   Catholici fideles (Benedict XV), 7:652

   Clericis laicos (Boniface VIII), 2:502, 3:803

   De fide catholica (Pius IX), 5:594, 11:387

   definition, 11:747

   Deus scientiarum dominus (Pius XI), 3:292, 4:700, 6:879, 10:434, 11:393, 394, 12:775

   Divinus perfectionis magister (John Paul II), 3:58, 63, 7:1001, 12:608

   Dominici gregis (Pius IV), 3:336

   Ecclesiam (Pius VII), 3:100

   Etsi pastoralis (Benedict XIV), 3:817, 7:651

   Ex corde ecclesiase (John Paul II), 1:54–55, 56, 3:58, 292, 5:498–499, 7:795, 1002

   Ex debito (John XXII), 4:950

   Excommunicamus (Gregory IX), 3:87

   Exiit Qui Seminat (Nicholas III), 5:902

   Exsul familia (Pius XII), 7:522, 11:482

   Fidei depositum (John Paul II), 3:245

   Fulgens Sicut Stella (Benedict XII), 3:748

   Gaudium et spes (John XXIII), 4:516, 8:358–359, 360, 417, 447, 549, 13:51–52, 117, 243, 259, 287, 14:826

   Humanae salutis (John XXIII), 6:869, 13:117

   Immensa dei (Sixtus V), 3:63, 349, 4:438

   In Suprema (Alexander VII), 3:748, 14:161

   Indulgentiarum doctrina (Paul VI), 7:439–440

   Inter multiplices (Alexander VII), 6:78

   Licet de vitanda discordia (Alexander III), 3:105, 11:499

   Magnum Matrimonii Sacramentum (John Paul II), 7:1006, 11:486

   Maxima vigilantia (Benedict XIII), 1:636

   Mirificus eventus (Paul VI), 14:415

   Munificentissimus Deus (Pius XII), 1:797, 799, 800, 3:623, 10:61–62, 11:399, 14:136

   Ne Romani electione (Clement V), 3:106

   Officiorum ac munerum (Leo XIII), 3:336

   Orientalium dignitas (Leo XIII), 3:817, 7:651, 9:681

   Parvus Fons (Clement IV), 3:748, 751

   Pastor bonus (John Paul II), 1:589, 3:57, 58, 4:438–440, 8:286, 10:853, 11:76, 480

   Poenitemini (Paul VI), 5:186, 635

   Postquam verus (Sixtus V), 3:105

   Praedecessores nostri (Leo XIII), 11:499

   Promulgandi (Pius X), 1:77

   Provida Mater Ecclesia (Pius XII), 11:400, 12:861–862

   Quae divinitus (Pius XI), 11:76

   Quia contingit (Clement V), 7:129

   Quo graviora (Leo XII), 3:101

   Regimini ecclesiase universae (Paul VI), 4:438, 5:480, 11:30

   Religiosa sanctorum (Sixtus V), 3:107

   Romanae Sedis (Gregory XV), 7:411, 10:408

   Romano pontifici eligendo (Paul VI), 3:106, 11:30, 500

   Romanus Pontifex (Pius IV), 7:650

   Sacra Rituum (Paul VI), 4:789, 12:256

   Sacrae disciplinae leges (John Paul II), 3:34, 56–57, 4:30

   Sacramentum Ordinis (Pius XII), 2:417, 4:551, 7:38, 11:400

   Sacri canones (John Paul II), 3:817

   Sapienti Consilio (Pius X), 1:116, 10:543, 11:390, 481, 751

   Sapientia Christiana (John Paul II), 5:498, 7:1002, 11:484, 12:688–689

   Sollicita ac Provida (Benedict XIV), 7:390–391

   Sollicitudo omnium ecclesiarum (Pius VII), 7:787

   Umbratilem (Pius XI), 3:194

   Universi dominici gregis (John Paul II), 2:910, 3:58, 106, 107, 4:60, 7:1001–1002

   Ut Periculosa (Boniface VIII), 12:100

   Ut si quis papa superstite (Symmachus), 3:104

   Ut sit (John Paul II), 11:527

   Vacante Sede Apostolica (Pius X), 11:499

   Verum sapientia (John XXIII), 11:488

   Veterum sapientia (John XXIII), 7:937, 8:365

   Vineam Domini (Clement XI), 7:718, 10:406

Apostolic Constitutions (c. 380), **1:581**

   clerical celibacy and marriage, 3:323, 324

   works of charity, 3:403

Apostolic councils, 5:22

Apostolic Delegation in the United States, **1:581–585**, 12:704

Apostolic exarch, 5:503

Apostolic exhortations, **1:585–586**

   Aspersis commitis anxietatibus (Pius XII), 1:585–586

   Catechesi tradendae (John Paul II), 6:127, 7:1003, 9:682

   Christifideles laici (John Paul II), 3:549, 7:1003

   definition, 11:747–748

   Dum Europe fere (Pius X), 11:391

   Evangelica Testificatio (Paul VI), 1:29, 3:393, 806

   Evangelii nuntiandi (Paul VI), 4:157, 5:39, 473–474, 478, 6:127, 9:682, 689, 11:32

   Familiaris consortio (John Paul II), 7:1003, 8:417, 10:179, 13:258

   Menti nostrae (Pius XII), 1:84, 586, 3:466

   On Evangelization in the Modern World (Paul VI), 11:616, 628

   Pastores dabo vobis (John Paul II), 4:157, 7:1003

   Reconcilatio et Paenitentia (John Paul II), 7:1003

   Redemptoris custos (John Paul II), 1:586

   Vita consecrata (John Paul II), 1:586, 7:1003

Apostolic Faith, **1:586–587**

Apostolic Fathers, **1:587–589**, 5:641
  apostolic prayers, 8:610
  biblical canon, 3:29, 30
  Byzantine theology, 2:820
  Canon Law, 3:37
  Christology, 3:559, 560
  Church history, 3:591
  Church property, 3:723
  Diognetus, Epistle to, 4:751
  disciple as term, 4:773–774
  Holy Trinity, 14:189
  studied, 8:585
  works of charity, 3:401–402, 578–579
  See also Clement, Epistles of; Clement I (Pope), St.; Early church; Ignatius of Antioch, St.; Patristic era; Polycarp (Bp. of Smyrna), St.; Pseudo-Barnabas; Shepherd of Hermas
Apostolic letters
  Ad Sanctam Beati Petri Sedem (Alexander VII), 7:717
  Aeterni patris (Pius IX), 1:147
  Amoris officio (Paul VI), 11:481
  Apostolicae curae (Leo XIII), 1:435, 438, 439, 592–594, 5:67–68, 252
  Apostolos suos (John Paul II), 3:58, 5:299, 301, 10:852–853, 14:315, 316
  Christifideles laici (John Paul II), 3:549, 7:1003, 8:289, 417, 14:826
  Cum Biblia sacra (Benedict XV), 11:485
  definition, 11:747
  Dies Domini (John Paul II), 7:1003
  Dominicae cenae (John Paul II), 7:1003
  Dum acerbissimas (Gregory XVI), 4:932, 6:508, 797
  Ecclesia Dei (John Paul II), 7:1005, 8:365, 14:182
  Ecclesiae sanctae (Paul VI), 10:460, 11:30
  Egregiae Virtutis (John Paul II), 7:998
  Euntes in mundum (John Paul II), 7:1003
  Explorata Res (Pius XI), 1:483
  Gravissimas inter (Pius IX), 6:778
  In Sublimi (Gregory XVI), 12:384
  In supremo (Gregory XVI), 2:44, 6:510
  Inde a primis (John XXIII), 11:642
  The Infinite Mercy of God (Pius XI), 12:206

  Laetamur magnopere (John Paul II), 3:238
  Longinqua oceani (Leo XIII), 1:585
  Magni Nobis Gaudii (Leo XIII), 3:290
  Maximum illud (Benedict XV), 3:500, 626, 8:429, 9:681
  Ministeria quaedam (Paul VI), 7:37, 38, 8:285, 443, 11:30, 525
  Mulieris dignitatem (John Paul II), 7:1003, 10:852, 14:826
  Multiplices inter (Pius IX), 14:404
  Novo millennio ineunte (John Paul II), 7:1003
  Octagesima adveniens (Paul VI), 4:157, 10:615, 11:32, 587, 12:396, 13:269
  Ordinatio sacerdotalis (John Paul II), 7:1003, 11:747
  Quae mari sinico (Leo XIII), 11:258
  Quod de fovenda (Benedict XV), 11:390
  Sacram Liturgiam (Paul VI), 4:165
  Sacrum diaconatus ordinem (Paul VI), 4:552, 553, 11:30
  Salvici doloris (John Paul II), 7:1003, 10:852
  Tertio Millennio Adveniente (John Paul II), 7:1003, 11:747, 13:692, 832–834
  Testem benevolentiae (Leo XIII), 1:84, 354, 356, 6:779, 13:838–839
  Ut ampliores et uberiores fructus (Pius IV), 11:490
  Vigilantiae (Leo XIII), 11:476
  Vinea electa (Pius X), 11:485
Apostolic Mission House (Washington, DC), 11:41
Apostolic sees, **1:589**, 4:155, 505, 10:484–486
Apostolic succession, **1:589–592**, 596, 597, 2:414, 10:448
Apostolic tradition. See Apostolic Fathers
Apostolic Tradition (canonical collection), 12:328, 467
  Anointing of the Sick, 1:482
  baptism, 2:62–63
  blessings, 2:439
  cantors, 3:75
  capital punishment, 3:85
  catechumenate, 3:250, 251
  consecration of a bishop, 10:636
  creedal statements, 4:350, 351
  Hippolytus of Rome, St., 6:859
  ordination of priests and deacons, 10:637

  priesthood, 11:693
  sources, 10:337–338
  subdiaconate, 10:639
Apostolic Tradition (church order), 8:651
Apostolica sedes (apostolic constitution, Pius XI), 7:652
Apostolica sollicitudo (motu proprio, Paul VI), 11:30, 13:683, 14:414
Apostolicae caritatis (motu proprio, Paul VI), 11:482
Apostolicae curae (apostolic letter, Leo XIII), 1:435, 438, 439, 592–594, 4:620, 5:67–68, 252
Apostolicae sedis (apostolic constitution, Pius IX), 1:470
Apostolicam actuositatem (decree, Vatican II), 10:616
Apostolici (heretical group), **1:594–595**, 4:821, 7:86, 11:572
Apostolici regiminis (papal bull, Leo X), **1:595**
Apostolicity, **1:579–580, 595–598**, 3:21, 29, 32–33, 9:189–191
Apostolicum Ministerium (papal bull, Benedict XIV), 4:734
Apostolicum pascendi munus (papal bull, Clement XIII), 3:792
Apostolines, 4:417
Apostolos Andreas, 6:460
Apostolos suos (apostolic letter, John Paul II), 3:58, 5:299, 301, 10:852–853, 14:315, 316
Apostolska Hrana (Apostolic Food, Slomšek), 13:218
Apostolus, 10:45
Apotactites, 1:365
Apothegms, 5:809–810, 811
Apotheosis, **1:598–599**
Les Apôtres (Renan), 12:126
Apparatus (John le Moine), 7:960
Apparatus ad Decretum (Guido de Baysio), 6:562
Apparatus ad Sextum (Guido de Baysio), 6:562
Apparatus decretalium (Richard de Mores), 12:229
Apparatus glossarum, 6:248–249
Apparatus super decretum florentinum unionis Graecorum (Torquemada), 14:112
Apparecchio alla morte (St. Alphonsus Liguori), 1:309
Apparitions, 14:562
Appasamy, A. J., 7:405
An Appeal to the Nobility of the German Nation (Luther), 8:881
Appeals to a future council, **1:599–600**

Appearance and Reality (Bradley), 6:712

Appellants, **1:600**, 847

Appendix Concilii Lateranensis III, 3:47

Appetite, **1:600–604**
  Aristotle, 1:682
  art, 1:749
  cogitative power, 3:823
  connatural knowledge, 8:205
  habit, 6:599
  human act, 7:170
  love, 8:825–830
  matter and form, 9:349
  motive, 10:24
  privation, 11:723
  Scholastics, 11:805

Appian of Alexandria, 12:308

Appian Way, 11:*73*

Appleby, Thomas (Bp. of Carlisle), 3:124

Appreciative love, 8:726

Apprehension, simple, **1:604–606**
  Aquinas, 8:24
  concept, 4:52–53
  definition, 4:609
  division, 4:792
  knowledge, 8:202

Appropinquante concilio (motu proprio, John XXIII), 14:408

Appropriation, **1:606–607**

Apreece, Robert. *See* Price, Robert, Ven.

Apsu (god), 4:337

Apuleius, 12:308

The Aquarian Conspriracy: Personal and Social Transformation in the 1980s (Ferguson), 10:273

Aquee, Blanche, 3:112

Aquila, Samuel J. (Bp. of Fargo), 5:625

Aquileia (Metropolitan See), **1:607–608**, 4:192, 13:30

Aquileia, Council of (381), 3:564

Aquileia Basilica, 1:*607*

Aquileian Rite, **1:608–609**

Aquilinus of Milan, St., **1:609**

Aquinas, Philippus, **1:609**

Aquino, Corazon, 11:260–261

Aquino, María Pilar, 8:369

Arab persecution of Christians (Spain), 4:261–263, 13:378, 379

Arabia, **1:609–620**
  Bible, 1:612–613
  Christianity, 1:619–620
  coinage, 10:480
  geography, 1:609–610
  history, 1:610–612
  paganism, 1:613–619

Saba (Sheba), 12:450–451

Arabian philosophy, **1:620–623**, 939
  Aristotelianism, 1:671–673
  atomism, 1:833
  Avempace, 1:622, 673, 932, 940
  Bernard Silvester, 2:317
  causality, 3:304
  Costa ben Luca, 4:287–288
  emanationism, 5:181–182
  existence, 5:533
  fideism, 5:711
  illumination, 7:319
  Liber de causis, 8:532–534
  metaphysics of light, 8:583
  neoplatonism, 10:241–242
  Rhazes, 12:210–211
  Sa'aida ben Joseph, Gaon, 12:449–450
  soul, 13:339
  See also Alfarabi (Fārābī, al-); Algazel (Ghazzālī, al-); Averroës; Avicenna

Arabic language
  Bible, 3:22
  Syriac language, 13:702

Arab-Israeli Conflict, 8:427

Arabs, history of the
  Constans II, 4:173
  Constantine IV (Byzantine Emperor), 4:173
  Constantine V (Byzantine Emperor), 4:174
  Constantine XI (Byzantine Emperor), 4:176
  Copts, 4:253–254, 255
  Cyprus, 4:461
  Demetrian of Khytri, 4:634
  Dhū-Nuwās, Masruk, 4:716
  divination by lots, 4:785
  Dwin (Armenian city), 4:957
  iconoclasm, 7:281
  invasion of Syria, 13:706
  scientific development, 12:809–810
  Spain, 4:261–262, 13:377–390

Aram I (Armenian Catholicos), 1:703

Aramaeans, **1:623–625**
  Abraham, 1:36
  sons of God, 13:321
  Tiglath-Pileser I, 9:530

An Aramaic Approach to the Gospels and Acts (Black), 5:522

Aramaic language, **1:625–627**
  disciple as term, 4:768
  Syriac language, 13:700

Aramaic language, biblical, **1:627**
  early languages, 8:361
  as liturgical language, 8:666–667
  Lord's Prayer, 8:783

Aramendía Gareía, Eutimio, Bl., 7:124

Aranda, Pedro Pablo, 3:792

Aranda Riera, Ana María, Bl., 1:4

Aranha, Francisco, 12:401

Āraṇyakas (Hindu scripture), 6:840, 842

Arator (6th c. Christian poet), **1:627–628**, 9:438

Araucanian people, 3:485, 486, 4:132, 13:213

Araújo, Antônio de, **1:628**

Araújo, Francisco de (Bp. of Segovia), **1:628**

Araújo, José Tomás Nabuco de, 2:595

Araújo, Juan Jacinto Rodriguez de. *See* Rodriguez de Araújo, Juan Jacinto

Arawak people, 3:113, 4:417, 7:698

Arba Turim (Ben Asher), 7:870

Die Arbeiterfrage un das Christentum (Ketteler), 8:160

Arbeo (Aribo) of Freising (Bp.), 5:192

Arbez, Edward Philip, **1:629**

Arbie, Karim, 7:794

Arbie, Karl Albrecht Karim (Father), 5:10

Arbiol y Diez, Antonio, **1:629**

Arbitrary symbols, 13:661

Arbogast of Strasbourg (Bp.), St., **1:629–630**

Arbor vitae crucifixae Jesu (Ubertino of Casale), 14:262

Arborelius, Anders (Bp. of Sweden), 13:638

Arbroath Abbey (Scotland), **1:630**

Arbuthnot Missal, 5:795

Arcadelt, Jakob, **1:630**, 930

Arcadius (Roman Emperor), **1:630–631**, 5:448, 12:321

Arcanum (encyclical, Leo XIII), **1:631**

Arce, José de, 2:465

Arcesillaus of Pitane, 13:201

Archabbeys, 1:11

Archaeology
  aerial photography, 11:436
  biblical exegesis, 4:791
  Constantinople, 4:188
  dictionary, 8:433
  dogmatic theology, 4:813
  hieroglyphics, 8:181
  Hippo Regius area, 6:854–855
  history of Israel, 8:186

Archaeology *(continued)*
  Israel and Palestine
    ancient Israelite sanctuaries,
      14:856
    biblical period, 10:794–796
    Bronze Age, 10:793–794
    Chalcolithic period, 10:792
    holy places, 10:797–799
    Jericho, 7:756–757
    Jerusalem, 2:284–285
    Mesolithic period, 10:790–791
    Neolithic period, 10:791–792
    Paleolithic or Early Stone Age,
      10:790
    Palestine pre-Israelite ethnology,
      10:796–797
    Palestine Proto-Urban Period,
      10:792
    precious stones, 11:646
    records on Palestine, 10:789–790
  Jung's orientation, 8:60–61
  Kraus, F. X., 8:246–247
  Mount of Olives, 10:33–34, 798
  Shechem, 13:71–72
  Sicily, 13:104
  work on Ugarit (Syrian coast),
    14:266–267, *268*
  See also Dead Sea Scrolls;
    Iconology; *specific historical*
    periods
The Archangel Leaving the Family of
  Tobias (Rembrandt), 11:*910*
Archangel Michael diptych, 2:727, *728*,
  729
Archangela Girlani, Bl., **1:631**
Archangelo of Calatafimi, Bl.,
  1:631–632
Archangels, 1:421, 425
  See also Gabriel (Archangel);
    Michael (Archangel); Raphael
    (Archangel)
Archangels, Feast of the, 6:41
Archbishop and Metropolitan of the
  Roman Province. *See* Pope (title)
Archbishops, **1:632–633**, 634
Archbishop's Commission on Human
  Relations, 8:250
Archchancellors, **1:633**
Archconfraternity of Charity, 3:418
Archconfraternity of Christian Mothers,
  3:536–537
Archconfraternity of Perpetual Adoration
  of the Blessed Sacrament and the
  Work of Need Churches, 5:435
Archconfraternity of St. Michael
  Archangel, 1:424

Archconfraternity of the Holy Hour,
  7:30
Archdeacons, **1:633–634**
  Church property, 3:724
  judicial vicar, 8:42–43
Archdioceses, **1:634**
L'Arche International, **1:634–635**, 8:416
Archer, Thomas, 3:707
Arches, Court of, **1:635**, 13:130
Archier, Pierre, 8:337–338
Archiereus, **1:635**
Archinto, Alberico, 3:791
Architecture
  Carolingian era, 3:154–155
  Cistercians, 3:749–750
  hospitals, 7:129–130
  mosques, 7:614–617
  See also Church architecture
Architecture as Space (Zevi), 3:680
Archiv für Literatur und
  Kirchengeschichte des Mittelalters,
  5:138
Archives, ecclesiastical, **1:635–642**
Archives, U.S. Catholic, **1:638–642**
Archivists of Congregations of Women
  Religious (ACWR), 1:639
Archivum Arcis (France), 14:399
Archivum Franciscanum Historicum,
  12:274
Archons (Manichaeism), 9:111–112
Archpriest controversy, 1:642, **642–643**,
  3:785
Archpriests, **1:642**
Arciconfraternita del Gonfalone
  (Gonfalonieri), **6:340**
Arcimboldi, Giovannangelo (Abp. of
  Milan), **1:643**
Arcosolia, **1:643–644**
Arcoverde de Albuquerque Cavalcanti,
  Joaquim (Card.), **1:644**
Arcudius, Peter, 6:458
Ardashir I (King of Persia), 11:137–138
Ardbraccan Abbey (Ireland), **1:644**
Ardchattan Priory (Scotland), **1:644–645**
Arden, Edward, **1:645**, 13:65
Ardenne Monastery (France), **1:645**
Arduum sane munus (*motu proprio*, Pius
  X), 3:55
Ardzivean, Abraham (Peter) (Catholicos-
  Patriarch of Sis), 3:733
Are Parochial Schools the Answer?
  (Ryan), 12:446
Aredius, St., **1:645**
Aregus (Bp. of Gap), 3:409
Arelatensis, 3:59
Arellan, Tristan de, 12:613

Arena Chapel (Padua, Italy), 1:575,
  6:230
Arendt, Hannah, 1:918
Areopagitica (Hilduin), 12:606
Areopagitica (Milton), 9:641–642
Areopagus, **1:646**
Aretas IV (Nabatean king), 6:801
Arethas (Abp. of Caesarea), **1:646–647**,
  2:756, 808, 846
Aretino, P., 3:484
Arévalo, Rodrigo Sánchez de (Bp. of
  Oviedo), **1:647**
Arezzo (Italy)
  Andrew of Strumi, Bl., 1:407
  Florentine hegemony over, 5:767
Arezzo, Geri d', 12:113
Argenteuil Abbey (France), **1:647–648**
Argentina, **1:648–657**, *651*, *653*
  Aneiros, León Federico, 1:410
  Byzantine Basilians, 2:144
  Castañeda, Francisco de Paula,
    3:210–211
  Catholic Church, 5:864
  Catholic social movement, 6:539
  Church reform, 12:260–261
  Clara, Jerónimo Emiliano, 3:759
  de Andrea, Miguel, 4:567
  demographic statistics, 1:648
  ecclesiastical organization, 1:649
  Esquiú, Mamerto, 5:360
  Fagnano, José, 5:589
  Falkner, Tomás, 5:611
  higher education, 5:864
  map, 1:*650*
  Marian shrines, 13:92
  mission, Augustinian, 9:714
  mission, Catholic, 1:648–649, *649*,
    9:714
  mission, Protestant, 1:657
  retreat houses, 12:651
  Sisters of Mercy, 13:184
Argentine Catholic Action (ACA), 1:653
Argentré, Charles du Plessis d' (Bp. of
  Tulle), **1:657**
Argimir, St., **1:657–658**, 4:262
Argüello, Kiko, 10:233
Argüello, Luis, 12:645
"Arguing Ethics" (Jonsen), 10:192
Argumentation, **1:658–659**, 11:947
  cosmological, 4:285–287
  demonstration, 4:651–654
  ex convenientia, 4:230–231
  from necessity, 4:231
  ontological, 10:600–603

Argyropoulos, John (Bp. of Florence), **1:659**
  Aristotelianism, 1:659, 676
  Eastern Schism, 2:762
Argyros, Isaac, **1:659–660**
Arialdo, St., **1:660**, 5:323
  Andrew of Strumi, Bl., 1:407
  Landulf, 8:322
Arianism, **1:660–664**, 685, 817–820
  abandonment, 8:453
  Acacius of Beroea, 1:50–51
  Acacius of Caesarea, 1:50, 663, 4:470, 471
  Agapetus I (Pope), St., 1:172
  agennētos, 1:175
  Alexander (Patriarch of Alexandria), St., 1:266
  Alexandria, 1:268
  Ambrose, St., 1:338, 339
  Amphilochius of Iconium, St., 1:365
  Anabaptists, 1:369
  Anthimus of Tyana, 1:503
  Antioch, 1:522
  Apollinarianism, 1:559
  Apollinaris of Laodicea, 1:559, 560
  Apollinaris of Valence, St., 1:561
  Aristotelianism, 1:660, 673
  Asterius the Sophist, 1:808–809
  Athanasius, 8:53
  Avitus of Vienne, St., 1:663, 946
  Basil of Ancyra, opposition to, 2:139
  Bobbio Abbey, 2:446
  Byzantine literature, 2:792
  Christmas, 3:552, 554, 555
  Church-State relations, 3:632, 633
  Clovis I (King of the Franks), 3:810
  Constans I, 4:173
  Constantine I (the Great) (Roman Emperor), 1:266–267, 661, 685, 4:181, 299
  Constantinople, 4:185
  Constantinople Council I, 4:190
  Constantius II, 4:185, 190, 197
  Council of Nicaea (325), 10:346–348
  Council of Sardica, 1:51, 662, 818, 3:38, 39, 12:692
  Cyril of Alexandria, 4:467
  Cyril of Jerusalem, 4:470, 471
  Damasus I (Pope), St., 4:504
  Eunomius of Constantinople, 5:448–449
  Eusebius of Caesarea, 5:45
  Eusebius of Emesa, 5:454
  Eusebius of Nicomedia, 5:454
  Eusebius of Samosata, St., 5:455

  Eustathius of Antioch, opponent of, 5:456
  exiles, 1:662, 817, 818, 3:594, 632
  Father of, 8:844
  Faustus of Riez, opponent of, 5:651
  France, 5:842
  historiography, 2:797
  homoousios, 4:197–198, 353
  hymnody, 7:252
  hypostasis, 7:263, 264
  influence on Newman's Oxford Movement, 10:734
  John I (Pope), St., 7:919
  Julian Sabas, St., 8:51
  Justin I, 8:92
  Liberius (Pope), 8:554
  Lithuania, 8:605
  liturgical apologies, 1:567
  Logos, 8:763
  Lombards, 1:664, 815
  Mary's Divine motherhood, 10:13
  opposition, 13:41
  Photinus (Bp. of Sirmium), 13:168
  School of Alexandria, 1:269, 273
  School of Antioch, 1:524, 527
  Sicily, 13:103
  Son of God, 4:890
  sources of Byzantine theology, 2:820
  Spain, 14:560
  subordinationism, 13:566
  Vandals, 1:663, 3:186–187, 189
  Victorinus, Marius, 9:182
  See also Nicene Creed
Arias, Francis, **1:664**
Arias de Ugarte, Fernando (Bp. of La Plata), 2:465
Arias Martín, Francisco, Bl., 7:125
Aribert (Abp.), 4:134
Aribert (King of the Lombards), 1:664
Aribo of Mainz (Abp.), **1:664**
Aridity, Spiritual, **1:665**
Arieta, Primo, 2:468
Ariminum, Council of (360), 2:621
Arintero, Juan González, **1:665**, 12:777
Ariosto, Ludovico, 1:761, *762*, 764
Aristarchus of Samos, 1:668
Aristenos, Alexios, 2:795, 3:46
Aristide, Jean-Bertrand, 6:621
Aristides (Greek philosopher), 1:567, **666–667**, 7:118
  See also Apologists, Greek
Arístides Zejas, Pedro, 2:468
Aristippus of Cyrene, 5:393, 6:701
Aristippus the Elder, 4:464

Aristippus the Younger, 4:464
Aristo of Pella, 1:567
Aristobulus I (King of Judea), 6:663–664
Aristobulus II (King of Judea), 6:664
Aristocles of Messene, 5:46
Aristocracy, **1:667–668**, 4:637
Aristocratic Psalters, 11:602
Aristocratic school, 4:393
Aristophanes
  afterlife, 1:167
  anthropomorphism, 1:510
  sacrifice, 12:509
Aristoteleskritik (Luther), 13:129
Aristotelianism, **1:668–679**, 684–685
  accident, 1:63
  act, 1:73, 74, 75, 678, 682
  Adam of Buckfield, 1:108
  Albert of Saxony, 1:224
  Albert the Great, St., 1:225–226
  alchemy, 1:237
  Alexander of Hales, 1:265–266
  Anatolius of Laodicea, St., 1:392
  animal rights, 1:456
  Argyropoulos, John, 1:659, 676
  Arianism, 1:660, 673
  art, 1:744, 746, 747
  atomism, 1:677, 832, 833, 834
  attacks on, 8:314, 12:657
  Augustinianism, 1:673, 878
  Averroës, 1:225, 622, 672, 674, 933
  Avicenna, 1:672, 940
  Bernard Silvester, 2:317
  biblical theology, 2:382
  Boethius of Sweden, 1:673, 674, 684, 935, 936, 2:454, 456, 457
  Bonaventure, St., 2:483, 484
  Brentano, Franz, 1:678, 2:604
  Bruno, Giordano, 1:677, 2:646
  Burke, Edmund, 1:678, 2:702
  Cajetan (Tommaso de Vio), 1:675, 677, 678, 2:854
  Cambridge University, 1:676, 2:906
  Christology, 3:560, 561
  Church-State relations, 1:675, 3:636
  concept of time under, 14:79–82
  controversies, 1:676–677
  cosmology, 12:813
  criteria for transcendental property, 2:185
  discursive power as term, 4:775
  Galileo, 6:58–59
  Greek, 1:668–671
  Greek philosophy, 13:919–920

Aristotelianism *(continued)*

humanism, 1:675–676

hylomorphism, 7:237–238

influence on neoplatonism, 10:240

Jewish philosophy, 4:360–361, 7:864–865

John of the Cross, St., 3:136

Kindī, 'Abd Al-Masiḥ Al-, 1:621, 671, 672

Latin, 1:673–675

Latin Averrorism, controversy over, 14:20–21

light symbolism, 3:674

modern, 1:678–679

Nicholas of Autrecourt's attacks against, 10:370–371

physics, 12:811–813

Platonism, 1:225, 669, 670, 675

School of Antioch, 1:524, 2:820

School of Nisibis, 1:805

science, 1:677–678, 681, 682–683, 685

Scotism vs., 12:824–825

Semitic, 1:671–673

Siger of Brabant, 13:112–113

Suarezianism compared to, 13:563

Thomas Aquinas, St., 9:551–552, 14:26

University of Bologna, 2:475

University of Paris, 3:603

See also Averroism, Latin

Aristotelicae animadversiones (Ramus), 12:124

Aristotelis opera quae extant omnia brevi paraphrasi ac litterae perpetuo inhaerente explanatione illustrata (Maurus), 9:374

Aristotle (Greek philosopher), **1:679–685**, 6:442, 11:*81*, 288

abortion, 1:26–27, 29

abstraction, 1:45, 683

accident, 1:59–60, 61, 63, 682, 683

act, 1:73, 74, 75

action and passion, 1:77, 78, 79

action at a distance, 1:80

Adam Pulchrae Mulieris, 1:110

aesthetics, 1:142, 143

Albert of Saxony, 1:223

Albert the Great, St., 1:224

Alcuin, Bl., 1:243

Amalric of Bène, 1:330

ambition, 1:334

analogy, 1:371, 376, 377

Anaxagoras, 1:393

angels, 13:423

Anscombe, Gertrude Elizabeth Margaret, 1:492

anxiety, 1:540

aporia, 1:570

Aquinas' proof of God, 6:304

Arianism, 1:660

aristocracy, 1:667

astral religion, 1:809, 812

astronomical theory, 11:723–724

authority of state, 13:251–252

beauty, 2:184

becoming, 2:195

Bessarion, Cardinal, 2:341

biology, 2:400, 404–405

Boethius, 2:454

Bonaventure, St., 2:488, 489

capital punishment, 3:87

categories of being, 3:255–257

cathedral and episcopal schools and, 3:441

causality, 3:297–298, 302–303, 304

central sense, 3:344–345

certitude, 3:352

chance, 3:375, 376

choice, 3:520

Christian philosophy, 3:540

Church-State relations, 3:636

civil authority, 1:921

classification of the sciences, 12:819

common good, 4:17

common sense, 4:22

Complutenses, 4:44–45

concept, 4:51, 52, 610

concept of truth, 14:222

consciousness, 4:152

continence, 4:211

contingency, 4:212–213

continuum, 4:215, 216, 217

contradiction, 4:223, 224

contributions to study of motion, 10:17, 21, 24

criteriology, 4:367

Dante Alighieri, 4:518

David of Dinant, 4:540

deliberation and free will, 5:937

democracy, 4:637–638

demonstration, 4:651–653

dialectics, 4:721–725, 726–727

distinction, 4:779

doctrine of forms, 5:803

double truth theory, 4:882

drama, 11:433–434

dreams, 4:903

dualism, 4:915

dynamism, 4:958, 959

early planetary systems, 12:803–804

educational philosophy, 5:89–90

Eliot, T. S., 5:160

Empedocles, 5:195, 196

entelechy, 5:267

epistemology, 5:301, 320

essence and existence, 5:361, 364

eternity, 5:380

ether, 8:583

ethics, 5:393

eudaemonism, 5:439

eutrapelia (recreation), 5:461

excluded middle principle, 5:503–504

exemplarism, 5:525

existence, 5:532–533

experience, 5:554

final causality, 5:723

first principles, 5:742–745

friendship, 6:6–7

geocentrism, 6:59

Gerard of Cremona, Latin translations of, 6:161

God, 6:307–308

good, 6:347

good as supreme value of man, 9:91

Grosseteste, Robert, 12:263–264

happiness, 6:347

Heidegger, Martin, 6:45

Heraclitus, 6:760

heroic virtue, 14:554

human will, 14:721

idea of Plato, 7:293

idealism, 7:296–297

identity principle, 7:304

immortality, 7:348

impetus, 7:363

individuation, 7:425

induction, 7:432–434

infinity, 7:456–457

intellectual life, 7:513, 8:461

intentionality, 7:517

introspection, 7:532

involuntarity, 7:539

John Buridan, 7:942

John of Jandun, 7:970

John Philoponus, 7:1008

judgment, 8:21

leisure, 8:460

location, 8:742

logic, 8:748, 753

love analyzed, 8:825

love and hate, 5:195

luck, 8:848

lust, sin of, 8:872–873

lying, 8:900

Maimonides, 9:53–54

man, concept of, 9:89

man, natural end of, 9:96–97, 98

mathematics, 9:326

matter, 9:340–342

matter and form, 5:802, 9:346–350

mechanism, 9:415

memory, 9:486

metaphysics, 9:549

methodology, 9:564–565

mirror of princes literature, 9:671–672

moderate realism, 11:942–943

monarchy, 9:781

moral circumstances, 3:742

music, consideration of, 10:70–71

natural law doctrine, 10:180

natural law in political thought, 10:201

noumena concept, 10:463

ontological perfection, 11:118

ontology and metaphysics, 10:605–606, 607

opinion and knowledge, 8:205, 214–217, 10:610, 12:1

origins of necessity, 10:225

participation, 10:905–906

phenomena, 11:229

philosophy of nature, 10:208, 209–210, 11:302

physical laws, 11:314–315

place, 11:401, 402

possibility, 11:550–551

potency and act, 11:555–558

power of governance, 6:376

predicates and predicables, 11:660

privation, 11:722, 723

providence of God, 11:781

prudence, 11:787, 789

psychology, 11:803

pure acts, 11:821

Pythagoreans, 11:844

quality, 11:848–849

quantity, 11:853

quiddity, 11:864–865

Ramus, Peter, 11:905

relation, 12:41

Richard Rufus of Cornwall, 12:236

scholasticism, 12:759, 13:905

scientific method, 12:748

similarity, 13:126

society, 1:918–919

Socrates, 13:293

solipsism, 13:303

soul, 13:334–335, 338–339, 355

soul-body relationship, 13:357

species, 13:408

spontaneous generation, 13:460

substantial change, 13:580

synderesis, development of, 13:679

synthesis, 13:698

theism, 13:862–863

transcendentals, 14:150

unity, 14:317

unity of intellect, 7:508, 510

universal essences, 14:322

utopia and utopianism, 14:360

voluntarity, 14:583

wisdom, 14:784, 785

wonder, 14:832

words, 14:836

world soul, 14:843

zoology, 12:806

See also Aristotelianism

Aristotle in the West (van Steenberghen), 14:388

Aristoxenus of Tarentum, 1:668

Arithmetic, continuum and, 4:216

Arithmetica speculativa (Bradwardine), 14:29

Arius (Alexandrian priest), 1:660, *661*, **685–686**, 3:559, 560, 5:454, 456

Alexander (Patriarch of Alexandria), 1:266, 268, 661, 685

condemnation, 4:191

Constantine I (the Great) (Roman Emperor), 4:181

Council of Nicaea (325), 10:346–348, 14:193

homoousios, 7:65

Lucian of Antioch, St., 1:527, 685

MacArius of Jerusalem, St., 9:2

mystery of God, 6:281

St. Athanasius's opposition to, 10:13

theology of Christ, 7:812

See also Arianism

Arizona, **1:686–688**, 8:180, 316, 9:716–717

See also specific dioceses and archdioceses

Ark of the Covenant, **1:688–690**, *689*

temple for, 13:808–809

Yahweh Sabaoth, 12:451

Arkansas, **1:690–693**

African Americans, 8:613, 614

creationism vs. evolution, 4:347

Epperson v. Arkansas (1968), 3:667

See also specific dioceses and archdioceses

Arkansas, Epperson v. (1968), 3:667

'Arkus, Ignatius Philip (Patriarch of Syria), 13:709

Arlegui, José, **1:693–694**

Arles (France), **1:694–695**

Arles, Councils of (314-813), 1:694–695

Agricius of Trier, St., 1:187

Arianism, 1:662, 818

Britain, 2:620–621

catechesis, 3:230, 240

Confirmation, 4:84

Constantine I (Roman Emperor), 3:594

exemption, 5:529

rebaptism, 3:186

symbols of the faith, 4:352

usury, 14:354

Arles, Synod of (473), 5:651

Arma Veritatis (Ottaviani), 10:710

Armageddon, Jehovah's Witnesses on, 7:751

Armagh, Primatial See of, 1:697, **697–698**

Armagnac, Georges d' (Card.), 1:943

Armand, Abraham (Father), 6:669

Armarius (scriptoria directors), 12:843

Armellini, Mariano, **1:698**

Armenia, **1:699–704**, *701*

cities, 1:453, 4:957–958

demographic statistics, 1:699

history, 1:398, 703, 3:593

map, 1:*700*

monasticism, 1:535, 9:801

Armenia, martyrs of, BB., **1:698–699**

Armenian Apostolic Church, 1:699, **704–706**

Catholicos title, 3:294

Communist collapse, 1:703

liturgy, 3:553, 556

See also Armenia

Armenian Apostolic liturgy, **1:707–711**

Armenian Catholic Church (Eastern Catholic), 1:699, 704, **706**

All Souls' Day, 1:290

Armenians, Decree of, 1:711–712

origins, 5:18, 19

Patriarchate, 3:732–733

Armenian Christianity

Constantine I (the Great) (Roman Emperor), 4:180

Council of Catholic Patriarchs of the Orient, 4:295–296

the cross, 4:383, 385

Armenian Christianity (continued)
    Crusades, 4:401
    holy lance, 7:31
    Holy Orders, 7:38
    hymnody, 7:243
    iconoclasm, 7:280
    Justin II, 8:93
    monophysitism, 4:477
    Nestorianism, 4:957–958
Armenian Creed, 2:72
Armenian liturgy, 1:707–711, 3:553, 556, 8:713
Armenians, Decree of (*Exsultate Deo*) (Eugene IV), **1:711–712**, 4:221, 12:470
Armentia, Nicolás, **1:712**
Armer, Elizabeth, 12:647
Arminianism, **1:712–713**, 2:894, 5:469, 471, 12:108–109
    baroque spirit, 2:112
    Calvinist defense, 13:406
    Cameron, John, 2:911
    Church-State relations, 3:638
    confessions of faith, 4:79
    heresy, 6:776
Arminius, Jacobus, 1:712, *713*, **713–714**
    predestination, 11:655–656
    Remonstrants followers, 12:108–109
    supralapsarianism, 2:894
Armonia della religione con la civiltà (newspaper), 9:151–152
Armstrong, Garner Ted, 14:847, 848
Armstrong, Gibson v., 3:658
Armstrong, Herbert W., 14:847
Arnáiz Barón, Rafael, Bl., **1:714**
Arnaldus Amalrici (Abp. of Narbonne), **1:714**
Arnauld, Anne de Sainte Eugénie de l'Incarnation, 1:715
Arnauld, Antoine, 1:716, 3:614, 11:524, 525
    Alexander VII (Pope), 1:262
    Cartesianism, 3:184–185
    Charles of the Assumption, 3:436
    Duvergier de Hauranne, Jean, 4:955
    grace controversy, 7:716, 717
Arnauld, Henri (1485-1564), 1:714–715
Arnauld, Henri (Bp. of Angers, 1597-1692), 1:432, 716–717, 9:74, 12:29
Arnauld, Jacqueline Marie Angélique (Mother), 1:715–716, 3:745
Arnauld, Jeanne Catherine Agnès (Mother Agnès de Saint-Paul), 1:715, *715*, 716, 7:*716*
Arnauld, Madeleine de Sainte-Christine, 1:715

Arnauld, Marie de Sainte-Claire, 1:715
Arnauld d'Andilly, Robert, 1:717
Arnauld family, **1:714–717**, 3:614
Arni Thorlaksson (Bp.), 7:275
Arno of Reichersberg, 12:33
Arno of Salzburg (Abp.), 1:289
Arnobius the Elder, **1:717–718**, 3:186
    Cicero, Marcus Tullius, 3:730
    immortality, 7:353
    soul, 13:342
    symbols, 4:352
Arnobius the Younger, **1:718**
Arnold, Gottfried, **1:718**
Arnold, Matthew, 2:908, 4:426
Arnold, Thomas, 2:624
Arnold II (Abbot of Gembloux), 6:124
Arnold of Bonneval (Marmoutier), **1:718–719**
Arnold of Brescia, **1:719**
    Adrian IIV (Pope), 1:126, 719
    Bernard of Clairvaux, 1:719, 2:309
    excommunication, 5:444
    Lucius III (Pope), 1:231
Arnold of Hiltensweiler, Bl., **1:719**
Arnold of Lübeck, 1:463
Arnoldi, Alberto, 12:488
Arnoldi, Bartholomaeus, **1:719–720**, 889, 12:764
Arnoldi, Wilhelm, 12:369
Arnoldists, 1:719
Arnulf (Holy Roman Emperor), 3:171, 5:815
Arnulf I (Count of Flanders), 6:160
Arnulf of Gap (Bp.), St., **1:720**
Arnulf of Lisieux (Bp.), **1:720**
Arnulf of Louvain (Abbot of Villers), 12:631
Arnulf of Metz (Bp.), St., **1:720–721**, 2:338, 3:161
Arnulf of Milan, **1:721**
Arnulf of Soissons, St., **1:721**
Aron, Petru Pavel (Bp.), 12:338
Aron, Raymond, 6:884
Arpad (Aramaean state), 1:624
Árpád (Hungarian hero), 7:209
Árpád Dynasty (Hungary), 7:210
Arpe, Agostina, 1:880
Arrabal, Fernando, 1:48, 5:544
Arras, Councils of, **1:721–722**
Arras, Jean d', 4:401
Arras, Martyrs of, BB., **1:722**, 5:973
Arras College, 13:234
Arregui, Antonio María, **1:722**
Arriaga, Pablo José de, **1:723**
Arriaga, Rodrigo de, **1:723**, 12:767

Arrian (Flavius Arrianus), 12:309
Arricivita, Juan Domingo, **1:723**
Arrieta, Franciso Sales de (Abp. of Lima), **1:723–724**
Arrillaga, Basilio, **1:724**
Arrowsmith, Edmund, St., **1:724–725**, *725*, 5:235
Arroyo de la Cuesta, Felipe, 2:865
Arrupe, Pedro, **1:725–727**, *726*, 5:3, 7:793–794
Ars Antiqua, 8:683–684
Ars cantus mensurabilis (Franco of Cologne), 5:911
Ars disserendi (Adam of Balsham), 8:750
Ars lectoris (Aimeric of Angoulême), 9:449
Ars moriendi, **1:727–734**, 2:522, 3:698, 4:10, 5:486, 848
Ars nova era
    Ciconia, Johannes, 3:731
    Landini, 8:320–321
    liturgical music history, 8:684–686
Ars praedicandi, **1:734–735**
Ars praedicandi (Baglioni), 2:115
Ars vivendi, 1:727–728, 732, 733
Arsacids, 5:311, 11:136–137
Arscinus (Abbot), 12:585
Arsenite Schism, 2:762
Arsenius Autorianus (Patriarch of Constantinople), 1:735, **735–736**, 2:762
Art, **1:736–745**
    aesthetics, 1:142–143, 746
    aureoles, 1:896–897
    baroque period, 2:114, 4:397
    Bible cycles, 2:368–376, *369*, *370*, *371*
    catacombs, 1:37, 573, 753, 754, 2:368–369, 3:223
    Christianity, 1:742–745
    Christocentrism, 3:558
    Church, 3:*576*, *577*, 629–630
    Counter Reformation, 4:313
    creation, iconography of, 4:*337*, *338*, 342
    cross, 4:379–380
    crucifixion, 4:391–398
    diptychs, 4:758–759
    fish as symbol of Christ, 5:746–747
    Gothic, 12:485–486
    as human nature, 7:323–324
    humanism, aesthetic, 7:196–197
    images, veneration of, 7:323–325
    Inquisition's influence, 7:491
    Irish, 4:395

mannerism, 2:424, 3:674

miniaturist art, 9:129

as natural to man, 7:323–324

as opposite to nature, 11:303

orans motif, 10:621

philosophy, 11:280

Reichenau school of, 10:720

religion, 1:736–742

Ruskin, John, 12:414–415

sacramental iconography, 12:485–488

secular iconography, 7:286–287

Transfiguration, 14:155

See also Architecture; Church architecture; Iconology and iconography; Religious art; *specific artists, artworks, art periods, and forms of art*

Art, philosophy of, **1:745–749**, 3:298

creative imagination, 4:347–349

liberal arts, Thomism, 8:537

transcendental principle, 4:372–374

L'Art de mourir (Matthew of Cracow), 3:241

Art d'Église (periodical), 3:713, 12:533

The Art of Life (Kolbe), 8:229

Art of Love (Ovid), 12:307, 310

The Art of Teaching Christian Doctrine (Ryan), 12:446

Art of War (Machiavelli), 12:124

Art poétique (Boileau), 2:115

L'Art poétique (Claudel), 3:768

L'Art sacré, 8:623

Art sacré Movement, 1:803–804, 3:713

Artaxerxes I (King of Persia), 11:135

Artaxerxes II (King of Persia), 11:135

Artaxerxes III (King of Persia), 11:135

El Arte adivinatoria (Sahagún), 12:529

Arte breve da Lingoa japoa, 12:282

Arte da Lingoa de Japam, 12:282

Arte de amar a Dios y al projimo (Orozco), 10:674

Arte de Artes (Rosa y Figueroa), 12:371

Arte de la lengua mexicana (Olmos), 10:586

Arte de lengua Tarasca (Basalenque), 2:132

Arte de Tañer Fantasía, assi para Tecla como para Vihuela (Tomás), 14:106

L'Arte della guerra (Machiavelli), 9:21

Artemis (deity), 4:729–730

Artes dictandi (medieval writing instructions), 9:459

Arthur, Roger. *See* Filcock, Roger, Bl.

Arthurian legends, **1:759–762**, *760, 761,* 6:142

Articles of 1682 (France), 3:524

Articles of Baden (1834), 6:509

Articles of faith, **1:764–765**

Articula fidei catholicae (Revetor), 9:881

Artificial insemination, 11:399–400

Artificial intelligence (AI), **1:765–766**

Artificial sign, 13:116

An Artist's Letters from Japan (LaFarge), 8:276

Artusi, Giovanni Maria, **1:766**

Arundel, John (Bp. of Chichester), 3:481

Arundel, Thomas (Abp.), **1:766–767**, 3:72, 4:317, 14:894

Arundel, Thomas Howard, Earl of, 10:424

Arver v. United States (1918), 3:660

"Aryan invasion theory," 6:840

Ås (Asylum) Abbey (Sweden), **1:767**

Asa (King of Judah), 7:639, 766

Asbury, Francis (Bp.), **1:767–768**, 2:454, 5:469, 472, 9:560

Ascanio, Nicanor, 4:503

Ascellino (Dominican priest), **1:768**

Ascension, era of, 5:314

Ascension of Isaiah, 1:550, 558, 3:592

Ascension of Jesus Christ, **1:768–772**, *769,* 8:39, 858

The Ascent of Mount Carmel - The Dark Night (St. John of the Cross), 7:988

Ascetical theology, 9:854

Asceticism, **1:772–776**

Augustinian Recollects, 1:873

Basil, St., 2:138

baths and bathing and, 2:154

cenobitism, 9:789

charity, notion of, 8:832

chastity, 3:444

Christian, 12:354, 787

contemplation, 4:204–205, 208

Cornaro, Elena Lucrezia Piscopia, 4:270

cynics, 4:455–457

De institutione virginum (Leander), 8:426

deadly sins, 4:565–566

early church, 3:594

Evagrius Ponticus, 5:465

Institutiones theologiae dogmaticae (Lercher), 8:511

Lancicious, N., 8:317

Lausiac history, 8:380–381

Les voies de l'orasion mentale (Lehodey), 8:455–456

Low Countries, 13:455

martyr concept broadened, 8:720

monasticism, 9:790

mortification, 13:434

Pelagianism, 1:860

Sergius of Radonezh, St., 13:15–16

Sperandea, St., 13:415

Spiritual Combat, 13:429–430

spiritual theology, 13:433–436

theology, 2:310, 13:434

Asceticism, theology of, **1:777–778**

Asceticism in the New Testament, **1:776–777**

Asceticon (St. Basil), 2:136–137, 140

See also Basilian monasticism

L'Ascétique chrétienne (Ribet), 12:221

Ascham, Roger, 1:762, 5:163

Asclepas of Gaza, 1:662, 818

Asclepiades

atomism, 1:833

Council of Sardica, 12:692

Aseity (*aseitas*), **1:778–781**, 13:138–139

Asensio Barroso, Florentino (Bp. of Barbastro), **1:781**

Ash Wednesday, 1:782

Ash'arī, Abū al-Hasan 'Alī, 1:620–621, **781–782**, 7:611

Algazel, 1:281

Mu'tazilism, renouncement of, 13:613–614

See also Ash'arism

Ash'arism, 1:781–782

Ashby, Thomas, Ven., 5:227

Asher ben Jehiel, 3:76, 148

Asherah (Canaanite deity), 14:270, 855

Ashes, liturgical use of, **1:782**, *783*

Ashley, B., 1:29

Ashley, Ralph, Bl., **1:782–783**, 5:234

Ashmole, Elias, 12:382

Ashot I (prince of Iberia), 6:153

Ashram Movement, 7:404

Ashtar (deity), 14:271

Ashton, Roger, Ven., 5:232

Ash-Wednesday (Eliot), 5:160, 161

Asia. *See specific countries*

Asia, Roman Province of, **1:784**

Asia Minor

early Church, **1:784–786**, 4:50, 5:312–313

iconoclasm, 7:281

Khazars, 8:163–164

patron saints, 10:975

Asian Americans, liturgical inculturation and, 7:387

Asian Bishops' Conferences, Federation of (FABC), 5:660–662

Asian patron saints, 10:975

Asidaeans. *See* Hasidaeans

Askarī, Hasan al-' (d. 874), 9:48

Aske, Robert, **1:786**, 5:244, 11:341, 12:8–9

Askew Codex, 6:257

Asociación Católica de la Juventud Mexicana, 6:344

Asoka (King), 2:660

Aspasius, 1:669

Asperges (liturgical rite), **1:786**, 14:661

Aspersion, baptism, 2:76

Aspersis commitis anxietatibus (apostolic exhortation, Pius XII), 1:585–586

Aspilcueta, Martin (Doctor Navarrus), **1:786–787**, 12:716

Assama ibn Zeid, 4:253

Assault, **1:787**

Assemani, Joseph Aloysius, **1:787**, 3:790

Assemani, Joseph Simon, 9:198–199

Assemblée des évêques du Québec (Canada), 3:8

Assemblées du Seigneur series, 12:533

Assemblies of God, **1:788–790**, *789*

Assemblies of the French Clergy, 1:262, **787–788**

Assertio septem sacramentorum (Henry VIII), 12:7

Assertoric propositions. *See* Modal propositions

Asses, Feast of, **5:654**

Assidua (Thomas of Pavia), 14:36

Assisi (Italy), **1:790–791**, *791*

Associates of Mary, Queen of the Apostles, 7:22

L'Association catholique, 8:371

Association for Christian Art, 3:710–711

Association of Catholic Colleges, 10:160

Association of Catholic Diocesan Archivists (ACDA), 1:639, 640

Association of Catholic Professors (Brazil), 5:840

Association of Evangelical Lutheran Churches (AELC), 5:470–471

Association of Pius V, 3:289

Association of Professors and Researchers in Religious Education (APRRE), 12:97, 98

Association of Professors of Missions (APM), **1:794**

Association of the Innocents (Valencia, Spain), 3:418

Association of Theological Schools (ATS), **1:794–795**

Association of Universal Prayer for the Conversion of England, 4:630

Associationism, **1:795–797**
    atomism, 1:831
    causality, 3:302

Associations, **1:791–794**
    See also specific associations

Associative symbols, 13:661

Associazione Archivistica Ecclesiastica, 1:636

Assumpta Est Maria (Palestrina), 10:803

Assumption Cathedral (Baltimore), 3:709

Assumption of Mary, 1:*797*, **797–801**, *798*, 9:157, 171–172
    Bernard of Clairvaux, 2:310
    Dormition of the Virgin, 4:875–876
    Munificentissimus Deus, 1:797, 799, 800, 3:623, 10:61–62
    papal decrees, 9:284

Assumption of the Virgin (fresco), 8:*481*

Assumptionists, 1:801, **801–802**, 3:621, 4:502

Assumptus homo theology, **1:802–803**

Assur (Babylonia), excavation of, 8:395

Assur (Mesopotamian god), 9:535

Assy, Notre-Dame-de-Toute-Grâce (France), **1:803–804**, 4:324, 8:623

Assyria, **1:804**, 9:530–531
    apocalyptic style, 1:546
    Aramaeans, 1:623
    art, 1:*804*
    capital punishment, 3:84
    Church-State relations, 3:631
    control of Judah (8th c. B.C.), 14:918–919
    covenants, 4:326
    cult of Nebo, 10:220
    deportation, 4:674
    diaspora of Jews, 4:730
    laws, 8:394–395
    Middle Assyrian period, 9:530

Assyrian Church, 10:681

Assyrian Church of India, 7:400–401

Assyrian Church of the East, **1:805–808**, 5:3, 18–19
    Catholicos title, 3:294
    Chaldean Catholic Church, 1:808, 3:366, 367–368
    China, 1:806, 807, 3:489, 491–492
    See also East Syrian liturgy

Assyrian Code, 3:84

Assyrian law on flagellation, 5:756

Astarte (goddess), **1:808**, 5:174

Asterius (Abp. of Milan), 2:408

Asterius (martyr), 3:770

Asterius of Amasea, St., 1:50, **808**, 5:449

Asterius the Sophist, 1:527, **808–809**

Astesano, 3:52

Aston, Francis William, 1:836

Astons, Roger d', 3:717

Astorch, María Angela, Bl., **1:809**

Astrain, Antonio, **1:809**

Astral religion, **1:809–810**, 811, 812, 6:454

Astree (Urfé), 2:115

Astrology, **1:811–813**
    astral religion, 1:810
    Babylonia, 1:810, 811, 3:370
    fatalism, 5:636–637
    Firmicus Maternus, Julius, 5:739–740
    history, 4:785, 786
    horoscopes, 7:112–114
    Letter on Astrology (Maimonides), 9:52–53
    in the Middle Ages, 12:809
    See also Magic

Astronomia nova (Kepler), 6:60, 8:155

Astronomical Discourses (Chalmers), 3:372

Astronomical theory (Pythagoras), 11:845–846

Astronomy
    Albion (astronomical clock), 12:236
    Arabic development, 12:809
    Copernicus, Nicolaus, 4:249–251
    Egypt, 12:799
    Gerson, L., 8:521
    Kepler, Johann, 8:154–155
    in the Middle Ages, 12:813–814
    in the Renaissance, 12:815–816

Astros, Paul Thérèse David d' (Card.), **1:813–814**

Astruc, Jean, **1:814**, 3:710
    exegesis, 5:519
    higher criticism, 6:825
    pentateuchal studies, 11:89

Asunción, Pedro de la, Bl., 7:732

Asylum, cities of, **1:814–815**, 2:444

Asylum, right of, **1:815**

Atala (abbess of Hohneberg), St., 5:446

Ateneo de Manila University, 5:3

L'Ateneo Italiano (Tosti), 14:120

'Ateret Zeqenim (Abrabanel), 1:36

Athala of Bobbio, St., **1:815**, 2:446

Athanasian Creed, **1:815–817**, *816*

Athanasius (Coptic Patriarch), 4:255

Athanasius (Görres), 3:846

Athanasius, St., 1:268, 273, *817*, **817–820**, 5:137, 399, 402, 12:354
    Ambrose, St., 1:337
    Apollinarianism, 1:559, 560
    Arian controversy, 8:554
    Asterius the Sophist, 1:808
    Athanasian Creed, 1:816

Basil of Ancrya, 2:139

biblical canon, 3:31

Byzantine literature, 2:792

Cassian, John, 3:207

catechumenate, 3:250

Christology controversies, 3:559, 561

Church history, 3:594

clerical dress, 3:801

as confessor, 4:83

Constans I, 4:173

Constantine I (the Great) (Roman Emperor), 1:662, 817, 3:632, 4:181

Constantius II, 4:197

Copts, 4:255

Council of Sardica, 12:692

creedal statements, 4:352, 354

death, 12:404

Desert Fathers, 4:686

Divine indwelling, 7:441

divinity of the Son and Holy Trinity, 14:195

Epiphanius of Salamis, 5:292

Eusebius of Nicomedia, 5:454

Eusebius of Vercelli, St., 5:455

exegetical works, 5:510

exile by emperor, 8:51

Frumentius, St., 6:17

Holy Week, 7:56

homoousios, 4:198, 7:65

lenten fasting, 8:468

Liberius (Pope), 8:554–555

life of St. Anthony, 12:606

liturgical history, 8:651

Mary's Divine motherhood, 10:13–14

Meletian Schism, 2:137–138

monasticism, 3:594

Nicene Creed, 1:662, 817

priesthood, 11:694–695

Serapion letters, 13:7

simplicity of God, 13:137

studies, 8:429

Athanasius I (Patriarch of Constantinople), **1:820–821**

Athanasius II (Abp. of Ohrid), 1:214

Athanasius III (Patriarch of Antioch), 1:525

Athanasius of Alexandria, 9:787, 788

Athanasius of Naples, St., **1:821**

Athanasius the Athonite, St., **1:821–822**, 10:31

Atharva Veda, 6:840

Atheism, **1:822–826**, 6:312, 11:285

absurdity, 1:49

agnosticism vs., 1:180

anti-Christian, 8:840

atomism, 1:831

conscience, 4:142

contemporary reflection, 8:840

deism, 4:617

existentialism, 5:546–547

idealism, 7:297

Lavater, J. K., 8:387

Loisy, J., 8:766

Loménie de Brienne, 8:770

miracles, 9:667

as modern rejections of transcendence, 14:143

morality, 9:865

sensism, 4:73

Athelney Abbey (England), **1:826**

Athelstan (King of England), **1:827–828**, 5:240, 9:80

Athena (Greek deity), 6:452

Athenagoras (Christian apologist), **1:828**

apologetics, 1:567

capital punishment, 3:85

Divine judgment, 8:30–31

Roman persecutions, 3:593

School of Alexandria, 1:272

soul, 13:339–340

Athenagoras I (Patriarch of Constantinople), **1:829**, 10:851, 965

catechesis, 3:228

demonology, 4:646, 647–648

Paul VI (Pope), 11:31

Athens (Greece), as center of Greek philosophy, 6:442

Athens, Schools of, **1:829**

Atienza, Juan de, **1:829**

Atilla (King of the Huns), 8:*475*

Atkins, William, 5:238

Atkinson, James, 5:237

Atkinson, Matthew (Paul of St. Francis), **1:830**

Atkinson, O'Brien, 11:625

Atkinson, Thomas, Bl., **1:830**, 5:235

Atlanta Archdiocese (GA), **1:830–831**, 8:903, 12:710

Atlantic Canada, 3:9

Atlantic Episcopal Assembly (Canada), 3:8

Atlantic School of Theology (Canada), 3:9

Atlas Hierarchicus (Streit, Karl), 13:547

Ātman, 7:410

Atomism, **1:831–836**, 4:644, 5:284, 6:441–442

action at a distance, 1:80, 834, 4:960–961

Aristotelianism, 1:677, 832, 833, 834, 4:959

Ash'arī, Al-(Abū Al-Hasan) 'Alī, 1:620–621

Cartesianism, 3:185

causality, 3:298

dynamism, 4:958–961

knowledge, 8:213

mechanism, 9:415

motion, 10:17

See also Dynamism; Hylomorphism

Atoms, 9:318–319

Aton (Egyptian god), 1:198–199

Atonal music, 3:525

Atonement, **1:836–838**

Atonement, Day of. *See* Yom Kippur (Day of Atonement)

Atonement Sisters, 5:883

Attaleiates, Michael, 2:776, 800

Attention, 4:152, 11:595

Atthis, 1:460

Attici Versio, 3:40

Atticus of Constantinople (Patriarch), St., **1:839**

Attigny, Councils of, **1:840**

Attigny, Synod of (870), 6:837

Attila the Hun, 7:*224*

Leo I (Pope), St., 8:475, 476

reign, 7:224

Attilanus, St., **1:840**

Attimis, Tristano d', 3:498

Attitude scales of measurement, 9:411

Attitudes, **1:840–841**

Atto of Mainz (Abp.), 3:44

Atto of Milan, 1:721, **841–842**

Atto of Vercelli (Bp.), **1:842**, 3:45, 9:448

Attraction, friendship and, 6:7

Attrition, **1:842–843**, 4:224, 225–229

Attritionists, 1:843

Attwater, Donald, **1:843–844**

Atum-Re. *See* Ra (Atum-Re) (Egyptian deity)

Atwater, William (Bp. of Lincoln), **1:844**

Au milieu des sollicitudes (encyclical, Leo XIII), 5:855, 11:900

Aubazine Abbey. *See* Obazine Abbey (France)

Aubenas, Martyrs of, BB., **1:844–845**

Aubert, Jean-Marie, 3:88

Aubert, Stephen (Card.). *See* Innocent VI (Pope)

Aubert of Avranches, St., **1:845**, 12:566

Aubeterre, Marquis d', 3:794, 795

Aubigné, Jean Henri Merle d', **1:845**

Aubry, Nicholas, 2:552, 3:3–4

Aubusson, Pierre d' (Card.), **1:846**

Auclert, Hubertine, 5:671

Auctor beate saeculi (hymn), 5:201

Auctor of Metz (Bp.), **1:846**

Auctorem Fidei (papal bull, Pius VI), **1:846–847**, 3:204, 5:659, 6:78, 11:364, 377, 12:225

Auctoritas, 10:834

Auctoritas contra praedeterminationem physician pro scientia media (Charles of the Assumption), 3:435–436

Audet, Nicholas, 3:134, 142

Audi Benigne Conditor (hymn), **1:847**

Audience cults, 4:424–425

Audita tremendi (papal bull, Gregory VIII), 4:411, 6:495

Audo, Joseph (Chaldean Patriarch), 3:369

Audoenus of Rouen. *See* Ouen of Rouen (Bp.), St.

Audoin of Rouen. *See* Ouen of Rouen (Bp.), St.

Audras, Jean-Baptiste, 3:374

Aue, Hartmann von, 4:400

Auf den Trümmern des Panbabylonismus (Kugler), 10:820

Aufklärung, 1:564. *See also* Enlightenment

Augenspiegel (Reuchlin), 12:181

Auger, Edmond, **1:847–848**, 3:233, 242

Augmentation, 10:18

Augouard, Prosper, 3:344

Augsburg, **1:848–849**

Augsburg, Diet of (1530)
    Arnoldi, Bartholomaeus, 1:720
    Augsburg Confession, 1:850
    Charles V (Holy Roman Emperor), 3:430–431

Augsburg, Peace of (1555), 1:848, **849**, 3:431, 638, 5:688, 12:18
    Commendone, Giovanni Francesco, 4:11
    German Lutheranism, 8:888

Augsburg, Synod of (952), 3:326

Augsburg, War of League of, 8:803

Augsburg Cathedral (Germany), 13:473

Augsburg Confession (1530), 1:849, **850**, 4:78
    Anglican Confessions, 4:80
    Austria, 1:911
    Calixtus, Georg, 2:873
    Calvin, John, 2:891
    church and state, 8:894
    church as assembly of believers, 8:894
    Cochlaeus, Johannes, 3:816

    Concord Formula and Book and, 4:60
    Edict of Restitution, 12:144
    Finland, 5:732–733
    Greek Orthodox rejection, 6:456
    Latomus, B., 8:370
    Lutheran revival, 8:886
    Moravian Church, beliefs of, 9:885
    Protestant Reformation religious reconciliation, 12:18
    Sweden, accepted in, 13:636

Augsburg Interim (1548), 7:520–521

Augury, **1:850**

August, Clemens (Abp. of Cologne), 3:843

Augusta, John (Bp.), 2:461, 4:482

Augusta Synod (1860), 5:330

Auguste, Jacques de, 14:61

Augustine (Bp. of Hippo), St., **1:850–868**, *851*, *852*, 5:651
    absolute, 1:41
    abstraction, 1:45
    accident, 1:61
    acrostics, 1:72
    active life, 1:83
    Acts of the Martyrs, 1:92
    Adam, 1:104–105
    Aelred, St., 1:138
    aesthetics, 1:142
    Aeterne Rerum Conditor, 1:147
    Albert the Great, St., 1:225
    Alexander of Hales, 1:266, 878
    Alger of Liége, 1:282
    Alipius, St., 1:288
    allegory, 1:292
    Alphonsus Liguori, St., 1:309
    Ambrosiaster, 1:347
    analogy, 1:371–372
    angels, 1:419, 422, 423
    Anglo-Saxons, 1:448
    Anointing of the Sick, 1:481–482
    Anselm of Canterbury, St., 1:496
    Anthony of Padua, St., 1:506
    antipodes question, 1:529
    Apocalypse iconography, 1:544
    Aristotelianism, 1:673
    art, 1:743, 744
    aseity, 1:779
    Assumption of Mary, 1:800
    astrology, 1:812–813
    Athanasian Creed, 1:816
    Augustinian Heritage Institute, 1:871
    Augustinians, 1:886–888
    baptism of Ethelbert of Kent, 5:*385*

baths, 2:154

beatific vision, 2:171–172, 173

beatitudes, 2:178

beauty, 2:184

Bernard of Clairvaux, 2:311

biblical canon, 3:21, 26, 32

biblical theology, 2:382

birth imagery in baptism, 2:75

Blondel, Maurice, 2:441

Boethius, 2:456

Boniface I (Pope), St., 2:498

burial, 2:699, 700

Byzantine theology, 2:762

Calvin, John, 2:891

Canons Regular of St. Augustine, 3:67

capital punishment, 3:86

Cartesianism, 3:185

Carthage, 3:186

casuistry, 3:220

catechesis, 3:228, 229, 239, 240–241, 242, 243

Catechism of the Council of Trent, 3:239

catechumenate, 3:250, 251

Catharism, 1:230

cathedral and episcopal schools and, 3:262, 263

Catherine of Siena, St., 3:273

causality, 3:303, 304–305

Celestine I (Pope), St., 3:316

censorship, 3:336

certitude, 3:352

charity, 1:83, 3:395, 396

Charlemagne, 3:166

chastity, 3:444

choice, 3:520

Christian anthropology, 3:531

Christian philosophy, 3:538, 539, 541

Christmas, 3:554

Christology, 1:864–865, 874

chronicle, 1:461

Church-State relations, 1:123, 884, 3:633, 635

Cicero, Marcus Tullius, 1:852, 3:729, 730

City of God, 13:252

civil authority, 1:921

Clarenbaud of Arras, 3:762

Claudianus, Mamertus, 3:769

common good, 4:17–18

concept of time, 14:77–78

concupiscence, 4:66, 69, 5:488

as confessor, 4:83

Confirmation, 4:87

conformity, 4:92

congruism, 4:120, 121

conscience, 4:147

consciousness, 4:152

conservation, 4:160–161

contemplation, 4:205, 207

contraception, 4:218–219, 220

conversion, 4:237, 240

conversion of Anglo-Saxons, 2:267, 273

Coustant, Pierre, 4:323

creation, 8:574

Crusades, 4:407

Cyprian, St., 4:459

de auxiliis controversy, 4:112

death, 1:867, 5:273

Demetrias, St., 4:635

demonology, 4:647

descent of Christ into hell, 4:684

dialectics, 4:725

Donatism, 1:858–859, 866–867, 3:594, 633, 4:862–864

dreams, 4:904

Easter Vigil, 5:14, 15

empiricism, 5:197

Epiphany, 5:294

eschatology, 5:343

essence, 5:361

eternity, 5:380, 383

ethics, 5:393–394

evil, 5:489–491

evolution, 5:495–496

exegetical works, 5:512

exemplarism, 5:525, 533

expiation, 5:565

faith, 1:862–863, 876, 5:594

fatalism, 5:638

Fathers of the Church, 5:640, 642

Felix of Nola, 5:670

flagellation, 5:754

following of Christ, 5:788

free will and grace, 5:929–930, 934

freedom of conscience, 4:148

funeral rites, 6:31

gifts of Holy Spirit, 7:48

good, 6:347–348

grace, 4:240, 6:385–387, 401–402

grace and nature, 6:411

Greco-Roman schooling, 6:431–432

happiness, 6:636, 637

heresy, 6:770, 771, 773

hexaemeron, 6:815

Holy Trinity, 14:195–196

homily, 7:62

hope as based in Christ, 7:96

human nature, pessimistic view of, 9:860

human will, 14:721

hymns, 7:244

hypostatic union, 7:264–265

idea, 7:293

immortality, 7:348, 349, 353

infant baptism, 2:68

infinity, 7:458

influence of Optatus, 10:612

I-Thou mysticism, 10:117–118

John of the Cross, St., 3:136

Joseph, St., 7:1039–1040

justification, 8:81–82

just-war tradition, 14:636

Kingdom of God, 8:174

Latin use, 8:364

lay spirituality, 8:414

liberal arts, 8:537

liturgical history, 8:652

lying, 8:900

Madaura (Africa), Martyrs of, 9:28

man, natural end of, 9:97–98

Manichaeism, 1:852, 856–857, 858, 862, 864, 866, 3:186, 4:218–219

Marcellinus, Flavius, 9:135–136

marriage, 1:151

matter, 9:343

memory, 8:214, 9:486

mental reservation, 9:499

metaphysics of light, 8:583

Middle Ages, origins of term, 9:609

Monica, St., 9:810

music, contributions to doctrine, 10:71–72

mystery of God, 6:281–282

mystical body of Christ, 10:102, 103

natural law, 10:181, 201

nature, 13:618

notion of truth, 14:222

order of universe, 14:329

pacifism, 10:746, 747

pagan festivals, 3:556

patristic philosophy, 10:959

Pelagianism, 1:859–861, 877, 2:498, 3:206–207, 594, 9:511, 10:431, 11:61, 62

persecution of Donatists, 10:431

person, 11:149

pilgrimage, 11:354

Platonism, 1:857, 862, 865, 5:90

political dualism, 13:252

political theology, 11:459–460

Possidius, St., 11:554

preaching, 11:610–611, 618, 627

predestination, 5:783, 11:647, 649

priesthood, 11:696–697

Prosper of Aquitaine, St., 11:772

providence of God, 11:782

prudence, 11:789

reading of Scripture in liturgy, 11:126–127

reflection, 12:1

relics of saints, 12:51, 52, 55

reordination, 12:128

repentance, 4:225

rhetoric, 12:212

Roman primacy, 3:317

sacraments, 1:867, 878, 12:206, 467

schism, 12:737–738

Scripture, 1:865, 874

secular learning, 10:756

self, concept of, 12:882

seminal reasons, 12:892

Semi-Pelagianism, 1:877, 3:206–207, 12:899

sin, 13:149, 155, 158

Sixtus III (Pope), 13:195

slavery, 13:211–212

society, Church as, 13:285

soul, 1:865–866, 876, 13:342–343

soul of the Church, 13:358

speculative-practical cognition, 3:825

spiration, 13:421

spiritual direction, 4:760

spiritual life, 13:433

substance, 13:575

symbolism, 3:673, 674

symbols of the faith, 4:352

table of works, 1:853–856t

as teacher, 12:83

Ten Commandments, 4:6, 7, 8, 9

theological symbolism, 13:670–671

theological terminology, 13:890

theology, 13:904

theology of Church, 1:866–867, 3:584–585

theology of history, 6:888

theory of illuminations, 8:583

theory of knowledge, 1:866, 7:319–320, 8:214

Trinitarian processions, 11:734

universality of Christianity, 3:275, 293

universals, 14:323

virtue, 14:548

voluntarism, 14:581

will and willing, 14:721

wisdom, 14:785

Augustine (Bp. of Hippo), St.
(continued)
words, 14:836
works, 1:861–862
world soul, 14:844
See also Augustine, Rule of St.;
Augustinian spirituality;
Augustinianism; Patristic era
Augustine (Triumphus) of Ancona,
1:870–871
Augustinianism, 1:879, 883, 884, 888
Church-State relations, 1:884, 3:636
Augustine, Rule of St., **1:868–870,**
3:67–68, 5:761, 793
Altmann of Passau, St., 1:322
Ambrosians, 1:346
Augustinian union, 1:886
Dominican order, 4:828
hospitallers, 7:119
Knights of Malta, 8:193
Knights of St. James, 8:196
Lindau Convent, 8:593
order of the Holy Cross, 4:415
Servites, 13:26, 27
women's orders, 1:871–872
works of charity, 3:412
Augustine Kažotić (Bp.), Bl., **1:870**
Augustine Novellus, Bl., **1:870**
Augustine of Canterbury, St., **1:871,**
3:70, 598
Anglo-Saxons, 1:449, 2:621
bishops of Wales, 14:610
Canterbury Cathedral, 3:72
cathedral and episcopal schools and,
3:263
Celtic Rite, 3:331
Christianity in England, 5:239
Divine judgment, 8:32
Easter date controversy, 5:14
Eulogius (Patriarch of Alexandria),
St., 5:448
Gregory the Great, St., 1:871, 3:596
Saint Augustine Abbey, 12:536
Augustine of Tarano, Bl., 1:889
Augustinian Heritage Institute, **1:871**
Augustinian Hermits
Carmelite spirituality, 3:130–131
Colombia, 3:848
Honorius IV (Pope), 7:86
Augustinian missions
Argentina, 9:714
Mexico, 9:572
Peru, 9:714
South America, 9:714
Tanzania, 13:755–756

Augustinian Recollects, **1:873–874**
Colombia, 3:850
founding, 1:324
Augustinian Rule. *See* Augustine, Rule
of St.
Augustinian spirituality, **1:874–875,**
13:444–445
Augustinianism, **1:875–886**
Adam of Saint-Victor, 1:109
analogies, rejection of, 13:898–899
Aristotelianism, 1:673, 878
Bonaventure, St., 1:878, 2:482, 488,
492
Campanella, Tommaso, 2:917
Cassiodorus Senator, Flavius Magnus
Aurelius, 1:877, 3:208
devout humanism, 7:194
Dominicans, 8:497
Greek philosophy, 13:919–920
Hugolino of Orvieto, 7:163
idealism, 7:297
Innocent X (Pope), 4:436
Jansenism, 1:716, 880, 884, 892
Malebranche, Nicolas, 9:74–75
modern, 1:880–882
participation, 10:907
revival, 4:310
See also Augustine (Bp. of Hippo),
St.
Augustinianism, theological school of,
1:879–880, **882–886,** 888, 8:188,
10:968–969, 13:28
Augustinians, **1:886–892,** 14:743
Ancient See of Carlisle, 3:124
Antolínez, Agustín, 1:532
archives, 1:641
Armenia, 1:703
Austria, 1:910
Bolivia, 2:466
Brictinians, 2:614
Carroll, John, 3:181
Chile, 3:485
China, 3:495
Counter Reformation, 3:611
England, 5:242
founding, 1:886, 3:175
hierarchical insignia, 6:764
hospital work, 3:412, 7:137, 138
Klosterneuburg Monastery, 8:188
Latin America, 3:415
as mendicant order, 9:491
Mexico, 9:572
origins, 3:602
Poverty Movement, 11:573
Recollects, 1:324, 873–874, 3:850

scholasticism, 12:764–765
Scottish religious orders, 12:833
South America, 9:714
Spain, 12:529
spirituality, 1:875
Tanzania, 13:755–756
Villanova University, founding of,
14:514
women's orders, 1:871–873
Augustinians of the Assumption. *See*
Assumptionists
Augustinis, Aemilio de, 1:438, **892**
Augustinus (Jansen), 1:716, **892–893,**
3:614, 4:4, 5:555, 7:714, 715–716
Ad sanctam beati petri sedem, 1:97
Alexander VII (Pope), 1:262
Bossuet, Jacques Bénigne, 2:550
Augustinus Beroius, 3:52
Augusto Andrés, Br., 14:247
Augustus (Gaius Octavius) (Roman
Emperor), 12:299, 301–304, *324*
Aulard, François Alphonse, 5:969
Aulén, Gustaf, 10:239
Aulneau, Jean Pierre, Rev., 8:382
Aulne-sur-Sambre Abbey (Belgium),
1:893, 13:131
Aunarius of Auxerre (Bp.), St.,
1:893–894, 927
Aunemund of Lyons, St., **1:894,** 2:153
Auraeus, St., **1:894**
Aurea luce et decore roseo (hymn),
5:108
Aurea of Córdoba, St., **1:894–895,** 4:262
Aurelian (Father), Ven., 7:406
Aurelian (Roman Emperor)
astrology, 1:812
Castel Sant'Angelo, 3:212
Christian persecution under, 1:171,
264, 12:351
reign, 12:313
Aurelian of Arles, St., 1:694, **895,** 5:754,
7:244
Aurelian of Réomé, **1:895,** 6:466
Aurelius (Bp. of Carthage), 3:186, 188
Aurelius and Sabigotona, SS., **1:896,**
4:262
Aurelius of Armenia (Bp.), St.,
1:895–896
Aureoles (nimbus), **1:896–897,** 6:688
Aurevilly, Barbey d', 2:445
Auria, Bernardino d' (Mother), 12:551
Auric, Georges, 11:562
Auriel, Antoine, 12:276
Aurillac Abbey (France), **1:897**
Aurora (Peter Riga), 9:457, 11:206
Aurora consurgens, 1:239

Aurora Iam Spargit Polum (hymn), **1:897**

Aurora Lucis Rutilat (hymn), **1:897–898**

Aurora University (Zhendan University) (China), 3:500

Aus Kirche und Welt (Hettinger), 6:813

Auschwitz-Birkenau Concentration Camp (Poland), 7:13, *15*, 8:229

Ausculta fili (papal bull, Boniface VIII), **1:898**, 2:503

Ausdruck, 14:852

Ausonius, 12:320

Auspicato concessum (encyclical, Leo XIII), 8:491

Die ausserordentlichen Heilswege für die gefallene Menschheit (Schmid), 12:743

Austin, John, **1:898**, 10:184, 11:545–547

Austin Canons. *See* Canons Regular of St. Augustine

Australia, **1:899–907**, *902*, *903*
  Anglican-Episcopalian Religious Orders, 12:103
  catechesis, 3:245
  Chisholm, Caroline, 3:517–518
  cults and myths, 5:155
  demographic statistics, 1:899
  ecclesiastical organization, 1:900
  hospice movement, 7:117
  Knox, James Robert, 8:223–224
  map, 1:*901*
  Mercy Pacific, 13:187
  Sisters of Loretto, 8:787
  Sisters of Mercy, 13:184, 186

Australian Consultation on Liturgy (ACOL), 5:253

Australian Religion: An Introduction (Eliade), 5:155

Austrasia, 9:518

Austreberta, St., **1:907**

Austregisilus (Outril) (Bp. of Bourges), St., **1:907**

Austria, **1:908–918**, *911*
  Canons Regular of St. Augustine, 3:69
  Carthusians, 3:194
  catechesis, 3:243–244, 245
  church architecture, 3:706, 707, 712
  Church-state relations, 12:794
  classical music, 8:692–693
  comparative religion, 8:231–232
  demographic statistics, 1:908
  Josephinism, 3:54, 92, 615, 616, 639–640
  Kulturkampf, 8:255
  liturgical movement, 8:673

  Los-von-Rom Movement, 8:794
  map, 1:*909*
  scholasticism, 12:773–774
  Slovenia, 13:225–226
  social philosophy, 13:407

Austrian Chronicle (Ebendorfer), 5:29

Austrian Empire
  anti-Semitism, 1650-1750, 7:872
  Church-State system, 7:1041–1042, 1045–1046
  Revolutions of 1848, 6:640–641
  rule of Poland, 11:446–447
  Succession (1740-48), 6:640
  See also Hapsburg, House of

Austro-Hungarian Empire, 8:794

Authority, **1:918–920**
  Authority in the Church (McKenzie), 9:402
  community churches and rejection, 4:39
  conscienctious objection, 4:151
  Considérations sur la France (Maistre), 9:60–61
  Divine right of kings, 4:788
  dogmatic definition, 4:611
  Duranti, William the Younger, 4:950
  as foundation of obedience, 10:503
  law, 8:398–399
  Leo XIII (Pope) encyclicals, 8:492
  society, 13:277
  in the state, 13:483

Authority, civil, **1:921–922**, 3:631
  England, 13:79
  papal social thought, 13:266
  Renaissance ideals, 4:376–377

Authority, ecclesiastical, **1:922–923**
  conciliarism, 4:53–58, 171
  Constance Council, 4:171
  Ecumenical councils, theology of, 4:303–306
  jurisdiction, 4:309

Authority in the Church (McKenzie), 9:402

Authority of clergy, 6:226–227

Autobiography (Gāndhi), 6:87

Autobiography (Gerard), 6:158

Autocephalous Orthodox Churches, 10:679

Autocephaly, **1:924**, 2:744, 4:196

Autochthonous Greek cults, 10:85–89

Autokinetic Movement, 10:20

Autonomous Orthodox Churches, 10:679

Autonomy, Syro-Malabar Church, 13:714, 715, 716

L'Autorité en matière de foi et la nouvelle école (Doumerque), 5:711

Autos sacramentales, **1:924–925**

Autos-da-fé, **1:923–924**, 7:490, 491

Autour d'un petit livre (Loisy), 9:754

Autpert, Ambrose, St., **1:925–926**, 12:656

L'autre Parole (Québec, Canada), 3:10

Autun (France), **1:926**

Autun, Councils of, **1:926–927**

Auvray de Saint-André, Jean Prosper, 5:442

Auxentius (Bp. of Milan), 4:504

Auxentius, Mercurinus (Bp.), 1:338, 342, 343

Auxerre (France), **1:927**

Auxerre, School of, 5:515

Auxerre, Synod of (578 or 588), 1:894

Auxilius of Naples, **1:927–928**, 13:15

Auzou, Abbé, 3:449

Avancini, Nikolaus, 1:429, 7:782

Avarice, **1:928–929**, 7:305

Avars, **1:929**, 7:209, 13:13

Ave Maria (antiphon), **1:929–930**

Ave Maria (periodical), 7:147, 14:60

Ave Maria (Schubert), 12:788

Ave Maria (Verdi), 14:446

Ave Maris Stella (hymn), **1:930**, 9:449, 10:856

Ave Regina Caelorum (antiphon), **1:930–931**, 9:449, 10:522

Ave Verum Corpus (hymn), **1:931**

Aveling, F., 5:802

Avellana Collectio, **1:931**, 3:40, 60

Avellaneda, Diego, 1:325

Avellino, Andrew, St., **1:931–932**

Avempace (ibn Bājjah, Abū Bakr Muhammad ibn Yahyā), 1:622, **932**
  Aristotelianism, 1:673
  Avicenna, 1:940

Avendaño, Diego de, **1:932**

L'Avenir (Lamennais), 6:778–779

L'Avenir (periodical), 4:324, 5:854, 8:271, 309, 309–310, 12:290

Avenir de la Science (Renan), 12:126

Averbode Abbey (Flanders), 3:706

Averroës (Ibn Rushd), **1:932–934**, *933*, 940
  Adam of Buckfield, 1:108, 935
  Alumbrados, 1:323
  Aristotelianism, 1:225, 622, 672, 674, 933
  astrology, 1:813
  atomism, 1:833, 834
  causality, 3:304

Averroës (Ibn Rushd) *(continued)*
Cavalcanti, Guido, 3:310
cogitative power, 3:822–823, 824
concept of time, 14:78
double truth theory, 4:882
Duns Scotus, John, 4:936, 937
emanationism, 5:182
essence and existence, 5:364
immortality, 7:349, 353
influence, 1:623
knowledge, 8:216
naturalism, 1:677
overview, 1:622
rationalism, 11:922
scholasticism, 12:761
Themistius, 1:670
unity of intellect, 7:510
See also Averroism, Latin
Averroism, Latin, 1:623, **934–937**
Albert the Great, St., 1:224, 225, 674, 934, 935
Alexander of Aphrodisias, 1:676, 677
Aristotelianism, 1:672, 676
atomism, 1:834
Boethius of Sweden, 1:674, 935, 936, 2:457, 12:761
Bonaventure, St., 1:935, 936, 2:483
Christian philosophy, 3:540
immortality, 7:349
mendicant controversy, 2:483
role of Aquinas in controversy over, 14:20–21, 44
scholasticism, 12:761–762
Siger of Brabant, 12:761, 13:112–113
Sorbon, R., 13:326
soul, 13:339
See also Aristotelianism
Averroist Movement, 5:816
Aversa, Raphael, **1:937**
Avertissement Pastoral (1682), 8:804
Avery, Martha Moore, 6:336
Avery, Oswald T., 2:404
Avesta, **1:937–938**, 11:142–143, 12:145
Aviat, Francesca Salesia, Bl., **1:938**, *939*
Aviau, Charles d' (Abp. of Vienne), 2:141
Avicebrol. *See* Avicebron (ibn Gabirol, Solomon ben Judah)
Avicebron (ibn Gabirol, Solomon ben Judah), **1:938–939**
Albert the Great, St., 1:225
Aristotelianism, 1:673
Bombolognus of Bologna, 2:476
cabala, 1:938, 2:833
God as first principle, 8:8
Jewish Neoplatonism, 7:863
light symbolism, 3:674
pantheism, 10:826
soul, 13:344
Thomism and *Fons vitae*, 14:43–44
Avicenna (Ibn Sīnā, Abū), **1:939–941**
Adam of Buckfield, 1:108
Adam Pulchrae Mulieris, 1:110
Albert the Great, St., 1:225, 226, 674
Algazel, 1:281, 622, 940
Aristotelianism, 1:672, 940
astrology, 1:813
beauty, 2:184
biology, 2:401
causality, 3:304
Cavalcanti, Guido, 3:310
cogitative power, 3:822
concept of time, 14:78
distinction, 4:781
Dominic Gundisalvi, 4:830
Duns Scotus, John, 4:936
emanationism, 5:182
essence and existence, 5:364
estimative power, 5:374
existence, 5:533
God, 1:934
idealism, 7:297
I-It mysticism, 10:117
influence, 1:623
as inspiration to John Blund, 7:941
intellect, 1:621–622, 672, 933, 940
intentionality, 7:517
knowledge, 8:215–216
light symbolism, 3:674
mechanics, 12:809–810
pantheism, 10:826
possibility, 11:551
Siger of Brabant, 1:935
soul, 13:339, 343–344
unity of intellect, 7:510
universals, 14:324
Avigad, N., 2:379
Avignon (France), **1:941–943**, *942*
Alexander VIII (Pope), 1:262
Casoni, Filippo, 3:204
Concordat of 1801, 4:63
French influence, 5:846
Avignon papacy, 1:941, **943–945**, *944*, 3:603–604, 7:666
Adam Easton, 1:107
anointing, 1:479
Carmelite privileges, 13:99
Clement V (Pope), 1:943, 3:603, 780
French Revolution, 5:972
Ghibelline-Guelf conflict, 1:943, 3:855
leading diplomat, 13:130
Lupold of Bebenburg, 8:869
Nicholas of Clamanges's role, 10:371
papacy development during, 10:839
papal taxation, 1:941, 3:726–727
popes, 12:357
Protestant Reformation, 12:13
Richard Fitzralph sermons, 12:230
Richard of Bury, 12:231
role of Orsini family, 10:676
Saint Paul-Outside-the-Walls Abbey, 12:577
Shepey, J., 13:79
See also specific popes
Avignonese Registers, 10:859
Ávila, Francisco de, **1:945–946**
Ávila, Pedro de, Bl., 7:733
Avisamenta (Nieheim), 10:388
Avisamentia vel Reformationis methodus (Nicholas of Dinkelsbühl), 10:376
Avisso salutevole (Fauré), 5:647
Avitus (Avy), St., **1:946**
Avitus of Vienne, St., **1:946–947**, 3:596, 5:842, 9:440
Arianism, 1:663, 946
Sigismund conversion, 13:115
Aviz, Order of, 5:687
Avogadro, A., 1:835
Avranches, Council of (1172), **1:947**
Avril, Philippe, **1:947**
Avrillot, Barbé. *See* Marie de l'Incarnation, Bl.
Avvakum, **1:947–948**, 12:424
Awareness, 4:151, 153
Awe, wonder and, 14:833
Awful Disclosures of the Hotel Dieu Nunnery of Montreal (Monk), 10:170
Axiology, **1:948**
Axiomatic system, **1:948–950**
continuum, 4:216–217
logic, history of, 8:747–752
symbolic logic, 8:752–755
Axioms, 5:742–743
See also First Principles
Axum (Ethiopia) church, *5:400*
Ayala, Juan Manuel, 12:644
Ayala Niño, Arturo, Bl., 7:123
Ayer, Alfred Jules, 4:252, 5:397, 11:297
British moralists, 2:624
knowledge, 8:221
phenomenalism, 11:230
'Ayiṭ Ṣāvû'a (The Hypocrite) (Mapu), 6:663

Aylesford Monastery (Kent, England), 3:*141*

Aylmer, Walter, 7:579

Aymard, Bl., **1:950**

Aymer de la Chevalerie, Henriette, **1:950**, *951*, 4:293, 12:497

Aymer de Lusignan (Bp. of Winchester), **1:950–951**

Al-'Ayn, Qurrat, al-Bāb and, 2:3

Aynard (Abbot), 12:581

Azaria (Armenian Catholicos), 1:702

Azariah (King of Judah), 5:87, 7:640–641

Azeglio, Massimo Taparelli d', 7:672, 673

Azevedo, Ignacio de, Bl., **1:951–952**

Azevedo, Luiz de, **1:952**

Azevedo, Silvestro de, 2:901

Azitawwadu Inscription, 3:3

Azor, Juan, **1:952**

Azpilicueta, Martin de, 3:176, 828

Azpuru, Thomas (Abp.), 3:794, 795

Azriel of Gerona, 2:832

Aztec people, 3:246, 248
  Clavigero, Francisco Javier, 3:771
  conquistadores, 4:130–131
  religion, 12:507–508, 13:205

Aztec religion, **1:952–953**

Azymes, 2:651, 763
  See also Passover

B

Baader, Franz Xaver Von, **2:1**, 3:624, 6:183

Baal (Canaanite deity), **2:1–2**, *2*, 5:191, 14:269
  Astarte, 1:808
  Dagon, 4:493

Baal Cycle (Uagritic text), 14:267

Ba'al Shem Tov (Rabbi Israel), 6:660, 662, 7:872, 8:9

Baasha (King of Israel), 7:766

Al-Bāb (Muslim leader), 2:2–3, 12, 4:254, 255

Baba, Louis, Bl., 7:734

Baba Ram Dass (Richard Alpert), 10:273

Bābai the Great, 1:806

Babenstuber, Ludwig, 12:765, 14:51

Babgen I (Armenian Catholicos), 4:957–958

Babism, **2:2–3**, 12, 11:141
  See also Baha'ism; Shī'sm

Bablmann, Amando (Bp.), 5:885

Bābôe (Assyrian Catholicos), 1:806

Babolinus (Abbot), St., 12:566

Babylas, St., 1:522, 12:52

Babylon, city of, **2:3–4**
  Abdias of Babylon, St., 1:13–14
  archeological excavation of site of, 10:225
  Chaldeans, 3:369–370
  First dynasty (c. 1830-1531 B.C.), 9:529, 534–535
  Marduk, patron deity of, 5:267–269

Babylon Gate, 9:*526*

Babylon of the Chaldeans, Patriarchate of, **2:4–5**

Babylonia, **2:5**, 9:527–530
  afterlife, 1:164
  Akkad Dynasty (2360-2180 B.C.), 9:528, 534
  Aramaeans, 1:623–624
  astral religion, 1:809–810
  astrology, 1:810, 811, 3:370
  Berossus, 2:329–330
  books, 2:510
  capital punishment, 3:84
  covenant treaties, 4:325
  creation accounts, 4:337
  cult of Nebo, 10:220
  Cyrus the Great, 4:477–478
  Daniel, 4:509
  Diaspora, 7:867
  Early Dynastic period (c. 2800-2360 B.C.), 9:527–528
  First dynasty of Babylon (c. 1830-1531 B.C.), 9:529, 534–535
  genealogies of antediluvian kings of, 10:951
  Isin period (c. 1958-1733 B.C.), 9:529
  Jewish diaspora, 4:730
  Kassite period (c. 1531-1150 B.C.), 9:529
  Larsa period (c. 1961-1699 B.C.), 9:529
  Manichaeism, 9:107–109
  martyrs, 1:14
  Neo-Babylonian period, 9:529–530
  rabbinic academies, 8:8
  sacred prostitution, 11:774
  sons of God, 13:321
  Third dynasty of Ur (c. 2060-1950 B.C.), 9:528–529
  See also Mesopotamia, ancient

Babylonian Chronicle, 1:460

Babylonian codes, 8:393–394

Babylonian Exile, 8:179

Babylonian Targum. *See* Onkelos Targum

Bacchae (Euripides), 10:93

Bacchides, 9:11

Bacchus temple ruins, 10:*753*

Bacchylus (Bp. of Corinth), 6:436

Baccilieri, Ferdinando Maria, Bl., **2:5**

Bach, Carl Philipp Emmanuel, 2:5, 6–7

Bach, Johann Christian, **2:5–6**, 6, 6–7, *6*

Bach, Johann Christoph Friedrich, 2:6

Bach, Johann Sebastian, **2:6–8**, *7*, 114
  Buxtehude, Dietrich, 2:722
  as cantor, 3:75
  Chopin, Frédéric François, 3:525

Bach, Wilhelm Friedmann, 2:6

Bacha, Constantine, **2:8**

Bachelot, Alexis, 6:669, 12:497

Bachiarius (Spanish monk), **2:8**

Bachmann, Anna Maria (Mother Mary Francis), 5:888, 890

Backer, Alois, 2:9

Backer, Augustin de, **2:9**

Back-to-the-land movements, 4:782–783

Backus, Isaac, 2:79

Baclaran Church (Philippines), 10:*466*

Bacon, David William (Bp. of Portland, ME), **2:9**, 9:57, 11:531

Bacon, Francis, 2:9, **9–10**, 11:293, 14:360
  analysis and synthesis, 1:382
  aristocracy, 1:667
  Aristotelianism, 1:676
  atomism, 1:834
  causality, 3:300, 306
  educational philosophy, 5:91, 92
  Enlightenment, 5:254, 255
  influence on Comte, Auguste, 11:542
  mechanism, 9:415
  philosophy and science, 11:298–299
  writings, 5:207

Bacon, Leonard, 2:199

Bacon, Robert. *See* Robert Bacon

Bacon, Roger. *See* Roger Bacon

Badajóz, Antonio de, 5:875

Baden School (Neo-Kantian), 8:220, 10:237–238

Badia, Tommaso (Card.), **2:10–11**

Badía Mateu, José María, 2:92

Badilon of Marmoutier (Abbot), 12:585

Badin, Stephen Theodore, **2:11**, 5:757
  Chicago Archdiocese, 3:475
  first U.S. ordination, 2:39
  Indiana, 7:414
  Kentucky missions, 8:147–148
  St. Mary's Seminary, 3:181

Baducing. *See* Benedict Biscop, St.

Baeck, Leo, 8:13

Baena, Alphonsus de, Bl., 1:951

Baer, S., 2:355

Baeumker, Clemens, 12:776

Bagai, Council of, 4:862

Bagatti, B. B., 2:380, 10:217

Baghdad (Iraq), Chaldean Catholic Church in, **2:11–12**

Bagshaw, Christopher, **2:12**

Bagshawe, Edward G. (Bp.), 12:556

Bahā'-Allāh. *See* Bahā'-Ullāh (Muslim leader)

Baha'ism, **2:12–13**, 11:141

Bahamas, **2:13–15**, *14*, 3:120–121, 8:161

Bahā'-Ullāh (Muslim leader), 2:3, **12–13**

Bahir, Book of, 6:266–267

Bahira Legend, **2:15–16**, 10:51

Bahrain, **2:16**, *17*

Bahrām (King of Persia), 9:108

Bai jia (Hundred Schools), 3:508–510, 513

Baibars (Mamluk sultan), 4:405

Bailey, Benjamin, 7:403

Bailey, Laurence, Ven., 5:234

Baillargé, Jean, 3:714

Baillet, Abbé Maurice, 5:51

Baillief, Claude, 3:714

Bailly, L., 12:771

Bailly, Vincent de Paul, **2:16–17**, *18*, 12:591

Baily, D. Sherwin, 7:66

Bain, Alexander, 1:796

Bainbridge, Christopher (Card.), **2:17–18**, 14:894

Baines, Peter Augustine (Bp. of Siga), **2:18**

Baini, Giuseppe, 2:841

Bainvel, Jean Vincent, **2:18**

Bainville, Jacques, 1:81

Baird, Bellotti v., 1:33

Baius and Baianism, **2:18–21**, 5:499–500, 555, 12:621

    Augustinianism, 1:880, 884

    beatific vision, 2:169–170

    Comma pianum, 4:4

    concept of justice, 8:75

    concupiscence, 4:69

    destiny, supernatural, 4:694

    heresy, 6:776

    Lessius, L., 7:194, 8:518

Baixeras Berenguer, Juan, 2:92

Baizhang Huaihai, 3:511

Baja, California Jesuit Mission, 9:709–710

Bajocensis, Amadeus, 11:622

Bajothny (Prince of the Tatars), 13:132

Bakanja, Isidore, Bl., **2:22**

Baker, Augustine, 1:365

Baker, Charles. *See* Lewis, David (Charles Baker), St.

Baker, David Augustine, **2:22–23**, 102

Baker, Francis Asbury, **2:23**, 6:700, 11:40

Baker, Geoffrey, 1:464

Baker, Henry, 7:403

Baker, Henry, Sir, 7:257

Baker, Nelson Henry, **2:24**

Baker Diocese (OR), **2:23**

Bakhita, Giuseppina, St., **2:24**, *25*

Bakócz, Tamás (Card.), **2:24**, *26*

Bakunin, Mikhail, 1:384, 3:620

Balaam (Oriental seer), **2:26**

    oracles of, 9:541

Baladites. *See* Basilian Order of St. John Baptist

Balak (King of Moab), 2:26

Balas, Alexander, 9:11

Balassa, Bálint, **2:26**

Balat, Théodoric, St., **2:27**

Balbi, Giovanni, 5:206

Balbinus (Roman Emperor), 12:312

Balbo, Cesare, 7:672

Balboa, Vasco Nuñez de, 4:132

Balbuena, Bernardo de, 3:110

Balbus, John, 4:850

Baldachinos, 1:317, **2:27**, *28*, 8:348

Baldassaro di S. Catarina di Siena, 3:137

Baldeschi, Federico (Card.), 3:856

Baldi, Gerard, 12:765

Baldinucci, Antonio, Bl., **2:27–28**, 7:782

Baldo, Giuseppe, Bl., **2:28–29**

Baldus de Ubaldi

    Canon Law, 3:49

    Western Schism, 3:51

Baldwin (Abp. of Canterbury), 1:206

Baldwin (Kings of Jerusalem), **2:29–30**

Baldwin, William, 12:569

Baldwin I (King of Jerusalem), 2:29, 7:770, 774

    Crusades, 4:401

    Daniel Palomnik, 4:513

    Fulcher of Chartres, 6:21

    Ida of Boulogne, 7:289

Baldwin I of Flanders (Latin Emperor), 8:366

Baldwin II (King of Jerusalem), 2:29, 7:770, 774

    crown of thorns, 4:388

    holy lance, 7:31

Baldwin III (King of Jerusalem), 2:29, 4:403, 7:770, 774

Baldwin IV (King of Jerusalem), 2:29–30, 4:404, 7:774

Baldwin V (King of Jerusalem), 2:29–30, 7:774

Baldwin of Boulogne. *See* Baldwin I (King of Jerusalem)

Baldwin of Bury-St.-Edmunds, 2:713

Baldwin of Canterbury (Abp.), **2:30**

    Bartholomew of Exeter, 2:125

    Hubert Walter, 7:145

Baldwin of Edessa, 4:402

Baldwin of Hainault (Latin Byzantine Emperor), 2:787

Bale, John (Bp. of Ossory), 2:508, 637, 4:900

Bales, Christopher, Bl., **2:30**, 428, 5:231, 7:112

Balfour Declaration (Great Britain, 1917), 2:250, 7:645

Balić, C., 12:776

Balkan countries

    eras, 5:313

    Hapsburg interests in, 6:641

Ball, Eleonora Birmingham, Bl., 7:580

Ball, Frances Mary Teresa, **2:30–31**, 8:787, 10:68

Ball, John, **2:31**

Ballerini, Antonio, 1:311, **2:31**, 716, 12:462

Ballerini, Pietro and Girolamo, **2:31–32**

Ballou, Hosea, 14:321

Balmaceda, Francisco, **2:32**

Balmerino Abbey (Scotland), **2:32**

Balmes, Jaime Luciano, **2:32–33**

    apologetics, 3:624

    certitude, 3:352

    ideology, 12:770

    Thomistic revival, 12:773

Balsamon, Theodore, **2:33–34**, 10:415

    Canon Law, 2:773, 795, 3:46

    chorbishops, 3:526

    pentarchy theory, 2:825

Baltfrid (Bp. of Bayeux), 2:163

Balthasar, Hans Urs von, **2:34–35**, 4:31

    apologetics, 1:566

    atheism, 1:826

    Christian anthropology, 3:532

    descent of Christ into hell, 4:685

    eucharistic theology, 5:430

    foundational theology, 5:828

    Holy Trinity, 14:199

    International Theological Commission, 7:528

    natural order, 10:193

sacramental theology, 12:473

Speyr visions, 13:415–416

A Theological Anthropology, 9:814

transcendental Thomism, 14:56

Balthasar, N., 12:776

Balthasar Crossa (Card.). *See* John XXIII (Antipope)

Balthasar of St. Catherine of Siena, **2:35–36**

Baltic region deities, **2:36**

Baltimore, Barron v. (1833), 3:660

Baltimore, Councils of, 2:39, **41–47**, 10:541

　　Conwell, Henry, 4:245

　　Elder, William Henry, 5:144

　　England, John, 5:223

　　General Chapters of the Clergy (1783-89), 2:41–42

　　Meeting of American Bishops (1810), 2:43

　　Rosati, Joseph, 12:376

　　Society for the Propagation of the Faith, 11:753

　　plenaries (1852-84)

　　　　African American Catholics, 1:157

　　　　agreement, 13:405

　　　　Alemany, Joseph Sadoc, 1:249, 250, 12:647

　　　　Amat, Thaddeus, 1:332

　　　　apostolic delegation in the United States, 1:582, 585

　　　　Bouquillon controversy, 2:564

　　　　cathedrals, 3:262

　　　　Catholic grade schools, 8:132

　　　　clerical dress, 3:801–802

　　　　Dwenger, Joseph Gerhard, 4:957

　　　　fast and abstinence, 5:634

　　　　Feehan, Patrick Augustine, 5:663

　　　　Fitzgerald, Edward, 5:752

　　　　Lamy (Abp. of Santa Fe), 8:316

　　　　Loughlin, J., 8:798

　　　　Riordan, Patrick William, 12:250, 648

　　　　Robot, Isidore, 12:275

　　　　Ryan, Patrick John, 12:446

　　　　Sabetti, Luigi, 12:462

　　　　secret societies, 8:132

　　　　Seton, R., 13:35

　　provincials (1829-1849), 2:39, 43–45, 5:42, 796, 7:334, 12:646

Baltimore, George Calvert, Lord, 2:886, 3:649

　　Maryland, founding of, 9:299

　　missions, 9:724

Baltimore, Synod of (1791), 2:42–43

Baltimore Archdiocese (MD), **2:36–41**, 3:179

　　archives, 1:639, 639–640

　　Curtis, Alfred Allen, 4:445

　　Kenrick, F. P., 8:145

　　Keough, F. P., 8:153–154

　　Shehan, L. J., 13:76–77

　　See also Baltimore, Councils of

Baltimore Catechism, 2:41, 3:243, 244, 4:9

Baltimore Cathedral (Maryland), 2:*37*, 3:715, 717

Baltimore Catholic Review, 2:40

Balue, Jean (Card.), 5:659

Baluffi, Gaetano, **2:47**, 12:659

Baluze, Étienne, **2:47–48**, 4:192

Bamber, Edward, Bl., **2:48**, 5:236

Bamberg Cathedral (Germany), 3:601

Bamberg Diocese (Germany), 8:256–257

Banco Ambrosiano collapse, 8:250, 14:128

Banda, Hastings Kamuzu, 9:67–68

Bandas, Rudolph G., **2:48–49**

Bandinelli, Roland. *See* Alexander III (Pope)

Bandrés Jimémenez, Javier Luis, 2:92

Bandrés y Elósegui, María Antonia, Bl., **2:49**

Banerjee, K. M., 7:405

Báñez and Bañezianism, **2:49–51**, 5:935, 936

　　Ambrosius Catharinus, 1:347

　　Charles of the Assumption, 3:436

　　congruism, 4:120

　　de auxiliis controversy, 4:111

　　Divine concurrence, 4:71

　　free predetermination, 5:936

　　free will and grace, 5:935, 938

　　Ledesma, P., 8:443

　　omnscience controversy over, 10:597–598

　　predestination, 11:652

　　scholasticism, 12:764

　　speculative theology, 3:613

　　vision of God, desire for, 4:691

　　works, 2:51

Bangha, Béla, 7:218

Bangladesh, **2:51–54**, *52*, 7:21

Bangor (Wales), Ancient See of, **2:54**

Bangor Abbeys (Ireland and Wales), **2:54**, 3:864, 4:3

Bangor Antiphonary (St. Comgall), 1:577, 3:331

Bangor Fawr yn Arfon (Wales). *See* Bangor Abbeys (Ireland and Wales)

Bangor in the Ards of Ulster (Ireland). *See* Bangor Abbeys (Ireland and Wales)

Bangor Use, **2:55**

Bangorian controversy, 8:403

Bangor-ys-coed (Wales). *See* Bangor Abbeys (Ireland and Wales)

Banks, Nathaniel, 3:378

Banks, Robert J. (Bp. of Green Bay, WI), 14:783

Bannassat, Antoine, 12:276

Banners, as ecclesiastical symbol, 6:763

Bannon, John B., **2:55**

Bannwart, Clemens, 4:671

Banquet (Thalia) (Arius), 10:347

Bantus (brother of St. Beatus of Trier), 2:182

Baouardy, Maríam, Bl., **2:55–56**

Bapst, John (Father), **2:56**, 557, 9:56

Baptism

　　conditional baptism, 2:67

　　Councils of Carthage, 3:186, 188

　　deaconesses, 7:37

　　forced, 9:203, 204–205

　　God's spirit, 13:427–428

　　in the Holy Spirit, 3:393

　　iconography, 8:*619*, *622*

　　by immersion, 7:37

　　imposition of hands, 7:365–366

　　incorporation in Christ, 7:380

　　incorporation into the Church, 7:381–382

　　Judaism, 2:57

　　oils, 7:34–35

　　ordination candidates, 7:39

　　pagan, 2:56–57

　　Radical Reformation, 3:608

　　rebaptism, 3:186, 593

　　sponsors, 13:459

　　water, liturgical use of, 14:660–661

　　See also Baptism, Sacrament of

Baptism, Eucharist, and Ministry (World Council of Churches Commission on Faith and Order), 2:76–77, 12:477

Baptism, in the Bible, **2:56–60**

　　New Testament, 2:57–60

　　Old Testament, 2:57

　　terminology, 2:56

Baptism, Sacrament of, **2:60–67**

　　adult baptism, 2:64–65

　　affusion, 2:75–76

　　Alger of Liége, 1:283

　　Armenian liturgy, 1:709–710

　　aspersion, 2:76

Baptism, Sacrament of *(continued)*

Baptism, Eucharist, and Ministry (World Council of Churches Commission on Faith and Order), 2:76–77

Baptists, 2:78

Canon Law, 3:35

catechesis, 3:228, 229, 231

catechumenate, 3:249–254

Christian (term), 3:529

Confirmation, 4:84–88, 90

Coptic, 4:257

creeds, 4:349–355

death, 4:583

Donatism, 4:863–864

during Easter Vigil, 5:12, 15, 17

East Syrian rite, 5:5

ecumenism, 4:241

Ephpheta Rite, 5:276

Evira Council, 5:178

exorcism before, 5:552

Gallican rites, 6:72

heresies, 13:195

history, 2:61

iconography, 2:61, 12:485–486

immersion, 2:75

Jewish children, 5:948

Justin Martyr, St., 8:94–95

laity, 8:295

laity's mission, 8:291–292

lay spirituality, 8:416

Leo I (Pope), St., 8:477

Lima Text, 8:588, 589

liturgical history, 8:653–654

liturgical rituals, 2:62–64

man, creation of new, 9:87

mutual recognition, 2:66–67

mystagogy period in process of adult, 10:77

Novatianist Schism, 4:457–458

Pentecostalists, 11:106

People of God, 8:291

reviviscence, 12:206

Roman Rite of Christian Initiation of Adults, 2:76

sacramental theology, 2:59–60, 65–66

significance of Sunday, 13:608

sin, 13:146

sponsors, 13:459

submersion, 2:75

suffering, 13:587–588

Zwingli, Huldrych, 14:941

See also Anabaptists

Baptism Movement, 7:873

The Baptism of Christ (Gerard David), 7:*50*

The Baptism of Christ (Perugino), 2:*71*

The Baptism of Christ (Pisano), 7:*812*

The Baptism of Ethelbert of Kent by St. Augustine (Dyce), 5:*385*

Baptism of infants, 2:65, **67–70**, *69*

exorcism, 5:553

justification, 8:81

limbo, 8:591

liturgical rituals, 2:64, 70

Middle Ages, 8:658

objections to, 2:68–70

sacramental grace, 6:408

Servetus, M., 13:25

shift to, 8:656

unbaptized infants, fate of, 2:70

Baptism of the Lord, **2:70–73**, 8:857, 14:202

Baptismal names, 10:139–141, 971

Baptist Missionary Society, 9:697

Baptist of Mantua (Spagnoli), Bl., **2:73–74**, 551, 3:134, 142

Baptist Union, 5:928

Baptista, Mariano, 2:468

Baptisteries and baptismal fonts, 1:754, 2:*74*, **74–77**, 3:262, 685–686, 8:*619*, *622*, 13:196

Baptists, **2:77–81**

Christian Church (Disciples of Christ), 3:534

Christian Church merger, 4:117

colonial America, 3:646, 647, 652

confessions of faith, 4:82

England, 13:462–463

fundamentalism, 6:27

General Missionary Convention, 12:227

hymnody, 7:257–258

infant baptism, 2:69

mission, 3:108, 7:403, 8:46

Radical Reformation, 3:608

revivalism, 12:204

U.S. church membership, 3:719, 720

''Baptizers.'' *See* Mandaean religion

Bar, Cathérine de, **2:81**

Bar, François de, 1:396

Bar Archdiocese (Montenegro), 13:9

Bar Cocheba, Simon. *See* Bar Kokhba, Simon

Bar Kokhba, Simon (Bar Cocheba), 1:199, **2:83–84**, 7:867, 8:6

Bar Madani, John, 2:82

Bar mitzvah, **2:84–85**, 3:*76*, 8:11–12

Barabbas (Jewish insurgent), **2:85–86**

Barace, Cipriano, 2:465

Baradai, Jacob, 5:19

Baradai, James, **2:86**

Jacobites (Syrian), 7:691

Justinian I (Byzantine Emperor), 3:596

Monophysitism, 1:523, 525

Baradai, James (Bp. of Edessa), 5:82, 137

Baraga, Frederic (Bp. of Marquette, MI), **2:86–87**, *87*, 8:504

Baraldi, Teodora, 2:95

Barat, Madeleine Sophie, St., **2:87–88**, *88*, 3:622, 9:78, 12:493

Barba, John (Bp. of Teramo), 1:879

Barbados, 3:111, 120

Barbal, Diego. *See* Barbal Cosan, Jaime (James) Hilario, St.

Barbal Cosan, Jaime (James) Hilario, St., **2:88**, 633

Barbantini, María Domenica Brun, Bl., **2:88–89**

Barbara, St., **2:89**, 8:*621*

See also Fourteen Holy Helpers

Barbara Celarent (Gilby), 6:217

Barbarigo, Giovanni Francesco (Card.), **2:90**

Barbarigo, Gregory, St., **2:89**, 90, 3:791

Barbarigo, Marc' Antonio (Card.), **2:89–90**, 5:722, 12:101

Barbaro, Daniele, 2:90–91

Barbaro, Ermolao (1454-93, the Younger), 2:90

Barbaro, Ermolao (ca. 1410-71, the Elder), 2:90, *91*

Barbaro, Ermolao (d. 1622), 2:91

Barbaro, Francesco (d. 1454), 2:90

Barbaro, Francesco (d. 1616), 2:91

Barbaro, Nicolo, 2:90

Barbaro family, **2:90–91**

Barbastro (Spain), Martyrs of, **2:91–92**

Barbastro, Francisco Antonio, **2:91**

Barbatia, Andreas de (Andreas Siculus), **2:92–93**, 3:52, 91

Barbatus, St., **2:93**

Barbeaux Abbey (France), **2:93**

Barbelin, Felix Joseph, **2:93**

Barbelo-Gnostics, 6:260

Barber, Abigail. *See* St. Francis Xavier (Sister)

Barber, Daniel, 2:93–94, 3:472

Barber, Edward. *See* Stransham, Edward, Bl.

Barber, Jerusha. *See* Mary Austin (Sister)

Barber, Josephine, 2:94

Barber, Mary, 2:94

Barber, Samuel Joseph, 2:94

Barber, Susan. *See* Mary St. Joseph (Sister)

Barber, Virgil Horace, 2:94

Barber family, **2:93–94**

The Barber of Seville (Paisiello), 10:758

The Barber of Seville (Rossini), 12:389

Barberi, Domenico, Bl., **2:94**, *95*, 4:500, 5:251, 10:734

Barberini, Antonio (Card., 1569-1646), 2:95

Barberini, Antonio (Card., 1607-1671), 2:94–95

Barberini, Carlo, 2:94

Barberini, Cornelia, 2:95

Barberini, Francesco (Card.), 4:49

Barberini, Francesco (Card., 1597-1679), 2:94–95

Barberini, Francesco (Card., d. 1738), 2:95

Barberini, Francesco (fl. 1540), 2:94

Barberini, Maffeo (1568-1644). *See* Urban VIII (Pope)

Barberini, Maffeo (fl. 1650), 2:95

Barberini, Taddeo, 2:95

Barberini, Urbano, 2:95

Barberini family, 1:716, **2:94–95**

Barberino, Andrea da, 1:764

Barbier, Emmanuel, 7:503

Barbieri, Clelia Maria Rachel, St., **2:95–96**

Barbieri, Dominic, 12:632

Barbo, L., 12:577

Barbo, Pietro. *See* Paul II (Pope)

Barbosa, Agostino (Bp.), **2:96**

Barbosa, Januário da Cunha, **2:96**

Barcelona, Councils of, 4:87

Barcelona, Martyrs of, 7:124

Barcelona, Treaty of (1529), 7:669

Barcelona Pavilion, 3:680

Barclay, John, **2:96–97**

Barclay, Robert, **2:97**, 5:838

Barclay, W., 10:500

Barclayites. *See* Barclay, John

Bar-Cursus (Bp. of Tella), **2:82**

Bardas (brother of Empress Theodora), 7:309, 310, 11:310, 311

Bardas Sclerus, 1:504

Bardesanes (Bar-Daisān), **2:97–98**, 3:593, 6:260

Bardet, Gaston, 1:803

Bardili, C. G., 8:125

Bardo of Oppershoffen, St., **2:98**

Bardstown. *See* Louisville Archdiocese (KY)

Bardy, Gustave, **2:98**, 5:510, 10:963

Barelli, Armida, 9:731

Bar-Hebraeus (Gregorius Ibn Al-Ibri), **2:82–83**, 3:259

Bari, Council of (1098), 1:495

Baril II Ibn, 4:255

Barili, Agostino, 5:191

Barker, E., 1:679

Barking Abbey (England), **2:98–99**, 4:449

Barkworth, Mark, Bl., **2:99**, 5:233, 718

Barlaam and Joasaph

    Acts of the Martyrs, 1:93

    Aristides, 1:666

Barlaam and Joasaph (St. John Damascene), **2:100–101**

Barlaam Monastery (Greece), 2:*100*

Barlaam of Calabria, **2:99–100**

    Argyros, Isaac, 1:659

    controversy with Palamas, 10:765–766

    Dishypatos, David, 4:776

    Gregorius Akindynos, 6:475–476

    hesychasm, 2:763, 771, 794, 826, 827, 837

    papal primacy, 12:620

Barlow, Ambrose, Bl., **2:101**, 5:235

Barlow, Edward. *See* Barlow, Ambrose, Bl.

Barlow, William (Bp.), **2:101**, 12:544

Barlow, William Rudesind, **2:101–102**

Barmen Declaration (1934), 2:120, 4:81

Barnabas (Brother), 3:279

Barnabas, Epistle of, **2:102**, 5:509

    Canon Law, 3:37

    canonicity, 3:31

    catechesis, 3:228

    contraception, 4:220

    disciple as term, 4:774

    discovery, 2:652

    Lord's Day, 8:782

    Old Testament, 3:29

    Son of David, 13:310

Barnabas, St., 1:502, **2:102–103**, *103*

    Antioch, 1:521, 523

    Council of Jerusalem, 7:773

    Cyprus, 4:461

    journeys with St. Paul, 11:6, 7, 13–14, 15

    Mark, Evangelist, St., 9:182

Barnabas of Terni

    Bernardino of Feltre, Bl., 2:322

    works of charity, 3:414

Barnabites, **2:103–104**, 4:310

    Burma, 2:706

    Ferrari, Bartolomeo, Ven., 5:692

    founding, 3:610, 782

    Lambruschini, L., 8:307

    Sauli, Alexander, St., 12:708

    Zaccaria, St. Anthony Mary, St., 14:902

Barnabò, Alessandro (Card.), 5:81

Barnard of Vienne, St., **2:104**, 5:443

Barnes, Barnabe, 13:320

Barnes, Robert, 5:749

Barnette, West Virginia Board of Education v. (1943), 3:661–662

Barns, J. W. B., 3:465

Barocci, Federico, 2:114

Barolo, Giulia Falletti, 3:419

Baron, Hans, 7:193

Baron, Vincent, **2:104–105**, 3:102

Barone, Domenico, 8:356

Baronius, Caesar, Ven., 2:*105*, **105–106**, 5:754, 10:248, 12:248

    Borromeo, Federigo, 2:541

    censorship, 3:336

    Centuriators of Magdeburg, 3:348

    chronicles, 1:465

Baronius Club, 8:798

Barontus, St., **2:106**

Baroque architecture, 2:113–114, 3:*693*, *695*, 702–707

    altars, 1:317

    Altenburg Abbey, 1:321

    Cologne, 3:845

    liturgy, 3:670

    North American mission, 3:714

    St. Peter's Basilica, 3:701

    symbolism, 3:674–675

Baroque art, 2:114, 4:397

Baroque music, 1:1, 293, 766, 2:214–215, 353–354, 8:689–691

Baroque period, **2:106–117**

    Austria, 1:912–913

    Bohemia, 4:483

    Catholic revival, 4:313

    choirs, 3:523

    Church art patronage, 2:111

    government art patronage, 2:112

    literary language, 2:116

    literature, 2:115

    movement growth and spread, 2:107

    philosophy, 2:116–117

    religious order founders and reformers, 2:109

    spirit and motifs, 2:113

    theater and stagecraft, 2:115–116

    vestments, 8:636

Baroque period (continued)

See also Baroque architecture; Baroque art; Baroque music

Barozzi, Giacomo, 3:701

Barr, James, 14:83

Barradas, Constantino (Bp.), 2:590

Barré, Nicholas, Bl., **2:117**, 6:232, 12:291

Barreneche, Juan, 2:863

Barrera Izaquirre, Josefa Maria (1881-1936), 14:564, 566

Barret, C., 3:741

Barreto, Francisco (Father), 5:10

Barrett, C. K., 5:522, 523

Barrière, Jean de la, **2:117–118**, 3:747, 4:808, 5:707

Barriere, Peter, 3:51

Barrios, Juan de los (Bp. of Santa Marta), 3:848

Barrios, Justo Rufino, 12:372

Barron, Edward (Bp.), **2:118**, 8:551, 556, 12:709

Barron, Geoffrey, 7:582

Barron v. Baltimore (1833), 3:660

Barros Cámara, Jaime de, 5:840

Barruel, Augustin de, **2:118**, 5:969

Barry, Colman James, **2:119**

Barry, Gerald (Mother), **2:119**

Barry, John E. (Bp. of Savannah), **2:119–120**, 9:56, 12:709

Barry, Richard, 7:581

Barth, Karl, 2:120, **120–121**, 5:172

  analogy, 1:373, 379

  analogy of faith, 1:380–381

  Anselm of Canterbury, St., 1:496

  antimysticism, 10:115

  atheism, 1:825

  Barmen Declaration, 4:81

  Bultmann, Rudolf Karl, 2:690

  death of God, 4:584

  deconstructionism, 4:594

  dialectical theology, 4:721

  dogmatic theology, 4:812

  Ecumenical Movement, 5:74

  exegesis, 5:521

  existentialist faith, 5:596

  fatalism, 5:639

  fideism, 5:712

  Holy Trinity, 14:197

  humanism, 7:195–196, 198

  infant baptism, objection to, 2:69–70

  justification, 8:88

  neo-orthodoxy, 10:238

  predestination, 11:656–657

  religious experience, 5:556

scientia media doctrine, 5:935

Barthélemy, Dominque, 5:51

Bartholomaeus Anglicus, **2:121–123**, 343, 14:177

Bartholome, Peter W., 12:543

Bartholomeus de Martyribus. See Bartholomew of Braga, Ven.

Bartholomeus Hominis de Taiuti. See Bartholomew of Urbino (Bp.)

Bartholomew, Apostle, St., **2:123–124**

  Afghanistan, 1:153

  conversion of Tiridates III (Armenian king), 5:18

  shrine, 13:94

Bartholomew, Gospel of St., 1:559, 4:684

Bartholomew of Braga, Ven., **2:124**

Bartholomew of Brescia, **2:124–125**, 3:48, 49

Bartholomew of Byzantium, 2:825

Bartholomew of Exeter (Bp.), 2:30, 125

Bartholomew of Lucca (Bp. of Torcello), 1:465, **2:126**, 14:19, 47

Bartholomew of Marmoutier, St., **2:126**

Bartholomew of Pisa. See Bartholomew of San Concordio

Bartholomew of Rome, **2:126**, 3:69

Bartholomew of San Concordio, **2:126–127**, 3:52, 14:47

Bartholomew of Simeri, St., **2:127**, 12:656

Bartholomew of Trent, **2:127**

Bartholomew of Urbino (Bp.), 1:870, 875, 879, 883, 888, **2:127–128**

Bartholomew of Vicenza, Bl., **2:128**

Bartholomew the Englishman. See Bartholomaeus Anglicus

Bartholomites, **2:128**, 7:58

Bartning, Otto, 3:678, 711

Bartók, Béla, **2:128–129**, 129

"Bartolists," 2:129

Bartolo, Domenico di, 1:119

Bartolo of Sassoferrato, **2:129**, 3:52

Bartolocci, Giulio, **2:129–130**

Bartolomeo (Serafini) de Ravenna, 3:192

Barton, Elizabeth, **2:130**, 451, 5:749, 12:8, 210

Bartsch, H. W., 5:522, 7:850

Baruch (friend of prophet Jeremiah), **2:130–131**

Baruch, Book of, 1:552–553, **2:131**, 211, 8:396

Al-Baruni, 1:672

Barzana, Alonso, 1:649

Barzyński, Vincent, **2:132**

Al-Bāša. See Bacha, Constantine

Basalenque, Diego, **2:132**

Bascio, Matteo Serafini da, **2:132–133**, 3:611

Basedow, Johann Bernhard, 5:93, 263

Basel, Councils of (1431-49), **2:133–135**, 5:243

  Ambrose Traversari, Bl., 1:340

  anti-Semitic regulations, 7:871

  Bernardine of Siena, St., 2:321

  Brouns, Thomas, 2:635

  Capranica, Domenico, 3:91

  cardinalate, 3:105

  Cesarini, Giuliano, 3:357

  Communion, 7:231

  composition of, 4:302

  conciliarism, 1:647, 3:604, 4:56

  convocation of, 4:301

  Denmark, 4:665

  Escobar's abandonment, 5:352, 353

  Eugene IV (Pope), 1:647, 3:195, 197, 604, 5:444, 668

  Holy Innocents' Day, 2:574

  Hussites, 3:604, 605, 4:481, 7:231

  Langdon, J., 8:325

  Nicholas of Cusa's participation, 10:372

  papal taxation, 1:466

  Pragmatic Sanction of Bourges, 11:581–582

  recognition of Utaquists as Christians, 14:363

  regarding neophytes, 10:239

  Sheen Charterhouse protested, 13:75

  Sigismund convoking, 13:116

Basel Compact, 14:363

Basel Confession (1534), 10:77

Basel Missionary Society, 7:403

Basel-Ferrara-Florence, Council of, 3:51–52

Baseline, Theodore, 4:440

Basic Christian Communities, 1:655, **2:135**

  Bolivia, 2:469

  Catholic social thought, 13:257

  evangelization, 9:727–728

  lay spirituality, 8:417–418

  liberation theology, 8:547

Basic Norms for the Formation of Permanent Deacons, 4:553

Basil, Mary (Sister Mary Francis), 5:880

Basil I (Armenian Catholicos), 1:453, 701

Basil I (Byzantine Emperor), 2:754, 823

  Constantinople Council IV, 4:194, 195

  Damasus I (Pope), St., 4:504

histories written, 4:175
Ignatius of Constantinople, 7:310
Photian Schism, 5:23
Photius, 7:310, 11:311–312
political support, 2:785
unity of Church, 4:194
Basil II (Byzantine Emperor)
  Anthony III (Patriarch), 1:504
  Bulgaria, 2:746, 786
  early Russian Church, 12:421
  Eastern Schism, 2:757
  political support, 2:785–786
Basil of Ancyra (Bp.), **2:139–140**, 5:457
  Arianism, 1:663
  chorbishops, 3:526
  Council of Sardica, 12:692
  Cyril of Jerusalem, 4:471
  Synod of Ancyra (358), 1:398
Basil of Cilicia, 2:797
Basil the Bogomil, 1:276
  See also Bogomilism
Basil the Great, St., **2:135–139**, *136*,
  144–145, 846, 5:455
  alleged works, 2:137
  Ambrose, St., 1:337
  Amphilochius of Iconium, St., 1:365
  Anthimus of Tyana, 1:503
  Apollinaris of Laodicea, 1:560
  apophatic theology, 1:568
  Aredius, St., 1:645
  Arianism, 1:663, 2:792
  baptism, 2:67
  baptism of the Holy Spirit, 3:393
  beatific vision, 2:169, 172
  biblical canon, 3:32
  biblical catenae, 3:258
  Book of Common Prayer, 2:524
  Carthusian spirituality, 3:190
  Cassian, John, 3:207
  cenobitism, 3:334, 335
  charity, 3:395
  Christmas, 3:553
  conformity, 4:92
  creedal statements, 4:353, 354
  Cynics, 4:456
  death, 3:594
  devotion to Trinity, 14:205
  Dionysius (Pope), St., 4:753
  Divine personal properties, 11:755
  doctrine, development of, 4:804
  dogma as term, 4:811
  eucharistic epiclesis, 5:279
  Eustathius of Sebaste, 5:457
  grace, 6:401

Hellenistic culture, 2:772
hexaemeron, 6:814–815
Holy Trinity, 2:137
homiletics, 2:773
homilies, 5:510, 7:62
hospitals, 7:127
human will, 9:859
images, veneration of, 7:325
influence on Great Lavra Rule, 10:31
liturgy, 2:811, 812–813
Macrina the Elder, 9:25
marriage, 1:151
order of universe, 14:329
preaching, 11:609, 618
relics, 12:51
religious habit, 12:99
religious obedience, 10:506
School of Alexandria, 1:272
schools of Athens, 1:829
Ukrainian translation, 13:80
works, 2:136
works of charity, 3:406, 411
  See also Basilian monasticism;
    Cappadocians
Basile of Soissons, **2:140**
Basilian Fathers in America, 2:142
Basilian monasticism, 2:127, **140–141**,
  142–143
  See also specific Basilian orders
Basilian Order of Aleppo, 2:144
Basilian Order of Grottaferrata, 2:143
Basilian Order of St. John Baptist, 2:144
Basilian Order of St. Josaphat, 2:141,
  143–144
Basilian Order of St. Saviour, 2:144
Basilian Orders of the Melkite Greek
  Catholic Church, 2:141, 144
Basilians, **2:141–142**, 8:139
Basilians (Byzantine), 2:140–141,
  142–144
  Albania, 1:214
  Bessarion, Cardinal, 2:341
  Russia, 3:265
  Ruthenian Catholics, 12:422
  Ṣaifi, Euthymios, 12:529
  Saint Alexander of Orosh Abbey,
    12:532
  Santa Maria di Polsi Abbey (Italy),
    12:679
  Sheptyts'kyĭ, 13:79
  Shuwairite Order, 1:13
  superiors, 1:9
Basilians (Sisters of the Order of St.
  Basil the Great), **2:144–145**
Basilica (law code), 4:175

Basilica Julia (Rome), 2:145
Basilica of Aquileia (Italy), 2:*146*
Basilica of St. John Lateran (Rome),
  2:146, 3:261, 8:347–348, *351, 352*
  art, 3:*790*
  Clement XII (Pope), 3:790
  erection of, 1:754
  facade, 8:358
  importance, 3:686
  restoration, 13:15
  Sergius IV (Pope), epitaph, 13:*16*
  suburbicarian bishops, 13:140
Basilica of St. Paul-Outside-the-Walls
  (Rome), 11:*5*
Basilica of St. Peter (Rome), 2:146
Basilica of the Nativity (Bethlehem),
  1:757, 2:347, *349*
Basilica of the Sacred Heart (South
  Bend, IN), 7:*414*
Basilica Portiana (Milan), 1:338
Basilicas, **2:145–148**
  cathedrals, 3:262
  Constantine I (the Great) (Roman
    Emperor), 3:594, 684
  early church, 1:752, 754, 756–757,
    758, 3:594, 684–686
  Egypt, 1:758
  as martyria, 9:231–232
  See also Church architecture; *specific
    churches*
Basilides (Gnostic teacher), **2:148–149**,
  6:259
  Abraxas, 1:40
  Alexandria, 1:268
  Antioch, 1:521
  emanationism, 5:181
Basilides, SS., **2:149**
Basiliscus (Byzantine Emperor), **2:149**,
  150
  Acacian Schism, 1:49
  Simplicius (Pope), St., 13:140
  Zeno, 14:916
"The Basis of Union" (1957), 14:306
Baskerville, John, 2:523
Basly, D. M. de, 1:802
Basotho people, 8:515
Basques, first saint canonized, 12:659
Bassi, Metteo di, 3:782
Bassianus of Ephesus (Bp.), **2:151**
Bassus continuus, 2:114, 115
Bastille, taking of, engraving by
  Berthault, 5:*970*
Bastnagel, Clement, 3:58
Bataille, George, 1:412
Bataille, Nicolas, 1:544

Bataillon, Pierre Marie, **2:151**, 3:378

Bates (Battie), Antony, Ven., 5:234

Bath, John, 7:581

Bath, Thomas, 7:581

Bath Abbey (England), **2:151**

Bath and Glastonbury, Ancient See of (England), 2:152, 12:711

Bath and Wells, Ancient See of (England), **2:152–153**, 3:262, 13:467

Bathildis (Queen), 1:894, 2:334

Bathildis, St., **2:153**, 5:793
    Chelles Convent, 3:463
    Leodegar of Autun, 8:496
    works of charity, 3:409

Báthory, Andrew (Bp. of Nagyvárad), 2:153

Báthory, Andrew (Card.), 2:153

Báthory, Ladislaus, Bl., 2:153

Báthory, Sigismund, 2:153–154

Báthory, Stephen. *See* Stephen Báthory (King of Poland)

Báthory family, **2:153–154**

Baths and bathing, in Christian antiquity, **2:154–155**

Bathsheba (Queen of Israel), 4:537, 6:126

Batiffol, Pierre, **2:155**, 409, 9:78, 10:963

Batista, Cícero Romão, **2:155**

Batista, Fulgencio, 4:418

Batiz Sainz, Luis, St., **2:155–156**, **6:545**, 12:292

Baton Rouge Diocese (LA), **2:156**

Batons, as ecclesiastical symbol, 6:763

La Battaglia di Legnano (Verdi), 14:446

Batten, Samuel Zane, 2:80

Batteux, C., 1:142

Battini, Constantine, 12:765

Battle Abbey (England), **2:156**, *157*, 3:481

Battle of Lepanto (fresco by Giorgio Vasari and Daniele da Volterra), 8:505

Battle Standards, Cult of, **2:156–157**

Bauch, Bruno, **2:157–158**, 10:236

Baudon, Adolphe, 5:581

Baudot, Anatole de, 3:710

Baudouin, Louis Marie, Ven., **2:158**

Baudouin I (King of Belgium), 2:220, 221

Baudrillart, Henri Marie Alfred (Card.), **2:158**

Baudry (Abp. of Dol), 9:450–451

Baudry, Charles, 8:388

Baudry of Bourguilen-Vallée, 1:432

Bauer, André, St., **2:158–159**

Bauer, Bruno, **2:159**, 385, 5:521, 6:709

Bauer, Georg Lorenz, 2:383–384

Baum, William (Card.), 3:237, 14:658

Baumann, J., 10:121

Baume, Henry de la, Bl., 3:833

Bäumer, Suitbert, **2:159**

Baumgarten, Alexander Gottlieb, 1:141, 746, 3:679, 5:47, 263, 534

Baumgartner, M., 12:776

Baumstark, Anton, **2:159–160**, 5:5, 6, 8:722, 10:963

Bauny, Étienne, **2:160**

Baur, Ferdinand Christian, **2:160–161**, 5:521, 9:114, 12:256, 14:234

Baur, Hermann, 3:712

Bautain, Louis Eugène Marie, **2:161**
    Bonnetty, Augustin, 2:508
    faith, 5:596
    fideism, 5:712
    Sisters of St. Louis founder, 12:562

Bautista, Pedro, St., 7:732

Bautista de Morales, Juan, 3:495

Bautista Jiménez, Eduardo, Bl., 7:125

Bauzan, Jean (abbé), 5:796

Bavo, St., **2:161**, 12:587

Bawden, William, **2:161–162**

Baxter, Richard, **2:162**

Bay, Michel de. *See* Baius and Baianism

Bay Psalm Book, **2:162**, 7:257

Al-Bayān (The Manifestation) (al-Bāb), 2:3

Bayazid II, 7:31

Bayer, Xaver, 5:681

Bayeux Diocese (France), **2:162–164**

Bayeux Tapestry, 2:*163*, 164

Bayle, Pierre, **2:164–165**, 5:255
    conservation, 4:162
    skepticism, 13:203

Bayley, James Roosevelt (Abp. of Baltimore), 2:39, **165–166**, 10:282, 323, 329

Bays, Marguerite, Bl., **2:166**

The Bazaaar of Heracelides (Nestorius), 10:252, 254

Bazaine, J., 1:803, 3:713

Bazianus (12th c. canonist), **2:166**

Bazin, John Stephen (Bp. of Vincennes, IN), **2:166–167**, 7:413

Bazin, René, 1:432

Bazzi, J. A., 3:484

Be Not Afraid: Studies in Personalist Sociology (Mounier), 10:31

Bea, Augustin (Card.), **2:167**, 3:625, 13:19

Beachy, Moses M., 1:361

Beagle, 4:531

Beale, Genevieve (Mother), 12:562

Beasley, Abraham, 2:167–168

Beasley, Mathilda (Mother), **2:167–168**

Beason, Davis v. (1890), 3:660

Beata nobis gaudia (hymn), **2:168**

Beata Virgo Maria (Roskoványi), 12:383

Beati Urbani papae II vita, Dissertatio de pallio archiepiscopali (Ruinart), 12:407

Beatific vision, **2:168–177**
    (im)possibility, 2:168–170
    Augustinianism, 1:883, 885
    Baianism, 2:20
    Benedict XII (Pope), 2:243–244
    characteristics, 2:175–176
    Christ, 7:819, 822–823, 828
    Christ our life, 8:572
    church teachings, 2:172–174
    created actuation by uncreated act, 4:335–336
    deprivation, 11:826
    desire to see God, 4:690–691
    destiny, supernatural, 4:694–695
    Divine judgment, 8:33
    good, 6:353
    heaven, 6:686–688
    holiness, 7:10
    immortality, 7:354
    Incarnation, 7:374
    ineffability of God, 7:446
    John XXII (Pope), 3:604, 7:932, 947, 948
    light of glory, 8:585
    Mary, Blessed Virgin of, 9:253–254
    mysteries of faith, 2:176
    natural order and call to, 10:204
    nature, 2:174–175
    New Testament, 2:170, 171–172
    Old Testament, 2:170–171
    potency-act model, 8:833
    Réponse (Malebranche), 9:74
    See also Glorified body

Beatification, **2:177**
    canonization, 3:65–66
    Congregation of Sacred Rites and Ceremonies and, 12:256
    cult (worship), 4:426
    heroic virtue, 14:554
    hope as neccesity for, 7:102
    See also specific blesseds

Beatitudes, Christian life, **2:178–179**, 3:546, 5:31, 9:99, 100
    See also Goodness

Beatitudes, in the Bible, **2:177–178**

Beaton, David (Card.), 1:630, 2:179

Beaton, James (1473-1539, Abp. of Glasgow), **2:179**

Beaton, James (1517-1603, Abp. of Glasgow), **2:180**

Beatrice, Dante Alighieri and, 4:517, 520

Beatrice Cenci (Reni), 2:107

Beatrice d'Este I, Bl., **2:180**

Beatrice d'Este II, Bl., **2:180**

Beatrice of Nazareth, Bl., **2:180–181**

Beatrice of Tuscany, **2:181**

Beatus, St., **2:181**

Beatus Apocalypse, 9:129

Beatus of Liébana, **2:181–182**, 5:161–162, 775

   Apocalypse iconography, 1:543, 545

   Elipandus, 13:379

   Silos Abbey, 13:120

Beatus of Trier, St., **2:182**

Beatus qui intelligit (Richard of Conington), 12:232

Beauchamp, Richard (Bp. of Salisbury), **2:182–183**

Beaucousin, Richard, 3:192

Beauduin, Lambert, **2:183**

   active lay participation, 8:673

   Chevetogne Monastery, 3:472

   liturgical history, 8:663–664

   liturgical movement, 8:672–673

   living the liturgy, 8:628

Beaufort, Henry (Card.), **2:183**

   Bourgchier, Thomas, 2:566

   Chichele, Henry, 3:481

Beaufort, Lady Margaret, **2:184**

Beaulieu, Edict of, 7:167

Beaulieu, Treaty of (1576), 8:424

La Beaume, monastery (France), 8:63

Beaupré, Anne de, Ste., 8:383

Beausobre, Isaac de (fl. 1734), 9:114

Beauty, **2:184–188**

   as a transcendental, 2:184–186

   aesthetics, 2:186–187

   art, 1:743, 746

   nature of, 2:187–188

   as property of being, 14:152

Beauvais (France), **2:188–189**

Beauvais, Buzenvol de (Card.), 3:786

Beauvais Cathedral (France), 3:696, 697

Beauvoir, Simone de, 5:388, 398

   Angela of Foligno, Bl., 1:412

   existentialism, 5:544

   feminism, 5:672, 677

Beaven, Thomas (Bp. of Boston), 9:307

Bec Abbey (France), 2:*189*, **189–190**

Becanus, Martin, **2:191**

Beccadelli, Leonardo, 12:117

Beccaria, Cesare Bonesana, **2:191**, 3:87–88

Beccerra Tanco, Luis, **2:191–192**

Beche, John, Bl., **2:192**, 5:226, 14:456

Beck, J. S., 8:125, 12:345

Becker, Christopher Edmund, **2:192**

Becker, Thomas Andrew (Bp.), **2:192–193**

   as Bp. of Savannah, GA, 2:168, 12:709–710

   as Bp. of Wilmington, DE, 4:625, 14:764

   Catholic University of America, 3:290

Becket, Thomas, St., **2:193–194**, 3:*71*, 5:240

   Bartholomew of Exeter, support of, 2:125

   Celestine III (Pope), 3:319

   Eliot's play about, 5:161

   feast of, 3:556

   Foliot, Gilbert, 5:787–788

   Henry II, 6:738

   martyrdom, 2:*193*, 5:241, 787

   relics of, 3:72, 73, 761

   Roger de Pont l'Évêque, 12:286

   Roger of Worcester, supporter of, 12:289

   See also Becket affair

Becket affair, 3:72

   Alan of Tewkesbury, 1:206

   Alexander III (Pope), 1:255–256, 947

   Arnulf of Lisieux, 1:720

   Carthusians, 3:194

   Clarendon Constitutions, 3:72, 762

   Council of Avranches, 1:947

Beckett, Samuel

   absurdity, 1:48, 49

   existentialism, 5:544, 546

Beckington, Thomas. *See* Bekynton, Thomas (Bp.)

Beckman, Francis J. L. (Bp. of Dubuque, IA), 4:923

Beckx, Pieter, 1:65, 7:789

Becoming, **2:194–195**, 6:289

   being vs., 5:99, 101

   continuum, 4:215

   contradiction, 4:224

   nature as principle, 10:208

   See also Being

Becon, Thomas, 1:733

Béda, Noël, 5:847

Bede, St., **2:195–197**, 9:*609*

   Acca of Hexham, St., 1:57

   Aidan of Lindisfarne, St., 1:192

   Aldhelm, St., 1:246

   Anglo-Saxon origins, 1:449

   annals, 1:460

   biblical catenae, 3:258

   biblical theology, 2:382

   cantors, 3:75

   catechesis, 3:230

   Cedd, St., 3:316

   Ceolfrid of Wearmouth, St., 3:348

   chronicles and annals, 1:461, 462

   chronology, 3:571

   computus, 4:46

   Cuthbert of Wearmouth, 4:449

   denotation of Sundays, 4:832

   Ely Abbey, 5:179

   exegetical works, 5:514, 515

   Honorius I (Pope), 7:80

   hymns, 7:245

   Latin literature, 9:442

   martyrologies, 9:233

   monastic bishops, 2:422

   multiplication of martyrologies, 8:643

   preaching, 11:611, 619

   science, 12:807–808

   Solemnity of All Saints, 1:289

   writings, 5:239

   writings of Pseudo-Dionysius, 11:801

Bedell, William (Bp. of Kilmore), 2:368

Bedingfeld, Frances, **2:197**

Bedingfeld, Thomas, Ven., 5:236

Bedini, Cajeton, 3:659

Bedini, Gaetano (Card.), **2:197**

   apostolic delegation in the United States, 1:581

   Purcell, John Baptist, 11:820

   visit to Milwaukee, 9:646–647

Bedjan, Paul, **2:198**

Bedloe, William, 3:830

Bedón, Pedro, **2:198**, 424

Bedyll, Thomas, **2:198**

Bee, St. *See* Bega, St.

Beecher, Harriet, 2:*199*

Beecher, Henry Ward, 2:199–200

Beecher, Lyman, 2:199, 5:467, 10:169, 13:797

Beecher family, 2:*199*, **199–200**

Beelen, Jan Theodoor, **2:200**

Beelzebub. *See* Beelzebul

Beelzebul, **2:200**, 5:174

Beersheba, 1:36

Beesley, George, Bl., **2:200–201**, 5:231

Beethoven, Caspar Anton Karl van, 2:201, 202

Beethoven, Johann van, 2:201

Beethoven, Karl van, 2:202

Beethoven, Ludwig van, 2:*201*, **201–203**

    Albrechtsberger, Johann Georg, 1:234

    Cherubini, Luigi, 3:468

    liturgical music history, 8:693

Beethoven, Maria Magdalena van, 2:201

Beethoven, Nikolaus Johann van, 2:202

Bega, St., **2:203**

Begel, John Joseph, 7:207

Begg, Christopher, 7:528

Begga, St., **2:203**

    Gertrude of Nivelles, St., 6:191

    Iduberga, Bl., 7:306

Beggar (Theodoret of Cyr), 13:879

Begging, 3:417

Bégin, Louis Nazaire (Card.), **2:204**

Begin Here (Sayers), 12:716

Beginnings in Ritual Studies (Grimes), 12:258

Beginnings of Christianity (Lake and Jackson), 8:298

Begley, Michael J. (Bp. of Charlotte), 3:437

Begon of Murat, 2:322

Begriffsschrift (Frege), 8:752

Begu, St., 2:203

Béguelin, N. de, 12:769

Beguignot, Claude, 12:276

Béguin, Albert, 2:303

Béguinage Church (Malines, Flanders), 3:706

Beguines and Beghards, **2:204–205**, *205*, 5:45, 889

    Belgium, 2:217

    destiny, supernatural, 4:694

    Douceline of the Midi, 4:885

    hospitals, 7:120

    persecution, 2:205

    Poverty Movement, 11:572

    rise in the Low Countries, 10:258

    Soubiran, M., 13:331

    works of charity, 3:413

    See also Picards

Behavior sciences, moral theology and, 9:856

Behaviorism, associationism and, 1:797

Beheim, Lorenz, **2:206**

Behemoth and Leviathan engraving (Blake), 10:*130*

Behm, Johannes, 2:874

Behm, Michel, 2:874

Behrens, Peter, 3:679, 712

Behrensmeyer, Christopher (Father), 5:884

Die beiden Grundprobleme der Ethik (Schopenhauer), 12:785

Beijing Convention (1860), 3:498

Being, **2:206–209**, 11:284

    accident, 1:60

    act, 1:74

    agnosticism, 1:182

    analogy, 1:371, 372, 376

    Averroës, 1:933

    Bergson, Henri Louis, 2:297

    Boethius, 2:456

    categories, 1:59–60, 77, 670, 681, 3:255–258, 300

    continuum vs., 4:215

    contradiction, 4:223

    criteriology, 4:368

    deconstructionism, 4:593

    Divine concurrence, 4:70

    Duns Scotus, John, 4:936

    eros and agape, 8:826

    freedom, 5:940

    Gioberti, Vincenzo, 6:229–230

    God as, 8:209

    good, 6:348

    identity principle, 7:303–304

    immutability of God, 7:356–357

    intelligibility, 7:515–516

    Lavelle, L., 8:387

    matter, 9:339–340

    metaphysics, 9:549, 550–551

    nothingness, 12:696–697

    now related to mobile, 10:470

    Peter Thomae, 11:208

    rational love, 8:825

    Siva, 13:194

    Spinoza, 13:419

    Thomistic thought on static structure, 10:908

    transcendental properties, 14:151

    Truth, 8:399

    wisdom, 14:786

    See also Becoming; Possibility

Being (*causa essendi*), 5:99

Being and Nothingness (Sartre), 1:541, 12:697

Being and Time (Heidegger), 1:540, 6:789, 10:607

Beis, R. H., 10:194

Beitang (Northern) Cathedral (China), 3:*497*

Bek, Anthony (Bp.), **2:209**

Bek, Thomas (Bp.), 12:544

Bekken, Dean, 8:539, 540

Bekker, J., 1:678

Bekynton, Thomas (Bp.), **2:209–210**

Bel (Mesopotamian deity), **2:210**

Bel and the dragon (Bible story), **2:210–211**, 4:509

Bel canto, 3:525

Béla III (King of Hungary), 5:108, 7:210

Béla IV (King of Hungary), 7:210

Bélanger, Dina, Bl., **2:211**

Belarus, 2:143, *211*, **211–214**

Belasyse, John, **2:214**

Belaunzarán, José María de Jesús (Bp.), **2:214–215**

Belchiam, Thomas, Ven., 5:226

Belcourt, George Anthony, **2:215**

Belgian Congregation. *See* Annunciation Congregation

Belgic Confession, 3:543

Belgium, **2:215–222**

    catechesis, 3:244, 245

    Catholic Action, 3:277

    church architecture, 3:713

    Church-state relations, 3:641

    Corpus Christi feast, 4:272

    demographics, 2:217, 5:615

    education, 8:491

    Jocism, 7:889

    Josephinism, 5:913–914

    Lateau, Louise, 8:346–347

    liturgical movement, 8:672–673

    Loos, Cornelius, 8:777

    Louvain, American College, 8:820–823

    Lutgardis, St., 8:877

    map, 2:*216*

    mission, early Church, 8:322

    onanism, 4:222

    social justice, 3:620

Beliaev, N. J., 12:434

Beliefs, **2:222–224**, 5:198

    See also Faith

Beliefs and Opinions (*Kitāb al-Amanāt wal-I'tiqadāt*) (Sa'adia ben Joseph), 7:863, 12:450

Belisarius (Byzantine general), **2:224**

    Agapetus I (Pope), St., 1:172

    Sicily, 13:103

    Silverius (Pope), St. implicated, 13:123

Belize, **2:224–225**, *226*

Bell, Alden J. (Bp.), 2:872

Bell, Arthur, Bl., **2:225–226**, 5:236

Bell, Clive, 1:143, 144

Bell, Endorus N., 1:789

Bell, Francis. *See* Bell, Arthur, Bl.

Bell, James, Bl., **2:226**, 5:228

Bella, Giano della, 5:767

Bellacci, Thomas, 1:507

Bellah, Robert, 2:223, 3:755–756

Bellamera, Aegidius, 3:52

Bellamy, Edward, 14:361

Bellarmine, Robert, St., **2:226–228**, 7:782

   absolutism, 1:44

   Acquaviva, Claudius, 1:72

   Aloysius Gonzaga, St., 1:305

   Andrewe, Richard, 1:408

   apologetics, 1:564

   Aristotelianism, 1:678

   ars moriendi, 1:733–734

   Borromeo, Federigo, 2:541

   catechesis, 3:234–235, 242, 244

   choice, 3:521

   Church-State relations, 3:639, 5:395

   Comitli, Paolo, 4:4

   congruism, 4:120–121

   democracy, 4:640

   distinguishing between body and soul, 10:104

   Divine right of kings, 4:788

   ecclesiology, 5:37

   faith, 5:597

   free will, 5:938

   Galileo, 6:62–63

   heliocentrism, 6:61

   James I, 7:705

   Oath of Allegiance (or Obedience) of 1606, 10:500

   papal Antichrist, 1:517

   patristic studies, 10:963

   preaching, 11:621

   priesthood, 11:704

   reform, 4:312

   Reformation exegesis, 5:518

   relics of saints, 12:55

   Roman Breviary, 5:820

   Sarpi, Paolo, 12:694

   scholasticism, 12:766

   social contract, 13:240

   society (church as), 13:286

   soul of the Church, 13:359

   Thomistic principles, 14:49

   transubstantiation, 14:160

Belleli, Fulgenzio, 1:884, 889

Bellesini, Stefano, Bl., **2:228**

Belleville, Jeanne de, 12:486

Bellevue Hospital, 7:132

Le Bellezze della fede (Ventura), 14:442

Bellini, Gentile, 2:228–229

Bellini, Giovanni, 2:229, *229*, 12:*146*

Bellini, Jacopo, 2:228

Bellini, Vincenzo, **2:229–230**, *230*

Bellini family, **2:228–229**

Bellino, G., 3:259

Bellinzaga, Isabella Cristina, **2:230**, 6:48

Belloc, Joseph Hilaire Pierre, **2:230–231**, *231*, 5:252

   Chesterton, Gilbert Keith, 3:470

   distributism, 4:782

Bellot, Paul, **2:231–232**, 3:713

Bellotti v. Baird, 1:33

Bellovacensis. *See* Vincent of Beauvais

Belloy, Jean Baptiste de (Card.), **2:232**

Bells, **2:232–234**, 8:700

Belluschi, Pietro, 3:717

Belmont, François Vachon de, **2:234**

Belmont Abbey (North Carolina), 3:437

Belo, Carlos Filipe Ximenes (Bp.), 5:9–10, *9*

Belorussian Autocephalous Orthodox Church, 2:212, 214

Belorussian Orthodox Church, 2:213

Belostoksky, Gavril, 9:436

Belson, Thomas, Bl., **2:234**, 5:231

Belsunce de Castlemoran, Henri François Xavier de (Bp.), **2:234**

Belthandros and Chrysantza, 2:806

Beltrán, Aurelio, 2:468

Beltrán, Edgar, 5:203

Beltran, Eusebius J. (Bp. of Tulsa), 14:235

Beltrán, Louis, Bl., 7:734

Beltrán, Luis, **2:234–235**

Beltrán Llorca, Enrique, Bl., 7:123

Bêmâ, 5:5, 7

Bembo, Pietro, 3:484, 12:526

Ben Asher, Aaron ben Moses, 2:355, 356, 357

Ben Chayyim, Jacob, 2:355

Ben Ezra, Juan Josafat. *See* Lacunza y Díaz, Manuel de

Ben Hakana, Neḥunya, 2:831

Ben Joseph, Akiba, Bar Kokhba and, 2:83

Ben Naphtali school, 2:357, 358

Benaglio, Giuseppe, 12:490

Der Benan-Brief (Planitz), 7:852

Benard, Edmond D., 11:625

Bénard, Laurent, **2:235**

Benardo, St. (statue), 10:*970*

Benavides, Alonso de, **2:235**, 10:285, 12:674

Benavides, Miguel de (Abp. of Manila), **2:235–236**

Bencivieni di Pepo (Cimabue), 2:374

Benda, Václav, 4:487

Ben-Dov, M., 2:379–380, 381

Benê Mikrā (Sons of the Scriptures), 7:868

Benedicamus Domino, **2:236**

Benedicenda (Schulte), 12:789

Benedicite Dominum (Canticle of the Three Youths in the Fiery Furnace), 3:73, 4:890

Benedict (Card.) (papal legate), 2:761

Benedict (hermit), St. *See* Zoërardus and Benedict, SS.

Benedict, Ruth, 4:430

Benedict, St., **2:236–238**

   Compline, 4:44

   compunction, 4:45

   flagellation, 5:754

   lauds, 8:380

   manifestation of conscience, 9:115–116

   painting by Il Sodoma, 5:*552*

   relics, 12:*53*, 539

   shrine, 13:94

   See also Benedictine Rule

Benedict I (Pope), **2:238–239**, 3:596

Benedict II (Pope), St., **2:239**, 4:193, 719

Benedict III (Pope), **2:239**

Benedict IV (Pope), **2:239–240**

Benedict V (Pope), 1:102, **2:240**, 5:856, 8:484

Benedict VI (Pope), **2:240**, 500, 3:213, 4:362

Benedict VII (Pope), 1:504, **2:240–241**, 4:362

Benedict VIII (Pope), **2:241**

   Aribo of Mainz, 1:664

   clerical celibacy and marriage, 3:326

   early life, 14:249

   Ethelnoth of Canterbury, 5:386

   filioque, 5:24

Benedict IX (Pope), 1:466, **2:241–242**, 14:249

Benedict X (Antipope), **2:242**, 3:777, 11:502

Benedict XI (Pope), Bl., 1:943, **2:243**, 3:803, 10:416

Benedict XII (Pope), **2:243–244**

   Andronicus III Palaeologus (Byzantine Emperor), 1:410

   Apostolic Penitentiary, 11:76

   beatific vision, 2:244, 276

      baptism of saints, 2:173

      before resurrection, immediately after death, 6:687, 7:354, 10:900

Benedict XII (Pope) *(continued)*
Divine essence, 6:297
rebirth in grace, 2:169
Bertrand of Aquileia, St., 2:337
Canons Regular of St. Augustine, 3:68
Cistercians, 3:748
Durandus of Saint-Pourçain, 4:948
monastic reform, 2:271, 12:589
Benedict XIII (Antipope), **2:245–247**
Álvarez of Córdoba, Bl., 1:326
Boniface IX (Pope), 2:504
Brevicoxa, 2:611
Charles VI, 6:74
Council of Pisa, 11:360, 361
Disputation of Tortosa, 1:232
Fillastre, Guillaume, 5:722
in Frangipani family, 5:912
Gerson, Jean, 6:190
Gregory XII (Pope), 6:500
papal taxation, 1:466
Salamanca University, 12:611
sorrows of Mary, 13:328
Western Schism, 1:258, 14:693
Benedict XIII (Pope), **2:244–245**, *245*
Alexandre, Noël, 1:267
Canon Law, 3:51
Clement VIII (Antipope), 3:785
deposition, 4:170, 171
ecclesiastical archives, 1:636
Knights of Montesa, 8:195
transubstantiation, 5:280
Benedict XIV (Antipope), 3:785
Benedict XIV (Pope), **2:247–248**
Alexandre, Noël, 1:267
All Souls' Day, 1:290
Angela of Foligno, Bl., 1:412
Apostolic Penitentiary, 11:76
appeals to a future council, 1:599
Aquileia, 1:608
Augustinianism, 1:885
Basilians, 2:143, 144
Bernis, François Joachim de Pierre de, 2:326
Canon Law, 3:53
canonization, 3:63
catechesis, 3:234, 244
Catherine de' Ricci, St., 3:267
Ceillier, Remi, 3:316
clerical celibacy and marriage, 3:324
Colosseum, 3:860
Communion outside the liturgy, 4:37
Confirmation, 4:91

Congregation of the Most Holy Redeemer, 1:307, 308, 9:154–155
controveries on grace, 6:404
cross feast, 4:383
Divine judgment, 8:33
Eastern Catholic churches, 3:817
English mission rules, 4:734
episcopal duties, 5:205
exemptions of congregations, 5:530
Fruttuaria Abbey, 6:17
Garampi, Giuseppe, 6:92
Index of Prohibited Books, 7:390–391
Indian Rites controversy, 7:402
Institute of the Most Holy Savior, 1:307
Italo-Albanian Church, 7:651
Maria Theresa, 9:154–155
marriage, juridical form of, 10:218–219
Mt. Lebanon, Synod of, 9:199
papal writings, 1:308
plenary indulgences and Carnival, 13:98
poverty of religious, 4:59
promoter of the faith, 4:705–706
Redemptorists, approval of, 11:993
Roman martyrology, 9:233, 234
scholastic doctrine, 2:32, 14:354
secret societies, 12:857
supernatural powers, 10:107
suppression of Jesuits, 1:58–59
sweet odors classified as miraculous, 10:109
usury, 2:32
on writings of Pseudo-Dionysius, 11:801
Benedict XV (Pope), **2:248–251**, *249*
Action Française, 1:82
All Souls' Day, 1:290
anti-Catholic propaganda, 8:191
Apostolic Penitentiary, 11:76
Bendictine Oblates, patronage of, 6:41
biblical exegesis, 5:523
biblical study, 13:457–458
Canon Law, 3:55
Catholic Near East Welfare Association, 3:286
censorship, 3:336
Church-State relations, 3:642
Congregation of the Oriental Church, 5:22
Eastern churches, 5:22
ethnocentrism, missionary, 9:681

Hugon, Éouard, 7:164
integralism, 7:504
Italo-Albanian Church, 7:652
mission, 3:428, 500, 626, 8:429
modern biblical criticism, 2:250
Muslims, 2:688
papal writings
Sodalitium pianum, 13:295
Spiritus Paraclitus (encyclical), 13:457–458
Pontifical Bible Institute, 11:485
Pontifical Council for the Interpretation of Legislative Texts, 11:482
St. Columban's Foreign Mission Society, approval of, 6:83
Sodalitium pianum, 13:295
Thomistic revival, 12:775
upholding principles of Aquinas, 11:390
Benedict Biscop, St., 1:448, **2:251**, 5:239, 14:665
Benedict of Aniane, St., **2:251–252**, 268–269, 10:743, 12:549
Adalard, St., 1:98
Anointing of the Sick, 1:485
Ansegis of Fontenelle, St., 1:493
Apostles' Creed, 1:577
Aurelian of Arles, St., 1:895
Carolingian reform, 3:157, 168, 600
Cluniacs, 3:813, 815
Conques Abbey, 4:129
conscience, 4:147
Smaragdus influenced, 13:228
Benedict of Benevento, St., **2:252**
Benedict of Canfield. *See* Fitch, William Benedict
Benedict of Nursia, St., 9:787
Agapetus I (Pope), St., 3:596
Alleluia, 1:293
angels, 1:423
Cassian, John, 3:207
Monte Cassino Archabbey, 9:830
See also Benedictine Rule
Benedict of Peterborough, **2:252–253**
Benedict the Levite, **2:253**
Ansegis of Fontenelle, St., 1:494
Canon Law, 1:494, 3:42, 60, 90
capitularies of (false decretals), 5:615, 616–617
Benedict the Moor, St., **2:253–254**
Benedictine abbeys and priories, U.S., **2:254–256**
Benedictine Armenian Antonines. *See* Mechitarists

Benedictine edition of the Bible, 14:597–598

Benedictine liturgical conference. *See* Liturgical conference

Benedictine medals, 2:238

Benedictine missions
Colombia, 7:290
post-Reformation, 2:259

Benedictine Nuns and Sisters, **2:256–261**, *257, 258, 271*
among martyrs of Orange, 10:620–621
South Dakota, 13:368

Benedictine Nuns of the Blessed Sacrament, 2:81

Benedictine Rule, 2:256, **261–263**, 264–265, 5:456, 793
abbesses, 1:8
Abbots, 1:9–10, 3:334
Aelred, St., 1:138
Agapetus I (Pope), St., 3:596
Ambrosian hymns, 8:365
Ansegis of Fontenelle, St., 1:493
Aurelian of Arles, St., 1:895
baths, 2:154
Benedict Biscop, St., introduction to England, 2:251
Bernard of Clairvaux, 2:308, 309
blessing for Abbots, 1:11
Carolingian reform, 3:157, 168, 600
Celestines, 3:321
cenobitism, 3:334, 335
chapter of faults, 3:386
Chautard, Jean Baptiste, 3:458
Chrodegang of Metz, St., 3:564
church architecture, 3:811
Cistercians, 3:745, 746, 748, 749–750
Cluniac reform, 3:813
Cluniacs, 3:811, 812, 813, 815
Compline, 4:44
compunction, 4:45
Councils of Chalon-Sur-Saône, 3:373
direction, spiritual, 4:761
hospitallers, 7:119
hours for prayers, 8:610–611
hymns, 7:240, 244
idleness, 7:305
influences, 8:511
Italy, 7:665
Knights of Alcántara, 8:189
lauds, 8:380
Luxeuil Abbey, 8:899
manuscript illumination, 3:812

medieval Latin literature works, 9:438
model for, 8:730
monasteries, 9:782–783
Obazine Abbey adoption, 10:503
poverty, 11:569
prayers, 8:656
priors, 11:716
reform at Kastl Abbey, 8:131
wide acceptance, 3:600
works of charity, 3:411, 412
See also Benedictine spirituality; *specific Benedictine orders*

Benedictine Sisters of Charity, 6:41

Benedictine Sisters of Providence, 5:920

Benedictine Spirituality, **2:263–267**

Benedictines, **2:267–273**, *268*, 9:*784*
12th-century increase, 3:601
Alaska, 1:209
Ancient See of Carlisle, 3:124
Apostolic Penitentiary, 11:76
Arkansas, 1:692
Australia, 1:902–903
Austria, 1:910, 12:670
Bohemia, 4:479
Brittany, 8:41
Butler, Edward Cuthbert, 2:720
Canons Regular of St. Augustine, 3:68
Caribbean, 3:116
Carolingian Renaissance, 9:791
Celestines, 1:428, 3:320, 321–322, 762
church architecture, 3:716
Colombia, 7:290
Conques Abbey, 4:129
contemplation, 4:207–209
cowl, 4:332
Durham See, 4:951
Fintan Mundwiler, 10:60
Fontfroide Abbey, 5:794
Gregory the Great, St., 3:596
hierarchical insignia, 6:764
Idaho, 7:290, 291
Jumièges Abbey, 8:59–60
monasteries, 9:783
19th-20th century overview, 3:621
Olivetan, 2:318
Regula Magistri, 12:32
religious conversion of Germanic tribes, 9:691
represented in Nebraska, 10:223
scholasticism, 12:765
Ut In Omnibus Glorificetur Deus motto, 14:355

See also Camaldolese; Celestines; English Benedictines; Olivetan Benedictines; Sylvestrine Benedictines

Benediction of the Blessed Sacrament, **2:275**

The Benedictional of John Longlande, Bishop of Lincoln, 8:776

Benedictionale Friburgense, 6:70

Benedictionalia, Gallican rites, 6:70

Benedict's Rule: A Translation and Commentary (Kardong), 2:263

Benedictus (Canticle of Zechariah), **2:275–276**, 3:73, 4:327–328

Benedictus Capra de Benedictis, 3:52

Benedictus Christianus, 11:326

Benedictus Deus (apostolic constitution, Benedict XII), 2:173, 244, **276**, 8:33, 37, 10:900

Benedictus Deus (papal bull, Pius IV), 14:174

Benedictus Dominus (papal bull, Gregory XIII), 2:143

Benediktbeuern Abbey (Germany), **2:276**, *277*

Benefatti, Giacomo (Bp.). *See* James de Benefactis, Bl.

Benefice of Christ (Valdés), 14:369

Benefices
annates, 1:267, 466–467, 3:726
Carolingian Dynasty, 3:163, 170
Church property, 3:725
Clement IV (Pope), 3:778
papal provision, 3:602–603, 780
works of charity, 3:410, 414

Beneke, F. E., 11:802

Benelli, Giovanni, **2:276–278**

Benet of Canfield, 4:93

Beneventan Chant, **2:278**

Beneventan Rite, **2:278–279**

Benevento, Councils of
(1087), 7:151
(1108), 10:916

Benevento, Synod of (1091), 1:782

Benevento, Treaty of (1156), 1:126, 8:847

Benevolent love, 8:826

Bénézet, St., **2:279**, 11:572

Bengel, J. A., 2:366

Bengoa Aranguren, Juan Pedro, Bl., 4:494

Benigni, Umberto, **2:279–280**, 7:503

Benignitas et humanitas (Pius XII), 3:642

Benignus of Dijon, St., **2:280**

Bénilde, Bl., **2:280**

Benin, **2:280–282**, *281*

Benincasa, Ursula, Ven., **2:282**

Bénisson-Dieu Abbey (France), 3:751

Benito de Jesús, Br., 14:247

Benito Nozal, Anacario, Bl., 4:494

Benizi, Philip, St., 13:26, 29

Benjamin (biblical figure), 2:282

Benjamin (Jacobite Patriarch), 4:253

Benjamin (tribe), **2:282–283**

Benjamin, W., 5:914

Benjamín Julián, Br., 14:247

Bennet, William, 5:238

Bennett, J. C., 10:192

Bennett, John G. (Bp. of Lafayette, IN), 7:416

Bennett, William Harper, 1:286

Bennett Law (WI, 1889), 8:132

Benni, Ignatius Behnam (Patriarch of Syria), 13:709–710

Benno II of Osnabrück, Bl., **2:283**

Benno of Meissen, St., **2:283**, 5:200

Benno of Metz (Bp.), **2:283–284**, 5:29

Benoît, Michel, **2:284**

Benoit, Pierre, **2:284–285**, 5:50, 51, 523

Benson, Edward (Abp.), 4:543

Benson, Nelson v. (1873), 3:657

Bentham, Jeremy, **2:285–286**, 5:107, 396, 440

    Anglicanism, 1:444

    British moralists, 2:624

    common good, 4:19

    hedonism, 6:701

    Mill, John Stuart, 3:832

    postivism, 10:184

Bentivoglio, Anna Maria. *See* Bentivoglio, Maria Maddalena

Bentivoglio, Annibale (Abp.), 2:286

Bentivoglio, Domenico, 2:286

Bentivoglio, Guido (Card.), 2:286, *286*

Bentivoglio, Marco Cornelio (Card.), 2:286

Bentivoglio, Maria Maddalena, **2:286–287**

Bentivoglio family, **2:286**

Bentley, J. F., 3:709

Bentley, Richard, **2:287–288**

    Cambridge University, 2:906

    higher criticism, 6:825

    philology, 11:274

Bentzen, A., 3:338

Benvenutus Scotivoli, St., **2:288**

Benxing, 9:487

Benzi, B., 5:647

Benziger, Alfred F., 2:288

Benziger, Bernard A., 2:288

Benziger, Bernard C., 2:288

Benziger, Charles, 2:288

Benziger, J. N. Adelrich, 2:288

Benziger, Joseph Charles, 2:288

Benziger, Louis G., 2:288

Benziger, Nicholas C., 2:288, *289*

Benziger, Xavier N., 2:288

Benziger family, **2:288**

Benzinger, Immanuel, 5:520

Benzo of Alba (Bp.), **2:288–289**

Beornrad of Echternach (Abbot), 5:42

Beowulf (epic poem), **2:289–290**

Ber, Rabbi Dov, 7:872

Berab, Jacob, 3:148

Berakhot, **2:290–291**

    See also Mishnah

Beran, Joseph (Card.), **2:291**, 3:200, 4:485

Berard of Carbio and Companions, SS., **2:292**

Bercharius, St., **2:292**

Bercheure, Pierre, 5:206

Berchmans, Jan (John), St., **2:292–293**, 4:626

Berçot, P., 1:803

Berdiâev, Nikolai Aleksandrovich, **2:293**, 5:773, 12:437

    Bulgakov, Sergeĭ Nikolaevich, 2:679

    existentialism, 5:544

    philosophy of history, 6:884

Bere, Richard, Bl., 5:226, 7:1019

Bereans. *See* Barclay, John

Bereavement, 13:854

Beregis, St., 12:549

Berengar of Verdun (Bp.), 5:760

Berengarius of Tours, **2:293–294**, 14:158

    Bernold of Constance, 2:327

    Canon Law, 3:47

    cathedral and episcopal schools, 1:432, 3:441

    dialectics, 4:725–726

    Durandus of Troarn, 4:949

    Eucharist, 1:64

    eucharistic controversy, 5:423–424

    Humbert of Silva Candida, 7:199

    Latin literature, 9:450

    Leo IX (Pope), St., 8:485

    orthodox position versus, 8:323

    scholasticism, 12:758

Bérenger, Raymond, 8:519

Bérénice (Racine), 11:887

Berettini. *See* Humiliati

Berg, Karl (Card.), 1:917

Bergen Abbey (Germany), 4:60

Berger, Benedict (Abbot), 5:886

Berger, Elisabeth, 12:565

Berger, Mary Odilia, 5:881

Berger, Peter, on beliefs, 2:223

Berger, Wilhelm, Rev., 5:883

Berghold, Alexander, 10:309

Bergier, Nicolas Sylvestre, **2:295**

Bergin, Luke, 7:582

Bergson, Henri Louis, 2:*295*, **295–296**, 5:398

    Alexander, Samuel, 1:252

    Augustinianism, 1:881

    Blondel, Maurice, 2:441

    Boutroux, Étienne Émile Marie, 2:570

    Bureau, Paul, 2:696

    causality, 3:307

    concept of time, 14:79

    conceptualism, 4:53

    contributions to theory of motion, 10:19–20

    creative imagination, 4:348, 349

    existence of God, 6:314

    form, 5:803

    freedom of spirit, 5:939

    good, 6:350

    irrationalism, 7:586–587

    knowledge, 8:219

    Le Roy influenced, 8:513

    matter, 9:344

    nonbeing, 10:417

    philosophy and science, 11:301

    pragmatism, 12:71

    pragmatism and religious experience, 5:556

    Sertillanges, A., 13:23–24

    simple apprehension, 1:605

    soul, 13:348

    substance, 13:579

    universals, 14:326

    vital impulse (*élan vital*) doctrine, 10:824

Bergson, James, 10:630–631

Bergsonisme, 9:177–178

Berichte der Lepoldinene Stiftung im Kasierthume Oesterreichs, 8:504

Berington, Charles, **2:297–298**

Berisha, Sali, 1:217

Berkeley, George (Bp.), **2:298–300**, *299*, 11:294

    accident, 1:62

    being, 2:206

    Bradley, Francis Herbert, 2:577

    British moralists, 2:623

    concept, 4:52

    continuum, 4:215

empiricism, 5:198, 7:297, 12:47

idea, 7:295

idealism, 7:297, 301

image and concept, 7:506

Johnson, Samuel, 7:301

knowledge, 8:218

matter, 9:344

metaphysics, 9:553

moral philosophy, 12:34

phenomenalism, 11:229–230

quality, 11:849, 850

quality in substance, 13:578

rejection of abstraction, 14:325–326

solipsism, 13:303

soul, 13:346

world soul, 14:845

Berkeley, William, 3:645

Berlage, H., 3:679

Berlière, Ursmer, **2:300**

Berlin Codex, 6:257

Berlioz, Louis Hector, 2:*301*, **301–302**, 580

Bermondsey Settlement, 8:561

Bermuda, 3:120–121

Bermudez, João, **2:302**

Bernadine of Feltre, Bl., 3:414

Bernadot, Marie Vincent, **2:302**, *303*

Bernadot, V., 1:82

Bernal Díaz del Castillo, 4:130

Bernalte Calzado, Pedro de Alcántara, Bl., 7:125

Bernanos, Georges, 1:412, **2:302–305**, *304*, 5:857

Bernard, Claude, 2:402, 406, 4:316–317

Bernard, St.

    Conrad of Bavaria, 4:135

    Mariology, 9:170

    monastic theology, 13:905

    spiritual life, 13:433, 445–446

Bernard de Ager (Abbot), 12:680

Bernard Gui (Bp. of Túy), **2:305**, 14:47

Bernard Lombardi, **2:305–306**

Bernard Marangon, 1:463

Bernard of Aosta, St., **2:306**, 3:813

Bernard of Auvergne (Alvernia), **2:306**

Bernard of Besse, **2:306–307**, 482

Bernard of Chartres, **2:307**

    cathedral and episcopal schools, 2:307, 3:264, 441

    Gilbert de la Porrée, 6:213, 214

    Latin literature, 9:453

    School of Chartres, 12:758

Bernard of Clairvaux, St., **2:307–312**, *308*

    Abelard, Peter, 1:18, 19, 2:308–309

Achard, Bl., 1:67

Adalgott II, St., 1:103

Aelred, St., 1:138

Alexander of Hales, 1:266

Alvastra Abbey, 1:327

Amadeus of Lausanne, St., 1:328

Anacletus II (Antipope), 1:370

angels, 1:419, 423

apostolici, 1:594

architecture, 3:750

Arnold of Bonneval, 1:718

Arnold of Brescia, 1:719, 2:309

Arnulf of Lisieux, 1:720

biblical theology, 2:382

Catherine of Siena, St., 3:273

Celestine I (Pope), St., 3:318

Celestine III (Pope), 3:319

charity, 3:395

Chautard, Jean Baptiste, 3:458

chivalry, 3:519

Church property, 3:727

Church-State relations, 3:635

Cistercians, 3:746, 747, 751, 9:792

Cîteaux Abbey, 3:746, 751

Clairvaux Abbey, 3:746, 758

Cluniac art, 3:812

Cluniac reform, 3:814

Cluny Abbey, 2:308

courtly love, 4:320, 321

Crusade preaching, 5:844

Crusade propaganda, 4:408, 410–411

decadence, 3:413

denunciation of Abelard, 5:844

dialectics, 4:726

direction, spiritual, 4:761

exegetical works, 5:514

Fastred, Bl., 5:636

following of Christ, 5:788

Fountains Abbey, 5:832–833

freedom, 5:937–938

Geoffrey of Clairvaux, 6:141

Gerard of Clairvaux, 6:161

Holy Name, 7:31

Humbeline (sister of), 7:198

hymns of, 7:248, 253, 12:631

Imitation of Christ, 7:329

Latin literature, 3:601, 9:453

Les Dunes Abbey, 8:513

Liber de laude novae militiae, 9:625

manuscript illumination, 3:750

Mellifont Abbey, 9:481

mysticism, 2:310–311, 3:749, 5:45, 10:118

Poverty Movement, 11:571

preaching, 11:619

relics, 12:54

Robert of Bruges, Bl., 12:267

Second Crusade, 5:443–444

verse composition, 10:591

will and willing, 14:722

William of Saint-Thierry, 14:752–753

works of charity, 3:412, 413

Bernard of Cluny, **2:312**

Bernard of Compostella (the Elder), **2:312–313**

Bernard of Compostella (the Younger) (Bp.), **2:313**, 3:48

Bernard of Corleone, Bl., **2:313**

Bernard of Fontcaude, **2:313–314**

Bernard of Montmirat, **2:314**, 3:48

Bernard of Offida, Bl., **2:314**

Bernard of Parma (Canonist), St. (*ca.* 1200-1264), **2:314–315**

    Canon Law, 2:314–315, 3:48

    glossa ordinaria, 6:247

Bernard of Parma (Card.), St. (*ca.* 1055-1133), 2:*315*, **315–316**

Bernard of Pavia, 12:229

    Canon Law, 3:47, 48

    decretals, 4:597, 601, 603

Bernard of Saisset (Bp.), 2:503

Bernard of Salvetat, 6:157

Bernard of Tiron, St., **2:316**

Bernard of Trille, **2:316–317**

Bernard Silvester, **2:317–318**, 14:2

    Alan of Lille, 1:205

    cathedral and episcopal schools, 3:441

    Latin literature, 9:453

    School of Chartres, 12:758

Bernard Tolomei, Bl., **2:318**

Bernardes, Manoel, **2:318**

Bernardi, Prosper, 13:328

Bernardian reform, 5:843–845

Bernardin, Joseph Louis (Card.), 1:831, **2:318–320**, *319*, 3:480, 737, 10:572

    Charleston Diocese, 13:367

Bernardine of Fletre, 1:455

Bernardine of Siena, St., 2:*320*, **320–321**, 5:876, 896, 902, 921–922

    Albert of Sarteano, Bl., 1:223

    Assumption of Mary, 1:800

    Caracciolo, Landolf, 3:96

    Caracciolo, Roberto, 3:94

    Devotio Moderna, 3:605

    Holy Name, 7:32–33

    John Capistran, St., 7:944

    mediation of Mary, 9:263

    penance and anti-materialism, 13:108

Bernardine Sisters of the Third Order of
St. Francis, 5:876–877

Bernardines, 3:744, 745

Bernardino of Busti, 3:96

Bernardino of Feltre, Bl., **2:321–322**,
8:805

Bernardino of Laredo, **2:322**, 12:234

Bernay Abbey (France), **2:322–323**

Bernetti, Tommaso (Card.), **2:323**

Bernger, Bl., **2:323–324**

Bernhard (Count of Sponheim), 14:512

Bernier, Étienne Alexandre (Bp. of
Orléans), **2:324**

    Caprara, Giovanni Battista, 2:324,
3:92

    Concordat of 1801, 4:61, 62

Bernier, Francis, 12:390

Bernier of Nivelles, 1:935

Bernières-Louvigny, Jean de, **2:324–325**

    Chrysostom of Saint-Lô, John, 3:573

    Laval influenced, 8:382

Bernini, Giovanni Lorenzo, 2:*325*,
325–326, 3:705, 706, 14:341,
395–396

    Alexander VII (Pope), 1:262

    Barberini family patronage, 2:95

    Castel Gandolfo villa, 3:212

    saint images in paintings, 12:601

    St. Peter's Basilica, 12:580

    symbolism, 3:675

Bernis, François Joachim de Pierre de
(Card.), 1:229, **2:326**, 3:794, 795

Berno, Bl., **2:327**, 3:814, 12:32–33

Berno, Peter, 12:401

Berno of Reichenau, **2:327**

Bernold of Constance, **2:327–328**

    Canon Law, 3:45, 47, 60

    false decretals, 5:618

    Latin literature, 9:451

    liturgical gestures, 8:647

    Seventy-Four Titles, Collection,
13:39

Bernold of Ottobeuren, Bl., **2:328**

Bernoulli, Johann, 14:73

Bernstein, Richard, 5:829

Bernulf, St., **2:328**

Bernward of Hildesheim (Bp.), St.,
2:328–329, 9:448

Bernward's cross, 4:395

Berossus, **2:329–330**

Berquin, Louis de, **2:330**

Berrigan, Daniel J., 7:794

Berrio, Antonio de, 3:113

Berrio-Ochoa, Valentín (Bp. of Central
Tonkin), 14:491–492

Berrotarán, Nicolás, 3:759

Berruyer, Isaac Joseph, **2:330**, 3:792

Berry, Jean de, 2:374

Berry, Thomas, 5:54

Berse, Gaspar (Barzeo), **2:330–331**

Bertha of Blangy, St., **2:331**

Bertha of Val d'Or, St., **2:331**

Bertharius, St., **2:331–332**, 7:246

Berthelot, P. E. M., 12:126

Berthémy Convention (1865), 3:498

Berthier, Guillaume François, **2:332**

Berthier, Jacques, **2:332–333**, 13:735

Berthier, Jean Baptiste, **2:333**, 7:23–24

Berthold Missal, 3:*552*

Berthold of Chiemsee (Berthold
Pürstinger) (Bp.), **2:333**

Berthold of Garsten, Bl., **2:333**

Berthold of Mosburg, 1:226

Berthold von Reichensberg, 3:413

Bertholet, Pierre. *See* Dionysius of the
Nativity, Bl.

Berti, Giovanni Lorenzo, 1:884–885,
2:334

    Augustinianism, 1:875, 880, 889

    scholasticism, 12:764, 767

Bertier, Ferdinand de, 8:197–198

Bertieri, Giuseppe, **2:334**

Bertilla of Chelles, St., **2:334**, 3:463

Bertinus, St., **2:334–335**, **12:539**

Bertoni, Gaspare (Caspar) Luigi Dionigi,
St., **2:335**, 13:529

Bertonio, Ludovico, **2:335**

Bertram, G., 5:812

Bertram of Le Mans (Bp.), St.,
2:335–336

    Julian of Le Mans, 8:48

    Licinius of Angers, 8:561

Bertrand, Louis, St., **2:336**, 3:851, 4:852

Bertrand, Pierre (Card.), **2:336–337**

Bertrand de Garriga, Bl., **2:337**

Bertrand de Got. *See* Clement V (Pope)

Bertrand of Aquileia (Patriarch), St.,
2:337

Bertrand of Comminges (Bp.), St.,
2:337–338

Bertulf of Bobbio, St., **2:338**, 446

Bertulf of Renty, St., **2:338**

Bérulle, Pierre de (Card.), 2:109,
338–339

    Bossuet, Jacques Bénigne, 2:550

    Bourgoing, François, 2:568

    Carmelites, 1:468, 3:136

    Carthusian spirituality, 3:192

    Condren, Charles de, 4:74

    consecration to Mary, 4:156

    Coton, Pierre, 4:291

    Counter Reformation, 3:612

    Fitch, William Benedict, 5:750

    Francis de Sales, St., 5:850, 867, 868

    French School, 13:451

    Gibieuf, Guillaume, 6:208

    Oratory, 2:568, 714

    priesthood, 11:704

    scholasticism, 12:765

Beryl, alleged magical properties of,
11:646

Beryllus of Bostra (Bp.), **2:339**

Besançon, Diet of (1157)

    Alexander III (Pope), 1:254

    Celestine III (Pope), 3:319

Besançon, Synod of (1571), 3:234

Besant, Annie, 13:935–936

Beschi, Costanzo Giuseppe, **2:339–340**

The Besht. *See* Ba'al Shem Tov (Rabbi
Israel)

Besozzi, Alber, 1:346

Bessarabian Orthodox Church, 9:767

Bessarion (Byzantine theologist), 2:141

Bessarion, Cardinal, **2:340–341**, *341*

    Aristotelianism, 1:676, 2:341

    Chrysoberges, Andrew, 3:572

    Council of Florence, 2:340, 828

    Eastern Schism, 2:762, 794

    eucharistic epiclesis, 5:279

    Platonism, 11:416

    Plethon, George Gemistos, 2:340,
810

    San Salvatore di Messina Monastery,
12:656

Bessarion of Egypt, St., **2:341–342**

Bessarione (periodical), 10:812

Bessay, Jean de, 2:190

Bessette, André, Bl., **2:342**

Bessin, Guillaume, 2:190

Bestès, Theodore, 3:46

Bestiaries, **2:342–344**

Besuzzi, Alessandro, 5:191

Bet Shearim, 8:2

Bêt Yehûdâ (The House of Judah)
(Levinsohn), 6:663

Beta Israel. *See* Falashas (Jewish sect)

Betancur (Bethancourt), Pedro de San
José, Bl., **2:344–345**, *345*, 12:372

Betanzos, Domingo de, **2:345–346**

Betanzos, Pedro de, **2:346**, 4:288

Beth Alpha synagogue (Galilee, Israel),
13:677

Beth Yoseph (Caro), 3:148

Bethany of the Sacred Heart, 3:763

Betharius, St., 3:441

Betharram Fathers, **2:346**, 6:98

Bethel, 1:36, 2:346, **346–347**

Bethesda, **2:347**

Bethlehem, **2:347–348**, *348*, *349*, 10:798

Bethlehem (Faber), 5:582

Bethlehem Fathers, **2:348–349**, 494

Bethlehem Mission Immensee (SMB).
See Bethlehem Fathers

Bethlehemites, **2:349–350**, 12:372

Beth-Rehob (Aramaean state), 1:624

Bethulia citadel, 8:44

Béthune, Conon de, 4:400

Bethune, James. See Beaton, James
(1473-1539, Abp. of Glasgow);
Beaton, James (1517-1603, Abp. of
Glasgow)

Bethune-Baker, J., 10:252

Betto di Biago (Pinturicchio), 1:261,
2:375

Beukels, John, 1:368

Beurel, Jean-Marie, 13:161

Beuron Abbey (Germany), **2:350**, 3:711,
8:671

Beuronese art, **2:350–352**, *351*, 8:471,
12:601

Beuronese Congregation, 2:273

Beverini, Bartolomeo, 3:804

BeVier, Charles, 3:722

Bevilacqua, Anthony J. (Abp. of
Philadelphia), 1:25, 11:241–242, 367

Beyond All Appearances (Weiss), 10:608

Beyond God the Father (Daly), 5:677

Beza, Theodore, **2:352**, 5:317
Assemblies of the French Clergy,
1:787
Bolsec, Jérôme Hermès, 2:475
Castellio, Sebastian, 3:214
Catherine de Médicis, 3:266
Conference of Poissy, 7:167, 11:437
Psalters, 7:255
supralapsarianism, 2:894

Bezpopovtsi, 2:745

Bhadrabāhu (Jain leader), 7:697

Bhagavad Gītā, 6:844–845, 7:407,
14:366, 892

Bhakti tradition, 10:299

Bhaktivedanta Swami Prabhupada, A.
C., 10:299

Bhāskara, 7:408–409

Bhedābheda, 7:408

Bhutan, **2:352–353**, *354*

Bialkowski, Mary Clara (Mother), 5:890

Bianchi, Francesco Saverio Maria, St.,
2:353

Bianchi, Francis Xavier, St., 2:104

Biard, Pierre, 3:4

Bibel und Liturgie (periodical), 8:188,
673, 10:903

Bibel und Natur (Reusch), 12:182

Biber, Heinrich Johann Franz Von,
2:353–354

Bible, **2:354–355**
adultery, 1:131–133
afterlife, 1:164–165
altars, 1:319–320
angels, 1:415–418, 422, 425–427
anger, 1:430–431
animal symbolism, 1:457–458
anointing, 1:477
Anointing of the Sick, 1:480–481
anthropomorphism, 1:511–512
Antichrist, 1:513, 515–516
apocalyptic style, 1:545–547
apologetics, 1:563
Apostles, 1:570–572
Augustine, St., 1:865
authorship, 1:487–488
blasphemy, 2:434–435
blessings, 2:437–439
blood, 2:443–444
book of life, 2:525–526
canticles, 3:73, *74*
catenae, 3:258–259, 770
censuses, 3:337–339
charisms, 3:389–390, 578
Church, 3:575, 578–580, 581–583,
629
conscience, 4:140–141, 142,
143–145, 146
contemplation, 4:205
conversion, 4:231–234, 239, 240
cosmogonic myths in the, 10:127,
129
cosmogony, 4:284
curses, 4:442–443
Dead Sea Scroll texts, 4:562–563
death, 4:569–571
demonology, 4:645–646
didactic literary artifices, 10:950
Divine truth, 14:230–231
dream interpretation, 4:903
early use, 8:638, 639
Greek Orthodox use of Protestant
Bibles, 6:459
Holy Trinity in the, 14:201–202
instances of parenesis, 10:882
as Jehovah's Witnesses' source of
faith and conduct, 7:751
justification, 8:76–80
Knox edition, 8:226
Latin translations, 8:362–364

lectionaries, 8:435
leprosy, so-called, 8:508–510
literary myth found in, 10:123–124
meditative commentaries, 13:416
midrashic method of exegesis, 9:619
modesty, 9:758
moral obligation in the, 10:519
morality, 9:866
morality of thoughts, 14:62
names for Palestine, 10:777–778
natural history of Palestine,
10:785–786, 788
New American, 10:275–277
19th-20th century piety, 3:623
nudity in the, 10:473
numerology in the, 10:243, 476–478
oils, 7:34
omnipotence of God, 10:592
omnipresence of God, 10:593
oracles in the, 10:619
original sin, 10:664
papacy foundations in the,
10:829–830
Parousia in the, 10:894–899
patriarchs in the, 10:948–951
as Pentecostal church authority,
11:105
political geography of Palestine,
10:782–784
Protestant mission translation, 9:697
as Puritans' source of faith and
conduct, 11:837
reading in liturgy, 11:124–127
Reform Judaism, 8:10
repentance, 4:225
Resurrection of Christ, 1:799
spiritual life, 13:435
spiritual reading, 11:941
stars, 1:810
theology of history, 6:887
tithes in the, 14:91–92
Tower of Babel story of, 10:129,
14:128–130
translations, 1:296, 3:214, 623
unicity of the Church, 14:297
unleavened bread, 10:933–934,
14:332–*333*
virgin birth, 14:533, 535–536
ways of reading, 8:435
works of charity, 1:300, 3:400–401
See also New Testament; Old
Testament; *specific Bibles*; *specific
books of the Bible*

Bible, canon, **3:20–34**
apostolic succession, 1:591, 592

Bible, canon (continued)
    criteria, 3:20–22, 32–33
    criticism, 3:33–34
    Dead Sea Scroll, 4:562–563
    defined, 3:20
    deuterocanonical sections, 4:509, 562–563
    New Testament, 3:27–33
    Old Testament, 3:22–27, 565
    Son of Man, 13:316
Bible, exegesis. See Biblical theology; Exegesis, biblical
Bible, historical/geographical context of
    Amorrites, 1:362–363
    Arabia, 1:612–613
    Aramaeans, 1:623–625
    archaeology, 2:377–381
    Bethel, 2:346–347
    Bethesda, 2:347
    Bethlehem, 2:347–348
    Book of Amos, 1:364
    burial, 2:697–699
    Calvary, 2:885–886
    Cana of Galilee, 3:1
    Canaan and Canaanites, 3:1–3
    Capernaum, 2:380, 3:83
    Cenacle, 3:332–333
    Dead Sea, 4:558–560
    Decapolis, 4:588
    deportations, 4:674
    Galatia, 6:51–52
    Genesis' theological interpretation of history, 6:132
    Isaiah, Book of, 7:597
    Jacob (Hebrew Patriarch), 7:686–687
    Jericho, 7:756–757
    Jerusalem, 7:765–769
    John's Gospel, 7:904–905
    Jordan River, 7:1028–1029
    Joshua, Book of, 7:1052–1053
    Old Testament books, 6:863
    Philistines, 11:265–266
    Red Sea, 11:962
    See also Israel, ancient
Bible, inspired books of, 4:6
Bible, piety in the, 2:377
Bible, texts and versions, 2:355–367
    Acts of the Apostles, 1:88
    Benedictine edition, 14:597–598
    Bomberg, Daniel, 2:355, 475–476
    Bryennios, Philotheus, 2:652
    Clementine edition, 14:596
    English, 5:244
    German, 5:256

Icelandic, 7:277
    illustrations, 2:355, 356, 357, 358, 359, 360
    Irish, 2:368
    King James Bible (1611), 3:27, 14:253, 254
    Latin, 12:453, 14:591
    liberalized requirements for, 4:792
    New Testament, 2:362–367
    New Testament of Wordsworth-White-Sparks (WWS), 14:597
    Old Testament, 2:355–362
    Rheims-Douay New Testament, 1:296, 9:213
    Septuagint, 12:920–924
    Sistine edition, 14:596
    by Theodulf (Abp. of Orléans), 14:595
    Vulgate, 12:449, 14:591–600
    Welsh, 12:536
    See also Catholic Bible
Bible, textual criticism
    Baruch, Book of, 2:131
    Bauer, Bruno, on Gospels, 2:159
    definition, 6:794
    Geddes, Alexander, on Pentateuch, 6:115
    Gunkel, Hermann on Old Testament, 6:582–583
    higher criticism, 6:825
    Isaiah, Book of, 7:595–597
    Jeremiah, Book of, 7:754–755
    Job, Book of, 7:887
    Jonah, Book of, 7:1021–1022
    Joshua, Book of, 7:1052–1055, 1056
    Psalms, Book of, 11:795–796
    Simon, Richard, 13:127
    Stephen Langton, St., 13:524
    See also Hermeneutics, biblical
Bible Christians, 9:559
Bible Cycles in art, 2:368–376, 369, 370, 371
Bible de Jérusalem (Jerusalem Bible), 2:284, 5:51, 8:906, 12:262
Bible historiale, 5:848
Bible Moralisée, 2:376–377, 3:577
Bible Story (O'Connell), 10:542
Bible Today (periodical), 12:552
Bibles, rabbinical, 11:883–884
Biblia Hebraica, 14:234
Biblia pauperum, 2:377, 522
Biblia virginea (Tenorio), 13:824
La Biblia y la cienca (González y Díaz), 6:346
Biblica sacra (Osiander), 10:705

Biblical archaeology, 2:377–381, 5:50–51
Biblical chronicler, 3:338, 564–569
    covenant, 4:327
    Levites, 8:524
    Nathan, 10:155
    See also Chronicles, Books of; Ezra, Book of; Nehemiah, Book of
Biblical glosses, 5:507, 6:247–248
Biblical languages, 1:627, 2:381
"Biblical" literary hand style, 10:769–770
Biblical sortes. See Sortes Homericae, Vergilianae, Biblicae
Biblical studies, 4:790–791, 814, 8:280–281, 13:457–458
Biblical theology, 2:381–390, 3:623
    dogmatic theology, 4:815–817
    early period, 2:382–385
    Lutheran influence, 8:449–450
    modern period, 2:385–390
    speculative theology, 13:898
    See also Bible, canon
Bibliocentrism, 14:941
Bibliografía filosófica mexicana (Valverde), 14:380
Bibliographical Dictionary of English Catholics (Gillow), 14:111
Bibliorum Codex Sinaiticus Petropolitanus (Tischendorf, ed.), 14:90
Bibliorum sacrorum Latinae versiones antiquae, seu Vetus Italica (Sabatier), 12:454
Biblioteca Angelica (Rome), 12:275
Biblioteca Cattolica series, 12:671
Biblioteca graeco-latina veterum Patrum antiquorumque scriptorum ecclesiasticorum (Gallandi), 6:67
Biblioteca historica medii aevi. . . (Potthast), 11:560
Biblioteca mística carmelitana (Silverio de St. Teresa), 13:122
Biblioteca universale sacro-profano (Coronelli), 5:207
Bibliotheca (Photius), 5:448, 10:962
Bibliotheca Corvina, 7:213
Bibliotheca graeca (Vatican Archives), 14:398, 420
Bibliotheca latina (Vatican Archives), 14:398, 420
Bibliotheca magna rabbinica de scriptoribus et scriptis hebraicis (Bartolocci), 2:130
Bibliotheca Missionum (Streit, Robert), 13:548

Bibliotheca sacra (Sixtus of Siena), 13:199

Bibliotheca scriptorum S. Ordinis Cisterciensis (Visch), 14:557

Bibliotheca scriptorum Societatis Jesu (Ribadeneyra), 13:369

Bibliotheca secreta (Vatican Archives), 14:398, 420

Bibliothèque de théogie historique, 14:241

Bibliothèque des écrivains de la Compagnie de Jésus (Backer), 2:9

Biblische Geschichte der Welterlöserung durch Jesum der Sohn Gottes (Galura), 3:243

Biblische Geschichte des Alten und Neuen Testamentes zum Gebrauch der katolischen Schulen (Neumann), 10:265

Biblische Geschichte des Alten und Neuen Testaments (Overberg), 3:243

Bichi, Antonio (Card.), 3:484

Bichier des Ages, Jeanne Élisabeth, St., **2:390–391**, 5:835

Bickerdike, Robert, Bl., **2:391**, 5:229

Bickersteth, Edward, 5:467

Biddle, John, **2:391**, 14:303

Biel, Gabriel, **2:391–392**, 5:425, 14:233

Bieler, L., 10:955

Bien Hoa, Vietnam, 14:*505*

Biffi, Eugenio (Bp. of Cartagena), **2:392**

Bigandet, Paul (Bp.), 2:706

Biggs, Robert, 3:280

Biglia, Andrea, 1:888

Bigordi, Domenico (Ghirlandaio), 2:375, 13:*193*

Bigotiana, 3:40

Bihlmeyer, Karl, **2:392**

Bihn, Joseph (Father), 5:882

Bijns, Anna, **2:392–393**

Bilbo, Theodore G., 10:172

Bilderdijk, Willem, 1:218

Bildhausen Abbey (Germany), 1:108

Bilfinger, G. B., 5:263

Bilhem, Louise Josson de, 3:536

Bilhild, St., **2:393**

Bilio, Luigi (Card.), **2:393**

Bill of Rights (English), 4:590

Billerbeck, Paul, **2:393–394**

Billiart, Julie (Marie Rose), St., 2:*394*, **394**, 10:458

Billick, Eberhard, **2:394–395**, 3:142

Billings, Evelyn, 10:176

Billings, John, 10:176

Billot, Louis (Card.), **2:395**, 14:136, 160
    Action Française, 1:82, 2:395

person, 11:149

sacrifice, 4:624

Billuart, Charles René (Card.), **2:396**, 14:51
    Ambrosius Catharinus, 1:347
    attrition-contrition distinction, 4:227
    relics of saints, 12:55

Billy, Jacques de, **2:396**

Bilocation, **2:396**, 10:108

Bilocation, mystical, **2:397**

Biloxi Diocese (MS), **2:397**

Bilson, Thomas (Bp. of Winchester), 3:152

Bin-bir-Kilissé Churches, 1:756, 757

Binchois, Gilles, **2:397–398**, *398*, 4:940

Binding and Loosing, **2:398–399**, 8:162–163

Binet, Étienne, **2:399**

Bingham, Joseph, **2:399**

Bini, G., 4:302

Binius, Severin, **2:399–400**

Binz, Leo (Abp.)
    Dubuque Archdiocese (IA), 4:924
    St. Paul Archiocese, 12:574–575

Bio-bibliografía eclesiástica mexicana (Valverde), 14:381

Biographia Literaria (Coleridge), 3:832

Biographie universelle des musiciens et bibliographie générale de la musique (Fétis), 5:701

Biographies (medieval Latin literature works), 9:448

Biography as theology, 10:153–154

Biography of Bishop MacCaughwell (Fleming), 5:760

Biological mechanism, 9:418–421

Biological sciences. *See* Biology

Biology, **2:400–408**, 12:806–807
    Greek period, 2:400, 404–405
    Middle Ages, 2:401
    in the Middle Ages, 12:814
    philosophy, 2:406–408
    Renaissance, 2:401–402, 12:816–817
    Roman period, 2:400–401
    scientific method, 2:405–406

Biondo, Flavio, **2:408**

Biopesis, theories of, 8:574–576

Biran, A., 2:379

Biran, Maine de, **9:59–60**, *60*
    efficient causality, 5:101, 102
    idealism, 7:300
    introspection, 7:532
    irrationalism, 7:586
    will and willing, 14:723

Bird (Bird or Beard), James, Bl., 5:232

Biretta, **2:408**

Birge, E. A., 2:404

Birinus (Bp.), St., **2:408–409**, 4:874, 5:239

Birkett, Richard, 5:238

Biró, Ferenc, 7:218

Birth control. *See* Abortion; Contraception

Birth imagery in baptism, 2:75

Bis saeculari (apostolic constitution, Pius XII), 13:295

Bisazza, Felice, 5:865

Bischler, M. Anastasia (Mother), 5:883–884

Bischoff, Bernhard, 6:120, 10:775

Ein bischöfliches Wort... über die Kontroverspunkte (Martin, Konrad), 9:213–214

Bishop, Edmund, **2:409**, 8:673, 11:604

Bishop, William (Bp. of Chalcedon), 1:642, **2:409–410**, 4:912, 5:248, 10:580

Bishop, William Howard (Father), **2:410**, 6:238, 239

Bishop of Rome. *See* Pope (title)

Bishops, **2:411–417**, *413*
    academic freedom, 1:55–56
    African American, 1:161
    anointing, 1:478–479
    apostolic succession, 1:589–592, 596, 597, 2:414
    archiereus term, 1:635
    authority per Leo IV (Pope), St., 8:483
    canonization, 3:63, 64
    cardinal bishops, 3:105
    cathedral and episcopal schools, 3:262–263
    Ceremonial of Bishops, 1:290, 3:349
    Church property, 3:656–657, 724, 725, 726, 727
    coats of arms, 8:637–638
    collegiality, 2:414–415, 418–419, 3:837–838
    conciliarism, 4:54–58
    consecration, 10:635–637
    Council of Trent, 2:418, 3:53
    Council of Trent on residence and jurisdiction of, 14:170
    declaration of presumed death, 11:717
    dismissorial letters, 4:747
    distinguishing between spiritual and secular functions, 7:537
    duties, 2:415–417
    early church, 2:411–414
    ecclesiastical hierarchy, 11:698

Bishops *(continued)*
  Holy orders, 7:36
  Ignatius of Antioch, 7:311
  Leo I (Pope), St., instructions to,
    8:476
  Liber regulae pastoralis, 3:229
  martyrdom, 8:720
  Merovingian era, 3:810
  as minister of Holy Orders, 7:38
  miters, 9:743–744
  origin of order, 7:36
  papal appointment, 3:602
  Paul VI (Pope), 3:627
  preaching specific to, 11:631
  priests, relationships to, 13:779–780
  religious conversion of chiefs and
    kings, 9:691
  rings, 8:637
  Roman Empire, 3:632
  sanctoral cycle, 12:662
  secularizing church property, 12:869
  Spanish reform, 13:391–392
  Vatican Council II, 2:414, 415, 418,
    420, 3:626
  works of charity, 3:415
  See also specific bishops
Bishops, auxiliary, **2:419**
Bishops, College of. *See* College of
  Bishops
Bishops, diocesan, **2:419–422**
Bishops, in the Bible, **2:410–411**
Bishops, monastic, **2:422**
Bishops, sacramental theology of,
  2:417–419
Bishops, Synod of. *See* Synods of
  Bishops; Synods of Bishops,
  assemblies
Bishops' Committee for the Spanish
  Speaking, 5:203, 8:843
Bishops' Committee on the Liturgy of
  the United States National, on sacred
  spaces, 12:503–504
Bishops' conferences, 4:13–15
Bishops for Hispanic Affairs, 5:203
Bishops of U.S., 4:149, 151
Biskup, George J. (Abp. of Indianpolis),
  7:418
Bismarck, Otto Eduard Leopold von
  Center Party, 3:340
    restoration of states of Church, 8:444
  See also Kulturkampf
Bismarck Diocese (ND), **2:422–424**, *423*
Bisset, James, 12:533
Bissolo, Pier Francesco, 3:273
Bissy, H. de (Card.), 1:57
Bistrita Abbey (Moldavia), **2:424**

Bistrita Abbey (Wallachia), **2:424**
Bit-Adini (Aramaean state), 1:624
Bitti, Bernardo, **2:424**
Bittle, Celestine N., 7:239, 12:777
Black, William, **2:424–425**
Black Baptists, U.S., 2:80, 81
Black Catholic Congress, 1:162
Black Catholic Theological Symposium,
  1:162
Black Death
  clergy depletion in Scotland, 12:833
  Dominicans, 4:851
  England, 13:130
  Siena, 13:108
  See also Plagues
"The Black Legend," 7:491, 8:341
Black Madonna, 5:140, 13:*379*
Black magic, 9:37
Black Mother (Madre Moretta). *See*
  Bakhita, Giuseppina, St.
*Black Popes—Authority: Its Uses and
  Abuses* (Roberts), 12:272
Black theology, 8:544, 545
Blackburn, William. *See* Thomson,
  William, Bl.
Blackening, as term, 4:696
Blackfoot people, 4:692, 8:270
Blacklo (Blacklow), Thomas. *See* White,
  Thomas
Blackman, John, **2:425**
Blacks in America. *See* African
  Americans
Blackstone, William, Sir
  Aristotelianism, 1:678
  *Commentaries on the Laws of
    England*, 14:816–817
Blackwell, George, **2:425**, 5:247
  archpriest controversy, 1:642, 643
  Garnet, Henry, 6:100
  Oath of Allegiance (1606), 10:500
Blahoslav, John, 2:461
Blaine, James Gillespie, 2:425–427,
  3:654, 660
Blaine Amendment (U.S), **2:425–428**,
  3:653, 654, 660
Blaise of Sebaste (Bp.), St., **2:428**,
  12:668
Blaise of the Conception, 4:44
Blaj (Romania), Councils of, 12:338–339
Blake, Alexander, Bl., 2:30, **428**, 5:231
Blake, Eugene Carson, 4:199, 5:299
Blake, William, **2:428–429**, *429*
  Behemoth and Leviathan engraving,
    10:*130*
  Christian symbolism, 12:601
  death of God theology, 4:585

deconstructionism, 4:594
I-It mysticism, 10:117
Soul parts with dead body, 13:*337*
Blakely, Paul Lendrum, **2:429–430**
Blanc, Anthony (Abp. of New Orleans),
  2:430, 3:129–130, 8:811, 10:292,
  12:640, 14:220
Blanchard, Louis, 5:441
Blanche of Castile (Queen of France),
  3:440, 8:799, 800, *800*, 9:365
Blanchet, Augustin Magliore (Bp. of
  Walla Walla, WA), 12:851,
  14:654–655
Blanchet, Francis Norbert (Abp. of
  Oregon City, OR), **2:430–431**, 7:34,
  10:644, 645, 11:529, 12:850–851,
  14:654
Blanco, Francisco, St., 7:732
Blandina of Lyons, St., 1:93, **2:431**,
  3:593
Blandrata, Giorgio, **2:431–432**
Blanes Giner, Marino, Bl., **2:432**
Blanshard, Paul, 10:172
Blarer, Ambrosius, 1:312, 2:433
Blarer, Diethelm, 2:433
Blarer, Gerwig, 2:433
Blarer, Jakob Christoph (Bp. of Basel),
  2:433
Blarer, Ludwig, 2:433, 5:139
Blarer, Thomas, 2:433
Blarer family, **2:433**
Blasco Juan, José Marí, 2:92
Blasphemy, **2:433–434**, 11:739, 13:411
Blasphemy, in the Bible, **2:434–435**,
  13:158
Blass, Maria, 6:166
Blastares, Matthew, **2:435**, 795
Blaurock, Georg, 1:368
Blauvelt (NY), 4:840
Blavatsky, Helena Petrovna, 13:934, 935
Blenk, James Hubert (Bp. of New
  Orleans), 8:813, 10:294
Blenkinsop, Catherine, 2:436
Blenkinsop, Peter (b. late 18th cent.),
  2:40, 435
Blenkinsop, Peter J. (1818-1896),
  2:435–436
Blenkinsop, William A., 2:436
Blenkinsop family, **2:435–436**
Blessed Are the Merciful, 9:505
Blessed Rage for Order (Tracy), 12:203
Blessed Sacrament
  devotion to, 13:326
  exposition, 9:818–819
  tabernacles, 13:726, *726*
The Blessed Sacrament (Faber), 5:582

Blessed Sacrament Church (Holyoke, MA), 3:672, 716

Blessed Sacrament Fathers, 2:436, 437, **437**, 3:621, 5:572

Blessed Virgin. *See* Mary, Blessed Virgin

Blessed Virgin, Feasts of the, 9:159

Blesseds, **2:436**

> *See also* Beatification; *specific blesseds*

Blessings

> for Abbots, 1:11–12
>
> apostolic, 1:580
>
> Judaism, 8:11
>
> *See also* Magic

Blessings, in the Bible, **2:437–439**

Blessings, liturgical, **2:439–440**, 816

> collect of blessings, 8:470
>
> of the cross, 4:382
>
> of the New Fire, 5:16

Blicking Homilies, 11:632

Blin de Bourdon, Francoise, 10:458

Bliss, F. I., 7:763

The Blithedale Romance (Hawthorne), 14:149

''Blob'' literary hand style, 10:772

Bloch, Ernst, 13:925–926, 14:361

Bloch, Marc, 5:704

Blome, Leopold T., 14:459

Blomevenna, Peter, 3:192

Blondel, François, 3:675

Blondel, Maurice, **2:440–442**, 11:296, 14:52

> apologetics, 1:565, 566
>
> aseity, 1:780
>
> Boutroux, Étienne Émile Marie, 2:570
>
> Bremond, Henri, 2:601
>
> Christian philosophy, 3:541
>
> doctrine, development of, 4:808
>
> existence of God, 6:315
>
> pragmatism, 12:71
>
> privation, 11:722
>
> Sangnier, March, 12:666

Blondin, Marie-Anne Sureau, Bl., **2:442**, 12:534

Blood, religious significance of, **2:442–444**

> altars, 1:319
>
> Shroud of Turin, 13:95–97
>
> sin offering, 13:159

Blood Drenched Altars (Kelley), 8:138

Blood jasper, alleged magical properties of, 11:646

Blood of St. Januarius, 7:723

The Blood of the Redeemer (Bellini), 11:*640*

Blood prodigies, 10:109

Blood vengeance, 1:814, 2:443, 444, **444–445**, 5:264

Blosi, Francis, 10:723

Blosius, Francis Louis (De Blois), **2:445**, 8:565, 12:491

Blosset, Françoise de, 3:417

Blouet de Camilly, Jean Jacques, 5:441

Blount, Richard, 1:467

Blouzawi, Gabriel, 1:534–535

Blowick, John, Rev., 3:864, 12:543

Bloy, Léon Henri Marc, **2:445**

Blue Nuns. *See* Little Company of Mary

Blueprint for the Christian Reshaping of Society (periodical), 14:252

Bluet, Thomas, 5:247

Blume, C., 7:254

Blyth, Stephen Cleveland, 2:553, 3:472

B'nai B'rith, **2:446**

Boa Vontade Church (Brazil), 2:592

Board of Education, Brown v. (1954), 10:296, 521

Board of Education, Everson v. (1947), 3:660, 665, 667

Board of Education, McCollum v. (1948), 3:666

Board of Education v. Allen (1968), 3:667

Board of Education v. Mergens (1990), 3:664

Board of Public Works, Roemer v. (1976), 3:667

Boas, Franz

> afterlife, 1:163
>
> culture, 4:435
>
> symbolism, 1:740

Bobadilla, Francisco de, 3:867

Bobadilla, Nicolás Alfonso de, **2:446**

Bobbio, N., 10:194

Bobbio Abbey (Italy), 2:338, **446–447**, 3:600

Bobbio Missal, 1:343, 577, 2:447, 3:331, 6:69

Bobola, Andrew, St., **2:447**

Bobolenus of Bobbio, 2:446

Boccaccio, Giovanni, **2:447–450**, *448*

> Chaucer, Geoffrey, 3:450, 452, 456
>
> poetry, 12:110
>
> Renaissance humanism, 12:114

Boccardo, Giovanni Maria, Bl., **2:450–451**, 5:90

Boccasini, Niccolo. *See* Benedict XI (Pope), Bl.

Boccherini, Luigi, **2:451**

Bochachevsky, Constatine (Bp. for Ukrainians), 5:20

Bocheński, I. M., 1:668

Bockelson, Jan, 9:637

Bocking, Edward, 2:130, **451–452**

Böddeker, Melchior, 2:710

Bodel, Jehan, 4:401

Bodey, John, Bl., **2:452**, 5:228

Bodhidharma (Indian monk), 14:915

Bodhisattvas, **2:452**, *453*, 661, 9:47

Bodin, Jean

> absolutism, 1:44
>
> democracy, 4:640, 641
>
> Renaissance philosophy, 12:124
>
> sovereignty, 13:371

Bodmer Papyri, 2:363–364

Bodo-Eleazar (deacon), 11:43

Bodoni, Giambattista, 2:523

Body of Christ. *See* Mystical body of Christ

Boece, Hector, 12:533

Boehm, John Philip, **2:452**, 5:468, 12:739

Boehm, Martin, **2:452**, **454**, 606, 5:471, 10:711, 14:305

Boehner, Philotheus Heinrich, **2:454**, 12:541

Boel, Henricus, 5:969

Boeringer, Hans, 4:201

Boethius (Roman philosopher), **2:454–457**, *455*

> Alan of Lille, 1:205
>
> Alexander of Hales, 1:266
>
> Aristotelianism, 1:673, 684, 2:454, 456
>
> Aristotle, 5:90
>
> cathedral and episcopal schools, 3:441
>
> Chaucer, Geoffrey, 3:452, 453
>
> Cicero, Marcus Tullius, 3:730
>
> Clarenbaud of Arras, 2:457, 3:761
>
> classification of the sciences, 12:819
>
> death, 3:595
>
> Divine love, 4:321
>
> dualism, 4:915
>
> eternity, 5:380–381, 383
>
> glosses by Remigius of Auxerre, 12:107
>
> happiness, 6:636
>
> hypostasis, 7:264
>
> inclence on Thierry of Chartres, 14:2
>
> incommunicability, 7:379
>
> individuation, 7:425
>
> influence of neoplatonism, 10:241

Boethius (Roman philosopher)
(*continued*)
  knowledge, 8:214–215
  Latin literature, 9:438
  lay philosophy, 10:959
  liberal arts, 8:537
  logic, 8:749, 750
  man, natural end of, 9:97–98
  music, consideration of, 10:72
  number symbolism, 3:674
  person, 11:146, 149
  Platonism, 11:414
  prescholasticism, 12:757
  providence of God, 11:782
  schools of Athens, 1:829
  science, 12:807
  Syrianus, 1:670
Boethius of Sweden (Dacia), **2:457–458**
  double truth theory, 4:882
  Latin Averroism, 1:674, 935, 936, 2:457, 12:761
Boethus of Sidon, 1:669
Boff, Leonardo, 2:598, 3:590, 12:477–478
  atheism, 1:825
  liberation of poor, 8:547
  liberation theology, 12:729
Bogards. *See* Beguines and Beghards
Bogarín, Juan Sinforiano (Abp. of Paraguay), **2:458**, 10:879
Bogomilism, **2:458–460**
  Bosnia-Herzegovina, 2:545
  Bulgaria, 2:680
  Catharism, 1:230, 2:458, 3:259
  Hungary, 7:211
  Manichaeism, 2:458, 459, 759
Bogomils, 4:219
  See also Catharism
Bogumił of Gniezno (Abp.), St., **2:460**
Bohemia
  Catholic revival, 4:483–484
  Crusades, 4:413
  Czech Republic, 4:478, 479
  Dusek, Jan Ladislav, 4:954
  Enlightenment, 4:483
  Hussites, 4:480–482, 7:228, 230–231
  Reformation and Counter Reformation, 4:482–483
  Wyclif doctrines, 4:170
Bohemia Manor, **2:460**
Bohemian Brethren, **2:460–461**, 4:482, 7:230
Bohemian War (1618-23), 14:8–9
Bohemond IV (King of Cyprus), 4:403, 405

Bohemond of Taranto
  Alexius I Comnenus, 1:275
  Crusades, 4:401, 403, 413
Bohic, Henri, 3:52
Bohier, Antoine (Card.), 5:659
Bohier, François, 2:322–323
Böhm, Dominikus, 3:710, 711, 712
Böhm, Hans, **2:461–462**, 9:637
Böhme, Jakob, **2:462**, *463*
  Angelus Silesius, 1:429
  influence on mysticism, 10:826
  influence on Schelling, 12:733
  Renaissance philosophy, 12:124
  theosophy, 12:784
Böhmer, H., 1:489
Boiardo, M., 1:764
Boileau, L. A., 3:709
Boileau-Despréaux, Nicolas, 3:186
Boisgelin de Cucé, Jean de Dieu, Raymond de (Card.), **2:462–463**
Boisil, St., 4:449
Boismard, Marie-Emile, 2:366, 5:51, 523, 7:904
Bojanowski, Edmund Wojciech Stanislas, Bl., **2:464**
Bojaxhiu, Teresa (Mother). *See* Mother Teresa of Calcutta
Bojko, Konstanty, 11:583
Bojko, Łukasz, 11:583
Bokusai, Magdalena, Bl., 7:733
Bokusai, Simon Kiyota, Bl., 7:733
Boland, J. Kevin (Bp. of Savannah), 12:710
Boland, Thomas Aloysius, 10:330
Bolaños, Luis de, 1:649, **2:464**
Boleslaw I (the Great) (King of Poland), 1:102
Boleslaw II (Sovereign of Lesser Poland), 8:172
Boleyn, Anne (second Queen of Henry VIII), 2:507, 3:268, 269, 782, 6:739, 741
  marriage, 5:163, 244, 12:5, 7, 8
  Mary Tudor, 9:292
Bolívar, Simon, 7:875, 14:*439*
Bolivia, **2:464–471**, *468, 469*
  demographic statistics, 2:465
  ecclesiastical organization, 2:465, 466
  map, 2:*467*
  mission, 1:712, 2:465–466, 9:712, 714
  missions and missionaries, 1:712, 9:735
Boll, Barbara (Sister Margaret), 5:888
Bolland, Jean, 2:471

Bollandists, **2:471–472**
  Acta Sanctorum, 6:615
  Amatus of Nusco, St., 1:333
  Atticus of Constantinople, St., 1:839
  Carmelites, 3:143
  Concina, Daniel, 4:59
  Delehaye, Hippolyte, 4:626
  hagiography, 12:607
  iconography, 7:285
  Saint imagery, 12:598
  Smedt, C., 13:230
Bologna, School of, 12:228
Bologna, University of (Italy), **2:472–475**, *473, 474*
Bologna National Church Architecture Congress (Italy), 3:712
Bolognetti, Alberto, 11:442
Bolotov, V. V., 12:435
Bolsec, Jérôme Hermès, **2:475**, 889
Bolsheviks, 8:467–468
Bolton, Doe v. (1973), 1:32, 14:315
Bolton, Herbert, 9:718
Boltzmann, L., 3:302
Bolzano, Bernhard, 1:80, 678
Bombay, See of, 12:271–272
Bomberg, Daniel, 2:355, **475–476**, 11:883
Bombolognus of Bologna, **2:476**
Le Bon confesseur (St. Eudes), 5:441
Bona, Giovanni (Card.), **2:477**, 4:766
Bona, St., **2:476–477**
Bona, Stanislaus (Bp. of Green Bay, WI), 10:222, 14:782
Bona Anima, William (Abp. of Rouen), 1:489
Bona Mors, 3:98
Bonacum, Thomas, 10:222
Bonagratia of Bergamo, 7:932
Bonal, François de, **2:477**
Bonal, Raymond, **2:477–478**
Bonald, Louis Gabriel Ambroise de, **2:478–479**, 508, 3:624, 5:854, 12:290, 14:138
  Donoso Cortés, Juan, 4:869
  political theology, 11:460
Bonalists. *See* Priests of St. Mary
Bonaparte, Joseph, 10:146
Bonaparte, Josephine de Beauharnais, 10:146, 148–149
Bonaparte, Napoleon. *See* Napoléon I (Napoléon Bonaparte) (Emperor of France)
Bonaventure, St., 2:*479*, **479–493**
  Albert the Great, St., 1:224
  Alexander IV's support, 14:16, 17

Alexander of Hales, 1:265, 479

analogy, 1:372, 378

on analogy, 1:378

Angelus, 1:427

Anointing of the Sick, 1:482

Anselm of Canterbury, St., 1:496

Arabian philosophy, 1:623

Arbiol y Diez, Antonio, 1:629

aseity, 1:780

Assumption of Mary, 1:800

attrition, 1:842–843

Augustinianism, 1:878, 2:482, 488, 492

Avicebron, 1:939

Bernard of Besse, 2:306, 482

causality, 3:304

censorship, 3:336

Christian philosophy, 3:540, 541

Christocentrism, 2:484, 493, 3:558

cogitative power, 3:823

conservation, 4:161

contemplation, 2:491–492, 4:206, 207

devotion to Holy Trinity, 14:205

direction, spiritual, 4:761

docta ignorantia, 4:798

eucharistic sacrifice, 5:425

exegetical works, 5:517

exemplarism, 5:526

following of Christ, 5:788

Franciscan Spiritual-Conventual conflict, 3:603

Franciscan spirituality, 5:895, 896

Franciscans, First Order, 5:901–902

illumination, 2:489, 7:320

immortality, 7:349

incommunicability, 7:379

individuation, 7:425

indulgences, 7:437

infinity, 7:458–459

influence of Richard of Saint-Victor, 12:234

John of the Cross, St., 3:136

knowledge, 8:217

Latin Averroism, 1:935, 936, 2:483

legendae, 5:737

liberal arts, 8:537

manifestation of conscience, 9:116

mysticism prose, 10:118

Paris School (Franciscan), 5:899

prayer, 11:595

priesthood, 11:701

purgatory, 11:827

reflection, 12:1

relationship to Aquinas, 14:20

scholasticism, 12:761

soul, 13:344

spirituality, 13:446

on the three ways, 14:65

understanding of faith, 13:907

University of Paris, 2:479, 481, 3:603

venial sin, 13:155

Bonaventure of Peraga, 1:888

Bonavia, 3:706

The Bond of Love in Proclaiming the Good News (pastoral letter), 11:260

Bondol of Bruges, Jean, 1:544

Bondolfi, Pietro, 2:348, 494

Bondonnet, Jehmann, 3:473

Bone-Dry Law (OK, 1917), 10:574–575

Bonet, Juan Pablo, 3:418

Bonet, Nicholas, 2:494

Bonfrère, Jacques, 2:494, 5:518

Bongo, Omar, 6:39–40

Bonherba, Raffaelo, 12:765

Bonhoeffer, Dietrich, 1:825, 4:584

Boni homines, 3:259

Boni Pastoris (motu proprio, John XXIII), 7:936

Boniface, 2:494–497

Boniface (priest), 3:363

Boniface, John (Abbot-bishop), St., 12:670

Boniface, St., 2:61, 494–497, 495, 3:445

activities in Germany, 6:172–173

Adalar, St., 1:98

Aldebert and Clement, 1:244

Aldhelm, St., 1:246

Alto, St., 1:322

Anglo-Saxon origins, 1:449

antipodes question, 1:529

Burchard of Würzburg, St., 2:695–696

Carolingian reform, 2:496, 3:124, 155, 156, 159, 164

catechesis, 3:229–230

Charles Martel, 2:495, 3:163, 434

Cologne, 3:842

Confirmation, 4:88

Cuthbert of Canterbury, 4:448

Cuthbert of Wearmouth, 4:449

Eoban, 5:269

Gregory II (Pope), St., 6:485

Gregory III (Pope), St., 6:486–487

Hesse and Thuringia, evangelization of, 2:268

Latin literature, 9:442

Lioba, St., 8:596

Pepin III (King of the Franks), 1:478

Pepin III, 11:110, 111

pilgrimage, 11:354

relics, 4:672

religious conversion of the Franks, 9:691

shrine, 13:94

works of charity, 3:410

Zachary (Pope), St., 14:904

Boniface I (Pope), St., 2:497, 497–498, 3:316, 317, 5:447–448, 7:87

Boniface II (Pope), 2:498–499

Agapetus I (Pope), St., 1:172

Dioscorus (Antipope), 4:756

grace and free will, 5:668

in Liber pontificalis, 8:535

Pelagianism, rejection in Gaul, 6:113

predestination, 11:649–650

Boniface III (Pope), 2:499

Boniface IV (Pope), 1:289, 314, 2:499–500

Boniface V (Pope), 2:500, 3:229

Boniface VI (Pope), 2:500

Boniface VII (Antipope), 2:500–501

Anthony III (Patriarch), 1:504

Benedict VI (Pope), death of, 2:500, 3:213

Crescentii family land, 4:362

Crescentius I, 2:240

John XIV (Pope), death of, 3:213

Salamanca University, 12:611

Boniface VIII (Pope), 2:501, 501–504

Anfredus Gonteri, 1:410

apostolic administrators, 1:116

Apostolic Penitentiary, 11:75

Avignon papacy, 1:943

Benedict XI (Pope), Bl., 2:243

Bernard of Auvergne, 2:306

Canon Law, 1:219, 3:48, 4:273, 12:410

cardinalate, 3:105

Celestine V (Pope), 2:501–502, 3:321

Church-State relations, 1:207, 898, 2:501, 502–503, 3:636, 727

Clareni, 1:428, 3:762

Clement V (Pope), 3:779

clerical celibacy and marriage, 3:326

cloister, 4:210

coinage, 10:481

commissaries apostolic, 4:13

conciliarism, 4:55

Congregation for the Propagation of the Faith, 11:749

Dante Alighieri, 4:518

Franciscan Celestines, 3:321–322

as Gaetani family member, 6:47

Ghibelline-Guelf conflict, 3:854

Boniface VIII (Pope) *(continued)*
Holy Year, 7:57
Jacopone da Todi, 7:692
James II (King of Aragon), 7:705
laicism, 8:282
in *Liber sextus*, 8:536
mendicant controversy, 2:501, 3:141
mendicant privileges restricted, 4:850
nepotism, 10:247
papal primacy, 3:603
Philip IV (King of France), 2:502,
3:727, 5:846, 10:839
pilgrimage, 11:354
posthumous trial, 5:928
reign, 12:357
religious garb, 12:100
taxation, 3:803, 11:246
taxing of French clergy, 11:246
Unam Sanctam, 14:287–288
wearing papal tiara, 14:*70*
Boniface IX (Pope), **2:504**, 14:693
Acciaioli, Angelo, 1:58
Avignon papacy, 12:357
Bartholomites, privileges granted to,
2:128
Castel Sant'Angelo, 3:213
Charles VI's nonrecognition, 6:74
Clareni, 3:762
Boniface of Savoy (Abp. of Canterbury),
Bl., 1:107, **2:505**, 3:72, 481
Bonifatius de Vitalinis, 3:52
Bonilli, Pietro, Bl., **2:505**
Bonino, Giuseppina Gabriella, Bl., **2:505**
Bonino, J. Miguez, 1:826
Boniscambi de Montegiorgio, Fra
Ugolino, 5:736
Bonitus of Clermont (Bp.), St., **2:506**
Bonitz, H., 1:678
Bonizo of Sutri (Bp.), **2:506**, 3:45, 60,
518–519
Bonlieu Abbey (France), 3:751
Bonmont Abbey (Switzerland), 3:750
Bonnard, Jean Louis, 14:492
Bonnard, Pierre, 1:803, 3:713
Bonnault d'Houet, Marie Madeleine
Victoire de, 13:171
La Bonne volonté (Schrijvers), 12:787
Bonneau, Norman, 8:434, 437
Bonnecamps, Joseph (Father), 11:82
Bonnechose, Henri Marie Gaston de
(Card.), **2:507**
Bonne-Espérance Monastery (Belgium),
2:506–507
Bonnefoy, J. F., 3:558, 7:836–837
Bonnemere, Edward, 1:162

Bonner, Edmund (Bp.), **2:507–508**, 569
Bonner, Edward (Bp.), 1:436
Bonner, Elena, 7:998
Bonnet, Charles, 2:407
Bonnetty, Augustin, **2:508**, 14:138
faith, 5:596
God's existence, 5:712
heresy, 6:778
Bonneuil, Étienne de, 3:696
Bonomelli, Geremia (Bp. of Cremona),
1:228, **2:508–509**, *509*, 7:673
Bononius, St., **2:509**
Bonsirven, Joseph, **2:509–510**
Bonte, Guilelmus, 3:52
Bontempi, Gaudentius, 12:764
Bonucci, Agostino, 13:28
Bonum certamen (Orozco), 10:674
Bonum est diffusivum sui (Good is
diffusive of itself), 12:754–755
Bonum ex integra causa (Good results
from integral totality), 12:755
Bonvicino, Ambrogio, 14:340
Bonville, Anthony. *See* Terill, Anthony
Bony, Paul, 1:803
Bonzano, Giovanni, 1:585
Bonzano, John, 12:648
Bonzel, Aline (Mother Maria Theresia),
2:510, 5:888
Bonzi, Clement de, 1:454
Bonzi, Pierre de (Card.), 1:454
Book of Adam (Mandaean religion),
9:104
Book of Advertisements (Parker),
1:135–136
A Book of Architecture (Gibbs), 3:714
Book of Bahir, 2:831–832
Book of Blessings, 2:440
Advent, 1:134
All Souls' Day, 1:290
Book of Cerne (prayer book),
11:603–604
Book of Changes (*Yijing*), 3:508
Book of Classes (*Kitāb al-ṭabaqāt*),
7:624
Book of Common Prayer, 1:444,
2:524–525, 5:245
Anglican Communion, 1:433
Anglican orders problem, 1:434
Anglican Reformation, 1:442, 443,
3:608–609
Anglo-Catholics, 1:446, 447
Athanasian Creed, 1:817
Black Rubric, 8:225
Cartwright, Thomas, 3:197
confessions of faith, 4:80

Cranmer, Thomas, 4:333–334
creedal statements, 4:356
cursus rhythm, 4:444
Episcopal Church of the United
States, 5:297, 298
introduction, 12:9
low church, 8:836
principles of theology, 8:660
Reformed Episcopal Church,
12:25–26
revision, 8:677
Ridley, Nicholas, 12:243
Book of Concord, 12:191
Book of Confutation (Flacisu Illyricus),
5:754
The Book of Consolation (*El libro del
conorte*) (Juana de la Cruz), 7:1061
Book of Dimma, 12:378
Book of Durrow, 1:448, 9:127
The Book of Gems (Marbod), 9:132
Book of Giants (Mānī), 9:113
Book of Guidance (*Kitāb al-Hudā*),
9:195
Book of Heraclides of Damascus
(Bedjan), 2:198
The Book of Hierotheus (Stephen
Bar-Sūdhailē), 13:522
Book of Hours, 2:522–523, 8:611,
11:604–605
Book of James, 9:274
Book of John (Mandaean religion), 9:104
Book of Kells. See Kells, Book of
Book of Life, **2:525–526**
The Book of Margery Kempe, 8:141
Book of Morals (St. Gregory I), 6:482
Book of Mysteries (Mānī), 9:113
Book of Principles (*Sefer ha-Ikkarim*)
(Albo), 1:232
The Book of Resolution (Persons), 5:750
Book of Sentences (Peter Lombard),
3:220, 5:344, 516, 517, 11:190–191,
12:468, 919, 14:18, 24
Adam Pulchrae Mulieris, 1:110
Albert the Great, St., 1:224
Alexander of Hales, 1:265
Alger of Liége, 1:283
Almain, Jacques, 1:298
Anfredus Gonteri, 1:410
Anselm of Laon, 1:498
ars moriendi, 1:728
attrition, 1:842
Augustinianism, 1:877
Bacon, Roger, 12:285
Bernard Lombardi, 2:305, 306
Bombolognus of Bologna, 2:476
Bonaventure, St., 2:479

Caracciolo, Landolf, 3:95–96

casuistry, 3:220

Cowton, Robert, 12:263

Durandus of Saint-Pourçain, 4:947, 948–949

Holcot, Robert, 12:265

Hugh of Newcastle, 7:154

introduction into curriculum, 5:899

relics, 12:54

Richard of Middleton, 12:234

Richard Rufus of Cornwall, 12:236

Robert of Melun, 12:268

systemization of theology, 6:282–283

Book of Splendors (Bar-Hebraeus), 2:83

Book of Sports (Charles I), 12:454

Book of Sports (James I), 12:454

The Book of Stones (Marbod), 9:132

Book of the Bees (Thomas of Cantimpré), 14:32

The Book of the Courtier (*Il Libro del Cortegiano*) (Castiglione), 3:215–216

Book of the Covenant, **2:526–527**

covenant relationship with Yahweh codified, 10:7

as group of laws, 8:397

Sabbath Year, 12:460

Book of the Dead, **2:527–529**, *528*, 13:149

Book of the Dove (Bar-Hebraeus), 2:82

The Book of the Duchess (Chaucer), 3:450, 452, 456–457

Book of the Laws of the Countries (Bardesanes), 2:97

The Book of the Lover and the Beloved (Lull, R.), 8:866

Book of the Nativity of Mary, 9:274

The Book of the Resurrection of Christ by Bartholomew the Apostle, 2:124

The Book of the Sparkling Stone (Ruysbroeck), 10:118, 12:439

Book of the Title (*Kitāb al-'Unwān*) (Agapios of Hierapolis), 1:172

Book of the Translator (Elias Bar Shināyā), 5:156

The Book of the Twelve Beguines (Rutherford), 12:439

Book of Vocalization (*Sefer ha-Nikkud*) (Gikatilla), 6:211

Book of Yeḥirah, 10:135

The Book of Zhuangzi, 14:924

Book on the Proof of the Truth of the Faith (Elias Bar Shināyā), 5:156

Book on the Removal of Suffering (Elias Bar Shināyā), 5:156

Bookbinding, 2:519–520

Books, ancient, **2:510–515**

Books, medieval, 2:*515*, **515–520**, *516*, 773, 817–818

Books, printed, **2:520–524**

Books concerning Fiefs, 5:702

The Books of Dialogues on the Life and Miracles of the Italian Fathers (Libri dialogorum) (Gregory the Great), 3:229

Books of the Bible. *See specific books*; *specific Gospels and Epistles*

Boole, George, 8:751–752

Boolean logic, 8:751–753

Boone, Joseph, 3:646

Boonen, Jacques (Abp. of Malines), **2:529**

Boos, Martin, 5:681

Booth, Lawrence (Abp. of York), **2:529–530**

Booth, William (Abp. of York), **2:530**

Booth, William (Salvation Army founder), **2:530**, 12:626

Booths (Tabernacles), Feast of, 2:131, **530–533**, 4:607, 5:656

Bopp, Pauline (Mother Anselma), 5:890

Borda, Andrés de, **2:533**

Borderlands (U.S.), 9:715–718

Borders, William D. (Abp. of Baltimore), 2:39

Bordoni, Francesco, **2:533**

Boretski, Job, 12:422

Boretta, Beatrice, baptism of, 2:*68*

Borgess, Caspar Henry (Bp.), **2:533–534**, 9:606

Borghese, Agostino, 2:534

Borghese, Camillo. *See* Paul V (Pope)

Borghese, Camillo (1775-1832), 2:535

Borghese, Camillo (Abp. of Siena), 2:534

Borghese, Enrico (Bp. of Alife), 2:534

Borghese, Francesco (1776-1839), 2:535

Borghese, Francesco (Card.), 2:534

Borghese, Galgano, 2:534

Borghese, Giambattista, 2:534

Borghese, Girolamo (Bp. of Pienza), 2:534

Borghese, Giulio, 2:535

Borghese, Ippolito (Bp. of Montalcino), 2:534

Borghese, Lucio (Bp. of Chiusi), 2:534

Borghese, Marcantonio (17th cent.), 2:534

Borghese, Marcantonio (1814-1886), 2:535

Borghese, Niccolò, 2:534

Borghese, Paolo, 2:535

Borghese, Pier Maria (Card.), 2:534

Borghese, Pietro, 2:534

Borghese, Scipione (Card., 18th cent.), 2:534–535

Borghese, Scipione (Card., 1576-1633), 2:534

Borghese, Tiberio, 2:535

Borghese family, **2:534–535**

Borghi, H. A., 12:765

Borgia (Borja) family, **2:535–538**, 10:247

Borgia, Cesare (Card.), 1:259, 261, 2:537, 12:118, 220

Ghibelline-Guelf conflict, 3:855

Julius II (Pope), 8:56

Pius III (Pope), 11:370–371

Borgia, Francis, St., **2:538–539**, 11:621

Borgia, Joan, 2:537

Borgia, Jofré, 2:537–538

Borgia, Lucrezia, 2:*536*, 537

Borgia, Pere-Lluís, 2:536–537

Borgia, Rodrigo (Card.). *See* Alexander VI (Pope)

Borgia, Rodriquez. *See* Innocent VI (Pope)

Borgo San Donnino, Gerard de, 10:554, 14:16

Borgsleben, Christian, 11:619

Boril (Czar), 2:458

Boris I (King of Bulgaria), **2:539**, 679–680, 745, 10:683–684

Adrian II (Pope), 1:124

Byzantine Church, 2:754, 775, 785, 823

Ermenrich of Passau missionary expedition, 5:324

Photius, 11:311

Borja, Francesc de (Card.), 2:535

Born to Sing: An Interpretation and World Survey of Bird Song (Hartshorne), 6:657

Bornati, Gabriella Echenos, 6:633

Borneo, 9:69–70, 71

Bornkamm, Günther, 5:522

Corinthians Epistles, 4:268

Historical Jesus, 6:865

Borralho Mendes, Álvaro, Bl., 1:951

Borrás Román, Robías, Bl., 7:125

Børresen, Kari, 5:677

Borromeo, Charles (Card.), St., 2:*539*, **539–541**

Ambrosian Rite, 1:344

Ambrosians, 1:346

Barnabites, support of, 2:103

Boonen, Jacques, 2:529

catechesis, 2:714, 3:235

Catholic revival, 4:313

Borromeo, Charles (Card.), St.
(continued)
church architecture, 3:701, 705
Church property, 3:727
Clement XIII (Pope), 3:791
*Compagnia dei servi de' puttini
carità*, 3:214
Confraternity of Christian Doctrine,
3:234, 4:94
Councils of Milan, 1:196
Counter Reformation, 3:612
Felix of Cantalice, friendship with,
5:669
Humiliati, 7:205
Oratory, 10:249
preaching, 11:621
Sarpi, Paolo, 12:694
Sauli, Alexander, St., 12:708
Shroud of Turin, 13:96
vestments, 8:636
works of charity, 3:415, 418
Borromeo, Federigo (Card.), **2:541–542**
Borromini, Francesco, 3:671, 705, 706
Borsi, Pier Luca, 3:413
Borysthenic discourse (Dio Chrysostom),
10:96
Bosanquet, Bernard
Alexander, Samuel, 1:252
idealism, 7:299–300
Bosatta, Chiara (Clare) Dina, Bl., **2:542**
Bosatta, Marcellina (Sister), 4:534
Bosboom-Toussaint, Anna Louisa
Geertruida, **2:542**
Boscana, Gerénimo, 2:865
Boscardin, Maria Bertilla, St.,
2:542–543, *543*
Bosch, David J., 9:676, 10:623
Bosch, Hieronymus
alchemy, 1:239
Bible cycles, 2:371
works, 4:*566*
Bosco (Duke of Arles), 7:923
Bosco, Johannes (Belgian recollect),
12:764
Bosco, John, St., **2:543–544**, *544*, 3:419,
622, 5:865, 12:247
Albert, Federico, Bl., 1:221
Allamano, Giuseppe, Bl., 1:291
Cafasso, St. Joseph, 2:543, 851
Cagliero, Juan, 2:852
direction, spiritual, 4:763
Fagnano, José, 5:589
Rosaz, Edoardo Giuseppe, Bl.,
12:377
Salesian Sisters, founder of,
12:613–614

Salesians, founder of, 12:614–615
Savio, Dominic, St., 12:712
Boscovich, Ruggiero, 7:782
action at a distance, 1:80
atomism, 1:831, 835, 4:960
dynamism, 9:416–417
scholasticism, 12:768
Bosgrave, Thomas, Bl., 4:271, 5:232
Bosio, Antonio, 3:224, 12:387
Bosnia-Herzegovina, **2:544–547**, *546*,
4:413
Boso, Cardinal, **2:547–548**, 8:532
Bosque, Juan de Dios, 2:467
Bossanquet, B., 5:939
Bossi, Matteo, 5:32
Bossilkov, Evgenij (Bp.), Bl., **2:548**,
683, 684
Bossuet, Jacques Bénigne (Bp. of
Meaux), 2:115, **548–551**, *549*, 5:496,
6:589, 590
Ágreda, Mary of, 1:187
Alphonsus Liguori, St., 1:310
Angela of Foligno, Bl., 1:412
Assemblies of the French Clergy,
1:788
catechesis, 3:235, 243
Caussade, Jean Pierre de and, 3:309
charity, 3:398
Choiseul du Plessis Praslin, Gilbert
de, 3:524
Compagnie du Saint-Sacrement, 4:41
Declaration of the French Clergy,
4:591
doctrine, 4:804
Fénelon, François de Salignace de la
Mothe, friendship with, 5:682
Fleury, Claude, 5:762
Gallicanism, 2:550, 3:615
Jansenist opponent, 5:851
Lamy, F., 8:315
precursors, 8:495
Quietism, 2:550, 3:614
Simon, R. opposed, 13:127
Boste, John, St., **2:551**, 5:232, 12:273
Bostius, Arnold, **2:551**, 3:133
Boston Archdiocese (MA), **2:551–557**
archives, 1:639–640, 640
Fenwick, Benedict Joseph, 5:685
Boston College, **2:557–558**, 9:309, 396
Boston Quarterly Review, 14:149
Bostra, Synod of (244), 3:593
Boswell, James, **2:558–559**, *559*
Botany, in the Renaissance, 12:817
Botelho, Diogo de, 2:590
Bothwell, James Hepburn, Earl of, 9:291

Botswana, **2:559–560**, *561*
Botte, Bernard, 3:552, 4:83
Botticelli, Sandro
"Madonna and Child," 13:*311*
Renaissance paintings, 12:117
Sistine Chapel fresco, 13:*192*
The Last Communion of St. Jerome,
5:*415*
Botulph of Icanhoe, St., **2:560**
Boturini Benaduci, Lorenzo, **2:560–562**,
3:246
Botvid, St., **2:562**
Boucart, Jean, 2:189
Boucat, Minim Antoine, 12:767
Bouchard, Claude Florent, 2:553
Bouchard, James, **2:562–563**
Boucherat, Nicholas, 3:748, 751
Bouciant Hours (prayer book), 11:605
Boudinhon, Auguste, 1:438
Boudon, Henri de, 3:573
Bouillard, Henri, 5:827, 6:389
Bouillier, François, 3:183
Bouillon, Emmanuel Théodose de la
Tour d'Auvergne (Card.), **2:563**
Boulainvilliers, Henri de, 5:702
Boulay, César Égasse, **2:563**
Boulbon, Edmond, 6:12
Bound, Nicholas, 12:454
Boundaries (Feeney), 5:663
Bouquillon, Thomas Joseph, **2:563–564**
Americanism, 1:354
Catholic University of America,
3:291, 12:787
Bouquillon controversy, **2:564–565**
Bourbon, Edward Chaix, 6:196
Bourdaloue, Louis, 2:*565*, **565–566**,
5:762, 7:782
Bourdelle, E. A., 3:713
Bourdier-Delpuits, Jean Baptiste, 4:113
Bourdin, Pierre, 3:185
Bourdoise, Adrien (Father), 2:478, 3:235
Bourdon, Jean, 12:276
Bourgade, Peter (Bp. of Tucson), 1:688,
12:676
Bourgchier, Thomas (Bourchier) (Card.),
2:566, 3:72
Bourgeois, Louis, 7:255, 256
Bourgeoisie, 7:719
Bourgeoys, Marguerite, St., **2:566–567**,
567, 3:4, 8:432, 10:458
Bourget, Ignace (Bp. of Montreal),
2:567–568, 3:8, 517, 12:534, 14:471
Misericordia Sisters, 9:672
Sisters of the Holy Names of Jesus
and Mary, 7:33–34

Bourgignon, Antoinette, 2:462

Bourgoing, François, **2:568**

Bourgueil-en-Vallée Abbey (France), **2:568–569**

Bourne, Francis (Card.), 2:*569*, **569**, 5:252, 9:78

Bourne, Gilbert (Abp. of Bath and Wells), 2:152, **569**

Boursier, L. F. (1679-1749), 9:74

Bouscaren, T. Lincoln, 1:28

Bousset, Wilhelm, **2:570**
   apotheosis, 1:599
   biblical theology, 2:385
   biographies of Christ, 7:849
   scholasticism, 12:765

Bouteflika, Abdelaziz, 1:286

Bouteiller, Marthe le, Bl., **2:570**

Boutelou, Charles, 3:129

Boutroux, Étienne Émile Marie, **2:570–571**
   contingency, 4:214
   idealism, 7:300

Bouvet, Joachim, **2:571**

Bouvier, Jean Baptiste (Bp. of Le Mans), 2:*571*, **571–572**

Bouyer, Louis, 5:860
   International Theological Commission, 7:528
   sacramental theology, 12:473, 474

Bova, St., **2:572**

Bover, Joseph, 2:367, 10:14

Bover Olivio, Isidoro, 12:408

Boville, Terill. *See* Terill, Anthony

Bovillus, Carolus (Charles de Bouelles), **2:572**

Bovincourt, Gaspard de, 1:396

Bovius, Antonio, 4:112

Bowen v. Roy (1986), 3:663

Bower, Walter, 12:533

Bowers, Henry F., 1:352, 7:542

Bowes, Marmaduke, Bl., **2:573**, 5:228

Bowet, Henry (Abp. of York), **2:573**

Bowman, Thea (Sister), 1:162, **2:573–574**

Bowne, Borden P., 2:617, 12:70

Bows, liturgical gestures, 8:649

Boxadors, J. T. (Card.), 12:772

Boxer Rebellion, Martyrs of, 1:367–368, 400, 3:99, 464, 498, 500, 7:625, 14:884, 921–924

Boxing. *See* Prizefighting

Boy Bishop, **2:574**

Boyer, André, 3:244

Boyer, Charles, 12:748, 777

Boyer, Pierre Denis, 12:771

Boyes, George, 2:460

Boyid Dynasty, 11:139

Boyle, Hugh C. (Bp. of Pittsburgh), 11:87, 367

Boyle, Michael (Bp. of Mandeville, Jamaica), 3:113

Boyle, Robert, 1:*832*, 834, 2:368, 9:416

Boyle, Roger (Early of Orrery), 1:76

Boyle Abbey (Ireland), **2:574–575**, *575*

Boynes, Norbert de, 7:792

Boys' choirs, 3:524

Boys Town (NE), 5:758, 10:223, 463

Boyton, William, 7:581

Brabantinus. *See* Thomas of Cantimpré

Bracaloni, L., 4:387

Bracco, Teresa, Bl., **2:575**

Bracken, Joseph, 11:731

Bracton, Henry de, **2:575–576**

Brader, Caritas (Mother), 5:881

Bradford, William, **2:576**, 4:115

Bradford-on-Avon Church (England), 1:448

Bradley, Denis Mary (Bp. of Manchester), **2:576**, 10:278–279

Bradley, Francis Herbert, **2:576–577**, 5:160, 161, 504, 11:296
   on the Absolute, 10:827
   Alexander, Samuel, 1:252
   British moralists, 2:624
   freedom, 5:939
   idealism, 7:299
   identity, 7:302–303
   Neo-Hegelianism, 6:712
   relativism, 12:48
   self, concept of, 12:883

Bradley, Richard, 5:238

Bradley, Ritamary, **2:577–578**, 13:170

Bradshaw, P., 3:250

Bradwardine, Thomas, 5:91, 242
   Albert of Saxony, 1:223
   determinism and free will, 5:938
   mechanism, 9:415
   Pelagianism, 12:265
   scholasticism, 12:760

Brady, Ignatius Charles, **2:578**

Brady, Matthew Francis (Bp. of Burlington), **2:578–579**, 14:455

Brady, Nicholas and Genevieve, 11:87

Brady, William Maziere, **2:579**, 10:279

Brady, William O. (Abp.), 12:574, 13:164–165

Braga, Councils of
   first (563)
      Church property, 3:724
      contraception, 4:219

second (573)
      Confirmation, 4:87
      demonology, 4:649
   fourth (675)
      cult of relics, 12:52
      God the Holy Spirit, 6:293

Bragadino, Marcantonio, 7:670

Bragan Rite, **2:579–580**

Bragança Dynasty, 11:538

Braganza, Theotonio de (Bp.), 3:416

Brahe, Tycho, 8:154, 12:815–816
   heliocentrism and, 6:60

Brahmā (Hindu deity), 6:848

Brahman (Hindu concept), **2:580**, 6:842–843
   Nimbārka, 6:847
   Rāmānuja, 6:847
   Śaṅkara, 6:846
   soul, 13:337–338
   Vallabha, 6:847

Brāhmaṇas (Hindu scripture), 6:840, 842

Brahms, Johannes, **2:580–581**, *581*, 8:247

Brainard, Daniel, 12:562

Bramante, Donato, 3:96, 671, 701–702, 12:578–579, 580, 14:394–395

Brameld, Theodore, 5:94

Bramhall, John (Abp. of Armagh), 3:152

Brancati, Lorenzo, **2:581–582**, *582*, 12:764

Branch Davidians, 4:541–543

Branch Theory of the Church, **2:582–583**

Branco, Rio, 2:596

Brandis, C. A., 1:678

Brandom, Robert, 5:829

Brandsma, Titus, Bl., 2:*583*, **583–584**, 3:130, 139

Brandy trade, 9:722
   colonial America, 9:723

Brann, Henry Athanasius, **2:584**

Branner, Robert, 3:694

Bransiet, Philippe (Brother), 2:632

Branstad, Terry, 7:543

Brant, Robert, 2:551

Brant, Sebastian (Brandt), **2:584–585**

Brantôme Abbey (France), 3:473

Braque, Georges, 1:803

Braschi, Giovanni Angelo. *See* Pius VI (Pope)

Brask, Hans (Bp. of Linköping), **2:585**

Bratulić (Bp. of Zagreb), 4:370

Braulio, St., **2:585–586**, 4:87, 5:445

Braun, Joseph, **2:586**

Braun, Placidus, 1:848

Braun, Victor (Father), 12:498

Braunfeld v. Brown (1961), 3:662, 663

Brauns, Heinrich, 6:185

Braunsberger, O., 3:16

Brautmystik (Nuptial mysticism), 6:191

Brauweiler Abbey (Germany), **2:586–587**

Brave New World (Huxley), 14:361

Bray, Thomas, 5:296, 13:288–289

Bray, William D., 2:366

Brazil, **2:587–599**, *592, 593, 595*

  abolition of slavery, 13:214

  Anchieta, José de, Bl., 1:394–395

  Arcoverde de Albuquerque Cavalcanti, Joaquim, 1:644

  Byzantine Basilians, 2:144

  Camara, Helder Pessoa, 2:899–901

  Carmelites, 3:143

  Carnival, 13:98

  cultural contributions, 13:163

  demographic statistics, 2:588

  ecclesiastical organization, 2:589–590

  Figueiredo, Jackson de, 5:717

  history, 12:622–623

  intellectuals, 8:465

  Leme da Silveira, 8:465–466

  map, 2:*591*

  military repression, 8:546

  mission, Catholic, 5:43

    Abbeville, Claude d', 1:8

    aldeiamento system, 1:244–245

    Anchieta, Bl. José de, 1:394–395

    Araújo, Antônio de, 1:628

    Capuchins, 9:719

    Franciscans, 9:718–720

    Jesuits, 2:588, 593–594, 597, 3:417, 5:43

    Lisboa, Cristóvão de, 8:597

    Macedo Costa, Antônio de, 9:14

    Misericordia, 3:417

    as threat to colonial interest, 2:588, 590–592

  mission, Protestant, 9:700–701

  missionaries, 1:8, 394–395, 628, 5:43

  missions, 1:244–245, 3:417, 8:597

  religious education, 5:840

  Sardinha, Pedro Fernandes, 12:692–693

  spiritualism, 13:437

Brazil, Martyrs of, BB., **2:587**

Brazilian Congregation, 2:273

Brazilian Plenary Council (1939), 1:644, 8:466

Bread, liturgical use of, **2:599**

  Lord's Prayer symbolism, 8:784

showbread, 13:88

Bread-basket Law (1875), 8:255

Breaking of Bread, **2:599–600**, 8:785

  See also Eucharist

Breakspear, Nicholas. *See* Adrian IV (Pope)

Breast-beating, 8:650

"Breastpiece of decision," 11:646

Breath control, yoga and, 14:891

Brébeuf, Jean, St., 2:164, 9:*227*, 10:435

Breck, James L., 5:297

Breckinridge, John, 7:160

Bregno, Andrea, 10:373

Bréhier, Louis, **2:600–601**

Bremond, Henri, **2:601**, 7:194

Brems, Josef (Bp. of Denmark), 4:667

Brendan, SS., **2:601–602**

Brendan of Birr, St., 2:602

Brendan of Clonfert, St., 2:601–602

Brengaret Pujol, José, 2:92

Brennan, Andrew J. (Bp. of Richmond, VA), 14:543

Brennan, Francis (Card.), **2:602–603**

Brennan, Thomas F. (Bp. of Dallas, TX), 13:846

Brennan, William J., 5:327

Brenner, Scott F., 4:201

Brent, Charles Henry (Bp.), 2:*603*, **603–604**, 5:299, 606, 14:841

Brent, Giles, 3:645

Brent, Margaret, **2:604**

Brent, Robert, 2:460

Brentano, Clemens M., 5:193, 7:847

Brentano, Franz, **2:604–605**, 5:362, 398

  Aristotelianism, 1:678, 2:604, 12:732

  associationism, 1:796

  Husserl, Edmund, 7:229

  intentionality, 7:516–517, 518

  judgment, 8:24, 26–27

Brenz, Johann, **2:605**

Bresee, Phineas, 3:722

Brest, Union of (1595-1596), **2:605–606**, 747, 3:613, 785, 5:19, 6:456, 14:273, 275, 279

  Lucaris, C., 8:842

  Smotryts'kyi, M., 13:237

Brest-Litovsk Peace Treaty, 8:468

Brethren, **2:606–607**

  See also specific churches

Brethren in Christ Church, 12:261

Brethren of Dominic, 9:491

Brethren of Francis, 9:491

Brethren of the Common Life, **2:607–609**, 3:605

  Devotio Moderna, 4:707–708, 12:590

Erasmus, 5:314

Florentius, Radewijns, 5:774

humanism, 7:190

Luther's early years, 8:877

Brethren of the Cross, **2:609–610**

Breton, Raymond (Father), 3:118

Bretton, John, Bl., **2:610**, 5:233

Breuddwyd Pabydd Wrth Ei Ewyllys (A Papist's Wishful Dream) (Emrys Ap Iwan), 5:199

Breuer, Marcel, 3:678, 717, 12:552

Bréuf, Jean de, 9:*227*

Breul, Jacques du, 3:473

Brevarium causae Nestorianorum et Eutychianorum (Liberatus), 8:550–551

Breve compendio intorno alla perfezione cristiana (Abrégé de la perfection) (Bellinzaga), 2:230, 6:48

Breve instucción de comme se ha administrar el Sacramento de la Penitencia (Medina, Bartolomé), 9:465

Breve noticia de las Misiones vivas de la Compañía de Jesús en la provincia del Paraguay (Muriel), 10:66

Breviarium (Alaric), 3:40

Breviarium (Atto of Vercelli), 3:45

Breviarium (Hippo), 3:40

Breviarium apostolorum, 12:681

Breviarium Syriacum, 3:556

Breviarum extravagantium (Bernard of Pavia), 3:48, 12:229

The Breviary Explained (Parsch), 10:903

Breviatio canonum (Fulgentius Ferrandus), 3:40, 60, 5:691

Brevicoxa (Jean Courtecuisse), **2:610–611**

Breviloquium (Bonaventure), 5:425

Brevis explicatio sensus literalis totius Sacrae Scripturae ex optimis quibusque auctoribus per epitomen collecta (Menochio), 9:496–497

Brevísima relación (Las Casas), 8:341, 10:29

Brewer, Johannes, 3:192

Brianchon, M., 1:803

Briand, Jean Olivier (Bp. of Quebec), **2:611**, 3:7, 179

Briande, Aristide, 5:*849*, 855

Briant, Alexander, St., **2:611–612**, 922, 5:227

Bribery, **2:612**

Brice of Tours (Bp.), St., **2:612–613**

Briceño, Alonso (Bp.), **2:613**

Bricero, Alphonsus, 12:764

Briçonnet, Guillaume (Bp. of Meaux, 1472-1534), 2:613, 5:849

Briçonnet, Guillaume (Card., *ca.* 1445-1514), 2:613

Briçonnet, Robert (Abp. of Reims), 2:613

Briçonnet family, **2:613–614**

Brictinians, **2:614**

Bridal mysticism, 3:132

Bridal symbolism, 3:629

Brideshead Revisited (Waugh), 14:663

The Bridge (Institute of Judeo-Christian Studies), 10:559

Bridgeman, Elijah, 3:499

Bridget of Sweden, St., **2:614**, 5:732

    Adam Easton, 1:107

    Alvastra Abbey, 1:327

    Avignon papacy, 1:943

    Bridgit Abbey, 2:615

    Brigittine Sisters, 2:614, 618

    Devotio Moderna, 3:605

    Hemming, Bl., 6:731

    mysticism literature, 10:118

    private revelations, 12:200

Bridgett, Thomas Edward, **2:614–615**, *615*

Bridgewater, John, **2:615**

Bridgit Abbey (Sweden), **2:615–616**

Bridgman, P. W., 5:142, 10:609

Brie, Simon de. *See* Martin IV (Pope)

Brief Declaration of the Sacraments (Tyndale), 14:253

Brief Outline of the Evidences of the Christian Religion (Alexander), 1:251

Brief Sketch of the Early History of the Catholic Church on the Island of New York (Bayley), 2:165

Briega Morales, Rafael, 2:92

Brieuc, St., **2:616**

Brigéat de Lambert, Scipion-Jérôme, 12:276

Briggs, Charles Augustus, **2:616–617**

Bright, John, 5:408, 520

Brightman, Edgar Sheffield, **2:617**, 5:397, 10:827, 12:70

Brightman, F. E., 2:811–812

Brighton Rock (Greene), 6:461

Brigid of Ireland, St., 1:698, **2:617**, 8:167

Brigidines, **2:618**

Brigittine Sisters, 2:614, **618**, 5:320, 353

Brignole, Emmanuele, 3:348

Brignoline Sisters, 3:348

Brinckerinck, John, 2:607

Brindholme, Edmund, Ven., 5:227

Brinkley, Stephen, **2:618–619**

Brinkmann, B. R., 12:475

Brion, Simon de. *See* Martin IV (Pope)

Brisacier, Jacques Charles de, **2:619**

Brisson, Louis Alexandre, **2:619**, 10:516

Bristol Cathedral (England), 1:448

Bristow, Richard, **2:619–620**

Britain, early church in, **2:620–621**, 3:596

    Anglo-Saxons, 1:448–449

    Canon Law, 3:41, 42

    Celestine I (Pope), St., 3:317

    See also England; Northern Ireland; Scotland; Wales; *specific saints*

Britannica, 3:45, 60

Britannicus (Racine), 11:887

Brithwald of Canterbury (Abp.), St., **2:621–622**

Brithwald of Wilton (Bp.), St., **2:622**

British and Foreign Bible Society, 3:27, 486, 5:472

British Council of Churches (BCC), **2:622**, 5:928

British Criminal Law Amendment Act (1885), 11:774

British Critic (Newman), 10:333, 734

British Guyana, 3:112

British Moralists, **2:622–624**, 6:349

British Museum Bible texts, 2:357

British Psalters, 11:603

British Society of Franciscan Studies, 8:609

Britt, M., 4:349, 7:252–253

Britten, Benjamin, 3:151–152

Britto, John de, St., 7:406

Broad Church, 1:444, **2:624–625**, 8:370

Brock, Dominic (Brother), 1:275

Brockie, Marianus, 12:765

Brockmeyer, Henry Conrad, 7:301

Brodrick, J., 3:16

Broere, Cornelis, 10:261

Broglie, Albert de, 5:855

Broglie, Charles de, 12:496

Broglie, L. de, 1:836

Broglie, Maurice Jean de, **2:625**, 12:496

Brogne Abbey (Belgium), **2:625–626**

Brogne Reform Movement, 2:269

The Broken Covenant (Bellah), 3:755

Brollo, Basilio, **2:626**, 4:630

Brondel, John Baptist (Bp. of Helena, MT), **2:626**, 9:826

Bronescombe, Walter (Bp. of Exeter), 5:530

Bronisława, Bl., **2:626–627**

Brook Farm, **2:627**

Brooke, Ferdinand. *See* Green, Hugh, Bl.

Brooke, James, Sir (fl. 1844), 9:69–70

Brookes, James (Brooks) (Bp. of Gloucester), **2:627–628**

Brooks, Phillips (Bp. of Massachusetts), **2:628**

Brorby (Brookby), Antony, Ven., 5:226

Brosig, Moritz, 2:842

Brossar, Ferdinand (Bp. of Covington), 4:331

''Brother Courtesy.'' *See* Gárate, Francisco, Bl.

Brother in Christ, **2:628**

Brother Leo. *See* Leo of Assisi

Brotherhood of Charity (Poland), 13:200

Brotherhood of St. Lazarus of Bethany (Poland), 13:200

Brotherhood of St Luke. *See* Nazarenes

Brotherhood of the Holy Cross, 7:678

''Brotherhood of Theologians.'' *See* Zoe Movement

Brothers and Sisters of Jesus, **2:627–628**, 8:17

Brothers and Sisters of the Free Spirit, 1:384, **2:629**, 3:413, 11:572

Brothers and Sisters of the Third Order of St. Francis Servants of the Poor, 3:520

Brothers and Sisters to Us, 1:161

Brothers Hospitallers, 7:968, 969

Brothers of Charity, **3:400**, 622, 14:185

Brothers of Christian Instruction of Ploërmel (La Mennais Brothers), **2:630**, 4:687

    Alaska, 1:209

    founding, 3:622, 8:311

    Seychelles, 13:53

Brothers of Christian Instruction of St. Gabriel, **2:630**, 3:622

Brothers of Death, 6:800

Brothers of Divine Providence, 10:672

Brothers of Mercy, **9:504**

Brothers of Mercy of Montabaur. *See* Brothers of Mercy

Brothers of Our Lady Mother of Mercy, **10:721–722**

Brothers of Penance, 13:26

Brothers of St. Francis of Assissi, 4:687

Brothers of St. Francis Xavier. *See* Xaverian Brothers

Brothers of St. John of God, 3:415, 14:186

Brothers of St. Patrick, Congregation of the (FSP), 10:951

Brothers of St. Vincent, 4:292

Brothers of the Christian Schools, **2:630–634**, *631*, 3:188, 8:316, 12:394

Brothers of the Common Life, 4:147

Brothers of the Poor of St. Francis, **12:546–547**

Brothers of the Presentation of the Blessed Virgin Mary. *See* Presentation Brothers

Brothers of the Sword. *See* Knights of the Sword

Brothers of Tilburg, 10:721–722

Brothers' Voice (newsletter), 12:95

Brottier, Daniel Jules Alexis, Bl., **2:634–635**, *635*

Brou, Alexandre (Father), 1:95, **2:635**

Broue, Pierre de la (Bp. of Mirepoix), 1:600

Brouillet, John, **2:635–636**

Brouillet, John Baptist (Father), 12:646

Brouns, Thomas (Bp.), **2:636**

Brouwer, Adriaen, 1:539

Brouwer, Christoph, **2:636**

Brouwer, L. E. J., 4:216

Brouwers, Theodore, 11:366

Browe, Peter, **2:637**

Brown, Braunfeld v. (1961), 3:662, 663

Brown, Elizabeth A. R., 5:706

Brown, George (Abp. of Dublin), **2:637**

Brown, Grayson, 1:162

Brown, Jerry, 3:460

Brown, John Newton, 4:82

Brown, R., 5:522, 523

Brown, Raymond Edward, **2:637–638**

Brown, Robert (Augustinian missionary), 1:890–891

Brown, Robert McAfee, 10:153, 12:729

Brown, Tod David (Bp. of Idaho), 7:291

Brown v. Board of Education (1954), 8:252, 10:296, 521

Browne (Card.), 5:*434*

Browne, Borden Parker, 7:301–302

Browne, Patrick, 7:580

Browne, Robert (1550-1633), **2:638–639**, 4:114, 6:66

Browne, Robert (American priest), 1:582

Browne, William, Bl., 5:234

Brownlee, William C., 10:170, 313

Brownson, Josephine Van Dyke, **2:639**

Brownson, Orestes Augustus, **2:639–641**, 10:313, 14:146–147, 454

    Cummings, Jeremiah Williams, 4:437

    de Courcy, Henry, 4:596

    Hecker, Isaac Thomas, 6:700

    scholasticism, 12:777

Broychot, Lazaruss, 3:328

Bruce, Frank M., 2:641

Bruce, William C., 2:641

Bruce, William George, 2:641

Bruce Codex, 6:257

Bruce family, **2:641**

Bruchési, Louis Joseph Paul Napoléon (Abp. of Montreal), **2:641**

Brück, Heinrich, **2:642**

Bruckner, Anton, 2:580, **642, 643**, 10:775, 12:669

Ein Bruderzwist in Habsburg (Grillparzer), 6:533

Brueghel, Pieter, 2:114

Brueghel family, 1:539, 2:375

Bruguès, Jean-Louis, 7:528

Bruillard, Philibert de (Bp.), 8:337–338, 338, *339*

Brulard, Michel-Louis, 12:276

Brun, Padraig de, 2:368

Brun Arará, Cosme, Bl., 7:124

Bruneau, Joseph, **2:642–643**

Brunei, **2:643–644**, *645*

Brunel de Grammont, 12:535

Brunelleschi, Filippo, 3:699–700, 701, 12:115

Brunet, A. M., 3:565, 567

Brunet, Jean Louis, 6:76

Brunett, Alexander J. (Abp. of Seattle, WA), 9:827, 12:853

Brunfels, Otto, 2:401

Brunhilde (Queen of France), 4:689

Brunhilde (Visigothic princess), 9:518

Bruni, Leonardo Aretino, 12:110–111, 115, 116, 622

Brüning, Heinrich, 3:341, 6:185

Brunini, Joseph B. (Bp. of Jackson, MS), 2:397, 7:686, 9:739–740

Brunner, Francis de Sales, **2:644**, 11:643

Brunner, Heinrich Emil (theologian), 1:381, 825, **2:644–645**

    dialectical theology, 4:721

    infant baptism, objection to, 2:69–70

Brunner, Maria Anna (Mother), 11:644

Bruno, Giordano, **2:645–647**, *646*

    Aristotelianism, 1:677, 2:646

    atomism, 1:834

    identity principle, 7:303

    monistic concept of substance, 10:826

    privation, 11:722

    relativism, 12:46

    Renaissance philosophy, 12:123

    soul, 13:345–346

    world soul, 14:844

Bruno de Jésus-Marie, **2:647**

Bruno of Asti, 9:452

Bruno of Augsburg (Bp.), 12:671

Bruno of Cologne, St., **2:647**, 3:843, 10:719

    Agapetus II (Pope), 1:172

    biography, 9:448

    Corvey Abbey, 4:280

Bruno of Querfurt (Bp.), St., 1:102, **2:648**

Bruno of Segni (Bp.), St., **2:648**

Bruno of Toul (Bp.). *See* Leo IX (Pope)

Bruno of Würzburg (Bp.), St., **2:648–649**

Bruno the Carthusian, St., 2:*649*, **649–650**, 3:191–192, 193

Brunschvicg, Leon, **2:650**

    Aristotelianism, 1:678

    Blondel, Maurice, 2:441

Brunswick Cathedral (England), 3:697

Bruskewitz, Fabian (Bp.), 2:877

Bruté, Simon (Bp. of Vincennes, IN), 13:188

Bruté de Rémur, Simon William Gabriel (Bp. of Vincennes), **2:650–651**, 5:441, 757, 7:417, 13:33–34, 174

Bruun. *See* Candidus of Fulda

Bruxelles, Jean-Baptiste de, 12:277

Bruyère, Jeanne Henriette Cécile, 2:565, **651**

Bruyn, Barthel, 3:845

Bryan, William Jennings, 4:*346*, 347, 5:495, 6:28, 30

Bryant, William Cullen, 3:379

Bryce, J., 1:678

Bryennios, Joseph, **2:651**, 827

Bryennios, Philotheus (Metropolitan), **2:651–652**

Bryennius, Nicephorus, 2:800

Brzozowki, Tadeusz, 7:787–788

Buber, Martin, **2:652**, *652*

    communication, 4:24–25

    community, 4:39

    existentialism, 5:544, 12:70

    fideism, 5:712

    ''I-Thou'' relationship, 12:70

    I-Thou religious vision, 10:116

    Jesus, 8:13

    modern Jewish philosophy, 7:865

    self, concept of, 12:884

Bubwith, Nicholas (Bp.), **2:652–653**

Bucer, Martin (Butzer), **2:653–654**

    Billick, Eberhard, 2:394

    Calvin, John, 2:653, 889, 891

    Latomus, B., 8:370

    Protestant Reformation, 12:15, 20

    sacramentals, 12:481

    Wittenberg Concord, 8:889

Buchanan, George, 3:638

Buchanan, John R., 1:210

Buchez, Philippe Joseph Benjamin, **2:654**

Buchier, Maximilien, 2:716

Buchman, Frank Nathan Daniel, **2:654**

Büchner, Ludwig (1824-1899), 9:320

Buck, V. de, 2:472

Buckfast Abbey (Devon, England), **2:654–655**, *655*, 5:*420*, 8:816

Buckland Abbey (England), **2:655–656**, *656*

Buckler, Reginald, **2:656–657**

Buckley, James (Bp. of Trinidad), 3:115, 118

Buckley, John. *See* Jones, John, St.

Buckley, Joseph, 9:101

Buckley, Sigebert, 1:365, 12:271

Budde, K. F. R., 5:520

Buddha, 9:*47*

Buddhism, **2:657–674**, 11:287

   Amidism, 1:358

   apophatic theology, 1:568

   asceticism, 1:774

   Assyrian Church of the East, 3:491

   Bhutan, 2:352

   Bodhisattvas, 2:452, *453*, 661

   Burma, 2:670–671, 706

   Cambodia, 2:672–673

   Cao Dai, 3:79

   chain of causation, 3:361

   China, 2:*660*, 662–664, 3:510–511

   community, 4:38

   Confucianism, 4:98

   Daoism as amalgamated with, 10:111

   dharma, 4:714–715

   elements of existence, 5:147–148

   Hinayana, 6:836–837

   hospitality, 7:118

   India, 2:658–661, *659*

   Japan, 1:358, 2:*658*, 664–666, 7:736–737

   Korea, 2:668–669, 8:238

   Lamaism compared, 8:299

   Laos, 8:331

   liberation thinking, 8:549

   Mahayana, 9:46–48

   Malaysia, 9:69

   Mongolia, 9:805

   moral guidance, 4:760

   Nirvāṇa, 10:399

   Nostra aetate: Declaration on the Relation of the Church to Non-Christian Religions, 9:687

   Pali Canon, 10:803–804

   pessimism, 11:169

   Pure Land, 1:358, 2:453, 663, 664, 665, 668

   Shintoism compared, 13:87

   Soka Gakkai, 13:298

   soul, 13:338

   Sri Lanka, 2:661–662

   temples, 13:*807*

   Thailand, 2:*657*, 671–672

   Tibet, 2:666–668

   Vietnam, 2:669–670

   Western, 2:673–674

   See also Zen

Buddy, Charles Francis, 2:869

Budé, Guillaume, 10:482–483, 12:119

Buechlein, Daniel M. (Abp. of Indianpolis), 7:418, 13:824

Buenaventura, Alonso de, 1:649

Bufalo, Gaspare del, St., **2:674–675**, 11:642

Buffier, Claude, **2:675**, 12:771

Buffon, George-Louis Leclerc de, 5:210, 260

Bufi, Ylli, 1:216

Bugenhagen, Johann, **2:675**, 4:666, 8:888

Bughetti, B., 4:387

Buglio, Ludovico, **2:675–676**

Bugnini, Annibale (Abp. of Diocletiana), **2:676–677**

Buh, Joseph, Rev., 12:542

Buil Lalueza, Manuel, 2:92

Building Our Future (Malawi, pastoral letter), 9:68

Bukhtīshū' (d. 870), 2:678

Bukhtīshū', Abu Sa'id 'Ubaidallah ibn Jibrīl, 2:678

Bukhtīshū', 'Alī ibn Ibrahim ibn, 2:678

Bukhtīshū', Jabrīl ibn, 2:678

Bukhtīshū', Jibrīl ibn 'Ubaid Allāh, 2:678

Bukhtīshū', Jūrjīs ibn Jibrīl ibn, 2:677

Bukhtīshū', 'Ubaid Allāh, 2:678

Bukhtīshū' family, **2:677–678**

Bukhtīshū' ibn Jūrjīs, 2:677–678

Bulfinch, Charles, 2:553

Bulgakov, Macarius (Metropolitan of Moscow), **2:678–679**, 12:425

Bulgakov, Sergeĭ Nikolaevich, **2:679**, 5:773, 12:345

Bulgaria, **2:679–684**, *682*, *683*, *685*

   Bogomilism, 4:219

   Bossilkov, Evgenij, Bl., 2:548

   Byzantine Church, 2:680, 754, 755, 775, 786

   Catharism, 3:259

   Constantine V (Byzantine Emperor), 4:174

   demographic statistics, 2:680

   history, 4:173, 187, 412

   John XXIII (Pope), Bl., 7:933–934

   Macedonia, 9:14–15

   map, 2:*681*

   mission, 5:814, 9:110

   missions and missionaries, 5:814, 9:110

   monasticism, 9:801–802

   Orthodox Church, 2:680, 684, 745–746, 4:196, 10:683–688

   See also Cyril and Methodius, SS.

Bulgarian Catholic Church (Eastern Catholic), 2:539, 680–681, **685–686**, 748

Bulgarian Orthodox Church, **10:683–688**

   early history, 10:683–685

   post-communist era schism, 10:687–688

   stand against Jewish deportation, 10:685–686

   under communism, 10:686–687

   under Turkish rule (1396-1878), 10:685

Bulgaris, Eugenius, **2:686–687**

Bulhões, Miguel de, 2:594

Bulla, **2:687–688**

Bulla cruciata (papal bull, Eugene III), **2:688**, 5:443

Bullaker, Thomas, Bl., **2:688**, 5:235

Bullarium Maronitarum (Anaissi), 9:195–196

Bulletin d'Ancienne Littérature et d'Archéologie Chrétienne, 8:268

Bulletin of Medieval Canon Law, 8:257

Bullinger, Heinrich, **2:689**

   confessions of faith, 4:79

   Consensus Tigurinus, 4:416

Bullock, Texas Monthly v. (1989), 3:661

Bullough, E., 1:145

Bulls, papal. *See* Papal bulls

Bülow, Hans von, 12:28

Bulozi. *See* Black magic

Bulter, Marie Joseph (Mother), 9:302–303

Bultmann, Rudolf Karl, **2:689–691**, 5:338, 521, 522, 523, 6:865

   analogy, 1:379

   apothegms, 5:809–810, 811

   biblical theology, 2:387

   biographies of Christ, 7:849

   Bousset, Wilhelm, 2:570

   christological titles, 4:564

   death of God theology, 4:584

Bultmann, Rudolf Karl (*continued*)
  deconstructionism, 4:594
  dialectical theology, 4:721
  existential theology, 5:543–544
  fideism, 5:712
  form criticism, 5:807, 811–812
  Gadamer, Hans-Georg, 6:44
  John's Gospel, 7:902–903
  mythical character of the New Testament, 5:809, 10:124
  New Testament scholarship, 10:303
  transcendence and immanence of God, 6:322
  See also Demythologizing
Bulto (statue), 12:685
Bunderius, Jan (Van Den Bundere), **2:691**
Bundy, W. E., 7:850
Bungaku kai (periodical), 13:85
Bunge, Alejandro, 1:652
Bunsen, Christian Karl Josias Von, **2:691–692**
Bunyan, John, 1:292, 2:*692*, **692–693**
La Buona Stampa (periodical), 10:65
Buonaccorsi, Filippo, **2:693**
Buonafede, Appiano, 12:770
Buonaiuti, Ernesto, **2:694**, 7:673, 9:755
Buonarroti, Filippo, 3:101
Buoncompagni, Ugo. *See* Gregory XIII (Pope)
Buong Viet Tong, Paul, 14:492
Buonpensiere, Enrico, 12:777
Burali-Forti, C., 1:520–521
Burchard (prior of Mt. Carmel), 1:222
Burchard of Worms (Bp.), **2:695**, 3:325, 12:30
  See also Decretum (Burchard of Worms)
Burchard of Würzburg (Bp.), St., **2:695–696**, 8:168
Burckhardt, Jacob
  humanism, 7:193
  Renaissance, 9:611–612
  Renaissance concept, 12:112–113
Burden, Edward, Bl., **2:696**, 5:230
Bureau, Paul, **2:696**
Bureau International Catholique de l'Enfance (BICE), **2:696–697**
Burel, Gilbert, 3:4
Buren, Paul van, 4:584
Burgersdijck, F. P., 12:768
Burghhardt, Walter, 7:528
Burgkmair, Hans, 1:545
Burgo, Bonaventure de, 7:582
Burgo, Honoria de, 7:582

Burgo, Theobald de, 7:582
Burgoa, Francisco de, **2:697**
Burgos, laws of (1512-1513), 5:358
Burgundians
  Arianism, 1:663
  Church in Gaul, 6:112
  Germany, 6:171, 172
Burial
  banquet after (*refrigerium*), 12:26–27
  Canon Law, 3:332
  ceremonies and loculus, 8:746
  charnel houses, 3:437
  coffin, 12:690–691
  cremation vs., 4:358–360
  Early Christian, 3:221–225
  images, 7:324
  Jewish ceremonies, 8:12
  sarcophagus, 12:690–691
  use of light in ceremonies, 8:582
  works of charity, 3:404
  See also Catacombs; Death
Burial, early Christian, **2:699–700**
Burial, in the Bible, **2:697–699**
Burial of Count Orgaz (El Greco), 6:427
Burigny, Jean Lévesque de, **2:700–701**
Burin, Jacques, 8:384
Burke, Edmund, 2:*701*, **701–702**, 10:757
  aesthetics, 1:145
  architecture, 3:678
  aristocracy, 1:667
  Aristotelianism, 1:678, 2:702
  British moralists, 2:622, 624
  Catholic Relief Acts, 5:183, 250
  Fallon, Michael Francis, 5:614
  sovereignty, 13:372
Burke, Honoria, **2:702–703**
Burke, John, Sir, **2:703**
Burke, John J., **2:703–704**, 7:580
Burke, Maurice Francis (Bp. of Cheyenne, WY), 14:869–870
Burke, Raymond L. (Bp. of La Crosse, WI), 3:59, 8:273–274, 14:783
Burke, Thomas, **2:704**, 3:652, 4:424, 10:436, 12:385
Burkina Faso, **2:704–705**, *705*
Burkitt, Francis Crawford, 2:366, **705–706**
Burley, Walter. *See* Walter Burley
Burma (Myanmar), 2:670–671, **706–707**, *707*, *708*, 3:174
Burne-Jones, Edward, 1:851, 13:475
Burnet, Gilbert, 3:830
Burnet, J., 1:678
Burnett, Peter Hardeman, **2:707–708**, 868

Burnier, Joâo Penido, 7:794
The Burning Bush (Undset), 14:295
Burns, James Aloysius, **2:708–709**, *709*, 10:461
Burnt offerings, **2:709–710**
Burró Más, Juan Antonio, Bl., 7:124
Burrows, M., 5:520
Burses, **2:710**
Bursfeld Abbey (Germany), 1:152, **2:710**, 5:107, 8:324
Bursfeld Union, 8:564
Burtsell, Richard Lalor, **2:710–711**
Burundi, 2:*711*, **711–712**
Bury, John Bagnell, **2:712–713**, 10:954–955
Bury-St.-Edmunds Abbey (England), 1:464, 2:*713*, **713–714**, 5:86, 12:267
Bus, César de, Bl., 1:943, **2:714**
Busa, R., 12:778
Busaeus (de Buys), Johannes, **2:715**, 14:209
Busaeus (de Buys), Petrus, **2:714–715**, 3:242
Busch, John, 2:607
Busch, Joseph F., 12:542–543
Büsching, Anton Friedrich, 2:383
Busenbaum, Hermann, **2:715–717**, 7:782, 12:462
  Alphonsus Liguori, St., 1:310, 2:715–716
  casuistry, 3:221
  scholasticism, 12:766
Bush, George H., 1:34
Bushnell, Horace, 2:*717*, **717**
  anti-Catholicism, 4:122
  religious education, 4:116–117
  social gospel, 13:241–242
Business ethics
  just price, 8:64
  moral theology, 9:869
  patristic opinion, 13:252
Busnois, Antoine, **2:717–718**
Bussche, Hermann von dem, 5:306
Bustamante, Carlos María, **2:718**
Buswell, Charles A. (Bp. of Pueblo), 3:859
Le But de la guerre et de la paix, ou discours du chancelier l'Hospital pour exhorter Charles IX à donner la paix à ses sujets (L'Hôpital), 8:531
Butin, Romanus, **2:718**
Butiño, Francisco, 12:553–554
Butler, Alban, **2:718–719**, *719*
Butler, Benjamin, 1:156
Butler, Charles, **2:719–720**, *720*, 5:183, 250

Butler, Edmond J., 3:279

Butler, Edward Cuthbert, 2:263, **720**, 4:208, 6:890, 7:582

Butler, James (Abp. of Cashel), 3:243

Butler, Joseph (Bp. of Durham), 1:676, 2:623, **720–721**, *721*, 10:338

Butler, Leo T., 7:699

Bütler, María Bernarda, Bl., **2:721**

Butler, Marie Joseph (Mother), **2:721**, 12:496

Butler, Richard, 7:581

Butler-Bowden Cope, 8:635

Butsi, Cecilia, 13:848

Butt, Isaac, 7:563

Butterfield, William, 3:709

Buttigeg, Ambrose, 3:367

Buttimer, Charles Henry (Brother), 2:633

Buxtehude, Dietrich, **2:722**

Buxton, Christopher, Bl., **2:722**, 922, 5:230

Buxtorf, Johannes the Elder, 3:25, 6:697

Buyl, Bernal (Boyl), **2:722–723**

Buytaert, Eligius, 12:541

Buzenval (Bp. of Beauvais), 1:717

Buzzetti, Vincenzo, 12:770, 772

Byblos, **2:722–723**, *723*

Byrd, William, **2:724–725**, *725*, 3:150

Byrne, Andrew (Bp. of Little Rock), 1:691, **2:725**, *726*, 8:612

Byrne, Barry, 3:716

Byrne, Edmund (Abp. of Dublin), **2:725**

Byrne, Edwin Vincent (Abp. of Santa Fe, NM), 10:287–288, 12:676

Byrne, James J. (Abp. of Dubuque, IA), 4:924, 7:291, 12:574

Byrne, Leo C. (Bp. of St. Paul and Minneapolis, MN), 12:575–576, 13:295

Byrne, Patrick James, **2:726**

Byrne, Thomas S. (Bp. of Nashville, TN), 13:823

Byrne, William, **2:726**

Byrne, William, Rev., 5:144, 12:174

Byron, William J., 3:292

Bytown (Canada). *See* Ottawa (Canada)

Byzantinae historiae scriptoribus (Labbe), 8:265

Byzantine art, **2:727–741**, 769
angels, 1:425
Apocalypse iconography, 1:544, 545
Bible cycles, 2:370–371
Christology controversies, 2:731, 733
Constantinople, 4:189
crucifixion depictions, 4:393–395
development of mosaics, 10:3–4
doors of churches, 4:872–873

early period, 2:727–731, *728*, *732*
iconoclasm, 2:733, 821
iconography of Last Supper, 8:344
late period, 2:*731*, 739
Mary, Blessed Virgin, 9:276, 277–278, 280, 281
middle period, 2:*729*, *730*, 733–739, *733*, *734*, *735*
mosaics, 1:754, 2:*735*, *812*, *819*
precursors, 1:756

Byzantine Catholic Churches. *See* Eastern Catholic churches

Byzantine Chant, 1:197–198, **2:741–744**, 802–803
See also Liturgical music

Byzantine Christianity, **2:744–748**
Manichaeism mission vs., 9:109–110
monothelistism, 4:193
Romania, 12:330
See also Eastern Catholic churches; Eastern churches; Orthodox and Oriental Orthodox Churches

Byzantine Church, **2:748–764**
Adrian II (Pope), 1:124, 2:754–755
Albania, 1:213
All Souls' Day, 1:290
Anastasius the Librarian, 1:389–390
Armenian liturgy, 1:708, 709
Arsenite Schism, 1:735–736
biblical canon, 3:26–27
Bulgaria, 2:680, 754, 755, 775, 786
Canon Law, 2:773, 795, 3:45–46
Council of Chalcedon, 1:271, 3:365
diptychs, 4:758, 759
history, 2:748–762, 13:293
as area of study, 6:880
facing the east, 8:649
liturgical language, 8:667
Octoechos musical system of, 10:548–549
pre-Lent period, 13:98
Simeon of Syracuse, St., 13:125
vestments, art of, 8:634
hymnology, 7:242–243
Melkite Greek Catholic Church, 9:479–480
names, calling out of, 4:758
ruins (Crete), 14:*94*
works of charity, 3:413
See also Byzantine Empire; Eastern Catholic churches; Eastern Schism (1054); Iconoclasm; *specific Patriarchs*

Byzantine civilization, **2:764–777**
ancient Near East, 2:772
coinage, 10:480

environment, 2:768–769
evalution, 2:774–775
Hellenistic culture, 2:765–766, 775
historiography, 2:775–776
intolerance, 2:771–772
languages, 2:770, 774, 790
literary production, 2:773–774
paganism, 2:767–768
periodization, 2:771, 777
self-consciousness, 2:766–767
terminology, 2:764–765
Western civilizations, 2:770
See also Byzantine art; Byzantine Empire

Byzantine Empire, **2:777–789**
Adrian II (Pope), 1:124
Adrian III (Pope), 1:125
Adrian IV (Pope), 1:126
anti-Semitism, 7:868
apocrisiarius, 1:548
architecture, 2:816, 3:686–689
astrology, 1:813
Bulgarian Church, 10:684–685
Bury, John Bagnell, 2:713
Carolingian Dynasty, 3:167, 426, 427
Carthage, 3:187
ceremonies, 2:780–781
Church-State relations, 2:773, 820–822, 851, 3:633, 634
cities, 2:768, 782–783
Constans II, 4:173
Constantine IV, 4:173
Constantine IX, 4:175
Constantine V, 4:174
Constantine VII, 4:174–175
Constantine XI, 4:175–176
Coptics, 4:252–253
Croats, 4:370
Crusades, 4:401, 403, 410, 413
Cyprus, 4:461
Demetrius Chomatianus, 4:636
Donation of Constantine, 4:861
economy, 2:781–782
Egypt during, 5:117
historical sources, 2:777–778
historiography, 2:775–776, 778–779, 788–789, 795–802
Khazars, 8:164
Kingdom of God, 8:174
legislation, 8:99–100
military conflicts, 2:783–785, 786–787
military policies, 2:775, 781
Monophysitist strength, 13:13

Byzantine Empire *(continued)*
 Nicaean period, 2:760–762, 787
 political geography of Palestine
  during, 10:784
 religious policy, 8:97
 reorganization, 8:96
 Russia, 12:419
 secularization of Church property,
  12:870
 Sicily, 13:103
 See also Byzantine Church;
  Constantine I (the Great) (Roman
  Emperor); Constantinople;
  Constantinople, Councils of;
  Iconoclasm; *specific emperors*
Byzantine indiction, 7:419
Byzantine literature, **2:789–811**
 epistography, 2:807
 general character, 2:791
 history, 2:795–802
 philosophy, 2:807–810
 poetry, 2:802–806
 romance, 2:806–807
 satire, 2:807
 scope, 2:789–790
 theological, 2:791–795
Byzantine liturgy, **2:811–818**
 Andrew of Crete, St., 1:405, 2:742,
  803
 Antiochene liturgy, 1:528
 chant, 1:197–198, 2:741–744,
  802–803
 Christmas cycle, 3:556
 history, 2:811–813
 litanies, 8:600
 poetry, 2:802–803
 Scripture reading, 11:125
 Solemnity of All Saints, 1:289
Byzantine minuscule literary hand style,
 10:*769*, 771, 772
Byzantine monasticism, 9:797–803
Byzantine Orthodox Church
 icon veneration, 7:278–279
 unity, 4:255
 See also Iconoclasm
Byzantine Redemptorists, 11:995
Byzantine theology, 2:762, 791–795,
 818–829, 13:905, 910
 Cabasilas, Nicolas, 2:827–828,
  836–837
 Canon Law, 2:773, 795, 3:45–46
 Council of Florence, 2:828
 early church, 2:772–773
 Eastern Schism, 2:794, 823–828
 encyclopedias, 2:775, 794–795, 808
 Epiclesis, 2:763, 827–828

 homiletics, 2:795
 Incarnation, 2:766
 Justinian age, 2:793, 820–822
 Mariology, 2:766, 823, 828
 mysticism, 2:793–794
 Nicaean period, 2:761–762
 Photian period, 2:822–823
 Platonism, 2:818–819, 824
 sources, 2:819–820
 See also Christology controversies
  (patristic era); Hesychasm;
  Iconoclasm; Palamism
Byzantium. *See* Constantinople
Bzommar, Synod of (1867), 1:706

C

Cabala, **2:831–836**
 Avicebron, 1:938, 2:833
 Caro, Joseph ben Ephraim, 3:148
 described, 8:8–9
 Luria, I., 8:870–871
 revival, 13:56–57
Cabala, Gikatilla, 6:211
Caballero y Góngora, Antonio (Abp. of
 Bogotá), 2:465, **736**, 3:495, 851
Cabasilas, Nicolas, **2:836–837**, 5:426
 Dishypatos, David, 4:776
 Epiclesis, 2:827–828
 Palamism, 2:827
Cabasilas, Nilus, **2:837–838**
 Palamism, 2:826, 837
 papal primacy, 12:620
Cabassut, A., 7:32
Cabassut, Jean, **2:838**
Caberet, M. Bernardine (Mother), 12:537
Cabezón, Antonio de, **2:838**
Cabot, Richard, 8:901
Cabra, Dublin (Ireland), 4:843
Cabrini, Frances Xavier (Mother), St.,
 2:838–839, *839*, 3:859, 9:734, 12:718
Cabrini Sisters. *See* Missionary Sisters
 of the Sacred Heart
Cabrol, Fernand, **2:839–840**, 5:629
Cacciaguerra, Bonsignore, **2:840**
Caccini, Guilio, 2:115
Caccioli, Andrew, Bl., **1:403–404**, **2:840**
Cadalus (Antipope), 1:472
Cadeoldus (Bp. of Vienne), 3:766
Cadouin Abbey (France), **2:840**, *841*
Cadoux, C. J., 7:850
Cadwalla (King of Wessex), 3:481
Cadwallador, Roger, Bl., **2:840–841**,
 5:234
Caecilian (Bp.), 4:180, 861–862, 864

Caecilian Movement, **2:841–843**
 a cappella style, 3:523
 Bruckner, Anton, 2:642
 congregational singing, 4:119,
  7:254–255
 Liszt, F., 8:599
 music in Midwest, 8:698–699
Caeciliani Versio, 3:40
Caedmon, St., **2:843**
Caedwalla (King of Wessex), St.,
 2:843–844
Caelestis Agni Nuptias (hymn), **2:844**
Caelestis Aulae Nuntius (hymn), **2:844**
Caelestis pastor (apostolic constitution,
 Innocent XI), 11:866
Caelestis Urbs Jerusalem (hymn), **2:844**
Caelestius, 1:859, 860, 3:317
 See also Pelagius and Pelagianism
Caeli Deus Sanctissime (hymn), **2:844**
Caelitum Joseph Decus (hymn),
 2:844–845
Caelius Sedulius, 7:253, 843
Caen, Guillaume de, 2:13
Caen Hermitage, 8:382
Caerols Martínez, Florencia, Bl., 1:4
Caesar, Gaius Julius, 2:145, 3:571,
 6:664, 12:299, 301
Caesarea (Palestine), 2:845–846,
 846–847, *847*, 4:470–472, 10:653
Caesarea, School of, **2:845–846**, 847
Caesarea in Cappadocia, 1:785, **2:846**,
 10:653
Caesarea Maritima, 2:380
Caesarea Philippi, **2:847**
Caesarean indiction. *See* Indiction of
 Bede
Caesaria, SS., **2:848**
Caesaria the Elder, St., 2:848
Caesaria the Younger, St., 2:848
Caesarius of Arles, St., 1:694,
 2:848–849, 3:596, 5:668, 754, 10:620
 Aeonius of Arles, St., 1:140
 Aeterne Rerum Conditor, 1:147
 Apostles' Creed, 1:577
 ars moriendi, 1:728
 Athanasian Creed, 1:816
 Augustinianism, 1:877
 Aurelian of Arles, St., 1:895
 baths, 2:154
 contraception, 4:220
 Cyprian of Toulon, 4:460
 Gaul, 6:113
 hymns, 7:244
 preaching, 11:611
 Semi-Pelagianism, 2:499, 12:900

Caesarius of Heisterbach, **2:849–850**, *850*, 5:220, 529

  Dialogus Miraculorum, 2:850, 3:749

  Latin literature, 9:462

  preaching, 11:620

Caesarius of Nazianzus, St., **2:850**

Caesaropapism, **2:851**

  Anglicanism, 3:638

  Arcadius, 1:631

  Byzantine civilization, 2:773, 3:634

  Caprara, Giovanni Battista, 3:92

  Carolingian reform, 1:123, 3:425

  Charlemagne, 8:480

  development of papal rights, 10:834–835

  Eusebius of Caesarea, 3:633

  Gallicanism, 3:639

  heresy, 6:777–778

  Justinian I (Byzantine Emperor), 2:820–821

  sacred kingship, 13:252

  tensions between papacy and Byzantine Emperors, 7:656

Caesarus of Arles, 5:842

Caetani, Benedict. *See* Boniface VIII (Pope)

Caetani, Gelasio, 6:47

Caetani family. *See* Gaetani family

Cafasso, Joseph, St., 2:543, 851, **851**, 4:166

Caffaro of Caschifelone, 1:463

Cagliero, Juan (Card.), **2:852**

Cagliostro, Alessandro, 3:213

Cagnaold of Laon, St., 5:622

Cahensly, Peter Paul, **2:852**, 6:185, 12:573

  Abbelen, Peter M., 1:7–8

  Americanism, 1:354, 2:852

  "Americanizing" of immigrants, 7:551

  St. Raphael's Society, 12:582

Cahenslyism, 4:279, 957

Cahier 4 (Maréchal), 14:53

Cahiers de doléances, 5:971

Cahill, Patrick, 5:761

Cai, Xavier, 7:793

Caiani, Maria Margherita del Sacro Cuore, Bl., **2:852–853**

Cailloux, André, 1:156

Cáin Adamnáin (*Canon of Adamnan*), 1:110

CAIP (Catholic Association for International Peace), 9:398

Caird, E., 3:183

Caird, John, 12:69–70

Cairo Prophets text, 2:357

Caius (Pope). *See* Gaius (Pope), St.

Caius Marius Victorinus. *See* Marius Victorinus; Victorinus, Marius

Cajetan (Gaetano da Thiene), St., **2:855–856**

  Clement VII (Pope), 3:782

  Latin Averroism, 1:937

  Theatines, 2:855–856, 3:610

Cajetan (Tommaso de Vio) (Card.), 2:*853*, **853–855**, 14:48–49, 213

  abstraction, 1:47, 48

  accident, 1:60

  action and passion, 1:77, 78, 79

  Almain, Jacques, 1:298

  analogy, 1:372–373, 378

  archpriest controversy, 1:642

  Aristotelianism, 1:675, 677, 678, 2:854

  beauty, 2:185–186

  biblical canon, 3:32

  concept, 4:51

  conservation, 4:161

  demonology, 4:648

  Ferrariensis (Francesco Silvestri), 5:693

  immanence, 7:340

  immortality, 7:349, 353

  individuation, 7:426

  Luther meeting, 8:880

  Luther recantation, 12:16

  person, 11:147, 149–150

  philosophy of nature, 11:302

  pure nature, 11:*23*

  Reformation exegesis, 5:518

  scholasticism, 12:762, 764

  Thomism, 2:854, 3:588

  vision of God, desire for, 4:691

Cajetan, Constantino, **2:855**

Cajetans. *See* Theatines

Calabria, Giovanni (John), St., **2:856**

Calabria, Italo-Albanian Church in, 7:650–651

Calafato, Eustochia, St., **2:856–857**

Calafell (Spain), Martyrs of, 7:122–123

Calancha, Antonio de la, **2:857**

Calas, Jean, **2:857–858**

Calasanctian Sisters. *See* Daughters of the Divine Shepherdess

Calasanctius, Joseph. *See* Joseph Calasanctius, St.

Calatrava Order, **2:858**, 5:751

  Cistercians, 3:747

  Knights of Alcántara, 8:189

  Knights of Montesa, 8:195

  Order of Aviz, 1:947, 2:858

Raymond of Fitero, founding of, 11:936

Calbezudo, Diego Nuno, 4:111

Calcidius, **2:858–859**

Calciuri, Nicholas, 3:134

Calculus, 8:751

Caldara, Antonio, **2:859–860**, *860*

Caldeira, Mark, Bl., 1:952

Calderón, 1:925

Caldey Abbey (Wales), **2:860**

Caldor, Inc., Estate of Thornton v. (1985), 3:662

Caldwell (NJ), 4:844

Caldwell, John. *See* Fenwick, John, Bl.

Caldwell, Mary Gwendoline, 2:860–861, **860–861**, 3:290

El Calendario (Sahagún), 12:529

Calendars

  Byzantine liturgy, 2:815

  Carthaginian, 3:556

  Celtic, 3:331

  Chaldeans, 12:799–800

  Chinese, 3:494–495

  Chronographer of 354, 3:569–570

  dominical letter, 4:832

  Gregorian, 2:715, 3:611, 771, 772

  Julian, 8:54

  mahzor prayer structure, 9:49–50

  Philocalian, 4:675–676

  Synaxary, 13:678–679

  See also Chronology; Martyrologies; Roman Calendar; *specific liturgical calendars*

Calénus, Henri, 1:893, **2:861**

Calepino, Ambrogio, 1:888, 2:861, **861**

Calepinus, 5:798

California, **2:861–873**

  Alemany, Joseph Sadoc, 1:249–250

  Amat, Thaddeus, 1:332

  American Protective Association (APA), 8:791, 12:648

  anti-Catholicism, 2:868

  Catholic Action, 12:649

  Catholic education, 7:339, 9:746

  Deymann, Clementine, 4:713

  Dominicans, 2:867, 14:513

  early history, 2:862–866

  ecclesiastical organization, 2:862, 865–866, 871

  first bishop, 12:645

  first ordination, 12:645

  Franciscans, 2:862–865, 867, 9:717, 12:644–645

  Immaculate Heart of the Blessed Virgin Mary, Sisters of, 7:339–340

California *(continued)*
    Jesuits, 1:65, 2:867, 12:623
    Ku Klux Klan, 12:648
    Mannix, Daniel (Abp.), 9:123
    Manogue, Patrick, 9:123–124
    Miller v. California (1973), 11:519
    19th century U.S. period, 2:866–869
    Passionists, 2:867
    Pious fund, 2:862, 12:251, 623, 645
    racial integration, 8:792
    religious orders (communities),
      2:867–868
    separation of dioceses by Gregory
      XVI (Pope), 6:93
    social issues and programs,
      2:871–872
    tax exemptions, 12:251
    20th century, 2:869–872
    *See also specific dioceses and
      archdioceses*
California, Miller v. (1973), 11:519
Caligula (Gaius Caligula) (Roman
    Emperor), 12:303, 304
Caliph, 7:327–328
Caliphs, 1:611, **2:873**, 13:613
Calixtines. *See* Utraquists
Calixtus, Georg, **2:873–874**
    Calov, Abraham, 2:874, 884
    Carpzov, Johann Benedikt (I), 3:174
    dogmatic theology as term, 4:812
    Lutheran humanism, 8:890–891
Calixtus II (Pope), 4:410
Call to Action Conference (CTA),
    2:874–876, 4:569
Callahan, Patrick Henry, **2:876**, 8:190
Callan, Charles Jerome, **2:876**
Calles, Plutarco Elías, **2:876–877**, *877*
    Díaz y Barreto, Pascual, 4:733
    laicism, 8:283
    persecution of Mexican Catholics,
      9:582
Calles Vive, Vicente de Paúl, 7:123
Callewaert, Camille, **2:878**
Calligraphy, Islamic, 7:617–618
Callimachus (Roswitha of Gandersheim),
    12:390
Callimachus and Chrysorrhoe
    (Byzantine poem), 2:806
Callinicum, 1:338
Callinicus (Patriarch of Constantinople),
    2:878
Callistus I (Patriarch of Constantinople),
    2:826, 878, **878**
Callistus I (Pope), St., 1:752, **2:879–880**,
    3:224, 560, 12:353

Callistus II (Pope), **2:880–881**
    Anchin Abbey, 1:396
    Cistercians, 3:748, 751
    Cluniacs, 3:815
    Concordant of Worms, 14:849
    First Lateran Council, 8:350
    French monarchy, 5:843
    Geoffrey of Vendôme, 6:142
    Gerhoh of Reichersberg, 6:167
    Gregory VIII (Antipope), 6:485
    investiture struggle, 7:539
    Muslims, 2:688
Callistus II Xanthopulus (Patriarch of
    Constantinople), **2:879**
Callistus III (Antipope), 1:254, 2:882,
    882
Callistus III (Pope), **2:881–882**
    Alexander VI (Pope), 1:259, 2:881
    Angelus, 1:428
    Clement VIII (Antipope), 3:786
    coinage, 10:481
    family, 2:535
    nepotism, 2:881, 3:91, 10:247
Callistus Angelicudes, 2:879, **882–883**
Callo, Marcel, Bl., **2:883**, 8:306
Callot, Jacques, 4:313
Callus, Daniel Angelo Philip, **2:883**
Calmet, Augustin (Antoine), **2:883–884**,
    5:519
Caloca Cortés, Agustín, St., **2:884**, 6:545
Calov, Abraham, **2:884**
    biblical theology, 2:383
    Calixtus, Georg, 2:874, 884
    Carpzov, Samuel Benedikt, 3:174
    confessions of faith, 4:81
Calumny, **2:884–885**, 4:696
Calungsod, Pedro, Bl., **2:885**, 12:657
Calvary, **2:885–886**
Calvary Basilica (Jerusalem), 3:685
Calvat, Melanie, 5:865
Calvert, Benedict Leonard, 3:649
Calvert, Cecil, 2:886–887, 3:649, 9:299,
    14:103, 104
Calvert, Charles, 2:887
Calvert, George, Lord Baltimore. *See*
    Baltimore, George Calvert, Lord
Calvert family, **2:886–887**, 10:321
Calvin, John, *2:887*, **887–890**, 14:159
    Apostles' Creed, 1:577
    ars moriendi, 1:733
    Beza, Theodore, 2:352
    biblical canon, 3:21
    Bucer, Martin, 2:653, 889, 891
    capital punishment, 3:87
    Castellio, Sebastian, 2:889, 3:214

    Church-State relations, 3:637–638
    clerical celibacy and marriage, 3:327
    confessions of faith, 4:79
    Crypto-Calvinism, 4:416
    Farel, Guillaume, 5:622, 7:166
    free will nonexistent, 5:930, 938
    French reform, 7:166
    grace, 6:403
    heresy, 6:776
    impact on liturgical reforms,
      8:659–660
    imputation of justice and merit, 7:368
    Institutes, 7:498–499
    intemediate judgment, 8:33
    justification, 8:84, 86–87
    laicism, 8:282
    Lord's Supper, 5:426–427, 521
    Luther, Martin, 3:608
    predestination, 11:650, 655,
      13:625–626
    Presbyterianism, 11:678
    priesthood, 11:703
    Protestant Reformation, 12:12, 15
    Reformation exegesis, 5:518
    religious experience, 5:555
    sacramentals, 12:481
    on the state, 13:483–484
    See also Calvinism
Calvinism, **2:890–896**, 3:608
    Amiens, 1:359
    Amyraut, Moïse, 1:367
    Andrewe, Richard, 1:408
    Aniane Abbey, 1:454
    Antwerp, 1:468, 538
    Aristotelianism, 1:676, 677
    Arminianism, 1:712–713, 2:894
    Aubigné, Jean Henri Merle d', 1:845
    Auger, Edmond, 1:847–848
    Augustinianism, 1:884
    Austria, 1:912, 913
    Belgium, 2:217
    Boers, 13:360
    Bolsec, Jérôme Hermès, 2:475
    Brazil, 2:587
    Bullinger, Heinrich, 2:689
    Calas case, 2:857–858
    Calvin, John, 2:889–890
    Cameron, John, 1:367, 2:911
    Catholic faith banned, 5:867
    Cayet, Pierre Victor, 3:314
    Christian Church formation, 4:117
    Christian Reformed Church, 3:543
    confessions of faith, 4:79
    Congregationalist questioning, 4:116

Cambridge Platonists, 2:908–910, 11:294, 416

CANADA

Coornhert, 4:248
covenant theology, 4:328–329
Drašcovič, Georg de, 4:902
Duperron, Jacques Davy, 4:943
Eastern churches, 8:841–842
Edwards, Jonathan, 5:97–98, 193
France, 4:314
Hungary, 7:213–214
hymnody, 7:255
Jansenism, 3:614
Lithuania, 8:605
Lutheranism, 3:608
Peace of Augsburg, 1:849
Protestant Reformation, 12:20–21
16th century Ruthenians, 12:422
Spanheim, E. and F., 13:406–407
spread, 10:842
theology, 2:890–891
Unitarians and Universalists, 5:193
Westminster Confession, 14:695
See also Calvin, John; Huguenots
Calvó, Bernard (Abbot), 12:680
Calvo, Gabriel (Father), 9:205
Calvo, Miguel, 12:641
Calvo Martínez, Sebastían (Father), 2:92
Calvo Sánchez, Fulgencio, Bl., 4:494
Calvo y Calvo, Antolíin María, 2:92
Cam, Dominic, 14:492
Camaiani, Pietro (Bp. of Ascoli Piceno), 2:896
Camaldolese, 2:896–898, 897, 899
Canons Regular of St. Augustine, 3:67
Carthusian spirituality, 3:191
contemplative life, 4:210
Counter Reformation, 3:611
as discalced order, 4:765
founding, 3:600
reform, 4:310
Servite friars, 13:27
solitude, 13:303
Camaldoli Abbey (Italy), 2:897–898, 898–899, 899, 5:755, 766, 792, 12:366–367, 367
Camara, Helder Pessoa (Abp. of Olinda and Recife), 2:899–901, 900, 4:157
Camaterus, Andronicus, 2:794, 825
Cambio, Arnolfo di, 1:128, 2:374
Cambodia, 2:672–673, 901–904, 902, 903, 9:700
Cambrai, Treaty of (1529), 7:669
Cambrai Archdiocese (France), 2:904–905, 8:565
Cambridge Platform, 2:907–908, 4:81, 115

British moralists, 2:623
Cartesianism, 3:185
Coleridge, Samuel Taylor, 3:832
latitudinarianism, 8:370
world soul, 14:844–845
Cambridge University (England), 2:905–907
Aristotelianism, 1:676, 2:906
Jesus College, 1:241
King's College, 8:837
Cambyses (King of Persia), 11:135
Camerarius, Joachim, 4:416
Camerlengo, 2:910–911, 4:60
Cameron, John (Bp.), 2:911–912
Cameron, John (Scottish theologian), 1:367, 2:911
Cameron, Richard, 2:912
Cameronians, 2:912, 4:330
Cameroon, 2:912–914, 915
Camillians, 2:914
Camillus de Lellis, St., 2:914–916
Camino interno dell'anima (St. Charles of Sezze), 3:435
Camisards, 2:916
Camisassa, James, 1:291
Campana, Emilio, 2:916–917
Campanella, Tommaso, 2:917, 14:360
aristocracy, 1:667
Aristotelianism, 1:677
empiricism, 5:197
heliocentrism, 6:61
world soul, 14:844
Campans, Bernard, 8:513
Campbell, Alexander, 2:917, 918, 3:534
Campbell, Frederic (Bp.), 12:577
Campbell, Joseph, 2:918–919, 919
Campbell, Thomas Joseph, 2:919–920, 3:534
Campbellites. See Christian Church (Disciples of Christ)
Campeggi, Camillo (Card.), 2:920
Diet of Nuremberg, 3:781
Henry VIII divorce, 3:268, 782
Campeggio, Lorenzo (Card.), 2:920–921, 5:244, 12:8
Campidelli, Pius (Pio), Bl., 2:921
Campion, Edmund, St., 2:921, 921–922, 5:227, 247, 799, 7:783
Brinkley, Stephen, 2:618
Bristow, Richard, 2:619
Flanders plot, 8:181
martyrdom, 2:611–612, 922
Recusant literature, 11:959

Sherwin, R. R., 13:82
Campion, Edward, Bl., 2:722, 922, 5:230
Camplo, Iacobus de, 3:51
Campo (Van de Velde), Heymericus de, 1:226
Campo, Almadóvar del. See John Baptist of the Conception, St.
Campo Santo Teutonico, 2:922–924, 923
Campomanés, Pedro, 3:792
Campos, Augutin de (Father), 1:687
Campra, André, 2:924
Camus, Albert
absurdity, 1:48, 49
existentialism, 5:544, 545, 7:197
Camus, Jean (Bp.), 5:850
Can Nguyen, Francisco Javier, 14:492
Cana of Galilee, 3:1, 9:245–246
Canaan and Canaanites, 3:1–3, 2
archeological work, 10:796
biblical name for Palestine, 10:777
Byblos, 2:724
circumcision, 3:739
creation, 4:337, 341
religion, 1:808
Ugaritic-Canaanite religion, 14:267–271
wisdom literature, 14:789
See also Phoenicians
Canada, 3:3–12
Basilians, 2:142, 144
capital punishment, 3:88
Charbonneau, Joseph, 3:388
Charbonnel, Armand François Marie de, 3:388
church architecture, 3:717
Coady, Moses Michael, 3:815–816
Colin, Frederic Louis, 3:834
Connolly, Thomas Louis, 4:128
cremation practices, 4:359
demographic statistics, 3:3
ecclesiastical organization, 3:4
education, 8:270
history, 3:3–9
Holy Cross Congregation, 7:21
Hutterites, 7:234
Lauzon, Pierre de, 8:382
Little Sisters of the Holy Family, 8:616
map, 3:5
Mennonite churches, 9:496
Methodist churches, 9:561
mission
addressing wrongs against natives, 3:11
end as missionary territory, 3:8

NEW CATHOLIC ENCYCLOPEDIA

225

Canada *(continued)*
    end of French rule, 3:6
      Maritime Provinces, 3:3–4, 9,
        8:464
      Protestant mission, 12:273
      Quebec, 3:388, 9:165
      Sisters of St. Anne, 12:534
    provinces and territories, 3:9–11
    Simon de Longpré, M., 13:129
    Sisters Adorers of the Precious
      Blood, 13:171
    Sisters of Loretto, 8:787
    Sisters of Mercy, 13:184
    Sulpicians, 13:600–601
    Ukrainian hierarchy, 13:80
Canadell Quintana, Enrique, Bl., **3:12**,
  10:816
Canadian Center for Ecumenism
  (Montréal), 3:9
Canadian Council of Churches (CCC),
  3:9
Canadian Martyrs Church (St. Boniface,
  MB), 3:717
Canal, José de la, **3:12**
Cañas y Calvo, Blas, **3:12–13**
Canavan, Patrick, Bl., 7:579
Cancius Camerarius. *See* Honorius III
  (Pope)
Candela, F., 3:676, 677
Candide ou l'Optimisme (Voltaire),
  10:613, 14:580
Candido, L., 3:740
Candido, Vincenzo, **3:13**
Candidus (Byzantine historian), 2:798
Candidus of Fulda, **3:13**, 12:757
Candlemas, **3:13–15**, *14*, 8:581
Candles, **3:15**, *16*
  altars, 1:318
  light, use of, 8:580–582
  paschal candle, 5:16
  See also Light, liturgical use of
Canelles Vives, Vicente de Paúl, Bl.,
  7:123
Canepanova, Peter (Bp. of Pavia). *See*
  John XIV (Pope)
Canevin, J. F. Regis (Bp. of Pittsburgh),
  11:367
Canfield, Benedict, 3:192
Canh Luong Hoang, José, 14:492
Canice of Derry. *See* Kenneth (Canince)
  of Derry, St.
Canigiani, Alexandre (Abp. of Aix),
  1:196
Canisius, Peter, St., **3:15–19**, *17*, 5:173,
  331, 7:782
    Augsburg, 1:848

Austria, 1:911
    Carthusian spirituality, 3:192
    catechesis, 2:714–715, 3:17–18, 233,
      242, 244
    catechisms, 4:9
    Counter Reformation, 3:611
    Faber, Peter, Bl., 5:584
    Lanspergius influence, 8:326
    St. Stanislaus, 8:243
    spiritual retreat, 13:430
Canning, George, 5:184
Cannon, Beekman C., 12:725
Cannon, W. B., 1:604
Cano, Francisco, 4:111
Cano, Melchior, 3:*19*, **19–20**, 14:49
    Báñez, Domingo, 2:49
    Carranza, Bartolomé, 3:176
    loci theologici, 8:743
    Louis of Granada condemned, 8:806,
      807
    positive theology, 3:614, 4:812
    scholasticism, 12:764
    successor, 13:330
Canon, biblical. *See* Bible, canon
Canon Law, 5:300
  (1209), 10:838
  Abbots, 1:10–11
  abortion, 1:31–32
  Admonitio generalis, 3:42, 156, 425
  Adrian IV (Pope), 1:127
  adultery, 1:131
  age, 1:174, 7:40
  Agustín, Antonio, 1:190
  Alanus Anglicus, 1:206–207, 3:48
  Alberic of Rosate, 1:219–220, 3:48
  Anselm II of Lucca, St., 1:494, 3:45,
    60
  Anselmo Dedicata, Collectio, 1:499
  Apostolic Constitutions, 1:581, 3:323,
    324, 403
  apostolic delegation in the United
    States, 1:583
  Armenia, 1:705–706
  beatification and canonization of
    saints, 12:608
  Bernard of Compostella, the Elder,
    2:312–313
  Bernard of Compostella, the
    Younger, 2:313
  Bernard of Montmirat, 2:314, 3:48
  Bernard of Parma, St., 2:314–315,
    3:48
  Bertrand, Pierre, 2:336
  blasphemy, 2:434
  Blastares, Matthew, 2:435

Byzantine Church, 2:773, 795,
  3:45–46
Catharism, 1:231
cathedrals, 3:261
cemeteries, 3:332
Chabham, Thomas, 3:358
Church-State relations, 3:635–636,
  643–645
Clementinae, 3:46, 48, 50, 780, 800
clerical misconduct and inquisition,
  7:487
communio, 4:30
conciliarism, 4:58
concubinage, 4:64–65
confessions of faith, 4:355
Confirmation, 4:88
Confraternity of Christian Doctrine,
  4:94
consecrated life, 4:154–156
Copts, 4:254–255
Corpus Iuris Canonici, 4:272–273
cremation, 4:359
cult worship, 4:426
deacons, 4:553
digamy, 4:744
Dionysiana collectio, 4:752
dowry, 4:888–889
dueling, 4:929
ecclesiastical heraldry, 6:762–763
enclosure, 3:806
English language, 8:905
epiclesis, 5:279
excommunication, 5:506
exemption, 5:529, 530
exorcisms, 5:552
force and fear, 5:796–797
funerals, 6:33–34
Gasparri, Pietro, 6:103
glosses, 6:248–249
Gregorian reform, 1:841, 3:44, 46,
  47, 60
heresy, 6:772
Hollweck, Josef, 7:11
homily, 7:63
Honorius III, 7:84–85
hospitals, 7:128–129
Joannes Andreae, 7:881
John Paul II (Pope), 7:1001–1002
judical vicar, 8:42–43
laicization, 8:284–287
laity, 5:39, 8:288–289
laity, rights and duties of, 5:39
Latin literature, 9:455
Latin Rite, 8:367–369
liturgical laws, authority, 8:669

mandatum, 9:104–105

manifestation of conscience, 9:116

Maria Theresa, 9:155

Maronite Church, 9:198–199

marriage legislation, 9:206–207

mission and evangelization,
9:682–683

monks, 4:58–59

papal legates, 8:451

Peru, 1:932

preaching, 11:620–632

prior marriage, 11:717

Provost, James H., 11:786–787

proxy, 11:787

public order, 11:808–809

religious life, 12:89–92

research and cataloging, 8:257–258

revision under John XXIII (Pope),
Bl., 7:936

sacred places, 12:500

Schmalzgrueber, 12:741

Summa parisiensis (anonymous),
13:604–605

team ministry, 13:782–783

University of Bologna, 2:474

See also Code of Canon Law (1917);
Code of Canon Law (CIC) (1983);
Code of Canons of the Eastern
Churches (CCEO) (1990);
Decretalists; Decretals; *Decretum*
(Burchard of Worms); Religious,
Canon Law of; Rules of Law
(*Regulae Iuris*)

Canon Law, history of, **3:37–58, 59–60**,
5:691, 6:881

9th-11th centuries, 3:44–46, 600, 601

1917 Code, 3:55

1983 Code, 3:56–58

Carolingian era, 3:41–44, 156–157,
158

classical period, 3:46–50

Council of Trent, 3:51, 53–54

Divine origins, 13:102

early church, 3:37–41

15th-16th centuries, 3:50–52

Lawrence of Spain, 8:408–409

Laymann, P., 8:419

Le Plat, J., 8:507

Legitimacy of children, 8:454–455

Leuren, P., 8:520

Liber sextus, 8:536

liturgical colors, 8:645

liturgical music, 8:699

pre-Gregorian collections, 8:324

servitude and slavery, 13:209, 211

17th-20th centuries, 3:54

Simon of Bisignano, 13:131–132

Third Lateran Council, 8:352

Canon Law, mission and evangelization,
9:682–683

Canon Law glosses, **6:248–249**

Canon Law Society of America (CLSA),
3:58–59

Concilium Monasticum Iuris
Canonici, 4:58–59

Krol, J. J., 8:250

Canon of Adamnan (*Cáin Adamnáin*),
1:110

Canon of Cyprian, 3:39

Canones Apostolorum, 3:37, 38, 59

Canones ecclesiastici Apostolorum, 3:37

Canones Hippolyti, 3:37–38

Canones paenitentiales apostolorum,
3:38

*Canones pseudo-synodi Antiochenae
apostolorum*, 3:38

Canonesses Regular of St. Augustine,
8:432

Canonical criticism, 6:795, 10:307–308

Canonical Epistle (St. Gregory
Thaumaturgus), 6:525

Canonical Prayerbook (Mandaean
religion), 9:104

Canonical shape, 3:33–34

Canonists, in Apostolic Penitentiary,
11:76

Canonization of Saints. *See specific
saints*

Canonization of Saints (history and
procedure), **3:61–66**

canonization ceremony, 10:856

Congregation of Sacred Rites and
Ceremonies, 12:256

cult worship, 4:426

devil's advocate (promoter of the
faith), 4:705–706

heroic virtue, 14:554

hope as necessity, 7:102

procedure, 3:63–66, 12:607–608

universal call to holiness, 7:7

See also specific saints

Canons, chapters of, **3:66–67**

Canons, Roman primacy, 8:53–54

Canons of Dort, 3:543

Canons of Hippolytus (canonical
collection), 1:170, 2:62

Canons Regular, 3:412, 564

See also specific groups

Canons Regular of Prémontré. *See*
Premonstratensians

Canons Regular of St. Augustine,
3:67–69, 601, 5:455

Ancient See of Carlisle, 3:124

Bernard of Aosta, St., 2:306

Celles-Sur-Belle Monastery,
3:328–329

Ireland, 8:138

Roduc Monastery (Netherlands),
12:292

Saint Andrews (Scotland), 12:533

Saint-Lô Monastery (France), 12:558

Santa Cruz Monastery (Portugal),
12:673

Servites replacing, 13:27

Solminihac, A., 13:305

Wales, 8:739

Canons Regular of St. Ruf, 3:191

Canons Regular of the Holy Cross,
2:609, 3:69

Canons Regular of the Immaculate
Conception, 3:69

Canons Regular of the Order of the Holy
Cross. *See* Crosier Fathers

Canons Regular of Windesheim,
4:707–708

Canori-Mora, Elisabetta, Bl., **3:69–70**

Canossa, Louis di (Bp. of Bayeux),
3:415

Canossa, Maddalena Gabriella, St., **3:70**,
12:127, 383, 384

Cansfield, Brian, Ven., 5:236

Cantacuzenus, John, 1:409, 410, 2:776

La Cantate à trois voix (Claudel), 3:768

Canterbury, Ancient See of (England),
3:70–73, 14:894

Arches Court, 1:635

burial of archbishops, 4:448

Courtenay, William, 4:317–318

Canterbury, Archbishop of

London as suffragan see, 8:770–772

Simon Islip, 13:130

Simon Langham, 13:130

Simon Mepham, 13:131

Simon of Sudbury, 13:133

Stafford, John, 13:467–468

synodal constitutions collected, 8:905

Canterbury, Convocation of, 4:243–244

Canterbury Cathedral (England), 3:*71*,
72–73, 73, 601, 13:*469*

Canterbury Psalter (prayer book),
11:603

Canterbury Tales (Chaucer), 3:*452*,
453–456, 457, 5:529

The Canticle of Brother Sun (St. Francis
of Assisi), 5:893

Canticle of Canticles, 8:104,
13:318–319. *See Also* Song of Songs

Canticle of Love (Bélanger), 2:211

Canticle of Mary (song), **9:43–44**

Canticle of Simeon. *See Nunc Dimittis* (Canticle of Simeon)

Canticle of Zechariah (Benedictus), **2:275–276**

Canticles, biblical, **3:73**, *74*

Cantilène de Saint Faron (ballad), 5:631

Canting arms (heraldry), 6:764

Le Cantique des Cantiques (Robert), 12:262

Cantor, Georg, 4:216
    antimonies, 1:520–521
    infinity, 7:459–460

Cantor, N. F., 1:489

Cantors in Christian liturgy, **3:73**, **75–76**, 522

Cantors in Jewish liturgy, **3:76**, 8:108

Cantù, Cesare, 7:673

Cantus firmi, 1:234

Cantwell, John Joseph (Abp. of Los Angeles), 2:869, **3:76–77**, 4:534, 8:791, 12:648

Cantwell v. Connecticut (1940), 3:660, 661

Canut de Bon, Juan Bautista, 3:486

Canute (King of England and Denmark), 1:306, **3:77–78**, 5:386, 14:*769*

Canute II (King of Denmark), 4:663–664

Canute IV (King of Denmark) St., 1:40, **3:77**, 4:664

Canute Lavard, St., **3:78–79**

Il Canzoniere (Petrarch), 11:215

Cao Dai, 3:*79*, **79–80**

Caoshan Benji, 3:511

Caouette, Catherine Aurélie, 13:171

Capdevila Miró, Tomás, 2:92

Cape Verde, 3:*80*, **80–81**, *81*

Capecelatro, Alfonso (Card.), **3:81–82**, 7:673

Capella, 3:382

Capella Greca (Roman catacomb of Priscilla), 12:485

Capelle, Bernard, 3:*82*, **82**, 6:121

Capello, Felice M., 7:792

Capéran, Louis, **3:82–83**

Capernaum (Israel), 2:380, **3:83**

Capernaum synagogue (Galilee, Israel), 13:677

Capgrave, John, 1:888, **3:83**, 8:103

Capillas, Francis de, Bl., **3:83–84**, 496

Capilulare generalis (789), 3:424

Capistran, John, 3:91–92, 197, 8:275

Capita doctrinae christianae compendio tradita. . . (Canisius), 3:242

"Capital grace" doctrine, 11:986

Capital punishment, **3:84–89**
    Catechism of the Catholic Church, 3:88, 238
    Chile, 3:488
    human rights, 10:199

Capital sins (deadly sins), 4:565–567

Capitalism
    democracy, 4:642–643
    distributism, 4:782–783

Capitanio, Bartolomea, St., **3:89**, 6:189

Capito, Wolfgang, **3:89**

Capitol Square Review and Advisory Board v. Pinette (1995), 3:664

Capitoline era, 5:311

Capitula (Remedius of Chur), 3:43

Capitula Angilramni, 5:615, 616

Capitulare, 5:466

Capitulare Evangeliorum, 11:124

Capitulare institutum (Louis I), 2:251–252

Capitulare missorum speciale (802), 3:424

Capitularia (Charlemagne), 3:240

Capitularia missorum generalis, 3:156

Capitularies, imperial and ecclesiastical, **3:89–91**
    Ansegis of Fontenelle, St., 1:494
    Canon Law, 3:41, 42
    Charlemagne, 3:166, 423
    France, 5:842
    hospital regulation, 7:128

Capitulate de imaginibus (Libri Carolini), 10:349, 350

Capitulations, **3:91**, 11:20

Cappadocians, 5:510–511
    Arianism, 1:663
    Armenia, 1:707, 708
    Christmas, 3:552
    Christology, 3:561
    contributions to Christian paideia, 10:755
    the cross, 4:383, 393
    Holy Trinity doctrine, 14:194–195
    homoousios, 4:198
    spirituality, 13:444
    See also Basil the Great, St.; Gregory of Nazianzus, St.; Gregory of Nyssa, St.

Cappel, Jacques, 5:518

Cappel, Louis, 5:518

Cappellari, Bartolomeo Alberto (Card.). *See* Gregory XVI (Pope)

Capponi, Gino, 7:673

Capranica, Angelo (Card.), **3:91–92**

Capranica, Domenico (Card.), **3:91**, 357

Caprara, Giovanni Battista (Card.), **3:92**
    appointment, 3:796
    Bernier, Étienne Alexandre, 2:324, 3:92
    Josephinism, 1:914, 3:92

Capreolus, John, **3:92–93**, 4:949, 12:762, 764, 14:47

Captivity Epistles, 1:784, **3:93**

Capuchin Congregation of Franciscan Missionaries of the Mother of the Divine Shepherd, 9:759

Capuchinesses. *See* Franciscan Sisters

Capuchins
    Armenia, 1:703
    Austria, 1:911
    Brazil, 2:590, 593, 595
    Cape Verde, 3:80
    Caribbean, 3:118
    Carthage, 3:188
    Central African Republic, 3:344
    Chad, 3:359–360
    Counter Reformation, 3:611
    Felix of Cantalice, St., 5:669–670
    Fitch, William Benedict, 5:750–751
    Forbes, John, 5:795
    founding, 3:54, 782
    Franciscan friars, 5:*903*
    Knoll, A., 8:199
    Latvia, 8:376
    Lawrence of Brindisi, 8:406
    Louis of Besse, 8:805
    Louisiana, 8:8–9
    missions, 9:719, 721
    19th-20th century overview, 3:621
    origin, 5:902–903
    reform, 4:310
    Seraphino, St., 13:6–7
    Sheehan, L., 13:73–74
    Somalia, 13:308
    Trinidad, 3:113–114

Caputiati, **3:93**

Caputo, Maddalena, 12:551

CARA (Center for Applied Research in the Apostolate), 10:576

CARA (Medieval Academy of America, Committee on Centers and Regional Associations), 9:436

Carabanchel Alto (Spain), Martyrs of, 7:123–124

Carabantes, José de, **3:94**

Caracalla. *See* Antoninus, Marcus Aurelius (Caracalla)

Caracci brothers (painters), 4:313

Caracciolo, Bernardo (Card.), 3:94

Caracciolo, Diego Innico (Card.), 3:94

Caracciolo, Domenico, 3:94

Caracciolo, Francesco, 3:94

Caracciolo, Francis, St., **3:95**

Caracciolo, Galeazzo, 3:94

Caracciolo, Giacomo, 3:94

Caracciolo, Giovanni Costanzo (Card.), 3:94

Caracciolo, Innico (Card.) (d. 1685), 3:94

Caracciolo, Innico (Card.) (d. 1730), 3:94

Caracciolo, Landolf, 3:94, **95–96**

Caracciolo, Marino (Card.), 3:94

Caracciolo, Nicolò (Card.) (d. 1389), 3:94

Caracciolo, Nicolò (Card.) (d. 1728), 3:94

Caracciolo, Roberto, 3:94

Caracciolo, Sergianni (Giovanni), 3:94

Caracciolo family, **3:94–95**

Carafa (Caraffa) family, **3:96–98**, 4:11

Carafa, Alfonso (Card.), 3:97

Carafa, Antonio, 3:97

Carafa, Carlo (Card.), 3:96–97

Carafa, Carlo II, Ven., 3:97

Carafa, Carlo III, 3:98

Carafa, Carlo IV, 3:98

Carafa, Gian Pietro. *See* Paul IV (Pope)

Carafa, Giovanni, 3:96

Carafa, Oliviero (Card.), 3:96, *97*, 11:23–24, 12:526

Carafa, Pierluigi, 3:98

Carafa, Rosa di Traetto, Ven., 3:98

Carafa, Vincenzo, 3:97–98

Caraman, Philip, 1:467

Caramuel, Juan Lobkowitz, **3:98–99**, 8:411, 12:768, 14:51

Caravaggio, Michelangelo Mirisi da, 2:114, 375

Caravario, Callisto (Kalikst), St., **3:99**, 12:615

Carayon, Auguste, **3:99**

Carberry, John Joseph (Abp. of St. Louis), 3:868, 7:416, 12:561

Carbonari (Italian secret society), **3:99–101**, *100*, 10:150, 12:666

Carbonnelle, I. J. J., 1:80

Carceller Galindo, Francisco, Bl., **3:101**, 10:816

Carda Sporta, José Pascual, 12:408

Cardano, Geronimo, 1:677, 7:239, 10:823

Cardello, Gaspar, 1:236

Cárdenas, Bernardino de (Bp. of Paraguay), **3:101–102**

Cárdenas, Juan de, **3:102**

Cárdenas, Lázaro, 9:583

Cardenas, Rafael Salzar, 7:528

Cardiel, José, **3:102**

Cardijn, Joseph (Card.), 2:219, **3:102–103**, 7:889

Catholic Action, 3:277

Jocist technique, 3:536

Cardinal

consistories, 4:165–166

Papal Election Decree (1059), 10:365, 836, 857–858

papal elections, 11:498–501

Cardinal Cagliero Institute, 12:247

Cardinal Consalvi and Anglo-Papal Relations, 1814-1824 (Ellis), 5:170

Cardinal Cusa with St. Peter in Chains (Bregno), 10:*373*

Cardinal Major Penitentiary, 11:76

Cardinal Newman Award, 8:153

Cardinale, Beda, 4:567

Cardinals, **3:103–108**

capitulations, 3:91

John Paul II (Pope) creation of, 3:628

See also Curia, Roman; Papal elections; *specific cardinals*

Cardona Meseguer, Matias, Bl., **3:108**, 10:816

A Careful and Strict Enquiry into the Modern Prevailing Notions of That Freedom of Will . . . (Edwards), 5:98

Carette, Louis, 1:691

Carey, George (Abp. of Canterbury), 1:442, 5:253

Carey, John, Bl., 4:271, 5:232, 7:579

Carey, Thomas F., 10:134

Carey, William, 2:78–79, **3:108**, 7:403, 9:697

Carhart, Stenberg v., 1:35

Cariattil, Joseph (Abp. of Cranganore, India), 7:399

Carib people, 3:108, 109, 110, 113, 118, 119

Caribbean, **3:108–122**, *109*

See also specific nations

Caribbean Islands mission, 9:692

Carileffus (Calais), St., 1:946, **3:122–123**, 12:541

Carissimi, Giacomo, 3:123, *123*, 438

Carissimis Russiae populis (papal decree, Pius XII), 11:400

Carità (periodical), 8:806

Caritas (papal brief, Pius VI), 11:377

Caritas Centers (Hong Kong), 7:76

Caritas Christi urgens (Pallotti), 8:415

Caritas International, 13:110

Caritas-Secours (Belgium), 2:221

Caritate Christi (encyclical, Pius XI), 11:393, 12:491

Carlini, Armando, 1:881–882

Carlisle, Ancient See of (England), **3:123–124**

Carloman (Frankish mayor of the palace), 1:121, **3:124–125**, 165, 172, 11:111

Canon Law, 3:41

Carolingian reform, 3:124, 156, 424

consolidation of power, 3:164

Council of Attigny, 1:840

Pepin III, 11:108–109

Stephen III (IV) (Pope), 13:518

Carlone, C. A., 12:668

Carlone, Carlo Antonio, 1:913

Carlyle, Thomas, 5:188, 189

aristocracy, 1:667

Brownson, Orestes Augustus, 2:640

Samson, 12:636

Carmathians, 1:612

Carmel, Mount, **3:125**, 131, 140, 141, 145

Carmel Mission (CA), 3:714

La carmelita perfecta (Silverio de St. Teresa), 13:122

Carmelite Nuns, Discalced, 3:127–128

Carmelite Rite, **3:125–126**, 140–141

Carmelite Rule, 7:156

Carmelite Sisters, **3:126–130**, 134–135, 144, 8:807

See also Carmelites

Carmelite Sisters for the Aged and Infirm, 3:128

Carmelite Sisters of Charity, 3:128–129

Carmelite Sisters of Corpus Christi, 3:129

Carmelite Sisters of St. Thérèse of the Infant Jesus, 3:129

Carmelite Sisters of the Divine Heart of Jesus, 3:129

Carmelite spirituality, **3:130–140**

Brandsma, Titus, Bl., 3:130, 139

Decem Libri, 3:134

Devotio Moderna, 3:134

Elian character, 3:133

Elizabeth of the Trinity, Bl., 3:130, 138–139

French School, 3:136–137

John of the Cross, St., 3:130, 132, 134, 135–136, 137

Marian character, 3:133, 137, 141, 143

origins, 3:130–132

Carmelite spirituality (continued)
preaching and hearing confessions, 13:99
reforms, 3:134–135, 142–143
Scholasticism, 3:137–138
Stein, St. Edith, 3:130, 139
Teresa of Avila, St., 3:130, 135, 139
Thérèse de Lisieux, St., 3:130, 138
Carmelite Third Order (Secular), 3:144
Carmelites, **3:140–144**
Albert of Jerusalem, St., 1:222, 3:125, 140, 141
Ancient See of Carlisle, 3:124
Antolínez, Agustín, 1:532
Armenia, 1:703
Bolivia, 2:466
Brazil, 2:593, 3:143
Caribbean, 3:118, 143
Carroll, John, 3:180
Colombia, 3:850
contemplation, 4:206, 207
Counter Reformation, 3:142–143, 611, 4:310
as discalced order, 4:765
Doswald, Hilary Joseph, 4:879
England, 5:242
general, 13:134
hierarchical insignia, 6:764
history, 8:530
Honorius IV (Pope), 7:86
Hunt, Walter, 7:225
Indian mission, 13:713–714
liturgy, 3:125–126, 140–141
Massachusetts, 2:555
as mendicant order, 9:491
missionaries in India, 13:713–714
origins, 3:602
Poverty Movement, 11:573
reform, 7:156, 13:326
scholasticism, 12:765
Scottish religious orders, 12:833
slavery, 1:156
solitude, 13:303
Syro-Malabar Church, 3:130, 146–147, 459
Western Schism, 1:194, 3:141–142
See also Carmelite Sisters; Carmelite spirituality
Carmelites, Discalced, **3:144–146**
Carmelite Sisters, 3:127–128
Colombia, 3:850
Compiègne martyrs, 4:43–44
Counter Reformation, 3:611
general, 13:122
historian, 13:122

John of the Cross, St., founding of, 7:986
Lawrence of the Resurrection, 8:409
Louisiana, 8:812
martyr of the confessional, 8:111–112
Mount Carmel, 3:141
nuns, 3:127–128
restoration in Poland, 8:112
Salamanca University, 12:612
Teresa of Avila, St., 3:142–143, 144–145, 611, 13:828–829
Carmelites of Mary Immaculate, **3:146–147**, 459
Carmen de bello Actiaco (ancient Latin papyrus), 10:774
Carmen de vita sua (St. Gregory of Nazianzus), 6:516
Carmina Abdinhofensia, 1:14
Carmina Burana (collection of poems), 9:458
Carmina natalicia (St. Paulinus of Nola), 11:39
Carmina Nisibena (St. Ephrem), 10:400
Carnap, Rudolf, **3:147**, 302, 5:397, 8:220
Carneades of Cyrene (Greek philosopher), 1:812, 5:46, 13:201
Carnesecchi, Pietro, **3:147–148**
Carney, Thomas A., 11:625
Carnival of the Animals (Saint-Saëns), 12:584
Carnival Season, 13:97–98
Carnot, Maurus, 4:775
Caro, Joseph ben Ephraim, **3:148**, 8:9, 12:140
Caro Rodríguez, José María (Card.), **3:148–149**
Carocci, Horacio, **3:149**
Caroline Divines, 1:444, **3:152–153**
Andrewe, Richard, 1:409
Coleridge, Samuel Taylor, 3:832
Hooker, Richard, 7:90
Caroline Islands dispute, 8:493
Caroline minuscule literary hand style, 10:776–777
Carolingian architecture, 3:691, 12:669
Carolingian art, 1:448, 543, **3:153–155**, 161
Corbie Abbey, 4:258
crucifixion, 4:395
illumination of books, 8:436
Carolingian Dynasty, **3:162–173**, 5:916–917
Adalbero of Augsburg, Bl., 1:99
Adrian I (Pope), 1:121

anointing, 1:478
Byzantine Empire, 3:167, 426, 427
Charlemagne's role, 3:165–168
chronicles, 5:923
consolidation of power, 3:124, 163–165, 421, 433–434, 598
end, 3:170–173, 411, 562, 600
Folcwin, St., 5:787
Golden Book of Prum, 3:162
Louis the Pious' role, 3:168–170
Merovingian family, 9:518
origins, 1:720, 3:40, 162–163
papal rule, 12:356
secularization of Church property, 12:870
See also Charlemagne (Holy Roman Emperor); specific kings
Carolingian era
Anointing of the Sick, 1:482, 485
Apocalypse iconography, 1:543
apocrisiarius, 1:548
archchancellors, 1:633
Austria, 1:908–909
Byzantine theology, 2:821–822
Canon Law, 3:41–44, 156–157, 158
capitularies, 1:494, 3:41, 42, 89–91, 166, 423
catechesis, 3:229
catechisms, 3:239
Chartres, 3:441
Church property, 2:496, 3:725
conscience, 4:142
Disentis Abbey, 4:775
Disticha catonis, 4:778
historical works, 8:741
hospitals, 7:128
hymns, 7:244, 245–247
Leo IV (Pope), St., 8:482
liturgical music history, 8:682–683
Lombard influence, 8:768
martyrology, 8:643
omniscience question during, 10:595–596
palace schools during, 10:763
spirituality, 13:445
works of charity, 3:410–411
See also Carolingian reform; Carolingian Renaissance; Middle Ages
Carolingian legends, 1:762–764, 762
Carolingian miniscule, 1:448, 3:154, 167, 426
Carolingian reform, **3:155–159**
adoptionism, 1:123, 3:156, 425, 561, 599

Adrian I (Pope), 1:122

Alcuin, Bl., 1:243, 3:156, 425, 599

altars, 1:315

Ambrosian Rite, 1:343

Apostles' Creed, 1:577

Barnard of Vienne, St., 2:104

Belgium, 2:216

Boniface, St., 2:496, 3:124, 155, 156, 159, 164

Canon Law, 3:42–43, 60, 156–157, 158

Carloman, 3:124, 156, 424

Carolingian consolidation of power, 3:164, 165

Carolingian Renaissance, 3:155, 157, 159

Charlemagne, 3:156–157, 166, 424–425, 599, 600

Chrodegang of Metz, St., 1:840, 3:156, 157, 410, 563–564

Church-State relations, 1:122–123

Communion outside the liturgy, 4:37

Council of Attigny, 1:840

Dacheriana collectio, 4:491–492

decretal collections, 4:602

drama, 4:893

filioque, 2:821–822, 3:599

France, 5:842–843

heresy, 6:773

images, worship of, 8:557

Italy, 7:657, 659

literature, 12:30

liturgical history, 8:654–655

monastic orders, 3:157, 168, 600

works of charity, 3:410–411, 412

See also Alcuin, Bl.

Carolingian Renaissance, **3:159–161**

Adalard, St., 1:98

Alberic of Utrecht, St., 1:220

Alcuin, Bl., 1:98, 243, 3:153, 159, 166–167, 425

Angilbert of Saint-Riquier, St., 1:98, 432, 3:160, 12:583

Benedictines, 9:791

Bible cycles, 2:371, 373

biblical catenae, 3:258–259

capitularies, 3:91

Carolingian reform, 3:155, 157, 159

Charlemagne, 3:159, 166–167, 425–426

Christian of Stablo, 3:537

Church-State relations, 3:634

dialectics, 4:725

exegesis, 5:515

German religious centers and leaders, 6:175

hymnary, 7:240–241

Latin literature, 9:442–446

liturgical music history, 8:683

Louis the German, 3:171

manuscript illumination, 9:128

Saint-Germain-des-Prés Abbey, 12:547–548

scholasticism, 12:758

theology, 13:904–905

See also Carolingian art

Carols, **3:149–152**, *150*, *151*, 557

Caron, Redmond, **3:173–174**

Carpaccio, Vittore, 14:347

Carpani, Melchiorre, **3:174**

Carpentarius (Charpentier), J., 1:676

Carpentras, Council of (*c.* 527), 3:410

Carpio, Felix de Vega, 1:236

Carpocrates (Gnostic teacher), 1:268, **3:174**, 4:218, 6:259

Carpzov, Benedikt, 3:174

Carpzov, Johann Benedikt (I), 3:174

Carpzov, Johann Benedikt (II), 3:174

Carpzov, Johann Benedikt (III), 3:175

Carpzov, Johann Gottlob, 3:174

Carpzov, Samuel Benedikt, 3:174

Carpzov family, **3:174–175**

Carr, Anne E., 5:677, 678

Carr, Henry, **3:175**

Carr, Thomas Matthew, 1:890, **3:175**, 181, 11:237

Carracci, Annibal, 10:138

Carracedo Ramos, Honorino, Bl., 4:494

Carradini, F., 5:798

Carranza, Bartolomé (Abp. of Toledo), **3:175–176**

Aspilcueta, Martin, 1:786

Cano, Melchior, 3:19

Council of Trent, 1:347, 3:175

Carranza, Miguel de, 3:135

Carrasquer Fos, Julián, Bl., 7:123

Carrberry, John (Card.), 3:58

Carrell, George Aloysius (Bp. of Covington), 4:331, 625

Carrier, Jean (Card.), 3:785

Carrière, Joseph, **3:76**

Carrighy, Hugh, 7:581

Carroll, Charles, 2:36, **3:176–177**, 652

Maryland, independence of, 9:301

religious freedom, 5:960

St. Omer College, 12:569

Carroll, Coleman F. (Abp. of Miami, FL), 9:592

Carroll, Daniel, II, **3:177–178**, 5:960

Carroll, Howard Joseph (Abp. of Altoona-Johnstown, PA), **3:178**

Carroll, John (Abp. of Baltimore), 2:37, 38, 40, **3:178–181**, *179*, 4:697, 14:453

African American Catholics, 1:155–156, 159

Baltimore seminary, 8:521

Bohemia Manor, 2:460

Carr, Thomas Matthew, 3:175

catechesis, 3:243

Charleston Diocese, 13:363, 364

Cheverus, Jean Louis Lefebvre de, 3:472

church architecture, 3:715

Church-State relations, 3:640

Councils of Baltimore, 2:39, 42–43

Egan, Michael, 5:103

Fenwick, Edward Dominic, 5:686

Flagett, Benedict Joseph, 5:757

Gallagher, Simon, 6:66

Georgetown University, 6:145–146

Kentucky missions, 8:147–148

Louisiana supervision, 8:810

Pennsylvania, 11:82, 236–237

religious freedom, 5:960

Rhode Island, 12:214

St. Louis Archdiocese, 12:559

St. Omer College, 12:569

seminary education, 12:895

Seton, Elizabeth Ann, St., 13:32, 173

Carroll, John P. (Bp. of Helena, MT), 3:*182*, **182**, 9:826, 10:282

Carroll, Walter Sharp, **3:182**

Carroll family, 5:960

Carroll Institute, 8:134

Carson, Edward, Sir, 7:564

Carta apologética (Muzi), 10:76

Carta dirijida a los Españoles Americanos (Vizcardó, Juan Pablo), 14:576

Carta marina (Olaus Magnus), 9:45

Cartae latinae antiquiores (Bruckner and Marichal), 10:775

Cartas (Figueiredo), 5:717

Cartas a un escéptico (Balmes), 2:33

Carte générale du cours du Gange et du Gogra dressée par les cartes particulières du P. T. (Anquetil-Duperron), 14:72–73

Cartel, Marie Anne, 8:311

Carter, Gerald Emmett (Bp.), 3:9

Carter, Samuel (Abp. of Jamaica), 3:112

Carter, William, Bl., **3:182–183**, 5:228

Cartesianism, **3:183–186**

action at a distance, 1:80

Cartesianism *(continued)*
architecture, 3:675
biological mechanism, 9:420
causality, 3:301
Cogito ergo sum, 4:680–681
doubt, 4:680, 883–884
free will, 4:681–682
Geulincx, Arnold, 6:196–197
Lamy, F., 8:315
Maine de Biran, 9:60
Malebranche, Nicolas, 9:74–75
mechanism, 4:681
method, 4:678–680
necessity, 10:227
scholasticism, 12:770–771
substance, 13:577, 578
theory of extension, 8:314
See also Descartes, René
Carthage, **3:186–188**, 5:313
Algeria, 1:284
lapsi, 8:333
Carthage, Councils of (225-534), 3:186,
188–189, 10:620, 11:62
Anastasius I (Pope), St., 1:387
apostolic administrators, 1:116
Augustine, St., 1:859, 860
conversion and grace, 4:239
cult of relics, 12:52
Donatism, 4:862–863
Ecumenical as term, 4:190
usury, 14:354
Carthage, Synods of
(256), 1:785, 3:593
(419), 13:885
(421), 13:885
Carthusian Church (Cologne), 3:844
Carthusian Rite, **3:189–190**
Carthusian spirituality, **3:190–193**, 8:465
Carthusians, 3:*190, 191, 193*, **193–197**
Austria, 1:910, 3:194
contemplative life, 4:210
England, 5:243
founding, 2:649
Hugh of Lincoln, 7:153–154
solitude, 13:303
*Cartilla para enseñar a leer a lost
Indios* (Sanctis), 12:661
Cartography, 13:389
Cartography, ecclesiastical, 13:547–548
Cartuja church (Granada, Spain), 3:707
Cartwright, Edmund, 5:260–261
Cartwright, Thomas, **3:197**
Browne, Robert, 2:638
Church-State relations, 3:638, 646

Puritans, 11:836
Sabbatarianism, 12:454
Carus (Roman Emperor), 12:313
Carushomo, Benedict, 3:319
Caruso, J. A., 4:140
Carvajal, Bernardino Lopez de (Card.),
3:197
Carvajal, Gaspar de (Father), **3:197–198**,
5:62
Carvajal, Juan de (Card.), 2:881, **3:197**
Carvajal, Luisa de, **3:198**
Carvalho, Diogo, Bl., 7:734
Carvalho, Miguel, Bl., 7:734
Carvalho, Vincent, Bl., 7:735
Casa, Giovanni Della, **3:198–199**
La Casa de María (Chile), 3:12
Casa Sollievo della Sofferenza (Padre
Pio's hospital), 10:751
Casadevall Puig, Esteban, 2:92
Casamari Abbey (Italy), 3:750
Casamassa, Anthony, 1:889
Casanate, Girolamo, **3:199**
Casanate, Jerome, 1:438
Casanatense Library, 3:199
Casani, Pietro (Peter), Bl., **3:199–200**
Casanovas Perramón, Ignacio, Bl.,
3:200, 10:816
Casaroli, Agostino (Card.), **3:200–202**,
201, 7:1004, 10:850
Las Casas (Gutierrez), 10:623
Casas, Felipe de Jesús de las, St., 7:732
Casas Martínez, Felipe de Jesús, St.,
3:202
Casati (Bp. of Mondovì), 3:243
Casaubon, Isaac, 12:620
Case, John, 1:676
Case, Shirley Jackson, 6:884
Case, Thomas, 1:684
The Case of the Catholics in Ireland
(Nary), 10:154
The Case of the Officers of Excise
(Paine), 10:757
Casel, Odo, 2:159, **3:202**, *203*, 5:430
liturgical movement, 8:671–672
mystery theology theory, 10:97–99
Caselius, Johannes, 12:768
Caselli, Carlo, 4:61
Casey, James V. (Abp. of Denver),
3:859, 4:670
Casey, Planned Parenthood v., 1:34, 35,
11:88
Casey, Solanus, **3:203**
Cashel, Synod of (1172), 3:331
Cashwell, G. B., 1:788
Casimir, St., **3:203–204**

Casimir III (King of Poland), 11:439
Casimir IV (King of Poland), 11:439
Casimiri, R. C., 3:380
Caslon, William, 2:523
Caso, Prisco (Brother), 3:857
Casoni, Filippo (Card.), **3:204**
Casoni, Giambattista, 7:673
Casoria, Ludovico da (Father), 3:419
Cass, Lewis, 13:797
Cassander, George, 2:874, **3:204–205**
Cassandra, 13:100
Cassanges, Gesselin de, 3:800
Cassant, Marie Joseph, **3:205**
Cassel, Dom Odo, 12:777
Cassian, John (Johannes Cassianus),
3:205–207, 5:513, 651, 6:112, 14:144
Abraham the Simple, St., 1:39
acedia, 1:66–68, 3:399
Alleluia, 1:293
Aredius, St., 1:645
Augustinianism, 1:861, 877
burial, 2:699
Carthusian spirituality, 3:190
chastity, 3:444
collatio, 3:836
Compline, 4:44
compunction, 4:45
continence, 4:211
creedal statements, 4:352
de auxiliis controversy, 4:112
diaconia, 4:719
direction, spiritual, 4:760–761
discernment, spiritual, 4:765
grace, 6:402
pilgrimages, 3:594
religious habit, 12:99
Saint-Victor in Marseilles Abbey,
12:590
Semi-Pelagianism, 12:899
spiritual abandonment, 1:5
spirituality, 13:445
works of charity, 3:407–408, 411
Cassian, St., 12:582
Cassian of Nantes, Bl., **3:207**
Cassiano da Macerata, **3:208**
Cassiano dal Pozzo, 12:488
Cassidy, Edward (Card.), 1:441, 5:68
Cassidy, Francis P., 3:283
Cassidy, James E., 5:612
Cassinese Congregation, 2:272
Cassiodorus Senator, Flavius Magnus
Aurelius, **3:208–209**
Adrianus, 1:130
Alcuin, Bl., 1:243

Augustinianism, 1:877, 3:208

Boethius, 2:454

Canon Law, 3:41

chronicle, 1:461

dialectics, 4:725

Gregory the Great, St., 3:597

Junilius' Introduction, 8:63

Latin literature, 9:438

music, consideration of, 10:72

preaching, 11:619

prescholasticism, 12:757

Cassirer, Ernst, 3:*209*, **209–210**, 5:47, 10:237, 12:65

literary myth, 10:120–121

mythical consciousness, 3:672, 673

origin and development of mythology, 10:128

Cassius Dio. *See* Dio Cassius

Cassocks, **3:210**, *211*, 801

Cassou, Jean, 1:803

Cassuto, M. D., 2:356, 357

Castaðeda, Jacinto, 14:492

Castagno, Andrea del, 1:58

Castán Messeguer, Francisco (Brother), 2:92

Castañeda, Carlos, 12:385

Castañeda, Francisco de Paula, **3:210–211**

Caste system (India), **3:211**, *212*, 6:851, 853

Castel Gandolfo villa (Italy), **3:211–212**, 793, 12:711

Castel Sant'Angelo (Rome), **3:212–214**, *213*

Alexander VI (Pope), 1:261, 3:213

Boso, Cardinal, 2:548

Clement XII (Pope), 3:789

sack of Rome, 3:430, 782

Castel Sant'Elia Church (Nepi), 1:336

Castelberg, Christian de, 4:775

Castelet, Domingos, Bl., 7:734

Castellani, Albert, 12:258

Castellano, Julius, 14:470

Castellano, Nicéforo, 3:759

Castelli, Benedetto (Father), 6:61

Castelli, Juan José, 1:650

Castellino da Castelli, **3:214**

Castellio, Sebastian (Châteillon), 2:889, **3:214**

Castellis, Guido de. *See* Celestine II (Pope)

Castello, Albert da, 12:375

Castelnovo, Leopold da. *See* Mandic, Leopold Bogdan, St.

Casti connubii (encyclical, Pius XI), 1:28, **3:214**, 4:221, 11:392–393, 14:825

birth control, 13:258

intercourse during infertile times, 10:178

Castigationes (Barbaro the Younger), 2:90

Castiglione, Baldassare, 3:*215*, **215–216**

Castiglione, Giuseppe, **3:216–217**, 498

Castiglioni, Francesco Saverio. *See* Pius VIII (Pope)

Castiglioni, Goffredo. *See* Celestine IV (Pope)

Castillo, Juan del, 6:342, 10:876

Castillo Lara, Rosalio (Card.), 3:35

Castillo y Guevara, Francisca Josefa Del, **3:217**

Castle of Perseverance (play), 9:881, 882

Castner, Gaspar, **3:217–218**

Castor, Northamptonshire, 4:454

Castorena y Ursúa, Juan Ignacio de (Bp. of Yucatán), **3:218**

Castrati, 3:523

Castriota, George (Prince of Albania), 1:213, 2:881

Castro, Agustín Pablo, **3:218**

Castro, Alfonso de, 3:609

Castro, Bento de, Bl., 1:951

Castro, Fidel, 4:418–421

Castro, Mateo de, **3:219**

Castronovo, A., 3:824

Castronovo, Leopold da. *See* Mandic, Leopold Bogdan, St.

Castropalao (moral theologian), 1:311

Casuistry, **3:219–221**

consequentialism, 4:159–160

Diana, Antonino, 4:729

moral theology, 9:854

Near East law, 8:392

scholasticism, 12:766

Casus conscientiae in praecipuas quaestiones theologiae moralis (Gury), 6:585

Casus decretalium (Richard de Mores), 12:229

Casus decretorum (Bartholomew of Brescia), 2:125

Casus s. Galli, 5:142

Casus sancti Galli (Ekkehard IV of St. Gall), 9:449

Catacombs, 1:752, **3:221–225**, *222*, *223*, *224*, *225*, *226*, 11:*51*

ampullae, 1:366

archeological explorations, 12:387

arcosolia, 1:643

art, 1:37, 573, 753, 754, 2:368–369, 3:223

Christian archaeology, 12:387

Christian persecutions, 12:352–353

Damasus I (Pope), St., 4:505

Egypt, 1:758

iconography as science, 7:285

iconography of Last Supper, 8:344

lamps and lighting, 8:314

relics of saints, 12:53

shrines for martyrs, 13:88

Catafalques, **3:225–226**

Cataldino, José, **3:226**

Cataldo, Joseph Mary, 1:208, **3:226**

Cataldo Mission (Coeur d'Alene, ID), 3:227, 7:289, *291*

Cataldus of Rachau, St., **3:226–227**

Catalina Hills School District, Zobrest v. (1993), 3:668

Catalogue des manuscrits datés, 10:775

Catalogues des manuscrts de la bibliothèque franciscaine provinciale (Ubald), 14:261

Catalogus musei Caesari Vindobonensis nummorum veterum (Eckhel), 5:46

Catalogus sanctorum ordinis sancti Benedicti (Lang), 8:324

Catalogus scriptorum ecclesiasticorum (Trithemius), 14:209

Catanoso, Gaetano (Cajetan), Bl., **3:226**

Cataphyrgians. *See* Montanism

Cateau-Cambrésis, Treaty of (1559), 5:849, 7:669

Catechesi tradendae (apostolic exhortation, John Paul II), 6:127, 7:1003, 9:682

Catechesis, 3:*238*

art, 1:753

Brownson, Josephine Van Dyke, 2:639

Bus, Bl. César de, 2:714

catechists, 3:248–249

catechumenate, 3:249–253

Collins, Joseph Burns, 3:839

conversion, 4:237–238, 241–242

doctrine, 4:802–803

implications of narrative theology for, 10:154

renewal, 8:62

salvation history, 12:630

School of Alexandria, 1:272

solidarity, 13:301, 302

Ten Commandments, 4:8–9

See also Catechisms

Catechesis (Cyril of Jerusalem), 10:755

Catechesis (Theodore of Mopsuestia), 10:755

Catechesis, early Christian, **3:227–228**

Catechesis, medieval, **3:228–232**, 239–240, 241

Catechesis, Reformation era, **3:232–236**, 241–244

Catechesis Weissenburgensis, 3:239

Catechetical Directories, National, **3:236**

Catechetical Leadership, 10:163

Catechetical Methods (Bandas), 2:48

Catechetical Movement, U.S., 2:48–49

Catechism for Filipino Catholics, 3:245

A Catechism of Catholic Education (Ryan), 12:444–445

Catechism of the Catholic Church, **3:237–239**, 5:429, 861

  animal rights, 1:456

  baptism name, 10:971

  capital punishment, 3:88, 238

  casuistry, 3:221

  communion of saints, 4:34

  creation, 4:341

  cremation, 4:360

  descent of Christ into hell, 4:685

  homosexuality, 7:67

  indulgences, 7:440

  John Paul II (Pope), 3:237, 245

  limbo of children, 8:591

  liturgical inculturation, 7:385–386

  meditation, 9:466

  original sin, 10:670

  taking saint's name at baptism, 10:140–141

  teachings on birth regulation, 10:179

  Ten Commandments, 4:8, 9

  on the two ways, 14:251

Catechism of the Council of Trent (Roman Catechism), 3:233–234, **239**, 242–243

  Anglican orders problem, 1:437

  capital punishment, 3:87

  Catechism of the Catholic Church, 3:237, 245

  Spanish mission in the Americas, 3:246

Catechism of the Metropolitan Philaret of Moscow, 10:701

Catechism of the Third Plenary Council of Baltimore. See Baltimore Catechism

Catéchisme du sens commun (Rohrbacher), 12:290

Catéchisme historique (Fleury), 3:243, 5:762

A Catechisme of Christian Doctrine necessarie for children and ignorante people (Vaux), 3:233, 243

Catéchisme pour adultes, 3:245

Catechisms, **3:239–246**

  Augustine, St., 3:240–241

  Bellarmine, Robert, St., 3:234–235, 242, 244

  Canisius, St. Peter, 2:714–715, 3:17–18, 233, 242, 244

  Deharbe, Joseph, 4:612–613

  Felbiger, Johann Ignaz von, 5:665

  Imperial, 3:236–237, 244

  Middle Ages, 3:239–240, 241

  national, 3:244–245

  patristic era, 3:239–241

  Post-Reformation, 4:9

  post-Tridentine, 3:243–244

  Reformation, 4:9

  Reformation era, 3:232–236, 241–243

  teachings on eschatology, 5:346–347

  See also Catechesis; *Catechism of the Catholic Church*; *Catechism of the Council of Trent*

Catechisms, colonial Spanish America, 3:234, **246–248**, *247*, 252

Catechisms, Protestant, 4:78

Catechismus catholicus (Gasparri), 3:244

Catechismus minimus (Canisius), 3:18, 233, 242

Catechismus Romanus. See Roman Catechism

The Catechist of the Missions (Le Roy), 8:512

Catechistical Instruction on the Doctrines and Worship of the Catholic Church (Lingard), 3:243

Catechists, **3:248–249**

Catechumenate, **3:249–254**

  baptism, 2:63

  blessings, 2:439

  doctrine, 4:803

  Elvira Council, 5:178

  lenten fasting, 8:468

Catecismo real (San Alberto), 12:639

Catedral Primada de Colombia (Bogota), 3:*852*

Categorical imperative, **3:254–255**, 5:388

  free will, 5:931

  justice, 8:400

  Kantianism, 8:125

  natural law, 10:183

Categorical propositions, 11:769

Categorical syllogisms, 13:654–655

Categories (Aristotle), 12:41, 14:322

Categories of being, **3:255–258**

  accident, 1:59–60

  action and passion, 1:77

  Aristotelianism, 1:670, 681

  causality, 3:300

  concept, 4:51

  dialectics, 4:722

  Location (Ubi), 8:742

  relatives, 12:41

  similarity, 13:126

Catelinus. *See* John III (Pope)

Catena aurea (Aquinas), 3:258–259, 14:18–19, 25

Catena evangelica (Rubino), 12:399

Catenae, biblical, **3:258–259**, 770, 5:507

Catez, Elisabeth. *See* Elizabeth of the Trinity, Bl.

Catgui, Giovanni-Ignacio, 9:524–525

Cathari, 5:496, 769, 845, 7:665

  Crusade against, 4:413

  Humiliati, 7:204

  infant baptism, objection to, 2:69

  lay role, 8:295

  Lombers, Council of, 8:770

  procreation, repudiation of, 4:219–220

  transmigration of souls doctrine, 14:157

Catharinus, Ambrose, 3:609

Catharism, 1:230–231, **3:259–260**

  Albi Archdiocese, 1:229

  Bogomilism, 1:230, 2:458, 3:259

  cabala, 2:831

  clerical celibacy and marriage, 3:326

  Innocent III (Pope), 3:602

  See also Albigensians

Catharsis, 11:434

Cathecismo en lengua castellana y timuquana (Pareja), 10:882

Cathecismo y brevo exposición de la doctrine Christiana (Pareja), 10:882

Cathecismo y examen para los que comulgan en lengua castellana y timuquana (Pareja), 10:882

Cathecyzon (Colet), 3:241

Cathedral and episcopal schools, **3:262–264**

  academic freedom, 1:51

  Aldric of Le Mans, St., 1:248

  Angers, 1:432

  Bernard of Chartres, 2:307, 3:264, 441

  Carolingian Renaissance, 3:161, 167

  Chartres, 3:441

Cicero, Marcus Tullius, 3:730

Councils of Chalon-Sur-Saône, 3:373

exegesis, 5:515–516

Cathedral College of the Sacred Heart (Chicago, IL), 3:478

Cathedral High School (NY), 8:387

Cathedral Metropolitana (Brazil), 2:595

Cathedral of Le Mans, 8:48

Cathedral of Mary Our Queen (Baltimore), 2:39, 8:154

Cathedral of Notre Dame (Luxembourg), 8:898

Cathedral of Our Lady (Antwerp), 1:539, 539

Cathedral of Our Lady (Viborg, Denmark), 8:187

Cathedral of Our Lady of Guadalupe (Dodge City, KS), 8:115

Cathedral of St. John and St. Finbar (Charleston, SC), 8:904

Cathedral of St. John the Divine (New York), 5:296

Cathedral of San Francisco de Asis (Sante Fe, NM), 8:316

Cathedral of the Assumption of the Blessed Virgin Mary (Baltimore), 2:39

Cathedral of Uppsala (Sweden), 5:320, 320

Cathedral Office, 8:656, 730

Cathedrale-St.-Front (Perigueux, France), 3:691

Cathedrals, **3:260–262**, 261, 262

chapters of canons, 3:66–67

choirs, 3:523, 524

Church property, 3:726

Magistri Comacini, 9:39

symbolism, 3:630

See also Church architecture; *specific cathedrals and churches*

Cathemerinon (Prudentius), 11:792

Cather, Willa, 3:489, 10:287, 571

Catherick, Edmund, Bl., **3:264**, 5:235

Catherine (Queen of Castile), 1:327

Catherine, Bl. (17th c. Japanese martyr), 7:733

Catherine I (Russian Empress), 11:182

Catherine II (the Great) (Empress of Russia), 1:252, **3:264–266**, 795

Belorussia, 2:211–212

bull of suppression, 5:43

confiscation of Church property, 12:424

Georgia, relations with, 6:156

Order of St. George, 12:547

Polish ecclesiastical affairs, interference in, 11:444

Catherine de Médicis (Queen of France), **3:266–267**

Bartholomew's Day Masscre, 12:537–538

Conference of Poissy, 11:437

Protestants, 7:167

regent of France, 5:849

Catherine de' Ricci, St., **3:267**

Catherine of Alexandria, St., **3:267–268**, 268

Catherine of Aragon (Queen of England), **3:268–269**, 269

Barton, Elizabeth, 2:130

divorce proceedings, 6:739–740

marriages, 5:163, 244, 749, 8:57, 12:5–8

Mary Tudor, 9:292

See also Henry VIII (King of England), divorce of

Catherine of Bologna, St., **3:269**, 9:460

Catherine of Genoa, St., **3:269–272**, 270, 606, 4:787, 11:827

Catherine of Lorraine (abbess), 12:108

Catherine of Portugal (Queen), 8:806

Catherine of Racconigi, Bl., **3:272**

Catherine of St. Susan (Sister), 7:716

Catherine of Siena, St., 3:62, **272–274**, 273

Avignon papacy, 1:943

canonization, 3:62, 192, 273

Catherine of Sweden, St., 3:274

Clare Gambacorta, Bl., 3:759

Columba of Rieti, Bl., 3:863

Devotio Moderna, 3:605

as Doctor of the Church, 11:32

Dominici, John, 4:855

Flete, William, 5:761

following of Christ, 5:789

hierognosis, 3:759

John de Cellis, correspondence with, 5:921

mystical experience interpreted, 10:114

mystical quality of writings, 10:117, 118

private revelations, 12:200, 201

Raymond of Capua, 11:935

Rose of Lima, St., 12:378

Siena's internal discord, 13:108

spirituality, 13:46

Western Schism, 3:273, 783

Catherine of Sweden, St., 2:618, **3:274**

Bridgit Abbey, 2:615

Devotio Moderna, 3:605

Western Schism, 3:783

Catherine Tegahkwitha, the Saint of Caughnawaga (Rouquette), 12:391

Catherine the Great. See Catherine II (the Great) (Empress of Russia)

Catherine the Little Nun (Catinon Menette). See Jarrige, Catherine, Bl.

Catherine Thomas, St., **3:274**

Catholic (diocesan newspaper), 10:547

Catholic (term), **3:274–275**, 292

See also Universality of Christianity

Catholic Action, **3:275–278**, 276, 5:857, 12:366

active life, 1:83

Africa, 8:899

Australia, 1:904

Austria, 1:915, 916

Brazil, 2:598, 8:465

California, 12:649

Catholic social thought, 13:257

Church-State relations, 3:643

Communion and Liberation, 4:32

Czechoslovakia, 4:486

France, 8:564

Italy, 8:357

lay spirituality, 8:416

Mexico, 8:334

mission of laity, 8:290

Pius XI (Pope), 11:392

role of the laity, 12:790

St. Pampuri's role, 10:817

Spain, 13:397, 400

Summer School of Catholic Action (SSCA), 8:779, 13:294

Catholic Actors Guild, 13:234

Catholic Advocate (periodical), 8:149, 13:404

Catholic Almanac, **3:278**, 14:314

Catholic Anthropological Conference, 8:430

Catholic Apostolic Church, **3:278–279**

adventism, 1:135

Irving, Edward, founding of, 7:587–588

New Apostolic Church resulting from schism, 10:277–278

Catholic Archives of Texas, 1:640

Catholic Association (Ireland), 3:619

Catholic Association for International Peace (CAIP), 9:398

Catholic Association of Apprentices (*Katholischer Lehringsverein*), 12:793

Catholic Association of French Youth, 5:857

Catholic Banner (periodical), 13:367

Catholic Bible College (Canmore, Canada), 3:11

Catholic Biblical Association of America, 4:437, 5:523, 10:277, 12:34

Catholic Biblical Quarterly, 4:814, 10:566, 12:34

Catholic Bishops Conference of India, 7:403

Catholic Bishops Conference of the Philippines, 11:259, 263

Catholic Campaign for Human Development, 1:288

Catholic Campus Ministry Association (CCMA), 10:345

Catholic Central Association, 6:226

Catholic Charities and Kindred Activities of St. Louis, 6:240

Catholic Charities of Idaho, 7:292

Catholic Charities Review, 12:445

Catholic Charities USA, **3:279–280**, 478
  Alinsky, Saul David, 1:288
  Mundeleini's organization, 10:60
  New York leadership, 8:136

The Catholic Christian Instructed (Challoner), 3:243

''The Catholic Church and Civil Society'' (Ireland), 7:550

The Catholic Church and German Americans (Barry), 2:119

Catholic Church Expansion Fund, 10:50

Catholic Church Extension Society of the United States of America (CCES), 3:478, 8:114, 137

The Catholic Church in the United States (Roemer), 12:283

Catholic Churches of the Middle East, 9:616

The Catholic Citizen (periodical), 12:551

Catholic Clergy Conference on the Interracial Apostolate, 1:161

The Catholic Collegian, 10:161

Catholic Commission on Intellectual and Cultural Affairs (CCICA), **3:280–281**

Catholic Confederation of Rio de Janeiro, 8:465, 466

Catholic Conference for Ecumenical Questions, 5:74

Catholic Conference on Industrial Problems (CCIP), 9:398

Catholic Congress of 1871, 12:582

Catholic Congress of 1889, 8:412

Catholic Counter Reformation (Catholic traditionalism), 3:289

Catholic Daughters of the Americas (CDA), **3:281–282**, 622, 4:930

Catholic Diary, 10:313

Catholic Diocesan Archivists (ACDA), 1:639

Catholic Directory (Ireland), 13:233

The Catholic Directory for the Clergy and Laity in Scotland, 9:24–25

Catholic Directory. See *Official Catholic Directory*

Catholic education. See Education, Catholic; Parochial schools; *specific educational institutions*

Catholic Education Association of the U.S. (CEA), 10:159, 160, 13:59

Catholic Educational Review, **3:282–283**, 10:740, 13:83

Catholic Electoral League (Brazil), 8:466

Catholic Emancipation (Britain, 1829), 2:719, 3:619, 641

Catholic Encyclopedia, 5:207, 208, 684, 821, 12:274, 418, 445, 789
  (1907-14), 10:316, 323, 341
  (1922), 10:806
  Shahan contributions, 13:58
  supplement, 13:69

Catholic Encyclopedia for School and Home, 13:412

Catholic encyclopedias and dictionaries, **5:206–208**

Catholic Epistles, 3:274, **283–284**, 5:305–306
  canonicity, 3:21, 28, 31, 32
  Church history, 3:593
  See also specific epistles

Catholic Evidence Guild, 8:430, 13:73

Catholic Expositor (periodical), 10:313

Catholic Foreign Mission Society of America. See Maryknoll Fathers and Brothers

Catholic Forum of the Air, 14:291

Catholic Foundation controversy, 10:342–343

Catholic Health Association, **3:284**

Catholic Herald, 8:144

Catholic Historical Review, 10:550, 14:246

Catholic Home Bureau, 10:57

Catholic Homilies (Aelfric Grammaticus), 1:136

Catholic Institute for the Blind, 8:388

Catholic Interracial Councils (CIC), 3:479, 10:158

Catholic Kolping Society of America, 8:231

Catholic League, 5:42, 849

Catholic Library Association (CLA), **3:284–285**, 5:787

Catholic Magazine, 13:233

Catholic Medical Association (CMA), **3:285–286**, 7:67

Catholic Mirror (periodical), 2:40, 10:67

Catholic Miscellany (periodical), 2:192, 5:223, 8:904

Catholic Mission Organization, 12:744

Catholic Moral Teaching and Its Antagonists (Mausbach), 9:376

Catholic Music Educator, 10:157

Catholic Near East Welfare Association (CNEWA), **3:286**

Catholic News (periodical), 12:243

Catholic News and Herald, 10:438

Catholic organizations. See Youth organizations; *specific organizations*

Catholic organizations, 19th-20th century overview, 3:622

Catholic Party (Belgium), 2:219

Catholic Periodical Index, 5:787

Catholic Press Association (CPA), 8:430, 10:159, 12:243

The Catholic Priest in the United States: Historical Investigations (Ellis), 5:170

Catholic Priests' Association for Justice (Korea), 8:239

Catholic Publication Society, 11:41

Catholic Readings (periodical), 12:615

Catholic Relief Act (England, 1778), 3:371, 6:361, 10:501, 502

Catholic Relief Act (England, 1791), 10:502

Catholic Relief Services (CRS), 10:429, 761, 14:312

Catholic Review, 10:315, 13:234

Catholic revival, England, 14:796

Catholic School Journal, 5:753

Catholic School of Economics (Tilburg), 10:262

Catholic Sentinel (periodical), 10:645, 11:529

Catholic Social Movement, 7:673

Catholic Social Service Conference, 9:407

Catholic Social Thought: As I Have Lived It, Loathed It and Loved It (Land), 8:318

Catholic Social Welfare Bureau, 9:407

Catholic Standard (periodical)
  Ghana, 6:198
  Guyana, 6:588
  U.S., 6:66

Catholic Students Mission Crusade (CSMC), **3:286–287**

Catholic Summer School (Plattsburg, NY), 8:388

Catholic Summer School of America, 8:798, 13:234

Catholic Theological Society of America (CTSA), **3:287–288**

Catholic Theological Union at Chicago, **3:288**, 480

Catholic Times (periodical), 8:303

Catholic Total Abstinence Union of America (CTAUA), 5:169, 8:134, 153, 13:801

Catholic Traditionalism, **3:288–289**

Catholic Truth Guild, 6:336

Catholic Truth Society, 8:791, 11:530, 13:81

Catholic Union of Germany, 6:184

Catholic Universe (periodical), 6:226

Catholic University Bulletin, 13:58

Catholic University chapel (Vienna), 3:712

Catholic University of America (Washington, DC), 3:*290*, **290–292**, 10:316

  academic freedom, 1:53–54

  African American Catholics, 1:160, 3:291

  Americanism, 1:354–355

  archives, 1:637, 640, 641

  Brazilian collection, 8:588

  Caldwell, Mary Gwendoline, 2:860–861, 3:290

  Canon Law, 8:257, 258

  Catholic Sisters' College, 13:169

  church history and patrology, 13:58

  Collins, R., 8:822

  Conaty, Thomas James, 4:49

  education department, 13:83

  Ellis, John Tracy, 5:170

  establishing, 12:572, 573

  Fenlon, John F., 5:684

  Fenton, Joseph Clifford, 5:684–685

  founding, 8:134, 13:402–403

  Gibbons, James, 6:205

  inauguration, 12:704

  Ireland, John, 7:551

  Keane rectorship, 8:134, 135

  mission, 13:58

  Paulists, 11:41

  physical structures, 13:59

  psychology, 13:83

  rectorship, 13:58–59

  Religious Education Movement, 12:97

  Ryan, James Hugh, 12:444–445

  Ryan, John Augustine, 12:445–446

  scholasticism, 12:777

  School of Philosophy, 13:232

  Semitic languages, 13:200

  Sisters College, 13:403

  sociology, 8:155–156

  theology and philosophy of religion, 13:74

  Thomist center of U.S., 13:232

Catholic University of Beijing (Fujen University), 3:500

Catholic University of Ecuador, 5:*65*

Catholic University of Nijmegen (Netherlands), 10:262

Catholic University of Rio de Janeiro, 8:466

Catholic War Council, 12:786

Catholic Welfare Organization, 11:259

Catholic Woman, 10:164

Catholic Women's Suffrage Society, 12:550

The Catholic Worker (newspaper)

  Day, Dorothy, 4:546

  distributism, 4:782

  Maurin, Aristide Peter, 9:369

Catholic Worker Movement, 3:824, 11:573, 13:257

Catholic World (periodical), 6:225, 700, 10:314

Catholic Writers Guild, 13:234

Catholic Young Men's National Union, 8:134

Catholic Youth Magazine, 10:67

Catholic Youth Organization (CYO), 4:667, 12:243, 13:77

Catholica monarchia Christi (Baldi), 12:765

Catholicae ecclesiae (papal letter, Leo XIII), 9:681

Catholicam Christi ecclesiam (*motu proprio*, Paul VI), 11:481

Catholici fideles (apostolic constitution, Benedict XV), 7:652

Catholic-Islamic dialogue, 7:683, 1004

Catholicisme (Lubac), 2:34, 8:840

Catholicisme hier, aujourd'hui, demain, 5:207

Catholicity, 3:274–275, **292–294**, 9:189–191

  See also Universality of Christianity

Catholicity in Philadelphia (Kirlin), 8:184

Catholic-Jewish dialogue, 7:1004

Catholicon (Balvi), 5:206

Catholicos, 1:700, **3:294**

Catholic-Protestant dialogue, 9:283–284

  England, 14:796

  Lutherans, 5:69–70, 9:284

  Virginia, 14:542

Catholics, persecution of. *See specific countries*; *specific martyrs and saints*

Catholics in Colonial America (Ellis), 5:170

Catholics in Media, 8:793

Catholics United for the Faith (CUF), 13:504

Cathrein, Viktor, **3:294**, *295*, 5:397, 13:242

Catinon Menette (Catherine the Little Nun). *See* Jarrige, Catherine, Bl.

Cato the Elder, 4:778

El Catolicismo en presencia de sus disidentes (Eyzaguirre), 5:573

Católicos por la Raza, 8:792

Catrik, John (Bp.), **3:294–295**

Catrou, François, **3:295**

Catroux, Jean Maurice, 12:495

Cattaneo, Lazzaro, **3:295–296**

Cattedrale de Santa Eufemia (Grado, Italy), 12:*106*

Cattell, J. McK., 5:587

Cauchie, Albert, 8:823–824

Cauchon, Pierre (Bp. of Beauvais, France), 7:879

Cauchy, Augustin Louis, 5:581

Caulet, François Étienne (Bp. of Pamiers), 1:717, **3:296**, 8:803, 804

Caulites, **3:296**

Caum, Vicente Kahyōye, Bl., 7:734

Caunton, Richard, **3:296–297**

Causa cessante cessat effectus (The cause ceasing the effect ceases), 12:755

Causa finalis, 10:27

Causal participation, 10:908–909

Causality, **3:297–302**

  abstraction, 1:46, 3:308

  accident, 1:61

  act, 1:75, 3:307

  action and passion, 1:78, 79

  agent, 1:175, 3:297, 302

  agnosticism, 1:181

  analogy, 1:376

  analysis, 3:299–300

  Aristotle, 9:342

  cogitative power, 3:823, 824

  condition for, 4:73

  contingency, 4:212–214

  cosmological argument, 4:285–287

  creation, 4:344

  demonstration, 4:651–654

  dialectics, 4:723

  direction, speed, 10:20

  Divine concurrence, 4:70–72

  double effect principle, 4:880–881

  Ducasse, Curt John, 4:925

  efficient, 5:98–102

  exemplary, 5:528

Causality *(continued)*
  final, 5:99, 528, 723–727
  formal, 5:806
  Greek philosophy, 3:297–298,
    302–303
  Hume, David, 7:201–202
  hylomorphism, 7:238
  justification, 3:298–299
  knowledge of necessity, 8:210,
    10:225
  modern thought, 3:300–302
  moral, 5:99, 12:469
  naturalism's solution to problems,
    10:207
  occasion for opportunity, 10:525
  panentheism, 10:821
  participation, 10:908–909
  patristic era, 3:303
  phenomenology, 11:233
  physical, 5:99, 12:469
  physical premotion, 11:671
  privation, 11:724
  Scholasticism, 1:175, 3:298, 303–306
  as solution to problem of normality,
    10:425
Causality, Divine, 3:300, **302–307**,
  4:160–163, 239–241
Causality, principle of, **3:307–308**, 4:73,
  5:101, 745, 8:88–89
Causation, effective, 9:60
Cause, first, 4:70, 10:26
Caussade, Jean Pierre de, **3:309–310**,
  4:763
Caussin, Nicholas, 7:783, 11:622
Cautio criminalis (Spee), 13:410
La Cava Abbey (Italy), 1:277,
  4:167–168, **8:268–269**, 494–495
Cava Diocese, 8:268
Cavalcanti, Guido, **3:310–311**, 4:517,
  518
Cavalier, Jean, 2:916
Cavalli, Francesco, **3:311**
Cavallini, Pietro, 2:374
Cavallo, G., 10:775
Cavanaugh, Agnes, 3:129
Cavanaugh, John Joseph, **3:311–312**
Cavazzoni, Girolamo, **3:312**
Cave, William, **3:312**
Cavendish, Henry, Sir, 5:260
Caverel, Philip de, 4:888, 12:588
Cavestany y Anduaga, Teresa Maria,
  14:564, 566
Cavo, Andrés, **3:313**
Cavour, Camillo Benso di, 3:*313*,
  313–314
  Bosco, St. John, 2:543

Victor Emannuel II, 14:481
Caxton, William, 2:523, 5:206
Cayet, Pierre Victor, **3:314–315**
Caylus, Charles G. (Bp. of Auxerre),
  1:927
CCD (Confraternity of Christian
  Doctrine), **4:94–95**, 9:189, 10:162
CCEE (Council of European Bishops'
  Conferences), **4:296–298**
CCEO. *See* Code of Canons of the
  Eastern Churches (CCEO) (1990)
CCES. *See* Catholic Church Extension
  Society of the United States of
  America
CCIP (Catholic Conference on Industrial
  Problems), 9:398
CCMA (Catholic Campus Ministry
  Association), 10:345
CCT. *See* Consultation on Common
  Texts
CCT (Consultation on Common Texts),
  4:201
CEA (Catholic Education Association of
  the U.S.), 10:159, 160
Ceauşescu, Nicolae, 10:691, 692
Cebrol, Ferdinand, Dom, 8:433
Cecaumenus (Byzantine historian), 2:799
Ceccano, Annibale de, 6:47
Cecil, William (1st baron Burghley),
  12:11
Cecilia, St., 3:*315*, **315**, 12:387, 600
Cecilia Romana, Bl., **3:315**
Cedd (Cedda) (Bp. of the East Saxons),
  St., **3:316**, 4:330
CEE. *See* Spanish Episcopal Conference
Ceillier, Remi, **3:316**, 5:760, 10:963
CELAM (Consejo Episcopal Latino-
  Americano). *See* Consejo Episcopal
  Latinoamericano (CELAM)
Celano, Venantius, 12:540
Celebret, **3:316**
*The Celestial and Ecclesiastical
  Hierarchy* (Pseudo-Dionysius), 1:414,
  425, 3:674, 11:801
Celestial Masters Sect (Daoism), 4:524
Celestial phenomena, 9:52–53
''The Celestial Railroad'' (Hawthorne),
  14:149
Celestine I (Pope), St., **3:316–318**
  Council of Ephesus, 5:273
  Ecumenical as term, 4:190
  General Council of Ephesus, 10:14
  Nestorianism, 1:390
  papal authority, 12:354
  religious habit, 12:99
  St. Sabina Church (Rome), 12:462
Celestine II (Antipope), **3:318**, 7:82

Celestine II (Pope), **3:318**
Celestine III (Pope), 1:701–702,
  3:318–319, 4:600–601, 7:144, 12:832
Celestine IV (Pope), **3:320**
Celestine V (Pope), **3:320–321**, *321*
  Boniface VIII (Pope), 2:501–502,
    3:321
  Clareni, 1:428, 3:762
  Clement V (Pope), 3:779
Celestines, 3:320, **321–322**
  Clareni, 1:428, 3:762
  founding, 5:897
  See also Benedictines
Celestis altitudo potentie (Nicholas IV),
  10:367
Celestius, 3:188
Celibacy
  Basil, St., 2:140
  ordination requirements, 7:40
  reform under Gregory VII (Pope),
    St., 6:471–472, 492
  virgines subintroductae, 14:539
  See also Clerical celibacy/marriage
Celis Santos, Eufrasio de, Bl., 4:494
Cell theory, 2:402–403
Celles, Theodore de, 4:415
Celles-Sur-Belle Monastery (France),
  3:328–329
Cellier, Elizabeth, 10:495
Celsus (Greek philosopher), **3:329–330**,
  592
  apologetics, 1:567
  biblical theology, 2:382
  Catholic mission in the Roman
    Empire, 9:690
Celtic Church (Scotland), 12:830
Celtic monks, confession and, 4:77
Celtic people, Wales, 14:610
Celtic religion, **3:330–331**
  Culdees, 12:533, 831–832
  Earth-Mother worship, 5:2
Celtic Rite, **3:331–332**
  history, 8:713
  sacramentaries, 12:483
Celtis, Conrad, 12:119
CEM (Mexican Episcopal Conference),
  9:583
Cemeteries
  as church property, 11:756–757
  early Christian funerals, 6:30
  early use for celebration of rites,
    2:146
  See also Burial; Catacombs; *specific
    cemeteries*
Cemeteries, Canon Law of, **3:332**

Cenacle (Jerusalem), **3:332–333**

Cenacle (papal bull), 3:54

Cencius, 3:319

Cendoya Araquistain, Maria Cecilia (1910-1936), 14:564, 566

"The Cenobiarch." *See* Theodosius of Palestine, St.

Cenobitic communities, 9:788

Cenobitism, **3:334–335**

   asceticism, 9:789

   Asceticon (St. Basil), 2:136–137, 142–143

   Athanasius the Athonite, St., 1:821

   contemplative life, 4:210

   Desert Fathers, 4:686

   Germain of Auxerre, St., 6:168

   lauras, 8:281

   monasticism, 9:799

   See also specific religious orders

Censers, 1:320, **3:335–336**, 8:716

Censorship of books, **3:336–337**

   burning of heretical books (St. Paul's Cross, 1521), 5:749

   Carter, Bl. William, 3:182–183

   Clement XIII (Pope), 3:792–793

   Clement XIV (Pope), 3:796

   French Reformation, 7:166

   obscenity and pornography, 5:326–327

   Pfefferkorn-Reuchlin controversy, 5:306, 12:12

   religious encyclopedias, 5:209

   See also Index of Prohibited Books

Censura (Huet), 3:186

Censure, theological, **3:337**

Censure of Toulouse, 8:309

Censure philosophiae cartesianae (Fabri), 12:771

Census, in the Bible, **3:337–339**, 8:856

Centelles Abad, Recaredo, 12:408

Center for Applied Research in the Apostolate (CARA), 10:576

Center for Muslim-Christian Understanding, 6:146

Center for the Study of Democratic Institutions, 3:824–825

Center Moriches Union Free School District, Lamb's Chapel v. (1993), 3:664

Center of Concern, 8:317, 318

Center Party (Germany), **3:339–342**, 619, 6:184, 185

   Kaas, Ludwing, 8:107

   Kulturkampf, 8:253–255

Centering prayer, **11:601**, 13:450

Centesimus annus (encyclical, John Paul II), **3:342–343**, 620, 643, 5:206, 7:998, 10:852, 11:567, 13:568, 14:643

   social justice, 13:244

   solidarity, 13:301–302

Cento concerti ecclesiastici. . .Con il basso continuo per sonar nel'organo (Viadana), 14:468

Le Cento e dieci considerazioni. . . (Valdés), 14:369

Centonization, 10:45

Central African Republic, **3:343–344**, *345*

Central Conference of American Rabbis, 8:10

Central sense, **3:344–347**

   cogitative power, 3:346, 823

   consciousness, 4:152

   creative imagination, 4:348

   sensation, 12:908

   senses, 12:913

   simple apprehension, 1:604

Centro di Studio e Informazione per l'Architettura Sacra (Italy), 3:712

Centro Intercultural de Documentación (CIDOC), 9:583–584

Centuria di lettere de S. Francesco di Paola (Preste), 5:874

Centuriators of Magdeburg, 3:*347*, **347–348**, 5:754

   Canisius, St. Peter, 3:18

   chronicles, 1:465

Centuries. See Centuriators of Magdeburg

Centurione Bracelli, Virginia, Bl., **3:348**

Centurions, **3:348**, 12:301

Century (Callistus II Xanthopulus and Ignatius Xanthopulos), 2:879

Ceolfrid of Wearmouth, St., **3:348–349**

Cepeda, Francisco, **3:349**

Cepeda y Ahumada, Teresa de. *See* Teresa of Avila, St.

Cerbonius, St., **3:349**

Cercamon, 4:400

Cercle Saint-Jean Baptiste, 4:516

Cere, M. Madeleine (Sister), 7:34

Cerejeira, Manuel Gonçalves (Card.), 11:539

Ceremonial of Bishops (liturgical book), 1:290, **3:349**

   Council of Trent, 12:328

   origins, 8:640

   See also Bishops

The Ceremonies of the Roman Rite Described (Fortescue), 5:821

Cerfaux, Lucien, **3:350**, 5:813, 8:143

Cerinthus, 1:304

Cerioli, Costanza, Bl., **3:350**

Cerqueira, Luís de (Bp. of Japan), **3:351**, 7:739

Certitude, **3:351–356**

   Balmes, Jaime Luciano, 2:33

   causality, 3:302

   doubt, 4:883–884

   in morality, 9:877

   similarity, 13:126

   skepticism, 13:200–205

   Thomist view, 8:538

   truth, 5:743, 14:223

Certitude of Faith, **3:357**, 5:600–601

Cerularius, Michael, 8:485

Cervantes, Miguel de, 2:116

Cervini, Marcello. *See* Marcellus II (Pope)

Cesarini, Alessandro (Card.), 3:357

Cesarini, Giuliano (Card.) (d. 1444), 2:133, 3:357

Cesarini, Giuliano (Card.) (d. 1510), 3:357

Cesarini family, **3:357**

Cesina, Teresa Adelaida. *See* Manetti, Teresa Maria della Croce, Bl.

Ceslaus of Silesia, Bl., **3:357–358**, 7:236

Cevoli, Florida, Bl., **3:358**

Ceylon. *See* Sri Lanka

Chaadaev, Peter Yakovlevich, 13:216

Chabanel, Noël, 10:436, 12:554

Chabham, Thomas, **3:358**

Chabot, Jean Baptiste, **3:358–359**

Chad, **3:359–361**, *360*

Chad (Ceadda), St., **3:359**

   Aidan of Lindisfarne, St., 1:192, 3:359

   Cedd, St., 3:316

   Coventry and Lichfield See, 4:330

   shrine, 13:94

Chaduiz, Durand, 3:93

Chadwick, George W., 12:212

Chafer, Lewis Sperry, 4:776

Chagall, Marc

   Bible cycles, 2:376

   crucifixion art, 4:397

   Notre-Dame-de-Toute-Grâces Church, 1:803, 3:713

Chahapivan, Council of (447), 1:705

Chain of Causation, **3:361**

La Chaine d'or sur les psaumes (Péronne), 3:259

Chair of Peter, **3:361**

Chair of Unity Octave (prayer crusade), 5:874

Chaise-Dieu Abbey (France), 1:454, **3:361–362**, *362*

Chakkarai, V., 7:405

Chalcedon (Turkey), **3:362**

  martyrs, 5:449

  Neochalcedonians, 8:503

  schism in Syrian Church, 13:705–706

  simony, 13:136

Chalcedon, Council of (451), 2:820, **3:363–366**, *364*, 559, 561, 595, 4:300, 5:3, 83

  Alexandria, 1:269

  Alexandria Patriarchate, 1:271

  Alexandrian liturgy, 1:273

  Anabaptists, 1:369

  Anastasius I (Byzantine Emperor), 1:386

  Anatolius of Constantinople, 1:392, 3:363, 365

  Antioch Patriarchate, 1:525

  Armenia, 1:700, 701, 704–705, 712, 4:958

  Athanasian Creed, 1:815

  Atticus of Constantinople, St., 1:839

  autonomy of Patriarchate of Jerusalem, 7:775

  Bassianus of Ephesus, 2:151

  biblical theology, 2:386

  Byzantine art, 2:731

  Caesarea in Cappadocia, 2:846

  caesaropapism, 2:851

  Canon Law, 3:38

  Christocentrism, 3:558

  Cilicia, 3:733

  communication of idioms, 4:26

  Constantinople, 4:185

  Constantinople Council II, 4:191, 192

  consubstantiality, 4:197–199, 7:66

  Coptic Church, 5:19

  Copts, 4:252–253

  Council of Ephesus, 5:274, 275

  Council of Orléans, 1:895

  Councils of Anse, 1:493

  creedal statements, 4:352, 353–354

  crucifixion, 4:379

  Cyprus, 4:461

  Cyril of Alexandria, 4:467

  Diadochus of Photice, 4:720

  Dionysiana collectio, 4:752

  Dioscorus (Patriarch of Alexandria), 4:756

  diptychs, 4:759

  Eastern Schism, 5:22

  Ethiopian Catholic Church, 5:403

  Euphemia, St., 5:449

Euthymius the Great, St., 5:460–461

Eutyches condemned, 5:462

exemption, 5:529

Hormisdas (Pope), St., 3:595

hypostasis, 7:263, 264

Leo I (Pope), St., 8:472

Leontius of Byzantium, 8:502

Liberatus, 8:550

Maronite Church, 9:194–195

Monophysitism, 4:195–196, 252, 379

Monothelitism, 7:80

One Person of the Son of God doctrine, 10:967

primacy of Constantinople, 2:744, 821

Robber Council of Ephesus, 1:523, 3:363

St. Euphemia Basilica, 3:362

Schwart, Eduard, 12:793

Son of God, 13:315

Song of Songs, 13:318

Timothy Aelurus, 14:86

two natures in Christ, 13:705

works of charity, 3:409

See also Acacian Schism

Chalcondyles, Demetrius, 12:119

Chaldaic Oracles (Roman era poem), 10:240, 241

Chaldean Antonines of St. Hormisdas, 1:535

Chaldean Catholic Church (Eastern Catholic), **3:366–369**

  ancient Persia, 7:395

  Assyrian Church of the East, 1:808, 3:366, 367–368

  Babylon of the Chaldeans Patriarchate, 2:4–5

  Baghdad, 2:11–12

  chorbishops, 3:526

  clerical celibacy and marriage, 3:324

  Council of Catholic Patriarchs of the Orient, 4:295–296

  influence in Iraq, 7:548

  Iran, 7:543

  liturgy, 1:528, 5:3–7

  Syro-Malabar Church, 13:714

  See also East Syrian liturgy

Chaldeans, **3:369–370**, 5:19

  Antonine monasticism, 1:535

  Aramaeans, 1:624

  astronomy, 12:799

  Syro-Malabar Church, 13:716–717

  See also Chaldean Catholic Church (Eastern Catholic)

Chalices, **3:370**, *371*, 8:630–631, 10:*720*

The Challenge of Peace: God's Promise and Our Response (NCCB), 2:319, 3:480, 10:544, 14:315

Challoner, Richard (Bp. of London), 3:243, **370–372**, *372*, 5:250, 11:960

Chalmers, Thomas, **3:372**

Chalmers, William (Camerarius), **3:372**

Chalon-sur-Saône, Councils of, **3:373**

Chambers, Ephraim, 5:207, 208

Chambers, Marsh v. (1983), 3:668

Chambiges, Pierre, 3:689

Chambon, Jean Alexis (Abp. of Tokyo), 3:515–516

Chaminade, Guillaume Joseph, Bl., **3:373–374**, 4:763, 9:160

Champagnat, Marcellin Joseph Benoît, St., **3:374–375**, 9:175

Champagne, Thibaut de, 4:400

Champion de Cicé, Jérôme (Abp. of Aix), 1:197, 927

Champlain, Samuel de, 9:721

Chance, **3:375–377**

  accident, 1:59

  atomism, 1:833

  contingency, 4:212–213

  fortune, 5:824

  Hume's denial, 10:227

  luck related, 8:848

  as opposite to nature, 11:303–304

  origin of life, 8:576

  randomness, 3:376–377

  See also Randomness

Chancellor, Diocesan (Eparchial), **3:377–378**

Chancels, 1:317

Chancery, Avignon papacy and, 1:945

Chanche, John Joseph (Bp. of Natchez, MS), 7:685, 9:738

Chandler, Joseph Ripley, **3:378**

Chandragupta (Mauryan Emperor), 7:697

Chanel, St. Peter Louis Marie, 3:374, *378*, **378–379**

Change

  act, 1:75

  Aristotle, 1:682, 746, 832, 9:340–341

  art, 1:746

  atomism, 1:832

  causality, 3:298, 307

  privation, 11:722–723

Channing, William Ellery, 3:*379*, **379**, 472, 4:116, 14:146, 148

Channing, William Henry, 14:149

Chanones, Jean, 7:312

Chanson, courtly love and, 4:318–322

La Chanson d'Antioche, 4:400

Chanson de Roland, 8:683

Chansons de geste, 2:806, 3:518

Chant

    Alma Redemptoris Mater, 1:297–298

    antiphons, 1:297–298, 529

    Beneventan, 2:278

    Byzantine, 1:197–198, 2:741–744, 802–803

    Carolingian Renaissance, 3:161

    Melismatic, 6:466

    Mozarabic, 1:294, 7:245, 10:41–42

    Old Roman, 4:32, 33, 6:464, 10:581–582

    Russian, 12:431

    Stabat Mater, 13:467

    Syllabic, 6:466

    See also Ambrosian Chant; Gregorian Chant; Liturgical music; Sarum Use

Chant books, **3:379–381**, *380*

    See also Kyrie Eleison

Chant traditions, 8:681, 682, 13:2

Chantal, Jane Frances de, St., *3:381*, **381–382**

    Binet, Étienne, 2:399

    Bonal, Raymond, 2:478

    Condren, Charles de, 4:74

    Duvergier de Hauranne, Jean, 4:955

    Francis de Sales, St., friendship with, 5:868, 869

    humanism, 7:194

    Visitation nuns, founding of, 14:563

Chanvallon, Harlay, 4:591

Chapdelaine, Auguste, 3:498

Chapelle, Placide Louis (Abp. of New Orleans), **3:382, 384**, 8:812–813, 10:293–294

Chapels, 1:633, **3:382**, *383*

Chaplain, William, 5:237

A Chaplain Looks at Vietnam (O'Connor), 10:544

Chaplains, 13:803

    Army chaplains, 9:627

Chapman, J. L., 10:168

Chapman, John, **3:384**

    contemplation, 4:208

    Monothelitism, 7:81

Chappotin de Neuville, Helénè de, **3:384**, *385*, 5:878

Chappuis, Jean, 4:273

Chappuis, Maria Salesiav, Ven., 2:619, **3:385**

Chapt de Rastignac, Armand, Bl., **3:385**

Chapter of Faults, **3:385–386**

Chapters, Religious, **3:386–387**

Chapters of canons, 3:66–67

Chaput, Charles J. (Abp. of Denver), 3:859, 4:670

Character, **3:387–388**, 8:514

Charbonneau, Joseph (Abp. of Montreal), 3:388

Charbonnel, Armand François Marie de (Bp. of Toronto), **3:388**

Chardon, Louis, **3:388–389**

Chardon, Mathias Charles, **3:389**

Charisma, 12:78–79

Charismatic churches in China, 3:501

Charismatic Movement, 8:240, 10:288

Charismatic prayer, **3:391–392**

Charismatic renewal, Catholic, **3:392–393**

    Australia, 1:906

    baptism in the Holy Spirit, 7:45

    spirituality, 13:449

    Suenens, Leon-Joseph, 13:585

Charisms, **3:389–391**, 14:562

    cenobitism, 3:335

    Church, 3:578

    classification of mystical phenomena as, 10:106–107

    God's spirit, 13:427

    list of principal, 10:107–109

    renewal of religious communities, 13:176

Charisms, in religious life, **3:393–394**

    ecstasy, 5:60

    private revelations, 12:200

Charistikion, 13:13

Charitable Address to All Who Are of the Communion of Rome (Nary), 10:154

Charité-sur-Loire Abbey (France), 3:259, **394**, 4:536

Charity, **3:395–400**

    active life, 1:83

    ambition, 1:334

    Baianism, 2:20–21

    beatific vision, 2:171

    Boniface, St., 3:230

    commitment, 4:15

    communication, 4:24

    Compagnie du Saint-Sacrement, 4:40–41

    contemplation, 4:204–205

    contrition, 4:224, 226, 227, 228, 230

    courtesy, 4:318

    courtly love compared to, 4:320–321

    created actuation by uncreated act, 4:336

    during difficult times, 8:311

    flame of, 13:5–6

    fraternal correction, 4:273–274

    heroic virtue, 14:554

    hope compared to, 7:92, 94, 96, 100–101

    idolatry opposed to, 7:305

    I-Thou model for understanding, 8:833

    kindness, 8:171

    law of, 8:403–404

    Lawrence Justinian, St., 8:405–406

    laws, conflict of, 8:410

    love, virtue of, 8:832

    lukewarmness, 8:865–866

    models for understanding, 8:832–833, 832–834, 833–834

    moral theology, 9:852–853, 854, 855

    obedience, 10:506

    spiritual perfection, 11:121–122

    spiritual reading, 11:941

    spirituality, 13:440

    Ten Commandments, 4:8

    virginity, 14:547

    See also Charity, works of

Charity, St., 5:608–609

Charity, works of, **3:400–421**

    Ambrose, St., 1:338, 3:406

    Antoninus, St., 1:533

    apostolic tradition, 3:401–402, 578–579

    Australia, 3:518

    Bible, 1:300, 3:400–401

    China, 3:504

    Christian Rome, 3:406–408

    Council of Trent, 3:415

    early Church, 3:546, 547, 724

    French Revolution, 3:419

    Knights of Malta, 8:195

    laity, 3:413, 416, 419–420

    liberality, 8:544

    Little Missionary Sisters of Charity, 8:611

    Middle Ages, 3:408–414

    mission, 3:415–417

    19th-20th centuries, 3:622

    paupers, 3:417

    Protestant Reformation, 3:414

    Roman persecution era, 3:402–406

    specialized institutions, 3:417–419

    See also Church property

Charlemagne (Holy Roman Emperor), 1:*121*, 3:*421*, **421–428**, 5:842, 9:*610*

    Aachen, 1:1

    Adalard, St., 1:98

    adoptionism condemned, 5:162

    Adrian I (Pope), 1:121–122, 3:422, 425

Charlemagne (Holy Roman Emperor)
(continued)
Amalberga, St., 1:329
Ambrosian Rite, 1:343
Angilramnus of Metz, 1:433
art, 3:153, 155
Austria, 1:908
Autpert, St. Ambrose, 1:925
Byzantine Church, 2:752, 785
Canon Law, 3:43
capella, 3:382
Carolingian dynasty, 3:165–168
Carolingian reform, 3:156–157, 166,
424–425, 599, 600
Carolingian Renaissance, 3:159,
166–167, 425–426
catechisms, 3:240
Christology, 3:561
Church-State relations, 1:122–123,
3:166, 634–635
computus, 4:46
Confirmation, 4:88
coronation, 1:243, 478, 3:167,
426–427, 554, 598, 634, 8:479–480
Council of Attigny, 1:840
Council of Nicaea and conversion of,
10:349–350
Councils of Chalon-Sur-Saône, 3:373
cross, 4:380
Einhard biographer of, 5:139
empire divided between three sons,
14:7
filioque, 2:752, 822
forced religious conversion, 9:691
German Church, 6:174–175
governance, 3:165–166, 422–424
hymns in court, 7:245–246
iconoclasm, 2:752
inheritance laws, 7:42
Irene (Byzantine Empress), 7:572
lay spirituality, 8:415
legal position in papal state, 8:479
legends, 1:762–764
Leidradus, 8:458–459
Leo III (Pope), St., 8:479–480
Liturgy of the Hours, 8:730
Lombards defeated, 8:767
Ludger to Frisia, 8:851
metropolitan constitution, 3:42
military operations, 3:165, 421–422
palace school founded, 10:763, 764
papal alliance, 7:656–657
Patriciius Romanorum title, 10:952
Paulinus II (Patriarch), 1:607
personal life, 3:427–428

Peter of Pisa, 11:201–202
Rolendis, St., 12:293
Roman Rite, 12:328
rule over Low Countries, 10:255
Second Council of Nicaea, 1:123
Slovene conversion, 13:225
Stephen III (IV) (Pope), 13:518
Theodulf (Abp. of Orléans), 13:886
works of charity, 3:410
See also Carolingian Dynasty;
Carolingian reform; Carolingian
Renaissance; Palace schools
*Charlemagne Departing for Spanish
Crusade with Roland and Archbishop
Turpin of Reims* stain glass window
(Chartres Cathedral), 14:*249*
Charles (Archduke), 1:911
Charles (Duke of Mayenne), 6:579
Charles, Josephine, 1:158
Charles, Paul-Jean, 12:276
Charles, Pierre, **3:428–429**
Charles, Sydney (Bp. of Granada), 3:120
Charles I (Card. of Lorraine),
6:578–579, 8:787
Charles I (Emperor of Austria), 6:642
Charles I (Holy Roman Emperor). *See*
Charlemagne (Holy Roman Emperor)
Charles I (King of England), **3:432**
anti-Catholicism, 3:612
Bahamas land grant, 2:13
Church in England under, 5:248
Church of Ireland, 7:548
Con, George, 4:49
Covenanters, 4:329
Divine right of kings, 4:788
Irish Catholic Confederacy, 12:724
Irish confessors and martyrs, 7:577
Laud, W., 8:377–378
marriage, 2:339
martyrs persecuted under, 5:235–236
Sabbatarianism, 12:454
Charles I (King of Hungary), 2:153,
7:211
Charles I (King of Spain). *See* Charles V
(Holy Roman Emperor)
Charles II (Card. of Lorraine), 8:788
Charles II (King of England), **3:433**
Bahamas land grant, 2:13
Church in England under, 5:248
Church of Ireland, 7:548
Church-State relations, 2:502, 3:648
Covenanters, 4:329–330
Huddleston, John, 7:148
Irish Church, 7:560
James II, 7:706

Oates Plot over succession following,
10:492–496
Pickering, Thomas, 11:322–323
Remonstrance, 3:173
Charles II (King of Naples-Sicily),
3:320, 7:86
Charles II (the Bald) (Holy Roman
Emperor), 3:157, 4:450, 8:*796*, 9:*127*
Ado of Vienne, St., 1:117
Adrian II (Pope), 1:124
Aldric of Le Mans, St., 1:248
Carolingian Dynasty, 3:170, 171
Carolingian Renaissance, 3:154, 161
Chartres, 3:441
John VIII (Pope), 7:923
Lothair II, 8:795, 796
Charles III (King of Spain)
Acquaviva, Trojano, 1:71
autos sacramentales, 1:925
Jesuits, 1:688, 3:792, 795, 9:717,
13:754
Tanucci, Bernardo, 13:754
Charles III (the Fat) (Holy Roman
Emperor)
Adrian III (Pope), 1:125
Carolingian Dynasty, 3:170, 171, 172
Charles III (the Simple) (King of the
West Franks), 3:172
Charles III de Bourbon, 4:364
Charles IV (Holy Roman Emperor)
advisors, 8:869
anointing, 1:479
Clement VI (Pope), 3:780
Golden Bull, 1:633, 3:843
succession, 6:640
Charles IV (King of Bohemia), 4:479
Charles IV (King of Spain), 2:91, 3:204
Charles IV (King of the Two Sicilies),
7:671
Charles V (Holy Roman Emperor),
3:*429*, **429–432**, 7:669, 10:258
Adrian VI (Pope), 1:129, 3:429
anointing, 1:478
Bobadilla, Nicolás Alfonso de, 2:446
Castiglione, Baldassare, 3:215
Catherine of Aragon, 3:268
Clement VII (Pope), 3:430, 609, 781,
782
confessions of faith, 4:77
confessors, 13:330
Contarini, Gasparo, 4:201–202
Council of Trent convocation, 14:168
election, 8:487, 12:737
empire plan, 13:392–393

friendship with Ernest of Pardubice, 5:325

Fugger family, 6:20

Gattinara, Mercurino Arborio di, 6:108–109

Granvelle, Antoine Perrenot de, 6:418

Hapsburg-Valois rivalry, 6:639

Henry VIII's divorce, 12:8

Inquisition, 2:217

Knights of Alcántara, 8:189

Lutheran suppression, 12:741

mausoleum (El Escorial, Spain), 5:353

Paul III (Pope), 11:22

Protestant Reformation, 1:849, 850, 2:889, 3:430–431, 638, 12:16–17

Protestant relations, 4:312

Salamanca University, 12:611

secularization of Church property, 12:872

Sicily, 13:104

Spanish hegemony, 13:390

swearing his oath upon Gospels miniature, 10:497

Charles V (King of France), 3:784

Charles VI (Emperor of Germany), 7:216

Charles VI (Holy Roman Emperor), 7:32

Charles VI (King of France), 7:878
Benedict XIII (Antipope), 2:246
Gallicanism, 6:74
Western Schism, 4:136

Charles VII (King of France)
Albergati, Niccolò, Bl., 1:219
Council of Basel, 2:134
Estouteville, Guillaume d', 5:379
Felix V (Antipope), 5:669
Joan of Arc, St., 7:878
Pragmatic Sanction, 6:75

Charles VIII (King of France)
Alexander VI (Pope), 1:259
humanism, 7:190
invasion of Italy, 7:668
Julius II (Pope), 8:56
Pragmatic Sanction, 11:581–582

Charles IX (King of France), 5:849

Charles IX (King of Sweden), 5:733

Charles X (King of France), 3:448

Charles Edward Stuart (pretender to the English throne), 7:690, 691

Charles Emmanuel II (Duke of Savoy), 7:670

Charles Emmanuel III (Duke of Savoy), 7:670–671

Charles Martel (Frankish mayor of the palace), **3:433–435**, 5:438, 9:519
Adalard, St., 1:98
Boniface, St., 2:495, 3:163, 434
Canon Law, 3:41
Carolingian Dynasty chronicle, 5:923
Carolingian reform, 5:842
Chrodegang of Metz, St., 3:563
confiscations of church property, 12:36
consolidation of power, 3:163–164, 433–434
Flavigny-sur-Ozerain Abbey (France), 5:760
Gregory III (Pope), St., 6:486–487
Leidradus of Lyons, 8:458
Lombards, 8:768
Pepin III, 11:108
Reichenau Abbey (Germany), 12:32
Remigius of Rouen, St., 12:108
secularization of Church property, 12:870
succession, 3:124, 164
works of charity, 3:410, 411

Charles of Anjou (King of Sicily), 2:502, 3:778, 4:414
Byzantine Empire, 2:762, 787
Honorius IV (Pope), 7:85
Michael VIII Palaeologus, 9:597

Charles of Blois, Bl., **3:435**

Charles of Lorraine-Vaudemont (Card. of Lorraine, 1559-1587), 8:788

Charles of Sezze, St., **3:435**

Charles of the Assumption (Charles de Bryas), **3:435–436**

Charles of Valois, 4:518

Charles of Villers, Bl., **3:436**

Charles the Great. See Charlemagne (Holy Roman Emperor)

Charles University (Prague), 4:480, 5:325

Charles-Michel l'Épée, 3:418

Charleston Diocese (SC), 5:223
creation, 2:38, 13:362–364
Georgia as part, 6:150–151

Charlesworth, J. H., 14:858

Charlevoix, Pierre François Xavier de, **3:436–437**

Charlotte Diocese (NC), **3:437**

Charlotte of the Resurrection, Bl., 4:44

La Charmoye Abbey (France), 3:751

Charnel houses, **3:437–438**, 438

Charnock, Robert, 1:642

Charpentier, Marc Antoine, 3:123, 438, **438–439**, 439, 10:12

Charron, Pierre, **3:439**, 11:293, 13:202

Charroux, Council of (989), 3:518

Charta Caritatis (St. Stephen), 14:161

Chartae latinae antiquiores (Cavallo and Nicolaj, eds.), 10:775

Chartier, Roger, 1:732

Chartrand, Joseph (Bp. of Indianapolis), 7:415, 417–418

Chartres (France), **3:441–442**

Chartres, School of, 5:516
Amalric of Bène, 1:330
art, 1:743
Bernard Silvester, 2:317
Boethius, 2:457
Calcidius, 2:859
liberal arts, 8:537
number symbolism, 3:674
scholasticism, 12:758–759, 776

Chartres Cathedral (France), **3:439–441**
Apocalypse iconography, 1:544
architecture, 3:440, 601, 695–696
Charlemagne Departing for Spanish Crusade with Roland and Archbishop Turpin of Reims (stained glass), 14:249
relics, 13:91
Sacristan standing near Virgin's Veil, 12:522

Chartularies, **3:442**

Chase, Martha, 2:404

Chase, Philander, 5:297

Chastan, Jacques Honoré, martyr, 8:234, 239

The Chastising of God's Children, 10:119

Chastity, **3:442–445**, 444
among the married and unmarried, 11:514
Basil of Ancyra, 2:139–140
continence, 4:211–212
as evangelical counsel, 4:306–307
lust opposed to, 8:871–877
means of grace, 8:876
modesty, 9:758
religious vow, 12:88
rightly ordered sex life, 8:873–874
See also Sex; Virginity

Chasubles, **3:445–446**, 446, 8:633–634

Chatard, Francis Silas (Bp. of Vincennes), **3:446**, 7:415, 417

Chateaubriand, François René de, **3:446–449**, 447, 624
lack of social perspective, 13:256
Renaissance concept, 12:113

Chatel, Ferdinand Toussaint, **3:449**

Châtillon Abbey (France), 3:751

Chatilloon, Jean, 1:67

Chaucer, Geoffrey, **3:449–457**, 5:529
  Canterbury Tales, 3:452, 453–456, 457
  early works, 3:452–453
  life, 3:449–451
  religious faith, 3:605
Chaumette, Pierre, 5:974
Chaumont, Henri, **3:457**
Chaurand, Père, 3:417
Chautard, Jean Baptiste, **3:457–458**
Chautauqua Movement, **3:458**
Chauvet, Louis Marie, 12:475, 476, 570–571
Chavara, Kuriakose (Cyriac) Elias, Bl., 3:146, **459**, 7:406
Chavasse, Antoine, 6:120–121
Chaves de la Rosa, Pedro José (Bp. of Arequipa), **3:459–460**
Chávez, César Estrada, 2:872, 3:*460*, **460–461**, 5:203
Chávez Orozco, María Vicenta of Santa Dorotea, Bl., **3:461**
Chavoin, Jeanne Marie, 3:835, 9:177
Cheating, **3:461–462**
Checa y Barba, José Ignacio, 3:*462*, **462**
Cheevers, Edward, 7:579
Cheevers, James, 7:581
Cheffontaines, Christophe de, **3:462–463**
Chelčický, Petr, 1:384, 2:461
Chelidonia, St., **3:463**
Chelles Convent (France), **3:463**
Chelsea, Council of, 4:88
"Le Chemin de la Croix" dans l'histoire et dans l'art (Ubald), 14:261
Chemistry, in the Renaissance, 12:816
Chemnitz, Martin, **3:463–464**
  Busaeus, Johannes, 2:715
  Concord Formula, 4:60, 61, 78
Ch'en, Rose and Teresa, SS., **3:464**
Chen Ximan, **3:464–465**
Chenchaiah, P., 7:405
Cheng Hao (Ch'eng Hao), 3:511
Cheng Yi (Ch'eng Yi), 3:511, 4:98
Chengo Hao, 4:98
Chénier, Marie Joseph, 4:587
Chenoboskion Gnostic texts, **3:465–466**
Chenu, Marie-Dominique, **3:466**
  scholasticism, 4:818, 12:776, 777
  Vatican Council II, 4:853
Cherez, Reynold, 7:78
Chernishevsky, Nikolai G., 10:394, 395
Chernobyl nuclear plant disaster (Ukraine, 1986), 2:213
Chertes, Ioan, 12:339

Cherubim, **3:466–467**, *467*
Cherubin of Avigliana, Bl., **3:467–468**
Cherubini, Luigi, 3:*468*, **468**
Cherzo, Francesco Patrici da, 8:584
Chester, Ancient See of (England), **3:468–469**
Chester Beatty Papyri, 2:363
Chesterton, Gilbert Keith, **3:469–471**, 4:782, 5:252
Chevalier, Jules, Rev., **3:471**, 12:494
Chevalier, Ulysse, **3:471**, 12:246
Chevallier, P., 1:532
Cheverus, Jean Louis Lefebvre de (Card.), 2:39, 43, 3:180, **471–472**, 9:305, 12:214, 14:453
  apostolic delegation in the United States, 1:582
  Boston Archdiocese, 2:553
  missionary work in Maine, 9:55
Cheverus, John, Rev., 12:297
Chevetogne Monastery (Belgium), **3:472–473**
Chevreul, Louis, 2:901
Chevrier, Antoine Marie, Bl., **3:473**
Cheyenne Diocese (WY), 14:869–871
Chezal-Benoît Abbey (Bourges, France), **3:473–474**, 12:548
Chézard de Matel, Jeanne Marie (Mother), **3:474**, 7:370
Chhmar Salas, Joseph, 2:903
Chiaramonti, Barnaba. *See* Pius VII (Pope)
Chiaramonti Museum (Vatican City), 14:397
Chiarito Convent (Regina Coeli), 3:765
Chiasm, 6:694
Chibcha people, **3:475**, 847, 848
Chicago Archdiocese (IL), **3:475–481**, *476*
  Alinsky, Saul David, 1:287–288
  archives, 1:640
  Barzyński, Vincent, 2:132
  Bernardin, Joseph Louis, 2:318–320
  Cody, John Patrick, 3:479–480, 821–822
  Daughters of St. Mary of Providence, 4:534
  founding, 1:155
  Friendship House headquarters, 6:10
  religious education, 12:785
  Schorsch, Dolores, 12:785
  See also Chicago Archdiocese (IL)
Chicago Back-of-the-Yards Neighborhood Council, 13:77
Chicago Bible Institute, 9:843
Chicago Historical Society, 10:599, 600

Chicago Resurrectionists, 2:132
Chichele, Henry (Abp. of Canterbury), 3:72, **481**, 13:467–468
Chichele, Henry (Bp.), 12:544
Chichen-Itza (Mexico), 9:*381*
Chichester, Ancient See of (England), **3:481–482**
Chidwick, John Patrick, **3:482**
Chief Priests, **3:482**
Chieregati, Francesco (Bp. of Teramo), **3:482–483**
Chiesa Nuova Church (Rome), 2:110, 3:703
La Chiesa Russa (Palmieri), 10:812
Chieu van Do, Francisco, 14:492
Chigi, Agnes, 3:484
Chigi, Agostino (founder of Chigi-Albani family), 3:484
Chigi, Agostino (the Elder), 3:483
Chigi, Agostino (the Magnificent) (1464-1520), 3:483–484
Chigi, Angela, Bl., 3:483
Chigi, Fabio. *See* Alexander VII (Pope)
Chigi, Flavio (Card.), 3:484
Chigi, Flavio the Younger (Card., 1711-1771), 3:484
Chigi, Giovanni da Lacceto, Bl., 3:483
Chigi, Giuliana, Bl., 3:483
Chigi, Mariano, 3:483
Chigi, Sigismondo (1479-1525), 3:*483*, 484
Chigi, Sigismondo (Card., 1649-1678), 3:484
Chigi family, **3:483–484**
Chigi-Albani, Flavio (Card.), 3:484
Chigi-Zondadari, Antonio Felice the Elder (Card., 1665-1737), 3:484
Chigi-Zondadari, Antonio Felice the Younger (Card., 1740-1823), 3:484
Chihamba, the White Spirit: A Ritual Drama of the Ndembu (Turner), 14:245
Child guidance, 9:191
Child Jesus Society, 1:2
Child pornography, 11:519
Childbearing, 14:817–818
Childebert I (King of the Franks), 12:547
  Aurelian of Arles, St., 1:895
  Germain, St., 6:168
  Pelagius I (Pope), 11:59
  works of charity, 3:409
Childeric I (King of the Salian Franks), 3:809
Childeric III (King of the Franks), 3:124, 11:109

Childhood (Tolstoi), 14:105

Children
duties, 11:335
Lewis, C. S., 8:527
limbo, 8:590, 591
oblate, 10:512
Piaget, Jean, on moral judgment of, 11:319

Children with a Shell (Murillo), 10:66

Children's Crusade, 3:275

Childs, Brevard S., 3:33, 11:98

Chile, 3:12, **484–488**, *488*, 12:282
Caro Rodríguez, José María, 3:148–149
Church-state relations, 5:328, 7:999
Cienfuegos, José Ignacio, 3:732
demographic statistics, 3:485
Donoso, Justo, 4:869
ecclesiastical organization, 3:486
Eyzaguirre, José Alejo, 5:572–573
Eyzaguirre, José Ignacio Víctor de, 5:573
fascist influences, 5:326
Hurtado Cruchaga, Alberto, 7:226–227
Lacunza y Díaz, Manuel de, 8:274
laicism, 8:284
map, 3:*487*
mission, 3:485, 486, 9:712

Chiliasm, 1:547, **3:488**
heaven, 6:687
millenarianism, 9:636, 637
Taborites, 13:728
See also Millenarianism

Chillenden, Thomas, **3:488–489**

Chilperic II (Merovingian King), 3:433–434

Chimayó Santuário (NM), **3:489**

China, **3:489–507**, *492*, *494*, *496*
ancestor worship, 1:394, 3:497, 500, 507, 513–517
books, 2:522
Boxer Rebellion (1900), 5:651, 683
Buddhism, 2:*660*, 662–664, 3:510–511
Communism, 2:664, 665, 3:501–503, 864
Cultural Revolution, 3:502–503
democracy movement, 4:*637*
demographic statistics, 3:489
early 20th century, 3:500–501
ecclesiastical organization, 3:490
historical works, 9:51
Holy See, relations with, 3:502, 505–506

Jesuit mapping, 6:1
Macau, sovereignty over, 9:4
Manichaeism mission, 9:108
map, 3:*491*
martyrs
Boxer Rebellion, 1:367–368, 400, 3:99, 464, 500, 14:884, 921–924
canonization, 3:506
Capillas, Francis de, Bl., 3:83–84, 496
Díaz del Rincón, Francisco, 4:732
Dierkx, Anne Catherine, 4:741
Dong Bodi, Patrick, 4:865
18th century, 1:240–241, 3:498
Feng De, Matthew, St., 5:683
Jesuits, 1:400
mission, Assyrian Church of the East, 1:806, 807, 3:489, 491–492
mission, Catholic
Aleni, Giulio, 1:250
Amiot, Jean Joseph Marie, 1:359–360
Bouvet, Joachim, 2:571
Brollo, Basilio, 2:626
Buglio, Ludovico, 2:675–676
Caballero, Antonio, 2:836
Castiglione, Giuseppe, 3:216, 217, 498
Castner, Gaspar, 3:217–218
Cattaneo, Lazzaro, 3:295–296
Cibot, Pierre Martial, 3:729
Columban Fathers, 3:864
Confucianism, 4:95, 96, 98, 101
Costantini, Celso, 4:290–291
Cruz, Gaspar da, 4:415–416
Daughters of the Holy Spirit, 7:46
d'Elia, Pasquale, 4:628
Della Chiesa, Bernardino, 4:630
Díaz, Manuel, 4:731–732
Díaz del Rincón, Francisco, St., 4:732
Dierkx, Anne Catherine, 4:741
Favier, Alphonse, 5:651
Filippucci, Alessandro Francesco Saverio, 5:722
Ford, Francis Xavier, 5:798
Franciscans, 2:836, 3:492–493, 495, 499, 513
Galvin, Edward, 6:83
Grassi, St. Gregorio, 6:420
Hinderer, Roman, 6:839
Hong Kong, 7:75
Huc, Évariste Régis, 7:146
Immaculate Heart of Mary, Congregation of, 7:337–338

Jesuits, 3:493–496, 497, 7:784
John of Monte Corvino, 7:975–976
Le Gobien, Charles, 8:455
Lebbe, Frederic Vincent, 8:428–429
Martini, Martino, 9:225
Maryknoll Fathers and Brothers, 9:295, 296
Maryknoll Sisters, 12:289
19th century, 3:498–499
Perboyre, St. Jean-Gabriel, 11:112
Pereira, Tomás, 11:114
Pro Mundi Vita (Brussels), 11:726–727
Rho, Giacomo, 12:214
Ricci, Matteo, 12:223–225
Ricci, Vittorio, 12:226
Ripa, Matteo, 12:251
Rodriguez Tçuzu, João, 12:281–282
Rougemont, François, 12:390–391
Rubino, Antonio, 12:399
Russian Orthodox, 3:501
Schall von Bell, Johann Adam, 12:727–729
Sisters of Mercy and Holy Cross, 7:22
Sisters of Providence, 13:189
Xavier, St. Francis, 14:878–879
mission, Manichaean, 9:108
mission, Orthodox, 9:694–695, *695*
mission, Protestant, 3:499–500, 9:699
post-1980, 3:503–506
Providence Catechist Society, 13:189
religions, **3:512–513**
Russian Orthodox Church, 3:501
Vincentians, persecution of, 14:528
women, status of, 14:813–814
See also Chinese philosophy; Chinese rites controversy

China Christian Council, 3:503

Chinard-Durieux, Anne of the Holy Spirit (Mother), 7:371

Chinese American Catholics, 2:868–869

Chinese Catholic Patriotic Association (CCPA), 3:502, 503, 504–505, 506

Chinese Independent Church, 3:501

Chinese philosophy, **3:507–512**
Confucianism and Neo-Confucianism, 4:95–99
Daoism, 4:523–524
soul, 13:337

Chinese Rites controversy, 3:497–498, **513–517**, 613, 789, 4:98, 5:722, 7:385, 9:692, 12:281, 399
 Alexander VII (Pope), 1:262
 Alexandre, Noël, 1:267
 Brisacier, Jacques Charles de, 2:619
 Castner, Gaspar, 3:218
 Clement XI (Pope), 3:514, 515, 789
 Clement XII (Pope), 3:515, 790
 Della Chiesa, Bernardino, 4:630
 Le Gobien, C., 8:455
 Visdelou, Claude de, 14:557
Chínipas Jesuit Mission (Mexico), 9:709
Chiniquy, Charles Pascal, 3:477, **517**
Chinmoku (Silence) (Shusaku), 5:219
Chiona, James (Abp.), 9:67–68
Chippewa Exercises: Being a Practical Introduction into the Study of the Chippewa Language (Verwyst), 14:461
Chippewa people, 12:552, 572
 Baraga, Frederic, 2:86
 mission to, 4:364
 Pierz, Francis Xavier, 11:329
Chi-Rho, 2:699, **3:474**, *475*, 4:180, *379*, 7:*33*
 Constantine I (the Great) (Roman Emperor), 8:263
 Holy Name, 7:33
Chirico, G. de, 1:545
Chirographs, 4:758
Chirurgia (Theodoric Borgognoni of Lucca), 13:880
Chisholm, Caroline, 1:904, 3:517–518, *517*
Chistkatholisches Religions-Handbuch (Overberg), 10:726
Chitimacha people, 8:808
Chittagong Diocese (Bangladesh), 2:53
Chivalry, 1:762, **3:518–519**, 8:866
Chlodulf of Metz, St., **3:519–520**
Chlotar II (King of Neustria), 9:518
Chlotar II (King of the Franks), 2:336, 3:163, 8:869
Chlotar III (King of Neustria), 2:153
Chmielowski, Albert, St., **3:520**, 7:685
Chōbyōye, Peter Araki, Bl., 7:734
Chōbyōye, Susana, Bl., 7:734
Choctaw people, 8:159, 12:274, 391
Choice, **3:520–522**
 act, 7:172–173
 character, 3:387
 deliberation, 4:629–630
 Honorius of Autun, 7:89
 Kierkegaard, 8:166–167
 pluralism in society, 13:277

Choirs, 3:*522*, **522–524**
 altars, 1:317
 architecture, 3:686, 711
Choiseul du Plessis Praslin, Gilbert de (Bp. of Tournai), 3:436, **524**
Chollet, A., 5:101
Cholleton, Claude (Father), 12:555
Cholmogory Abbey (Russia), **3:524**
Ch'ondogyo (Religion of the Heavenly Way), 8:238
Chong Hasang, Paul, 8:233, 234, 239
Chong Zhen (Ch'ung-chen) (Emperor of China), 3:496
Choniates, Michael (Abp. of Athens), 2:795
Chopin, Frédéric François, 3:524–525, *525*
Chora Monastery. *See* Kariye Cami
Choral polyphony, 10:13
Choralis Constantinus (Isaak), 7:591–592
Chorbishops, 1:785, **3:525–526**
 Caesarea in Cappadocia, 2:846
 Eoban, 5:269
 Lull of Mainz, 8:867
Chorisantes, **3:526**
Choron, Alexander, 2:841
Chosen people. *See* Election, Divine
Choses Passées (Loisy), 8:766
Chosroes I (Sassanian King of Persia), 1:806
Chosroes II (Sassanian King of Persia), 2:783
Chosroid Dynasty, 9:671
Chossat, M., 5:365
Chou Tun-i (Zhou Dunyi), 3:511
Chouteau, Charles Pierre, 12:562
Chouteau, François and Berenice, 8:118
Chōzaburō, John Mutsunoo, Bl., 7:735
Chrestomathia rabbinica et Chaldaica (Beelen), 2:200
Chrétien de Troyes, 7:26, 28
Chrétiens desunis (Congar), 4:102
Chrism, 4:87, 90, 7:34–35
Chrism Mass, **3:526–527**
Chrismation. *See* Confirmation, Sacrament of
Christ. *See* Jesus Christ
The Christ (Schoonenberg), 12:783
Christ (term), **3:527**
Christ (title), 7:833
Christ Among the Doctors (Luini), 7:*801*
Christ and the Church (O'Connell), 10:542
Christ Before Pilate (Master of Cappenberg), 11:*40*

Christ Child Society, 9:520
Christ Church (Philadelphia), 3:714
Christ Church Cathedral (Canterbury, England), 3:72, 263, 488–489
Le Christ dans le banlieu (Daniel and Godings), 5:857
Christ Explaining a Parable to the Disciples illumnination (Predis), 10:*868*
Christ Giving the Keys to Saint Peter (Catena), 8:*163*
Christ Healing the Paralytic (Predis), 6:*679*
Christ Healing the Sick Presented to Him by the Pharisees (Cristoforo de Predis), 9:*665*
Christ of Daphni, 4:393
Christ on the Cross with Three Angels (Dürer), 11:*638*
Christ Preaching (Rembrandt), 11:*08*
Christ Removed from the Cross (Carracci), 10:*138*
Christ the King, Feast of, **3:527**, 11:857
Christ the King Cathedral (Liverpool, England), 5:*249*
Christ the King Church (Gloggnitz, Austria), 3:712
Christ the King Church (Seattle), 3:716
Christ the King Church (Tulsa), 3:716
Christ the Redeemer statue (Rio de Janeiro), 8:465
Christadelphians, **3:527–528**
 apocatastasis, 1:548
 pacifism, 10:746
Christanus alter Christus (Tertullian), 5:788
Christe sanctorum decus angelorum (hymn), **3:528**
Christen, Ulrich, 12:568
Christenspiegel (Kolde), 3:241
Christi Matri (encyclical, Paul VI), 11:32
Christian (Faithful of Christ), **3:528–529**, 5:272
Christian (term), **3:528–530**, 578
Christian II (King of Denmark), 1:643, 4:665
Christian III (King of Denmark), 4:666, 7:276
Christian III (King of Norway), 10:448
Christian IV (King of Denmark), 14:9
Christian and Missionary Alliance, **3:530**
Christian anthropology, **3:530–533**, 589, 14:827
Christian archaeology, 6:880
Christian base communities. *See* Basic Christian Communities

Christian Brethren. *See* Plymouth Brethren

Christian Brothers, 2:867, 3:621

See also Brothers of the Christian Schools

Christian Brothers Institute. *See* Irish Christian Brothers

Christian Charity, Sisters of, 8:108

Christian Church (Disciples of Christ), 2:917, 3:527, **534–535**, 4:117, 199–200, 6:27

Christian Conference of Asia, 9:698

Christian democracy, 8:492, 9:755

Christian Democratic Party (Italy), 7:674, 935

Christian Democratic Union (Germany), 6:186

Christian Directory (Persons), 11:960

Christian education. *See* Catholic education; Parochial schools

Christian Education of Youth (encyclical, Pius XI), 10:650

Christian Eloquence in Theory and Practice (Gisbert), 11:622

Christian Endeavor Society, **3:535–536**

Christian era, 5:313–314

Christian Ethics (Hildebrand), 6:831

The Christian Examiner (Hedge), 14:147

The Christian Faith (Schleiermacher), 12:740

Christian Family Movement (CFM), **3:536**

Christian Federation of Malaysia (CFM), 9:72

Christian History (Philip, presbyter of Side), 13:169

Christian humanism, 7:182, 193–194, 197–198

Christian Initiation, General Introduction, 3:253

Christian Initiation for Adults, 8:724, 784

Christian Initiation of Adults, Order of, 5:741

The Christian Knight (Fitch), 5:750

Christian life, 6:8, 7:799, 801

Christian Life and Worship (Ellard), 5:168

Christian Liturgy (Kilmartin), 8:169

A Christian Manifesto (Lewis), 8:529

Christian Mercy Program, 14:888

Christian Methodist Episcopal Church (U.S.), 9:562

Christian Methodist Episcopal Church (U.S), 4:199–200

The Christian Occupation of China, 3:500

Christian of Prussia (Bp.), **3:537**, 8:192

Christian of Stablo, **3:537–538**

Christian oratory, 6:431

Christian papyri, 10:864

Christian philosophy, **3:538–542**

communication, 4:24

existential metaphysics, 5:540–541

Gratry, Auguste Joseph Alphonse, 6:424

Greek influence, 6:442–443

Platonism, 11:413–416

Simon, Y., 13:127–128

Christian Reformed Church, **3:542–543**, 12:24–25

Christian Religious Education (Groome), 12:98

Christian Science (Church of Christ, Scientist), **3:544–546**, *545*, 716, 5:80, 10:110, 308

Christian Science before the Bar of Reason (Lambert), 8:303

Christian Science Monitor (newspaper), 5:80

Christian Spirituality (La Spiritualité chrétienne) (Pourrat), 11:564

Christian Topography (Cosmas Indicopleustes), 1:270

Christian Union (periodical), 2:199–200

Christian Union, Conference on (Liverpool, 1846), 5:467

Christian Virtues and Perfection (Rodriguez), 12:240

Christian way of life (Early Church), 1:588, 3:228, **546–548**

See also Early Church

Christiana of Lucca, Bl., **3:548**

Christiane persecutiones (Simonetta), 13:134

Christian-Hindu relations (India), 7:396–397, 405

Christianikē topographia (Indicopleustes), 7:676

Christianity at the Crossroad (Tyrrell), 7:790

Christianopolis (Andrea), 14:360

Christie, Alexander (Abp. of Oregon City), 11:530

Christifideles laici (apostolic exhortation, John Paul II), **3:549**, 7:1003, 8:289, 417, 14:826

Christina (Queen of Sweden), 1:262, 3:786

Christina of Hamm, Bl., **3:550**

Christina of Markyate, St., **3:550**

Christina of Spoleto, Bl., **3:550**

Christina of Stommeln, Bl., **3:550**, 11:221

Der Christliche Glaube (The Christian Faith) (Schleiermacher), 8:542, 12:740

Das christliche Kultmysterium (Casel), 8:671–672

Die christliche Lehre von der Rechtfertigung und Versöhnung (Ritschl), 12:257

Christliche Schriften (Herder), 6:768

Christlijke Gereformeerde Kerk (CGK), 10:264

Christmas, **3:551–557**

Advent, 1:133–134

Armenian liturgy, 1:707, 710, 3:553, 556

calendar, 3:552–553, 8:642, 719, 721

crib, 4:364, 895

European customs, 3:557

forbidden in colonial America, 3:647

light, use of, 8:581

liturgy, 3:554–557

Middle Ages, 3:553–554, 4:895–896, 897–898

origins, 3:551–553

Polish popular piety and, 11:511

precursors, 3:14

Protestant Reformation, 3:554, 557

as veneration of Mary, 9:157

Christmas Carols or Sacred Songs, 3:151

Christmas Oratorio (Saint-Saëns), 12:584

Christocentrism, **3:557–559**

Aelred, St., 1:138

Alphonsus Liguori, St., 1:309

anonymous Christian, 1:489

biblical theology, 2:387

Bonaventure, St., 2:484, 493, 3:558

catechesis, 3:230

Catherine of Siena, St., 3:273

church architecture, 3:711

liturgy, 3:558–559

Louis of Granada, 8:807

19th-20th centuries, 3:623

Christodoulos (Patriarch of Alexandria), 4:255

Christology, **3:559–560**

Augustine, St., 1:864–865, 874

biblical theology, 2:387

Bonaventure, St., 2:484–485, 486–487

cantors, 3:75

circumincession, 3:741

controversies, 5:788

creation doctrine, 4:345

creedal statements, 4:351

Christology (continued)
 Cyril of Alexandria, 4:468–469
 Dead Sea Scrolls and titles, 4:564
 Duns Scotus, John, 4:938
 Epistles of St. Paul, 3:560, 861–862
 eschatology, 5:346, 349–350
 Ethiopia, 5:400–401
 eucharistic, 8:840–841
 feminism, 5:679–680
 Following of Christ, 5:788–789
 liberation theology, 8:547
 Lukan, 8:864
 Mary, Blessed Virgin, 9:247–248
 Schoonenberg, Piet, 12:783
 Son of God, 13:315
 soteriology, 13:329
 soul, 13:352
 subsistence, 13:573–574
 Theodore (Bp. of Mopsuestia in
  Cilcia), 13:875
 Theodoret (Bp. of Cyr), 13:878
 theology of Logos, 8:761
 titles, 7:808–809, 833–834
 universe as Christ-like, 8:840
 See also Christology controversies
  (patristic era); Consubstantiality;
  Humanity of Christ
Christology controversies (patristic era),
 2:792–793, 3:559, **560–562**, 595
 Armenian liturgy, 1:707
 Assyrian Church of the East, 1:805,
  806
 Byzantine art, 2:731, 733
 Byzantine Church, 2:748–750
 Byzantine Empire, 2:783
 Byzantine literature, 2:792
 historiography, 2:797
 homoousios, 7:65–66
 Leontius of Byzantium, 8:502
 School of Alexandria, 1:272, 273
 School of Antioch, 1:524, 527
 Second Council of Constantinople,
  1:343, 607, 805, 2:499–500, 820,
  3:561, 595, 596
 sources of Byzantine theology, 2:820
 Theodore of Mopsuestia, 1:119, 523,
  3:365, 561
 See also Acacian Schism;
  Adoptionism; Apollinarianism;
  Arianism; *Henoticon* (Zeno);
  Hypostasis; Monophysitism;
  Monothelitism; Nestorianism
Christomonistic theologies, 8:169
Christophany, 12:152–156
Christopher (Antipope), **3:562**, 8:483
Christopher, St., **3:562**, 12:599

Christopher Maccassoli, Bl., **3:562–563**
Christopher News Notes (Keller), 8:137
Christopher of Mytilene, 2:805
Christopher of Padua, 1:879
Christopher of Romandiola, Bl., **3:563**
The Christophers, **3:563**, 8:137
Christopherson, John (Bp. of
 Chichester), 3:481
Christophorus (papal chancellor), 4:178,
 11:243
Christotokos, Mary as, 9:815
Christ's Blueprint of the South
 (periodical), 14:252
Christ's Church (Oxford), 8:182
Christ's Poor (periodical), 8:360
*Christus, das Evangelium in seiner
 weltgeschichtlichen Bedeutung*
 (Schell), 12:732
Christus als Prophet (Schmid), 12:743
Christus Coelestis Medicus
 (iconography), 7:860
Christus Dominus (*Decree on the
 Bishops' Pastoral Office in the
 Church*) (Vatican Council II), 2:420,
 3:236, 5:38, 300
Christus und die Cäsaren (Bauer), 2:159
Chrodegang of Metz, St., **3:563–564**,
 12:413, 540
 Carolingian reform, 1:840, 3:156,
  157, 410, 563–564
 cathedral and episcopal schools,
  3:263
 Gorze Abbey, 6:366
 model for Leidradus, 8:458
 works of charity, 3:410
Chromatius of Aquileia, St., **3:564**, 594,
 12:404
Chrondegang, 8:656
Chronica (Gervase of Canterbury), 6:193
Chronica (*Monumenta Germanica
 Scriptores*) (Sigebert of Gembloux),
 13:112
Chronica Casinensis monasterii (Leo
 Marsicanus), 8:494
*Chrónica de la Orden de N.P.S. Agustín
 en las provincias de la Nueva
 España en quatro edades desde el
 año de 1533 hasta el de 1592*
 (Grijalva), 6:532–533
*Chrónica do Felicíssimo Rei Dom
 Emanuel* (Góis), 6:334
Chrónica do Principe Dom Ioam (Góis),
 6:334
Chronica Montis Sanctae Agnetis (Á
 Kempis), 14:13
*Chronicka und Beschrybung von Anfang
 des nüwen Ungloubens* (Salat),
 12:612

Chronicle (George Hamartolus), 6:144
Chronicle (George Syncellus), 6:145
Chronicle (St. Hippolytus of Rome),
 6:859
Chronicle (Salimbine), 12:615
Chronicle of 754, 9:445–446
Chronicle of Alfonso III, 9:445–446
Chronicle of Arbela, **1:628**
Chronicle of Edessa, 1:461
Chronicle of Roda, 9:445–446
*Chronicle of St. Peter's Monastery in
 Ratisbon* (Fleming), 5:760
Chronicle of the Emperors (Ebendorfer),
 5:29
Chronicle of the Morea, 2:806
Chronicle of William of Sandwich,
 14:754
Chronicler, Biblical. *See* Biblical
 chronicler
Chronicles. *See* Annals and chronicles;
 specific titles
Chronicles (Eusebius of Caesarea),
 5:148, 453
Chronicles (Julius Africanus), 8:58–59
Chronicles, Books of, 3:566–567
 altars, 1:320
 Ark of the Covenant, 13:88
 Baal, 2:2
 Benjamin (tribe), 2:283
 Edomites, 5:87
 exile of Judah, 13:40
 Hezechiah's tunnel, 13:120
 inheritance, 7:464
 Kingdom of God, 8:172
 kingship, 8:179
 lamentations, 8:312
 leprosy, 8:509
 Lord's Prayer, 8:782
 magic, 9:39
 showbread, 13:88
 sin, 13:144
 slavery, 13:206
 Solomon, 13:305
 See also Biblical Chronicler;
  Paralipomenon, Books of; *specific
  titles*
*Chronicles of John Skjlitzes: Persecution
 of the Monk Lazarus de Theophanes
 and his brother Theodoros*, 13:928
Chronicles of Narnia (Lewis), 8:527
Chronicon (Frutolf of Michelsberg), 6:17
Chronicon (Hermannus Contractus),
 6:784
Chronicon (Hugh of Saint-Victor),
 12:235

Chronicon (Prosper of Aquitaine),
10:805

Chronicon (Regino of Prüm), 6:873,
12:30

Chronicon (St. Isidore of Seville), 7:604

Chronicon Bohemorum (Cosmas of
Prague), 6:873

Chronicon ecclesiasticum (Bar-
Hebraeus), 2:82

Chronicon ex chronicis (Florence of
Worcester), 5:772

Chronicon Paschale, 1:461, 5:191

Chronicon Syriacum (Bar-Hebraeus),
2:82

Chronicum Edessenum (Chronicle of
Edessa), 5:82, **83**

*Chronicum sive Breviarum de sex mundi
aetatibus ab Adamo usque ad annum
869* (Ado of Vienne, St.), 1:117–118

Chronike Syngraphe (Acropolites),
2:800

Chronograph (Philocalus), 3:551

Chronographer of 354, 1:460–461,
3:*569*, **569–570**, 9:*232, 234*

birth date of Jesus, 8:54

Depositio Martyrum, 4:675–676

Liberian Catalogue, 8:553

Chronographia (Psellus), 4:177

Chronography (Elias Bar Shināyā),
5:156

Chronography, Christian, 8:58–59

Chronologie septennaire (Cayet), 3:314

Chronology, medieval, **3:570–571**

See also Chronicles, Books of

Chronology, use in division of
philosophies, 11:285–286

Chrysanthus, St., 2:146

Chrysanthus and Daria, SS., **3:571–572**

Chrysaphius, 3:363

Chrysippus, 5:393

Chrysoberges, Andrew (Abp. of
Rhodes), **3:572**

Chrysoberges, Maximus, 2:762, 827

Chrysococcus, Manuel, 2:340

Chrysogonus, St., **3:572–573**

Chrysoloras, Demetrius, 2:827

Chrysoloras, Manuel, 2:810

Chrysopassus (Eck), 5:43

Chrysostom, John, St. *See* John
Chrysostom, St.

Chrysostom of Saint-Lô, John (French
Franciscan), 2:324, 3:*573*, **573**

Chthonic Divinities, Worship of,
3:573–574

Chu, Francis, 7:793

Chuang Tzu. *See* Zhuangzi (Chinese
philosopher)

Chugoku, John, Bl., 7:733

Chu-Hsi (Zhu Xi), 3:511–512, 4:98

Chulalongkorn (King of Thailand),
13:849

Chur Diocese (Switzerland), patron of,
5:782, 8:845

Chur Monastery (Switzerland), **3:574**

The Church (Nevin), 10:272

Church, Alonzo, 14:326

Church, historical overviews

early church, **3:590–597**, 8:174,
10:141

early modern era, **3:607–616**,
8:131–132, 184–185, 294, 10:141

late modern era, **3:616–629**, 5:170,
10:141

Middle Ages, **3:597–606**, 8:174–175,
421, 10:141, 13:124–125

Church, symbols of, **3:629–630**

Church, theology of, **3:580–590**

Apostles, 1:573

apostolicity, 1:596

Aquinas, 3:581–582, 586–588

Augustine, St., 1:866–867, 3:584–585

Bible on, 3:575, 578–580, 581–583,
629, 5:271, 8:174

as Bride of God, 14:827

branch theory, 2:582–583

communio as mission, 4:27–31

Divine judgment, 8:36

Mary, Blessed Virgin, relationship
between, 9:254–258

modern era, 3:588–590

New Testament, 3:575, 578–580,
581–583, 629

patristic era, 3:583–586

as the People of God, 5:37

role in the contemporary world,
5:33–34

unity and universality, 8:94–95

as witness of Jesus Christ, 14:802

*Church, World, Mission: Reflections on
Orthodoxy in the West* (Schmemann),
12:742

Church Alert, 13:296

The Church and Modern Society
(Ireland), 7:550

Church and Republic (Schroeder),
12:787

Church and State, **3:630–643**

Action Française, 1:81–82, 3:617

Alanus Anglicus, 1:207

Alvaro Pelayo, 1:327

Ambrose, St., 1:338, 339, 922, 3:633

Amette, Léon Adolphe, 1:357

Anabaptists, 3:637

Anglicanism, U.S., 3:645–646, 647,
648, 651, 652

anticlericalism, 1:518

Antiochus IV Epiphanes (King of
Syria), 3:631

Aquinas, 1:675, 3:637

Argentina, 1:654, 6:34, 12:260–261

Arianism, 3:632, 633

Aristotelianism, 1:675, 3:636

Arminianism, 3:638

Assyria, 3:631

Augustine (Triumphus) of Ancona,
1:884, 3:636

Augustine, St., 1:123, 884, 3:633,
635

Augustinianism, 1:883–884

Ausculta fili, 1:898, 2:503

Austria, 1:914, 917, 9:154–155,
12:794

Church-state system, 7:1041–1042

Maria Theresa (Empress of
Austria), 1:913, 3:615, 639,
7:216

Belgium, 3:641

Bellarmine, Robert, St., 3:639, 5:395

Berkeley, William, 3:645

Bernard of Clairvaux, St., 3:635

Bonnechose, Henri Marie Gaston de,
2:507

Bossuet, Jacques Bénigne, 2:549,
550, 3:615

Brazil, 2:597, 6:339

Buchanan, George, 3:638

Byzantine Empire, 2:773, 820–822,
851, 3:633, 634

Calvin, John, 3:637–638

Canada, 3:8, 10–11, 4:887

Canon Law, 3:635–636, 643–645,
644–645

Carolingian reform, 1:122–123

Carolingian Renaissance, 3:634

Carroll, John (Abp. of Baltimore),
3:640

Carthusians, 3:195

Cartwright, Thomas, 3:638, 646

Catholic Action, 3:643

Caulet, François Étienne, 3:296

Cavour, Camillo Benso di, 3:313,
314

Charlemagne, 1:122–123, 3:166,
634–635, 8:480, 558

Chile, 3:486–487, 5:328, 7:999

Church of Jesus Christ of the Latter
Day Saints, 3:653

Church property, 3:656–657, 662,
727

Church and State (continued)
  civil authority, 1:922
  civil religion, 3:755–757
  Clarendon Constitutions, 3:72, 762
  clericalism, 3:802
  Cologne mixed marriage dispute, 3:845–846
  Commission of the Bishops' Conferences of the European Community (COMECE), 4:13–15
  common good, 4:16–22
  conciliarism, 3:636, 4:55
  Congregational churches, 3:638, 640, 647, 650, 4:115
  Conrad of Gelnhausen, 3:636
  conscientious objection, 3:660, 661
  constitutionalism, 3:640–641
  Costa Rica, 4:289–290
  Counter Reformation, 4:312, 313–314
  covenant theology, 3:646
  Croatia, 4:371–372
  Cuba, 4:418–421, 7:999
  Cyrus II (King of Persia), 3:631
  Czech Republic, 4:483–484, 484–488
  Dante Alighieri, 1:675, 3:636
  Darius I, the Great (King of Persia), 3:631
  Davies, Samuel, 3:646
  Decius (Roman Emperor), 3:632
  deism, 3:639
  democracy, 3:640–641
  Denmark, 4:665
  Diocletian persecution, 3:632
  Divine right of kings, 3:637
  donatism, 3:632
  Dupanloup, Félix Antoine Philibert (Bp. of Orléans), 3:641
  Ecuador, 5:65–66
  Ecumenical Patriarchate, 4:196–197
  Egypt, 3:630
  England, 7:472
    Charles II (King of England), 2:502, 3:648
    Convocations of Canterbury/York, 4:243–244
    De heretico comburendo act (1401), 4:550
    Edward I (King of England), 2:502, 3:636, 803
    Henry II (King of England), 3:636
    James II (King of England), 3:648
  Enlightenment, 3:54, 639, 640, 5:257
  Erastus, 5:318

Eusebius of Caesarea, 3:633
evolution, 3:667
False Decretals (Pseudo-Isidorian forgeries), 3:635
Ferdinand I (King of Portugal), 11:534
flag salutes, 3:661–662
France, 7:472, 9:723, 824
  Assemblies of the French Clergy, 1:788
  Concordat of 1801, 4:61–63
  Concordat of Fontainebleau, 4:63–64
  La Congrégation, 4:113
  Declaration of the French Clergy, 4:591
  Francis I, 3:639, 4:312
  Louis XIV (King of France), 4:591
  Philip IV the Fair (King of France), 2:502, 503, 3:636, 727, 803
Frederick I Barbarossa (Holy Roman Emperor), 3:636, 7:42–43
Frederick II the Great (Holy Roman Emperor), 3:636, 639
Free Churches views, 5:928
French Revolution, 3:92, 441, 472, 617, 640, 753–754
fundamentalism, 3:638
Gaston, William Joseph, 3:652
Gelasian Letter, 6:119–120
Germany
  Diepenbrock, Melchior von, 4:741
  Geissel, Johannes von, 6:119
  Hirscher, Johann on, 6:861
  investiture, 6:176–177
  Kulturkampf, 8:253–256
  Nazism, 3:642
  Otto I, 6:175–176
Gerson, Jean, 3:636
Ghibelline-Guelf conflict, 1:257, 943, 3:778, 853–856
Giles of Rome, 3:636
Gomułka, Władysław, 11:451
Gratian (Roman Emperor), 3:632
Greece, ancient, 3:630–631, 634
Gregorian reform, 3:600–601, 635
Guatemala, 6:554
Haiti, 12:377
Henry II (King of England), 3:636
Henry IV (Holy Roman Emperor), 1:100, 3:635, 639, 7:43
Henry V (Holy Roman Emperor), 7:43

Henry Heinbuche of Langenstein, 3:636
Heraclius (Byzantine Emperor), 3:634
Hincmar of Reims (Abp.), 3:634
Hobbes, Thomas, 3:638
Holy Alliance, 7:17
Hooker, Richard, 3:638, 7:91–92
Hooker, Thomas, 3:647
Humbert of Silva Candida (Card.), 3:635
Hungary, 7:216–217, 219–223, 9:650
Isidore of Seville, St., 3:634
Israel, 7:657–658
Italy, 9:152, 753, 14:481–482
  Conon, 4:128
  Lateran Pacts (1985), 8:357–360
  Risorgimento, 12:253–255
  20th century, 7:673, 673–674
James II (King of England), 3:648
Jansenism, 3:639, 753, 7:719
Jefferson, Thomas, 3:641, 652
Jehovah's Witnesses, 3:661
John of Paris, 3:636
Johnson, Lyndon Baines, 1:358
Jonas (Bp. of Orléans), 3:634
Judaism, 3:631
jurisdictional conflict, 8:295
Justinian I the Great (Byzantine Emperor), 2:820–821, 851, 3:633, 634
Knox, John, 3:638
Korea, 8:238–239
Kuwait, 8:258–259
Lamennais, F., 8:309
Lanfranc (Abp. of Canterbury), 4:243
Laos, 8:330–331
Latin Averroism, 1:937
Latvia, 8:375–377
Laud, William (Abp. of Canterbury), 3:645
liberalism, 1:914, 3:618–619, 640–643
Liberia, 8:552–553
Liechtenstein, 8:562–563
Lithuania, 8:605, 606, 607–608
Locke, John, 3:638, 646
Louis I (the Pious) (Holy Roman Emperor), 5:615
Luther, Martin, 3:637
Lutheranism, 8:894
Machiavelli, Niccolò, 3:637
Malawi, 9:68
marriage, 3:644, 845–846
Marsilius of Padua, 3:636, 637

Mennonites, 3:652

Mexico, 7:999, 9:576–586, 726, 11:395

Middle Ages, 3:634–637, 4:638–640, 13:253

Moravian Church, 3:648

Murray, John Courtney (Father), 3:643

Nantes, Edict of (1598), 3:639

Native North Americans, 3:663–664

Nazism, 3:642

Nicaea Councils, 3:632

Nicholas I (Emperor of Russia), 12:424

Nicholas II (Emperor of Russia), 12:424

Nicholas of Cusa (Card.), 3:636

oaths, 3:646, 648–649, 651, 652

Old Testament, 1:123

papal legates, 8:450–452, 451

parousia (return of Christ), 3:631

Penn, William, 3:641, 648, 651

Persia, 3:631

Peru, 11:164–165

Philippines, 6:658

 Church-State separation, under U.S., 11:258

 colonial period, 11:257

 during Philippine Revolution, 11:254

Pithou, Pierre, 3:639

Plato (Greek philosopher), 3:631

Pobedonostev, Konstantin Petrovich, 12:424

Poland, 11:451, 452

popes

 Adrian I, 1:122–123

 Alexander IV, 3:636

 Benedict XIII (Antipope), 2:246

 Boniface VIII, 1:207, 898, 2:501, 502–503, 3:636, 727, 803

 Clement IV, 3:778

 Clement V, 3:779

 Clement XI, 3:788–789

 Gelasius I, 1:122, 922, 3:595, 633–634, 643

 Gregory I the Great, 3:635, 6:481

 Gregory II, 3:635

 Gregory III, 3:635

 Gregory IX, 7:44

 Gregory VII, 1:100, 3:635, 7:43

 Gregory XIII, 6:501, 503

 Gregory XVI, 6:508

 Innocent XI (Pope), 4:591

 Innocent III, 3:636, 7:43–44

Innocent IV, 2:501, 3:636, 7:44

John Paul II, 3:643, 4:487–488, 7:999–1000

John XXIII, 3:642–643, 7:937

Leo I the Great, 3:633

Leo III, 3:635

Leo IX, 3:635

Leo X, 8:487

Leo XIII, 3:642, 7:346–347, 8:492

Nicholas I, 3:635

Nicholas II, 7:43

Pius IX, 3:642

Pius V, 11:374

Pius VI, 11:376

Pius X, 3:642, 4:63, 11:390–391

Pius XI, 3:642, 11:394–395

Pius XII, 2:502

Simplicius, 3:633

Symmachus, 3:633

Portugal, 7:402, 11:539

 Sancho I (King of Portugal), 11:534

 Sancho II (King of Portugal), 11:534

Pradt, El Abate de, 11:577–578

prayer, 3:666–667, 668

pre-Roman world, 3:630–631

Presbyterianism, 3:638

proprietary churches, 3:600, 725

 Belgium, 2:216

 conflicts with laity, 8:294

 Czech lands, 4:479

 England, 5:240

 Gregorian reform, 6:472

proselytism and proselytizing, 3:661

Prussia, 8:253–255

Puritanism, 3:638, 640, 645

Quakers (Religious Society of Friends), 3:646, 647, 648, 651, 652

rationalism, 3:639, 640

Reformation, 3:612, 637–639, 640

Remigius of Lyons, St., 12:107

Renaissance, 3:637, 4:376–377

Richer, Edmond, 3:639, 753, 12:239

Russia

 Doukhobors, 4:886–887

 Holy Synod, 7:53–54

 Peter I, 11:182

 Russian Orthodox Church, 7:53–54

sabbath, 3:662

schism, 3:657–658

Sedulius Scotus, 3:634

17th-18th century overview, 3:615

Smaragdus of Saint-Mihiel, 3:634

social contract, 3:635, 639

South Africa, 13:360–361

Soviet Union, 2:745, 3:642

Spain, 3:204, 11:248, 13:393–394, 395, 397–399

 Philip II (King of Spain), 3:639

States of the Church, 3:637, 641, 642

Suárez, Francisco, 3:639

Syria, 3:631

Theodosius I (Roman Emperor), 3:632

totalitarianism, 3:642

Trent, Council of, 3:638

trusteeism, 3:656

Unam sanctam, 2:503, 3:603, 636

Vatican Council I, 1:914

Vatican Council II, 1:356–357, 3:642–643, 644

Venezuela, 6:559

Vietnam, 8:385, 835

Westminster Confession, 3:647

Westphalia, Peace of, 3:639

William of Ockham, 3:636

Williams, Roger, 3:647, 648

works of charity, 1:303

World War I, 3:642, 660

Wyclif, John, 3:636

Wyszyński, Stefan (Card.), 11:451, 452

Zabarella, Francesco, 3:636

Zambia, 14:907–908

Zeno (Byzantine Emperor), 2:851, 3:634

Zoroastrianism, 3:631

Zwingli, Huldrych, 3:638

See also Caesaropapism; Church and State, Canon Law; Church and State, U.S.; Civil Constitution of the Clergy; Concordat of 1801 (France); Education and State; Febronianism; Gallicanism; Holy Roman Empire; Investiture struggle; Josephinism; Laicism; Roman Empire; Roman persecution era; specific countries; specific popes and rulers

Church and State, Canon Law, 3:635–636, 643–645

John Murray's defense of views, 10:68

non expedit policy, 10:415–416

Thomistic doctrine of separation of, 14:46

Vatican Council I, 14:404

Church and State, U.S., 3:640, 641, 644,
645–669

    Americans United for Separation of
    Church and State, 1:356–357

    Blaine Amendment, 2:425–427,
    3:653, 654, 660

    colonial period, 3:645–649

    Connecticut, 3:647, 650

    Delaware, 3:649

    disestablishment period (1776-1834),
    3:649–653

    Georgia, 3:646, 652

    Maryland, 3:641, 649, 651–652

    Massachusetts, 3:646–647, 650

    New Hampshire, 3:647–648, 651

    New Jersey, 3:648, 651

    New York, 3:648, 651

    19th century, 3:653–659

    North Carolina, 3:646, 652

    Oregon School Case, 2:429,
    10:646–650, 11:530

    Pennsylvania, 3:641, 648–649, 650,
    651

    Rhode Island, 3:641, 648, 650, 651

    South Carolina, 3:646, 652

    20th century, 3:659–668

    Virginia, 3:641, 645–646, 652

The Church and the Country Community
(O'Hara), 10:566

The Church and the Second Sex (Daly),
5:677

Church architecture, **3:669–718**

    altars, 1:316, 317, 318, 3:671, 705,
    711, 712, 715

    ambos, 1:334–336

    ambries, 1:347–348

    baptisteries, 2:75

    basilicas, 2:145–148

    belfries, 2:232

    Catholic revival, 4:313

    cornerstone, 4:271

    diaconicum, 4:720

    doors, 4:871–874, *872*

    early church, 1:752, 754, 756–757,
    3:683–686, 699

    fish as symbol of Christ, 5:746–747

    form, 3:678–681

    grass churches (Hawaii), 6:*668*

    house churches, 2:145–146

    iconography, 1:576, 12:598–602,
    14:205

    liturgy, 3:669–672, 684–685, 710,
    711, 712, 715, 716, 717

    rococo, 3:675, 679, 707–708

    sacristy, 12:522

    social and cultural considerations,
    3:669

    stained glass, 13:472–473

    structure, 3:676–678

    symbolism, 1:576, 3:630, 672–676,
    688, 694, 812

    See also Baroque architecture;
    Cistercians, art and architecture of;
    Cluniac art and architecture; Gothic
    architecture; Medieval architecture;
    Renaissance architecture;
    Romanesque architecture; *specific
    cathedrals and churches*

Church architecture, history of

    arrangement of shrines and relics,
    13:93

    identified as Mozarabic, 10:47

    Leubus Abbey, 8:520

    Lincoln, Ancient See of, 8:592

    liturgical reform, 8:626

    Magistri Comacini, 9:39

    modern art, 8:627

    modern radical innovations,
    8:622–623

    relics of the Passion, 13:89–90

    Silos Abbey, 13:121

    term sacred, 8:618

Church at Jerusalem, 3:546

Church cantatas (Bach), 2:7

Church Dogmatics (Barth), 2:120–121,
10:238, 14:197

Church Fathers

    exegesis on parables of Jesus,
    10:865, 867–868

    tradition in theology, 14:135

    unicity of God, 14:296

Church government, monarchical
episcopate and, 9:781

Church hierarchy

    Apostolic Fathers, 1:588

    theology of Church, 3:586, 587–588

Church History (Eusebius of Caesarea),
10:962

Church History (Milner), 10:332

*Church History of England from 1500 to
1688* (Tootell), 14:111

The Church Incarnate (Schwarz), 3:672

Church membership, 2:77, 80, 221, 6:4

Church membership, U.S., **3:718–721**

Church Missionary Society, 5:472

Church Missionary Society (Anglican),
7:403

Church Music Association of the United
States, 8:704

Church music reform, 14:604, 646–647

Church of Annunciation (Nazareth),
10:*778*

Church of Athens, 6:435

Church of Christ (China), 3:501

Church of Christ, Scientist. *See* Christian
Science (Church of Christ, Scientist)

Church of Christ the King (Seattle),
3:671

Church of England

    comparative liturgics, 8:723

    Hooker, Richard, 7:90–92

    justification, 8:87

    latitudinarianism, 8:370

    liturgical calendar, 8:644

    low church, 8:836

    moral theology, 8:181–182

    Roman practices, 8:226

    Thirty-Nine Articles, 14:7–8

    in the United States, 5:295–296

    women deacons, 4:554

    women in priesthood, 7:203

    See also Anglicanism

Church of God (Abrahamic Faith), 1:135

Church of Ireland, 7:555–556

Church of Jerusalem, 5:105

Church of Jesus Christ of Latter-day
Saints, 10:169, 277–278, 14:356,
356–357

    adventism, 1:135

    Church-State relations, 3:653,
    654–655

    U.S. church membership, 3:719, 720

Church of New France, 3:4

Church of North India, 7:403

Church of Our Lady of the Assumption
(Palayakottai, India), 7:*398*

Church of Resurrection (St. Louis),
3:671

Church of S. Apollinare Nuovo
(Ravenna, Italy), 11:*28*, 932–933

Church of S. Vitale (Ravenna, Italy),
11:933

Church of St. Agnese (Rome), 2:*110*

Church of St. Euphemia, 5:449

Church of St. Gall (Prague), 6:*65*

Church of Saint John (Byblos), 2:*723*

Church of Saint Joseph (Nazareth),
10:*217*

Church of Saint Maryam (Lalibal,
Ethiopia), 5:*402*

Church of Saint Remi (Reims, France),
12:*36*, 37

Church of Saint Sebastian (Kerala,
India), 7:*396*

Church of Saints Cosmas and Damian
(Rome), 5:668, *668*

Church of San Francesco frescoes
(Assisi, Italy), 6:230, *231, 232*

Church of San Ignazio (Rome), 2:113–114

Church of San Philippo (Nagasaki, Japan), 7:741

Church of San Sepolcro (Bologna, Italy), 7:668

Church of Scientology, Belgian concern of, 2:220

Church of Scotland, **12:828–829**

Church of Seventh Day Adventists (Chicago), 1:135

Church of South India, 5:72, 7:403, 8:678–679

Church of the Apostles (Constantinople), 1:574–575, 576, 5:759

Church of the Apostles (Milan), 1:575

Church of the Ascension, 3:677–678

Church of the Assumption (Cologne), 3:845

Church of the Brethren (Dunkers), 2:606, 3:652, **721–722**, 12:261

Church of the Brothers of St. Anthony (Cologne), 3:844

Church of the Czech Bretheren. *See* Moravian Church

Church of the Holy Child (Jacksonville, NC), 11:899

Church of the Holy Ghost (Wolfsburg, Germany), 3:697

Church of the Holy Sepulcher (Jerusalem), 7:797

Church of the Holy Sepulcher (Old City, Jersualem), 12:925

Church of the Nazarene, **3:722**, 7:7

Church of the Resurrection (St. Louis), 3:716

Church of the United Brethern in Christ, 5:471

Church of the United Brethren, 10:711

The Church of the Word Incarnate (L'Église du Verbe incarné) (Jounet), 7:1058

Church Progress (periodical), 10:806

Church property, **3:723–728**
  Canon Law, 3:644
  Church-State relations, 3:656–657, 662, 727
  early church, 3:723–725
  lay interference, 8:294
  Middle Ages, 2:496, 3:603, 604, 725–727
  midwestern United States, 3:734–735
  proprietary churches, 3:725
  secularization, 3:727, 843, 845
  See also Charity, works of; Papal taxation

Church rectors, 11:957

Church reform
  Contarini, Gasparo, 4:202
  Gregorian, 10:257, 836, 857–858
  impact on monasteries by Cluniac, 10:719
  Mysterium fidei (''Mystery of the Faith'') on liturgical, 10:77–79
  need for, 4:309
  ordination rites by Clement VIII, 10:640
  ordination rites by John XXIII (Pope), Bl., 10:640
  papacy development during 1536, 10:842–843
  Patarine campaign for, 10:940–942
  Vatican Council II, 10:43, 564, 640
  See also Counter Reformation; The Reformation

Church Truth (Ekklesiastike Alethia), 6:459–460

Church World Service (CWS), 10:166

Churches. *See* Church architecture; *specific churches*

Churches, neighborhood. *See* Basic Christian communities

Churches in Covenant Communion: the Church of Christ Uniting (COCU), 4:200

Churches of Christ, 5:468

Churches Together in Britain and Ireland (CTBI), 2:622

Churches Uniting in Christ (CUIC), 4:200

The Churches' Year of Grace (Parsch), 10:903

The Church-Idea, An Essay Towards Unity (Huntington), 5:299

Churchill, Thomas, 3:111, 7:699

Church's Missionary Activity, Decree on the (Ad gentes) (Vatican Council II), 5:480, 741

Churriguera, José, 3:706, 707

Chylinski, Rafał Melchoir, Bl., **3:728**

Chymische Hochzeit (Andrea), 12:382

Chytraeus, David, 4:60

Ci riesce (Pius XII), 3:642

Ciampi, Mario, 3:716

Ciasca, Agostino, 1:889, **3:728**

Cibo, Giovanni Battista (Card.). *See* Innocent VIII (Pope)

Ciboria, **3:728–729**, 8:631–632

Cibot, Pierre Martial, **3:729**

CIC. *See* Catholic Interracial Councils; Code of Canon Law (CIC) (1983)

Cicé, Marie Adelaide de, 6:682

Cicero, Marcus Tullius, **3:729–730**
  Aelred, St., 1:138

Aristotelianism, 1:673

Augustine, St., 1:852, 3:729, 730

Canon Law, 3:36

common good, 4:17

conscience, 4:143

divination, 4:784

dreams, 4:903

eclecticism, 5:47

friendship, 6:7

logical history, 8:749

moral circumstances, 3:742

natural law doctrine, 10:180

natural law in political thought, 10:201

Platonism, 11:412–413

political authority, 13:239

Cicognani, Amleto Giovanni (Card.), 1:585, **3:730**, 13:175

Ciconia, Johannes, **3:731**

Los Cículos de estudios sociales (Franceschi), 5:864

CIDOC (Centro Intercultural de Documentación), 9:583–584

Ciempozuelos (Spain), Martyrs of, 7:124–125

La Ciencia Tomista (periodical), 12:774

Cienfuegos, Álvaro, **3:731–732**

Cienfuegos, José Ignacio (Bp.), **3:732**

Cieplak, Jan (Abp.), **3:732**, 12:429

Cilicia of the Armenians, Patriarchate of, **3:731–732**
  See also Armenia

Cimabue. *See* Bencivieni di Pepo

Cimabue, Giovanni (Cenni di Pepo)
  Female Saint (fresco painting), 12:598
  Vasari, Giorgio, 12:111
  Villani, Filippo, 12:110

Cimarosa, Domenico, 3:733, **733–734**

Cimatti, Maria Raffaella, Bl., **3:734**

Cimatti, Vicenzo, 3:99

Les cimetrìres sacrés (Spondanus), 13:459

Cincinnati Archdiocese (OH), **3:734–738**, 10:569–570
  bankruptcy action, 5:145
  Brothers of the Poor of St. Francis, 12:546–547
  diocesan synod, 5:145
  Lasance, F. X., 8:340
  provincial council, 5:145

Cincture, 8:633

Cingoli, Gentile da, 1:675

Cingria, Alexandre, 3:711

Cinq grandes odes (Claudel), 3:768

Cinthius, Sanctes, 3:328

Cinti, Giacomo. *See* James Cinti de Cerqueto, Bl.

Cipitria y Barriola, Cándida María de Jesús, Bl., **3:738–739**

Cipo Zhenke, 3:511

Ciquard, François, 12:227

Circa modum praedicandi (Fifth Lateran Council), 11:613–614

Circles of the Living Rosary, 8:246

Circuit riders, 9:560–561, 14:541

Circular letters, 11:748

Círculo de Cultura Cristiana (Circle of Christian Culture), 12:281

Circumcellions, 4:862, 864

Circumcision, *3:739*, **739–741**, *740*
  al-Kindī refutation, 8:170
  covenant, 4:327
  feasts, 3:556
  Islam, 7:610
  justification, 8:79
  prohibition by Hadrian, 2:83
  replaced by baptism, 2:59

Circumcision, Feast of the, 5:654

Circumincession, **3:741–742**

Circumstances, moral, **3:742–743**
  end justifying the means, 5:212–213
  sins, 13:152

Las Circunstancias sociales de Pío XI (Franceschi), 5:864

Cirer Carbonnel, Francinaina, Bl., **3:743–744**

Cirilo Bertrán, Br., 14:247–248

Cisalpine Club, 5:183

Cisneros, Francisco (Card.), 14:435

Cisneros, García de, **3:744**

Cistercian Monastery of Les Feuillants (Toulouse, France), 5:707

Cistercian Nuns, **3:744–745**, 10:620–621

Cistercian Order of the Strict Obervance, 14:161

Cistercian Rite, **3:745–746**, 4:837, 838

Cistercians, **3:746–749**
  12th-century increase, 3:601
  Abbots, 1:10
  Anacletus II (Antipope), 1:370
  Ancient See of Carlisle, 3:124
  Austria, 1:910
  Benedictine Rule, 2:265
  Canada, 3:9
  Canons Regular of St. Augustine, 3:68
  Carthusian spirituality, 3:191
  Church property, 3:726

Cîteaux Abbey, 3:744, 746, 747, 748, 749, 751–752
  Cluniac reform, 3:813
  contemplation, 4:208–209
  Czech lands, 4:479
  de Lisle, Ambrose, 4:630
  Deer Abbey, 4:608
  England, 5:240
  founding, 12:268
  Germany, 5:29, 30
  Holland, 5:192
  hymns, 7:244
  Italian expansion, 7:665
  Kinloss Abbey, 8:180
  Kirkstall Abbey, 8:183
  Lucius III (Pope), 8:848
  Melleray Abbey, founding of, 9:481
  patrons, 8:799
  Poverty Movement, 11:572
  power struggle among abbeys, 8:279
  Prussia, 3:537
  Robert of Molesme and Stephen Harding, founding of, 9:792
  San Galgano Abbey, 12:650
  San Giovanni Abbey, 12:651
  Simon of Aulne, 13:131
  Sora Abbey, 13:325
  soul, 13:343
  Spain, 5:751
  works of charity, 3:412
  See also Feuillants; Trappists; *specific people*

Cistercians, art and architecture of, **3:749–751**, 750–751, 4:450, 12:601

Ciszek, Walter J., 7:793

Cîteaux, Order of, 8:195

Cîteaux Abbey (France), 3:744, 746, 747, 748, 749, **751–752**
  first daughter abbey, 8:279
  founded, 5:844
  Robert of Molesme, St., founder of, 12:268

Citizens Organized for Political Service (COPs), 12:642, 643

Citizenship
  rights and duties, 13:481
  Vitoria, Francisco de, 14:571

Cittadini, Caterina, Bl., **3:752**

Il Cittadino di Brescia (newspaper), 14:128

City of Boerne v. Flores (1997), 3:664

City of God (Porphyry), 12:327

The City of God (St. Augustine). *See De civitate Dei* (St. Augustine)

City of Struthers, Martin v. (1943), 3:661

The City of the Sun (Campanella), 1:667, 14:360

Civezza, Marcellino da, **3:752**

Cividale, Synod of (796), 11:38

Civil authority, 1:921–922, 3:631

Civil Constitution of the Clergy (France, 1790), 3:617, 640, **753–754**
  Angers, 1:432
  Bernier, Étienne Alexandre, 2:324
  Boisgelin de Cucé, Jean de Dieu, Raymond de, 2:462
  Bonal, François de, 2:477
  Brothers of the Christian Schools, 2:632
  Caprara, Giovanni Battista, 3:92
  Chartres, 3:441
  Cheverus, Jean Louis Lefebvre de, 3:472
  Clermont-Tonnerre, Anne Antoine Jules de, 3:804
  Concordat of 1801, 4:62, 63
  Coudrin, Pierre Marie Joseph, 4:293
  Émery condemnation of, 5:190
  enactment, 5:853
  Fesch, Joseph (Card.), 5:699
  Fournet, André Hubert, St., 5:835
  French Revolution, 5:972, 12:276–278
  Gallicanism, 6:77
  Grégoire, Henri Baptiste, 6:462
  laicism, 8:282
  Loménie de Brienne, 8:770
  Marty, Antoine, 12:279
  martyrs of Laval, 8:384
  martyrs of Paris, 10:884
  oath taken by Joseph Fesch, 10:146
  Pius VI (Pope), 10:845, 846
  religious liberalism, 8:541
  Romagné, James René, 12:297

Civil disobedience, **3:754–755**, 6:87

Civil Disobedience (Thoreau), 3:755, 14:147, 149

Civil justice, 9:211

Civil religion, **3:755–757**

Civil Rights Movement
  African American Catholics, 1:160–161
  Arkansas, 1:693

Civil society, 8:36

Civil War, U.S. *See* American Civil War (1861-65)

Civil wars. *See specific countries; specific wars*

Civilization, culture as term and, 4:427

The Civilization of Christianity (McKenzie), 9:402

La Civiltà Cattolica (periodical), **3:757–758**, 7:788, 8:550, 12:774

Civis (citizen), 8:296

Civitas Dei concept, 10:716

Civories, 1:317

Claggett, Thomas John (Bp. of Maryland), 5:297

Clairvaux Abbey (France), 1:327, 3:746, 748, 751, **758**, 14:517

Clairvoyance, spiritual, **3:758–759**, 13:100

Clancy, Thady, 7:580

Clancy, Visitation Bridget (Mother), 12:551

Clapham Sect, 3:372

Clara, Jerónimo Emiliano, 1:*652*, **3:759**

Clare, Mary Frances. *See* Cusack, Margaret Anna

Clare Gambacorta, Bl., **3:759–760**

Clare of Assisi, St., **3:760**
   Agnes of Bohemia, St., 4:479
   Franciscan spirituality, 5:892, 893–894
   Franciscan theology, 5:898
   Poor Clares, 11:494
   rule of, 12:288

Clare of Montefalco, St., 1:872, 888, **3:760–761**

Clare of Rimini, Bl., **3:761**

Clarenbaud of Arras, **3:761–762**
   Boethius, 2:457, 3:761
   cathedral and episcopal schools, 3:441
   Latin literature, 9:453
   School of Chartres, 12:758

Clarendon Constitutions, 3:72, **762**

Clareni, 1:428, 3:762, **762–763**, 5:921

Clareno, Angelo, 13:129

Claret, Anthony Mary, St., **3:763**, 764, 835, 12:659

Claret de la Touche, Louise, **3:763**

Claretian martyrs, Spanish Civil War, 2:91–92

Claretians, 3:621, 763, **764–765**

Clari, Robert de, 4:401

Clarís Vilaregut, Wenceslao María, 2:92

Claritus, Bl., **3:765**

Clark, Alan (Bp. of East Anglia), 1:440

Clark, Francis, 3:535

Clark, Gordon, 5:473

Clark, Mark, 1:356

Clark, Robert B., 3:286–287

Clark, Stephen, 1:456

Clarke (Abp. of Kingston), 3:113

Clarke, Catherine Goddard, 5:663, 664

Clarke, John, 2:79

Clarke, Mary Frances (Mother), 3:*765*, **765**

Clarke, Maura, 8:133

Clarke, R. F., 12:775

Clarke, Richard, 1:351

Clarke, Samuel, **3:766**

Clarorum virorum epistolae (Letters of Famous Men) (Reuchlin), 5:306

Clarus, St., **3:766**

Class distinction
   Church property, 6:175
   Corinthians Epistles, 4:267
   Crusades, 4:409
   democracy, 4:638, 639, 641

Classes, logical, 13:407–408

Classical cyclicism, 6:882

Classical music, 2:451

Classical Republicans, 4:640–641

Classici auctores (Mai), 9:50

Clauberg, J., 3:184

Claude (Duke of Guise), 6:577

Claudel, Paul Louis, 3:711, **766–769**, *767*, 5:857

Claudian (Latin poet), 12:110, 320

Claudianus, Mamertus, 3:208, **769**, 5:651

Claudin. *See* Sermisy, Claude de

Claudius (Bp. of Turin), 3:258, 9:444

Claudius I (Tiberius Claudius Drusus Nero Germanicus) (Roman Emperor), 12:304

Claudius II (Marcus Aurelius Claudius) (Roman Emperor), 12:312

Claudius and Companions, SS., **3:770**

Claudius of Condat, St., **3:769**, 12:542

Claudius of Turin (Bp.), **3:769–770**, 5:783

Claudius Ptolemaeus. *See* Ptolemy (Greek astronomer)

Clauson, Zorach v. (1952), 3:666

Claustral priors, 11:716

Clave historical (Flórez), 5:775

Claver, Peter, St., 3:417, **770–771**, *771*, 851, 8:195–196, 12:280

Claverie, Pierre (Bp. of Oran), 1:286

Clavigero, Francisco Javier, **3:771**

Clavis Prophetarum (Vieira), 14:489

Clavis regia sacerdotum casuum conscientae sive theologiae moralis thesauri (Sayer), 12:716

Clavis scripturae sacrae (Flacius Illyricus), 6:787

Clavius, Christopher, **3:771–772**, *772*, 6:60, 7:782, 12:223, 399

Claxton (Clarkson), James, Bl., 5:230

Claxton, Henry. *See* Morse, Henry, St.

Cleary, Patrick (Bp. of Hanzhong), 3:864

Cledonomancy, 4:785

Clemency, **3:772**

Clemens, Flavius, 3:592

Clemens, Franz Jacob, 12:774

Clemens, Joseph (Abp. of Cologne), 3:843

Clemens Non Papa, Jacobus, **3:772–773**, 8:342

Clemens Wenzeslaus (Abp. of Trier), **3:773**

Clement (pseudosaint). *See* Aldebert and Clement (pseudosaints)

Clement, Caesar, **3:773**

Clement, Epistles of, 3:774–775
   Apostles, 3:29, 30
   apostolic succession, 1:591
   canonicity, 3:22, 31
   Christian way of life, 3:546–547
   Church history, 3:591–592
   discovery, 2:652
   Old Testament, 3:29

Clement I (Pope), St., **3:773–775**, *774*
   anchor symbolism, 1:396
   as Apostolic Father, 1:587
   biblical canon, 3:26
   Dionysius of Corinth, 4:755
   ecclesiastical archives, 1:636
   Gauderich of Velletri, 6:111
   hospitality, 7:118
   martyrs and martyrdom, 9:227
   nature of Church government, 10:830–831
   presbyters, 11:673
   works of charity, 3:402, 405
   See also Apostolic Fathers; Clement, Epistles of

Clement II (Pope), **3:775–776**, 6:745–746

Clement III (Antipope), **3:777–778**
   Anselm II of Lucca, St., 1:494
   Carthusians, 3:193
   Council of Autun, 1:926, 927
   Henry IV, 6:746, 7:43
   Hugh of Remiremont, 7:155

Clement III (Pope), 1:222, 3:319, 324, **776–777**, 11:666

Clement IV (Pope), **3:778**
   Adrian V (Pope), 1:127
   Cistercians, 3:748, 751
   Holy Name, 7:31
   intervention in sentencing of Naḥmanides, 10:135

Clement IV (Pope) *(continued)*
  papal provision, 3:602
  Roger Bacon, 12:284
Clement V (Pope), **3:778–780**, *779*
  Avignon papacy, 1:943, 3:603, 780,
    12:357
  Beguines and Beghards, 2:205
  cardinalate, 3:105, 106
  Chinese mission, 3:492–493
  coinage, 10:481
  Corpus Christi feast, 4:272
  decretal legislation, 3:46, 48, 800
  Durandus of Saint-Pourçain, 4:947
  election, 5:846
  Frédol, Bérenger, 5:928
  Ghibelline-Guelf conflict, 3:854
  hospitals, 7:129
  Jacques de Molay, 7:693
  liturgical language, 8:668
  papal taxation, 1:466
  Philip IV (King of France), 2:503,
    3:779, 11:246
  poverty, 11:570
  reform of Church in France, 1:898
  Salamanca University and, 12:611
  taxes, 3:803
  Templars, 1:194–195, 3:603, 779,
    13:804–805
  Vienne, Council of (1311-1312),
    14:489
Clement VI (Pope), **3:780–781**, *781*
  Cenacle, 3:333
  Chaise-Dieu Abbey, 3:362
  Fécamp Abbey, 5:659
  flagellation, prohibition of, 5:755
  Holy Year, 7:57
  Jansenism, 5:851, 12:454
  Olivetan Benedictines, approval of,
    2:274
  Rienzo, Cola di, 3:780, 828
Clement VII (Antipope), **3:783–784**
  Avignon papacy, 5:846
  Boniface IX (Pope), 2:504
  Charles VI, 4:136
  Contarini, Gasparo, 4:202
  Despenser, Henry, 4:692–693
  election, 5:846
  Low Countries denial of claims,
    10:258
  reform, 4:310
  See also Western Schism (1378-
    1417)
Clement VII (Pope), **3:781–783**, *782*
  Acciaioli, Angelo, 1:58
  Acquaviva, Claudius, 1:72

Barnabites, approval of, 2:103
Bascio, Matteo Serafini da, 2:132
Castel Sant'Angelo, 3:213
Castiglione, Baldassare, 3:215
Charles V (Holy Roman Emperor),
  3:430, 609, 781, 782
conciliarism, 3:609
Congregation for Matters of the Holy
  Faith and Catholic Religion and,
  5:21
dueling, 4:929
Ethiopia, 1:325
Forty Hours devotion, 5:435
Ghibelline-Guelf conflict, 3:855
Henry VIII's divorce, 12:7–8
Holy Name feast, 7:32
Index of Prohibited Books, 7:390
indulgences, 7:438
Łaski, J., 8:342
Last Judgment (Michaelangelo),
  commission of, 2:111
League of Cognac, 7:669
Michelangelo Buonarroti, 9:603
papacy development under, 10:842
Peter of Ailly, 11:193
sack of Rome, 3:268, 430, 781–782
Shroud of Turin, 13:96
Western Schism, 14:691–693
works of charity, 3:418
Clement VIII (Antipope), **3:785–786**
  See also Western Schism (1378-
    1417)
Clement VIII (Pope), **3:784–785**
  archpriest controversy, 1:642, 3:785
  Baronius, Caesar, 2:106
  Bellarmine, St. Robert, 2:227
  Canon Law, 3:53
  catechesis, 3:234
  Church in England, 5:247
  Church union with Kiev, 12:422
  Clerks Regular of the Mother of
    God, 3:803
  Congregatio, 4:110, 111–112
  Congregation for the Propagation of
    the Faith, 11:749
  Congregation of Claustrales,
    reformation of, 2:272
  de auxiliis controversy, 4:111–112,
    6:404
  Discalced Carmelites, 3:145
  ecclesiastical archives, 1:636
  efficacious grace dispute, 8:466–467
  family, 1:246
  Gagliardi, Achille, 6:48
  Henry VIII's divorce, 6:740

Italo-Albanian Church, 7:650
James I (King of England), 1:467,
  3:785
papal decline, 3:612
Piarists, 7:1043
reform of ordination rites, 10:640
Roman Pontifical, 11:474
Ukranian Catholic Church (Eastern
  Catholic), 14:278
Union of Brest, 2:606
Vatican construction under, 14:395
Clement IX (Pope), **3:786**
  Charles of Sezze, St., 3:435
  Clement X (Pope), 3:788
  Congregation of St. George, founding
    of, 2:126
  indulgences, 7:439
  Jesuati, 7:777
Clement X (Pope), 3:368, **786–788**, *787*
Clement XI (Pope), **3:788–789**, *789*
  Albania, 1:213
  Anglican orders problem, 1:438
  appellants, 1:600
  Chinese Rites controversy, 3:514,
    515, 789
  Congregation for Editing the Books
    of the Oriental Church, 5:21
  Ellis, Philip, 5:171
  Emperor Joseph I, 10:63
  family, 1:212
  French Bourbons, 10:844
  Indian Rites controversy, 7:411–412
  Jansenism, 3:788–789, 790, 7:718,
    8:804, 10:406, 14:301–302
  Louis XIV, 8:804
  Luther's denial, 8:880
  promoter of the faith office, 4:706
  providence of God, 11:784
  Quesnel condemned, 8:804
  theological censure, 3:337
  theological error, 5:330
  works of charity, 3:417
Clement XII (Pope), **3:789–790**, *790*
  Antonines, 1:534
  Chinese rites controversy, 3:515, 790
  family background, 4:279
  Forty Hours devotion, 5:435
  secret societies, 12:857
Clement XIII (Pope), **3:790–793**
  Abondance Monastery, 1:24
  catechesis, 3:244
  Caulites, 3:296
  Hontheim, Johann Kikolaus von,
    7:90
  Jesuit expulsion, Portugal, 11:467

Jesuit suppression, 7:787

Jesuits, defenders of, 12:222

Tanucci, Bernardo, 13:754

Clement XIV (Pope), **3:793–797**, *794*

Antonines, 1:534

Apostolic Penitentiary, 11:76

Cordell, Charles, 4:260

Cuxa Abbey, 4:450

Garampi, Giuseppe, 6:92

Jesuit expulsion, Portugal, 11:467

Jesuit suppression, 7:787, 12:426

Passsionists, 10:931

Pontificia Facoltà Teological "San Bonaventura," 11:490

suppression of Jesuits, 2:218, 3:92, 265, 615, 794–796, 12:221–223

Tanucci, Bernardo, 13:754–755

Clement of Alexandria, St., 3:797, **797–799**, 5:293, 11:*282*, 290

Alexander of Jerusalem, St., 1:266

anchor symbolism, 1:396

apologetics, 1:567

Arnobius the Elder, 1:717

Berossus, 2:329

Bible texts, 2:366

biblical canon, 3:30–31

bilocation, 2:397

Carpocrates, 3:174

casuistry, 3:220

catechumenate, 3:250

causality, 3:303

charity, 3:395

Christian paideia, 10:755

Christmas, 3:551

Christocentrism, 3:558

Christology, 3:560

clerical celibacy and marriage, 3:323

cult of Magna Mater, 10:92

descent of Christ into hell, 4:684

devotion to Trinity, 14:205

docetism, 4:797

Epistle of Barnabas, 2:102, 103

exegetical works, 5:510

faith, 5:594

Gnosis, 6:255

Greco-Roman schooling, 6:429

ineffability of God, 7:445

John of the Cross, St., 3:136

lauds, 8:380

liturgical history, 8:651

Luke's Gospel, 8:859

luxurious dress and ornaments, 11:645

marriage procreation, 4:218

martyr, as term, 4:83

order of universe, 14:328–329

patristic theology, 10:965, 967

penitential controversy, 11:73

Platonism, 11:414

presbyters, 11:673–674

rings, 12:249

rites of Eleusinian mysteries, 10:90

School of Alexandria, 1:268, 269, 272, 3:797

schools of Athens, 1:829

similarity, 13:126

soul, 13:340

spiritual life, 13:435

spirituality, 13:444

theology of history, 6:887–888

See also Patristic era

Clement of Ireland, St., 3:160, **799**

Clement of Osimo, Bl., 1:889

Clement of Rome, St.

Holy Trinity, 14:189

Sanctus (hymn), 12:664

works of charity, 3:403, 404

Clement the Bulgarian, St., **3:799–800**

Clementinae, 3:46, 48, 50, 780, **800**, 4:273, 604

Clementine edition of the Bible, 14:596

Clementine peace (1653), 10:844

Clemintine Homilies, 4:646–647

Clenock, Maurice (Clynnog), **3:800**

Cleopas, **3:801**

Cleopatra (Queen of Egypt), 6:803

Cleray, Philip, 7:581

Clergy

celibacy, 12:14, 26, 182

clerical ranks, 5:288

concubinage, 4:64, 65, 12:14

indigenous Protestants as, 9:698

marriage, 12:14

marriage of, 4:62, 486, 488

in the Middle Ages, 9:613–614

patron of diocesan clergy, 12:387–388

salaries, 4:62

secularization, 5:258

sexual misconduct, 12:678

See also Priesthood

Clergy, indigenous

Congo, 4:105

Mexico, 4:416

Clergy, scarcity of

Ireland, 7:566

Peru, 11:162, 163

Portugal, 11:540

Zambia, 14:908–909

Clergy sex scandals, 12:678

Austria, 1:917

Bernardin, Joseph Louis, 2:319, 3:737

Boston archdiocese, 2:557

Ireland, 7:568–569

Clerical celibacy/marriage, **3:322–328**

abolishment, 12:26, 182

Altmann of Passau, St., 1:322

Bernold of Constance, 2:327

Canons Regular of St. Augustine, 3:67

Clement III (Antipope), 3:778

First Lateran Council, 2:880, 3:326

Georgian reform, 12:14

history of

dispensations from, 8:285–287

laicization, 8:285–287

Paul VI (Pope), 3:627

proprietary churches, 3:600

William I (King of England), 3:72

Wyclif, John, 3:605

Clerical dress, 3:210, **801–802**

albs, 1:211–212

Ambrosian Rite, 1:345

amices, 1:358

biretta, 2:408

Byzantine, 2:817

cassocks, 3:210, *211*

chasubles, 3:445–446, *445*

tonsure as distinguishing, 8:293

See also Liturgical vestments; Religious habits

Clerical reform (Gregorian reform), 6:471–472

Clericalism, **3:802–803**

Clericis Laicos, **3:803**, 8:293, 12:270

Clericis laicos (apostolic constitution, Boniface VIII), 2:502, 3:803

Clericis laicos (papal bull, Boniface VIII), 11:246

Cleric-laity dualism

Gratian, Jerome, 8:293, 414–415

Gregorian reform, 8:293, 294

liberation theology, 8:545

Clerics Regular of St. Paul. *See* Barnabites

Clericus, J., 1:587

Clerk, John (Bp. of Bath and Wells), **3:803**

Clerks Regular of Religious Schools. *See* Piarists

Clerks Regular of St. Paul. *See* Barnabites

Clerks Regular of Somaschi, 4:310

Clerks Regular of the Mother of God, **3:803–804**, 8:498, 499

Clermont, Council of (1095), 7:437

Clermont-Tonnerre, Anne Antoine Jules de (Card.), **3:804–805**

Clermont-Tonnerre, Isabelle de, 1:802

Cleromancy, 4:785

Clerselier, Claude, 3:185

Clerus saecularis et reularis (Schmalzgrueber), 12:741

Cletus of Bologna, 2:609

Cleveland, Grover, 10:171

Cleveland Diocese (OH), 10:570–571
    Catholic education, 5:179
    Koudelka, J. M., 8:243
    Krol, J. J., 8:249–250

Clichtove, Josse, 3:609

Clichy, synod of (626-627)
    Acharius of Noyon, St., 1:68
    Arnulf of Metz, St., 1:720

Client cults, 4:425

Clifford, John, 5:928

Clifford, R. J., 11:767

Clifford, Richard (Bp. of London), **3:805**

Climacus, John, 4:237

Clines, A. J. H., 11:98

Clinton, William, 1:35

Clitherow, Margaret, Bl., **3:805–806**, 5:229

Clodius Albinus. *See* Albinus, Decimus Clodius Septimus

Cloister, 4:210
    See also Enclosure

Cloister, Canon Law on, **3:806**

Cloning, 7:178, 178–179, 13:356

Clonmacnois Monastery (Ireland), **3:806–807**, *807*

Clorivière, Joseph Pierre Picot de, **3:807–808**
    Charleston (SC), 13:364
    Daughters of the Heart of Mary, founding of, 6:682
    Gallagher, Simon, 6:66
    Georgetown Visitation Convent, 6:147–148
    Institute of the Heart of Jesus, founding of, 6:682

Clothing
    cowl, 4:332
    discalced orders, 4:764–765
    See also Clerical dress; Liturgical vestments; Religious habits

Clotilde (Queen of the Franks), St., **3:808**, 809

Clotilde, St., 12:107, 14:126

Cloud, St., **3:808**

Cloud of Unknowing, **3:808**, 4:762
    apophatic theology, 1:568
    Carthusian spirituality, 3:192
    mysticism, 3:605, 808

The Cloud of Unknowing (anonymous), 10:118, 119

The Cloud of Unknowing (Cassian), 14:144

The Cloud of Unknowing (Hilton), 5:243, 6:835, 12:297

Clovesho, Councils of
    (747), 3:230, 240
    (803), 5:386

Clovis I (King of the Franks), 3:161, *809*, **809–811**, 6:172, 14:126
    Albi Archdiocese, 1:229
    baptism, 12:107–108
    Charlemagne, 3:421
    conversion, 3:441, 596, 809–810, 5:841, 12:107
    Deodatus of Blois, 4:672
    Merovingians, 5:916
    works of charity, 3:410

Clovis II (King of Neustria), 2:153, 12:566

Clowesites, 9:559

The Clue to Christian Education (Miller), 12:98

Cluniac art and architecture, 3:692, 750, **811–812**, 814, 815, 12:672

Cluniac reform, 2:270, 3:600, **812–814**, 5:530
    Adalbero II, 1:100
    Albert of Pontida, St., 1:222
    Anchin Abbey, 1:396
    Aribo of Mainz, 1:664
    Austria, 1:909–910
    Autun, 1:926
    Aymard, Bl., 1:950
    Bernard of Cluny, 2:312
    Berno of Reichenau, 2:327
    Brauweiler Abbey, 2:586
    Conrad of Constance, 4:136
    Cuxa Abbey, 4:450
    Domingo de la Calzada, 4:827
    Ferrières-en-Gâtinais Abbey, 5:695
    Flavigny-sur-Ozerain Abbey, 5:760
    Hugh of Cluny, 7:150
    Hugh of Remiremont, 7:155
    Leo VII (Pope), 8:484
    Leo IX (Pope), St., influenced, 8:485
    Leonius, 8:502
    monasticism, 2:257, 269, 9:792, 10:719

Saint-Bertin Abbey, 8:304, 12:540

Saint-Maur-des-Fossés Abbey, 12:566

Saint Paul-Outside-the-Walls Abbey, 12:577

Spain, 13:385

spirituality, 13:445

    See also Hugh of Cluny, St.

Cluniacs, 1:117, 290, 3:601

Cluny Abbey (France), 3:*814*, **814–815**
    Abbots, 1:10
    Abdinghof Abbey, 1:14
    Bernard of Clairvaux, St., 2:308
    Berno, Bl., 2:327
    Charité-sur-Loire Abbey, 3:394
    church architecture, 1:926, 3:692, 750, 811–812, 814
    Cistercians, 3:748
    Councils of Anse, 1:493
    end of Carolingian reform, 3:158
    Hugh, St., 7:150–151
    La Cava Abbey, 8:268
    Order of the Holy Sepulcher of Jerusalem, 3:68
    restoration, 5:844
    works of charity, 3:412
    See also Cluniac reform; Cluniacs

Clusa, Jacobus de, 1:729

Clut, Isidore (Bp.), 1:207

Clynnog, Morys (Bp. of Bangor, Wales), 2:54

Clypeus theologiae thomisticae contra novos ejus impugnatores (Gonet), 6:340

Clypeus Thomistarum (Nigri), 14:48

CMC (Congregation of the Mother Co-Redemptrix), **4:114**

CMC (Dòng Đồng Công), 4:114

CMR (Congregation of Mary, Queen), **4:113–114**

CMR (Trinh Vương), 4:113–114

CMSM (Conference of Major Superiors of Men). *See* Conference of Major Superiors of Men

CMSWR (Conference of Major Superiors of Women Religious), **4:298**, 8:422, 13:170

CND (Sisters of the Congregation de Notre Dame), 2:566–567, 10:458, **458**

Cnossos (Greece), 4:362–363

CO (Confederation of the Oratory of St. Philip Neri), 10:621–623

Coady, Moses Michael, **3:815–816**

Çoba, Ernest (Bp.), 1:216

Cobb, John, 11:731

Cobden Treaty (1860), 10:150

Cobden-Sanderson, T. J., 2:523

Cobos Celada, Benjamín, Bl., 7:124

Cocceius, Johannes, 2:383

Cocchetti, Annunciata, Bl., **3:816**

Cocchi da Fiesole, Angelo, 3:495

Cochet, Jean, 12:771

Cochin China (Vietnam), 12:218, 219

Cochlaeus, Johannes (Johann Dobeneck), 3:609, **816**, 5:43

Cochran v. Louisiana State Board of Education (1930), 3:660

The Cocktail Party (play, Eliot), 5:161

Cocteau, Jean, 11:562

COCU (Consultation on Church Union), **4:199–200**

Codd, Kevin A., 8:822

Codde, Pieter (Coddaeus) (Abp. of Sebaste), **3:816–817**, 14:363

See also Utrecht, Schism of

Code Noir, 1:155

Code of Canon Law (1917), 3:55

  abortion, 1:31

  beatification and canonization of saints, 12:608

  candles, 3:15

  cardinalate, 3:107

  Carthusians, 3:194

  censorship, 3:336

  Chinese rites controversy, 3:515, 516

  church titles, 10:971

  clerical dress, 3:801

  Code of Canons of the Eastern Churches, 3:817

  confession of mortal sins, 13:152

  diocesan synods, 2:41

  dueling, 4:929

  ecclesiastical archives, 1:636

  ecclesiastical office, 10:559–563

  ecclesistical ordinaries, 10:633–634

  establishment of espiscopal conferences, 14:310

  illegitimate children, 8:455

  indulgences, 7:440

  Jesuit constitution, 8:445

  laicization, 8:285

  laity, 8:288–289

  Lovers of the Holy Cross, 8:834–835

  marriage, 1:152

  mention of Aquinas, 14:23

  Ne Temere decree, 10:218–219

  papacy legal position, 10:849

  philosophical pluralism, 11:428

  plenary councils, 2:41

  preaching, 11:631

precursors, 3:46

  sacred art, 8:621

  time, 14:82–83

  translations, 3:35

  unity of the Church, 14:356

  vernacular use, 8:365

  Woywod, Stanislas, 14:860

  See also Canon Law

Code of Canon Law (CIC) (1983), **3:34–37**, 56–58

  abortion, 1:31

  academic freedom, 1:55

  acolytes, 1:68

  Acta Apostolicae Sedis, 1:77

  Ad tuendam fidem, 1:97–98, 3:58

  age, 1:174

  Anointing of the Sick, 1:484

  Apostolic See, 1:589

  appeals to a future council, 1:599

  candles, 3:15

  canonization, 3:63

  cardinalate, 3:106

  Carthusians, 3:194

  celebret, 3:316

  censorship, 3:336

  Church-State relations, 3:644–645

  Code of Canons of the Eastern Churches, 3:818–820

  diocesan consultors, 3:66

  ecclesiastical archives, 1:636

  enclosure, 3:806

  episcopal conferences, 14:310

  freedom of inquiry, 7:391

  Holy orders, 7:40

  indulgences, 7:440

  laicization, 8:286

  laity, 8:288–289, 418

  marriage, 1:150, 152, 174–175

  novitiate period, 10:467–470

  poverty, 11:570

  preaching, 11:630–632

  presbyteral councils, 11:674

  Profession of Faith and Oath of Fidelity, 11:740

  on sacred spaces, 12:500–501

  schism, 12:738

  secular institutes, 12:862–863

  seminary education, 12:898

  Sunday observance, 13:612

  time, 14:82–83

  translations, 3:35, 56

  unity of the Church, 14:356

  women's position, 3:549

  See also Canon Law

Code of Canons of the Eastern Churches (CCEO) (1990), 3:36–37, 57, **817–820**

  abortion, 1:32

  Ad tuendam fidem, 1:97–98, 3:58

  appeals to a future council, 1:599

  Carmelites, 3:130

  consecrated life, 4:155–156

  convents, 4:231

  ecclesiastical archives, 1:636

  enclosure, 3:806

  marriage, 1:150, 175

  patriarchate office, 10:947

  reservation of sins, 11:76–77

  women, role of, 14:821

Code of Eshnunna, 8:393

Code of Hammurabi, 4:389, 6:631, 11:774

Code of Lipit-Ishtar, 8:393

Code of Rubrics, 8:641

Code of Ur-nammu, 8:392–393

Codex, 12:294–295

Codex Alexandrianus, 2:364–365, 8:842

Codex Amiatinus (Tischendorf, ed.), 14:90

Codex Aureus, 3:154, 9:128, 128–129, 10:*866*

Codex Bezae, 2:365

Codex Calixtinus, 8:683

Codex canonum Ecclesiorum Africanae. See *Collectio concilii Cartaginensis*

Codex Canonum Ecclesiarium Orientalium, 10:947

Codex Claromontanus, 2:365

Codex Claromontanus (Tischendorf, ed.), 14:90

Codex Compilationis (Laborans), 8:266

Codex Egberti (book), 5:32, 9:128–129

Codex Ephraemi Rescriptus, 2:365, 10:*805*, 14:90

Codex Frederico-Augustinus, 14:90

Codex Gregorianus, 12:295

Codex Hermogenianus, 12:295

Codex iuris canonici. See Code of Canon Law

Codex Koridethi, 2:365

Codex Salemitanus, 5:30

Codex Sinaiticus, 2:364, 367, 10:305, 14:90

Codex Theodosianus, 3:39, 724

Codex Vaticanus, 2:364

Codex Vercellensis, 5:455

Codex Washingtonianus, 2:365

Códice de autos viejos, 1:925

Codices latini antiquiores (Lowe), 10:774

Codina Millá, Eusebio María, 2:92
Codinachs Tuneau, Juan, 2:92
Codrington, Thomas, **3:820–821**
Cody, John (Card.), 2:875, 3:479–480, **821–822**, 7:318, 8:816, 10:296, 12:412
Coe, George Albert, 12:96
Coeffeteau, Nicolas, **3:822**
Coelestius (5th c. heretic), 11:61, 62
Coelho, Feliciano de, 2:590
Coelho, Gaspar, 7:726
Coelibatus, et brevarium: duo gravissima clericorum officia (Roskoványi), 12:383
Coercion, governmental use of, 6:375–376
Coetus 11 study group, 8:438
Le Coeur admirable de la très sacrée Mère de Dieu (St. Eudes), 5:441
Coeur d'Alène people, 3:226
Coffin, Charles (Father), 7:254
Coffin, Edward, **3:822**
Cogitative power, **3:822–824**
   central sense, 3:346, 823
   discursive power as term for, 4:775
   perception of time, 14:81
   senses, 12:913
Cogito ergo sum (Descartes), 4:680–682
Cogley, John, **3:824–825**
Cognition, speculative-practical, **3:825–826**, 10:188
Cognitive development, 11:318
Cogolludo, Diego López de, **3:826**
Coguin, Charles, 1:396
Cohen, Gustav, 4:900
Cohen, Hermann (Augustine Mary of the Blessed Sacrament), **3:826–827**, 5:435, 10:237
   Cassirer, Ernst, 3:209
   ethical formalism, 5:388
   knowledge, 8:220
   modern Jewish philosophy, 7:865
Cohen, M. R., 10:185
"Coherent Christology," 2:120–121
Coimbra University (Portugal), 2:609, 3:*827*, **827–828**
Coimbricenses, 14:51
Coinage
   Christian monogram, 4:180
   Constantinople, 4:189
   Copernicus' theory, 4:250
   labarum, 8:263
COINCAT (International Council for Catechesis), **7:526–527**
Coindre, André, Rev., 12:494
Coindre, Vincent, Rev., 12:494

Coinred (King of Mercia), 4:178
Coke, Edward, Sir, 7:705, 12:271
Cola di Rienzo (Roman revolutionary), **3:828–829**, 5:921
Colani, Timothée, 10:896
Colautti v. Franklin, 1:33
Colbert, Jean Baptiste, 8:802
Colbert, Joachim (Bp. of Montpellier), 1:600
Cold War
   aristocracy, 1:667
   Australia, 1:904
   Lithuania, 8:608
   See also Communism; *specific countries*
Colder, Winebrenner v. (1862), 3:658
Cole, Henry, **3:829**
Colección diplomatica de varios papeles antiguos y modernos sobre dispensas matrimoniales y otros puntos de disciplina ecclesiástica (Llorente), 8:740
Colegio de Santo Tomás (Manila), 2:236
Colegio Seminario Conciliar de San Carlos (Paraguay), 10:878
Colegio-Seminario de San Luis (Colombia), 14:910
Coleman, Edmund, 10:492, 493, 494
Coleman, Edward, Bl., **3:829–830**, 5:236
Coleman, Walter, **3:830**
Colenso, John William (Bp. of Natal), 1:444–445
Coleridge, Henry James, **3:830**
Coleridge, Samuel Taylor, **3:830–832**, *831*
   Emerson, 5:188, 189
   I-It mysticism, 10:117
Coleridge, William (Bp. of Barbados), 3:120
Colet, John, 3:606, **832–833**, *833*
   catechesis, 3:232, 241
   humanism, 7:190, 191
   St. Paul's Cathedral, 8:771
   St. Paul's School (London), 12:119
   Warham, William, 3:72
Coleti, Giacomo, 5:627
Colette, St., 3:783–784, **833**
Colgan, John, **3:833–834**, 5:833
Coligny, Gaspard de, 3:267, 12:537–538, *537*
Colin, Frederic Louis, **3:834**
Colin, Jean Claude Marie, Ven., **3:834–835**
   Champagnat, St. Marcellin Joseph Benoît, 3:374
   Marist Fathers, founding of, 9:176

Marist Sisters, founding of, 9:177
Coll Guitart, Francisco, Bl., **3:835**
Coll y Prat, Narciso (Abp. of Caracas), **3:835–836**, *836*
Collas du Bignon, Charles-René, 12:276
Collatio, **3:836**, 4:*706–707*
Collationes (St. Odo of Cluny), 10:555
Collationes XXIV (Cassian), 3:206, *206*, 207
Collations (Cassian), 6:112
Collations on the Six Days (St. Bonaventure), 5:899, 6:815
Collectanea (Peter Lombard), 11:190
Collectanea Anglo-Minoritica, or a Collection of the Antiquities of the English Franciscans or Frairs Minors Commonly Called Gray Friars (Parkinson), 10:892
Collectanea rerum memorabilium (Gaius Julius Solinus), 12:620
Collectanea sacra (Fleming), 5:760
Collected Papers of Charles Sanders Peirce (Peirce), 11:57
Collected Writings/Elizabeth Bayley Seton (Seton), 13:177
Collectio V Librorum, 3:60
Collectio Andegavensis I, 3:40, 41
Collectio Andegavensis II, 3:41
Collectio Anselmo Dedicata, 3:44, 60
Collectio Arelatensis, 3:40
Collectio Caesaraugustana, 3:60
Collectio canonum (Anselm of Lucca), 1:494, 3:45, 60
Collectio concilii Cartaginensis, 3:40, 59
Collectio de novis erroribus (Argentré), 1:657
Collectio documentorum Maronitarum (Anaissi), 9:195–196
Collectio Hispana chronologica (Isidoriana). See Hispana Collectio Versio (canonical collection)
Collectio Ingilrami (Teatina), 3:39
Collectio L titulorum (John Scholasticus), 3:60
Collectio libre quinque, 3:44
Collectio Libri Duo, 3:45
Collectio Parisiensis (Bernard of Pavia), 3:48
Collectio Rituum, 8:675
Collectio Romana, 4:601
Collectio S. Mauri, 3:40
Collectio Trullana, 3:38–39
Collection (Ivo of Chartres), 3:60
Collection de la Bibliothèque des Exercices (Watrigant), 13:431
Collection ecclésiastique (Barruel), 2:118

Collection in 60 Titles, 3:46

Collection maxima (Hardouin), 6:876

Collection of 87 Chapters (John III Scholasticus), 7:915–916

Collection of Atto (Atto of Milan), **1:841**

Collection of Saint-Amand, 3:40

Collectiones in epistolas et evangelia (Smaragdus), 13:228

Collections catholicae et canonicae scripturae (William of Saint-Amour), 14:*751*

Collective guilt, 6:567, 570

Collective unconscious, 8:60–61

College chapels, 3:523

Collège de France, 12:126

Collège de Ste. Anne la Royale (France), 7:575

Collège Notre Dame du Perpé Secours (Haiti), 8:157

College of Bishops

    authority in the Church, 5:39

    infallibility, 7:449–450

    pope, relationship to, 13:778–779

    as teaching authority of the Church, 13:775

College of Cardinals, 11:499–501

    Western Schism, 14:691–693

College of Consultors, 11:674–675

College of Holy Cross (Belgium), 7:576

College of St. Anthony (Belgium), 7:576

College of St. Bonaventure. *See* Quaracchi (college)

College of St. Scholastica (Duluth, MN), 9:*656*

College of St. Teresa (Winona, MN), 9:774

College of St. Teresa and St. John of the Cross (Rome), 3:145

College of Santa Clara (CA), 9:493

College of Santa Cruz (Mexico), 12:528

College of the Congregation for the Propagation of the Faith (Rome), 11:*750*

College of the Immaculate Conception (New Orleans), 10:292

College of the Sacred Heart (Denver), 9:19

Collège Ste. Anne (Nova Scotia, Canada), 3:9

College Theology Society, **3:836–837**, 13:289–290

Colleges and universities. *See specific cities and countries*; *specific colleges and universities*

Collegiality, episcopal, 2:414–415, 418–419, **3:837–838**, 5:39, 11:30

Collegiate Church (Salzburg, Austria), 3:706

Collegio Corsini Seminary (Italy), 7:650, 651

Collegio Sant'Anselmo (Rome), 2:273

Collegium Germanicum, 8:58

Collegium Nepomucenum, 4:484

Collegium universi juris canonici . . . (Engel), 5:220

Colli, Bonifacio de', 13:857–858

Collier, Peter Fenelon, **3:838**

Collins, Anthony, 4:617, 5:967

Collins, Dominic, Bl., **3:838**, 7:580

Collins, John J. (Bp. of Kingston, Jamaica), 3:112

Collins, Joseph Burns, **3:839**

Collins, Mary, 5:677

Collins, Raymond F., 3:93, 8:822

Collins, Thomas Aquinas (Raymond), **3:839**

Colliot, Louis-Felix, 8:319

Collirium fidei adversus hereses (Alvaro Pelayo), 1:327

Collius, Francesco (Collio), **3:840**

Cölln, D. G. C. von, 2:384

The Colloquies (Pazzi), 11:47

Colloquium Biblicum Lovaniense, 8:824

Colloredo, Hieronymus, **3:840**

Collot, A., 1:545

Colman (fl. early 9th c.), 3:160

Colman, SS., **3:840–841**

Colman Elo, St., 3:840–841

Colman Macduach, St., 3:841

Colman of Cloyne (Bp.), St., 3:840

Colman of Dromore (Bp.), St., 3:840

Colman of Lindisfarne (Bp.), St., 3:841

Colmerauer, Alain, 1:766

Cologne (Germany), **3:841–845**

    art, 3:844–845

    Confirmation, 4:89

    Napoleon I's ambitions, 8:489

Cologne (Germany) mixed marriage dispute, 1:328, 2:691, 3:843, **845–846**

    antecedents, 13:416

    Döllinger, Johannes, 4:823

    Droste zu vischering, Clems, 4:909

    Dunin, Martin von, 4:933–934

    protests, 8:160

    Prussian Catholics, 8:253

    Reisach, Karl August von, 12:40

Cologne, School of, **3:846–847**, 856

Cologne Cathedral (Germany), 3:*688*, 696, 709, 710, *841*, *842*, 844, 6:*174*, *178*

    art, 3:844–845

    Engelbert I (Abp.), 5:220

    precursors, 3:844

Coloman, St., **3:847**

Colombia, **3:847–853**, *851*, *852*

    Biffi, Eugenio, 2:392

    Castillo y Guevara, Francisca Josefa Del, 3:217

    charismatic renewal movement, 3:392

    Chibcha religion, 3:475

    conquistadores, 4:132

    demographic statistics, 3:848

    diplomacy, 12:658–659

    Domínguez, Isidoro, 4:827

    ecclesiastical organization, 3:848

    education, 8:869, 12:661

    encomendero abuses, 8:777

    Euse Hoyos, Mariano de Jesús, Bl., 5:450

    Lasso de la Vega, 8:343–344

    map, 3:*849*

    mission, 3:770–771, 847–851, 7:290, 9:711, 14:909–910

    social action programs, 8:869–870

Colombière, Claude de la, St., 1:203, **3:853**

Colombini, John, Bl., 7:777

Colombo, Giuseppe, 7:528

Colonialism. *See* Slavery; *specific countries*; *specific mission entries*

Coloniensis, 3:40

Colonization Realty Company, 6:240

Colonna, Agapito (Card.), 3:855

Colonna, Antonio Branciforte, 3:856

Colonna, Ascanio (Card.) (d. 1608), 3:856

Colonna, Ascanio (d. 1559), 3:855

Colonna, Fabrizio, 3:855

Colonna, Francis, 4:850

Colonna, G. P., 3:123

Colonna, Giacomo (Card.) (d. 1318), 3:854

Colonna, Giovanni (Card.) (d. 1244), 3:854

Colonna, Giovanni (Card.) (d. 1348), 3:855

Colonna, Giovanni (Card.) (d. 1508), 3:855

Colonna, Girolamo (Card.) (d. 1666), 3:856

Colonna, Girolamo (Card.) (d. 1763), 3:856

Colonna, James (Card.), 2:502

Colonna, John, 3:320

Colonna, Lorenzo, 3:855

Colonna, Marco Antonio (Card.) (d. 1803), 3:856

Colonna, Marco Antonio IV (Card.), 3:856

Colonna, Marco Antonio II, 3:855, 856

Colonna, Margaret, Bl., 3:854

Colonna, Oddo. *See* Martin V (Pope)

Colonna, Pietro (Card.) (d. 1326), 3:854

Colonna, Pietro de (1064-1118?), 3:854

Colonna, Pietro Pamphili, 3:856

Colonna, Pompeo, 3:855

Colonna, Prospero (Card.) (d. 1463), 3:855

Colonna, Prospero (Card.) (d. 1743), 3:856

Colonna, Prospero (Card.) (d. 1765), 3:856

Colonna, Prospero (d. 1523), 3:855

Colonna, Sciarra, 2:503, 3:854–855

Colonna, Stefano (d. 1379), 3:855

Colonna, Stefano (d. after 1347), 3:854, 855

Colonna, Vespasiano, 3:855

Colonna, Vittoria, **3:856–857**, *857*

Colonna di Stigliano, Niccolò, 3:856

Colonna family, **3:853–856**

Alexander VI (Pope), 1:259

Boniface VIII (Pope), 2:502, 503

See also Guelfs and Ghibellines

Colorado, **3:857–860**, 4:668, 670, 8:316

See also specific dioceses and archdioceses

Colored Methodist Episcopal Church (U.S.), 9:562

Colossae, **3:860**

Colosseum (Rome), **3:860**, *861*

Colossians, Epistle to the, 3:93, 860–863, **860–863**

authorship, 4:704

baptism, 2:59

beatific vision, 2:171

captivity epistles, 3:93

Christian law, 8:403

Christocentrism, 3:558

Church, 3:578–579, 582–583, 862

clerical celibacy and marriage, 3:322

death imagery in baptism, 2:75

Divine election, 5:146

edification, 5:84–85

glory of God (end of creation), 6:245

God the Son, 6:295

guilt, 6:571

justice of men, 8:74

justification, 8:79

Lord's Day, 8:782

Luke, 8:855

lying as sin, 8:900

man, creation of new, 9:87

merit, 6:383

mystical body of Christ, 10:100, 101

ransom, 11:909

Scripture readings, 8:435

sin, 13:147

slavery, 13:207, 208

social principle, 13:251

wisdom, 14:791

world, 14:840

Columba and Pomposa, SS., **3:863**, 4:262, 12:830

Columba of Iona, St., 2:54, **3:863**, 7:553, 12:830

Colman Elo, St., 3:841

Comgall, St., 4:3

hymns, 7:245

Kells Abbey, 8:138

Kenneth of Derry, 8:143

Columba of Rieti, Bl., **3:863**

Columban, St., 2:54, 3:598–599, 600, **863–864**, 5:842

Abondance Monastery, 1:23

Agil, St., 1:176

Amatus of Remiremont, St., 1:333

Austria, 1:908

Bobbio Abbey, 2:446

Boniface IV (Pope), 2:500

Celtic Easter date controversy, 5:14

Comgall, St., 4:3

the discpline, 4:775

exemption, 5:529–530

exile, 5:456

Gall, St., 6:64–65

Irish monastic exegesis, 5:514–515

Jonas of Bobbio, 7:1024

Latin literature, 9:441

Luxeuil Abbey, 8:899

Columban Fathers, **3:864**

founding, 3:622

mission, 3:622, 864, 6:83

represented in Nebraska, 10:223

Columban Sisters, 12:543

Columbel, Nicholas, 1:133

Columbia University (New York), 1:52

Columbian College (Washington, DC), 6:146

Columbianism. *See* Knights of Columbus

Columbo, R. R., 1:30

Columbus, Christopher, **3:864–867**, *865*, 10:350

Alexandrine bulls, 1:273, 274

antipodes question, 1:530

discovery of Bahamas, 2:13

discovery of Jamaica, 7:698

Dominican Republic, 4:834

symbolism, 8:189–190

Columbus Diocese (OH), **3:867–868**, 4:843, 10:571

Columbus Platform (1937), 8:10

Columcille, St. *See* Columba of Iona, St.

Column of Trajan, 12:*300*

Colvin, Patrick, 10:281

Colwell, E. C., 2:365–366

Combes, Justin Émile, 5:855, 8:283

Comblin, José, 8:549

Comboni, Daniele, Bl., **4:1**

Comboni Missionaries of the Heart of Jesus, **4:1–2**

COMECE (Commission of the Bishops' Conferences of the European Community), **4:13–15**, 297

Comenius, John Amos (Komenský) (Bp. of Moravian Brethren), **4:2–3**

Bohemian Brethren, 2:461

educational philosophy, 5:90, 92

world soul, 14:844

Comensoli, Gertrude Caterina, Bl., **4:3**, 12:484, 13:417

Comentarios a pensmientos religiosos de Luis Veillot (Elguero), 5:154

Comes (books), 11:124

Comes of Murbach, 1:289

Comes of Würzburg, 1:289

Il comforto dell'anima divota (Frassinetti), 5:920

Comgall, St., 1:577, 2:54, 3:596, **4:3–4**

Comites Christi, 3:555–556

Comitoli, Paolo, **4:4**

Comittal, Rite of, 4:359–360

Comma pianum, 2:19, **4:4**, 5:500

Commandments. *See* Ten Commandments

Commedia della Ninfe (Boccaccio), 2:448

Commen, in XII libros metaphysicorum Aristotelis ad mentem Scoti (Fabri), 5:585

Commenda and commendatory Abbots, 2:271

Commendation, 3:616, **4:9**

Abbots, 1:10

Abondance Monastery, 1:23

Airvault Monastery, 1:196

Alcobaça Abbey, 1:240

Anchin Abbey, 1:396

Aniane Abbey, 1:454

Arbroath Abbey, 1:630

Aurillac Abbey, 1:897

Celles-Sur-Belle Monastery, 3:329

Chaise-Dieu Abbey, 3:362

Church property, 3:726

Cistercians, 3:747, 751

Cluny Abbey, 3:815

Conques Abbey, 4:129

Jacques d'Amboise attacks, 5:847

La Cava Abbey, 8:268

Lagny-sur-Marne Abbey, 8:280

Luxeuil Abbey, 8:899

Order of Aubrac, 1:846

Sesto de Réghena Abbey, 13:30

Settimo Abbey, 13:36

Solesmes Abbey, 13:300

Commendation of the Dying, **4:9–10**

Commendone, Giovanni Francesco
(Card.), **4:10–11**, 11:442

*Commentaria absolutissima in quinque
libros Decretalium* (Fagnani), 5:588

*Commentaria in b. Pauli Epistolam ad
Romanos* (Musso), 10:73

*Commentaria in libros Aristoteles de
ortu et interitu* (Rubio), 12:399

*Commentaria in octo libros Aristoteles
de physico auditu* (Rubio), 12:399

*Commentaria in omnes Divi Pauli
Epistolas* (Lapide, C. A.), 8:332

Commentaria in psalmos (Vega), 14:430

*Commentaria in universam Aristotelis
Logicam* (Rubio), 12:399

Commentaries (Pius II), 11:370

Commentaries on the Laws of England
(Blackstone), 14:816–817

Commentaries on the Psalms (Eusebius
of Caesarea), 5:455

*Commentarii in libros Metaphysicorum
Aristotelis* (Fonseca), 5:790

Commentarii in Zachariam (St. Jerome),
5:571

*Commentarii lucidissimi in textum Petri
Hispani* (Mercado), 9:500

*Commentarii rerum getarum Francisci
Sfortiae* (Simonetta), 13:134

Commentariolus (Copernicus), 4:250,
251

*Commentariorum theologicorum tomi
quatuor* (Gregory of Valencia), 6:524

*Commentariorum urbanorum libri
XXXVIII* (Maffei), 5:207

*Commentarios sobre el Catecismo
Cristiano* (Carranza), 3:20

Commentarium (Tudeschis), 14:235

*Commentarium in Bullam Paul III
(Fauré),* 5:647

Commentarium in s. Mattheum (St.
Hilary of Poitiers), 6:112

Commentarium theologicorum
(Passaglia), 10:919

Commentarius historico-apologeticus
(Concina), 4:59

Commentarius in symbolum (Rufinus of
Aquileia), 3:243

*Commentarius litteralis et historicus in
omnes Psalmos et selecta Veteris
Testamenti cantica cum versione
nova ex Hebraico* (Simon de Muis),
5:518–519

Commentary (Thomas of Buckingham),
14:31

Commentary illustrations, 2:182

Commentary of the Apocalypse, 9:129

Commentary on Aristotle's Politics (St.
Albert the Great), 10:72

Commentary on Job (Hesychius of
Jerusalem), 6:812

Commentary on John (Origen), 6:256,
10:658

Commentary on Leviticus, 12:548

Commentary on Psalm 32 (Aquinas),
10:72

Commentary on the Apocalypse (Beatus
of Liébana), 5:775

A Commentary on the Divine Liturgy
(Cabasilas), 5:426

Commentary on the Galatians (Luther),
3:327

Commentary on the Hebrews (St. Cyril
of Alexandria), 11:695

*Commentary on the Law of Prize (De
iure praedae commentarius)*
(Grotius), 6:540

Commentary on the Metaphysics
(Thomas Aquinas), 12:43

Commentary on the New Testament
(Schaff), 12:726

Commentary on the Psalms
(Cassiodorus), 3:208

*Commentary on the Psalms from
Primitive and Medieval Writers*
(Neale and Littledale), 3:259

Commentary on the Sentences
(Bonaventure), 5:899

Commentary on the Sentences (Thomas
Aquinas), 5:390

Commentary on the Sentences (Thomas
of Bungey), 14:32

*Commentary on the Sermon on the
Mount* (Luther), 14:253

Commenting and Commentaries
(Spurgeon), 13:463

*Commentum super Boethii librum de
Trintate* (Thierry of Chartres), 14:2

Commer, Ernst, **4:11–12**

Commer, F., 2:842

Commingling, **4:12**

Commissa nobis (papal bull, Pius VI),
7:651

Commissariat of the Holy Land, **4:12**

Commissariate for the Byzantine-
Slavonic rite, 5:648

Commissary Apostolic, **4:12–13**

Commission for Catholic Missions
Among the Colored and Indians,
12:642

Commission for Sacred Art, 12:790

Commission for the New Martyrs, 8:418

Commission of Regulars, 1:196, **4:13**

Commission of the Bishops'
Conferences of the European
Community (COMECE), **4:13–15,**
297

Commission on Religious Life and
Ministry, 8:424

Commission on World Mission and
Evangelism, 9:698

Commissum divinitus (apostolic brief,
Gregory XVI), 6:509

Commissum nobis (Adrian IV), 1:127

Commissum nobis (papal bull, Pius X),
11:499

Commitment, **4:15–16**

certitude, 3:357

dimensions, 13:274

recruitment and conversion research,
13:274

Commitment (newsletter), 10:158

Commitment to Truth (Ellis), 5:170

Committee against the Extension of
Race Prejudice in the Church, 14:243

*Committee for Public Education v.
Nyquist* (1973), 3:668

Commodus, Lucius Aelius Aurelius
(Roman Emperor), 12:304

Common good, **4:16–22**

associations, 1:791

human act, 7:171

John XXIII (Pope), Bl. on the,
10:850

law, final cause of, 8:390

Leo XIII (Pope), 8:492

papal social thought, 13:266–267

society, 13:276

solidarity, 13:300–302

in the state, 13:486–488

*Common Lectionary: The Lectionary
Proposed by the Consultation on
Common Texts* (1983), 4:201, 8:441

Common life, according to St. Augustine, 3:67

Common Rules of the Daughters of Charity, 13:33, 172

Common sense, **4:22**
  causality, 3:301
  certitude, 8:308
  cogitative power, 3:822
  See also Central sense

Common Sense (Paine), 5:262, 10:757

Commonitoria (St. Vincent of Lérins), 6:112, 14:136, 524

Commonitorium de errore Priscillianistarum et Origenistarum (Orosius), 10:673

Commonweal (periodical), **4:22–23**
  editor, 13:99
  Scharper, Philip J., 12:729
  Skillin, E., 13:205
  Williams, Michael, 14:759

Communal living
  communes, 8:164–165
  history of, 10:153
  monasteries, 9:782
  Sadocites, 3:546

Communautés de base. See Basic Christian communities

Communication, philosophy of, **4:23–25**
  law, 8:399
  lying, 8:902
  society, 13:278
  spirit, 13:423

Communication of idioms, **4:25–26**
  Crypto-Calvinism, 4:416
  described, 10:13
  Severus of Antioch, 13:44

Communio, **4:27–31**
  apostolicity, 1:597
  Christian anthropology, 3:532
  founding, 8:840
  mission of laity, 8:293
  natural order, 10:193
  unity of laity, 8:416, 418
  universality of Christianity, 3:293
  Vatican II, 3:293, 10:852

Communio: International Catholic Review, 2:34, **4:31**, 5:861

Communion
  altars, 1:319
  apostolic faith, 1:586
  Canon Law, 3:35
  Commingling, 4:12
  Communione e Liberazione, 4:31–32
  as concept, 4:27–31
  definitive exclusion from, 5:178

devotion to Eucharist, 3:623

Egan, Edgar Michael (Abp. of New York) delivering, 12:*328*

hierarchical, 4:29–30

Hussites, 7:231

infants, 4:86, 89

Justin Martyr on the Eucharist, 5:421

outside the liturgy, 4:36–38

saints, 4:34–36

sequence, 4:89–90

songs, 4:32–34

theology of Church, 3:580, 582, 583, 584–586, 587, 590

See also First Communion

Communion (communio) of churches, 14:298

Communion, First. *See* First Communion

Communion and Liberation, **4:31–32**

Communion antiphon, **4:32–34**, *33*

Communion of Apostles, 8:345

Communion of Infants, 4:86, 89

Communion of saints, **4:34–36**, 556–557

Communion service, **4:36–38**
  Buckfast Abbey (England), 5:*420*
  Council of Trent, 14:172
  Good Friday, 6:356

Communione e Liberazione, 4:31–32

Communism and Communist bloc, 3:620, 5:93–94
  Albania, 1:214–216
  Assumptionists, 1:801
  atheism of, Pius XI, 4:790
  Augustinians, 1:890
  Bosnia-Herzegovina, 2:545–547
  Bulgaria, 2:548, 682–684
  Bulgarian Orthodox Church under, 10:686–687
  Catholic Church in Tibet under, 14:72
  China, 2:664, 665, 3:501–503, 864
  Cistercians, 3:748
  collapse, 1:705, 3:627
  Cuba, 4:417, 418–421
  Czechoslovakia, 4:485–488
  Dibelius, Otto, 4:734
  economic democracy, 4:643
  European collapse, 4:296–297
  excommunication, 4:418
  freedom of religion, 5:946
  Holy See relations with, 3:200–201, 625, 627
  Hong Kong, 7:76
  Hungary, 7:218, 219–223
  John Paul II (Pope), 3:342, 627, 7:997–998

Labadists, 8:263

Laos, 8:329–330

Latvia, 8:375–376

persecution, 3:620

Polish Church, 11:450–451

Romanian Byzantine Catholic Church, 12:339

Romanian Latin Catholics, 12:333–335, 339

Russian Catholic Church, 12:427–430

Russian Orthodox Church, 10:694–695, 13:12

secular humanism, 7:196, 197

Serbian Orthodox Church under, 10:698

Slovakia, 13:222–223

Ukrainian Church, 14:275–276, 280

Vietnam, 3:79–80, 8:385–386, 835

Yugoslavia, 4:371–372, 13:10

See also Cold War; Soviet Union; *specific countries*

Communist Manifesto (Engels, Marx), 5:222, 14:361

Communitarians, 7:233–235

Community, **4:38–39**
  Acts of the Apostles, 1:89
  Augustine, St., 1:874–875
  friendship, 6:7
  intimate community and justice, 8:65–66
  justice, 8:67–69
  law vs. custom, 8:670
  leisure, 8:461
  Lent, 8:470
  life, concept of, 8:567–569
  liturgical catechesis, 8:645
  love for fellow human, 8:831
  Marsilius of Padua, 9:211
  missiology, 9:677
  political theory, 8:182
  prophecy, 11:764
  spirituality, 13:438–439
  Vatican Council II, 8:832

Community churches, **4:39–40**, 199–200

Community living. *See* Communal living

Community of Sant'Egidio, 12:672–673

Community of True Inspiration. *See* Amana Society

Community organizing, 1:287–288

Commutative justice, 8:67
  Aquinas, 8:72
  social justice vs., 13:243
  taxation and moral obligation, 13:768

Comoros, **4:40**, *41*, *42*

Compactata, 4:481

Compacts (Council of Basel), 2:134, 7:231

Compagnia dei servi de' puttini carità (Milan, Italy), 3:214

Compagnie du Saint-Sacrement, 2:324, **4:40–41**

A Companion to Summa (Farrell), 5:631

Companion to the Greek Testament (Schaff), 12:726

Company of Divine Love, 3:415

Company of Jesus, 14:776

Company of Mary, **4:41**, 8:518

Company of St. Jerome, 3:415

Company of St. Ursula, 9:508

Company of the elect, 6:689

Comparatio sensibilium (Thomas of York), 14:39

Comparative Liturgy (Liturgie comparée) (Baumstark), 2:159

Comparative religion
  "dimensions" approach, 13:229
  interactive pluralism, 13:229
  Smart, R., 13:228–230
  Smith, W.C., 13:235–236
  Smith, W.R., 13:236
  worldview analysis, 13:229

Comparative theology, 8:110

Compassion
  Franciscan spirituality, 5:896
  Mahayana Buddhism, 9:47
  mercy, 9:504

Compendio della dottrina cristiana (Casati), 3:243

Compendio della dottrina cristiana (Pius X), 3:244

Compendio della telogia dogmatica (Frassinetti), 5:920

Compendio della teologia morale de S. Alfonso (Frassinetti), 5:920

Compendio y descripción de las Indias Occidentales (Vázquez de Espinosa), 14:428

Compendium annalium ecclesiasticorum regni Hiberniae (Porter), 11:526

Compendium iuris Publici Ecclesiastici (Ottaviani), 10:710

Compendium philosophiae (Hugh of Strassburg), 5:206

Compendium philosophiae (Roger Bacon), 12:285

Compendium philosophiae scholasticae (Urráburu), 14:344

Compendium phiosophiae moralis (Bartholomew of San Concordio), 14:47

Compendium studii (Roger Bacon), 5:517

Compendium theologiae (Aquinas), 3:241

Compendium theologiae (Hugh of Strassburg), 5:206

Compendium theologiae ad fratrem Reginaldum socium suum carissimum (Aquinas), 14:27

Compendium theologiae moralis (Gury), 6:585

Compendium theologiae moralis (Sabetti), 12:462

Compenetration of bodies, 10:108–109

Compensation, Occult, **4:41–43**

Compensationism, **4:43**, 9:880

Compère, Loyset, **4:43**

Compertum exploratumque (apostolic brief, Clement XII), 7:412

Competentibus ad baptismum instructionis libelli sex (Nicetas of Remesiana), 10:356–357

Compiègne, Council of (833), 1:186

Compiègne, Martyrs of, **4:43–44**, 5:973

Compilatio III Antiqua (Petrus Collivaccinus), 11:220

Compilatio secunda antiqua (John of Wales), 7:990

Complete substances, 13:576–577

Compline, **4:44**

Complutenses, 1:677, **4:44–45**, 14:51

Complutensian Polyglot, 7:187, 12:12

Complutensis, 3:137

Complutum Monastery (Spain), 6:16

Compost ou Kalendrier des bergiers, 3:241

Compotus (John de Sacrobosco), 7:956

Compound propositions, 11:769, 770

Compromise of the Nobles (1566), 2:217

Compulsion, **4:45**

Compunction, **4:45–46**

Compurgation, **4:46**

Computus, **4:46**, *47*, *48*
  chronology, 3:571
  computation of Easter, 8:642

Comte, Auguste, **4:46–49**, 11:295
  agnosticism, 6:312
  authority, 1:919
  Bonald, Louis Gabriel Ambroise de, 2:478
  causality, 3:306
  classification of the sciences, 12:821
  cultural evolution, 4:433
  demonstration, 4:654
  humanism, 7:195
  influence on Mill, 11:544
  laicism, 8:283
  logical positivism, 8:756

mechanism, 9:417
  methodology, 9:566
  philosophy and science, 11:299
  physical laws, 11:315
  society, 13:280–281
  sociology founding, 13:279
  See also Positivism

Comunidades eclesiasles de base. See Basic Christian communities

Comunidades Eclesiasles de Base (CEB). *See* Basic Christian communities

Comus (Milton), 9:642–643

Con, George, **4:49**

Con, John Baptist, 14:492

Conant, J. B., 7:196

Conant, K. J., 3:812, 814

Conarini, Anthony, 12:717

Conaty, Thomas James (Bp. of Monterey-Los Angeles), **4:49**
  Los Angeles diocese, 8:791
  role in NCEA, 10:160

Concanen, Richard Luke (Bp. of New York), 2:43, 3:180, 10:311–312

Conceição, Apolinário da, **4:49–50**

Concelebration, 1:318, **4:50–51**, 8:906

Concept, **4:51–53**
  composite, and judgment, 8:205
  definition, 4:610
  idea distinguished from, 7:294, 295
  intellect, 7:506
  intention, 13:408
  knowledge, 8:202, 209
  sign related, 13:117
  simple apprehension, 1:604

The Concept of Dread (Kierkegaard), 1:540, 8:166

The Concept of Mind (Ryle), 8:221

Conceptionist Handmaids of the Divine Heart, 13:417, 418

Conceptionist Missionaries, 12:618

Conceptualism, **4:53**, 5:361
  causality, 3:302
  Ockhamish, 10:535
  realism, 11:942

Concerning the Lord's Body and Blood (Paschasius), 10:918

Concertato style, *a cappella* style, 1:1

Concerto a cinque (Respighi), 12:139

Concetti, G., 3:88

Conchobuir, Ultan moccu, 1:644

Du Concile général et de la paix religieuse (Maret), 9:147–148

Conciliabulum. *See* Pisa, Councils of (1409-1512)

Conciliar fellowship, 14:298

Conciliarism, 3:604, 637
  Almain, Jacques, 1:298
  appeals to a future council, 1:599
  appellants, 1:600
  Arévalo, Rodrigo Sánchez de, 1:647
  Brevicoxa, 2:611
  Canon Law, 3:51
  Catholic responses to Protestant Reformation, 3:609
  Chrysoberges, Andrew, 3:572
  Church-State relations, 3:636
  Conrad of Gelnhausen, 4:136
  England, 5:243
  Febronianism, 3:614–615
  Fifth Lateran Council, 8:354–355
  Fillastre on superiority of councils over the pope, 5:722
  papal authority, 12:13
  theology of Church, 3:589
  Western Schism, 3:784, 14:693
  See also Basel, Councils of (1431-49); Constance, Councils of; Councils, General (ecumenical); Florence, Councils of; Gallicanism

Conciliarism, history of, **4:53–56**

Conciliarism, theological aspects of, **4:56–58**, 10:376

La Conciliazione pamphlet (Tosti), 14:120

Conciliengeschichte (Hefele), 6:704

Concilio, J. de, 3:244

Il Concilio Vaticano (Scalabrini), 12:718

Conciliorum collectio regia maxima: Act conciliorum et epistolae decretales, ac constitutiones summorum pontificum (Hardouin), 6:643–644

Concilios provinciales, I, II, III de México (Lorenzana), 8:786

Concilium: Theology in the Age of Renewal (periodical), 5:207, 8:840

Concilium Germanicum, 3:42

Concilium Monasticum Iuris Canonici, **4:58–59**

Concina, Daniel, 1:311, **4:59**, 5:647

Conciones 100 supra Christi passionem coram D. Carlo Borromeo recitatae (Panigarola), 10:822

A Concise Dictionary of Early Christianity, 5:208

A Concise Historical Account of the Unitas Fratrum (Spangenberg), 13:406

Conclaves, **4:60**, 8:907, 11:499–500
  See also Papal elections

Concomitant mystical phenomena, 10:106

Concord, Formula and Book of, **4:60–61**, 78–79, 11:655
  Chemnitz, Martin, 3:464
  doctrinal controversy, 8:889
  logical method, 8:86
  purpose, 8:890
  redaction, 8:890
  revival by Lutherans, 8:886
  Scriptures, role, 8:895
  sinful nature, 8:893

"Concord on the Merrymaking" (Joyce), 14:149

Concordantia discordantium (Gratian), 9:455

Concordat of 1516 (France), 3:612, 639

Concordat of 1801 (France), **4:61–63**, 5:699, 853, 976, 10:846
  Albi Archdiocese, 1:229
  anticlericalism, 1:518
  Antwerp, 1:539
  Auxerre, 1:927
  Bernier, Étienne Alexandre, 2:324
  Boisgelin de Cucé, Jean de Dieu, Raymond de, 2:462
  Caprara, Giovanni Battista, 3:92
  Chartres, 3:441
  Chateaubriand, François René de, 3:448
  Church and state, 3:640, 641
  Church history, 3:618
  Civil Constitution of the Clergy, 3:754
  Consalvi, Ercole, 4:138
  Émery, Jacques André support for, 5:190
  Imperial Catechism, 3:236
  Liège, 8:563
  Luxembourg, 8:898
  Napoleon I, 10:147–148
  negotiating, 13:417
  opposition to, 8:309
  Pius VII (Pope), 11:379
  signing, 5:847
  See also Petite Église

Concordat of 1860 (Haiti). *See* Petite Église

Concordat of Austria, 1:914

Concordat of Fontainebleau, **4:63–64**, 138, 10:149, 11:380–381

Concordat of Haiti (1860), 6:619

Concordat of Latvia, 8:376

Concordat of Spain, 13:395–397, 396–397

Concordat of Yugoslavia, 13:10

Concordats of Italy (1929, 1983), 8:356–360

Concordia canonum, 3:40, 60

Concordia Diocese (KS), 8:113

Concordia discordantium canonum. See Gratian, Decretum of

Concordia evangelistarum (William of Notingham), 14:746

Concordia liberi arbitrii cum gratiae donis (Molina), 2:50, 4:111–113, 5:935, 6:403, 9:769, 14:49

Concordia regularum (Benedict of Aniane), 10:743

Concordism, 6:132–133

Concubinage, **4:64–65**, 11:809, 12:14

Concubine, in the Bible, **4:65–66**

Concupiscence, **4:66–69**, 5:218, 488
  Augustinianism, 1:879–880, 884, 885
  Council of Trent, 8:85
  defined, 13:150
  gift of integrity, 7:504–505
  inclination to sin, 13:144
  Jansenism, 1:892
  justification, 8:82
  sphere of sex, 13:46

Concupiscent love, 8:826

Concurrence, Divine, **4:70–72**
  causality, 3:300
  free will, 5:930

Condat Abbey. *See* Saint-Claude Abbey (France)

Condé, Louis I de. *See* Louis I de Bourbon (Prince of Condé)

El Condenado por desconfiado (Molina), 2:116

Condillac, Étienne Bonnot de, **4:72–73**, 5:261, 12:765

Conditae a Christo (papal constitution, Leo XIII), 5:530, 12:100

Condition, 1:61, 62, **4:73**

The Condition of the Working Class in England (Engels), 5:222

Condon, William J. (Bp. of Great Falls, MT), 9:826–827

Condorcet, Marie Jean Antoine Caritat, **4:73–74**, 5:210, 261

Condorcet, Marquis de. *See* Condorcet, Marie Jean Antoine Caritat

Condotta ammirabile della divina Providenza (St. Alphonsus Liguori), 1:310

Condren, Charles de (Father), **4:74**, 5:440
  Chrysostom of Saint-Lô, John, 3:573
  Compagnie du Saint-Sacrement, 4:41
  Counter Reformation, 3:612
  French School, 13:451

Conduct, human, 9:870–871, 874, 14:551–552, 789

The Conduct of Life (Emerson), 5:188, 14:147

Condulmaro, Gabriel. *See* Eugene IV (Pope)

Cone, James, 1:162, 5:677, 8:545, 10:153

Confédération française de Travailleurs chrétiens, 5:857

Confederation of the Oratory of St. Philip Neri (CO), 10:621–623

Confederazione Latina, 3:100

A Conference about the Next Succession (Verstegan), 14:460

Conférence des évêques du Canada/Canadian Conference of Catholic Bishops (CCCB), 3:8

Conference for Pastoral Planning and Council Development (CPPCD), **4:75**

Conference of Catholic Seminary Faculties, 10:159

Conference of Charity (Society of St. Vincent de Paul), 10:735

Conference of Major Superiors of Men, 8:423, 424, 14:309

Conference of Major Superiors of Women Religious. *See* CMSWR (Conference of Major Superiors of Women Religious)

Conference of Mother Seton's Daughters, 13:35

Conference of Religious of Ireland, 7:567

Conference of Roman Catholic Cathedral Musicians (CRCCM), **4:75**

Conference of St. Vincent de Paul. *See* St. Vincent de Paul Society

Confernity of Christian Doctrine (CCD), 10:162

Confessio (Albar), 9:446

Confessio (anonymous), 9:458

Confessio (St. Patrick), 9:441, 10:954

Confessio Amantis (Gower), 6:378

Confessio Augustana (Melanchthon), 8:882

Confessio Belgica (1561), 10:264

Confessio Bohemica, 4:482

Confessio catholica (Gerhard), 6:166

Confessio catholicae et apostolicae in Ecclesia oriente (Metrophanes Critopoulos), 9:569

Confessio catholicae fidei christianae vel potius explicatio quaedam confessionis (Hosius), 3:242

Confessio christiana de via Domini (Nielsen), 10:388

Confessio Tetrapolitana, 12:18, 20

Confession, 11:*69*, 70, *74*
   annual, 3:231

lay confession, 8:411

Spanish mission in the Americas, 3:248

Ten Commandments, 4:8–9

See also Exomologesis

Confession (Dositheus of Jerusalem), 6:457–458

Confession (Lucari), 6:457

Confession (Moghila), 6:457

Confession, auricular, **4:75–77**, 76–77

Confession, seal of, 8:228

Confession of Augsburg (1530)
   condemnation of Anabaptists, 2:69
   saints as intercessors, 12:596–597

Confession of Czenger, 4:80

Confession of Dositheus of Jerusalem (Patrirach), 10:701

Confession of Faith of the Catholic and Apostolic Oriental Church (Critopoulos), 6:457

Confession of Gennadius II Scholarius, 10:700, 701

Confession of Metrophanes Critopoulos, 10:700

Confession of Peter Moghila (Metropolitan of Kiev), 10:700–701

Confessionario en lengua castellana y timuquana (Pareja), 10:882

Confessions (Rousseau), 12:393

Confessions (St. Augustine), 1:138, 857, 860, 864, 5:512

Confessions of Faith, **4:77–82**
   common, 4:82, 355
   creeds, 4:349–356
   doctrine, 4:802
   Helvetic Confessions, 2:689
   Knox, J., 8:226
   Orthodox, 4:355
   Protestant, 10:264, 13:406
   revival, 8:886

Il confessore diretto per le confessioni della gente di compagna (St. Alphonsus Liguori), 1:311

Confessores fidei, 3:61

Confessors, **4:82–84**, 12:661–662
   lay confession, 8:411–412
   martyr's honors, 8:720

The Confidential Clerk (play, Eliot), 5:161

Confirmation, Sacrament of, **4:84–92**
   age of, 4:86, 87, 88–89, 90
   Baptism, 4:84–88
   Christian witnesses, 14:803
   Coptic, 4:257
   death, 4:576
   Elvira Council, 5:178

historical development, 4:85–90, 91

for Holy orders, 7:40

laity's mission, 8:291–292

Middle Ages, 8:658

oils, 7:34–35

ordination candidates, 7:40

origin of term, 4:84

other denominations, 4:92

post-baptismal annointing, 2:64, 66

Reform Judiasm, 2:84

reviviscence of sacramental power, 12:206

rite, 4:87, 91–92

sequence, 4:89–90

sponsors, 13:459

theology, 4:90–91

Confirmation of Infants, 4:87, 88

Conformity of the Jansenists and the Thomists concerning the Five Propositions (Nicole), 10:384–385

Conformity to the Will of God, **4:92–94**

Conforti, Guido Maria, Bl., **4:94**, 14:877

Confraternities
   African American Catholics, 1:159
   angels, 1:424
   Campo Santo Teutonico, 2:922–924
   Christian Doctrine, 4:94–95
   Communione e Liberazione, 4:31–32
   lay spirituality, 8:414
   See also specific confraternities

Confraternities of the Calends, 8:111

Confraternities of the Rosary, 1:204

Confraternity of Catholic Colleges for Women, 9:774

Confraternity of Christian Doctrine (CCD), **4:94–95**, 5:179, 10:275, 12:97, 574
   Bandas, Rudolph G., 2:49
   Castellino da Castelli, 3:214
   catechesis, 3:234, 244
   Catholic Action, 3:277
   Collins, Joseph Burns, 3:839
   founding, 8:499
   Lucey, R., 8:843
   Marks, Miriam, 9:189
   New American Bible, 1:190
   New Orleans, 8:814, 816
   San Francisco, 12:649

Confraternity of Gonfalone, 3:418

Confraternity of Mercy, 3:419

Confraternity of Misericordia, 3:416, 417

Confraternity of Our Lady of Help, 1:159

Confraternity of Our Lady of Loreto, 3:418

Confraternity of Our Lady of Mount Carmel, 1:159
Confraternity of Pietà, 3:418
Confraternity of the Holy Rosary, 1:159
Confraternity of the Sorrows of Mary. *See* Servants of Mary
Confraternity Version (CV), 10:276
Confucianism and Neo-confucianism, **4:95–99**, *96*, 7:736
  Assyrian Church of the East, 3:491
  Buddhism, 3:510–511
  Chinese mission, 3:491, 493–494, 497–498, 500, 513–517
  ethics and law, 8:391
  Han Dynasty revival, 3:510
  Korea, 8:238
  Laozi, 8:332
  Le Tellier defense of Jesuits, 8:519
  natural law, 10:186
  origins, 3:508
  women, status of, 14:813–814
Confucius (Kongfuzi), 3:508–509, 4:*99*, **99–101**, 11:287
  See also Confucianism
Confucius Sinarum Philosophus, sive Scientia Sinesis exposita studio et opera Prosperi Intorcetta, Christiani Herdtrich, Francisci Rougemont, Philippi Couplet, P.P. Soc. Jesu (Herdtrich), 6:768
Confutation of Tyndale (More), 14:253, 254
Congar, Yves Marie-Joseph (Card.), **4:101–103**
  biblical canon, 3:21
  ecclesiology, 5:37
  Ecumenical Movement, 5:73
  International Theological Commission, 7:528
  Journet, Charles, 7:1058
  mission and missions, 9:684
  New Theology, 5:859
  priesthood, 11:705
  scholastic theology, 12:777
  theology of Church, 3:589
  theology of history, 6:891
  Vatican Council II, 4:853
Congo, Democratic Republic of, **4:103–108**, *105*, 9:674–676
Congo, Republic of, **4:108–110**, *109*, *110*
Congregacion de Religiosas Hijas de San José, 12:554
Congregación de Santa Mariana de Jesús, 9:769
Congregatio de auxiliis, **4:110–113**
  Acquaviva, Claudius, 1:72

Álvarez, Diego, 1:326
Báñez, Domingo, 2:50
Clement VIII (Pope), 3:785
conflict over grace during, 14:48
Salas, Juan de, 12:612
Thomism, 14:50
Congregatio de Propaganda Fide. See Congregation for the Propagation of the Faith
Congregatio de Propaganda Fide pro Negotiis Ritus Orientalis (Congregation for the Propagation of the Faith for the Matters of the Oriental Rites), 5:21
Congregatio pro Ecclesia Orientali (Congregation for the Oriental Church), 5:21, 22
Congregatio pro Ecclesiis Orientalibus (Congregation for the Eastern Churches), 5:21–22
Congregatio pro Gentium Evangelizatione (Congregation for the Evangelization of Peoples), **5:480–481**
Congregatio prosarum, early cycle, 13:3, 4
Congregatio Sanctae Mariae Montis Oliveti Ordinis Sancti Benedicti. See Olivetan Benedictines
La Congrégation, **4:113**, 5:796
Congregation Centorbi, 6:551
Congregation de Notre Dame (Canada), 8:432
Congregation for Catholic Education, 4:553
Congregation for Divine Worship and the Discipline of the Sacraments (CDWDS), 7:525
Congregation for Institutes of Consecrated Life and Societies of Apostolic Life (CICLSAL), 8:423, 424
Congregation for the Doctrine of the Faith, 11:518
  Christocentrism, 3:558
  homosexuality, 7:66, 71–73
  Sixtus V (Pope), 3:611
  teaching authority of the Church, 13:780
Congregation for the Evangelization of Peoples. *See* Congregation for the Propagation of the Faith; Evangelization of Peoples, Congregation for the (CEP)
Congregation for the Oriental Church, 12:790
Congregation for the Propagation of the Faith, 10:976, **11:749–752**
  African American Catholics, 1:160

Alexander VII (Pope), 1:262
American Board of Catholic Missions, 1:350
Antioch Patriarchate, 1:525
apostolic delegation in the United States, 1:582–583, 584
Bouquillon controversy, 2:564
Burma, 2:706
California, 2:866, 867
Canada, 3:9
Caribbean, 3:119
Carthage, 3:188
catechumenate, 3:252
China, 3:494, 497, 498, 514, 516
Confirmation, 4:88
Congo, 4:104
Conwell, Henry, 4:245
Copts, 4:255
Discalced Carmelites, 3:145
Dominicans, 4:844–845
Eastern Churches and the, 5:21–22
Fidelis of Sigmaringen, St., 5:713
founded by Gregory XV, 5:21
founding, 3:53, 613
Gregory XV (Pope), 6:505
Ledóchowski, M. H., 8:444
liturgical language, 8:668
Massachusetts, 2:554
Matters of the Oriental Rites, 5:21, 22, 12:251
Melkite Catholic Church, 1:195
Oregon, 2:430–431
Ripa, Matteo, correspondence with, 12:251
Rist, Valerius in Indochina, 12:255
Saint Alexander of Orosh Abbey, 12:532
  See also Evangelization of Peoples, Congregation for the (CEP)
Congregation of Benedictine Sisters of Perpetual Adoration, 2:260
Congregation of Bursfeld, 2:272
Congregation of Canons Regular of St. John Lateran, 2:126
Congregation of Cellites. *See* Alexian Brothers
Congregation of Ceremonies, **3:349–350**
Congregation of Christian Brothers. *See* Irish Christian Brothers
Congregation of Christian Workers of St. Joseph Calasanz (*Kalasantiners*), 12:793
Congregation of Clerks Regular Minor, 3:94, 95
Congregation of Clerks Regular of St. Paul. *See* Barnabites

Congregation of Clerks Regular of Somascha, 3:415

Congregation of Fathers of the Sacred Heart, 8:228

Congregation of France, 8:336

Congregation of Friars Pilgrims for Christ among the Gentiles, 4:851

Congregation of Holy Cross, **7:18–21**

Congregation of Incarnate Word and Blessed Sacrament, **7:370–373**

Congregation of Jesus and Mary (CJM) (France), 5:440, 441

Congregation of Justina of Padua, 12:643

Congregation of Lyons, 4:113

Congregation of Maria Auxilium Christianorum, 3:420

Congregation of Mariannhill Missionaries, 2:559, 3:621, **9:163**, 11:223

Congregation of Marians of the Immaculate Conception of the Blessed Virgin Mary. *See* Marian Fathers

Congregation of Mary, Queen (CMR), **4:113–114**, 8:834

Congregation of Minims of the Sorrowful Mother, 2:95–96

Congregation of Missionary Benedictine Sisters of Tutzing, 2:260

Congregation of Missionary Sisters, Servants of the Holy Spirit, 13:539

Congregation of Monte Corona (Umbria), 2:898

Congregation of Notre Dame, 8:431–432

Congregation of Notre Dame de Sion, **10:460**, 11:923

Congregation of Our Lady of Charity of the Refuge (Caen, France), 5:440

Congregation of Our Lady of Mt. Carmel, 3:129–130

Congregation of Our Lady of the Retreat in the Cenacle. *See* Religious of the Cenacle

Congregation of Our Lady of the Rosary, 4:838–839

Congregation of Our Lady of the Sacred Heart, 4:839

Congregation of Our Saviour, 5:834

Congregation of Perpetual Adorers, 5:435

Congregation of Piccola Opera della Divina Providenza, 10:672

Congregation of Portugal, 2:272

Congregation of Priests of St. Basil. *See* Basilians (Byzantine)

Congregation of Primitive Observance. *See* Subiaco Congregation

Congregation of Regular Clerics. *See* Theatines

Congregation of Religious, 8:223

Congregation of Rites, 12:790

  candles, 3:15

  canonization, 3:63, 64

  chasubles, 3:446

  Consilium, 4:164, 165

  founding, 8:640, 662

Congregation of Sacred Rites and Ceremonies, 12:256

Congregation of Saint Adalbert, 2:273

Congregation of St. Brigid. *See* Brigidines

Congregation of St. Catharine of Siena, 4:839–840

Congregation of St. Catherine de Ricci, 4:839

Congregation of St. Cecilia, 4:840

Congregation of St. Dominic, 4:840

Congregation of St. George, 2:126

Congregation of Saint Joseph (CSJ), 12:554

Congregation of St. Justina, 3:473

Congregation of St. Marcellina, 12:609

Congregation of St. Mary, 4:840

Congregation of St. Maur. *See* Maurists

Congregation of St. Peter, 8:308, 311

Congregation of St. Rose of Lima, 4:841, 8:360

Congregation of St. Thomas Aquinas, 4:841

Congregation of Sainte-Geneviève, 8:336

Congregation of Sankt Ottilien, 2:273

Congregation of Senanque, 8:512

Congregation of Servants of the Sacred Heart, 9:364–365

Congregation of Sisters of St. Agnes, **12:531**

Congregation of Sisters of St. Dorotea, 5:921

Congregation of Sisters of the Holy Cross, **7:21–22**

  Gillespie, Angela, 6:224

  Moreau, Basil Anthony, 9:893

Congregation of Sisters of the Holy Family, **7:23**

Congregation of Sisters of the Holy Infant Jesus, 2:117, **7:30**

Congregation of Sisters of the Immaculate Conception, 9:364–365

Congregation of Sisters of the Third Order of St. Francis of Perpetual Adoration, 5:877

Congregation of the Annunciation, 2:255–256

Congregation of the Apostolic Missions, 12:694

Congregation of the Brothers of St. Patrick. *See* Patrician Brothers

Congregation of the Cenacle, 4:292–293

Congregation of the Daughters of Mary Immaculate. *See* Marianist Sisters

Congregation of the Daughters of St. Camillus, 13:848

Congregation of the Holy Cross, 4:841

Congregation of the Holy Ghost

  Le Roy, A., 8:512

  Leen, E., 8:445–446

  Poullart des Places, Claude François, 11:563

Congregation of the Holy Office, 7:491

Congregation of the Holy Roman and Universal Inquisition (Holy Office). *See* Roman Inqusition

Congregation of the Immaculata, 12:680

Congregation of the Immaculate Heart of Mary (Missionhurst), 3:499, 621, **7:337–338**

Congregation of the Lateran, 3:69

Congregation of the Little Sisters of Divine Providence, 9:600

Congregation of the Mission. *See* Vincentians

Congregation of the Missionaries of Saint Charles, 12:717

Congregation of the Missionary Servants of the Poor, 4:447

Congregation of the Most Holy Name, 4:841–842

Congregation of the Most Holy Redeemer, 1:307–308

Congregation of the Most Holy Rosary, 4:295, 842

Congregation of the Mother Co-Redemptrix (CMC), **4:114**

Congregation of the Mother of Carmel (Syro-Malabar), 3:130, 459

Congregation of the Observance, 13:27

Congregation of the Oratory, 2:105, 10:249, 13:127

Congregation of the Penitents of St. Mary Magdalen, 3:413

Congregation of the Priests of Mercy. *See* Fathers of Mercy

Congregation of the Queen of the Holy Rosary, 4:840–841

Congregation of the Religious Missionaries of Our Lady of Perpetual Help, 9:377–378

Congregation of the Religious of Jesus and Mary, 13:942

Congregation of the Resurrection, 12:174

Congregation of the Sacred Hearts of Jesus and Mary, **12:497–498**

Congregation of the Sacred Stigmata. *See* Stigmatine Fathers

Congregation of the Servants of the Most Sweet Name of Mary, 12:291

Congregation of the Servants of the Sacred Heart of Jesus and the Poor, 14:888

Congregation of the Sisters of St. Dominic of the Immaculate Heart of Mary, 4:842

Congregation of the Sisters of St. Veronica of the Holy Face, 3:227

Congregation of the Sisters of the Holy Family, 9:118

Congregation of the Sisters of the Holy Names of Jesus and Mary, 4:953, **7:33–34**

Congregation of the Sisters of the Immaculate Conception of the Blessed Virgin Mary, 4:530

Congregation of the Sisters of the Third Order of St. Francis of Assisi, Servants of the Poor. *See* Albertines

Congregation of the Sons of the Holy Family, 9:130

Congregation of the Third Order of St. Francis of Mary Immaculate, 5:878

Congregation of the Visitation of Holy Mary, 5:868

Congregation of Valladolid, 2:272

Congregation of Vincentian Sisters of the Immaculate Conception. *See* Albertines

Congregation of World Mission, 8:232

Congregational churches, **4:114–118**
  Baptist emergence from, 2:78
  Browne, Robert, 2:638, 639
  Bushnell, Horace, 2:717
  Church-State relations, 3:638, 640, 647, 650
  covenant theology, 4:328–329
  Massachusetts, 9:304
  missions, 4:116
  origins, 4:114–116
  unity, 4:114–115, 116, 117–118

Congregational singing, **4:118–120**
  Credos, 4:356, 357
  folk music, 7:260
  hymnology, 7:252, 254, 255, 260

Congregations, local (Baptist), 2:77–78

Congregations and laicism, 8:283

Congregations of oblates, 10:512

Congrès Eucharistique de Montreal (Emard), 5:186

Congress (U.S.), 12:228

Congress of Latvian Catholics, 8:375

Congress of Mantua (1459), 10:373

Congress of Vienna (1814-15), 10:846

Congruism, **4:120–121**
  Divine concurrence, 4:72
  Molinism, 9:772
  predestination, 11:652–653
  Suárez, Francisco, 13:559

Conicaris Jesuit Mission (Mexico), 9:709

Conimbricenses, 1:677

Coninck, Giles de, **4:121**

Conjectures sur les mémoires originaux dont il parait qu'il Moise s'est servi pour composer le livre de la Genese (Astruc), 5:519

La Conjuration du Compte Jean-Louis de Fièsque (Retz), 12:179

Conlaed (Bp. of Kildare), 8:167

Conn, Joann Wolski, 5:680

Connaissance de l'est (Claudel), 3:768

Connaturality, 8:205–206

Connecticut, **4:121–126**
  Cantwell v. Connecticut (1940), 3:660, 661
  Catholic colleges and universities, 6:654
  Church-State relations, 3:647, 650
  Daughters of Isabella, 4:533–534
  Fundamental Agreement (1639), 3:647
  Saybrooke Platform (1708), 3:647
  temperance movments, 13:797
  Toleration Acts of Connecticut (1784), 3:650
  See also specific dioceses and archdioceses

Connecticut, Cantwell v. (1940), 3:660, 661

Connecticut Catholic (periodical), 6:55

Connell, Francis J., 3:287, **4:126**
  catechesis, 3:244
  criticism of John Murray's views, 10:68

Connelly, Cornelia (Mother), **4:126–127**
  religious habit, 12:100
  Society of the Holy Child Jesus, 7:17–18

Connelly, J., 4:349

Connery, J., 1:24, 27

Conniat, Marie Hyacinthe (Mother), 4:534

Connolly, James L., 5:612

Connolly, John (Bp. of New York), **4:127**, 10:312

Connolly, Myles, **4:127**

Connolly, Thomas A. (Abp. of Seattle, WA), 12:852–853

Connolly, Thomas J. (Bp.), 2:23

Connolly, Thomas Louis (Abp. of Halifax), **4:127–128**

Conolly, Phillip, 1:900

Conon (Pope), **4:128–129**, 719, 8:535, 12:355

Conques Abbey (France), 3:691, **4:129**

La Conquistadora (Our Lady of Peace) (Santa Fe, NM), 10:285, 12:674, 675

Conquistadores, **4:129–133**
  Argentina, 1:648
  Costa Rica, 4:288–289
  Cuba, 4:417
  encomienda condemned, 8:340–341

Conrad (14th c. monk), 5:29, 32

Conrad (Abp. of Salsburg), 3:67

Conrad (prior of Canterbury), 3:72

Conrad, Frowin, 2:255, 12:568

Conrad, Joseph, **4:133–134**

Conrad II (Holy Roman Emperor), 2:327, **4:134–135**
  John XIX (Pope), 7:929
  Leo IX (Pope), St., 8:485
  Lucius II (Pope), 8:846

Conrad III (King of Germany), 1:126, 4:410, 5:444

Conrad Bosinlother, Bl., **4:135**

Conrad of Bavaria, Bl., **4:135**

Conrad of Constance, St., **4:135–136**

Conrad of Eberback, 3:749

Conrad of Gelnhausen, 3:636, 784, 4:55, **136**

Conrad of Marburg, 5:165

Conrad of Masovia, 3:537

Conrad of Montferrat, 7:774

Conrad of Offida, Bl., **4:136–137**, 5:736

Conrad of Ottobeuren, Bl., **4:137**

Conrad of Parzham, St., 1:323, **4:137**, 6:185

Conrad of Querfurt (Bp. of Hildesheim and Wü), **4:137**

Conrad of Waldhausen, 7:230

Conradin (Prince), 3:778

Conradine of Brescia, Bl., 4:197

Conring, Herman, 2:874

Conrius, F., 1:893

Conroy, George (Bp. of Ardagh), 1:583

Conroy, Hilary, 7:581

Consalvi, Ercole (Card.), **4:137–139**, 7:672
  Concordat of 1801, 4:61, 138
  Congress of Vienna, 3:618
  Lambruschini, L., 8:307

opposition to, 8:489

Severoli, A., 13:42

Conscience, **4:139–147**, 11:948

Bible, 4:140–141, 142, 143–145, 146

character, 3:387

deliberation, 4:629

as general concept, 4:139–140

Heidegger, M., 12:885

judgment, 7:173–174

Malebranche, Nicolas, 9:75

manifestation, 9:115–117

objection to military service, 4:149–151

philosophy, 4:139–140, 141–143

syndersis, 13:681

theology, 4:141–147

universality, 4:139

Conscience, Council of, 8:269

Conscience, examination of, **4:147–148**, 8:399, 410–411

Conscience, freedom of, **4:148–149**, 5:949, 8:541

Conscientious objection, 3:660, 661, **4:149–151**, *150*, 14:641

Consciousness, **4:151–154**

agnosticism, 1:184

central sense, 3:346

cogitative power, 3:823

contradiction, 4:224

dreams, 4:905

epistemological, 4:151–152

existentialism, 5:545–546

free will and unconscious influences, 5:933

James, William, 7:703

knowledge compared, 8:202

philosophical thought, 4:153–154

psychological, 4:153, 154

self-knowledge, 8:206

subsistent truth, 14:230

Consecranda (Schulte), 12:789

Consecrated Life (Canon Law), **4:154–156**

Consecrated Phrases: A Latin Theological Dictionary, 5:208

Consecration, 4:257, 7:34, 35

Consecration, personal, **4:156**

Consejo de la Suprema y General Inquisición (The Council of the Supreme and General Inquisition). *See* Inquisition

Consejo Episcopal Latinoamericano (CELAM), 1:654, 655, 3:121, 627, **4:157–158**

first (1955), 9:726

second (1968), 8:544, 546, 870, 9:426, 688, 726

third (1979), 9:726–727

fourth (1992), 9:727, 12:685–686

Bolivia, 2:469

Camara, Helder Pessoa, 2:900

liberation theology, 1:655

Consensus of Sandomierz, 4:80

Consensus Sandomiriensis (1570), 2:461

Consensus Tigurinus (1549), 4:416

Consent, Moral, **4:158–159**

Consequences, teleological ethics and, 13:791

Consequentialism, **4:159–160**

Conservation, Divine, **4:160–162**

annihilation, 1:471

causality, 3:303

Conservatism and Liberalism, Political, 8:182

Conservatism and Liberalism, Theological, **4:163**

Lambruschini, L., 8:307–308

Lefebvre, M., 8:446–449

Conservative Baptist Movement, 2:80

Conservative Judaism, 8:10

Consideraciones políticas sobre la situación de España (Balmes), 2:32–33

Considerateness, familial piety and, 11:332, 334

Considerations on Painting (LaFarge), 8:276

Considérations sur la France (de Maistre), 5:969, 9:60–61

Considine, John J. (Father), **4:163–164**

Consilia seu responsa iuris (Schmalzgrueber), 12:741

Consilium, **4:164–165**

Congregation for Divine Worship, 4:789

Jungmann's role, 8:61

revision of service books, 8:641

Consilium cuiusdam ex animo cupientis esse consultum et R. pontificis dignitati et christianae religionis tranquillitati (Faber), 5:583

Consilium de emendanda Ecclesia (Contarini), 4:202

Consilium for the Implementation of the Constitution on the Liturgy

described, 8:665

Ecumenical aspects, 8:679

liturgical movement, 8:676

Consilium on Sacred Liturgy, 12:258

Consistory, 1:945, 3:106–107, **4:165–166**

Consobrino, João (Sobrinho), **4:166**

Consociatio Internationalis Musicae Sacrae, 8:704

Consolata Missionaries, **4:166**

founding, 1:291, 3:621

Kenya, 8:150

Somalia, 13:308

Consolata Missionary Sisters, 4:166

Consolation of Philosophy (Boethius), 2:454, 9:438, 10:756, 959

Consolations, Spiritual, **4:166–167**

Consolatorium piorum (Maes), 9:30–31

Consors Paterni Luminis, **4:167**

Consortium Perfectae Caritatis, 8:422

Constabilis, St., **4:167–168**, 8:268

Constable, Benedict, 5:238

Constable, Cuthbert, **4:168**

Constable, Henry

Recusant literature, 11:960

religious sonnets, 13:320

Constance, Bl., 4:44

Constance, Councils of, **4:168–173**, 5:243

Escobar, Andrés de, 5:352

Eugene IV (Pope), 5:444

exemption, 5:530

Protestant Reformation, 12:13

(1414-18), 3:604, 4:203

Assemblies of the French Clergy, 1:788

authenticity of decrees of, 4:171–172

Canon Law, 3:51

cardinalate, 3:105

Catrik, John, 3:295

Chrysoberges, Andrew, 3:572

Clifford, Richard, 3:805

composition of, 4:302

conciliarism, 4:56–57, 136, 168–170, 171–172

convocation of, 4:301

Dominici, John, 4:855

Gerson, Jean, 6:190

Gregory XII (Pope), 6:500

Haec sancta (decree), 6:607–608

heresy, 4:170–171

Hus, John, 3:604, 605, 4:480–481, 7:228–229

Hussite opposition, 13:132

Johann Nider's participation in, 10:386

John XXIII (Antipope), 7:939

Julius II, 8:486

monastic reform, 2:272

papal reform, 2:133

papal taxation, 1:466

Constance, Councils of (continued)
reform, 4:171
regarding tyrannicide, 14:256
Sigmismund convoking, 13:116
theological censure, 3:337
tyrannicide, 7:884
Western Schism, 4:168–170, 203
See also Western Schism (1378-1417)
Constance, Treaty of (1153), 1:126, 8:847
Constancy. See Long-suffering
Constans (Bp. of Ancyra), 1:398
Constans I (Roman Emperor), 4:173
Council of Sardica, 12:692
Nicene Creed, 1:662
Roman militia, 4:128
Constans II (Emperor)
Martin I (Pope), St., 9:216
Vitalian (Pope), St., 14:568
Constans II Pogonatus (Byzantine Emperor), 4:173
Armenia, 1:700, 4:958
Eugene I (Pope) St., 5:442
Monothelitism, 2:750, 7:656
Constantin Order of St. George, 12:547
Constantine (Pope), 4:177–178
Constantine I (Armenian Catholicos), 1:702
Constantine I (the Great) (Roman Emperor), 4:179, 179–183
architecture, 1:754, 3:594, 684
Arianism, 4:181, 299, 470
Arianism exiles, 1:662, 817, 818, 3:594, 632
Arianism intervention, 1:266–267, 661, 685
Athanasianism, 4:470
Canon Law, 3:37
Christmas, 3:553
Constantinople, 2:777, 3:594, 4:181–182
conversion, 2:780, 3:250, 474, 594, 4:179–180, 12:316
Council of Nicaea (325) role, 10:347–348
cross, 4:379, 383
crucifixion, 4:389
death, significance, 8:53
donation of property to the Church, 11:757
Donatism, 1:859, 3:594, 632, 4:180, 299, 862
Emperor cult, 4:182, 186
empire, 12:316–318, 353–355
Eusebius of Caesarea, 5:451–453

Eusebius of Nicomedia, 5:454
hospitals, 7:127
labarum banner, 8:263
lamps and lighting, 8:314
Lateran, 8:347
Milan, Edict of, 9:625
monogram, 4:180
Nicene Creed, 1:661–662
pilgrimage, 11:344
relics, 13:89
religious policy, 4:299, 749
Sylvester I (Pope), St., 13:655–657
Sylvester legend, 4:182–183, 860, 861
tomb of St. Peter, 12:578
Constantine II (Antipope), 4:178–179, 11:243
Constantine II (Patriarch of Constantinope), 7:281, 282
Constantine II (Pope), 13:517
Constantine II (Roman Emperor), 4:173
Constantine III Leichudes (Patriarch of Constantinople), 4:176–177
Constantine IV (Byzantine Emperor), 4:173–174
Benedict II (Pope), St., 2:239
Constantinople Council III, 4:186, 193
Donus (Pope), 4:870
Irene (Byzantine Empress), 7:572
Monothelitism, 7:81
Third Council of Constantinople, 1:174, 2:750
Constantine V (Byzantine Emperor), 4:174
Anastasius (Patriarch of Constantinople), 1:388
iconoclasm, 2:733, 751, 759, 785, 793, 7:281–282
monasticism, 7:282
Paul I (Pope), St., 11:19
Zachary (Pope), St., 14:904
Constantine VI (Byzantine Emperor), 2:752, 785
Constantine VI (Emperor), 9:759
Constantine VII Porphyrogenitus (Byzantine Emperor), 2:775, 4:174–175
Byzantine chant, 2:743
historiography, 2:798–799
Constantine IX Monomachus (Byzantine Emperor), 4:175, 176
Constantine III (Byzantine Emperor), 4:176
Eastern Schism, 2:758, 824, 4:187
triple alliance, 8:485

Constantine X (Byzantine Emperor), 4:176–177
Constantine XI Palaeologus (Byzantine Emperor), 4:175–176, 177
Eastern Schism, 2:764
Ottoman invasions, 2:788
rebuked by Nicetas Stethatos, 10:357
Constantine XII (Byzantine Emperor), 4:188
Constantine Cephalas, 2:804
Constantine Chrysomallus, 2:759
Constantine of Barbanson, 4:183
Constantine of Nakoleia (Bp.), 7:280
Constantine of Rhodes, 2:805
Constantine the African, 3:187, 4:183–184, 184
cathedral and episcopal schools, 3:441
Latin literature, 9:450
Constantinian basilicas, 2:146, 148, 14:391–392
Constantinople (Byzantium, Istanbul)
Alexander II (Pope), 1:253
Alexandria, 4:185, 195–196, 252–254
Andrew legend, 4:185, 195
Antioch, 4:195–196, 285
Arab seige (717), 8:473
archaeology, 4:188
arts and architecture, 1:756, 757, 2:727, 4:188–189
Byzantine art and civilization, 2:739, 770, 782, 12:317
Constantine I (the Great) (Roman Emperor), 2:777, 3:594, 4:181–182, 184–185
Crusades, 4:188, 402–403, 409, 413
early history of Church, 4:184–185
fall of (1453), 1:659, 676, 702, 2:764, 788, 828, 881
holy lance, 7:30–31
Latin Empire, 2:761, 787, 823, 3:602, 688–689, 8:366–367
liturgical history, 8:652
local councils, 4:302
monasticism, 4:188, 9:790, 797–798
Muslim rule, 4:176, 196–197
patriarchal school, 2:820, 826
precedence, 4:190, 195, 196
primacy, 1:523, 2:744, 821, 3:595
Rome, 4:185–188
sack of (1204), 2:738–739, 745, 760, 787, 3:602
stational liturgy, 8:652
Studion Monastery, 13:554–555
See also Byzantine Church
Constantinople, Colloquy of (532), 1:503

Constantinople, Councils of
communication of idioms, 4:26
creedal statements, 4:185, 190,
353–355
Cyril of Jerusalem, 4:470
Damian of Pavia, 4:506
Ecumenical status, 4:194–195
first (381), 4:185, **190**, 195, 300,
5:22, 292, 12:317
Acacius of Beroea, 1:50
African bishops, 10:432
Alexandria Patriarchate, 1:271
Amphilochius of Iconium, St.,
1:365
Apollinarianism, 1:559, 560
apostolicity, 1:595
Arianism, 1:663
Armenia, 1:705
Canon Law, 3:38
Copts, 4:255
Damasus, 4:504–505
Diodore of Tarsus, 4:750
as ecumenical, 7:111
Gregory of Nazianzus, St., 6:515
homoousios, 4:198, 7:65
Justinian I, 8:98–99
Leontius of Byzantium, 8:502
Liberatus of Carthage, 8:550
Origenism, 10:660–661
primacy of Constantinople, 1:523,
2:744, 821, 3:595, 10:945
Roman Empire, 3:594
second (553), 1:607, 2:499–500, 820,
4:191–193, 300, 5:274, 463
Ambrosian Rite, 1:343
Assyrian Church of the East,
1:805
Christology, 3:561, 595, 596
demonology, 4:649
Didymus the Blind, 4:738
Evagrius Ponticus, 5:464
Holy Trinity dogma, 14:196
Justinian I, 4:186
Theodore of Mopsuestia, 5:511
Three Chapters controversy,
14:64
third (678-81), 2:750, 821, 3:559,
4:186, **193–194**, 300, 10:968
Agatho, St., 1:174
Andrew of Crete, St., 1:405
Armenia, 1:712
Benedict II (Pope), St., 2:239
Christ with two volitions, 7:361
Christocentrism, 3:558
Dionysiana collectio, 4:752

Justinian II, 4:128
Leo II, 8:478
Monothelitic controversy, 4:173,
7:80–81
fourth (869-70), **4:194–195**
Adrian II (Pope), 1:124, 2:755
Anastasius the Librarian, 1:390
Bulgaria, 2:679–680
Byzantine Church, 2:755
Canon Law, 3:46
Honorius I, 4:193
Photian Schism, 4:187, 5:23,
7:310
religious habit, 12:100
Constantinople, Ecumenical Patriarchate
of, 2:744–745, 4:195–197, 5:18, 22
Serbia, 13:8
Sergius I (Pope), St., 13:13
Sergius II (Pope), 13:13
Sicily, 13:103
Sinnius I, 13:169
Sinnius II, 13:169
Constantinople, Synods of (360-1351)
Acacius of Caesarea, 1:51
Andrew of Crete, St., 1:405
apocatastasis, 1:548
Arianism, 1:663
hesychasm, 2:763, 837
iconoclasm, 2:821
pentarchy theory, 2:825
Constantinople, Univerisity of, 6:433,
13:882–883
Constantinople, University of the
Imperial Palace of, 2:822
Constantinople-Rome rivalry
Anatolius of Constantinople, 1:392
Andrew, St. Apostle, 1:403
Council of Chalcedon, 1:392
First Council of Constantinople,
3:595
Constantinopolitan Creed, 1:712, 4:185,
190, 353–355, 356–357
Constantius II (Roman Emperor), 2:784,
4:197
Arianism, 1:662, 663, 818, 2:139,
3:632, 8:51, 554, 13:7
Byzantine Empire, 2:780
Christian persecution, 4:749, 750
Church law, 12:318
Council of Sardica, 12:692
death, 5:455
Donatism, 4:862
Honorius (Roman Emperor), 7:87
Liberius (Pope), 5:666
Nicene Creed, 1:662

Senate in Constantinople, 12:319
Serapion of Thmuis, 13:7
Constantius of Fabriano, Bl., **4:197**
Constitutia Cypria, 4:402
Constitutio Olonensis (Lothair I), 5:766
Constitutio Romana, 3:169, 5:443,
10:915
Leo IV (Pope), St., 8:482
Sergius II (Pope) consecration, 13:14
A Constitution Based on Social Justice
(Rosmini-Berati), 12:384
Constitution on the Sacred Liturgy
(*Sacrosanctum concilium*) (Vatican
Council II), 11:615, 12:468,
471–472, 475, 478–481, 14:415
ambos, 1:336
Anointing of the Sick, 1:486
blessings, 2:439–440
Bugnini, Annibale, 2:676–677
cantors, 3:75
catechumenate, 3:252
church architecture, 3:522, 717
Church history, 3:626
Compline, 4:44
concelebration, 4:50
congregational singing, 4:118, 119
ecclesiology, 5:38
faith and liturgy, 8:715
homily, 7:63
hymnody and hymnals, 7:259–262
liturgical art, 8:625–626
liturgical catechesis, 8:645
liturgical languages, 8:668–669
liturgical movement, 8:676
liturgical year, 8:716
nature of penance, 8:469
Office reformed, 8:731
Sacramental theology, 12:256
sacred music code, 8:701–702,
704–705
sanctoral cycle, 12:663
spiritual life, 13:435
Constitutionalism, Church-State relations
and, 3:640–641
Constitutione Apostolica (instruction,
Paul VI), 14:182
Constitutiones Aegidianae, 1:233
Constitutiones Apostolurum, 3:37, 59,
336
See also Apostolic constitutions
Constitutiones Narbonnenses, 3:336
Constitutiones per Hippolytum or
Epitome, 3:38

Constitutions

  Essai sur le principe générateur des constitutions politiques (Maistre), 9:61

  Maine, 9:55

  Malaysia, 9:71

  Malta, 9:82–83

  Massachusetts, 9:304–305

  Mexico, 9:579–580

Constitutions (Loyola), 7:313–314

Constitutions of Melfi (Frederick II), 7:488

Constituto Romana of 824, 7:924

Constitutum (Justinian I), 3:596

Constitutum I and II (Vigilius), 4:*191, 192,* 8:*98–99,* 14:*510, 510–511*

Constructing Local Theologies (Schreiter), 10:623

Consubstantiality, **4:197–199**

  Constantine I (the Great) (Roman Emperor), 4:181

  God the Son, 6:296

  homoousios as term, 7:65

  Logos, 8:763

  Luther, 3:608

  Nicea Council I (324-325), 8:763, 10:354, 14:193

  Nicetas of Remesiana's defense of, 10:357

  theological terminology, 13:889

  See also Homoousios

Consuetudines (Guigo I), 3:192, 193, 194

Consuetudines Castellenses, 8:131

Consultatio de Articulis Religionis inter Catholicos et Protestantes Controversis (Cassander), 3:205–206

Consultation on Church Union (COCU), **4:199–200**

  Consultation on Common Texts, 4:201

  liturgical calendar, 8:644

Consultation on Common Texts (CCT), **4:201,** 5:253

  Common Lectionary: The Lectionary Proposed by the Consultation on Common Texts, 8:441

  lectionary consensus, 8:440–441

Consumers and Wage Earners: The Ethics of Buying Cheap (Ross), 12:385

Consummated fullness of grace, 9:253

Contagious magic, 9:37–38

Contarini, Eleanore, 1:346

Contarini, Gasparo (Card.), **4:201–204,** *202,* 12:526

  Bucer, Martin, 2:653

Colonna, Vittoria, 3:856

Cortese, Gregorio, 4:280

Ecumenical councils, 4:302

School of Cologne, 3:846

Contarini, Giovanni (Patriarch of Constantinople), **4:203**

Conte, Noël-Hilaires le, 12:276

Contemplation, **4:203–209**

  action, 13:442

  art, 1:747, 748–749

  Benedictine, 4:207–209

  Bernardino of Laredo, 2:322

  Berthier, Jean Baptiste, 2:333

  Bonaventure, St., 2:491–492

  Cassian, John, 3:207

  Denis the Carthusian, 4:661–662

  Dominican, 4:204, 206, 846, 848–849

  Guigo de Ponte, 6:566

  happiness, 5:439, 9:96–97

  Hugh of Balma, 7:150

  Philo Judaeus, 11:269–270

  Plotinus, 11:422

  spirituality, 13:449

  supernatural, 4:204–205

  See also Meditation; Prayer

Contemplative Hermit Sisters, 2:282

Contemplative life, **4:209–211**

  active life vs., 1:83

  Evagrius Ponticus, 5:465

  religious, 12:88–89

Contemporary Christian Art Galley (NY), 8:386

Contenet (Mother), 4:293

Contenson, Guillaume Vincent de, **4:211,** 14:51

Content psychology. *See* Associationism

La Contessa Matilda e i romani Pontefici (Tosti), 14:120

Contextual theologies, 9:728–729

Conti, Gregory. *See* Victor IV (Antipope, fl. 1138)

Conti, Michelangelo de' (Card.). *See* Innocent XIII (Pope)

Continence, **4:211–212,** 11:514–515

  See also Sex; Temperance

Contingency, **4:212–214**

  agnosticism, 1:183

  cosmological argument, 4:285–287

Continuum, **4:214–218**

  paradoxes of Zeno solved by analysis of, 10:18

  time as, 14:79–80

Contra academicos (St. Augustine), 3:352

Contra adversarium perfectionis Christinae (Gerard of Abbeville), 6:159

Contra Arianos (Fulgentius of Ruspe), 6:24

Contra astronomos judiciarios (Oresme), 10:380

Contra Celsum (Origen), 1:564, 10:653

Contra errores Graecorum (Aquinas), 14:19, 27

Contra Eunomium (St. Gregory of Nyssa), 6:518

Contra Eutychen (Haring), 14:2

Contra gradus et pluralitates formarum (Giles of Rome), 5:818

Contra Graecorum opposita (Ratramnus of Corbie), 11:924

Contra impugnantes Dei cultum et religionem (Aquinas), 14:17, 27

Contra Judaeos et Gentiles (St. John Chrysostom), 7:948

Contra Marcionem (Tertullian), 5:509

Contra Monophysitas (Leontius of Jerusalem), 8:503

Contra Noetum (Discourse against the Heresy of Noetus) (St. Hippolytus of Rome), 6:859

Contra Novatianos (Pacian), 10:744

Contra Parmenianum Donatistam (St. Optatus), 10:612

Contra pestiferam doctrinam retrahentium pueros a religionis ingressu (Aquinas), 14:20, 27

Contra pluralitatem formarum, de productione formae substantialis (Thomas of Sutton), 5:818, 14:37, 45

Contra quatuor labyrinthos Franciae (Abelard), 1:19

Contra simoniam (Peter the Painter), 11:207

Contra Symmachum (Prudentius), 11:792

Contra Thomam et Pecham (Nicholas of Lisieux), 14:20

Contra Vigilantium (St. Jerome), 12:51

Contra Wiclevistas (Robert Waldby of York), 12:271

Contraception, **4:218–223,** 11:514–516

  anovulants, 1:489–491

  Argentina, 1:657

  artificial birth control, 12:272, 13:47

  Austria, 1:916

  basal body temperature method (BBT), 10:176

  Casti connubii, 3:214

  Catharism, 4:219–220

  coitus interruptus, 4:218, 219

  de Koninck, Charles, 4:618

  disordered conscupiscence, 8:875

Germany, 6:187

gnosticism, 4:218

Humanae vitae (encyclical, Paul VI), 5:40, 860, 7:179–181, 12:272

hysterectomy, 7:265–266

Ireland, 7:568

Manichaeism, 4:218–219

modern problem, 4:221–222

natural family planning vs., 10:176–179

papal social thought, 13:258

Paul VI (Pope), 3:627

rhythm method, 13:258

values of Church, 4:220–221

Contraception and Holiness, 12:272

Contractus germanicus, 3:18

Contradiction, principle of, **4:223–224**, 5:745

absolute, 1:43

criteriology, 4:367–368

demonstration, 4:652

excluded middle principle, 5:503–504

identity, 7:304

logical necessity, 10:227

Contradictiones iuris civilis cum canonico (Blasio), 3:52

Contraposition, 11:770

Contrarietates et diversitates seu differentiae inter ius canonicum et romanum (Galvanus), 3:52

Le Contrat de l'homme avec Dieu par le saint baptême (St. Eudes), 5:441

Contreras, Miguel, 3:416

Contrition, **4:224–229**

attrition, 1:842–843

attrition distinguished from, 4:224, 225–229

compunction compared to, 4:45

justification, 8:89

occasions of sin, 13:157

Contritionism, 1:843, 4:226, **229–230**

Controversia anglicana de potestate regis et pontificis (Becanus), 2:191

Controversia de valore baptismi haereticorum (Schwane), 12:793

Controversial theology, 13:909

Controversias antiguas y modernas (Navarrete), 10:215

Controversies (Bellarmine). *See Disputationes de Controversiis Christianae Fidei adversus hujus temporis haeretios* (Bellarmine)

Contumely, **4:230**, 677, 7:502

See also Insult

Convenientia, Argumentum Ex, **4:230–231**

Convent, **4:231**

Convent of the Assumption (Daphni, Greece), 3:689

Convent of Unterlinden (France), **14:333–334**

Conventionalism, physical laws and, 11:315–316

Conventual Franciscan Order, 8:229, 12:690

Conventual priors, 11:716

Conversano Monastery (Italy), 1:8

Conversation, 6:45–46

Conversations on the Gospels (Alcott), 14:148

Conversion

catechumenal process for, 4:237–238, 241–242

chiefs and kings, 9:691

to Christianity in the Roman Empire, 9:690

concept, 13:272

grace, 4:239–241

Igatius of Loyola, St., 13:430, 431

Jeremiah, 7:755

in the Middle Ages, 9:613–614

neophytes to describe, 10:239

Nobili's method, 10:407–408

numbers, 4:242

paradigm conflict in research, 13:272, 273

pastoral practice, 4:237–238, 242

proselytism, 4:241–242

Protestant denominations to Eastern Orthodoxy, 9:696

seven-step description, 13:271–272

socialization, religious, 13:271–275

Soka Gakkai, 13:298

as term, 4:234, 241

See also Mission and evangelization; Mission and missions

Conversion: The Old and the New in Religion from Alexander the Great to Augustine of Hippo (Nock), 10:409

Conversion, in the Bible, 3:546, **4:231–234**, 239, 240

Conversion, psychology of, **4:238–239**

Conversion, theology of, **4:234–238**

atheism, 1:826

Augustine, St., 1:875

God's self-communication, 8:775

loe as state, 8:833

Lutheranism, 8:894

radical intellectual conversion, 8:775

Conversion and converts, **4:241–242**, 13:25

Conversion and grace, controversies of, **4:239–241**

Conversion en Piritú (Ruíz Blanco), 12:407

The Conversion of the Pagan World (Manna), 9:119–120

Conversos, Inquisition and, 1:304

Convert, as term, 4:241

Convertini, Francis (Father), 7:406

Converts. *See* Conversion and converts

Convivio (Dante), 4:518

Convocation of the English Clergy, **4:243–244**, 5:245, 6:740

Courtenay, William, 4:318

direct to approve Thirty-Nine Articles, 14:7–8

Convulsions, children, patron of, 12:413

Conway, John, 7:794

Conway, William (primate of Ireland), **4:244–245**

ecumenism, 7:566

Northern Ireland violence, 7:568

Conwell, Henry (Bp. of Philadelphia), 4:*245–246*, 11:82–83, 238

Conwell, Russell H., 2:80

Conybeare, F. C., 7:850

Conzelmann, Hans G., 2:386, 5:522, 7:850, 10:303

Cook, David, 11:252

Cook, James, 6:669, 10:324

Cook Islands, 10:531

Cooke, George, 5:*285*

Cooke, Henry, 7:549

Cooke, Terence J. (Card.), **4:246–247**, 7:70, 10:318–319

Cooley, Charles Horton, 13:282

Cooper, Anthony Ashley

British moralists, 2:623

Platonism, 11:416

Cooper, James Fenimore, 14:149

Cooper, John Montgomery, **4:247–248**, 5:237

Cooper, Samuel Sutherland, 13:33, 173

Cooperation

God's action, 8:89

solidarity and collaboration, 13:267–268

Cooperators (Salesians). *See* Salesian Cooperators

Coornhert, Dirck Volkertszoon, 2:894, **4:248**

Cope (great mantle), 10:857

Cope, Marianne (Mother), **4:248–249**, 5:891, 6:671

Cope and Humeral Veil, 4:*249*, **249**

Copeland, M. Shawn, 3:288, 5:677, 678

Copernicus, Nicolaus, **4:249–251**, *250*
    Aristotelianism, 1:678
    astronomy, 12:815–816
    geocentrism, 6:59
    relativism, 12:46
    space, 13:373, 374
Copleston, Frederick C., **4:251–252**, 7:792
Copley, Thomas, 2:887
Coppens, Joseph, 5:519, 13:21
Coptic art, 1:270, 758
Coptic Christianity, 2:744, **4:252–255**, 5:19, 322
    Abū 'L-Barakāt, 1:49
    Chalcedon, Council of, 1:271
    clerical celibacy and marriage, 3:324, 325
    Council of Catholic Patriarchs of the Orient, 4:295–296
    Dioscorus (Patriarch of Alexandria), 4:756
    Hyvernat, Henri, 7:266–267
    martyrs, 3:207
Coptic Gospel of Thomas, 14:12
Coptic literature, 5:643
Coptic liturgy, 1:273, 4:253, **256–267**, 13:42–43
Copyists, 2:512–513, 845
Cor Arca Legem Continens (hymn), **4:257**, 5:201
Cor nostrum (encyclical, Alexander III), 1:256
Cor Unum, 2:705, 3:81
Corban, **4:257**
Corbeiensis, 3:40
Corbeil, William of (Abp. of Canterbury), **4:258**
Corbie, Ralph, Bl., 5:236
Corbie Abbey (France), 1:359, 3:154, **4:258**
Corbington, Ralph. *See* Corbie, Ralph, Bl.
Corbinian of Freising, St., **4:258–259**, 5:192
Corbishley, Thomas, **4:259**
Corbo, V., 2:380
Corbon, Jean, 3:237, 7:528
Corby, Ralph John, Bl., 7:579
Corby, William, 10:461
Corcoran, James Andrew, **4:259–260**
Cordell, Charles, **4:260**
Cordemoy, Géraud de, 3:185
Cordeses, S., 1:326
Cordeyro, Antonio, 12:767
Cordier, Jean-Nicolas, Bl., **4:261**, 12:276
Cordi-Marian Missionary Sisters, **4:261**

Córdoba (Spain), **4:261–263**
Córdoba, Antonio de, **4:263**
Córdoba, martyrs of, 3:863
Córdoba, Pedro de, **4:263–264**
Córdoba Belda, Társila, Bl., 1:4
Córdova, Matías de, **4:264**
Córdova y Salinas, Diego de, **4:264**
Cordovero, Moses, 2:834–835
Coredemptrix, Mary, Blessed Virgin as, 9:259–263
Corelli, Arcangelo, **4:264–265**
Coressios, George, 6:458
Cori spezzati, 3:523
Corinth Basilica, 1:756
Corinthians, Epistles to the, **4:265–268**
    activism, 1:84
    agility, 1:176
    altars, 1:320
    Amen, 1:348
    anamnesis, 1:383
    asceticism, 1:776, 777
    Assumption of Mary, 1:799
    atonement, 1:837
    attire in and hairstyle, 4:267
    authorship, 4:265–266, 267–268
    baptism, 2:59, 60, 61, 65
    Barnabas and Paul, 2:103
    beatific vision, 2:169, 170, 171, 174
    birth imagery in baptism, 2:75
    blesseds, 2:436
    celibacy, 3:322, 327
    charisms, 3:389, 578
    charity, 3:396, 397
    Christian healing, 6:678
    Christian law, 8:403, 404
    Christian paideia expression, 10:754
    Christian way of life, 3:546
    Church of Christ, 13:439
    Church property, 3:724
    class distinctions, 4:267
    clerical celibacy and marriage, 3:322
    conscience, 4:141, 148
    contraception, 4:220
    covenant, 4:328
    Divine indwelling, 7:441
    Divine judgment, 8:40
    Divine plan, 5:58
    divorce, 13:49
    ecclesiastical authority, 1:923
    edification, 5:84–85
    eschatology, 5:340–341
    eucharistic liturgy, 5:410–411
    faith, 5:592, 6:382

faith, profession through baptism, 2:59, 60
friendship with God, 6:11
gifts of Holy Spirit, 7:45
glorified body, 6:242, 243
glory, 6:245
glory of God (end of creation), 6:245
glossolalia, 3:391, 6:249
gluttony, 6:251–252
Gnosis, 6:254, 255
God the Son, 6:295
God's spirit, 13:427, 428
grace, 6:381, 382
heaven, 6:685
Holy Spirit, 13:440, 441
homosexuality, 7:66
house churches, 2:146
human sexuality, 13:48
ignorance sinful, 13:36
incest, 7:378, 13:50
infant baptism, 2:67
infused knowledge, 8:207
Jesus as Lord, 8:781
Jesus as sacrificial lamb, 10:936–937
Judith, Book of, 8:43
justification, 8:78, 79, 80
kenosis, 8:143
kerygma, 8:157, 158
kindness, 8:172
Kingdom of God, 8:174
kiss of peace, 8:185
Lamb of God, 8:301
lamps and lighting, 8:314
lay spirituality, 8:413
life of grace, 13:441
likeness of Christ, 13:440
Lord's Day, 8:781, 782
Lord's Supper, 8:784, 785
manna, 9:118–119
maranatha, 9:130
meat offered to idols, 4:266–267
merit, 6:383
mystical body of Christ, 10:100, 101
on the Parousia, 4:266, 10:896
Paul's third missionary journey, 11:7
peace, 11:50
penance, 11:68
perseverance, 11:133
preaching and teaching, 11:627
Precious Blood, 11:638
presbyters, 11:673
promiscuity, 8:872
ransom, 11:909
rapture, 11:912

rebirth, 11:951

resurrection of Christ, 12:148–149

self-denial, 13:443

sexual mores, 13:48–49

sexuality, 4:266

Silas (Silvanus), 13:119

sin, 13:147, 148

sins of Adam, 9:87

slavery, 13:207, 208, 211

social principle, 13:249

Son of God, 13:314

Son of Man, 13:317, 318

soul of the Church, 13:359

spirit, 13:425

Spirit of God, 4:266

spirituality, 13:438

structure, 4:265–266, 268

suffering servant, songs of the, 13:591

transcendent God, 13:441

veiled heads for women, 8:596

vices, 9:315–316

virgines subintroductae, 14:539

virginity, 4:306–307

women, role of, 14:831

works of charity, 1:301, 302, 3:401, 402, 403, 404, 405, 724

works of the flesh, 8:871

world, 14:840

Corippus (medieval poet), 9:439

Corker, James Maurus, **4:269**

Cormier, Hyacinthe-Marie, Bl., **4:269–270**, 854

Cornaro, Catarina, 4:461–462

Cornaro, Elena Lucrezia Piscopia, **4:270**

Cornay, Jean-Charles, 14:492

Cornbury, Lord, 9:63

Corneille, Pierre, 2:115, 116

    Catholic revival, 4:313

    Racine, Jean Baptiste, 11:887

Cornelius (Pope), St., 3:403, 408, **4:270–271**, 7:38, 8:*53*, 10:464, 12:387

Cornelius, John, Bl., **4:271**, 5:232, 7:579, 580

Cornelius of Zierikzee, **14:924–925**

Cornerstone, Church, **4:271**

Cornerus, Christopher, 4:60

Cornoldi, Giuseppe, 12:772

Cornu, Marie, 5:623

Corona Christi capitis, 1:147

Coronado, Francisco Vásquez de, 1:686–687, 10:284

Coronation Book of Charles V (miniature, 1365), 10:*497*

Coronation of Saint Rose of Lima (Cignani), 12:*380*

Coronel, Juan, **4:271–272**

Coronelli, Vincenzo Maria, 5:207

Coronets, as ecclesiastical symbol, 6:763

Corónica y historia religiosa de la provencio de la compañía de Jesús de Mexico en la Nueva España (Pérez de Rivas), 11:116

Corpa, Pedro de (Father), 5:875, 6:148

Corporatism, 2:1, 8:371

Corporativism. *See* Corporatism

Corporeal visions, 14:562

Corpus canonum Africanum, 3:39, 40

    See also Hispana Versio (canonical collection)

Corpus canonum orientale, 3:40, 59

Corpus Christi. See Corpus et Sanguis Christi, Solemnity of

Corpus Christi, an Encyclopedia of the Eucharist, 5:208

Corpus Christi Church (Aachen, Germany), 3:711

Corpus Dictionary of Western Churches (O'Brien, ed.), 5:208, 10:524

Corpus et Sanguis Christi, Solemnity of, **4:272**, 5:463, 12:486

    autos sacramentales, 1:924–925

    ceremony (Venezuela), 14:*441*

    cycles (plays), 4:897–900

    origins of feast, 7:156, 8:52

    Sequence, 13:1

Corpus Hermeticum (Nock and Festugière), 10:409

Corpus Hermeticum (Reitzenstein), 12:40

Corpus Iuris Canonici, 3:46, 50, 59, **4:272–273**

    Boniface VIII (Pope), 2:504

    Council of Trent, 3:53

    Latin Rite, 8:368

    Liber sextus, 8:536

    period, 4:602–604

Corpus Iuris Civilis (Justinian I), 3:39

Corpus Mysticum, 12:486

Corpus Scriptorum Christianorum Orientalium, 5:5–6, 8:429

Correa de Vivar, Juan, 14:110

Correa Magallanes, Mateo, St., **4:273**

Correction, fraternal, **4:273–274**

    accusation, 1:66

    courtesy withholding, 4:318

Correctoria, **4:274–278**

Correctoria corruptorii Thomae (Dominican text), 4:275

Correctorium (John of Paris), 7:978–979

Correctorium (William de la Mare), 12:761–762

Correctorium "Circa" (John of Paris), 4:277, 14:46

Correctorium corruptorii "Quaestione" (William of Macclesfield), 14:45–46

Correctorium Corruptorii "Quare" (Dominican text), 4:275–276, 12:230–231, 14:45

Correctorium fratris Thomae (William de la Mare), 4:275, 5:818, 14:43

Correctorium "Quaestione" (Dominican text), 4:275, 276–277

Correctorium "Sciendum" (Dominican text), 4:275, 276, 12:269, 14:45

Correggio, Claudio da. *See* Merulo, Claudio

Correia, Antony, Bl., 1:951

Correia, Louis, Bl., 1:951

Correr, Angelo. *See* Gregory XII (Pope)

Correspondance de Rome (periodical), 2:279

Le Correspondant (periodical), 14:465

"Correspondences" (Cranch), 14:148

Correspondenza di Roma. See Correspondance de Rome (periodical)

Corrierre della Serra (Tyrrell as anonymous), 14:258

Corrigan, Michael Augustine (Abp. of New York), 3:290, 4:*278–279*, 5:82, 10:315, 329

    Americanism, 1:354

    apostolic delegation in the United States, 1:582

    Bahamas mission, 2:14

    Bouquillon controversy, 2:564, 7:1

    Doane, George Hobart, 4:796

    Farley, John (Card.), 5:628

    Salesians, 12:615

Corrigan, Patrick, **4:279**

Corsetus Siculus, Antonius, 3:52

Corsini, Andrea (Card.), 4:280

Corsini, Andrew (Bp. of Fiesole), St., **1:404**

Corsini, Lorenzo. *See* Clement XII (Pope)

Corsini, Neri (Card.), 4:279–280

Corsini, Pietro (Card.), 4:279

Corsini family, **4:279–280**

Cort, Thomas, Ven., 5:226

Corté, Hernán, 4:*129*, 130–131, 5:175

Cortés, Fernando, 3:415

Cortés, Juan Donoso

    Christian political theory, 12:773

    philosophy of history, 6:884

    political theology, 11:460

Cortese, Enzo, 11:97–98

Cortese, Gregorio, **4:280**

Cortona, Pietro da, 2:114, 3:705

Corvey Abbey (Saxony), 1:98, **4:280–281**, 912, 8:852

Corvinus, Matthias, 7:213

Coscia, Niccolò (Card.), 2:245, 3:789

Cosgrove, Henry (Bp. of Davenport, IA), **4:281**, 535

Cosimo, Piero di, 2:375

Cosin, John (Bp. of Durham), 3:152

Cosmas (Bulgarian priest), 2:458

Cosmas II Atticus (Patriarch of Constantinople), 2:759

Cosmas and Damian, SS., 4:282, **282–283**, 719

Cosmas Indicopleustes, 1:270, 2:807–808, 5:399

Cosmas of Maiuma, 2:742, 803

Cosmas of Prague, 1:463

Cosmas the Melodian, 2:803, **4:281–282**

Cosmas the Priest, 3:259

Cosmic Religion (Einstein), 5:141

Cosmogonic myth, 10:127

Cosmogony, **4:283–284**

    Bible, 4:284

    Gnosticism, 6:258

    Manichaeism, 9:110–111

    Shāpūraqān (Mānī), 9:113

Cosmographia (Bernard Silvester), 2:317, 14:2

Cosmological Argument, **4:285–287**

Cosmological transcendence, 14:141–142

Cosmology, **4:287**

    Empedocles theories, 5:195

    Rhazes, 12:211

    scientific cosmologies and eschatolgies, 5:332, 350–351

Cosmos

    as potential from God, 9:93

    redemption in order, 9:95

Cosmozoic processes, 8:574

Cossa, Baldassare. *See* John XXIII (Antipope)

Costa, Duarte de, 2:588

Costa, Simon da, Bl., 1:952

Costa ben Luca, **4:287–288**

Costa Lopes, Martinho, 5:9

Costa Rica, **4:288–290**, *289*, 9:707, 12:290, 372

Costantini, Celso (Card.), 1:803, 3:500, **4:290–291**

Costanzo, Camillo, Bl., 7:734

Costanzo, John J., 8:822

Costelloe, Peter, 7:581

Côté, Dom Claude, 2:232

Cote, Michael (Bp.), 9:59

Cotesmore, Thomas, 5:237

Cotham, William, 7:699

Cotolendi, Ignace, 3:497

Coton, Pierre, **4:291**, 7:783

Cotta, Landulph, 1:660

Cottam, Thomas, Bl., **4:291–292**, 5:228, 717

Cotten, Edward, 10:346

Cotter, Joseph (Bp. of Winona, MN), 14:774

Cottiaux, Jean, 1:19

Cottier, Georges, 7:528

Cottolendi, Ignace, 1:197

Cottolengo, Giuseppe Benedetto, St., 3:419, **4:292**

Cotton, Bartholomew, 1:464

Cotton, Francis R. *See* Nevill, Francis, Ven.

Cotton, John, **4:292**

Couderc, Marie Victoire Thérèse, Bl., 3:334, **4:292–293**, 12:31

Coudrin, Pierre Marie Joseph, 1:950, 4:293, **293–294**, 10:528, 12:497

Coughlin, Charles Edward, 4:294, **294–295**, 10:172, 13:77

Coughlin, Mary Samuel (Mother), **4:295**

Coulanges, Numa Fustel de, 5:703

Coulomb, C. A., 1:835

Council for Social Action, 4:117

Council for the Implementation of the Constitution on the Sacred Liturgy (Concilium), 4:164–165

Council of Catholic Patriarchs of the Orient (CPCO), **4:295–296**

Council of Churches in Malaysia (CCM), 9:72

Council of Community Churches, 4:39

Council of European Bishops' Conferences (CCEE), **4:296–298**

Council of European Churches (KEK), 4:297, 298

Council of Major Superiors of Women Religious (CMSWR), **4:298**

The Council of the Supreme and General Inquisition (Consejo de la Suprema y General Inquisición). *See* Inquisition

Council of Trent (Zuccarelli), 8:76

Council on the Laity, 3:626–627

Councilors (Apostolic Penitentiary), 11:76

Councils, General (ecumenical)

    conciliarism, 4:56–58, 136

    history, 5:642

        appeals to a future council, 1:599

        conciliarism, 4:53–56

Constantinople Council I, 4:190

    frequency of, 4:171

    number of, 4:302

    See also Conciliarism

Councils, General (ecumenical), history of, **4:298–303**

Councils, General (ecumenical), theology of, **4:303–306**

Counsel, Gift of, **4:306**

Counsels, evangelical, **4:306–307**

    ascetical theology, 8:832

    religious, 12:88

Counter Reformation, 3:610–612, **4:308–314**

    Abercromby, Robert, 1:20–21

    Aguado, Pedro de, 1:189

    among 16th century Ruthenians, 12:422

    Angelus Silesius, 1:429

    attrition-contrition distinction, 4:226–227, 229, 230

    Australia, 1:903, 905, 906

    Austria, 1:911–912

    baroque period, 2:109–112

    Billick, Eberhard, 2:394–395

    Blarer, Jakob Christoph, 2:433

    Carmelites, 3:142–143, 611

    Castellino da Castelli, 3:214

    Catherine de' Ricci, St., 3:267

    chapter of faults, 3:386

    church architecture, 3:701, 703

    Church property, 3:727

    Church's affirmation of free will, 2:110

    Clement VII (Pope), 3:782

    Clement VIII (Pope), 3:785

    Clerks Regular of the Mother of God, 3:803–804

    condition of the Church, 4:309

    conversions of Protestants, 8:431

    Council of Autun, 1:926

    Czechs, 4:482–483

    devotional renewal, 4:311

    ecclesiology, 5:37

    Echter von Mespelbrunn, 5:42

    Estonia, 5:377

    Ferdinand II (Holy Roman Emperor), 5:688

    German leaders, 6:181

    Holy League, 8:424–425

    Hosius, Stanislaus, 7:117

    humanism, 7:191–192

    Hungary, 7:214, 216

    hymnology, 7:250

    indulgences, 7:438–439

influence of second Thomism, 14:48
Latomus, B., 8:370
Lawrence of Brindisi, 8:407
lay spirituality, 8:415–416
Lithuania, 8:605
Low Countries, 8:777
mission, 3:613
papacy development during,
  10:842–843
papal reform, 4:311–312
penance, 11:71
Poland, 8:342, 11:441–443
popular devotions, 4:709–710, 711
Protestant writers censured, 8:265
reform attempts, 8:487
renewal of religious orders,
  4:309–311
Seripando, G., 13:17
Slovakia, 13:220–221
Slovenia, 13:225
social contract, 13:240
Soto, P., 13:330–331
Spain, 13:391
Switzerland, 13:649
as term, 4:308
theology, renewal in study of, 13:909
Ukraine, 14:273
Vulgate translation of Bible, 8:364
Wales, 14:612
See also Jesuits
Counts, George, 5:94
*County of Allegheny v. American Civil
  Liberties Union* (1989), 3:668
Couperin, François, **4:314–315**, *315*
Couppé, Louis, **4:315**
Courage, 1:602, 3:388, **4:315–316**, 7:70
Courcelle, P., 1:337
Courianne, Samuel de (Abbot), 12:541
Courier, Paul Louis, 5:199
Cournot, Antoine Augustine, **4:316–317**,
  7:300
Couroyer, Bernard, 5:50
Cours de philosophie (De Wulf), 12:776
Cours de philosophie positive (Comte),
  4:47, 10:609
*Cours entier de philosophie ou système
  général selon les principes de M.
  Descartes* (Regis), 12:31
*A Course in Religion for Elementary
  Schools* (Schorsch), 12:785
Coursins, William (Bp. of Milwaukee,
  1902-1988), 14:783
Court, Antoine, 2:916
Courtenay, Peter (Bp.), **4:317**, 5:530

Courtenay, Richard (Bp. of Norwich),
  4:317
Courtenay, William (Abp. of
  Canterbury), 3:72, **4:317–318**
  condemnation of Wyclif, 12:131
  Crumpe, Henry, 4:400
  Lollards, 8:766
  Simon of Sudbury, 13:133
  Wyclif, John, 3:605, 4:170, 317–318
Courtesy, **4:318**
Courtly love, **4:318–322**
  Bijns, Anna, 2:393
  Chaucer, Geoffrey, 3:456
Courveille, Jean Claude, 9:176
Cousin, Pierre, 5:441
Cousin, Victor, 4:*322*, **322–323**
  Cartesianism, 3:186
  eclecticism, 5:47, 48
  laicism, 8:283
  neoscholastic revival, 12:776
  spiritualism, 13:436
Coussa, Acacius (Card.), **4:323**
Coustant, Pierre, **4:323**
Couturier, Pierre Marie Alain,
  4:323–324, *324*
  art innovations, 8:623
  Notre-Dame-de-Toute-Grâces
    Church, 1:803, 3:713
Coux, Charles de, **4:324**
Covenant, in the Bible, **4:324–328**,
  7:629
  anger, 1:430
  apologetics, 1:563
  blood, 2:443
  Church, 3:575
  curses, 4:442–443
  Deuteronomy, 4:703
  God's call to faith, 6:271–273
  justice of men, 8:73
  justification, 8:77–78
  leadership, 8:179
  marriage as, 9:337
  mediator role of Moses in Israel and
    Yahweh, 10:6
  messianic message as, 9:540
  oath taken to establish, 10:498
  punishment for infidelity to, 7:597
  puritan theology, 4:328–329
  sin, 13:143
  Ten Commandments, 4:4, 6–7, 9
Covenant code. *See* Book of the
  Covenant
Covenant theology, **4:328–329**
  biblical theology, 2:385–386
  Calvinism, 2:894

Church-State relations, 3:646
  law, relation of, 8:396
  social contract, 13:240
Covenanters, 2:912, **4:329–330**
Coventry and Lichfield, Ancient See of
  (England), **4:330**
Coventry Cathedral (England),
  4:330–331
Coverdale, Miles (Bp. of Exeter), **4:331**,
  5:531, 7:255–256
Coverdale Bible, 3:27
Covington Diocese (KY), **4:331**
Cowardice, **4:332**
Cowardice of spirit. *See* Pusillanimity
Cowl, **4:332**
Cowley, Leonard, 12:574
Cowley Fathers, **4:332–333**
Cox, Harvey, 11:890
Cox, John. *See* Sugar, John, Bl.
Cox, Robert, 5:238
Cox, Samuel H., 5:467
Cozza-Luzi, Giuseppe, 2:143
CP (Passionist Sisters of the Cross and
  Passion), 10:930–931
CP (Religious of the Passion of Jesus
  Christ), 10:930
CPA (Catholic Press Association),
  10:159
CPCO (Council of Catholic Patriarchs of
  the Orient), **4:295–296**
CPPCD (Conference for Pastoral
  Planning and Council Development),
  4:75
Crackenthorpe, Richard, 1:676
''Cradle of Bishops'' (Mount St. Mary's
  College and Seminary), 10:35
Craft of the Wise. *See* Wicca
Craftsmen, preservation of, 4:782–783
Craig, A. C., 5:74
Craig, Thomas, 5:702
Crainquebille (France), 5:841
Cram, Ralph Adams, 3:715, 716
Cranach, Lucas (the Elder), 1:544–545
Cranch, Christopher, 14:148
Cranmer, Thomas (Abp. of Canterbury),
  3:72, 268–269, 4:*333*, **333–334**
  Anglican orders problem, 1:434, 436,
    593
  Barton, Elizabeth, 2:130
  Bonner, Edmund, 2:507
  Book of Common Prayer, 1:442,
    2:524
  Brookes, James, 2:627
  Bucer, Martin, 2:653
  confessions of faith, 4:80
  execution, 12:10

Cranmer, Thomas (Abp. of Canterbury) (continued)
    Gardiner, Stephen, 6:95–96
    Henry VIII's divorce, 6:740
    Lasco, J., 8:342
    marriage and coronation of Anne Boleyn, 5:244, 12:8
    Pilgrimage of Grace, 1:786
    Protestant Reformation, 12:9, 20
    Ridley, Nicholas, chaplain to, 12:243
Crashaw, Richard, 11:960
Crasset, Jean, **4:334**
Crastone, John, 3:142
The Crater (Cooper), 14:149
Crates (Cynic philosopher), 4:455–456
Crathorn, John, **4:334–335**
Crawley-Boevey, Mateo, **4:335**, 12:492
Crayer, Caspar de, 1:539
CRCCM (Conference of Roman Catholic Cathedral Musicians), **4:75**
Creagh, Richard (Bp. of Armagh, Ireland), 1:698, 7:557, 580
Cream. See Science of Sciences (Bar-Hebraeus)
Created Actuation by Uncreated Act, **4:335–336**, 624
Creating an Inclusive Church program (NCCIJ), 10:158
Creatio ex nihilo, 4:342, 343
Creation, **4:336–345**
    annihilation, 1:470–471
    Aquinas' philosophy, 5:525
    art, 1:742–743
    Avicenna's views on essence and existence, 5:364
    Barth, Karl, 2:121
    Bible, 4:336–342, 344
    Bonaventure, St., 2:488
    Book of Genesis, 8:574
    cabala, 2:834, 8:871
    causality, 3:303, 304, 307
    Christian anthropology, 3:530
    Clarenbaud of Arras, 3:762
    conservation contrasted with, 4:162–163
    cosmogonic myths, 10:127, 129
    development by man, 9:93
    doctrine, 5:180
    Enuma Elish, 5:267–269
    Eve, 5:483
    evolution, 4:345, 347
    feminist theology and eschatology, 5:679
    God, 6:273–274
    Hinduism, 6:852–853

    iconography, 4:*337, 338*, 342
    identity principle, 7:304
    Liber de causis, 8:533
    literary myths on the, 10:124
    matter and form, 9:349–350
    origin of life, 8:574
    out of nothing, 10:416–417
    purpose, 6:246
    Resurrection of Christ, 12:165
    sin, mythical and cultic aspects, 13:149
    sin's effect, 13:144–145
    stoicism, 13:537
    terminology, 4:341
    theology, 4:342–345
    Thierry of Chartres, 14:3
    women, 14:828
Creation-centered theology, 5:55
Creationism, **4:346–347**
    Greek philosophy, 13:918–919
    soul, human, 13:353
    soul's origin, 13:353
Creative Evolution (Bergson), 2:296
Creative imagination, 1:746, **4:347–349**
    See also Imagination
The Creative Mind (Bergson), 10:20
Creative Ministry (Nouwen), 13:774
Creative Synthesis and Philosophic Method (Hartshorne), 6:657
Creativity
    imagination, 7:327
    theology, 13:917
    Treatise on Logic (Maimonides), 9:53
    Whitehead, Alfred North, 14:705
Creator, will of, 13:276
Creator alme siderum (hymn), **4:349**
The Creator and the Creature (Faber), 5:582
La Crédibilité et l'apologétique (Gardeil), 6:94
Credit Union Movement (Korea), 10:56
Credo of the People of God (Paul VI), 10:670
Credos, 4:356–357
Cree people, 8:270
Creed in eucharistic liturgy, **4:356–357**
Creed or Chaos? (Sayers), 12:716
Creeds, **4:349–356**
    Antioch, Creed of, 4:352
    Apostolic Fathers, 1:588
    Armenian Creed, 2:72
    articles of faith, 1:764
    Athanasian Creed, 1:815–817, *816*, 3:279, 4:685, 5:384

    catechesis, 3:228, 230, 231, 234, 242, 251
    Constantinopolitan Creed, 1:712, 4:185, 190, 353–355, 356–357
    Fourth Formulary of Sirmium, 1:663
    iconography of Apostles, 1:576
    Jerusalem Creed, 4:190
    Orthodox Creed of 1678 (General Baptists), 2:78
    redemption, 11:975
    Roman Baptismal Creed (R), 4:35
    Roman Creed, 4:351
    Second Creed of Antioch, 1:662
    Syriac Creed, 2:72
    See also Apostles' Creed; Nicene Creed
The Creeds of Christendom (Schaff), 12:726
Creighton, Edward, 4:357
Creighton, John, 4:357–358
Creighton, Mandell, **4:358**
Creighton family, **4:357–358**
Crell, Nicaolaus, 4:416
Cremation, **4:358–360**, 557, 6:33, 13:215
Cremona Cathedral (Italy), 3:*690*
Crépy, Treaty of (1544), 7:669
Crescas, Ḥasdai ben Abraham, **4:360–362**
    Albo, Joseph, 1:232
    Aristotelianism, 1:673, 7:865
    Spinoza, 13:418
Crescens (Bp. of Ancyra), 1:398
Crescens the Cynic, 3:592
Crescentia, St. *See* Vitus, Modestus and Crescentia, SS.
Crescentii family, **4:362**, 6:491, 7:926, 927
Crescentius, John (patrician of Rome), 4:362
Crescentius I de Theodora, 2:500, 4:362
Crescentius II (Roman consul), 4:362
Crescentius de Caballo Marmoreo, 4:362
Cresconius (Bp.), 3:40
Crespi, Juan (Father), 12:644
Crespin, Jean, 12:538
Cresswell, Arthur and Joseph, 8:269
Cretan-Mycenaean religion, **4:362–363**, 10:86
Crete (Greece), 3:786
Crétin, Joseph (Bp. of St. Paul, MN), **4:363–364**, 9:654–655, 12:542, 551–552, 572, 573
    Cosgrove, Henry, 4:281
    Loras, Jean Mathias, 4:921
Crib, Christmas, **4:364**, 895
Crichton, William, 1:20

Crick, Francis, 2:404

Crimea (Russia), 8:164

Crimen for ecclesiastici (Schmalzgrueber), 12:741

Criminali, Antonio, Ven., **4:364–365**

Criminology, 2:191

Crimont, Joseph R. (Bp. of Alaska), 1:208

Crisis, theology of, 4:721

Crisis and Closure of the Council of Trent (Jedin), 7:750

Crisis theologica bipartita (Cárdenas), 3:102

Crisógono de Jesús Sacramentado, **4:365**

Crispin, Gilbert. *See* Gilbert Crispin

Crispin, Miles, 2:190

Crispin of Viterbo, St., **4:365**

Crispina, Crispin, and Crispinian, SS., **4:366**

Crispolti, Filippo, **4:366**

Crispus, 4:182

Críst, Gilla (Bp. of Clogher, d. 1138), 9:65

Il Cristiano santificato (Sarnelli), 12:694

El Cristo de Valazquez (Unamuno), 14:289

Cristobal (Martyr of Tlaxcala), 14:95

Cristobal Magallanes. *See* Guadalajara (Mexico), Martyrs of, SS.

El Criterio (Balmes), 2:33

Criterio (periodical), 5:864

Criterion (Criteriology), **4:366–368**

Criterion (periodical), 5:160

Crites, Steven, 10:152

La Critica (periodical), 4:372

Crítica filosófica (Valverde), 14:380

Critica Sacra (Jacques and Louis Cappel), 5:518

Critical ontology, 6:656

Critical realism, 11:316, 12:915

Critical theory, Frankfurt School, 5:914

Criticism, biblical. *See* Bible, textual criticism

Criticism, philosophical, **4:368–369**, 8:120–125

Criticisms (Hassagoth) (Gikatilla), 6:211

Critique de la recherche de la vérité (Desgabets), 9:74

Critique de la recherche de la vérité (Foucher), 9:74

Critique de la science (movement), 4:316–317

Critique of Judgment (Kant), 12:346

Critique of Practical Reason (Kant), 1:42, 3:254, 5:390, 8:120, 12:256, 345

Kantianism, 8:128

morality, 8:219

Critique of Pure Reason (Kant), 6:349, 10:236, 237, 12:47, 345, 14:150

agnosticism, 1:42, 181

antimony, 1:520

categorical imperative, 3:254

cosmological argument, 4:285

reviewed, 8:125

revolution in philosophy, 8:219

Crito (Plato), 4:16

Critopoulos, Metrophanes, 6:457

Crivelli, Alexander, 1:346

Croagh Patrick, **4:369**

Croatia, **4:360–372**, *373*

Croce, Benedetto, **4:372–374**, *374*, 5:397, 11:296

aesthetics, 1:142

irrationalism, 7:587

Neo-Hegelianism, 6:712, 7:300

philosophy of history, 6:885

Crockaert, Peter, **4:374**, 14:48

Crockett, Ralph, Bl., **4:374–375**, 5:230

Croesus (King of Lydia), 4:478

Cróica de la provincia de la Visitación de Ntra. Sara. de la Merced redención de cautivos, de Nueva España (Pareja), 10:881–882

La Croix (periodical), 2:16–17, 8:157

La Croix-Saint-Ouen Abbey (France), 8:520

Croke, James, 10:645, 12:646

Croke, Thomas William (Abp. of Cashel and Emly), **4:375**

Crolly, William, 1:698

Cromer, George, 1:698

Cromer, Martin. *See* Kromer, Martin

Cromwell, Oliver, **4:375–376**, *376*, 5:248

anti-Catholicism, 3:612

Caribbean settlement, 3:111

Congregationalism, 4:114

Irish Act of Settlement, 1:75–76

Cromwell, Thomas, **4:376–377**, *377*, 5:244

Barton, Elizabeth, execution of, 2:130

Bonner, Edmund, 2:507

Faringdon, Hugh, Bl., 5:627

Henry VIII's adviser, 12:8

Henry VIII's divorce, 12:210

Houghton, John, 7:140

Pilgrimage of Grace, 1:786

Rich, Richard, 12:227

Crónica de la Provincia del Santo Evangelio de México (Vetancurt), 14:465

Crónica miscelánea de la sancta provincia de Xalisco (Tello), 13:792

Cronin, Daniel A. (Abp. of Hartford), 4:126, 5:612, 6:654

Cronin, Donough, 7:580

Cronin, Eugene, 7:579

Cronycles (Nicholas Trevet), 10:381

Crosier Fathers, 2:609, **4:377–378**, 415

Crosiers, as ecclesiastical symbol, 6:763

Crosiet, Jean, 12:491

Cross, **4:378–383**, *379–380*, *380*

Anglo-Saxon art, 1:448

church architecture, 1:318, 3:675

Crusades, 4:407–408

as ecclesiastical symbol, 6:763

relics of the Holy Cross, 4:379, 383, 7:18, 12:735

sacramental significance, 12:520

shrines of the Holy Cross, 13:89

significance, 4:391

as symbol for martyrs, 7:731

symbols, 13:666–667

veneration, 6:355–356

Way of, devotion, 8:498

See also Crucifixes; Crucifixion; Maltese Cross

Cross, F., 10:79

Cross, finding of the Holy, 4:379, **383–386**

Cross Moline, 4:380

The Cross of Jesus (Chardon), 3:389

Cross Potent, 4:380

Crossan, John Dominic, 6:876, 10:869

Crostarosa, Maria Celeste (Sister), Ven., 11:*993*

Alphonsus Liguori, St., 1:307

Redemptoristines, founding of, 11:992

Crotus Rubianus. *See* Jäger, Johann (Crotus Rubianus)

Crouzet, J., 5:405

Crow, Alexander, Bl., **4:386**, 5:229

Crowland Abbey (England), 1:22, **4:386–387**, *387*

Crowley, Jeremiah, 3:478, 5:663

Crown, Franciscan, **4:387–388**

A Crown for Our Queen (Ryan), 12:443

The Crown of Thorns (Dore), 7:815

Crown of Thorns (relic), 4:*388*, **388**

feast of, 1:147

Notre Dame Cathedral shrine, 13:90

Solesmes Abbey, 13:299

Crowns, symbols of, 13:665–666

Crowns of Martyrs (Peristephanon) (Prudentius), 11:792

Crowther, Thomas, 5:237

La Croyance, 9:60

Crozier, origins and use, 8:637

CRS (Catholic Relief Services), 10:429, 761, 14:312

Cruce, Petrus de, 10:13

Cruchaga, Alberto Hurtado, Bl., 7:793

Crucial Problems of Modern Philosophy (Hawkins), 6:672

Cruciati, 2:609

Crucifixes, **4:388**, *389*

  altars, 1:318

  history of use of, 4:378–380

  See also Cross

Crucifixion, **4:388–391**, *390*, 7:*802*

  Christ, 4:390–391

  controversies, 4:378–379

  cross, significance in, 4:391

  history, 4:388–390

  holy nails and connection to, 10:137

  representation, 4:378–380

  represented in baptismal fonts, 2:76

  See also Cross

Crucifixion, in art, 3:155, 4:378–379, **391–398**, *399*, 5:*567*

Crucifixion, theological significance of, 1:5, 4:391, **398**

Cruciform and *quatrefoil* baptismal fonts, 2:75, 76

Cruciger, Caspar, 4:416

Cruets (liturgical vessels), 8:716

Crumpe, Henry, **4:398–400**, 12:271

Crusaders' States, **4:401–405**

  Carmelites, 3:131, 140, 141

  Latin Empire of Constantinople, 8:366–367

Crusades, **4:405–414**

  Adam of Ebrach, Bl., 1:108

  Alexander II (Pope), 1:253

  Alexander VI (Pope), 1:261

  Alexandria Patriarchate, 1:271

  Alexius I Comnenus, 1:275, 2:738, 787

  Antioch Patriarchate, 1:525

  anti-Semitism during, 7:869–870

  Armenia, 1:701, 702, 705–706, 708, 709

  Bogomilism, 2:459

  Brethren of the Cross, 2:609

  bulla cruciata, 2:688

  Byzantine art, 2:738–739

  Byzantine Empire, 2:787, 4:188, 401, 403, 410, 413

  Callistus III (Pope), 2:881

  Catharism, 3:259

  Catherine of Siena, St., 3:272, 273

  Cesarini, Giuliano, 3:357

  Children's (1212), 4:409, 411

  chivalry, 3:518, 519

  Christians as targets, 4:410, 412–414

  chronicles, 1:464

  church architecture, 3:690

  Clement V (Pope), 3:779

  Council of Anse, 1:493

  criticism, 4:410

  Despenser, Henry, 4:692–693

  Eastern Schism, 1:276, 2:760, 823, 10:837–838

  Fourth Lateran Council, 8:353

  German, 3:319, 4:137

  Gregorian reform, 4:406–407

  Gregory X (Pope), Bl., 8:907

  El-Hakem biamr Allah, 4:253

  Hroznata, 7:144

  Hubert Walter, 7:144

  Hungary, 7:210

  Hussites as targets, 7:231

  indulgences, 7:437

  Innocent III (Pope), 2:688, 3:602

  as institution, 4:405–410

  Jews as targets, 4:410

  John Capistran, St., 7:944–945

  Kingdom of Jerusalem, founding of, 7:774–775

  knightly elite, 4:405–406, 407, 412, 414

  Knights of Malta, 8:193–195

  Louis IX, 8:800

  Low Countries contributions to, 10:257–258

  Maronite Church, 9:195

  medieval Latin literature, 9:451, 456

  Mongols, 4:405, 414

  Muslims as targets, 4:404, 405, 407, 410–412

  northeastern Europe, 4:414

  Order of the Holy Sepulcher of Jerusalem, 3:68

  origins, 4:405–407

  Palestine during period of, 10:784

  papal enemies as targets, 4:413–414

  Pastoureaux, 10:940

  Pius II (Pope), 11:369–370

  professionalization of military, 4:409

  propaganda for, 4:408, 409, 413, 414

  relics, 12:54

  relics of the Passion, 13:89

  Robert of Courçon died during, 12:267

  Saladin, 12:609–610

  Shepherds (1254, 1309, 1320), 4:409, 411

  Spain, 4:401, 409, 412

  states created through, 4:401–405

  Urban II (Pope), Bl., 1:276, 2:760, 3:518, 601, 14:335–336

  William II Rufus, 14:730

  First (1095-99), 4:407, 408, 410, 5:843

    Adjutor, St., 1:115

    Arnold of Hiltensweiler, Bl., 1:719

    bulla cruciata, 2:688

    Byzantine Empire, 2:787

    Crusaders' states, 4:401–402, 403–404

    Eastern Schism, 1:276, 2:760

    literature of, 4:400, 401

  Second (1146-48), 4:410–411, 5:443–444, 844, 12:544

    Armenia, 1:701

    Bernard of Clairvaux, 2:309

    bulla cruciata, 2:688

    Celestine III (Pope), 3:319

    Leonius, 8:502

    literature of, 4:400–401

  Third (1188-92), 4:411

    Armenia, 1:701

    Clement III (Pope), 3:776

    destruction of, 10:355

    Gregory VIII (Pope), 6:494–495

    literature of, 4:400–401

    Theodore of Celles, 4:377

  Fourth (1202-4), 4:188, 411, 413

    Adam of Perseigne, 1:109

    Crusade tax, 7:84

    Crusaders' states, 4:402–403

    failure of, 7:471

    literature of, 4:400, 401

    sack of Constantinople, 2:738–739, 745, 760, 878, 3:602

  Fifth (1213-21), 4:411

    Colonna, Giovanni, 3:854

    Honorius III, 7:84

  See also Crusaders' States

Crusades, literature of, **4:400–401**

Crusius, Christian, 5:47, 263, 534

Crutched Friars (Friars of the Cross), **4:415**

Cruz, Bernardo de la, 2:143

Cruz, Gaspar da, **4:415–416**

Cruz, Mancio de la, Bl., 7:734

Cruz Alvarado, Atilano, St., **4:416**

Crypto-Calvinism, **4:416**

Cryptoscopy, 3:759

Crystal Cathedral (Garden Grove, CA), 3:*702*

CTAUA (Catholic Total Abstinence Union of America), 13:801

Ctesiphon, Synod of (*ca.* 614), 1:700

Cualladó Baixauli, Francisca, Bl., 1:4

Cuartero Gascón, Jose Maria, Bl., 4:494

Cuartero Gascón, Tomas, Bl., 4:494

Cuba, 3:112, **4:416–421**, *420*

    Church-state relations, 4:418–421, 7:999

    Claret, Anthony Mary, 3:763

    ecclesiastical organization, 4:417

    Espada y Landa, Juan José Díaz de (Bp. of Havanna), 5:357

    Law, Bernard F., 2:557

    map, 4:*418*

    mission, 4:417–418, 9:706–707

Cubagua, 3:109

Cudworth, Ralph, 3:185, 5:395

    British moralists, 2:622, 623

    Cambridge Platonists, 2:908, 910

    hylozoism, 7:239–240

    world soul, 14:844

Cuenca. *See* Montemayor, Juan Francisco

Cuénot, Étienne-Théodore (Bp.), 14:492

Cuero y Caicedo, José de (Bp. of Quito, Ecuador), **4:422**, 5:63

Cuesta Redondo, Justiniano, Bl., 4:494

Cuevas, Mariano, 2:718, **4:422**

CUF (Catholics United for the Faith), 13:504

Cujas, Jacques, 5:702

Culdees, **4:422–424**, 608, 8:597, 12:533, 831–832

Cullen, Paul (Abp. of Dublin), **4:424**, 7:562, 9:18, 10:333

Cullen, Paul (Card.), 1:698, 903

Cullmann, Oscar, 3:559, 12:195, 14:83

    gates of hell, 6:107

    immortality, 7:354

Culpable ignorance, 14:585

Cult Decalogue, 8:397

Cult of Mary. *See* Devotion to Mary

Cult of St. Patrick, 10:955

Cult of the Martyrs and Confessors, 5:288–289, 12:596

Cult of the Supreme Being, 5:853, 974, 12:273, **13:626**

Cult worship, **4:426**, 14:853

    Great Mother, 10:91–92

myth, 10:125–126

Nebo (Nabu), 10:220

Ugaritic-Canaanite religious, 14:271

Cults, **4:424–426**

    churches compared, 13:274

    of the dead, 12:66–67

    Decadi, 4:586–587

    fertility and vegetation, 5:746

    France, 5:853

    New Religious Movements (NRMs), 10:298–302

    of the nude, 12:601

    pre-Christian symbolism of fish, 5:746

    relics, 12:50–51

    religious socialization, 13:271–275

    Roman religion, 12:325–326

    of the Supreme Being, 13:626

    Unification Church as, 14:299

Cultura sociale (periodical), 10:69

"Cultural" Christians Movement (China), 3:503

Cultural pessimism, 11:168

Cultural Revolution (China), 3:502–503

Culture, **4:426–436**, 7:388

    change, 4:434, 436

    as concept, 4:426–427

    deism and exposure to, 4:616–617

    elements, 4:427–430

    individiual vs. society, 4:431–433

    integration, 4:430–431

    leisure, 8:460

    mission theology, 9:729

    positivist history, 13:414

    rites of passage, 14:245

    shame, 13:68

    spirit, 13:423

    theories, 4:433–436

Culture Protestantism, 8:175

Cum Biblia sacra (apostolic letter, Benedict XV), 11:485

Cum de quibusdam mulieribus (papal decree, Clement V), 2:205

Cum ex officii nostri (papal decree, Innocent III), 7:488

Cum gravissima (motu proprio, John XXIII), 3:106, 7:936

Cum iuris canonici (motu proprio Benedict XV), 11:482

Cum nulla (papal bull, Nicholas V), 3:126, 134–135

Cum nuper (papal bull, John XXII), 3:800

Cum occasione (papal bull, Innocent X), 1:97, 717, 893, **4:436**, 7:716

Cum postquam (papal decree, Leo X), 7:438

Cum primum (encyclical, Gregory XVI), 6:509

Cum sanctissimus (Sacred Congregation for Religious), 12:862

Cumaean Sibyl, 13:100

Cuman people, 7:210

Cumberland, Richard, 2:622–623, 5:395

Cummings, James E., 3:283

Cummings, Jeremiah Williams, **4:436–437**

Cummings, Jonathan, 1:135

Cummins, George David (Bp. of Kentucky), 12:25

Cummins, Patrick, **4:437**

Cumont, Franz, 1:20, **4:437–438**, 10:96

Cunctipotens dominator (trope), 14:217

Cunegund. *See* Kinga, St.

Cunhill Padrós, Pedro (Father), 2:92

Cunialati, Fulgenzio, **4:438**

Cunibert of Cologne, St., 3:842, **4:438**

Cunnigham, William, 5:95

Cunningham, Daniel F., Rev., 12:785

Cunningham, Mary, 2:40

Cuno, Bl., 6:188–189

Cupertino, Joseph, St., 2:397

Cur Deus homo (*Why God Became Man*) (St. Anselm of Canterbury), 1:496–497, 12:129, 700

Curacao (West Indies), 3:116–117

Curaeus, Joachim, 4:416

Curci, Carlo Maria, 7:673, 12:772

Curé d'Ars, 1:311

Cure of the Pagan Evils (Theodoret of Cyr), 13:878

Curia, Roman, **4:438–440**

    1983 Code of Canon Law, 3:57

    abbreviators, 1:12–13

    administrative norms, 8:670

    Apostolic See, 1:589

    canonization, 3:63

    congregations of, generally, 4:439

    Council of Trent, 3:53

    history, 4:438

    John Paul II (Pope), 7:1004

    Lambruschini, L., 8:307

    Liber diurnis, 8:534–535

    liturgical history, 8:657

    organization, 4:438–440

    origins, 8:730

    pre-Reformation spiritual hunger, 3:607

    reorganization (1588), 3:611

    seal, 13:114

Curia, Roman *(continued)*

    See also Cardinals

Curial declarations, 11:748

Curiosity, **4:440**

Curley, Michael Joseph (Abp. Baltimore), 2:39, **4:440–441**

Curlin, William J. (Bp. of Charlotte), 3:437

Curran, Charles E., 1:53, 54, 3:292, 7:1004, 8:821

Currier, Charles Warren (Bp. of Matanzas, Cuba), 3:119, **4:441**

Curry, H. B., 1:948–949

Curse of Artemisia (epigraphical style, 4th c. B.C.), 10:*768*

Curses, 2:437, **4:441–443**

    See also Magic

Cursillo Movement, 1:906, **4:443–444**, 8:116

Curso de filosogia elemental (Balmes), 12:773

Cursus, **4:444–445**

Cursus artium (Complutenses), 4:44–45, 14:51

Cursus Curiae Romanae, 4:444

Cursus moralis, 1:311

Cursus philosophiae (Frassen), 12:764

Cursus philosophicus (Oviedo), 12:767

Cursus philosophicus (Sichem), 12:764

Cursus philosophicus thomisticus (John of St. Thomas), 7:984, 12:776, 14:51

Cursus theologiae (Goudin), 6:372–373

Cursus theologiae moralis (Babenstuber), 12:619, 14:51

Cursus theologiae moralis tripartitus (Sasserath), 12:698

Cursus theologicus (John of St. Thomas), 7:984, 12:777, 14:51

Cursus Theologicus Summam d. Thomae Complectens, 12:612, 618–619

Curtis, Alfred Allen (Bp. of Wilmington, DE), **4:445**, 14:764

Curtis, Patrick (Bp. of Armagh), 4:245

Curtis, Walter W. (Bp. of Norwich), 4:125

Curtiss, Elden F. (Abp. of Omaha, NE), 9:827

Cusack, Christopher, 7:575

Cusack, Margaret Anna, **4:445–446**, 12:556

Cusack, Thomas Francis (Bp. of Albany), **4:446**

Cushing, Richard (Card.), 2:556, 3:622, **4:446–447**, *447,* 9:309, 735

Cushites, 5:406–407, *407*

Cusmano, Giacomo (Abp.), **4:447–448**, 5:865

Cuspinian, Johannes, 12:119

Cusson, Catherine, 6:528

Custodes Hominum Psallimus Angelos (hymn), **4:448**

Custody of the Holy Gospel, 10:28

Custody of the Senses, **4:448**

Cuthbert of Canterbury (Abp. of Canterbury), **4:448–449**

Cuthbert of Lindisfarne, St., 3:598, **4:449**, 5:239, 629

    Elfleda of Whitby, 5:153

    Iona spirituality, 8:593

    "miracle of the heavenly loaves," 12:253

Cuthbert of Wearmouth (Abbot), **4:449**

Cuthburga, St., **4:449–450**, 14:766

Cuvier, Georges, 2:402

Cuxa Abbey (France), **4:450**

Cuzco City (Peru), 11:*161*

CV (Confraternity Version), 10:276

CWS (Church World Service), 10:166

Cyaxares (founder of the Medes), 9:428

Cybekks Minguell, Protasio, Bl., 7:124

Cybele (deity), **4:450–451**, *451*

Cybernetics, **4:451–453**

Cycle plays. *See* Drama

Cyclic history

    philosophy of history, 6:885–886

    theology of history, 6:886–887

Cyclopaedia; or an Universal Dictionary of Arts and Sciences (Chambers), 5:207, 208

Cydones, Demetrius, **4:453–454**

    Cabasilas, Nilus, 2:837

    Chrysoberges, Andrew, 3:572

    Eastern Schism, 2:794

    hesychasm, 2:762, 827

Cydones, Prochorus, 2:827, **4:454**

Cyneburg, St., **4:454**

Cynegils (King of the West Saxons), 2:409

Cynewulf, **4:454–455**, *455*

Cynics, **4:455–457**, 6:442, 11:288

    asceticism, 1:773–774

    early Christian theology, 3:591

    philosophy as a school for life, 6:447

    Socrates, 13:293

    as teachers and missionaries, 6:446

Cyparissiota, John, 2:827

Cyprian of Carthage, St., 3:186, 4:*457,* **457–460**, 9:228–229

    altars, 1:314

    Antichrist, 1:516

    Apocalypse iconography, 1:543

    biblical canon, 3:32

    birth imagery in baptism, 2:75

    Canon Law, 3:37

    Church property, 3:723

    Confirmation, 4:86

    Cornelius (Pope), St., 4:270

    corpus, 4:458

    Councils of Carthage, 1:785, 3:188

    creedal statements, 4:350, 351

    Donatism, 4:862, 863

    ecclesiology, 4:458–459, 5:36

    Fabian (Pope), 5:584

    Firmilian of Caesarea, 5:740

    following of Christ, 5:788

    hospitality, 7:118

    life of, by Deacon Pontius, 12:606

    liturgical history, 8:652

    martyr, as term, 4:83

    names, calling out of, 4:758

    papal primacy, 3:593

    patristic theology, 10:967

    penance, 4:225, 11:68

    penitential controversy, 11:73

    presbyters, 11:674

    priesthood, 11:693–694, 699

    provincial assemblies, 4:299

    relics, 12:51

    reordination, 7:39, 12:128

    Spain, 13:376

    Stephen I (Pope), St., 13:514

    taking Christian name practice, 10:139

    theology of Church, 3:586

    works of charity, 3:405

Cyprian of Toulon, St., 1:577, **4:460**

Cyprien de la Nativité, 3:137

Cypriot Orthodox Church, **10:688**

Cyprus, **4:460–464**, *462*

    Anthemius of Constantia, 1:502

    Antioch, 1:523

    Byzantine Empire, 4:461

    Crusades, 4:402, 403, 404–405

    ecclesiastical organization, 4:460

    map, 4:*461*

Cyrenaics, **4:464–465**, 5:107, 11:289, 13:293

Cyrene Edicts, 12:303

Cyriacus, cemetery of (Rome), 3:224

Cyricus (Bp. of Ancyra), 1:398

Cyril (Seraphim) of Turiv (Patriarch of Antioch), 1:525–526

Cyril II of Jerusalem (Greek Orthodox Patriarch), 6:459

Cyril III (metropolitan of Kiev), 14:277–278

Cyril III Ibn Loklok, 4:253–254, 255

Cyril IV (Patriarch of Antioch), 4:254

Cyril V (Patriarch of Antioch), 1:525, 4:254

Cyril and Methodius, SS., 3:599, 4:*474*, **474–477**, 479, 7:922

  Adrian II (Pope), 1:125

  Anastasius the Librarian, 1:389

  Austria, 1:908

  Boris I of Bulgaria, 2:539

  Christianity in Russia, 12:419

  Clement the Bulgarian, St., 3:799

  Photius, 2:755, 775

  Slavorum Apostoli, 13:216–217, *217*

  Slovenes, 13:225

  University of the Imperial Palace of Constantinople, 2:822

  vernacular, 3:231

Cyril Jehunla (Melchite Patriarch), 1:195

Cyril of Alexandria, St., 4:*465*, **465–470**

  Act of Union, 4:859

  biblical catenae, 3:258

  Cassian, John, 3:206

  Christology, 1:273, 391, 3:317, 363, 559

  Christology and Apollinarianism, 1:391, 559, 561, 2:792–793

  Christology and Nestorianism, 1:268, 390–391, 523, 2:793, 3:561, 595

  computing Easter, 8:642

  conflict between Nestorius, 10:254

  Council of Ephesus, 5:273–275

  the cross, 4:385

  defense of incarnation, 10:14

  descent of Christ into hell, 4:684

  Diodore of Tarsus, 4:750

  Divine indwelling, 7:441

  Easter date controversy, 5:13–14

  Ethiopian Catholic Church, 5:403

  Eutyches friendship with, 5:461, 462

  exegetical works, 5:511

  expiation, 5:565

  Fathers of the Church, 5:640

  friendship with God, 6:10

  grace, 6:401

  homoousios, 4:198

  Isidore of Pelusium, St., 7:601

  Monophysitism, 2:793, 820, 3:595, 7:263

  Nestorianism, 4:191, 195, 10:252

  physis of the Incarnate Word, 14:203

  priesthood, 11:694–696

  relics, 13:89

  Roman primacy, 3:317

  Severus of Antioch, 13:43

  Shenoute of Atripe, 13:78

  theology of Church, 3:576

  two natures of Christ, 7:816, 818, 13:196

Cyril of Constantinople, St., **4:470**

Cyril of Jerusalem, St., **4:470–472**, 5:279

  Acacius of Caesarea, 1:51

  Ambrose, St., 1:337

  baptism in the Holy Spirit, 3:393

  catechesis, 3:228, 239

  catechumenate, 3:251

  creedal statements, 4:352

  on the cross, 4:383

  death imagery in baptism, 2:75

  exorcism, 5:551

  liturgical history, 8:651

  priesthood, 11:699

Cyril of Scythopolis, **4:472–473**, 5:461, 12:452

Cyril of Turiv (Bp.), **4:473–474**

Cyrilli Versio, 3:40

Cyrion (Kyrion), **4:477**

Cyrus (Bp. of Phasis), 2:749

Cyrus (Patriarch of Alexandria), 4:253, 7:80

Cyrus II (King of Persia), 2:210–211, 3:631, **4:477–478**, 11:135

Cyrus the Great. *See* Cyrus II (King of Persia)

Cyzicus, Council of (376), 5:457

Czech Confession, 4:80

Czech Republic, **4:478–488**, *481*

  Czech National Church, 7:230, 8:156

  ecclesiastical organization, 4:479–480, 483, 484–485, 488

  Hussitism, 4:480–482, 7:230–231

  map, 4:*480*

  Romanticist music, 13:230–231

  See also Czechoslovakia

Czechoslovak Church, 4:484

Czechoslovakia, 7:227–229, 8:241–242

  See also Czech Republic; Slovakia

Czechoslovakian Orthodox Church, 13:219

Czepko, Daniel Von, 1:429

Czerski, Johann, 3:624, **4:488**, 12:369

Częstochowa (Poland), **4:488–490**

Częstochowa, Our Lady of (Poland), 13:92

D

D. Thomas sui intepres (Baron), 2:105

Da, Peter, 14:492

"Da Qin" (China), 3:491

Da Rho, Antonio, 5:445

Da Silva, Samuel, 1:69

Da Vinci, Leonardo. *See* Leonardo da Vinci

Dabin, Paul, 11:705

Dablon, Claude, **4:491**, 9:722

Dabrowski, Joseph, **4:491**, 10:624–626

Dac Nguyen, Matthew, 14:492

Dachau concentration camp

  Kozal, M., 8:245

  Leisner, K. F., 8:459

  Lichtenberg, B., 8:561

Dacheriana Collectio, 3:42, 60, 4:492

Dacia, **4:492**

  See also Denmark; Romania

Dadisho' (Assyrian Catholicos), 1:805, 806

Dado of Rouen. *See* Ouen of Rouen (Bp.), St.

Daeger, Albert T., 10:287, 12:676

Daemen, Marie Catharina (Mother Magdalen), 5:887

Daems, Edward Francis (Fr.), 4:378, 5:888–889

Daēvas, **4:492–493**

Dagaeus, 4:494

Dagobert I (King of the Franks), 1:99, 3:163, 9:518, 12:544

Dagobert II (King of Austrasia), St., **4:493**

Dagon (god), **4:493**

Daguessea, H. F., 1:57

Daher, Ignatius Michael IV (partriarch of Syria), 13:708

Dahlmann, Joseph, **4:493–494**

Dahm, Innocent, 12:541

Dahomey, 1:162

Daig MacCairill, St., **4:494**

Daillé, Jean, **4:494**, 12:856

Daimbert (Patriarch of Pisa), 2:29

Daimiel, Martyrs of, BB., **4:494–495**

Daimon, **4:495–498**, *496*

  See also Demons

Dalai Lama, 14:72

  John Paul II (Pope), 7:*994*

  Lamaism, 8:299

Dalberg, Adolf von, 4:498, *499*

Dalberg, Johann Friedrich Hugo Nepomuk Eckenbrecht von (Bp. of Worms), 4:498, 499, 12:119

Dalberg, Karl Theodor von (Abp. of Mainz), **4:499–500**, 6:183, 12:668

Dalberg, Wolfgang von (Abp. of Mainz), 4:498

Dalberg family, **4:498–499**

Dalby, Robert, Bl., 5:230

Dalgairns, John Dobree, **4:500**

Dalí, Salvador, **4:500–501**, *501*

Dalit community, Christianity and, 7:402

Dall, Gerhard Bernhard, Rev., 5:890

Dalman, Gustav, 2:385

Dalmatic, **4:501–502**, 8:634

Dalmau Rosich, Antonio María, 2:92

D'Alton, Edward Alfred, **4:502**

Dalton, J., 1:835

Daly, Edward, 10:443

Daly, Mary, 5:677

D'Alzon, Emmanuel, 1:801, **4:502–503**

Damas, Arturo Rivera (Abp. of San Salvador), 5:177

Damascene, John, St.
   systematic theology, 13:904
   theological terminology, use of, 13:890
   will and willing, 14:721–722

Damascius, 1:670, 10:241

Damascus, 1:624, 4:402, **503**, 513

Damascus, Martyrs of, **4:503**

Damascus Affair (1840), 7:874

Damasus I (Pope), St., **4:503–505**
   Agnes, St., 1:178
   Alleluia, 1:294
   Apollinarianism, 1:559, 560
   ascetism, 12:354
   Chrysanthus and Darius, SS., 3:572
   Church history, 3:594
   clerical celibacy and marriage, 3:325
   Constantinople Council I, 4:190
   epigrams, 5:287
   hymnody, 7:243
   hypostasis, 7:263
   Lapsi controversy, 5:450
   liturgical languages, 8:667
   Meletian Schism, 2:137–138
   poem honoring martyrs, 5:665
   practice of taking Christian names, 10:139
   soul of Christ, 7:813
   Theodore of Mopsuestia, 4:192

Damasus II (Pope), 1:910, **4:505**

Dambo, Gabriel, 3:368

Damen, Arnold, 2:563, 3:477

Damian of Finario, Bl., **4:505**

Damian of Pavia, St., **4:505–506**

Damiano, Celestine (Bp. of Camden, NJ), 5:879

Damien, Joseph, Fr., 2:219, 4:954–955, 14:466–467, *468*

Damnation, **4:506**

Damus el-Carita Basilica, 1:754

Dan (Israel), 2:379

Danby, Thomas Osborne, Earl of, 10:493–494

Dance madness, 3:526

Dance of Death, 3:698, **4:506–508**, 5:485–486, *485*, 12:584

Dandoy, George, **4:508**

Danforth, Planned Parenthood v., 1:33

Dangerfield, Thomas, 10:495

Dangi, Thomas, St., 7:732

Dani people, 4:*558*

Daniel (biblical figure), **4:508–509**
   composition, 4:511–512
   Cyrus II, 2:210–211
   Darius the Mede, 4:529
   deuterocanonical sections, 4:509
   Gabriel, 6:40
   interpretation, 4:511
   language use in, 4:509–511
   literary genre, 4:512
   protocanonical sections, 4:511
   Son of Man, 13:316

Daniel, Antoine, 3:4, 10:435

Daniel, Book of, **4:509–513**
   abomination of desolation, 1:22–23
   angels, 1:427
   Antichrist, 1:515
   apocalyptic style, 1:546
   Aramaic language, 1:627
   Babylonia, 2:5
   beatific vision, 2:171
   Bel and the dragon, 2:210–211
   biblical canon, 3:24
   Chaldeans, 3:370
   Divine judgment, 8:29
   eschatology, 5:336
   Gabriel, 6:40
   Gentiles, 6:140
   glory of God (end of creation), 6:246
   God's spirit, 13:426
   Jesus as Lord, 8:781
   justification, 8:77
   Kingdom of God, 8:172–173
   Magi, 9:34
   magic, 9:39
   seventy weeks of years, 13:39–40
   Son of Man, 9:544–545
   Susanna (heroine), 13:629
   works of charity, 1:301

Daniel, Gabriel (Father), 1:267, 3:186

Daniel, Norman, 1:493

Daniel, Walter, 1:137, 12:244

Daniel de la Vierge-Marie, 3:137, 143

Daniel of Belvedere, St., **4:513**

Daniel Palomnik (Abbot), **4:513**

Daniel the Stylite, 2:149

Daniélou, Jean (Card.), **4:514–516**
   angelology, 1:415
   Christian philosophy, 3:541
   incarnation, 9:684
   Jewish Gnosticism, 6:263
   New Theology, 5:859, 860

Daniel-Rops, Henri, **4:514**

Danish War (1625-29), 14:9–10

Danites, 7:323

Danse macabre. See Dance of Death

Dante Alighieri, **4:516–522**, *517–519*, 5:767, 14:47
   alchemy, 1:239
   allegory, 1:291
   astrology, 1:813
   Boccaccio, Giovanni, 2:450
   Cavalcanti, Guido, 3:310
   Chaucer, Geoffrey, 3:450
   Church-State relations, 1:675, 3:636
   influence of Remigio de' Girolami, 12:106
   influence on T. S. Eliot, 5:160
   language use, 8:364
   poetry, 12:110
   religious faith, 3:605
   translations by Emerson, 5:189

Daochuo, 3:510

Daode Jing (Laozi), 4:523–524, 8:332

Daoguang (Tao-kuang) (Emperor of China), 3:498

Daoism, **4:522–525**
   alchemy, 1:238
   as amalgamated with Buddhism, 10:111
   apophatic theology, 1:568
   Buddhism, 3:510–511
   Confucianism, 4:98
   mysticism, 10:111
   origins, 3:510
   pantheism, 10:825
   sky gods, 13:206

Daojia. See Daoism

Daquin, Louis Claude, **4:525–526**

Darboy, Georges (Abp. of Paris), **4:526**, 5:855

Darby, John Nelson, **4:526–527**, 776

D'Arcy, Brigid, 7:582

D'Arcy, Martin Cyril, **4:527**, 6:890, 7:792

Dare the Schools Build a New Social Order? (Counts), 5:94

Daria, St., 2:146, 3:571–572

Darin, Synod of, 5:7

Darius I, the Great (King of Persia),
3:631, **4:527–529**, *528*, 8:43–44,
11:135

Dark Ages, **4:529–530**
Latin literature, 9:446
Petrarch, 12:110

The Dark Knowledge of God (Journet),
7:1058

Dark Night of the Soul, **4:530**

Darkness. *See* Light and darkness

Darmashāstras (Hindu scriptures),
6:843–844

Darnley, Henry Stewart, Lord, 9:291

Darowska, Marcelina Kotowicz, Bl.,
4:530

Darrow, Clarence, 4:*346*, 347

Darstellung meines Systems (Schelling),
12:733

Darwin, Charles Robert, 3:623,
4:530–532, *531*, 5:492, 495, 496
biology, 2:403, 404
causality, 3:306
creation doctrine, 4:345
cultural evolution, 4:433
evolutionary theory, 12:64
liberal theology, 8:543
origin of living things, 8:576–577
See also Darwinism; Evolution

Darwinism, 1:12, 9:320–321

Dasein, 1:540–541, 3:521, 6:714–715,
715, 789, 8:221

Dasius, St., 12:705

Dat, Juan, 14:493

Dat Dinh, Domingo Nicolás, 14:492–493

Date of the Redemption (Naḥmanides),
10:135

Dated Creed. *See* Fourth Formulary of
Sirmium

Datheus (archpriest in Milan), 3:411

*Datos cronológicos para la historia
eclesiástica de Costa Rica durante el
siglo XIX* (Thiel), 14:1

Daublain, Bonaventure, 2:506

Daude de Pradas, 2:343–344

Daudet, Léon, 1:81, 82, 2:303,
4:532–533

Dauferius (Daufari). *See* Victor III
(Pope)

Daughters of Anne of Providence, 3:419

Daughters of Charity of Canossa (Italy),
3:70

Daughters of Charity of St. Vincent de
Paul, 3:417, 419
California, 2:868
founding, 8:807, 13:172, 178, 14:518,
519
Labouré, C., 8:267

Los Angeles, 8:790
merger, 13:35, 175
Michigan, 8:449
19th-20th century overview, 3:621
Sisters of Charity of St. Joseph's
join, 13:175

Daughters of Divine Charity, **4:786**

Daughters of Divine Providence, 3:419

Daughters of Divine Zeal, 5:865

Daughters of Isabella, 3:622, **4:533–534**

Daughters of Jesus (Hijas de Jesús),
3:738–739

Daughters of Mary. *See* Marianist Sisters

Daughters of Mary and Joseph, **4:534**

Daughters of Mary Health of the Sick,
6:96

Daughters of Mary Help of Christians.
See Salesian Sisters

Daughters of Mary Immaculate for
Domestic Service, 8:778

Daughters of Mary of the Immaculate
Conception, **7:335**

Daughters of Mary of the Pious Schools,
9:823

Daughters of Our Lady Help of
Christians, 9:389

Daughters of Our Lady of Mercy, **4:534**,
12:386

Daughters of Our Lady of the Garden,
6:203

Daughters of Our Lady of the Sacred
Heart, 3:471, **10:725**

Daughters of Providence of Saint-Brieuc,
3:417, 8:311

Daughters of St. Géneviève, 3:417

Daughters of St. Joseph (Gerona),
12:553–554

Daughters of St. Mary of Mount
Calvary. *See* Brignoline Sisters

Daughters of St. Mary of Providence,
4:534, 6:549

Daughters of Saint Rosario of Pompeii,
8:776

Daughters of Temperance, 13:799

Daughters of the Blessed Virgin Mary of
the Immaculate Conception. *See*
Sisters of Christian Charity

Daughters of the Charity of the Sacred
Heart of Jesus, **12:495**

Daughters of the Cross, **4:534**

Daughters of the Divine Redeemer,
5:307

Daughters of the Divine Shepherdess,
9:624

Daughters of the Heart of Mary, **6:682**

Daughters of the Holy Cross of Liège,
4:535, 6:678

Daughters of the Holy Cross of St.
Andrew, 2:390, 5:834

Daughters of the Holy Family, 3:417

Daughters of the Holy Spirit, **7:45–46**

Daughters of the Immaculate
Conception, 14:561

Daughters of the Sacred Heart, 4:633

Daughters of the Sacred Heart
(Bergamo), **12:490**

Daughters of Wisdom, 4:687, **14:793**

Daure, Warnier de, 1:396

Daveluy, Antoine (Bp.), 8:235, 239

Davenport, John, 3:647

Davenport Diocese (IA), **4:535**

Davenport League for Social Justice,
7:542

Daventry Priory, **4:535–536**

David (King of Israel), **4:536–538**, *537*
Benjaminite dissatisfaction with,
2:282
biblical Chronicler, 3:566, 568
covenant with God, 9:541
God's spirit, 13:426
Jerusalem, 7:765
messianism, 9:541, 543
Moabites, 9:748
Philistines, 11:266
power of keys, 8:162–163
reign, 7:638–639
sin, offense against God, 13:142
Son of David, 13:310
tribe of Judah, 8:1

David, Armand, **4:538**

David, Canticle of, 3:73

David, Franz, 2:432, **4:538**, 14:303

David, John Baptist Mary (Bp. of
Bardstown, KY), **4:538–539**, *539*,
5:757, 13:174

David, Lucien (Abbot), 5:793

David I (King of Scotland), **4:539**, *540*
Melrose Abbey, 9:482
Scottish Church reform, 12:832

David Comnenus, 2:787

David of Angers, 1:432

David of Augsburg, 1:848, **4:539–540**

David of Dinant, **4:540–541**
Albert the Great, St., 1:225
Aristotelianism, 1:677
pantheism, 10:826

David of Himmerod, Bl., **4:541**

David of Västmanland, St., **4:541**

David Punishing Ammonites
(anonymous), 14:*634*

David the Jew (Ibn Daoud), 8:533

Davidek, Felix (Bp.), 4:486

Davidians (Adventist Reform Movement), **4:541–543**

Davidic descent, 10:175–176

Davidson, Randall Thomas (Abp. of Canterbury), **4:543**

Davies, B., 5:384

Davies, Samuel, 3:646

Davies, W. D., 5:331, 508

Davies, William, Bl., **4:543–544**, 5:232

Davignon, Veronica (Mother), 7:34

Dávila y Padilla, Agustín (Abp. of Santo Domingo), **4:544**

Davis, Henry, **4:544–545**

Davis, James (Bp. of Davenport, IA), 4:535

Davis, James Peter (Abp. of Santa Fe, NM), 10:287, 288, 12:677

Davis, S., 3:675

Davis v. Beason (1890), 3:660

Davitt, T. E., 8:400

Davost, Ambroise, 3:4

Davy, John, Bl., 5:226, 7:1019

The Dawn of Humanism in Italy (Weiss), 12:113

Dawson, Christopher, **4:545**, 5:252, 6:890

Day, Dorothy, 3:824, **4:545–546**

Day, George (Bp. of Chichester), 3:481, **4:546**

Day, Victor, **4:546**

Day of Atonement. *See* Yom Kippur (Day of Atonement)

Day of the Lord (Eschatology), **4:547–549**, 7:890

apocalyptic style, 1:546

Book of Obadiah, 10:502

concept of time, 14:83

Divine judgment, 8:29–30

Pauline letters, 5:340–341

Day of the sun (Sunday), 13:607

Dayton, University of, **4:549–550**

De abstinentia (Porphyry), 11:521

De accentibus et orthographia linguae hebraicae (Reuchlin), 12:181

De Actibus Apostolorum (Arator), 1:627–628

De actibus humanis moroliter consideratis (Frins), 6:12

De actibus humanis ontologice et psychologice consideratis (Frins), 6:12

De adulteratione librorum Origenis (Rufinus of Aquileia), 12:405

De Adventu Christi (Nicholas of Strassburg), 10:378

De Aeternitate mundi contra murmurantes (Thomas Aquinas), 14:21, 27

De allegoria et historia (Theodore of Mopsuestia), 5:511

De amore (Ficino), 5:710

De Andrea, Miguel (Bp. of Temnos, Argentina), **4:567**

De anima (Aristotle), 7:508, 510

Averroist commentary, 13:339

soul, 13:338–339

De anima (Dominic Gundisalvi), 5:816

De anima (Gilbert Crispin), 6:213

De anima (Hugh of Saint-Victor), 12:716

De anima (Tertullian), 13:342

De anima et resurrectione (St. Gregory of Nyssa), 11:414

De anima et vita libri tres (Vives), 12:124

De Antichristo (Adso of Montier-en-der), 1:130

De antiquis ecclesiae ritibus (Mabillon, Martène), 6:876

De Anulo et baculo (Rangerius), 9:450

De Apice theoriae (Nicholas of Cusa), 10:374

De arca Noe morali (Hugh of Saint-Victor), 7:158

De arte bene moriendi (Bellarmine), 1:733–734

De arte cabalistica (Reuchlin), 12:181

De arte sacra (Instruction, Sacred Congregation of the Holy Office), 8:620–621

De articulis fidei et ecclesiae sacramentis (Thomas Aquinas), 12:470

De aspectibus (Al-Kindī), 8:171

De Asse et partibus eius (Budé), 10:482

De Assumpto homine (Vacarius), 14:365

De astrolabio (Hermannus Contractus), 6:784

De auctoritate ecclesiae et conciliorum generalium adversus Thomam de Vio (Almain), 1:298

De auxiliis controversy, 4:110–113, 6:390–391, 403–404

De Baptismo (Pacian), 10:744

De beata vita (St. Augustine), 10:756

De Beatificatione et Canonizatione Servorum Dei (Benedict XIV), 10:107

De bellis, libri VIII (History of the Wars) (Procopius of Caesarea), 11:738

De bellis parisiacae urbis (Abbo), 12:548

De bello (Martinus Laudensis), 3:52

De bello (On War) (Joannes de Ligano), 7:883

De bello (Segobiensis), 3:52

De Beryllo (Nicholas of Cusa), 10:374

De bono communi (Remigio de' Girolami), 12:106

De bono et malo (William of Auvergne), 2:184

De bono pacis (Rufinus), 12:403

De Brébeuf, Jean, 3:4

De Bruyne, D., 3:30

De Bruyne, E., 3:674

De Buggenoms, Louis (Father), 3:119

De caeremoniis et ritibus ecclesiasticis (Reiffenstuel), 12:34

De Canonicis Scripturis, 3:32

See also Trent, Councils of (1543-63)

De cantu et musica sacra a prima ecclesiae aetate usque ad praesens tempus (Gerbert von Hornau), 6:164

De captivitate babylonica (Luther), 6:403

De caritate (Aquinas), 3:396

De casto connubio Verbi et animae (St. Lawrence Justinian), 8:405

De casu diaboli (Gilbert Crispin), 6:213

De catechizandis rudibus (St. Augustine), 3:229, 240, 243, 250, 10:755

De catholicae ecclesiae unitate (Cyprian), 5:36

De Causa Dei contra Pelagium et de virtute causae causarum ad suos Mertonenses (Bradwardine), 14:29

De causa formosiana libellus (Eugenius Vulgarius), 5:447

De Causis, statu, cognitione ac fine praesentis schismatis et tribulationum futurarum (Telesphorus of Cosenza), 13:792

De Christiana expeditione apud Sinas (Trigault), 14:186

De christliche Moral als Lehre von der Vewirklichung des göttlichen Reiches in der Menschheit (Hirscher), 6:861

De Cibis Judaicis (Novatian), 10:465

De civitate Dei (St. Augustine), 1:859, 877, 878, 879, 3:633, 674, 730, 5:343, 6:872, 882, 888, 10:381, 629, 673, 716, 11:697, 12:403, 13:252, 14:360, 373

De clave David (Sander), 12:665

De Clerck, Paul, 12:328

De coelibatu sacerdotum ad Nicolaum II (Peter Damian), 3:326

De commendatione fidei (Baldwin of Canterbury), 2:30

De comparatione auctoritatis papae et concili (Cajetan), 1:298

De computo (Richard of Wallingford), 12:236

De Conciliis oecumenicis, theses (Passaglia), 10:919

De concilio (Jacobazzi), 7:688

De Concilio, Januarius Vincent, 2:41, **4:591–592**

De concordantia catholica (Nicholas of Cusa), 4:55, 10:372

De Concordantia sacerdotii et imperii (Marca), 9:133

De concordia (St. Anselm of Canterbury), 1:497

De concordia sacerdotii et imperii seu de libertatibus ecclesiae gallicanae (Baluze), 2:48

De concordia temporum (Summa de temporibus) (Giles of Lessines), 6:219

De confesione (Sorbon), 13:326

De confessione mollicei (Gerson), 3:232

De Coniecturis (Nicholas of Cusa), 10:374

De conscientia (Sorbon), 13:326

De consensu Evangeliorum (St. Augustine), 5:512

De Consequentiis (Roger of Swyneshed), 12:288

De consideratione libri quinque ad Eugenium III (Bernard of Clairvaux), 2:310

De consolatione philosophiae (Boethius), 12:107

De Constantia (Lipsius), 12:125

De contemptu mundi (Bernard of Cluny), 2:312, 10:591

De contemptu mundi (Hermannus the Lame), 9:449

De contemptu mundi (St. Eucherius of Lyons), 5:438

De contractibus (Rolevinck), 12:293

De controversiis (Bellarmine), 5:37

De Corpore Christi (St. Odo of Cluny), 10:555

De corpore domini (Engelbert of Admont), 5:221

De corpore et sanguine Christi (Haymo of Halberstadt), 6:677

De corpore et sanguine Christi (Paschasius Radbertus, St.), 9:444–445

De corpore et sanguine Domini (Lanfranc), 1:64

De corpore et sanguine Domini (Ratramnus of Corbie), 11:924

De corpore et sanguine Domini (St. Paschasius Radbertus), 1:64

De corporis et sanguinis Domini veritate (Guitmond of Aversa), 6:579

De Correctione rusticorum (Martin, St.), 9:219, 439

De correptione et gratia (St. Augustine), 6:386

De Courcy, Henry, **4:596**

De Culta feminarum (Tertullian), 13:836

De Cultu adorationis libri tres et disputationes contra errores Felicis et Elipandi (Vázquez), 14:427

De cultu sacrosancti Cordis Dei ac Domini nostri Jesu Christi (Gallifet), 6:79

De Cultu sanctorum dissertationes decem (Trombelli), 14:213

De cura gerenda pro mortuis (St. Augustine), 5:670

De cursu temporum (Hilarianus), 1:461

De Deo et natura (Polignac), 8:849

De Deo Trino (Franzelin), 5:919

De Deo Uno (Franzelin), 5:919

De Deo Uno et Trino (Musso), 10:73

De Differentiis (St. Isidore of Seville), 7:604

De diligendo Deo, 3:395

De disciplina ecclesiastica (Rabanus Maurus), 3:230

De disciplinae arcani antiquitate et usu (Scholliner), 12:779

De Diversis artibus (Theophilus), 13:930–931

De divina charitate et septem ejus gradibus (Van seven manieren van Heiligher Minnen) (Beatrice of Nazareth), 2:181

De Divina Historia Libri III (Musso), 10:73

De divina Traditione et Scriptura (Franzelin), 5:919

De divinis instit. (Lactantius), 5:15

De divinis nominibus (Thomas Gallus of Vercelli), 2:184

De divisione naturae (John Scotus Eriugena), 3:161, 7:1010–1011, 9:445, 12:757

De divortio Lotharii (Hincmar of Reims), 6:838

De doctrina Christiana (St. Augustine), 3:730, 5:516, 6:787

De Doctrina institutione monachorum (Horsiesi), 10:743

De Doctrina spirituali (Othlo of Sankt Emmeram), 9:449, 10:709

De documentis antiquorum (Bartholomew of San Concordio), 2:126

De dono perserverantiae (St. Augustine), 5:343

De duabus naturis in Christo. . . (Chemnitz), 3:464

De Duobus praeceptis caritatis et decem legis praeceptis (Aquinas), 14:22, 28

De duodecim abusivis saeculi (anonymous Irish author), 3:634, 9:441

De duodecim gemmis (Epiphanius of Salamis), 5:293

De ebrietate (Philo Judaeus), 11:270

De Ecclasticis Officiis (St. Isidore of Seville), 7:603

De Ecclesia Christi (Murray), 10:69

De ecclesia Christi (Passaglia and Schrader), 3:589, 10:919

De Ecclesia triumphanti (Bellarmine), 12:55

De ecclesiae catholicae unitate (Cyprian), 4:457, 459

De Ecclesiae officiis (Isidore of Seville), 12:52

De ecclesiastica et civili potestate (Richer), 12:239

De eclipsi solis et lunae (Richard of Wallingford), 12:236

De Educatione liberorum et eorum claris moribus (Vegius), 14:430

De Electione cononica tractatus (Passerini), 10:919

De electione regis Rudolfi (Engelbert of Admont), 5:221

De elegantia linguae latinae (Valla), 12:120

De eloquentia patrum libri xiii (Weissenbach), 11:622–623

De Emmanuele (Richard of Saint-Victor), 12:235

De Ente et essentia (Aquinas), 14:16, 27, 46

De Ente et Uno (Pico Della Mirandola), 11:323

De ente supernaturali disputationes in universam theologiam (Ripalda), 12:251

De Eodem et diverso (Adelard of Bath), 9:453

De errore profanarum religionum (Firmicus Maternus), 5:740

De eruditione interioris hominis (Richard of Saint-Victor), 12:235

De eruditione praedicatorum (Humbert of Romans), 11:619

De esse intelligibili (Peter Thomae), 11:208

De essentia, motu et significantione cometarum (Giles of Lessines), 6:219

De esterminatione mali et promotione boni (Richard of Saint-Victor), 12:235

De eucharistia eiusque adoratione (Espence), 5:358

De Eucharistiae sacramento et sacrificio (Franzelin), 5:919

De excidio et conquestu Brittaniae (St. Gildas), 6:217–218, 9:442

De Exhortatione castitatis (Tertullian), 13:836

De fabrica ecclesiae (Borromeo), 3:705

De facto (in fact), 12:750

De Fallaciis ad quosdam nobiles artistas (Aquinas), 14:27

De Falso credita et ementita Constantini donatione declamatio (Valla), 14:377

De fato (Salutati), 12:622

De felicitate (Siger of Brabant), 13:113

De Fide (Ambrose), 10:967

De fide ad Petrum (Fulgentius of Ruspe), 6:24

De fide catholica (apostolic constitution, Pius IX), 5:594, 11:387

De fide catholica contra Judaeos (Isidore of Seville), 5:773

De Fide sanctae et individuae Trinitatis (Alcuin), 9:444

De Fideli dispensatore (Á Kempis), 14:13

De Filio prodigo (Nicholas of Clamanges), 10:372

De fletu Ecclesiae (Lignano), 3:51

De Forma absolutionis (Aquinas), 14:27

De formanda conscientia (Frins), 6:12

De Fructu eremi (Nicholas of Clamanges), 10:371

De Fructu rerum adversarum (Nicholas of Clamanges), 10:371

De Futuris contingentibus (Bradwardine), 14:29

De gaudio paradisi (Peter Damian). *See Ad perennis vitae fontem*

De Genesi ad litteram imperfectus liber (St. Augustine), 5:512

De Genesi ad litteram libri 12 (St. Augustine), 5:512

De Genesi contra Manichaeos libri 2 (St. Augustine), 5:512

De genuina missae notione (Hirscher), 6:861

De gestis domini salvatoris (Simon Fidati of Cascia), 13:129

De gestis Pelagii (St. Augustine), 11:62

De Gestis Pontificium Anglorum (Deeds of the Archbishops and Bishops of the English) (William of Malmesbury), 9:80–81

De Gestis Regem Anglorum (Deeds of the Kings of the English) (William of Malmesbury), 9:80–81

De gloria martyrum (Gregory of Tours), 12:52

De Godsdienstvriend (Le Sage ten Broek), 10:261

De Goesbrian, Louis (Bp. of Burlington), 14:455

De gradibus humilitatis et superbiae (Bernard of Clairvaux), 2:310

De gratia Dei (Faustus of Riez), 5:651

De gratia efficaci (Lessius), 8:518

De gratia et auxiliis (Salas), 12:612

De gratia et libero arbitrio (Bernard of Clairvaux), 2:310

De gratis et virtutibus beatae Mariae virginis (Engelbert of Admont), 5:221

De Groot, J. V., 12:777

De gubernatione Dei (Salvian of Marseilles), 6:112, 12:633

De haeresibus et synodis (St. Germanus I), 6:170

De haereticis, an sint persequendi? (Castellio), 3:214

De harmonica institutione (Regino of Prüm), 12:30

De heretico comburendo (1401), **4:550**

De hierarchia ecclesiae catholica (Scholliner), 12:779

De Hominum statibus et officiis (Passerini), 10:919

De Hueck Doherty, Catherine, **4:614–615**, 6:9, 10

De Humani corporis fabrica (Versalius), 12:817

De Iesu puero duodenni (St. Aelred), 1:138

De illa quae. . .filium adamavit (Peter the Painter), 11:207

De imagine Dei (Wizo), 3:13

De imagine peccati (The Image of Sin) (Hilton), 6:834–835

De immaculata Deiparae semper virginis conceptu (Passaglia), 10:919, 12:786

De immaculato B. Marina conceptu (Perrone), 11:132

De Immortalitate animae (Nifo), 10:391

De Immutabilitate traditionis contra modernam haeresim evolutionismi (Billot), 14:136

De Inani gloria et de educandis liberis (St. John Chrysostom), 10:755

De Incarnastionis diss. (Billuart), 12:55

De Incarnatione (Cassian), 3:206, 6:112

De incarnatione Domini (De Lugo, J.), 8:854

De Incendio Amoris (Rolle de Hampole), 12:295, 297

De incertitudine et vanitate omnium scientiarum (Agrippa), 13:202

De Indiarum iure (Solórzano Pereira), 10:978

De Indis (Vitoria), 14:570–571

De instauranda aethiopum salute (Sandoval), 3:770

De institutione clericorum (Philip of Harvengt), 11:250

De institutione harmonica (Hucbald of Saint-Amand), 3:161

De institutione inclusarum (St. Aelred), 1:138

De institutione laicali (Jonas of Orleans), 3:230

De institutione virginum et contemptu mundi (Leander of Seville), 5:773, 8:426

De Institutis coenobiorum et de octo principalium vitiorum remediis libri XII (Cassian), 3:205, 207

De Intellectu (Nifo), 10:391

De intellectu (Siger of Brabant), 13:113

De inventione dialectica (Agricola), 3:20, 9:565, 12:123

De ira Dei (Lactantius), 8:274

De Irreformabili Romani pontificis in definiendis fidei controversiis iudicio (Orsi), 10:676

De iure (by right), 12:750

De iure belli ac pacis libri tres (On the Law of War and Peace) (Grotius), 6:540

De iure praedae commentarius (Commentary on the Law of Prize) (Grotius), 6:540

De iure sacerdotali (Egbert of York), 5:103

De Iustificatione, gratia, fide, operibus et meritis (Vega), 14:430

De iustitia et iure (De Lugo, J.), 8:855

De Jesu puero duodenni (Aelred of Rievaulx), 9:454

De Jure belli Hispanorum in barbaros (Vitoria), 14:570–571

De Jure et justitia (Soto), 14:49

De Jure publico ecclesiastico commentaria (Ventura), 14:442

De justitia distributiva (Zapata y Sandoval), 14:910

De justitia et jure (Lessius), 8:518

De Katholiek, 10:261

De katholieke Encyclopaedie, 5:207

De Koninck, Charles, **4:618–619**, 11:301

De la Certitude morale (Ollé-Laprune), 10:585

De la connaissance de soi-même (Lamy, F.), 8:315

De la Croix, Charles, **4:619**, 8:112

De la Forge, Louis, 3:185, 186

De la Fréquente communion (Arnauld), 1:716, 8:855

De la littératre (Staël), 3:447

De la Mare, William. *See* William de la Mare

De la orden que en algunos pueblos de España se ha puesto en la limosína para remedio de los verdaderos pobres (Medina), 3:417

De la perfección del cristiano en todos sus estados (La Puente, L.), 8:334

De la philosophie scolastique (Hauréau), 12:770

De la providence (Touron), 14:125

De la Recherche de la Vérité (Malebranche), 9:74

De la Sagesse (Charron), 3:439

De la sainteté et des devoirs de la vie monastique (Rancé), 11:907

De la Salle, John Baptist, St., **4:620–623**

  catechesis, 3:235

  Christian Brothers, 2:630, 12:647

  rule, 3:543

De la suavidad de Dios (Orozco), 10:674

De la Taille, Maurice, **4:623–624**

  Divine indwelling, 7:442–443

  grace, 6:397

  supernatural quality of Divine gift, 10:15

De la valeur des ordinations anglicanes (Gasparri), 6:103

De laboribus Herculis (Salutati), 12:622

De laude eremi (St. Eucherius of Lyons), 5:438

De laude Flandriae (Peter the Painter), 11:207

De laude veteris Saxoniae nunc Westphaliae dictae (Rolevinck), 12:293

De laudibus philosophiae (Sadoleto), 12:526

De laudibus S. Annae (Trithemius), 14:209

De laudibus Sanctae Crucis (Rabanus Maurus), 3:154

De laudibus sapientiae divinae (Alexander Neckham), 9:456

De lege (Cicero), 3:36

De legibus (Cicero), 10:201

De l'Église gallicane dans son rapport avec les Souverains Pontifes (Maistre), 9:61

De l'Esprit (Helvétius), 3:792

De l'Excellence de la dévotion au Coeur adorable de Jésus-Christ (Gallifet), 6:79

De libertate christiana (Luther), 6:403

De libertate Dei et creaturae (Gibieuf), 6:208

De Lisle, Ambrose Lisle March Phillipps, **4:630**

De Lisle, Henriette, 7:23

De Lobera, Jean, 3:327, 328

De locis sanctis (Adamnan and Bede), 7:676–677, 9:441, 11:353

De locis theologicis (Cano), 3:20, 14:49

De los nombres de Cristo (León), 8:498

De Ludegna, John, 3:328

De ludo globi (Nicholas of Cusa), 10:374, 375

De Luna, Pedro. *See* Benedict XIII (Pope)

De magistratum ecclesiasticorum origine et creatione (Scholliner), 12:779

De Magnete (William Gilbert), 12:816

De magnete, magneticisque corporibus, et de magno magnete tellure; Physiologia nova, plurimis et argumentis, et experimentis demonstrata (Gilbert), 6:212–213

De Maio, R., 3:97

De malignis cogitationibus (Evagrius Ponticus), 10:397

De Mari, Agostino (Bp. of Savona), 4:534

De matrimoniis mixtis (Roskoványi), 12:383

De matrimonio (Sorbon), 13:326

De Meester, Marie Louise (Mother), **4:633**

De Mello, Anthony, **4:634**

De mensuris et ponderibus (Epiphanius of Salamis), 5:293

De methodis (Zabarella), 14:901

De Methodo (Aconcio), 9:565

De methodo philosophandi (Ventura), 14:442

De Meulemeester, P., 1:308

De mirabilibus sacrae Scripturae, 5:514

De miseria humane conditionis (*On the Misery of the Human Condition*) (Innocent III), 7:470

De moderno Ecclesiae schismate (Ferrer), 3:51

De modis rerum (Remigio de' Girolami), 12:106

De modo bene vivendi (Nider), 10:386

De modo componendi sermones (Thomas Waleys), 14:40

De monarchia (Dante), 1:675, 3:636

De monogamia (Tertullian), 13:836

De morali disciplina libri quinque (Sforza), 12:115

De morali systemate s. Alphonsi M. de Ligorio (Ballerini), 2:31

De Moreau, É., 1:331

De Morgan, Augustus, **4:655**

  logic of relatives, 8:751

  syllogistic, 8:748, 753

De Morte Peregrini (Lucian), 12:635

De mortibus persecutorum (Lactantius), 8:274

De motibus naturalibus (Roger of Swyneshed), 12:288

De Motu (Berkeley), 2:298

De Mundi universitate (Bernard Silvestris), 9:453

De Musica (St. Augustine), 3:673–674

De nativitate Christi (Ratramnus of Corbie), 11:924

De natura boni (St. Albert the Great), 1:224

De natura et dignitate amoris (William of Saint-Thierry), 14:753

De natura et gratia (Soto), 13:330, 14:49

De natura et origine animae (Albert the Great), 10:391

De natura et statibus perfectionus (Le Gaudier, A.), 8:452

De natura hominis (Nemesius of Emesa), 10:958

De natura rerum (On the Nature of Things) (Thomas of Cantimpré), 14:32

De natura rerum (St. Isidore of Seville), 7:604

De naturis rerum (Neckham), 5:206, 9:456

De Neve, John, **4:659**

De Nieuwe Gemeenschap (Netherlands), 10:262

De nieuwe Katechismus, 3:245, 12:783

De nihilo et tenebris (Fredegisus), 12:757

De nomimun analogia (Cajetan), 1:378

De Nominibus utensilium (Alexander Neckham), 9:456

De non aliud (Nicholas of Cusa), 10:374

De Norzi, Shlomo Yedidiah, 2:355, 357

De Nouë, Anne, 3:4

De novis festitatibus non instituendis (Nicholas of Clamanges), 10:372

De novissiumis, 5:342, 344

De Nugis curialium (Walter Map), 14:624

De Nuptiis Christi et Ecclesiae (Fulcoius of Beauvais), 9:457

De nuptiis Mercurii et Philologiae (Martianus Capella), 12:107, 757

De obligationibus et insolubilibus (Roger of Swyneshed), 12:288

De octo vitiis principalibus (Hermannus Contractus), 6:784

De officiis (St. Ambrose), 1:339, 3:407, 730, 5:393

De officio episcopi (Contarini), 4:202

De officio militari (Ullerston), 14:282

De Officio Pii ac Publicae Tranquillitatis vere Amantis Viri in hoc Religionis Dissidio (Cassander), 3:204–205

De officio sacerdotis (Albert of Brescia), 14:47

De operibus supererogatoriis et consilis evangelicis (Schwane), 12:793

De Opificio Dei (Lactantius), 8:274

De opificio hominis (St. Gregory of Nyssa), 6:*519*

De oratione (Evagrius Ponticus), 10:397

De ordine intelligendi (Zabarella), 14:901

De ordine iudiciario (Giles of Foscarari), 6:219

De origine, natura, jure, et mutationibus monetarum (Oresme), 10:380

De origine ac progressu schismatis anglicani (Sander), 12:665

De origine et gestis Francorum compendium (Gaguin), 6:49

De origine et rebus gestis Polonorum (Kromer), 8:251

De origine nobilitatis (Rolevinck), 12:293

De origine urbis Venetiarum (Giustiniani), 6:234

De ortu, progressu et fine Romani imperii (Engelbert of Admont), 5:221

De ortu scientiarum (Robert Kilwardby), 12:265

De Orygnale Cronykil of Scotland (Andrew of Wyntoun), 12:533

De pace (On Peace) (Joannes de Ligano), 7:883

De pace fidei (Nicholas of Cusa), 10:374

De Pascha Computus, 3:551

De Pauw, Gommar, 3:289

De peccato originali (Odo of Cambrai), 10:553

De peccato usurae (Remigio de' Girolami), 12:106

De perfectione operum contra allegoricos (Theodore of Mopsuestia), 5:511

De perfectione vitae spiritualis (Aquinas), 14:27

De perfectionibus status clericorum (Nicholas of Lisieux), 14:20

De periculis novissimorum temporum (William of Saint-Amour), 14:16, 17

De Petter, Dominic, 14:57

De Philosophia mundi (William of Conches), 9:453

De pignoribus sanctorum (Guibert of Nogent), 6:560, 12:54

De Planctu naturae (Alan of Lille), 1:205, 9:457

De pontificis romani clave (Henríquez), 6:735

De porestate papae (Barclay), 10:500

De potentia (Thomas Aquinas), 12:43

De Potestate civili (Vitoria), 14:570–571

De Potestate ecclesiae (Vitoria), 14:570–571

De potestate papae et imperatoris respectu infidelium (Vladimiri), 11:439

De potestate regia et papali (John of Paris), 5:36, 14:46

De praedestinatione (Mirabilibus), 14:47

De praedestinatione (Ratramnus of Corbie), 11:924

De praeparatione ad missam (Nicholas of Dinkelsbühl), 10:376

De Praepartione ad mortem (Erasmus), 1:733

De praescriptione hereticorum (Tertullian), 13:836, 837

De praesulibus simoniacis (Nicholas of Clamanges), 10:371

De predestinatione (John Scotus Eriugena), 7:1009

De Pressuris ecclesiasticis (Atto), 9:448

De primatu Petri, et Pontificis Romani (Fabri), 5:585

De primatu Romani Pontificis eiusque iuribus (Rosković), 12:383

De principiis (Origen), 1:269, 548, 5:510, 12:404

De principiis (Theophilus), 14:157

De principiis moralibus actuum humanorum (De Lugo, F.), 8:854

De principiis naturae (John de Seccheville), 7:957

De principiis naturae ad fratrem Sylvestrum (Aquinas), 14:16, 27

De probatis Sanctorum historiis (Surius), 13:628

De processione mundi (Dominic Gundisalvi), 5:816

De procuranda indorum salute (Acosta), 1:70

De procuranda salute omnium gentium (Thomas of Jesus), 14:36

De productione formae substantialis (Thomas of Sutton), 5:818

De profectu spirituali (Venturino of Bergamo), 14:443

De professione religiosorum (Valla), 12:118

De propositionibus modalibus (Aquinas), 14:27

De proprietatibus rerum (Bartholomaeus Anglicus), 2:*122*, 123, 14:177

De prudentia (Pontano), 12:116

De pudicitia (Tertullian), 13:836

De quatuor gradiabus violentae charitatis (Richard of Saint-Victor), 12:235

De quinque septenis seu septenariis (Hugh of Saint-Victor), 3:239

De Raeymaeker, Louis, **4:676**

De ratione temporum (Bede), 3:571

De Raymaeker, Louis, 12:776

De re diplomatica (Mabillon), 10:773

De re militari (Albensis), 3:52

De re militari (Paris a Puteo), 3:52

De re uxorio libri II (Barbaro), 2:*90*

De rebus naturalibus (Zabarella), 14:901

De recta doctrina morum, quatuor libris distincta, quibus accessit (Elizalde), 5:168

De reformatione ecclesiae suasoria . . . ad Hadrianum VI (Ferreri), 5:694

De reformtione religionis christiana (Nielsen), 10:388

De rege et regis institutione (Mariana), 14:256

De regimine Christiano (Bl. James of Viterbo), 7:710

De regimine principum (Engelbert of Admont), 5:221

De regimine principum (Thomas Aquinas), 9:781

De regimine rectoris (Paulinus of Venice), 11:39

De regimine rusticorum (Rolevinck), 12:293

De regno (De regimine principum) ad regem Cypri (Aquinas), 14:27

De regressu (Zabarella), 14:901

De regressu animae (Porphyry), 11:521

De reliquiis preciosorum martirum Albini et Rufini (Silver and Gold) (Garcí of Toledo), 6:93–94

De remediis contra temtationes (Flete), 5:761

De remediis schismatis (Arévalo), 1:647

De renuntiatione papae (Giles of Rome), 6:220

De reparatione lapsi (Bachiarius), 2:8

De republica (Cicero), 10:201

De rerum inuentoribus (Vergil), 14:449

De rerum natura (Lucretius), 5:283, 8:848–849, 9:319

De rerum natura (Telesio), 12:122

De Restitutione et contractibus tractatus sive codex, nempe de rerum dominio atque earum restitutione et de aliquibus contractibus, de usura, de cambiis, de censibus (Medina, Juan), 9:465

De revelatione ab ecclesia proposita (Garrigou-Lagrange), 6:102

De revolutionibus orbium coelestium (Copernicus), 4:250–251, 6:59, 62, 10:705

De' Ricci, Maria Catherine (Mother), 4:839

De Rosario B. Mariae Virginis (Vallgornera), 14:377

De Rossi, Giovanni Bernardo, 2:356, 357

De rudimentis Hebraicis (Reuchlin), 6:696, 12:181

De ruina et reparatione ecclesiae (Nicholas of Clamanges), 10:371

De sacerdotio (St. John Chrysostom), 7:948

De sacra coena (Berengarius of Tours), 2:294

De sacra Eucharistia (Peter the Painter), 11:207

De sacra Ordinatione (Gasparri), 6:103

De sacramentis (St. Ambrose), 6:67

De sacramentis ac personis sacris..Theologiae moralis (Bauny), 2:160

De sacramentis in communi (Sayer), 12:716

De Sacramentis in genere (Franzelin), 5:919

De sacramento altaris (Baldwin of Canterbury), 2:30

De sacrarum electionum jure (Génébrard), 6:127

De Sainctes, Claude, 3:327, 328

De Sanctissima Eucharistia (Gasparri), 6:103

De sanctitate meritorum et gloria miraculorum beati Caroli Magni, 14:248

De Sancto Matrimonii Sacramento (Sanchez), 12:658

De sapientia veterum (Bacon), 2:10

De scriptoribus ecclesiasticis (Bellarmine), 2:227, 10:963

De scriptoribus ecclesiastiis quos attigit card. Robertus Bellarminus (Labbe), 8:265

De scripturis et scriptoribus sacris (Hugh of Saint-Victor), 7:157–158

De secreto (Aquinas), 14:27

De seculo et religione (Salutati), 12:622

De servo arbitrio (Luther), 5:316, 6:403, 8:882, 12:124

De servorum Dei beatificatione et beatorum canonizatione (Benedict XIV), 2:247, 3:63, 267, 9:665

De simoniacis (Gilbert Crispin), 6:213

De sinubus et arcubus (Richard of Wallingford), 12:236

De Smet, Pierre Jean (Father), 2:219, **4:692**, 7:789, 10:440, 644, 12:562, 851

    Accolti, Michael, 1:65

    Blanchet, Francis Norbert, 2:430

    Clarke, Mary Frances, 3:765

    Idaho, 7:289

    Oregon Territory, 11:529

    St. Joseph Mission, 10:220–221

    Wyoming, 14:869

De Soto, D., 3:417

De Soto, Hernando, 1:690, 13:820

De spectaculis (Tertullian), 13:836

De spiritali amicitia (St. Aelred), 1:138

De spiritu et anima (Alcher of Clairvaux), 1:239–240

De Spiritu Sancto (Faustus of Riez), 5:651

De Spiritu Sancto (Gilbert Crispin), 6:213

De Spiritu Sancto (St. Basil), 2:136

De Spirituali amicitia (Aelred of Rievaulx), 9:454

De Spirtu Sancto adversus Latinos (Planudes), 11:406

De Squaloribus curiae romanae (Matthew of Cracow), 9:361

De statu animae (Claudianus), 3:769, 5:651

De statu Ecclesiae (Hontheim), 2:218

De statu ecclesiae et legitima potesate Romani Pontificis (Hontheim and Febronius), 3:792–793, 5:257, 658

De statu et planctu ecclesiae (Alvaro Pelayo), 1:327

De Stijl Movement, 3:680

De studio theologico (Nicholas of Clamanges), 10:372

De substantiis separatis, seu de angelorum natura (Aquinas), 14:27

De subventione pauperum, sive de humanis necessitatibus (Vives), 3:417, 418

De summa felicitate (Pistoia), 3:310

De summo bono hominis in hac vita (Engelbert of Admont), 5:221

De synodis (St. Hilary of Poitiers), 6:828–829

De Theologicis institutis (Sgambati), 13:55

De Tijd (daily), 10:261

De transitu Beatae Mariae Virginis, 1:559

De translatione Imperii Romani (Bellarmine), 2:227

De tribus dietis (Sorbon), 13:326

De Trinitate (Eusebius of Vercelli, St.), 5:455

De Trinitate (Novatian), 10:464, 967, 14:192

De Trinitate (St. Augustine), 10:967, 968–969, 11:734–735

De Trinitate (St. Hilary of Poitiers), 6:112, 828

De triumphis Christi Antiochae gestis (Flodoard of Reims), 5:763

De triumphis Christi apud Italiam (Flodoard of Reims), 5:763

De triumphis Christi sanctorumque Palestinae (Flodoard of Reims), 5:763

De unico vocationis modo (Las Casas), 8:341

De unitate (Dominic Gundisalvi), 5:816

De unitate formae (Giles of Lessines), 5:818, 6:219, 14:44

De unitate formarum (William de Hothum), 14:45

De unitate intellectus contra Averroem (St. Albert the Great), 7:511

De unitate intellectus contra Averroistas (Aquinas), 14:21, 27

De unitate Romana (Schrader), 12:786

De universo (Rabanus Maurus), 5:206

De universo creaturarum (William of Auvergne), 5:364

De usuris (Giles of Lessines), 6:219–220

De utilitate et prerogativis religionis (The Advantages and Privileges of Religious Life) (Hilton), 6:834

De Valera, Éamon, 7:565

De Van Nguyen, Tomás, 14:493

De vanitate librorum, sive de amore coelestis patriae libri tres (Haymo of Halberstadt), 6:677

De Vaux, Roland, 5:50, 51, 520, 12:457–458

De vera praesentia corporis Christi in sacramento Eucharistiae (Garet), 6:97

De Vera y falsa magia (Loos), 8:777

De Verbo Incarnato (Franzelin), 5:919

De verbo mirifico (Reuchlin), 12:181

De Vere, Aubrey, 3:271

De veritate (Aquinas), 14:17

De veritate conceptionis B.V.M. (Torquemada), 14:112

De veritate fidei Christiane (Vives), 12:124

De veritate prout distinguitur a revelatione, a verisimili, a possibili, et a falso (Herbert of Cherbury), 6:765

De vetusis canonum collectionibus dissertationum sylloge (Gallandi), 6:67

De via paradisi (Remigio de' Girolami), 12:106

De virginibus velandis (Tertullian), 13:836

De viris illustribus (Gennadius of Marseilles), 6:137

De viris illustribus (Petrarch), 11:215

De viris illustribus (St. Jerome), 10:962, 12:606

De viris illustribus (Sigebert of Gembloux), 9:451, 13:112

De viris illustribus Germaniae (Trithemius), 14:209

De viris illustribus Ordinis S. Benedicti (Trithemius), 14:209

De virtutibus et vitiis (Alcuin), 3:241

De virtutibus impiorum (Baius), 2:20

De visibili monarchia ecclesiae (Sander), 12:665

De Visionibus (Othlo of Sankt Emmeram), 9:449

De vita beata (Baptist of Mantua), 2:74

De vita contemplativa (Philo Judaeus), 11:269–270

De vita contemplativa (Pomerius), 11:469

De vita et miraculis sanctii Trudonis (Thierry), 12:587

De vita Josephi Juliani Parreni (Cavo), 3:313

De vita Pilati (Peter the Painter), 11:207

De vita solitaria (Petrarch), 12:269

De Vita spirituali (Vincent Ferrer), 9:461

De vocatione omnium gentium (St. Prosper of Aquitaine), 11:772

De voluptate (Bruni), 12:117

De voluptate (Valla), 14:376

De votis monasticis (Luther), 3:327

De Vries, Hugo, 2:403

De vulgari eloquentia (Guido), 3:310

De Waelhans, Alphonse, 12:776

De Wette, Wilhelm M. L., 5:519
  biblical theology, 2:384–385
  pentateuchal studies, 11:89

De Witt, N. W., 5:285

De Wulf, Maurice, **4:712**, 10:244, 12:748, 776

Deacon Benedict. *See* Benedict the Levite

Deaconesses, **4:554–555**
  Carthusians, 3:195
  Holy orders, 7:37
  origin of order, 7:37

Deacons, **4:550–554**
  African American, 1:161
  cardinalate, 3:105
  Church property, 3:723
  Holy orders, 7:36
  Jamaica, 3:112
  ordination, 10:637–639, 641–642
  origin of order, 7:36
  preaching specific to, 11:631
  role, 5:39
  works of charity, 3:402, 403, 546
  See also Archdeacons

The Dead
  cults, 12:66–67
  diptychs, 4:758–759
  names, calling out of, 4:758, 759
  Requiem Mass, 12:134–136
  resurrection from, Greco-Oriental, 12:145

The Dead, prayers for, **4:555–557**, 7:438, 8:107–108, 11:829

The Dead, worship of, **4:557–558**, *558*, 12:66–67

Dead Christ (Pinacoteca di Brera), 7:*814*

The Dead Christ (Sammartino), 7:*858*

The Dead Risen Out of Their Sepulchres (Cristoforo de Predis), 5:*214*

Dead Sea, **4:558–560**, *559*, 5:408

Dead Sea Scrolls, 4:*560*, **560–565**
  American Schools of Oriental Research, 1:353
  Benoit, Pierre, editing of, 2:285
  Bethesda, 2:347
  biblical canon, 3:25–26
  biblical texts, 2:356, 4:562–563
  biblical theology, 2:386
  bishops, 2:411
  Book of Isaiah, 7:595–596

concept of mystery, 10:80
  discovery and excavation, 4:559, 560–561
  École Biblique publication project, 5:51
  Enoch literature, 5:266
  Jewish Gnosticism, 6:264
  Skehan, P., 13:200
  See also Qumran Community

Deadly Sins, **4:565–567**

Deaf mutes, 3:418, 13:228

Dean, William, Bl., **4:567**, 5:229, 684, 14:668

Deane, Henry (Abp. of Canterbury), 2:54, **4:567–568**

Dear Remembrances (Seton, E.), 13:30, 34

Dearborn Independent, 10:171

Dearden, John Francis (Card.), 2:874, **4:568–569**, 698–699, 11:367

Dease, Mary Teresa (Mother), **4:569**

Death
  Abraham's bosom, 1:39
  ars moriendi, 1:727–734, 3:698
  Augustine, St., 1:867
  Commendation of the Dying, Rite for, 4:9–10
  concupiscence, 4:68
  dance of (motif), 4:506–507
  education, 13:855
  as evil, 5:489
  hospice movement, 7:117
  Mesopotamia, ancient, 9:537
  Socrates, 13:293
  thanatology, study of, 13:852–855
  viaticum, 14:470–471
  See also Burial; The Dead; Euthanasia; Immortality

Death, Grief, and Mourning (Gorer), 13:854

Death, in the Bible, **4:569–571**
  conflict with, 8:566
  Judas Iscariot, 8:15–16
  life, concept of, 8:566
  paradise in Jewish thought, 13:37
  raising from dead, 8:420, 422
  Sheol, 13:79

Death, preparation for, **4:582–583**, 14:470–471

Death, theology of, **4:571–582**
  mystery, 4:573–577, 577–581
  particular judgment of God, 8:37–39
  problem of death, 4:571–573

Death, Where Is Thy Victory? (Daniel-Rops), 4:514

Death Comes for the Archbishop (Cather), 3:489, 10:287, 571

Death of God theology, 1:825, **4:583–586**, 594, 6:322

Death of Saint Nicholas of Tolentino (da Rimini), 10:*379*

Death of the Beast and the Enemies of God, 9:635

Death of the Virgin (Giambono), 10:2

Death penalty. *See* Capital punishment

DeBecker, Jules, 8:821

El Deber actual de los Católicos (Franceschi), 5:864

Deborah (Hebrew prophetess), 11:765

Debrosse, Robert, 7:30

Debt, guilt and, 6:571

Debussy, Achille Claude, 3:525, **4:586**, 587, 8:696

Decadence
Avignon papacy, 3:604
Carolingian era, 3:410, 600
works of charity, 3:410, 412–413, 414

La Decadence de l'art sacré (*Der Verfall der kirchlichen Kunst*) (Cingria), 3:711

Decadence of monasteries (1125-1408), 2:271

Decadi, cult of, **4:586–587**, 5:853, 975

Decadicon (John Klenkok), 7:959

Decalogue. *See* Ten Commandments

Decameron (Boccaccio), 2:448–449, 12:114

Decapolis (ancient Palestine), **4:587–588**, *588*

Decapolis, deaf mute of, 5:276

Deceit, **4:588–589**

Decem Libri (Ribot), 3:134

Il Decennale primo (Machiavelli), 9:21

Il Decennale secondo (Machiavelli), 9:21

Decet Romanum Pointficem (apostolic letter, Clement VIII), 14:278

Dechamps, Victor Auguste (Bp. of Malines), 3:624, **4:589**

Dechant, Virgil C., 8:191–192

Dechristianization, 5:972–975

Decius (Roman Emperor), **4:590**
Cornelius (Pope), St., 4:270
persecution under, 3:594, 5:766, 7:654, 10:430, 12:315, 353
Alexandria, 1:268
Asia Minor, 1:785
chorbishops, 3:525–526
Church-State relations, 3:632
Lapsi, 1:785, 2:879, 3:186, 188

Decius, Phillipus (Philippe de Dexio), **4:589–590**

Decker, Jeremias V. de, 12:771

Declaratio brevis (Fludd), 12:382

Declaratio de Libertate Relgiosa (Vatican Council II), 5:946

Déclaration des droits de l'homme (1789), 5:943

"A Declaration of a Global Ethic" (World's Parliament of Religion), 14:847

Declaration of 1660 (Ireland), 1:76–77

Declaration of Independence (U.S., 1776), 10:203, 322

Declaration of Indulgence for Catholics and Dissenters (1687), 7:560, 707

Declaration of Nuremberg (1323), 7:931

Declaration of Principles (International Alliance), 10:308–309

Declaration of Rights (England, 1689), 3:645–646, 647, 648, **4:590–591**, 8:541

Declaration of the French Clergy, **4:591**, 5:796, 6:77
appeals to a future council, 1:599
Gallicanism, 8:803
Innocent XII (Pope), 7:482

Declaration of the Rights of Man (France, 1789), 5:262, 10:203

Declaration of the Rights of Man (Massachusetts, 1780), 3:650

Declaration of the Rights of Man (United Nations, 1948), 1:793

Declaration on Certain Questions Concerning Sexual Ethics (Sacred Congregation for the Doctrine of the Faith), 6:26

Declaration on Christian Education (Vatican Council II), 14:418

Declaration on Euthanasia, 5:458, 560

Declaration on Religious Freedom (Vatican Council II). *See Dignitatis humanae* (Declaration on Religious Freedom) (Vatican Council II)

Declaration on the Admission of Women to the Ministerial Priesthood, 12:551

Declaration on the Church's Attitude toward Non-Christian Religions (Vatican Council II), 14:417–418

Declaratory creeds, 4:349, 350–352

Decline and Fall of the Roman Empire (Gibbons), 12:310

Decline of the West (Spengler), 6:885–886

Deconstructionism, **4:592–595**, 6:794

Decora lux aeternitatis (hymn), **4:595**, 5:108

Decorations, Papal, **4:595–596**, 6:763

Decorative art, 8:138–139, 436–437

Decourtray, A. (Abp. of Lyon), 5:861

Decree for the Armenians. See Armenians, Decree of (*Exsultate Deo*) (Eugene IV)

Decree of Gelasius, 3:32

Decree of Gratian, 12:468

Decree on Church's Missionary Activity (*Ad gentes*) (Vatican Council II), 5:480, 741

Decree on Eastern Catholic Churches (*Orientalium Ecclesiarum*) (Vatican Council II), 5:20

Decree on Ecumenism (*Unitatis redintegratio*) (Vatican Council II), 3:590, 626, 4:30, 5:70, 75–76, 12:197, 700, 14:416

Decree on Education for the Priesthood (Vatican Council II), 14:416–417

Decree on Priestly Formation (Vatican Council II), 2:387–388

Decree on the Apostolate of the Laity (Vatican Council II), 8:291, 11:615, 14:417

Decree on the Bishops' Pastoral Office in the Church (*Christus Dominus*) (Vatican Council II), 2:420, 3:236, 5:38, 300

Decree on the Media of Social Communication (Vatican Council II), 14:417

Decree on the Ministry and Life of Priests (Vatican Council II), 14:416

Decree on the Missionary Activity of the Church (Vatican Council II), 11:615, 14:417

Decree on the Oriental Catholic Churches (Vatican Council II), 14:416

Decree on the Pastoral Office of Bishops (Vatican Council II), 11:615, 14:416

Decree on the Up-to-date Renewal of the Religious Life (Vatican Council II), 14:417

Decretales (Canon Law collection), 6:496–497

Decretales Pseudo Isidorianae et capitula Angilramni, 5:619

Decretalists, 3:48, **4:595–599**
Bernard of Compostella, the Elder, 2:312–313
Hostiensis, 7:134–135
Huguccio, 7:164–165

Decretals, **4:599–601**
Alanus Anglicus, 1:206
definition, 11:747
Gilbertus Anglicus' collection, 6:217
Gregory IX (Pope), 2:314, 3:46, 6:511–512, 8:284, 11:936

Decretals *(continued)*
  Lancelotti's notes, 8:216
  papal registers, 4:604
  Quinque Compilationes Antiquae (collection), 11:869
  Reiffenstuel, Anacletus, 12:34
  Rufinus' writings, 12:403
  Third Lateran Council, 8:352
  Venerabilem, (Innocent III), 7:43
  See also Extravagantes; False Decretals (Pseudo-Isidorian Forgeries); Gratian, Decretum of; Gregory IX (Pope), decretals of
Decretals, collections of, 3:47–48, **4:601–604**, 5:570
Decretists, 3:47, **4:604–607**
  Alanus Anglicus, 1:206
  Honorius Magister, 7:88
  Laborans, 8:265–266
  Lawrence of Spain, 8:408
Decretum (Burchard of Worms), **2:694–695**, 3:44, 46, 60, 11:75
  ars moriendi, 1:728
  clerical celibacy and marriage, 3:326
  Ivo of Chartres, 3:45
Decretum (Gratian), **6:420–422**, 9:455
Decretum (Ivo of Chartres), 1:282, 3:45, 46, 7:680
Decretum (Joannes Teutonicus), 4:54
Decretum de Sponslibus et matrimonio cum declaratione (Noldin), 10:410
Decretum Gelasianum
  Canon Law, 3:37
  censorship, 3:336
Decretum super lectione et praedicatione (Council of Trent), 11:614
Decretum super scripta (John Paul II), 10:672
Dedal, Adrian Florensz. *See* Adrian VI (Pope)
Dedekind, R., 4:216
Deden, D., 10:98
Dederoth, Johann, 2:710
Dedham Case, 4:116
Dedication Council, 8:54
Dedication of the Temple, Feast of, **4:607–608**, 8:43, 580
Dedieu, Stanislaus (Mother), 7:372
Deduction, **4:608**, 11:948
  argumentation, 1:658
  axiomatic system, 1:948–950
  Cartesian method, 4:679
  knowledge, 8:203
  liberal arts, 8:538
  symbolic logic, 8:752
Dee, John, 1:239

Deeds of Frederick Barbarossa (Otto of Freising), 10:716
Deeds of the Archbishops and Bishops of the English (De Gestis Pontificium Anglorum) (William of Malmesbury), 9:80–81
Deeds of the Kings of the English (De Gestis Regem Anglorum) (William of Malmesbury), 9:80–81
Deep River (Shusaku), 5:219
Deer Abbey (Scotland), **4:608**
Defamation, **4:608–609**
Defence of Origen (Eusebius of Caesarea and Pamphilius), 5:453
Defence of the English Catholics (Allen), 1:296
Defender of the Faith, 1:445, **4:609**
Defenestration, 8:765
Defense du christianism (Frayssinous), 5:922
A Defense of Free-Thinking in Mathematics (Berkeley), 2:298
"Defense of Marriage" referendum (Nebraska), 10:224
The Defense of the Seven Sacraments (Henry VIII), 3:803, 6:739
The Defense of the Standard of the Cross (Francis de Sales), 5:868
Defense of the Three Chapters (Facundus of Hermiane), 10:968
Defensio doctrinae fr. Thomae (Harvey Nedellec), 14:46
Defensio Fidei Catholicae adversus Anglicanae sectae errores (Suàrex), 10:500
Defensio synodi Florentinae (Joseph of Methone), 7:1045
Defensiones theologiae Divi Thomae (Capreolus), 3:92–93, 14:47
Defensor (Bp. of Angers), 1:431
Defensor civitatis, **4:609**
Defensor pacis (Marsilius of Padua), 3:636, 8:282, 9:210, 463, 12:871
Defensorium dotacionis ecclesiae (Ullerston), 14:282
Defensorium ecclesiastice potestatis (Adam Easton), 1:107
Definition, **4:609–611**, 5:742
  Aristotelian-Thomist, 13:349
  axiomatic system, 1:949
  causality, 3:298
  concept, 4:53
  definitum distinguished from, 4:610
  demonstration, 4:652
  dialectics, 4:723
  distinction compared to, 4:778–779
  God, 13:139

  logical parts, 10:905
  soul, 13:334
  understanding distinguished from, 14:293
Definition, Dogmatic, **4:611–612**
Definitor, Religious, **4:612**
DeGioia, John J., 6:147
Degradation penalty, 8:285, 286
Les Degrés de la vie spirituelle (Saudreau), 12:708
Deharbe, Joseph, 3:244, **4:612–613**
Dehille, Henriette, 10:292
Dehon, Léon Gustave, Ven., **4:613–614**, 12:495
Dei delitti e delle pene (Beccaria), 3:87
Dei diritti dell'uomo (Spedalieri), 13:410
Dei Providentis (motu proprio, Benedict XV), 5:22
Dei Providentis (motu proprio, Pius X), 12:100
Dei Verbum (Vatican Council II), 2:167, 8:439, 12:191–192
Deicolus of Lure, St., **4:615**
Deidre of Killeedy, St. *See* Ita of Killeedy, St.
Deiniol, St.
  Bangor Abbey, founding of, 2:54
  Bangor Use, founding of, 2:55
Deir, Thomas, 7:582
Deism, **4:615–618**, 5:262, 852, 974, 12:72
  Alexander I (Emperor of Russia), 1:252
  apologetics, 1:564
  Butler, Joseph, 2:721
  causality, 3:306
  Church-State relations, 3:639, 640
  conservation, 4:162
  Divine concurrence compared to, 4:70
  Église catholique française, 3:449
  Encyclopedists, 3:791
  Holbach, Paul Heinrich Deitrich, 7:1
  miracles, 9:667
  opposition, 8:403
  philanthropy, 13:930
  theism, 4:615, 13:862
  Voltaire, 14:579
  See also Theism
Le Déisme réfuté par lui-même (Bergier), 2:295
Del Bene (Pallavicino), 10:806
Del gran mezzo della preghiera (St. Alphonsus Liguori), 1:309
Del Prado, Norbert, 12:777

Del Primato Morael e Civile degli Italiani (Gioberti), 10:234

Del sagrificio di Gesù (St. Alphonsus Liguori), 1:309

Del sentimiento trágico de la vida (Unamuno), 14:288

Delahaye, Karl, 3:573–574, 4:36

Delahoyde, Henry, 7:579

Delaissé, L. M. J., 7:329

Delaney, Daniel (Bp. of Kildare and Leighlin), 2:618, 7:582

Delanoue, Jeanne, St., **4:619**

Delanoue, Joan, St. *See* Delanoue, Jeanne, St.

Delany, Selden Peabody, **4:619–620**

Delaware, 3:649, 651, **4:624–626**

Delectable good, 6:352–353

Delectatio victrix, 6:387

Delehaye, Hippolyte, 1:90, 2:471, 472, 3:860, **4:626**

De'Lelli, Teodoro, 3:91

Deleplace, François, 7:29–30

Delfini, John Anthony, **4:626–627**

Delfino, Daniello (Abp. of Aquileia), 4:627

Delfino, Giovanni, 4:627

Delfino, Giovanni (Card., b. 1545), 4:627

Delfino, Giovanni (Card., b. 1617), 4:627

Delfino, Pietro (Abbot), 2:898, 4:627

Delfino, Zaccaria (Card.), 4:627

Delfino family, **4:627**

Delgado, Alexis, Bl., 1:951

Delgado, José Matías (Bp. of Honduras), **4:627–628**, 12:290

Delgado Pastor, Juan de la Cruz, Bl., 7:122

Delgado Vilchez, Hilario, Bl., 7:125

Delgado y Cebrian, Ignacio (Bp. of East Tonkin), 14:493

Delhaye, Philippe, 7:528, 10:194

D'Elia, Pasquale, **4:628**

Deliberacion en la causa de los pobres (de Soto), 3:417

Deliberate acts, 6:398

Deliberatio (Dubois), 9:463

Deliberation, free will and, 5:932, 937

Deliberation and Morality, **4:629–630**

Delilah (Biblical figure), 8:19

Delille, Henriette, 1:157–158

Delisle, Léopold, 10:773

Delitzsch, Friedrich, 5:520

Deliverance from Error (Algazel), 1:622

Della Casa, Giovanni. *See* Casa, Giovanni Della

Della Chiesa, Bernardino (Bp. of Beijing), 2:626, **4:630**

Della Chiesa, Giacomo. *See* Benedict XV (Pope)

Della Francesca, Piero, 2:375

Della guerra di Flandria (Bentivoglio), 2:286

Della historia (Patrizi), 12:122

Della poetica (Patrizi), 12:122

Della Porta, Giacomo, 1:247, 12:580

Della Quercia, Jacopo, 2:374

Della Robbia family, **4:631**
    Bible cycles, 2:375
    terra cotta figures, 12:679

Della Robia, Andrea, 4:631

Della Robia, Giovanni, 4:631

Della Robia, Luca, 4:631

Della Rocca, Charles, 2:901

Della Rovere, Bartolomeo (Bp. of Massa), 4:631

Della Rovere, Clemente Grosso (Card.), 4:631

Della Rovere, Cristofero (Card.), 4:631

Della Rovere, Domenico (Card.), 4:631

Della Rovere, Francesco. *See* Sixtus IV (Pope)

Della Rovere, Francesco Maria I, 4:632

Della Rovere, Francesco Maria II, 4:632

Della Rovere, Galeotto (Card.), 4:631

Della Rovere, Giovanni, 4:631

Della Rovere, Girolamo (Card.), 4:631

Della Rovere, Guidobaldo II, 4:632

Della Rovere, Guilio (Card.), 4:632

Della Rovere, Leonardo Grosso (Card.), 4:631

Della Rovere, Sisto (Card.), 4:631

Della Rovere family, **4:631–632**, 10:247

Della Somaglia, Giulio Maria (Card.), **4:632**

Della Valle, William, 12:717

Dello spirito della rivoluzione e dei mezzi per farla cessare (Ventura), 14:442

Delon, Philip I., 1:210

Delp, Alfred, 7:792

Delphi, Oracle of, **4:632–633**, *633*, 784, 10:87, 94

Delphina of Signe, Bl., **4:633**, 5:180

Deluge. *See* Flood

Le Déluge (Saint-Saëns), 12:584

Deluil-Martiny, Marie de Jésus, Bl., **4:633**

Deluol, Louis-Regis, 13:174–175

Demaisières, Marí, St., 6:633

Dematrakopoulos, A., 2:825

Dembo, Gabriel, 1:535

Demers, Catherine, 6:528

Demers, Modeste (Bp. of Vancouver Island, WA), 1:207, 2:430, 11:529, 12:850–851

Demetrian of Khytri, St., **4:634–635**

Demetrias, M. (Mother), 9:689

Demetrias, St., **4:635**

Demetrius (Bp. of Alexandria), St., 1:272, 4:635

Demetrius, SS., **4:635–636**

Demetrius I, 9:11

Demetrius Basilica (Salonika), 1:756

Demetrius Chomatianus (Abp. of Ochrida), **4:636**

Demetrius II, 4:254, 9:11–12

Demetrius of Phaleron, 1:668

Demetrius the Megalomartyr (Great Martyr), 4:635–636, *635*

La Democracia y la iglesia (Franceschi), 5:864

Democracy, **4:636–644**
    American theory, 4:641–642
    aristocracy, 1:667
    Catholic social thought, 13:255
    Catholic viewpoint, 4:636, 643–644
    Church, 13:489–490
    Church-State relations, 3:640–641
    civil religion, 3:756
    conciliarism, 4:57
    Congregationalism, 4:115
    early modern period, 4:640–641
    economics, 4:642–643
    freedom, 5:944
    freedom of conscience, 4:149
    Greek theory, 4:636–638
    Lamennais, F., 8:310
    Middle Ages, 4:638–640
    papal social thought, 13:259
    religious revival, 4:642
    Roman theory, 4:638
    See also Liberalism

La Democrazia cristiana; concetti e indirizzi. . . (Toniolo), 14:109

Democritus (Greek philosopher), **4:644–645**, 11:287
    afterlife, 1:167
    analysis and synthesis, 1:381
    atomic theory, 12:211
    atomism, 1:831, 832, 834, 4:958, 5:803
    atoms, 12:803
    chance, 3:375, 377
    conscience, 4:142
    contingency, 4:213
    continuum, 4:217

Democritus (Greek philosopher)
(continued)
  free will, 5:929
  immortality, 7:348
  knowledge, 8:213
  materialism, 9:318–319
  matter, 9:339–340
  mechanism, 5:805, 9:415
  skepticism, 13:201
  soul, 13:332, 334, 338
Demonology, **4:650–651**
Demons and spirits, 13:425
  exorcism, 5:551–553
  iconography, 4:645, 646, 650
  Shintoism, 13:86–87
  Son of God, 13:313
  See also Daimon; Diabolical
    possession; Satan
Demons and spirits, in the Bible,
  4:645–646, 5:551
Demons and spirits, theology of,
  4:646–650
Demonstratio Evangelica (Eusebius of
  Caesarea), 5:451, 453
Demonstration, **4:651–654**, 11:947
  argumentation, 1:659
  Aristotle, 1:681–682
  axiomatic system, 1:949
  causality, 3:298
  connatural knowledge, 8:205
  dialectics, 4:723
  logical necessity, 10:227
  soul defined, 13:335
  Thomist view, 8:538
Demonstratio (Kitāb al-Burhān)
  (Eutychios of Alexandria), 5:463
La Démonstration de la prédication
  apostolique de St. Irénée (Tixeront),
  14:95
Démonstration de la véritié et de la
  sainteté de la morale chrétienne
  (Lamy), 8:315
Demonstration of the Apostolic Teaching
  (St. Irenaeus), 7:570
Dempsey, Mary Joseph (Sister), **4:655**
Dempsey, Timothy, **4:655**
Demythologizing, **4:655–659**
  caution regarding, 10:124
  exegesis, 5:522
Denatura deorum (Firmicus Maternus),
  5:740
Dene people (Canada), 3:11
Dengel, Anna, **4:659–660**
  McLaren, Agnes, 9:402–403
  Medical Mission Sisters, founding of,
    9:432

Denial of Church funerals, 6:33–34
Denifle, Heinrich Seuse, 4:660, **660**,
  5:138, 6:184, 12:776
Denis, M., 3:713
Denis, Maurice, 12:601
Denis, Stephen (Father), 7:371
Denis of Antioch, 2:82
Denis of Paris, St., **4:660–661**
  burial at Saint-Denis-en-France
    Abbey, 12:544
  Fourteen Holy Helpers, 5:836
Denis the Carthusian (Denys of Ryckel),
  3:192, **4:661–662**, 14:47
  angels, 1:424
  ars moriendi, 1:729
  beauty, 2:185
  exegetical works, 5:518
Denis the Little. See Dionysius, Exiguus
Denison, George, 1:447
Denji, James, Bl., 7:733
Dēnkart (Persian encyclopedia), 11:143
Denmark, **4:662–668**, 664
  Absalon of Lund, 1:40
  Canute, 3:77–78
  Canute IV, 1:40, 3:77
  Canute Lavard, St., 3:78–79
  Caribbean, 3:119–120
  Dacia as term for, 4:492
  Danish National Church, 8:166
  ecclesiastical organization,
    4:662–664, 666–667
  Kjeld, St., 8:186–187
  Lutheranism, 8:888, 12:19
  map, 4:663
  Protestant Reformation, 4:309,
    665–666
Denver Archdiocese (CO), **4:668–670**,
  669
Denver Catholic Register, 4:669–670
Denys of Ryckel. See Denis the
  Carthusian
Denzinger, Heinrich Joseph, 3:589,
  4:672, 5:729
  grace, 6:394
  justice of God, 8:70, 72, 75
Denzinger collection, **4:670–672**
Deochar, St., **4:672**
Deodatus of Blois, St., **4:672**
Deodatus of Nevers, St., **4:672–673**
Deogratias (Bp. of Carthage), 3:186
Deontologism, **4:673–674**, 11:768
Deontology (Bentham), 2:285
DePaul University (Chicago), 3:480
Dependency theory, 8:544–545
DePetter, Dominic, 6:311

Deploige, Simon, 12:776
Deportation, in the Bible, **4:674–675**
Deposit of faith, 3:357, **4:675**
  Apostles, 1:572
  dogma development, 4:811
  liberal theology, 8:543
Depositio Episcoporum, 4:676
Depositio Martyrum, **4:675–676**
Deposition from the Cross (Caravaggio),
  12:701
Deposition penalty, 8:285, 286
Deprecatio Gelasii, 8:600
Deprecatio Gelasii (Gelasius), 12:328
Derand, François, 3:706
Dêr-Balyzeh Papyrus, 1:273
Derby, Thomas Stanley, Earl of, 2:184
Derham, W., 12:768
Derision, **4:676–677**
Dermot O'Hurley and 16 Companions,
  BB., 7:579
Le Dernier mot du fidéisme
  (Doumerque), 5:711
Derniers Mélanges (Veuillot), 14:466
Derrida, Jacques, 4:592–595, 6:794
Dervishes, **4:677**, 678
Des colonies et de la révolution actuelle
  de l'Amérique (Pradt), 11:577
Des Doctrines philosophiques sur la
  certitude, dans leurs rapport avec les
  fondements de la théologie (Gerbet),
  6:165
Des Grâces d'oraison (Poulain), 11:562
Des Influences franciscaines sur l'auteur
  du "Combat Spirituel" (Ubald),
  14:261
Descamps, Albert (Bp.), 3:350, 11:477,
  478
Descartes, René, 3:183, 183, 184,
  4:677–683, 679, 5:47, 91, 11:293
  absolute, 1:42
  accident, 1:62, 63
  act, 1:74
  Algazel, 1:281
  analysis and synthesis, 1:382
  Anselm of Canterbury, St., 1:496
  antipodes question, 1:530
  apologetics, 1:564
  Aristotelianism, 1:677
  aseity, 1:780
  atomism, 1:834, 4:959–960
  Avicenna, 1:672
  biology, 2:401, 407
  Bufalo, St. Gaspare del, 2:675
  Cambridge Platonists, 2:909
  causality, 3:300, 306
  certitude, 3:352

choice, 3:521

Christian philosophy, 3:538, 540, 541

Claudianus, Mamertus, 3:769

concept, 4:52

concept of substance, 14:143

consciousness, 4:153

conservation, 4:162

contingency, 4:214

criteriology, 4:367

critical realism, 11:944

critique and evaluation, 4:682

demonstration, 4:654

dualism, 9:91

Enlightenment, 5:254, 255

epistemology, 5:302

exemplarism, 5:526–527

existence, 5:533

extension, 5:569

form, 5:803

free will, 5:931, 938

infinity, 7:459

innate ideas, 8:456

innatism, 7:466

intuition, 7:533

judgment, 8:23, 26

knowledge, 4:883–884, 8:217

Malebranche, Nicolas, 9:74

materialism, 9:319–320

matter, 9:344

mechanism, 9:416

metaphysic, 12:770–771

method, 4:678–680

methodology, 9:566

necessity, 10:227

ontological argument, 10:600–601, 603

ontological perfection, 11:119

personality, 11:155

philosophy and science, 11:298–299

possibility, 11:551

quality, 11:849

rational contentment, 5:395

rationalism, 11:920

reason and faith, 6:286

reflection, 12:2

Regis, Pierre Sylvain, 12:31

scientific method, 12:748

self, concept of, 12:882

skepticism, 13:203

soul, 13:346

space, 13:374

study of motion, 10:19

substance, 13:577

truth, 14:227

truth and certitude, 14:223

unity, 14:317

universals, 14:325

See also Cartesianism

Descent into Limbo (Fiesole), 8:590

Descent of Christ into Hell, 1:559, 4:683–686

Descent of Christ into Hell (Firenze), 4:683, 683

Deschner, John, 5:606

Descoqs, P., 13:593

Descriptio nummorum Antiochiae (Eckhel), 5:46

Description de la Chine et de la Tartarie Chinoise (Halde), 10:903

Description de la Louisiana (Hennepin), 6:732

A Description of Patagonia (Falkner), 5:611

Descrizione del modo tenuto dal Duca Valentino nell' ammazzarre Vitellozzo Vitelli, Oliverotto da Fermo, il signor Paolo e il duca di Gavina Orsini (Machiavelli), 9:20–21

Desegregation

    Mississippi Catholic schools, 9:739–740

    Tennessee, 13:823

    Washington, DC, 14:658

    See also Racial discrimination

Desert Clarion (Las Vegas, NV), 8:346

Desert Fathers, 4:686

    Abraham the Simple, St., 1:39

    Aelred, St., 1:138

    Carthusian spirituality, 3:190

    John Climacus, St., 2:826

    Macarius the Egyptian, St. as, 9:3

    martyrdom category, 8:720

    poverty, 11:569

    St. Moses the Black as, 10:7–8

    works of charity, 3:407–408

Desgabets, Robert

    Malebranche, Nicolas, 9:74

    scholasticism, 12:771

Desgardin, Augustine-Joseph, 12:277

Deshayes, Gabriel, 2:630, 4:686–687

Deshon, George, 2:23, 4:687, 6:700, 11:40

Desideratus of Bourges (Bp.), St., 4:687–688

Desiderius. See Victor III (Pope)

Desiderius (King of the Lombards), 4:688

    Adrian I (Pope), 1:121, 122

    Charlemagne, 3:421, 422

    Constantine II (Antipope), 4:178

Paul I (Pope), St., 11:19

    Stephen III (IV) (Pope), 13:517, 518

Desiderius of Cahors, St., 4:688, 10:735

Desiderius of Langres (Bp.), St., 4:688

Desiderius of Monte Cassino. See Victor III (Pope)

Desiderius of Vienne, St., 4:688–689

    Ado of Vienne, St., 1:118

    Councils of Chalon-Sur-Saône, 3:373

Desiderius Rhodonensis, St., 4:689

Desing, Anselm, 12:769

Desire, 1:602, 4:689–690

Desire to see God, natural, 1:883, 4:690–691, 695

Desjardins, Paul, 12:666

Desmaisières, María Miguela of the Blessed Sacrament, St., 4:692

Desmond, Daniel F. (Bp. of New Orleans), 1:270

Despenser, Henry (Bp. of Norwich), 2:573, 4:413, 692–693

Despierres, Jean, 1:396

Desposorio espiritual (Orozco), 10:674

Desprez, Josquin, 2:398, 717, 4:693, 8:342, 687, 688

Dessau, Moses. See Mendelssohn, Moses

Dessauer, Friedrich, 13:785

Destiny, in Greek religion, 6:452

Destiny, supernatural, 4:693–695

    justice, 8:75

    life, concept of, 8:572

Destiny of man, 9:92–93

Destombes, Emile, 2:904

Destrez, Jean, 11:54

Desurmont, Achille, 4:695–696

Desvallières, George, 3:713, 12:493, 601

The Detection and Overthrow of the False Gnosis. See Adversus haereses (St. Irenaeus)

Determinatio compendiosa (Bartholomew of Lucca), 2:126

Determinatio contra emulos et detractores fratrum predicatorum (Thomas of Sutton), 14:37

Determinism

    free will, 5:931

    law, 8:399

    Loci communes (Melanchthon), 13:681

    miracles, 9:667, 669

    physical laws, 11:316

Detraction, 4:230, 696, 13:411

Detroit Archdiocese (MI), 4:491, 568–569, 696–699

Detstvo (Tolstoi), 14:105

Deus, tuorum militum (hymn),
 4:700–701

Deus scientiarum dominus (apostolic
 constitution, Pius XI), 3:292, **4:700**,
 6:879, 10:434, 11:393, 394, 12:775

Deusdedit, Collection of (Gregory VII),
 3:45, 60, **4:701**

 Collection of Atto, 1:841

 Liber diurnis, 8:534, 535

 tax documents, 8:532

Deusdedit I (Pope), St., **4:701**

Deusdedit of Monte Cassino, St.,
 4:701–702

Deuterocanonical books, 3:20, 26, 27, 28

 See also Bible, canon

Deutero-Isaiah (anonymous poet-
 prophet), 4:478, 5:335–336, 7:595,
 597–598

Deuteronomist documents, 11:91

Deuteronomists, **4:702**

 Judges, Book of, 8:20

 Kings, Books of, 8:177

 Shechem covenant, 13:72

Deuteronomy, Book of, **4:702–704**

 adultery, 1:131, 13:50

 Baal, 2:2

 beatific vision, 2:170

 book of the covenant, 2:527

 canonical criticism, 3:33

 canonicity, 3:23

 as code of laws, 8:397

 convenant, 4:327

 conversion, 4:233

 creation, 4:341

 cross-dressing, 13:49

 curses, 4:442

 demons, 13:429

 Divine election of Israel, 5:145

 Edomites, 5:86–87

 flagellation, 5:755

 Gentiles, 6:140

 gluttony, 6:251

 God, name of, 6:298

 God as redeemer, 11:965

 guilt, 6:570

 heaven, 6:684

 holiness of man, 9:87

 imposition of hands, 7:364

 incest, 7:378

 inheritance, 7:464

 justice of men, 8:73

 justification, 8:76

 Kingdom of God, 8:173

 kingship, 8:179

 laity, 8:290, 293

leprosy, 8:509

levirate marriage, 8:522

Levites, 8:523

Logos, 8:760

love, 8:831

magic, 9:39

manna, 9:118–119

messianism, 9:545

names for God, 8:780, 13:77

Passover, 10:933

pilgrimages, 11:342

purification, 11:832

rape, 13:50

redemption, 11:964

retaliation, 8:394

Sabbath Year, 12:461

serpent as symbol, 13:20

sin, 13:144

Sinai, Mt., 13:159

slavery, 13:206, 207, 250

social principle, 13:248

sons of God, 13:322

suffering servant, songs of the,
 13:588

temple liturgy, 8:434

Ten Commandments, 4:4–9

Deutero-Pauline Literature, **4:704**

Deutero-Zechariah, 5:336

Deutsch, Alcuin (Abbot), 12:552

Deutschkatholizismus, 3:624

DeVaux, R., 2:380

*The Development of Capitalism in
 Russia* (Lenin), 8:467

*Development of Socialism from
 Utopianism* (Engels and Marx), 5:222

Developmental psychology, conversation
 and, 4:238–239

Devémy, Jean, 1:803

Devenandan, P. D., 7:405

Dever, W. G., 2:378–379

Devereux, Nicholas, 12:540

Devil

 exorcism, 5:*551*

 iconography of Last Supper, 8:345

 locutions, 8:747

 serpent as symbol, 13:19

 test in Lord's Prayer, 8:784

 See also Satan

Devil worship, **4:705**

Devil's advocate (promoter of the faith),
 4:705–706

The Devil's Advocate (West),
 14:685–686

Devil's rights theory, 11:984–985

Devine, Arthur, **4:706**

Devolution, Right of, **4:706–707**

Devolution, War of, 8:802

Devos, Adrian. *See* Gabriel of St. Mary
 Magdalen

Devotio Moderna, 3:605, **4:707–708**,
 5:243, 774, 847, 12:15

 À Kempis, Thomas, 7:328, 329

 À Kempis as representative, 14:13

 Brethren of the Common Life, 2:607,
 608, 12:590

 Canisius, St. Peter, 3:16, 18

 Carmelite spirituality, 3:134

 Cassian, John, 3:207

 Cisneros, García de, 3:744

 Crosier Fathers, 4:378

 Czechs, 4:480

 David of Augsburg, 4:539

 devotion to Passion, 10:925

 Groote, Gerard, 4:707

 humanism supporting, 10:258–259

 Low Countries, 13:454

 Protestantism, 7:330

 Rolevinck, Werner, 12:293

 scholasticism, 12:767

 Servites, 13:27

 spirituality, 13:446

Devotion, 3:232, **4:708–709**

 consolation compared to, 4:167

 to Holy Spirit, 7:46

 19th-20th century overview,
 3:622–623

 as quality of prayer, 11:595

 Stations of the Cross, 13:500

 virtue of religion, 12:85

 See also Devotions, popular; *specific
 devotions*

Devotion to Mary, **9:266–271**

Devotions, Popular, **4:709–712**

 to Holy Spirit, 7:46

 Lasance, F. X., 8:340

The Devout Christian (Hay), 3:243

Devout humanism, **7:194**

DeVries, Hugo, 4:531–532

Devshirme system, 10:718

Dewanto, Tarcisius (Father), 5:10, 7:794

Dewart, L., 1:566

Dewey, John, 11:296–297

 academic freedom, 1:52

 activism, 1:83

 aesthetics, 1:145

 appetite, 1:603

 civil religion, 3:756

 educational philosophy, 5:88, 91, 92,
 94

 empiricism, 5:198

experience, 5:554

form, 5:803

functionalism, 6:24–25

instrumentalism, 7:501–502

knowledge, 8:220

naturalism, 10:205

Neo-Hegelianism, 6:712

philosophy and science, 11:300

pragmatism, 5:397, 12:48, 71

theory of truth, 14:228

understanding, 14:294

Dexios, Theodore, 1:659, **4:712–713**

Deymann, Clementine, **4:713**

Dezcoll, Bernat, 1:465

Dezza, Massimiliano, 3:804

Dezza, Paolo (Card.), **4:713–714**, *714*, 7:794

Dhaka Seminary (Bangladesh), 2:53

Dharma, **4:714–715**, 6:837

Dhikr, 7:620

Dhimmi, **4:715–716**, 8:558

Dhorme, Paul, 5:50

Dhū-Nuwās, Masruk (King of South Arabia), 1:619, **4:716**, 10:137–138

Di Noia, Joseph, 7:528

Di Rosa, Maria Crocifissa, St., **4:764**, 6:633

Diabolical obsession, **4:716–717**

Diabolical possession, the Bible and, **4:717–718**

Diabolical possession, theology of, **4:718**

Diaconate, 4:550–554

See also Deacons

Diaconia, 3:407–408, **4:718–720**, 5:418, 7:118, 126

Diaconicum, **4:720**, 8:599

Diadema monachorum (Smaragdus), 13:228

Diadochus. *See* Proclus (Greek philosopher)

Diadochus of Photice (Bp.), 2:794, **4:720–721**

Diakonia. *See* Diaconia

The Dial (periodical), 14:58, 149

Dialectic of Enlightenment (Adorno, Horkheimer), 5:914

Dialectica (Abelard), 1:18, 8:749–750

Dialectica (Logica) (Ramus), 11:906

Dialectica (St. John Damascene), 7:951

Dialectica resolutio (Vera Cruz), 14:444

Dialecticae institutiones (Ramus), 12:767–768

Dialecticae partitiones (Ramus), 12:124, 125

Dialectical disputations (Valla), 12:121, 14:376

Dialectical materialism, 9:322–324, 11:300

See also Historical materialism

Dialectical theology, **4:721**

analogy of faith, 1:380

Brunner, Heinrich Emil, 2:644–645

Bultmann, Rudolf Karl, 2:690

duty as dialectic, 8:514

Neo-Hegelianism, 6:712

revelation theology, 8:253

See also Neo-Orthodoxy

Dialectics, **4:721–725**

Abelard, Peter, 1:15, 18, 3:47

argumentation, 1:659

Aristotle, 1:682

Canon Law, 3:47

contradiction, 4:223

controversy of using, 13:905

problems, 4:723–724

study, 8:536

See also Materialism, dialectical

Dialectics in the Middle Ages, **4:725–728**

Dialectique du monde sensible (Lavelle), 8:287

Dialexis (Nicetas Stethatos), 10:357

Diálogo de doctrina critiana (Valdés), 14:368, 369

Diálogo de la lengua (Valdés), 14:369

Dialogo del Purgatorio (Ochino), 10:535

Dialogue (Literary Genre), **4:728**

Dialogue (St. Catherine of Siena), 3:273

Dialogue Against Trypho (Justin the Martyr, St.), 5:509

Dialogue and Proclamation, 8:175

Dialogue between Ratius and Everard (Everard of Ypres), 5:484

Dialogue Concerning Heresies (More), 14:254

Dialogue of the injuste usurped primacie of the Bishop of Rome (Ochino), 10:535

Dialogue on Orators (Tacitus), 12:308

Dialogue on the Sack of Rome (Alphonse of Valdes), 3:215

Dialogue on the Two Great World Systems (Galileo), 6:62, 63, 9:415

Dialogue with Heraclides (Origen), 10:659

Dialogue with Trypho the Jew (Justin Martyr), 8:93

Dialogues (Gregory the Great), 3:597, 12:606

Dialogues (Plato), 10:240, 906

Dialogues (Rousseau), 12:393

Dialogues (St. Gregory I), 2:236–237, 6:482–483

Dialogues des Carmélites (Bernanos), 2:304

Dialogues des morts (Fénelon), 5:682

Dialogues on Eloquence (Fénelon), 11:622

Dialogues on the Procession of the Holy Spirit (Nicetas of Maronia), 10:355

Dialogus (Prierias), 8:880

Dialogus (Thomas of Pavia), 12:288

Dialogus (William of Ockham), 4:55

Dialogus de gesis ss. Fratrum Minorum (Thomas of Pavia), 14:36

Dialogus de schismate (Nieheim), 10:388

Dialogus de tribus quaestionibus (Othlo), 10:709

Dialogus de vita Sancti Joannis Chrysostomi (Palladius of Helenopolis), 10:805

Dialogus inter militem et clericum (Trevisa), 14:177

Dialogus inter philosophum, Judaeum et Christianum (Abelard), 1:19

Dialogus miraculorum (Caesarius of Heisterbach), 2:850, 3:749

Dialogus..contra perfidiam Judaeorum (Paul of Burgos), 11:33

Diamond, Charles, **4:728**

Diamonds, alleged magical properties of, 11:646

Diamper, Synod of (1599), **4:728–729**, 7:398–399, 13:713

Diana (Artemis) of the Ephesians (deity), **4:729–730**

Diana (Montemayor), 2:115

Diana, Antonino, **4:729**, 14:51

Dianetics: The Modern Science of Mental Health (Hubbard), 12:823

El Diario de la Marina (Elguero), 5:154

Diario delle S. Missioni (Leopold of Gaiche), 8:504

Diarioi y derrotero de sus viajes (Parras), 10:903

Diarium (Ebendorfer), 5:29

Diary (St. Veronica Giuliani), 6:234

The Diary of Bathsheba (Roberts), 12:272

Dias, André, 3:51

Diaspora, Jewish, **4:730–731**

biblical canon, 3:25

postexilic period, 8:5

Roman and Byzantine periods, 7:867–868

Diaspora synagogues, 13:676

Diatessaron (Tatian), 3:30, **4:731**, 7:843, 13:764

Diatriba circa methodum Wolfianum (Desing), 12:769

Diatribe de libero arbitrio (Erasmus), 12:123

Diaz, Joachim Hiryama, Bl., 7:733

Diaz, Juan, 2:863

Díaz, Manuel, Jr., **4:731–732**

Díaz, Porfirio, 9:580–581

Díaz Arias, García (Bp. of Quito, Ecuador), 5:62

Díaz de Cerio, Braulio María Corres, Bl., 7:123

Díaz del Rincón, Francisco, St., 3:498, **4:732**

Díaz Gandía, Carlos, Bl., **4:732–733**

Díaz Nosti, Juan (Father), 2:92

Diaz Sanjurjo, José (Bp.), 14:493

Díaz y Barreto, Pascual (Abp. of Mexico), **4:733**

Díaz-Stevens, Ana María, 11:510

Dibdale, Robert, Bl., 1:112, 4:733, 5:229

Dibelius, Martin, **4:733–734**, 5:521
    form criticism, 5:807, 811, 812
    mythical style of the Bible, 5:809

Dibelius, Otto (Lutheran Bp. of Berlin), **4:734**

Dicaearchus of Sicilian Messene, 1:668

Diccionario español cumanagoto (Ruíz Blanco), 12:407

Dicconson, Edward (Bp. of Ghent), **4:734–735**

Dich Nguyen, Anthony, 14:493

Dichiarazione più copiosa della dottrina cristiana (Bellarmine), 2:227

Dichiarazione piu copiosa della dottrina cristiana (Bellarmine), 3:234

Dichiarazione più copiosa della dottrina cristiana (Bellarmine), 3:242

Dichtung und Wahrheit (Goethe), 6:332

Dickens, Charles, 14:149

Dickenson (Dicconson), Roger, Bl., **4:735**, 5:231

Dickenson, Francis, Bl., 5:231, 6:159

Dickie, A. C., 7:763

Dickinson, Emily, 14:149

Dickson, Anthony (Bp. of Bridgetown), 3:120

Dicta (Golden Sayings) (Giles of Assisi), 6:218

Dicta (Sayings of Patrick) (Book of Armagh), 10:954

Dicta adversus pelagianam haeresim (Gelasius I), 11:63

Dicta Candidi (Monumenta Germaniae Historica: Epistolae) (Wizo), 3:13

Dicta Pirminii (Scarapsus) (St. Pirmin), 11:360

Dictatus Papae, 3:44, 45, **4:735–736**, 6:470, 10:859

Dictionaries, Catholic. *See* Encyclopedias and dictionaries

Dictionarium seu linguae latinae thesaurus (Estes), 5:374

Dictionary of Christian Biography, 5:208

Dictionary of Fundamental Theology, 5:208

Dictionary of the Bible (McKenzie), 9:402

Dictionary of the Liturgy, 5:208

Dictionnaire apologétique (Jaugey), 14:365

Dictionnaire Apologétique de la Foi Catholique, 1:251

Dictionnaire d'archéologie chrétienne et de liturgie (Leclercq, H.), 8:433

Dictionnaire de la Bible, 5:207

Dictionnaire de spiritualité ascétique et mystique, 5:207

Dictionnaire de théologie catholique, 5:207

Dictionnaire de Trévoux, 5:209

Dictionnaire des cas de conscience (Pontas), 11:472

Dictionnaire d'histoire et de géographie ecclésiques (Baudrillart), 2:158

Dictionnaire historique et critique (Bayle), 5:255

Dictionnaire Philosophique (Voltaire), 14:361

Dictionnaire théologique (Bergier), 2:295

Dictionnarium bovis (Thomas of Pavia), 14:36

Didache, **4:736**
    abortion, 1:26
    agape, 1:170
    Antichrist, 1:516
    Apostolic Church Order, 1:580
    Apostolic Constitutions, 1:581
    Apostolic Fathers, 1:587, 588
    baptism, 2:59, 61
    biblical canon, 3:30, 31
    breaking of bread, 2:599
    Canon Law, 3:37, 59
    catechesis, 3:228
    catechumenate, 3:249, 250
    Christian way of life, 3:547
    Church property, 3:723
    contraception, 4:220
    discovery, 2:652
    house churches, 2:146

    literary form, 3:591
    Lord's Day, 8:781
    Lord's Prayer, 8:782, 784
    maranatha, 9:130–131
    two ways method of parenesis, 14:251
    universality of Christianity, 3:274

Didacus of Alcalá, St., **4:736–737**, *737*

Didacus of Azevedo (Bp. of Osma), Bl., **4:737**

Didascalia apostolorum, **4:737–738**
    Apostolic Constitutions, 1:581
    Canon Law, 3:37, 59

Didascalicon (Hugh of Saint-Victor), 7:157, 12:235

Diderot, Denis, 14:361
    anarchism, 1:384
    anticlericalism, 1:518
    Catherine the Great, 3:264
    censorship, 3:792
    Enlightenment, 5:255, 261
    religious encyclopedias, 5:207, 208–210, 255

Didier, Peter Joseph, 3:734

Didier, R., 12:478

Didymus the Blind, **4:738–739**
    Ambrose, St., 1:337
    apocatastasis, 1:548
    exegetical works, 5:510
    James, St., 12:681
    pilgrimages, 3:594
    School of Alexandria, 1:272, 273

Diedo, Francis, 12:276

Diego de Jesús, 3:137

Diego de Osma (Bp.), 1:231

Diego of Cádiz, Bl., 4:263, **739**

Diego of Estella, **4:739**, 11:621

Diego y Moreno, Francisco Garcia (Bp. of California), 2:862, 866, 12:645

Diekamp, Franz, **4:739–740**

Diekmann, Godfrey, **4:740**

Diem The Nguyen, Vincent, 14:493

Diepenbrock, Melchior Von (Card.), **4:741**

Dier of Muiden, Rudolph, 2:607

Dieric Bouts the Elder, 9:*228*

Dieringer, Franz Xaver, **4:741**

Dierkx, Anne Catherine, St., **4:741**

Dies Domini (apostolic letter, John Paul II), 7:1003

Dies irae (Thomas of Celano), **4:742**, 9:460

Dietary Laws, Hebrew, **4:742–743**, 8:11

Dietenberger, J., 3:241

Dieterich, A., 1:20

Dietmar of Merseburg. *See* Thietmar (Bp. of Merseburg)

Dietrich, Bishop of Verdun, To Hildebrand the Pope (Wenrich of Trier), 14:680

Dietrich of Freiberg. *See* Theodoric of Freiberg

Dietrich of Nieheim, 4:55, **10:388**

Dietrichstein, Franz von (Card.), 12:693

Dietz, Peter Ernest (Bp. of Milwaukee), 1:352, **4:743–744**, 10:56

Dieu, son existence et sa nature (Garrigou-Lagrange), 6:102

Les Dieux ont soif (France), 5:841

Dievs (Baltic region deity), 2:36

Diez, José Ricardo, 10:29

Díez de Games, Gutierre, 1:465

Díez Laurel, Bartolomé, Bl., **4:744**

Díez Macho, A., 2:357

Díez Sahagún, Clemente, Bl., 7:125

Diez Tejerina, Nicefero, Bl., 4:494–495

Diez y Bustos de Molina, Vitoria, Bl., **4:744**

Difesa del giudizio formato dalla Santa Sede Apostolica (Rubino), 12:399

Difféance (in deconstructionism), 4:593–594

Difference, as predicable, 11:659–660

Digambaras (Jains), 7:697, 698

Digamy, **4:744–745**

Digby, Everard, Sir, 1:676, 4:*745*, **745**

Digby, Kenelm, Sir, 12:382

Digenis Akritas, 2:773, 806

Digest (Tribonian), 8:100

Digesta Iustiniani Augusti (Ferrini), 5:696

Digestum sapientiae (Yves de Paris), 14:898

Diggers (Puritan sect), 11:838

Dignitatis humanae (Declaration on Religious Freedom) (Vatican Council II), 1:356–357, 3:643, 644, 4:149, 7:422, 14:103, 417

   conservatives on, 8:447

   papal social thought, 13:259

Dignity of man, 13:853

Dignity/USA, **4:745–746**

Dignum est (Adrian IV), 1:127

Dijon, Guiot de, 4:400

Dilati (martyrs), 5:224, 237–238

Dilatio inferni theory, 6:726

Dilectio, 3:399

Dilectissima nobis (encyclical, Pius XI), 11:395

Dilling, Elizabeth, 10:172

Dillmann, August, 2:384

Dillon, Dominic, 7:581

Dillon, Gerard, 7:581

Dillon, John J., 10:35

DiLorenzo, Francis X. (Bp. of Honolulu), 6:671–672

Dilthey, Wilhelm, **4:746–747**, 11:295–296

   Arnold, Gottfried, 1:718

   demythologizing, 4:656

   hermeneutics, 6:788–789, 796

   knowledge, 8:220

   life philosophies, 8:578–579

   Max Scheler, 12:731

   methodology, 9:566

   Neo-Hegelianism, 6:712

   Neo-Kantian Baden School, 10:*235*, 237, 238

   philosophy of history, 6:885

   psychologism, 11:802

   understanding, 14:292, 293

Dimensions (periodical), 10:159

Diminution, 10:18

Dimissorial Letters, **4:747**, 11:353

Dimock, Robert, 5:237

Al-Din, Bab. *See* al-Bab (Muslim leader)

Dinajpur Diocese (Bangladesh), 2:53

Dinand (Bp.), 3:112

DiNardo, Daniel, 13:164

Dinet, Jacques (Father), 3:185

Dingley, Thomas, Ven., 5:226

Dinis, Nicholas, Bl., 1:952

Dinkel, Pancratius von (Bp.), 1:848

Dintilhac, Jorge (Louis Eugene), **4:747**

Dio Cassius, 12:319

Dio Chrysostom (Greek philosopher), 4:456, 6:446, 10:96

Diocesan archives, 1:639–640

Diocesan consultors, 3:66

Diocesan Cooperators, 4:417

Diocesan Parish Council Personnel, 4:75

Diocesan synods, 2:41

Diocese, creation of, 7:654–656

Diocletian (Roman Emperor), **4:750**, 10:430

   Constantine I (the Great) (Roman Emperor), 4:179

   ecclesiastical organization of Roman Empire, 5:17–18

   era of, 5:312, 12:313–316

   Galatia, reorganization of, 6:51

   Galerius, 6:57

   Silvanus (Bp. of Emesa), 5:191

   See also Diocletian persecution

Diocletian persecution, 3:594, **4:748–750**, 7:654, 12:315–316

   Alexandria, 1:268

   Antioch, 1:522

   Asia Minor, 1:785

   catacombs, 3:223–224

   Church-State relations, 3:632

   Donatism, 1:858, 3:186, 4:861, 863

   Forty Martyrs, 5:825

   Four Crowned Martyrs, 5:833

   Spanish marytrs, 13:376

   works of charity, 3:406

Diodore of Tarsus (Bp.), **4:750–751**

   apocatastasis, 1:548

   Apollinarianism, 1:560

   Apollinaris of Laodicea, 1:560

   Aristotelianism, 1:669

   Christology, 1:523, 3:561

   Christotokos, Mary as, 9:815

   exegetical works, 5:511

   School of Antioch, 1:524, 526, 527, 2:820

   schools of Athens, 1:829

Diodorus Cronus of Iasus, 8:749

Diogenes Laertius

   analysis and synthesis, 1:381

   Empedocles, 5:195

   life of Epicurus, 5:285

   Platonism, 11:413

   soul, 13:33, 332, 334

Diogenes of Sinope, 4:455, 456, *456*

Diogense of Appolonia (fl. 5th c. B.C.), 9:89

Diognetus, Epistle to (St. Justin Martyr), **4:751–752**

   Aristides, 1:666

   Christian way of life, 3:547–548

   disciple as term, 4:774

Dion Cassius, 4:859

Dion Chrysostom (Synesius of Cyrene), 13:683

Dionigi da Piacenza, **4:752**

Dionigi da San Sepolero, 11:213

Dionisio de Sanctis (Bp. of Cartagena), 3:848

Dionysiaca (Nonnus of Panopolis), 10:419

Dionysian era, 5:313

Dionysiana Collectio, 3:39, 59–60, 4:601–602, **752–753**

Dionysio-Hadriana, 3:42, 60, 157

Dionysius (Bp. of Corinth), St., **4:755**, 6:435–436

   Christian way of life, 3:547

   Church history, 3:593

Dionysius (Bp. of Corinth), St.
  (continued)
  works of charity, 3:405
Dionysius (Bp. of Milan), 1:342
Dionysius (Denis) of Alexandra (Bp.),
  St., **4:755**, 5:136
  atomism, 1:833
  biblical canon, 3:31
  Christology, 1:273, 3:560
  Dionysius (Pope), St., 4:753
  exegetical works, 5:510
  homoousios, 4:197, 353, 753, 7:65
  hypostasis, 7:263
  Sabellianism, 12:462
  School of Alexandria, 1:272
  taking Christian name practice,
    10:139
  works of charity, 3:404–406
Dionysius (Pope), St., **4:753–754**
  cardinalate, 3:103
  homoousios, 4:353
  Sabellianism, 12:462
Dionysius, Exiguus, **4:754**
  Apostolic Constitutions, 1:581
  birth of Jesus Christ calculations,
    10:173
  Canon Law, 3:39, 40, 42
  chronology, 3:571
  Collection of Atto, 1:841
  Computus of Easter, 8:642
  Constantinople Council, 4:190
  decretal collection, 4:601–602
  Dionysiana collectio, 4:752, 754
  Easter computus, 4:46
  Easter date controversy, 5:13–14
  era of, 5:313
  Latin literature, 9:439
Dionysius bar Ṣalībī (Bp.)
  biblical catenae, 3:259
  Christmas, 3:552
Dionysius of Halicarnassus, 12:308
Dionysius of St. John, 12:770
Dionysius of the Nativity, Bl., 3:145,
  4:755
Dionysius the Areopagite. *See* Pseudo-
  Dionysius (unknown author)
Dionysus (Greek god), 12:145
Dionysus, cult of, **4:753**
  mysteries, 10:92–94
  as part of Autochthonous Greek
    cults, 10:85
Dionysus of Borgo San Sepulchro, 1:888
Dioscorides (Greek physician), 2:401
Dioscorus (Antipope), 1:171–172,
  4:755–756, 8:476

Dioscorus (father of St. Barbara), 2:89
Dioscorus (Patriarch of Alexandria),
  4:756, 5:275, 759
  Apollinarianism, 1:559
  Boniface II (Pope), 2:498–499
  Council of Chalcedon, 1:269, 271,
    392
  Monophysitism, 4:196, 252, 756, 860
  Robber Council of Ephesus, 1:392,
    3:363
Diospolis, Synod of (415), 3:188, 11:62
Diplomacy, religious conversion and,
  9:691
Diplomata, Canon Law and, 3:41
Diplomatics, ecclesiastical, **4:756–758**
  Leo X (Pope), 8:487
  Leo XIII (Pope), 8:493
  papal legates, 8:450–452
  sigillography, 13:114–115
Diplomatics, secular
  Lee, E., 8:445
  sigillography, 13:114–115
Diptychs, **4:758–759**
  Byzantine art, 2:727
  liturgical use, Armenia, 1:708
  necrology originating from,
    10:228–229
Direct certainty (morality), 9:877
Direction, Spiritual, **4:759–763**
Directionality, philosophy of nature,
  11:306
*Directions spirituelles de Saint François
  de Sales* (Chaumont), 3:457
Directoire spirituel (Lehodey, V.), 8:456
Directorium novitiorum (Le Masson),
  8:465
Directory for the Application of
  Principles and Norms on Ecumenism.
  See Ecumenical Directory
*Directory for the Ministry and Life of
  Permanent Deacons*, 4:553
*Directory for the Ministry and Life of
  Priests* (1994), **4:763–764**
A Directory of Catholic Colleges, 12:444
Direttoria mistico (Scaramelli), 12:31,
  724
Direttorio Ascetico (Scaramelli), 12:724
Dirigierrolle (Passion plays),
  10:927–928
Disabled persons
  L'Arche International, 1:634–635
  Cushing, Richard, 4:447
Discalced orders, **4:764–765**
  See also Carmelites, Discalced
Disce Mori, 10:119

Le Discernement du corps et de l'âme
  (Cordemoy), 3:185
Discernimento degli Spiriti (Scaramelli),
  12:724
Discernment, spiritual, **4:765–767**
  Ignatian exercises, 13:430
  Loyola, 7:308
  revelations, 10:108
  spiritual director, 4:759
Disciple, as term, **4:767–774**, 8:857
Disciples of Christ. *See* Christian Church
  (Disciples of Christ)
Disciples of Christ-Roman Catholic
  Dialogue, 5:69
Discipleship, 9:187, 14:830–831
Disciplina apostolico-monastica
  (Concina), 4:59
Disciplina Arcani, 10:337
Disciplina Ordinis Cartusiensis (Le
  Masson), 3:192, 8:465
Disciplinati (religious groups), 5:755
The Discipline, **4:774–775**
Discipline of Sacraments, Sacred
  Congregation on, 4:89
Discorsi sulla prima Deca di Tito Livio
  (Machiavelli), 9:21
*Discorso sobre a Vinda de Jesus
  Christo, a Krista-Purana* (Stephens),
  13:526
Discours de la méthode (Descartes),
  12:748
*Discours de la réformation de l'homme
  intérieur* (Jansen), 7:714
*Discours pour le sacre de l'Electeur de
  Cologne* (Fénelon), 5:683
*Discours su les affaries d'Allemange et
  sur le vicariat de l'Empire*
  (Spanheim), 13:406
*Discours sur les libertés de l'Église
  gallicane* (Fleury), 5:762, 6:76
Discours sur les sciences et les arts
  (Rousseau), 12:392
*Discours sur l'origine de l'inégalité
  parmi les hommes* (Rousseau),
  12:392
*Discourse against the Heresy of Noetus
  (Contra Noetum)* (St. Hippolytus of
  Rome), 6:859
Discourse Chrétiens (Charron), 3:439
*Discourse of Free Thinking, Occasion'd
  by the Rise and Growth of a Sect
  called Freethinkers* (Collins), 5:967
*Discourse of Matters Pertaining to
  Religion* (Parker), 10:892, 14:148
"Discourse of the Transient and
  Permanent in Christianity" (Parker),
  14:148

The Discourse on Method (Descartes), 4:677–680

Discourse on Universal History (Bossuet), 6:888–889

Discourses (Epictetus), 5:282

Discourses concerning Two New Sciences (Galileo), 6:63, 9:415

Discourses on the First Decade of Livy (Machiavelli), 12:118

Discovery and Exploration of the Mississippi Valley (Shea), 13:70

Discretio, 3:190

Discrezione degli spiriti (Sarnelli), 12:694

Discrimination. *See* Human rights abuses; Racial discrimination

''Discrimination and Christian Conscience'' (NCCIJ), 10:158

Discursive knowledge, 8:203

Discursive Power, 3:822, **4:775**

Discurso de las Duenas (León), 8:497

Discurso sobre la elección de successor del pontificado en vida del pontifice (Ripalda), 12:252

Discursos del amparo de los legitimos pobres y reducción de los fingidos. . . (Pérez de Herrera), 3:417

Disease, demons and, 4:498

Disentis Abbey (Switzerland), **4:775–776**

Disequilibrium, 2:187

Disertaciones selectae in primam aetatem historiae ecclesiasticae (Smedt), 13:230

Dishypatos, David, 2:826, **4:776**

Disinterested Love, 8:828–829

Dispensational theology, 4:527, **776**

''Dispensationalist millennialism,'' 11:913

Display oratory, 12:855–856

Disposition, **4:776–778**
  character, 3:387
  condition, 4:73

Dispositions of matter, 9:349

Disputatio Christiani cum gentili (Gilbert Crispin), 6:213

Disputatio de mundi officio (Zachary the Rhetor), 14:905

Disputatio Iudaei et Christiani (Gilbert Crispin), 6:213

Disputatio puerorum per interrogationes et responsiones, 3:230, 239

Disputation Between a Christian and a Heretic (Eutychios of Alexandria), 5:463

Disputation of Tortosa (1413-1414), 1:232

Disputationes, Expositio super simbolum (Simon of Tournai), 13:133

Disputationes contra Astrologiam (Pico Della Mirandola), 11:323

Disputationes de Controversiis Christianae Fidei adversus hujus temporis haeretios (Bellarmine), 2:227

Disputationes in 2am2ae D. Thomae: De fide, spe, charitate et prudentia (Torres), 14:115

Disputationes in primam secundae D. Thomas (Pallavicino), 10:806

Disputationes metaphysicae (Suárez), 1:378, 12:767, 768

Disputationes theologicae (Fabri), 5:585

Disputations
  dialectics, 4:727
  scholastic method, 12:747–748

Disputed Questions, 5:899

Disquisitio metaphysica (Gassendi), 6:105

Dissertatio de causis majoribus ad caput concordatorum (Gerbais), 6:77

Dissertation on the Epistles of Phalaris (Bentley), 2:287

Dissertationes in concilia generalia et particularia (Thomassin) (Louis d'Eynac), 14:40

Dissident Catholic Movement (Lithuania), 8:608

Dissimulation, 3:186, **4:778**

Distance, perception of, 9:74

Disticha catonis, **4:778**

Distinctio librorum (Bartholomew of Urbino), 2:127–128

Distinction, kinds of, **4:778–782**
  See also Formal distinctions

The Distinguishing Marks of a Work of the Spirit of God (Edwards), 5:97

Distributism, 3:470, **4:782–783**

Distributive justice, 8:67, 13:244

Distributive Justice (Ryan), 12:445

Ditchling, Guild of St. Joseph and St. Dominic, **4:783**

Diversarum hereseon liber (Filastrius of Brescia), 5:294

Diversorum patrum sententie. See Seventy-Four Titles, Collection of

Dives in misericordia (encyclical, John Paul II), 3:627, **4:783–784**, 10:852

Divided Christendom (Congar), 5:73

Le Divin ami (Schrijvers), 12:787

Divina (brief, Pius VI), 1:297

Divina Commedia (Dante), 1:291, 3:310, 4:519–522

Divina Proportione (Pacioli and Leonardo da Vinci), 10:749

Divinae institutiones (Lactantius), 8:274

Divination, **4:784–786**
  China, 3:507, 512
  Christianity, 4:786
  dreams, 4:903–905
  Greece, 1:811
  Hittite religion, 6:895
  Islam, 4:786
  Judaism, 4:785–786
  Mesopotamia, ancient, 9:536–537
  occult, 3:759
  Oracle of Delphi, 4:632
  Sortes Homericae, Vergilianae, Biblicae, 13:328
  spiritism, 13:428–429
  See also Magic

Divine and Catholic faith theological note, 10:453–454

Divine attributes, 6:319

Divine causality, 6:752, 11:657–658

Divine choice and election. *See* Election, Divine

Divine concurrence, **4:70–73**

Divine economy. *See* Economy, Divine

Divine essence, 6:319–320

Divine faith theological note, 10:454

Divine grace, 12:899

Divine Grace and Man (Fransen), 5:918

Divine illumination, 13:898–899

Divine intelligence, 6:321

Divine intervention, **7:530**
  See also Miracles, in the Bible; Miracles, theology of

Divine judgment, ordeal and, 10:626–627

Divine judgment in theology. *See* Judgment, Divine, in theology

Divine knowledge, omniscience and, 10:593–599

Divine love, 8:49

Divine maternity of Mary, 9:173–174, 257–258

Divine Mercy, Apostle of, 8:243–245

Divine Mercy Sunday, 8:245

The Divine Milieu (Teilhard de Chardin), 10:116

Divine missions. *See* Missions, Divine

The Divine Names (Pseudo-Dionysius), 11:800–801

Divine Office
  early liturgical books, 8:640
  Little Hours, 8:610–611
  Little Office of the BVM, 8:611
  readings for, 8:437–438
  See also Liturgy of the Hours

Divine perfection, 11:118–119

Divine Person, 7:373–374, 11:149, **151–152**

Divine plan. *See* Economy, Divine

Divine predilection, 11:648

Divine Principle (Young Oon Kim), 14:299

Divine providence, 14:942

Divine Redeemer, Daughters of the, 5:307

The Divine Relativity (Hartshorne), 6:658

Divine revelation, 9:857, 13:892–893, 914

Divine right of kings, **4:788**
   Church-State relations, 3:637
   democracy, 4:640
   law's origin, 8:398
   scholasticism, 12:766
   social contract vs., 13:240
   and the state, 13:484

Divine will, 6:321–322, 7:864, 10:536, 14:724–725

Divine wisdom, 14:790

Divine Word, Society of the (SVD), 6:185, 7:431, 10:529, 14:98

Divine World Missions (SVD), 5:10

Divine Worship and the Discipline of the Sacraments, Sacred Congregation for, **4:789–790**
   Confirmation, 4:89
   dispensation from celibacy, 8:287
   lauds, 8:379
   liturgical books, 8:638
   liturgical laws, 8:669
   origin, 4:165

Divine Zeal, Daughters of, 5:865

Divini illius magistri (encyclical, Pius XI), 11:392

Divini redemptoris (encyclical, Pius XI), 1:823, 3:642, **4:790**, 11:393, 394, 13:243

Divinity, concept of, 12:58–59

"Divinity School Address" (Emerson), 14:147

Divinius Magister Perfectionis (apostolic constitution, John Paul II), 3:58, 63, 7:1001, 12:608

Divinization, doctrine of, 8:81, 82

Divino afflante spiritu (encyclical, Pius XII), 2:167, **4:790–792**, 5:523, 6:793, 10:303, 11:399, 478
   Catholic scholarship, 11:95
   Church history, 3:623
   Fundamentalism, 6:29
   Genesis, Book of, 6:133

Divinum illud munus (encyclical, Leo XIII), **4:792**, 6:294, 7:442

Divinus perfectionis magister (apostolic constitution, John Paul II), 3:58, 63, 12:608

Divisio Apostolorum, feast of, 1:575

Division (Logic), 4:53, **792–794**

The Division of Labor (Durkheim), 4:952

Divison of Nature (Eriugena), 10:826

Divorce
   in the Bible, 13:49
   Catholic views, 5:253
   Chile, 3:488
   Ireland, 7:568
   Israelites, 13:249
   Italy, 7:674
   Jewish, 8:12
   sex, in the Bible, 13:49–50

Divus Thomas (periodical), 12:774

Divus Thomas Doctor angelicus contra Liberalismum invictus veritatis catholicae assertor (Schäzler), 12:730

Dix, Dorothea, 7:132

Dix, Gregory, **4:794**

Dixon, James, 1:900

Dizionario degli Istituti de Perfezione, 5:208

Dizionario di erudizione (Moroni), 5:207

Dizionario Patristico e de Antichità Cristiane, 5:208

Djibouti, Republic of, **4:794–795**

Djidjov, Pavel, 2:548

Djoundrin, Samuil (Bp. of Sofia-Plovdiv), 2:683

Długosz, Jan, 3:203–204, **4:795–796**

Dmitrovica (ancient city), 13:168

Doane, George Hobart, **4:796**

Dobmayer, Marianus, 12:770

Dobrizhoffer, Martin, **4:796**

Dobromil (Galicia), Basilian reform in, 2:144

Docetism, **4:796–797**
   Bogomilism, 2:458
   Christology, 3:559, 560
   Clement of Alexandria, St., 3:799
   definition, 10:13
   hypostasis, 7:264
   Ignatius of Antioch, St., 2:820, 7:311
   theology of Christ, 7:811

Dochkus v. Lithuanian Benefit Society of St. Anthony (1903), 3:658

Docility, **4:797**

Docta ignorantia (Nicholas of Cusa), **4:797–798**, 9:461, 10:374, 12:121

Doctor (scholastic title), 4:798–801, **798–801**

Doctor Angelici (*motu proprio*, Pius X), 11:*390*

Doctor Eximius. *See* Suárez, Francisco

Doctor mellifluus (encyclical, Pius XII), 2:309

Doctor of the Church, **4:801–802**

Doctor perspicuus. *See* Walter Burley

Doctor planus. *See* Walter Burley

Doctoris gentium (papal bull, Eugene IV), 2:134

Doctors without Borders (MSF), 10:615

Doctrina XII Apostolorum. See Didache

Doctrina breve, 3:246

Doctrina christiana y catecismo para instrucción de los indios, 3:246

Doctrina cristiana, 5:202

Doctrina cristiana para los Indios (Sanctis), 12:661

Doctrina nummorum veterum (Eckhel), 5:46

Doctrina S. Thomae Aquinatis de cooperatione Dei (Frins), 6:12

Doctrinae eius (quam certorum articulorum damnatio postulare visa est) brevis et quoad fieri potest ordinata et cohaerens explicatio (Baius, et al), 2:19

Doctrinaires, 2:714

Doctrinal tolerance, 14:102

Doctrinale fidei catholicae contra Wiclevistas et Hussitas (Netter), 10:264

Doctrine, **4:802–803**

Doctrine, development of, **4:803–809**, 8:405–406

La Doctrine ascétique des premiers maâtres égyptiens de quatrième siècle (Resch), 12:137

"Doctrine of Addai," 1:112

The Doctrine of Faith According to St. John of the Cross (Wojtyła), 7:993

Doctrine of the Faith, Congregation for the
   creedal statements, 4:355
   de Mello, Anthony, 4:634
   Dechamps, Victor Auguste, 4:589
   development, 4:809
   dogmatic theology, 4:814
   Ecumenical dialogues, 5:67
   eschatology, 5:346
   evolution, 4:347
   theologians censured, 5:40

Documents, papal and curial
   abbreviators, 1:12–13
   diplomatics, 4:756–758

types of, generally, 4:757–758
See also specific document types
Documents of American Catholic History, 5:170
Dodd, Charles Harold, **4:809–810**, 5:331–332, 338, 508, 522, 7:850
  Constable, Cuthbert, 4:168
  revelation, 12:195
  Sabran, Louis de, 12:464
Dodena, 3:230
Dodge City Diocese (KS), **4:810**, 8:115–116
Dodo of Asch, Bl., **4:810**
Dodona ruins, 10:*754*
Doe, Santa Fe Independent School District v. (2000), 3:667
Doe v. Bolton (1973), 1:32, 14:315
Doenmeh, 13:57
Doerfler, Bruno (Abbot), 12:578
Does Civilization Need Religion? (Niebuhr), 10:387
Dogma, **4:810–811**
  heresies vs., 13:897
  history, 6:880, 8:188
  liberal theology, 8:543
  Mary, Blessed Virgin, perpetual virginity of, 14:532
  modernism, 9:754–755, 755
  moral dogmatism, 8:265
  Seeberg, Reinhold, 12:875
Dogmata theologia (Petau), 11:172
Dogmata theologica (Thomassin) (Louis d'Eynac), 14:40
Dogmatic Constitution on Divine Revelation (Vatican Council II), 2:388, 10:304, 12:191–192, 14:415
Dogmatic Constitution on the Church (Lumen gentium) (Vatican Council II), 3:626, 7:380–381, **380–381**, 10:559–560, 12:865, 14:415
  bishops, 2:414, 415, 418, 420
  canonization of saints, 12:608
  Catholic Action, 3:278
  charisms, 3:393
  Christocentrism, 3:558
  communio as concept, 4:27
  communion, 3:590
  communion of saints, 4:34
  conciliarism, 4:57
  deacons, 4:552
  ecclesiology, 5:37, 39
  Ecumenical councils, 4:303, 304, 305
  ecumenism, 5:40
  episcopal collegiality, 3:837
  Episcopal conferences, 5:299
  eschatology, 5:346

  laity, 8:290, 291–292
  saints, 12:604
  social justice, 4:157
Dogmatic definition, **4:611**
Dogmatic facts, 1:390, **4:811**
Dogmatic Memoir (Basil of Ancyra), 2:139
Dogmatic process of methodology, 9:568
Dogmatic theology, **4:812–821**, 9:853–854, 13:895–896, 910
  biblical studies, 4:814, 816–817
  historical challenges to the Church, 5:36
  historical theology, 6:870
  history, 4:812–814
  intentionality analysis, 8:773–774
  justice of God, 8:71–72
  justice of men, 8:74–75
  kerygma, 8:158
  Ledesma, P., 8:443
  loci theologici, 8:743
  Marian, 8:506–507
  moral theology, 4:812
  orthodoxy, 8:199
  point of departure of, 4:815
  positive theology, 4:812, 815–817
  scholastic errors, 8:432
  Schwane, Joseph, 12:792–793
  scientific dialectic, 8:253
  speculative theology, 4:813–814, 818–820
  spiritual theology, 13:435
  as term, 4:811, 812
  thematization, process of, 13:896
Dogmatic theology of the Eastern Catholic Church (Amphiteatrov), 6:459
Dogmatics (Petavius), 10:919
Dogmatik (Schell), 3:589
Dogmatism, **4:821**, 883, 11:284–285
Le Dogme de la Rédemption: Étude historique (Rivière), 12:262
Le Dogme de la Rédemption: Étude théologique (Rivière), 12:262
Dogme et critique (Le Roy), 9:755
Dogmengeschichte (Schwane), 12:792
Doheny, William, 3:58
Doi, Peter Tatsuo (Card.), 7:*740*, 12:534
Doisy, Edward A., 12:563
Dokkum (Netherlands), martyrs of, 5:269
Doktor Faustus (Mann), 5:650
Dolan, Albert, 11:625
Dolbeau, Jean, 3:4

Dolcino, Fra, **4:821**
  apocalyptic movements, 1:548
  apostolici, 1:594
  Crusade against, 4:413
Dold, Alban, 2:350, **4:821–822**
Dold, Louis (Father), 3:119
Dolejsi, Edward, 2:871
Dolentium hominum (*motu proprio*, John Paul II), 11:482
Dölger, Franz Joseph, 1:20, 3:552, **4:822**, 10:963
Dollfuss, Engelbert, 1:915
Döllgast, Hans, 3:711
Döllinger, Johannes Joseph Ignaz Von, 3:624, **4:822–824**, *823*, 6:183
  Acton, John Emerich Edward Dalberg, 1:85
  heresy, 6:778
  Hergenröther, Joseph, 6:780
  papal infallibility, 12:730
Döllingerites (Ullathorne), 14:282
Dolly (cloned sheep), 7:178
The Dolorous Passion of Our Lord and Saviour Jesus Christ (Brentano), 5:193
Dom St. Rupert (Salzburg, Austria), 12:*413*
Dôme des Invalides church (Paris), 3:706
Dome of the Rock (Jerusalem), 7:*618*, 10:10
Domenec, Michael (Bp. of Pittsburgh), **4:824–825**, 11:85–86, 367
Domenech, Emmanuel, **4:825**
Il Domenechino, 4:313
Doménikos Theotokópoulos (Domenico Theotocopuli). *See* El Greco (painter)
Domes, Islamic, 7:617
Domesday Book, 3:469, **4:825–826**, *826*
Domestic Prelate, **4:826**
Domestic Work. *See* Servants of Our Lady Queen of the Clergy
Domingo de la Calzada, St., **4:826–827**
Domíngo de Santa Teresa, 12:618
Domingo y Sol, Manuel, Bl., **4:826**
Domingos de S. Francisco, Bl., 7:734
Domingos del S. Rosario, Bl., 7:733
Dominguez, Atanasio, 10:267
Domínguez, Isidoro (Abp. of Santa Fe de Bogotá, Colombia), **4:827**
Dominguito of Saragossa, St., **4:827**
Dominic, St., 4:*828*, **828–829**, 5:845, 12:29
  Bertrand de Garriga, Bl., 2:337
  Cecilia Romana, Bl., 3:315
  Church property, 3:727

Dominic, St. (continued)
  direction, spiritual, 4:761
  Dominican Rite, 4:837
  founding of Dominicans, 4:828–829, 848–851
  Innocent III (Pope), 3:602
  life, 13:121
  Life of St. Dominic (Lacordaire), 8:272
  mysticism prose, 10:118
  Rosary, 12:374–375
  shrine, 13:94
  Silos Abbey, 13:121
  spirituality, 13:446
  spirituality teachings, 4:845–847
  Theodore of Celles, 4:377
Dominic Gundisalvi (Gundissalinus), 4:829–830
  Arabian philosophy, 1:622
  Avicebron, 1:938
  unicity thesis, 5:816
Dominic Loricatus, St., 4:830, 5:792
Dominic of Flanders, 1:677, 4:831
Dominic of Prussia, 3:192, 4:831
Dominic of Silos, St., 4:831, 13:120
Dominic of Sora, St., 4:732, 13:325
Dominic of the Most Holy Sacrament. See Iturrate Zubero, Domingo, Bl.
Dominic of the Mother of God (Domenico della Madre di Dio). See Barberi, Domenico, Bl.
Dominica, 3:117–119
Dominica of Flanders, 14:48
Dominicae cenae (apostolic letter, John Paul II), 7:1003
Dominical Letter, 4:832
Dominican Daughters of Saint Rosario, 8:776
Dominican Nuns (Nuns of the Order of Preachers), 4:832–833
Dominican Order of France, 8:271, 272
Dominican Order of the United States, 8:147
The Dominican Province of St. Joseph (O'Daniel), 10:550
Dominican Reformed Congregation of Italy, 8:408
Dominican Republic, 4:833–837, 835, 836, 8:340–341
Dominican Rite, 4:837–838
Dominican Rural Missionaries, 4:842
Dominican School, 12:760–761
Dominican Sisters, 4:838–845
Dominican Sisters, St. Mary of the Springs, 4:843

Dominican Sisters Congregation of Holy Cross, 4:842
Dominican Sisters of Charity of the Presentation of the Blessed Virgin Mary, 4:842
Dominican Sisters of Great Bend, 4:842–843
Dominican Sisters of Hope, 4:843
Dominican Sisters of Houston, Texas, 4:843
Dominican Sisters of Our Lady of the Rosary and of St. Catherine of Siena, Cabra, 4:843
Dominican Sisters of St. Catharine, 8:148
Dominican Sisters of Springfield, 4:843
Dominican Sisters of the Annunciation, 3:835
Dominican Sisters of the Presentation, 11:564
Dominican spirituality, 3:605, 4:845–848
Dominican Third Order of Teachers, 8:272
Dominican University (River Forest, IL), 3:480
Dominicans, 4:848–855
  active life, 1:83
  Alberto Castellani, 1:229
  Albigensians, 1:229, 231
  alternativa, 1:321
  Ancient See of Carlisle, 3:124
  Anointing of the Sick, 1:482
  Apostolic Penitentiary, 11:76
  Aristotelianism, 1:674–675
  Armenia, 1:702, 706
  art sacré movement, 1:803, 3:713
  Augustinianism, 1:878
  Austria, 1:910
  Bolivia, 2:466
  Byzantine Church, 2:762
  California, 2:867
  Caribbean, 3:116, 117, 118
  Carroll, John, 3:181
  Carthage, 3:187–188
  catechesis, 3:231
  Catharism, 1:229, 231, 3:260
  Chile, 3:485
  China, 3:83–84, 495, 499, 513
  chronicles, 1:464
  Clare Gambacorta, Bl., 3:759–760
  Colombia, 3:848, 849
  Concina, Daniel and poverty, 4:59
  Congregatio de auxiliis conflict over grace between Jesuits, 14:48
  contemplation, 4:204, 206
  Cormier, Hyacinthe-Marie, 4:269

  correctoria of Thomism, 4:273–278
  Counter Reformation, 4:310
  Crosier Fathers, 2:609
  Cuba, 4:417
  de auxiliis controversy, 4:111–113
  direction, spiritual, 4:761–762
  dispute with Oxford University, 7:961
  disputes with Augustinians, 8:497
  Divine concurrence, 4:71
  Dominic, St., 4:828–829, 845–847, 848–851
  following of Christ, 5:789
  Franciscan rivalry with, 3:603
  free will, 5:930
  Gregory IX (Pope), 6:497
  hierarchical insignia, 6:764
  Hugh of Saint-Cher, 7:156
  Humbert of Romans, 7:198–199
  Hungary, 7:210–211
  Hyacinth, St., 7:236
  Indonesia, 7:428
  Jerusalem, 7:775
  medieval preaching, 11:612
  membership by Aquinas, 14:14–15, 17–18
  Mexico, 2:345–346
  missions
    Africa, 12:686
    Baja California, 12:644
    China, 12:226
    East Timor, 5:8
    England, 5:242
    France, 5:760
    Mexico, 9:571–572
    Mozambique, 10:38
    Panama, 10:817–818
    Philippines, 12:226
    Taiwan, 12:226
    U.S., 9:715, 14:513
  moral obligation and 1932 constitutions, 10:520
  19th-20th century overview, 3:621
  nuns, 4:832–833
  Ohio, 3:734–735
  Order of Magdalens, direction of the, 9:33
  Panama missionary work, 10:817–818
  Peru, 11:159
  poverty, 11:569, 570
  Poverty Movement, 11:573
  Prussia, 3:537
  religious orders in Scotland, 12:833
  Rosary, 12:373–376

scholasticism, 12:760–761, 764

sisters, 4:838–845

slavery, 1:156

Spain, 13:384

suppression, 4:853

Third Orders, 3:413, 418

See also Dominican spirituality

Dominicans, English, 12:265–266

The Dominicans in Early Florida (O'Daniel), 10:550

Dominicans Thomistic teaching promoted by, 14:45

Dominici, John, Bl., 1:536, **4:855–856,** 5:90, 9:461

Dominici gregis (apostolic constitution, Pius IV), 3:336

Dominicianus ordo (*motu proprio*, John XXIII), 11:487

Dominicus de Sancto Geminiano, 3:52

Dominicus Germanus, **4:856**

Dominicus Prutenus, 4:*831*

Dominion, 14:865

Dominis, Marcantonio de, 2:874, **4:856**

Dominque de Saint-Albert, 3:137

Dominum et vivificantem (encyclical, John Paul II), **4:856–857**

Dominus ac Redemptor (apostolic brief, Clement XIV), 3:92, 795–796, 5:43, 7:787

Dominus Iesus (Congregation for the Doctrine of the Faith, 2000), 7:842, 8:175

Dominus vobiscum (Peter the Painter), 11:207

Domitian (Roman Emperor), 3:592, **4:857–858,** *858,* 12:304, 351

Domitian of Ancyra (Bp.), **4:858**

Domitian of Maastricht (Bp.), St., **4:858–859**

Domitilla, catacomb of (Rome), 3:224

Domitilla, Flavia, SS., 3:592, **4:859,** 12:351

Domna Ebba. *See* Ermenburga (Anglo-Saxon queen), St.

Domnall Mór O'Brien (King of Thomond), 7:18

Domneva. *See* Ermenburga (Anglo-Saxon queen), St.

Domnina (martyr), 3:770

Domninus of Antioch, 4:191

Domnolus of Le Mans (Bp.), St., **4:859**

Domnus of Antioch (Bp.), 3:365, 4:859, **859–860**

Doms, Herbert, 4:221

Domus Aurea (Golden House) (Antioch), 1:524

Domus ecclesia. See House churches

Domus Sanctae Marthae, **4:860**

Don Bosco Union, 12:248

Le Don de soi (Schrijvers), 12:787

Don Quixote (Cervantes), 2:115

Donaghoe, Terence J., 3:765

Donahue, Patrick J. (Bp. of Wheeling, WV), 14:688

Donatello (Italian artist), 1:507

ambos, 1:335, 336

Bible cycles, 2:374

iconography of Apostles, 1:575

Donati, Orsola, 2:95

Donation of Constantine, 3:635, **4:860–861,** 12:120–121

Alexander II (Pope), 1:253

Alexandrine bulls, 1:274

Augustine (Triumphus) of Ancona, 1:870

Carolingian consolidation of power, 3:164–165

forgery, 9:445, 10:714

Leo IX (Pope), St., 8:485

Nicholas of Cusa, 10:375

States of the Church, 10:835

Sylvester legend, 4:183

Valla, Lorenzo, 7:187

Donation of Pepin (756), 1:121–122, 3:165, 635

Donatism, **4:861–864**

African Church, 10:430–431

Algeria, 1:284

Anabaptists, 1:368

Augustine, St., 1:858–859, 866–867, 3:594, 633

Christmas, 3:553

Church-State relations, 3:632

Constantine I (the Great) (Roman Emperor), 1:859, 3:594, 632, 4:180, 299, 862

Councils of Carthage, 3:186, 188

Donatus, 4:861–862, 864

Honorius (Roman Emperor), 7:87

ordination ministers, 7:39

Sicily, 13:103

universality of Christianity, 3:275, 293

Donato, St., reliquary bust of, 12:*105*

Donatus (Bp. of Carthage), 1:859, 3:188, **4:864**

commentary on manual, 13:228

Constans I, 4:173

Donatism, 4:861–862, 864

Miltiades, 9:640

See also Donatism

Donatus of Besançon, St., **4:864**

Donceel, Joseph, 7:64

Donders, Peter, Bl., **4:864–865,** *865*

Dondeyne, Albert, 12:776

Dong Bodi, Patrick, St., **4:865**

Dòng Đồng Công (CMC), 4:114

Dongan, Thomas, 3:648, 10:281, 321

Dongshan Liangjie, 3:511

Donizetti, Gaetano, **4:866**

Donne, John, **4:866–869,** *867,* 10:629–630, 13:320

Le Donné révélé et la théologie (Gardeil), 6:94

Donnellan, Thomas A. (Abp. of Atlanta), 1:831

Donnelly, Bernard, 8:118

Donnelly, Francis P., 11:625

Donnelly, Lynch v. (1984), 3:668

Donoghue, John Francis (Abp. of Atlanta), 1:831, 3:437, 10:438

Donoso, Justo, **4:869**

Donoso Cortés, Juan Francisco María de la Salud, **4:869–870**

Donoso Murillo, Arturo, Bl., 7:125

Donovan, Jean, 8:133

Donum vitae: Instruction on Respect for Human Life in its Origin and on the Dignity of Procreation (1987), 1:29, 13:356

Donus (Pope), **4:870**

Dooley, Thomas Anthony, 4:*871,* **871,** 8:*331*

Doors, Church, **4:871–874**

Döpfner, Julius (Card.), 4:222, **874**

Dorchester Abbey (England), **4:874**

Dordrecht on predestination (1619), 10:264

Dore, Gustave, 3:275

Jesus Walking on Water, 9:*666*

Satan's Flight Through Chaos, 9:*634*

Doré, Joseph, 7:528

Doria, Niccolò, 1:468

Doria, Nicholas, 7:972

Dorival, Bernard, 1:803

Dorland, Peter (Dorlandus), **4:874–875**

Dormi secure (Sleep without Anxiety) (Johannes of Werden), 11:613

Dormition of the Virgin, 1:800, **4:875–876**

Dorn, Anna (Sister Bernardine), 5:888

Dorn, Mary Bernardine (Mother), 5:891

Dorothea von Montau, St., **4:876**

Dorotheans, **4:876,** 5:921

Dorotheus of Antioch, 1:526–527, 2:820, 4:876–877, **876–877**

Dorotheus of Gaza, 4:877

Dorotheus of Mytilene, 4:877

Dorothy, St., 4:*877*, **877**

D'Ors, Eugenio, 13:423

Dort, Synod of (1618-19), 1:713, 2:894, 8:84

Dortel-Claudot, Madame, 11:45

Dositeo patriarcha greco di Gerusalemme (Palmieri), 10:812

Dositheus of Jerusalem (Patriarch), 6:457–458, 10:701

Dositheus of Samaria, **4:877**

Dossetti, Giuseppe (Father), 7:674

Dostoevskiĭ, Fëdor Mikhaĭlovich, 4:*878*, **878–879**, 13:307

Doswald, Hilary Joseph, **4:879**

Dothan, M., 2:379

Dottrina cristiana breve (Bellarmine), 2:227, 3:234, 242

La Dottrina de San Giovani della Croce (Scaramelli), 12:724

Douai (Douay) (France), **4:879–880**, 888

Douai (Douay) University (France)
Anchin Abbey, 1:396
Andleby, William, Bl., 1:400
English exiles, 13:369
founding, 1:295–296

Douai, Graindor de, 4:400

Al-Douaihi, Stephan (Maronite Patriarch), 1:534

Douay Bible, 2:43

Double effect, principle of, **4:880–881**, 11:767
compensationism, 4:43
hysterectomy, 7:266
sin, cooperation in, 13:156–157

Double righteousness, 8:85

Double truth theory, **4:881–883**
Apostolici regiminis, 1:595
Latin Averroism, 1:674, 936
Siger of Brabant, 13:113

Doubt, **4:883–884**
aporia, 1:570, 4:883
biological mechanism, 9:420
certitude, 3:351, 4:883–884
Hermes, Georg, 4:932
law vs. fact, 4:883, 884
methodical, 4:680, 883–884
skepticism, 13:200–205

Doubt, moral, 4:883, **884–885**
compensationism, 4:43
laxism, 8:410–411

Doubtful law, 9:878–879

Douceline of the Midi, St., **4:885**

Dougherty, Dennis (Abp. of Philadelphia), **4:885–886**, 11:87, 240

Douglas, Archibald (Earl of Angus), 2:179

Douglas, Gawin, 2:179

Douglas, George, Bl., **4:886**, 5:229

Douglas, Mary, 12:87, 259

Doukhobors, **4:886–887**, 12:425

Doumerque, E., 5:711

Douzy, Synod of (871), 6:837

Dove, as symbol, 7:49, 51

Doway Catechism, 3:243

Dowdall, George (Abp. of Armagh), 1:698, 4:887, **887**

Dowdall, James, **4:887**, 5:233

Dowdall, John Baptist, 7:582

Dowling, Austin (Abp. of St. Paul, MN), **4:887–888**, 12:573

Down Syndrome, 8:463–464

Downside Abbey (England), **4:888**, 8:222–223

Downside Review, 8:222

Dowry, 4:65

Dowry for women religious, **4:888–889**

Doxai, 8:213

Doxology, biblical, **4:889–890**

Doxology, liturgical, **4:890–891**

Doxopaties, Neils, **4:891**

Doxopatres, Johannes, 4:891

Doxopatres, Neilos, **4:891**

Doyle, James Warren (Bp. of Kildare and Leighlin, Ireland), **4:891**

Dozier, Carroll T. (Bp. of Memphis, TN), 13:823–824

Drabik, Richarch, Rev., 10:159

Dracontius, 3:186, 9:439

Dragmaticon (William of Conches), 14:739

Dragovitsa, Church of, 3:259

Drake, Francis, Sir, 5:295

Drake constitution (MO), 8:145–146

Drakestein, Yvonne Bosch van, **4:891–892**

Drama
Aristotle, 11:433–434
baroque period, 2:115–116
criticism, 8:516–517
liturgical, 4:893–896
religious, 9:457
Shakespeare, 13:60–66
See also Theater

Drama, medieval, **4:892–902**

Dramas, Fields, and Metaphors (Turner), 14:245

Draškovič, Georg de Trakosćan (Card.), **4:902–903**

Dražic, John (Bp. of Prague), 4:480

The DRE Book (Harris), 12:97

Dream literature. *See* Vision literature

The Dream of Gerontius (Newman), 3:271, 10:340

The Dream of Gerontius (oratorio by Elgar), 5:153

The Dream of Pope Innocent III (Giotto), 7:*471*

The Dream of St. Ursula (Carpaccio), 14:*347*

The Dream of the Rood, 10:119

Dreams, **4:903–906**
imagination, 7:326–327
interpretation, 4:784, 903–905
Jungian interpretation, 8:60
moral questions about, 4:905
use of, spiritual, 4:905

Dresser, Julius A., 10:308

Dreves, G. M., 12:246

Drexel, Jeremias, 4:94, **906**, 7:782

Drexel, Katharine Marie, St., **4:906–907**, *907*, 10:588, 11:240
African American Catholics, 1:157, 162
Beasley, Mathilda, 2:168
beatification, 11:241
Mary Mission, 13:368
prominence, 11:87
Savannah Archdiocese, 12:710
Sisters of the Blessed Sacrament, 2:437, 8:813
Xavier University of Louisiana, founding of, 14:879, 880

Drey, Johann Sebastian von, **4:907–908**
apologetics, 5:827
doctrine, development of, 4:807

Driesch, Hans
Aristotelianism, 1:678
concept of entelechy, 5:267
life philosophy, 8:579

Drinan, Robert F., 7:794

Drioton, E., 1:199

Driscoll, James F., **4:908**

Driscoll, Justin A., 5:625

Driscoll, Michael P. (Bp. of Idaho), 7:291

Driver, S. R., 5:519, 13:19

Drobka, Frank J., 3:283

Drogo of Metz (Bp.), **4:908–909**
Aldric of Le Mans, St., 1:248
Council of Attigny, 1:840
Councils of Chalon-Sur-Saône, 3:373
manuscript illumination, 3:154

Drolin, Gabriel (Brother), 2:632

Drossaerts, Arthur Jerome, 12:642

Droste zu Vischering, Clemens August von (Abp. of Cologne), 3:843, **4:909**, 6:185
  Döllinger, Johannes, 4:823
  Fourth Baltimore Provincial Council (1840), 2:44
  mixed marriage dispute, 3:845–846
Drouin, Hyacinthe René (Drouven), **4:909**
Drozdov, Filaret, 12:434
Drozdov, Vasiliĭ Mikhailovich. *See* Filaret (Russian theologian)
Druids, 3:330–331
  Chartre, 3:439, 441
  Samhain, 1:290
Druillettes, Gabriel (Father), 4:491, 9:55
Druim-Cetta, Assembly of (575), 3:863
Drumgoole, John Christopher (Father), **4:909–910**, 5:890
Drummond, Henry, 3:278
Drunkenness, **4:910–912**, 14:771–772
Drury, Robert, Bl., **4:912**, 5:234
Druthmar, St., **4:912**
Drużbicki, Gaspar, **4:912–913**
Druzes, **4:913**, 8:427
Dryburgh Monastery (Scotland), **4:913–914**
Dryden, John, 10:494
  Chaucer, Geoffrey, 3:453
  Corker, James Maurus, 4:269
D'Souza, Agnel (Father), Ven., 7:406
D'Souza, Jerome, 7:793
DSP (Pious Society of the Daughters of St. Paul), **12:570**
Du Bos, Charles, **4:919**
Du Contrat Social (The Social Contract) (Rousseau), 12:392, 393
Du Hamel, Jean Baptiste, **4:931**
  opponent of Descartes, 12:31
  scholasticism, 12:765
Du Houx, Jeanne, **4:931**
Du Pac, Gabriel de Bellegarde, **4:941**
Du pape (Maistre), 9:61
Du Pape et de ses droits religieux (Barruel), 2:118
Du Pin, Louis Ellies, **4:944**
Du Pre, Richard, 3:328
Du Ru, Paul, 10:290
Du Sollier (Bollandist), 2:472
Du Tertre (Father), 3:118
Du Viet Dinh, Tomás, 14:493
Dualism, **4:914–916**
  absolute, 1:42
  accident, 1:63
  Albigensians, 1:230

Alfarabi, 1:276–277
Anaxagoras, 1:393
asceticism, 1:774
Cartesianism, 3:184, 185, 4:681, 916
Catharism, 3:259–260
Clement of Alexandria, St., 3:799
concupiscence, 4:69
demonology, 4:646
early theories, 4:914–915
Gnosticism, 6:262–263
identity principle, 7:303–304
Kantian, 4:916
Maine de Biran, 9:60
male and female, 13:59, 194
man, relations of, 9:89
Manichaeism, 9:110, 111
monism vs., 4:914–915, 9:812
Plato, 11:409–410
De la Recherche de la Vérité (Malebranche), 9:74
sensation, 12:907
soul-body relationship, 13:358
theodicy, 13:868
Thomistic conception, 4:915, 9:90
Zoroastrianism, 4:914, 11:144, 145
See also Manichaeism
Dualists (heretical group), 11:572
Duality, philosophy of nature and, 11:306
Duarte y Quirós, Ignacio, 1:649
Dubarle, A. M., 8:44
DuBay, William (Father), 2:872
Dubček, Alexander, 4:486–487
Dublin Archdiocese (Ireland)
  Ryan, Dermot, 12:443–444
  Sisters of Mercy, founding of, 13:182
Dublin Review, **4:916–917**, 5:251
Dub-Litter (Abbot of Finglas), 4:423
Dubois, Guillaume (Card.), **4:917**
Dubois, John (Bp. of New York), 2:44, **4:917–919**, *918*, 10:34–35, 313, 14:540
Dubois, Louis Ernest (Card.), 4:919
Dubois, Nicolas (Abbot), 12:532
Dubois, Pierre, 9:463
DuBois, W. E. B.
  African American Catholics, 1:161
  McGhee, Fredrick, 1:160
Dubourg, Louis William Valentine (Bp. of Louisiana), **4:919–920**, 9:741, 10:291–292, 12:559, 562
  Brothers of the Christian Schools, 2:633
  Georgetown University, 6:145
  Louisiana, 8:810–811

Sedella, Antonio de, 12:874
Seton, E., 13:32–33, 173
slavery, 1:156
Dubreuil de Pontbriand, Henri Marie, 3:5–6
Dubuis, Claude Marie (Bp. of Galveston, TX), 12:641
  Fifth Baltimore Provincial Council (1843), 2:45
  Sisters of Charity of the Incarnate Word, 7:369
Dubuque, Julien, 4:921
Dubuque Archdiocese (IA), **4:920–925**
  first bishop (Loras), 4:921–922, 8:778–779
  Keane, J. J. (Abp.), 8:135
  Sioux City Diocese, 13:164
Duby, Georges, 5:706
Ducas, Michael Angelos, 2:787, 801
Ducasse, Curt John, **4:925**
Duccio (artist), 2:374, 4:396
Duchemin, M. Theresa Maxis (Mother), **4:925–927**, 7:338
Duchesne, Louis, 3:553, **4:927**, 8:63, 10:252, 963
  Ambrosian Rite, 1:342–343
  Andrieu, Michel, 1:409
  Anglican orders problem, 1:438
  Bishop, Edmund, 2:409
  Epitaph of Abercius, 1:20
  Gallican rites, 6:67, 68, 71
  Loisy's teacher, 8:765
Duchesne, Rose Philippine, St., **4:928**, 12:494
  Barat, St. Madeleine Sophie, 2:87
  Kansas missions, 8:112, 117
  Louisiana, 8:810
Duchesneau, Claude, 14:321
Ducitus (Roswitha of Gandersheim), 12:389
Duckett, James, Bl., 5:234
Duckett, John, Bl., 5:236
Dudley, John (Earl of Warwick). *See* Warwick, John Dudley, Earl of
Dudley, John, Duke of Northhumberland. *See* Northumberland, John Dudley, Duke of
Dudo of Saint-Quentin, 12:582
Dudum dum charissima (papal bull, Julius III), 1:436
Dudum ecclesiae eboracensis (papal bull, Paul IV), 1:436
Dudum sacrum (papal bull, Eugene IV), 2:133
Dudzik, Josephine (Mother Mary Theresa), 5:880

Due Van Vo, Bernardo, 14:493

Dueling, **4:928–929**

Duèse, Jacques. *See* John XXII (Pope)

Duetto Comico (Paisiello) manuscript page, 10:*758*

Dufay, Guillaume, 2:*398*, **4:929–930**, 10:13

    Dunstable, John, 4:940

    liturgical music history, 8:686–687

Duff, Alexander, 7:405

Duffey, William R., 11:625

Duffy, Francis Patrick, **4:930**

Duffy, James A., 10:222–223

Duffy, Mary C., 3:281, **4:930**

Dufour, Charles (Bp. of Montego Bay), 3:113

Dufresne, M. Agnes (Sister), 7:34

Dufresse, Jean Gabriel, 3:498

Duggan, James (Bp. of Chicago), 3:477, 478, 517

Duglioli, Helena, Bl., **4:930–931**

Duhem, P., 1:678, 2:570, 10:207

Duhm, Bernhard, 5:519

Duke, Edmund, Bl., **4:931**, 5:231

Dulany, Daniel, 3:177

Dulau, Jean Marie (Abp. of Arles), 1:694

Dulia, **4:931–932**

Dulles, Avery, 5:38, 7:528

Dum acerbissimas (apostolic letter, Gregory XVI), **4:932**, 6:508, 797

Dum attenta (papal bull, Sixtus IV), 3:144

Dum Europe fere (apostolic exhortation, Pius X), 11:391

Dumas, A., 8:282

Dumézil, Georges, 12:87

Duminique, Ferdinand von, 3:773

Dummermuth, A. M., 12:777

Dumonet, Claude, 12:277

Dumont, Henri, 12:29

Dumont, Pierre, 5:441

Dumontet de Cardaillac, Florent, 12:277

Dumoulin, Charles, 5:702

Dumoulin, Heinrich, 7:743

Dumoulin, Jean (Joannes Molinaeus), **4:932**

Dumoulin, Severe, 10:439

Dumoulin-Borie, Pierre, 14:493

Dun Ġorġ (Father George). *See* Preca, George, Bl.

Dunash ben Labrat, 5:509

Dundrennan Abbey (Scotland), **4:932**

Dunfermline Abbey (Scotland), **4:932–933**, 12:832

Dung Lac An Tran, Andrew, 14:493–494

Dung Van Dinh, Peter, 14:494

Dungal (Irish poet, fl. 855), **4:933**

Dungal of Bobbio, **4:933**

    Bobbio Abbey, 2:447

    Carolingian Renaissance, 3:159–160, 425

    Claudius of Turin, 3:769–770

Dungal of Pavia, **4:933**

Dungal of Saint-Denis, **4:933**

Dungan, Edmund (Bp. of Down and Conor), 7:581

Dũng-Lạ, Andrew, 14:491

Dunin, Martin Von (Abp. of Gneizno and Poznań), 1:328, 2:44, 3:846, **4:933–934**

Dunkers. *See* Church of the Brethren (Dunkers)

Dunlevy, Christopher, 7:581

Dunn, J. D. G., 3:93, 11:242–243

Dunne, Edward Joseph (Bp. of Dallas, TX), 13:846

Dunne, M. Frederic (Abbot), **4:934**, 6:196

Dunne, Peter Masten, **4:934**

Dunne, Robert (Abp. of Brisbane), 1:903

Dunot (Abbot of Bangor Abbey), 2:54

Duns Scotus, John, Bl., **4:934–940**, *935*, 5:242, 367, 394, 528

    act, 1:74

    action and passion, 1:78

    Adam Wodham, 1:110

    Alexander of Hales, 1:266

    on analogy, 1:372, 378

    Anfredus Gonteri, 1:410

    annihilation, 1:471

    Anointing of the Sick, 1:482

    Antonius Andreas, 1:538

    appetite, 1:602–603

    Arabian philosophy, 1:623, 941

    aseity, 1:780

    Assumption of Mary, 1:800

    assumptus homo theology, 1:802

    attrition, 4:226, 230

    Avicebron, 1:939

    beauty, 2:185

    Biel, Gabriel, 2:391

    Bonet, Nicholas, 2:494

    Calvin, John, 2:891

    Caracciolo, Landolf, 3:96

    causality, 3:305

    contemplation, 4:207

    contingency, 4:213

    Cowton, Robert, 12:263

    critical editions of writings of, 12:778

    demonology, 4:648

    dialectics, 4:727

    distinction, 4:781–782, 14:4

    Divine essence, 6:320

    Divine infinity, 4:937

    division, 4:793

    Eucharist, 5:425

    Fabri, Filippo, 5:585

    final causality, 5:724, 727

    following of Christ, 5:788

    formal distinction, 4:937

    Franciscan spirituality, 5:895, 12:232

    free will, 5:938

    God's existence, 4:937

    Hugh of Newcastle, 7:154–155

    human will, 14:722

    immortality, 7:353

    impenetrability, 7:362

    individuation, 4:936–937, 7:426–427

    knowledge, 8:217

    matter and form, 4:936

    morality and freedom, 4:937–938

    natural law, 10:182

    necessity of the Incarnation, 7:375–376

    notional acts, 1:86

    ordination, 7:39

    Oxford School (Franciscan), 5:900

    Palamism, 2:827

    panentheism, 10:820

    penance, 11:70

    person, 11:146–147

    plurality of forms, 5:803

    possibility, 11:551

    potency and act, 11:559

    primacy of Christ, 7:836

    procreation, 4:221

    relation, 12:42

    Richard of Campsall, 12:232

    Richard Rufus of Cornwall, 12:236

    Roger Marston, 12:286

    scholasticism, 12:762

    Scotism, founding of, 12:824–828

    soul, 13:344, 345

    subsistence, 13:572

    theology, 4:938–939

    Thomism, 3:93

    two natures of Christ, 7:818

    understanding of faith, 13:907

    universals, 14:324

    univocity of being, 4:936

    voluntarism, 14:581

on will and willing, 14:722

works edited by Maurice O'Fihely, 10:564

writings, 12:541

See also Scotism

Dunstable, John, **4:940**, 8:686, 10:13

Dunstan of Canterbury, St., 1:306–307, 449, 3:70, 71, **4:940–941**, 14:694

Duodi, Veronica, 1:346

Duong, Paul, 14:494

Duong, Vincent, 14:494

Duong Van Truong, Peter, 14:494

Dupanloup, Félix Antoine Philibert (Bp. of Orléans), **4:941–943**, *942*, 5:855, 12:539

  catechesis, 3:244

  Church-State relations, 3:641

  Darboy, Georges, 4:526

  Döllinger, Johannes, 4:824

  preaching, 11:623

  Sisters of St. Anianus, 1:454

  slavery, 1:156

Dupas, Jacques-Morellus, 12:277

Duperron, Jacques Davy (Card.), **4:943–944**, *944*, 5:850

Dupeyron, James E., 7:699

Duplessis, Maurice, 3:388

Duplessis, Pacifique, 3:4

Duplessis-Mornay, Philippe, **4:944**

  Daillé, Jean, 4:494

  Dupperon, Jacques Davy, 4:943

Dupont, Jacques, 3:350, 5:813

Dupont, Joseph, 7:699

Duprat, Guillaume (Card.), **4:944–945**

Dupuy, Pierre, 6:76

Dura-Europos (Syria), 1:37, 752, 755–756, 2:74, 76, 3:593, 683–684, **4:945–946**, 12:704, 13:677–678

Durán, Diego, **4:946**

Durán, Narciso, 2:862, 865

Duran, Profiat (Ephodi), **4:946–947**

Duran, Simeon ben Tzemah, 1:232

Durand, Guillaume, 4:91

Durand de Maillane, Pierre Toussaint, 6:76

Durandellus, 14:47

Durandus, William, 1:119, 3:676

Durandus of Aurillac, **4:947**, 14:47

Durandus of Saint-Pourçain (Bp. of Meaux), **4:947–949**

  Bernard Lombardi, 2:306

  causality, 3:305

  Divine concurrence, 4:70

  hope, 7:94

  John of Naples, 7:976–977

Launoy, J., 8:381

Durandus of Troarn (Abbot), 2:164, **4:949**

Duranti, William the Elder (Bp. of Mende), **4:949–950**, 10:642

  Canon Law, 3:48, 49

  chivalry, 3:518

  comites Christi, 3:555–556

  computus, 4:46

  cornerstone of church, 4:271

  Roman Pontifical, 11:474

Duranti, William the Younger, 4:55, **950**

Durbin, Elisha John, **4:950**

Dürer, Albrecht, 5:33

  Apocalypse iconography, 1:544, 545

  book illustration, 2:522

  Christ in art, 7:859

  works, 4:*705*

Durey, Louis, 11:562

Durham, Ancient See of (England), 3:124, **4:951**, 13:124–125

Durham, Council of, 4:88

Durham Cathedral (England), 3:601, 693

Durick, Joseph A. (Bp. of Nashville, TN), 13:823–824

Durier, Antoine (Bp. of New Orleans), 1:270

Düring, I., 1:679

Durkheim, Émile, **4:951–953**

  animism, 1:459

  Bureau, Paul, 2:696

  civil religion, 3:755

  Comte, Auguste, 11:544

  conscience, 4:140

  ethics, 5:396

  evolution of religion, 12:64

  magic, 1:737

  society, 13:281

  sociology of knowledge, 8:211

  totemism, 14:120

  worship, 14:852

Durocher, Eulalie, 7:34

Durocher, Marie Rose, Bl., **4:953**, 7:34

Durrow, Book of, **4:953–954**

Durrwell, F. X., 11:983–984

Dušan the Great (ruler of Serbia), 13:8

Dusek, Jan Ladislav, 3:525, **4:954**

Dusmet, Giuseppe Benedetto, Bl., **4:954**

Dušna Paša (Spiritual Food) (Baraga), 2:86

Dutch Catechism (1966), 10:670

Dutch East India Company, 7:428, 429

Dutch Islands, 3:116–117

Dutch mission, 12:395

Dutch Psalter, 11:798

Dutch Reformed Church of South Africa, 13:361

Duties of a Christian (La Salle), 3:235, 4:623

Duties of the Heart (Pāqūdā), 7:864, 869

Dutton, Joseph (Brother), **4:954–955**

Dutton, Paul, 2:307

Duty

  as dialectic, 8:514

  ethics, 4:673–674

  moral theology, 9:855

  voluntarism, 14:582

Duval, André, 2:338, 12:239

Duvalier, François "Papa Doc," 6:619–620

Duvalier, Jean-Claude "Baby Doc," 6:620

Duvergier de Hauranne, Jean (Abbot of Saint-Cyran), 1:716, 3:614, 745, **4:955–956**

  Jansen, Cornelius Otto, 7:713–714, 715–716

  Jansenism, 5:851

  Le Maistre, A., 8:464

  Port-Royal Abbey, 11:523–524

  scholasticism, 12:764

  See also Jansenism

Duverneuil, Jean Baptiste, 12:277

Duvoisin, Jean Baptiste (Bp.), 12:771

Dux dubiorum, Dux neutrorum (Môrēh Nᵉbûkîm) (Maimonides), 9:52–53

Dux perplexorum (Justinianus), 9:52–53

Duyen, Godfrey Van, 6:364

Dva Gusara (Tolstoi), 14:105

Dvaita Madhva, 7:409–410

Dvaitādvaita (Hindu doctrine), 6:847

Dvin, Synod of (506-507), 1:704–705

Dvořák, Antonín, 4:*956*, **956**

Dvornik, F., 2:755, 822

Dwenger, Josesph Gerhard (Bp. of Fort Wayne, IN), 1:582, **4:956–957**, 7:415

Dwight, Timothy, **4:957**, 7:257

Dwin (Armenian city), **4:957–958**

Dwin, Council of (649), 1:700

Dworschak, Baldwin (Abbot), 12:553

Dworschak, Leo F., 5:625

Dwyer, Robert Joseph (Abp. of Portland, OR), 10:271, 11:530, 12:127

Dyer, Thomas. *See* Tunstal, Thomas, Bl.

Dying, care of the, 13:853

Dympna, St., **4:958**

Dynamic power, 14:723

Das Dynamische in der Kirche (Rahner), 5:538

Dynamism, **4:958–961**

  Leibniz, G. W., 4:958, 960, 8:457

Dynamism (continued)

matter and form, 4:958–961, 9:351

mechanism, 4:958, 9:416

theory of motion, 10:19

See also Atomism; Hylomorphism

Dynasty of Akkad. *See* Akkad Dynasty (2360-2180 B.C.)

Dyophysitism, 1:700, 7:262

Dyson, Freeman, 5:351

Dziennik Chicagoski (periodical), 2:132

Dziwisz, Stanislaw (Bp.), 2:*412*

E

E supremi Apostolatus (encyclical, Pius X), 11:388–389

Eadmer of Canterbury, **5:1**

Anselm of Canterbury's biographer, 12:607

Canterbury Cathedral, 3:72

Lanfranc, 3:72

Latin literature, 9:455

works, 5:772

Eadwald of Kent (Anglo-Saxon king), 5:788

Ealdred (Aldred) (Abp. of York), **5:1**

Ealing Abbey (England), **5:1–2**

Eanswith, St., 5:788

Early Catholic Americana (Parsons), 10:904

Early Christian art, **1:749–759**

architecture, 3:683–686, 699

Bible cycles, 2:368–370

Chi-Rho monogram, 7:33

Church symbolism, 3:629–630

Eastern overview, 1:755–758

Egyptian overview, 1:758–759

iconography, 7:285

images, veneration of, 7:325

manuscript illumination, 9:127

Mary, Blessed Virgin, 9:272, 274

Western overview, 1:749–755

Early Church

abortion, 1:26

accommodation to state political organization, 4:299

altars, 1:315

arrangement of shrines and relics, 13:93

Asia Minor, 1:784–785

bishops, 2:411–414

blessings, 2:439

brother in Christ, 2:627

burial, 2:699–700, 3:221–225

Byzantine theology, 2:772–773

cantors, 3:73

capital punishment, 3:85–86

catechesis, 3:227–228

catechumenate, 3:249–250

cathedrals, 3:260–261

chalices, 3:370

Christian way of life, 1:588, 3:228, 546–548

Church property, 3:723–725

circumcision, 3:741

Colossae, 3:860

communion of saints, 4:34–36

Confession, 4:75–77

confessors, 4:83

Confirmation, 4:85–87

congregational singing, 4:118

conscience, 4:148

contemplative life, 4:210

conversion, 4:239–240

Copts, 4:254–255

cross and crucifixion, 4:378–379, 391, 398

Cyprus, 4:460–461

deacons, 4:550–551

Dead Sea Scrolls, 4:563–564

diaconia, 4:718–719

direction, spiritual, 4:760–761

divinity of Jesus, 13:312

dogma as term, 4:811

dogmatic theology, 4:812

doors of churches, 4:872

ecclesiastical authority, 1:922–923

Egypt, 1:758–759, 3:30–31, 335

episcopal elections, 8:294

episcopate, 1:590–591

eschatology, 5:342–343

gifts of the Holy Spirit, 7:47–48

history, 3:590–597, 8:433

Holy Orders, 7:35–38

homily, 7:62

hospitals, 7:126–128

Hungary, 7:209

Hyginus (Pope), St., 7:237

hymnology, 7:241–242

iconoclasm, 7:280

images, veneration of, 7:325

kerygma, 8:157

lamps and lighting, 8:313–314

lapsi, 8:333

Latin Rite, 8:367

lauds, 8:380

Lawrence of Canterbury, 8:407–408

lay education, 8:296

lay spirituality, 8:413

lectionaries, 8:434–435

lector, 8:442–443

lenten fasting, 8:368

litanies, 8:599

liturgical history, 8:650–654

liturgical music history, 8:680–681

Liturgy of the Hours, 8:729

martyrs, 3:61

morning prayer, 8:380

mosaics, 10:3

natural law doctrine, 10:181

North Africa, 10:430

order of universe thought during, 14:328–329

Palestine, 3:31, 553, 555

position on pacifism, 10:745–746

Protoevangelium Jacobi, 1:469

reform in England, 8:323–324

rites of initiation, 8:724

Sibylline Oracles, 13:100

Silas (Silvanus), 13:119

Silverius (Pope), St., 13:122–123

slavery, 13:207–208, 211–212

Slovenes, 13:224–225

Soter (Pope), St., 13:328–329

soul of the Church, 13:358–359

spirituality, 13:443, 444

standing, 8:647–648

theater of Rome, 4:893

theology, 5:339–340

tithing and the, 14:92

tradition, 14:132–133

vestments, 8:634

See also Apologists, Greek; Apostolic Fathers; Britain, early church in; Christian Way of Life (early church); North Africa, early church in; Patristic era; Roman Empire; Roman persecution era

Early Dynastic period (c. 2800-2360 B.C.), 9:527–528

The Earth, the Temple and the Gods (Scully), 3:669

Earth and human dominion, 5:49, 52–53

Earth goddesses. *See* Fertility and vegetation cults

Earth-Mother, Worship of the, **5:2–3**, 13:753

"Earth's Holocaust" (Hawthorne), 14:149

East, facing the, 8:649

East Asian Christian Conference. *See* Christian Conference of Asia

East Asian Pastoral Institute (EAPI, Philippines), **5:3**, 13:80

East Syrian Church. *See* Chaldean Catholic Church (Eastern Catholic)

East Syrian liturgy, 1:528, **5:3–7**

East Timor, **5:7–10**, *9*

See also Indonesia

Easter, **5:10–13**, *11*

    Armenian liturgy, 1:711

    catechesis, 3:231, 250, 251

    Celtic Rite, 3:331

    computus, 4:46

    date, 5:11–12, 13–14, 12:460

    Gallican rites, 6:70

    lauds, 8:379–380

    light, use of, 8:581–582

    liturgical calendar, 8:641, 718

    Low Sunday (2nd Sunday), 5:13

    Paschaltide, 5:12–13

    plays for, 4:94, 96

    Polish popular piety during, 11:511

    preparation for, 8:718–719

    Sequence, 13:1

    Shrove Tuesday, 13:97–99

    See also Easter date controversy; Easter Vigil; Holy Thursday; Holy Week; Lent

Easter confession, 8:470

Easter date controversy, 5:12, **13–14**, 656

    Celtic, 1:110, 140, 192, 460, 3:864, 5:14

    computation of Easter, 8:642

    Council of Nicaea I (325) over, 10:347–348

    Dionysius, Exiguus, 4:754

    Egbert of Iona, St., 5:103

    Laodicea, 8:328

    Quartodeciman, 1:455, 785, 3:593, 5:12

    Roman-Alexandrian, 5:13–14

Easter Rebellion (Ireland, 1916), 7:564

Easter Vigil, **5:14–17**

    baptism during, 2:63

    Kyrie eleison, 8:259

    liturgical year, 8:718

Easter Week, 5:12

Eastern Catholic churches, 2:746–748, 5:19–20

    baptismal sponsors, 13:459

    Bulgarian, 2:539, 680–681, 685–686, 748

    Italo-Albanian Catholic Church, 2:747, 7:648–652

    Melkite Catholic Church, 1:195, 525, 526, 2:746–747

    rebaptism policies, 13:195

Romanian Catholic Church, 2:747–748, 12:337–340

Ruthenian Catholic Church, 2:141, 747

    soul, origins of, 13:354

Syrian Catholic Church (Eastern Catholic), 13:706–710, 708–709

    See also Armenian Catholic Church (Eastern Catholic); Chaldean Catholic Church (Eastern Catholic); Code of Canons of the Eastern Churches (CCEO) (1990); Greek Catholic Church (Eastern Catholic); Ukrainian Catholic Church (Eastern Catholic)

Eastern Catholic Copts, 4:255

Eastern churches, **5:17–20**

    altars, 1:317

    anchorites, 1:397

    Anointing of the Sick, 1:484

    Antonines, 1:534–535

    Athanasian Creed, 1:817

    autocephaly, 1:924, 2:744

    biblical canon, 3:26–27, 28

    bread, 2:599

    Calvinism, 8:841–842

    Canon Law, 3:38–39, 45–46

    canonical governance, 10:947

    Chevetogne Monastery, 3:472–473

    chorbishops, 3:525–526

    Christmas, 3:552, 553

    Christology, 8:502, 503

    chronology, 3:570–571

    clerical celibacy and marriage, 3:324–325

    clerical dress, 3:801

    Communion outside the liturgy, 4:37

    concelebration, 4:50

    Confession, 4:77

    Confirmation (Chrismation), 4:84, 85–86, 90, 91, 92

    congregational singing, 4:118

    consecrated life, 4:155–156

    Council of Catholic Patriarchs of the Orient (CPCO), 4:295–296

    creedal statements, 4:351–352, 353–355

    Croatia, 4:370–371

    cross, 4:380, 382–383

    crucifixion art, 4:391–395

    Crusades' states, 4:402

    deaconesses, 7:37

    development of the, 5:18–20

    diocesan chancellors, 3:377

    direction, spiritual, 4:760

    Divine judgment, 8:32, 33

Easter Vigil, 5:15

Eastern-rite Catholics in U.S., 13:87

ecclesiastical organization of the empire, 5:17–18

Ecumenical engagement, 8:232

formation of the, 5:18

grace, 3:533

Greek Melchite mission, 8:389

Holy Orders rite, 7:38

homoousios, 4:197–198

hospitals, 7:128

hypostasis, 7:263

Immaculate Conception, 7:332–333

Italo-Albanian Catholic Church, 7:648–652

justification, 8:81

Kuwait, 8:259

Kyrie eleison, 8:259

lamb as icon, 8:302

lay confession, 8:411

lay theologians, 8:296

lector as order, 7:37

Lent, 8:468, 470

Leo I (Pope), St. on orthodox faith, 8:472

Leo XIII (Pope), 8:492

litanies, 8:600

liturgical languages, 8:667

liturgical music history, 8:681

liturgical rites, 8:712–713

liturgy, comparative, 8:722

martyr, as term, 4:83

Mary as Theotokos, 2:766, 823, 3:317

monastic superiors, 1:9

names, calling out of, 4:758, 759

patriarchate in the, 10:947–948

profound bow, 8:648

Roman primacy, 8:53

Russia, 3:265

Singidunum, marytrs of, 13:161

subdiaconate, 7:38

theocentrism, 1:508

tonsure, 7:37

in the U.S., 5:20

Week of Salvation (Holy Week), 7:56

See also Assyrian Church of the East (Persia); Byzantine Church; Coptic Christianity; Eastern Catholic churches; Ecumenism; Orthodox and Oriental Orthodox Churches

Eastern Churches, Congregation for the, 3:473, **5:21–22**, 12:339

Eastern Jesuit Philosophical Association, 8:430

Eastern monasticism, 9:797–803

Eastern Schism (1054), 2:745, 757–758, 760–762, 3:817, **5:22–27**

  Albania, 1:213, 214

  Alexandria Patriarchate, 1:271

  Alexius I Comnenus, 1:276

  Byzantine art, 2:738

  Byzantine Empire, 2:787–788

  Byzantine theology, 2:794, 823–828

  clerical celibacy and marriage, 3:324

  Council of Florence, 2:762, 788, 828

  Crusades, 1:276, 2:760, 823, 10:837–838

  filioque doctrine, 5:719

  Fourth Lateran Council, 8:353

  intermediate state of judgment, 8:32

  justification, 8:81

  Justinian II, 8:102

  Leo IX (Pope), St., 8:485

  Michael Cerularius, 4:187–188

  mutiplication of patriarchates after, 10:945

  Nicetas Stethatos's role, 10:357

  papal primacy, 1:526

  Photian schism, 2:755, 4:186–187, 5:23–24, 13:169

  Romanian Orthodox Church influence, 12:330–331

  Sergius I (Pope), St., 13:13

  Sergius IV (Pope), 13:15

  See also Eastern Schism (1054); Western Schism (1378-1417)

Eastre (Anglo-Saxon goddess), 5:10

East-West unity (ecclesial reconciliation)

  Gregory X (Pope), Bl., 6:498–499

  Isidore of Kiev, 7:601

  John XI Beccus, 7:917–918

  John of Parma, 7:979–980

  John Paul II (Pope), 7:1003

Easy Essays (Maurin), 9:369

Eata, St., 1:192, 4:449

Eaubonne, Françoise d', 5:48

Ebba, SS., **5:27**

Ebba the Elder, St., 5:27

Ebba the Younger, St., 5:27

Ebbinghaus, Hermann, **5:27**

Ebbo of Reims (Abp.), 1:840, 4:662, **5:28**, 6:837–838, 12:36

Ebbo of Sens, St., 1:248, **5:28**

Ebelign, Gerhardon historical theology, 6:870

Ebendorfer, Thomas, **5:29**

Eber, Paul, 4:416

Eberbach Abbey (Germany), 3:750, **5:29**, *30*

Eberhard of Einsiedeln, Bl., **5:29**, 139

Eberhard of Rohrdorf, Bl., **5:30**

Eberhard of Tüntenhausen, St., **5:31**

Eberlin, Johannes, **5:31**

Ebertran (Abbot), 12:582

Ebionites (Jewish Christian sect), 3:559, 560, **5:31–32**

Ebner, Margaretha, Bl., 1:455, **5:32**

Eborius (Bp. of York), 2:620

Ebrach Abbey (Germany), 1:108, 3:750, **5:32**

Ebroin, 1:894, 3:163

Ebroinus (French mayor of the palace), 2:153

Ebrulf. *See* Évroul

Ecbasis captivi (poem, anonymous), 9:447

Ecce Ego Joannes (Palestrina), 10:803

Ecce Homo, **5:32–33**

Ecce Homo (Chmielowski), 3:520

Ecce Homo (Dürer), 5:*33*

Ecce iam noctis tenuatur umbra (hymn), **5:33**

Ecce quam bonum (Gradual), 6:414

Ecce Sacerdos Magnus (Palestrina), 10:802

Ecclesfield, Francis, 2:551

Ecclesia (periodical), 4:514

Ecclesia, a Theological Encyclopedia of the Church, 5:208

Ecclesia Dei (apostolic letter, John Paul II), 7:1005, 8:365, 14:182

Ecclesia Mater, 3:583–584, 585, *598*

Ecclesia Parisiensis vindicata (Ruinart), 12:407

Ecclesiae occidentalis monumenta iuris antiquissima (Turner), 14:242

Ecclesiae orientalis et occidentalis concordia in transubstantiatione (Scholliner), 12:779

Ecclesiae Sanctae (apostolic letter, Paul VI), 5:480, 10:460, 483, 11:30

Ecclesiam (apostolic constitution, Pius VII), 3:100

Ecclesiam (papal bull, Pius VII), 12:857

Ecclesiam Dei (encyclical, Pius XI), 11:393

Ecclesiam suam (on the Church in the Contemporary World) (encyclical, Paul VI), 1:823, **5:33–34**, 10:850–851, 855, 11:32, 12:858

Ecclesiastes, Book of, **5:34–36**

  canonicity, 3:25

  judgment, Divine, 8:28

  original sin, 10:664

  pessimism, 11:169

  retribution, 12:177

  sin, 13:145

  spirit, 13:424

  venial sin, 13:155

Ecclesiastes sive de ratione concionandi (Erasmus), 11:620–621

Ecclesiastica historia.... See Centuriators of Magdeburg

Ecclesiastica historia... (Flacius Illyricus), 5:754

Ecclesiasticae historiae liber primus (Harlay), 6:647

Ecclesiastical archives. *See* Archives, ecclesiastical

Ecclesiastical authority, 1:922–923

Ecclesiastical cartography, 13:547–548

Ecclesiastical discipline. *See* Excommunication

Ecclesiastical faith theological note, 10:454

Ecclesiastical finance, Fugger family and, 6:20

Ecclesiastical History (Eusebius of Caesarea), 5:136, 148, 452, 453, 12:606

Ecclesiastical History (Evagrius Scholasticus), 5:465

Ecclesiastical history (Gelasius of Caesarea), 6:123

Ecclesiastical History (Ordericus Vitalis), 12:546

Ecclesiastical History (Pamphilus), 10:815

Ecclesiastical History (Xanthopulus), 14:875

Ecclesiastical History (Zachary the Rhetor), 14:904–905

Ecclesiastical History of the English People (Historia Ecclesiastica gentis Anglorum) (St. Bede), 2:195–196, 9:442, 12:606

Ecclesiastical jurisdiction, 9:78

Ecclesiastical learning, 13:911–913

Ecclesiastical organization

  Alaska, 1:207

  Albanian Orthodox Church, 1:213

  Anglicanism, 1:445–446

  Angola, 1:450

  archdioceses, 1:634

  Argentina, 1:649

  Arles, 1:694

  Asia Minor, 1:785

  Australia, 1:900

  Austria, 1:913

  autocephaly, 1:924, 2:744

  Bolivia, 2:465, 466

  Brazil, 2:589–590

  California, 2:862, 865–866, 871

Cameroon, 2:914

Canada, 3:4

Carolingian era, 3:41

Carolingian reform, 3:156

Chile, 3:486

China, 3:490

Cologne, 3:842–843

Colombia, 3:848

Colorado, 3:858, 4:668, 670

the Comoros, 4:40

Congo, Democratic Republic of, 4:104

Congo, Repuglic of, 4:108–110

Constantinople, 4:185

Costa Rica, 4:288–290

Croatia, 4:370–372

Cuba, 4:417

Cyprus, 4:460

Czech Republic, 4:479–480, 488

Delaware, 4:625

Denmark, 4:492, 663–664, 666–667

Djibouti, 4:795

East Timor, 5:10

Ecuador, 5:62–63

El Salvador, 4:628

Equatorial Guinea, 5:310

Eritrea, 5:321–322

Finland, 5:731

First Council of Nicaea, 3:594

Florida, 5:775

France, 4:62–63

Germany, 6:172

Ghana, 6:198

Guatemala, 6:553–554

Honduras, 7:74

Hong Kong, 7:75–76

Hungary, 7:209, 218, 222

India, 7:393

Indiana, 7:413

Indonesia, 7:429

Iowa, 7:541

Iraq, 7:545

Ireland, 7:554

Israel, 7:646

Italy, 7:653–654, 654–656

Ivory Coast, 7:681

Japan, 7:737

Kansas, 8:113

Kentucky, 8:147

Kenya, 8:150

Korea, 8:239

Lebanon, 8:428

Liberia, 8:551

Libya, 8:558, 560

Liechtenstein, 8:562, 563

Lithuania, 8:606–607

Little Rock, 8:614

Los Angeles Archdiocese, 8:788–789

Louisiana, 8:809

Louisville Archdiocese, 8:816, 819

Lovers of the Holy Cross (LHC), 8:835

Lutheran churches in North America, 8:885

Luxembourg, 8:897

Macedonia, 9:15–16

Madagascar, 9:28

Malawi, 9:69

Mali, 9:77–78

Malta, 9:83

Mauritania, 9:371

Mauritius, 9:373

Mexico, 9:576, 586

Moldova, 9:767

Monaco, 9:777

Morocco, 9:899

Mozambique, 10:41

Namibia, 10:144

Nepal, 10:245

New Orleans Archdiocese, 8:814

New Zealand, 10:325

Nicaragua, 10:353

Niger, 10:391

Nigeria, 10:393–394

Norway, 4:492, 664, 10:450–451

Oman, 10:590

Panama, 10:819

Paraguay, 10:879–880

Pennsylvania, 11:80

Peru, 11:159

Philippines, 11:256

Poland, 11:440

Portugal, 11:534

Roman Empire, 5:17–18

Russia, 1:252

Sengal, 12:905

Serbia and Montenegro, 13:11

Seychelles, 13:53

Siena, 13:105–106

Sierra Leone, 13:110

Singapore, 13:161

Sioux Falls Diocese, 13:165

Slovakia, 13:219, 221, 222, 224

Slovenia, 13:225

Somalia, 13:308

South Africa, 13:361

South Carolina, 13:362

Spain, 13:377

Sri Lanka, 13:466–467

Sudan, 13:584–585

Suriname, 13:628

Swaziland, 13:633–634

Sweden, 4:492, 664

Tanzania, 13:756

Thailand, 13:850–851

Togo, 14:98

Tunisia, 14:236–237

Turkey, 14:239

Uganda, 14:265–266

Ukraine, 14:276

U.S., under Jesuits, 2:41

Uruguay, 14:351–352

Venezuela, 14:438

Vietnam, 14:501

Wales, 14:610–611, 612

Western Sahara, 14:691

See also Ancient sees; *specific dioceses and archdioceses*

Ecclesiastical Sonnets (Wordsworth), 13:320

Ecclesiastical typology, 3:670–672

L'Ecclesiastico santificato (Sarnelli), 12:694

Ecclesiasticus (Wisdom of Ben Sira), **5:36**, 14:794–796

See also Sirach, Book of

Ecclesiological Society, 3:709

Ecclesiologist (periodical), 3:709

Ecclesiology, **5:36–41**

    Church and the world, 5:38

    Church symbolism, 3:630

    collegiality, 5:39–40

    communio, 4:27, 30

    dominated by Augustine thought, 10:102, 103

    ecumenism, 5:40–41

    history, 5:36–37

    Khomiakov, Alexius Stepanovich, 12:435

    laity, theology of, 8:290–291

    local and universal Church, 5:38

    Lutheran, 8:894

    magisterium and disagreement, 5:40

    ministries and mission, 5:39

    modernism, 9:752

    Mystici Corporis (Pius XII) response to, 10:104, 110

    nature of the Church, 5:37–38

    primacy, 5:39–40

    sacramental, 5:426

Eccleston, Samuel (Abp. of Baltimore), 2:39, 44, 45, **5:41–42**

Ecernis (Mussato), 12:113

Ecgbert. *See* Egbert of York (Abp.)

L'Échange (Claudel), 3:768

Echarri Vique, Juan, 2:92

L'Écho de Rouen (periodical), 14:465

Echo of Africa (periodical), 8:443

Echter Von Mespelbrunn, Julius (prince-Bp. of Würzburg), **5:42**

Echternach Abbey (Luxembourg), **5:42**, 8:897

Eck, Johann, 3:609, **5:42–43**
  Adrian VI (Pope), 1:129
  Amerbach, Veit, 1:349
  Augsburg Confession, 1:850
  Sachatzgeyer, Kaspar, 12:730

Eckart, Anselm Von, **5:43**

Eckbert of Schönau, **5:43–44**, 166

Eckhart, Meister, **5:44–46**
  Albert the Great, St., 1:226
  apophatic theology, 1:568
  conformity, 4:93
  doctrine, 5:45
  exegetical works, 5:518
  German mysticism, 12:783
  hope as necessity, 7:101
  influence, 5:45–46
  inquisition, 5:44
  Latin literature, 9:461
  mysticism, 3:605
  Neoplatonism, 12:121
  panentheism, 10:820
  pantheism, 10:826
  Rhenish spirituality, 13:453, 454
  Tauler, Johannes, 13:765

Eckhel, Joseph Hilarius Von, **5:46**

Éclaircissement (Charles of the Assumption), 3:436

Eclecticism, **5:46–48**, 6:442, 11:284
  Cousin, Victor, 4:322–323
  critique, 5:47–48
  history, 5:46–47

Eclipse of God (Buber), 12:70

Eclipse of Reason (Horkheimer), 5:914

Eclogae Propheticae (Eusebius of Caesarea), 5:452

Eclogues (Baptist of Mantua), 2:73

Ecofeminism and Ecofeminist theology, **5:48–50**

École Biblique et Archéologique Française de Jérusalem, **5:50–51**
  biblical archaeology, 2:380, 381
  Lagrange, M. J., 8:280, 281

Une École de théologie: Le Saulchoir (Chenu), 3:466

École des Chartres. See Chartres, School of

L'École et la famille (periodical), 14:471

École Pratique d'Études Bibliques (The Practical School of biblical Studies, Jerusalem), **5:50–51**

Ecological theology, 5:52–58

Ecology, 2:404, 5:48–50, **51–58**

Econe problem, 8:447–449

Economic development
  medieval Church, 8:296
  population, 11:513–514
  social progress, 13:263
  Sollictudo rei socialis, 13:304
  subsidiarity, 13:568–569

Economic justice, 8:64, 13:263

Economic Justice for All (U.S.Catholic bishops pastoral letter), 4:21–22, 10:616, 14:315, 362

Economic thought, Catholic
  intelligibility of economy, 8:774
  just price, 8:64
  work, 13:261–264

Economic Trinitarianism, 11:734

Economics
  De moneta (Oresme), 13:254
  democracy, 4:642–643
  John Paul II (Pope), 3:342–343
  laissez-faire liberalism, 13:232, 413
  Marx, Karl, 9:237
  in the papal state, 13:492, 493–494
  Smith, Adam, 13:231–232, *232*
  social principle, 13:250
  solidarism, 13:300–301

Economics, Politics, and Justice (pastoral letter), 14:908

L'Économie de la vraie religion (Leo of St. John), 8:495

Economy, Divine, 3:531, **5:58–59**, 13:941–942

Ecotheology, 8:317

Ecstasy, 4:205, **5:59–60**, 12:601
  See also Mystics

Ecstasy, in the Bible, **5:60–61**

The Ecstasy of St. Theresa (Bernini), 12:601

Ecstatic Doctor (Denis the Carthusian), 4:661–662

Ecthesis (Heraclius), 2:749–750, 14:255–256

Ectopic pregancy, 1:28

Ecuador, **5:61–66**, *65*, *66*
  Cuero y Caicedo, José de, 4:422
  map, 5:*64*
  mission, 5:62–63, 9:711, 735, 12:372

Ecumenical Association of Third World Theologians (EATWOT), 5:677

Ecumenical Councils. *See* Ephesus, Council of (431); *specific councils*

Ecumenical Councils of the Catholic Church: An Historical Outline (Jedin), 7:750

Ecumenical dialogues, **5:66–70**
  Anglican-Roman Catholic dialgue, 5:67–68
  Commission for Christian Unity, 13:76
  Disciples of Christ-Roman Catholic Dialogue, 5:69
  Evangelical-Roman Catholic Dialogue on Mission, 5:69
  Germany, 8:743
  Hotchkin, John Francis, 7:136
  Kentucky, 8:817
  Korea, 8:240
  lectionary use, 8:440, 441
  Lima Text, 8:589
  liturgical conference, 8:646
  Lutheran-Catholic dialogues, 5:69–70
  Pentecostal-Roman Catholic Conversations, 5:69
  reversing secularism, 8:868
  Roman Catholic-Orthodox in U.S., 8:168
  Roman-Catholic participation, 5:77–78
  Shehan, L., 13:76
  Societas Liturgica, 13:275
  See also Anglican-Catholic dialogue

Ecumenical Directory, **5:70–71**, 14:356

Ecumenical Forum (Toronto, Canada), 3:9

Ecumenical Institute, 10:387

Ecumenical Movement, **5:71–79**
  art and architecture, 8:386
  Brent, Charles Henry, 2:603
  California, 8:793
  defined, 5:71
  early efforts, 8:673
  Episcopal Church (U.S.), 5:299
  Germany after 1850, 8:892
  Hotchkin, John Francis, 7:136–137
  Kansas, 8:118–119
  Kenya, 8:151–152
  lay spirituality, 8:418
  life and work, 8:577–578
  liturgical consensus, 8:678
  liturgical movement, 8:678–680
  liturgical year, 8:643–644
  Lutherans in U.S., 8:887
  missiology, 9:677
  origins, 10:262
  Reformation martyrs, 8:242

SODEPAX, 13:296

Söderblom, N., 13:296

Solov'ev, V. S., 13:307

Spínola, C., 13:417

U.S. leaders, 8:250

Visser't Hooft, Willem Adolf, 14:566–567

world theology, 13:236

Ecumenical Patriarchate, Orthodox churches dependent on, 10:679–680

Ecumenical Patriarchate of Constantinople, 10:945–947

Ecumenical Society of the Blessed Virgin Mary, 9:172, 283–284

Ecumenism, 3:625

1983 Code of Canon Law, 3:35

academic freedom, 1:54

Albania, 1:217

Alter, Karl J., 3:737

American Council of Christian Churches, 1:351

Anglican orders problem, 1:438–439

Apostles' Creed, 1:577

apostolicity, 1:597

Baader, Franz Xaver von, 2:1

baptism, 4:241

Brent, Charles Henry, 2:603–604

British Council of Churches, 2:622

Calixtus, Georg, 2:873–874

Canada, 3:9

charismatic renewal movement, 3:392–393

Chevetogne Monastery, 3:472–473

Christian (term), 3:528

communio, 4:30

Congar, Yves Marie-Joseph, 4:102

Constantinople Council I, 4:190

Consultation on Common Texts, 4:201

Corbishley, Thomas, 4:259

Council of European Bishops' Conferences, 4:297–298

Honduras, 7:74

Hong Kong, 7:77

Hume, George Basil, 7:203

Ireland, 7:569

Jamaica, 3:113

Japan, 7:743–744

John XXIII (Pope), Bl., 3:625, 626

John Paul II (Pope), 5:40, 7:1003–1004

McQuaid, John Charles, 9:407–408

movements toward, 12:22

Paul VI (Pope), 11:31

sacraments, 12:476–477

Scotland, 12:838

See also Anglican-Catholic dialogue; Ecumenical dialogues

Eddington, Arthur, 3:302, 11:300

Eddy, Mary Baker, 3:544, 5:80, 80, 10:308

Edelbrock, Alexius (Abbot), 12:552

Eden, Garden of, 5:80–81, 81, 13:18–22

Edersheim, A., 7:850

Edes, Ella B., 5:81–82

Edessa (Mesopotamia), 5:4, 82–83

Egeria's pilgrimage to, 5:104

Syriac liturgy, 8:667

See also Antioch

Edessa, Chronicle of, 5:82, 83

Edessa, School of, 1:527, 805, 2:820, 5:82, 83, 642

Edgar the Peaceful (King of the English), 5:83–84

Bath Abbey, 2:151

Christianity in England, 5:240

Dunstan of Canterbury, 4:941

Ely Abbey, 5:179

Ethelwold of Winchester, 5:387

Edgeworth de Firmont, Henry Essex, 5:84

Edict of April 1679 (France), 10:889

Edict of Diocletian, 3:32

Edict of January 1562, 3:266

Edict of Milan. See Milan, Edict of

Edict of Nantes (1598), 8:282

Edict of Toleration (Roman), 4:749

Edictum Theodorici, 3:40

Edification in the Bible, 5:84–85

Edigna, Bl., 5:85

Edinburgh, Treaty of (1560), 8:225

Edinburgh Catholic Magazine, 13:233

Edinburgh Conference on Faith and Order, 8:678

Edinburgh Missionary Conference (1910), 5:71

Editae saepe (encyclical, Pius X), 11:391

Edith (Queen of England), 6:650

Editing the Books of the Oriental Church, Congregation for, 5:21

Edmonds (WA), 4:842

Edmund I (King of England), 2:151, 4:940

Edmund of Abingdon, St., 3:72, 5:85–86, 242

Albert II of Riga, 1:221

Alexander of Hales, 1:265

Ancient See of Chichester, 3:481

Robert Bacon, 12:262

Edmund the Martyr (King of East Anglia), St., 5:86, 87

Edomites, 1:36, 5:86–87, 10:502

The Educatin of Sisters (Meyers), 13:169–170

Education

activism, 1:83

Alain, 1:203–204

Australia, 1:904–905, 906–907

Bosco, St. John, 2:543–544

Bouquillon controversy, 2:564–565

Brazil, 2:597

Brothers of the Christian Schools, 2:630–634

Burns, James Aloysius, 2:708–709

China, 3:499, 500, 506

Church-State relations, 3:655–656, 663, 665–668

compulsory, in Europe, 8:342

Congo, 4:107

Congregationalism, 4:115–116

Constantine VII, 4:174–175

Constantinople, 4:188

Cooke, Terence, 4:246–247

creationism, 4:346–347

Curley, Michael, 4:440–441

Daughters of Isabella, 4:533

docility, 4:797

France, 8:432

free public schools, 8:256

functionalism, 6:24–25

Greco-Roman schooling, 6:428–433

higher education, 12:38–39

historical development, 5:88–92

Hungary, 7:214, 216

importance, 9:120–121

Ireland, 4:424, 14:621

Jesuit code, 5:790

kindergarten system, 6:13–14

Kulturkampf, 8:254

La Salle, John Baptist de, 4:620–623

Luxembourg, 8:898

mission schools, 8:160

Montessori Method, 9:836–837

for Native Americans, 12:528

as parental duty, 11:335

Pestalozzi, Johann Heinrich, 11:170–171

Philo Judaeus, 11:269, 270

Poland (1492-1650), 7:871

Poughkeepsie Plan (NY), 1:352, 10:315, 11:561–562

procreation, 4:221

Quebec, 8:383

religion teachers, 12:82–84

Education *(continued)*
  responsibility of institutions, 11:513
  Sagan method of teaching, 5:665
  Shields, T., 13:83
  sister formation movement, 13:169–170
  Sisters of Loretto, 8:786
  South Africa teachers, 8:228–229
  term defined, 5:88
  U.S.
    Alaska, 1:210
    Brook Farm, 2:627
    Connecticut, 4:124, 125
    history, 1840-1900, 8:115–116, 118
    Lowell Plan, 8:837–838
  Walsh, Mary Rosalia (Sister), 14:619
  working class, 8:230–231
  See also Education, Catholic; Education and State; Moral education; Parochial schools; Religious education
Education: To Whom Does It Belong? (Bouquillon), 2:564
Education, Catholic, 5:95
  Belgium, 2:219, 221
  Belize, 2:225
  Canada, 8:270
  Connelly, Cornelia, 7:17–218
  early parish schools, 6:433
  educational philosophy, 5:95
  England, 12:569–570
  Faribault Plan, 1:352, 354, 584, 2:564, 584, 5:625–626, 7:551, 8:798, 13:403
  Felbiger, Johann Ignaz von, 5:664–665
  France, 9:160
  General Directory for Catechesis, 6:127–128
  Germany, 6:36
  Haiti, 6:622
  integration, 12:257, 412
  Ireland, 7:562, 566–567, 9:18
  Japan, 7:742–743
  Jesuit ''Nativity Schools,'' 7:795
  Malta, 9:83
  Marist Brothers of the Schools, 9:175
  Metropolitan Readers (Catholic textbooks series), 12:524
  Mexico, 9:573, 12:408
  moral education, 9:847
  National Catholic Educational Association (NCEA), 12:96–97
  On Our Way series (Catholic textbooks), 12:524

Peru, 12:280–281
Philippines, 11:262–263
Reinert, Paul C., 12:38–39
Roger Bacon, 12:283–285
Ryan, Mark Perkins, 12:446
Scotland, 12:837–838
for slaves, 12:394
Switzerland, 9:160
Taiwan, 13:734
teaching, 13:775
U.S.
  Baltimore Archdiocese, 2:40
  California, 7:339
  Cincinnati, 9:405
  Cleveland, 5:179
  Denver, 9:19
  Gibbons, James, 6:206
  Henni, John Martin, 6:733–734
  Idaho, 7:292
  Illinois, 7:317–318
  Indiana, 7:414, 415
  Jesuit institutions, 7:788–789, 790, 791
  Kentucky, 9:31
  Maine, 9:57
  Marianists, 9:161–162
  Massachusetts, 5:751, 9:307–308
  Michigan, 7:338–339
  Milwaukee, 9:647–648
  Minnesota, 7:551
  Mississippi, 9:739–740
  Montana, 9:827
  New York, 9:406
  Philadelphia, 12:447
  Poughkeepsie Plan, 11:561–562
  public funds debate, 6:226
  Rhode Island high schools, 12:216–217
  St. Mary's School (Philadelphia), 12:565–566
  San Francisco, 9:746
  Texas, 13:847
  Twin Cities, 12:574
  Winona (KS), 14:774
  Wisconsin, 5:753, 14:780–781
See also Parochial schools; Pontifical Roman universities; *specific countries*; *specific educational institutions*; *specific religious orders*
Education, scholastic, **5:95–96**, 10:10–11
Education and State, 3:665–668
  Amish people, 3:663
  Blaine Amendment (U.S.), 2:425–428, 3:653, 654, 660

Canada, 3:10–11, 11
Ireland, 7:562
Oregon School Case, 2:429, 10:646–650, 11:530
parochial schools, 3:655
public schools, 3:655–656
See also Church and State
Education for Modern Man (Hook), 10:205
Education of clergy. *See* Seminary education
The Education of Henry Adams (Adams), 1:112
The Education of Man (Fröbel), 6:13
The Education of the Virgin (painting), 2:*108*
Education of women, 5:676–677, 682, 834, 12:291
  Sisters of the Holy Cross, 7:22
  Society of St. Teresa of Jesus, 12:587
Educational philosophy, **5:88–96**
  Comenius, John Amos, 4:2–3
  Dominici, John, 4:855–856
  Giussani, Luigi, 4:31–32
  liberal arts, 8:536
Edward I (King of England)
  Bek, Anthony, 2:209
  Church revenues, 12:270
  Church-State relations, 2:502, 3:636, 803
  common law, 8:401
  Convocations, 4:243–244
  with his bishops, 5:*244*
  John le Romelyn (Abp. of York), 7:960
  Robert of Winchelsea, 12:270
Edward II (King of England)
  barons opposing, 13:128
  Robert of Winchelsea, 12:270
Edward III (King of England)
  Adam of Orleton, 1:109
  Chaucer, Geoffrey, 3:450
  John de Saint-Pol, 7:956
  Mepham as key figure, 13:131
  nuncio, 13:133
  Order of the Garter, 12:547
  papal provision, 3:780
  seal, 5:*245*
Edward IV (King of England)
  Bourgchier, Thomas, 2:566
  Goldwell, James, 6:337
  Russell, John, 12:416
  Shirwood, J., preferment, 13:88

Edward VI (King of England)
Anglican orders problem, 1:435–436
Anglican Reformation, 1:442, 3:608
Church of England, 5:245, *246*, 12:9
confessions of faith, 4:80
heresy, 6:777
Irish confessors and martyrs, 7:577
Mary Tudor, 9:292, 293

Edward VI and the Book of Common Prayer (Gasquet), 6:104

Edward the Confessor (King of England), St., **5:96**
Brithwald of Wilton, St., 2:622
church architecture, 3:693

Edward the Martyr (King of England), St., **5:96–97**, *97*

Edwards, Bede, 3:132

Edwards, James Fenwick, 1:641

Edwards, Jonathan, 4:115, **5:97–98**, *98*
Emmons defense, 5:193
Great Awakening, 6:425
I-It mysticism, 10:117
influence on Emerson, 5:189
revivalism, 12:204

Edwards, Justin, 13:797

Edwards, R., 3:673

Edwards v. Aguillard (1987), 3:667

Edwig (King of England), 4:941

Edwin (King of Northumbria), St., 2:500, **5:98**, 386, 10:707, 11:40

Effendi, 'Abbās. *See* 'Abd-al-Bahā (Muslim leader)

Effendi, Shoghi, 2:13

Efficient causality, types of, 3:297, 302, 305, **5:98–102**
accidental, 1:61
action and passion, 1:78
agent, 1:175
cogitative power, 3:823
condition for, 4:73
first cause of motion, 10:23–24
Hume, David, 7:201–202
physical vs. moral, 12:469
See also Causality

Efficient instrumentality, 7:499–500

Effraenatam (papal bull, Sixtus V), 4:221

Egan, Boetius (Bp. of Ross), 7:581

Egan, Dominic, 7:582

Egan, Edward (Card.), 4:125, 10:319–320, *546*, 12:*328*

Egan, Jack, 1:288

Egan, Michael (Bp. of Philadelphia), 2:39, 43, 3:180, **5:102–103**, 11:82, 237–238

Egan, William A., 1:211

Egbert (King of Mercia), 1:479

Egbert of Iona (Abbot Bp.), St., **5:103**

Egbert of Liège, 9:449

Egbert of Schönau. *See* Eckbert of Schönau

Egbert of York (Abp.), 1:289, 2:195, **5:103**, 385

Eger (Armenian Catholicos), 1:700

Egeria (4th c. Christian pilgrim), 3:14–15, 555

Egeria, Itinerarium of, **5:104–106**

Egher van Kalkar, Heinrich, 3:192

Egidio Maria of St. Joseph, Bl., **5:106**

Egino, Bl., **5:106**

Egino of Verona (Bp.), 12:32

Église catholique française, 3:449

Église catholique gallicane, 8:838

L'Église chrétienne (Renan), 12:126

L'Église du Verbe incarné (The Church of the Word Incarnate) (Jounet), 7:1058

Egmond (Egmont) Abbey (Netherlands), **5:106–107**

Egmont (Goethe), 6:330–331

Egoism, **5:107–108**
Absolute, 4:369
consciousness, 4:153, 154
God as moral order, 10:827
self-love, 12:887
wei wo, 3:509

Egozcuezábal Aldaz, Juan Bautista, Bl., 7:124

Egregiae Virtutis (apostolic letter, John Paul II), 7:998

Egregie doctor Paule (hymn), **5:108**

Egres Abbey (Hungary), **5:108**

Egwin (Bp. of Worcester), St., 5:486

Egypt, ancient culture of, **5:119–136**
architecture and art, 5:129–132
burial practices, 4:358
clergy, 5:127
creation concept, 4:337
cult, 5:125–128
feasts and daily rituals, 5:127–128
gods, 5:121, 123
heart as conscience, 4:139
immortality, 7:347
kingship concept, 8:178
language and literature, 5:133–136
law, 8:395
leprosy, 8:509
myths, 5:125
papyri, 5:510–511, 10:863–864
prototype of evil, 13:149

pyramids, 5:130
religion, 5:119–129
Rosetta Stone, 12:381, *381*
Son of God, 13:311
soul, 13:337
sun worship, 13:606
syncretist cults, 12:68
temples, 5:*120, 122*, 125–126, *126*, 131–132
theological systems, 5:123–125
tombs, 5:130

Egypt, early Church in, **5:136–138**
art and architecture, 1:758–759
biblical canon, 3:30–31
cenobitism, 3:335
Christian persecution, 5:136–137
concelebration, 4:50
Confirmation, 4:86
Constantinople Council, 4:192
Coptic literature, 13:42–43
creedal statements, 4:352
diaconia, 4:719
liturgical history, 8:651
liturgical rites, 8:713
Liturgy of St. Mark, 8:713
monasticism, 9:789, 797, 800
Serapion of Thmuis, 13:7

Egypt, history to present, **5:108–119**
Akhnaton, reform under, 1:198–199
astrology, 1:812
Byblos, 2:723–724
Canaanites, 3:1
demographic statistics, 5:109
Jews, 7:874
Manichaeism mission, 9:109
map, 5:*110*
millennium celebrations, 13:*832*
origin of the name, 5:109
as part of Roman Empire, 12:299
physical sciences, in antiquity, 12:799
Sudan, rule of, 13:581
wisdom literature, 14:789
See also Alexandria; Coptic Christianity

Egypt, plagues of, 11:402–405

Egyptian indiction, 7:419

Egyptian Recital (Synesius of Cyrene), 13:683

Ehler, S. Z., 6:119

Ehrenfels, C. von, 1:678, 5:398

Ehrhard, Albert, **5:138**, 6:184, 12:26

Ehrle, Franz (Card.), **5:138–139**, 865, 6:184, 12:766, 776, 827

Eichhorn, Johann Gottfried, 5:519
  Coleridge, Samuel Taylor, 3:832
  demythologizing, 4:656
  documentary hypothesis, 1:814
Eichmann, Adolf, 7:12–13
Eichorn, Joachim, 5:139
Eichrodt, Walther, 2:385–386, 5:520
Eigenkirchen, 3:44
Eighteenth Amendment (U.S.
  Constitution), 13:802
Eighth Day. *See* Resurrection of Christ
Eigil of Fulda, 1:290, 3:13
Eijl, Edouard van, 4:4
Eilmer (monk), 9:80
Einführung in die Missionswissenschaft
  (Schmidlin), 12:744
Einhard, **5:139,** 12:54
  Ansegis of Fontenelle, St., 1:493
  Candidus of Fulda, 3:13
  Carolingian legends, 1:762, 763
  Carolingian Renaissance, 3:160
  Charlemagne's coronation, 3:426
  chronicles, 1:461
  Clement of Ireland, St., 3:799
  Latin literature, 9:443
  sculpture, 3:153
Die Einheit in der Kirche (Möhler),
  9:763, 10:104
Einleitung in das Alte Testament
  (Reusch), 12:181
*Einleitung in die christkatholische
  Theologie: Philosophische Einleitung*
  (Hermes), 6:797
Einleitung in die Philosophie
  (Frohschammer), 6:15, 12:901
Einsiedeln, Maria, 12:568
Einsiedeln Abbey (Switzerland), 4:136,
  5:29, **139–140,** *140*
Einstein, Albert, **5:140–142,** *141*
  Alexander, Samuel, 1:252
  chance, 3:375, 377
  continuum, 4:217
  mechanism, 9:417–418
*Der einzig mögliche Beweisgrund zu
  einer Demonstration des Daseins
  Gottes* (Kant), 8:120
Eirenicon (Pusey), 11:842
Eirik the Red, 10:446
Eisendrath, Maurice, 8:13
Eisengrein, Martin and William, **5:142**
Eisenman, Robert H., 4:563
Eissfeldt, Otto, 2:385, 5:520
Eitan, A., 2:381
Eitrem, S., 3:573
Eiximenis, Francesco, 1:424

*Ejercicio de perfección y virtudes
  cristianas* (The Practice of Perfection
  and of Christian Virtues)
  (Rodríguez), 12:279
Ejercitatorio de la vida espiritual
  (*Exercises for the Spiritual Life*)
  (Cisneros), 3:744
Ekkehard I (monk of Sankt Gallen),
  5:142, 12:669
Ekkehard II (monk of Sankt Gallen),
  5:142, 7:247, 12:669
Ekkehard IV (monk of Sankt Gallen),
  1:664, 5:142, *142,* 9:449, 12:669
Ekkehard of Aura, 1:462
Ekklesiastike Alethia (Church Truth),
  6:459–460
*Ekthesis (Exposition of the Orthodox
  Faith)* (St. John Damascene), 7:952
Ekthesis (Heraclius), 3:634
El (God), 4:337, 341, **5:143,** 14:269
El Paso Diocese (TX), **5:174,** 175,
  12:641
El Paso Interreligious Sponsoring
  Organization (EPISO), 5:174–175
El Salvador, 4:628, **5:175–178,** *177*
  Aguilar, Nicolás, 1:189
  Delgado, José Matías, 4:627–628
  demographic statistics, 5:175
  map, 5:*176*
  Romero, Oscar A., 12:365–366
  Ursuline martyrs, 8:132–133
  war of 1980s, 8:548
El Santa Cruz y Loydi, Manuel Ignacio,
  7:699
Elagabalus (Varius Avitus Bassianus)
  (Roman Emperor), 12:312
Elbel, Benjamin, **5:143**
ELCA. *See* Evangelical Lutheran Church
  in America
Eldad ha-Dani, **5:143–144**
Eldarov, G., 2:684
Elder, George, **5:144**
Elder, William Henry (Abp. of
  Cincinnati), 3:736, **5:144–145,** 7:685,
  12:647
The Elder Statesman (play, Eliot), 5:161
Elderly, care of, 8:47, 616–617
Eldrad, St. (Abbot of Novalese, France),
  5:145
Eleanor (Queen of Portugal), 3:416
Eleanor of Aquitaine, 8:799
Eleatics, 4:367, 11:441, 13:324
Eleazar the Priest, 2:83
Election, Divine, **5:145–146**
Electricity, 6:212–213
Elegantiarum latinae linguae libri sex
  (Valla), 14:376

Elegia di Madonna Fiammetta
  (Boccaccio), 2:448
Element, **5:146–147**
*Elementa philosophiae aristotelico-
  thomisticae* (Gredt), 6:433, 12:776
Elementa philosophiae christianae
  (Lepidi), 8:507
Elementa philosophiae sive Ontosophia
  (Clauberg), 10:606
Elementarism, associationism and, 1:795
The Elementary Forms of Religious Life
  (Durkheim), 1:459, 4:952
Elemente der Psychophysik (Fechner),
  5:27
Elements (Euclid), 12:805, 13:374
Elements, four basic "roots," 5:195
Éléments de Botanique (Tournefort),
  10:773
Elements of Existence, **5:147–148**
Elements of Popular Theology
  (Schmucker), 12:745
Elements of Theology (Proclus),
  11:736–737
Eleousa (Virgin of Tenderness), 9:272
Elephantine Temple (Egypt), 13:811
Elert, W., 3:586
Eleusinian Mysteries
  celebration, 10:89–90
  early history, 10:89
  evaluation and later history, 10:91
  fertility aspects of rites, 10:90–91
  prehistoric origins, 10:86
Eleusis, Cretan-Mycenaean culture and,
  4:363
Eleusius of Cyzicus, 2:139
Eleutherius (Pope), St., 3:263, **5:148**
Eleutherius of Tournai (Bp.), St., **5:148**
Elevatio Crucis (medieval drama), 4:894
Elevation of man, **5:148–153**
  destiny, supernatural, 4:694
  immortality, 7:352
  life, concept of, 8:572–573
Eleventh-century Ottonian chalice,
  10:*720*
Elfleda of Glastonbury, St., 5:153
Elfleda of Ramsey, St., 5:153
Elfleda of Whitby, St., **5:153**
Elfodd (Bp. of Bangor, Wales), 2:54
Elgar, Edward, Sir, 5:*153,* **153–154**
Elguero, Francisco, **5:154,** 13:121
Eliade, Mircea, **5:154–155**
  afterlife, 1:163
  alchemy, 1:239
  death of God theology, 4:585
  literary myth, 10:121
  myth, 4:658

mythical consciousness, 3:672

Elias (Abp. of Nicosia), 1:807

Elias (Bp. of Cyprus), 3:366

Elias (Patriarch of Jerusalem), St., **5:155**

Elias III (Patriarch), 5:6

Elias Asmar, Ḥabīb (Bp.), 3:367

Elias Bar Shināyā, **5:155–156**

Elias Ekdikos (Greek theologian), **5:156**

Elias of Cortona, **5:156–157**

    Andrew Caccioli, Bl., 1:404, 2:840

    Franciscan Orders, 5:870

    S. Francesco Basilica, 1:790

    Salimbene, 12:616

Elias of Reggio, St., **5:157**, 8:865

Elias of Thessalonika, St., **5:157**

Elias Peter Abūlyonan (Chaldean
    Patriarch), 3:369

Elias Spelaiotes (d. 960), 5:157

Eliezer, Rabbi Israel ben. *See* Ba'al
    Shem Tov (Rabbi Israel)

Eliezer ben Yose (Rabbi), 5:508

Eligius of Noyon, St., **5:157–158**

    Antwerp, 1:538

    Brittany dispute, 8:41

    catechesis, 3:230

    slavery, 13:212

    Solignac Abbey, 13:302

    Souillac Abbey, 13:332

Elihu (biblical figure), 7:886–887

Elijah (Hebrew prophet), 5:*158*, **158–159**

    Baal cult, opposition to, 2:2

    Carmelite spirituality, 3:133, 143

    disciple as term, 4:768

    sacrifice, 3:125

Elijah (Hebrew prophet), Second
    Coming of, **5:159**

Elin, St. *See* Helen of Skövde, St.

Eliot, John, 2:162, 4:115, 11:*606*

Eliot, Thomas Stearns, 4:868,
    5:159–161, *160*, 14:271

Elipandus of Toledo (Abp.), **5:161–162**

    adoptionism, 1:119, 243, 9:446

    Beatus of Liébana, 2:182

    conversion, 8:458

Elisabethcellencia et Oosterhofensia
    (Scholliner), 12:779

Elisha (Hebrew prophet), 1:402, 478,
    4:768, **5:162**, *163*

Elites, 1:667

Elizabeth, St., **5:162**, *164*, 7:1012–1013,
    14:564

Elizabeth I (Queen of England), 3:72,
    5:163–165, *165*

    Acts of Uniformity and church
        settlement, 10:418, 14:300–301

Allen, William, 1:296

Ancient See of Chichester, 3:481

Anglican orders problem, 1:437

Anglican Reformation, 1:442, 3:608,
    638

Arden, Edward, 1:645

Bahamas land grant, 2:13

Bible texts, 2:368

birth, 5:244

Bonner, Edmund, 2:507

Book of Advertisements, 1:136

Book of Common Prayer, 2:524

Catherine de Médicis, 3:266

Church in England under, 4:912,
    5:245, 247–248

Church of Ireland, 7:548

Cole, Henry, 3:829

confessions of faith, 4:80

De heretico comburendo act, 4:550

excommunication, 5:163, 224–225,
    247, 670–671, 10:842

expulsion of Jesuits, 1:21

Holy Cross Abbey, 7:18

Irish Church, 7:557–558

Irish confessors and martyrs, 7:577

James I, 7:705

martyrs persecuted under, 5:224–225,
    227–234

persecution of Catholics, 12:665

Pius V (Pope), St., 3:609, 611

Protestant Reformation, 12:5–6,
    10–11

Puritans, 2:689

revisions to Thirty-Nine Articles,
    14:7–8

Spanish Armada, 1:696

See also The Reformation in the
    British Isles

Elizabeth of Hungary, St., **5:165–166**,
    166, 7:120

Elizabeth of Portugal, St., **5:166**

Elizabeth of Ranfaing, Ven., **11:907–908**

Elizabeth of Schonau, St., **5:166–167**

Elizabeth of the Trinity, Bl., 3:128, 130,
    138–139, **5:167–168**, 7:444

Elizabeth of Valois, 11:247

Elizabeth Rose, St., 3:463

Elizalde, Miguel de, 1:564, **5:168**

Elizondo, Virgilio, 5:203, 11:510,
    12:642

Elkins Park (PA), 4:839

Ella, Rabbi Gaon, 7:872

Ellard, Gerald, **5:168**, *169*

ELLC. *See* English Language Liturgical
    Consultation

Ellerker, Clare. *See* Mary of the Blessed
    Sacrament

Elling, William (Father), 11:236

Elliott, Walter, 1:354, 355, **5:168–169**

Ellis, John Tracy, **5:169–171**, 12:462

Ellis, Philip (Michael) (Bp. of Segni,
    Italy), **5:171**, 250

Ello of Brauweiler, 2:586

Ellul, Jacques, **5:171–172**, 13:783–784,
    785

Ellwangen Abbey (Württemberg,
    Germany), 4:475–476, **5:172–173**,
    324

Elmo, St., **5:173**, 12:545

Elne, Council of (1027), 3:518

Elohim, **5:173–174**, 13:58

Elohist, **5:174**

    documents, 11:91

    tradition, 1:3, 36, 2:526

Eloisa to Abelard (Pope), 11:497

Elphinstone, James, Sir, 2:32

Elphinstone, William (Bp.), **5:175**,
    12:832

Der Elsässer (daily), 10:75

Elsensohn, M. Alfreda (Sister),
    7:290–291

Elsner, J. K., 3:525

Elucidarium (Honorius of Autun), 3:239

Elvira, Council of (300-303 or 309),
    3:593, **5:178**

    capital punishment, 3:85–86

    catechumenate, 3:250

    clerical celibacy and marriage, 3:325

    marriage, 1:150

    works of charity, 3:404

Elwell, Clarence E. (Bp. of Columbus),
    3:868, **5:178–179**

Ely, Ancient See (England), **5:179–180**

Ely Abbey (England), 1:22, 241, 3:693,
    5:179–180

Elyot, Thomas, Sir, 5:206

Elzéar of Sabran, St., 1:197, 4:633,
    5:180

Emanation, 11:422

Emanationism, **5:180–182**

    Avicebron, 1:939

    causality, 3:303

    creation doctrine, 4:343

    soul's origin, 13:353

Emancipation, Catholic, **5:182–185**,
    250–251

    Act of Union, 5:183

    Daniel O'Connell advocation,
        10:538–540

    Hughes, John Joseph, 7:160

    Relief Acts, 5:182–185, 250–251

Emancipation, Catholic *(continued)*
　role of Daniel Murray during, 10:68
　Smith, James support, 13:233
Emancipation, Jewish (1750-1948),
　7:872–875
Emancipation Act (1829), 5:182, 10:502
Emard, Joseph Médard (Abp.), 5:*185*,
　185–186
Ember Days, **5:186–187**
　Callistus I (Pope), St., 2:879
　liturgical cycles, 8:718
　readings in liturgy, 8:437
Emblemata mosaics, 10:2
Embolism, **5:187**
Embroyonic research, 13:355
Embury, Philip, **5:187–188**
Emden catechism, 8:342
Emebert of Cambrai, St., **5:188**
Emerald Table of Hermes, 1:238
Emeralds, alleged magical properties of,
　11:646
The Emerging Layman (Thorman), 14:60
Emeric of Hungary, St., **5:188**
Emerson, Ralph Waldo, **5:188–189**, *189*
　aristocracy, 1:667
　Channing, William Ellery, 3:379
　I-It mysticism, 10:117
　transcendentalism, 14:146, 147
Émery, Jacques André, **5:190–191**, 974,
　6:77
Emesa (Homs), **5:191**
Emila (martyr of Córdoba), 4:262
Emile ou Traité de l'Éducation
　(Rousseau), 3:792, 12:392, 393
Emiliani, Jerome, St., 4:310, **5:191**
　Somascan Fathers, 3:418, 610, 782,
　13:309–310
　works of charity, 3:415, 418
Eminenter (eminently), 12:751
In Eminenti (papal bull, Clement XII),
　1:893, 3:790
Emma (Queen of England). *See*
　Aelfgyfu (Queen of England)
Emmanuel (Bp. Cremona), Bl., **5:192**
Emmanuel (periodical), 8:184
Emmanuel, Book of, 7:596
Emmanuel, in the Bible, **5:192**,
　9:542–543
Emmanuel II Thomas, 5:6
Emmanuel of Jesus, 3:436
Emmanuel Philibert (Duke of Savoy).
　See Savoy, Emmanuel Philibert,
　Duke of
Emmeram, St., **5:192**, 319, 12:668, 670
Emmerich, Anne Catherine, 3:759, **5:193**
Emmons, Nathanael, **5:193**

Emotion, moral aspect, **5:193–195**
　emotive meaning, 8:757
　human control, 5:194
　influence on responsibility,
　5:194–195
　love, 8:825–830
　morality, 5:194
　subject of sin, 13:153
　use and misuse, 5:193–194
　virtue, 5:195
Emotivism, 5:397
Empedoclean elements, 6:441
Empedocles (Greek philosopher),
　5:195–196, 6:306, 441, 11:287,
　14:156
　atomism, 1:832
　causality, 3:297, 4:958
　matter, 9:339–340
　nature of matter, 12:802
　panpsychism, 10:823
　soul, 13:333
　transmigration of the soul, 7:347
Emperor Honorius Holding a Labarum
　(ivory diptych), 8:264
Empirical pessimism, 11:168
Empiricism, **5:196–199**, 11:294
　abstraction, 1:45
　accident, 1:62, 63
　agnosticism, 1:181
　argumentation, 1:659
　associationism, 1:796
　Bacon, Francis, 5:91
　Berkeley, George, 7:297
　Brentano, Franz, 2:605
　British moralists, 2:624
　Carnap, Rudolf, 3:147
　Cartesianism, 3:184
　causality, 3:301
　certitude, 3:352
　choice, 3:521
　conscience, 4:140
　Hobbes, 3:184
　Hume, David, 7:200–202
　idealism, 7:297–298
　illuminism, 7:321
　James, William, 7:703–704
　knowledge, 8:222
　Locke, John, 5:91, 197–198, 261
　logical positivism, 8:756
　naturalism, 10:206
　necessity, 10:227
　nominalism and modern, 10:413
　opposition to, 13:407
　relation, 12:42

Royce, Josiah, 12:397–398
　secular humanism, 7:196
　Spencer, Herbert, 13:413
　Thomasius, Christian, 5:262
　verfication notion in modern, 14:451
　See also Sensism
Employment, occult compensation and,
　4:42–43
Employment Division v. Smith (1990),
　3:663–664
Empyromancy, 4:785
Emrys Ap Iwan, **5:199**
Ems, Congress of (1786), **5:199–200**,
　258
　Caprara, Giovanni Battista, 3:92
　Clemens Wenzeslaus, 3:773
　Cologne, 3:843
　Febronianism, 3:639
Emser, Hieronymus, **5:200–201**
Emūnōt weDē'ōt (Beliefs and Opinions)
　(Sa'adia ben Joseph), 7:863, 12:450
Emygdius of Ancona, St., **5:201**
En Clara Vox Redarguit (hymn), **5:201**
En el humo del incendio (Franceschi),
　5:864
En Ut Superba Criminum (hymn), **5:201**
Enantiophanes, 3:46
Enarrationes in Psalmos (St. Augustine),
　5:512
Enchiridion (Eck), 5:43
Enchiridion (Epictetus), 5:282
Enchiridion (St. Augustine), 3:240, 4:8,
　93
Enchiridion militis christiani (Erasmus),
　5:315, 12:123
Enchiridion of Counsels (Nicodemus),
　10:382
Enchiridion symbolorum (Denzinger),
　5:729
Enciclopedia cattolica, 5:207
Enciclopedia ecclesiastica e morale
　(periodical), 14:442
Enclosure, 3:126, 134, 806
Encomienda-doctrina system in Spanish
　America, 2:864–865, 3:246, 485,
　5:201–203
　Las Casas against, 8:340–341, 12:613
　mission vs., 9:701
　San Martín opposed to, 12:654
Encomium Moriae (More), 7:190, 192
Encratism, 3:323, 325
Encratites, 1:365, 3:323
Encuentros, National Pastoral,
　5:203–205
Encyclical letters, **5:205–206**
　Acerba animi (Pius XI), 12:408

Acerbo nimis (Pius X), 4:94, 11:390, 391

Ad apostolorum principis (Pius XII), 1:823, 3:502

Ad beatissimi Apostolorum (Benedict XV), 7:504

Ad caeli Reginam (Pius XII), 11:399

Ad Catholici Sacerdotii (Pius XI), 11:393

Ad Petri cathedram (John XXIII), 7:936

Aeterna Dei (John XXIII), 7:937

Aeterni patris (Leo XIII), 1:74, 147, 592, 678–679, 3:624, 5:712, 6:287, 7:503, 8:188, 492, 499, 824, 9:752, 10:244, 440, 11:301, 12:774, 14:23

Allatae sunt (Benedict XIV), 3:817

Annum sacrum (Leo XIII), 8:491, 12:491, 492, 493

Arcanum (Leo XIII), 1:631

Au milieu des sollicitudes (Leo XIII), 5:855, 11:900

Caritate Christi (Pius XI), 11:393, 12:491

Casti Connubii (Pius XI), 1:28, 3:214, 4:221, 10:178, 11:392–393, 13:258, 14:825

Centesimus annus (John Paul II), 3:342–343, 620, 643, 5:206, 7:998, 10:852, 11:567, 13:244, 301–302, 568, 14:643

Christi Matri (Paul VI), 11:32

Christian Education of Youth (Pius XI), 10:650

Cor nostrum (Alexander III), 1:256

Cum primum (Gregory XVI), 6:509

definition, 11:747

Dilectissima nobis (Pius XI), 11:395

Dives in misericordia (John Paul II), 3:627, 4:783–784, 10:852

Divini illius magistri (Pius XI), 11:392

Divini redemptoris (Pius XI), 1:823, 3:642, 4:790, 11:393, 394, 13:243

Divino afflante spiritu (Pius XII), 2:167, 3:623, 4:790–792, 814, 5:523, 968, 6:29, 133, 793, 10:303, 11:95, 399, 478, 13:913

Divinum illud munus (Leo XIII), 4:792, 6:294, 7:442

Doctor mellifluus (Pius XII), 2:309

Dominum et vivificantem (John Paul II), 4:856–857

E supremi Apostolatus (Pius X), 11:388–389

Ecclesiam Dei (Pius XI), 11:393

Ecclesiam suam (Paul VI), 1:823, 5:33–34, 10:850–851, 855, 11:32, 12:858

Editae saepe (Pius X), 11:391

Evangelium vitae (John Paul II), 1:24, 456, 3:88, 238, 5:205, 459, 476–477, 560, 7:998, 1003, 10:179, 852, 13:302

Fidei donum (Pius XII), 9:681

Fides et Ratio (John Paul II), 3:542, 5:714–715, 7:1002, 10:185, 852, 11:475, 487, 950, 12:198, 778

Grata recordatio (John XXIII), 7:937

Gravissimo officii munere (Pius X), 11:390

Haurietis aquas (Pius XII), 5:565, 12:490, 491–492, 493

Humanae vitae (Paul VI), 1:196, 490, 3:627, 4:222, 5:40, 860, 6:645, 7:179–181, 450–451, 10:178, 521, 11:32, 12:272, 575, 13:258

Humani generis (Pius XII), 1:64, 422, 3:466, 541–542, 624, 4:345, 347, 649, 691, 815–816, 5:496, 712, 6:394, 412, 7:181–182, 10:667, 849, 11:399, 824, 12:775, 14:23–24, 159

Humanum genus (Leo XIII), 3:101

Il fermo proposito (Pius X), 9:755, 10:415, 11:389, 390–391

Immortale Dei (Pope Leo XIII), 7:346–347

In Suprema Petri Apostoli Sede (Pius IX), 6:459

Inscrutabili (Leo XIII), 13:258

Inter multiplices (Pius IX), 14:285

Inter omnia (Alexander III), 1:256

Jamdudum in Lusitania (Pius X), 11:391

Jucunda sane (Pius X), 11:389

Laborem exercens (John Paul II), 3:620, 627, 5:206, 7:1002, 8:266, 548, 10:852, 11:744, 13:263–264, 14:90, 826

Lacrimabili statu (Pius X), 11:391

Libert as praestantissimum (Leo XIII), 11:784

Mater et magistra (John XXIII), 1:793, 823, 3:620, 625, 626, 4:16, 21, 7:936–937, 9:317, 11:566, 13:260, 567

Maximam gravissimamque (Pius XI), 11:395

Mediator Dei (Pius XII), 2:676, 3:589–590, 9:428, 11:400, 705, 12:500

Mens nostra (Pius XI), 11:393

Mense maio (Paul VI), 11:32

Mirae caritatis (Leo XIII), 4:34, 556

Miranda prorsus (Pius XII), 11:400

Mirari vos (Gregory XVI), 2:218, 3:619, 643, 5:854, 6:507, 779

    Lamennais censured, 8:309

    ultramontism rejected, 8:271–272

Miserentissimus Redemptor (Pius XI), 11:393, 12:491, 492, 493

Mit brennender Sorge (Pius XI), 3:642, 5:352, 6:186, 11:393, 395

Mortalium animos (Pius XI), 5:72, 6:29, 9:903

Musicae sacrae (Pius XII), 11:400

Mysterium fidei (Paul VI), 10:77–79, 11:32

Mystici corporis (Pius XII), 3:589–590, 5:37, 948, 950–951, 7:380, 442, 9:428, 10:104, 110–111, 11:399, 12:471, 625, 13:286–287

Nobilissima Gallorum gens (Leo XIII), 11:900

Non abbiamo bisogno (Pius XI), 3:277, 642, 11:393

Non amgigimus (Benedict XIV), 4:59

Nova impendet (Pius XI), 11:393

Pacem in terris (John XXIII), 3:88, 625–626, 642–643, 755, 5:206, 7:937, 8:586, 10:741–742, *741*, 747, 850, 11:566, 13:117, 259, 261, 567–568, 14:642, 825

    association, 1:792, 793

    common good, 4:16, 20

    conscientious objection, 4:151

    freedom of religion, 5:952

    intellectual freedom, 5:943

Paenitentiam agere (John XXIII), 7:937

Pascendi dominici gregis (Pius X), 2:395, 694, 3:336, 5:789, 968, 6:313, 779, 7:503, 8:311, 10:912–913, 12:775, 14:139

    Modernism, 9:755

    Pius X, 11:389

Pieni l'animo (Pius X), 9:755, 11:389

Populorum progressio (Paul VI), 3:627, 4:157, 5:206, 9:688, 11:32, 516–517, 566, 13:244, 260, 303–304, 14:362, 638

Praeclara gratulationis (Leo XIII), 1:503, 6:459

Princeps Pastorum (John XXIII), 3:626, 7:936, 937, 9:681

Providentissimus Deus (Leo XIII), 5:523, 6:793, 7:494–495, 8:492, 10:335, 11:478, 784–785, 13:457, 458

Encyclical letters *(continued)*

Quadragesimo anno (Pius XI), 1:915, 3:420, 620, 5:95, 206, 10:850, 11:393, 512–513, 847–848, 13:243, 246–247, 259, 262, 14:251, 453
   common good, 4:19
   poverty, 11:566
   subsidiarity, 13:567, 569

Quanta Cura (Pius IX), 3:619, 620, 5:855, 968, 11:387, 852

Quas primas (Pius XI), 7:164, 8:284, 11:393, 857, 12:493

Qui pluribus (Pius IX), 3:101, 5:712, 11:384–385, 14:139

Redemptor hominis (John Paul II), 3:627, 7:1002, 10:852, 853, 11:989–990

Redemptoris Mater (John Paul II), 7:1003, 9:173, 10:234, 11:990

Redemptoris Missio (John Paul II), 5:39, 478, 7:1002–1003, 8:175, 9:678–679, 682, 11:990–992

Rerum ecclesiae (Pius XI), 9:681, 11:393, 753

Rerum novarum (Leo XIII), 1:792–793, 2:219, 3:342, 420, 643, 5:205–206, 8:161, 190, 193, 371, 466, 492, 9:317, 10:184, 440, 850, 12:136–137, 667, 793, 13:241, 256–257, 14:109, 251, 824
   Catholic labor movement, 11:367
   common good, 4:19
   democratic priests, 5:855
   John XXIII, 3:625
   poverty, 11:566
   Quanta cura, 3:620

Rerum orientalium (Pius XI), 11:393

Respicientes ea omnia (Pius IX), 12:322

Sacerdotalis caelibatus (Paul VI), 3:627, 11:32

Sacerdotii Nostri primordia (John XXIII), 7:936

Sacra Virginitas (Pius XII), 12:464–465

Satis cognitum (Leo XIII), 1:592, 12:700

Singulari nos (Gregory XVI), 3:619, 6:508, 8:310

Singulari quadam (Pius X), 11:389

Slavorum apostoli (John Paul II), 3:627, 7:1003, 9:682, 13:216–217, 14:107

Sollicitudo rei socialis (John Paul II), 5:206, 7:1001, 10:616, 11:566–567, 13:244, 258–259, 269, 301, 303–305

Spiritus Paraclitus (Benedict XV), 2:250, 5:523, 13:457–458

Studiorium ducem (Pius XI), 6:287

Summi Pontificatus (Pius XII), 10:191, 956, 11:395, 13:605

Traditi humilitati nostrae (Pius VIII), 11:382

Ubi arcano (Pius XI), 11:392

Ubi nos (Pius IX), 6:549

Ubi primum (Benedict XIV), 5:205

Ubi primum (Leo XII), 8:489, 10:433, 12:789

Ut unum sint (John Paul II), 5:40, 205, 7:1002, 10:853, 12:700, 14:355–356

Vehementer nos (Pius X), 4:63, 11:390

Veritatis splendor (John Paul II), 3:219, 220, 221, 627, 743, 4:160, 5:205, 560, 6:26, 7:998, 1002, 10:185, 852, 14:451–452

Vix pervenit (Benedict XIV), 2:32, 14:354

Encyclical of Anthimus VII, 6:459

Encyclical of Oriental Patriarchs, 6:459, 10:701

Encyclical of the Four Patriarchs (Constantius I). *See* Encyclical of Oriental Patriarchs

The Encyclicals of Pius XI (Ryan), 12:445

Encyclopaedie van het Katholicisme, 5:207

Encyclopedia Britannica, controversial articles in, 13:236

Encyclopedia Dictionary of Religion, 10:524

The Encyclopedia of American Catholic History, 5:208

Encyclopedia of Religion, 5:155

Encyclopedia of the Early Church, 5:208

Encyclopedia of the Philosophical Sciences (Hegel), 12:346

Encyclopedias and dictionaries, 2:775, 794–795, 808

Encyclopedias and dictionaries, Catholic, **5:206–208**

Encyclopedic Dictionary of Religion, 5:208

Encyclopedie (Alembert), 1:518, 3:792, 5:207

Encyclopédie, ou Dictionnaire raisonné des sciences, des arts et des métiers, par une société de gens de lettres, 5:208–209, *209*, 255
   censorship, 5:209
   contents and contributors, 5:209–210
   origins, 5:208–209

Encyclopédie des sciences religieuses, 5:207

Encyclopédie Méthodique (Bergier), 2:295

Encyclopédie théologique (Migne), 5:207

Encyclopedists, **5:208–210**
   antipodes question, 1:530
   apologetics, 1:564
   atheism, 1:823
   Berthier, Guillaume François, 2:332
   Bufalo, St. Gaspare del, 2:675
   Catherine the Great, 3:264
   Catholic social thought, 13:255
   Clement XIII (Pope), 3:791
   deism, 4:617
   Holbach, Paul Heinrich Dietrich, 7:1
   hylozoism, 7:240
   Journal de Trévoux, 3:295
   Lambert of Saint-Omer, 8:304
   scholasticism, 12:768

End, **5:210–213**
   Aristotelian analysis on nature as, 10:210
   Aristotle, 1:682
   damnation and loss, 4:506
   law, 8:401
   object of the will as universal, 10:24–25
   society, 13:276
   See also Final causality

The End of the Affair (Greene), 6:461

End of the world, 1:516, **5:213–219**, *214*
   See also Millenarianism

The End Times (Schedel), 8:*32*

Endo, Shusaku, 5:*219*, **219–220**

Enea Silvio de' Piccolomini. *See* Pius II (Pope)

Engberding, H., 3:553

Engel, Hans Ludwig, **5:220**

Engel, Peter (Abbot), 12:552

Engel v. Vitale (1962), 3:666

Engelbert I of Cologne (Abp.), St., 3:843, **5:220**

Engelbert of Admont, 1:117, **5:220–221**

Engelbert of Sankt Paul (Abbot), 12:670

Engelbrecht, A., 5:651

Engelhardt, Zephyrin, **5:221**

Engels, Friedrich, 3:620, **5:221–222**, 222, 703, 14:223, 361
   dialectical materialism, 9:323
   ideology as superstructure, 8:211
   Marx, Karl, 9:236–237

Engjulli, Pál (Abp. of Durrës), 1:216

England, **5:238–253**
   Acts of Uniformity, 2:524, 3:72
   Alfred the Great, 1:279–281

Anglican-Episcopalian Religious Orders, 12:102–103

Anglicans, 9:78

Anne of Denmark, 1:467

anointing, 1:478, 479

archpriest controversy, 3:785

Athelstan, 1:827–828

Barons' War, 12:233

Bishop, William, 2:409–410

Calvinism, 2:895

Canon Law schools, 3:49

Canons Regular of St. Augustine, 3:67, 68

capital punishment, 3:87

Carmelites, 3:129, 141

carols, 3:150

Cartesianism, 3:185

catechesis, 3:243

Charles I, 3:432

Charles II, 2:502, 3:173, 433, 648

chronicles and annals, 1:462, 464

church architecture, 3:696, 697, 707, 709

Church-state relations, 7:472

Clement VIII (Pope), 3:785

colonialism, 9:697

colonialism, African, 9:67–68, 371–372, 13:582, 755

colonialism, American, 9:55, 724–726, 737–738

colonialism, Maltese, 9:82–83

colonialism, Southeast Asian, 9:69–70

confessions of faith, 4:79–80

Confirmation, 4:87

contraception, 4:221

control of Palestine, 7:771

Convocations of the clergy, 4:243–244

Counter Reformation, 2:259, 4:49, 313, 9:293–294

crib custom, 4:364

Crusades, 4:411

culture as term, 4:426–427

De heretico comburendo act (1401), 4:550

decretals, 4:597, 603, 605–606

deism, 4:616, 617

demographic statistics, 5:239

Douai seminaries, 4:879–880

ecclesiastical organization, 5:240, 251, 252

Enlightenment, 5:254, 259–262

evangelicalism, 5:472–473

Free Churches, 5:928

Glorious Revolution (1688), 12:207–208, 463

Gregory I (Pope), St., 6:481–482

Gregory XII (Pope), 6:501

Honorius III (Pope), 7:84

Horner, Nicholas, 7:112

humanism, 7:190, 191

hymnology, 7:255–257, 258

iconography, 7:286

idealism, 7:299–300

investiture, 7:538

Jacobites, 7:690

Jesuits, 7:783

Kuwait, 8:258

Lollards, 8:766–767, 836–837

map, 5:241, 12:831, 14:611

medieval Church reorganization, 3:598, 8:323–324

medieval drama and literature, 4:896, 897, 898–901, 9:442

Methodist churches, 9:556–560

mission, 3:714–715, 9:680–681

mortmain (law), 9:904–905

music, 8:685–686

new morality, 8:868

Oates Plot, 8:140, 325

Old Catholics, 8:539

Peace of God Movement, 11:50

Pilgrimage of Grace (1536-1537), 1:786

Popish Plot (1678), 5:481, 686, 12:396

Presbyterianism, 11:679–680

Puritanism, 11:838–839

Reformation, 12:5–11

Regalia, 12:27

religious education, 8:787, 12:98

Renaissance, 8:689, 12:119

Ridolfi Plot, 5:752

secularization of Church property, 12:8

Sees, ancient, 8:770–772, 12:278

Servants of the Paracletes, 13:25

Simeon of Durham, 13:124–125

Simon de Ghent, 13:128

Simon Hinton, 13:129

slavery, 13:212

Smith, Richard, 13:234

social justice issues, 3:620

Spanish Armada, 1:696–697

succession and Catholic prohibition, 12:396

temperance movements, 13:796

Trinidad, 3:114–116

Union of Sisters of Mercy, 13:186

works of charity, 3:408, 411

See also Anglican Reformation; Anglicanism; Anti-Catholicism, England; Britain, early church in; England, Scotland, and Wales, Martyrs of; Gunpowder Plot (1605); Mission in colonial America, English

England, John (Bp. of Charleston, SC), 5:222–223, 10:437, 14:220

accomplishments, 13:364–365

Baltimore Councils, 2:43–44

Liberia missions, 8:551

Savannah Archdiocese, 12:709

slavery, 1:156

writings collected, 8:904

England, Scotland, and Wales, Martyrs of, 5:224–238

See also Gunpowder Plot (1605); Irish confessors and martyrs; specific confessors and martyrs

English anti-Catholicism. See Anti-Catholicism, England

English Benedictines, 2:255, 256, 272, 273–274

English Civil War, 3:432, 433

Anglicanism, 1:444

apocalyptic movements, 1:548

Cambridge University, 2:906

Ireland, 1:75–76

English College (Douai), 4:879–880

English College (Rome), 13:82, 370

English Congregation of the Order of St. Benedict. See English Benedictines

English for the Mass (ICEL), 7:524

English language, use in U.S. liturgy, 2:43, 7:523–525

English Language Liturgical Consultation (ELLC), 5:253–254

Consultation on Common Texts, 4:201

founding, 8:441

inclusive language use, 8:439–440

The English Liturgist (periodical), 6:366

English Liturgy Society, 6:366

English Martyrs (feast day), 5:225

See also England, Scotland, and Wales, Martyrs of

English mission, colonial America, 9:724–726

English Peasants' Revolt (1381), 2:31

English Secular Clergy Chapter, 13:11

English Traits (Emerson), 5:188

The English-American, his Travail By Sea and Land or a New Survey of the West Indies (Gage), 6:48

Engnell, Ivan, 11:766

Enkidu (literary character), 6:222–223

Enlart, Camile, 3:694

"Enlightened Catholicism," 10:63

Enlightenment, **5:254–259**

  anticlericalism, 1:518

  architecture, 3:708

  Australia, 1:899, 905

  biblical hermeneutics, 6:793

  biblical theology, 2:384

  blasphemy, 2:434

  Bonald, Louis Gabriel Ambroise de, 2:478

  Brazil, 2:593–594

  Brück, Heinrich, 2:642

  Castro, Agustín Pablo, 3:218

  catechesis, 3:244

  charnel houses, 3:437

  Church in France, 5:254–255, 259–262, 852–853

  Church-State relations, 3:54, 639, 640

  Clemens Wenzeslaus, 3:773

  Cologne, 3:843

  education, 5:256

  England, 5:254, 259–262

  evaluation, 5:259

  Finland, 5:723

  foundational theology, 5:827

  Germany, 5:262–263, 6:182

  historical theology, 6:869

  Hungary, 7:216

  illuminism, 7:321–322

  impact on papacy, 10:844

  Jesuits, 7:786

  Jewish emancipation, 7:872

  Jewish response, 8:9

  Josephinism, 1:910, 913, 3:615

  liberal theology, 8:542, 543

  Liège, 8:563

  literature, 5:258–259

  Lutheranism, 8:891

  Middle Ages, 9:611

  monastic orders, 3:747

  monasticism, 9:794

  natural law, 13:484

  nature and history, 5:254–255

  19th-20th centuries, 3:624

  papacy, 5:257–258

  political theology, 11:460

  politics, 5:261–262

  religion, attitude toward, 5:261

  Russian Church influence and the, 12:424

  scientific developments, 5:261, 262

  secularization of Church property, 12:872–873

  secularization of the clergy, 5:258

  Slovenia, 13:225

  Spain, 13:394

  Spiegel, F. A., 13:416

  the State and Church, 5:257

  the State and society, 5:256–257

  theology of history, 6:889

  theories of man, 5:261

Enlightenment (Sirāj) (Maimonides), 9:52

Enlightenment, philosophy of, 5:255–256, **259–264**

  common good, 4:18

  Comte, August, 4:47

  Condorcet, Marie Jean Antoine Caritat, 4:73–74

  Czechs, 4:483

  deism, 4:617–618

  Lemennais, F., 8:308

  Lessing, G., 8:516–517

  liberal Protestantism, 8:87

  natural law, 10:183–184

  ontology, 10:606–607

  religious liberalism, 8:541

Enlightenment through baptism, 2:66

Enlil (Mesopotamian deity), 2:210

Enmity in the Bible, **5:264**

Ennarrationes in Epist. ad Ephesios (Nacchianti), 10:133

Ennarrationes in Epist. and Romanos (Nacchianti), 10:133

Enneads (Plotinus), 5:47

Ennodius, Magnus Felix (Bp. of Pavia), **5:264–265**

  Arator, 1:627

  hymnody, 7:244

  Latin literature, 9:438

  life of Epiphanius of Pavia, 5:264, 292

  prohibition of pagan books, 6:432–433

Enoch (son of Cain)

  in the Bible, 5:265

  Elijah' story, 5:159

  extraordinary characteristics, 10:951

  literature, 5:266

Enoch, Book of, 1:551–552

  celestial man, 13:316

  demonology, 4:646, 647, 648

  Gehenna, 6:116

  God's spirit, 13:427

  Jewish Gnosticism, 6:264

Enquiry into the Effects of Spirituous Liquors on the Human Body and Mind (Rush), 13:796–797

Ens actu (actual being), 12:750–751

Ens et unum convertuntur (Being and one are convertible), 12:755

Ens potentia (potential being), 12:750–751

Ens rationis (being of reason), 12:751

Ens reale (real being), 12:751

L'Enseignement de Jésus (Batiffol), 2:155

Entelechy, **5:267**

  alchemy, 1:237

  Aristotle, 1:682

  immortality, 7:348

  monad concept, 8:457

  soul, 13:334

Entheticus (John of Salisbury), 9:453

Entitative habits, 6:598

Entos hymon translated, 8:174

Entretien avec M. de Sacy sur Epictète et Montaigne (Pascal), 10:911

Entretien d'un philosophe chrétien et d'un philosophe chinois (Malebranche), 9:74

Entretiens de philosophie (Rohault), 3:185

Entretiens sur la métaphysique et la religion (Malebranche), 9:74

Entretiens sur la mort (Malebranche), 9:74

Entrusted secrets, 12:859–860

Die Entstehung der altkaholischen Kirche (Ritschl), 12:256

Enuma Elish (Babylonian epic), **5:267–269**, 6:815

  Berossus, 2:329

  creation concept, 4:337, 341

  role of myth, 10:122

Enumeration of problems, 11:286

Environment

  art in sacred spaces, 12:503–504

  ethics, 5:57–58

  term defined, 5:48

  See also Ecofeminism and ecofeminist theology

Environment and Art in Catholic Worship, 12:503, 503–504

Envy, 3:399, **5:269**, 14:473

Eoban, St., **5:269**

Éon of Stella, 1:219, **5:269–270**

Epact, 4:46

Epaon, Council of (517)

  altars, 1:314

  Apollinaris of Valence, St., 1:561

Confirmation, 4:87

Eparchia, 5:502

Eparchius, St., **5:270**

Ephemerides Theologicae Lovanienses, 8:824

Ephemerides Theologicae-Carmeliticae (periodical), 6:42

Ephesians, Artemis cult of, 4:729–730

Ephesians, Epistle to the, **5:270–273**

  aeons, 1:140

  asceticism, 1:776, 777

  atonement, 1:837

  authorship, 4:704, 5:273–274

  baptism, 2:61, 65

  beatific vision, 2:171

  beatitudes, 2:178

  birth imagery in baptism, 2:75

  Body of Christ, 13:440

  as captivity epistle, 3:93

  captivity epistles, 3:93

  Christian law, 8:403

  Christian way of life, 3:546

  Christocentrism, 3:558

  Church, 3:578–579, 582–583, 13:440

  Church of Christ, 13:438

  clerical celibacy and marriage, 3:322

  contents and doctrine, 5:270–272

  covenant, 4:328

  date of writing of, 5:272

  deacons, 4:550

  Divine indwelling, 7:441

  Divine plan, 5:58

  divorce, 13:49–50

  edification, 5:85

  faith, 6:382

  faith, profession through baptism, 2:59, 60

  friendship with God, 6:11

  glory of God (end of creation), 6:245

  Gnosis, 6:255

  God's spirit, 13:427

  grace, 6:381

  guilt, 6:571

  Hades, 6:604

  heaven, 6:684

  justification, 8:79

  kingdom of Christ, 13:440

  laity, 8:290

  life of grace, 13:441

  Lord's Day, 8:782

  Lord's Prayer, 8:783

  lying as sin, 8:900, 903

  man, creation of new, 9:87

  marital bond, 8:871

  marriage, 13:319

  merit, 6:383

  Precious Blood, 11:638

  rebirth, 11:951

  sanctification through baptism, 2:59

  Scripture readings, 8:435

  sharing goods, 8:544

  sin, 13:147

  slavery, 13:207, 208, 211

  Son of God, 13:314

  soul of the Church, 13:359

  spirituality, 13:438

  venial sin, 13:155

  world, 14:840

Ephesus, Council of (431), 1:268, 523, 2:820, 3:559, 595, 4:300, 5:3, 137, **273–275**

  Anathemas of Cyril, 1:391

  Antioch Patriarchate, 1:525

  Apollinarianism, 1:559

  Armenia, 1:700, 704, 705

  Atticus of Constantinople, St., 1:839

  Canon Law, 3:38

  communication of idioms, 4:26

  Copts, 4:255

  Council of Chalcedon, 3:363

  creedal statements, 4:352

  crucifixion, 4:379

  Dioscorus (Patriarch of Alexandria), 4:756

  doctrine of Nestorius preserved, 10:252

  dogma, 5:274

  Eastern Schism, 5:22

  Euthymius the Great, St., 5:460

  Felix I (Pope), St., 5:666

  history, 5:273–274

  Liberian Basilica, 3:555

  Mother of God doctrine, 7:332, 10:14, 254

  Nestorius condemned, 4:195, 466

  Pelagianism, 11:63

  primacy of Constantinople, 2:744, 3:595

  Roman primacy, 3:317

  Schwartz, Eduard, 12:793

  Shenoute of Atripe, 13:78

  significance, 5:274–275

Ephesus, Robber Council of (449), 5:82, 83, 137, **275–276**

  Anatolius of Constantinople, 1:392

  Assyrian Church of the East, 1:805

  Council of Chalcedon, 1:523, 3:363

Ephesus, Seven Sleepers of, 13:38

Ephesus, Synod of (*ca.* 190), 1:785

Ephpheta, **5:276**

Ephraem of Edessa, 3:594

Ephraim, in the Bible, **5:276–277**

Ephrem the Syrian, St., **5:277–278**

  baptism of Jesus, 2:72, 73

  biblical canon, 3:32

  Diatessaron, 4:731

  dogma, 5:277–278

  free will, 5:929

  liturgical history, 8:652

  relics, 12:52

  School of Antioch, 5:511

  School of Edessa, 5:82, 83, 277

  School of Nisibis, 1:805

  works, 5:278

Epiclesis, Eucharistic, **5:279–282**

  Commingling, 4:12

  controversy over, 5:279–280, 426

  Eastern Schism, 2:763, 827–828

  eucharistic prayers, 5:280–282

  Orthodox theology, 5:281

  place in the Eucharist, 5:279

  Roman Catholic theology, 5:281, 422

  Serapion's contribution, 13:7

  term defined, 5:279

Epictetus, **5:282–283**, 12:309

  asceticism, 1:773

  Cynics, 4:456

Epicureanism, 5:107, **283–285**, 6:442, 11:289

  Aristotelianism, 1:669

  atheism, 1:822

  atomism, 1:832–833

  certitude, 3:352

  Cyrenaics, 4:464–465

  early Christian theology, 3:591

  ethics, 5:285, 393

  God, 6:308

  good, 6:347

  identity principle, 7:303

  knowledge, 8:214

  logic, 8:537

  philosophy as a school for life, 6:447

  philosophy of nature, 8:849

  state, 13:239

Epicurus (Greek philosopher), 5:*285*, **285–286**

  afterlife, 1:167

  analysis and synthesis, 1:381

  atomism, 4:644

  causality, 3:303

  contingency, 4:213

  empiricism, 5:197

  ethics, 5:393

Epicurus (Greek philosopher)
(continued)
exclluded middle principle, 5:504
free will, 5:937
hedonism, 6:701
immortality, 7:348
materialism, 9:319
providence of God, 11:781
religious veneration, 6:445
soul, 13:339
as teacher and missionary, 6:447
Epicycles, 11:807
Epidaurus Basilica, 1:756
Epideixis, in the Second sophistic,
12:855–856
Epigrams, 1:429
Epigraphical literary hand style,
10:767–768
Epigraphy, Christian, **5:286–290**
Epikeia (reasonableness), 3:772,
5:290–291, 8:66
Epikeia (reasonableness), in the Bible,
5:291
Epileptics, patron of, 8:869
Epimachus, St. *See* Gordian and
Epimachus, SS.
Epiphanius (Patriarch of Constantinople),
5:291–292
Epiphanius of Pavia (Bp.), St., **5:292**
Ennodius' life of, 5:265, 292
works of charity, 3:406
Epiphanius of Salamis (Constantia), St.,
4:461, **5:292–293**
Alogoi, 1:304
apocrypha, 1:558
apostolici, 1:594
Arius, 1:266
biblical canon, 3:32
Cenacle, 3:333
Clement I (Pope), St., 3:774
creedal statements, 4:353
Ebionites, 5:32
heresy, 6:773
iconoclasm, 7:280
Jerome, St., 3:595
liturgical history, 8:651
pilgrimages, 3:594
Protoevangelium Jacobi, 1:469
Saturnalia, 12:705
Epiphany, **5:293–295**
Feast of, 1:134, 2:73, 3:14, 557
lessening importance, 8:642
origins, 8:719
Episcopal Chapel, Illinois Institute of
Technology (Chicago), 3:716

Episcopal Church (U.S.), **5:295–299**
church membership, 3:719
church union, 4:199–200
Consulation on Common Texts,
4:201
doctrine, 5:298
Ecumenical relations, 5:299
fundamentalism, 6:27–28
General Convention, 5:67
history, 5:295–298
hymnals, 7:261
Lambeth Quadilateral, 8:306
liturgical movement, 8:677
liturgical reforms, 5:298
ordination of women, 1:447
organization structure, 5:298–299
Polish National Catholic Church,
11:459
Seton, Elizabeth, St., 13:30–31
Episcopal Church of the Redeemer
(Baltimore), 3:717
Episcopal Commission on Catechesis
and Catholic Education, 11:262
Episcopal Committee on Motion
Pictures, Radio and Television, 13:76
Episcopal Conferences, 2:415,
5:299–301
Canada, 3:8
Canon Law, 3:35, 36, 57
Caribbean, 3:121
collegiality, 5:39–40, 299
Episcopal Gallicanism, 6:75
Episcopalianism, 8:644
Episcopate. *See* Bishops
Episcopius (Biscop), Simon, 12:109
Episkepsis, 9:274
Epistemological transcendence, 14:142
Epistemology, **5:301–304**
abstraction, 1:45
consciousness, 4:151–152
intentional species, 13:409
intuitivism, 8:794
knowledge, 8:203, 212
naturalism, 10:205–206
positions with respect to thing, 14:5
similarity, 13:125–126
skepticism, 13:200–205
truth, 14:224–228
uncertainty principle in context,
14:289–290
Epistemology (Van Steenberghen),
14:388
Epistle of Barnabas, 14:251
Epistle to Diognetus (Athenagoras),
8:413, 10:965

Epistle to Dr. Arbuthnot (Pope), 11:497
The Epistle to the Romans (Barth), 2:120
Epistles, as form, 4:757
Epistles, New Testament, **5:304–306**
commentaries, 8:585
Divine judgment, 8:30
on the Parousia, 10:895–896
type and antitype in the, 14:255
Epistles of Phalaris, dispute on, 2:287
Epistles to Virgins (exhortations), 11:799
*Epistola de Indicis gentibus et de
Bragmannibus* (Palladius of
Helenopolis), 10:805, 806
Epistola de litteris colendis
(Charlemagne), 3:159, 425
Epistola fidei catholicae (Facundus of
Hermiane), 5:587
Epistola tractoria (Zosimus), 11:62
*Epistola...ad RR. Provinciales et ad
Definitores.* (Mandatum) (Barlow),
2:102
Epistolae, orationes et carmina (Barbaro
the Younger), 2:90
Epistolae ad ecclesiam triumphantem
(Ricoldus de Monte Croce), 12:242
Epistolae Decretales. See Decretals
Epistolae obscurorum virorum (*Letters
of Obscure Men*), **5:306**, 12:181
Epistolae theologiae (Le Clerc, J.),
8:432
Epistula Apostolorum, 5:14
Epitaphium Adalheidae (St. Odilo of
Cluny), 10:552
Epithets, Divine, **5:306–307**
Epitome, 12:191
*Epitome juris canonici cum
commentariis* (Vermeersch), 14:452
Epitomes (early Christian writings),
11:800
Epperson v. Arkansas (1968), 3:667
Eppinger, Elisabeth, 5:*307*, **307–308**
Eptadius, St., **5:308**
Equatorial Guinea, **5:308–310**, *309*
Equestrian Order of the Holy Sepulchre
of Jerusalem. *See* Knights of the
Holy Sepulcher
Equidem verba (Pius XI), 3:472
Equipollence, 11:770
Equiprobabilism, **5:310**, 9:880
Alphonsus Liguori, St., 1:311, 363,
9:864
Amort, Eusebius, 1:363
Equivocation (Logic), **5:310–311**
Eranistes (Theodoret of Cyr), 5:461,
13:879
Eras, historical, **5:311–314**

Erasistratus (Greek physician), 2:400, 12:806

Erasmus, Desiderius, **5:314–317**
  Adrian VI (Pope), 1:129
  Albrecht of Brandenburg, 1:233
  Ambrosiaster, 1:346–347
  anticlericalism, 1:517
  Aristotelianism, 1:675
  ars moriendi, 1:733
  Bible, 2:366, 5:518, 7:187, 12:12
  Bostius, Arnold, 2:551
  Bucer, Martin, 2:653
  Calixtus, Georg, 2:874
  Cambridge University, 2:906
  catechesis, 3:232, 241
  Church property, 3:727
  clerical celibacy and marriage, 3:327
  Coimbra University, 3:828
  Colet, John, 3:832, 833
  contributions, 12:119
  devout humanism, 13:447
  educational philosophy, 5:90, 92
  Faber, Johannes, 5:583
  Fisher, John, St., 5:749
  humanism, 12:15
  Hutten, Ulrich von, 7:233
  Latomus, B., 8:370
  Lee, E., controversy with, 8:445
  Luther's letters, 8:882
  methods of study, 7:182, 188, 190
  More, Sir Thomas, 9:888
  pilgrimage, 11:354
  positive theology, 3:613
  Reformation, 5:316, 12:15
  reforms in France, 5:847
  reliquary, 12:*106*
  Renaissance philosophy, 12:123–124
  skepticism, 13:202
  tomb, 7:188
  Warham, William, 3:72
  works, 5:315–316

Erasmus, George, 1:912

Erastianism, 3:637, 638, **5:317–318**

Erastus, Thomas, 5:317, 317–318

Erc of St. Finian's Clonard, 2:601

Erchempert, **5:318**

Erchinoald (French mayor of the palace), 2:153

Erconwald of London, St., 2:98, **5:318–319**, 8:771

Erdington Abbey (England), **5:319**

L'Ère nouvelle (periodical), 5:854, 14:465

Eremitical life, 4:155

Erfahrung und Urteil (Husserl), 11:232

Die Erfuellung (periodical), 10:558

Erhard, St., 5:*319*, **319**

Eric IX Jedvardsson (King of Sweden), St., **5:319–320**, 320, 732

Erikson, Erik
  conversion, 4:238, 239
  dysfunctional family relationships, 7:69
  guilt, 6:568

Eritrea, **5:320–322**, *321*

Eritrean Orthodox Church (Oriental Orthodox), **5:322**

Erkembodo, St., **5:322**

Erlach, Johann Fischer von, 3:706

Erlangen School (Germany), **5:322–323**, 557

Erlembald, St., 1:660, **5:323**

Erlolf of Langres (Bp. of Ellwangen), 5:173

Erluin II (Abbot of Gembloux), 6:124

Ermelinde, St., **5:323–324**

Ermenburga (Anglo-Saxon queen), St., **5:324**

Ermenegildo martire (Pallavicino), 10:806

Ermengarde (Queen of Scotland), 2:32

Ermenrich of Passau (Bp.), 5:173, **324**
  hymns, 7:246
  Methodius, 4:475–476

Ermin (Abbot Bp. of Lobbes), St., **5:324**

Erminfrid, St., **5:324–325**

Erminold of Prüfening, Bl., 5:325, **325**

Erminus of Lobbes (Abbot), 5:787

Ernani (Verdi), 14:446

Ernest (Archduke), 1:911

Ernest of Pardubice (Pardubitz) (Abp. of Prague), **5:325**, 7:230

Ernest of Zwiefalten, St., **5:325–326**

Ernesti, Johann August, 2:383

Ernst of Bavaria (Abp. of Cologne), 3:843

Ernulf (prior of Canterbury), 3:72

Erotic Literature, **5:326–327**

Erp, Harphius van. *See* Henry of Herp

Errázuriz y Valdivieso, Crescente (Abp. of Santiago, Chile), 3:487, **5:327–329**, *328*

Errington, George, Bl., 5:232, **329**

Error, **5:329**
  certitude, 3:351
  criteriology to determine, 4:366–368
  doubt as preventing, 4:883
  freedom of conscience, 4:148–149
  See also Falsity

Error, theological, **5:330**

Error in measurement, 9:413

Erster Entwurf eines Systems der Naturphilosophie (Schelling), 12:732

Erthal, Franz Ludwig Von (prince Bp. of Würzberg and Bamberg), **5:330**

Erthal, Friedrich Karl Joseph von (Abp. of Mainz), 5:200, 300, **330**

Ervigius (King of Visigoths), 7:81

Erzberger, Matthias, 3:341

Die Erzieherische Bedeutung der Kulturgüter (Bauch), 2:157

Esbjörn, Lars Paul, **5:330**, 8:886

Escalante, Silvestre de, 10:267

Esch, Nicholas Van, **5:330–331**

Eschatological myths, 10:128

Eschatologism, **5:331–332**
  John of Parma, 7:979
  liberal theology, 8:543

Eschatology
  apocalyptic movements, 1:547–548
  Apostolic Fathers, 1:588
  ars moriendi, 1:728
  asceticism, 1:777
  Assumption of Mary, 1:799
  Bonaventure, St., 2:481, 492–493
  chiliasm, 1:547, 3:488
  Christian anthropology, 3:530, 531, 533
  damnation, 4:506
  destiny, supernatural, 4:695
  dispensational theology, 4:776
  iconography of Apostles, 1:576
  Israelite development, 7:633–634
  Sukkot, 2:532
  theology of Church, 3:589
  theology of history, 6:890
  See also Apocalyptic style; Eschatology, in the Bible

Eschatology, in the Bible, **5:332–342**
  abomination of desolation, 1:23
  aeons, 1:139
  Book of Revelation, 12:186
  Christocentrism, 3:558
  conversion, 4:233
  Day of the Lord, 4:547–549
  death, attitudes toward, 4:571
  early Christian way of life, 3:546
  of the Eucharist, 5:412–413
  Jesus as fulfillment, 3:28
  in the New Testament, 5:338–341, 349–350
  in the Old Testament, 5:333–338
  patience, 10:944
  redemption, 11:972

Eschatology, in theology, **5:342–352**, 13:916–917
    Catholic Catechism, 5:346–347
    Catholic theology, 5:345–352
    Christological focus, 5:346, 349–350
    ecological theology, 5:55–57, 58
    historical perspectives, 5:342–345
    post-modernity movement, 5:348
    principles of interpretation, 5:347
    Resurrection debates, 5:350
    sacred time, 12:505–506
    scientific cosmologies, 5:350–351
    Shāpūraqān (Mānī), 9:113
    term defined, 5:56
    See also Parousia
Eschenbach, Wolfram von, 4:401, 7:26, 28
Eschmann, Ignatius T., **5:352**
Escobar, Andrés de, **5:352–353**
Escobar, Diego de, 4:288
Escobar, Marina de, Ven., **5:353**
Escobar y Mendoza, Antonio de, 14:51
El Escorial Palace and Monastery (San Lorenzo, Spain), **5:353–354**, *354*
Escribano, Gregory, Bl., 1:951
Escrivá de Balaguer y Albás, Josemaría, Bl., **5:355**, *356*, 10:*617*, 11:526, 527
Esdras, Books of. *See* Ezra, Book of
Esglis, Louis Philippe Mariaucheau d' (Bp. of Québec), 3:7, **5:355**
Eskil, St., 4:664, 665, **5:357**
Eskil of Lund (Abp.), **5:357**
    Adrian IV (Pope), 1:127
    Alvastra Abbey, 1:327
    Ås Abbey, 1:767
Esmond, John, 7:581
Espada y Landa, Juan José Díaz de (Bp. of Havana), **5:357**
Espań sagrada, 5:774
Espelage, Bernard T. (Bp. of Gallup, NM), 6:81
Espen, Zeger Bernhard, **5:357–358**, 658
Espence, Claude Togniel de, **5:358**
Espín, Orlando, 11:510
Espinal, Luis, 2:470
Espinar, Alonso de, **5:358–359**
Espinareda, Pedro de, **5:359**
Espínola Doria, Próspero, 1:236
Espinosa, Isidro Félix de, **5:359**
L'Espirit humain et ses facultés (Bautain), 2:161
Espíritu Santo (laity association), 3:416
Espolio (El Greco), 6:427
Esposizione storica e dottrinale del diritto penale romano (Ferrini), 5:696

L'Esprit de Leibnitz (Émery), 5:190
L'Esprit de Sainte Thérèse (Émery), 5:190
Esqueda Ramírez, Pedro, St., **5:359–360**
Esquisse d'un tableau historique des progrès de l'esprit humain (Condorcet), 4:74, 5:261
Esquiú, Mamerto (Bp. of Córdoba), 1:651, **5:360**
Esquivel, Adolfo Pérez, 1:655
Essai pour les coniques (Pascal), 10:910
Essai su l'indifférence en matière de religion (Lamennais), 8:308
Essai sur la théologie mystique de l'Église d'Orient (Lossky), 12:436
Essai sur le principe générateur des constitutions politiques (de Maistre), 9:61, 14:139
Essai sur l'indifférence en matière de religion (de Lamennais), 14:138
Essai sur l'origine des connaissances humaines (Condillac), 4:73
Essai sur l'origine des idées (Ventura), 14:442
Essais (Montaigne), 2:115, 9:822, 12:125
Essay Concerning Education (Locke), 5:91
An Essay Concerning Human Understanding (Locke), 3:183, 5:97, 7:295, 8:744, 10:202
Essay on Crimes and Punishments (Tratto dei Delitti e delle Pene) (Beccaria), 2:191
Essay on Greek Architecture (Laugier), 3:679
Essay on Man (Pope), 11:497
Essay on Population (Malthus), 9:83–84
Essay on the Development of Christian Doctrine (Newman), 6:878, 10:333, 339, 734, 812
Essay on the Manners and Mind of Nations (Voltaire), 6:889
An Essay Towards a New Theory of Vision (Berkeley), 2:298
Essays (Emerson), 5:188
Essays, Chiefly Theological (Murray), 10:69
Essays and Poems (Very), 14:148
Essays and Reviews, 1:445
Essays Catholic and Critical (Kirk), 8:182
Essays in Seminary Education (Ellis), 5:170
Essays on the Law of Nature (Locke), 10:202
Essence, **5:360–363**
    accident, 1:60

    activity of intellect, 8:208
    agnosticism, 1:184
    being, 2:206–207
    contemporary thought, 5:362
    contingency, 4:212–214
    definition, 4:610
    distinction, 4:779–780
    freedom, 5:940
    Giles of Rome, 6:220–221
    Greek philosophy, 5:360
    historical development, 5:360–362
    human beings, 5:363
    intellection, 8:204
    material beings, 5:362–363
    Medieval thought, 5:361
    modern thought, 5:361–362
    spiritual beings, 5:363
    Theodoric of Freiberg, 13:881
    Thomistic metaphysics, 10:908, 909–910
    thought, 13:422
    universals, 13:408
    See also Individuation; Substance
Essence and existence, **5:363–368**, 531, 534–536, 539
    Arabian philosophy, 1:672
    contingency, 4:212–214
    dualism, 4:915–916
    Durandus of Saint-Pourçain, 4:948
    simplicity of God, 13:138
Essence of Christianity (Feuerbach), 12:70
Essenes (Jewish sect), **5:368–370**
    Book of Jubilees, 1:549
    early Christian theology, 3:591
    influence, 8:6
    ritual bathing and purification, 2:58
    virginity, 3:322
Esser, Ignatius (Abbot), 12:568
Esta es nuestra fe. Esta es la fe de la iglesia, 3:245
Estalayo García, José, Bl., 4:494
Estate of Thornton v. Caldor, Inc. (1985), 3:662
Estcourt, E. E., 1:438
Este, Alexander (Card.), 5:372
Este, Louis (Card.), 5:371–372
Este family, **5:370–372**
Estepa, José (Bp.), 3:237
Estevao, Padre. *See* Stephens, Thomas
Estevez, Jorge Medina, 7:528
Esther, Book of, **5:372–374**
    canonicity, 3:25
    catechumenate, 3:250
    peace, 11:49

Purim, 11:834–835

Estienne (Étienne) family, **5:374**

Estienne, Henry, 5:374

Estienne, Henry II, 5:374

Estienne, Paul, 5:374

Estienne, Robert, 2:366, 5:374, 518

Estimative power, **5:374–375**, 7:497–498, 13:409

Estissac, Geoffroy d', 3:329

Estius, Gulielmus, **5:375**, 523

Estonia, **5:375–379**, *377*, *378*

Estonian Orthodox Church, 2:746

Estouteville, Estout d', 2:190

Estouteville, Guillaume d' (Card.), **5:379**, 659

Estrada, José Manuel, 1:651

Estrees, César d' (Card.), 3:788

Estudio sobre los Cañaris (González Suárez), 6:345

Estudios sobre la filosofía de S. Tomás (González y Díaz), 12:773

Esztergom family, 7:210

Étaix, R., 3:564

État de la France (Boulainvilliers), 5:702

L'État mystique, sa nature (Saudreau), 12:708

L'État sans Dieu (Nicolas), 10:384

Etchécopar, Auguste (Father), 2:346

Eterianus, Hugo, 2:761, 762

The Eternal Priesthood (Manning), 9:121–122

Eternal truths, phenomenology and, 11:233

Eternal Word Television Network (EWTN), **5:379–380**

Eternity, 1:673, **5:380–383**, 7:349

Eternity of God, **5:383–384**

Ethelbald of Mercia, 4:386

Ethelbert (King of East Anglia), St., **5:384**, 12:531

Ethelbert (King of Kent), St., 3:70, 5:239, **384–385**, *385*

Augustine of Canterbury, St., 1:871

baptism by St. Augustine, 12:536

St. Paul's Cathedral, 8:771

Ethelbert of York (Abp.), 5:103, **385–386**

Ethelburga (Queen of Northumbria), 2:500

Ethelburga, St., 5:386, 14:801–802

Ethelburga, SS., **5:386**

Ethelburga of Barking, St., 5:386

Ethelburga of Lyminge, St., 5:386

Etheldreda, St., 14:801–802

Ethelfeda. *See* Elfleda of Whitby, St.

Ethelhard (Aethelheard) of Canterbury (Abp.), **5:386**

Ethelnoth of Canterbury (Abp.), St., **5:386–387**

Ethelreda (Queen of Northumbria), St., 5:179, 239, *387*, **387**

Ethelwold of Winchester, St., **5:387–388**

Abingdon Abbey, 1:22

Aelfric Grammaticus, 1:136

Alphege of Winchester, St., 1:306

Ely Abbey, 5:179

Hyde Abbey, 7:237

Ether, continuum and, 4:217

Etherius (Bp. of Osma), 5:162

Ethica (Geulincx), 3:184

Ethica amoris, sive theologia sanctorum (Henry of St. Ignatius), 6:756

Ethical and Religious Directives for Catholic Care Services (United States Conference of Catholic Bishops), 5:459

Ethical formalism, 3:254–255, **5:388**, 14:581

Ethical guilt, 6:567

Ethical hedonism, 6:701

Ethical pessimism, 11:168

Ethics, **5:388–392**

Aristotle, 1:683

art, 1:736

asceticism, 1:773

characteristics, 5:388–389

controversy over usury, 14:353

Cyrenaics, 4:464

deontologism, 4:673–674

egoism, 5:107–108

emotive meaning, 8:757

Epicureanism, 5:284–285

existential, 5:537–538

faith in higher power, 8:166

genetic technologies, 7:175–179

Hartmann, Nicolai, 6:656

Hugh of Saint-Victor, 7:158

illuminist, 7:321–322

law related, 8:390–391, 401

Locke's empiricism, 8:745

logical positivists, 8:757

modern thought, 5:394–398

moral necessity, 10:226

moral theology, 5:390, 9:857

naturalism, 10:206

Nichomachean, 1:334, 3:396, 5:439, 10:201, 232, *380*

opposing theories, 5:390

philosophy, 11:280

political, 11:460

professional, 11:743–745

relativism, 12:49

religion, 12:416

Rhazes, 12:211

schools, 5:392

social, 9:867

stoicism, 13:535–536

teleological, 4:160, 13:791

Thomistic conception, 9:90

triage, 14:177–178

womanist theology, 14:823

See also Business ethics; Existential ethics; Medical ethics

Ethics (Abelard), 1:19

Ethics (Bar-Hebraeus), 2:82

Ethics, history of, **5:392–398**

The Ethics of Freedom (Ellul), 5:172

Ethiopia, **5:398–402**

ecclesiastical organization, 5:402

Falashas (Jewish sect), 5:609–700

map, *5:399*

martyrs, 3:207

mission, 1:952, 5:400, 401, 7:689–690, 8:742

monasticism, 9:800

See also Eritrea

Ethiopia Oriental (Santos), 12:686

Ethiopian (Ge'ez) Catholic Church, **5:402–406**

clerical celibacy and marriage, 3:324–325

liturgy, 1:273

Ethiopian (Ge'ez) liturgy, 1:273, 5:400, **406**, 8:713

Ethiopian Orthodox Church, 5:19, 320–321, 398, 401

Ethiopians (Cushites), **5:406–407**, 407

Ethiopic literature, 5:643

Ethnic cleansing, Kosovo, 13:11

Ethnic issues, Knights of Columbus and, 8:190

Ethnic violence, Cyprus, 4:463

Ethology, 2:404

Ethos, as concept, 4:430

Étienne de Bourbon, 5:529

Etimasia (Pentecostal symbols), 11:104

Etiology, **5:407–409**, 14:129

Etruria francescana (Papini Tartagni), 10:861

Etruscan religion, **5:409–410**

Etsi animarum (papal bull, Innocent IV), 14:16

Etsi apostolici principatus (brief, Pius VII), 4:62

Etsi de statu (papal bull, Boniface VIII), 2:502

Etsi pastoralis (apostolic constitution, Benedict XIV), 3:817, 7:651

Ett, Kaspar, 2:842

Étude historique et critique sur le P. Lacordaire (Nicolas), 10:384

Étude sur saint Vincent de Paul (Veuillot), 14:466

Études Bibliques (monograph series), 5:50, 8:280

Études d'ésthétique médiévale (de Bruyne), 3:674

Études d'histoire et de théologie positive (Batiffol), 2:155

Études franciscaines (periodical), 14:261

Études inédites (Sabatier), 12:453

Études philosophiques sur le Christianisme (Nicholas), 10:384

Etudes théologiques sur les constitutions du Concile du Vatican de'après les Acres du Concile (Vacant), 14:365

Etymologiae (St. Isidore of Seville), 7:604–605, 9:439–440, 12:757

Etymologiarum ibri XX (Etymologies) (St. Isidore of Seville), 5:206

Eubel, Konrad, **5:410**

Eubulides of Miletus, 1:681

Eucaristia per la chiesa (Giraudo), 5:430

Euch, Johannes von (Bp. of Denmark), 4:667

Eucharist
  Abraham, 1:37
  accident, 1:60, 64–65
  Aelfric Grammaticus, 1:136
  agape, 1:170
  Agnus Dei, 1:184–186
  Alger of Liége, 1:283
  Alphonsus Liguori, St., 1:309, 312
  altars, 1:314, 318, 320
  anamnesis, 1:382–383
  Anglican and Catholic dialogue, 1:441
  Anglican Reformation, 3:609
  annihilation, 1:471
  Anthroposophy, 1:513
  Armenian liturgy, 1:709
  in the Bible, 5:410–415
  bilocation, 2:396
  bishops, 2:415, 418
  blessings, 2:439
  bread, 2:599
  as breaking of bread, 2:599–600
  burial, 2:700
  Calvinism, 3:608
  Christian (term), 3:529
  Christ's memorial command, 5:420

church architecture, 3:712

Cienfuegos, Álvaro, 3:731

communio, 4:29, 30–31

communion of saints, 4:35, 36

contemporary spirituality, 13:448–449

Copts, 4:256, 257

Council of Trent, 1:64, 65, 3:610

creed, 4:356–357

death, 4:576, 583

devotion to, 3:623, 5:434–436

Durandus of Saint-Pourçain, 4:948

elevation, 5:436

epiclesis, 5:279–282, 422, 426

Epitaph of Abercius, 1:20

eschatology, 5:412–413

extension, 5:569

fasting, 5:437–438

fermentum (eucharistic bread), 5:689

fish as eucharistic symbol, 5:747

Glycas, Michael, 2:759–760

Hus, John, 7:228

iconoclasm, 7:281

Ignatius of Antioch, 7:311

Luther, 3:608

mystagogy, 5:421

names, reading of, 4:758–759

origin of the term, 5:410

outside mass, worship of the, 4:36–38

Paschasius' teaching, 10:918

processions in honor, 11:732

Radical Reformation, 3:608

as sacrament, 5:351–352, 411–412, 416–418

theology of Church, 3:582, 585, 586, 588, 589

unity, 5:413

Utraquists, 3:605

wine, use of, 14:772

Wyclif, John, 3:605

Zwingli, Huldrych, 14:941

See also Breaking of Bread; Eucharist, devotion to; Lord's Supper

Eucharist: Sacrament of the Kingdom (Schmemann), 12:742

Eucharist, exposition of the, **5:415**
  Carolingian reforms, 8:656
  Justin Martyr, St., 8:94–95
  Latin use, 8:364
  Leo I (Pope), St., 8:477
  liturgical history, 8:654
  Middle Ages, 8:658–659
  minor elevation, 8:658

vernacular, 8:365

Eucharist as sacrifice, 5:420, 422, 425

Eucharist in contemporary Catholic tradition, **5:415–430**

The Eucharist in the West (Kilmartin), 5:430

Eucharist Outside Mass, Worship of the, **5:431–433**, 435–436, 824

Eucharistia (Kramp), 8:246

Eucharistic Congresses, 3:623, 5:432–433, **433–434**, 8:224

Eucharistic controversies
  Luther, 8:882
  Lutheranism, 8:895
  Protestantism, 8:129
  Ratramnus, 4:258, 725–726

Eucharistic devotion, 3:623, 764, **5:434–436**, 13:189, 190, 417
  Eucharistic Heart of Jesus, 8:507
  Eucharistic League of Priest Adorers and Women Adorers, 13:228
  kiss of peace, 8:185
  lay spirituality, 8:413, 415, 418
  Louise of France, 8:807
  Sibyllina Biscossi, 13:100

Eucharistic elevation, **5:436–437**
  Ave Verum Corpus, 1:931

Eucharistic epiclesis. *See Epiclesis,* Eucharistic

Eucharistic Fast, **5:437–438**

Eucharistic liturgy
  Basil, St., 2:138
  East Syrian rite, 5:7–8
  healing, 6:680
  reforms and revisions, 5:415–416
  sources, 5:410–411

Eucharistic mission societies, 6:344

Eucharistic Missionaries of Nazareth, 6:344

Eucharistic Missionaries of St. Dominic, 4:843–844

Eucharistic Movement, 8:184

The Eucharistic Mystery (Power), 5:430

Eucharistic prayers, 5:280–282, 421–422
  liturgics, 8:723
  Preface, 11:661, 662
  Sanctus (hymn), 12:664–665

Eucharistic theology, 2:293–294

Eucharisticon de vita sua (Ennodius), 5:265

L'Eucharistie: la Présence réelle et la Transubstantiation (Batiffol), 2:155

Die eucharistische Opferhandlung (Schwane), 12:793

Eucherius of Lyons, St., 1:197, **5:438**, 513, 12:587

Eucherius of Orléans, St., **5:438**

Euchologion (St. Serapion of Thmuis), 1:273, 13:7

Euchologium seu Rituale Graecorum (Goar), 6:268

Eucken, Rudolf, 1:678, 8:579, 12:731

Euclid (Greek mathematician)
analysis and synthesis, 1:381
Elements, 12:805
geometry, 12:804, 13:374
logic, 8:747

Euctemon (Bp. of Smyrna), 1:785

Eudaemonism, **5:439–440**

Eudaemonistic pessimism, 11:168

Eudemus of Rhodes, 1:668

Eudes (King of West Franks). See Odo (King of West Franks)

Eudes, John, St., 2:109, 163, **5:440–441**, 12:491, 499
Bernières-Louvigny, Jean de, 2:325
catechesis, 3:235
Chrysostom of Saint-Lô, John, 3:573
Compagnie du Saint-Sacrement, 4:41
Counter Reformation, 3:612
French School, 13:451
preaching, 11:622
priesthood, 11:704

Eudes I (Duke of Burgundy), 3:751

Eudes Rigauld
See Odo Rigaldus

Eudist Fathers, 3:9

Eudists, **5:441–442**, 8:556

Eudoxia (Byzantine Empress), 2:774, 804, 7:946, 947

Eudoxus of Cnidos
Arianism, 1:663
Aristotelianism, 1:669
astrology, 1:812
early planetary systems, 12:803
School of Antioch, 1:527

Eugendus of Condat, St., **5:442**, 8:63, 12:542

Eugene (Bp. of Carthage), 3:186–187

Eugene I (Pope), St., 2:750, **5:442–443**

Eugene II (III) of Toledo, St., 4:720, **5:445–446**

Eugene II (Pope), 2:753, 3:169, **5:443**

Eugene III (Pope), Bl., **5:443–444**
Armenia, 1:701
Arnold of Brescia, 1:719, 5:444
cardinalate, 3:105
Celestine III (Pope), 3:319
Celles-Sur-Belle Monastery, 3:329
Chaise-Dieu Abbey, 3:361
Clairvaux Abbey, 3:758

Crusades, 2:688, 4:410, 414
Gerlach, St., 6:167
Gilbertines, approval of, 6:216
influence, 3:601
Treaty of Constance, 1:126

Eugene IV (Pope), 5:*444*, **444–445**
Albergati, Niccolò, Bl., 1:219
Albert of Sarteano, Bl., 1:223
Ambrosians, 1:346
Antoninus, St., 1:536, 537
Armenia, 1:702, 706, 711–712
Armenian Church and See of Rome, 1:711–712
Assyrian Church of the East, 1:807
Bourgchier, Thomas, 2:566
Camaldolese, 2:898
Canons Regular of St. Augustine, 3:69
cardinalate, 3:105, 107
Carmelites, 3:134, 145
Charles VII, 6:75
Chichele, Henry, 3:481
Chrysoberges, Andrew, 3:572
Clareni, 3:763
Council of Basel, 1:647, 2:133, 133–134, 3:195, 197, 604, 5:668
Crusades, 3:357
Escobar, Andrés de, 5:353
German Church, relations with, 6:178
Ghibelline-Guelf conflict, 3:855
hospitality, 7:52
Hussites, 7:231
marriage, 4:221

Eugenia (abbess of Hohenberg), St., **5:446**

Eugenianus, Nicetas, 2:806

Eugenics, 5:93–94, 7:177

Eugenicus, Mark (Metropolitan of Ephesus), **5:446–447**
Apostles' Creed, 1:577
Bessarion, Cardinal, 2:340, 341
Chrysoberges, Andrew, 3:572
Council of Florence, 2:828

Eugenius II (Pope), 10:915

Eugenius III (Pope), 6:213–214

Eugenius Vulgarius, **5:447**
Auxilius of Naples, 1:928
Latin literature, 9:448
Sergius III (Pope), 13:15

Euhemerus, **5:447**

Eulalius (Antipope), 3:316, **5:447–448**, 7:87

Eulogius (9th c. monk), 3:863, 7:246, 11:43, 44

Eulogius (Patriarch of Alexandria), St.
Córdoba, 4:261, 262
death, 4:262
manuscript painting, 5:*448*

Eulogius of Córdoba, 12:606

Eunapius of Sardis, 2:798

Eunomius of Constantinople, **5:448–449**
apophatic theology, 1:568
Arianism, 1:663
beatific vision, 2:169, 6:687
knowledge of God, 10:960–961
mystery of God, 6:281

Euntes in mundum (apostolic letter, John Paul II), 7:1003

Euphemia, St., 5:*449*, **449**

Euphemius (Patriarch of Constantinople), 1:50, 386

Euphrasia (Sister), 7:406

Euphrasia, St., **5:449–450**

Euphrasia of the Immaculate Conception, Bl., 4:44

Euripides (Greek playwright), 1:510, 10:93

Eurocentrism, 11:393

Europäismus, 14:212

Europe, patron saints of, 10:975–976

Europe and the Faith (Belloc), 2:231

European civil codes, Islamic adoption of, 7:622

European Convention of the Rights of Man (1950), 1:793

European political model, 8:174

European Society of Women in Theological Research (ESWTR), 5:677

European Union (EU)
Commission of the Bishops' Conferences of the European Community (Comece), 4:13–15
Council of European Bishops' Conferences (CCEE), 4:297–298

European Values Study, 11:727

Euse Hoyos, Mariano de Jesús, Bl., **5:450**

Eusebia of Hamay, St., **5:450**

Eusebia of Saint-Cyr, St., **5:450**

Eusebius (Pope), St., **5:450–451**, 12:387

Eusebius of Caesarea, **5:451–454**, 14:204
Acacius of Caesarea, 1:51
Acts of the Martyrs, 1:92, 93
Agapios of Hierapolis, 1:172
anti-Athanasianism, 4:470
apocrypha, 1:558
Arianism, 1:661, 662, 2:796
Arius, 1:266, 685

Eusebius of Caesarea (*continued*)
Baptism, 4:86
Berossus, 2:329
biblical canon, 3:31
Byzantine civilization, 2:767
Christian way of life, 3:548
Chronicle, 1:460
Chronicles as source, 8:59
church architecture, 1:756
Church history, 3:593
Church of Alexandria, 5:136
Church-State relations, 3:633
Clement I (Pope), St., 3:774
Clement of Alexandria, 3:797
clerical celibacy and marriage, 3:323
Constantine I (the Great) (Roman Emperor), 3:474, 594, 4:180, 181, 182
Constantinople, 4:185
creedal statements, 4:350, 352–353
on the cross, 4:383, 384, 385
Dionysius of Corinth, 4:755
Divisio Apostolorum, 1:575
Domitilla, Flavia, 4:859
editions of works, 13:168
Eleutherius (Pope), 5:148
fermentum (Eucharistic bread), 5:689
historiography, 2:796–797
iconoclasm, 2:796, 7:278, 280
Jerome, St., 3:594
Kingdom of God, 8:174
Lamb of God, 8:30
legends of Abgar, 1:21
life of, 5:451–452
Macarius of Jerusalem, St., 9:2
martyr, as term, 4:83
Neronian persecution, 12:350
Nicene Creed, 1:662
pilgrimages, 11:343–344
sacred kingship, 13:252
School of Antioch, 1:526
School of Caesarea, 2:846, 847
theology of history, 6:888
writings of, 5:452–453, 510, 12:316, 318, 320, 606
Eusebius of Doryleum (Bp.), 3:363, 5:461, 462, 10:254
Eusebius of Emesa (Bp.), 5:82, 83, **454**
Eusebius of Milan, 1:49
Eusebius of Nicomedia (Bp.), 4:181, **5:454–455**
Arianism, 1:266, 661, 662, 685, 817
Athanasius in exile, 8:53
Constantine I (Roman Emperor), 3:594

Nicene Creed, 1:662
School of Antioch, 1:527
Eusebius of Samosata (Bp.), St., **5:455**
Eusebius of Vercelli, St., **5:455**
Arianism, 3:632
cathedral and episcopal schools, 3:262
Liberius (Pope), 8:554
Eusebius Pamphili. *See* Eusebius of Caesarea
Euspicius (founder of Micy Abbey), 9:608
Eustace. *See* Eustathius
Eustace, Bartholomew, 10:282
Eustace, Christopher, 7:579
Eustace, James, 7:581
Eustace, Maurice, **5:455**, 7:579
Eustace, Thomas, 7:579
Eustace, Walter, 7:579
Eustace of Luxeuil, St., 5:325, **455–456**
Acharius of Noyon, St., 1:68
Agil, St., 1:176
Amatus of Remiremont, St., 1:333
Austria, 1:908
Bertulf of Bobbio, St., 2:338
Luxeil Abbey, 8:899
Eustachia a S. Paolo (French Cistercian), 12:768
Eustachius of Jerusalem, 4:191
Eustathios (Bp. of Khytri), 4:634
Eustathius Dyrrachiensis, 2:825
Eustathius of Antioch (Bp.), St., **5:456**
Christology, 1:527, 3:561
Constantine, 4:181
Eusebius of Caesarea, 5:452
Eusebius of Nicomedia, 5:454
homoousios, 4:198, 353
Nicene Creed, 1:662, 817, 4:352
School of Antioch, 5:511
Eustathius of Sebaste (Bp.), **5:456–457**
Arianism, opposition to, 2:139
Atticus of Constantinople, St., 1:839
monasticism, 9:789
Eustathius of Thessalonica (Abp.)
philosophy, 2:809
poetry, 2:803, 804
Eustochia of Padua, Bl., **5:457**
Eustochium, St., **5:457**, 11:344
Eustratius of Nicaea, 2:759, 825
Euthanasia, **5:457–459**
Catholic moral teaching, 5:458–459
Germany, 6:187
history, 5:458
legalization, Belgium, 2:221–222

Euthymius (Abbot of Iviron), 2:100
Euthymius I (Patriarch of Constantinople), 1:646, 2:756, **5:460**, 8:474
Euthymius Saifi (Abp. of Tyre and Sidon), 1:525
Euthymius the Great, St., 1:707, **5:460–461**, *461*
Cyril of Scythopolis, 4:473
Gerasimus, St., 6:163
lauras, 8:381
Eutrapelia (recreation), **5:461**, 7:305
Eutyches (Abbot), **5:461**
Acacian Schism, 1:49, 50
Apollinarianism, 1:559
Christology, 1:273, 3:561
condemnation and deposition, 5:462, 759
consubstantiality, 4:198, 7:66
Council of Chalcedon, 1:525
Council of Orléans, 1:895
Dioscorus (Patriarch of Alexandria), 4:756
Domnus of Antioch, 4:859–860
Hormisdas (Pope), St., 3:595
Robber Council of Ephesus, 1:392, 3:363, 5:275, 461, 462
School of Alexandria, 1:272, 273
two natures of Christ, 7:816–817
See also Monophysitism
Eutychian (Pope), St., **5:461–462**
Eutychianism, 1:268–269, 816, **5:462**
Eutychios of Alexandria, **5:462–463**
Eutychius (Patriarch of Constantinople), **5:463**
Constantinople Council II, 4:191–192
Julianists, 8:52
Euzoius, 2:846
Eva of Liège, Bl., **5:463–464**
Evagrius Ponticus, **5:464–465**, 10:397, 659
acedia, 1:66
apocatastasis, 1:548
Byzantine theology, 2:793
Cassian, John, 3:207
Church history, 3:594
doctrine, 5:465
Letter to Melania, 5:464, 465
life, 5:464
Oriental moral theology, 9:860
translated into Syriac, 13:16
works, 5:464
Evagrius Scholasticus, 2:797, **5:465–466**, 6:872, 12:320
Evangelary (Book of Gospels), **5:466–467**, 8:436–437

Evangeliarium (Ebbo of Reims), 5:28

Evangeliary of Otto III, 9:128–129

Evangelica Testificatio (apostolic exhortation, Paul VI), 1:29, 3:393, 806

Evangelical Alliance, **5:467–468**, 8:597, 12:726

Evangelical Alliance for the U.S., 5:467

Evangelical and Reformed Church, 4:117–118, **5:468**

Evangelical Brethren Church, 5:469

Evangelical Church, 1:234, **5:468–469**, 471, 14:306–308

Evangelical Church in Germany (EKD), **5:469–470**, 8:186

Evangelical churches, Jamaica, 3:112–113

Evangelical Congregational Church, 5:472

Evangelical Czech Brethren Church, 2:461

Evangelical Foreign Mission Society, 5:473

Evangelical Lutheran Church in America (ELCA), **5:470–471**, 8:887

Evangelical Protestant Missionary Union, 8:597

Evangelical Synod of North America, 4:117, 5:468

Evangelical Union, 8:794

Evangelical United Brethren (EUB), 2:606, 4:199, 200, 5:469, **471–472**, 9:561, 14:308

Evangelicalism, **5:472–474**

    Anglicanism, 1:444

    Knox, J., 8:225

    monasticism, 9:787

    origins, 8:370

    Waldenses, 14:607–608

    Wesley, J., 8:87

Evangelical-Roman Catholic Dialogue on Mission, 5:69

L'Évangelie et l'Église (Loisy), 8:766

Evangelii nuntiandi (On Evangelization in the Modern World) (apostolic exhortation, Paul VI), 4:157, 5:39, **473–474**, 478, 6:127, 9:682, 689, 11:32

Evangelii praecones (papal letter, Pius XII), 9:681

El Evangelio en triunfo o historia de un filósofo desengañado (Olavide y Jauregui), 10:579

Evangelistarium, 5:466

Evangelists, **5:474–475**

Evangelists, iconography of, **5:475–476**

Evangelium, 10:45

Evangelium Infantiae Salvatoris arabicum, 1:559

Evangelium Pseudo-Matthaei, 1:558–559

Evangelium vitae (encyclical, John Paul II), 3:88, 238, 5:205, 459, **476–477**, 560, 7:998, 1003, 10:179, 852

    abortion, 1:24

    animal rights, 1:456

    solidarity, 13:302

Evangelization

    Community of Sant'Egidio, 12:672–673

    conversion, 4:240–241

    Dominicans, 4:847, 850–851

    Europe, 4:296

    Illig, Alvin Anthony, 7:316

    McPherson, Aimee Semple, 5:835–836

    papal writings, 5:39

    See also Mission and evangelization; Mission and evangelization, Canon Law; Mission and evangelization, papal writings on

Evangelization, new, **5:477–480**

Evangelization of Peoples, Congregation for the (CEP), **5:480–481**, 9:682, 687, 692, 693

    Albania, 1:217

    Zago, Marcello, 14:905

    See also Congregation for the Propagation of the Faith

L'Évangile et L'Église (Loisy), 9:754

Évangiles des domées (Sunday Gospels), 5:846

Les Évangiles et la seconde géneration chrétienne (Renan), 12:126

Evanglii nuntiandi (papal exhortation, Paul IV), 8:417

Evans, Hiram Wesley, 8:252

Evans, Philip, St., 5:237, **481–482**, 10:495

Evans, Warren F., 10:308

Evans-Pritchard, E. E., 12:65

Evansville Diocese (IN), 7:416

Evaristus (Pope), St., 3:103, **5:482**

Eve, **5:482–484**

    Adam, 1:104

    Adam and Eve, engraving by William Morris, 5:*483*

    in the Bible, 5:408, 482–483

    etiology of her name, 5:408

    iconography of serpent, 13:*21*

    iconography of temptation, 13:*141*

    Manichaeism, 9:112

    Mary, Blessed Virgin, compared to, 9:168–169, 174, 255, 258, 265–266, 14:536

    Mary as new, 13:37

    sex as primordial sacrament, 13:46

    theology, 5:483–484

    Tree of Knowledge of Good and Evil, plucking apple from (bas relief), 5:*484*

Eve of St. Martin, 4:272

Everard of Ypres, **5:484–485**, 13:102

Everett, Edward, 3:472

Evergislus (Bp. of Cologne), St., **5:485**

Evergreen (sexual reorientation group), 7:69

Evermode, St., 11:666

Evers, Christopher. *See* Bales, Christopher, Bl.

Everson v. Board of Education (1947), 1:356, 3:660, 665, 667

Everwin (prior of Steinfeld), 1:594

Everyman (morality play), **5:485–486**, 9:882

Everything That Rises Must Converge (O'Connor), 10:547

Evesham Abbey (England), **5:486–487**

Evidence, 8:203, 10:18

Evidentia Durandelli contra Durandum (Durandellus), 14:47

Evil, **5:487–491**

    causality, 3:303

    as disorder, 14:331–332

    distinguishing nonbeing from, 10:416–417

    Honorius of Autun, 7:89

    Manichaeism, 1:852, 856–857

    moral circumstances, 3:743

    morality, 9:875

    New Age Movement failure to address, 10:275

    Philo Judaeus, 11:270–271

    sin, external causes, 13:154

    theism, 13:863

    theodicy, 13:867

    See also Demons and spirits; Good and evil

Evil Eye, **5:491**

Evil gods (Mesopotamia), 9:533

Evocative symbols, 13:661

Evodius of Antioch (Bp.), St., **5:491–492**

Evolution, 3:623, 5:260, 397–398, **492–496**

    Adam, 1:105–106

    Bergson, Henri, 2:295–297, 5:398

    biology, 2:403, 404, 407

    Church-State relations, 3:667

    creation doctrine, 4:345, 347

    creationism, 4:346–347

Evolution *(continued)*
    cultures, theories of, 4:433–434
    Darwin, Charles, 4:531–532, 5:492, 495, 496
    hominisation, 7:64–65
    Humani generis, 7:181
    hylozoism, 7:250
    monogenism and polygenism, 9:813
    phenomenology, 8:513
    religions, 12:64–65
    Scopes trial, 6:28, 30
    soul's origins, 13:354
    Spencer, Herbert, 5:397
    See also Evolutionism
L'Evolution homogéne du dogme catholique (Marín-Sola), 9:166–167
Evolutionary conversion, 4:235–238
Evolutionary historicism, irrationalism and, 7:586
Evolutionary Naturalism (Sellars), 10:204
Evolutionism
    Alexander, Samuel, 1:252
    animism, 1:458–459
    causality, 3:306–307
    Cournot, Antoine Augustine, 4:316
    man, concept of, 9:91
    man, natural end of, 9:99
    social, 13:413
Evrard of Béthune, **5:496–497**
Évroul (Ebrulf), St., **5:497**, 12:545
Évroul of Ouche, 5:497
Évroul of Saint-Fuscienau-Bois, St., **5:497**
Ewald, Black, St., 5:497
Ewald, Black and White, SS., **5:497**
Ewald, G. H. A., 5:519, 11:90
Ewald, White, St., 5:497
Ewing, Charles and Thomas, **5:497–498**
Ex cathedra, 3:361, **5:498**, 10:453
Ex corde ecclesiase (apostolic constitution, John Paul II), 3:58, 292, **5:498–499**, 7:1002
    Catholic education, 1:54–55, 56
    Jesuits, 7:795
Ex debito (apostolic constitution, John XXII), 4:950
Ex illa die (papal decree, Clement XI), 3:498, 515
Ex iniuncto (brief, Clement XIV), 1:534
Ex more docti mystico (hymn), **5:499**
Ex nihilo nihil fit (From nothing, nothing comes), 12:755
Ex omnibus afflictionibus (papal bull, Pius V), 2:19, 4:4, **5:499–500**
Ex opere Christi, 12:469

Ex opere operantis, **5:500–501**
Ex opere operantis Ecclesiae, 5:500
Ex opere operatis, 5:500, **501–502**, 6:406, 406–407, 12:469
Ex quo singulari (papal decree, Benedict XIV), 3:498, 515, 516
Exaemeron (Bartholomew of Lucca), 2:126
Exafernon pronosticorum temporis (Richard of Wallingford), 12:236
Exaltation of the Cross, 4:383
Examen concilii Tridentini (Chemnitz), 3:463
Examen de conscience sur les devoirs de la royauté (Fénelon), 5:683
L'Examen de la philosophie de Bacon (Maistre), 9:61
Examen philosophicotheologicum de ontologismo (Lepidi), 8:507
Examen vanitatis doctrinae gentium (Pico Della Mirandola), 11:324
Examens particuliers sur divers sujets propres aux ecclésiastiques (Tronson), 14:214
Example acripturae epigraphicae latinae (Hübner), 10:774
Exarch, **5:502**
    apostolic, 5:503
    independent, 5:503
    patriarchal (archiepiscopal), 5:503
    See also Feodorov, Leonid (Russian Byzantine exarch)
Exarchy, **5:502–503**
Excerpta (canonical collection), 6:862
Excerpta legum edita a Bulgarino Causidico, 10:642
Excerpts from the works of Theodotus and the school called Oriental from the time of Valentinus (Theodotus), 13:885
Exchange of hearts, 10:108
Excluded middle, principle of the, 4:213, **5:503–504**, 745
Excommunicamus (apostolic constitution, Gregory IX), 3:87
''Excommunicamus'' (Fourth Lateran Council), 1:231
Excommunication, **5:504–506**
    Basil, St., 2:138
    communists, 4:418
    Council of Trent, 3:54
    Elivra Council, 5:178
    Erastus, 5:317
    Lefebvre, M., 8:448
    Mayer, A. Castro de, 8:448
    Protestant Reformation, 3:637
Executive Newsletter, 10:164

Executive powers, 6:374
Exegesis, biblical, **5:506–524**
    Africa, 8:63
    allegory, 1:292, 337, 5:507–508
    Amalarius of Metz, 1:329
    Ambrose, St., 1:337, 339
    analogy of faith, 1:380
    Andrew of Saint-Victor, 1:406–407
    Arethas, 1:646–647
    Berruyer, Isaac Joseph, 2:330
    Bible Moralisée, 2:376
    biblical theology, 2:389–390
    Bonfrère, Jacques, 2:494
    Bossuet, Jacques Bénigne, 2:884
    Brown, Raymond Edward, 2:638
    Bultmann, Rudolf Karl, 2:690–691
    Burkitt, Francis Crawford, 2:705
    Cajetan (Tommaso de Vio), 2:854, 855
    Calmet, Augustin, 2:883–884
    Christian of Stablo, 3:537
    Claudius of Turin, 3:769–770
    Coleridge, Samuel Taylor, 3:832
    documentary hypothesis, 1:814
    Húgel, F. von, 9:755
    Hugh of Saint-Victor, 7:157–158
    Ibn Ezra, Abraham ben Meír, 7:271–272
    Isidore of Seville, St., 7:604
    Jerome, St., 7:759
    Jewish, 1:35–36, 5:508
    Lamb of God, 8:299–301
    Lapide, C. A., 8:332
    Leo XIII, 8:492
    Lightfoot, J. B., 8:585
    literal, 1:406–407
    19th and 20th centuries, 3:623, 5:519–523, 521–523
    Pentateuch, 8:129
    Pius XII, 4:790–792
    progressive, 3:174
    Rashi, 11:914–915
    School of Alexandria, 1:269, 272, 524
    School of Antioch, 1:269, 272, 524, 527, 8:844
    seventy weeks of years, 13:40
    Smith, W.R., 13:236
    spiritual sense, 5:513–514
    theology, 13:914–915
    See also Biblical theology
Exegetes, 12:181–182, 405, 449–450
Exegetica (Basilides), 2:148
Exemplarism, **5:524–527**
    Augustinianism, 1:878

Bonaventure, St., 2:486
causality, 3:303
idea, 7:293
Exemplarity of God, **5:527–528**
Exemplary Causality, 3:298, **5:528**
Exemplum, **5:528–529**
Exemption
 Abbots, 1:10
 annates, 1:466
 Bobbio Abbey, 2:338, 446
 Canons Regular of St. Augustine, 3:68
 Monte Cassino Archabbey, 2:331
Exemption, history of, 4:450, **5:529–530**, 8:788
Exercises for the Spiritual Life (Ejercitatorio de la vida espiritual) (Cisneros), 3:744
Exercitations paradoxicae adversus Aristoteleos (Unpopular Essays against the Aristotelians) (Gassendi), 6:105
Exercitia Conventualia (1615), 14:122
Exercitia spiritualia (St. Gertrude the Great), 6:191
Exeter, Ancient See of (England), 4:317, **5:530–531**
Exeter, Synod of, 4:88
Exeter Cathedral (Devon, England), 5:530, *531*
Exhortation to Martyrdom (Origen), 10:655
"An Exhortation to Peace in Response to the Twelve Articles of the Swabian Peasants" (Luther), 11:53
Exhortation to the Greeks (Clement of Alexandria), 11:414
Exigitordo or *Satis exigit ordo* (Nicholas of Autrecourt), 10:370
Exiit Qui Seminat (apostolic constitution, Nicholas III), 5:902
Exile, conversion in, 4:232–233
Exile of Israel, 7:643
Eximeno y Pujader, Antonio, 12:770
Existence, **5:531–537**
 accident, 1:60
 act, 1:73
 agnosticism, 1:183
 Aquinas, 8:25, 26, 13:575
 causality, 3:300, 304
 conservation, Divine, 4:160–163
 contingency, 4:212–214
 created actuation by uncreated act, 4:335–336
 existential psychology, 5:541
 form, 5:802–806
 history of the concept of, 5:532–534

human soul, 13:349
the individual, 5:544–545
intentional levels, 5:531–532
notion, 5:531
participation, 5:526
Siger of Brabant, 13:113
Theodoric of Freiberg, 13:881
truth in judgment, 14:227
Existenialism and Humanism (Sartre), 12:697
Existential ethics, **5:537–538**
 evaluation and critique, 5:538
 "I-Thou" relationship, 5:537–538
 situational ethics, 5:537
Existential metaphysics, **5:538–541**
Existential phenomenology, 11:232–233
Existential psychology, **5:541–543**
Existential theology, 4:25, **5:543–544**, 11:460
Existentialism, **5:544–547**, 11:284, 298
 absurdity, 1:48–49
 activism, 1:83
 agnosticism, 1:184
 anthropocentrism, 1:508
 Aristotelianism, 1:678
 atheism, 1:823
 Augustinianism, 1:882
 bridging gap between subject and object, 10:510
 Buber, Martin, 2:652
 Christian philosophy, 3:539
 communication, 4:25
 community, 4:38–39
 consciousness, 4:154
 critique, 5:547
 development, 4:808
 dogmatic theology, 4:820
 eclecticism, 5:47
 educational philosophy, 5:94–95
 essence, 5:362
 ethics, 5:398
 existence of God, 6:315
 Hegelianism influence, 6:712–713
 Humani generis, 7:181
 humanism, 7:182, 186
 influence, 9:865
 irrationalism, 7:587
 knowledge, 8:219, 221–222
 as life philosophy, 8:580
 Maine de Biran, 9:60
 man, concept of, 9:91
 Marcel, Gabriel, 9:133–134
 metaphysics, 9:549–550
 Nietzsche's influence, 10:390

nonscholastic realism, 11:944–945
notion of order, 10:630
notion of truth, 14:223
phenomenology, 12:3
philosophy and science, 11:300
philosophy of religion, 12:70
precursors, 8:165–167
Sartre, Jean-Paul, 12:695–697
soul, 13:348
universals, 14:327
Existentialism and Humanism (Sartre), 7:197
Exmew, William, Bl., 5:225, **547**, 9:617
Exodus, 7:636–637, 8:5
Exodus (sexual reorientation group), 7:69
Exodus, Book of, 1:*3*, **5:547–550**
 Aaron, 1:2–3
 adultery, 1:131, 13:50
 aseity, 1:779
 beatific vision, 2:170, 171
 book of the covenant, 2:526–527
 "breastpiece of decision," 11:646
 contents, 5:548–549
 covenant, 4:327
 Covenant, Book of, 8:397
 cult Decalogue, 8:397
 Dead Sea Scrolls version, 4:562
 Divine election of Israel, 5:145, 146
 El (God), 5:143
 enmity, 5:264
 friendship with God, 6:10
 Gentiles, 6:140
 glory, 6:243–244
 God, name of, 6:298
 God as redeemer, 11:965
 God's spirit, 13:426
 grace, 6:381
 guilt, 6:570
 heaven, 6:684
 ineffability of God, 7:445
 infused knowledge, 8:207
 justification, 8:76
 Kingdom of God, 8:173
 laity, 8:290
 Lamb of God, 8:302
 leprosy, 8:509
 Lord as honorific title, 8:780
 magic, 9:39
 manna, 9:118–119
 names for God, 13:77
 origin, 5:549–550
 on the Passover, 10:933, 934, 935
 Passover vigil, 5:15

Exodus, Book of (continued)
 peace, 11:49
 pesach, 5:11
 pilgrimages, 11:342
 plagues of Egypt, 11:403–405
 Priestly Code, 8:397
 pure and impure, 11:822
 Red Sea, 11:962
 redemption, 11:963
 retaliation, 8:394
 royal priesthood, 11:692
 Sabbath, 12:456
 seraphim, 13:5–6
 serpent as symbol, 13:20
 Shaddai, 13:58
 Shechem covenant, 13:72
 showbread, 13:88
 simplicity of God, 13:137
 sin, 13:144
 slavery, 13:206, 207, 456
 spirit, 13:424
 Ten Commandments, 4:4–9
 theology, 5:550
 word of God, 14:836–837
Exomologesis, 4:75, 77, **5:550–551**
Exorcism, **5:551–553**
 baptism, 2:63
 dance madness, 3:526
 of the devil, manuscript illustration of, 5:*551*
 Saint Benedict Exorcises a Demon from a Possessed Man (Il Sodoma), 5:*552*
Exorcists, holy orders of, 7:37
Exordium magnum Cisterciense (Conrad), 5:29
Exordium parvum, 12:268
Exoticon (Alexander of Hales), 1:265
Experience, **5:553–555**
 criteriology, 4:368
 empiricism, 5:196
 first principles, 5:743–744
 identity principle, 7:304
 Locke, J., 8:744
 Maine de Biran, 9:60
 Schleiermacher, Friedrich Daniel Ernst, 9:752
 Wolff, Christian, 14:807
Experience, religious, **5:555–557**
Experience and Nature (Dewey), 10:205
Experience theology, **5:557**
Experiences and Expectations: The Fortieth Anniversary of the Institue of the Institute of Judeo-Christian Studies (Oesterreicher), 10:559

Experimental psychology, 6:14–15
Experimentation, medical, **5:558–561**
 for the benefit of others, 5:558–559
 Catholic teaching, 5:560–561
 governmental regulation, 5:560
 informed consent, 5:561
 medical and public concern, 5:559–560
 for the subjecct's benefit, 5:558
Expiation, **5:561–562**
 avoiding sin, 13:148
 sin offering, 13:159
 spiritual theology, 5:566
 See also Satisfaction of Christ; Soteriology
Expiation, in the Bible, **5:562–565**
 religious significance of blood, 2:444
 sin offering, 13:159
Expiation, in theology, **5:565–566**
Explanation of the Sayings of the Lord (Eusebius), 10:861
An Explanation of the Thirty-Nine Articles of the Church of England (Forbes), 5:795
Explantory laws, 6:882–883
Explicanción del catecismo de la doctrina cristiana (Thiel), 14:1
Explicatio Apologetica in Hexaemeron (St. Gregory of Nyssa), 5:510, 6:519
L'Explication des Maximes des Saints sur la vie intérieure (Fénelon), 5:682
Explorata Res (apostolic letter, Pius XI), 1:483
Exploration. *See specific countries; specific explorers; specific missions*
Exploring a Theology of Education (Fitzpatrick), 5:753
The Explusion from Eden (Masaccio), 6:*132*
Exponi nobis (apostolic brief, Urban VIII), 2:143
Exponi nobis (papal brief, Clement XIII), 11:467
Exposcit debitum (papal bull, Julius III), 7:313
Exposición de varios pasajes de la Sagrada Escritura (Sorazu), 13:325
Expositio antiquae liturgiae gallicanae, 8:653
Expositio brevis antiquae liturgiae Gallicanae, 6:71
Expositio continua (St. Albert the Great), 5:517
Expositio epistolae ad Romanos (Cassiodorus), 3:208
Expositio in canticum canticorum (Aquinas), 14:25

Expositio in Dionysium de divinis nominibus (Aquinas), 14:27
Expositio in evangelium Joannis (Aquinas), 14:25–26
Expositio in evangelium s. Matthaei (Aquinas), 14:25
Expositio in isaiam prophetam (Aquinas), 14:25
Expositio in Jeremiam prophetam (Aquinas), 14:25
Expositio in Job ad litteram (Aquinas), 14:25
Expositio in librum Boethii de hebdomadibus (Aquinas), 14:26
Expositio in Psalmis (Gerhoh of Reichersberg), 6:167
Expositio in Psalterium Davidis (Ludolf), 8:853
Expositio in regulam s. Benedicti (Smaragdus), 13:228
Expositio in s. Pauli epistolas (Aquinas), 14:26
Expositio in threnos Jeremiae prophetae (Aquinas), 14:25
Expositio moralis et mysticia in Canticum Canticorum (La Puente), 8:334
Expositio quattuor magistrorum super regulam fratrum minorum, 1241-1242 (Oliger), 10:584
Expositio regulae quatuor magistrorum (Odo Rigaldus), 10:555
Expositio super librum Boethii de Trinitate (Aquinas), 14:26
Exposition de la doctrine chrétienne. . . (Mésenguy), 3:792
Exposition des principes sur la Constitution civile (1790), 10:846
Exposition of 1 John (Tyndale), 14:253
Exposition of Aristotle's Nicomachean Ethics (Aquinas), 5:389
Exposition of Matthew 5, 6, 7 (Luther), 14:253
''An Exposition of the Canticle of Canticles'' (Bartholomew of Vicenza), 2:128
Exposition of the Orthodox Faith (Ekthesis) (St. John Damascene), 7:952
Exposition thrones, 1:317
Expositiones missae, 8:656
Expositions on the First Book of Kings (St. Gregory I), 6:482
Expression, as transcendental principle, 4:372–374
Expressionism, aesthetics and, 1:142
Expressive leadership, men vs. women, 14:813

Expugnatio Hibernica (Giraldus Cambrensis), 6:231

Exsecrabilis (papal bull, Pius II), 4:58, 6:608, 11:369

Exsufflation, during baptism, 2:63

Exsul familia (apostolic constitution, Pius XII), 7:522, 11:482

Exsultate Deo (papal bull, Eugene IV), 1:711–712, 4:221, 12:470

Exsultet Iam Angelica Turba (hymn), 5:16, **566–568**

Exsultet Orbis Gaudiis (hymn), **5:568**

Exsurge Domine (papal bull, Adrian VI), 1:66, 3:482, 609

Exsurge Domine (papal bull, Leo X), 7:438

    excommunication of Luther, 5:43

    Luther condemned, 8:488

Extension, **5:568–570**

    accident, 1:61

    causality, 3:306

    continuum, 4:214–215

    Leibniz, 8:457

    mathematical space, 13:374

    matter, 9:344

    simplicity of God, 13:138

Extension Magazine, 8:137–138

External Religion (Tyrrell), 14:258

The Extinction of Pauperism (Napoleon), 10:150

Extispicy, 4:785

Extractio (Gallus), 14:30

Extraordinary ministers, priests as, 7:38–39

Extraordinary processions, 11:732

Extraordinary Synod of 1985, 7:1001

Extravagantes, **5:570**

Extravagantes (John XXII), 4:273

Extravagantes Communes, 3:50

Extravagantes Ioannis XXII, 3:50

Extreme Unction. *See* Anointing of the Sick, Sacrament of

Extrinsic modes, 9:751

Extrinsicism, **5:570–571**, 12:621, 622

Exuperious (Bp. of Bayeux), St., 2:163

Exuperius of Toulouse (Bp.), St., **5:571**

Eybler, Joseph von, 1:234

Eyes, patroness of, 8:849

Eymard, Pierre Julien, St., 2:436, 437, 5:435, **571–572**

Eymerie, Nicholas, 1:239

Eynon, John, Bl., 5:226, 627, 12:406

Eynsham Abbey (England), 1:136

Eyraud, Françoise (Sister), 12:554

Eyre, Thomas, **5:572**

Eyston, Charles, **5:572**

Eyzaguirre, José Alejo, **5:572–573**

Eyzaguirre, José Ignacio Víctor de, **5:573**

Ezekiel (Hebrew prophet), **5:573–575**, 11:*759*, *766*

    altarpiece by Buoninsegna, 5:*574*

    Baal cult, opposition to, 2:2

    deportation, 4:674

Ezekiel, Book of, **5:575–578**

    Antichrist, 1:515

    apocalyptic style, 1:546

    authenticity, 5:575

    Baal, 2:2

    Babylonia, 2:5

    beatific vision, 2:171

    canonicity, 3:24

    cherubim, 3:466–467

    conversion, 4:233

    covenant, 4:327

    curses, 4:442

    Day of the Lord, 4:548

    El (God), 5:143

    eschatlogy, 5:335

    exile of Judah, 13:40

    Gentiles, 6:140

    God's spirit, 13:426, 427

    guilt, 6:570

    holiness of the Temple, 14:857

    Kingdom of God, 8:173

    literary character, 5:577–578

    Lord as honorific title, 8:780

    magic, 9:39

    on the Passover, 10:934

    peace, 11:49

    precious stones, 11:646

    prophecies, 9:543

    pure and impure, 11:822

    ritual bathing and purification, as symbol of baptism, 2:57–58

    serpent as symbol, 13:20

    sin, 13:143, 145, 153

    slavery, 13:207

    Son of God, 13:310

    Son of Man, 13:316

    Song of Songs, 13:319

    spirit, 13:424

    structure and contents, 5:575–576

    theology, 5:578

    virginity, 14:544

    word of God, 14:837

Ezekiel, Canticles of, 3:73

Ezquerra, Pablo, 3:136

Ezra (Hebrew priest), **5:578–579**

    biblical canon, 3:23, 25

    Judaism origins, 8:2–3

    reform under, 7:644

Ezra, Book of, 1:549–550, 552, 3:567–568, **5:579**

    Aramaic language, 1:627

    biblical canon, 3:25

    canonicity, 3:26

    censuses, 3:338

    Gentiles, 6:140

    God's spirit, 13:427

    inheritance, 7:464

    slavery, 13:207

    Son of Man, 13:317

    See also Biblical Chronicler

F

Faà di Bruno, Francesco, Bl., **5:581**

Faber, Frederick William, 3:271, **5:581–582**, *582*

Faber, Geoffrey, 5:160

Faber, Johann Augustanus, **5:583**

Faber, Johannes (Bp. of Vienna), **5:583**

Faber, Peter, Bl., 3:16, **5:583–584**, *584*, 8:326, 12:280, 14:877

Faber and Faber, 5:160, 161

Fabian (Pope), St., 1:636, 3:105, 222, **5:584**

Fabiola (Wiseman), 14:797

Fabiola, St., 3:406, **5:585**, 7:127

Fabius (Bp. of Antioch), 4:270

Fable of the Bees (Mandeville), 5:107

Fables (Fénelon), 5:682

Fables, nature of, 8:516

Fabré-Palaprat, Bernard, 3:449

Fabri, Filippo (Faber), **5:585**

Fabri, Honoré, 12:771

Fabri, Johannes, 1:848, 3:609

Fabro, C., 1:378, 5:539, 12:776

Fachinetti, Giovanni Antonio (Card.). *See* Innocent IX (Pope)

Facism, 5:328

Faculties of the soul, **5:585–587**

    Alexander of Hales, 1:266

    basic principle, 13:408

    creative imagination, 4:348

    Duns Scotus, John, 4:937

    origin of human soul, 13:337

    parts of soul, 13:335

    power parts, 13:351

    See also Sensation

Facundus of Hermiane (African Bp.), 3:596, 4:192, **5:587–588**

FADICA (Foundations and Donors Interested in Catholic Activities), **5:588**

Faeroe Islands, 4:666–667

Fagaras (Romanian ecclesiastical province), 12:331

Fage, Marie-Antoinette, 1:802, 8:616

Fagius, Paul, 6:697

Fagnani, Prospero, **5:588–589**

Fagnano, José, **5:589**

Fahey, Leo F. (Bp.), 2:23

Faidit, Gaucelm, 4:400

The Fairest Argument (Noll), 10:410

Faith, **5:589–604**

   as a habit, 6:599

   abiding in Christ, 1:22

   achieving, 8:476

   Alger of Liége, 1:283

   analogy, 1:380–381

   Anselm of Canterbury, St., 1:495–496

   apostolic, 1:586–587

   articles, 1:764–765

   Ascension of Jesus Christ, 1:771

   Augustine, St., 1:862–863, 876

   in the Bible, 5:589–593

   Calvin, John, 2:892

   Catholic teaching, 5:594–595

   certitude, 3:355–356, 357

   Christian philosophy, 3:539

   commitment, 4:15–16

   contemplation, 4:204–205

   conversion, 4:240–241

   created actuation by uncreated act, 4:336

   death, 4:575

   denial, 11:740

   deposit, 4:675

   doctrine, development of, 4:803–806

   dogmatism, 4:611–612, 815, 816–817

   Durandus of Saint-Pourçain, 4:948

   dynamics, 13:235–236

   evidence, 9:667

   God as subject of, 6:310

   grace, 6:382

   growth and meaning (Christ's divinity), 7:824–826

   Hermesianism, 6:798

   hope compared to, 7:92, 94, 96, 100–101

   idolatry opposed to, 7:305

   infallibility, 7:448–449

   Isaiah's message, 7:597–598

   Judaism, 5:590–591

   kerygma, 8:158

   liturgy, relationship, 8:715

   Lutheranism, 8:893–894

   Maine de Biran, 9:60

   man, renewal of, 9:87

   moral theology, 9:869

   Ockhamish on role, 10:536

   ontological argument to understand, 10:602, 603

   Patristic tradition, 5:593–594

   profession through baptism, 2:59

   reason, 6:311

   role apostolic tradtion, 7:801–802

   Rule of Faith, 12:409–410

   science linked in theology, 13:923

   Semi-Pelagianism, 12:899–900

   as soul source of justification, 8:87, 88, 881, 892

   spiritual reading, 11:941

   as supernatural gift, 8:202

   teaching authorities of the Church, 13:775–778

   theology, 2:223–224, 5:595–596, 10:83, 84, 13:925–927

   unity, 14:319

   Weltanschauung (world view), 14:677

   See also Beliefs; Conscience

Faith, act of, **5:603–604**

Faith, beginning of, 4:239–240, **5:604–605**

Faith, Hope, and Charity, SS., **5:608–609**

Faith, St., 5:608–609

Faith and Morals, **5:605–606**

Faith and Order Commission, World Council of Churches, 5:40, 67, **606–608**

   filioque, 5:721

   Lima Text, 8:588–590

   revelation, 12:191

   sacraments, 12:477

Faith and Order Conferences

   (1925) Lausanne, 5:72

   (1937) Edinburgh, 5:72, 73

   (1960) St. Andrews, Scotland, 5:73

   (1963) Montreal, 5:73

Faith and Order Movement, 5:71, 72, 606, 14:841

Faith and practice, Islam distinction between, 7:608

Faith and Reason. See Fides et Ratio (Faith and Reason) (encyclical, John Paul II); *Fides et Ratio (Faith and Reason)* (encyclical, John Paul II)

Faith expressions. *See* Popular piety

Faith in Action (Santa Fe, NM), 12:678

Faith of Jesus, Society of the (Paccanarists), 10:528, 740

The Faith of Our Fathers (Gibbons), 6:204, 10:67

The Faith of the Millions (1901), 14:258

Faithful, **5:609**, 12:202

A Faithful Narrative of the Surprising Work of God (Edwards), 5:97

The Faithful Wife (Undset), 14:295

Les Faits extraordinaires de la vie spirituelle (Saudreau), 12:708

Fajia (legalism), 3:509–510

Fakenham, Nicholas de, 3:51

Fakhr al-Dīn al-Rāzī, 1:782

Falashas (Jewish sect), **5:609–700**

Falāsifa. See Arabian philosophy

Falco, Pietro, 12:234

Falco of Benevento, 1:463

Falcoia, Thomas (Bp. of Castellamare di Stabia), 1:307

Falconieri, Alessandro (Card.), 5:610

Falconieri, Alexius, St., 5:610, 13:26

Falconieri, Juliana, St., 5:610, 13:24

Falconieri, Lelio (Card.), 5:610

Falconieri family, **5:610**, *611*

Falconio, Diomede (Card.), 1:160, 585, 5:880

Falda, 10:856–857

Falgarona Vilanova, Jaime, 2:92

Falk, Adalbert, 6:184, 7:789

Falkland Islands War (1982), 7:1000

Falkner, Tomás, **5:611**

Fall of Man

   Baianism, 2:20

   justification, 8:81

   literary myths on the, 10:124, 129

   Paradise Lost (Milton), 9:644

   sexual relationship, 13:46

The Fall of Man (Goltzius), 8:*872*

Fall River Diocese (MA), **5:611–612**

Falla, Manuel de, **5:612**, *613*

Fallacy, **5:612–614**

   ambiguity, 1:334

   argumentation, 1:658

   equivocation, 5:310

   Sophists, 13:323

Fallon, Michael Francis (Bp. of London, Ontario), **5:614–615**

Fallon, Valère, **5:615**

Falloux, Frédéric de, 1:432

Falloux Law, 4:942, 5:854–855

Falqera, Shem Tob, 7:864

False Decretals (Pseudo-Isidorian forgeries), 3:599, 5:200, **615–619**, 9:445

    Angilramnus of Metz, 1:433

    Anselmo Dedicata, Collectio, 1:499

    Benedict the Levite, 2:253

    Canon Law, 3:42, 44, 60

    Carolingian reform, 3:158

    Church-State relations, 3:635

    Collection of Atto, 1:841

    Dacheriana collectio, 4:492

    importance in history, 4:601, 602

    marriage, 1:151

    papacy, 10:836

    Seventy-Four Titles, Collection, 13:39

False statements (*falsiloquium*), 8:901

Falsity, 5:329, **619–621**, 8:202

Falstaff (Verdi), 14:446

Falun Gong (China), 3:503, 504, 505

Falzon, Ignatius, Bl., **5:621**

Fama fraternitatis (Andrea), 12:382

Famian, St., **5:621**

Familia a Deo instituta (*motu proprio*, Paul VI), 11:481

Familial piety, **11:332, 334–335**

Familiar Instructions (Fitton), 5:751

Familiaris consortio (apostolic exhortation, John Paul II), 7:1003, 8:417, 10:179, 13:258

Family

    as basic unit, 13:482

    benefits for, advocated, 8:466

    Confucianism, 4:97–98, 100–101

    culture, 4:431

    Divine judgment, 8:36

    Jesus, 9:239–240

    legitimacy of children (Canon Law), 8:454–455

    Old Testament, 14:828–829

    papal social thought, 13:258

    preservation, 13:249

    private ownership, 13:265

    size of, contraception, 4:221

    social contract, 13:241

    social justice, 8:68

    Synoptic Gospels, 14:830

The Family Digest, 10:410

Family of Love (Puritan sect), 11:838

Family Rosary Crusade, 11:222

Famuli vestrae pietatis. See Gelasian Letter

Fan Xueyan (Bp. of Baoding), 3:505

Fancher, Mollie, 3:759

Fani, Mario, 7:673

Fanning, Dominic, 7:582

Fanon (liturgical garment), **5:621–622**, *622*

Fantuzzi, Joannes, 3:52

Fanzago, Cosimo, 3:705

Fara, St., **5:622**, 623, 631

Al Fārābī. *See* Alfarabi (Fārābī, al-)

Faraday, Michael, 1:80, 835, 4:*959*, 960–961

Faradj, Gregory Abou'l. *See* Bar-Hebraeus (Gregorius Ibn Al-Ibri)

Farcicius of Abingon, 5:240

Fardella, Michelangelo (1650-1718), 9:75–76

Farel, Guillaume, 2:889, **5:622–623**, 7:166

Faremoutiers Abbey (France), 5:622, **623**, 631

Farfa Abbey (Italy), 5:*623*, **623–624**

Farges, Albert, **5:624**

Fargo Diocese (ND), **5:624–625**

Faribault School Plan (MN), 1:352, 354, 584, 2:564, 584, 5:625–626, **625–626**, 7:551, 8:798, 10:541, 13:403

    Bouquillon controversy, 2:564

    Brann, Henry Athanasius, 2:584

    opposition, 7:1, 8:798, 13:403

Farina, Giovanni Antonio, Bl., **5:626–627**

Faringdon (Farington), John. *See* Woodcock, John, Bl.

Faringdon, Hugh, Bl., 5:226, **627**, 12:406

Faringdon, John. *See* Woodcock, John, Bl.

Farington, John. *See* Woodcock, John, Bl.

Farlati, Daniele, 3:793, **5:627**

Farley, John Murphy (Card.), 3:534, 5:*627*, **627–628**, 10:316

Farmer, Ferdinand (Father), **5:628–629**, 10:281, 311, 11:81, 12:566

Farnborough Priory (England), 5:*629*, **629**

Farne (island), 4:449, **5:629**

Farneland. *See* Farne (island)

Farnese, Alessandro (1468-1549). *See* Paul III (Pope)

Farnese, Alessandro (d. 1592), 5:630

Farnese, Alexander, 1:539

Farnese, Constanza, 11:21

Farnese, Francesco Maria (Card.), 5:630

Farnese, Girolamo (Card.), 5:630

Farnese, Ottavio, 5:629, 630

Farnese, Paolo, 11:21

Farnese, Pierluigi, 5:630, 631, 11:21

Farnese, Ranuccio (d. 1460?), 5:629

Farnese, Ranuccio (d. 1509), 11:21

Farnese, Ranuccio I (d. 1622), 5:630

Farnese, Ranuccio II (d. 1694), 5:630

Farnese family, **5:629–631**, *630*

Faro of Meaux (Bp.), St., 5:622, **631**, 8:167

Farouk (King of Egypt), 5:118

Farrar, F. W., 7:850

Farrell, Thomas, 2:711

Farrell, Walter, **5:631**, 9:100

Farther Thought on Tar-Water (Berkeley), 2:298

Fasani, Francesco Antonio, St., **5:631–632**

Fasani, Rainier, 5:755

Fasce, Maria Teresa, Bl., 1:872, 888, **5:632**

Fasciculus rerum expetendarum ac fugiendarum (Gratius), 6:424

Fasciculus temporum (Rolevinck), 12:293

Fascism

    economic democracy, 4:643

    Hungary, 7:219

    Schuster, Alfredo Ildefonso (Card.) response to, 12:790

Fast and abstinence, **5:632–635**

    Ember Days, 5:186–187

    lenten season, 8:468–470

    liturgical cycles, 8:718

    Manichaeism, 9:111, 113

    sobriety, 13:239

    temperance movements, 13:239, 799

Fasti (Ovid), 10:727

Fasti Campililienses (Hanthaler), 6:635

Fasti novi orbis et ordinationum apostolicarum ad Indias pertinentium breviarium (Muriel), 10:66

Fasting, 1:774, 775, 6:252

    Eucharist, 3:623

    as one of the Five Pillars of faith, 7:609

Fastorum libri duodecim (Baptist of Mantua), 2:73

Fastred, Bl., **5:636**

Fate and fatalism, **5:636–639**

    causality, 3:303

    kismet, 8:185

The Fates Gathering in the Stars (Vedder), 5:*637*

Father (Religious Title), **5:639**

Father Mateo, 4:335

Father Ryan's Poems (Ryan), 12:443

Father Smith Instructs Jackson (Noll), 10:410

Fathers and Sons (Turgenev), 10:394

Fathers of Jura, **8:63**

Fathers of Mercy, 5:796, **9:505**

Fathers of Mérida, **9:510**

Fathers of Sion, **5:640**, 11:923

Fathers of the Church, **5:640–643**

  Abelard, Peter, 1:19

  ambos, 1:336

  astrology, 7:114

  Byzantine theology, 2:818

  Catechism of the Council of Trent, 3:239

  Catholic social thought, 13:251–253

  common good, 4:17–18

  communication of idioms, 4:25–26

  compunction, 4:45

  conformity, 4:92

  contemplation, 4:205

  contraception, 4:218–219, 220

  cursus, 4:444

  death, 4:576

  demonology, 4:646–648

  descent of Christ into hell, 4:684–685

  digamy, 4:744–745

  discernment, spiritual, 4:765

  divination, 4:786

  Divine judgment, 8:31–32

  doctrine, 4:804

  dreams, 4:904

  Eucharist, 1:64

  gifts of the Holy Spirit, 7:47–48

  hominisation, 7:64

  Immaculate Conception, 7:332–333

  immortality, 7:347–349

  immutability of God, 7:355

  Jesus-Logos, 8:762

  John Climacus, St., 2:826

  Kingdom of God, 8:174

  Lent, 8:469

  levels of Latin, 8:363–364

  light of glory, 8:584–585

  list of "holy fathers," 5:640

  liturgical music history, 8:680–681, 699

  mystical body of Christ, 10:100–101

  patristic studies, 10:962–963

  penance, 4:225

  practices of penance, 11:66

  regarding licitness of oaths, 10:496–497

  schism and heresy, 12:737–738

  School of Alexandria, 1:272

  Severus of Antioch writings, 13:43

  simplicity of God, 13:137

  sin against Holy Spirit, 13:158

  Siricius (Pope), St., 13:166

  Sisinnius (Pope), 13:168

  Sixtus I (Pope), St., 13:194

  social justice, 8:69

  sorrows of Mary, 13:327

  Soter (Pope), St., 13:328–329

  soul, 13:342–343

  soul of the Church, 13:358

  standing versus kneeling, 8:647–648

  works of charity, 1:302

  See also Desert Fathers; Early church; Patristic era; *specific people*

"Fathers of the Church" (Canisius), 3:16

Fathers of the Incarnate Word, 7:370

Fathers of the Sacred Hearts, 4:293, 10:528–529, 531

Fátima (Portugal), 3:623, 5:*643*, **643–644**, 13:93

Fatima Church (Graz, Austria), 3:712

Fatimids, 7:624

Faubel Cano, Juan Bautista, Bl., **5:644–645**

Faulhaber, Andreas, **5:645**

Faulhaber, Michael von (Card.), **5:645–646**

  church architecture, 3:711

  Nazism, opposition to, 6:186

Fault, **5:646**

Faure, François (Bp. of Amiens), 1:359

Fauré, Gabriel Urbain, 3:525, **5:646–647**, *647*

Faure, Giovanni Battista, **5:647**

Faust (Goethe), 6:330–331, 332–333

Faust, Johann. *See* Faust legend

Faust, Mathías, **5:647–648**

Faust legend, **5:648–650**

Fausta (Roman Empress), 4:182

Faustino of the Incarnation. *See* Míguez, Faustino, Bl.

Faustinus (Bp.), 3:317

Faustinus of Lyons (Bp.), 6:111

Faustus of Mileve, 10:13

Faustus of Riez (Bp.), **5:651**, 12:900

  Apostles' Creed, 1:577

  Augustinianism, 1:877

  Claudianus, Mamertus, 3:769

  Confirmation, 4:84

Favarola, John C. (Bp. of Alexandria, LA), 1:270

Favaroni, Augustine, 1:883, 888

Faverge, Pierre-Sulpice-Christophe, 12:277

Faverge, Roger, Bl., 2:632

Favier, Alphonse, **5:651**

Favre, Peter. *See* Faber, Peter, Bl.

Fay, Charles, 10:194

Fay, Cyril Sigourney Webster, **5:651–652**

Fayrfax, Robert, **5:652**

FCJ. *See* Sisters, Faithful Companions of Jesus

FDLC. *See* Federation of Diocesan Liturgical Commissions

FDP (Sons of Divine Providence), 10:672, **13:320–321**

Fear, **5:652–653**

  anxiety, 1:540

  appetite, 1:602

  compunction, 4:45

  courage, 4:316

  cowardice, 4:332

  force and (Canon Law), 5:796–797

  involuntary acts, 14:584–585

Fear of the Lord, **5:653–654**

Feast of the Holy Innocents, 9:*673*

Feasts, religious, **5:655–657**, 9:157–159

  Advent, 1:133–134

  All Souls' Day, 1:290–291

  ancient Israelite worship, 14:857–858

  Annunciation, Feast of the, 1:197, 476–477

  Archangels, Feast of the, 6:41

  Ash Wednesday, 1:782

  Booths, Feast of, 2:131, 530–533, 4:607, 5:656

  Candlemas, 3:13–15

  ceremonies, 12:61

  Christ the King, Feast of, 3:527, 11:857

  Christmas, 3:551–557

  Christ's crown of thorns, Feast of, 1:147

  classification, 8:717

  of the cross, 4:382–383, 385

  Day of the Dead (Michoacan, Mexico), 9:*581*

  Dedication of the Temple, 4:607–608, 8:43, 580

  Depositio Martyrum listing, 4:675–676

  Divisio Apostolorum, 1:575

  Dormition of the Virgin, Feast of the, 1:800

  Epiphany, 1:134, 2:73, 3:14, 557, 5:293–295

  Holy Innocents' Day, 2:574, 3:556, 5:654, 7:484

  Holy Name, Feast of the, 7:32

  Indiction (Byzantine), 7:419

Islamic, 7:610

John, Apostle, St., 7:897

Joseph, St., 7:1040–1041

liturgical history, 8:662–663

liturgical year in Roman Rite,
8:716–722

Low Countries, 13:455

martyrologies, 9:232–234

New Year Feast (ancient
Mesopotamia), 9:536

Orthodoxy, Feast of, 2:753, 766,
7:283

pagan, 1:289, 3:229, 526, 5:655

Precious Blood, Feast of the, 5:700,
11:642

Protoevangelium Jacobi, 1:469

Purim, 5:408, 11:834–836

religious processions, 11:732

Sacred Marriage (ancient
Mesopotamia), 9:536

sanctoral cycle, 12:662

Saturnalia, 12:705

Seven Sorrows of Mary, Feast of the,
13:327–328

Solemnity of All Saints, 1:288–290

Sunday observance, 13:611

Trinity, Feast of the, 14:205

Unleavened Bread, Feast of the,
5:656, 10:933–934, 14:332–333

Virgin Mary, Feast of the, 1:263,
3:556

Visitation, Feast of the, 9:158,
14:564

See also Corpus et Sanguis Christi,
Solemnity of; Easter; Marian feasts;
Passover; Sabbath; Sunday; Yom
Kippur (Day of Atonement)

Febres Cordero Muñoz, Miguel
Francisco, St., 2:633, **5:657**

Febronianism, 3:614–615, 5:257,
657–659

Argentina, 1:650

Austria, 1:914

Caprara, Giovanni Battista, 3:92

Church-State relations, 3:639

Clement XIII (Pope), 3:791

conciliarism, 4:56

Dalberg, Karl Theodor von,
4:499–500

disappearance, 3:616

Döllinger, Johannes, 4:823–824

Gallicanism, 3:54

heresy, 6:778

Hontheim, Johann Kikolaus von,
7:89–90

Pius VI (Pope), 11:376

Spiegel, F. A., 13:416

theology of Church, 3:589

Febronius. *See* Febronianism; Hontheim,
Johann Nikolaus von

Febronius, Justinius (pseudonym). *See*
Hontheim, Johann Nikolaus von

Fécamp Abbey (France), 3:813,
5:659–660, 14:633

Fechner, Gustave T., 3:679, 5:27,
10:821, 824

Fecunda ratis (Egbert of Liège), 9:449

Fede e Scuola (periodical), 14:128

Federal Council of Churches in the U.S.,
5:467

Federal Council of Churches of Christ in
America, 10:157, 165

Federal Council of Evangelical Free
Churches, 5:928

Federal system of government, 6:377

Federalism. *See* Federal system of
government

Federated Colored Catholics, 1:160,
5:660, 14:243–244

Fédération des Institutions de l'Enfance
Inadaptée (Belgium), 2:221

Fédération des Institutions
Hospitaliéreres (Belgium), 2:221

Fédération des Services Médico-sociaux
(Belgium), 2:221

Federation of Asian Bishops'
Conferences (FABC), **5:660–662**,
13:161

Federation of College Catholic Clubs,
10:342

Federation of Diocesan Liturgical
Commissions (FDLC), **5:662**, 8:676

Federation of St. Benedict, 2:260

Federation of St. Gertrude, 2:260

Federation of St. Scholastica, 2:260

Federation of the Daughters of Blessed
(later Saint) Elizabeth Ann Seton,
13:175–180

Feehan, Daniel F. (Bp. of Fall River,
MA), 5:611–612, 9:308

Feehan, Patrick Augustine (Abp. of
Chicago), 3:478, **5:662–663**, 7:317,
8:412, 10:55–56, 13:822–823

Feeling, appetite and, 1:600

Feeney, Bernard, 11:625

Feeney, Daniel Joseph (Bp. of Portland,
ME), 9:59, 11:532

Feeney, Helen Margaret (Sister), 4:125

Feeney, Leonard, **5:663–664**

Feet, bare (discalced orders), 4:764–765

Feijó, Diogo Antônio (Father), 2:595,
5:*664*, **664**

Feijóo y Montenegro, Benito Jerónimo,
12:770

Feine, H. E., 3:42

Feirgil, St. *See* Virgilius of Salzburg, St.

Feirgil of Salzburg, St. *See* Virgilius of
Salzburg, St.

Felbiger, Johann Ignaz von, 1:913,
3:243, 244, **5:664–665**

Felici, Pericle (Card.), 3:56, **5:665**,
14:409

Felician sisters, 4:491

*Felicidad de Mexico en la admirable
aparicíon de la Virgen Marí Nuestra
Señora de Guadalupe* (Beccerra
Tanco), 2:192

Felicissimus, and Agapitus, SS.,
5:665–666

Felicitas (martyr), 1:93, 3:594

Felicity, St. *See* Perpetua and Felicity,
SS.

Felinus Sandeus, 3:52

Félire of Oengus, 1:289

Felix (Bp. of Urgel), 1:119, 186

Felix, Kelvin (Bp. of St. Lucia), 3:120

Felix, Marcus Antonius, **5:666**, 700

Felix I (Pope), St., **5:666**

Felix II (Antipope), 4:504, **5:666–667**,
12:354

Felix II (Pope), 6:121

Felix III (II) (Pope), St., 1:50, 3:633,
4:186, **5:667**, 6:119

Felix IV (III) (Pope), St., 4:282,
5:667–668, 12:355

Felix V (Antipope), 2:134, 5:445,
668–669, 10:841

Felix of Acci (Bp.), 5:178

Felix of Cantalice, St., 1:346, **5:669–670**

Felix of Dunwich, 5:239

Felix of Nicosia, Bl., **5:670**

Felix of Nola, St., **5:670**

Felix of Urgel

adoptionism, 9:446

Alcuin, Bl., 1:243

author of adoptionism, 5:161

Beatus of Liébana, 2:182

Claudius of Turin, 3:769

Felix of Valois, St., **5:670**

Fellenberg, Philip Emmanuel von,
11:171

Felner, Carolone and Koloman, 8:303

Felton, Aguilar v. (1986), 3:668

Felton, John, Bl., 5:227, 238, **670–671**

Felton, Thomas, Bl., 5:230, **671**

Female Society of St. Vincent de Paul,
3:420

Feminism, **5:671–674**

Angela of Foligno, Bl., 1:412

language use, inclusive, 8:439–440

Feminism *(continued)*
    United States, 9:868
    womanist theology, 14:822
    See also Ecofeminism and
      ecofeminist theology
Feminist Christologies, 7:839–840
Feminist hermeneutics, **5:674–675**,
    10:307
Feminist theology, **5:675–681**
    abba (term), 1:6
    femininity of God, 8:545
    Land, P., 8:317
    Latina theology, 8:369–370
    as liberation theology, 8:544–545
    Luke-Acts, 8:862
    praxis, 11:585
    sexism, 13:51–52
    See also Ecofeminism and
      ecofeminist theology
Feminist Theology (periodical), 5:680
Femmes de l'eglise Populaire (Québec,
    Canada), 3:10
Femmes en Eglise (Québec, Canada),
    3:10
Femmes en Minsterem (Québec,
    Canada), 3:10
Les Femmes Savantes (Molière), 3:186
Feneberg, Johann Michael, **5:681**
Fénelon, François de Salignac de la
    Mothe (Abp. of Cambrai), 5:90, *681*,
    681–683, 6:589, 590–591
    anarchism, 1:384
    Angela of Foligno, Bl., 1:412
    Argenté, Charles du Plessis d',
      1:657
    Bouillon, Emmanuel Théodose de la
      Tour d'Auvergne, 2:563
    Bourdaloue, Louis, 2:565
    Caussade, Jean Pierre de, 3:309, 310
    charity, 3:397–398
    conformity, 4:93
    direction, spiritual, 4:763
    hope, 7:101
    Lawrence of the Resurrection, 3:137
    preaching, 11:622
    Quietism, 3:614, 5:851
    spirituality, 13:447–448
Feng De, Matthew, St., **5:683**
Fenian Movement, 4:128
Fenianism, 9:647
Fenlon, John F., **5:684**
Fenn, James, Bl., 5:228, **684**
Fenn, Joseph, 7:403
Fenton, Joseph Clifford, **5:684–685**,
    10:68

Fenwick, Benedict Joseph (Bp. of
    Boston), 2:554, 557, 4:122, **5:685**,
    6:652, 9:305, 10:312, 12:497
    immigrant colony in Maine, 9:56
Fenwick, Edward Dominic (Bp. of
    Cincinnati), 3:734–735, **5:685–686**,
    10:568, 569
    Carroll, John, 3:181
Fenwick, John, Bl., 5:236, **686**
Fenwick, Joseph, 14:454
Feodorov, Leonid (Russian Byzantine
    exarch), 2:748, **5:687**, 12:429
Ferall, John, 7:582
Ferchius, Mattheus, 12:764
Ferdinand (Abp. of Cologne), 3:843
Ferdinand (Archduke), 1:911
Ferdinand, Bl., **5:687**
Ferdinand I (Holy Roman Emperor)
    Bohemian Brethren, 2:461
    Carbonari, 3:100
    clerical celibacy and marriage, 3:327
    Hapsburg-Valois rivalry, 6:639
    Jesuits, 1:911, 3:17
Ferdinand I (King of Castile), 10:978
    accomplishments, 13:390
    Mudejar ceiling, 13:*380*
    Reconquest, 13:380
Ferdinand I (King of Portugal), 11:534
Ferdinand I (King of the Two Sicilies),
    7:671
Ferdinand II (Holy Roman Emperor),
    5:*687*, **687–688**
    Austria, 1:912
    Becanus, Martin, 2:191
    Bohemia, 4:482–483
    Bohemian War (1618-23), 14:8–9
    Córdoba, 4:261
    election of son, 8:433
    spiritual counselor to, 8:313
Ferdinand II (the Catholic) (King of
    Spain), 3:110, 14:881, 882
Ferdinand III (King of Castile), St.,
    4:412, **5:688–689**, 12:610
Ferdinand IV (King of Castile and
    León), 12:611
Ferdinand V (King of Castile), 1:259,
    274
Ferdinand the Catholic. *See* Ferdinand II
    (the Catholic) (King of Spain)
Ferēmenatos. *See* Frumentius, St.
Fergal of Salzburg, St. *See* Virgilius of
    Salzburg, St.
Ferguson, Marilyn, 10:273
Feria Quinta in Coena Domini. See
    Holy Thursday

Feriman, Francis. *See* Rawlins,
    Alexander, Bl.
Fermentum (eucharistic bread), **5:689**
Fermo Cathedral (Italy), 7:*664*
Il Fermo propositio (encyclical, Pius X),
    9:755, 11:389, 390–391
Il fermo proposito (encyclical, Pius X),
    10:415
Fernan, Walter, 7:580
Fernand, Charles, 3:473
Fernandes, Ambrosio, Bl., 7:732
Fernandes, Antony, Bl., 1:951
Fernandes, Dominic, Bl., 1:951
Fernandes, John, Bl. (b. *ca.* 1547), 1:952
Fernandes, John, Bl. (b. *ca.* 1551), 1:951
Fernandes, Manuel, Bl., 1:951
Fernández, Benito, 3:112, 7:699
Fernandez, John (Brother), 7:737
Fernandez, John James, 4:503
Fernández, José, 14:494
Fernandez, Oliviera, 14:540–541
Fernández Crespo, Zacarias, Bl., 4:494
Fernández de Agüero, Julián, 1:649
Fernández de la Torre, Pedro (Bp. of
    Río de la Plata), 1:649
Fernández de Piedrahita, Lucas (Bp.),
    5:689
Fernández de Recalde, Pedro, 3:145
Fernández Solar, Teresa de los Andes,
    St., **5:690**
Fernández Truyols, Andrés, **5:690**
Fernando, Stephen (Bp.), 7:406
*Ferndinand II, Romanorum Pimperatoris
    virtutes* (Lamormaini), 8:313
Férotin, Marius, **5:690**
    Farnborough Priory, 5:629
    work on Mozarabic codices, 10:44
Ferragud Girbés, José Ramón (Joseph
    Raymond), Bl., **5:690–691**
Ferragut, Roig, María Teresa, Bl., 1:4,
    5:691
Ferrandus of Carthage, 3:186, **5:691–692**
Ferrar, Nicholas, 3:152, 12:101
Ferrar, Robert, 12:10
Ferrara, Council of (1438), 1:340
Ferrara-Florence, Council of. *See*
    Florence, Councils of
Ferrari, Andrea Carlo (Card.), Bl., **5:692**
Ferrari, Bartolomeo, Ven., 2:103, **5:692**
Ferrari, M. Giovanni (Sister), 9:125
Ferraria v. Vascanelles (1860), 3:658
Ferrariensis (Italian philosopher),
    5:692–693, 14:49
    action and passion, 1:78
    analogy, 1:373
    Aristotelianism, 1:677

individuation, 7:426

scholasticism, 12:764

vision of God, desire for, 4:691

Ferrario, Joseph A. (Bp. of Honolulu), 6:671

Ferraris, Lucio, **5:693**

Ferrata, Domenico (Card.), **5:693–694**

Ferrata, Ercole, 3:787

Ferratéte, Eusebio, 7:123

Ferreira Viana, Antônio, 2:596

Ferreolus of Uzè (Bp.), St., **5:694**

Ferrer, Boniface, 3:51

Ferrer, Bonifacio, 12:486

Ferrer, Rafael, 5:62

Ferrer, Vincent, St.

flagellants of, 5:848

private revelations, 12:201

Western Schism, 3:51, 783–784

Ferrer Botella, José Pascual (Father), 5:691

Ferrer Esteve, José, Bl., **5:694**, 10:816

Ferreri, John, 8:180

Ferreri, Zaccaria (Bp.), **5:694–695**

Ferretti, Gabriele (Card.), **5:695**

Ferretti, Giovanni Maria Mastai. *See* Pius XI (Pope)

Ferrières-en-Gâtinais Abbey (France), **5:695**

Ferrini, Contardo, Bl., **5:695–696**, *696*

Ferro, Ambrósio Francisco, Bl., 2:587

Ferrua, A., 3:224

Ferry, Jules, 7:789

La Ferté Abbey (France), 3:748, 751, **8:279**

Fertility and vegetation cults, **5:696–698**, 13:21

Fertility and vegetation cults, in the Bible, **5:698–699**

Fesch, Joseph (Card.), **5:699**, 10:146

Fessler, Joseph (Bp. of St. Pölten), 1:914, 8:255, 12:730

Festa, Costanzo, **5:699–700**

Festal Sermons (Anthony of Padua), 5:894

Festivals. *See* Feasts, religious

Festivis resonent compita vocibus (hymn), 5:700

Festugière, A. M. J., 5:285

Festus, Porcius, **5:700**

Fetherston, Richard, Bl., 5:226, **700**

Fétis, François Joseph, **5:700–701**

Feudal Society (Bloch), 5:704

Feudalism, **5:701–706**

abbesses, 1:8

abbots, 1:10

aristocracy, 1:667

Bogomilism, 2:458

Church property, 3:725–726

coinage, 10:480

democracy, 4:639

Ghibelline-Guelf conflict, 3:853, 855

growth in Italy, 7:657, 659

investiture struggle, 7:536

monasteries, 2:269, 271

proprietary churches, 3:600, 725

servitude, 13:212

social thought, 13:253

works of charity, 3:411

Feudalism (Ganshof), 5:704

Feuerbach, Ludwig Andreas, **5:706–707**, 11:294–295

anarchism, 1:384

humanism, 7:195–196

materialism, 12:70

pantheism thought, 10:827

self, concept of, 12:883

theology, 6:286

Young Hegelians, 6:710

Feuillants, 3:747, **5:707–708**

Abondance Monastery, 1:23

Barrière, Jean de la, 2:117–118

as discalced order, 4:765

Feuillet, André, 7:528

Fey, Clara (Mother), 1:2, **5:708**, 6:185, 11:493

Les FF. Mineurs et les débuts de la Réforme à Port Royal (Ubald), 14:261

Les FF. Mineurs et l'Université d'Angers (Ubald), 14:261

Ffrench, Charles (Father, fl. 1835), 9:56

Fiacre, St., 8:167

Fiadonibus, Bartholomew de. *See* Bartholomew of Lucca (Bp. of Torcello)

Fibonacci, Leonardo, 12:814

Fichet, William, 2:341

Fichte, Johann Gottlieb, **5:708–709**, *709*, 11:294

absolute, 1:42

aesthetics, 3:679

conscience, 4:140

critical idealism, 4:368, 369

ethics and morality, 5:361, 396

freedom, 5:939

idealism, 7:298, 10:227

intuition, 7:533

Kantianism, 8:126–127

noumenal principles, 12:397

philosophy of history, 6:885

philosophy of religion, 12:69

Schelling defense of, 12:732

Schopenhauer, Arthur, 12:784

self, concept of, 12:883

system of reason, 12:346

Fichter, Joseph H., **5:709–710**

Ficino, Marsilio, **5:710–711**, 768, 847, 11:*283*, 292

Anabaptists, 1:369

Aristotelianism, 1:675

Colet, John, 3:832

influence on Johann Reuchlin, 12:181

music as art, 10:72

personal immortality, 13:345

Platonism, 11:415–416

Renaissance cultural developments, 12:117

Renaissance philosophy, 7:186, 12:121

world soul, 14:844

Ficker, G., 1:20

Fiddes, P., 5:384

Fidei depositum (apostolic constitution, John Paul II), 3:245

Fidei donum (encyclical, Pius XII), 9:681

Fideism, **5:711–713**

Bautain, Louis Eugène Marie, 2:161

Bayle, Pierre, 2:164–165

Bonald, Louis Gabriel Ambroise de, 2:478

Bonnetty, Augustin, 2:508

Huet, Pierre Daniel, 7:148

religious liberalism, 8:541

symbolic, 12:453

Fidelis of Sigmaringen, St., **5:713**

Fidelity, **5:713–714**, 10:656, 11:746

Fides, Religio, Moresque Aethiopum (The Manners, Lawes, and Customes of All Nations) (Góis), 6:334

Fides et ratio (Faith and Reason) (encyclical, John Paul II), 3:542, **5:714–715**, 7:1002, 11:475, 950, 12:198, 778

Fides News Service, 11:754

Fides qua creditur and *fides quae creditur*, 2:222

Fides Quaerens Intellectum, 4:726, **5:715–716**

Fiefs, 3:170

Fiefs and Vassals (Reynolds), 5:706

Field, John, 3:525

The Field Afar (periodical), 9:294, 295, 12:289

Fierens, John F., 10:645

Fiery Arrow (Ignea Sagitta) (Nicholas Gallicus), 3:132, 133

The Fiery Darts of Satan (Tela Ignea Satanae) (Wagenseil), 7:588

Fieschi, Ottobuono. *See* Adrian V (Pope)

Fieschi, Sinibaldo dei. *See* Innocent IV (Pope)

Fiesole, Guido da (Fra Angelico), Bl., 1:536, **5:716**, 10:174
    Bible cycles, 2:374
    crucifixion art of, 4:396
    St. Lawrence in fresco cycle *The Lives of Saint Stephen and Lawrence*, 13:*196*

Fifth Monarchy Men, 1:548

Figliucci, Felix (Filliucius), **5:716–717**

Figueiredo, Jackson de, **5:717**

Figuero Beltrán, José, 2:92

Figueroa, Francisco de, 2:533, 5:62–63

Figulus, P. Nigidius, 10:243

Fiji Islands, 10:531

Filaret (Russian theologian), 4:355, **5:717**, 10:*680*, 12:424

Filastrius of Brescia (Bp.), 5:294

Filby, William, Bl., 5:228, **717–718**

Filcock, Roger, Bl., 5:233, **718**

Filelfo, Francesco, 12:115–116

Filiae Mariae. *See* Marianist Sisters

Filial piety, 3:516

Filiation, **5:718–719**, 8:758–764

Filicchi, Antonio, 13:32

Filioque, 4:187, **5:719–722**
    Adalard, St., 1:98
    Adrian I (Pope), 1:123, 2:752, 821
    Athanasian Creed, 1:817
    Bessarion, Cardinal, 2:340
    Bryennios, Joseph, 2:651
    Byzantine Church, 2:752, 754, 762
    Carolingian reform, 2:821–822, 3:599
    Council of Florence, 3:26, 572, 5:426
    Eugene IV (Pope), 5:445
    Eugenicus, Mark (Metropolitan of Ephesus), 5:446
    Frankish position, 13:228
    Holy Trinity dogma, 14:200
    Italo-Albanian Church, 7:651
    John XI Beccus, 7:917–918
    Methodius, 4:476
    Michael Cerularius, 2:824
    Photian Schism, 5:23, 24, 719
    Sergius IV (Pope), 13:13

Filipino Americans, 6:672

Filippini, Lucy, St., **5:722**, 12:101

Filippucci, Alessandro Francesco Saverio, **5:722**

Fillastre, Guillaume (Card.), 1:197, 5:722, 722–723, **722–723**

Fillmore, Millard, 8:200

Filmer, Robert, Sir, 4:788

Filocolo (Boccaccio), 2:448

Filosofía elemental (Balmes), 2:33

Filosofía fundamental (Balmes), 2:33, 12:773

Filson, F. V., 5:520

Fin dalla prima (*motu proprio*, Pius X), 11:*389*

Fina, St. *See* Seraphina, St.

Final causality, 3:297, 302, 5:99, 528, **723–727**
    act, 1:75
    Aristotelianism, 1:669
    cogitative power, 3:823
    as solution to problem of normality, 10:425

Final Commendation, 6:32

Final events, Judaism, 8:5

Final perseverance, **11:133–134**

The Final Report of the Extraordinary Synod of Bishops of 1985, 4:30

Finality, principle of, 1:748, **5:727–728**

Fínán Cam, St., **5:728**

Finan of Lindisfarne (Bp.), St., 3:316, **5:728–729**

Finch, John, Bl., 5:228, **729**

Finding the Relics of St. Stephen (fresco painting), 12:52

Fingesten, P., 3:676

Finglas Abbey (Ireland), 4:423

Fingley (Finglow), John, Bl., 5:229, **729**

Finis operantis, **5:729**

Finis operis, **5:729–730**

Finite and Eternal Being (Stein), 13:506

Finite being, **5:730–731**
    agnosticism, 1:184
    contingency, 4:212
    contradiction, 4:224
    metaphysics, 9:551–552

Fink, Louis Mary (Bp. of Kansas City), **5:731**, 8:113, 117–118, 12:539

Fink, Michael. *See* Fink, Louis Mary (Bp. of Kansas City)

Fink, Tom, 1:211

Finke, Heinrich, 6:184

Finland, **5:731–735**, *734*
    ancestor worship, 1:394
    demographic statistics, 5:732
    ecclesiastical organization, 5:731
    Lutheranism, 8:889, 12:19
    map, 5:*733*

Finn, Francis James, **5:735**

Finney, Charles Grandison, **5:735**, 12:204

Finnian of Clonard (Abbot), 4:494, 5:735–736, **735–736**

Finnian of Moville (Abbot), 5:735–736

Finnigan, George J. (Bp. of Helena, MT), 9:826

Finnis, John, 7:528

Finnish Orthodox Church, 2:746

Fintan, **5:736**

Fintan, Chapel of, 12:211

Fintan of Cloneagh (Abbot), 5:736

Fintan of Rheinau (Abbot), 5:736

Fintan of Taghmon (Abbot), 5:736

Fiorentino, Francesco, 10:238

Fiorenza, Francis Schüssler, 6:791

Fiorenza, Joseph (Bp.), 7:73

Fioretti (*I Fioretti di San Francesco*) (The Little Flowers of St. Francis), 4:136, **5:736–737**, 898

Fire, use and symbolism of, 5:16, **737–739**, 13:535

Fire of Judgment, 5:739, 8:40

Fire ordeal, 10:626

Firenze, Andrea da, 4:396, *683*

Firestone, Shulamith, 5:672

Firmian, Leopold Anton Eleutherius (Abp. of Salzburg), 1:912, 5:739

Firmian, Leopold Ernst (Card.), 5:739

Firmian, Leopold Max (Bp. of Passau), 5:739

Firmian family, **5:739**

Firmicus Maternus, Julius, **5:739–740**

Firmilian of Caesarea (Bp.), 1:785, 2:846, 4:350, 351–352, 458, **5:740**

Firmin of Amiens (Bp. of Amiens), St., 1:359, **5:740–741**, 760

Firmus, 4:862

First act, 1:73, **75**

First Baptist Meeting House (Providence, RI), 3:715

First Book of Homilies, 12:9

First Catholic Slovak Union, 12:609

First cause, **3:308–309**
    act, 1:75
    action and passion and, 1:80
    annihilation, 1:471
    Aristotle, 1:682
    causality, 3:304

First Church of Christ Scientist (Berkeley, CA), 3:715–716

First Communion, Sacrament of, **5:741–742**
    age of, 4:89
    Lambertini, I., 8:305
    Lent, 8:469

First Considerations (Weiss), 10:608

First Epistle to the Corinthians (Pope Clement I), 5:509, 11:673

First Formulary of Sirmium, 1:662

The First Freedom (NCWC), 14:312

The First Freedom (Parsons), 10:904

The First Life (Vita Prima) (Thomas of Celano), 14:33

First Mass in Maryland, 9:302

First Presbyterian Church (Princeton, NJ), 3:715

First Presbyterian Church (Stamford, CT), 3:675, 716, 11:*675*

First principles, **5:742–745**
  Aquinas, 5:303–304, 8:26
  awareness of necessity included, 10:225
  axiomatic system, 1:949
  causality, 3:299
  certitude, 3:354
  contradiction, 4:223–224
  criteriology, 4:368
  demonstration, 4:652
  knowledge, 8:203, 204
  Liber de causis, 8:533
  See also Finality, principle of

First Trullan Council. *See* Constantinople, Councils of

First truths, syndersis and, 13:679

First Unitarian Church (Rhode Island), 14:*303*

First Universalist Church (Chicago), 3:680, 716

Fisac, Miguel, 3:713

Fischer, Bonifatius, 2:350

Fischer, G. H., 3:245

Fischer, Johann Bernhard, 1:913

Fischer, Johann Kaspar Ferdinand, **5:746**

Fish, symbolism of, 1:458, **5:746–748**, 7:277, 8:344, 13:667–668
  See also Fisherman's Ring

Fish on Friday (Feeney), 5:663

Fisher, Geoffrey (Abp. of Canterbury), 1:440, 5:74

Fisher, John (Card.), St., 5:225, 244, **748–750**, *749*, 12:8
  Barton, Elizabeth, 2:130
  Bp. of Rochester, 12:278
  Cambridge University, 2:905–906
  execution under Henry VIII, 12:227, 278
  Lutheranism, 3:609

Fisher, Robert, 6:100

Fisherman's Ring, **5:750**, *751*

Fishta, Antonin (Bp.), 1:216

Fitch, R. E., 10:192

Fitch, William Benedict, **5:750–751**

Fitero Abbey (Spain), **5:751**

Fitton, James, 4:122, **5:751**, 13:462

Fitzalan, Henry, **5:751–752**

Fitzalan-Howard, Bernard Marmaduke (Duke of Norfolk). *See* Norfolk, Bernard Marmaduke Fitzalan-Howard, Duke of

Fitzalan-Howard, Henry (Duke of Norfolk). *See* Norfolk, Henry Fitzalan-Howard, Duke of

Fitzgerald, Edward M. (Bp. of Little Rock), 1:691–692, **5:752**, 8:612–613, 10:569, 12:274

FitzGerald, Francis, 7:581

Fitzgerald, Gerald Michael Cushing, 13:25

Fitzgerald, John, 10:222

Fitzgerald, Nicholas, 7:579

Fitzgerald, Robert, 7:579

FitzGerald, Thomas, 7:581

Fitzgerald, Walter J. (Bp. of Alaska), 1:209

Fitzgibbon, Gerald, 7:581

Fitzgibbon, Mary Irene (Sister), **5:752–753**

Fitzmaurice, Charles F., 4:921

FitzMaurice, John Edmond (Abp. of Tomi, DE), 4:625, 14:765

Fitzmyer, Joseph, 8:861, 863–864

Fitzpatrick, Brian, 7:582

Fitzpatrick, Edward Augustus, 5:*753*, **753**

Fitzpatrick, John Bernard (Bp. of Boston), 1:158, 2:554–555, 557, 640, 9:306–307, 14:454

Fitzsimon, Edmund, 7:579

Fitzsimon, Henry, **5:753**

Fitzsimon, Michael, 7:580

Fitzwilliam, Earl, 5:183

Five Books on Architecture (Serlio), 3:672

The Five Considerations of the Holy Stigmata, 5:737

Five Elements (*Wu xing*), 3:508

"Five fundamentals," 6:27, 29–30

Five Mile Act (1727) (United States), 3:647

Five Patriarchates, 10:945

Five Pillars of faith (Islam), 7:609–610, 622

"Five Polish Brothers," 2:252

The Five Wounds of the Church (Rosmini-Serbati), 12:384

Flacius Illyricus, Matthias, **5:754**, 6:253
  Centuriators of Magdeburg, 3:347
  Chemnitz, Martin, 3:464

Crypto-Calvinists, 4:416
  ecclesiastical historiography, 6:874–875
  fragmentation of Luthern Movement, 4:60
  hermeneutics, 6:787
  Lutheran doctrine, 5:740, 8:889, 892

Flag salutes, Church-State relations and, 3:661–662

Flagellation, **5:754–755**, 848
  apocalyptic movements, 1:547
  the discipline, 4:774–775
  Jesus Christ, 5:756, *756*

Flagellation, in the Bible, 4:390, **5:755–757**

The Flagellation of Christ (Caravaggio), 7:*810*

Flagellation of Christ (painting), 5:*756*

Flaget, Benedict Joseph (Bp. of Bardstown, KY), 2:39, 43, 5:757, **757–758**, 796, 12:559
  Badin, Stephen, 2:11
  David, John Baptist Mary, 4:538, 539
  Kentucky missions, 8:148–149
  Louisville Archdiocese, 8:816
  Sisters of Loretto, 8:786
  slavery, 1:156
  Spalding, M. J. influenced, 13:404

Flahiff, George Bernard (Abp. of Winnipeg), 3:8–9

Flamarique Salinas, Rafael, Bl., 7:123

Flamboyant Gothic architecture, 3:697–698

Flames of love, 10:108

Flaming Bible Children's Church (Sierra Leone), 13:*112*

Flanagan, Bernard J. (Bp. of Norwich), 4:125, 5:664

Flanagan, Edward Joseph (Father), **5:758**, *759*, 10:223, *587*

Flanagan, Joseph (Bp. of Worcester, MA), 9:309

Flanders, church architecture, 3:706

Flandrin, Petrus (Card.), 3:51

Flasch, Kilian Caspar (La Crosse, WI), 8:273, 14:781

Flathead people, 14:869

Flathers, Matthew, Bl., 5:234, **758**

Flatisbury, Philip, 7:582

Flavian (Patriarch of Constantinople), St., **5:759–760**
  death of, 5:275
  Dioscorus (Patriarch of Alexandria), 4:756
  Eutyches condemned, 5:275, 461, 462
  Leo I (Pope), St., 8:476

Flavian (Patriarch of Constantinople), St. *(continued)*
  Robber Council of Ephesus, 3:363
Flavigny-sur-Moselle Abbey (France), **5:760**
Flavigny-sur-Ozerain Abbey (France), **5:760**
Flavius Arrianus. *See* Arrian (Flavius Arrianus)
Flay Abbey (France), 6:188
Fléché, Jesse, 3:4
Flectamus genua (Let us kneel), 10:651
Fleege, Urban J., 3:283
Fleming, David, 1:438
Fleming, Patrick, 3:834, **5:760–761**
Fleming, Thomas (Abp. of Dublin), **5:761**
Flemish art, crucifixion in, 4:396
Fletcher, Albert Lewis (Bp. of Little Rock), 1:692, 693, 8:614–615
Fletcher, Joseph, 12:49
Flete, William, 1:888, **5:761**
Fleury, André Hercule de (Card.), **5:761–762**, 8:804
Fleury, Claude, **5:762**, 10:676, 12:290
  catechesis, 3:235, 243
  censorship, 3:796
  Gallicanism, 6:76
Fleury, Joachim, 11:682
Fleury-Sur-Loire. *See* Saint-Benoît-sur-Loire Abbey (France)
Fliche, Augustin, **5:762–763**
Fliedner, Theodor, 4:554
Das Fliessende Licht der Gottheit (Mechtild of Magdeburg), 9:423
Fliss, Raphael M. (Bp. of Superior, WI, b. 1930), 14:783
Flodoard of Reims, 1:462, **5:763**, 9:447, 10:554–555, 12:607
Floersh, John A. (Bp. of Louisville), 8:818
Flood, **5:763–765**, 11:712–713
  Gilgamesh, 6:223–224
  Hittite texts, 11:712
  myths, 2:329–330, 10:124, 129
  Noah, 10:*403, 404*
Flor, Michael, 1:321
Flora (martyr of Córdoba), 4:262
Floreffe Monastery (France), **5:765–766**
Florence (Italy), **5:766–769**
  city skyline, 5:*768*
  early Christian history, 5:766
  frescoes and paintings of Fiesole, 5:716
  humanism, 7:186
  martyrs of, 5:766

Medici family, 5:768–769, 12:116–117
  Renaissance cultural developments, 12:117
  Renaissance political developments, 12:116–117
  Savonarola, Girolamo, 12:714
  Siena rivalry, 13:108
  See also Guelfs and Ghibellines
Florence, Councils of (1431-45), **5:770–772**
  Amadeus' excommunication, 5:669
  Copts, 4:255
  Cyprus, 4:462
  dead, prayers for the, 4:556
  Divine judgment, 8:32
  Eastern Schism, 4:188
  as Ecumenical council, 4:302
  Escobar, Andrés de, 5:352
  Ethiopian delegation, 5:403
  eucharistic controversy, 5:423, 425–426
  eucharistic epiclesis, 5:279, 280
  Eugene IV (Pope), 5:445
  filioque, 5:426, 720
  Holy Orders, 7:38, 41
  Romanian Orthodox Church, 12:330, 338
  Russian rejection of, 12:419
  sacramental teaching, 12:470
  water with wine, 8:661
  first (1438-39), 3:604
    Alexandria Patriarchate, 1:271
    Ambrose Traversari, Bl., 1:340
    Antoninus, St., 1:536
    Apostles' Creed, 1:577
    Argyropoulos, John, 1:659
    Aristotelianism, 1:671, 676
    Armenia, 1:702, 706, 711–712
    Bessarion, Cardinal, 2:340, 828
    biblical canon, 3:26, 32
    Cesarini, Giuliano, 3:357
    Chrysoberges, Andrew, 3:572
    Eastern Schism, 2:762, 788, 828
    Epiclesis, 2:828
    Melkite Catholic Church, 1:526
  second (1439-45)
    Albert of Sarteano, Bl., 1:223
    beatific vision, 2:169, 174, 6:297
    doctrine of personal properties ratified, 14:196
    God the Holy Spirit, 6:294
    heavenly bliss, 6:688
    primacy of the pope, 11:708
    purgatory, 11:825

    purpose of amendment, 11:840
Florence of Worcester, 1:463, 464, **5:772**, 10:708
Florenskii, Pavel Aleksandrovich, 2:679, **5:772–773**
Florensz, Adrian. *See* Adrian VI (Pope)
Florentina, St., **5:773**, 6:23
Florentine Histories (Machiavelli), 12:124
Florentini, Theodosius, **5:773–774**, 7:22, 12:734
Florentius (Bp. of Ancyra), 1:398
Florentius, Radewijns, **5:774**
Florentius, St., 12:546
Flores, City of Boerne v. (1997), 3:664
Flores, Luis, Bl., 7:733
Flores, Patricio F. (Bp. of San Antonio, TX), 5:174, 203, 12:642, 13:847
Flores, Patrick F. *See* Flores, Patricio F. (Bp. of San Antonio, TX)
Flores epitaphii sanctorum (Thiofrid of Echternach), 14:6
Flores García, Margarito, St., **5:774**
Flores Varela, José (Joseph) Isabel, St., **5:774**
Flórez, Enrique, **5:774–775**
Florian, St., 1:908, 12:668
Florians (Floriacenses), **5:775**
Florida, **5:775–780**
  African American Catholics, 1:155
  ecclesiastical organization, 5:775
  missions, 6:148–149, 7:785, 9:707, 715
  See also specific dioceses and archdioceses
Floridus aspectus (Peter Riga), 9:457
Florilegia, Christian, 5:640, **780–782**
  biblical catenae, 3:258
  Carolingian reform, 3:157
  Carolingian Renaissance, 3:161
Florimonte, Galeazzo, 3:198
Florinus, St., **5:782**
Floris de Vriendt, Cornelius, 1:539
Florovsky, George, **5:782–783**, 12:436, 742
Florus of Lyons, **5:783**
  Ado of Vienne, St., 1:118
  Agobard of Lyons, St., 1:186
  Canon Law, 3:43
  Carolingian Renaissance, 3:160, 161
  hagiography, 3:161
  hymns of, 7:246
Flos Sanctorum (Lives of the Saints) (Ribadeneyra), 12:220
Flotte, Pierre, 2:502, 503
Flower, J. Roswell, 1:789

Flower, Richard, Bl., 5:230, **783–784**

Flower, William. *See* Way, William

Flowers, symbolism of, **5:784**

Floyd, John, **5:784**

Fludd, Robert, 12:382

Flumen aque vive (papal bull, John XXI), 7:930

Flynn, Harry J. (Abp.), 12:576

Flynn, Thomas, 11:625

Focher, Juan, **5:785**, 14:367

Focillon, Henri, 3:750

Focillon, J., 3:679

Focolare Movement (Work of Mary), **5:785–786**, 8:416

Foigny Abbey (France), 3:758

Foik, Paul Joseph, **5:786–787**

Folcwin of Lobbes (Abbot), **5:787**, 7:247, 12:540

Folcwin of Thérouanne (Bp.), St., **5:787**

Foley, E., 3:75

Foley, John Samuel (Bp. of Detroit), 4:698, 9:606–607

Foley, Thomas (Bp. of Chicago), 3:477–478, 5:882, 7:317

Foliot, Gilbert, 5:240, **787–788**

Folk art, 4:364

Folk music, 7:260

Folk religion, China, 3:513

Folkstone Abbey (England), **5:788**

Follett v. McCormick (1944), 3:661

Following of Christ (In the Christian Life), **5:788–789**

Following the Conquistadores (Zahm), 14:906

Folmar of Trier, 1:119

The Folowyng of Cryste (Whitford), 14:706

Fonck, Leopold, **5:789**

Fons philosophiae (Godfrey of Saint-Victor), 6:328, 9:457

Fons vitae (Fountain of Life) (Avicebron), 7:863–864, 14:43

Fonseca, Peter da, **5:789–790**
    action and passion, 1:78
    Aristotelianism, 1:677
    scholasticism, 12:766, 767

Fonseca, Pinto de, 3:792

Font, Pedro, 12:644–645

Font covers, 2:77

Fontaine, Marie Madeleine, Bl., 1:722

Fontainebleu, Concordat of (1813), 5:854

Fontaines Abbey (France), 3:864

Fontaines de Neuilly, Guy de, 5:441

Fontana, Carlo, 3:706

Fontana, Domenico, 3:704, 12:580

Fontana di Trevi (Rome), 3:790, 793

Fontbonne, Saint Jeanne. *See* Fontbonne, Saint John (Mother)

Fontbonne, Saint John (Mother), **5:790–791**, 12:555

Fontbonne, Saint Teresa (Marie) (Sister), 5:790

Fonte, Pedro José (Abp. of Mexico), **5:791–792**

Fonte Avellana Monastery (Italy), 2:897–898, 5:755, *792*, **792**

Fontenay Abbey (France), 3:749, 750, 758

Fontenelle, Bernard le Bovier (1657-1757), 9:74

Fontenelle Abbey (France), **5:793**, 14:632

Fontevrault, Order of, 12:266

Fontevrault, Reform of (1498-1500), 3:463

Fontevrault Convent (France), 1:8, 432, 5:623, **793–794**

Fontevrault Monastery, 12:266

Fonteye, Henri, 7:788

Fontfroide Abbey (France), 5:*794*, **794–795**

Fontignano Abbey (Italy), 1:333

Fontou, Marie Thérèse, Bl., 1:722

Fontoura, Peter, Bl., 1:951

Food and Agriculture Organization (United Nations), 8:586

"Fool letter," 6:480

Foolhardiness, **5:795**

Fools, Feast of, **5:654**

The Foot of the Cross (Faber), 5:582

For the Life of the World: Sacraments and Orthodoxy (Schmemann), 12:742

Forbes, Alexander Penrose, **5:795**

Forbes, George Hay, 5:795

Forbes, John, **5:795**

Forbes, William (Bp. of Edinburgh), 3:152

The Forbidden Forest (Eliade), 5:155

Forbin-Janson, Charles de (Bp.), 5:*796*, **796**

Forcades Ferraté, Eusebio, Bl., 7:123

Force and fear (Canon Law), **5:796–797**

Force and moral responsibility, **5:797–798**, 8:398

The Force of Truth (Scott), 10:332

Forcellini, Egidio, **5:798**, *799*

Forces, the supernatural and, 13:620

Ford, Francis Xavier (Bp.), **5:798–799**, 9:295, 12:289

Ford, Ita, 8:133

Ford, John C., 7:180

Ford, Joseph F., 7:699

Ford, Thomas, Bl., 5:227, **799**

Fordun, J. de, 12:533

Foreign Mission Institute of Milan (PIME), 3:499

Foreiro, Francisco, **5:799**

Forel, F. A., 2:404

Forer, Laurence, 7:845, 847

Forest, Aimé, 5:539

Forest, John, Bl., 5:226, **799–800**

Forest, John Anthony, 12:641

Forgery of decretals, 4:600–601, 602, 860–861

Forget, J., 3:358

Forgiveness of sins, **5:800**
    communio, 4:29
    impenitence and lack of, 7:362
    See also Repentance

Forgiveness of sins, in the Bible, 4:225, **5:800–802**, 13:36

Forgoret, Peter di (Abbot), 12:528

Foriero, Francisco, 3:328

Form, **5:802–806**
    act, 1:73
    Aristotle, 1:682, 10:210
    art, 1:746
    certitude, 3:352
    knowledge, 8:201, 209–210, 213–214
    monad concept, 8:457
    Plato, 11:408–409
    soul, 13:345
    substantial and accidental, 8:209
    Thomistic thought, 10:907–908

Form and Content in the Christian Tradition (Sanday), 12:665

Form criticism, biblical, 5:521–522, **806–814**
    biblical hermeneutics, 6:794
    biblical theology, 2:385
    Dibelius, Martin, 4:733–734
    literature survey, 5:812–813
    pentateuchal studies, 11:92, 93

Form criticism, biographies of Christ, 7:849

Form in Gothic (Worringer), 3:676

Form of Life (St. Clare of Assisi), 5:898

Forma verae religionis quaerrendae et inveniendae (Elizalde), 5:168

Formal and Transcendental Logic (Husserl), 9:567, 10:607

Formal distinctions, 4:781–782, 937

Formal intellectual locutions, 8:747

Formal Sign, 13:116

Formalism
    aesthetics, 1:142–143
    axiomatic system, 1:948

Formalism *(continued)*
    categorical imperative, 3:254–255
Formalism (mathematics), 9:327
Der Formalismus in derEthik und die materiale Wertethik (Scheler), 12:731
Formalistic ethics. *See* Ethical formalism
Formaliter (formally), 12:751
The Formative Years of Catholic University of America (Ellis), 5:170
Formbach Monastery (Bavaria), 2:323
Die Formgeschichte des Evangelium (Dibelius), 5:521, 812
Formicarius (Nider), 9:461, 10:386
Formigão, Manoel, 5:644
Formosus (Pope), **5:814–816**, 7:923–924
    Bulgaria, 2:679
    Carolingian Dynasty, 3:171
    Eugenius Vulgarius, 5:447
    posthumous trial, 5:815, 8:305, 12:346
    Sergius III (Pope), 13:15
    Stephen VI (VII) (Pope), 13:520
Forms, unicity and plurality of, **5:816–819**
    controversy, 12:230–231, 266
    correctoria, 4:275, 276–277
    distinction, 4:782
    soul, 13:339–345
    See also Plurality of forms
Formula of Concord (1577), 14:263
Formulae spiritalis intelligentiae (Eucherius of Lyons), 5:438, 513
Formularies, 3:41, 4:757
Fornari-Strata, Maria Victoria, Bl., **5:819**
Fornication, 1:131, 4:64–65, 221, **5:819**, 8:875
Fornication, in the Bible, **5:820**
Forrest, Nathan Bedford, Ku Klux Klan, 8:251
Forrestal, Mary Pacifica (Mother), 5:889
Fors Clavigera (Ruskin), 12:414
Forst, Marion F., 4:810
Forster, Johann, 6:697
Fort Augustus Abbey (Scotland), **5:820**
Fort Wayne Diocese (IN), 4:956–957, 7:415
Fortalitium Fidei (Alonso de Espina), 1:304
Forte, Bruno, 7:528
Fortem virili pectore (hymn), **5:820–821**
Fortescue, Adrian (1476-1539), Bl., 5:226, **821**
Fortescue, Adrian (1864-1923), **5:821**
Fortis, Luigi, 7:788
Fortitude, gift of, 5:822, **822**, 9:44

Fortitude, virtue of, 1:334, 4:315–316, 332, **5:822–823**
Fortunatus, Venantius Honorius Clementianus (Bp. of Poitiers), 1:180, 645, 3:596, **5:823**, 7:253
Fortune, **5:824**, 9:22, 14:585–586
The Forty Days (Pazzi), 11:47
Forty Hours Devotion, 4:711, 5:435–436, **824**, 8:145, 267–268
Forty Martyrs, SS. (Roman Empire), **5:825**
Forty-eighters (political party, U.S.), 9:646–647
The Forty-Two Articles of Religion, 12:9
Forty-two line Bible. *See* Gutenberg Bible
Foscarini, Paolo Antonio, **5:825**, 6:61
Fosdick, Harry Emerson, 2:80, 6:30
Fossanova Abbey (Italy), 3:750, 5:825, **825–826**
Foster, Augustus, 3:180
Foster, Kenelm, 4:320–321
Fotterell, Edward, 2:36
Foucauld, Charles Eugène de, 4:763, 5:826, **826–827**
Foucauld Rule, 8:610, 616
Fouché, Joseph, 5:974
Foucher, Abbé Simon, 9:74
Fouille, Alfred, 5:396, 7:300
Foundation for International Cooperation (FIC), 3:536
Foundational theology, **5:827–831**, 11:461, 13:915
Foundationalism, 5:829–830, **831–832**
Foundations and Donors Interested in Catholic Activities (FADICA), 5:588
Foundations of Christian Education (Fitzpatrick), 5:753
Foundations of Christian Faith (Grundkurs) (Rahner), 5:827–828, 11:894
Foundations of the Metaphysics of Morals (Kant), 9:566
Founding Church of Scientology, 12:823
Foundling Asylum Society (New York City), 5:752
Fountain of Life (Fons vita) (Avicebron), 7:863–864
Fountainbleau, Treaty of, 8:809
Fountains Abbey (England), 3:749, 750, 5:832, **832–833**, 8:183
The Fountains of Rome (Respighi), 12:139
Fouquet, Jean, 11:605
Four Articles of 1682, 3:615, 4:591
Four Articles of Prague (1420), 14:363

The Four Books of Dialogues on the Life and Miracles of the Italian Fathers and on the Immortality of Souls. See Dialogues (St. Gregory I)
Four Crowned Martyrs, **5:823**, 12:52, 13:167–168
Four Dissertations (Hume), 7:200
Four ends of life, 6:844
Four Gallican Articles of 1682, 6:778
Four Masters, Annals of the, **5:833–834**
Four Quartets (Eliot), 5:160, 161
Fourier, Charles, 2:627, 5:397
Fourier, Peter, St., **5:834**, 8:432, 12:780
Fourier, Rule of, 8:432
Fournet, André Hubert, St., 2:390, **5:834–835**
Fournier, Jacques. *See* Benedict XII (Pope)
Fournier John (Mother), St., **5:835**, 12:555
Foursquare Gospel, International Church of the (Los Angeles), **5:835–836**
Fourteen Holy Helpers, 2:428, 3:268, 5:173, **836–837**
Fourteenth Amendment (U.S. Constitution), 3:660
Fourth Ecumenical Council. *See* Chalcedon, Council of
Fourth Formulary of Sirmium (Dated Creed), 1:663
The Fourth Gospel (Sanday), 12:665
Fowler, James W., 2:223
Fox, George, 2:462, 4:39, **5:837–838**, *838*, 6:3, 8:87
Fox, James, 6:196
Fox, Joseph (Bp. of Green Bay, WI), 14:780
Fox, Matthew, 5:55
Foxe, John, 2:508, 5:838
Foxe, Richard (Fox) (Bp. of Winchester), 1:402, **5:838**
Foxe's Book of Martyrs, **5:838–839**
Foy, Francis, 3:279
Foy, St., 4:129, 5:839, **839**
Fra Angelico. *See* Fiesole, Guido da, Bl.
Fracastoro, Girolamo, 1:677, 2:403
Frachet, Gerard de, 14:33
Fraction Rite, 4:12
Fragment Targum, 13:761
Fragmente eines Wolfenbüttelschen Ungenannten (Reimarus), 12:35
Franca (virgin), St., 5:840
Franca, Leonel, 5:717, **840**
Franca, SS., **5:840–841**
Franca Visalta of Piacenza (abbess), St., 5:840–841
Francart, Jacques, 3:706

France, **5:841–863**, 922

　Action Française, 1:81–82, 3:617

　anointing, 1:478–479

　anticlericalism, 1:518–519

　anti-Semitism, 7:874

　Assemblies of the French Clergy, 1:262, 787–788

　Assembly of 1755, 2:232

　baroque period, 2:107

　Benedictine monasteries, 2:256–257

　cabala, 2:831

　Calvinism, 2:895, 12:20

　capital punishment, 3:87

　Carmelites, 3:126, 129, 141, 143

　Cartesianism, 3:184–185, 186

　catechesis, 3:243, 244, 245

　Catholic revival, 4:40–41, 61–64, 113, 314

　Chateaubriand, Françios René de, 3:446–449

　Christian workers organizations, 6:647–648

　Christmas, 3:554

　chronicles and annals, 1:463–464

　church architecture, 3:691–693, 695–696, 706, 708, 713

　Church-State relations, 7:472, 9:723, 824

　colonialism, African, 9:76–77, 898–899

　colonialism, Indian Ocean, 9:26, 371

　colonialism, Maltese, 9:82

　colonialism, North American, 9:54–55, 720–721, 737–738, 740–741, 13:820–821

　colonialism, Vietnamese, 14:500, 501

　commission of regulars, 4:13

　Communio edition, 4:31

　Communion antiphon, 4:32

　concelebration, 4:50

　confessions of faith, 4:79

　Confirmation, 4:87

　Congregation of the Incarnate Word and Blessed Sacrament, 7:370–371

　contraception, 4:221–222

　Convent of Unterlinden, 14:333–334

　Council of Trent, 4:312, 313

　Counter Reformation, 2:259

　Crusades, 4:400–401, 410, 411, 413

　deism, 4:617

　Dominicans, 4:853

　Dubois, Guillaume, 4:917

　dueling, 4:928

　Durkheim, Émile, 4:951

　ecclesiastical organization, 4:61–63, 5:843

　Ecumenical Movement, 5:73–74

　education, 3:49, 9:160, 175, 12:773

　Enlightenment, 5:254–255, 259–262

　Fénelon, François de Salignac de la Mothe, 5:681–683

　Gallicanism, 6:73–78

　Gregory VII (Pope), St., 6:493–494

　Gregory XII (Pope), 6:501

　Gregory XVI (Pope), 6:508–509

　heraldry, 6:764

　Honorius III (Pope), 7:84

　humanism, 7:190

　iconography, 7:285–286

　idealism, 7:300

　investiture struggle, 7:537, 538

　Jesuits, 3:792–793, 7:786–787

　John XXIII (Pope), Bl., 7:934–935

　law, 5:702–703, 9:386–387

　liturgical movement, 8:671, 674

　Lutheranism, 12:18

　Lyons martyrs, 4:83

　map, 5:*844*

　medieval drama, 4:894, 897, 898, 900, 901–902

　medieval literature, 9:455

　Mexico, 9:579

　mission

　　Eudes, St. John, 5:440–441

　　Francis de Sales, St., 5:867

　　medieval mission, 3:599

　　Protestant mission, 12:30–31

　　20th century, 5:858

　modernism, 9:753–754

　music, 7:255, 259, 8:690–691, 696

　papal state, 7:488–489, 13:494–496

　Peace of God Movement, 11:50

　Pius X (Pope), St., 11:390

　Pius XI (Pope), 11:395

　politics, 3:619, 9:753, 12:666

　preaching, 11:621–622

　Presbyterianism, 11:678–679

　Prône, 11:746–747

　Protestant toleration, 4:309

　ralliement policy, 8:389, 11:900–901

　Red Mass, 11:961

　Reformed churches, 7:166, 12:23–24

　Regalia, 12:27

　Renaissance, 12:119

　sacramental theology, 12:478

　St. Bartholomew's Day Massacre, 12:537–538

　Servites, 13:28

　Sidonius Apollinaris, St., 13:104

　social justice, 3:417–418, 620, 13:256

　Solesmes, 13:299–300

　structuralism, 13:551

　Vincentians, 14:527

　wars of religion, 3:612

　worker priests, 14:838

　See also Avignon papacy; Carolingian era; French art; French Revolution; Gallicanism; Huguenots; Jansenism; Mission in colonial America, French

France, Anatole, 5:*841*, **841**

France Pagan (Ward), 5:857

France pays de mission? (Godin), 14:838

Frances, Bl. (17th c. Japanese martyr), 7:734

Frances d'Amboise, Bl., 3:126, **5:863**

Frances of Rome, St., 3:605, 759, **5:863–864**

Franceschi, Gustavo Juan, 1:652, **5:864**

Francesco de Osuna, 5:896

Francesco Forgione. *See* Padre Pio (Bp. of Mérida), St.

Francesco Maria of Camporosso, St., **5:864–865**

Francesco of Siena, 5:911

Francesco Silvestri. *See* Ferrariensis (Italian philosopher)

Franchi de' Cavalierio, Pio, **5:865**

Francia, Annibale Maria di, Bl., **5:865–866**

Francinaina de los Dolores de María. *See* Cirer Carbonnel, Francinaina, Bl.

Francis (Bp. of Ancyra), 1:398

Francis (Duke of Guise), 6:577–578, *578*

Francis, Norman C., 14:881

Francis, St. (carpenter, 17th c. Japanese martyr), 7:732

Francis, St. (physician, 17th c. Japanese martyr), 7:732

Francis I (King of France)

　Adrian VI (Pope), 1:129

　Charles V (Holy Roman Emperor), 3:429, 430, 781

　Church-State relations, 3:639, 4:312

　Clement VII (Pope), 3:781–782

　Concordat of, 5:847, 849

　hospitals, 7:137

　invasion of Italy, 7:669

　Paul III (Pope), 11:22

　Pragmatic Sanction, 6:75

Francis II (Holy Roman Emperor), 1:*910*, 914

Francis II (King of France), 5:849, 7:167

Francis Antony of Lucera. *See* Fasani, Francesco Antonio, St.

Francis Cardinal Bourne (Oldmeadow), 10:583

Francis de Sales, St., 2:109, 5:850, **866–869**
Abondance Monastery, 1:23
Alphonsus Liguori, St., 1:310
Angela of Foligno, Bl., 1:412
apologetics, 1:564
Arnauld, Jacqueline Marie Angélique, 1:716
Binet, Étienne, 2:399
Bonal, Raymond, 2:478
Bosco, St. John, 2:543
Bossuet, Jacques Bénigne, 2:550
Brisson, Louis Alexandre, 2:619
Cambridge Platonists, 2:909
catechesis, 3:234, 235
Caussade, Jean Pierre de, 3:310
Chantal, St. Jane Frances de, 3:381
Chaumont, Henri, 3:457
Clement VIII (Pope), 3:785
Coton, Pierre, 4:291
Counter Reformation, 3:612
Denis the Carthusian, 4:661
friendship with God, 6:11–12
humanism, 7:194
lay spirituality, 8:415
painting by Tiepolo, 5:*867*
Sisters of the Visitation, 12:554
skepticism, 13:202
Spiritual Combat, 13:429
spiritual direction, 4:762
spirituality, 13:47
Vincent de Paul, St., 14:518–519
Visitation nuns, 14:563

Francis Joseph (Emperor of Austria), 1:914

Francis of Assisi, St., **5:870–871**
Agnellus of Pisa, Bl., 1:177
Andrew Caccioli, Bl., 1:403–404, 2:840
Anthony of Padua, St., 1:506
bare feet of, 4:764
bilocation, 2:397
biographies, 5:871, 896, 898, 899, 12:453
Bonaventure, St., 2:479, 485, 489–490, 492, 493
Carmelite spirituality, 3:130
Catharism, 1:231
Christmas, 3:557
Christopher of Romandiola, Bl., 3:563

Clare of Assisi, St., 3:760
crib devotion, 4:364
devotion to Passion, 10:925, 926
Divine Office for, 8:50
Elias of Cortona, 5:156–157, 870–871
Fioretti, 5:736–737
following of Christ, 5:788
Franciscan spirituality, 5:892, 893
Giles of Assisi, 6:218
Honorius III (Pope), 7:84
images of, 12:600
Innocent III (Pope), 3:602
lay fervor, 8:295
Life written, 8:50
Luchesius of Poggibonsi, 8:844
Luke Belludi, 8:865
mystical quality of writings, 10:117
painting by Giotto, 5:*870*
"Pardon of Assisi," 11:527–528
patron of Santa Fe Archdiocese, 12:675
poverty, 11:569
relics, 5:871
religious conversion of Muslims, 9:691
religious habit, 12:99
Roger of Todi, Bl., 12:288
Rule of Life, 5:901
Sacred Heart devotion, 12:499
St. Francis Receiving the Stigmata (van Eyck), 13:*531*
Solano modeling life after, 13:299
spirituality, 13:446
stigmata, 5:871, 893
works of charity, 3:413

Francis of Geronimo, St., **5:871–872**, 7:782

Francis of Jesus Mary Joseph. *See* Palau y Quer, Francisco, Bl.

Francis of Marchia, 7:363
Francis of Meyronnes, 12:762, 825
Francis of Osuna, 3:135, **5:872**
Francis of Pamplona, **10:816**
Francis of Paola, St., 3:606, **5:872–874**, *873*, 874, 9:650

Francis Xavier Mission Society, 1:2
Franciscan Annunciades, 7:879–880
Franciscan Church (Cologne), 3:844
Franciscan Church of Muna (Mexico), 9:*702*

Franciscan crown, 6:42
Franciscan Friars of the Atonement, **5:874–875**
Franciscan Handmaids of Mary, 5:878

Franciscan Handmaids of the Most Pure Heart of Mary, 1:158, 162, 5:878
Franciscan Hospitaller Sisters of the Immaculate Conception, 5:878
Franciscan Martyrs of Georgia, **5:875**
Franciscan Missionaries of Mary, 3:384, 8:156
Franciscan Missionaries of Mary (Rome), 5:878
Franciscan Missionaries of Our Lady, 5:878–879
Franciscan Missionaries of St. Joseph (Rome), 5:879
Franciscan Missionary Sisters of Our Lady of Sorrows, 5:879
Franciscan Missionary Sisters of the Divine Child, 5:879
Franciscan Missionary Sisters of the Infant Jesus, 5:879
Franciscan Missionary Sisters of the Sacred Heart of St. Francis, 5:882
Franciscan Observants, 3:462–463, 5:897, 902, 903, 904, 7:932
Franciscan Order at the Friary of Our Lady of Grace, 8:409
Franciscan Regula Breviary, 1:486
Franciscan Ritual of the Last Sacraments, 4:10
Franciscan School, 8:83, 12:760
Franciscan Sisters, **5:875–892**
African American, 1:158
founding of, 2:510
Hawaiian mission, 6:671
Maria Laurentia Longo, founding of, 9:153
Saint Felix of Cantalice (Felicians), 8:246
Franciscan Sisters, Daughters of the Sacred Hearts of Jesus and Mary (Rome), 5:879
Franciscan Sisters of Allegany, 5:880
Franciscan Sisters of Baltimore, 5:880
Franciscan Sisters of Chicago (Rome), 5:880–881
Franciscan Sisters of Christian Charity, 5:881
Franciscan Sisters of Little Falls (MN), 5:881
Franciscan Sisters of Mary, 5:881
Franciscan Sisters of Mary Immaculate (Rome), 5:881
Franciscan Sisters of Mill Hill, 5:880
Franciscan Sisters of Oldenburg, 5:881–882
Franciscan Sisters of Our Lady of Lourdes (Rome), 5:882
Franciscan Sisters of Our Lady of Perpetual Help (Rome), 5:882

Franciscan Sisters of Peace, 5:882

Franciscan Sisters of Penance and Charity of Tiffin (OH), 5:882–883

Franciscan Sisters of Perpetual Adoration, 5:877

Franciscan Sisters of St. Joseph of Hamburg (NY), 5:883

Franciscan Sisters of the Atonement, 5:874

Franciscan Sisters of the Atonement (Rome), 5:883

Franciscan Sisters of the Holy Cross, 4:378

Franciscan Sisters of the Poor, 3:419, 12:735

Franciscan Sisters of the Poor (Rome), 5:883

Franciscan Sisters of the Sacred Heart (Rome), 5:883–884

Franciscan Sisters of the Sorrowful Mother (Rome), 5:884

Franciscan Spirituality, 2:374, 578, **5:892–897**

Franciscan Spirituals, 3:321–322, 603, 604, **5:897–898**, 7:876, 932

    Angela of Foligno, Bl., 1:412

    Angelus Clarenus, 1:428

    apocalyptic movements, 1:548

    Boniface VIII (Pope), 2:502

    Church property, 3:727

    Clareni, 1:428, 3:762–763

    Clement VI (Pope), 3:780

    Joachim of Fiore, 8:174

    John XXII persecution of, 5:897, 902

    Richard of Conington, 12:232

Franciscan theological tradition, **5:898–900**

    aseity, 1:780

    Avicebron, 1:939

    Bernard of Clairvaux, 2:311

    British Society of Franciscan Studies, 8:609

    histories of, 8:609–610

    Latin Averroism, 1:936

    See also Bonaventure, St.

Franciscan University of Steubenville (OH), 10:572

Franciscans

    active life, 1:83

    Agnellus of Pisa, Bl., 1:177

    Albania, 1:213

    Albigensians, 1:229, 231

    Alexander IV (Pope), 1:257

    alternativa, 1:321

    Ancient See of Carlisle, 3:124

Andrew Caccioli, Bl., 1:403–404, 2:840

Anointing of the Sick, 1:482, 486

Anthony of Padua, St., 1:506

archaeology, 2:380, 3:83

Argentina, 1:649, 650

Arizona, 1:687

Augustinianism, 1:878–879

Austria, 1:910

Avicebron, 1:673

Bogomilism, 2:459

Bolivia, 1:712, 2:466

Brazil, 2:588, 590, 595

Canada, 3:5

Cape Verde, 3:80

Carthage, 3:187–188

catechesis, 3:231

Catharism, 1:229, 231, 3:260

Celestines, 3:321–322

Cenacle, 3:333

censorship, 3:336

Central American mission, 9:707

Chile, 3:485

China, 2:836, 3:492–493, 495, 499, 513

choice, 3:521

Christmas carols, 3:557

Christocentrism, 3:558

chronicle, 5:899

chronicles, 1:464

Civezza, Marcellino da, 3:752

Clareni, 1:428, 3:762–763

Colorado, 3:857

Commissariat of the Holy Land, 4:12

contemplation, 4:207

correctoria of Thomism, 4:273–278

Counter Reformation, 3:611

Deymann, Clementine, 4:713

as discalced order, 4:765

Dominican rivalry with, 3:603

Elbel history of, 5:143

Elias of Cortona, 5:156–157

Engelhart histories of, 5:221

England, 5:242

European missions, 5:905

following of Christ, 5:788

Fraticelli, 3:337, 762

Gonsalvus Hispanus, on poverty, 6:341

Gregory IX (Pope), 6:497

hierarchical insignia, 6:764

Honorius III (Pope), 7:84

Horgan, Thaddeus Daniel, 7:110

Hugh of Digne, 7:151

Hugh of Newcastle, 7:155

Hungary, 7:210–211

Italian expansion, 7:665–666

John XXII (Pope), 3:603–604, 7:931–932

John of Parma, on poverty, 7:980

Knights of of Holy Sepulcher, 8:198

lay allegiances, 8:295

lay brothers of, 4:49–50

medieval preaching of, 11:612

Mexico, 1:723, 2:533

mission

    abandoned Jesuit missions, reuse of, 9:707

    Arizona, 9:717

    California, 9:717, 12:644–645

    Central America, 9:707

    Colombia, 3:762–763, 850, 9:711

    colonial America, 9:701–702

    Costa Rica, 12:290

    Detroit, 9:723

    Ecuador, 9:711

    Europe, 5:905

    Florida, 9:707, 715, 12:613

    Guatemala, 12:290–291

    Indochina, 12:255

    Mexico, 5:785, 12:371–372, 528–529

    Mongolia, 9:805–806

    New Mexico, 9:716

    New York state, 12:540–541

    Nicaragua, 12:290

    North American missions, 5:903–904

    Paraguay, 10:877

    Peru, 9:710–711, 12:240–241, 616

    Texas, 9:716, 13:845

    Venezuela, 9:711, 12:407

    See also specific Franciscan missionary societies

monk, watercolor by Martinez Compañ, 5:*901*

monks, 5:*902*

Observant reform, 5:902

opposition to Thomism, 14:44–45

Peru, 11:159

poverty, 5:895–896, 902, 11:569, 570

Poverty Movement, 11:572–573

reform under John Capistran, St., 7:944

Roger of Todi, Bl., 12:288

rule of St. Francis, 12:730

St. Bonaventure University, 12:540–541

Franciscans *(continued)*
Santo Domingo, Cuba, 9:706–707
Schaaf, Valentine Theodore, 12:726
scholasticism, 12:760, 764
Scotism, as followers of, 12:825–826
Scottish religious orders, 12:833
Sixtus V (Pope), 13:198
Spain, 13:384
Spiritual-Conventual conflict, 3:132, 603, 780
stations of the Cross, 13:500
Strict Observance, 13:461
Third Orders, 1:413, 3:413, 520
Wyoming, 14:870
Zambia, 14:907
See also Bonaventure, St.; Capuchins; Franciscan Spirituals; Franciscan theological tradition
Franciscans, Conventuals, 5:897, 902, 903
Franciscans, Discalced, 5:903
Franciscans, First Order, 4:764–765, **5:900–905**
Franciscans, Recollects, 5:903
Franciscans, Reformed, 5:903
Franciscans, Second Order, 5:870, **905–906**
Franciscans, Third Order Regular, 1:413, **5:906–908**
Franciscan Friars of the Atonement, 5:874–875
Franciscan Sisters, 5:875–892
Luchesis and Buona, 8:844
Shen Jihe, St., 13:78
Stigmatine Sisters, 8:333
Franciscans, Third Order Secular, 2:168, **5:909**
The Franciscans in Arizona (Engelhardt), 5:221
The Franciscans in California (Engelhardt), 5:221
Francisco, Antonio, 12:401
Francisco de Jesús Maria, 12:619
Francisco de los Angeles. *See* Quiñones, Francisco de
Francisco de S. Buenaventura, Bl., 7:734
Francisco de S. Maria, Bl., 7:734
Francisco de San Tómas, 3:137
Francisco de Toledo, 5:513
Franciscus de Accoltis, 3:52
Franck, César Auguste, **5:909–910**, *910*
Franck, Sebastian, 1:369, 718
Francke, August Hermann, **5:910–911**
Carpzov, Johann Benedikt (II), 3:174
Pietism, 11:330
Pietist groups, 8:891

Franco, Apollinar, Bl., 7:733–734
Franco, Boniface. *See* Boniface VII (Antipope)
Franco, Francisco (Gen.), 13:205, 395–396, 396–397
Franco Gómez, Canuto, Bl., 7:124
Franco Lippi, Bl., **5:911**
Franco of Cologne, **5:911**, 8:684
Franco of Liège, 12:808
Francogallia (Hotman), 5:702
François, Armand (Bp. of Toronto), 2:142
François, François, 12:277
François de Fontenay, 8:59–60
François de la Purification (Bp. of Beijing), 3:515
François Joseph de la, Bl. (1755-92), 8:336
Franco-Prussian War, 8:254
Franczuk, Ignacy, 11:583
Frangipani, Aldruda, 5:912
Frangipani, Cencius, II, 6:123
Frangipani, Fabio Mirto, 5:912
Frangipani, Giovanni, 5:912
Frangipani, Jacoba, 5:912
Frangipani, Muzio, 5:912
Frangipani, Ottavio Fraja, 5:912
Frangipani, Ottavio Mirto, 5:912
Frangipani family, 1:370, **5:911–913**
Franipani, Silvester (Ignatius Ciantes), 5:912
Frank, Franz Hermann von, 5:323
Frank, Jacob, 2:835, **5:913**, 13:57
Frank, Phillip, 3:302, 5:142
Frankel, Zacharias, 7:873
Frankenberg, Bernard Frank de, 4:775
Frankenberg, Johann Heinrich (Abp. of Malines), **5:913–914**
Frankfort, H., 3:672, 673
Frankfurt, Council of (794)
adoptionism, 1:119
Alcuin, Bl., 1:243
Canon Law, 3:42
Carolingian reform, 3:156, 425
catechesis, 3:230, 240
Frankfurt, Diet of (1791), 3:92
Frankfurt Institute of Social Research, 5:914
Frankfurt School (Germany), **5:914–915**
Frankish kingdom, 9:517–519
in the Middle Ages, 9:614
papal state, protection of, 13:491
patron saint of, 12:413
Frankish penitentials, 11:75

Frankish Reform. *See* Carolingian Reform
Frankish-papal alliance
Stephen II (III) (Pope), 13:516
Stephen III (IV) (Pope), 13:517
Stephen IV (V) (Pope), 13:519
Frankl, Paul, 3:676, 694, 697
Franklin, Benjamin, 4:617–618, 5:260, 262, 10:484
Franklin, Colautti v., 1:33
Franklin, William (Bp. of Davenport), 4:535
Franklin's Tale (Chaucer), 3:456
Franks (people of Germanic origin), **5:915–917**
Byzantine Empire, 4:174
Canon Law, 3:40–41
Carolingian Dynasty, 5:916–917
chronicles, 5:922
Church in Gaul, 6:112
Constantine II (Antipope), 4:178
conversion of, 3:229
Crusaders' states, 4:401, 402, 403–405
Merovingians, 5:916
Methodius, 4:475, 476
Normandy occupied, 10:426
Pelagius II (Pope), 3:596
rites of death, 4:10
Siena, city of, 13:106
synodic practice of, 4:302
tribal migrations, 5:915–916
works of charity under, 3:408
Zachary (Pope), St., relations with, 14:904
See also Carloman (Frankish mayor of the palace); Carolingian Dynasty; Carolingian era; Carolingian reform; Charlemagne (Holy Roman Emperor); *specific kings*
Fransen, Pieter Frans, **5:918–919**, 6:400, 401
Franz, John B., 4:810
Franzelin, Johannes Baptist (Card.), **5:919**, 7:789
affinity of spirit between Möhler, 10:104
Anglican orders problem, 1:438
dogmatic theology, 4:814
ecclesiology, 5:37
Schmid, Franz, 12:743
Vatican Council I, 5:919
Franziska of Hegne, Bl. *See* Nisch, Ulrika Franziska, Bl.
Franzoni (Abp. of Turin), 2:543

Frassati, Pier Giorgio, Bl., **5:919–920**

Frassen, C., 12:764

Frassinello, Benedetta Cambiagio, Bl., **5:920**

Frassinetti, Giuseppe, **5:920–921**

Frassinetti, Paola Angela Maria, St., 5:920, **921**

Frasso, Pedro, 10:978

Fraternal Appeal to the American Churches, with a Plan for Catholic Union (Schmucker), 12:745

Fraternal organizations, 1:285–286, 3:281, 622

Fraternité Sacerdotale de Saint Pie X, 3:289, 8:447

Fraternity Jeanne Jugan, 8:617

Fraternity of Diocesan Worker Priests, 4:827

Frati Bigi, 10:812

Fraticelli (heretical sects), **5:921–922**

Anthony of Stroncone, Bl., 1:507

apocalyptic movements, 1:548

Clareni, 3:762

papal Antichrist, 1:517

Paul II (Pope), 11:20

theological censure, 3:337

Fraticelli de Opinione, 5:921–922

Fraticelli de Paupere Vita, 5:921

Fratis Simonis historia (Simon of Saint-Quentin), 13:132

Frauenfriedenskirche (Frankfurt am Main, Germany), 3:711

Frauenkirche (Dresden, Germany), 3:707

Fravashi (protective spirits), **5:922**

Fravita (Patriarch of Constantinople), 1:50

Frayssinous, Denis (Bp.), 5:854, **922**

Frazee v. Illinois Department of Employment Sec. (1989), 3:663

Frazer, James George, Sir

animism, 1:459

biblical theology, 2:385

evolution of religion, 12:64

Freculf (Bp. of Lisieux), 1:462

Fredegarius, **5:922–923**

Fredegisus (d. 834), 12:757

Fredegund (d. 597), 9:518

Frederick (Duke of Austria), 4:169, 170

Frederick (the Wise)

Charles V (Holy Roman Emperor), 3:429

Luther's extradition, 8:880

Wittenberg University, 14:803

Frederick I (King of Denmark), 4:665

Frederick I Barbarossa (Holy Roman Emperor), 5:166, 444, **924–926**, *925*

Adalgott II, St., 1:103

Adrian IV (Pope), 1:126, 127

Albert of Jerusalem, St., 1:222

Alexander III (Pope), 1:254

Arnold of Brescia, 1:719

Callistus III (Antipope), 2:882

Church-State relations, 3:636, 7:42–43

Clement III (Pope), 3:776

Cologne, 3:843

Colonna family, 3:854

conflict between Urban III (Pope), 14:336

Cremona's independence, 13:101

Crusades, 2:609, 4:411

destruction caused by Crusade armies, 10:355

Distentis Abbey, 4:775

Gerhoh of Reichersberg, 6:167

Holy Empire as term, 7:42, 43

Hugh of Honau, 7:153

imperial power in Italy, 7:663

Lateran Councils, 12:356

Lombard League, 8:767

Low Countries bishops appointed, 10:258

Low Countries lords in army of, 10:257–258

Lucius III (Pope), 8:847

papacy, 3:601

Sankt Gallen Abbey (Switzerland), 12:669

Treaty of Constance, 1:126

University of Bologna, 2:472

Frederick II the Great (Holy Roman Emperor), **5:926–928**, *927*

Albert Behaim, 1:222

apocalyptic movements, 1:548

bestiaries, 2:344

capital punishment, 3:87

Celestine IV (Pope), 3:320

Church-State relations, 3:636, 639

Colonna family, 3:854

conciliarism, 4:55

conflict between papacy, 14:14

constitution on *Ortolevos* heresy, 10:702

Crusades, 4:400, 403, 404–405, 414

Gregory IX (Pope), 6:496–497, 7:474

Guelfs and Ghibellines, 6:555–556

heresy charge, 8:907

Herman of Salza, 6:783

Innocent III (Pope), 3:602

Innocent IV (Pope), 3:603, 7:475

Lombard League, 8:767

Papal States, 7:664

prince-bishops, 11:714

Frederick II the Great (King of Prussia), 5:*923*, **923–924**

deism, 4:617

Jesuits, 3:795

Order of the Swan, 10:631–632

Frederick III (Austrian Emperor), 5:29

Frederick III (Holy Roman Emperor), 6:639

Council of Basel, 2:134

Crusades, 2:881

Zamometič, Andrea, 14:909

Frederick V (elector of the Palatinate), 1:912

Frederick of Isenberg, 5:210

Frederick William III (King of Prussia), 3:845, 4:81, 7:17

Frederick William IV (King of Prussia), 3:846

Fredeswinda, St. *See* Frideswide of Oxford, St.

Frédol, Bérenger (Berengarius Fredoli) (Card.), **5:928**

Free and Faithful in Christ (Häring), 6:646

Free associations, in the state, 13:487

Free choice (*liberum arbitrium*). *See* Free will

Free Church Federal Council, 5:928

Free Churches, 2:622, **5:928**

Free Methodist Church (U.S.), 7:7, 9:562

Free music, 2:115

Free Spirit Movement, 4:876

Free will, **5:928–934**

appetite, 1:602

Augustine, St., 1:877

Cartesianism, 4:681–682

Concordia liberi arbitrii cum gratiae donis (Molina, Luis de), 9:769

consent, 4:158–159

Counter-Reformation's affirmation of, 2:110

death, 4:578–581

Duns Scotus, John, 4:937–938

efficient causality, 5:99, 102

Kierkegaard, 8:166

Lutheranism, 3:608

Malebranche, Nicolas, 9:75

Methodism, 14:684

molinism, 9:771

Mu'tazilite school, 10:74

natural causes vs., 5:99

Free will *(continued)*

New Haven theology (Taylorism), 10:280

occasionalism, 10:527

Origen's defense of, 10:656

Pico della Mirandola, 7:186

predetermination, 11:658–659

Spinoza, 13:420

spirituality, 13:440

sufficient reason vs., 13:593

theodicy, 13:868

Thomistic conception of, 9:90

See also Choice; Human act; Pelagius and Pelagianism; Will and willing

Free will and grace, **5:934–935**

congruism, 4:120–121

conversion, 4:239–241

de auxiliis controversy, 4:110–113

Durandus of Saint-Pourçain, 4:948

See also Baptism of infants

Free will and providence, **5:935–936**

Free Will Baptists, 2:80

Freedman, D. N., 3:565, 566

Freedmen, evangelization of (U.S.), 9:738

Freedom, **5:936–942**

absolute, 1:42

agnosticism, 1:184

anguish, 12:696

anxiety, 1:540

in the Bible, 5:944–945

Catholic social thought, 13:255

Christian anthropology, 3:532, 533

communication, 4:24

Divine concurrence, 4:72

exercise, 7:172

existentialism, 5:545–546, 725, 8:166–167, 12:695–697

French ideas, 8:272

grace, 6:385, 386–387, 389, 399–400

Gregory of Nyssa, St., 6:520

history of, as transcendental principle, 4:373

human act, 7:172–173

limitations of, 7:172–173

Maine de Biran, 9:60

Maritain, Jacques, 9:179

Mary, Blessed Virgin, from sin, 9:250–251

motion, 10:25–26

physical premotion, 11:671

Piaget, Jean, 11:318

redemption in patristic thought, 10:961

specification, 7:172

will and willing, 14:720, 723

See also Choice

Freedom, intellectual, **5:942–944**

See also Academic Freedom

Freedom, spiritual, **5:944–945**, 8:828, 881

Freedom and Nature (Ricoeur), 12:241

The Freedom of a Christian (Luther), 12:16

Freedom of choice, 4:152

Freedom of religion, 3:641–643, **5:946–954**

Anglicanism, 1:445

Baptists, 2:78

Castellio, Sebastian, 3:214

colonial Pennsylvania, 11:79

community churches, 4:39

Comoros, lack of, 4:40

conscience, 4:148–149

Constantine I (the Great) (Roman Emperor), 4:179–182, 185

Croatia, 4:371

democracy, 4:640

Denmark, 4:666–667

Edict of Milan, 12:316

France, 8:309

Germany, 8:517

Hungary, 7:214, 216, 222

Iceland, 7:277

Israel, 7:647

Japan, 7:741

Korea, 8:239

Lateran Pacts (1985), 8:359

Latvia, 8:376

liberalism, 3:619

Lithuanian dissidents, 8:608

Malaysia, 9:71

Malaysian Consultative Council of Buddhism, Christianity, Hinduism, and Sikhism, 9:72

Moldova, 9:767

Pacification of Amboise, 3:266

papal social thought, 13:259

Slovenia, 13:227

Sweden, 13:638

Transylvania, 7:214

U.S. law

Barron v. Baltimore, 5:961

McCollum v. Board of Education, 5:961

state legislation, 5:963–964

Terret v. Taylor, 5:963

See also Church and State; Church and State, U.S.; *specific countries*

Freedom of religion in the U.S. Constitution, **5:954–964**

Freedom of speech, Catholic teaching on, 5:944, **964–966**

Freeland (Hertzka), 14:361

Freeman, William, Bl., 5:232, **966**

Freeman's Journal and Catholic Register (newspaper), 8:303, 9:403, 10:314

Freemasonry

Argentina, 1:651

Brazil, 2:595–596

Carbonari, 3:99

Christian Reformed Church, 3:543

Clement XII (Pope), 3:790

illuminism, 7:321

opposition to, 8:197

Rosicrucians, 12:381–382

The Freethinker (periodical), 5:967

Freethinkers, 1:823, **5:966–967**

Frege, Gottlob, 1:520, 8:752, 753, 12:415

Frei, Hans, 5:829

Freiburg Archdiocese (Germany), 8:255, 304

Freire, Paolo, 8:549, 11:585

Freising Collection. See *Quesnelliana Collectio*

Freitas, Luzia de, Bl., 7:733

Freking, Frederick W. (Bp. of La Crosse, WI), 8:273, 14:783

Frelichowski, Stefan Wincenty, Bl., **5:969**

FRELIMO (political party), 10:39, 40

Frelinghuysen, Theodore Jacobus, **5:969**, 6:425

French, Richard, 7:579

French Americans in Georgia, 6:151

French and Indian War (1754-63), 11:82, 235

See also Québec Act (Canada, 1774)

French art, 4:*394*, 397

French Association for Parapsychological Studies, 11:463

French Canadian nationalism, 8:280

French Episcopal Conference, 5:859–860

French Modernism, 12:453

French Passion plays, 10:928

French Polynesia, 10:531–532

French Revolution (1789), **5:969–977**

Abondance Monastery, 1:24

Anchin Abbey, 1:396

Angers, 1:432

anticlericalism, 1:518, 519

Assemblies of the French Clergy, 1:788

Avignon, 1:942

Boisgelin de Cucé, Jean de Dieu, Raymond de, 2:462

Bollandists, 2:472

Bonal, François de, 2:477

Brothers of the Christian Schools, 2:632

Buchez, Philippe Joseph Benjamin, 2:654

Burke, Edmund, 2:702

Calas case, 2:858

Canada, 3:7, 9–10

Canon Law, 3:54

Caprara, Giovanni Battista, 3:92

Caribbean, 3:115, 118

Carmelites, 3:128, 143

Carthusians, 3:195

Casoni, Filippo, 3:204

Caulites, 3:296

Chaise-Dieu Abbey, 3:362

Chaminade, Guillaume Joseph, Bl., 3:373

Chateaubriand, François René de, 3:447

Cheverus, Jean Louis Lefebvre de, 3:472

Chinese mission, 3:498

Church history, 3:616–617

Church-State relations, 3:92, 441, 615, 617, 640, 753–754

Cistercians, 3:747, 751, 758

Comte, Auguste, 4:47

Cuxa Abbey, 4:450

Daughters of the Holy Spirit, 7:45

dechristianization, 5:972–975, 8:282

Émery, Jacquesré, 5:190

fears of, 13:255

Feuillants, 3:747

fugitive priests, 8:778

Goddess of Reason, 11:945–946

Hapsburgs, 6:640

ideals inspiring, 8:271

Jansenism, 7:718–719

Jewish emancipation, 7:872–873

Knights of Malta, 8:194

Knights of the Faith, 8:197–198

laicism, 8:282

Lettres d'un royaliste savoisien (Maistre), 9:60–61

liberalism, 3:618, 619

Loménie de Brienne, 8:770

Luxembourg, 8:897, 898

Luxeuil Abbey, 8:899

Lyonese Rite, 8:905

martyrs, 1:722, 2:632, 3:128
    of Compiègne, 4:43–44
    of Laval, 8:384
    of Orange, 10:620–621
    of Paris (September Martyrs), 10:884–885
    Rogue, Pierre René, Bl., 12:290
    Sacramintine nuns, 12:484
    Saint-Germain-des-Prés, 12:548
    Sisters of St. Joseph, 12:554–555
    of Valenciennes, 14:371

papacy during, 10:845–846

papal social thought, 13:257

persecution of Catholic priests, 2:158

Pius VI (Pope), 11:377

Premonstratensians, 11:667

priests immigrating, 13:364

reaction, 13:410

Reign of Terror, 5:974

restoration of religion following, 4:61–63

Robespierre, Maximilien François de, 5:974, 12:273

Rome, 12:359–360

Sanfedists, 12:666

secularization of Church property, 12:873

Sisters of Bon Secours, 2:476

Sisters of Divine Providence, 13:181–182

Sisters of Providence, 13:188

socialism, 3:620

Solignac Abbey, 13:302

Spain, 4:739, 13:394–395

suppression of religious, 5:707, 12:548
    Commission of Regulars and, 4:13
    Compiègne martyrs, 4:43–44
    Conques Abbey, 4:129
    Coudrin, Pierre Marie Joseph and, 4:293
    Courdier, Jean-Nicolas, 4:261
    Crozier Fathers and, 4:378
    Decadi cult and, 4:586–587
    Holy Ghost Fathers, 7:25
    holy lance and, 7:31
    Hospitallers of St. John of God, 7:122
    Hospitallers of St. Lazarus of Jerusalem, 7:126
    Savigny Abbey, 12:711

Trappists, 3:745

University of Bologna, 2:475

Vincentians, effect, 14:527

works of charity, 3:419
    See also Civil Constitution of the Clergy

French School. See Spirituality, French school of

French Solesme Congregation, 2:255

A Frenchman's Thoughts on the War (Sabatier), 12:453

Frente Faravundo Marti de Liberación (FMLN), 5:175, 177

Freppel, Charles Émile (Bp. of Angers), 1:432, 5:977–978, 978

Frequens (Council of Constance), 3:604, 4:171

Frere, Rudolph Walter Howard (Bp.), 1:437, 5:978, 9:78

Frescobaldi, Girolamo, 2:115, 5:978–979, 979, 6:14

Freud, Sigmund
    appetite, 1:603
    conscience, 4:140
    consciousness, 4:153
    deconstructionism, 4:592–593
    dreams, 4:904, 905, 7:327
    evolution of religion, 12:64
    guilt, 6:568
    imagination, 7:326–327
    Jung relationship, 8:60
    sexual orientation, 7:68
    symbolism of mythology, 10:129

Frévisse, St. See Frideswide of Oxford, St.

Frey, Gerard L. (Bp. of Savannah), 12:710

Friars, 6:1, 2
    See also Mendicant orders

Friars Minor, Order of. See Franciscans, First Order

Friars Minor Capuchin, 2:132–133

Friars Minor Conventual, 5:902

Friars Minor of the Eremetical Life, 5:902

Friars Minor of the Regular Observance, 5:902

Friars of Unity, 1:706

Frías Cañizares, Luisa María, Bl., 1:4

Fribourg Union, 13:256

Frick, Carolo, 10:607

Friday, Christian week, 8:718

Fridelli, Xaver Ehrenbert, 6:1

Frideswide of Oxford, St., 6:1–2

Fridolin of Säckingen, St., 6:2

Friedel, Francis, 6:2

Friedel, Xaver. See Fridelli, Xaver Ehrenbert

Friedhofen, Peter, Bl., 6:2–3

Friedman, R. E., 11:96

Friedrich, Johann, 4:824, **6:3**
See also Old Catholics

Friend, William B. (Bp. of Alexandria-Shreveport, LA), 1:270

Friends, Religious Society of. *See* Quakers (Religious Society of Friends)

Friends of God, **6:5–6**, 13:453–454

Friends World Committee on Consultation, 6:5

Friendship, **6:6–9**
Aristotle, 8:826–827
charity, 3:396
communication, 4:24
courtesy compared to, 4:318

Friendship, particular, **6:9**

Friendship House, 4:614, **6:9–10**

Friendship with God, **6:10–12**
Adam (biblical figure), 1:106
Divine judgment, 8:35
reparation, 12:128–130

Fries, J. F., 11:802, 12:345

Friess, Mary Caroline (Mother), 12:781

Frigidian of Lucca, St., **6:12**

Frigolet Monastery (France), **6:12**

Frings, Josef Cardinal, 10:*485*

Frins, Victor, **6:12**

Frisians, mission to, 1:220, 2:494–495, 496

Friso, Master Reiner, 5:44

Frithonas (Abp. of Canterbury), 3:70

Fritz, Samuel, 5:62–63, **6:12–13**

Friuli, Council of (796), 1:119

Fröbel, Friedrich Wilhelm, 5:91, 93, **6:13–14**

Froben, Johann, 2:523, **6:14**

Froberger, Johann Jakob, 5:979, **6:14**

Fröbes, Joseph, **6:14–15**

Frobisher, Martin, Sir, 5:295

Frodoard of Reims. *See* Flodoard of Reims

Frodobert, St., **6:15**

Froger, J., 1:185

Froget, Bartholomé, 12:777

Fröhling, Friedrich, 12:582

Frohschammer, Jakob, 3:624, 5:599, **6:15**, 778, 12:770, 901–902

Froidmont, Liber, 1:893

Froilán, St., 1:840, **6:15**

Froissart, Jean, 1:464

From Darkness to the Light (Hartshorne), 6:657

From First Adam to Last (Barrett), 5:523

From Out the Flaminian Gate (Newman), 10:333

From Quebec to New Orleans (Schlarman), 12:739

From the Stone Age to Christianity (Albright), 1:235

From Tradition to Gospel (Dibelius, tr. by Woolf), 5:521

Fromm, Erich, 5:914

Fronde revolt, 5:850, 8:801, 803, 12:179–180

Fronto, 3:592

Fronzola, Robertus de, 3:51

Frost, Shannon v. (1842), 3:658

Froude, Richard Hurrell, **6:15–16**, 8:135–136, 10:332, 732, 733
See also Oxford Movement

Fru Marta Oulie (Undset), 14:295

Fructuosos (Abp. of Braga), St., **6:16**
Apostles' Creed, 1:577
Cassian, John, 3:207
martyrdom of, 1:92
medieval Latin literature works of, 9:440
Spain, 13:376

Fructuosus of Tarragona, St., **6:16**

Frumentius, St., 5:399, 402, **6:16–17**

Frutolf of Michelsberg, 1:462, **6:17**

Fruttuaria Abbey (Italy), **6:17**
Alpirsbach Abbey, 1:312
Cluniac reform, 3:813
William of Saint-Bénigne of Dijon, 14:752

Fry, Elizabeth, **6:17–18**, *18*

FSP (Congregation of the Brothers of St. Patrick), 10:951

Fuad I (King of Egypt), 5:118

Fuchs, E., 7:849

Fuchs, Josef, **6:18–19**
existential ethics, 5:538
natural law doctrine, 10:193
sex, 8:873

Fuchs, Joseph. *See* Fuchs, Josef

Fuchs, Leonhard, 2:401

Fuente, Michael de la, 3:136, 143, **6:19**, 8:530

Fuente, Miguel de la. *See* Fuente, Michael de la

Fueros (privileges, franchises, and immunities), 13:381

Fugger, Andreas, 6:19

Fugger, Anton, 6:20

Fugger, Georg, 6:19

Fugger, House of, 8:879

Fugger, Jacob, I, 6:19

Fugger, Jacob, II, 1:233, 6:19–20

Fugger, Johann, 6:19

Fugger, Raymund, 6:20

Fugger, Ulrich (fl. 1367), 6:19

Fugger, Ulrich, I, 6:19

Fugger, Ulrich, II, 6:20

Fugger family, 1:848, **6:19–20**

Fuhrmann, David, 12:668

Fujishima, Denis, Bl., 7:734

Fulbert (Bp. of Chartres), 3:441, 5:516, **6:20**, 7:247–248, 9:450, 12:758

Fulcher of Chartres, **6:20–21**

Fulcodi, Guy. *See* Clement IV (Pope)

Fulcoius of Beauvais, **6:21**, 9:457

Fulcran of Lodève, St., **6:21**

Fulda Abbey (Germany), 3:13, **6:21–22**
archchancellors, 1:633
Boniface, St., 2:496
Carloman, 3:124
Sturmi, St., founding of, 13:556

Fulfillment, personal
I-Thou model of grace, 8:833
love of self and others, 8:829

Fulgens Sicut Stella (apostolic constitution, Benedict XII), 3:748

Fulgentius Ferrandus, 3:40, 12:606

Fulgentius of Astigi, 3:409

Fulgentius of Écija, St., **6:23**

Fulgentius of Ruspe (Bp.), 3:186, **6:23–24**, 10:431
Augustinianism, 1:877
editions of works, 13:168
Fulgentius Ferrandus, 12:606
hymns of, 7:244
incommunicability, 7:379

Fulk (Bp. of Beauvais), 2:190

Fulk V (King of Anjou), 2:29, 7:770

Fulk Nerra (Count of Anjou), 1:432

Fulk of Neuilly, Bl., **6:24**

Full Gospel Central Church (Korea), 8:240

Full incorporation, 7:383

Fuller, Andrew, 2:78

Fuller, Margaret, 14:148

Fuller, Samuel, 4:115

Fullerism, 2:78–79

Fulthrop, Edward, Bl., 5:233

Fumasoni-Biondi, Pietro (Card.), 1:585, 3:516

Fumo, Bartholomeus, 3:52

Funcken, Eugene (Father), 12:174

Functional processions, 11:732

Functionalism, **6:24–26**
activism, 1:83
associationism, 1:796–797
sociology of religion, 12:75–78

Fundación social de la propiedad privada en la República Argentina (Franceschi), 5:864

Fundamental Agreement (1639) (Connecticut), 3:647

Fundamental Agreement (1993), 7:1000

Fundamental Law (Belgium), 2:218

Fundamental Law of the Church. *See Lex ecclesiae fundamentalis*

Fundamental option (morality), 4:236, **6:26**, 9:868

Fundamental theology, 3:19–20, **6:26–27**

Fundamentalism, **6:27–29**
American Council of Christian Churches, 1:351
Baptists, 2:80
Church-State relations, 3:638
creationism, 4:346–347
fundamentalist-modernist dispute, 13:411
Holiness churches, 7:7–8
literal interpretation of patriarch ages as, 10:950
Pentecostal Movement, 1:788
rapture, 11:912–913

Fundamentalism, biblical, **6:29–30**

The Fundamentals: A Testimony to the Truth (Stewart), 6:27

Fundamentum Theologiae Moralis (González de Santalla), 6:343

Fundamentum totius theologiae moralis seu tractatus de conscientia probabili (Terrill), 13:831

Funeral rites, **6:30–33**, *31*
acrostics, 1:72
All Souls' Day, 1:290
catafalques, 3:225
cremation, 4:359–360
dead, worship of, 4:557–558
loculus, 8:746
Slavic religion, 13:215
See also Burial; Cemeteries; Requiem Mass

Funerals, Canon Law, **6:33–34**

Funerary monuments and crypts, early Christian usage, 2:146

Funes, Deán Gregorio, 6:*34*, **34–35**

Die 15 Bundgenossen (The Fifteen Confederates) (Eberlin), 5:31

Funk, Franz Xaver Von, **6:35**, 10:963, 14:234

Funk, Philipp, 12:26

Fur trade, 8:383

Fürbass, Simon, 12:735

Furet, Louis Théodore, 7:741

Furey, Patrick (Abp. of San Antonio, TX), 12:642–643

Furius Dionysius Philocalus, 4:675, 8:642

Furlong, Thomas (Bp. of Wexford), **6:35**, 12:551

Furman v. Georgia, 3:88

Furseus, St. *See* Fursey, St.

Fursey, St., 1:139, 5:239, **6:35–36**, 8:280

Fürstenberg, Franz and Wilhelm Egon von, **6:36–37**

Fürstenberg, Franz von (1729-1810), **6:36**

Furtenbacher, Burckhard, 1:912

Fusai, Gonzales, Bl., 7:733

Fusco, Alfonso Maria, 12:551

Futuna Islands, 10:534

Futuribles, **6:37**
congruism, 4:121
molinism, 9:770
scientia media, 12:821
theology of hope, 13:926–927

Futurology, 13:785

Fux, Johann Joseph, 1:234, **6:37–38**

G

Gabala, Harith Ibn, 2:86

Gabet, Joseph, 7:146

Gabilhaud, Pierre, 12:277

Gable, Miller v. (1845), 3:658

Gabler, G. A., 6:709

Gabler, Johann Philipp, 2:383

Gabon, **6:39–40**, *41*

Gaboury, J., 3:717

Gabra Micha'el. *See* Ghebremichael, Bl.

Gabriel (archangel), 1:420, 424, 425, **6:40–41**, *42*

Gabriel, Colomba Joanna, Bl., **6:41**

Gabriel, St. (17th c. Japanese martyr), 7:732

Gabriel de S. Magdalena, Bl., 7:735

Gabriel Ferretti, Bl., **6:41–42**

Gabriel Marcel et Karl Jaspers: philosophie du mystère et philosophie du paradoxe (Ricoeur), 12:241

Gabriel of Our Lady of Sorrows, St. *See* Possenti, Gabriel, St.

Gabriel of St. Mary Magdalen, 4:205, 206, **6:42**

Gabriel Sionita, 1:37, **6:42**

Gabrieli, Andrea, 1:766, **6:42–43**

Gabrieli, Giovanni, **6:43–44**, 12:792

Gabriella Marie (Sister). *See* Joan of France, St.

Gabriol, Solomon ibn. *See* Avicebron (ibn Gabirol, Solomon ben Judah)

Gaby, Pierre, 2:913

Gadamer, Hans-Georg, **6:44–45**
apologetics, 1:565
biblical hermeneutics, 6:796
hermeneutics, 6:789–790, 10:306
praxis, 11:586

Gaddi, Taddeo, 1:933

Gadsby, Beatrice, 12:550

Gaelic Society of Dublin, 8:326

Gaetani, Antonio I (Card., d. 1412), 6:47

Gaetani, Antonio II (Card., d. 1624), 6:47

Gaetani, Benedetto. *See* Boniface VIII (Pope)

Gaetani, Camillo, 6:47

Gaetani, Enrico (Card.), 6:47

Gaetani, Francis (Card.), 6:47

Gaetani, Honorato, 6:47

Gaetani, James II, 6:47

Gaetani, Leone, 6:47

Gaetani, Michelangelo, 6:47

Gaetani, Onorato I (fl. 1370), 6:47

Gaetani, Onorato IV (fl. 1570), 6:47

Gaetani, Tommaso, 5:247

Gaetani family, **6:47**
Boniface VIII (Pope), 2:501, 502
Boniface VIII (Pope) nepotism, 10:247
Colonna family, 2:502, 3:854

Gaffney, Evangelista (Mother), 12:556

Gagarin, Ivan Sergeevich, **6:47**, 12:426

Gage, Thomas, **6:48**

Gagelin, François, 14:494

Gager, John G., 10:307

Gagliardi, Achille, 2:230, **6:48**, 13:429

Gagnot, Jacques, 12:277

Gaguin, Robert, 2:551, 5:847, **6:48–49**

Gaia (Greek goddess), 5:2–3

Gaichiès, Jean, 11:622

Gailhac, Pierre Jean Antoine, **6:49**, 12:496

Gaillard, J., 10:99

Gainas, 1:631

Gairdner, James, 2:508

Gaiseric. *See* Geiseric (King of the Vandals)

Gaius (Pope), St., **6:49–50**

Gaius Caligula. *See* Caligula (Gaius Caligula) (Roman Emperor)

Gaius Julius Solinus, 12:620

Gajo, Bl. (17th c. Japanese martyr), 7:734

Galaktotrophousa (The Nursing Madonna), 9:272

Galand, Agnès of Jesus, Bl., **6:50**

Galano, Clemente, **6:50**

Galantini, Hippolytus, Bl., **6:51**

Galateo (Casa), 3:198

Galatia, **6:51–52**

Galatians, Epistle to the, **6:52–55**

    aeons, 1:140

    baptism, 2:60, 61

    Barnabas and Paul, 2:103

    beatific vision, 2:171

    "carnal" activities, 13:442

    catechumenate, 3:249

    Christian law, 8:403

    Church in, 3:578–579, 582–583

    circumcison, 6:53

    covenant, 4:328

    development of Gospel tradition on Passion, 10:921

    Divine indwelling, 7:441

    ecclesiastical authority in, 1:923

    faith, 5:592

    faith, profession through baptism, 2:59, 60

    fraternal correction in, 4:274

    freedom, 6:400

    Galatia, 6:52

    Gnosis, 6:254

    God, encounter with, 13:438

    God, sons of, 13:322

    God's spirit, 13:427, 428

    grace, 6:381, 382

    Hagar, 6:608–609

    Holy Spirit, 13:441

    justice of men, 8:74

    justification controversy, 8:78–80

    kerygma, 8:157

    kindness, 8:172

    life of grace, 13:441

    magic, 9:39

    Mary, Blessed Virgin, 9:238–239

    meekness, 9:468

    merit, 6:383

    Paul's first missionary journey, 11:7, 13–14

    rebirth, 11:951

    sacrifice of self, 13:439

    sexual equality, 13:51

    Simon the Apostle, 13:126

    sin, 13:147, 148, 155

    slavery, 13:207, 208

    social principle, 13:25

    Son of God, 13:314

    spiration, 13:420

    spirit, 13:425

    supernatural life, 13:438

    virtuous works, 13:438

    works of charity, 3:401, 402

    works of the flesh, 8:871

Galberry, Thomas (Bp. of Hartford), 1:891, **6:55**, 653

Galbis Gironés, Vicente, Bl., **6:55–56**

Galdinus, St., **6:56**

Galen, Clemens Augustinus von (Card.), 3:592, **6:56–57**

    Aristotelianism, 1:669

    Nazism, opposition to, 6:186

    spirit vs. soul, 4:288

    translation into Latin, 8:592

Galen of Pergamum

    biology, 2:401, 402, 405, 407

    medicine, 12:309, 806–807

    temperament, 13:793

Galeotto del Carretto, Marchese Biagio, 12:679

Galerius (Roman Emperor), 3:594, 632, **6:57**, 7:654

    Diocletian, 4:750

    Milan, Edict of, 9:625

    persecution of Christians, 4:748, 749, 750

Gales, Louis, Rev., 12:574

Galfrido. *See* Walfrid, St.

Galgani, Gemma, St., **6:58**

Galicia

    Basilians in, 2:144

    Priscillianism in, 11:720

A Galick and English Vocabulary (MacDonald), 9:12

Galilee, topography of, 10:779–780

Galilei, Galileo, 2:227–228, **6:58–64**, *59*, 11:293

    Aristotelianism, 1:678

    atomism, 1:834, 4:959

    contribution to study of motion, 10:18–19

    empiricism, 5:197, 12:47

    mechanism, 9:415

    quality, 11:849

    Reusch, Franz Heinrich, 12:182

    scholasticism, 12:768

    space, 13:373

Galitzin, Elizabeth, **6:64**

Gall, St., **6:64–65**

    Austria, 1:908

    catechesis, 3:229

    hymns of, 7:245

    role in palace school education, 10:763

    Sankt Gallen Abbey, 12:669

Gall of Clermont, St., **6:65**

Gallagher, Hugh Patrick, **6:66**

    California missions, 12:647

    Carson Valley mssion established, 10:267

Gallagher, Mary E., 10:57

Gallagher, Michael James (Bp. of Detroit), 4:294, 698, 9:607

Gallagher, Redmund (Bp. of Derry), 7:580

Gallagher, Simon Felix, 3:807, **6:66**, 13:363–364

Gallandi, Andrea, **6:67**

Gallant, G. Edgar (Father), 1:210

Gallemant, Jacques, 2:338

Gallet (Cenacle Sister), 4:293

Galletti, Pier Luigi, 3:793

Gallican Articles, 4:591

Gallican Lectionaries, 6:70–71, 11:126

Gallican Liberties, 3:524

Gallican Psalter, 14:592

Gallican Rites, **6:67–72**

    Advent, 1:134

    Agnus Dei, 1:185

    Ambrosian Rite, 1:343

    apologies, 1:566

    Book of Common Prayer, 2:524

    Carolingian reform, 3:563–564

    feast of the Holy Innocents, 3:556

    Gregorian Sacramentary, 1:243

    hymns of, 7:245, 253

    Introit, 4:893

    origins, 2:62, 8:713

    sacramentaries, 12:483

Gallican Rites, chants of, **6:72–73**

Gallicanism, 3:605, 615, 639, 5:257, **6:73–78**

    acolytes, 7:37

    Alexander VIII (Pope), 1:262, 3:54

    Alexandre, Noël, 1:267

    Almain, Jacques, 1:298

    anointing, 1:478

    appeals to a future council, 1:599

    Assemblies of the French Clergy, 1:788

    Astros, Paul Thérèse David d', 1:813–814

    Baluze, Étienne, 2:48

    beginnings of, 5:847, 12:544

    Bossuet, Jacques Bénigne, 2:550, 3:615

    Bourget, Ignace, 2:567

    Bouvier, Jean Baptiste, 2:572

    Canon Law, 3:54

    Catherine de Médicis, 3:266

    Church property, 3:727

Cistercians, 3:747

Clement X (Pope), 3:788

Conciliarism, 1:600, 3:54, 4:56

Concordat of Fontainebleau, 4:63

confessions of faith, 4:79

Darboy, Georges, 4:526

disappearance of, 3:616

Döllinger, Johannes, 4:824

forerunner, 13:132

French Revolution, 3:615, 753, 5:971

heresy of, 6:777–778

Holden, Henry, 7:2

Hontheim, Johann Kikolaus von, 7:90

impact of French Revolution, 10:845–846

influence on Joseph Semashko, 14:274

Innocent XI (Pope), Bl., 7:481

Launoy, J., 8:381

Le Tellier, C., 8:519

Louis XIV, 8:803

Pius XI (Pope), undermining of, 10:848

political consequences of, 10:843

Pragmatic Sanction, 11:582

Québec Diocese, 8:383

Romanism in context of, 14:284

Russian Orthodox Church, 12:425

theology of Church, 3:576, 589

Le Gallicanisme politique et le clergé de France (Martin), 6:76

Gallicanus (Roswitha of Gandersheim), 12:389

Gallienus (Roman Emperor), **6:78**, *79*, 12:312–313

cardinalate, 3:103

Church property, 3:723

emancipation of Christians, 4:753

Gallifet, Joseph François de, **6:78–79**, 12:491

Galling, K., 3:566

Gallitzin, Amalia, **6:79**

Gallitzin, Demetrius Augustine, **6:80**, 11:83

Carrolltown founding, 8:466

conversion to Catholicism, 12:426

Pittsburgh Diocese, 11:366

Gallo, Andrés María, **6:80**

Gallo, Maria Francesca of the Five Wounds, St., 2:353, **6:80–81**

Galloni, Francesco, 2:548

Gallup Diocese (NM), **6:81**

Galluppi, Pasquale, **6:81**

Gallus (Roman Emperor), 8:846

Gallus, Nikolaus, 5:754

Galtier, Lucien (Father), 12:572

Galtier, Paul, 4:227, **6:82**, 7:80

Galtieri, Leopoldo, 1:656

Galuppi, Baldassare, **6:82**

Galura, B. (Bp. of Brixen), 3:243

Galván Bermúdez, David, St., **6:82**, 545

Galvanus de Bettino de Bononia, 3:52

Galvão, Henrique Noronha, 7:528

Galvão de França, Antônio de Sant'ana, Bl., **6:83**

Galveston (TX), 4:843

Galvez, Francisco, Bl., 7:734

Galvin, Edward J. (Bp.), 3:864, **6:83**

Galway, Geoffrey, 7:582

Gam Van Le, Matthew, 14:494

Gamaliel (Palestinian rabbis), **6:83–84**

Gamaliel I (Palestinian rabbi), 6:83–84

Gamaliel II (Palestinian rabbi), 6:84

Gamaliel III (Palestinian rabbi), 6:84

Gambacorta, Peter, Bl., **6:84**

Gambetta, Léon, 3:802

Gambia, **6:84–85**, *86*

Gambling, 5:178, **6:85**

Gamelbert, Bl., 9:570

Gammurrini, J. F., 5:104

Gams, Pius, **6:86**

Gandersheim Convent (Germany), 1:664, **6:86–87**

Gāndhi, Mohandas Karamchand, **6:87–88**, *88*, 852

Gandolf of Binasco, Bl., **6:88**

Gandulpus (canonist), 3:50

Gangala, Giacomo. *See* James of the Marches, St.

Ganganelli, Giovanni Vincenzo Antonio (Card.). *See* Clement XIV (Pope)

Gangolf, St., **6:88**

Gangra (Paphlagonia), **6:88–89**

Gangra, Councils of, 3:38, 5:456, 12:52, 13:212

Gangra, Synod of (*c.* 345), 3:323

Ganguly, Theotontius Amol (Abp. of Dhaka, Bangladesh), 2:53

Gannon, Arthur, 1:578

Gannon, John Mark (Bp. of Erie), 11:87

Gans, Eduard, 6:709

Gansfort, Johannes Wessel, **6:89**

Ganshof, François Louis, 5:704

Ganss, Henry George, 9:203

Gante, Pedro de, 3:246, 247, 248, **6:89–90**, 12:528

Ganter, Bernard J. (Bp. of Tulsa), 14:235

Gapp, Jakob, Bl., **6:90–91**, 10:*268*

Garabito, Juan de Santiago y León (Bp. of Guadalajara, Mexico), **6:91**

Garakonthie, Daniel, **6:91**, 8:383

Garampi, Giuseppe (Card.), 1:914, 3:793, **6:91–92**

Gárate, Francisco, Bl., **6:92**

Garatenses, Catharism and, 3:259

Garcés, Francisco Tomás Hermenegildo, 2:863, **6:92–93**

Garcés, Julián (Bp. of Tlaxcala, Mexico), **6:93**

Garcí Molina, Diego De Cádiz, 7:125

García, Gonsalo, St., 7:406, 732

García, Margarito Flores, St., 6:545

García Bernal, Pedro, 2:92

García Diego y Moreno, Francisco (Bp. of the Californias), **6:93**, 10:269

García Montaña, Rafael, 3:759

García Moreno, Gabriel, 5:64

García Nozal, Ildefonso, Bl., 4:494

García of Toledo, **6:93**

García Sampedro, Melchoir, 14:494

García Villada, Zacarias, **6:94**

García Xerez, Nicolás (Bp. of Nicaragua), **6:94**

Gardeil, Ambroise, **6:94–95**

Crusade literature, 4:400

dogmatic theology, 4:814

scholasticism, 12:777

Garden of Delights (Syriac biblical catena), 3:259

Garden of Eden. *See* Eden, Garden of

Garden of Nuts (*Ginnath Egoz*) (Gikatilla), 6:211

Gardiner, German, Bl., 5:227, **6:95**

Gardiner, Harold Charles, **6:95**

Gardiner, Robert H., 5:606

Gardiner, Stephen (Bp. of Winchester, England), **6:95–96**

Bonner, Edmund, 2:507

branch theory of the Church, 2:582

chancellor to Mary Tudor, 12:9

Garesché, Edward Francis, 2:556, **6:96**, 13:323

Garesché, Julius Peter, **6:97**

Garet, Jean, **6:97**

Garetius. *See* Garet, Jean

Gargantua (Rabelais), 11:885

Garibaldi, Giuseppe, 3:314, **6:97–98**

Garicoïts, Michael, St., **6:98**

Betharram Fathers, 2:346

Bichier des Ages, St. Jeanne Élisabeth, 2:390

Garin, André, **6:98**

Garlick, Nicholas, Bl., 5:229, **6:98–99**

Buxton, Christopher, Bl., 2:722

Garlick, Nicholas, Bl. *(continued)*
Ludlam as fellow martyr, 8:851
Simpson as fellow martyr, 13:141
Garnerius of Rochefort, **6:99**
Garnet, Henry, 5:237, 718, 6:*99*, **99–100**, 10:727
archpriest controversy, 1:642
Ashley, Ralph, Bl., 1:783
Recusant literature of, 11:959
Garnet, Thomas, St., 5:234, **6:100–101**, *101*, 12:569
Garnett, Porter, 2:524
Garnier, Bernard. *See* Benedict XIV (Antipope)
Garnier, Charles, 10:435–436
Garnier, T., 8:622
Garraghan, Gilbert Joseph, **6:101**, 884
Garrelon, Ephrem M., 2:56
Garrigan, Philip J., 3:291, 13:164
Garrigou-Lagrange, Réginald, **6:101–102**, *102*, 10:112, 14:66
angelology, 1:415
Chenu, Marie-Dominique, 3:466
Christocentrism, 3:558
contemplation, 4:205
existential metaphysics, 5:539
freedom of religion, 5:951
scholasticism, 12:777
sufficient reason, 13:593
Garstang, J., 13:159
Garter, Order of the, 12:547
Gartland, Frances X. (Bp. of Savannah), 12:709
Gärtner, B., 8:300
Garucci, R., 10:774
Garufalov, Ivan, 2:682
Garve, Christian, 5:47, 8:125
Garvin, John E., **6:103**
Gary Diocese (IN), 7:416
Gasca, Pedro de la, 4:132
Gascoigne, Thomas, 2:530
Gaspais, Augustin Ernest Pierre, 3:516
Gaspar de Abalos, 12:684
Gaspar de Zúñiga, 12:684
Gaspar of Coimbra (Bp.), 1:879
Gasparri, Pietro (Card.), 2:150, 6:*103*, **103–104**
Anglican orders problem, 1:438
Canon Law, 3:55
catechesis, 3:244
Code of Canons of the Eastern Churches, 3:817
social justice, 13:243
Gasperi, Alcide de, 6:*104*, **104**
Gasquet, Adrian, 1:438

Gasquet, Francis Neil Aidan (Card.), **6:104–105**
Gassendi, Pierre, **6:105–106**
Aristotelianism, 1:677
atomism, 1:834
Cartesianism, 3:185
egoism, 5:107
Enlightenment, 5:107, 852
mechanism, 9:416
physical space, 13:374
skepticism, 13:203
world soul, 14:845
Gasser, Vinzenz Ferrer (prince-Bp. of Brixen), **6:106**
Gasson, Thomas I., 2:557
Gaston, William Joseph, 3:652, **6:106**, *107*, 146
Gastoué, A., 1:185
Gates of Hell, **6:107**
The Gates of Hell (Rodin), 6:*108*
Gates of Light (Sha'are Orah) (Gikatilla), 6:211
Gath (Philistine city), 11:266
Gāthās (Persian poems), 1:938, **6:107–108**, 11:142, 144, 14:935
Gatterer, Michael, **6:108**
Gatti, Vicenzo, 12:773
Gattinara, Mercurino Arborio di (Card.), 3:429, **6:108–109**
Gattorno, Anna Rosa. *See* Gattorno, Rosa Maria Benedetta, Bl.
Gattorno, Rosa Maria Benedetta, Bl., **6:109**
Gaucherius, St., **6:109–110**
Gaudaire, Louis, 5:441
Gaudentius of Brescia, St., 1:344, **6:110**, 12:52
Gaudentius of Gniezno, St., **6:110**
Gauderich of Velletri (Bp.), **6:110–111**
Gaudí, Antonio, 3:672, 678, 681, 709, 8:622, 13:*383*
Gaudin, Juliette, 1:158, 7:23
Gaudium et spes (apostolic constitution, John XXIII), 4:516, 14:825, 826
anti-discrimination, 13:51–52
Church in the world, 13:287
democracy, 13:259
lay spirituality, 8:417
liberation theology, 8:549
opposition, 8:447
political community relations, 8:358–359, 360
signs of the times, 13:117
social justice, 13:243

Gaudium et spes (Pastoral Constitution on the Church in the Modern World) (Vatican Council II), 10:670, 11:615, 14:416
act of faith, 5:603–604
atheism, 1:823, 826
Catholic Action, 3:278
Christian anthropology, 3:532
civil disobedience, 3:755
ecclesiology, 5:37, 38
eschatology, 5:346
feminism, 5:676–677
John Paul II (Pope), 3:643
Thomism, 3:466
Gaufridi, Raymond, 1:428
Gaughan, Norbert F. (Bp. of Gary, IN), 7:416
Gaugin, Paul, 4:397
Gaul, 5:841–842, **6:111–113**
Canon Law, 3:40
Christmas, 3:553
Church property, 3:724
Confirmation in, 4:87
creedal statements, 4:356
cross, feast of, 4:383
Gregory I (Pope), St., relations with, 6:481
liturgical history, 8:653, 654
medieval Latin literature works of, 9:440–441
Reims, 12:35–38
Roman primacy, 3:317
Gaulli, G. B., 7:33
Gaunilo of Marmoutiers, 1:496
Gautbert (Bp. of Sweden), 1:500
Gautier, Léon, 5:519
Gautrelet, Francis X., 1:578
Gauzelin of Toul, St., **6:113**, 12:539
Gavan, John, Bl., 5:236, **6:113**
Gavardi, Federico Nicola, 1:880, 12:765
Gay, Charles Louis, **6:114**
Gay men. *See* Homosexuality
Gāyatrī (mantra), 9:125
Gay-Lussac, J. L., 1:835
Gayo, Ribeiro (Bp.), 12:686
A Gazeta do Povo (periodical), 8:465
Gazette du livre médiéval, 10:776
GDC. *See General Directory for Catechesis*
Geb (Babylonian deity), 4:337
Geber (alchemist), 1:238
Gebhard (Abp. of Salzburg), Bl., 1:116–117, **6:114–115**
Gebhard II of Constance, St., **6:114**, 11:210

Gebhard III of Constance (Bp.), 1:312, **6:114**, 12:211

Gebizo, St., **6:115**, 14:674

Die Geburt der Tragödie aus dem Geiste der Musik (Nietzsche), 10:389

Gedanken eines Denkers über Tod und Unsterblichkeit (Feuerbach), 5:707

Geddes, Alexander, **6:115**
exegesis, 5:519
higher criticism, 6:825
pentateuchal studies, 11:89

Gedy, John, 1:630

Geertz, Clifford, 12:65, 475

Ge'ez (Semitic language), 5:19

Gefahren im heutigen Katholizismus (Rahner), 5:538

Geffré, Claude, 11:586

Gehenna, **6:116**
nether world, 13:79
Orphan's Kaddish, 8:107
See also Sheol

Gehlen, Arnold, 4:24

Gehring, Rose Bernard, 7:22

Geiger, Abraham, 7:607, 873

Geiger, L. B., 5:539, 8:829, 12:776

Geikie, J. C., 7:850

Geiler von Kayserberg, Johannes, 1:729, **6:116–118**

Geiselmann, J. R., 3:589, 14:137

Geiseric (King of the Vandals), **6:118**

Geissel, Johannes von (Card.), 3:843, 846, **6:118–119**

Geisteswissenschaften (Sciences of the Spirit), 3:301–302, 11:802

Gelasian Decree, 5:640, **6:119**, 7:390

Gelasian Letter, **6:119–120**

Gelasian Sacramentary, 3:231, **6:120–121**, 122, 474
Advent in, 1:134
Ambrosian Rite, 1:343
Anointing of the Sick in, 1:482
catechumenate, 3:252
Christmas cycle, 3:555, 556
liturgical books, 8:639

Gelasianum Vetus (Old Gelasian Sacramentary). *See* Gelasian Sacramentary

Gelasius I (Pope), St., **6:121–123**
Acacian Schism, 1:50, 387
Canon Law, 1:841, 3:39
Church property, 3:724
Church-State relations, 1:122, 922, 3:595, 633–634, 643
Confirmation, 4:87
diaconia, 4:719
Dionysius, Exiguus, 4:754

Ember Days, 5:186
hardline approach, 8:404
hymns of, 7:244
Mass formulations, 8:532
Pelagianism, 11:63
prohibited books, 7:390
Roman Rite, 12:328

Gelasius II (Pope), **6:123**
Concordat of Worms, 3:601
exile at Cluny, 8:799
Gregory VIII (Antipope), 6:485
investiture struggle, 2:880
Kyrie eleison, 8:259
litanies, 8:600

Gelasius of Caesarea (Bp.), 4:471, **6:123–124**

Gelati Gospel, 3:*21*

Gelin, A., 5:520

Gelineau, Joseph, 2:332, 3:73

Gelineau, Louis E. (Bp.), 12:218

Gelmírez, Diego (Abp.), 12:683

Gemarah, 5:508, **6:124**, 8:7, 13:746–747

Gembloux Abbey (Belgium), **6:124**

Gemelli, Agostino, **6:124–125**
Duns Scotus, John, 4:939
Men's Institute of Missionaries, founding of, 9:732
Missionaries of the Kingship of Christ, founding of, 9:731
Secular Institute of Priest Missionaries of the Kingship of Christ, founding of, 9:732
Thomistic revival, 12:774

Geminus, St. *See* Ingenuin (Bp. of Sabiona), St.

Geminus of Antioch, 1:526

Gender
congregational singing, 4:119
formation of, 7:68
homosexuality, 7:67, 68

Gendron, Odore, 10:279, 280

Genealogies, biblical, **6:125**, 11:712

Genealogy of Jesus, **6:125–127**, 8:857

Génébrard, Gilbert (Abp. of Aix), 1:197, **6:127**

General Association of Regular Baptists, 2:80

General Baptists, 2:78, 79

General Chapters of the Clergy (Baltimore, 1783-89). *See* Baltimore, Councils of

General Councils. *See* Councils, General (ecumenical)

General Directory for Catechesis, 3:248, 249, **6:127–128**

General Elementary Introduction (Eusebius of Caesarea), 5:452

General History of the Spanish in the Indies in Eight Decades (Herrera y Tordesillas), 6:807

General Hospital (Paris), 3:417

General Instruction of the Liturgy of the Hours (1971), 8:731

General Instruction of the Roman Missal, 1:336, 3:75, 8:618, 705, 12:142

General Intercessions, **6:128**

General Introduction to the Study of the Holy Scriptures (Gigot), 6:211

General judgment
apocalyptic descriptions, 8:39
biblical concept, 8:29–30
Catholic tradition, 8:30–33
establishment of heavenly society, 8:38–39
names and aspects, 8:39
one consummating intervention, 8:40
revelation in judgment, 8:40–41
victory and purification, 8:40

General Missionary Convention of the Baptist Denomination, 12:227

The General Statutes of the Order of Knights of the Red Cross of Rome and Constantine, 12:382

General Theological Seminary (New York), 5:297

General Theory of Employment, Interest and Money (Malthus), 9:84

Generatio fit in instanti (Generation is instantaneous), 12:755

Generatio unius est corruptio alterius (The generation of one thing is the corruption of another), 12:755

Generation of the Word, 5:718–719, **6:129**, 8:758–764

Generation-corruption, 1:682, **6:128–129**

Genesis, Book of, **6:130–134**
Adam, elevation of, 5:149
Adam in, 1:103–104
antifeminist attitudes, 4:321
Babylon, 2:3
Babylonia, 2:5
Babylonian myth, 2:329–330
beatific vision, 2:170
begetting children, 8:394
Benjamin (biblical figure), 2:282
Benjamin (tribe), 2:282
Christian law, 8:403
concupiscence, 4:68
covenant, 4:326–327
covenant with Israel, 6:133–134
creation, 8:574

Genesis, Book of (continued)

creation account, 4:337–340

creation doctrine, 5:49, 52, 218

demonology, 4:646–648

Divine election, 5:146

Edomite genealogy, 5:87

El (God), 5:13

Enoch, 5:265

eschatology, 5:333–334

Eve's role in the Fall, 5:482–484

flood, 5:763–765

Garden in Eden, 5:80–81

Gilgamesh flood narrative, comparison to, 6:223–224

God, sons of, 13:321–322

God's spirit, 13:426, 427

Hagar, 6:608

heaven, 6:684, 685

as history, Church stance, 7:182

homosexuality, 7:66, 67

human sexuality, 13:47–48

humans dominion over the Earth, 5:49, 52–53

Immaculate Conception, 7:331

infused knowledge, 8:207

inheritance, 7:464

Israel's election, 8:3

justification, 8:79, 80

Levi, tribe of, 8:523

literary myths in the, 10:123

Logos, theology of, 8:761

man, 9:85, 87

man as image of God, 4:27

marriage, 7:67

Memra, 8:759

messianic blessings, 9:63

messianism, 9:540

onanism, 9:315

origin of man, 5:495

original sin, 10:664

Paradise of primeval age, 10:874–875

patriarch genealogies in, 10:948, 950

peace, 11:49

precious stones, 11:646

primeval age in the Bible, 11:709–713

Proto-evangelium, 11:775–776

retaliation, 8:394

Sabbath, 12:455–456

salvation, 6:133–134

serpent as symbol, 13:18–21

Shaddai, 13:58

Shechem, 13:71

significance of Tower of Babel story in, 14:129–130

sin, notion of, 13:*142*, 143, 145

sin, origin of, 13:144

slavery, 13:207

soul, 13:336

spirit, 13:424

temptation, 13:815

twin brothers Jacob and Edom-Esau stories, 5:86

Tyndale's translations of, 14:253

unity in diversity in, 4:28

word of God, 14:836, 837

Genesius (Bp. of Clermont), St., 6:135

Genesius (Bp. of Lyons), St., 6:135

Genesius, SS., **6:135**

Genesius of Arles, St., 6:135

Genesius the Comedian, St., 6:135

Genest, Mark. *See* Mark of the Nativity

Genet, F., 1:311

Genet, Jean, 1:48, 49, 5:544, 546

Genethlialogy, 7:112–113

Genethlius (Bp.), 3:188, 4:862

Genetics, 2:403–404

cloning, 7:178–179

counseling, 7:177

discrimination and testing, 7:175–177

Down's syndrome, 8:463–464

soul's origins, 13:355

therapies based on, 7:177–178

Geneva (Switzerland), 7:166

Genevan Psalter, 11:798

Geneviève, St., 1:482, 3:409, **6:134–135**, *135*, 12:595–596

Genghis Khan, 11:685

Gengorō, James Bunzo, Bl., 7:733

Gengorō, Mary, Bl., 7:733

Gengorō, Thomas, Bl., 7:733

Génicot, Édouard, **6:135**

Génie du Christianisme (*Genius of Christianity*) (Chateaubriand), 3:447–448, 624, 12:113

Geniza, 2:357, 358, **6:135–136**

Gennadius (Abp. of Novgorod), 12:423

Gennadius II Scholarius (Patriarch of Constantinople), **6:136–137**

Bessarion, Cardinal, 2:340

Confession of, 10:700, 701

confession of faith, 4:355

Eastern Schism, 2:794, 828

Gennadius I, St., **6:136**

Gennadius of Astorga, St., **6:137**

Gennadius of Marseilles, **6:137–138**

Canon Law, 3:59

lives of saints, 12:606

Salvian of Marseilles, 12:632

Statuta ecclesiae antiqua, 13:501

Gennings, Edmund, Bl., 5:231, 6:*138*, **138**

Gennings, John, **6:138–139**

Genoa (Italy), patroness of, 12:131

Genome. *See* Human Genome Project

Genome research, 13:356

Genovefa, St. *See* Geneviève, St.

Genovesi, Antonio, 12:770

Genseric. *See* Geiseric (King of the Vandals)

Gentile, Giovanni, 5:397, **6:139**, 11:296

act, 1:74

irrationalism, 7:587

Neo-Hegelianism, 6:712, 7:300

Gentiles, **6:139–140**

early church, 3:575, 578

Mary, Blessed Virgin, 9:242

not bound by Mosaic Law, 7:772–773

as recipients of John's Gospel, 7:909

sexual mores of, 13:48–49

Gentili, Luigi, 5:251, 12:385

Gentilly, Synod of (767), 5:720

Gentilone Pact (1913), 7:673

Gentis Polonae Gloria, **6:140**

Genuflection, 8:648–649

Genuinus, St. *See* Ingenuin (Bp. of Sabiona), St.

Genus, **6:140–141**

Aristotle, 1:681

categories of being, 3:256

dialectics, 4:723

God's primacy of being, 13:139

parts signifying, 10:905

as predicable, 11:659–660

similarity, 13:126

Gény, F., 10:184

Geocentrism, 6:59

Geoffrey (Bp. of Auxerre), 3:394

Geoffrey (Bp. of Avignon), 1:942

Geoffrey III (Count of Anjou), 2:126

Geoffrey Hardeby, **6:141**

Geoffrey of Aspall, 1:225

Geoffrey of Auxerre. *See* Geoffrey of Clairvaux

Geoffrey of Clairvaux, 3:758, **6:141**

Geoffrey of Dunstable, **6:142**

Geoffrey of Monmouth (Bp.), 1:464, **6:142**, 12:536

Arthurian legends, 1:759–761, 762

medieval Latin literature works of, 9:455

Geoffrey of Vendôme, **6:142–143**, 7:539

Geoffrey of Vigeois, 1:463

Geoffrey of York (Abp.), **6:143**

Geoffrey the Bearded. *See* Geoffrey III (Count of Anjou)

Geography, as division of philosophies, 11:286

Geomagnetism, 6:212–213

Geometria speculativa (Bradwardine), 14:29

Geometry
  Cartesian method, 4:679–680
  continuum, 4:216
  space, 13:373–374
  truth, 13:419

Georg, E., 1:545

George (Bp. of Ani-Gamakh), 1:453

George, Francis (Abp. of Chicago), 3:480, 7:70, 11:531

George, Henry, 6:206, 9:397–398

George, St., 6:*143*, **143–144**, 8:196, 12:32

George, Stefan, 6:44

George II (King of England), 2:14

George III (King of England), 5:182

George IV (King of England), 5:184

George VIII (King of Georgia), 6:154

George XIII (King of Georgia), 6:156

George Akropolites, 2:776

George Hamartolus, **6:144**

George of Cappadocia (Bp. of Alexandria), 1:662, 818

George of Iconium, 1:398

George of Laodicea, 1:663, 4:471

George of Nicomedia, 1:469

George of Pisida, 2:804

George of Saxony, **6:144–145**

George of Trebizond, 1:676, 2:810

George Poděbrad (King of Bohemia), 2:881

George Syncellus, 2:329, **6:145**

George the Monk. *See* George Hamartolus

George Washington University (Washington, DC), 12:227

Georgetown Lutheran Church (Washington, DC), 8:*884*

Georgetown University (Washington, DC), **6:145–147**
  archives, 1:637, 642
  Kohlmann, A., 8:228
  Rey, Anthony, 12:209
  sodality, 13:294

Georgetown Visitation Convent (Washington, DC), **6:147–148**, 14:563

Georgia (Europe), ancient Church in, **6:151–156**, 9:801

Georgia (U.S.), **6:148–151**
  African Americans, programs for, 2:168
  Church-State relations, 3:646, 652
  French Americans, 6:151
  Furman v. Georgia, 3:88
  martyrs of La Florida, 5:875
  mission, 5:875
  See also specific dioceses and archdioceses

Georgia, Furman v., 3:88

Georgian architecture, 3:707, 714–715

Georgian Byzantine Church, 6:154–155, **156–157**

Georgian Orthodox Church, 2:746, 3:294, 6:156, **10:688–690**

Georgius III Bardanes (Metropolitan of Corfu), 2:825

Gerald of Aurillac, St., **6:157**

Gerald of Braga, St., **6:157**

Gerald of Mayo, St., **6:157**

Geraldini, Alejandro (Bp. of Santo Domingo, Italy), **6:157–158**

Geraldinist controversy, 14:20

Gérard, Jeanne, Bl., 1:722

Gerard, John (Father), 4:745, **6:158**, 12:245

Gérard, Josef Valencia, Bl., **6:158–159**

Gerard, Miles, Bl., 5:231, **6:159**

Gerard, Richard, **6:159**

Gerard d'Haméricourt (Abbot), 12:540

Gerard of Abbeville, 2:483, **6:159–160**, 12:286

Gerard of Bologna, 3:141

Gerard of Borgo San Donnino, 1:548, 2:481, 5:897

Gerard of Brogne, St., 2:217, 625, **6:160**, 12:540, 583

Gerard of Cambrai (Bp.), 1:722, 927, **6:160–161**

Gerard of Clairvaux, Bl., **6:161**

Gerard of Cremona, 1:674, **6:161**, 8:533

Gerard of Csanád, St., 4:726, **6:161–162**

Gerard of Sauve-Majeure, St., **6:162**

Gerard of Siena, 1:883

Gerard of Toul, St., **6:162**

Gerard of Villamagna, Bl., **6:162–163**

Gerard of York (Abp.), 1:489, **6:163**

Gerasim (Syrian monk), 2:144

Gerasimus, St., **6:163–164**

Geraty, L. T., 2:379

Gerbais, Jean, 6:77

Gerbel, Nikolaus, 5:306

Gerber, Eugene J. (Bp. of Wichita, KS), 4:810, 14:711

Gerberon, Gabriel, **6:164**

Gerbert. *See* Sylvester II (Pope)

Gerbert of Aurillac. *See* Sylvester II (Pope)

Gerbert of Reims, 10:714, 715

Gerbert von Hornau, Martin, **6:164**, 12:668

Gerbet, Olympe Philippe (Bp.), **6:164–165**
  Bonnetty, Augustin, 2:508
  Coux, Charles de, 4:324
  liberalism, 3:619

Gerbillon, Jean François, 3:497, **6:165**

Gercke, Daniel James (Bp. of Tucson), 1:688

Gerdil, Hyacinthus Sigismond (Card.), 9:75–76, 12:769

Gereformeerde Kerke in Nederland (GKN), 10:264

Gerety, Peter Leo (Bp. of Portland, ME), 9:59, 10:330, 11:532

Gerganos, Zachary, 3:27

Gergy, Languet de (Abp. of Sens), 1:57

Gerhard, Johann, **6:165–166**, 8:86, 890, 10:962

Gerhardinger, Karolina Elizabeth Frances, Bl., 3:217, **6:166**, 10:462, 12:780, 781

Gerhoh of Reichersberg, **6:166–167**, 12:33
  Abelard, Peter, 1:19
  Celestine III (Pope), 3:319
  dialectics, 4:726
  medieval Latin literature works, 9:454
  Peter of Vienna, 11:204

Gerken, Rudolph Aloysius (Abp.), 5:881, 12:676

Gerlach, St., **6:167**

Gerlach of Tübingen, Stephen, 2:715

Germain of Auxerre (Bp.), St., 1:927, **6:168**

Germain of Paris, St., 2:621, 3:596, 5:823, **6:168**, 12:547

Germaine of Pibrac, St., **6:168–169**

German II (Patriarch of Nicaea), 4:636

German Americans
  Henni, John Martin, ministry to, 6:733
  Iowa, 7:541
  Josephinum, 7:1046
  Raffeiner, John Stephen, 11:891
  Redemptorists, 11:996

German Baptists. *See* Church of the Brethren (Dunkers)

German Catholic Conclave (Fulda),
10:*485*

"German Catholics" (schismatic sect),
12:368–369

German Crusade of 1197, 4:137

German Ideology (Engels and Marx),
5:222

German language, confessions of faith
in, 4:77

German materialism, 9:320

German Passion play manuscript page,
10:*927*

German Question, U.S., 8:132

German Reformed Church, 9:502

German Reformed Church, U.S., 8:678

German Reformed Church v. Seibert
(1846), 3:658

German Requiem (Schubert), 12:788

German transcendentalism, 14:146

Germani, St., 8:314

Germania (Tacitus), 12:308

Germania sacra (Gerbert von Hornau),
12:668

Germanic religion, **6:169**

Germanic tribes, 9:691

Germanus (Bp. of Auxerre), 3:317

Germanus I (Patriarch of
Constantinople), St., **6:169–170**
    iconoclasm, 2:751, 793, 7:280, 281,
    8:473
    Protoevangelium Jacobi, 1:469

Germanus II (Patriarch of
Constantinople), **6:170**

Germanus of Münster-Granfelden, St.,
6:170

Germany, **6:171–188**
    academic freedom, 1:51, 52
    Amana Society, 1:330
    ancestor worship, 1:394
    anointing, 1:479
    anti-Catholicism, 7:26
    anti-Semitism, 7:12–16, 870–874
    baroque period, 2:107
    Benedictines, 2:256
    Calvinism, 2:895, 12:20–21
    Canisius, St. Peter, 3:15–19, 233, 242
    catechesis, 3:243–245
    Catholic reforms, 2:270, 4:11,
    8:324–325
    Catholic youth movement, 8:246
    Center Party, 3:339–342, 619
    chronicles and annals, 1:463,
    464–465
    church architecture, 3:710–712, 8:628
    Communio edition, 4:31
    confessions of faith, 4:78–79, 81

contraception, 4:222

Counter Reformation, 2:259

Credos, 4:356

Crusades, 4:400, 401, 410, 411, 414

culture as concept, 4:427, 436

deism, 4:617

demographic statistics, 6:171

Dieringer, Franz Xaver, 4:741

Döllinger, Johannes, 4:822–824

Dominicans, 4:853

dueling, 4:928

early Church, 3:593

ecclesiastical organization, 6:172,
183–184

Ecumenical Movement, 5:73

education, 12:773–774, 14:233–234

Enlightenment, 5:255, 262–263

Friends of God, 6:5

Gregory XVI (Pope), 6:509

Haskalah Movement, 6:662

humanism, 7:190, 192

iconography, 7:286

idealism, 7:297–299, 300

investiture, 7:537, 538–539

Kalands, 8:111

liturgy, 8:668, 671

Liutbirg, St., 8:736

Lutheranism, 8:888

map, 6:*173*

medieval drama, 4:894, 896, 897,
898, 900

Mennonite churches, 9:496

mission, 3:498, 599, 8:430–431, 853

modernism, 9:755

music, 7:254–255, 258, 8:689

Nazi regime, 3:342, 619, 642,
5:93–94

Peace of God Movement, 11:50

Pius XI (Pope), 11:394–395

Pius XII (Pope), 11:396–397

Poland, 11:447–448, 452

political reactionism, 9:753

popular devotions, 4:711

preaching, 11:622–623

Reformation, 4:309, 12:23

Reformkaktholizismus, 12:26

Regalia, 12:27

Renaissance, 8:689, 12:119

Servites, 13:28

Sibert of Beka, 13:99

Siffrin, Peter, 13:110–111

Sisters of Divine Providence, 13:181

social justice, 3:620, 13:256

synodal practices, 4:302

See also Holocaust (Shoah); Holy
Roman Empire; Nazism

Germerius, St., **6:188**

Germier, St. *See* Germerius, St.

Germigny des Prés Church (France),
3:155

Gernrode Abbey (Germany), 3:691

Gero of Cologne, St., **6:188**

Gerold, St., **6:188–189**

Gerondi, Nissim ben Reuben, 4:361

Gerónimo de Santa Fe, 1:232

Gerosa, Vincenza, St., 3:89, 6:*189*, **189**

Gerow, Richard Oliver (Bp. of Natchez-
Jackson, MS), 7:686, 9:739

Gerry, Elbridge, 3:472

Gerry, Joseph John (Bp. of Portland,
ME), 9:59, 11:532

Gerson, Jean, **6:189–190**
    Alexander V (Antipope), 1:258
    ars moriendi, 1:729, 730, 732
    art of dying, 5:486
    catechesis, 3:232, 235, 241
    Church-State relations, 3:636
    conciliarism, 4:55, 5:847
    education theory, 5:847
    exegetical works, 5:518
    Gallicanism, 6:75
    Imitation of Christ, 1:363, 7:328, 329
    mystical experience, 10:114
    mystical theology, 13:434
    pantheism, 2:629
    theory of devolution, 5:694
    tyrannicide, 4:171
    Western Schism, 3:51

Gerstenberger, E. S., 14:858

Gertken, Severin, 12:578

Gertrude of Hackeborn, 3:744

Gertrude of Helfta, St., 8:327

Gertrude of Nivelles, St., 3:519,
6:191–192, 7:306

Gertrude of the Blessed Sacrament. *See*
Comensoli, Gertrude Caterina, Bl.

Gertrude the Great, St., 3:744,
6:190–191, 12:200, 201

Gerulf, St., **6:192**

Gervaise, François Armand, **6:192**

Gervase, George, Bl., 5:234, **6:192–193**

Gervase, Henry, 6:192

Gervase and Protase, SS., **6:194**, 8:48

Gervase of Canterbury, 1:464, **6:193**

Gervase of Chichester, 11:667

Gervase of Reims (Abp.), **6:193**

Gervase of Tilbury, **6:193–194**

Gervin of Oudenburg, St., **6:194**

Géry of Cambrai, St., 1:721, 2:904, **6:194–195**

Gesché, Adolphe, 7:528

Geschichte der Päpste (Pastor), 6:880

Geschichte der Philosophie (Hegel), 12:111

Geschichte der Philosophie des Mittelalters (Stöckl), 12:774

Die Geschichte der synoptischen Tradition (Bultmann), 5:521, 812

Geschichte der syrischen Literatur (Baumstark), 2:159

Geschichte des Breviers (Bäumer), 2:159

Geschichte des deutschen Volkes (Janssen and Pastor), 10:938

Geschichte des Vatikanischen Konzils (Granderath), 6:416

Geschichte des Volkes Israel (Kittel), 8:186

Geschichtlichkeit (History and historicity), **6:893**

Gesenius, Heinrich Friedrich Wilhelm, 6:697

Geshichte der Religion Jesu Christi (Stolberg), 6:877

Geshur (Aramaean state), 1:624

Gesner, Konrad, 2:401

Gesta abbatum Fontanellensium, 5:793

Gesta archiepiscoporum Mediolanensium (Arnulf of Milan), 1:721

Gesta Caroli (Notker), 10:455

Gesta de Piquer, 7:125

Gesta Dei per Francos (Guibert of Nogent), 6:560, 9:452

Gesta Friderici imperatoris (Otto of Freising), 10:716

Gesta Henrici II (manuscript), 2:253

Gesta Karoli (Notker Balbulus), 9:446–447

Gesta Normannorum ducum (William of Jumièges), 12:270

Gesta Othonis (Roswitha of Gandersheim), 9:447

Gesta regum (Gervase of Canterbury), 6:193

Gesta Romanorum, 5:529, **6:195**

Gesta Treverorum, 14:185

Gestalt psychology, 1:796

Gestis Caroli Magni (St. Gall), 10:763

Gestures, symbols vs., 13:661

Gesù Church (Rome), 2:113, 3:701, 703

Gesù Cristo nelle S. Scritture e nei SS. Padri e Dottori (Bellino), 3:259

Gesù Cristo regola del sacerdote (Frassinetti), 5:921

Gesualdo, Carlo, 1:766, **6:195–196**

Gesvres, Léon Potier de, 2:323

Geta, Publius Septimus (Roman Emperor), 12:312

Gethsemani (Gethsemane), 8:14

Gethsemani Abbey (Bardstown, KY), **6:196**, 8:149, *817*, 14:162

Die Getreide politik der Päpste (Benigni), 2:279

Gettysburg College (PA), 12:745

Geulincx, Arnold, 3:184, **6:196–197**

Géza I, 7:209

Géza II, 7:210

Gezelinus, Bl., **6:197**

Gezer (Canaanite city), 2:379

Gezzelinus, Bl., **6:197**

Ghaerbald of Lüttich, 3:43

Ghana, **6:197–201**, *199, 200*

Ghazzālī, Al-. *See* Algazel (Ghazzālī, al-)

Ghebremichael, Bl., **6:201**

Ghettos, **6:201**, 8:9

Ghibelline-Guelf conflict. *See* Guelfs and Ghibellines

Ghibellines. *See* Guelfs and Ghibellines

Ghiberti, Lorenzo, 2:374

Ghirlandaio. *See* Bigordi, Domenico

Ghislain, St. *See* Gislenus, St.

Ghisleri, Paolo, 13:857–858

Ghislieri, Antonio. *See* Pius V (Pope)

Ghose, Aurobindo, 6:*202*, **202**, 852, 10:116

Giaccardo, Timoteo, Bl., **6:202–203**

Giaccone, G. M., 3:243

Giacomo Bianconi of Mevania. *See* James of Bevagna, Bl.

Giambono, Michele, 10:2

Gian Giacomo the Great, 14:210, 211

Gianboniti, 1:886

Gianelli, Anthony, St., 2:446, 6:*203*, **203**

Giani, Arcangelo, 13:29

Gibault, Pierre, **6:203–204**, 12:558

Gibbon, Augustine, 1:889

Gibbon, Edward, 3:434, 12:310, 312

Gibbons, James (Card.), 5:880, 10:167, 170, 437, 14:542

    as Abp. of Baltimore, 2:39, 165, 5:880

    activism, 1:84

    Americanism, 1:354, 355, 356

    ''Americanist'' controversy, 12:573

    apostolic delegation in the United States, 1:582, 584

    Catholic University of America, 3:290

    Curtis, Alfred Allen, 4:445

Gilmour, Richard, 6:226–227

    Josephites, 7:1047

    Knights of Labor, 7:551–552

    labor unions, 8:192–193

    lay congresses, 8:412

    preaching, 11:625

    Price, Thomas Frederick, 11:688

    Russell, William Thomas, 12:418

    Sabetti, Luigi, 12:462

    Sisters of Bon Secours, 2:476

    social justice issues, 3:620

    temperance, 13:802

    Third Baltimore Plenary Council (1884), 2:46

    as vicar apostolic of Raleigh (NC) Diocese, 11:899

Gibbs, James, 3:707, 714

Giberti, Gian Matteo (Bp. of Verona), 3:415, 610, **6:207–208**

Gibieuf, Guillaume, **6:208**

Gibney, Matthey (Bp. of Perth), 12:551

Gibson, William, Bl., 5:233, 329, 572, **6:208**

Gibson v. Armstrong (1847), 3:658

Gibson v. Morris (1903), 3:658

Gideon (Hebrew judge), 1:319, **6:208–209**

Giedion, S., 3:680

Gierek, Edward, 11:452

Giese, Tiedmann (Bp. of Kulm), 4:251

Giet, Rose, 12:495

Giffard, Bonaventure (Bp.), 5:250, **6:209–210**

Giffard, William (Bp. of Winchester), 14:663

Gifford, William (English party leader), 6:100, **210**

Gigli, Giovanni (Bp.), **6:210–211**

Gigli, Silvestre (Bp. of Worcester), 2:17

Gignac, F. T., 10:276

Gihon spring (Jerusalem), 7:762–763, 765

Gikatilla, Joseph ben Abraham, **6:211**

Gil Arano, Carmelo, Bl., 7:124

Gil de Federich, Francisco, 14:494

Gil de Hontanon, Juan and Rodrigo, 13:*381*

Gil Valls, Encarnación, Bl., 1:4, **6:212**

Gil Valls, Gaspar, 6:212

Gilbert, Creighton, 7:284

Gilbert, Davies, 3:151

Gilbert, Humphrey, Sir, 2:13

Gilbert, William, **6:212–213**

Gilbert Crispin, 2:190, **6:213**

Gilbert de la Porrée, 5:444, 484, 516, **6:213–215**, 12:268
  Abelard, Peter, 1:19
  adoptionism, 1:119
  Alexander of Hales, 1:266
  Anselm of Laon, 1:498
  Bernard of Clairvaux, 2:308–309
  Boethius, 2:457
  cathedral and episcopal schools, 3:441
  Celles-Sur-Belle Monastery, 3:329
  Clarenbaud of Arras, 3:761
  dialectics, 4:726
  distinction, 4:781
  Geoffrey of Clairvaux, 6:141
  Hugh of Honau, 7:153
  individuation, 7:425
  medieval Latin literature works of, 9:453
  School of Chartres, 12:758
  subsistence in Christology, 13:573–574
Gilbert of Holland, 3:749, 758, **6:215**
Gilbert of Hoyland. *See* Gilbert of Holland
Gilbert of Neuffontaines, St., **6:215**, 11:666
Gilbert of Poitiers
  Alan of Lille, 1:205
  Bernard of Chartres, 2:307
  Laborans, 8:266
Gilbert of Sempringham, St., 3:601, **6:215–216**
  See also Gilbertines
Gilberti, Gian Matteo (Bp. of Verona), **6:207–208**
Gilbertines, 3:69, 6:215–216, **216**
  England, 5:240
Gilbertus Anglicus, 1:206, 207, **6:216–217**
Gilby, Thomas, **6:217**, 8:206
Gildas, St., 1:759, **6:217–218**, 12:544, 548
Giles, St., **6:218**, 12:548
  See also Fourteen Holy Helpers
Giles Mary of St. Joseph. *See* Pontillo, Egidio Maria di San Giuseppe, St.
Giles of Assisi, Bl., **6:218**
Giles of Foscarari, **6:218–219**
Giles of Lessines, **6:219–220**, 14:44
  Albert the Great, St., 1:226, 936
  Latin Averroism, 1:936
  unity thesis, 5:818
Giles of Orléans, 1:935
Giles of Rome, **6:220–221**
  Aristotelianism, 1:675

Augustine (Triumphus) of Ancona, 1:870
  Augustinianism, 1:875, 879, 882, 888
  Church-State relations, 3:636
  correctoria, 4:275
  distinction, 4:780
  essence and existence, 5:364–365
  Ghibelline-Guelf conflict, 3:855
  Latin Averroism, 1:936
  matter, 9:344
  Robert of Orford commentary, 12:269
  scholasticism, 12:762, 764
  unity thesis, 5:818
Giles of Santarem, Bl., **6:221**
Giles of Viterbo (Card.), **6:221–222**
  Alexander V (Antipope), 1:258
  Augustinianism, 1:875, 883, 888
  Counter Reformation, 3:611
  revival, 4:310
Das Gilgamesch-epos in der Welt-literatur (Jensen), 10:820
Gilgamesh (epic poem), 1:164, 4:647, **6:222–224**, 14:164, 167
Gilgamesh (King of Uruk). *See Gilgamesh* (epic poem)
Gilij, Filippo Salvatore, **6:224**
Gilkey, L., 12:475
Gill, Eric
  Attwater, Donald, 1:844
  distributism, 4:782–783
  Westminster Cathedral, 12:602
Gil-Leonis, Antonio Martínez, Bl., 7:125
Gilles de Duremont, 5:659
Gilles of Reims (Bp.), 12:36
Gillespie, Angela (Mother), **6:224–225**, 225, 7:33, 13:327
Gillet, Louis Florent, 4:926, 7:338
Gillis, James Martin, **6:225**
Gillman, Florence Morgan, 11:252
Gillow, Joseph, 14:111
Gillow y Zavalza, Eulogio Gregorio (Abp.), **6:225–226**
Gillows, Thomas (Father), 3:115
Gilmore, Joseph M. (Bp. of Helena, MT), 9:827
Gilmore, Ronald M., 4:810
Gilmour, Richard (Bp. of Cleveland), **6:226–227**, 12:537, 786
Gilmour v. Pelton (1883), 6:226
Gilson, Étienne Henri, **6:227–228**
  analogy, 1:378
  Blondel, Maurice, 2:441
  Christian philosophy, 3:540, 541
  Cistercian architecture, 3:749

  existential metaphysics, 5:539–540
  naturalism of, 10:207
  neoscholasticism and neothomism, 10:244
  Thomistic metaphysics, 12:776
  unity of intellect, 7:511
Giménez Malla, Ceferino, Bl., **6:228–229**
Ginnath Egoz (Garden of Nuts) (Gikatilla), 6:211
Ginneken, Jacques van, 6:415, 7:328–329
Ginoulhiac, Jacques Marie Achille (Bp.), **6:229**
Ginsburg, C. D., 2:355
Ginseng, tract on, 8:279
Gioberti, Vincenzo, **6:229–230**, 7:672, 12:346
  beatific vision, 2:169
  existence of God, 6:313
  heresy, 6:778
  Neo-Guelfism, 10:234
  ontologism, 10:603, 604
  panpsychism thought, 10:824
Giorgi, Luis, 10:62
Giornale dell'assedio di Constantinopoli (Barbaro), 2:90
Giotto di Bondone, 1:769, **6:230–231**
  Bible cycles, 2:374
  crucifixions, 4:396
  mosaic works, 10:4
  paintings, 12:110
  Saint Francis of Assisi Presenting His Rule to Pope Innocent III, 5:870
Giovanna of Orvieto. *See* Joan of Orvieto, Bl.
Giovanni da Pian Del Carpini. *See* John da Pian del Carpine
Giovanni di Fidanza. *See* Bonaventure, St.
Giovanni Medda, Bl. *See* Nicola da Gesturi, Bl.
Giovio, Paolo, 1:325, 3:484
Giraldus Cambrensis, **6:231**, 8:167, 9:455–456, 12:544
Giraldus of Salles, Bl., **6:231–232**
Girard of Angers, St., **6:232**
Giraud, Sylvain, 8:338
Giraudo, Cesare, 5:430
Girls and Boys Town (Nebraska), 10:223
Girolomini, Church of the (Naples, Italy), 3:81
Girouard v. United States (1946), 3:660
Giry, François, **6:232**

Gisa (Bp. of Wells), 2:152

Giscard, Robert (Brother), 2:332, 13:735

Gisela (Queen of Hungary), Bl.,
6:232–233, 7:209

Gish, Duane, 4:347

Gislebert of Mons, 1:463

Gislenus, St., **6:233**

Giuliani, Marianna, St., **6:233–234**

Giuliani, Veronica, St., 3:358, **6:234**

Giunta Pisano, 4:396

Giuseppe figlio di Giacobbe (Rossi),
12:388

Giussani, Luigi, 4:31–32

Giustiani, Paolo, 3:611

Giustiniani, Agostino (1551-90), 6:235

Giustiniani, Agostino (Bp., d. 1536),
6:235

Giustiniani, Allesandro (Card.),
6:235–236

Giustiniani, Angelo (Bp.), 6:236

Giustiniani, Antonio (Abp.), 6:236

Giustiniani, Benedetto (1551-1622),
6:235

Giustiniani, Benedetto (Card., 1554-
1621), 3:804, 6:235

Giustiniani, Bernardo, 6:234

Giustiniani, Gerolamo (Bp.), 6:235, 236

Giustiniani, Giacomo (Card.), 6:235

Giustiniani, Giorgio, 6:235

Giustiniani, Giovanni, 6:235

Giustiniani, Innocenzio, 6:235

Giustiniani, Lawrence. *See* Lawrence
Justinian, St.

Giustiniani, Leonardo (Abp.), 6:234, 236

Giustiniani, Lorenzo, 6:235

Giustiniani, Michele, 6:235

Giustiniani, Nicholas, Bl., 6:234

Giustiniani, Nicolò Antonio (Bp.), 6:235

Giustiniani, Olimpiuccia, 2:95

Giustiniani, Orazio (Card.), 6:235

Giustiniani, Ottaviano, 6:235

Giustiniani, Paolo, Bl., 2:898, 6:235

Giustiniani, Pietro, 6:235

Giustiniani, PietroMario (Bp.), 6:236

Giustiniani, Timoteo (Bp.), 6:236

Giustiniani, Vincenzo (1593-1661),
6:235

Giustiniani, Vincenzo (Card., d. 1582),
6:235

Giustiniani, Vincenzo (d. 1599), 6:235

Giustiniani family, **6:234–236**

Gjini, Francis, 12:532

Gjonali, J., 12:532

Glaber, Radulphus, 3:812, 9:451

Gladbach Abbey (Germany), 6:188

Gladden, Washington, 1:352, 4:117

Gladstone, William Ewart, 1:85, 2:579,
6:236–237, *237*, 7:563–564, 10:334

Glagolitic Mass (Janáček), 7:712

Glanfeuil Abbey. *See* Saint-Maur-sur-
Loire Abbey (Angers, France)

Glaphyra (Cyril of Alexandria, St.),
5:511

Glasgow, Ancient See of (Scotland),
3:124

Glass, Joseph Sarsfield (Bp. of Salt Lake
City), 14:358

Glastonbury Abbey (England), 5:84,
6:237–238, *238*, 13:90

Gleeson, Francis D. (Bp. of Alaska),
1:209, 210

Die Gleichnisreden Jesu (Jülicher),
10:865

Glen, Paul, 12:777

Glen Riddle Franciscans, 5:888, 890

Glendalough Monastery (Ireland), **6:238**

Glenmary Home Mission Sisters, **6:238**

Glenmary Home Missioners, 2:410,
6:239, 10:728

Glenmary's Challenge (periodical),
6:239

Glennon, John Joseph (Card.),
6:239–240, 12:257, 560

Gligorov, Kiro, 9:15

Globalization, effect on Eurocentric
classicism, 7:840–841

Glodesindis, St., **6:240**

Gloria, 4:890–891, **6:240–241**

Gloria, Laus et Honor (hymn) (Theodulf
of Orléans), 1:431, **6:241–242**

Gloria in excelsis (papal bull, Adrian II),
4:475

Gloriam virginalem (papal bull, Gregory
IX), 2:205

Le Glorie di Maria (St. Alphonsus
Liguori), 1:310

*Le Glorie e grandezze della divina
Madre* (Sarnell), 12:694

Glorieux, Alphonse Joseph (Bp. of
Idaho), 7:290

Glorified body, 1:104, 176, **6:242–243**,
689–690

Glorious Revolution. *See* Revolution of
1688 (England)

Glory, in Jewish Gnosticism, 6:264–265

Glory, in the Bible, 3:466, **6:243–245**

Glory, personal, 8:802

Glory and Praise (hymnal), 7:260

Glory of God (End of Creation),
6:245–246, 13:151

Glory of the Confessors (Gregory of
Tours), 12:606

Glory of the Martyrs (Gregory of
Tours), 12:606

Gloss on the Sentences, 5:899

Glossa, 4:604–605

Glossa in 4 libros sententiarum
(Alexander of Hales), 1:265

Glossa Ordinaria, 2:314–315, 3:800,
6:246–247, 249, 8:408

Glossa ordinaria (St. Anselm), 5:517

Glossa ordinaria Decreti (Bartholomew
of Brescia), 2:125

Glossa ordinaria on the Decretum of
Gratian (Joannes Teutonicus), 7:885

Glossa Palatina, 8:408

Glossa super Boethii librum de Trinitate
(Thierry of Chartres), 14:2

Glossaria (Stephen Langton), 5:517

Glossary of the New Testament (Flacius
Illyricus), 5:754

Glosses, biblical, 5:507, **6:247–248**

Glosses, Canon Law, **6:248–249**

Glossolalia, 3:391, **6:249–250**

Gloucester Abbey (England), **6:250**

Gloucester Cathedral (England), 3:697

Glubokovskii, Nikolai Nikanorovich,
6:250, 12:435

Gluck, Christoph Willibald, 3:468,
6:250–251, *251*

Glueck, N., 5:86

Gluttony, **6:251–252**

Glycas, Michael, 2:759–760, **6:252–253**

Glycon cult, 1:264

Glykophilousa, 9:272

Gmeiner, John, 12:777

Gnanopadesam (Nobili), 10:408

Gnecchi Soldo, Organtino, **6:253**

Gnesiolutheranism, **6:253–254**

    Concord Formula and Book, 4:60, 61

    Crypto-Calvinism, 4:416

    Flacius Illyricus, Matthias, 5:754

    Majoristic controversy, 9:62–63

    Melanchthon's adiaphorism, 8:890

    See also Philippism

Gniezno (Poland) archbishopric, 11:438,
439

Gnilka, Joachim, 7:528

Gnome, 11:791

Gnoseology, **6:254**

    See also Knowledge

Gnosiological magic, 9:38

Gnosis, **6:254–255**

    Christian paideia education,
    10:753–756

    Clement of Alexandria, 4:472

    Cyril of Jerusalem, 4:472

Gnosis (continued)

    See also Gnosticism; Gnosticism, Jewish

Gnostic Centuries (Evagrius Ponticus), 5:464, 465

Gnosticism, 5:136, 522, **6:255–261**

    Abraxas, 1:40

    afterlife, 1:168

    alchemy, 1:237

    Antioch, 1:521

    apostolic succession, 1:590–591, 592

    apostolici, 1:594

    apostolicity, 1:595

    Bardesanes, 2:97

    Basilides, 2:148–149

    bishops, 2:414

    Bousset, Wilhelm, 2:570

    Buddhism, 2:660–661

    Burkitt, Francis Crawford, 2:706

    Carpocrates, 3:174

    Catharism, 1:230

    causality, 3:303

    Chenoboskion texts, 3:465

    Christology, 3:560, 561

    Clement of Alexandria, St., 3:798–799

    contraception, 4:218

    cosmogony, 6:258

    docetism, 4:797

    doctrines, 6:257–259

    emanationism, 5:181

    Epistles of St. Paul, 3:861

    Gnostic works, 6:255–256, 257

    grace, 6:401

    heresy, 6:256

    Hippolytus of Rome, St., 2:149

    homoousios, 4:197

    hymnody, 7:241

    illuminism, 7:320

    influence on John's Gospel, 7:905

    Judaism, 2:831, 3:465

    Jude, Epistle of, 8:16

    leaders and sects, 6:259–261

    Marcion, 9:142

    New Age Movement, 10:274–275

    patristic works against, 6:256–257

    Plotinus, 1:669

    regarding the flesh, 10:13

    Rome as intellectual center, 7:237

    spirituality, 13:443–444

    theology of Christ, 7:811

    See also Manichaeism

Gnosticism, Jewish, 2:831, 6:256, 260–261, **261–267**

Goa (Portuguese colony), **6:267–268**

    China, 3:497

    Criminali, Antonio, 4:364

    historical churches, 6:268

    works of charity, 3:416

Goan, St. See Godo, St.

Goan Schism of 1838, 6:268, 7:402

Goar, Jacques, **6:268**

Goar of Trier, St., **6:268–269**

Gobat, George, **6:269**

Gobel, Jean Baptiste Joseph (Bp. of Paris), 3:754, **6:269–270**

Gobelinus Persona, 5:618

Gobierno de los regulares de la América (Parras), 10:903

Gobitis, Minersville School District v. (1940), 3:661–662

Goch, Mechitar, 1:705–706

Göckel, R., 10:606

God, **6:270–290**, 11:285

    absence of, 9:7–8

    absolute spirit, 13:423

    action of, 8:565–566

    as addressee of prayer, 11:596

    analogy, 1:376–377

    anthropomorphic qualities of, 6:271, 288–289, 318

    anthropomorphism, 1:512

    Augustine, St., 1:863

    Averroës, 1:934

    basis for theology of, 6:271

    as being, 8:209

    Bradwardine on sovereignty, 14:29

    cabala, 2:832, 833

    Christian tradition, history, 6:280–290

    confidence in, 11:595

    continuous judgment of, 8:34–37

    covenant and, 6:271–273

    creation, 4:339, 340–345

    as creator, 6:273–274

    death of, theology, 4:583–586

    Divine concurrence, 4:70–73

    Divine missions of, 9:735–736

    Divine Paternity of, 10:942

    Egypt, 8:178

    as Father, 6:277–280

    first cause of motion, 10:23–24

    friendship with, 6:10–12

    as future hope, 6:275–276

    future of, theology of hope, 13:926

    futuribles, 6:37, 9:770

    gender attribution, 5:49, 679

    glory of, 10:213

Gregory of Nyssa, St. on image of, 6:520

growth of man in likeness of, 9:93

as head of Islamic community, 7:621

holiness of, 7:3–4, 8–9

hope, 7:94–97, 102–103

ideas, human, 8:218

Ignatian spirituality, 7:307–308

immutability, 7:354–357

ineffability, 7:445–446

infinity, 7:459, 460–461

Israel's disobedience and God's anger, 6:274–275

jealousy of, 7:749

Judaistic concept, 8:3

as judge, 8:27

justice of, 14:788–789

liberation theology, 8:546–547

living, 8:567

Lord as honorific title, 8:780

Maccabees, Books of the, 9:9

Maimonides, 9:53–54

as main agent, 8:862

Maine de Biran, 9:60

as maker of man, 9:87

Malebranche, Nicolas, 9:75

man, natural end of, 9:102

Marcion, 9:142–143

Marcionists/Manichaeans on nature of, 10:666

Mary, Blessed Virgin, bestowing grace on, 9:251

mercy of, 9:504, 506–508

Mesopotamia, 8:178

metaphysics, 2:208–209

mysteries of, 13:892

mystical marriage with, 10:105

mystical union with, 10:109

mystic's knowledge of, 10:113–114

Naḥmanides, 10:135–136

name of, 5:679

nature of, theosophy on, 13:934–935

Nicholas of Cusa on human nature of, 10:375

oath witnessed, 10:496–497

obedience of superior and subject before, 10:507–508

occasionalism and existence of, 10:527

omnipotence, 10:591–592

omnipresence, 10:593

omniscience, 10:593–599

Pastorals and theological understanding of, 10:940

permission of evils, 13:867–869

presence in world through participation, 14:141

prophecies of, 9:247

as redeemer, 11:694–967, 978

revelation, 6:270–280, 13:663–664

scientia media doctrine on knowledge of, 10:598, 14:50

scrupulosity, as cause of, 12:847

sin as rejection of, 9:902–903

social life under, 8:568

as spirit, 13:425

stoicism on matters relating to, 13:537

sufficient reason, 13:593

supernatural as new relationship with, 13:620

supernatural order, 13:623

supreme good, 6:354

technology and need for, 13:787

temptation and obligations toward, 13:814–815

tempting by believers, 13:818

theism, 13:862

theocentrism, 13:865

theophany, 13:929–930

Thierry of Chartres, 14:3

trancendental Thomism, 14:55–56

transcendence of, 13:765

union with, 2:492, 13:620–621, 14:792

via negativa tradition and knowledge of, 10:113

vows to, in the Bible, 14:590

Whitehead, Alfred North, 14:705

widows, sustainment of, 14:713

wisdom of, 14:790

Yahweh, meaning of, 6:272–273

See also Contemplation; God (Father); God, existence of; Yahweh

God (Christological title), 7:809

God (Father), 1:118, 6:277–280, **290–292**, 8:762, 9:780, 13:566

God (Father), iconography of, **6:323–324**, *324*

God (Holy Spirit), **6:292–295**

God (Son), **6:295–296**

Divine origins debated, 8:763

Leo I (Pope), St., 8:477

Logos, 8:761

sacramental worship, 8:728

santification in, 8:301

God, impassibility of, **7:357–360**

God, intuition of, **6:297–298**

See also Beatific vision

God, knowledge of. *See* Beatific vision

God, Name of, **6:298**

Hebrew, 13:77–78

Islam, 7:271

Logos, 8:758–764

The Lord, 8:779–781

Memra, 8:759

Seven Last Words, 13:38

Shaddai, 13:58

Spirit of God, 13:426–428

God, proofs for the existence of

contingency, 4:213

cosmological argument, 4:285–287

Descartes, 4:680–681

Dicta Candidi, 3:13

Duns Scotus, John, 4:937

fideism, 5:712–713

first cause of motion as, 10:23

"five ways" (Aquinas), 6:298–305, 315–317, 14:142, 143

proof from contingency, 6:302–303

proof from efficiency causality, 6:301–302

proof from grades of perfection, 6:303–304

proof from motion, 6:300–301

proof from order, 6:304–305

Hermesianism, 6:798

Hume, David, 7:202

Kant's theory, 8:122, 124

Locke, J., 8:745

Lonergan, B., 8:773

Sertillanges, A., 13:23

simplicity of God, 13:138, 139

God, providence of

in the Bible, 11:780–781

theology of, 11:781–784

God and Intelligence in Modern Philosophy (Sheen), 13:74

God and Ourselves (Godfrey), 6:325

God at Auschwitz? (Oesterreicher), 10:559

God Glorified in the Work of Redemption (Edwards), 5:97

God in Pagan thought, **6:305–309**

God in philosophy, **6:309–323**

existence of, 6:310–318

nature of, 6:318–323

place of, 6:309–311

God Warning Adam and Eve stained glass (Chartres Cathedral), 14:*166*

Godard of Hildesheim, St., 1:664, **6:324–325**

Godden, Thomas, **6:325**

Godden v. Hales (1686), 10:501

Goddesses. *See* Gods and goddesses

Godeau, Antoine (Bp.), **6:325**

Godeberta, St., 5:157

Godefroy (Bp. of Amiens), St., 1:359

Godefroy, Maximilian, 3:715

Godehard, St. *See* Godard of Hildesheim, St.

Gödel, K., 8:753

Godet des Marais, Paul (Bp. of Chartres), 12:572

Godfrey, C. J., 2:621

Godfrey, William (Card.), 5:252, **6:325**

Godfrey II (Duke of Lorraine), 2:242, 7:83, 13:521

Godfrey Giffard, **6:325–326**

Godfrey of Amiens, St., **6:326**

Godfrey of Bouillon, 2:217, **6:326**, 7:770

Alexius I Comnenus, 1:275

Crusaders' states, 4:401–402

Crusades literature, 4:400

Ida of Boulogne, 7:289

Knights of the Holy Sepulcher, 8:198

Godfrey of Fontaines, 2:306, **6:327**, 13:99

Godfrey of Saint-Victor, **6:327–328**, 9:457, 12:589, 14:323

Godfrey of Savigny (Abbot), 12:711

Godfrey of Trani, 3:48

Godfrey the Bearded. *See* Godfrey II (Duke of Lorraine)

Godhead, 8:762

Godin, Abbé H., 14:838

God-Man, **6:323**, 13:856–857

God-Man relationship (Lutheranism), 8:893

Godo, St., **6:328**

Godoy, Manuel, 3:204

Godoy, Pedro de, **6:328–329**, 14:51

Godric of Finchale, 10:119

Gods and goddesses

ancient Persian religions, 11:143

in the Bible, 5:173–174

Divine ephithets for, 5:307

ecofeminism and goddess worship, 5:49

Egyptian pantheon, 5:121, 123

Epicureanism, 5:284

fertility, 5:696–697

Mesopotamia, ancient, 9:532–534

pagan Slavic, 13:215

Roman religion, 12:309–310

sky gods, 5:696–697

sun-god (*Sol Invictus*), 5:191

temples of, 13:808

Gods and goddesses *(continued)*

  See also specific gods and goddesses; specific religions

God's Orders Noah to Build the Ark (Raimond), 10:*404*

God's World in the Making (Schoonenberg), 10:667

Godwin, William, 1:384

Gody, Peter, 6:340

Goemaere, Mary of the Cross (Mother), 2:867, 12:646–647

Goesbriand, Louis de (Bp.), **6:329**

Goethe, Johann Wolfgang von, **6:329–333**

  aesthetics, 3:679

  Arnold, Gottfried, 1:718

  Faust legend, 5:650

  Kantianism, 8:126

Goetz, John, 11:236

Goeze, Johann Melchior, 8:517, 12:35

Gogarten, Friedrich, 4:721, **6:334**

El-Gohari, Guiguis, 4:254

El-Gohari, Ibrahim, 4:254

Góis, Damião de, 1:324, **6:334–335**

Góis e Vasconcelos, Zacarías, 2:596

Gold chain (*Catena aurea*) (Aquinas), 14:18–19, 25

Golden Age, **6:335**

Golden Book of Prum, 3:*162*

The Golden Bough (Frazer), 1:459, 12:64

Golden Bull of 1356, 1:633, 3:843, 8:869

Golden Epistle (William of Saint-Thierry), 3:190

Golden Militia, 4:596

Golden Number, computus and, 4:46

Golden Rose, **6:335–336**, *336*, 10:856

Golden Sayings (Dicta) (Giles of Assisi), 6:218

"Golden Sequence." *See Veni sancte spiritus* (sequence)

Golden Spur, 4:596

Das Goldene Vliess (Grillparzer), 6:533

Goldstein, David, 1:352, **6:336–337**, 10:543

Goldwell, James, **6:337**

Goldwell, Thomas, 5:247

Goldziher, I., 1:781

Golgotha, 4:384–385

Goliathismus profligatus (Sinnich), 13:163

Goltzius, Hendrick, 8:*872*

Gomarists, 12:109

Gomarus, Franciscus, 1:712, 2:894, **6:337**, 12:109

Gombert, Nicholas, **6:337–338**

Gomensoro, Tomás Xavier de, **6:338**

Gomer, St. *See* Gummar, St.

Gomes, Antonio Carlos, **6:338**

Gomes, António Ferreira (Bp. of Oporto, Portugal), 11:539

Gomes, Francis Anthony (Bp. of Mymensingh, Bangladesh), 2:53

Gomes de Lisboa, 3:52

Gomez, José Valentín, **6:338**

Gomez, Martin, Bl., 7:734

Gomez, Miguel, 12:645

Gómez Farías, Valentin, 2:215

Gomułka, Władysław, 11:451, 452

Gonçalves, Andrew, Bl., 1:951

Gonçalves, Vital María Oliveira de (Bp.), **6:339**

Gonçalves de Oliveira, Vital María, 2:596

Gonçalves Ledo, Joaquim, 2:96

Gondeberga (Queen of the Lombards), 1:664

Gondulf (Bp. of Rochester), 2:189

Gondulphus of Metz, St., **6:339**

Gonet, Jean Baptiste, 2:396, 3:102, **6:339–340**, 14:51

Gonfalonieri (*Arciconfraternita del Gonfalone*), **6:340**

Gong Pinmei (Ignatius Kung) (Bp.), 3:502

Góngora y Argote, Luis de, 2:116

Gonsalvus Hispanus, **6:340–341**

Gonsalvus of Curiola (Bp. of Ancyra), 1:398

Gonson, David, Bl., 5:227

Gontard (Abbot), 8:59

Gonzaga, Annibale, 6:342

Gonzaga, Carlo, 6:342

Gonzaga, Ercole (Card.), 6:342

Gonzaga, Federico (Card.), 6:342

Gonzaga, Federigo, II, 6:341

Gonzaga, Ferdinando (Card.), 6:342

Gonzaga, Ferrante, 6:341

Gonzaga, Francesco (1484-1519), 6:341

Gonzaga, Francesco (Card., d. 1483), 6:342

Gonzaga, Francesco (Card., d. 1566), 6:342

Gonzaga, Gianfrancesco, 6:341

Gonzaga, Gianvincenzo (Card.), 6:342

Gonzaga, Guglielmo, 6:341

Gonzaga, Ludovico, 6:341, 342

Gonzaga, Pirro (Card.), 6:342

Gonzaga, Scipione (Card.), 6:342

Gonzaga, Sigismondo (Card.), 6:342

Gonzaga, Vincenzo (Card., d. 1627), 6:342

Gonzaga, Vincenzo, I (1587-1612), 6:341–342

Gonzaga family, **6:341–342**

  See also Aloysius Gonzaga, St.

González, de Marmolejo, Rodrigo, 3:485

González, John. *See* Sahagún, John of, St.

González, Roque, St., **6:342**

González, Tirso, 7:782

González, Toribio Romo, St., 6:545

González Dávila, Gil, 4:288, **6:343**

González de Santalla, Tirso, **6:343**

González Dorado, Antonio, 12:478

González Flores, Anacleto, **6:343–344**

González García, Manuel, Bl., **6:344–345**

González Holguín, Diego, **6:345**

Gonzalez Rubio, Jose Maria de Jesus, 2:866, 12:645, 646

González Suárez, Federico (Bp.), 6:*345*, **345–346**

González y Díaz, Tuñón, Ceferino (Card.), **6:346**, 12:773

Gonzalo Gonzalo, Gonzalo, Bl., 7:124

Good, **6:346–354**

  analogy, 1:376

  Aristotle, 1:683

  axiology, 1:948

  beauty, 2:187

  choice, 3:520

  Christ's influence, 10:668

  common good, 4:16

  duty vs., 4:673–674

  God as transcendent, 8:832

  Honorius of Autun, 7:89

  human act, 7:170

  laws, conflict of, 8:410

  Lonergan, B., 8:773

  man's capacity for, 10:667–668

  moral good, 6:348–349, 350–354

  object of the will as universal, 10:24–25

  ontological, 6:346–350

  ontological argument, 10:601

  Philo Judaeus, 11:270

  Plato, 8:826

  practical reason, 8:389–390

  Spinoza, 13:420

Good, supreme, 6:353, **354–355**

Good acts. *See* Salutary acts

Good and evil, 5:282–283

Good Cousins, 3:99

Good Friday, **6:355–356**
  cross veneration, 4:382
  Hispanic American popular piety, 11:510
  liturgical year, 8:718
Good Friday Agreement (1998), 7:569
Good Friday prayer
  Oremus, 10:45, 46, 651
  revisions, 10:559
Good habits, 6:500
A Good Man Is Hard To Find (O'Connor), 10:547
Good News Club v. Milford Central School (2001), 3:664
Good Shepherd, 2:699, **6:356–357**, 7:856–857
The Good Shepherd (*Pastor bonus*) (apostolic constitution, John Paul II), 3:57, 58, 4:438–440, 5:480–481, 10:853, 11:76, 480
Good Shepherd Institute (Poland), 8:129
Good Shepherd Sisters of Quebec, **6:358**
Good works, **6:358–359**
  justice of men, 8:75
  Luther, Martin, 3:608
  Pentecostal churches, 11:105
  Wesley, John, 8:87
  works of charity, 3:414
Goodenough, E. R., 7:909
Goodier, Alban (Abp.), **6:359–360**
Goodman, Godfrey (Bp. of Gloucester), **6:360**
Goodman, John, Ven., 5:235
Goodman, Nelson, 11:552, 14:327
Goodness
  man, natural end of, 9:101
    Aquinas, 9:98
    Aristotle, 9:97
    Plato, 9:96
  as property of being, 14:152
  See also Beatitudes, Christian life
Goodrich, Thomas (Bp. of Ely), 5:180
Goossens, Pierre Lambert (Abp. of Mechelen), 1:170, **6:360–361**
Goral, Wladyslaw (Bp. of Lublin), 11:450
Gorbachev, Mikhail, 7:998, 10:686, 695, 12:429, 14:280
Gordian I (Roman Emperor), 12:312
Gordian II (Roman Emperor), 12:312
Gordian III (Roman Emperor), 12:312
Gordian and Epimachus, SS., **6:361**
Gordis, R., 5:35
Gordman, Thomas K., 10:270
Gordon, Charles (Bp. of Kingston, Jamaica), 3:112

Gordon, George, 6:361, 362
Gordon, James Clement (Bp.), 1:438, 592
Gordon, Judah Leib, 6:663
Gordon, Lord George (1751-93), 5:250
Gordon Riots (London, 1780), 5:183, 250, **6:361–362**
Gore, Charles, 8:896
Gore, Charles (Bp.), 6:*363*, **363**, 9:78
Gorer, Geoffrey, 13:854
Goretti, Maria, St., **6:363–364**
Gorgias (Plato), 5:88
Gorgias of Leontini, 3:351, 13:324
Gorgonia, St., **6:364**
Gorham, George C., 10:734
Gorham, Joseph A., 3:283
Gorkum (Holland), Martyrs of, **6:364**
Gorman, Daniel Mary (Bp. of Idaho), 7:290
Gorman, Thomas K. (Bp. of Reno), 10:270, 271, 12:127
Görres, Johann Joseph von, **6:364–365**
  Cologne mixed marriage dispute, 3:846
  Döllinger, Johannes, 4:823
  Munich Circle, 6:183
Görres-Gesellschaft, 1:328, 3:622, 6:184, **365**
Gorriti, Juan Ignacio de, **6:365**
Gorze Abbey (France), **6:365–366**
  Adalbero I, 1:99
  Chrodegang of Metz, St., 3:563
  Kremsmünster Abbey influenced, 8:248
  reform promoted, 8:484
  St. Paul-Outside-the-Walls Abbey, 1:172
Gosling, Samuel, **6:366**
Gospel harmonies, 7:845
Gospel hymns. *See* Gospel songs
Gospel music. *See* Gospel songs
Gospel of Life (Mānī), 9:113, 115
The Gospel of Life. See *Evangelium vitae* (encyclical, John Paul II)
Gospel of the Ebionites, 5:31
Gospel of the Nativity of Mary (Radbert), 9:274–275
Gospel of the Truth, 5:82
Gospel of Thomas
  iconography, 1:559
  parables, 10:871, 872
  scholarship, 10:305
Gospel of Truth (Valentinus), 14:374
Gospel Questions and Solutions (Eusebius of Caesarea), 5:452
Gospel songs, **6:368**, 7:257, 8:694–695

Gospels, **6:366–368**
  apologetics, 1:563, 565
  asceticism, 1:776
  base ecclesial communities, 8:417–418
  canonicity, 3:28, 31
  Capernaum, 3:83
  casuistry, 3:220
  composition of, 3:29–30
  Diatessaron, 4:731
  inspiration of, 3:21
  kerygma, 8:157
  Kingdom of God, 8:173–174
  liberation theology, 8:547
  Lutheranism, 8:893
  mission theology, 9:729
  Pharisees, 8:6
  references in the Qur'ān, 7:608
  See also Bible, textual criticism; *specific gospels*
Gospels of Godescalc, 3:154, 9:128
Gospels of Saint-Médard-de-Soissons, 3:154, 9:128
Gospels of Speyer, 9:128–129
Gossé, François Joseph. *See* Gossec, François Joseph
Gossec, François Joseph, **6:368–369**, 10:439
Gossman, F. Joseph (Bp. of Raleigh, NC), 11:900
Goswin, St., 1:396, **6:369**
Goswin of La Chapelle, 1:935
Got, Betrand de. *See* Clement V (Pope)
Gothard, St. *See* Godard of Hildesheim, St.
Gother, John, 5:572
Gothic architecture, 3:*687*, *688*, *690*, *693–699*, *701*, *704*
  altars, 1:317
  Apocalypse iconography, 1:544
  Bible cycles in, 2:373–374
  Cistercians, 3:750
  revival, 3:*701*, 709, 715
  Ruskin, 12:414
  social considerations, 3:669
  structure, 3:601, 677
  symbolism, 3:674, 676
  theories, 3:694–695
Gothic Architecture and Scholasticism (Panofsky), 3:669, 676
Gothic art, 12:485–486
The Gothic Cathedral (Simpson), 3:674
Gothic Cathedrals and Sacred Geometry (Lesser), 3:674
Gothic peoples, 1:631, 663, 3:596

Gothic Revival, 8:636

Gothic rite. *See* Mozarabic Rite

Gothicus. *See* Claudius II (Marcus Aurelius Claudius) (Roman Emperor)

Goths, 4:590, **6:369**

Gotō, John Soan de, St., 7:732

Gottfried of Admont, 1:117

Gotthard, St. *See* Godard of Hildesheim, St.

Gotti, Vincenzo Lodovico, **6:370**, 14:51

Göttingen, University of (Germany), 5:256, 8:137

Gottschalk, St., **6:370**, 402

Gottschalk of Limburg, **6:370–371**, 7:248

Gottschalk of Orbais, 5:783, **6:371–372**

    Carolingian reform, 3:158, 599

    Carolingian Renaissance, 3:160

    dialectics, 4:725

    hymns of, 7:246

    medieval Latin literature works of, 9:443

    predestination, 9:445, 11:650

    prescholasticism, 12:757

    Remigius of Lyons, St., 12:107

Gottsched, J. C., 5:263

Göttweig Abbey (Krems, Austria), 1:322, 909, **6:372**

Götz von Berlichingen (Goethe), 6:330

Gouda, Nicholas de, 1:20

Goudimel, Claude, **6:372**

Goudin, Antoine, **6:372–373**, 12:767, 772, 14:51

Gouine, Claude, 2:188

Gounod, Charles François, 6:*373*, **373**

Goupil, René, 10:310, 434–435

Goussen, H., 4:385

Gousset, Thomas Marie Joseph (Card.), 1:311, 3:619

Gouthe-Soulard, François Xavier (Abp. of Aix), 1:197

Governance, power of, **6:373–375**, 8:476, 477

Government, **6:375–377**

    authority, 4:151

    Church law versus, 8:410

    classification, 4:637

    common good, 4:16–22

    Confucianism, 4:100–101

    forms of, 13:487–488

    Leo XIII (Pope), 7:346–347, 8:492

    Mayflower Compact, 9:382

    monarchy, 9:781–782

    papal legates, 8:450–452

    social justice, 8:68

    sovereignty, 13:371–372

    taxation, 13:769

    See also Church and State; Church and State, U.S.; State

The Government in Charity (Mulry), 10:57

The Governour (Elyot), 5:206

Gower, Henry (Bp.), 12:544

Gower, John, **6:377–378**, 9:462

Goyau, Georges, **6:378**

Goyeneche y Barreda, José Sebastián de (Bp.), **6:378–379**

Gozbert (Abbot), 12:669

Gozbert, Thuringian duke, 8:168

Gozzoli, Benozzo, 5:766

Grabmann, Martin, 3:586, 587, 5:365, 6:184, 379–380

    Adam of Buckfield, 1:108

    Adoro Te Devote, 1:120

    neoscholastic revival, 12:776

Grace

    administration of Holy orders, 7:38–39, 41

    ascetical and mystical, 13:434

    beatific vision, 2:176

    conflict of Jesuits and Dominicans over, 14:48

    Consummation in Christ, 9:253

    controversies, 6:401–405

        Báñez, Domingo, 2:50–51, 6:390, 391

        Bellarmine, St. Robert, 2:227

        conversion, 4:239–241

        De auxiliis controversy, 6:390–391

        Jansenism, 7:715–718

        medieval period, 6:402

        Molina, Luis de, 2:50, 51

        patristic era, 6:401–402

        Paul V (Pope), ban on discussion, 11:26

        Reformation and Counter Reform, 6:402–403, 8:86

    Duns Scotus, John, 4:939

    free will, 5:934–935

    freedom in, 5:945

    good works, 6:358–359

    Hermesianism, 6:798

    heroic virtue, 14:554

    human act, 7:172

    hylomorphism, 7:238

    hypostatic union, 7:264–265

    immortality, 7:352

    I-Thou model, 8:833

    life of, 13:441–442

    man, natural end of, 9:96, 99

    Mary, Blessed Virgin, 7:331–334, 9:250–253

    merit, 9:513

    molinism, 9:770, 771, 772

    moral theology, 9:851–852

    Mystici Corporis (Pius XII), 10:104, 110

    mysticism and role of, 10:112–113

    ordination, 7:39, 41

    Palamas's doctrine, 10:766

    participation in life of God through, 10:909

    reunion in, 11:982–983

    sovereignty of, 5:934

    spirituality, 13:440

    supernatural as example, 13:621

    supernatural existential, 13:622

    virtue, 14:551–552

Grace, actual, 6:397–398

Grace, controversies on conversion and, **4:239–241**

Grace, created and uncreated, 6:396, **405**

Grace, efficacious, **6:405**

    congruism, 4:120–121

    de auxiliis controversy, 4:110–113

    Lemos, T., 8:466–467

    Lessius, L., 8:518

Grace, free will and, **5:934–935**

Grace, in the Bible, 5:934, **6:380–383**

    Adam, 1:104

    Corinthians, Epistles to the, 9:87

    man, renewal of, 9:87

    Timothy, Books of, 9:87

Grace, sacramental, **6:406–409**

Grace, sanctifying, 6:406–407, 7:45

Grace, state of, **6:410–411**, 11:133–134

Grace, sufficient, 4:120–121, **6:409–410**

Grace, theology of, **6:383–401**

    accident, 1:64

    Alphonsus Liguori, St., 1:309

    Álvarez, Diego, 1:326

    analogy, 1:379

    Augustinianism, 1:860, 861, 866, 874, 876–877, 880–881, 883, 885

    charisms, 3:390

    Charles of the Assumption, 3:435–436

    chastity as means, 8:876

    Christian anthropology, 3:532–533

    Christian philosophy, 3:538, 541

    communio, 4:28

    contemplation, 4:207, 208

    contemporary, 6:392–393

contrition-attrition distinction, 4:226, 227, 228–229

created actuation by uncreated act, 4:335–336

de auxiliis controversy, 4:110–113

Divine concurrence, 4:70, 72

Divine judgment, 8:35

doctrine, development of, 4:807

double justice, 8:69

Fransen, Pieter Frans, 5:918

generous love, 8:830

Greek Fathers, 6:385

habitual vs. actual, 8:86

Holy Spirit, baptism in, 7:45

hope, 7:97–98

hypostatic union caused by sanctifying, 10:14

Jansenism, 1:881, 892–893, 3:614

justice as gift, 8:74–75

justification, 8:82, 86, 89

life, concept of, 8:572

man, concept of, 9:92

Molina, Luis de, 3:785

neoscholastic, 8:89

nominalist tradition, 6:389–390

original justice, 1:105

patristic era, 6:384–385

theology of Church, 3:586–587

treatment of grace, 6:393–401

Grace, Thomas Langdon (Bp. of St. Paul, MN), 5:882, 9:655–656, 12:572–573

Grace and nature, **6:411–413**

Grace Cathedral (Episcopal) (San Francisco), 3:717

Grace Church (New York), 3:715

Grace of union, 7:264–265

Graces of Interior Prayer (Poulain), 12:201

Gracia Real de Santa Teresa de Mose, 1:155

Gracián de la Madre de Dios, 3:136

Gradines, 1:317

Gradual, **6:413–415**

Gradus ad Parnassum (Fux), 6:37–38

Graebner, F., 12:744

Graecismus (Evrard of Béthune), 5:496

Graecorum affectionium curatio (Theodoret of Cyr), 13:878

Graetz, Heinrich, 7:873

Graf, Joseph, 3:291

Graf, Karl Heinrich, 5:519

Graffiti, cross and, 4:380, 381

Graffiti de Pompei (Garucci), 10:774

Graft, **6:415**

Graham, Stone v. (1980), 3:666

Graham, William Franklin (Billy), 12:205

Grahmann, Charles, 7:523

The Grail (Catholic Movement), **6:415–416**

Grail (lay women's group), **4:891–892**

The Grail (periodical), 8:625, 12:568

Gramich, Jeannine (Sister), 7:73

Grammar, Aquinas on, 8:538

The Grammar of Assent (Newman), 10:334, 338, 339

El Gran teatro del mundo (Baraca), 2:116

Granada, Treaty of (1500), 7:669

Granado, Francisco María del, 2:467

Le Grand dictionnaire historique (Moréri), 5:207

Grande, Rutilio, 7:794

Grande Román, Juan, St., **6:416**

Granderath, Theodor, **6:416–417**

Le Grandezze delle misericordie di Dio (St. Charles of Sezze), 3:435

Grandgent, C. H., 4:520

Grandin, Vital (Bp. of St. Albert), **6:417**

Grandmaison, Léonce de, **6:417**, 7:790

Grandmont Abbey (France) and order, **6:417–418**, 11:572

Grandmontines, 3:191

Grandrue, Claude de, 12:590

Granier, Claude de (Bp. of Geneva), 5:866–867

Granjon, Henri (Bp. of Tucson), 1:688, 11:753

Granjon, Jean Marie, 3:374

Grannan, Charles P., 1:354

Grant, F. C., 7:850

Grant, Madison, 10:171

Grant, Ulysses S., 2:425, 3:660

Granvelle, Antoine Perrenot de, 2:605, **6:418**

Granzotto, Claudio, Bl., **6:418–419**

Grass churches (Hawaii), 6:*668*

Grassel, Lorenz, **6:419**

Grassi, Achilles (Bp.), 6:420

Grassi, Achilles (the Elder), 6:419

Grassi, Anthony, Bl., **6:420**

Grassi, Antonio (Bp.), 6:419

Grassi, Giovanni A., 7:788

Grassi, Gregorio, St., **6:420**, 13:78

Grassi, Horatio, 6:62

Grassi, John, 3:181

Grassi, Paris de, 3:349, 6:419–420

Grassi family, **6:419–420**

Grass-roots communities. *See* Basic Christian communities

Grata recordatio (encyclical, John XXIII), 7:937

Gratiae gratis datae, 10:107

Gratian (monk), 9:455

Gratian (Roman Emperor), 3:594, 5:455, **6:422–423**, 12:301, 318, 354

altar of Victory, 1:337–338

Arianism, 1:522, 663

Church-State relations, 3:632

contraception, 4:219, 220

Decretum of (Concordia Discordantium Canonum), 5:618

Ecumenical councils, 4:302

Gratian, Decretum of (Concordia Discordatium Canonum), 3:42, 47, 49–50, **6:420–422**, 7:663–664

Alanus Anglicus, 1:207

Alger of Liége, 1:283

Ansegis of Fontenelle, St., 1:494

apparatus, 8:408

capital punishment, 3:86

computus, 4:46

cornerstone of church, 4:271

Corpus Iuris Canonici, 4:272–273

Councils of Chalon-Sur-Saône, 3:373

Cyprian, St., 4:459

decretal as form, 4:599, 600

Decretists, 8:265

dialectics, 4:726

First and Second Laterans, 8:350–351

Laborans, 8:265–266

natural law, 10:181

plan as model, 13:101–102

precursors, 3:60

Simon of Bisignano, 13:132

Sixtus V (Pope), 13:197

University of Bologna, 2:474

works of charity, 3:411

Gratian, Jerome, 3:145, **6:422**, 8:293, 414–415, 10:627

Gratiano, John de. *See* Gregory VI (Pope)

Gratitude, 4:318, **6:423**

Gratius, Ortwin, **6:423–424**

Gratry, Auguste Joseph Alphonse, 1:881, **6:424**, 7:848

Grattan, Henry, 5:184, 7:561

Gratus of Carthage (Bp.), 3:188, 4:862

Grau, Micaela, 13:180

Gravamina, 5:658, **6:424–425**

Grave markers, 13:*665*

Gravener, John, 7:786

Graves, James, 2:80

Graves, Lawrence P. (Bp.), 1:693

Graves et diuturnae (Pope Clement VII), 5:435

Gravestones, 13:507

Gravier, Jacques, 1:691

Graviora (papal bull, Leo XII), 12:857

Gravissimas inter (apostolic letter, Pius IX), 6:778

Gravissimo officii munere (encyclical, Pius X), 11:390

Gray, John. *See* Tatham, John

Gray, Robert (Abp. of Capetown), 1:445

Gray, William (Bp. of Ely), **6:425**

Gray League Republic, 4:775

Gray Ursulines, 8:444

Graymoor Sisters, 5:883

Gréa, Adrien, 3:69

Great and Little Rules for cenobitic life. *See Asceticon* (St. Basil)

Great Awakening, 5:472, 969, **6:425–426**

　Boehm, Martin, 2:454

　Congregationalism, 4:115

　Dwight, Timothy, 4:957

　Edwards, Jonathan rejection of, 5:97

　growth of Baptist churches, 2:79

　Presbyterian Church, 11:676

　revivalism, 12:204

　Shakers, 13:60

　spirituals, 13:456

　Whitefield, George, 14:703–704

Great bells, 2:233

Great Bend (KS), 4:842–843

Great Bet Din, 8:7

Great Bible of Demeter Neksei-Lipocz (Book of Nahum), 10:*136*

Great Britain. *See* Britain, early church in; England; Northern Ireland; Scotland; Wales

Great Catechism (Gregory of Nyssa), 10:755

Great Catechism (Moghila), 10:700–701

The Great Chain of Being (Lovejoy), 10:630

Great Depression, 8:115

Great Dispute and Christian Policy (Solov'ev), 13:307

Great Malvern priory. *See* Malvern Abbey (Worcester, England)

Great mantle or cope, 10:857

Great Mosque (Mecca), 6:*623*

Great Mother cult, 10:91–92

Great Rift Valley, 7:1027

Great Saint Bernard Hospice (Switzerland), 3:67, 69, **6:426**

Great St. Martin Church (Cologne), 3:844

Great Schisms. *See* Eastern Schism (1054); Western Schism (1378-1417)

"Great Vehicle" (Buddhism), 9:46–48

Greater Antilles. *See* Caribbean

Greater Doxology. *See* Gloria

Greater Week. *See* Holy Week

Greaton, Joseph (Father), 11:80, 234–235

Greban, Arnoul, 10:928

Grebel, Conrad, 1:368, **6:426**

El Greco (painter), 2:114, 4:397, 6:*427*, **427–428**, 12:600

Greco, Charles P. (Bp. of Alexandria, LA), 1:270

Greco-Roman Schooling, **6:428–433**

Gredt, Joseph August, **6:433**, 12:748, 776

Greece, **6:434–437**, *435*, 9:801

　anti-Catholic legislation, 7:934

　demographic statistics, 6:434

　interfaith relations, 6:437

　John XXIII (Pope), Bl., as diplomat to, 7:934

　map, 6:*435*

　monasticism, 9:801

　nonrecognition of Roman Catholic Church, 6:437

　physical sciences, 12:800–801

　prostitution in ancient, 11:773

　wisdom, 14:784

　See also Greece, ancient

Greece, ancient

　prostitution, 11:773

　sciences, 12:799–807

　wisdom, 14:784

　See also Greek philosophy

Greek Anthology, 2:804

Greek Catholic Church (Eastern Catholic), 2:748, 5:21, **6:437–438**

　ambos, 1:336

　cross feast, 4:383

　history, 13:372

　hymnology, 7:241–242

　imposition of hands, 7:366

　lay confession, 8:411

　Romania, 12:334, 336, 339–340

　Slovakia, 13:219

　Ten Commandments in, 4:6

Greek Fathers. *See* Fathers of the Church; Patristic era

Greek Grammar (Constantine Lascaris), 10:772

Greek hymnology, 7:241, 242

Greek language

　European study of, 12:622

　humanism, 7:185

　translation of word grace, 6:380, 381

Greek language, biblical, **6:438**

　Maccabees, Books of the, 9:7

　Septuagint, 12:920

　translation of word gospel, 6:366–367

Greek language, early Christian and Byzantine, 2:769, 774, 790, **6:438–439**

　early languages, 8:361

　as lingua franca, 8:667

　as liturgical language, 8:666

　as second language, 8:361

　translations to Latin, 8:363, 364

　use in Roman Church, 7:652

Greek menologies, 6:614

Greek mythology, 9:89

Greek naturalists, 6:6

Greek Orthodox Church, **10:690**

　biblical canon, 3:27, 28, 30–31

　Bulgaris, Eugenius, 2:686

　Crusades against, 4:413

　Cyprus, 4:461–463

　Latin Empire of Constantinople, 8:367

　Muslim rule, 4:196

　United States, 3:717

　See also Byzantine chant; Byzantine Christianity

Greek philosophy, **6:439–443**

　accident, 1:59–60, 61

　action at a distance, 1:80

　Alexandria, 1:268, 269

　Alfarabi, 1:277

　allegory, 1:292, 6:786–787

　analogy, 1:371, 376, 377

　analysis and synthesis, 1:381

　antimonies, 1:519–520

　Arabian philosophy, 1:620

　art, 1:743, 745–746

　asceticism, 1:772–773

　atheism, 1:822

　atomism, 1:832–833, 4:644

　biblical canon, 3:25

　biology, 2:400

　capital punishment, 3:87

　categories of being, 3:255–257

　causality, 3:297–298, 302–303

　central sense, 3:344–345

　certitude, 3:351–352

　chance, 3:375, 376

　conscience, 4:139–140, 142

　consciousness, 4:151–152

　contingency, 4:212–213

continuum, 4:215, 216, 217
contradiction, 4:223, 224
cosmogony of, 4:283
criteriology, 4:367
Cynics, 4:455–457
Cyrenaics, 4:464–465
Dionysus cult, 4:753
disciple as term, 4:768, 772–773
division, 4:792
dogmatism, 4:821
dualism, 4:914–915
dynamism, 4:958–960
essence, 5:260–261, 364
final causality, 5:723–724
freethinkers, 5:967
human will in, 14:721
hylozoism, 7:239
idea, 7:292–293
identity, 7:302, 303
immanence, 7:340
immortality, 7:347–348
impact on Roman religion, 12:326
influence of Parmenides, 10:893
influence on John's Gospel,
    7:905–906
influence on theology, 13:918–921
intellectualism, 7:514
knowledge, theories of, 8:213
leisure, 8:461
light, notions of, 8:583
materialism in, 9:318
mathematics, 9:325–326
matter in, 9:339
mechanism, 9:415
metaphysics in, 9:548–549
methodology in, 9:564–565
motion in, 10:16–17
music, 10:70–71
natural law doctrine, 10:180
nature, 13:618
notion of order, 10:630
number symbolism, 3:673
optimism of, 10:613
participation, 10:905–906
relativism, 12:46
self, concept of, 12:882
Sophists, 13:323–324
soul, 13:332–334, 338–339
soul-body relationship, 13:357
substance in, 13:574–575
substantial change, 13:580
will and willing, 14:721
Wisdom, Book of, reflected in,
    14:792

wonder in, 14:832
See also Aeschylus; Anaxagoras;
    Anaximander; Anaximenes;
    Aristides; Aristotelianism; Aristotle;
    Carneades of Cyrene; Celsus;
    Democritus; Dio Chrysostom;
    Empedocles; Epicurus; Heraclitus;
    Iamblichus; Melissus of Samos;
    Neoplatonism; Parmenides; Plato;
    Platonism; Plotinus; Porphyry;
    Poseidonius; Proclus; Socrates;
    Speusippus; Syrianus; Thales;
    Theophrastus; Xenocrates;
    Xenophanes of Colophon; Zeno of
    Citium; Zeno of Elea
Greek philosophy, religious aspects of,
    6:307, **443–450**
    explanation of the world and way of
        salvation, 6:448–450
    kindness, 8:171
    main aspects and historical facts,
        6:443–444
    philosopher as superior being,
        6:444–445
    philosopher as teacher and
        missionary, 6:445
    philosophic syncretism, 6:449
    philosophy as a school for life,
        6:447–448
    Sextus, Sentences of, 13:52
    unity and multiplicity opposition,
        10:58–59
    veneration of philosophers, 6:445
Greek religion, **6:450–455**
    Aesculapius cult, 1:140–141
    afterlife, 1:165–167
    anthropomorphism, 1:510
    Artemis cult, 4:729–730
    chthonic divinities, 3:573–574
    Cretan-Mycenaean, 4:362–363
    Cybele, 4:450
    daimones, 4:495–497
    Delphi, Oracle of, 4:632–633
    Dionysus cult, 4:753
    divination, 4:784–785
    Divine epithets, 5:306–307
    dream interpretation, 4:903
    earth worship, 5:2
    hospitality, 7:118
    immortality, 7:347
    prayer, 11:590
    resurrection, 12:145
    sacrifice, 12:508–510
    soul, 13:338
Greek theology, 4:237, **6:455–460**,
    8:81–82, 13:910
Greek theoretical science, 12:807–809

Greeks, Congregation for the Affairs of
    the, 5:21
Greeley, Horace, 14:148
Green, Francis J. (Bp. of Tucson), 1:688
Green, Hugh, Bl., 5:235, **6:460–461**
Green, Joseph (Bp.), 4:444, 12:127
Green, Richard. See Reynolds, Richard
    (Thomas) (d. 1642), Bl.
Green, Robert, 5:238
Green, Thomas (Father), Bl., 5:226,
    7:1019
Green, Thomas Hill, 2:624, 6:712,
    7:299, 12:48
Greene, Graham, 6:461, **461–462**,
    14:686
Greene, R. L., 3:149–150
Greenhill, W. A., 12:210
Greening, Bruce, 1:161–162
Greenland, 1:261, 4:664, 666
Greenlee, J. G., 2:366
Greenwood, William, Bl., 5:226, 7:1019
Grégoire, Henri Baptiste (Bp. of Loir-et-
    Cher), 3:754, 4:180, 5:974,
    6:462–463, 12:541
Gregoras, Nicephorus
    hesychasm, 2:794, 826, 827
    historiography, 2:776, 800
Gregori, Luigi, 10:461
Gregorian calendar, 6:503
    Easter date, 4:46
    introduction to Poland, 2:153
    liturgical aspects, 8:642
Gregorian Chant, 5:701, **6:463–468**
    adapting to vernacular, 8:705
    Alleluia, 1:294–295
    Ambrosian chant, 1:341
    Aurelian of Réomé, 1:895
    Berthier, Jacques, 2:333
    Carolingian reform, 3:563–564
    church architecture, 3:812
    Communion antiphons, 4:33–34
    comparison of Old Roman, 10:581
    Fontenelle Abbey, 5:793
    liturgical music history, 7:253,
        8:682–683
    medieval Latin literature, 9:439
    Mocquerau, André, founding of,
        9:750
    origins of, 3:75
    printed books, 3:379–380
    Remigius of Rouen, St., 12:108
    responsorial and antiphonal, 6:465
    restoration, 4:119, 120, 13:300
    revival, 3:523–524
    theories of Jewish origins, 8:680

Gregorian Chant (continued)
Tract section of, 14:130–131
Ward, Justine Bayard Cutting, reform of, 14:646
Gregorian College of St. Benedict, 2:855
Gregorian reform, 3:600–601, **6:468–473**, 492–493
Alberic of Ostia, 1:219
Alger of Liége, 1:283
Anonymous of York, 1:489
Anselm II of Lucca, St., 1:494
Anselm of Canterbury, St., 1:495
Arialdo, St., 1:660
Arnulf of Gap, St., 1:720
Bonizo of Sutri, 2:506
Bruno the Carthusian, St., 2:649
Canon Law, 1:841, 3:44, 46, 47, 60
Canons Regular of St. Augustine, 3:67
capital punishment, 3:86
Carolingian reform, 3:158
Catharism, 3:259
Church property, 3:725, 726
Church-State relations, 3:600–601, 635
Clement III (Antipope), 3:777–778
clerical celibacy/marriage, 3:326–327
clericalism, 3:802
cleric-laity dualism, 8:293, 294
concubinage, 12:14
Council of Anse, 1:493
Council of Autun, 1:926, 927
Crusades, 4:406–407
Czech Republic, 4:479
decretals of, 4:602
Deusdedit Collection, 4:701
English reforms, 8:324
Fliche, Augustin, scholar of, 5:762–763
France, 5:843–845
Hugh of Die, 7:151
Hugh of Remiremont, 7:155
Humbert of Silva Candida, 7:199–200
Hungary, 7:210
Low Countries, 10:257
opposition of Tusculani family to, 14:249
papal elections, 10:836, 857–858
Rule of St. Augustine, 1:869
Gregorian Sacramentary, **6:473–475**, 480
Alcuin, Bl., 1:243
baptism, 2:62
Christmas cycle, 3:555, 556
Gregorian University (Rome), 8:187

Gregorii Episcopi Turonensis opera (Ruinart), 12:407
Gregorius II (Patriarch), 2:826
Gregorius Akindynos, 4:776, **6:475–476**, 10:766
Gregorius praesul, 6:464
Gregory (Abp. of Canterbury), 1:449
Gregory (exarch of North Africa), 11:843–844
Gregory (Patriarch of Antioch), 5:465
Gregory (Vahrām Pahlav) (Armenian Catholicos), 1:701
Gregory, C. R., 2:363, 367
Gregory, Lady Isabella Augusta, 14:885
Gregory, Wilton D. (Bp. of Belleville, IL), 7:317
Gregory I the Great (Pope), St., **6:478–484**
acedia, 1:67
active life, 1:83
Advent, 1:134
Alleluia, 1:294
Anastasius I (Patriarch of Antioch), 1:388
angels, 1:419, 420
Anglo-Saxons, 1:449
apostolic administrators, 1:116
Armenia, 1:700
Augustine of Canterbury, St., 1:871, 3:596
beatific vision, 2:173
Benedictines, 3:596
biblical canon, 3:26
biblical theology, 2:382
blessing for Abbots, 1:12
Boniface III (Pope), 2:499
Byzantine Church, 2:750, 751–752
Canon Law, 1:841
cardinalate, 3:104
Carolingian reform, 3:156
Castel Sant'Angelo, 3:213
catechesis, 3:229
catechumenate, 3:252
Catholicism in England, 5:239
charity, 3:395
Christmas, 3:555
Church property, 3:724
Church-State relations, 3:635
civil authority, 1:921
clerical celibacy/marriage, 3:325
compunction, 4:45
Confirmation, 4:87
Consors Paterni Luminis ascribed to, 4:167
Constantinople Council, 4:190

Constantinople Council II, 4:192
contemplation, 4:205, 206
contraception, 4:219
creation of monasteries, 7:665
decretals as form, 4:600, 604
diaconia, 4:719
Donatism, 4:863
Easter controversy, 3:864
Ecumenical councils, 4:302
Ecumenical Patriarch as term, 4:196
Eulogius (Patriarch of Alexandria), St., 5:448–449
Eutychius (Patriarch of Constantinople), 5:463
exemption, 5:529
four senses, 5:513
friendship with God, 6:10, 479
gifts of Holy Spirit, 7:48
Gregorian chant, 6:463–464
homily, 7:63
hospitals, 7:127
hymns, 7:244, 253
jealousy, 7:748
Jews, 1:253
Kyrie eleison, 8:259
lay spirituality, 8:414
Leander of Seville, 8:426
life of the saints, 12:606
London, 3:70
London See, 8:771
Lucy, St., 8:849
manuscript illumination, 3:750
Maurice, 9:367
medieval Latin literature works of, 9:438–439
Middle Ages, 3:597
mission and evangelization, 9:680–681
notaries, 4:757
papacy development under, 10:835
persecution of Jews, 7:867
Peter the Deacon of Rome, 11:206
preaching of, 11:611, 619
pro-monastic policies opposed, 13:42
prudence, 11:789
psalmody, 1:57
relations with the East, 6:480–481
relics, 1:314, 12:53
representation in art, 6:483
Sabinian (Pope), 12:463
Sicily, 13:103
simony, 13:135, 136
soul, 13:343
spirituality, 13:445

spread of Benedictine rule, 2:256, 267

virtue, 14:548

works of, 6:482–483

works of charity, 3:408, 409

writings of Pseudo-Dionysius, 11:801

Gregory II (Pope), St., **6:484–486**

Boniface, St., 2:495

catechesis, 3:230

Church-State relations, 3:635

diaconia, 4:719, 720

iconoclasm, 2:751, 7:281, 656

papacy development under, 10:835

Gregory II Cyprius (Patriarch of Constantinople), 2:762, **6:477–478**

Gregory II Jusof (Melkite Patriarch), 1:526

Gregory II Vkajaser, 6:476

Gregory III (Armenian Catholicos), 1:701

Gregory III (Patriarch of Constantinople), **6:478**

Gregory III (Pope), St., **6:486–487**

Anastasius (Patriarch of Constantinople), 1:388

Carolingian Dynasty, 3:164, 434

Church-State relations, 3:635

Congregation for the Affairs of the Greeks, 5:21

iconoclasm, 7:281, 656

Leo III (Pope), St., 4:720

Solemnity of All Saints, 1:289

Gregory III Pahlav (Armenian Catholicos), 6:477

Gregory IV (Pope), **6:487–489**

Lothair I supported, 8:795

papacy development under, 10:835

Solemnity of All Saints, 1:289

Gregory IV Tegha (Armenian Catholicos), 1:701, **6:477**

Gregory V (Pope), **6:489**

Cluniacs, 3:813

Corvey Abbey, 4:280

Crescentius II, 4:362

crowning of Otto III, 10:714

papal name, 10:141

Gregory VI (Antipope), **6:491**

Gregory VI (Pope), **6:489–491**

Lateran Councils, 12:356

simony, 13:136

Gregory VI Apirat (Armenian Catholicos), 1:453, 706

Gregory VII (Pope), St., 6:491, **491–494**

Alexander II (Pope), 1:253

Algeria, 1:284

Alphanus of Salerno, St., 1:306

Apostles' Creed, 1:577

Armenia, 1:701

Arnulf of Milan, 1:721

authority, papal, 8:657

Beatrice of Tuscany, 2:181

Benedict X (Antipope), 2:242

Bernold of Constance, 2:327

Bishopric of Rome, 4:735, 10:859

Bruno of Segni, St., 2:648

Canon Law, 3:45

Canons Regular of St. Augustine, 3:67

Chaise-Dieu Abbey, 3:361

Christmas, 3:555

Church-State relations, 1:100, 3:635, 7:43

clerical celibacy/marriage, 3:326

clerical misconduct, 7:486–487

Cluniacs, 3:813

Croatia, 4:370

Crusade history, 4:407

decretals as form, 4:600, 604

Eucharist, 1:64

Fulcoius' letters on reform, 6:21

Gebhard of Salzburg, 6:115

Henry IV, excommunication of, 6:746

hierocratic theme, 13:252

importance, 3:601

investiture struggle, 7:537, 662–663

laicism, 8:282

Lateran Councils, 12:356

in *Liber pontificalis*, 8:535

papacy development under, 10:834, 837

papal primacy, 6:470–471

Philip I, 11:244

proprietary churches, 11:771

Solemnity of All Saints, 1:289

Victor III (Pope), 14:479

See also Deusdedit, Collection of; Gregorian Reform

Gregory VII Vkajaser (Armenian Catholicos), **6:477**

Gregory VIII (Antipope), 2:880, 6:123, **495**

Gregory VIII (Pope), 1:127, 4:411, **6:494–495**

Gregory IX (Armenian Catholicos), 1:702

Gregory IX (Pope), **6:496–498**

Agnes of Bohemia, St., 1:179

Albert Behaim, 1:222

Andrew Caccioli, Bl., 1:404, 2:840

Angelus, 1:427

Armenia, 1:702

Assyrian Church of the East, 1:807

Baius, condemnation of works of, 2:19

Beguines and Beghards, 2:205

canonization, 3:63, 12:607

capital punishment, 3:87

Carmelites, 3:132

Church-State relations, 7:44

Clare of Assisi, St., 3:760

conciliarism, 4:55

contraception, 4:219–220

Coventry and Lichfield See, 4:330

Dominic, St., 4:847

Elias of Cortona, 5:157

Frederick II the Great, 5:926–927, 7:664, 14:14

monastic reform, 2:271

papal arbitration code in writings of, 10:855

papal judges-delegate, 7:488–489

Paris, University of, 10:886

prostitution, 11:773–774

Roger of Todi, Bl., 12:288

Rusudan, 6:155

works of charity, 3:414

Gregory IX (Pope), decretals of, 3:46, 48, 5:570, **6:511–512**, 11:936

Church legislation, 4:273

Latin Rite, 8:368

productions based on, 4:598

Gregory X (Pope), Bl., **6:498–499**

Canon Law, 3:48

Celestines, 3:320, 321

conclaves, 4:60

Crusades, 4:411

Dominicans, 4:850

Duranti, William the Elder, 4:949

election of popes, 6:499, 11:499

Holy Name, 7:31

Honorius IV (Pope), 7:86

mendicant controversy, 2:483

Second Council of Lyons, 2:484, 826, 8:907–908

Gregory XI (Pope), **6:499–500**

Ambrosians, 1:346

Avignon papacy, 12:357

Benedict XIII (Antipope), 2:246

Catherine of Siena, St., 3:273, 5:761

Clement VII (Antipope), 3:783

Eastern Schism, 2:763

return to Rome, 1:943, 3:604

Sirmium made diocese, 13:168

Wyclif, John, bulls against, 14:866

Gregory XII (Pope), **6:500**, *501, 502*
  abdication of, 4:170
  Constance Council, 4:172
  Contarini, Giovanni, 4:203
  Dominici, John, 4:855
  Escobar, Andrés de, 5:352
  Pisa Council, 11:360, 361
  Western Schism, 1:258, 14:693
Gregory XIII (Pope), **6:501, 503**
  Ambrosians, 1:346
  Anne and Joachim, SS., 1:469
  Armenia, 1:702
  Baius, condemnation of, 2:19
  beatific vision, 2:169, 170
  Bellarmine, St. Robert, 2:227
  in *bulla cruciata*, 2:688
  Canisius, St. Peter, 3:17
  Canon Law, 3:53
  Carranza, Bartolomé, 3:176
  chant books, 3:379
  Chinese mission, 3:493, 495
  chronology, 3:571
  Church legislation, 4:273
  Congregation for the Propagation of
    the Faith, 11:749
  Congregation of Ceremonies, 3:349
  Congregation of the Oratory
    approved, 10:249
  Counter Reformation, 3:611
  Divine judgment, 8:32–33
  Gorze Abbey, secularization of,
    6:366
  house for neophytes, 10:239
  Innocent IX (Pope), 7:478–479
  Italo-Spanish Basilian Congregation,
    2:143
  Lateran baptistery, 8:349
  Lazarites, 7:126
  papacy development under, 10:842
  papal diplomacy, 8:451
  Possevino, Antonio, 11:549–550
  reform, 4:498
  Roman martyrology, 9:233, 234
  Sixtus V (Pope) relations, 13:197
  Vatican construction under, 14:396
Gregory XIV (Pope), **6:503–504**
Gregory XV (Pope), **6:504–505**
  Bishop, William, 2:409
  Brahmin converts, 10:408
  capitulations, 3:91
  Clerks Regular of the Mother of
    God, 3:803
  Congregation for the Propagation of
    the Faith, 5:21, 11:750

  Contemplative Hermit Sisters,
    approval of, 2:282
  Immaculate Conception, 7:334
  Indian Rites controversy, 7:411
  mission and evangelization,
    9:680–681
  witchcraft, punishment for,
    14:799–800
Gregory XVI (Pope), **6:505–511**, *506*
  American slavery condemned, 10:168
  Articles of Baden (1834), 6:509
  Basilians, 2:141
  Bautain, L. E. M., 5:712
  Belgian constitution, 2:218
  censure of Lamennais, Hugues, 8:309
  Cologne mixed marriage dispute,
    3:845, 846
  Colonna family, 3:856
  England, John, 5:223
  existence of God, 6:287
  Forbin-Janson, Charles de, 5:796
  Goa and Goan Schism, 6:268, 510,
    7:402
  Hermes, Georg condemned, 4:932
  independence of New Granada, 2:47
  liberalism, 3:619, 642
  Melkites, 1:271
  mission, 3:624
  mission in newly-independent areas,
    6:510
  Multa praeclare, 10:977, 978
  Oregon, 2:430
  papacy development under, 10:847
  papal authority, 6:507
  papal decorations, 4:596
  papal state reform, 13:496
  Polish bishops, 10:358
  rationalism, 6:507–508, 797
  religious freedom, 5:951
  religious liberalism, 8:542
  Roman revitalization, 12:359–360
  Russia, 1:84, 6:509
  separation of California dioceses,
    6:93
  separation of Church and State, 5:854
  slavery, 1:156, 2:44, 6:510, 13:209
  Society of the Sacred Heart reform,
    6:64
  ultramontism, 8:271–272
Gregory Dekapolites, 6:476
Gregory Magistros, 6:476
Gregory Narek, 6:477
Gregory of Agrigentum, 6:476
Gregory of Antioch, 6:476
Gregory of Bergamo, **6:512**

Gregory of Cappadocia, 8:53, 54
Gregory of Cerchiara, St., **6:512**
Gregory of Cyprus, 1:409, 2:776
Gregory of Einsiedeln, Bl., **6:512**
Gregory of Elvira, St., **6:513**, 11:610
Gregory of Montelongo (Patriarch of
  Aquileia), 1:608
Gregory of Nazianzus, St., 5:455,
  6:513–517
  apocatastasis, 1:548
  Apollinarianism, 1:560
  apophatic theology, 1:568
  Arianism, 2:792
  asceticism, 3:594
  baptism of, 2:67
  baptism of the Holy Spirit, 3:393
  Basil, St., 2:135, 136, 6:513
  beatific vision, 2:172
  biblical canon, 3:32
  charity, 3:395
  Christmas, 3:553
  circumincession, 3:741
  Constantinople Council, 4:190
  correspondence with Nemesius of
    Emesa, 10:232
  Cosmas the Melodian, 4:281
  Cynics, 4:456
  doctrine, development of, 4:804
  Ecumenical as term, 4:190
  exegetical works, 5:510
  Gorgonia, St., 6:364
  homiletics, 2:773
  hypostasis, 7:263
  influence of, 6:516–517
  poetry, 2:803
  preaching, 11:618
  preaching of, 11:609
  relics, 12:52
  School of Alexandria, 1:272
  schools of Athens, 1:829
  theotokos, 13:936
  use of pagan rhetoric, 6:439
  works of, 6:515–516
  See also Cappadocians
Gregory of Nyssa, St., 5:279, 343,
  6:517–521, 10:586, 11:290
  Adam, 1:104
  apocatastasis, 1:548
  Apollinarianism, 1:560
  apophatic theology, 1:568
  Arianism, 2:792
  asceticism, 3:594
  Basil, St., 2:135, 136, 6:517
  beatific vision, 2:169

biblical canon, 3:32

biblical catenae, 3:258

Cappadocian Fathers, 10:755

catechumenate, 3:250

chastity, 3:444

Christmas cycle, 3:556

church architecture, 1:756, 757

Daniélou, Jean, 4:515

evolution, 5:495

exegetical works, 5:510–511

friendship with God, 6:11

grace, 6:401

hexaemeron, 6:815

immortality, 7:349

ineffability of God, 7:445

Macrina the Younger, 9:25

Platonism, 11:414

preaching, 11:609, 618

similarity, 13:126

simplicity of God, 13:137

slavery, 13:211

soul, 13:341

spirituality, 13:444

Synod of Ancyra (375), 1:398

The Three Ways, 14:65–66

transubstantiation, 14:158

trinitarian doctrine, 14:195

works of, 6:518–519

See also Cappadocians

Gregory of Ostia, St., 4:826–827, **6:521**

Gregory of Rimini, **6:521–522**

    Augustinianism, 1:879, 880, 883, 884, 888

    conservation, 4:162

Gregory of Tat'ew, 6:477

Gregory of Tours, St., 3:596, 5:842, **6:522–523**

    Abraham of Clermont, St., 1:38

    Abrunculus of Trier, St., 1:40

    Amabilis, St., 1:328

    biographies of saints, 8:63

    bishops of Gaul, 6:111

    catechesis, 3:229

    chronicles, 1:461, 5:922

    Chrysanthus and Darius, SS., 3:572

    Clovis I (King of the Franks), 3:809

    confessors, as term, 4:83

    Domnolus of Le Mans, 4:859

    Eparchius, cult of, 5:270

    Evergislus, St., 5:485

    Fortunatus, Venantius Honorius Clementianus, 5:823

    holy nails, 10:137

    Leobard of Tours, 8:496

    lives of saints, 12:606

    relics, 12:52

    Saint-Calais Abbey, 12:541

    St. Denis, 4:660

    taking baptismal name practice, 10:140

    works of, 6:111–112, 522–523, 9:440–441

Gregory of Utrecht, St., **6:523**, 8:851

Gregory of Valencia, **6:523–524**, 7:782, 12:766

Gregory Pidzak (Armenian Catholicos), 1:702

Gregory Sinaites, 2:826, 878, **6:524**

Gregory Thaumaturgus, St., **6:524–525**

    Alexander of Comana, St., 1:264

    Christology, 3:560

    Decian persecution, 1:785

    Origen, 2:845

    Origen's advice on paideia, 10:755

    School of Alexandria, 1:272

    School of Caesarea, 2:845

Gregory the Illuminator, St., 1:453, 699, 704, 707, 3:732, **6:525–526**

Gregory the Wonder Worker, St., 8:720

Greifenberg, Bernard (Father), 12:495

Gremillion, Joseph Benjamin, **6:526**

Grenada, 3:120

Grenier, Pierre, 12:590

Greshake, Ghisbert, 5:346

Gressman, H., 5:520

Greswold, Robert. *See* Grissold, Robert, Bl.

Greteman, Frank, 13:164

Grétry, André Ernest Modeste, **6:526–527**, *527*

Gretser, Jakob, **6:527**, 7:782

Greutungi. *See* Ostrogoths

Grew, Nehemiah, 2:402

Grey, Charles, 10:540

Grey, Lady Jane, 1:435, 436, 2:689, 9:293, 12:243

Grey, Lord Leonard, 7:556

Grey, Mary, 5:677

Grey Brothers, 3:419

Grey Nuns, 3:6, **6:527–528**, 14:896–897

Grey Nuns of Quebec, 6:528

Grey Nuns of St. Hyacinthe, 6:528

Grey Nuns of the Cross, 6:528

Grey Nuns of the Immaculate Conception, 6:528

Grey Nuns of the Sacred Heart, 6:528

Greytak, William, 8:822

Griaule, M., 1:740

Gribaldi, Matteo, 2:431–432

Grief, 13:940–941

Grienberger, Christopher, 12:399

Griesbach, J. J., 2:366

Griesbacher, Peter, 2:843

Griffe, Élie, 6:67

Griffin, Bernard William (Card.), **6:528–529**, 14:849

Griffin, James A. (Bp. of Columbus), 3:868

Griffin, Martin Ignatius Joseph, 1:351–352, **6:529**

Griffith, John, Ven., 5:226

Griffith, Patrick Raymond, **6:529**

Griffiths, Ambrose (Bp.), 1:366

Griffiths, Bede, **6:529–531**, *530*, 7:405

Griffiths, Thomas, **6:531**

Grignion de Montfort, Louis Marie, St., 2:109, 5:344, **6:531–532**, *532*

    Brothers of Christian Instruction, 2:630

    Carmelite spirituality, 3:137

    consecration to Mary, 4:156

    Daughters of Wisdom, founding of, 14:793

    French School, 13:451

    Legion of Mary, 8:453

    Montfort Fathers, founding of, 9:839

Grigos, 9:50

Grijalva, Juan de, **6:532–533**

Grillmeier, Alois, 4:684–685, 751

Grillparzer, Franz, 6:*533*, 533

Grimald (Abbot of Sankt Gallen), 12:669

Grimaldi, Jérôme de (Abp. of Aix), 1:197

Grimaldi, Marqués de, 3:792

Grimbald, St., **6:533–534**

Grimes, Ronald, 12:258

Grimmelshausen, Hans Jakob von, 2:115

Grimmelsman, Henry J. (Bp. of Evansville, IN), 7:416

Grimoald (Frankish aristocrat), 3:163

Grimston, Ralph, Bl., 5:233, **6:534**

Grimstow, Ralph. *See* Grimston, Ralph, Bl.

Grimwoald (Duke of Bavaria), 4:259

Grisar, Hartmann, **6:534–535**

Grisez, Germain, 7:180, 181, 10:186

Grissold, Robert, Bl., 5:234, **6:535**

Griswold, Alexander V., 5:297

Griswold, Robert. *See* Grissold, Robert, Bl.

Grivot, Irma, St., 5:878, **6:535**

Grodziecký, Melichar, 8:241

Groenendael Abbey (Brussels), **6:535**

Groer, Hans Hermann (Card.), 1:917

Groome, Thomas, 12:98

Groote, Gerard, 3:69, 605, 5:774, **6:535–536**
  Brethren of the Common Life, 2:607
  Devotio Moderna, 4:707
  Imitation of Christ, 7:329, 330
  pantheism, 2:629
  spiritual direction, 4:762

Gropper, J., 2:394, 3:846

Grosjean, Paul, **6:536**, 10:955

Grosoli, Giovanni, **6:536–537**

Gross, Nikolaus, Bl., **6:537**

Gross, William Hickley (Abp. of Portland), **6:537–538**, *538*, 11:530, 12:565, 709

Der Grosse Catechismus (Luther), 8:889

Der Grosse Herder, 5:207

Grosseteste, Robert, 5:242
  appointed University of Oxford chancellor, 10:729
  beauty, 2:185
  evolution of science, 12:798
  existence, 5:533
  metaphysics of light, 8:583–584
  Oxford School (Franciscan), 5:899
  Richard Fishacre, 12:229
  scholasticism, 12:760
  study of music, 10:72

Grossi, John, 3:142

Grossolano, Peter, 2:761

Grösz, József (Abp. of Kalocsa, Hungary), 7:220

Grote, Federico, 1:652, **6:539**

Grotius, Hugo, **6:539–541**, 10:182, 855
  apologetics, 1:564
  Aristotelianism, 1:678
  lying, 8:901
  natural law, 5:395
  papal Antichrist, 1:517
  Reformation exegesis, 5:518

Grottaferrata Monastery (Rome), 2:143, **6:541–542**

Grotto of the Nativity (Bethlehem), 3:*554*

Grou, Jean Nicolas, 4:763, **6:542–543**, 7:782

Group 4 architects, 3:712

Groupe des Six, 11:562

Groups des Dombes, 9:284

Grove, John, Bl., 5:236

Growth in Holiness (Faber), 5:582

Gruber, Augustin (Abp. of Salzburg), 3:243–244, 12:794

Grüber, Eberhard, 1:330

Gruber, Gabriel, 3:265

Grueber, Johannes, **6:543**

Gruenthaner, Michael, 5:523, **6:543**

Grundkurs (Foundations of Christian Faith) (Rahner), 11:894

Grundmann, W., 7:850

Grundner, Wikterp (Abbot), 12:671

Grundtvig, Nikolai Frederik Severin, **6:543–544**

Grundzüge der Ethik (Bauch), 2:158

Die Grundzüge der Psychologie (Ebbinghaus), 5:27

Gruner, Anton, 6:13

Grünewald, Mathis Gothart Nithart. *See* Grünewald, Matthias

Grünewald, Matthias, 4:396–397, **6:544**, *545*

Grutka, Andrew G. (Bp. of Gary, IN), 7:416

Grützmacher, R. H., 3:22

Grynaeus, Simon, 2:689

Gryphius, Sebastian, 1:545

Gua de Malnes, Jean Paul, 5:208

Gúa espiritual (La Puente, L.), 8:334

Guadagni, Bernardo Gaetano (Card.), **6:544**

Guadalajara (Mexico), Martyrs of, SS., 1:189, 326, **6:545**
  Esqueda Ramírez, Pedro, 5:359
  Flores Varela, José Isabel, 5:774
  Lara Puente, S., 8:334
  Reyes Salazar, Sabás, St., 12:209
  Robles Hurtado, José María, 12:274

Guadaloupe (West Indies), 3:117–119

Guadalupe, Our Lady of, **6:545–548**, *546*, *547*, 7:1060, 8:*790*, 9:*579*
  chapel (Guadalupe Hidalgo, Mexico), 9:*268*
  coronation of statue, 8:264
  shrines, 2:560–562, 7:*1061*, 8:274, 13:*90*, 93
  Silva, A., 13:121

Guadalupe Hidalgo, Treaty of (1848), 10:286

Guaiferius (medieval writer), 9:450

Gual, Pedro, **6:548**

Guala of Bergamo, Bl., **6:548**

Guale people, 6:148–149, 12:709

Gualfard. *See* Wolfhard of Verona, St.

Gualfredus. *See* Walfrid, St.

Guallensis, John. *See* John of Wales

Gualtmannus. *See* Waltman of Antwerp, Bl.

Guam, missions, 12:657

Guanella, Luigi, Bl., 2:542, 4:534, **6:548–549**

Guaraní people, 2:593–594, 7:785

Guarantees, Law of (1871), **6:549–550**
  Castel Gandolfo villa, 3:212
  Lateran Pacts, 8:356
  See also Roman question

Guardian angels, 1:422, 423–424, **425–427**, *426*

Guardini, Romano, **6:550**
  liturgical movement, 3:711
  Mystical Body, 5:37
  religious experience, 5:556
  scholastic theology, 12:777
  theology of Church, 3:589

Guarducci, M., 14:391

Guarini, Guarino, 3:675, 705, 706

Guarinus (Abbot of Cuxa), 4:450

Guarinus of Palestrina, St., **6:550**

Guarinus of Sion, St., **6:550–551**

Guarna, Giovanni. *See* John of Salerno, Bl.

Guarnerius (jurist). *See* Irnerius (jurist)

Guarracino, Antonio (Card.), 1:657

Guastalla, Council of (1106), **6:551**, 10:916

Guasto, Andrea del, **6:551**

Guatemala, 2:344–345, **6:551–554**, *553*, 8:340
  demographic statistics, 6:551
  ecclesiastical organization, 6:553–554
  map, 6:*552*
  mission, 3:349, 6:552–553, 9:707, 12:290–291

Guazzo, Stefano, 1:675

Gubbio, Giovanni da, 1:790

Gubernaculum conciliorum (Escobar), 5:352

Gubernatis, Domenico de, **6:554–555**

Gudula, St., 5:188, **6:555**

Gudwal, St., **6:555**

Guébriant, Jean-Baptiste Budes de, 3:500

Guelfia, 3:100

Guelfs and Ghibellines, 3:853–856, **6:555–556**
  Alexander IV (Pope), 1:257
  Avignon papacy, 1:943, 3:855
  Cavalcanti, Guido, 3:310
  Clement IV (Pope), 3:778
  Dante Alighieri, 4:517–519
  Engelbert of Admont, 5:221
  Florence, 5:767–768
  penitential processions, 5:755
  Siena, 13:106, 108

Guénolé, St., 8:319

Le Guêpier italien (Veuillot), 14:465

Guéranger, Prosper, 2:259, 273, **6:557**
  Astros, Paul Thérèse David d', 1:814

Bruyère, Jeanne Henriette Cécile, 2:651

    chant books, 3:380

    liberalism, 3:619

    liturgical history, 8:663

    liturgical movement, 3:623, 8:670, 671

    Solesmes Abbey, 13:300

Guéric of St. Quentin, 1:224

Guerin (prior of Gembloux), 6:124

Guérin, Theodore (Mother), Bl., **6:557–558**, 13:188–189, *189*

Guerra, Elena, Bl., **6:558**

Guerrero, Lobo (Abp.), 3:850

Guerrero González, Angela de la Cruz, Bl., **6:558**

Guerric of Igny, Bl., 3:749, 758, **6:558–559**, 9:454

Guerric of Saint-Quentin, 2:479

Guerrilla wars, just-war principles in, 14:638

Guertin, George A., 10:279

Guest houses (*hospitale hospitum*), 3:411–412

Guevara y Lira, Silvestre (Abp. of Caracas), **6:559**

Guevarre, Père, 3:417

Guí espiritual (Molinos), 6:777

Guí práctica del catequista (Ossó y Cervelló), 10:706

Guía espiritual (Molinos), 10:844

Guibert (Wibert) of Ravenna. *See* Clement III (Antipope)

Guibert, J. H. (Card.), 1:197

Guibert, Joseph de, 4:334, **6:559–560**, 7:791, 13:433, 14:66

Guibert of Nogent, **6:560**

    Crusades, 4:407

    medieval Latin literature works of, 9:452

    preaching, 11:619

    relics, 12:54

Guibert of Tournai, **6:560–561**

Guiborat, Weibrath. *See* Wiborada, St.

Guicciardini, Francesco, 6:*561*, **561–562**

Guide des Écoles (Champagnat), 3:374

Guide for the Perplexed (Maimonides), 7:864, 869, 9:52–53, 10:135

Guide to the Manuscript and Printed Book Collections and Numismatic Cabinet of the Vatican Library (2002), 14:422

Guide to the Perplexed (Maimonides), 5:509

Guidiccioni, Alessandro (Bp.), 3:803

Guido. *See* Witelo

Guido (Guy) of Spoleto, 5:814–815

Guido II (Bp. of Assisi), 1:790

Guido da Siena, 13:109

Guido de Baysio, 3:48, 52, 320, **6:562**

Guido de Monte Richerii, 3:50

Guido di Pietro. *See* Fiesole, Guido da, Bl.

Guido Maramaldi, Bl., **6:562–563**

Guido of Anderlecht, St., **6:563**

Guido of Arezzo, **6:563–564**

Guido of Cortona, Bl., **6:564**

Guido of Ferrara, 7:537

Guido of Pomposa, St., **6:564–565**

Guido of Velate (Abp.), 1:407, 660

Guido Papa, 3:52

Guido the Lombard, Bl., **6:565**

Guigo I (Carthusian legislator), 3:189, 192, 193, 194, **6:565**, 9:455

Guigo II (Carthusian writer), 3:191, **6:565–566**, 9:455

Guigo de Ponte, 3:192, **6:566**

Guigue du Pont. *See* Guigo de Ponte

Guild for the Tabernacle for Perpetual Adoration, 9:820

Guild of St. Sebastian, 5:834

Guilday, Peter K., 1:350, 5:169, **6:566–567**, *567*, 10:550

Guililmus Alvernus (Arvernus). *See* William of Auvergne

Guillaume, Jean-Baptiste, 12:277

Guillaume, Uldaric, Bl., 2:632

Guillaume de Grimoard (Abbot), 12:590

Guillaume de Nogaret, 3:779

Guillaume de Sens, 3:696

Guillelmus de Monserrat, 3:52

Guillement, M. Françoise (Sister), 12:537

Guillerand, Augustin, 3:192

Guillet, Urban, 6:196, 14:162

Guillot, Marguerite, 2:436

Guilt, **6:567–569**

    in the Bible, 6:569–572, 13:141–148

    guilt cultures, 13:67–68

    shame compared, 13:67

Guilt, theology of, **6:572–573**, 13:155

Guinea, **6:574**, *575*

Guinea-Bissau, **6:575–576**, *577*

Guinizelli, G., 3:310

Guiraud, Jean, **6:576–577**

Guise (House of Lorraine), **6:577–579**, 7:167

Guitmond of Aversa, **6:579–580**

Guitton, Jean, 1:565

Guízar Valencia, Rafael, Bl., **6:580–581**, *581*

Guizot, François Pierre Guillaume, 5:864

Guldines Tugendbuch (Spee), 13:410

Gulielmites. *See* Augustinians; Williamites

Gullini, Pia (Mother), 12:527

Gulliver's Travels (Swift), 13:641–642

Gumbert of Ansbach, St., **6:581**

Gumilevsky, Filaret, 12:434

Gumilla, José, 3:851

Gummar, St., **6:582**

Gundebert, St. *See* Gumbert of Ansbach, St.

Gundecar, Bl., **6:582**

Gundecarianum (Gundecar), 6:582

Gundert, Hermann, 7:403

Gundisalvi, Dominic

    Arab influence, 13:384

    beauty, 2:184

    immortality, 7:349

Gundlach, Gustav, **6:582**, 7:792

Gunkel, F., 8:313

Gunkel, Hermann, 2:689, 5:520, 807, **6:582–583**, 11:92

Gunlind (abbess of Hohenberg), 5:446

Gunn, John E. (Bp. of Natchez, MS), 7:686, 9:739

Gunnar's Daughter (Undset), 14:295

Gunpowder Plot (1605), 1:21, 22, 408, 4:745, 10:843

    Anne of Denmark, 1:467

    Ashley, Ralph, Bl., 1:783

    Bawden, William, 2:162

    Garnet, Henry, 6:100

    Narrative of the Gunpowder Plot (Gerard), 6:158

    Oath of Allegiance, 2:425, 5:248, 758

Guntbert of Saint-Bertin, **6:583**

Gunter, William, Bl., 5:230

Günther, Anton, 1:914, 3:624, 6:184, **583**, 14:204

    Christian Hegelianism, 12:773

    faith, 5:596, 599

    heresy, 6:778

    idealistic philosophy, 12:770

    influence on Schwarzenberg, 12:794

    semirationalism, 12:901

Günther of Niederaltaich, Bl., **6:584**

Gunther of Pairis, **6:584**

Gunthildis, SS., **6:584–585**

Gunthilidis of Eichstätt, 6:584

Gunthilidis of Plankstetten, 6:584

Gunthilidis of Wimborne, 6:585

Gunzo (architect), 3:812

Gurney, Joseph John, 6:5

Gurney, Marion (Mother Marianne of Jesus), 3:535

Gury, Jean Pierre, 3:221, 4:881, **6:585**, 12:462

Gustavus I Vasa (King of Sweden), 1:327

Gustavus Adolphus (King of Sweden), 14:9, 10

Gustavus Adolplus Union (Austria), 8:794

Gutberlet, K., 1:80

Gutenberg, Johann, 2:521, 6:585–586, 10:772

Gutenberg Bible, **6:585–586**, 586

Guthlac, St., 5:239, **6:586**

Gutiérrez, Gustavo, 5:677, 10:623, 14:361, 362
    A Theology of Liberation, 13:245
    atheism, 1:825
    faith, 2:222–223
    institutionalized injustice, 13:245
    liberation theology, 9:688, 12:729
    praxis, 11:584
    Ratzinger instruction, 8:549

Gutierrez, Menoyo, 4:419

Gutierrez, Rafaél Alonso, Bl., 4:733

Gutiérrez Rodríguez, Bartolomé, Bl., **6:586–587**

Guttée, V., 12:434

Guttierez, Bartholomeo, Bl., 7:735

Gützlaff, Karl Friedrich, 3:499

Guy (Bp. of Beauvais), 2:188

Guy de Lusignan (King of Jerusalem), 4:461

Guy de Montpellier, **6:587**, 7:129

Guy of Bazoches, 1:463

Guy of Lusignan (King of Jerusalem), 4:402, 7:770

Guyana, **6:587–588**, 589

Guyon, Jeanne Marie Bouvier de la Motte, 3:614, 5:396, 682, **6:588–591**
    Bossuet, Jacques Bénigne, 2:550
    heresy, 6:777
    private revelations, 12:201
    Quietism, 5:851
    writings of Lawrence, 8:409

Guyot, Henri Daniel, 3:418

Guzmán, Augusto, 3:102

Guzman, Dominic de, St., 1:231, 13:384

Guzmán y Lecaros, Joseph Javier, **6:591**

Guzzetta, Giorgio (Father), 7:651

Gwatkin, H., 1:661

Gwyn, Richard, Bl., 5:228, **6:591–592**

H

Haas, Francis Joseph (Bp.), **6:593**, 12:531

Habakkuk (Hebrew prophet), 2:210–211

Habakkuk, Book of, **6:593–594**, 7:105

Habakkuk, Canticle of, 3:73

Haberl, F. X., 2:842, 3:380

Habermas, Jürgen, 5:677, 914

Habersbrunner, Dionys, 11:624

Habert, Isaac, 4:121, **6:594–595**, 7:716

Habert, J. E., 2:842

Habets, Jean, 4:535

Habiru, **6:595–598**

Habit, **6:598–602**
    accident, 1:61, 62
    act, 1:73
    for attaining truth, 14:225–226
    charisms, 3:390
    disposition, 4:777
    first principles, 5:744–745
    formation of, 14:720–721
    human act, 7:170–171
    immortality, 7:350
    soul, 13:351
    speculative intellect, 5:744–745
    and will, 14:720–721

Habit, in theology, **6:602–604**, 8:88, 13:150, 161–162

Habit, religious (dress). *See* Religious habits

Habitual grace, 6:397

Habsburg, House of. *See* Hapsburg, House of

Hachizō, Lawrence Kaida, Bl., 7:735

Hackelmeier, Theresa (Sister), 5:881

Hacker, Hilary B. (Bp. of Bismarck), 2:423

Hackshott (Hawkshaw), Thomas, Ven., 5:234

Hadalinus, St., **6:604**

Hadelauga, St. *See* Hadeloga, St.

Hadelin, St. *See* Hadalinus, St.

Hadeloga, St., **6:604**

Hades, 1:166, **6:604–605**
    See also Hell

Hadewijch, Bl., **6:605**, 13:455

Ḥadīth. *See* Islamic tradition

Hadoindus, St., **6:605**

Hadrian (Roman Emperor), **6:605–606**, 606, 12:310
    apologists, 1:567
    Castel Sant'Angelo, 3:212
    persecutions, 3:592
    rebuilding of Jerusalem, 7:767

    second Jewish revolt against Rome, 2:83, 84

Hadrian of Canterbury, St., 1:246, 3:70, 5:239, **6:606**

Hadriana Collectio (canonical collection), 1:499, 3:42, 43, 4:492, 752, **6:606–607**

Hadrian's villa ruins (Vatican City), 14:401

Hadrianum, 6:474–475, 8:655

Hadrumetum (Phoenician colony), **6:607**

Haec dies (Gradual), 6:414

Haec sancta (decree), **6:607–608**

Haeckel, Ernst, 5:51, 7:240, 9:320–321

Haecker, Theodor, 6:185

Haereses (Panarion) (St. Epiphanius of Salamis), 6:256–257

Hafey, William J. (Bp. of Raleigh, NC), 10:438, 11:899

Hagar (biblical figure), 1:118, 4:328, **6:608–609**

Hagarty, Paul Leonard (Bp. of Nassau), 2:14

Hagen, Johann von, 2:710

Hagenau, Council of (1540), 2:394

Hagerty, James Edward, 1:352

Haggadah, 5:508, 6:609, **609–610**
    Annunciation, 1:473–474
    apocalyptic style, 1:546
    Eucharist, 5:410
    Susanna as, 13:629
    See also Talmud

Haggai, Book of, 4:529, 5:336, **6:610–611**

Haghiorita, Nicephorus, 2:826

Hagia Eirene (Constantinople), 3:687

Hagia Sophia (Byzantine church), 2:767, 778, **6:611–612**, 612
    archaeology, 4:188
    architecture, 1:756, 3:671, 687, 689
    building of, 4:188–189
    Byzantine art, 2:735, 737–738
    challenge to Nestorianism nailed to door, 10:254
    Constantine I (the Great) (Roman Emperor), 4:182
    iconoclasm, 7:282
    Justinian I, 8:96
    mosaics, 10:3
    officials of the, 10:946–947
    stational liturgy, 8:652

Hagia Sophia, Easter Synod of (815), 2:753

Hagiography, **6:613–616**
    Butler, Alban, 2:718–719
    Byzantine hagiography, 2:795

Carolingian Renaissance, 3:161

Colgan, John, 3:833–834

Ehrhard studies, 5:138

Franchi de' Cavalieri, 5:865

historical theology, 3:614

history, 6:880

John Damascene, St., 7:942

Muratori's conflict with ecclesiastical opinion, 10:63

Silician sources, 13:104

Spain, 13:383

spiritual abandonment, 1:5

See also Martyrologies; Saints

Hagiopolites. *See* Cosmas the Melodian

Hagiorite Tome, 10:766

Hagleitner, Kaspar (1779-1836), 9:106

Hagleitnerianer. *See* Manharter

Hague Convention (1899), 10:747

Hague Court (1907), 10:747

Hahn, Helana Petrovna. *See* Blavatsky, Helena Petrovna

Haid, Leo Michael (Bp.), **6:616**, 10:437

Haida people, 1:209, 13:206

Hail Mary, 1:204, 3:234, **6:616–617**

Hailandière, Celestine de la (Bp. of Vincennes, IN), 7:413, 417

Haile, John, Bl., 5:225, 12:8

Haimburg, Conrad, 3:192

Haimhramm. *See* Emmeram, St.

Haimo of Auxerre, 5:515, **6:617**

Haimo of Landecop, Bl., **6:617–618**

Hainmar of Auxerre, St., **6:618**

Hair shirts, **6:618**, 11:66

Hairstyles, 4:267

Haiti, **6:618–622**, *621*

   Church-state relations, 12:377

   demographic statistics, 6:619

   Dominican Republic, 4:835, 836

   England, John, 5:223

   Kersuzan, F. M., 8:156–157

   map, *6:620*

   mission, 6:622, 12:534

   slave revolt, 1:157, 3:111, 13:214

   South Carolina refugees, 13:363

   U.S. occupation, 8:157

   voodoo, 14:587

Hajj, **6:623–624**

   See also Mecca

Hakai (Breach of the Code, Shimazaki), 13:85

El-Hakem biamr Allah, 4:253

Halakah, 1:199, 5:143, 508, **6:624**, 8:2

   See also Haggadah

Haldane, Robert, 1:845

Halde, J. B. du, 10:903

Haldenston, John, 12:533

Hales, Godden v. (1686), 10:501

Ha-Levi, David. *See* Ibn Daud (Jewish philosopher)

Ha-Levi, Judah ben Samuel, 2:833, 7:864

Half-Way Covenant, 3:647, 4:115, 5:97, **6:624–625**

Halifax, Charles Lindley Wood, 4:543, 5:252, **6:625**, 9:78

Halifax Cathedral (Nova Scotia), 3:716

Halkes, Catharina, 5:677

Hall, Bruckhard von, 3:697

Hall, Granville Stanley, 5:93

Hallahan, Margaret Mary, **6:625–626**

Al-Hallāj (Persian mystic), 1:621, 7:620

Halle, University of (Germany), 5:256, 910–911

Hallel (hymn), 4:890

Haller, Carl Ludwig von, 2:843, 11:460

Haller, Johannes, **6:626**

Haller, Leonhard, **6:626**

Hallinan, Paul J. (Abp. of Atlanta), 1:831, **6:627**, 10:344, 345

Hallische Jahrbücher für deutsche Wissenschaft und Kunst (periodical), 6:710

Halloie, St. *See* Hadeloga, St.

Hallum, Robert (Bp.), 3:481, **6:627**

Hallvard Vebjörnsson, St., **6:627–628**

Halmont, J. B. van, 7:239

Haloes, 1:896, 6:*628*, *628*, *629*, *630*

Haltigar (Bp. of Cambrai), 3:42–43

Halton, John de (Bp. of Carlisle), 3:124

Hamann, Johann Georg, 5:263, **6:628–629**, 7:586, 8:126, 891, 12:345

Hamartia (tragic flaw), 11:434

Hamartigenie (Prudentius), 11:792

Hamartolus, George. *See* George Hamartolus

Hamath (Aramaean state), 1:624

Hambley, John, Bl., 5:229, **6:629**

Hamel, Edouard, 7:528

Hamelin, O., 1:678, 8:514

Hamer, Jean Jérome (Card.), **6:629–630**

Hamilton, Patrick, 2:179, **6:630**

Hamilton, William, Sir, **6:630**, 11:890

   agnosticism, 1:183

   appetite, 1:603

   death of God theology, 4:584

   methodology, 9:566

   relativism, 12:48

   Scottish School of Common Sense, 12:840–841

Hammarstrom, Olaf, 3:716

Hammes, George A. (Bp. of Superior, WI), 14:783

Hammond, Henry, 3:152

Hammond, Peter, 3:717

Hammurabi (King of Babylon), 3:84, 4:442, **6:631**, 8:*391*

Hammurabi, Code of, 8:393–394, 12:140–141

Hammurapi. *See* Hammurabi (King of Babylon)

Hamon, André J. M., 11:623

Hampton Court Conference (1604), 1:444

Ḥanafite school, 7:622

Ḥanbalite school, 7:622–623

Hanc igitur, 5:279

Handbook of Scriptural Reference (Lambert, tr.), 8:303

Handbook to the University of Oxford, 10:732

Handbuch der allgemeinen Kirchengeschichte (Hergenröther), 6:779–780

Handbuch der katholischen Liturgik (Thalhofer), 13:852

Handbuch Tehologischer Grundbefrifle, 5:207

Handel, George Frideric, 2:7, 722, 3:123, **6:631–633**, *632*, 12:725

Handmaids of Charity, **6:633**

Handmaids of Mary. *See* Sisters Servants of Mary

Handmaids of the Blessed Sacrament and of Charity, 4:692

Handmaids of the Blessed Sacrament and of Charity, Sisters Adorers, **6:633**

Handmaids of the Holy Child Jesus, 4:127, 7:18

Handmaids of the Sacred Heart of Jesus, **6:633**, 11:522

Hands, liturgical gestures, 8:649–650

Handspiegel (Pfefferkorn), 12:181

Haneberg, Daniel Bonifatius, 2:263, **6:633–634**

Hanh, Paul, 14:494

Hanh Van Nguyen, Domingo, 14:494

Hanifen, Richard C. (Bp. of Colorado Springs), 3:859

Hanmer, Meredith, 5:753

Hanna, Edward Joseph (Abp. of San Francisco), 2:869, **6:634**, 12:648–649

Hanna, Jacob, 4:254

Hannan, Philip Matthew (Abp. of New Orleans), 8:815, 10:296–297

Hannibaldus de Hannibaldis (Card.), **6:634–635**

Hanse, Everard, Bl., 5:227, **6:635**

Hansen's disease. *See* Leprosy

Hanshan Deqing, 3:511

Hanslick, Eduard, 1:143, 2:580, 642, 10:73

Hanslik, Rudolph, 2:263

Hanson, Stig, 3:582

Hanssens, J. M., 10:98

Hanthaler, Chrysostomus, **6:635**

Hanukkah, 4:607, 9:497, *498*

Hanus, Charles-Arnaud, 12:277

Hanus, Jerome (Abbot), 12:543

Hanus, Jerome George (Abp. of Dubuque, IA), 4:925

Hanxleden, Johan Ernst, **6:635–636**

Haoma, **6:636**

Haplucheir, Michael, 2:805

Happiness, **6:636–637**

    Aquinas, 2:170

    Aristotle, 6:347

    common good, 4:17

    communication, 4:23–24

    freedom of will and determination to, 10:25–26

    heaven, 6:686–687

    immortality, 7:352

    man, natural end of, 9:96–102

    Old Testament, 2:171

    See also Beatific vision; Eudaemonism

Happy Days in Norway (Undset), 14:295

Hapsburg, House of, 4:482, 6:180, **637–642**, 642, 7:213–218

Harald Blaastand (King of Denmark), 4:663

Haran, M., 14:858

Harbor, Rawn, 1:162

Harcott, Thomas. *See* Whitbread, Thomas, Bl.

Harcourt, Philip d' (Bp. of Bayeux), 2:190

Harcourt, William, Bl., 5:236, **6:642–643**

Hard Sayings (Tyrrell), 14:258

Hardeby, Geoffrey. *See* Geoffrey Hardeby

Hardesty, Robert, Bl., 5:231, **6:643**

Hardey, Mary Aloysia (Mother), **6:643**, 12:494

Hardin, Garrett, 14:178

Harding, Robert (Father), 11:81

Harding, Stephen, 5:240

Harding, Thomas, 1:437

Hardouin, Jean, **6:643–644**, 7:782

Hare, R. M., 2:624, 5:398

Hare Krishnas, **6:644–645**, *645*, 10:298, 299, 301

Harenc, Geoffrey, 6:189

Harent, Étienne, **6:645**

Hargreaves, James, 5:260

Häring, Bernard, 5:538, **6:645–646**

Haring, Nikolaus, 14:2

Hariolf of Langres (Bp. of Ellwangen), 5:173

Al-Ḥarīzī, Judah, 2:833

Harkins, Matthew, 12:216

Harlay, Achille de (1536-1619), 6:646

Harlay, Achille de (1581-1646), 6:646–647

Harlay, François de, 6:647

Harlay family, **6:646–647**

Harlay-Chanvallon, François de (Abp.), 6:647

Harless, Gottlieb Adolph von, 5:322

Harley, David, 1:796

Harmel, Léon, **6:647–648**, 8:371

Harmenopulos, Constantinus, 2:795

Harmonia (Köndig and Hüber), 14:51

Harmonia, sive concordia quatuor evangelistarum (Lamy), 8:315

Harmonia evangelica graece et latine (Osiander), 7:845

Harmonia Macrocosmica (Cellario), 11:*807*

Harmonics (Ptolemy), 11:808

Die Harmonie der Welt (Hindemith), 6:839

Harmony of Anglican Doctrine with the Doctrine of the Eastern Church (Palmer), 10:812

A Harmony of the Reformed Confessions (Schaff), 12:726

Harmony Society, 11:912

Harnack, Adolf von, 5:521, **6:648**, 10:252, 12:257, 462

    Bousset, Wilhelm, 2:570

    Bultmann, Rudolf Karl, 2:690

    Christology, 3:559

    doctrine development, 4:805–806

    gates of hell, 6:107

    homoousios, 4:198

    liberal theology, 8:543

    Schlatter, Adolf, 12:739

Harnack, Theodosius, 5:323

Harney, Eucharia (Mother), 7:339

Harold, Francis, **6:649**

Harold, James (Father), 11:237–238

Harold, William Vincent, 4:245, 5:103, **6:649**, 11:83, 237–238

Harold II (King of England), 5:1, **6:649–650**

Harold II Bluetooth (King of Denmark), 4:*235*

Harold of Gloucester, St., **6:650–651**

Harper, Edward (Bp. of Virgin Islands), 3:120

Harper, James, 10:314

Harper, William Rainey, 3:458, 12:96

The Harper-Collins Encyclopedia of Catholicism, 5:208

Harphius van Erp. *See* Henry of Herp

Harrington, James, 4:641, 14:360

Harrington, William, Bl., 5:232, **6:651**

Harris, Barbara C. (Bp. of Massachusetts), 5:298

Harris, Howell, **6:651**, 11:680

Harris, J. R., 1:666

Harris, Maria, 12:97

Harris, Paul, 5:761

Harris, Robert L., 3:722

Harris, Thaddeus M., 3:472

Harris, William, 7:301

Harrison, Benjamin, 6:206

Harrison, James, Ven., 5:234

Harrison, John, 5:237

Harrison, Matthew, 5:237

Harrison, Wallace Kirkman, 3:675

Hart, Daniel A. (Bp. of Norwich), 4:125

Hart, H. L. A., 11:546

Hart, John, 2:79

Hart, Joseph (Bp. of Cheyenne, WY), 14:871

Hart, Luke E., 8:191

Hart, William, Bl., 5:228, **6:651**

Hartford Archdiocese (CT), **6:652–654**

Hartig, Emmanuel, 10:222

Hartley, D., 8:745

Hartley, James J. (Bp. of Columbus), 3:868

Hartley, William, Bl., 5:230, **6:654–655**

Hartman (1440-1514), 12:119

Hartman, L. F., 5:523

Hartmann, Anastasius, Ven., **6:655**

Hartmann, Eduard von, 1:948, **6:655–656**, 10:827, 11:169, 14:151

Hartmann, Nicolai, 5:398, **6:656–657**

    axiology, 1:948

    conscience, 4:140

    freedom, 5:940

    irrationalism, 7:587

    possibility, 11:552

Hartmann, Thomas (Abbot), 12:539

Hartmann of Brixen (Bp.), Bl., 1:910, **6:657**

Hartmut (Abbot of Sankt Gallen), 12:669

Hartshorne, Charles, **6:657–658**, 10:821, 11:729, 731, 12:71

Hartwich of Salzburg, Bl., **6:658**

Harty, Jeremiah James (Abp.), 3:864, **6:658–659**, 10:223

Hartzer, Marie Louise, 10:725

Hartzheim, Joseph, 7:782

Harun, Tun Mustapha, 9:71

Harun-al-Rashid (Caliph of Baghdad), 1:763, 3:422

Harvard, John, 12:768

Harvard University (MA), 4:115, 12:398

Harvengt, Philippe de, 2:506

The Harvest of Justice Is Sown in Peace (pastoral statement), 14:643

Harvey, James (Bp.), 2:*412*

Harvey, William, 2:402, 405, 407

Harvey Nedellec, 4:947, **6:659**, 12:762, 14:46

Has the Immigrant Kept the Faith? (Shaughnessy), 13:69

Hase, K. A. von, 7:848

Hāshimi, 'Abdallah ibn Ismāīl al-, 8:170

Hasidaeans, 1:529, **6:659–660**

Hasidism, 2:831–832, 835–836, **6:660–662**, *661*, 7:872, 8:9

Haskalah, 4:617, **6:662–663**

Haskell, Martin, 1:34

Hasler, August, 7:451

Hasmonaeans, 4:587–588, **6:663–665**

See also Maccabees

Hassagoth (Criticisms) (Gikatilla), 6:211

Hassard, John Rose Greene, **6:665**

Hasse, Johann Adolph, **6:665–666**

Hassoun, Anthony (Card.), 1:535

Hastrich, Jerome J. (Bp. of Gallup, NM), 6:81, 14:782

Hatha yoga, 14:892

Hathaway, Frederick, 7:699

Hatred, **6:666**

Hats, as ecclesiastical symbol, 6:763

Hatshepsut's Temple (Egypt), 5:131

Hattin, Battle of (1187), 3:131, 140

Hatto (Abp. of Mainz), 1:103

Hau, M. John (Mother), 5:889

Hauck, F., 3:583

Haulin, St. *See* Hadalinus, St.

Hauréau, Jean Barthélemy, 3:13, 12:770, 776

Haurietis aquas (encyclical, Pius XII), 5:565, 12:490, 491–492, 493

Hauser, Berthold, 12:769

Haussmann, G. E., 10:151

Hautecombe Abbey (Savoy, France), **6:666–667**, *667*

Hauterive Abbey (Switzerland), 3:750, **6:667–668**

Haüy, R. J., 1:835

Havel, Václav, 4:487

Hawaii, 4:248–249, 954–955, **6:668–672**

See also Honolulu Diocese (HI)

Hawgood, John, 3:783

Hawkins, Denis John Bernard, 5:554, **6:672**

Hawks, Edward, **6:672–673**

Hawksmoor, Nicholas, 3:707

Hawryluk, Maksym, 11:583

Hay, George (Bp.), 3:243, 5:183, **6:673**

Hay, John, 1:20

Hayashi, James, Bl., 7:734

Haydn, Franz Joseph, 1:234, 2:201, 3:468, 6:*673*, **673–674**, 8:692–693

Haydn, Michael, **6:674–675**

Haydock, George, Bl., **6:675–676**

Hayen, A., 1:378

Hayes, Elizabeth (Mother Mary Ignatius). *See* Ignatius of Jesus, Mary (Mother)

Hayes, Patrick Joseph (Card.), 1:158, 3:128, 6:*676*, **676**, 7:579, 10:316–317, 323

Hayes, Ralph Leo (Bp. of Helena, MT), 4:535, 9:826

Hayes, Rutherford B., 2:425, 427

Hayhurst, Richard. *See* Herst, Richard, Bl.

Haymann, Carl, 2:383

Haymarket Square riot (Chicago, 1886), 8:192, 10:170

Haymarus Monachus, **6:676–677**

Haymo of Faversham, 2:610, 5:899, **6:677**

Haymo of Halberstadt (Bp.), **6:677–678**

Haynald, Ludwig (Card.), **6:678**

Haynes, B. F., 3:722

Hayy ibn-Yaqzān (Tufail), 7:612

Hayyim, Jacob ben, 11:883–884

Hazard, Paul, 1:518

Haze, Maria Theresia, Bl., 4:535, **6:678**

Hazor (Canaanite City), 2:379

Hazzān, 3:76

He That Cometh (Mowinckel), 10:36–37

Head and ear maladies, patroness of, 8:854

Head of Christ Crowned with Thorns (Reni), 7:*854*

Headlam, A. C., 12:665

Healey, Patrick Joseph, **6:681**

Healing, Christian, 5:80, **6:678–680**, 13:449

The Healing of the Paralytic (Cyril of Jerusalem), 4:472

Health, 9:102–103, 11:348, 350

Health care

 Catholic Health Association, 3:284

 Catholic hospitals, 7:133–134

 Catholic Medical Association, 3:285–286

 See also Hospitals, history of

Healy, Alexander Sherwood, 1:158

Healy, Eliza. *See* St. Mary Magdalen (Sister)

Healy, James Augustine (Bp. of Portland, ME), 1:158, 2:554, **6:680**, 9:57, 11:531

Healy, Michael Morris, 1:158

Healy, Patrick Francis (Father), 1:158, 6:146, 9:57

Healy, Sherwood (Father), 9:57

Healy, Timothy S., 6:147

Hear the Cry of the Poor (pastoral letter), 14:908

Hearne, Thomas, 5:572

Hearst, William Randolph, 10:172

Heart, in the Bible, **6:681**, 8:566

Heart of the Admirable Mother, 8:47

The Heart of the Matter (Greene), 6:461

Hearts, Exchange of, 8:877

Heath, Henry, Bl., 5:235, **6:682**

Heath, James, 2:460

Heath, Nicholas, **6:683**

Heath, Robert, Sir, 2:13

Heaven, in the Bible, **6:683–685**, 8:584–585

Heaven, theology of, **6:685–690**, 8:584–585

Heaven and sky gods, 13:205

Heavenly Ladder (St. John Climacus), 7:949

Hebblethwait, Peter, **6:690**

Hebdomadibus (Boethius), 14:2

Hebert, A. G., 8:663

Hébert, François, 5:441

Hébert, Jacques, 1:518, 5:974

Hébert, Marcel, **6:690–691**, 9:753–754

Hébert-Stevens, A., 1:803

Hebga, Meinrad, 2:913

Hebräische Grammatik (Gesenius), 6:697

Hebrew language, **6:691–692**

 Dead Sea Scrolls, 4:563

 disciple as term, 4:768

 Duran, Profiat, 4:947

 modern times, 8:9, 11

 names for God, 13:77

 revival of, 7:186–187

 Sheol (death), 13:79

 shibboleth, 13:83

Hebrew language *(continued)*
  translation of grace, 6:380, 381
Hebrew poetry, **6:692–695**
Hebrew scriptures, **6:695–696**, 8:599,
  13:145
  See also Old Testament
Hebrew studies (in the Christian
  Church), **6:696–697**, 8:680
Hebrews, 6:597–598, **697–698**, 8:580
Hebrews, Epistle to the, **6:698–700**
  altars, 1:320
  anchor symbolism, 1:396
  Ark of the Covenant, 13:88
  Ascension of Jesus Christ, 1:770
  Assumption of Mary, 1:800
  baptism, 2:59, 60
  beatific vision, 2:171
  canonicity, 3:28, 31, 32
  catechesis, 3:227
  Christian law, 8:403
  Christ's priesthood, 8:728, 11:691
  the Church, 3:579
  Confirmation, 4:85
  conscience, 4:143
  covenant, 4:328
  creedal statements, 4:349
  divine judgment, 8:40
  faith, 5:592–593
  glory of God (end of creation), 6:245
  God the Son, 6:295, 296
  guilt, 6:572
  heaven, 6:685
  justice of God, 8:72
  Lamb of God, 8:301
  papyrus fragment of, 10:*862*
  penance, 11:68
  Precious Blood, 11:639, 641
  redemption, 5:58
  sin, 13:148, 151
  sin offering, 13:159
  spirit, 13:425
  Suffering Servant, Songs of the,
    13:591–592
  supernatural knowledge, 8:202
Hebrich, Samuel, 7:403
Hebron (Israel), 1:36, 7:*628*
*Hechos de la Orden de Predicadores en
  el Imperio de China* (Ricci), 12:226
Hecker, Isaac Thomas, 5:169, **6:700**,
  10:314, 11:40, 41, 14:149
  Americanism, 1:354, 355, 356
  Brook Farm, 2:627
  Catholic University of America,
    3:290
Hedda, St., **6:701**

Hedge, Frederick Henry, 14:147
Hedonism and hedonists, 2:577,
  4:464–465, 5:107, 193, **6:701–702**,
  11:418
Hedwig of Anjou, St., **6:702**, *703*
Hedwig of Poland, St. *See* Jadwiga of
  Poland, St.
Heelan, Edmond, 13:164
Heenan, John (Card.), 12:272
Heereboord, Andriaan, 3:184, 12:768
Heeswijk Monastery (Netherlands),
  6:702, **704**
Hefele, Carl Joseph von (Bp.), 3:624,
  6:399, **704**
Hefele, K. J., 14:234
Hegel, Georg Wilhelm Friedrich, 5:91,
  6:704–709, *705*, 11:294
  absolute, 1:43
  absurdity, 1:48
  act, 1:74
  aesthetics, 1:142, 3:679
  Alain, 1:203
  analogy, 1:379
  Anselm of Canterbury, St., 1:496
  aristocracy, 1:667
  aseity, 1:780
  atheism, 1:823
  authority, 1:918
  Böhme, Jakob, 2:462
  Burke, Edmund, 2:702
  Bury, John Bagnell, 2:713
  Cartesianism, 3:183
  causality, 3:301, 306
  certitude, 3:352
  Christian philosophy, 3:539
  consciousness, 4:154
  contradiction, 4:224
  Cousin, Victor, 4:322
  creation doctrine, 4:345
  death of, 12:784
  death of God theology, 4:585
  determinism's influence, 8:399
  essence, 5:361–362, 368
  eternity, 5:381
  ethics and morality, 5:396
  exegesis, 5:519, 520
  existence, 5:533, 534
  existentialism, 5:544
  feudalism, 5:703
  Feuerbach, Ludwigreas, 5:706–707
  freedom, 5:939
  good, 6:349–350
  idealism, 7:298, 300, 8:219
  identity, 7:302
  influence on Hermann Schell, 12:732

  inner necessity, 10:227
  irrationalism, 7:586
  Kantianism, 8:127
  knowledge, theories of, 8:219
  Kuhn influenced, 8:253
  matter, 9:344
  metaphysics, 9:554–555
  methodology, 9:566
  monism, 9:811
  ontology, 10:607, 11:119
  personalism, 11:152–153
  philosophical romanticism, 12:345
  philosophy and science, 11:299
  philosophy of religion, 12:69
  philosophy of spirit, 13:347
  quiddity, 11:865
  relation, 12:43
  Renaissance concept, 12:111–112
  self, concept of, 12:883
  society, 13:279
  substantial change, 13:581
  system of reason, 12:346, 784
  transcendentals, 14:150
  truth, 14:227
  universals, 14:326
  Wellhausen School, 5:519
Hegelianism and Neo-Hegelianism,
  2:384, 385, 5:707, 6:139, **709–713**,
  8:253
Hegemonius (Christian writer), **6:713**
Hegesias (Cyrenaic philosopher), 11:169
Hegesippus (ecclesiastical writer), 1:455,
  591, **6:714**
Hegumens, 1:9
Heidegger, Martin, 5:94, 362, 368, 398,
  6:714–716, 11:298
  agnosticism, 1:184
  anxiety, 1:540–541
  Augustinianism, 1:882
  biblical hermeneutics, 6:796
  Bultmann, Rudolf Karl, 2:690
  choice, 3:521
  communcation, 4:25
  concept of time, 14:79
  conscience, 4:140, 12:885
  deconstructionism, 4:592, 593
  existence of God, 6:315
  existentialism, 5:543, 544, 545, 828
  free will, 5:931
  Gadamer, Hans-Georg, 6:44–45
  hermeneutics, 6:789
  Kant, 8:124, 127–128
  knowledge, theories of, 8:221
  leisure, 8:461

notion of truth, 14:223

ontology, 10:607–608

phenomenology development, 14:54

philosophy of technology, 13:785

praxis, 11:586

religous experience, 5:556

spirit, 13:348

Heidelberg Catechism (1563), 3:543, 4:79, **6:716**, 10:264, 272

Heider, C., 1:678

Heilbron, John, 11:236

Das Heilige (Otto), 10:711

Die Heilige Schrift und die Tradition (Geiselmann), 14:137

Heiligenkreuz Abbey (Austria), 3:750, **6:716–717**, *717*, 8:503

''Heiligenstadt Testament'' (Beethoven), 2:201

Heiligenthal, Cistercian convent of, 8:104

Heilsbronn Abbey (Ansbach, Germany), 1:108, **6:717**

Heilsgeschichte. See Salvation history (*Heilsgeschichte*)

Heimerad, St., **6:717–718**

Heimo of Michelsberg, **6:718**

Heineman, Barbara, 1:330

Heinemann, J., 14:859

Heinke, Franz Joseph, 7:1041–1042

Heinrich, Johann Baptist, **6:718**

Heinrich, Maximilian (Abp. of Cologne), 3:843

Heinrich IV Schmid (Abbot), 12:568

Heintschel, Donald E., 3:59

Heiric of Auxerre, 1:927, 5:515, **6:718–719**, 12:106

Heisenberg, Werner Karl, 1:836, 5:102

Heisenberg Principle of Uncertainty, 10:19

Heiss, Michael (Abp.), 1:7, **6:719**, 8:132, 273, 14:780

Heisterbach Abbey (Germany), 3:412, **6:719–720**

Heitmüller, W., 2:570

Heiu of Hartlepool, 2:203

Helbron, Peter, 11:366

Heldanus (A. van der Heiden), 3:184

Heldrade. *See* Eldrad, St. (Abbot of Novalese, France)

Helen of Skövde, St., **6:720**

Helen of Udine, Bl., **6:720**

Helena, Marie (Mother), 7:55–56

Helena, St., **6:720–721**

church building by, 4:181

Constantine I (the Great) (Roman Emperor), 4:179, 182–183

cross relics, 4:384–385, 10:137, 13:89

pilgrimage of, 11:344

Helena Maria Espirito Santo (Sister), 6:83

Helentrudis, St., **6:721**

Helfta Convent (Eisleben, Germany), 3:744, **6:721**

Helga (Princess of Kiev). *See* Olga, St.

Helgesen, Povl, 3:142, **6:722**

Heliae, Paulus. *See* Helgesen, Povl

Heliand (poem), 6:722

Hélinand of Froidmont, 1:463, **6:722–723**

Heliocentric religions, 3:551–552

Heliocentrism, Galileo and, 6:59–63

Hell, 6:*723*, *725*

in *Beowulf*, 2:290

damnation, 4:506

Divine Comedy, 4:520–521

Divine judgment, 8:28

See also Hades

Hell, in the Bible, **6:723–724**, 8:28

Hell, theology of, 4:506, **6:724–728**

Hellenic Republic. *See* Greece

Hellenism

cult of the Great Mother, 10:91

deities, 10:88–89

ethics, 9:858–859

mosaics, 10:1–3

motion in early Greek philosophers, 10:16–17

natural law doctrine, 10:179–180

natural law in political thought, 10:201

philosophy of nature, 10:208–209

transmigration of souls doctrine, 14:157

Hellenistic culture

Abraxas, 1:40

adultery, 1:133

afterlife, 1:167

alchemy, 1:237

Alexandria, 1:270

Anima naturaliter christiana, 1:455

Antiochus IV Epiphanes, 1:528–529

Apostolic Fathers, 1:588

architecture, 1:757

Arianism, 1:661

Aristotelianism, 1:668–669, 672

Asia Minor, 1:784

astrology, 1:812

Avicenna, 1:940

biblical theology, 2:382

bishops, 2:411

Book of Jubilees, 1:549

Bousset, Wilhelm, 2:570

Byzantine civilization, 2:765–766, 775

catechesis, 3:228

Celsus, 3:329–330

Christology, 3:559

Church-State relations, 3:634

Ignatius of Antioch, 7:311

School of Alexandria, 1:272

symbolism in, 3:629

Hellenistic mystery religions. *See* Mystery religions, Greco-Oriental

Hellenistic philosophy, 4:299, 550

Die hellenistischen Mysterienreligionen (Reitzenstein), 12:40

Hellenists, **6:728**

Hellenization of Judea, 9:9–10

Hellensim, 11:136

Hellfire, **6:728–729**

Hello, Ernest, 1:412

Hellriegel, Martin, 5:168

Helmes, Thomas. *See* Tunstal, Thomas, Bl.

Helmold of Bosau, 1:463

Helmont, J. F., 3:845

Helms, Mitchell v. (2000), 3:668

Héloïse (abbess of the Paraclete), 1:15, *16*, 18, 648, 6:729, **729**

Helpers of the Holy Souls, **6:729**, 13:230

Helsinki Accords, 3:200–201

Helt, Julius, 12:382

Helvetic College, 8:609

Helvetic Consensus Formula, 4:79

Helvétius, Claude Adrien, 3:792, 5:107, 255, 263

Helviennes ou Lettres provinciales philosophiques (Barruel), 2:118

Helwys, Thomas, 2:78

Hematidrosis (tears of blood and bloody sweat), 10:108

Hemerford, Thomas, Bl., 5:228, **6:729–730**

Hemingway, Ernest, 6:*730*, **730–731**

Hemma, Bl., **6:731**

Hemmer, Hippolyte, 9:78

Hemming (Bp. of Finland), Bl., 5:732, **6:731**

Hemor, sons of, 13:71–72

Hempel, C. G., 14:451

Henana (Syriac theologian), **6:731–732**

Henares, Domingo (Bp.), 14:494–495

Henderson, Donald, 1:252

Hendrick, Thomas Augustine (Bp.), **6:732**

Hendricken, Thomas F. (Bp. of Rhode Island), 12:214, 216

Hendriksen, W., 3:741

Hengenstenberg, E. W., 12:726

Hengsbach, Franz (Card.), 4:14

Henneguier, Jerome, 3:436

Hennel, C. C., 7:850

Hennepin, Louis, **6:732–733**, 7:317, 14:778

Hennessy, John (Bp. of Dubuque, IA), 4:922–923

Henni, John Martin (Abp. of Milwaukee, WI), 6:*733*, **733–734**, 12:531, 633, 14:779–780

  Abbelen, Peter, 1:7

  Caecilian Movement, 2:842

  School Sisters of Notre Dame, 12:781

Hennig, J., 1:289

Henno (Reuchlin), 12:181

Henotheism, **6:734**, 14:297

Henoticon (Zeno), 2:748, 4:253, 5:23, **6:734–735**

  Acacian Schism, 1:50, 3:595, 4:186, 10:834

  Anastasius I (Byzantine Emperor), 1:386

  Anastasius II (Pope), 1:387

  Armenia, 1:700, 704

  caesaropapism, 2:851, 3:634

  events leading to compromising, 14:64

  Iberia, 4:477

  Severus of Antioch, 13:43

  Simplicius (Pope) St., 13:140

Henri de Maupas (Bp. of Le Puy), 12:554

Henrick, O'Connor v. (1906), 11:562

Henricus Aristippus, 1:673, **6:735**, 11:415

Henricus Gallus. *See* Henry of Clairvaux, Bl.

Henrietta Maria (Queen of England), 4:49, 11:267

Henrietta of Jesus, Bl., 4:44

Henrik, St., 5:732

Henriques, António-José, 3:498

Henriques, Gonçalo, Bl., 1:951

Henriques, Henrique, **6:735**

Henríquez, Enrique, **6:735–736**

Henry (Abp. of Cologne), 2:205

Henry (Duke of Gloucester), 3:481

Henry (Duke of Guise), 8:424–425

Henry (Latin Emperor of Constantinople), 2:761

Henry, Carl F. H., 5:473

Henry, Hugh T., 11:625

Henry, P., 8:143

Henry I (Duke of Guise), 6:579

Henry I (King of England), 6:*736*, **736–737**

  Ancient See of Carlisle, 3:123

  Anselm of Canterbury, St., 1:495

  Bayeux Cathedral reconstruction, 2:164

  as benefactor to abbeys, 6:737

  Callistus II (Pope), 2:881

  Canons Regular of St. Augustine, 3:67

  Church in England under, 5:241

  dispute between Anselm of Canterbury, 10:916

  Gerard of York, 6:163

  investiture struggle, 3:72

Henry I (King of Germany), 2:284

Henry I (King of the East Franks), 3:172

Henry II (Holy Roman Emperor), St., **6:744–745**, 7:661

  Adalbero II, 1:100

  Albuin of Säben-Brixen, St., 1:235

  Alexander III (Pope), 1:254

  Benedict VIII (Pope), 2:241

  Bobbio Abbey, 2:446

  Gerard of Cambrai, 6:160

  Poppo of Stavelot, St., 11:508–509

Henry II (King of England), 6:*737*, **737–738**

  anointing, 1:479

  Baldwin of Canterbury, 2:30

  Becket, St. Thomas, 2:193–194

  Church in England under, 5:241

  Church-State relations, 3:636

  English common law, 6:738

  Fontevrualt Convent, 5:793

  Geoffrey of York, 6:143

  Grandmont Abbey, 6:417–418

  Hilary of Chichester, 6:828

  hospitals, 7:121

  Hugh of Lincoln, 7:154

  Irish Church, 7:554

  John of Oxford, 7:978

  Magna Carta, 9:40

  St. Thomas controversy, 5:788

  Witham Charterhouse, founding of, 14:801

  See also Becket affair

Henry II of Admont, 1:117

Henry II of Bursfeld, 2:710

Henry III (Holy Roman Emperor), St., **6:745–746**

  Adrian V (Pope), 1:127

Berno of Reichenau, 2:327

Bernulf, St., 2:328

Clement II (Pope), 3:775–776

Gregory VI (Pope), 6:490

papacy, 7:662

Henry III (King of Castile), 1:326

Henry III (King of England)

  Adam Marsh, 1:107

  Albert II of Riga, 1:221

  anointing, 1:479

  Church in England under, 5:241

  Edmund of Abingdon, 5:85

  representative government, 4:639

Henry III (King of France), 5:849, 8:424–425

Henry III (King of Poland), 2:153

Henry IV (Holy Roman Emperor), **6:746–747**

  Adalbert of Bremen, 1:100

  Albert (Antipope), 1:220

  Alexander II (Pope), 1:253

  Altmann of Passau, St., 1:322

  Andrew of Strumi, Bl., 1:407

  Anselm II of Lucca, St., 1:494

  Bernold of Constance, 2:327

  Church-State relations, 1:100, 3:635, 639, 7:43

  Clement III (Antipope), 3:777, 7:43

  Clifford, Richard, 3:805

  creation of Hohenstaufen empire, Italy, 7:663

  excommunication, 2:283, 6:493

  Gebhard of Salzburg, 6:114–115

  Honorius II (Antipope), 1:253

  investiture struggle, 1:926, 927, 2:506, 6:176, 7:537, 663

  Lazarites, 7:126

Henry IV (King of England), 3:451, 600–601, 4:317, 550, 943, 944

Henry IV (King of France), **6:742–744**, *743*

  abjuration of Protestantism, 6:743

  Acquaviva, Ottavio (the elder), 1:71

  anointing, 1:478

  assassination, 5:850

  Church reforms, 5:849–850

  Coton, Pierre, 4:281

  Edict of Nantes, 7:167–168, 10:144–145

  Francis de Sales, St., 5:867

  Génébrard, Gilbert, 6:127

  Holy League, 8:425

  hospitals, 7:137, 139

  La Rochefoucauld, 8:336

  wars of religion, 3:612, 784

Henry V (Holy Roman Emperor), 6:*747*, **747–748**
 Alpirsbach Abbey, 1:312
 Church in England under, 5:243
 church-state relations, 7:43
 Concordant of Worms, 7:82, 14:849
 Gelasius II (Pope), 6:123
 Gregory VIII (Antipope), 6:485
 investiture struggle, 2:880, 7:538
 Pascal's condemnation of, 10:916
Henry V (King of England), 3:481, 4:317, 8:275, 13:75
Henry V (King of France), 2:189–190
Henry VI (Holy Roman Emperor), 4:403, 411, 7:144
Henry VI (King of England), 1:408, 2:425, 6:216
Henry VII (Holy Roman Emperor), **6:747–748**, *748*
 anointing, 1:479
 Avignon papacy, 1:943
 Celestine III (Pope), 3:319
 Dante Alighieri, 4:519
 Elzéar of Sabran opposition to, 5:180
 Ghibelline-Guelf conflict, 3:854
 Lombard League, 8:767
Henry VII (King of England), 1:130, 402, 3:866, 4:317, 5:244–245, 12:6–7
Henry VIII (King of England), **6:738–742**, *739*
 Adrian of Castello, 1:130
 Ancient See of Chester, 3:469
 Ancient See of Chichester, 3:481
 Anglican Reformation, 3:72, 608, 638, 782
 Brown, George, 2:639
 Campeggio, Lorenzo, 2:920
 chaplain, 8:445
 Charles V (Holy Roman Emperor), 3:429, 430
 Church in England under, 5:244
 Church of Ireland, 7:548
 Clerk, John, 3:803
 confessions of faith, 4:80
 confessors to, 8:592, 775
 Coventry and Lichfield See, 4:330
 Cromwell, Thomas, 4:376–377
 Day, George, 4:546
 De heretico comburendo act, 4:550
 as Defender of the Faith, 4:609, 8:405
 dispensation to marry, 8:57
 divorce of, 3:268–269, 6:739–740, 8:775–776
  Abell, Thomas, Bl., 1:19–20
  Barton, Elizabeth, 2:130, 451
  Bedyll, Thomas, 2:198
  Bonner, Edmund, 2:507
  Campeggio, Lorenzo, 2:920
  Clement VII (Pope), 3:781, 782
  Clerk, John, 3:803
  Cranmer, Thomas, 3:72
  Forest, John, Bl., 5:800
  Luther, 8:883
  Powell, Edward, 11:574
 doctrine of royal supremacy, 8:445
 Dowdall, George, 4:887
 Faringdon, Hugh, Bl., 5:627
 Fisher, John, St., 5:749–750
 Fitzalan, Henry, 5:751
 France, relations with, 6:738
 French invasions of Italy, 7:669
 Gardiner, Stephen, 6:95–96
 Gilbertines, 6:216
 Glastonbury Abbey, 6:237–238
 Irish confessors and martyrs, 7:576–577
 Kirkstall Abbey, 8:183
 Lewes Priory, 8:527
 Lutheranism, 3:609
 marriage with Catherine of Aragon, 5:163, 244, 749, 800, 12:5–8, 210
 martyrs persecuted under, 5:224, 225–227, 8:772
 Mary Tudor, 9:292
 More, Sir Thomas, 9:888–890, 12:227
 Oath of Supremacy, 13:75
 Pilgrimage of Grace, 1:786
 Pole, Reginald, 11:456
 Protestant Reformation, 12:5–6
 Ridley, Nicholas, chaplain to, 12:243
 royal physician, 8:592
 Scottish politics of, 12:834
 Submission of the Clergy, 4:244
 Ten Articles, 14:7
 Warham, William, 14:651–652
 Wolsey, Thomas, 14:811
Henry VIII and the English Monasteries (Gasquet), 6:104
Henry Bradshaw Society, 8:673
Henry de Marcy, 1:256
Henry Heinbuche of Langenstein, 3:636, 784, 4:136, **6:748–749**
Henry IV (Shakespeare), 13:*61*, *64*
Henry Murdac (Abp. of York), 5:832, **6:749**
Henry of Albano (Card.), 6:141
Henry of Blois (Bp. of Winchester), 6:237, **749–750**
Henry of Bolzano, Bl., **6:750**
Henry of Bonn, Bl., **6:750**
Henry of Champagne, 7:774
Henry of Clairvaux, Bl., 3:758, **6:750**
Henry of Friemar, 1:875, 883, 887, **6:750–751**
Henry of Ghent, 5:365–366, 533, **6:751–752**
 analogy, 1:372
 Arabian philosophy, 1:623
 Bernard of Auvergne, 2:306
 conservation, 4:162
 distinction, 4:781
 individuation, 7:425
 scholasticism, 12:762, 765
 Thomism, 3:93
 unity thesis, 5:818
Henry of Gorkum, **6:753**
Henry of Hainault (Latin Emperor), 8:366, 367
Henry of Hane, 3:133
Henry of Harclay, 1:410, **6:753**
Henry of Heisterbach, Bl., **6:753**
Henry of Herp, **6:753–754**, 13:455
Henry of Huntingdon, 1:464, **6:754–755**
Henry of Kalkar, **6:755**
Henry of Lausanne, 1:219, **6:755–756**
Henry of Navarre. *See* Henry IV (King of France)
Henry of Newark (Abp. of York, England), **6:756**
Henry of Nördlingen, 5:32
Henry of Peine, 1:14
Henry of Poiters, 13:96
Henry of Raperswil (Count), 14:696–697
Henry of St. Ignatius, **6:756**
Henry of Segusio. *See* Hostiensis (Card.)
Henry of Uppsala, St., **6:756–757**
Henry of Virneburg (Abp. of Cologne), 5:44
Henry of Vitskól, Bl., **6:757**
Henry of Zwiefalten, Bl., **6:757**
Henry Stuart (Card.), 7:690
Henry Suso, Bl., 3:605, **6:757–758**
 Albert the Great, St., 1:226
 apophatic theology, 1:568
 Dominican mysticism, 5:789
 Holy Name, 7:32
 mystical union, 4:847
 pantheism, 2:629
Henry the Lion (Duke of Bavaria), 6:*179*
Henry the Navigator, 10:631
Henry the Quarrelsome, Duke of Bavaria, 10:713, 714
Henschenius, Godefroid, 2:471
Hensel, Luise, 1:2

Hentten, J., 12:186

Heortology, **6:759**

Hepburn, James, Earl of Bothwell. *See* Bothwell, James Hepburn, Earl of

Hepburn, John, 12:533

Heptaplomeres (Bodin), 12:124

Heptaplus (Pico Della Mirandola), 11:323, 12:122

Heptateuchon (Thierry of Chartres), 9:453, 14:2

Hera (Greek deity), 6:452

Heraclas (Bp. of Alexandria), 1:272

Heracleides of Pontos, 12:803

Heracleon (Gnostic teacher), **6:759**

Heraclitus (Greek philosopher), 6:441, **759–760**, 7:239, 292, 10:94, 11:287

  Anaxagoras, 1:393

  atomism, 1:832

  beauty, 2:184

  becoming, 2:195

  certitude, 3:351

  consciousness, 4:151–152

  creator-gods, 6:306

  existence, 5:533

  intellectual life, 7:513

  monism of, 10:825

  pantheism of, 10:825

  soul, 13:338

Heraclius (Antipope), **6:761**

Heraclius (Byzantine Emperor), **6:761**

  anti-Semitism, 7:868

  Armenia, 1:705

  Church-State relations, 3:634

  Council of Chalcedon, 1:700

  Ekthesis demands, 13:42

  Monophysitism, 2:499

  Monothelitism, 1:271, 2:749, 783, 3:561, 7:81, 656

  Persia, 2:783

  Sergius I (Patriarch), 13:13

Heraclius II (King of Georgia), 6:156

Heraldry, 4:380, 8:637–638, 13:114–115

Heraldry, ecclesiastical, **6:761–765**

Herbart, Johann Friedrich, 5:91, 93, 388, 7:299, 10:61, 13:347

Herbermann, Charles George, **6:765**

Herbert, George, 1:409, 3:152, 5:161

Herbert I (Bp. of Auxerre), 1:927

Herbert of Bosham, 1:407

Herbert of Cherbury, Edward, 4:*615*, 617, 5:255, **6:765–766**

Herbet, Frumence (Brother), 2:632

Herbigny, Michael d', **6:766**, 7:791, 12:429

Hercules, Charles, 9:75–76

Herder (publishing house), **6:766–767**

Herder, Bartholomew, 6:766

Herder, Benjamin, 6:766

Herder, Hermann, 6:766

Herder, Johann Gottfried von, 5:263, 6:*767*, **767–768**

  Arnold, Gottfried, 1:718

  biography of Christ, 7:847

  form criticism, 5:812

  Goethe, Johann Wolfgang von, 6:330

  I-It mysticism of, 10:117

  irrationalism, 7:586

  Kantianism, 8:126, 12:345

  literary myth, 10:120

  neo-Lutheranism, 8:891

  world soul, 14:844

Herder and Herder (company), 6:767

Herder-Dorneich, Theophil, 6:766–767

Herdtrich, Christian Wolfgang, **6:768**

Heredity, 9:488

Hereford, Ancient See of (England), **6:768**

Hereford, Nicholas, **6:768–769**, 12:131

Hereford Cathedral (England), 5:384

Hereford Use, **6:769**

L'Hérésie convainçue (Baron), 2:104

Heresy, **6:769–772**, 7:487

  Alexandria, 1:268–269, 272

  anathema, 1:390

  Antichrist, 1:516

  apocrypha, 1:558

  apostasy, 1:570

  Apostolic Fathers, 1:588

  capital punishment, 3:86, 87

  Celestine I (Pope), St., 3:317

  Church property, 3:727

  conciliarism, 4:54–58

  Constance Council, 4:170–171

  De heretico comburendo act (1401), 4:550

  dogmas vs., 13:897

  Gregory IX (Pope), 6:497

  Isidore of Seville, St., 7:603–604

  Italy, 11th century, 7:664–665

  legislative responses to, 7:487–488

  Manichaeism, 9:108–110, 114

  monarchianism, 9:780

  monothelitism, 9:816–817

  schism, 12:737

  spiritism, 13:429

  subordinationism, 13:566

  theological censure, 3:337

  universality of Christianity, 3:275

  Waldenses, 14:608

  See also Index of Prohibited Books; Inquisition; *specific heresies*

Heresy, Canon Law, **6:772**

  See also Apostasy

Heresy, history of, **6:772–779**

  Council of Lombers, 8:770

  Crusades, 4:412

  during later patristic period, 10:968

  early church, 6:772–773, 13:166

  first comprehensive papal policy, 8:847

  Fourth Lateran Council, 8:353

  lay preaching, 8:295

  Lollards, 8:766

  Louis IX reign, 8:800–801

  medieval period, 6:773–775

  modern period, 6:775–779

  Nestorian heresy, 4:26

  suppression methods, 8:295

Heretical presumption, 11:686

Heretics, denial of Church funeral, 6:33

Hergenröther, Joseph, **6:779–780**

Heribert of Cologne (Abp.), St., 3:843, **6:780**, 8:563

Heriger of Lobbes, 1:498, **6:780–781**, 7:247, 9:448

Herimannus Augiensis, 3:562

Herincx, William (Bp. of Ypres), **6:781**

Heristal, Council of (779), 3:42

Herkommer, Hans, 3:710, 711

Herkumbert, St., **6:781–782**

Herluin of Bec, Bl., 2:189, **6:782**

Herluka of Bernried, Bl., **6:782**

Herman (15th c. German scholar), 12:119

Herman (Bp. of Ramsbury), 12:616

Herman, Nicholas. *See* Lawrence of the Resurrection

Herman II (Abp. of Cologne), 1:102–103, 3:843

Herman Joseph of Steinfeld, St., **6:782–783**, 11:666

Herman of Carinthia, 14:2

Herman of Dalmatia, 3:441

Herman of Reichenau. *See* Hermannus Contractus

Herman of Salza, **6:783**

Herman of Scheda, **6:783**, 9:454–455

Herman of Schildesche, **6:783–784**

Herman the German, Bl., **6:784**

Herman the Jew. *See* Herman of Scheda

Herman the Lame. *See* Hermannus Contractus

Hermanas de Nuestra Señora de la Consolación. *See* Sisters of Our Lady of Consolation

Hermanas Franciscanas de la Inmaculada Concepcion, 5:879

Hermaniuk, Maxime (Abp.), 3:350

Hermann, A. C., 12:765

Hermann, Wilhelm, 2:690

Hermann und Dorothea (Goethe), 6:331

Hermannus Contractus, 1:297, 462, 6:177, **784**, 12:32

Hermannus the Lame, 9:449

Hermenegild, St., **6:786**, 8:426

Hermeneutics, **6:786–791**, 13:916
  crisis of Christianity, 8:774
  doctrine development, 4:808
  feminist, 5:674–675
  philosophy, 6:45–46
  theology, 11:586–588
  See also Exegesis

Hermeneutics, biblical, **6:791–799**
  advocacy criticism, 6:796
  biblical theology, 2:383, 389–390
  demythologizing, 4:655–658
  scholarship, 10:306
  ''suspicion,'' 8:862

Hermes (Greek deity), 3:573–574

Hermes, Georg, 3:624, **6:797–798**
  Cologne mixed marriage dispute, 3:845, 13:416
  condemnation, 4:932
  Droste zu Vischering, Clemens, 4:909
  faith, 5:596, 599
  heresy, 6:778
  religious liberalism, 8:541
  scholasticism, 12:770
  semirationalism, 12:622, 901
  See also Hermesianism

Hermesianism, 3:624, 4:741, **6:798–799**

Hermetic literature, 1:168, **6:799**, 13:311

Herminus, 1:669

Hermits, **6:799–800**
  anchorites vs., 1:397
  cenobitism, 3:334
  lay movements (12th-13th c.), 3:130–131, 140
  Martin V (Pope), 1:631–632
  solitude, 13:303
  See also Augustinian Hermits; Recluses

Hermits of Divine Providence, 10:672

Hermits of Morrone. *See* Celestines

Hermits of St. Damian. *See* Celestines

Hermits of St. Paul, 1:534, **6:800–801**

Hermits of St. William. *See* Augustinians; Williamites

Hermosilla, Jeronimo (Bp. of East Tonkin), 14:495

Hermosillo Archdiocese (Mexico), **6:801**

Hermylus and Stratonicus, SS., 13:161

Hernández de Córdoba, Francisco, 10:350

Hero of Alexandria, 1:834

Herod Agrippa I (King of Judea), 7:768

Herod Agrippa II, 5:700

Herod Antipas, 5:87, **6:801**, 803, 804, 7:1014

Herod the Great (King of Judea), **6:801–803**, 7:645
  Antigonus, 6:665
  birth of Christ, 10:173
  censuses, 3:339
  Edomites, 5:87
  Jerusalem construction projects, 7:767–768
  palace of, 11:579
  slaughter of innocents, 7:483, 484

Herodians, **6:803–804**

Herodias (wife of Herod Antipas), **6:804**, 7:1014

Herodotus (Greek historian), 4:389, 9:33, 11:145, 14:156

Herod's Temple, 13:810

Heroic virtue. *See* Virtue and virtues, heroic

Heroides (Ovid), 10:727

Herolt, Johannes, 3:241

Herondas, 12:509

Herophilus (Greek physician), 2:400, 12:806

Herovalliana, 3:40, 41

Herp, Hendrik, 3:134

Herr, Jacob, 11:624

Herrad of Hohenburg, 5:206

Herrad of Landsberg, **6:805**, 9:454

Herranz, Miguel (Father), 3:738

Herrera, Bartolomé (Bp.), 6:805, **805–806**

Herrera, Juan de, **6:806**, *807*

Herrera y Tordesillas, Antonio de, **6:806–807**

Herrero, Andrés, **6:807–808**

Herrero, Valerio Bernardo, Bl., 1:298

Herrisvad Abbey (Sweden), **6:808**

Herrlichkeit (Balthasar), 2:34–35

Herrmann, Edward J. (Bp. of Columbus), 3:868

Herrmann, Wilhelm, 4:656

Hersfeld Abbey (Germany), **6:808**

Hershey, Alfred D., 2:404

Herst, Richard, Bl., 5:235, **6:808–809**

Hertfelder, Bernhard (Abbot), 12:671

Hertford, Council of (672), **6:809**

Hertling, Georg von, 6:365, 12:776

Hertz, H. R., 1:80

Hertzberg, H. W., 5:520

Hertzka, Theodroe, 14:361

Hervaeus Natalis. *See* Harvey Nedellec

Hervas, Juan (Bp. of Ciudad Real, Spain), 4:443

Hervás y Panduro, L., 3:418

Hervé (dean of Canterbury), 2:190

Hervey (Archdeacon of Salisbury), 12:617

Herwegen, Ildefons, 6:185, **809**

Hérzelo (architect), 3:812

Hesburgh, Theodore M., 10:461

Hesiod (Greek poet), 14:360
  aesthetics, 1:142
  allegory, 1:292
  cosmogeny, 4:283
  daimones, 4:495
  earth cult, 5:2
  Golden Age, 6:335

Hesius, Willem, 3:706

Hesketh, Ildephonse, 5:238

Heskyn, Thomas, 2:372

Heslin, Thomas (Bp. of Natchez, MS), 7:686

Hess, Bede Frederick, **6:809–810**

Hesse (Germany), 2:495

Hesselblad, Elisabeth, Bl., 2:618, 6:*810*, **810–811**

Hessels, Jan, 2:18–19

Hessing, Jacob, 6:712

Hesychasm, 2:762, 763–764, 771, 794, 826–827, **6:811**
  Andronicus III Palaeologus, 1:410
  Argyros, Isaac, 1:659
  Barlaam of Calabria, 2:99
  Cabasilas, Nilus, 2:826, 837
  Callistus I (Patriarch), 2:826, 878
  Callistus II Xanthopulus, 2:879
  Century, 2:879
  Chrysoberges, Andrew, 3:572
  Cydones, Prochorus, 4:454
  Eastern Schism, 2:788
  Manuel Calecas, 9:126–127
  monasticism, 9:799

Hesychastic monks, 10:765–766

Hesychius Illustrios of Miletus, 2:798

Hesychius of Jerusalem, **6:812**

Heterodoxy, 7:487

Hettinger, Franz, **6:812–813**, 11:623

Het'um I (Armenian Catholicos), 1:702

Het'um II (Armenian Catholicos), 1:702

Heusden, Joannes Vos de, 4:708

Heuser, Herman Joseph, **6:813**

Heussgen, Johannes. *See* Oecolampadius, Johannes

Hewett, John, Bl., 2:696, 5:230, **6:813–814**

Hewit, Augustine Francis, 2:23, 3:291, 4:260, 6:700, **814**, 11:40

Hexaemeron (Bonaventure), 4:338–339, **6:814–815**, 12:761

Hexagonal baptismal fonts, 2:76

Hexapla (Origen), 2:845, 847, 3:258, **6:816**, 10:654

Hexateuch, **6:817**, 13:72

Hexham Monastery (England), 6:*817*, **817**

Heyden, Thomas, 1:582

Heylyn, P., 12:454

Heymans, G., 8:514

Heynen, William (Father), 1:208

Heythrop College (England), **6:817**

Heythrop Pontifical Athenaeum (England), 6:*818*

Heywood, Ellis, 6:818

Heywood, Jasper, 6:818–819

Heywood, John, 6:817–818, *819*

Heywood family, **6:817–818**

Hezekiah (King of Judah), 7:641–642, 766, 13:*20*, 120

Hibernensis Collectio (canonical collection), 3:60, **6:819–820**

Hickel, Walter J., 1:211

Hickey, Antony, **6:820**

Hickey, J. S., 12:748, 776

Hickey, James A. (Card.), 1:*25*, 14:658

Hickey, Joseph Aloysius, 1:891, **6:820**

Hickey, William A. (Bp.), 7:581, 12:216, 217

Hicks, Elias, 6:5

Hidalgo y Costilla, Miguel, **6:820–821**, *821*

The Hidden God (Van Steenberghen), 14:388

Hidulf, SS., **6:821–822**

Hidulf of Lobbes, St., 6:821

Hidulf of Regensburg, St., 6:821

Hien Quang Do, José, 14:495

Hierarchal Personalism, 8:794

Hierarchia caelestia (Pseudo-Dionysus), 8:583

Hierarchia catholica medii aevi (Eubel), 5:410

Hierarchical insignia, of clergy, 6:764

Hierarchy of the Catholic Church in the U.S. (Shea), 13:70

Hierarchy of Truths, **6:822**, 8:533

Hieria, Iconoclast Council of (754), 5:23, 7:281, 282

Hieria, Synod of (754), 2:751, 753, 4:174, 5:23

Hierocles (Byzantine historian), 2:799

Hieroglyphics, 6:*898*

Hierognosis, 3:759, 10:108

Hieron, St. *See* Jeron, St.

Hieronymian Martyrology, 9:233

Hieronymite Monastery (Madrid), 6:*823*

Hieronymites (Los Jerónimos), **6:822–823**

Hierophany, 5:154–155, 696–697

Hierotheus II of Alexandria (Greek Orthodox Patriarch), 6:459

Hieu Van Nguyen, Peter, 14:495

Higden, Ralph, 14:177

Higgins, George G., 10:545

Higgins, Peter, Bl., 7:581

Higginson, Thomas Wentworth, 13:456–457

High Church, 1:446–447, **6:823–824**
　Charles I (King of England), 3:432
　Delany, Selden Peabody, 4:619–620
　Low Church, 8:836
　Lux Mundi attacked, 8:896
　origins, 1:444
　See also Anglicanism; Anglo-Catholics; Tractarianism

High God (traditional African religion), 12:67

High Priest (Christological title), 3:482, 7:809

High priests (of Israel), **6:824–825**

High School Movement (KS), 8:118

Higher Catechectical Institute, 12:783

Higher criticism, **6:825**

Higher education. *See specific universities and colleges*

Highlights, 10:164

Higinio Durán, José, 10:818

Hijas de Jesús. *See* Daughters of Jesus

Hijas de la Sagrada Familia, 9:130

Hijas de Maria, Religisas de las Escuelas Pias. *See* Daughters of Mary of the Pious Schools

Hijos de la Sagrada Familia, 9:130

Hijra, 1:611, 5:314, **6:825**, 10:51, 53–54

Hikojirō, Caspar, Bl., 7:732

Hilarianus, Quintus Iulius (Bp.), 1:461

Hilarion, St., 4:83, **6:825–826**, *826*, 12:606

Hilarus of Mende, St., **6:826–827**

Hilary I (Pope), St., **6:827**, 12:353

Hilary of Arles (Bp.), St., 1:694, **6:827–828**, 10:620
　censure by Leo I (Pope), St., 6:112
　correspondence with Eucherius of Lyons, St., 5:438
　divine indwelling, 7:442
　Leo I (Pope), St., 8:476
　Prosper of Aquitaine, St., 11:771–772
　Semi-Pelagianism, 12:899

Hilary of Chichester (Bp.), **6:828**

Hilary of Poitiers (Bp.), St., **6:828–830**, 10:755
　acrostics, 1:72
　Arianism, 1:662, 818, 3:594, 632, 5:455, 642
　aseity, 1:779
　baptism in the Holy Spirit, 3:393
　baptism of Jesus, 2:72
　beatific vision, 2:172
　biographies of, 5:823
　on the Church, 6:829
　controversies in Gaul, 6:112
　divine judgment, 8:32
　exegetical works, 5:512
　exile of, 4:197
　friendship with God, 6:10
　God and the Trinity, 6:829
　homily, 7:62
　hymnody, 7:243, 252
　hymns of, 5:104
　influence of, 6:829
　Leobin of Chartres, 8:496
　Martin of Tours, St., 9:220
　mystery of God, 6:281
　Nicene Creed, 4:353
　preaching, 11:610
　works of, 6:828–829

Hilbert, David, 9:327

Hilbert, M. Colette (Mother), 5:883

Hilda of Whitby, St., 1:192, 2:203, 5:239, **6:830**, 14:699–700

Hildebert of Lavardin (Abp. of Tours), **6:830**, 7:248, 9:451, 459, 12:29

Hildebrand. *See* Gregory VII (Pope)

Hildebrand, Dietrich von, 4:221, **6:830–831**, 11:*231*

Hildebrandine Reform. *See* Gregorian Reform

Hildebrandt, Lukas von, 3:706

Hildegar of Meaux (Bp.), 5:631

Hildegard of Bingen, St., 5:166, 444, **6:831–832**
　Adam of Ebrach, Bl., 1:108
　Jutta, Bl., 8:104

medieval Latin literature works of, 9:454

mysticial writings of, 10:118

private revelations, 12:200

Hildegard of Kempten, Bl., **6:832**, 8:596

Hildegunde of Meer, Bl., **6:832**

Hildegunde of Schönau, **6:832–833**

Hildelide, St., 2:98, 4:449, **6:833**

Hildesheim Cathedral (Germany), 12:485–486

Hildigrim, St., **6:833**

Hildradus. *See* Eldrad, St. (Abbot of Novalese, France)

Hilduin of Saint-Denis, 5:514, **6:833**, 12:544

Hilgenfeld, Adolf, 14:234

Hilgers, Thomas, 10:176

Hill, Laurence, 5:238

Hill, Richard, Bl., 5:231, **6:834**

Hill, William Joseph, **6:834**, 11:629

Hillebrand, Fr., 10:176

Hillel (Jewish sage), 5:508

Hillquit, Morris, 12:445

Hiltalinger, John, 1:883, 888

Hilton, Walter, 5:243, **6:834–835**, 10:118, 119, 12:297

　divine love, 8:49

　mysticism, 3:605

Himiko (Japanese queen), 7:736

Himmels-und Weltenbild der Babylonier als Grundlage der Weltanschauung und Mythologie aller Völker (Winckler), 10:820

Himmerod Abbey (Germany), 1:67, 4:541, **6:835–836**, *836*

Himonoya, Michael, Bl., 7:734

Himonoya, Paul, Bl., 7:734

Hīnayāna Buddhism, 2:657, **6:836–837**

Hincmar of Laon (Abp.), 1:840, **6:837**, 838, 10:362

Hincmar of Reims (Abp.), **6:837–839**

　Adrian II (Pope), 1:124

　annals, 1:461

　art, 3:153

　asperges, 1:786

　Benedict III (Pope), 2:239

　Canon Law, 3:43

　Carolingian Dynasty, 3:171, 434

　Carolingian reform, 3:158, 599

　Carolingian Renaissance, 3:160

　Church-State relations, 3:634

　Council of Attigny, 1:840

　false decretals, 5:618

　four propositions of, 11:865

　Gottschalk of Orbais, 6:371

grace, 6:402

Leo IV (Pope), St., 8:482

Lothair II's annulment, 8:796

prescholasticism, 12:757

Reims Cathedral, rebuilding of, 12:36

Remigius of Lyons, St., 12:107

Sanctorum meritis (office hymn), 12:664

works of, 6:838

Hind Swaraj (Gāndhi), 6:*87*

Hindemith, Paul, 6:*839*, 839, 10:73

Hinderer, Roman, **6:839–840**

Hindi, Augustine, 3:368

Hindu Renaissance Movement, 7:405

Hinduism, **6:840–853**

　anthroposophy, 1:513

　apophatic theology, 1:568

　Brahman, 2:580

　Buddhism, 2:661

　Caribbean, 3:116

　caste system, 3:211, 6:851, 853

　comparison with Christianity, 6:852–853

　conscience, 4:139

　daēvas, 4:492

　dharma, 4:714

　interpretations of Jesus, 7:842

　Kālī, 8:111, *111*

　karma, 8:130

　legends and manuals, 6:848–850

　mantras in, 9:125

　metaphysics, 9:548

　Nostra aetate: Declaration on the Relation of the Church to Non-Christian Religions, 9:687

　philosophy, 6:845–846

　reform, 6:851–852

　reincarnation, 12:38

　sacred writings, 6:840, 842–845

　Siva, 13:193–194

　sutras, 13:631–632

　teachers, 6:846–848

　temples, 6:*841*, 850–881

　wedding ceremony, 6:*842*

　See also Yoga

Hines, Vincent J. (Bp. of Norwich), 4:125

Hinojosa Naveros, Maria Gabriela de (1872-1936), 14:564, 566

Hinrichs, H. F., 6:709

Hinschius, P., 1:433

Hinsley, Arthur (Card. of Westminster), 5:252, 6:*853*, **853–854**, 13:651

Hintenach, Andrew (Archabbot), 12:591

Hipparchus of Nicaea, 1:812, 12:804–805

Hippias of Elis, 8:536, 13:324

Hippo, Council of, 1:858, 3:323

Hippo Regius (African bishopric), **6:854–855**

Hippocrates (Greek physician), 2:400, 4:184, 6:*855*, **855–856**, 12:806

Hippocratic Oath, **6:856**, *857*

Hippolyte I (Card.), 5:371

Hippolyte II (Card.), 5:371

Hippolytus, cemetery of (Rome), 3:224

Hippolytus of Rome, St., **6:858–860**, 14:191, 192

　agape, 1:170

　Alogoi, 1:304

　Ambrose, St., 1:337

　Antichrist, 1:516

　Apostolic Constitutions, 1:581

　Basilides, 2:149

　biblical canon, 3:31

　Callistus I (Pope), St., 2:879

　Canon Law, 3:37–38, 59

　Christology, 3:560

　chronicles, 1:460

　Chronographer of 354, 3:569

　Church order, 12:328, 467

　contraception, 4:220

　creedal statements, 4:350, 351

　divine judgment, 8:31

　doxology, 4:890

　Easter date controversy, 4:46, *47*, *48*, 5:13

　Ebionites, 5:31

　exegetical works, 5:512

　Fabian (Pope), 5:584

　heresy, works, 6:773, 858–859

　lauds, 8:380

　other works, 6:859

　papal primacy, 3:593

　penitential controversy, 11:73

　relics of, 12:655

　Roman Rite, 12:328

　theology of history, 6:887

　Zephyrinus (Pope), St., 14:919

Hirsau Abbey (Germany), 1:312, 909–910, 6:*860*, **860–861**, 8:248

Hirsau reform, 12:211

Hirsch, Samson Raphael, 7:873

Hirschboeck, George, 7:742

Hirscher, Johann Baptist, 3:244, **6:861**

His praecipue (brief, Innocent III), 7:51–52

Hishām, 14:286

Hispana (St. Isidore of Seville), 7:603

Hispana Collectio Versio (canonical collection), 3:39, 40, 42, 43, 60, **6:861–862**

Dacheriana collectio, 4:492

described, 13:377

Hispana Gallica Augustoduensis, 5:615–619

Hispana Systematica (canonical collection), 3:40, 6:862

Hispana Versio (canonical collection), **6:862**

Hispanic Americans

Bishops' Committee for the Spanish Speaking, 8:843

El Paso Diocese, 5:175

Encuentros in Washington, DC, 5:203–205

Flores, Patricio, 5:203

hymnals, 7:261

Idaho, 7:292

Iowa, 7:543

Kansas, 8:115, 116

Latina theology, 8:369–370

lay leadership programs, 8:290

liturgical inculturation, 7:387

Louisiana, 8:816

popular piety, 11:509–510, 541–542

San Antonio Archdiocese, 12:639–642

South Dakota, 13:369

women religious, 8:424

Hispanic Women: Prophetic Voice in the Church (Isasi-Díaz and Tarango), 5:677

Hispano-Mozarabic rite, 10:42–43

Histoire ancienne de l'Église (Duchesne), 7:503

Histoire critique du Vieux Testament (Simon), 5:519, 13:127

Histoire de Béarn (Marca), 9:133

Histoire de Fr. Morsini (Ruinart), 12:407

Histoire de France (Michelet), 12:112

Histoire de la philosophie médiévale (De Wulf), 12:776

Histoire de la théolgie positive (Turmel), 14:241

Histoire de la théologie au XIXe siècle (Hocedez), 6:901

Histoire de l'Abbé de Rancé et de sa réforme (Gervaise), 6:192

L'Histoire de origines du christianism (Renan), 12:126

Histoire des auteurs sacrés et ecclésiastiques (Ceiller), 5:760

Histoire des empereurs (Tillemont), 14:75

Histoire des hommes illustres de l'ordre de Saint-Dominique (Touron), 14:125

Histoire des langues sémitque (Renan), 12:126

Histoire des sacrements (Chardon), 3:389

Histoire des variations des églises protestantes (Bossuet), 5:496

Histoire du Bréviaire romain (Batiffol), 2:155

Histoire du dogme catholique pendant les trois premier siècles (Ginoulhiac), 6:229

L'Histoire du droit Française (Fleury), 5:762

Histoire du peuple de Dieu (Berruyer), 2:330, 3:792

Histoire d'une âme (*The Story of a Soul*) (Thérèse de Lisieux), 3:138

Histoire ecclésiastique (Eusebius), 12:793

Histoire ecclésiastique (Fleury), 5:762, 10:676

''Histoire ecclesiastique'' (Tillemont), 14:75

Histoire généalogique de la maison d'Auvergne (Baluze), 2:47

Histoire générale de la musique depuis les temps les plus anciens (Fétis), 5:701

Histoire générale de la réforme de l'order de Citeaux (Gervaise), 6:192

Histoire générale de l'Amérique depuis sa découverte (Touron), 14:125

Histoire générale du jansénisme (Gerberon), 6:164

Histoire naturelle, générale et particulìre (Buffon), 5:260

Histoire naturelle de l'ăme (La Mettrie), 9:319–320

Histoire religieuse de la France (Goyau), 6:378

Histoire universelle de l'Église catholique (Rohrbacher), 12:290

Historia (Nicholas Trevet), 10:381

Historia Acephala, 13:885

Historia anglorum et dacorum (Simeon of Durham), 13:124–125

Historia Apollonii, regis Tyri (anonymous), 9:447

Historia Augusta (Salmasius), 12:620

Historia calamitatum (Abelard), 1:15, 9:452

Historia civil y política de Méjico (Cavo), 3:313

Historia Compostelana (history of Santiago de Compostela, Spain), 12:684

Historia congregationum de auxiliis (Sperry), 14:50

Historia Constantinopolitana (Gunther of Pairis), 6:584

História da Igreja de Japam (Rodriguez Tçuzu), 12:281

Historia de duabus civitatibus (Otto of Freising), 6:873, 10:716

Historia de filosofia (González y Díaz), 12:773

Historia de la Compañía de Jesús de la Provincia del Paraguay (Lozano), 8:839

Historia de la provincia de San Nicolás de Tolentino de Michoacán del orden de N. P. S. Agustín (Basalenque), 2:132

Historia de la Provincia de San Vicente de Chiapa y Guatemala (Remesal), 12:105–106

Historia de las Indias (Durán), 4:946

Historia de las Indias (Las Casas), 8:341

Historia de los indios de Neuva España (Motoloní), 10:28

Historia de los triumphos de nuestra sante fee entre gentes los má barbaros y fieros del Nuevo Orbe (Pérez de Rivas), 11:116

Historia de Nueva España escrita por su esclarecido conquistador Hernán Cortés aumentada con otros documentos (Lorenzana), 8:786

Historia del Carmen Descalzo en España, Portugal y América (Silverio de St. Teresa), 13:122

Historia del Concilio Tridentino (Sarpi), 10:806

História do Brasil (Salvador), 12:622

Historia ecclesiae dunelmensis (Simeon of Durham), 13:124

Historia ecclesiastica (Eusebius of Caesarea), 6:871–872

Historia ecclesiastica (St. Gregory of Tours), 6:873

Historia ecclesiastica (Socrates, Byzantine historian), 13:293

Historia ecclesiastica (Theodore Lector), 13:873–874

Historia Ecclesiastica gentis Anglorum (*Ecclesiastical History*) (St. Bede), 2:195–196

Historia eclesiástica (Mendieta), 9:492

Historia eclesiástica, política y literaria de Chile (Eyzaguirre), 5:573

Historia eclesiástica de España (Garcia Villada), 6:94

Historia eclesiástica indiana (Torquemada), 14:113

Historia Eliensis (Ely), 5:179

Historia Florentiae (Poggio Bracciolini), 11:435

Historia Francorum (Aimon of Fleury), 9:448

Historia Francorum (Gregory of Tours), 3:229, 5:922

Historia general de las conquistas del Neuvo Reino de Granada (Fernández de Piedrhita, Lucas), 5:689

Historia general de las cosas de Nueva España (Sahafún), 12:529

Historia Henrici I regis Anglorum (Robert of Torigny), 12:270

Historia Hierosolymitana (Fulcher of Chartres), 6:21

Historia iuris ecclesiastici universi libri tres (Barbosa), 2:96

Historia Julii Caesaris (Petrarch), 12:114

Historia Langobardorum (Paul the Deacon), 11:36

Historia Lausiaca (Palladius of Helenopolis), 10:805, 806

Historia monachorum, 3:594

Historia natural y moral de las Indias (Acosta), 1:70

Historia naturalis (Pliny the Elder), 5:206

Historia Normanorum (Dudo of Saint-Quentin), 12:582

Historia Novella (Recent History) (William of Malmesbury), 9:80–81

Historia novorum (Eadmer of Canterbury), 5:1, 9:455

Historia orientalis et occidentalis (Jacques de Vitry), 7:693

Historia Ottonis (Liutprand of Cremona), 8:737

Historia persecutionis Vandalicae (Ruinart), 12:407

Historia pontificalis (John of Salisbury), 7:985, 9:453

Historia reformationis Polonicae (Lubieniecki), 8:841

Historia Regibus Gothorum (St. Isidore of Seville), 7:604

Historia regum Britanniae (Geoffrey of Monmouth), 1:464, 759–761, 762, 6:142

Historia regum Francorum ab origine gentis ad annun, 12:548

Historia religiosa (Theodoret of Cyr), 6:613

Historia Remensis ecclesiae (Flodoard), 5:763

Historia rerum Anglicarum (William of Newburgh), 14:745

Historia scholastica (Peter Comestor), 5:517

Historia septem tribulationum (Angelus Clarenus), 5:897

Historia sui temporis (Thou), 14:61

Historia Tartaro-Sinica nova (Rougemont), 12:391

Historia theologiae christiani saeculi primi (Scholliner), 12:779

Historia tripartita (Theodore Lector), 13:873–874

Historia von D. Johann Fausten (Spies), 5:650

Historiae (Tacitus), 13:729–730

Historiae ecclesiasticae repertorium (Benigni), 2:279

Historiae sacrae epitome (Haymo of Halberstadt), 6:677

Historiae super libro Decretorum (Bartholomew of Brescia), 2:125

Historiale (Vincent of Beauvais), 14:522

Historiarum adversus paganos libri VII (Orosius), 10:673

Historiarum Florentini populi libri xii (Bruni), 12:111

Historica ecclesiastica (Bartholomew of Lucca), 2:126

Histórica relación del reino de Chile (Ovalle), 10:726

Historical and Critical Dictionary (Bayle), 2:164–165

Historical books of the Old Testament, 4:702, **6:863**

Historical criticism, 6:794–795, 8:862, 13:230

Historical Dictionaries of Religions, Philosophies, and Movements, 5:208

The Historical Dictionary of Catholicism, 5:208

Historical eras, **5:311–314**

Historical Evidence for the Resurrection of Jesus Christ (Lake), 8:297

Historical Jesus, 2:690, 3:623, **6:863–868**, 7:804–808, 837–838
   See also Jesus Christ, biographical studies of

Historical materialism, 9:324–325
   See also Dialectical materialism

Historical method (liberal arts), 8:539

Historical Path of Eastern Orthodoxy (Schmemann), 12:742

Historical Records and Studies, 12:243

Historical research, 8:62

Historical Review of the State of Ireland (Plowden), 11:423

Historical theology, 3:614, **6:868–871**, 13:910

Historical-Biographical Studies (O'Daniel), 10:550

Historiche Politische Blätter (periodical), 6:183

Historicism, 4:372–374, **6:871**, 7:181–182

Historicity, 1:596

Historiography
   Arnold, Gottfried, 1:718
   Byzantine Empire, 2:775–776, 778–779, 788–789, 795–802
   chronicles, 1:461, 465

Historiography, ecclesiastical, **6:871–881**
   Catholic Church in U.S., 13:70
   Church history, 16th to 18th century
      editions and methodology, 6:875–876
      papal, diocesan and institutional history, 6:876–877
      professional studies in, 6:877
   Delehaye, Hippolyte, 4:626
   early Christianity, 6:871–873
   Historia Ottonis (Liutprand), 8:737
   Lea, H. C., 8:421
   Lebreton, J., 8:430
   Lezana, J. B., 8:530
   Llorente, J. A., 8:739–740
   medieval papacy, finances, 8:532
   Middle Ages, 6:873–874
   scientific Church history
      new interpretation, 6:877–878
      reference works and periodicals, 6:878–879
      source collections, 6:878–879
      special areas of church history, 6:880–881
      textbooks and special monographs, 6:878–880

Historiola Langobardorum Beneventi degentium (Erchempert), 5:318

History, philosophy of, 1:43, 4:372–373, 6:706–707, **881–886**, 8:578–579, 13:414

History and Future of Theocracy (Solov'ev), 13:307

The History and Genius of the Heidelburg Catechism (Nevin), 10:272

History and historicity (*Geschichtlichkeit*), **6:893**

History of Dogmas in Christian Antiquity (Tixeront), 14:94–95

History of England (Belloc), 2:231

History of England (Hume), 7:200

History of England (Lingard), 5:251

History of England, from the First Invasion by the Romans to the Accession of William and Mary in 1688 (Lingard), 8:595–596

A History of Freethought in the Nineteenth Century (Robertson), 5:968

History of ideas, 8:120–121

History of Latin Christianity down to the Death of Pope Nicholas V (Milman), 6:878

The History of Love (Rosmini-Serbati), 12:383

History of Medieval Philosophy (De Wulf), 8:824

History of My Calamities (Thierry of Chartres), 14:2

History of Philosophy (Copleston), 4:252

History of Philosophy (Turner), 14:246

History of Religion (Eliade), 5:154

History of religions hypothesis (date of Christmas), 3:551–552

A History of Religious Ideas (Eliade), 5:155

The History of the Apostolic Church (Schaff), 12:726

History of the Bishops of Hamburg (Bernold of Constance), 9:451

A History of the Catholic Church (Mourret), 10:36

History of the Catholic Church in New York (Smith), 13:234

A History of the Catholic Church in the Dioceses of Pittsburgh and Allegheny (Lambing), 8:306

History of the Catholic Church in the U.S. (Shea), 13:70

History of the Catholic Melkhite Community and of the Salvatorian Order (Tārîḫ Taifat ar-Rūm al-Malakîyat war Rahbānīat alMuḥalliṣītat) (Bacha), 2:8

History of the Christian Church to 600 A.D. (Schaff), 12:726

History of the Church (Hughes), 7:162

History of the Church (Jedin), 7:750

History of the Church of Reims (Flodoard of Reims), 9:447

History of the Corruptions of Christianity (Priestley), 5:260

History of the Diocese of Fort Wayne (Noll), 10:410

A History of the Dynasties (Bar-Hebraeus), 2:83

History of the English College at Doway (Tootell), 14:111

History of the Expansion of Christianity (Latourette), 8:372

History of the Famous Preacher Friar Gerund of Campazas (Isla), 11:622

History of the Franks (Gregory of Tours, St.), 6:113, 9:440, 12:606

The History of the Jesuits in England (Taunton), 13:766

History of the Jewish War (Justus of Tiberias), 8:103–104

History of the Jewish War against the Romans (Josephus), 12:308

A History of the Martyrs of Gorcum (Estius), 5:375

History of the Martyrs of Palestine (Eusebius of Caesarea), 12:606

History of the Monks of Egypt (Rufinus of Aquileia), 12:606

History of the Patriarchs (Severus), 13:42–43

History of the Popes from the Close of the Middle Ages (Pastor), 10:937–938, 12:743

History of the Princes of Carrara (Vergerio), 14:448

The History of the Protestant Reformation (Spalding), 13:404

History of the Reformation in Scotland (Knox), 8:226

A History of the Roman Catholic Church in the United States (O'Gorman), 10:565

The History of the Sabbath (Heylyn), 12:454

History of the Synoptic Tradition (Bultmann, tr. by Marsh), 5:521, 812

History of the Wars (De bellis, libri VIII) (Procopius of Caesarea), 11:738

History of the Y.M.C.A. in North America (Hopkins), 10:30

History of Vatican II (Gutierrez), 10:*623*

Hitchcock, George S., 11:625

Hitchcock, Henry Russell, 3:709, 715

Hitler, Adolf, 5:93, 6:185–186, 7:874–875, 8:108, 13:99

Hittinger, Russell, 10:186

Hittite and Hurrian religions, 1:118, **6:893–896**, 10:86–87

Hittites, 3:732, **6:896–898**, 8:395, 10:796–797

Hittorp, Mechior, **6:898**

HIV. *See* AIDS

Hiver, Angelique of the Incarnation (Mother), 7:371

Hiver, Rosalie. *See* Hiver, Angelique of the Incarnation (Mother)

Ḥiyya, Abraham Bar, 2:833, 7:864

Ḥizzuk Emunah (Strengthening of the Faith) (Isaac ben Abraham), 7:588

Der hl. Thomas v. Aquin (Werner), 12:774

Hlinka, Andrew, 13:221–222

Hlond, Augustyn (Card.), **6:898–899**, 11:450

Hmong people, 8:330

Hoa Dac Phan, Simon, 14:495

Hoan trinh Doan, John, 14:495

Hoban, Edward F. (Bp.), 12:786

Hoban, M. J. (Bp.), 12:609

Hobart, John H., 5:297

Hobbes, Thomas, 5:107, 255, 256, 6:*899*, **899–900**, 11:293
  absolutism, 1:44
  Alphonsus Liguori, St., 1:310
  Aristotelianism, 1:676
  atomism, 1:834
  Austin, John, 1:898
  British moralists, 2:622, 623
  Cambridge Platonists, 2:909
  Cartesianism, 3:184, 185
  causality, 3:306
  Church-State relations, 3:638
  common good, 4:18–19
  democracy, 4:640, 642
  demonstration, 4:653–654
  determinism and free will, 5:931, 938
  ethics, 5:395
  experience, 5:554
  freedom defined, 10:227
  judgment, 8:23, 25
  knowledge, theories of, 8:218
  Leibniz's opposition, 8:458
  Locke on state of nature, 8:745
  mechanism, 9:415–416
  metaphysics, 9:553
  moral goodness, 6:351
  natural law doctrine, 10:183, 202
  social contracts, 13:240, 483
  sovereignty, 13:371
  universals, 14:325

Hobbie v. Unemployment Appeals Comm'n of Florida (1987), 3:663

The Hobbit (Tolkien), 14:105

Hocedez, Edgar, **6:900–901**

Hoch, Lambert A. (Bp. of Bismarck), 2:423

Hochland (monthly), 10:75

Hockelmann, Anskar (Abbot), 5:319

Hocking, W. E., 12:70

Hodge, Charles, 6:*901*, **901**

Hodges, Joseph H. (Bp. of Wheeling, WV), 14:688–689

Hodgson, Sydney, Bl., 5:231, **6:901**

Hodgson v. Minnesota, 1:34

Hodoeporicon (Willibald, St.), 14:761

Hodur, Francis (Father), 11:86, 458–459

Hoell, Alexia (Mother), 5:885

Hoensbroech, Paul de, 5:213

Hoever, Johannes, 12:546

Hofbauer, Clement Mary, St., 1:914, 4:483–484, 6:902, **902**, 11:994, 12:530

Hofenstaufen, House of, 8:796

Höfer, Josef, 12:730

Hoffaeus, Paul, 1:72, 3:18

Höffding, H., 5:941

Hoffman, Melchior, 1:368, **6:902–903**, 12:795

Hoffmeister, Johannes, 1:889

Hofinger, Johannes, 5:3, **6:903**

Hofmann, Augustine, 5:139

Hofmann, Fritz, 3:584, 585

Hofmann, Johann IV of Admont, 1:117

Hofmann, Johann Christian von, 5:322–323

Hofstadter, Richard, 10:173

Hogan, John Baptist, 2:555, 3:291, **6:903–904**

Hogan, John Joseph (Bp.), **6:904**, 8:118

Hogan, William, Rev., 4:245, 5:223, **6:904**, 11:82–83

''Hoganism,'' 6:904

Hogarth, William, 3:678

Hoger of Bremen-Hamburg, St., **6:904–905**

Hogg, John, Bl., 5:231, **6:905**

Hohenbaum Van Der Meer, Moritz, **6:905**, 12:211

Hohenburg. See Mont Sainte-Odile Convent (Alsace)

Hohenheim, Theophrastus Bombastus von. See Paracelsus, Philippus Aureolus

Hohenstaufen family, 8:847, 907, 13:103

Holaind, René, 1:355, 2:564–565, **7:1**

Holbach, Paul Heinrich Dietrich, 5:107, 210, 255, 261, **7:1**, 9:320

Holbein, Hans (the Younger), 1:545, 2:522, 4:508

Holcot, Robert, 4:334, 10:412

Holden, Henry, **7:1–2**

Holdheim, Samuel, 7:873

Holey, K., 3:712

Holford, Thomas, Bl., 5:230

Holiday, Richard, Bl., 5:231, **7:2**

Holiness, **7:2**
    Fathers of the Church, 5:641
    Immaculate Conception, 7:331–334
    man, 7:3, 4, 9:87
    marks of the Church, 9:189–191
    Mary, Blessed Virgin, 9:249–253, 256
    as term, 7:2

Holiness (Papal Title), **7:4**

Holiness, in the Bible, **7:2–4**, 3–4, 8, 9–10, 8:525

Holiness, law of, **7:4–5**, 8:397, 525

Holiness, universal call to, **7:5–7**

Holiness Churches, 1:788, 3:722, **7:7–8**

Holiness of God, **7:8–9**, 8:71

Holiness of the Church, **7:9–10**

Holinshed, Raphael, 1:465

Holland. See Netherlands

Holland, Sharon L. (Sister), 3:59

Holland, Thomas, Bl., 5:235

Hollaz, David, **7:10**

Hollis, (Maurice) Christopher, **7:10–11**

Hollman, Henricus, 4:378

Hollweck, Josef, **7:11**

Holmes, Oliver Wendell, 3:379, 7:197

Holmes, Robert, 5:237, 519

Holocaust (sacrifice), **7:11–12**

Holocaust (Shoah), **7:12–16**, 874–875
    Brandsma, Bl. Titus, 3:139
    Church on moral failures of Catholics, 7:14–15, 647
    Hungary, 7:219, 223
    John Paul II (Pope), denouncement of, 7:13–15, 10:853
    Leviticus, Book of, 8:525
    Lithuania, 8:608
    papal response to, 3:758, 11:398
    restitution for, 7:223
    Stein, St. Edith, 3:139

Holofernes (biblical figure), 8:43, 44

Holscher, Gustav, 3:23, 5:520

Holste (Holstenius), Lukas, 1:534

Holstenius, Lucas, 8:534

Holtzmann, Heinrich Julius, 2:384, 5:521, **7:16**, 848, 13:695

Holtzmann, Walther, **7:16**

Holweck, Frederick G., **7:17**

Holy Alliance (Russia, 1815), 1:252, 2:1, **7:17**

Holy Angels Benedictine community (Jonesboro, AK), 2:261

Holy Apostles Church (Cologne), 3:844

Holy Childhood, Pontifical Association of the, 5:796

Holy Childhood Association, 5:796

Holy Chrism, 9:196

Holy Church of the Gesu at Marquette University (Milwaukee, WI), 14:779

Holy Communion and Worship of the Eucharist outside Mass, 4:37

Holy Cross. See Cross

Holy Cross Abbey (Ireland), **7:18**

Holy Cross Brothers, 8:311

Holy Cross Cathedral (Boston), 2:552, 553, 3:715

Holy Cross College (MA), 9:309

Holy Cross Congregation, 3:621, 9:893

Holy Cross convent (Poitiers), 1:180

Holy Cross Fathers, 3:9

Holy Cross Foreign Mission Seminary, 9:330

Holy Cross Friary (Mt. Calvary, Wisconsin), 5:904

The Holy Cross Hymnal (O'Connor), 10:544

Holy Cross Mission (Alaska), 1:209

Holy Cross of St. Andrew, Daughters of the, 5:834

Holy Cross Seminary (La Crosse, WI), 8:273

Holy Dying (Taylor), 13:770

The Holy Family (Engels and Marx), 5:222

Holy Family, feast of, 3:556–557

Holy Family Church (Kapfenberg-Hafendorf, Austria), 3:712

Holy Family Missionaries, **7:23–24**

Holy Family of Villefranche, Sisters of the, 12:279

Holy Family Sisters, 12:647

Holy Garment, 14:185

Holy Ghost Catholic Church (Denver), 3:859

Holy Ghost Fathers, **7:25–26**, 10:294
    Botswana, 2:559
    Cameroon, 2:913
    Cape Verde, 3:80
    Central African Republic, 3:344
    Chad, 3:359
    Congo, 4:104
    founding of, 3:621
    Kenya, 8:150
    Kulturkampf, 8:254
    Laval, J. D., 8:383
    Lefebvre, M., 8:446
    Liberia missions, 8:552
    Liberman's society, 8:556
    Sierra Leone, 13:110

Holy Ghost Hospital, 8:300

Holy Grail, 1:761–762, 4:401, 7:26–28, **26–29**, 27

Holy Hour, **7:30**

Holy House of Loreto, 3:471

Holy Innocents, **7:483–484**

Holy Innocents' Day, 2:574, 3:556

Holy Lance, **7:30–31**

Holy League, 7:216, **8:424–425**

Holy League of Nuremberg, 6:145

Holy Leagues, 4:410, 6:742–743

Holy Mosque of Mecca, 10:9

Holy Name, devotion to, 2:321, 3:557, **7:31–32**

Holy Name, iconography of, **7:32–33**

Holy Name Journal, 10:134

Holy Name of Jesus hospital (Paris), 3:417

Holy Name Society, 3:622

"Holy Negro." *See* Benedict the Moor, St.

Holy Office (Congregation of the Holy Roman and Universal Inquisition). *See* Roman Inqusition

Holy oils, **7:34–35**

Holy orders, Sacrament of, **7:35–42**
    categories, 7:36–38
    character conferred, 7:41
    Coptic, 4:257
    force and fear (Canon Law), 5:797
    minister of, 7:38–39
    recipient of, 7:39–41
    rite of, 7:38–41
    sacramental grace, 7:41
    sale of (simony), 13:136
    scripture, 7:35, 36

Holy Roman Empire, **7:42–44**
    anointing, 1:479
    Church history, 3:594
    conflicts, 3:637
    Eastern Schism and creation of, 5:23
    emperors of, authority, 7:42–44
    end of, 3:843, 845, 7:44
    as Germanic, 7:42
    humanism in, 7:190, 191–192
    liturgical music history, 8:682
    mission, Christian, 9:690
    papacy, 3:602, 603
    papal authority, 7:43–44, 8:294
    prince-bishops, 11:713–714
    as term, 7:42, 42–43
    See also Carolingian Dynasty; Carolingian era; Church and State; Hapsburg, House of; Investiture struggle; *specific emperors*

Holy Rood Abbey (Scotland), **7:44**

Holy Saturday. *See* Easter Vigil

Holy See, **7:44**
    China, relations with, 3:502, 505–506
    Communist bloc, relations with, 3:200–201, 625, 627
    diplomatic corps, 8:224
    France, 13:198
    India, diplomatic posts, 9:843
    Kuwaiti relations, 8:259
    Lateran Pacts, 8:356–357, 357–358

Latin American independence, 8:343–344

liturgical laws, 8:670

Mariology, 9:172

Maronite Church, relations with, 9:195, 197–198

Papal Secretariate of State, 8:194

prerogatives of, 13:54

rapprochement with France, 8:389

representatives of, 9:779–780

Shroud of Turin, 13:96

Slovak accord (2000), 13:224

U.S., diplomatic relations with, 1:585, 3:627, 659

See also Vatican

Holy Sepulcher, **12:924–926**, *926*

Holy Sepulcher Basilica (Jerusalem), 1:757

Holy Spirit
    in Canon Law, 3:36
    charismatic prayer, 3:391
    Church and the, 14:134–135
    Constantinople Council I, 4:190
    contemplation, 4:206, 207, 208, 209
    creeds, 4:349–355
    Cyril and Methodius, 13:217
    divine mission of, 9:735–736, 737
    gift of understanding, 14:295
    Holiness churches, 7:7
    holiness of, 7:4
    John Paul II (Pope), 4:856–857
    Leo XIII (Pope), 4:792
    ministries as gift from, 9:652
    monarchianism, 9:780
    Origen's theology, 10:657
    as paraclete-advocate and paraclete-defender, 10:873
    sin against, 13:158
    soul of the Church, 13:358–359
    spiration, 13:420–421
    Spirit of God, 13:426–428
    subordinationism, 13:566
    teaching authorities of the Church, as guide for, 13:775–776
    theology of Church, 3:584, 587, 589
    tradition regarding role of, 14:133

Holy Spirit, baptism in, 3:393, **7:45**

Holy Spirit, devotion to, **7:46**, 13:100

Holy Spirit, fruits of, **7:46–47**

Holy Spirit, gifts of, **7:47–49**, 14:793
    charisms, 3:390
    consecrated life as, 4:154, 155
    Corinthians Epistles, 4:267
    counsel, gift of, 4:306
    Fear of the Lord, 5:653–654

imposition of hands, 7:365–366

knowledge, 8:207

Holy Spirit, iconography of, **7:49–51**

Holy Spirit, University of (Kalik), 8:427

Holy Spirit Church, 3:711

Holy Spirit Missionary Sisters, **7:53**

Holy Spirit Monastery (Italy), 8:560

Holy Synod, 4:196–197, 5:717, **7:53–54**, 10:692–693, 694, 12:424

Holy Thursday, **7:54–55**, 8:718

Holy Trinity. *See* Trinity, Holy

Holy Trinity Fathers. *See* Trinitarians

Holy Union Sisters, **7:55–56**

Holy War, 8:6, 170, 14:634–635

Holy water, blessing of, 14:661

Holy Week, 7:*56*, **56**
    Hereford Use, 6:769
    Lent, 8:468–470
    litanies, 8:601
    Ordinal of Pius XII (Pope), 4:37, 5:16, 17, 10:811
    reformed liturgical books, 8:641
    themes, 8:470

Holy Wisdom, Church of. *See* Hagia Sophia

Holy Year, 1:259, **7:56–57**, 11:354

Holyday observance. *See* Sunday and holyday observance

Holywood, Christopher (Father), 5:753, **7:58**

Holzhauser, Bartholomew, **7:58**

Holzinger, Franz Josef, 1:321

Holzklau, Thomas, 14:776

Holzmeister, Clemens, 3:711, 712

Homage, 7:525–536

Homans, George, 13:283

Home Missioners of America (*Societas Missionarium Domesticorum Americas*). *See* Glenmary Home Missioners

Home Rule Movement (Ireland), 10:441

Homelessness, religious, 5:53, 56

Homer (Greek poet)
    aesthetics, 1:142
    afterlife, 1:166
    allegory, 1:292
    anthropomorphism, 1:510
    anxiety, 1:540
    Byzantine poetry, 2:804
    daimones, 4:495
    earth cult, 5:2
    sacrifice in, 12:508–509
    soul, 13:337

Homeric religion, 6:451, 10:88–89

Homestead Act (1862), 7:290

Homicide, 4:220

Homiletics, 2:773, 795, 5:507, **7:58–61**, 8:61

See also Preaching, homiletic theory

Homiletics, teaching of, **7:61–62**, 8:61

Homilies. *See* Homily; Preaching

Homilies (early Christian writings), 11:799

Homilies (Gregory the Great), 3:229

Homilies of James of Kokkinobaphos, 9:275, 276–277, 279

Homilies on Ezekiel (St. Gregory I), 6:482

Homilies on the Canticle of Canticles (St. Gregory I), 6:482

Homilies on the Gospel (St. Gregory I), 6:482

Homily, **7:62–64**, 948, 8:666, 11:631, 737

See also Preaching; Sermon

Homily for Palm Sunday (Eulogius [Patriarch of Alexandria], St.), 5:448

Homily on Luke (Titus of Bostra), 14:93

Homily on Palm Sunday (Titus of Bostra), 14:93

Homily Service, 8:646

Homines Intelligentiae, **7:64**

Hominisation, **7:64–65**

L'Homme machine (La Mettrie), 5:261, 9:319–320

Hommer, Joseph von (Bp.), 3:845

Homoeans, 1:663

Homoeousians, 1:663

Homoousios, 4:197–198, **7:65–66**

Acacius of Caesarea, 1:51

Alexander (Patriarch of Alexandria), St., 1:267

Cyril of Jerusalem, 4:471, 472

Eusebius of Caesarea, 5:451–452

Eusebius of Nicomedia, 5:454

First Council of Nicaea, 1:267, 661, 662, 3:560–561, 594

Holy Trinity controversy, 14:203

Nicene Creed, 4:353

Synod of Ancyra (358), 1:398

See also Arianism; Christology controversies (patristic era); Consubstantiality; Nicene Creed

Homophobia, 7:71, 72, 73

Homosexuality, **7:66–71**

Canadian law, 3:11

Catholic higher education, 3:11

causes of, 7:67–69, 71–72

Dignity/USA, 4:745–746

Greece (ancient), 14:814

Paul, St. on, 13:49

Romans, Epistle to the, 13:49

Homosexuality and pastoral care, 7:69–70, **71–73**

Homosexuality and Western Christian Tradition (Baily), 7:66

Hompesch, Ferdinand von, 8:194

Homs. *See* Emesa (Homs)

Honan, John, 7:581

Honduran mission, 9:707

Honduras, **7:73–75**, *75*, *76*, 9:707

Honegger, Arthur, 11:562

Hong Kong, **7:75–77**, 13:80

Hong Xiuquan (Hung Hsiu-ch'üan), 3:499

L'Honnête femme (Veuillot), 14:466

Honolulu Diocese (HI), 6:671

Honor, 4:230, 677, 928, **7:78**

Honorat a Biala Rat. *See* Kozka, Karolina, Bl.

Honorati T. cursus theologicus scholastico-dogmaticus et moralis (Tournely), 14:123

Honoratus of Amiens, St., **7:78**

Honoratus of Arles (Bp.), St., 1:694, 3:206, 7:79, *79*, 8:502, 511

Honoratus of Lérins (Bp. of Arles). *See* Honoratus of Arles (Bp.), St.

Honoré, Jean (Bp.), 3:237

Honorée de Sainte-Marie, 3:137

Honorius (Roman Emperor), 7:*17*, **87–88**

Britain, 2:621

Donatism, 1:859

Eulalius (Antipope), 5:447–448

Pelagianism, 1:860, 3:188

works of charity, 3:409

Honorius I (Pope), **7:79–82**, *80*

Birinus, St., 2:408

Braulio, St., 2:585

churches in Rome, 12:356

condemnation, 4:193

Eastern Schism, 5:23

exemption, 5:529

Leo II (Pope), St., 8:478

Monoenergism, 2:749

St. Agnes Basilica, 1:178

Third Council of Constantinople, 1:174, 2:750

Honorius II (Antipope), 1:253, 3:777, **7:83**, 155

Honorius II (Pope), 3:318, 5:912, **7:82**

Honorius III (Pope), 7:*83*, **83–85**

Apostolic Penitentiary, 11:75

Bogomilism, 2:459

Canon Law, 3:49

Carmelites, 3:*127*, 132

Caulites, 3:296

Chaldean Catholic Church, 3:366

Christian of Prussia, 3:537

Crosier Fathers, 2:609

Frederick II, 5:926, 14:14

Herman of Salza, 6:783

Jacques de Vitry, 2:205

monastic reform, 2:271

Rusudan, 6:155

Savelli family, 12:711

taxes, 8:532

Honorius IV (Pope), 1:594, 6:220, **7:85–86**, 12:711

Honorius Augustodunensis, 9:454

Honorius Magister, 3:49, 4:597, **7:88**

Honorius of Autun, 3:239, 4:357, 5:206, **7:88**, 12:758

Honorius of Canterbury, St., 3:70, **7:89**

Hontheim, Johann Nikolaus von (Bp. of Trèves), 3:614–615, 639, **7:89–90**

absolutism, 6:182

Caprara, Giovanni Battista, 3:92

Clemens Wenzeslaus, 3:773

Clement XIII (Pope), 3:791

Febronianism, 5:257, 657–659

Gallicanism, 3:54, 615

See also Febronianism

Hoogewerff, G. H., 7:284

Hooght, E. van der, 2:356

Hooghvorst, Emilie Olympe Marie Antoinette van der Linden d' (Baroness). *See* Oultremont, Emilie d', Bl.

Hoogstraten, Jacob van, 5:306

Hook, Sidney, 10:205

Hook literary hand style, 10:768

Hooke, Richard, 1:834

Hooke, Robert, 2:402

Hooker, J. D., 4:531, 532

Hooker, Richard, 1:443, 5:318, **7:90–92**

Aristotelianism, 1:676, 678

British moralists, 2:622

Caroline Divines, 1:409, 3:152

Church-State relations, 3:638

scholasticism, 12:768

Hooker, Thomas, 3:647, 4:121–122, **7:92**

Hooper, John, 2:507, 12:10

Hoople, William, 3:722

Hoorn, Peter, 2:607

Hope, **7:92–102**

act of, 7:99–100

appetite, 1:602

certitude, 3:356

courage, 4:316

death, 4:575

Hope *(continued)*
  despair as sin against, 7:102
  faith and charity compared to, 7:92,
    94, 96, 100–101
  Isaiah's message, 7:597–598
  motives, 7:96–98
  necessity, 7:101–102
  object of, 7:91–96
  presumption as sin against, 7:102,
    11:686
  spiritual reading, 11:941
  subject of, 7:98–99
  theology of, 13:925–927
  virtue and habit, 7:94, 100
Hope, in the Bible, 7:92–103, **102–103**
Hope, St., 5:608–609
Hope in Time of Abandonment (Ellul),
  5:172
Hope of salvation, **7:103–107**
Höpfl, Hildebrand, 2:350
Hopkins, C. Howard, 10:30
Hopkins, Gerard Manley, 1:120, 5:880,
  7:*107*, **107–110**, 13:320
Hopkins, John, 3:150, 7:256
Hopkins, Samuel, 5:193
Hoppe, Norbert Strotmann, 7:528
Horae Paulinae (Paley), 10:803
Horan, Ellamay, 12:524
Horby, C. H. St. John, 2:523
Horeb, Mount, **7:110**
  See also Sinai, Mount
Horgan, Paul, 10:287
Horgan, Thaddeus Daniel, **7:110**
Hori, Michael Diaz, Bl., 7:733
Horkheimer, Max, 5:914
Hormannseder, Anselm, 1:880
Hormez, John. *See* John IX Hormizd
  (Chaldean Patriarch)
Hormisdas (Pope), St., 5:264, **7:110–112**
  Acacian Schism, 1:50, 7:111
  Canon Law, 3:39
  Dioscorus (Antipope), 4:756
  Epiphanius' profession of faith, 5:291
  Justin I (Byzantine Emperor), 3:595,
    8:92
  relics, 1:314
Horne, Herman, 5:94
Horne, William, Bl., 5:227, 7:1019
Horner, Nicholas, Bl., 2:30, 428, 5:231,
  7:112
Horner, Richard, Ven., 5:233
Horney, Conrad, 2:874
Horoscopes, 1:811, **7:112–114**
Horrors of Transportation (Ullathorne),
  14:281

Horses, in the Bible, 6:898
Hort, Fenton John Anthony, 2:367
Horton, Douglas, **7:114**
Hortulana, Bl. *See* Ortolana, Bl.
Hortulanus, 4:894
Hortulus animae, **7:114–115**
Hortulus reginae (Meffreth), 11:613
Hortus deliciarum (Herrad of
  Landsberg), 5:206, 6:805, 9:454
Horus (Egyptian deity), 7:605
Horus-Harpocrates, 3:174
Horváth, Mihály (Bp. of Csanád), 7:217
Hosanna, **7:115**, 8:617
Hosea (King of Israel), 4:674
Hosea, Book of, **7:115–117**
  Baal, 2:2
  beatific vision, 2:171
  beatitudes, 2:178
  covenant, 4:327
  El (God), 5:143
  eschatology, 5:334
  Gentiles, 6:140
  love, Divine elective, 8:831
  sin, 13:143
  Song of Songs, 13:319
  spirit, 13:424
Hosius, Stanislaus (Card.), **7:117**, 11:442
  Abercromby, Robert, 1:20–21
  catechesis, 3:242
  Council of Trent, 12:665
  Counter Reformation, 3:613, 7:117
Hosius of Córdoba (Bp.)
  Arianism mission, 1:266–267, 661,
    685
  clerical celibacy/marriage, 3:323, 325
  Constantine I (the Great) (Roman
    Emperor), 3:594, 4:181
  Council of Sardica, 1:818, 12:692
  exile of, 1:662, 818, 3:632, 4:197
  homoousios, 4:198
  Nicene Creed, 1:661–662
Hospice Movement, **7:117–118**, 13:853
Hospital Brothers of St. Anthony, 12:535
Hospital de Nuestra Señora de la Paz
  (Seville, Spain), 3:*695*
Hospital del pobres (Lisbon, Portugal),
  3:416
Hospital del Rei (Lisbon, Portugal),
  3:416
Hospital Progress (1924-37)
  (Fitzpatrick), 5:753
Hospital Sisters of the Third Order of St.
  Francis, 5:884
Hospitality, **7:118–119**
  Benedictines, 2:266

  kindness, 8:171
  religious, 12:88
  works of charity, 3:405, 407,
    411–412, 414
Hospitaller Sisters of St. John of
  Jerusalem, 8:194
Hospitaller Sisters of the Sacred Heart of
  Jesus, 9:494
Hospitallers and Hospital Sisters,
  7:119–122
  Bethlehemites, 2:349
  Canada, 3:9
  Crusaders' states, 4:402
  first U.S. Catholic hospital, 13:174
  Order of the Holy Spirit, 7:51–52
  Poverty Movement, 11:572
  Scottish religious orders, 12:833
Hospitallers of St. John of God, **7:122**
  Bolivia, 2:466
  Chile, 3:485
  Colombia, 3:848, 850
  entered by St. Pampuri, 10:817
Hospitallers of St. John of God, Martyrs
  of the, BB., **7:122–125**
Hospitallers of St. John of Jerusalem,
  3:412, 8:197
Hospitallers of St. Lazarus of Jerusalem,
  1:846, 7:121, **125–126**
Hospitals. *See* Hospitallers; *specific
  dioceses and archdioceses; specific
  hospitals; specific religious orders*
Hospitals, history of, **7:126–134**
Höss, Crescentia, Bl., **7:134**
Hostiensis (Card.), 3:48, **7:134–136**,
  8:295–296, 13:102
Hot iron ordeal, 10:626
Hotchkin, John Francis, **7:136–137**
Hôtel-Dieu (Montréal), 3:4, 9:103
Hôtel-Dieu (Québec), 3:4
Hôtel-Dieu de Paris, 3:412, 417–418,
  7:127–128, **137–139**, 8:322
Hotho, Heinrich Gustav, 6:709
Hotman, François, 5:702
Houben, Charles of Mount Argus, Bl.,
  7:139
Houbigant, Charles F., 5:519
Houck, George Francis, **7:139**
Houck, William R. (Bp. of Jackson,
  MS), 7:686
Houdon, Jean-Antoine, 2:649
Houghton, John, St., 5:225, 547,
  7:139–140, 12:8, 210
  Act of Succession, 8:772
  Middlemore, Humphrey, 9:617
"The Hound of Heaven" (Thompson),
  14:58

Hours of Étienne Chevalier (prayer book), 11:605

The Hours of the Passion of Our Lord Jesus Christ, 5:865

House churches, 2:145–146, 3:503–504, 11:718–719

House Committee on Un-American Activities, 10:172

House of Fame (Chaucer), 3:452

House of Jesus of Bethlehem. *See* Sheen Charterhouse

The House of Judah (Bêt Yehûdâ) (Levinsohn), 6:663

House of Livig (Palatine Hill, Rome), 12:*509*

Houselander, Frances Caryll, 4:891, **7:140**

Houteff, Florence, 4:542

Houteff, Victor T., 4:541–542

Houtin, Albert, **7:141**

Hovda, Robert W., **7:141**

Höver, Johannes, 12:735

Höver, Philipp, 1:2

Hovhannes IV Otznetzi. *See* John of Otzun

How the Pope Became Infallible: Pius IX and the Politics of Persuasion (Hasler), 7:451–452

How to Educate Human Beings (Fitzpatrick), 5:753

How to Find Heaven Upon Earth (Elizabeth of the Trinity), 5:167

Howard, Bernard Edward (12th Duke of Norfolk). *See* Norfolk, Bernard Edward Howard, 12th Duke of

Howard, Bernard Edward (13th Duke of Norfolk). *See* Norfolk, Bernard Edward Howard, 13th Duke of

Howard, Charles (10th Duke of Norfolk). *See* Norfolk, Charles Howard, 10th Duke of

Howard, Charles (11th Duke of Norfolk). *See* Norfolk, Charles Howard, 11th Duke of

Howard, Edward (9th Duke of Norfolk). *See* Norfolk, Edward Howard, 9th Duke of

Howard, Edward Daniel (Abp. of Portland, OR), 10:646, 11:530

Howard, Francis William (Bp. of Covington), 4:331, **7:141–142**

role in NCEA, 10:160

Howard, Henry (6th Duke of Norfolk). *See* Norfolk, Henry Howard, 6th Duke of

Howard, Henry (7th Duke of Norfolk). *See* Norfolk, Henry Howard, 7th Duke of

Howard, Henry Granville (14th Duke of Norfolk). *See* Norfolk, Henry Granville Howard, 14th Duke of

Howard, John, 3:418

hospital reform, 7:131

Howard, John (Duke of Norfolk). *See* Norfolk, John Howard, Duke of

Howard, Philip, St., 5:232, **7:142**, 10:423

Howard, Philip Thomas (Card.), 5:171, **7:142–143**, *143*

Howard, Thomas (5th Duke of Norfolk). *See* Norfolk, Thomas Howard, 5th Duke of

Howard, Thomas (8th Duke of Norfolk). *See* Norfolk, Thomas Howard, 8th Duke of

Howard, Thomas (Earl of Arundel). *See* Arundel, Thomas Howard, Earl of

Howard, Thomas, Duke of Norfolk. *See* Norfolk, Thomas Howard, Duke of

Howard, William (Viscount Stafford), 10:495–496

Howard, William, Bl., 5:237

Howell, Vernon (David Koresh), 4:541, 542–543

Howison, George Holmes, 7:301, 12:70

Howlett, William Joseph, **7:143**

Howman, John. *See* John of Feckenham

Howze, Joseph L. (Bp. of Biloxi), 2:397

Hoxha, Enver, 1:216

Hoyos, Fermín (Father), 5:450

Hoyuelos Gonzalo, Jacinto, Bl., 7:124

Hromcla, Synod of (1179), 1:701

Hrotswitha. *See* Roswitha of Gandersheim

Hroznata, Bl., **7:144**, 11:666, 13:825

Hryciuk, Anicet, 11:584

Huangbo (Chinese scholar), 3:511

Huangdi (Emperor of China), 3:507

Hubbard, L. Ron, 12:823

Hüber, Benedict, 14:51

Huber, Josef, 1:117

Hubert, Jean François (Bp. of Quebec), 5:355, **7:144**

Hubert, Liège, St. *See* Hubert of Maastricht, St.

Hubert of Maastricht, St., 2:216, **7:144**, *145*, 10:255, 12:549, 550

Hubert Walter (Abp. of Canterbury), 7:88, **144–145**

Hubmaier, Balthasar, 1:368, **7:145**

Hübner, E., 10:774

Huc, Évariste Régis, **7:145–146**

Hucbald of Saint-Amand, 1:99, 3:161, **7:146**, 246, 12:246, 607

Hucke, Helmut, 10:581

Huddleston, John, 3:433, 5:248, **7:146–147**

Ḥûdrâ (liturgical book), 5:5, 6

Hudson, Daniel Eldred, 7:*147*, **147**

Hudson, Henry, 10:320

Hudson, Winthrop, 3:756

Huelgas de Burgos Abbey (Spain), 1:8, 3:744, **7:147–148**

Huerta, Dolores, 2:872

Huet, Pierre Daniel (Bp. of Avranche), 3:186, 5:852, **7:148**, 12:31, 13:203

Hügel, Friedrich von, **7:148–149**, 9:755

Hugenberg, Alfred, 3:341

Hugh (Earl of Chester), 3:469

Hugh, SS., **7:154**

Hugh II of Northwold, 2:714

Hugh Bonnevaux, St., **7:149**

Hugh Capet (King of France), 3:172, 7:927, 12:588

Hugh Cavellus, 12:764

Hugh of Amiens (Abp. of Rouen), 1:115, 5:514, **7:149–150**

Hugh of Anzy (Abbot), 12:585

Hugh of Auxerre (Bp.), 1:927

Hugh of Balma, 3:192, **7:150**, 14:65

Hugh of Bayeux (Bp.), 2:163

Hugh of Cluny, St., 3:813, **7:150–151**

Charité-sur-Loire Abbey, 3:394

church architecture, 3:811, 814

Councils of Chalon-Sur-Saône, 3:373

Lewes Priory, 8:527

Robert I (Duke of Burgundy), 1:927

See also Cluniac Reform

Hugh of Die (Abp.), 1:493, 927, 2:649, 5:843, **7:151**, 12:268

Hugh of Digne, **7:151**, 12:615, 616

Hugh of Flavigny, 1:462

Hugh of Fleury, **7:152**, 12:539

Hugh of Fosse, Bl., **7:152**, 11:665–666

Hugh of Fouilloy, **7:152**, 9:455

Hugh of Grenoble (Bp.), St., 2:649, 3:193, **7:152–153**, 153

Hugh of Honau, **7:153**

Hugh of Leicester (Bp. of Daventry), 4:535–536

Hugh of Lincoln, St., 3:192, 194, 7:153–154, 154

Hugh of Lobbes, 1:396

Hugh of Newcastle (Novocastro), **7:154–155**, 12:762

Hugh of Orléans, 9:457

Hugh of Pisa. *See* Huguccio

Hugh of Remiremont (Card.), 1:253, **7:155**

Hugh of Saint-Cher, 1:407, 2:376, 3:132, **7:156**, 437, 8:52

Hugh of Saint-Lô (Bp.), 12:558
Hugh of Saint-Victor, 3:68, 5:516, **7:156–159**
  Adam of Saint-Victor, 1:109
  Albert the Great, St., 1:224
  Andrew of Saint-Victor, 1:406–407
  Anointing of the Sick, 1:482
  atomism, 1:833
  Augustinianism, 1:877
  Bernard of Clairvaux, 2:311
  biblical theology, 2:382
  Bonaventure, St., 2:482
  catechesis, 3:239, 240
  Clarenbaud of Arras, 3:761
  faith, 5:597
  influence on Richard of Saint-Victor, 12:234–235
  mysticism, 12:759
  restored use of reason in study of Scripture, 13:905–906
  sacraments, 12:468
  Saint-Victor Monastery, 12:589–590
  soul, 13:343
  William of Champeaux, 14:485
  works of, 9:452–453, 12:716
Hugh of Strassburg, 1:226, 5:206
Hugh of Vermandois (Abp.), 12:583
Hughes, Alfred C. (Bp. of Baton Rouge), 2:156
Hughes, Angela (Mother), **7:159–160**
Hughes, Hugh Price, 5:928
Hughes, John Joseph (Abp. of New York), 2:165, 5:82, 7:*160*, **160–162**, 10:313–314
  apostolic delegation in the United States, 1:582
  Cummings, Jeremiah Williams, 4:437
Hughes, Philip, 1:296, 2:507, **7:162**
Hughes, William A. (Bp. of Covington), 4:331
Hugo, Charles Hyacinthe, **7:162–163**
Hugo, Victor, 3:669, 5:874
Hugo Candidus. *See* Hugh of Remiremont
Hugolino. *See* Gregory IX (Pope)
Hugolino of Gualdo Cattaneo, Bl., **7:163**
Hugolino of Orvieto, 1:888, 7:163, **163**
Hugon, Édouard, 3:823, **7:163–164**, 12:748, 776
Huguccio (Hugh of Pisa), **7:164–165**, 12:403
  Alanus Anglicus, 1:207
  Canon Law, 1:207, 3:47, 50
  conciliarism, 4:54
  decretals as form, 4:600, 606

Huguenots, **7:165–169**
  Amiens, 1:359
  Beza, Theodore, 2:352
  Caribbean, 3:118
  Carthusians, 3:194
  Catherine de Médicis, 3:266–267
  Celles-Sur-Belle Monastery, 3:329
  Chartres, 3:441
  Civil War in France, 5:849
  colonial United States, 3:646
  doctrine of, 7:166
  Duplessis-Mornay, Philippe, 4:944
  Francis (Duke of Guise), 6:578
  Holy League, 8:424
  L'Hôpital, 8:530–531
  Louis XIV, 8:803–804
  martyrs, 1:844–845, 951–952
  persecution of, 7:166
  political infuence, 7:166–167
  refugees in Berlin, 13:406
  sacking of Bayeux, 2:163
  St. Bartholomew's Day Massacre, 5:849, 12:537
  Sixtus V (Pope), 13:198–199
  social contract, 13:240
  as term, 7:166
  wars of religion, 7:167
  See also Nantes, Edict of; Wars of religion
Hugues (Abp. of Lyons), 1:926
Huizar, Pedro, 3:715
Huldah (Hebrew prophetess), 11:765
Hull, Ernest Reginald, **7:169**
Hull, John, 12:98
Hulsbosch, Ansfridus, 12:783
Hulst, Maurice d', 7:503
Human act, **7:169–173**, 420
  acts of man distinguished from, 7:169
  analysis, 7:173–174
  dead, prayers for, 4:556–557
  deliberation, 4:629, 5:932
  dogmatic definition, 4:611–612
  external principles, 7:171–172
  freedom, 7:172–173
  internal principles, 7:169–171
  moral circumstances, 3:742–743
  moral quality, 5:390–391
  sin as, 13:150
Human anatomy, 12:806
Human destiny, 12:863–866
Human dignity, 9:867
"Human Evolution: A Challenge to Thomistic Ethics" (Fay), 10:194

Human genome project, 1:765–766, **7:174–179**, 11:475
Human Immunodeficiency Virus (HIV). *See* AIDS
Human life amendment, 1:32–33
Human mind, 9:90
Human nature, 9:486–487, 13:619
Human race, 13:787
Human respect, **7:179**
Human rights, 1:456, 8:552–553, 9:867, 10:199–200, 13:467–468
Human rights abuses, 2:213, 7:502, 996–997, 9:68
  See also Slavery
Human sacrifice, 12:506–508, **506–508**, *507*
Human Sexuality, 7:69–70
Human soul, 9:95, 348, 735–736, 14:739–740
Human will, 14:582, **719–723**
  See also Will and willing; Will power
Humanae salutis (apostolic constitution, John XXIII), 6:869, 13:117
Humanae salutis (papal letter, Leo XIII), 9:681
Humanae vitae (encyclical, Paul VI), 5:40, 860, 6:645, **7:179–181**, 450–451, 11:32
  Austria, 1:916
  birth control, 1:490, 4:222, 13:258
  natural family planning, 1:490, 10:178
  opposition to, 10:521, 12:575
Humani generis (encyclical, Pius XII), 5:496, 712, 6:394, **7:181–182**, 10:667, 849
  demonology, 4:649
  evolution, 4:345, 347
  opposition to théologie nouvelle, 3:624, 6:412, 12:775
  scholasticism, 3:466
  support for Thomism, 14:23–24
  transubstantiation, 1:64, 14:159
  truth in theology, 4:815–816
  vision of God, desire for, 4:691
Humanism, **7:182–193**
  Ambrose Traversari, Bl., 1:340
  Amerbach, Veit, 1:349
  Anabaptists, 1:369
  anthropocentrism, 1:508
  Arévalo, Rodrigo Sánchez de, 1:647
  Aristotelianism, 1:675–676
  ars moriendi, 1:733
  astrology, 1:813
  Augsburg, 1:848

Augustinians, 1:888

Bessarion, Cardinal, 2:341

Biondo, Flavio, 2:408

Boccaccio, Giovanni, 2:449–450

Bostius, Arnold, 2:551

Brant, Sebastian, 2:584

Byzantine civilization, 2:776

Callistus III (Pope), 2:881

Canisius, St. Peter, 3:18–19

Carmelites, 3:142

Cassander, George, 3:204–205

catechesis, 3:232, 241, 242

Chaucer, Geoffrey, 3:450

Christian, 7:182, 193–194, 197–198

civic, 12:114–115

Colet, John, 3:72, 232, 241, 606, 832–833

Crockaert, Peter, 4:374

Dalberg, Johann von, 4:498

Devotio Modern supported, 10:258–259

Florence (Italy) circle of, 12:622

Gaguin, Robert, 6:49

Greek revival, 7:185–186, 187

Hebrew revival, 7:185, 186–187

hymnody, 7:250, 254

Jansenism, 3:614

Jesuits, 3:611

Latin, 7:184, 188

links between New Age Movement, 10:274

manuscripts and libraries, 7:185

Maritain, Jacques, 9:179

Middle Ages, 7:184, 193

New Order Movement, 4:514

Nietzsche's influence, 10:390

origin of the term, 12:15

Petrarch, 7:184–185, 190

positive theology, 3:613

Reformation and Counter Reformation, 7:191–192

Renaissance, defined, 7:182, 184

Renaissance art, 12:115–116

Renaissance humanists, 12:5, 15, 113–116

Reuchlin, Johann, 12:180–181

scholasticism, 7:182, 184, 191, 192–193

secularism, 12:863–866

Shirwood, J., 13:88

Sinzig, Pedro, 13:163–164

speculative theology, 13:898

spread of, 7:190

study methods, 7:188–189

as term, 7:182

textual scholarship, 7:187

typography, 7:187–188

vernacular, 7:189–190

Humanism, Christian, 7:182, **193–194**, 197–198, 8:541

Humanism, devout, **7:194**

Humanism, secular, 7:182, **194–198**

Humanism and, 7:196

"The Humanist Manifesto," 7:194–195

Humanity of Christ, 13:573–574

Aelred, St., 1:138

art, 1:743

ascension, 1:771

assumptus homo theology, 1:802–803

Athanasian Creed, 1:816

Carmelite spirituality, 3:134, 136

Christian anthropology, 3:531

Christmas, 3:555

Cistercian spirituality, 3:749

Clare of Assisi, St., 3:760

iconography of, 7:859–860

See also Apollinarianism; Arianism; Christocentrism; Christology; Eutychianism; Incarnation; Monophysitism; Monothelitism

Humankind, 8:759–760, 893

Humanum genus (encyclical, Leo XIII), 3:101

Humbeline, Bl., **7:198**

Humbert, Jean-Baptiste, 2:380, 5:51

Humbert of Maroilles, St., **7:198**

Humbert of Romans, Bl., 4:837–838, **7:198–199**, 11:619

Humbert of Silva Candida (Card.), 3:600, 5:843, **7:199–200**, 10:37

Church-State relations, 3:635

Constantine IX (Byzantine Emperor), 4:175

Deodatus of Nevers, St., 4:673

reordination, 12:128

simony, 13:136

Hume, David, **7:200–202**, *201*, 11:294

abstraction, 1:45

accident, 1:62

agnosticism, 1:181–182, 184

analysis and synthesis, 1:382

associationism, 1:796

atomism, 1:831

biology, 2:407

Bradley, Francis Herbert, 2:577

British moralists, 2:622, 623–624

causality, 1:78, 79, 3:300–301, 302, 308

certitude, 3:352

choice, 3:521

Clarke, Samuel, 3:766

consciousness, 4:153

continuum, 4:215

cosmological argument, 4:285

"disposition theory," 14:326

efficient causality, 5:101, 102, 197, 7:201–202

empiricism, 5:197, 198, 7:201–202, 12:47

Enlightenment, 5:255

essence, 5:361

existence, 5:533

experience, 5:554

free will, 5:931, 939

God, 7:202

idea, 7:295

induction, 7:434, 435

influence on Comte, Auguste, 11:542–543

judgment, 8:23, 25

knowledge, theories of, 8:218

law of causality, 8:120

Locke's influence, 8:745

metaphysics, 9:554

methodology, 7:200–201, 9:566

miracles, 9:667

moral philosophy, 12:34

natural rights, 10:203

necessary causes in nature, 10:227

occasionalism doctrine of, 10:526–527

origin and development of mythology, 10:128

pessimism, 11:169

philosophy of religion, 12:69

physical laws, 11:315

quality, 11:849

relation, 12:42, 43

Rousseau, Jean-Jacques, 12:392

self, concept of, 12:882–883

skepticism, 7:200–202, 13:203

social contract, 13:240

solipsism, 13:303

soul, 13:346

substance, 7:201, 13:578

works of, 7:200

Hume, George Basil (Card.), 1:366, **7:202–204**

Humeral veil, 4:*249*, **249**

Humiliana de Circulus, Bl., **7:204**

Humiliati (lay poverty movement), **7:204–205**, 665

Borromeo, St. Charles, 2:541

Guido the Lombard, 6:565

Lucius III (Pope), 1:231

Humiliati (lay poverty movement)
  (*continued*)
    preaching of, 11:612
    Sauli, Alexander, St., 12:708
Humility, 2:265, 5:896, **7:205–207**, 9:42, 11:941–942
Hummel, Johann Nepomuk, 1:234, **7:207–208**
Hummel, Maria Innocentia, **7:208**
Humphrey (Duke of Gloucester), 2:183
Humphrey, Edward, 5:960
Humphrey, Laurence, Bl., 5:231
Humphrey ap Richard. *See* Pritchard, Humphrey, Bl.
Hundred Schools, 3:508–510, 513
Hundred Years' War
    Airvault Monastery, 1:196
    Angers, 1:432
    Church history, 3:604
    Cistercians, 3:751
    Clement VI (Pope), 3:780
    clerical celibacy/marriage, 3:327
    hospital history, 7:130
Hunegundis, St., **7:208**
Huneric (King of the Vandals), 3:189
Hunermann, Peter (Bp. Thérouanne), 4:671
Hunfried, St., **7:208–209**
Hungary, **7:209–223**, *212, 213, 214, 215*
    Apor, Vilmos, Bl., 1:569
    Byzantine Basilians, 2:144
    Church-State relations, 9:650
    Cistercians, 5:108
    Communism, 3:200, 7:219–222
    Counter Reformation, 3:613, 4:314
    Croatia, 4:370
    Crusades, 4:412, 413
    demographic statistics, 7:209
    Draškovič, Georg de, 4:902
    ecclesiastical organization, 7:210, 218–219
    folk music, 8:227–228
    incursions into Freising, 8:327
    Lutheranism, 8:889
    map, 7:*211*
    Reformed churches, 4:80, 12:24
    Sigismund (Holy Roman Emperor), 13:115–116
    Simor, János, 13:136–137
    Slovak nationalism, 13:221–222
    Stephen I (King of Hungary), St., 13:513
Hunkeler, Edward J., 10:222
Hunnius, Aegidius, 6:253
Hunnius, Nikolaus, 6:253

Hunot, François, 12:277
Hunot, Jean, 12:277
Hunot, Sebastian-Loup, 12:277
Huns, 1:454, 3:595, 6:369, **7:223–224**
Hunt, Duane Garrison (Bp. Salt Lake City), **7:224**
Hunt, Eleanor, 5:237, 14:697
Hunt, Ralph, Rev., 12:648
Hunt, Robert, 5:295
Hunt, Thomas, Bl., 5:233, **7:225**
Hunt, Thurstan, Bl., 5:233, **7:225**
Hunt, Walter, **7:225**
Hunt v. McNair (1973), 3:667
Hunthausen, Raymond G. (Abp. of Seattle, WA), 9:827, 12:853
Huntington, William E., 5:299
Hunyadi, John, 2:881, 3:357, 7:211, 213
Huonder, Anton, **7:225–226**
Huong Van Nguyen, Lawrence, 14:495
Hupfeld, Hermann, 5:519, 11:90
Huppy, Louis Wulphy, 12:277
Hurezi (Horezi) Abbey (Moldovia), **7:226**
Hurley, Francis (Abp. of Anchorage), 1:209, 396
Hurley, Michael, 1:890, **7:226**
Huron people, 3:4, 8:697
Hurrian religion. *See* Hittite and Hurrian religions
Hurst, Richard. *See* Herst, Richard, Bl.
Hurtado, Caspar, **7:226**
Hurtado, José María Robles, St., 6:545
Hurtado Cruchaga, Alberto, Bl., **7:226–227**
Hurtado de Mendoza, Pedro, 12:767
Hurter, Hugo Von, **7:227**
Hus, John, 2:606, 3:605, **7:227–229**, *232*
    Constance Council, 4:170–171, 7:228–229
    death of, 4:480–481, 7:229, *232*
    heresy, 6:774
    papal Antichrist, 1:517
    relics, 12:55
    Simon of Cramaud, 13:132
    theological censure, 3:337, 604
    as Wyclifite, 7:229, 230
    See also Hussites
Ḥusayn (Islamic figure), 7:610
Husbands, duties of, 11:334
Husschyn, Johannes. *See* Oecolampadius, Johannes
Hussein (King of Jordan), 7:1029, 1030
Hussein, Saddam, 7:545–546
Al Hussein Mosque (Karbala, Iraq), 13:*84*

Husserl, Edmund, 5:362, 556, **7:229–230**, 10:510–511, 607, 11:297
    Aristotelianism, 1:678
    Brentano, Franz, 2:605
    intentionality, 7:518
    intuition, 7:534
    knowledge, theories of, 8:219, 220
    methodology, 9:567
    moral goodness, 6:351
    phenomena, 11:229
    phenomenology and existenialism, 12:3, 241
    philosophy and science, 11:300
    possibility, 11:552
    Scheler, Max, 12:731
    self, concept of, 12:884
    soul, 13:347
    transcendental Thomism, 14:54
    See also Phenomenology
Hussey, Anthony, 7:581
Hussgen, Johannes. *See* Oecolampadius, Johannes
Hussites and Hussitism, 2:606, **7:230–232**, *231*
    Black Madonna vandalization, 4:490
    Böhm, Hans, 2:461
    Church property, 3:727
    Council of Basel, 2:134, 3:604, 605
    Crusades against, 4:409, 413
    Czechs, 4:480–482
    Dominici, John, 4:855
    heresy, 6:774
    Hungary, 7:211
    John Capistran, St., 7:944
    prehistory, 7:230–231
    Taborites, 13:728
    See also Hus, John
Hutcheson, Francis, 1:145, 2:622, 623, 3:678
Hutchins, Robert Maynard, 5:92, 94, 10:194
Hutchinson, Anne, 3:647
Hutten, Christoph Franz von (Prince-Bp. of Würzburg), 7:233
Hutten, Christoph von (Bp. of Speyer), 7:233
Hutten, Moritz von (Bp. of Eichstätt), 7:233
Hutten, Ulrich von, 3:430, 816, 5:306, 7:232–233, *233*
Hutten family, **7:232–233**
Hutter, Jakob, **7:233–234**
Hutterites, 1:368, 369, 2:606, **7:234–235**, *235*
Huvelin, Henri, 7:148

Huxley, Aldous J., 5:397, 10:111, 14:361

Huxley, Julian, Sir, 7:196

Huxley, T. H., 3:623, 4:532
  agnosticism, 1:180
  Alexander, Samuel, 1:252
  evolutionary theory, 5:397, 495, 12:64

Huy Viet Phan, Augustin, 14:495

Huyen, Dominic, 14:495

Huygens, C., 1:834

Huysman, Roelof. *See* Agricola, Rodolphus (Roelof Huysman)

Huysmans, Camille, 2:445

Huyssens, Peter, 3:706

Hyacinth (Apostle of the Slavs), St., **7:236**, 12:54

Hyacinth (Mother) (Zahalka, Magdalene), 5:886

Hyckescorner (play), 9:882–883

Hydatius (Bp.), 1:461, **7:236**

Hyde Abbey (England), **7:236–237**

Hy-Dinh-Ho, Michael, 14:495

Hydromancy, 4:785

Hygebert of Lichfield (Abp.), 5:386

Hyginus (Pope), St., **7:237**

Hygrade Provision Company v. Sherman (1925), 3:660

Hyksos Period, 3:1, 13:71

Hyland, Francis E. (Bp. of Atlanta), 1:830–831

Hyle, Michael William (Bp. of Wilmington, DE), 4:625, 14:765

Hylomorphism, **7:237–238**
  Aristotelianism, 1:677
  Augustinianism, 1:878
  Bonaventure, St., 1:878, 2:488
  disposition, 4:777
  as dualistic, 7:237–238
  hylosystemism compared to, 7:238, 239
  knowledge theories, 8:214
  matter and form, 9:352
  Palmieri's opposition, 10:813
  sacraments, 12:468
  scholasticism, 12:770
  soul, 13:344
  soul-body relationship, 13:357
  temperament, 13:793
  Thomistic denial of universal, 14:44
  See also Atomism; Dynamism

Hylosystemism, 7:238, 239, **239**, 9:352

Hylozoism, 1:677, **7:239–240**, 340, 10:823

Hymmonides, John. *See* John the Deacon of Rome

Hymn to Demeter (Homer), 10:90

Hymnary, **7:240–241**

Hymni novi eccelesiastici (Ferreri), 5:694

Hymni otius anni (Victoria), 14:*483*

Hymnology, **7:241–251**
  Armenian, 7:243
  contemporary works, 6:615–616
  Early Church, 7:241
  Greek and Byzantine, 7:242–243
  Latin, 7:243–250, 251–254
    Ambrosian school, 7:243–244, 252–253
    beginnings of, 7:243, 251–252
    Carolingian period, 7:245–247
    early Middle Ages, 7:244
    fourteenth and fifteenth centuries, 7:250
    Sequence and, 7:247, 253–254
    seventh and eighth centuries, 7:244–245
    tenth and eleventh centuries, 7:247–248
    thirteenth century, 7:249–250
    twelfth century, 7:248–249
  Syriac, 7:241–242
  vernacular, 7:254–259
    African American, 7:261–262
    Catholic, 7:254–255, 258–262
    folk music, 7:260
    Hispanic, 7:261
    Protestant, 7:255–258, 262
    traditional hymns, 7:260–261, 262
    translations and texts, 7:261
  See also Hymns and hymnals

Hymns Ancient and Modern, For Use in the Services of the Church, 7:257

Hymns and hymnals, **7:251–262**
  Ad regias agni dapes, 1:97
  Adeste Fideles, 1:115
  Aeterna Caeli Gloria, 1:146
  Aeterna Christi Munera, 1:146
  Aeterne Rerum Conditor, 1:147
  Aeterne Rex Altissime, 1:147
  African American Catholics, 1:162, 7:261–262
  Akathistos, 1:197–198, 2:742, 12:348
  Ambrose, St., 1:97, 146, 147, 339
  Ancient Egypt, 5:135
  Andrew of Crete, St., 1:405
  Auctor beate saeculi, 5:201
  Audi Benigne Conditor, 1:847
  Aurea luce et decore roseo, 5:108
  Aurora Iam Spargit Polum, 1:897
  Aurora Lucis Rutilat, 1:897–898

Austin, John, 1:898

Ave Maris Stella, 1:930, 9:449, 10:856

Ave Verum Corpus, 1:931

Beata nobis gaudia (hymn), **2:168**

Caelestis Agni Nuptias, 2:844

Caelestis Aulae Nuntius, 2:844

Caelestis Urbs Jerusalem, 2:844

Caeli Deus Sanctissime, 2:844

Caelitum Joseph Decus, 2:844–845

Christe sanctorum decus angelorum, 3:528

Cor Arca Legem Continens, 4:257, 5:201

Creator alme siderum, 4:349

cross, 4:380

Custodes Hominum Psallimus Angelos, 4:448

Decora lux aeternitatis, 4:595, 5:108

Deus, tuorum militum, 4:700–701

doxology, 4:889–891

Ecce iam noctis tenuatur umbra, 5:33

Egregie doctor Paule, 5:108

En clara vox redarguit, 5:201

En ut superba criminum, 5:201

Ex more docti mystico, 5:499

Exsultet Iam Angelica Turba, 5:16, 568

Exsultet Orbis Gaudiis, 5:568

Festivis resonent compita vocibus, 5:700

Fortem virili pectore, 5:820–821

Gloria, Laus et Honor, 1:431, 6:241–242

Glory and Praise (hymnal), 7:260

Hallel (hymn), 4:890

historical developments
  Byzantine Ochotechos, 10:548–549
  origins, 8:639–640
  sequence, 13:1–5
  U.S., 7:256–259, 8:697–698

hymnary, 7:240–241

Iam Christus Astra Ascenderat, 7:269

Iam Sol Recedit Igneus, 7:269

Iam Toto Subitus Vesper, 7:269

Iste Confessor Domini Colentes (hymn), 7:648

Jesu, Corona Virginum (hymn), 7:776–777

Jesu, Dulcis Memoria (hymn), 7:777

Jesu, Redemptor Omnium (hymn), 7:777

Lead Me, Guide Me (hymnal), 7:261

Lift Every Voice and Sing (hymnal), 7:261

Hymns and hymnals *(continued)*

meter of, 7:253, 254, 256, 258

Nocte surgentes vigilemus omnes (hymn), 5:33

Nunc Dimittis (Canticle of Simeon), 10:483, *484*

Nunc Sante (hymn), 12:136

O Deus ego amo te, 10:490

O filii et filiae, 10:490

O gente felix hospita (hymn for Lauds), 12:464

O lux beam caelitum (hymn for Vespers), 12:464

O Roma nobilis, 10:490–491

Omni die dic Mariae, 10:591

Pange lingua gloriosi laureaum certaminis, 5:823, 10:822

as Psalm genre, 11:795

Quem Terra, Pontus, Sidera (hymn), 11:860

Quicumque Christum Quaeritis (hymn), 11:863–864

recommended, 4:119–120

Rector Potens, Verax Deus (hymn), 11:956–957

Regina Caeli Laetare (Marian antiphon), 12:29

Rerum Deus Tenax Vigor (office hymn), 12:136

Rex Gloriose Martyrum (office hymn), 12:208–209

Rex Sempiterne Caelitum (office hymn), 12:209

Rimed Office (rhythmic offices), 12:246–247

Sacra iam splendent (office hymn for Matins), 12:464

Sacris solemnis (office hymn), 12:521

Salve Mundi Sautare (hymn), 12:631

Salve Regina (Marian antiphon), 12:631

Salvete Christi vulnera (office hymn), 12:632

Sanctorum meritis (office hymn), 12:664

Sanctus, Sanctus, Sanctus (Holy, Holy, Holy), 12:664–665

spirituals, 13:456–457

Stabat Mater, 13:467

standardized, 4:120

Te Lucis Ante Terminum (anonymous), 13:773

Urbs Beata Jerusalem Dicta Pacis Visio, 14:342

Ut Queant Laxis Resonare Fibris, 14:355

Veni creator spiritus, 14:439

Verbum supernum prodiens, 14:445

Vexilla Regis Prodeunt, 5:823, 14:467–468

Vox clara ecce intonat, 5:201

See also Ambrosian Chant; Beneventan Chant; Byzantine Chant; Gallican Rites, chants of; Gregorian Chant; Hymnology; Liturgical music; Music; *Te Deum*

Hymnus angelicus. See Gloria

Hyōzaemon, Matthias Araki, Bl., 7:734

Hypatia, 1:268, 4:465

Hypatius of Ephesus (Bp.), 2:793, **7:262**, 8:502

Hyperaspistes (Erasmus), 5:316

Hypocrisy, **7:263**

The Hypocrite ('Ayiṯ Ṣāvûʾa) (Mapu), 6:663

Hypognosticon (Lawrence of Durham), 9:457

Hypostasis, **7:263–264**

Anathemas of Cyril, 1:391

Council of Chalcedon, 3:365

Cyril of Alexandria, 4:468

Heraclius (Byzantine Emperor), 2:749

homoousios, 7:65

Medieval theology, 3:559, 561

Mystici corporis (Pius XII), 10:104, 110

Nicene Creed, 1:662

School of Alexandria, 1:273

subsistence, 13:570

See also Christology controversies (patristic era); Hypostatic Union

Hypostatic Union, **7:264**, 822–823

communication of idioms, 4:25–27

communio, 4:28

community, 4:38

created actuation by uncreated act, 4:335–336

divine motherhood and realization of, 10:14

French school, 13:451

Incarnation, 7:374

Seven Last Words, 13:37

Severus of Antioch, 13:43–44

supernatural as example of, 13:621

Hypostatic Union, grace of, **7:264–265**

''Hypotheses of the Planets'' (Ptolemy), 11:807

Hypothesis, 5:742

See also Postulates

Hypothetical syllogisms, 13:655

Hypsis (Bp. of Parnassus), 1:398

Hyrcanus II (Jewish high priest), 6:664–665

Hysterectomy, **7:265–266**

Hystoria Albingensis (Peter of Vaux-de-Cernay), 11:204

Hyūga, Dominic Magoshichi de, Bl., 7:733

Hyvernat, Henri, 3:291, 358, **7:266–267**

I

I Believe in Education (Fitzpatrick), 5:753

I Défense invincible (Basile of Soissons), 2:140

I Fioretti di San Francesco (The Little Flowers of St. Francis). *See Fioretti*

I Fondement inébranlable (Basile of Soissons), 2:140

I Lombardi (Verdi), 14:446

I miei trentacinque anni di missione nell'alta Etiopia (Massaja), 9:310

I Moscoviti nella California o sia dimostrazione della veritá del passo all'America Settentrionale nuovamente scoperto dei Russi (Torrubia), 14:118

I primitivi cemeteri (*motu proprio* Pius XI), 11:490

I Prolegomini alla storia universale della Chiesa (Tosti), 14:120

I Scrittori dei chierici regolari detti teatini (Vezzosi), 14:468

I Shih Pao (People's Welfare Daily, China), 8:428–429

Iacobus de Zocchis de Ferraria, 3:52

Iacobus episcopus Laudensis, 3:51

Iacobus Fontanus, 3:52

Iacobus Ioannes de Canis, 3:52

Iacobus Radwicz, 3:52

I͡Avorskiĭ, Semen. *See* Stefan (Bp. of Riazan)

I͡Avorskiĭ, Stefan. *See* Stefan (Bp. of Riazan)

Iam Christus Astra Ascenderat, **7:269**

Iam Christus Astra Ascenderat (hymn), 7:269

Iam Sol Recedit Igneus (hymn), 7:269, **269**

Iam Toto Subitus Vesper (hymn), 7:269, **269**

Iamblichus (Greek philosopher), 5:47, **7:269–270**

Aristotelianism, 1:670

Byzantine philosophy, 2:807

emanationism, 5:181

influence on neoplatonism, 10:241

Mount Carmel, 3:125
as teacher and missionary, 6:446
Iaroslav the Wise (Prince of Kiev), 3:634
Iban, Gumiel de, 12:612
Ibáñez, Pedro, 3:128
Ibaraki, Louis, St., 7:732
Ibarra y González, Ramón (Abp. of Puebla, Mexico), **7:270**
Ibas of Edessa (Bp.), 4:191, 192, 5:83
Assyrian Church of the East, 1:805
Council of Chalcedon, 3:365
Council of Orléans, 1:895
Three Chapters controversy, 14:64
Iberian Church, 6:152–153
Iberville, Pierre Le Moyne d', 9:723
Ibn Al-'Assāl, **7:270**
Ibn 'Arabī, **7:270–271**
Ibn Daud (Jewish philosopher), 7:874
Ibn Ezra, Abraham ben Meïr, 5:143, 509, **7:271–272**, 12:450
Ibn Hazm, 12:211
Ibn Kabar, 4:254, 255
Ibn Khaldun, 1:672, 813
Ibn Paqūda, **7:272–273**, 8:8
Ibn Tibbon, Jacob ben Makhir, 7:274
Ibn Tibbon, Judah ben Saul, 7:273
Ibn Tibbon, Moses ben Samuel, 7:274
Ibn Tibbon, Samuel ben Judah, 7:273–274
Ibn Tibbon family, 2:831, **7:273–274**
Ibn-Ṭufail, Abū-Bakr, 1:622
Al-Ibri, Gregorius ibn. *See* Bar-Hebraeus (Gregorius Ibn Al-Ibri)
ICDA (International Catholic Deaf Association), **7:521**
ICEL. *See* International Commission on English in the Liturgy (ICEL)
Iceland, 4:309, 667, **7:274–277**, *276*
ICET (International Consultation on English Texts), 4:201, 5:253–254, **7:525–526**, 8:679
Ichizayemon, Mancio Yukimoto, Bl., 7:735
Ichthus, **7:277–278**
ICMC (International Catholic Migration Commission), **7:521–522**, 10:429
Iconoclasm, 2:793, 3:598, **7:280–283**
Adrian I (Pope), 1:123, 2:751, 752
Aemilian, St., 1:139
Anastasius (Patriarch of Constantinople), 1:388
Andrew of Crete, St., 1:405
Byzantine art, 2:733, 821
Byzantine Church, 2:751, 752, 753, 754

Byzantine civilization, 2:766, 7:325
Byzantine liturgical poetry, 2:803
Carolingian art, 3:153
Carolingian Dynasty, 3:426
Carolingian reform, 3:156, 599
Catherine of Alexandria, St., 3:268
church architecture, 3:686, 687
Constantine V (Byzantine Emperor), 4:174
Constantinople, 4:186, 189
Constantinople Council IV, 4:194
controversy, 5:23, 12:53, 600
crucifixion art, 4:393
decline and disappearance of, 7:282–283
Dungal of Saint-Denis, 4:933
Eusebius of Caesarea, 2:796
Gregory II (Pope), St., 6:485
Gregory III (Pope), St., 6:486
John Damascene, St., 2:751, 793, 821, 7:951
Leo III (Pope), St., 8:473
Libri carolini, 8:558
Manichaeism, 2:759
monastic persecutions, 7:281, 282
Muslim invasions, 2:785, 7:281
papal state, 13:490–491
Paul I (Pope), St., 11:19
second period, 8:473
Iconoclastic Synod (815), 1:504
Iconology and iconography, **7:283–288**
Andrew, Apostle, St., 1:403
angels, 1:424–425
Anne and Joachim, SS., 1:469–470, 9:275–276
of the Annunciation, 9:278–279
Anthony of Padua, St., 1:506–507
Apocalypse, 1:543–545, *545*
apocrypha, 1:558–559
Apostles, 1:573–577, 8:14–16
baptism, 2:61
Benedict, St., 2:238
Christ, 7:853–861
Ecce Homo, 5:32
Elijah, 5:159
Evangelists, 5:475–476
God the Father, 6:323–324, *324*
Holy Innocents, 7:484
Holy Name, 7:32–33
Holy Spirit, 7:49–51
Holy Trinity in, 14:205–208
Ignatius of Loyola, 7:314
Immaculate Conception, 7:*332*, 334
Isaiah (Hebrew prophet), 7:594

Jeremiah (Hebrew prophet), 7:752–753
Jesus Christ, 1:270, 4:391–398, 5:32–33, 7:853–861
John, Apostle, St., 7:897
John of God, St., 7:969
John the Baptist, St., 7:1015–1016
Joseph, St., 9:278
Joshua, 7:1056
Lamb of God, 8:302
Last Supper, 8:14–16, 334–345, 12:485
Mary, Blessed Virgin, 4:395–397, 488–490, 8:345, 9:271–281
miracles, 9:281
Moses, 10:7
paintings by Andrei Rublëv, 12:400
Paul, Apostle, St., 11:12
Pentecost, 7:49, 51, 11:103–104, *103*
Peter, Apostle, St., 11:176
Presentation of Mary, 11:683
sacraments, 12:485–488
Sacred Heart, 12:493
saints, 12:598–602
secular, 7:286–287
Stephen, St., 13:512
Transfiguration represented in, 14:155
vices and virtues, 14:555–557
woman clothed in the sun, 14:822
Zaccaria, St. Anthony Mary, 14:902
Iconostasis, 1:317
Icons, **7:278–280**, *279*
church architecture, 3:688
hodegetria, 13:91, 92
shrines possessing, 13:91–92
ICSC (International Catholic Stewardship Council), **7:522–523**
Ictus, 6:466
Ida, BB., **7:288**
Ida Elisabeth (Undset), 14:295
Ida of Boulogne, Bl., **7:289**
Ida of Herzfeld, St., **7:289**
Ida of Killeedy, St. *See* Ita of Killeedy, St.
Ida of Leeuw, Bl., 7:288
Ida of Louvain, Bl., 7:288
Ida of Nivelles, Bl., 7:288
Ida of Toggenburg, Bl., **7:289**
Idaho, **7:289–292**
See also specific dioceses and archdioceses
Idea, **7:292–296**
Aquinas, 7:293–294
Aristotle, 7:293

Idea (continued)
  Berkeley, George, 7:295
  causality, 3:306
  Chesterton, Gilbert Keith, 3:470
  Descartes, 4:682, 7:294–295
  divine ideas, 7:294
  dualism, 4:914–915
  Hume, David, 7:295
  knowledge, 8:202
  Locke, John, 7:295
  Platonic concept, 7:292–293
  practical concepts, 7:294
  realism, 7:295
  sign related, 13:117
  speculative concepts, 7:294
  subjectivism, 7:295
*Idea de la Hermandad de Sacerdotes
  Operarios Diocesanos* (Ruiz de los
  Paños), 12:407
The Idea of a University (Newman),
  10:334, 339, 340
Idea of the Holy (Otto), 12:70
L'Idéal de l'âme fervente (Saudreau),
  12:708
*The Ideal of a Christian Church,
  Considered in Comparison with
  Existing Practice* (Ward), 5:251,
  14:650
Idealism, **7:296–302**, 11:284, 296
  absolute, 1:42, 7:299–300, 301
  actual, 6:139
  antimonies, 1:520
  Aristotelianism, 1:678, 7:296–297
  Bergson, Henri, 8:513
  Berkeley, G., 7:297, 301
  Bradley, Francis Herbert, 2:576–577
  Brentano, Franz, 2:604
  Brunschvicg, Leon, 2:650
  Bulgakov, Sergeĭ Nikolaevich, 2:679
  choice, 3:521
  consciousness, 4:154
  contradiction, 4:224
  Cournot, Antoine Augustine,
    4:316–317
  criteriology, 4:368
  critical, 4:368, 369
  criticized, 7:300, 8:201
  Fichte, Johann Gottlieb, 5:708, 7:298
  France, 8:269–270
  Frohschammer, Jakob, 6:15
  German
    inductive metaphysics, 8:797
    Kantianism, 8:126
  Hegelian idealism, 7:298, 8:219
  Husserl, Edmund, 7:229–230

  James, William, 7:704
  Kant, Immanuel, 7:297–298
  knowledge, theories of, 8:222
  Lachelier influence, 8:269–270
  Leibniz, G. W., 7:297
  liberal theology, 8:543
  Locke's influence, 8:745
  Medieval thought, 7:297
  mythology and influence of German,
    10:128
  naturalism as alternative to, 10:204
  necessity, 10:227
  Neo-Confucian, 4:98
  Neoplatonism, 7:297
  objective in, 10:510
  pantheism development, 10:827
  personalism, 7:301–302
  phenomenology, 11:*232*
  philosophy and science, 11:299, 300
  philosophy of history, 6:884–885
  Plato, 7:296
  post-Hegelian, 7:298–300
  realism vs., 7:302, 11:941–942
  religion, 12:69–70
  Royce, Josiah, 12:397–398
  Schelling, F. W. J. von, 7:298,
    12:42–43
  Schopenhauer, A., 7:298–299
  solipsism, 13:303
  Sophists, 7:296
  soul, 13:347
  spiritualism, 13:436
  truth and transcendental, 14:223
*Ideas for a Pure Phenomenology and
  Phenomenological Philosophy*
  (Husserl), 10:607
Ideen I (Husserl), 12:*241*
*Ideen zur Philosophie der Geschichte
  der Menschheit* (Herder), 6:767–768
*Les Idées de St. François sur la
  pauvreté* (Ubald), 14:261
Identity, 4:223, **7:302–303**, 351
Identity, principle of, 5:745, **7:303–304**
Ideologie und Utopie (Mannheim), 8:211
Ideology, 8:211, 547–548
Ideology and Utopia (Mannheim),
  14:361
Idesbald, Bl., **7:304**
Idioms. *See* Communication of idioms
Idiorhythmia, 3:335
Idiota dialogues (Nicholas of Cusa),
  10:374
Idleness, Moral Aspects of, **7:304–305**
Idol worship, Bible's ridicule of, 2:211

Idolatry, **7:305**, 14:793
  fertility and vegetation cults, 5:698
  Hezekiah image, 13:*20*
  Islamic opposition to, 7:615
  Knox, J., 8:225
  liberation theology, 8:546–547, 548
  Spanish mission in the Americas,
    3:248, 848, 850–851
Idolatry, in the Bible, **7:305–306**, 8:3
Ibn-Idrīs, Aḥmad, 7:613
Iduberga, Bl., **7:306–307**
Iero, St. *See* Jeron, St.
La Iglesia (Franceschi), 5:864
Iglesia del Carmen (Church of Carmen)
  (Panama City), 10:*819*
Iglesia Filipina Independiente. *See*
  Philippine Independent Church
Ignatian Council (869-70), 4:302
Ignatian School, 4:207
Ignatian spirituality, 3:610, **7:307–309**
  Caussade, Jean Pierre de, 3:310
  God, concept of, 7:307–308
  lay spirituality, 8:415
  Ledóchowski, W., 8:445
  love, 7:309
  prayer, 7:308–309
  spiritual man, 7:308
  See also Ignatius of Loyola, St.;
    Jesuits
Ignatius (Patriarch of Constantinople),
  St., 2:755, **7:309–310**, 11:310
  Adrian II (Pope), 1:124
  Leo IV (Pope), St., 7:309, 8:482
  Michael III, 4:187, 7:309, 310
  Photius, 2:754, 7:309–310
  unity of Church, 4:194
Ignatius III (Patriarch of Antioch), Bar-
  Hebraeus and, 2:82
Ignatius Elias III, St., 7:406
Ignatius Loyola, 3:16
Ignatius Michael III (Patriarch of Syria),
  13:707–708
Ignatius of Antioch, St., 1:*521*, 5:491,
  7:310–312, 9:227–228
  agape, 1:170
  Antioch, 1:521–522
  Apostles, 3:29
  as Apostolic Father, 1:587
  apostolic succession, 1:591
  apostolicity, 1:579, 595
  Asia Minor, 1:785
  baptism of Jesus, 2:73
  beatific vision, 2:172
  bishops, 2:411, 413, 7:311
  Canon Law, 3:37

charity, 3:395

Christian way of life, 3:547

Christocentrism, 3:558

Christology, 3:560

Christ's descent into hell, 4:684

Church history, 3:592

Church property, 3:723

communion of saints, 4:36

creedal statements, 4:350–351

deacons, 4:551

Docetism, 2:820, 4:797, 7:311, 811

Eucharist, 7:311

following Christ, 5:788

hospitality, 7:118

marriage, 7:311

martyrdom of, 3:592

martyrs and martyrdom, 9:227

Mary's motherhood, 10:13

mystical body of Christ, 10:102

Old Testament, 3:29

Pauline epistles, 3:30

Polycarp, St., 11:464

practice of taking Christian names, 10:139

priesthood as order, 7:36

theology of Church, 3:584

transubstantiation, 14:158

universality of Christianity, 3:274, 292

virgin birth, 14:533

works of charity, 3:403, 406

See also Apostolic Fathers; Patristic era

Ignatius of Jesus, Mary (Mother), 5:884–885, 12:542, 709

Ignatius of Laconi, St., **7:312**

Ignatius of Loyola, St., 2:109, 5:344, 7:307–309, **312–314**, *313, 779*

Ad Majorem Dei Gloriam, 1:95, 96

Alphonsus Liguori, St., 1:309, 310

Anima Christi, 1:455

Bobadilla, Nicolás Alfonso de, 2:446

Carthusian spirituality, 3:192

Casa dei neofiti (Rome), 10:239

Cassian, John, 3:207

Cisneros, García de, 3:744

conformity, 4:93–94

Counter Reformation, 3:610, 611, 782

Daughters of Jesus, 3:738

Denis the Carthusian, 4:661

discernment, spiritual, 4:766

disciple as term, 4:774

eucharistic devotion, 5:435

Faber, Peter, Bl., friendship with, 5:583, 584

iconography of, 7:314

Jesuits, 4:310, 311

Laínez, D., 8:287, 288

missions to Ethiopia, 5:400

mysticism, 7:309, 313–314

patron of Baltimore Archdiocese, 2:41

preaching, 11:621

Religious of the Cenacle, 3:334

Ribadeneyra, Pedro de, disciple of, 12:220

Rules for Thinking with the Church, 14:6

Salmerón, 12:620

scholasticism, 12:765

shrine, 13:94

spirituality, 13:446–447

Thomism, 14:49

University of Alcalá, 1:236

visions, 13:415

Xavier, Francis, St., 14:877

See also Ignatian spirituality; *Spiritual Exercises* (St. Ignatius of Loyola)

Ignatius Peter VI (Patriarch of Syria), 13:707

Ignaz von Döllinger (Freidrich), 6:3

Ignea Sagitta (*Fiery Arrow*) (Nicholas Gallicus), 3:132, 133

Ignorance, **7:314–315**

innocence, 14:585–586

morality of, 7:315

types, 7:539–540

wonder, 14:832–833

Igny Abbey (France), 3:758

I-It mystics, 10:117

Ījī, 1:782

Ilarion, St., 2:*749*

Ildefonso de Los Angeles, 12:619

Ildefonsus of Toledo, St., 1:577, 4:87, 5:445, **7:316**, 12:606

Ilerus, St. *See* Hilarus of Mende, St.

Ilga, Bl., **7:316**

Ilgen, K. D., 1:814

Iliad (Homer), 1:140, 12:508

Illa Salvía, Ramón, 2:92

Illatio sancti Benedicti (Thierry of Fleury), 14:3

Illich, Ivan, 9:583–584

Illig, Alvin Anthony (Father), 4:242, **7:316**, 11:42

Illinois, 3:663, **7:317–319**, 8:521, 9:571, 722

See also specific dioceses and archdioceses

Illinois Catholic Historical Review, 7:318–319

Illinois College (Jacksonville), 4:116

Illinois Department of Employment Sec., Frazee v. (1989), 3:663

Illinois Institute of Technology Chapel, 3:669

Illinois people, mission to, 1:296

Illtud, St., **7:319**, 12:543

Illuminati. *See* Alumbrados

Illumination, **7:319–320**

abstraction, 1:45

Augustine, St., 1:866, 876, 7:293

Bonaventure, St., 2:489

Books of Hours, 11:604–605

knowledge, theories of, 8:216

Pucelle, Jean, 11:811

See also Manuscript illumination

Illuminés, 7:320–321

Illuminism, **7:320–322**, 8:583–584

Illustriorum disquisitionum moralium (Candido), 3:13

Illustrium Germaniae scriptorum catalogus (Loos), 8:777

Illuyankas myth, 6:895

Illyrian Movement, 4:371

Illyricum sacrum (Farlati and Coleti), 5:627

Illyricus, Thomas, **7:322**

Im Bannkreis Babels (Kugler), 10:820

Image and Pilgrimage in Christian Culture: Anthropoligcal Perspectives (Turner), 14:246

Image of God, 4:24, **7:322**, 10:211–212, 961–962, 13:51

The Image of Sin (*De imagine peccati*) (Hilton), 6:834–835

Imagery, in Hebrew poetry, 6:693

Images, biblical prohibition of, **7:322–323**

Images, concept and, 7:506

Images, symbol and, 13:661

Images, veneration of, **7:323–326**

doctrine concerning, 7:325–326

Libri carolini, 8:557

as natural, 7:323–324

New Testament, 7:324–325

Old Testament, 7:324

older and recent instructions, 8:626

paganism, 7:324

papal prohibition of, 5:443

shrines, 13:92

Imagination, **7:326–327**
 art, 1:746, 748
 cogitative power, 3:822, 7:326
 control of, 7:326–327
 creative, 4:347–349
 Freud, Sigmund, 7:326, 327
 memory, 7:326
 perception of time, 14:81
 phenomena of movement, 10:21
 sensation, 12:908
 senses, 7:326, 12:913
 soul, 13:351
Imagination (Sartre), 12:697
Imagines et elogia virorum illustrium et eruditorum (Orsini), 10:482
Imaging Sign, 13:116
Imago Dei, 3:531, 532
Imago mundi (Honorius of Autun), 5:206
Imām, 7:*327–328*, **327–328**, 10:589, 13:83–84
Imamura, John, Bl., 7:734
Imberios and Margarona, 2:806
Imbert, Joseph, Bl., **7:328**, 12:277
Imbert, Laurent Joseph Marius, martyr, 8:234, 239
IMC (International Missionary Council), 5:71–72, **7:527**, 9:697
IMCS (Pax Romana-International Movement of Catholic Students), 10:161
Imitation, 4:768, 7:188–189, 323–324, 11:433–434
Imitation of Christ (Thomas À Kempis), 3:69, 605, **7:328–331**, 14:12
 Amort, Eusebius, 1:363
 authorship debate, 7:328–329, 8:381
 Bernard of Clairvaux, 2:311
 Devotio Moderna, 4:708
 friendship with God, 6:11
Imma, Bl., **7:331**
Immaculate Conception, **7:331–335**, *332*, 9:158, 173
 Alphonsus Liguori, St., 1:310, 312
 Alva y Astorga, Pedro de, 1:323
 Anselm of Canterbury, St., 1:497
 Aquinas, 7:333–334
 Bernard of Clairvaux, 2:310, 7:333
 Bombolognus of Bologna, 2:476
 Cajetan, 7:334
 Caracciolo, Landolf, 3:96
 Carmelite spirituality, 3:133
 doctrine definition (1854), 1:310, 3:623, 7:334–335
 Dominican Thomism opposition to, 14:43

Duns Scotus, John, 4:939, 7:334
Eadmer of Canterbury's writings, 5:1
Early Church, 7:332–333
 feast proclaimed, 7:149, 333, 334, 13:131
 Hugh of Newcastle, 7:155
 Ineffabilis Deus defining, 10:61–62
 literary contest (Mexico), 13:121
 Lourdes Shrine, 8:819
 Mariology, 9:171
 Middle Ages, 7:333–334
 papal decrees, 7:334–335, 9:284
 Pius IX (Pope), Bl., pronouncement (1854), 10:848
 teaching of, 7:331–332
 Torquemada's opposition to, 14:112
Immaculate Conception, Cathedral of the (Portland, ME), 9:57
Immaculate Conception Academy and Convent (Columbia, GA), 8:903
Immaculate Conception Brothers, 3:622, **7:335**
Immaculate Conception Church (Audincourt, France), 3:713
Immaculate Conception Society, 5:834
Immaculate Heart of Mary, 3:764, **7:335–337**, *336*, 9:158
Immaculate Heart of Mary Parish (Cleveland, OH), 8:249
Immanence, **7:340–342**
 absolute historicism, 4:372–374
 causality, 3:304
 of Christ, 13:25
 cosmological, 7:341
 critique, 7:341–342
 defined, 8:209
 epistemological, 7:341
 God, 6:322
 history of, 7:340
 kinds of, 7:340–341
 knowledge, 8:201
 liberal theology, 8:543
 ontological, 7:341
 psychological, 7:341
 Thomism, 4:53, 8:209
 transcendence, 7:340
Immanence apologetics, 1:565, 566, 7:341, 342–343, 12:732
Immanentism, 7:342, 342–343, **343–344**, 9:755, 10:827
Immanuel Kant (Bauch), 2:157
Immateriality, 7:340, **344–346**, 345–346, 8:201, 209
Immensa aeternae Dei (apostolic constitution, Sixtus V), 3:63, 349, 4:438

Immersion, baptism, 2:75
Immigration and emigration
 Americanism, 1:354
 Argentina, 1:657
 Arkansas, 1:691, 692
 Buddhism, 2:673
 California, 2:868–870, 872
 church architecture, 3:715, 716
 Church membership, U.S., 3:720, 721
 Eastern-rite Catholics, 13:87, 366
 Germany, 8:736, 765, 885
 Indiana, 1:251
 Iowa, 8:778–779, 13:164
 Ireland, 8:778–779, 837–838, 9:56, 13:402
 Italy, 8:812
 Japan, 13:298
 Kentucky, 8:817
 Knights of Columbus, 8:191
 Knights of St. George, 8:196
 Know-Nothingism, 8:199–200
 language controversy, 1:7–8, 354
 lay missionaries, 8:18
 liturgical movement, 8:6, 675
 Loughlin, J., 8:798
 Louisiana, 8:811, 812, 816
 Lutheran, 8:883–884
 Massachusetts, 2:553, 554, 555, 9:308, 13:462
 national parishes, 4:123, 124
 St. Raphael's Society, 2:852
 Sisters of Providence, 13:189
 South Carolina, 13:366
 Vietnam, 8:816
 West Virginia, 14:688
 Wisconsin, 8:256
 See also Nativism
Immo of Reichenau, 2:327
Immortale Dei (encyclical, Pope Leo XIII), **7:346–347**
Immortality, **7:347–354**
 afterlife, 1:165, 7:350–351
 ancient thought, 7:347–348
 Bible, 7:351–352, 353, 354
 Cajetan (Tommaso de Vio), 2:854–855
 Daoism, 4:524
 Patristic teaching, 7:347–349
 philosophical analysis, 7:349–351
 retribution, 7:353, 354, 12:178
 Scholasticism, 7:349
 theology of, 7:352–354
Immortality of the soul, 13:339–342, 352–353, 353–356, 626
Immutability of God, **7:354–357**

Impassibility of God, 1:104–105, 6:689, **7:357–360**

Impeccability, **7:360–361**

Impeccability of Christ, 7:265, **361**

Impenetrability, **7:361–362**, 8:742

Impenitence, **7:362–363**

Imperial Catechism (France), **3:236–237**, 244

Imperial cult, 3:631

Imperial Dalmatic (Byzantine garment), 8:*620*

Imperium christianum, 3:167, 168

Impersonal mind, 8:270

Impetus, 1:223, 670, **7:363–364**, 9:415, 10:18

Imposition of hands, **7:364–366**
    Church, 3:575
    consecration of a bishop, 10:636
    deacons, 4:551
    Holy Orders, 7:35, 38
    women, 4:554

Improperia, **7:366–367**

Improperia (Palestrina), 10:802

Imprudence, 11:789

Impugnatio Alcorani (Ricoldus de Monte Croce), 12:243

Impugnatio Henrici de Gandavo (Robert of Orford), 12:269

Impure. *See* Pure and impure

Imputability, 8:876

Imputation of Justice and Merit, **7:367–368**, 8:70, 85

In I sententiarum (Scotus), 14:213

In agro domini (papal bull, Benedict XII), 11:76

In Cantica Canticorum (St. Bernard of Clairvaux), 5:514

In catholicum catechismum libri sex (Nausea), 3:242

In coena Domini (papal bull, Gregory XIII), 4:498

In cotidianis precibus (*motu proprio* Pius XII), 11:400

In decem libros ethicorum expositio (Aquinas), 14:26

In Defense of the Three Chapters (Facundus of Hermiane), 3:596, 5:587

In defensione trium capitulorum (Pelagius), 14:64

In duodecim libros metaphysicorum expositio (Aquinas), 14:26

In eligendis (papal bull, Pius IV), 3:91, 11:499

In Eminenti (papal bull, Clement XII), 1:893, 3:790, 12:857

In Eminenti (papal bull, Urban VIII), 4:4, 7:715, 14:342

In facto esse (made), 12:751

In fieri (becoming in the process of being made), 12:751

In libros de anima expositio (Aquinas), 14:26

In libros de caelo et mundo expositio (Aquinas), 14:26

In libros de generatione et corruptione expositio (Aquinas), 14:26

In libros meteorolgicorum expositio (Aquinas), 14:26

In libros peri hermeneias expositio (Aquinas), 14:26

In libros politicorum expositio (Aquinas), 14:26

In libros posteriorum analyticorum expositio (Aquinas), 14:26

In librum de memoria et reminiscentia expositio (Aquinas), 14:26

In librum de sensu et sensato expositio (Aquinas), 14:26

In Memory of Her (Schlusser-Florenza), 5:677, 10:307

In Nomine Domine (papal decree, Nicholas II), 3:105

In octo libros physicorum expositio (Aquinas), 14:26

In omnes beati Pauli et septem catholicas apostolorum epistolas commentarii (Estius), 5:375

In Pauli Epistolam ad romanos commentariorum libritres (Sadoleto), 12:526

In plurimis (papal letter, Leo XIII), 9:681

In Sublimi (apostolic letter, Gregory XVI), 12:384

In summam theologiae S. Thomae Aquinatis enarratio (de Toledo), 14:102

In Suprema (apostolic constitution, Alexander VII), 3:748, 14:161

In Suprema Petri Apostoli Sede (encyclical, Pius IX), 6:459

In supremo (apostolic letter, Gregory XVI), 2:44, 6:510

In Towns and Little Towns (Feeney), 5:663

In vitro fertilization, 1:656

Inalienability, 4:860

Inca people, 3:484–485, 4:*130*, 131–132, 11:158
    See also Peru

Inca religion, **7:368–369**

Incantations, **7:369**

Incarnate Wisdom, 8:405

Incarnation, **7:373–375**
    art, 1:743–744
    assumptus homo theology, 1:802–803
    Athanasian Creed, 1:815–816
    atonement, 1:837
    Bonaventure, St., 2:486–487
    Byzantine theology, 2:766
    Christmas, 3:554, 555
    Christocentrism, 3:558
    Christology, 3:560
    communication of idioms, 4:25, 26
    community as extension of, 4:38
    Constantinople Council II, 4:191
    consubstantiality, 4:198–199
    Council of Chalcedon, 3:365
    creation doctrine, 4:345
    Cyril of Alexandria, St., 10:14
    Daniélou, Jean, 9:684
    death of God theology, 4:585
    divine missions, 9:736
    doctrine, development of, 4:807
    Duns Scotus, John, 4:938
    Gregory of Nyssa, St., 6:520
    holiness, 7:8
    iconoclasm, 7:281
    impassibility of God, 7:359
    Islamic denial of, 7:608
    kenosis, 8:143
    Mary's Divine brideship, 10:14
    mystery of the, 10:84
    Nicene Creed (325), 10:354
    patristic philosophy, 10:961
    Radical Reformation, 3:608
    redemption, 11:983–984
    as remedy for disorder of evil, 14:331–332
    Resurrection of Christ, 12:160–161
    sacramental worship, 8:728
    sacramentalizing the human body, 8:647
    subsistence and union in, 13:571
    substance, 13:577
    temporal values, 13:812
    theology in nature, 10:212
    theology of man, 9:94
    union as relation to God, 13:139
    See also Humanity of Christ

Incarnation, necessity of the, **7:375–376**

Incarnationis mysterium (papal bull, John Paul II), 7:440

Incendium Amoris (Rolle), 10:119

Incense, 1:320, 3:335, **7:376–377**

Incest, **7:377–378**, 13:85

Incest, in the Bible, **7:378**, 13:50

Inchausti, Leon, 10:29

The Incoherence of the Incoherence (Averroës), 7:613

Incommunicability, **7:379–380**

Inconstancy, 8:775

Incorporation in Christ, 4:38, **7:380**

Incorporation into the Church (Membership), **7:380–383**

Incubi, 4:648

Inculturation, liturgical, **7:383–388**
    evangelization, 9:689
    Ghana, 6:198
    India, 7:404–405
    Indonesia, 7:430
    Ivory Coast, 7:681–682
    Jesuits, 7:784
    Sri Lanka, 13:465–466
    Vatican Council II, 9:678
    Zairean Episcopal Conference, 4:106
    Zambia, 14:907

Inculturation, theology of, **7:388–389**

Inde a Pontificatus (*motu proprio*, John Paul II), 11:479

Inde a primis (apostolic letter, John XXIII), 11:642

Indecent speech, 13:411

Indefectibility, **7:389**

Indeliberate acts, 6:398

Independent African American Catholic Rite, 1:161–162

Independent Catholicism. *See* Liberal Catholic Church

Independent Order of Good Templars, 13:800–801

Index der verbotenen Bücher (Reusch), 12:182

Index of Christian Art, 7:286

Index of Pope Pius IV. *See* Tridentine Index

Index of Prohibited Books, 5:647, 750, 825, **7:389–391**, 10:978, 11:518
    abolishment, 11:30, 12:26
    Ágreda, Mary of, 1:187
    Alexandre, Noël, 1:267
    Autour d'un petit livre (Loisy), 9:754
    Barbier, Emmanuel, works of, 7:503
    Barbosa, Agostino, 2:96
    Bauny, Étienne, works of, 2:160
    Berruyer, Isaac Joseph, 2:330
    Bibliothèque (Du Pin), 4:944
    Breve compendio intorno alla perfezione cristiana (Abrégé de la perfection) (Bellinzaga), 2:230, 6:48
    Buonaiuti, Ernesto, 2:694
    Cassander, George, 3:205

Cave, William, 3:312

Cayet, Pierre Victor, 3:314

Cochlaeus, Johannes, 3:816

Concio (Kenrick), 8:146

Congar, Yves Marie-Joseph, works of, 4:102–103

Controversia anglicana de potestate regis et pontificis (Becanus), 2:191

Copernicus, Nicolaus, works of, 4:251

De concordantia sacerdotii et imperii (Marca), 9:133

De concordia sacerdotii et imperii seu de libertatibus ecclesiae gallicanae (Baluze), 2:48

De corpore et sanguine Domini (Ratramnus of Corbie), 11:924

De divisione naturae (John Scotus Eriugena), 7:1010–1011

De pontificis romani clave (Henríquez), 6:735

Diego of Estella, 4:739

Dogme et critique (Le Roy), 9:755

Une école de théologie: Le Saulchoir (Chenu), 3:466

Einleitung in die Philosophie (Frohschammer), 12:901

L'Eucharistie: la Présence réelle et la Transubstantiation (Batiffol), 2:155

L'Évangile et L'Église (Loisy), 9:754

Fasciculus rerum expetendarum ac fugiendarum (Gratius), 6:424

Foreiro, Francisco, 5:799

Gerbais, Jean, 4:591

Gioberti, Vincenzo, 6:778

Glasgow Free Press, 8:133–134

Grégoire, Henri Baptiste, works of, 6:463

Günther, Anton, works of, 6:583, 778

heliocentric works, 6:62, 11:26

Hermes, Georg, works of, 4:932, 6:797

Hirscher, Johann, works of, 6:861

Histoire ancienne de l'Église chrétienne (Duchesne), 4:927, 7:503

History of the Famous Preacher Friar Gerund of Campazas (Isla), 11:622

Hontheim, Johann Kikolaus von, works of, 7:90

Hus, John, works of, 7:390, 12:658

Joachim of Fiora, works of, 7:390

John Scotus Eriugena, works of, 7:390

Kardec, A., 8:128

Laberthonnière, L. (works of), 8:265

Libri carolini, 8:557

Loisy, Alfred, works of, 7:149, 8:765–766

Louis of Granada, 8:806

Le Martyre de Saint Sébastien, (Annunzio), 4:586

Molina, Luis de, works of, 4:111–113

Montlosier, François de, 1:519

Montpellier Catechism, 11:561

Noris, Henry, 1:885

Olivi, Peter Jean, works of, 7:390

Paroles d'un croyant (Lamennais, F.), 8:310

Pentalogus diaphoricus (Charles of the Assumption), 3:436

Pigge, Albert, works of, 11:336

Protestant Reformation, 3:637

Quaternuli (David), 4:540

Quesnel, Pasquier, works of, 11:861

Raynaud, Théophile, works of, 11:939

Riforma cattolica (Gioberti), 6:230

Rosmini-Serbati, Antonio, 12:384

Rubino, Antonio, 12:399

Sa, Manoel, 12:449

Sabatier, Paul, 12:453

Sanctificatio S. Joseph Sponsi Virginis in utero asserta (Marcant, Pierre), 9:140

Sarpi, Paolo, 12:694

Simon, Richard, works of, 11:89

Sixtus V (Pope), order for new, 13:198

Theologia naturalis (Raymond of Sabunde), 11:937

Über die Freiheit der Wissenschaft (Frohschammer), 12:901

Venida del mesías (Lacunza), 8:274

La vie de Jesus (Steinmann), 7:391

Les vies des saints (Baillet), 6:615

Wyclife, John, works of, 7:390

See also Censorship of books

Index of Valdes, 13:447

Index Omnium (Shields), 13:83

Index Thomisticus (Busa), 12:778

Indexing, history of, 7:188

India, **7:391–406**, 8:*111*
    Brahmanism, 13:337–338
    Carmelites, 3:130, 146–147, 459
    caste system, 3:211, *212*, 6:851, 853
    Castro, Mateo de, 3:219
    demographic statistics, 7:392
    Diamper, Synod of (1599), 4:728–729

ecclesiastical organization, 7:393

map, 7:*394*

mission

    Anglican mission, 13:288–289

    Beschi, Costanzo Giuseppe, 2:339–340

    British education and, 7:405

    Carey, William, 3:108

    Dandoy, George and, 4:508

    de Mello, Anthony and, 4:634

    Dengel, Anna and, 4:659–660

    Holy Cross Sisters and, 7:22

    Jesuits and, 7:784

    Manichaeism and, 9:108

    Nobili, Roberto do, 9:692

    padroado and Propaganda missionaries, 3:219, 10:977

    Portuguese establishment of, 7:397–398, 401–402

    Roth, Heinrich, 12:390

    under Gregory XVI (Pope), 6:510

    Xavier, St. Francis and, 14:878

Roberts, Thomas d'Estene, 12:271–272

Rudolf Acquaviva and Companions, BB., 12:401

Sikhism, 13:118–119

Tantrism, 13:753

women, status of, 14:813

See also Buddhism; Hinduism; Syro-Malabar Church

Indian and White in the Northwest: A History of Catholicity in Montana (Palladino), 10:804

Indian philosophy, 1:833, **7:406–410**, 8:130, 11:287, 13:149

The Indian Prayer Book (Romagné), 12:297

Indian religion, 5:747–748, 922

Indian Rites controversy, 7:402, **410–412**, 9:692

Indian theology. *See* Native American theology

Indian Wars, 9:721–722

Indiana, 1:250–251, **7:412–416**, 13:123

    See also specific dioceses and archdioceses

Indianapolis Archdiocese (IN), **7:416–418**, 12:257

Indiction, 3:571, **7:418–420**

Indiction of Bede, 7:419

Indiculus luminosus (Paulus Albarus), 9:446, 11:44

Indifferent Acts, **7:420–421**

Indifferentism, 5:932, **7:421–422**, 8:489, 541

Indigenous art, 4:291

Indigenous peoples. *See* Native Australians; *specific countries*; *specific peoples*

The Indissolubility of Christian Marriage in the Case of Adultery (Fransen), 5:918

Individual eschatology, 5:333, 337–338, 340, 342

Individualism

    common good vs., 4:19–21

    communication philosophy, 4:25

    community vs., 4:38

    Ignatian exercises, 13:432–433

    individuality, 7:422

    irrationalism, 7:586

    Spencer, Herbert, 13:413

Individuality, **7:422–423**

Individuation, 7:422, 423, **424–427**

    abstraction, 1:46

    Crathorn, John, 4:335

    Duns Scotus, John, 4:936–937

    Durandus of Saint-Pourçain, 4:948

    Jung's theory, 8:60

    mutiplication, 5:362–363

    simplicity of God, 13:138

    soul, 13:350

Individuum est incommunicabile (The individual is incommunicable), 12:755

Indivisible, 4:215, 780, **7:427**

Indochina, 12:218–219, 255

Indonesia, 4:*558*, **7:428–432**, *430*

    See also East Timor

Indonesian Catholic Student Association, 7:431

Indo-Portuguese Schism. *See* Goan Schism of 1838

Indorum republicae descriptio (Valadés), 14:368

Indrechtach, St., **7:432**

Induced Movement, 10:20

Induction, **7:432–436**

    argumentation, 1:658

    Aristotle, 1:681

    axiomatic system, 1:949

    causality, 3:308

    certitude, 3:353

    deduction compared to, 4:608

    demonstration, 4:652

    first principles, 5:744

    knowledge, 8:203

    liberal arts, 8:538

    matter and form in, 9:346

    philosophy of nature, 11:305–306

    reasoning, 11:948

    uniformity in nature as basis of, 14:300

    See also Deduction

Indulgences, **7:436–441**

    controversy, 12:14

    Council of Trent decree on reform, 14:173–174

    Crusades, 4:407, 408, 409, 410, 412, 413, 693

    dead, prayers for, 4:556

    Holy Name, 7:31

    Luther, Martin, 8:879, 12:15–16

    papal taxation, 3:726

    "Pardon of Assisi," 11:527–528

    St. Peter's Basilica, financing, 8:487, 879

    See also Plenary indulgences

Indulgences, Sacred Congregation of, 4:556

Indulgentiarum doctrina (apostolic constitution, Paul VI), 7:439–440

Industriae Tuae (papal bull, John VIII), 4:370, 476

Industrial Citizenship (Fitzpatrick), 5:753

Industrial Revolution, 14:817

Industrial Workers of the World (IWW), 10:171

Industrialism, 4:642–643, 782–783, 783, 13:241–242, 255

L'Industrie du papyrus dans l'Égypte Greco-Romaine (Lewis), 10:862

Indwelling, Divine, 4:335–336, **7:441–444**, 9:736, 13:441

Indy, Vincent d', **7:444–445**

Ine (King of Wessex), **7:445**

Inedia, 10:109

Ineffabilis Deus (papal bull, Pius IX), 1:799

Ineffability of God, **7:445–446**

Inerrancy, biblical, **7:446–447**

Infallibility, 5:37, **7:448–452**

    conciliarism, 4:53–58

    Connolly, Thomas Louis, 4:128

    D'Alzon, Emmanuel, 4:502

    Darboy, Georges, 4:526

    Dechamps, Victor Auguste, 4:589

    Declaration of the French Clergy, 4:591

    Dieringer, Franz Xaver, 4:741

    Ecumenical councils, 4:305

    ex cathedra, 5:498

    faith and morals, 5:605–606

    growing support (1850s) for declaration of papal, 10:334

Infallibility (continued)
    Purcell, John Baptist, 11:820
    Vatican Council I, 5:855, 10:848,
      12:182, 417, 14:404, 405–406
Infallibility of the Pope. See Papal
    infallibility
Infancy narratives, **7:452–454**
    Annunciation, 1:473
    criticism, 3:34, 5:810
    historicity debates, 8:863
    iconography, 1:558–559
    as literary form, 7:484
    Luke's Gospel, 8:856
    Mary as primary source, 8:860
Infant baptism. See Baptism of infants
Infant Jesus of Prague, **7:455**
Infanticide, 4:220
Infidels, **7:455,** 8:75
Infinite in All Directions (Dyson), 5:351
The Infinite Mercy of God (apostolic
    letter, Pius XI), 12:206
Infinity, 4:216–217, 6:320–321,
    7:455–460
Infinity of God, 4:937, 938, 7:459,
    460–461
''The Influence of Habit on Thought''
    (Biran), 9:59–60
The Influence of the Catholic Layman
    (Onahan), 10:599
Information (periodical), 7:316
Infralapsarians (Sublapsarians), 2:894,
    7:461
    Arminianism, 1:712, 2:894
    predestination, 11:650, 655
    reprobation, 12:132
    See also Calvinism
Infused contemplation, 11:955
Infused knowledge. See Knowledge,
    infused
Infused knowledge of Christ, 7:829
Infused virtues, 14:550–551
Ingarden, Roman, 1:143
Inge, Hugh (Abp. of Dublin), **7:461–462**
Inge, William Ralph, 7:*462,* **462**
Ingelheim, Synod of (948), 1:172, 5:763
Ingenbohl Sisters, 12:735
Ingenuin (Bp. of Sabiona), St., 1:908,
    7:462
Ingersoll, Robert Green, 1:*181,* 5:968,
    8:303
Inghan, Alice (Mother Mary Francis),
    5:879
Ingleby, Francis, Bl., 5:229, **7:462–463**
Inglis, Charles (Bp.), **7:463**
Ingoldsby, John, 12:646
Ingoli, Francesco, 11:750

Ingram, John, Bl., 2:551, 5:232, **7:463**
Ingravescentem aetatem (*motu proprio,*
    Paul VI), 3:106–107, 11:30
Inheritance, in the Bible, 7:42, **463–465,**
    13:249, 14:829
Iñiguez Guzmán, Rodrigo, 13:121
Initiation Biblique, 12:262
*Initium, incrementum et exitus
    Geraldinorum* (O'Daly), 10:550
Injury, Moral, **7:465–466**
La Inmaculada (Elguero), 5:154
Innatism, 4:223–224, 5:743, 7:294–295,
    466, 10:131
Inner Light, 4:39
Innichen Abbey (Austria), 1:908
Innitzer, Theodor (Card.), **7:466–467**
Innocent, St., **7:467**
Innocent I (Pope), St., **7:467–469**
    Ambrosian Rite, 1:343
    Anointing of the Sick, 1:481, 7:35
    biblical canon, 3:32
    Canon Law, 3:39
    clerical celibacy/marriage, 3:323
    Confirmation, 4:86, 87
    correspondence of, 7:467–468
    decretals, legal force of, 4:600
    Ember Days, 5:186
    Exuperius of Toulouse, St., 5:571
    John Chrysostom, St., 7:947
    papal authority, 12:354
    Pelagianism, 3:188, 11:62
    Sicily, 13:103
    simony, 13:136
Innocent II (Pope), 7:469, **469–470**
    Abelard, Peter, 1:18, 19, 719
    Alberic of Ostia, 1:219
    Anacletus II (Antipope), 1:370
    Armenia, 1:701
    Arnulf of Lisieux, 1:720
    Celestine I (Pope), St., 3:318
    election of, 5:844
    Lothair III, 8:797
    Louis VI, 8:799
    Malachy, St., 9:65
    Second Lateran Council, 8:350
Innocent III (Antipope), **7:473**
Innocent III (Pope), 5:*870,* **7:470–473,**
    14:*69*
    abbesses, 1:8
    abbreviators, 1:13
    Adam of Perseigne, 1:109
    Adam of Saint-Victor, 1:109
    Adrian IV (Pope), 1:127
    Albert of Jerusalem, St., 1:222
    Albigensians, 1:713, 2:688

    Alexander III (Pope), 1:255
    Amalric of Bène, 1:330
    ambries, 1:348
    Ancient See of Canterbury, 3:72
    anointing, 1:478–479
    Bulgaria, 2:680, 685
    Canon Law, 1:207, 3:48
    Caulites, 3:296
    Christian of Prussia, 3:537
    Church wealth, 8:294
    Church-State relations, 3:636,
      7:43–44
    Clare of Assisi, St., 3:760
    clerical celibacy/marriage, 3:324
    clerical misconduct, 7:485–486
    colors for liturgical use, 8:645
    conciliarism, 4:54
    Conrad of Querfurt, 4:137
    Constantine I (the Great) (Roman
      Emperor), 4:861
    Crosier Fathers, 2:609
    cross, sign of, 4:382
    Crusades, 2:688, 3:602, 4:409, 410,
      413
    decretals of, 4:600–601, 7:471–472
    defense of infant baptism, 2:69
    Eastern Schism, 2:760–761
    Eberhard of Rohrdorf, 5:30
    Engelbert I of Cologne, 5:220
    Fulk of Neuilly, 6:24
    Greek patriarchs, 4:188
    heresy, 7:472, 488
    Honorius Magister, 7:88
    Huguccio, 7:164
    Humiliati, 1:231, 7:204
    importance of, 3:602
    John (King of England), 5:242, 7:914
    John de Grey, 7:954
    lay confession, 8:411
    legitimacy, 7:472
    liturgical reform, 8:714
    Maronite Church, 9:196
    medieval Latin literature, support of,
      9:462
    monastic reform, 2:271
    Monastic Republic of Mount Athos,
      10:31–32
    nepotism of, 10:247
    Norbert's support of, 10:420–421
    Order of Aviz, 1:947
    Order of the Holy Spirit, 7:51–52
    papal development under, 10:838
    Peter of Castelnau, 11:198
    Poverty Movement, 11:571–573
    on priesthood, 11:700

prostitution, 3:413, 11:773

reordination, 7:39

right of pope to act in secular disputes, 7:472

Roman Breviary, 2:610

works of, 7:470

works of charity, 3:412

Innocent IV (Pope), 7:*464*, **473–476**

Albert Behaim, 1:222

Armenia, 1:702

Augustinians, 1:886

Canon Law, 3:48

cardinalate, 3:105

Carmelites, 3:132, 141

Chaldean Catholic Church, 3:366

Church-State relations, 2:501, 3:636, 7:44

Clare of Assisi, St., 3:760

conferrment of red hats on cardinals, 6:763

Crosier Fathers, 2:609

Eastern Schism, 2:761

Franciscans, 7:980

Frederick II the Great, 7:664

heresy, 7:488

Isabelle of France, 7:593

Joannes de Deo, 7:883

as jurist, 7:475

in *Liber sextus*, 8:536

Lyons Council, 8:906–907

mendicant controversy, 2:479

mendicant privileges, 14:16

papal taxation, 3:603

reign of, 12:357

Richard Fishacre, encouraging teachings of, 12:229

society, 13:278

Sylvestrine Benedictines, approval of, 2:275

torture sanctioned, 14:118

Innocent V (Pope), Bl., 1:878, 2:484, **7:476**, *477*

Innocent VI (Pope), 1:232, 2:128, 3:91, 493, 829, **7:476–477**

Innocent VII (Pope), **7:477**

Innocent VIII (Pope), **7:477–478**, *478*

Adrian of Castello, 1:130

Angelo Carletti di Chivasso, Bl., 1:413

Annecy Monastery, 1:470

censorship, 3:336

election, 8:54

holy lance, 7:31

pre-Reformation spiritual hunger, 3:606

prohibited books, 7:390

Roman Pontifical, 11:474

Innocent IX (Pope), **7:478–479**

Innocent X (Pope), 7:*479*, **479–480**

Ambrosians, 1:346

Barberini family pardon, 2:95

Bartholomite decline, 2:128

Charles of Sezze, St., 3:435

China, 3:514

Clement X (Pope), 3:788

de auxiliis controversy, 4:113

grace controversy, 7:716

Jansenism, 1:97, 262, 717, 4:436, 13:781

papal decline, 3:612

Piarists, 7:1043

Retz, Jean François Paul de Gondi de, 12:180

Innocent XI (Pope), Bl., 3:615, **7:480–481**

Alexandre, Noël, 1:267

Busenbaum, Hermann, 2:716

Caulet, François Étienne, 3:296

Church-State relations, 4:591

Declaration of the French Clergy, 4:591, 6:77

English vicariates, 8:771

Fürstenberg, Wilhelm, 6:36–37

Gallicanism, 2:550, 6:76

González de Santalla, Tirso, 6:343

Huguenots, 3:639

laxism condemned, 8:411

Mary of Ágreda, 1:187

occult compensation, 4:42

papacy development under, 10:843–844

papal authority, 5:851

quietism, 1:84, 11:866

Innocent XII (Pope), 3:143, 417, 4:591, 5:171, **7:481–482**, *482*

Innocent XIII (Pope), 1:220, 7:32, **482–483**

Innocent of Le Mans, St., **7:483**

Innocents, Holy, **7:483–484**, 13:*4*

Innocenzo of Berzo, Bl., **7:484**

Innsbruck, University of (Austria), 8:61, 13:28

Inocencio de la Immaculada, Fr., 14:248

An Inquiry Concerning Human Understanding (Hume), 7:295

An Inquiry into the Nature and Causes of the Wealth of Nations (Smith), 14:361

Inquisitio de fide (Erasmus), 5:316

Inquisition, 3:603, 5:845, **7:485–492**

Acton, John Emerich Edward Dalberg, 1:85

Alberti, Leandro, 1:228

alchemy, 1:239

Alonso de Espina, 1:304

Alumbrados, 1:323

Anthony Pavonius, Bl., 1:508

autos-da-fé, 1:923–924

Bollandists, 2:471

Bruno, Giordano, 2:646

Carranza, Bartolomé, 3:20, 176

Catharism, 1:231

Charles V, 2:217

Chinese rites controversy, 3:497–498, 514

Clareni, 3:762

Córdoba, 4:263

Crusades against heretics, 4:413

de auxiliis controversy, 4:111–113

Dominicans, 4:851

Dominis, Marcantonio, 4:856

Fauré, Giovanni Battista, 5:647

France, 13:113

Fraticelli persecuted, 5:921–922

Histoire critique de l'Inquisition d'Espagne (Llorente), 8:740

Honorius IV (Pope), 7:86

Index of Prohibited Books, 7:390

Jews, 7:869–870

Köllin, 8:230

León, L., 8:497–498

Mexico, 8:318

origins of, 7:485–487

Paul IV (Pope), 11:24

Portugal, 9:65–66, 204

Protestant Reformation, 3:637

Remesal imprisoned, 12:105

Rienzo, Cola di, 3:829

Sixtus V (Pope), 13:197

Spain, 7:489–490, 491, 9:82, 204, 572–573, 13:383, 393

Spinozas, 13:418

suppression of heresy, 8:295

Torquemada role during, 14:113–114

torture use, 8:855

Inscriptiones Pompeianae (Wordsworth), 10:774

Inscriptions. See Epigraphy, Christian

Inscrutabili (encyclical, Leo XIII), 13:258

Inscrutabili Divinae (papal bull, Gregory XV), 9:680–681

Insight, 1:181, **7:492**

Insight. A Study of Human Understanding (Lonergan), 14:292

Insimulator et actor (Eugenius Vulgarius), 5:447

Insinuationes (St. Gertrude the Great), 6:191

Insolubilia (Roger of Notingham), 12:287

Inspiration, biblical, 2:354, 3:20, 28, 32, 174, **7:492–496**

Inspiration, prophecy as, 11:763

Instant, **7:496–497**

Instauratio magna (Bacon), 5:207

Instinct, **7:497–498**, 12:908, 13:44–45

Instituciones iuris canonici, quibus ius pontificium singulari methodo libris quatuor comprehenditur (Lancelotti), 8:316

Instituciones theologiae dogmaticae (Klupfel), 8:188

Institut Catholique (Paris), 12:228

Institut für die Wissenschaften vom Menschen, 8:232

Institut Supérieur de Philosophie, 9:503

Instituta regularia divinae legis (Junilius Africanus), 8:63

Institute for Black Catholic Studies, 1:162

The Institute for Continuing Theological Education, 10:434

Institute for Missionary Apologetics (Philippines), 5:3

Institute of Catholic Education, 8:224

Institute of Charity (IC), 3:419, 12:383–385, 385

Institute of Christian Doctrine, 6:51

Institute of Daughters of St. Anne, 6:109

Institute of Daughters of Saint Joseph, 9:140

Institute of Holy Guardian Angels, 14:885

Institute of Mary, 14:648

Institute of Medieval Canon Law, 8:257

Institute of Mme. d'Youville, 3:6

Institute of Perpetual Adoration (Ireland), 6:35

Institute of Sisters of the Immaculata, 12:377–378

Institute of Social Order, 8:317

Institute of Spiritual Theology (Rome), 3:145

Institute of the Blessed Virgin Mary, 2:30–31, 4:569

Institute of the Brothers of the Christian Schools, 4:620–621

Institute of the Daughters of Mary Help of Christians, 12:614

Institute of the Good Shepherd, 8:149

Institute of the Heart of Jesus (Paris), **6:682**

Institute of the Most Holy Savior, 1:307

Institute of the Prado, 3:473

Institute of the Sisters of Charity of St. Anne, 11:891

Institute of the Sisters of Mercy (RSM). *See* Sisters of Mercy

Institute of the Sisters of St. Joseph of the Sacred Heart, 9:23

Institute Saint Pierre de Sion (Jerusalem), 5:640

Institutes (Cassian), 6:112

Institutes (Cassiodorus), 10:756

Institutes (Dorotheus), 8:100

Institutes of Calvin, 2:887, 888–889, **7:498–499**

   Church and State, 3:637–638

   Eucharist, 5:427

   Huguenots, 7:166

   justification, 8:84, 86

   predestination, 11:655

   religious experience, 5:555

Institutes of Justinian, 8:316

Institutes of the Christian Religion (Calvin). *See Institutes* of Calvin

Institutio astronomica (Gassendi), 6:105

Institutio canonicorum, 3:68

Institutio de arte grammatica (Priscian), 9:439

Institutio Philosophae (Legrand), 3:185

Institution du prince chrétien (Espence), 5:358

Institution of the Rosary (Tiepolo), 12:374

Institutional Commodity Services, 13:412

Institutiones apologeticae (Gatti), 12:773

Institutiones divinarum et humanarum lectionum (Cassiodorus), 3:208–209, 12:757

Institutiones divinarum et saecularium litterarum (Cassiodorus), 9:438, 12:757

Institutiones Iuris Publici Ecclesiastici (Ottaviani), 10:710

Institutiones logicae (Burgersdjck), 12:768

Institutiones logicae (Sanseverino), 12:671

Institutiones logicae (Storchenau), 12:769

Institutiones metaphysicae (Storchenau), 12:769

Institutiones philosophiae (Liberatore), 12:772

Institutiones philosophiae (Palmieri), 10:813

Institutiones philosophicae (Tamagna), 12:770

Institutiones philosophicae (Tongiorgi), 14:109

Institutiones philosophicae (Urráburu), 14:344

Institutiones philosophicae auctoritte D. C. Archiepiscopi Lugdunensis (Valla), 12:771

Institutiones sanae philosophiae iuxta divi Thomae atque Aristoles inconcussa dogmata (Buzzetti), 12:772

Institutiones theologiae dogmaticae generalis (Knoll), 8:199

Institutiones theologiae moralis, 3:220–221

Institutiones theologicae (Bouvier), 2:572

Institutiones theologicae ad mentem D. Thomae (Puig), 12:773

Institutiones theologicae dogmaticae ad textum S. Thomae Concinnatae (Lépicier), 8:507

Institutions ad Fundamenta Linguae Hebraeae (Schultens), 6:697

Institutions liturgiques (Guéranger), 6:557, 8:671

Institutionum biblicarum pars prima (Lanigan), 8:326

Institutionum christianae pietatis libri 4 (Rovenius), 12:395

Institutionum omnis generis doctrinarum tomis VII comprehensarum syntaxis (Foscarini), 5:825

Instituto de Hermanas Adoratrices Esclaves del Santísimo Sacramento y de la Caridad. *See* Handmaids of the Blessed Sacrament and of Charity, Sisters Adorers

Instituto de Liturgia Hispana, 5:204

Institutum Historicum Societatis Iesu (publication), 7:791

Instiuones theolgiae mysticae (Schramm), 12:31

Instrucción de sacerdotes, en que se dá doctrina muy importante para conocer la alteza del sagrado oficio sacerdotal, y para exercitarle debidamente (Molina, Anthony de), 9:768–769

Instructio super ritibus Italo-graecorum (Clement VIII), 7:650

Instruction du chrétien (Richelieu), 12:237

Instruction for the Proper Implementation of the Constitution on the Sacred Liturgy (Vatican Council II), 1:318

Instruction of the Sacred Congregation of Rites on Sacred Music and Sacred Liturgy, 4:118, 119

Instruction on Certain Aspects of the "Theology of Liberation" (Congregation for the Doctrine of the Faith), 11:585

Instruction on Christian Freedom and Liberation (Congregation for the Doctrine of the Faith), 11:587

Instruction on Respect for Human Life in Its Origin and on the Dignity of Procreation (*Donum Vitae*), 5:560–561

Instruction on Sacred Music and Sacred Liturgy, 3:380, 8:646

Instructiones Fabricae Ecclesiasticae (Borromeo), 3:701

Instructiones praedicationis verbi Dei (St. Charles Borromeo), 11:621

Instructions générales en forme de catéchisme (Pouget), 3:243

Instructions to the Holy (Valdés), 14:368

Instructionum libri duo (St. Eucherius of Lyons), 5:438

Instrumental causality, 1:46, 3:824, 4:71–72, 5:100, **7:499–501**

Instrumental leadership, 14:813

Instrumental power, 7:500

Instrumental signs, 13:116

Instrumentalism, 7:196, **501–502**, 14:228
  See also Pragmatism

Insult, **7:502**
  See also Contumely

Insurance programs, 7:176, 8:191

Intavolatura cioè Ricercari, Canzoni, Hinni, Magnificati (Cavazzoni), 3:312

Integrae servandae (*motu proprio*, Paul VI), 11:30

Integral Humanism (Maritain), 9:179

Integralism, 5:856, **7:503–504**, 10:262

Integrists, 1:803

Integrity, gift of, 1:104–105, **7:504–505**

Intellect, **7:505–508**
  abstraction, 1:45
  activity per Thomism, 8:208
  agnosticism, 1:180–181
  appetite, 1:602
  Aristotle, 1:682
  Averroës, 1:622, 676, 933
  Avicenna, 1:621–622, 672, 933, 940
  central sense, 3:346

certitude, 3:351
character, 3:387
cogitative power, 3:822–823
concept, 4:51–53
conversion of, 4:235, 236, 237–238
creative imagination, 4:348–349
criteriology, 4:367–368
human act, 7:170, 173–174
illumination, 7:320
immortality, 7:350
Kant's study of, 8:122, 124
Latin Averroism, 1:224, 935–936
reflection, 12:1
Siger of Brabant, 13:113
simple apprehension, 1:604
soul, 13:351
speculative, habits of, 5:744–745
spiritual acts, 13:422
William of Ockham, 14:747

Intellect, unity of, 4:882, **7:508, 510–512**, 13:339

Intellection, 8:204, 218

Intellectual consciousness, 4:152

Intellectual freedom, **5:942–944**

Intellectual knowledge, 8:202, 13:351

Intellectual life, **7:512–514**, 8:461

Intellectual pleasure, 11:417

Intellectual preference, 14:723

Intellectualism, 1:876, **7:514–515**, 8:83, 13:151

L'Intellectualisme de saint Thomas (Rousselot), 12:394

Intellectuality of metaphysics, 9:552

Intellectus fit omnia (The intellect becomes all things), 12:756

Intelligence, 7:505, 8:208, 9:54

Intelligent Theology (Fransen), 5:918

Intelligibility, principle of, 5:745, **7:515–516**, 12:3

Intention, 13:137, 409

Intention (Anscombe), 1:492, 493

Intention, purpose of, **7:516**

Intentional species. *See* Species, intentional

Intentionality, **7:516–519**
  Aristotelianism, 1:678
  bridging subject and object gap, 10:510
  concept, 4:52
  distinction, 4:781
  knowing, 8:201
  ordination, 7:39–40
  phenomenology's reaction to objectivity, 10:511
  Thomism, 8:209–210

Intentions (Holy orders), 7:39

Inter cunctas (papal bull, Martin V), 6:608

Inter mirifica (decree, Paul VI), 3:626, 10:546

Inter multiplices (apostolic consititution, Alexander VII), 6:78

Inter multiplices (encyclical, Pius IX), 14:285

Inter multiplices (papal bull, Alexander VIII, 1690), 1:262

Inter multiplices (papal bull, Innocent VIII, 1487), 3:336

Inter multiplicis (papal bull, Leo X), 9:835

Inter omnia (encyclical, Alexander III), 1:256

Inter plura illa mala (brief, Pius VII), 4:62

Interarium catholicum (Focher), 5:785

Intercession, **7:519–520**

Intercourse. *See* Sexual relations

Interdict, 3:637

Los Intereses católicos en América (Eyzaguirre), 5:573

Interest (moneylending), 2:322, 3:18, 19

Interfaith Center, Brandeis University (Waltham, MA), 3:717

Inter-Faith Peace Movement (Kenya), 8:151–152

Interfaith relations, Greece, 6:437

Interimism, 9:62

Interims (doctrinal formulas), 3:431, **7:520–521**, 13:330

Interior Castle (St. Teresa of Avila), 3:136, 13:829–830

Interlude on the Nature of the Four Elements (Rastell), 9:882

Intermediate state of judgment, 8:32–33

Internal security (McCarran) Act (1951), 10:172

International Catholic Deaf Association (ICDA), **7:521**

International Catholic Migration Commission (ICMC), **7:521–522**, 10:429

International Catholic Stewardship Council (ICSC), **7:522–523**

International Catholic-Orthodox Theological Commission, 5:69

International Charismatic Renewal Services, 3:393

International Church of the Foursquare Gospel, 9:405

International College in Rome, 13:122

International Commission on English in the Liturgy (ICEL), 1:483, 5:253, **7:523–525**, 10:524

Consultation on Common Texts, 4:201

Diekmann, Godfrey, 4:740

Ecumenical aspects, 8:679

founding of, 8:439

liturgical books, 8:641

liturgical movement, 8:676

International Community, 8:68, 13:260

International Confederation of Christian Family Movements (ICCFM), 3:536

International Consultation on English Texts (ICET), 4:201, 5:253–254, **7:525–526**, 8:679

International Convention of Humanistic Studies, 10:191

International Council for Catechesis (COINCAT), **7:526–527**

International Council of Community Churches, 4:199–200

International Eucharistic Conference, 1:652, 8:250, 13:76

International Eucharistic Congresses, Pontifical Committee for, 5:433

International Federation of Catholic Historical Associations, 13:59

International General Assembly of Spiritualists, 13:437

International Group of Fathers (Coetus Internationalus Patrum), 8:447

International Guild of Nurses, 6:96

International Joint Lutheran/Roman Catholic Commission, 8:90

International law, 13:561, 14:570–572

International Lutheran/Roman Catholic Working Group, 14:320

International Metapsychical Institute, 11:463

International Missionary Conference (1910), 9:677

International Missionary Council (IMC), 5:71–72, **7:527**, 9:697

International Old Catholic Congress, 10:580

International Order of Alhambra, **1:286–287**

International Register of Cultural Works under Special Protection in case of Armed Conflict (UN), 14:397

International Society for Krishna Consciousness. *See* Hare Krishnas

International Style (architecture), 3:680–681

International Theological Colloquium, 5:69

International Theological Commission (ITC), 2:34, 5:347, **7:527–529**, 8:840

International Union of Social Studies, 9:503–504

International Union of Superiors General (Women) (UISG), **7:529**

Internelle Consolacion, 5:848

Interpersonal life, 13:438–439

The Interpretation of the Bible in the Church (Pontifical biblical Commission), 6:29, 11:478

Interpretation of the Psalms (Athanasius, St.), 5:510

Interpretationists, 11:850

Interpretations of Poetry and Religion (Santayana), 12:680

Interpretative history, 6:883

Interracial Justice: A Study of the Catholic Doctrine of Race Relations (LaFarge), 8:278

Interracial Review, 10:158

Interreligious dialogue, 9:688–689

See also Ecumenical dialogues; Religious pluralism

Interrogatory creed, 4:349

Intervention, Divine, **7:530**

Intestinal troubles, patron saint of, 5:173

Intorcetta, Prospero, **7:530**, 12:391

Intrinsic modes, 9:751

Introductio ad Encyclopediam arcanam; sive initia et specimina scientiae generalis (Leibniz), 10:606

Introductio ad libros canonicos bibliorum VT (Carpzov), 3:174

Introductio ad theologiam (Abelard), 1:19

Introduction á la philosophie de l'histoire (Gerbet), 6:165

Introduction à l'étude de la philosophie médiévale (Van Steenberghen), 14:387

Introduction à l'ontologie du connaître (Simon), 13:128

An Introduction or Preparative to a Treatise on the English Mission (Baker), 2:102

Introduction to a Devout Life (Francis de Sales), 5:868

Introduction to Early Christian Symbolism (Palmer), 10:812

Introduction to Holy Scripture (Adrianus), 5:511

Introduction to Liturgical Theology (Schmemann), 12:742

Introduction to Orthodox Theology (Bulgakov), 6:459

An Introduction to Philosophy (Ryan), 12:445

Introduction to Romans (Luther), 14:253

Introduction to the Devout Life (St. Francis de Sales), 10:516

The Introduction to the Devout Life (Sales), 8:415

Introduction to the Eternal Gospel (Gerard of Borgo San Donnino), 5:897

Introduction to the Principles of Morals and Legislation (Bentham), 2:285

Introductiones parvulorum (Abelard), 1:18

Introductorius in Evangelium Aeternum (Borgo San Donnino), 14:16

Introductory Papers on Dante (Sayers), 12:717

Introit, 4:32, 893–894, **7:530–531**

"Introit of the Third Mass of Christmas" (liturgical music), 14:215

Introspection, 1:796, **7:531–533**, 13:349

See also Reflection

Intuition, **7:533–535**

Bergson, Henri Louis, 2:296

British moralists, 2:624

Cartesian method, 4:679

categories of being, 3:257

causality, 3:307

certitude, 3:354

deontologism, 4:673–674

Kant's theory, 8:124

knowledge, 8:203, 205, 210

Le Roy, E., 8:513

Neo-Kantian Marburg School, 10:237

objective order of values, 14:380

simple apprehension, 1:605

William of Ockham, 14:747

Inuit people, 1:210, 13:66–67

Inuvik (Canada), 3:3.6

Invectiva de sui ipsius ignorantia (Petrarch), 11:216

Invective Orations against Julian (Gregory of Nazianzus), 10:755

Invention, 9:565

Inventions to the Book of Job (Blake), 10:130

Inversion, 11:770

Investiture, **7:535–536**

Gregory VII (Pope) St., 6:493

Henry I, 6:736

Henry IV, 6:176–177

laicism, 8:282

papal prohibition of, 10:837

symbols of, 7:536

Investiture struggle, 3:635, 5:323, **7:536–539**

Adalbero of Würzburg, St., 1:100

Alexander II (Pope), 1:253

Altmann of Passau, St., 1:909

Ancient See of Canterbury, 3:72

anointing, 1:479

Anonymous of York, 1:489

Arnulf of Milan, 1:721

Bernard of Parma, St., 2:315

Bernold of Constance, 2:327

Bonizo of Sutri, 2:506

Brauweiler Abbey, 2:586

Callistus II (Pope), 2:880

Canon Law, 3:46

chronicles, 1:462

Cluniacs, 3:813

Concordat of Worms, 3:601

Council of Anse, 1:493

Council of Autun, 1:926, 927

Cyprian, St., 4:459

Ecumenical councils, 4:300

First Lateran, 8:350

forged Leonine documents, 8:484

Honorius II (Pope), 7:83

Hugh of Die, 7:141

Hugh of Fleury, 7:152

Ivo of Chartres, St., 7:679

Ladislaus of Hungary, 8:275

Leopold III, 8:503

Low Countries, 10:257

Matilda (Countess of Tuscany), 9:332

nature of power, 13:253

Regalia, 12:27

restoring the empire, 8:767

Sigebert of Gembloux, 13:112

See also Worms, Concordat of (1122)

Invice nos Stephani (trope), 14:216–217

Invicta Veritas (Abell), 1:20

Invocation of Mary, Blessed Virgin, 9:284

Involuntarity, **7:539–540**, 14:584

See also Voluntarity

Inwood, W. H., 3:709

Ioannes Antonius de Sancto Georgio, 3:52

Ioannes Baptista de S. Blasio, 3:53

Ioannes Baptista Trovamala, 3:52

Ioannes Berberius, 3:52

Ioannes Cagnazzo de Tabia, 3:52

Ioannes de Anaia, 3:52

Ioannes de Chapuis, 3:52

Ioannes de Imola, 3:51

Ioannes de Lignano, 3:51

Ioannes de Palaciis Rubeis, 3:52

Ioannes de Prato, 3:52

Ioannes de Vico Mercato, 3:52

Ioannes Franciscus de Pavinius, 3:52

Ioannes Koelnet de Vanckel, 3:52

Ioannes Milis, 3:52

Ion (Plato), 5:89

Iona Abbey (Scotland), 1:110–111, 7:*540*, **540**, 12:830

Ionata, Ninetta (Mother), 12:104

Ionesco, Eugène, 1:48, 49, 5:544, 546

Ionia (Greece), 6:440

Ionians, 4:367

Iowa, 4:281, 888, **7:540–543**, 8:778

See also specific dioceses and archdioceses

Iows, immigration, 8:778–779, 13:164

Iphigénie (Racine), 11:888

Iphigénie auf Tauris (Goethe), 6:331

Iqbāal, Muḥhammad, 7:613, 10:821

Iqtiṣad (al-Ghazzālī), 8:110

IRA (Irish Republican Army), 7:569, 10:442

Iran, 1:6, **7:543–545**, *544*

See also Persia

Das iranische Erlösungsmysterium (Reitzenstein), 12:40

Iraq, **7:545–548**, *547*

   Baghdad, 8:170

   Chaldean Catholic Church, 2:4–5, 11–12

   demographic statistics, 7:545

   ecclesiastical organization, 7:545

   Kuwait, 8:258

   map, 7:*546*

Ireland, **7:553–570**, *556, 557, 558, 559*

   Aarosian rule, 8:409

   Act of Settlement (1662), 1:75–77

   Act of Union, 5:183

   archdeacons, 1:634

   Australia, 1:899, 900, 903

   Brown, George, 2:637

   Canons Regular of St. Augustine, 3:67

   Carmelites, 3:143

   Catholic emancipation (1829), 7:549

   Catholic *vs.* Protestant conflict, 4:245

   Celtic religion, 3:330

   chronicles and annals, 1:464

   Church history, 8:326

   Cistercian abbey reform, 8:529

   Colgan, John, 3:834

   Colman, SS., 3:840–841

   Columba of Iona, St., 3:841, 863

   Columban, St., 3:598–599, 600, 863–864

   Confederate Catholics, 12:250

Conway, William, 4:245

creedal statements, 4:356

Croagh Patrick, 4:369

Croke, Thomas William, 4:375

Cromwell, Oliver, 4:375

Culdees, 4:422–424

Cullen, Paul, 4:424

D'Alton, Edward Alfred, 4:502

demographic statistics, 7:553

Diamond, Charles, 4:728

Dublin Archdiocese, 12:443–444

ecclesiastical organization, 7:554

England, 8:379

Fleming, Thomas, 5:761

Gladstone, William, 6:236

Gregory XVI (Pope), 6:509

hospice movement, 7:117

independence movement, 9:24, 123

Innocent X (Pope), 7:479–480

Jesuits, 7:783

Kevin, St., 8:161–162

Kilian of Aubigny, St., 8:167–168

Kilian of Würzburg, St., 8:168

Leen, Edward, 8:445–446

Legion of Mary, 8:453–454

liturgical movement, 8:674

map, 7:*555*

medieval literature, 9:441

''Mercy Ireland,'' 13:187

mission, 5:753, 7:567, 10:953, 954

monks, 2:422, 5:514

nationalism, 4:375, 424

19th-20th century religious orders, 3:622

Patrick, St., 10:953, 954

Presbyterianism, 11:680

Protestant Reformation, 3:612–613

Rinuccini, Giovanni Battista, 12:250

Scotland, 8:133–134

Sisters of Loretto, 8:787

Sisters of Mercy, 13:182, 187

Solemnity of All Saints, 1:289–290

See also Art, Irish; Irish confessors and martyrs; Patrick, St.

Ireland, Church of (Anglican), **7:548–549**

Ireland, John (Abp. of St. Paul, MN), 7:549, **549–552**, 12:572, 573

   Abbelen, Peter, 1:7

   Americanism, 1:354, 355

   apostolic delegation in the U.S., 1:583, 584

   Bouquillon controversy, 2:564, 12:787

   Faribault plan, 5:625

Ireland, John (Abp. of St. Paul, MN) (continued)
lay congresses, 8:412
McQuaid, Bernard John, 9:406
parochial schools, 1:354, 584
relations with other ethnic leaders, 9:656–657
St. John's Abbey and University, 12:552
See also Irish Catholic Colonization Association of the U.S.
Ireland, John (martyr), Bl., 5:227, **7:552–553**
Ireland, Seraphine (Mother), **7:553**
Ireland, William, Bl., 5:236, 686
Irenaeus, St., **7:570–571**, 10:966, 14:134, 158, 189
 Acts of the Martyrs, 1:93
 Adam, 1:104
 Alogoi, 1:304
 anonymous Christian, 1:489
 Antichrist, 1:516
 apocrypha, 1:558
 Apostolic Fathers, 1:587, 588
 apostolic succession, 1:591
 apostolicity, 1:595
 Ascension of Jesus Christ, 1:771
 atonement, 1:837
 authorship of John's Gospel, 7:910
 Basilides, 2:148–149
 beatific vision, 2:172
 biblical canon, 3:21, 26, 31
 birth imagery in baptism, 2:75
 bishops, 2:413
 catechesis, 3:228
 causality, 3:303
 Christocentrism, 3:558
 Christology, 3:560
 church architecture, 1:756
 Clement I (Pope), St., 3:774
 conservation, 4:160
 creedal statements, 4:350
 divine judgment, 8:31
 early church in Gaul, 6:111
 Easter controversy, 3:593
 exegetical works, 5:509
 fermentum (eucharistic bread), 5:689
 heresy, 6:773
 immortality, 7:348, 353
 impassibility of God, 7:358
 infant baptism, 2:67
 Lenten fasting, 8:468
 liturgical history, 8:653
 Luke's Gospel, 8:859
 Montanism, 5:148
 presbyters, 11:673
 priesthood, 11:693
 pseudo-gnosis, 13:443–444
 public Confession, 4:76
 recapitulation in Christ, 11:952–953, 983
 sacraments, 12:467
 similarity, 13:126
 soul, 13:340
 theology of history, 6:887
 works of, 7:570–571
 works of charity, 3:402
 See also Patristic era
Irenaeus of Tyre, 2:797
Irene (Byzantine Empress), **7:572**
 iconoclasm, 2:751, 753, 785, 793, 821, 7:282
 papal selection of Emperors, 8:480
 Roman primacy, 2:752–753, 3:167, 426
 worship of images, 8:557
Irene of Portugal, St., **7:572**
Irenicism, 3:472, 7:421–422, **572–573**
Irénikon (periodical), 2:183
Ireton, Peter Leo (Bp. of Richmond, VA), 14:543
Irigiray, Luce, 1:412
Irimbert of Admont, 1:117
Irish Americans
 Connecticut Church, 4:122–123, 124
 Georgia, 6:150–151
 Iowa, 7:541
 Maine, 9:56
 Massachusetts, 9:305–306, 307
 See also Immigration and emigration
Irish Capuchins, 13:74
Irish Catholic Colonization Association of the U.S., **7:573**, 13:402
Irish Catholic Confederacy, 12:724
Irish Catholicism, 5:184
Irish Christian Brothers, 3:622, **7:573–574**, 11:682, 12:226
Irish College in Paris, 7:575
Irish College in Rome, 7:575
Irish College of Bordeaux (France). See Collège de Ste. Anne la Royale (France)
Irish College of Compostella (Spain), 7:574–575
Irish College of Lisbon (Portugal), 7:574
Irish College of Nantes (France), 7:575
Irish College of Poitiers (France), 7:575
Irish College of Seville (Spain), 7:574–575
Irish College of Toulouse (France), 7:575
Irish Colleges on the Continent, **7:574–576**
Irish confessors and martyrs, **7:576–582**
Irish Crosses, 4:379, 7:583, **583–584**, 8:138
Irish mission, 5:753
Irish Oath (1774-1829), 10:501–502
Irish penitentials, 11:74–75
Irish pilgrims to Rome, 11:353
Irish Republican Army (IRA), 7:569, 10:442
Irish Sisters of Charity, 7:117, 10:68
Irish Theological Quarterly, 9:26
Irish versions of the Bible, **2:368**
Irmandades, 2:595–596
Irmengard, Bl., **7:584**
Irmgard of Hammerstein, 1:664
Irmgardis of Cologne, St., **7:584**
Irmhart, Öser, **7:584**
Irmina, St., **7:584**
Irnerius (jurist), 3:47, **7:584–585**
Iroquois people
 Canadian mission, 3:4, 5, 8:279, 382, 383
 Idaho, 7:289
 Jesuits, 9:721
 liturgical language, 8:668
 sky and sky gods, 13:205–206
Irrationalism, **7:585–587**, 10:390
Irreligious indifferentism, 7:421
Irving, Edward, 3:278, **7:587–588**
Isaac (Hebrew Patriarch), 1:37, 37, 5:408, 10:948
Isaac I Angelus (Byzantine Emperor), 2:787, 4:176
Isaac II Angelus, 12:547
Isaac ben Abraham, **7:588**
Isaac Israeli, 4:184, **7:589**, 863, 8:583
Isaac of Monte Luco, St., **7:589**
Isaac of Spoleto. See Isaac of Monte Luco, St.
Isaac of Stella, 3:749, **7:589–590**, 9:454, 13:343
Isaac Saggi Nehor, 2:831
Isaac the Good of Langres, St., **7:590**
Isaac the Great, St., 1:700, **7:590–591**
Isaak, Heinrich, 2:717, **7:591–592**
Isabel (Queen of Jerusalem), 7:774
Isabella I (Queen of Castile), 7:592, 592, 10:978, 14:881, 882
 accomplishments, 13:390
 Alexander VI (Pope), 1:259
 Columbus, Christopher, 3:865, 866
 Mudejar ceiling, 13:380
 Reconquest, 13:380

works of charity, 3:416
Isabella of Brienne, 4:411
Isabelle of France, Bl., **7:592–593**
Isagoge (Porphyry), 11:520, 14:323
Isaiah (Hebrew prophet), **7:593–594**
 afterlife, 1:165
 Alma prophecy, 1:297
 altarpiece by Buoninsegna, 5:*574*
 disciple as term, 4:768
 Jesus as savior, 2:58
 wife of, 11:765
Isaiah, Book of, **7:594–599**
 altars in, 1:320
 angels, 1:425
 apocalyptic style, 1:546
 authorship, 7:595
 Babylon, 2:4, 5
 beatific vision, 2:170, 171
 beatitudes, 2:178
 canonicity, 3:24
 Christmas, 3:555
 contents, 7:594–595
 conversion in, 4:232–233
 creation, 4:341, 342
 Day of the Lord in, 4:548
 Dead Sea Scroll version of, 4:562
 divine election, 5:146
 Emmanuel as the Messiah, 5:192
 eschatology, 5:334
 Eusebius's commentaries, 5:452
 exile of Judah, 13:40
 gates of hell, 6:107
 Gehenna, 6:116
 Gentiles, 6:140
 gifts of the Holy Spirit, 7:47
 glory, 6:244
 glory of God (end of creation), 6:245, 246
 God, name of, 6:298, 8:780, 13:77
 God as redeemer, 11:965
 God's ineffability, 7:445
 God's spirit, 13:426, 427
 guilt, 6:570, 570–571
 Hades, 6:604
 heaven, 6:684, 685
 holiness of man, 9:87
 hope of salvation, 7:105–106
 Jesus' possession of the Spirit, 2:58
 justice of God, 8:70
 justice of men, 8:73
 justification, 8:76, 80
 kenosis, 8:143
 Kingdom of God, 8:173
 kingship, 8:179

laity, 8:290
Lamb of God, 8:299, 300, 301
liturgy, 9:63
magic, 9:39
man, terms for, 13:316
messianism, 9:63, 542–543, 544
peace, 11:49
prophetic word, 8:4
ritual bathing and purification, as symbol of baptism, 2:57–58
seraphim, 13:5
serpent as symbol, 13:19, 20
Seven Last Words, 13:37
sin, 13:143, 144, 145, 146, 148
social principle, 13:248
Song of Songs, 13:319
soul, 13:336
spirit, 13:424
spiritual renewal, 9:87
Suffering Servant, Songs of the, 13:588, 591–592
word of God, 14:836
Isaiah, Canticles of, 3:73
Isaias Boner of Cracow, Bl., **7:599–600**
Isasi-Díaz, Ada María, 5:677, 678, 8:369
Is-Baal (son of Saul), 2:282
Isenheim Altarpiece (Grünewald), 6:544
Isfahānī, 1:782
Isfried, St., **7:600**
Ishaq ibn-Hunayn, 1:671
Isĥ-cyahb III, 5:5–6, 7
Ishida-Pinto, Anthony, Bl., 7:735
Ishimoto, Rufus, Bl., 7:733
Ishmael ben Elisha (Rabbi), 5:508
Īshō'dād of Merv (Bp.), **7:600**
Ishō'yab bar Maldon, 3:366
Isidore Mercator. *See* Pseudo-Isidore
Isidore of Kiev (Card.), **7:600–601**, 14:273, 278
 Eastern Schism, 2:762, 828
 eucharistic epiclesis, 5:279
 Lithuanian union with Rome, 12:421
Isidore of Pelusium, St., **7:601–602**
Isidore of Seville, St., 5:640, 773, 6:23, 7:*602*, **602–605**
 acedia, 1:67
 anti-Jewish legislation, 7:604
 atomism, 1:833
 Augustinianism, 1:877
 bestiaries, 2:342, 343
 Braulio, St., 2:585
 Cassian, John, 3:207
 catechesis, 3:240
 Christian paideia study, 10:756

chronicle of, 1:461
Church-State relations, 3:634
civil authority, 1:921
dialectics, 4:725
docility, 4:797
encyclopedia of, 5:206
following of Christ, 5:788
Fourth Council of Toledo, 3:325
heresey, 7:603–604
Justus of Urgel, 8:104
lives of saints, 12:606
medieval Latin literature works of, 9:439–440
natural law, 10:181
preaching, 11:619
prescholasticism, 12:757
priesthood, 11:699
relics, 12:52
sacraments, 12:467–468
Silos Abbey, 13:120
Vulgate, commendation of, 14:594
works of charity, 3:409
Isidore the Farmer, St., **7:605**
Isidorian Renaissance, 3:159
Isidoriana. See Hispana Collectio Versio (canonical collection)
Isin period (c. 1958-1733 B.C.), 9:529
Isis and Osiris (Egyptian deities), **7:605**, 10:87
Isis Unveiled (Blavatsky), 13:935
Islam, **7:606–614**
 'Abbāsids, 1:6–7
 African mission, 3:624–625
 Aḥmadiyya, 1:191
 Albania, 1:213
 alchemy, 1:237
 Alfarabi, 1:276, 277
 Algazel, 1:281–282
 Algeria, 1:284, 286
 Ali ('Alī Ibn Abī Tālib), 1:287
 al-Kindī's refutation, 8:170
 Arabia, 1:611–612
 Aristotelianism, 1:671–673
 Ash'arī, Al-(Abū Al-Hasan) 'Alī, 1:281, 620–621, 781–782
 Assyrian Church of the East, 1:806–807
 astrology, 1:813
 Baghdad as center, 8:170
 biblical archaeology, 2:381
 biology, 2:401
 Bogomilism, 2:459
 Brunei, 2:644
 bulla cruciata, 2:688
 Burkina Faso, 2:704

Islam *(continued)*
Byzantine civilization, 2:767
caliphs, 1:611, 2:873
Caribbean, 3:116
church architecture, 3:811, 812
circumcision, 7:610
Córdoba martyrs, 3:863
creed, 7:608–609
Crusades, 4:404, 405, 407, 410–412
dervish orders of, 4:677
devshirme system, 10:718
dhimmi, 4:715–716
divination, 4:786
dreams, 4:904
Druzes, 4:913
Ecumenical Patriarchate, 4:196–197
Five Pillars of faith, 7:609–610, 622
fundamentalism, 1:153, 286
hajj, 6:623–624
hospitality, 7:118
Ibn 'Arabī, 7:270–271
iconoclasm, 2:751
interpretations of Jesus, 7:842
Jewish and Christian influence, 7:607
jihād, 7:610
Kalām, 8:109–111
law, theology, and mysticism,
7:610–613
liberation thinking, 8:549
Mahdism, 9:48
Malaysia, 9:69, 71
Mali, 9:76
Mauritania, 9:371
Meccan pagnism incorporated,
10:51–52, 53
modern trends in, 7:613–614
mosques of, 10:8–11
Mu'tazilite school of, 10:74
mysticism, 13:594–595
Nizārīs sect of, 10:402
origins, 7:606–608
philosopher of the Arabs, 8:170–171
prayer in, 11:591
Sicily, 13:103
slavery, African, 13:215
Spain, 13:378–381
spread throughout Nubia, 10:472
Sunnites, 13:612–615
U.S., 3:718, 719–720
Wahhābis, 14:605
See also Arabian philosophy;
Babism; Baha'ism; Catholic-Islamic
dialogue; Imām; Muslim invasions;
Shī'sm
Islamic art, **7:614–619**

Islamic Call Society, 8:560
Islamic confraternities, 4:677, **7:619–620**
Islamic education, 8:537
Islamic era, 5:314
Islamic fundamentalism, 7:545
Islamic law, 7:610–611, **620–623**, 8:110
Islamic studies, 13:235–236
Islamic tradition, **7:623–624**, 8:110,
10:10–11, 51
Isle of Man, 13:297–298
Isleifur Gizurrasson (Bp. of Skalholt),
7:275
Ismā'īlīs, 1:612, **7:624–625**, 13:84–85
Isnard of Chiampo, Bl., **7:625**
Isochristes of Egypt, 4:192
Isocrates, 1:773, 5:88, 8:536
Isolanis, Isidore de, 3:92
Isoré, Remi, St., 1:400, **7:625**
Ispoved (Tolstoi), 14:105
Israel, ancient, **7:625–645**
chosen people, 8:3–4
cities and towns, 7:*628, 629, 631*
covenant with God, 9:541
David (King), 4:536–537
Day of the Lord, 4:547–548
diaspora, 4:674, 730–731
dispensational theology, 4:776
early religions, 7:628–635, 13:142,
14:855–859
family of nations, 8:568–569
feasts, 5:655–656
history, 7:635–645, 13:509–511
Judah (tribe), 8:1
Kingdom of God, 8:173
landscape, 7:*626, 627*
law, 8:396
magic, 9:39
monarchy, 7:*630*, 8:175–176,
178–179
name, 7:625–626
providence of God, 14:792–793
punishment from God, 13:815
salvation, 9:241, 244–245, 247
slavery, 13:206
Songs of the Suffering Servant,
13:590
sons of God, 13:321–322
temples, 7:*632, 633*
wisdom, 14:788
Yahweh, 7:464, 9:540
Israel, modern, **7:645–648**, *647*
demographic statistics, 7:646
ecclesiastical organization, 7:646
Holocaust, 7:13
map, 7:*646*

Israelites
afterlife, 1:164
altars, 1:319–320
angels, 1:425, 427
anointing, 1:477–478
ark of the covenant, 1:688–690, *689*
blood vengeance, 2:444
circumcision, 3:739, 741
cities of asylum, 1:814, 2:444
God as director of history, 9:539
law, 1:118, 2:526–527
miracles, 9:663
temples, 13:808–809
tents of meeting, 13:825
vows to God, in the Bible, 14:590
women, role of, 14:828
See also Bible,
historical/geographical context;
Judaism; Old Testament; Palestine
Issenmann, Clarence G. (Bp. of
Columbus), 3:868
Isserles, Moses, 12:140
Istanbul (Turkey), 14:*242*
See also Constantinople
ISTC (Vatican Library database), 14:422
Iste Confessor Domini Colentes (hymn),
7:648
Istituzioni harmoniche (Zarlino), 14:910
Istoria del concilio Tridentino (Sarpi),
12:694
Istoria diplomatica (Maffei), 10:773
Istoria ecclesiastica (Orsi), 10:676
Istorie florentine (Machiavelli), 9:21
Istoriia veherasnego dnia (Tolstoi),
14:105
Istrian Schism, 2:499–500
Istruzione e pratica per un confessore
(St. Alphonsus Liguori), 1:311
Īsvaratva, 7:408
Ita of Killeedy, St., 2:601, **7:648**
Itala Collectio-Versio (Prisca), 3:39
Itala Versio. See Prisca Versio
(canonical collection)
Italia sacra (Ughelli), 6:876
Italian Americans, 2:93
See also Immigration and emigration
Italian art, 4:395–397
Italian Camaldolese Congregation, 2:256
Italian Concordat (1803), 11:379–380
The Italian Journal (Seton), 13:24, 32
Italian Olivetan Congregation, 2:256
Italian Popular Party, 6:537
Italian Sylvestrine Congregation, 2:256
Italian unification, 3:314
See also Roman question

Italicus, Tiberius Catius Silius. *See* Silius Italicus

Italo-Albanian Catholic Church (Eastern Catholic), 2:747, **7:648–652**

Italy, 5:871–872, **7:652–675**

  Albanian immigrants, 7:649

  anticlericalism, 1:519

  architecture, 3:696, 703–708, 712–713, 7:*657, 660, 661, 662, 663, 664, 668*

  art, 4:395–397

  baroque period, 2:107, 112–113

  Basilians, 2:140–141

  Benedictine monasteries, 2:257

  Byzantine Basilians, 2:143

  Carbonari, 3:99–101

  Carmelites, 3:126, 143, 145

  Carolingian Dynasty, 3:171

  Carthusians, 3:195

  catechesis, 3:243

  Catharism, 3:259

  Catholic Action, 3:277

  Christmas customs, 3:557

  chronicles and annals, 1:462, 463, 465

  Church-state relations, 9:753, 14:481–482

  Communio edition in, 4:31

  Confirmation, 4:87

  Counter Reformation, 3:610, 4:310, 314

  Crusades, 4:401, 404, 413–414

  demographic statistics, 7:652

  ecclesiastical organization, 7:653–654

  education, 3:49, 5:865

  fascist regime, 3:619, 642

  freedom of religion, 5:947

  Greek philosophy, 6:441

  Gregory I (Pope), St., 6:481, 484

  Gregory XVI (Pope), 6:508

  Henry II, St., 6:744

  Honorius I (Pope), 7:79

  idealism, 7:300

  Jerusalem (Kingdom), 7:775

  Knights of Columbus, 8:191

  Landulf, 8:322–323

  Lateran Pacts, 8:356–360

  lauda spirituale, 3:150

  Lentini, Domenico, Bl., 8:471

  literature, 4:372–374, 9:438–439

  liturgy, 8:6, 652–653, 673

  Lombard League, 8:767

  Lutheranism, 12:19

  map, 7:*655*

  Marian shrines, 13:93

  mission, 3:498, 5:201, 9:109

  modernism, 9:755

  music, 8:685, 690, 692

  nationalism, 6:97, 12:253

  Peace of God Movement, 11:50

  Pius X (Pope), St., 11:390–391

  Pius XI (Pope), 11:394

  politics, 4:366, 12:116–117

  Redemptorists, 11:993–994

  Sanfedists, 12:666

  Sicily, 13:102–104

  Siena, 13:105–109

  works of charity, 3:418

  See also Italian unification; Renaissance; Renaissance architecture; Risorgimento; Roman question; States of the Church

ITC (International Theological Commission), **7:527–529**

Ite, missa est, **7:675**

Iter litterarium in Alsatiam et Lotharingiam (Ruinart), 12:407

Ithacius (Bp.), 3:86

I-Thou model of charity, 8:833

I-Thou mystics, 10:117–118

I-Thou relationship, 4:24–25, 10:116, 12:70, 14:199

I-Thou-We relationship, 14:199

Itineraria (pilgrim guide book), **7:675–677**, 11:353

Itinerario para párrocos (Peña Montenegro), 5:62

Itinerarium (Ricoldus de Monte Croce), 12:242

Itinerarium ad regiones sub aequinoctiali plaga constituas (Geraldini), 6:158

Itinerarium Antonini, 7:676

Itinerarium Cambriae (Giraldus Cambrensis), 6:231

Itinerarium catholicum (Focher), 14:367

Itinerarium Egeriae (Pilgrimage of Egeria), **5:104–106**

Itinerarium Einsidilense, 5:286, 7:677

Itinerary of William of Malmesbury, 7:677

Ittig, L., 1:587

Iturbide, Agustín de, 2:718, 5:791

Iturrate Zubero, Domingo, Bl., **7:677**

Ius canonicum universum (Reiffenstuel), 12:34

Ius divinum, 14:172–173

Ius publicum, 3:644, **7:677**

Iustitiam et pacem (*motu proprio* Paul VI), 11:481

Ivan IV (the Terrible), 12:423

Ivan VI (Czar of Russia), 11:549–550

Ivanios, Mar (Abp. of Trivandrum), **7:677–678**, 13:719–721

Ivanovich, Ivan (Abp. of Novgorod), 3:524

Ives, Charles, 3:*523*

Ives, Levi Silliman (Bp.), 7:*678*, **678–679**, 10:437

Ivo, St., **7:679**

Ivo Hélory, St., **7:679**

Ivo of Chartres (Bp.), St., 2:190, 3:441, **7:679–680**, 10:627

  Alger of Liége, 1:282

  Bernard of Tiron, St., 2:316

  Canon Law, 1:282, 3:45, 46, 47, 60

  Charles of Blois, Bl., 3:435

  Decretum of, 5:618

  influence of, 3:601

  investiture theology, 5:843

Ivo of Chartres (Bp.), St., collection of, 4:726, **7:680**

Ivo of Wardon, 1:138

Ivory Coast, **7:680–683**, *682*

Iwanaga, John, Bl., 7:732

IWW (Industrial Workers of the World), 10:171

Iyemitsu (Japanese Shōgun), 7:730

Iyo, Jerome de la Cruz, Bl., 7:735

Izard, Francis (Abbot), 5:319

Izquierdo, José Maria, 2:467–468

J

Jâbir ibn Hayyân, 1:237

Jablonska, Bernardina, Bl., **7:685**

Jaccard, François, 14:495

Jackson, Barbara. *See* Ward, Barbara

Jackson, Thomas, 3:152

Jackson Diocese (MS), **7:685–686**

Jacob (Hebrew Patriarch), 1:36, 319, 7:626, **686–687**, 10:948, 13:71

Jacob, Edmond, 3:27

Jacob ben Asher, 3:148

Jacob ha-Nazir of Lunel, 2:831

Jacob of Sarug (Bp.), **7:687–688**

Jacob of Serugh, 2:72

Jacobazzi, Domenico (Card.), **7:688**

Jacobellus, 4:481

Jacobellus (at Prague), 7:231

Jacobi, Friedrich Heinrich, 5:263, 7:586, **688–689**, 8:126, 12:345

Jacobina of Pisa, Bl., **7:689**

Jacobini, Ludovico (Card.), **7:689**

Jacobis, Giustino de, St., **7:689–690**

Jacobis, Justin de, 5:404

Jacobite Church of Antioch (Syrian), 5:19

Jacobites (English), **7:690–691**, 10:418–419

Jacobites (Syrian), 5:19, **7:691–692**
  Antiochene liturgy, 1:528
  biblical canon, 3:32
  Catholics vs., 13:704–705, 707
  Cilicia, 3:733
  controversy of 819, 8:170
  Melkites, 4:254
  Monophysitism, 1:523, 525
  See also Syrian Church

Jacob's Well (Myrc), 11:633

Jacobsen, T., 5:268

Jacopone da Todi, **7:692–693**
  Adoro Te Devote, 1:120
  Boniface VIII (Pope), 2:502
  Catherine of Genoa, St., 3:270
  Franciscan spirituality, 5:892, 894, 897

Jacques de Molay, **7:693**

Jacques de Vitry (Card.), 5:529, **7:693–694**
  Caesarius of Heisterbach, 2:850
  Carmelites, 3:131–132, 133
  Mary of Oignies, 2:204–205
  preaching, 11:620

Jadot, Jean, 1:585, **7:694**

Jadwiga, St. *See* Hedwig of Anjou, St.

Jadwiga of Poland, St., **7:694–695**, *695*

Jaegen, Jerome, **7:695**

Jaeger, Lorenz (Card.), **7:695–696**

Jaeger, Werner, 1:679, 684

Jaffree, Wallace v. (1985), 3:666

Jäger, Johann (Crotus Rubianus), **4:386**, 5:306

Jagiełło (King of Poland), 4:482, **7:696**, 8:604–605, 11:439

Jagiellonian Dynasty, 11:439–440

Jahouvey, Anna M., 3:419

Jahrbuch für Liturgiewissenschaft (periodical), 2:159

Jahrbuch für Philosophie und spekulative Theologie (periodical), 12:774

Jahwe und Christus (Schell), 12:732

Jainism, 1:833, **7:696–698**, 13:631–632

Jalāl al-Dīn Al-Rūmī, 1:621

Jalloutz, Dorothée, 3:296

Jamaica, 3:110–113, **7:698–700**, *700*

Jamdudum in Lusitania (encyclical, Pius X), 11:391

James (Bp. of Nisibis), 1:805

James (Duke of York), 10:492, 493, 494

James (son of Alphaeus), St., **7:700–701**, 769, 8:17, 74, 196–197, 13:155

James (son of Zebedee), Apostle, St., 3:556, **7:701**, 12:681, 683, 13:385

James, E. O., 12:68

James, Edward, Bl., 5:230

James, Epistle of, St., **7:701–703**
  Anointing of the Sick, 1:481
  canonicity, 3:21, 28, 31, 32
  catechesis, 3:227
  Christian law, 8:403
  Church in, 3:580
  date and authorship, 7:702
  divine election, 5:146
  faith and works, 7:702
  grace, 6:381
  guilt, 6:572
  inner moral demand of the law, 7:702
  Jewish wisdom of, 7:703
  justification, 8:80
  literary form, 3:591
  presbyters, 11:673
  rebirth, 11:951
  works of charity in, 1:300, 3:401

James, John A., 5:467

James, Roger, Bl., 5:226

James, William, 5:94, 7:*703*, **703–704**, 10:114, 115, 11:296
  Alcoholics Anonymous, 1:242
  appetite, 1:603
  Brightman, Edgar Sheffield, 2:617
  choice, 3:521
  empiricism, 5:198
  existence of God, 6:312
  form, 5:803
  free will, 5:939
  functionalism, 6:24
  humanism, 7:196
  idea, 7:295
  influence of, 7:*704*
  philosophy and science, 11:300
  pragmatism, 5:397, 556, 9:566–567, 12:48, 70
  Royce, Josiah, 12:397–398
  Santayana, George, 12:681
  self, concept of, 12:883–884
  soul, 13:348

James I (King of Aragon), 4:412

James I (King of England), 3:432, 7:*705*, **705–706**
  Abercromby, Robert, 1:21
  Andrewe, Richard, 1:408
  anti-Catholicism, 3:612
  branch theory of the Church, 2:582

  Church in England under, 5:248
  Clement VIII (Pope), 1:467, 3:785
  Digby, Sir Everard, 4:745
  divine right of kings, 4:788
  Donne, John, 4:868
  Ellis, Philip, 5:171
  Hampton Court Conference, 1:444
  Irish Church, 7:558–559
  Irish confessors and martyrs, 7:577
  martyrs persecuted under, 5:234–235
  Oath of Allegience, 4:912, 10:499–501
  Sabbatarianism, 12:454
  universality of Christianity, 3:293

James II (King of Aragon), 2:502, **7:704–705**, 12:547

James II (King of England), 7:*706*, **706–707**
  Anglican orders problem, 1:438
  anti-Catholicism, 3:433
  Barclay, Robert, 2:97
  Caribbean, 3:111
  Church of Ireland, 7:548
  Church-State relations, 3:648
  Codrington, Thomas, 3:820–821
  Declaration of Rights (1689), 4:590
  English Church, 5:249
  Glorious Revolution of 1688, 12:207–208, 463
  Irish Act of Settlement, 1:77
  Irish Church, 7:560
  Petre, Sir Edward, 11:217–218
  Puritans, 11:839
  Sabran, Louis de, 12:463

James III (King of Scotland), 1:130, 5:175

James V (King of Scotland), 2:179

James VI (King of Scotland). *See* James I (King of England)

James Cinti de Cerqueto, Bl., **7:707**

James de Benefactis, Bl., **7:707**

James della Marca. *See* James of the Marches, St.

James Francis Edward Stuart (pretender to the English throne), 7:690

James Gaetani Stefaneschi (Card.), **7:707–708**

James Griesinger of Ulm, Bl., **7:708**

James of Albenga, 6:247, **7:708**

James of Bevagna, Bl., **7:708–709**

James of Certaldo, Bl., **7:709**

James of Douai, 1:935

James of Edessa, 5:82

James of Massa (Brother), 5:736

James of Metz, **7:709**

James of Nisibis (Bp.), St., 5:277

James of St. Dominic, 3:102

James of Sarug. *See* Jacob of Sarug (Bp.)

James of the Marches, St., 2:321, 3:414, **7:709–710**, *710*

James of Venice. *See* James Salomonius, Bl.

James of Viterbo, Bl., **7:710**
    Augustine (Triumphus) of Ancona, 1:870
    Augustinianism, 1:879, 883, 888
    Bernard of Auvergne, 2:306
    laity, 8:295
    universality of Christianity, 3:293

James of Vitry, 3:413

James of Voragine, Bl., 7:312, **711**, 12:605

James Salomonius, Bl., 1:673, **7:711**

James the Greater, St. *See* James (son of Zebedee), Apostle, St.

James the Just, 3:546

James the Less, St. *See* James (son of Alphaeus), St.

Jameson, J. Franklin, 1:350

Jamet, Denys, 3:4

Jamet, Pierre-François, Bl., **7:711–712**

Jammo, S., 5:5

Jamnia (Jabneel), Jewish synod, 3:25, 26

Janáček, Leoš, 7:*712*, **712**

Jandel, Alexandre, 8:272

Jandel, Vincent, 4:853

Janequin, Clément, **7:712–713**

Janet, Paul, 5:47

Janin, Pierre, 1:691

Jankola, Matthew (priest), 12:609

Janov, Matthias, 4:480

Jansen, Cornelius (the Elder), 7:*713*, **713**

Jansen, Cornelius Otto (Jansenius) (Bp. of Ypres), 1:892–893, 3:614, **7:713–715**, 715
    Alexander VII (Pope), 12:28–29
    Comma pianum, 4:4
    concupiscence, 4:69
    Duvergier de Hauranne, Jean, 4:955
    grace, 6:404
    predestination, 11:650
    religious experience, 5:555
    Rovenius, Philippus, 12:395
    scholasticism, 12:764
    teaching authority of the Church, 13:781
    theology of, 5:851
    See also Jansenism

Jansenism, 3:614, **7:715–720**
    Ad sanctam beati petri sedem, 1:97, 893
    Aix Archdiocese, 1:196
    Alexander VII (Pope), 1:97, 262, 843, 3:786, 816, 12:28–29
    Alexander VIII (Pope), 1:262
    Alexandre, Noël, 1:267–268
    Alphonsus Liguori, St., 1:309, 312
    Amiens, 1:359
    Angers, 1:432
    appeals to a future council, 1:599
    Arnauld family, 1:714–717, 3:614
    Assemblies of the French Clergy, 1:788
    atonement, 1:837
    attrition, 1:843
    Auctorem Fidei, 1:846–847, 3:204
    Augustinianism, 1:716, 880, 884, 892
    Augustinius, 1:716, 892–893, 3:614
    Auxerre, 1:927
    beatific vision, 2:169–170
    Belgium, 2:218
    Belsunce de Castlemoran, opposition to, 2:234
    Berti, Giovanni Lorenzo, 2:334
    Billuart, Charles René, 2:396
    Boonen, Jacques, 2:529
    Bossuet, Jacques Bénigne, 2:550
    Bourgoing, François, 2:568
    Bouvier, Jean Baptiste, 2:572
    Brancati, Lorenzo, 2:581
    Brazil, 2:594
    Brothers of the Christian Schools, 2:632
    Buffier, Claude, 2:675
    Cafasso, St. Joseph, 2:851
    Calénus, Henri, 2:861
    Candido, Vincenzo, 3:13
    Carthusians, 3:195
    casuistry, 3:221
    Caulet, François Étienne, 3:296
    Ceillier, Remi, 3:316
    chapter of faults, 3:386
    Charles of the Assumption, 3:436
    Choiseul du Plessis Praslin, Gilbert de, 3:524
    Church-State relations, 3:639, 753
    Clement IX (Pope), 3:786
    Clement XI (Pope), 3:788–789, 790
    Clement XII (Pope), 3:790
    Codde, Pieter, 3:816
    Colombière, St. Claude de la, 3:853
    Crasset, Jean, 4:334
    Cum occasione, 1:97, 717, 893
    Descartes, 4:682, 5:91
    destiny, supernatural, 4:694
    Dicconson, Edward, 4:734
    Duvergier de Hauranne, Jean, 4:955
    encyclopedias of religion, 5:209
    fate of, 5:851
    Fleury, André Hercule de, 5:761–762
    French Revolution, 5:971
    grace, 1:881, 892–893, 3:614, 6:391–392
    heresy, 6:776–777
    Innocent X (Pope), 4:436, 7:480
    Innocent XII (Pope), 7:482
    Innocent XIII (Pope), 7:483
    Jesuits, 1:715, 893, 7:786
    Josephinism, 1:913
    Journal de Trévoux, 3:295
    Lallemant, J. P., 8:298
    Le Maistre, A. and I., 8:464–465, 465
    Le Plat, J., 8:507
    Le Tellier, M., 8:519
    limbo, 8:590–591
    Llorente, J. A., 8:740
    Louis XIV (King of France), 8:804
    Louvain, Catholic University of, 8:823
    Lugo, J. de, 8:855
    Mariology, 9:171
    piety, 3:622
    Port-Royal Convent, 3:524, 614, 744–745
    Pouget, François Aimé, 11:561
    religious experience, 5:555–556
    Ricci, Scipione de', 12:225–226
    Sinnich, J., 13:162–163
    Solitaries of Port-Royal, 11:525
    Synod of Pistoia, 11:363–365
    Theologia moralis condemned, 8:273
    theology of Church, 3:589

Jansenistic Piety, **7:720–721**

Jansenius, Cornelius. *See* Jansen, Cornelius Otto (Jansenius) (Bp. of Ypres)

Janski, Bogdan, 12:174

Janssen, Arnold, Bl., 4:789, 6:185, **7:721**, 11:131, 13:539–540

Janssen-Poppel, Nicholas, 6:364

Janssens, Aloysius, **7:721–722**

Janssens, Francis (Bp. of New Orleans), 7:685–686, 8:812, 10:293

Janssens, John Baptist, 7:792–793

Janssens, Louis, **7:722**

Janssoone, Frédéric Cornil, Bl., **7:723**

Jantzen, Hans, 3:694, 697

Janua Linguarum reserata (Comenius), 4:2

Januarius, St., **7:723–724**

Japan, **7:736–744**
  ban on Christianity (1616), 7:729–730
  Banishment, Decree of (1587), 7:728, 738–739
  Buddhism, 1:358, 2:*658*, 664–666, 13:87, 14:916
  Dahlmann, Joseph, 4:493
  dead, worship of the, 4:557
  demographic statistics, 7:736
  early peoples, 13:85–86
  ecclesiastical organization, 7:737
  Endo, Shusaku, 5:219–220
  imperialism in Korea, 8:238
  map, 7:*738*
  mission, 7:737–739
    Cerqueira, Luís de, 3:351
    Jesuits, 3:416, 5:722, 7:784, 12:281–282
    Maryknoll Fathers and Brothers, 9:295, 296
    Orthodox mission, 9:695
    Sisters of the Holy Names of Jesus and Mary, 7:34
    works of charity and, 3:417
    Xavier, St. Francis, 9:692, 14:878
  O'Connell, William, 10:543
  resistance to Christianity, 7:724–725
  Shimazaki, Tōson, 13:85
  Shintoism, 1:394, 459, 2:665, 3:515–516, 13:85–87
  Soka Gakkai, 13:298

Japan, Martyrs of, **7:724–736**

Japanese Orthodox Church, 9:695

Jaricot, Pauline, 5:796, **7:744**, 11:752–753

Jarlath of Tuam, St., 2:601

Jarrett, Bede, **7:744–745**, *745*

Jarrige, Barthélémy, 12:277

Jarrige, Catherine, Bl., **7:745**

Jarrige, Jean François, 12:277

Jarrige, Pierre, 12:277

Jarrow Abbey (England), 3:348, **7:745–746**

Jaruzelski, Wojciech, 11:453, 454

Jarweh, Michael. *See* Ignatius Michael III (Patriarch of Syria)

Jashar, Book of, **7:746**

Jaskulski, Mary Felicia (Mother), 5:890

Jasna Góra (Poland), 4:488–490

Jason of Cyrene, 9:8

Jasov Abbey (Košice, Slovakia), **7:746**

Jaspers, Karl, 5:94, 362, 398, **7:746–747**, 11:298
  agnosticism, 1:184
  Augustinianism, 1:882
  communication, 4:25
  conscience, 4:140
  existence of God, 6:315
  existentialism, 5:544, 545
  fideism, 5:712
  free will, 5:931
  knowledge, theories of, 8:221
  literary myth, 10:121
  philosophy and science, 11:300
  religious experience, 5:556
  Ricoeur, Paul, 12:241
  self, concept of, 12:884
  soul, 13:348

Jaucourt, Chevalier de, 5:210

Jauffret, Gaspard Jean André Joseph (Bp. of Metz), 12:595

Jaussen, Marius Antonin, 5:50

Java. *See* Indonesia

Javelli, Giovanni Crisostomo, 1:677, **7:747–748**, 14:49

Javouhey, Anne Marie, Bl., **7:748**

Jayme, Luis, 2:863

Jealousy, 5:269, **7:748–749**

Jealousy of God, **7:749**

Jean de Batheries, 1:396

Jean de Bourbon, 3:394

Jean de Craticula. *See* John of Châtillon, St.

Jean de Vandières. *See* John of Gorze, St.

Jeanmard, Jules B., 8:278

Jeanne Marie de Maillé, Bl., **7:749**

Jeanneret, Charles-Édouard. *See* Le Corbusier

Jeans, James, 11:300

Jedburgh Monastery (Roxburghshire, Scotland), **7:749–750**

Jedin, Hubert, 1:879, **7:750**

Jefferson, Thomas, 3:179–180, 5:193, 262, 10:484, 14:187
  architecture, 3:715
  Aristotelianism, 1:678
  Church-State relations, 3:641, 652
  civil religion, 3:755
  deism, 4:617–618
  democracy, 4:641
  Locke's theory, 8:746

Jeffrey, Gabrielle, 12:550

Jehoahaz (King of Judah), 7:642

Jehoash (King of Judah), 7:640

Jehoiachin (King of Judah), 7:642

Jehoiakim (King of Judah), 2:130, 7:642, 752, 753

Jehovah, **7:750–751**

Jehovah's Witnesses, 1:135, 3:661, **7:751–752**, 12:416, 438

Jehu (King of Israel), 7:640

Jehuda ben Baba, 1:94

Jeningen, Philipp, Ven., 5:173, **7:752**

Jenison, Thomas, 5:238

Jenner, Edward, 5:260

Jenny (Undset), 14:295

Jensen, A. E., 10:121

Jensen, P., 10:820

Jensen, S. S., 2:457

Jenson, Nicholas, 2:522

Jeremiah (Hebrew prophet), **7:752–753**
  Baal cult opposition, 2:2
  Baruch, 2:130
  Book of Lamentations, 8:312, 313
  fundamental option, 6:26
  Gehenna, 6:116

Jeremiah (Jeremy) of Valachia. *See* Kostistk, Geremia of Valachia

Jeremiah, Book of, **7:753–755**
  apocalyptic style, 1:546
  Baal, 2:2
  Babylon, 2:4, 5
  Baruch, 2:130
  beatific vision, 2:171
  canonicity, 3:24
  conversion, 4:233
  creation, 4:341
  curses, 4:442
  Dead Sea Scrolls version of, 4:562
  deportation, 4:674
  divine election, 5:146
  edification, 5:84
  eschatology, 5:334–335
  Gehenna, 6:116
  God, name of, 6:298
  God as redeemer, 11:965, 966
  God's spirit, 13:427
  guilt, 6:570, 570–571
  heart, 6:681
  heaven, 6:684
  holiness of man, 9:87
  hope of salvation, 7:105
  inheritance, 7:464
  justice of God, 8:70
  justice of men, 8:73
  kingship, 8:179
  laity, 8:290
  lamentations, 8:313
  magic, 9:39

peace, 11:49

seventy weeks of years, 13:39–40

sin, 13:143

sin, gravity of, 13:153

slavery, 13:206

Son of David, 13:310

Song of Songs, 13:319

soul, 13:336

spirit, 13:424, 425

Spirit of God, 13:426

textual criticism, 7:754–755

word of God, 14:837

Jeremiah, Canticles of, 3:73

Jeremiah, Letter of, **7:755**

Jeremiah II (Patriarch of
    Constantinople), 10:700

Jeremias (martyr of Córdoba), 4:262

Jeremias, Alfred, 10:820

Jeremias, Joachim, 1:6, 2:70, 398, 6:107,
    8:300

Jeremias II (Patriarch of Constantinople),
    4:355

Jeremias II (Patriarch of Moscow),
    2:745, 6:456

Jericho (ancient city), **7:755–757**

Jeroboam I (King of Israel), 7:639

Jeroboam II (King of Israel), 7:640–641,
    8:177

Jerome, St., 3:594–595, 5:*415*, 7:*757*,
    757–760, 8:*363*

    Alipius, St., 1:288

    Anastasius I (Pope), St., 1:387

    Antioch, 1:522

    apocrypha, 1:558

    Apollinaris of Laodicea, 1:560

    ars moriendi, 1:728

    asceticism, 3:594

    aseity, 1:779

    Assumption of Mary, 1:800

    Asterius the Sophist, 1:809

    Augustine, St., 1:852

    baptism of, 2:67

    baths, 2:154

    biblical canon, 3:26

    biblical Chronicler, 3:566

    biblical theology, 2:382

    bishops, 2:417

    Carthusian spirituality, 3:190

    Cassian, John, 3:207

    censorship, 3:336

    Christian paideia study, 10:755, 756

    Chromatius of Aquileia, St., 3:564

    chronicles, 1:460

    Cicero, Marcus Tullius, 3:730

clerical celibacy/marriage, 3:323,
    324, 327

clerical dress, 3:801

contraception, 4:220, 221

on the cross, 4:384

cult of relics, 12:51

Cyril of Jerusalem, 4:470

Dagon, 4:493

Dydymus the Blind, 4:738

Easter Vigil, 5:15

Eustochium, St., 5:457

exegetical works, 5:512, 515

expulsion from Rome, 13:167

Exuperius of Toulouse, St., 5:571

Fabiola, St., 5:585

Fathers of the Church, 5:640, 642

freedom of conscience, 4:148

friendship between St. Pammachius,
    10:815

Greco-Roman schooling, 6:431

heresy, 6:771

Hilarion, St., 6:826

homily, 7:63

John of Jerusalem, 7:971

Judith, Book of, 8:43

lamps and lighting, 8:314

Latin Bible, 8:362–363

literary career of, 7:757–758

lives of saints, 12:606

manger-crib, 4:364

Marcella, St., 9:135

Mary, Blessed Virgin, 9:240

Origen controversy, 5:292, 12:404,
    405

Paula of Rome, St., 5:457

Pelagianism, 11:61–62

pilgrimage, 11:344, 354

prudence, 11:789

schism, 12:738

School of Alexandria, 1:272

as scripture scholar, 7:758–759

soul, 13:343

spiritual direction, 4:760

Spiritus paraclitus, 13:457–458

studies about, 8:268

syndersis, 13:680

Ten Commandments, 4:6

Vulgate, 14:591–593

women, status of, 14:815

works of charity, 1:301, 3:406, 407

Jerome, St., Martyrology of. *See*
    Martyrology of St. Jerome

Jerome of Ascoli. *See* Nicholas IV
    (Pope)

Jerome of Prague, 3:605, 4:480, **7:760**,
    10:376

Jeron, St., **7:760**

Los Jerónimos. *See* Hieronymites

Jerusalem, **7:760–772**

    archaeology, 2:284–285, 7:763–765

    biblical archaeology, 2:379–380, 381

    biblical history of, 7:765–769

    Christian era, 7:769–772

    Christian population of, 7:772

    Crusaders' states, 4:401–402, 403,
        404

    David, 4:536

    deportations, 4:674

    destruction of (587 B.C.), 7:765, 866

    Ethiopian Church interior, 5:*406*

    fall of, 4:547, 548

    holy lance relics, 7:30

    as liturgical center, 5:4

    liturgical history, 8:650–651

    liturgical year, 5:105

    Muslims, conquered, 13:803–804

    name of, 7:760–761

    Nehemiah's role in rebuilding wall
        of, 10:230, 231

    reconstruction models, 7:*761*

    relic of the cross, 13:89

    religious life of Christian community,
        5:104–105

    as sacred city for major faiths, 7:647

    Siloam inscription, 13:120

    Sophronius (Patriarch), 13:324

    temples, 13:809–810

    topography and water supply,
        7:761–763

    Turkish period, 7:770–771

    walls of, 7:767–769

    Western Wall, 8:*4*

Jerusalem, Church of, 4:470–472

Jerusalem, Council of, 1:685, 3:578,
    4:298–299, **7:772–774**, 11:7

Jerusalem, Kingdom of, **7:774–775**

Jerusalem, Patriarchate of, 4:196,
    295–296, 7:769–772, **775–776**

Jerusalem, Synod of (1849), 1:526

Jerusalem Bible (Bible de Jérusalem),
    2:284, 5:51, 8:906, 12:262

Jerusalem Creed, 4:190, 470

Jerusalem Patriarchate, 1:525

Jervaulx Abbey (East Witton, England),
    7:776, **776**

Jesu, Corona Virginum (hymn),
    7:776–777

Jesu, Dulcis Memoria (hymn), **7:777**

Jesu, Redemptor Omnium (hymn), **7:777**

Jesuati, **7:777–778**, 950, 13:108

Jesuit Anthropological Association, 8:430

Jesuit Anthropological Conference, 8:430

Jesuit Conference of East Asia and Oceania (JCEAO), 5:3

Jesuit *Relations*, **7:778–779**

The Jesuit Relations and Allied Documents, 7:778

Jesuit Volunteer Corps, 1:210

Jesuits, **7:779–795**

    Acquaviva, Claudius, 1:71–72

    active life, 1:83

    Ad Majorem Dei Gloriam, 1:95–96

    Alexandre, Noël, 1:267

    anticlericalism, 1:519

    antipodes question, 1:530

    Apostleship of Prayer, 1:578

    apostolic delegation in the United States, 1:584

    archives, 1:641, 642

    archpriest controversy, 1:642, 643

    Arregui, Antonio María, 1:722

    Arrupe, Pedro, 1:725–727

    ars moriendi, 1:733–734

    Attritionists, 1:843

    Bérulle, Pierre de, 2:339

    Blarer, Gerwig, 2:433

    Borgia, St. Francis, 2:538

    Canisius, St. Peter, 3:15–19

    Carroll, John, 3:181

    Cartesianism, 3:185

    choice, 3:521

    choral celebration abandoned, 8:730

    church architecture, 3:701, 703

    code of education, 5:790

    Coimbricenses of, 14:51

    colonial United States, 3:649

    Concina, Daniel, 4:59

    Congregatio de auxiliis conflict over grace between Dominicans, 14:48

    La Congrégation, 4:113

    contemplation, 4:207

    Counter Reformation, 3:610–611, 782, 4:310–311

    de auxiliis controversy, 4:111–113

    Dezza, Paolo, 4:713

    dissolution, 5:258, 10:844

    distinctive features of, 7:780–781

    divine concurrence, 4:72, 73

    Dunne, Peter Masten, 4:934

    ecumenicism, 8:168–169

    encyclopedias of religion, 5:209

    ends justifying the means, 5:213

    English Reformation, 1:296

    expulsion, 1:21, 8:8–9, 9:717, 11:337–338, 12:221

    founding, 3:54, 782, 7:312–314, 8:287

    German scholastic method, 8:187–188

    government, 7:779

    hierarchical insignia, 6:764

    history, 1540-1773, 7:781–786

    history, 1814 to 21st century, 7:787–795

    Holy Name, 7:33

    homiletic theory, 8:61

    Hungary, 7:214, 222

    increase in Third World activity, 7:794

    Jansenism, 1:715, 893

    John Paul II (Pope) on governance, 7:1004

    Julius III (Pope), 8:58

    Kentucky colleges, 8:148

    Košice martyrs, 8:241–242

    Kulturkampf, 8:254, 255

    Lutheranism, 3:463

    membership, 7:779–780

    mission, 9:692

        Africa, 13:122

        Alaska, 1:208, 209, 210

        Albania, 1:213

        Algeria, 1:285

        Argentina, 1:649

        Arizona, 1:687, 688, 8:180, 9:717

        Armenia, 1:702–703

        Austria, 1:911, 3:17

        Brazil, 2:593–594, 597, 3:417, 5:43

        California, 1:65, 2:867, 8:180

        Canada, 3:4, 6, 9

        Caribbean, 3:116

        Caroline Islands, 10:530

        Chile, 3:485

        China, 3:493–496, 497

        Colombia, 3:850, 851

        colonial America, 9:701–702

        Colorado, 3:858

        Delaware, 4:625

        East Timor, 5:8

        England, 5:247

        Ethiopia, 5:400, 403–404

        Florida, 9:715

        Hong Kong, 13:80

        Illinois, 9:722

        India, 12:390, 399, 401

        Indochina, 12:218–219

        Indonesia, 7:428, 429

        Ireland, 5:753

        Jamaica, 3:112

        Japan, 3:416, 5:722, 7:784, 12:281–282

        Kansas, 8:112, 117, 14:711

        Laos, 8:329

        Lithuania, 8:605

        Louisiana, 8:809, 9:723

        Luxembourg, 8:897–898

        Macau, 9:4

        Maine, 9:721

        Malawi, 9:67

        Maryland, 2:460, 887

        Mexico, 1:249, 724, 9:573, 707–710, 12:623

        Michigan, 9:604

        mission history, 7:783–786, 13:70

        Montana, 9:826

        Mozambique region, 10:38

        Nebraska, 10:223

        New Mexico, 9:716, 12:462

        New Spain, 12:623

        New York, 9:721–722

        Nicaragua, 10:351, 352–353

        North America, 13:757–758

        Ohio, 10:568–569

        Oklahoma, 10:574

        Oregon, 10:644–645

        Pakistan, 10:759

        Paraguay, 8:839, 10:877, 12:408

        Peru, 9:711–712

        Philippines, 7:784–785

        Poland, 5:43, 11:442

        Portugal, 7:786, 11:466–468, 537

        Russia, 1:252, 3:265, 795

        South America, 9:713–714

        Spain, 12:220, 399–400

        suppression and restoration, 1:688, 723, 3:485, 498, 624

        Wisconsin, 9:722

        Wyoming, 14:869

        Vietnam, 14:500

        Zambia, 14:907

    moral theology, 8:139

    mysticism, 7:309, 8:16

    New Orleans Archdiocese, 10:291

    19th-20th century overview, 3:621

    Oates Plot, 10:492–496

    Oath of Allegiance, 10:499, 500–501

    patrons, 8:130

    Pious fund, 11:357–358

    prayer, 1:325, 326

    preaching, 11:621, 623, 13:80–81

Ratio Studiorum, 1:952, 2:110–111

reductions, 2:464, 465, 3:101–102, 226, 613, 11:997–998

retreats, 13:430–431

Russia, 12:422

Salmerón, Alfonso influenced, 12:620

scholasticism, 12:765–766

science teaching, 8:181

seminary programs of, 12:896

slavery, 1:156

social justice, 8:772–775

Society of Mary Aux., 13:331

Society of Mary Reparatrix under spiritual direction of, 10:721

spirituality, 8:333–334

Suarezianism, 13:563

superior general, 8:445

suppression and restoration, 3:265, 618, *794*, 7:786–787, 9:693

    Acciaioli, Filippo, 1:58–59, 3:791

    Alma Adophina, 4:498

    Argentina and, 1:649

    Austria, 1:913–914, 9:155

    Bernis, François Joachim de Pierre de, 2:326

    Berthier, Guillaume François, 2:332

    Cárdenas, Bernardino de, 3:102

    Clement XIII (Pope), 3:791–792

    Clement XIV (Pope), 3:92, 265, 615, 794–796, 12:221, 222–223

    Conclave of 1769, 3:794–795

    Denmark, 4:666

    England, 1:21

    Enlightenment, 3:621

    France, 4:261, 7:328

    Latin America, 9:726

    Ricci, Lorenzo and, 3:213

    U.S., 1:688, 723, 9:725, 12:369–370

U.S., early ecclesiastical organization, 2:41

U.S. politics, 7:794

universities (U.S.)

    Marquette University, 12:370

    St. Louis University, 12:562–564

    St. Omer College, 12:569–570

women, 7:313

works of charity, 3:416–417

See also Bollandists; Ignatian spirituality

Jesu-Maria Course in Religion (Schorsch), 12:785

Jesus: A Revolutionary Biography (Crossan), 6:867

Jesus (Bousset), 7:849

Jesus (the Name), **7:795**

Jesús, Francisco de, Bl., 7:735

Jesus, Society of. *See* Jesuits

Jesus Christ

    Adam as countertype of, 10:100

    as Apollo-Helios, 4:180

    baptism of, 7:49

    Cana of Galilee, 9:245–246

    communication of idioms, 4:25–27

    consciousness of Divine sonship, 13:312–313, 313

    contemplation, model of, 4:205

    crown of thorns, feast of, 1:147

    divinity of, 9:815

    false teaching regarding body of, 10:13

    fish as symbol of, 5:746–747

    flagellation of, 5:756–757, *756*

    Francisan spirituality, 5:896–897

    genealogy of, 14:829–830

    hope, 7:96, 106

    humanity of, 13:573–574

    Ignatius of Antioch, 7:311

    Ignatius Loyola, 7:307–308

    impeccability of, 7:361

    as Logos-Son, 8:764

    Mary, Blessed Virgin, 9:264–265, 14:532

    matter, theology of, 9:345

    medieval Latin literature, 9:460–461

    mercy, 9:504, 507–508

    as Messiah, 9:538–539, 545–546

    millenarianism, 9:633

    ministries, origin of, 9:651–652

    miracles of, 9:*661*, 662, 663–664

    moral teaching of, 9:858

    Moses compared to, 7:892–893

    mystical body of, 10:99–104

    Origenism on preexistence, 10:658

    our life, 8:572

    as the paraclete, 10:873

    pleroma of God, 9:94

    priesthood, creation of, 7:36

    in the Qur'ān, 7:608–609, 11:879–880

    Redemption of, 9:256–257

    Resurrection, 9:238–239, 13:608

    sacrifice as self-oblation, 12:888

    sayings of, 5:809

    self-abandonment of, 12:885

    as sin offering, 13:159

    suffering of, 13:587

    as suffering servant, 13:591

    supremacy of, 5:270–271

    teachings of, 5:338–339, 13:592, 14:790–791

    temptations of, 13:816–818

    theandric acts of, 13:856–857

    transubstantiation doctrine, 14:158–160

    Trier's claim to Holy Garment of, 14:185

    virgin birth, glory of, 14:536

    will of God, 14:724

Jésus Christ: sa personne, son message, ses épreuves (Grandmaison), 6:417

Jesus Christ, biographical studies of, **7:843–853**

    biographies based on faith

        early Christianity, 7:843–845

        18th century, 7:847

        15th to 17th century, 7:845, 847

        middle ages, 7:845

    Catholic development, 19th to 20th century, 7:851–852

    critics, 7:847–851

    imaginative lives of Christ, 7:853–854

    Leben-Jesu-Forschung, 8:542, 543

    liberal theology, 8:542–543

    Ludolf of Saxony, 8:853–854

    theological works, 20th century, 7:851–852

    "third quest," 8:173

    20th century works, 7:850–851

Jesus Christ, iconography of, **7:853–861**

    acheiropoietic images, 7:857

    Alexandria, 1:270

    Christus Coelestis Medicus, 7:860

    crucifixion, 4:391–398

    the Dead Christ, 7:858–859

    Ecce Homo, 5:32–33

    ethnic Christ, 7:860

    Humanity of Christ, 7:859–860

    Majestas Domini, 7:857–858

    Man of Sorrows, 7:859

    physical types, 7:853, 855–856

    Sacred Heart of Jesus, 7:860

    thematic types, 7:856–857

Jesus Christ, in the Bible, **7:797–810**

    anointing with Holy Spirit, 4:85

    baptism of, 2:58, 70–73, 13:427

    beatific vision, 2:171

    biblical sources, 7:797, 799, 801–804

    brothers and sisters of, 2:628–629

    charity, teaching on, 3:400–401

    Christological titles, 7:808–809

    circumcision of, 3:741

Jesus Christ, in the Bible *(continued)*

comparison of Passover lamb to, 10:936–937

Davidic Descent of Christ, 10:176

difference in Gospels' presentation of, 7:892–893

as Divine Person, 11:151

early Christian way of life, 3:546

foretold in the Old Testament, 3:28–29

genealogy of, 6:125–127

historical Jesus, 7:804–808

holiness of, 7:3–4

hope, 7:106

Joseph, 7:1036

justification for infant baptism, 2:67

kindness, 8:171

lament on the Cross, 13:37

life as possessed by, 8:570–571

Lord's Prayer, 8:782–783

love, concept of, 8:831

mystery of the Trinity, 2:172

names used for, 8:780–781

Nazareth birthplace, 10:216–217

as the New Israel, 7:453–454

prayer, 11:592

presentation at the Temple, 3:14

priesthood of, 11:626, 691–693

profession of faith, 11:739

redemption, 11:967–972

scholarship on teaching of Parousia, 10:898

Seven Last Words, 13:36–38

Son of Man, 13:316–318

trial of, 14:178–181, *179*

works of charity, 3:400–401

See also New Testament; Resurrection of Christ

Jesus Christ, in theology, **7:810–843**

death of, 7:823–824

divine judgment, 8:34, 40

divinity, 7:824–826

early controversies, 7:811–812

feminist Christologies, 7:839–840

formation of classical dogma, 7:810–814, 816–817

Historical Jesus, 7:837–838

holiness, sinlessness, and freedom of, 7:818–819

human knowledge of, 7:819

humanity of, 7:826–827

imitation of, 2:489–490, 491

intercession of, 7:519

Judaism, 8:12–13

kenosis, 8:143

knowledge of, 7:828–830

Lamb of God, 8:299–302

lay spirituality, 8:418

liberal theology, 8:543

liberation theology, 7:838–839

as Logos, 8:761–762

manual theology, 7:819–820

medieval and modern Scholasticism, 7:817–822

messianic consciousness of, 7:833–834

natural human defects of, 7:827–828

Nicene Creed on nature, 10:666

paradigm shift, 7:820–822

power and theandric acts of, 7:832–833

as priest-victim, 11:987

primacy of, 7:836–837

as prophet, priest, and king, 7:835–836

psychological unity of, 7:834–835

recapitulation in, 11:952–953

as redeemer, 11:978–979, 985–987

special questions, 7:822–843

as Theophoros, 1:391

as victor, 11:984–985

will of, 7:830–832

world religions, 7:840–843

See also Ascension of Jesus Christ; Christology; Christology controversies (patristic era); Humanity of Christ

Jésus Christ et les croyances messianiques de son temps (Colani), 10:896

Jesus Crucified, Bl., 4:44

Jesus Family (Chinese Christian group), 3:501

Jesus Nazareno hospital (Mexico), 3:415

Jesus of Nazareth: The Hidden Years (Robert), 7:850

Jesus of Nazareth (Bornkamm), 6:865

Jesus of Nazareth (Klausner), 7:850

Jesus Prayer, 4:720, **7:861**

Jesus' Proclamation of the Kingdom of God (Weiss), 8:175

Jesus Seminar (1985), 6:866–867

Jesus the Jew (Vermes), 6:866

Jesus von Nazareth (Bornkamm), 7:849

Jesus Walking on Water (Dore), 9:666

Jésus-Christ (The Life of Jesus) (Goguel), 7:850

Jethro (biblical figure), 10:6

Jetté, Julius, 1:209

Jetté, Rosalie, 9:672

Jetter, John, 5:237

Jettons (medals), 9:424

Le Jeu de saint Nicolas (Bodel), 4:401

Jeunesse Ouvrière Chrétienne, 5:857, 7:889

Jeuris, Pauline, St., **7:861–862**

Jewel, John (Bp. of Salisbury, England), 1:437, **7:862**

The Jewish Antiquities (Josephus), 7:1049, 10:863

Jewish Christians, 7:907–908, 8:7, 497–498, 556, 13:199

Jewish law, 4:358, 359, 389–391

Jewish literature, 4:385

Jewish liturgy, 3:24, 76, 4:607, 889–890, 7:5

Jewish philosophy, **7:862–866**

adaptation of Islamic ideals, 7:868

Aristotelianism, 1:673, 4:360–361

Avicebron, 1:225, 673, 938–939, 2:476, 833, 3:674

demons, 4:497

disciple as term, 4:768, 772–773

dreams, 4:904

emanationism, 5:182

Ibn Paqūda, 7:272–273

Levi ben Gerson, 8:521

metaphysics of light, 8:583

order of universe, 14:328

Philo Judaeus, 11:289

providence of God, 11:781–782

Spinoza, 13:418

See also Covenant; Judaism; Law, Mosaic; Old Testament

Jewish religious communities, 13:937–938

Jewish Revolt against Rome (67-70), 7:866

Jewish Revolt against Rome (132-35), 2:83–84, 7:866–867, 867

Jewish Sybilline Oracles, 1:553–554

Jewish theology, 10:965

The Jewish War (Josephus), 7:1048–1049

Jewish world era, 5:314

Jewish-Arabic symbiosis (622-1096), 7:868–869

Jews

Alexander II (Pope), 1:253

Antiochus IV Epiphanes, 1:528–529

apologists, 1:567

baptism of children, 5:948

Callinicum affair, 1:338

Caribbean, 3:116–117, 118

civil rights in U.S., 5:256

colonial United States, 3:648, 651, 652

Crescas, Ḥasdai ben Abraham, 4:360–362

Cyrus the Great, 4:478

Decapolis, 4:587–588

diaspora of, 4:730–731

expelled from Spain, 9:204

forgiveness to Catholics for past offenses, 9:686–687

independence, Maccabees, 9:9

Inquisition, 1:304

Marranos, 4:946–947, 9:203–205

martyrdom of medieval Christian boys, 9:436

Portuguese inquisition, 7:490

rebellion, Maccabees, 9:5–6, 8

as recipients of John's Gospel, 7:907

religious education, 12:98

Sabbath Day, 12:454, 456–457

Sadducees, 12:522–523

sexual mores of (biblical), 13:48–49

See also Anti-Semitism; Jewish philosophy; Jews, persecution of; Jews, post-biblical history of; Judaism

The Jews (Belloc), 2:231

Jews, persecution of, 1:304, 846

allegations of ritual murder, 7:154

Hungary, 7:218, 219, 223

post-biblical history, 4:465, 731

Spain, 4:263, 13:377

See also Anti-Semitism; Holocaust (Shoah)

Jews, post-biblical history of, **7:866–875**

Bulgarian Church protest against World War II deportation of, 10:685–686

confined to Rome ghetto, 8:489

Crusades and Spanish Inquisition, 4:410, 7:869–870

Cyprus, 4:461

divination, 4:785–786

early modern era (1650-1750), 7:872

emancipation (1750-1948), 7:872–875

Fourth Lateran legislation against, 8:354

ghettos, 6:201

Hanukkah feast, 4:607

Islamic period (622-1096), 7:868–869

literature confiscated, 8:488

Patristic Fathers, 8:484

Renaissance and Reformation (1492-1650), 7:870–872

Roman and Byzantine periods (67-622), 7:866–868

See also Holocaust (Shoah)

Jibril. *See* Gabriel (Archangel)

Jihād (holy war), 7:610, 10:54

Jiménez de Enciso, Salvado (Bp. of Popayán, Colombia), **7:875**

Jiménez de Quesada, Gonzalo, 4:132

Jimeno, José Joaquín, 2:862

Jingu (Tsinku) University (China), 3:500

Jinyemon, Caius, Bl., 7:734

Jinyemonō, Thomas, Bl., 7:734

JLG. *See* Joint Liturgical Group

Joab (general), 4:537

Joachim (Abp. of Cyprus), 4:463

Joachim (Hovakim) (Armenian Patriarch), 1:702

Joachim (King of Judah), 8:44, 10:224

Joachim, St. *See* Anne and Joachim, SS.

Joachim I of Brandenburg, 7:875

Joachim II of Brandenburg, 7:875–876

Joachim da Fiore. *See* Joachim of Fiore

Joachim of Brandenburg, **7:875**

Joachim of Fiore, **7:876–877**, 14:204

anti-Christian atheism, 8:840

apocalyptic movements, 1:547–548, 2:481, 492–493

apostolici, 1:594

Arnold, Gottfried, 1:718

bare feet of, 4:764

bibilical hermeneutics, 6:793

Book of Revelation, 12:186

Celestine V (Pope), 3:320

Czechs, 4:481

eschatological prophecies, 5:343–344, 755, 12:284

Florians, 5:775

Hugolino of Orvieto, 7:163

influence on Franciscans, 5:897, 902

Kingdom of God, 8:174–175

medieval Latin literature works of, 9:455

prophecy, 11:760

Salimbene, 12:616

San Giovanni Abbey, 12:651

theology of history, 6:888

works of, 7:876–877

Joachim of St. Anne (Brother). *See* Wall, John, St.

Joachimites. *See* Franciscan Spirituals

Joachin (King of Judah), 4:674

Joahaz (King of Israel), 7:640

Joakim (King of Judah), 4:674

Joan (Popess), Fable of, 2:239, **7:877**

Joan del Milà, Lluís, 2:881

Joan of Arc, 9:229

Joan of Arc, St., 5:379, 659, **7:878–879**, 9:229, 12:599

French victories following martyrdom, 10:427

Holy Name, 7:32, 33

trial of, 7:489

Joan of Aza, Bl., 7:879

Joan of France, St., 5:819, **7:879–880**

Joan of Orvieto, Bl., **7:880**

Joan of Portugal, Bl., **7:880**

Joan of Santa Lucia, Bl., **7:880**

Joan of Signa, Bl., **7:880–881**

Joan of the Cross. *See* Delanoue, Jeanne, St.

Joana Angélica de Jesús, **7:881**

Joannes Andreae, 3:38, **7:881–882**

Bartholomew of Urbino, 2:127

Canon Law, 3:48, 49

Clementinae, 3:800

glossa ordinaria, 6:247

lay education, 8:296

Liber sextus, 8:536

Joannes de Deo, **7:882–883**

Joannes de Lignano, 3:51, **7:883**

Joannes de Podio, 3:52

Joannes Fasanus. *See* John XVIII (Pope)

Joannes Faventinus, **7:883–884**

Joannes Lapus Castilioneus, **7:884**

Joannes Parvus, 4:171, **7:884–885**, 14:256

Joannes Quaglia, 3:52

Joannes Tellensis. *See* Bar-Cursus (Bp. of Tella)

Joannes Teutonicus, 3:39, 48, 4:54, 6:247, **7:885**

Joannis Launoii opera omnia, 8:381

Joannis Trithemii opera historica (Trithemius), 14:209

Joannis Trithemii opera pia et spiritualia (Trithemius), 14:209

João II (King of Portugal), 7:490

João III (King of Portugal), 1:324

Joash (King of Israel), 7:766

Job (Patriarch of Antioch), 1:504

Job, Book of, **7:885–888**

creation, 4:341

Dead Sea Scrolls version of, 4:563, 564

El (God), 5:143

Elohim, 5:173

enmity, 5:264

exegesis, 8:332

God, name of, 6:298

God as redeemer, 11:965

guilt, 6:569

Job, Book of (continued)
Hades, 6:604
heaven, 6:684
Job's skin disorder, 8:510
Leviathan, 8:522
maker of man, 9:87
pessimism, 11:169
retribution, 12:177
serpent as symbol, 13:19
simplicity, 13:137
sin, 13:142, 144, 145
spirit, 13:424
Jocelin, Reginald Fitz (Bp.), 2:153
Jocelin of Brakelond, 1:464, **7:888**, 12:267
Jocelin of Glasgow, **7:888–889**
Jocelin of Wells (Bp.), 2:152, 153, **7:889**
Jocham, Magnus, **7:889**
Jocism, 3:277, **7:889**
Jocist technique, 3:536
Joel, Book of, 1:546, **7:890**, 8:39, 470, 782, 864
Jogues, Isaac, 10:*435*
Johanan ben Zakkai, 1:199, 7:866, **890–891**, 8:7
Johann Adam Möhler, Der Symboliker (Freidrich), 6:3
Johann-Adam-Möhler-Institut für Konfessions and Diasporakunde, 7:696
Johannes Adam. See Hanthaler, Chrysostomus
Johannes Clericus. See Jocham, Magnus
Johannes Cornubiensis, **7:891**
Johannes Monachus, 3:320
Johannesgemeinschaft (secular institute), 2:34
Johannesverlag publishing house, 2:34
Johannine Comma, **7:891–892**
Johannine studies, 5:522
Johannine writings, 3:283, **7:892–897**, 10:305, 898–899, 14:178–181
See also John, Epistles of; John, Gospel According to
Johannitius (Ḥunayn ibn Isḥāq), 1:620, 671
John (Card. of Lorraine, 1498-1550), 8:787
John (King of England), **7:913–914**, *914*, 9:40–41, *41*
Adam of Perseigne, 1:109
Ancient See of Canterbury, 3:72
Church in England under, 5:242
excommunication, 5:242
Holy Cross Abbey, 7:18
Innocent III (Pope), 3:602

John (martyr), St., 11:17
John (martyr of Córdoba), 4:261
John (Patriarch of Alexandria), 1:223
John (Quidort) of Paris, 1:674, 4:55, 277, 14:46
John, Apostle, St., 5:*475*, **7:895–897**
abiding in Christ, 1:21–22
Annunciation, 1:473, 474
Christmas cycle, 3:556
circumincession, 3:741
divine indwelling, 8:49
God's spirit, 13:428
iconography of, 5:475
Laodicea, 8:328
painting by Francisco de Ribalta, 5:*476*
Risen Christ, 13:439
shrine, 13:94
sin, 13:146, 148
unicity, 14:297
works on, 7:896–897
See also Revelation, Book of
John, Bl. (17th c. Japanese martyr), 7:733
John, Epistles of, **7:897–902**
Antichrist, 1:515–516
Asia Minor, 1:784–785
authorship, 7:897
canonicity, 3:28, 30, 31, 32
children of God, 13:441
Church of Christ, 13:438
comparison to John's Gospel, 7:897–898, 901–902
docetism, 4:797
early language use, 8:361
glorified body, 6:243
God, sons of, 13:322
God's spirit, 13:427, 428
God's word-made-flesh, 14:837
grace, 6:381
hatred, 6:666
humanity of Jesus, 7:894
life of grace, 13:441
message of, 7:899, 900–901
Precious Blood, 11:641
redemption, 5:214
social principle, 13:248
Son of David, 13:310
Son of God, 13:313, 314–315
Son of Man, 13:317
sorrows of Mary, 13:327
soul, 13:336
spirit, 13:425
Spirit, concept, 13:420

spiritual life, 13:438
textual criticism, 7:894–895
Word of God, 13:438
work, 13:262
John, Gospel According to, 7:892–894, **902–913**
Andrew, Apostle, St., 1:402–403
anointing in, 4:85
apostolate, 1:579
apostolic faith, 1:587
Ascension of Jesus Christ, 1:771
authorship, 7:892, 902–904, 910–911
baptism, 2:56, 60, 65
Barabbas, 2:85
Bartholomew, Apostle, St., 2:123, 124
beatific vision, 2:169, 170, 171, 172, 174
Christian law, 8:403
Christmas, 3:555
Christocentrism, 3:558
Christology, 1:273
Christ's response to death of Lazarus, 5:193
Christ's wounds, 13:95
chronological sequence, 8:760
Church in, 3:579
comparison/relationship to Synoptic Gospels, 7:892–893, 904
comparison to Epistles of John, 7:897–898, 901–902
date of, 7:909–910
disciple as term, 4:768–773
divine indwelling, 7:441
divine judgment, 8:30, 35, 40
Elijah's Second Coming, 5:159
eschatology, 5:339
eucharistic doctrine, 5:413–414
faith, 6:382
freedom, 6:400
friendship with God, 6:10
glorified body, 6:242
glory, 6:245
glory of God (end of creation), 6:245, 246
Gnosis, 6:255
God the Father, 1:118
God the Son, 6:295–296
God's word-made-flesh, 14:837
grace, 6:381, 382
guilt, 6:572
heaven, 6:684, 684–685
historical tradition, 7:904–905
influences, 7:905

Jesus Christ
   baptism of, 2:57, 72
   baptisms performed, 2:57–58
   as Lord, 8:780
   prayer, 11:592
   prophecies, 9:546
   as street preacher, 11:626
   wisdom of, 14:791
John the Baptist, St., ministry of,
   7:1013–1014
justice of God, 8:72
justice of men, 8:74
justification, 8:80
Kingdom of God, 8:174
Lamb of God, 8:299, 300, 301–302
lay spirituality, 8:417
Lazarus of Bethany, 8:419–420
Logos, 8:760–761, 10:899
Lord's Day, 8:781
Lord's Prayer, 8:784
love, 7:898
love, Divine, 8:831–832
manna, 9:118–119
Mary, Blessed Virgin, 9:245–247
Mary Magdalene, St., 9:287
miracles, 9:664
outline, 7:911–912
parables of, 10:871
on the Parousia, 10:898–899
Passion, 10:922, 923–924
peace, 11:49
penance, 11:68
Peter, Apostle, St., 11:173–175
praetorium, 11:579
Precious Blood, 11:638, 642
purpose of, 7:906–909
rebirth, 11:951
rites of death, 4:10
salvation through baptism, 2:58
serpent as symbol, 13:19, 21
Seven Last Words, 13:36, 37, 38
Simon the Apostle, 13:126
simplicity of God, 13:137
sin, 13:145, 147, 148, 153
textual criticism, 7:892–894
theological symbolism in, 13:669
water to wine miracle in, 3:1
woman clothed in the sun,
   14:821–822
Word become flesh, 5:52
word of God, 14:837
works of charity, 1:302, 303, 3:401
world, 14:840
John I (King of Aragon), 4:450

John I (Pope), St., 3:595, 4:765, **7:919**
John I Tzimisces (Byzantine Emperor),
   2:759
John II (Armenian Catholicos), 1:700
John II (King of Castile), 1:326–327
John II (King of Portugal), 1:273–274
John II (Metropolitan of Kiev), 3:777
John II (Pope), 4:752, 5:291, **7:919–920**,
   10:141
John II Comnenus (Byzantine Emperor),
   2:458, 759
John II of Bursfeld, 2:710
John III (Armenian Catholicos), 1:700
John III (King of Portugal), 3:828, 866
John III (King of Sweden), 5:733,
   11:549
John III (Pope), 3:596, **7:920–921**
John III Ducas Vatatzes (Byzantine
   Emperor), 6:170, **7:913**
John III Scholasticus (Patriarch of
   Constantinople), 1:50, **7:915–916**
John III Sobieski (King of Poland),
   7:914–915, *916*, 11:443
John III Vatatzes (Byzantine Emperor),
   2:761
John IV (Pope), 2:749, 4:370, 7:81, **921**
John IV (the Faster) (Patriarch of
   Constantinople), 2:750, 751, 4:196,
   5:448, **7:916**
John IV Lascarius (Byzantine Emperor),
   2:762
John V (King of Portugal), 11:538
John V (Palaeologus) (Byzantine
   Emperor), 2:763, 788
John V (Pope), 4:719, **7:921**, 12:355
John V of Ypres (Abbot), 12:540
John VI (Cantacuzenus) (Byzantine
   Emperor)
   Argyros, Isaac, 1:659
   Callistus I (Patriarch), 2:878
   hesychasm, 2:763, 788, 794, 827
   historiography, 2:800–801
   Palamite theology upheld, 10:766
John VI (Pope), **7:921–922**
John VII (Pope), 2:750, 5:814, **7:922**
John VII Grammaticus (Patriarch of
   Constantinople), 4:474, **7:916–917**
John VIII (Abp. of Ravenna), 10:362
John VIII (Antipope), **7:923**, 13:14
John VIII (Pope), **7:922–923**
   Adrian III (Pope), 1:125
   Anastasius the Librarian, 1:390
   Byzantine Church, 2:755
   Carolingian Dynasty, 3:171
   concelebration, 4:50
   Constantinople Council IV, 4:195

   decretals as form, 4:604
   Gauderich of Velletri, 6:110
   Ignatius of Constantinople, 7:310
   instructions on petitioning for
      pallium, 10:807
   Methodius, 4:476
   Photius, 4:187, 11:312
   slavery, 13:209
   Slavonic liturgy, 4:370
   unity of the church, 3:170
John VIII (Xiphilinus) (Patriarch of
   Constantinople), 2:823
John VIII Palaeologus (Byzantine
   Emperor), 2:651, 764, 788,
   6:136–137
John IX (Pope), 2:500, **7:923–924**,
   12:356
John IX Hormizd (Chaldean Patriarch),
   2:5, 3:368
John X (Camateros) (Patriarch of
   Constantinople), 2:760, **7:917**
John X (Pope), 3:213, 4:370, 5:24,
   7:924–925
John XI (Beccus) (Patriarch of
   Constantinople), **7:917–918**
   Andronicus II Palaeologus, 1:409,
      2:826
   Bessarion, Cardinal, 2:341
   Eastern Schism, 2:762, 825, 826
   Nicephorus Blemmydes, 2:825
   Palamas's writings against, 10:767
John XI (Pope), 3:813, **7:925**
John XII (Pope), 3:172, 4:362,
   7:925–926, 8:484, 10:141, 12:356
John XIII (Pope), 3:34, 4:362, 5:142,
   7:926
John XIV (Pope), 2:501, 3:213, 4:362,
   7:926–927, 10:141
John XIV Calecas (Patriarch of
   Constantinople), 2:826, **7:918–919**
John XV (Pope), 4:362, **7:927**
John XVI (Antipope), 4:362, 6:489,
   7:927–928
John XVII (Pope), **7:928**
John XVIII (Pope), **7:928–929**
John XIX (Pope), 3:813, **7:929**, 14:249
John XX (Pope), **7:929**, 11:502, 12:611
John XXI (Pope), 1:936, 3:48,
   7:929–931, 8:750, 11:502, 14:44
John XXII (Pope), **7:931–932**
   abbreviators, 1:13
   academic freedom, 1:51
   Adam of Orleton, 1:109
   alchemy, 1:239
   Alvaro Pelayo, 1:327
   Angelus, 1:427

John XXII (Pope) *(continued)*
Armenia, 1:702, 708
Avignon papacy, 1:943
Barlaam of Calabria, 2:99
Bartholomew of Lucca, release of, 2:126
beatific vision, 2:173, 243–244, 276, 4:947, 948
Beguines and Beghards, 2:205
Bonet, Nicholas, 2:494
Canon Law, 3:48
Carmelites, 3:141, 142
Chaldean Catholic Church, 3:366
Clareni, 1:428
Clement VI (Pope), 3:780
coinage issued, 10:481
conciliarism, 4:55
Council of Vienne, 3:800
Crosier Fathers, 2:609
decretals of, 4:604
divine judgment, 8:33
Duranti, William the Younger, 4:950
Flanders, 5:846
Franciscan doctrine on poverty, 5:921
Franciscan Spirituals, persecution of, 5:897, 902
Fraticelli, 3:762
Georgian Church, 6:155
Ghibelline-Guelf conflict, 3:855
immortality, 7:354
importance of, 3:603–604
investiture, 6:177
Knights of Montesa, 8:195
Louis IV (Holy Roman Emperor), 1:327, 3:603
Mepham suspension, 13:131
Nicholas V (Antipope), 10:369
Order of Christ, 4:596
papal administration, 1:944
papal taxation, 1:466, 3:726
Philip VI of France, 4:948
poverty, 11:570–571
Scottish declaration of independence, 12:832
theological censure, 3:337
William of Ockham, 14:746–747
John XXIII (Antipope), 7:938–939
Boniface IX (Pope), 2:504
communists, 4:418
Constance Council, 4:168–170, *169*, 171–172
cross feast, 4:383
Fillastre, Guillaume, 5:722
Gregory XII (Pope), 6:500
Hus, John, 7:228

Western Schism, 2:246, 6:608, 14:693
Zabarella, Francesco, 14:901
John XXIII (Pope), Bl., 3:625–626, 7:932–939
agriculture, 8:586
The Angelicum, 11:487
Anglican-Catholic dialogue, 1:440
Apostleship of the Sea, 1:578
as archbishop, 7:933–935
associations, 1:792, 793
atheism, 1:823
authority of governments, 4:151
Beauduin, Lambert, 2:183
birth control commission of, 7:179–180
as bishop of Rome, 7:937
Bulgaria, 2:680, 683–684
canonizations, 7:937
capital punishment, 3:88
as cardinal, 7:935
cardinalate, 3:106, 107
cardinals' attention to curial affairs, 7:936
Catholic Action, 3:276
Church-State relations, 3:642–643
Code of Canons of the Eastern Churches, 3:818
common good, 4:16, 20–21
Communist bloc, 3:200
contemporary life of priests, 7:936
contraception, 4:222
cultural diversity, 9:681
Daniélou, Jean, 4:516
Ecumenical council, 8:250
Ecumenical Movement, 5:74
ecumenism, 3:625, 626, 7:937
episcopal dignity of cardinals, 7:936
Focolare Movement, 5:785
freedom, 5:943
Good Friday prayer revisions, 10:559
growth of missions, 7:937
historical theology, 6:869
Index of Prohibited Books, 7:391
indulgence for prayer, 11:600
inspiration of charity, 7:936
international peace, 5:206, 943, 952, 10:741–742, 747, 850
liturgical languages, 8:667
medical research, 5:560
mothers' roles in families, 14:826
music innovation condemned, 8:685
native hierarchy and clergy, 7:936
papal commission for telecommunications, 7:936

papal development under, 10:849–850
Passionists, 10:932
peace, 14:642
Pontifical Academy of Our Lady Immaculate, 11:476
poverty and social issues, 7:936–937, 11:566
preaching, 11:628
Precious Blood, 11:642
promotion of study of Latin, 7:937
reform of ordination rites, 10:640
rights and duties of public authorities, 13:567
role of the state, 13:567–568
Roman Pontifical, 11:474
rosary recitation, 7:937
signs of the times, 13:117
social conditions, 9:317
social progress, 10:850
vacancies of the Holy See, 7:936
Vatican construction under, 14:397
Vatican Council II, 2:676, 3:56, 626, 14:408
vernacular, 8:365, 667
women's rights, 14:825
works of, 7:933
World Council of Churches, 7:937
John Anagnostes, 2:801
John and Paul (Roman martyrs), SS., 7:1018
John Anglicus (Pope). *See* Joan (Popess), fable of
John Baconthorp, 3:141, 7:939–940, 12:232–233, 14:46
Carmelite spirituality, 3:133, 143
Latin Averroism, 1:937
unity thesis, 5:818
John Baptist of Saint Aignan, 3:368
John Baptist of the Conception, St., 7:940, *941*, 14:208
John Bassandus, Bl., 7:940–941
John Bekkos (Patriarch), 2:787
John Beleth, 1:289
John Benincasa, Bl., 7:941
John Blund, 1:225, 7:941–942
John Bonus of Milan, St., 7:942
John Buridan, 1:223, 675, 7:942–943, 10:18, 12:762
John Camateros of Constantinople, 2:825
John Cameniates, 2:799
John Cananus, 2:801
John Cantius, St., 7:943
John Capistran, St., 5:876, 7:943–945
anti-Semitism, 7:871

Antonia of Florence, Bl., 1:533
Böhm, Hans, 2:461
Canon Law, 3:53
Capranica, Angelo, 3:92
Crusades, 2:881, 4:412
Holy Name, 7:32
works of charity, 3:414
John Chrysostom, St., **7:945–949**
Acacius of Beroea, 1:50
Adrianus, 1:130
altars, 1:317
anamnesis, 1:383
Anthemius, 1:502
Antioch, 1:522, 7:945–946
Antiochene liturgy, 1:528
Arcadius, 1:631
Atticus of Constantinople, St., 1:839
baptism, 2:62
baptism in the Holy Spirit, 3:393
baptism of, 2:67–68
beatific vision, 2:172–173
Bible texts, 2:366
biblical canon, 3:32
bishops, 2:417
Book of Common Prayer, as source
of, 2:524
cantors, 3:75
capital punishment, 3:86
Cassian, John, 3:205, 206, 207
catechisms, 3:239
catechumenate, 3:251
character of, 7:947
charity, 3:395
Chi-Rho, 3:474
Christmas, 3:552, 553
clerical dress, 3:801
condemnation of, 4:185
congregational singing, 4:118
conscience, 4:147
conservation, 4:160
contraception, 4:221
on the cross, 4:385
Cyril of Alexandria, 4:465
demonology, 4:646–647, 648
divine conformity, 4:92
divine indwelling, 7:441
dogma as term, 4:811
Epiphanius of Salamis, 5:292
eucharistic epiclesis, 5:279
evolution, 5:495
as exegete and doctor, 7:948–949
exegetical works, 5:511
exile and death of, 7:947
freedom of conscience, 4:148

Genesis, Book of, 7:948
Gospels, 7:948
homiletics, 2:773, 795, 7:62
Honorius (Roman Emperor), 7:88
hospitality, 7:118
hospitals, 7:127
Innocent I (Pope), St., 7:468
Isidore of Pelusium, St., 7:601
lay spirituality, 8:414
liturgical history, 8:652
liturgy, 2:811–812
narrative practice, 8:863
natural law, 10:181
as patriarch of Constantinople, 7:946
patristic theology, 10:968
Pauline Epistles, 7:948
pedagogy among Fathers, 10:755
penance, 4:225
pilgrimage, 11:354
preaching, 11:610, 618
Precious Blood, 11:642
priesthood, 11:696
property, 11:758
prophecy, 11:761
Psalms, Book of, 7:948
relics, 12:51, 52
School of Antioch, 1:524, 527
Severian of Gabala, 13:40–41
Solemnity of All Saints, 1:289
Synod of the Oak, 1:839, 3:564, 595
synodos endēmousa convoking of,
10:946
transubstantiation, 14:158
use of pagan rhetoric, 6:439
works of, 7:947–948
works of charity, 3:407
John Cinnamus, 2:800
John Climacus, St., **7:949–950**
Byzantine theology, 2:794, 826
Carthusian spirituality, 3:190
chastity, 3:444
discernment, spiritual, 4:765
hesychasm, 2:763
spiritual abandonment, 1:5
John Codonatus (Bp. of Apamea), 1:49
John Colombini, Bl., 7:32, **950**
John Comnenum (Emperor of
Byzantium), 4:403
John Crescentius II (Patricius
Romanorum), 7:927
John Cunningham. *See* John Kynyngham
John da Pian del Carpine, 7:474–475,
950–951, 12:616

John Damascene, St., 5:279, 449, 640,
7:951–953, 10:548
Aristides, 1:666
Aristotelianism, 1:670–671
ascetical and exegetical works,
7:942–953
biblical canon, 3:26
Byzantine chant, 2:742, 803
Christology, 2:820, 821, 3:561
circumincession, 3:741
Cosmas the Melodian, 4:281
Didymus the Blind, 4:738
dogmatic works of, 7:951–952
human will, 14:721–722
hypostasis, 7:264
iconoclasm, 2:751, 793, 821, 7:281
infinity, 7:458
order of the universe, 14:329
Protoevangelium Jacobi, 1:469
relics, 12:53
traditionalism of, 2:791
transubstantiation, 14:158
John de Britto, St., **7:953–954**
John de Grey (Bp. of Norwich), **7:954**
John de Offord, **7:955**
John de Ridevall, **7:955**
John de Sacrobosco, 6:59, **7:955–956**
John de Saint-Pol (Abp. of Dublin),
7:956
John de Seccheville, **7:956–957**
John de Valle, 5:897
John Dewey: An Intellectual Portrait
(Hook), 10:205
John Diacrinomenus, 2:797
John Discalceatus, Bl., **7:957**
John Drungarios, 3:258
John Frederick of Saxony, 12:741
John Gilbert (Bp.), **7:957**
John Gualbert, St., 3:600, 5:766, 7:661,
957–958, *958*, 13:36
John Henry Cardinal Newman Honorary
Society, 8:153, 10:343–344
John Hymmonides. *See* John the Deacon
of Rome
John Hyrcanus, 2:360, 6:663, 13:72
John Italus, 2:758, 758–759, 759, 809,
824, **7:958–959**
John Joseph of the Cross, St., **7:959**
John Klenkok, 1:883, **7:959**
John Koukouzeles, 2:743
John Kynyngham, **7:959–960**
John Kyriotes, 2:805
John Lackland. *See* John (King of
England)

John Lancaster Spalding: First Bishop of Peoria, American Educator (Ellis), 5:170

John le Moine (Card.), 3:48, **7:960**

John le Romeyn (Abp. of York), **7:960**, 14:894

John Lobedau, Bl., **7:960–961**

John Lutterell, **7:961**

John Malalas, 1:461, 5:491, **7:961–962**, 12:320

John Mark, St. *See* Mark, Evangelist, St.

John Mary Irenaeus St. Cyr, 3:475

John Mauropus, 2:824

John Milíč, **7:962**, 11:320

John of Acton, **7:962**

John of Antioch (Bp.), 4:466, 859, 5:273, **7:962–963**, 13:196

John of Apamea, 2:73

John of Appleby, **7:963**

John of Arbela (Bp.), 1:628

John of Asia, 12:320

John of Avila, St., 1:236, 4:263, **7:963–964**

John of Bastone, Bl., **7:964**

John of Belna, 11:570

John of Beverley, St., **7:964–965**, 14:894

John of Biclaro (Bp. of Gerona), **7:965**, 10:472

John of Brandenburg, 7:875–876

John of Bridlington, St., **7:965**

John of Bromyard, 3:50, 5:529, **7:965**

John of Brussels. *See* Mombaer, John

John of Caramola, Bl., **7:965–966**

John of Chalcedon, 2:33

John of Châtillon, St., **7:966**

John of Coudenberg, 13:327

John of Damascus, 7:856–857

John of Dukla, St., **7:966**

John of Dumbleton, **7:966–967**, 12:812

John of Egypt, St., **7:967**

John of Ephesus (Bp.), 5:399, **7:967**

John of Falkenberg, 4:171, 172, **7:967–968**

John of Féchamp, 9:452, 13:445

John of Feckenham, **7:968**

John of Freiburg (Rumsik), 1:226, 3:50, **7:968**

John of Gaeta. *See* Gelasius II (Pope)

John of Garland, 1:265

John of Gaunt, 4:413, 14:865

John of Gerona, 3:409

John of God, St., **7:968–969**, *969*

John of Gorze, St., **7:969–970**

John of Grandisson (Bp. of Exeter), 5:530, **7:954**

John of Hispanus. *See* John of Spain

John of Hollywood. *See* John de Sacrobosco

John of Hoveden, **7:970**

John of Höxter, 2:607

John of Jandun, 1:675, 936–937, 4:882, **7:970–971**

John of Jenštein (Abp. of Prague), 7:977, 14:678

John of Jerusalem (Bp.), 3:595, 4:472, 5:292, 585, **7:971–972**, 12:404

John of Jesus Mary, **7:972**

John of Kilkenny, 11:620

John of la Rochelle, **7:972**

    Alexander of Hales, 1:265

    Augustinianism, 1:878

    beauty, 2:185

    Bonaventure, St., 2:479

    cogitative power, 3:823

    Paris School (Franciscans), 5:899, 12:760

    preaching, 11:619

John of La Verna, Bl., 5:736, **7:973**

John of Langton (Bp.), **7:973**

John of Lichtenberg, 1:226, **7:973**, 14:46

John of Lodi, St., 5:792, **7:973–974**

John of Matera, St., **7:974**

John of Matha, St., 3:414, 5:670, **7:974**

John of Mecklenberg, St., **7:974–975**

John of Mirecourt, **7:975**, 10:412, 536, 537, 13:201–202

John of Monte Corvino, 1:702, 3:492–493, **7:975–976**

John of Monte Marano, St., **7:976**

John of Montfort, Bl., **7:976**

John of Montmirail, Bl., **7:976**

John of Musca. *See* John de Ridevall

John of Naples, 1:27, 3:96, **7:976–977**

John of Nepomuc, St., 4:480, **7:977**

John of Otzun (Armenian Catholicos), **7:978**

John of Oxford (Bp. of Norwich), **7:978**

John of Palomar, **10:814**

John of Paris, 1:675, 678, 2:481, 3:636, 5:36, **7:978–979**

John of Parma, Bl., 1:404, 2:840, 5:897, **7:979–980**, 12:616

John of Plano Carpini. *See* John da Pian del Carpine

John of Prado, Bl., **11:577**

John of Pulsano. *See* John of Matera, St.

John of Ragusa, 3:293, **7:980–981**

John of Ravenna (Abp.), **7:981**, 8:482

John of Réôme, St., **7:981**

John of Ripa, 3:93, **7:981–982**

John of Rodington, **7:982**

John of Sabina. *See* Sylvester III (Pope)

John of Sahagún, St., 1:888

John of Saint-Samson, 3:137, 143, **7:982–983**

John of St. Thomas, **7:983–984**, 14:51

    abstraction, 1:47, 48

    accident, 1:60

    action and passion, 1:79

    analogy, 1:373

    connatural knowledge, 8:205, 206

    continuum, 4:215

    divine concurrence, 4:71

    divine essence, 6:320

    idea, 7:294

    immanence, 7:340

    individuation, 7:424, 426

    intelligible species, 13:409

    judgment, 8:23

    location (ubi), 8:742

    scholasticism, 12:764, 776, 777

    speculative theology, 3:613

    transcendental properties, 2:186

John of Salerno, Bl., **7:984**

John of Salisbury (Bp. of Chartres), 5:240, **7:984–985**, 14:2, 324

    Abelard, Peter, 1:19

    Bartholomew of Exeter, 2:125

    Bernard of Chartres, 2:307

    Bernard of Clairvaux, 2:311

    body politic, 13:253

    cathedral and episcopal schools, 3:264, 441

    chivalry, 3:519

    chronicle of, 1:463, 464

    Cicero, Marcus Tullius, 3:730

    Gilbert de la Porrée, 6:214

    Latin literature, 3:601

    medieval Latin literature works of, 9:453

    nominalism, 12:377

    School of Chartres, 12:758

John of Scythopolis (Bp.), **7:986**

John of Segovia (Card.), **12:878**

John of Seville, 11:44

John of Spain, 1:938, 4:288, 847, **7:986**

John of Sterngassen, **7:986**, 14:46

John of Texeda, 12:449

John of the Anunciation, 4:44

John of the Cross, St., 2:109, 115, **7:986–989**, *987*

    acedia, 1:67

    Alphonsus Liguori, St., 1:310

    Antolínez, Agustín, 1:532

    apophatic theology, 1:568

    Arbiol y Diez, Antonio, 1:629

Carmelite spirituality, 3:130, 132, 134, 135–136, 137

contemplation, 4:204, 205, 206

critical editions, 13:122

dark night of the soul, 4:530

Discalced Carmelites, 3:143, 144, 145

locutions, 8:747

mystical quality of writings, 10:117, 118

private revelations, 12:201

reform, 4:310, 311

spiritual direction, 4:762

spiritual purification, 11:832–833

spirituality, 13:47

tepidity, 8:866

transforming union, 13:441–442

universal holiness, 7:6, 7

works of, 7:988

John of Thilrode, 1:465

John of Thoresby (Abp. of York), **7:989**

John of Tossignano. *See* John X (Pope)

John of Tours. *See* Villula, John de

John of Tynemouth, 1:206, 3:49, 83

John of Valence, St., **7:989**

John of Vercelli, Bl., 1:226, **7:989–990**

John of Waldby, **7:990**, 12:271

John of Wales (Bolognese canonist), 1:207, **7:990–991**

John of Wales (English theologian, d.1285), **7:991**, 11:619

John of Wales (English theologian, fl. 1349), **7:991**

John of Worcester, 1:463, 5:772

John Otznetzi (Armenian Catholicos), 1:705

John Pagus, 1:110, 265

John Parenti, **7:991**

John Paul I (Pope), 1:726, 3:627, **7:991–992**, 10:851–852, 11:475

John Paul II (Pope), 1:*31*, 3:*211*, **7:992–1006**, *993*

abortion, 1:24, 28, 29, 30, 6:187

as Abp. of Kraków, 7:996

Communio (periodical), 4:31

Czech catholicism, 4:487

academic freedom, 1:54–55

acolytes, 1:68

Afghanistan, 1:153

Africa visits of, 4:106, 109

AIDS, 1:193

Albania, 1:216, 217

Algeria, 1:286

The Angelicum, 11:487

Anglican-Roman Catholic dialogue, 1:439, 441, 442, 5:67

Angola, 1:451–452

animal rights, 1:456

Apostolic Penitentiary, 11:76

L'Arche International, 1:635

Argentina, 1:653, 655, 656

Armenia, 1:703, 704

art of Guido da Fiesole, 5:716

Asian Synod of Bishops, Special Assembly of (1999), 13:*687*

assassination attempt, 5:644

Assisi, 1:790

Assyrian Church of the East, 1:805, 808

atheism, 1:824

Augustine, St., 1:852

Auschwitz, 11:*445*

Austria, 1:917

authority of Rome, 10:852–853, 14:315, 316

Bahrain, 2:16

Balthasar, Hans Urs von, 2:34

Baltimore, 2:41

Barbastro (Spain) martyrs, 2:92

beatification ceremonies, 7:*660*, 10:*268*, *736*

Belgium, 2:220

Bernardin, Joseph Louis, 2:319

birth control, 7:180

as bishop, 7:994

body, nuptial meaning of, 13:46

Bonino, Bl. Giuseppina Gabriella, 2:505

Boretta, Beatrice, baptism of, 2:*68*

Bridget, St., 6:810–811

Bulgaria, 2:684

Burkina Faso, 2:704

Burma, 2:707

Burundi, 2:712

Camara, Helder Pessoa, 2:*900*

camerlengo, 2:910

Canada, 3:11

canonization, 3:63

Canossa, St. Maddalena Gabriella, 3:70

capital punishment, 3:88, 238

as cardinal, 7:995–996, 11:*28*

cardinalate, 3:106, 107

Casaroli, Agostino, 3:201

catechesis and evangelization, 6:127

catechism, 3:237, 245

Catholic university, 5:498–499

CELAM IV (Santo Domingo), 12:686

celibacy, dispensations from, 8:286

Central African Republic, 3:344

Cevoli, Bl. Florida, 3:358

Chad, 3:361

challenge to Communism, 7:997–998

Chávez Orozco, Bl. María Vicenta of Santa Dorotea, 3:461

Chevrier, Bl. Antoine Marie, 3:473

China, 3:505

Christian anthropology, 3:532

Christian philosophy, 3:542

Church teaching, 5:205, 459, 476–477, 560, 10:179, 852

Church's missionary mandate, 11:990–992

Church-State relations, 3:643, 4:487–488, 7:999–1000

Cimatti, Bl. Maria Raffaella, 3:734

Code of Canon Law (CIC) (1983), 1:97–98, 3:34, 35, 36, 56–57, 58

Code of Canons of the Eastern Churches, 3:817, 818, 819

communio, 4:30

Communists in Poland, 8:250

conclaves, 4:60

consequentialism, 4:160

consumerism, 10:852

controversies, 7:1004–1005

Cor Unum charity, 2:705, 3:81

Cuba, 4:420–421, *421*

Curia, 4:438–440

Cyril and Methodius, SS., 13:216–217, 14:107

Częstochowa, 4:*489*, 490

Daimiel martyrs, 4:495

with the Dalai Lama, 7:*994*

democratic principles, 13:259

Denver (CO) visit of, 4:670

dialectical approach, 13:245

Discalced Carmelites, 8:112

Divine Mercy, devotion to, 8:245

ecclesiastical education, 12:688–689, 689–690

ecclesiastical facilities and universities, 5:498–499

ecclesiology, 5:40, 205, 10:853, 12:700, 14:355–356

economic interdependence, 13:260

ecumenism, 5:40, 7:1003–1004

election, 8:232

enclosure, 3:806

episcopal conferences, 5:299, 301

eucharistic congresses, 5:433

euthanasia, 5:459, 560

evangelization, 5:39, 478, 9:682

John Paul II (Pope) *(continued)*

evolution, 4:345

Faà di Bruno, 5:581

faith and reason, relationship between, 5:714–715, 10:185, 852, 12:198, 778

family, 14:826

Fátima pilgrimages, 11:540

fifth ordinary assembly of bishops (1980), 13:690

fundamental option, 6:26

Gambia, 6:85

German reunification, 6:186

Ghana, 6:*200*, 201

Greece, 6:437

Greek Catholic Church in Romania, 12:339

Guinea-Bissau, 6:576

Haiti, 6:620–621

health of, 7:1005

Holocaust, 7:13–15

in the Holy Land, 7:648

Holy Spirit, 4:856–857

homosexuality, 7:72

human labor, 13:263–264

Hume, George Basil, 7:203, 204

Hungary, 7:222

interpretation of the Bible, 11:478

Iowa, 7:543

Iraqi embargo, 7:548

Iturrate Zubero, Domingo, 7:677

Janssens, Louis, 7:722

Japan, 7:742

Jesuits, 1:726, 727, 7:794, 795

John Paul II (Pope) Institute, 11:486

Jordan, 7:1032

Jubilee Year 2000, 7:1002, 11:747, 989–990

justice, 4:236

Korean martyrs, 8:233, 239

Kosovo issue, 13:11

laity, 3:549, 8:292–293

Lateran Pacts (1985), 8:360

Latin American pilgrimages, 7:999–1000

Latvia, 8:377

lay evangelism, 4:487

lay spirituality, 8:417

Lebanon, 8:427–428

Lefebvre, M., 8:448

liberation theology, 2:598

Lithuanian pilgrims, 8:606

liturgical inculturation, 7:383, 384

Los Angeles (CA), 13:*19*

magesterium of, 7:1002–1003

Mali, monetary donation to, 9:77–78

man, nature of, 9:91–92

marriage, sacrament of, 9:338

martyrologies, 9:233–234

martyrs of Pratulin, 11:584

Marxism, 4:158

Mary, Blessed Virgin, 11:990, 14:826–827

medical research, 5:560–561

mercy, 4:783–784

military services, USA, archdiocese for, 9:629

mission theology, 5:480–481, 9:678

modern Russian Church issues, 12:430

modernization of Rome, 12:362–363

moral circumstances, 3:743

moral obligation of free societies, 7:998

moral theology, 10:185, 852, 14:451–452

Mozambique region, 10:39–40

Native Australians, 1:907

natural family planning, 10:179

Neocatechumental Way recognized, 10:233–234

new evangelization, 5:477–478, 7:1001–1002, 11:629–630

New York, 2:*600*, 10:319

New Zealand, 10:328

Nicaraguan, 10:352

Ninth ordinary assembly of Bishops (1994), 13:691, *693*

Oceania Synod of Bishops, Special Assembly for, 10:*529*

ordination of women, 5:68

Orione, Luigi, 10:672

Our Lady of Częstochowa Shrine, 11:512

Our Lady of La Vang, 8:385–386

papal development under, 10:852–853

papal social thought, 13:258–259

partisan politics prohibition, 5:38

peace, 10:747, 14:643

personalist ethics, 11:153–155

Peter To Rot, Bl., 11:209

Philippines, 11:260

Polanco Fontecha, Anselmo, 11:438

Polish pilgrimages, 11:*344*, 453, 454

pontifical councils, 11:479, 482

poverty, 11:566–567

power of governance, 6:375

Prat y Prat, Mercedes, Bl., 11:583

Prelature of the Holy Cross and Opus Dei, 11:527

presbyteral councils, 11:674

as priest, 7:993–994

procession to St. Peter's Basilica, 11:*733*

Reformation martyrs, 8:242

refugees, 4:668

regulating ecclesiastical faculties and seminaries, 11:484

religious directory, 4:763, 764

right to life, 7:1003

Roman Curia, 5:480, 10:853

Roman Curia reorganization, 11:480

saints, causes of, 12:608

Salinas, Carlos Gortari, 9:585

San Salvador, 5:177

Schuster, Alfredo Ildefonso, 12:790

Second extraordinary assembly of bishops (1985), 13:690

secularization in Puerto Rico, 11:814

sexism condemned, 13:52

sinful institutions, 13:245

Sistine Chapel restoration, 13:191

social issues, 3:342–343

social justice, 13:244

Socialism, 8:266, 10:852, 14:90

solidarity, 13:301–302, 304

Spain, 13:3, 400

subsidiarity, 13:568

suffering in love, 10:852

Synod of American Bishops (1997), 13:*686*

Synod of Bishops, 13:*684*, *690*, *691*, 692

Syro-Malabar Catholic Church, 7:400

theology of Church, 3:590

Thérèse de Lisieux, St., 3:138

Thomism, 11:950

treatment of the poor, 10:616, 13:303–305

Tridentine Mass, 14:182

Ugandan bishops, 14:265

Union of Brest, 2:606

value of human life, 5:205, 459, 476–477

Vatican construction under, 14:397

Vatican Council II, 7:994–995

Vatican Library, expansion of, 14:422

Western Wall (Jerusalem), 7:*632*

Willebrands, Johannes Gerardus Maria, 14:728

women

denigration of, 10:852

dignity of, 14:827

in the priesthood, 11:747

role in Church, 1:68, 3:549
  role of, 14:826–827
  status of, 14:819
work, 11:744
world religions, 10:852, 853
with Wyszyński, Stefan (Card.), 14:872
Year of Jubilee (2000), 13:832–834
Zambia, 14:908
John Paul II Cultural Center (Washington, DC), **7:1006**
John Paul II Foundation for the Sahel, 2:704, 3:81
John Paul II Institute on Marriage and Family (Rome), **7:1006–1007**, 11:486
John Pecham. See John Peckham (Abp. of Canterbury)
John Peckham (Abp. of Canterbury), 3:72, 5:242, **7:1007–1008**
  Arabian philosophy, 1:623
  Aristotelianism, 1:674
  Augustinianism, 1:878
  Boniface of Savoy, Bl., 2:505
  Confirmation, 4:89
  correctoria, 4:276, 277
  dispute with Aquinas over hylomorphism, 14:44
  Gerard of Abbeville, 6:160
  medieval Latin literature works of, 9:460
  Richard of Gravesend (Bp. of Lincoln), rebuked, 12:233
  Richard of Gravesend (Bp. of London), opposition to, 12:233
  Roger Marston, student of, 12:286
  scholasticism, 12:760
  sermon collections of, 11:633
  unicity thesis, 5:816, 818, 12:231
  University of Paris, 3:603
  works of, 7:1007
John Pelingotto, Bl., **7:1008**
John Philagathos. See John XVI (Antipope)
John Philoponus, **7:1008–1009**
  Ammonius Hermeae, 1:670
  Aristotelianism, 1:670
  atomism, 1:833
  impetus, 7:363
  logical history, 8:749
  School of Alexandria, 1:270
  thoery of impetus, 10:18
John Phurnensis, 2:825
John Plusiadenus. See Joseph of Methone
John Prandota of Cracow, Bl., **7:1009**
John Scholasticus, 3:60

John Scotus Eriugena, **7:1009–1012**, 10:83
  Albert the Great, St., 1:225
  Amalric of Bène, 1:330
  apophatic theology, 1:568
  art, 3:153
  Carolingian reform, 3:158, 599
  Carolingian Renaissance, 3:160, 161
  causality, 3:303–304
  dialectics, 4:725–726
  emanationism, 5:181
  exegetical works, 5:514, 515
  Florus of Lyons, 5:783
  knowledge, theories of, 8:215
  Lull influenced, 8:866
  Neoplatonism, 12:121
  panentheism, 10:820
  pantheism, 2:629, 10:826
  prescholasticism, 12:757
John Scylitzes, 2:800
John Sicco. See John XVII (Pope)
John Stratford (Abp. of Canterbury), 1:109, **7:1012**
John Studios Church (Constantinople), 1:756
John Talaya, 4:253
John the Almsgiver, St., 1:269, 4:253, **7:1012**
John the Archcantor, 3:75
John the Baptist, St., 5:*164*, **7:1012–1015**, *1013*
  Agnus Dei, 1:185
  baptism of, 2:57–58, 60
  beheading of, 6:804, 7:*1014*
  disciple as term, 4:768–769
  Elizabeth, St., 5:162–163
  followers of, as recipients of John's Gospel, 7:906–907
  God's spirit, 13:427
  head of at Emesa, 5:191
  imprisonment and death, 7:1014
  Knights of St. John, 8:197
  in the New Testament, 5:159
  Qumran community, 7:1014–1015
John the Baptist, St., iconography of, **7:1015–1016**
John the Deacon of Naples, **7:1016**
John the Deacon of Rome, 3:251–252, 6:111, **7:1017**
John the Fearless (Duke of Burgundy), 7:884
John the Good (King of France), 7:137
John the Grammarian. See John Philoponus
John the Grammarian of Caesarea, 2:773, 3:561, **7:1017**, 13:43

John the Hesychast. See John the Silent, St.
John the Jew (Bp. of Italian Cathari), 3:259
John the Merciful, St. See John III Ducas Vatatzes (Byzantine Emperor)
"John the Monk" (Octoechos author), 10:548
John the Sabaite. See John the Silent, St.
John the Scholastic. See John Climacus, St.
John the Scholastic III, 3:38
John the Silent, St., **7:1017**
John the Sinner (Juan Pecador). See Grande Román, Juan, St.
John the Solitary, 4:473
John the Teuton (Abbot), 12:589
John Vianney, St., 8:337, 471
John Vincentius, St., **7:1017–1018**, 12:527–528
John Vitalis, 3:96
John Welles, **7:1018**
John Wesley Ecumenical Award, 8:250
John Xiphilinos (Patriarch), 2:759
Johnannes Janseen, ein Lebensbild (Pastor), 10:938
Johns Hopkins University (MD), 5:911
Johnson, Albert, 10:171
Johnson, George, 3:283, **7:1018–1019**
Johnson, J. Neely, 2:868
Johnson, John. See Wall, John, St.
Johnson, Lyndon Baines, 1:358
Johnson, M., 1:30
Johnson, Philip, 3:716
Johnson, Robert, Bl., 5:228, 799, **7:1019**
Johnson, Samuel, 2:558, 559, 624
Johnson, Thomas, Bl., 5:226, **7:1019**
Johnston, William, 10:115
Johon of Naples, 12:762
Joint Declaration on the Doctrine of Justification, 5:40, 70, 8:91
Joint Declaration on the Doctrine of Justification, 8:885
Joint Doctrinal Commission of Anglicans and Orthodox, 5:721
Joint Liturgical Commission on English in New Zealand, 5:253
Joint Liturgical Group (JLG) of Great Britain, 5:253, 8:440
Joinville, Jehan de, 4:401
Jolenta of Hungary, Bl., **7:1019–1020**
Joliet, Louis, 3:5, 475, 9:722, 12:558
Joliet-Marquette Expedition, 9:722
Jommelli, Niccolò, 7:*1020*, **1020**
Jon Arason (Bp.), 7:276
Jón Ögmundsson, St., **7:1020–1021**

Jonah (Metropolitan of Moscow), 2:745

Jonah (sexual reorientation group), 7:69

Jonah, Book of, 6:140, **7:1021–1022**

Jonah, Sign of, **7:1022–1023**

Jonah ben Jiṣḥaq, Jehudah, **7:1023**

Jonas (Bp. of Orléans), 3:43, 230, 634, 769–770, **7:1024**

Jonas, Justus, 1:850, **7:1023**

Jonas of Bobbio, 1:331, 5:456, 7:245, **1023–1024**

Jonatus, St., **7:1024–1025**

Jones, Edward, Bl., 5:231, **7:1025**

Jones, G. V., 7:851

Jones, Inigo, 1:467, 3:678, 12:577

Jones, Jim, 10:301

Jones, John, St., 5:233, **7:1025**, 12:245

Jones, Leander, 10:501

Jones, Robert, 3:681, 717

Jones, Robert Ambrose. *See* Emrys Ap Iwan

Jones, Watson v. (1871), 3:657, 658

Jones, William Ambrose (Bp. of San Juan), 1:891, **7:1025–1026**

Jones v. Wolf (1979), 3:662

Jonestown (People's Temple), 4:*425*

Jong, Johannes de (Card.), **7:1026**

Jonker, J. T., 10:264

Jonnes, Jill, 10:318

Jonsen, A. R., 10:192

Joram (King of Israel), 5:87, 7:640

Jordá Botella, María, Bl., 1:4

Jordaens, Jacob, 1:539

Jordan, **7:1029–1032**, *1030*

Jordan, Edward Benedict, **7:1026**

Jordan, Francis Mary of the Cross, 4:788, **7:1026–1027**, *1027*, 12:630

Jordan, Fulgentius, 7:581

Jordan Forzatè, Bl., **7:1032**

Jordan of Giano, **7:1032**

Jordan of Paderborn, 9:462

Jordan of Quedlinburg, **7:1032–1033**

Jordan of Saxony, Bl., 1:224, 875, 887, 2:337, **7:1033**, 12:607

Jordan River, **7:1027–1029**, *1028*

Jorge, Domingos, Bl., 7:732

Jorge, Ignacio, Bl., 7:733

Jorge, Isabel Fernandez, Bl., 7:733

Joris, David, **7:1033**

Jornet e Ibars, Teresa, Bl., **7:1033–1034**

Josaphat (King of Edom), 5:87

Josaphat Kuncevyč, St., 2:141, 143, **7:1034**

Josbert, Bl. *See* Joscio, Bl.

Joscio, Bl., **7:1034**

Joscius, Bl. *See* Joscio, Bl.

José de Jesús Maria (Aravalles, d. 1609), 3:136

José de Jesús Maria (Quiroga, 1562-1629), 3:136

José de Jesús Maria (Sampedro, 1564-1615), 3:136

José del Espíritu Santo (Baroso, 1609-74), 3:137

José del Espíritu Santo (d. 1736), 3:137–138

Joseph (Aghovan Catholicos), 1:453

Joseph (Armenian Catholicos), 1:700

Joseph (Bp. of Diarbekir), 3:368

Joseph (Robert de Boron), 7:26, 28

Joseph, St., **7:1034–1037**, 9:241–242, 244, 248, 278, 12:599

Joseph, St., devotion to, **7:1037–1041**

Joseph I (Chaldean Patriarch), 3:368

Joseph I (King of Portugal), 3:791, 11:467, 468, 538

Joseph I (Patriarch of Constantinople), **7:1043**, 10:63

Joseph II (Holy Roman Emperor), 5:258, **7:***1041*, **1041–1042**

Bohemia/Moravia, 4:483

Carthusians, 3:195

Church-state relations, 7:216

Enlightenment, 7:216

See also Josephinism

Joseph II Ṣlībā (Chaldean Patriarch), 2:764, 3:368

Joseph III (Chaldean Patriarch), 3:368

Joseph IV (Chaldean Patriarch), 3:368

Joseph V (Audo) (Chaldean Patriarch), 2:5

Joseph Calasanctius, St., 2:541, 3:199, **7:1043**, 11:319, 12:247

Joseph de S. Jacinto, Bl., 7:733

Joseph Emmanuel II Thomas (Chaldean Patriarch), 3:369

Joseph Genesius, 2:798

Joseph of Arimathea, 7:28, 29

Joseph of Christ, 3:144

Joseph of Cupertino, St., **7:1044**

Joseph of Leonessa, St., **7:1044**

Joseph of Methone, **7:1044–1045**

Joseph of Paris. *See* Le Clerc du Tremblay, François

Joseph of Studion, 2:742, 743

Joseph of the Holy Spirit, 4:206, **7:1045**

Joseph the Hymnographer, 2:803

Josephine, Amanda, 1:158

Josephinism, 3:615, 639–640, **7:1045–1046**

Argentina, 1:650

Austria, 1:910, 913–914, 3:54, 92, 615, 616, 639–640

Belgium, 5:913, 8:507

Bertieri, Giuseppe, 2:334

Caprara, Giovanni Battista, 1:914, 3:92

Chile, 3:732

disappearance of, 3:616

Enlightenment, 5:257

Gallicanism, 3:54

heresy of, 6:778

Hungary, 7:216, 13:136

liturgical music history, 8:693

Pius VI (Pope), 11:376

reform in the Low Countries, 2:218

Rudigier, Franz Josef, 12:400–401

Severoli, A., 13:42

Josephinist Marriage Act of 1783, 7:1042

Josephite Fathers. *See* Josephites

Josephite Missionaries. *See* Josephites

Josephite Sisters, 9:23

Josephites, **7:1047**, 10:294

African Americans, 13:405

Alabama, 1:295

founding of, 3:622

Russian monasteries, 12:423

Josephium. *See* Pontifical College Josephinum (Columbus, OH)

Josephology, 7:1039

Josephus, Flavius, **7:1047–1050**, 14:68–69

Berossus, 2:329

biblical canon, 3:22–23, 24

Capernaum, 3:83

censuses, 3:338, 339

chief priests, 3:482

defenses of Jerusalem, 7:767

disciple as term, 4:769, 773

on the Essenes, 5:369–370

Feast of the Dedication, 4:607

Justus of Tiberias, 8:103

leprosy, 8:509

Letter of Aristeas, 1:666

misanthropia, 3:592

providence of God, 11:781–782

20th century scholarship, 7:1050

writings of, 12:308

Joshua (son of Nun), 7:364, **1055–1056**, 13:72

Joshua, Book of, **7:1050–1055**

Baal, 2:2

Balaam, 2:26

Benjamin (tribe), 2:282

conquest and settlement of Israel, 7:637

creation, 4:341

God's spirit, 13:426

grace of God, 9:87

Judah (tribe), 8:1

justice of men, 8:73

Lord as honorific title, 8:780

Lord's Day, 8:782

Passover, 10:933, 934

Shechem covenant, 13:72

sin, 13:142

slavery, 13:206, 207

spirit, 13:424

word of God, 14:836

Josiah (King of Judah), 4:703, 7:642

Josippon (Hebrew chronicle), **7:1056–1057**

Jouarre-en-Brie Abbey (France), **7:1057**

Joubert, Eugénie, Bl., **7:1057–1058**

Joubert de la Muraille, Jacques, 1:157

Jouffret de Bonnefont, Claude-Joseph, 12:277

Jouffroy, Theodore, 5:47

Jounel, P., 5:860

Jourdain, E. F., 3:759

Journal de dom Ruinart, 12:407

Journal de Trévoux, 3:295

Le Journal d'un curé de campagne (Bernanos), 2:303

Journal ecclésiastique, 2:118

Journal of Classic and Sacred Philology, 8:585

Journal of Feminist Studies in Religion, 5:678, 680

A Journal of Meditations for Every Day of the Year: Gathered out of Divers Authors (Southwell), 13:369

Journal of Ritual Studies, 12:260

Journal of Speculative Philosophy, 7:301

Journal of Theological Studies, 14:242

Journet, Charles (Card.), 3:589, 5:37, 7:440, **1058**

Journey East, Journey West: 1907-1937 (Eliade), 5:155

"Journey of the Magi" (Eliot), 5:160, 161

The Journey of the Mind into God (St. Bonaventure), 2:481–482, 5:899

Journeyman associations, 8:230

Jouvenaux, Guido, 3:473

Jovian (Roman Emperor), 1:268, 2:139, 8:263

Joy, 1:602, 778, **7:1059**

Joyce, James, 1:292, 14:149

Joyce, Robert F. (Bp. of Burlington), 14:456

Joyeuse, François de, 5:659

Joyeuse, Henri, Duc de, **7:1059–1060**

Juan (Martyr of Tlaxcala), 14:95

Juan Carlos I (King of Spain), 13:397, 398

Juan de la Anunciación, 12:618, 619

Juan de Los Angeles, **7:1060**

Juan de S. Domingo, Bl., 7:732

Juan de Santo Matía, Fray. *See* John of the Cross, St.

Juan de Ugarte, 12:623

Juan del Valle (Bp. of Popayán), 3:848

Juan Diego, Bl., 6:545–546, **7:1060–1061**

Juan Pecador (John the Sinner). *See* Grande Román, Juan, St.

Juana de la Cruz, Sor, **7:1061–1062**, 8:369

Juanillo (Guale chief), 6:148–149

Juarez, Jesus (Bp.), 2:471

Juazeiro (Brazil), pilgrimage to, 2:155

Jubani, Simon, 1:216

Jubilee Year 1450, 10:368

Jubilee Year 2000, 7:440, 1002, 11:747, 989–990

Jubilee years (Israelite tradition), 1:838, 2:502–503, **7:1062–1063**, 10:856, 12:458, 13:206

Jubilees (Essenes), 5:370

Jubilees, Book of, 1:549

Jucunda sane (encyclical, Pius X), 11:389

Juda (rabbi), 4:385

Judah (kingdom), 4:529, 674, 7:639–643

Judah (Patriarch), 8:1

Judah, Rabbi Gershom ben, 7:869

Judah, Tribe of, 8:1, 313

Judah ben David Hayyuj, 5:509

Judah ben Samuel ha-Levi, 8:8

Judah Ha-Nasi, 1:199, **8:2**, 7

Judaism, 8:2–14

  Abraham's bosom image, 1:39

  Acosta, Gabriel, 1:69–70

  Adonai, 1:118

  afterlife, 1:164–165

  Akiba ben Joseph, 1:94, 199

  Albo, Joseph, 1:232

  angels, 1:416–417, 418–419, 425, 427, 476

  Antichrist, 1:516

  Antioch, 1:521, 523

  apocalyptic style, 1:546

  art, 1:743, 752

  asceticism, 1:775–776

ashes, 1:782

biblical archaeology, 2:380

biblical canon in, 3:20, 22–26, 565

biblical criticism, 1:35–36

Billerbeck, Paul, 2:393–394

casuistry, 3:220

catechesis, 3:228

catechumenate, 3:249

chief priests, 3:482

Christian view, 8:13–14

Church, 12:184–185

church architecture, 3:715

Church-State relations, 3:631

confirmation, 2:84

conscience, 4:140–141, 143, 148

corban, 4:257

covenant with God, 9:687

Dead Sea Scrolls, 4:563

Dedication, Feast of, 4:607–608

deism, 4:617

dietary laws, 4:742–743

divination, 4:785–786

early Christian prayers, 8:380

early Christian theology, 3:591

Epistles of St. Paul, 3:860–861

Ethiopia, 5:699–700

faith, 5:590–591

first Christian centruy, 8:5–7

fish symbolism, 5:748

Gnosticism, 2:831, 3:465

God's spirit, 13:427

Ḥasidism, 6:660–662, 7:872

Haskalah Movement, 6:662–663

images, 7:324

imposition of hands, 7:365

influence on John's Gospel, 7:906

interpretations of Jesus, 7:842

Jesus, 8:12–13

Jewish Hellenism, 6:261–263

Judith, Book of, 8:43

Justinian I attitudes, 8:97

Kaddish, 8:107–108

Khazars, 8:163–164

law, Mosaic, 8:396–397

liberation thinking, 8:549

mahzor prayer structure in, 9:49–50

Maimonides, works of, 9:52–53

Marranos, 1:69

marriage, 1:150

martyr literature, 1:94

meaning of term, 8:2

medical ethics, 9:429

menorah, use of, 9:497

Messiah, 3:527, 529

Judaism (continued)

metaphysics, 9:548

Mezuzah, 9:591

Midrash, 9:618–619

millenarianism, 9:635

mixed marriages in the Book of Malachi, 9:63

modern times, 8:9–12

Mortara case, 9:903–904

Mountain Jews, 8:164

Muḥammad's attitude toward, 10:52

mysticism, 8:870–871

Naḥmanides, 10:135–136

oral law, significance of, 13:743–745

origins, 8:2–3

postexilic Judaism, 7:634–635

prayer, 11:591

primitive religions, 12:68

prophetic Judaism, 8:11

prophets, readings from, 8:434

purgatory, 11:825

rabbinic, 8:7–9

rabbis, 11:882–883

reform, 8:9–10, 11

reform movement, 19th century, 7:873

religious significance of blood, 2:443–444

ritual bathing and purification, 2:57

School of Alexandria, 1:272

Scriptures, use of, 8:434

seminal ideas, 8:3–5

seventy weeks of years, 13:39–40

Shabbataiïsm, 13:56–57

Shechem, 13:71–72

sin, 13:145

Spanish letters, 13:383–384

Spinoza, 13:418

spirit, 13:424–425

Sukkot, 2:530–533

synagogues, ancient, 13:675–678

Talmud, 13:742–747

Ten Commandments, 4:6–7

United States, 3:718, 719–721

wine, liturgical use of, 14:772

wisdom teaching in, 14:795

Yom Kippur, 1:838–839

See also Apocrypha; Catholic-Jewish dialogue; Covenant; Israelites; Jewish liturgy; Jews; Old Testament; Qumran Community; Talmud; specific people

Judas Barsabbas, 13:119

Judas Cyriacus, 4:384, 385

Judas Iscariot, 1:728, **8:14–16**, *15*, 344–345

Judas Maccabee, 7:644, 766

Judde, Claude, **8:16**

Jude, Epistle of St., **8:16–17**

agape in, 1:170

canonicity, 3:28, 31, 32

the Church, 3:580

creedal statements, 4:349–350

Enoch, 5:265

Gehenna, 6:116

Gnosis, 6:254

homosexuality, 7:66

wickedness, 8:16, 17

Jude Thaddeus, St., 8:*17*, **17–18**

Judeo-Christian symbolism, 13:664–665

Judge, Thomas Augustine, **8:18**, 9:732, 733

Judge, William Q., 13:934, 935–936

Judgement of Adam and Eve, 9:88

Judges, Book of, **8:18–21**

Baal, 2:2

beatific vision, 2:170

Benjamin (tribe), 2:282

conquest and settlement of Israel, 7:637

divine judgment, 8:29

Gideon, 6:208–209

Gideon cycle, 8:20

Judah (tribe), 8:1

Judith, Canticle of, 8:45

Kingdom of God, 8:173

Nazirites, 10:218

Othniel, 8:19

peace, 11:49

Samson, 8:19, 12:635

shibboleth, 13:83

social principle, 13:248

spirit, 13:424

Judges, in the Bible, **8:18**, 13:71, 72, 322

Judgment, **8:21–27**, 22

act of knowledge, 8:209

Book of Obadiah, 10:502

certitude, 3:351

contradiction, 4:223

definition, 4:609

discernment, spiritual, 4:766–767

division, 4:793

doubt and suspension of, 4:883–884

error, 5:329

false, 5:620

identity, 7:302

intentional, 13:422

logic, 9:565

notion of, 8:27

objectivity, 14:227

ordeal method to determine, 10:626–628

reflexive, 13:422

scrupulosity, 12:847

simple apprehension, 1:604

spirituality, 13:422

theology as, 13:893–894

truth in, 14:224–225, 226–227

validity of, 8:204–205

value, 14:379–380

Judgment, Divine

fire of, 5:739

sanction, 12:660–661

Judgment, Divine, in the Bible, **8:27–30**

Day of the Lord, 4:547–549

end of the world, 5:215

general judgment, 8:29–30

God as judge, 8:27

ordeal in the, 10:626–627

particular judgment, 8:27–29

Judgment, Divine, in theology, **8:30–41**

Catholic tradition, 8:30–33

continuous judgment of God, 8:34–37

definition, 8:34

essential idea, 8:33–34

general judgment of God, 8:38–41

names for, 8:39

particular judgment of God at death, 8:37–38

The Judgment of Jonah (Ellul), 5:172

Judicaël of Quimper, St. (King of Brittany), **8:41**

Judicatum (Vigilius), 14:64, 509–510

Judicial powers, 6:374

Judicial Vicar (officialis), 3:53, **8:42–43**

Judiciary reform, 9:144

Judicium ecclesiasticum (Schmalzgrueber), 12:741

Judith (Biblical figure), 8:*44*

Judith (Queen of the Franks), 3:169

Judith, Book of, **8:43–45**, 44

Achior, 1:191

canonicity, 3:26

catechumenate, 3:250

Gentiles, 6:140

God, friendship with, 6:10

God's spirit, 13:426

Hebrews, 6:698

Judith, Canticle of, 3:73, **8:45**

Judith of Niederaltaich, Bl., **8:45–46**

Judson, Adoniram, 2:79, **8:46**, *46*

Judson, Ann, 2:79

Judson, Edward, 2:80

Jugan, Jeanne, Bl., 3:419, **8:46–47**, 47, 616–617

Juge de Saint-Martin, Jean-Joseph, 12:277

Jugie, M., 3:26

Juicio político de los daños y reparos de cualquiera monarquía (Palafox), 10:765

Juizo da verdadeira causa do Terremoto (Malagrida), 9:65–66

Julian (Abp. of Toledo), St., **8:50–51**

Julián Alfredo, 14:248

Julian calendar, 8:54

Julian of Cuenca, St., 8:*47*, **47**

Julian of Eclanum (Bp.), **8:48**
   Augustine, St., 1:859–860, 3:207
   Boniface I (Pope), St., 2:498
   Nestorius, 3:317
   Pelagianism, 11:62
   Sixtus III (Pope), St., 13:196

Julian of Halicarnassus, 1:700, 2:793, 3:596, **8:48**, 13:43

Julian of Le Mans, St., **8:48–49**

Julian of Norwich, 3:605, 5:243, **8:49–50**, 10:118, 120

Julian of Speyer, 8:50

Julian Sabas, St., **8:51**

Julian the Apostate (Roman Emperor), 8:*51*, **51–52**, 12:318, 319
   Antioch, 1:522
   Apollinaris of Laodicea, 1:560
   Arianism, 1:818
   Byzantine civilization, 2:767
   Celsus, 3:330
   Church history, 3:594
   the cross, 4:383
   Cyril of Jerusalem, 4:471
   desecration of church of Emesa, 5:191
   Donatism, 4:862
   Dura-Europos, 4:945
   persecution under, 3:553, 632, 6:430–431
   Persia, 2:780
   works of charity, 3:404, 407

Julian the Hospitaler, St., 3:412

Juliana of Liège, St., 2:217, 5:463, **8:52**, 563

Julianists (Aphthartodocetism), 8:48, 52, **52**

Julianna of Cornillon, 4:272, 12:201

Julianus, Didius, 12:304

Julianus Teutonicus. *See* Julian of Speyer

Jülicher, Adolf, 2:690, 10:865, 867

Julie of Jesus, Bl., 4:44

Julius I (Pope), St., **8:52–54**, *53*
   Alexandrian relations, 4:753
   Arianism, 1:818
   Canon Law, 3:39
   Christian converts, 12:354
   Council of Sardica, 12:692
   excommunication, 12:692
   notaries, 4:757

Julius II (Pope), **8:54–57**, *55*
   appeals to a future council, 1:599
   astrology, 1:813
   Cajetan (Tommaso de Vio), 2:853
   Caribbean, 3:110
   Carvajal, Bernardino Lopez de, 3:197
   Castel Sant'Angelo, 3:213
   Chigi, Agostino, 3:483
   coinage, 10:481
   Decius, Phillipus, 4:589
   dueling, 4:929
   election, 8:486
   family of, 4:631
   Ghibelline-Guelf conflict, 3:855
   Giles of Viterbo, 6:221
   Grassi family, 6:419
   Michelangelo, 9:603
   papacy development under, 10:841
   Patronato Real, 2:862, 10:978
   Pragmatic Sanction, 11:582
   pre-Reformation spiritual hunger, 3:606, 607
   Renaissance humanism, 12:118
   St. Peter's Basilica, 12:578
   Sixtus IV (Pope) benefice, 13:197
   states of the Church, 1:259
   Swiss Guards, formation of, 13:642–643
   urbanization of Rome, 12:359
   Vatican construction under, 14:396

Julius III (Pope), 8:*57*, **57–58**
   Anglican orders problem, 1:435, 437
   Chaldean Catholic Church, 3:367
   Commendone, Giovanni Francesco, 4:11
   Council of Trent, 3:610
   Figliucci, Felix, 5:717
   Italo-Greek Catholic Church, 7:649
   Jesuits reconfirmed, 7:313
   Order of Aviz, 1:947
   papacy development under, 10:842

Julius Africanus, Sextus, 1:21, 460, 3:551, 570, 5:453, **8:58–59**

Julius Caesar. *See* Caesar, Gaius Julius

July Revolution (France, 1830), 11:382

Jumièges Abbey (France), 3:473, 693, **8:59–60**, *60*, 13:2

Jung, Carl Gustav, 1:239, 242, 4:140, 904, **8:60–61**, 10:129

Jüngel, Eberhard, 14:198

Junger, Aegidius (Bp. of Seattle, WA), 12:852

Jungius, J., 1:677

Jungmann, Josef, **8:61**

Jungmann, Josef Andreas, **8:61–63**
   beauty, 2:186
   blessings, 2:439
   catechesis, 3:241
   liturgical movement, 3:711
   preaching, 11:623, 625–626, 628
   Vatican Council II, 1:916
   writings of, 8:61–62

Junilius Africanus, **8:63**, 9:439

Jupiter (martyr), 9:28

Jupiter (planet), 6:60

Jupiter temple ruins, 10:*753*

Jura Anglorum (Plowden), 11:423

Juravit Dominus (O'Connor), 10:544

Juridical guilt. *See* Legal guilt

Jurieu, Pierre, 2:164, 916

Jurisprudence, 7:622

Jurjānī, 1:782

Jus ecclesiasticum universum (Van Espen), 5:358

Jus ecclesiasticum universum (Schmalzgrueber), 12:741

Jus Feudale (Craig), 5:702

Just price, **8:64**, 13:263

The Just Vengeance (Sayers), 12:717

Justice, **8:64–69**
   character, 3:388
   characteristics, 8:69
   common good, 4:16, 21
   commutative, 8:67, 72
   conversions of Church, 4:236
   courtesy, 4:318
   distributive, 8:67
   general (legal), 8:67
   laws, conflict of, 8:410
   legal theories, 8:400–401
   occult compensation, 4:41–43
   remuneration for work, 13:263
   social. *See* Social justice and social justice issues
   in the state, 13:486–487

Justice, double, 1:880, 884, 3:846–847, 856, **8:69–70**

Justice and Peace Office of the Bishops' Conference (Japan), 7:743

Justice in the World (Synod of Bishops), 4:21

Justice of God, 8:27, **70–73**, 879

Justice of men, 8:27, 71–72, **73–75**

Justice theory, 13:768–769

Justificatio ducis Burgundiae (Joannes Parvus), 7:884

Justification, **8:75–91**
  Aquinas, 9:511–512
  Augustinianism, 1:884
  Baianism, 2:20–21
  Catholic and Lutheran consensus, 6:187
  Christian anthropology, 3:531–532, 533
  contrition-attrition distinction, 4:228, 230
  conversion, 4:240–241
  conversion and grace in, 4:240
  Council of Trent, 3:610, 14:170
  Dead Sea Scrolls, 4:564
  divine judgment, 8:35
  double justice, 8:69
  by faith, 1:349, 732, 3:608, 4:334, 5:244
  good works, 6:359
  hope as neccessity in, 7:101
  joint declaration, 8:91
  justice of men, 8:74
  Luther, M., 8:879
  Lutheranism, 8:881, 892
  merit, 9:512
  neo-orthodoxy, 8:88
  Osiandric controversy, 8:890
  Resurrection of Christ, 12:159
  Ritschl, Albrecht, 12:257
  Scholastic theology, 8:82–83
  theology, 8:81–83, 83–84

Justin I (Byzantine Emperor), 1:523, 7:111, **8:91–92**, 96, 12:322

Justin I (Roman Emperor), 1:50, 3:595, 13:705

Justin II (Byzantine Emperor), 1:388, 4:253, 356, 719, 7:915–916, **8:92–93**

Justin Martyr, St., 8:*93*, **93–95**
  agape, 1:170
  aid to orphans, 10:675
  Amen, 1:348
  Anicetus (Pope), St., 1:455
  apologetics, 1:563
  Ascension of Jesus Christ, 1:770–771
  aseity, 1:778
  baptism of Jesus, 2:72
  biblical canon, 3:21, 26, 28, 30
  catechesis, 3:228

catechumenate, 3:250
causality, 3:303
Christian way of life, 3:548
Christology, 3:560
Church history, 3:592
Church property, 3:723, 724
conservation, 4:160
creedal statements, 4:350, 351
demonology, 4:647
Diognetus, Epistle to, 4:*751–752*
divine judgment, 8:32
Ebionites, 5:31
on the Eucharist, 5:421
exegetical works, 5:509
exorcism, 5:551
faith, 5:594
general intercessions, 6:128
grace, 6:385
hell, 6:726
heresy, 6:773
homily, 7:62
house churches, 2:146
impassibility of God, 7:358
infant baptism, 2:67
liturgical history, 8:651
Luke's Gospel, 8:859
martyrdom of, 1:92, 567, 3:593
original sin, 5:651
preaching, 11:607
presbyters, 11:673
sacraments, 12:467
school of Christian philosophy (Rome), 12:351
sexual practices of Rome, 4:220
Simon Magus, 13:131
works of charity, 3:402, 724
See also Apologists, Greek

Justin Moisescu (Romanian Orthodox Church Patriarch), 10:692

Justina (Roman Empress), 1:338, 3:632

Justina of Arezzo, Bl., **8:95**

Justina of Padua, St., 12:577

Justinian I (Roman Emperor), 4:271, 14:509–510

Justinian I the Great (Byzantine Emperor), 3:595–596, 8:*95*, **95–102**, 12:322, 355
  Agapetus I (Pope), St., 1:172
  Alexandria, 1:269
  anchorites, 1:397
  Aphthartodocetism, 1:388
  architecture, 3:686, 687
  Byzantine theology, 2:793, 820–822
  Caesaropapism, 10:834–835
  Canon Law, 2:434, 3:39, 40, 46

church building, 4:188–189
Church-State relations, 2:820–821, 851, 3:633, 634
code of civil and ecclesiastical laws, 8:398, 12:365
Constantinople Council II, 4:191, 192
Constantinople/Rome relations, 4:186
Coptic Orthodox Church, 1:271
Council of Orléans, 1:895
defensor civitatis, 4:609
Dhū-Nuwās, Masruk, 4:716
diaconia, 4:719
diptychs, 4:759
Eutychius (Patriarch of Constantinople), 5:463
Hagia Sophia, 2:737
Hormisdas (Pope), St., 7:111
Hypatius of Ephesus, 7:262
Julianists, 8:52
Justin I, 8:92
Laodicea, 8:328
military conflicts, 2:783
Monophysitism, 1:503, 523, 525, 3:596, 7:262
Nestorianism, 2:820, 3:596
North Africa, 1:663, 3:187, 189
Pelagius I (Pope), 4:192, 11:59
St. Catherine Monastery, 13:160
schools of Athens, 1:829
Theodora (c. 497-548), 13:869–870
theopaschite formula, 7:920
Three Chapters condemned, 5:587

Justinian II (Byzantine Emperor), **8:102–103**
  Armenia, 1:705
  Callinicus, 2:878
  Constantine (Pope), 4:177–178
  Leo III (Pope), St., 8:472–473
  paganism, 12:321
  Quinisext Synod, 2:750, 11:868
  Sergius I (Pope), 13:14
  Sixth Ecumenical Council, 4:128

Justinian Marina (Romanian Orthodox Church Patriarch), 10:691

Justinianus, St., **8:103**

Justinus Febronius. *See* Hontheim, Johann Nikolaus von

Justus of Canterbury (Abp.), St., 2:500, 3:70, **8:103**

Justus of Tiberias, **8:103–104**

Justus of Urgel, St., **8:104**

Just-war principles, 14:637–640

Just-war tradition, 14:636–637

Jutta, Bl., **8:104**

Jutta of Fuchsstadt, Bl., **8:104**

Jutta of Sangerhausen, St., **8:104–105**

Juvara, Filippo, 3:706, 707–708

Juvenal (Bp. of Jerusalem), 5:460, 7:769, 12:308, 310

K

Kaas, Ludwig, 3:341, 342, **8:107**

Ka'b, 'Ubay ibn, 11:877, 878

Kadalikkattil, Mathew (Father), 7:406

Kaddish, 8:12, **107–108**, 783

Kadecismo cult (Brazil), 2:597

Kadowaki, Kakichi (Father), 7:742

Kafka, Franz, 1:48, 49, 292, 5:544

Kafka, Maria Restituta, Bl., **8:108**

Kagawa, Toyohiko, **8:108–109**

Kähler, Martin, 4:656–657, 5:521

Kahn, Louis, 3:716

Kahyōye, Thomas Terai, Bl., 7:735

Kain, John Joseph (Abp. of St. Louis), 8:146, 12:560, 14:688

Kairis, Theophilus, 6:459

Kaiser, G. P. C., 2:384

Kaiserchronik, 1:463

Kaiser-Wilhelm-Gedachtniskirche (Berlin), 6:*177*

Kajsiewicz, Jerome, 12:174

Kakubilla, St., **8:109**

Kalām, 5:533, 7:863, **8:109–111**, 10:74, 12:450

Kalands Brethren, **8:111**

Kalasantiners, 12:793

Kalat Siman Basilica (Syria), 1:756, 757

Kalckbrenner, Gerard, 3:16, 192

Kalendarium manuale utriusque ecclesiae orientalis et occidentalis (Nilles), 10:396

Kalendars of Scottish Saints (Forbes), 5:795

Kālī, 8:*111*, 111

Kalinowski, St. Rafał of St. Józef, 3:520, **8:111–112**

Kálmán I (King of Hungary), 7:210

Kalteisen, Heinrich, 5:618

Kalus, Michael, 12:771

Kamehameha III (Hawaiian king), 6:669, 670

Kandel, Isaac, 5:94

Kandjur (Lamaist texts), 8:299

K'ang-hsi. *See* Kangxi (Emperor of China)

Kangxi (Emperor of China), 3:497, 498, 6:165, 11:114

Kania, Stanisław, 11:453

Kaniecki, Michael J. (Bp. of Fairbanks), 1:209

Kannon (bodhisattva), 2:*453*

Kanons (chant), 2:742, 803

Kansas, 5:731, **8:112–117**, 12:274, 14:711

See also specific dioceses and archdioceses

Kansas City Archdiocese (KS), **8:117–118**

Kansas City-St. Joseph Diocese (MO), **8:118–119**

Kansas-Nebraska Bill (1854), 10:221

Kant, Immanuel, 4:*369*, 7:296, 8:*119*, **119–124**, 11:294

absolute, 1:42

accident, 1:62, 63

action at a distance, 1:80

aesthetics, 1:145, 3:679

agnosticism, 1:180, 184, 6:312

Alexander, Samuel, 1:252

analysis and synthesis, 1:382

Anselm of Canterbury, St., 1:496

antinomies, 1:520

apriority, 12:34

astral religion, 1:809

atheism, 1:823

atomism, 1:835

Bauch, Bruno, 2:157

biology, 2:407

categorical imperative, 3:254–255, 5:388, 396

categories of being, 3:257

causality, 3:301, 306, 307

certitude, 3:352

choice, 3:521

concept of time, 14:78–79

conceptualism of, 4:53

conscience, 4:140, 141

consciousness, 4:154

contingency, 4:214

continuum, 4:215, 216

contributions to theory of motion, 10:19

cosmological argument, 4:285

Cournot, Antoine Augustine, 4:316

criteriology, 4:367

critical idealism, 11:944

critical study of, 8:507

criticism, philosophical, 4:368–369

Critique of Pure Reason, 10:236, 237

deconstructionism, 4:592–593

demonstration, 4:654

disinterestedness, 8:829

dogmatism, 4:821

dualism, 4:916

dynamism, 9:416–417

educational philosophy, 5:91

Enlightenment, 5:254, 255, 261, 262

epistemology, 5:302

essence and existence, 5:361–362, 368

eternity, 5:381

ethical formalism, 5:388

ethics and moral law, 5:390, 396

exegesis, 5:520

existence, 5:533–534

extension, 5:569

faith, 5:596

Fichte, Johann Gottlieb, 5:708

final causality, 5:724

first principles, 5:743

forms of knowledge, 5:802

freedom, 5:939

geniza, 6:135–136

good, 6:349

Hume, David, 7:297

idealism, 7:297–298

influence on Comte, Auguste, 11:542–543

influence on Ritschl, 12:256

intuition, 7:533

irrationalism, 7:586

Jacobi, Friedrich Heinrich, 7:688

judgment, 8:23–24, 25–26

Kingdom of God, 8:175

knowledge, theories of, 8:218–219

law, classification of, 8:400

law of nature, 10:183, 203

mathematics, 9:327

matter, 9:344

metaphysical empiricism, 5:196

metaphysics, 9:554–555

methodology, 9:566

moral obligation, 10:517

music, nature of, 10:73

noumena notion, 10:463–464

noumenal principles, 12:397

ontology, 10:606, 607, 11:119–120

pessimism, 11:169

phenomena, 10:227, 11:229

philosophy and science, 11:299

philosophy of religion, 12:69, 72–73

physical laws, 11:315

Le Point de départ de la métaphysique (Maréchal, Joseph), 9:145–146

possibility, 11:551

principle of causality, 5:101

principles, 11:715

provenance of law's obiligation from God, 10:189–190

Kant, Immanuel (continued)
  quantity, 11:853
  rationalism, 11:921
  reason and faith, 6:286
  relation, 12:42, 43
  relativism, 12:47
  religious experience, 5:556
  self, concept of, 12:883
  simple apprehension, 1:605
  skepticism, 13:203
  social contract, 13:241
  soul, 13:346–347
  soul-body relationship, 13:358
  substance, 13:578
  sufficient reason, 13:593
  supreme good, 6:354
  transcendental Thomism, 14:52–53
  transcendentalism, 14:145, 146, 150
  truth, 14:223
  understanding, 14:292
  universals, 14:326
  voluntarism, 14:581
  Weltanschauung (world view),
    14:677
  will and willing, 14:723
  See also Kantianism; Transcendental
    (Kantian)
Kant und die Epigonen (Liebmann),
  10:236
Kantianism, 5:101, 396, **8:125–128**
  agnosticism, 1:181–183
  categorical imperative, 3:254–255
  Coleridge, Samuel Taylor, 3:832
  critique of, 12:345–346
  19th-20th centuries, 3:624
  phenomena and noumena, 14:5
  theory of motion, 10:19
  transcendental, 14:144
  See also Kant, Immanuel; Neo-
    Kantianism
Kapaun, Emil (Father), 14:711
Das Kapital (Marx), 5:222
Kappen, Sebastian, 7:405
Karaites, 5:143, 508, 8:8, 12:449
Karakunnel, George, 7:528
Karasumaru, Leo, St., 7:732
Kardec, Allan, **8:128**
Karekin I (Armenian Catholicos), 1:703
Karekin II Nersissian (Armenian
  Catholicos), 1:704
Kariye Cami (Istanbul), 2:*731*, 739, 826,
  3:*685*
Karl XIV (King of Norway), 10:450
*Karl Jaspers et la philosophie de
  l'existence* (Ricoeur), 12:241

Karlic, Estanislo Estaban (Bp.), 3:237
Karlovtsy Synod ("the Synod in
  Exile"), 10:683
Karlowitz, Treaty of (1699), 7:670
Karlowska, Maria, Bl., **8:128–129**
Karlskirche (Vienna), 3:706
Karlstadt, Andreas Rudolf Bodenstein
  von, 5:43, 200, **8:129**, 12:16, 481
Karma, 7:697, **8:130**, 12:38
Karmasz, Daniel, 11:584
Karmi, Nicephore, 2:144
Karmuz, catacomb of (Alexandria),
  1:270
Karnak Temple (Egypt), 5:131
Karnkowski, Stanisław (Abp. of
  Gniezno), **8:130**, 11:442
Karolingische Dichtungen (Traube),
  14:163
Karoljak, Zbigniew, 2:214
Karotemprel, Sebastian, 7:528
Karska, Josephine, 4:530
Kartashev, A. V., 12:742
Kasātē Berhān (Revealer of the Light).
  See Frumentius, St.
Kasatkin, Nicholas. *See* Kasatkin,
  Nikolai (Abp.)
Kasatkin, Nikolai (Abp.), 9:695, 12:425
Käsemann, Ernst, 3:283, 5:522, 6:865,
  7:849, 10:303
Kasia (Byzantine poet), 2:803
Kasimo, Ignatius Josep, 7:430
Kasper, Katharina, **8:130**, 11:494
Kasper, Walter, 3:590, 7:528
Kaspi, Joseph ibn, 7:864
Kassab, Nimatullah al-Hardini Yousef,
  Bl., **8:130–131**
Kassia (Byzantine poet), 2:774
Kassite period (c. 1531-1150 B.C.),
  9:529
Kastl Abbey (Germany), **8:131**
*Katalog der festländischen
  Handschriften des neunten
  Jahrhunderts* (Bischoff), 10:775
Katechetik (Hirscher), 3:244
*Katechismus der christkatholischen
  Lehre zum Gebrauche der grösseren
  Schüler* (Overberg), 10:726
Katerkamp, John Theodor Hermann,
  6:877, **8:131–132**
Katherine Group, 1:397, 10:119
Katholiek Niewsblad (newspaper),
  10:263
Katholiek Politieke Partij (KPP)
  (Netherlands), 10:263
Katholieke Arbeiders Beweging, 10:262
Katholische Dogmatik (Kuhn), 8:253
Katholische Dogmatik (Schell), 12:732

Katholische Missionsatlas (Streit),
  13:547
Katholische Missionsgeschichte
  (Catholic Mission History)
  (Schmidlin), 12:744
Katholische Missionslehre im Grundriss
  (Catholic Mission Theory)
  (Schmidlin), 12:744
Die Katholische Moral (Mausbach),
  9:376
Katholische Moraltheologie (Mausbach),
  9:376
Katholische Reformatoren (Pastor),
  10:938
Katholischer Erwachsenen-Katechismus,
  3:245
Katholischer Katechismus (Neumann),
  3:244–245, 10:265
*Katholischer Katechismus oder
  Lehrbegriff* (Deharbe), 4:612–613
*Der Katholizismus als Prinzip des
  Fortschrittes* (Schell), 12:732
Katolikku Daijiten, 5:207
Katzer, Frederick Francis Xavier (Abp.
  of Milwaukee, WI), 1:354, **8:132**,
  14:780, 781
Kauma, Misaeri (Bp.), 1:*443*
Kaunda, Kenneth J., 14:907
Kaunitz, Wenzel Anton von (Prince),
  1:913, 7:1041, 1045–1046
Kaupas, Casimira (Mother Maria),
  12:541–542
Kavādh I (King of Persia), 11:138
Kavādh II (King of Persia), 1:806
Kavanagh, A., 12:474
Kavanagh, Edward (fl. 1813), 9:55–56
Kavanaugh, John, 10:648, 649
Kavanaugh, Robert, 13:854–855
Kavukatt, Mathew (Bp.), 7:406
Kawara, Louis, Bl., 7:733
Kay, John, 5:260
Kayla. *See* Falashas (Jewish sect)
Kazania Sejmowe (Sermons Preached to
  the Diet, Skarga), 13:200
Kazel, Dorothy, **8:132–133**
Kazimierczyk, Stanislaw Yousef, Bl.,
  8:133
Keane, Augustus Henry, **8:133–134**
Keane, James John (Abp.), 4:923,
  14:870
Keane, John Joseph (Abp. of Dubuque),
  8:134–135, 10:437, 14:542
  Abbelen, Peter, 1:7
  Americanism dispute, 1:354, 355,
    356, 12:573
  Catholic University of America,
    3:290, 291, 12:787

Keane, Patrick (Bp. of Sacramento), 2:869

Keane, Richard, Sir, 10:33

Kearn, O., 10:88

Kearney, Denis, 2:869

Kearney, Elizabeth, 7:581

Kearney, John, Bl., 7:582

Kearney, Stephen Watts, 12:645–646

Keating, John, 7:582

Keating, Thomas R. (Bp. of Arlington, VA), 14:543

Keble, John, 1:444, 8:*135*, **135–136**, 10:732, 733, 735

Keckermann, Bartholomew, 1:677, 12:768

Kedermyster, Richard, **8:136**

Kedroff v. St. Nicholas Cathedral (1952), 3:662

Keefe, D., 10:671

Keegan, Robert Fulton, **8:136**

Keeler, William H. (Card.), 1:*25*, 2:*38*, 39, 4:*419*, 8:885

Keely, Patrick Charles, 2:555, 3:715, **8:136**

Keeping Hope Alive: Stirrings in Christian Theology (Lane), 5:350

Keghart Church (Armenia), 1:*702*

Kehr, Paul Fridolin, **8:137**

Keiley, Benjamin J. (Bp. of Savannah), 1:162, 12:710

Keilschriftbibliographie (Pohl), 11:435

Keim, Karl Theodor, 5:521, 7:848

KEK (Council of European Churches), 4:297, 298

Kelaytâ, J., 5:6

Kele, Richard, 3:151

Keller, Edward, 14:357

Keller, James, 3:563, **8:137**

Keller, Pius, 1:890

Kellogg-Briand Pact (1928), 10:*745*, 747

Kells, Book of, **8:138–139**, *139*, 9:127

Kells Abbey (Ireland), **8:138**

Kelly, Edward J. (Bp. of Idaho), 7:290–291

Kelly, Francis Clement (Bp. of Oklahoma City and Tulsa), 3:478, 8:114, **137–138**, 10:575–576

Kelly, Gerald Andrew, **8:139**, 10:195

Kelly, J., 3:245

Kelly, Michael Vincent, **8:139–140**

Kelly, Thomas Cajetan (Abp. of Louisville), 8:818–819

Kelsen, Hans, 8:400, 11:545–546

Kelso Abbey (Scotland), 8:169

Kemble, John, St., **5:237**, 8:140–141, *140*, 10:495

Kemp, Boniface, 5:237

Kemp, John (Card.), 3:72, 481, **8:141**

Kemp, Thomas (Bp. of London), **8:141**

Kempe, John. *See* Kemp, John

Kempe, Margery, **8:141–142**

Kemper, Jackson, 5:297

Kempf, Nikolaus, 3:192

Kempten Abbey (Germany), **8:142**

Ken, Thomas (Bp. of Bath and Wells), 3:153

Kendall, May, 12:550

Kendrick, Francis Patrick (Abp. of Baltimore), 8:144, 144–145, 169, 466

Kenkel, Frederick, 1:352

Kenmare Publications, 4:445

Kenna, John Edward, **8:143**

Kennedy, Aimee. *See* McPherson, Aimee Semple

Kennedy, Edward, 3:460

Kennedy, John Fitzgerald, 1:356, 693, 3:824, 4:447, 8:252, 10:172

Kennedy, Robert Francis, 3:460

Kenneth (Canince) of Derry, St., **8:143**

Kenney, Michael H., 1:209

Kenney, Peter, 7:788

Kennicott, Benjamin, 5:519

Kenny, Patrick, 4:625

Kenosis, 4:585, 5:430, **8:143**

Kenraghty, Maurice, **8:143–144**

Kenrick, Francis Patrick (Abp. of Baltimore), 2:39, **8:144–145**, 14:455

    apostolic delegation in the United States, 1:582, 583

    Baltimore Councils, 2:44, 45, 46

    Barron, Edward, 2:118

    as Bp. of Philadelphia, 4:245–246, 5:144, 835, 11:83, 84, 238–239

    Spalding, M. J., 13:404

Kenrick, Peter Richard (Abp. of St. Louis, MO), **8:145–146**, 9:742

    Anglican orders problem, 1:438

    Chicago Archdiocese, 3:476, 477

    St. Louis Archdiocese, 12:446, 559

    Seventh Baltimore Provincial Council (1849), 2:45

Kent, James, 10:191

Kentigern (Bp. of Glasgow), St., **8:146**, 12:535–536, 830

Kentucky, **8:146–149**

    American Civil War, 13:405

    anti-Catholicism, 13:404

    Catholic schools, 9:31

    Durbin, Elisha John, 4:950

    early ecumenical dialogues, 8:817

    ecclesiastical organization, 8:147

Fenwick, Edward Dominic, 5:686

Flaget, Benedict Joseph, 5:757

immigration, 8:817

Know-Nothingism, 13:405

mission, 5:686, 8:529

Sisters of Divine Providence of Kentucky, 13:181–182

Sisters of Loretto, 8:786

Spalding, C. (Mother), 13:401

Ursulines, 8:817, 14:349

See also specific dioceses and archdioceses

Kenya, 1:291, **8:149–152**, *151*

Kenyatta, Jomo, 8:150

Kenyon, K., 2:379, 7:764

Kenyon College (Ohio), 5:297

Keogh, James, **8:152–153**, 153, *153*

Keogh, John W., **8:153**, 10:343

Keogh, Raymond, 7:581

Keough, Francis Patrick (Abp. of Baltimore), 2:39, **8:153–154**, 12:217

Kephalaia (Glycas), 6:253

Kephalaia gnostica (Evagrius Ponticus), 10:659

Kephalaiai (Manichaean text), 9:115

Kepler, Johann, 1:530, 6:59–60, **8:154–155**, *155*, 9:415

Keppeler, Anton (Father), 5:877

Kerala (India), 13:712–713

Kerby, William Joseph, 2:703, 3:279, **8:155–156**, 12:385

Kerchove, Robert de, 3:82

Kerguin, Jeanne Marie, St., **8:156**

Kerll, Johann Kaspar von, 3:123

Kern, Cyprian, 12:436, 742

Kern, Jakob Franz, Bl., **8:156**

Kersuzan, Francois Marie, **8:156–157**

Kerwin, Larkin, 3:10

Kerygma, 5:507, 521, **8:157–158**

    Bultmann, Rudolf, 5:543

    catechesis vs., 3:227

    creedal statements, 4:349–351, 354

    crucifixion, 4:398

    death, 4:571

    descent of Christ into hell, 4:683–684

    Neocatechumental Way goal of replicating, 10:234

Kerygma and Myth I (Bartsch), 5:522

Kerygmatic theology, 4:815, 8:62, **158–159**, 13:903–904

Kessler, K., 9:114–115

Kestoi (Julius Africanus), 8:58–59, *59*

Ketcham, William Henry, 8:*159*, **159–160**

Ketteler, Wilhelm Emmanuel von (Bp. of Mainz), 6:184, **8:160–161**
  Catholic social thought, 13:256
  Kulturkampf, 8:253
  La Tour du Pin influenced, 8:371
  Sisters of Divine Providence founding, 13:181
  social justice issues, 3:620
  works of charity, 3:420
Ketteler Workers' Circle, 9:124
Kevenhoerster, John Bernard (Bp. of Bahamas), 2:14, **8:161**
Kevin, St., 6:238, **8:161–162**
Kevorkian, Jack, 5:458
Key (Sherburne), 11:729
Key to Sacred Scripture (Flacius Illyricus), 5:754
Keyes, Michael J. (Father), 12:710
Keynes, Simon, 1:280
Keys, as ecclesiastical symbol, 6:763
Keys, power of, **8:162–163**
Keyserling (Franceschi), 5:864
Khach'atur (Armenian Catholicos), 1:702
Al-Khalifa, Hamad bin Essa, 2:16
Kham Viet Pham, Dominic, 14:495
Khambang, Lucy, 13:848
Khamse, Jean (Bp. of Vientiane), 8:331
Khang Duy Nguyen, Jose, 14:495
Khanh, Peter, 14:495
Khanqah, 7:616
Khargeh (Egypt), 1:758
Khārijites, 2:873
Khazars, 8:102–103, **163–164**
Khnum (deity), 4:337
Khoan Khan Pham, Paul, 14:495
Kholstomer (Tolstoi), 14:105
Khomeini, Ayatollah Ruhollah, 7:545
Khomîakov, Aleksei Stepanovich, 5:773, **8:164–165**, 12:435
Khrushchev, Nikita, 8:607–608, 12:428
Khuastuanift (Manichaeism), 9:115
Khuong, Thomas, 14:495–496
Khusrau I (King of Persia), 11:138
Khusrau II (King of Persia), 11:138–139
Khwarizmian people, 4:405
Kidd, B. J., Rev, on Malines conversations, 9:78
Kieft, William, 10:321
Kieran, John, 7:579
Kierkegaard, Søren Aabye, 5:368, 8:*165*, **165–167**, 11:294–295
  absurdity, 1:48
  Alphonsus Liguori, St., 1:312
  analogy, 1:373, 379

analogy of faith, 1:380
anxiety, 1:540
Augustinianism, 1:882
Brunner, Heinrich Emil, 2:645
choice, 3:521
conscience, 4:140
consciousness, 4:154
eternity, 5:381
existence, 5:534
existentialism, 5:544, 545, 546, 596, 12:3, 70
fideism, 5:712
freedom, 5:939
Hegelianism, 6:711
irrationalism, 7:586
justification, 8:88
knowledge, theories of, 8:221
proof of God, 5:532
rationalism, 11:923
religious experience, 5:556
self, concept of, 12:884
will acts, 13:440
Kiev School (Russia), 12:433–434
Kilber, Heinrich, 14:776
Kildare Abbey (Ireland), 2:617, **8:167**
Kiley, Moses Elias (Bp. of Milwaukee, WI), 14:781
Kilian of Aubigny, St., **8:167–168**
Kilian of Würzburg, St., **8:168**
Kilmartin, Edward J., 5:430, 8:168–169, 12:474
Kilpatrick, G. D., 2:367
Kilwardby, Robert (Abp. of Canterbury), 5:242
  Convocations, 4:243
  correctoria, 4:275, 276
  unicity thesis, 5:817, 818, 12:231
Kilwinning Abbey (Scotland), **8:169**
Kim, Stephen (Card.), 8:239–240
Kim Tae-gon, Andrew, St., 8:233–234, *233*, 239
Kimbanguism, 4:109–110
Ķimchi, David, 2:355, 4:493, 5:509
Ķimchi, Joseph, 5:509
Ķimchi, Moses, 5:509
Kimpfler, Gregor, 12:735
Kimura, Anthony, Bl., 7:732
Kimura, Leonard, Bl., 7:732
Kimura, Sebastian, Bl., 7:733
Kind Words From Your Pastor (Noll), 10:410
Kindekens, Peter, **8:169**, 820–821
Kindergarten system, 6:13–14
Al-Kindī, 'Abd Al-Masih, 1:621, 671, 672, 813, 940, **8:169–170**

Al-Kindī, Abū Yūsuf Ya'qūb Ibn-Isḥāq, 3:674, **8:170–171**
Kindness, **8:171–172**
Kinematics, 9:415
King, Clifford J., 3:286–287
King, John (Bp. of London), 1:299
King, Martin Luther, Jr., 1:160, 161, 3:754–755, 756, 12:729
King James Bible. *See* Bible, texts and versions
King Jesus (Graves), 7:852–853
King Rànavàlona II, 9:26–27
Kinga, St., **8:172**
The Kingdom (oratorio by Elgar), 5:153
Kingdom and Community: The Social World of Early Christianity (Gager), 10:307
Kingdom of God, 7:806, **8:172–175**
  Cassian, John, 3:207
  death, 4:577
  doctrine development, 4:807
  end of the world, 5:215
  hell, 6:724–725
  imminence of, 5:338–339
  Isidore of Pelusium, St., 7:601
  kerygma, 8:157
  keys to heaven, 8:163
  laity, 8:291
  lay spirituality, 8:418
  life, concept of, 8:568
  Lord's Prayer, 8:783
  love as seeking, 8:834
  Mark's Gospel, 9:186
  Parousia, 10:901
  Resurrection of Christ, 12:157–159
The Kingdom of God in America (Niebuhr), 10:386
The Kingdom of Lovers (Rutherford), 12:439
Kingdom of the Antichrist (Malagrida), 9:65–66
Kingdom of the Serbs, Croats, and Slovenes (Yugoslavia), 10:698
  See also Yugoslavia
Kings, Books of, **8:175–177**
  altars in, 1:319–320
  Baal, 2:2
  Beelzebul, 2:200
  Benjamin (tribe), 2:282–283
  book of the Law, 8:397
  Canaanite ritual references in, 14:271
  Christian healing, 6:678
  deportations in, 4:674
  edification, 5:84
  Edomites, 5:87

Elijah, 5:158, 159, 9:63

Elisha's story, 5:162

Gehenna, 6:116

glory, 6:244

God, name of, 6:298

heart, 6:681

heaven, 6:684

Hezechia's tunnel, 13:120

high priests, 6:824

as history, 8:176–177

inheritance, 7:464

Judith, Canticle of, 8:45

justice of men, 8:73

leprosy, 8:509, 510

magic, 9:39

Passover, 10:933, 934

peace, 11:49

pilgrimages, 11:342

possession by God, 13:441

precious stones, 11:646

reading today, 8:177

religious reform in, 4:703

seraphim, 13:6

serpent as symbol, 13:20

Shechem, 13:72

sin, 13:143

slavery, 13:206

Solomon, 13:305

soul, 13:336

spirit, 13:424

temple liturgy, 8:434

as theology, 8:177

Kings and kingship, 1:477–478, 479, 3:424, 9:105–106, 534, 779–780

King's Book, 4:546

King's College Chapel (Cambridge, England), 3:697

King's School (Canterbury, England), 3:263

Kingship, in the ancient Near East, **8:178–180**, 392, 13:311–312

Kingston Archdiocese (Jamaica), 7:800

Kingu (Babylonian deity), 4:337

Kinloss Abbey (Scotland), **8:180**

Kinnamos (Byzantine historian), 2:776

Kinney, John F. (Bp. of Bismarck), 2:423

Kino, Eusebio Francisco, 1:687, 7:785–786, **8:180**

Kinsey, A., 5:397

Kinuya, Leo, St., 7:732

Kippley, John, 10:176

Kipystensky, Zachary, 12:433

Kirby, Luke, St., 2:922, 5:228, 717, **8:180–181**, 13:82

Der Kirchenfreund (periodical), 12:726

Kirchengeschichte Deutschlands (Freidrich), 6:3

Kirchengeschichte von Spanien (Gams), 6:86

Kirchenlexikon (Wetzer and Welte), 5:207

Kirchenzeitung (newspaper), 10:558

Kircher, Athanasius, 7:782, 8:181, **181**

Kircher Museum, 8:181

Kirchner, Timothy, 4:61

Kireev, A. A., 12:435

Kirget Shema' synagogue (Galilee, Israel), 13:678

Kiribati (Oceania), 10:531

Kiril (archbishop of Plovdiv), 10:685

Kirk, Kenneth Escott (Bp. of Oxford), **8:181–182**

Kirk, Russell Amos, **8:182**

Kirkby, Edward (Abbot), 12:245

Kirkman, Richard, Bl., 5:228, **8:183**

Kirkstall Abbey (England), 8:183, **183–184**

Kirland, John, 3:472

Kirlin, Joseph, **8:184**

Kirsch, Felix M., 3:283

Kirsch, Johann Peter, 8:184, **184–185**

Kiryluk, Filip, 11:584

Kisai, Diogo, St., 7:732

Kisaku, John, Bl., 7:734

Kisemanito (Great Spirit) Center (Alberta, Canada), 3:11

Kish (Sumerian city), 2:3

Kismet, **8:185**

Kiss of Peace, 1:185, **8:185**, 650

Kitāb al-Amanāt wal-I'tiqadāt (Beliefs and Opinions) (Sa'adia ben Joseph), 7:863, 12:450

Kitāb al-Asrār (The Book of Secrets) (Rhazes), 12:210

Kitāb al-Ḥāwī (Rhazes), 12:210

Kitāb al-Hudā (Book of Guidance), 9:195

Kitab al-Intiṣār (Nyberg, ed.), 10:74

Kitāb al-Ṭibb al-Manṣūrī (Rhazes), 12:210

Kitāb Jāmìaṣ-Ṣalawāt wal-Tasāabīḥ (Collection of Prayers and Praises) (Sàdia ben Joseph), 12:450

Kitbamrung, Nicholas Bunkerd, Bl., **8:185–186**

Kittel, Gerhard, 2:386, **8:186**

Kittel, Rudolf, 2:355–356, 384, 5:520, **8:186**

Kittel-Kahle Bible edition, 2:355–356, 357

Kiuni, Anthony, Bl., 7:733

Kivengere, Festo (Bp.), 1:443

Kiyemon, Luke, Bl., 7:734

Kiyota, Magdalene, Bl., 7:734

Kizaiyemon, Michael, Bl., 7:734

Kjeld, St., **8:186–187**

Klagenfurt seminary church (Austria), 3:712

Klages, Ludwig, 8:579–580

Klassen, John (Father), 12:553

Klauck, H. J., 14:858–859

Klausner, Joseph, 8:13

Klein, Félix, 1:355

Klein, Jacob, 6:44

Klein, Luise, 1:732

Klein, Melanie, 6:568–569

Kleinclausz, A., 1:243

Kleine geistliche Concerte (Schütz), 12:792

Kleiner Haussegen (Overberg), 10:726

Kleiner Katechismus (Neumann), 10:265

Kleinmariazell Abbey (Austria), 8:503

Klemm, Gustav Friedrich, 4:427, 433

Klesl, Melchior (Card.), 1:911, **8:187**

Kleutgen, Joseph, **8:187–188**, 11:623, 12:770, 774, 13:286, 14:405

Kloppenburg, Bonaventura, 7:528

Klostermann, Ferdinand, 1:916

Klosterneuburg Monastery (Austria), **8:188**, 503

Klotz, Christian Adolf, 8:517

Klotz, Petrus (ArchAbbot), 12:671

Kluckhohn, Clyde, 4:426, 427, 431

Kluetgen, J., 12:743

Klupfel, Engelbert, **8:188**

Kmiec, Edward U. (Bp. of Nashville, TN), 13:824

Knabenbauer, J., 3:741

Knaebel, Bonaventure (Archabbot), 12:568

Knapwell, Richard. See Richard Knapwell

Knaresbrough, John, 4:168

Knaus, Herman, 10:176, 177

Kneale, W. C. and M., 5:504

Knecht, F. J., 3:243

Kneeling (liturgical gestures), 8:648

Knight, Death, and the Devil (Durer), 4:705

Knight, William, Bl., 5:232, 329, **8:188–189**

Knights (papal decorations), 4:596

Knights and knighthood

Crusades, 4:405–406, 407, 412, 414

initiation, 3:518

military religious orders, 9:625

Knights and knighthood *(continued)*
   patron of, 12:547
   Templars, 13:803
   See also Chivalry
Knights Hospitaller. *See* Knights of
   Malta
Knights of Alcántara, 2:858, **8:189**
Knights of Columbus, 3:281, 622
   American Federation of Catholic
      Societies, 1:352
   Commission on Religious Prejudices,
      8:190
   founding of, 4:124
   Historical Commission, 8:191
   International Order of Alhambra,
      1:286
   McGivney, Michael Joseph, founding
      of, 9:397
Knights of Columbus Headquarters
   (New Haven, CT), 8:*190*
Knights of Dobrin, 3:537, **8:192**, 11:439
Knights of Labor, **8:192–193**
   Church toleration, 7:551–552
   condemnation, 12:462
   controversies centered, 10:541
   Gibbons, James, defense of, 6:206
   Keane, J. J., 8:134
   Pennsylvania, 11:87
   protests against, 10:170
Knights of Malta, **8:193–195**
   Aubusson, Pierre d', 1:846
   classes of members, 8:194
   Crusades, 4:412
   grand masters, 8:194–195, 384–385
   grand priories, 8:194–195
   hospitals, 7:120
   Jerusalem, 7:774
   900th anniversary, 9:83
   reign, 9:82
   Saint-Antoine-de-Vennois Abbey,
      12:535
Knights of Montesa, 2:858, **8:195**,
   12:547, 680
Knights of Peter Claver, **8:195–196**
Knights of St. Eulalia. *See* Mercedarians
Knights of St. George, **8:196**, 12:547
Knights of St. James, **8:196–197**, 197,
   12:683
Knights of St. John, 5:843, **8:197**
Knights of St. John of Jerusalem, 8:131,
   384–385
Knights of St. John of Jerusalem (coat
   of arms), 8:*193*
Knights of the Faith, 5:190, 854,
   8:197–198

Knights of the Holy Sepulcher, **8:198**,
   12:243
Knights of the Sword, 1:221, 222, 8:192,
   198–199, 603–604
   See also Teutonic Knights
Knights' Revolt (1522-1523), 3:430
Knight's Tale (Chaucer), 3:452
Knights Templars. *See* Templars
Knitter, P., 7:841
Knoll, Albert, **8:199**
Knoller, Martin, 10:247
Knöringen, Heinrich von, 1:848
Knorr, Nathan H., 7:751
Know Thyself (Scito Teipsum) (Abelard),
   5:394
Knowledge, **8:200–205**
   actual or habitual, 8:203
   appetite, 1:601
   Aristotle on, 1:682
   art, 1:746
   Augustine, St., 1:866
   certitude, 3:356
   classification, 8:202–203
   common notion, 8:200
   critique of, 8:121
   definition and characteristics,
      8:200–202
   discursive power of, 4:775
   docto ignorantia, 4:797–798
   epistemology, 5:301–304
   God, 12:821–822
   Henry of Ghent, 6:752
   ignorance, 7:314–315
   immateriality, 7:345–346
   Lucretius, 8:849
   Maritain, Jacques, 9:179
   Mary, Blessed Virgin, 9:253–254
   mediate, 5:532
   moral theology, 9:856–857
   nature of, 5:303
   Ockhamish, 10:536
   omniscience, 10:593–599
   opinion, 10:610
   patristic philosophy on God's
      knowledge, 10:960–961
   as perfection, 8:201
   as philosophical problem, 8:203–204
   Piaget, Jean, 11:318
   principles, 5:743, 744
   properties of, 5:303
   reflection, 5:199, 12:1–4
   relation of, 12:44
   Scholastics, 11:804–805
   sensation, 12:907
   sense, 8:121

   similarity, 13:125
   skepticism, 13:200–205
   spirit, 13:422
   studiousness, 13:555
   theology as, 13:923
   theory of reflection on activity,
      14:142–143
   Thomastic thought on participation,
      10:909
   truth of, 14:224–225
   See also Conscience; Contemplation;
      Experience; Illumination
Knowledge, connatural, **8:205–207**
Knowledge, gift of, **8:207**
Knowledge, infused, **8:207–208**
Knowledge, process of, **8:205–210**
   acquisition of knowledge, 8:208
   concept/conceptualism, 4:51, 53
   form in, 8:209–210
   immateriality, 8:209
   knowing, 8:210
   problem of knowledge, 8:203
   types of, 8:208–209
Knowledge, sociology of, **8:210–212**
Knowledge, theories of, **8:212–222**
   criteriology, 4:366–368
   criticism, philosophical, 4:368–369
   Cyrenaics, 4:464
   doubt and critique of, 4:883–884
   Greek origins, 8:212–214
   Leibniz, 8:456–457
   Locke, J., 8:744–745
   medieval, 8:214–217
   modern thought, 8:217–219
   self-transcendence model, 8:833
   sociology of knowledge, 8:210–212
   Thomistic notion, 13:408–409
   twentieth-century views, 8:219–222
   Whitehead, Alfred North, 14:704
   William of Ockham, 14:747
   Wolff, Christian, 14:808
Knowles, David, **8:222–223**
Know-Nothingism (United States),
   3:653, **8:199–200**, 10:170, 314, 437
   American Protective Association,
      1:352
   apostolic delegation in the U.S.,
      1:582
   Arkansas, 1:691
   Bapst, John, 2:56
   Blaine Amendment, 2:426
   Blanc, Anthony, 2:430
   Blenkinsop, William A., 2:436
   California, 2:868
   Catholic persecution, 12:562, 572

church architecture, 3:715
Connecticut, 4:122
Irish in public schools, 8:838
Kentucky, 13:405
Massachusetts, 2:555, 9:307
Tennessee, 13:822
Knox, James Robert (Card.), **8:223–224**
Knox, John, **8:224–226**, *225*
    Church of Scotland, development of, 12:828
    Church-State relations, 3:638
    Presbyterianism, 11:679, 12:24
    Protestant Reformation, 12:534
    Scottish political unrest, 12:834
Knox, Ronald Arbuthnott, 3:398, 470, 5:252, **8:226**
Knoxville Diocese (TN), **8:227**
Knudson, Albert Cornelius, **8:227**
Knutsen, Matthias, 4:142
Knutson, Kent Sigvart, **8:227**
Knutzen, Martin, 5:47, 263, 12:767
Kōan (Zen technique), 14:915
Koberger, Anton, 10:833
Kocel (Slavic chieftain), 4:475
Koch, Alfred (Archabbot), 12:591
Koch, Jodocus. *See* Jonas, Justus
Kodaly, Zoltan, **8:227–228**
Koehler, Walther, 1:718
Koetschau, P., 10:658
Koffler, Andreas Xavier, 3:496
Köhl, Helmut, 6:187
Kohlberg, Lawrence, 4:238, 239
Kohlmann, Anthony, 2:44, **8:228**, 10:312
Koichi, James, 7:734
Koinonia (communion), 5:426, 918–919
Kokov, Simeon (Bp. of Sofia-Plovdiv), 2:683, 684
Kolb of Elchingen, Robert (Abbot), 12:671
Kolbe, Frederick Charles, **8:228–229**
Kolbe, Maximilian, St., 8:229–230, *229*, **229**, 11:450
Kolde, Dietrich, 3:241
Koldewey, R., 10:225
Koliqi, Mikel (Card.), 1:217
Kolland, Engelbert, 4:503
Köllin, Conrad, **8:230**, 14:48
Kollonitsch, Leopold (Card.), 7:216
Kolluthus (Egyptian priest), 1:266
Kölnische Blätter (newspaper), 12:181
Kolping, Adolf, Bl., 3:420, 620, **8:230–231**, 13:256
"Kolping Families," 8:230
"Kolping Houses," 8:231
Kolping Society, Catholic, **8:231**

Kolvenbach, Peter-Hans, 7:794–795
Kombo, Ernest (Bp.), 4:108
Komeito (Clean Government Party, Japan), 13:298
Kómínski, Honorat, Bl., 8:246
Komposition des Hexateuchs (Wellhausen), 14:676
Konare, Alpha Oumar, 9:77
Köndig, Raphael, 14:51
König, Arthur, 5:27
König, E., 5:520
König, Franz Borgia (Card.), 1:916–917, 3:200, **8:231–233**, *232*
Königsberg, University of (Germany), 1:233–234
Königsegg-Rothenfels, Maximilian Friedrich von, 3:843
Koninck, Charles de, 4:20
Konings, Anthony, 1:311, **8:233**
Konishi Yukinaga, 7:739
Konrad of Vechta (Abp. of Prague), 14:363
Konstant, David (Bp.), 3:237
Kontakia, 1:197–198, 2:741–742, 773, 802
Kontakion, 7:242
Koonen Cross Oath (1653), 7:399
Kopp, Liliana, 13:171
Koppers, Wilhelm, 12:67
Koran. *See* Qur'ān (Islamic holy book)
Korea, **8:237–240**, *242, 243*
    Buddhism, 2:668–669
    demographic statistics, 8:238
    ecclesiastical organization, 8:239
    maps, 8:*240, 241*
    mission, 2:726, 9:295, 296, 699–700
Korea, Martyrs of, SS., **8:233–239**
Korean Foreign Mission Society, 8:239
Korean War, 8:239
Korec, Jan (Card.), 7:793, 13:223
Koresh, David (Vernon Howell), 4:541, 542–543
Die Korrespondenz des Kardinals Contarini während seiner deutschen Legation 1541 (Pastor), 10:938
Kosaki, Michael, St., 7:732
Kosaki, Thomas, St., 7:732
Kosher food laws, 4:742–743, 8:11
Košice, Martyrs of, SS., 8:241–242
Koslowski, Anton, 11:458
Kosovo (Serbia), 13:10–11
Kostistk, Geremia of Valachia, Bl., **8:242**
Kostka, Stanislausa, St., **8:242–243**
Koteda, Caspar, Bl., 7:733
Koteda, Thomas Kiuni, Bl., 7:732

Kôthar (God), 14:270
Koudelka, Joseph Maria (Bp. of Superior, WI), **8:243**, 14:782
Kowalska, Faustina, St., 3:61, **8:243–245**, *244*
Kowalski, Jan, 9:164
Koyanagi, Thomas, Bl., 7:733
Koyukon people, 1:459
Kozaka, Matthias, Bl., 7:732
Kozal, Michał, Bl., **8:245–246**
Kozka, Karolina, Bl., **8:246**
Kozłowska, Maria Felicja (Sister), 9:164
Koźminek, Union of (1555), 2:461
Kózmínski, Florence Wenceslaus John. *See* Kozka, Karolina, Bl.
Kózmínskiego, Florence Wenceslaus John. *See* Kozka, Karolina, Bl.
Kraemer, Fintan, 1:692
Kraft und Stoff (Büchner), 9:320
Krafft, Christian, 5:322
Krahn, J., 3:711
Kralice Bible, 2:461
Kralik, Richard von, 10:75
Kramp, Joseph, **8:246**
Kramp, K., 3:711
Kramreiter, Robert, 3:712
Kraus, Franz Xaver, **8:246–247**, 12:26
Kraus, H. J., 2:532, 14:857
Krause, H. G., 10:858
Krause, Karl, 10:820, 12:773
Krautbauer, Francis Xaver (Bp. of Green Bay, WI), 14:780
Krauth, Charles Porterfield, **8:247**
Krebs, Fritz, 10:277
Kreil, Benno, 1:117
Kreisler, Fritz, 8:247, **247–248**
Krementz, Philip (Card.), 3:844, 12:787
Kremsmünster Abbey (Austria), 1:908, 8:*248*, **248–249**
Kretschmer, P., 10:93
Krishna (Hindu deity), 6:849
Die Krisis der europäischen Wissenschaften und die transzendentale Phämenologie (Husserl), 11:232
Kristeller, Paul Oskar, 7:186, 12:113, 119, 120
Kristeva, Julia, 1:412
Kristin Lavransdatter (Undset), 14:295
Koslowski, Anton. *See above*
Kritik der evangelischen Geschichte der Synoptiker (Bauer), 2:159, 6:710
Kritik der evangelischen Geschichte des Johannes (Bauer), 2:159, 6:710
Kritik des hegelschen Staatsrechts (Marx), 6:710–711
Krivoshein, Vasily (Abp.), 12:436

Križanić, Juraj, **8:249**

Križín, Marek, 8:241

Kroeber, A. L., 4:426, 427, 428, 430, 431

Krol, John Joseph (Card.), 3:58, 8:*249*, **249–251**, 11:88, 241, 14:772

Kromer, Martin (Cromer) (Bp.), **8:251**

Kropotkin, Peter, 1:384

Krynen, J., 1:532

Krzycki, Andrzej (Abp.), 11:442

Ku Klux Klan, **8:251–253**, *252*

  Arkansas, 1:693

  California, 2:868, 12:648

  Denver, 4:669

  Iowa, 7:542

  Oklahoma, 8:138

  Oregon School Case, 10:647

  revival in 20th century, 10:171

  Sheehan, L., 13:74

  South Carolina, 13:366

Kuang I Lu (Public Benefit Record, China), 8:428

Kübler-Ross, Elisabeth, 7:117, 13:852–853

Kucera, Daniel W. (Abp. of Dubuque), 4:924–925

Kuchimeister, C., 1:465

Kuenen, Abraham, 5:519

Kugler, F. X., 10:820

Kuhn, Johannes, **8:253**, 12:729, 730

Kuhn, Thomas, 2:407

Kuhyōye, Francis, Bl., 7:734

Kūhyōye, Peter Sawaguchi, Bl., 7:735

Külpe, Oswald, 7:532

Die Kultur der Renaissance in Italien (Burckhardt), 12:112

Kulturkampf, 3:340, 642, 846, 5:708, 903, **8:253–256**

  associations, 1:792

  Austria, 1:914, 12:793

  Beuron Abbey, 2:350

  Bismarck, Otto Eduard Leopold von, 6:184, 8:254–255

  Brück, Heinrich, 2:642

  Cologne, 3:843–844

  heresy, 6:778

  impact on Sisters of Divine Providence, 13:181

  impact on Sisters of Notre Dame (SND), 10:457

  intellectual life of Church, 6:184

  Leo XIII (Pope), 8:492

  liberalism, 3:619

  opposition, 8:160

  Poland, 11:448

  Poor Handmaids of Jesus Christ, 8:130

  reconciliation proposed, 8:246

  Reformkatholizismus, 12:26

  Switzerland, 8:255–256, 269

Kumārajīva, 3:510

Kumarbi myths, 6:896

Kuṇḍalinī, 14:892

Kundek, Josef, Rev., 12:568

Kundig, Martin, **8:256**, 9:605, 14:779

Küng, Hans, 7:450–451, 1004, 12:729, 777

Kunigunde. *See* Kinga, St.

Kunigunde (German Empress), St., **8:256–257**

Kunike, Jakob, 3:192

Kuno of Trier, St., **8:257**

Kunschak, Leopold, 1:915

Kuntstudien (periodical), 10:236

Kurck, Arvid (Bp. of Finland), 5:732

Kurialacherry, Thomas (Bp.), 7:406

Kurobyōye, Francis, Bl., 7:734

Kursulas, Nicolaus, 6:458

Kurtev, Kiril (Bp.), 2:683, 684

Kurtz, Joseph E. (Bp. of Knoxville, TN), 13:824

Kurtzman, Lemon v. (1971), 3:667, 668

Kuryer Polski (newspaper), 9:647, 14:780

Kurz, Michael, 3:711

Kurz, Otto-Orlando, 3:711

Kuttner, Stephan George, 3:59, **8:257–258**

Kuwait, **8:258–259**, *259*

Kuyper, Abraham, 10:262

Kuzari (Ha-Levi), 7:864, 869

Kyneburg, St. *See* Cyneburg, St.

Kyong-Hwan Choi, Francis Ch'oe, martyr, 8:235

Kyrie Eleison, **8:259–261**

  hymns written to tune of, 7:254

  litanies, 8:599–600

  Roman Rite, 12:328

  use in West, 8:600

Kyrion (Abp. of Mts'khet'a), 1:700

Kyrios, as title, 4:564

Kyrios Christos (Bousset), 7:849

Kyriotissa, 9:272

Kyūyemon, Clement, Bl., 7:734

Kyūzaburō, Mancio Araki, Bl., 7:734

L

La Bruyère, Jean de, 5:762

La Chaize, François de, 1:502, 7:783, **8:269**

La Colombière, Claude de, Bl., 10:880, 12:491

La Combe, François (Father), 6:588–589

La Crosse Diocese (WI), **8:173–174**

La Farge, John, 1:111, 10:68

La Lande, Jean de, 10:435

La Mennais, Jean Marie Robert de, Ven., 2:630, **8:310–311**, *311*

La Mennais Brothers. *See* Brothers of Christian Instruction of Ploërmel

La Mettrie, Julien Offroy de, 5:107, 255, 261, 931, 9:319–320, 13:346

La Puente, Luis de, Ven., 1:325, 5:353, 7:782, 8:*333*, **333–334**

La Rochefoucauld, F. J. (Bp. of Beauvais), 2:188

La Rochefoucauld, Roger de, 2:189

La Rochefoucauld family, **8:335–336**

La Rochefoucauld Maumont, François Joseph de (Abp. of Arles), 10:884

La Rochefoucauld-Liancourt, François-Alexandre-Frederic de, 5:850, 8:*335*

La Rouchefoucauld-Bayers, Pierre Louis de, 10:884

La Rouge, Pierre, 2:523

La Rue, Pierre de, **8:336–337**

La Salette, 3:623, 5:857, **8:337**, 13:93

La Salle, John Baptist de. *See* De la Salle, John Baptist, St.

La Salle, Patron of All Teachers (Fitzpatrick), 5:753

La Salle, Robert Cavelier de, 1:270, 690–691, 6:732, **8:339–340**, 808

La Tour du Pin, Charles Humbert René (Marquis de la Charce), 5:855, **8:371**, 13:242

La Valette, Antoine de, **3:791**

La Valette, Jean Parisot de, 8:384–385

La Vang, Our Lady of, **8:385–386**

La Villeurnoy (Countess), 4:293

Labadie, Jean de, **8:263**

Labadists, 8:263

Laban the Aramaean, 7:484

Labarum, 3:474, 4:180, **8:263**

Labastida y Dávalos, Pelagio Antonio de (Abp. of Puebla), **8:263–264**

Labat, Jean Baptiste, 3:118, **8:264**

Labbe, Philippe, 7:782, **8:265**

Laberthonnière, Lucien, **8:265**

Labiche de Reignefort, Marcel-Gaucher, 12:277

Labor and trade unions

  Belgium, 2:219

  Pittsburgh, 11:87–88

  as socially defined, 8:460

Yorke, Peter Christopher, 14:895–896

See also Labor organizations

Labor issues
coal strike (U.S.), 13:403
Germany, 8:160
Japan, 8:108–109
labor's bishop, 13:77
Maguire, John William Rochfort, 9:46
social justice, 13:242–244
social principle, 13:250
Texas, 8:843

Labor Movement
Blakely, Paul Lendrum, 2:429
Chávez, César Estrada, 2:872, 3:460
John Paul II (Pope), 3:620, 627
See also Social issues and programs; Social justice and social justice issues

Labor organizations
Austria, 8:232
Congress of Industrial Organizations (CIO), 13:77
France, 8:564
Knights of Labor, 8:192–193
See also Labor and trade unions

Labor relations, 4:117, 743–744

Laborans (Card.), 3:50, 8:160, **265–266**

Laborem exercens (encyclical, John Paul II), 3:627, **8:266**, 11:744, 14:90, 826
amplification of Leo XII's teaching, 3:620
Latin American theologians, 8:548
right of workers to organize, 3:627
subordination of person to the State, 10:852
work, 13:263–264

Laborier du Vivier, Jean-Baptiste, 12:277

Labouré, Catherine, St., 3:623, **8:266–267**, 9:670, 13:93, 94

Labre, Benedict Joseph, St., **8:267–268**

Labriolle, Pierre de, **8:268**

Labrouche de Loborderie, Pierre-Yrieix, 12:277

Labruzzi, Pietro, 8:407

Labuschagne, C. J., 11:98

Labyrinth (Ochino), 10:535

Lacambra, Gregorio Chirivás (Brother), 2:92

Lacan, Jacques, 4:592

LACC. *See* Latin American Caribbean Conference

Lacedra, Pedro María de, 2:596

Lacey, Brian, Bl., 5:231

Lacey, William, Bl., 5:228, **8:269**

Lachat, Eugène (Bp. of Basel), 8:255, **269**

Lachelier, Jules, **8:269–270**

Lachenaie Church, 3:714

Lachmann, Karl, 2:366

Lackner, J., 3:712

Lacombe, Albert, **8:270–271**

Lacombe, Stephen, 4:851

Lacops, James, 6:364

Lacordaire, Jean-Baptiste Henri, 3:420, 5:854, **8:271–273**
L'Avenir censured, 8:209
Catholic social thought, 13:256
Dominican Order, 12:773
liberalism, 3:619
Resurrectionists, 12:174
spiritual direction, 4:763

Lacrimabili statu (encyclical, Pius X), 11:391

Lacroix, Claude, 2:715, 3:221, **8:273**

Lactantius (Christian writer), 3:186, **8:274**, 10:755
aseity, 1:778–779
astrology, 1:812–813
capital punishment, 3:86
Cicero, Marcus Tullius, 3:730
Constantine I (the Great) (Roman Emperor), 3:474, 4:180
Diocletian persecution, 4:750
Divine judgment, 8:31
Easter Vigil, 5:15
exorcism, 5:551
immortality, 7:348, 349
Lucretius, 8:849
property, 11:757
soul, 13:342
works of charity, 3:404

Lacunza y Díaz, Manuel de, **8:274**

Lacy, Edmund (Bp. of Exeter), 5:531, **8:275**

Lacy, Richard, 5:238

Lacy, William de, 8:739

Ladies of Charity, 3:417, 13:177

Ladies of Loretto. *See* Institute of the Blessed Virgin Mary

Ladies of Mary, 4:534

Ladies of St. Maur. *See* Congregation of Sisters of the Holy Infant Jesus

Ladislaus (King of Durazzo-Naples), 1:258, 7:938–939

Ladislaus (King of Hungary), St., 4:370, 7:210, **8:275**

Ladislaus II (King of Bohemia), 7:213

Ladislaus III (King of Poland), 3:357, 7:211

Ladislaus of Gielniów, Bl., **8:275**

Lady Lohengrin (Oldmeadow), 10:583

Laelius, 1:369

Laetamur magnopere (apostolic letter, John Paul II), 3:238

Laetare Jerusalem (papal bull, Paul III), 11:22, 14:168

Laetare Medal, 10:462

Laetentur coeli (Council of Florence), 2:174

Laetus, St., **8:275–276**

LaFarge, Christopher G., 8:276–277

LaFarge, John (1835-1910), 8:276

LaFarge, John (1880-1963), 1:160, 8:277–278, 13:475, 14:244

LaFarge, John L. B. (1865-1938), 8:277

LaFarge family, **8:276–278**

Lafayette Diocese (IN), 7:416

Lafayette Diocese (LA), **8:278**

Lafever, Minard, 3:715

Lafitau, Joseph François, **8:279**

Laflèche, Louis François Richer, **8:279–280**

Laforgue, Jules, 5:160

Lafortune, Bellarmine, 1:210

Lafosse, Louis François Martin, 3:535

Lagasca, Pedro, 1:236

Laghi, Pio (Card.), 1:585, 655

Lagny-sur-Marne Abbey (France), **8:280**

Lagrange, Joseph Louis, 11:543

Lagrange, Marie Joseph, 3:21, 5:50–51, **8:280–281**, *281*
Bible texts, 2:367
biblical archaeology, 2:380
biblical exegesis, 5:520
biblical interpretation, 4:792
pentateuchal studies, 11:94
serpent as symbol, 13:19

Lagrené, Théodore de, 3:498

Lagrime de S. Pietro (Lasso), 8:343

Lahaqat Nebi'im (Abrabanel), 1:36

Laharpe, Frédéric, 1:252

Laicism, 1:517, 518, 3:802, 5:855, 8:160, **281–284**
See also Church and State

Laicization (Loss of the Clerical State), **8:284–287**

Laïcs en premières lignes (Cardijn), 3:103

Laicus (laity), 8:293

Laikos (laity), 8:414

Laima (Baltic region deity), 2:36

Laimbeckhoven, Gottfried von, 3:498

Laínez, Diego, 7:782, **8:287–288**
Abercromby, Robert, 1:20

Laínez, Diego *(continued)*
    Poissy Conference, 7:167
    preaching, 11:621
    scholasticism, 12:766
    University of Alcalá, 1:236
Laistner, M. L. W., 4:529
Laity
    active life, 1:83
    African American, 1:159–160
    altars, 1:317
    Anointing of the Sick, 1:482
    ars moriendi, 1:728, 732
    Australia, 1:906–907
    Carmelites, 3:144
    catechists, 3:248–249
    Catholic Action, 3:275–278
    Christian Family Movement, 3:536
    Christifideles laici, 3:549
    church architecture, 3:712, 715
    Church property, 3:726
    Church-State relations, 3:643
    Council on the Laity, 3:626–627
    during Protestant Reformation,
        12:12–13
    holiness, universal call to, 7:5–7
    liturgical movement, 3:623, 716
    Middle Ages, 3:413
    mission, 3:624
    19th-20th century overview, 3:622
    papal decorations for, 4:595–596
    preaching, 11:631–632
    rights and duties of, 5:39
    sensus fidelium, 12:917
    sodalities federation, 13:294–295
    Vatican Council II, 1:916
    vocations of, 12:865
    women, role of, 14:820–821
    works of charity, 3:413, 416,
        419–420
Laity, Canon Law, 3:36, 57, **8:288–289**
    concept of, 8:290
    lay state, 8:295
    lay-clergy jurisdiction, 8:295
    power of governance, 6:374
Laity, formation and education of,
    8:289–290
Laity, theology of, **8:290–292**
    Church organization and life, 8:292
    liturgical movement, 8:674–675
    postconciliar developments,
        8:292–293
    royal priesthood, 8:292
    secular character, 8:292
    vocation and mission, 8:291–292

Laity in the Middle Ages, 8:293–297
Lakanal, Joseph, 5:975
Lake, Kirsopp, 2:367, **8:297–298**
Lake Huleh (Israel), 7:1027
Lalande, M. R., 3:438
Lalemant, Gabriel, 9:227, 10:435
Lallemant, Charles, 3:4
Lallemant, Jacques Philippe, **8:298**
Lallemant, Louis, 3:310, 7:309, **8:298**
Lalor, Juvenal, 12:540
Lalor, Teresa (Mother), 6:147, 8:299,
    299
Lamaism, **8:299**
Lamarca, Emilio, 1:652
Lamarck, J. B. de, 2:403, 5:260
Lamb, as symbol, 4:393
Lamb of God, **8:299–302**
    exegesis, 8:299–301
    iconography, 8:302
    theology, 8:301–302
Lambach Abbey (Austria), 1:909,
    8:302–303
Lambert (Bp. of Arras), 1:722
Lambert, Johann, 5:47
Lambert, Louis Aloysius, **8:303**
Lambert, Mark. *See* Barkworth, Mark,
    Bl.
Lambert, W. G., 5:268
Lambert de la Motte, Pierre (Bp. of
    Berith), 3:497, 4:113–114,
    8:303–304, 10:810, 977
Lambert le Bègue, 2:204
Lambert of Auxerre, 1:927
Lambert of Hersfeld, 1:462
Lambert of Maastricht, St., 7:144, **8:304**,
    563, 10:255, 12:246
Lambert of Saint-Bertin (Abbot),
    8:304–305, 12:540
Lambert of Saint-Omer, 5:206, **8:304**,
    12:540
Lambert of Spoleto (German Emperor),
    2:500, 7:923, 924, **8:305**
Lambertenghi of Como, Geremia, Bl.,
    8:305
Lamberti, Wynand (Abbot), 12:292
Lambertian charism of the Cross, 8:835
Lambertini, Imelda, Bl., **8:305**
Lambertini, Prospero Lorenzo. *See*
    Benedict XIV (Pope)
Lambeth, Council of (1281), 3:231, 240
Lambeth Conferences, 1:440–441, 577,
    2:525, 5:721, **8:305–306**
    See also Anglicanism
Lambeth Quadrilateral, 1:433, 445,
    8:306

Lambing, Andrew Arnold, **8:306–307**,
    307
Lambres, Benoît, 3:192
Lambruschini, Ferdinando (Abp.), 7:180
Lambruschini, Luigi (Card.), **8:307–308**
*Lamb's Chapel v. Center Moriches
    Union Free School District* (1993),
    3:664
Lambton, Joseph, Bl., 5:232, **8:308**
The Lame Shall Enter First (O'Connor),
    10:547
Lamennais, Hugues Félicité Robert de,
    8:308–310
    Assumptionists, 1:801
    Astros, Paul Thérèse David d',
        1:813–814
    L'Avenir founding, 8:271
    Bonald, Louis Gabriel Ambroise de,
        2:478
    Bonnetty, Augustin, 2:508
    Bruté de Rémur, Simon William
        Gabriel, 2:651
    Catholic liberalism, 5:854
    Church history, 6:877
    Döllinger, Johannes, 4:823
    Dupanloup, Félix, 4:942
    Gregory XVI (Pope), 6:507
    heresy, 6:778–779
    liberalism, 3:619, 642
    Montalembert, Charles Forbes René
        de, 9:824
    political theology, 11:460
    primitive revelation, 12:193
    religious liberalism, 8:541
    Rohrbacher, René François, 12:290
    traditionalism of, 14:138, 139
    Ultramontanism, 10:847
Lamennais, Jean Marie de, 1:311
Lament, Boleslawa Maria, Bl., **8:311**
Lamentabili sane exitu (papal decree,
    Pius X), 5:712, 6:779, **8:311–312**,
    11:389, 12:228, 774–775
Lamentatio peccatricis animae
    (Hildebert of Lavardin), 9:459
Lamentationes obscurorum virorum
    (Gratius), 6:424
Lamentations (Palestrina), 10:802
Lamentations, Book of, 8:*312*, **312–313**
    acrostics in, 1:72
    author, 8:312
    Day of the Lord, 4:547
    form and content, 8:312–313
    kingship, 8:179
    sin, gravity of, 13:153
    soul, 13:336
    spirit, 13:424

Laments, as Psalm genre, 11:795, 797

Laminne, J., 13:593

Lamoricière, Louis de, 14:937

Lamormaini, Wilhelm, 7:783, **8:313**

Lamourette, A. (Bp.), 8:905

Lamp of the Sanctuary (Bar-Hebraeus), 2:82

Lampadius (Roman consul), 3:406

Lampe, J. F., 3:151

Lampel, Antonia (Mother Frances), 5:886

Lampley, William, Bl., 5:230, **8:313**

Lamport, Matthew, Bl., 7:579

Lamps and Lighting, Early Christian, **8:313–314**

Lampsacus, synod of (365), 1:51

Lamy, Bernard, **8:314–315**, 9:75–76, 11:622, 12:765

Lamy, François, **8:315**, 9:74, 75–76, 12:770

Lamy, Jean Baptiste (John Baptist) (Abp. of Santa Fe), 3:857, **8:315–316**, 10:287, 12:675–676, *676*

Lamy of Santa Fe (Horgan), 10:287

Lana-Terzi, F., 3:418

Lancelot (Percy), 11:114

Lancelotti, Giovanni Paolo, **8:316–317**

Lanciani, R., 3:860

Lancicius, Nicholas, Ven., 7:782, **8:317**

Land, Philip S., **8:317–318**

Land O'Lakes statement (1967), 1:54–55

Landa, Diego de (Bp. of Yucatán), **8:318–319**

Landelin, SS., **8:319**, 741

Landersdorfer, Simon K. (Bp.), 3:711

Landévennec Abbey (France), **8:319–320**, *320, 321*

Landini, Francesco, **8:320–321**, 685

Landmark Baptist Movement, 2:80

Landnâmabôk (late twelfth century), 10:445

Lando (Pope), **8:321–322**

Lando of Sezze. *See* Innocent III (Antipope)

Landoald, St., **8:322**

Landos, Agapius, 6:458

Landrich, SS. *See* Landry, SS.

Landry, SS., **8:322**

Landry of Paris (Bp. of Paris), 8:322

Landry of Soiginies (Bp.), 8:322

Landsberg, Herrade de, 1:544

Landsberger, B., 12:458

Landskron, Stephan von, 1:729

Landuin (Carthusian prior), 3:193

Landulf (Patarine reformer), 8:322–323

Landulf of Cotta, 5:323

Landulf of Évreux, St. (Bp.), **8:323**

Lane, Dermot A., 5:350

Laneau, Louis (Bp. of Siam), 2:901

Lanel, Marie Françoise, Bl., 1:722

Lanfranc (Abp. of Canterbury), **8:323–324**, 10:447
    Aldhelm, St., 1:246
    Alexander II (Pope), 1:253
    Alphege of Canterbury, St., 1:306
    Ancient See of Canterbury, 3:70, 72
    Ancient See of Chester, 3:469
    Canon Law, 3:47
    Church-State relations, 4:243
    Eadmer's transformation under, 5:1
    Eucharist, 1:64
    eucharistic controversy, 5:423–424
    growth of the Church in England under, 5:240
    Hugh of Remiremont, 7:155
    influence of, 3:601
    investiture struggle, 7:538
    Scottish Benedictine reform, 12:832

Lanfranc (Italian prelate), 1:888, 2:163, 189, 190, 4:726, 6:782

Lang, Andreas, **8:324**

Lang, Matthäus (Card.), 1:910, 2:333, 5:583, **8:324–325**

Langdon, John (Bp. of Rochester, England), **8:325**

Langdon, S. H., 13:21

Lange, Carl, 1:603

Lange, Elizabeth, 1:157

Lange, J., 5:263

Langenmantel, Josef Maria von (Abbot), 12:671

Langenthal, Heinrich, 6:13

Langer, Suzanne, 12:65, 475

Langevich, Helena (Mother), 2:145

Langevin, Gilles, 7:528

Langheim Abbey (Germany), 1:108

Langhorne, Richard, Bl., 5:237, **8:325**

Langlais, Jean, 2:332

Langland, William, 1:292, 3:605, 5:243, 11:327

Langle, Pierre de (Bp. of Boulogne), 1:600

Langley, Richard, Bl., 5:229, **8:325–326**

Langres. *See* Garnerius of Rochefort

Langres, Councils of, **8:326**

Langton, John (Bp. of Chichester), 3:481

Langton, Stephen (Abp. of Canterbury), 3:72, 5:242
    as Abp. of Salisbury, 12:618
    Convocations, 4:243
    end justifying the means, 5:212

exegetical works, 5:517

Language, Truth and Logic (Ayer), 8:221

Languages
    Arabic, 3:22, 13:702
    Aramaic, 1:625–627, 8:361
        biblical, 1:627
        disciple as term and, 4:768
        as liturgical language, 8:666–667
        Lord's Prayer, 8:783
        Syriac language replacement, 8:361, 13:700
    Coptic, 4:253, 256
    English in U.S. liturgy, 2:43, 7:523–525
    Flemish and French at Leuven, 8:825
    Gadamer, Hans-Georg, 6:46
    Ge'ez, 5:19
    Greek
        biblical, 6:438
        contemporary, former predominant language, 8:366
        early Christian and Byzantine, 2:790, 6:438–439, 8:361, 363–364, 666, 667
        European study of, 12:622
        humanism and, 7:185
        Maccabees, Books of the, 9:7
        Septuagint, 12:920
        translation of word gospel, 6:366–367
        translation of word grace, 6:380, 381
        use in Roman Church, 7:652
    Hebrew, 6:691–692
        Dead Sea Scrolls and, 4:563
        disciple as term and, 4:768
        Duran, Profiat and, 4:947
        modern times, 8:9, 11
        names for God, 13:77
        revival of, 7:186–187
        Sheol (death), 13:79
        shibboleth, 13:83
        translation of grace, 6:380, 381
    inclusive terms, 8:439–440, 545, 13:51–52
    Justinian I, 8:101
    Latin
        Byzantine Empire, 2:770
        Lactantius, 8:274
        lexicography, 2:861
        as sole liturgical language, 6:366
        translation of word gospel, 6:366
    semantics, 12:889
    Slavonic liturgy, 4:370, 475–476

Languages *(continued)*
    study of, Comenius, 4:2
    Syriac, 13:700–702
        Aristotelianism, 1:671
        biblical catenae, 3:259
        Elias Bar Shināyā, 5:156
        father of literature, 13:16–17
        hymnody of, 7:241–242
        text publication, 2:198
    Tamil, 2:339–340
Lanigan, John, **8:326**
Lanspergius, Johannes Justus, 3:16, 192, **8:326–327**
Lantbert of Freising, St. (Bp.), **8:327**
Lanteri, Bruno, 1:311, 3:420
Lanteri, Pio Brunone, **8:327**
Lantrua, Giovanni of Triora, St., **8:327–328**
Las Lanzas (Velázquez), 2:116
Laodicea, 1:785, **8:328**
Laodicea, Councils of (343-80)
    biblical canon, 3:32, 38
    cantors, 3:73, 75
    clerical dress, 3:801
    Confirmation, 4:86
    lenten fasting, 8:468
    subdiaconate as order, 7:37
    symbols of the faith, 4:352
Laon Cathedral (France), 3:695
Laonicus Chalcocondyles, 2:801
Laos, **8:328–331**, *330*
Laozi (Lao-Tzu), 4:523–524, **8:332**, 10:111, 825
Lapide, Cornelius A., 5:523, **8:332–333**
Lapie, Paul, 1:948
Lapierre, Joseph Bouvier, 2:141
Lapini, Anna Maria, **8:333**
Laplace, Claude, 12:277
Laplace, P. S., 5:260
''Laplace's Manifesto,'' 6:669
Lapsi, **8:333**
    Asia Minor, 1:785
    Callistus I (Pope), St., 2:879
    controversy over, 5:450
    Cornelius (Pope), St., 4:270
    Councils of Carthage, 3:188
    Decius' persecution, 4:590
    libellatici, 8:531
    Lucius I (Pope) liberal policy, 8:846
    persecution under Decius, 1:785, 2:879, 3:186, 188
Lara, Rosalio Jose Castillo, 13:*685*
Lara, Salvador, St., 2:156, 12:292
Lara Puente, **8:334**

Larevellière-Lépeaux, Louis, 5:975
Large Catechism (Luther), 4:78
Largentier, Claude, 3:758
Largentier, Denis, 3:758
Largo Redondo, Pedro, Bl., 4:494
Larke, John, Bl., 5:227, **8:334–335**
Larkin, Clarence, 4:776
Larkin, John, **8:335**
Larmenier, Victoire. *See* St. Basil (Mother)
Laroche-Héron, C. de, 4:596
Larraín, Manuel (Bp.), 4:157
Larrea, Fray Alonso de. *See* Rea, Alonso de la
Larrey, Jean, 14:177
Larsa period (c. 1961-1699 B.C.), 9:529
Lartigue, Jean Jacques (Bp.), 3:8
Laruel, Bartholomeo, Bl., 7:734
Las Casas, Bartolomé de, **8:340–341**, *341*
    Acosta, José de, 1:70
    Balboa, 4:133
    Cuba, 4:417
    ecomienda-doctrina system, 12:613, 654
    native rights, 4:852
    Salazar, Domingo de, student of, 12:613
    slavery, 3:417, 13:213
Las Lomas Chapel (Cuernavaca, Mexico), 3:676, 677–678
Las Vegas Diocese (NV), **8:346**, 12:127
Lasalle, Enomiya, 7:743
LaSallian Christian School of Our Lady of Covadonga College (Turón), 14:247
Lasallian martyrs, 2:88
Lasance, Francis Xavier, **8:340**
Lascallian Institute of the Brothers of Christian Instruction (Ecuador), 5:657
Lasco, Jan. *See* Łaski, Jan (the Elder); Łaski, Jan (the Younger)
Lasheras Aizcorbe, Rugino, Bl., 7:124
Łaski, Jan (Abp. of Gniezno), **8:341–342**, 11:442
Łaski, Jan (the Elder), **8:341–342**
Łaski, Jan (the Younger), **8:341–342**
Łaski Statutes, 8:341
Lasso, Orlando di, 3:773, **8:342–343**, *343*
Lasso de la Vega, Rafael (Bp.), **8:343–344**
The Last Communion of St. Jerome (Botticelli), 5:*415*
Last Judgement (Giovanni and Niccolo), 8:*22*

The Last Judgement (Michelangelo), 9:*602*
Last Judgment, 8:174
Last Judgment (Cavillini), 8:*21*
The Last Puritan (Santayana), 12:*680*
Last Retreat on the Praise of Glory (Elizabeth of the Trinity), 5:167
Last Supper
    agape, 1:170
    Judas' treachery, 8:14
    Lord's Supper, 8:784–786
    painting by Salvador Dali, 12:*466*
    reconstruction of, 5:419
    Son of Man, 13:317
The Last Supper (Tintoretto), 8:*785*
Last Supper, iconography of, 8:*344*, **344–345**, 12:485
Last Supper scenes (stained glass), 10:*921*
The Last Temptation of Christ (Kazantzakis), 7:852–853
The Last Three Popes and the Jews (Lepide), 11:398
Lasuén, Fermín Francisco de, 2:862, 866, 8:345–346
Lateau, Louise, **8:346–347**
Lateran, **8:347–350**
    Baptistery, 8:348–349
    Basilica of St. John Lateran, 8:347–348, 351, 352
    choirmaster, 8:342
    Donation of Constantine, 4:860
    lamb icon, 8:302
    Lateran Palace, 8:349
Lateran, Easter Synod of (1099), 1:495
Lateran, John, St., 12:717
Lateran Concordat (1929), 12:790
Lateran Councils, 5:242, **8:350–355**, 12:356
    (649)
        Convocations of England, 4:243
        Divine and human natures of Christ, 9:216
    (1110), Paschal's condemnation of Henry V, 10:916
    Cathari and procreation, 4:219
    Dominican order, 4:828
    Gregory VII (Pope) St., 6:492–493
    Honorius II (Pope), 7:84
    Leo X (Pope), 8:486–487
    Maronite Church, 9:195
    Pisa group as basis for, 8:486
    prohibiting clergy from participating in ordeals, 10:627–628
    Robert of Winchelsea, 3:72

first (1123), 2:880–881, 8:350, 10:838

bulla cruciata, 2:688

clerical celibacy/marriage, 2:880, 3:326

convocation, 4:300

secularization of Church property, 12:871

second (1139), 8:350–351, 10:838

Alberic of Ostia, 1:219

apostolic administrators, 1:116

Arnold of Brescia, 1:719

chivalry, 3:518

clerical celibacy/marriage, 3:326

convocation, 4:300

heresy, 7:487

Innocent II (Pope), 7:470

secularization of Church property, 12:871

third (1179), 8:351–352, 10:838, 14:354

Alexander III (Pope), 1:256

Canon Law, 3:47

collation, 4:706–707

convocation, 4:300–301

heresy, 7:487

papal protection for Dublin, 8:410

Poverty Movement, 11:571

Rufinus' opening address, 12:403

secularization of Church property, 12:871

fourth (1215), 5:376, 424, 8:352–354, 12:12

absolute dualism defined, 10:614

abuse of indulgences, 7:438

Adam of Saint-Victor, 1:109

Amalricians, 1:330

annual obligation to sacraments, 8:297

Canon Law, 3:50

Canons Regular of St. Augustine, 3:68

capital punishment, 3:87

casuistry, 3:220

catechesis, 3:231

Catharism, 1:231

Church-State relations, 2:502

collation, 4:707

convocation of, 4:301

Crusades, 4:409, 7:84

decretals, 4:598

demonology, 4:649

descent of Christ into hell, 4:685

diocesan chancellors, 3:377

examination of conscience, 4:147

God the Holy Spirit, 6:293–295

immutability of God, 7:356

impact on papal power, 10:838

influence on Holy Trinity dogma, 14:196

Innocent III (Pope), 3:602, 7:472–473

inquisition, 7:486

integration of monastic communities, 2:273

lay confession, 8:412

marriage, 1:151

mystery of God, 6:283

"Pardon of Assisi," 11:528

penance, 11:71

Poverty Movement, 11:572

preaching, 11:619

pronouncements on origin, 10:667

relics, 12:54

religious habit, 12:100

Rule of St. Augustine, 1:869

simplicity of God, 13:137

transubstantiation, 14:159

fifth (1512-17), 5:530, 694, 8:56–57

Antichrist, 1:517

benefit of clergy, 8:136

Carvajal, Bernardino Lopez de, 3:197

catechesis, 3:232

censorship, 3:336

Clement VII (Pope), 3:781

commendation reform, 4:9

convocation, 4:301

immortality, 7:353

laity concerns, 8:297

Poland's rights to Prussia, 8:341–342

teaching on the human soul, 14:23

Lateran of Corpus Christi, 8:133

Lateran Pacts (1929), **8:356–357**

Bonomelli, Geremia, 2:509

Castel Gandolfo Villa, 3:212

Church-State relations, 3:621

diplomatic immunity, 8:347

establishing Vatican City, 12:323, 14:400

Lateran Pacts (1985), 3:627, **8:357–360**, 12:27

Lateran Palace, 8:349

Lateran Registers, 10:859

Lateran Synods

angels, 1:421

Canons Regular of St. Augustine, 3:67

election of Constantine II (Pope), 13:517

Nicholas II (Pope), 10:365

Latermann, Johannes, 2:874

Lathrop, Mother Alphonsa, **8:360**, *361*

Latimer, Hugh (Bp. of Worcester), 2:507, 627, **8:360–361**, *362*, 12:10, 243

Latin America. *See specific countries*

Latin American Bishops' Conference (1968), 10:351

Latin American Bishops' Council (CELAM), 5:66

Latin American Caribbean Conference (LACC), 13:187

Latin American Church, 4:157–158

Latin American Episcopal Conference, 5:203

Latin American Episcopal Council (Consejo Episcopal Latinoamericano) (CELAM). *See* Consejo Episcopal Latinoamericano (CELAM)

Latin American Pastoral Institute, 4:157, 158

Latin American Plenary Council (1899), 1:644

Latin Bible of 42 Lines, 9:387

Latin Empire of Constantinople, 2:739, 761, 787, **8:366–367**

church architecture, 3:688–689

Eastern Schism, 2:823, 825

Innocent III (Pope), 3:602

Lyons, Councils of, 8:907

Latin Fathers. *See* Fathers of the Church; Patristic era

Latin language

Byzantine Empire, 2:770

humanism, 7:184, 188

Lactantius, 8:274

lexicography, 2:861

translation of word gospel, 6:366

Latin language, in the Church, **8:361–366**

beginnings, 8:362

Cicero, style of, 8:364

clergy in Early Church, 8:296

congregational singing, 4:119

Damasus I (Pope), St., as standard, 4:505

drama, 4:896, 901

laity excluded, 8:296

liturgical features, 8:364–365

as sole liturgical language, 6:366

superseded as vernacular, 8:364

two levels, 8:363–364

Latin Rite, 4:92, **8:367–369**, 532, 12:331–336, 428–429

Latina theology, 5:678, **8:369–370**

Latinarum litterarum (*motu proprio*, Pius XI), 11:484

Latini, Brunetto, 2:344, 5:206

Latini, Filippo (Philip). *See* Bernard of Corleone, Bl.

Latinization, 13:713

Latitudinarianism, 1:444, 7:148, **8:370**, 836, 12:745

Latomus, Bartholomaeus (Steinmetz), **8:370**

Latomus, Jacobus, 3:609, **8:371**

Latourette, Kenneth Scott, **8:372**

Latrobe, Benjamin Henry, 2:39, 3:709, 715

Latter-Day Saints, Church of Jesus Christ of, **8:372–375**, 13:234, *235*

Latvia, **8:374–377**, *376*, *377*

Latz, Leo, 10:176

Lau d'Alleman, Jean Marie, 10:884

Laube, Clifford, 11:576

Lauchen, George Joachim von. *See* Rheticus (German astronomer)

Laud, William (Abp. of Canterbury), 1:444, 3:152, 6:*824*, **8:377–378**, *378*, 10:500

    Charles I (King of England), 3:432

    Church-State relations, 3:645

    High Church party, 6:823

    Puritan emigration to America, 11:839

Lauda (Jacopone da Todi), 7:692

Lauda sion salvatorem (St. Thomas Aquinas), 4:272, **8:378–379**, 9:460

Lauda spirituale, 3:150

Laudabiliter (papal bull, Adrian IV), **8:379**

Laudes, 10:45

Laudes Dei (Dracontius), 9:439

Laudes Deo concinat (Notker), 10:455

Laudes festivae (trope), 14:216

Laudomar, St., **8:379**

Lauds, **8:379–380**

    hymns for, 4:257, 5:33, 201, 12:208, 464

    importance, 8:732

    Liturgy of the Hours, 8:729

    Scripture reading, 8:733

    structure, 8:732

    Vatican Council II, 8:731

Laudus (Lô), St. (Bp. of Coutances), **8:380–381**

Laugier, M. A., 3:679

Laumer, St., 12:557

Launoy, Jean de, 1:267, 2:105, 8:381

Lauras (community of monks), 2:895, 3:335, **8:381**, 12:452

Laurence of Lindores, 8:594

Laurens, Honoré de (Abp. of Embrun), 1:197

Laurentian Schism, 13:672–673

Laurentius (Antipope), 13:673

Laurentius II (Bp. of Milan), 7:920

Laurentius de Pinu, 3:52

Laurentius Puldericus, 3:52

Lauresheimensis, 3:40

Laus angeli cum carmine. See Gloria

Laus angelorum. See Gloria

Lausanne Cathedral (France), 1:576

Lausiac History (Palladius of Helenopolis), 3:594, **8:381–382**, 10:805, 12:60

Lauzon, Pierre de, **8:382**

Lavaisse, Benjamín, 1:651

Laval, François de Montmorency (Bp. of Québec), 3:4–5, 9, 714, **8:382–383**, *383*, 14:453

Laval, Jacques Désiré, Bl., 8:383–384

Laval, Martyrs of, 5:973, 8:384

Laval, Synod of, 4:89

Laval University (Québec, Canada), 3:10, 12:391, 395

Lavanoux, Maurice Émile, **8:386**

Lavater, Johann Kaspar, 2:428, **8:386–387**

Lavaur catechism, 3:240

Lavelle, Louis, 4:24, 5:362, 398, **8:387**

    act, 1:74

    aseity, 1:780

    Augustinianism, 1:881

    axiology, 1:948

    Le Senne collaboration, 8:514

    religious experience, 5:556

Lavelle, Michael Joseph, **8:387–388**

Lavialle, Peter Joseph (Bp. of Louisville), 8:817

Lavigerie, Charles Martial Allemand (Card.), 8:*388*, **388–389**

    Algeria, 1:285

    Carthage, 3:188

    catechumenate, 3:252

    Missionaries of Africa, founding of, 9:730

    Missionary Sisters of Our Lady of Africa, 9:733

    ralliement, 11:900

    slavery, 13:209

    Tunisia, 14:236

Lavoisier, Antoine Laurent, 5:260

Law, **8:389–391**

    administration and positivism, 11:547

    apodictic, 4:6

    authority, 1:920

    book of the covenant, 2:526–527

    civil, 7:171

    common good, 4:16–17

    compensationism, 4:43

    compurgation, 4:46

    Constantine I (the Great) (Roman Emperor), 4:182

    English medieval common law, 2:576

    eternal, human act, 7:171–172

    ethics, 8:390–391

    France, early civil law, 8:801

    human act, 7:171–172

    identification of, 11:545–546, 547

    Jewish, 8:4–5

    liberty, dilemma between, 9:877–879

    Locke, J., 8:745

    meaning of, 11:546–547

    moral obligation, 10:520

    Mortmain on, 9:904–905

    nomocanon, 10:414–415

    obedience and human, 10:506–507

    occult compensation, 4:41–43

    as principle of order, 8:389–390

    regarding usury, 14:353

    Russia, 3:264

    smuggling, 13:237

    Spain, 13:379

    Suárez, Francisco, 13:560–561

    theory behind use of torture, 14:118–119

    Thomistic definition, 8:390

    vulgar, 8:453

    will and willing, 14:723

    See also Canon Law; Law, ancient Near-Eastern; Natural law; Public law; Roman law

Law, Bernard F. (Card.), 1:*25*, 2:556–557, 3:237, 4:114, 9:309

Law, William, **8:402–403**

Law, Ancient Near-Eastern, **8:391–395**

    Assyrian laws, 8:394–395

    Babylonian codes, 8:393–394

    book of the covenant, 2:527

    capital punishment, 3:84

    Ecloga code, 8:473

    Egyptian laws, 8:395

    Hittite laws, 8:395

    Sumerian laws, 8:392–393

    Ten Commandments, 4:6

Law, Divine positive, **8:395–396**

Law, Ecclesiastical, 8:100, 421, 450–452, 13:128

Law, Germanic, 8:452–453

Law, Mosaic, 7:629–630, **8:396–397**
  apodictic form, 8:396
  Code of Hammurabi compared, 8:394
  collections of, 8:396–397
    Book of Deuteronomy, 8:397
    Book of the Covenant, 8:397
    Decalogue, 8:397
    Priestly Code, 8:397
  as covenant, 4:324–327
  Covenant related, 8:396
  growth, 8:396
  justice of men, 8:73–74
  justification, 8:77–78, 79–80
  light, use of, 8:580
  Reform Judaism, 8:10
  social principle, 13:248
  tone of, 8:402
Law, New Testament, 4:7–8, 9
Law, philosophy of, **8:398–402**
  authority and law's origin, 8:398–399
  end of law, 8:401
  historical sources, 8:401–402
  inadequate theories, 8:399–400
  justice and law, 8:400–401
  law and force, 8:398
  morality, 10:196–198
  present need, 8:402
Law, Roman. *See* Roman law
"Law for a Defense of the Nation"
  (Bulgarian Church, 1940), 10:685
Law in Christian Life, 8:403–404
The Law of Christ (Häring), 11:153
Law of comparative judgment, 9:411
Law of Guarantees (Italy), 8:357
Law of nature school, 10:182
Law of purity, 11:831–832
Law of the Twelve Tables (451-450
  B.C.), 14:353
"Law of Three States," 11:543
Lawes, Henry, 3:151
Lawlor (Father), 1:95
Lawrence (Antipope), **8:404**
Lawrence (Bp. of Milan), 1:627
Lawrence (Opimus), 13:27
Lawrence, D. H., 5:326
Lawrence, Robert, St., 5:225, **8:405**,
  12:8, 210
Lawrence, St., 3:224, 723, **8:404–405**,
  13:*196*
Lawrence Justinian, St., 6:234,
  8:405–406
Lawrence of Brindisi, St., 1:911,
  8:406–407, *407*
Lawrence of Canterbury, St., 3:70,
  8:407–408, 12:536

Lawrence of Durham, **8:408**, 9:457
Lawrence of Riparfatta, Bl., **8:408**
Lawrence of St. Nicholas, 1:433
Lawrence of Spain, 3:48, **8:408–409**
Lawrence of the Resurrection, 3:136,
  8:409, 13:447
Lawrence of Villamagna, Bl., **8:409**
Lawrence O'Toole, St. (Abp. of Dublin),
  8:409–410
Laws (Plato), 5:89, 6:335
Laws, conflict of, 5:290–291, **8:410**
The Laws of Ecclesiastical Polity
  (Hooker), 3:638
Laws of physics, 9:667
"Laws of the Ancients" (Maimonides),
  10:135
Lawyers, patron saint of, 5:713
Lax, Robert, 12:540
Laxism, **8:410–411**, 9:863
  Alexandre, Noël, 1:267
  Augustinianism, 1:885
  Busenbaum, Hermann, 2:716
  Candido, Vincenzo, 3:13
  Caramuel, Juan Lobkowitz, 3:99
  Cárdenas, Juan de, 3:102
  casuistry, 3:221
  condemned by Alexander VII (Pope),
    10:844
  conscience, 4:145
  heresy of, 6:777
  Sánchez, Juan, 12:658
Lay apostolates, 3:276, 4:40–41, 335,
  443–444
Lay communion, 4:36–38
Lay confession, 8:295, **411–412**, 412
Lay congresses, American Catholic,
  1:160, 351–352, **8:412**
Lay documents, 11:92
The Lay Folks' Catechism, 3:231, 240,
  4:8
Lay formation, 8:289, 289–290
Lay hermit movements (12th-13th
  centuries), 3:130–131, 140
*The Lay Members of Christ's Faithful
  People* (apostolic exhortation, John
  Paul II), 8:292–293
Lay ministries, 8:289, 289–290, 9:652,
  653–654
Lay movements, 8:417–418, 453–454,
  454
Lay policy, 8:282
Lay spirituality, **8:412–419**
  early twentieth-century, 8:416
  historical survey, 8:413–414
  Middle Ages, 8:414–415
  New Testament foundations, 8:413

  postconciliar, 8:417–418
  Reformation to modern times,
    8:416–417
  twenty-first century, 8:418–419
  Vatican Council II, 8:413, 416–417
Lay trusteeism, 14:540–541
Laya, F. L., 2:858
Laymann, Paulus, 1:311, 7:782, **8:419**
Laynez, Francisco, 7:411–412
Lazarists
  China, 3:498, 499
  France, 7:126
  works of charity, 3:419
  See also Vincentians
Lazarus (biblical figure), 8:37, **419–421**
Lazarus (Schubert), 12:787
Lazarus the Confessor, St., **8:421**
Lazius, Wolfgang, 1:13–14
LBJ. *See* Little Brothers of Jesus (LBJ)
LCM. *See* Little Company of Mary
LCWR. *See* Leadership Conference of
  Women Religious in the U.S.A.
  (LCWR)
Le Bec-Hellouin Abbey. *See* Bec Abbey
  (France)
Le Brun, Pierre, 8:647
Le Camus, Étienne (Card.), **8:431**
Le Caron, Joseph, 3:4
Le Clerc, Alix, Bl., 5:834, **8:431–432**,
  432, 12:780
Le Clerc, Jean, 5:518, **8:432**, 11:416
Le Clerc du Tremblay, François,
  8:432–433
Le Coq, Pierre, 5:441
Le Corbusier, 3:669, 672, 680, 713,
  8:623, 12:*369*
Le Courayer, Pierre François, 1:438
Le Cun, Father, 3:111
Le Donné (architect), 3:713
Le Doré, Ange, 5:441–442
Le Fèvre, Jean, 3:51
Le Gaudier, Anthony, **8:452**
Le Gobien, Charles, **8:455**
Le Goff, Abbé, 3:115, 118
Le Gos de Foulques, Guy (Card.). *See*
  Clement IV (Pope)
Le Grand, Antoine, 12:771
Le Jay, Claude (Jajus), 1:37, **8:463**
Le Maistre, Antoine and Isaac,
  8:464–465
Le Mans Cathedral (France), 3:696
Le Masson, Innocent, 3:192, 195, **8:465**
Le Mercier, Olivier (Father), 6:150,
  12:709
Le Moyne, Jean Baptiste, 6:150, 10:291,
  12:709

Le Moyne, Simon, 6:91

Le Nain de Tillemont, Sebastian, 7:847

Le Parc Monastery. *See* Park Monastery (Belgium)

Le Plat, Jodocus, **8:507**

Le Play, Frédéric, 2:696

Le Quien, Michel, **8:510–511**

Le Quieu, Antoine, 12:484

Le Roy, Alexander, **8:512–513**

Le Roy, Édouard, 6:314–315, **8:513**, 9:754

Le Sage 'ten Broek, J., 10:261

Le Senne, René, 5:362, 398, 8:387, **514**

Le Tellier, Charles Maurice (Abp. of Reims), **8:519**, 12:291

Le Tellier, Michel, **8:519**

Le Thoronet Abbey (France), 3:750, **8:519–520**

Le Vacher, Jean, 3:188, **8:520–521**

Le Van Trung, 3:79

Lea, Henry Charles, 8:421, 423

Lea, Richard. *See* Sergeant, Richard, Bl.

Lead Me, Guide Me (Lyke), 1:162, 7:261, 8:903

Leadbetter, Charles W. (Bp. of the Old Catholic Church of Australasia), 13:936

The Leader (newspaper), 10:571

Leadership Conference of Women Religious in the U.S.A. (LCWR), 1:639, **8:421–424**, 14:309

League for Catholic Social Action, 9:124

League for Evangelical-Catholic Reunion, 8:892

League of Cambrai, 7:669

League of Cognac, 7:669

League of Dessau, 6:145

League of Halle, 6:145

League of the Good Shepherd, 12:418

Leahy, William P., 2:558

Leal, J., 3:741

Leander (Abp. of Seville), St., 5:773, **8:425–426**

    Arianism, 1:663–664

    Isidore of Seville, St., 7:602

    Pelagius II (Pope), 3:596

    works of charity, 3:409

Learned ignorance method, 10:374–375

Learning, theory of, 6:25

Least Brothers (*Hermanos Minomos*), 10:523

Leavenworth Diocese (KS), 8:113, 117–118

Lebanese Maronite Order of St. Anthony, 1:534

Lebanon, **8:426–428**, *429*

    Byzantine Basilians, 2:144

    demographic statistics, 8:427

    ecclesiastical organization, 8:428

    map, 8:*428*

    Maronite Church, 9:195

    Sharbel Makhlouf, St., 13:69

Lebbe, Frederic Vincent, 3:500, **8:428–429**

Lebedev, Alexander A., 12:435

Leben Jesu kritisch bearbeitet (Strauss), 6:709

Das Leben Jesu kritisch bearbeitet (The Life of Jesus Critically Examined) (Strauss), 7:848

Leben Schleiermachers (Dilthey), 10:238

Leben und Leiden Jesu Christi (Cochem), 7:847

Lebensbericht: Mit einem Dokumentenanhang (Jedin), 7:750

Lebenswelt, 11:232

Lebna Dengel (David II) (Ethiopian Emperor), 1:324–325

Lebon, Joseph, 1:722, **8:429**

LeBreton, André, 5:208, 209

Lebreton, Jules, 4:853, **8:430**

Lebrun, Louis-François, 12:277

Lebuffe, Francis Peter, **8:430**

Lebuinus, St., **8:430–431**

Lebwin, St. *See* Lebuinus, St.

Lebwohl, K., 3:712

Lecerf, A., 2:891

Lechner, Peter, 12:735

Leclercq, Henri, 2:839, 5:629, **8:433**, 12:705

Leclercq, Jacques, 12:776

Leclercq, Jean, 2:311, 3:813, 815, 5:397, **8:433–434**

Leclercq, Solomon, Bl., 2:632

Leçons d'histoire franciscaine (Ubald), 14:261

Lecorre, Auguste, 1:207

Lectionaries, 11:124

Lectionaries, contemporary Roman Catholic, **8:438–440**

Lectionaries, ecumenical, 8:437–438, **440–442**

Lectionaries, historical, **8:434–438**, 655

Lectionaries, Syriac, 5:5

Lectionary for Mass (LFM), 8:439, 440

Lectionary for Masses with Children (LMC), **8:442**

Lectionary of Luxeuil, 8:899

Lectiones super Boethii librum de Trintate (Thierry of Chartres), 14:2

Lectors, 7:37, **8:442–443**, 10:639

Lectura (Hostiensis), 3:48

Lectura (Tudeschis), 14:235

Lectura super Apocalipsim (Olivi), 5:897

Lectura Thomasina (William of Peter of Godin), 14:46

Lecturas Catolicas (periodical), 12:247

Lecture on the Apocalypse (Peter John Olivi), 5:899

Lectures on Revivals of Religion (Finney), 5:735

Lectures on the History of Philosophy (Hegel), 3:183

Lectures on the Philosophy of Religion (Hegel), 12:69

LeCun, William, 7:699

Lecuona Aramburu, Maria Engracia (1897-1936), 14:564, 566

Lécuyer, Joseph, 11:705

Leczna, M. Solana (Mother), 5:882

Leczycki, Nicholas. *See* Lancicius, Nicholas, Ven.

Ledesma, Pedro de, **8:443**

Ledóchowska, Maria Teresa, Bl., **8:443–444**

Ledóchowska, Urzula, Bl., **8:444**

Ledóchowski, Miescysław Halka (Card.), 1:584, 8:254, **444**

Ledóchowski, Wladimir, 7:791–792, **8:445**, 12:775

Leduin (Abbot), 12:588

Ledwith, Michael, 7:528

Lee, Ann, 13:59

Lee, Edward (Abp. of York), **8:445**

Lee, James Michael, 12:98

Lee, John, 7:575

Lee v. Weisman (1992), 3:666–667

Leen, Edward, **8:445–446**

Leeuw, Gerardus Van der, **8:446**

Leeuwenhoek, Antoni van, 2:402

LEF. *See* Lex ecclesiae fundamentalis

Lefebvre, Gaspar, 12:533

Lefebvre, Marcel (Abp.), 5:*850*, 859, 861, **8:446–449**, *447*

    excommunication of (1988), 10:853

    John Paul II (Pope), 7:1005

    Paul VI (Pope), 11:30

    traditionalist movement, 3:289

Lefevere, Peter Paul (Bp. of Detroit), 4:697, **8:449**, 9:605, 606

    African American Catholics, 1:157

    American College at Louvain, 8:821

    Duchemin, M. Theresa, 4:926, 7:338

    Kindekens, P., 8:169

Lefèvre, Michel, 5:441

Lefévre, Peter. *See* Faber, Peter, Bl.

Lefèvre d'Étaples, Jacques, 3:606, 5:847, **8:449–450**
  Aristotelianism, 1:676
  Bovillus, Carolus, 2:572
  Farel, Guillaume, 5:622
  humanism, 12:119
  St. Paul literature, 7:166
Lefranc, François, 5:441
Lega democratica nazionale, 9:755, 10:69–70
Legal guilt, 6:567
Legal positivism. *See* Positivism in jurisprudence
Legal price, 8:64
Legal process, 11:547
Legalism (*Fajia*), 3:509–510
Legates, papal, 3:72, **8:450–452**
Legatus divinae pietatis (St. Gertrude the Great). *See Insinuationes*
The Legend for Use in Choir (Thomas of Celano), 14:33
The Legend of Aqhat (Uagritic text), 14:267
Legend of the Holy Cross (Piero della Francesca), 7:*811*
Legenda (*passionarium*), 8:436, 639
Legenda aurea (James of Voragine), 6:613, 7:711
Legenda de vita et miraculis beatae Margaritae de Cortona (Giunta of Bevegnati), **9:148–149**
Legendaries, 6:613
La Légende de Saint Christophe (Indy), 7:444
Léger. *See* Leodegar of Autun (Bp.), St.
Léger, Fernand, 1:803, 3:713
Léger, Paul-Émile (Card., Abp. of Montréal), 3:8, 10, **8:452**, 12:493
Leges Langobardorum, 3:41, 8:768
Leges Romanae Barbarorum, 3:40, **8:452–453**
Legg, S. C. E., 2:367
Legion of Decency, 8:792
Legion of Mary, 3:501, 622, **8:453**
Legionaries of Christ, **8:454**
Legislated law. *See* Positive law
Legislation, religious, 9:293
La Législation primitive (de Bonald), 14:138
Legislative powers, 6:374
Legitimacy of children (Canon Law), **8:454–455**
Legnani, Callisto, 2:24
Legnano, Battle of, 8:767
Legrand, Anthony, 3:185
LeGrand, France Jacques, 1:888

Legroing de la Romagère, Pierre-Joseph, 12:277
Léhen, Édouard de, 13:242
Lehmann, Karl (Card.), 6:187
Lehmkuhl, August, **8:455**
Lehodey, Vital, 4:208, **8:455–456**
Lehrbuch der Kirchengeschichte (Funk), 6:35
Lehrbuch der Philosophie (Stöckl), 12:774
Die Lehre von den heiligenSakramenten der katholischen Kirche (Schanz), 12:729
Leia, Peter de (Bp.), 12:544
Leiber, Robert, 10:68
Leibniz, Gottfried Wilhelm von, 2:116, 8:*456*, **456–458**, 11:293
  accident, 1:62
  antimonies, 1:520
  appetite, 1:603
  Aristotelianism, 1:677
  atomism, 1:831, 835
  Bossuet, Jacques Bénigne, 2:550
  Calixtus, Georg, 2:874
  Cartesianism, 3:183, 4:682
  causality, 3:306
  chance, 3:377
  choice, 3:521
  Church unity, 13:417
  Clarke, Samuel, 3:766
  concept of time, 14:78
  contingency, 4:214
  continuum, 4:215, 216
  contributions to study of motion, 10:19
  cosmological argument, 4:285
  cosmology, 4:287
  criteriology, 4:367
  determinism, 5:395
  dynamism, 4:958, 960, 9:416
  eclecticism, 5:47, 48
  Enlightenment, 5:255, 262
  entelechy, 5:267
  exemplarism, 5:526, 527
  existence, 5:534
  extension, 5:569
  first principles, 5:743
  free will, 5:931, 938–939
  idealism, 7:297
  knowledge, theories of, 4:960, 8:217–218
  logic, 8:748, 750, 751, 753
  Malebranche, Nicolas, 9:74
  metaphysic, 12:767

  metaphysical evil, 5:488
  monads, 9:777–778
  music, nature of, 10:73
  ontological perfection, 11:119
  ontology, 10:606
  optimism of, 10:613
  panpsychic nature of reality theory, 10:824
  philosophy of religion, 12:73, 785
  Platonism, 11:416
  possibility, 11:551, 552
  potency, 11:557
  quality, 11:849
  quantity, 11:853
  rationalism, 11:920
  reflection, 12:3
  solipsism, 13:303
  soul, 13:346
  substance, 13:578
  sufficient reason, 12:784
  transcendentals, 14:150
  unity, 14:318
  will and willing, 14:723
  Wolff, Christian, 14:806, 807, 808
Leibold, Paul F. (Abp. of Cincinnati), 3:737, 7:416
Die Leiden des jungen Werthers (Goethe), 6:330
Die Leidengeschichte Jesu und der Christuskult (Bertram), 5:812
Leidradus (Abp. of Lyons), 1:186, 3:160, 769, 5:783, **8:458–459**, 905
Leif Ericson, 10:446
Leigh, Richard, Bl., 5:230, 783, **8:459**
Leimon (Moschus), 10:6
Leimonos Monastery (Lesbos, Greece), 2:*779*
Leipzig, Francis P. (Bp.), 2:23
Leipzig, Synod of (743), 3:240
Leipzig debates, 8:129
Leipzig Interim (1548), 7:521, 11:224
Leisler, Jacob, 10:321
Leisner, Karl Friedrich Wilhelm Maria, Bl., **8:459–460**
Leisure, **8:460–462**
Leitl, Alfons, 3:711
Lejeune, Jean, **8:463**
Lejeune, Jérôme, 1:*31*, **8:463–464**
Lejeune, Paul, 3:4
Leland, John, 2:79
Leloutre, Jean Louis, **8:464**
Lemaître, Antoine, 11:524
Lemarié, J., 3:564
Leme, Sebastian (Card.), 5:840

Leme da Silveira Cintra, Sebastião (Card.), **8:465–466**

Lemercier, Jacques, 3:706

Lemierre, T., 2:858

Lemire, Jules, **8:466**

Lemke, Peter Henry, **8:466**, 12:538

Lemon v. Kurtzman (1971), 3:667, 668

Lemos, Tomás de, 1:326, **8:466–467**

L'Empereur, Martin, 1:545

Lemuria, 1:289

Lenbach, Franz Seraph von, 1:85

Lenihan, Mathias C. (Bp. of Great Falls, MT), 9:826

Lenihan, Thomas Mathias (Bp. of Cheyenne, WY), 14:870

Lenin, Vladimir Ilich, 5:94, 7:196, 8:*467*, **467–468**

Leningrad Codex, 2:357

Leninism, 9:322, 323–324

Lent, **8:468–470**

  baptisms during, 2:63

  fasting, 8:468–469

  history, 8:468

  lectionaries, 8:435

  Leo I (Pope), St., 8:477

  litanies, 8:600–601

  liturgical calendar, 8:642, 721

  liturgical calendar, norms, 8:643

  Polish popular piety during, 11:511

  Shrove Tuesday, 13:97–99

  spirit, 8:469–470

  stational mass, 8:470

Lentini, Anselmo, 2:263

Lentini, Domenico, Bl., **8:471**

Lentner, L., 3:245

Lentrup, Leonarda (Mother), 7:53

Lenz, Desiderius, 2:351, 3:671, **8:471**, 671, 12:601

Lenzen, V., 5:142

Lenziniana, Mateo Alonzo, 14:496

Leo (the Thracian) (Emperor), 8:476, 477

Leo, Leonardo, **8:471–472**

Leo I (Byzantine Emperor), 8:*472*, **472**

  Agatho (Pope), St., 1:174

  Basiliscus, 2:149

  Monophysitism, 3:595

  Monothelitism, 7:80

  papal authority, 12:354

  Zeno, 14:916

Leo I (the Great) (Pope), St., **8:474–478**, *475*

  Anatolius of Constantinople, 1:392

  beatific vision, 2:173

  catechumenate, 3:251

Christmas, 3:552, 554, 555

Christology, 3:559, 561, 595

Church-State relations, 3:633

clerical celibacy/marriage, 3:325

communion of saints, 4:35

Confession, 4:77

Constabilis, St., 4:168

Constantinople Council II, 4:191

Constantinople precedence, 4:190

Council of Chalcedon, 3:363, 365, 595

creedal statements, 4:354

cursus leoninus, 4:444

decretals, legal force of, 4:600

demonology, 4:649

Dioscorus (Patriarch of Alexandria), 4:756

doctrine, 8:476–478

Easter date controversy, 5:13

Epiphany, 5:294

Eutyches, 4:860, 5:461

Father of the Church, 5:642

Hilary of Arles, St., 6:112, 827–828, 11:772

homilies, 7:62

hypostasis, 7:263

juristic function of papacy under, 10:832–833, 834

Leonine Sacramentary, 8:501

Manichaeism mission in Italy, 9:109

Marcian (Byzantine Emperor), 9:141

''orienting'' the basilica, 2:148

papal legates, 8:450

preaching of, 11:611

priesthood, 11:697

primacy of Constantinople, 2:821, 3:595

Prosper of Aquitaine, St., 11:772

Quinisext Synod, 11:868

relics, 12:52

simony, 13:136

soul, 13:343

theology of Church, 3:586

Vatican construction under, 14:393

Leo I (the Magnificent) (Armenian King), 1:701–702

Leo II (Byzantine Emperor), 14:916

Leo II (Leo of Cava), Bl., 8:494

Leo II (Pope), St., 3:733, 4:193, 7:81, **8:478–479**, 12:355

Leo III (Byzantine Emperor), 7:*280*, **8:472–473**

  diaconia, 4:720

  Eastern Schism, 5:23

  Gregory II (Pope), St., 6:484–485

  Gregory III (Pope), St., 6:486

  iconoclasm, 7:280–281

  Nicholas I (Pope), St., 10:360

Leo III (Pope), St., **8:479–481**

  Adalard, St., 1:98

  Anastasius (Patriarch of Constantinople), 1:388

  Charlemagne, 1:478, 3:167–168, 425, 426–427, 554

  Church-State relations, 3:635

  creedal statements, 4:356

  filioque, 2:822, 5:24, 720

  iconoclasm, 1:123, 2:733, 751, 793

  rebellion against, 3:167

  works of charity, 3:411

Leo IV (Pope), St., 8:*481*, **481–483**

  asperges, 1:786

  cardinalate, 3:106

  Eastern Schism, 2:825

  Hincmar of Reims, 6:838

  iconoclasm, 2:751

  John of Ravenna, 7:981

  Leonine wall around Vatican built, 14:394

Leo V (Byzantine Emperor), 7:282, 309, **8:473**, 10:914–915

Leo V (Pope), 1:139, 504, 2:753, 793, 3:562, **8:483**

Leo VI (Byzantine Emperor), **8:473–474**

  Byzantine chant, 2:743

  Euthymius I, 5:460

  fourth marriage of, 5:24, 460

  Photius, 2:755

  poetry, 2:805

  tetragamy dispute, 1:646, 2:756–757, 786, 823, 4:174

Leo VI (Pope), **8:483–484**

Leo VII (Pope), **8:484**

Leo VIII (Pope), **8:484**, 12:356

Leo IX (Pope), St., **8:485**

  Church-State relations, 3:635

  clerical celibacy/marriage, 3:326

  Constantine IX (Byzantine Emperor), 4:175

  Decius, Phillipus, 4:589

  Eastern Schism, 2:757–758

  Gervase of Reims, 6:193

  Gregorian reform, 5:843

  Humbert of Silva Candida, 7:199

  influence of, 3:601

  Lateran Councils, 12:356

  Michael Cerularius, 4:187–188

  miters, 9:743–744

  reform, 3:600

  reordination, 12:128

Leo X (Pope), **8:485–488**, *486*
    abbreviators, 1:13
    Adrian of Castello, 1:130
    appeals to a future council, 1:599
    Arcimboldi, Giovannangelo, 1:643
    astrology, 1:813
    Carvajal, Bernardino Lopez de, 3:197
    Castel Sant'Angelo, 3:213
    Charles V (Holy Roman Emperor),
        3:429, 781, 7:669
    Chigi, Agostino, 3:483
    Defender of the Faith title, 4:609
    dueling, 4:929
    election to papacy, 8:486
    foreign policies, 8:487
    Francis I, 6:75, 8:487
    Gallicanism, 6:78
    Ghibelline-Guelf conflict, 3:855
    Grassi, Paris, 6:419
    Greek Liturgical Rite among Latins,
        use of, 7:649
    on the human soul, 1:595
    indulgences, 7:438
    Lateran Councils, 8:486–487, 12:358
    Lazarites, 7:126
    Luther, Martin, 5:43, 8:880–881,
        14:168
    Michelangelo, 9:603
    montes pietatis, 9:835
    nepotism of, 10:247
    Petrucci's conspiracy against, 12:220
    Pragmatic Sanction, 11:582
    pre-Reformation spiritual hunger,
        3:607
    prohibited books, 7:390
    promoter of the faith office, 4:706
    Renaissance humanism, 12:118
    St. Peter's financing, 8:487–488
    University of Alcalá, 1:236
    works of charity, 3:414
Leo XI (Pope), **8:488–489**, *489*
Leo XII (Pope), **8:489–490**, *490*
    Alexander I (Emperor of Russia),
        1:252
    Carbonari, 3:101
    Consalvi, Ercole, 4:139
    Conwell, Henry, 4:245
    Della Somaglia, Guilio Maria, 4:632
    Holy Year, 7:57
    Order of the Holy Spirit, 7:52
    secret societies, 12:857
Leo XIII (Pope), **8:490–493**, *491*
    abbots, 1:11
    abolition of slavery, 9:61
    Alaska, 1:208

Alexian Brothers, 1:275
Americanism, 1:84, 354, 355, 356,
    6:779
angelic devotion, 1:424
Anglican orders, 4:620
Anglican ordinations, 5:67–68, 252
Anglicanism, 1:435, 438, 439,
    592–594
Anne and Joachim, SS., 1:469
Anthimus VII (Patriarch), 1:503
apostolic delegation in the United
    States, 1:584, 585
associations, 1:792–793
Balmes, Jaime Luciano, 2:33
Basilians, 2:141, 144
Belgian school question, 4:589
Belgium constitution, dispute, 2:219
Benedictine confederation
    organization, 2:254
Bible studies, 4:791
biblical exegesis, 5:523
biblical inerrancy, 7:446
biblical inspiration, 7:494–495
biblical studies, 5:523, 10:335
bishop as order, 7:36
Bonomelli, Geremia, 2:508
Bouquillon controversy, 2:565
bulls as form, 4:758
Carbonari, 3:101
Catholic social movement, 2:219,
    11:367, 566
Catholic University of America,
    3:290
censorship, 3:336
Chaldean Catholic Church, 3:369
chant books, 3:380
Chapelle, Placide Louis, 3:384
Chile, 3:486
Church-State relations, 3:642
Cicero, Marcus Tullius, 3:730
Cincinnati provincial council (1882),
    5:145
Collegio Sant' Anselmo, revival of,
    2:273
common good, 4:19
communion of saints, 4:34
Communism, 3:620
composer of hymns, 12:464
Confirmation, Sacrament of, 4:90
Cusack, Margaret Anna, 4:446
Czech Catholicism, 4:484
Daughters of the Heart of Mary,
    6:682
dead, prayers for, 4:556
democracy, 13:259

Denifle, Heinrich Seuse, 4:660
Discalced Carmelites, 3:145
Divine indwelling, 7:442
Eastern Catholic Churches, 3:817
ecclesiastical learning, 13:911–912
economic democracy, 4:643
encyclical errors condemned by
    Baltimore Council (1884), 2:46
encyclicals relating to political and
    social matters, 10:184
eucharistic congresses, 5:433
exemption of congregations, 5:530,
    12:100
existence of God, 6:287
Ferrata, Domenico, 5:693–694
historical studies, importance of,
    14:421
Holy Spirit, 4:792, 6:294, 7:46
Holy Year, 7:57
human rights, 5:205–206, 855,
    10:184, 850, 12:136–137, 667
Index of Prohibited Books, 7:391
influence of Aquinas on Council of
    Trent, 14:23
intercredal cooperation as form of
    sycnretism, 10:162
Italo-Albanian Church, 7:651
justice, 4:236
Knights of Malta, 8:194
Kulturkampf, 8:255
leading a Christian life, 13:838–839
Leonine prayers, 8:500
liberalism, 6:793
Louvain, Catholic University of,
    8:823
marriage, 1:631, 14:825
Melkite Catholic Church, 1:526
mission and evangelization, 9:681
mystery of dogma of the Trinity,
    10:84
natural and positive rules of law,
    10:187
natural law, 10:184
Neoscholasticism, 3:624
North American College (Rome),
    establishment of, 10:433
Opera dei Congressi suppressed,
    10:69
Our Lady of Good Counsel, 10:723
papacy under, 10:847
papal social thought, 13:257,
    259–260
Philippine hierarchy, 11:258
Pontifical Biblical Commission,
    11:476
providence of God, 11:784

Leo XIII (Pope) *(continued)*
  Raillement policy, 5:855, 11:900, 12:573, 667
  Rampolla del Tindaro, Marino, 11:904
  religious liberalism, 8:542
  Roman Catechism, 3:234
  Roman-Orthodox reunion, 6:459
  Russian repression of Poland, 11:446
  Sacred Heart, devotion to, 12:491, 492, 493
  St. Thomas Christians, 7:400
  scholastic philosophy, 9:684–685
  scholasticism, 5:712, 10:244, 440, 12:774, 14:23
  Sisters of the Blessed Sacrament, 2:437
  social issues, 2:429, 3:342, 420, 620, 643
  social justice, 5:205–206, 855, 12:136–137
  social thought, 13:257, 258
  society, church as, 13:286
  sovereignty, 13:371
  speculative theology, 4:813
  spiritual motherhood of Mary, Blessed Virgin, 9:264
  study of Holy Scripture, 11:874
  Thomism, 1:147, 592, 678–679, 2:395, 854, 3:624, 4:853
  unity of the Church, 12:700
  University of Bologna, 2:475
  Vatican Archives opened to researchers, 6:878, 14:399, 421
  workers' rights, 13:259, 261, 14:824
Leo Diaconus, 2:799
Leo Ebreo Spinoza, 13:418
Leo Luke, St., **8:493–495**
Leo Marsicanus, 1:463, **8:494**
Leo of Assisi, 4:136, 5:897, **8:494**
Leo of Cava. *See* Leo I (the Great) (Pope), St.
Leo of Chalcedon, 2:759, 825
Leo of Ochrida, 2:824
Leo of St. John, **8:495**
Leo of Vercelli (Bp.), 7:660, 661, **8:495**, 9:450
Leo Thaumaturgus, St. (Bp. of Catania, Sicily), **8:495**
Leo the Isaurian, 13:103
Leo the Mathematician, 2:773
Leo the Philosopher, 2:822
Leobard (Liberd) of Tours, 8:495–496
Leobard, SS., **8:495–496**
Leobard of Maursmúnster, 8:496
Leobin of Chartres, St., 3:441, **8:496**

Leodegar of Autun (Bp.), St., 1:926, **8:496–497**, *497*
Leofric (Bp. of Exeter), 5:530
Leofric of Mercia, 3:469
Leola, Mary (Mother), 5:879
Leon, Jean, 1:92
León, Luis de, 2:115, **8:497–498**
  Antolínez, Agustín, 1:532
  Augustinian Recollects, 1:873
  Augustinianism, 1:883, 889
  Reusch, Franz Heinrich, 12:182
  scholasticism, 12:764
León, Martín de, 3:246
Leon, Moses ben Shemtob de, 14:932
León Cathedral (Spain), 3:696
León de Saint-Jean, 3:137
Léonard, André-Jean, 7:528
Leonard, Vincent M. (Bp. of Pittsburgh), 11:367
The Leonard and Feeney Omnibus (Feeney), 5:663
Leonard of Gaffoni, 1:265
Leonard of Noblat, St., 12:557–558
Leonard of Port Maurice, St., 1:414, **8:498**
Leonardi, John, St., 3:803–804, **8:498–499**
Leonardini. *See* Clerks Regular of the Mother of God
Leonardo da Vinci
  anatomy, 12:817
  architecture, 3:701
  Bible cycles, 2:375
  biology, 2:401
  empiricism, 5:197
Leone, Alejandro (Father), 3:857
Leonides (father of Origen), 3:594
Leonides, St., **8:499**
Léonin, **8:499**, 684
Leonine Commission, **8:499–500**, *500*
Leonine prayers, **8:500**, 12:482
Leonine Sacramentary, **8:500–502**
  altars, 1:315
  Christmas cycle, 3:555, 556
  concentration of bishop prayer, 10:636
  Leo I (Pope), St. origins, 8:478
  Libelli Missarum, 8:531–532
  liturgical books, 8:639
Leonius, Bl., **8:502**
Leontius of Antioch, 1:527
Leontius of Byzantium, 1:560, 2:793, 820, 7:264, 8:102, **502**
Leontius of Fréjus, St., **8:502–503**
Leontius of Jerusalem, **8:503**

Leontopolis, Temple of (Egypt), 13:811
Leopold (Bp. of Passau), 1:912
Leopold, Fr., 3:130
Leopold I (Emperor of Austria), 7:216
Leopold I (Holy Roman Emperor), 1:262
Leopold II (Holy Roman Emperor), 3:92, 615, 640, 4:483
Leopold III (King of Belgium), 2:219
Leopold III of Austria, St., 1:910, 8:188, **503**
Leopold of Gaiche, Bl., **8:503–504**
Leopold Wilhelm (Bp. of Passau), 1:912
The Leopoldine Foundation and the Catholic Church in the United States (Roemer), 12:283
Leopoldine Society. *See* Leopoldinen Stiftung
Leopoldinen Stiftung, **8:504**, 10:222
Leovigild (Visigothic king of Spain), 6:786
Leovigildus, 9:446
Lepanto, Battle of (1571), 3:856, 8:193, **504–506**, *505*, 11:374
Lépicier, Alexis (Card.), 1:415, **8:506–507**, 12:765
Lepidi, Alberto, 1:356, **8:507**, 12:777
Lepidus, Marcus Aemilius (Roman Emperor), 12:301
Lepodius, (Bp.), 8:*53*
LePorte, Maurice, 3:192–193
Leprosy, 4:248–249, 6:670, 7:120–121, **8:507–510**, *508*, 11:832
LeProust, Pierre, 12:587
Leray, Francis Xavier (Bp. of New Orleans), 1:270
Lercaro, Giacomo (Card.), 2:676, 3:712
Lercher, Ludwig, **8:511**
Lérins Abbey (St. Honoratus Island), 8:502, *511*, **511–512**
Leroquais, Victor Martial, **8:512**
Leroux, Pierre, 2:640
Les Dunes Abbey (Belgium), 7:304, **8:513**
Lesbians. *See* Homosexuality
Leseur, Élisabeth, **8:514–515**
Lesotho, **8:515–516**, *516*
Lessard, Raymond W. (Bp. of Savannah), 12:710
Lesser, G., 3:674
Lesser Antilles, 3:108
  See also Caribbean
Lesser Brothers (*fratres minores*). *See* Franciscans, First Order
Lessing, Gotthold Ephraim, 5:263, 520, 532, **8:516–518**, *517*
  deism, 4:617

Faust legend, 5:650

Febronianism, 5:658

orthodoxy, attack, 8:891

Reimarus, Hermann Samuel, 12:35

Lessius, Leonard, 1:311, 4:71, 5:852, 7:782, **8:518**, 12:766

Lessons in Logic (Turner), 14:246

Lestonnac, Jeanne de, St., 4:41, **8:518–519**

Lestrange, Augustin de, 8:372

Letailleur, Jean, 1:396

Letter 211 (St. Augustine), 3:68

Letter Against Werner (Copernicus), 4:250

Letter of Aristeas, **1:665–666**, 10:965

Letter on Astrology (Maimonides), 9:52–53

Letter on the Magnet (Peter of Maricourt), 12:813

Letter on the Mixed Life (Hilton), 6:835

A Letter to a Professor of Anthropology (Tyrrell as anonymous), 9:754, 14:258

Letter to All the Faithful (St. Francis of Assisi), 5:909

Letter to Diognetus, 3:402, 592–593

Letter to Flora (Ptolemy), 5:509

Letter to Foscarini (Bellarmine), 6:61

Letter to Herodutus on Physics (Epicurus), 5:283

Letter to Maris (Ibas of Edessa), 4:191, 192, 5:83, 14:64

Letter to Mill (Bentley), 2:287

Letter to Paula (Jerome), 10:654

Letter to the Duke of Norfolk (Newman), 10:334

A Letter to the Grand Duchess Christina (Galileo), 6:61

Letter to the Philippians (St. Polycarp), 11:464–465

Lettera ad un religioso amico ove si tratta del modo di predicare (St. Alphonsus Liguori), 1:308–309

Lettera sopa l'opinione de' Pittagorici, e del Copernico della mobilitá della terra . . . (Foscarini), 5:825

Lettere diplomatiche di Guide Bentivoglio (Bentivoglio), 2:286

Letters (Hadewijch), 6:605

Letters (Pliny the Younger), 11:421

Letters (St. Gregory I), 6:483

Letters and Poems (Eugenius Vulgarius), 5:447

Letters and Social Aims (Emerson), 5:188

Letters of Mani (Mānī), 9:113

Letters on Sunspots (Galileo), 6:60–61

Letters to Agnes of Prague (St. Clare of Assisi), 5:898

Lettioni sopra dogmi dette calviniche (Panigarola sermon), 10:822

Lettra spirituale (Montursius), 13:28

Lettre à l'auteur de l'article jésuite dans le Dictionnaire Encyclopédique (Muriel), 10:66

Lettre aux Espangnols-Américains (Vizcardó), 14:576

Lettres de M. Cornelius Jansenius (Gerberon), 6:164

Lettres diverses (Litta), 8:609

Lettres d'un royaliste savoisien (Maistre), 9:60–61

Lettres édifiantes et curieuses (Halde), 10:903

Lettres édificantes, 8:455

Leu. *See* Lupus, St.

Leubus Abbey (Poland), **8:520**

Leuchteldis. *See* Lüfthildis, St.

Leucippus, 1:832, 4:217, 9:318, 12:803

Leufroy, St. *See* Leutfred, St.

Leuren, Peter, **8:520**

Leutfred, St., **8:520**

Levada, William Joseph (Abp. of Portland, OR), 2:871, 3:237, 11:531

Levadoux, Michael, **8:521**

Levasseur, Nicholas, 2:901

Levate (Rise), 10:651

Levellers (Puritan sect), 11:838

Lever, Ralph, 1:676

Leverrier, Urbain, 5:581

Leveson, Francis, Ven., 5:237

Lévesque, Georges-Henri, 3:10

Levi (biblical figure), 8:523

Levi ben Gerson, 7:864–865, **8:521–522**, 13:418

Leviathan, 4:341, **8:522**, 13:19

Leviathan (Hobbes), 2:623, 4:18–19

Levina, Emmanuel, 5:830

Levine, B. A., 14:856, 857

Levinsohn, I. B., 6:663

Levirate marriage, in the Bible, **8:522**, 10:600

Lévi-Strauss, C., 12:87

Levita, Elias, 3:25

Levita, Elijah, 6:222

Levitation, **8:522–523**, 10:108

Levites, 7:364, **8:523–525**

Leviticus, Book of, **8:525**

adultery, 1:131, 13:50

bestiality, 13:49

commentaries, 12:548

Dead Sea Scrolls version of, 4:563

demons, 13:429

enmity, 5:264

glory, 6:244

grace of God, 9:87

guilt, 6:570

Holiness Code of, 7:4–5

homosexuality, 7:66, 13:49, 50

imposition of hands, 7:364

incest, 7:378

leprosy, 8:509, 510

magic, 9:39

Passover, 10:933, 935

peace, 11:49

Priestly Code, 8:397

pure and impure, 11:822

purification, 11:832

purification of Mary, 3:14

redemption, 11:963, 964

retaliation, 8:394

Sabbath Year, 12:461

sacrifice, 9:63

serpent as symbol, 13:20

seventy weeks of years, 13:40

showbread, 13:88

sin, 13:142, 144

sin offering, 13:159

slavery, 13:206, 207, 250, 251

social principle, 13:249

Levy, Marion J., 13:280

Lévy-Bruhl, L., 10:120

Lewes Priory (England), 3:481, **8:527**

Lewis, Agnes, 2:367

Lewis, Charles Baker, St. *See* Lewis, David (Charles Baker), St.

Lewis, Clive Staples, 1:292, 3:470, **8:527–528**, 12:717

Lewis, David (Charles Baker), St., 5:237, **8:528**

Lewis, Edwin, **8:528–529**

Lewis, Frank J., **8:529**

Lewis, John, 1:288, 2:41

Lewis, John (Father), 3:179

Lewis, S. N., 10:862

Lewoniuk, Wincenty, 11:583, 584

Lex Alamannorum, 3:41

Lex Baïwarorum, 3:41

Lex barbara Burgunionum, 3:41

Lex barbara Visigothroum, 3:41

Lex Credendi (Bourdon), 14:258

Lex dubia non obligat, 12:726

Lex ecclesiae fundamentalis (LEF), 3:34, 36

Lex Francorum Chamavorum, 3:41

Lex Naturae zur Theologie des Naturrechts (Fuchs), 10:193

Lex Orandi (Bourdon), 14:258

Lex propria, 1:11

Lex Ripuaria, 3:41

Lex romana. See Roman law

Lex romana Burgundionum, 3:40

Lex romana Curiensis, 3:40

Lex romana Visigothorum, 3:40

Lex Salica, 3:41

Lex Saxorum, 3:41

Lex Thuringorum, 3:41

Lex Unciaria (88 B.C.), 14:353

Lexicon philosophicum (Göckel), 10:606

Lexikon der christlichen Ikonographie, 5:207

Lexikon der Pädagogik, 5:207

Lexikon für Theologie und Kirche, 5:207, 208

Lexington Diocese (KY), **8:529**

Lexinton, Stephen de, 3:758, **8:529–530**

Leyburn, John, 5:249

Leyden, University of, 3:184

Leymarie de Laroche, Élie, 12:277

Lezana, Juan Bautista de, 3:143, **8:530**

Lezcano, Juan Gabriel de, 1:648

LFM. *See* Lectionary for Mass

LHC. *See* Lovers of the Holy Cross

L'Hôpital, Michel de, 1:787, 3:266, 7:167, **8:530–531**

L'Huillier de Villeneuve, Marie, 4:534

Li livres dou trésor (Latini), 5:206

Li Zhizao (Li Chih-tsao), 3:494

Liang Fa, 3:499

Liar Paradox, 1:519–520

Libanius (rhetorician), 2:767

Libellatici, 4:590, **8:531**

Libelli, 8:639

Libelli duo de consuetudinibus et statutis monasterii Floriacensis (Thierry of Fleury), 14:3

Libelli Missarum, 8:500, 501, **531–532**

Libellus Coloniensis (prayer book), 11:603

Libellus contra capitula Gilberti Pictaviensis (Geoffrey of Clairvaux), 6:141

Libellus de dignitate conditionis humanae, 3:13

Libellus de formatione arche (Hugh of Saint-Victor), 7:158

Libellus de suis temptationibus, varia fortuna et scriptis (Othlo), 10:709

Libellus fidei (Bachiarius), 2:8

Libellus manualis (Othlo), 10:709

Libellus Parisinus (prayer book), 11:603

Libellus Sacrosyllabus (St. Paulinus of Aquileia), 11:38

Libellus Trecensis (prayer book), 11:603

Liber Abaci (Leonard of Pisa), 10:749

Liber adv. Origenem (*Letter to Mennas*) (Pelagius), 10:660

Liber apologeticus (Claudius), 9:444

Liber apologeticus (Gerard of Abbeville), 6:160

Liber apologeticus (Orosius), 10:673

Liber auctoritatum, 3:40

Liber benedictionum (Ekkehard IV of St. Gall), 5:142, 9:449

Liber calculationum (Richard of Swyneshed), 12:236

Liber censuum, 2:548, 3:319, **8:532**

Liber congestorum de arte praedicandi (Reuchlin), 11:620

Liber contra Mocianum (Facundus of Hermiane), 5:587

Liber contra multiplices et varios errores (Vacarius), 14:365

Liber creaturarum (*Theologia naturalis*) (Raymond of Sabunde), 11:937

Liber de antichristo et eius ministris (William of Saint-Amour), 14:16

Liber de apibus (Book of the Bees) (Thomas of Cantimpré), 14:32, 33

Liber de arte contrapuncti (Tinctoris), 14:87

Liber de causis (Aquinas), 1:226, **8:532–534**, 12:1, 14:26

Liber de civitatis Florentiae famosis civibus (Villani), 12:110

Liber de corpore et sanguine Domini (Lanfranc), 8:323

Liber de diligendo Deo (Bernard of Clairvaux), 2:310

Liber de duobus principiis, 3:260

Liber de honore ecclesiae (Placidus), 10:416

Liber de imaginibus (Claudius of Turin), 3:769–770

Liber de laude novae militiae (St. Bernard of Clairvaux), 3:519, 9:625

Liber de ludo arithomachia (Shirwood), 13:88

Liber de misericordia et de justitia (Alger of Liège), 3:45, 47, 60

Liber de moralizationibus (Robert Holcot), 12:265

Liber de natura et proprietate tonorum (Tinctoris), 14:87

Liber de oblatione puerorum (Rabanus Maurus), 10:512

Liber de occultis mysteriis domus Dei (Stephen Bar-Sūdhailē), 13:522

Liber de originali Virginis innocentia (Peter Thomae), 11:208

Liber de ortu beatae Mariae et infantia Salvatoris (Matthew, St.), 9:353

Liber de predestinatione (Scotus), 9:445

Liber de restauratione (Heriman), 12:565

Liber de sacramento baptismi (Leidradus of Lyons), 8:459

Liber de vera et falsa poenitentia, 8:411

Liber de vita christiana (Bonizo of Sutri), 3:45, 60, 518–519

Liber decem capitulorum (Marbod), 9:450

Liber derivationum (Huguccio), 7:164

Liber derivationum (*Panormia*) (Osbern of Gloucester), 10:704

Liber discipli de eruditione Christi fidelium (Herolt), 3:241

Liber diurnus romanorum pontificum, 3:41, 45, 4:757, **8:534–535**, 9:439, 12:577

Liber ecclesiasticorum dogmatum (Gennadius of Marseilles), 6:137

Liber epilogorum (Bartholomew of Trent), 2:127

Liber exceptionum (Richard of Saint-Victor), 12:235

Liber extra. See Decretales (Canon Law collection)

Liber facetiarum (Poggio Bracciolini), 11:435

Liber floridus (Lambert of Saint-Omer), 5:206, 8:304

Liber Gomorrhianus (Peter Damian), 3:326

Liber hymnorum (Notker), 7:242, 10:455, 13:2

Liber in partibus Donāti (Smaragdus), 13:228

Liber introductorius in evangelium eternum (de Borgo Dan Donnino), 10:554

Liber iudicum (Spain), 13:379

Liber Jesu Christi pro simplicibus, 3:241

Liber Landavensis, 8:739

Liber lapidum (Marbod), 9:450

Liber manualis (Dodena), 3:230

Liber manualis (prayer book), 11:604

Liber miraculorum, 12:548

Liber missarum, 10:44

Liber misticus, 10:44

Liber natalis pueri parvuli Jesu Christi (Lull), 9:461

Liber offerentium, 10:44

Liber officialis (Amalarius of Metz), 1:329, 14:131

Liber ordinum episcopal, 10:42, 44

Liber pauperum (Vacarius), 14:365

Liber poenitentialis (Robert of Flamborough), 12:267

Liber pontificalis (LP), 5:186, 451, 461, 8:*535*, **535**
  cardinalate, 3:103, 104, 105
  chronicles, 1:461
  Constantine (Pope), 4:177
  earliest version, 8:553
  Eleutherius (Pope), St., 5:148
  Evaristus (Pope), St., 5:482
  Fabian (Pope), 5:584
  Felix I (Pope), St., 5:666
  Felix II (Antipope), 5:667
  finding of the cross, 4:384
  Lombard history, 8:768
  Lucius, St., 8:845
  Lucius I (Pope), 8:846
  Paschal I (Pope), 3:411
  references to struggles between monks and clergy, 10:581
  Simplicius (Pope), St., 13:140
Liber pontificalis ecclesiae Ravennatis (Agnellus), 14:344
Liber primus missarum (Lobe, A.), 8:742
Liber promissionum et praedictorum Dei (St. Quodvultdeus), 11:874
Liber regulae pastoralis (Gregory the Great), 3:229, 597, 11:611
Liber s. Jacobi in Santiago de Compostela (Turpin), 14:248
Liber sacramentorum (Schuster), 12:481, 790
Liber sacredotalis (Alberto Castellani), 1:486, 12:258, 14:470
Liber sententiarum. See *Book of Sentences* (Peter Lombard)
Liber sextus (Boniface VIII), 1:219, 3:46, 48, 800, 4:603–604, **8:536**
Liber specialis gratiae (Mechtild of Hackeborn), 9:422
Liber Tarraconensis, 3:60
Liber 24 philosophorum (Alexander of Hales), 1:266
Liber usualis, 8:704
Liber viarum Dei (Elizabeth of Schönau), 5:166
Liber visionum (Othlo), 10:709
Liber vitae (the *Verbrüderungsbuch*), 12:671
Liberal arts, **8:536–539**
  Boethius on, 2:456
  cathedral and episcopal schools, 3:262
  Hugh of Saint-Victor, 7:157
  palace school education in the, 10:763
  philosophy of, 1:746
  scholastic education, 5:95–96

University of Paris curriculum based, 10:887
Liberal Catholic Church, 8:134, 308–309, 539–540, 13:256
Liberal Catholic Church International, **8:539–540**
Liberal Catholics, 3:641–642
Liberal feminism, 5:672
Liberal Party (Belgium), 2:219
Liberal theology, 2:120, 6:393, 8:891–892
Liberalism
  Anglo-Catholics, 1:446, 447
  Austria, 1:914
  Billot, Louis, 2:395
  Broad Church, 2:624
  Church-State relations, 1:914, 3:618–619, 640–643
  Donoso Cortés, Juan, 4:869–870
  economic, 13:232
  Hungary, 7:216
  individualism, 13:255
  overview, 3:618–619
  social justice issues, 3:620
  subsidiarity, 13:567
Liberalism, German, 8:253
Liberalism, opposition to
  Ketteler, 8:160
  La Tour de Pin, 8:371
  Lambruschini, L., 8:307
  Leo XII (Pope), 8:490, 492
  Leo XIII (Pope), 8:557
  Roman censure of *L'Avenir*, 8:309
Liberalism, religious, **8:540–542**
Liberalism, theological, 8:528–529, **542–543**, 12:739–740
Liberalism and conservatism, theology and, 4:163
Der Liberalismus in Theologie und Geschichte (Schroeder), 12:787
Liberality, virtue of, 8:544
Liberation theology, **8:544–546**
  Argentina, 1:655
  Brazil, 2:598
  Colombia, 3:852
  de-privatizing Christian message, 13:245
  ecclesiology, 5:38
  Gutiérrez, Gustavo, 9:688, 11:166
  Land, P., 8:317
  Luke-Acts, 8:862
  Maryknoll Fathers and Brothers, 9:297, 12:729
  Mexico, 9:574
  political theology, 11:461

Poverty Movement, 11:573
praxis, 11:584–585, 586–588
revisionist theology, 12:203–204
sacraments, 12:477–478
self-transcendence model of charity, 8:833
theology of Christ, 7:838–839
Vatican Council II, 4:820
Liberation theology, Latin America, 4:157–158, 8:175, **546–550**, 13:245
Liberatore, Matteo, 7:673, **8:550**, 12:772
Liberatus of Carthage, **8:550–551**
Liberia, **8:551–553**, *552*
Liberian Basilica (St. Mary Major), 3:555, 13:196
Liberian Catalogue, 5:482, **8:553**
Liberian Council of Churches, **8:553**
Liberius (Pope), **8:553–556**, *554*, *555*
  Arianism, 1:662, 818, 3:594, 632
  exile of, 4:197, 504
  homoousios, 7:65
Libermann, François Marie Paul, Ven., 7:25, 8:384, **556**
Libert as praestantissimum (encyclical, Leo XIII), 11:784
Libertas (encyclical, Leo XIII), 3:642, **8:556–557**, 10:184, 13:258
Les Libertés de l'Église gallicane prouvées et commentées suivant l'ordre et la disposition des articles dressés par M. Pierre Pithou (Durand de Maillane), 6:76, 11:365
Libertinism. See Freethinkers
Liberty of a Christian Man (Luther), 8:881
Liberty of Prophesying (Taylor, Jeremy), 13:770
Libor epistolaris (Richard of Bury), 12:231
Libre del orde de cauayleria (Lull), 3:519
Les Libres penseurs (Veuillot), 14:465
Libreville (Gabon) Vicariate, 6:39
Libri III adversus simoniacos (Humbert of Silva Candida), 3:635
Libri IV Sententiarum (Peter Lombard), 9:455
Libri V apologetici pro religione, utraque theologia, moribus ac juribus Ord. Praed. (Baron), 2:105
Libri VII ad Heinricum IV (Benzo of Alba), 2:288
Libri carolini, **8:557**, 9:444
  Adrian I (Pope), 1:123, 432
  Alcuin, Bl., 1:243
  Angilbert of Saint-Riquier, St., 1:432
  Charlemagne, 3:425

Libri carolini(continued)
 Charlemagne's commssion of,
  10:349, 350
 iconoclasm, 2:821, 3:156
*Libri duo de synodalibus causis et
 disciplinis ecclesiasticis* (Regino of
 Prüm), 3:44, 60, 12:30
Libri epigrammaton, 9:439
*Libri Feudorum (Books concerning
 Fiefs),* 5:702
Libri Sententiarum (Peter Lombard),
 14:329
Libri tres adversus simoniacos (Humbert
 of Silva Candida), 12:128
*Libro de las tres vidas del hombre
 corporal, racional y espiritual*
 (Fuente), 6:19
*El Libro del conorte (The Book of
 Consolation)* (Juana de la Cruz),
 7:1061
*Il Libro del Cortegiano (Book of the
 Courtier)* (Castiglione), 3:215–216
Libro siro-romano (Ferrini), 5:696
Los Libros del alma (Vera Cruz), 14:444
Liburinus (Gunther of Pairis), 6:584
Libya, **8:558–560,** *559*
Liccio, John, Bl., **8:560**
Licet de vitanda discordia (apostolic
 constitution, Alexander III), 3:105,
 11:499
Licet debitum (apostolic constitution,
 Paul III), 5:530
Licet ecclesiae catholicae (papal bull,
 Alexander IV), 1:886
Licet Heli (papal decree, Innocent III),
 7:485
Licet juris (Law, 1338), 2:244
Licheto, Francesco, 12:764
Li-Cheu. *See* Wang Li, Mary, St.
Lichfield Cathedral (England), 4:330
Lichtenberg, Bernhard, Bl., **8:560–561**
Lichtenberg, Georg Christoph, 5:263
Lichtenberger, Arthur, 5:74
Licinius (Bp. of Angers), St., 1:431,
 8:561, 9:625
Licinius (Roman Emperor), 4:180–181,
 749
Lidanus, St., **8:561**
Lidgett, John Scott, **8:561–562**
Lieber, Ernst, 3:340–341
Liebmann, Otto, 10:236–237, 12:731
Liechtenstein, 8:*562,* **562–563**
Liège (France), **8:563–564**
Liem de la Paz, Vicente, 14:496
Liénart, Achille (Card.), 5:859, 8:13, **564**
Lienhardt, Godfrey, 12:65
Liesborn Abbey (Germany), **8:564**

Liessies Abbey (France), **8:564–565**
Lietbert of Cambrai-Arras, St. (Bp. of
 Cambrai), **8:565**
Lietzmann, Hans, 3:552, **8:565,** 10:963
Lievens, Konstant, 2:219
Life (Peter of Monterubbiano), 10:378
Life, concept of
 contraception and value of,
  4:220–221, 222
 philosophies, 11:295–296
 Scholastics, 11:804
Life, concept of, in the Bible, **8:565–572**
 Divine judgment, 8:30
 living God, 8:572
 New Testament, 8:569–571
 Old Testament, 8:565–569
 soul, 13:335–336
Life, concept of, in theology, **8:572–573**
 Heaven, 8:573
 mechanism vs. vitalism, 13:335
 organicism theory, 10:652
 serpent as symbol, 13:21
Life, origin of, **8:573–577**
Life, purpose of, 7:697–698
Life after death, 5:57
 See also Afterlife
Life after Life (Moody), 13:853–854
Life and Advent Union, 1:135
*Life and Labors of Rt. Rev. Frederic
 Baraga* (Verwyst), 14:461
Life and Work Commission, 5:71
Life and Work Conference (Stockholm,
 1925), 5:72
Life and Work Movement, 5:72,
 8:577–578, 13:296, 14:841
Life as a dream motif, 2:116
Life beyond the grave. *See* Afterlife
The Life Divine (Ghose), 6:202, 852
Life of Alfred (Asser), 5:772
Life of Anthony the Hermit (St.
 Athanasius), 3:594, 9:787, 11:345
Life of Charlemagne (Einhard), 3:160,
 5:139, 9:443
Life of Christ (O'Connell), 10:542
The Life of Christ in Recent Research
 (Sanday), 12:665
Life of Constantine (Eusebius of
 Caesarea), 5:452, 453, 12:316, 318,
 320
The Life of Father Hecker (Elliott),
 5:169
*The Life of God, the Savior, from the
 Four Gospels* (Aleni), 1:250
*The Life of James Cardinal Gibbons
 Archbishop of Baltimore, 1834-1921*
 (Ellis), 5:170, 12:462

The Life of Jesus (Jésus-Christ)
 (Goguel), 7:850
Life of Jesus (La Vie de Jésus Christ)
 (Renan), 7:848, 852
Life of Jesus (Shusaku), 5:219
Life of Jesus (Strauss), 5:521
*The Life of Jesus Critically Examined
 (Das Leben Jesu kritisch bearbeitet)*
 (Strauss), 7:*848*
Life of Macrina (Gregory of Nyssa, St.),
 9:25
A Life of Mary, Co-Redemptrix (Resch),
 12:137
Life of Moses (Gregory of Nyssa), 5:343
Life of Peregrinus (Lucian), 10:800
Life of Petrarch (Vergerio), 14:448
*Life of Pope Martin I (Thierry of
 Fleury),* 14:*3*
Life of Reason (Santayana), 10:204
Life of St. Ann, Mother of Mary
 (Malagrida), 9:65–66
Life of St. Anthony the Hermit (St.
 Anthony of Egypt), 10:968
The Life of St. Clare (Robinson), 12:274
Life of St. Columba (Fleming), 5:760
Life of St. Eigil (Candidus of Fulda),
 3:13
The Life of Saint Francis (Thomas of
 Celano), 5:871, 898, 14:33
Life of Saint Lucy (Jacobello del Fiore),
 8:*850*
Life of St. Rictrude (Hucbald), 1:99
Life of St. Wilfrid of York (Frithegode),
 10:554
Life of Severus of Antioch (Zachary the
 Rhetor), 14:905
Life of Symeon the New Theologian
 (Nicetas Stethatos), 10:357
Life of the Blessed Virgin Mary
 (Brentano), 5:193
The Life of the Servant (Henry Suso),
 6:758
Life of Wulfstan (Coleman), 5:772
Life Philosophies, 8:578–580
Life Without Principle (Thoreau), 14:59,
 147
''Lifeboat ethics,'' 14:178
Life-communions. *See* Basic Christian
 communities
Lift Every Voice and Sing (hymnal),
 7:261
Liga Nacional Defensora de la Libertad
 Religiosa, 6:344
Ligarides, Paisy, 6:458
Light, liturgical use of, 1:318, 5:15,
 8:580–582, 13:472
Light, metaphysics of, 7:319, **8:583–584,**
 12:264

Light and darkness, 9:111–112,
13:819–820

Light of glory, 2:174–175, 4:336, 6:688,
8:572, **584–585**

Light of the East (periodical), 4:508

Light of the Lord (Crescas), 7:865

Light symbolism, 3:674

Lightfoot, John, 3:27, 5:518

Lightfoot, Joseph Barber, **8:585**

Lightfoot, Peter (monk of Glastonbury),
5:530

Lightfoot, R. H., 5:522

Lighthouse of International Foursquare
Evangelism (L.I.F.E.) Bible School,
5:835

Liguest, Pierre Laclède, 12:558

Ligugé Abbey (France), **8:585–586**

Ligutti, Luigi G., **8:586**

Lilienfeld Abbey (Austria), **8:586–587**,
587

Lill, Hansjakob, 3:712

Lilli of Cappadocia, Salvatore, 1:698

Lima, Alceu Amoroso, 5:717

Lima, Councils of (1567-81), 3:234, 246,
252, 485, 10:239

Lima, Manuel de Oliveira, **8:587–588**

Lima Text, 8:168, **588–590**

Lima Text on Baptism-Eucharist-
Ministry (BEM), 1:586

Limbo, 2:70, 8:*590*, **590–591**

Limbourg brothers, 11:605

Limburg staurotheke, 2:*730*, 735–736

Limburgsche Sermoenen (14th century
essays), 2:181

*Le Limes de Chalcis; organisation de la
Steppe en Haute-Syrie romaine*
(Poidebard), 11:436

Limitation, **8:591–592**

''Limit-situation,'' 7:747

Limoges, statutes of, 4:90

Limoges Abbey (France), 3:691

Limonite, alleged magical properties of,
11:646

Limpach, Bernard de, 12:558

Linacre, Thomas, 3:832, **8:592**, 12:119

Linckens, Hubert J., 9:734

Lincoln, Abraham, 3:755, 756, 5:144,
7:161, 13:*211*

Lincoln, Ancient See of (England),
8:592

Lincoln Agricultural School
(Lincolndale, NY), 9:395

Lincoln Cathedral (England), 3:601, 696,
7:154

Lincoln Diocese (NE), 10:223–224

Lind, James, 7:131

Lindau Convent (Germany), **8:592–593**

Lindbeck, George, 5:829

Lindblom, J., 5:520

Linderbauer, Bruno, 2:263

Lindisfarne Abbey (England), 1:449,
4:449, **8:593**, *594*

Lindisfarne Gospels, 5:239, **8:593–594**,
9:*127*, *129*

Lindores Abbey (Scotland), **8:594**

Lindsay, James, 1:21, 467

Line, Anne, St., 5:233, 718, **8:594–595**

The Line of Popes woodcut (Koberger),
10:*833*

Linforth, I. M., 10:95

Lingard, John, 3:243, 5:251, 572,
8:595–596

Linguistic analysis, 1:373–374, 3:352

Linguistic philosophy, 11:300

Linguistics, 9:555, 13:551–552,
14:804–805

Linji Yixuan, 3:511

Link, Wenzeslaus, 3:327

Linnaeus, Carolus, 2:402, 5:260, *260*,
493

Linton, Bernard de, 1:630

Linton, Moses L., 12:562

Linton, Ralph, 4:427, 428, 430

Linus, St. Pope, **8:596**

Lioba, St., **8:596–597**

Lion, John, Ven., 5:233

Lipchitz, J., 1:803, 3:713

Lippershey, Hans, 6:60

Lippert, G., 3:712

Lippert, J., 5:520

Lippi, Filippino, 1:475, 2:375, 3:96, 142

Lippomano, Luigi (Bp. of Verona),
6:614

Lipscomb, Oscar H. (Abp. of Mobile,
AL), 1:202, 9:749–750

Lipsiensis, 3:47

Lipsius, Justus, 5:394, 12:125

Lipsius, Richard Adelbert, 7:16, **8:597**

Liptak, Dolores (Sister), 4:125

Lire, Louis de, 3:142

Lisboa, Cristóvão de, 2:590, 591, **8:597**

Li-Shih. *See* Wang Li, Mary, St.

Lisieux Basilica, 3:710

Lismore Abbey (Ireland), **8:597–598**

Lissner, Ignatius (Father), 1:158, 162,
5:878, 12:710

Listening, 2:265

Liszt, Franz, 8:*598*, **598–599**

Brahms, Johannes, 2:580

Chopin, Frédéric, 3:525

sonata on Francis of Paola, St., 5:874

Litany, **8:599–602**

current images, 8:601–602

definition, 8:599

devotional, 8:601

Eastern liturgies, 8:599–600

Major Litany, 12:283

Minor Litany, 12:283

origin, 8:599

popularity, 8:602

Roman Rite, 12:328

of the saints, 8:601

Western litanies, 8:600–601

Litany of Loreto, **8:602–603**

Litany of the Saints, 10:856

Literae, as form, 4:757

Literalism, 4:776

Literary criticism, 7:185, 8:906, 11:92

Literary forms, biblical exegesis and,
4:791

Literary language, 2:116

Literary Sources of the Gothic (Frankl),
3:676

Literary theory, 2:115

Literature

baroque period, 2:115–116

Catholic revival, 4:313

cursus prose rhythm, 4:444–445

deconstructionism, 4:593–594

dialogue as genre of, 4:728

Greek language and Christian
literature, 6:439

history of Christian literature, 6:880

influence of sermons, 11:634–635

inquisition's influence, 7:491

popular, 8:527–528

profanity in, 11:739

Puritan influence, 11:840

spiritual elevations, 13:455

transcendental principle of,
4:373–374

See also Drama; Poetry; Prose;
specific authors

Lith, Francis van, 7:429

Lithuania, **8:603–609**, *605*, *606*, 12:421

Casimir, St., 3:203–204

conversion to Christianity, 7:696

Crusades, 4:414

demographic statistics, 8:603

ecclesiastical organization, 8:606–607

Lancicius, 8:317

map, 8:*604*

mission, 8:275

*Lithuanian Benefit Society of St.
Anthony, Dockhus v.* (1903), 3:658

Litta, Alfonso and Lorenzo, **8:609**

Littera inintelligibilis (Aquinas), 14:14

Litterae Decretales. See Decretals

Litteris altero (papal brief, Pius VIII), 11:382

Little, A., 12:776

Little, Andrew George, 8:609–610

Little, Robert Wentworth, 12:382

Little and Great Rules for cenobitic life. *See* Asceticon (St. Basil)

The Little Book of Enlightenment (Rutherford), 12:439, 441

Little Book of Eternal Wisdom (Henry Suso), 6:758

Little Book of Truth (Henry Suso), 6:757–758

Little Brothers and Little Sisters of Jesus, 11:573

Little Brothers of Jesus (LBJ), 5:826, **8:610**

Little Brothers of Mary. *See* Marist Brothers

Little Brothers of the Good Shepherd, 12:677

Little Church of Utrecht (OBC), 10:579

Little Company of Mary (LCM), 7:1, **8:610**, 11:560

"Little Constitution" (Poland), 11:455

Little Daughters of Saint Joseph, 2:28

Little Doxology, 4:890

Little Flock, 3:501

"The Little Flower of Lebanon." *See* Rafqa de Himlaya, St.

The Little Flowers of St. Francis. See Fioretti

Little Hours, **8:610–611**

Little House of Divine Providence (Turin, Italy), 3:419

"Little Jerusalem," 13:500

The Little Method, 11:621–622

Little Missionary Sisters of Charity (LMSC), 3:419, **8:611**, 10:672, 13:321

Little Office of the BVM, 4:710, **8:611**, 658

Little Rock Diocese (AR), **8:612–615**

Little St. John (Murillo), 10:66

Little Sisters of Jesus, 1:209, 5:826, **8:616**

Little Sisters of the Assumption, 1:802, **8:616**

Little Sisters of the Holy Family, **8:616**, 10:154, 155

Little Sisters of the Poor, 3:622, **8:616–617**, 10:293

  founding of, 8:47

  Los Angeles, 8:791

  Louisiana, 8:812

Massachusetts, 2:555

  Savannah (GA), 12:710

Little Sisters of the Poor and Aged, 3:419, 7:1033–1034

Little Walsingham Priory (Norfolk, England), 14:*621*

Little Work of Divine Providence, 10:672, 13:321

Littledale, Richard F., 3:259

Liturgia Horarum, 8:731–732

Liturgiarum orientalium collectio (Renaudot), 12:126

Liturgica Mozarabica (St. Isidore of Seville), 7:603

Liturgical acclamations, **8:617–618**

Liturgical art, 4:758–759

  See also Art; Church architecture

Liturgical art, history of, **8:618–638**

  Christian art, 8:618, 620

  definition, 8:618, 620

  function, 8:620

  legislation before Vatican Council II, 8:620–622

  renewal societies, 8:625

  Siena, 13:109

  Sistine Chapel, 13:190

  twentieth-century liturgical renewal, 8:622–624

Liturgical Arts Quarterly, 8:386

Liturgical Arts Society, 3:716, 8:386, 624, **638**, 675

Liturgical books of the Roman Rite, **8:638–641**

  books issued by Council of Trent, 12:328

  Evangelary (Book of Gospels), 5:466–467

  functions, 8:712

  Gelasian sacramentary, 12:482–483

  Gregorian sacramentary, 12:482–483

  Leonine Sacramentary, 12:482

  Liber Mozarabicus sacramentorum, 12:483

  Liber Sacramentorum, 12:481–482

  liturgics compared, 8:723

  Mass formulary, 12:482

  Middle Ages, 8:657–658

  Missale Gallicanum Vetus, 12:483

  Missale Gothicum, 12:483

  Missale Romanum, 12:484

  origins, 8:712

  Pontificale, 12:483

  reform at Trent, 8:662

  reform of, 4:165

  Ritual (*Rituale Romanum*), 12:258, 483

Sacramentaries

  contemporary, 12:483–484

  historical, 12:481–483

  Sacramentarium Bergomense, 12:483

  Sacrosanctum Concilium, 12:484

Liturgical calendar, Catholic, **8:641–643**

  computus, 4:46

  Ember Days, 5:186–187

  liturgical history, 8:655–656, 662

  liturgical year in Roman Rite, 8:716–722

  Palm Sunday, 10:810–811

  sanctoral cycle, 12:661–664

Liturgical calendar, Ecumenical, **8:643–644**

Liturgical calendar, Israelite, 12:512

Liturgical catechesis, 8:442, **644–645**

Liturgical colors, 8:634, **645–646**

Liturgical conference, 5:168, 8:625, **646**, 675

The Liturgical Dictionary of Eastern Christianity, 5:208

Liturgical drama, 4:893–896

Liturgical feasts. *See* Feasts

Liturgical gestures, **8:644–650**

Liturgical history, 8:512, 531–532, **650–666**

Liturgical languages, 8:364–365, **666–669**

Liturgical laws, authority of, **8:669–670**

Liturgical Movement, Anglican and Protestant, **8:677–678**

Liturgical Movement, Catholic, **8:670–677**

  Affligem Abbey, 1:152

  Americas, 8:674–676

  art and architecture, 8:386, 624, 626–628

  art renewal societies, 8:625

  Attwater, Donald, 1:844

  Austria, 8:673

  Beauduin, Lambert, 2:183

  Belgium, 8:672–673

  Capelle, Bernard, 3:82

  church architecture, 3:710, 711, 712, 716, 717

  Diekmann, Godfrey, 4:740

  France, 5:857, 8:671

  Germany, 8:671–672, 12:785

  Guéranger, Prosper, 3:623

  homily, 7:63

  Hovda, Robert W., 7:141

  laity, 8:290

  music reexamined, 8:699

  spirituality, 13:448

Vatican, 8:676
Liturgical Movement, Ecumenical convergences, **8:678–680**
Liturgical music
  antiphons, 1:297–298, 529, 929–930
  baroque period, 2:112
  cantors, 3:73, 75–76, 522
  gospel songs, 6:368, 7:257, 8:694–695
  Sarum Use, 1:446, 2:524, 8:682, 12:697–698, 14:895
  spirituals, 13:456–457
  See also Chant; Hymnology; Hymns and hymnals; *specific chants*; *specific musical pieces*
Liturgical music, history of, **8:680–702**
  Catholic revival, 4:313
  classical style, 8:692–693
  Cranmer's reform, 8:660
  early Christian music, 8:680–681
  litanic forms, contemporary, 8:602
  liturgical acclamations, 8:617–618
  monophonic music to 1200, 8:681–683
  opera, 8:471
  polyphonic music, 1450-1600, 8:686–689
  polyphonic music to 1450, 8:683–686
  post-Romanticism, 8:695–696
  pre-Vatican II legislation, 8:699–701
  Renaissance motets, 8:342
  Romanticism and aftermath, 8:693–695
  Sequence, 13:1–5
  Sermisy, C., 13:18
  trope, 14:214–217
  United States, 8:696–699
  use of organ, 10:651–652
  Vatican Council II, 8:701–702
  See also Chant; Hymnology; Hymns and hymnals
Liturgical music, theology and practice of, **8:702–711**
  development of motet, 10:11–13
  Lamb of God, 8:302
  Liturgy of the Hours, 8:734–735
  Mozarabic Chant, 10:41–42
  O antiphons, 10:489–490
  Universa Laus study group, 14:320–321
Liturgical Music Today (1982), 8:702, 708–709
Liturgical prayer, 1:309, 11:600
Liturgical press, 12:552, 553
Liturgical processions, 11:732

Liturgical reform
  Consilium, 4:164–165
  Cummins, Patrick, 4:437
  Jungmann, J. A., 8:61–63
    works by, 8:62
  liturgical conference, 8:646
  Löw, J., 8:836
  resource materials for, 8:646
  Vatican II
    major achievements, 8:665–666
    principles of, 8:664–665
    vehicles, 8:665
Liturgical rings, 12:249
Liturgical rites, **8:711–714**
  commemorating Mother of God, 10:15
  implications of narrative theology for, 10:154
  incense use, 7:376–377
  kiss of peace, 8:185
  lauds, 8:379–380
  lectionaries, 8:434
  light, use of, 8:581
  litanies, 8:599–602
  Lyonese Rite, 8:905–906
  Mysterium fidei (''Mystery of the Faith''), 10:77–79
  Ordines Romani on sequence, 10:632–*633*
  Oremus during, 10:45, 46, 651
  Orthodox Church of Georgia, 10:689
  Serbian Orthodox Church, 10:700
  sermon, 13:18
  use of palms in, 10:813
The Liturgical Singer, 10:157
Liturgical studies. *See* Liturgics
Liturgical texts, 5:253–254
Liturgical theology, 3:202, 8:168, **714–715**
Liturgical vessels, 3:335, 370, 728–729, **8:715–716**
  artistic structure, 8:630–632
  burse, 2:710
  Byzantine, 2:816–817
  sacristy, 12:522
Liturgical vestments, 5:621–622, **8:716**
  art, 8:634–636
  colors, 8:634
  cope, 4:249, *249*
  Coptic, 4:257
  dalmatic, 4:501–502
  domestic prelates, 4:826
  humeral veil, 4:249, *249*
  papal vestments, 10:856
  sacristy, 12:522

  styles, 8:632–634
  See also Clerical dress
Liturgical weeks, 2:183, 8:646
Liturgical year, 1:345, 710–711, 5:105, 656
Liturgical year in Roman Rite, **8:716–722**
  Feast of Mary (4th c.), 10:15
  Kramp, J., 8:246
  lay spirituality, 8:415
  Lent, 8:469
  Leo I (Pope), St., 8:475
  liturgical movement, 8:671
  research, 8:724–725
  sanctoral cycle, 8:717, 719–722
  temporal cycle, 8:717–719, 721
Liturgicam authenticam, 8:669
Liturgics, **8:722–725**
Liturgie comparée (Comparative Liturgy) (Baumstark), 2:159
Liturgiology. *See* Heortology
Liturgy, **8:727–729**
  Acts of the Martyrs, 1:94
  Adam of Saint-Victor, 1:109–110
  Advent, 1:134
  Agnus Dei, 1:184–186
  Alexandrian liturgy, 1:271, 273
  All Souls' Day, 1:290
  Alleluia, 1:293–295
  altars, 1:314–318
  ambos, 1:336
  Ambrosian Rite, 1:185, 342–346
  Amen, 1:348
  anamnesis, 1:383
  Andrieu, Michel, 1:409
  angels, 1:424
  Anglican liturgy, 3:608–609
  Anglo-Catholics, 1:447
  Anointing of the Sick, 1:482, 484–487, 710
  Antiochene liturgy, 1:527–528, 5:4, 8:435, 712
  antiphons, 1:297–298, 529
  apologies, 1:566–567
  apostolic blessing, 1:580
  Aquileian Rite, 1:608–609
  Arianism, 3:186
  Armenian liturgy, 1:707–711, 3:553, 556, 8:713
  ars moriendi, 1:728
  art, 1:753
  ashes in, 1:782, *783*
  asperges, 1:786
  Athanasian Creed, 1:816–817
  Australia, 1:906

Liturgy (continued)

basilica, 8:730

Baumstark, Anton, 2:159–160

Bona, Giovanni, 2:477

Bragan Rite, 2:579–580

bread in, 2:599

Bugnini, Annibale, 2:676–677

canonicity, 3:21–22, 32–33

canticles, 3:73

cantors, 3:73, 75

Carmelite Rite, 3:125–126, 140–141

Carthage, 3:186

Carthusians, 3:191

catechesis, 3:231

Celestine I (Pope), St., 3:318

Celtic rite, 3:331–332

Chaldean Catholic Church, 1:528

Christmas, 3:554–557

Christocentrism, 3:558–559

church architecture, 3:669–672, 710, 712

Cistercian Rite, 3:745–746

Cluniacs, 3:815

congregational singing in, 4:118–120

Consultation on Common Texts (CCT), 4:201

Coptic liturgy, 1:273, 4:253, 256–257, 13:42–43

death preparation, 4:582–583

definition, 8:727–728

eclogadic reading, 8:435

Ecumenical Movement, 5:79

Ethiopian (Ge'ez) liturgy, 1:273, 5:400, 406, 8:713

exorcism, 5:553

Federation of Diocesan Liturgical Commissions, 5:662

French reform, 5:860

Gregorian Sacramentary, 1:243, 3:555, 556

history of, 2:159, 6:880

history of word, 8:727

Holy Gospels, 3:29

Holy Thursday, 7:55

hope, 7:93–94

hosanna, 7:115

Jewish liturgy, 3:24, 76, 4:607, 889–890, 7:5

laity, role of, 8:288

as locus of encounter, 8:665

Lord's Prayer, 8:784

Maronite liturgy, 8:712–713, 9:201, 202

Mary, Blessed Virgin, redemption of, 9:263

meaning of term, 8:727

nature, 8:728–729

pastoral theology, 9:855

popular devotions, 4:710–712

as prayer of the whole people, 8:666

reading from the Gospels, 6:367

Ritual (Rituale Romanum), 12:258

ritual studies, 12:259

Ritualist Movement, 1:447

Russian liturgy, 12:431–432

sacramental theology, 12:474–475

Sacristan liturgy, 12:522

sermon, 13:18

Slavic liturgy, 4:370, 475–476

spiritual theology, 13:435

Syro-Malabar liturgy, 5:3, 13:713, 715–718

tradition in theology, 14:135

Tridentine liturgy, 3:288–289

use of Psalms in, 11:796–797

Vatican II reforms, 8:664–666

Vatican Council II call for reform of, 10:43, 564

veneration of relics, 12:54

See also Byzantine liturgy; Constitution on the Sacred Liturgy; East Syrian liturgy; Gallican Rites; Gelasian Sacramentary; Hymns; Liturgical Movement; Roman Rite; Syrian liturgy

Liturgy (periodical), 8:646

Liturgy, Carthusian Rite, 3:189–190

Liturgy and Christian Culture, 12:281

Liturgy and Tradition: Theological Reflections of Alexander Schmemann (Schmemann), 12:742

The Liturgy of the Church of the East (Kelaytâ), 5:6

Liturgy of the Hours, 6:128, 8:729–736, 10:564

canticles, 3:73

Communion on weekdays, 4:37

Compline, 4:44

descent of Christ into hell, 4:685–686

East Syrian rite, 5:7

lauds, 8:380

popular devotions, 4:711

research, 8:724–725

Sisters Adorers of the Precious Blood, 13:171

structure, 8:732–733

The Liturgy of the Mass (Parsch), 10:903

Liturgy of the Word, 10:855

Litz, Damian, 8:736

Liu Yuanren (Bp.), 3:495

Liu Ziyn, Peter, St., 8:736

Liudhard (Abp. of Mainz), 1:633

Liutbirg, St., 8:736–737

Liuthild. See Lüfthildis, St.

Liutprand (Lombard king), 6:486–487, 11:108

Liutprand of Cremona (Bp.), 8:737–738, 768, 9:447, 13:15

Liutwin of Trier, St., 8:738

Livarius of Metz, St., 8:738

Lives and Opinions of Eminent Philosophers (Diogenes Laertius), 11:413

Lives of the Eastern Saints (John of Asia), 12:320

Lives of the Fathers (Gregory of Tours), 12:606

Lives of the Fathers, Martyrs and Other Principal Saints (Butler), 6:614

Lives of the Fathers of Mérida (Paul of Merida), 12:606

Lives of the Painters (Vasari), 12:111

Lives of the Popes (Platina), 10:828

Lives of the Popes in the (Early) Middle Ages (Mann), 9:118

Lives of the Prophets, 1:550–551

Lives of the Saints (Aelfric Grammaticus), 1:136, 11:632–633

Lives of the Saints (Butler), 12:524

Lives of the Saints (Surius), 13:628

Lives of the Saints (Zwoty Swietych) (Skarga), 13:200

Lives of the Twelve Caesars (Suetonius), 12:308

Livia Drusilla (Julia Augusta), 12:303–304

Living City (periodical), 5:786

The Living Flame of Love (St. John of the Cross), 7:988

Living gnosis, 9:110–111

See also Gnosis

The Living Light (Ryan), 12:446

Living Our Faith (Malawi, pastoral letter), 9:68

A Living Wage: Its Ethical and Economic Aspects (Ryan), 12:445, 446

Livingstone, David, 14:906–907

Livonia (Russian province), 4:309

Livonian Knights. See Knights of the Sword

Livre de divinacions (Oresme), 10:380

Livre de la foi, 3:245

Livre des manières (Stephen of Fougères), 3:519

Livre du ciel et du monde (Oresme), 10:380

Livres des métiers (Guild Book), 5:846

Livy (Roman historian), 10:93, 12:307

Lizana y Beaumont, Francisco Javier (Abp. of Mexico), 5:791

Lizárraga, Reginaldo de, **8:738**

Lladó Teixidor, Luis, 2:92

Llandaff, Ancient See of (Wales), **8:738–739**

Llandaff Oratory (South Africa), 13:*364*

Llanthony Monastery (Wales), 8:*739*, **739**

Llauradó Parisi, Antonio, Bl., 7:123

Llaveneras, Calasanzio de, 1:438

Llibre d'amic e amat (Lull, R.), 8:866

Llibre de contemplació (Lull, R.), 8:866

Llibre de gentil e los tres savis (Lull, R.), 8:866

Llop Gayá, Guillermo, Bl., 7:125

Llorente, Juan Antonio, **8:739–740**

Llorente Martín, Hilario María, 2:92

Llosa, Cayetano de la, 2:467

Lloyd, John, St., 5:237, 482, **8:740**, 10:495

Lloyd, William, 5:238

Llull, Raymond, 12:765, 776

LMSC. *See* Little Missionary Sisters of Charity

Loan Va Vu, Luke, 14:496

Loarte, Gaspar, 1:305

Loaysa, Jerónimo de (Abp. of Peru), 3:246, **8:740–741**

Lobbes Abbey (Belgium), 5:324, 787, **8:741**

Lobe, Alfonso, 8:742

Lobedau, John, Bl., 8:105

Lobo, Duarte, **8:741–742**

Lobo, Jerónimo, **8:742**

Loc Van Le, Paul, 14:496

Local church and the universal Church, 5:38

Local motion (place), 10:17, 21

Location (category of being), 1:61, 2:396, **8:742**, 13:193

Loccum Abbey (England), **8:743**

Lochel. *See* Lohelius, Johann

Lochner, Stephen, 3:844

Loci communes (Melanchthon), 5:43, 12:16, 13:681

Loci theologici, **8:743**

Loci theologici (Gerhard), 8:86, 890

Lock of Berenice (Callimachus), 10:768

Locke, John, **8:744–746**, 11:294
    abstraction, 1:45
    accident, 1:62
    Alphonsus Liguori, St., 1:310
    Aristotelianism, 1:678
    associationism, 1:796

atomism, 1:831

Blake, William, 2:428

Bradley, Francis Herbert, 2:577

British moralists, 2:623

Bufalo, St. Gaspare del, 2:675

Cartesianism, 3:183, 4:682

causality, 3:300, 306

choice, 3:521

Church-State relations, 3:638, 646

common good, 4:19

conceptualism of, 4:53

deism, 4:616

democracy, 4:640, 642

demonstration, 4:654

educational philosophy, 5:91, 93

empiricism, 5:91, 197–198, 261, 12:42, 47

Enlightenment, 5:255, 256

eternity, 5:381

ethics and natural law, 5:395

experience, 5:554

form, 5:803

free will, 5:939

freedom defined, 10:227

freedom of religion, 5:947

freethinker, 5:966

idea, 7:295

influence on Jonathan Edwards, 5:97

judgment, 8:23, 25

knowledge, theories of, 8:218

natural law doctrine, 10:183, 202–203

ontological argument, 10:603

quality, 11:849, 850

reflection, 12:3

scholasticism, 12:765, 768

self, concept of, 12:882

sense knowledge, 12:910

Sergeant, J., 13:12

social contracts, 13:240, 483

solipsism, 13:303

soul, 13:346

substance, 13:578

understanding, 14:292

Lockwood, John, Bl., 3:264, 5:235, **8:746**

Lockyear, J., 3:673

Locnikar, Bernard (Abbot), 12:552

Loculus, **8:746**

Locutiones (St. Augustine), 5:512

Locutions, 8:409, **747**, 10:107–108

Lodigeri, Calistus, 12:765

Loetschert (1820–1886), 9:504

Loftus, Adam (Abp. of Dublin), 5:455, 7:548

Logic, 12:818
    ambiguity in, 1:334
    Aristotelianism, 1:668, 681–682
    art, 1:747
    cosmological argument, 4:285–287
    deduction, 4:608
    demonstration, 4:651–653
    dialectics, 4:726–727
    division, 4:792–794
    error and falsity, 5:329
    Hegel, Georg, 6:706
    identity principle, 7:303
    mathematics, 12:415–416
    Mill, John Stuart, 9:630–631
    philosophy, 11:278
    quantity in, 11:853–854
    relation in, 12:43
    Russell, Bertrand, 12:415–416
    species, 13:407
    stoicism, 13:534–535
    truth in, 14:224
    William of Ockham, 14:747
    See also Argumentation; Equivocation

Logic, G., 12:533

Logic, history of, **8:747–752**
    Abelard, Peter, 1:18
    Aristotle, 8:537, 748
    Cartesianism, 3:183–186
    Greco-Roman period, 8:747, 748–749
    Leibniz, 8:456–457
    Logic of Port Royal, 3:184
    logicism, 8:758
    Medieval period, 8:749–750
    modern period, 8:751–752
    post-Renaissance period, 8:750–751
    Thomist view, 8:538
    vernacular logics, 8:751

Logic, symbolic, **8:752–755**, 9:327
    axiomatic system, 1:948–950
    concept, 4:52
    constants and variables, 8:753
    contingency, 4:212
    intention, 13:410
    Leibniz, 8:457
    logic of predicates and class, 8:754–755
    logic of relations, 8:755
    propositional logic, 8:754
    sign, 13:117

Logic of Port Royal (Arnauld and Nicole), 3:184

Logic of predicates and class, 8:754–755

Logic of relations, 8:755, 13:139

The Logic of Scientific Discovery (Logik der Forschung) (Popper), 11:508

''Logic without Ontology'' (Nagel), 10:608

Logica (Dialectica) (Ramus), 11:906

Logica ingredientibus (Abelard), 1:18

Logica magna (Veneto), 14:435

Lógica Mexicana (Rubio), 12:399

Logica parva (Veneto), 14:435

Logica valde utilis et realis contra Ocham (Richard of Campsall), 12:232

Logical atomism, 12:415

Logical empiricism, 4:584

Logical instruments, 7:499

Logical Investigations (Husserl), 10:607

Logical necessity, 10:227

Logical positivism, 5:197, **8:755–758**, 11:297

    agnosticism, 1:183–184, 6:313

    British moralists, 2:624

    certitude, 3:352

    contradiction, 4:224

    death of God theology, 4:584

    Locke's influence, 8:746

    physical laws, 11:316

    relativism, 12:44, 48

    Russell, Bertrand, 12:416

    See also Empiricism; Positivism

Logicism, **8:758**

Logik der Forschung (The Logic of Scientific Discovery) (Popper), 11:508

Logische Untersuchungen (Husserl), 11:230

Logische Untersuchungen (Trendelenburg), 6:711

Logos, 5:180, **8:758–764**

    Alogoi, 1:304

    anonymous Christian, 1:489

    Arianism, 1:660

    Athanasius, St., 1:820

    Bible, 8:758–761

    Christ as, 8:93

    Christian paideia education to reach, 10:753–756

    Christology, 1:527, 3:560

    community, 4:38

    creation, 4:342

    filiation, 5:718–719

    Heraclitus, 7:513

    Holy Trinity dogma use of, 14:198, 200

    John's Gospel, 10:899

    patripassianism denial of, 10:409, 957

    Philo Judaeus, 11:271–272

    Precious Blood, 11:639–640

    revelation, 7:513

    School of Antioch, 1:527

    son of god, 13:311

    theology of, 8:761, 761–764

Löhe, Johann Konrad Wilhelm, **8:765**

Lohelius, Johann (Lochel) (Abp. of Prague), **8:765**

Loher, Dietrich, 3:192

Löhr, Aemiliana, 8:672

Loir, Jean-Baptiste Jacques Louis Xavier, 12:277

Loisy, Alfred, 5:331, 8:*765*, **765–766**, 9:754

    Bremond, Henri, 2:601

    doctrine, development of, 4:806

    Húgel, Friedrich von, 7:149

    religious experience, 5:556

    Richard de la Vergne, 12:228

Lollards, 3:605, **8:766–767**

    Archbishops of Canterbury, 3:72, 481

    Arundel, Thomas, 1:767

    Carmelites, 3:141

    Church property, 3:727

    Courtenay, Richard, 4:317

    De heretico comburendo, 4:550

    impact on Ancient See of Norwich, 10:452

    Lowe, J., 8:836–837

    Netter's criticism of, 10:264

    repression of, 8:775

    Wyclif, John, 8:766, 14:867

Lomax, James, 5:237

Lomazzi, Isabella Cristina. *See* Bellinzaga, Isabella Cristina

Lombard, Peter. *See* Peter Lombard

Lombard League, 5:925, 7:663, **8:767**

Lombard-Catalan architecture, 3:690–691

Lombardi, Riccardo, 7:792

Lombardie, Jacques, 12:277

Lombards, **8:767–770**

    Adrian I (Pope), 1:121, 122

    Arianism, 1:664, 815

    Byzantine Church, 2:750

    Byzantine Empire, 2:783

    Carolingian Dynasty, 3:124, 164, 421, 422, 434, 563, 598

    Constantine II (Antipope), 4:178

    Constantine V (Byzantine Emperor), 4:174

    Damian of Pavia, 4:506

    Desiderius (King), 4:688

    Deusdeit I, St., 4:701

    Donation of Constantine, 4:860–861

    driven back by Pepin, 10:835

    Germany, 6:171–172

    Gregory I (Pope), St., 6:479–480

    Gregory III (Pope), St., 6:486–487

    iron crown, 8:*768*

    Italian invasion (6th century), 7:920

    King Rachis, 8:768, *769*

    Paul I (Pope), St., 11:18–19

    Pepin III, 11:110–111

    Ravenna (Italy) capture, 11:929

Lombers, Council of, **8:770**

Loménie de Brienne, Étienne Charles de (Abp. of Paris), 3:753, 4:13, **8:770**

London, Ancient See of (England), 3:70, 8:141, **770–772**

London, Councils of (1075-1160), 1:254, 495, 3:469, 481

London Charterhouse, **8:772**

Lonergan, Bernard, 6:288, **8:772–775**, 14:54, 56, 199, 292–293

    biblical hermeneutics, 6:796

    conversion, 4:235

    faith and beliefs, 2:223

    foundational theology, 5:827

    humanity of Christ, 7:821

    induction, 7:435

    International Theological Commission, 7:528

    intuition, 7:534–535

Long, Melvin T., 8:822

Longe, Richard. *See* Sergeant, Richard, Bl.

The Longest Years (Undset), 14:295

Longfellow, Henry Wadsworth, 3:379

Longhaye, Georges, 11:623

Longhena, Baldassare, 3:705

Longinqua oceani (apostolic letter, Leo XIII), 1:585

Longissimae melodiae, 1:294–295

Longjumeau, André de, 3:492

Longjumeau, Treaty of (1568), 3:266

Longland, John (Bp. of Lincoln), **8:775–776**

Longley, Charles (Abp. of Canterbury), 8:306

Longo, Bartolo, Bl., **8:776**

Longpont Abbey (France), 3:696

Long-suffering (moral virtue), **8:775**

Loofs, Friedrich, 10:252, 963, 12:257

Looking Backward (Bellamy), 14:361

Loom of Years (Noyes), 10:471

Loomer, Bernard, 11:731

Loor, Isidore of Saint Joseph de, Bl., **8:776–777**

Loos, Cornelius, **8:777**

Lootens, Louis Aloysius (Bp. of Idaho), 7:290

Lopes, Simon, Bl., 1:951

Lopez, Domingo, 7:577

López, Francisco, 12:674

López, Ludovico, **8:777**

López Aguilar, Rubén de Jesús, Bl., 7:123

López de Ayala, Pero, 1:465

Lopez de Legazpi, Miguel, 11:255

López de Mendoza Grajales, Francisco, **8:777–778**

López López, Cecilio, Bl., 7:124

López Orbara, Manuel, Bl., 7:123

Lopez Portillo, Pablo Maria, Bl., 4:494

López Trujillo, Alfonso (Bp.), 4:158

López y Vicuña, Vicenta María, Bl., **8:778**

Lopuchin, A., 12:435

Loras, Jean Mathias Pierre (Bp. of Dubuque, IA), 3:765, 4:281, 363, 921–922, 7:541, **8:778–779**

The Lord, **8:779–781**
  apotheosis, 1:599
  Christological title, 1:599, 7:808–809
  as honorific title for God, 8:780
  Malachi, Book of, 9:63
  New Testament, 8:780–781
  Old Testament, 8:780
  substitution for Yahweh, 8:780
  used for God, 8:780
  used for Jesus Christ, 8:780–781

Lord, Daniel Aloysius, **8:779**, 13:294

The Lord of the Rings (Tolkien), 14:105

Lorde, Audre, 5:673

Lord's Day, **8:781–782**, 12:459–460, 13:607

Lord's Day Observance Act (England), 12:455

Lord's Prayer, **8:782–784**
  catechesis, 3:230, 231, 234, 240
  hope, 7:93, 99
  kiss of peace, 8:185
  outstretched hands, 8:649

Lord's Supper, **8:784–786**
  Baptists, 2:78, 80
  Pentecostalists, 11:106
  Phillipists, 4:416
  scriptural basis, 5:419
  See also Breaking of Bread; Eucharist

Lorenz, Konrad, 2:404

Lorenzana, Francisco Antonio de (Abp. of Mexico City and Toledo), 8:786

Lorenzelli, B., 4:121

Lorenzetti, Pietro, 1:791, 3:127, 4:396

Lorenzini, Francesco, 2:844

Lorenzo Maria of Saint Francis Xavier, 12:632

Loreto, Shrine at, 8:602–603

Loretto Chapel (Santa Fe, New Mexico), 12:*674*

Loretto Sisters (Institute of the Blessed Virgin), **8:786–787**
  See also Sisters of Loretto at the Foot of the Cross

Lori, William E. (Bp. of Norwich), 4:125

L'Orme, P. de, 3:675

Lorrain, Claude, 2:114

Lorraine, Cardinals of, 3:266, **8:787–788**

Lorraine Benedictine congregation, 8:142

Lorraine Dynasty, 5:768

Lorraine-Armagnac, François (Bp. of Bayeux), 2:163

Lorris, Guillaume de, 1:291

Lorry, Michel de (Bp. of Angers), 1:432

Lorsch Abbey (Germany), 1:99, 3:563, 5:325, **8:788**

Los Angeles Archdiocese (CA), 1:640, 3:76–77, **8:788–793**, 792, 836

Los Angeles Bible Institute (CA), 6:27, 30

Los Angeles Cathedral (CA), 3:716

Los Angeles Diocesan Archives (CA), 1:640

Losskiĭ, Nīkolaĭ Onufrievich, **8:794**

Lossky, Vladimir, 12:436

Lost articles, patron saint of, 5:670

Los-Von-Rom Movement, 1:915, 3:624, **8:794–795**

Lot and His Daughters (Krodel), 6:*131*

Lothair I (Carolingian Emperor), 3:170, **8:795**
  Alexander of Fiesole, St., 1:264
  Clement of Ireland, St., 3:799
  Drogo of Metz, 4:908
  Leo IV (Pope), St., 8:482
  Sergius II (Pope) consecration, 13:14

Lothair I (Holy Roman Emperor), 5:28, 139, 145, 443, 766, 6:488

Lothair II (Holy Roman Emperor), **8:795–796**
  Anacletus II (Antipope), 1:370
  divorce of, 1:117, 124, 840, 3:160, 171, 599
  Hincmar of Reims, 6:838
  Innocent II (Pope), 7:470

Lothair III (Holy Roman Emperor), 3:78, 7:82, **8:796–797**, 10:420, 421

Lothair IV (King of the East Franks), 3:172

Lothar of Cadolo, 13:36

Lotharingia, 8:795

Lotto, Lorenzo, 1:132

Lotze, Rudolf Hermann, 1:80, 603–604, **8:797**, 10:824

Loughlin, James F., **8:797–798**

Loughlin, John (Bp. of Brooklyn), **8:798**

Loughran, Neilan, 7:581

Louis (Duke of Orléans), 7:884

Louis I (Card. of Lorraine, 1527-1578), 8:787

Louis I (Holy Roman Emperor), 4:908

Louis I (the Great) (King of Hungary), 7:211

Louis I (the Pious) (Holy Roman Emperor), 3:*154*, 5:28, 14:7
  Adalard, St., 1:98
  Agobard of Lyons, St., 1:186
  Aldric of Le Mans, St., 1:248
  anointing, 1:478
  Barnard of Vienne, St., 2:104
  Benedict of Aniane, St., 2:251–252, 269
  Canon Law, 3:43
  capitularies, 3:91
  Carolingian Dynasty, role in, 3:168–170
  Carolingian reform, 3:157, 168, 599, 600
  Carolingian Renaissance, 3:160
  Church-State relations under, 5:615
  Council of Attigny, 1:840
  Council of Thionville, 1:248
  Euguene II (Pope), 5:443
  Gregory IV (Pope), 6:488
  Hilduin of Saint-Denis, 6:833
  iconoclasm, 2:753
  Leo III (Pope), St., 8:480
  Ordinatio imperii (817), 10:914
  Pactum Ludovicianum, 10:913–914
  works of charity, 3:410–411

Louis I de Bourbon (Prince of Condé), 3:266–267

Louis I de Guise, 3:266

Louis II (Card. of Lorraine, 1555-1588), 8:787

Louis II (King of Hungary), 7:213

Louis II (King of Naples), 1:258

Louis II (the German) (King of the East Franks), 3:170–171, 8:796
  Ado of Vienne, St., 1:117
  Adrian II (Pope), 1:124

Louis II (the German) (King of the East
Franks) *(continued)*
archchancellors, 1:632
John of Ravenna, 7:981
Leo IV (Pope), St., 8:482
Lothair II, 8:795, 796
Louis II (the Stammerer) (King of the
Franks), 3:171
Louis III (Card. of Lorraine), 8:788
Louis III (King of the Franks), 1:99,
3:171–172, 172
Louis IV (d'Outremer) (King of the East
Franks), 3:172
Louis IV (the Bavarian) (Holy Roman
Emperor)
appeals to a future council, 1:599
Avignon papacy, 1:943
Benedict XII (Pope), 2:244
Clement VI (Pope), 3:780
conciliarism, 4:55
excommunication of, 6:177
Ghibelline-Guelf conflict, 3:854
John XXII (Pope), 1:327, 3:603,
7:931
Lupold of Bebenburg, 8:869
Marsilius of Padua, 9:210
Louis V (King of the East Franks),
3:172
Louis VI (King of France), 8:798–799,
12:544
Louis VII (King of France), 8:799, 799
Alexander III (Pope), 1:254
Barbeaux Abbey, 2:93
Celestine I (Pope), St., 3:318
Celestine III (Pope), 3:319
Crusades, 4:410
Louis VIII (King of France), 1:229,
4:413, 7:84
Louis IX (King of France), St.,
8:799–801, 800, 801
Aeterne Rex Altissime, 1:147
anointing, 1:478
church architecture, 3:697
Clement IV (Pope), 3:778
Crusades, 4:401, 405, 411
holy lance, 7:31
Holy Name, 7:31
law, 8:401
North Africa, 3:187
Pastoureaux Crusade to free, 10:940
reform of French kingdom, 5:846
Sainte Chapelle for crown of thorns,
13:90
Louis XI (King of France)
Celles-Sur-Belle Monastery, 3:329
Cuxa Abbey, 4:450

Francis of Paola, 5:872
hospitals, 7:137
Paul II (Pope), 11:20
Pragmatic Sanction, 6:75, 11:582
Louis XII (King of France), 1:259, 261,
7:668, 8:56
Louis XIII (King of France)
Bérulle, Pierre de, 2:339
Chrysostom of Saint-Lô, John, 3:573
Church reform, 5:850
confessor to, 13:168
Edict of Alais, 10:145
La Rouchefoucauld, 8:336
Richelieu's relationship with, 12:238
Louis XIV (King of France), 8:801–804,
802
absolutism, 5:850–851
Alexander VII (Pope), 1:262
Alexander VIII (Pope), 1:262
appeals to a future council, 1:599
Assemblies of the French Clergy,
1:788
Baluze, Étienne, exile of, 2:47
baroque architecture, 2:107
Bossuet, Jacques Bénigne, 2:549
Bouillon, Emmanuel Théodose de la
Tour d'Auvergne, 2:563
Brogne Abbey, 2:625
Camisards, 2:916
Caribbean, 3:118
Church-State relations, 4:591
Clement X (Pope), 3:788
Clement XI (Pope), 3:788
closing of Calvinist academy at
Sedan, 2:164
Declaration of the French Clergy,
6:77
Edict of Alais, 10:145
Fénelon, François de Salignac de la
Mothe, 5:683
Fleury, Claude, court tutor, 5:762
Fürstenberg brothers, 6:36
Gallicanism, 3:615, 639, 788, 6:76
Hugo, Charles Hyacinthe, 7:162
Huguenots, 3:639, 7:168
Innocent XI (Pope), Bl., 7:481
Innocent XII (Pope), 7:482
Jesuit confessor, 8:269
Le Tellier, M., 8:519
Louisiana exploration, 8:340
Lully's opera, 8:867
Oates Plot, 10:496
Port-Royal Abbey, 11:525
Retz, Jean François Paul de Gondi
de, 12:180

slavery, 1:155
Unigenitus, 1:57
works of charity, 3:417
Louis XV (King of France), 3:791–792,
5:209, 761, **8:804–805**, *805*
Louis XVI (King of France), 5:84, 972,
7:130
Louis XVIII (King of France)
Carthusians, 3:195
Chateaubriand, François René de,
3:448
Cheverus, Jean Louis Lefebvre de,
3:472
Civil Constitution of the Clergy,
3:753
Concordat of 1801, 4:63
Edgeworth de Firmont chaplian to,
5:84
Imperial Catechism, 3:237
Louis d'Aleman (Card.), Bl., 1:694,
8:805
Louis of Besse, **8:805**
Louis of Casoria, Ven., **8:805–806**
Louis of Féterne, 1:23
Louis of Granada, 1:305, **8:806–807**,
11:621
Louis of Guise (Card.), 6:579
Louis of León, 2:50
Louis of Tech (Patriarch of Aquileia),
1:608
Louis of Udine. *See* Scrosoppi, Luigi, St.
Louis of Verona, 3:414
Louis the Bavarian. *See* Louis IV (the
Bavarian) (Holy Roman Emperor)
Louis the Pious. *See* Louis I (the Pious)
(Holy Roman Emperor)
Louise de Marillac, St., 3:235, 417,
8:807, 13:172
Louise of France (Thérèse de St.
Augustin), Ven., **8:807**
Louise of Savoy, Bl., **8:808**
Louisiana, **8:808–816**
*Cochran v. Louisiana State Board of
Education* (1930), 3:660
Congregation of Sisters of the Holy
Family, 7:23
Daughters of the Cross, 4:534
ecclesiastical organization, 8:809
exploration era, 8:339–340
French exploration, 8:340
Jesuits, 8:8–9, 809, 9:723
mission, 1:270, 9:715–716, 723,
12:274
Sisters of the Most Holy Sacrament,
13:190

See also Dubourg, Louis William Valentine; *specific dioceses and archdioceses*

Louisiana State Board of Education, Cochran v. (1930), 3:660

Louismet, Savinien, **8:816**

Louis-Philippe (King of France), 3:448, 472, 5:854

Louisville Archdiocese (KY), **8:816–819**

Loup. *See* Lupus, St.

Lourdes (France), 3:623, 5:857, **8:819–820**, *820*, 13:93, 331

Lourdes Basilica, 3:710

Lourdes Brothers, 3:622

Loutre, Jean Louis Le, 7:25

Louvain, American College at, 4:659, **8:820–823**

Louvain, Catholic University of (Belgium), 2:220, 227–228, 7:714, **8:823–825**, 12:540

   Boonen, Jacques, 2:529

   course in St. Thomas, 12:776

   Dechamps, Victori Auguste, 4:589

   neoscholastic revival, 12:776

   Sheen, F., 13:74

Lovatelli urn, 10:*86*

Lovati, Lovato dei, 12:113

Love, **8:825–830**

   appetite, 1:602

   appreciative love, 8:726

   Augustine, St., 1:875

   benevolent love, 8:826

   common good, 4:18

   communication, 4:23–24

   conjugal, 7:180, 13:45

   courage, 4:316

   courtly, 4:318–322

   creation, 4:343, 344

   death, 4:575

   depiction in Islamic art, 7:618

   duties in, 8:66

   effect on knowledge, 8:206–207

   existentialsim, 5:725

   familial piety, 11:332

   Ficino' theory of Platonic love, 5:710

   freedom, 5:725

   hate, 5:195

   historical development, 8:826–827

   John of Saint-Samson, 7:983

   John Paul II (Pope), 11:154

   John's Gospel, 7:898

   justice related, 8:64–66

   justice related, boundaries between, 8:68–69

   kinds of, 8:825–826

   level of reason, 8:828–830

   level of sense, 8:827–828

   Lucretius, 8:849

   man's fruitful nature, 8:873

   person, 11:148

   sexual urge, 13:44–45

   Song of Songs, 13:318–319

   spiration, 13:421

   supererogation, 4:307

   will and willing, 14:723

Love, in the Bible, 4:7–8, 9, **8:830–832**, 13:249

Love, in theology, 4:938, 939, 8:65–66

Love, virtue of, **8:832–834**

Love and Responsibility (Wojtyła), 13:44, 45

The Love of the Eternal Wisdom (Grignion de Montfort), 6:532

Lovejoy, Arthur, 1:52, 10:630

Loverde, Paul (Bp. of Arlington, VA), 14:543

Lovers of the Holy Cross (LHC), 4:113–114, 8:304, **834–836**

Löw, Joseph, **8:836**

Löw, Leopold, 2:84

Low Church, 1:444, **8:836**, 12:25

Low countries, 8:686, 820–823, 823–825, 13:454–456

Low Sunday (2nd Sunday of Easter), 5:13

Lowe, E. A., 10:774

Lowe, John (Bp. of Rochester, England), **8:836–837**

Lowe, John, Bl., 1:112, 5:229, **8:837**

Lowell, J. R., 3:379

Lowell, John, 3:472

Lowell Plan, **8:837–838**

Löwith, Karl, 6:882, 884

Loyola College (Baltimore), 2:40

Loyola Marymount University (CA), 8:791, 793, 9:303

Loyola University (Chicago), 3:480, 13:104

Loyola University (New Orleans), 8:813

Loyson, Charles, 8:*838*, **838**

Lozano, Pedro, **8:838–839**

Luanda (Angola), 1:*452*

Lubac, Henri de (Card.), 8:*839*, **839–841**

   atheism, 1:826

   Balthasar, Hans Urs von, 2:34

   Christian philosophy, 3:541

   Daniélou, Jean, 4:515

   destiny, supernatural, 4:694

   ecclesiology, 5:37

   integrity of natural order, 10:193

   International Theological Commission, 7:528

   man, natural end of, 9:101

   New Theology, 5:859

   sacramental theology, 12:473

   theology of Church, 3:589

   theology of history, 6:890

   World War I service, 7:791

Lubich, Chiara, 5:785, 786

Lubieniecki, Stanisław, **8:841**, 13:291

Lubin (Bp. of Chartres), 3:264

Lublin Comittee, 11:450

Lublin Lectures (John Paul II), 9:91

Lucan (Roman poet), 12:308, 311

Lucaris, Cyril (Patriarch of Constantinople), 2:820, 4:355, 6:457, **8:841–842**

Lucas, Albert, 5:442

Lucas, Fielding, Jr., **8:842**

Lucas, Frederick, **8:842**, 13:726–727

Lucas Cranach the Elder, 4:397, 5:*81*

Lucas of Hildebrand, 1:913

Lucas of Túy, 1:465

Lucayan people, 2:13

Lucca (Italy), 3:67

Lucci, Antonio Nicola, Bl. (Bp. of Bovino), **8:842–843**

Lucentius (Bp. of Ascoli), 3:363

Lucernarium (lighting of the lamps), 3:15, 5:16

Lucerne (Tolstoi), 14:105

Lucerno (Father), 3:247

Lucey, Robert Emmet (Abp. of San Antonio, TX), 5:203, 879, **8:843–844**, 12:642

Luchesius of Poggibonsi, Bl., **8:844**

Luchtel. *See* Lüfthildis, St.

Lucian (Greek satirist), 1:567, 3:592, 593, 12:309, 635

Lucian (Roman martyr), 2:188

Lucian of Antioch, St., 5:454, **8:844**

   Arius, 1:527, 685

   biblical canon, 3:32

   Christology, 3:560

   Creed of, 1:662

   influence on Arius, 10:346

   School of Antioch, 1:524, 526, 2:820, 5:511

   works of charity, 3:402, 406

Lucian of Samosata, 12:635

Luciani, Albino (Card.). *See* John Paul I (Pope)

Lucidus (Gallic priest), 11:650

Lucie-Christine, **8:844–845**

Lucifer of Cagliari, 3:632, 724–725, 4:504, **8:845**

Luciferians. *See* Satanism
Lucius, St., **8:845–846**
Lucius I (Pope), St., **8:846**
Lucius II (Pope), **8:846–847**
Lucius III (Pope), **8:874–878**
    Armenia, 1:701
    capital punishment, 3:86–87
    Catharism, 1:231
    decretal forgeries, 4:600–601
    heresy, 7:487–488
    heretics condemned, 8:847
    Humiliati, 7:204
    Humiliati and Waldenses,
      excommunication of, 11:612
    Inquisition, 7:665
    lay boycotts of concubinous priests,
      8:847–848
Lucius of Cyrene, 1:521
Luck, **8:848**, 14:585–586
Lucker, Raymond A., 10:309–310
Luckhardt, H., 3:680
Luckmann, Thomas, 2:223
Lucretius (Roman poet), **8:848–849**
    atheism, 1:822
    atomism, 1:833
    chance, 3:375, 377
    materialism, 9:319
    place, 11:401
    sensations, 5:283
Lucrezia (Respighi), 12:139
Lucula noctis (Dominici), 9:461
Lucy, St., **8:849**, *850*, 13:103
Ludanus, St., **8:851**
Ludger of Münster, St., 1:220, 8:431,
    851, 14:680–681
Ludi Apollinares, 12:325
Ludi Magni, 12:325
Ludi Megalenses, 12:325
Ludi saeculares, 12:326
Ludlam, Robert, Bl., 5:229, **8:851–852**,
    13:141
Ludmilla, St., 4:479, **8:852**, 14:677
Ludolf of Corvey, St., **8:852**
Ludolf of Fonte Avellana, 5:792
Ludolf of Ratzeburg, St., **8:852**
Ludolph of Saxony, 3:192, 5:789, 7:312,
    8:852–853, 9:460–461
Ludovicus de Cividale, 3:52
Ludovicus Gomesius, 3:52
Ludovisi, Alessandro. *See* Gregory XV
    (Pope)
Ludovisi, Ludovico (Card.), 7:575
Ludus breviter de Pasione
    (Benediktbeurern play), 10:927
Ludwig I (King of Bavaria), 4:823

Ludwig II (King of Bavaria), 4:824
Ludwig Missionsverein (Ludwig Mission
    Society), **8:853**, 10:222, 12:781
*The Ludwig-Missionverein and the
    Church in the United States*
    (Roemer), 12:283
Lueger, Karl, 1:914, 7:873–874
Luers, John Henry (Bp. of Fort Wayne,
    IN), 7:415
Luethen, Bonaventure (Father), 12:630
Lueven Scholars. *See* Louvain, Catholic
    University of
Lüfthildis, St., **8:853–854**
Lufthold. *See* Lüfthildis, St.
Lugdunensis, 3:40
Lugo, Francisco de, 8:854
Lugo, Juan de (Card.), 1:311, 7:782,
    8:854–855, 12:766
Luigi of Udine. *See* Scrosoppi, Luigi, St.
Luis de la Puente. *See* La Puente, Luis
    de, Ven.
Luisa, Bl. (17th c. Japanese martyr),
    7:734
Lukáš of Prague, 2:461, **8:855**
Lukashyenko, Aleksandr, 2:213, 214
Łukaszuk, Konstanty, 11:584
Luke, Evangelist, St., **8:855–856**, *856,
    857*
    Barnabas, 2:102–103
    God's spirit, 13:427
    as icon painter, 7:278
    iconography of, 5:475
    liberation of oppressed, 13:245
    See also Acts of the Apostles; Luke,
      Gospel According to
Luke, Gospel According to, **8:856–861**
    Acts of the Apostles, 1:87, 88
    Annunciation in, 1:473–475
    anointing, 4:85
    apostles, 9:363
    Ascension of Jesus Christ in,
      1:769–770
    baptism, use of word, 2:56
    Barabbas, 2:85
    Bartholomew, Apostle, St., 2:123
    beatitudes, 2:177, 178
    Beelzebul, 2:200
    biblical canon, 3:21, 24
    blessings in, 2:438
    breaking of bread in, 2:600
    censuses in, 3:338–339
    Christmas, 3:555
    contemplation, 4:210
    contents and division, 8:856–858
      infancy gospel, 8:856
      ministry in Galilee, 8:857

      ministry in Jerusalem, 8:858
      Passion narrative, 8:858
      preparation for public ministry,
        8:856–857
      Resurrection narrative, 8:858
      travel account, 8:857–858
    conversion in, 4:233–234
    criticism, 3:34
    descent of Christ into hell, 4:684
    disciple as term, 4:769–773
    discipleship of women, 14:830–831
    Divine indwelling, 7:441
    divorce, 13:49
    early Christian way of life, 3:546
    edification, 5:84
    Elijah's Second Coming, 5:159
    enmity, 5:264
    eschatology, 5:339
    family structure, 14:830
    final perseverance, 11:134
    forgiveness, 13:36
    friendship with God, 6:10
    Gabriel, 6:40
    Gehenna, 6:116
    glory, 6:245
    gluttony, 6:251
    God the Son, 6:295–296
    God's word-made-flesh, 14:837
    Hades, 6:604
    heart, 6:681
    hell, 6:724
    house churches, 2:145
    Immaculate Conception, 7:331–332
    infancy narrative of, 7:452–453, 454
    infused knowledge, 8:207
    Jesus Christ
      baptism of, 2:72
      genealogy of, 6:126, 14:829–830
      prayer, 11:592
      temptations of, 9:546
      trust and faith of, 13:38
    John the Baptist, St.
      birth and infancy of, 7:1012–1013
      ministry of, 7:1013–1014
    justification, 8:77
    kerygma, 8:157
    Kingdom of God, 8:173, 174
    laicism, 8:284
    Lazarus of Bethany, 8:420
    Lazarus the Poor Man, 8:421
    leprosy, 8:510
    Lord used for God, 8:780
    Lord's Day, 8:781
    Lord's Prayer, 8:782–784

love and justice, 8:65
Luke Evangelist, 8:855–856
Magnificat, 9:43, 243–244
Mary, Blessed Virgin, 9:242–244,
 248, 14:536
Mary Magdalene, St., 9:287
miracles, 9:664
Nazareth, 10:216
origins, 8:858–860
pacifism, 10:745
parables in, 10:870, 871
paradise, 13:36–37
on the Parousia, 10:897, 899
passage reading, 8:434
Passion, 10:920, 922, 923
peace, 11:49
Pharisees, 11:226
prayer times, 8:729
presentation of the Lord, 3:14
prodigal son, 13:145
publicans, 11:810
redaction criticism scholarship,
 10:304
rhetorical training, 8:861
St. John the Baptist, 5:159, 162
Seven Last Words, 13:36
ship symbolism, 3:630
sign of Jonah, 7:1022
Simon the Apostle, 13:126
simplicity of God, 13:137
sin, 13:146, 148
Son of David, 13:310
Son of God, 13:312
Son of Man, 13:317
sons of God, 13:322
sorrows of Mary, 13:327
soul, 13:340
spirit, 13:425
virgin birth, 14:534
virginity, 4:306
visitation of Mary, 14:564
women, role of, 14:830
works of charity in, 1:300
See also Synoptic Gospels
Luke Belludi, Bl., **8:865**
Luke of Armento, St., **8:865**
Luke-Acts, **8:861–865**
Lukewarmness, **8:865–866**
Lull, Raymond, Bl., **8:866–867**
 chivalry, 3:519
 Congregation for the Propagation of
  the Faith, 11:749
 Latin Averroism, 1:936

medieval Latin literature works of,
 9:461
 mystical literature, 10:118
 Tunisia, 3:188
Lull of Mainz (Bp.), St., 2:496, 4:449,
 8:867
Lully, Jean Baptiste, 5:746, 8:690–691,
 867–868, *868*
Lumbrozo, Jacob, 14:104
Lumen gentium (LG) (Dogmatic
 Constitution on the Church), 5:37,
 39, 40, 299, 346, 859
 lay spirituality, 8:416, 416–417
 society, Church as, 13:287
Lumen Gentium award, 4:75
Luna, Pedro de. *See* Benedict XIII
 (Antipope)
Lundy, Victor, 3:716
Lune, John, 7:580
Lunn, Arnold, **8:868–869**
Luo Wenzao (Bp.), 3:497
Lupicinus of Jura, St., 8:63
Lupold of Bebenburg (Bp. of
 Bebenburg), **8:869**
Lupus, St., 2:163, **8:869**, 9:444
Lupus of Ferrières, Servatus, 1:248,
 3:160, 730, 5:695, 7:246
Luque, Crisanto (Card.), **8:869–870**
Lurana (Mother). *See* White, Lurana
 Mary
Lurçat, Jean, 1:545, 3:713
Lure Abbey (France), 4:615
Luria, Isaac, 2:833, 834, 835,
 8:870–871, 13:56
Luria, Solomon, 12:140
Lust, **8:871–877**, 14:473
Lustiger, J. M., 5:861
Lutgardis, St., **8:877**
Luther, Martin, 5:36, 316, 8:*877*,
 877–883
 abuse of indulgences, 7:438
 Amsdorf, Nikolaus von, 1:366
 Angelo Carletti di Chivasso, Bl.,
  1:414
 Apocalypse iconography, 1:544–545
 Apostles' Creed, 1:577
 Aristotelianism, 1:675
 Arnoldi, Bartholomaeus, 1:719–720
 ars moriendi, 1:732–733
 attrition, 4:226
 Augustinians, 1:889
 Benno of Meissen, St., 2:283
 Berquin, Louis de, 2:330
 biblical canon, 3:21, 27, 32
 biblical Chronicler, 3:566
 biblical hermeneutics, 6:793

biblical translation, 5:518, 12:16
Bugenhagen, Johann, 2:675
capital punishment, 3:87
catechesis, 3:232–233, 241–242
Charles V (Holy Roman Emperor),
 3:430
Christian philosophy, 3:538
Church-State relations, 3:637
clerical celibacy/marriage, 3:327
Cochlaeus, Johannes, 3:816
confessions of faith, 4:78
Crotus Rubianus, 4:386
death of God, 4:583
defenders, 8:129
Denifle, Heinrich Seuse, 4:660
Diet of Nuremberg, 3:482–483
Diet of Worms, 3:430, 482
disagreement between Thomas
 Münzer, 10:62–63
ecclesiology, 5:36
excommunication of, 5:43,
 8:880–881, 12:16
faith, 2:222
free will and providence, 5:930, 936,
 938
Gansfort, Johannes Wessel, 6:89
George of Saxony, 6:144
grace, 6:397, 402–403
grave in Castle Church, 8:*888*
Grisar, Hartmann, 6:534
historical image of the Church, 6:874
humanism, 7:192
Hutten, Ulrich von, 7:233
hymnody, 7:255
impact on liturgical reforms, 8:659
impact on papacy, 10:841
imputation of justice and merit,
 7:367–368
indulgences, 12:15
indulgences issue, 8:487–488
infant baptism, defense of, 2:69
intermediate judgment, 8:33
justice of God, 8:71
justification, theology of, 8:83–84,
 90–91
laicism, 8:281–282
Leo X (Pope), condemnation of 41
 propositions from, 14:168
Lord's Supper, 5:426–427, 521
Mānī, 9:114
Mazzolini, Sylvester, 9:389–390
Melanchthon, Philipp, 13:681–682
merit (virtue), 9:512
Ninety-five Theses, 1:233,
 8:879–880, 888, 889, 12:5, 15–16

Luther, Martin *(continued)*
  nominalism, 12:12
  Norwegian Lutheranism, 10:448
  opponents
    Eck, Johann, 5:42–43
    Emser literary adversary,
      5:199–200
    Faber, Johann Augustanus, 5:583
    Faber, Johannes, 5:583
    Luevn theology faculty, 8:823
  papal Antichrist, 1:517
  partisan of, 13:401
  Paul, St., 3:608
  Paulus, Nikolaus, 11:42–43
  Peasants' War, 11:53
  penance, 11:71
  Philip of Hesse, 11:250
  Powell, Edward, reply to, 11:574
  predestination, 11:654
  priesthood, 11:702–703
  Quietism, 3:614
  reaction in Europe, 8:488
  religious experience, 5:555
  religious liberalism, 8:540–541
  Renaissance concept, 12:111
  sacerdotium et regnum, 11:703
  salutary acts, 12:621
  salvation, 13:908
  scholasticism, 12:762
  secularization of Church property,
    12:872
  on the state, 13:483
  Ten Commandments, 4:9
  theodicy, 13:868–869
  transubstantiation doctrine, 14:159
  Tyndale's translations of works,
    14:253
  ubiquitarian arguments, 14:263
  works of charity, 3:414
  See also Lutheranism; The
    Reformation
Lutheran Chapel for the Deaf (St. Paul,
  MN), 3:716
Lutheran Church in America (LCA),
  5:470, 471
Lutheran churches in North America,
  4:201, 356, 7:261–262, **8:883–887**,
  884
Lutheran Church—Missouri Synod (LC-
  MS), 5:470, 471, 8:765, 886, 887
Lutheran Evangelical Church, 8:376
Lutheran General Synod, 8:885
Lutheran Ministerium of North America,
  8:885
Lutheran Missouri Synod. *See* Lutheran
  Church—Missouri Synod

Lutheran Theological Seminary
  (Gettysburg, PA), 8:247, 12:744–745
Lutheran theology, 5:754
Lutheran World Federation, 8:90, 91,
  227, 887, 892
Lutheran-Anglican dialogues, 8:227
Lutheran-Catholic dialogues, 8:227
Lutheranism, 5:732, **8:887–896**, 892
  Adrian VI (Pope), 1:129
  Albrecht of Brandenburg-Ansbach,
    1:233–234
  Amana Society, 1:330
  Ambrosius Catharinus, 1:347
  Amsdorf, Nikolaus von, 1:366
  Anderson, Lars, 1:399
  anthropocentrism, 1:508
  Antwerp, 1:538
  Aristotelianism, 1:677
  Athanasian Creed, 1:817
  Augsburg, 1:848
  Augsburg Confession, 1:850
  Austria, 1:910, 912, 913, 914
  Belgium, 2:217
  Blarer, Ambrosius, 2:433
  Böhme, Jakob, 2:462
  Book of Common Prayer, 2:524
  Brask, Hans, 2:585
  Brenz, Johann, 2:605
  Bucer, Martin, 2:653
  Bugenhagen, Johann, 2:675
  Calixtus, Georg, 2:873–874
  Calov, Abraham, 2:383, 874, 884,
    3:174
  Calvin, John, 2:888, 891
  cantors, 3:85
  Carnesecchi, Pietro, 3:147
  Carpzov family, 3:174–175
  Carranza, Bartolomé, 3:176
  Catherine of Genoa, St., 3:271
  Centuriators of Magdeburg, 1:465,
    3:18, 347–348
  Chemnitz, Martin, 3:463–464
  Chile, 3:486
  Christian II (King of Denmark),
    1:643
  Clement VII (Pope), 3:782
  colonial United States, 3:646, 649
  comparative liturgics, 8:722–723
  Concord Formula and Book, 4:60–61
  confessions of faith in, 4:78–79, 81,
    82
  conservative, 8:247
  Council of Trent, 3:431
  Cranmer, Thomas, 4:334
  Denmark, 4:665–666, 12:19

Evangelical Lutheran Church in
  America (ELCA), 5:470–471
  Exsurge Domine on, 1:66, 3:482, 609
  Finland, 12:19
  France, 12:18
  fundamental doctrine, 8:892–895
  fundamentalism, 6:27–28
  General Council, 8:247
  Germany, 8:691, 892
  grace, 3:538
  heresy of, 6:775–776
  history of Lutheran institutions and
    church life, 8:888–892
  Hollaz, David, 7:10
  Hungary, 7:213–214
  Hussites, 4:482
  hymnody, 7:255
  Iceland, 7:274, 276
  impact on liturgical reforms, 8:659
  Indian mission, 7:403
  Italy, 12:19
  justification dialogues, 8:90–91
  Latvia, 8:375–376
  law and gospel, 8:893
  Lawrence of Brindisi, 8:407
  liberalism, 8:891–892
  liturgical calendar, 8:644
  liturgical movement, 8:677–678
  liturgical music history, 8:691
  Majoristic controversy in, 9:62–63
  Neo-Lutheranism, 8:891
  Netherlands, 12:18–19
  North America, 5:330
  Norway, 10:448–450
  orthodoxy, 8:765, 890–891
  overview, 3:608
  Peace of Augsburg, 3:431
  Pietism, 7:10, 8:891
  reforms, early, 8:881–882
  Schmalkaldic League, 12:741
  Seripando, G., 13:17
  Spain, 13:330
  Sweden, 9:45, 12:19, 13:636–637
  synods, proliferation of independent,
    8:886
  Ten Commandments, 4:6
  ubiquitarianism of, 14:263
  U.S. church membership, 3:719
  See also Gnesiolutheranism;
    Philippism
Lutheran-Roman Catholic Dialogue in
  the United States, 5:40
Lutyens, E., 3:672
Luu van Nguyen, Joseph, 14:496
Lux Mundi (Gore), **8:896**

Luxembourg, **8:896–899**, *897*, *898*

Luxeuil Abbey (France), 3:600, 864, 5:455–456, **8:899**

Luxeuil Lectionary, 6:70

Luxeuil Rule, 8:59–60

Luxor Temple (Egypt), 5:*120*, 131

Luzarches, Robert de, 1:359

Luzy, Joseph (Brother), 2:151

Lwanga, Charles, St., **8:899**

LXX. *See* Septuagint

Lycidas (Milton), 9:643

Lyco (Roman philosopher), 1:668

Lydus (Roman historian), 1:92

Lyell, Charles, 4:531, 532

Lying, 4:588–589, **8:899–903**, 9:499, 13:141

Lyke, James Patterson (Abp. of Atlanta), 1:831, **8:903**

Lyman, Theodore, 3:472

Lynch, Baptista, Mother, **8:903**

Lynch, John Joseph (Abp. of Toronto), **8:903–904**

Lynch, Kenny (Father), 9:*629*

Lynch, Patrick Nelson (Bp. of Charleston), **8:904**, 13:365–366

Lynch, William, 7:582

Lynch v. Donnelly (1984), 3:668

Lyndon, Maynard, 3:716

Lyndwood, William (Bp. of St. David's), 3:481, **8:904–905**

Lynes, Paul d'Albert (Card.), 3:794

Lyng v. Northwest Indian Cemetery Protective Association (1988), 3:663

Lyonese Rite, 4:50, **8:905–906**

Lyonnet, Stanislaus, 5:523, **8:906**

Lyons, Councils of, **8:906–908**

  filioque, 5:719, 721

  Franciscan suppression, 5:902, 12:464

  Honorius IV (Pope), 7:85

  Leo II (Pope), St., 8:494

  Robert Grosseteste on Church corruption, 12:263–264

  Robert of Winchelsea, 3:72

  veneration of relics prohibition, 12:54

  first (1244-45), 8:906–907

    Albert II of Riga and, 1:221

    Alexander of Hales and, 1:265

    Boniface of Savoy, Bl. and, 2:505

    Canon Law and, 3:48

    cardinalate and, 3:105

    convocation of, 4:301

    Holy Roman Empire and, 3:603

    Innocent IV (Pope) and, 7:474–475

  papacy development and, 10:838

  second (1274-75), 8:907–908

    Adrian V (Pope) and, 1:127

    Angelus Clarenus and, 1:428

    apostolici and, 1:594

    Bonaventure, St. and, 2:484

    Canon Law and, 3:48

    Carmelites and, 3:132, 141

    commendation reform, 4:9

    Confirmation, 4:87

    dead, prayers for, 4:556

    descent of Christ into hell and, 4:685

    Divine judgment, 8:32

    Eastern Schism and, 2:762, 763, 825–826, 4:188

    God the Holy Spirit, 6:294

    Gregory X (Pope) and, 6:498–499

    Holy Name and, 7:31–32

    Latin language and, 2:770

    papacy development and, 10:838

    purgatory, 11:825

    suppression of mendicant orders, 6:1

    transubstantiation, 14:159

    usury, 14:354

Lyons, Martyrs of, 4:83

Lyons, Rite of, 3:189

Lyons, Synods of, 1:561, 5:651

Lyons Archdiocese (France), 8:905–906

Lysias, 9:11

M

Ma mère (Schrijvers), 12:787

Ma Xiangbo, 3:500

Maacah (Aramaean state), 1:624

Maban (cantor), 1:57

Mabillon, D., 3:418

Mabillon, Jean, 2:471, 3:185, 4:757, 8:223, 379, **9:1**

Mac Giolla Choinne, Brian, 7:582

Mac O'Cagha, Loughlin, 7:580

Macarius (Patriarch of Antioch), 4:193

Macarius Magnes (Bp.), **9:1–2**

Macarius of Alexandria (Father), St., **9:2**

Macarius of Jerusalem, St., 1:685, **9:2**

Macarius of Pelecete, St., **9:2**

Macarius Scottus, Bl., **9:2–3**

Macarius the Egyptian, St., **9:3**

Macau, **9:4–5**, *5*

Macbeth (Shakespeare), 2:116

MacBriody, Bernard, 7:582

MACC. *See* Mexican American Cultural Center

Maccabee, Abaron. *See* Maccabee, Eleazar (d. 163 B.C.)

Maccabee, Apphus. *See* Maccabee, Jonathan (160-143 B.C.)

Maccabee, Eleazar (d. 163 B.C.), 9:10

Maccabee, Gaddis. *See* Maccabee, John (d. 160 B.C.)

Maccabee, John (d. 160 B.C.), 9:10

Maccabee, Jonathan (160-143 B.C.), 9:6, 11

Maccabee, Judas (166-160 B.C.), 9:5–6, 8, 9, *9*, 10–11

Maccabee, Simon (143-134 B.C.), 9:6, 11–12

Maccabee, Thasi. *See* Maccabee, Simon (143-134 B.C.)

Maccabees, 1:320, 529, **9:9–12**

Maccabees, Books of the, **9:5–9**, *7*

  altars in, 1:319

  beatific vision, 2:171

  biblical canon, 3:24

  creation, 4:342

  Galatia, 6:51

  God's spirit, 13:427

  Hebrews, 6:698

  martyr literature in, 1:94

  overview, 1:550, 557

  purgatory, 11:824–825

  Roman province of Asia in, 1:784

  seventy weeks of years, 13:40

  spirit, 13:425

MacCarthy, Dermot, 7:575

MacClanchy, Daniel, 7:582

MacColgan, Clement, 7:582

MacConnell, Rory, 7:579

MacCreid, Donough, 7:580

MacDonald, Alexander, **9:12**

MacDonell, Alexander (Bp.), 3:8, **9:12–13**

MacDonnell, Felix, 7:582

MacEachen, Evan, **9:13**

MacEachern, Angus (Bp.), 3:8

MacEagan, Eugene (Bp. of Ross, Ireland), 7:580

Macedo Costa, Antônio de (Bp.), 2:596, **9:13–14**

Macedonia, **9:14–16**

  Constantinople Council I, 4:190, 198, 354

  demographic statistics, 9:15

  ecclesiastical organization, 9:15–16

  map, 9:*16*

  Paul, St., 1:784

Macedonian Orthodox Church, 9:15, 13:10

Macedonianism, 13:566, 14:204

Macedonians. *See* Pneumatomachians

Macedonius, St., **9:16**

MacEgan, Cormac, 7:581

Macelwane, James Bernard (Father), **9:16–17**, 12:563

Macerata, Pietro da, 3:321

Macevilly, John (Abp.), **9:17**

MacGauran, Edmund (Bp. of Armagh, Ireland), 7:580

MacGinley, John B., 2:869

MacGoill, Hugh, 7:582

MacGollen, William, 7:581

MacGoran, Charles, 7:579

MacGrath, Myler, 7:581

MacGreith, Thomas, 7:580

Mach, C., 12:768

Mach, Ernst, 1:835, 3:302, 11:299, 315

Machado, João Bapt., Bl., 7:732

MacHale, John (Abp. of Tuam, Ireland), 2:368, 7:562, **9:17–18**

Machaut, Guillaume de, 8:685, **9:18–19**, *128*, 10:13

Machebeuf, Joseph Projectus (Bp. of Denver), 3:858, 859, 4:668, 8:316, **9:19**, 10:287

Mächen, 10:126–127

Machen, John Gresham, 5:473, 6:28

Machiavelli, Niccolò, **9:19–22**, 11:293
  absolutism, 1:44
  Buonaccorsi, Filippo, 2:693
  Catherine de Médicis, 3:266
  Church-State relations, 3:637
  Cromwell, Thomas, 4:377
  fortune, 5:824
  public vs. private morality, 5:394
  Renaissance humanism, 12:118
  Renaissance philosophy, 12:124
  republic as form, 4:640
  royal absolutism, 9:781–782

Machiavellian principle, 9:22

Macho Rodríquez, Maurilio, Bl., 4:494

Machutus. *See* Maclovius (Bp.), St.

Maciejowski, Bernard (Card.), 2:605

Maciel, Marcial, 8:454

MacInerny, Jeremiah, 7:582

Macintosh, Donald, 1:578

Macintosh, United States v. (1931), 3:660

MacIver, Robert, 13:283

Mack, Alexander, Sr., 3:721

Mackemie, Francis, 3:648

MacKenraghty, Maurice, Bl., 7:580

MacKenzie, R. A. F., 5:520

MacKeon, Hugh, 7:582

Mackey, R., 13:783

Mackey, William (Father), 2:353

MacKillop, Maria Ellen. *See* MacKillop, Mary Helen, Bl.

MacKillop, Mary Helen, Bl., 1:905, **9:23**

Maclagan, William (Abp. of York), 1:594

MacLaine, Shirley, 10:273

MacLeod, Colin, 2:404

Maclovius (Bp.), St., **9:23**

MacMahon, Ever (Bp. of Clogher, Ireland), 7:581, **9:24**

MacMahon, Hugh, 7:581

Macmillan, John, 2:912

MacNamara, Roger, 7:582

MacNeill, E., 10:955

MacNutt, Francis Augustus, **9:24**

MacNutt, Sylvester, 11:625

Macomber, William, 5:4, 5, 6

Mâcon, Councils of, 1:134, 3:409

Maconi, Stephen, 3:192

Macpherson, John (Father), **9:24–25**

MacQuhirrie, Alexander, 1:467

MacRae, G., 2:532

Macrembolites, Eustathius, 2:806

Macriana, Council of (419), 1:116

Macrina, St., 2:135, 144–145

Macrina, SS., **9:25**

Macrina the Elder, 9:25

Macrina the Younger, 9:25

Macrinus (Roman Emperor), 12:312

Macrobius, 3:161, 441, **9:25–26**, 12:320

Macrory, Joseph (Card.), **9:26**

MacSorley, Alexander, 7:581

Macuarta, Conor, 7:579

Madagascar, **9:26–28**, *27*

Madame Dorothea (Undset), 14:295

Madaura (Africa), Martyrs of, **9:28**

Madeira, Hilario (Father), 5:10

La Madeleine Church (Paris), 3:708

La Madeleine Church (Vézelay, France), 3:692

Madeleine de Saint Joseph, 3:136

Madeleva, Mary (Sister), 5:676, 680, **9:28–29**, *29*

Madelonnettes, 9:33

Maderno, Carlo, 3:703–705, 12:580

Madhva (Hindu teacher), 6:847

Madison, James (Bp. of Virginia), 5:297

Madison, James (U.S. president), 3:652, 4:641

Madison Square Presbyterian Church (New York), 3:716

Madonna, 9:*273*
  See also Mary, Blessed Virgin

Madonna and Child (Black Virgin), 13:*379*

Madonna and Child (Botticelli), 13:*311*

Madonna and Child (Tiepolo), 7:*665*

Madonna House (Combermere, ON), 4:614, 892

Madrasah, 7:616

La Madre di Dio madre degliuomini (Ventura), 14:442

Madre Moretta (Black Mother). *See* Bakhita, Giuseppina, St.

Madrigal, Justino Orona, St., 6:545

Madrigals, 1:630

Madruzzi (Card.), 2:51

Madruzzo, Carlo Emanuele (Bp., 1599-1658), 9:30

Madruzzo, Carlo Gaudenzio (Bp., 1562-1629), 9:29–30

Madruzzo, Cristoforo (Bp., 1512-1578), 9:29, *30*

Madruzzo, Lodovico (Bp., 1532-1600), 9:29

Madruzzo family, **9:29–30**

Maelor. *See* Maglorius (Bp.), St.

Maelruain, St., 13:739

Máel-Ruain of Tamlachta, 4:423

Maes, Boniface, **9:30–31**

Maes, Camillus Paul (Bp. of Covington), 4:331, **9:31**

Maffei, Bernardino (Card., 1514-53), 9:31

Maffei, Celso (c. 1425-1508), 9:31

Maffei, Francesco Scipione (1675-1755), 9:32

Maffei, Giampietro (1535-1603), 9:31–32

Maffei, Marcantonio (Card., 1521-83), 9:31–32

Maffei, Paolo (d. 1480), 9:31

Maffei, Paolo Alessandro (1653-1716), 9:32

Maffei, Raffaela (1451-1522), 9:32

Maffei, Timoteo (c. 1400-70), 9:31

Maffei family, **9:31–32**

Maffeo, 3:492

Magalhães, Francis de, Bl., 1:951–952, 12:728

Magallanes, Cristobal, 5:359, 774

Magallanes, Mateo Correa, St., 6:545

Magallanes Jara, Cristóbal, St., 6:545, **9:32**

Magan, Honoria, 7:582

Maganotto, Peter, 2:867

Magdalen Albrici, Bl., **9:32–33**

Magdeburg Cathedral (Germany), 1:315

Magdeline of Jesus, Little Sister, 8:616

Mageddo, 3:3, **9:469**

Magellan, Ferdinand, 1:648

Magennis, Elias, 3:144

Magennis, Terence, 7:580

Mager, Alois, 4:208

Maggiolini, Alessandro (Bp.), 3:237

Magi, 1:805, **9:33–35**

Magi (plays), 4:896

Magic, **9:35–39**

    alleged properties of precious stones, 11:646

    art, 1:736–737

    astrology, 1:812

    black, 9:37

    contagious, 9:37–38

    curses, 4:442

    gnosiological, 9:38

    Haiti, 8:157

    Hittite religion, 6:895

    incantations, 7:369

    Kakubilla, 8:109

    Magi, 9:34

    mantras, 9:125

    Mesopotamia, ancient, 9:536–537

    necromancy form of, 10:229–230

    object, 9:37

    primitive prayer, 11:589

    religion, 12:57–58, 64

    sympathetic, 9:38

    white, 9:37

    worship, 14:851–852

    See also Witchcraft

Magic, in the Bible, **9:39**

    example of necromancy, 10:230

    serpent as symbol, 13:20–21

    Simon Magus, 13:130–131

Maginnis, John, 12:646

Magister Adam Anglicus, 1:108

Magisterium, 7:93, 96, 13:247, 14:135–136, 159

Magisterium divinale (William of Auvergne), 14:736

Magisterium vitae (motu proprio, Paul VI), 11:487

Magistri, 8:848

Magistri Comacini, **9:39**

    See also Freemasonry

Magliano, Pamfilo da (Father), 5:878, 880, 12:540

Maglione, Luigi (Card.), **9:40**

Magloire. *See* Maglorius (Bp.), St.

Maglorius (Bp.), St., **9:40**

Magna Carta, 5:242, 7:914, **9:40–42**, *41*, 12:6, 263

Magna Mater, 5:2, 746

Magna Mater cult, 10:91–92

Magnanimity, 1:334, 7:179, 206–207, **9:42**

Magner, James A., 3:283

Magnericus of Trier (Abp.), St., **9:42**

Magni, Alessio A., 7:792

Magni, Valeriano (Father), **9:43**

Magni Nobis Gaudii (apostolic letter, Leo XIII), 3:290

Magnien, Alphonse, **9:43**

Magnificat (Lobo, D.), 8:741

Magnificat (song), 3:73, 8:687, **9:43–44**, 243–244, 13:249

Magnificence, **9:44**

Magnobod of Angers (Bp.), St., 1:431, **9:44–45**

Magnum Matrimonii Sacramentum (apostolic constitution, John Paul II), 7:1006, 11:486

Magnus, Johannes (Abp. of Uppsala), **9:45**

Magnus, Olaus (Abp. of Uppsala), 5:732, **9:45**

Magnus, Philip, 2:702

Magnus Dominus et laudabilis nimis (Clement VIII), 2:606, 14:278

Magnus liber organi. . . (Léonin), 8:499, 684

Magnus of Füssen, St., **9:45**

Magnus opus musicum (Lasso), 8:343

Magnyfycence (Skelton), 9:882

Maguire, Cathal, 1:464

Maguire, Charles Bonaventure (Father), **9:45–46**, 11:366

Maguire, Conor, 7:581

Maguire, John William Rochfort (Father), **9:46**

Magyars, 7:209–210, 213–214, 216

The Mahābhārata (Hindu epic), 6:844

Mahadī, 2:3

Maharishi, Ramana, 6:852

Maharishi Mahesh Yogi, 14:144

Mahāvīra (founder of Jainism), 7:697

Mahāyāna Buddhism, 2:452, 657, 661, **9:46–48**, 13:631–632

Mahbūb ibn Qustantin. *See* Agapios

Mahdī, Al-, 1:191, **9:48**

Maher, Michael, 12:775

Mahler, Gustav, **9:48–49**, *49*

Mahon, Roger (Bp.), 2:872

Mahoney, Dennis, 7:541

Mahoney, John, 7:528

Mahoney, William, 1:582

Mahony, Roger M. (Abp. of Los Angeles), 1:25, 8:793

Mahzor, **9:49–50**

Mahzor Vitry, 9:50

Mahzor Yannai (Yannai), 9:50

Mai, Angelo (Card.), **9:50**

Maida, Adam (Card.), 1:25, 3:58, 4:*697*, 699, 14:783

Maidalchini, Olimpia, 7:480

Maier, Anneliese, 1:678, 937, **9:50–51**

Maier, H., 1:834

Maignan, Minim Emmanuel, 12:771

Maignen, Charles, 1:355–356

Maigret, Louis (Bp.), 6:669, 670

Maigrot, Charles (Bp. of Fujian), 3:497, 514–515

Maildubh, 1:246

Maile, L., 12:31

Mailla, Joseph Anne Marie Moyria de (Father), **9:51**

Maillard, Olivier, 5:848

Maillard, Pierre, 7:25

Maillet, B. de, 5:260

Maimbourg, Louis (Father), **9:51–52**

Maimon, Moses ben. *See* Maimonides (Jewish philosopher)

Maimon, Saolmon, 8:125, 12:345

Maimonides (Jewish philosopher), 5:509, **9:52–54**, *53*

    Albo, Joseph, 1:232

    Alfarabi, 1:277

    Aristotelian philosophy, 7:864

    Aristotelianism, 1:673

    Bible texts, 2:356

    cabala, 2:833

    Caro, Joseph ben Ephraim, 3:148

    condemnation on works of, 7:870

    Crescas, Ḥasdai ben Abraham, 4:361

    debate over *Guide for the Perplexed*, 10:135

    free will, 5:929

    geniza, 6:135–136

    Gerson, 8:521

    Ibn Tibbon, Samuel, 7:274

    I-It mysticism of, 10:117

    immortality, 7:349

    messianism, 13:56

    Spinoza, 13:418

    thirteen principles, 8:8

La Main de Dieu sur les incrédules, ou histoire abrégée des Israélites (Touron), 14:125

Main National University of San Marcos. *See* San Marcos, Main National University of

Maine, 2:56, **9:54–59**, 721, 11:898
See also specific dioceses and archdioceses
Maine (battleship), 3:482
Maine Catholic Historical Society, 9:58
Maini, Giovanni Battista, 3:790
Mainz, Councils of, 3:412, 413
Mainz, Synods of
    (813), 1:68, 3:240
    (1049), 2:98
Mainz Cathedral (Germany), 3:691
Mainz Circle, 6:183
Mainz-Bischofsheim Church (Germany), 3:711
Mainzer Journal, 10:75
Maiora in dies (motu proprio, John XXIII), 11:476
Maistre, Claude Pascal, 1:157
Maistre, Joseph Marie de, 3:624, 5:854, 969, **9:60–61**
    political theology, 11:460
    traditionalism of, 14:138
    Ultramontanism, 10:847
Maitland, S. R., 2:508
Maiztegui, Joseph, 3:764–765
Majella, Gerard, St., **9:61–62**
Majestas Domini (iconography), 7:857–858
Majestas Mariae (Virgin in Majesty), 9:274
Majláth, Gusztáv, 7:218
Majolus of Cluny, St., 3:814, **9:62**, 12:577, 13:371
Major, Georg (Maier), 4:416, **9:62**
Major, Matthew. *See* Flathers, Matthew, Bl.
Major Francis (Bosboom-Toussaint), 2:542
The Major Life of Saint Francis (Bonaventure), 5:896, 899
Major orders (Holy orders), 7:37–38
Major prophets, 11:765
Major Superiors of Women's Religious Institutes, 2:119
Major Week. *See* Holy Week
Majorian (Roman Emperor in the West), 12:321, 355
Majoristic controversy, **9:62–63**
Makemie, Francis, 3:646, 9:63, **63**
Maki, John, Bl., 7:734
Maki, Louis, Bl., 7:734
Malabar Independent Syrian Church of Thozhiyur, 7:401
Malabar Rites controversy, 3:790
Malachi, Book of, **9:63–65**
    apocalyptic style, 1:546

Elijah, 5:159
eschatology, 5:336
heaven, 6:684
Lord as honorific title, 8:780
magic, 9:39
Malachy, St., 1:697, 7:554, **9:65**, 481
Malagrida, Gabriel (Father), **9:65–66**, 11:467
Malankara (Indian) Orthodox Syrian Church, 7:400
Malaspina, Germanico, **9:66**, 11:442
Malatesta, Carlo (d. 1429), 9:66–67
Malatesta, Domenico di Pandolfo (d. 1465), 9:66–67
Malatesta, Galeotto Roberto, Bl. (d. 1432), 9:66–67
Malatesta, Giovanni (d. 1304), 9:66
Malatesta, Giovanni (fl. 1237), 9:66
Malatesta, Malatesta da Verucchio (fl. 1312), 9:66
Malatesta, Malatestina (fl. 1312), 9:66
Malatesta, Novello. *See* Malatesta, Domenico di Pandolfo (d. 1465)
Malatesta, Pandolfo (d. ca. 1326), 9:66
Malatesta, Pandolfo, II (d. 1373), 9:66
Malatesta, Pandolfo, III, 9:66–67
Malatesta, Pandolfo, IV (d. 1523), 9:66–67
Malatesta, Paolo, 9:66
Malatesta, Roberto (d. 1482), 9:66–67
Malatesta, Salustio, 9:66–67
Malatesta, Sigismondo di Pandolfo (d. 1468), 9:66–67
Malatesta family, **9:66–67**
Malatesta Temple (Rimini, Italy), 3:692
Malaval, Francis, 11:866, 867
Malawi, **9:67–69**, 68
Malaysia, **9:69–72**, 70
Malaysian Catholic News, 13:80
Malaysian Consultative Council of Buddhism, Christianity, Hinduism, and Sikhism (MCCB-CHS), 9:72
Malberg, Mme. Carré de, 3:457
Malchion, 1:526
Malchus (Byzantine historian), 2:798
Malchus, St. (Syrian hermit), 12:29, 606
Malcolm, Norman, 10:603
Malder, John. *See* Malderus, John (Bp. of Antwerp)
Malderus, John (Bp. of Antwerp), **9:72**
Maldonado, José, 12:616
Maldonado, Juán de. *See* Maldonatus, Johannes (Father)
Maldonado Lucero, Pedro de Jesús (Father), St., **9:72**

Maldonatus, Johannes (Father), 5:518, 523, **9:73**, 12:29, 764
Mâle, Émile, 3:676, **9:73**
Malebranche, Nicolas, 2:116, 5:395, 9:73, **73–76**, 11:293
    absolute optimism, 10:613
    Augustinianism, 1:881
    beatific vision, 2:169
    Bufalo, St. Gaspare del, 2:675
    Cartesianism, 3:183, 184, 185
    causality, 3:306
    existence of God, 6:313
    free will, 5:931
    Lamy, B. as disciple, 8:315
    Lamy, F., 8:315
    Lamy, F. as critic, 8:315
    Le Clerc, J., 8:432
    occasionalism, 7:320, 10:526
    ontologism, 10:603–604
    opponent of Descartes, 12:31
    scholasticism, 12:765
Malecite people (Canada), 3:9
Malevansky, Silvester, 12:434
Malevez, Leopold, 6:891
Malevich, Kazimir Severinovich, 3:679–680
Mali, **9:76–77**, 77
Mālikite school, 7:622–623
Malines Conversations (1921-26), 3:625, 5:978, **9:78**
    Beauduin, Lambert, 2:183
    Benedict XV (Pope), 2:250
    Davidson, Randall Thomas, 4:543
    Mercier, Désiré Joseph, 2:183
Malinovsky, Nicholas, 12:434
Malinowski, Bronislaw, 4:427, 430, 10:122, 12:65, 867–868
Mallarmé, Stéphane, 3:767
Malleus in haeresim Lutheranum (Faber), 5:583
Mallinckrodt, Hermann von, 3:340
Mallinckrodt, Marie Bernadine Sophia Pauline. *See* Mallinckrodt, Pauline von, Bl.
Mallinckrodt, Pauline von, Bl., 1:2, 3:533–534, 533, 6:185, **9:78–79**
Malloy, Edward A., 10:462
Malmédy Abbey (Liège, Belgium), **9:79**, 13:111
Malmesbury Abbey (England), **9:79–81**, 80
Malo. *See* Maclovius (Bp.), St.
Malone, James (Bp.), 4:30
Malone, Sylvester (Father), **9:81**
Maloney, John Baptist, 5:250
Maloney, Thomas F., 8:821

Malory, Thomas, 1:762

Malpighi, Marcello, 2:402, 407

Malraux, A., 1:48

Malta, 8:193, 9:82, **82–83**

Maltese Cross, 4:392–393

Malthus, Thomas Robert, 4:531, **9:83–84**

Malvar, Sebastian (Bp.), 12:651

Malvenda, Tomás, **9:84**

Malvern Abbey (Worcester, England), **9:84**

Malvinas Islands War (1982). *See* Falkland Islands War (1982)

Mamelukes, 1:612, 9:196–197

Mamertus, Claudianus, 9:84

Mamertus of Vienne, St., **9:84–85**, 12:283

Mamilian, St. (274-295), 9:376–377

Mamluk people, 4:405, 412

Mammon, 7:305, 9:85

See also Wealth

Man

anthropogonic myths on origin, 10:127

authors as God's instruments, 7:495

in the Bible, 9:85, 87

capacity for good, 10:667–668

as changed by original sin, 10:614

concept of

William of Ockham on, 14:747–748

Wolff, Christian on, 14:808

Genesis creation account, 4:339–340

Logos image as Divine man, 8:759

myths of the primitive state of, 10:127

natural end of, 9:96–103

Nicholas of Cusa on nature of, 10:375

omniscience, 10:596

Origen's theology, 10:657

origin of sin, 13:144

Pacem in terris (encyclical, John XIII) on order, 10:741–742

philosophy, 9:87–92

primordial archetype, 13:316

scholastic definition of, 11:805–806

as social being, 13:246

in the state, 13:485

stoicism, 13:536–537

theology, 9:92–96

Man and Morals (Hawkins), 6:672

The Man Born to Be King (Sayers), 12:716

Man of Sorrows (iconography), 7:859

Manantiales de nuestra fe (Franceschi), 5:864

Mananzan, Mary John, 5:677

Manasseh (King of Judah), 7:642, 766

Manasseh (tribe), 5:276–277

Manasses, Constantine, 2:806

Manasses I (Abp. of Reims), 1:926, 927, 2:649, **9:103**

Mance, Jeanne, 3:4, **9:103**

Manchester Diocese (NH), 10:278–280

Manchukuo, 3:516

Manchuria, 9:108

Mandaean religion, 7:905, 8:565, **9:104**, 12:243

Mandart, Joseph (Father), 1:207–208

Mandate for Action, 12:782

Mandate of Heaven (*Tianming*), 3:507–508

Mandato, Pius de, 12:775

''Mandatum'' (*Epistola..ad RR. Provinciales et ad Definitores..*) (Barlow), 2:102

Mandatum, Academic, **9:104–105**

Mande, Hendrik, 4:708

Mandela, Nelson, 13:361

Mandelbaum, Maurice, 6:871

Mandeville, Bernard, 2:622, 623, 5:107, 395

Mandic, Leopold Bogdan, St., **9:105**

Mandonnet, Pierre, 5:365, **9:105**, 10:244, 12:776

Mandylion, 7:278

Manegold of Lautenbach, 3:635, **9:105–106**, 13:39, 239

Manegoldi ad Gebhardum liber (Manegold of Lautenbach), 9:105–106

Manehen, 1:521

Manenti, Orazio, 10:4

Manes. *See* Mānī (3rd c. missionary)

Manessier, Alfred, 2:524, 4:397

Manetti, Teresa Maria della Croce, Bl., **9:106**

Manger-crib, Christmas. *See* Crib, Christmas

Mangin, Leon, 1:400

Manharter, **9:106**

Mānī (3rd c. missionary), 9:106–108, *107*, 110, 112, 114, 11:782

Manichaeism, **9:106–117**

Aquilinus of Milan, St., 1:609

Augustine, St., 1:852, 856–857, 858, 862, 864, 866, 3:186

Bogomilism, 2:458, 459, 759

Buddhism, 2:660–661

Burkitt, Francis Crawford, 2:706

Byzantine theology, 2:759, 794

clerical celibacy/marriage, 3:326

creation doctrine, 4:343

demonology, 4:649

Diocletian, 4:748

dualism in, 1:230

Faustus of Mileve, 10:13

Hydatius, 7:236

list of sins, 13:149

procreation, 4:218–219

women's rights, 14:815

Zoroastrianism, 11:145

See also Albigensians

Manichaeus. *See* Mānī (3rd c. missionary)

Manifest sinners, denial of Church funeral, 6:33–34

The Manifestation (al-Bayān) (al-Bāb), 2:3

Manifestation of Conscience, **9:115–117**

Manifesto on Rural Life (Muench), 10:51

Maniple, 8:633, 9:*117*, **117–118**

Mankidiyan, Mariam Thresia Chiramel, Bl., 8:306, **9:118**

Mankudian, Thresia. *See* Mankidiyan, Mariam Thresia Chiramel, Bl.

Mankynd (play), 9:882–883

Mann, Horace Kinder (Father), 3:655, **9:118**

Mann, Thomas, 5:650

Manna, 5:413, **9:118–119**, *119*

Manna, Paolo, **9:119–120**

Mannerism, 2:107, 424, 3:674

The Manners, Lawes, and Customes of All Nations (Fides, Religio, Moresque Aethiopum) (Góis), 6:334

Mannheim, Karl, 8:211–212, 14:361

Mannheim School (Austria), 8:692–693, 12:240

Manning, Henry Edward (Card.), 5:251–252, **9:120–122**, *121*, 10:735, 12:417

Catherine of Genoa, St., 3:271

Gladstone, William, 6:236–237

Lemire, J., 8:466

Oblates of St. Charles, 10:515

papal infallibility, 2:507

preaching, 11:625

social justice issues, 3:620

works of charity, 3:420

Manning, Timothy (Card.), 8:792–793, **9:122–123**

Mannix, Daniel (Abp. of Melbourne), 1:904, 3:864, 9:*123*, **123**

Mannix v. Purcell (1888), 3:656

Manny, Walter, 8:772

Manogue, Patrick (Bp. of Sacramento), **9:123–124**, *124*, 10:270

Mañoso González, Benito José Labre, Bl., 7:123

Manríquez y Zárate, José de Jesús, **9:124–125**

Man's Last End (Buckley), 9:101

Man's Nature and His Communities (Niebuhr), 10:387

Man's Vision of God and the Logic of Theism (Hartshorne), 6:658

Mansart, François, 3:706

Mansart, Jules Hardouin, 3:706

Mansel, H. L., 1:676, 12:841

Mansi, Giovanni Domenico (Abp.), 3:804, **9:125**

Mansion, Auguste, 12:776

Manso, Alonso, 3:110

Manso, Pedro, 1:880

Manson, T. W., 7:850

Mansour, Tanios Bou, 7:528

Mansuetus a S. Felice, 12:769

Al-Manṣūr, 1:6

Mantegna, Andrea, 10:949

Mantellate Sisters, **9:125**, 13:24

Mantello, 10:856

Mantras, **9:125**

Mantua, Council of (1064), 1:253

Manual of Discipline (Qumran), 14:462

Manual para Catekizar (Ruíz Blanco), 12:407

Manuale controversiarum (Becanus), 2:191

Manuale di Pandette (Ferrini), 5:696

Manuale Parochorum (Engel), 5:220

Manuale pratico del parocho novello (Frassinetti), 5:920

Manucci, Teobaldo. *See* Manutius, Aldus (1450-1515)

Manucy, Dominic (Bp. of Mobile, AL), 1:201, 9:749

Manuductio ad stoicam philosophiam (Lipsius), 12:125

Manuductionis ad moralem theologian pars altera (Baron), 2:104–105

Manuel, State v., 6:106

Manuel I (King of Portugal), 11:536–537

Manuel I Comnenus (Byzantine Emperor), 1:126, 255, 813, 2:29, 759

Manuel II (Palaeologus) (Byzantine Emperor), 2:651, 4:454, **9:125–126**

Manuel II (Patriarch of Constantinople), 2:761, 826, **9:126**

Manuel Calecas, 2:762, 827, 4:454, **9:126–127**

Manuel Chrysoloras, 12:622

Manuel Comnenus (Emperor of Jerusalem), 4:403

Manuel de paléographie (Prou), 10:774

Manuel de spiritualité (Saudreau), 12:708

Manuel du droit public ecclésiastique française (Dupin), 6:77

Manug, Peter. *See* Mechitar (Father)

Manus quae contra omnipotentem (Thomas of York), 14:39

Manuscript illumination, 3:601, **9:127–129**

Apocalypse iconography, 1:543, 544

Bible cycles in, 2:370, 373

Carolingian art, 8:436

Carolingian era, 1:448, 543, 3:154, 167, 426

Charles II the Bald, 9:*127*

Cistercians, 3:750

Cluniacs, 3:812

courtly love, 4:320

crosses, 4:379

crucifixions, 4:395

Durrow, Book of, 4:953–954

Echternach Abbey school of, 5:42

embroidery compared, 8:635

Fiesole, Guido da, Bl., 5:716

The Hours of Jeanne d'Evreux, 8:*639*

Hyde Abbey, 7:*236*, 237

Joan of Arc. St., 9:*229*

Lindisfarne Gospels, 8:593

Louis IX and Queen Blanche, 8:*800*

Machaut, Guillaume de, 9:*128*

Mark, Evangelist, St., 9:*184*

Silos Abbey library, 13:120

Manutius, Aldus (1450-1515), 2:522, 9:129

Manutius, Aldus, II (1547-97), 7:186, 188, 9:130, 10:772

Manutius, Paulus (1512-74), 9:130

Manutius family, **9:129–130**

Manuzio, Aldo. *See* Manutius, Aldus (1450-1515)

Manyanet y Vives, José (Joseph), Bl. (Father), 7:23, **9:130**

Manz, Felix, 1:368

Manzù, 2:376

Mao Trong Ha, Dominic, 14:496

Maolíosa, Nicholas Mac, 1:697

Maori people (New Zealand), 10:324–325, 328

Map of the Jesuits, 4:491

Mapas. *See* Stylianos of Neocaesarea (Abp.)

Mappa Mundi (Gervase of Canterbury), 6:193

Maps

Afghanistan, 1:*154*

Albania, 1:*214*

Algeria, 1:*284*

Andorra, 1:*402*

Angola, 1:*451*

Argentina, 1:*650*

Armenia, 1:*700*

Australia, 1:*901*

Austria, 1:*909*

Bahamas, 2:*14*

Bahrain, 2:*17*

Bangladesh, 2:*52*

Belarus, 2:*211*

Belgium, 2:*216*

Belize, 2:*226*

Benin, 2:*281*

Bhutan, 2:*354*

Bolivia, 2:*467*

Bosnia-Herzegovina, 2:*546*

Botswana, 2:*561*

Brazil, 2:*591*

Brunei, 2:*645*

Bulgaria, 2:*681*

Burkina Faso, 2:*705*

Burma, 2:*707*

Burundi, 2:*711*

Cambodia, 2:*902*

Cameroon, 2:*915*

Canada, 3:*5*

Cape Verde, 3:*80*

Caribbean, 3:*109*

Central African Republic, 3:*345*

Chad, 3:*360*

Chile, 3:*487*

China, 3:*491*

Colombia, 3:*849*

Comoros, 4:*41*

Congo, Democratic Republic of, 4:*105*

Congo, Republic of, 4:*109*

Costa Rica, 4:*289*

Croatia, 4:*373*

Cuba, 4:*418*

Cyprus, 4:*461*

Czech Republic, 4:*480*

Denmark, 4:*663*

Djibouti, 4:*795*

Dominican Republic, 4:*835*

Ecuador, 5:*64*

Egypt, 5:*110*

El Salvador, 5:*176*

England, 5:*241*
Equatorial Guinea, 5:*309*
Eritrea, 5:*321*
Estonia, 5:*377*
Ethiopia, 5:*399*
Finland, 5:*733*
France, 5:*844*
Gabon, 6:*41*
Gambia, 6:*86*
Germany, 6:*173*
Ghana, 6:*199*
Greece, 6:*435*
Guatemala, 6:*552*
Guinea, 6:*575*
Guinea-Bissau, 6:*577*
Guyana, 6:*589*
Haiti, 6:*620*
Honduras, 7:*75*
Hungary, 7:*211*
Iceland, 7:*276*
India, 7:*394*
Indonesia, 7:*430*
Iran, 7:*544*
Iraq, 7:*546*
Ireland, 7:*555*
Italy, 7:*655*
Ivory Coast, 7:*682*
Jamaica, 7:*700*
Japan, 7:*738*
Jordan, 7:*1030*
Kenya, 8:*151*
Korea, 8:*240, 241*
Kuwait, 8:*259*
Laos, 8:*330*
Latvia, 8:*376*
Lebanon, 8:*428*
Lesotho, 8:*516*
Liberia, 8:*552*
Libya, 8:*559*
Liechtenstein, 8:*562*
Lithuania, 8:*604*
Luxembourg, 8:*897*
Macau, 9:*5*
Macedonia, 9:*16*
Madagascar, 9:*27*
Malawi, 9:*68*
Malaysia, 9:*70*
Mali, 9:*77*
Malta, 9:*82*
Mauritania, 9:*372*
Mauritius, 9:*374*
Mexico, 9:*577*
Moldova, 9:*766*
Monaco, 9:*778*

Mongolia, 9:*806*
Morocco, 9:*898*
Mozambique, 10:*40*
Nepal, 10:*246*
Netherlands, 10:*256*
New Zealand, 10:*326*
Nicaragua, 10:*352*
Niger, 10:*392*
Nigeria, 10:*395*
Norway, 10:*449*
Oman, 10:*589*
Pakistan, 10:*760*
Panama, 10:*818*
Paraguay, 10:*878*
Peru, 11:*160*
Philippines, 11:*257*
Poland, 11:*441*
Portugal, 11:*535*
Puerto Rico, 11:*815*
Romania, 12:*331*
Russia, 12:*420*
Rwanda, 12:*442*
San Marino, 12:*653*
São Tomé and Principe, 12:*688*
Saudi Arabia, 12:*707*
Scotland, 12:*831*
Senegal, 12:*905*
Serbia and Montenegro, 13:*9*
Seychelles, 13:*53*
Sierra Leone, 13:*111*
Singapore, 13:*162*
Slovakia, 13:*220*
Slovenia, 13:*226*
Somalia, 13:*309*
South Africa, 13:*362*
Spain, 13:*378*
Sri Lanka, 13:*463*
Sudan, 13:*583*
Suriname, 13:*628*
Swaziland, 13:*634*
Sweden, 13:*636*
Switzerland, 13:*647*
Syria, 13:*700*
Taiwan, 13:*734*
Tanzania, 13:*757*
Thailand, 13:*850*
Togo, 14:*99*
Tunisia, 14:*237*
Turkey, 14:*240*
Uganda, 14:*267*
Ukraine, 14:*274*
United Arab Emirates, 14:*306*
United Kingdom, 14:*611*
Uruguay, 14:*352*

Vatican City, State of, 14:*400*
Venezuela, 14:*437*
Vietnam, 14:*503*
Western Sahara, 14:*692*
world (Ricci), 12:*223*
Yemen, 14:*887*
Zambia, 14:*908*
Zimbabwe, 14:*927*
See also Cartography
Mapu, Abraham, 6:663
Maquart, F. X., 12:776
Mar 'Abdīshō of Jezirch (Chaldean
    Patriarch), 3:367
Mar Dinkha IV (Assyrian Patriarch),
    1:805, 808
Mar Gregorios of Parumala, St., 7:406
Mar Gregoriose Abdul Jaleel, St., 7:406
Mar Saba Monastery (Kidron Valley,
    Israel), 12:*451*
Mar Simon XXIII (Assyrian Patriarch),
    1:807–808
Mar Thoma Syrian Church of Malabar,
    7:401
Marabotto, Cattaneo, 3:270, 271
Marai, St., **1:112–113**
Maranatha, **9:130–131**
Maranges, Isabel de, 12:553–554
Marango, John, 2:748
Marañón, David Carlos, Bl., **9:131**
Marat, Jean, 5:974
Maratta, Carlo, 3:789
Marbach Abbey (Colmar, France), 3:68,
    9:131–132
Marbán, Pedro, 2:465
Marbeck, Pilgram, **9:132**, 12:795
Marbod (Bp. of Rennes), **9:132**
    Angers, 1:432
    Licinius, 8:561
    medieval Latin literature works of,
        9:450
Marburg School, 8:220, 10:237
    See also Neo-Kantianism
Marc, André, 5:539
Marc, C., 1:311
Marca, Pierre de (Abp. of Paris), 2:47,
    9:132–133
Marca Hispanica (Marca), 9:133
Marcabru (troubadour), 4:400
Marc-Aurèle et la fin du monde antique
    (Renan), 12:126
Marcel, Gabriel, 9:*133*, **133–135**, 11:298
    Augustinianism, 1:882
    consciousness, 4:154
    existentialism, 5:94, 398, 544, 545
    fideism, 5:712

Marcel, Gabriel *(continued)*
   free will, 5:931
   knowledge, theories of, 8:221
   Notre-Dame-de-Toute-Grâces
      Church, 1:803
   reflection, 12:3
   religious experience, 5:556
   Ricoeur, Paul, 12:241
   self, concept of, 12:884
   self-sufficient individualism, 5:348
   soul, 13:348
   soul-body relationship, 13:358
   technocratic world, 8:461
   technological civilizations, 13:785
Marcella, St., 5:457, **9:135**
Marcellian (Bp. of Auxerre), 1:927
Marcelline Sisters, 12:609
Marcellinus, 1:859, 860
Marcellinus (Pope), St., 4:749, **9:135**
Marcellinus, Flavius, **9:135–136**
Marcellinus and Peter, SS., **9:136**
Marcellinus Comes, 1:461
Marcello, Benedetto, **9:136–137**
Marcello of Seville. *See* Spínola y
   Maestre, Marcelo (Card. Abp.), Bl.
Marcellus (Bp. of Ancyra), **9:139**,
   12:692
Marcellus (martyr), 1:92
Marcellus, Publicius, 2:84
Marcellus, SS., **9:137**
Marcellus I (Pope), St., 3:103, 5:201,
   450, **9:137–138**, *138*, 13:*193*
Marcellus II (Pope), 3:610, **9:138–139**,
   13:167
Marcellus Akimetes, St., **9:139**
Marcellus of Ancyra, 5:452, 454
   Arianism, 1:685, 809, 818
   Constantine I (the Great) (Roman
      Emperor), 4:181
   creedal statements, 4:351
   Damasus I (Pope), St., 4:504
   homoousios, 4:353
   School of Antioch, 1:524
   Synod of Sirmium, 1:662
Marcellus of Chalon-sur-Saône, 9:137
Marcellus of Die, 9:137
Marcellus of Paris, 9:137
Marcellus the Centurion, 9:137
March Mesa, Nazaría Ignacia, Bl.,
   9:139–140
Marchand, Joseph, 14:496
Marchand, Michel-Bernard, 12:277
Marchandon, André-Joseph, 12:277
Marchant, Jacques, **9:140**
Marchant, Pierre, **9:140**

Marchena, Antonio de, 3:865
Marchetti-Selvaggiani, Francesco
   (Card.), 1:585
Marchi, G., 3:224
Marchionne, Gian Carlo. *See* Charles of
   Sezze, St.
Marchisio, Clemente, Bl. (Father),
   9:140–141
Marcian (Byzantine Emperor), 1:392,
   3:363, 365, 4:756, 7:224, **9:141**
Marcian of Cyr, St., **9:142**
Marciano, Rocky, 11:*725*
Marciano José, Br., 14:248
Marcianus (Bp. of Arles), 1:694
Marcion, 5:509, **9:142**, 12:351
   apostolicity, 1:595
   biblical canon, 3:30
   creedal statements, 4:351
   Dionysius of Corinth, St., 3:548,
      4:755
   false teachings of, 10:13
   Justin Martyr, St., 8:94
   Luke's Gospel, 8:859
   procreation, 4:218
Marcion (Gnostic teacher), 6:260, 11:782
*Marcion, Das Evangelium vom fremden
   Gott* (Harnack), 6:648
Marcionite sect, 9:142
Marcos, Ferdinand E., 11:259–260
Marcos de Niza, Fray, 1:686
Marcus Aurelius (Roman Emperor),
   5:191, 9:*143*, **143–144**, 12:304, 312
   Benignus of Dijon, St., 2:280
   persecution under, 2:431, 3:406, 592,
      593
Marcus Julius Eugenius (Bp. of
   Laodicea), 8:328
Marcus Mantuanus, 3:52
Marcus of Alexandria (Patriarch), 2:33
Marcus of Arethusa, 1:663
Marcus of Ephesus, 5:279
Marcuse, Herbert, 5:914, 13:784
Mardaga, Thomas J. (Bp. of
   Wilmington, DE), 14:765
Marduk (Babylonian god), 4:337, 341,
   5:267–269, 8:394, **9:144–145**,
   534–535
Maréchal, Ambrose (Abp. of Baltimore),
   2:39, 3:715, **9:145**, 12:227
   apostolic delegation in the United
      States, 1:582
   contemplation, 4:207
   First Baltimore Provincial Council
      (1829), 2:43
   lay trusteeism, 14:540–541
   Whitfield, James, 14:706

Maréchal, Joseph, 5:539, 8:127, 210,
   9:145–146, 14:53
Maredsous Abbey (Namur, Belgium),
   9:146
Marella, Paolo (Card.), 1:585
Marella, Paul, 3:516
Marello, Giuseppe (Bp. of Asti), Bl.,
   9:146
Marello, Joseph. *See* Marello, Giuseppe
   (Bp. of Asti), Bl.
Marengoni, John, 1:577
Marenzio, Luca, **9:146–147**
Marescotti, Hyacintha, St., **9:147**
Maret, Henri Louis Charles (Bp.), 3:420,
   6:78, **9:147–148**, 10:150
Margaret (Queen of Scotland), St.,
   4:932–933, **9:150**, 12:832
Margaret, SS., **9:148**
Margaret Colonna, Bl., **9:148**
Margaret Mary, St., 1:926
Margaret of Austria, 6:108
Margaret of Burgundy, 7:121
Margaret of Cashel, 7:581
Margaret of Cortona, St., 4:136,
   9:148–149
Margaret of Hungary, St., **9:149**
Margaret of Lorraine, Bl., **9:149**
Margaret of Metola, Bl., **9:149**
Margaret of Roskilde, St., 1:40, **9:150**
Margaret of Savoy, Bl., **9:150**
Margaret of the Blessed Sacrament,
   Ven., **9:150–151**
Margaret Tudor, 2:179
Margarita, 3:109
Margarita philosophica (Reisch), 5:206
Margil, Antonio, Ven., 5:359, 8:808,
   9:*151*, **151**, 12:290, 639
A Marginal Jew (Meier), 6:867
Margotti, Giacomo, **9:151–152**, 10:415
Marguinios, Maximus, 6:456
Marheinecke, P. K., 6:709
Marí Mercedes. *See* Prat y Prat,
   Mercedes, Bl.
Maria (martyr of Córdoba), 4:262
Maria, Bl. (17th c. Japanese martyr),
   7:733
Maria, Micahaele de, 12:775
Maria I (Queen of Portugal), 11:468
Maria Bernardina. *See* Jablonska,
   Bernardina, Bl.
Maria Chiara, St. *See* Nanetti, Clelia,
   St.
Maria Clara of the Child Jesus (Mother),
   5:878
Maria Clementina Sobieski (Princess),
   8:843

Maria Cristina of Savoy, Queen, Ven., **9:152**

Maria Crucifixa (Mary Crucified). *See* Satellico, Elisabetta Maria, Bl.

María de la Cabeza, St., 7:605

Maria della Pace (Mary of Peace). *See* Giuliani, Marianna, St.

Maria Egiziaca (Respighi), 12:139

Maria Euphrasia (Mother), 6:357

Maria Laach Abbey (Germany), 3:711, 8:671, 672, **9:152–153**, *153*

Maria Laurentia Longo, Ven., **9:153**

Maria of Pilar (Mother), 11:522

María of the Sacred Heart. *See* Porras y Ayllón, Rafaela María, St.

Maria Regina, 9:274

Maria Stella Adela Mardoscwicz (Sister) and Ten Companions. *See* Nowogródek, martyrs of, BB.

Maria Theresa (Holy Roman Empress), 4:483

Maria Theresa (Marie Thérèse) (Empress of Austria), 5:258, 664–665, **9:153–155**, *154*

　Bernis, François Joachim de Pierre de, 2:326

　catechesis, 3:244

　Church-State relations, 1:913, 3:615, 639, 7:216

　Joseph II, 7:1041, 1045, 1046

　Josephinism, 5:913

　Migazzi, Christoph Anton, 9:622–623

　War of Succession, 6:640

Maria Theresia of Jesus. *See* Gerhardinger, Karolina Elizabeth Frances, Bl.

Mariam Thresia (Sister), Ven., 7:406

Mariamme (Queen of Judea), 6:665, 802, 803

Maria-Mödingen, Convent (Dillingen, Bavaria, Germany), **9:153**

Marian antiphons, 4:710, 8:611, **9:155–156**, 12:631–632

Marian Antiphons Salve Regina (Obrecht), 10:522

Marian Church of Danzig, 1:315

Marian devotion. *See* Mary, Blessed Virgin, devotion to

Marian Fathers, **9:156–157**

Marian feasts, **9:157–159**

　Ave Maris Stella, 1:930

　Dormition of the Virgin, 4:875–876

　early, 8:642

　Immaculate Conception, 7:149, 333, 334

　Immaculate Heart of Mary, 7:335

　liturgical year, 8:720

　pilgrimages in Vietnam, 8:386

　sanctoral cycle, 12:663

　See also Feasts, religious

Marian priests, **9:159**

Marian theology. *See* Mariology

Mariana, Juan de, 1:72, **9:160**, 12:29, 13:240, 14:256

Marianas Islands, 12:657

Marianist Meditations (Resch), 12:137

Marianist Sisters, 3:373–374, 486, **9:160**

Marianists, **9:160–162, 176**

　archives, 1:641

　founding of, 3:373–374, 621

　Hawaiian mission, 6:670

　Litz, D., 8:736

　Resch, Peter Anthony, 12:137

Marianitas. *See* Congregación de Santa Mariana de Jesús

Marianites of the Holy Cross, 7:18, 21–22, **9:162–163**, 893

Marianito (Father). *See* Euse Hoyos, Mariano de Jesús, Bl.

Marianne of Jesus (Mother) (Marion Gurney), 3:535

Mariannist Missionaries. *See* Congregation of Mariannhill Missionaries

Mariano of Florence, 4:387

Marianus Scotus, Bl., 1:462, 5:772, **9:163–164**, 164, 451

Marianus Socinus, 3:52

Mariavites, **9:164**, 10:579

Marichal, R., 10:775

Marie Alphonse (Mother). *See* Eppinger, Elisabeth

Marie Amandine (Sister). *See* Jeuris, Pauline, St.

Marie de Guise-Lorraine. *See* Mary of Guise

Marie de Jésus Crucifié. *See* Baouardy, Maríam, Bl.

Marie de Jesus d'Oultremont (Mother). *See* Oultremont, Emilie d', Bl.

Marie de la Paix (Mary of Peace). *See* Giuliani, Marianna, St.

Marie de l'Incarnation, Bl. (Barbé Acarie), 2:109, 3:128, 136, 5:750, 867, **9:164–165**

Marie de Médicis, 5:850, 12:238

Marie Elisabeth de la Croix de Jesus. *See* Elizabeth of Ranfaing, Ven.

Marie Eugénie de Jésus (Mother), Bl. (Anne Eugénie Milleret de Brou), 1:797, 802

Marie Henrietta of Providence, Bl., 4:44

Marie Hermine de Jésus. *See* Grivot, Irma, St.

Marie Louise (Archduchess of Austria), 10:149

Marie Martin de L'Incarnation, Bl., **9:165**

Marie of Pau. *See* Baouardy, Maríam, Bl.

Marie of the Cross, 8:46–47

Marie of the Holy Spirit, Bl., 4:44

Marie of the Incarnation, Ven., 3:4

Marie Sainte-Cecile de Rome. *See* Bélanger, Dina, Bl.

Marie Thérèse (Empress of Austria). *See* Maria Theresa (Marie Thérèse) (Empress of Austria)

Marienbad Elegie (Goethe), 6:332

Marienberg Abbey (Italy), **9:165–166**

Marienwerder, Johannes, 4:876

Marie-Thérèse du Sacré-Cour de Jésus. *See* Haze, Maria Theresia, Bl.

Marietta College, 4:115

Marignolli, Giovanni de, 3:493

Marina, Justinian, 12:333

Marine, Council of (1717), 10:291

Marini, Piero (Bp.), 2:*412*

Marino, Eugene A. (Bp. of Atlanta), 1:831, *831*

Marín-Sola, Francisco, 1:309, 4:814, 9:*166*, **166–167**, 12:777

Marinus (papal legate), 1:172

Marinus, Jonah (Abū'l Walīd Ibn-Janah), 5:509

Marinus, St. *See* Anianus and Marinus, SS.

Marinus, SS., **9:167**

Marinus I (Pope), 1:125, 5:814, **9:167–168**

Marinus II (Pope), **9:168**

Marinus of Anazarbus, 9:167

Marinus of Caesarea, 9:167

Marinus of Rome, 9:167

Marinus of San Marino, 9:167

Mariological Society of America, 9:172–173

Mariology, **9:168–175**

　Bernard of Clairvaux, 2:309–310

　Byzantine theology, 2:766, 823, 828

　de Koninck, Charles, 4:618

　Dorland, Peter, 4:875

　Duns Scotus, John, 4:938–939

　feminist theology, 5:680

　John Damascene, St., 7:942–943

　Lawrence of Brindisi, 8:406

　Lebon, J., 8:429

　Lépicier, A., 8:506–507

　Munificentissimus Deus (papal bull), 10:61–62

Mariology (continued)
as New Eve, 1:799–800
19th-20th centuries, 3:623
See also Marian feasts; Theotokos
Marion, Jean-Luc, 12:476
Marion-Brésillac, Melchior Marie Joseph de, 1:162, 7:406, **9:175**, 13:110
Maris of Chalcedon, 1:527, 12:692
Marist Brothers, 3:374, 622, 8:311, 563, **9:175**
Marist Brothers of the Schools, **9:175**
Marist Fathers, **9:176**
Eymard, Pierre Julien, St., 5:571–572
founding of, 3:374, 621, 834–835
Western Oceania mission, 10:529
Marist Missionary Sisters, **9:176–177**
Marist Sisters, 3:834–835, **9:177**
Maritain, Jacques, 5:92, 95, 390, 397, 9:*177*, **177–180**
Action Française, 1:82
Alinsky, Saul David, 1:288
Alphonsus Liguori, St., 1:309
atheism, 1:824, 825
Camara, Helder Pessoa, 2:900
causality, 3:300
Christian philosophy, 3:540–541
common good, 4:20
contemplation, 4:204
creative imagination, 4:348–349
existential metaphysics, 5:539, 540
freedom, 5:940
humanism, 7:182, 194
intellective mode, 8:206
man, natural end of, 9:100
Maritain, Raïssa Oumansoff, 9:181
natural-law teaching, 10:185, 203
philosophy and science, 11:301
philosophy of history, 6:883
Thomistic metaphysics, 12:776
Maritain, Raïssa Oumansoff, 9:177–178, **181**
Maritime provinces (Canada), 3:9
Marius (Bp. of Avenches), St., **9:181**
Marius Mercator, **9:181**
Marius Victorinus, 3:186, 11:290
Aristotelianism, 1:670, 673
aseity, 1:779
Boethius, 2:454
hymnology, 7:243
Mark (Bp. of Arethusa), St., **9:188**
Mark (Bp. of Italian Cathari), 3:259
Mark (Pope), St., **9:187–188**, *188*
Mark, Evangelist, St., **9:182–183**, *183*, 184
Alexandria, 1:268

Alexandrian liturgy, 1:273, 528
Antiochene liturgy, 1:528
manuscript illumination of, 9:*184*
Paul, Apostle, St., 11:6, 13–14, 15
relics of, 12:32, 564
Mark, Gospel According to, **9:183–187**
abomination of desolation in, 1:23
adultery, 13:50
Andrew, Apostle, St. in, 1:402
Ascension of Jesus Christ in, 1:769–770
baptism, 2:56
baptism of children, 8:591
Barabbas, 2:85
Bartholomew, Apostle, St., 2:123
canonicity, 3:21
Christ's repsonse to death of Lazarus, 5:193
corban in, 4:257
dietary laws in, 4:743
disciple as term, 4:769–773
discipleship of women, 14:830–831
Divine judgment, 8:29
divorce, 13:49
early Christian way of life, 3:546
edification, 5:84
eschatology, 5:339
faith, 6:382
family structure, 14:830
final perseverance, 11:134
Gehenna, 6:116
glossolalia, 6:249
God the Son, 6:295–296
God's spirit, 13:427, 428
God's word-made-flesh, 14:837
heaven, 6:684, 685
house churches, 2:145
infant baptism, 2:67
Jesus Christ
baptism of, 2:57–58, 72
death as reconciliation with God, 11:970
genealogy of, 6:126, 14:829–830
temptations of, 9:546
John the Baptist, St., 5:159, 7:1013–1014
Judas Iscariot, 8:14
justice of God, 8:70
justice of men, 8:74
justification, 8:77
kerygma, 8:157
Kingdom of God, 8:173
law of love, 8:403
lay element in government, 13:248

Lazarus of Bethany, 8:420
leprosy, 8:510
Lord used for God, 8:780
Lord's Day, 8:781
Lord's Supper, 8:785
love as commandment, 4:8
Mary, Blessed Virgin, 9:239–241
Mary Magdalene, St., 9:287
Matthew's Gospel compared to, 9:357
miracles, 9:664
missionary work, 13:216
Monothelitism, 7:80
obedience, 4:307
parables, 10:870
on the Parousia, 10:896, 897, 898
Passion, 10:920, 921, 922, 923
peace, 11:49
penance, 11:68
Pharisees, 11:226
poverty in, 4:307
praetorium, 11:579
Precious Blood, 11:638, 641
publicans, 11:810
pure and impure, 11:822–823
rebirth, 11:951
redaction criticism scholarship, 10:303
repentence, baptism as sign of, 2:57
ritual bathing and purification, as symbol of baptism, 2:57–58
salvation through baptism, 2:58
Seven Last Words, 13:36, 37
sharing goods, 8:544
sign of Jonah, 7:1022
Simon the Apostle, 13:126
sin, 13:146, 147
Son of David, 13:310
Son of God, 13:312
Son of Man, 13:317
spirit, 13:425
virginity, 4:306
women, role of, 14:830
See also Synoptic Gospels
Mark Antony, 6:802–803
Mark Eugenicus (Bp. of Ephesus), 2:764, 794
Mark of Montefeltro, 2:482
Mark of the Nativity, 3:143, **9:188**
Mark the Apostle, 5:475
Mark the Hermit, **9:189**
Markabta, Synod of, 2:4
Markarios III (Abp. of Cyprus), 4:463
Markoe, William, 1:160, 14:244

Marks, Miriam, 4:95, **9:189**

Marks of the Church, **9:189–191**

Markward of Anweiler, 4:414

Marley, Hilda Gertrude. *See* Marley, Marie Hilda (Sister)

Marley, Marie Hilda (Sister), **9:191**

Marlowe, Christopher, 5:650

Marmaggi, Francesco (Card.), 2:694

Marmion, Joseph Columba, Bl., 4:208, 8:672, **9:191–192**

Marmoutier Abbey (Tours), **9:192**

Maro of Cyr, St., **9:192**

Maronite Antonine Order of St. Isaia, 1:534–535

Maronite Church, 5:19, **9:192–201**

    Ambarach, Peter, 1:333

    Clement XII (Pope), 3:790

    Council of Catholic Patriarchs of the Orient, 4:295–296

    early history, 8:426–427

    Kassab, Nimatullah, 8:130–131

    Tripoli, 4:402

Maronite liturgy, 8:712–713, **9:201**, *202*

Maronite missal, 9:201

Maronite Monastery (Deir el Nourieh, Lebanon), 9:*194*

Maronites, 1:534

Maroons, 3:111

Marot, Clément, 2:352, 7:255, 13:18

Marozia (Italian noblewoman), 3:213, 7:925, 8:483, **9:201–202**, 13:15, 520–521

Marquard of Randech (Patriarch of Aquileia), 1:608

Marquette, Jacques (Father), 3:475, **9:202–203**, *203*, 740, 12:558, 14:778

    Arkansas, 1:690

    as explorer, 7:786, 13:820

    Illinois, 9:722

    Mission of the Holy Ghost, 3:5

Marquette League, **9:203**, 13:87

Marquette University (Milwaukee, WI), 1:637, 641, 12:370, 14:783

Marracci, Ippolito, 3:804

Marracci, Ludovico, 3:804

Marranism, 9:203–205

Marranos, 1:69, 4:946–947, 7:870, 871, **9:203–205**, 13:391

Marriage

    abduction, 1:15

    Adam, 1:104

    affinity, 1:150–152, 13:169

    age, 1:174–175

    as analogy, 7:116

    Anne and Joachim, SS., 1:469

    Arcanum, 1:631

    Armenian liturgy, 1:710

    Austria, 1:917

    Canon Law, 1:150, 151, 152, 174–175

    Casti Connubii, 3:214

    chastity, 3:444–445

    Chaucer, Geoffrey, 3:455–456

    China (traditional), 14:813–814

    Christian Family Movement, 3:536

    Church-State relations, 3:644, 845–846

    circumcision, 3:741

    clerical continence in, 5:178

    contraception, 1:490

    Council of Trent, 3:54, 14:173

    deacons, 4:553

    death, preparation for, 4:583

    digamy (remarriage), 4:744–745

    duties of husbands, 11:334

    Elvira Council, 5:178

    force and fear (Canon Law), 5:797

    homosexuality, 7:66–67

    Hosea, Book of, 7:116

    Ignatius of Antioch, 7:311

    India, 14:813

    indissolubility of, 5:178

    Ivo of Chartres, 3:45

    Jesus Christ, 14:814

    Jewish ceremonies, 8:12

    King Henry VII's annulment, 5:163, 244

    lay spirituality, 8:414, 415, 416

    lust, 8:871–877

    Matrimonia quae in locis (Benedict XIV), 10:218–219

    medieval theology of, 4:321

    Old Testament, 3:28

    Pius XII (Pope) on obligations of state, 10:178

    polygamy, 3:248

    procreation, 4:218–222

    Protestant Reformation, as sacrament, 14:816–817

    public propriety, as impediment to, 11:809

    relationship of natural family planning (NFP) to, 10:178–179

    Sanchez, Thomas, 12:658

    sex in, 13:45–46

    sexual relationships (biblical), 13:50–51

    slavery, 3:117

    Song of Songs, 13:319

    Tertullian, 13:836

    tetragamy dispute (Leo VI), 1:646, 2:756–757, 786, 823, 4:174

    use of proxy, 11:787

    virginity, 14:546–547, 547

    wedding rings, 12:249

    women, role of, 14:829

    York Use vows, 14:895

    Zwingli, Huldrych, 14:941

    See also Adultery; Clerical celibacy/marriage; Divorce; Matrimony, Sacrament of; Mixed marriages

Marriage and Concupiscence (Augustine), 4:219

Marriage contracts, 8:12, 381

Marriage Encounter, 1:906, 5:203, **9:205–206**

    See also Worldwide Marriage Encounter

Marriage law reform, 10:218–219, 13:749–750

Marriage legislation (Canon Law), **9:206–207**, 335–336

    barren marriage, Luther on, 8:883

    fourth marriages, 8:474

    judicial vicar's role, 8:43

    laicized priests, 8:286

    Lateran Pacts (1985), 8:359

    legitimacy of children, 8:454

    legitimate vs. concubinage, 8:796

    Levirate marriage, 8:522

    People of God, 8:288–289

    See also Matrimony, Sacrament of

Marroquín, Francisco (Bp.), **9:207–208**

Mars gallicus (Jansen), 7:714

Marsden, William, Bl., 1:399, 5:229

Marseilles, **9:208–210**

Marset, R. R., 12:58

Marsh, Adam, 5:242, 899, 12:263

Marsh v. Chambers (1983), 3:668

Marshall, Thurgood, 1:161

Marshall, William, 2:79

Marshman, Joshua, 7:403

Marsili, Luigi, 1:888

Marsilius of Inghen, 7:363, **9:210**

Marsilius of Padua, 3:604, **9:210–212**

    Adam Easton, 1:107

    Aristotelianism, 1:675

    Augustinianism, 1:879

    Church-State relations, 3:636, 637

    conciliarism, 4:53–54, 55–56

    democracy, 4:639

    ecclesiastical liberalism, 8:540

    false decretals, 5:618

    John XXII (Pope), 1:327, 3:603

Marsilius of Padua (continued)
laicism, 8:282
Latin Averroism, 1:937
medieval Latin literature works of, 9:463
secularization of Church property, 12:871
sovereignty, 13:254
state vs. Church law, 10:839
Martel, Charles. See Charles Martel (Frankish mayor of the palace)
Martellange, E., 3:706
Marthonie, Geoffroy de la (Bp. of Amiens), 1:359
Martí, Mariano (Bp.), **9:212**
Martial (1st c. writer), 12:308, 311
Martiall, John Marshall, **9:212**
Martianus Capella, 1:673, 8:537, 12:107, 757
Martillo Morán, Narcisa de Jesús, Bl., **9:213**
Martimort, A. G., 5:860
Martin (Abp. of Braga), St., 1:577, 3:252, 4:219, **9:219**, 439, 13:376
Martin (Bp. of Tours), St., **9:220**, *221*
Amiens, 1:359
Anointing of the Sick, 1:482
Brice of Tours, St., 2:612
capella, 3:382
church dedicated to, 12:413
as confessor, 4:83
as conscientious objector, 4:150
evangelization of Gaul, 6:112
execution of Priscillian, 3:86
intercession for Fortunatus, 5:823
life of, Sulpicius Severus, 12:606
Ligugé Abbey, 8:585
Marmoutier Abbey, founding of, 9:192
works of charity, 3:407, 408
Martin, Auguste Marie (Bp. of New Orleans), 1:156, 270
Martin, C., 2:845
Martin, Gregory, **9:213**
Martin, J. M. (Abp. of Rouen), 5:70
Martin, Jacob T., 3:659
Martin, Konrad (Bp. of Paderborn), 5:889, **9:213–214**
Martin, Luis, 7:790
Martin, Marie Françoise Thérèse. See Thérèse de Lisieux, St.
Martin, Marie Helena. See Martin, Mary (Mother)
Martin, Mary (Mother), **9:214**
Martin, Raymond Joseph, **9:214–215**
Martin, Richard, Bl., 5:230, 784, **9:215**

Martin, Theresa (Mother), 7:34
Martin, Thérèse. See Thérèse de Lisieux, St.
Martin, Victor, 1:599, 5:762, 6:76, **9:215**
Martin, W. A. P., 3:499
Martin I (Abbot), 12:588
Martin I (Pope), St., **9:215–217**
Amandus, St., 1:331
communion of saints, 4:36
Constans II, 4:128, 173, 186
death of, 3:597, 5:442
diaconia, 4:719
exile of, 7:656
Monothelitism, 2:750, 821, 7:81, 9:215–216
patronage system used, 10:976
prohibited books, 7:390
theology of Church, 3:584
in writings of Pseudo-Dionysius, 11:801
Martin IV (Pope), 2:762, 826, 8:268, **9:217**, 11:502
Martin V (Pope), **9:217–219**
Albergati, Niccolò, Bl., 1:219
authority of Ecumenical councils over popes, 6:607–608
briefs as form, 4:758
Bryennios, Joseph, 2:651
cardinalate, 3:107
Chichele, Henry, 3:481
Clement VIII (Antipope), 3:785–786
Colonna family, 10:676
conciliarism, 4:56
confusion over numbering of, 11:502
Contarini, Giovanni, 4:203
Council of Basel, 2:133
Council of Constance, 3:572
election of, 3:604, 4:170
Escobar, Andrés de, 5:352
family of, 3:855
Fillastre, Guillaume (Card.), 5:722
hermits, 1:631–632
Holy Name, 7:32
Holy Year, 7:57
Hussites, 7:231
John Capistran, St., 7:944
Louis d'Aleman, 8:805
papacy development under, 10:839–840
reform decrees of, 4:171
Sacrosancta authenticity, 4:172
Salamanca University, 12:611
Martin Buber and the Christian Way (Oesterreicher), 10:559
Martin del Campo, Juana, 3:461

Martin of Alnwick, 12:232
Martin of León, St., **9:219–220**
Martin of Signa, 1:888
Martin of Troppau, 1:465, 7:877, **9:220**, **222**
Martin Sierra, Manuel, 10:29
Martin v. City of Struthers (1943), 3:661
Martina, St., **9:222**
Martindale, Cyril Charles, 5:252, 7:792, **9:222**
Martineau, James, **9:223**
Martinelli, Sebastiano, 1:585, 890
Martínez, Compañón y Bujanda, Baltasar Jaime (Abp. of Bogotá), **9:224**
Martínez, Juan de Prado, **9:223**
Martínez, Luis María (Abp. of Mexico), **9:223–224**
Martínez, Pedro, 7:785
Martínez Amigó, Herminia, Bl., 1:4
Martínez Compañón y Bujanda, Baltasar Jaime, 5:901
Martínez de Aldunate, José Antonio (Bp.), **9:224**, 12:282
Martínez Izquierdo, Isidoro, Bl., 7:125
Martínez Jarauta, Manuel (Brother), 2:92
Martinez Pascual, Martín, 12:408
Martini, Cornelius, 12:767
Martini, Giovanni Battista, 2:5–6, **9:224–225**, *225*
Martini, Jakob, 12:768
Martini, Martino, 3:514, **9:225–226**
Martini, Raymond, 13:384
Martini, Simone, 1:230, 791, 4:396, 5:*416*
Martiniana, Carlo della, 4:61
Martinique, settlement of, 3:117–119
Martins, Pedro (Bp.), 7:739
Martinus Laudensis, 3:52
Martinuzzi, György (Card.), 7:213, **9:226**
Martorana Church (Palermo), 1:*798*
Martorell, Joanot, 4:401
Marty, Antoine (Abbé), 12:279
Marty, Martin (Bp. of Sioux Falls), 2:255, **9:226**, 12:542, 568, 13:164, 165, 368
Martyr literature. See Acts of the Martyrs
Martyr Movement (9th century), 11:44
Martyrdom, **9:226–230**
as baroque art theme, 2:111
cross as symbol for, 7:731
inscriptions honoring Christian martyrs, 5:288–289
martyrologies, 9:232–234

Roman Christian legends, 12:363–364
 sentence of execution, 5:224
 term martyr defined, 5:224
Martyrdom, theology of, **9:230–231**
 lay spirituality, 8:418
 libellatici, 8:531
 ritual child murder, 13:133
 spirituality, 13:443
Martyrdom of Polycarp, 1:93–94, 579
Martyrdom of St. Maurice (El Greco), 6:427
Martyrdom of Saint Sebastian (Il Sodoma), 12:*854*
The Martyrdom of Saint Ursula and the 11,000 (Rubens), 14:*346*
Martyrdom of the Ten Thousand (Dürer), 13:*819*
Mártyres, Bartolomeo dos, 3:416
Martyribus, Bartholomeus de. *See* Bartholomew of Braga, Ven.
Martyrium, 3:685–686, **9:231–232**
Martyrologie (Crespin), 12:538
Martyrologies, **9:232–234**
 liturgical calendar, 8:642–643
 Philocalian calendar, 4:675–676
 Spain, 13:379
 Usuard, 9:233, 12:548, 14:352–353
 See also specific martyrologies
Martyrologium, 10:229
Martyrology, Roman, 9:233–234, **234**
 Delehaye, Hippolyte, 4:626
 Engelbert I of Cologne, 5:220
 Sidonius Apollinaris, 13:104
 Simon (Simeon) of Trent, 13:133
 Sixtus II (Pope), 13:194–195
 Sixtus III (Pope), St., 13:195–196
Martyrology of St. Jerome, 4:676, 927, 8:849, **9:234–235**, 13:104
Martyrology of Usuard, 9:233
Martyrs
 Acts of the Martyrs, 1:90, 92–94, 3:404
 burial, 3:222
 canonization, 3:61, 65
 confessor distinguished from, 4:83
 medieval boys, 4:827, 9:436–437
 passiones of life of, 10:919
 sanctoral cycle, 12:661
 shrines, 13:88
 See also Cult of the Martyrs and Confessors; Martyrdom; Roman persecution era; *specific martyrs*
Martyrs of Diocesean Worker Priests. *See* Ruiz de los Paños y Angel, Pedro and eight Companions, BB.

Martyrs of the Cristero Movement. *See* Guadalajara (Mexico), martyrs of, SS.
Marulić, Marko, **9:235–236**
Maruthas (Bp. of Martyropolis), 1:805, **9:236**
Maruthas of Tagrit, **9:236**
Marwān II, 14:287
Marx, Karl, 3:620, 5:91, 94, **9:236–238**, 11:294–295, 14:223
 atheism, 1:823, 825
 dialectical materialism, 5:397, 707
 essence, 5:362
 existence, 5:534
 fetishism concept, 8:548
 feudalism, 5:703
 friendship with Engels, 5:221–222
 Hegelianism, 6:710–711, 8:219
 historical materialism, 9:325
 ideology as superstructure, 8:211
 influence on Ellul, Jacques, 5:171–172
 praxis, 11:585
 religion, 6:286
 self, concept of, 12:883
 society, 13:279, 281–282
 See also Marxism
Marx, Wilhelm, 6:185
Marxism, 9:236, 237, 11:306
 arguments against, 8:549
 Austria, 1:915
 Bulgakov, Sergeĭ Nikolaevich, 2:679
 community, 4:38
 dialectical materialism, 9:322
 economic democracy, 4:643
 educational philosophy, 5:91
 existentialism, 5:534
 Hegelianism influence, 6:713
 humanism, 7:194, 196
 liberation theology, 8:547–548
 pragmatic nature of truth, 14:223–224
 social justice movement, 4:158
 soul, 13:348
 and the state, 13:484
 theological anthropology, 1:509
 See also Materialism, dialectical
Marxsen, Willi, 2:386, 5:522, 10:303
Mary, Bl. (17th c. Japanese martyr), 7:734
Mary, Blessed Virgin, 9:*169*
Mary, Blessed Virgin, 9:272
 angels, 1:425
 Anglican-Catholic dialogue, 1:442
 Annunciation, 1:473–477

consecration, 4:156
 Council of Ephesus, 5:273, 274
 courtly love and devotion, 4:321
 doctrine, 10:13–15
 dormition, 4:875–876
 hope, 7:98
 Immaculate Heart of, 7:335–337, *336*
 as intercessor, 11:596
 mediation of, 9:171, 174, 258–263
 Medjugorje, Yugoslavia apparition of, 9:466–467
 miraculous medal, 9:670
 nativity of, 10:175–176
 Nestorianism, 10:252–253
 parents of, 1:468–470
 as patroness, 2:41, 11:443
 Presentation of, 11:682–683
 processions in honor of, 11:732
 purification of, 11:834
 sorrows of, 13:327–328
 veneration, 9:266, 269
 virginity of, 1:476, 800, 2:629, 4:633, 14:532
 visitation to Elizabeth, St., 14:564
 as woman clothed in the sun, 14:822
 See also Assumption of Mary; Immaculate Conception; Madonna; Marian feasts; Mariology; Mother of God; Theotokos
Mary, Blessed Virgin, Canticle of. *See Magnificat* (song)
Mary, Blessed Virgin, devotion to, **9:266–271**, *267*
 Allamano, Bl. Giuseppe, 1:291
 Alphonsus Liguori, St., 1:310, 312
 Ambrose, St., 1:339
 Austria, 1:913
 Carmelite spirituality, 3:133, 137, 141, 143
 Carthusian spirituality, 3:195
 Cistercian spirituality, 3:749
 Dominicans, 4:847
 Immaculate Heart of Mary, 7:335–337
 Joachim and Anne, SS. and, 1:469
 litanies, 8:601, 13:327
 Litany of Loreto, 8:602–603
 Mary of Ágreda, 1:187
 19th-20th centuries, 3:623
 scapular, 13:134, 135
 Servites, 13:28–29
 shrines, 13:90–93
 Soubirous, B., 13:331–332
Mary, Blessed Virgin, iconography of, 4:395–397, 488–490, *489*, 8:345, **9:271–281**

Mary, Blessed Virgin, in Catholic-Protestant dialogue, **9:283–284**

Mary, Blessed Virgin, in the Bible, **9:238–249**

Magnificat, 9:43

marriage to Joseph, 7:1035–1036

Proto-evangelium, 11:776

purification of, 3:14, 15

Seven Last Words, 13:37

Mary, Blessed Virgin, in theology, **9:249–266**

intercession of, 7:519

primary source for Infancy Narratives, 8:860

See also Mariology

Mary, Blessed Virgin, Queenship of, **9:282–283**

Mary, Mother of God, Solemnity of, 3:556

Mary, University of (Bismarck), 2:423–424

Mary II (Queen of England, Ireland and Scotland), 3:648, 649, 12:207, *207*

Mary Austin (Sister), 2:94, 6:147–148

Mary Clare, St. See Nanetti, Clelia, St.

Mary de Cervellón, St., **9:285**

Mary in the New Testament, 9:283

Mary Magdalen (Mother). See Taylor, Frances Margaret

Mary Magdalene, St., 7:247, **9:285–288**, *286*, 12:150–152, 567, 14:831

Mary Magdalene of the Incarnation (Mother), 11:131

Mary of Ágreda, **1:187**, 363, 629

Mary of Bethany, 9:287

Mary of Brittany (Abbess of Fontevrault), 5:793

Mary of Egypt, St., **9:288**, *289*

Mary of Guise, 2:179, 6:577

Mary of Jesus (Mother). See Oultremont, Emilie d', Bl.

Mary of Jesus the Good Shepherd. See Siedliska, Franciszka, Bl.

Mary of Oignies, Bl., 2:204–205, **9:288, 290**

Mary of St. Joseph Salazar, **9:290**

Mary of St. Theresa Petijt, 3:143

Mary of the Angels, Bl., 3:128

Mary of the Blessed Sacrament (Mother) (Clare Ellerker), 3:129

Mary of the Cross. See MacKillop, Mary Helen, Bl.

Mary of the Passion (Sister), Ven., 7:406

Mary Reparatrix, Society of, 10:721

Mary St. Ignatius (Mother). See Thévenet, Claudine, St.

Mary St. Joseph (Sister), 2:94

Mary Stuart (Queen of Scots), 2:179, **9:290–292**, *291*, 12:*832*, 834–835

Abington, Thomas, 1:22

Babington Plot, 13:370

Church, 12:828

execution of, 12:11

imprisonment of, 5:752

Knox, J., 8:226

Northern Rising, 5:247

Sixtus V (Pope), 13:199

Spanish Armada, 1:696

Mary Teresa of St. Joseph (Mother), 3:129

Mary Tudor (Queen of England), **9:292–294**, *293*, 14:300

Ancient See of Canterbury, 3:72

Ancient See of Chichester, 3:481

Anglican Reformation, 1:434, 435, 442–443, 3:608

Book of Common Prayer, 2:524

Church in England under, 5:245

De heretico comburendo act, 4:550

Dowdall, George, 4:887

Fitzalan, Henry, 5:752

Gardiner, Stephen, 6:96

Knox exile, 8:225

Latimer execution, 8:361

marriage, 12:9

persecutions of Marian Regime, 12:10

Philip II, marriage to, 11:247

Pole, Reginald, 11:457

Protestant Reformation, 12:9–10

Protestantism in Ireland, 7:556–557

Scottish Church, 12:834

studies of, 8:596

Mary Veronica (Sister), 7:406

Mary Ward Sisters, 1:323

Maryknoll (periodical), 9:297

Maryknoll Fathers and Brothers, **9:294–297**, 10:623–624, 11:688, 12:289, 729, 14:617

Maryknoll Mission Association of the Faithful, 9:296–297, **297–298**

Maryknoll Missioners. See Maryknoll Sisters

Maryknoll School, 9:*295*

Maryknoll Sisters, 3:622, 5:798, 8:133, **9:298–299**, 12:289

Maryknoll Sisters of St. Dominic. See Maryknoll Sisters

Maryland, **9:299–302**

African Americans, 8:277

anti-Catholicism, 9:724–725

Bohemia Manor, 2:460

Brent, Margaret, 2:604

Calvert family, 2:886–887

Catholic colleges and universities, 2:40

church architecture, 3:714

Church-State relations, 3:641, 649, 651–652

mission, 2:460, 887, 8:277

slavery, 1:156

Toleration Acts (1639, 1649), 2:886–887, 3:641, 649, 14:103–104

See also Baltimore, George Calvert, Lord; *specific dioceses and archdioceses*

Maryland, Land of Sanctuary (Russell), 12:418

Marymount College (Tarrytown, NY), 9:302–303

Marymount Colleges and Universities, 9:302–303

Marymount Manhattan College (NY), 9:303

Marymount Palos Verdes (CA), 9:303

Marymount University (Arlington, VA), 9:303

Marys of the Tabernacles, 12:400

Marziale, Marco, 3:739

Masada (Israel), 2:379, 6:*804*

Masada synagogue (Israel), 13:678

Masaryk, Tomáš, 4:484

Mascall, Erich Lionel, 1:566, 676

Mascall, F. L., 10:113

Maschopulos, Manuel, 2:810

Mascloux, Claude-Barnabé de Laurent de, 12:277

Masdeu, Baltasar, 12:772

Masferrer Vila, Luis (Father), 2:92

Mashtotz. See Mesrop, St.

Masías, Juan, St., **9:303**

Maslow, Abraham, 7:197

Mason, C. H., 1:789

Mason, George, 3:652

Mason, John, Bl., 5:231

Masona of Emerita, 3:409

Masonic lodges, 9:576–577

Masonry. See Freemasonry

Masons, 6:339

Masoretic Text, 2:355, 3:26, 10:950, 950–951

See also Old Testament

The Mass (Fortescue), 5:821

The Mass for EveryDay in the Year (Pace), 10:741

Mass fragments, Gallican rites, 6:69–70

Mass in B Minor (Bach), 2:7

Mass in Transition (Ellard), 5:168

Mass Lectionary, 8:436

Mass of the Future (Ellard), 5:168

Massabki, 'Abd-al-Mūti, 4:503

Massabki, Francis, 4:503

Massabki, Raphael, 4:503

Massachusetts, **9:304–310**

    American Civil War, 2:555, 9:307

    anti-Catholicism, 2:552–553, 554

    Carmelites, 2:555

    Catholic education, 5:751, 9:307–308

    Church-State relations, 3:646–647, 650

    Congregation for the Propagation of the Faith, 2:554

    Congregationalism, 4:114–115, 9:304

    Declaration of the Rights of Man (1780), 3:650

    immigration, 2:553, 554, 555, 9:308, 13:462

    Know-Nothingism, 2:555, 9:307

    Prince v. Massachusetts (1944), 3:661

    Puritans, 9:304, 11:839

    Sisters of Providence, 13:188

    slavery, 9:307

    trusteeism, 2:554

    See also specific dioceses and archdioceses

Massachusetts, *Prince v.* (1944), 3:661

Massachusetts Catholic Conference (MCC), 9:309

Massachusetts Institute of Technology chapel, 3:716

Massachusetts Missionary Magazine, 5:193

Massachusetts Quarterly Review, 14:149

Massacio, 12:115

Massacres of Christians by Turks, 13:710

Massaja, Gugliemo (Card.), 1:291, 5:401, 404, 405, **9:310**, *311*

Massaja, Lorenzo. *See* Massaja, Gugliemo (Card.)

Massé, Ennemond, 3:4

Massenet, Damien, 12:639

Massenet, Jules, **9:310–311**, *312*

Masses, 3:*581*

    Ambrosian Rite, 1:344–345

    blessing for Abbots, 1:12

    candles in, 3:15

    Carthusian Rite, 3:189

    Christmas, 3:554–555

    Cistercian Rite, 3:745

    Council of Trent, 3:610

    Council of Trent on sacrifice of the, 14:172

    devotion to Passion, 10:926

    genuflection, 8:649

    Georgian Orthodox Church, 10:689

    Kyrie Eleison, 8:259–261

    lay participation, 8:295

    Leonine Sacramentary, 8:500–502

    Luther, 3:608

    Mozart's works for, 10:48

    music

        compositions, 8:336

        concerted mass, 8:694

        Renaissance, 8:687

    New Mass denounced, 8:447

    Palestrina's music for, 10:248, 801–803

    participation in, as moral obligation, 13:611

    pontifical, 10:855–856

    private, 8:657

    Requiem Mass, 12:134–136

    Roman Ordo calendar for, 10:643

    significance of Sunday, 13:608

    stipendiary system, 8:658–659

    sung and recited, 8:700

    Tridentine, 14:181–182

    Verdi's music for, 14:446

    See also Liturgy

Masses (population), **9:311–312**

Masses, dry, **9:303–304**

Masses, votive, 8:718, **9:312–313**

Massignon, Louis, 4:516

Massillon, Jean Baptiste (Bp.), 1:334, 9:*313*, **313–314**

Massip, González, Miguel, 2:92

Massoulié, Antonin, **9:314**, 14:51

Massuet, René, 2:190

Massys, Quinten, 1:539

Mastelloni, Andrea, 3:143

Master, as term, 4:798

Master Alcuin, Liturgist (Ellard), 5:168

The Master Idea of St. Paul's Epistles (Bandas), 2:48

Master of Ceremonies, **9:314**

Mastrius, Bartholomaeus, **9:315**, 12:764

Masturbation, 4:45, 8:871–877, **9:315–317**, 10:600

Masuda Shirō. *See* Amakusa Shirō

Masure, E., 10:99

Matagna people, 8:280

Matashichi, John, Bl., 7:733

Mateos, J., 5:5, 7

Mater et magistra (encyclical, John XXIII), 1:793, 823, 3:620, 625, 626, 4:16, 21, 7:936–937, **9:317**, 10:850, 11:566, 13:260, 567

Material sin, 9:878, 13:150

Material supposition, 13:625

Materialism, 9:*318*, **318–322**, 11:284

    Alphonsus Liguori, St., 1:310

    atomism, 1:831

    Cambridge Platonists, 2:909

    Coleridge, Samuel Taylor, 3:832

    conscience, 4:140

    Fouillée, Alfred, 7:300

    man, natural end of, 9:99

    matter, 9:342

    matter and form in, 9:352

    Milton, John, 9:643

    New Religious Movements and rejection of, 10:301

    religion, 12:70

    Royce, Josiah, 7:302

    soul-body relationship, 13:358

Materialism, Dialectical and Historical, 5:707, **9:322–325**

Maternus (Bp. of Cologne), 3:842

Maternus Pistoris, 12:119

Mateu, María Climet, Bl., 1:4

Mathathias (d. 167 B.C.), 9:10

Mathematical necessity, 10:226

Mathematical physics, 11:304

Mathematical Principles of Natural Theology (Newton), 12:768

Mathematical transcendence, 14:142

Mathematics

    Arabic development, 12:809

    Aristotle, 1:683

    Cartesian method, 4:678–680

    continuum, 4:215–217

    demonstration, 4:653

    infinity in, 7:459–460

    logic, 12:415–416

    mathematical extension, 5:569–570

    measurement in, 9:412–413

    philosophy, 11:279

    Pythagoreans, 11:844–845

    quantity in, 11:855

    Renaissance, 12:815

    Richard of Swyneshed, 12:236

Mathematics, philosophy of, **9:325–328**

    Aquinas, 8:538

    composite medicine, 8:171

    deduction from definitions, 8:218

    deductive vs. inductive, 8:538

    importance of, 8:537

    logicism, 8:758

    unity in, 14:318

    See also Logic, symbolic

Mathematicus (Bernard Silvester), 2:317–318

Mather, Increase and Cotton, 4:115,
9:328

Mather, Richard, 2:162

*Matheseos libri VIII (Firmicus
Maternus)*, 5:740

Mathew, Theobald (Father), 3:517,
9:328–329, 13:800

Mathews, Shailer, **9:329**, 13:242

Mathieu, François Désiré (Card.), 1:432,
9:329–330

Mathieu, Marie Hélène, 1:635

Mathiez, Albert, 5:969–970

Mathijs, John, 1:368

Mathis, Michael Ambrose, **9:330**

Mathis der Maler (Hindemith), 6:839

Matignon, Francis Anthony, 2:553,
3:472, **9:330–331**

Matignon, François, 12:227

Matilda (Countess of Tuscany), 9:*332*,
332

Matilda (Empress of England), **9:331**,
12:287, 13:512–513

Matilda (Queen of Germany), St.,
9:331–332

Matilda of Flanders, 5:1

Matilda of Hackeborn, St. *See* Mechtild
of Hackeborn, St.

Matilda of Tuscany, 2:181, 315, 506,
8:847, 12:643

Matins, **9:332–333**

   Consors Paterni Luminis, 4:167

   *Custodes Hominum Psallimus
   Angelos*, 4:448

   drama, 4:894

   Iam Toto Subitus Vesper, 7:269

   Liturgy of the Hours, 8:729

   office hymns of, 5:33, 7:269, 12:464

   Vatican Council II, 8:731

Matisse, Henri, 1:803, 3:713

Matocha, Josef (Abp. of Olomouc),
4:485

Matovalle, Julio María, 5:64

Matre, Anthony, 1:352

Matrimonia quae in locis (Benedict
XIV), 10:218–219

Matrimony, Sacrament of, **9:333–339**,
334, 335

   Coptic, 4:257

   Durandus of Saint-Pourçain, 4:948

   Hugh of Saint-Victor, 7:158

   Middle Ages, 8:295

   reviviscence of sacramental power,
   12:206

   Tametsi, 13:749–750

   See also Marriage; Marriage
   legislation (Canon Law)

Matsuo, Louis, Bl., 7:734

Matter

   abstraction, 1:46

   action at a distance, 1:80

   Aristotle, 1:682, 4:915

   Berkeley, George, 2:299–300

   causality, 3:297, 299

   dialectical materialism, 9:323

   identified with nature, 10:209

   nature of, 12:802–803

   parts of, 10:904–905

   Plotinus, 11:422

   privation, 11:723

   soul, 13:334

   substantial change, 13:580

Matter, philosophy of, **9:339–344**

Matter, theology of, **9:345–346**

Matter and form, **9:346–353**

   Aristotle, 1:682, 4:915, 5:802, 803

   disposition, 4:777

   distinction, 4:780

   Duns Scotus, John, 4:936

   human soul, 13:350–351

   hylosystemism, 7:239

   origins, 13:354

   origins of life, 8:576

   simplicity of God, 13:138

   soul, 13:334

   Suarezianism, 13:562

   theory of motion, 10:19–20

   unicity, 5:802–806

   See also Atomism; Dynamism; Form;
   Hylomorphism

Matter and Memory (Bergson), 2:296

Matters of the Holy Faith and Catholic
Religion, Congregation for, 5:21

Matthaean formula, baptism, 2:61–62

Matthew, Apostle, St., 5:475, *476*,
9:*353*, **353**, *355*, 358, 11:810

Matthew, Gospel According to, **9:354**,
356–360

   abomination of desolation in, 1:23

   adultery, 1:133, 13:49, 50

   Barabbas, 2:85

   Bartholomew, Apostle, St., 2:123

   beatific vision, 2:169, 171

   beatitudes, 2:177–178

   Beelzebul, 2:200

   charity, 13:439

   Christian law, 8:403, 404

   Christian monastacism, 2:264

   Christmas, 3:555

   Christ's wounds, 13:95

   criticism, 3:34

   death of traitors, 8:15–16

   descent of Christ into hell, 4:684

   dietary laws, 4:743

   disciple as term, 4:769, 771–772

   discipleship of women, 14:830–831

   Divine election, 5:146

   Divine indwelling, 7:441

   divorce, 13:49–50

   early Christian way of life, 3:546

   edification, 5:84

   Elijah's Second Coming, 5:159

   Elijah's story, 5:159

   end of the world, 5:215–216

   eschatology, 5:339

   family structure, 14:830

   final perseverance, 11:134

   gates of hell, 6:107

   Gehenna, 6:116

   Gentiles, 6:140

   glory, 6:245

   glory of God (end of creation), 6:246

   gluttony, 6:251

   Gnosis, 6:254

   God the Son, 6:295–296

   God's spirit, 13:427, 428

   God's word-made-flesh, 14:837

   Hades, 6:604

   hatred, 6:666

   heaven, 6:684, 684–685

   hell, 6:724

   human sexuality, 13:49–50

   infancy narrative of, 7:452–454

   infused knowledge, 8:207

   inner moral demand of the law,
   7:702

   Jesus Christ

      baptism of, 2:58, 72

      genealogy of, 6:126, 14:829–830

      as Lord, 8:781

      prayer, 11:592

      as street preacher, 11:626

      temptations of, 9:546

   John the Baptist, St.

      baptism of, 2:58

      ministry of, 7:1013–1014

   judgment, Divine, 8:28–30

   justice, 8:65, 72

   justice of men, 8:74

   justification, 8:77

   kerygma, 8:157

   kindness, 8:171

   Kingdom of God, 8:173–174

   Lamb of God, 8:300

   lay spirituality, 8:413

Lazarus of Bethany, 8:420

Lebanon, 8:426

leprosy, 8:510

Lord used for God, 8:780

Lord's Day, 8:781

Lord's Prayer, 8:782–784

love as commandment in, 4:8

Magi, 9:34, 35

marital bond, 8:871

Mary, Blessed Virgin, 9:241–242

Mary Magdalene, St., 9:287

miracles, 9:664

Nazareth, 10:216

parables in, 10:870–871

on the Parousia, 10:897–898

Passion, 10:920, 921, 922, 923

peace, 11:49, 13:249

penance, 11:68

perseverance, 11:133

Pharisees, 11:226

poverty in, 4:307

praetorium, 11:579

prayer, 13:439

Precious Blood, 11:641, 642

publicans, 11:810

rebirth, 11:951

redaction criticism scholarship, 10:304

repentence, baptism as sign of, 2:57

St. John the Baptist, 5:159

salvation through baptism, 2:58

sanctification through baptism, 2:59

Second Coming, 8:40

serpent as symbol, 13:20

Seven Last Words, 13:36, 37

Shekinah, 13:77–78

showbread, 13:88

sign of Jonah, 7:1022

signs of the times, 13:117

Simon the Apostle, 13:126

simplicity, 13:137

sin, 13:145, 147, 148

sixth beatitude, 2:172

slaughter of innocents, 7:484

social principle, 13:249

Solomon, 13:305

Son of David, 13:310

Son of Man, 9:547, 13:317

sons of God, 13:322

soul, 13:336

spiration, 13:420

spirit, 13:425

Stephen, St. in, 13:510

tradition of ancients, 8:5

Trinitarian formula, 2:61

virgin birth, 14:533

virginity in, 4:306

women, role of, 14:830

your Father, 13:312

See also Synoptic Gospels

Matthew of Albano (Card.), **9:360**

Matthew of Aquasparta (Card.), 1:878, **9:360–361**, 12:234, 760

Matthew of Cracow (Bp. of Worms), 3:241, **9:361**

Matthew of Gubbio, 1:937

Matthew Paris, 1:464, 4:444, **9:361–362**, 12:233, 532, 13:44

Matthews, Ann. *See* Matthews, Mary Bernardina (Mother)

Matthews, Mary Bernardina (Mother), **9:362**

Matthews, Shailer, 2:80

Matthews, William (Father), **9:362–363**, *363*

Matthias (Holy Roman Emperor), 5:688

Matthias, Apostle, St., **9:363–364**, *364*

Matthias, Bl. (17th c. Japanese martyr), 7:732

Matthias, St. (17th c. Japanese martyr), 7:732

Matthias Corvinus (Hunyadi) (King of Hungary), 2:881

Matthias of Janov, 7:230

Matthias of St. John, 3:143

Matthys, Jan (d. 1534), 9:637

Mattias, Maria de, Bl., 2:674, **9:364**, 11:643

Mattiussi, Guido, 12:775

Matulaitis-Matulewicz, Jurgis, Bl., **9:364–365**

Matulewicz, Jerzy. *See* Matulaitis-Matulewicz, Jurgis, Bl.

Maturin, Basil William, **9:365**

Matz, M. Ernestine (Mother), 5:882

Matz, M. Hilaria (Mother), 5:882

Matz, Nicholas Chrysostom (Bp. of Denver), 3:859, 4:668–669

Mau, Dominic, 14:496

Mau, Francisco Javier, 14:496

Mau Mau Movement, 8:150

Maubant, Pierre Philibert, martyr, 8:234, 239

Maubeuge Convent, 1:244

Maubuisson Abbey (France), **9:365**

Mauburnus, Joannes, 4:708

Mauburnus, John. *See* Mombaer, John

Mauger, Vincent. *See* Vincent Madelgarius, St.

Maundy Thursday. *See* Holy Thursday

Maunoir, Julien, Bl., **9:365–366**

Maupertuis, Pierre Louis Moreau de, 11:169

Maur, St. *See* Maurus of Subiaco, St.

Maur de l'Enfant Jésus, 3:137, 143

Maurdramnus (Abbot of Corbie), 4:258

Mauriac, François, 1:803, 2:303, 5:219, 857, 9:*366*, 366–367

Maurice (Byzantine Emperor), 6:153, 479–480, **9:367–368**

Armenia, 1:700

Dormition of the Virgin, 4:875

John IV the Faster, 7:916

Lombards, 2:750

Monophysitism, 2:748

papacy, 2:750–751

Maurice, Frederick Denison, **9:368**

Maurice, St., 12:567

Maurice of Carnoët, St., **9:368**

Maurice of Orange, 1:713, 12:109

Maurice of Saxony, 6:418, 12:741

Maurice of Sully (Bp. of Paris), **9:368–369**

Maurilius (Bp. of Angers), St., 1:431

Maurin, Aristide Peter, 3:824, 4:546, **9:369**

Maurinus (Bp. of Beauvais), 2:188

Maurists, 2:235, **9:176**, 369–370, 12:406

Abbots, 1:10

Aniane Abbey, 1:454

Bourgueil-en-Vallée Abbey, 2:568

Chaise-Dieu Abbey, 3:362

Chezal-Benoît Abbey, 3:473

Clement XII (Pope), 3:790

diplomatics, 4:757

Fécamp Abbey, 5:659

Ferrières-en-Gâtinais Abbey, 5:695

Flavigny-sur-Ozerain Abbey, 5:760

Fontenelle Abbey, 5:793

Pierre Nicole's defense of, 10:384

reform

Jumièges Abbey scholars, 8:60

Lagny-sur-Marne Abbey, 8:280

Landévennec Abbey, 8:319

Saint-Calais Abbey, 12:541

Saint-Évroult-d'Ouche Abbey, 12:545

Saint-Germain-des-Prés Abbey (Paris, France), 12:548

Saint Laumer of Blois Abbey (France), 12:557

Saint-Maixent Abbey (France), 12:564

Saint-Ouen Abbey (Rouen, France), 12:570

Saint-Pierre-sur-Dives Abbey, 12:581

Maurists *(continued)*
 Saint-Remi Abbey (Reims, France), 12:583
 Saint-Savin-sur-Gartempe Abbey, 12:585
 Saint-Server-de-Rustan Abbey, 12:585–586
 Saint-Sever Abbeys, 12:585
 Saint-Valery-sur-Somme Abbey, 12:588
 Solesmes Abbey, 13:300
 Solignac Abbey, 13:302
 Souillac Abbey, 13:332
Mauritania, **9:370–371**, *372*
Mauritius, 8:384, **9:371–373**, *374*
Mauritius Burindus. *See* Gregory VIII (Antipope)
Mauritius de Portu Fildaeo. *See* O'Fihely, Maurice
Maurois, André, 1:203
Mauron, Nicolas, 11:994
Maurras, Charles, 5:856, **9:373–374**
 Action Française, 1:81, 82, 2:303
 Bonald, Louis Gabriel Ambroise de, 2:478
 Pius X (Pope), St., 11:390
Maurus, Sylvester, 1:78, 677, 9:374–375, 14:51
Maurus of Subiaco, St., **9:375**, 12:566, 567
Maury, Jean Siffrein (Card.), 1:813, **9:375–376**, 10:149
Mausbach, Joseph, **9:376**
Mausoleum of Galla Placidia (Ravenna, Italy), 11:932
Mausoleums, Islamic, 7:617
Al-Mawlawi, 7:620
Mawson, John, 5:237
Maxentius, 4:179, 749
Maxentius (Patriarch of Aquileia), 1:608
Maxfield, Thomas, Bl., 5:235, **9:376**
Maxim I (Bulgarian Patriarch), 2:684
Maxima vigilantia (apostolic constitution, Benedict XIII), 1:636
Maximam gravissimamque (encyclical, Pius XI), 11:395
Maximes (La Rochefoucauld), 8:336
Maximian (Roman Emperor), 2:751
Maximilian (Archduke), 1:911–912
Maximilian (Bp. of Lorch), St., 9:377
Maximilian, Johann Baptist Joseph. *See* Reger, Max
Maximilian, St. (274-295), 9:376–377
Maximilian, SS., **9:376–377**
Maximilian I (Holy Roman Emperor), 6:108–109, 639

Maximilian II (Holy Roman Emperor), 1:911, 4:482, 7:213–214
Maximilian Franz of Austria (Elector of Cologne), 3:843
Maximilian Heinrich (Bavarian prince), 6:36–37
Maximilian of Austria (Emperor of Mexico), 8:264
Maximilian of Hapsburg, 9:579
Maximillian, St., 4:150
Maximinus, St., 9:608
Maximinus Daia (Roman Emperor), 1:268, 4:179, 180
Maximinus the Thracian (Roman Emperor), 12:312
Maximinus Thrax (Roman Emperor), 3:594
Maximlianus (martyr), 1:92
Maximos III (Maxlūm), 1:195, 271, 526, **9:377**
Maximos IV Sayegh (Card.), 1:526, **9:377–378**
Maxims of Christian Perfection (Rosmini-Serbati), 12:384, 385
Maxims of Perfection (Médaille), 12:554
Maxims of the Little Institute, 12:554
Maximum illud (apostolic letter, Benedict XV), 3:500, 626, 8:429, 9:681
Maximus (Bp. of Saragossa). St., **9:378**
Maximus (Bp. of Turin), St., **9:378–379**
Maximus (Roman Emperor), 3:86
Maximus of Alexandria, 4:456
Maximus of Jerusalem (Bp.), 4:470–471
Maximus of Madaura, 9:28
Maximus of Turin, St., 1:289, 344, 577, 3:407, 12:42, 51
Maximus the Confessor, St., 2:794, **9:379–380**
 apophatic theology, 1:568
 Christology, 2:749, 750, 793, 3:561
 Constans II, 4:186
 Monothelitism, 2:821, 7:81
 Nemesius of Emesa quoted, 10:232
 works of, 9:379
Maximus the Cynic (Bp. of Constantinople), 4:190
Maxis, Therese Duchemin, 1:157
Maxwell, J. C., 1:80
Maxwell, James (Father), 9:741, 12:558
Maxwell, Winifred (Countess), **9:380–381**
May, John C. (Abp. of St. Louis, MO, b. 1922), 9:749
May, John L. (Abp. of St. Louis), 1:202, 12:561
May, William, 7:528

May Day (Emerson), 5:188
May Laws (1873), 8:254–255, 444
Māyā, 7:408
Maya Gutiérrez, Esteban, Bl., 7:123
Maya religion, 8:318–319, **9:381**
Mayaudon, François, 12:277
Maybeck, Bernard, 3:715
Mayer, Alfred (prior), 12:578
Mayer, Antonio de Castro (Bp. of Campos, Brazil), 8:448
Mayer, Pius, 3:143
Mayer, Rupert, Bl., 7:792, **9:381–382**
Mayflower Compact, 3:647, 4:115, **9:382**, *383*
Mayhew, Thomas, 4:115
Maynard, Theodore, **9:382–383**
Mayne, Cuthbert, St., 5:227, **9:383–384**
Maynooth, Synod of (1875), 3:243
Mayorga, John de, Bl., 1:952
Mayos Jesuit Mission (Mexico), 9:709
Mazar, B., 2:379–380, 381
Mazarin, Jules (Card.), 9:386, **386–387**
 Ad sanctam beati petri sedem, 1:97
 Amyraut, Moïse, 1:367
 death of, 5:851
 and the Fronde, 5:850, 12:179–180
 Huguenots, 3:639, 7:168
 Louis XIV, 8:801–802
 Retz, Jean François Paul de Gondi de, 12:179–180
 secret meeting ban, 4:41
Mazarin Bible. *See* Gutenberg Bible
Mazdaism, 9:108, 14:920
Mazella, Andrew, 10:220
Mazenod, Charles Joseph Eugène de (Bp.), St., **9:387–388**, *388*
Mazenod, Eugène (Bp.). *See* Mazenod, Charles Joseph Eugène de (Bp.), St.
Mazlūm, Michael. *See* Maximos III (Maxlūm)
Mazu Daoyi, 3:511
Mazzarella, Modestino, Bl., **9:388–389**
Mazzarello, Maria Domenica, St., 2:543, **9:389**, 12:613, 614
Mazzella, Camillo (Card.), **9:389**
Mazzella, Marcello (Card.), 1:438
Mazzini, Giuseppe, 3:101, 7:672, 12:322
Mazzochio, Lorenzo, 13:28
Mazzoldi, Sixtus (Bp.), 1:577
Mazzolini, Sylvester, **9:389–390**
Mazzucconi, Giovanni Battista, Bl., **9:390**
Mazzuchelli, Samuel, 4:921, **9:390–391**, 14:778–779
McAddo, Henry (Abp. of Dublin), 1:440

McAuley, Catherine Elizabeth (Mother), 3:622, **9:391**, 10:68, 13:182–183, 187

McAuliffe, Maurice Francis (Bp. of Hartford), 4:124, 6:653–654, 12:245–246

MCC (Massachusetts Catholic Conference), 9:309

McCaffrey, John Henry, 3:243, **9:391–392**

McCann, Justin, 2:263

McCarran, Patrick, 10:172

McCarran-Walter Act (1952), 10:172

McCarrick, Theodore E. (Card.), 10:283, 330, 14:658

McCarthy, Edward Anthony (Bp. of Phoenix), 1:688, 9:592–593

McCarthy, John, 1:765, 766

McCarthy, Joseph (American senator), 10:172, 13:77

McCarthy, Joseph Edward (Bp. of Portland, ME), 9:59, 11:532

McCarty, MacLyn, 2:404

McCaughwell, Hugh, 1:698

McClatchy, C. K., 2:869

McClendon, James W., 10:154

McCloskey, John (Card.), 5:628, 752, 891, **9:392–393**, 10:314–315, 322

  Hughes, John Joseph, 7:162

  refusal of Poor Clares' entrance to NY Archdiocese, 2:287

  Third Baltimore Plenary Council (1884), 2:46

McCloskey, William George (Bp. of Louisville, KY), 8:149, 817–818, **9:393**

McClurkan, J. O., 3:722

McCollum v. Board of Education (1948), 3:666

McCormick, Follett v. (1944), 3:661

McCormick, Patrick J. (Bp.), 3:283

McCormick, Richard A., **9:393–395**

McCrystal, Teresa Vincent (Sister), 5:752

McCue, J., 1:595

McDevitt, John K., 8:191

McDevitt, John W., **9:395**

McDonald, Andrew J. (Bp. of Little Rock), 1:692, 693, 8:615

McDonald, Barnabas Edward (Brother), **9:395**

McDonald, Cuthbert (Abbot), 12:539

McDonald, William (Bp.), 3:291, 292

McDonnell, Kilian, 3:393

McDonnell, Thomas John (Bp.), **9:396**

McDonough, Thomas Joseph (Abp.), 8:818, 12:710

MCDP. *See* Missionary Catechists of Divine Providence

McEleney, John J. (Bp. of Kingston, Jamaica), 7:700

McElroy, John, 2:557, **9:396**

McEnerney, Garret, 10:649

McFague, Sallie, 5:49

McFarland, Francis Patrick (Bp. of Hartford, CT), 4:123, 6:652–653, **9:396–397**, 12:214

McFarland, Norman F. (Bp. of Reno), 10:271, 12:127

McGaen, Honoria, 2:702

McGavick, Alexander J., 3:478, 5:663, 8:273, 14:782

McGhee, Fredrick, 1:160

McGill, John (Bp. of Richmond, VA), 14:541, 542

McGill University, 3:9

McGivney, Michael Joseph (Father), 4:124, 8:189, **9:397**

McGlynn, Edward, 1:582, 2:711, 4:278–279, 6:206, **9:397–398**, 10:315–316

McGovern, James, 3:477

McGovern, Patrick Aloysius (Bp. of Cheyenne, WY), 14:870

McGowan, Raymond Augustine (Father), **9:398–399**

McGrath, James, **9:399**

McGrath, Joseph F. (Bp.), 2:23

McGroarty, Julia (Sister), **9:399**

McGucken, Joseph T. (Abp. of San Francisco), 2:872, 12:649

McGucken, William, 5:95

McGuiness, Eugene J. (Bp. of Raleigh, NC), 10:438, 11:900

McGuire, Martin R. P., **9:399–400**

McHale, John (Abp. of Tuam), 3:243

McHugh, Antonia (Sister), **9:400**

McInerney, Garrett, 12:251

McInerny, Ralph, 10:186

McIntyre, James Francis Aloysius (Card.), 2:870–871, 872, 8:792, **9:400–401**

McKenna, Charles Hyacinth, **9:401**

McKenzie, John Lawrence, 4:337, 5:146, 520, **9:401–402**

McKeough, Michael J., 3:283

McLaren, Agnes, **9:402–403**

McLaughlin, John J., 7:794

McLaughlin, Thomas H., 10:282

McMahan, Franklin, 3:476

McMahon, D. J., 3:279

McMahon, Franklin, 14:402

McMahon, Hugh, 1:698, 2:725

McMahon, Lawrence Stephen (Bp. of Hartford), 4:124, 6:653

Mcmahon, Thomas John, **9:403**

McManus, Frederick R., 3:59, 4:201

McMaster, James Alphonsus, **9:403**

McMullen, John, 3:477, 4:535, 12:640

McNabb, John (Bp. of Chulucanas), 1:891

McNabb, Joseph. *See* McNabb, Vincent

McNabb, Vincent, 3:129, 4:783, **9:404**

McNair, Hunt v. (1973), 3:667

McNamara, Lawrence J., 10:222

McNeil, Neil (Abp. of Toronto), **9:404**

McNicholas, John Timothy (Abp. of Cincinnati, OH), 2:410, 3:736, **9:404–405**

McPherson, Aimee Semple, 5:835, **9:405–406**

McQuaid, Bernard John (Bp. of Rochester, NY), 1:354, 3:290, 8:303, **9:406–407**

McQuaid, John Charles (Abp. of Dublin), 7:566, **9:407–408**

McReynolds, Justice, 10:648, 649–650

McShea, Joseph (Bp. of Allentown, PA), 11:88

McSweeney, Edward, 8:191

McSweeney, Patrick F., 11:561

McTaggart, John Ellis, 7:300

McVann, James, 11:625

McVinney, Russell J., 12:217

Meacham, Joseph, 13:59

Mead, George Herbert, 6:24, 12:884

Meagher, Paul Kevin (Father), **9:408**

Meal Tub Plot (1680), 10:495–496

The Meaning and End of Religion: A New Approach to the Religious Traditions of Mankind (Smith), 13:235

The Meaning of Revelation (Niebuhr), 10:152, 386

The Meaning of the City (Ellul), 5:172

The Meaning of Truth (James), 5:198

Meanness and magnificence, 9:44

Measurement, 8:201, **9:408–413**

Meaux Abbey (Beverley, Yorkshire, England), **9:413**

MECC (Middle East Council of Churches), **9:616–617**

Mecca, 5:325, **9:413–414**, *414*, 10:9, 51, 53–54

Mechanical necessity, 8:270

Mechanics, 12:809–810, 816

Die Mechanisierung des Weltbildes im 17. Jahrundert (Maier), 9:50–51

Mechanism, **9:414–418**

  action at a distance, 1:80

Mechanism *(continued)*
  atomism, 1:831, 4:958
  Cartesianism, 4:681
  illuminism, 7:321
  immanence, 7:340
  legal theory, 8:399
  materialism, 9:320
  matter and form in, 9:351
Mechanism, biological, **9:418–421**, 13:335
Mechitar (Father), **9:421**
Mechitarists, 1:535, **9:421–422**
Mechitarists of Venice, 9:421–422
Mechitarists of Vienna, 9:422
Mechtild of Hackeborn, St., 6:191, **9:422–423**, 10:114, 118
Mechtild of Magdeburg, 3:744, **9:423**, 12:440
Mechtilde of the Blessed Sacrament (Mother). *See* Bar, Cathérine de
Meda, Filippo, 1:228
Meda of Killeedy, St. *See* Ita of Killeedy, St.
Médaille, Jean-Pierre, 12:554
Medals, religious, 9:*423*, **423–424**
Médard (Bp. of Noyon), St., **9:424–425**
Medeiros, Humberto Sousa (Card. of Boston), 2:556, 5:664, **9:425–426**
Medellín, Diego de (Bp. of La Imperial), 3:485
Medellín Conference (1968), 4:157
Medellín Documents, 8:318, **9:426**, 13:245, 245–246
Medes, 4:477–478, **9:426**, *427*, **428**, 11:134–135
Medes Ferrís, José, Bl., 5:691
Media, 1:303
Mediaevalism (Tyrrell), 14:259
Mediator dei (encyclical, Pius XII), 2:676, 3:589–590, **9:428–429**, 11:400, 705, 12:500
Il mediatore (weekly), 10:918
Mediatrix, Mary, Blessed Virgin as, 9:258–263
Mediavilla Concejero, Julio, Bl., 4:494
Medical ethics, 5:458, 459, 558–561, **9:429–432**, 869
  See also Euthanasia
Medical International Corporation (MEDICO), 4:871
Medical Mission Institute of Würzburg (Germany), 2:192
Medical Mission Sisters (MMS), 4:659–660, 9:330, **432**
Medical Missionaries of Mary (MMM), 9:214, **432–433**

Medical research. *See* Experimentation, medical
Medical technology, 9:430, 13:852
Medici, Anna Caterina de, 1:912
Medici, Ardingo de', 9:433
Medici, Bonagiunta, 9:433
Medici, Cosimo de (1389-1464), 1:536, 5:768, 9:433, *434*, 11:415–416, 12:116–117
Medici, Cosimo de, I (1519-74), 7:670, 9:435
Medici, Cosimo de, II, 6:60
Medici, Giovanni Angelo de'. *See* Pius IV (Pope)
Medici, Giovanni di Bicci (fl. 1360-1429), 9:433
Medici, Giuliano (fl. 1453-78), 9:433, 12:118
Medici, Giulio de. *See* Clement VII (Pope)
Medici, Lorenzo (fl. 1492-1519), 9:435
Medici, Lorenzo il Magnifico (fl. 1449-92), 1:659, 3:781, 5:768, 7:186, 9:433
Medici, Piero (fl. 1416-69), 9:433
Medici, Piero (fl. 1471-1303), 9:435, 12:714
Medici, Salvestro (fl. 1331-88), 9:433
Medici Chapel (Florence), 9:*435*
Medici family, 5:768–769, **9:433–435**, 12:116–117
  Florence, 12:714
  Leo X (Pope), 8:485–486
  L'Hôpital, 8:530, 531
  Pazzi conspiracy, 12:118, 220
  as rivals of Pazzi family, 11:47
Medicina spiritualis contra temptationem concupiscentiae carnalis (St. Odilo of Cluny), 10:552
Medicinal grace, 6:399
Medicine
  Arabic development of, 12:810–811
  Constantine the African, 4:184
  Galen, 12:806–807
  history of, 12:210–211
  hysterectomy, 7:265–266
  in the Middle Ages, 12:814
  Renaissance, 12:817–818
  See also Medical ethics
Medicine Man. *See* Shaman and Medicine Man
Médicis, Catherine de. *See* Catherine de Médicis
Médicis, Marie de. *See* Marie de Médicis
MEDICO (Medical International Corporation), 4:871

Medieval Academy News (newsletter), 9:435
Medieval Academy of America (Cambridge, MA), **9:435–436**
Medieval Academy of America, Committee on Centers and Regional Associations (CARA), 9:436
Medieval architecture, 3:673–674
  See also Church architecture; Gothic architecture; Romanesque architecture
Medieval art, 12:357
Medieval books, **2:515–520**
Medieval boy martyrs, 4:827, **9:436–437**
Medieval era
  coinage of, 10:480–481
  concept of time during, 14:78
  controversy over universals during, 14:322–323
  development of names during, 10:142
  mosaics of, 10:3–4
  mystical body of Christ study during, 10:103–104
  notion of order during, 10:630
  notion of truth during, 14:222–223
  ordeals during, 10:627–628
  panentheism thought during, 10:820
  papacy development during, 10:835–840
  papal arbitration development during, 10:854–855
  Summa ideal of, 10:374
  transcendental doctrine during, 14:150
  transubstantiation doctrine during, 14:158–159
  See also Middle Ages
Medieval Latin literature, 3:159, 601, **9:437–464**
Medina, **9:464**, 10:53–54
Medina, Bartolomé de, 2:49, 50, 5:395, **9:464–465**, 12:716, 764
Medina, Jorge (Bp.), 3:237
Medina, Juan, 3:417, **9:465**
Medina, Miguel de, 3:327
Medina Olmos, Emmanuel (Bp. of Guadix), St., 1:298, 299
Meditaciones de los misterios de nuestra fe (La Puente, L.), 8:334
Meditatio de stau praelati (Simon de Ghent), 13:128
Meditation, **9:465–466**
  Carmelite spirituality, 3:134
  Daoist, 4:523
  Jesus prayer, 7:861
  movement, 13:449–450
  yoga, 14:891–892

Zen, 14:915–916

Meditationes seu contemplationes devotissimae (Torquemada), 14:*113*

Meditationes vitae Christi (biography of Christ), 7:845

Meditations (Descartes), 3:184, 185, 7:294–295

Meditations (Guigo I), 3:192

Meditations (Marcus Aurelius), 9:144

Meditations (St. Anselm), 10:119

Méditations chrétiennes (Malebranche), 9:74

Meditations on First Philosophy (Descartes), 12:771

Medium a quo (the means from which), 12:751

Medium quo (the means by which), 12:751

Medium quod (the means which), 12:751

Medium sub quo (the means under which), 12:751

Medjugorje (Croatia), **9:466–467**

Medrano, Mariano (Bp. of Buenos Aires), 1:650, 651, **9:467**

Medulla theologiae moralis (Busenbaum), 2:715–716, 3:221, 8:273

Medwall, Henry, 9:881

Meegan, Joseph, 1:288

Meehan, Charles (Father), Bl., **9:467–468**

Meehan, Charles, Bl., 5:237

Meehan, Thomas Francis, **9:468**

Meek v. Pittenger (1975), 3:667–668

Meekness, **9:468–469**

Meerschaert, Theophile, 10:574–575

Meet the American Catholic (Scharper), 12:729

Meeus, Anna de, 5:435

Megarian-Stoic school of logic, 8:749

Megiddo (Israel), 2:379, 9:*469*, **469**, 10:780

Mehegan, Catherine Josephine. *See* Mehegan, Mary Xavier (Mother)

Mehegan, Mary Xavier (Mother), **9:470**

Mehrerau Abbey (Bregenz, Austria), **9:470**

Meier, John P., 6:867

Mein Kampf (Hitler), 7:874

Meinhard (Bp. of Livonia, Germany), St., **9:470–471**

Meinhard of Holstein (Bp. of Livonia), 5:376

Meinong, Alexius, 1:678, 5:398, 7:518

Meinrad. *See* Meinhard (Bp. of Livonia, Germany), St.

Meinrad of Einsiedeln, St., 5:139, **9:471**, 13:369

Meinwerk (Bp. of Paderborn), Bl., **9:471**

Meir, Gaon ben, 12:449

Meiron Excavation Project, 2:380

Meistermann, Barnabas, **9:471**

Melancholy, 1:66–67

Melanchthon, Philipp, 5:43, 521, 732, **9:471–473**, *472*, 10:214, 14:233
adiaphorism, 8:890
Aristotelianism, 1:677
astrology, 1:810, 813
Augsburg Confession, 1:850, 4:78
Blarer, Ambrosius, 2:433
Bohemian Brethren, 4:482
Calixtus, Georg, 2:874
Calvin, John, 2:891
capital punishment, 3:87
Chemnitz, Martin, 3:463, 464
Confessio Augustana, 8:882
determinism, 13:681–682
Flacius Illyricus, opposition to, 5:754
fragmentation of Lutheran Movement, 4:60
humanism, 7:192
imputation of justice and merit, 7:368
Jesuits, 3:611
justification, 8:84
Latimer, H., 8:361
Luther, Martin, 9:62–63
Lutheran theology, 12:16
nonessentials, 5:754
predestination, 11:655
Protestant Reformation, 12:15, 16, 17
rationalism, 11:922
Reformation exegesis, 5:518
Sadoleto, Jacopo, 12:526
scholasticism, 12:767
See also Philippism

Meland, Bernard, 11:731

Mélanges (Veuillot), 14:465, 466

Mélanges de patrologie et d'histoire des dogmes (Trixeront), 14:95

Melania the Elder, 4:383, 5:464, **9:473**, 12:404

Melania the Younger, St., 5:449, **9:473**, 12:404

Melanie of Rennes, St., 8:380

Melbourne Overseas Mission, 8:224

Melcher, Joseph (Bp. of Green Bay, WI), 14:780

Melchers, Paulus (Card.), 3:843–844, **9:473–474**, *474*

Melchior, Nicholas, 1:239

Melchizedek, 1:37, **9:474–475**, *475*

Meleager of Gadara, 2:804

Meléndez, Juan de, **9:475–476**

Meléndez Sánchez, Martiniano, Bl., 7:125

Meletian Schism, 1:268, 3:561, 5:137, 292, **9:476**
Apollinarianism, 1:559
Arius, 1:685
Athanasius, St., 1:817
Basil, St., 2:136, 137–138
Constantine I (the Great) (Roman Emperor), 4:181
Lucifer of Cagliari, 8:845
Theodosius the Deacon, 13:885

Meletios IV Metaxakis (Patriarch), 10:682

Meletius (Bp. of Antioch), 4:190
Basil, St., 2:137–138
Canon Law, 3:38
Christology, 3:561
Cyril of Jerusalem, 4:471
Damasus I (Pope), St., 4:504
Diodore of Tarsus, 4:750
John Chrysostom, St., 7:945
Meletian schism, 9:476

Meletius of Lycopolis, 1:266
See also Meletian Schism

Meletius Syrigus, 12:433

Melfi, Councils of, **9:477**

Melisend (Queen of Jerusalem), 2:29

Melismatic Chant, 6:466

Melissus of Samos (Greek philosopher), 6:441, 11:117

Melitiniotes, Constantinus, 2:826

Melito of Sardes (Bp.), 1:785, **9:477–478**
apocrypha, 1:559
apologetics, 1:567
biblical canon, 3:30
descent of Christ into hell, 4:684
Roman persecutions, 3:593
works of, 9:477
works of charity, 3:405

Melk Abbey (Austria), 3:706, 8:248, 303, **9:478–479**, *479*

Melkite Greek Catholic Church, 1:195, 525, 526, 2:746–747, 5:19, **9:479–481**
Basilian orders, 2:141, 144
Cilicia, 3:733
Copts, 4:252–253, 254
Council of Catholic Patriarchs of the Orient, 4:295–296
Lebanon, 8:428
liturgy, 1:273

Melkite Greek Catholic Church
  (continued)
  Ottoman Turks, 1:271
  Sankt Ulrich von Augusburg Abbey,
    12:671
  Syria, 13:705
Melleray Abbey (Brittany), **9:481**
Mellifont Abbey (Ireland), 8:529, 9:*481*,
  481
Mellitus (Abp. of Canterbury), St.,
  1:871, 3:70, 8:771, **9:481–482**
Melos amoris (Rolle de Hampole),
  12:297
Melotto, Angelico (Bp. of Solala,
  Guatemala), 9:827
Melrose Abbey (Melrose, Scotland),
  3:749, **9:482**, *483*
Melsa Abbey (Beverley, Yorkshire,
  England), **9:413**
Melun, Armand de, 5:854, **9:482–483**
Mélusine (Arras), 4:401
Melville, Andrew, **9:483–484**,
  12:828–829
Melville, Annabelle McConnell, **9:484**
Membre, Zenobius, 1:270
Memling, Hans, 14:458
Memnon (Bp. of Ephesus), 2:151
*Mémoire sur la réform de la faculté de
  théologie* (Gerson), 6:190
Mémoires (La Rochefoucauld), 8:336
Mémoires de Trevoux (Le Tellier), 8:519
Mémoires d'Outre-tombe
  (Chateaubriand), 3:449
*Mémoires et lettres du P. Timothée de la
  Flèche, O. Cap* (Ubald), 14:261
Mémoires pour l'histoire du Jacobinisme
  (Barruel), 5:969
*Mémoires pour servir à l'histoire du
  Jacobinisme* (Barruel), 2:118
*Mémoires pour servir à l'histoire
  ecclésiastique des six premiers
  siécles* (Tillemont), 14:75
*Mémoires pour servir a l'histoire
  ecclésiastique des six premiers
  sièsiastiques* (Ceillier), 10:963
*Mémoires pour servir a l'Histoire
  religieuse de notre Temps, 1860-1931*
  (Loisy), 8:766
Memoirs (Hegesippus), 6:714
Memoirs (Syropoulos), 13:723
*Memoirs of the Rt. Rev. Simon Wm.
  Gabriel Bruté, D.D., First Bishop of
  Vincennes* (Bayley), 2:165
*Memorabilium omnis aetatis et omnium
  gentium chronici commentarii*
  (Nauclerus), 10:214
Memorare (prayer), **9:484–485**
Memorial (Angela of Foligno), 5:898

Mémorial (Pascal), 10:911
Memorial de Fray Matías Ruíz Blanco,
  12:407
Mémorial de la Dordogne (periodical),
  14:465
Le Mémorial de la vie ecclésiastique (St.
  Eudes), 5:441
Memoriale Sanctorum (Eulogius of
  Córdoba), 12:606
Memoriales (Motoloní), 10:*28*
*Memorials of Those Who Suffered for
  the Catholic Faith in Ireland*
  (O'Reilly), 7:579
Memorias de las reinas católicas
  (Flórez), 5:775
*Memorie ecclesiastichi e civili di Città
  di Castello* (Muzi), 10:76
Memory, 3:822, 4:453, 5:27, 12:913
*Memory and Reconciliation: The Church
  and the Sins of the Past* (ITC), 7:529
*Memory and Reconciliation: The Church
  and the Mistakes of the Past*, 3:628
Memory image, 8:209
Memory in Ancient and Medieval
  Thought, **9:485–486**
Memra (name for God), 8:759
Men at Work and Worship (Ellard),
  5:168
Men Like Gods (Wells), 14:361
Mena, Alonso de, Bl., 7:733
Menabuoi, Giusto de', 1:544
Menace (periodical), 10:171
Menachem ben Saruk, 5:509
Ménager (Bp.), 5:859
Menander, 1:521, 4:496–497
Menander Protector, 2:798
Menard, Eusebe M. (Father), 9:731
Ménard, René (Father), 14:778
Mencius (Mengzi), 3:508, 509, 4:97,
  9:486–487
Mendel, Gregor Johann, 1:889, 2:403,
  4:531–532, **9:487–489**, *488*
Mendeleev, Dmitri Ivanovich, 1:835
Mendelssohn, Moses, 4:617, 5:47, *261*,
  263, 6:662, 7:865, 872–873, 8:9
Mendelssohn-Bartholdy, Felix, 1:293,
  9:*489*, **489–490**
Mendelssohn-Bartholdy, Jacob Ludwig.
  See Mendelssohn-Bartholdy, Felix
Mendenhall, G. E., 3:338
Mendes, Alfonso (Patriarch), 5:403–404
Mendes de Almeida, Cândido, 2:596
Mendes de Almeida, Luciano (Abp.),
  12:686
Méndez, Ramón Ignacio (Abp. of
  Caracas), **9:490**
Méndez Montoya, Jesús, St., **9:490–491**

Mendez Pinto, Fernando, 2:901
Mendicant controversy (1269-70), 14:20
  Second Council of Lyons, 3:132, 141
  University of Paris, 2:479, 481, 483,
    501
Mendicant orders, 5:689, 845, **9:491**,
  14:187
  Albert the Great, St., 1:224
  Albigensians, 1:229
  Behemia, 4:479
  Catharism, 3:260
  Cistercians, 3:746–747
  contemplative life, 4:210
  Crumpe, Henry, 4:400
  Crusades, 4:414
  Dacia, 4:492
  expansion in Scotland of, 12:832–833
  Gerard of Abbeville, opposition to,
    6:159–160
  glorification of poverty, 11:565
  Honorius IV (Pope), 7:86
  hospital history, 7:120
  Inquisition, 1:231
  Italian expansion, 7:665–666
  medieval heresies, 8:295
  origins, 3:602
  suppression of, 6:1
  William of Saint-Amour, legitimacy
    of, 14:750–751
  work in the Low Countries, 10:258
  works of charity, 3:413, 414
  See also Carmelites; Dominicans;
    Franciscans; Mendicant controversy
Mendieta, Gerónimo de, **9:492**
Mendonça Furtado, Diogo de, 2:592,
  594
Mendoza, Amalio, St., 1:298
Mendoza, Antonio de, 1:686
Mendoza, Julio Alvarez, St., 6:545
Mendoza, Pedro González de (Card.),
  9:492
Ménégoz, Eugene, 5:711
Menem, Carlos Saúl, 1:656
Menéndez, Francisco, 1:155
Menéndez, Josefa (Sister), **9:492–493**
Meneses, Juan Francisco, **9:493**
Mēness (Baltic region deity), 2:36
Menestrel, Jean-Baptiste, 12:277
Menezes, Alexis de (Abp. of Goa),
  7:398–399
Menezes, Diogo, 2:590
Mengarini, Gregorio, **9:493**
Mengs, Anton Raphael, 3:793, 795
Mengzi. *See* Mencius

La Mennais Brothers. *See* Brothers of Christian Instruction of Ploërmel

Mennas (Patriarch of Constantinople), 1:172, **9:494**

Menni, Angel Hercules. *See* Menni Figini, Benedetto, St.

Menni, Angelo Ercolino. *See* Menni Figini, Benedetto, St.

Menni Figini, Benedetto, St., **9:494**

Mennonite churches, **9:495–496**

Mennonites, 9:*495*, 12:261
    Amish churches, 1:360
    Anabaptists, 1:368, 369, 2:606
    Church-State relations, 3:652
    pacifism of, 10:746
    See also Anabaptists; Hutterites; The Reformation

Menochio, Giovanni Stefano, 7:847, **9:496–497**

Menologion of Basil, 5:865

Menominee people, 5:221

Menophantes of Ephesus, 1:527, 662

Menorah, 4:607, **9:497**, *498*

Mens (Congregation for the Propagation of the Faith), 3:516

Mens nostra (encyclical, Pius XI), 11:393

Mense maio (encyclical, Paul VI), 11:32

Menstruation, 2:442

Mensurius of Carthage (Bp.), 4:861

The Mental Cure (Evans), 10:308

Mental illness, 3:418, 5:933–934, 7:132

Mental Medicine (Evans), 10:308

Mental prayer, 1:309, 323, 11:597–600

Mental reservation, 8:900, 902, **9:497, 499–500**

Mental test scales of measurement, 9:411

Menti nostrae (apostolic exhortation, Pius XII), 1:84, 586, 3:466

MEP. *See* Paris Foreign Missionary Society (MEP)

Merbot, Bl., **9:500**

Mercadé, Eustache, 10:928–929

Mercado, Tomás de, **9:500**

Mercati, Angelo, 5:865, **9:500–501**

Mercati, Giovanni (Card.), 2:358, **9:501**

Mercedarian Missionaries of Berriz, **9:501**

Mercedarians, **9:501–502**
    Argentina, 1:650
    Bolivia, 2:466
    Carthage, 3:187
    Chile, 3:485
    Colombia, 3:848

Mary de Cervellón, St., founding of, 9:285

Mercedarian Missionaries of Berriz, 9:501

Peter Nolasco, St., founding of, 11:193

works of charity, 3:419

Mercenaries, 13:642–644

Mercersburg Review, 10:272, 12:726

Mercersburg theology, **9:502–503**, 12:726

Mercians, 1:148

Mercier, Désiré Joseph (Card.), 5:252, **9:503–504**, 12:776
    certitude, 3:352
    chair at Leuven, 8:824
    Malines Conversations, 2:183, 9:78
    neoscholasticism, 12:748, 776
    philosophy and science, 11:301

Mercier, Francois X., 1:207

Merciless Parliament (England, 1388), 1:263

Mercurian, E., 1:325

Mercurius (Roman priest). *See* John II (Pope)

Mercy, 4:783–784, 5:152, **9:504**
    See also Alms and almsgiving

Mercy, works of, **9:505–506**

Mercy Brothers, 3:622

Mercy International Association (MIA), 13:187

Mercy killing. *See* Euthanasia

Mercy of God, **9:506–508**

Mercy Sisters, 1:691, 3:622

Merdes, Edward, 1:211

Mère Angélique. *See* Arnauld, Jacqueline Marie Angélique (Mother)

Meres, Thomas. *See* Pormort, Thomas, Bl.

Mergens, Board of Education v. (1990), 3:664

Meribanes. *See* Mirian (King of Iberia)

Merici, Angela, St., 3:610, 782, 4:310, **9:508**

Mérida, Spain, **9:508–510**, *509*

Meriman, Emily Butterfield, 8:838

Merino, Antolin, 3:12

Merit, **9:510–514**
    Baianism, 2:21
    in the Bible, 12:206
    conversion, 4:240
    created actuation by uncreated act, 4:336
    good, 6:353
    grace, 6:383
    restoration of, 12:206–207

Merk, Augustin, 2:367

Merkelbach, Benoît Henri, 4:159, **9:514**, 12:777

Merkle, Sebastian, 6:184

Merks, Thomas (Bp. of Carlisle), **9:514**

Merle d'Aubigne, J. H., 5:467

Merleau-Ponty, Maurice, 5:362, **9:514–515**, 11:297–298, 13:347–348

Merlini, Giovanni, **9:515**

Merlo, Teresa. *See* Thecla (Mother) (Teresa Merlo)

Merloni, Clelia (Mother), 12:495

Mermillod, Gaspard (Card.), 8:255, **9:515–516**, 13:256

Mérode, Frédéric Ghislain de (Abp.), **9:516**, 14:937

Merode, Monsignor de, 1:532

Merope (play) (Maffei, Francesco Scipione), 9:32

Merovingian era
    Angers, 1:431
    archchancellors, 1:633
    bishops, 3:810
    Canon Law, 3:41–42
    Carolingian Dynasty, 3:162–163, 164, 423, 434–435
    Carolingian reform, 3:155
    Chartres, 3:441
    clerical celibacy/marriage, 3:326
    hospitals, 7:127–128
    works of charity, 3:409, 410
    See also Clovis I (King of the Franks); Middle Ages

Merovingian family, **9:516–520**

Merovingians, 5:841–842, 916, 10:763

Merrick, Mary Virginia, **9:520**

Merry del Val, Rafael (Card.), 1:438, 2:249, 3:212, 8:766, **9:520–521**, *521*

Merry England (periodicial), 9:590

Mersch, Émile, 5:37, **9:521–522**

Mersen, Treaty of (870), 1:124

Mersenne, Marin (Father), 3:184, 6:105

Merten, Blandina, Bl., **9:522**

Merten, Maria Magdalena. *See* Merten, Blandina, Bl.

Merton, Robert, 13:283

Merton, Thomas, 8:*817*, **9:522–523**, *523*, 12:540
    Carthusian spirituality, 3:193
    contemplation, 4:208–209
    evangelical counsels, 4:307
    interest in contemplative spirituality, 10:116
    works of, 9:522

Merton College (Oxford, England)
    election of John Wylyot, 12:235–236

Merton College (Oxford, England)
  (continued)
  Richard of Campsall, 12:232
  Robert Kilwardby, 12:266
  Walter of Merton, founding of,
    12:266, 14:627
Merton Theorem, 12:812–813
Merulo, Claudio, **9:523**
Mesarites, John, 2:825
Mesarites, Nicholas (Metropolitan of
  Ephesus), 2:825
Meschler, Moritz, **9:523–524**
Mesdeu, Baltasar, 12:770
Meseguer, P., 4:905
Mésenguy, François Philippe, 3:792
Mesha Inscription, **9:524**, 13:120
Mesina, Antonia, Bl., **9:524–525**
Mesland, Pierre (Father), 3:185
Mesmerism, 8:387
Mesonzo, Peter (Bp.), 12:683
Mesopotamia, ancient, **9:525–538**
  architecture, 1:757
  creation, 4:337
  Dagon (god), 4:493
  deities of, 10:87–89
  double ax, 4:363
  excavations on Ugarit, 14:266–267
  geography, 9:526
  history, 9:526–531
  kingship, 8:178
  religion, 9:531–538
  science, 9:531
  Simeon Barsabae, 13:124
  wisdom literature, 14:789
  See also Assyria; Babylonia
Mesopotamian art, 9:*528*
Mesopotamian genealogies, 10:951
Mesrop, St., 1:700, 704, 705, 710, **9:538**
Le Message de Jésus à son Prêtre
  (Schrijvers), 12:787
Messager des Fidèles (periodical),
  14:381
Messalians and Messalianism, 1:365,
  700, 2:794, 4:720, 11:760
  See also Paulicians
Messe de Notre Dame (Machaut), 9:18
Messengers, Islamic, 7:608
Messengers of the Heart of Mary, 4:417
Messiaen, Olivier, 2:332
Messiah, 7:807, 833, 834, **9:538–539**
  Abrabanel, Isaac, 1:36
  Christ (term), 3:527
  Christian (term), 3:529
  Conservative Judaism, 8:10
  Day of the Lord, 4:548

  as ideal king, 8:179
  justice of men, 8:73
  Magi, 9:35
  Mark's Gospel, 9:185–187
  Son of God, 13:312
  superiority of, 3:28
  as title, Dead Sea Scrolls, 4:564
  virgin birth of Christ, 5:192
Messianic secret, 9:546
*The Messianic Secret in the Gospel of
  Mark* (Wrede), 6:865
Messianism, **9:539–547**
  Abrabanel, Isaac, 1:36
  Alma prophecy, 1:297
  Annunciation, 1:475–476
  cabala, 2:835–836
  development of, 7:634
  Divine judgment, 8:29
  end of the world, 5:214–215
  eschatology in the Bible, 5:337
  Micah, Book of, 9:594
  millenarianism, 9:635
  prophecies, 9:247
  redemption, 11:965–966
  Shabbataiïsm, 13:56–57
  Son of David, 13:310
  Son of Man, 13:316
  Sukkot, 2:532
Das Messiasgeheimnis in den Evangelien
  (Wrede), 7:840
Messina, Antonello da, 1:737
Messingham, Thomas, 3:834
Messmer, Sebastian Gebhard (Abp. of
  Milwaukee), 3:284, **9:547**, 646–647,
  14:780, 781
  Americanism, 1:354
  Premonstratensians, 11:668
Mestizos, 11:159–160
Metalogicon (John of Salisbury), 7:985,
  9:453, 14:2
Metamorphoses (Golden Ass)
  (Apuleisus), 12:308
Metamorphoses (Ovid), 10:727, 12:307
Metanoia, 3:546
Metaphysica vetus et nova (Osterrieder),
  12:770
Metaphysicae commentatio (Schegk),
  12:768
Metaphysical empircism, 5:196
Metaphysical irrationalism, 7:587
Metaphysical Meditations (Descartes),
  4:677, 680, 681
Metaphysical pessimism, 11:168
Metaphysics, **9:547–553**, 12:818
  action at a distance, 1:81

  Aristotle, 1:683
  being, 2:207–209
  Billot, Louis, 2:395
  Christian philosophy, 3:540
  contradiction, 4:223–224
  de Raeymaker, Louis, 4:676
  deconstructionism, 4:592–593
  demonstration, 4:653
  distinction, 4:781–782
  final causality, 5:726
  first principles, 5:745
  Florenskii, 5:772
  German idealism, 8:797
  history of, 9:548–550
  intellectual knowledge, 8:202
  judgments, 8:204
  Kant's theory, 8:124, 127
  matter and form in, 9:350–351
  Mill, John Stuart, 9:631–632
  modes in, 9:751–752
  monad per Leibniz, 8:457
  phenomenology, 11:233–234
  philosophy, 11:279–280
  philosophy of nature, 11:304
  quantity in, 11:854–855
  religious liberalism, 8:541
  Rhazes, 12:211
  science of, 9:550–553
  Scotism, 12:824
  similarity, 13:126
  simplicity of God, 13:138
  spirituality, 13:422
  Suárez, Francisco, 13:560
  theological reflection, 4:819–820
  Thomastic, 10:907–908
  Whitehead, Alfred North, 14:704,
    705
  wisdom in, 14:786
  Wolff, Christian, 14:807
  See also Existential metaphysics
Metaphysics (Aristotle), 5:554, 10:605,
  606, 607, 964, 12:41
  act and potency, 1:73
  Adam Pulchrae Mulieris, 1:110
  analogy in, 1:371
  aporia, 1:570
  causality, 3:298, 376
  contingency, 4:212–213
  immortality, 7:348
Metaphysics, validity of, 8:755–758,
  797, **9:553–556**
Metaphysics and the Existence of God
  (O'Brien), 10:524

Metempsychosis, 1:166, 5:929, 8:871, **9:556**, 10:658, 13:355
See also Reincarnation; Transmigration of souls
Meterological divination, 4:785
Metham, Thomas, 5:237
Method in Theology (Lonergan), 8:773
"Method of concretion," 11:305
Methodenbuch für Lehrer der deutschen Schulen (Felbiger), 5:665
Methodios (Patriarch of Constantinople), 2:742
Methodism
abolitionism, 1:156
Albright, Jacob, 1:234
Asbury, Francis, 1:767–768
Assemblies of God, 1:788
basic doctrines of, 9:558–559
Black, William, 2:424–425
Boehm, Martin, 2:454
Chile, 3:486
Christian Church merger, 4:117
colonial United States, 3:646
confessions of faith, 4:81–82
Evangelical Church, 5:468–469
Holiness churches, 7:7, 8
hymnody, 7:256, 257–258
origins, 1:444
U.S. church membership, 3:719
Wesley, Charles, founding of, 14:682
Wesley, John, founding of, 14:682
women deacons, 4:554
Methodist Church of Canada, 9:561
Methodist churches, **9:556–562**
Canada, 9:561
England, 9:559–560
latitudinarianism, 8:370
Lewis, E., 8:528–529
Lidgett, J. S., 8:561–562
liturgical calendar, 8:644
liturgical movement, 8:678
United States, 9:560, 561–562
Methodist Episcopal Church (U.S.), 9:560, 561
Methodist Episcopal Church, South (U.S.), 9:561, 562
Methodist New Connection, 9:559
Methodist Protestant Church (U.S.), 9:561
Methodists, 6:27, 7:403, 12:204
Methodius, St., 4:370, *474*, **474–477**, 479
Methodius I (Patriarch of Constantinople), St., 2:753, 7:282–283, 309, 353, **9:562–563**

Methodius of Antioch (Greek Orthodox Patriarch), 6:459
Methodius of Olympus, St., 1:785, **9:563–564**
Methodius Seminary (Detroit), 10:625
Methodology (philosophy), 6:63, 8:758, **9:564–567**, 631, 12:818–819
Methodology (theology), 8:743, 773–774, 774, 823–824, **9:567–569**
Methodus ad facilem historiarum cognitionem (Bodin), 12:124
Methodus confessionis. . .seu epitome (Soto), 3:243
Métis people, 8:270
Metlinger, Peter, 3:746
Metochites, George, 2:826, **9:569**
Metochites, Theodore, 2:739, 776, 810
Metochites literary hand style (14th c.), 10:770
Metodo della dottrina che i padri della Compagna de Gesú insegnano ai neofiti nelle missioni della Cina con las risposta alle obiettioni di alcuni moderni che la impugnano (Rubino), 12:399
Metrodorus of Lampsacus, 1:292
Metrophanes Critopoulos (Patriarch of Alexandria), 4:355, **9:569–570**, 10:700
Metrophanes of Smyrna, 1:390, **9:570**
Metropolitan (periodical), 2:40
Metropolitan Cathedral (Mexico City), 9:*578*
Metropolitan Catholic Almanac and Laity's Directory, 8:842, 10:67
Metropolitan Interreligious Task Force, 14:847
Metropolitan Musem of Art (NY), 8:276
Metropolitan Readers (literature series), 6:224
Metropolitan Record, 10:314
Metropolitans, 1:632, 634
Metten Abbey (Bavaria, Germany), **9:570**
Mettenleiter, J. G., 2:842
Metternich, Klemens W. N. L. von, 3:101, 618
Mettinger, T. N. D., 11:767
Metulla (Israel), 7:*629*
Metz, Christian, 1:330
Metz, Johann-Baptist, 5:345, 351, 828–829, 10:153, 11:460, 585
Metz, Ken, 3:393
Metzger, F., 3:712
Metzger, Joseph, 12:671
Metzger, Paul, 12:671
Metzger, Sidney M. (Bp.), 5:174

Meunand, Jean de, 1:291–292
Meurers, Heinrich Von, **9:570–571**
Meurin, Sébastien Louis, **9:571**, 12:558
Mexía de Trillo, Pedro, 4:417
Mexican American Catholics, 2:869–870
Mexican American Cultural Center (MACC), 5:203, 8:290
Mexican Episcopal Conference (CEM), 9:583
Mexican Martyrdom (Parsons), 10:904
Mexican Revolution, 9:581–583
Mexico, a Land of Volcanoes (Schlarman), 12:739
Mexico, colonial, **9:571–575**
independence, 5:791
La Salle expedition, 8:339–340
Mexican War, 12:209
mission
Arricivita, Juan Domingo, 1:723
Betanzos, Domingo de, 2:345–346
Carocci, Horacio, 3:149
catechisms, 3:234, 246, *247*, 248
Espinareda, Pedro de, 5:359
Focher, Juan, 5:785
Gante, Pedro de, 6:89–90
Landa, Diego de, 8:318–319
Margil, Antonio, 9:151
overview, 9:571–573, 692
Sahagún, Bernardino de, 12:528–529
sodality, 13:294
Spanish civilization, 5:154
See also Mission in colonial America, Spanish
Mexico, Council of (1585), 3:234, 246, 252
Mexico, Martyrs of, 4:273, 6:545
Mexico, modern, 5:791–792, **9:575–586**, *581*, *582*
anti-Catholicism, 4:416, 441, 854
architecture, 9:*578*, *580*
Arrillaga, Basilio, 1:724
Borda, Andrés de, 2:533
Burgoa, Francisco de, 2:697
Bustamante, Carlos María, 2:718
California, 2:865–866
Calles, Plutarco Elías, 2:876–877
Carocchi, Horacio, 3:149
Castorena y Ursúa, Juan Ignacio de, 3:218
Castro, Agustín Pablo, 3:218
Catholic Crusades, 9:124
Cavo, Andrés, 3:313

Mexico, modern (continued)

Church of Santo Domingo (Oaxaca), 13:89

Church-state relations, 7:999, 11:395

Clavigero, Francisco Javier, 3:771

Congregation of the Incarnate Word and Blessed Sacrament, 7:371–372

conquistadores, 4:130–131

Cristero Revolt, 8:334

demographic statistics, 9:575

Díaz y Barreto, Pascual, 4:733

ecclesiastical organization, 9:576, 586, 14:938

Guízar Valencia, Rafael, Bl., 6:580–581

historiography, 4:422

Ibarra y González, Ramón, 7:270

Jesuits, 7:785, 12:623

Labastida (Abp. of Puebla), 8:263–264

laicism, 8:283

Legionaries of Christ, 8:454

map, 9:577

martyrs of Guadalajara, 1:189, 326

mission

    Baja California, 12:644

    catechumenate, 3:252

    Guízar Valencia, Rafael, 6:580

    Pious Fund, 8:789

    secularization of, 6:93

Our Lady of Guadalupe, 2:560–562, 9:579

persecution of the Church, 5:174

Pious Fund, 8:789, 11:357–358

Revolution, 8:138

Silva Atenógenes, 13:121–122

sun worship, 13:606

See also Aztec people; Mexico, colonial; Mission in postcolonial Latin America

Mexico City (Mexico), 9:579

Mey, Claude, 12:771

Mey, Gustav, 3:243, 9:586–587

Meyenbert, Albert, 11:624

Meyendorff, John, 5:607, 9:586, 12:436

Meyer, Albert Gregory (Card.), 3:479, 9:586–589, 14:782

Meyer, Bernard F. (Father), 9:295

Meyer v. Nebraska (1923), 10:647–648

Meyers, Bertrande, 13:169–170

Meyers, C., 2:380

Meyers, E., 2:380

Meyerson, Emile, 11:301

Meyler, Peter, 7:580

Meyler, Robert, Bl., 7:579

Meynard, André, 9:589

Meynell, Alice C. and Wilfrid, 9:589–590

Meynell, Wilfrid. See Meynell, Alice C. and Wilfrid

Mey-Pichler Method (cathechism), 9:586

Mezger, Franz, 9:590–591

Mezger, Joseph, 9:591

Mezger, Paul, 9:591, 12:765, 14:51

Mezger family, 9:590–591

Mézière, Françoise, 8:384

Mezuzah, 9:591

Mezzabarba, Carlo Amrogio (Patriarch of Alexandria), 2:706, 3:515, 9:591–592

Mezzofanti, Giuseppe (Card.), 9:592

MHS. See Sisters of the Most Holy Sacrament

Miami (FL), 9:592–593

Micah, Book of, 9:593–595, 594

hope of salvation, 7:105

justice of God, 8:70

Lord as honorific title, 8:780

magic, 9:39

peace, 13:249

sin, 13:143, 145

spirit, 13:424

Micarelli, Barbara (Sister Mary Joseph of the Infant Jesus), 5:879

Michael (Archangel), 1:420, 423, 424, 425, 9:595, 595

Michael (Armenian Catholicos), 1:702

Michael (Bp. of Ancyra), 1:398

Michael, Abba Ghebré, 5:401

Michael I (the Syrian) (Patriarch of Antioch), 1:172, 9:597

Michael II (Byzantine Emperor), 2:753, 7:282, 10:915

Michael III (Byzantine Emperor), 9:596, 10:360

iconoclasm, 2:753, 821, 5:23

murder of, 2:754, 5:23

Photius, 7:310, 11:311–312

Theodora (2), 7:309

Michael III (Patriarch of Constantinople), 9:598

Michael IV (Autorianus) (Patriarch of Constantinople), 2:759, 760

Michael VII Ducas (Byzantine Emperor), 1:253

Michael VII Parapinakes (Byzantine Emperor), 2:799

Michael VIII Palaeologus (Byzantine Emperor), 2:739, 4:176, 8:907–908, 9:596–597

Arsenius Autorianus, 1:735, 2:762

Eastern Schism, 2:762, 787, 825, 826

Michael Cerularius (Patriarch of Constantinople), 9:597–598

conflict with Pope Leo IX (Pope), St., 5:24, 7:199

Eastern Schism, 2:757–758, 760, 823–824, 4:175, 187–188

excommunication, 1:253

Michael da Calci, 5:922

Michael de Massa, 1:883

Michael de Northburgh (Bp. of London), 9:598–599

Michael de Sanctis, de, St., 9:599

Michael Italicus, 2:824

Michael of Cesena, 1:428, 3:603–604, 5:736, 921, 7:932, 9:599–600

Michael of Ephesus, 1:671

Michael of Maleinos, St., 9:600

Michael of St. Augustine, Ven., 3:137, 143

Michael of the Most Holy Trinity, 4:44

Michael of Thessalonica, 2:825

Michael Palaeologus (Byzantine Emperor), 7:917

Michael Psellus, 2:773, 809

Aristotelianism, 1:671

Eastern Schism, 2:824

historiography, 2:776, 799

Homer, 2:804

John Italus, 2:758–759

Michael Scotus, 1:813

Michaelis Baii..opera (Gerberon), 6:164

Michaelsbrüder. See Manharter

Michalski, Konstanty, 12:776

Michel, Anton, 10:857–858, 13:39

Michel, George. See Michel, Virgil

Michel, Jehan, 1:432

Michel, Maddalena Grillo. See Michel, Teresa Grillo, Bl.

Michel, Teresa Grillo, Bl., 9:600

Michel, Virgil, 3:716, 5:168, 8:672, 674, 9:600–601, 12:552

Michel de Bay. See Baius and Baianism

Michel of Northgate, Dan, 12:716

Michelangelo Buonarroti, 9:601–603, 603

Alexander VI (Pope), 1:261

architecture, 3:703

beauty, 1:743

Bible cycles, 2:375

Clement VII (Pope), 3:782

Colonna, Vittoria, 3:857

"Creation of Adam," 1:104, 106

genius rediscovered, 13:192–193

Jacopo della Quercia influencing, 13:109

The Last Judgement, 9:*602*, 13:190, 192

Paul III (Pope), 11:21

St. Peter in Chains Church, 8:*55*

Saint Peter's Basilica, 12:*579*, 580, *580*

Sistine Chapel decorated, 13:190–191, 14:396

    chapel ceiling, 13:190–191, *191*

    frescoes restored, 13:*195*

work on new St. Peter's Basilica, 14:395

''Michelangelo's Youth'' exhibit (Florence, Italy), 7:*659*

Michelet, Jules, 1:18, 519, 9:611–612, 12:112

Michelet, K. E., 6:709

Michelsburg Abbey (Germany), 8:324

Michelucci, G., 3:713

Michieli family, 2:24

Michigan, 7:338–339, 8:449, **9:603–608**

    Catholic education, 7:338–339

    Lefevere, Peter Paul, 8:449

    mission, 2:86–87

    See also specific dioceses and archdioceses

Michigan Essay or Impartial Observer (newspaper), 12:228

Michotte, Albert, 5:101, 102, 10:20, 12:776

Micklegate Bar Convent, 8:787

Micmac people, 3:9, 7:25, 8:464

Mico, Edward, Ven., 5:236

Micon of Saint-Riquier, 3:161

Microcosmus (Godfrey of Saint-Victor), 6:328

Micrologus, **9:608**

Micu-Klein, Innocent (Bp.), 12:331

Micy Abbey (France), 1:946, **9:608**

Mida of Killeedy, St. *See* Ita of Killeedy, St.

Mid-America (periodical), 5:787, 7:319

Mid-American Province of Saint Conrad, 8:113

Middle Ages, **9:609–616**

    abbesses, 1:8

    abbots, 1:10

    Abelard, Peter, 1:18

    abortion, 1:26–27, 29

    Abraham, images of, 1:37

    aesthetics, 1:142

    All Souls' Day, 1:290

    Alleluia, 1:294

    annals and chronicles, 1:459–465

    anointing, 1:478–480

    anticlericalism, 1:517

apologetics, 1:564

ars moriendi, 1:727–734

astrology, 7:114

asylum, 1:815

atomism, 1:833–834

bestiaries, 2:342–344

biblical canon, 3:32

biblical theology, 2:382

biology, 2:401

Boethius as founder of, 2:454

books, 2:515–520

Canon Law, 3:44–50

Canons Regular of St. Augustine, 3:68–69

Canterbury, 3:72

capital punishment, 3:86–87

Carmelites, 3:141–142

casuistry, 3:220

catechesis, 3:228–232, 239–240, 241

catechisms, 3:239–240, 241

Catholic social thought, 13:253–254

chalices, 3:370

chapter and verse, 8:435

chartularies, 3:442

Chi-Rho, 3:474

chivalry, 3:518–519

choirs, 3:522–523

Christian philosophy, 3:538

Christmas, 3:553–554

Christology, 3:559, 561

chronology, 3:570–571

Church in Rome, 12:356–357

Church property, 2:496, 3:603, 604, 725–727

Church symbolism, 3:630

Church-State relations, 3:634–637

coinage issued during, 10:481–482

commendation as practice in, 4:9

Communion antiphons of, 4:32–34

communion of saints, 4:36

conciliarism, 4:53–56

Confirmation, 4:86–89

conformity, 4:92–94

conscience, 4:148

consciousness, 4:152

conservation, 4:161, 162

contemplative life, 4:210

contingency, 4:213–214

continuum, 4:215

contraception, 4:220

contrition and attrition, 4:225–226

conversion, 4:240

Convocations of English clergy, 4:243–244

courtly love, 4:318–322

Credos of, 4:357

Crosier Fathers, 4:377–378

cross, 4:379–382

crucifixion depictions, 4:393–397

Culdees, 4:422–424

cursus, 4:444

Dante Alighieri, 4:516–522

Dark Ages as derogatory term for, 4:529–530

democracy, 4:638–640

demonology, 4:648–649

Denmark, 4:662–665

devotion to Sacred Heart, 12:491

diaconia, 4:719–720

Disticha catonis, 4:778

doctor as title in, 4:798

drama of, 4:892–902

dueling, 4:928–929

Durandus of Saint-Pourçain, 4:948–949

dynamism of, 4:959

flowering of mysticism during, 10:118

form and matter, 5:803

gifts of Holy Spirit, 7:48

heraldic art, 8:638, 13:114–115

historical overview, 3:597–606

Holy Name, 7:31–32

Holy Spirit, devotion to, 7:46

homily, 7:63

hospices, 7:117

hospitallers, 7:119–121

hospitals, 3:412, 413, 726, 7:128–129, 130

humanism, 7:184, 193

hymnology of, 7:244–249

idealism, 7:297

illumination of books, 8:436

Immaculate Conception, 7:333–334

immutability of God, 7:355–356

kiss of peace, 8:185

laity, 3:413, 8:293–297, 412, 414–415

lectionaries, 8:435, 436

legends, 1:759–764, 12:606–607

lenten fasting, 8:469

liturgical calendar, 8:643

liturgical history, 8:654–659

liturgical language, 8:667

logic, field of, 8:749–750

Logos, theology of, 8:764

master as term in, 4:798

millenarianism, 9:636–637

Middle Ages *(continued)*

 mission, 3:41, 155, 158, 163–164, 434

 miters, 8:637

 monarchy in, 9:781

 mosaics of, 10:3–4

 motets of, 10:11, 13

 natural law doctrine during, 10:202

 papal legates, 8:450

 relics, 12:52–54

 Rochester, Ancient See of, 12:278

 Sacramentary, 8:640

 sacraments, 12:468

 saints, legends of, 12:606–607

 salutary acts, 12:621

 science in, 12:807–815

 scriptoria in, 12:843

 secularization of Church property in, 12:870–871

 simony, 13:136

 slavery, 13:212

 slavery, evolution of term, 13:212

 Slovakia, 13:219–220

 Spain, 13:377–390

 spiritual direction, 4:761–762

 spirituality, 13:445–446

 stained glass, 13:469–470, 472–475

 stoicism in, 13:538

 treatment of neophytes during, 10:239

 universality of Christianity, 3:293

 vestments, 8:716

 war, morality of, 4:150

 women, role of, 14:816

 works of charity, 3:408–414

 See also Carolingian era; Feudalism; Medieval era; Merovingian era; Scholasticism

Middle Assyrian period, 9:530

Middle Byzantine period, 9:798

Middle East Council of Churches (MECC), **9:616–617**

Middle Eastern mission (Protestant), 9:700

Middle knowledge. *See Scientia Media*

The Middle Span (Santayana), 12:680

Middlemore, Humphrey, Bl., 5:225, 547, 7:140, **9:617**

Middleton, Antony, Bl., 5:231, **9:617**

Middleton, Conyers, 3:371

Middleton, Robert, Bl., 5:233, **9:617–618**

Middleton, Thomas Cooke, **9:618**

Midrash, **9:618–619**, 12:605

Midrashic literature, 2:832, 5:508, **9:619–620**, 12:699

Midrokosmus (Lotze), 8:797

Miège, John Baptist (Bp. of Kansas), 3:858, 4:668, 8:113, **9:620–621**, 10:221, 14:869

Mier, Servando Teresa de, 9:*621*, **621–622**

Miera y Pachecho, Bernardo, 12:685

Mies van der Rohe, Ludwig, 3:669, 680–681, 716

Mieszko I (Prince of Poland), 11:438

Migazzi, Christoph Anton (Abp. of Vienna), 1:914, **9:622–623**

Migdol Yeshu'ot (Abrabanel), 1:36

Migeot, Antoine, 12:771

Migetius, 1:119

Miggin (martyr), 9:28

Migliorati, Cosimo de' (Card.). *See* Innocent VII (Pope)

Mignano, Treaty of (1139), 3:318

Migne, Jacques Paul, 2:494, 3:601, 5:207, **9:623**, 10:963, 969

Mignot, Eudoxe Irénée (Abp. of Albi), 1:229, 7:504, **9:623–624**

Migrant worker issues, 8:843

Míguez, Faustino, Bl., **9:624**

Míguez, Manuel. *See* Míguez, Faustino, Bl.

Miguez-Bonino, José, 5:607

Mihan, Charles. *See* Meehan, Charles (Father), Bl.

Mihan, Charles, Ven., **9:624**, 10:495

Mikaelites, 5:400

Milan (Italy), 3:724, 4:192, 7:121, 129, 9:231, 12:116

Milan, Agreement of. *See* Milan, Edict of

Milan, Councils of

 Arianism, 1:662, 818

 Borromeo, St. Charles, 1:196

 Liberius (Pope), 8:554

 third provincial, 3:377

Milan, Edict of (313), 1:749, 752, 2:620, 3:262, **9:625**, 13:136

Milan, Galeazzo Maria Sforza, Duke of, 12:220, 13:55

Milan liturgy, 11:125–126

Milanese Patraines, 10:941–942

Milburga, St., 14:679

Mildred, St., 5:324

Miles, Richard Pius (Bp. of Nashville, TN), 13:821

Miles Christi Jesu (Vermeersch), 14:452

Milesians, 1:393

Milevis, Council of (416), 11:62

Milford Central School, Good News Club v. (2001), 3:664

Milgrom, J., 14:856, 857

Milhaud, Darius, 11:562

Milíč, John, 4:480, 7:230

Milik, Josef T., 2:347, 5:51, 266

Military dictatorships (Latin America), 8:546

Military Order of the Cross with a Red Star, 2:609

Military Order of the Red Star Crucifers, 3:69

Military orders, **9:625–626**

 chivalry, 3:519

 Crusades, 4:402, 410

 hospitals of, 7:129

 Huguenots, 7:166–167

 iconoclasm, 7:281, 282

 pope elections, 4:128

 Portugal, 11:534–535

 Roman, and Christian persecution, 4:748

 See also specific orders

Military service, 4:149–150, 409, **9:626–628**, *627*

Military services (U.S.), Archdiocese for, **9:628–630**, *629*

Milites, 4:405

Militia Immaculatae, 8:229

Militia of Jesus Christ, 2:128

Milk and honey, use in baptism, 2:63

Mill, James, 1:796, 5:396, **9:630**

Mill, John Stuart, 5:361, 396, 440, **9:630–632**, *631*, 11:295

 associationism, 1:796

 Bradley, Francis Herbert, 2:577

 British moralists, 2:624

 categories of being, 3:257

 Coleridge, Samuel Taylor, 3:832

 Comte, Auguste, 4:48, 11:544

 form, 5:803

 freedom, 5:939

 Locke's influence, 8:745

 methodology, 9:566

 phenomenalism, 11:230

 relativism, 12:48

 sevice to others, 8:829

 true or false premise, 5:504

Mill Hill Missionaries, 7:1047, **9:632–633**

 African American Catholics, 1:157

 Cameroon, 2:913

 founding of, 3:622, 10:515, 583, 14:423

 Kenya, 8:150

New Zealand, 10:325
origins of, 10:808
Pakistan, 10:759–760
Uganda, 14:265
See also Society of St. Joseph of the Sacred Heart
Millar, John, 5:703
Milleloquium veritatis s. Augustini (Bartholomew of Urbino), 2:127
Millenarianism, 1:547, **9:633–637**
Catholic Apostolic Church, 3:278–279
chiliasm, 1:547, 3:488
chronicles, 1:460
Divine judgment, 8:31
early adherents to, 10:900
heaven, 6:687
Holy Office ban, 8:274
Mormon doctrine, 8:374
See also Eschatology
Millenary Petition (England, 1603), 11:839
Millenial Church. *See* Shakers
Millennialism, 4:542–543
Millennium celebrations (2000), 13:*832*
Miller, George Elias, 1:796
Miller, Lewis, 3:458
Miller, Randolph Crump, 12:98
Miller, William, 1:135, 4:542, **9:637–638**, 13:38–39, *39*
Miller v. California (1973), 11:519
Miller v. Gable (1845), 3:658
Milleret de Brou, Anne Eugénie. *See* Marie Eugénie de Jésus (Mother), Bl.
Millet, Kate, 5:672
Millet-bashi, 4:196
Mills, John, 5:208
Mills, Samuel J., 4:116, **9:638**
Millvale Franciscans, 5:889
Milman, Henry Hart, **9:638**
Milne, William, 3:499
Milner, John (Bp. Castabala), 2:719, **9:638–639**, *639*
Milner, Ralph, Bl., 4:735, 5:231, **9:639–640**
Milo (Bp. of Nanteuil), 2:188
Milo of Saint-Amand, 3:161
Milone, Anthony M. (Bp. of Great Falls-Billings, MT), 9:827
Miltiades (Pope), St., 3:593, 594, 4:180, 862, **9:640**, 12:353
Miltitz, Karl von, **9:640–641**
Milton, John, 2:112, 9:*641*, **641–645**, 14:378
Arthurian legends, 1:762
freedom of religion, 5:947

republicanism, 4:641
works of, 9:642–645, 12:620
Milwaukee Archdiocese (WI), 6:733–734, 8:256, **9:645–649**
Milwaukee Symposia for Church Composers: A Ten-Year Report (Universa Laus), 8:70, 14:321
Mīmāmsā, 7:408
Mimes (Theocritus), 12:509
Mimoso Pires, James, Bl., 1:951
The Mind and Heart of Love (d'Arcy), 4:527
The Mind of the Maker (Sayers), 12:717
Mind-body problem, 4:681
Mindszenty, József (Card.), 1:569, 916, 3:200, 7:219–220, 222, **9:649–650**
Minersville School District v. Gobitis (1940), 3:661
Minerva Medica Temple (Rome), 3:699
Ming, Dominic Tang Yee (Abp. of Canton), 7:793
Minh Mang (Emperor of Vietnam), 14:500–501
Minh Van Phan, Philip, 14:496
Miniaturist art, 9:129
Minima Moralia (Adorno), 5:914
Minims, **9:650–651**, *651*
Capernaum, 10:798
as discalced order, 4:765
Francis of Paola, St., 5:872
hierarchical insignia, 6:764
of the Sacred Heart, 2:852–853
Mini-parishes. *See* Basic Christian communities
Ministeria quaedam (apostolic letter, Paul VI), 7:37, 38, 8:285, 443, 11:30, 525
Ministers of the Sick of St. Camillus, 3:415
Ministers to the Sick. *See* Servants of Mary, Sisters
Ministry (ecclesiology), 5:39, 8:588, 589, **9:651–654**, 13:774
Ministry and Life of Priests, Decree on the (Vatican II), 5:741
Minkowski, H., 4:217
Minnerath, Roland, 7:528
Minnesota, **9:654–657**
Catholic education, 7:551
Dowling, Austin, 4:887–888
Hodgson v. Minnesota, 1:34
mission, 11:934, 12:542, 552
See also Faribault School Plan (MN); *specific dioceses and archdioceses*
Minnesota, Hodgson v., 1:34
Minoan-Mycenaean culture, 5:2

The Minoan-Mycenaean Religion and Its Survival (Nilsson), 10:86
Minocchi, Salvatore, 7:673, 9:755
Minor, William T., 4:122–123
Minor Church of Poland, 2:431, 432
Minor Litanies. *See* Rogation Days
Minor orders (Holy orders), 7:37–38
Minor prophets, 9:63, **657–658**, 11:765
Minoriten Church (Cologne), 8:231
Minsart, Nicolas Joseph, 12:565
Minsteria quaedam (*motu proprio*, Paul VI), 1:68
Minucius Felix, Marcus, 1:717, 2:146, 3:186, 730, 4:220, **9:658**
El Minuto di Dios (Colombia), 3:392
Miquel Garriga, Alfonso (Brother), 2:92
Mirabilibus, Nicholas de, 14:47
Miracle of the Host (Uccello), 5:*418*
Miracle plays, 3:231, 4:401, 900–902
''The Miracle Window'' (Canterbury Cathedral, England), 3:*71*
Miracles, 11:687
canonization, 3:65
certitude, 3:353
charisms, 3:390
Christ, 5:218
Christ feeding the five thousand (Roslin), 5:*417*
Christ healing the sick presented to him by the Pharisees (Cristoforo de Predis), 9:*665*
''City of Mary,'' Italy, 8:776
De servorum Dei beatificatione et beatificatione et beatificationis canonizatione (treatise, Benedict XIV), 9:665
detecting, 8:387
Elisha's story, 5:162
Empress Kunigunde, 8:257
Fátima ''Miracle of the Sun,'' 5:643–644
heroic virtue in, 14:554
Jesus Walking on Water, 9:*666*
Julian of Cuenca, St., 8:47
La Salette, 8:337
Lacy's tomb at Exeter, 8:275
Landulf of Éreux, St., 8:323
Lateau, L., 8:346–347
Lawrence of Villamagna, 8:409
levitation, 8:522–523
Locke, John, 8:745
Louis IX's tomb, 8:801
Lourdes, 8:819, 820
Lüfthildis, St., 8:853–854
Mary, Blessed Virgin in, 9:281
Sergius of Radonezh, St., 13:16

Miracles *(continued)*
  Seton, E., 13:34, 176
  Sharbel Makhlouf, St., 13:69
  Sigismund, St., 13:115
  Simeon of Polirone, St., 13:124
  supernatural vs., 13:620
Miracles, in the Bible, **9:661–664**
Miracles, moral, **9:658–659**
Miracles, moral (the Church), **9:659–661**
Miracles, theology of, **9:664–670**, 10:509
Miracles Nostre Dame (Walter of Coincy), 14:627
Miracles of St. Julian (Gregory of Tours), 12:606
Miracles of St. Robert (Jocelin of Brakelond), 12:267
Miraculous Mass (fresco by Simone Martini), 5:*416*
Miraculous medals, 3:623, 7:334, 8:266–267, **9:670**
Mirae caritatis (encyclical, Leo XIII), 4:34, 556
Miraeus, Aubert le Mire, **9:670–671**
Miraeus, J. (Bp. of Antwerp), 1:539
Miramion, Maria, 3:417
Miranda prorsus (encyclical, Pius XII), 11:400
Mirari vos (encyclical, Gregory XVI), 2:218, 3:619, 642, 5:854, 6:507, 779, 8:271–272, 309
Miriam (sister of Moses), 11:765
Miriam, Canticle of, 3:73
Miriam of the Holy Spirit (Sister). *See* Powers, Jessica
Mirian (King of Iberia), **9:671**
Mirian III (King of Iberia), 6:152
Mirificus eventus (apostolic constitution, Paul VI), 14:415
Miroir Historial (Vincent of Beauvais), 14:*523*
Mirour de l'Omme (Gower), 6:378
Mirror of Eternal Blessedness (Rutherford), 12:440
Mirror of Holy Church (St. Edmund), 10:119
Mirror of Love (St. Aelred), 10:119
Mirror of Princes (literary genre), **9:671–672**
The Mirrour of Vertue in Worldly Greatness (Roper), 12:370
Mirylo Pravednoie, 14:278
Misanthropia, 3:592
Misere (Leo, L.), 8:471
Miserentissimus Redemptor (encyclical, Pius XI), 11:393, 12:491, 492, 493

Misericordia. See Confraternity of Misericordia
Misericordia Sisters, **9:672**
Mishael ben Uzziel, 2:357
Mishnah, 5:508, **9:672**, 13:745–747
  Akiba ben Joseph, 1:199
  biblical canon, 3:25
  Dedication, Feast of in, 4:607
  described, 8:7
  Judah Ha-Nasi, 8:2
Mishneh Torah (Repetition of the Law) (Maimonides), 9:52
Misioneras Hijas de la Sagrada Familia de Nazaret, 9:130
Missa ad prohibendum ab idolis, 3:557
Missa canonica (Fux), 6:37
Missa Cellensis (Haydn), 6:674
Missa Fors seulement (Okeghem), 10:573
Missa Laetare in contrapuncto posita (Richter), 12:240
Missa Mi-Mi (Okeghem), 10:573
Missa pro Defunctis (Okeghem), 10:573
Missa Prolationum (Okeghem), 10:573
Missa Sacra (Schumann), 12:789
Missa Sanctae Cecilae (Haydn), 6:674
Missa sicca. See Masses, dry
Missa solemnis (Beethoven), 2:202–203
Missae votivae, 9:312
Missal, Roman, **9:672–674**, *674*
  Council of Trent, 12:328
  kiss of peace, 8:185
  lectionaries, 8:436
  liturgical history, 8:657–658
  Mass formularies for Lent, 8:470
  Pius V (Pope), St., 8:437
  Tridentine reform, 8:661–662
  Vatican Council II, 8:365
Missal for the Dioceses of Zaire, **9:674–676**, *675*
"Missal of St. Corneille de Compiègne," 3:*371*
Missale Francorum ritual, 10:639–640
Missale Gallicanum Vetus, 6:68–69
Missale Gothicum, 1:343, 6:68
Missale Hispano-Mozarabicum, 10:44
Missale romanum (constitution of 1969, Paul VI), 14:182
Missarum Sollemnia: Eine genetische Erklärung der römischen Messe (Jungmann), 8:62
Misse Petri de la Rue (Petrucci), 8:336
Missel des fidèles (periodical), 12:785, 14:381
Missel romain pour les diocèses du Zaïre, **9:674–676**

Missett, Luke, 11:625
Missi dominici, 3:166, 410, 423
Missia, Francis A., Rev., 12:574
MISSIO München (Munich). *See* Ludwig Missionsverein (Ludwig Mission Society)
Missiology, 1:353–354, 3:428–429, 6:881, **9:676–680**
  See also Mission and evangelization
Mission, African. *See* African mission; African Missions, Society of (SMA); Missionaries of Africa
Mission, Protestant
  Angola, 1:450
  Argentina, 1:657
  Brazil, 9:700–701
  Cambodia, 9:700
  Canada, 12:273
  Caribbean, 3:115
  China, 3:499–500, 9:699
  France, 12:30–31
  Ghana, 6:198
  Hawaii, 6:669
  history of, 9:697–701
  India, 3:108, 7:402–403
  Indonesia, 7:428–429
  Korea, 9:699–700
  Macau, 9:4
  missiology, 1:353
  Mongolia, 9:806
  North America, 13:289
  Philippines, 11:258
  Presbyterian, 13:411
  South Africa, 9:700
  U.S., Methodists, 9:560
  Vietnam, 9:700
  Washington, 14:654–655
Mission and evangelization, Canon Law, 1:932, 5:39, **6:682–683**
Mission and evangelization, papal writings on, 5:39, **9:680–682**
Mission and missions, **9:683–689**
  church architecture and (North America), 3:714–715
  colleges training for, 4:313, 8:820–823
  community type of mission, 13:289
  Counter Reformation, 3:613
  hymnody, 7:258
  idolatry, 3:248, 848, 850–851
  indigenous leadership in missions, 11:752
  liberation theology, 8:545
  medical mission, 4:659–660
  mission aid societies, 3:622

music, 8:697, 710

19th-20th century overview, 3:624–625

North American foundations, 8:338–339

pastoral work vs., 9:679

polygamy, 3:248, 848

purpose of, 5:39

reductions, Spanish missions, 1:649, 2:464, 465, 3:101–102, 226, 613

shrines, 13:94

spirituality, 13:448

theology of, 9:684

theology of inculturation, 7:388–389

works of charity, 3:415–417

See also African mission; Congregation for the Propagation of the Faith; Conversion; Missiology; Mission, Protestant; Mission history, Catholic; Mission history, Orthodox; Mission history, Protestant; specific countries; specific missionary groups and organizations; specific religious orders

Mission Concepcion (San Antonio, TX), 13:846

Mission de France. See Worker Priests

Mission Dolores (San Francisco), 3:714, 12:644, 645

Mission Helpers of the Sacred Heart, 2:40, 9:689–690

Mission history, Catholic, 9:690–693

See also specific countries; specific religious orders

Mission history, Orthodox, 9:693–969

See also specific countries

Mission history, Protestant, 9:697–701

See also specific countries; specific mission groups

Mission in colonial America, English, 9:724–726

See also specific countries; specific mission groups

Mission in colonial America, French, 9:720–724

See also specific countries; specific religious orders

Mission in colonial America, Portuguese, 9:718–720

See also specific countries; specific religious orders

Mission in colonial America, Spanish, 9:701–718

See also Alternativa; Catechisms, colonial Spanish America; Encomienda-doctrina system in Spanish America; specific countries; specific religious orders

Mission in postcolonial Latin America, 9:726–728

See also specific countries; specific religious orders

Mission of the Holy Ghost (Canada), 3:5

Mission of the Immaculate Virgin, 4:910

Mission San Carlos Borromeo del Rio Carmelo (California), 2:865

Mission San Gabriel (CA), 9:251

Mission San Jose (CA), 4:840–841

Mission San Jose (San Antonio, TX), 3:715

Mission San Miguel (Arizona), 1:687

Mission San Xavier del Bac (Arizona), 1:687

Mission theology

The Conversion of the Pagan World (Manna), 9:119–120

The Workers Are Few (Operarii autem pauci) (Manna), 9:119–120

Missionaries of Africa, 9:730–731

Algeria, 8:388–389, 520–521

Burkina Faso, 2:704

Burundi, 2:712

Cameroon, 8:452, 564

Carthage, 3:188

catechumenate, 3:252

Congo, 4:104–105

Ethiopia, 8:742

founding of, 3:622

Lesotho, 8:515

Liberia, 8:551

Monomotapa people, 13:122

Mozambique region, 10:38–39, 41

Nigeria, 10:393

Nubia, 10:471–472

Seychelles, 13:53

Sierra Leone, 13:110

visiting missionaries from California, 8:793

See also African mission; African Missions, Society of (SMA)

Missionaries of Charity, 1:217, 8:224, 9:582, 732, 10:15–16, 12:100

Missionaries of France. See Fathers of Mercy

Missionaries of Our Lady of La Salette, 3:621, 8:337–339

Missionaries of St. Charles, 12:717, 718–719

Missionaries of the Blessed Sacrament, 6:35

Missionaries of the Company of Mary. See Montfort Fathers

Missionaries of the Holy Apostles, 9:731

Missionaries of the Kingship of Christ, 9:731–732

Missionaries of the Precious Blood, 11:642–643

Missionary Catechists of Divine Providence (MCDP), 13:172

Missionary Cenacle Apostolate, 8:18

Missionary Crusaders of the Church, 9:139–140

Missionary Daughters of the Holy Family of Nazareth, 9:130

Missionary Franciscan Sisters of the Immaculate Conception, 5:884–885

Missionary Labors of Fathers Marquette, Menard, and Allouez in the Lake Superior Region (Verwyst), 14:461

Missionary of Charity Sisters, 3:437

Missionary Servants of the Most Blessed Trinity, 8:18, 9:732–733, 733, 10:543

Missionary Servants of the Most Holy Trinity, 8:18, 9:732, 733, 10:543, 13:69

Missionary Sisters of Mary Help of Christians, 2:721

Missionary Sisters of Our Lady of Africa, 8:388, 9:733

Missionary Sisters of St. Augustine, 4:633–634

Missionary Sisters of St. Charles Borromeo, 12:717, 718

Missionary Sisters of St. Columban (MN), 12:543

Missionary Sisters of St. Peter Claver, 8:443, 9:733–734

Missionary Sisters of the Holy Cross, 1:323

Missionary Sisters of the Holy Family, 8:311

Missionary Sisters of the Holy Ghost, 8:512–513

Missionary Sisters of the Holy Rosary, 8:446, 9:734

Missionary Sisters of the Immaculate Conception, 7:335

Missionary Sisters of the Immaculate Conception of the Mother of God, 5:885

Missionary Sisters of the Most Sacred Heart of Jesus of Hiltrup, 9:734

Missionary Sisters of the Precious Blood, 9:734, 11:223

Missionary Sisters of the Sacred Heart, 2:838–839, 9:734–735

Missionary Sisters of the Society of Mary. *See* Marist Missionary Sisters

Missionary Sisters of the Third Order of St. Francis (Rome), 5:885

Missionary Society of Lyons. *See* Society for the Propagation of the Faith

Missionary Society of St. James the Apostle, 2:556, 3:622, 4:447, **9:735**

Missionary Teaching Sisters of the Immaculate Conception (*Concepcionistas Misioneras de la Enseñanza*), 12:618

Missionary Union of the Clergy, 3:622

Missionary Zelatrices of the Sacred Heart (MZSH), 12:495

Missionnaires de France, 5:796

Missions, Divine, **9:735–737**

Missions, Protestant, 8:150

Missions and Missionaries of California (Engelhardt), 5:221

Mississippi, 2:397, **9:737–740**

> *See also specific dioceses and archdioceses*

Mississippi Religious Leadership Conference, 9:739–740

Misson theology, **9:728–730**

Missouri, 4:928, **9:740–743**

> *See also specific dioceses and archdioceses*

Missouri Watchman (periodical), 11:228

Mistra, 2:776

Mit brennender Sorge (encyclical, Pius XI), 3:642, 5:352, 6:186, 11:393, 395

Mitcham, C., 13:783

Mitchell v. Helms (2000), 3:668

Miters, 6:763, 8:636–637, **9:743–744**

Mithradates I (King of Persia), 11:136

Mithradates II (King of Persia), 11:136

Mithras and Mithraism, **9:744–745**

> anthropomorphism, 1:510
> astral religion, 1:810
> Christmas, 3:551
> Mithraic myth, 10:95–96
> ritual of, 10:96
> Roman persecutions, 3:594
> sources of, 10:95

Mithridate (Racine), 11:888

Mitigated realism, 4:120

Mitrale (Sicardus), 13:101

Mittarelli, Giovanni Benedetto, **9:745**

Mitteis, Heinrich, 5:704

Mittendorf, Wilhelm, 6:13

Mitterer, Albert, 7:239

Mitty, John Joseph (Abp. of San Francisco, CA), 2:869, **9:745–746**, 12:649

Mivart, George Jackson, St., 4:532, **9:746–747**

Mixed marriages
> *Arcanum*, 1:631
> Caribbean, 3:116
> children of, 4:261, 262
> Cologne dispute, 1:328, 2:691, 3:843, 845–846
> Council of Trent, 3:54
> Malachi, Book of, 9:63
> Schlarman, Joseph Henry, 12:739

Mixed marriages, prohibition of, **9:747**

Mlada (Princess of Bohemia), 4:479

MMM (Medical Missionaries of Mary), **9:432–433**

MMS (Medical Mission Sisters). *See* Medical Mission Sisters (MMS)

Mnemonics, 9:485, 13:655

Mo Ti. *See* Mozi (Mo Tzu)

Moabites, 1:36, **9:747–748**

Moberly, C. A. E., 3:759

Mobile Archdiocese (AL), **9:748–750**

Mobile Christian-Jewish Dialogue, 1:202

Mobuti Sese Seko, 4:106–107

Mockery. *See* Derision

Mocquereau, André, 3:380, 9:*750*, **750**

Modal distinction, 4:779–780

Modal propositions, 11:769, 771

Modalism, 3:560, 8:763, **9:750–751**, 11:734

Modalists, 9:780

Modena, Rinaldo de, 2:17

Moderate realism, 4:53, 367, 368, 654, 7:302

The Modern Catholic Encyclopedia, 5:208

Modern Churchmen's Union, 2:624

Modern Devotion. *See* Devotio Moderna (Modern Devotion)

Modern Painters (Ruskin), 12:414

Modern Utopia (Wells), 14:361

Modernism, 3:624, **9:752–757**
> Arbez, Edward Philip, 1:629
> Benigni, Umberto, opposition to, 2:279
> Billot, Louis, 2:395
> Blondel, Maurice, 2:441
> Buonaiuti, Ernesto, 2:694
> causality, 3:307
> censorship, 3:336
> *La Civiltà Cattolica*, 3:757, 12:774
> Comte, Auguste, 4:47
> Cormier, Hyacinthe-Marie, 4:269

> doctrine development, 4:806, 808, 14:136
> dogmatic theology, 4:813–814
> Duchesne, Louis, 4:927
> errors condemned, 8:663
> existence of God, 6:313
> French, 5:856
> Garrigou-Lagrange, Réginald, opposition to, 2:279
> heresy, 6:779
> history and spirit, 8:841
> Houtin, Albert, 7:141
> Húgel, Friedrich von, 7:149
> hypostasis, 7:264
> inegralism promoted by reaction against, 10:262
> Italy, 7:673
> Joseph Turmel's contributions to, 14:240–241
> *Lamentabili*, 8:311–312
> *Lamentabili* condemnation of, 12:774–775
> *Pascendi dominici gregis*, 2:395, 694, 3:336, 12:775
> Petre, Maude Dominica, 11:218
> Pius X (Pope), St., 10:849, 912, 11:389, 391
> Pontifical Bible Commission, 11:477
> propositions of *Lamentabili*, 5:712, 789, 12:228
> religious liberalism, 8:541, 542
> Sodalitium Pianum, 13:295–296
> Söderblom, N., 13:296
> Thomistic revival, 12:774–775
> Tyrrell's excommunication for support of, 14:259

Modernism, French, 12:453

Modernism, oath against, 2:694, 4:355, **9:757–758**

Le Modernisme dans l'Église: Étude d'histoire religieuse contemporaine (Rivière), 12:262

Modernist crisis, 13:912

Modernization, political, 9:584–585

Modes, 4:779–780, 8:742, **9:751–752**, 13:562

Modes of Being (Weiss), 10:608

Modestino of Jesus and Mary. *See* Mazzarella, Modestino, Bl.

Modestus of Fulda, 3:799

Modesty, 4:318, **9:758–759**

> *See also Sex*

Modo di conversare continuamente ed alla familiare con Dio (St. Alphonsus Liguori), 1:310

Moechian controversy, 2:752, **9:759**

Móel Brigte. *See* Marianus Scotus, Bl.

Moeller, Henry (Abp. of Cincinnati), 3:736, 868

Moes, Catherine (Sister Barbara), 5:881

Moes, Maria Catherine (Mother Alfred), 5:878, 881

Moeslein, Mark, 11:625

Les Moeurs des Israélites (Fleury), 5:762

Moeurs des sauvages américains comparés aux moeurs des premiers temps (Lafitau), 8:279

Mogas Fontcuberta, María Ana, Bl., **9:759–760**

Moghila, Peter, 4:355, **9:760–761**, 10:700–701, 12:422, 433

Mogila Abbey (Poland), 3:750

Mogrovejo, Toribio Alfonso de (Abp. of Lima), St., 1:829, 946, **9:761–762**, 12:378

Mohammed II (Ottoman Sultan), 10:*719*

Mohammed Ali. *See* al-Bāb (Muslim leader)

Mohan, Glaudens, 12:541

Mohawk people, 8:668

Mohlberg, Kunibert, **9:762**, *763*

Möhler, Johann Adam, 3:624, 6:183, **9:763**, 10:104, 14:234

communion of saints, 4:36

doctrine, development of, 4:807

Döllinger, Johannes, 4:823

ecclesiology, 5:37

theology of Church, 3:589

Moholy-Nagy, L., 3:679

Mohyōye, Bartholomew, Bl., 7:733

Moi, Daniel arap, 8:150–151

Moi Van Nguyen, Agustín, 14:496

Moine, Claudine, **9:764**

Moisescu, Justin, 12:333

Moism (*Mojia*), 3:509

Moissac Abbey (France), **9:764**

Moist philosophy, 10:49

Mojia (Moism), 3:509

Molanus, Gerhard Wolter, 2:874, 8:743, 13:417

Molanus, Johannes, 7:285

Molas y Vallvé, María Rosa Doloribus Francisca (Sister), St., **9:764–765**

Moldova, **9:765–767**, *766*

Moldovan Orthodox Church, 9:767

Moldoviṭa Abbey (Moldova), **9:767**

Molé, Édouard (Bp. of Bayeux), 2:163

Moleschott, Jakob, 9:320

Molesme Abbey (France), **9:767–768**

Moleyns, Adam (Bp.), **9:768**

Molière (French playwright), 3:186, 11:887

Molière et Bourdaloue (Veuillot), 14:466

Molina, Alonso de, 3:246, 8:466, **9:768**

Molina, Anthony de, **9:768–769**

Molina, Luis de, 9:*769*, **769**

Acquaviva, Claudius, 1:72

Clement VIII (Pope), 3:785

congruism, 4:120, 121

de auxiliis controversy, 4:111–113

Divine concurrence, 4:71

grace controversies, 2:50, 51, 6:390–391, 403–404

molinism, 9:770

physical premotion, 11:669

predetermination, 2:50

predestination, 11:651–652

primacy of Christ, 7:836

radical new views of, 14:49

scientia media, 5:790, 935, 936, 938, 10:598, 12:766

University of Alcalá, 1:236

Molina, Mercedes de Jesús, Bl., **9:769–770**

Molinism, **9:770–773**

Alexandre, Noël, 1:267, 268

Chalmers, William, 3:372

Charles of the Assumption, 3:436

Descartes, 4:682

Divine concurrence, 4:71–72

free will, 5:930, 938

Jansenism, 1:892

predetermination, 11:658

reprobation, 12:132

Struggl, Marc, 12:765

Molinos, Miguel de, **9:773**, 10:844

Arbiol y Diez, Antonio, 1:629

conformity, 4:93

private revelations, 12:201

quietism, 1:84, 3:614, 5:851, 11:866, 867

spiritual direction, 4:763

Molitor, R., 3:380

Molla, Gianna Beretta, Bl., **9:773–774**

Molla, Joan Beretta, Bl. *See* Molla, Gianna Beretta, Bl.

Molloy, Aloysius (Sister), **9:774**

Molloy, Francis, **9:774**

Molloy, Thomas Edmund (Abp. of Brooklyn, NY), **9:774–775**

Moloney, Daniel, 7:580

Moloney, Francis, 7:528

Molony, Patrick, 2:142

Moltmann, Jürgen, 5:345, 351, 6:890, 13:925–927, 14:198–199

Molyneux, Robert, **9:775**, 11:235, 236, 12:566

Molyneux, William, 5:966

Mombaer, John, 1:729, **9:775–776**

Mombritius, Boninus, **9:776**

Mommsen, T., 3:569

Monachorum Silvestrunorum, OSB. See Sylvestrine Benedictines

Monachus (monk), 9:812–813

Monachus, Joannes, 8:536

Monaco, **9:776–777**, *778*

Monaco Cathedral (Monaco), 9:*779*

Monadology (Leibniz), 8:751

Monads, **9:777–778**

appetite, 1:603

atomism, 1:835, 4:960

causality, 3:306

knowledge, theories of, 4:960, 8:218, 457–458

Monaghan, John James (Bp. of Wilmington, DE), 4:625, 14:764–765

Monaghan, John Patrick, **9:778–779**

Monan, J. Donald, 2:558

Monarchia (Dante), 4:518–519

Monarchia sicula, **9:779–780**

Monarchianism, **9:780**

Asia Minor, 1:785

Beryllus of Bostra, 2:339

Callistus I (Pope), St., 2:879

Christology, 3:560

Holy Trinity controversy, 14:203

homoousios, 7:65

Nicene Creed, 1:662

See also Modalism

Monarchical Episcopate, **9:781**

Monarchy, 5:683, 8:175–176, **9:781–782**

See also Democracy; Divine right of kings

Monarchy, French, 5:683

Monasteries, 3:725, 726, 8:635, 656, **9:782–784**

See also Commendation; *specific monasteries*

Monasteries, Double, **9:784–785**

Monastery of St. Maron, 9:192–194

Monastery of St. Mary Magdalen, 9:150

Monastery of San Francisco (CA), 9:*703*

Monastic art, 4:393

Monastic Constitutions (Lanfranc), 3:72

Monastic Institute (Rome), 11:488

Monastic office, 8:656

The Monastic Order in England; a History of its Development from the Times of St. Dunstan to the Fourth Lateran Council, 943-1216 (Knowles), 8:222

Monastic orders
  abbesses, 1:8
  Anglo-Saxons, 1:449
  Carolingian reform, 3:157, 168, 600
  chapters of faults, 3:385–386
  chronicals/annals, 1:465
  Enlightenment, 3:747
  medieval importance, 3:600, 601
  19th-20th century overview, 3:621
  Spain, 13:377
  works of charity, 3:411–412
  *See also specific orders and monastic
    houses*
Monastic psalters, 11:602
Monastic regulation, 13:877–878
Monastic Rules (Bail of Caesarea),
  10:755
Monastic schools, 3:827, 5:514–516,
  9:785–786, 12:83–84
Monastic theology, 13:905
Monasticism, **9:786–803**
  African Church, 10:431–432
  Alfred the Great, 1:280
  apocalyptic movements, 1:547–548
  Apophthegmata patrum, 1:568–569
  Assyrian Church of the East, 1:806
  Austria, 1:909–910
  Bernard of Clairvaux, 2:308, 309
  Byzantine Church, 2:752
  Byzantine civilization, 2:772
  Canon Law for Religious, 4:58–59
  Catharism, 1:230
  Church history, 3:594
  Cluniac reform of, 10:719
  Constantinople, 4:188
  Cortese, Gregorio, 4:280
  definitor, 4:612
  the discipline, 4:774–775
  Dominicans, 4:846
  early Britain, 2:621
  Egyptian, 5:137
  eschatology, 5:343
  Georgia, 6:153
  Georgian Orthodox Church,
    10:689–690
  Greco-Roman schooling, 6:432
  Gregory VII (Pope) St., 6:494
  hymns, 7:253
  iconoclasm, 7:281, 282
  *Institutiones divinarum et
    saecularium litterarum*
    (Cassiodorus), 9:438
  Italy, 2:140–141, 143, 7:665–666
  knighthood, 9:625
  lauras, 8:381

Lausiac history, 8:381–382
lay spirituality affected, 8:414
Lazarus the Confessor, St., 8:421
Liturgy of the Hours, 8:730
monasteries, 9:782
Monastic Republic of Mount Athos
  practice of, 10:32
Palestinian origins of, 10:800
Poland, 11:439
Portugal, 11:534, 536
poverty, 11:569–570
Ravenna (Italy), 11:930
reform
    Bénard, Laurent and, 2:235
    Benedictines, 2:268–270, 271–273
    Bessarion and, 2:141
    Cluniac reform movement, 2:257
    Dunstan, St. and, 4:941
    George of Saxony and, 6:144–145
    Gerard of Brogne, St. and, 2:217,
      6:160
    Gerhoh of Reichersberg and,
      6:167
    under Joseph II (Holy Roman
      Emperor), 7:1042
  revival of, 5:84
  Roman empire, 9:690
  Rule of St. Augustine, 1:322, 346,
    868–869, 871–872, 3:67–68, 412
  Serbian Church, 10:698–699
  solitude, 13:303
  spirituality, 13:444–445
  supported by St. Otto of Bamberg,
    10:715
  Syria, 13:704
  virginity, 14:545
  See also Benedictine Rule; Desert
    Fathers; *specific monasteries;
    specific religious orders*
Monasticism, early Irish, **9:803–804**
Monasticism, non-Christian, 7:612, 698
Monasticon belge (Berlière), 2:300
Monchanin, Jules, 8:839
Monck, George (Duke of Albemarle),
  1:76
Il Mondo riformato (Sarnelli), 12:694
Il Mondo santificato (Sarnelli), 12:694
Mondonville, J. J. de, 3:438
Mondrian, Piet, 3:679, 680
Mondsee Abbey (Austria), 1:908
Mone, Franz Joseph, 1:147, 6:68,
  9:804–805
Mone, Jean, 12:488
Moneda, Andreas de la, 12:765
Monergism, 3:561

Money and magnificence, 9:44
Mongolia, 3:491–492, 8:299, **9:805–807**,
  806
Mongols, 9:805, **807–810**, *808*
  Arabia, 1:611
  Assyrian Church of the East, 1:807
  Crusades, 4:405, 414
  Hungary invasions, 7:210, 211
  Persian rule, 11:140
  Russian invasion, 1:263
  sky and sky gods, 13:205
Monica, St., 1:888, 9:*810*, **810**
Moniño, José, 3:792, 795
Monism, **9:811–812**, 11:284
  Avicenna, 1:941
  Bradley, Francis Herbert, 2:577
  dialectical materialism, 9:322
  dualism vs., 4:914–915
  identity principle, 7:303
  immanence, 7:340
  Milton, John, 9:643
*Monita privata Societatis Jesu. See
  Monita secreta*
Monita secreta, **9:812**
The Monitor (NCDC report), 10:159
Monk, Maria, 10:170
Monk of Farne, **9:813**
Monks, **9:812–813**
Monkton Priory. *See* Pembroke Priory
  (Wales)
Monod, Adolphe, 5:467
Monoenergism, 2:749, 793, 6:761
Monogenism and polygenism, 4:347,
  9:813–814, 10:667
Monologion (St. Anselm of Canterbury),
  1:496, 10:601, 602
Monomotapa people (Africa), 13:122
Monophyletic polygenism, 9:813
Monophysitism, 3:561, 595, **9:814–816**
  adopted by Timotheus I, 14:85–86
  Agapetus I (Pope), St., 1:172
  Alexandria, 1:268–269, 4:196
  Alexius the Studite, 1:276
  Anastasius I (Byzantine Emperor),
    1:386, 523
  Anathemas of Cyril, 1:391
  Anatolius of Constantinople, 1:392
  Ani, 1:453
  Anthimus of Trebizond, 1:503
  Antioch, 1:523, 525, 4:196
  Apollinarianism, 1:559, 560
  Armenia, 1:700, 704–705, 707
  Arnobius the Younger, 1:718
  attacks of Nerses Gratiosus against,
    10:251

Boniface IV (Pope), 2:499

Byzantine art, 2:731

Byzantine Church, 2:748–749

Carthage, 3:187

Chalcedon Council, 4:195–196, 379

condemned, 13:122–123

Constantine V (Byzantine Emperor), 4:174

Constantinople, 4:185

Constantinople Council II, 4:192

creedal statements, 4:356

cross, 4:379, 382

Cyril of Alexandria, 4:467, 468

Cyril of Alexandria, St., 2:793, 820, 3:595

Diadochus of Photice, 4:720

Dioscorus (Patriarch of Alexandria), 4:196, 250, 756, 860

Domnus of Antioch, 4:859–860

early Palestinian, 10:800–801

Eastern Schism, 5:22

Edessa, 5:82

Egypt, 5:137–138

Ethiopia, 5:399, 400, 403

Eutyches father of, 5:461

Felix III (Pope), St., 5:667

founding of, 13:43

historiography, 2:797

history, 8:429

Hypatius of Ephesus, 7:262

hypostasis, 7:263–264

Ibn Al-'Assāl, 7:270

iconoclasm, 7:281

influence on Newman's Oxford Movement, 10:733–734

Jacob of Sarug, 7:687

John Philoponus, 1:670

Julian of Halicarnassus, 8:48, 52

Justian I, 4:186

Justin II, 8:93

Justinian I, 1:503, 523, 525, 3:596, 7:262, 8:97

Leo I (Pope), St., 8:472

Leontius of Byzantium, 8:502

Liberatus, 8:550–551

Nilus, 2:759

School of Alexandria, 1:269–270, 273, 2:820

Sergius I (Patriarch), 13:13

Sergius of Resaina, 13:17

Simplicius (Pope), St., 13:140

Syria, 13:704, 705

Syrian Jacobite Church, 5:19

Theodora, 13:123

Theodosius, 13:882

See also Acacian Schism; Chalcedon, Council of; Eutychianism; Monothelitism; Severus (Patriarch of Antioch)

Monotheism

afterlife, 1:163

Akhnaton, 1:199

Albright, William Foxwell, 1:235

Book of Amos, 1:365

theandric acts of Christ in, 13:857

Monothelitism, 2:821, 3:598, 7:817, **9:816–817**

Adeodatus (Pope), 1:115

Agatho (Pope), St., 1:173–174

Alexandria, 1:269, 271

Byzantine Church, 2:749–750

Carthage, 3:187

Christology, 3:559, 561

Constans II Progonatus, 4:173, 186

Constantine (Pope), 4:178

Constantine IV (Byzantine Emperor), 4:173, 186

Constantinople Council III, 4:193, 300

Damian of Pavia, 4:506

Donus (Pope), 4:870

favored by Byzantine Emperors, 10:432

Heraclius (Byzantine Emperor), 1:271, 2:749, 783, 3:561, 6:761

Honorius I (Pope), 7:80–81

hypostasis, 7:264

John IV (Pope), 7:921

Julian of Toledo, 8:50

Justinian II, 4:128

Leo II (Pope), St., 8:478

Maronite Church, 9:194–195

Monoenergism, 2:793

Pyrrhus I, 11:843–844

Sergius I (Patriarch of Constantinople), 4:193

Sergius I (Pope), St., 13:13

Severinus (Pope), 13:42

Sophronius, St., 13:324

Typos decree (648) supporting, 14:256

Monroe, Francis M., 1:209

Monroy É Hijar, Antonio (Abp. of Santiago de Compostela, Spain), **9:817**

Monsabré, Jacques Marie, 9:*817*, **817–818**, 11:624

Monsabré, Louis. *See* Monsabré, Jacques Marie

Monsen Canon, 3:32

Monsignors, **9:818**

Monstrances, 8:632, **9:818–819**

Mont Sainte-Odile Convent (Alsace), **9:820**

Montagnes, B., 1:378

Montagny, Aymon de (Abbot), 12:535

Montague, George, 3:393

Montague, Richard (Bp. of Chichester), 3:152

Montaignac de Chauvance, Louise-Thérèse de, Bl., **9:820**

Montaigne, Claude-Louis de, 1:309

Montaigne, Michel Eyquem de, **9:820–823**, 11:293

Charron, Pierre, 3:439

Renaiassance philosophy, 12:125

skepticism, 5:394, 12:47, 13:202

Montal, Fornés, Paula, St., **9:823**

Montalembert, Charles Forbes René de, 5:854, 855, 9:*823*, **823–825**

L'Avenir censured, 8:309

Catholic social thought, 13:256

Dupanloup, Félix, 4:942

liberalism, 3:619

negotiations between Napoleon III, 10:150

Resurrectionists, 12:174

Montana, 2:626, **9:825–827**

See also specific dioceses and archdioceses

Montanism, 5:148, **9:828–829**

Ancyra, 1:398

apocalyptic movements, 1:547

Apollinaris of Hierapolis, St., 1:560, 785

Asia Minor, 1:785

biblical canon, 3:22

chorbishops, 3:525

Church history, 3:593

digamy, 4:745

history of, 8:268

laicism, 8:281

millenarianism, 9:636

Parousia, 1:135

prophecy, 11:760

Tertullian, 1:547, 3:186

Montavon, William F., **9:829**

Montazet, A. de, 8:905

Mont-César Abbey (Louvain, Belgium), 3:82

Montcheuil, Yves de, 7:792, **9:829**

Mont-Cornillon Monastery (Liège, Belgium), **9:819**

Monte, Bartolomeo Maria dal (Father), Bl., **9:829**

Monte, Guidobaldo del, 6:58, 59

Monte, Philippe de, **9:829–830**

El Monte Carmelo, 13:122

Monte Cassino Archabbey (Italy), 2:237–238, 5:755, 9:*783*, **830–832**, *831*

    Alphanus of Salerno, St., 1:306

    art, 2:350, *351*, 8:471

    chronicler of, 8:494

    exemption, 2:331

    founding of, 3:596

    Lidanus, 8:561

Monte Senario, 13:27, 29

Monteagudo, Ana de los Angeles, Bl., **9:832**

Monteagudo, Bernardo, 1:650

Montecchi e Capuletti (Romeo and Juliet) (Bellini), 2:229

Montefiore, Claude Joseph Goldsmid, 8:13, **9:832–833**

Monteiro, Ignace, 12:770

Monteiro da Vide, Sebastião (Abp.), **9:833**

Montemayor, Juan Francisco, **9:833–834**

Montemayor, Prudentius, 2:50

Montemayor Córdoba de Cuenca. *See* Montemayor, Juan Francisco

Montemayor of Cuenca. *See* Montemayor, Juan Francisco

Montenegro. *See* Serbia and Montenegro

Montereau, Pierre de, 12:544

Montereuil, Bernard de, 7:847

Monterey-Fresno Diocese (CA), 8:791

Montes Pietatis, **9:834–835**

    Angelo Carletti di Chivasso, Bl., 1:413

    Bernardino of Feltre, Bl., 2:322

    Fifth Lateran Council, 8:355

    Urban VII (Pope), regulation of, 14:340

    works of charity, 3:414, 416

Montesino, Antonio, 5:358, **9:835**

Montesinos Orduña, María Luisa, Bl., 1:4–5

Montesquieu, Baron de. *See* Secondat, Charles-Louis de

Montesquieu, Charles de, 1:667, 678, 3:88, **9:835–836**, *836*

Montesquieu, Charles Louis Joseph de Secondat, Baron de la Brède et de. *See* Montesquieu, Charles de

Montessori, Maria, 1:83, 5:91, **9:836–837**, *837*

Montessori Method, 9:836–837

Monteverdi, Claudio, 1:766, 2:114, 3:311, **9:837–838**, *838*

Montfaucon, Bernard de, 4:757, 5:519, **9:839**

Montfort Fathers, 3:329, 621–622, 4:687, 6:531, **9:839**

Montgomery, Charles Pius, 12:646

Montgomery, George (Bp. of Monterey-Los Angeles), 8:791, 12:648

The Month (periodical), **9:839–840**, 14:258

Months, Special Devotions for, **9:840**

Montier-la-Celle Monastery (France), 6:15

Montigny, Francis de, 1:270

Montini, Giorgio, 14:128

Montini, Giovanni Battista Enrico Antonio Maria (Card.). *See* Paul VI (Pope)

Montlosier, François de, 1:519

Montmajour Abbey (France), 1:197, **9:840–841**, *841*

Montmartre Paris Abbey (France), 8:798, **9:841**

Montmayor, Prudencio de, 4:111

Montovano, Pomponio, 12:118

Montoya, Jesús Méndez, St., 6:545

Montpellier Catechism, 11:560–561

Montréal (Canada), 3:4, 5, 6, 7, 8, 9

Montreal, University of, 2:567

Montreuil, Jean de, 7:190

Montreuil Abbey (France), **9:841–842**

Montreuil-Les-Dames Abbey (France), **9:842**

Mont-Saint-Elois Monastery (France), 3:67

Mont-Saint-Michel Abbey (France), 1:845, 9:*819*, **819–820**, 12:270

Mont-Saint-Michel and Chartres (Adams), 1:112

Montserrat Abbey (Barcelona, Spain), 3:744, 8:673–674, **9:842**, 13:*379*, 384

Montúfar, Alonso de (Abp. of Mexico), 6:547

Montumenta Germaniae (St. Odilo of Cluny), 10:552

Monument of Bude (Chalgrin), 12:112

Monument of Pope Benedict XIV (Bracci), 2:247

Monument of Pope Leo XI (Algardi), 8:489

Monument of Pope Leo XII (Fabris), 8:490

Monument to Pope Pius VII (Tenarani), 14:*391*

Monument of Pope Pius VIII (Tenerani), 11:*383*

Monument of Pope Urban VII (Bonvicino), 14:*340*

Monumenta Boica (Scholliner), 12:779

Monumenta catholica pro independentia potestatis ecclesiasticae ab imperio civili (Roskoványi), 12:383

Monumenta Germaniae Historica (St. Odilo of Cluny), 10:552

Monumenta Germaniae Historica: Auctores antiquissimi (Magnobod of Angers), 9:44

Monumenta graphica medii aevi ex archivis et bibliothecis imperii Austriaci collecta (von Sickel), 10:774

Monumenta iuris canonici (Kuttner), 8:257

Monumenta Niederaltacensia (Scholliner), 12:779

Monumenta Oberalticensia (Scholliner), 12:779

Monumental archway (Tyre, Lebanon), 8:*429*

Moody, Dwight Lyman, 7:257, **9:842–843**, 12:205

Moody, Ernest A., 12:541

Moody, Raymond, 13:853–854

Moody Bible Institute. *See* Chicago Bible Institute

Mooney, Edward Francis (Card.), 3:516, 4:294–295, 698, **9:843–844**

Moonies. *See* Unification Church

Moore, Edward Roberts, **9:844**

Moore, G. E., 5:397, 10:190, 11:297, 12:415

    Alexander, Samuel, 1:252

    British moralists, 2:624

    sense knowledge, 12:910–911

Moore, Richard C., 5:297

Moore, Thomas Verner, 3:192, **9:844–845**

Moore, Wilbert, 13:284

Moore, Willis S., 10:649

Moosbrugger, Caspar, 5:139

Moosmüller, Oswald, 2:168

Mopinot, Jean, 12:277

Mopinot, León, Bl., 2:632

Mopsuestia, 3:732, **9:845**

Mora, Francis, 8:790–791

Mora, J. E., 12:767

Mora, Melchior de, 7:726

Mora, Michael de la, St. *See* Mora, Miguel de la, St.

Mora, Miguel de la, St., 6:545, **9:845–846**, *846*

Mora Velasco, José, Bl., 7:125

Mora y del Rio, José (Abp. of Mexico), **9:846**, *847*

Moraga, José Joaquin, 12:645

Moragas Cantarero, María Sagragio of San Luis Gonzaga, Bl., **9:846–847**

Moral absolutes, 9:875–876

Moral causality, 5:99, 12:469

Moral education, 4:759–763, 797, 5:195, **9:847–848**

Moral Essays (Pope), 11:497

Moral evil, 5:490, 6:352

Moral guilt. *See* Ethical guilt

Moral instruments, 7:499

Moral limitations, 9:781

Moral Man and Immoral Society (Niebuhr), 10:387

Moral minimum, 3:220

Moral monism, 9:811

Moral necessity, 10:226

Moral objectivity, 6:352

Moral obligation and taxation, **13:768–769**

Moral obligations, 9:876, 13:237, 611, 768–769

Moral philosophy, 4:937–938, 5:108, 9:866, 12:33

Moral Philosophy (Rickaby), 12:240

Moral precepts (Neo-Pythagorean), 10:243

Moral Re-Armament (MRA). *See* Oxford Group

Moral responsibility, 5:797–798

Moral theology, 6:351, **9:848–858**

    absolutism, 1:44

    academic freedom, 1:53

    accusation, 1:66

    Aertnys, Jozef, 1:140

    Alphonsus Liguori, St., 1:310–311

    American culture, 9:868

    Angelo Carletti di Chivasso, Bl., 1:413–414

    Anglican, 8:182

    assault, 1:787

    Bauny, Étienne, 2:150

    Bautain, Louis Eugène Marie, 2:161

    Bouquillon, Thomas Joseph, 2:563–564

    Busenbaum, Hermann, 2:715–717, 12:766

    Cafasso, St. Joseph, 2:543, 851

    Caramuel, Juan Lobkowitz, 3:98–99

    casuistry, 3:219–221

    Civil War (U.S.), 8:145

    compensationism, 4:43

    Coninck, Giles de, 4:121

    Connell, Francis J., 4:126

    consequentialism, 4:159–160

    continence, 4:211–212

    Davis, Henry, 4:544–545

    deliberation, 4:629–630

    demonstration, 4:653

    discernment, spiritual, 4:767

    dogmatic theology, 4:812

    double effect principle, 4:880–881

    ethics, 5:390, 394

    feminist ethics, 5:680

    formal and material cooperation in sin, 13:156–157

    Fuchs, Josef, 6:18–19

    Geiler von Kaysersberg, Johannes, 6:117

    Génicot, Édouard, 6:135

    German anti-Reformation, 8:230

    Gregory I (Pope), St., 6:483

    Häring, Bernard, 6:646

    imputability, 8:876

    Janssens, Louis, 7:722

    Jesuit development of, 7:782

    Johannes Clericus, 7:889

    Laymann, P., 8:419

    Lehmkuhl, A., 8:455

    lying as sin, 8:901

    moral philosophy, 9:866

    morality of thoughts, 14:62

    occult compensation, 4:41–43

    as official doctrine of the Church (19th century), 14:285

    papal social thought, 13:266

    patristic literature, 10:882–883

    proportionality, 11:767

    Prümmer, Dominikus, 11:794

    Redemptorist, 8:233

    Reginald, Valerius, 12:29

    restitution, 12:142–144

    retribution, 12:174–179

    Reusch, Franz Heinrich, 12:182

    Schwane, Joseph, 12:792–793

    spiritual theology, 13:435

    Sporer, Patritius, 13:461

    standards of conduct, 9:852

    Suárez, Francisco, 13:559

    taxation and moral obligation, 13:768

    Ten Commandments, 4:6–8

    virginity, 14:546

    See also Conscience; Epikeia (reasonableness); Scandal

Moral theology, history of

    to 700, **9:858–861**

    700 to Vatican Council I, **9:861–864**

    20th century, **9:864–865**

    contemporary trends, 8:139, **9:865–870**

Moral theology, methodology of, **9:870–872**

Moral virtue, 5:195

    charity, 14:553

    human act, 7:171

    religion as, 12:84–85

    respect, 12:138–139

    reverence (*observantia*), 12:203

    spirituality, 13:438

La Morale et la loi de l'histoire (Gratry), 6:424

Morales, Cristóbal de, 8:88, **9:872–873**, *873*

Morales, Francisco de, Bl., 7:733, **9:873**

Morales, Juan Bautista, 3:514, **9:873**

Morales, Manuel, St., 2:156, **9:873–874**, 12:292

Moralia (Gregory the Great), 3:597

Moralia (Plutarch of Chaeronea), 11:413

Moralia (St. Basil), 2:136

Moralia in Genesim (Guibert of Nogent), 9:452

Moralia in Job (Gregory the Great), 3:750

Moralia in Job (St. Odo of Cluny), 10:555

Moralist theory on redemption, 11:984

Moralitates (Thomas Waleys), 14:40

Moralitates in Psalmos (Edmund of Abingdon), 5:86

Morality, **9:874–876**

    Alphonsus Liguori, St., 1:311

    Ancient Egypt, 5:128

    art, 1:748

    Clement of Alexandria, St., 3:798

    concubinage, 4:65

    courage, 4:316

    detraction, 4:696

    dreams, 4:905

    drunkenness, 4:910–911

    emotion, 5:194

    end justifying the means, 5:212–213

    fear, 5:652–653

    Gnosticism, 6:259

    homosexuality, 7:67, 72

    human respect, 7:179

    idleness, 7:305

    ignorance, 7:315

    immortality, 7:350

    indifferent acts, 7:420

    lust and sexual order, 8:873–874

    moral circumstances, 3:742–743

    natural law, 10:196–198

    obedience, 10:507

    perfectional trend, 13:423

    reflex principles, 12:4–5

    relativism, 12:49–50

Morality *(continued)*
    religion, 12:62–63, 86
    Roman religion, 12:309–310
    sadness, 12:525
    Schopenhauer's pessimism, 7:299
    suicide, 13:598–599
    superstitions, 13:624
    Thomistic conception of, 9:90
    tutiorism system of, 14:250
    Veritatis Splendor (John Paul II), 10:185, 852, 14:451–452
    See also Doubt, moral; Faith and morals; Moral theology
Morality, systems of, **9:876–880**
    compensationism, 4:43
    Concina, Daniel, 4:59
    deontologism, 4:673–674
    equiprobabilism, 5:310
    Kant's theory, 8:122–123
    laxism, 8:410–411
    rigorism, 12:246
Morality and religion, 12:62–63, **86**
Morality of consequences, 6:352
Morality plays, 3:231, 4:899, 5:485–486, **9:880–883**
    See also Drama
Morall, J. B., 6:119
Morals, 4:235, 236, 237–238, 7:448–449, 9:849–850
The *Morals of the Catholic Church* (Augustine), 4:219
The *Morals of the Manichaeans* (Augustine), 4:219
Moran, James, 7:581
Moran, Patrick Francis (Card. of Sydney, Australia), 1:903, 904, 905, **9:883–884**
Morandus, St., **9:884**
Morano, Maddalena Caterina, Bl., **9:884**
Moranvillé, John, 7:25
Moravia
    Clement the Bulgarian, St., 3:799
    Cyril and Methodius, SS., 4:475, 476
    Czech Republic, 4:478, 479
    Hubmaier, Balthasar, 7:145
    Hutterites, 7:234
    martyrs of, 12:693
    Orthodox Church, 3:599
    patron of, 12:693
    See also Cyril and Methodius, SS.; Moravian Church
Moravian Brethren, 4:2–3
Moravian Church, **9:884–886**
    Bohemian Brethren, 2:461
    Carpzov, Johann Gottlob, 3:174

Church-State relations, 3:648
dress of members, 9:*885*
Hussites, 2:606
justification, 8:87
Lutheran Pietism, 8:891
organizer in U.S., 13:406
Zinzendorf, Nikolaus, 14:928–929
Moravians, 1:548
More, Gertrude, 2:259, **9:886**
More, Henry, 3:185, 5:395
    Cambridge Platonists, 2:908, 909–910
    hylozoism, 7:239–240
    Maryland, 2:887
    world soul, 14:844
More, Hugh, Bl., 5:230, **9:886–887**
Moré, Marcel, 4:516
More, School of, **9:887**
More, Sir Thomas, St., 5:225, 749, 750, **9:887–893**, *889*
    aristocracy, 1:667
    Barton, Elizabeth, 2:130
    British moralists, 2:622
    Colet, John, 3:833
    Forty Martyrs, 12:210
    Gaguin, Robert, 6:49
    humanism, 7:189–190, 191
    influence on Recusant literature, 11:959
    Lord Chancellor for Henry VIII, 12:8
    Lutheranism, 3:609
    Roper, William, 12:370–371
    Russell, John, 12:416
    trial and execution of, 5:244, 12:8, 227
    utopianism, 14:360
    works of, 9:892
Moreau, Anne Françoise, St., **9:893**
Moreau, Basil Anthony, 7:18–19, 21–22, 9:162–163, **893**
Moreau, Louis-Zéphyrin, Bl. (Bp. of St. Hyacinthe, Québec, Canada), **9:893–894**
Moreau, Patrick, 10:325
Môrēh Nᵉbûkîm (Dux dubiorum, Dux neutrorum) (Maimonides), 9:52–53
Morel, Thomas, 12:595
Morello, Brigida di Gesù, Bl., **9:894**
Moreno, Juan Ignacio (Card.), **9:894**, 12:280
Moreno, Julian Benigno, 10:29
Moreno, Manuel D. (Bp. of Tucson), 1:688
Moreno, Matías, 2:863
Moreno, Rafael, 2:862

Moreno y Díaz, Ezequiel, St. (Bp. of Pasto, Colombia), **9:894**
Moreno y Maisanove, Juan de la Cruz. *See* Moreno, Juan Ignacio (Card.)
Moréri, Louis, 5:207
Moreruela Abbey (Spain), **9:894–895**
Moreville, Richard de, 8:169
Morfi, Juan Agustín de, **9:895**
Morgair, Máel Máedoc Úa. *See* Malachy, St.
Morgan, C. Lloyd, 1:252
Morgan, Edward, Ven., 5:235
Morgan, Henry, 3:111
Morgan, Lewis Henry, 4:433
Morgan, Philip. *See* Powel, Philip, Bl.
Morgan, Philip (Bp. of Worcester), **9:895**
Morgan, T. H., 2:403
Morgan, William (Bp.), 10:169, 12:536
Morgott, Franz, 12:774
Mori, Paolo, 1:582
Moriarty, Bernard, 7:580
Moriarty, Patrick Eugene, **9:895–896**
Moriarty, Tadhg, 7:582
Morigia, Catherine, 1:346
Morigia, James, Ven., 2:103
Morimond Abbey (France), 1:108, 3:747, 748, 751, 5:32, **9:896**
Morin, Germain, 1:718, 5:740, **9:896**, 10:744, 963
Morin, Jean, 1:333, **9:896–897**
Morinière, Jérôme Louis de la, 5:441
Mörlin, Joachim, 6:253
Morlino, Robert C. (Bp. of Helena), 9:827
Mormon Church. *See* Church of Jesus Christ of Latter-day Saints
Mormonism. *See* Church of Jesus Christ of Latter-day Saints
Morocco, 7:874, **9:897–899**, *898*, 14:*692*
Morone, Giovanni (Card.), 3:610, **9:899–900**
Moroni, Gaetano, 3:854, 5:207, **9:900–901**
Morosini, Andrea (d. 1618), 9:901
Morosini, Domenico (fl. 1148-58), 9:901
Morosini, Dorothea, 1:346
Morosini, Francesco (fl. 1688-94), 2:89–90, 7:670, 9:901
Morosini, Gianfrancesco (d. 1596), 9:901
Morosini, Giovanni (fl. 10th c.), 9:901
Mórosini, Marino (fl. 1249-53), 9:901
Morosini, Michele (fl. 1382), 9:901
Morosini, Petrina. *See* Morosini, Pierina, Bl.

Morosini, Pierina, Bl., **9:901**

Morosini, Pietro (Card., fl. 1408), 9:901

Morosini, Tomaso (Patriarch of Constantinople), 2:760, 8:367, 9:901

Morosini family, **9:901**

Morra, Alberto de. *See* Gregory VIII (Pope)

Morrill Law (1873), on polygamy, 8:373

Morris, Gibson v. (1903), 3:658

Morris, Henry, 4:347

Morris, John B. (Bp. of Little Rock), 1:692, 5:752, 8:613–614

Morris, William, 2:523, 5:483, 13:475

Morrisey, Francis G., 3:59

Morrison, H. C., 12:785

Morrison, Robert, 3:499

Morrissey, Thomas, 7:581

Mors Pilati, 14:457

Morse, Henry, St., 5:*247*, **9:902**, 13:370

Morse, Samuel, 10:313

Mortal sin, 4:273–274, 7:230, 231, **9:902–903**, 904, 11:825

See also Sin

Mortalium animos (encyclical, Pius XI), 5:72, 6:29, **9:903**

Mortara, Edgar (b. 1851), 9:903–904

Mortara Case, **9:903–904**

Le Morte d'Arthur (Malory), 1:762

Mortification, 4:774–775, **9:904**, 10:742–743, 13:429, 434

Mortimer, Roger, 1:109

Mortmain (law), 3:419, 5:*242*, **9:904–905**, 12:542

Morton, John (Card. of Canterbury), 3:72, **9:905**

Morton, Robert, Bl., 5:230, **9:905**

Morton, Thomas (Bp.), 4:868

Mosaic law. *See* Law, Mosaic

Mosaic of the Last Supper (S. Apollinaire Nuovo), 8:344

Mosaics, 1:*751*, 754–755, 757, **10:1–5**

Bible cycles in, 2:369–370, 371

Byzantine, 2:*735, 812, 819*

Christocentrism, 3:558

Death of the Virgin (Giambono), 10:*2*

depicting Trinitarian seal (13th century), 14:*187*

early history of, 10:1

National Shrine of the Immaculate Conception, 10:168

Moscardó Montalvá, Josefina, Bl., 1:4

Moscati, Giuseppe Mario Carolo Alphonse, St., **10:5**

Moscati, S., 3:1

Moschabarus, George, 2:826

Moschus, John (Eucratas), 10:6, **6**, 12:606, 13:324

Moscow, 2:745, 8:164–165, 12:420–421, 433, 434

Moseley, G. H. J., 1:836

Moser, Karl, 3:710

Moses, **10:6–7**

Aaron, 1:2–3

covenants, 4:326

crucifixion prefigured, 4:391, 398

God's spirit, 13:426

graven images, 13:137

historical information, 10:6

holding tablets of Ten Commandments, 10:9, 13:*160*

iconography of, 10:7

Jesus as Moses-like prophet, 8:864

Jesus compared to, 7:892–893

Joshua, 7:1055

Levitical priesthood, 8:523

manna gathering, 9:*119*

messianic message, 9:540

Mount Horeb (Sinai), 7:110

Mount Nebo memorial to, 10:7

in the Qur'ān, 7:608, 11:879–880

with the tablets, 5:*548*

Ten Commandments, 4:5, 6–7

Moses, Canticles of, 3:73

Moses II (Armenian Catholicos), 1:700, 4:958

Moses and the Burning Bush (Raphael), 10:*8*

Moses ben Maimon. *See* Maimonides (Jewish philosopher)

Moses ben Nahman. *See* Naḥmanides (Talmudist)

Moses de Leon, 2:832, 833

Moses of Narbonne, 7:864

Moses the Black, St., **10:7–8**

Mosheim, Johann Lorenz von, 1:718

Moskwa, Jerzy, 7:793

Mosque of Medina, 10:10

Mosque of the Sultan Hassan (Egypt), 10:*10*

Mosquera, Manuel José, **10:11**

Mosques, 7:614–617, **10:8–11**

The Most Holy Book (Kitāb-i Aqdas) (Bahā'-Ullāh), 2:12

Most Holy Sacrament Sisters, 8:278

Môt (God), 14:269

Mota y Escobar, Alonso de la, **10:11**

"Motet for a Long Offertory" (Charpentier), 10:*12*

Motets, 3:438, **10:11–13**

Mothe, François Frison de, 7:25

Mothe-Arnauld, Antoine de, 1:715

Mothe-Arnauld, Antoine II, 1:715

Mother Clare (Nun of Kenmare), 4:445–446

Mother Earth. *See* Fertility and vegetation cults

Mother goddesses, 8:111

Mother Immaculata of Jesus, 5:885

Mother of God, **10:13–15**

See also Mary, Blessed Virgin; Theotokos

Mother Teresa of Calcutta, 1:217, 7:406, 9:731, **10:15–16**, 12:100

Mother-goddesses

Baltic region, 2:36

sacred prostitution, 11:774

Śakti of Śiva, 2:36

serpents, 11:776

Motion, **10:16–21**

accident, 1:61

act, 1:73, 75

action and passion, 1:80

Aristotelian physics in, 12:811–813

Aristotle, 1:682

causality, 3:305

as continnum, 4:215

cosmological argument, 4:285–287

Divine concurrence, 4:71–72

freedom of, 10:25–26

generation-corruption, 6:129

motive and freedom of, 10:25–26

natural time, 14:79, 80–81

Ockhamish, 10:535–536

physical premotion as, 11:669–670

soul, 13:334

of the will, 10:24–25

Zeno of Elea, 14:917

See also Matter and Form; Substantial Change

Motion, first cause of, **10:21–24**, 14:81–82

Motion Picture Code, 8:779

Motive, **10:24–26**

Motive, unconscious, **10:26–28**

Motolinía, Toribio de Benavente, 2:346, 3:248, **10:28–29**

Motoyama, John, Bl., 7:732

Motoyama, Peter, 7:733

Motoyama, Romanus, Bl., 7:732

Motril, Martyrs of, BB., **10:29**

Mott, John Raleigh, 9:697, 10:*30*, **30**, 13:554

Motu proprios, 4:758

Ad hoc usque tempus (Paul VI), 3:106

Motu proprios(continued)

Ad purpuratorum (Paul VI), 3:106

Ad tuendam fidem (John Paul II), 1:97–98, 3:58

Apostolatus peragendi (Paul VI), 11:481

Apostolica sollicitudo (Paul VI), 11:30

Apostolicae caritatis (Paul VI), 11:482

Apostolos suos (John Paul II), 3:58

Arduum sane munus (Pius X), 3:55

Boni Pastoris (John XXIII), 7:936

Catholicam Christi ecclesiam (Paul VI), 11:481

Cum gravissima (John XXIII), 3:106, 7:936

Cum iuris canonici (Benedict XV), 11:482

definition of, 11:747

Doctor Angelici (Pius X), 11:390

Dolentium hominum (John Paul II), 11:482

Dominicianus ordo (John XXIII), 11:487

Familia a Deo instituta (Paul VI), 11:481

Fin dalla prima (Pius X), 11:389

I primitivi cemeteri (Pius XI), 11:490

In cotidianis precibus (Pius XII), 11:400

Inde a Pontificatus (John Paul II), 11:479

Ingravescentem aetatem (Paul VI), 3:106–107, 11:30

Integrae servandae (Paul VI), 11:30

Iustitiam et pacem (Paul VI), 11:481

Latinarum litterarum (Pius XI), 11:484

Magisterium vitae (Paul VI), 11:487

Maiora in dies (John XXIII), 11:476

Minsteria quaedam (Paul VI), 1:68, 7:37, 38, 8:285

Pastorale munus (Paul VI), 3:56

Postquam apostolicis litteris (Pius XII), 1:534

Praeclara inter opera (Pius X), 11:488

Praestantia (Pius X), 11:389

Primo feliciter elapso (Pius XII), 11:400

Quod maxime (Pius XI), 11:485

Recognito iuris canonici codice (John Paul II), 3:35, 11:482

Romanorum Pontificum (Pius XI), 11:753

Rubricarum instructum (John XXIII), 7:936

sacred music (1903), 3:523

Sacro Cardinalium Consilio (Paul VI), 3:107

Sanctitatis clarior (Paul VI), 3:63

Socialum scientiarum (John Paul II), 11:475

Studia latinitatis (Paul VI), 11:488

Suburbicariis sedibus (John XXIII), 3:106, 7:936

Summi Pontificis electio (John XXIII), 7:936

Superno Dei mutu (John XXIII), 7:937

Tra le sollecitudini (Pius X), 4:118, 11:390

Vitae mysterium (John Paul II), 11:475

See also Apostolic letters; Encyclicals

Moulinier, Charles B., 3:284

Mounier, Emmanuel, 5:931, **10:30–31**, 11:153

Mount Athos (Greece), 3:335

Mount Athos, Monastic Republic of, **10:31–32**

Mount Herman (Israel), 7:*629*

Mount Lebanon, Synod of (1736), 9:198–199

Mount Mary College (Milwaukee, WI), 5:753, 13:165

Mount Melleray Abbey (Ireland), **10:33**

Mount of Olives (Jerusalem), **10:33–34**, *34*, 798

Mount St. Bernard Seminary (Iowa), 8:779

Mount St. Mary's College and Seminary (Emmitsburg, MD), 2:40, 4:918, 5:144, 145, **10:34–35**, 13:601

Mount St. Mary's College and Seminary (Los Angeles), 8:793

Mount Tabor (Israel), 4:713, **13:727–728**, 14:153–154

Mount Zion. *See* Zion

Mountain Sanctuary: Mother Mary of the Church, 9:*274*

Moura, Antônio de, 2:595

Mourning, 8:12

Mourret, Fernand, **10:36**

Mouskés, Philippe, 1:764

Mousson, synod of (948), 1:172

Mouth of Truth in Santa Maria (Italy), 10:*619*

Mouvement Républicaine Populaire (France), 3:619

Movement for a Better World, **10:36**

Movement for Reunion of the Bulgarian Orthodox Church (1992), 10:687

Movement perceptions, 10:20

The Moviegoer (Percy), 11:114

Movizzo, Catalina Sordini. *See* Mary Magdalene of the Incarnation (Mother)

Mowbray, John de (First Duke of Norfolk). *See* Norfolk, John de Mowbray, 1st Duke of

Mowbray, John de (Second Duke of Norfolk). *See* Norfolk, John de Mowbray, 2nd Duke of

Mowbray, John de (Third Duke of Norfolk). *See* Norfolk, John de Mowbray, 3rd Duke of

Mowbray, John de (Fourth Duke of Norfolk). *See* Norfolk, John de Mowbray, 4th Duke of

Mowbray, Thomas de, 10:421

Mowinckel, Sigmund, 2:531, 5:520, **10:36–37**, 11:766, 14:857–858

Moyë, John Martin, Bl., 10:37, 13:181–182, 182

Moyenmoutier Abbey (France), 5:843, 10:37

Moyes, James, 1:438, 4:917

Moyne de Bienville, J. B. le, 1:270

Moysan, Jeanne Marie, 7:30

Moyses, Rabbi. *See* Maimonides (Jewish philosopher)

Moyses sanctus (Matthew of Cracow), 9:361

Moysis libri quinque (Le Clerc), 5:518

Mozambique, **10:38–41**, *40*

Mozarabic Chant, 1:294, 7:245, **10:41–42**

Mozarabic Rite, 8:437, **10:42–47**

approval, 13:381

Bragan Rite, 2:579

Dominic of Silos, St., 4:831

Elipandus, 13:378–379

Elipandus of Toledo, 5:162

Eucharist, 10:44–47

Férotin, Marius, 5:690

Hugh of Remiremont, 7:155

Ildefonsus of Toledo, 7:316

invasiosn, 13:380

litanies, 8:601

liturgical history, 8:653, 713

revisions, 8:50

sacramentaries, 12:483

sources of, 10:43–44

Spain, 13:377

Mozarabs, 4:261, 356, 357

Mozart, Wolfgang Amadeus, 1:293, 931, 3:525, 796, 8:692–693, **10:47–49**

Mozi (Mo Tzu), **10:49**

Mozley, J., 4:331

MRA (Moral Re-Armament). *See* Oxford Group

Mrak, Ignatius, **10:49–50**

MSF (Doctors without Borders), 10:615

Muard, Marie Jean Baptiste, 10:50, 12:545

Mu'āwiya, 14:286

Mubarak, Hosni, 5:119

Much Wenlock. *See* Wenlock Abbey (Hereford, England)

Müeller, Gerhard, 7:528

Mueller, Joseph Maximilian, 13:164

Mueller v. Allen (1983), 3:668

Muench, Aloisius Joseph, 5:625, 10:50–51, 440, *485*

Muench, Robert W. (Bp.), 2:156, 4:331

Muerte en vida y vida en muerte (Basalenque), 2:132

Mugabe, Robert, 14:926, 927

Muḥammad (Muslim prophet), 1:611, **10:51–55**

    Bahira legend, 2:15–16

    buried at Mosque of Medina, 10:10

    death of, 11:877

    early life of, 10:51–52

    hijra, 6:825

    Jews, 7:868

    Meccan period of, 10:52–54

    Medinese period of, 10:54–55

    prophetic dignity refuted, 8:170

    Qur'ān, 11:874, 876, 878

    Shi'a Islam, 13:83

Muhammad Alī (Muslim leader). *See* al-Bāb (Muslim leader)

Mühlenberg, Henry Melchior, 8:885, 10:55

Muhlenberg, William A., 5:473

Muirchertach Mac Robartaig. *See* Marianus Scotus, Bl.

Muiredach's Cross (Monasterboice, Ireland), 7:*557, 583*

Muisis, Giles Li (Abbot), 12:565

Mujerista theology, 8:369

Mujica, Carlos, 1:654

Mújica Goiburu, Lázaro, Bl., 7:125

Muktafi II (Caliph), 10:252

Muldoon, Peter James (Bp.), 1:352, 3:478, 5:663, 9:46, **10:55–56**

Mulherin, Mary Gabriella, 10:56

Mulieris dignitatem (apostolic letter, John Paul II), 7:1003, 10:852, 14:819, 826

Mullanphy, John, 12:559

Mullany, Azarias of the Cross (Brother), **10:57**

Mullen, Arthur, 10:648

Muller, Dom, 4:276–277

Muller, H. J., 2:403

Müller, Josef, 12:26

Müller, Karl, 2:689

Müller, Max, 10:120

Müller, Ulrich. *See* Munier, Ulrich (d. 1759)

Mulligan, Edmund, 7:581

Mulloy, William Theodore (Bp. of Covington), 4:331

Mulry, Thomas Maurice, 3:279, **10:57**

Multa praeclare (apostolic brief, Gregory XVI), 6:268, 510, 10:977, 978

Multiplication of the Loaves Church (Et-Tabgah), 1:757

Multiplices inter (apostolic letter, Pius IX), 14:404

Multitudes, 5:525–526, 7:302, 303–304, **10:58–59**, 14:80

Multum ad movendos animos (brief, Pius IX), 2:842

Muluzi, Bakili, 9:69

Mulvee, Robert E. (Bp. of Wilmington, DE), 12:218, 14:765

Mumford, Lewis, 13:784–785

Mun, Albert de, 5:855, 13:242

Munárriz, Felipe (Father), 2:92

Muñatones, Juan de (Bp. of Segarbe), 1:879

Munck, J., 3:797, 5:331, 523

Mundelein, George William (Card.), 1:350, 3:478–479, 7:317, 10:*59*, **59–60**, 270

Munden, John, Bl., 5:228

Mundus et Infans (play), 9:881, 882

Mundwiler, Fintan (Abbot), 2:255, **10:60**, 12:568

Mungenast, Joseph, 1:321, 913

Mungo, St. *See* Kentigern (Bp. of Glasgow), St.

Munguía, Clemente de Jesús, **10:61**

Munich Circle, 2:1, 6:183

Munich Method in Catechetics, **10:61**

Munier, Ulrich (d. 1759), 14:776

Munificentissimus Deus (apostolic constitution, Pius XII), 1:797, 799, 800, 3:623, **10:61–62**, 11:399, 14:136

Muñoz, Peter (Abp.), 12:684

Muñoz, Vicente, 10:62

Al-Munqidh min aḍ-ḍalāl (Algazel), 1:281

Münster, Sebasian, 6:697

Münster circle, 6:79

Münzer, Thomas, 1:368, **10:62–63**, *63*, 11:53, 12:16

Al-Muqtadir (Caliph), 1:7

Murat, Joachim, 3:100

Muratori, Lodovico Antonio, 1:310, **10:63**

Muratorian Canon, 3:21, 31, **10:64**

    Alogoi, 1:304

    censorship, 3:336

    Luke's Gospel, 8:859

    prohibited books, 7:390

Murbach Abbey (France), **10:64**

Murchertagh, Brian, 7:580

Murder in the Cathedral (play, Eliot), 5:161

Murdoch, William, 1:20

Murdock v. Pennsylvania (1943), 3:661

Mure, G. R., 1:679

Mureşan, Lucian (Bp.), 12:339

Muri Abbey (Italy), **10:65**

Murialdo, Leonardo, Bl., **10:65**, 12:553

Muriel, Domingo, **10:65–66**

Murillo, Bartolomé Esteban, 2:114, 4:313, 10:*66*, **66**

Muris, Johannes de, 8:685

Murkowski, Frank, 1:211

Murner, Thomas, 2:584, **10:66–67**

Murnion, P., 12:478

Murphy, Bridey, 3:759

Murphy, John, **10:67**

Murphy, John Joseph, **10:67**

Murphy, Joseph, 3:716

Murphy, Margaret Mary Healy (Mother), 7:53

Murphy, Mary Paul (Mother), 5:880

Murphy, R. E., 5:523

Murphy, Thomas J. (Abp. of Seattle, WA), 9:827, 12:853

Murphy-O'Connor, Cormac, 1:441

Murray, Daniel (Abp. of Dublin), 1:194, 2:31, 7:562, **10:67–68**

Murray, John Courtney (Father), 1:55, 3:280, 643, 5:950, **10:68–69**, 12:729

Murray, John Gregory (Abp. of St. Paul), 9:58–59, 11:531–532, 12:573

Murray, Margaret Courtney, 10:68

Murray, Michael John, 10:68

Murray, Patrick, **10:69**

Murri, Romolo, 7:673, 9:755, **10:69–70**

Mursili II (Hittite king), 6:894–895

Murton, John, 2:78

Musculus, Andrew, 4:60

Museo intelectual (Elguero), 5:154

Music

    a cappella style, 1:1, 2:842, 3:523

Music *(continued)*

ars nova-era compositions,
8:320–321

art, 1:748

Byzantine Octoechos system,
10:548–549

Caecilian Movement, 2:642,
841–843, 3:523

carols, 3:149–152, 557

choirs, 3:522–524

choral polyphony, 10:13

Cluniacs, 3:811

Communion antiphon, 4:32–34, *33*

congregational singing, 4:118–120

Credos, 4:356–357

Crusade songs, 4:400

dodecaphony, or serialism, 12:745

Kyrie eleison, 8:259–261

mensural music, 8:171

motet arrangements, 10:11–13

Mozarabic Chant, 10:41–42

patron saint of, 12:600

revival movement, 8:697

stile antico, 1:1, 234, 293, 3:123

stile moderno, 1:234, 3:123

as will and power, 7:196

See also Caecilian Movement;
Carols; Hymns and hymnals;
Liturgical music; Polyphony;
specific composers and musicians;
specific musical periods

Music (philosophy), 8:171, **10:70–73**

Music, religious. *See* Liturgical music

Music, sacred

Gregorian Chant, 5:701, 793, 12:108

Kontakion, 12:348

Koukoulion, 12:348

Laus perennis (continuous chanting),
12:108

rimed office (rhythmic offices),
12:246–247

Russian Chant, 12:431

Schola Cantorum, 12:746

stile antico, 12:240

Music and Liturgy (periodical), 14:321

*Music and Liturgy—the Universa Laus
Document and Commentary*
(Duchesneau and Veuthey), 14:321

Music in Catholic Worship (MCW),
8:706–707, 709

''Music in Christian Celebration''
(1980), 8:707–708

Music in Christian Celebration
(Universa Laus), 14:321

Music theory, 5:911

Musica enchiriadis, 8:683

Musica reservata, 8:343

Musicae sacrae (encyclical, Pius XII),
11:400

Musical bells, 2:233

Musicam sacram (Vatican Council II),
3:75, 8:704–705

Musicology, 8:695

Muslim invasions, 3:164, 187, 599

Byzantine Empire, 2:783–785

fall of Constantinople (1453), 1:659,
676, 702, 2:764, 788, 828, 881

Monophysitism, 2:749

See also Ottoman Turks

Muslims

forgiveness to Catholics for past
offenses, 9:687

freethinkers, 5:967

invasions of Nubia (640-710) by,
10:472

occasionalism philosophy, 10:526

occupied by Nazareth, 10:217

persecution of, 2:3

relationship between Christians and
Pakistan, 10:762

See also Islam

Musnier, François, 13:151

Mussato, Albertino, 12:113

Musso, Cornelius, **10:73**

Mussolini, Benito, 3:619, 7:674, 8:356,
357

Musurgia universalis (Kircher), 14:372

Mutakallimūn (loquentes), 8:109–110

Mu'tazilism, 13:613–614

Mu'tazilites, 1:620, 781, 7:611, 8:110,
10:74

Muth, Carl, 6:184, **10:75**, 12:26

Muth, Placidus, 12:770

Mutinensis, 3:40

Mutis, José Celestino, 3:851

Muttathupandatu, Alphonsa, Bl.,
10:75–76

Mutual recognition of baptism, 2:66–67

Mutuca Picante (periodical), 2:96

Muzi, Giovanni (Bp. of Cittá di
Castello), **10:76**

Muzi, Juan, 3:732

My Confession (Tolstoi), 14:105

My Host the World (Santayana), 12:680

My Huy Nguyen, Michael, 14:496

My Lord Leicester's Commonwealth,
13:78

My Van Nguyen, Paul, 14:496

Myanmar. *See* Burma

Myconius, Friedrich, **10:76**

Myconius, Oswald, 2:689, **10:77**

Myers, John Joseph, 10:330

Mynd, Wyll, and Understanding (play),
9:882–883

Myrc, John, 11:633

Myriobiblon (Photius), 10:962

Myrrour of the World (Caxton), 5:206

Myslenta, Coelstinus, 2:874

Mystagogical Catecheses (Cyril of
Jerusalem), 2:64, 4:472, 7:971

Mystagogy, 3:253, 8:644, **10:77**

Le Mystère du Temple (Congar), 4:103

Die Mysterien des Christentums (The
Mysteries of Christianity)
(Scheeben), 12:730

*Das Mysteriengedächtnis der
Messliturgie im Lichte der Tradition*
(Casel), 5:430

The Mysteries of Christianity
(Scheeben), 12:731

Mysteries of faith, 2:176

Mysterii paschalis (motu proprio, Paul
VI), 8:720–721

Mysterium Cosmographicum (Kepler),
8:154

Mysterium ecclesiae (Congregation for
the Doctrine of the Faith), 4:809,
814, 11:950

Mysterium fidei (encyclical, Paul VI),
4:623–624, **10:77–79**, 11:32

Mysterium Filii Dei, 12:783

Mystery, 5:417–418

Mystery, in the Bible, **10:79–85**

destiny, supernatural, 4:694

mystery of Christ, 13:439–441

New Testament, 10:81–82

non-biblical Jewish thought, 10:80

Old Testament, 10:79–80

Origen, 10:655–656

satisfaction of Christ, 12:700, 702

Mystery, in theology, **10:82–85**

death, 4:573–581

ecclesiology, 5:36, 37

French School, 13:451

history of, 10:82–84

sacramental theology, 12:466–467

The Mystery of Christian Worship
(Casel), 10:97, 98

Mystery of life, 5:35

''Mystery of the Faith'' (*Mysterium
fidei*), 10:77–79

Mystery plays

acting of, 4:899

authorship of, 4:899–900

catechesis, 3:231

Christmas, 3:557

origins of, 4:896–900

staging of, 4:898–899

Mystery religions, Greco-Oriental, **10:85–97**
  afterlife in, 1:167, 168
  Alexander of Abonoteichos, 1:264
  apotheosis, 1:599
  asceticism, 1:773
  Casel, Odo, 3:202
  cult of the Great Mother, 10:91–92
  Cybele cult, 4:450
  Dionysus, 10:92–94
  discipline of the secret, 3:251
  early Church, 1:784
  Eleusianian, 10:89–91
  Mithraism, 10:95–96
  Mysteries of Isis, 12:326, *326*
  Orphism, 10:94–95
  relations with Christianity, 10:96–97
  religious and moral sin, 13:149
  Roman Empire, 12:309–310, 326–327
Mystery theology, **10:97–99**
Mystic numbers, 10:478
Mystica theologia divi Thomae (Vallgornera), 14:377
The Mystical Art (Benjamin minor) (Richard of Saint-Victor), 12:235
Mystical aureoles and illuminations, 10:109
Mystical Body of Christ, **10:99–105**
  Church as, 1:880, 3:28, 578, 580, 13:278
  Divine judgment, 8:36
  ecclesiology, 5:36, 37
  Ecumenical councils, 4:306
  French School, 13:451, 452
  grace, 8:572–573
  laity, 8:290
  Legion of Mary, 8:453
  life, concept of, 8:570–571
  liturgical movement, 8:670
  Mersch, Émile on, 9:521
  Mystici Corporis (Pius XII), 10:104, 110, 12:625, 626
  Patristic Fathers, 10:101–103
  priestly worship, 8:728
  St. Paul, 10:100–101
  soul of the Church, 13:358–359
  theology from medieval to modern times, 10:103–104
  ubiquitarianism, 14:263
The Mystical City of God and the Divine History of the Virgin Mother of God (Mary of Ágreda), 1:187, 363
Mystical marriage, 4:205, 206, 208–209, 5:45, 8:405, **10:105**
Mystical mill, 1:575–576

Mystical phenomena, 4:209, **10:105–109**
Mystical poetry, 7:970
The Mystical Presence (Nevin), 10:272
Mystical sermons, 11:612
Mystical theology, 9:30, 854, 12:31, 13:909–910
Mystical Theology (Pseudo-Dionysius), 11:801
Mystical Theology or Spiritual Life (Mystieke Theologie ofte verborghen Godtsgheleertheyt) (Maes), 9:30
Mystical union, **10:109–110**
Mystici corporis (encyclical, Pius XII), 3:589–590, 5:37, 948, 950–951, 7:380, 442, 9:428, 10:104, **110–111**, 11:399, 12:471, 625
  society, church as, 13:286–287
Mysticism, **10:111–117**
  Albert the Great, St., 1:226
  Alcher of Clairvaux, 1:239–240
  Alfarabi, 1:277
  Alumbrados, 1:323
  Alumbrados, 13:392
  Amelry, Francis, 1:348
  Angela of Foligno, Bl., 1:411–413
  Angelus Silesius, 1:428–429
  apophatic theology, 1:568
  art, 1:755, 3:844
  Bernard of Clairvaux, 2:310–311, 3:749
  Bernardes, Manoel, 2:318
  Bernières-Louvigny, Jean de, 2:324–325
  Böhme, Jakob, 2:462, 10:826
  Bremond, Henri, 2:601
  bridal, 3:132
  Byzantine, 2:793–794
  cabala, 2:831–836
  Cavalcanti, Guido, 3:310
  Cistercians, 3:749
  Cloud of Unknowing, 3:192, 605, 808
  consolations, 4:167
  contemplation, 4:204–209
  developments in theology, 10:115–116
  Eckhart, Meister influence, 5:45–46
  ecstasy, 5:60
  Evagrius Ponticus, 5:465
  experience of, 10:111–112
  grace in, 10:112–113
  irrationalism, 7:585
  Islamic, 7:611–612
  Jesuits, 7:309, 8:16
  Judaism, 8:8–9, 870–871
  knowledge of God, 10:113–114

Lawrence of the Resurrection, 8:409
Lepidi, A., 8:507
Louismet, S., 8:816
love, estatic conception of, 8:829
Low Countries, 13:455
Lucie-Christine, 8:844–845
Lull, R., 8:866–867
Lutgardis, 8:877
Miraculous Medal devotion, 8:266–267
natural, 4:204
non-Christian, 10:111
Origen, 10:655–656
Poland, 8:243, 245
scholasticism, 12:759
School of Alexandria, 1:269, 272
significance for Christian spirituality, 10:116
Solov'ev, V. S., 13:306–307
Sorazu, Ángeles, 13:325, *325*
soul, 13:343
Spain, 13:392
speculative theology, 13:908
Speyr, Adrienne von, 13:415–416
spiritual theology, 13:433–436
Stagel, Elsbeth, 13:468
Sufi, 8:866
validity of experiencing, 10:114–115
See also Hesychasm; *specific mystics*
Mysticism (Underhill), 14:291
Mysticism in Literature, **10:117–118**
Mystics, Bavarian, 5:681
Mystics, Chilean, 5:690
Mystics, English, 8:49–50, 141–142, 403, 10:118, **119–120**
Mystics, Flemish, 5:193, 12:439–441
Mystics, French, 5:167–168, 307–308, 12:221
Mystics, German, 5:32, 44–46, 166–167, 12:727
Mystics, Spanish, 5:353
Mystieke Theologie ofte verborghen Godtsgheleertheyt (Mystical Theology or Spiritual Life) (Maes), 9:30
La Mystique divine distinguée des contrefaçons diaboliques et des analogies humaines (Ribet), 12:221
Myth, literary, **10:120–124**
  the Bible, 5:809, 10:123–124
  ritual, 10:122–123
  Ugaritic, 14:267
Myth and mythology, **10:124–129**
  analogy, 1:373
  Ancient Egypt, 5:125
  art, 1:741

Myth and mythology *(continued)*
  aspects of sin, 13:149
  Babylonian, 2:329–330
  blood in, 2:442–443
  Campbell, Joseph, 2:918–919
  classification of, 10:127–128
  distinguishing saga and legend from,
    10:126
  fatalism, 5:636
  Kakubilla, 8:109
  life, concept of, 8:567
  Manichaeism, 9:110–112
  Märchen, 10:126–127
  Mesopotamia, ancient, 9:535
  mythical consciousness, 3:672–673
  nudity in, 10:472–473
  origin and development of,
    10:128–129
  rehabilitation of, 4:658
  religion, 12:61
  serpent as symbol, 13:21
  Shea on ambition of, 10:152
  See also Demythologizing
Myth and mythology, in the Bible,
  8:543, 10:123–124, **129**, **131**
Myth and reflective thought, **10:131–132**
Myth and ritual, 5:154–155
Myth of Sisyphus (Camus), 7:197
Mythic theology, 11:459
Mythical consciousness, 3:672–673
Mythological systems, 10:128
Mythologiques (Lévi-Strauss), 12:87

N

NAAL. *See* North American Academy
  of Liturgy
Naassenes, 6:260
NAB. *See* New American Bible
Nabataeans, 1:613, 614, 624–625
Nabu. *See* Nebo
Nabucco (Verdi), 14:446
Nabuna'id (King of Babylon),
  4:477–478
NAC. *See* North American Conference
Nacchianti, Giacomo, **10:133**
Nachapostolische Zeitalter (Schwegler),
  14:234
Nacimiento, Cecilia de, 3:136
Nack, K., 10:247
Naclantus. *See* Nacchianti, Giacomo
Nadal, Cyprien, 11:623
Nadal, Gerónimo, **10:133**
Nadīm, an- (fl. 987), 9:114

NAfIM. *See* National Apostolate for
  Inclusion Ministry
Nagaishi, Paul, Bl., 7:733
Nagel, Ernest, 10:205, 608
Nagle, Edward J. *See* Nagle, Urban
Nagle, Nano Honoria, **10:133–134**,
  11:684, 13:183
Nagle, Urban, **10:134**
Nagot, Francis Charles, **10:134–135**
Nagy, Imre, 7:220, 222
Naḥmanides (Talmudist), 2:832, 5:509,
  10:135–136
Nahum, Book of, 10:*136*, **136–137**
Nails, Holy, **10:137**
Nairobi Archdiocese (Kenya), 8:150
Naitan (King of Scotland), 5:14
Naizen, John Onizuka, Bl., 7:734
Naizen, Louis, Bl., 7:734
Naizen, Monica, Bl., 7:734
Najran, Martyrs of, 5:399, **10:137–138**
Nakamura, Alexis, Bl., 7:732
Nakanishi, Leo, Bl., 7:732
Nakano, Dominic, Bl., 7:733
Nakano, Matthias, Bl., 7:732
Nakashima, Michael, Bl., 7:735
Nam, James, 14:496
Namatianus. *See* Rutilius Namatianus,
  Claudius
Name of God, 8:3
Names, Christian, **10:138–141**, *139–140*
Names, Medieval, **10:142–143**
Namibia, **10:143–144**
Namphano, 9:28
NAMRP. *See* National Apostolate with
  Mentally Retarded Persons
Nānak, Gurū, Sikhism, 13:118, *119*
Nanetti, Clelia, St., **10:144**
Nanni di Banco, 4:631
Nantes, Council of, 1:728
Nantes, Edict of (1598), 5:682, 849,
  7:167–168, **10:144–145**
  Amyraut, Moïse, 1:367
  Angers, 1:432
  Bossuet, Jacques Bénigne, 2:549–550
  Camisards, 2:916
  Chartres, 3:441
  Church-State relations, 3:639
  Clement VIII (Pope), 3:784
  clericalism, 3:802
  revocation of, 5:851, 7:168, 12:208
  strict interpretation, 8:803–804
  wars of religion, 3:612, 784
Napier, George, Bl. *See* Napper, George,
  Bl.
Naples (Italy), 5:872

Naples, University of (Italy), 5:926
NAPMR. *See* National Apostolate with
  People with Mental Retardation
Napoléon I (Napoléon Bonaparte)
  (Emperor of France), 5:975–976,
  10:*145*, **145–150**
  anointing, 1:478
  anticlericalism, 1:518
  Astros, Paul Thérèse David d', 1:813
  Barnabites, suppression of, 2:103
  Belgian Catholics, 2:218
  Bernier, Étienne Alexandre, 2:324
  Broglie, Maurice Jean de, 2:625
  Caprara, Giovanni Battista, 3:92
  Chateaubriand, François René de,
    3:448
  Cherubini, Luigi, 3:468
  Church history, 3:617–618
  Concordat of 1801, 4:61–63
  Concordat of Fontainebleau, 4:63–64
  La Congrégation, 4:113
  Consalvi, Ercole, 4:138
  Dalberg, Karl Theodor von, 4:499
  Fesch, Joseph (Card.), 5:699
  Illyrian Movement, 4:371
  Imperial Catechism, 3:236–237, 244
  Malta, 8:194, 9:82
  marriage to Marie Louise, 4:632
  papal state, relations with, 13:494,
    495–496
  Papal States, 8:503–504
  Pius VI (Pope), 11:377
  Pius VII (Pope), 10:148–149,
    11:379–381
  relations with Jews, 7:873
  religious restoration in France
    supported, 10:147–148
  Talleyrand-Périgord, Charles Maurice
    de, 13:740–741
  Vatican Archives transferred to Paris,
    14:399
  See also Concordat of 1801 (France)
Napoléon III (Emperor of France),
  1:532, 3:314, 802, 10:*150*, **150–151**
Napoleonic Code, 3:176
Napoleonic Ideas (Napoleon), 10:150
Napoleonic Wars, 6:640
Napper, George, Bl., 5:234, **10:151**
Narbonne, Council of (990), 3:518
Nardin, Ernestine, 6:682
Nardins. *See* Daughters of the Heart of
  Mary
Narrative analysis, 10:306–307
Narrative criticism, 6:794
Narrative of the Gunpowder Plot
  (Gerard), 6:158

"The Narrative Quality of Experience" (Crites), 10:152

Narrative theology, 8:862–863, **10:151–154**

Das Narrenschiff (Brant), 2:584

Narsai, 5:5, 8:314

Narses (Byzantine general), 7:920

Narses of Edessa, 5:83

Nary, Cornelius, **10:154**

Nascimbeni, Giuseppe, Bl., **10:154–155**

Nashotah Hall (Wisconsin), 5:297

Nasi, Judah ha-, 13:745–746

Al-Nāṣir (Caliph), 1:7

Nāṣir-al-Dīn, Shah, 2:3

Nasoraeans. *See* Mandaean religion

Nasser, Gamal Abdel, 5:118–119

Natalis, Alexander, 2:396

Natalis Solis Invicti (Roman festival), 10:173

Natalitiae noctis Responsoria (Lobo, D.), 8:741

Natchertanie Khristianskavo nravooutchenia (An Outline of Christian Moral Teaching) (Zatvornik), 14:911

Natchez Diocese (MS), 7:685–686

Natchitoches Diocese (LA), 10:292

Nathan (prophet), 4:536, 8:179, 9:541, **10:155**

Nathan Berating David (17th century), 10:*156*

Nathan of Gaza, 13:57

Nathanael, Apostle. *See* Bartholomew, Apostle, St.

"National Apostasy" sermon (Keble), 10:732

National Apostolate for Inclusion Ministry (NAfIM), **10:155–156**

National Apostolate with Mentally Retarded Persons (NAMRP), 10:155

National Apostolate with People with Mental Retardation (NAPMR), 10:155

National Assembly of Religious Brothers, 12:94

National Association of Catholic Diocesan Gay and Lesbian Ministries, 7:70

National Association of Evangelicals, 1:351, **10:156–157**

National Association of Pastoral Musicians (NPM), 8:676, 707, **10:157**

National Association of Religious Brothers, 12:94

National Association of Women Religous (NAWR), 8:422

National Baptist Convention. *See* National Baptist Convention, U.S.A., Inc.

National Baptist Convention, U.S.A., Inc., 2:80, 81

National Black Catholic Clergy Caucus, 1:161

National Black Catholic Seminarians' Association, 1:161

National Black Sisters' Conference (NBSC), 1:161, **10:157–158**

National Catholic Coalition for Responsible Investment (NCCRI), **10:158**

National Catholic Conference for Interracial Justice (NCCIJ), 8:277, **10:158–159**

National Catholic Congress, 7:431

National Catholic Council for Hispanic Ministry (NCCHM), 5:204–205

National Catholic Development Conference (NCDC), **10:159**

National Catholic Educational Association (NCEA), **10:159–161**, 342, 12:96–97

academic freedom, 1:53

Conaty, Thomas James, 4:49

Howard, Francis William, 7:142

Peterson, John Bertram, founding of, 11:211

Shehan, L. J., 13:76

sister formation, 13:170

National Catholic Office of Motion Pictures (NCOMP), 10:563

National Catholic Pharmacists Guild of the U.S., **10:161**

National Catholic Reporter (newspaper), 8:119, 14:60

National Catholic Rural Life Conference (NCRLC), 7:542, 8:273, 586, 12:739

National Catholic School of Social Service (NCSSS), 10:164, 12:27–28

National Catholic Stewardship Council (NCSC), 7:522–523

National Catholic Student Coalition (NCSC), **10:161**

National Catholic War Council, 6:240, 12:418

National Catholic Welfare Conference, 2:703, 3:178, 622, 10:56, 163, 410, 12:27, 243, 412, 418, 445, 14:310–312

American Federation of Catholic Societies, 1:352

founding of, 2:47, 8:388

Hanna, Edward J., first chairman, 12:649

Keough, F. P., 8:153–154

Krol, J. J., 8:250

National Federation of Sodalities of Our Lady, 13:294

papal authority for, 12:786

Shehan, L. J., 13:76

Siedenburg F., 13:104

National chaplain post, 10:344

National Christian Council (China), 3:501

National Conference for Community and Justice (NCCJ), **10:162**

National Conference of Catechetical Leadership (NCCL), **10:162–163**

National Conference of Catholic Bishops (NCCB) (United States), 5:67, 300, 14:309, 313–315

American Board of Catholic Missions, 1:350

American College at Louvain, 8:822

Anglican-Catholic dialogue, 1:439

archives, 1:639

Bernardin, Joseph Louis, 2:319

Call to Action Conference, 2:874–876

capital punishment, 3:88–89

catechisms, 3:236, 238

The Challenge of Peace, 3:480

clerical dress, 3:802

Encuentros, 5:204

environment and art, 12:503

homily, 7:63–64

homosexuality, 7:69–70

lectionary for masses with children, 8:442

penitential discipline, 5:635

Priestly Life and Ministry Committee, History Subcommittee, 5:171

The Program of Priestly Formation (PPF), 12:898

Ratio fundamentalis, 12:898

Secretariat of African American Catholics, 1:161

vernacular lectionary, 8:439

National Conference of Catholic Bishops (NCCB)/United States Catholic Conference (USCC) (1966-2001), 14:313–315

National Conference of Catholic Charities, 8:156, 12:594, 13:59

National Conference of Christians and Jews (NCCJ), 8:250, 12:386, 13:76

National Conference of Diocesan Directors of Religious Education (NCDD), 10:162

The National Conversation of Race, Ethnicity, and Culture (NCCJ), 10:162

National Council for Catholic Evangelization, 4:242

National Council of Catholic Laity (NCCL), 10:163

National Council of Catholic Men (NCCM), **10:163–164**, 14:312

National Council of Catholic Women (NCCW), **10:164**, 12:27, 14:312

National Council of the Churches of Christ in the U.S.A. (NCCC-USA), 1:351, 8:887, 10:157, **165–166**, 13:242

National Councils of Catholic Men and Women (United States), 3:277

National Directory for the Formation, Ministry, and Life of Permanent Deacons in the United States, 4:553–554

National Episcopal Commission for Social Affairs (Canada), 3:9

National Evangelical Christian Fellowship (NECF), 9:72

National Free Church Council, 5:928

National Incentive Congress on Evangelization (Japan), 7:742

National Interracial Conference (Washington, 1920), 12:27

National League for the Protection of American Interests (N.L.P.A.I.), 10:323

National Legion of Decency, 8:779

National Lutheran Commission for Soldiers' and Sailors' Welfare, 8:887

National Lutheran Council, 8:887

National Newman Alumni Association, 10:344

National Newman Association of Faculty and Staff, 10:345

National Newman Chaplains Association, 10:344

National Newman Club Federation, 8:153

National Newman Foundation, 10:344–345

National Office of Black Catholics, 1:161

National Organization for Continuing Education of Roman Catholic Clergy (NOCERCC), **10:166–167**

National Pastoral Consultation on Church Renewal (Philippines), 11:263–264

National Pastoral Plan for Hispanic Ministry (NPPHM), 5:204

National Pastoral Planning Conference, 4:75

National Religious Retirement Office (NRRO), 8:424

National Shrine of the Immaculate Conception (Washington, DC), 3:716, 10:*167*, **167–168**

blessing the congregation, 13:*91*

construction, 13:59

Our Mother of Africa Chapel, 8:196

patroness of U.S., 13:94

National Socialist Party (Germany). *See* Nazism

National Society for the Education of the Poor in the Principles of the Established Church, 1:446

National Spiritual Alliance, 13:437

National Spiritualist Association, 13:437

National Sunday School Association, 5:473

National Temperance Society, 13:800–801

National Union for Social Justice, 4:294

National Union of Catholic Young Men's Societies, 8:798

National Union Theological Seminary (Nanjing, China), 3:503

National Women's Temperance Union, 13:801

Nationalism, 13:481

Aristotelianism, 1:678

civil religion, 3:756

Croatia, 4:371–372

Czech music, 13:230–231

educational theory, 5:91–92

Ghibelline-Guelf conflict, 3:855–856

Hungary, 7:214, 216–217

Hus, 4:170–171

Hus, John, 7:228

Ireland, 4:375, 424

Hughes, John Joseph and, 7:161

MacHale, John, 9:17

Kulturkampf, 8:253–254

Macedonia, 9:15

Milwaukee (WI), 9:647

Minnesota, 9:656–657

population increase, 4:222

Protestant Reformation, 3:637

Slavophilism, 13:216

Slovakia, 13:221–222

Slovene, 13:225–226

Western Sahara, 14:691

See also Americanism; Americanization Movement

Nationalism and Religion in America (Humphrey), 5:960

Nationalization, 13:568

Nation-states, 13:481

Native American Democratic Association (Morse), 10:313

Native American Party, 10:170

Native American theology, 9:574

Native Australians, 1:907

Native North Americans. *See* Mission in colonial America, English; Mission in colonial America, French; Mission in colonial America, Spanish; *specific countries*; *specific native peoples*

Native South Americans. *See* Mission in colonial America, Portuguese; Mission in colonial America, Spanish; *specific countries*; *specific native peoples*

Native traditions, use in liturgy. *See* Inculturation

Nativism (United States), 3:653, **10:168–173**

apostolic delegation in the United States, 1:582

Blaine Amendment, 2:426

Blanc, Anthony, 2:430

church architecture, 3:715

Connecticut, 4:122–123

Iowa, 7:542

Know-Nothingism, 8:199–200

Ku Klux Klan, 8:251

Milwaukee (WI), 9:646

New Hampshire, 2:576

North Carolina, 10:437

Pennsylvania, 11:84

See also Know-Nothingism

The Nativity (lectionary), 8:*858*

Nativity of Christ, 8:856, 858, **10:173**

The Nativity of Jesus Christ (Angelico), 10:*174*

Nativity of Mary, 9:157, **10:175–176**

Nativity scene, 4:364

"Nativity Schools," 7:795

Natorp, Paul, 5:388, 10:237

Natura naturans, 12:751–752

Natura naturata, 12:751–752

Natural family planning (NFP), 4:218, 222, 7:180–181, **10:176–179**

Natural History (Pliny the Elder), 12:308

Natural law, **10:179–196**

Burke, Edmund, 2:702

Catholic social thought, 13:247

Christian faith, alteration of, 9:866

communication, 4:24

contemporary theology and philosophy, 10:191–195

definition of, 10:179

Durandus of Saint-Pourçain, 4:948

existential ethics, 5:537
Grotius, Hugo, 6:540
history of, 10:179–186
Hooker, Richard, 7:91–92
Hostiensis, 7:135
human act, 7:171
McCormick, Richard A., 9:394–395
miracles beyond power of, 9:668, 669
Sabbath, 12:458–459
society, 13:276
sovereignty, 13:372
in the state, 13:483
syndersis, 13:681
Thomistic anlaysis of, 10:186–191
Natural Law: A Theological Investigation (Fuchs), 6:18
Natural law and jurisprudence, **10:196–200**
Divine positive law compared, 8:395–396
human law, 8:390, 557
inalienable human rights, 10:199–200
Leo XIII (Pope) on, 8:557
Liberatore, M., 8:550
morality, 10:196–198
sanction, 12:660
sexual appetites, 8:872
truth and being, 8:398–399
Natural Law and Practical Reason (Rhonheimer), 10:186
Natural law in political thought, 4:640, 642, 644, 8:64, **10:201–203**, 13:240
Natural mysteries, 10:84
Natural necessity, 10:226
Natural order, 4:694–695, **10:203–204**
Natural philosophy. *See* Cosmology; Nature, philosophy of
Natural religion, 12:273
Natural Rights (Ritchie), 10:194
Natural science, 14:804
Natural secrets, 12:859
Natural selection, 4:532
See also Evolution
Natural signs, 13:116
Natural Symbols (Douglas), 12:87, 259
Natural theology, 11:459, 12:72, **13:921–923**
See also Philosophical theology; Theodicy
Natural Theology (Paley), 10:803, 12:768
A Natural Theology for Our Time (Hartshorne), 6:658
Natural time, 14:79–80
Natural virtures, 14:551–552

Naturaleza, policía sagrada y profana, costumbres, ritos y supersticiones de todos los Etíopes (Sandoval), 3:770
Naturalism, **10:204–207**
activism, 1:84
Alexander, Samuel, 1:252
anthropocentrism, 1:508
Aristotelianism, 1:677
art of Ancient Egypt, 5:132
characteristics of, 10:205–207
critique of, 10:207
destiny, supernatural, 4:694
history of, 10:204–205
idealism vs., 7:302
immanence, 7:340
moral goodness, 6:351
Neo-Kantianism, 3:209–210
Rousseau's philosophy of, 5:91, 93
Naturalism (Pratt), 10:204
Naturalist School, 8:220
Naturalization Act (1798), 10:169
Nature
appetite, 1:600
Aristotle, 1:682
art, 1:746
Boethius, 1:673
causality, 3:298, 302
Christian anthropology, 3:532
Christian philosophy, 3:538, 541
cogitative power, 3:822
Council of Chalcedon, 10:967
demons of, 4:497
Duns Scotus, John, 4:939
emanationism and the four stages of, 5:181
eschatological interpretation, 5:55–57
with female subordination, 5:48
final causality, 5:725–726
five different possible states of, 10:213
grace, 6:394–395, 411–413
identified with the Absolute, 14:146
John Scotus Eriugena, 7:1011
laws, 8:399
Leonardo da Vinci, 5:197
Mistress of Nature, 5:2
natural causes, 5:99
normality, 10:425
original sin and corruption of, 10:195, 201
as principle of motion and rest, 10:19
sacramentality of, 5:49–50, 54
state of, 13:482–483
subsistence, 13:570
substance vs., 13:575

and the supernatural, 13:618, 619–620
theology of, 5:52
Thoreau on literary use, 14:147–148
William of Ockham, 14:747–748
Nature (Emerson), 5:188, 14:147, 148
Nature (Medwall), 9:881
Nature, in philosophy, **10:208–211**, 11:278–279
Aristotelian analysis of, 10:209–210
concept of time, 14:80
courtly love, 4:321–322
demonstration, 4:653
first cause of motion, 10:23
Greek development of, 10:208–209
theory of motion, 10:19
See also Philosophy
Nature, in theology, **10:211–213**
Nature, philosophy of, 6:706, 752, **11:301–307**, 14:80
See also Cosmology
Nature and Historical Experience (Randall), 10:205
Nature and Mind (Woodbridge), 10:204
The Nature of Destiny of Man, 2 v. (Niebuhr), 10:387
The Nature of True Virtue (Edwards), 5:98
Nature worship, 13:86
Nature's Divine Revelations (Davis), 13:437
Nauclerus, John, **10:214**, 14:233
NAU-OLC. *See* North American Union Sisters of Our Lady of Charity
Nausea (Sartre), 12:697
Nausea, Friedrich (Bp.), 3:242, 609, **10:214**
Nausea, Grau (Bp.). *See* Nausea, Friedrich (Bp.)
Nausiphanes, 5:285
Naval Girbes, Josefa, Bl., **10:214**
Naval weaponry, 8:504, 506
Navarete, Alonso, Bl., 7:732
Navarre, Henry de. *See* Henry IV (King of France)
Navarre, University of (Spain), **10:215**
Navarrete, Domingo Fernández, **10:215**
Navarro, Pedro Paul, Bl., 7:734
Navarro Miguel, Carlo, Bl., **10:216**, 816
Navarro Miguel, Charles, Bl. *See* Navarro Miguel, Carlo, Bl.
NAWR. *See* National Association of Women Religious
Naya, Florentí Felipe, Bl., **10:216**
Nayarit Jesuit Mission (Mexico), 9:710
Nayler, James, 5:838

Nazarenes, **10:216**

Nazareth, **10:216–217**

archeological sites in, 10:798

biblical archaeology, 2:380

as Mary's birthplace, 10:175–176

photograph of Church of Annunciation, 10:*778*

Statue of Holy Family (Church of Saint Joseph), 10:*217*

Nazareth (NC) project, 11:688

Nazaría Ignacia of Santa Teresa of Jesús. *See* March Mesa, Nazaría Ignacia, Bl.

Nazarius, J. P., 1:78

Nazarius of Lérins, St., **10:217**

Nazirites, **10:217–218**, 12:635

Nazism, 2:883, 3:619

Altaner, Berthold, 1:313

Apor, Vilmos, Bl., 1:569

Austria, 1:915, 916, 917

Bracco, Teresa, Bl., 2:575

Brandsma, Titus, Bl., 2:583

Bultmann, Rudolf Karl, 2:690

Center Party, 3:342

church architecture, 3:711–712

Church-State relations, 3:642

community vs. individuality, 4:38

confessions of faith, 4:81

criticism from U.S., 8:614

Czechoslovakia, 4:485

Czechs, 4:485

Denmark, 4:667

Dibelius, Otto, 4:734

France, 4:514

Galen, Clemens, opposition to, 6:57

Gapp, Jakob, opposition to, 6:90–91

German Church, 6:185–186

Holy Family Missionaries under, 7:24

Hungary, 7:219

Jesuit activity against, 7:792

Kaas, L., 8:107

Lambach Abbey, 8:303

Latvia, 8:375

Lithuania, 8:607

Lutheranism, 8:892

martyrs and martyrdom

Kolbe, M., 8:229

Kozal, M., 8:245

Leisner, K. F., 8:459

Mayer, Rupert, spoke out against, 9:382

Pius XI (Pope), 11:394–395

political prisoners, 13:407

Slovakia, 13:222

See also Holocaust; Holocaust (Shoah)

NCCB. *See* National Conference of Catholic Bishops

NCCIJ. *See* National Catholic Conference for Interracial Justice

NCRLC. *See* National Catholic Rural Life Conference

Ndayen, Joachim (Abp. of Bangui), 3:344

Ne Romani electione (apostolic constitution, Clement V), 3:106

Ne super his (papal bull, John XXII), 2:276

Ne Temere (papal decree, Pius X), 3:54, **10:218–219**

Nea Ecclesia Church (Constantinople), 3:687

Neale, Benedict, 2:36, 460

Neale, Charles, 3:181

Neale, Edward, 2:460

Neale, J. E., 3:266, 267

Neale, John Mason, 3:151, 259, 675, 7:257

Neale, Leonard (Abp. of Baltimore), 2:38–39, 460, 3:180, 6:66, 147, **10:219**

Neamtu Abbey (Romania), **10:219**

Neander, J. A. W., 7:848, 12:726

Neander, William, 1:845

Near East, ancient

Byzantine civilization, 2:772

law, 2:527, 3:84

love poems, 13:319

religions, 1:624

Son of God, 13:311

sons of God, 13:321

wisdom literature, 1:190–191

Near-death experiences, 13:853–854

Nebo, **10:220**

Nebraska, **10:220–224**, 463

See also specific dioceses and archdioceses

Nebraska, Meyer v. (1923), 10:647–648

Nebreda, Alfonso, 5:3

Nebridius, 1:852, 856–857, 858, 3:406

Nebrija, Antonio de, 1:236, 12:119

Nebuchadnezzar (King of Babylon), 3:369, **10:224–225**

concept of mystery and dream, 10:79

Daniel, 4:508–509, 511, 512

deportations, 4:674

invasion of Palestine, 7:642, 643

Judith, Book of, 8:43–44

Nec insolitum (papal bull, Alexander IV), 14:16

Necessity, 3:354, 4:212, 231, 10:225–227, **225–228**

Necessity of means, 10:228

Necessity of precept, 10:228

Necker, Jacques, 5:210

Neckham, Alexander, 5:206

Necrology, **10:228–229**, 229

Necromancy, **10:229–230**, 619

Nectarius (Bp. of Autun), 1:926

Nectarius (Bp. of Constantinople), 4:190, 7:946

Nederlandse Hervormde Kerk (NHK), 10:263–264

Neefe, Christian Gottlob, 2:201

Neemtallah El Hardini, Bl., 13:69

Neercassel, Joannes Van (Bp. of Castoria), **10:230**

Neerlandia franciscana (periodical), 14:261

Negation, knowing God as, 6:318

Negative infidels, 7:455

Negative propositions, 11:769

Negative theology, 7:1011

"Negro Plot" (New York, 1741), 10:311

Nehemiah (Hebrew leader), 7:644, 766, 10:230–231

Nehemiah, Book of, 3:567–568, **10:231**

apocalyptic style, 1:546

biblical canon, 3:24

censuses in, 3:338

God's spirit, 13:426

inheritance, 7:464

justice of men, 8:73

slavery, 13:206

temple liturgy, 8:434

See also Biblical Chronicler

Neher, Peter, 1:730

Neighborhood churches. *See* Basic Christian communities

Neill, Charles P., 3:280

Neill, Stephen Charles, **10:231**

Nelis, C. F. (Bp. of Antwerp), 1:539

Nell-Breuning, Oswald von, 7:792

Neller, G. C., 5:658

Nellessen, Leonhard, 1:2

Nelson, John, Bl., 5:227, **10:231–232**

Nelson, Leonard, 10:236

Nelson, Richard K., 1:459

Nelson, Smith v. (1846), 3:658

Nelson v. Benson (1873), 3:657

Nemania, Stephen (Serbian prince), 2:458

Nemesius (Bp. of Emesa), 1:670, 7:349, **10:232**, 11:290, 13:341–342

Nemo dat quod non habet (No one gives what he does not have), 12:756

Nemore, Jordanus de, 12:813

Nengapete, Marie-Clémentine Anuarite, Bl., **10:233**

Neno, Pacifico, 1:890

Neo-Assyrian empire, 9:530–531

Neo-Babylonian period, 9:529–530

Neocaesarea (bishoprics), **10:233**

Neocaesarea (Bithynia), 10:233

Neocaesarea (Northern Syria), 10:233

Neocaesarea (Pontus Polemoniacus), 10:233

Neocaesarea, Council of (314-325), 1:150, 3:38, 4:50

Neocatechumenal Way, **10:233–234**

Neo-Chalcedonianism, 4:192

Neoclassical architecture, 3:707, 708

Neo-Confucianism. *See* Confucianism and Neo-Confucianism

Neo-Friesian School, 10:236

Neo-Guelfism, 5:695, **10:234–235**

Neo-Hegelianism, 9:752

Neoidealism, 6:885

Neo-Kantianism, **10:235–238**
  Bauch, Bruno, 2:157–158
  Cassirer, Ernst, 3:209–210
  knowledge, theories of, 8:219, 220
  life philosophies, 8:578
  Lipsius, R., 8:597
  metaphysics, 8:127
  natural right doctrine of, 10:185
  See also Marburg School

Neo-Lutheranism, 8:891

Neon (martyr), 3:770

Neo-Orthodoxy, 2:120–121, 6:889–890, 8:528–529, **10:238–239**

Neo-Pentecostalism, 6:249, 11:106, 107

Neophyte, **10:239**

Neoplatonism, 6:442, 450, **10:240–242**, 11:289
  afterlife, 1:168
  Albert the Great, St., 1:226
  Alfarabi, 1:276–277
  allegory, 1:292
  Ambrose, St., 1:337
  Anselm of Canterbury, St., 1:496
  Arabian philosophy, 1:621, 935
  Aristotelianism, 1:670, 671, 673, 674
  art, 1:743
  Augustine, St., 9:97
  Augustinianism, 1:878
  Avicebron, 1:938–939
  Byzantine theology, 2:758–759, 794, 807

cabala, 2:832, 833
  Calcidius, 2:858–859
  Carolingian Renaissance, 3:161
  causality, 3:298, 303–304
  chastity, 3:444
  Christian philosophy, 3:539
  Christology, 3:560
  church architecture, 3:694, 703
  Claudianus, Mamertus, 3:769
  Colet, John, 3:832
  conservation, Divine, 4:160
  educational philosophy, 5:90
  emanationism, 5:180–181
  final causality, 5:724
  Greek philosophy, 13:919
  homoousios, 4:197
  Iamblichus, 7:269
  idea, 7:293
  idealism, 7:297
  identity principle, 7:303
  immortality, 7:348
  infinity, 7:457
  influence on Eckhart, 5:45
  Jewish philosophy, 7:863–864
  John Climacus, St., 2:826
  John of the Cross, St., 3:136
  Liber de Causis, 8:532–534
  man, natural end of, 9:99
  metaphysics of lights, 7:319
  Nicholas of Cusa, 3:604
  notions of light, 8:583
  pantheism of, 10:825
  participation, 10:906–907
  Plotinus, 5:47, 12:1
  Rhenish spirituality, 13:453
  School of Alexandria, 1:268, 2:820
  schools of Athens, 1:829
  soul, 13:339
  soul origins, 13:355
  transmigration of souls, 14:157
  world soul, 7:239, 14:843
  See also Platonism

Neopositivism, 8:220–221, 11:316, 13:348

Neo-Pythagoreanism, 1:168, 6:449–450, 8:170, **10:242–243**, 11:846, 13:52

Neorealism, 4:52, 8:220

Neos Paradeisos (Moschus), 10:6

Neoscholasticism and Neothomism, 4:676, 5:397, 7:182, **10:244**
  Aristotelianism, 1:678–679
  dogmatic theology, 4:813
  Germany, 6:184
  humanism, 7:182

justification, 8:88–89
  Kantianism, 8:127–128
  Leo XIII (Pope), 3:624
  Lépicier, A., 8:507
  Lepidi, A., 8:507
  scientific method, 12:748–749
  theology of Christ, 7:821

Neostoicism, 12:903

Neot, St., **10:244**

Neothomism. *See* Neoscholasticism and Neothomism

Nepal, **10:245–246**, *246*

Nepos (Bp. of Arsinoë), **10:246–247**

Nepotism, **10:247**, 843
  Avignon papacy, 5:846
  Boniface VIII (Pope), 2:502
  Callistus III (Pope), 2:881, 3:91
  Capranica, Domenico, 3:91
  Clement V, 3:780
  Counter Reformation, 3:612
  Innocent XII (Pope), 7:482
  Leo X (Pope), 8:487
  Paul III (Pope), 3:609
  Pius IV (Pope), 11:372
  Sixtus IV (Pope), 12:118

Neraz, John Claude, 12:641

Neresheim Abbey (Germany), **10:247**

Neri, Philip, St., 10:*248*, **248–249**
  Ambrosians, 1:346
  Baronius, Caesar, 2:105, 106
  Borromeo, Federigo, 2:541
  Cacciaguerra, Bonsignore, 2:840
  catechesis, 2:714
  Chiesa Nuova, 2:110
  church architecture, 3:703
  Clement VIII (Pope), 3:784
  Felix of Catalice, 5:669
  spiritual direction, 4:762
  works of charity, 3:418

Nerinckx, Charles, 8:786, **10:249**

Nero (Roman Emperor), 1:752, 3:591, 592, 10:*250*, 250, 12:304, 310
  See also Roman persecution era

Néron, Pierre-François, 14:496–497

Nerses, **10:250–251**

Nerses II (Armenian Catholicos), 1:700, 10:251

Nerses III (Armenian Catholicos), 4:957, 10:251

Nersēs IV of Glayec'i. *See* Nerses Gratiosus (Armenian Catholicos)

Nerses Bedros XIX (Armenian Patriarch), 1:704

Nerses Gratiosus (Armenian Catholicos), 1:701, 709, **10:251**

Nersēs Lampronac'i, 1:709

Nerses of Kla. *See* Nerses Gratiosus (Armenian Catholicos)

Nerses of Lambron, St., 10:251

Nerses Šnorhall. *See* Nerses Gratiosus (Armenian Catholicos)

Nerses the Great, St. (Armenian Catholicos), 1:699, 10:250–251

Nerva, Marcus Cocceius (Roman Emperor), 12:304

Neslon, John, Bl., 10:231–232

Nesmond, François de (Bp. of Bayeux), 2:163

Nestle, Eberhard, 2:367

Nestorian heresy
  communication of idioms, 4:26
  Constantinople, 4:185
  Constantinople Council II, 4:191–192
  Cyprian, St., 4:459
  Cyril of Alexandria, 4:465–469
  Diodore of Tarsus, 4:750
  Dionysius, Exiguus, 4:754
  Ephesus Council, 4:195

Nestorianism, 3:561, **10:252–254**
  Alexandria, 1:268–269, 523
  al-Kindī's apology, 8:169–170
  Anathemas of Cyril, 1:390–391
  Antioch, 1:523
  Armenian Church, 1:700, 4:957–958
  assumptus homo theology, 1:802
  Assyrian Church of the East, 1:805–806
  Cassian, John, 3:206
  Christmas, 3:554
  Christology, 3:559
  Clement XIV (Pope), 3:796
  East Syrian liturgy, 5:3, 4
  Eastern Schism, 5:22
  Edessa, 5:82, 83
  hypostasis, 7:264
  influence on Persian Church, 2:4
  Justinian I (Byzantine Emperor), 2:820, 3:596
  Leo I (Pope), St., 8:474
  Marius Mercator, 9:181
  Mary's Divine motherhood, 10:13
  Robber Council of Ephesus, 1:392, 3:363
  School of Alexandria, 1:269
  School of Antioch, 1:527
  See also Ephesus, Council of (431)

Nestorius (Patriarch of Constantinople), 3:561, 5:5, **10:254**
  Acacian Schism, 1:49, 50
  adoptionism, 1:119

Celestine I (Pope), St., 3:317

Christotokos, Mary as, 9:815

condemnation of, 4:181, 195, 352

consubstantiality, 7:66

Council of Chalcedon, 3:365

Council of Ephesus condemnation, 5:273–275

Council of Orléans, 1:895

Cyril of Alexandria, 1:390–391, 2:793

denial of Mary's Divine motherhood, 10:14

disciple of Theodore of Mopsuestia, 10:14

Eusebius of Doryleum, 5:462

Hormisdas (Pope), St., 3:595

John of Antioch, 7:963

Julian of Eclanum, 8:48

Pelagianism, 3:317

primacy of Constantinople, 3:595

School of Antioch, 1:524, 527

teachings of, 10:252–253

Theodore of Mopsuestia, 1:523

two natures of Christ, 7:816

works of, 10:254

See also Nestorianism

Netherlands, **10:254–263**
  Calvinism, 2:893–894, 895
  Cartesianism, 3:184
  catechism, 3:245
  colonialism
    Caribbean, 3:110–111, 116–117
    Malaysia, 9:70
    Suriname, 13:627–628
  ecclesiastical organization, 10:255
  Gorkum martyrs, 6:364
  Jewish refugees in (1492-1650), 7:871–872
  Lutheranism, 12:18–19
  map, 10:*256*
  music, 8:689
  Presbyterianism, 11:679
  Reformed churches, 12:23
  Remonstrants, 12:109
  wars of religion, 3:612

Netherlands Reformed Church, **10:263–264**, 12:23

Netsch, Walter, 3:716–717

Netschayev, Sergei, 1:384

Netsvetov, Jacob, 10:682

Netter, Thomas, 3:141, **10:264**

Netterville, Robert, 7:581

Nettesheim, Agrippa von, 11:851

Neubauer, Ignaz (d. 1795), 14:776

Neue Leipziger Zeitschrift für Musik, 12:789

Die neue Zeit und der alte Glaube (Schell), 12:732

Neues Testament und Mythologie (Bultmann), 5:522

Neuf Leçons (Maritain), 9:100

Neufchâteau, François, 4:587

Neufmarché, Council of (1160), 1:254

Neufville, Jean, 2:263

Neuhof experiment, 11:171

Neumann, Asam, 3:707

Neumann, B., 3:671, 675, 10:247

Neumann, J. B., 3:707

Neumann, John Nepomucene (Bp. of Philadelphia), St., 5:835, 888, 890, **10:265**, 11:84–85, 239
  Leopoldine Society, 8:504
  School Sisters of Notre Dame, 12:781

Neumann, Theresa, **10:265–267**, *266*

Neumeister, Erdmann, 8:691

Neuner and Dupuis handbook, 4:671

Neunheuser, B., 10:98

Neururer, Otto, Bl., **10:267**, *268*

Neuter (Fulcoius of Beauvais), 6:21

Nevada, 6:66, **10:267–272**
  See also specific dioceses and archdioceses

Nève, Theodore (Abbot), 12:533

Nevill, Francis, Ven., 5:236, 10:728

Neville, George A., 13:87–88

Nevin, John Williamson, **10:272**, 12:726

New Abbey (Scotland), **10:272**, *273*

New Advent Theological Institute, 4:670

New Age Movement, **10:272–275**

New Alliance, 10:519

New American Bible (NAB), 1:190, 4:437, 8:439, **10:275–277**, 13:200

New Apostolic Church, 1:135, 3:278, **10:277–278**

The New Atlantis (Bacon), 1:667, 14:360

New Britain, 10:532

New Caledonia, 10:532

New Catholic Dictionary (1929), 10:806

New Catholic Encyclopedia (1967), 5:207, 208, 10:521, 524, 13:412, 14:70

New Connection General Baptists, 2:79

The New Creation in Christ (Griffiths), 6:530

New Criticism, 1:143

The New Demons (Ellul), 5:172

The New Dictionary of Catholic Social Thought, 5:208

The New Dictionary of Catholic Spirituality, 5:208

The New Dictionary of Sacramental Worship, 5:208

The New Dictionary of Theology, 5:208

New Economic Policy (NEP, Lenin), 8:468

The New Encounter between Christians and Jews (Oesterreicher), 10:559

New England Fellowship, 10:157

New England Psalm Book, 2:162

New England way, 4:115

New evangelization, **5:477–480**

New Eve, 1:799–800

New France, 8:279, 339–340, 382–383, 13:129

New Granada. *See* Colombia

New Hampshire, **10:278–281**

   Church-State relations, 3:647–648, 6451

   nativism, 2:576

   Toleration Acts (1819), 3:651

   See also specific dioceses and archdioceses

New Hampshire Confession, 4:82

New Haven theology, **10:280**

New History (Zosimus), 12:319

New History of the World (Nary), 10:154

New Ireland, 10:533

New Jersey, 2:79, 3:648, 651, **10:281–283**

   See also specific dioceses and archdioceses

New Jersey Sisters of Charity, 9:470

New Jerusalem Church (Swedenborgian Church), 10:283

New Laws of the Indies, 8:340

New Life of Grace (Fransen), 5:918

New Light Congregationalists. *See* Separate Congregationalists

New/Living City (periodical), 5:786

New Mexico, 3:489, 8:315–316, 9:716, **10:284–289**, 12:462, 674

   See also specific dioceses and archdioceses

The New Morality (Lunn), 8:868

New Natural-Law Theory, 10:185–186

New Norcia Abbey (Australia), **10:289**

New Notes (NOCERCC newsletter), 10:167

New Order (Movement), 4:514

New Orleans Archdiocese (LA), **10:290–298**

   archives, 1:640

   diocesan archives, 1:640

Dominicans, 4:840

ecclesiastical organization, 8:814

expansion of Church, 8:811

Lafayette Diocese, 8:278

Rummel, Joseph Francis, 12:411–412

Shrove Tuesday, 13:98

Sisters of the Most Holy Sacrament, 13:190

sodality, 13:294

"New Poems" (Thompson), 14:58

A New Quest of the Historical Jesus (Robinson), 5:522

New Religious Movements (NRMs), **10:298–302**, 300–301, 301–302

New Revised Standard Version, 10:277

New Sacristy of S. Lorenzo (Florence), 9:*435*

New Scholasticism (periodical), 10:740, 12:444, 777

"New School" (New Haven theology), 10:280

New Spain. *See* Mexico

New Testament Abstracts, 8:168

New Testament Books, **10:302–303**

   Abba (term) in, 1:5–6

   abiding in Christ, 1:21–22

   abortion, 1:26

   account of Transfiguration in, 14:153–154

   Adam in, 1:104–105

   adoption in, 1:118

   adultery in, 1:133

   aeons in, 1:139–140

   afterlife in, 1:164, 165

   agape in, 1:169–170

   Alma prophecy, 1:297

   altars in, 1:319, 320

   Amen in, 1:348

   Andrew, Apostle, St. in, 1:402–403

   angels in, 1:417–418, 423, 427

   anger in, 1:430–431

   Antichrist in, 1:513, 515–516

   apocalyptic style, 1:546–547

   apocrypha, 1:558

   apologetics in, 1:563

   Apostolic Tradition in, 10:337–338

   Ascension of Jesus Christ in, 1:768–770

   asceticism, 1:776–777

   atonement in, 1:837

   authorship, 1:488

   avarice in, 1:928

   Balaam, as symbol of false teachers, 2:26

   based on apostolic tradition, 7:802

beatific vision, 2:170–172

in the bible, 12:189–190

biblical inspiration, 7:493

binding and loosing, 2:398

bishops, 2:410–411

blasphemy in, 2:434–435

blessings in, 2:438–439

book of life in, 2:526

brother in Christ in, 2:627

Bultmann, Rudolf Karl, 2:690–691

Canon Law, 3:37

canonicity, 3:30–33

casuistry, 3:220

catechesis, 3:227–228

censuses in, 3:338–339

centurions in, 3:348

Cerfaux, Lucien, 3:350

charisms in, 3:389–390

chastity in, 3:444

cherubim in, 3:467

chief priests in, 3:482

Christ (term), 3:527

Christian (term) in, 3:528–529, 530

Christocentrism, 3:557–558

Christology, 3:559

Church in, 3:575, 578–580, 581–583, 629

civil authority in, 1:921

Cleopas, 3:801

clerical celibacy/marriage, 3:322

communion of saints, 4:34–35

concept of time in, 14:84

confessors in, 4:83

Confirmation, 4:85

Confraternity revisions of, 10:275–276

conscience in, 4:141, 142, 143–145, 146

conscientious objection, 4:149

contemplation, 4:205

contraception in, 4:218, 220

conversion in, 4:231–232, 233–234, 239, 240

corban in, 4:257

covenant in, generally, 4:327–328

creation, 4:342, 344

creedal statements, 4:349–350

crucifixion in, 4:390–391, 398

curses in, 4:443

Cyril, 4:467

Davidic descent of Christ, 10:176

Day of the Lord in, 4:548–549

Dead Sea Scrolls, 4:563–564

death in, 4:570, 571

New Testament Books *(continued)*

death of God theology, 4:584

demonology in, 4:646, 649, 716–718

deposit of faith in, 4:675

descent of Christ into hell, 4:683–684

destiny, supernatural in, 4:693–694

devil as term in, 4:704

dietary laws, 4:743

digamy, 4:744–745

discernment, spiritual, 4:765, 766

disciple as term, 4:767–774

Divine truth, 14:231

dogma as term, 4:810

doxology, 4:89–90

drunkenness, 4:911

eschatology, 5:338–341, 349–350

eucharist, 5:410–411

evangelical counsels in, 4:306–307

events at Nazareth, 10:216–217

excommunication, 5:505

expiation, 5:564

faith in the, 5:591–593

form criticism, 5:806–814

formation of, 3:29–30

Gentiles, 6:139, 140

glory, 6:244–245

gluttony, 6:251

gnostic influence, 6:254

God in revelation, 6:276–280

God the Father, 6:291–292

Greco-Oriental mystery religions, 10:96–97

Greek language, 6:438

guilt, 6:571–572

hell, 6:723–724

historians on acuracy, 7:803–804

holiness in, 7:3–4, 8, 9, 10

Holy Orders in, 7:35–36

Holy Trinity in the, 14:202

homosexuality, 7:66

hope, 7:93–102, 103

hope of salvation, 7:106–107

hospitality, 7:118

human sexuality, 13:48–49

humility in, 7:205, 206

hypostasis, 7:264

idolatry, 7:305–306, 323

images, veneration of, 7:324–325

immortality, 7:352

impassibility of God, 7:360

impeccability, 7:360, 361

imposition of hands, 7:365–366

incense use, 7:376

incest, 7:378

information on birth of Christ, 10:173

inheritance, 7:465

I-Thou mysticism in, 10:118

Jesus, priesthood of, 11:691–992

Jesus as sacrificial lamb, 10:936–937

Jewish frame of reference for, 7:802–803

justice of God, 8:70–71

justice of men, 8:74

kerygma, 8:157

leprosy references, 8:510

life, concept of, in the Bible, 8:569–571

light, use of, 8:581

literary myth found in, 10:123, 124

man, 9:85, 87

marriage in, 1:150

martyrdom, 9:227

Mary, Blessed Virgin, 9:238–247, 247–248

devotion to, 9:266

merit, 9:510–511

messianism, 9:545–547

ministries, 9:652

miracles, 9:662, 663–664

moral obligation in the, 10:519

Mount of Olives in, 10:33

Muratorian Canon as oldest canon of, 10:64

mystery in the, 10:81–82

mystical body of Christ, 10:100–101

myth, 4:656–658

names for Palestine used in, 10:778

Nazirites, 10:218

nudity in the, 10:473

oaths in the, 10:498

obedience in, 10:504–505

oils used in, 7:34

omniscience, 10:594

original sin in, 10:664

pacifism, 10:745

papacy foundations in the, 10:829–830

papyri fragments of, 10:864

parables of Jesus in, 10:865–872

Paradise in the, 10:875

Parousia in the, 10:894–899

Passion, 10:920–924

patience, 10:943–944

peace, 11:49–50

Pharisees, 11:226

poverty, 11:568

prayer, 11:592–593

presbyters, 11:672–673

prophecy, 11:759

prophetesses, 11:765

providence of God, 11:780–781

purgatory in, 11:825

quotations from the Old Testament, 5:507

rabbis, 11:882

read in the liturgy, 11:124

rebirth, 11:951–952

reference to Old Testament in, 1:272, 292, 3:26, 28–29

repentance in, 4:225

Resurrection of Christ, 12:145, 147–157

Resurrection of the Dead, 12:170–172

retribution, 12:178–179

sacred space, 12:502–503

Sadducees, 12:523–524

salvation history, 12:628

Samaritans, 12:634

sin, 13:145–146, 146–148

spirit, 13:425

suffering of Christ, 13:587

Suffering Servant, Songs of the, 13:591–592

Sukkot in, 2:532

symbolic numbers used in, 10:477–478

temptation, 13:816

Ten Commandments, 4:7–9

texts, 2:362–367

theology, 13:903

theophanies, 13:930

tradition in the, 14:132–133

trial of Jesus related in, 14:178–181

Trinitarian processions roots in, 11:733

on the triumphalism, 14:210

Tyndale's translations of, 14:252–253

unicity of God, 14:296

use of word gospel, 6:366–367

use of word grace, 6:380

utopianism, 14:360

virgines subintroductae, 14:539

virginity, 14:544–545

virtue, 14:548

war, 14:635

water, liturgical use of, 14:660

widows, 14:713

wisdom, 14:790–791

women, role of, 14:829–832

women deacons in, 4:554

word of God, 14:837

works of charity, 1:300, 301, 3:395, 400–401

See also specific Gospels and Epistles

New Testament Introduction (Wikenhauser), 5:522

New Testament law. *See* Law, New Testament

New Testament of Wordsworth-White-Sparks (WWS), 14:597

New Testament scholarship, 8:465, **10:303–308**, 938–940

New Testament Theology Today (Schnackenburg), 5:523

New Theology Movement (La nouvelle théologie), 5:827, 859, 12:775

New thought, **10:308–309**

New Ulm Diocese (MN), **10:309–310**

"New Views of Christianity, Society, and the Church" (Brownson), 14:147

New Ways Ministry, 7:73

New Year Feast (ancient Mesopotamia), 9:536

New Year Festival, 8:178

New York, **10:320–324**

    Catholic Charities USA, New York leadership, 8:136

    Catholic education, 9:406, 10:315, 316, 319, 324

    Church-State relations, 3:648, 651

    Franciscan missionaries, 12:540–541

    history of, 13:234

    Jesuit missionaries, 9:721–722

    statistics of, 4:246

    See also specific dioceses and archdioceses

New York Archdiocese, **10:310–320**

    Cooke, Terence, 4:246–247

    as diocese, 10:311–313

    Dubois, John, 4:917–918

    Hughes, John Joseph, 7:161

    Sisters of Divine Compassion, 4:786–787

    social agencies, 8:136

    Spellman, Francis Joseph (Card.), 13:411–412

New York Catholic Charities, 10:520–521

New York City Orphan Asylum, 13:174

New York Foundling Hospital, 5:752–753

New York General Hospital, 7:132

New York Tablet (periodical), 12:524

New Zealand, **10:324–329**, *327*

    Book of Common Prayer, 2:525

    demographic statistics, 10:325

    ecclesiastical organization, 10:325

map, 10:*326*

Mercy Pacific, 13:187

Newark Archdiocese (NJ), 2:165, **10:329–331**

Newbattle Abbey (Scotland), **10:331**

Newbigin, Lesslie, 9:676

Newbottle Abbey (Scotland). *See* Newbattle Abbey (Scotland)

Newdigate, Roger, Sir, 5:182

Newdigate, Sebastian, Bl., 5:225, 547, 9:617, **10:331**

Newell, Hubert Michael (Bp. of Cheyenne, WY), 14:870–871

Newfoundland (Canada), 9:724

Newman, John Henry (Card.), **10:331–340**, *332*

    Acton, John Emerich Edward Dalberg, 1:85

    Alphonsus Liguori, St., 1:309

    Anglo-Catholics, 1:444

    Antichrist, 1:517

    apologetics, 1:565, 3:624

    Augustinianism, 1:881

    Bremond, Henri, 2:601

    Bridgett, Thomas Edward, 2:614

    Bunsen, Christian Karl Josias von, 2:691

    Butler, Joseph, 2:721

    Catherine of Genoa, St., 3:271

    Catholic conversion, 5:251, 467

    Catholic higher education, 5:251–252

    Cherubini, Luigi, 3:468

    Coleridge, Henry James, 3:830

    conscience, 4:140

    Cullen, Paul, 4:424

    Dalgairns, John Dobree, 4:500

    doctrine, development of, 4:807–808

    doctrines of, 10:335–338

    dogmatic theology, 4:814

    ecclesiology, 5:37

    An Essay in Aid of a Grammar of Assent, Longergan influenced, 8:772

    Faber, Frederick William, 5:582

    influence on John Ellis, 5:170

    Keble influence, 8:135–136

    lay spirituality, 8:415

    literary influence, 10:339–340

    Manning, Henry Edward, 9:121

    oratorio of poem of, 5:153

    organization of Irish hierarchy, 7:534, 563

    Oxford Movement, 10:332, 732–734

    preambles of faith, 11:635

    religious communities revival, 12:101

"Second Spring" sermon, 5:251

on the Thirty-Nine Articles, 14:8

Newman Apostolate, 3:622, 8:153, **10:340–346**, 12:643

Newman Chaplains' Association, 8:153

Newman Clubs, 8:814

Newman Quarterly, 10:343

Newman Theological College (Edmonton, Alberta), 3:11

Newman's Apolgia: A Classic Reconsidered (symposium), 10:340

New-Moon feast, Hebrew, **10:289**

Newport, Richard, Bl., 5:235

Newton, Isaac, Sir, 3:306, 7:340, 9:416, 10:19, 23, 11:293

    atomism, 1:834–835, 4:960

    Blake, William, 2:428

    Cambridge University, 2:906

    Clarke, Samuel, 3:766

    deism, 4:616

    induction, 7:434

    scholasticism, 12:768

    space, 13:373, 374

Newtonianism, 1:80, 3:183

Newtown Manor School (Maryland), **10:346**

Nez Percé people, 3:226

Ngan Nguyen, Paul, 14:497

Nghi, José, 14:497

Ngo Dinh Diem, 3:79

Ngo Van Chieu, 3:79

Ngon, Lorenzo, 14:497

NGOs. *See* Non-governmental organizations (NGOs)

Nguyen, Domingo, 14:497

Nguyen, Huu Nam Anthony, 14:497

Nguyễn, Văn Lưu, 14:497

Nguyen Van Vinh, Esteban, 14:497

Nhi, Domingo, 14:497

Niagara Bible Conference (1878), 6:27

Nicaea, Councils of

    hypostasis, 7:263, 264

    immutability of God, 7:356

    I (324-325), 1:*661*, **10:346–348**

        Alexander (Patriarch of Alexandria), St. and, 1:267, 2:821

        alleged second council (327), 1:685

        Anabaptists, 1:369

        Anatolius (Bp. of Emesa), 5:191

        Antichrist, 1:516

        Antioch Patriarchate, 1:525, 2:821

        Arianism, 1:660, 661–662, 685, 5:454

Nicaea, Councils of *(continued)*
  Armenia, 1:705
  Athanasius, St., 1:817
  Byzantine art, 2:731
  Canon law, 3:38, 39
  Christmas, 3:552
  Christology, 3:559, 560–561
  Church-State relations, 3:632
  clerical celibacy and marriage, 3:323, 325
  Constantine I (Roman Emperor), 2:780, 3:594, 4:181, 182, 299, 12:318
  Constantinople Church authority, 4:185
  consubstantiality, 4:197–199, 14:193
  Copts, 4:255
  Council of Chalcedon, 3:363
  cross, 4:382
  Cyprus, 4:461
  deacons, 4:551
  Dionysiana collectio, 4:752
  divinity of the Son, 8:763
  Easter controversy, 4:754
  Eastern Schism, 5:22
  ecclesiastical provinces, 12:364–365
  Eustathius of Antioch (Bp.), St., 5:456
  God the Son, 6:296
  homoousios, 7:65
  honorary patriarchate of Jerusalem, 10:945
  hospitals, 7:127
  lenten fasting, 8:468
  ordination of neophytes, 10:239
  Peperius (Bp.), 12:635
  senatorial procedure, 4:299
  standing, 8:648
  subordinationist theology, 14:193
  Trinity, 8:845, 10:966, 14:192–194, 204
  usury, 14:354
 II (787), 4:300, **10:348–350**
  Adrian I (Pope), 1:123
  alleged second council (327), 1:685
  Anastasius the Librarian, 1:390
  Armenia, 1:705
  Byzantine Church, 2:751–752
  Canon Law, 3:46, 817
  Carolingian reform, 1:243, 3:425
  Cyprus, 4:461
  diptychs, 4:759

  Eastern Schism, 5:23, 12:53
  iconoclasm, 2:733, 751, 821
  images, 7:281–283, 325, 8:473, 557, 621
  See also Nicene Christians; Nicene Creed
Nicaean-Chalcedonian theology, 11:148–149
Nicaragua, **10:350–354**, *353*
  demographic statistics, 10:351
  ecclesiastical organization, 10:353
  John Paul II (Pope), 7:999
  liberation theology, 8:548
  map, 10:*352*
  mission, 9:707, 10:350–351, 352–353, 12:290
  Sandinista government, 8:548
Niccoli, Niccolò de', 12:117, 622
Nicene Christians, 3:552, 555
  See also Nicaea, Councils of; Nicene Creed
Nicene Creed, **10:354**
  Acacius of Caesarea, 1:51
  Adrian I (Pope), 1:123
  agennētos, 1:175
  Alexander (Patriarch of Alexandria), St., 1:267
  Anglicanism, 8:306
  apostolic faith, 1:587
  Arianism, 1:661–662, 685, 4:173
  Athanasius, St., 1:661, 662, 817
  Byzantine literature, 2:792
  Catholic Apostolic Church, 3:279
  Constantine I (the Great) (Roman Emperor), 4:181
  Divine judgment, 8:39
  filioque, 2:752, 5:23, 24, 719–722, 8:480
  language use, 8:362
  origin of, 4:352–353, 354, 10:347–348
  original sin, 10:666
  Orthodox churches, 4:354–355
  redemption, 11:975
  School of Alexandria, 1:273
  Synod of Alexandria, 1:818
  See also Arianism; Nicaea, Councils of
Nicephorus I (Byzantine Emperor), 3:259
Nicephorus I (Patriarch of Constantinople), St., 1:504, 2:753, 793, 7:282, 8:473, **10:354–355**
Nicephorus Blemmydes, 2:761–762, 776, 803, 809, 825, **10:355**

Nicephorus Callistus Xanthopoulos, 2:797, 803, 828, 5:491
Nicephorus Chumnus, 2:810
Nicetas (Catharist Bp. of Constantinople), 3:259
Nicetas, St., 12:330
Nicetas Acominatus, 2:825
Nicetas Choniates, 2:794–795, 800, **10:355–356**
Nicetas David, 2:803, **10:356**
Nicetas of Heraclea, 3:258
Nicetas of Maronia, 2:825
Nicetas of Remesiana (Bp.), 1:97, 577, **10:356–357**, 13:771–773
Nicetas Seides, 2:825
Nicetas Stethatos, 2:794, 824, **10:357**
Nicetius of Lyons, 3:407
Nicetius of Trier (Bp.), St., 1:645, **10:357**
Nichiren Buddhism, 2:665
  See also Soka Gakkai
Nichoás, M. J., 10:14
Nicholaikirche (Hamburg, Germany), 3:709
Nicholas, St., 3:557, 4:401
Nicholas, Studite Abbot, St., **10:358**
Nicholas I (Emperor of Russia), 1:84, 10:358, *359*, 12:424, 13:216, 14:274
Nicholas I (Patriarch of Constantinople), 10:359
  Alans, 1:206, 2:755
  Euthymius I (Patriarch of Constantinople), 5:460
  iconoclasm, 7:282
  tetragamy dispute, 1:646, 2:756–757, 823
Nicholas I (Pope), St., **10:360–364**, *361*
  Ado of Vienne, St., 1:117
  Adrian II (Pope), 1:124
  Boris of Bulgaria's allegiance to, 10:683–684
  Bulgaria, 2:679, 823
  Canon Law, 3:42, 43, 44
  capital punishment, 3:86
  Carolingian reform, 3:158
  censorship, 3:336
  Church-State relations, 3:635
  decretals, legal force, 4:600
  Formosus (Pope), 5:814
  Gottschalk of Orbais, 6:371
  Hincmar of Reims, 6:838
  Ignatius of Constantinople, 7:310
  John of Ravenna, 7:981
  Photian Schism, 5:23
  Photius, 2:754, 822, 3:599, 4:187, 194, 11:311

Roman primacy, 3:599–600

unity of the church, 3:170

Nicholas I Mysticus. *See* Nicholas I (Patriarch of Constantinople)

Nicholas II (Emperor of Russia), 11:916, 12:424

Nicholas II (Patriarch of Constantinople), 2:757

Nicholas II (Pope), **10:365**

  Alexander II (Pope), 1:253

  Benedict X (Antipope), 2:242

  cardinalate, 3:105

  Church-State relations, 3:635, 7:43

  clerical celibacy/marriage, 3:326

  Crescentii family, 4:362

  designation of new popes, 6:469

  German bishops, 10:857

  Humbert of Silva Candida, 7:199

  investiture, 7:537

  papal elections, 11:498–499

  simony, 13:136

  William I's marriage dispensation, 2:189

Nicholas III (Patriarch of Constantinople), 2:823, **10:360**

Nicholas III (Pope), **10:365–367**

  capitulations, 3:91

  Castel Sant'Angelo, 3:213

  Colonna family, 3:854

  Franciscan poverty, 5:902

  Orsini family, 10:676

  poverty, 11:570

  reign, 12:357

Nicholas IV (Pope), **10:367–368**

  apostolici, 1:594

  Armenia, 1:702

  Coimbra University, 3:828

  Colonna family, 3:854

  Orsini family, 10:676

  papal revenues, 10:367

  Roger Bacon, 12:285

Nicholas V (Antipope), **10:369–370**

Nicholas V (Pope), **10:368–369**, 841

  Ambrosians, 1:346

  Capranica, Domenico, 3:91

  Carmelites, 3:126, 134–135

  Carvajal, Juan de, 3:197

  Castel Sant'Angelo, 3:213

  Clareni, 3:763

  Council of Basel, 2:134

  Estouteville, Guillaume d', 5:379

  Felix V (Antipope), 5:669

  Ghibelline-Guelf conflict, 3:855

  Holy Year, 7:57

  Renaissance, 3:606, 12:117–118

St. Peter's Basilica (Rome), 12:578

Vatican Library, 14:420

Nicholas Francis (Card. of Lorraine), 8:788

Nicholas Gallicus, 3:132

Nicholas Hermansson (Bp.), St., **10:370**

Nicholas of Aarhus, Bl., **10:370**

Nicholas of Autrecourt, **10:370–371**, 412, 536, 537

  atomism, 1:833

  principle of causality, 5:101

  skepticism, 13:202

  universal essences, 5:361

Nicholas of Basel, **10:371**

Nicholas of Clamanges, 8:381, **10:371–372**

Nicholas of Cusa (Card.), 10:*372*, **372–375**

  Andechs Abbey, 1:398

  Bovillus, Carolus, 2:572

  Cesarini, Giuliano, 3:357

  Church-State relations, 3:636

  conciliarism, 3:604, 636, 4:55

  Denis the Carthusian, 4:661

  docta ignorantia, 4:798

  Donation of Constantine, 4:860

  double truth theory, 1:595

  geocentrism, 6:59

  Lefèvre influenced, 8:449

  medieval Latin literature works, 9:461

  pantheism, 10:821, 826

  privation, 11:722

  Renaissance philosophy, 11:292, 12:121

  skepticism, 13:202

  social contract, 13:240

  utopianism, 14:360

Nicholas of Dinkelsbühl, **10:376**

Nicholas of Flüe, St., **10:376–377**

Nicholas of Guilford, 10:728–729

Nicholas of Lisieux, 14:20

Nicholas of Lyra, 1:407, 3:26, 5:517, 518

Nicholas of Methone, 2:825

Nicholas of Myra (Bp.), St., 8:327, 10:*377*, **377–378**, 13:94

Nicholas of Prussia, Bl., **10:378**

Nicholas of Strassburg, **10:378**, 14:46

Nicholas of Tolentino, St., 1:888, **10:378–379**

Nicholas of Winghe, 7:328

Nicholas Oresme (Bp. of Lisieux), **10:379–380**

  Albert of Saxony, 1:223

Aristotelianism, 1:675

  geocentrism, 6:59

  mechanism, 9:415

  motion, 12:811–812

  scholasticism, 12:762

Nicholas Paglia, Bl., **10:380**

Nicholas Trevet, 1:464, 5:518, **10:381**, 14:46

Nichols, George, Bl., 5:231, **10:381**

Nicholson, E. W., 11:766–767

Nichomachean ethics, 1:334

Niclaes, Hendrik, **10:382**

Nicod, Jean, 7:434

Nicodemus, Gospel of, 1:559, 4:684

Nicodemus of Mammola, St., **10:382**

Nicodemus the Hagiorite, **10:382**

Nicola da Gesturi, Bl., **10:383**

Nicolai, Christoph, 5:255

Nicolaites, 10:382, **383**

Nicolaj, G., 10:775

Nicolantonio, Mariano da Roccacasale, Bl., 10:383–384

Nicolas, Jean Jacques Auguste, **10:384**

Nicolás de Jesús María, 3:137

Nicolas of Cabasilas, 5:279

Nicolaus ab Auximo, 3:52

Nicolaus of Damascus, 1:669

Nicole, Pierre, 3:184, 8:315, 10:384–385

Nicolò, Donato Antonio Giovanni. *See* Fasani, Francesco Antonio, St.

Nicomachean Ethics (Aristotle), 3:396, 5:439, 10:201, 232, *380*

Nicomedia (Asia Minor), **10:385**

Nicopolis, Crusade of, 2:764

Nicopolis Basilica, 1:756

Nidal, Gerónimo, 11:621

Nider, Johann, 1:729, 9:461, **10:386**

Niebla (Unamuno), 14:288

Niebuhr, Helmut Richard, 1:826, 10:152, **386**, 12:861

Niebuhr, Reinhold, 5:468, 10:192, **386–387**, *387*

Niederaltaich Abbey (Bavaria), 8:45–46, **10:387**

Niederbronn (France), Ecstatic of. *See* Eppinger, Elisabeth

Niedergeses, James D. (Bp. of Nashville, TN), 13:824

Niedermünster Convent (Alsace), **10:388**

Niehaus, Hermann, 10:277

Niel, Francis, Rev., 12:562

Nielsen, Laurentius, **10:388**

Niem, Dietrich of. *See* Dietrich of Nieheim

Niemeyer, O., 3:677

Nietzsche, Friedrich Wilhelm, 5:107, **10:388–390**, *389*, 11:295
    aesthetics, 1:145, 3:679
    aristocracy, 1:667
    atheism, 1:823
    death of God, 4:583, 585
    deconstructionism, 4:592, 593
    evolution and egoism, 5:397
    existentialism, 5:546
    human will, 14:582
    insignificance of God, 6:286
    irrationalism, 7:586–587
    philosophy of history, 6:885
    philosophy of music, 10:73
    transcendentals, 14:150–151
Nieuwe Kirk bells (Netherlands), 2:*233*
Nieves, Elías del Socorro, Bl., 1:888, **10:390**
Nifo, Agostino, 1:676, 834, 935, **10:391**
Niger, **10:391–392**, *392*
Niger, Donough, 7:581
Niger, Gaius Pescennius (Roman general and rival Emperor), 12:305
Niger, Roger (Bp. of London), 8:771
Nigeria, **10:392–394**, *395*, *396*
Night, Death, and the Devil (Durer), 4:*705*
Night office issue, 8:272
Night prayer, 8:735
Nightingale (John Peckham), 9:460
Nihachi, Dominic, Bl., 7:734
Nihachi, Francis, Bl., 7:734
Nihachi, Louis, Bl., 7:734
Nihil est causa sui ipsius (Nothing is the cause of itself), 12:756
Nihil est in intellectu quod prius non fuerit in sensu (Nothing is in the intellect that was not first in the sense), 12:756
Nihil obstat (There is nothing standing in the way), 3:336, **10:394**
Nihilism, 1:384, 823, **10:394–395**
Nika Revolt (532), 8:96
Niketas Choniates, 2:776
Nikolin, I., 12:434
Nikon (Patriarch of Moscow), 1:948, 2:745, **10:396**, 12:424
Nikopeia (Our Lady of Victory), 9:272
Nilan, James, 11:562
Nilan, John Joseph (Bp. of Hartford), 4:124, 6:653
Nilles, Nikolaus, **10:396**
Nilsson, M. P., 3:573, 5:2, 10:86
Nilus (monk), 2:759
Nilus of Ancyra, St., 5:464, **10:396–397**

Nilus of Rossano, St., 2:143, 7:928, **10:397**
Nilus the Archimandrite. *See* Doxopaties, Neils
Nimbārka (Hindu teacher), 6:847
Nimbarka school, 7:409
Nimeiry, Jafaar Muhammad al-, 13:582
Nimwegen, Chapter of (806), 3:410
Nina, Lorenzo (Card.), **10:397–398**
Nineteen (19), mystical meaning, 2:3
1984 (Orwell), 14:*361*
Ninety-Five Theses (Luther), 7:438
Nineveh (Assyria), 8:43–44, 10:136–137, *136*, **398**
Ninfale fiesolano (Boccaccio), 2:448
Ninguarda, Feliciano, 1:912, **10:398–399**
Ninh, Dominic, 14:497
Ninian (Bp. of Whithorn), St., 2:621, **10:399**, 12:830
Nino, St., 6:152
Niño Pérez, Cesáreo, Bl., 7:124
Niphon of Cyzicus, 1:409
Nirvāṇa, 3:361, **10:399**
Nisch, Franziska, Bl. *See* Nisch, Ulrika Franziska, Bl.
Nisch, Ulrika Franziska, Bl., **10:399–400**
Nishga people, 3:11
Nisibis (Turkey), 1:805, **10:400**
Nisibis, School of, 1:805–806, 2:820, 5:5, 277, 642, **10:400–401**
Nissen, H., 3:673
Nithard (Bp. of Liège), 1:500, 2:625, 3:160
Nivard (Bp. of Reims), St., 12:36
Nivard, Bl., **10:401**
Niweindt, Mathinus (Father), 3:116
Niza, Marcos de, 10:284, **401–402**, 12:674
Niẓām al-Mulk, 1:281
Nizārīs, 7:624, **10:402**
Nizolio, M., 1:677
N.L.P.A.I. *See* National League for the Protection of American Interests
No Other Man (Noyes), 10:471
No Souvenirs: Journal (Eliade), 5:155
Noack, B., 5:522
Noadiah (prophetess), 11:765
Noah, 4:326–327, 5:763–765, **10:402–405**, *403*
Noah's Ark, 10:*403*
Noailles, Louis Antoine (Card.), 1:57, 268, 3:789, 8:519, **10:405–406**
Noailles, Pierre Bienvenu, **10:406**
Nobili, John, 1:65, **4:407**, 12:646–647
Nobili, Roberto de, 3:613, 7:402, 410–411, 784, 9:*690*, **10:407–408**

Nobilissima Gallorum gens (encyclical, Leo XIII), 11:900
Nobill, John, 10:407
Noble Guards, 4:596
Nóbrega, Manuel da, 1:245, 2:588, 7:785, **10:408–409**
NOCERCC. *See* National Organization for Continuing Education of Roman Catholic Clergy
Noches en los jardines de España (Nights in the Gardens of Spain) (Falla), 5:612
Nock, Arthur Darby, **10:409**
Nocoes da História da Filosofia (Franca), 5:840
Nocte surgentes vigilemus omnes (hymn), 5:33
Nocturnal Adoration Society, 5:435
Noël, Leon, 12:776
Noël, Pierre-Michel, 12:277
Noeldeke, Theodor, 5:519
Noëli (religious song), 3:150
Noëtus of Smyrna, 3:560, 10:409
Nogaret, Guillaume de, 2:503, 3:603, 854, 5:846
Noguera Albelda, María del Olvido, Bl., 1:4
Noldin, Hieronymus, **10:409–410**, 12:777
Noli, Fan, 1:214
Noll, John Francis (Bp. of Fort Wayne), 1:350, 7:415–416, 10:168, **410**
Nollau, Louis, 5:468
Nomenclautre School ("taxonomists"), 10:773
Nomina Sacra (Traube), 14:163
Nominales school, 10:411–412
Nominalism, 5:361, 732, **10:410–414**
    Abelard, Peter, 1:19
    absolute realism, 11:942
    agnosticism, 1:180–181
    Aiguani, Michele, 1:194
    Albert of Saxony, 1:223
    Biel, Gabriel, 2:391
    causality, 3:301
    certitude, 3:352
    Church history, 3:604
    concept, 4:51, 52
    conscience, 4:141, 145
    contingency, 4:213–214
    Crathorn, John, 4:334–335
    criteriology, 4:367
    Crockaert, Peter, 4:374
    Duns Scotus, John, 4:781–782
    Durandus of Saint-Pourçain, 4:949
    free will, 5:934, 938

Germans, 7:228

grace, 6:389–390

grace and nature, 6:411

humanism, 7:195

intentional species, 13:409–410

John XXII (Pope), 3:603

John Buridan, 7:942–943

Ockhamism, 9:862

origins in logicism, 8:758

Protestant Reformation, 12:12

Roscelin of Compiègne, 12:377

scholasticism, 12:762

society, 13:278

soul, concept of, 13:348

Thomism, 4:51, 335

unity and multiplicity opposition, 10:58

universals, 14:326–327

William of Ockham, 12:762

See also Scotism

Nomocanon (Balsamon), 2:33

Nomocanon (Bar-Hebraeus), 2:82

Nomocanon XIV titulorum (canonical collection), 10:415

Nomocanon in 14 Titles (Enantiophanes), 3:46

Nomocanon L. titulorum (canonical collection), 10:415

Nomocanons (canonical collections), 3:39, 46, 60, 9:195, **10:414–415**

Nomōn Syngraphē (Plethon), 11:420

Non abbiamo bisogno (encyclical, Pius XI), 3:277, 642, 11:393

Non amgigimus (encyclical, Benedict XIV), 4:59

Non expedit (it is not expedient), 2:508, 3:642, 8:492, **10:415–416**

Non Mediocri (papal bull, Eugene IV), 3:105

Non sine magno (brief, Pius VII), 14:220

Nonadorantism, 2:432

Nonantola Abbey (Italy), 1:498–499, **10:416**, *417*

Nonbeing, 4:25, 223, 7:346, 457, **10:416–417**

Non-Christian mysticism, 10:111

Noncombatant immunity (just-wars), 14:639–640

Nonconformists, 5:182, 928, **10:418**

Nonduality (*Advaita*), 6:846, 7:408

Nondum erant abyssi (Peter Aureoli), 3:96

Non-governmental organizations (NGOs), 9:583–584, 13:177

Nonimaging signs, 13:116

Nonjurors, English, **10:418–419**

Nonmaterial reality, 9:550–551

Nonnberg Abbey (Austria), 1:908, **10:419**

Nonnus of Panopolis, 2:804, **10:419**

Nonscholastic realism, 11:300–301

Nonviolence, 7:698, 14:636, 641, 642–644

Norbert, St., 1:538, 3:601, 4:764

Norbert of Magdeburg, 3:601

Norbert of Xanten, St., 1:594, 3:68, 6:177, 7:152, **10:419–421**, 11:665

Norbertines. *See* Premonstratensians

Norden, E., 3:553

Norfolk (line of English peers), **10:421–425**

Norfolk, Bernard Edward Howard, 12th Duke of, 10:424

Norfolk, Bernard Edward Howard, 13th Duke of, 10:424

Norfolk, Bernard Marmaduke Fitzalan-Howard, Duke of, 10:424

Norfolk, Charles Howard, 10th Duke of, 10:424

Norfolk, Charles Howard, 11th Duke of, 10:424

Norfolk, Edward Howard, 9th Duke of, 10:424

Norfolk, Henry Fitzalan-Howard, Duke of, 10:424

Norfolk, Henry Granville Howard, 14th Duke of, 10:424

Norfolk, Henry Howard, 6th Duke of, 10:424

Norfolk, Henry Howard, 7th Duke of, 10:424

Norfolk, John de Mowbray, 1st Duke of, 10:421

Norfolk, John de Mowbray, 2nd Duke of, 10:421

Norfolk, John de Mowbray, 3rd Duke of, 10:421

Norfolk, John de Mowbray, 4th Duke of, 10:421

Norfolk, John Howard, Duke of, 10:422

Norfolk, Thomas Howard, Duke of, 9:291, 10:422, 422–423, 11:341–342

Norfolk, Thomas Howard, 5th Duke of, 10:424

Norfolk, Thomas Howard, 8th Duke of, 10:424

Norgaud (Bp. of Autun), 1:926

Norinaga, Motoori, 1:459

Noris, Henry (Card.), **4:425**

Alphonsus Liguori, St., 1:309

Augustinianism, 1:875, 880, 881, 884, 885, 889

scholasticism, 12:764

Norma (Bellini), 2:229

Norma Vitae (Papczyński), 10:860

Normae servandae in inquisitionibus ab episcopis faciendis in causis sanctorum (John Paul II), 12:608

Normality, **10:425–426**

Normandy, **10:426–427**

Normandy, Geoffrey Plantagenet, Duke of, 9:331

Normans, 1:253, 464, 3:161, 4:175, **10:427–429**, 480–481

Normoyle, Roger, 7:581

Norreys, Roger, 5:487

Norris, James Joseph, **10:429**

Norris, John, 9:75–76

Norris, Thomas, 7:528

North Africa, early Church in, 3:593, **10:429–432**

architecture, 1:754, 3:685

Augustine, St., 1:852

Canon Law, 3:40–41

Carthage, 3:186–188

liturgical history, 8:652

mosaics, 1:754–755

Novatianist schism, 4:457–459

Roman primacy, 3:317

Vandal invasions, 1:663, 3:40, 186–187, 189

See also Donatism

North America, 4:31, 9:560–562, 795, 10:974–975

North American Academy of Liturgy (NAAL), 8:679, 10:432–433, **432–433**, 12:259

North American College (Rome, Italy), **10:433–434**, 12:788, 13:405

North American Conference (NAC), 13:29

North American Forum on the Catechumenate, 4:242

North American martyrs, 7:786, **10:434–436**, 13:94

North American Union Sisters of Our Lady of Charity (NAU-OLC), **10:722**

North Carolina, 3:437, 646, 652, **10:436–439**

See also specific dioceses and archdioceses

North Carolina Catholic (newspaper), 10:438

North Dakota, 2:215, **10:439–441**

See also specific dioceses and archdioceses

North Korea. *See* Korea

Northampton, Battle of, 8:141

Northeast Pastoral Formation Institute, 8:290

Northern Baptist Convention, 2:80

Northern Ireland, **10:441–444**, *442*

  Anglican-Episcopalian Religious
    Orders, 12:102–103

  demographic statistics, 10:441

  maps, 5:*241*, 12:*831*, 14:*611*

  ''Troubles,'' 7:569

  See also Britain, early church in

Northern kingdom, 8:177, 178

Northmen, **10:444–447**

Northrop, Henry P., 13:366

Northumberland, John Dudley, Duke of,
  9:293

*Northwest Indian Cemetery Protective
  Association, Lyng v.* (1988), 3:663

Norton, John, Bl., 5:233, **10:447**

Norton, Thomas, 2:611

Norway, **10:447–451**, *450*

  demographic statistics, 10:448

  ecclesiastical organization, 4:664,
    10:450–451

  map, 10:*449*

  Protestant Reformation, 4:309

  stave churches, 13:502–503, *503*

Norway, Church of, 8:886

Norwich, Ancient See of (England),
  4:317, **10:451–452**

Nossa Senhora da Graca Church (Evora,
  Portugal), 3:*694*

Nossa Senhora da Serra (penitent home)
  (Lisbon, Portugal), 3:416

Nossa Senhora de Piedade (laity
  association), 3:416

Nossa Senhora de Rocamador (laity
  association), 3:416

*Nostra aetate: Declaration on the
  Relation of the Church to Non-
  Christian Religions* (decree),
  9:686–687

Notabilia (Notes) (Richard Knapwell),
  12:230

Notae in programma quoddam
  (Descartes), 3:184

Notary (Canon Law), 4:757, **10:452**

Notationes in totam Scripturam Sacram
  (Sa), 12:449

Notburga, St., **10:452**

Note agiografiche (Franchi de'
  Cavalieri), 5:865

Notes, theological, 8:743, **10:453–455**

Notes on a Visit to the Russian Church
  (Palmer), 10:812

Notes on Ingersoll (Lambert), 8:303

Notes on Moral Theology, 1965-1980
  (McCormick), 9:394

Notes on Moral Theology, 1981-84
  (McCormick), 9:394

Notes on the New Testament (Wesley),
  4:81–82

Noth, Martin, 2:385, 3:565–566, 5:408,
  520, 7:1054, 11:93

Noticias Catolicas (Spanish and
  Portuguese edition), 14:312

Noticias de la Nueva California (Palóu),
  10:815

Notitia ecclesiarum orbis Romae
  (Salzburg Itinerary), 7:676

Notker Balbulus, Bl., **10:455–456**, *456*

  Adam of Saint-Victor, 1:109

  medieval Latin literature works,
    9:446–447

  Notker Sequences, 7:247, 13:1, 2, *2*,
    3

  Sankt Gallen Abbey, 12:669

Notker Curti, 4:775

Notker Labeo, 4:778, 5:142, 6:177,
  9:449, **10:456–457**, 12:669

Notker of Liège (Prince, Bp.), Bl.,
  10:457, 719

Notre Dame Cathedral (Reims), 12:37

Notre Dame Church (Montreal), 3:715

Notre Dame College of Maryland, 2:40

Notre Dame de Saigon Cathedral (Ho
  Chi Minh City, Vietnam), 14:*504*

Notre Dame de Sion Abbey
  (Diepenveen), 5:192

Notre Dame d'Espinay Abbey (France),
  12:581

Notre Dame du Calvaire (Calvairiennes),
  8:432–433

Notre Dame du Lac, University of
  (South Bend, IN), 1:641, 7:416,
  10:461–462

  archives, 1:637, 640

  Burns, James Aloysius, 2:709

  Cavanaugh, John Joseph, 3:311–312

  founding, 13:327

  Shuster, G., 13:99

  Summer School of Liturgy, 8:675

Notre Dame la Grande Church (Poitiers,
  France), 3:693, 5:*848*

Notre Dame Sisters, 10:223, **462–463**

Notre Père qui êtes aux cieux
  (Schrijvers), 12:787

Notre-Dame Cathedral (Isle de la Cité,
  Paris), 5:*851*, *852*, 8:*31*, 499,
  9:368–369, 13:90

Notre-Dame Cathedral (Senlis, France),
  3:*689*

Notre-Dame Church (Jumièges, France),
  3:*695*

Nôtre-Dame de Chartres. *See* Chartres
  Cathedral

Notre-Dame de la Garde (Marseilles),
  9:*209*

Notre-Dame du Haut Cathedral
  (Ronchamp), 3:669, 680, 712, 713

Notre-Dame du Haut Ronchamp
  (pilgrimage chapel), 12:368, *369*

Notre-Dame du Raincy Church (France),
  3:669, 710, 713, **11:897**, *898*

Notre-Dame du Travail Church (Paris),
  3:710

Notre-Dame-de-Bethléem chapel
  (France), 5:695

Notre-Dame-des-Domes Cathedral
  (Avignon), 1:942

Notre-Dame-De-Toute-Grâce Assy
  (France), **1:803–804**, 4:324, 8:623

Notre-Dame-de-Toutes-Grâces Church
  (Assy, France), 1:545, **803–804**,
  3:713

Notre-Dame-du-Port Church (Clermont-
  Ferrand, France), 3:693

Notre-Dame-en-vaux (Chalons-sur-
  Mame, France), 5:*846*

Nouet, Jacques, 7:782

Noumena (Kantianism), **10:463–464**

  accident, 1:59

  agnosticism, 1:182

  causality, 3:301, 307

  demonstration, 4:654

  Royce, Josiah, 12:397

Nous, 2:148–149

Nouveau guide de Terre Sainte
  (Meistermann), 9:471

Nouveau Testament (Erasmus), 5:847

Nouveau traité de diplomatique (Tassin,
  Toustain), 10:773

Nouveau voyage aux Isle de l'Amerique
  (Labat), 8:264

Le Nouvel athéisme (Lamy), 12:770

La Nouvelle Atala (Rouquette), 12:391

*Nouvelle bibliothèque des auteur
  ecclésiastiques* (Dupin), 6:876

Nouvelle découverte (Hennepin), 6:732

La Nouvelle Héloïse (Rousseau), 12:392,
  393

La Nouvelle histoire de Mouchette
  (Bernanos), 2:304

Nouvelle Voyage (Hennepin), 6:732

Nouvelles Ecclesiastiques, 8:507

*Nouvelles Études philosophiques sur le
  Christianisme* (Nicolas), 10:384

Nouwen, Henri, 13:774

Nova Cruzada Movement (Brazil), 5:717

Nova de universes philosophia (Patrizi),
  10:823

Nova et Vetera (Tyrrell), 14:258

Nova impendet (encyclical, Pius XI),
  11:393

Nova Nada (Spiritual Life Institute of America), 3:9

Nova patrum bibliotheca (Mai), 9:50

Nova Scotia (Canada), 2:424–425, 3:9

Novak, Francis A., 7:523

Novak, Michael, 14:361–362

Novarina, Maurice, 1:803, 3:713

Novatian (Antipope) and Novatianism, **4:464–466**

  Arles, 1:694

  burial site, 3:224

  Celestine I (Pope), St., 3:317

  Cornelius (Pope), St., 4:270

  Cyprian, St., 4:457–458

  Cyprian of Carthage, St., 3:186

  lapsi, 8:333, 846

  papal primacy, 3:593

  penitential controversy, 11:73

  works, 10:464–465

Novatianist churches, 10:465

Novatianist Schism, 4:457–459, 10:465

Novecosky, Peter, 12:578

Novella Commentaria (Joannes Andreae), 7:881

Novels (Leo VI), 8:474

Novena, 10:466–467

Novich Rabionet, Ramón, 2:92

Novit ille (papal decree, Innocent III), 3:636, 7:472

Novitiate, Canon Law of, **10:467–470**

Novo millennio ineunte (apostolic letter, John Paul II), 7:1003

Novum instrumentum (Erasmus), 5:316

Novum organum (Bacon), 1:676, 2:10

Novus thesaurus veterum inscriptionum (Muratori), 10:63

Now, **10:470**

Now I See (Lunn), 8:868

Nowell-Smith, P. H., 5:398

Nowogródek, Martyrs of, BB., **10:470–471**

Nowowiejski, Antoni (Abp. of Plock, Poland), 11:450

Noyes, Alfred, 2:693, **10:471**

NPM. *See* National Association of Pastoral Musicians

NRMs. *See* New Religious Movements (NRMs)

NRRO. *See* National Religious Retirement Office

Nubia, 4:1, **10:471–472**

Nuclear families, 14:814–815

Nuclear war, 14:642

Nudity, **10:472–473**

Nuestra Señora de la Soledad chapel, 3:677

Nuestra Señora de Los Desamparados hospital (Mexico), 3:416

Nuestra Señora de Monserrate Church (Puerto Rico), 11:814

Nugae curialium (Walter Map), 9:456

Nugent, Andrew, 10:311

Nugent, Francis, **10:473–474**

Nugent, Robert (Father), 7:73

Nulato Mission (Alaska), 1:209

Number symbolism, 1:740–741, 3:673–674, 812, 10:243, 13:333

Numbers, Book of, **10:474–475**

  Balaam, 2:26

  beatific vision, 2:170, 171

  censuses, 3:337–338

  conquest and settlement of Israel, 7:637

  El (God), 5:143

  enmity, 5:264

  eschatology, 5:333–334

  God's spirit, 13:426

  heart, 6:681

  heaven, 6:684

  imposition of hands, 7:364

  inheritance, 7:464

  Jesus as Lord, 8:781

  Kingdom of God, 8:173

  leprosy references, 8:509

  Magi, 9:35

  manna, 9:118–119

  Nazirites, 10:217–218

  Passover, 10:933, 935

  peace, 11:49

  pesach (28.16), 5:11

  Priestly Code, 8:397

  purification, 11:832

  redemption, 11:963, 964

  serpent as symbol, 13:20

  sin, 13:142

  sin offering, 13:159

  slavery, 13:206

  social principle, 13:249

  sources and literary form, 10:474

  spirit, 13:424

  tale of the talking ass, 2:26

  terms for man, 13:316

Numbers, natural and real, 4:216

Numerius of Trier, 3:519

Numerology, **10:475–476**, 12:458, 14:317

Numerology, in the Bible, 10:243, **476–478**

Numerus numerans (number counting), 12:752

Numerus numeratus (number enumerated), 12:752

Numismatics, 5:46, **10:478–483**, *479*, 13:406

Nun (Egyptian theology), 4:337

"Nun of Kent." *See* Barton, Elizabeth

Nunc Dimittis (Canticle of Simeon), 3:73, 10:483, *483*, *484*

Nunc Sante (hymn), 12:136

Nuncio, Apostolic, 8:451, **10:484–486**

Nunes, Peter, Bl., 1:951

Nunes Barreto, João (Patriarch of Abyssinia), 8:58, **10:486–487**

Nuñez de Cáceres, José (Abp. of Dominican Republic), 4:835

Nünning, Hermann, 2:716

Nunraw Abbey (Scotland), **10:487**

Nuns and sisters, 2:256, **10:483**

  See also specific orders

Nuns of St. Ambrose, 1:346

Nuns of the Order of Preachers, **4:832–833**

Nuns of the Perpetual Adoration of the Blessed Sacrament, **11:131**

Nuptial mysticism (*Brautmystik*), 6:191

Nureddin (Sultan of Syria and Egypt), 2:29

Nuremberg, Diet of (1522), 1:233, 3:482–483

Nuremberg, Diet of (1524), 3:781

The Nursing Madonna (*Galaktotrophousa*), 9:272

Nursing orders, 7:119–121, 8:610, 616

Nutiature controversy, 3:843

Nutter, John, Bl., 5:228

Nutter, Robert, Bl., 5:233, **10:487**

Nyasaland. *See* Malawi

Nyāya (Hindu philosophy), 6:845

Nyāya and Vaiśeṣika, 7:407

Nyel, Adrien, 2:630

Nyel, M., 4:620

Nymphs, 4:497

Nyquist, Committee for Public Education v. (1973), 3:668

Nys, Désiré, 12:776

O

O Antiphons, **10:489–490**, *490*

O Dei verbum, Patris ore proditum (Beatus of Liébana), 2:182

O Deus ego amo te (hymn), **10:490**

O Divórcio, A Psicologia da Fé, A Crise do Mundo Moderno (Franca), 5:840

O filii et filiae (hymn), **10:490**

O gente felix hospita (hymn), 12:464

O Livro dos Salmos (Franca), 5:840

O lux beam caelitum (hymn), 12:464

O Roma nobilis (hymn), **10:490–491**

O Sacrum Convivium (Palestrina), 10:803

Oak, Synod of the (403), 1:839, 3:564, 595, 7:947, **10:491–492**, 13:41

Oastea Domnului (Army of the Lord), 12:335

Oates, Titus, 3:433, 5:248, 481, 10:*492*, 493

Oates Plot (1678), 3:433, 5:248, 481, 686, **10:492–496**, 12:396, 14:612

    Coker, James Maurus, 4:269

    Coleman, Edward, Bl., 3:829, 830

    Colombière, St. Claude de la, 3:853

    Howard, Philip Thomas, 7:143

    Kemble, John, St., 8:140

    Lewis, David, St., 8:528

    Lloyd, John, St., 8:740

    Sergeant, J., 13:12

    Test Oaths (1672 and 1678), 10:501

Oath of 16 Points, 7:412

Oath of Abjuration (1643-1655), 10:501

Oath of Allegiance (England), 4:912, 5:758, 10:499–501, 13:11–12

Oath of Supremacy (1534-1559), 5:224, 244, 245, 700, 10:498–499, 13:75

Oaths, **10:496–497**

    allegiance to the pope, 5:248

    Church-State relations, 3:646, 648–649, 651, 652

    compurgation, 4:46

    feudalism and oath-taking, 5:704

    Royal Declaration, 12:396–397

    vows and oaths (Canon Law), 5:797

    See also Civil Constitution of the Clergy

Oaths, English Post-Reformation, **10:498–502**

Oaths, in the Bible, **10:498–502**, 626

Obadiah, Book of, 4:548, **10:502**

Obazine Abbey (France), 3:751, **10:503**, 13:525

OBC (Little Church of Utrecht), 10:579

OBC (Rooms-Katholieke Kerk der Oud-Bisschoppelijke Clerezie), 14:363

Obedience, **10:503–508**

    Basil, St., 2:140

    Benedictines, 2:265–266

    Catholic social thought, 13:247

    as evangelical counsel, 4:306–307

    religious vow, 12:88

    as responsibility of children, 11:335

Obedience of a Christian Man (Tyndale), 14:253, 254

Obediential active potency, 13:563

Obediential potency, **10:508–510**, 11:557

    beatific vision, 2:169

    capacity in human nature, 10:213

    created actuation by uncreated act, 4:335–336

    destiny, supernatural, 4:694–695

    grace, 6:394–395

    instrumental causality, 7:500

Obedientiary priors, 11:716

O'Beirne, Edmund, 7:581

Obelisci (Eck), 5:43

Oberammergau (Upper Bavaria), **10:510**

Obermann, Julian, 7:608

Obicini, Thomas, 3:367

L'Obituaire et le nécrologe des Cordeliers d'Angers (Ubald), 14:261

Object magic, 9:37

Objections Answered (pamphlet), 14:104

Objections to Roman Catholicism, 12:272

Objective happiness, 6:636

Objective redemption, 9:259, 260

Objective right (*ius*), 8:66

Objectivity, **10:510–511**, 14:227

    categories of being, 3:257

    consciousness, 4:154

    Hartmann, Nicolai, 6:656

    knowledge, 8:209–210

    love, 8:827

    sensibles, 12:914–915

    Thomism, 8:209–210

Objects, **10:510**

Objectum formale (formal object), 12:752

Objectum materiale (material object), 12:752

Oblate Fathers of Texas, 12:676

Oblate of St. Francis de Sales, 10:512, 516–517

Oblate Sisters of Misericordia. *See* Misericordia Sisters

Oblate Sisters of Providence, 1:157, 158, 2:40, 4:926, 8:812, 10:292–293, 513

Oblate Sisters of St. Francis de Sales (OSFS), 2:619, 3:385, **10:513**

Oblate Sisters of the Assumption, 4:502

Oblate Sisters of the Holy Spirit, 6:558

Oblate Sisters of the Most Holy Redeemer (OSSR), **10:513**

Oblates, **10:512**

Oblates of Mary Immanculate (OMI), **10:513–515**

    agreement on spiritual direction, 10:406

    Alaska, 1:207

    Botswana, 2:559

    Burma, 2:706

    Cameroon, 2:913

    Canada, 3:8

    entrusted with Great Namaqualand, 10:143

    founding, 3:622, 9:387–388

    Laos, 8:330

    Lesotho, 8:515

    New Orleans, 8:813

    northern missions, 8:270

    Solignac Abbey, 13:302

    South Africa, 13:360

Oblates of St. Ambrose, 1:346, 3:415

Oblates of Saint Benedict, 6:41

Oblates of St. Charles (OSC), 1:346, 2:540, **10:515–516**

Oblates of St. Charles Borromeo, 10:512

Oblates of St. Francis de Sales, 1:938, 2:619, 3:385, 622, **10:516–517**

Oblates of St. Joseph (OSJ), 9:146, 10:512, **517**

Oblates of the Assumption, 1:802

Oblates of the Blessed Sacrament, 13:165

Oblates of the Immaculate Conception, 2:282

Oblates of the Sacred Heart, 4:613

Oblates of the Sacred Heart of Jesus, 9:820

Oblates of the Virgin Mary (OVM), 8:327, 10:512

Oblationaries of St. Ambrose, 1:346

Obligation, moral, **10:517–520**

O'Boyle, Patrick A. (Card.), 10:168, **520–521**, 14:658

O'Boyle, Thady, 7:580

O'Brady, Patrick, 7:580

Obras literarias, pastorales y oratorias (Silva), 13:122

Obras propias, y traduccines latinas, griegas, y italianas (León), 8:498

Obrecht, Edmond, 6:196

Obrecht, Jakob, 2:717, **10:521–522**

Obrecht, M. Edmond, **10:523**

Obregonians, **10:523**

O'Brien, Bernard, 7:582

O'Brien, Daniel (d. 1651), 7:582

O'Brien, Daniel (d. 1653), 7:582

O'Brien, Donough, 7:582

O'Brien, Henry Joseph (Abp. of Hartford), 4:125, 6:654

O'Brien, James, 7:582

O'Brien, John, 8:838

O'Brien, Matthew Anthony, **10:523–524**

O'Brien, Maurice (Bp. of Emly, Ireland), 7:580

O'Brien, Terence Albert, Bl., 7:581, **10:524**

O'Brien, Thomas C., **10:524**

O'Brien, Thomas J. (Bp. of Phoenix), 1:688

O'Brien, Timothy (Father), 14:541

O'Brien, William D. (Bp. of Chicago), 1:350

O'Brien, William F. X., 11:366

O'Brien, William Vincent, 10:311, **524–525**

O'Bruadair, Anthony, 7:582

Obscenity, 5:326–327, 11:517, 519

Observant Reform Movement, 5:897, 902, 903, 904, 12:15

Obsessive-compulsive neurosis, 4:45

Obversion, 11:769–770

O'Byrne, Dominick, 6:150

OCA (Orthodox Church of America), 2:744, 745, 3:717, **10:681–683**, 12:742

O'Cahan, Eugene, 7:582

O'Cahill, Ambrose Aeneas, 7:581

O'Callaghan, Jeremiah, **10:525**, 14:454

O'Callaghan, José, 4:563

O'Caraghy, Tadhg, 7:581–582

O'Carolan, Bernard, 7:580

O'Cathan, John, 7:581

Occasion, **10:525**

Occasionalism, **10:526–527**
    Cartesianism, 3:184, 185, 4:681
    causality, 3:306
    conservation, 4:162
    defined, 13:346
    Divine concurrence compared to, 4:70
    Lamy, F., 8:315
    Malebranche, Nicolas, 7:320, 9:74, 74–75
    philosophical implications, 10:527

Occult compensation, **4:41–43**

Occult qualities, 11:851–852

Occultism, 3:758–759, **10:527**, 13:935

Occupatio (St. Odo of Cluny), 10:555

Oceana (Harrington), 14:360

Oceania, 3:378–379, 4:315, **10:527–535**, 528–534, 976

Ochino, Bernardino, 2:856, 3:611, 856, **10:534–535**, 13:108

Ochoa, Armando X., 5:174

Ochoa Ugandarín, Jerónimo, Bl., 7:122

Ockhamism, 5:711, **10:535–537**
    Adam Wodham, 1:110
    nominalism, 10:412–413, 13:908

occasionalism, 10:526

School of Cologne, 3:846

study of motion, 10:18

Thomism, 3:93

See also William of Ockham

Ockham's razor principle, 10:412

O'Clery, Michael (Brother), 3:834, 5:833, 834, **10:537**

O'Clery, Peregrine, 5:833

O'Conga, Murtagh, 2:368

O'Connell, Anthony (Sister), **10:538**

O'Connell, Anthony J. (Bp. of Palm Beach, FL), 8:227, 13:824

O'Connell, Daniel, **10:538–541**, *539*
    Butler, Charles, 2:719
    Doyle, James Warren, 4:891
    emancipation, 5:184, 251
    Fallon, Michael Francis, 5:614
    Irish Catholics, 1:75
    liberalism, 3:619, 641
    MacHale, John, 9:17
    Murray, Daniel, 10:68
    Repeal Movement, 10:441
    slavery, 1:156

O'Connell, Denis Joseph (Bp. of Richmond, VA), 10:160, **541–542**, 12:573, 14:542–543
    Americanism, 1:354, 355
    apostolic delegation in the United States, 1:584
    Catholic University of America, 3:291, 12:648
    North American College rector, 12:789
    Richmond Diocese, 12:648

O'Connell, Eugene, 2:867, 10:269, 12:647

O'Connell, John Patrick, 10:542

O'Connell, Tadhg, 7:581

O'Connell, William Henry (Card.), 1:640, 2:555–556, 9:57–58, 308–309, **10:542–544**, 11:531

O'Connor, Bede, 12:568

O'Connor, Cornelius, 7:581

O'Connor, Denis (Abp. of Toronto), 2:142

O'Connor, Felix, 7:582

O'Connor, James (Bp. of Omaha), 7:573, 10:587–588, 14:869

O'Connor, John Joseph, 10:319, 329, **544–546**, *545*

O'Connor, Martin John (Abp.), 3:279, **10:546**

O'Connor, Mary Catharine (Sister), 1:727, 730

O'Connor, Mary Flannery, **10:547**

O'Connor, Michael (Bp.), **10:547–548**, 11:83–84, 85, 366, 12:591, 647

O'Connor, Patrick, 7:580

O'Connor, Rory (Irish king), 7:554

O'Connor, Thomas Francis, **10:548**

O'Connor, William P. (Bp. of Madison, WI), 7:581, 14:782

O'Connor v. Henrick (1906), 11:562

O'Connor-Kerry, John, 7:582

O'Connor-Sligo, Tadhg, 7:582

Oconór, Hugh, 1:687

Ocotlán Church (Mexico), 3:707

Octagesima adveniens (apostolic letter, Paul VI), 4:157, 10:615, 11:32, 587, 12:396, 13:269

Octagonal baptismal fonts, 2:76

Octateuchus Clementis, 3:38

Octavian. *See* John XII (Pope)

Octavian of Monticelli. *See* Victor IV (Antipope, fl. 1159-1164)

Octavius (Minucius), 9:658

Octavius, Gaius. *See* Augustus (Gaius Octavius)

Octoechos, **10:548–549**

O'Cullen, John, 7:581

O'Cullenan, Gelasius, 7:579, **10:549**

O'Cullenan, Glaisne. *See* O'Cullenan, Gelasius

Oda Nobunaga, 7:726

Oda of Canterbury, St. *See* Odo of Canterbury, St.

O'Daly, Daniel, **10:549–550**

O'Daly, Eugene, 7:581

O'Daly, John, 7:580

O'Daly, Thady, 7:579

O'Daniel, Victor Francis, **10:550**

Odd Fellows, 12:462

Oddi, Diego, Bl., **10:550–551**, 12:275

Oddi, Giuseppe. *See* Oddi, Diego, Bl.

Oddo of Colona. *See* Martin V (Pope)

"Ode to the Setting Sun" (Thompson), 14:58

O'Dea, Edward J. (Bp. of Seattle), 12:852, 14:655

O'Deery, Patrick, 7:581

Oderisius (Card.), Bl., **10:551**

Odermatt, Adelhelm (Father), 2:255

Odes (Verstegan), 14:460

Odes of Solomon, 1:555, 556, 5:82

Odescalchi, Benedetto (Card.). *See* Innocent XI (Pope), Bl.

Les Odeurs de Paris (Veuillot), 14:465

O'Devany, Cornelius (Bp. of Downs and Connor, Ireland), Bl., 7:580, **10:551**

Odile, St., 3:409

Odilia, St., 5:446, 9:820, **10:551**

Odilienberg. *See* Mont Sainte-Odile Convent (Alsace)

Odilo of Cluny, St., 3:813, 814, **10:552,** 12:544

  Alferius, St., 1:277

  All Souls' Day, 1:290

  Councils of Anse, 1:493

  relics, 12:286

  Souvigny Abbey, 13:371

Odin, Jean-Marie (Abp.), **10:292–293,** 552–553, 13:846

  Louisiana administration, 8:811–812

  New Orleans Archdiocese, 1:157, 9:741, 14:528

  San Antonio Archdiocese, 12:640

Odin, John Mary (Abp.), **10:552–553,** 13:846

Odo (Bp. of Bayeux), 2:163, 164

Odo (King of West Franks), 3:172

Odo of Bayeux, 3:72

Odo of Cambrai (Bp.), Bl., **10:553,** 11:700, 12:565

Odo of Canterbury, St., 3:70, **10:554**

Odo of Châteauroux (Card.), 1:265, **10:554,** 708

Odo of Cluny, St., 2:269, 3:813, 814, **10:554–555,** *555,* 12:106

  Leo VII (Pope), 8:484

  music, 3:811, 7:247

  Saint Paul-Outside-the-Walls Abbey, 12:577

Odo of Ostia. *See* Urban II (Pope)

Odo of Soission, 13:133

Odo of Tournai. *See* Odo of Cambrai (Bp.), Bl.

Odo Rigaldus, 1:110, 265, 2:189, 479, 5:899, **10:555–556,** 13:344

Odoacer (barbarian king of Italy), 12:321

O'Dogherty, Cornelius, 7:580

O'Donaghue, Denis (Bp. of Louisville), 8:818

O'Donnell, Anne M., 14:254

O'Donnell, Cletus F. (Bp. of Madison, WI, 1917-1992), 14:783

O'Donnell, Edmund, 7:579, **10:556**

O'Donnell, Hugh Roe, 7:18, 557, **10:556**

O'Donnell, James, 3:715

O'Donnellan, Rory, 7:579

O'Donnoghue, Margaret E., 10:67

O'Donohugh, Sean, 1:687

O'Donovan, John, 5:834

Odoric of Pordenone, Bl., 3:493, **10:556–557**

O'Dowd, John, 7:579

O'Dowd, W. B., 11:625

O'Duignan of Leitrim, Peregrine, 5:833

Odysseus, **10:557**

Odyssey (Homer), 12:509

Oecolampadius, Johannes, **10:558,** 12:481

Oeconomia (Swedenborg), 13:639

Oehler, G. F., 2:384

Oerebro, Council of (1529), 1:399

Oertel, John James Maximilian, **10:558**

Oesterly, W., 2:385

Oesterreicher, John M., **10:558–559**

Oeuvres complétes de Louis Veuillot (Veuillot), 14:466

Les Oeuvres et la doctrine de Siger de Brabant (Van Steenberghen), 14:386

Les Oeuvres inédites (Van Steenberghen), 14:386

Oeuvres spirituelles du P. Judde (Lenoir-Duparc), 8:16

Of the Laws of Ecclesiastical Polity (Hooker), 5:318, 7:90

Of the Patagonias (Falkner), 5:611

Of Water and the Spirit: A Liturgical Study of Baptism, 12:742

O'Falvey, Donough, 7:580

O'Farrell, Bernard, 7:581

O'Farrell, Geoffrey, 7:580

O'Farrell, Laurence, 7:581

O'Feral, Anthony, 7:582

Offa (King of Mercia), 2:151, 3:70

Offa (Prince of East Saxony), 4:178

Offering of the Jews (painting), 8:526

Offerings by pilgrims, 11:349

Office, ecclesiastical, **10:559–563**

Office, Hymns. *See* Hymns and hymnals

Office for Film and Broadcasting, **10:563**

Office of Governmental Affairs (Washington, DC), 10:157

Office of the Dead, 8:658, **10:563–564**

Office of the Lamp, 4:257

Official Catholic Directory, **3:282,** 717, 10:159

Officialis. *See* Judicial Vicar

Officiorum ac munerum (apostolic constitution, Leo XIII), 3:336

Officious Lies (*mendacium officiosum*), 8:900

Officium pastorum, 1:925

Offray de la Mettrie, Julien, 3:795

O'Fihely, Maurice, 4:936, **10:564,** 12:764

O'Flanagan, Dermot (Bp. of Alaska), 1:209

O'Flaverty, John, 7:581

O'Flynn, Jeremiah, 1:900

O'Fury, Manus, 7:580

O'Gallagher, Eugene, 7:580

Ogata, Dominica, Bl., 7:733

Ogden, Schubert, 11:731

Ogilvie, John, St., **10:564–565,** 12:835

Ogilvie, William, 1:21

Ogino, Kyusako, 10:176, 177

Oglethorpe, James, 3:652, 6:149, 12:709

Ogmund (Bp. of Hólar, Iceland). *See* Jón Ögmundsson, St.

Ognibene. *See* Salimbene (Franciscan chronicler)

Ogorman, James Miles (Bp.), 10:221–222, 587, 14:869

O'Gorman, Juan, 10:5

O'Gorman, Thomas, **10:565–566**

O'Gormley, Brian, 7:581

O'Grady, John, 1:288, 3:279, 280, 7:579–580

O'Hair, Madalyn Murray, 1:822

O'Hanlon, Rory, 7:579

O'Hanrahan, Daniel, 7:579

O'Hara, Edwin Vincent (Abp. of Kansas City, MO), 4:95, 9:189, 826, 10:275, **566,** 11:391

O'Hara, Gerald Patrick (Abp.), 1:830, 12:339, 710

O'Hara, John (Card. of Philadelphia, PA), 9:628–629, **10:567,** 11:240–241

O'Hara, Phelim, 7:579

O'Hara, Stettler v. (Oregon, 1913), 10:566

O'Hara, William (Bp. of Philadelphia), 11:85

O'Heagarty, Father (17th c. Irish martyr), 7:582

O'Healy, Patrick, Bl., 7:579

Oheix, A., 8:319

O'Hely, Patrick, Bl., **10:567–568**

O'Higgin, Augustine, 7:581

O'Higgin, Daniel, 7:582

O'Higgin, Thomas, 7:581

Ohio, **10:568–573**

  anti-Catholicism, 7:139

  Congregationists, 4:115

  Dominicans, 3:734–735

  Fenwick, Edward Dominic, 5:686

  Franciscan Sisters of Penance and Charity of Tiffin, Ohio, 5:882–883

  mission, 2:11, 3:735, 5:686, 6:558, 7:413, 9:161

  Ohio v. Akron Center for Reproductive Health, 1:34

  religious orders (communities), 3:735

  See also specific dioceses and archdioceses

Ohio Catholic Conference, 10:572–573

Ohio v. Akron Center for Reproductive Health, 1:34

Ohio Valley Catholic Historical Society, 8:306–307

O'Hurley, Dermot (Abp.), Bl., 7:557, 579, **10:573**

O'Hurley, Donough, 7:580

Oil and Wine (Tyrrell), 14:258

Oil economies, 8:258, 259

Oils, holy, **7:34–35**

Oingt, Marguerite d', 3:192

Ojo, Anthony, 7:528

O'Kane, Godfrey, 7:581

O'Kane, Rory, 7:581

O'Keefe, George, 2:14

O'Keefe, Gerald F. (Bp. of Davenport), 4:535

O'Keefe, Vincent, H., 7:794

Okeghem, Jan van, 2:398, **10:573**

O'Kelly, Brian, 7:582

O'Kelly, John, 7:580

O'Kelly, Malachy, 7:580

O'Kelly, Thomas, 4:117

O'Kenna, Patrick, 7:579

O'Kennedy, Donough, 7:582

Oklahoma, 8:137–138, 816, **10:574–575**

See also specific dioceses and archdioceses

Oklahoma City Archdiocese (OK), **10:575–576**

Olaf (King of Sweden), St., 1:500, 10:446

Olaf I Tryggvessøn (King of Norway), 7:274–275, **10:577**

Olaf II (King of Norway), St., **10:577, 578**

Olaf the Fat (King of Sweden). *See* Olaf (King of Sweden), St.

Oláh, Miklós (Abp. of Gran, Hungary), 7:214, **10:577–578**

O'Lahy, John, 7:579

Olai, Erik. *See* Olsson, Erik

Olaizola Garagarza, Maria Angela, 14:564, 566

Olav Audunsson (Undset), 14:295

O'Laverty, Laughlin, 7:581

Olavi, Peter, 1:327

Olavide y Jauregui, Pablo de, **10:578–579**

Olbert (Abbot of Gembloux), 6:124

Olcott, Henry Steele, 13:934, 935

Old Believers. *See* Raskolniks (Russian schismatics)

Old Catholic Congress in Vienna (1909), 10:579

Old Catholics, 3:624, **10:579–580**

Acton, John Emerich Edward Dalberg, 1:85

Döllinger, Johannes, 4:824

Germany, 6:184

heresy, 6:778

Kulturkampf, 8:254

Liberal Catholic Church, 8:539

Los-von-Rom Movement, 8:794

Loyson, C., 8:838

Mariavites, 9:164

Reusch, Franz Heinrich, 12:182

Old Chapter, 2:410, **10:580**

Old Czech party, 4:484

Old Deluder Satan Act (1647), **10:580–581**

Old Gelasian Sacramentary (*Gelasianum Vetus*). *See* Gelasian Sacramentary

Old Religion. *See* Wicca

Old Ritualists. *See* Raskolniks (Russian schismatics)

Old Roman Chant, 4:32, 33, 6:464, **10:581–582**

Old Saint Joseph's Church (Queen Anne, MD), 9:*300*

Old St. Peter's Church (Detroit), 3:715

"Old School" (New Haven theology), 10:280

Old School Baptist Movement, 2:80

Old Ship Meeting House (Hingham, MA), 3:714

Old South Meeting House (Boston), 3:714

Old Testament

Aaron, 1:2–3

abortion, 1:26

adoption, 1:118

adultery, 1:131–132

aeons, 1:139

afterlife, 1:164–165

Alma prophecy, 1:297

altars, 1:319

Amen, 1:348

Amorrites, 1:362–363

Angel of the Lord, 1:411

angels, 1:416–417, 423, 425, 427

anger, 1:430

Annunciation, 1:475–476

anthropomorphism, 1:511

Antichrist, 1:513, 515

apocalyptic style, 1:546

apocrypha, 1:549, 551, 554

apologetics, 1:563

Aramaeans, 1:623, 624

Aramaic language, 1:627

ark of the covenant, 1:688, 690

ashes, 1:782

Astarte, 1:808

atonement, 1:837

authority, 3:28–29

authorship, 1:488

bare feet, 4:764

beatific vision, 2:170–171

biblical Chronicler, 3:338, 564–569

bishops, 2:411

blasphemy, 2:434

blessings, 2:437–438

blood, 2:443–444

book of life, 2:526

burnt offerings, 2:709

Canaanite ritual references, 14:271

canonicity, 3:25–27, 565

capital punishment, 3:84

Catharism, 3:260

censuses, 3:337–338

charisms, 3:390

cherubim, 3:466

Christ (term), 3:527

Church concept, 3:575, 629

Church-State relations, 1:123

concubines, 4:65–66

Confraternity revisions, 10:276

conscience, 4:140–141, 143, 146

contemplation, 4:205

conversion, 4:231–233

corban, 4:257

covenant, 4:325–327

creation, 4:336–342, 344

crucifixion, 4:398

curses, 4:442

Cyril, 4:467

David (King of Israel), 4:536–537

Day of the Lord, 4:547–548

Dead Sea Scrolls, 4:562–564

death, 4:569–571

demonology, 4:645–646, 649, 716, 717

demons, 4:497

deportations, 4:674

descent of Christ into hell, 4:684

devil as term, 4:704

disciple as term, 4:768

divination, 4:785

Divine Person, 11:151

Divine truth, 14:230–231

double effect principle, 4:881

doxology, 4:89–90

eschatology, 5:333–338

exegesis, 12:181–182

Old Testament *(continued)*
    expiation, 5:563–564
    faith, 5:589–590
    Feast of Passover, 10:933–935
    food prohibitions, 10:465
    as foretelling, 3:28–29
    formation, 3:22–24
    genealogies, 6:125
    Gentiles, 6:139–140
    glory, 6:243–244
    gluttony, 6:251
    God in revelation, 6:271–276
    God the Father, 6:290–291
    Greek language, 6:438
    guilt, 6:569–570
    happiness, 2:171
    heaven, 6:684
    Hebrew language, 6:691–692
    hell, 6:723–724
    Hexateuch, 6:817
    historical books, 6:863
    holiness, 7:3, 8
    Holy Trinity, 14:201–202
    Holy War, 14:634–635
    homosexuality, 7:66, 67
    hope, 7:92–94, 96–99, 102–103, 103–106
    hospitality, 7:118
    humility, 7:205
    idolatry, 7:305–306, 324
    images, veneration of, 7:324
    images prohibited, 7:322–323
    immortality, 7:351–352
    immutability of God, 7:354–355
    impassibility of God, 7:357–358
    imposition of hands, 7:364
    incense use, 7:376
    incest, 7:378
    infinity, 7:458
    interpretations, 5:507–508
    intrinisic power of the spoken word, 2:26
    justice of God, 8:70–71
    justice of men, 8:73–74
    justification, 8:76–77
    leprosy references, 8:509
    life, concept of, 8:565–569
    light, use of, 8:581
    man, 9:85, 87
    Marcion on lack of Christian God, 9:142
    marriage, 7:67
    martyrdom, 9:227
    merit, 9:510

    miracles, 9:662
    moral obligation, 10:519
    Mount of Olives, 10:33
    mystery, 10:79–80
    names for Palestine, 10:777–778
    natural history of Palestine, 10:785–786, 788
    Nazirites, 10:217–218
    Nebo (Nabu) worship, 10:220
    Nebuchadnezzar, King of Babylon, 10:79, 224–225
    New Testament reference to, 1:272, 292, 3:26, 28–29
    nudity, 10:473
    O antiphons text from Prophetic and Sapiential books, 10:489
    oaths, 10:498
    obedience, 10:503–504
    omniscience, 10:593–594
    oracles, 10:619
    Origen on revelation nature, 10:654
    original sin, 10:664
    papyri fragments, 10:864
    Paradise, 10:875
    Passion narratives, 10:923–924
    passion plays, 4:893–894, 897–898, 900
    patience, 10:944
    peace, 11:49
    political geography of Palestine, 10:782–784
    poverty, 11:568
    prayer, 11:591–592
    presentation of the Lord, 3:14
    prophecies, 9:246, 247, 545
    prophecy, 11:759, 764–765
    Prophetic Books of the, 11:766
    providence of God, 11:780
    punishment, 11:817–818
    purgatory, 11:824–825
    quotations, 5:507
    read in the liturgy, 11:124–125
    rebirth, 11:951
    references in Matthew's Gospel, 9:357–358
    references in the Qur'ān, 7:608
    repentance, 4:225
    Resurrection of the Dead, 12:168–170
    retribution, 12:175–176
    sacred spaces, 12:501–502
    salutary acts, 12:621
    salvation history, 12:627–628
    Septuagint, 12:920–924
    sexuality, 3:444

    sin, 13:143–145
    spirit, 13:424–425
    suffering, 13:586
    suffering servant, songs of the, 13:588–591
    Sukkot, 2:532
    symbolic numbers, 10:477–478
    Targums version, 13:760–762
    temptation, 13:815–816
    Ten Commandments, 4:4–9
    texts, 2:355–362
    theology, 13:903
    theophanies, 13:929–930
    time, 14:83
    tradition, 14:132
    Tree of Knowledge, 14:164, 166
    Tree of Life, 14:166–167
    The Twelve, 14:250
    Tyndale's translations, 14:253
    use of word grace, 6:380, 381
    utopianism, 14:360
    virginity, 3:322, 14:544
    virtue, 14:548
    votive offerings, 14:589–590
    water, liturgical use of, 14:660
    widows, 14:712–713
    wisdom, 14:788–789
    women, role of, 14:828–829
    word of God, 14:836–837
    works of charity, 1:300, 301, 302
    Yom Kippur, 1:838
    See also Historical books of the Old Testament; Sapiential books; *specific books*; *specific books of the Bible*

The Old Testament and the Critics (Coppens), 5:519
The Old Testament in the Jewish Church (Smith), 6:825
Old Testament Law, 9:238–239
Oldcastle, John, 8:766
Oldcorne, Edward, Bl., 1:783, 5:234, 784
Oldegar, St., **10:582**
Oldmeadow, Ernest James, **10:582–583**
Oldrado de Ponte, 1:239, 3:52
O'Leary, Edward Cornelius (Bp. of Portland, ME), 9:59, 11:532
O'Leary, Henry Joseph (Abp. of Edmonton, Alberta, Canada), **10:583**
O'Leary, Peter (Father), 2:368
Oleśnicki, Zbigniew (Card.), 4:795–796, 11:440
Olevianus, Caspar, 4:79
O'Leyn, Matthew, 7:580

OLG (Sisters of Our Lady of the Garden), 10:724

Olga, St., **10:583**

Oliba (Bp. of Vich), 4:450

Olier, Jean Jacques (Father), 5:850, **10:583–584**

    Angela of Foligno, Bl., 1:412

    catechesis, 3:235

    Chrysostom of Saint-Lô, John, 3:573

    Compagnie du Saint-Sacrement, 4:41

    Counter Reformation, 3:612

    French School, 13:452

    Galand, Agnès of Jesus, 6:50

    priesthood, 11:704

    Sulpicians founding, 13:599, 600

Oliger, Livarius, **10:584**

Oliva Abbey (Poland), **10:584**

Olivétan, Pierre Robert, **10:585**, 13:230

Olivetan Benedictines, **2:274**, 318

Olivi, Petrus, 4:517

Ollé-Laprune, Léon, **10:585–586**

Oller, Bernard, 3:141–142

Olmos, Andrés de, **10:586**

O'Lochran, John, 7:579

Olot, Esteban de, 3:129

O'Loughran, Patrick, Bl., 7:580

Olsson, Erik, **10:586**

O'Luin, Donough, 7:580

O'Luin, John, 7:580

OLVM (Our Lady of Victory Missionary Sisters), 10:726

Olwell, Robert, 3:717

Olympiad era, 5:311

Olympias, St., **10:586**

Olympiodorus of Alexandria, 1:670, 3:258

Olympiodorus of Thebes, 2:797

Omaha Archdiocese (NE), 10:587–589

O'Mahoney, Francis, 7:581

O'Malley, Raymond, 7:582

O'Malley, Sean (Bp.), 5:612

Oman, **10:589–590**, *590*

Omar, Mohammad, 1:153

Omar II (Caliph), 2:751

O'Meara, Edward (Abp. of Indianpolis), 7:418

Omega. *See* Alpha and Omega

Omer of Thérouanne (Bp.), St., 1:68, 2:334, 5:787, **10:590**, 12:539

O'Meran, Thady, 7:579

OMI (Oblates of Mary Immanculate). *See* Oblates of Mary Immanculate (OMI)

Omission, **10:590–591**

Omne agens agit propter finem (Every agent acts for an end), 12:756

Omne quod movetur ab alio movetur (Everything moved is moved by another), 12:756

Omnebene. *See* Omnibonus (Bp.)

Omni die dic Mariae (hymn), **10:591**

Omnia opera (Slipyj), 13:218

Omnibonus (Bp.), 1:482, **10:591**

Omnipotence, 4:161, **10:591–593**, 11:553

Omnipresence, 10:593

Omniscience, **10:593–599**

L'Omniscienza di Dio (The All-Knowing God) (Pettazzoni), 11:221

Omnium sollicitudinum (papal bull, Benedict XIV), 7:412

O'Molloy, John, 7:580

O'Moore, Lawrence, 7:579

O'Moore, Raymond, 7:582

Omri (King of Israel), 7:640

Omrid Dynasty, 8:176

O'Mulconny of Roscommon, Farfassa, 5:833

O'Mulroney, Dermot, 7:580

OMV (Oblates of the Virgin Mary), 10:512

On Common Prejudice Concerning the Effectiveness of Witchcraft (Sterzinger), 13:528

On Consulting the Faithful in Matters of Doctrine (Newman), 10:334

On Divine Providence (Synesius of Cyrene), 13:683

On Dreams (Synesius of Cyrene), 13:683

On Evangelizatoin in the Modern World (apostolic exhortation, Paul VI), 11:616, 628

On Evil (Thomas Aquinas), 5:390

On Faith and the Principles of the Catholic Faith (Patrologia Graeca) (Manuel Calecas), 9:126–127

On Free Will (Valla), 12:121

On Generation and Corruption (Aristotle), 14:22

On His Return (Rutilius Namatianus), 12:320

On Immortality (Pomponazzi), 12:122

On Interpretation (Aristotle), 3:257

On Orthodox Faith (Damascene), 9:94

On Papal Infallibility (Spalding), 13:405

On Peace (De pace) (Joannes de Ligano), 7:883

On Philosophy (Aristotle), 1:669

On Pleasure (Valla), 12:121

On Prayer (Origen), 10:659

On Restoring Unity in the Church (Vergerio), 14:448

On Royalty (Synesius of Cyrene), 13:683

On the Babylonian Captivity of the Church (Luther), 5:427, 8:881, 12:16

On the Church and the World Today (Vatican Council II), 1:778

''*On the Church Music of the Future*'' (Liszt), 8:598–599

On the Coming of the Friars Minor to England (Thomas of Eccleston), 5:899

On the Death of His Brother (St. Ambrose), 12:705

''*On the Duty of Civil Disobedience*'' (Thoreau), 14:59

On the Edge of the Bush: Anthropology as Experience (Turner), 12:259

On the Education of Children and Their Moral Training (Vegius), 14:430

On the Epiphany (Titus of Bostra), 14:93

On the Eternal in Man (Scheler), 12:70

On the First Principle (Duns Scotus), 5:900

On the Gods and the World (Sallust), 10:241

On the Governance of Rulers (Machiavelli), 12:124

On the Heavens and Earth (Aristotle), 14:22

On the Hexameron (St. Basil), 2:136, 5:510

On the Immorality of the Soul (Pomponazzi), 11:470

On the Incarnation (St. Athanasius), 11:695

On the Law of War and Peace (De iure belli ac pacis libri tres) (Grotius), 6:540

On the Manners of a Gentleman and Liberal Studies (Vergerio), 14:448

On the Martyrs of Palestine (Eusebius), 6:613

On the Martyrs of Palestine (Pamphilus), 10:815

On the Misery of the Human Condition (De miseria humane conditionis) (Innocent III), 7:470

On the Nativity I (Romanus Melodus, St.), 12:348

On the Nature of Man (Nemesius of Emesa), 10:232

On the Nature of Things (Thomas of Cantimpré), 14:32

On the Origin of Species (Darwin), 4:532

On the Pastoral Care of Homosexual Persons (Congregation for the Doctrine of the Faith), 7:66, 71–73

On the Priesthood (St. John Chrysostom), 7:945

On the Procession of the Holy Spirit (St. Anselm of Canterbury), 1:497

On the Promises (St. Dionysius), 5:510

On the Promulgation of Laws (Espen), 5:658

On the Properties of Things (De proprietatibus rerum) (Bartholomaeus Anglicus), 2:*122*, 123

On the Redemption of Mankind (St. Anselm of Canterbury), 1:497

On the Resurrection (Methodius), 9:563

On the Spirit (St. Basil), 2:136

On the Theology of the Church (Eusebius of Caesarea), 5:452

On the True Purity of Chastity (Basil of Ancyra), 2:139–140

On the Truth of the Catholic Faith (Aquinas). *See Summa contra gentiles* (St. Thomas Aquinas)

''On the Vigilance of the Church's Pastors Regarding Books'' (Vatican Council II), 3:336

On the Virginal Conception and Original Sin (St. Anselm of Canterbury), 1:497

On the Virtues (Thomas Aquinas), 5:390

On the Way of Life (Synesius of Cyrene), 13:683

On the Witch of Endor against Origen (Eustathius of Antioch), 5:456, 511

On Virginity (Basil of Ancyra). *See On the True Purity of Chastity* (Basil of Ancyra)

On War (De bello) (Joannes de Ligano), 7:883

Onahan, William James, 8:412, **10:599–600**

Onanism, 4:219, 222, **9:315–317**, **10:600**

Oñate, Juan de, 1:687, 10:284

137 Chapters of Spiritual Mediations (Gregory Sinaites), 6:524

One Hundred Years of Educational Foundations by the Brothers of Mary in America (Resch), 12:137

O'Neaghtan, Donall, 7:581

O'Neil, Leo E., 10:280

O'Neil, Mary Anne (Sister Mary Theresa), 5:880

O'Neilan, Daniel, 7:579

O'Neilan, Denis, 7:581

O'Neill, Art, 7:581

O'Neill, Arthur Barry, 11:625

O'Neill, Brian, 7:581

O'Neill, Hugh, 7:18, 557

O'Neill, Owen Roe, 9:24, 12:250

O'Neill, Phelim, Sir, 7:582

O'Neill, Sara Benedicta, **10:600**

O'Neill, Thomas J., 2:39

One's Self as Another (Ricoeur), 5:349

Onganía, Juan Carlos, 1:654

Onias III (high priest), 1:528, 9:10

Onizuka, Peter, Bl., 7:734

Onkelos Targum, 13:760–761

Only Son (Farrell), 5:631

Ono, Anthony, Bl., 7:733

Ono, Clement, Bl., 7:733

Onomasticon (Eusebius of Caesarea), 5:452

Onondaga people, 8:383

Onphitak, Philip Siphong, 13:848–849

Ontario (Canada), 3:10–11

Ontario Conference of Catholic Bishops (Canada), 3:8

Ontinyent martyrs, Spanish Civil War, 6:56

Ontologia sive Metaphysica Generalis (Frick), 10:607

Ontological argument, **10:600–603**
    Anselm of Canterbury, St., 1:496
    aseity, 1:779, 780
    dualism, 4:916
    Duns Scotus, John, 4:937
    Hartshorne, Charles, 6:657–658
    Leibniz, 8:458
    Richard Rufus of Cornwall, opposition to, 12:236

Ontological transcendence, 14:142

Ontologism, 3:624, **10:603–605**
    beatific vision, 2:169
    destiny, supernatural, 4:694
    existence of God, 6:313
    Lepidi, A., 8:507
    Malebranche, Nicolas, 9:75
    truth, 14:223

Ontology, 7:303, **10:605–608**, 14:228–230, 290

Ontology (Van Steenberghen), 10:607, 14:388

Oosterhout Abbey (Netherlands), 2:231

Oosterwyk, John Van, 6:364

OP. *See* Dominicans

Opata people, 2:91

Open Catholic Church (China), 3:504–505

Open communion, 2:80

Open Letter to Dr. Hyde (Stevenson), 14:467

An Open Letter to His Eminence Cardinal Gibbons (Sabatier), 12:453

Open Letter to the Christian Nobility (Luther), 8:281–282

Opening Procession of Vatican Council I (McMahon), 14:*402*

Opera, 2:112, 6:250–251, 12:725

Opera, sacred, 8:471, 867

Opera dei Congressi e Comitati Cattolici (social organization), 6:537, 7:673, 10:69, 14:128

Opera Dionysii (Gallus), 14:30

Opera dommatica contro gli eretici pretesi riformati (St. Alphonsus Liguori), 1:310

Opera moralia (Gobat), 6:269

Opera omnia (Lawrence of Brindisi), 8:406, 407

Opera omnia (Luther), 14:234

Opera omnia (Pohle, ed.), 14:13

Opera omnia (St. John Damascene), 8:511

Opera Patrum Apostolicorum (Funk), 6:35

Operarii autem pauci (The Workers Are Few) (Manna), 9:119–120

Operation Resuce organization, 8:116

Operationalism, 5:142, 9:418, **10:608–609**

Operative habits, 6:598–599, 600

Ophites, 6:260

Opinion, 3:302, 351, 4:366–368, 7:179, **10:609–610**

Oppenheim, Philipp, **10:610**

Oppose America-Aid Korea Movement (China), 3:501–502

Opposition, 4:793, 5:503–504, **10:611**

Optatianus Porphyrius, 1:72

Optatus of Milevis (Bp.), St., 3:275, 293, 553, 4:83, 10:431, **611–612**

Optatus of Thamugadi (Bp.), 4:862, 863

Optics, 12:810, 813, 13:881

Optics (Newton), 10:19

Optics (Ptolemy), 11:808

Optimism, **10:612–614**

Optimism, theological aspects of, **10:614**

Option for the poor, **10:615–616**

Optiz, Martin, 2:115

Opus Anglicanum, 8:635

Opus de natura rerum (Thomas of Cantimpré), 9:462

Opus Dei (organization), **10:616–618**
    Escrivá de Balaguer y Albás, Josemaría, Bl., founding, 5:355, 356
    lay spirituality, 8:416
    Portillo, Alvaro del, 11:526–527

precursors, 8:198

Spain, 13:397, 400

University of Navarre, 10:215

Opus maius (Roger Bacon), 12:284

Opus metaphysicum (Scheibler), 12:768

Opus metricum (James Gaetani Stefaneschi), 7:707

Opus nonaginta dierum (William of Ockham), 5:900

Opus prophetale (St. Jerome), 7:759

Opus tessellatum mosaics, 10:2

Opus theologicum morale in Busembaum medullam (Ballerini), 2:31

Opus tripartitum (Eckhart), 5:45

Opus vermiculatum mosaics, 10:2

Opuscula moralia (Váquez), 14:427

Opuscula Sacra (Boethius), 12:107

Opúsculos de San Pascual Bailón (Paschal Baylon), 10:917

Opusculum contra Wolfelmum Coloniensem (Manegold of Lautenbach), 9:105–106

Opusculum de vita sua (Herman of Scheda), 6:783

Opusculum tripertitum (Gerson), 3:232, 241

O'Queeley, Malachy (Abp. of Tuam, Ireland), 7:581

O'Quillan, Peter, 7:579

Or Adonai (Crescas), 4:361

Oracle, in the Bible, 1:297, **10:619–620**

Oracles, 1:264, 4:632, *633*, 784, **10:618–619**

See also Sibylline Oracles

Oracles of the Twelve Tribes, 9:540–541

O'Rahilly, T. F., 10:955

Oral history, 6:132

Oral law, 8:2, 13:742–743

Oral traditions, 8:20, 13:742

Orange, Councils of (441-529), **10:620**

beginning of faith, 5:604–605

clerical celibacy/marriage, 3:325

Confirmation, 4:84, 87

conversion, 4:239, 240–241

destiny, supernatural, 4:694

predestination, 11:649–650, 12:900

Semi-Pelagianism, 1:877, 2:499, 3:206, 8:82

Orange, Martyrs of, 5:973, **10:620–621**, 12:484

Orans, 4:391, 392, 8:649, 9:272, **10:621**, 12:600

Orant symbolism, 3:630

Orate Fratres (periodical), 12:552

Oratio (Pico Della Mirandola), 11:324

Oratio ad Graecos (Tatian), 13:764

Oratio Admonitionis, 10:45

Oratio catechetica magna (St. Gregory of Nyssa), 6:518

Oratio contra poetas (Barbaro the Elder), 2:90

Oratio de imaginibus (St. John Damascene), 5:449

Oratio in funere Caroli V (Seripando), 13:*17*

Oratio Post Gloriam (prayer), 10:44–45

Oratio Post Nomina (prayer), 10:45

Oratio Post Sanctus (prayer), 10:46

Oratio super populum (prayer), **10:621**

Oration Against the Arians (St. Athanasius), 11:695

Oration of the Dignity of Man (Pico Della Mirandola), 12:117, 122

Orationum ac epistolarum libri XV (Barbaro), 2:90

Oratorians, 3:185, 243, **10:621–623**, 12:765, 13:464–465

Oratorio catechetica (St. Gregory of Nyssa), 3:250

Oratorio delle Missioni (Italy), 5:871

Oratorio habita Thuronii (Ferreri), 5:694

Oratorio per la Settimana Santa (Rossi), 12:388

Oratorios, 3:123, 438, 8:694

Oratory, 10:248–249

Oratory of Divine Love, 3:610, 782, **4:787**

Oratory of Pierre de Bérulle, 2:568, 714

See also Bérulle, Pierre de (Card.)

Orban, Alexis, 3:291

Orbis Books (NY), **10:623–624**, 12:729

Orbis sensualium pictus (Comenius, John Amos), 4:2, *3*

Orbis Seraphicus (Gubernatis), 6:554–555

Orbona (goddess), 12:679

Orchard Lake Schools (MI), **10:624–626**

Ordained ministries, 9:653

Ordeal, 4:46, 442, 8:354, **10:626–629**

Ordeal by water, 10:626

Order, 1:59, 747, 3:302, **10:628–631**, 12:206, 13:485–486

Order and History (Voegelin), 10:630

Order of Arrouaise, 3:68

Order of Aubrac, **1:845–846**

Order of Aviz, 1:240, 947, **947**, 2:858

Order of Brothers of Mercy of Mary the Helper, 6:3

Order of Celebrating Marriage (Rome, 1990), 9:338

Order of Christ, 1:240, 4:596, **10:631**

The Order of Christian Funerals. See Funeral rites

Order of Cluny, 3:68

The Order of Communion, 12:9

Order of Friar Servants of St. Mary. *See* Servites

Order of Friars Minor. *See* Franciscans, First Order

Order of Friars of the Sack, 7:151

Order of Friars Preachers. *See* Dominicans

Order of Friars Unitors of St. Gregory the Illuminator, 4:851

Order of Grandmont, 13:525

Order of Hospitalers of the Holy Spirit, 6:587

Order of Lebanese Monks, 8:427

Order of Magdalens, **9:33**

Order of Mercy, 3:414

Order of Our Lady of Mercy. *See* Mercedarians

Order of Our Lady of Ransom. *See* Mercedarians

Order of Poor Clerics Regular of the Mother of God of the Pious Schools. *See* Piarists

Order of St. Anthony, 9:421

Order of St. Augustine. *See* Augustinians

Order of St. Basil the Great. *See* Basilians (Byzantine)

Order of St. Clare. *See* Poor Clares

Order of St. Gregory the Great, 4:596

Order of St. Gregory the Illuminator, 8:668

Order of Saint Hubert, **12:549–550**

Order of St Jerome Aemilian. *See* Somascan Fathers

Order of St. John. *See* Knights of Malta

Order of St. John of Jerusalem. *See* Knights of Malta

Order of St. Sylvester Pope, 4:596

Order of Santa Inés de Montepulciano, 3:850

Order of Sempringham. *See* Gilbertines

Order of Suwayr. *See* Basilian Order of St. John Baptist

Order of the Blessed Virgin Mary for the Ransom of Captives. *See* Mercedarians

Order of the Company of Our Lady (La Enseñanza), 3:850

Order of the Holy Cross, 4:415

Order of the Holy Cross with a Red Heart, 2:609

Order of the Holy Sepulcher of Jerusalem, 3:68

Order of the Holy Spirit, 3:412, **7:51–52**, 120, 129

Order of the Holy Spirit, Guy de Montpellier, 6:587

Order of the Most Holy Redeemer. *See* Redemptoristines

Order of the Most Holy Savior of Saint Brigit, 6:810

Order of the Most Holy Saviour. *See* Brigittine Sisters

Order of the Poor Clerics Regular of the Mother of God of the Pious Schools. *See* Piarists

Order of the Savior and of the Blessed Virgin, 7:371

Order of the Star-Spangled Banner. *See* Know-Nothingism

Order of the Swan (1440), **10:631–632**

Order of the Visitation, 5:866

Order of the Visitation of Holy Mary, 3:381

Ordericus Vitalis, 1:463, 5:497, 772, **10:632**, 12:546

Orders, Holy. *See* Holy Orders, Sacrament of; Ordination

Orders of St. George, **12:547**

Ordinal for Holy Week (Pius XII), 5:16

Ordinal numbers, in pope's names, 11:502, 507

Ordinals, Roman, **10:632–633**, *633*

Ordinamenti di giustizia (Giano della Bella), 5:767

Ordinances (Torquemada), 14:114

Ordinaries, ecclesiastical, **10:633–634**

Ordinary (ordinal) time, 8:719

Ordinary magisterium, 2:172–173, 13:353

Ordinatio, 10:634

Ordinatio (Duns Scotus), 5:895, 900

Ordinatio imperii (Lothair I), 8:795

Ordinatio imperii (Louis the Pious), 3:169, 10:914

Ordinatio sacerdotalis (apostolic letter, John Paul II), 7:1003, 11:747

Ordination
    age requirements, 7:40
    Anglicanism, 5:67–68
    anointing, 7:35
    Armenian liturgy, 1:710
    Baptist minsters, 2:81
    canonical impediments, 7:40–41
    dismissorial letters, 4:747
    imposition of hands, 7:364, 365
    ministers, 7:38–39
    reception and requirements, 7:39–41
    See also Holy Orders

Ordination Anointings in the Western Church before 1000 A.D. (Ellard), 5:168

Ordination of women
    Anglicanism, 1:*435*, 439, 441, 447
    Ecumenical dialogues, 5:68
    Episcopalianism, 5:298
    Roman Catholicism, 5:710
    Synod of Bishops, 12:551
    Women's Ordination Conference (WOC), 5:677

Ordinationes et exercitia quotidiaan (Foscarini), 5:825

Ordinations in the Roman Rite, **10:634–642**, 13:166

Ordinem vestrum (papal bull, Innocent IV), 7:980

Ordines Judiciarii, **10:642–643**

Ordines Romani, 3:45, 10:632–633, *633*

Ordo, 10:634

Ordo, Roman, **10:643**
    adoption, 8:440
    catechesis, 3:231
    early liturgical books, 8:640
    English translation, 8:439
    liturgical history, 8:655
    liturgical music history, 8:682
    RCL compared, 8:441
    second edition, 8:439–440, 442
    Vatican Council II, 8:440

Ordo ad catechumenum faciendum, 3:251

Ordo cluniacensis, 10:555

Ordo compendiosus, 1:486

Ordo concilii. . .celebrandi (Paul VI), 14:411

Ordo executionis (order of execution or accomplishment), 12:752

Ordo intentionis (order of intention), 12:752

Ordo iudiciarius (Bartholomew of Brescia), 2:125

Ordo iudiciarius Bambergensis (1182-85), 10:642

Ordo iudiciarius Causa II, quaestio I (1171), 10:642

Ordo Missae (liturgical right), 9:672–673, 674–676, 10:43

Ordo Missae of the Missale Ambrosianum, 4:356

Ordo monasterii, 3:68

Ordo querimoniae (Valerio of Bierzo), 14:375

Ordo Regularium Matris Dei. See Clerks Regular of the Mother of God

Ordo Romanus Antiquus (Hittorp), 10:633

Ordo Romanus I, 4:118

Ordo Romanus III, 4:50

Ordo Romanus Primus, 12:328

Ordo Romanus VII, 4:354

Ordo Romanus XLIX, 4:9–10

Ordo Sancti Benedicti de Monte Fano. See Sylvestrine Benedictines

Ordo XI, 4:86

Ordonnances cabochiennes (1413), 10:888

L'Ordre et les ordinations (Trixeront), 14:95

Oré, Luis Gerónimo de (Bp.), **10:643**

O'Regan, Anthony (Bp. of Chicago), 3:477, 517

Oregon, **10:644–647**
    anti-Catholicism, 11:529, 530
    Blanchet, Francis Norbert, 2:430–431
    Congregation for the Propagation of the Faith, 2:430–431
    De Smet, Pierre Jean (Father), 11:529
    Sheehan, Luke Francis, 13:73–74
    Sisters of St. Mary of Oregon, 12:565
    Stettler v. O'Hara (1913), 10:566
    Whitman massacre (1847), 2:431, 635
    See also specific dioceses and archdioceses

Oregon City Archdiocese (OR). *See* Portland Archdiocese (OR)

Oregon School Case, 2:429, **10:646–650**, 11:530

O'Reilly, Bernard (Bp. of Hartford), 6:652, **10:650**, 12:214

O'Reilly, Charles B. (Bp.), 2:23

O'Reilly, Edmund (Bp. of Armagh), 1:698, **10:650–651**

O'Reilly, Edmund (Bp. of Hartford), 4:122

O'Reilly, Hugh (Abp. of Armagh), 1:698, 3:834

O'Reilly, James, 5:624

O'Reilly, John, 11:366

O'Reilly, Patrick Thomas (Bp.), 9:307, 13:462

O'Reilly, Richard, 1:698

O'Reilly, Thomas (Father), 1:830

Oreintalium Ecclesiarum (Decree on Eastern Catholic Churches), 5:20

Orel, Anton, 1:915

Orellana, Francisco, 3:198

Oremus (Let us pray), 10:45, 46, **651**

Oresme, Nicholas, 13:254

Orfali, Gaudenzio, 3:83

Orfanel, Jacinto, Bl., 7:733

Orfeo (Rossi), 12:388

Organ, liturgical use of, 8:694, **10:651–652**

Organic articles, 3:92, 618, 4:61, 63

Organicism, **10:652**

Organization for African Unity (OAU), 2:712

Organon (Aristotle), 1:377, 670, 8:748, 12:40

Oriel College (Oxford University), 10:*730*

Oriens Christianus (periodical), 2:159

Oriental Canon Law, 10:415

Oriental Christians, 13:711–715

Oriental Church, Congregation for the, 5:21, 22

　See also Eastern Churches, Congregation for the

Oriental churches. *See* Eastern churches

Oriental cults, 10:85–89

Oriental hagiography, 6:614–615

Oriental moral theology, 9:860

Oriental Orthodox copts, 4:255

Oriental studies, 9:114

Oriental theology, 5:58

Orientalium dignitas (apostolic constitution, Leo XIII), 3:817, 7:651, 9:681

Orientalium ecclesiarum (Vatican Council II), 3:626, 818

Oriental-Orthodox dialogue, 8:168

''Orienting'' the basilica, 2:147–148

Origen and Origenism, 5:292, 10:*653*, **653–661**, 11:290

　6th century overview, 10:660–661

　active life, 1:83

　Alexander (Patriarch of Alexandria), St., 1:266

　Alexander of Jerusalem, St., 1:266

　allegory, 1:292, 337

　Ambrose, St., 1:337, 339

　Anastasius I (Pope), St., 1:387

　angels, 1:419

　Antichrist, 1:516

　apocatastasis, 1:548

　apocrypha, 1:558

　apologetics, 1:564, 567

　Arianism, 1:660

　Assumption of Mary, 1:800

　Basil, St., 2:136, 137

　Beryllus of Bostra, 2:339

　Bible texts, 2:358, 366

　biblical canon, 3:21, 31

　Byzantine theology, 2:793

　Caesarea, 10:800

　Carpocrates, 3:174

　casuistry, 3:220

　catechumenate, 3:250

　causality, 3:303

　Celsus, 3:329

　Christian paideia, 10:755

　Christmas, 3:551

　Christology, 3:560

　church architecture, 1:756

　Church property, 3:723, 724

　Clement of Alexandria, St., 3:797

　clerical celibacy/marriage, 3:323

　condemnation, 4:191, 192

　contemplation, 4:205

　contemporary state, 10:661

　controversies, 5:292, 10:659–660, 12:404, 405, 452

　creedal statements, 4:350, 353

　death imagery in baptism, 2:75

　demonology, 4:648, 649

　descent of Christ into hell, 4:684

　Didymus the Blind, 4:738

　dogmatic definition, 4:611

　Domitian of Ancyra, 4:858

　early Palestine, 10:800–801

　eschatology, 5:343

　exigetical works, 5:509–510, 512–513

　exorcism, 5:551

　fidelity, 10:656

　Firmilian of Caesarea, 5:740

　Gnosis, 6:255

　grace, 6:401

　Greco-Roman schooling, 6:429–430

　hell, 6:726–727

　Holy Trinity, 14:192, 203

　homily, 7:62

　homoousios, 4:197, 7:65

　hypostasis, 7:263

　Immaculate Conception, 7:332

　immortality, 7:353

　impassivity of God, 7:358

　Jerome, St., 3:594, 7:758–759

　John Italus, 2:758

　Julius Africanus, 8:58–59

　Justinian I (Byzantine Emperor), 3:595–596

　Kingdom of God, 8:174

　Leontius of Byzantium, 2:820, 8:502

　liturgical history, 8:651

　martyrs, 4:83

　mysticism and mystery, 10:655–656

　Origen's father, 8:499

　patristic theology, 10:967

　penitential controversy, 11:73

　Platonic theory, 5:90

　preaching, 11:608–609, 617

　presbyters, 11:674

　priesthood, 11:694, 699

　public confession, 4:76

　relics, 12:51

　Rufinus of Aquileia, 12:406

　School of Alexandria, 1:268, 269, 272–273

　School of Antioch, 1:527

　School of Caesarea, 2:845, 847

　similarity, 13:126

　simplicity of God, 13:137

　soul, 13:340–341

　speculative theology, 10:657–659

　spiritual life, 13:435–436

　spirituality, 13:444

　theology, 10:656–657

　theology of history, 6:888

　Theophilus of Alexandria, 13:932

　works, 10:654–655

　works of charity, 3:403

　See also Patristic era

Origen milagroso del Santuario de Nuestra Señora de Guadalupe (Beccerra Tanco), 2:192

Origin of the Species (Darwin), 5:492, 495

Original integrity of man, 2:19–20

Original justice, 1:105, 4:68–69, 8:74–75, **10:661–664**

Original sin, **10:664–672**

　Ambrosius Catharinus, 1:347

　Augustine, St., 1:860, 876–877

　Baianism, 2:20

　De Baptismo (Pacian), 10:744

　Catholic faith and theology, 10:665–671

　Christian philosophy, 3:538

　concupiscence, 4:68–69

　conversion, 4:240

　Council of Trent, 14:170

　death, 4:573–574

　defined, 13:150

　Hermesianism, 6:798

　justice of men, 8:75

　lay spirituality, 8:414

　liberal theology, 8:543

　Machiavelli, Niccolo, 9:21

　Malebranche, Nicolas, 9:75

　man as changed by, 10:614

　Mariology, 9:170–171

　nature corrupted by, 10:195, 201

　Protestant view, 8:166

　reprobation, 12:132

　Rosmini-Serbati, Antonio, 12:384

Original sin *(continued)*
 Semi-Pelagianism, 1:877, 3:206
 sin of Adam, 10:665–667, 668–669,
  670
 sphere of sex, 13:46
 suffering, 13:586
 supernatural endowments, 9:93–94
 See also Sin, in the Bible

Origines (Isidore of Seville, St.),
 9:439–440

*Les Origines de l'Église d'Éesse et la
 légende d'Abgar* (Tixeront), 14:95

Les Origines du dogme de la Trinité
 (Lebreton), 8:430

Oriol, Joseph, St., **10:672**

Orione (Bach), 2:6

Orione, Luigi, Bl., 3:419, 8:611, **10:672**,
 13:320–321

Orlandini, Niccolò, 8:317

Orléans, Councils of (511-549), 1:895,
 3:325, 409, 409–410, 410

Orléans, Synods of (533-541), 1:232,
 3:409

Orléans de la Motte, François Gabriel d'
 (Bp. of Amiens), 1:359

Orléans-Longueville, Antoinette d',
 10:672–673

Orléansville Basilica, 1:754

Ormaneto, Niccolò, 3:145, 214

Ormanian, Malachy (Father), 1:706

Ormo Seró, José María, 2:92

Ormonde, James, 7:560

Ormulum (Orm), 11:633

Ornacieux, Beatrice d', 3:192

Ornithomancy, 4:785

Orona Madrigal, Justino, St., **10:673**,
 12:366

Orosius (Spanish priest), **10:673–674**,
 11:61

Orosius, Paul, 1:461, 784, 877

O'Rourke, Donough, 7:579

O'Rourke, K. D., 1:29

Orozco, Alfonso de, Bl., 1:875, **10:674**

Orozco y Jiménez, Francisco (Abp.),
 10:674

Orphanotrophia, 10:675

Orphans and orphanages, 14:*348*
 diaconia and care, 4:718–720
 Italy, 5:632, 865, 872
 social principle, 13:249–250
 Somascan fathers, 13:309–310
 United States, 5:752, 758, 759, 835,
  13:174

Orphans and orphanages, in the early
 church, **10:674–675**

Orphic passports, 10:95

Orphism, **10:675–676**
 asceticism, 1:773
 history and evaluation, 10:94–95
 mysteries, 10:85, 86
 soul, 13:338
 transmigration of souls, 14:156

Orsi, Giuseppe Agostino (Card.), **10:676**

Orsini, Alessandro, 10:677–678

Orsini, Bobone, 10:677

Orsini, Domenico, 10:677–678

Orsini, Flavio, 10:677–678

Orsini, Francesco, 10:677–678

Orsini, Franciotto, 10:677–678

Orsini, Fulvio, 10:482

Orsini, Giacinto. *See* Celestine III (Pope)

Orsini, Giacomo, 10:677–678

Orsini, Giambattista, 10:677–678

Orsini, Gian Gaetano, 10:677–678

Orsini, Giordano (d. 1165), 10:677

Orsini, Giordano (d. 1287), 10:677

Orsini, Giordano (d. 1438), 10:677–678

Orsini, Giovanni Gaetano. *See* Nicholas
 III (Pope)

Orsini, John, Bl., 10:676

Orsini, Latino (d. 1477), 10:677–678

Orsini, Latino Frangipane Malabrance
 (d. 1294), 10:677

Orsini, Matteo (d. 1340), 10:677–678

Orsini, Matteo Rosso (Card.), 3:320,
 10:676

Orsini, Napoleone, 10:677

Orsini, Nicholas (Card.), 3:321

Orsini, Pietro (d. 1181), 10:677

Orsini, Pietro Francesco. *See* Benedict
 XIII (Pope)

Orsini, Poncello, 10:677–678

Orsini, Raimondello, 10:677–678

Orsini, Rinaldo, 10:677–678

Orsini, Tommaso, 10:677–678

Orsini, Vincenzo Maria. *See* Benedict
 XIII (Pope)

Orsini, Virginio, 1:259, 10:677–678, *677*

Orsini d'Aragona, Domenico (Card.),
 3:794

Orsini family, 1:58, 259, 3:854,
 10:676–678

Orsucci, Angelo Ferrer, Bl., 7:733

Ortega García, Secundino María
 (Father), 2:92

Ortega y Alamino, Jaime (Abp. of
 Havana), 4:*419*

Ortega y Gasset, José, 5:544,
 10:678–679, 11:*284*

Orthodox and Oriental Orthodox
 Churches, 5:19, **10:679–681**
 Albania, 1:213, 214, 215, 2:746

angelic devotion, 1:424

Bulgaria, 2:680, 684, 745–746

Byzantine art, 2:731

China, 9:695

Christology, 8:503

Coptic, 1:271, 273

creedal statements, 4:354–355

Crusades, 4:402, 413

Easter service (Kiev), 10:*702*

Estonian, 2:746

Finland, 2:746

Georgia (Europe), 2:746, 3:294

history, 8:510–511

Latvia, 8:376

light of glory, 8:585

liturgy, 1:273

Moldova, 9:765

Moravia, 3:599

Orthodox Church of America, 2:744,
 745, 3:717

overview, 2:744–746

philetism, 4:196

Romanian, 2:745

Serbian, 2:547

seven great councils, 4:300

Shehan, L. J., 13:76

synthesis of opposites, 13:238

Ukrainian, 1:533–534, 10:696

Vatican Council II, 1:829

World Council of Churches
 members, 14:842

Yugoslavia, 13:10

See also Armenian Apostolic Church;
 Eastern churches; Greek Orthodox
 Church; Russian Orthodox Church

Orthodox Baptistery of S. Giovanni
 (Ravenna, Italy), 11:932

Orthodox Church of America (OCA),
 2:744, 745, 3:717, **10:681–683**,
 12:742

The Orthodox Confession of Faith
 (Moghila), 9:760–761

Orthodox Creed of 1678 (General
 Baptists), 2:78

Orthodox doctrine, 5:641

Orthodox Dogmatic Theology
 (Staniloae), 13:477

The Orthodox Eastern Church
 (Fortescue), 5:821

Orthodox Greco-Russian theology,
 13:910

Orthodox Judaism, 8:10–11

Orthodox Roman Catholic Movement,
 3:289

Orthodox symbolic books, **10:700–701**

Orthodox theology, 13:911, 912

Orthodoxia, 6:460

Orthodoxy, **10:701**, 13:55–56

Orthodoxy, Feast of (843), 2:753, 766, 7:283

Orti y Lara, Juan Manuel, 12:773

Ortio synodalis de primatu (Torquemada), 14:112

Ortiz, Diego, 1:889

Ortiz de Zárate, Pedro, Ven., **10:701–702**

Ortlibarii, 2:629, **10:702–703**

Ortlieb of Strasbourg. *See* Ortlibarii

Ortolana, Bl., **10:703**

Orton, William Aylott, **10:703–704**

Ortus et progressus ordinis minorum S. Francisci ultra quinque saecula (Elbel), 5:143

Ortynsky, Soter (Bp.), 2:145, 5:20, 11:86

Orval Abbey (Luxembourg), 3:751, **10:704**

Orvieto Cathedral (Italy), 1:544, 12:601

Orwell, George, 1:292, 14:361

Os trabalhos de Jesus (Thomas of Jesus), 14:35

Osage people, 8:113, 117

Osbaldeston, Edward, Bl., 5:232, **10:704**

Osbern of Gloucester, **10:704**

Osborne, K., 12:473

Osborne, Thomas (Earl of Danby). *See* Danby, Thomas Osborne, Earl of

OSC (Oblates of St. Charles), 10:515

O'Scanlan, Maolpadraig, 1:697

O'Scanlon, Maurice, 7:579

Oscott, Synod of (1852), 5:251

Osei-Bonsu, Joseph, 7:528

Osés Sáinz, Jose, Bl., 4:494

OSFS (Oblate Sisters of St. Francis de Sales), 10:512, 513

O'Shea, Philip, 7:579

Oshida, Shigeto, 7:743

Osiander, Andreas, **10:704–705**, 14:159

Albrecht of Brandenburg-Ansbach, 1:233, 234

Copernicus, Nicolaus, 4:251

justification controversy, 8:890

Schatzgeyer, Kaspar, 12:730

Osiris (Egyptian deity). *See* Isis and Osiris (Egyptian deities)

OSJ (Oblates of St. Joseph), 10:512, 517

OSM (Servants of Mary). *See* Mantellate Sisters

Osmund (Bp. of Salisbury), St., **10:705**, 12:617

Osoba y czyn (Person and Act) (Wojtyła), 7:995

Osrhoene, **10:705–706**

Osservatore Cattolico, 1:228

L'Osservatore Romano (newspaper), 14:402

Ossius of Córdoba. *See* Hosius of Córdoba (Bp.)

Ossó y Cervelló, Enrique (Henry) de, St., **10:706**, 12:587

OSSR (Oblate Sisters of the Most Holy Redeemer), 10:513

Ossuaries, 2:698, 10:33, **707**

Östborn, G., 3:24

Osterrieder, Hermann, 12:770

Ostia synagogue (Rome, Italy), 13:678

Ostiensis. *See* Leo Marsicanus

Ostliffe, George (Father), 5:729

Ostpolitik, 11:31

Ostracon, **10:707**

Ostrogoths, 1:172, 663, 6:171, 369, 7:223

Ostrozhski, Constantine, 12:422

Ostwald, W., 1:835

O'Sullivan, Francis, 7:582

O'Sullivan, Jeremiah (Bp. of Mobile, AL), 1:201, 9:749

Oswald (King of Northumbria), St., 1:192, **10:707–708**

Oswald of York (Bp.), St., **10:708**, 11:905, 12:253, 539, 14:894

"Oswego Movement," 11:171

Oswiu (King of the Anglo-Saxons), 1:449

Oswy (King of Northumbria), 5:14, 153

Osypiuk, Bartołomiej, 11:584

Ot, Guiral, 1:265

Ota, Augustine, Bl., 7:733

L'Otage (Claudel), 3:766, 768

Otbert (Bp. of Liège), 12:549

O'Teevan, Eugene, 7:581

Oteiza Segura, Faustino, Bl., **10:708**, 816

Otello (Tancredi), 12:389

Otello (Verdi), 14:446

Otey, James H., 5:297

Othbert of Liége (Bp.), 12:293

Otherness, 4:592–595

Othlo of Sankt Emmeram, 7:248, 9:449, **10:708–709**

Othmar, St., **10:709**, 12:669

Otia imperialia (Gervase of Tilbury), 6:194

Otis, Harrison Gray, 3:472

Ōtomo Yoshishige, 7:726

O'Toole, George Barry, **10:709–710**

O'Toole, James, 1:640

O'Treivir, Bernard, 7:580

O'Treivir, Donegal, 7:580

Ott, Michael, **10:710**, 12:578

Ott, Stanley J. (Bp. of Baton Rouge), 2:156

Ottaviani, Alfredo (Card.), 10:68, 710–711

Ottaviano of Monticello. *See* Victor IV (Antipope)

Ottawa (Canada), 3:8

Ottawa, University of, 5:614–615

Ottawa people, 2:86, 3:5

Otterbein, Philip William, 5:468, 471, **10:711**, 14:305, 308

Boehm, Martin, 2:454

River Brethren, 2:606

Otto, Rudolf, 5:331, **10:128**

existence of God, 6:314

experience of the holy, 13:68

irrationalism, 7:587

mystery in theology, 10:85

phenomenology, 12:70

sacred and profane, 12:57

theological doctrine, 10:711

Otto, Rudolph. *See* Otto, Rudolf

Otto, W., 1:664, 5:2

Otto I (the Great) (Holy Roman Emperor), 3:172, 600, **10:711–713**, *712*, 836

Adalbero I, 1:99

Adaldag, St., 1:102

anointing, 1:479

Bruno of Cologne, St., 2:647

Cologne, 3:843

Conrad of Constance, 4:136

Council of Ingelheim, 1:172

Gerold, St., 6:188

hereditary duchies, 6:175–176

Historia Ottonis, 8:737

Italy, 7:660

John XII (Pope), 4:362, 7:925–926

John XIII (Pope), 7:926

Lantbert of Freising, 8:327

Liutprand of Cremona, 8:737

prince-bishops, 11:714

Ratherius of Verona, 11:918

Otto II (Holy Roman Emperor), 1:235, 2:500, 7:42, 660, 8:852, **10:713–714**

Otto III (Holy Roman Emperor), **10:714–715**, 720

Adalbert of Prague, 1:102

Bernward of Hildesheim, St., 2:328

Brogne Abbey, 2:625

Donation of Constantine, 4:860

Gregory V (Pope), 4:362, 6:489

John XVI (Antipope), 7:927–928

Leo of Vercelli, 8:495

Otto III (Holy Roman Emperor)
(continued)
 papal relations, 7:660–661
Otto IV (Holy Roman Emperor),
 6:193–194
Otto of Bamberg, St. (Bp.), 4:88, 5:325,
 10:715
Otto of Cappenberg, Bl., **10:716**
Otto of Freising (Bp.), 1:463, *912*,
 2:309, 3:601, 749, 5:325, **10:716**
Otto of Ostia. *See* Urban II (Pope)
Ottobeuren Abbey (Germany), 4:137,
 10:*717*, **717**
Ottoboni, Pietro Vito. *See* Alexander
 VIII (Pope)
Ottoman Sultan Mohammed II (Bellini),
 10:*719*
Ottoman Turks, **10:717–719**
 Adrian VI (Pope), 1:129
 Albania, 1:213
 Alexander VI (Pope), 1:261
 Andronicus III Palaeologus
  (Byzantine Emperor), 1:410
 Anthony IV (Patriarch), 1:504
 Arabia, 1:612
 Armenians, 1:706
 Bogomilism, 2:459
 Bulgaria, 2:685, 10:685
 Byzantine Empire, 2:788
 Charles V (Holy Roman Emperor),
  3:431
 church architecture, 3:706
 Clement VIII (Pope), 3:785
 Clement IX (Pope), 3:786
 Clement XI (Pope), 3:788
 conquest of Palestine, 10:784
 control of Jerusalem, 7:770–771
 Ecumenical Patriarchate, 4:196
 Hapsburgs' war against, 6:639
 Hungary, 7:211–216
 Innocent XI (Pope), Bl., 7:481
 Melkites, 1:271
 Otranto recaptured, 13:197
 Paul II (Pope), 11:20
 policy toward Christianity, 14:239
 Polish victory against invasion, 7:915
 reign over Malta, 9:82
 Rhodes, 8:193
 Serbian Orthodox Church, 10:698
 Sigismund's difficulties, 13:116
 Slovenes, 13:225
 Syria, 13:699
 Turkish history, 14:238–239
 Urban V (Pope), 14:337
 Venetian surrender, 7:670

 See also Muslim invasions
Ottonian Renaissance, **10:719–720**
 Carolingian Renaissance, 3:159
 hymns, 7:247
 illumination of books, 8:437
 Leo VIII (Pope), 8:484
 manuscript illuminations, 9:128–129
 medieval Latin literature, 9:447–448
Ottonianum (Otto I), 10:836
Oudinot de la Boissière, François d',
 12:278
Ouen of Rouen (Bp.), St., 2:334, 5:157,
 793, 8:41, **10:721**, 12:570
Ouevres des écoles d'Orient, 8:388
Ouevres spirituelles du P. Judde (1898-
 1910), 8:16
Oultremont, Emilie d', Bl., 9:290,
 10:721
Our Blessed Mother (Resch), 12:137
*Our Catholic Heritage in Texas, 1519-
 1950* (Folk, ed.), 5:787
Our Dear Lady's Psalter, 12:375
Our Faith and Our Flag (Onahan),
 10:599
Our Father. *See* Lord's Prayer
Our God's Brother (John Paul II), 3:520
Our Lady, Comfort of the Afflicted,
 8:896
Our Lady, Feasts of, 9:159, 13:467
*Our Lady Guide of Wayfarers (The
 Virgin Odigitria)*, 9:272
Our Lady Mother of Mercy Brothers,
 3:622
Our Lady of Assumption Church (Santa
 Fe, New Mexico), 12:674
Our Lady of Charity of the Refuge
 (Caen, France), Congregation of,
 5:440
Our Lady of Consolation. *See* Stanbrook
 Abbey (Worcester, England)
Our Lady of Częstochowa (Poland),
 13:92
Our Lady of Fátima, 5:644
Our Lady of Good Counsel, **10:722–723**
Our Lady of Good Health statue
 (Pátzcuaro, Mexico), 13:122
Our Lady of Grace hospital (Saragossa,
 Spain), 3:418
Our Lady of Grace orphanage (Oporto,
 Portugal), 3:416
Our Lady of Guadalupe. *See* Guadalupe,
 Our Lady of
Our Lady of Guadalupe (tile mosaic),
 9:*251*
Our Lady of Hope orphanage (Oporto,
 Portugal), 3:416
Our Lady of Latvia icon, 8:*377*

Our Lady of Lourdes, 8:819
Our Lady of Montréal, 3:4
Our Lady of Peace Church (Suresnes,
 France), 3:713
Our Lady of Perpetual Help (Succour),
 10:723–724
Our Lady of Pompeii, 13:228
Our Lady of Pompeii Shrine, 8:776
Our Lady of Prompt Succor, 8:812, 813
Our Lady of Refuge, 11:907–908
Our Lady of Sorrows, 8:471, 13:1
Our Lady of Tamiche monastery
 (Lebanon), 8:130–131
Our Lady of the Angels, 3:126, 416,
 8:904
Our Lady of the Angels Cathedral
 Center, 8:793
Our Lady of the Conception of the
 Divine Providence Convent (São
 Paulo), 6:83
Our Lady of the Incarnation (retreat)
 (Lisbon, Portugal), 3:416
Our Lady of the Lake Church (Seattle),
 3:716
Our Lady of the Rosary, 9:158
Our Lady of the Snow, 10:725
Our Lady of Victory (Nikopeia), 9:272
Our Lady of Victory Homes of Charity
 (Lackawanna, NY), 2:24
Our Lady of Victory Missionary Sisters
 (OLVM), **10:726**
Our Martyrs (Murphy), 7:579
*Our Rights and Duties as Catholics and
 Citizens* (Onahan), 10:599
Our Sunday Visitor (periodical), 10:410
*An Outline of Christian Moral Teaching
 (Natchertanie Khristianskavo
 nravooutchenia)* (Zatvornik), 14:911
Outlines of a Philosophy of Religion
 (Sabatier), 12:453
Ouyi Zhixu, 3:511
Ovalle, Alfonso de, **10:726**
Ovariotomy, **10:726**
Overall, John (Bp. of Norwich), 3:152
Overbeck, Johann Friedrich, 10:216
Overberg, Bernard, 3:243, 6:79, **10:726**
Oveton, Richard, 7:581
Ovid. *See* Publius Ovidius Naso
Ovid in Christian culture, **10:727**
Oviedo, Andre de (Bp.), 5:403
Oviedo, Carlos (Card.), 3:488
Oviedo, Francisco de, 12:767
OVM (Oblates of the Virgin Mary),
 8:327, 10:512
Ovulation method (OM), 10:176
Owen, Nicholas, St., 1:783, 5:234,
 10:727–728, 12:245

Owen, Robert, 5:968

Owen of Rouen. *See* Ouen of Rouen (Bp.), St.

Owens, J., 1:60, 3:308

Owensboro Diocese (KY), **10:728**

The Owl and the Nightingale, **10:728–729**

Ownership, 2:65, 11:548

Oxenstierna, Axel, 14:10

Oxford (MI), 4:841

Oxford Group, 1:242, 2:654

Oxford Movement, 5:251, 467, 472, **10:733–735**

    Anglo-Catholics, 1:446

    branch theory of the Church, 2:582–583

    Caroline Divines, 3:153

    carols, 3:151

    church architecture, 3:715

    Church of Ireland, 7:549

    convocation, 4:244

    Cusack, Margaret Anna, 4:445

    de Lisle, Ambrose, 4:630

    Devine, Arthur, 4:706

    Faber, Frederick William, 5:582

    Forbes, Alexander Penrose, 5:795

    Fortescue, Adrian, 5:821

    hymnody, 7:257

    John Newman's role in, 10:332

    leadership, 8:135–136

    liturgical movement, 8:677

    nonjurors as forerunners, 10:419

    Pusey, Edward Bouverie, 11:841–842

    ''Romanizing'' tendencies, 8:896

    spirituality, 13:448

    Tract 90, 10:734, 14:131

    Wiseman, Nicholas Patrick, 14:796

    See also Tractarianism

Oxford School (Franciscan), 5:242, 899–900

Oxford University, **10:729–732**, *730*

    Aristotelianism, 1:672, 675, 676, 679

    Canterbury Hall, 13:130

    Courtenay, Richard, 4:317

    Courtenay, William, 4:318

    Dominican priory, 13:129

    Dominicans, 7:961

    instructional methods, 13:129

    organization of, 10:730–732

    Robert Bacon, 12:262–263

    Robert Grosseteste, 12:263–264

    Ruskin, John, 12:414–415

    Rygge, Robert, 12:447–448

Oxford University Sermons (Newman), 10:338

Oxyrhynchus, **10:735**

Oxyrhynchus era, 5:312

Ozanam, Antoine Frédéric, Bl., 3:622, **10:735–737**

    Catholic social thought, 13:256

    Coux, Charles de, 4:324

    lay spirituality, 8:416

    Resurrectionists, 12:174

    St. Vincent de Paul Society, 12:591

    works of charity, 3:420

Ozenfant, A., 3:680

P

Pacca, Bartolomeo (Card.), 4:64, 8:309, **10:739**

Paccanarists, 3:181, 10:528, **740**, 12:496

La Pace (daily), 10:918

Pace, Edward Aloysius, 1:355, 3:282, **10:740–741**, 12:777

Pacelli, Eugenio Maria Giuseppe Giovanni. *See* Pius XII (Pope)

Pacelli, Francesco, 8:356

Pacem in terris 132 (encyclical, John XXIII), 3:625–626, 4:16, 20, 151, 5:206, 943, 952, 7:937, 10:*741*, **741–742**, 747, 850, 11:566, 13:567–568, 14:642, 825

    agriculture, 8:586

    associations, 1:792, 793

    capital punishment, 3:88

    Church-State relations, 3:642–643

    civil disobedience, 3:755

    democracy, 13:259

    dignity of person, 13:261

    freedom of religion, 13:259

    signs of the times, 13:117

Pachecho, Alfonso, 12:401

Pacheco, Francisco, Bl., 7:734

Pacheco, Manuel, Bl., 1:951

Pacher, Michael, **10:742**

Pachomius, St., 5:754, **10:742–743**

    baths, 2:154

    cenobitism, 3:334–335, 9:788

    conformity, 4:92

    contemplative life, 4:210

    as Desert Father, 4:686

    the discipine, 4:774–775

    lauras, 8:381

    religious habit, 12:99

Pachymeres, George, 2:776, 800, **10:743**

Pacian (Bp. of Barcelona), St., **10:743–744**

Pacific of Cerano. *See* Pacificus of Novara, Bl.

Pacific of Cexedano. *See* Pacificus of Novara, Bl.

Pacific School of Religion, 10:192

Pacification of Amboise (1563), 3:266

Pacificator (Blome and Walsh, eds.), 14:459

Pacifico of San Severino, St., **10:744**

Pacificus of Novara, Bl., **10:744**

Pacifism, 3:45, 379, **10:744–748**

Pacioli, Luca, 10:*748*, **748–749**

Pacius, Julius, 1:676

Pactum (St. Fructuosus of Braga), 6:16

Pactum Ludovicianum (Louis I the Pious), 3:169, 10:913–914

Padberg, Rudolf, 3:241

Paderewski, Ignacy Jan, 10:*749*, **749**

Padilla, Antonio de, 4:111

Padilla, Diego Francisco, **10:749–750**

Padilla, Ernesto E., 1:652

Padilla, Juan de, 10:284, **750**

    Carthusian spirituality, 3:192

    death of, 12:674

    Kansas missions, 8:112, 14:711

    New Mexico missions, 12:674

Padilla y Estrada, Ignacio de, 10:750

Padre Pio (Bp. of Mérida), St., **10:750–752**, *751*

Padres Asociados por los Derechos Religiosos, Educativos y Sociales (PADRES), 5:203

Padroado of Portugal, 10:976–977, 977–978

Paedagogus (Clement of Alexandria, St.), 3:798, 5:510

Paenitentiam agere (encyclical, John XXIII), 7:937

Paez, Alvaro, 1:428

Paéz, Pedro (Father), 5:400, 403

Páez Perdomo, Gaspar, Bl., 7:123

Pagan baptism, 2:56–57

Pagan festivals, 3:229, 526

    Christmas cycle, 3:551–552, 556

    Lemuria, 1:289

    Samhain, 1:290

    Saturnalia, 12:705

''Pagan humanism,'' 2:110

Pagan temple ruins, 10:*753*, *754*

Paganism, 10:*752*

    Antioch, 1:523–524

    Arabia, 1:613–619

    Byzantine civilization, 2:767–768

    dangers of, 9:105–106

    Emesa (Homs), 5:191

    icons, 7:278

    idols, 7:323, 324

Paganism *(continued)*
    Roman Empire, 12:320–321
    wisdom, 14:784
    See also Greek religion; Pagan festivals; Roman Empire; Roman religion
Pagans, **10:752**
    Constantine I (the Great) (Roman Emperor), 4:180, 181–182, 185
    cross as symbol, 4:378–379
    Cyprus, 4:461
    demonology of Christians, 4:646, 647
    lapsi, 8:333
    light, use of, 8:580–581
    moral guidance, 4:760
Page, Anthony, Bl., 5:232, **10:752**
Page, Francis, Bl., 5:234
Pageant of Letters (Noyes), 10:471
Pagnani, G., 5:736, 737
Pagnini, Santes, 5:518, **10:753**
Pagnino, Santes. *See* Pagnini, Santes
Pahlavi Dynasty, 11:141
Paidagogos (Clement of Alexandria), 10:755
Paideia, Christian, **10:753–756**
Le Pain dur (Claudel), 3:766, 768
Paine, John, St., 5:227, **10:756**, *757*
Paine, Thomas, 4:617, 5:262, 10:756–757
Painting, 1:753, 754, 756, 2:114, 3:844–845
    See also Art; Icons
Paisiello, Giovanni, **10:758**
Pakistan, 7:22, **10:759–762**, *760*
Palace schools, 3:153, 159–160, **10:762–764**
    Aldric of Sens, St., 1:248
    Amalarius of Metz, 1:329
    Angilbert of Saint-Riquier, St., 1:432
    cathedral and episcopal schools, 3:264
    Clement of Ireland, St., 3:799
    See also Carolingian reform
Palacios, Deogracias, 10:29
Palacios, Manuel Antonio (Bp.), **10:764**
Palacios, Pedro, 2:588
Palaeologus, Helen, 4:462
Palafox y Mendoza, Juan de (Bp. of Mexico), Ven., 3:792, 795, **10:764–765**
Palamas, Gregory, St., 7:919–920, **10:765–767**
    Andronicus III Palaeologus, 1:410
    Argyros, Isaac, 1:659
    Barlaam of Calabria, criticism of, 2:99

    Bessarion, Cardinal, 2:341
    Byzantine civilization, 2:769
    Cydones brothers, 4:454
    Dishypatos, David, 4:776
    distinction between Divine essence and uncreated Divine, 14:200
    Gregorius Akindynos, 6:475–476
    hesychasm, 2:763, 771, 788, 794, 6:811
    monasticism, 9:798–799
    synaxary, 12:606
    See also Palamism
Palamism, 1:659, 2:826–827, 837, 4:712–713
    See also Hesychasm; Palamas, Gregory, St.
Palaser, Thomas, Bl., 5:233, **10:767**
Palatine chapel (Aachen, Germany), 3:154–155, 382, *383*
Palau y Quer, Francisco, Bl., **10:767**
Palazzi, Raphael Angelo (Bp.), 5:879
Il palazzo incantato (Rossi), 12:388
The Pale, 7:555, 556
Paleae, 6:421
Palencia Monastery (Spain), 1:8
Palentinus Pastor, 5:720
Paleography, Greek, **10:767–772**, *769*
Paleography, Latin, **10:772–777**
Palermo (Italy), patroness of, 12:373
Palestine, **10:777–799**
    Alt, Albrecht, 1:313
    ancient center of tribe of Dan, 10:*780*
    archeology work, 1:235, 10:789–799
    basilicas, 9:232
    Commissariat of the Holy Land, 4:12
    crucifixion art, 4:392
    Decapolis, 4:587–588
    holy places, 10:797–799
    hydrography, 10:781–782
    Jewish population, 1:188, 7:874, 8:2, 6, 10
    monasticism, 9:797, 801
    natural history, 10:785–789
    physical geography, 10:778–781
    political geography, 10:782–785
    Shechem, 13:71–72
    Tel Hazor, 10:*779*
    See also Bible, historical/geographical context; Crusaders' States; Israelites
Palestine, early Church in, 3:31, 553, 555, **10:799–801**, 13:90
Palestine Archaeological Museum Gallery Book (PAMGB), 10:789
Palestine Liberation Organization (PLO), 8:427

Palestinian Targum, 13:761–762
Palestra críticomédica (Rodríquez), 14:460
Palestrina, Giovanni Pierluigi da, 1:1, 3:379–380, 4:313, 10:248, *801*, **801–803**
Palestrina tradition, 1:293, 2:841
Palevi, Muhammad Reza Shah, 11:141
Paley, William, 2:407, 4:531, **10:803**, 12:768
Pali Canon, **10:803–804**
Palimpsest manuscripts, 2:363, 705, **10:804**
Palladino, Lawrence Benedict, **10:804**
Palladio, Andrea, 3:674, 701, 706, 707
Palladis Tamia: Wits' Treasury (Meres), 13:62
Palladius (Bp. of Heleneopolis), St., 8:381–382, **10:805–806**, 12:606
Palladius (Bp. of Ireland), St., 3:207, 317, 596, 4:738, **10:805**
Pallau, François, 12:219
Pallavicino, Pietro Sforza (Card.), **10:806**, 12:694
Pallegoix, Jean-Baptiste (Msgr.), 13:850
Pallen, Condé Benoist, 1:355, **10:806–807**
Pallium, 1:172, 3:180, 5:240, 6:763, 8:484, **10:807–808**
Palliyogams, 7:396
Pallota, Maria Assunta, Bl., **10:808**
Pallotti, Vincent, St., 8:415, **10:808–809**
Pallottine Missionary Sisters, 10:808, **809**
Pallottine Sisters of the Catholic Apostolate, **10:809**
Pallottines, 3:622, 10:808, **809–810**
Pallu, François (Bp. of Heliopolis), 3:497, 8:303, **10:810**, 977
Palm Sunday, 8:718, **10:810–811**, 813
Palmentieri, Ludovico da Casoria, Bl., **10:811–812**
Palmer, Elihu, 10:757
Palmer, William, 2:582, **10:812**
Palmieri, Alexander, 1:*939*
Palmieri, Aurelio, **10:812**
Palmieri, Domenico, 10:813, 12:743
Palms, liturgical use of, **10:813**, 13:665–666
Palmyra, 1:625, **10:813–814**
Palóu, Francisco, 2:865, **10:815**, 12:644–645
Paltz, Johann von, 1:729
Pamfili, Giovanni Battista. *See* Innocent X (Pope)
Pamfili, John Baptist. *See* Innocent X (Pope)

PAMGB (*Palestine Archaeological Museum Gallery Book*), 10:789

Pamiers, Caulet (Card.), 3:786

Pammachius (Roman senator), St., 3:406, 5:585, 7:127, **10:815**

Pamphilus, St., 2:845, 5:451, 510, 10:800, **815–816**

Pamphilus cemetery (Rome), 3:224

Pamplona, Dionisio and Companions, BB., **10:816**

Pampuri, Riccardo, St., **10:817**

Pan (Arcadian god), 4:497

Panaetius of Rhodes, 5:46

Panaghia Kera Church (Crete), 2:*780*

Panama, 9:707, **10:817–820**, *818*

Panaretus, Matthew Angelus, 2:827

Panarion (Epiphanius of Salamis), 5:292

Panarion (Haereses) (St. Epiphanius of Salamis), 5:293, 6:256–257

Panbabylonism, 8:186, 10:820

Die Panbabylonisten (Jeremias), 10:820

Pan-Caucasian Empire, 6:153–154

Panchen Lama, 8:299

Pane, Ramón (Father), 3:246

Panegyric for Origen (St. Gregory Thaumaturgus), 6:525

Panegyric on Basil (Gregory of Nazianzus), 10:755

Panentheism, **10:820–822**

Pange Lingua Gloriosi Laureaum Certaminis (hymn), 5:823, **10:822**

Pangrazio, Andrea (Abp.), 6:822

Panigarola, Francesco, **10:822**

Panikervirtis, Givergis Thomas. *See* Ivanios, Mar (Abp. of Trivandrum)

Panikkar, Raimundo, 7:405, 841

Pannartz, Arnold, 2:522

Pannenberg, Wolfhart, 5:346, 351, 6:870–871, 14:199

Pannini, Giuseppe, 3:793

Pannonhalma Abbey (Hungary), 10:*823*, **823**

Panofsky, Erwin, 3:669, 676, 694, 7:283, 284, 287–288

Panoplia contra schisma Graecorum (Le Quien), 8:511

Panoplia Dogmatike (Zigabenus), 14:925

Panopolia gratiae (Lemos), 8:467

Panormia (St. Ivo of Chartres), 7:680

Panormitanus. *See* Tudeschis, Nicolaus de

Panpsychism, 7:239, 240, 340, 8:457, **10:823–824**

Pan-Slavism, 8:249

Pansophia (universal wisdom), 5:92

Pantaenus, St., 1:266, 268, 272, 3:797, 5:510, **10:824–825**

Pantaleoni, Diomede, 3:314

Pantheism, **10:825–828**, 11:285

  absolute, 1:42

  accident, 1:64

  Albert the Great, St., 1:225, 2:629

  Alexander, Samuel, 1:252

  Amalricians, 1:330, 2:629

  Angelus Silesius, 1:429

  Brothers and Sisters of the Free Spirit, 2:629

  causality, 3:302, 303

  contradiction, 4:224

  Cousin, Victor, 4:322

  creation doctrine, 4:343

  David of Dinant, 4:540

  man, natural end of, 9:99

  transcendental theism, 13:139

  unity and multiplicity opposition problem, 10:58

  See also Emanationism

Pantheologia (Raynerius of Pisa), 14:47

Pantheon (Rome), 12:*352*

Panthéon Littéraire (Le Gobien), 8:455

Pantin, Anthony (Abp. of Port of Spain), 3:116

Pantocrator, Christ as, 2:*733*, 737, 3:558

Pantocrator Monastery (Constantinople), 3:413

Panvinio, Onofrio, 1:888–889, **10:828–829**

Panzani, Gregorio, 3:152, **10:829**

Paoli, Sebastiano, 3:804

Paolina del Cuore Agonizzante di Gesú. *See* Visintainer, Amabile Lucia, Bl.

Paolo de Moneglia, 6:235

Papa a nemine judicatur, 10:833–834

Papacy, **10:829–854**

  Antichrist, 1:517

  Carolingian Dynasty, 3:164–165, 167–168, 169, 170

  Castel Gandolfo villa, 3:211–212

  coinage issued, 10:481

  College of Bishops, 13:778–779

  consecration, 1:479–480

  Enlightenment, 5:257–258

  episcopal elections, 8:294

  Ex Cathedra definitions, 10:453

  Frederick I Barbarossa, 3:601

  Germany, 8:253

  Ghibelline-Guelf conflict, 1:257, 3:778, 853–856

  history

    contemporary (1958-2001), 10:849–853

    early period, 10:829–835

    medieval period, 10:835–840

    modern period (1789-1958), 10:845–849

    19th-20th century, 3:620–621

    Renaissance, 10:840–844, 12:117–118

    17th-18th century, 3:615

  infallibility, 10:334, 848, 14:404, 405–406

  Jesuits, 3:610

  mission, 3:624

  Muratori's conflict with ecclesiastical opinion, 10:63

  nepotism, 10:247, 843

  papal authority, 12:354–355

  power of Ecumenical council, 4:305

  pre-Reformation spiritual hunger, 3:604, 605, 606

  Roman Question, 12:322–323

  sovereignty, 10:913–914

  taxation, 3:603, 726–727

  theology of Church, 3:586

  tool of Roman factions, 7:659

  Ultramonianism, 10:847

  works of charity, 3:408

  See also Avignon papacy; Church and State; Conciliarism; States of the Church; *specific popes*

Papadopoulos, Chrysostomos (Orthodox Abp.), **10:854**

Papal absolutism, 9:463

Papal arbitration, **10:854–855**

Papal authority, 7:134–135, 13:166, 491, 496

Papal briefs

  Ad pastoralis dignitatis fastigium (Benedict XIV), 1:307, 308

  Caritas (Pius VI), 11:377

  Exponi nobis (Clement XIII), 11:467

  Litteris altero (Pius VIII), 11:382

  Quod aliquantum (Pius VI), 11:377

Papal bulls, 2:687, 4:757–758

  Abbatia nullius diocesis (Pius X), 10:437–438

  Ad decorem (Benedict XII), 3:68

  Ad decorum militantis Ecclesiae (Sixtus IV), 14:396, 420

  Ad sanctam beati petri sedem (Alexander VII), 1:97, 893, 7:717

  Admonet nos (Pius V), 10:247

  Aeterni Patris (Gregory XV), 3:91, 5:588

Papal bulls (*continued*)

against Wyclif (Gregory XI), 14:866

Alexandrine bulls (Alexander VI),
1:259, 261, 273–274

Antiquorum habet (Boniface VIII),
7:57

Apostolici regiminis (Leo X), 1:595

Apostolicum Ministerium (Benedict
XIV), 4:734

Apostolicum pascendi munus
(Clement XIII), 3:792

Auctorem Fidei (Pius VI),
1:846–847, 3:204, 5:65, 659, 6:78,
11:364, 377, 12:225

Audita tremendi (Gregory VIII),
4:411, 6:495

Ausculta fili (Boniface VIII), 1:898,
2:503

Benedictus Deus (Pius IV), 14:174

Benedictus Dominus (Gregory XIII),
2:143

Bulla cruciata (Eugene III), 2:688,
5:443

Cenacle, 3:54

Clericis Laicos (Boniface VIII),
11:246

Commissa nobis (Pius VI), 7:651

Commissum nobis (Pius X), 7:651,
11:499

Cum nulla (Nicholas V), 3:126,
134–135

Cum nuper (John XXII), 3:800

Cum occasione (Innocent X), 1:97,
717, 893, 4:436, 7:716

Decet Romanum Pontificem (Leo X),
8:488

Doctoris gentium (Eugene IV), 2:134

Dudum dum charissima (Julius III),
1:436

Dudum ecclesiae eboracensis (Paul
IV), 1:436

Dudum sacrum (Eugene IV), 2:133

Dum attenta (Sixtus IV), 3:144

Ecclesiam (Pius VII), 12:857

Effraenatam (Sixtus V), 4:221

Etsi animarum (Innocent IV), 14:16

Etsi de statu (Boniface VIII), 2:502

Ex omnibus afflictionibus (Pius V),
2:19, 4:4, 5:499–500

Exposcit debitum (Julius III), 7:313

Exsecrabilis (Pius II), 4:58, 6:608,
11:369

Exsultate Deo (Eugene IV),
1:711–712, 4:221

Exsurge Domine (Adrian VI), 1:66,
3:482, 609

Exsurge Domine (Leo X), 5:43,
7:438, 8:488

Flumen aque vive (John XXI), 7:930

Gloria in excelsis (Adrian II), 4:475

Gloriam virginalem (Gregory IX),
2:205

Graviora (Leo XII), 12:857

In agro domini (Benedict XII), 11:76

In coena Domini (Gregory XIII),
4:498

In eligendis (Pius IV), 3:91, 11:499

In Eminenti (Clement XII), 1:893,
3:790, 12:857

In Emineti (Urban VIII), 4:4, 7:715,
14:342

Incarnationis mysterium (John Paul
II), 7:440

Industriae Tuae (John VIII), 4:370,
476

Ineffabilis Deus (Pius IX), 1:799

Inscrutabili Divinae (Gregory XV),
9:680–681

Inter cunctas (Martin V), 6:608

Inter multiplices (Alexander VIII,
1690), 1:262

Inter multiplices (Innocent VIII,
1487), 3:336

Inter multiplicis (Leo X), 9:835

Laetare Jerusalem (Paul III), 11:22,
14:168

Laudabiliter (Adrian IV), 8:379

Licet ecclesiae catholicae (Alexander
IV), 1:886

Ne super his (John XXII), 2:276

Nec insolitum (Alexander IV), 14:16

Non Mediocri (Eugene IV), 3:105

Omnium sollicitudinum (Benedict
XIV), 7:412

Ordinem vestrum (Innocent IV),
7:980

Parens scientiarum (Gregory IX),
1:265, 10:886

Pastor aeternus (Leo X), 6:78

Praeclara charissimi (Paul IV),
1:436

Primitiva (Leo X), 8:487

Providas (Benedict XIV), 12:857

Provisionis nostrae (Gregory XIII),
2:19

Quae honorem Conditoris (Innocent
IV), 3:132, 141

Quantum praedecessores (Eugene
III), 2:688, 4:410

Qui major (Innocent III), 2:688

Quod divina sapientia (Leo XIII),
2:475, 8:490

Racio recta non patitur (John XXII),
2:205

*Regesta pontificum romanorum ab
condita ecclesia ad annum post
Christum natum 1198* (Leo IX),
9:743–744

Regimini militantis Ecclesiae (Paul
III), 4:311, 7:313, 779

Regimini universalis ecclesiae (Paul
IV), 1:436–437

Regiminis apostolici (Alexander VII),
7:717, 12:28–29

Regnans in Excelsis (Pius V), 1:437,
443, 5:163, 224–225, 247,
670–671, 12:10–11

Relatio nimis implacida (John XXI),
7:930

Religionis zelus (Clement VII), 4:310

Romana Ecclesia (Gregory XIII),
1:702

Romanus Pontifex (Clement IX),
7:777

Sacratissimo uti culmine (John
XXII), 12:723

Sacrosancta romana (John XXII),
2:205

Sacrosanctum fidei (Clement VII),
7:390

Salvator noster (Sixtus IV), 7:438

Sancta Romana (John XXII), 3:762

Sollicitudo ecclesiarum (Gregory
XVI), 6:509, 510

Sublimis Deus (Paul III), 11:22

Super cathedram (Boniface VIII),
4:850

Super Petri solio (Boniface VIII),
2:503

Super universas (Urban VIII), 2:12,
10:259

Supremi Apostolatus (Clement XIV),
10:931

Transiturus de hoc mundo ad Patrem
(Urban IV), 5:463, 12:521

Ubi periculum (Gregory X), 6:499,
11:499

Unam sanctum (Boniface VIII),
1:207, 2:503, 3:603, 636, 4:518,
14:287–288

Unigenitus (Clement XI), 1:57, 268,
600, 3:789, 790, 4:944, 7:718,
10:406, 844, 14:124

Unigentius Dei Filius (Clement VI),
5:851, 12:454

Universalis ecclesiae (Julius II),
10:978

Vineam Domini (Clement XI), 3:789,
5:358

Vixdum Poloniae (Pius XI), 11:448

Vota per quae vos (Clement VII), 5:692

Vox in excelso (Clement V), 13:804

Papal ceremony and vesture, **10:855–857**

Papal constitutions

Conditae a Christo (Leo XIII), 5:530

Quamis iusto (Benedict XIV), 5:530

Papal court, 3:349–350

Papal decrees

Ad abolendam (Lucius III), 1:231, 3:86–87, 7:488

Ad extirpanda (Innocent IV), 7:488

Ad nostrum qui desideranter (Clement V), 2:205

Armenians, Decree of, 1:711–712

Carissimis Russiae populis (Pius XII), 11:400

Cum ex officii nostri (Innocent III), 7:488

Cum postquam (Leo X), 7:438

Ex illa die (Clement XI), 3:498, 515

Ex quo singulari (Benedict XIV), 3:498, 515, 516

In Nomine Domine (Nicholas II), 3:105

Lamentabili sane exitu (Pius X), 6:779, 8:311–312, 11:389

Licet de vitanda (Alexander III), 3:105, 11:499

Licet Heli (Innocent III), 7:485

Ne Temere (Pius X), 3:54, 10:218–219

Novit ille (Innocent III), 3:636, 7:472

Per venerabilem (Innocent III), 7:472

Plane compertum est (Pius XII), 3:498, 500, 516

Quae maiori (John Paul II), 7:400

Quam singulari (Pius X), 11:390

Sacra Tridentina Synodus (Pius X), 11:390

Sane (Innocent III), 1:348

Vergentis in senium (Innocent III), 1:231, 7:472, 488

See also Decretals

Papal Election Decree (1059), 1:253, 3:600, 7:662, 10:365, 836, **857–858**

Papal elections

accessus, 1:57

antipopes, 1:530

camerlengo, 2:910–911

capitulations, 3:91

cardinalate, 3:106

Papal Election Decree (1059), 1:253, 3:600

See also specific popes

Papal elections, veto power in, **10:858**

Papal Foundation, 8:250

Papal indiction, 7:419

Papal infallibility

Du concile général et de la paix religieuse (Maret), 9:147

Du pape (Maistre), 9:61

See also Vatican Council I (1869-70)

Papal judges-delegate, 7:488–489

Papal letters

Ad extremas orientis plagas (Leo XIII), 9:681

Catholicae ecclesiae (Leo XIII), 9:681

Evangelii praecones (Pius XII), 9:681

Humanae salutis (Leo XIII), 9:681

In plurimis (Leo XIII), 9:681

Maximum illud (Benedict XV), 9:681

Sancta Dei civitas (Leo XIII), 9:681

Papal names, 10:141

Papal patrimony, 6:480

Papal penitentiary, 10:859

Papal power. *See* Primacy of the pope

Papal primacy. *See* Primacy of the pope

Papal recognition, 6:335–336

Papal reform, 2:133, 134, 276–277, 6:468–473, 505, 11:374

Papal registers, **10:858–859**

Papal rescripts, *Primo feliciter* (Pius XII), 12:862

Papal scene (illuminated manuscript), 10:*832*

Papal states. *See* States of the Church

Papal supremacy, 4:887, 9:61, 133, 211

Papal taxation, 3:726–727, 784

annates, 1:267, 466–467, 3:726

Avignon papacy, 1:941, 3:726–727

Boniface IX (Pope), 2:504

Constance Council, 4:171

Innocent IV (Pope), 3:603

Papal Volunteers for Latin America (PAVLA), **10:859–860**, 12:574

Papczynski, Mary, 9:156

Papczyński, Stanislaus, 9:156, **10:860**

Du Pape (de Maistre), 14:139

Le Pape et la diplomatie (Veuillot), 14:465

Papenbroek, Daniel van, 2:471, 6:*873*

Paper, early use of, 2:516–517, 773

Paperbroch, Danial van. *See* Papenbroek, Daniel van

Papers on Literature and Art (Fuller), 14:148

Paphnutius (Roswitha of Gandersheim), 12:390

Paphnutius the Anchorite, St., 10:861

Paphnutius the Bishop, St., 3:323, 10:860, **860–861**

Paphnutius the Buffalo, 10:860

Papias (fl. 11th C.), 9:449

Papias of Hierapolis (Bp.), 1:172, 587–588, 785, **10:861**

Papini Tartagni, Niccolò, **10:861–862**, 12:717

Papon, Philippe, 12:278

Der Papst und die modernen Ideen (periodical), 12:786

Papua New Guinea, 10:532–533

Papyrology, **10:862–865**

Papyrus, 2:510–511, 515, 724, 12:293–295

Papyrus Codex (Cyril of Alexandria), 10:770

Papyrus Gurob, 10:95

Paquin, Ulric, 1:209

Para du Phanjas, François, 12:771

Parabeln des Herrn im Evangelium (Fonck), 5:789

Parable of the Unjust (Titus of Bostra), 14:93

Parable of the Wicked Mammon (Luther), 14:253

Parables of Enoch, 13:316–317

Parables of Jesus, **10:865–872**

eschatology, 5:339

form criticism, 5:809

John's Gospel, 10:871

Kingdom of God, 8:173

literary dimension, 10:868–869

Luke's Gospel, 8:857, 858

Matthew's Gospel, 9:356

The Parables of the Gospels (Fonck), 5:789

Paracelsus, Philippus Aureolus, 1:238, 11:851, 12:124, 816, 817–818

Paraclete (Holy Spirit), 7:908, **10:872–873**

Paraclitus (Warnerius of Basel), 9:449

Das Paradies und die Peri (Schumann), 12:789

Paradis, Alodie Virginie, 8:616

Paradis, Marie-Léonie, Bl., **10:874**

Paradise, 1:103, 5:80–81, **10:874–876**, 13:36–37

Paradise (Lucas Cranach the Elder), 5:*81*

Paradise Lost (Milton), 2:112, 9:644, 14:378

Paradise Regained (Milton), 9:645

Paradoxes, 1:519, 5:612, 8:749, **10:876**

Parafrasi: Institutionum graeca paraphrasis Theophilo antecessori vulgo tributa (Ferrini), 5:695

Paraguay, **10:877–880**
  Bogarín, Juan Sinforiano, 2:458
  demographic statistics, 10:877
  ecclesiastical organization,
    10:879–880
  map, 10:*878*
  Mennonite churches, 9:496
  mission, 2:464, 3:101–102, 226, 613,
    8:839, 12:408
  reductions, 2:464, 3:101–102, 226,
    613, 11:997–998, 12:408
Paraguay, Jesuit Martyrs of, SS.,
  10:876–877
Parahaṁsa, Rāmakrishna, 6:852
Paralipomenon, Books of, **10:880**
Parallel Lives (Plutarch), 12:308
Parallèle de l'incrédule et du vrai fidèle
  (Touron), 14:125
Parallelism, in Hebrew poetry,
  6:693–694
Paralogism, 5:612
Paraphrase of St. John's Gospel
  (Nonnus of Panopolis), 10:419
*Paraphrasis et compendiosa expositio ad
  nonnullas epistolas S. Pauli*
  (Váquez), 14:427
Parareschi, Gregory. *See* Innocent II
  (Pope)
Paravicino, Hortensio Felix, 2:115
Paray-le-Monial (France), 5:855, **10:880**,
  881, 13:94
Parchment, 2:511–512, 515–516, 773
"Pardon of Assisi," 11:527–528
Paredes y Flores, Mariana de Jesús, St.,
  10:880–881
Pareja, Francisco, **10:881–882**
Pareja, Francisco de, **10:882**
Parekklesion Dome (Kariye Camii,
  Istanbul), 14:*243*
Paremindes (fl. 470 B.C.), 12:802
Paremmakkal, Thomas, 7:399
Parenesis, **10:882–883**
Parens scientiarum (papal bull, Gregory
  IX), 1:265, 10:886
Parent, Alphose-Marie, 3:10
Parenti, John, 2:123
Parents
  duties, 11:334–335
  marriage related, 13:47
  participation in baptismal liturgy,
    2:70
  People of God, 8:288–289
  social justice, 8:68
Parentucelli, Tommaso. *See* Nicholas V
  (Pope)
Parerga und Paralipomena
  (Schopenhauer), 12:785

Pareto, Vilfredo, 13:282–283
Le Parfum de Rome (Veuillot), 14:465
Parham, Charles F., 1:788
Paris, Councils of (829-1210), 1:330,
  3:42, 4:87
Paris, Count of Lodron (Abp. of
  Salzburg), 1:912
Paris, Gaston, 4:318
Paris, Institut Catholique de, **10:883–884**
Paris, Martyrs of, 5:973, **10:884–886**
Paris, Synod of (614), 2:336
Paris, Treaty of (1259), 8:800
Paris, University of (France), 3:603,
  10:886–890
  academic freedom, 1:51
  Alexander of Hales, 1:265–266,
    3:603
  Avicebron, 1:939
  Bouillon, Emmanuel Théodose de la
    Tour d'Auvergne, 2:563
  Everard of Ypres teacher at, 5:484
  gifts of Holy Spirit, 7:48
  mendicant controversy, 2:479, 481,
    483, 501
  Robert of Courçon, 12:267
  Saint-Victor of Paris, 3:68
  scholasticism, 12:760
  Western Schism, 14:693
  See also Averroism, Latin
Paris a Puteo, 3:52
Paris Adult Theater v. Slaton (1973),
  11:519
Paris Cathedral (France), 1:544, 3:695
Paris Foreign Missionary Society (MEP),
  10:890–891
  Burma, 2:706
  Cambodia, 2:901
  China, 3:495, 497, 499, 513
  Compagnie du Saint-Sacrement, 4:41
  Japan, 7:741–742
  Korea, 8:233, 234, 235, 239
  Laos, 8:329, 330
  Leloutre, J. P., 8:464
  Louisiana, 8:808
  Moyë, John Martin, 10:37
  origins and development, 10:890–891
  Quebec, 8:382
  Singapore, 13:161
  Tibet, 14:71–72
Paris Missions Seminary, 8:303
Paris pendant les deux sièges (Veuillot),
  14:466
Paris psalter, 2:733, *734*, 735
Paris School (Franciscan), 5:898–899

Parish and Diocesan Council Network,
  4:75
Parish and People Movement, 8:663
Parish catechesis, 8:733–734
Parish School Conference, 10:160
*Parish Stewardship Educational
  Program*, 7:522–523
Parish Visitors of Mary Immaculate
  (PVMI), **10:891**
Park Monastery (Belgium), **10:891**
Parke, Herbert, 8:*139*
Parker, Horatio, 12:212
Parker, Matthew (Abp. of Canterbury),
  10:891–892
  Anglican orders problem, 1:437, 438,
    593–594
  Book of Advertisements, 1:135–136
  Bourne, Gilbert, 2:569
  confessions of faith, 4:80
Parker, Peter, 3:499
Parker, Samuel (Bp. of Oxford), 3:185
Parker, Theodore, **10:892**, 14:146, 148
Parker, Thomas. *See* Sprott, Thomas, Bl.
Parker Society, 5:472–473
Parkinson, Anthony, **10:892**
Parkminster (Charterhouse), **10:892–893**
Parlement of Foules (Chaucer), 3:453,
  457
Parlement of Provence, 1:196
Parliamentary system of government,
  6:376
Parma (Italy), 8:58
Parmenides (Greek philosopher), 6:441,
  10:893–894, 11:287
  Anaxagoras, 1:393
  atomism, 1:832, 13:374
  becoming, 2:195
  Bradley, Francis Herbert, 2:577
  concept of truth, 14:222
  Empedocles' theories, 5:195
  existence, 5:533
  Greek religion, 6:453
  idealism, 7:296
  identity, 7:302, 303
  intellectual life, 7:513
  knowledge, 8:212–213
  matter, 9:339–340
  nonbeing, 10:417
  ontological perfection, 11:117
  pantheism, 10:825
  possiblity of change denied, 10:16,
    17
Parmenides (Plato), 10:417
Parnell, Charles Stewart, 7:563

Parochial and Plain Sermons
(Newman), 10:333, 733
Parochial schools
Americanism, 1:354
anti-Catholicism, 1:352
apostolic delegation in the United
States, 1:584
Australia, 1:904, 905
BLOCS (Business Leaders Organized
for Catholic Schools), 8:250
Church-State relations, 3:655
controversy, 13:99
desegregation, 3:821
Laos, 8:330
Lateran Pacts (1985), 8:359
Lesotho, 8:515
Poughkeepsie Plan (NY), 1:352,
10:315, 11:561–562
South Africa, 8:228–229
United States
California, 2:871
Cincinnati (OH), 3:738
Colorado, 3:858–859
Everson v. Board of Education
(1947), 1:356, 3:660, 665, 667
Faribault Plan (MN), 1:352, 354,
584, 2:564, 584
Know-Nothing nonsupport, 8:200
Native-American riots, 8:144–145
Poughkeepsie Plan, 1:352
Sisters of Notre Dame,
12:780–782
taxation issue, 8:792
works, 13:403
See also Education, Catholic
Paroikia, 5:502
Paroisse et liturgie (periodical), 12:533
La Parola Catolica (periodical), 5:865
Paroles d'un croyant (Lamennais, F.),
8:310
Parousia (return of Christ), 5:412,
8:39–40, 9:635–636, **10:894–902**,
14:631–632
Adventists, 1:135
afterlife, 1:165
agape, 1:170
angels, 1:418
Antichrist, 1:517
apocalyptic movements, 1:547
Ascension of Jesus Christ, 1:769
in the Bible, 10:896–899
burial, 2:700
Christian and Missionary Alliance,
3:530
Church, 3:578
Church-State relations, 3:631

Day of the Lord, 4:548–549
Divine judgment, 8:29–30
early Christian way of life, 3:547
end of the world, 5:216
Epistle of Clement, 3:775
eschatology, 5:332, 344, 350
immortality, 7:352–354
Lord's Supper, 8:785
Resurrection of Christ, 12:157
Son of Man, 13:317
terminology, 10:894
theology, 10:900–902
time of the, 10:895–896
virginity/celibacy, 4:306
See also Eschatology; Eschatology,
in theology; Millenarianism
Parras, Coahuila Jesuit Mission
(Mexico), 9:708
Parras, Pedro José, **10:902–903**
Parrenin, Dominique, **10:903**
Parreño, José Julián (Father), 3:313
Parsch, Pius, 1:916, 3:712, 8:673,
10:903
Parsees (India), 1:937–938, **10:903–904**
Parsons, Talcott, 13:283–284
Parsons, Wilfrid, 10:68, **904**
Parson's Prologue and Tale (Chaucer),
3:456
Partage de midi (Claudel), 3:768
Parte Saiz, Alfredo, Bl., 10:816, **905**
Parthenice Mariana (Baptist of Mantua),
2:73–74
Parthenon (Athens, Greece), 13:*806*
Partial birth abortion, 1:34–35
Participation, **10:905–910**
act, 1:74–75
analogy, 1:373, 375–376
Augustinianism, 1:881
being, 2:209
causality, 3:297
conservation, 4:161
dualism, 4:915–916
existential, 5:526, 539
God's presence in world through,
14:141
good in itself, 10:601
history, 10:906–907
identity principle, 7:304
Marcel, Gabriel, 9:134
patristic philosophy on forms, 10:960
simplicity of God, 13:138
Thomistic theory, 10:907–910,
12:394
truth justified through, 14:222
Particular Baptists, 2:78, 79

Particular friendship. *See* Friendship,
particular
Particular judgment, 8:27–29, 31, 31–33,
37–39
Partito Populare Italiano, 2:250
Parts (philosophy), **10:904–905**
Parvis, M. M., 2:367
Parvus Catechismus Catholicus
(Canisius), 3:18, 233, 242
Parvus Fons (apostolic constitution,
Clement IV), 3:748, 751
Parzival (Eschenbach), 4:401, 7:26, 28
Pascal, Blaise, 2:117, 10:417, **910–912**,
911
Augustinianism, 1:881
Brunschvicg, Leon, 2:650
Cartesianism, 3:186
casuistry, 3:221
end justifying the means, 5:213
existence of God, 6:314
free will, 5:931
Jansenism, 5:851
religious experience, 5:556
scholasticism, 12:768
skepticism, 13:202–203
voluntarism, 14:581
Pascal e a Inquietaçâo Moderna
(Figueiredo), 5:717
Pascendi dominici gregis (encyclical,
Pius X), 2:395, 694, 3:336, 5:789,
968, 6:313, 779, 7:503, 9:755,
10:912–913, 11:389, 14:139
modernism condemned, 12:775
modernism criticized, 8:311
Paschal (Antipope), 1:254, **10:913**
Paschal I (Pope), St., 3:169, 411,
10:913–915, *914*, 12:52, 356
Paschal II (Pope), 3:*746*, **10:915–916**,
916
Alpirsbach Abbey, 1:312
Bernard of Parma, St., 2:315
Bruno of Segni, St., 2:648
Canon Law, 3:45
Chaise-Dieu Abbey, 3:361
Charité-sur-Loire Abbey, 3:394
Cistercians, 3:746, 751
Council of Guastalla, 6:551
Crusades, 1:275, 276
Eastern Schism, 1:276, 2:760
Gebhard III of Constance, 6:114
Geoffrey of Vendôme, 6:142
Gerard of York, 6:163
Gregorian reform, 3:601
Gregory VIII (Antipope), 6:485
investiture struggle, 2:880, 7:538
Knights of Malta, 8:193

Paschal II (Pope) *(continued)*
  Regalia, 12:27
  reordination, 7:39
Paschal III (Antipope), 1:255,
  10:916–917
Paschal Baylon, St., **10:917–918**
Paschal candle, 5:16
Paschal cycle, 7:919
Paschal Epistle (Athanasius), 3:31
Paschal epistle (St. Peter of Alexandria),
  11:195
Paschal feast, 5:14
Paschal Lamb, 5:14
Paschal Letter (719), 10:770
The Paschal Liturgy and the Apocalypse
  (Shepherd), 12:186–187
Paschal mystery, 8:644, 728,
  12:163–165, 467, 13:439
Paschal sacrifice, 8:301
Paschal tables, 1:460
Paschal time, 8:719, 721
Paschal vigil. *See* Easter Vigil
Paschal Week. *See* Holy Week
Paschaltide, 5:12–13, 12:29
Paschang, John L., 10:222
Paschasinus (Bp. of Lilybeum), 3:363
Paschasius Radbertus, St., 3:599, 4:258,
  10:918, 14:158
  Carolingian reform, 3:158
  Eucharist, 1:64
  eucharistic controversy, 5:423
  exegetical works, 5:515
  medieval Latin literature works,
    9:444–445
  prescholasticism, 12:757
  Ratramnus of Corbie, 4:725–726
Pascualigo, Theatine Z., 12:767
Pasion des jongleurs (c. 1200), 10:926
Pasquier, Étienne, 1:478
Passaglia, Carlo, 3:314, 589, 5:37,
  10:104, **918–919**, 12:786
Passau Anonymus (*Pseudo-Rainer*),
  10:703
Passeri, Cinzio (Card.), 1:246
Passerini, Pietro Maria, **10:919**
The Passing of the Great Race (Grant),
  10:171
Passio (martyr account), **10:919**
Passio Acaunensium martyrum (St.
  Eucherius of Lyons), 5:438
Passio Perpetuae et Felicitatis, 11:130
Passio SS. Perpetuae et Felicitatis
  (Cyprian), 1:93, 4:83
Passion, 1:601–602, 4:391–397,
  681–682, 685, 8:828, **10:919–920**
  See also Action and passion

Passion According to St. John (Bach),
  2:7–8
Passion According to St. Matthew
  (Bach), 2:7–8
Passion d'Arras (Mercadé), 10:928
Passion of Christ
  Álvarez of Córdoba, Bl., 1:327
  iconography, 1:559, 5:32–33, 14:208
  literal exegesis, 5:513
  narratives, 5:810
  shrines, 13:89–90
  stations of the Coss, devotion to,
    13:500
  stigmatization, 13:530
  voluntary suffering, 13:588
  See also Stations of the Cross
Passion of Christ, devotion to,
  10:924–926
Passion of Christ, in the Bible, 8:15,
  857, 858, 10:137, **920–924**,
  11:579–580, 13:317
The Passion of Our Lord (O'Connor's
  translation), 10:544
Passion of the Theban Martyr Legion
  (Sigebert of Gembloux), 13:111
Passion plays, 4:897–898, 897–900,
  5:848, 10:510, **926–929**
Passionaries. *See* Legendaries
Passionary of Cunegonde, 12:486
Passionei, Domenico (Card.),
  10:929–930
Passionist Nuns, **10:930**
Passionist Sisters of the Cross and
  Passion, **10:930–931**
Passionists, **10:931–933**
  Botswana, 2:559
  California, 2:867
  Caribbean, 3:116
  as discalced order, 4:765
  Loor, I., 8:776–777
  Paul of the Cross, St., 11:34, 35
  Santamaria, Grimoaldo of the
    Purification, 12:680
  Silvestrelli, B., 13:124
Passive potency, 11:556
Passmore, John, 5:53, 12:47
Passover, feast of, 5:11, **10:933–936**,
  937
  agape, 1:170
  Christian calendar, 8:641
  eucharistic traditions, 5:411
  martyrdom of medieval Christian
    boys, 9:436
  night vigil, 5:15
  unleavened bread used during,
    14:333

See also Azymes
Passover lamb, 2:443, 5:11, **10:936–937**,
  937
Past and Present (Carlyle), 12:636
Pasteur, Louis, 2:403, 8:573–574, 10:151
Pastor, Ludwig von, 3:327, **10:937–938**,
  12:743
Pastor aeternus (papal bull, Leo X),
  6:78
Pastor bonus (The Good Shepherd)
  (apostolic constitution, John Paul II),
  1:589, 3:57, 58, 4:438–440,
  5:480–481, 8:286, 10:853, 11:76, 480
Pastor selection, 6:472
Pastoral Care (St. Gregory I), 6:482
*Pastoral Care of the Sick: Rites of
  Anointing and Viacticum*, 4:9–10
Pastoral College of Douai (France),
  7:575
Pastoral College of Louvain (Belgium),
  7:575
Pastoral Constitution on the Church in
  the Modern World (*Gaudium et spes*)
  (Vatican Council II). *See Gaudium et
  spes* (Pastoral Constitution on the
  Church in the Modern World)
  (Vatican Council II)
Pastoral Epistles, 2:410, 4:551, 8:318,
  10:938–940
Pastoral issues, 1:193, 483, 2:416–417,
  540, 3:557
*Pastoral Letters of the United States
  Catholic Bishops* (USCCB), 14:314
Pastoral liturgy, 8:664, 666
Pastoral manuals, 3:358
Pastoral Music (periodical), 8:707,
  14:321
Pastoral practice, 8:703–704, 711, 734
*The Pastoral Provisions: Married
  Catholic Priests* (Ficher), 5:709
Pastoral renewal, 8:62
Pastoral theology, 9:856, 13:910
  justification doctrine, 8:89–90
  Latina theology, 8:369–370
  liberation theology, 8:547
  liturgical theology, 8:714–715
  liturgy, 9:855
Pastorale munus (motu proprio, Paul
  VI), 3:56, 14:412
Pastoralis officii (brief, Clement XI),
  1:600
Pastores dabo vobis (apostolic
  exhortation, John Paul II), 4:157,
  7:1003
Pastoureaux, Crusade of the, **10:940**
Patarine Movement (11th century),
  10:940–942

Patarines (religious group), 7:662, **10:940–942**

  Alexander II (Pope), 1:253

  Arialdo, St., 1:660

  Atto of Milan, 1:841

  Bogomilism, 2:458

  Bonizo of Sutri, 2:506

  Bosnia heresy, 13:168

  clerical celibacy/marriage, 3:326

  condemnation, 5:769

  Erlembald, St., 5:323

  Humiliati, 7:204

  Landulf, 8:322–323

Patens, 3:370, 8:630–631

Patenson, William, Bl., 5:232, **10:942**

Pater Noster (Our Father). *See* Lord's Prayer

Pater Noster Church (Jerusalem), 8:*783*

Pater Noster plays. *See Speculum: Liber de Pater Noster* (play)

Paternity, Divine, **10:942**

Pathet Lao, 8:329–330

Pathway into the Holy Scripture (Luther), 14:253

Patience, **10:943**

Patience, in the Bible, **10:943–944**

Patients' rights, 9:430–431

Paton, H. J., 5:397

The Patriarch Nicon and the Tsar (Palmer), 10:812

Patriarch of Alexandria, 10:944–945

Patriarch of the West. *See* Pope (title)

Patriarchal exarch, 5:503

Patriarchate of Antioch, 10:944–945

Patriarchate of Rome, 10:944–945

Patriarchates, **10:944–948**

  Eastern Catholic Churches, 10:947–948

  Ecumenical Patriarchate of Constantinople, 10:945–947

  history, 10:944–945

  Latin Church, 10:948

  Latin Rite, 8:367

Patriarchates, ecumenical, 4:186, 187, **195–197**, 196

Patriarchs, 1:104, 118, 632, 634, 9:540

Patriarchs, biblical, **10:948, 950–951**

Patrician Brothers, 3:622, **10:951**

Patricius Romanorum, **10:951–952**, 14:249

Patrick, St., 2:621, 3:596, **10:952–955**, *953*

  Ardbraccan Abbey, 1:644

  Croagh Patrick, 4:369

  medieval Latin literature works, 9:441

  monasticism in Ireland, 9:803

  Palladius, 3:317

  Primatial See of Armagh, 1:697

  works, 10:954

  See also Ireland; *Rigail Pátraic*

Patriotism, 6:207, 7:551, **10:955–957**

Patripassianism, 3:560, 8:763, **10:409**, 957

  See also Modalism

Patripassians, 9:780

Patristic administration, 8:42, 294, 367–369, 442–443, 484

Patristic era, 3:594–595

  Abelard, Peter, 1:18

  Aelred, St., 1:138

  allegory, 1:292

  angels, 1:414, 423

  Anointing of the Sick, 1:481–482

  Antichrist, 1:516–517

  Assumption of Mary, 1:800

  biblical canon, 3:29

  biblical theology, 2:382

  Carthusian spirituality, 3:190

  casuistry, 3:220

  catechisms, 3:239–241

  Catholic social thought, 13:251–253

  causality, 3:303

  censorship, 3:336

  charity, 3:395–396

  chastity, 3:444

  Christian philosophy, 3:539

  Christocentrism, 3:558

  Christology, 3:559, 560–561

  clerical celibacy/marriage, 3:322–324

  communion of saints, 4:35–36

  Confession, 4:75–77

  congregational singing, 4:118

  conscience, 4:144–145

  contraception, 4:220

  dating of, 5:640–641

  Day of the Lord, 4:549

  discernment, spiritual, 4:765

  Divine conservation, 4:160–161

  grace, 3:533

  homily, 7:62–63

  hypostasis, 7:263

  immortality, 7:348–349

  papal social thought, 13:257

  preaching, homiletic theory, 11:617–618

  priesthood, 11:693–696

  Sisinnius (Pope), 13:168

  society (Church as), 13:285

  soul, 13:339–342

  spirituality, 13:443–445

  theology of Church, 3:583–586

  works of charity, 3:402–406

  See also Apologists, Greek; Augustine (Bp. of Hippo), St.; Basil the Great, St.; Clement of Alexandria, St.; Jerome, St.; Origen; Polycarp (Bp. of Smyrna), St.; Rufinus of Aquileia; Tertullian

Patristic Institute Augustinianum (Rome), 11:486

Patristic literature, 5:509–511, 641–643, 7:5, 12:467–468, 491, 516

Patristic philosophy and doctrine, 6:887–888, **10:957–962**

  biblical inspiration, 7:493–494

  Divine indwelling, 7:441–442

  general movements, 10:958–959

  general synthesis, 10:959–962

  Gnosis, 6:255

  God the Holy Spirit, 6:293

  heresy, 6:770–771

  history, 11:289–291

  infinity, 7:457–458

  meaning of Old Testament, 6:792

  mystery of God, 6:280–282

  notion of truth, 14:222–223

  order of universe, 14:329

  prayer, 11:593

  property, 11:757–758

  providence of God, 11:782–783

  prudence, 11:789

  purgatory, 11:826

  redemption, 11:976–977

  spiritual reading, 11:941

  works against gnosticism, 6:256–257

  world soul, 14:843–844

Patristic studies, 5:641, **10:962–963**

  Daniélou, Jean, 4:515

  Diekamp, Franz, 4:739–740

  Labriolle, P., 8:268

  Lawrence of Durham, 8:408

  Lebon, J., 8:429

  omniscience, 10:594–595

  Sirmond, J., 13:168

  Soto, Pedro de, 13:330–331

Patristic theology, 5:641, **10:964–969**, 13:903–904

  dogmatic theology, 4:817

  kenosis, 8:143

  laity, 8:293, 411

  lying as sin, 8:900

  mystical body of Christ, 10:102–103

  patristic homilies, 8:436

  similarity, 13:126

Patristic theology *(continued)*
speculation, 10:965–966
transubstantiation, 14:158
Patristic voluntarism, 14:580–581
Patrizi, Francesco, 1:677, 10:823, 12:122–123
Patrocinio de San José (Chile), 3:12–13
Patrologia Graeca (Cyril), 4:467
Patrologia Graeca (On Faith and the Principles of the Catholic Faith) (Manuel Calecas), 9:126–127
Patrologia Latina (Marbod), 9:132
Patrologia Latina (Migne), 11:604
Patrologia Latina (St. Odilo of Cluny), 10:552
Patrologiae cursus completus (Migne), 10:963
Patrologica Graeca (Migne), 9:94
Patrology (Migne), 3:601
Patrology (Quasten), 11:858
Patron saints, 6:764, **10:969–976**
Patronato real (royal patronage), **10:976–980**, 978–979
Alexander VI (Pope), 1:259, 2:862
Bolivia, 2:466
Brazil, 2:594
California, 2:862
Cambodia, 2:901
creation, 9:680–681
Leo XII (Pope), 8:490, 491
mission history, Catholic, 9:691–692
Philippines, 11:255–257
Patterns in Comparative Religion (Eliade), 5:154
Patuzzi, Giovanni Vincenzo, 1:311
Paucapalea (writer), 3:47, **11:1**
Paucar, Hernando, 1:946
Paul (martyr), St., 11:17
Paul (Roman martyr), St. *See* John and Paul (Roman martyrs), SS.
Paul, Apostle, St., 1:*87*, **11:1–12**, *4*
as a writer, 11:9
active life, 1:83
Acts of the Apostles, 1:89–90
Adam, 1:104
analogy of faith, 1:380
Ancyra, 1:398
anger, 1:430
Antioch, 1:521
Apollos, 1:562
apostolate, 1:579
apostolic faith, 1:586, 587
apotheosis, 1:599
appropriation, 1:606
Areopagus speech, 1:646

Asia Minor, 1:784
baptism, 2:60, 61, 66
Barnabas, St., 2:102–103, 11:6, 7, 13–14, 15
beatific vision, 2:171
birthplace, 3:733
body theme, 13:359
censorship, 3:336
charity, 4:307
Christmas cycle, 3:556
Church history, 3:591
civil authority, 1:921, 3:631
companion Silas (Silvanus), 13:119–120
congregational singing, 4:118
conscience, 4:141, 142, 143–144, 148
contemplation, 4:205
contraception, 4:220
conversion, 4:234, 239, 240, 11:3, 5
conversion and ecstatic visions, 5:61
Council of Jerusalem, 7:773
covenant, 4:328
cross, devotion to, 4:382
crucifixion, 4:398
curses, 4:443
Cyprus, 4:461
Day of the Lord, 4:548
death of, 11:8, 16
democracy, 4:638–639
demonology, 4:646, 716–717
descent of Christ into hell, 4:684
diaconia, 4:719
discernment, spiritual, 4:765
disciple as term, 4:768, 769, 770
Divine judgment, 8:30
Divine love, 8:49
drunkenness, 4:911
Ebionite opposition to teachings, 5:31
episcopate, 1:590
eternal law concept, 8:456
faith and works, 7:702
fraternal correction, 4:274
friendship with God, 6:11
fruits of the Holy Spirit, 7:46
fundamental option, 6:26
Galatia, 6:51–52
general intercessions, 6:128
gifts of Holy Spirit, 7:45
God's spirit, 13:428
gospel, 11:10–12
grace of Holy Orders, 7:41
Greece, 6:424
Holy Name, 7:31
homosexuality, 7:66

hope, 7:103
house churches, 2:145–146
iconography, 11:12
immortality, 7:354
imprisonment, 11:7–8
infant baptism, 2:67
James the Just, 3:546
jealousy, 7:748
justice, 8:70–71, 74
justification, 4:564, 8:77–80
kindness, 8:171–172
Kingdom of God, 8:174
language use, 8:362
Laodicea, 8:328
Lebanon, 8:426
letter to Philemon, 13:207, 208, 211
Lord's Day, 8:781
Lord's Supper, 8:784, 785
Mark, Evangelist, St., 9:182
ministries, 9:652
mystery of Christ, 13:439
pagan lust, 8:871
personality, 11:8–9
Philippians, 11:253
power of preaching, 11:627
predestination, 11:647
Prisca and Aquila, 11:718
prisoner at Caesarea, 5:666, 700
prisoner in Rome, 12:350
public penance, 7:436
purgatory, 11:825
reasoning, 11:949
recapitulation in Christ, 11:952
redemption, 11:970–971, 980
repentance, 4:225
reversal of values, 11:253
Sicily, 13:103
slavery, 13:211
Son of God, 13:313–314
sons of God, 13:322
sovereignty, 13:371
supernatural knowledge, 8:202
taxation and moral obligation, 13:768
teaching, 13:773
theology, 11:9–10
tomb, 11:352, 12:577
vices, catalog of, 13:48–49
women as deacons, 4:554
Paul, Apostle, St., missionary journeys, 11:*3*, 6–7, **12–17**, 12:340–341

Paul, Epistles of St. *See* Colossians, Epistle to the; Corinthians, Epistles to the; Ephesians, Epistle to the; Galatians, Epistle to the; Hebrews, Epistle to the; Philemon, Epistle to; Philippians, Epistle to the; Thessalonians, Epistles to the

Paul, John J. (Bp. of La Crosse, WI), 8:273, 14:783

Paul, SS., **11:17**

Paul I (Czar of Russia), 3:265, 6:156

Paul I (Pope), St., 10:*939*, **11:18–20**
  iconoclasm, 7:282
  I-Thou mysticism, 10:118
  Knights of Malta, 8:194
  mysteries in the Bible, 10:81–82
  natural law, 10:181
  ordination of neophytes, 10:239
  rabbinical training, 14:133
  transfer of relics, 12:52
  unicity, 14:297
  use of *mysterion*, 10:96
  works of charity, 3:411
  in writings of Pseudo-Dionysius, 11:801

Paul I of Constantinople, St., 11:17

Paul II (Patriarch of Constantinople), 2:750, **11:17**

Paul II (Pope), **11:20–21**, *21*
  Ammanati de' Piccolomini, Jacopo, 1:361
  assassination plot, 12:118
  Buonaccorsi, Filippo, 2:693
  cardinalate, 3:105
  carnival season, 13:98
  common good, 4:21
  George of Poděbrady, 4:481
  Holy Year, 7:57
  Renaissance humanism, 12:118
  simony, 13:136

Paul III (Pope), **11:21–23**, *22*
  Argentina, 1:648
  astrology, 1:813
  Charles V (Holy Roman Emperor), 3:431
  church reform, 11:21–22
  Contarini, Gasparo, 4:202
  Cortese, Gregorio, 4:280
  Council of Trent, 3:609, 610, 638, 14:168, 168–171
  Faber, Peter, Bl., 5:583
  Inquisition, 5:647
  Italo-Greek Catholic Church, 7:649
  Jesuits, 2:11, 3:610, 4:311, 5:530, 7:313, 779
  Michelangelo, 9:603

Order of St. George, 12:547
papacy development under, 10:842
reform, 4:311, 312
slavery, 13:209
Society of the Servants of the Poor, 5:191
Ursulines, 3:610
Vatican construction, 14:396

Paul IV (Patriarch of Constantinople), St., **11:18**

Paul IV (Pope), 11:*23*, **23–24**
  Anglican orders problem, 1:436–437
  Armenia, 1:702
  Charles V (Holy Roman Emperor), 3:431
  Commendone, Giovanni Francesco, 4:11
  Council of Trent, 3:610
  family, 3:96–97
  Ghibelline-Guelf conflict, 3:855
  Index of Prohibited Books, 7:389–390
  lay spirituality, 8:417
  litanies, 8:601
  Mary Tudor, 12:9
  papacy development, 10:842
  papal legates, 8:451
  Philip II (King of Spain), 3:20, 96
  Philip Neri, St., 10:248
  redemption, 11:976
  reform, 4:311
  reorganization of Low Countries' ecclesiastical hierarchy, 2:217
  sexism condemned, 13:52
  Theatines, 3:610, 782, 13:857–858

Paul V (Pope), **11:24–26**
  Abondance Monastery, 1:23
  Anne and Joachim, SS., 1:469
  Bellarmine, St. Robert, 2:227
  Bérulle, Pierre de, 2:338
  Chinese mission, 3:494
  Confraternity of Christian Doctrine, 4:94
  Congregatio de auxiliis under, 14:50
  de auxiliis controversy, 4:112–113, 6:404
  ecclesiastical archives, 1:636
  family, 2:534
  Galileo, 6:60, 61–62
  Oath of Allegiance (1606, England), 10:499–500
  Order of the Visitation of Holy Mary, 3:381
  papal decline, 3:612
  Piarists, 7:1043

Vatican construction, 14:395–396

Paul VI (Pope), 7:*763*, **11:26–33**, *27*, 14:*264*
  as Abp. of Milan, 11:28–29
  acolytes, 1:68
  Anglican-Catholic dialogue, 1:440
  Anointing of the Sick, 1:484
  Arrupe, Pedro, 1:726, 7:793–794
  atheism, 1:823, 824, 916
  Athenagoras I (Patriarch), 1:829
  beatifications, moratorium, 2:92
  Benelli, Giovanni, 2:276–277
  Beran, Josef, 4:486
  birth control, 5:40, 860, 7:179–181, 12:272, 575
  bishops' privileges, 14:412
  Bulgaria, 2:684
  Canon Law, 3:36, 56, 818
  canonization, 3:63
  as cardinal, 11:29
  cardinalate, 3:105, 106, 107
  cardinals voting in papal elections, 11:30
  catechesis and evangelization, 6:127
  Catholic traditionalism, 3:289
  charismatic renewal movement, 3:392
  charisms, 3:393
  Christocentrism, 3:558–559
  church architecture, 3:712
  clerical celibacy, 8:285, 11:32
  Code of Canons of the Eastern Churches, 3:818
  collegiality, 11:30
  common good, 4:21
  Confirmation, Sacrament of, 4:90
  Congregation for Divine Worship, 4:789, 790
  Congregation of Ceremonies, 3:350
  Congregation of Rites, 12:256
  congregational singing, 4:118
  Consilium, 4:164
  contraception, 1:490, 916, 4:222, 6:645, 11:32
  cooperation of curial offices, 11:30
  coronation ceremony, 10:*856*
  Corpus Christi mass, 4:272
  creedal statement, 4:355
  Cursillo Movement, 4:443–444
  Częstochowa, 4:490
  deacons, 4:552, 553
  diplomatic relations with Communist countries, 11:31–32
  ecumenism, 11:31
  enclosure, 3:806
  episcopal collegiality, 3:837

Paul VI (Pope) *(continued)*

Episcopal conferences, 5:39–40

Eucharist, 10:77–79

eucharistic fast, 5:437

evangelization, 5:39, 473–474, 478, 480, 9:682, 688–689

extraordinary assembly of Bishops (1969), 13:688–689

Feast of Christ the King, 3:527

Francis de Sales, St., 5:869

Greek Orthodox Church, 6:437

Hungary, 7:222

Index of Prohibited Books, 7:389–390, 391

indulgences, 7:439–440, 9:684–685

International Council for Catechesis, 7:526

International Theological Commission, 7:527

international travel, 11:30–31

Jadot, Jean, 7:694

Jesuits, 1:726

Jubilee celebrations (1966), 14:415

just-war, 14:638

laymen as lectors and acolytes, 11:30

lectors, 8:443

lenten observances, 8:469

liturgy, 2:676–677

Liturgy of the Hours, 8:731

''majority report'' rejection, 6:18

married deacons, 11:30

media of social communications, 10:546

medical research, 5:560

Mindszenty, József, 7:219

modernization of Rome, 12:361–362

Mother Teresa, 10:16

mystery of the Holy Eucharist, 11:32

Neocatechumental communities, 10:233

New York visit (1965), 10:318

option for the poor, 10:615, 12:396

orders redefined, 7:37, 38

ordination rituals suppressed, 10:639

original sin, 10:670

papacy development, 10:850–851

penitence, 5:186, 635

Pontifical Commission for the Neo-Vulgate, 14:598

pontifical councils, 11:477, 481–482

Pontifical Mission for Palestine, 11:484

pontifical Roman universities, 11:487, 488

poor nations, 13:260

porters, 11:525

praxis, 11:587

preaching, 11:616, 628

procreation, 10:178, 521, 13:46–47

religious freedom, 5:946, 952

religious houses, 4:231

religious unity, 5:75

resignation of bishops and cardinals, 11:30

revised Roman calendar, 8:720–721

rites of ordination, 2:417, 10:640, 641

Roman Curia, 4:438, 5:480

sacraments, 2:417

Secretariat for Non-Believers, 12:858

Secretariat for Non-Christians, 12:858

Seton canonization, 13:176

signs of the times, 13:117

social challenges and social justice, 11:32, 516–517, 566

social justice, 4:157

Synod of Bishops, 5:39, 13:683, 688, 14:414

Tridentine Mass, 14:182

Vatican construction, 14:397

Vatican Council II, 2:676–677, 3:626, 11:29–30, 33, 14:411–418

vernacular in the liturgy, 8:365, 11:30

Villot, Jean, 14:517–518

women as mothers, 14:826

world religions, 5:33–34, 10:850–851, 855

world solidarity and world peace, 11:32

Paul and the Salvation of Mankind (Munck), 5:523

Paul de Samosate (Bardy), 2:98

Paul of Aegina, 2:808

Paul of Ancona, 4:476

Paul of Burgos (Bp.), **11:33**

Paul of Caen (Abbot), 12:531

Paul of Canopus, **11:33–34**

Paul of Emesa, 3:553

Paul of Merida, 12:606

Paul of Persia, 1:671

Paul of St. Magdalen. *See* Heath, Henry, Bl.

Paul of Samosata (Bp. of Antioch), 1:521, **11:34**

Christology, 1:119, 524, 3:560

deposition, 5:666, 740

homoousios, 4:197, 353, 7:65

Lucian of Antioch, 8:844

preaching, 11:609

School of Antioch, 1:526, 2:820

Paul of Tarsus. *See* Paul, Apostle, St.

Paul of the Cross, St., 10:930, **11:34–36**, *35*, 13:124

Paul of Thebes, 4:686, 12:606

Paul the Deacon, 5:842, **11:36–37**

Adalard, St., 1:98

Carolingian Renaissance, 1:98, 3:159, 425

chronicles, 1:461

hymns, 7:245, 253

Lombard history, 8:768

Paul the Hermit, St., 11:17

Paul the Simple, St., 11:17

Paula of Rome, St., 5:457, 7:757, 758, **11:37**, 344

Paula of St. Joseph Calasanctius. *See* Montal, Fornés, Paula, St.

Paúles. *See* Vincentians

Paulicians, 1:700, 2:458, 759, **11:37**

See also Messalians

Paulina of the Agonizing Heart of Jesus (Mother). *See* Visintainer, Amabile Lucia, Bl.

Pauline (daughter of Paula), 3:406

Pauline Fathers and Brothers, **11:37–38**

Pauline privilege, 8:507, **11:38**

Pauline Rule, 8:771

Pauline writings, 10:81–82, 304–305, 896–897, 921–922, 14:202

Paulines. *See* Pious Society of the Daughters of St. Paul (DSP)

Paulinus (poet), 12:320

Paulinus I (Patriarch of Aquileia), 1:607

Paulinus II (Patriarch of Aquileia), St., 1:608, 3:160, 425, 4:356, 7:246, **11:38**

Paulinus of Antioch, 2:137

Paulinus of Milan, 12:606

Paulinus of Nola, St., 5:449, 6:112, **11:38–39**

Anastasius I (Pope), St., 1:386–387

cross, 4:383, 384

Easter Vigil, 5:15

Felix of Nola, 5:670

hymns, 7:244

''invention'' of bells, 2:232

lamps and lighting, 8:314

pilgrimage, 11:352

relics, 12:52

Siricius distance, 13:167

works, 12:320

works of charity, 3:406, 407

Paulinus of Tyre (Bp.), 1:662, 5:451

Paulinus of Venice (Bp.), 1:888, **11:39**

Paulinus of York, St., 2:500, 5:98, 239, 386, 7:89, **11:39–40**

Paulist Fathers Renewal Chapter (1967-68), 11:41–42

Paulist National Catholic Evangelization Association, 4:242

Paulist Press, 7:316, 11:*40*, 42

Paulist Young Adults Ministry (2000), 11:42

Paulists, 5:169, **11:40–42**
  church architecture, 3:716
  Deshon, George, 4:687
  founding, 2:23, 3:622, 6:700
  publishing ventures, 6:700

Paulus, Heinrich E. G., 5:521, 7:847–848

Paulus, Nikolaus, **11:42–43**

Paulus Albarus, **11:43–44**

Paulus de Aretio, 3:52

Paulus de Liazariis, **11:44–45**

Paulus Euergetinos, **11:45**

Paulus Silentiarius, 2:804, 805, 4:189

Paulus Vladimirus, 3:51–52

Pavillon, Nicolas (Bp. of Alet), 1:717, 8:431, **11:45**, 12:29

PAVLA (Papal Volunteers for Latin America), 10:859–860

Pavo de natura saeculi (Jordan of Paderborn), 9:462

Pavón Bueno, José (Father), 2:92

PAX (Persatuan Agama Katolik Sabah), 9:71–72

Pax Christi International, 1:918, **11:45–46**

Pax Romana (Roman Peace), 12:305

Pax Romana-International Movement of Catholic Students (IMCS), 10:161

Paxton, Frederick, 1:485

Payens, Hugh de, 9:625

Payeras, Mariano, 2:862

Payne, John, 5:250

Payne, Peter, **11:46**

Payrus fragment (4th century), 10:*862*

Paz, Luis, 2:468

Paz en la guerra (Unamuno), 14:288

Pazheparambil, Aloysius, 3:130

Pázmány, Péter (Card.), 3:613, 7:214, **11:46**, 13:220

Pazzi, Andrea, 11:46

Pazzi, Giangirolamo, 11:47

Pazzi, Guglielmo, 11:46–47

Pazzi, Jacopo, 11:46

Pazzi, Maria Maddalena de', St., 3:126, **11:47–48**

Pazzi, Piero, 11:46

Pazzi Chapel (Florence, Italy), 7:*661*

Pazzi conspiracy, 12:118, 220, 13:197

Pazzi family, **11:46–47**

Peabody, Elizabeth, 14:149

Peace, **11:48–49**
  Caussade, Jean Pierre de, 3:310
  De Indis (Vitoria), 14:570–571
  De jure belli Hispanorum in barbaros (Vitoria), 14:570–571
  Justice and Peace Commission, 12:396
  military service, 9:627–628
  papal social thought, 13:260
  SODEPAX, 13:296
  Söderblom, N., 13:297

Peace, Council of (1031), 11:50

Peace, in the Bible, **11:49–50**

Peace of God, 1:815, 2:880–881, 3:45, 411, 518

Peace of God Movement, **11:50–51**

"Peace of the Church" (1669), 7:717

Peace of Venice, 7:149

Peace offerings, in the Bible, 8:525, **11:51**

Peano, G., 12:415

The Pearl (poem), 3:605, **11:51–53**

Pearson, Karl, 11:299

Pearson, Wolstan, 5:2

Peasant Revolt (1381), 4:317, 692

Peasants' War (1524-25), **11:53**, 12:17
  Alpirsbach Abbey, 1:312
  Altdorf Abbey, 1:320
  Anabaptists, 1:368
  Berthold of Chiemsee, 2:333
  Böhm, Hans, 2:461
  Charles V (Holy Roman Emperor), 3:430
  Lutheran reform, 8:881–882
  Salzburg, 8:324

Pecia, **11:53–54**

Peckham, John. *See* John Peckham (Abp. of Canterbury)

Pecock, Reginald (Bp. of Chichester), 3:481, 8:837, **11:54**, 12:536

Pectorius, Epitaph of, 5:286, 7:277, **11:54–55**

The Pedalion (Nicodemus the Hagiorite), 6:458

Pedalion or *Rudder of the Ship of Knowledge* (Nicodemus), 10:382

Pedemonte, Manuel José (Father), 6:805

Pedro I (Emperor of Brazil), 2:594, 595

Pedro II (Emperor of Brazil), 2:596, 597

Pedro IV (King of Aragon), 3:780, 4:361

Pedro de S. Clara, Bl., 7:734

Pedro de S. Maria, Bl., 7:734

Peel, Robert, Sir, 7:562, 10:540

Peers, Edgar Allison, 11:*55*, **55**

Peeters, P., 2:472

Pegis, Anton Charles, **11:55–56**

Pégues, Thomas, **11:56**

Péguy, Charles Pierre, **11:56–57**

Peio Clementine Museum (Vatican City), 14:396

Peirce, Charles Sanders, 5:94, 11:*57*, **57–58**, *299*
  Boolean algebra, 8:751–752
  causality, 3:301–302
  characteristics of belief, 5:198
  empiricism, 5:198
  panpsychism, 10:824
  philosophy and science, 11:296, 300
  pragmatism founder, 5:198
  Royce, Josiah, 12:398

Peitz, W. H., 3:39, 40

Pekah (King of Israel), 4:674

Pékin, Histoire et Déscription (Favier), 5:651

Pelagia, SS., 5:*449*, **11:58–59**

Pelagia of Antioch, St., 11:58

Pelagia of Jerusalem, St., 11:58

Pelagia of Tarsus, St., 11:58

Pelagia the Penitent. *See* Pelagia of Jerusalem, St.

Pelagius I (Pope), **11:59–60**
  Ambrosian Rite, 1:343
  Anastasius I (Patriarch of Antioch), 1:388
  appointment, 8:99
  Demetrias, St., 4:635
  Justinian I, 3:595, 596, 8:97
  Origenism, 3:595
  porters, 7:37
  Three Chapters, 4:191, 192
  works of charity, 3:408

Pelagius II (Pope), **11:60**, 12:356
  Byzantine Church, 2:750, 751
  Constantinople Council II, 4:192
  Ecumenical Patriarch as term, 4:196
  Franks, 3:596

Pelagius and Pelagianism, **11:60–63**
  anthropocentrism, 1:508
  Arminianism, 2:894
  Augustine, St., 1:859–861, 877, 2:498, 3:206–207, 594, 9:511
  Boniface I (Pope), St., 2:498
  Britain, 2:621
  Cassian, John, 3:206–207
  Cassiodorus, 3:208
  Celestine I (Pope), St., 3:317
  conversion, 4:239–240

Pelagius and Pelagianism *(continued)*
 Council of Antioch, 1:523
 Councils of Carthage, 3:186, 188
 devout humanism, 7:194
 Durandus of Saint-Pourçain,
  4:947–948
 Eastern Schism, 2:761
 England, 2:621
 freedom, 5:937
 grace, 6:402
 grace and nature, 6:411
 Honorius (Roman Emperor), 7:87
 hope, 7:95
 infant baptism, 2:68
 Innocent I (Pope), St., 7:468
 Jansenism, 1:893
 John IV (Pope), 7:921
 Julian of Eclanum, 8:48
 justification, 8:82
 Marius Mercator, 9:181
 predestination, 11:648–649, 650–651
 rejection in Gaul, 6:113
 St. Augustine, 10:431
 St. Palladius, 10:805
 salutary acts, 12:621
 Sixtus III (Pope), St., 13:195
 sovereignty of Grace, 5:934
 See also Caelestius; Semi-
  Pelagianism
Pelayo, Alvaro, 13:384
Pelczar, Jósef Sebastian, Bl., **11:63**
"El Pele." *See* Giménez Malla,
 Ceferino, Bl.
Le Pèlerin (periodical), 2:16
Pèlerinages en Suisse (Veuillot), 14:465
Peletier, Jean, 3:327, 328
Pelican symbolism, 1:458
Pelicans, as symbol of Christ the
 Redeemer, **11:63–64**
Pelissier, Appollonie Cure (Mother),
 12:496
Pellegrino, Edmund D., 3:292
Pelletier, Maria Euphrasia, St., 3:419,
 11:64
Pellicanus, Konrad, 6:696, **11:64–65**
Pellicer, Anthony Dominic (Bp. of San
 Antonio, TX), 13:846
Pelotte, Donald E. (Bp. of Gallup, NM),
 6:81
Pelster, Frantz, 4:275–276, 12:230, 776
Pelton, Gilmour v. (1883), 6:226
Pelzer, August, 12:776
Pembroke Priory (Wales), **11:65**
Peña, Pedro de la (Bp. of Quito,
 Ecuador), 5:62

Peña, Raymundo J., 5:174
Peña Montenegro, Alonso de la (Bp. of
 Quito), 5:62, **11:65**
Penal law theory, 13:768
Penal laws, 2:701, 719
Peñalver y Cárdenas, Luis Ignacio (Bp.
 of Louisiana), 8:809–810, 10:291,
 11:65–66, 12:559
Penance, practices of, 6:421, **11:66**, 68
 Apostolic Fathers, 1:588
 Canon Law, 3:41–42
 Carolingian era, 8:657
 commutations, 7:436
 Lambertenghi of Como, 8:305
 lenten fasting, 8:468–470
 Middle Ages, 13:445
 pilgrimage as, 11:348, 353–354
 prostration as liturgical gesture, 8:649
 public to private, 8:657
 redemptiones, 8:659
 sins, 9:861
 Tertullian, 13:836
 See also Penitentials
Penance, Sacrament of, 8:650, **11:66–72**,
 13:97
 ancient penance, 11:68–69
 Armenian liturgy, 1:710
 attrition, 1:843
 catechesis, 3:231
 confession, 4:75–77
 contrition-attrition distinction, 4:226,
  227–230
 Coptic, 4:257
 dead, prayers for, 4:556–557
 death, 4:576
 examination of conscience, 4:148
 lay confession, 8:412
 lay spirituality, 8:415
 medieval penance, 11:69–71
 modern penance, 11:69–72
Penet, Mary Emil, 13:170
Penido, M. T. L., 12:776
Penitêncîa (laity association), 3:416
Penitentes (New Mexico), 8:316, 10:286
Penitential controversy, **11:72–73**
Penitential prayer, 11:592
Penitential psalms, 4:225, **11:73–74**
Penitentials, **11:74–75**
 Canon Law, 3:41–43, 45, 60
 canons of Robert of Flamborough,
  12:267
 casuistry, 3:220
 Columban, St., 3:864
 processions of flagellants, 5:755
Penitentiary, apostolic, 7:439, **11:75–78**

Penitents. *See* Order of Magdalens
Penn, William, 5:468, 10:321, 746,
 11:78, 80
 Barclay, Robert, 2:97
 Church-State relations, 3:641, 648,
  651
 Society of Friends, 5:838
Pennings, Bernard Henry, **11:78**, *79*, 668
Penn's Charter of Liberties, **11:78–80**
Pennsylvania, **11:80–88**
 Baptists, 2:79
 Church-State relations, 3:641,
  648–649, 650, 651
 Duchemin, M. Theresa, 4:916–927
 German Reformed Church, 12:739
 history, 8:306
 missions, 6:80, 9:725, 11:60
 Moravian Church, 9:885
 Polish National Catholic Church,
  11:458
 Sisters of Divine Providence, 13:181
 See also Penn's Charter of Liberties;
  specific dioceses and archdioceses
Pennsylvania, Murdock v. (1943), 3:661
Pennsylvania, Synod, 12:739
Pennsylvania Abortion Control Act of
 1989, 11:88
Pennsylvania Catholic Conference, 11:88
Pennsylvania Magazine, 10:757
Penny, Aeneas, 7:579
Penobscot people, 9:55
Pentalogus diaphoricus (Charles of the
 Assumption), 3:436
The Pentarchy, 10:945
Pentarchy theory, 2:757, 822, 824, 825
Pentateuch, 1:814, 3:23, 5:519–520,
 13:760–761, 14:253
 See also Exodus, Book of
Pentateuchal studies, **11:88–100**
 1965 to present, 11:96–98, 98–99
 composition problem, 13:127
 Elohist, 5:174
 life, concept of, 8:566
 Lutheran exegetes, 8:129
 Moses and the Pentateuch, 11:95
 origins until 1965, 11:92–95
 role of law, 8:396
Pentecost, 5:12, **11:100–103**, 13:1
 Annunciation, 1:476
 ecstasy of the Holy Spirit, 5:61
 God's spirit, 13:427
 speaking in tongues, 5:136
 Veni sancte spiritus sequence,
  14:440–441

Pentecost, iconography of, 7:49, 51, 11:*103*, **103–104**

Pentecostal churches, 1:135, 788–790, 3:487, **11:104–106**, 14:842

See also Assemblies of God; Foursquare Gospel

Pentecostalism, 3:113, 4:241–242, **11:106–108**

Pentecostal-Roman Catholic dialogue, 5:69

People of God, **11:107–108**

baptismal identity, 8:291

Church as the, 5:37

communio, 4:29–31

conciliar ecclesiology, 8:291

laity as, 8:288, 416

married couples, 8:288

New Testament ecclesiologies, 8:290

social principle, 13:248

theology, 8:290

See also Covenant, in the Bible

People's Eucharistic League, 5:435

People's Mass Book, 7:261

People's Temple (Jonestown), 4:*425*

Pepe, Joseph A. (Bp. of Las Vegas), 8:346

Pepin I (Mayor of the Palace), 3:163–164

Pepin I of Aquitaine, 12:550

Pepin II (King of the Franks), 3:163, 9:518–519, 10:835

Pepin III the Short (King of the Franks), 3:124, 4:178, 5:842, 917, 9:519, **11:108–112**, *109*

Adalard, St., 1:98

anointing, 1:478

Burchard of Würzburg, St., 2:696

Canon Law, 3:41

Carolingian reform, 2:496, 3:156, 424

Carolingian Renaissance, 3:159

Chrodegang of Metz, St., 3:563

consolidation of power, 3:164–165, 421, 598

donations, 1:121–122, 3:165, 635

Paul I (Pope), St., 11:18–19

Roman Rite, 12:328

Saint-Germain-des-Prés Abbey, 12:547

Stephen II (III) (Pope), 13:515–516

works of charity, 3:410

Pequenos na terra, grandes no céu (Conceição), 4:49–50

Per accidens (through another), 12:752

Per se (through itself), 12:752

Per venerabilem (papal decree, Innocent III), 7:472

Peraudi, Raimondo (Card.), 5:200

Perboyre, Jean-Gabriel, St., 11:*112*, **112**

Perception

cybernetics, 4:452–453

defined, 8:208

movement, 10:20

Scottish School of Common Sense, 12:840

sensation, 12:906

sense knowledge, 12:910

sensibles, 12:914

theories, 10:20–21

Perceptionists, 11:850

Perceval (Chrétien), 7:26, *27*, 28

Perché, Napoléon Joseph (Abp.), 8:812, 10:293, 12:274

Perctarit (King of the Lombards), 1:664

Percy, Thomas, Bl., 5:227, **11:112–113**

Percy, Walker, 11:*113*, **113–114**

Peregrinatio ad loca sancta (itinerary), 7:676

Peregrinatio Aetheriae (Aetheria's Pilgrimage), 5:104–106, 12:681

Peregrine Chapel at Mission San Juan Capistrano (CA), 9:*705*

Peregrini (play), 4:894

Peregrinus (Bp. of Auxerre), 1:927

Peregrinus (Cynic), 4:456

Peregrinus of Sankt Paul (Abbot), 12:670

Pereira, Benedict, 1:677

Pereira, Jacob Rodriguez, 3:418

Pereira, Solórzano, 12:616

Pereira, Tomé, 3:497, **11:114–115**

Pereira y Castellón, Simeón (Bp.), **11:115**

Pérez, Esteban, **11:115**

Perez, Joaquín, 3:498

Pérez, Juan (Father), 3:866, **11:115–116**

Pérez de Herrera, Christoval, 3:417, 418

Pérez de Rivas, Andrés, **11:116**

Pérez Florido, Petra de San José, Bl., **11:116–117**

Pérez García, Faustino, 2:92

Pérez Godoy, Francis, Bl., 1:952

Pérez Jiménez, German, Bl., 4:494

Pérez Ramos, Leoncio (Father), 2:92

Perfect gnosis, 9:111

See also Gnosis

Perfect Sublime Masters, 3:101

La Perfecta Casada (León), 8:498

Perfectae caritatis (Vatican Council II), 3:393, 806, 10:460, 483, 13:186

Perfection

Aquinas, St., 13:575

Bellinzaga, Isabella Christina, 2:230

Consolatorium piorum (Maes), 9:30–31

controversies, 13:326

creation by man, 9:93

heroic virtue, 14:554

man, concept of, 9:92

man, natural end of, 9:96

Mary, Blessed Virgin, 9:253

Molinos, Miguel de, 9:773

Perfection, ontological, 8:201, 460–461, **11:117–120**

Perfection, spiritual, 8:461, 775, 829, **11:120–121**, 13:52, 450

Perfective good, 6:352

Perfectus (martyr of Córdoba), 4:261–262

Pergaud, Gabriel, 12:278

Pergolesi, Giovanni Battista, **11:122**, *123*

Peri Archon (Origen), 10:653, 657–658, 660, 967

Perichoresis, Christological, 4:28–29, **11:122–123**

Pericopes, **11:123–128**

See also Lectionaries

Périès, Georges, 1:354, 355

Périgueux Cathedral (France), 3:693

Perin, G., 5:798

Périn, Henri Charles Xavier, **11:128**

Periodica de re canonica et morali (periodical), 14:452

Peripatetics, 1:668, 680, 682

Periplus Ponti Euxini (Mariner's Chart) (Arrian), 12:309

Peris Polo, José Maria, 12:408

Peristephanon (Crowns of Martyrs) (Prudentius), 11:792

Perizonium, 4:393

Perjury, 8:901, **11:128–129**

Perko, Franc, 7:528

Pērkons (Baltic region deity), 2:36

Permanence du droit naturel (Delhaye), 10:194

Pernet, Étienne Claude, 1:802, 8:616, 11:*129*, *129*

Pernicious lies (*medacium perniciosum*), 8:900

Perón, Juan Domingo, 1:652, 654

Perón, María Estela ''Isabelita,'' 1:654

Péronne, J. M., 3:259

Pérotin (French composer), **11:129–130**

Perpendicular Gothic architecture, 3:698

Perpetua, St., 11:130–131, 12:26

Perpetua, Vibia (martyr), 1:93, 3:403–404, 594

Perpetua and Felicity, SS., 3:403–404, **11:130–131**, 12:26

Perpetual Adorers of the Blessed Sacrament, 13:321

Perpetuité de la foi catholique de l'Église (Renaudot), 12:126

Perpetuus of Tours, St., 3:553, **11:131**

Perpignan, Guy Terrena de, 3:141

Perrault, C., 3:675

Perrers, Alice, 3:450

Perret, Auguste, 3:669, 672, 677–679, 710, 713, 8:622–623, **11:131–132**

Perrone, Giovanni, 1:565, 3:244, 5:37, **11:132**

Perrone, P., 2:678

Perry, Harold (Bp. of New Orleans), 1:161, 8:815

Persatuan Agama Katolik Sabah (PAX), 9:71–72

Perseverance, 8:775, **11:132–133**, 595

Perseverance, final, **11:133–134**

Persia, **11:134–141**

　Achaemenid Dynasty, 11:135–136

　Arsacid Dynasty, 11:136–137

　Boyid, Turkish, and Mongol Dynasties, 11:139–140

　Church-State relations, 3:631

　crucifixion, 4:389

　Cyrus the Great, 4:477–478

　Darius I, 4:527–529

　demonology, 4:646

　Discalced Carmelites in, 3:145

　dualism, 4:914

　Dura-Europos, 4:945

　fire altars, 11:*143*

　immortality, 7:347

　invasion of Christian Jerusalem (614), 7:770

　Justin II, 8:92–93

　Kalām, 8:109–110

　Pahlavi Dynasty, 11:141

　Qajar Dynasty, 11:141

　rise of Islam, 11:139

　Roman invasion, 2:780

　Roman wars, 8:51

　Safavid Dynasty, 11:140–141

　Sasanian Dynasty, 11:137–139

　See also Assyrian Church of the East (Persia)

Persian fire altars, 11:*143*

Persian Gulf War (1991), 7:545–546, 1000, 13:260

Persian religions, ancient, 4:492–493, 5:2, **11:142–145**

　See also Zoroastrianism

Persian Revolution (1905), 11:141

Persico, Ignatius (Card.), **11:145–146**, 12:709

Persius (writer), 12:308

Person, concept of, 5:941–942, 9:735–736, 13:570, 577

Person, Divine, 7:374, 11:149, **151–152**

Person, in philosophy, **11:146–148**

　Boethius, 1:673, 2:456

　character, 3:387

　consciousness, 4:152

　nature, 8:399

　normality, 10:426

　papal social thought, 13:261

　principles of action, 10:26

　spirit, 13:422

Person, in theology, **11:148–151**

　common good, 4:20

　incarnation doctrine on nature, 10:961

　love, 8:825–830

　mystical union between God, 10:109

　notional acts, 1:85

　obedience and personal responsibility, 10:507

　Trinitarian doctrine, 10:960

　See also Hypostasis

Person and Act (Osoba y czyn) (Wojtyła), 7:995

Person of Jesus Christ, 13:315

Personal consecration, **4:156**

Personal gods in ancient Mesopotamia, 9:533

Personal guilt, 6:573

Personal idealism, 11:296

Personal morality, 9:867–868

Personal responsibility, 10:507

Personal sin, 9:902

Personal supposition, 13:625

Personal tolerance, 14:102–103

Personalism, 7:301–302, **11:152–153**

　anthropocentrism, 1:508

　associations, 1:793

　Brightman, Edgar Sheffield, 2:617

　Christian philosophy, 3:539

　community, 4:38–39

　doctrine, 4:808

　Knudson, A. C., 8:227

　laicism, 8:283

　love, concept of, 8:827

　Maritain, Jacques, 4:20

　Mounier's development, 10:30–31

　religion, 12:70

　See also Materialism

Personalism (Mounier), 10:31

Personalisme en democratisering (Janssens), 7:722

Personalist ethics, **11:153–155**

A Personalist Manifesto (Mounier), 10:31

Personality, 4:431–433, 5:942, 8:60–61, **11:155–157**

Personality in Christ and in Ourselves (Sanday), 12:665

Personé, Salvador (Father), 3:857

Persons, Robert, 5:165, 750, 6:100, 7:783, 11:*157*, **157–158**, 12:569

　Allen, William, 1:296

　Briant, Bl. Alexander, 2:611

　Brinkley, Stephen, 2:618

　Campion, Edmund, 2:921

　Gifford, William, 6:210

　Recusant literature, 11:959

Persons and Places (Santayana), 12:680

Perspectiva (Witelo), 14:801

Perspectives in American Catholicism (Ellis), 5:170

Pertinacity, 8:775

Peru, **11:158–167**, *161*, *162*, *164*

　Canon Law, 1:932

　catechesis, 3:234, 246, 248, 252

　conquistadores, 4:131–132, 11:*165*

　demographic statistics, 11:158

　ecclesiastical organization, 11:159

　educational reform, 12:280–281

　independence, 6:378–379, 11:161–162

　map, 11:*160*

　missions, 11:158–160

　　catechisms, 3:234, 246, 248

　　catechumenate, 3:252

　　Discalced missionaries, 11:115

　　Franciscans, 9:710–711, 12:240–241, 616

　　Iquitos and Chulucanas centers (Augustinians), 9:714

　　Ocopa center (Jesuits), 9:711–712

Perugia, Andrea da, 3:493

Perugino (Umbrian painter), 2:375, 4:*399*, 11:*167*, **167**

Perulles Estivill, Antonio, 12:408

"Peruvian Revolution" (1968), 11:166

Peruzzi, Baltasar, 3:484

"A Perverted Devotion" (Tyrrell), 14:258

Pesach (passage of Yahweh), 5:11

Pesch, Christian, **11:168**, 12:777

Pesch, Heinrich, 13:300

Pesch, Tilmann, **11:168**

Pesellino, Francesco, 3:443

Peshitta (Bible text of Syrian Christianity), 3:32, **11:168**

Pessimism, 7:298–299, **11:168–170**

Die Pest des Laizismus und ihre Erscheinungsformen (Galen), 6:57

Pestalozzi, Johann Heinrich, 5:91, 93, 255, 263, **11:170–172**, *171*

Petau, Denis, 6:392, 404, *872*, 7:782, 10:963, **11:172–173**

Petavius. *See* Petau, Denis

Peter (17th c. Irish martyr), 7:581

Peter (Bp. of Alexandria), 1:272, 6:515

Peter (Bp. of Lichfield), 3:469

Peter (Czar of Bulgaria), 3:259

Peter (Patriarch of Aquileia), 1:607

Peter (Roman martyr), St. *See* Marcellinus and Peter, SS.

Peter, Apostle, St., 1:*87*, **11:173–176**

    Antioch, 1:521

    burial site, 3:224

    Christmas cycle, 3:556

    connection of three patriarchates, 10:944–945

    Council of Jerusalem, 7:773

    death of, 11:176

    iconography, 11:176

    John, Apostle, St., 7:896

    kerygma, 8:157–158

    keys to heaven, 8:162–163, *163*

    Kingdom of God, 8:174

    kiss of peace, 8:185

    language use, 8:361

    lay spirituality, 8:413

    leadership, 11:175–176

    Leo I (Pope), St., 8:475, 478

    Mark, Evangelist, St., 9:184

    messiahship of Jesus, 9:546

    pagan peoples, 8:4

    primacy of, 11:175, 495–496

    successor, 8:596

    tomb, 2:146, 4:181, 11:352, 12:578, 14:390–391

    See also Peter, Epistles of St.

Peter, Bl. (17th c. Japanese martyr), 7:733

Peter, Carl Joseph, 7:528, **11:176–177**

Peter, Epistles of St., **11:177–180**

    Babylon, as symbol for Rome, 2:4

    baptismal symbolism, 2:60

    beatific vision, 2:171

    birth imagery in baptism, 2:75

    canonicity, 3:21, 28, 30, 31, 32

    catechesis, 3:227

    Christian (term), 3:530

    Church, 3:580

    conscience, 4:143, 144

    Divine election, 5:146

    Divine judgment, 8:40

    docetism, 4:797

    end of the world, 5:215, 216

    Galatia, 6:51

    Gnosis, 6:254

    grace, 6:381

    guilt, 6:572

    heaven, 6:685

    justification, 8:80

    laity, 8:290, 292

    life of grace, 13:441

    long-suffering, 8:775

    Parousia, 10:896

    Precious Blood, 11:638, 641

    presbyters, 11:673

    ransom, 11:909

    rebirth, 11:951

    royal priesthood, 8:728, 11:692

    Silas (Silvanus), 13:119

    sin, 13:147, 148

    slavery, 13:207

    social principle, 13:248

    spirit, 13:425

    suffering servant, songs of the, 13:591–592

    See also Catholic Epistles

Peter, Sarah Worthington King, **11:180**

Peter I (Armenian Catholicos), 1:701

Peter I (Emperor of Russia), 7:53–54, **11:180–183**, *181*, 12:*422*, 424, 13:216

    Moscow Patriarchate, 2:745

    Russian theology, 12:434

Peter I (King of Hungary), 6:233

Peter III (Patriarch of Antioch), 2:757, 824

Peter IV Saulnier (Bp. of Autun), 1:926

Peter VII (Patriarch of Alexandria), 4:254

Peter IX Hassun (Armenian Patriarch), 1:703

Peter Acotanto, Bl., **11:183**

Peter and Paul Hermitage, SS., 13:69

Peter Arbués, St., **11:183**

Peter Armengol, Bl., **11:183**

Peter Aureoli (Abp. of Aix), 1:197, 410, 3:96, 4:162, **11:183–184**

Peter Cadalus. *See* Honorius II (Antipope)

Peter Cansius, St., 7:439, 8:602

Peter Cantor, 3:727, 5:516, **11:184**, 12:267

Peter Cathanii, 5:870

Peter Chrysologus, St., **11:184–185**

    Ambrosian Rite, 1:344

    Apostles' Creed, 1:577

    Euphemia, St. relics, 5:449

    exegetical works, 5:512

    Holy Name, 7:31

    mystery of Divine motherhood, 10:14

    Ravenna (Italy), 11:928

Peter Comestor, 1:407, 5:516, 517, 618, **11:185**

Peter Crassus, 3:49

Peter Crisci of Foligno, Bl., **11:185–186**

Peter Damian, St., 3:600, **11:186–187**

    Ad perennis vitae fontem, 1:96–97

    adopting the common life, 7:661

    Adraldus (Abbot), 12:655

    Alexander II (Pope), 1:253

    Alger of Liége, 1:282

    atonement, 1:837

    Camaldolese, 2:897

    Canons Regular of St. Augustine, 3:67

    Cassian, John, 3:207

    Church property, 3:727

    clerical celibacy/marriage, 3:326

    Councils of Chalon-Sur-Saône, 3:373

    dialectics, 4:726

    the discipline, 4:775

    Dominic Loricatus, St., 4:830

    flagellaion, 5:755

    following of Christ, 5:788

    Fonte Avellana Monastery, 5:792

    Humbert of Silva Candida, 7:200

    hymns, 7:248

    Little Office of the BVM, 8:611

    medieval Latin literature works, 9:450, 452

    reordination, 12:128

    scholasticism, 12:758

    simony, 13:136

Peter des Roches (Bp. of Winchester), **11:187**, 12:262

Peter Geremia, Bl., **11:187**

Peter González, St., **11:188**, 12:545

Peter Grossolano (Abp. of Milan), **11:188**

Peter Guetadartz (Armenian Catholicos), 1:453

Peter Ignatius VII (Patriarch of Syria), 13:708–709

Peter Igneus, Bl. (Card.), **11:188**

Peter John Olivi, 7:932, **11:189–190**, 14:23
  condemnation, 5:897
  Conrad of Offida, 4:136
  Franciscan poverty, 5:896
  mechanism, 9:415
  papal infallibility, 7:451
  Paris School (Franciscan), 5:899
  soul, 13:344–345
  works, 5:900
Peter Lombard (Bp. of Paris), 5:43, 44, 344, **11:190–192**, *191*, 14:18, 24, 329
  Abelard, Peter, 1:19
  Anointing of the Sick, 1:482
  assumptus homo theology, 1:802
  Bernard of Clairvaux, 2:311
  charity, 3:396
  conformity, 4:92–93
  contraception, 4:219, 220
  contrition, 4:225
  dialectics, 4:726
  end justifying the means, 5:212
  Eucharist, 5:424
  exegetical works, 5:514, 516, 517
  exile, 1:698
  grace, 6:396
  hell, 6:727
  Hugh of Newcastle, 7:154
  hypostatic union, 7:265
  indifferent acts, 7:420
  Mariology, 9:170
  medieval Latin literature works, 9:455
  Paris School, 5:899
  priesthood, 11:701
  reason, 13:906
  relics, 12:54
  sacraments, 12:468
  virtue, 14:549
  works, 11:190–191
  See also Book of Sentences (Peter Lombard)
Peter Martyr, St., 5:769, 11:*192*, **192**, 13:26
Peter Moghila (Metropolitan of Kiev), 10:700–701
Peter Mongus (Patriarch of Alexandria), 1:50, 3:595, 4:253
Peter Monoculus, Bl., **11:192**
Peter Nigri, **11:192–193**, 14:48
Peter Nolasco, St., 9:501, **11:193**
Peter of Abano, 1:675
Peter of Ailly (Card.), 5:722, 10:413, **11:193–195**
  antipodes question, 1:530

Columbus, Christopher, 3:865
conciliarism, 4:55
Gallicanism, 6:75
Homines Intelligentiae condemnation, 7:64
Western Schism, 3:51
Peter of Alcántara, St., 3:128, 135, **11:195**
Peter of Alexandria, St., 1:685, **11:195–196**
Peter of Alliaco. *See* Peter of Ailly (Card.)
Peter of Amalfi, 4:175
Peter of Anagni, St., 1:253, **11:196**
Peter of Apamea (Bp.), **11:196**
Peter of Aquila, 3:96
Peter of Auvergne (Bp. of Clermont), **11:196–197**
Peter of Bergamo, **11:197**, 14:48
Peter of Blois, 3:730, 9:456
Peter of Bonagenta, 4:93
Peter of Bruys, **11:197**, 12:549
  See also Petrobrusians
Peter of Candia. *See* Alexander V (Antipope); Alexander V (Pope)
Peter of Castelnau, Bl., 1:231, 714, 5:794, **11:198**, 12:549
Peter of Celle (Bp. of Chartres), 3:441, **11:198**
Peter of Conflans, 5:818
Peter of Corbara. *See* Nicholas V (Antipope)
Peter of Dieburg, **11:198**
Peter of Dives, 2:190
Peter of Fossombrone, 3:762
Peter of Iberia, 10:690
Peter of Ireland, **11:198–199**
Peter of Jerusalem (Patriarch), **11:199**
Peter of Jully, Bl., **11:199**
Peter of La Palu, 4:947, **11:199–200**, 14:46
Peter of Lamballe, 1:110
Peter of Luxemburg, Bl., **11:200**
Peter of Macerata, 1:428, 3:762
Peter of Maricourt, 12:813
Peter of Mas, 3:473
Peter of Mogliano, Bl., **11:201**
Peter of Morrone. *See* Celestine V (Pope)
Peter of Onesti, **11:201**
Peter of Pisa (deacon), **11:201–202**
Peter of Pisa (hermit). *See* Gambacorta, Peter, Bl.
Peter of Poitiers, 1:19, 4:726, 5:500, 516, **11:202–203**
Peter of Ruffia, Bl., **11:203**

Peter of St. Eucharius, 4:541
Peter of Spain. *See* John XXI (Pope)
Peter of Tarentaise (Card.). *See* Innocent V (Pope), Bl.
Peter of Tarentaise, St., 11:203
Peter of Tiferno, Bl., **11:203**
Peter of Todi, 13:26–27
Peter of Treia, Bl., 4:136
Peter of Trevi, St., **11:203**
Peter of Vaux-de-Cernay, **11:204**
Peter of Vienna, **11:204**
Peter of Walcourt, 2:609, 4:377
Peter Orseolo, St., **11:204–205**
Peter Pappacarbone, St., 8:268, **11:205**
Peter Pascual, St., **11:205**
Peter Petroni, Bl., **11:205**
Peter Riga, 9:457, **11:205–206**
Peter Schwarz. *See* Peter Nigri
Peter the Chanter, 1:407, 3:86
Peter the Deacon of Monte Cassino, 1:463, **11:206**
Peter the Deacon of Rome, Bl., **11:206–207**
Peter the Fuller (Bp. of Antioch), 1:49, 523, 525, 2:149, 3:595, 4:356
Peter the Great. *See* Peter I (Emperor of Russia)
Peter the Hermit, 1:275, 359, 2:760, 4:410, **11:207**
Peter the Little. *See* Peter the Hermit
Peter the Painter, **11:207**
Peter the Stammerer (Coptic Patriarch), 1:269
Peter the Venerable, Bl., **11:207–208**
  Abelard, Peter, 1:18
  Alberic of Ostia, 1:219
  Alger of Liége, 1:283
  art, 3:811
  Bernard of Clairvaux, St., 2:308
  Bernard of Cluny, 2:312
  Celestine I (Pope), St., 3:318
  Cluniac reform, 3:813, 814
  medieval Latin literature, 9:454
Peter Thomae, **11:208**, 12:233, 762
Peter To Rot, Bl., **11:208–209**
Peter Trigosus (Pedro Trigoso de Calatayud), 12:764
Peterborough Abbey (England), 1:22, 4:454, **11:209**
Peterborough Church (England), 3:693
Peterfy, Ida (Sister), 12:493
Peterich, E., 5:2
Peters, Gerlac, 4:692, 707–708
Peter's Pence, 1:206, 388, 5:240, **11:209–210**

Petersen, Norman, 11:242

Petershausen Abbey (Constance, Germany), 6:114, **11:210**

Peterson, John Bertram (Bp.), **11:211**

Petiniaud de Jourgnac, Raymond, 12:277

Petit, Jean. *See* Joannes Parvus

Petit, Louis (Abp.), **11:211**

Petit, Stephen, 7:581

Petit-Didier, Matthieu, **11:211–212**

Petite Église, 4:62, 5:835, 853, **11:212**

Petite Messe Solennelle (Rossini), 12:389

Petites méditations pur se disposer à l'humilité et à la pénitence (Malebranche), 9:74

Petition prayer, 11:592, 594

Petitiones pro ecclesiae militantis reformatione (Ullerston), 14:282

Petitot, Émile (Father), 1:207

Peto, William. *See* Peyto, William (Card.)

Petra fidei (Yavorsky), 12:434

Petrarch, Francesco, **11:212–217**, *213*

   Augustinians, 1:888

   Avignon papacy, 1:943

   Bartholomew of Urbino, 2:127

   Boccaccio, Giovanni, 2:449, 450, 12:110

   Bruni, Leonardo, 12:110, 115

   Chaucer, Geoffrey, 3:450, 456

   Christianity and culture theme, 11:214

   Clement VI (Pope), 3:780

   Colonna, Giovanni, 3:855

   Dark Ages concept, 12:110

   humanism, 7:184–185, 190

   Latin Averroism, 1:937

   Middle Ages, origins of term, 9:609, 611

   numismatic study, 10:482

   religious faith, 3:605

   Renaissance humanism, 12:114

   Renaissance philosophy, 12:120

   Richard of Bury, 12:231

   Rienzo, Cola di, 3:828

Petre, Benjamin (Bp. of London), 3:371, 5:250, 11:218

Petre, Edward, Sir, 11:217–218

Petre, Maude Dominica, **11:218**

Petre, William (1602-77), 11:217

Petre, William (1627-84), 11:217

Petre, William, Sir (ca. 1505-72), 11:217, *217*

Petre family, **11:217–218**

Petri, Olaus, 1:399, 2:585, 8:888–889, **11:218–219**, 12:19

Petrilli, Savina, Bl., **11:219**

Petroaldus of Bobbio, 2:446

Petrobrusians, **11:219**

Petronax of Brescia, St., **11:219–220**

Petronilla, St., **11:220**

Petronius (playwright), 12:307–308

Petrucci, Alfonso (Card.), 1:130, 12:220

Petrus ab Apostolis, 3:125

Petrus and Paulus in Rom (Lietzmann), 8:565

Petrus Bertrandus, 3:48

Petrus Bonus, 1:239

Petrus Collivaccinus (Card.), **11:220**

Petrus de Ancherano, 3:51

Petrus de Cruce, 8:684, **11:220–221**

Petrus de Dacia, **11:221**

Petrus de Monte, 3:52

Petrus Hispanus. *See* John XXI (Pope)

Petrus Juliani. *See* John XXI (Pope)

Petrus Leonis, Jr., 11:326

Petrus Leonis, Sr., 11:326

Petrus Maurocenus, 3:52

Petrus Pictor. *See* Peter the Painter

Petrus Quesvel, 3:52

Pettazzoni, Raffaele, 10:121, **11:221**

Petuchowski, J., 14:859

Peucer, Caspar, 4:416

Peukert, Helmut, 5:829

Le Peuple juif et ses Saintes Ecritures dans la Bible chrétienne, 11:478

Peutinger, Conrad, 12:119

Peyto, William (Card.), 5:800, **11:221–222**

Peyton, Patrick Joseph, **11:222**

Pezel, Christoph, 4:416

Pfaender, Maria Clara (Mother), 5:879

Pfäfers Abbey (Ragaz, Switzerland), **11:222–223**

Pfanner, Franz, 9:734, **11:223**

Pfefferkorn, Ignaz, **11:223**

Pfefferkorn, Johannes, 5:306, 7:187, **11:223–224**, 12:12, 181

Pfegginger, Johann, 4:416

Pfeiffer, R. H., 3:565, 567, 568, 5:520

Pflug, Julius von (Bp.), **11:224**

Pforta Abbey (Germany), **11:224**

Phaedrus (Plato), 5:89, 10:96, 12:307

Pham, Trong Ta Joseph, 14:497

Pham Cong Tac, 3:79

Phan, Peter C., 3:288

Die Phantasie als Grundprinzip des Weltprozesses (Frohschammer), 6:15

Phantasm, 1:45–46, 604, 3:823–824, 4:367, 7:507, 8:203, **11:225–226**, 12:2, 910

   See also Dream

Pharisees, **11:226–228**

   apocalyptic style, 1:546

   disciple as term, 4:773

   influence, 8:6

   justification, 8:77–78

   Publican parable, 4:225

   regimen of the Law, 8:5–6

   strength, 8:6–7

Pharos Church (Constantinople), 3:687

Pharus Galliae Antiquae (Labbe), 8:265

Phébus, Gaston, 2:344

Phèdre (Racine), 2:116, 11:888

Phelan, Gerald Bernard, **11:228**, *229*, 12:776

Phelan, Gerard (Mother), **11:228–229**

Phelan, James Duval, 2:869

Phelan, Marie Gerard (Mother), 12:496

Phelan, Richard (Bp. of Pittsburgh), 11:367

Phelen, David Samuel, **11:228**

Phelps v. Reagan, 10:486

Phenomena, **11:229**

   agnosticism, 1:182

   causality, 3:301, 306, 307

   contingency, 4:214

   existence, 5:533

   Kant, 8:125, 10:227, 14:5

   sufficient reason in, 13:593

   thing dissociated from, 14:5

Phenomenalism, 3:352, 4:654, 7:201–202, **11:229–230**, 12:47

Les Phénomènes mystiques, distingués de leurs contrefaçons humaines et diaboliques (Farges), 5:624

Phenomenological transcendence, 14:142

Phenomenology, **11:230–234**, 297

   aesthetics, 1:143

   agnosticism, 1:184

   Aristotelianism, 1:678

   Augustinianism, 1:881

   Brentano, Franz, 2:604–605

   bridging gap between subject and object, 10:510

   Carmelite spirituality, 3:139

   Carnap, Rudolf, 3:147

   categories of being, 3:258

   causality, 3:306

   concept, 4:52

   consciousness, 4:154

   Descartes, 4:682

   existence of God, 6:315

Phenomenology *(continued)*

  existentialism, 12:3

  history of religion, 8:446

  humanism, 7:197

  Husserl, Edmund, founding, 7:229–230

  John Paul II (Pope), 9:91–92

  knowledge theories, 8:219, 220

  new personalism, 8:827

  objectivity in Husserl's, 10:510–511

  ontology in contemporary, 10:607–608

  Peirce, Charles Sanders, 11:58

  philosophy and science, 11:300

  philosophy of religion, 12:70

  Ricoeur, Paul, 12:241–242

  Scheler, Max, 12:731

  self, concept of, 12:884

  soul, 13:347

  soul-body relationship, 13:358

  value of theological mysteries, 10:85

Phenomenology (Hegel), 12:69

Phenomenology of man, 13:789

Phenomenology of Spirit (Hegel), 6:706, 12:346

Phenomenology of the Mind (Schelling), 12:733

Pherecydes of Syros, 4:283

Phidia and Christian basilica workshop ruins (Olympia, Greece), 2:*145*

Phila, Agnes, 13:848

Philadelphia Archdiocese (PA), **11:234–242**

  anti-Catholicism, 7:161

  archives, 1:640

  Catholic parochial education, 12:565–566

  Catholicity in Philadelphia (Kirlin), 8:184

  colonial and Revolutionary era, 11:234–236

  creation, 2:38

  as diocese, 2:38

  Dougherty, Dennis, 4:885–886

  ecclesiastical organization, 8:250

  Egan, Michael, 5:103

  Hogan schism, 5:223

  Hughes, John Joseph, 7:160–161

  Kenrick, F. P., 8:144–145

  Krol, J. J., 8:250

  Nativism violence, 11:84

  Ryan, Patrick John, 12:446–447

  Schulte, Augustine Joseph, 12:789

  shift in Catholic population, 11:241

Philadelphia Baptist Association, 2:79

Philadelphia Catholic Standard, 8:152

Philadelphia Confession, 4:82

Philadelphia Diocesan Archives (PA), 1:640

Philalethes (Severus of Antioch), 13:43

Philaret (Metropolitan of Moscow), 10:701

Phileas (Bp. of Thmuis), St., 1:93, **11:242**

Philemon, Epistle to, **11:242–243**

  canonicity, 3:31

  captivity epistles, 3:93

  edification, 5:85

  epikeia, 5:291

  God's spirit, 13:428

  house churches, 2:146

  Luke's Gospel, 8:855

  slavery, 13:207, 211

Philes, Manuel, 2:805–806

Philetism, 4:196

Philibert II (Duke of Savoy), 6:108

Philibert of Rebais, St., **11:243**

Philip II (King of Spain), 5:245

Philip (Antipope), **11:243–244**

Philip (Roman Emperor), 1:268

Philip, Apostle, St., 2:123, 124, **11:244**

Philip I (King of France), 3:45, 5:353, **11:244**

Philip II (Holy Roman Emperor), 2:217

Philip II (King of France), 2:163

Philip II (King of Spain), 10:11, 11:*247*, **247–249**, *248*

  Allen, William, 1:296

  Aspilcueta, Martin, 1:786

  Carmelites, 3:143, 144, 145

  catechesis, 3:234

  Chile, 3:486

  Church-State relations, 3:639

  eucharistic vigil, 5:435

  Granvelle, Antoine Perrenot de, 6:418

  hegemony, 13:390

  Holy League, 8:424, 425

  Jesuits, 1:72

  marriage to Mary Tudor, 12:9

  Paul IV (Pope), 3:20, 96

  reign described, 13:393

  Spanish Armada, 1:696–697

Philip II Augustus (King of France), 5:845, **11:244–245**

  Adam of Perseigne, 1:109

  Boniface VIII (Pope), 4:518

  Crusades, 3:776

  Honorius II (Pope), 7:84

  John (King of England), 7:914

Philip III (King of France), 7:86

Philip III (King of Spain), 4:112, 544

Philip IV (King of France), 11:*245*, **245–246**

  conciliarism, 4:55

  conflict between Boniface VIII (Pope), 10:839

  excommunication, 5:846

  laicism, 8:282

  religious policy, 5:846

  Rojas, Simon de, St., 12:291

Philip IV (King of Spain), 8:855

Philip IV the Fair (King of France)

  appeals to a future council, 1:599

  Boniface VIII (Pope), 1:410, 2:502, 3:321, 603, 727

  Church-State relations, 2:502, 503, 3:636, 727

  Clement V (Pope), 2:503, 3:779

  Ghibelline-Guelf conflict, 3:854

  Templars, 1:943, 13:804–805

Philip V (King of Spain), 1:220

Philip VI (King of France), 3:780, 4:948

Philip Benizi, St., 1:405, **11:249**

Philip of Ancyra (Bp.), 1:398

Philip of Grève, **11:249**

Philip of Harvengt, 9:454, **11:249–250**

Philip of Heinsberg, 3:843

Philip of Hesse, 8:882, 883, **11:250**, *251*, 12:741

Philip of Macedonia, 3:99

Philip of Opus, 1:812

Philip of Seitz, 3:192

Philip of the Blessed Trinity, **11:250**

Philip the Chancellor, 1:265, 674, 934, 2:184, **11:250–251**

Philip the Deacon, 4:550–551, **11:251–252**, 13:130–131

Philip the Evangelist. *See* Philip the Deacon

Philip the Good (Duke of Burgundy), 1:219

Philipp II (King of France), 4:411

Philipp of Flanders, 4:411

Philippa Mareri, Bl., **11:252**, 12:288

Philippe, Thomas (Father), 1:635

Philippe de la Trinité, 3:137

Philippians, Epistle to the, **11:252–254**

  asceticism, 1:776

  authorship, 7:310

  baptism, 2:60

  beatific vision, 2:171

  bishops, 2:410, 411–412

  Catholic Action, 3:277

  charity, 3:396, 397

Christocentrism, 3:558

Church, 3:578–579, 582–583

deacons, 4:551

Divine indwelling, 7:441

Divine judgment, 8:40

edification, 5:85

faith, 2:59, 6:382

gluttony, 6:251–252

God the Son, 6:295

grace, 6:381, 382–383

heaven, 6:685

hope, 3:356

immortality, 7:354

justification, 8:78, 79

kenoticism, 8:143

Lord's Day, 8:782

missionary journeys, 11:13

peace, 11:50

praetorium, 11:580

sin, 13:147

suffering servant, songs of the, 13:591

works of charity, 3:401, 402

world, 14:840

See also Captivity Epistles

Philippicus (Byzantine Emperor), 2:748, 750, 4:178

Philippine Independent Church, **11:254**, 258

Philippines, **11:255–264**, *258, 259, 260*

Aduarte, Diego Francisco, 1:131

Augustinian Recollects, 1:873

Carmelites, 3:130

catechesis, 3:245

demographic statistics, 11:255

Dougherty, Dennis, 4:886

ecclesiastical organization, 11:256

Hendrick, Thomas, 6:732

map, 11:*257*

missions, 11:255–256

Dominicans, 12:226

Jesuits, 7:784–785

Maryknoll Fathers and Brothers, 9:296

Protestants, 11:258

Philippines, Second Plenary Council of the (1991), 11:263

Philippism, 2:873, 4:60, 416, 8:889, 9:62, **11:264**

Philippson, Ludwig, 7:873

Philips, Ambrose, 5:967

Philips, Gerard, 7:528

Philipus Franchus de Franchis, 3:52

"Philistine ware," 11:266

Philistines, 3:2, 4:493, **11:264–267**

Phillimore, John S., **11:267**

Phillip, Robert, **11:267**

Phillip of the Blessed Trinity, 12:767

Phillips, George, 6:183, **11:267–268**

Philo Judaeus (philosopher of Alexandria), 7:862–863, 10:83, 117, 965, 11:*268*, **268–272**

Alexandria, 1:268, 269, 272

allegory, 1:292, 337

Ambrose, St., 1:337, 339

another God, 8:94

art, 1:743

biblical canon, 3:24

causality, 3:303

Clement of Alexandria, St., 3:799

disciple as term, 4:773

emanationism, 5:180

Essenes, 5:368–369

exegetical works, 5:512

free will, 5:929

infinity, 7:458

Letter of Aristeas, 1:666

Logos, 8:758–760

priesthood, 11:694

Philo of Alexandria. *See* Philo Judaeus (philosopher of Alexandria)

Philo of Byblos, **11:273**

Philo of Larissa, 5:46

Philobiblon (Richard of Bury), 12:231

Philocalia (Macarius of Corinth and Nicodemus), 10:382, 14:431

Philocalia (Origen anthology), 2:136

Philocalian calendar, 4:675–676

Philochorus, 10:93

Philokalia (aesetical writings), 6:458

Philology, 5:518, 7:192, 8:565, 585, **11:273–274**

Philomena (John Peckham), 9:460

Philomena, St., legend of, **11:274**, 12:56

Philoponus, John, 12:805–806, 808–809

Philosophes médiévaux (Van Steenberghen), 14:386

Philosophia Christiana cum antiqua et nova comparata (Sanseverino), 12:671, 772

Philosophia elementaris (González y Díaz), 12:773

Philosophia juxta inconcussa tutissimaque divi Thomae dogmata (Goudin), 6:372

Philosophia Lugdunensis (Valla), 12:773

Philosophia methodo scientiis propria explanata (Stattler), 12:769

Philosophia mundi (William of Conches), 9:453, 14:739

Philosophia naturalis (Fabri), 5:585

Philosophia perennis, 10:244, 471, 11:428

Philosophia prima sive ontologia (Wolff), 10:606

Philosophia rationalis electica (Monteiro), 12:770

Philosophia thomisstica (Babenstuber), 14:51

Philosophia Thomistica Salisburgensis (Babenstuber), 12:765

Philosophiae universae institutiones (anonymous), 12:770

Philosophical and Classical Seminary of Charleston (South Carolina), 5:223

Philosophical Commentary (Bayle), 2:164

Philosophical Fragments (Kierkegaard), 5:712

Philosophical sin, 13:151–152

Philosophical theology, 13:921–923

See also Natural theology

Philosophically oriented history, 6:883

Philosophie, psychologie expérmentale (Bautain), 2:161

La Philosophie au XIIIe siècle (Van Steenberghen), 14:388

La Philosophie chrétienne (Ventura), 14:442

Philosophie de Lyon (Valla), 12:771

La Philosophie de Malebranche (Ollé-Laprune), 10:585

Philosophie der Geschichte (Hegel), 12:111

Philosophie der Mythologie (Schelling), 12:733

Philosophie der Offenbarung (Schelling), 12:733

Philosophie der Vorzeit (Kleutgen), 12:774

La Philosophie du Christianisme (Bautain), 2:161

Philosophie du christianisme (Bautain), 5:712

Philosophie morale (Bautain), 2:161

Philosophie vetus et nova (Du Hamel), 10:606

Philosophie zoöogique (Lamarck), 5:260

Der Philosophische Kritizismus (Riehl), 10:236

Philosophische Untersuchungen über das Wesen der menschlichen Freiheit (Schelling), 12:733

Philosophische Weltanschauung (Scheler), 12:731

Philosophisches Jahrbuch (periodical), 12:774

Philosophumena (Refutation of All Heresies) (St. Hippolytus of Rome), 6:858–859

Philosophy, **11:275–281**

  afterlife, 1:168

  art, 1:745–749, 3:298

  baroque period, 2:116–117

  biology, 2:406–408

  concept/conceptualism, 4:51–53

  consciousness, 4:153–154

  contingency, 4:212–214

  continuum, 4:214–216

  contradiction, 4:223–224

  critical theory, 5:914

  deconstructionism, 4:592–595

  demonstration, 4:653–654

  freedom, 7:172–173

  hierarchical personalism, 8:794

  historicty, 11:282–283

  idealism, 8:269–270

  knowledge, 8:200, 217–219

  limitation, 8:591–592

  logic, 8:747–755

  logical positivism, 8:755–758

  metaphysics, 9:549–550

  moral dogmatism, 8:265

  motion in modern, 10:19–20

  natural law, 10:183–184, 193

  ontologism, 10:604–605

  orthodoxy and rationalism, 8:517

  philosophical systems, 11:284–285

  religion, 2:440–441

  role of logical positivists, 8:757

  skepticism, 13:200–205

  spirit, 8:387, 514, 13:421

  superstitious fear, 8:848–849

  transcendental method, 14:145

  uncertainty principle, 14:289

  understanding, 14:292

  unwarranted assumptions, 8:400

  See also Eclecticism; Educational philosophy; Epistemology; Ethics; Greek philosophy; Nature, in philosophy; Philosophy of art; *specific philosophers, movements, schools, and theories*

Philosophy, ancient, 8:21, 93–94

Philosophy, history of, 11:275–277, **281–298**

  ancient philosophy, 11:286–289

  contemporary, 13:347–348

  Copleston, Frederick, 4:252

  Descartes, 4:682

  dialectics, 4:725

  Dilthey, Wilhelm, 4:746

  divisions, 11:285–286

  Husserl, Edmund, 7:229

  Leibniz, G. W., 8:456–458

  life philosophies, 8:578–580

  medieval, 11:289–292

  metahistory, 11:286

  modern, 11:292–294

  modernization, 8:797

  Neo-Kantian Movement, 10:235–238

  neoplatonism, 10:240–242

  19th century overview, 11:294–295

  notion of order, 10:629–631

  philosophical problems, 11:283

  philosophical systems, 11:284–285

  Siger of Brabant, 13:112–113

  20th century overview, 11:295–298

Philosophy and Religion (Schelling), 12:69

Philosophy and science, **11:298–301**

  element, 5:147

  Leibniz, G. W., 8:456–458

  mechanism, 4:681

  metaphysics of light, 8:583–584

  spontaneous generation, 13:459–460

Philosophy and the Mirror of Nature (Rorty), 10:205

"Philosophy Drawn from the Oracles" (Porphyry), 11:520–521

Philosophy of art, **1:745–749**, 3:298, 4:347–349, 372–374, 8:537

Philosophy of Being, The (De Raeymaeker), 4:676

Philosophy of St. Bonaventure (Gilson), 12:776

Philosophy of science, 2:570–571, 4:618

Philosophy of Structures (Torroja), 3:677

The Philosophy of Symbolic Forms (Cassirer), 3:209–210

Philosophy of the spirit, 11:296

Philostorguis (Church historian), 1:266, 527, 661, 2:797, **11:307**

Philostratus II, 1:562

Philotheus Coccinus (Patriarch of Constantinople), 2:826–827, 10:766, **11:307–308**

Philoxenus of Mabbugh (Bp.), **11:308–309**

  baptism of Jesus, 2:72–73

  creedal statements, 4:354

  Monophysitism, 1:386, 3:595

  Severus of Antioch, 13:43

  studies, 8:429

Philpot, Clement, Ven., 5:227

Phlorios and Platizphlora, 2:806

Phocas (Byzantine Emperor), 2:499, 749, 750, 783

Phoenician art, 3:2–3

Phoenicians, **3:1–3**, 467, **11:309**

  See also Canaan and Canaanites

Phoenix (mythical bird), **11:309**

The Phoenix and the Turtle (Gilby), 6:217

Phon, Mary, 13:848

Photian Schism, 4:186–187, 194–195, 370, 5:23–24, 719

Photian Synod, condemnation of, 4:194, 195

Photinus (Bp. of Sirmium), 1:387, 662, 3:593

Photius (Patriarch of Constantinople), 2:773, 4:186–187, 194–195, 300, 10:360, **11:309–313**, *310*

  Adrian II (Pope), 1:124, 2:754–755

  Adrian III (Pope), 1:125

  Adrianus, 1:130

  Anastasius the Librarian, 1:389, 390

  Anthony II (Patriarch), 1:504

  Aristotelianism, 1:671

  Balkan mission, 2:755, 775

  Bulgaria, 2:679, 823

  Canon Law, 3:46

  Christianity in Russia, 12:419

  deposed as Patriarch, 5:814

  Eastern Schism, 5:23

  Ignatius of Constantinople, 7:309–310

  John VIII (Pope), 7:923

  John IX (Pope), 7:924

  Metrophanes of Smyrna, 9:570

  Nicaean period theology, 2:761, 762

  Nicholas I (Pope), St., 7:310

  philosophy, 2:808

  Protoevangelium Jacobi, 1:469

  Roman primacy, 2:754–755, 822–823, 3:599

  Stylianos of Neocaesarea, 13:557

  University of the Imperial Palace of Constantinople, 2:822

Photius Patriarch von Constantinopel, sein Leben, seine Schriften und gas griechische Schisma (Hergenröther), 6:779

Phrygians. *See* Montanism

Phung van Le, Emmanuel, 14:496

Phutta, Agatha, 13:848

Phylacteries, 8:11, **11:313–314**, *314*

Physica speculatio (Vera Cruz), 14:444

Physical laws, philosophical aspects of, 3:353, **11:314–316**

Physical premonition, 11:658

Physical sciences, 12:799–806, 13:581

Physician-assisted suicide, 5:458, 459

Physics, 1:746, 2:299, 4:212–213, 9:667, 12:816, 13:535

Physics (Aristotle), 1:73, 3:298, 375, 10:425, 11:303, 304, 12:768

The Physics of Immorality (Tipler), 5:351

Physiognomische Fragmente zur Beförderung der Menschenkenntnis und Menshliebe (Lavater), 8:386

Physiologia stoicorum (Lipsius), 12:125

Physiologus (animal book), 2:342, 343, **11:316–317**

Physiology in the Renaissance, 12:817

Physis. *See* Hypostasis

Pia Desideria (Spener), 11:330, 13:414

Piae Cantiones (Swedish carols), 3:151

Piaget, Jean, 4:238, 5:102, **11:317–319**

Piamarta, Giovanni Battista, Bl., **11:319**

Piano del Carpini, Giovanni dal, 3:492

Piano Order, 4:596

Piaristen Church (Vienna), 3:706

Piarists, 3:804, 7:104, 216, 1043, **11:319–320**, 12:793

Piazza di San Pietro fresco (Vatican Library), 14:*395*

Pibush, John, Bl., 5:233, **11:320**

Picansel, Léorat, Basilians and, 2:141

Picard, François, 1:802

Picard, Jean, 12:590

Picards, **11:320**

Picasso, Pablo, 1:803

Piccirillo, M., 2:380

Piccolomini, Aeneas Silvii, 3:52

Piccolomini, Aeneas Sylvinus. *See* Pius II (Pope)

Piccolomini, Alessandro (Bp.), **11:321**

Piccolomini, Ambrogio, Bl., 11:321

Piccolomini, Celio (Card.), 11:321

Piccolomini, Francesco (Card.), 1:676, 11:321

Piccolomini, Francesco Todeschini. *See* Pius III (Pope)

Piccolomini, Octavio, 11:321

Piccolomini family, 11:*321*, **321**, 13:108

Pichler, Johann and Wilhelm, **11:322**

Pichler, Vitus, **11:322**

Pickering, Thomas, Bl., 5:236, **11:322–323**

Pico Della Mirandola, Gianfrancesco, II, 11:324

Pico Della Mirandola, Giovanni, 11:292, 323–324, *323*

  Bovillus, Carolus, 2:572

  Colet, John, 3:832

  eclecticism, 5:47

  Johann Reuchlin, 12:181

Platonism, 5:710, 11:416

Renaissance cultural development, 12:117

Renaissance philosophy, 7:186–187, 12:121–122

Savonarola, Girolamo, 12:714

Pico Della Mirandola, Poliziano, 5:768

Pico Della Mirandola family, **11:323–324**

Picot de Clorivière, Pierre-Joseph, 7:788

Picpus Sisters, 4:293

Picts, 2:621

Picturesque, 3:678

Pidal y Chico de Guzmán, María Maravillas de Jesús, Bl., **11:324**

Pidou, Louis, 6:50

Pie, Louise François Désiré (Card.), 5:855, **11:324–325**

Pieck, Nicholas, 6:364

Piedra Abbey (Spain), **11:325**

Pieni l'animo (encyclical, Pius X), 9:755, 11:389

Pieper, J., 8:460

Pierce, Charles, 5:829

Pierce, Cyril, 3:192

Pierce, Franklin, 1:582

Pierce, Walter M., 10:648–649

Pierce v. Society of Sisters (1925), 3:660

Pierius, St., 1:272, **11:325–326**

Pierleoni, Anacletus, II (Card.), 11:326

Pierleoni, Jordan, 8:846

Pierleoni, Peter. *See* Anacletus II (Antipope)

Pierleoni family, 1:370, 3:777, **11:326**

Piero della Francesca, 12:*147*

Pierotti, Rafaele, 1:438

Pierre d'Ailly. *See* Peter of Ailly (Card.)

Pierre de la Châtre (Abp. of Bourges), 3:318

Pierre de la Résurrection, 3:137

Pierre Saintive (Veuillot), 14:466

Pierres vivantes (Conference of Bishops), 5:861

Pierron, Jean, 14:453

Piers Plowman (Langland), 1:292, 5:243, **11:326**

Pierson, Walter, Bl., 5:226, 7:1019

Pierz, Francis Xavier, 4:364, 8:504, **11:329**, 12:542, 551

Pietà (iconographic theme), 11:*329*, **329–330**

Pietà (Michelangelo), 1:261

Pietá (Titian), 7:*799*

Pietà hospital and orphanage (Evora, Portugal), 3:416

La Piété à travers les âges (Saudreau), 12:708

La Piété de l'Église (Beaudin), 2:183, 8:673

Pietism, **11:330–332**

  Amana Society, 1:330

  Arnold, Gottfried, 1:718

  biblical theology, 2:383

  Carpzov, Johann Benedikt, II, 3:174

  Carpzov, Johann Gottlob, 3:174

  Church of the Brethren, 3:721

  doctrine, 4:805

  Finland, 5:733

  founding, 13:414

  Francke's theories of education, 5:910

  Frelinghuysen, 5:969

  German immigration to U.S., 8:885

  Guilds of Piety, 13:414

  humanism, 7:191

  justification, 8:87

  Lutheranism, 7:10, 8:891

  Protestant theology in, 13:911

  Wolff School, 5:262

Pietrantoni, Agostina Livia, St., **11:332**, *333*

Pietrasancta, Anthony, 1:346

Pietro, Sano de, 4:396

Pietro Vannucci. *See* Perugino (Umbrian painter)

Piety, 2:377, 7:32, 8:296–297, 11:941

Piety, familial, **11:332–335**

Piety, gift of, **11:336**

Piffl, Friedrich Gustav (Card.), 1:915, **11:336**

Pigas, Meletius, 6:456

Pigem Serra, Salvador, 2:92

Pigge, Albert, 3:846, **11:336–337**

Pighius. *See* Pigge, Albert

Pighius, Albert. *See* Pigge, Albert

Pignatelli, Antonio (Card.). *See* Innocent XII (Pope)

Pignatelli, Bernardo. *See* Eugene III (Pope), Bl.

Pignatelli, Joseph Mary, St., 3:792, 7:787–788, **11:337–338**

Pigott, F. W., 8:540

Pii Operarii (missionary congregation), 3:97

Pii Papae VI responsio super nuntiaturis apostolicis (anonymous), 5:200

Pike, N., 5:384

Pike, William, Bl., 5:231, **11:338–339**

Pilar, Francisco del, 2:465

Pilarczyk, Daniel E. (Abp. of Cincinnati), 3:737–738

Pilate, Pontius, 2:85–86, **11:339**
  See also Trial of Jesus
*Pilate Liberating Barabbas and
  Crucifying Christ* (Predis), *2:85*
Pilato, Leonzio, 2:449
Pilcher, Thomas, Bl., 5:229, **11:339**
Pilgram, Friedrich, 3:589
Pilgrim (Abp. of Cologne), 3:843
Pilgrim guide books, 11:353
Pilgrim Holiness Church, 7:7, **11:341**
Pilgrim of Bordeaux, 4:383
Pilgrim of Passau (Bp.), 1:909, **11:341**
Pilgrimage of Grace (England), 1:786,
  4:377, 5:244, 8:445, **11:341–342**,
  12:8–9
Pilgrimage of the Abbot Daniel (Daniel
  Palomnik), 4:513
Pilgrimages, 9:*414*, **11:342–351**
  Aachen, 1:2
  Altötting Monastery, 1:322–323
  Argentina, 1:654–655
  Assisi, 1:790
  Austria, 1:912–913
  in the Bible, 11:342–343
  Bolivia, 2:466
  Bury-St.-Edmunds Abbey, 2:713
  Carolingian legends, 1:763
  Chartres, 3:441–442
  Chaucer, Geoffrey, 3:455
  chronology, 11:347–348
  church architecture, 3:690, 704
  Croagh Patrick, 4:369
  Częstochowa, 4:490
  early Christian, 3:594, 596
    Egypt and Rome, 7:676–678,
     11:345
    Holy Land, 7:676, 11:343–345
    local pilgrimages, 11:345–346
  Egeria's *Intinerarium Egeriae*,
    5:104–106
  Fortunatus, 5:823
  goals, 11:346
  guidebooks for pilgrims, 12:53
  Holy Land, 8:565, 13:134
  indulgences, 7:437
  Louis VII of France, 8:799
  Lourdes Shrine, 8:819–820
  to Mecca, 7:609–610, 8:170
  motives, 11:348
  19th-20th centuries, 3:623
  origins of shrines, 11:346–347
  penance, 11:348
  pilgrim ritual, 11:349–350
  pilgrim roads, 11:348–349
  pilgrims' return home, 11:350–351

Polish popular piety, 11:512
  reaction to pilgrims, 11:351
  relics, 12:54
  religious homelessness, 5:53, 56
  routes, precrusade, 13:125
  St. Patrick's Purgatory, 11:829–830
  St. Willibrord's tomb (Echternach
    Abbey), 5:42
  Silos Abbey, 13:120
  statistics, 11:349
  works of charity, 3:412
  See also Santiago de Compostela;
    World Youth Days
Pilgrimages, Roman, 11:345, **351–354**
  Blessed Sacrament, 13:417
  hostels within Vatican for,
    14:393–394
  Labre, B. J., 8:267–268
  Lawrence, St., 8:404
  Ludanus, St., 8:851
  Ludolf of Corvey, 8:852
  Lull of Mainz, 8:867
  Sixtus IV (Pope), 13:197
Pilgrims, 8:141–142, 193, 198, 9:304
  See also Pilgrimages; Pilgrimages,
    Roman
The Pilgrim's Progress (Bunyan), 1:292,
  2:693
The Pilgrim's Regress (Lewis), 8:527
Pillai, Devasagayam, 7:406
Pillan, James, 7:579
*The Pillar and Foundation of Truth: An
  Essay on Orthodox Theodicy in
  Twelve Chapters* (Florenskii), 5:772
Pilot (newspaper), 10:544
Piloti, Eugenio, 3:498
Pima people, 8:180
Pimen I (Bulgarian Patriarch), 2:684
Pimenta, Silvério Gomes (Abp.), **11:355**
Pimería Alta, 8:180
Pin, L. Ellies do, 2:550
Piña Piazuelo, Acisclo, Bl., 7:124
Pinard de la Boullaye, Henri,
  11:355–356
Pinazo, Francis, 4:503
Pinckaers, Servais, 3:221
Pinckney, Charles, 3:653
Pineda, Juan de, **11:356**
Pinel, Philippe, 7:132
Pinell, Dom Jordi, 10:43, 44
The Pines of Rome (Respighi), 12:139
Pinet, François, 3:475
*Pinette, Capitol Square Review and
  Advisory Board v.* (1995), 3:664
Pingusson, G., 3:713

Pinilla, Vicente, 10:29
Pinochet, Augusto, 3:487
Pinot, Noël, Bl., 1:432, **11:356**
Pinsard, P., 3:713
Pinten, Joseph (Bp. of Superior, WI),
  14:782
Pinter, Harold, 1:48, 5:544
Pinto, Manuel Vieira (Bp. of Manpula,
  Mozambique), 11:539
Pinturiccio. *See* Betto di Biago
Piny, Alexander, **11:356**, 12:767
Pinytos (Bp. of Cnossos), 3:548
Pinzoni, Faustino, 6:633
Pio IX (Balmes), 2:33
Piombo, Sebastiano del, 3:780
Piona Abbey (Italy), **11:356–357**, *357*
Pioneer Capuchin Letters (Roemer),
  12:283
Pioneer Catholic Journalism in the U.S.
  (Folk), 5:787
Pionius of Smyrna, 1:93, 785
Piosistratus, Sextus Amaricius, 9:449
Pious Congregation of St. Joseph
  (Turin), 10:65
Pious Congregation of St. Xavier for
  Foreign Missions, 4:94
Pious Disciples of the Divine Master,
  6:202, **11:357**
Pious fund, **11:357–358**
  Alemany, Joseph Sadoc, 1:249
  Amat, Thaddeus, 1:332
  California, 2:862, 867, 12:251, 623,
    645
  Mexican independence period, 8:789
Pious Society of the Daughters of St.
  Paul (DSP), **12:570**
Pious Union of Sisters, 1:186
Pious Union of the Sisters of Charity,
  2:88
Pious Workers. *See Pii Operarii*
  (missionary congregation)
Pious Works of Saint Zita (*Opera Pia
  Santa Zita*) (Italy), 5:581
Piper, John, 4:331
Piracy, 3:414, 419
Piranesi, Giovanni, 3:793
Pirhing, Ehrenreich, **11:358**
Pirke Avoth, **11:358–359**
Pirkheimer, Charitas, **11:359**
Pirkheimer, Willibald, **11:359**, 12:119
Pirmin, St., 3:163, **11:359–360**, 12:32
Pirminius of Reichenau, 1:577
Pirrotti, Pompilius, St., **11:360**
Pisa, Councils of (1409-1512), 5:694,
  8:354–355, **11:360–361**
  Alexander V (Antipope), 1:258

Canon Law, 3:51

Carmelites, 3:142

Chillenden, Thomas, 3:489

Crusades, 4:413–414

John XXIII (Antipope), 3:604

John XXIII (Pope), Bl., 4:168

president, 13:132

Wenceslaus IV, 7:228

Western Schism end, 14:693

See also Lateran Councils; Western Schism (1378-1417)

Pisa, Pseudo-Council of, 1:298

Pisa Baptistery (Italy), 2:75

Pisani, Mary Adeodata, Bl., **11:361**

Pisano, Andrea, 2:374, 12:488

Pisano, Giovanni, 2:374, 4:396

Pisano, Niccolò, 2:374, 4:396, 13:*106*, 109

Pise, Charles Constantine, **11:361–362**, *362*

Pisidia, Laodicea in, 8:328

Pissini, Andreas, 12:771

Pistis Sophia, 6:257

Pistoia (Italy), **11:362**

Pistoia, G. da, 3:310

Pistoia, Synods of, **11:362–365**

(1786), 10:844

(1794), 14:159

Pistoia, Synods of (1794)

attrition, 1:843

condemned by Pius VI, 12:225

Jansenism and, 1:846–847

limbo, 8:590

liturgical movement, 8:671

liturgical reform, 8:663

Pius VI (Pope) and, 11:376–377

religious liberalism, 8:541

Pitarch Gurrea, Domingo, 7:123

Pitaval, John Baptist (Abp.), 12:676

Pithou, Pierre, 1:599, 3:639, 6:76, **11:365**

Pithouensis, 3:40

Pitra, Jean Baptiste (Card.), **11:365–366**

Pitt, William (1st earl of Chatham), 5:182

Pittenger, Meek v. (1975), 3:667–668

Pitts, John, **11:366**

Pittsburgh Catholic (periodical), 8:152

Pittsburgh Diocese (PA), **11:366–368**

Pittsburgh Platform, 8:10

Pius, Antonius, 3:212

Pius I (Pope), St., 11:*368*, 368, 12:351

Pius II (Pope), 3:*62*, 5:669, **11:368–370**

abbreviators, 1:13

Alexander VI (Pope), 1:259

Ammanati de' Piccolomini, Jacopo, 1:361

appeals from pope to council, forbiddin gof, 6:608

appeals to a future council, 1:599

conciliarism, 4:56

Crusade, 11:369–370

Louis XI, 6:75

Renaissance, 3:606, 12:118

works of charity, 3:414

Pius III (Pope), **11:370–371**

Pius IV (Pope), **11:371–373**, *372*

Anglican orders problem, 1:437

Apostolic Penitentiary, 11:76

Basilians, 2:143

Canisius, St. Peter, 3:17

capitulations, 3:91

Carafa family, 3:97

censorship, 3:336

clerical celibacy/marriage, 3:327

Commendone, Giovanni Francesco, 4:11

Council of Trent, 3:610, 14:171–174

dueling, 4:929

La Valette recognized, 8:385

papacy development under, 10:842

papal elections, 11:499

Pontificia Facoltà Teological "San Bonaventura," 11:490

reform, 4:311, 482

Tridentine Index, 7:390

Tridentine Profession of faith, 11:740

Pius V (Pope), St., 11:*373*, **373–375**

Acquaviva, Giulio, 1:70

Ambrosian Rite, 1:344

Ambrosians, 1:346

Anglican orders problem, 1:437

Anne and Joachim, SS., 1:469

Apostolic Penitentiary, 11:75, 76

Armenia, 1:702

Baius, 5:499–500

Baius, condemnation of works of, 2:19

beatific vision, 2:170

Canisius, St. Peter, 3:17, 18

Carranza, Bartolomé, 3:176

catechism, 3:234, 239

Catechismus Romanus, 14:50

Cheffontaines, Christophe de, 3:463

Colonna family, 3:856

comma pianum controversy, 4:4

Commendone, Giovanni Francesco, 4:11

Communion outside the liturgy, 4:37

Confraternity of Christian Doctrine, 3:234

Congregation for the Propagation of the Faith, 11:749

Counter Reformation, 3:611, 4:310, 311–312

cross on altar, 4:388

Easter Vigil, 5:15

Elizabeth I, 3:609, 611, 5:163, 224–225, 227, 670–671, 12:10–11

Humiliati, 7:205

indulgences, 7:439

Knights of Malta, 8:385

Lepanto, Battle of, 8:504, 506

litanies controlled, 8:603

Missal, 8:437

nepotism, 10:247

papacy development under, 10:842

providence of God, 11:784

Roman Breviary, 2:610

Roman Missal, 1:120, 243, 336, 501, 3:745

Roman Pontifical, 11:474

sin, 13:155

Society of the Servants for the Poor, 5:191

Pius V Association, 3:289

Pius VI (Pope), 11:*375*, **375–377**

Alma prophecy, 1:297

Brothers of the Christian Schools, 2:632

Caprara, Giovanni Battista, 3:92

Carroll, John, 3:179

Carthusians, 3:195

Catholicism and science, 5:951

Congress of Ems, 5:200

Consalvi, Ercole, 4:137

death of, 3:615, 617, 11:377

Focolare Movement, support for, 5:785

French captivity, 4:137

French Revolution, 3:204, 640, 753, 5:972

Gallicanism, 6:78, 11:377

Italo-Albanian Church, 7:651

Jansenism, 1:846–847

Jesuits, 3:265, 12:222

Joseph II, 7:1042

Josephinism, 1:914, 3:615

limbo, 8:590–591

liturgical languages, 8:667

papacy development, 10:845

Pignatelli, St. Joseph Mary, 11:338

Pistoia Synod condemned, 8:663

Redemptorists, 11:993

Pius VI (Pope) *(continued)*
    Synod of Pistoia, 12:225
    Treaty of Tolentino, 5:976
Pius VII (Pope), 11:*378*, **378–382**, 14:*391*
    abbesses, 1:8
    abbreviators, 1:13
    Bernetti, Tommaso, 2:323
    as bishop of Tivoli and of Imola, 11:378–379
    Bobbio Abbey, 2:446
    caesaropapism, 3:92
    Caprara, Giovanni Battista, 3:92
    captivity, 11:380
    Carbonari, 3:100
    Caribbean, 3:115
    Carroll, John, 3:180
    Casoni, Filippo, 3:204
    Concordat of 1801, 4:61–63, 5:976, 10:147–148, 846
    Concordat of Fontainebleau, 4:63–64
    Consalvi, Ercole, 4:138–139
    Daughters of the Heart of Mary, 6:682
    Émery, Jacques André, 5:190
    French bishops, 2:232
    French hierarchy, 11:212
    Holy Alliance, 1:252, 7:17
    Immaculate Heart of Mary feast, 7:335
    Jesuit restoration, 7:787
    Jesuits, 3:265, 618
    Lanteri's support, 8:327
    Marist Fathers, 3:835
    Missionaries of the Precious Blood, 11:642
    Napoleon I, 3:237, 618, 640–641, 754, 10:148–149, 13:298, 495–497
    papacy, 10:845–846
    papal primacy, 10:847
    Passionists, 10:932
    St. Mary's Seminary (Baltimore), 2:40
    secret societies, 12:857
Pius VIII (Pope), 2:44, 3:845, 11:382, **382–384**, 384
Pius IX (Pope), Bl., **11:384–387**, *385*
    Alexian Brothers, 1:275
    Antonelli, Giacomo, 1:532, 533
    apologetics and prophecy, 11:762
    apostolic delegation in the United States, 1:582–583
    appeals to a future council, 1:599
    Armenia, 1:706
    Baltimore Council (1849), 2:45

Baltimore Council (1866), 2:46
Basilians, 2:141
Brazil, 2:596
Caecilian Movement, 2:842
Carbonari, 3:101
Castel Gandolfo villa, 3:212
Catholic organizations, 1:351
Catholicism and science, 5:855, 968, 10:261, 13:651–652
chant books, 3:380
Church-State relations, 3:642
Claretians, 3:764
Colosseum, 3:860
Communism, 3:620
deism, 11:387
existence of God, 6:287
Feast of Christ the King, 11:857
freedom of conscience, 4:149
Frohschammer, Jakob, 6:778
Gillow y Zavalza, Eulogio Gregorio, 6:225–226
Holy Year, 7:57
Huelgas de Burgos Abbey, 7:148
Hughes, John Joseph, 7:161
Immaculate Conception, 1:310, 799, 7:331, 334–335
indifferentism, 7:421
Irish cause, 8:842
Italian unification, 3:314, 7:672
Kulturkampf, 8:254
Law of Guarantees, 6:549
liberalism, 3:641, 11:384–385
Lyonese Rite, 8:905
man's reason, 5:712
Melkite Catholic Church, 1:526
Mérode, Frédéric Ghislain de, 9:516
monogenism, 10:667
Mosquera's activities, 10:11
natural family planning, 10:178
New Orleans as Province, 8:811
New York visit (1850), 10:322–323
non expedit policy accepted, 10:415
North American College, 10:433
Order of the Holy Spirit, 7:52
papacy development, 10:848–849
papal primacy, 3:621
papal state reform, 13:496–497
Poor Clares, establishment in U.S., 2:287
Precious Blood Sisters, 11:644
rationalism, 11:922
Redemptorists, 11:994
religious liberalism, 8:542
Republic of 1849, 12:360

restoration of society, 11:387, 852
Roman Question, 12:322, 322–323
Roman-Orthodox reunion, 6:459
Rossi, Pellegrino, 12:388
Scalabrini, Giovanni Battista, Bl., 12:717–718
social justice issues, 3:620
sovereignty, 13:371
on Thomas Aquinas, St., 14:23
Tridentine Profession of faith, 11:740
ultramontanism, 14:285
U.S.-Holy See relations, 3:659
Ursulines, 3:752
Vatican Council I, 1:147, 14:404
Victor Emannuel II, 14:481–482
See also Syllabus of Errors (Pius IX)
Pius X (Pope), St., **11:387–392**, *388*
    abbreviators, 1:13
    Action Française, 1:82
    African Missions Society, 1:162
    agnosticism, 6:313
    American liberalism, 11:391
    anticlericalism in France, 11:390
    apostolic administrators, 1:116
    Apostolic Penitentiary, 11:76
    Basilians, 2:141
    Bendictine Oblates, 6:41
    Benedict XV (Pope), 2:249
    Bethlehem Fathers, 2:494
    bishops founding institutions, 12:100
    Borromeo, St. Charles, 11:391
    Briggs, Charles Augustus, 2:616
    Canon Law, 3:54, 55
    canonization, 3:63
    cardinalate, 3:105–106
    Carmelite Rite, 3:126
    catechesis, 3:234, 244
    catechism, 4:94, 11:390, 391
    Catholic Action, 3:276
    censorship, 3:336
    chant books, 3:380
    Church internal affairs, 11:390
    Church-State relations, 3:642, 4:63
    condemned propositions, 8:311–312
    Conforti, Guido Maria, 4:94
    Confraternity of Christian Doctrine, 4:94
    Congregation for the Propagation of the Faith, 11:751
    congregational singing, 4:118, 119
    Cormier, Hyacinthe-Marie, 4:269
    Crawley-Boevey, Mateo, 4:335
    "cultuelles," 8:283
    devotion to the Eucharist, 11:390

dogma, 9:755

estrangement from God, 11:388–389

eucharistic epiclesis, 5:280

eucharistic fast, 5:437

existence of God, 6:287

faith and morals in political affairs, 11:389

ferial Masses, 8:470

First Communion, 11:390

Franciscan Sisters, 5:880

Holy Name feast, 7:32

importance of religious instruction, 11:390

improvement of life of Latin American natives, 11:391

insubordination of clergy, 9:755

inter-confessional groups, 11:389

Italian popular action groups, 11:389

laity, 3:716

laity participation, 8:663

Lega democratica nazionale, 10:70

Little Sisters of the Poor, 8:47

liturgical languages, 8:667

liturgical movement, 3:710

liturgical music, 8:621, 704, 705

liturgy as indispensable, 8:673

marriage, juridical form, 10:218, 218–219

Merry del Val, Rafael, 9:520

missions, 1:116, 10:543, 11:390, 481, 751

modern music, 8:695–696

Modernism, 5:968, 9:755–757, 10:849, 912–913, 12:775, 14:139

music, 2:842, 8:699, 700–701

National Shrine of the Immaculate Conception, 10:167–168

Office of the Dead, 10:563

ordination, 5:627

papal elections, 1:57, 11:499

Pontifical Bible Commission, 11:477, 485

Pontifical Council for the Laity, 11:481

Pontificia Ateneo di S. Anselmo, 11:488

Portugal's separation of Church and State, 11:391

pre-papal career, 11:388

Raillemont policy renounced, 5:856

religious liberalism, 8:542

rules, 4:757

secular elections and voting, 10:415

Sillonists, 12:667

social role of the Church, 11:389

spiritual motherhood of Mary, Blessed Virgin, 9:264–265

Tridentine Profession of faith, 11:740

unicity thesis, 12:231

upholding principles of Aquinas, 11:390

Vatican construction, 14:397

workers' circles dissolved, 5:855

working class, 3:620

World War I, 11:391

Pius X Basilica (Lourdes, France), 3:713

Pius X School of Liturgical Music (Purchase, NY), 8:674–675, **11:400–401**

Pius XI (Pope), 11:*392*, **392–396**

abortion, 1:28, 11:515

Action Française, 1:82

American Board of Catholic Missions, 1:350

anti-Semitism, 11:395

Anton Günther's teaching on Absolute, 14:204

Apostolic Penitentiary, 11:76

Assumption of Mary, 6:685, 11:399

atheism, 1:823

Basilians, 2:141, 143, 144

Bea, Augustin, 2:167

beatifications and canonizations, 11:393

Benedictines, 2:273

Billot, Louis, 2:395

birth control, 13:258

Brothers of the Christian Schools, 2:634

canonization, 3:63

Cardijn, Joseph, 3:103

Carthusians, 3:194

catechesis, 3:234, 244

Catholic Action, 3:276–277, 11:392

Catholic Near East Welfare Association, 3:286

Chesterton, Gilbert Keith, 3:470

Chile, 3:486

Chinese rites controversy, 3:516

Christian activity, 11:393

Christian education, 10:650, 11:392

Christian exegesis and application to Scripture, 6:29, 133, 793

Christian social order and social reform, 11:393

Church-State relations, 3:642

Code of Canons of the Eastern Churches, 3:817, 818

common good, 4:19

communism and atheism, 4:790

concordats, 11:394

Confirmation, Sacrament of, 4:88

Confraternity of Christian Doctrine, 4:94

continence, 11:515

contraception, 4:222

Divine definitions, 10:454

Eastern Catholic churches, 11:393

East-West reunion, Benedictine mediation, 2:183

ecclesiastical faculties, 10:434

economic democracy, 4:643

Ecumenical Movement, 5:72, 73, 9:903

ecumenism, 3:472

effective liturgy, 8:664

Emiliani, Jerome, St., 5:191

eucharistic congresses, 5:433

existence of God, 6:287

family wage, 14:824

Feast of Christ the King, 3:527

feminism, 14:825

France, 11:395

fundamental articles, 6:29

Gabriel as patron of telecommunications workers, 6:40

Gasparri, Pietro, 6:103

grace and nature, 6:412

Holy Year, 7:57

Holy Year (1925), 12:206

human rights, 5:95, 206, 10:850, 14:251, 453

Ignatian exercises, 13:433

indigenous clergy, 9:681

Italo-Albanian Church eparchies, 7:652

Jubilee Years, 11:393

Lateran Pacts, 8:356, 357

Malines conversations, 9:78

marriage, 3:214, 11:392–393

missions, 3:428, 625

Muslims, 2:688

natural law doctrine, 10:193

Nazis, 6:186

Orthodox Churches, 5:72–73

Paul VI (Pope), 11:27–28

pentateuchal studies, 11:95

persecution in Mexico, 11:395

Polish ecclesiastical order, 11:448

Pontifical Bible Institute, 11:485

Pontifical Oriental Institute, 11:485

Pontificio Istituto di Archeologia Cristiana, 11:490

population, 11:512, 512–513

prepapal career, 11:396–397

radio, TV, and films, 11:400

Pius XI (Pope) *(continued)*
  Raillement policy, 5:856
  Sacred Heart, 3:623
  Sacred Heart, devotion to, 12:491, 492, 493
  School Sisters of Notre Dame, 6:166
  seminary studies, 12:775
  sisters as doctors, 4:659
  social issues, 1:915, 3:420
  social justice, 13:243
  social order and poverty, 11:566, 847–848
  Society for the Propagation of the Faith, 11:753
  solidarity and collaboration, 13:267–268
  Spanish separation of Church and State, 11:395
  spiritual exercises, 13:433
  sterilization, 11:515
  study of historical method, 6:879
  subsidiarity, 13:567, 569
  supernaturality, 6:394
  Syro-Malabar Catholic Church, 7:400
  Thérèse de Lisieux, St., 3:128
  totalitarianism, 11:393
  Ugon, Édouard, 7:164
  Ultramonianism, 10:847
  Vatican Library expansion, 14:421–422
  world mission, 11:393
Pius XII (Pope), 1:*96*, **11:396–400**, *397*
  abortion, 1:28
  Action Française, 1:82
  African mission, 9:681
  angels, 1:422
  Apostleship of the Sea, 1:578
  art in liturgy, 8:621
  Assumption of Mary, 1:797, 799, 800, 10:61–62
  atheism, 1:823
  Bible studies, 4:790–792, 814
  biblical exegesis, 5:523
  biblical interpretation, 10:303, 12:637
  biblical intrepretation, 5:523, 968, 12:637
  biblical theology, 3:623, 839
  Buonaiuti, Ernesto, 2:694
  cardinalate, 3:106
  Catholic Action, 3:275–276, *276*
  Catholic exegesis, 13:913
  Catholic Near East Welfare Association, 3:286
  certitude, 3:355
  China, 3:500, 502

Christian philosophy, 3:541–542
Church as Body of Christ, 8:290
Church-State relations, 2:502
Code of Canons of the Eastern Churches, 3:817
collective guilt, 11:400
Communion outside the liturgy, 4:37
Communism, 11:400
Communists excommunicated, 4:418
concordant with Germany, 11:396–397
conjugal act, 8:874
conjugal love, 13:45
conscientious objection, 4:151
contemplative life, 4:210
contraception, 1:490, 4:222
democracy, 3:642, 4:636, 13:259
demonology, 4:649
destiny, supernatural, 4:694
devotion to the Sacred Heart, 12:490
diaconate, 4:551, 552
dignity of Mary, 11:399
diplomatic repudiation of Ottaviani, 10:68
Divine indwelling, 7:442
Divine missions, 9:737
Easter Vigil restoration, 5:14, 15, 16
Eastern liturgies, 8:667
economic democracy, 4:643
Ellis, John Tracy, 5:171
Eucharist, 1:64
eucharistic fast, 5:437
evolution, 1:105–106, 4:345, 347
expiation, 5:565
ferial Masses, 8:470
functions of the state, 13:605
Holocaust, 3:758
Holy Thursday, 7:54, 55
holy virginity, 12:464–465
Holy Week Ordinal, 7:56, 10:811
human law, 8:390
Immaculate Heart of Mary feast, 7:335, 337
imputability, 8:876
incorporation in Christ, 7:380
Jesus Christ, expiation, 5:565, 12:490, 491–492, 493
Jews, 11:398
lay participation in the liturgy, 11:400
liturgical languages, 8:668
liturgical movement, 11:400
liturgy, 2:676
Liturgy of the Hours, 8:732
love, nature of, 13:47

Maglione, Luigi, 9:40
medical ethics, 9:430
medical research, 5:560
mission and evangelization, 9:681
Movement for a Better World, 10:36
music, 8:704, 705
mystical body, 9:428
Mystical Body of Christ, 5:948, 950–951, 10:110, 12:625
natural law, 10:191, 956
Ne Temere exception, 10:219
necessity of self-defense, 10:748
needs of migrants and refugees, 7:521–522
obligations of state of marriage, 10:178
ordination rites, 7:38
ordinations, 11:400
papal charities, 11:398
papal development under, 10:849
personality, 11:156
Pontifical Council for the Pastoral Care of Migrants and Itinerant Peoples, 11:482
priesthood, 11:705
religious habit, 12:100
Resurrectionists, 12:174
Roman Pontifical, 11:474
sacraments, 2:417
sacred liturgy, 12:500
sacred spaces, 12:500
secular institutes, 11:400, 12:861–862
sin, nature of, 13:150
slavery, 13:209
social issues, 11:399
on the soul, 11:399
Taylor, Myron Charles, 13:770–771
as teacher, 11:398–399
teaching sisters, 13:170
theology of Church, 3:589–590
translation of Psalms, 11:400
transubstantiation, 5:496, 712, 10:849, 12:775, 14:23–24, 159
truth in theology, 4:815–816
Vatican construction, 14:397
Vatican Library expansion, 14:422
virginity, 12:464–465, 14:546–547
vision of God, 4:691
war and peace, 11:399
women, dignity of, 14:825
women, role of, 14:825
women, status of, 14:819
World War II, 1:585–586, 11:397–398
Piyyutim (liturgical piety), 3:76, 9:49–50

Pizan, Christine de, 5:672

Pizarro, Francisco, 4:131–132, 11:*165*

Pizarro, Gonzalo, 4:132

Pizarro, Hernando, 2:465

Pizolpasso, Francesco (Abp.), 1:344

Pizzaro, Juan, 4:288

Place, **11:401–402**

    accident, 1:62

    Aristotle, 4:959

    bilocation, 2:396

    disposition, 4:776–777

    local motion, 10:17

    location (ubi), 8:742

    prayer, 11:597

    situation (situs), 13:193

Placher, William, 5:830

Placida, Galla, 12:321

Placidus, St., 4:775

Plagues

    Abraham of Sancta Clara, 1:38

    Alexian Brothers, 1:275

    Ancient See of Chichester, 3:481

    ars moriendi, 1:732

    Augustinians, 1:889

    Byzantine Empire, 2:788

    Canon Law, 3:48–49

    Canons Regular of St. Augustine, 3:69

    Carafa, Vincenzo, 3:97–98

    Carthusians, 3:194

    Castel Sant'Angelo, 3:213

    Church history, 3:604

    Church property, 3:726

    Cistercians, 3:751

    clerical celibacy/marriage, 3:327

    Ghibelline-Guelf conflict, 3:855

    Gregory I (Pope), St., 6:479

    Justinian I, 8:101

    land leasing, 3:488–489

    London, 13:370

    mission, 3:493

    works of charity, 3:404, 415

Plagues of Egypt, 10:933, **11:402–405**

Plain Truth (periodical), 14:847

Plains of Esdraelon (Israel), 7:*647*

Plan de Estudios (Funes), 6:34

Plan for Parish Action (NCCIJ), 10:158

Plan for Pro-Life Activities (NCCB/USCC), 14:315

Plan of Ayutla, 8:264

Plane compertum est (papal decree, Pius XII), 3:498, 500, 516

Planetary motion, laws of, 8:154–155

Planets and Greek philosophy studies, 12:801

Planisphere (Herman of Carinthia), 14:2

Planned Parenthood v. Casey, 1:34, 35, 11:88

Planned Parenthood v. Danforth, 1:33

Planque, Augustin (Father), 1:162

Plant life, fertility and vegetation cults and, 5:697

Plant life, philosophical aspects, **11:405–406**

Plantagenet, Geoffrey (Duke of Normandy). *See* Normandy, Geoffrey Plantagenet, Duke of

La Plante de Dieu (Pollien), 11:462

Plantin, Christophe, **11:406**

Planudes, Maximus, 2:762, 804, 809–810, 826, 4:778, **11:406–407**

Plasden, Polydore (Father), St., 5:231, 6:138, **11:407**

Plaskow, Judith, 5:677

Plassmann, Hermann, 12:774

Plassmann, Thomas, 12:540

Plasticism (architecture), 3:681

Platina, Bartolomeo, 1:258, 2:341, 12:118

Plato (Greek philosopher), 6:442, 11:288, *407*, **407–411**

    absolute, 1:41

    abstraction, 1:45, 47

    accident, 1:59, 63

    aesthetics, 1:142, 145

    afterlife, 1:167

    Alexander, Samuel, 1:252

    Alfarabi, 1:277

    analogy, 1:371

    Anaxagoras, 1:393

    anthropocentrism, 1:508

    anthropomorphism, 1:510

    anxiety, 1:540

    Aquinas' proof of God, 6:303–304

    aristocracy, 1:667

    Aristotle, 1:680, 684

    art, 1:746

    asceticism, 1:773

    astral religion, 1:810, 812

    atomism, 1:832

    Averroës, 1:933

    Avicenna, 1:940

    beauty, 2:184

    becoming, 2:195

    Cappadocians, 2:792

    cathedral and episcopal schools, 3:441

    causality, 3:297, 302, 303, 304

    certitude, 3:352

    Church-State relations, 3:631

    Claudianus, Mamertus, 3:769

    common good, 4:16–17

    concept of truth, 14:222

    consciousness, 4:152

    contemplation, 4:204

    criteriology, 4:367

    daimones in, 4:495

    democracy, 4:636, 637, 638

    dialectics, 4:721–722

    dialogue as form, 4:728

    Dialogues, 10:240

    disciple as term, 4:768

    distinction, 4:779, 780–781

    doctrine of forms, 5:803

    dreams, 4:903

    dynamism, 4:958–959

    educational philosophy, 5:88–89

    emanationism, 5:181

    error, 12:398

    essence, 5:360–361, 364

    eternity, 5:380

    ethics, 5:393

    exemplarism, 5:524–525

    faith, 1:876

    free will, 5:929

    freedom, 5:937

    freedom of conscience, 4:148

    Gnostic texts, 3:465

    God, 6:307

    Golden Age, 6:335

    good, 6:346–347

    Good versus love, 8:826

    Greek religion, 6:453–454

    Heidegger, Martin, 6:45

    Heraclitus, 6:760

    human will, 14:721

    idea, 7:292–293

    idealism, 7:296

    I-It mysticism, 10:117

    immortality, 7:347–348

    infinity, 7:456

    innatism, 7:466

    intellectual life, 7:513

    judgment, 8:21

    knowledge theories, 8:213

    liberal arts, 8:536–537

    logic and syllogism, 8:748

    Logos as image of God, 8:759

    lying, 8:900

    man, concept of, 9:89–90

    man, natural end of, 9:96

    mathematics, 9:326

    matter, 9:340

Plato (Greek philosopher) *(continued)*
   matter and form, 5:803, 9:350
   metaphysics, 9:549
   monads, 9:777
   motion, 10:17
   music, 10:70
   natural law, 10:201
   natural law doctrine, 10:180
   nominalism vs. absolute realism, 11:942
   noumena concept, 10:463
   number symbolism, 3:673
   ontological perfection, 11:118
   opinion and knowledge, 10:610
   participation, 10:905, 906
   philosophy of nature, 10:208
   possibility, 11:550
   power of governance, 6:376
   providence of God, 11:781
   relation, 12:40–41
   religious veneration of, 6:445
   sacrifice, 12:509, 510
   soul, 13:333
   species, 13:407
   substance, 13:574–575
   as teacher and missionary, 6:446
   theism, 13:862–863
   transcendentals, 14:149–150
   uniformity, 14:300
   unity, 14:316–317
   unity and multiplicity opposition, 10:58
   universal essences, 14:322
   usury, 14:353
   utopia and utopianism, 14:360
   wisdom, 14:784
   wonder, 14:832
   works, 11:408
   world soul, 14:843
   See also Neoplatonism; Platonism
"Plato and the Poets" (Gadamer), 6:44
Platonic Academy (Florence), 5:710
Platonism, **11:411–417**
   Abelard, Peter, 1:19
   absolute, 1:41
   act, 1:75
   Albert the Great, St., 1:225
   analogy, 1:371, 373
   Apollinarianism, 1:559
   Aquinas, St., 9:551–552
   architecture, 3:700–701
   Aristotelianism, 1:225, 669, 670, 675
   Athenagoras, 1:828
   Augustine, St., 1:857, 862, 865

   Bernard of Chartres, 2:307
   Boethius, 2:456
   Byzantine theology, 2:818–819, 824
   Cambridge Platonists, 2:623, 908–910, 3:185, 832
   Celsus, 3:329
   charity, 3:395
   Clement of Alexandria, St., 3:798, 799
   Coleridge, Samuel Taylor, 3:832
   Ficino, Marsilio, 5:710
   humanism, 7:186
   Justin Martyr, St., 8:93–94
   knowledge theories, 8:214–215
   liberal arts, 8:537
   Lull, 8:866
   mysticism, 6:449
   School of Alexandria, 1:269, 272, 524
   Seripando, G., 13:17
   skepticism, 13:201
   soul, 13:342, 351
   soul-body relationship, 13:358
   See also Cambridge Platonists; Neoplatonism
Plato's Dialectical Ethics (Gadamer), 6:44
"Plato's Educational State" (Gadamer), 6:44
Plaza de Mayo Cathedral (Buenos Aires), 1:*651, 653*
Plaza Hernández, Guillermo, 12:408
Plazaola Artola, Julián, Bl., 7:125
Pleasure, **11:417–418**
   appetite, 1:601
   Epicurean conception, 5:284–285
   finality of action, 8:874
   friendship, 6:6
   lust related, 8:873
   Réponse (Malebranche), 9:74
Pledge, in the Bible, 13:251
Plegmund of Canterbury (Abp.), 5:530, **11:418–419**
Plenary indulgences, 7:30, 56–57, 437
Plenkers, Heribert, 2:263
Plenty Good Romm: The Spirit and Truth of African American Catholic Worship, 8:709
Plenum, 4:217, 9:318
Pleroma, theology of man in, 9:93–95
Plerophoriai (John of Maiuma), 10:548
Plessington, John, St., 5:237, 10:495, **11:419**
Plessington, William, St. *See* Plessington, John, St.

Plessis, Joseph Octave (Bp. of Quebec), 1:582, 3:7–8, **11:419–420**, 14:453
Plethon, George Gemistos, 2:773, 776, **11:420**
   Bessarion, Cardinal, 2:340, 810
   Council of Florence, 2:828
   philosophy, 2:810, 7:186
   traditionalism, 2:791
Pleutschau, Henry, 7:402–403
Pley, Celestin, 12:765
Plinianae exercitationes (Salmasius), 12:620
Pliny the Elder, 2:400–441, 5:206, 369, 12:305, 308
Pliny the Younger, 1:170, 2:342–343, 3:529, 4:588, **11:420–421**, 12:308
PLO. *See* Palestine Liberation Organization
Ploscaru, Ioan, 12:339
Plotinus (Greek philosopher), **11:421–423**
   absolute, 1:41
   aesthetics, 1:142
   Alfarabi, 1:277
   Ambrose, St., 1:337
   Aristotelianism, 1:669
   art, 1:743
   aseity, 1:779
   Augustine, St., 1:857, 862, 864
   Avicebron, 1:939
   Avicenna, 1:941
   beauty, 2:184
   Byzantine philosophy, 2:807
   causality, 3:303
   concept of time, 14:77
   consciousness, 4:152
   contemplation, 4:204
   eclecticism, 5:47
   eternity, 5:380
   existence, 5:533
   faith, 1:876
   free will, 5:929
   God, 6:308
   good, 6:347
   Greek religion, 6:442, 450
   idealism, 7:297
   I-It mysticism, 10:117
   illumination, 7:319
   infinity, 7:457
   influence of, 11:422–423
   irrationalism, 7:585
   John Italus, 2:758
   knowledge of self, 12:1
   matter, 9:342
   metaphysics of light, 8:583

music, consideration of, 10:71

neoplatonism, 12:327

the One, 5:180–181

pantheism, 10:825–826

participation, 10:906–907

prophecy, 11:760

relation, 12:41

soul, 13:339

teacher and missionary, 6:446

theism, 13:863

transcendentals, 14:150

world soul, 7:239

See also Neoplatonism

Plowden, Charles and Francis, **11:423**

Plowden, Edmund, **11:423–424**

Plows, symbols of, 13:668

Plummer, Alfred, **11:424**

Plummer, Charles, **11:424**

Plumpe, Joseph Conrad, **11:424–425**

Plumtree, Thomas, Bl., 5:227

Plunket, Oliver (Abp. of Armagh), St., 1:698, 7:560, 579, 10:496, **11:425–426**, 12:725

Corker, James Maurus, 4:269

Oates Plot, 5:248

relics, 4:888

Pluralism, philosophical, 11:283–284, 284, **426–430**

Augustinianism, 1:878

monism, 9:811

society, 13:277

Zeno of Elea, 14:917

Pluralism, religious

Anglo-American theology, 13:236

anonymous Christian, 1:489

Smith, W.C., 13:236

Plurality of forms, 1:108, 2:488–489

Pluries instanterque (Congregation for the Propagation of the Faith), 3:516

Plus, Raoul, **11:430**

Pluscarden Priory (Elgin, Scotland), **11:430–431**, *431*

Plutarch of Athens, 1:829, 5:47, 12:308

Plutarch of Chaeronea, 11:413

Plymouth (MA), 4:116

Plymouth Brethren, 2:606, 4:526–527, 10:746, **11:431–432**

Pneuma, 14:200

Pneumatology, 14:200–201

Pneumatomachians, 1:818, 4:190, 354, **11:432**

Pobedonostev, Konstantin Petrovich, 7:54, **11:432**, 12:424

Poblet Abbey (Spain), 3:750

Podlasie, Martyrs of. *See* Pratulin (Poland), martyrs of, BB.

Poe, Edgar Allan, 14:149

Poems: Patriotic, Religious, Miscellaneous (Ryan), 12:443

Poems (Emerson), 5:188

Poems (Hadewijch), 6:605

Poems (Santayana), 12:680

Poems (Tabb), 13:725

Poems in Stanzas (Hadewijch), 6:605

Poems of the New World (Noyes), 10:471

Poenitemini (apostolic constitution, Paul VI), 5:186, 635

Poenitemini (Gerson), 6:190

''The Poet'' (Emerson), 14:147

Poeta Saxo, **11:432–433**

Poetae Latini Aevi Carolini (Traube), 14:163

Poeticarum Institutionum liber variis ethicorum christianorumque exemplis illustratus (Rubio), 12:399

Poetics (Aristotle), 1:659, 675, 683–684, 685, 8:538, **11:433–435**

Poetics (Possevino), 2:115

Poetry

alphabetic psalms, 1:305–306

baroque period, 2:115

Carolingian Renaissance, 3:159, 160

meditation, 13:320

sonnet, religious use of, 13:319–320

See also Byzantine literature; Hebrew poetry; Hymns; Recusant literature; Religious poetry; *specific poets*

Pogedaïeff, G. de, 1:545

Poggio Bracciolini, Giovanni Francesco, 2:341, **11:435**, 12:622

Pohl, Alfred, **11:435**

Pohle, Joseph, 1:354, 3:291, **11:436**

Pohle, M. J., 14:13

Poidebard, Antoine, **11:436**

Poincaré, J. Henri, 2:570, 11:299, 315–316

Point, Nicholas, 7:289

Le Point de départ de la métaphysique (Maréchal), 9:145–146, 14:53

Point du Sable, Jean-Baptiste, 1:155

Poiret, Pierre, 3:137

Poirino, Giacomo da (Father), 3:314

Poirters, Adriaen, **11:436–437**

Poisidonius of Apamea, 5:46

Poison ordeal, 10:626

Poisson, André, 3:192

Poisson, Paul du, 1:691

Poissy, Conference of (1561), 2:352, 3:266, 7:167, **11:437**

Poitiers, Council of (1000), 3:325

Poitiers Cathedral (France), 3:697

Pokagon, Leopold and Simon, **11:437**

Pokrov (Protection of the Mantle of Our Lady), 9:274

Polanco, Anselmo, Bl., 1:888

Polanco, Juan de, 1:733, 3:514

Polanco Fontecha, Anselmo (Bp. of Teruel), Bl., **11:437–438**, 12:252

Poland, **11:438–455**

Byzantine Basilians, 2:143

Counter Reformation, 3:613

demographic statistics, 11:439

ecclesiastical organization, 11:440, 454–455

Gregory XVI (Pope), 6:509

history

foreign domination (1815-1918), 11:445–448

martial law, 11:453–454

Middle Ages, 11:438–440

partitions, 11:444

Republic of (1918-1930), 11:448–449

under German rule, 11:447–448

Jewish population

1650-1750, 7:872

during the Crusades, 7:871

post-World War I, 7:874

John Paul II (Pope), 3:627

Ledóchowski, Miescysław Halka, 8:444

map, 11:*441*

patron saints, 7:236, 8:242–243

Pratulin Martyrs, BB., 11:583–584

public demonstrations, 11:*443, 444*

Reformation, 11:440–444

Reformed churches, 12:24

religious discrimination and persecution, 11:443–446, 449–450

Union of Brest, 2:605–606

Poland, popular piety in, **11:510–512**

Polansdorf, Polanus von, 12:768

Polding, John Bede (Abp. of Sydney), 1:900, 902, 903–904, 11:455

Pole, Edward, 5:237

Pole, Margaret Plantagenet, Bl., 5:227, **11:455–456**

Pole, Reginald (Card.), 3:72, 5:245, 11:455, **456–458**, *457*, 12:9–10

Agustín, Antonio, 1:189

Anglican orders problem, 1:434, 435–436

Colonna, Vittoria, 3:856

Ecumenical councils, 4:302

Polemics, 13:836

Die Polemik des Islam (Palmieri), 10:812

Police officers, 3:764

Policraticus sive de nugis et vestigiis curialium (John of Salisbury), 3:519, 7:985, 9:453

Polignac, Melchior de (Card.), 8:849, **11:458**

Polish Americans, 2:132

Polish Apostles of Divine Mercy, 8:243, 245

Polish Crier (daily newspaper), 9:647, 14:780

Polish National Catholic Church, 3:624, 11:86, **458–459**

    church union, 4:199

    disunity, 13:462

    Old Catholics influence, 10:579

    trusteeism, 14:221

Polish Seminary (Detroit), 10:624

Polish United Workers' Party, 11:452, 453, 454

Political authority, 13:239–241, 266, 371–372, 484, 488–489

Political conservatism (France), 9:753

Political ethics, 11:460

The Political Illusion (Ellul), 5:172

Political modernization, 9:584–585

Political parties, 3:619, 642

    Austria, 1:914, 915

    Center Party (Germany), 3:339–342

    government, 6:377

    Leo XIII (Pope), 8:493

    See also specific political parties

Political philosophy, 6:707, 14:570–571

Political power, 13:488–489

Political reactionism, 9:753

Political theology

    civil religion, 3:756–757

    de-privatizing Christian message, 13:245

    foundational theology, 5:828–829

    Lemire, J., 8:466

    praxis, 11:585

    theology of society, 13:288

Political theology, **11:459–461**

    See also Theology

Political theory

    conservative, 8:182

    constitutions and law, 8:390

    Gaudium et spes, 8:358–359, 360

    Locke, J., 8:745

    man as social being, 8:855

    Marxism, 8:467–468

    populists, 8:467

Simon, Y., 13:128

social contract, 13:239–241

Wolff, Christian, 14:808

Politicoethical dualism, 11:410

Politicorum (Lipsius), 12:125

Politics (Aristotle), 1:678, 3:636, 4:17, 10:70–71, 13:253, 14:360

The Politics of God and the Politics of Man (Ellul), 5:172

Politika (Križanić), 8:249

Politique, Église et Foi (Conference of Bishops), 5:860

Poliziano, Angelo, 12:119

Polk, James K., 3:659, 7:161

Pollaiuolo, Antonio del, 1:91

Pollaiuolo, Piero del, 1:91

Pollen, John Hungerford, 5:684, **11:461–462**

Pollien, François de Sales, 3:192, **11:462**

Pollo, Secondo, Bl., **11:462**

Pollock, F., 5:914

Polo, Marco, 3:491, 865

Polo, Nicolò, 3:492

Polonia sive de situ, populis, moribus, magistratibus et republica reni Poloniae (Kromer), 8:251

Pols, Edward, 11:730

Poltergeists, **11:462–464**

Polton, Thomas (Bp.), **11:464**

Poltzmacher, Johann, **11:464**

Polycarp (Bp. of Smyrna), St., **11:464–465**

    Anicetus (Pope), St., 1:455

    Apostles, 3:29

    as Apostolic Father, 1:587

    apostolic succession, 1:591

    biblical canon, 3:26

    bishops, 2:413

    burial of, 3:222

    Canon Law, 3:37

    catechesis, 3:228

    charity, 3:395

    Christian way of life, 3:547

    creedal statements, 4:351

    deacons, 4:551

    disciple as term, 4:774

    docetism, 4:797

    Easter controversy, 1:785, 3:593

    Ignatius of Antioch, 7:310

    martyrdom of, 1:92–93, 12:606

    martyrs and martyrdom, 9:228

    Pauline epistles, 3:30

    relics, 12:50–51

    universality of Christianity, 3:274

    works of charity, 3:403, 405

    See also Apostolic Fathers

Polycarpus (Canon Law collection), **11:465**

Polycarpus (Cardinal Gregory), 3:45, 60

Polychronicon (Ralph Higden), 11:901, 14:177

Polychronius of Apamea, 5:511

Polycrates (Bp. of Ephesus), 1:785, 3:593, 5:13

Polygamy, 3:248, 653, 654–655, 848, 8:373–374

Polygenism. *See* Monogenism and polygenism

Polyglot Bibles, 1:236, 2:355, 366, 5:518, 6:42, **11:465–466**

Polyphemus and Galatea (Carracci), 6:*305*

Polyphony, 1:1, 234, 2:397–398, 3:523–524, 7:254, 255

Polyphyletic polygenism, 9:813

Polysyllogisms, 13:655

Polytheism, 12:67, 14:297

Poma de Ayala, Huamán, 1:946

Pombal, Marquês de, 2:593–594

Pombal, Sebastião José de Carvalho e Mello, **11:466–468**, *467*

    Clement XIV (Pope), 3:795

    Coimbra University, 3:828

    Eckart missionary work in Brazil, 5:43

    Jesuits, 1:58, 3:791, 12:222

Pombeiro Abbey (Spain), **11:468**

Pomeiana (Vegius), 14:430

Pomerius (African ascetical writer), **11:469**

Pommerel, Celestine (Mother), **11:469**

"Pomp and Circumstance" marches (Elgar), 5:153

Pompallier, Jean Baptiste François (Bp.), 2:151, **11:469–470**

Pompeii (Italy), 10:87, 93–94

Pompey (Roman general), 6:664

Pomponazzi, Pietro, 1:676, **11:470**

    Apostolici regiminis, 1:595

    double truth theory, 4:882

    immortality, 7:349

    Latin Averroism, 1:937

    Renaissance philosophy, 12:122

    skepticism, 13:202

    soul, 13:345

Pomponius Laetus, 12:118

Pomposa, St., **3:863**

Pomposa Abbey (Codigoro, Italy), 11:*471*

Ponce, Alonso, **11:471**

Ponce, Manuel María, **11:471–472**, *472*

Ponce Cathedral (Puerto Rico), 11:*816*

Ponce de León, Juan, 4:132–133

Ponce de León, Pedro, 3:418

Poncelet, A., 2:472

Pongrácz, Stefan (Stephen), 8:241–242

Pons asinorum (asses' bridge), 12:752

Pons de Lubières (Abp.), 12:708

Pons de Melgueil, 3:814

Ponsa Casallach, Francisco Javier, Bl., 7:124

Pontano (orator), 12:116

Pontanus Romanus, Ludovicus, **11:472**

Pontas, Jean, **11:472–473**

Pontello, Francesco. *See* Egidio Maria of St. Joseph, Bl.

Pontianus (Pope), St., 5:584, **11:473**

Ponticus (martyr), 1:93, 3:593

Pontifex, Charles, 5:2

Pontiffs, **11:473**

Pontifica Ateneo di S. Anselmo (Rome), 11:488–489

Pontifica Università della Santa Croce (Rome), 11:488

Pontifica Università di S. Tommaso d'Aquino in Urbe (Angelicum) (Rome), 11:487

Pontifica Università Lateranense (Rome), 11:485–486

Pontifica Università Salesiana (Rome), 11:487–488

Pontifica Università Urbaniana (Rome), 11:486–487

Pontifical, Roman, 3:53, 4:50, 165, 271, 553, **11:474**

altars, 1:318

blessings, 2:440

Council of Trent, 12:328

liturgical history, 8:655

modern ritual for conferring Sacrament of Holy Orders in, 10:635

origins, 8:640

Pontifical Academies, **11:474–476**

Pontifical Academy for Life, 1:31, 11:475

Pontifical Academy of Our Lady Immaculate, 11:476

Pontifical Academy of Roman Archaeology, 11:476

Pontifical Academy of St. Thomas, 11:475

Pontifical Academy of Science, 11:475

Pontifical Academy of Social Sciences, 11:475

Pontifical Academy of the Arts, 11:476

Pontifical Academy of the Cult of Martyrs, 11:476

Pontifical Association of the Holy Childhood, 3:622, 5:796

Pontifical Biblical Commission, 5:789, **11:476–479**

anti-discrimination, 13:52

approving modern translation of Bible, 10:276

biblical method, 13:457

founding, 8:492

pentateuchal studies, 11:94–95

serpent as symbol, 13:19

Pontifical Biblical Commission on the Historical Truth of the Gospels, 10:304

Pontifical Biblical Institute (Rome), 5:789, 11:390, 485, 12:402

Pontifical Catholic University (Rio de Janeiro, Brazil), 5:840

Pontifical College Josephinum (Columbus, OH), **7:1046–1047**, 10:572

Pontifical Commission for Authentically Interpreting the Canons of the Code, Confirmation, 4:89

Pontifical Commission for Latin America, 4:158

Pontifical Commission for the Cultural Heritage of the Church, 1:639

Pontifical Commission for the Neo-Vulgate, 14:598

Pontifical Commission for the Revision of the Code of Canon Law, 4:58–59

Pontifical Commission Justice and Peace, 6:526, 8:317, 13:296

Pontifical Council for ''Cor Unum,'' 11:481–482

Pontifical Council for Culture, 1:824–825, **11:479**, 482

Pontifical Council for Interreligious Dialogue, **11:479–480**

Pontifical Council for Justice and Peace, 11:481

Pontifical Council for Promoting Christian Unity, 3:393

Pontifical Council for Social Communications, 11:482–483

Pontifical Council for the Family, 11:481

Pontifical Council for the Interpretation of Legislative Texts, 11:482

Pontifical Council for the Laity, 11:481

Pontifical Council for the Pastoral Assistance to Health-Care Workers, 11:482

Pontifical Council for the Pastoral Care of Migrants and Itinerant Peoples, 11:482

Pontifical Council for the Promotion of Christian Unity, 8:91, 11:481

Pontifical Councils, 4:439–440, 5:70, **11:480–483**

Pontifical equestrian orders. *See* Decorations, papal

Pontifical Institute for Foreign Missions (Rome), 3:622, 10:529, **11:483**

Pontifical Institute of Mediaeval Studies (Toronto, Canada), 3:175

Pontifical Liturgical Institute (Rome), 11:488–489

Pontifical mass, 10:855–856, 13:499

Pontifical Mission for Palestine, 3:286, **11:483–484**

Pontifical Missionary Union of the Clergy, 4:94, 9:119

Pontifical of the Roman Curia, 1:486

Pontifical Oriental Institute (Rome), 5:72, 11:485

Pontifical Roman Universities, **11:484–492**

Pontifical University of Salamanca, 12:612

Pontifical University of the Holy Cross (Rome), 10:618

Pontifical vespers, 14:*463*

Pontificale Durandi, 10:641

Pontificale Romano-Germanicum, 10:640, 641, 642

Pontificale Romanum (1485), 4:949

Pontificale Romanus, 8:658

Pontificalis Romani Recognitio (constitution, Paul VI), 2:417, 10:640, 641

Il pontifice ed il principe (Passaglia), 10:918

Pontificia Facoltà di Scienze dell'Educazione ''Auxilium'' (Rome), 11:491–492

Pontificia Facoltà Teologica e Pontificio Instituto di Spiritualità ''Teresianum'' (Rome), 11:490–491

Pontificia Facoltà Teologica ''Marianum'' (Rome), 11:491

Pontificia Facoltà Teological ''San Bonaventura'' (Rome), 11:490

Pontificia Università Gregoriana (Rome), 11:484–485

El Pontificiado romano (Franceschi), 5:864

Pontifical Society for the Propagation of the Faith, 8:810

Pontificio Ateneo ''Antonianum'' (Rome), 11:489

Pontificio Ateneo ''Regina Apostolorum'' (Rome), 11:489

Pontificio Istituto di Archeologia Cristiana (Rome), 11:490

Pontificio Istituto di Musica Sacra (Rome), 11:489

Pontificio Istituto di Studi Arabi e d'Islamistica (Rome), 11:491

Pontigny Abbey (France), 1:109, 3:746, 748, 751, 5:86, **11:492**, *493*

Pontillo, Egidio Maria di San Giuseppe, St., **11:492–493**

Pontius of Balmey, Bl., **11:493**

Pontius of Faucigny, Bl., **11:493**

Poor, 4:620–622, 718–720, 8:843, 860, 896, 9:834–835

Poor Brothers of St. Francis, 12:735

Poor Brothers of St. Francis Seraph, 12:546–547

Poor Caitiff, The, 10:119

Poor Clares, 5:166, **11:494**

    Agnes of Assisi, St., 1:178

    Brazil, 2:593

    Carroll, John, 3:180

    Clare of Assisi, St., 3:760

    Colette, St., 3:833

    Creighton, John, 4:357

    Cusack, Margaret Anna, 4:445

    as discalced order, 4:764

    establishment in U.S., 2:287

    hospitals, 7:120

    Louise of Savoy, 8:808

    Louisiana, 8:812

    Massachusetts, 2:555

    monastery at Orbe, Switzerland, 8:808

    Nebraska, 10:223

    Satellico, Elisabetta Maria, Bl., 12:699

    Seraphina Sforza, Bl., 13:6

    Stary Sacz Abbey, 8:172

Poor Clares of Perpetual Adoration (PCPA), 5:379

Poor Daughters of St. Cajetan, 2:451

Poor Daughters of the Holy Stigmata of St. Francis, 8:333

Poor Fellow-Soldiers of Christ and the Temple of Solomon. *See* Templars

Poor Handmaids of Jesus Christ, 8:130, **11:494**

Poor Infirmarians. *See* Obregonians

Poor Jesuatesses of the Visitation of the B.V.M., 7:777

Poor Ladies. *See* Poor Clares

Poor Ladies of San Damiano, 3:760

"Poor Man of Anderlecht." *See* Guido of Anderlecht, St.

Poor Servants of Divine Providence, 2:856

Poor Servants of the Mother of God, **11:494–495**, 13:769

Poor Sisters of Jesus Crucified and the Sorrowful Mother, **11:495**

Poor Sisters of Nazareth, **11:495**

Poor Sisters of St. Francis Seraph of Perpetual Adoration, 2:510, 5:888

Poor souls, **11:495**

    See also Purgatory

Pope (title), 7:4, **11:495–496**

Pope, Alexander, **11:496–498**, 497

Pope, Charles Alexander, 12:562

Pope, Hugh, **11:498**

Pope, primacy of. *See* Primacy of the pope

The Pope and Italy (Parsons), 10:904

Pope John XXIII Peace Prize, 10:16

Pope Paul VI Institute (Nebraska), 10:224

Pope Sylvester I Carried in the Sedia Gestatoria, with His Retinue (Raphael), 13:656

Popes, election of, **11:498–501**

    conclave for, 4:60

    Constance Council, 4:170

    Humbert of Silva Candida, 7:199

    imperial military establishment, 4:128

    John Paul II (Pope), 7:1001–1002

    Third Lateran Council, 8:352

Popes, list of, 8:535, 553, **11:501–506**

Popes, names of, **11:506–507**

Pope's Day, 2:552–553

Popiełuszko, Jerzy, 11:*448*

Popish Plot. *See* Oates Plot (1678)

Popovtsi in Russian churches, 2:745

Poppe, Edward Johannes Maria, Bl., 2:219, **11:507**

Popper, Karl, 1:667, 670, 2:407, 6:871, **11:507–508**

Poppo (Bp. of Brixen). *See* Damasus II (Pope)

Poppo of Stavelot, St., 1:498, 2:586, 9:79, **11:508–509**

"Popular church," 8:547, 602

Popular conviction, 14:723

"Popular Liturgical Apostolate" (Parsch), 10:903

Popular piety, 4:709–712, 11:510–512, 541–542

Popular piety of Hispanic Americans, **11:509–510**

Popularism, 4:366

Population, 4:222, **11:512–516**, 566

Population theory, 9:83–84

Populorum progressio (encyclical, Paul VI), 3:627, 4:157, 5:206, 9:688, 10:851, 11:32, **516–517**, 566, 14:362, 638

    John Paul II (Pope), 13:303–304

    poor nations, 13:260

    social justice, 13:244

Porion, Jean-Baptiste, 3:192

Pormort, Thomas, Bl., 5:232, **11:517**

Pornography, 5:326–327, **11:517–520**

Porphyrian trees, 4:52, 780–781, 8:749, **11:520**

Porphyry (Greek philosopher), **11:520–521**, 12:327

    Aristotelianism, 1:669–670

    Boethius, 2:456

    Byzantine philosophy, 2:807

    Celsus, 3:330

    Methodius of Olympus, St., 1:785

    neoplatonism, 10:240

    ontological status of universals, 14:322–323

    species, 13:407

    teacher and missionary, 6:446

Porphyry of Gaza, St., **11:521**

Porpora, Nicola Antonio, **11:521–522**

Porras y Ayllón, Rafaela María, St., **11:522**, *523*

Porrée, Gilbert de la. *See* Gilbert de la Porrée

Porres, Diego de, 2:465

Porres, Martin de, St., 2:397, **11:522–523**

Port Royal Logic (Descartes), 9:566

Porta, Giacomo della, 3:213, 703

Porta Lucis. See Sha'are Orah (Gates of Light) (Gikatilla)

Portal, Fernand, 1:438, 9:78

Portalis, Jean, 4:62, 6:77

Porter, A. K., 3:694

Porter, Francis, **11:526**

Porters, 7:37, **11:525–526**

Portier, Michael (Bp. of Mobile, AL), 1:156, 200–201, 2:45, 9:748, **11:526**

Portillo, Alvaro del (Bp.), **11:526–527**

"Portinari Altarpiece" (van der Goes), 1:*315*

Portiuncula chapel (Assisi, Italy), 4:400, **11:527–528**

Portland Archdiocese (OR), 10:645, **11:528–531**

Portland Diocese (ME), **11:531–532**, 13:182–183

Portrepticus (St. Clement of Alexandria), 3:797–798

Port-Royal, 8:464–465, 804

Port-Royal Abbey (Versailles, France), 7:715–716, 717, **11:523–525**, *524*

Port-Royal Convent (Paris), 1:715–716, 717, 2:550, 3:524, 614, 744–745

Port-Royal-des-Champs convent (France), 3:614

Portugal, **11:532–541**, *536, 537*
  Alexandrine bulls, 1:259, 261, 273–274
  Angola, 1:450
  Brazil, 8:597, 9:65–66
  Carthusians, 3:195
  China, 3:497
  church architecture, 3:707
  Congregation for the Propagation of the Faith, 11:750, 751–752
  Council of Trent, 4:312
  crib-making, 4:364
  de auxiliis controversy, 4:111
  demographic statistics, 11:533
  ecclesiastical organization, 11:534
  Gregory XVI (Pope), 6:508
  Jesuits, 1:58–59, 3:792
  laicism, 8:283
  liturgical music history, 8:741–742
  Lobo, Jerónimo, 8:742
  Macau, 9:4
  Malaysia, 9:70
  map, 11:*535*
  monastic schools, 3:827
  Morocco, 9:898–899
  Pius X (Pope), St., 11:391
  Pius XI (Pope), 11:395
  Reconquest, 13:380
  works of charity, 3:416–417
  See also Brazil; Mission in colonial America, Portuguese

The Portuguese and Dutch in South Africa (Welch), 14:675

Portuguese Catholic University, 11:539

Portuguese Inquisition, 7:490, 9:65–66

The Porvoo Common Statement, 1:597

Posada y Gardüno, Manuel (Abp. of Mexico), **11:541**

Posadas, **11:541–542**

Poschmann, B., 4:76–77

Poseidon (sea god), 3:573

Poseidonius (Greek philosopher), 7:585, 13:339

''The Position and Duties of the American Scholar'' (Parker), 14:148

The Position of Liberal Theology (Sanday), 12:665

''Positive hierarchy'' of the sciences, 11:453

Positive infidels, 7:455

Positive law, 8:66

Positive Polity (Comte), 4:48

Positive theology, 3:613–614, 4:812, 815–817, 13:894, 895–898
  Alzog, Johann Baptist, 1:328
  Batiffol, Pierre, 2:155
  Bulgakov, Macarius, 2:678
  Byzantine, 2:824–825
  speculative theology, 13:900–901

Positivism, **11:542–545**
  analogy, 1:373–374
  causality, 3:301–302, 306, 307
  certitude, 3:352
  Christian philosophy, 3:538
  classification of the sciences, 12:821
  Comte, Auguste, 4:46–48, 5:396, 9:555–556, 10:184, 609, 12:47, 70
  Cournot, Antoine Augustine, 4:316
  demonstration, 4:654
  Dilthey, Wilhelm, 4:746
  Einstein, Albert, 5:142
  idealism, 7:300
  Leo XIII (Pope), 10:187
  mechanism, 9:417
  moral goodness, 6:351
  natural law doctrine, 10:184
  operationalism variation of, 10:608–609
  philosophy and science, 11:299
  philosophy of history, 6:884
  religion, 12:70
  religious liberalism, 8:541
  secularism, 12:865
  society, 13:279
  See also Empiricism; Logical positivism

Positivism in jurisprudence, 8:400, **11:545–548**, 13:484–485

Pospishil, Victor, 3:59

Possenti, Gabriel, St., **11:548**

Possessors in good, bad, or dubious faith, **11:548–549**

Possevino, Antonio, 2:606, **11:549–550**, 12:425

Possibility, 1:540, 4:212, **11:550–553**
  See also Being

Possidius, St., 1:481, 888, 3:67, **11:553–554**, 12:606

The Possition of Liberal Theology (Sanday), 12:665

Post-baptismal annointing. *See* Confirmation, Sacrament of

Post-Bultamannians, 10:303

Postel, Marie Madeleine, St., 3:543, **11:554**, *555*

Posterior Analytics (Aristotle), 5:160, 12:263, 748

Postexilic period, 10:79–80

Postgate, Nicholas, Bl., 5:237, **11:554–555**

Postilla litteralis (Nicholas of Lyra), 11:613

Postilla super librum sapientiae (Robert Holcot), 12:265

Postillae perpetuae in Vetus et Novum Testamentum (Nicholas of Lyra), 5:518

Post-modernity Movement, 5:348

Postquam apostolicis litteris (*motu proprio*, Pius XII), 1:534

Postquam verus (apostolic constitution, Sixtus V), 3:105

Postulates, 5:742, **11:555**

Postures, 11:597, 14:891

Potamiaena, St., 2:149

Potawatami people, 4:928, 8:112, 117, 12:274

Pote, Josephine, 2:476

Potency, **11:555–557**
  agnosticism, 1:184
  Aristotle, 1:682, 9:342
  created actuation by uncreated act, 4:335–336
  simplicity of God, 13:138
  Thomistic thought, 10:907
  See also Faculties of the Soul

Potency and act, 1:73–74, 75, 8:591, 828, **11:557–560**, 12:41

Potentia absoluta-potentia ordinata principle, 6:390

Potentia et actus dividunt omne ens (Potency and act divide all being), 12:756

Potentiae specificantur per actus et obiecta (Potencies are specified through their acts and objects), 12:756

Potentior principalitas, 7:571

Potestas, 10:834

Potgieter, E. J., 1:218

Pothier, Joseph, 5:793

Pothinus (Bp.), 1:93

Potter, Mary, 8:610, **11:560**

Potter, Philip, 14:842

Potter, Thomas J., 11:623, 624

Potthast, August, **11:560**

Pottier, Claude, 5:441

Pottier, François, 3:498

Pottmeyer, Hermann, 7:528

Pouget, François Aimé, 3:243, **11:560–561**

Poughkeepsie Plan (NY), 1:352, 10:315, **11:561–562**

Poulain, Augustin (Father), 8:845, 10:113, **11:562**, 12:201

Poulenc, Francis, **11:562–563**, *563*

Poullart des Places, Claude François, 7:25, **11:563**

Poulton, Thomas, 2:460

Pound, Ezra, 5:160

Pounde, Thomas, **11:563–564**

Poupard, Paul (Card.), 13:*685*

Pour l'Histoire du problème de l'amour au moyen âge (Rousselot), 12:394

Pourrat, Pierre, **11:564**

Poussepin, Marie, Bl., **11:564**

Poveda, Peter. *See* Poveda Castroverde, Pedro, Bl.

Poveda Castroverde, Pedro, Bl., **11:564–565**, 13:830

Poverty, **11:565–567**
  Basil, St., 2:140
  Basilian Fathers of America, 2:142
  begging, 3:417
  evangelical counsel, 4:306–307
  Franciscan spirituality, 5:895
  Hugh of Digne, 7:151
  Humiliati, 7:204–205
  Ireland, 7:567
  Japan, 8:109
  John XXII condemnation of Franciscan doctrine, 5:897, 902, 921
  Psuedo-Apostles, 4:821
  religious vow of, 12:88
  Seton, E. pilgrimage, 13:34
  social justice issues, 3:620
  socialism, 3:619
  See also Poor; Poverty, religious

Poverty, religious, **11:567–570**
  Basel Council, 7:231
  Catharism, 3:259, 260
  Church property, 3:725
  Cistercians, 3:750
  Clare of Assisi, St., 3:760
  Francis of Assisi, St., 3:413
  Hussites, 7:230, 231
  Vita Apostolica, 3:131
  See also Poverty Movement

Poverty controversy, 4:59, 5:897, 902, 921, **11:570–571**

Poverty Movement, 1:594, 3:259, 7:665, **11:571–573**, 13:383

Powderly, Terence Vincent, 8:192–193, 10:170, 11:87

Powel, Philip, Bl., 5:236, **11:573–574**

Powell, Edward, Bl., 5:226, 700, **11:574**

Power, Cornelius Michael (Abp. of Portland, OR), 11:530–531

Power, David, 5:430, 12:475

Power, Edmund, **11:574**

Power, Emily (Mother), **11:574–575**, *575*

Power, George, 7:580

Power, John, 10:312–313, **11:575**

Power, Lionel, **11:575–576**

Power and government, 6:375–376

The Power and the Glory (Greene), 6:461

The Power and the Wisdom: An Interpretation of the New Testament (McKenzie), 9:402

Power of governance, 6:373–375

Power of jurisdiction. *See* Power of governance

The Power of Naming (Fiorenza), 5:677

Power of orders, 6:374

Powers. *See* Faculties of the Soul

Powers, Jessica, 3:139, **11:576**

Poynter, William, **11:576**, *577*

Pozzo, Leopoldo del, 10:4

PPF (The Program of Priestly Formation) (National Conference of Catholic Bishops), 12:898

Prá ctica de la theolgía mystica (Godinez), 12:31

Prabhupada, A. C. (Bhaktivedanta Swami), 6:644

Práctica de las misiones (Carabantes), 3:94

Practice of Prelates (Tyndale), 14:254

Practice of the Presence of God (Lawrence of the Resurrection), 3:136–137

Prades, Jean Marie de, 12:770

Prades, Jean Martin de, 3:796

Pradt, El Abate de, **11:577–578**

Praeceptorium divinae legis (Nider), 10:386

Praeclara charissimi (papal bull, Paul IV), 1:436

Praeclara gratulationes (encyclical, Leo XIII), 1:503, 6:459

Praeclara inter opera (motu proprio, St. Pius X), 11:488

Praedecessores nostri (apostolic constitution, Leo XIII), 11:499

Praelectiones dogmaticae (Pesch), 11:168

Praelectiones theologicae (Tournely), 14:123

Praelectiones theologicae ad usum studii communis congregatiionis Benedictiono-Bavaricae (Scholliner), 12:779

Praemunire, Statute of (1353, England), 3:604, 5:242, 244, **11:578**, 12:6, 8
  Beaufort, Henry, 3:481
  Courtenay, William, 4:318

Praenotamenta (Gratius), 6:424

Praeparatio (Eusebius of Caesarea), 5:453

Praepositinus of Cremona, **11:578**

Praepositus (canonist), **11:578**

Praestantia (motu proprio, St. Pius X), 11:389

Praeterita (Ruskin), 12:414

Praetextatus, catacombs of, 3:224

Praetextatus of Rouen, St., **11:579**

Praetorian Guard, 12:301–302

Praetorium, **11:579–581**

Praetorius, Michael, 11:*581*, **581**

Pragmatic Sanction of Bourges (1438), 6:74, 11:581–582

Pragmatic Sanction of Bourges (1439), 1:599, 3:605, 639

Pragmatic sanctions, 5:847, **11:581–582**
  abolition (1516) of, 10:841–842
  Fifth Lateran, 8:354–355
  Justinian I, 7:655–656, 8:99
  Louis IX, 8:801
  Louis XII's reinforcement of, 10:841
  union of Hapsburg domains, 9:153–154

Pragmatism, 5:397
  Alexander, Samuel, 1:252
  causality, 3:301
  idea, 7:295
  James, William, 7:704
  man, natural end of, 9:99
  methodology, 9:566–567
  naturalism, 10:206
  Peirce, Charles Sanders, 11:58
  philosophy and science, 11:300
  philosophy of religion, 12:70–71
  relativism, 12:48
  religious experience, 5:556
  voluntarism, 14:582

Prague, Synod of (1386), 1:427

Prague Cathedral (Czech Republic), 3:697

Praise of Folly (Erasmus), 5:315, 12:123

Prakriti, 7:407–408

Prandtauer, Jakob, 1:913, 3:706

Prat, Ferdinand, **11:582**

Prat y Prat, Mercedes, Bl., **11:582–583**

Pratensis, Felix, **11:583**

Pratica del confessore per ben esercitare il suo ministero (St. Alphonsus Liguori), 1:311

Pratica di amar Gesù Cristo (St. Alphonsus Liguori), 1:309

La Pratique de la dévotion à Notre Dame de la Salette (Giraud), 8:338

La Pratique de l'oraison (Saudreau), 12:708

Pratique du droit canonique au gouvernement de l'Église (Bauny), 2:160

Prato Cathedral (Italy), 1:*335*, 336

Pratovecchio, Antonio de, 3:52

Pratt, James B., 10:204

Pratulin (Poland), Martyrs of, BB., **11:583–584**

Pratum spirituale (Moschus), 12:606

Praxedes, St. *See* Pudens, Pudentiana, and Praxedes, SS.

Praxis, 8:544, 545, 832, **11:584–588**

Praxis, 10:157

Praxis theologiae mysticae, opusculum selectum auctore P. Michaele Godinez. . . (Reguera), 12:31

Prayer, **11:588–591**

    Alphonsus Liguori, St., 1:309–310

    altars, 1:316

    Alumbrados, 1:323

    Álvarez de Paz, Diego, 1:326

    ancient religions, 11:590–591

    Anima Christi, 1:455

    Baker, David Augustine, 2:22

    Basil, St., 2:140

    Benedictine spirituality, 2:264

    Carmelite spirituality, 3:134, 135

    charismatic, 3:391–392

    Church-State relations, 3:666–667, 668

    communal, 8:729

    daily, 8:656

    for the dead, 4:555–557

    eucharistic prayers, 5:279–282, 421–422

    family, 8:735

    Five Pillars of faith, 7:609

    form of worship, 14:852–853

    French School, 13:452

    Greek religion, 6:452–453

    hesychasm, 6:811

    hope, 7:93, 98, 99

    Hortulusa animae, 7:114–115

    Ignatian, 7:308–309

    intercession, 7:519

    interior struggle, 13:431

    Jesuits, 1:325, 326

    Jesus Prayer, 13:450

    Kaddish, 8:107–108

    Leonine Prayers, 8:500

    Leonine Sacramentary, 8:500–502

    Libelli missarum, 8:531–532

    liturgical gestures, 8:647

    Liturgy of the Hours, 8:729

    mahzor structure, 9:49–50

    matins, 9:332–333

    meditative, 9:773

    Memorare, 9:484–485

    Middle Ages, 8:658

    motives for, 11:589–590

    Novena practice of, 10:466–467

    Oratio super populum, 10:621

    Oremus, 10:45, 46, 651

    Psalms, 11:797

    religion, 12:58, 60

    revisions of Good Friday, 10:559

    Roman Rite, 12:328

    Rosary, 12:373–376

    solitude, 13:303

    spirituality, 13:441, 442

    types, 11:592

    vespers, 14:462–463

    virtue of religion, 12:85

    World Day of Prayer for Peace (Assissi, 1986), 12:672

    See also Contemplation; Hail Mary; Lord's Prayer; Mental prayer

Prayer, centering, **11:601**, 13:450

Prayer, in the Bible, 2:377, 8:860, **11:591–593**

Prayer, theology and, **13:923–924**

Prayer, theology of, **11:593–601**

    contemplation, 4:204–205, 208

    for the dead, 4:556–557

    ends and efficacy, 11:594

    lay spirituality, 8:413–414

    mental prayer, 11:597–600

    necessity and obligation, 11:594

    objects and circumstances, 11:596–597

    psychology of, 11:595–596

    qualities, 11:595

    symbolic action, 8:715

    transforming and ecstatic union, 10:109

    value of, 11:593–594

    vocal prayer, 11:600

Prayer and theology, **13:923–924**

Prayer Book (O'Connell), 10:542

Prayer books, 1:455, 9:50, **11:601–606**

    See also Book of Common Prayer

The Prayer Life of a Religious (Resch), 12:137

Prayer of Manasseh, 1:556–557

Prayer of quiet, **11:866**

Prayer of the faithful. *See* General intercessions

Prayers of consecration, 10:636, 637, 638

Prayers of the people. *See* General intercessions

Prayers We Have in Common (ICET), 5:253, 7:525–526

Praying Madonna, 9:272

Praying Together: English Language Liturgical Consultation, 5:254

Preaching, 1:734–735, 2:565–566

    See also Homiletics

Preaching, Canon Law, **11:630–632**

Preaching, history of, **11:606–616**

    6th-9th centuries, 11:611–612

    apostles, 11:606–607

    Greek preaching, 11:609–610

    Honorius III (Pope), 7:84

    Latin preaching, 11:610–611

    medieval period, 11:612–614

    Patristic era, 11:607–611

    Reformation, 11:614

    17th to 19th centuries, 11:614

    Vatican II, 11:615–616

Preaching, homiletic theory of, **11:617–626**

Preaching, medieval English, **11:632–635**

Preaching, theology of, 8:806–807, **11:626–630**

Preambles of Faith, 5:827, **11:635–636**

Preca, George, Bl., **11:636**

Precepts, 7:101–102, **11:636–637**

Precepts, canonical, **11:637–638**

Precepts of Stewardship (NCDC), 10:159

Preces Gertrudianae (St. Gertrude the Great). *See* Insinuationes

The Precious Blood (Faber), 5:582

Precious Blood, devotion to, 3:273, 623, **11:641–642**

Precious Blood, Feast of the, 5:700, 11:642

Precious Blood, in the Bible, **11:638–639**

Precious Blood, theology of, **11:639, 641**

Precious Blood Sisters, 2:644, 674, 8:563, **11:643–645**

    See also Sisters Adorers of the Precious Blood

Precious Blood Society, 2:644, 674–675, 867, 3:622

Precious stones, **11:645–646**

Precious stones, in the Bible, **11:646**

Preconscious, 4:153

Precursor of the Messiah, 7:1013
Predefinition, **11:646–647**
Predermination, 2:50
Predestination
　Francis de Sales, St., 5:866
　Hus, John, 7:228
　Luther, 5:930
　medieval Latin literature, 9:445
　molinism, 9:771–772
　Qur'ān, 7:609
　Remigius of Lyons, St., 12:107
　Semi-Pelagianism, 12:899–900
　Supralapsarians, 13:625–626
Predestination, in Catholic theology,
　6:24, 371, **11:647–653**
　astrology, 1:813
　Augustine, St., 1:861, 883
　Carolingian Renaissance, 3:160
　Charles of the Assumption,
　　3:435–436
　Council of Trent, 8:86
　Divine concurrence, 4:71–72
　Origen, 10:656
　Semi-Pelagianism, 3:206
Predestination, in non-Catholic theology,
　11:653–657, 14:942
　Arminianism, 1:712, 2:894
　Calvinism, 1:712, 2:892–893, 894
　covenant theology, 2:894, 4:328–329
　Daillé, Jean, 4:494
　deism, 4:618
　kismet, 8:185
Predetermination, 4:71–72, 111–113,
　120–121, 10:598, **11:657–659**
Predicables, 1:59, 670, 3:256, 4:52,
　11:659–660, 13:407
　See also Property (logic)
Predication, 1:391, 4:723–724,
　5:310–311, **11:660–661**
Predictamental relations, 12:42
Prediction, 9:340
Die Predigt Jesu vom Reiche Gottes
　(Weiss), 5:331, 7:849
Predis, Cristoforo de, 5:214, 10:868
Preexile period, 10:79
Preexistence, 8:762–763
Preexistence of souls, 10:658
Preface, **11:661–663**
Prefecture of the Papal Household, 3:350
Preferential Option for the Poor, 8:369,
　546–550, 548, 13:244
Pre-Hadrian Sacramentary. *See* Primitive
　Sacramentary
Preininger, Mathias von, 1:117
Prejean, Helen (Sister), 3:85

Prejudice, 7:71, 72, 73, 8:190
Prelates, **11:663**
Prelatial dress, 10:856
Preludes (Meynell, Alice), 9:590
Prémare, Joseph Henri de, **11:663**
*La Premiére idée du Collége de la
　Propagande, ou méoire présenté en
　1589 par Jean Vendville, évêque de
　Tournai, au souverain pontife Sixte V
　(Vendville)*, 14:434
Premonstratensian rite, **11:664–665**
Premonstratensians, 3:68, 69, 601,
　11:665–668
　Anacletus II (Antipope), 1:370
　Antwerp, 1:538
　Austria, 1:910
　Bernard of Fontcaude, 2:313–314
　Conques Abbey, 4:129
　Dodo of Asch, 4:810
　Dominicans, 4:846
　Dryburgh Monastery, 4:913
　England, 5:240
　Floreffe monastery, 5:765–766
　Gregorian reform, 4:479
　hierarchical insignia, 6:764
　Honorius II (Pope), 7:82
　Hroznata, 7:144
　Hugh of Fosse, 7:152
　Kern, J. F., 8:156
　Lucius II, 8:846
　Ludolf of Ratzeburg, 8:852
　Rule of St. Augustine, 1:869
　Scottish religious orders, 12:833
Prémontré Monastery (France), 3:68,
　11:668–669
Premotion, physical, **11:669–672**
　act, 1:75
　Báñez, Domingo, 2:50–51
　Chalmers, William, 3:372
　Divine concurrence, 4:72
　free will, 5:930, 935
　Medina, Bartolomé de, 2:51
　Suárez, Francisco, 4:120
Prendergast, Edmond Francis (Abp. of
　Philadelphia), 11:240, **672**
Prendergast, John J., 12:647
Prephilosophical knowledge of God,
　6:313–314
Prepositinus of Cremona, 3:260
Pre-Quietist mystical movement (Low
　Countries), 10:473
Pre-Reformation crisis, Germany,
　6:178–179
Pres. Church of John's Island, Wilson v.
　(1846), 3:657
Presbyter, Benedict, 8:532

Presbyteral Councils, **11:674–675**
Presbyterian Board of Foreign Missions,
　13:411
Presbyterian Church of the Confederacy,
　11:676
Presbyterian churches in Canada, 12:273
Presbyterian churches in United States,
　11:675–677, 677
　Christian Church merger, 4:117
　church union, 4:199–200
　Congregationalists, 4:11, 115
　Consultation on Common Texts,
　　4:201
Presbyterian missions in Canada, 12:273
Presbyterianism, **11:677–680**
　abolitionism, 1:156
　Anglican Reformation, 1:443
　Briggs, Charles Augustus, 2:616–617
　Cameronians, 2:912
　Campbell, Thomas Joseph, 3:534
　Chalmers, Thomas, 3:372
　Chiniquy, Charles Pascal, 3:517
　Church of Scotland, 12:828–829
　Church-State relations, 3:638
　colonial United States, 3:646, 647,
　　652
　confessions of faith, 4:79, 82
　Covenanters, 4:329–330
　fundamentalism, 6:27
　Indian mission, 7:403
　liturgical calendar, 8:644
　Makemie, Francis, 9:63
　origins, 2:893, 895
　Reformed churches, 12:22
　Scotland, 12:837
　Speer, R. E., 13:411
　Sweden, 1:399
　U.S. church membership, 3:719
　Westminster Confession in, 14:695
Presbyterorum Ordinis (Third Council of
　Baltimore), 3:801–802
Presbyters, **11:672–674**
Presbytery of Philadelphia, 11:675
Prescription, theological use of,
　11:680–681
Presence of God, practice of,
　11:681–682
The Presence of the Kingdom (Ellul),
　5:172
The Present, **11:682**
Presentation Brothers, 3:622, **11:682**,
　12:226
Presentation of Mary, 9:157–158,
　11:682–683
Presentation of the Lord, 3:13–14

Presentation of the Lord, Feast of the. *See* Candlemas

Presentation of the Virgin in the Temple (Titian), 11:*683*

Presentation Order, 10:133, 134, 13:183

Presidential system of government, 6:376–377

Preslav, National Synod of (918), 10:684

Pre-Socratic philosophy, on creator-gods, 6:306–307

Pressensé, E. D. de, 7:848

Preste, F., 5:874

Prester John (mythical Eastern ruler), 5:143, **11:684–685**

Preston, Thomas, 1:355, **11:685**

Preston, Thomas Scott, **11:685–686**

Presumption, 7:102, 9:42, **11:686**

Preternatural, 10:213, **11:686–687**

Pretiosa margarita novella (Petrus Bonus), 1:239

Prêtres Auxiliaires, Missionaires de St. Edmund, 12:545

Prêtres du Sacre-Coeur de Jesus (PSCJ). *See* Betharram Fathers

Preuss, Arthur, 1:355, **11:687–688**

''The Previous Question'' (Gaston), 6:106

La prevue de l'existence de Dieu et l'éternité du monde (Sertillanges), 13:23

Preysing, Konrad von (Bp. of Berlin), 6:186

Pribil, Clement, 8:822

Price, H. H., 4:53

Price, Robert, Ven., 5:236

Price, Thomas. *See* Pormort, Thomas, Bl.

Price, Thomas Frederick, 9:294, 295, **11:688–689**, 12:289, 14:617

See also Maryknoll Fathers and Brothers

Prichard, A. A., 4:673

Prichard, H. A., 2:624

Pricilla (evangelist). *See* Prisca and Aquila

Pride, 7:205, 206, 207, **11:689–690**

Pride of Life (play), 9:882

Prierias, Sylvestro, 8:880

Priest and People (Fichter), 5:709

Priesthood in Christian tradition, **11:690–707**
    Carolingian era, 8:657
    formation of clergy, 8:511
    laicization, 8:284–287
    Latin West, 11:696–698
    Lichtenberg, B., 8:560
    liturgical developments, 11:698–699

    Lutheranism, 8:894
    medieval period, 11:699–701
    modern era, 11:704–706
    New Testament texts, 11:691–693
    ordinations, 10:635–639
    Patristic teaching, 11:693–696
    Serra International, 13:23
    16th century overview, 11:702–704

Priestley, Joseph, 1:835, 5:260

Priestly documents, 11:91–92

Priestly Society of the Holy Cross, 10:617–618

Priestly worship, 8:728

Priestly writers, pentateuchal, **11:707–708**
    Aaron, 1:3
    Abraham, 1:36
    Book of Numbers source, 10:474
    censuses, 3:337–338
    circumcision, 3:737
    corporate life, 8:567
    creation account, 4:337–338
    Deuteronomists, 4:702
    Judah (tribe), 8:1
    Levites, 8:524
    Leviticus, Book of, 8:525
    unleavened bread usage, 14:332–*333*

Priests and priesthood
    African Americans, 1:158–159
    anointing, 1:477
    bishops, 2:415, 416, 417
    celebret, 3:316
    Chrism Mass, 3:526–527
    clerical training in U.S., 13:234
    Holy orders, 7:35, 36
    Marians, 9:159
    messianism, 9:543–544
    19th-20th century overview, 3:621
    ordinations, 7:38–39, 10:637–639
    origins, 7:36
    preaching, 11:631
    religion, 12:62
    religious significance of blood, 2:444
    See also Clerical celibacy/marriage

Priest's Eucharistic League (periodical), 8:184

Priests for the Third World, 1:654, 655

Priests' League for Adoration of the Blessed Sacrament, 5:435

Priests of Chavagnes. *See* Sons of Mary Immaculate of Luçon

Priests of Sacred Heart of Jesus, **12:495–496**

Priests of St. Mary, 2:477–478

Priests of the Good Shepherd, 6:49

Priests of the Sacred Heart of Jesus, 4:613

Priest-worker Movement, 3:466, 13:439

Prignano, Bartolomeo. *See* Urban VI (Pope)

Prignaud, P., 2:380

Prima Clementis, 3:37

Prima Primaria Sodality, 13:294

The Primacy of Charity in Moral Theology (Gilleman), 11:153

Primacy of Jesus Christ, 7:836–837

Primacy of the pope, **11:708–709**
    Amerbach, Veit, 1:349
    Anglican-Catholic dialogue, 1:441–442
    Arévalo, Rodrigo Sánchez de, 1:647
    Augustine of Ancona, 1:870
    Ballarmine's *Controversies*, 2:227
    bishops, 2:414, 3:627
    Boniface VIII (Pope), 3:603
    capitulations, 3:91
    Carolingian reform, 3:599
    conciliarism, 3:604–605, 4:53–58
    Cyprian, St., 4:459
    Donation of Constantine, 4:861
    early Church conflicts, 3:593
    ecclesiology, 5:39–40
    Febronianism, 5:658
    Gallicanism, 3:54
    Gasser, Vinzenz Ferrer, 6:106
    Gelasius I (Pope), St., 6:122
    Gregorian reform, 3:44–45, 47, 600–601, 6:469–471
    Henry III, St., 2:227
    Humbert of Silva Candida, 7:199
    Hus, John, 7:228
    Innocent I (Pope), St., 7:468
    Innocent IV (Pope), 7:475
    John X Camateros, 7:917
    Pithou, Pierre, 6:76
    Pius IX (Pope), Bl., 11:386
    Restoration era, 3:618
    Vatican Council I, 1:85, 526, 2:414, 3:621, 10:848
    See also Febronianism

Primal heavenly man, 10:100

Primal man (Manichaeism), 9:111

Primary and secondary senses (being), 2:207

Primary Chronicle (Nestor), 10:583

Primary matter, 6:327, 9:341–342, 347–348

Primas. *See* Hugh of Orléans

Primasius (Bp. of Hadrumentum), 8:63

Primate of Italy. *See* Pope (title)

Primative Methodists, 9:559

Prime (hours for prayer), 8:610–611

Prime Mover, 4:959

Primeau, Ernest, 10:279

Primer or Office of the Blessed Virgin Marie (Verstegan), 14:460

Primeval age in the Bible, **11:709–713**, 13:143

Primitiva (papal bull, Leo X), 8:487

Primitive, concept of, 8:446

Primitive Advent Christian Church, 1:135

Primitive Culture (Tylor), 1:458–459, 12:64

Primitive sacramentary, 6:473–474

Primitive state, 13:482

Primo felicite elapso (*muto proprio*, Pius XII), 11:400, 12:862

Primo feliciter (papal rescript, Pius XII), 12:862

Primo libro de Motetti (Lasso), 8:342–343

Prímoli, Juan Bautista, **11:713**

Primordia coenobii Gandeshemensis (Roswitha of Gandersheim), 6:86, 9:447

The Prince (Il Principe) (Machiavelli), 4:377, 9:21, 22, 12:118, 124

Prince v. Massachusetts (1944), 3:661

Prince-bishops, **11:713–714**, 12:14

Princeps Pastorum (encyclical, John XXIII), 3:626, 7:936, 937, 9:681

Princes, 9:671

La Princess de Cleves (La Fayette), 2:115

Principatus Romanae ecclesiae, 10:833

Il Principe (The Prince) (Machiavelli), 4:377, 9:21, 22, 12:118, 124

Principe, Walter, 7:528

Principes de la critique historique (Smedt), 13:230

Les Principes de la vie spirituelle (Schrijvers), 12:787

Principia juris publici ecclesiastici (Neller), 5:658

Principia Mathematica (Russell and Whitehead), 8:752, 753, 9:327, 12:415

Principles, 4:780, 915, 5:742–745, **11:715–716**

Principles and Guidelines for Fund Raising in the United States (NCCB), 10:159

Principles of Government (Erthal), 5:330

The Principles of Human Knowledge (Berkeley), 2:298

Principles of Logic (Bradley), 6:712

The Principles of Moral and Political Philosophy (Paley lectures), 10:803

Principles of Philosophy (Descartes), 4:677–678, 680, 681, 12:771

The Principles of Psychology (James), 7:703

Principles of Sociology (Spencer), 13:412, 413

Pringle-Pattison, A. Seth, 11:153

Prinknash Abbey (Gloucester, England), **11:716**

Printed books, **2:520–524**

Printing in the Renaissance, 7:188, 12:118

Printing press, 8:142

Das Prinzip der Hoffnung (Bloch), 14:361

Prior marriage, as impediment to marriage, **11:717**

Prior Park Seminary (England), 2:18

Prioress' Tale (Chaucer), 3:454

Prioresses, **11:717–718**

Priories, **11:718**

Priority of physical premotion, 11:670

Priors, 9:783, **11:716–717**

Priorum quatuor de cultu sanctorum dissertationum vindiciae (Trombelli), 14:213

Prisca, St. *See* Priscilla, St.

Prisca and Aquila (evangelists), 1:562, **11:718–719**

Prisca. See Itala Collectio-Versio

Prisca Versio (canonical collection), **11:719**

Priscian (author), 9:439

Priscilla, St., **11:719**

Priscillian (Bp. of Avila), 3:86

Priscillian (Spanish nobleman), **11:719–720**

Priscillianism, 4:219, 7:236, **11:720–721**, 13:166, 376

Prisco, G., 12:671

Priscus (martyr), 1:927

Priscus of Panion, 2:797–798

Prison reform, 6:18

Prisoners, assistance for, 3:403–404, 409–410, 418–419

Pritchard, Humphrey, Bl., 5:231, **11:722**

Privacy (Weiss), 10:608

Private chapels, 3:523

Private property. *See* Property, private ownership

Privation (philosophy), 5:52, 816, 9:348, **11:722–724**

Privatus of Lambaesis, 5:584

Privilegia, as form, 4:757

Privilegia monasteriorum ex jure communi deducta (Engel), 5:220

Le Prix de la vie (Ollé-Laprune), 10:585

Prizefighting, **11:724–725**

Pro causa italica ad episcopos catholicos (Passaglia), 10:918

Pro ecclesiasticae unitatis defensione (Pole), 11:456

Pro Juárez, Miguel Agustín, Bl., 4:273, 5:174, 7:791, **11:725–726**, *726*

Pro Mundi Vita (Brussels), **11:726–727**

Pro Oriente foundation, 8:232

Pro Ssma. Eucharistia (Skarga), 13:199

Proaño, Leonidas (Bp. of Riobamba, Ecuador), 4:157

Proaño Cuesta, Laurino, Bl., 4:494

Probabiliorism, 1:311, 4:438, **11:727**, 12:726, 14:51

Probabilism, 5:168, 9:863, 879, **11:727**

    Alexandre, Noël, 1:267

    Alphonsus Liguori, St., 1:311, 9:864

    Amort, Eusebius, 1:363

    Ballerini, Antonio, defense of, 2:31

    Caramuel, Juan Lobkowitz, 3:98–99

    casuistry, 3:221

    Comitoli, Paolo, 4:4

    Concina, Daniel, 4:59

    Fagnani, Prospero, 5:588

    forerunners, 8:443

    Medina, Bartolomé de, 9:465

    Sasserath, Rainer, 12:698

Probability, 4:316–317, 7:975

Probable theological notes, 10:455

The Probation (Pazzi), 11:47

Das Problem der Naturrechtslehre (Wolf), 10:194

The Problem of God (Murray), 10:69

The Problem of Method (Sartre), 12:697

"Le Problème de diue d'après M. Edourard Le Roy" (Maréchal), 14:53

Le Problème de l'Église et de l'État au temps de Philippe le Bel (Rivière), 12:262

Le Problème de l'existence de Dieu dans les écrits de s. Thomas d'Aquin (Van Steenberghen), 14:388

Problems of Religious Freedom (Murray), 10:69

Probst, Ferdinand, **11:727–728**

The Proceedings of the North American Academy of Liturgy, 10:433

Procés de Paradis (dramatization), 10:928

Process and Reality (Whitehead), 10:652

Process philosophy, 5:52, 7:356, 359, **11:728–730**

Process theology, 5:52, **11:730–732**

Procession of the Relics of Saint Benedict through the Streets of Valladolid, 12:53

Processions, religious, **11:732–733**, 12:53, 54, *113*, 283

Processions, Trinitarian, **11:733–736**, 12:45, 13:421

Processus and Martinian, SS., cemetery of (Rome), 3:224

Proclus (Greek philosopher), **11:736–737**

  analysis and synthesis, 1:381

  Aristotelianism, 1:670

  Byzantine theology, 2:758, 794, 807, 820

  Liber de causis, 8:533–534

  pantheism, 2:629

  place, 11:401

  Sixtus III (Pope), St., 13:196

Proclus (Patriarch of Constantinople), St., **11:737–738**

  as bishop of Constantinople, 5:759

  Byzantine liturgy, 2:812

  eclecticism, 5:47

  emanationism, 5:181

  existence, 5:533

  knowledge of self, 12:1

  neoplatonism, 10:241

  participation, 10:907

  works, 12:321

Proconsular Acts of Cyprian, 1:92

Procopius of Caesarea, 2:776, 798, 4:189, 8:100–101, **11:738**, 12:320

Procopius of Gaza, 3:258, **11:738–739**

Procreation, 4:218–222, 7:67, 265–266, 13:46–47

Prodigal Son parable, 4:225

Prodigality, 1:928, 9:44

Prodramus, Theodore, 2:803, 805, 806, 824, 3:46

Prodromus Reginae Artium (Papczyński), 10:860

Product scales of measurement, 9:411

Proeve van een Program (Schaepman), 10:262

Profanity, 2:433, **11:739**

  See also Speech, indecent and vulgar

Professio fidei Tridentina (1564), 14:174

Profession of faith, 2:59, **11:739–740**

Profession of faith and oath of fidelity, 1:97, 98, **11:740–743**

Professional ethics, **11:743–745**

Profuturus (Bp.), 2:579

A Program of Catholic Rural Action (O'Hara), 10:566

The Program of Priestly Formation (PPF) (National Conference of Catholic Bishops), 12:898

Les Progrès de l'Amour divin (Yves de Paris), 14:898

Progress and Religion (Dawson), 4:545

Progressive Spiritual Church, 13:437

Progressivism (education), 5:94

Progressivist theory, 6:883–884

Prohetiae Sibyllarum (Lasso), 8:343

Prohibition of alcohol, 13:801

  See also Temperance Movements

Project North (Canada), 3:11

Prokop the Great, 7:231

Prokopovich, Feofan (Abp.), 7:53–54, **11:745–746**, 12:424, 434

Prolegomena (Kant), 9:566

Prolegomena (Wellhausen), 14:676

Pro-life Movement, 7:543, 8:464

Prologus galeatus (St. Jerome), 10:880

Promise, moral obligation of, **11:746**

Promised secrets, 12:859

Promissory oath, 10:497

Promoter of the faith. *See* Devil's advocate

Prompa bibliotheca canonica, juridica, moralis, theologica necnon ascetica, polemica, rubristica historica (Ferraris), 5:693

Promptuarium (Rouille), 10:482

Promulgandi (apostolic constitution, Pius X), 1:77

Prône (vernacular service), **11:746–747**

Pronouncements, papal and curial, **11:747**

Proof, 4:651–654, 5:262, 267, **11:748–749**

Proof of the Apostolic Preaching (St. Irenaeus), 6:112

Propaganda, **11:749**

Propaganda (Ellul), 5:172

Propaganda Fide. *See* Congregation for the Propagation of the Faith

Propagation of the Faith, Congregation for the. *See* Congregation for the Propagation of the Faith

Propassions of Christ, **11:754–755**

Propempticon (Paulinus of Nola), 10:356

Proper of the saints, 8:721

Proper of the time, 8:721

Properties, Divine personal, **11:755**, 14:195–196

Property

  distributism, 4:782–783

  land reform, 13:266

  as predicable, 11:660

private ownership, 8:266

  Church Fathers, 13:252

  Middle Ages, 13:254

  papal social thought, 13:259, 260, 264–266

  St. Thomas, 13:254

  social mortgage, 13:304

  solidarism, 13:300–301

  See also Church property; Poverty

Property (logic), 4:652, 723, **11:755–756**

Property, early church, **11:756–758**

Prophecies, 1:169, 7:631–632, 9:247

Prophecies, in the Bible, 1:363, 545–546, 9:594, **11:758–759**, 13:426, 14:533

Prophecies, theology of, **11:759–764**, 13:1, 100

Prophet, Christ as, 7:807–808, 835

Prophetesses, 11:765

Prophetia, 10:45

Prophetic books of the Old Testament, **11:766**

  authorship, 1:488

  canonicity, 3:24, 25

  covenant, 4:327

  as foretelling, 3:29

  O antiphons text, 10:489

Prophetic Chronicle (Spanish medieval literature work), 9:445–446

The Prophetical Office of the Church (Newman), 10:733

Prophetism, in the Bible, **11:766–767**

Prophetism and religion, 12:62

Prophets, 7:608, 8:179, 9:542–543, 10:79–80, **11:764–765**, 13:762

Prophets, Procession of (play), 4:895–896, 897–898

Propitation, 11:594

Proportionalism, 4:160

Proportionality (morality), 9:867–868

Proportionality, Principle of, **11:767–769**

Proposals against Tradition (Acosta), 1:69

Proposals for the Edition of the Greek Testament (Bentley), 2:288

Proposition 63 (*Syllabus* of Pius IX), 14:256–257

Propositional logic, 8:754

Propositions, 5:742, **11:769–771**

  art, 1:747

  axiomatic system, 1:949

  categories of being, 3:255

  doctrine of propositions, 8:756

  identity, 7:302, 303

  supposition, 13:624

Propositum monasticum de Codice iuris canonici recognoscendo, 4:58–59

Proprietary churches, 3:600, 725, **11:771**
  Belgium, 2:216
  conflicts with laity, 8:294
  Czech lands, 4:479
  England, 5:240
  reform under Gregory VII (Pope) St., 6:472

Proprium theory, 7:443–444

Propter quid (on account of which), 4:651–652, 653, 12:752

Propter quod unumquodque tale et illud magis (Whatever makes a thing to be in a certain way, is that and more so), 12:756

Prosdocimus de Comitibus, 3:52

Prose Writers of Germany (Hedge), 14:148

Prosecution of witches, 14:798–800

Proselytism and proselytizing, 3:661, 4:241–242

Proske, Karl, 2:842

Proslogion (St. Anselm of Canterbury), 1:496, 5:715, 10:601–602

Prosopon union, 10:253

Prospect (monthly), 10:757

Prospects on the Rubicon (Paine), 10:757

Prospectus for the Triumph of Realism (Russman), 5:831

''Prospectus of the Scientific Works Required for the Reorganization of Society'' (Comte), 4:47

Prosper of Aquitaine, St., **11:771–772**
  Augustine, St., 6:112
  Augustinianism, 1:877
  chronicles, 1:461
  Demetrias, St., 4:635
  grace, 6:402
  Patrick. St., 10:954
  predestination, 11:649
  works, 11:772

Prosper of the Holy Spirit, 3:145

Prosser, Philip. *See* Powel, Philip, Bl.

Prost, Joseph (Father), 3:119

Prostitution, **11:772–774**
  contraception, 4:221
  Corinthians Epistles, 4:266
  Israel's traditions, 13:50
  Paul's reflections, 13:48
  rehabilitation, 8:128–129
  sins against sexual order, 8:873–874

Prostitution, sacred, **11:774**, 14:855

Prostration, 8:648

Prosula texts, 13:4

Protagoras (Plato), 5:88

Protagoras of Adbera, 3:351, 7:195, 12:46, 13:323

Protase, St. *See* Gervase and Protase, SS.

Protasov, Nicholas Alessandrovich, 6:459, 12:434

Protection of the Mantle of Our Lady (Pokrov), 9:274

Protée (Claudel), 3:768

Proterius (Patriarch of Alexandria), St., 4:252, **11:775**

Protest (Protestant Oath, 1788), 10:501–502

Protestant churches, 8:694–695, 697, 698, 722, 794, 13:108

Protestant Episcopal Church (U.S.), 5:297

Protestant ethic, 13:255

The Protestant Ethic and the Spirit of Capitalism (Weber), 2:895, 14:667

Protestant Evangelicalism, 9:616

Protestant Methodists, 9:559

Protestant Missionary Societies, 9:693

Protestant Reformation. *See* The Reformation

Protestant Reformation in the British Isles. *See* Anglican Reformation; The Reformation

Protestant Vindicator (newspaper), 10:*169*

Protestant-Catholic dialogue, 9:283–284

Protestant-Catholic relations, 14:542, 796

Du Protestantisme et de toutes les hérésies dans leur rapport avec le socialisme (Nicolas), 10:384

El Protestantismo comparado con el Catolicismo en sus relaciones con la civilización europea (Balmes), 2:33

Protestants and Protestantism
  abolitionism, 1:156, 7:75, 76, 77
  Alphonsus Liguori, St., 1:310
  analogy, 1:373, 379
  Apocalypse iconography, 1:544–545
  apostolic succession, 1:589, 591
  Argentina, 1:650
  biblical canon, 3:20, 21–22, 27, 32
  Bossuet, Jacques Bénigne, 2:550
  Bucer, Martin, 2:653
  Bunsen, Christian Karl Josias von, 2:691–692
  Camisards, 2:916
  capital punishment, 3:87
  Caribbean, 3:112, 114, 115, 116, 118, 120
  Chile, 3:486, 487
  China, 3:499–500, 503–504
  Christian and Missionary Alliance, 3:530
  Christian Endeavor Society, 3:535–536
  Christology, 3:561
  church architecture, 3:711
  civil religion, 3:756
  Civil Rights Movement, 1:160
  confessions of faith, 4:77–82
  conversion to Eastern Orthodoxy, 9:696
  Croatia, 4:370
  deconstructionism, 4:594–595
  dogmatic theology, 4:812
  Europe, 10:841
  expression of baroque spirit, 2:112
  Franciscan Observants, 3:463
  free will, 5:930
  fundamentalism, 6:27–29
  German culture, 6:183
  Great Awakening, 6:425–426
  Henry VIII, 6:741
  Honduras, 7:74
  hope as unnecessary, 7:101
  Hussitism, 7:230
  hymns and hymnals, 7:255–258, 262
  incorporation into the Church, 7:382
  Journal de Trévoux, 3:295
  Lawrence of the Resurrection, 3:137
  Mary Tudor, 9:293–294
  medical ethics, 9:429
  Methodism, 9:558
  Mexico, 9:579
  natural law doctrine, 10:191–192
  neo-orthodoxy movement, 10:238–239
  Poland, 11:443–444
  Protestant ethic, 13:255
  Puerto Rico, 11:814
  sexual reorientation, 7:69
  social gospel, 13:241–242
  Socianism, 13:290–291, *291*
  spirituals, 13:456–457
  Sweden, 13:636
  Ten Commandments, 4:6
  theology, 3:589, 13:910, 911, 912
  tradition and scripture, 14:137
  U.S. church membership, 3:719
  Wales, 14:612
  women as deacons, 4:554

See also Calvinism; *Institutes* of Calvin; Lutheranism; Mission, Protestant; Puritans; The Reformation; The Reformation in the British Isles; The Reformation on the Continent; *specific Protestant sects*

Protestation of Allegiance (1603), 10:499

"Protestation of St. Louis," 6:424

Protmann, Regina, Bl., **11:775**

Proto-Byzantine era, 5:313

Protocanonical books, 3:20, 26, 28

Protocol of London (1830), 6:436

Proto-Evangelium, 10:62, **11:775–777**

Protoevangelium Jacobi, 1:468–469, 558–559

Protoevangelium of James, 9:274–275

Protoiereus (ranks of married clergy), 1:635

Protonica (Empress of Rome), 4:384–385

Protoromanticism, 12:345

Protrepticus (Clement of Alexandria), 5:510

Protus and Hyacinth, SS., **11:777**

Prou, E., 10:774

Proudhon, Pierre Joseph, 1:384, 3:620, 5:397, 13:128

Prouerbiorum libellus (Vergil), 14:449

Proulx, Armadee Wilfrid (Bp. of Portland, ME), 11:532

Proust, Eutropius, 6:196

Proust, J. L., 1:835

Provencher, Joseph Norbert, 2:215, 3:8, 11:*777*, **777–778**

Proverbia (Othlo), 10:709

Proverbia (Wipo), 9:449

Proverbs, Book of, **11:778–780**
  beatitudes, 2:177
  creation, 4:341
  enmity, 5:264
  erotic love, 13:50
  Fortem viril pectore (office hymn), 5:820
  hatred, 6:666
  lying as sin, 8:900
  serpent as symbol, 13:20
  sheol (death), 13:79
  simplicity, 13:137
  sin, 13:145
  social principle, 13:248
  soul, 13:336
  spirit, 13:424
  wisdom personified, 8:760

Proverbs of Solomon. *See* Proverbs, Book of

Provida (Pius X), 10:218

Provida Mater Ecclesia (apostolic constitution, Pius XII), 11:400, 12:861–862

Providas (papal bull, Benedict XIV), 12:857

Providence, method of, 4:589

Providence College (RI), 12:*215*

Providence Diocese (RI), 6:653

Providence of God, in the Bible, **11:780–781**

Providence of God, theology of, 4:344, 9:61, 10:178, **11:781–784**

Providential history, 6:882

Providentissimus Deus (encyclical, Leo XIII), 5:523, 6:793, 7:494–495, 10:335, 11:478, **784–785**
  biblical exegesis, 8:492
  biblical study, 13:457, 458

Provinciale (seu Constitutiones Angliae) (Lyndwood), 8:905

Provinciale ordinis fratrum minorum (Paulinus of Venice), 11:39

Provinciales (Pascal), 5:851

The Provisional Regulations for Saint Joseph's Sisters, 13:173

Provisionis nostrae (papal bull, Gregory XIII), 2:19

Provisions, **11:785–786**
  conciliarism, 4:54–55, 171
  impact on nepotism, 10:247
  Louis IX, 8:801
  papacy, 3:602–603, 780, 5:242
  Sewal de Bovill, 13:44

Provisors, Statute of (England, 1351), 3:604, 4:318, 5:242, **11:786**, 12:6

Provoost, Samuel (Bp. of New York), 5:297

Provost, James H., 4:30, **11:786–787**

Proximate to faith theological note, 10:454

Proxy (Canon Law), **11:787**

Prudence, **11:787–792**
  art, 1:746
  Burke, Edmund, 2:702
  character, 3:388
  cogitative power, 3:824
  conscience, 4:145
  deliberation, 4:629
  discernment, spiritual, 4:765–766
  docility, 4:797
  gift of counsel, 4:306
  man, natural end of, 9:97

Prudentius (Spanish poet), 11:352, **792–793**

Prudentius of Troyes, St., 1:461, 4:*565*, 7:253, 8:314, **11:793**

Prüm Abbey, (Germany), 1:491, 3:572, **11:793**

Prümm, K., 10:98

Prümmer, Dominikus, 4:43, **11:793–794**, 12:4, 777

Prussia, 3:845–846, 8:253–255, 11:376
  See also Germany

Prussia, Albrecht of Brandenburg-Ansbach, Duke of, **1:233–234**, 8:889

Prussian Academy of Sciences (Berlin), 5:256

Prussian Union, 4:81

Psallendum, 10:45

Psalmenstudien (Mowinckel), 10:36

Psalmody, 1:57, 3:318, 8:733

In Psalmos Davidis expositio (Aquinas), 14:25

Psalms, 1:305–306, 809, 2:812
  alphabetic, 1:305–306
  penitential, 4:225, 11:73–74
  responsorial, 3:75, 6:413, 12:142
  royal, 9:541–542

Psalms, Book of, **11:794–797**
  acrostics, 1:72
  beatific vision, 2:171
  beatitudes, 2:177, 178
  Canticle of Judith, 8:45
  Christian law, 8:403
  Communion antiphons, 4:32
  creation, 4:341
  curse of enemy, 4:442
  Diodore of Tarsus, 4:750
  Divine judgment, 8:27–28, 32
  edification, 5:84
  El (God), 5:143
  enmity, 5:264
  Eusebius' commentaries, 5:452
  exegesis, 8:332
  glory, 6:244
  glory of God (end of creation), 6:245, 246
  heart, 6:681
  heaven, 6:684
  Hebrew poetry, 6:692–695
  holiness of man, 9:87
  hope of salvation, 7:106
  ineffability of God, 7:445
  inheritance, 7:464
  Jesus as Lord, 8:781
  justice of God, 8:70, 72
  justice of men, 8:73–74

Psalms, Book of (continued)

justification, 8:76

Kingdom of God, 8:172, 173

kingship, 8:179

lauds, 8:379, 380

Leviathan, 8:522

light of glory, 8:584

Lord as honorific title, 8:780

Lord's Day, 8:782

love and justice, 8:65

lying as sin, 8:900

Magi, 9:34

maker of man, 9:87

name of God, 6:298

names for God, 13:77

peace, 11:49

prayer times, 8:729

redemption from sin, 11:966

resurrection of the dead, 12:177

rites of death, 4:10

ritual bathing and purification, as symbol of baptism, 2:57–58

Seton, E., 13:34

Seven Last Words, 13:37, 37–38

Shaddai, 13:58

Shechem, 13:72

sin, 13:142, 144, 145

Son of David, 13:310

soul, 13:336

spirit, 13:424

spirit of God, 13:426, 427

temptation, 13:815

terms for man, 13:316

Word of God, 8:759

See also Penitential Psalms

The Psalms Hymns and Spiritual Songs of the Old and New Testament, Faithfully Translated into English Metre. See New England Psalm Book

The Psalms in Israel's Worship (Mowinckel), 10:36

The Psalms of David Imitated in the Language of the New Testament (Watts), 11:798

Psalms of Solomon, 1:555–556

Psalms of Thomas, 5:82

Psalmus abededarius contra partem Donati (St. Augustine), 1:72

The Psalter. *See* Psalms, Book of

Psalter, common, 4:201

Psalterium Romanum (Jerome), 14:593

Psalters, 4:393

Psalters, metrical, 7:255–256, **11:797–798**, 13:456

PSCJ (*Prêtres du Sacre-Coeur de Jesus*). *See* Betharram Fathers

Pseaume, Nicholas, **11:798–799**

Psellus, Michael, 4:176, 177

Pseudo-Ambrose. *See* Ambrosiaster

Pseudo-Apostles. *See* Apostolici

Pseudo-Aristotle, 13:100

Pseudo-Barnabas, 1:587

See also Apostolic Fathers

Pseudo-Chrysostom, 5:279

Pseudo-Clementines (early Christian writings), **11:799–800**

Pseudo-Dionysius (unknown author), 11:290, **800–802**

Adam Pulchrae Mulieris, 1:110

Albert the Great, St., 1:226

Alexander of Hales, 1:266

analogy, 1:371

angels, 1:414, 419, 420, 425

apophatic theology, 1:568

Aristotelianism, 1:670

art, 1:743

beauty, 2:184

Bonaventure, St., 2:482, 485, 491, 492

burial, 2:699

Byzantine theology, 2:769, 793–794

Carthusian spirituality, 3:192

connatural knowledge, 8:205

contemplation, 4:206

Denis of Paris, St., 4:660–661

emanationism, 5:181

exemplarism, 5:533

happiness, 6:637

Hugh of Saint-Victor, 7:158

Hypatius of Ephesus, 7:262

John Scotus Eriugena, 7:1009–1010

Lefèvre influenced, 8:449

light symbolism, 3:674

Maximus the Confessor, 2:821

mysticism, 2:826

notions of light, 8:583

order of universe, 14:329

priesthood, 11:697–698

prophecy, 11:760

publication of works, 13:300

schools of Athens, 1:829

Sirmond's distinction, 13:168

spiritual life, 13:433, 436

spirituality, 13:444, 446

three ways, 14:65

translated into Syriac, 13:16

Pseudo-Gelasian Decree, 1:558

Pseudo-Grosseteste, **6:538–539**

Pseudo-Isidore, 5:615–619

Pseudo-Isidorian collection. *See* False Decretals (Pseudo-Isidorian Forgeries)

Pseudo-Isidorian forgeries. *See* False Decretals (Pseudo-Isidorian Forgeries)

Pseudo-Marcellus, 13:131

Pseudonymity, **1:487–488**

Psychics, **11:802**

Psychoanalytic iconology, 7:287

Psychoanalytic reading approach, 10:307

Psychological hedonism, 6:701

Psychologism, 7:229, **11:802–803**

Psychology

Aristotelianism, 1:678

associationism, 1:795–797

attrition, 4:226, 227

Bruno de Jésus-Marie, 2:647

Christian philosophy, 3:540

consciousness, 4:153, 154

conversion, 4:238–239

courage, 4:316

culture, 4:430, 431–433

direction, spiritual, 4:763

dreams, 4:904–905

educational theories, 5:91

existential, 5:541–543

freedom, 7:172–173

guilt, 6:567–568

habits, 6:602

homosexuality, 7:67–69

man, natural end of, 9:99–100

measurement in, 9:410–412

philosophy, 11:278–279

philosophy of nature, 11:305

sadness, 12:525

space, 13:373

Treasure of Life (Mānī), 9:113

Psychology (Sartre), 12:697

Psychology, classical, 4:45, 10:20–21, **11:803–807**

Psychomachia (Prudentius), 4:565, 11:792, 14:556

Psychometry, 3:759

Psychophysical scales of measurement, 9:411

Ptah (Egyptian god), 4:337

Ptolemaic astronomy, 12:804–805, 813

Ptolemaic rulers (Egypt), 5:116

Ptolemaic Dynasty, 7:644

Ptolemy (Greek astronomer), **11:807–808**, 12:308

Almagest, 12:805

Aristotelianism, 1:669, 674

astrological fatalism, 5:636

astrology, 7:114

astronomy, 12:805

Columbus, Christopher, 3:865

Decapolis, 4:588

exegetical works, 5:509

geocentrism, 6:59

space, 13:374

Ptolomeo of Lucca. *See* Bartholomew of Lucca (Bp. of Torcello)

Public law, 13:480

Public morality, 10:198

Public office, 3:651, 652, 653–654, 9:304–305

Public order (Canon Law), **11:808–809**

Public peace, 13:486–487

Public propriety, impediment to marriage, 4:65, **11:809**

Public schools, 3:655–656

See also Education

The Public Servant (Fitzpatrick), 5:753

Public Worship Regulation Act (England, 1874), 1:444, 447

Publicans, **11:809–810**

Publishing

Hong Kong periodicals, 7:77

liturgical movement, 8:672, 673

liturgical music, 8:687, 706

Sheed and Ward, 13:73

Skillin, E., 13:205

United States, 8:842

Publius Lentulus, 7:857

Publius Ovidius Naso, 10:727, 12:307, 310

Pucci, Antonio Maria, St., **11:810**

Puccini, Giacomo, **11:810**

Pucelle, Jean, 11:604–605, **811**, 12:486

Pudendorf, Samuel von, 10:182

Pudens, Pudentiana, and Praxedes, SS., **11:811–812**

Pudens, St, 11:811–812

Pudentiana, St. *See* Pudens, Pudentiana, and Praxedes, SS.

Pudsey, Hugh, 8:408

Puebla (CELAM meeting, 1972), 8:547, 548

Puebla (Mexico) Conference (1979), **11:812–813**

Puebla Document (DP), 10:615–616

Pueblo people, 3:714

Pueblo Revolt (1680), 1:687

Puech, Abbé Emile, 5:51

Puerto, Nicolás del (Bp. of Oaxaca, Mexico), **11:813**

Puerto Rico, 3:110, 112, **11:813–814**, 12:281

demographic statistics, 11:814

map, 11:*815*

missions, 8:18

Pufendorf, Samuel von, 5:255, 256, 262, 8:901

Pugin, A. C., 3:709

Pugin, Augustus Welby, **11:814–815**

Gothic architecture, 1:745, 3:694

Gothic revival, 3:709, 715

Renaissance architecture, 3:699

symbolism, 3:675

Puig, Narciso, 12:773

Pujo, Maurice, 1:82

Pulcheria, St., 3:363, **11:815**

Pulci, L., 1:764

Puliat, Adrian, 3:10

Pulpit Law (1871), 8:254

Pulpits. *See* Ambos

Punch, John, **11:815–816**

Puniet de Parry, Pierre de, **11:817**

Punishment, **11:817–818**

Assyrian law, 8:395

Babylonian law, 8:395

clemency, 3:772

damnation, 4:506

the discipline, 4:774–775

Juizo da verdadeira causa do Terremoto (Malagrida), 9:65–66

penal justice, 8:69

sanction, 12:660

sanction, Divine, 12:660–661

suffering for sin, 13:586

vengeance, 14:438–439

witchcraft, 14:798–800

Pupienus Maximus (Roman Emperor), 12:312

Purāṇas (Hindu legends), 6:848

Purcell, Edward, Rev., 5:145, 11:820

Purcell, Harold, **11:818**

Purcell, Henry, 2:114, **11:818–819**, *819*

Purcell, John Baptist (Abp. of Cincinnati), 3:735–736, 5:144–145, 796, 10:569, **11:819–821**, 12:546–547

Burnett, Peter Hardeman, 2:708

Campbell, Alexander, 2:917

Civil War, 13:405

Precious Blood Society, 2:644

slavery, 1:156

Purcell, Mannix v. (1888), 3:656

Purcell, Patrick, 7:582

Pure acts, 1:73, **11:821**

Bonaventure, St., 2:488

causality, 3:302

concept of God, 13:139

exercise of will's freedom, 10:26

God as being, 14:230

identity principle, 7:303–304

immutability of God, 7:356

impassibility of God, 7:359

Leibniz, 8:458

living God, 8:572

omnipotence of God, 10:592

Pure and impure, 4:742–743, 8:509, 525, **11:821–823**, 13:148–149, 159

Pure Land Buddhism, 1:358, 2:453, 663, 664, 665, 668

Pure nature, state of, 1:883, 892, 4:68, 694, 10:213, **11:823–824**

Pure potency, 11:556–557

Purgative contemplation, 11:833–834

Purgatorio (Dante), 14:246

Purgatory, **11:824–829**

in the Bible, 11:824–825

Catherine of Genoa, St., 3:271

charnel houses, 3:437

Council of Florence, 3:26, 572

Divine judgment, 8:32–33, 38

hope as necessity in, 7:101

immortality, 7:354

prayers for the dead, 4:556–557

Reformation, 5:344

souls praying, 11:596

theology, 11:825–829

Purgatory, St. Patrick's, **11:829–830**

Purification, 8:40, **11:830–831**, 14:660, 853–854

Purification, in the Bible, **11:831–832**

Purification, spiritual, 4:530, 8:469–470, 10:106, **11:832–834**, 13:148

Purification in the Temple (Memling), 7:*453*

Purification of Mary, 3:14, 15, 8:642–643, 856, **11:834**

Purim, Feast of, 5:408, **11:834–836**

La Purisima Concepción (San Antonio, TX), 12:639

Purism (architecture), 3:680–681

Puritans, **11:836–840**, *837*

Anglican Reformation, 1:443–444

Baptist branches, 2:78

Book of Advertisements, 1:136

Bradford, William, 2:576

Bunyan, John, 1:292, 2:692–693

Calvinism, 2:894, 895

Cambridge Platform, 2:907–908

Cambridge University, 2:906

Caribbean, 3:111, 120

Puritans *(continued)*
   Cartwright, Thomas, 3:197
   Christmas, 3:554
   Church-State relations, 3:638, 640, 645
   Congregationalism, 4:114–115
   Cotton, John, 4:292
   covenant theology, 4:328–329
   Coverdale, Miles, 4:331
   crib customs, 4:364
   Dwight, Timothy, 4:957
   Elizabeth I, 2:689, 12:11
   Hooker, Richard, 7:90–92
   Hooker, Thomas, 7:92
   hymnody, 7:256–257
   latitudinarianism, 8:370
   Laud, W., 8:377
   Massachusetts, 9:304
   Milton, John, 9:641, 643
   repression under Elizabeth I, 11:679
   Sabbatarianism, 12:454–455
   Seekers, 12:875–876
   United States, 3:640, 645, 646–647
"Purple Christ," 11:*164*
"Purple Rose." *See* Rafqa de Himlaya, St.
Purpose of Amendment, **11:840–841**, 13:157
Pursley, Leo A. (Bp. of Indianapolis), 7:416
Pūrva Mīmāṁsā (Hindu philosophy), 6:845–846
Pūrvas (Jain texts), 7:697
Purvey, John, **11:841**
Pusey, Edward Bouverie, 5:795, 10:733, 735, 11:*841*, **841–842**
   Anglo-Catholics, 1:444
   branch theory of the Church, 2:582
Pusillanimity, 9:42, **11:842**
Pustet, Anton, 11:842
Pustet, Friedrich, 3:380, 11:842
Pustet family, **11:842**
Puthenparampil, Thommachan, 7:406
Putin, Vladimir, 12:430
Putman, J. (Father), 3:117
Putnam Bill (United States, 1855), 8:200
"Putting on the new man" through baptism, 2:66
Putzer, Joseph, **11:842–843**
Puvis de Chavannes, P., 3:713
PVMI (Parish Visitors of Mary Immaculate), 10:891
Pynson, Richard, 2:523
Pyramid of the Sun (Teotihuacon, Mexico), 13:*808*

Pyromancy, 4:785
Pyrrho of Elis, 11:843
Pyrrhonism, 6:442, **11:843**, 12:47, 13:201
Pyrrhus I (Patriarch of Constantinople), 2:749, 7:81, **11:843–844**, 13:872
Pytel, Ronald, 3:*61*
Pythagoras and the Pythagoreans, **11:844–846**
   afterlife, 1:166, 167
   Anaxagoras, 1:393
   asceticism, 1:773, 773–774
   astrology, 1:811
   atomism, 1:831, 832
   causality, 3:297
   Clarenbaud of Arras, 3:762
   deification, 6:444–445
   dualism, 4:914
   early Christian theology, 3:591
   infinity, 7:456
   mathematics, 9:325–326
   metempsychosis, 5:929
   number symbolism, 3:673, 812
   order of universe, 14:328
   physical sciences, 12:801–802
   teacher and missionary, 6:446
   transmigration of souls, 7:347, 14:156
Pythagorean theorem, 11:845
Pyx, 8:632, **11:846**

Q

Q Document (Synoptic Gospels), 13:696–697
Qajar Dynasty, 11:141
Qalat Sem'an Monastery (Syria), 3:685
Qarqafel, Synod of (1806), 1:195, 526
Qatar, **11:847**
Qatrāyâ, Abraham Bar Lipāh, 5:6
Qatrāyâ, Gabriel Bar Lipāh, 5:5
Qianlong (Ch'ien-lung) (Emperor of China), 3:498
Qin Shi Huangdi (Shih Huang-ti) (Emperor of China), 3:509
Qoheleth, words of. *See* Ecclesiastes, Book of
QS. *See* Dead Sea Scrolls
Quadhalf, Mu'ammar Abu Minyar al-, 8:559
Quadragesimo anno (encyclical, Pius XI), 1:915, 3:420, 620, 4:19, 5:95, 206, 10:850, 11:393, 512–513, 566, **847–848**, 13:567, 569, 14:251, 453
   morality and social order, 13:246–247

   social justice, 13:243
   subsidiarity, 13:259
   work, 13:262
Quadratus, St., 1:567, 587, 666, **11:848**
   See also Apologists, Greek; Apostolic Fathers
Quadripartitum (Claudius Ptolemaeus), 5:636
Quadripartitum (Richard of Wallingford), 12:236
Quadrivium, 3:262
Quadrupani, Carlo Giuseppi, **11:848**
Quae divinitus (apostolic constitution, Pius XI), 11:76
Quae honorem Conditoris (papal bull, Innocent IV), 3:132, 141
Quae maiori (papal decree, John Paul II), 7:400
Quae mari sinico (apostolic letter, Leo XIII), 11:258
Quaestio, as form, 4:605–606
Quaestio disputata de virtutibus (St. Thomas of Aquinas), 12:748, 14:21, 25
Quaestio Episcopus et quidam rector curatus (Tudeschis), 14:235
Quaestiones (St. Augustine), 5:512
Quaestiones (Seripando), 13:17
Quaestiones (Thomas of Buckingham), 14:31
Quaestiones de quolibet (Aquinas), 14:25
Quaestiones de sacramentis (William of Melitona), 14:744
Quaestiones disputatae (Nicholas Trevet), 10:381
Quaestiones disputatae (Richard of Conington), 12:232
Quaestiones disputatae (Richard of Middleton), 12:234
Quaestiones disputatae (Simon Hinton), 13:129
Quaestiones disputatae (Thomas of Wilton), 14:39
Quaestiones disputatae 'antequem esset frater' (Alexander of Hales), 1:265
Quaestiones disputatae et de quolibet (Gonsalvus Hispanus), 6:340–341
Quaestiones duodecim ss. theologiae studiosis (Rolevinck), 12:293
Quaestiones hebraicae in Genesium (St. Jerome), 5:515
Quaestiones Mellicenses (Nicholas of Dinkelsbühl), 10:376
Quaestiones Mercuriales (Joannes Andreae), 7:881–882
Quaestiones metaphysicales (Trombetta), 14:213

Quaestiones naturales (Adelard of Bath), 9:453

Quaestiones ordinariae (Thomas of Sutton), 14:37

Quaestiones selectae ex theologica dogmatica (Schmid), 12:743

Quaestiones statutorum (Alberic of Ostia), 1:219

Quaestiones super libros Sententiarum (Robert Holcot), 12:265

Quaestiones super librum Priorum Analyticorum (Richard of Campsall), 12:232

Quaestiones super librum sextum metaphysicorum (Thomas of Sutton), 14:37

Quaestiones theologiae (Remigio de' Girolami), 12:106

Quaestiones veneriales and *dominicales* (Bartholomew of Brescia), 2:125

Quaestionum philosophicarum libri quinque (Maurus), 9:374

Quakers (Religious Society of Friends), **6:3–5**

   abolitionism, 1:156

   Anabaptists, 1:369

   capital punishment, 3:87, 88

   Church-State relations, 3:646, 647, 648, 651, 652

   community churches, 4:39

   discrimination and persecution, 6:3

   Fox, George, 5:837–838

   justification, 8:87

   pacifism, 10:*746*

Qualitative measurement, 9:409–410

Qualitative motion (alteration), 10:17–18

Quality, 1:61, 78, 4:777, 8:201, 10:17–18, **11:848–852**

   See also Being

Quam singulari (papal decree, St. Pius X), 11:390

Quamis iusto (papal constitution, Benedict XIV), 5:530

Quanta cura (encyclical, Pius IX), 3:620, 5:855, 968, 10:261, 11:387, **852**

   liberalism, 3:619

Quantitative measurement, 9:409, 410–411

Quantity, **11:853–855**

   abstraction, 1:48

   accident, 1:61

   motion in category, 10:18

   quality, 11:850–851

   Suarezianism, 13:562

   See also Being

Quantum praedecessores (papal bull, Eugene III), 2:688, 4:410

Quantum theory, 4:217, 9:418

Quaracchi (college) (Florence, Italy), **11:855–856**

Quarantotti, G. B., 5:184

Quaresmio, Francesco, **11:856**

Quarles, Francis, 2:162

Quarr Abbey (Isle of Wight), 2:231, **11:856**, *857*, 13:300

Quarter, William (Bp. of Chicago), 3:475–476, **11:856–857**

Quarterly Review, 10:314

Quartodecimans, 3:592, 5:13, 8:642, **11:857**, 12:351

Quas primas (encyclical, Pius XI), 7:164, 8:284, 11:393, **857**, 12:493

Quasten, Johannes, **11:857–858**

Les Quatre concordats (Pradt), 11:577–578

Quatrefoil and cruciform baptismal fonts, 2:75, 76

Quattor abhinc annos (indult, John Paul II), 8:365

Quattro Libri (Palladio), 3:701

Quattuour libri sententiarum Petri Lombardi (Estius), 5:375

Québec (Canada), 3:4–6, 7, *8*, 9–10, 7:144, 9:721

Québec, plenary council (1909), 5:186

Québec Act (Canada, 1774), 3:7, 177, 5:182, 10:322, 501, **11:858–859**

Québec Archdiocese (Canada), 2:204, 8:382, 383

Quebec Cathedral (Anglican), 3:715

Quedlinburg Convent (Germany), **11:859–860**

Quedlinburg Synod (1085), 7:155

Queen Hatshepsut, Temple of (Luxor, Egypt), 13:*805*

Queen Isabella Foundation, 4:533

Queen Mary's Psalter (prayer book), 11:*603*

The Queen's Work (periodical), 6:96, 8:779, 13:294

Queenship of Mary, 9:158

Quélen, Hyacinthe Louis de (Abp. of Paris), 2:476, 5:854, 8:271, 272, 11:*860*, **860**

Quellinus, Artus, 1:539

Quem queritis in presepe?, 4:895

Quem Terra, Pontus, Sidera (hymn), **11:860**

Quenstedt, Johann Andreas, **11:861**

Quentin, Henri, **11:861**

Quentin, St., 12:582

Querbes, Louis Joseph, 14:471

Quercia, Jacopo della, 13:109

Querini, Angelo Maria (Card.), 14:902–903

Querini, Pietro, 2:898

Quesnel, François, 3:337

Quesnel, Pasquier (Paschase), 3:614, **11:861–862**, 14:51

   Alexandre, Noël, 1:268

   Anthelmi, Joseph, 1:502

   Arnauld, Antoine, 7:717

   attrition, 1:843

   battle of pamphlets, 8:804

   censure, 5:761

   Clement XI (Pope), 3:789

   laicism, 8:282

   religious experience, 5:555

   Sabran, Louis de, 12:464

   supernatural destiny, 4:694

   See also Jansenism

Quesnelliana Collectio (canonical collection), 3:39, 40, 42, 59, **11:862–863**

The Quest: History and Meaning in Religion (Eliade), 5:155

The Quest for Being (Hook), 10:205

The Quest for Certainty (Dewey), 7:501, 10:205

The Quest of the Historical Jesus (Schweitzer, tr. by Montgomery), 5:521

La Question Américaine (Rouquette), 12:391

Questions and Solutions Concerning First Principles (Damascius), 10:241

Les Questions liturgiques (Beauduin), 2:183, 8:672

Questions on Evangelical Perfection (Peter John Olivi), 5:899

Quétif, Jacques, **11:863**

Quevedo, Francisco de, 1:236, 2:115

Quevedo, Juan de (Bp. of Darien, Panama), 4:288, **11:863**

Qui major (papal bull, Innocent III), 2:688

Qui pluribus (encyclical, Pius IX), 3:101, 5:712, 11:384–385, 14:139

Quia (because the fact that), 4:652, 12:752

Quia contingit (apostolic constitution, Clement V), 7:129

Quickborn Youth Movement, 3:711

Quicumque Christum Quaeritis (hymn), **11:863–864**

Quicumque-vult. See Athanasian Creed

Quiddity, 11:659, **864–865**

   abstraction, 1:46

   Avempace, 1:932

Quiddity *(continued)*
    categories of being, 3:256
    cogitative power, 3:823
    concept, 4:51
    God's primacy of being, 13:139
    reflection, 12:2
    species, 13:407
    time, 14:83
Quidquid recipitur ad modum recipientis recipitur (Whatever is received is received after the mode of the one receiving), 12:756
Quiercy, Councils of (754-858), 11:783, **865**
Quierzy, Synod of (838), 1:329
Quiet, prayer of, 4:205, **11:866**
Quiet Revolution (Canada), 3:10
Quietism and Semiquietism, 3:614, 5:682, **11:866–867**
    activism, 1:84
        Argentré, Charles du Plessis d', 1:657
        Billuart, Charles René, 2:396
        Bossuet, Jacques Bénigne, 2:550, 3:614
        Brancati, Lorenzo, 2:581–582
        Brisacier, Jacques Charles de, 2:619
        condemnation, 5:851–852, 10:844
        conformity, 4:93
        heresy, 6:777
        hope as unnecessary, 7:101
        Innocent XII (Pope), 7:482
        Lawrence of the Resurrection, 3:137
        Le Masson, 8:465
        Malebrance, Nicolas, 9:74
        Réponse générale (Malebranche), 9:74
        Traité de l'amour de Dieu (Malebranche), 9:74
        voluntarism, 14:582
Quigley, James Edward (Abp. of Chicago), 3:478, 12:541–542
Quigley Prepatory Seminary South (IL), 9:588
Quigly, Anthony, 3:111, 7:699
Quimby, Phineas P., 10:308–309
Quimperlé Abbey (France), **11:867–868**
Quinctian of Clermont, St., **11:868**
Quincy, Josiah, 3:472
Quine, W. V. O., 11:552, 14:326–327
Quinet, Camille, 3:244
Quinet, Edgar, 1:519, 5:969
Quinisext Synod (691-692), 4:186, **11:868**
    Byzantine Church, 2:750, 760
    Canon Law, 3:37, 41, 45–46

    clerical celibacy/marriage, 3:324
    condemnation of Honorius I (Pope), 4:193
    deacons, 4:551
    Justinian II, 8:102
    primacy of Constantinople, 2:821
    Sergius I (Pope), St., 13:14
Quinlan, John (Bp. of Mobile, AL), 1:201, 9:748–749
Quinlan, Karen Ann, 5:458
Quinn, John J. (Abp. of San Francisco), 2:871, 3:58
Quinn, John R., Rev., 12:647, 649–650
Quiñones, Francisco de (Card.), 2:524, 8:661, 730, **11:868–869**
Quinque Compilationes Antiquae (decretal collections), 2:314–315, 3:48, 8:352, **11:869**
Quinque viae ("Five ways"). *See* God, proofs for the existence of
Quintana, Andrés, 2:863
Quintillian, 5:90
Quirinal Palace (Rome), 3:793
Quiroga, Facundo, 2:468
Quiroga, Gaspar de, 4:111
Quiroga, Vasco de (Bp. of Michoacán), 3:415, 11:*870*, **870–871**
Quis dives salvetur? (St. Clement of Alexandria), 3:798
Quis sit orationis et paentitentiae usus (Acquaviva), 1:72
Quispel, Gilles, 6:263
Quivil, Peter, 5:530
Qumran community, 4:561, **11:871–873**
    Abba (term), 1:6
    agape, 1:170
    Annunciation, 1:476
    apocalyptic style, 1:546
    Bible texts, 2:359, 360
    biblical archaeology, 2:380
    biblical canon, 3:25–26
    bishops, 2:411
    Book of Jubilees, 1:549
    catechumenate, 3:249
    communal life, 3:546
    Dead Sea Scrolls discovery, 4:561, 563–564
    described, 8:6
    discernment, spiritual, 4:765
    early Christian theology, 3:591
    Essenes, 8:6
    Johannine studies, 5:522
    John the Baptist, St., 7:1014–1015
    Kingdom of God, 8:172, 173
    leprosy, 8:510
    midrashic literature, 9:619–620

    New Testament scholarship, 10:305
    Paul, St., 11:9
    ritual bathing and purification, 2:58
    sacred meals, 5:413
    See also Dead Sea Scrolls
Qumran Scrolls (QS). *See* Dead Sea Scrolls
Quo est (that which by which a thing is), 12:752–753
Quo graviora (apostolic constitution, Leo XII), 3:101
Quo Vadis? (Where are you going?), **11:873–874**
Quod aliquantum (papal brief, Pius VI), 11:377
Quod de fovenda (apostolic letter, Benedict XV), 11:390
Quod divina sapientia (papal bull, Leo XII), 2:475, 8:490
Quod est (that which is), 12:752–753
Quod maxime (*motu proprio*, Pius XI), 11:485
Quod nemo laeditur (St. John Chrysostom), 7:948
Quod omnis probus liber sit (Philo Judaeus), 5:368–369
Quodlibet (Peter Thomae), 11:208, 12:748
Quodlibeta (Richard of Conington), 12:232
Quodlibeta (Richard of Middleton), 12:234
Quodlibeta (Robert of Orford), 14:45
Quodlibeta I-V (Nicholas Trevet), 10:381, 14:46
Quodlibetal Questions (Duns Scotus), 5:900
Quodlibetal Questions (William of Ockham), 5:900
Quodvultdeus, St., 1:577, **11:874**
Quomodo legendum sit in rebus visibilibus (Othlo), 10:709
Qur'ān (Islamic holy book), 1:611, 7:606, **11:874–880**
    authority for Muslims, 7:610–611, 621–622
    calligraphy, 7:617
    disassociation of Islam from Judaism and Christianity, 7:607–608
    early chapters of the, 10:52–53
    imām, 7:327
    Jesus Christ, 7:843, 845
    Kalām, 8:109–111
    kinds of law, 8:170
    Mu'tazilite school teachings on the, 10:74

revelations delivered to Muḥammad, 10:52, 54–55

Quy Cong Doan, Pedro, 14:497

R

Ra (Atum-Re) (Egyptian deity), 4:337, 6:305, 8:178, **11:881**, 12:723

Rabanus Maurus, Bl., 3:599, 5:206, 10:512, 763–764, **11:881–882**
  acrostics, 1:72
  Aldric of Sens, St., 1:248
  art, 3:153, 154
  Augustinianism, 1:877
  biblical catenae, 3:258
  Canon Law, 3:43
  Carolingian reform, 3:158
  Carolingian Renaissance, 3:160
  Cassian, John, 3:207
  catechesis, 3:230, 240
  exegetical works, 5:515
  hymns, 7:246, 12:664
  medieval Latin literature works, 9:443
  preaching, 11:619
  prescholasticism, 12:757
  relics, 12:54

Rabban Ara, 3:366

Rabbinic literature, 1:39, 2:398, 532
  See also Talmud

Rabbinical Assembly of America, 8:10

Rabbinical Bibles, 2:355, 5:508, 7:271–272, **11:883–884**

Rabbinical Council of America, 8:11

Rabbinical Judaism, 8:7–9

Rabbinical literature, 5:508, 8:173, 12:139–140

Rabbis, 6:264–265, **11:882–883**, 14:132

Rabbula (Bp. of Edessa), 1:805, 5:83, **11:884**

Rabelais, François, 1:384, 517, **11:884–886**

Rabi`a, 1:621

Rabut, Facile (Brother), 2:633

Raccolta (document collections), **11:886**

Race relations
  Arkansas, 1:693
  Arrupe, Pedro, 1:726
  Boston Archdiocese, 2:556
  Chicago Archdiocese, 3:479, 821
  Cincinnati Archdiocese, 3:737
  Mississippi, 9:739
  Washington, DC, 14:658
  See also African Americans

Rachis (King of Lombards), 8:768, 769

Racial discrimination
  apartheid, 13:360–361
  genetics, 7:175, 177
  Holocaust, 7:12–13, 15
  insult, 7:502
  Ireland, John, 7:552
  Japan, 7:743
  Keough, F. P., 8:154
  papal social thought, 13:258
  Zimbabwe, 14:926

Racial integration
  California, 8:792
  Charleston (SC), 13:367
  founding of interracial movement, 8:277–278
  Knights of Columbus, 8:191
  Knights of Peter Claver, 8:195–196
  Krol, J. J., 8:250
  Little Rock Diocese, 8:614
  papal social thought, 13:258
  Rummel, J. F., 8:815
  Shehan, L. J., 13:76

Racicot, M. Félix, 2:232

Racine (WI), 4:840

Racine, Jean Baptiste, 2:115, 116, **11:886–889**

Racio recta non patitur (papal bull, John XXII), 2:205

Racisme, Antisémitisme, Antichristianisme (Oesterreicher), 10:558

Raclot, Mathilde, **11:889**

Racovian Catechism, 4:80

Rad, Gerhard von, 1:425, 427, 2:386, 3:565–566, 4:341, 5:520

Rada, José, 10:29

Rada, Rodrigo-Jiménez de, 1:465

Radbod (Bp. of Utrecht), St., 3:161, 7:247, **11:889**

Radcliffe-Brown, A. R., 4:430–431, 12:65, 14:120

Radegunda, St., 1:179–180, 3:409, 5:823, **11:889**

Rademacher, Joseph (Bp. of Fort Wayne, IN), 13:823

Radewijns, Florentius, 2:607, 4:707

Radhakrishnan, Sarvepalli, 10:821

Radical reformation, 3:608, 4:80–82

Radical sanction, 8:454

Radical theology, **11:889–891**

Radin, Paul, 1:163, 12:66, 68

Radio broadcasts
  Alaska, 1:209
  Catholic Hour, 13:74
  Coughlin, Charles Edward, 4:294
  Family Theater, 11:222
  Radio Liberty, 12:742
  Radio Veritas, 13:80
  Spain, 13:400

Radio Church of God. *See* Worldwide Church of God

Radulph (Latin Patriarch), 1:219

Raffaella o Dialogo della creanze aelle donne (Piccolomini), 11:321

Raffeiner, John Stephen, 8:504, **11:891**

Rafols, María, Bl., **11:891**

Rafqa de Himlaya, St., **11:892**

Ragembert (Bp. of Vercelli), 1:387–388

Ragny, Claude de (Bp. of Autun), 1:926

Rahab (biblical figure), 6:126

Rahmani, Ignatius Ephrem II (Patriarch of Syria), 13:710

Der Rahmen der Geschichte Jesu (Schmidt), 5:521, 812

Rahner, Hugo, **11:892**

Rahner, Karl, 4:671, 5:38, 346, 351, 6:288, **11:892–895**, *893*, 14:362
  angelology, 1:415
  angels, 4:649
  anonymous Christian, 1:488–489
  Antichrist, 1:516
  apologetics, 1:565, 566
  apostolicity, 1:596
  atheism, 1:825
  beatific vision of Christ, 7:823
  biblical canon, 3:21
  Christocentrism, 3:558
  conversion, 4:235
  eucharistic theology, 5:430
  existential ethics, 5:538
  foundational theology, 5:827–828
  Frassati, Pier Giorgio, 5:920
  fundamental theology, 6:27
  grace, 6:395, 397, 398
  Holy Trinity, 14:197–198
  humanity of Christ, 1:802–803, 7:821
  indulgences, 7:440
  International Theological Commission, 7:528
  kerygma, 8:158
  missiology, 9:678
  mission and missions, 9:684
  mysteries, 10:84, 85
  natural order, 10:204
  original sin, 10:667
  preaching, 11:628–629
  preambles of faith, 11:635
  private revelations, 12:201
  prophecy, 11:763
  religious experience, 5:556

Rahner, Karl (*continued*)
 sacramental theology, 12:471, 472, 474, 475
 scholastic theology, 12:777
 theology of Christ and world religions, 7:841
 theology of history, 6:891–892
 theology of hope, 13:927
 transcendental Thomism, 14:54, 55, 56
 Trinitarian processions, 11:735–736
 Vatican Council II, 1:916
 works, 12:729
Rahosa, Michael (Metropolitan of Kiev), 2:605, 606
Railing. *See* Insult
Railroad chapel cars, 8:114
Raimond, Marcantonio, 10:404
Raimondi, Giovanni Battista, 3:379–380
Raimondi, Luigi (Card.), 1:585, **11:895–896**
Raimondi, Pietro, 2:841
Rainald of Bar, Bl., **11:896**
Rainald of Dasel (Abp. of Cologne), 1:127, 3:843, **11:896**
Rainald of Ravenna, Bl., **11:896–897**
Rainald of Saint-Calais, 1:248
Rainaldi, Carlo, 3:693, 705
Rainerius of Pomposa, **11:897**
Rainier of Sacconi, 3:260
La Raison et le rationalisme (Ollé-Laprune), 10:585
Raisons (Triest), 14:185
Ra'ita, Abu, 8:170
Ralbag. *See* Levi ben Gerson
Rāle, Sebastian, 2:552, 9:55, **11:897–898**
Raleigh, Walter, Sir, 5:295
Raleigh Diocese (NC), **11:899–900**
Ralliement, 1:355, 3:617, 5:694, 855, **11:900–901**, 12:228
Ralph (King of the West Franks), 3:172
Ralph de Luffa (Bp. of Chichester), 3:481
Ralph Higden, 1:464, **11:901**
Ralph of Coggeshall, 1:464
Ralph of Dicteo, **11:901–902**
Ralph Strode, **11:902**
Rāma (Hindu deity), 6:848–849
Ramaḍān, 7:610, 10:9, **11:902**
Rāmānuja (Indian philosopher), 6:846–847, 7:409, 10:820
The Rāmāyaṇa (Hindu epic), 6:844
Ramban. *See* Naḥmanides (Talmudist)
Rambert of Bologna (Bp.), **11:902–903**, 14:46
The Rambler (periodical), 10:334

Rameau, Jean Philippe, 4:526, 11:*903*, **903**
Ramée, Pierre de la. *See* Ramus, Peter
Ramière, Henri, 1:578, 3:309
Ramírez, Pedro Esqueda, St., 6:545
Ramírez, Pedro Pablo, 1:652
Ramirez, Santiago, 9:100, 12:776
Ramírez Salazar, Eugenio, Bl., 7:123
Ramírez Zuloaga, Melquídes, Bl., 7:123
Ramiro of Aragon, 2:688
Ramism, 11:906
Ramist controversy, 8:751
Ramm, Bernard, 5:473
Ramos Arizpe, Miguel, **11:903–904**
Ramos Ramos, Abilio, Bl., 4:494
Ramos-Horta, Jose, 5:9–10
Ramousse, Yves-Georges-René, 2:903, 904
Rampolla del Tindaro, Mariano (Card.), 2:249, 11:904, *905*
Ramsay, W., 1:20
Ramses II and II Temples (Egypt), 5:131–132
Ramsey, Michael (Abp. of Canterbury), 1:440, 11:31
Ramsey, Paul, 14:177
Ramsey Abbey (England), **11:905**
Ramus, Peter, 5:90, **11:905–906**
 analysis and synthesis, 1:382
 Aristotelianism, 1:676
 humanism, 7:190
 quality, 11:851
 Renaissance philosophy, 12:124–125
 St. Bartholomew's Day Massacre, 12:538
 scholasticism, 12:767–768
Ramwold of Sankt Emmeram (Abbot), 12:668
Rànavàlona I (Queen), 9:26
Ranbeck, Ägidius, 12:735
Rancé, Armand Jean le Bouthillier de, 3:747, 8:372, **11:906–907**, 14:161
Ranconis, Adalbert, 4:480
Rand, E. K., 10:727
Randall, Benjamin, 2:80
Randall, John Herman, Jr., 10:205
Randomness, **11:907**
 See also Chance
Rangerius (Bp. of Lucca), 9:450
Ranke, Leopold von, 4:823, 11:*908*, **908–909**
Ransom, **11:909**, 968, 975
Ranters (Puritan sect), 11:838
Rape, in the Bible, 13:50
The Rape of the Lock (Pope), 11:496

Raphael (Archangel), 1:420, 427, **11:909–911**
 Bible cycles, 2:375
 Castiglione, Baldassare, 3:215
 Chigi family, 3:483
 Clement VII (Pope), 3:782
 devotion to, 1:424
 iconography, 1:425, 574, 575
 mosaic cartoons, 10:4
 Moses and the Burning Bush, 10:*8*
 Resurrection of Christ, 13:*312*
 The Transfiguration, 14:*153*
 Virgin and Child, 12:*109*
Raphael I Bidawid (Chalden Patriarch), 1:808
Rapheal, St., 8:275
Rapid City Diocese (SD), **11:911**
Rapin, René, 11:622, **911–912**
Rapp, Johann Georg, **11:912**
Rappe, Amadeus (Bp. of Cleveland), 12:537
Rapson, Ralph, 3:716
Rapture, 4:527, **11:912–913**
Raquette, Gabriel de (Bp. of Autun), 1:926
Rash judgment, **11:913–914**
Rashbam (Samuel ben Meír), 5:509
Rashi (Rabbi Shelomoh ben Yishaq) (medieval commentator), 1:36, 2:833, 5:143, 509, 7:869, **11:914–915**
Al-Rashīd, al-Ma'mūn, 1:7
Al-Rashīd, Harūn, 1:7
Raskolniks (Russian schismatics), 1:948, 5:717, **11:915–916**, 12:424
Rasoamanarivo, Victoria, Bl., **11:916**
Rasputin, Grigorii Efimovich, **11:916**, *917*
Rassegna Sociale, La (periodical), 2:279
Rassler, Christoph, **11:916–917**
 See also Equiprobabilism
Rastafarians, 3:113
Rastell, John, 9:882, **11:917**
Rastell, William, 11:917
Rastislav (Duke of Greater Moravia), 4:475, 476, 479
Ratdolt, Erhard, 2:522
Rath Melsigi (Irish monastery), 5:103
Rathbreasail, Synod of (1111), 1:697, 2:422
Ratherius of Verona (Bp.), 8:563, 9:448, **11:917–918**
Ratio fundamentalis (National Conference of Catholic Bishops), 12:898

Ratio Studiorum (Jesuit methods guide), 1:952, 4:311, 5:790, 6:145, **11:918–919**
  Franca study of, 5:840
  Nadal's role in development, 10:133
Rational appetite, 14:723
Rational distinction, 4:780–781
Rational love, 8:825, 826, 828
Rationalism, 5:395, 11:294, **919–923**
  absurdity, 1:48
  accident, 1:62, 63
  agnosticism, 1:181
  Alphonsus Liguori, St., 1:312
  angels, 1:422
  Anselm of Canterbury, St., 1:496
  anticlericalism, 1:518
  argumentation, 1:659
  Arianism, 1:660
  autos sacramentales, 1:925
  Bautain, Louis Eugène Marie, opposition to, 2:161
  biblical theology, 2:383–384
  Bonald, Louis Gabriel Ambroise de, 2:478
  Bonaventure, St., 2:483
  Cambridge Platonists, 2:910
  Cartesianism, 3:183
  certitude, 3:352
  Chesterton, Gilbert Keith, 3:469
  Christian philosophy, 3:538, 540
  Church-State relations, 3:639, 640
  Clarke, Samuel, 3:766
  community, 4:38
  Cousin, Victor, 4:323
  destiny, supernatural, 4:694
  dialectical materialism, 9:322
  Dilthey, Wilhelm, 4:746
  doctrine, 4:808
  Église catholique française, 3:449
  exegesis, 5:520, 521
  French philosophers, 8:580
  German opposition, 8:230
  Gregory XVI (Pope), 6:507–508
  hypostasis, 7:264
  idealism, 7:297
  illuminism, 7:321
  law, 8:399
  laws of reality, 14:223
  literary myth, 10:120
  metaphysics, 9:549–550
  Montaigne, Michel Eyquem de, 9:821
  natural law doctrine, 10:182
  necessity, 10:227
  Neo-Confucian, 4:98

  papal social thought, 13:257
  Protestant theology in, 13:911
  religious liberalism, 8:542
  Spencer, Herbert, 13:413
  Spinoza, Baruch, 13:418–420, *418*
  unconscious motivation, 10:28
  Voltaire, 14:580
  Wolff, Christian, 14:807
Rationalist philosophy, 8:175, 557
Ratisbon, Council of (1541), 3:846, 9:512
Ratisbonne, Marie Théodore and Marie Alphonse, 5:640, 10:460, **11:923–924**, 13:93
Ratold of Verona (Bp.), 12:32
Ratramnus of Corbie, 3:599, **11:924**
  Aelfric Grammaticus, 1:136
  Cranmer, Thomas, 4:334
  dialectics, 4:725
  eucharistic controversies, 4:258, 334, 5:423
  prescholasticism, 12:757
  reality of symbolic presence, 8:656
Ratsiraka, Didier, 9:27
Rattazzi Bill (Italy, 1855), 3:313–314
Ratti, Ambrogio Damiano Achille. *See* Pius XI (Pope)
Ratzel, F., 12:744
Ratzinger, Joseph (Card.), 3:237, 590, 837, 7:528
Ratzinger Instruction, 8:547, 548, 549
Raumer, Karl von, 5:322
Raus, Matthias, 11:994
Rausch, James S. (Bp. of Phoenix), 1:688, **11:924–925**
Rauschenbusch, Walter, 2:80, **11:925**, 13:242
Rauscher, Joseph Othmar von (Card.), 1:914, 8:255, **11:925**
Rautenstrauch, Franz Stephan, 1:914, 5:258, **11:925–926**
Rauzan, Jean Baptist, 9:505
Ravaisson-Mollien, F., 1:678
Ravalli, Antonio, **11:926**
Ravanello (composer), 2:843
Ravaschieri, Balthasar, Bl., **11:926**
Ravenna (Italy), **11:926–933**
  art and architecture, 3:710, 11:931–933, 12:691
  Bible cycles, 2:369
  Constantine (Pope), 4:177–178
  Exarchate, 11:931
  history, 11:927–930
  monasteries, 11:930
Ravenna, Church of, 8:478, 768
Raverdy, Jean, 3:858

Ravestyn, Josse, 2:18–19
Ravignan, Gustave François Xavier de, **11:933–934**, *934*
Ravoux, Augustin, **11:934**
Rawlings, Jerry, 6:198
Rawlins, Alexander, Bl., 5:232
Rawlinson, A. E. J., 7:850
Rawls, John, 3:754–755, 10:205
Ray, John, 2:402, 12:768
Raymond (Abp. of Toledo), 1:623
Raymond (Count of Toulouse), **11:938**
Raymond (prince of Antioch), 4:403, 404
Raymond, Antonin, 3:677, 12:534–535
Raymond IV (Count of Toulouse), 7:31, 11:198, 938
Raymond VI (Count of Toulouse), 1:714, 11:938
Raymond VII (Count of Toulouse), 11:938
Raymond de Podio (du Puy), 8:193
Raymond Martini, **11:934–935**
Raymond Nonnatus, St., **11:935**
Raymond of Capua, Bl., 3:273, 4:851, 855, 8:408, **11:935–936**, 14:47
Raymond of Fitero, Bl., **11:936**
Raymond of Peñafort, St., 3:50, 6:511, **11:936–937**, 13:382
Raymond of Roda-Barbastro, St., **11:937**
Raymond of Sabunde, 9:821, **11:937**
Raymond of St. Gilles, 4:402
Raymond of Toulouse, St., **11:938**
Raymund of Puis, 3:412
Raynaud, Théophile, **11:938–939**
Raynerius of Pisa, 14:47
RCIA. *See Rite of Christian Initiation of Adults* (RCIA)
Re (Egyptian deity). *See Ra (Atum-Re) (Egyptian deity)*
Re rege et regis institutione (Mariana), 9:160
Rea, Alonso de la, **11:939**
Reader-response criticism, 6:795–796
Reading, spiritual, **11:939–941**
Reading Abbey (England), **11:939**
Reading of hearts, 3:759, 10:108
Ready, Michael J. (Bp. of Columbus), 3:868
Reagan, American United for Separation of Church and State v., 10:486
Reagan, Phelps v., 10:486
Reagan, Ronald, 1:34
The Real St. Francis (Robinson), 12:274
Realino, Bernardine, St., **11:941**
Realism, 11:284, **941–945**
  Alexander, Samuel, 1:251–252

Realism *(continued)*
    antimonies, 1:520
    art, 1:744
    cathedral and episcopal schools, 3:441
    causality, 3:302
    concept, 4:51–53
    criteriology, 4:367
    Czechs, 7:228
    idea, 7:295
    idealism, 7:302
    mitigated, 4:120
    objectives, 10:510
    philosophy and science, 11:299–300
    scientific determinism, 8:270
    Thomism, 4:51–53
    unity and multiplicity opposition, 10:58
    universals, 14:326, 327
    Wyclif, John, 3:605
    See also Moderate realism
Realism of Being (Santayana), 12:681
Reality, **11:945**
    monistic conception, 10:824
    motion, 10:18
    qualities, 11:850
    society, 13:276
    supreme good, 6:354
    will and willing, 14:723
Reality (Weiss), 10:608
Reason
    Albert the Great, St., 1:226
    distinction, 4:780–781
    drunkenness, 4:910–911
    faith, 5:595, 599–600, 13:899
    God as subject, 6:310–311
    happiness, 9:96–97
    Hugh of Saint-Victor, 13:905–906
    religion, 12:72–73
    Thomas Aquinas, St., 13:906–907
Reason, cult goddess of, 8:282, **11:945–946**
Reason, Social Myths, and Democracy (Hook), 10:205
Reason, use of, **11:946**
    common good, 4:17
    contemporary thought on natural law, 10:192–193
    Locke, J., 8:745
    love, concept of, 8:828
    nature of law, 8:390
    speculative and practical, 8:389–390
    Thomistic analysis, 10:187–188
Reason: The Only Oracle of Man (Allen), 1:295

Reasoning, **11:946–949**
    definition, 4:609–610
    deliberation, 4:629–630
    demonstration, 4:651–654, 679
    discursive, 10:17
    Kant's theory, 8:121–122
    See also Deduction; Dialectics
Reasoning, theological, **11:949–950**
Rebais Abbey (France), 1:176
Rebaptism, 3:186, 593
Rebecca ar-Rayyes. *See* Rafqa de Himlaya, St.
Rebirth, in the Bible, 8:569, 571, 572, **11:951–952**
Rebirth through baptism, 2:66
Rebuschini, Enrico, Bl., **11:952**
Recapitulation in Christ, 1:489, 6:385, 7:571, **11:952–953**
Recaredo, conversion of, 3:40
Reccared (King of the Visigoths), 1:663–664, 3:596
Recemundus (Bp. of Elvira), 4:262–263, 13:379
Recent History (Historia Novella) (William of Malmesbury), 9:80–81
Receptivity theory, 9:259
Rèche, Arnold, Bl., 2:633
Rèche, Jules-Nicolas, Bl., **11:953–954**
Recherches (Bernoulli), 14:73
Recherches de science religieuse (periodical), 8:430
Recherches hist. et géogr. sur l'Inde (Anquetil-Duperron), 14:72
Recherches philosophiques sur les premiers objects de nos connaissances morales (de Bonald), 14:138
Recherches sur le texte du 'De Principiis' d'Origène (Bardy), 2:98
Rechtfertigungsschrift (Justificative Report) (Eckhart), 5:44–45
Recluses, **11:954**
    See also Anchorites; Hermits
Recognitio summularum (Vera Cruz), 14:444
Recognitions (early Christian writings), 11:799
Recognito iuris canonici codice (*motu proprio*, John Paul II), 3:35, 11:482
Recolhimento de Nossa Senhora da Luz (*Recollects of Our Lady of Light*) (Galvão de França), 6:83
Recollect Tertiaries of St. Augustine, 3:850
Recollection, **11:954–955**, 13:303
    See also Prayer

Recollections of the Last Four Popes (Wiseman), 14:797
Recollects of Our Lady of Light (*Recolhimento de Nossa Senhora da Luz*) (Galvão de França), 6:83
Reconcilatio et Paenitentia (apostolic exhortation, John Paul II), 7:1003
Reconciliation, ministry of, **11:955–956**
Reconciliation, Sacrament of. *See* Penance, Sacrament of
Reconciliation with God, 2:121
Reconnaissance au Maroc, 1883-1884 (Foucald), 5:826
Reconquista, 4:412, 13:380–381, 391
Reconstruction (U.S.), 8:251
The Reconstruction of Religious Thought in Islam (Iqbāl), 7:613–614
Reconstructionist Movement (Judaism), 8:10
Recovery of temporalities, 6:472–473
Recreation (eutrapelia), 5:461, 7:305
Rectangular baptismal fonts, 2:76
Rectangulum (Richard of Wallingford), 12:236
Rector Potens, Verax Deus (hymn), **11:956–957**, 12:136
Rectors, **11:957–958**
Rectors and Visitors of the University of Virginia, Rosenberger v. (1995), 3:664–665
Recueil de toutes les réponses... à M. Arnauld (Malebranche), 9:74
Recusant literature, 3:150, **11:958–961**
Recusants, 4:866–867, **11:958**, 13:370
"Red kit." *See Parish Stewardship Educational Program*
Red Mass, **11:961–962**
Red River (Canada), 3:7, 8
Red Sea, 11:*962*, **962–963**
Redaction, 6:795
Redaction criticism of New Testament, 10:303–304
Reddentes honorem (Justinian I), 7:920
Rede, Robert (Bp. of Chichester), 3:481
Redeemer and large apple (19th c. illustration), 10:666
Redemption, in the Bible, **11:963–973**
    Christ, 11:967–972
    creation, 4:342
    end of the world, 5:214–215
    God as redeemer, 11:964–967
    Isaiah, 7:599
    liberal theology, 8:543
    Mary, Blessed Virgin, 4:939, 9:256–257, 259–263
    ransom, 11:963–964
    repentance of man, 9:94–95

Redemption, theology of, **11:973–989**
  Anselm of Canterbury, St., 1:497
  atonement, 1:837
  Augustine, St., 1:864
  Baianism, 2:20–21
  Christ as victor, redeemer, and victim, 11:984–988
  constitutive aspect, 13:439
  creation, 4:342, 343–344
  Cyril of Alexandria, 4:469
  doctrinal context, 11:977–983
  dogmatic formulations, 11:975–976
  Duns Scotus, John, 4:938, 939
  Immaculate Conception, 7:334
  incarnation, 11:983–984
  mystical marriage related, 10:105
  Patristic Fathers, 11:976–977
  patristic philosophy, 10:961–962
  Precious Blood, 11:639
  redeemed nature through, 10:213
  Scotism, 3:558
  scriptural themes, 11:973, 975
  soteriology, 13:329
  See also Salvation
Redemptive history. *See* Salvation history (*Heilsgeschichichte*)
Redemptor hominis (encyclical, John Paul II), 3:627, 7:1002, 10:852, 853, **11:989–990**
Redemptoris custos (apostolic exhortation, John Paul II), 1:586
Redemptoris Mater (encyclical, John Paul II), 7:1003, 9:173, 10:234, **11:990**
Redemptoris missio (encyclical, John Paul II), 5:39, 478, 7:1002–1003, 8:175, 9:678–679, 682, **11:990–992**
Redemptoristines, **11:992**
Redemptorists, **11:993–996**
  Alphonsus Liguori, St., 1:311
  Caribbean, 3:116, 119, 120
  Desurmont, Achille, 4:695
  Konings, A., 8:233
  Kulturkampf, 8:254
  Lefevere in controversy, 8:169
  New Orleans, 8:811
  reestablishment of Catholicism in Norway, 10:450
  Schrijvers, Joseph, 12:787
  seminary programs of, 12:896
  Sheeran, J., 13:75
  spiritual direction, 4:763
  Sportelli, C., 13:461
Redemptus of the Cross, Bl., 3:145
Reden an die deutschen Nation (Fichte), 5:708

Redfield, Robert, 1:163, 4:430
Redi, Anna Maria. *See* Teresa Margaret of the Sacred Heart, St.
Reding, Augustine (Abbot), 5:139, 12:767
Redlhamer, Joseph, 12:769
Redman, Richard (Bp.), 12:536
Redmond, John, E., 7:564
Redon, O., 3:713
Redon Abbey (France), **11:996–997**
Reducción de las letras y arte para enseñar a hablar los mudos (Bonet), 3:418
Reductions (South America), 1:649, 2:465, 7:785
  See also Aldeiamento system (Brazil)
Reductions of Paraguay, 2:464, 3:101–102, 226, 613, **11:997–998**
Reductorium, repertorium, et dictionarium morale utriusque testamenti (Bercheure), 5:206
Redyng, Thomas, Bl., 5:226, 7:1019
Reed, Victor, J., 10:576
Rees, Seth C., 3:722
Referentialism, 1:142
Reflection (knowlege), 4:73, 152, 5:199, 8:205, **12:1–4**, 14:142–143
  See also Introspection
Reflections on the French Revolution (Burke), 10:757
Reflex action and behavior, 7:498
Reflex principles (morality), 8:410–411, 9:877–879, **12:4–5**, 726
Reflexiones (Gorriti), 6:365
Réflexion morale sur le Nouveau Testament (Quesnel), 7:717, 718
Reflexions morales (Le Tellier), 8:519
Réflexions morales (Noailles), 10:406
Réflexions sur la prémotion physique (Malebranche), 9:74
Réflexions sur le Nouveau Testament (Quesnel), 8:804
Reflexions sur l'état de l'Église en France au XVIIIe siècle (La Mennais), 8:308, 311
Réflexions sur l'évangile du salut (Ménégoz), 5:711
Reform Congregation of St. Justina, 8:268
Reform Judaism, 8:9–10, 11
Reform theology, 2:227
The Reformation
  academic freedom, 1:51
  Adrian VI (Pope), 1:129, 3:609
  apologetics, 1:564
  archdeacons, 1:633–634
  Aristotelianism, 1:685

ars moriendi, 1:732–733
attrition, 4:226
biographical studies of Christ, 7:845, 847
bishops, 2:417
cantors, 3:75
carols, 3:150–151
Carthusians, 3:192, 194
catechesis, 3:232–236, 241–244
catechisms, 4:9
Catholic responses, 3:233, 609–610, 638–639
charnel houses, 3:437
Christian anthropology, 3:531–532, 533
Christmas, 3:554, 557
Church property, 3:727, 12:872
Church-State relations, 3:637–638, 640
Clement VII (Pope), 3:781, 782
clerical celibacy/marriage, 3:327
confessions of faith, 4:77–82, 355
Congregationalism, 4:114
conscience, 4:149
Covenanters, 4:329–330
Crosier Fathers, 2:609
Crusades, end of, 4:410
democracy, 4:640
devotion to the saints, 12:596–598
Dominicans, 4:852
drama, 4:896
emphasis on preaching, 11:614
exegesis, 5:518
financial abuses, 8:294
grace and nature, 6:411
historical theology, 6:869
humanism, 7:192–193
hymnody, 7:255–256
Iceland, 7:275–276
intermediate judgment, 8:33
liturgical history, 8:659–662
Mary, Blessed Virgin, devotion to, 9:269
millenarianism in, 9:637
mixed marriages, 3:54
natural law doctrine during, 10:182–183
nominalism during, 10:413
overview, 3:608–609
purgatory, 5:344
religious authority, 6:286
religious liberalism, 8:540
sacraments, 12:470–471
spiritual hunger, 3:603, 604, 605, 606, 607–608

The Reformation *(continued)*
  studies, 8:184
  suppression of monasteries, 2:258
  theology of creation, 6:285
  transubstantiation doctrine during, 14:159
  vernacular languages, 8:667, 668
  vestments destroyed, 8:635
  women, role of, 14:816
  works of charity, 3:414
  See also Calvinism; Counter Reformation; Huguenots; Luther, Martin; Lutheranism; Mennonite churches; Protestants and Protestantism; Radical Reformation
The Reformation in the British Isles, **12:5–11**
  Browne, Robert, 2:638–639
  Cambridge University, 2:906
  Convocations of English clergy, 4:243, 244
  Cranmer, Thomas, 4:333–334
  Douai, 4:879–880, 13:234
  drama, 4:896
  Knox, J., 8:225–226
  Latimer, H., 8:360–361
  Lawrence, R., 8:405
  litany of saints, 8:601
  nonconformists, 10:418
  Smith, Richard, 13:234
  See also The Reformation
The Reformation on the Continent, **12:11–22**
  Albrecht of Brandenburg, 1:233
  Alpirsbach Abbey, 1:312
  Alvastra Abbey, 1:327
  Ambrosius Catharinus, 1:347
  Antwerp, 1:538–539
  Assemblies of the French Clergy, 1:787
  Austria, 1:910–912
  Bavaria, 8:326
  Belgium, 2:217–218
  Bursfeld Abbey, 2:710
  Capito, Wolfgang, 3:89
  Carmelites, 3:142
  Cassander, George, 3:204–205
  Catholic defenders, 8:230
  Charles V (Holy Roman Emperor), 1:849, 850, 2:889, 3:430–431, 638
  Chartres, 3:441
  Cologne, 3:842, 843
  confessional debate, 6:180–181
  conversions to Catholicism, 8:406
  Council of Trent as Church's answer to, 14:174–175

Crotus Rubianus, 4:386
Czechs, 4:482–483
Denmark, 4:665–666
Disentis Abbey, 4:775
Eberlin, Johannes, 5:31
Erasmus, 5:316
Estonia, 5:376–377
Farel, Guillaume, 5:622–623
Faust legend, 5:648–650
Finland, 5:733
Hungary, 7:213–214
Hussites, 3:605
Ireland, 7:555–558
Knights of Malta, 8:193–194
Košice martyrs, 8:241–242
Łasco, J., 8:342
Low Countries during, history, 10:258–260
Luxembourg, 8:897
Norway, 10:448–450
opposition, 8:324
Peace of Augsburg, 1:848, 849, 3:431, 638
Poland, 11:440–441
pre-Reformation crisis, 6:178–179
Regensburg talks, 4:202
16th century Ruthenians, 12:421–422
Slovakia, 13:220
Slovenia, 13:225
Sweden, 1:327, 399, 643, 13:635–636
Switzerland, 13:648–649
Zwingli, Huldrych, 14:940–941
See also The Reformation
Reformed Bernardines (Italy), 5:707
Reformed Church in America, 2:452, 895, 3:542, 543, 5:468, 12:24–25
Reformed Church of England. *See* Anglicanism
Reformed churches
  Bohemia/Moravia, 4:483
  Brenz, Johann, 2:605
  Calvinism, 8:678
  Caribbean, 3:116
  Christian Reformed Church, 3:542–543
  confessions of faith, 4:79–80
  Congregational union, 4:117–118
  Remonstrants, 12:109
  United Church of Christ from union of Evangelical and Reformed Church, 14:306–308
Reformed churches, **12:22–25**
Reformed Episcopal Church, **12:25–26**
Reformed Mercedarians, 4:765

Reformed Mourning Church (*Gereformeerde Kerk*), 10:264
The Reformed Pastor (Baxter), 2:162
Reformed Roman Missal (1570), 14:174
Reform-Katholizismus, 3:624
Reformkatholizismus, 9:755, **12:26**
Refrigerium (Refreshment), **12:26–27**
Refugees, 4:667–668, 7:522, 13:308
Refutation and Apology (Dionysius of Alexandria), 12:462
Refutation of All Heresies (Philosophumena) (St. Hippolytus of Rome), 6:858–859
Refutation of the Allegorists (Nepos of Arsinoë), 10:246
Regalia, 6:76, **12:27**
Regalis institutio (Orozco), 10:674
Regalism, 11:538
Regan, Agnes Gertrude, **12:27–28**
Regan, Tom, 1:456
Regensburg, Diet of (1540-1541), 2:394, 653, 889
Regensburg Interim (1541), 7:520
Regensburg Liturgical Publications, 11:842f
Regents (Apostolic Penitentiary), 11:76
Reger, Max, 12:*28*, **28**
Regesta Pontificum Romanorum (Kehr), 8:137
Regesta pontificum romanorum ab condita ecclesia ad annum post Christum natum 1198 (papal bull, Leo IX), 9:743–744
Regestrum visitationum (Odo Rigaldus), 10:555
Regestum super negotio Romani imperii (Innocent III), 10:859
Regia in matrimonium potestas (Launoy), 8:381
Regime of the Solitary (Avempace), 1:622, 932
Regimienot del alma (Orozco), 10:674
Regimini ecclesiae universae (apostolic constitution, Paul VI), 4:438, 5:480, 11:30
Regimini militantis Ecclesiae (papal bull, Paul III), 4:311, 7:313, 779
Regimini universalis ecclesiae (papal bull, Paul IV), 1:436–437
Regiminis apostolici (papal bull, Alexander VII), 7:717, **12:28–29**
Regina Caeli Laetare (Marian antiphon), 9:449, 12:*29*, **29**
Regina College (Campion, Canada), 3:11
Reginald, Valerius, **12:29**
Reginald of Canterbury, 7:248, 8:304, 9:457, **12:29**

Reginald of Orléans, Bl., **12:29–30**

Reginald of Piperno, 4:848, **12:30**

Reginbert (Bp.), 1:909, 910

Reginensis latinus 316. *See* Gelasian Sacramentary

Regino of Prüm, 1:99, 462, 3:44, 60, 9:447

Regino of Prüm, collection of, **12:30**

Regis, John Francis, St., 4:292, 7:782, **12:30–31**, 554, 694

Regis, Pierre Sylvain, 3:185, 9:74, **12:31**

Regius (Henri de Roy), 3:184

Regius, Charles, 11:622

Réglements de la Compagnie (Tronson), 14:213

Regli, Aniceta (Mother), 7:22

Regnans in Excelsis (papal bull, Pius V), 1:437, 443, 5:163, 224–225, 247, 670–671, 12:10–11

Régnon, Theodore de, 6:392

Regnum Christi Movement, 8:454

Regressus in infinitum (infinite regress), 12:753

Reguera, Emmanuel de la, **12:31–32**

Regula Cassiani, 12:590

Regula communis (St. Fructuosus of Braga), 6:16

Regula Magistri (Rule of the Master), 2:262, 263, 3:411, **12:32**

Regula monachorum (St. Fructuosus of Braga), 6:16

Regula monachorum (St. Isidore of Seville), 7:603

Regula morum (Terrill), 13:831

Regula Tarnatensis, 10:743

Regula Vigilii (*Regula Orientalis*), 10:743

Regula vitae eremiticae (Giustiniani), 6:235

Regulae Iuris. See Rules of Law (*Regulae Iuris*)

Regulae Studiorum (St. Gregory Barbarigo), 2:89

Regulare Tribunale (Passerini), 10:919

Regularis Concordia (Ethelwold of Winchester), 5:387

Rehm, Jean-Georges, 12:278

Rehrl, Caspar, 8:504, 12:531

Reichenau Abbey (Germany), 4:168, **12:32–33**

Reichenau school of Art (Germany), 10:720

Reichenbach, Hans, 5:142, 8:220, 14:289

Reichensperger, Peter, 3:340

Reichersberg Monastery (Austria), 1:322, 3:67, **12:33**

Reichstag Sessions (1566, 1576), 3:17

Reid, Thomas, 4:22, 12:*33*, **33–34**

Bufalo, St. Gaspare del, 2:675

Cartesian philosophy, 12:771

causality, 3:301

induction, 7:434

judgment, 8:23, 25

Scottish School of Common Sense founding, 12:839–841

Reiffenstuel, Anacletus (Johann Georg), **12:34**

Reign of Terror, 5:974

Reihm, Eduard Karl August, 5:519

Reilly, Daniel Patrick (Bp. of Norwich), 4:125

Reilly, James, 7:581

Reilly, Lambert (ArchAbbot), 12:568

Reilly, Patrick, 1:691, 4:625

Reilly, Wendell, 5:523, **12:34–35**

Reimarus, Hermann Samuel, 5:255, 263, 521, 7:847, **12:35**

Reims (France), **12:35–38**

Reims, Councils of, 1:720, 2:309, 11:611–612

Reims Archdiocese (France), 7:927, 8:738, 12:37

Reims Cathedral (France), 3:601, 696, 698

Reincarnation, 1:867, **12:38**

See also Metempsychosis

Reine (Regina) of Alise, St., 5:760

Reiner, chronicle of, 1:463

Reinert, Paul C., 7:794, **12:38–39**

Reinhold, Hans A. (Father), 3:717, **12:39**

Reinhold, K. L., 8:125, 12:345

Reinkas, Joseph, 12:182

Reinstadler, Sebastian, 12:748, 775

Reipublicae christianae libri 2 (Rovenius), 12:395

Reisach, Karl August Von (Card.), **12:40**

Reisch, Gregor, 5:206

Reitzenstein, Richard, 1:20, **12:40**

Relación de la vida y milagros del Venerable P. Fray Francisco Solano (Oré), 10:643

Relación de las cosas de Yucatan (Landa), 8:318–319

Relación de los mártires de la Florida (Oré), 10:643

Relación histórica de la vida y apostólicas tareas del Venerable Padre Fray Junípero Serra (Palóu), 10:815

Relatio nimis implacida (papal bull, John XXI), 7:930

Relation, 1:42, 61, 180, 10:18, **12:40–44**, 13:139

Relations, des Jésuites (1648-49), 10:436

Relations, Trinitarian, **12:45–46**

Rélations des déliberations due clergé de France (Marca), 9:133

Relations des Jésuites. See Jesuit Relations

Relations Spirituelles (Moine), 9:764

Relationum historicarum de rebus Angliae (Pitts), 11:366

Relative latria, 4:382

Relative perfection, 11:117

Relativism, 11:285, **12:46–49**

absolute, 1:43

Christian philosophy, 3:542

Einstein's theory of relativity, 5:141

man, natural end of, 9:96

mechanism, 9:417–418

narrative theology, 10:152

Sophists, 13:323

Relativism, moral, 3:627, **12:49–50**

Das Relativitaets-prinzip in Herbert Spencer's psychologischer Entwicklungslehre (Pace), 10:741

Relics, 3:65, **12:50–56**

Aachen, 1:2

altars, 1:314–315, 316

Athelstan, 1:827–828

Córdoba, 4:262

crown of thorns, 4:388, *388*

holy lance, 7:30–31

Roman, 11:352–353

saints, 12:598

shrines, 13:89–90

Shroud of Turin, 13:95–97

Relief Action for Refugee Jews, 13:527

Relief Acts (England), 5:182–185, 250–251

Les Religieuses de Nôtre Dame du Sacré-Coeur, 13:178, 179

Religio-Historical School (19th century), 10:128

Religion, **12:56–64**

art, 1:736–742

asceticism, 1:773–774

blasphemy, 2:434

Cretan-Mycenaean, 4:362–363

defined, 12:56–57

Enlightenment, 5:261

legal definitions of, 3:660–661

magic, 9:36, 37

Religion, philosophy of, 2:440–441, 8:123–124, **12:69–73**, 13:229, 236

Religion, sociology of, 5:172, **12:73–82**

Religion, teachers of, **12:82–84**

Religion, virtue of, **12:84–85**

Religion and morality, 12:62–63, **86**

Religion as a Factor of Life (Engels), 14:258

Religion des Volkes Israel (Kittel), 8:186

Die Religion in Geschichte und Gegenwart, 5:812–813

Religion in primitive cultures, **12:64–69**
 Durkheim, Émile, 4:951–952
 shamans and medicine man, 13:66–67
 sin (phenomenology of), 13:148–149
 sky and sky gods, 13:205–206
 Slavic religion, 13:215

Religion of Light. *See* Manichaeism

The Religion of the Primitives (Le Roy), 8:513

Religion und Offenbarung (Schell), 12:732

Religion within the Limits of Reason Alone (Kant), 8:175

Religionis zelus (papal bull, Clement VII), 4:310

Religions, comparative study of, 4:437–438, **12:87**

Religions of Authority and the Religion of the Spirit (Sabatier), 12:453

Religionsgeschichtliche Schule, 6:582

Religionsphilosophie (Hartmann), 6:655–656

Religiosa sanctorum (apostolic constitution, Sixtus V), 3:107

Religious (men and women), **12:87–89**
 commitment, 4:15–16
 contemplative life, 4:210
 Cuba, 4:417
 enclosure for women, 13:172, 183
 French Revolution, 4:43–44
 Hungary, 7:218–219
 Idaho, 7:290–291
 Lawrence Justinian, St., 8:405
 Leadership Conference of Women Religious (U.S.), 8:421–423
 National Black Sisters' Conference support for female African Americans, 10:157–158
 New Hampshire, 10:279–280
 reform, 8:432–433
 religious obedience, 10:505–506
 Serra International, 13:23
 Sister Formation Movement, 13:169–170
 Sisters Survey, 8:422–423
 universal call to holiness, 7:5, 7
 See also Nuns and sisters; Priests and priesthood; *specific clerical titles*; *specific religious orders*

Religious, Canon Law of, **12:89–92**
 apostolate, 12:91

consecrated life, 4:154–156

contemplative life, 4:210

convents, 4:231

Directory for the Ministry and Life of Priests, 4:763–764

Eastern law code, 12:92

force and fear, 5:797

governance, 12:90

membership and formation, 12:90–91

monks and monasteries, 4:58–59

obligations and rights, 12:91

separation, 12:91

Religious, constitutions of, **12:92–93**

Religious, exemption of, **12:93–94**

Religious affiliation. *See* Church membership

Religious art
 Church patronage, baroque period, 2:111
 Good Shepard theme, 6:356–357
 liturgy research, 8:725
 nimbus (cloud) of the saints, 12:598–599
 sarcophagal art, 12:691
 Satan, 12:699
 Siena, 13:109
 vestments, 8:634–636
 Woman Clothed with the Sun, 14:822
 See also Church architecture

Religious Art in France of the Thirteenth Century (Mâle), 9:73

The Religious Aspect of Philosophy (Royce), 12:70

Religious Brothers Conference, **12:94–95**

Religious Cabinet (periodical), 2:40

Religious communities. *See* Religious orders (communities)

Religious conservatism in France, 9:753

The Religious Crisis in France (Onahan), 10:599

Religious dissent, 13:25

Religious drama, 9:457

Religious education, **12:95–96**
 Brazil, 5:840
 Bushnell, Horace, 4:116–117
 Confraternity of Christian Doctrine, 4:94
 Dearden, John Francis, 4:568
 ecclesiastical education, 12:688–689
 history of Christian paideia, 10:753–756
 New Hampshire, 10:280
 New Jersey, 10:283
 New Mexico, 10:287

New Orleans, 10:295, 296

New York, 10:315, 316, 319, 324

Newark (NJ) Archdiocese, 10:330–331

Newman Apostolate, 10:341–342

Nicaragua, 10:352–353

Ohio, 10:571–572

Oregon, 10:646

Pius XII (Pope), 4:790–792
 role of Viatorians in U.S., 14:471
 teachers of religion, 12:82–84
 See also Education

Religious Education (periodical), 12:97

Religious Education and Instruction (Bandas), 2:48

Religious Education Association (REA), **12:96–97**

Religious Education Association of the U.S. and Canada, 12:729

Religious education movement, **12:97–98**

Religious experience. *See* Experience, religious

Religious Formation Conference (RFC), 13:170

Religious freedom. *See* Freedom of religion

Religious Freedom Restoration Act (RFRA) (U.S., 1993), 3:664

Religious guilt, 6:567

Religious habits, **12:98–101**, *99*, 721–723

Religious language and theology, 13:915–916

Religious leadership, 13:614

Religious Liberty, An End and A Beginning (Murray), 10:69

Religious Mission of the Irish People and Catholic Colonization (Spalding), 13:402

Religious music. *See* Liturgical music

Religious names, 10:141

Religious obedience, 10:505–506

Religious of Christian Education, **3:535**

Religious of Jesus and Mary, **12:101**

Religious of Our Lady of Sion, 5:640

Religious of the Assumption, **1:797**, 802

Religious of the Cenacle, **3:334**, 12:31

Religious of the Order of the Blessed Sacrament and of Our Lady, 12:484

Religious of the Passion of Jesus Christ. *See* Passionist Nuns

Religious of the Sacred Heart of Mary (RSHM), 6:49, 8:112, 254, 793, 9:302–303, **12:496–497**

Religious orders (communities)
 African Americans, 1:157–158

Alaska, 1:209–210

angelic devotion, 1:424

Anglicanism-Episcopalianism, 12:101–103

archives, 1:637, 641–642

Argentina, 1:649

Arkansas, 1:692

Australia, 1:905

Bolivia, 2:466

Brazil, 2:593–594, 595, 597

California, 2:867–868

Caribbean, 3:116, 118, 121

Carlisle See, 3:124

Carroll, John, 3:180

Cavour, Camillo Benso di, 3:313–314

cenobitism, 1:821, 3:334–335

Chicago, 3:477–478

Council of Major Superiors of Women Religious, 4:298

Council of Trent, 3:53–54

Counter Reformation, 3:611

Cuba, 4:417, 418–419

Czech restoration, 4:487

definitor, 4:612

discalced, 4:*764–765*

France, suppression of, 4:13

higher education, 1:53

Hungary, 7:210–211

laicism, 8:283

19th-20th century overview, 3:621–622

Ohio, 3:735

pre-Reformation conditions, 12:14–15

renewal of, 4:309–310

Scotland, 12:832–833, 838–839

shrines, 13:94

solitude, 13:303

Switzerland, 13:647–648

United States, development in, 12:896

See also Monasteries; Monasticism; *specific orders*; *specific orders and monastic houses*; *specific religious orders*

Religious Organization Bill (Japan, 1939), 7:742

Religious pluralism, 9:687, 12:858–859

Religious poetry, 2:26, 12:389–390

Religious psychology, 2:647

Religious rationalism, 11:921–922

Religious reform, 9:580, 614–615

Religious seals, 6:762

Religious Society of Friends. *See* Quakers (Religious Society of Friends)

Religious studies, 13:289–290

Religious symbols, 13:661–662

Religious Teachers Filippini, 5:722, **12:101**, **104**

Religious Tract Society, 5:472

Religous feasts. *See* Feasts, religious

Reliquaries, 2:*813*, *814*, *815*, **12:104–105**, *605*

Reliquiae Baxterianae (Baxter), 2:162

Relly, James, 14:321

Remaclus, 9:79

Remains (Froude), 6:16

Remarks (Bentley), 2:288

Rembert (Abp. of Bremen-Hamburg), St., 1:102, **12:105**

Rembrandt (Dutch painter), 14:96

Abraham, images of, 1:37

Bible cycles, 2:376

Christ in art of, 7:860

crucifixion art, 4:397

Faust in His Study, 5:*649*

The Raising of Lazarus, 12:*166*

religious art, 2:112

Remedius of Chur (Bp.), 3:43

The Remembrance of the Desire of a Soul (Thomas of Celano), 14:33

Remer, Vincent, 12:775

Remesal, Antonio de, **12:105–106**

Remigio de' Girolami, **12:106**, 14:47

Remigius of Auxerre, 1:927, 2:457, **12:107–108**

Remigius of Lyons, St., 5:783, 8:326, **12:107**

Remigius of Reims, St., 3:596, 808, **12:107–108**

Remigius of Rouen (Abp.), St., **12:108**

"Reminiscences" (Verwyst), 14:461

Remiremont Abbey (France), 1:23, 333, **12:108**

Remonstrance, 3:173

Remonstrance of 1610, 1:713

Remonstrants, 2:894, **12:108–109**

Removens prohibens, 4:73

Renaissance, **12:109–120**

Adrian VI (Pope), 1:129

aesthetics, 1:142, 746

altars, 1:317

analysis and synthesis, 1:382

angels, 1:424

Apocalypse iconography, 1:544–545

Arabian philosophy, 1:672

Aristotelianism, 1:671, 672, 685

astrology, 7:114

Augustinians, 1:888–889

benevolent despotism, 4:376–377

Bessarion, Cardinal, 2:341

Bible cycles, 2:374–375

biology, 2:401–402

Carolingian legends, 1:764

Carolingian Renaissance, 3:159

Castiglione, Baldassare, 3:215–216

catacombs, 3:224

catechesis, 3:232

choirs, 3:523

Christianity and art, 1:743

Church history, 3:605–606

Church-State relations, 3:637

Cicero, Marcus Tullius, 3:730

clerical celibacy/marriage, 3:327

coinage during, 10:481–482

Cologne, 3:845

contrast with baroque period, 2:113

crucifixion art, 4:397

Dark Ages, 4:529

democracy, 4:640

doors of churches, 4:873

exegesis, 5:518–519

hospitals, 7:129–131

hylozoism, 7:240

hymnody, 7:254

iconography of saints, 12:601–602

Leo X (Pope) as personification, 8:486

liturgical music history, 8:687, 688

metaphysics of light, 8:584

mosaics, 10:4–5

motets, 10:11, 13

Nicholas V (Pope), 10:369

panentheism thought, 10:821

papacy development, 10:840–844

papacy stimulus for birth, 10:840

pre-Reformation spiritual hunger, 3:606

printing in, 7:188, 12:118

religious liberalism, 8:540

science, 12:815–818

soul, 13:345–346

spirituality, 13:446–447

study of music, 10:72–73

Transfiguration, 14:155

University of Alcalá, 1:236

vestments, 8:635

See also Renaissance architecture

La Renaissance (Michelet), 12:112

Renaissance architecture, 3:699–702

Renaissance art, 12:115–116, 357–358, 13:192–193

Renaissance philosophy, 8:867, **12:120–125**

Renaissance Trinity College chapel (Washington, DC), 3:716
RENAMO (political party), 10:40
Renan, Joseph Ernest, 5:521, 841, **12:126**
   aristocracy, 1:667
   biographies of Christ, 7:848
   Claudel, Paul Louis, 3:767
   historical Jesus, 3:623
   laicism, 8:283
   liberal theology, 8:543
   mythical character of the New Testament, 10:124
   supernatural, 1:565
Renard, Henri, 12:777
Renaudot, Eusèbe, 1:438, **12:126–127**
Rendtorff, Rolf, 11:97
René (Marquis d'Elbeuf), 6:579
René, Georges Edme, 12:278
René, John B., 1:208
Renelda, St., 5:188
Reneri, Henri, 3:184
RENEW program, 8:116, 819, 10:297, 12:678
Renewed Church of the Brethren. *See* Moravian Church
"Renewing the Earth" (American Catholic Bishops), 5:53, 56
Reni, Guido, 2:114
Renier of Huy, 12:486
Reno Diocese (NV), 8:346, 10:271, **12:127**
Renoirte, Fernand, 12:776
Renouveau catholique, 10:75
Renouvier, Charles Bernard, 5:939, 7:300, 10:238
Renovatio Romanorum imperii (renovated Roman Empire), 10:715
The Renovation of the Church (Pazzi), 11:47
Renunciation, 2:138
Renwick, James, Jr., 3:709, 715
Renzi, Elisabetta, Bl., **12:127**
Reordination, 1:928, 7:39, **12:127–128**
Reparation, **12:128–130**
Reparatus of Ravenna (Abp.), 4:870
Repeal Association, 10:540
Repentance, 2:57, 4:224–225, 7:362, 9:94–95, **12:130**, 13:147
   See also Contrition
The Repentant St. Mary Magdalene, 9:*285*
Repertorium Decreti (Bartholomew of Brescia), 2:125
Repertorium utriusqe iuris (Ioannes Milis), 3:52

Repertorum Hymnologicum (Chevalier), 12:246
Repetition of the Law (Mishneh Torah) (Maimonides), 9:52
Repetto, Maria, Bl., **12:130–131**
Repington, Philip (Repyngdon) (Card.), **12:131–132**
Repkow, Eike von, 1:464–465
Réponse (Malebranche), 9:74
Réponse générale (Malebranche), 9:74
Report on Church, Community, and State in Relation to the Economic Order (1937), 8:578
Reporter (newspaper), 14:60
Representation, principle of, 4:639, 641
Representative Men (Emerson), 5:188
Reprobation, 1:883, **12:132**
Reprobationes dictorum a fratre Aegidio in sententiarum libros (Robert of Orford), 12:269
Reproductive Health Services, Webster v., 1:34
Reproductive technology, 1:656
   artificial insemination, 11:399–400
   cloning, 7:178, 178–179, 13:356
Republic (Plato), 5:89, 929, 10:201, 14:316, 360
   Alfarabi, 1:277
   aristocracy in, 1:667
Reputation, defamation of, 4:608–609
Reputation, moral right to, **12:132–134**
Requiem (Schumann), 12:789
Requiem (Verdi), 14:446
Requiem Mass, 1:185, 3:225, **12:134–136**
Requieum (Fauré), 5:646
Rerum Aethiopicarum Scriptores Occidentales, 5:400
Rerum Deus Tenax Vigor (office hymn), 12:136, **136**
Rerum ecclesiae (encyclical, Pius XI), 9:681, 11:393, 753
Rerum Italicarum scriptores (Muratori), 10:63
Rerum novarum (encyclical, Leo XIII), 1:792–793, 2:219, 3:342, 420, 620, 625, 643, 4:19, 5:205–206, 855, 9:317, 10:184, 440, 850, 11:367, 566, **12:136–137**, 793, 14:109, 251, 824
   Catholic social thought, 13:256–257
   described, 8:492
   Ketteler's influence, 8:161
   Knights of Columbus, 8:190
   labor organizations, 8:193
   Raillement policy, 12:667
   social gospel, 13:241
   spreading the word, 8:466

studies beforehand, 8:371
Rerum orientalium (encyclical, Pius XI), 11:393
"Res publica" (Muth), 10:75
Resch, Peter Anthony, **12:137**
Rescripts, 4:758, **12:137–138**
Résé, Frederic (Bp. of Detroit), 4:697, 8:504, 853, 9:605
Resende, Sebastião Sores de (Bp. of Beira, Mozambique), 11:539
Resheph (God), 14:270
Resolutiones (Luther), 8:879–880
Respect, **12:138–139**
Respicientes ea omnia (encyclical, Pius IX), 12:322
Respighi, C., 3:380
Respighi, Ottorino, 12:*139*, **139**
Responsa, Jewish, **12:139–140**
Response (Apocriticus) (Macarius Magnes), 9:1
Response to Julius Africanus (Origen), 10:654
"Responses" (Nicholas I), 10:361
Responsibility, 5:194–195
Responsibility, in the Bible, **12:140–142**
Responsio ad Apologiam Cardinalis Bellarmini (Andrewes), 1:408
Responsio ad librum: Triplici nodo, triplex cuneus (Bellarmine), 10:500
Responsio. . .de articulis CVIII ex opere Petri de Tarentasia (Aquinas), 14:27
Responsio. . .de articulis XLII (Aquinas), 14:27
Responsiones ad conclusiones domini papae (Richard of Conington), 12:232
Responsorial psalms, 3:75, 6:413, **12:142**
Rest, 10:21, **12:142**, 13:610–611
Restaurus Cataldus Perusinus, 3:52
Restitution, 1:787, 2:612, **12:142–144**
Restitution, Edict of (1629), 5:688, 8:313, **12:144**
Restitution of Decayed Intelligence in Antiquities (Verstegan), 14:460
Restitutus (Bp. of London), 2:620, 8:770
Restitutus of Carthage (Bp.), 4:862
Restoration (1660-1700), 3:618, 7:577, 11:460
Resurrection, Greco-Oriental, **12:145**
Resurrection of Christ, 5:218, **12:145–165**, *146*, *147*, 13:*312*
   Assumption of Mary, 1:799
   Christophanies, 12:152–156
   Cleopas, 3:801
   death of God theology, 4:585
   demythologizing, 4:657

elevation of man, 5:149–151
eschatology, 5:350
impenetrability, 7:361–362
lauds, 8:379
Lent, 8:469
liturgical calendar, 8:641
Lord's Day, 8:781, 782
narratives, 5:810
Nicene Creed (325), 10:354
redemption, 11:971–972, 975, 988
represented in baptismal fonts, 2:76
sacrifice of the cross, 12:518–520
Son of God in power, 13:313
Son of Man, 13:317
Sunday as weekly celebration, 13:608
theology, 12:157–161
women's visit to the tomb, 12:150–152
The Resurrection of the Ancient Scottish Language (Ais-Eiridh na Sean Chánoin Albannaich) (MacDonald), 9:12
Resurrection of the dead, **12:165–174**
Adam, 1:104
afterlife, 1:165
in the Bible, 12:165, 167–172
burial, 2:700
Corinthians Epistles, 4:267
cremation, 4:360
death, 4:577
Divine judgment, 8:27
early Judaism, 8:5
end of the world, 5:*214*, 218
Jesus' reference to Old Testament, 3:28
in the Qur'ān, 7:609
represented in baptismal fonts, 2:76
retribution, 12:177–178
theology, 12:172–174
See also Glorified body
Resurrectionists, **12:174**
Retables, 1:316–317
Retablo, 12:685
El Retablo de Maese Pedro (Falla), 5:612
Rethinking Missions, 13:411
Reticius (Bp. of Autun), St., 1:926
Retórica christiana (Valadés), 14:367–368
Retouret, Jacques, 12:278
Retraction (Chaucer), 3:456
Retribution, **12:174–179**
afterlife, 1:164–165
Divine judgment, 8:27
Ecclesiastes, 5:35

individual eschatology, 5:337–338
Paradise, 10:876
sin, 13:143
wisdom literature, 14:788–789
Rettenpacher, Simon, 8:248–249
Return to the Future (Undset), 14:295
Retz, Jean François Paul de Gondi de, **12:179–180**
Reuchlin, Johann, 6:696–697, **12:180–181**, *181*
Argyropoulos, John, 1:659
biblical philology, 5:518
Crotus Rubianus, 4:386
humanism, 7:187, 12:119, 180–181
Pfefferkorn controversy, 5:306, 12:12, 181
Renaissance philosophy, 12:123
Reuental, neidhart von, 4:400
Reun Abbey (Germany), 1:108
Reunion Movement (Syro-Malankara Church), 13:719–721
The Reunion of Christendom (Schaff), 12:726
Reusch, Franz Heinrich, **12:181–182**
Reuss, E. G. E., 5:519, 521
Reuss, Maternus, 12:770
Reussner, Adam, 12:795
Reuwich, Erhard, 2:522
Revealer of Hidden Things (Tsofnath Pa'aneah) (Gikatilla), 6:211
Revealer of the Light (Kasātē Berhān). *See* Frumentius, St.
Reveille for Radicals (Alinsky), 1:288
Revelation
Albert the Great, St., 1:226
Catholic social thought, 13:247
Christian law, 10:201
dogma, 9:754
Gioberti, Vincenzo, 6:230
heaven, 6:685
intellect, 7:506–507
judgment, 8:40–41
need for, 10:195
prophecy, 11:762–764
religious freedom, 5:953–954
Son of Man, 13:317
soteriology, 13:329
soul, 13:336
spirit, 13:425
Thomistic analysis on natural law, 10:190–191
Revelation, Book of, **12:182–187**, *183*
adultery, 1:133
altars, 1:320
Amen, 1:348

angels, 1:417–418, 427
Antichrist, 1:515
apocalyptic style, 1:546, 12:182
Assumption of Mary, 1:799
authorship, 7:895
authorship and canonicity, 3:31, 32, 12:182–183
baptism, 2:56
beatific vision, 2:171
canonicity, 3:28
cherubim, 3:467
Christocentrism, 3:558
Church, 3:579
contents, 12:184
curses, 4:443
date of composition, 12:184
Divine judgment, 8:30, 40
Elijah's Second Coming, 5:159
eschatology, 5:341
Gehenna, 6:116
glory of God (end of creation), 6:246
Gnosis, 6:254
Hades, 6:604
heaven, 6:687
holiness, 7:10
iconography, 1:543–545
I-Thou mysticism, 10:118
Johannine work, 7:895
justice of God, 8:71, 72
Kingdom of God, 8:173, 174
Lamb of God, 8:301, 302
lamps and lighting, 8:314
Laodicea, 8:328
letters to the churches of Asia Minor, 5:306, 12:184
Logos, 8:760
lukewarmness, 8:865
magic, 9:39
martyrs and martyrdom, 9:227
Mary, Blessed Virgin, 9:244–245
methods of interpretation, 12:186–187
millenarianism, 9:633, 635
Paradise, 10:875
Parousia, 10:899
Precious Blood, 11:639, 641
precious stones, 11:646
right and justice, 8:65
Roman persecutions, 3:592
royal priesthood, 11:692–693
serpent as symbol, 13:19
Sukkot, 2:532
wisdom, 14:791
women, role of, 14:831–832

Revelation, concept of, in the Bible, **12:187–190**

Revelation, fonts (sources) of, **12:190–193**

Revelation, primitive, **12:193**

Revelation, the Birth of a New Age (Spangler), 10:273

Revelation, theology of, 3:355, 8:253, 10:190–191, 12:57, **193–198**, 13:892

Revelation, virtual, **12:198–200**

Revelation of Peter, 3:31

Revelationes (St. Gertrude the Great). *See* Insinuationes

Revelations, 10:108

Revelations, private, **12:200–203**

Revelations and Intelligences (Pazzi), 11:47

Revelations of Divine Love (Julian of Norwich), 10:118, 120

Revérbero Constitucional Fluminense (periodical), 2:96

Reverence (*Observantia*), **12:203**

Rêveries du promeneur solitaire (Rousseau), 12:393–394

Reverman, Theodore (Bp. of Superior, WI, 1877-1941), 14:782

Reversion, Daoism and, 4:523

Revetor, William, 9:881

Review Board, Thomas v. (1981), 3:663

Review for Religious, 8:139

Reviling. *See* Contumely

Reville, Albert, 5:521

Revised Common Lectionary (RCL), 5:254, 8:441

Revised Lateran Pacts. *See* Lateran Pacts (1985)

Revised Version of the Bible (1885), 13:236

Revisionist theology, **12:203–204**

La Revista Catolica (periodical), 12:675–676

Revista de Occidente (Ortega y Gasset, ed.), 10:679

Revista do Instituto histórico e geográfico brasileiro (periodical), 2:96

Revista la Sagrada Familia (periodical), 9:130

Revista Maryknoll (periodical), 9:297

Revius (Jacques de Rèves), 3:184

Revivalism, **12:204–205**

   Bushnell, Horace, 4:116–117

   Finney, Charles Grandison, 5:735

   hymnology, 7:257–258

   justification, 8:87

   liberal theology, 8:542

   Lutherans, 8:885–886

spiritual music, 13:456

The Revivification of Religious Sciences (Algazel), 7:612

Reviviscence, sacramental, 6:408, **12:205–206**

Reviviscence of Merit, **12:206–207**

Revocatus (martyr), 1:93

La Révolution (Quinet), 5:969

Revolution of 1688 (England), 5:249, 7:707, **12:207–208**, 463

   Anglicanism, 1:444

   Catholic sympathies in Scotland, 12:835

   Declaration of Rights (1689), 4:590

   Maryland, 2:887, 9:300

   Test Oaths enforced after, 10:501

Revolution of 1848 (Austria), 1:914

Revolution Settlement (1689), 4:330

Revue Biblique (periodical), 5:50, 8:280

Revue biblique 1980: The Rule of St. Benedict with Notes, 2:263

Revue d'histoire ecclésiastique (periodical), 8:824

Revue du clergé; français, 14:241

Revue Musicale (periodical), 5:700

Revue néoscolastique de philosophie (periodical), 12:774

Revue Sacerdotale (periodical), 14:261

Revue Thomiste (periodical), 6:94, 12:774, 13:23

Rex Gloriose Martyrum (office hymn), **12:208–209**

Rex Sempiterne Caelitum (office hymn), **12:209**

Rey, Anthony, **12:209**

Rey, Joseph, 3:751

Reyes, Antonio de los (Bp.), 2:866

Reyes, Isabelo de los, Sr., 11:254

Reyes Salazar, Sabás, St., **12:209**

Reynal, Jeanne, 10:5

Reynald of Châtillon, 4:403

Reynolds, Ignatius A., 13:365

Reynolds, J., 3:678

Reynolds, Joshua, 13:474

Reynolds, Richard (d. 1535), St., 5:225, 12:8, **209–210**

Reynolds, Richard (Thomas) (d. 1642), Bl., 5:235

Reynolds, Susan, 5:706

Reynolds v. United States (1878), 3:655, 661

Rezzonico, Carlo della Torre. *See* Clement XIII (Pope)

RGP. *See* Romano-Germanic Pontifical

Rhapsodomacy, 13:328

Rhazes (Razes, Al-Rāzī), 1:238, 833, **12:210–211**

Rheims, School of, 1:448

Rheims-Douay New Testament, 1:296, 9:213

Rheinau Abbey (Switzerland), **12:211**

Rheinberger, Josef Gabriel Von, **12:212**

Rheticus (German astronomer), 4:251

Rhetoric, **12:212–214**

   argumentation, 1:659

   Aristotle, 1:684

   art, 1:747

   Byzantine literature, 2:773, 791

   dialectics, 4:723, 727

   Galatians, 6:54

   preaching, 11:617

   Second sophistic, 12:855

   study, 8:536

   teaching, 6:428

Rhetorica (Alcuin), 10:763

Rhetorica ecclesiastica (Panigarola), 10:822

Rhetorical criticism, 6:794

Rho, Giacomo, 3:495, **12:214**

Rhode, Peter Paul (Bp. of Green Bay, WI), 3:478, 14:782

Rhode Island, **12:214–218**

   Baptist church founding, 2:79

   Church-State relations, 3:641, 648, 650, 651

   Williams, Roger, founding, 14:759

   See also specific dioceses and archdioceses

Rhodes, Alexandre de, 1:407, 408, 10:977, **12:218–219**

Rhodes, Island of, 8:193

Rhodes, Mary, 8:786

Rhodes scholarships (Oxford University), 10:732

Rhonheimer, Martin, 10:186

Rhymed sermons, 11:612

Riario, Alessandro, 12:220

Riario, Girolamo, 3:855, 12:219–220, 13:197

Riario, Pietro (Card.), 12:219

Riario, Raffaele, 12:220

Riario family, **12:219–220**

Ribadeneyra, Pedro de, **12:220**, 13:369

Ribalta, Francisco de, 5:476

Ribat (Islamic institution), 7:616

Ribeiro, Bras, Bl., 1:951

Ribera, Francisco de, 12:186

Riberi, Antonio, 3:502

Ribero, Juan, 3:851

Ribet, Jérôme, **12:221**

Ribot, Philip, 3:133, 4:470

Ricaldone, Peter, 12:614

Ricardo, Antonio, 3:246

Riccardi, Alessandro (Bp.), 12:386

Riccardi, Andrea, 12:672

Riccardi, Placido, Bl., 5:624, 12:221

Ricceri, Luigi, 12:614

Ricchini, A., 2:844

Ricci, Lorenzo, 3:213, 792, 793, 7:787, **12:221–223**

Ricci, Matteo, 3:493–494, 613, 12:214, *223*, **223–225**

    Cattaneo, Lazzaro, 3:296

    Chinese mission, 7:784, 9:692

    Chinese rites controversy, 3:498, 514

    Clavius, Christopher, 3:772

    Indian Rites controversy, 7:402

Ricci, Scipione de' (Bp. of Pistoia-Prato), 12:225, **225–226**

    Josephinism, 3:615

    Synod of Pistoia, 1:846–847, 8:663, 11:363, 364

Ricci, Sebastiano, 10:4

Ricci, Vittorio, **12:226**

Rice, Edmund Ignatius, Bl., 7:573–574, 11:682, **12:226–227**

Rice, Joseph J. (Bp. of Burlington), 14:455

Rice, Luther, 2:79, **12:227**

Riceputi, Filippo, 5:627

Ricerche istoriche concernenti le due canoniche di S. Maria di Reno e di S. Salvatore (Trombelli), 14:213

Rich, Edmund (Abp. of Canterbury), St., 12:545

Rich, Richard, 5:749–750, **12:227**

Richar (Bp.), 12:549

Richard (Bp. of Chichester), 3:481

Richard, Claude, 12:278

Richard, Gabriel, 4:697, 8:521, 9:604–605, **12:227–228**

Richard I (Lionheart) (King of England), 7:145

    Celestine III (Pope), 3:319

    Crusades, 3:776, 4:400, 402, 411

    Cyprus, 4:461

    Fonevrault Convent, 5:793

    Garnerius of Rochefort, 6:99

    Geoffrey of York, 6:143

    Philip II Augustus, 11:244–245

Richard II (King of England)

    Alexander Neville, 1:263

    Arundel, Thomas, 1:766, 767

    Chaucer, Geoffrey, 3:451

    Clifford, Richard, 3:805

    Courtenay, William, 4:318

Robert Waldby of York, 12:271

    Western Schism, 13:79

Richard III (King of England), 4:317, 13:88

Richard III (More), 9:892

Richard de Clare, 1:433

Richard de la Vergne, François Marie (Card.), 1:357, **12:228**

Richard de Mores (Ricardus Anglicus), 3:48, **12:228–229**

Richard Fishacre, 1:878, 3:50, **12:229–230**, 262, 285

Richard Fitzralph (Abp.), 1:697, **12:230**, 234

Richard Grant of Canterbury (Abp.), **12:230**

Richard Knapwell (Clapwell), 4:275–276, 5:818, **12:230–231**, 14:45

Richard of Bury (Bp. of Durham), 4:444, **12:231–232**, 234, 265

Richard of Campsall, **12:232**

Richard of Canterbury (Abp.), 2:125, **12:232**

Richard of Chichester (Bp.), 4:88, 5:242

Richard of Conington, **12:232–233**

Richard of Cornwall, 4:411

Richard of Fountains, 1:219

Richard of Gravesend (Bp. of Lincoln, d. 1279), **12:233**

Richard of Gravesend (Bp. of London, d. 1303), **12:233**

Richard of Kilvington, **12:233–234**

Richard of Middleton (Mediavilla), 1:878, 2:391, 10:602, **12:234**

Richard of Saint-Vanne, 12:540

Richard of Saint-Victor, 3:68, **12:234–235**

    Andrew of Saint-Victor, 1:407

    Bonaventure, St., 2:485

    efficient causality, 5:101

    incommunicability, 7:379

    love, concept of, 8:827

    mysticism, 12:589, 759

    mysticism prose, 10:118

    Victorine spirituality, 14:485

Richard of St. Leger, 2:190

Richard of Swyneshed, **12:235–236**, 812

Richard of Thetford, 11:619

Richard of Verdun (Abbot), 12:588

Richard of Wallingford (Abbot), **12:236**

Richard Rufus of Cornwall, **12:236**

Richard the Bishop, 2:307

Richard the Lion-Hearted. *See* Richard I (Lionheart) (King of England)

Richardot, Francis (Bp. of Arras), 1:722

Richards, I. A., 1:143

Richardson, Alan, 12:195

Richardson, E., 4:385

Richardson, H. H., 3:670, 700, 709, 715

Richardson, Laurence, Bl., 5:228, 717, **12:236–237**

Richardson, Tilton v. (1971), 3:667

Richardson, William (c. 1550–90). *See* Gerard, Miles, Bl.

Richardson, William, Bl. (d. 1603), 5:234, **12:237**

Richelieu, Armand Jean du Plessis de (Card.), 12:*237*, **237–239**

    as Abp. of Aix, 1:197

    adviser, 8:432–433

    Amyraut, Moïse, 1:367

    Bérulle, Pierre de, 2:339

    Canada, 3:4

    Chaise-Dieu Abbey, 3:362

    Chézard de Matel, Jeanne Marie, 3:474

    Chrysostom of Saint-Lô, John, 3:573

    Church reform in France, 5:850

    Cistercians, 3:747

    domestic policy, 12:238

    Duvergier de Hauranne, Jean, 4:955

    Edict of Alais (1629) issued on advice of, 10:145

    foreign policy, 12:238–239

    Huguenots, 3:639, 7:168

    papal power, 12:680

    plots against, 8:336, 12:179

    religious character, 12:239

    Richer, Edmond, 12:239

    rule during Swedish Intervention (1630-35), 14:10

    Smith's patron, 13:234–235

    as Sorbonne headmaster, 10:889

Richelmy, A. (Abp.), 1:291

Richeome, Louis, 12:488

Richer (d. after 998), 9:447–448

Richer, Edmond, 3:639, 753, 10:843, **12:239–240**

Richer of Metz, 9:457

Richet, Charles, 11:463

Richier, Germaine, 1:803, 4:397

Richmond Diocese (VA), 2:37–38

Richter, Franz Xaver, **12:240**

Richter, Henry Joseph (Bp. of Grand Rapids, MI), 4:839

Richtlinien für die Gestaltung des Gotteshauses aus dem Geiste der römischen Liturgie, 8:621–622

Ricimer the Goth, 12:355

Rickaby, John, 12:775

Rickaby, Joseph, 2:624, **12:240**, 775

Ricke, Jodoco, **12:240–241**

Ricken, David Laurin (Bp. of Cheyenne, WY), 14:871

Rickert, H., 5:398

Ricoeur, Paul, 5:349, 10:869, **12:241–242**
 guilt, 6:568
 hermeneutics, 6:790, 796, 10:306
 literary myth, 10:121
 myth, 4:658
 sacramental theology, 12:475

Ricoldus de Monte Croce, **12:242–243**

Ricvera of Clastre, Bl., 11:666

Ridder, Charles H., **12:243**

Riddle, D. W., 2:365–366

Riddle and Reverie (Feeney), 5:663

Rider, John, 5:753

Ridley, Nicholas (Bp. of Rochester and London), 12:9, 10, **243**
 Anglican orders problem, 1:435, 436
 Brookes, James, 2:627
 Cranmer, Thomas, 4:334

Ridolfi, Laurentius, 3:51

Ridolfi Plot, 5:752

Riedl, Paul D., 8:821–822

Rieger, Karl (Father), 12:727

Riehl, Alois, 10:236

Riel, Louis, 8:270

Rienzo, Cola di, 1:548, 3:780, **828–829**, 855

Riepp, Benedicta (Mother), 2:259

Riera Coromina, Sebastián, 2:92

Riess, Bruno, 12:552

Rietveld, Gerrit Thomas, 3:680

Rietzenstein, Richard, 2:385

Rieux, René de (Bp. of Lyon), 2:160

Rievaulx Abbey (England), 1:137–138, 3:601, 749, *750*, 5:832, **12:243–245**, *244*

Riez, Council of (439), 1:116, 4:84

Al-Rifā'i, 7:620

Riforma cattolica (Gioberti), 6:230

Rig Veda, 6:840

Rigail Pátraic, 2:422

Rigali, Justin Francis (Abp. of St. Louis), 12:561

Rigaux, B., 5:523

Rigby, John, St., 5:233, **12:245**

Riggs, Thomas Lawrason, **12:245–246**

Righetti, M., 1:185

Right and rights, 8:65–67, 294

Righteousness. *See* Justification

Rights of Man (Paine), 5:262

The Rights of Man (Paine), 10:757

Rigobert (Bp. of Reims), 12:36

Rigoletto (Verdi), 14:446

Rigord of Saint-Denis, 1:463

Rigorism, 9:879–880, **12:246**
 Alexander VIII (Pope), 10:844
 Alphonsus Liguori, St., 1:311
 Cárdenas, Juan de, 3:102
 casuistry, 3:221
 Elvira Council, 5:178

Rijn, Rembrandt Harmensz van. *See* Rembrandt (Dutch painter)

Rilke, M., 5:544

Rilke, Rainer Maria, 1:429, 7:196–197

Rimbaud, Arthur, 3:767

Rimed Office, 8:682, **12:246–247**

Rimini, Council of, 8:555–556

Rinaldi, Filippo, Bl., **12:247–248**

Rinaldi, Odorico (Raynaldus), **12:248**

Rinaldi, Philip, 12:614

Rinaldi, Stephen, 12:717

Rinaldo (Card., 1618-1672), 5:372

Rinaldo (Card., 1655-1737), 5:372

Ringeltaube, W. T., 7:403

Rings, liturgical use of, 8:637, **12:248–249**, *249*

Il Rinovamento civile d'Italia (Gioberti), 6:229

Rinsei, Peter, Bl., 7:734

Rinuccini, Giovanni Battista (Abp. of Fermo), 1:77, 7:559, **12:249–250**, 724

Rinzai School, 14:916

Río de la Plata Diocese (Argentina), 1:648–649

Rio de la Plata mission (South America), 9:712–713

Riobé, G. (Abp. of Paris), 5:861

Riobó, Juan, 1:207

Riordan, Michael Augustine (Brother), 7:*573*, 11:682

Riordan, Patrick William (Abp. of San Francisco), 1:250, 2:867, **12:250–251**, 615, 647–648

Ripa, Cesare, 7:283

Ripa, Matteo, **12:251**

Ripalda, Juan Martînez de, 3:233, 242, **12:251–252**

Ripley, George, 2:627

Ripley, Sophia Dana, 2:627

Ripoll Abbey (Spain), **12:252**

Ripoll Diego, Eduardo, 2:92

Ripoll Morata, Felipe, Bl., **12:252**

Ripon Abbey (England), 4:449, 8:430, **12:253**

Rishanger, William, 12:532

Risorgimento, 3:100, 313–314, 7:672, 10:151, **12:253–255**

Risso Patron, Buenaventura (Bp. of Salta), 1:651

Rist, Valerius, **12:255**

Rita of Cascia, St., 1:872, 888, 5:632, **12:255**

Ritchie, D. G., 10:194

Rite of Baptism for Children, 2:65, 70

Rite of Christian Initiation of Adults (RCIA), 1:906, 3:253, 5:17, 553
 Confirmation, 4:84, 88, 90, 91, 10:77
 conversion, 4:237, 238, 242
 lay formation, 8:289

Rite of Confirmation, 4:88, 91

Rite of Consecration, 14:546

Rite of Penance, 8:650, 11:71–72

Rites, Congregation of, **12:256**, 493

Rites of committal, 6:32–33

Ritschl, Albrecht, 5:323, 332, 6:314, **12:256–257**, *257*, 14:234
 Christomonism, 12:739
 doctrine, 4:805
 ethics and a moral life, 5:396
 experience theology, 5:557
 justification, 8:88
 Knudson, 8:227
 liberal theology, 8:543
 Lipsius dialogue, 8:597

Rittelmayer, Friedrich, 1:513

Ritter, Joseph E. (Card.), 7:416, 418, **12:257–258**, 560–561

Ritual, Roman (*Rituale Romanum*), 4:9, 10, 11:26, **12:258**
 Anointing of the Sick, 1:486, 487
 blessing of lamb, 8:302
 catechumenate, 3:252
 celebration of the Hours, 8:735
 Council of Trent, 12:328
 Middle Ages, 8:658

Ritual bathing and purification, 2:57–58, 11:830–831

Ritual pattern theory, 8:178

The Ritual Process: Structure and Anti-Structure (Turner), 14:245

Ritual studies, 8:724, 12:87, **258–260**, 14:245–246

Rituale Sacramentorum Romanum (Santori), 1:486, 14:470

Ritualist Movement, 1:446–447

Rituals, nature of myth and, 10:122–123

Ritus Servandus in Celebratione Missae (1965), 10:640

Rivadavia, Bernardino, 1:650, 3:211, **12:260–261**, *261*

Rivail, Hippolyte Léon Denizard. *See* Kardec, Allan

River Brethren, 2:606, **12:261**

Rivera, Norberto (Abp.), 1:*632*

Rivero, Mariano, 12:280

Rivers, Clarence, 1:162

Rivier, Anne Marie. *See* Rivier, Marie-Anne, Bl.

Rivier, Marie-Anne, Bl., 11:683–684, **12:261–262**

Rivière, Jean, 11:976, 977, **12:262**

Rivista di cultura, 10:70

Rivista di Vita Spirituale (periodical), 6:42

Rivista internazionale di scienze sociali e ausiliarie (periodical), 14:109

Rivista Liturgica (periodical), 12:679

Rivists Italiana di filosofia neoscoloastica (periodical), 12:774

Rizal, José, 11:*260*

Rizo Patron, Buenaventura (Bp.), 3:759

Rizzo, Rita Frances. *See* Angelica (Mother)

RNA, 8:575–576

RNDM (Sisters of Our Lady of the Missions), 10:724

Roach, John (Abp. of St. Paul-Minneapolis), 2:875, 12:576

Road to Heaven, 3:232

Roads to Freedom (Sartre), 12:697

Robaut, Aloysius, 1:208, 209

Robert, André, **12:262**

Robert I (Duke of Burgundy), 1:927

Robert I (King of the West Franks), 3:172

Robert II (King of France), 1:9

Robert Bacon, 12:229, **262–263**

Robert Bellarmine, St. (d. 1621), 13:909

Robert Cowton, **12:263**

Robert Grosseteste (Bp. of Lincoln), 4:46, 11:633, **12:263–264**, 285

Adam Marsh, 1:107

Adam of Buckfield, 1:108

Agnellus of Pisa, Bl., 1:177

Albert the Great, St., 1:225

Alexander of Hales, 1:265

Aristotelianism, 1:674

light symbolism, 3:674

Robert Holcot, **12:265**

Robert Kilwardby (Card.), 3:72, **12:265–266**, 14:44

Albert the Great, St., 1:225

Aristotelianism, 1:674

Latin Averroism, 1:936

scholasticism, 12:760

University of Paris, 3:603

Robert of Arbrissel, Bl., 5:793, 10:503, **12:266**

Angers, 1:432

apostolici, 1:594

Bernard of Tiron, St., 2:316

Vitalis of Savigny, 12:711

Robert of Basevorn, 11:619

Robert of Bruges (Abbot), Bl., **12:267**

Robert of Bury Saint Edmunds, **12:267**

Robert of Chester, 1:238

Robert of Colletorto, 4:276

Robert of Courçon (Card.), 4:540, **12:267**

Robert of Courtonne (Card.), 12:582

Robert of Flamborough, 3:50, **12:267–268**

Robert of Geneva. *See* Clement VII (Antipope)

Robert of Hereford, 1:219

Robert of la Bassée, 1:265

Robert of Melun (Bp. of Hereford), 5:516, 9:455, **12:268**, 289

Robert of Molesme, St., 2:649, 3:746, 751, 9:767, 792, **12:268–269**

Robert of Newminster (Abbot), St., **12:269**

Robert of Orford (De Colletorto), 4:276, 5:818, **12:269**, 14:45

Robert of Soleto, Bl., **12:269**

Robert of Stratford (Bp. of Chichester), 3:481

Robert of Torigny, 1:462, 2:190, **12:269–270**

Robert of Torote, 8:52

Robert of Turotte (Bp.), 4:272

Robert of Walsingham, 12:232

Robert of Winchelsea (Abp. of Canterbury), 2:502, 3:72, 803, **12:270**

Robert Pullen (Card.), **12:270**

Robert Waldby of York (Abp.), **12:271**

Roberts, J. Deotis, 8:545

Roberts, John, St., 3:198, 5:234–235, **12:271**

Roberts, Thomas d'Esterre (Abp. of Bombay), **12:271–272**

Robertson, J. MacKinnon, 7:850

Robertson, James, **12:273**

Robertson, John M., 5:967, 968

Robespierre, Maximilien François de, 5:974, 10:146, **12:273**, 13:626

Robin, L., 1:678

Robinson, Armitage, 9:78

Robinson, Christopher, Bl., 5:233, **12:273**

Robinson, H. W., 10:79

Robinson, James M., 3:465, 4:657, 5:522

Robinson, John, 4:115

Robinson, John, Bl., 5:230

Robinson, John A. T., 4:585–586, 1:666, 7:909, 11:890

Robinson, Paschal (Charles), **12:273–274**

Robinson of Carlisle (Bp.), 12:273

Robles, Tranquilino Ubiarco, St., 6:545

Robles Hurtado, José María, **12:274**

Robot, Isidore (Abbot), **12:274–275**

Robusti, Jacobo, 1:37, 2:370, 375, 4:397, 8:345, 12:564

Roca, Julio A., 1:651

Roca Huguet, Constancio, Bl., 7:123

Roca Huguet, Cristino, Bl., 7:124

Rocca, Angelo, 1:889, **12:275**

Roccacasale, Mariano da, Bl., **12:275**

Roch, St., 12:*275*, **275–276**

Roche, Aloysius, 11:625

Roche, Christopher, 7:580

Roche, Daniel, 1:732

Roche, David, 7:582

Roche, John, Bl., 5:230, 784, 7:579

Rochefort Ships, Martyrs of, BB., **12:276–278**

Rochefort-Lucay, Lucrèce de (abbess), 12:390

Rochefoucauld, François de la (Card.), 3:747

La Rochelle (France), 7:168

Rochester, Ancient See of (England), 3:70, 8:103, 325, **12:278**

Rochester, John, Bl., 5:226, **12:278–279**

Rochester Sisters of St. Joseph, 9:406

Rochette, Gabrielle Charlotte Ranfray de la, 2:158

Rochford, Joseph, 7:581

Rochmarius, Andrew, 12:764

Rock, Johann, 1:330

Rockos, Thomas (Bp.), 7:400

Rococo architecture, 2:106, 3:675, 679, 707–708

Roda y Arrieta, Manuel de, 3:792, 794

Rodat, St. Émilie de, 7:24, **12:279**

Roden, Ben, 4:541, 542

Roden, George, 4:542

Rodie, Thomas (Bp. of Biloxi), 2:397

Rodolphus Agricola. *See* Agricola, Rodolphus (Roelof Huysman)

Rodotà, Felice Samuele, 7:650

Rodrigo de la Cruz, 4:289

Rodrigo del Padrón (Bp.), 12:684

Rodrígues, Alonso, 6:342

Rodrígues, Blas de (Father), 6:148

Rodrigues, Louis, Bl., 1:952

Rodrigues, Manuel, Bl., 1:951

Rodríguez (Bp. of Santiago), 3:485

Rodríguez, A. J., 14:460

Rodriguez, Agustin, 12:674

Rodríguez, Alfonso, 1:310, 7:782, 10:876, **12:279–280**

Rodríguez, Alphonsus, St., 3:770, 771, 4:94, **12:280**

Rodríguez, Blas, 5:875

Rodríguez, Edmigio, St., 1:298

Rodríguez, Joao, 3:112

Rodríguez, José Cecilio, St., 1:298

Rodríguez, Miguel, 5:63

Rodriguez de Araújo, Juan Jacinto, 3:112, 7:699

Rodríguez de Mendoza, Toribio, **12:280–281**

Rodríguez Santiago, Carlos Manuel, Bl., **12:281**

Rodriguez Tçuzu, João, **12:281–282**

Rodríguez Zorrilla, José Santiago (Bp.), 3:732, **12:282**

Roe (Rowe), Alban (Bartholomew), St., 5:235, **12:282–283**

Roe v. Wade (1973), 1:32, 34, 12:575, 14:315

Roemer, Theodore, **12:283**

Roemer v. Board of Public Works (1976), 3:667

Roerig, Gabriel, 2:14

Roey, Joseph van (Card.), 9:78

Rogation Days, 9:84, **12:283**

Rogationist Fathers of the Heart of Jesus, 5:865

Rogellus (martyr of Córdoba), 4:262

Roger (Archdeacon of Wiltshire), 12:617

Roger, Gaspar, 2:625

Roger, Peter. *See* Clement VI (Pope)

Roger, Pierre. *See* Clement VI (Pope)

Roger I (Norman king), 13:103

Roger II (Count of Sicily), 3:318, 7:469–470, **12:287–288**

Roger II (King of Sicily), 1:370, 371, 4:891, 7:82

Roger Bacon, 4:46, 5:242, 517, **12:283–285**, *284*

   Adam Marsh, 1:107

   Albert the Great, St., 1:225

   alchemy, 1:239

   Alexander of Hales, 1:265

   Arabian philosophy, 1:623

   astrology, 1:813

   Averroës, 1:935

   evolution of science, 12:798

   experimental science, 5:554

   Franciscan theology, 5:899

   individuation, 7:425

   Liber de causis, 8:533

   music, study of, 10:72

   optics, 12:813

   Robert Grosseteste, 12:263

   scholasticism, 12:760

Roger de Limesey (Bp. of Chester), 3:469

Roger de Pont L'Évêque (Abp. of York), **12:286**

Roger le Fort (Abp. of Bourges), Bl., **12:286**

Roger Marston, 1:878, **12:286–287**, 760

Roger of Conway, 12:234

Roger of Élan, Bl., **12:287**

Roger of Hoveden, 1:464

Roger of Lewes (Bp. of Wells), 2:152

Roger of Notingham, **12:287**

Roger of Salisbury (Bp.), **12:287**, 617

Roger of Swyneshed, **12:288**

Roger of Todi, Bl., **12:288**

Roger of Wendover, 1:464, 12:532

Roger of Worcester (Bp.), 2:125, **12:289**

Rogers, Bruce, 2:524

Rogers, Carl, 7:197

Rogers, John (architect), 3:715

Rogers, Mary Joseph (Mother), **12:289–290**

Rogers, Woodes, 2:14

Rogerus. *See* Theophilus (Benedictine writer)

Rogier, L. J., 10:263

Rogue, Pierre René, Bl., **12:290**

Rohan, A. G. de (Card.), 1:57

Rohault, Jacques, 3:185

Rohault de Fleury, 13:89

Rohde, E., 2:443

Rohling, Canon, 7:873

Rohlman, Henry P. (Bp. of Dubuque), 4:535, 923–924

Rohrbacher, René François, 3:619, **12:290**

Roifus, Karl, 11:644

Rojas, José Ramón, **12:290–291**

Rojas, Simon de, St., **12:291**

Rojas Pinilla military government, 8:870

Rokusuke, Lawrence, Bl., 7:733

Rokycana, John, 2:460–461

Roland, Nicolas, Bl., **12:291**

Roland of Cremona, **12:291–292**, 14:5

Roldán Lara, David, St., 2:156, 6:545, **12:292**

Rolduc Monastery (Netherlands), **12:292–293**

The Role of Knowledge in Western Religion (Randall), 10:205

Rolendis, St., **12:293**

Role-taking, in conversion, 13:272–273

Rolevinck, Werner, **12:293**

Rolin, Nicolas, 1:926

Roll and Codex, **12:293–295**

Rolle de Hampole, Richard, 5:243, **12:295–297**, *296*

   direction, spiritual, 4:762

   Holy Name, 7:32

   mysticism, 3:605, 10:118, 119

Rollini, Giuseppe, 2:544

Rollo (Hrolf the Ganger), 10:427–428

Rollo (Viking leader), 3:172

Rolly, Miguel (Father), 3:857

Roma sotteranea (Bosio), 3:224

Romagné, James René, 9:55, **12:297**

Romaillon, J. B., 2:714

Romain, Lenoir le, 3:751

Romain of Luxeuil, St., 3:409

Romainmôtier Abbey (Switzerland), **12:297–298**, *298*

Roman aristocracy, 13:493

Roman Baptismal Creed (R), 4:35

Roman baths, 2:*152*, 154

Roman Breviary, 1:97, 147, **2:610**, 3:73, 11:374

   Ambrosian hymns, 8:365

   Belleville Breviary, 12:486

   Council of Trent, 8:661, 12:328

   Dominican Rite, 4:838

   origins, 8:640, 730

   Quiñones, Francisco de, 11:869

   revisions of 1632, 12:208, 209

   revisions of Clement VIII, 5:820

   See also Hymns; Hymns and hymnals

Roman calendar, 3:571

   feasts, fixed and moveable, 8:644

   Marian feasts, 9:158–159, 12:663

   norms, 8:643–644

   reforms, 8:717

   saints, 8:643, 721, 12:662

   sanctoral cycle, 12:662, 663–664

   Saturnalia, 12:705

   Sunday, 13:608–609

   Vatican II reforms, 8:720, 12:663–664

Roman Catechism. *See Catechism of the Council of Trent* (Roman Catechism)

Roman Catechism for Pastors (1566), 14:174

Roman Catholic Church

   attitude toward usury, 14:354

   Holy Spirit, 14:134–135

   Mystici Corporis (Pius XII), 10:110

   natural family planning (NFP), 10:177–178

natural law doctrine, 10:193–195

necessity for salvation, 10:228

New Religious Movements and response, 10:302

original sin, 10:665–671

papal nuncio diplomatic representation of, 10:484–486

torture, 14:118

The Roman Catholic Church (McKenzie), 9:402

Roman Catholicism, **12:298–299**

Roman Catholic-Orthodox dialogue in U.S., 8:163

Roman Catholic-Pentecostal dialogue, 4:241–242

Roman Catholics of America, 3:289

Roman College (Italy), 8:181, 12:449

Roman Creed, 4:351

Roman de la Rose (Lorris and Meunand), 1:291–292, 3:452

Roman Empire, **12:299–322**

    altar of Victory, 1:337–338

    Ammianus, Marcellinus, 1:361–362

    architecture, 3:671, 673

    Aristotelianism, 1:673

    art, 1:749

    Asia Minor, 1:784

    augury, 1:850

    Babylon, 2:4

    biology, 2:400–401

    books, 2:512–513

    capital punishment, 3:86

    centurions, 3:348

    Chaldean astrology, 3:370

    Christian art under, 1:752–754

    Christian burial, 3:222–225

    Christian communities, 9:690

    Christian persecution, 7:653–654

    Christmas, 3:551

    Chronographer of 354, 3:569–570

    Church property, 3:724–725

    Church-State relations, 3:595, 630–634, 632–634

    Cilicia, 3:732

    civil authority, 1:921

    coinage, 10:478–480

    Constantinople, 4:185–188

    contraception and infanticide, 4:220

    cremation vs. burial, 4:358

    crucifixion, 4:389–391

    cult of emperor, 4:182, 186

    cult of Magna Mater, 4:450, 10:91–92

    Cynics, 4:456

    days and hours, 8:610

Dead Sea Scrolls, 4:561

Decapolis, 4:587–588

defensor civitatis, 4:609

democracy, 4:638

Dionysus cult, 10:93

dream interpretation, 4:903

dyptychs, 4:758

ecclesiastical organization, 5:17–18

Egypt during, 5:116

Equestrian Order (*ordo equestris*), 12:302–303

fall of, 3:40, 6:182–183

Galatia, 6:51

genuflection, 8:648

Germany, 6:171

Huns, 7:224

Iberian slaves, 13:*210*

Israel, 7:644–645

Jewish diaspora, 4:730–731, 7:867–868

Judaism, 3:631

Julian the Apostate, 8:51–52

literature and art, 12:307–309, 319–320

liturgical history, 8:654

military, 8:101, 12:301–302

Moldova, 9:765

mosaics, 10:1–3

natural law doctrine during, 10:180–181

Palestine, 10:784

Persia, 11:137

prostitution, 11:773

publicans, 11:809

ruler cult, 4:748, 750

secularization of Church property, 12:869–870

Senate, 12:302

Serbia, early, 13:8

sexual practice, 4:220

slavery, 12:306–307, 13:209, 211

Spain, 13:375–376

succession of emperors, 12:303–305, 310–313

theater, 4:893

vestal virgins, 14:464

women, status of, 14:814

works of charity, 3:406–408

See also Byzantine Empire; Carolingian Dynasty; Carolingian era; Church and State; Hapsburg, House of; Holy Roman Empire; Investiture struggle; Roman law; Roman persecution era; *specific emperors*; *specific Roman provinces and colonies*

Roman History (Dio Cassius), 12:319

Roman Inqusition, 7:490–491

Roman law, 10:42

    Acts of the Martyrs, 1:92

    Agustín, Antonio, 1:190

    archives, 1:636

    Canon Law, 3:40, 45, 49

    capital punishment, 3:84

    Church property, 3:723, 724

    Church-State relations, 3:636

    flagellation and scourging, 5:756

    marriage, 1:150

    natural law in political thought, 10:201

    relics, 1:314

    slavery, 1:155

    torture, 14:118

Roman martyrology, 2:106

Roman Missal (Pius V), 1:120, 243, 336, 501, 3:745, 11:374

Roman Missal for the Dioceses of Zaire, **9:674–676**

Roman Oration (Aelius Aristides), 12:308–309

Roman oratory of Divine love, 4:310

Roman persecution era, 1:*91, 92*

    Acts of the Martyrs, 1:90, 92–94, 3:404

    Alexandria, 1:268

    art, 1:752

    Aurelian, 1:171, 264, 3:406, 592, 593, 12:351

    canonization, 3:61

    capital punishment, 3:85–86

    cardinalate, 3:103

    chorbishops, 3:525–526

    Christmas, 3:553

    Church history, 3:591, 592–594

    Church property, 3:723–724

    Church-State relations, 3:632

    Colosseum, 3:860

    Constantius II, 4:749, 750

    Domitian, 4:858

    Galerius, 3:594, 632, 4:748, 749, 750, 7:654

    Julian the Apostate, 3:553, 632, 6:430–431

    Licinius, 4:749

    Marcus Aurelius, 2:431, 3:406, 592, 593

    Nero, 1:752, 3:591, 592

    Philip, 1:268

    Septimius Severus, 1:266, 268

    Valerian, 1:268, 3:103, 223–224, 594, 10:430

Roman persecution era *(continued)*
 works of charity, 3:402–406
 See also Decius (Roman Emperor);
  Diocletian persecution; *specific
  martyrs and saints*
Roman philosophy, 5:46–47
Roman pontifical and missal. *See*
 Pontifical, Roman
Roman primacy, 2:751–753
 Celestine I (Pope), St., 3:317
 Council of Chalcedon, 3:365–366
 Eastern Schism, 2:762–763, 824,
  825–826
 iconoclasm, 2:751–752
 Nicholas I (Pope), St., 3:599–600
 Palamism, 2:827
 Paschal II (Pope), 1:276
 pentarchy theory, 2:757, 822, 824,
  825
 Photius, 2:754–755, 822–823, 3:599
 Theophylactus (Metropolitan of
  Bulgaria), 2:824
 See also Byzantine Church; Eastern
  churches; Eastern Schism (1054)
Roman question, **12:322–323**
 Antonelli, Giacomo, 1:532–533
 Bonomelli, Geremia, 2:508–509
 Cavour, Camillo Benso di, 3:314
 Kulturkampf, 8:254
 Lateran Pacts, 3:621, 8:357
 Lavigerie, C. M. A., 8:388
 Leo XIII (Pope), 8:492
 Mussolini regime, 3:619
 Pius X (Pope), St., 3:642
 Pius XI (Pope), 11:394, 12:718
Roman religion, **12:323–327**
 afterlife, 1:165–166, 167–168
 anthropomorphism, 1:510
 Divine epithets, 5:307
 public morality, 12:309–310
 sacrifice, 12:510
Roman rite, **12:327–329**
 Agnus Dei, 1:185
 Ambrosian Rite, 1:343
 Aquileian Rite, 1:608
 ashes, 1:782
 Carmelite Rite, 3:126
 Carolingian reform, 3:563
 concelebration, 4:50
 cross, 4:382
 Ember Days, 5:186–187
 history, 8:714
 Kyrie eleison, 8:259–261
 Latin Rite, 8:367–369
 Liège, 563 acclamations, 8:617

 liturgical books, 8:638
 liturgical colors, 8:645
 liturgical Latin, 8:364–365
 liturgical year, 8:716–722
 Liturgy of the Hours, 8:729
 Lyonese Rite compared, 8:905–906
 responsorial psalm, 12:142
 Sequence, 13:1–5
 sermon, 13:18
 Servites, 13:26
*Roman Rite of Christian Initiation of
 Adults*, 2:76
Roman Union of the Order of St. Ursula,
 14:347–348
Roman Union Ursulines, 14:348
Romana Ecclesia (papal bull, Gregory
 XIII), 1:702
Romanae Sedis (apostolic constitution,
 Gregory XV), 7:411, 10:408
Romance, medieval, 4:401
Romancon, Benilde, St., 2:633
Romanesque architecture, 3:601,
 689–693
 Andorra, 1:401
 Apocalypse iconography, 1:543–544
 Bible cycles, 2:373
 Cluniacs, 3:811–812, 814
 Cologne, 3:844
 iconography of Apostles, 1:575
 illustrations, 3:*682, 686, 690*
 liturgy, 3:669–670
 revival, 3:709, 715
 Spain, 13:382
Romanesque art, 4:873, 9:129
Romani Pontifices et Cardinales
 (Panvinio), 10:828
Romani Pontificis (apostolic brief, Leo
 XIII), 7:391
Romania, **12:329–337**
 Basilians, 2:141
 Byzantine Basilians, 2:144
 Communism, 12:332–335, 337, 339
 demographic statistics, 12:330, 335
 Greek-Catholic Church, 12:334–335,
  336, 339–340
 Kostistk, Geremia of Valachia, Bl.,
  8:242
 map, 12:*331*
 monasticism, 9:801–802
Romanian Catholic Church (Eastern
 Catholic), 2:747–748, **12:337–340**
Romanian Orthodox Church, 2:745,
 10:690–693, 12:336, 337
 during Communist rule, 12:330–331,
  332, 333, 334, 335
 founding, 4:196

 membership, 13:10
 Moldova, 9:765–766, 767
Romanians, 7:214, 216
Romano, Ezzelino da, 12:291
Romano, Giulio, 12:643
Romano, Julius, 3:484
Romano of Rome, **12:340**
Romano pontifici eligendo (apostolic
 constitution, Paul VI), 3:106, 11:30,
 500
Romanoff, P., 5:520
Romano-Germanic Pontifical (RGP),
 8:655
Romanorum Pontificum (*motu proprio*,
 Pius XI), 11:753
Romanos, 2:741–742
Romans, ancient, 4:139–140, 142–143,
 9:565
Romans, Epistle to the, **12:340–344**
 Abraham, 1:37
 addresses, 12:342
 asceticism, 1:776
 atonement, 1:837
 authenticity and integrity,
  12:341–342
 baptism, 2:59, 60, 61, 65
 beatific vision, 2:169, 171
 Beelen, Jan Theodoor, 2:200
 capital punishment, 3:84–85
 charisms, 3:389, 578
 Chaucer, Geoffrey, 3:456
 choice, 13:440
 Christian law, 8:403
 Christian way of life, 3:546
 Christology, 3:560
 Church, 3:582–583
 conscience, 4:141, 144–145
 content analysis, 12:343–344
 covenant, 4:328
 creation in crisis, 5:52
 creation of new man, 9:87
 death imagery in baptism, 2:75
 descent of Christ into hell, 4:684
 development of Gospel tradition on
  Passion, 10:921
 dietary laws, 4:743
 Divine election, 5:146
 Divine judgment, 8:35, 37
 Divine plan, 5:58
 edification, 5:85
 enmity, 5:264
 eternal law concept, 8:456
 exegesis, 5:522–523
 faith, profession through baptism,
  2:59

glory, 6:244

glory of God (end of creation), 6:246

glossolalia, 6:249

Gnosis, 6:255

God's spirit, 13:427, 428

grace, 6:381, 382, 382–383

guilt, 6:571–572

Hades, 6:604

heaven, 6:684, 685

Holy Name, 7:31

Holy Spirit, 13:438

homosexuality, 7:66, 13:49

house churches, 2:146

ineffability of God, 7:445

Jesus, baptism of, 2:72

justice of God, 8:71, 72

justice of men, 8:74

justification controversy, 8:78–80

kenosis, 8:143

kerygma, 8:157, 158

Kingdom of God, 8:175

kiss of peace, 8:185

law, 13:438

law of love, 8:403

law vs. spirit, 13:425

lay spirituality, 8:413

life of grace, 13:441

Lord's Day, 8:782

love as fulfillment of law, 8:400

merit, 6:383

Monothelitism, 7:80

mystical body of Christ, 10:100, 101

natural law origins, 8:399

original sin, 9:93, 10:664

outline, 12:342–344

pacifism, 10:745

Paul's second and third missionary
    journeys, 11:14–16

peace, 11:49–50

preaching and teaching, 11:627

Precious Blood, 11:638, 641

predestination, 11:651

purpose and provenance, 12:340–341

ransom, 11:909

redaction criticism scholarship,
    10:303–304

redemption, 9:95, 11:967

religious homelessness, 5:56

Sanday, William, 12:665

significance of, 12:344

sin, 13:145–146, 148

sins of Adam, 9:87

Son of David, 13:310

Son of God, 13:314

Son of Man, 13:318

sons of God, 13:322

soul, 13:336

sovereignty, 13:371

spirit, 13:425

suffering servant, songs of the,
    13:591

union with Christ, 13:439

universality of Christianity, 3:274

vengeance, 14:438–439

wisdom, 14:791

women, role of, 14:831

women as deacons, 4:554

works of charity, 1:300, 301, 302,
    3:401, 402, 405

Romansh Mustér, 4:775

Romantic love, 11:332

Romantic theology, 13:911

Romanticism, 11:294

    aesthetics, 1:142

    Angelus Silesius, 1:429

    Anglo-Catholics, 1:444

    Catholic revival, 4:483–484

    Middle Ages, 9:611

    philosophy of history, 6:884

Romanticism, literary, 5:189

Romanticism, philosophical, 8:271,
    598–599, 693–695, 10:128,
    12:344–346, 732–734

Romanum decet pontificem (1692),
    10:247

Romanus (Pope), **12:346–347**

Romanus, SS., 8:63, **12:347**, 599–600

Romanus I (Lecapenus) (Byzantine
    Emperor), 2:757, 798, 4:174,
    12:347–348

Romanus Melodus, St., 2:802, 5:191,
    12:348–349, *349*, 13:327

Romanus of Auxerre, 12:347

Romanus of Caesarea, 12:347

Romanus of Le Mans, 12:347

Romanus of Moscow, 12:347

Romanus of Nepi, 12:347

Romanus of Reims, 12:347

Romanus of Rouen, 12:347

Romanus of Subiaco, 12:347

Romanus of Tusculum. *See* John XX
    (Pope)

Romanus Ostiarius, 12:347

Romanus Pontifex (apostolic
    constitution, Pius IV), 7:650

Romanus Pontifex (papal bull, Clement
    IX), 7:777

*Romanus Pontifex tamquam primas
    ecclesiae* (Roskoványi), 12:383

Romanus the Hermit, 12:347

Romaric, 1:333

Romary, St., 12:108

Romay, Tomás, 5:357

Rome (Italy), **12:349–363**

    as Apostolic See, 1:589

    basilicas, 9:231

    catacombs, 3:222, *223*, 224–225, *224*

    Church property, 3:724

    Community of Sant'Egidio
        evangelization, 12:672–673

    early Christianity, 7:237, 12:349–350

    early Roman Christians, 12:350–351

    hymnody, 7:242–243

    Jewish diaspora, 4:730, 731

    liturgical history, 8:651

    liturgical languages, 8:667–668

    Manichaeism mission, 9:109

    Middle Ages, 9:613

    public buildings for church use,
        13:140

    rebuilding, 13:197

    Rienzo, Cola di, 3:827–828

    stational churches in, 13:498–499

    World War II, 11:397–398

    See also Church architecture; Guelfs
        and Ghibellines; Roman law; Sack
        of Rome

Rome, Councils of (340-1079)

    adoptionism, 1:119

    Apollinarianism, 1:560

    Arianism, 1:662

    Eucharist, 1:64

    God the Holy Spirit, 6:293

    marriage, 1:150–151

Rome, legends of Christian, **12:363–364**

Rome, Patriarchate of, **12:364–365**

Rome, Synod of (372-769), 1:151, 574,
    3:104, 595, 13:885

Rome, Synod of (1960), 7:936

Rome et Lorette (Veuillot), 14:465

Rome Peace Accord (1992), 10:40

Rome pendant le Concile (Veuillot),
    14:466

*Romeo and Juliet (Montecchi e
    Capuletti)* (Bellini), 2:229

Romero, Francisco, 3:851

Romero, Juan, **12:365**

Romero, Oscar A. (Abp. of San
    Salvador), 5:176–177, **12:365–366**,
    366

Romillon, Jean-Baptiste, 1:943

Romilly, Samuel, 3:88

Römisch Elegien (Goethe), 6:331

*Römischen Päpste in den letzten vier
    Jahrhunderten* (Ranke), 6:879–880

Rommen, Heinrich, 10:185

Romo González, Toribio, St., **12:366**

Romuald, St., 3:600, 5:766, 792, 7:661, **12:366–367**

    Adalbert of Prague, 1:102

    Bruno of Querfurt, St., 2:648

    Camaldolese, 2:895–896

    chronicle of, 1:463

    Cuxa Abbey, 4:450

Romulus Augustus (Roman Emperor), 3:633, 12:321–322

Ronan, St., 12:*367*, **367–368**

Roncagli, Diet of (1158), 1:127

Roncalli, Angelo (Card.). *See* John XXIII (Pope), Bl.

Roncalli, Giovanni. *See* John XXIII (Pope), Bl.

Ronchamp, Notre-Dame du Haut (France), 4:324, 8:623, 627, **12:368**, *369*

Ronge, Johann, 3:624, **12:368–369**

Ronsin, Pierre, 4:113

Rooms Katholieke Staatspartij, 10:262

Rooms-Katholieke Kerk der Oud-Bisschoppelijke Clerezie (OBC), 14:363

Rooney, William (Father), 3:281

Roosevelt, Franklin Delano, 1:667, 2:429–430, 3:458, 4:294–295

Roosevelt, Theodore, 6:*205*, 207

Roothaan, Johann Philipp, 3:757, **12:369–370**

Roothan, Jan, 7:788

Roper, William, **12:370–371**

Rore, Cipriano de, 1:766, 12:*371*, **371**

Rorty, Richard, 5:829, 10:205

Ros Florensa, José María, 2:92

Rosa, Carmen Francisca. *See* Sallés y Barangueras, María del Carmen, Bl.

Rosa y Figueroa, Francisco de la, **12:371–372**

Rosal Vásquez, María Vicente, Bl., **12:372**

Rosales, Román Adame, St., 6:545, **12:372–373**

Rosalia, St., **12:373**

Rosario do Porto do Cachoeira, Church of (Brazil), 9:*719*

Rosary, 12:*373*, **373–376**

    Alan de la Roche, 1:204–205

    development, 3:192

    Domincans, 4:847

    Dominic of Prussia, 4:831

    Fifteen Saturdays (Longo), 8:776

    Franciscan crown, 4:387, 6:42

    popular devotion, 4:710

    See also Hail Mary

Rosary Basilica (Lourdes, France), 8:819, 820

The Rosary of the Glorious Virgin (Castello), 12:375

"Rosary Priest." *See* Peyton, Patrick Joseph

Rosas, Juan Manuel, 1:650–651

Rosati, Joseph (Bp. of St. Louis, MO), 2:44, 3:475, 8:810–811, 9:741, 12:*376*, **376–377**, 555, 559, 14:528

Rosaz, Edoardo Giuseppe (Bp. of Susa), Bl., **12:377**

Roscelin of Compiègne, 1:15, 19, 496, **12:377**, 14:204

Roscelli, Agostino, St., **12:377–378**

Roschini, G. M., 3:558

Roscrea Abbey (Ireland), **12:378**

Rose, G. L., 2:379

Rose, V., 1:678

Rose of Baba and Guayaquil. *See* Molina, Mercedes de Jesús, Bl.

Rose of Lima, St., **12:378–379**, *380*

Rose of Viterbo, St., **12:379–380**

Rosecrans, Sylvester (Bp. of Cincinnati), 3:868, 10:571, 11:820

Roseline, St., **12:380**

Roselli, Salvatore Maria, **12:380–381**, 771

Rosellis, Antonio, 3:52

Rosemont College (Philadelphia), 11:*238*

Rosen-Ayalon, M., 2:381

Rosenberger v. Rectors and Visitors of the University of Virginia (1995), 3:664–665

Rosencreuz, Christian, 12:381–382

Rosenkranz, Karl, 6:709

Rosenzweig, Franz, 7:865

Rosetta Stone, 12:*381*, **381**

Rosicrucians (occult sect), 7:321, **12:381–382**

Roskoványi, Augustus (Bp.), **12:383**

Roslin, Thoros, 5:*417*

Rosminians, 4:630, **12:385**

Rosmini-Serbati, Antonio, 7:673, 12:346, *383*, **383–385**

    Antonelli, Giacomo, 1:532

    existence of God, 6:313

    reflex principle, 12:726

    works of charity, 3:419, 420

Rospigliosi, Giulio. *See* Clement IX (Pope)

Ross, Fred, 3:460

Ross, Johannes (Bp.), 3:515

Ross, John Elliot, **12:385–386**

Ross, W. D., 1:679, 2:624, 4:673

Rossano Gospel, 2:729, 731, *732*

Rosselino, Bernardo, 3:213, 12:578

Rosselli, C., 2:375

Rossello, Maria Giuseppa, St., 4:534, **12:386**

Rosseter, John, 1:890

Rossetti, Carlo (Card.), **12:386–387**

Rosshirt of Ebrach (Abbot), 5:32

Rossi, Giovanni Battista de, 3:142, **12:387**

    Castel Gandolfo villa, 3:212

    catacombs, 3:224

    Cecilia, St., 3:315

    Church property, 3:723

    Discalced Carmelites, 3:144

    Epitaph of Abercius, 1:20

    exegesis, 5:519

Rossi, John Baptist, St., 12:*387*, **387–388**

Rossi, Luigi, **12:388**

Rossi, M. Filomena (Sister), 9:125

Rossi, Pellegrino, **12:388**

Rossignoli, Bernardino, 3:207

Rossini, Gioacchino, **12:389**

Rostagnus (Abp. of Arles), 1:694

Rostaing (Abp. of Arles), 1:453–454

Rostan, L. L., 13:793–794

Rostovtzeff, M. I., 10:94

Rosweyde, Leribert, 2:471

Rosweydus, Heribert, 7:328

Roswitha of Gandersheim, 9:447, **12:389–390**

Rotelle, John E., 1:871

Roth, Cecil, 3:454

Roth, Heinrich, **12:390**

Roth v. U.S. (1957), 11:519

Rothstein, J. W., 3:565–566

Rotlandus (Abp. of Arles), 1:694

Rotta, Angelo, 7:219

Rotulo de Giosué, 5:865

Rouault, Georges, 1:803, 2:376, 3:713, 4:397

Rouchouze, Stephen (Bp.), 6:669–670

Rougemont, François, **12:390–391**

Rougemont Abbey (France), **12:390**

Rouille, Guillaume, 10:482

Rouleau, Felix Raymond Marie (Card.), **12:391**

Round baptismal fonts, 2:76

Rouquette, Adrien Emmanuel, **12:391**

Roura Farró, Francisco, 2:92

Rouse, Stephen. *See* Rowsham, Stephen, Bl.

Rousseau, Jean-Bernard. *See* Rousseau, Scubilion, Bl.

Rousseau, Jean-Jacques, **12:391–394,** *392*

  absolutism, 1:44

  Alexander I (Emperor of Russia), 1:252

  authority, 1:920

  censorship, 3:792

  civil authority, 1:921

  civil religion, 3:755, 11:460

  community, 4:38

  deism, 4:617, 5:974

  Enlightenment, 5:255, 256, 262

  ethical formalism, 5:388

  ethics, 5:395–396

  freedom of religion, 5:947

  humanism, 7:195, 196

  Hume, David, 7:200

  Lacordaire influenced, 8:271

  law of nature, 10:183

  religious encyclopedias, 5:91, 93, 210

  Robespierre, 12:273

  social contracts, 5:256, 13:241, 483

  society, 13:279

  sovereignty, 13:371

  will and willing, 14:723

Rousseau, Scubilion, Bl., 2:633, **12:394**

Rousselet, Louis de (Father), 2:553

Rousselot, Pierre, 7:791, 8:829, **12:394–395**

Roux, Benedict, 8:118

Roux-Lavergne, Pierre, 12:773

Rovenius, Philippus (Abp. of Philippi), **12:395**

Rovere, Francesco della. *See* Sixtus IV (Pope)

Rowe, Nicholas, 13:60

Rowland, Thomas, 1:22

Rowley, H. H., 5:520

Rowsham, Stephen, Bl., 5:229, **12:395**

Roy, Bowen v. (1986), 3:663

Roy, Maurice (Card.), 3:8, 10, **12:395–396**

Royal absolutism. *See* Monarchy

Royal College of Physicians, 8:592

Royal Declaration (England), **12:396–397**

Royal Dublin Society, 8:326

Royal Gallicanism, 6:75–76

Royal psalms, 9:541–542

Royal Society of London, 5:256

Royaumont Abbey (Paris), 3:749

Roybal, Santiago, 10:286

Royce, Josiah, 11:296, 12:*397*, **397–398**

  Brightman, Edgar Sheffield, 2:617

  ethical formalism, 5:388

idealism of, 7:302

panpsychism, 10:824

philosophy of religion, 12:69–70

Santayana, George, 12:681

self, concept of, 12:883

Royer-Collard, P. P., 7:434

Royo Pérez, Joachim, 4:732

Rozario, Patrick d' (Bp. of Rajshahi, Bangladesh), 2:53

Rozycki, J., 1:19

RSHM (Religious of the Sacred Heart of Mary), 9:302–303

RU-486 (abortion pill), 3:11

Rua, Michael, 12:614

Ruaidhrí O'Conchobhair, 8:410

Rubatto, Maria Francesca, Bl., **12:398**

Rubeis, Leonardo de (Rossi), **12:398–399**

Ruben, Leonard, 1:14

Rubens, Peter Paul, 2:114

  Abraham, images of, 1:37

  Antwerp, 1:539

  architecture, 3:706

  crucifixion art, 4:397

  The Martyrdom of Saint Ursula and the 11,000, 14:*346*

  Peter Paul and Philip Rubens with Justus Lipsius and John van Woverius, 12:121

  St. Norbert of Xanten, 10:420

Rubert of Deutz, 7:836

Rubies, alleged magical properties of, 11:646

Rubino, Antonio, 12:219, **399**

Rubio, Alfredo (Bp. of Giradot, Columbia), 4:157

Rubio, Antonio, **12:399**

Rubio Alonso Dositeo, Bl., 7:124

Rubio Alvarez, Federico, Bl., 7:122

Rubio y Peralta, José María, Bl., **12:399–400**

Rublëv, Andrei, **12:400**

Rubricarum instructum (*motu proprio,* John XXIII), 7:936

Rubroek, Willem van, 3:492

Rucki, Lambert, 12:493

Rudd, Daniel, 1:159–160, 10:570

Rudhart, J., 12:508

Rüdiger, Andreas, 5:47, 263

Rudigier, Franz Josef (Bp. of Linz), Ven., 1:914, 8:255, **12:400–401**

Rudimenta Juris Naturae et Gentium (Muriel), 10:66

Rudloff, Leo (Father), 2:256

Rudolf (Bp. of Würzburg), 2:461

Rudolf, Kurt, 6:263

Rudolf, Rainer, 1:729

Rudolf II (Holy Roman Emperor), 2:153

Rudolf Acquaviva and Companions, BB., **12:401**

Rudolf of Worms, 9:33

Rudolph (Archduke of Austria), 2:201–202

Rudolph, Joseph (Father), 5:881

Rudolph, W., 3:566

Rudolph I (Holy Roman Emperor), 6:638, 7:85, 86

Rudolph II (Holy Roman Emperor), 1:911, 4:482, 6:639

Rudolph of Vauserier, 1:23

Rueda Mejías, Miguel, Bl., 7:125

Ruelens, Charles, 2:9

Ruether, Rosemary Radford, 5:49, 677, 678

Ruffini, Ernesto (Card.), **12:401–402**

Ruffo, Fabrizio (Card.), **12:402,** 666

Rufina, SS., **12:402–403**

Rufina of Caesarea, 12:403

Rufina of Sirmium, 12:403

Rufinianus, St., 2:163

Rufinus (Abp.), **12:403–404**

Rufinus (Armenian calligrapher), 1:700

Rufinus (Bp. of Assisi), 1:256, 790, 3:47

Rufinus of Aquileia, 3:594, **12:404–406**

  Apostles' Creed, 1:577

  Cassian, John, 3:207

  catechisms, 3:239, 243

  Chromatius of Aquileia, St., 3:564

  chronicles of, 12:320

  creedal statements, 4:351, 352

  Cyril of Jerusalem, 4:470

  descent of Christ into hell, 4:685

  Dydimus the Blind, 4:738

  Fabiola, St., 5:585

  Jerome, St., 1:387, 3:595, 5:292, 12:404–405

  John of Jerusalem, 7:971

  legends of Abgar, 1:21

  life of, 12:404–405

  property, 11:758

  translations of, 12:405

  works, 12:405

Rufus, Tineius, 2:84

Rugambua (Card.), 5:*434*

Rugerus. *See* Theophilus (Benedictine writer)

Rugg, John, Bl., 5:226, 627, **12:406**

Ruggieri, Michele, 3:493–494

Ruhuna, Joachim (Abp. of Gitega), 2:712

Ruinart, Thierry, **12:406–407,** 453

Ruiz, Emmanual, 4:503

Ruiz, Samuel (Bp. of San Cristobal de las Casas, Mexico), 9:585

Ruíz Blanco, Matías, **12:407**

Ruiz Cascales, Proceso, Bl., 7:124

Ruiz Cuesta, José, Bl., 7:125

Ruiz de Larrinaga García, Teodoro, 2:92

Ruiz de los Paños y Angel, Pedro and eight Companions, BB., **12:407–408**

Ruíz de Montoya, Antonio, **12:408**

Ruíz del Corral, Felipe, 12:105

Ruiz Fraile, Felipe, Bl., 4:494

Ruiz Martínez, Jose Maria, Bl., 4:494

Ruíz y Flores, Leopoldo (Abp.), **12:408–409**

Rule and Constitutions (Passionist Community), 10:931, 932

Rule and Exercise of Holy Living (Taylor, Jeremy), 13:770

Rule for Monks (Benedictine). *See* Benedictine Rule

Rule of Échtgus Úa Cúanáin, 12:378

Rule of faith, 4:349, 611–612, **12:409–410**

The Rule of Perfection (Fitch), 5:750

Rule of St. Anthony, 1:534

Rule of St. Augustine. *See* Augustine, Rule of St.

Rule of St. Benedict. *See* Benedictine Rule

Rule of the Master (Regula Magistri), 2:262, 263

"Rules and Statutes" (1612), 14:122

Rules of Law (*Regulae Iuris*), **12:410–411**

The Rules of Sociological Method (Durkheim), 4:952

Al-Rūmī, Jalāal al-Dīn, 7:612

Rummel, Joseph Francis (Abp. of New Orleans), 8:814–815, 10:295–296, 588, **12:411–412**

Rumschlag, Mary Catherine (Mother), 6:238

Runcie, Robert (Abp. of Canterbury), 1:*435*, 441, *443*, 5:67, 68

Ruotger of Trier (Abp.), 4:87

Ruotmann of Hausen, 1:312

Rupert of Deutz (Abbot), 2:625, 9:454, **12:412**

Rupert of Ottobeuren, Bl., **12:412–413**

Rupert of Salzburg, St., 1:908, **12:413–414**, 670–671

Ruppert, Frederick A., 1:210

Rural dean. *See* Vicar Forane

Rural life conference. *See* National Catholic Rural Life Conference (NCRLC)

Rural sociology, Catholic, 8:586

Rusati, F., 8:555

Rush, Benjamin, 3:88, 13:796–797, *796*

Rushworth, John, 4:376

Ruskin, John, 3:669, 694, 699, 701, 709, 12:*414*, **414–415**

Russell, Bertrand, 5:95, 397, 11:297, **12:415–416**

  agnosticism, 1:180

  Alexander, Samuel, 1:252

  ambiguity, 1:334

  antimonies, 1:520, 521

  atomism, 1:831

  classes, 13:408

  Copleston debate, 4:252

  experience, 5:554

  form, 5:803

  identity, 7:302

  knowledge, 8:220

  phenomenalism, 11:230

  realism, 14:326

  sense knowledge, 12:910–911

  soul, 13:348

Russell, Charles Taze, 1:135, 7:751, **12:416**

Russell, David S., 5:337

Russell, John (Bp. of Richmond, VA), **12:416**, 14:543

Russell, Mary Baptist (Mother), 2:868, **12:416–417**

Russell, Odo, **12:417**

Russell, Richard, **12:417**

Russell, William Thomas (Bp. of Charleston, SC), **12:417–418**, 13:366

Russia, 5:687, **12:418–430**, *421*, *422*

  Byzantine Church, 2:775

  caesaropapism, 2:851

  Catherine II (The Great), 1:252, 3:264–266, 795

  church architecture, 3:689

  Communism, 12:427–430, 429

  Daniel Palomnik, 4:513

  demographic statistics, 12:419

  ecclesiastical organization, 1:252, 12:419

  Georgia (nation), 6:155–156

  Grand Priory of Knights of Malta, 8:194

  Gregory XVI (Pope), 1:84, 6:509

  Haskalah Movement, 6:662–663

  Jesuits, 1:252, 3:265, 795

  Jews, 7:873, 8:13

  Khazars, 8:164

  Latvia, 8:375

  Lithuania, 8:606

  Losskiĭ, Nīkolaĭ Onufrievich, 8:794

  map, 12:*420*

  missions, 1:252, 3:265, 795, 8:249, 9:694–695

  monasticism, 9:802–803

  Mongol invasion, 1:263

  Peter I (Emperor), 11:181–182

  Pius VI (Pope), 11:376

  Poland, 11:445–446

  Raskolniks, 11:915–916

  Sergius (Patriarch of Moscow), 13:12

  Slavophilism, 13:216

  sobornost, 13:238

  Solov'ev, Vladimir Sergeevich, 13:306–307

  See also Russian Byzantine Catholic Church; Russian Orthodox Church; Soviet Union

Russian Academy of Sciences (St. Petersburg), 5:256

Russian Alaska, 9:695

Russian art, 12:400

Russian Byzantine Catholic Church, 2:748

Russian Chant, **12:431**

Russian Holy Synod (1870), 10:682

Russian liturgy, **12:431–432**

Russian Orthodox Church, **10:693–696**

  Antonii, 1:533–534

  Armenia, 1:703

  Belorussia, 2:212

  biblical canon, 3:27

  Bulgakov, Sergeĭ Nikolaevich, 2:679

  China, 3:501

  Church-State relations, 7:53–54

  Communism, 2:745

  Confession, 4:*76*

  creedal statements, 4:355

  Crusades against, 4:413

  establishment, 4:196

  Georgia, 6:156

  Japan, 7:743

  Knights of Malta, 8:194

  Moldova, 9:765–766

  monastic superiors, 1:9

  Moscow Patriarchate, 2:745

  Sergius (Patriarch of Moscow), 13:12

  Sergius of Radonezh, St., 13:15–16

  Slavophilism, 13:216

  Soviet government, 2:212

  split within, 13:12

Russian Primary Chronicle, 10:447

Russian Revolution (1917-21), 3:501, 8:468, 9:695

Russian theology, 5:782–783, **12:432–437**

Russman, T., 5:831

Russo, Nicholas, 12:777

Rusticus (Bp. of Trier), 6:269

Rusticus Diaconus, 2:797

Rusudan (Queen of Georgia), 6:155, 156

Rutebeuf, 4:400

Ruth (biblical figure), 6:126

Ruth, Book of, **12:437–438**

Ruthenian Catholic Church (Eastern Catholic), 2:141, 747

Ruthenians, 1:252, 3:613, 785

See also Brest, Union of

Rutherford, E., 1:836

Rutherford, Joseph Franklin, 7:751, **12:438**, *439*

Rutilius Namatianus, Claudius, 12:320

Rutski, Velamin (Abp. of Kiev), 2:143, 12:422

Ruysbroeck, Jan van, Bl., 2:217, 12:*439*, **439–441**

    Albert the Great, St., 1:226

    apophatic theology, 1:568

    Carthusian spirituality, 3:192

    influence, 13:454, 455

    mystical theology, 5:918

    mysticism, 3:605

    mysticism literature, 10:118

    pantheism, 2:629

    spiritual direction, 4:762

    three ways, 14:66

Rwanda, 4:107, **12:441–443**, *442*

Ryan, Abram Joseph (poet), **12:443**

Ryan, Dennis (Father, fl. 1817), 9:56

Ryan, Dermot (Abp. of Dublin), **12:443–444**

Ryan, Edward F. (Bp. of Burlington), 14:455–456

Ryan, James (Bp. of Alton, IL), 1:584

Ryan, James Hugh (Abp.), 10:223, 12:*444*, **444–445**, 777

Ryan, John Augustine, 12:*445*, **445–446**

Ryan, Joseph (Abp. of military services USA), 9:629

Ryan, Joseph T. (Abp. of Anchorage), 1:209, 396

Ryan, Mary Perkins, **12:446**

Ryan, Patrick John (Abp. of Philadelphia), 8:146, 11:240, **12:446–447**

Ryan, Vincent J. (Bp. of Bismarck), 2:423

Rycerz Niepokalanej, 8:229

Rycharde Rolle hermyte of Hampull (Wrode), 12:*296*

Ryder, Henry (Bp. of Gloucester), 5:472

Ryder, James, 6:146

Rygge, Robert, 12:131, **447–448**

Ryken, Francis Xavier (Brother), 12:*448*, **448**, 14:876

Ryken, Theodore James. *See* Ryken, Francis Xavier (Brother)

Ryle, Gilbert, 7:295, 8:221

Ryrie, Charles C., 4:776

Rythmes du Monde (periodical), 12:533

S

Sá, Mem de, 2:588

Sa'adia ben Joseph, Gaon, 2:359, 5:508–509, 7:863, 8:8, **12:449–450**

Saarinen, E., 3:681, 716

Saavedra, Cornelio, 1:650

Saavedra, Sylvester de, 10:14

Saba (Sheba) (South Arabia), **12:450–451**

Sabaeans. *See* Mandaean religion

Al-Sabah family, 8:258

Sabaoth, **12:451**

Sabas, St., 4:472–473, 636

Sabas, SS., 8:381, **12:451–452**

Sabas of Palestine, 12:451–452

Sabas the Goth, 12:452

Sabas the Martyr, 12:452

Sabas the Younger, St., **12:452–453**

Sabatier, Louis Auguste, 5:711, 9:753–754, **12:453**

Sabatier, Paul, 5:737, **12:453**

Sabatier, Pierre (Bp. of Amiens), 1:359, 5:519, **12:453–454**

Sabbatarianism, **12:454–455**

Sabbath, **12:455–460**

    Church-State relations, 3:662

    covenant, 4:327

    Genesis creation account, 4:340

    Judaic significance, 8:8

    Lord's Day, 8:782

    origin of the term, 12:457–458

    prohibitions against working, 12:457

    servile work, 12:460

    Seventh-Day Adventists, 13:38–39

    Sunday, 8:641–642, 13:609–610

Sabbath Year, **12:460–461**

Sabeans, 12:450–451

Sabellianism, 5:161, 279, 452, **12:462**

    Asterius the Sophist, 1:809

    Christology, 3:560

    Clarenbaud of Arras, 3:761

    Dionysiana collectio, 4:752

    Dionysius (Pope), St., 4:753

    homoousios, 4:197, 198, 7:65

    hypostasis, 7:263

    Synod of Ancyra (358), 1:398

    See also Modalism

Sabellius, 2:879, 12:462

Sabetti, Luigi, **12:462**

Sabev, Christophor, 2:684, 10:686–687

Sabina of Rome, St., **12:462–463**, *463*

Sabinian (Pope), **12:463**

Sabran, Louis de, **12:463–464**

Sabrīshō' V (Assyrian Catholicos), 1:807

Sabrishō'ibn-al-Masīhī, 3:366

SABS. *See* Sisters of the Adoration of the Blessed Sacrament

SACBC. *See* South African Catholic Bishops' Conference

Sacchini, Francesco, 1:305

Sacerdotalis caelibatus (encyclical, Paul VI), 3:627, 11:32

Sacerdotes, 8:284

Sacerdotii Nostri primordia (encyclical, John XXIII), 7:936

Sacerdotium et regnum, 11:700

Sachenhausen Appellation (1324), 7:931

Sachenspiegel, 7:959

Sack Friars, **12:464**

Sack of Rome (1527)

    Augustine, St., 1:859

    Borghese, Giambattista, 2:534

    Castiglione, Baldassare, 3:215

    Clement VII (Pope), 3:268, 430, 781–782

Sackville, John, 1:935

Sacra iam splendent (office hymn), **12:464**

Sacra iam splendent (office hymn for Matins), 12:464

Sacra Rituum (apostolic constitution, Paul VI), 4:789, 12:256

Sacra Tridentina Synodus (papal decree, Pius X), 11:390

Sacra Virginitas (encyclical, Pius XII), **12:464–465**

Sacrae cantiones (Gesualdo), 6:195

Sacrae disciplinae leges (apostolic constitution, John Paul II), 3:34, 56–57, 4:30

    See also Code of Canon Law (CIC) (1983)

Sacrae Scripturae medulla (Nacchianti), 10:133

Sacrae Theologiae Summa Ioannis Duns Scoti... et Commentaria quibus eius doctrina elucidatur, comprobatur, defenditur (Vulpes), 14:600

Sacram Liturgiam (apostolic letter, Paul VI), 4:165

The Sacrament of Matrimony (Pisano), 9:*335*

The Sacrament of the Last Supper (Dalí), 12:*466*

The Sacrament of the True Body and Blood of Christ and the Brotherhoods (Luther), 5:426–427

Sacramental grace, **6:406–409**, 7:41

Sacramental theology, **12:465–479**, 13:670–671

   communion of saints, 4:34–36

   Lutheranism, 8:894–895

   as *mysterium*, 10:99

   ontology of *communio*, 4:27–31

   sacramental worship, 8:728

Sacramentals, **12:479–481**

   blessings, 2:439–440

   Carolingian era, 8:656

   Fourth Lateran Council, 8:353

   laity, 8:295

   litanies, 8:602

   liturgical catechesis, 8:644

   paschal candle, 5:16

Sacramentarians, 3:608, **12:481**, 14:263

Sacramentaries, contemporary, **12:483–484**

Sacramentaries, historical, **12:481–483**

   characteristics, 8:639

   Hadrianum, 8:655

   index created, 13:110–111

   Leroquais, V., 8:512

   Libelli missarum, 8:531–532

   liturgical history, 8:655

   Low Countries, 10:259

   Mohlberg, Kunibert, 9:762

   Sarapion, 8:651

   transubstantiation doctrine, 14:159

Sacramentarium Gregorianum (Hadrianum), 3:157

Sacramentary of Corbie, 1:289

Sacramentary of Drogo, 9:128

Sacramentary of Henry II, 9:128–129

Sacramentary of Rodradus, 1:485

Sacramentary of Verona. *See* Leonine Sacramentary

Sacramentine Nuns, 10:620–621, **12:484**, 13:417

Sacramentine Sisters of Bergamo (*Suore Sacramentine di Bergamo*), 4:3, **12:484**

Sacraments

   Alger of Liége, 1:283

   Alphonsus Liguori, St., 1:309, 311

   Ambrosian Rite, 1:345

   Armenian liturgy, 1:709–710

   ars moriendi, 1:733

   Augustine, St., 1:867, 878

   autos sacramentales, 1:925

   Bernard of Clairvaux, 2:310

   bishops, 2:415

   Byzantine liturgy, 2:815–816

   Calvinism, 2:893

   Catharism, 3:260

   Coptic, 4:257

   Council of Trent, 14:170

   death, 4:575–577, 582–583

   definition of sacrament, 12:465

   devotion to Passion, 10:926

   ex opere operato, 5:500, 501–502, 12:469

   feminist theology, 5:680

   homily, 7:63–64

   Hugh of Saint-Victor, 7:158

   Methodism, 9:561

   reviviscence of sacramental power, 12:205–206

   seven sacraments, 12:470–471

   theology of, 2:59–60, 65–66, 4:948, 7:238

   viaticum, 14:470–471

   See also Anointing of the Sick, Sacrament of; Baptism, Sacrament of; Confirmation, Sacrament of; First Communion, Sacrament of; Holy Orders, Sacrament of; Matrimony, Sacrament of; Penance, Sacrament of

Sacraments, conditional administration of, **12:484–485**

Sacraments, iconography of, **12:485–488**

Sacraments and Orthodoxy (Schmemann), 12:742

Sacramentum extremae unctionis, 4:10

Sacramentum Mundi, 5:207

Sacramentum Ordinis (apostolic constitution, Pius XII), 2:417, 4:551, 7:38, 11:400

Sacramentum Verbi, 5:207

Sacratissimo uti culmine (papal bull, John XXII), 12:723

Sacre-Coeur Basilica (Paray-le-Monial, France), 10:*881*

Sacré-Coeur Church (Paris), 3:709

Sacred and profane, 4:585, 8:525, 12:57, 61, **488–490**

Sacred and Profane Love (Titian), 4:*319*

Sacred art, 8:618

Sacred College, 3:91

   See also Papal elections

Sacred Congregation for Divine Worship, 4:50, 8:224

Sacred Congregation for the Doctrine of the Faith, 7:491

Sacred Congregation for the Oriental Church, 2:250

Sacred Congregation of Rites (1948), 10:558

Sacred Congregation on Discipline of Sacraments, 4:88

Sacred Doctrine Notes, 13:290

Sacred Heart, devotion to, **12:490–492**

   Alacoque, St. Margaret Mary, 1:203

   Carthusian spirituality, 3:192

   Chevalier, Jules, 3:471

   Christocentrism, 3:623

   Claret de la Touche, Louise, 3:763

   Clement XIII (Pope), 3:793

   Jutta of Sangerhausen, 8:105

   Lanspergius, J. J., 8:327

   Leo XIII (Pope), 8:491

   Louis of Casoria, 8:806

Sacred Heart, enthronement of the, **12:492–493**

Sacred Heart, iconography of, **12:493**

Sacred Heart Brothers, 3:622, **12:494**

Sacred Heart Catholic Church (Tampa, Florida), 5:*776*

Sacred Heart Church (Audincourt, France), 3:713

Sacred Heart Missionaries, 2:913, 3:471, 10:529, **12:494–495**

Sacred Heart of Jesus (iconography), 7:860

Sacred Heart Society, 2:87, 3:622

Sacred Hearts Missionaries (of Issoudun), 3:622

Sacred Hearts of Jesus Priests (of Saint-Quentin), 3:621

Sacred humanity, devotion to the, **12:498–500**

Sacred marriage, 8:178, 9:536

Sacred music. *See* Chant; Liturgical music; Music, sacred

Sacred penitentiary, 1:311

Sacred Record (Euhemerus), 5:447

Sacred spaces, **12:500–504**

Sacred theology, 9:848–849, 13:921

Sacred time, **12:504–506**

The Sacred Wood (Eliot), 5:160

Le Sacrement de Pénitence dans l'antiquité chrétienne (Tixeront), 14:95

Sacri canones (apostolic constitution, John Paul II), 3:817

Sacrifice

   ancient Israelite worship, 14:856–857

   de la Taille, Maurice, 4:624

holocaust, 7:11–12

Jesus' death, 11:968–970

offerings, 4:266–267, 13:159

redemption, 11:975, 987–988

religion, 12:60–61

worship, 14:853

See also Eucharist as sacrifice

Sacrifice, Christian theology of, 4:257, 8:301, 531, 895, **12:515–518**, 13:159

Sacrifice, Greco-Roman, **12:508–510**

Sacrifice, human, 12:506–508, *507*

Sacrifice in Israel, 8:525, 526, **12:510–515**, 13:159

The Sacrifice of Isaac (Mantegna), 10:*949*

Sacrifice of the Cross, 12:159, **518–520**

atonement, 1:837

Commingling, 4:12

Lord's Supper, 8:785

Soterichus Panteugenus, 2:759

theology of, 4:398

Sacrifices, 2:443, 709, 9:63, 12:888, 14:589

Sacrificum, 10:45

Sacrilege, **12:520–521**, 13:135

Sacris solemnis (office hymn), **12:521**

Sacristan, 12:*522*, **522**

Sacristies, 1:348, **12:522**

Sacro Cardinalium Consilio (*motu proprio*, Paul VI), 3:107

Sacrobosco, John de, 4:46

Sacrosancta (Council of Constance), 4:56–57, 170, 171–172, 6:875–876

See also Haec sancta (decree)

Sacrosancta romana (papal bull, John XXII), 2:205

Sacrosancta Romanae ecclesiae (papal decree, Julius II), 5:694

Sacrosanctum concilium. See *Constitution on the Sacred Liturgy* (*Sacrosanctum concilium*) (Vatican Council II)

Sacrosanctum fidei (papal bull, Clement VII), 7:390

Sacrum diaconatus ordinem (apostolic letter, Paul VI), 4:552, 553, 11:30

Sadamatsu, Caspar, Bl., 7:734

Sadat, Anwar, 4:254, 5:118

Sadducees (Jewish sect), 1:165, 8:5, **12:522–524**

Sadlier, Annie Cassidy, 12:524

Sadlier, Frank X., 12:524

Sadlier, James, 12:524

Sadlier, Mary Anne, 12:524

Sadlier, William H., 12:524

Sadlier family, **12:524**

Sadness, **12:525**

Sadocites, 3:546

Sadoleto, Jacopo (Card.), 4:280, **12:525–526**, *526*

Saepenumero (Leo XIII), 14:421

Safavid Dynasty, 10:718–719, 11:140–141

Safavids (Shī'ite Muslims), **12:526–527**

Safed school, 7:871

Al-Saffāḥ, Abū al-'Abbās, 1:6

Saga, 10:126

Saga of Saints (Undset), 14:295

Sagaris (Bp. of Laodicea), 1:785, 8:328

Saggio di Storia Americana (Gilij), 6:224

Saggio teoretico di diritto naturale appogiato sul fatto (Taparelli d'Azeglio), 13:756

Sagheddu, Maria Gabriella, Bl., **12:527**

Sagra di San Michele Abbey (Italy), **12:527–528**

Sagrada Biblia, 10:542

Sagrada Familia Church (Barcelona), 3:709, 13:*383*

Sahag the Great (Armenian Catholicos), 1:705

Sahagún, Bernardino de, 3:246, 248, **12:528–529**

Sahagún, John of, St., **12:529**

Sahak I (Armenian Catholicos), 1:707

Ṣaḥīḥ, 7:623

Sahlin, M. R., 3:150

Ṣaifi, Euthymios, 2:144, **12:529–530**

Sailer, Johann Michael (Bp. of Regensburg), 6:183, **12:530–531**, *531*, 770

Caecilian Movement, 2:842

catechesis, 3:244

catechetical instruction of children, 12:743

preaching, 11:623

Zimmer, Patrick, 14:928

Sailors, patron saint of, 12:545

Sailors' Chapel (Quebec, Canada), 12:595

Le Saint abandon (Lehodey), 8:456

St. Agnes Basilica (Rome), 1:178, 754, 3:224

St. Agnes Le Thi Thanh Parish (New Orleans, LA), 10:297

St. Agnes-Outside-the-Walls Church (Rome), 1:8

Saint Alban Psalter, 1:*816*

St. Alban Theological Seminary (U.S.), 8:539

Saint Albans Abbey (England), **12:531–532**, *532*

St. Albans Chronicle (Walsingham), 14:622

St. Albert Mission, 8:270

Saint Alexander of Orosh Abbey (Albania), **12:532**

Saint-Allyre Abbey (Clermont, France), 3:473

Saint-Amand Abbey (Flanders, Belgium), 1:248

Saint-Amand-les-Eaux Abbey (France), **12:532–533**

St. Ambrose Cathedral (Des Moines, IA), 7:*542*

St. Ambrose University (IA), 4:535

The Saint and the Saviour (Spurgeon), 13:463

Saint-André-lez-Bruges Abbey (Belgium), **12:533**

Saint-André of Villeneuve-les-Avignon Abbey. *See* Villeneuve-les-Avignon Abbey (France)

St. Andreas Church (Cologne), 3:844

St. Andrew Abbey (Bruges, Belgium), 3:713

St. Andrews Cathedral (Singapore), 13:*163*

Saint Andrews Priory (Scotland), **12:533–534**, 831

St. Andrews University (Scotland), 12:533

St. Anne Church (Vilnius, Lithuania), 3:*687*

St. Anne Monastery (Altötting, Germany), 1:323

St. Anne's Hospital (Manila, Philippines), 3:416

Saint Ann's Academy (KS), 8:113

St. Anselm Priory (Tokyo), 3:678, **12:534–535**

St. Anselm's Priory (Washington, DC), 14:617

St. Ansgar's Scandinavian Catholic League, 4:668, **12:535**

St. Anthony Monastery (Egypt), 5:*111*

St. Anthony the Abbot Church (Italy), 3:678

St. Anthony's Almanac, 3:278

St. Anthony's Superior Church (WI), 3:717

Saint-Antoine-de-la-Mothe Church (France), 12:535

Saint-Antoine-de-Viennois Abbey (France), 7:119, **12:535**

St. Antonius Church (Basel, Switzerland), 3:710

Saint Apollinare Nuovo, 12:600

Saint Asaph, Ancient See of (Wales), **12:535–536**

Saint-Aubin Abbey (Angers, France), 1:431

St. Augustine, Canons Regular of, 12:833

St. Augustine, Sisters of Charity of (CSA), **12:537**

Saint Augustine Abbey (Canterbury, England), **12:536–537**, 13:131

St. Augustine Psalter. See Canterbury Psalter

St. (Ayois) Titus Byzantine church ruins (Crete), 14:*94*

St. Bail's on Red Square (Moscow), 10:*694*

St. Barbara, Charterhouse (Cologne), 8:326–327

St. Barbara Chapel (Turkey), 14:*241*

St. Bartholomew Cathedral (Liège, Belgium), 12:486

St. Bartholomew's Day Massacre (France, 1572), 1:715, 2:689, 3:267, 5:849, 8:531, **12:537–538**

St. Bartholomew's Hospital (London), 3:69

St. Basil (Mother), 11:495

St. Bavon Church (Ghent), 1:544

Saint-Bavon monastery (Belgium), 2:161

St. Benedict and His Times (Schuster), 12:790

Saint Benedict Exorcises a Demon from a Possessed Man (Il Sodoma), 5:*552*

Saint Benedict Presents the Rule of the New Order (Vanni), 2:*262*

Saint Benedict Supervising the Construction of Twelve Monasteries (Il Sodoma), 2:*237*

St. Benedict's Abbey (Atchison, KS), **12:538–539**

Saint-Benoit-du-Lac Abbey (Canada), 2:232

Saint-Benoît-sur-Loire Abbey (France), 1:9, 5:842, 12:539, **539**

St. Bernardo statue (Italy), 10:*970*

St. Bernard's Abbey (AL), 1:201

Saint-Bertin Abbey (France), 3:813, 5:787, 7:289, 8:304–305, 502, **12:539–540**

St. Birgitta's Church (Vadstena, Sweden), 13:*637*

St. Bonaventure University (New York), 10:324, **12:540–541**

Saint-Calais Abbey (France), 1:248, **12:541**

Saint Calasanctius-Blätter (periodical), 12:793

St. Callistus, Catacombs of (Rome), 3:224, *225*

St. Catharine (KY), 4:839–940

St. Catherine Monastery (Sinai, Egypt), 3:*438*

St. Catherine's Church (Vilnius, Poland), 8:*605*

St. Catherine's Institute (Baltimore), 6:225

St. Cecilia Church (Cologne), 3:844

St. Cecilia Monastery (Sezze, Italy), 8:561

Saint-Chamond, Jean de (Abp. of Aix), 1:196

St. Charles Borromeo Church (Antwerp, Belgium), 3:706

St. Charles Borromeo Seminary (Philadelphia, PA), 8:144, 250

St. Charles Church (Antwerp), 1:539

St. Charles College (Baltimore), 5:42

St. Charles Seminary (PA), 8:152

Saint-Claire-sur-Epte, Treaty of (911), 10:426

St. Clare Grieving Over the Body of St. Francis (Giotto), 11:*494*

Saint-Claude Abbey (France), 3:769, **12:542**

St. Clement's Episcopal Church (Alexandria, VA), 3:671, 716

St. Cloud Diocese (MN), **12:542–543**

St. Columban's Foreign Mission Society (SSC), 6:83

See also Columban Fathers

Saint Cronan's Church (Roscrea, Ireland), 12:*379*

St. Cyprian's Basilica (Carthage), 3:685

Saint-Cyran, Abbé de. *See* Duvergier de Hauranne, Jean

St. Cyriacus Basilica (Italy), 2:*765*

Saint Davids, Ancient See of (Wales), **12:543–544**

Saint-Denis Abbey (France), 1:18, 248, 3:154, 382, 693, 695

Saint-Denis Cathedral (Paris), 3:697, 706

Saint-Denis-en-France Abbey (France), **12:544–545**

St. Edward's Seminary (Seattle), 5:684

St. Elia Church (Bulgaria), 2:*685*

St. Elizabeth Healing the Sick (Murillo), 10:66

St. Elmo's Fire, 5:173, **12:545**

St. Engelbert Church (Cologne-Riehl, Germany), 3:711

Saint-Étienne Church (Caen, France), 3:693, 695

Saint-Éugene Church (Paris), 3:709, 710

St. Euphemia, Basilica of (Chalcedon), 3:362, 363

Saint-Évroult-d'Ouche Abbey (France), 1:463, 5:497, **12:545–546**

Saint-Florent-le-Vieil Abbey (Angers, France), 1:431, **12:546**

Saint-Florent-lès-Saumur Abbey (France), **12:546**

St. Florian Abbey (Austria), 1:908

St. Florian's Church (Hamtramck, Michigan), 9:*605*

Saint-Foi Cathedral (Conques, France), 3:812

St. Francis (Sister), Bl., 4:44

Saint Francis de Sales (Tiepolo), 5:*867*

Saint Francis Industrial and Boarding School for Girls (Savannah, GA), 2:168

St. Francis Mission Community, 5:892

Saint Francis of Assisi Presenting His Rule to Pope Innocent III (Giotto de Bondone), 5:*870*

St. Francis Receiving the Stigmata (van Eyck), 13:*531*

St. Francis with the Crucified Christ (Murillo), 10:66

St. Francis Xavier (Sister), 2:94

St. Francis Xavier Church (Kansas City, MO), 3:716

Saint Francis Xavier Foreign Mission Society. *See* Xaverian Missionary Fathers

St. Francis Xavier Society. *See* Society for the Propagation of the Faith

St. Francis Xavier University (Antigonish, Canada), 3:9

St-Front Church (Périgeux), 3:671

Saint Gall Repertory, 14:214–216

St. Gall's Monastery (Devil's Lake, ND), 14:669

St. Gatien Cathedral (France), 14:*126*

St. George and the Dragon (Dürer), 6:*143*

St. George the Great (Venice), 5:463

St. George's Cathedral (India), 7:*397*

Saint George's United Methodist Church (Pennsylvania), 14:*308*

St. Gereon Church (Cologne), 3:844

Saint-Germain-des-Prés Abbey (Paris, France), 3:473, 695, 4:258, **12:547–548**

Saint-Gildas-de-Rhuys Abbey (France), 1:18, **12:548**

Saint-Gilles (Nîmes, France), 12:548, **548–549**

Saint-Gilles-du-Gard Church (France), 3:693

St. Gregory of Nazianzus (Rubens), 6:*514*

Saint-Guilehm-du-Désert Abbey (France), 1:453, **12:549**

St. Hedwig's Cathedral (Berlin), 6:*176*

St. Helen Church (Munich), 3:712

St. Hermagoras Society, 13:218, 226

St. Honoratus Island (France), 8:511

Saint-Hubert Abbey (Luxembourg), **12:549**

St. Ignatius Church (San Francisco), 2:*864*

St. James Cathedral (Seattle, WA), 12:*851*

St. James Church (Antwerp), 1:539

St. James Hospital (Rome), 3:418

St. James Monastery (Pontida), 1:222

St. James Shrine (Italy), 3:691–692

St. James the Fisherman Chapel (Wellfleet, MA), 3:672

Saint-Jean-Baptiste Abbey (France), 8:41

Saint-Jean-d'Angély Abbey (France), **12:550**

Saint-Jean-de-Losne, Council of (673-675), 3:40

Saint-Jean-de-Montmartre Church (France), 3:710

Saint-Jean Hospital (Angers, France), 3:697, 698

St. Joachim Mission (Edmonton), 8:270

St. Joan's International Alliance, **12:550–551**

St. John Baptist Church (Neu-Ulm, Germany), 3:711

St. John Lateran. *See* Basilica of St. John Lateran

St. John Lateran Cathedral (Rome), 8:*358*

St. John of Ephesus Cathedral, 1:757, 3:687, 689

St. John the Baptist (Savannah, GA), 12:709

St. John the Baptist Cathedral (Chester, England), 3:469

St. John the Divine Cathedral (New York City), 3:715, 8:276

St. John the Evangelist Cathedral (LA), 8:278

St. John the Evangelist Cathedral (Milwaukee, WI), 9:649

St. John the Evangelist Church (Hopkins, MN), 3:*703*

Saint John the Theologian University (Moscow), 10:695

St. John Vianney and Ugandan Martyrs Seminary (Trinidad), 3:116

St. John's Abbey and University (Minnesota), 3:717, 8:161, 624, **12:551–553**

St. John's Cathedral (KY), 8:148

St. John's Catholic Church (North Cambridge, MA), 3:716

St. John's City (NB), 10:221

St. John's College (Belize), 2:225

St. John's College (Fordham, NY), 8:335

St. John's College (KY), 8:148

St. John's University (Collegeville, MN), 1:637

St. Joseph (Mother) (Françoise Blin de Bourdon), 2:394

St. Joseph, Congregation of (*Congregatio Sancti Joseph*), **12:553**

St. Joseph, Sisters of Cluny, 13:53, 110

St. Joseph, University of (Beruit), 8:427

St. Joseph Hospital (Mexico), 3:415

St. Joseph in Appleton (Roemer), 12:283

St. Joseph Mission (Nebraska), 10:220–221

St. Joseph Sisters, 7:748

St. Joseph Sisters of Peace of the Immaculate Conception, 12:556

St. Joseph's College (Bardstown, Kentucky), 5:144

St. Joseph's College (London), 9:*633*

St. Joseph's College (NS), 3:9, 11

St. Joseph's College (Philadelphia), 11:*235, 236*

St. Joseph's Hospital (CO), 9:19

St. Joseph's Manual (Fitton), 5:751

St. Joseph's Missionary Society of Mill Hill. *See* Mill Hill Missionaries

St. Joseph's Provincial Seminary (New York), 10:323

St. Joseph's Society of the Sacred Heart. *See* Josephites

Saint-Jouin-de-Marnes Abbey (France), **12:557**

Saint-Juré, Jean Baptiste, 1:310, 7:782, **12:557**

St. Justina (Donatello), 7:*656*

St. Justina of Padua, Congregation of, 12:643

St. Kevin Monastery tower (Ireland), 6:*239*

Saint Kevin's Church (Ireland), 8:161, *162*

St. Kitts, 3:120

St. Kunibert Church (Cologne), 3:844

Saint Laumer of Blois Abbey (France), **12:557**

St. Laurence Monastery (Dielouard, France), 1:365

St. Laurent Church (Île d'Orleans), 3:714

Saint-Lazare Cathedral (Autun, France), 1:926, 3:692

St. Lazarus hospital (Mexico), 3:415

Saint-Léonard-le-Noblat Monastery (France), **12:557–558**

St. Leonard's College (Scotland), 12:533

Saint-Lô Monastery (France), **12:558**

Saint Louis (MO), 12:376–377

St. Louis, Bl., 4:44

St. Louis, Sisters of, **12:562**

St. Louis Archdiocese (MO), 8:118–119, 145, 145–146, **12:558–559**

St. Louis Basilica (NO), 10:290

St. Louis Cathedral (NO), 8:809, 10:*290*

St. Louis University (MO), 1:637, 9:743, 12:38–39, **562–564**

St. Lucia (West Indies), 3:118–119, 120

St. Luke's Church (Smithfield, VA), 3:714

St. Lupicin Monastery (France), 8:63

St. M. de la Visitation Church (France), 3:706

Saint-Maclou Cathedral (Rouen, France), 3:697–698

Saint-Maixent Abbey (France), **12:564**

St. Maria della Pietà confraternity, 3:418

St. Maria im Kapitol Church (Cologne), 3:844, 845

St. Maria Lyskirchen (Cologne), 3:844

St. Maria on Schnurgasse Church (Cologne), 3:845

Saint-Marie d'Abondance Abbey. *See* Abondance Monastery (France)

St. Marien Convent. *See* Lindau Convent (Germany)

St. Mark hospital (Braga, Portugal), 3:416

St. Mark's Cathedral (Venice), 3:671, 689

St. Mark's Church (Burlington, VT), 3:716

St. Mark's Church (Kenosha, WI), 8:256

Saint Mark's Church (Venice, Italy), 4:*337*, **12:564–565**, 600

St. Mark's College (Vancouver, BC), 3:11

St. Martha (Sister), Bl., 4:44

Saint-Martial Cathedral (Limoges, France), 3:812

St. Martial Repertory, 14:214

Saint-Martin Abbey (Sées, France), 3:473

Saint-Martin-aux-Jumeaux Abbey (Amiens, France), 1:359

St. Martin Church (Landshut, Germany), 3:697

Saint-Martin-des-Champs Monastery (France), 3:813

Saint-Martin-du-Canigou Church (France), 3:690

St. Martin-in-the-Fields Church (London), 3:707, 715

Saint-Martin of Tournai Abbey (Belgium), **12:565**

St. Martin's Lent, 1:134

See also Advent

St. Mary Abbey (Paris), 8:433

St. Mary Church (Fleury), 1:543

St. Mary Magdalen (retreats) (Castillo Branco and Coimbra, Portugal), 3:416

St. Mary Magdalen (Sister), 1:158

St. Mary Magdalene monastery (Altötting, Germany), 1:323

St. Mary Major Basilica (Rome), 1:37, 3:555, 686, 4:364

angels, 1:425

mosaics, 1:754, 2:369

St. Mary of the Angels Church. *See* Portiuncula chapel (Assisi, Italy)

St. Mary of the Martyrs Church (Rome), 1:314

St. Mary of the Portiuncula, 5:892–893

See also Portiuncula chapel (Assisi, Italy)

Saint Mary's Cathedral (Gdansk, Poland), 3:*704*

St. Mary's Cathedral (San Francisco), 12:647, 648

St. Mary's Cathedral (Sydney), 1:*902*

St. Mary's Church (New York), 10:323

St. Mary's College (Detroit), 10:625

Saint Mary's College (KS), 8:113

St. Mary's College (KY), 8:148, 12:174

St. Mary's College (MD), 5:41

St. Mary's College (Notre Dame, IN), 7:22

St. Mary's Hospital (CA), 12:417

St. Mary's Hospital (Rochester, NY), 4:655

Saint Mary's Jesuit Mission, 8:113

St. Mary's Mission (Stevensville, MT), 9:*825*

St. Mary's of Grottaferrata Monastery (Italy), 2:747

St. Mary's Orphan Boys' Home (New Orleans), 10:292

St. Mary's School (Philadelphia), **12:565–566**

St. Mary's Seminary (Baltimore), 2:40, 41, 3:181, 715, 8:521

St. Mary's Seminary (Cleveland, OH), 8:250

St. Mary's Seminary (Perryville, MO), 14:*526*

St. Mary's Seminary of Theology (Baltimore), 5:684, 757, 12:227

Saint Matthew and Saint John the Evangelist (Francisco de Ribalta), 5:*476*

St. Maur Chapel, 2:351, 8:471

Saint-Maur-des-Fossés Abbey (France), **12:566**

Saint-Maur-sur-Loire Abbey (Angers, France), 1:431, **12:567**

St. Maurice Abbey (Switzerland), 1:23, 3:69, **12:567**, 13:115

St. Maurice Church (Duvernay, Quebec), 3:717

Saint-Maximin Abbey (France), 1:403, **12:567–568**

St. Meinrad Archabbey (Indiana), **12:568**

St. Michael Abbey (Antwerp), 1:539

St. Michael Church (Farnborough Priory, England), 5:629

St. Michael Church (Hildesheim, Germany), 3:691

St. Michael's Church (Charleston, SC), 3:707

St. Michael's Seminary (PA), 8:152

St. Michel de Frigolet Abbey (France), 6:*13*

Saint-Mihiel Abbey (Verdun), **12:568–569**, 13:228

Saint-Nicholas Abbey (Angers, France), 1:432

St. Nicholas Cathedral, Kedroff v. (1952), 3:662

St. Nicholas' Chest (Polish charity), 13:200

Saint Nicholas Church (Tallinn, Estonia), 5:*378*

St. Nicomedes, cemetery of, 3:224

St. Norbert Abbey (De Pere, WI), 11:*665*

St. Norbert of Xanten (Rubens), 10:*420*

St. Omer College, **12:569–570**

St. Oswald and King Aidan seated at dinner (illumination), 10:*707*

Saint-Ouen Abbey (Rouen, France), **12:570**, *571*

St. Palais, Maurice de (Bp. of Vincennes, IN), 7:413–414, 417, 12:568

St. Pancras Church (London), 3:709

St. Pancratius cemetery (Rome), 3:224

St. Pantaleon Church (Cologne), 3:844, 845

St. Panteleimon Church (Yugoslavia), 2:729, 738

St. Panteleimon Monastery (Ochrida), 3:799

St. Patrick Fathers, 12:570

St. Patrick's Cathedral (Dublin), 7:*559*

St. Patrick's Cathedral (NY), 3:709, 715, 8:387, 10:*312*, 313

St. Patrick's Church (Oklahoma City), 3:681, 717

St. Patrick's College (Maynooth, Ireland), **9:384–386**

St. Patrick's Missionary Society, 3:622, 8:150, **12:570**

St. Patrick's Purgatory, **11:829–830**

St. Patrick's Seminary (Menlo Park, CA), 12:251

St. Paul (Nock), 10:409

Saint Paul (Renan), 12:126

St. Paul and Minneapolis Archdiocese (MN), 7:550, **12:572–577**, 13:164–165

St. Paul Basilica (Rome), 12:51

St. Paul Bazire (Mother), 3:130

St. Paul Cathedral (MN), 3:716

St. Paul Monastery (Egypt), 5:*115*

St. Paul of the Cree mission (Brousseau, AB), 8:270

Saint Paul-Outside-the-Walls Abbey (Rome), 1:172, 5:623, 12:221, **577**

St. Paul-Outside-the-Walls Basilica (Rome), 1:543, 754, 2:369, 3:793, 13:166

St. Paul–St. Louis Church (Paris), 3:706

St. Paul Seminary (MN), 7:551

St. Paul the Apostle Church (New York City), 11:*41*

St. Paul's Basilica (Rome), 3:686, 699

St. Paul's Cathedral (London), 3:707, 832, 5:385, **12:577–578**

center of early see, 8:771

Erconwald of London burial site, 5:318

liturgical rite *Usus S. Pauli*, 8:771

rebuilding by Bp. Maurice, 8:771

St. Paul's Cathedral (Macau), 9:*6*

St. Paul's Church (Antwerp), 1:539

St. Paul's Church (Wickford, RI), 3:714

Saint Paul's Cloister, 4:864

St. Paul's College (Winnipeg, MB), 3:11

St. Paul's First Epistle to the Corinthians (manuscript), 8:*323*

St. Peregrine Shrine, 13:27

St. Peter (Ramses II's temple, Egypt), 10:*471*

St. Peter Abbey (Italy), 14:613

St. Peter Church (Cologne), 5:485

St. Peter Church (Moissac, France), 1:543

St. Peter in Chains Cathedral (Cincinnati, OH), 3:715, 736–737

St. Peter in Chains Church (Rome), 8:55

St. Peter of Muenster Abbey (Saskatchewan, Canada), **12:578**

St. Peter statue (Vatican), 10:*831*

St. Peter's Abbey (Austria), 1:908

St. Peter's Basilica (Vatican City), 2:*635*, **12:578–581**, *579, 581*, 14:390–391, *390, 394–396, 403*

Aachen Cathedral, 1:1

archaeological investigations, 8:107

architectural drawings, 12:*580*

architecture, 3:670, 671, 701, 703, 704, 705

art, 3:606, *787*

Bernini, Giovanni Lorenzo, 2:325

catacombs, 3:224

Christmas, 3:555

erection of, 1:754

excavations, 11:398

indulgences for, 8:487–488

martyrium, 3:685, 686

Michelangelo, 1:261

official status, 3:261, 8:348

priests to assist, 13:140

relics, 12:51

St. Faustina Kowalska, 8:244

Sylvester legend, 4:183

tomb of Sixtus IV (Pope), 13:197

St. Peter's Church (Baltimore), 2:39

St. Peter's Church (Linda del Mar, CA), 3:716

Saint Peter's Church (Vatican City), 12:*350*

St. Petersburg codex, 2:358

Saint-Philibert Church (Tournus, France), 3:692

St-Philibert-de-Grandlieu (France), 3:*694*

St. Philip Neri Seminary (TX), 8:138

St. Philip's Home, 9:395

Saint-Pierre Cathedral (Beauvais, France), 2:188–189, *188*

Saint-Pierre Church (France), 8:59

Saint-Pierre-et-Saint-Paul Cathedral (Troyes, France), 3:*261*

St. Pölten Abbey (Austria), 1:909

Saint-Polyeucte (Metz), 8:738

St. Pudentiana Basilica (Rome), 1:754

Saint-Quentin Monastery (Beauvaise, France), 3:67, **12:582**

St. Raphael's Society, 2:852, **12:582**

St. Raymond Nonnatus Preaching (Saraceni), 11:*935*

Saint-Remi Abbey (Reims, France), 1:478, 3:695, 12:108, *583*, **583**

St. Remigius of Reims Chapel (France), 12:583

Saint-Riquier Abbey (France), 1:359, 3:155, 160, **12:583–584**

St. Rita Church (Madrid), 3:713

Saint-Robert-de-Cornillon Priory (France), **12:584**

Saint Ronan sculpture (Thompson), 12:*367*

St. Rose of Lima Church (Ste. Rose du Lac, MB), 3:717

Saint-Ruf monastery (Avignon, France), 1:942, 3:67, 69

St. Sabina Basilica (Rome), 1:754, 12:462–463

Saint-Saëns, Camille, **12:584**

St. Sargius Coptic Church (Egypt), 5:*116*

Saint-Sauveur, Synod of (1790), 1:195

Saint-Savin-De-Bigorre Abbey (France), **12:584–585**

Saint-Savin-sur-Gartempe Abbey (France), 1:543, 2:*316*, 3:693, **12:585**

St. Scholastica Abbey (Subiaco, Italy), 13:*565*

St. Sebastian, Basilica of (Rome), 3:*222, 223, 223, 224*

Saint-Serge Abbey (Angers, France), 1:431

St. Sergius Institute (Paris), 12:436

Saint-Sernin Church (Toulouse, France), 3:692

Saint-Sever Abbeys (Italy, France), **12:585**

Saint-Sever-de-Rustan Abbey (France), **12:585–586**

St. Severin Church (Cologne), 3:844

Saint Simeon Monastery (Jebel Shaikh Barakat, Syria), 13:*703*

Saint-Simon, Claude Henri de Rouvroy, 3:620, 5:397, 703, 12:*586*, **586–587**

Bonald, Louis Gabriel Ambroise de, 2:478

Buchez, Philippe Joseph Benjamin, 2:654

Comte, Auguste, 4:47

Napoleon III, 10:150

St. Stephen Distributing Alms (Angelico), 13:*510*

St. Stephen's Cathedral (Vienna), 1:909

St. Stephen's Catholic Church (Boston), 9:*305*

Saint-Sulpice Abbey (Bourges, France), 3:473, 5:190

Saint-Suplice Church (Paris), 3:708

St. Symphorian Abbey (Belgium), 1:100

St. Teresa's Catholic Church (Albany, GA), 6:*149*

St. Thomas Aquinas Foundation, 8:500

St. Thomas Christians, 1:14, 13:718

See also India; Syro-Malabar Church; Syro-Malankara Church

St. Thomas Church (Episcopal) (New York), 3:715

St. Thomas College (KY), 8:147

St. Thomas Evangelic Church of India, 7:401

St. Thomas' Hospital (London), 3:69

St. Thomas More College (Saskatoon, SK), 3:11

St. Thomas Seminary (KY), 8:148

St. Thomas Seminary of Detroit, 8:169

St. Thomasblätter (periodical), 12:774

Saint Tikhon of Moscow Theological Institute, 10:695

Saint-Trond Abbey (Belgium), 3:563, 5:438, **12:587**

Saint-Trophime Church (Arles, France), 1:*695*, 3:693

St. Ubald of Gubbio with St. Sebastian and the Virgin and Child (Perugia), 14:*262*

Saint Ulrich von Augsburg Abbey (Germany), **12:671**

Saint-Urbain Church (Troyes, France), 3:697

St. Ursula Church (Cologne), 3:844

Saint-Vaast Abbey (France), 3:154, **12:588**

Saint-Valery-sur-Somme Abbey (France), **12:588**

Saint-Vallier, Jean Baptiste de la Croix Chevrières de, 3:5, **12:588–589**

St. Veronica (Memling), 14:*458*

Saint-Victor Abbey (Marseilles), 5:450, **12:590–591**

Saint-Victor Abbey (Paris), 5:516, 12:267, 589, 759

Saint-Victor Monastery (Paris), 3:68, 8:798, **12:589–590**

Saint-Vincent Abbey (Mans, France), 3:473

St. Vincent College and Archabbey (Latrobe, PA), 8:624, 11:*81*, **12:591**, *592*

Saint Vincent de Paul Quarterly, 8:156

St. Vincent de Paul Society, 3:420, 622, **12:591, 593–594**

Australia, 1:904

Catholic Charities USA, 3:279, 280

Legion of Mary, 8:453

Los Angeles, 8:791

Louise de Marillac, 8:807

Mulry, Thomas, 10:57

origins of, 10:735

St. Vincent Ferrer's Union, 9:401

St. Vincent's Female Orphan Asylum, 9:362–363

St. Vincent's Hospital (New York), 10:314

St. Vitus Cathedral (Prague), 5:325

St. Vladimir's Seminary Quarterly, 5:782

St. Vladimir's Theological Seminary (New York), 12:742

Saint-Wandrille Abbey. *See* Fontenelle Abbey

St. Werburgh Abbey (Chester, England), 3:469

St. Werburgh Church (Chester, England), 3:469

St. Wolfgang Altarpiece (Pacher), 10:742

Saint Xavier University (Chicago, IL), 3:480

St. Xavier's College, 3:480

St. Yrieix Abbey (France), 1:645

Sainte Anne de Beaupré Shrine (Quebec, Canada), **12:594–595**, *595*

La Sainte Bible en latin et en français (Le Maistre), 8:465, 10:542

Sainte-Cécile Cathedral (Albi, France), 1:229

Sainte-Cécile de Solesmes Abbey (France), 2:651

Sainte-Chapelle Church (Paris), 1:147, 3:382, 697, 5:*845*

Sainte Chrétienne, Sisters of (SSCH), **12:595**

Sainte-Colombe Abbey (Sens, France), 3:473

Saint-Étienne Church (Caen, France), 3:693, 695

Sainte-Geneviève-de-Paris Monastery (France), 3:708, 8:519, **12:595–596**

Sainte-Radagone Monastery (Poitiers), 1:927

Sainte-Trinité Church (Caen, France), 3:693

La Sainte Volonté Convent (Switzerland), 3:745

Sainthood. *See* Saints

Saints, 8:436, **12:605–607**

attributes, 12:598, 599

Bollandists, 1:333, 839, 2:471–472, 3:143

Catholic theology, 12:602–604

comites Christi, 3:555–556

Communion of, 4:34–36

confessor, 4:82–83

definition, 12:602

feasts, 12:662

first U.S., 13:176

Irish, 5:760

nimbus (cloud) surrounding the head of saints, 12:598–599

sanctoral cycle, 12:661–664

See also Canonization of saints; Feasts, religious; Hagiography; *specific saints*

Les Saints (hagiography), 6:615

Saints, devotion to the, **12:596–598**

in the Bible, 12:597

consecration, personal, 4:156

dulia, 4:932

litanies, 8:601

liturgical year, 8:717, 719–722

shrines, 13:93–94

theology of, 12:597

Saints, iconography of, 7:51, **12:598–602**

Saints, intercession of, 7:519–520, 10:969–976, **12:602–605**

Saints and Beati, **12:607–608**

SS. Cosmas and Damian Church (Sardinia), 3:*683*

Saints Cyril and Methodius, Sisters of, **12:609**

SS. Cyril and Methodius Seminary (Orchard Lake, MI), 10:625

Saints' Everlasting Rest (Baxter), 2:162

SS. Justo y Pastor Church (Madrid), 3:706

SS. Martina and Luca Church (Rome), 3:705

SS. Peter and Marcellinus Basilica (Rome), 1:754

SS. Peter and Paul Church (Brooklyn, NY), 3:715, 9:81

SS. Peter and Paul Church (Cluny, France), 3:811–812

Saints Peter and Paul Church (Cracow, Poland), 11:*446*

SS. Sergius and Bacchus, Justinian's building, 8:100

SS. Sergius and Bacchus Church (Constantinople), 3:687

SS. Sindone Church (Turin, Italy), 3:705

SS. Teuteria e Fosca Chapel (Verona, Italy), 1:*317*

SS. Trinitá Abbey. *See* La Cava Abbey (Italy)

Säiz, Teodomiro Joaquín, St., 1:298

Sakaguchi, Michael, Bl., 7:732

Sakakibara, Joachim, St., 7:732

Sakramentalien der katholischen (Schmid), 12:743

Śakti of Śiva, 2:36

Sala, Maria Anna, Bl., **12:609**

Sala Picó, José, 12:408

Saladin (Muslim hero), 1:612, 3:776, 4:404, 411, **12:609–610**

Salamanca (Spain), 12:529

Salamanca, University of (Spain), 1:236, **12:610–612**

Salamanca College (Spain), 7:574

Salas, Juan de, **12:612**

Salas Toro, José Hipólito, 3:486

Salat, Hans, **12:612–613**

Salat, Jacob, 12:770

Salawa, Aniela, Bl., **12:613**

Salazar, António de Oliveira, 11:539

Salazar, Domingo de, **12:613**

Salazar, Sabás Reyes, St., 6:545

Salem Abbey (Baden, Germany), 5:30–31

Salem Witch Trial, 14:*800*

Salès, James, Bl., 1:844–845

Salesian Cooperators, 12:614

Salesian Fathers, 3:419, 622

Salesian Sisters, 2:543, 3:419, 622, 9:389, 12:248, **613–614**

Salesians, 12:614–615, **614–615**

Argentina, 1:649, 5:589

Cape Verde, 3:80

Chile, 3:486

East Timor, 5:8–9

Fagnano, José, 5:589

founding, 2:543, 4:687

Italy, 7:673

missions, 9:714, 12:247

Rinaldi, Filippo, Bl., 12:247–248

Saliceto, Bartholomew de, 3:51

Saliège, Jules (Card.), 1:518, 3:277

Salimbene (Franciscan chronicler), 1:465, 9:461–462, 12:464, **615–616**, 13:101

Salinas, Carlos Gortari, 9:584–585

Salinas y Córdova, Buena Ventura, Bl., **12:616**

Salisbury, Ancient See of (England), **12:616–618**, *617*, 13:128

Salisbury Cathedral (England), 3:263, 696, 5:242

Salle, John-Baptiste de la, St., 14:247

Salle, Robert Cavelier de La, 9:722

Sallés y Barangueras, María del Carmen, Bl., **12:618**

Salliceto, Guglielmo di, 7:121

Salmanasar V (King of Assyria), 4:674

Salmanticenses (Disclaced Carmelite authors), 1:311, 3:137, **12:618–619**

Ambrosius Catharinus, 1:347

Complutenses, 4:44

hope, 7:94

Salamanca University, 12:612

Salmasius, Claudius, **12:620**

Salmerón, Alfonso, **12:620**

Salmon, Patrick, 4:271, 5:232, 7:579

Salome, Marie (Mother), 9:733

Salome, St., 8:45–46

Salome Receiving the Head of Saint John the Baptist (Guercino), 7:*1014*

Salona Basilica (Greece), 1:757

Salpointe, Jean Baptiste (Abp.), 1:688, 3:858, 8:316, 12:676

Salt, H. S., 1:456

Salt, Robert, Bl., 5:226, 7:1019

Salt Lake City Diocese (UT), 12:720

SALT Treaty of 1979, 8:250

Saltarellil, Michael A. (Bp. of Wilmington, DE), 14:765

Salteaux people, 13:66

Salterio del soldato (Tosti), 14:120

Saluhaku, Albino (Father), 1:452

Salutary acts, 4:121, 6:359, **12:620–622**

Salutati, Coluccio, 12:113, 114–115, **622**

Salutiferos Cruciatus (brief, John XXIII), 10:932

Salva Regina (Aimar), 9:449

Salvado, Rosendo, 10:289

Salvador, Vicente do, **12:622–623**

Salvador del Río, Nicéforo, Bl., 7:124

Salvati, Scipione (Borghese), 2:535

Salvatierra, Juan María, **12:622**

Salvation, **12:627–630**

  Apostles, 1:572

  Ascension of Jesus Christ, 1:771–772

  baptism, 2:65

  in the Bible, 12:627–628

  Bonaventure, St., 2:486–487

  communio, 4:27, 30

  crucifixion, 4:398

  Day of the Lord, 4:547–549

  death transformed, 4:574–577, 581

  Divine economy/plan, 5:58–59

  doctrinal proofs, 12:625

  evangelization, 9:688

  historical development, 12:624–625

  hope, 7:101, 103–107

  human virtues, 6:133–134

  Jansenism, 1:892–893

  lay spirituality, 8:418–419

  Luther, Martin, 13:908

  Lutheranism, 8:891

  Manichaeism, 9:111

  merit, 9:510–511

  Mesopotamia, ancient, 9:537

  messianism, 9:540

  Philo Judaeus, 11:271–272

prayer, 11:594

predestination, 11:647

religions, 12:63

Resurrection of Christ, 12:161–165

social morality, 13:246

soteriology, 13:329

theology, 12:57

votum, 14:590

See also Redemption

Salvation, necessity of Church for, 3:580, 10:228, **12:624–626**

''Salvation and the Church'' (ARCIC II), 5:68

Salvation Army, 2:530, **12:626–627**, *627*

Salvation history (*Heilsgeschichichte*), 5:323, 523, 6:886, **12:623–624**

  Abraham, 1:37

  in the Bible, 12:627–628

  biblical theology, 2:386

  catechesis, 12:630

  chronicles, 1:460

  covenant, 4:324–328, 328–329

  creation, 4:337–338, 340, 341

  Divine judgment, 8:33

  dogmatic theology, 12:628–629

  hope, 7:103–107

  Ignatian exercises, 13:432

  ignorance sinful, 13:36

  kerygmatic theology, 8:157, 158

  Lamb of God, 8:301

  Logos, 8:764

  Luke's Gospel, 8:860

  New Testament, 12:628

  Old Testament, 2:386, 3:28, 12:627–628

  passion narratives, 10:921–922

  Paul, St., 10:100

  purpose of Bible, 2:354

  sin, 13:142

  three stages, 8:174

  Transfiguration, 14:155

Salvator Mundi (Previtali), 7:*846*

Salvator noster (papal bull, Sixtus IV), 7:438

Salvator of Horta, St., **12:630**

Salvatore, Giovanni Angelo, Bl. *See* Nicola da Gesturi, Bl.

Salvatorians, 3:622, 7:1026, 12:529–530, 530, **630–631**

Salve Mundi Sautare (hymn), **12:631**

Salve Regina (Marian antiphon), **12:631–632**

Salve Regina (Obrecht), 10:*522*

Salve Regina (Palestrina), 10:*803*

''*Salve Regina*'' (Schlick), 10:*651*

Salve Regina (Valentini), 14:372

Salvete Christi vulnera (office hymn), **12:632**

Salvi, Lorenzo Maria, Bl., **12:632**

Salvian of Marseilles, 6:112, 11:757, **12:632–633**

Salvici doloris (apostolic letter, John Paul II), 7:1003, 10:852

Salvius (Bp. of Albi), St., 1:229

Salzburg, University of (Austria), 12:671

Salzburg Itinerary (*Notitia ecclesiarum orbis Romae*), 7:676

Salzmann, Joseph, 8:504, **12:633**

Sāma Veda, 6:840

Samāj, Brāhma, 6:851–852

Samaria, fall of, 7:641

Samaritan Pentateuch, 2:359–360, 4:562

Samaritan Targum, 13:761

Samaritan Temple (Mt. Garizim), 13:811

Samaritans, 3:23, **12:633–634**, 13:130–131

Samhain, 1:290

Samore, Antonio (Card.), 1:655

Samosata, 12:635, **635**

Samperio, José M., 1:652

Sampo, Peter, Bl., 7:733

Sampson, Richard (Bp. of Chichester), 3:481

Samson, 8:19, 9:446, 10:218, **12:635**

Samson Agonistes (Milton), 9:645

Samson and Dalila (Saëns), 12:584

Samson Captured by the Philistines (Guercino), 11:*265*

Samson of Bury-Saint-Edmunds (Abbot), 2:713, **12:636**

Samuel (biblical figure), **12:636**

Samuel, Arthur, 1:765

Samuel, Books of, **12:636–639**

  Baal, 2:2

  Balaam, 2:26

  Benjamin (tribe), 2:282

  censuses, 3:338

  content and organization, 12:637

  creation, 4:341

  David, 4:536–537

  Dead Sea Scroll version, 4:562

  edification, 5:84

  Edomites, 5:87

  grace of God, 9:87

  heart, 6:681

  heaven, 6:684

  history, 12:637, 637–638

  inheritance, 7:464

  Judah (tribe), 8:1

  justice of men, 8:73

Samuel, Books of (*continued*)
kindness, 8:171
Kingdom of God, 8:173
kingship, 8:179
leprosy, 8:509
magic, 9:39
name and division, 12:636–637
name of God, 6:298
peace, 11:49
salvation, 7:105
serpent as symbol, 13:20
Shaddai, 13:58
showbread, 13:88
sin, 13:142, 144
Solomon, 13:305
soul, 13:336
spirit, 13:424
theology, 12:638

Samuel, Hillel ben, 7:864

San Alberto, José Antonio de (Bp.), **12:639**

San Ambrosii de Nabuthae: A Commentary with an Introduction and Translation (McGuire), 9:399

San Andrea al Quirinale Church (Rome), 2:325, *326*, 3:675, 705

San Andrea della Valle Church (Rome), 3:*693*, 703

San Andrés, Inocencio de, 3:136

San Antonio Archdiocese (TX), 8:843–844, **12:639–643**

San Antonio Mission (TX), 12:*640*

San Benedetto di Polirone Abbey (Lombardy, Italy), **12:643–644**

San Benito de Valladolid Monastery (Spain), 3:744

San Biagio Church (Montepulciano, Italy), 3:701

San Carlo alle Quattro Fontane (Rome), 3:671, 705

San Clemente Basilica (Rome), 1:*336*

San Diego Mission (CA), 3:*698*

San Domenico Convent (Pisa), 3:760

San Fernando Church (San Antonio, TX), 12:640

San Francesco Basilica (Assisi), 1:790, *791*

San Francisco, University of (CA), 12:*644*

San Francisco Archdiocese (CA), 2:869, 8:345–346, **12:644–650**, 14:895–896

San Francisco Cathedral (CA), 3:717

San Francisco de la Espada (San Antonio, TX), 12:639

San Francisco Diocesan Archives (CA), 1:640

San Frediano monastery (Lucca, Italy), 3:67

San Fruttuoso Abbey (Capodimonte, Italy), **12:650**

San Gabriel Mission (Los Angeles), 8:*789*

San Galgano Abbey (Tuscany, Italy), **12:650**

San Giovanni a Campi Bisenzio (Italy), 3:713

San Giovanni in Fiore Abbey (Italy), **12:651**

San José, Hernando de, Bl., 7:732

San José de Guadalupe (Oakland, CA), 12:645

San José de la Paz, María Antonia, **12:651**

San José Mission (San Antonio, TX), 12:639

San Juan, Catarina de, **12:651**

San Juan Archdiocese (Puerto Rico), 11:814

San Juan Bautista Mission (CA), 3:714

San Juan Capistrano (San Antonio, TX), 12:639

San Lorenzo Church (Florence, Italy), 3:699

San Lorenzo Church (Turin, Italy), 3:705

San Lorenzo of Ulcio monastery (Italy), 3:67

San Luis de la Paz Jesuit Mission (Mexico), 9:708

San Manuel Bueno y martir y historias más (Unamuno), 14:289

San Marcello, Church of (Corso, Rome), 12:*351*

San Marco Convent (Florence, Italy), 1:536–537

San Marcos, Main National University of (Valladolid, Spain), **12:651–652**

San Marino, **12:652–654**, *653*

San Martín, John de, Bl., 1:952

San Martín, José Francisco de, 2:234–235

San Martín, Tomás de, 2:465, **12:654**

San Martin Church (Fromista, Spain), 3:*686*

San Martino al Monte Cimino Abbey (Italy), **12:654**

San Michel Church (Louvain), 3:706

San Miguel, Andrés de, **12:654–655**

San Miguel, Antonio de (Bp. of Santiago), 3:485

San Miguel, Francisco de, St., 7:732

San Pedro y Ustarroz, Juan. *See* John of Jesus Mary

San Pietro Abbey (Assisi), 1:790

San Pietro Church (Rome), 3:701–702

San Pietro in Breme Abbey (Italy), **12:655**

San Rafael (CA), 4:841–842

San Rafael (Spain), Martyrs of, 7:124

San Rufino Cathedral (Assisi), 1:790

San Salvatore Abbey (Maggiore, Italy), **12:655–656**

San Salvatore di Messina Monastery (Italy), **12:656**

San Sebastiano Church (Mantua), 3:700, 701

San Tomaso di Villanova Church (Italy), 3:705

San Vincenzo al Volturno Abbey (Italy), **12:656**

San Vitale Church (Ravenna, Italy), 1:1, 2:369–370, *766*, 3:154–155, 687, 8:100

San Vitores, Diego Luis de, Bl., 2:885, **12:657**

Sanam (martyr), 9:28

Sanblasiana, 3:39

Sanches, Francisco (Sánchez), **12:657**, 13:202

Sánchez, Diego, 1:925

Sánchez, Ferdinand, Bl., 1:951

Sánchez, José Bernardo, 2:862

Sánchez, Juan, 8:411, **12:658**

Sanchez, Lourdes (Sister), 1:324

Sanchez, Robert Fortune (Father), 10:288, 12:677

Sánchez, Thomas (Tómas), 11:808, **12:658**, 14:51

Sanchez de Arevolo, Rodrigo, 3:52–53

Sánchez de Tejada, Ignacio, **12:658–659**

Sánchez Delgadillo, Jenaro, St., 6:545, **12:659**

Sánchez Munárriz, Juan, 2:92

Sanchez Muñoz y Carbón, Gil. *See* Clement VIII (Antipope)

Sanchiz Silvestre, Bl., 7:123

Sanchiz Silvetre, Antonio, 7:123

Sancho I (King of Portugal), 11:534

Sancho II (King of Portugal), 11:534

Sancho III (Garcés the Great) (King of Spain), 13:385

Sancho IV (King of Castile), 12:611

Sancho de Guerra, María Josefa del Corazón de Jesús, St., **12:659**

Sancia, St., **12:659–660**

Sancrosanctum concilium (Vatican II), 7:385, 386

Sancta Dei civitas (papal letter, Leo XIII), 9:681

Sancta Mater ecclesia (1964), 10:304

Sancta Romana (papal bull, John XXII), 3:762

Sancta Sanctorum Chapel (Rome), 13:90

Sanctificatio S. Joseph Sponsi Virginis in utero asserta (Marcant, Pierre), 9:140

Sanctification, 3:531–532, 533, 8:85, 715

Sanction, Divine, **12:660–661**

Sanctions, **12:660**, 14:63

Sanctis, Dionisio de, **12:661**

Sanctis, F. de, 4:520

Sanctitatis clarior (*motu proprio*, Paul VI), 3:63

Sanctity. *See* Holiness

Sanctoral Cycle, 8:719–722, **12:661–664**

Sanctorum meritis (office hymn), **12:664**

Sanctorum patrum Trias (Sinnich), 13:163

Sanctus (hymn), 10:46, 11:662, **12:664–665**

Sanctus (martyr), 1:93

Sand, Josephine, 12:565

Sandanha, Francesco, 3:791

Sanday, William, 7:850, **12:665**

Sander, Nicholas (Sanders), **12:665–666**

Sanders, James A., 2:359, 3:33

Sanderson, John, 1:676

Sandoval, Alonso de, 3:770, 851

Sandusky, Adelaide (Mother), 5:887

Sandys, John, Bl., 5:229, **12:666**

Sandys, W., 3:151

Sane (papal decree, Innocent III), 1:348

Sanfedists, 3:101, 12:402, **666**

Sanga, Anthony, Bl., 7:733

Sanga, Magdalene, Bl., 7:733

Sangallo, Antonio da, 3:213, 701, 12:579

Sangallo, Giuliano da, 3:701

Sangnier, Marc, 2:303, 5:855, **12:666–667**

Sanhedrin, 3:482, 14:179–180

Śaṅkara (Hindu teacher), 6:846

Sankey, Ira David, 7:257, 12:205

Sāṅkhya (Hindu philosophy), 6:845

Sankichi, Paul, Bl., 7:733

Sankt Blasien Abbey (Switzerland), 1:114, 312, 909, 5:106, **12:667–668**

Sankt Emmeram Abbey (Germany), 5:192, **12:668**

Sankt Florian Monastery (Austria), 1:322, **12:668–669**

Sankt Gallen Abbey (Switzerland), 3:155, **12:669–670**

    Adalbero of Augsburg, Bl., 1:99

    Altdorf Abbey, 1:321

    Communion antiphons of, 4:32

    Conrad of Constance, 4:136

    Constance jurisdiction, 4:168

    monks, 5:142

Sankt Lambrecht Abbey (Austria), 1:321, **12:670**

Sankt Maxim Abbey (Trier, France), 5:42

Sankt Nikola Abbey (Austria), 1:322

Sankt Paul Abbey (Carinthia), **12:670**

Sankt Peter Abbey (Salzburg, Austria), 5:220, **12:670–671**

Sankt Peter Monastery (Salzburg, Austria), 12:413

Sankt Pólten Monastery (Austria), 1:322

Sankt Ulrich Von Augsburg Abbey (Germany), 5:106

Sanseverino, Gaetano, **12:671–672**, 772–773

Santa Anna, Ricardo de, Bl., 7:733

Santa Barbara Mission (California), 2:863

Santa Bibiana Church (Rome), 3:705

Santa Catalina Catholic Church (Colombia), 3:850

Santa Caterina all rota (Rossi), 12:388

Santa Chiara Basilica (Assisi), 1:790

Santa Claus, 3:557

Santa Coloma de Farnés, 12:630

Santa Costanza Church (Rome), 3:687

Santa Croce Basilica (Rome), 3:686

Santa Croce Church (Rome, Italy), 4:181, 5:769

Santa Croce frescoes (Florence), 6:230

Santa Croce monastery (Mortara), 3:67

Santa Cruz Monastery (Coimbra, Portugal), 3:68–69, 827, **12:673**

Santa Fe Archdiocese (NM), 1:637, 640, 8:315–316, **12:673–679**, 13:25

Santa Fe Independent School District v. Doe (2000), 3:667

Santa Justa y Rufina, Sancho de (Abp. of Manila), 11:257

Santa Maria, Juan de, 12:674

Santa María Church (Ripoll), 3:690

Santa Maria Convent (Campitelli, Italy), 3:803, *804*

Santa Maria d'Arabona Abbey (Abruzzi, Italy), **12:679**

Santa Maria degli Angeli (Florence), 3:699

Santa Maria degli Angeli Basilica (Assisi), 1:790–791

Santa Maria del Popolo Church (Rome), 1:887

Santa Maria della Salute Church (Venice, Italy), 3:705

Santa Maria della Vittoria Church, 2:325

Santa Maria dell'Assunzione Church (Ariccia, Italy), 3:705

Santa Maria de'Miracoli (Rome), 3:705

Santa Maria di Finalpia Abbey (Italy), **12:679**

Santa Maria di Monte Santo Church (Rome), 3:705

Santa Maria di Polsi Abbey (Italy), 12:679

Santa Maria Egiziaca Church (Naples), 3:705

Santa Maria Foras Portas Church (Castelseprio), 2:371, 373

Santa Maria in Dominica Church (Rome), 1:571

Santa Maria in Porto monastery (Ravenna, Italy), 3:67

Santa Maria Magdalena (penitent home) (Lisbon, Portugal), 3:416

Santa Maria Maggiore Basilica (Rome), 1:426, 474, 543, 751, 2:28, 8:555, 556

Santa Maria Maggiore Cathedral (Assisi), 1:790

Santa Maria Novella Church (Florence), 1:933, 3:696

Santa Maria Odigitria monastery (Italy), 2:127

Santa Maria sopra Minerva Church (Rome), 1:740

Santa Marta, Juan de, Bl., 7:732

Santa Prisca Church (Taxco, Mexico), 3:696

Santa Pudenziana Church (Rome), 1:425

Santa Sabina, 3:317–318

Santa Susanna Cathedral (Rome), 3:704

Santa Teresa de Jesús (periodical), 10:706

Sant'Agnese Church (Rome), 3:705

Sant'Agnese Monastery (Bologna, Italy), 3:315

Santamaria, B. A., 1:904

Santamaria, Grimoaldo of the Purification, Bl., **12:680**

Sant'Ambrogio Cathedral (Milan), 3:691

Sant'Andrea Church (Mantua), 3:700–701

Sant'Andrea Church (Rome), 3:701

Sant'Anselmo (Rome), 4:437

Sant'Antimo Abbey (Siena, Italy), 10:380, **12:672**

Sant'Apollinare Nuovo Church (Italy), 12:463, 599, 600

Santarelli, Anton, **12:680**

Santas Creus Abbey (Spain), 3:750, **12:680**

Santayana, George, 3:670, 5:440, 11:296, **12:680–681**, *681*

    aristocracy, 1:667

    form, 5:803

    knowledge, theories of, 8:220

Santayana, George *(continued)*
    naturalism, 10:204, 12:71
    nonscholastic realism, 11:944
Sant'Egidio, 7:1000
Sant'Egidio, Community of, **12:672–673**
Sant'Eligio Church (Rome), 3:701
Santer, Michael (Bp. of Kensington),
    1:441
Santero, 12:685
Sant'Eutizio di Norcia Abbey (Italy),
    12:673
Santi, Giovanni, 12:*275*
Santiago de Compostela, 4:129,
    12:681–684
    archdiocese, 12:683–684
    Knights of St. James, 8:196–197, 197
    pilgrimage shrine, 12:584, 681, 683
    relics of St. James, 12:681, 683
    Saint Davids (Wales), 12:544
    Saint-Gilles Abbey, 12:548
    Saint-Savin-de Bigorre Abbey,
      12:584
    shrine, 13:94
    university, 12:684
Santiago de Compostela Cathedral
    (Spain), 3:691, 707, 12:*682*
Santini, Fortunato, 2:841
Santissima Trinidade (laity association),
    3:416
Sant'Ivo Church (Rome), 3:705
Santo, **12:685**
Santo Domingo (West Indies), 4:544,
    5:358
Santo Domingo CELAM meeting
    (1992), 2:469, **12:685–686**
    See also Consejo Episcopal
      Latinoamericano (CELAM)
Santo Domingo Church (Brazil), 2:*596*
Santo Domingo Church (San Cristobal
    las Casas), 3:714
Santo Domingo de Silos (Spain), 8:*681*
Santori, Julius, 1:486, 14:470
Santos, João dos, **12:686**
Santos, Paulo dos, 7:727
Santos Machicao, José, 2:468
Santuario de Chimayo (New Mexico),
    12:677
Sanz, José Aparicio, Bl., 1:5
Sanz, Juan, 3:135
Sanz y Jordá, Pedro Mártir, St., 3:498,
    12:687
Sanzio, Raphael, 3:484
Sao Salvadore, Church of (Portugal),
    12:*523*
São Tomé and Principe, **12:687–688**,
    688

Sapieha, Adam Stefan (Card.),
    11:449–450, **12:688–689**
Sapienti consilio (apostolic constitution,
    Pius X), 1:116, 10:543, 11:390, 481,
    751
Sapientia (Roswitha of Gandersheim),
    12:390
Sapientia Christiana (apostolic
    constitution, John Paul II), 5:498,
    7:1002, 11:484, **12:689–690**
Sapiential books, 3:250, 775, 8:28,
    10:489, **12:690**, 13:305
Sapiential literature, 14:788
Sapientiale (Thomas of York), 14:39
Sapinière. See Sodalitium; Sodalitium
    Pianum
Sapor I (King of Persia), 3:593
Sapphires, alleged magical properties of,
    11:646
Saraceni, Maurus, **12:690**
Saracens
    Carolingian legends, 1:763
    John VIII (Pope), 7:923
    John X (Pope), 7:924
    Leo IV (Pope), St., 7:659, 8:481–482
    protection for Rome, 13:14
    wars of conquest against, 3:51, 52
Saragossa, Council of (380), 1:134,
    5:178
Sarah (wife of Abraham), 1:118
Sarajevo (Yugoslavia), 7:1000
Sarapis (Egyptian deity), 7:605
Sarcophagus, **12:690–691**
Sardica, Councils of (343-421), 1:662,
    12:692
    Acacius, 4:470
    Acacius of Caesarea, 1:51
    Athanasius, St., 1:818
    Canon Law, 3:38, 39
    Cyprus, 4:461
    primacy of Rome, 8:54
    summons, 4:173
    Theodosius the Deacon, collection of,
      13:885
    See also Arianism
Sardinha, Pedro Fernandes (Bp. of
    Bahia), 2:588, **12:692–693**
Sardinia Confirmation, 4:87
Sardis synagogue (Turkey), 13:678
Sardonyx, alleged magical properties of,
    11:646
Sargis I (Armenian Catholicos), 1:453
Sargon II (Assyrian king), 7:641
Sargon II (King of Babylon, 722-706
    B.C.), 9:531
Sarkander, Jan, St., **12:693**

Särkilax, Peter, 5:732
Sarnelli, Gennaro Maria, Bl., **12:694**
Sarpi, Paolo, 10:806, **12:694–695**, *695*,
    13:29
Sarrasin, Jean (Abp. of Cambrai), 12:588
Sarriá, Vicente Francisco de, 2:862
Sart, Giuseppe, 3:468
Sartain, J(ames) Peter (Bp. of Little
    Rock), 8:615
Sarto, Andrea del, 1:562, 2:315
Sarto, Giuseppe Melchiorre. *See* Pius X
    (Pope), St.
Sartre, Jean-Paul, 5:94, 11:298,
    12:695–697, *696*
    absurdity, 1:48
    agnosticism, 1:184
    anxiety, 1:541
    atheism, 1:823
    Augustinianism, 1:882
    being-in-itself vs. being-for-oneself,
      14:4–5
    communication philosophy, 4:25
    consciousness, 4:154
    essence and existence, 5:362, 368
    essences denied, 13:348
    existentialism, 5:398, 544, 545, 546
    free will, 5:931
    freedom, 5:725, 939
    good, 6:350
    humanism, 7:197
    knowledge theories, 8:219, 221–222
    nonbeing, 10:417
    self, concept of, 12:884
    social structure, 14:245
Sarum. *See* Salisbury, Ancient See of
Sarum ritual, 3:252
Sarum Use, 1:446, 2:524, 8:682,
    12:697–698, 14:895
Sasada, Louis, Bl., 7:734
Sasanian Dynasty, 11:137–139
Sassanian persecution, 1:37–38
Sasserath, Rainer, **12:698**
Sastre Corporales, Angel, Bl., 7:125
Satan, **12:698–699**
    afterlife, 1:164
    angels, 1:417, 419–420
    death, 4:575, 576, 582
    defined, 4:704
    demonology and conceptions,
      4:645–648, 649, 717
    evil, 5:490–491
    Jewish literature, 12:698–699
    millenarianism, 9:633
    New Testament, 12:699
    Old Testatment, 12:698

scrupulosity, 12:847

serpent as symbol, 13:19

temptation, 13:813

See also Evil

Satan Tries to Tempt Christ in the Forest (painting), 13:*817*

Satanism, 4:705, **12:699**

Satan's Flight Through Chaos (Dore), 9:634

Satellico, Elisabetta Maria, Bl., **12:699**

Satie, Erik, 11:562

Satis cognitum (encyclical, Leo XIII), 1:592, **12:700**

Satisfaction of Christ, **12:700–703**

Sato, Michael, Bl., 7:733

Satolli, Francesco (Card.), 12:*704*, **704**

　Americanism, 1:355

　anti-Catholicism, 1:352

　apostolic delegation in the United States, 1:584, 585

　Bouquillon controversy, 2:565

　congruism, 4:121

Sator Arepo ("magic square" cryptogram), **12:704–705**

Satornilus (gnostic teacher), 1:521

Satsuma, Leo de, Bl., 7:733

Sattler, Michael, 4:81

Saturday, 8:718

Saturnalia (Macrobius), 3:551–552, 9:25, 12:320, **705**

Saturninus of Toulouse (Bp.), 6:111

Saturus Saturninus, 1:93

Satutua Ecclesiae Antiqua, 10:639

Satyrica gestarum rerum regum atque regnorum (Paulinus of Venice), 11:39

Satyrus of Milan, St., 1:337, **12:705**

Saudi Arabia, 8:258, **12:705–707**, *707*

Saudreau, Auguste, 4:209, **12:707–708**

Saul (King of Israel), 2:282, 4:536, 7:638

Saul, James, 7:581

Saul of Tarsus. *See* Paul, Apostle, St.

Saule (Baltic region deity), 2:36

Sauli, Alexander, St., 2:104, **12:708**

Saultemouche, William, Bl., 1:845

Saulus Exrex (Sinnich), 12:246, 13:163

Sauma, Rabban, 3:492

Saumur, Assembly of (1611), 7:168

Saunders, Dame Cicely, 7:117

Saunders, Joseph, 3:716

Saur, Wunibald, 11:210

Saussure, Ferdinand de, 13:551–552

Sauvé Joseph-Mignault-Paul, 3:10

Sauvecanne (Silvacane) Abbey (France), **12:708**

Sava, St., 10:697

Savannah Archdiocese (GA), **12:709–711**

Savannah Diocese (GA), 6:151

Les Savannes, poésies américaines (Rouquette), 12:391

Savaric of Bath (Bp.), 2:152, **12:711**

Savelli, Cencio (Card.), 12:711

Savelli, Fabrizio (Card.), 12:711

Savelli, Giacomo (Card.), 12:711

Savelli, Giovanni Battista (Card.), 12:711

Savelli, Giulio (Card.), 12:711

Savelli, Paolo (Card.), 12:711

Savelli, Silvio (Card.), 12:711

Savelli family, 3:854, **12:711**

Savi, Niccolò, 3:793

Savignac, Antoine Raphael, 5:50

Savigny, Friedrich Karl von, 10:184, 12:530

Savigny Abbey (France), 8:372, 513, **12:711–712**

Savinus, St., 12:584, 585

Savio, Dominic, St., 12:615, **712**

Savior, 8:18, **12:712–713**, 13:310

　See also Jesus Christ

Savior (Christological title), 7:809

Savior myths, 10:127–128

Savitri (Ghose), 6:202

Savonarola, Girolamo, 5:768, **12:714–716**

　Alexander VI (Pope), 1:259

　Ambrosius Catharinus, 1:347

　apocalyptic movements, 1:548

　ars moriendi, 1:729

　Catherine de' Ricci, St., 3:267

　direction, spiritual, 4:762

　Leo X (Pope), 8:486

　Louis of Granada influenced, 8:806

　pre-Reformation spiritual hunger, 3:606

Savouret, Nicolas, 12:278

Savoy, Emmanuel Philibert, Duke of, 7:670

Savoy, House of, 13:96

Savoy, Synod of, 4:114

Savoy, Victor Amadeus I, Duke of, 7:670

Savoy, Victor Amadeus II, Duke of, 7:670

Savoy, Victor Amadeus III, Duke of, 7:671

Sawles Award (Guardian of the Soul), **12:716**

Sawtre, William, 4:550

Saxo Grammaticus, 1:40, 463, 4:665

Saybrook Articles, 4:81

Saybrooke Platform (1708) (Connecticut), 3:647

Sayer (Seare), Robert Gregory, **12:716**

Sayers, Dorothy Leigh, **12:716–717**

Sayle, William, 2:13–14

Sbaraglia (Sbaralea), Giovanni Giacinto, **12:717**

Sbaretti, Donato (Card.), 1:585

Scala Claustralium. See Scala Paradisi (Guigo II)

Scala Paradisi (Guigo II), 3:192, 6:565

Scalabrini, Antonio, 2:89

Scalabrini, Giovanni Battista (Bp.), Bl., 1:228, 12:495, 717–718, *717*

Scalabrinians, 12:717, **718–719**

The Scale of Perfection (Hilton), 6:835, 10:118, 119

Scaliger, J. C., 1:834

Scaliger, J. J., 12:620

Scamozzi, O., 3:675

Scanaroli, G. Battista, 3:418

Scandal, **12:719–720**

　as cause of sin, 13:154, 156

　charity, 3:399

　double effect principle, 4:881

　lying as mortal sin, 8:901

Scandinavia

　Adalbert of Bremen, 1:100

　ancestor worship, 1:394

　Ansgar, St., 1:500

　Arcimboldi, Giovannangelo, 1:643

　Canons Regular of St. Augustine, 3:67

　Christianization, 10:446–447

　Lutheranism, 8:888–889

　migratory movements, 10:444

　See also specific countries

Scandinavian Catholic League, St. Ansgar's. *See* St. Ansgar's Scandinavian Catholic League

Scandinavian School, 10:131

Scanlan, John J. (Bp. of Honolulu), 6:671

Scanlan, Lawrence, 10:270, **12:720**, *721*, 14:357–358

Scannell, Richard, 10:588

Scannell, T. B., 1:438

Scapegoats, 1:838, **12:720–721**

Scapulars, **12:721–723**

Scarab, **12:723–724**

Scarabelli, Celestine, 3:420

Scaramelli, Giovanni Battista, 1:310, 7:782, 12:31, **724**, 13:434

Scarampi, Pier Francesco, 12:250, **725–726**

Scarapsus (Dicta Pirminii) (St. Pirmin), 11:360

Scarcity of clergy, 1:906, 3:11, 487

Scarlatti, Alessandro, **12:725**

Scarlatti, Domenico, **12:725–726**

Scarpa, John, 1:346

Scarpari, Jerome, 12:765

Scavini, Pietro, **12:726**

Scenes from the early life of Christ and the Madonna (13th century), 10:*175*

Sceptism and Animal Faith (Santayana), 12:681

Schaaf, Valentine Theodore, **12:726**

Schabel, M. (Father), 3:116

Schädel, Hans, 3:713

Schaepman, Hermann, 10:262

Schaezler, Karl, 10:75

Schaff, Philip, 5:467, 473, **12:726–727**, *727*

Schäffer, Anna, Bl., **12:727**

Schaff-Herzog Encyclopedia of Religious Knowlege, 12:726

Schaffner, Martin, 1:545

Schäler, Konstantin von, **12:730**

Schall Von Bell, Johann Adam, 3:495, 496–497, 613, 7:784, 12:214, **727–729**

Schanz, Paul, **12:729**

Scharper, Philip J., **12:729**

Schatzgeyer, Kaspar, **12:729–730**

Schaufelein (artist), 1:545

Schaumberg, Adolf von (Abp. of Cologne), 2:394

Schautheet, Fulgentius, 12:765

Schechter, Solomon, 4:560

Scheeben, Matthias Joseph, **12:730–731**
  affinity between Möhler, 10:104
  created actuation by uncreated act, 4:336
  death of, 12:787
  dogmatic theology, 4:813
  ecclesiology, 5:37
  grace, 6:392, 404
  Precious Blood, 11:639
  theology of Church, 3:589
  Thomism philosophy, 12:619
  Trinity as mystery of mysteries, 10:84

Schegk, Jakob, 1:382, 677, 12:768

Scheibler, Christoph, 12:768

Scheicher, Joseph, 1:914

Scheler, Max, 5:398, 10:711, 11:297, **12:731–732**, 14:380
  Aristotelianism, 1:678

Augustinianism, 1:881

Brentano, Franz, 2:605

communication theory, 4:24

conscience, 4:140

existence of God, 6:315

Husserl, Edmund, 7:229

phenomenology, 12:70

sociology of knowledge, 8:211

soul, 13:347

Schelkle, K. H., 5:523, 813

Schell, Hermann, 3:589, 4:11, 6:184–185, 12:26, **732**

Schelle, Augustinus, 12:770

Scheller, Emil J., 11:705

Schelling, Friedrich Wilhelm Joseph von, 11:294, **12:732–734**, *733*
  absolute, 1:42–43
  aesthetics, 3:679
  aseity, 1:780
  Böhme, Jakob, 2:462
  eclecticism, 5:47
  essence, 5:361
  free will, 5:931, 939
  Hegel, Georg Wilhelm Friedrich, 6:704–705
  idealism, 7:298
  identity, 7:302, 303
  inner necessity, 10:227
  Kantianism, 8:127
  literary myth, 10:120
  pantheism, 10:821, 827
  philosophy of religion, 12:69
  relation theory, 12:42–43
  spirituality, 13:423
  system of reason, 12:346
  teaching, 5:708

Schells kleinere Schriften (Schell), 12:732

Schema constitutionis de parvo catechismo (Vatican Council I), 3:244

Schempp, Abington School District v. (1963), 3:666, 667

Schenke, H. M., 3:465

Schenoudi. *See* Shenoute of Atripe

Scherer, George, 1:911

Scherer, Maria Theresia, Bl., **12:734–735**

Schervier, Franziska, Bl., 1:2, 5:883, 6:185, **12:735**

Scherzer, J. A., 12:768

Scheut Fathers. *See* Congregation of the Immaculate Heart of Mary

Scheyern Abbey (Bavaria, Germany), **12:735–736**, *736*

Schiaparelli, Luigi, 10:774

Schiarimenti sulla questione della certezza. . .Osservazioni sulle dottrine dei de Bonald, de Maistre, de la Mennais e Laurentie (Ventura), 14:442

Schick, E., 5:813

Schiedermayer (composer), 2:841, 842

Schiffini, Biagio, 12:777

Schillebeeckx, Edward Henry, 5:556, 6:311, 10:99
  Christology, 12:783
  grace, 6:395–396
  hermeneutics, 6:790–791
  preaching, 11:629
  sacramental theology, 12:471, 472, 475
  scholastic theology, 12:777
  works, 12:729

Schiller, F. C. S., 7:196, 12:48

Schiller, Johann Christoph Friedrich von, 3:679, 6:331–332, 8:126

Schindler, Franz, 1:914

Schiner, Matthäus (Card.), **12:736–737**, *737*

Schinina, Maria of the Sacred Heart, Bl., **12:737**

Schinner, Augustine Francis (Bp. of Superior, WI), 14:781

Schism of Antioch. *See* Meletian Schism

Schismatics, denial of Church funeral, 6:33

Schisms, **12:737–738**
  African American Catholics, 1:161–162
  Apostolic Fathers, 1:588
  Arsenite Schism, 2:762
  Church-State relations, 3:657–658
  Goan Schism, 6:268, 7:402
  heresy, 6:769, 770, 773, 12:737
  Istrian Schism, 2:499–500
  Laurentian Schism, 13:672–673
  Milan Schism, 4:192
  19th-20th centuries, 3:624
  Novatianist Schism, 4:457–458, 10:465
  Photian, 4:186–187, 370, 5:23–24, 194–195, 719
  Syrian Church, 13:705–706
  theology of Church, 3:586, 587–588
  Utrecht Schism, 3:614, 816, 9:164, 10:260, 579
  See also Church and State; Eastern Schism (1054); Meletian Schism; Western Schism (1378-1417)

Schlarman, Joseph Henry (Abp.), **12:738–739**

Schlarman, Stanley G., 4:810

Schlatter, Adolf, **12:739**, 14:234

Schlatter, Michael, 5:468, **12:739**

Schlegel, Friedrich, 10:73

Schleiden, Matthias, 2:403

Schleiermacher, Friedrich Daniel Ernst, **12:739–741**, *740*

    aesthetics, 3:679

    apocatastasis, 1:548

    biblical hermeneutics, 6:796

    biographies of Christ, 7:848

    Bushnell, Horace, 2:717

    Coleridge, Samuel Taylor, 3:832

    confessions of faith, 4:81

    doctrine, 4:805

    Erlangen School, 5:322, 323

    ethics and moral life, 5:396

    existence of God, 6:314

    experience theology, 5:557, 9:752

    Father of Liberal theology, 8:542

    Hegelian approach, 8:597

    hermeneutics, 6:787–788

    justification, 8:87–88

    Knudson influenced, 8:227

    philosophy of religion, 12:69

    rationalism, 11:922–923

    religious experience, 5:556

    Schopenhauer, Arthur, 12:784

    system of reason, 12:346

Schleiniger, Nikolaus, 11:623

Schleitheim Confession, 1:368

Schlick, Moritz, 3:301, 5:397, 504

Schlink, Edmund, 4:612

Schlusser-Fiorenza, Elisabeth, 10:307

Schmalkaldic Articles, 4:78

Schmalkaldic League, 1:849, 2:605, 3:431, 637, 12:18, **741**

    Bascio, Matteo Serafini da, 2:133

    Charles V, 1:848

    Philip of Hesse, 11:250

Schmalzgrueber, Franz, 7:782, **12:741**

Schmaus, Michael, 6:399

Schmemann, Alexander, 12:474, **742–743**

Schmid(ius), Sebastian, 2:383

Schmid, Alfons (Mother), 5:885

Schmid, Christoph von, 3:243, 5:681, **12:743**

Schmid, Franz, **12:743**

Schmid, Heinrich, 1:289, 5:139

Schmid, Josef, 6:107

Schmidlin, Joseph, **12:743–744**

Schmidt, Edmund, 2:263

Schmidt, J., 2:363

Schmidt, K. L., 5:521, 812

Schmidt, Wilhelm, 1:163, 4:436, 12:67, 193, **744**

Schmiedel, P. W., 7:16

Schmithals, Walter, 4:265

Schmitt, Athanasius (Abbot), 12:568

Schmitt, H. C., 11:97

Schmucker, Samuel Simon, 1:850, 5:467, 473, 8:885, **12:744–745**

Schnackenburg, Rudolf, 5:523, 7:528

Schneemann, Gerhard, **12:745**, 777

Schneider, Gabriel, 10:462

Schneider, Mary L., 3:756

Schneider, Theodore, 11:81

Schneiders, S., 4:767

Schnerr, Leander, 12:591

Schnürer, Gustav, 6:184

Schoeffler, Agustin, 14:497

Schoenberg, Arnold, 12:*745*, **745–746**

Schola Cantorum, 1:185, 3:75, 522, 8:260, 682, **12:746**

Scholastic education, **5:95–96**, 10:10–11

Scholastic method, 1:19, 4:726–727, 5:95–96, 8:591–592, 663–664, **12:747–749**

Scholastic philosophy, 3:355, 8:265, **12:749–750**

Scholastic terms and axioms, **12:750–757**

Scholastic theology, 13:905, 906–907

    German Catholic, 8:187–188

    kerygmatic theology, 8:158

    Liber de causis, 8:532–534

    Louis of Granada, 8:806

    Robert Bellarmine, St., 13:909

    schism, 12:738

Scholasticism, 5:394–395, 7:340, 11:298, **12:757–779**

    Abelard, Peter, 1:19

    Abrabanel, Isaac, 1:36

    accident, 1:62

    act, 1:73–75

    Aelfric Grammaticus, 1:136

    agility, 1:177

    Alexander of Hales, 1:265

    Alphonsus Liguori, St., 1:309

    analogy, 1:372–373, 378–379

    angels, 1:414–415, 423–424

    Anglican orders problem, 1:592–593

    Anointing of the Sick, 1:482–483

    anonymous Christian, 1:489

    apostolicity, 1:596

    architecture, 3:694

    Aristotelianism, 1:671

    aseity, 1:779

    Assumption of Mary, 1:800

    astrology, 1:813

    Athanasian Creed, 1:815

    Augustinianism, 1:879

    Avicenna, 1:941

    Báñez, Domingo, 2:50

    bilocation, 2:396

    Boethius, 1:673

    Brentano, Franz, 2:604

    calculationes of, 4:727

    Carmelite spirituality, 3:137–138

    Catechism of the Council of Trent, 3:239

    Catholic social thought, 13:254

    causality, 1:175, 3:298, 303–306

    central sense, 3:345–347

    certitude, 3:352

    charity, 3:395–400

    Christian philosophy, 3:539–540

    Christology, 3:561

    Cistercians, 3:749

    Claudianus, Mamertus, 3:769

    conscience, 4:144–145

    conservation, 4:161

    conversion, 4:240

    cosmology, 4:287

    courtly love, 4:321–322

    criteriology, 4:367

    de Wulf, Maurice, 4:712

    decline of, 4:727

    demonstration, 4:651–653

    dialectics, 4:726–727

    discernment, spiritual, 4:765–766

    disputations, 4:727, 12:747–748

    distinctions, 4:778–782

    division, 4:793–794

    doctors, listing of, 4:798–801

    dogmatic theology, 4:813

    Döllinger, Johannes, 4:823

    doubt, 4:883–884

    Drey, Johann Sebastian von, 4:907

    dualism, 4:915–916

    effect on preaching, 11:612

    Eucharist, 5:423–425

    exegesis, 5:516–518

    existence, 5:533

    Fonseca, Peter da, 5:790

    France, 5:847

    free will, 5:930

    Gilson, Étienne Henri, 6:228

    Godfrey of Fontaines, 6:327

    history, 11:291–292

    Humani generis, 3:466, 12:775

    humanism, 7:181, 182, 184, 192–193

    hylomorphism, 7:238

Scholasticism *(continued)*
  idealism, 7:297
  immortality, 7:349
  immutability of God, 7:355–356
  impetus, 7:363
  Incarnation, 7:373–374
  incommunicability, 7:379–380
  infinity, 7:458–459
  Jansenism, 3:614
  John Lutterell, 7:961
  judgment, 8:23, 26
  justification, 8:82–83
  knowledge, theories of, 8:212, 222
  law, philosophy of, 8:398–402
  Modernism, 2:694
  moral goodness, 6:351–352
  motto of, 5:715–716
  personalism, 4:20
  philosophical pluralism, 11:427
  philosophy and science, 11:301
  priesthood, 11:701–702
  psychology, 11:804–806
  quality, 11:850
  relation, 12:41–42
  relics, 12:54–55
  sacraments, 12:468–469
  sin, 13:155, 158
  soul, 13:343–345
  soul-body relationship, 13:356–358
  University of Salamanca, 1:236
  works of charity, 1:302
  See also Kalām; Neoscholasticism
    and Neothomism; Scotism; Thomas
    Aquinas, St.; Thomism
Scholasticism Old and New (De Wulf),
  10:244
Scholasticus, **12:779**
Scholia in Quaturo Evangèlica (Sa),
  12:449
Scholiast, 12:779
Scholium, 5:507, **12:779**
Scholliner, Hermann, **12:779–780**
Scholz, H., 5:504
Schomann, George, 4:80
Schönbert, Nikolaus von (Card.), 4:251
Schönborn, Christoph (Card.), 1:917,
  3:237
Schönborn, Christophe von, 7:528
Schönborn, Damien Hugo (Card.),
  12:780
Schönborn, Franz (Card.), 12:780
Schönborn, Franz Georg (Prince Bp. of
  Würzburg), 12:780
Schönborn, Friedrich Karl (Prince Bp. of
  Würzburg), 12:780

Schönborn, Johann Philipp (Prince Bp.
  of Würzburg), 12:780
Schönborn family, **12:780**
Schonbrunn Palace (Vienna), 6:*638*
Schöner, Johann, 4:251
Schönerer, Georg von, 7:874
Schonmetzer, Adolf, 4:671
School of Baden (Neo-Kantain),
  10:237–238
School of Chartres, 11:291
School of Marburg (Neo-Kantian),
  10:237
School of the Mind (*Xinxue*), 3:512
School Sisters of Notre Dame, 3:622,
  6:166, 8:432, **12:780–782**
School Sisters of St. Francis, 5:885
School Sisters of St. Francis of Christ
  the King (Rome), 5:885–886
School Sisters of the Third Order
  Regular of St. Francis, 5:886
Schools of Charity, 2:117
Schoondonch, Giles, 12:569
Schoonenberg, Piet, 10:667, **12:782–783**
Schopenhauer, Arthur, 11:295,
  12:783–785, *784*
  aesthetics, 1:142, 145, 3:679, 7:196
  appetite, 1:603
  aseity, 1:780
  ethics, 5:396
  free will, 5:931, 939
  Hegelian idealism, 8:219
  human will, 14:582
  idealism, 7:298–299
  intuition, 7:533–534
  irrationalism, 7:586
  pessimism, 11:169–170
  philosophy of music, 10:73
  soul, 13:347
  transcendent will, 10:827
  will and willing, 14:723
Schorsch, Alexander, Rev., 12:785
Schorsch, Dolores, **12:785**
Schott, Anselm, 3:710, **12:785**
Schott Messbuch, 12:785
Schott Missal, 3:710
Schrader, Klemens, 3:589, 5:37, **12:786**
Schramm, Dominikus, 12:31
Schramm, P. E., 10:715
Schreck, Johann (Terrentius), 3:495
Schreibmayr, F., 3:245
Schreiner, Chrysostom, 2:14
Schreiter, Robert, 10:623
Schrembs, Joseph (Bp.), 2:842,
  12:786–787
Schrevogel, Erenbert, 8:248

Schriften zur Theologie, I-XVI (Rahner),
  11:893–894
Schrijvers, Joseph, **12:787**
Schrödinger, E., 1:836
Schroeder, Peter Joseph, 1:354, 355,
  3:291, **12:787**
Schroll, Beda, 12:670
Schubert, Franz, 8:693, **12:787–788**, *788*
Die Schule des hl. Thomas (Plassmann),
  12:774
Schuler, Anthony J. (Bp.), 5:174
Schulte, Augustine Joseph, **12:788–789**
Schulte, Francis Bible (Abp. of New
  Orleans), 2:156, 8:815, 10:297
Schulte, Karl Joseph (Card.), 3:844
Schulte, Paul C. (Abp. of Indianpolis),
  7:418
Schultes, Reginald, 12:777
Schultheiss, Michael Hieronymus. *See*
  Praetorius, Michael
Schultz, Charles H., 11:625
Schultz, Hermann, 2:384
Schulz, S., 5:522
Schulze, G. E., 8:126, 12:345
Schumann, Robert, 12:*789*, **789–790**
Schürer, Emil, 2:385
Schurmans, Maurice, 7:792
Schüssler Fiorenza, Elisabeth, 5:677, 678
Schuster, Alfredo Ildefonso (Card.), Bl.,
  12:533, **790–792**, *791*
Schuster, Eldon B. (Bp. of Great Falls,
  MT), 9:827
Schütz, Heinrich, 12:*792*, **792**
Schwab, Charles Michael, 11:87
Schwabach Articles, 4:78
Schwally, F., 5:520
Schwane, Joseph, **12:792–793**
Schwann, Theodor, 2:403
Schwanzer, K., 3:712
Schwartz, Anton Maria, Bl., **12:793**
Schwartz, Eduard, **12:793–794**
Schwartz, F. W., 10:277
Schwarz, Peter. *See* Peter Nigri
Schwarz, Rudolf
  influence of, 3:711
  interdenominational study, 3:717
  spatial consciousness, 3:679
  structure as expression, 3:678
  succession of architecture styles,
    3:671
  symbolism of church architecture,
    3:675
  typology theory, 3:672
Schwarz, Sebastian (Father), 5:888
Schwarzenau Brethren. *See* Church of
  the Brethren (Dunkers)

Schwarzenberg, Friedrich Joseph von (Card.), 12:*794*, **794**

Schwarzenberg, Johann von, 12:730

Schwebach, James (Bp. of La Crosse, WI), 8:273, 14:781

Schwegler, Albert, 2:385, 14:234

Schweikher, Paul, 3:680, 716

Schweitz, Roger L. (Abp. of Anchorage), 1:209, 396

Schweitzer, Albert, 5:331, 338, 521, 6:863–864, 7:849

Schwenckfeld, Caspar, 1:368, 369, 12:794–795, *795*

Schwenckfelder Church (Silesia, Germany), 1:369, **12:794–795**

Schwertschlager, J., 1:80

Schwetz, Johann Baptist, **12:795**

Schwippert, Hans, 3:711

Sciacca, M. F., 1:881

Science

    abstraction, 1:47

    action at a distance, 1:80, 81

    Adam, 1:105, 106

    Albert the Great, St., 1:226

    alchemy, 1:238

    antipodes question, 1:529, 530

    Aristotelianism, 1:677–678, 681, 682–683, 685

    art, 1:746

    atomism, 1:834–836

    axiomatic system, 1:949

    Bible studies, 4:790–792

    cosmogony of Bible, 4:284

    creationism, 4:346–347

    cybernetics, 4:451–453

    Darwin, Charles Robert, 4:530–532

    deism, 4:616

    demonology, 4:649

    demonstration, 4:651, 652–654

    dialectics, 4:724–725, 726–727

    Enlightenment, 5:260–261

    experimental science, 5:554

    faith linked in theology, 13:923

    Humani generis, 7:181–182

    humanism, 7:195–196

    intellectual habit, 5:744

    magic, 9:38

    moral theology, 9:865–866

    philosophy, 4:47–48, 316–317, 11:276–277

    practical science, 12:797

    reduction of God's role, 6:285

    speculative science, 12:796–797

    spontaneous generation, 13:459–460

    theology, 3:623

William of Ockham, 14:747

See also Anatomy; Biology; Physical sciences; Zoology

Science *(scientia)* (in the Aristotelian-Thomistic tradition), 8:538, 12:795–796, **795–799**

    activity, 8:461

    causality, 3:297–298, 301–302

    habit, 14:293–294

    judgments, 8:204

    liberal arts, 8:538

    motion, 10:18–19

    nature (in philosophy), 10:208–209

    object specifying knowledge, 10:510

    operationalism, 10:608–609

    similarity, 13:125–126

    truth, 14:225–226

    uniformity in nature, 14:300

    unity, 14:318

Science, classification of, 1:47, 2:10, 5:260, **12:818–821**

Science, in antiquity, **12:799–807**

Science, in the Middle Ages, 8:521, 10:18–19, **12:807–815**

Science, in the Renaissance, **12:815–818**

Science, philosophy of, 2:300

Science and Health with Key to the Scriptures (Eddy), 3:544, 5:80

Science and the Modern World (Whitehead), 10:630

Science of Sciences (Bar-Hebraeus), 2:82

The Science of the Cross (Stein), 13:506

Sciences. *See* Anatomy; Biology; Physical sciences; Zoology

Sciences of the spirit *(Geisteswissenschaften)*, 11:802

Scientia media ad examen revocata (Charles of the Assumption), 3:436, 5:790, **12:821–822**

    congruism, 4:120–121

    Divine concurrence, 4:72

    Molina's concept of, 5:935, 936, 6:391, 10:598, 14:50

    Suarez, 5:938

Scientific cosmologies, 5:350–351

Scientific creationism, 4:347

Scientific determinism, 8:270

Scientific empiricism, 5:197

Scientific hagiography, 6:615–616

Scientific method, 5:260, 261

Scientific status of theology, 13:913–914

Scientific syntheses, 13:900

Scientism, 5:93, 8:212, 9:322, **12:822–823**

Scientology, 10:299, **12:823**

La Scienza e la Fede (periodical), 12:671, 772

La Scienza nuova (Vico), 6:889, 12:345, 14:476

Scillium, Martyrs of, 3:30, 186

Scioppius, Kaspar, **12:823–824**

Scito Teipsum (Know Thyself) (Abelard), 5:394

Scivias (St. Hildegard of Bingen), 5:166, 6:831

Scofield, Cyrus Ingerson, **12:824**

The Scofield Reference Bible (Scofield), 4:776, 12:824

Scolari, Paolo. *See* Clement III (Pope)

Scopes, John, T., 3:667, 4:346, 5:495, 6:28, 30

Scot, Michael, 1:239, 674

Scot, Monford. *See* Scott, Montford, Bl.

Scotism, 5:394, **12:824–828**

    action and passion, 1:78

    adoptionism, 1:119

    anonymous Christian, 1:489

    Antonius Andreas, 1:538

    Christocentrism, 3:558

    Fabri, Filippo teachings, 5:585

    lying, 8:900

    realism, 11:942

    scholasticism, 12:762

    sin, 13:152

    soul, 13:344, 345

    studies, 12:827

    See also Nominalism; Scholasticism; Thomism

Scotland, **12:829–839**, *832*, *833*

    Anglican-Episcopalian Religious Orders, 12:102–103

    Calvinism, 2:895

    Canons Regular of St. Augustine, 3:67

    The Catholic Directory for the Clergy and Laity in Scotland, 9:24–25

    Catholic Relief Acts, 5:182–183

    Counter Reformation, 1:20–21

    Covenanters, 4:329–330

    Culdees, 4:422–423

    David I (King of Scotland), 4:539

    demographic statistics, 12:830

    English Book of Common Prayer, 8:377–378

    Free Press incident, 8:133–134

    hymnology, 7:256

    Irish-born Catholics, 8:133–134

    Jacobites, 7:690–691

    Kentigern (Mungo), St., 8:146

    Laud, William, 8:38–77

Scotland *(continued)*
  map, 5:*241*, 12:*831*, 14:*611*
  miracle plays, 4:902
  Presbyterianism, 11:680, 12:24
  Reformation, 2:179, 180, 4:309,
    8:224–226, 12:834–836
  Sisters of Mercy, 13:184
  Smith, William Robertson,
    13:236–237
  See also Britain, early church in;
    England; Northern Ireland; Wales
Scotland, Church of, 4:329–330, 554,
  12:828–829
Scott, George Gilbert, 3:679, 709
Scott, Montford, Bl., 5:231, **12:839**
Scott, Thomas, 10:332
Scott, William, Bl., 5:235
Scottish Psalter, 11:798
Scottish School of Common Sense,
  2:675, 4:22, 322, 11:294, 12:33–34,
  839–841
Scotus, Adam (d. ca. 1210), 9:454–455
Scotus, Jacobus Martinus, 1:676
Scotus academicus (Frassen), 12:764
Scotus Erigena, John, 9:445
The Scoundrel: A Romance
  (Oldmeadow), 10:583
Scourging. *See* Flagellation
Scribes, in the Bible, **12:841**
Scripta super libros Sententiarum
  (Aquinas), 14:24
*Scriptores ecclesiastici de musica sacra
  potissimum* (Gerbert von Hornau),
  6:164
Scriptorium, **12:841–845**, *842*
  Bobbio Abbey, 2:447
  Brethren of the Common Life, 2:608
  Bury-Saint-Edmunds Abbey, 2:714
  Carolingian Renaissance, 3:161, 167,
    425–426
  Cava, 8:494
  Clonmacnois Monastery, 3:806
  Luxeuil, 8:899
  Spain, 13:382
Scriptorium (periodical), 10:776
Scriptum contra Basileense concilium
  (Palomar), 10:814
Scriptures. *See* Bible
Scrittura latina nell'eta romana
  (Schiaparelli), 10:774
Scrolls, 2:512, **12:845–846**
Scrope, Richard (Abp. of York), **12:846**,
  14:894
Scrosoppi, Luigi, St., **12:846**
Scrupulosity, **12:846–848**
Scrutinies, 3:251–252, 253

Scryven, Thomas, 5:226, 7:1019
Scully, V., 3:669, 673
Sculpture
  Anglo-Saxon, 1:448
  baroque period, 2:114
  Bible cycles, 2:373
  Carolingian era, 3:153
  Chartres Cathedral, 3:440–441
  cherubim, 3:*467*
  Cluniac, 3:812
  Cologne, 3:844
  early Christian, 1:753–754, 757
Scuola Italiana Moderna (periodical),
  14:128
Scupoli, Lorenzo, 3:207, **12:848–849**,
  13:429
SDP. *See* Sons of Divine Providence
Se aliquis (Gregory IX), 4:219–220
Se conditiones (Gregory IX), 4:219
Sea of Galiee, 7:626, 1027
Seabury, Samuel (Protestant Episcopal
  Bp.), 5:297, **12:849**
Seafarers, patron saint of, 5:874
Seals, **12:849–850**, *850*, 13:114–115
''The Search for Divine Love''
  (Bartholomew of Vicenza), 2:128
Searle, George M., 3:291
*Seasons of Change: Reflections on Half
  a Century* (Reinert), 12:39
Seasons of Grace (Parsch), 10:903
Seattle Archdiocese (WA), 1:640,
  12:850–853, 13:69
Seattle Cathedral (WA), 3:716
Se-Baptist. *See* Smyth (Smith), John
Sebastian, St., 1:*91*, **12:853**
Sebastian de San Joaquin, 12:619
Sebastiani, Joseph, 7:399
Sechnall, St., 7:244
Seckau Abbey (Styria, Austria), **12:853**,
  855
Le Second catéchisme (Bossuet), 3:243
Second Collection (Lonergan),
  8:773–774
The Second Coming (Percy), 11:114
Second Coming of Christ. *See* Parousia
Second Council of Lyons (1274). *See*
  Lyons, Councils of
Second Creed of Antioch, 1:662
*Second Epistle of Clement ot the
  Corinthians*, 11:608
Second Formulary of Sirmium, 1:663
Second General Conference of the Latin
  American Episcopate. *See* Consejo
  Episcopal Latinoamericano
  (CELAM)

Second Isaiah. *See* Deutero-Isaiah
  (anonymous poet-prophet)
Second Order of the Incarnate Word.
  See Order of the Savior and of the
  Blessed Virgin
The Second Sex (Beauvoir), 5:672
Second Sophistic, 1:829, **12:855–856**
Second Timothy, Epistle of. *See*
  Timothy, Epistles to
Second Vatican Council. *See* Vatican
  Council II
Secondary matter, 9:347–348
Secondat, Charles-Louis de (baron de la
  Brède et de Montesquieu), 5:210,
  255, 262
Secret, discipline of the, 1:20, 3:251,
  12:856–857
The Secret Doctrine (Blavatsky), 13:935
Secret History (Procopius of Caesarea),
  11:738
Secret marriages, 13:749–750
Secret of the Electrum (Sod ha-Hashmal)
  (Gikatilla), 6:211
*The Secret Policy of the English Society
  of Jesus* (Tootell), 14:111
Secret societies
  Carbonari, 3:99–101
  Compagnie du Saint-Sacrement,
    4:40–41
  France, 4:41
  Gibbons, James, 6:206
  Isma'iliya, 13:84–85
  Knights of the Faith, 8:197–198
  Know-Nothingism, 8:199–200
  Ku Klux Klan, 8:251
  Leo XII (Pope), 8:489
  Pennsylvania, 11:86–87
  Pius VIII (Pope), 11:382
  Sodalitium pianum, 13:295
Secret societies, church policy on,
  12:857–858
Secret Treaty of Dover (1670), 10:492
Secrétan, C., 5:940–941
Secretariat for Non-Believers, 1:824,
  916–917, 8:232, 11:30, **12:858**
Secretariat for Non-Christians,
  9:688–689, 11:30, **12:858–859**
Secretariat for Promoting Christian
  Unity, 2:167, 3:625
Secretariat of State (Roman Curia),
  4:439
Secrets, 4:778, 8:902, **12:859–860**
*Secrets of the Commandments (Sodoth
  ha-Mitzvoth)* (Gikatilla), 6:211
Secretum (Petrarch), 11:214–215
Sects, **12:860–861**
  See also Cults

"Sects or New Religious Movements: Pastoral Challenge" (Vatican report, 1986), 10:302

Secular arm, **12:861**

Secular education, 13:614–615

Secular Franciscan Missionary Sisters of Susa, 12:377

Secular Franciscan Order. *See* Franciscans, Third Order Regular

Secular humanism, 7:182, **194–198**

Secular Institute of Priest Missionaries of the Kingship of Christ, 9:732

Secular institutes, 3:144, **12:861–863**

Secular oblates, 10:512

Secular pilgrims, 11:354

Secular world, 5:33–34, 38

Secularism, 1:906, 8:868, 10:509, **12:863–866**, 867, 13:256

See also Laity

Secularity, 9:334–335, **12:866–867**

Secularization, 3:727, 843, 845, **12:867–869**

   Belgium, 2:221

   Cologne, 3:843, 845

   First dynasty of Babylon (c. 1830-1531 B.C.), 9:534

   Gibbons, James, 6:207

   Gogarten, Friedrich, 6:334

   grace, 6:393

   monasticism, 9:794

   Puebla Conference, 11:812

Secularization of Church property, 8:565, 789, 12:532, **869–874**

Seculius Scotus, 3:160–161

Secunda Pars (Thomas Aquinas), 9:862

Secundum quid (after a fashion), 12:753

Sed Festival (Egypt), 8:178

Sedding, Edmund, 3:151

Sede vacante jurisdiction, 10:580

Sedecia (King of Judah), 10:224–225

Sedella, Antonio de, 8:809, 810, **12:874–875**

Seder Ray Amram (Rav Amram bar Sheshna), 9:50

Sedero Luminoso. See Shining Path (guerilla group)

Sedlmayr, Hans, 3:694, 7:284

Sedula Cura (apostolic brief, Paul VI), 11:477

Sedulius Scotus, 1:72, 3:634, 7:246

Sée, Henri, 5:704

See Zhuangzi (Chinese philosopher), 4:523, 524

See Zoroaster (Persian religious leader), 4:492, 529, 9:*34*

Seeberg, Reinhold, 5:557, **12:875**

Seeger, United States v. (1965), 3:661

Seekers (Puritan societies), 11:838, **12:875–876**

Seelos, Francis Xavier, Bl., **12:876**

Sefer ha-Ikkarim (*Book of Principles*) (Albo), 1:232

Sefer ha-Nikkud (*Book of Vocalization*) (Gikatilla), 6:211

Seffrid II (Bp. of Chichester), 3:481

Segarelli, Gerard, 1:594

   See also Poverty Movement

Seger, J. D., 2:379

Segesser, Philipp, **12:876**

Seghers, Charles John (Abp.), 1:208, 10:645, 11:529–530, **12:876–877**

Segneri, Paolo, 7:782, 11:622, 12:*877*, **877–878**

Segneri, Paolo the Younger, **12:878**

Segobiensis, Joannes Lupi, 3:52

Segovia Cathedral (Spain), 13:*381*

Segregation. *See* Desegregation; Racial discrimination

Seguar, Juan, 7:785

Séguin, Jean, 1:207

Segundo, Juan Luis, 8:547, 548, 12:477–478, 729

Ségur, Louis Gaston de, **12:878–879**

Segura López, Manuel, Bl., 9:131, 10:816, **12:879**

Segura y Sáenz, Pedro (Card. of Toledo and Seville), 12:*879*, **879–880**

Seheult, Paul, 14:440

Die Sehnsucht nach dem ganz Anderen (Longing for the Entirely Other) (Horkheimer), 5:915

Seibert, German Reformed Church v. (1846), 3:658

Seidenbusch, Rupert (Abbot), 12:542, 552

Seiller, L., 1:802

Seinsheim, August Graf von, 12:*531*

Seipel, Ignaz, 1:915, **12:880**

Seir documents, 11:92

Seitenstetten Abbey (Austria), **12:880–881**, *881*

Seiter, Clara (Sister), 5:885

Seixas, Romualdo Antônio de (Abp. of Bahia), 2:595, **12:881–882**

Seki, Bartholomew, Bl., 7:732

A Select Bibliography of the History of the Catholic Church in the United States (Ellis), 5:170

Selecta historiae capita et in loca ejusdem insignia dissertationes historicae, chronologicae, criticae, dogmaticae (Alexandre), 1:267

Selectae et practicae disputationes de rebus in administratione sacramentorum (Sánchez), 12:658

Seleucia, Council of (359), 4:471

Seleucia, Synods of (410-486), 1:805, 806, 5:4

Seleucid Dynasty, 1:784, 5:311

The Self, **12:882–885**

   absolute, 1:42

   Biran, Maine de, 9:60

   eschatology, 5:349

   Hume, David, 7:201

   idealism, 7:296–302

   solipsism, 13:303

Self-abandonment, spiritual, **12:885–886**

Self-abuse. *See* Masturbation

Self-awareness. *See* Conscience; Consciousness

Self-deception, 10:27

Self-denial, **12:886**, 13:42–43

Self-determination, 9:90

Self-examination, 4:147–148

Self-flagellation, 9:636–637

Self-government, 9:382

Selfishness, 13:440

Self-knowledge, 8:206, **12:887**

Self-love, 8:829–830, **12:887–888**

Self-oblation, **12:888**

Self-perception, 6:81

Self-pollution. *See* Masturbation

Self-transcendence model of charity, 8:833, 833–834

Seligman, Edwin R., 1:52

Selim II (Sultan), 8:504

Seljuk Turks, 1:7, 2:738, 4:175, 10:784, 11:139, **12:888–889**

Sellars, Roy Wood, 10:204

Sellars, Wilfrid, 5:829

Sellin, Ernst, 2:385

Sellius, Gottfried, 5:208

Selmer, C., 2:602

Selneccer, Nicholas, 4:60, 61

Selva di materie predicabili. . . (St. Alphonsus Liguori), 1:308

Semantics, 4:52, 8:757, **12:889–892**

Semashko, Joseph, 14:274

Semen Îâvorskiĭ. *See* Stefan (Bp. of Riazan)

Semenenko, Peter, 12:174

Semhairy, Antony (Syrian Orthodox Bp.), 13:708–709

Semi-Arianism, 1:818, 13:566

Seminal reasons, 1:876, 878, **12:892–893**

Seminar (periodical), 8:257

Seminaries. *See specific houses*
Seminary education, **12:893–899**
  African Americans, 1:160
  Catholic Theological Union at
    Chicago, 3:181, 288, 478
  China, 3:503
  Colombia, 3:849–850
  Council of Trent, 14:173
  Counter Reformation, 3:610, 612
  Dues scientiarium dominus
    governing, 4:700
  East Asia Pastoral Institute (EAPI),
    5:3
  homiletics, teaching of, 7:61
  Hungary, 7:214
  Jamaica, 3:113
  St. Mary's Seminary, 3:181
  Scotland, 12:835–836
  20th century overview, 3:621
Seminary rectors, 11:957
Seminominalism, 1:194
Semi-Pelagianism, 1:861, 5:651,
  11:62–63, **12:899–901**
  accusations of reviving, 8:518
  Cassian, John, 1:861, 3:206–207
  Celestine I (Pope), St., 3:317
  conversion, 4:239–240, 239–241
  Council of Trent, 12:622
  Cyprian of Toulon, 4:460
  Jansenism, 1:893
  justification, 8:82
  predestination, 11:648–649, 650–651
  Second Council of Orange, 1:877,
    2:499, 3:206
Semiquietism. *See* Quietism and
  Semiquietism
Semirationalism, **12:901–902**
Semitic languages, 1:625–627
Semitic people, 9:747–748
Semler, Johann Salomo, 1:718, 2:383,
  4:805, 5:520, 12:35
Semmes, M. Oliver, 7:699
Sempiternus Christus rex (papal bull,
  Pius XII), 10:251
Sen, K. C., 7:405
Señán, José, 2:862
Senan, St., **12:902**
Seneca, Lucius Annaeus, 12:307, 311,
  902–904
  Aristotelianism, 1:673
  aseity, 1:779
  civil authority, 1:921
  conscience, 4:139–140, 143
  Corinthians Epistles, 4:266
  Nero, 10:250

slavery, 13:209
Senegal, **12:904–905**, *905*
Senestrey, Ignaz von (Abp.),
  12:905–906, *906*
Senfl, Ludwig, **12:906**, *907*
Sengler, O., 12:732
Senilias poéticas (Elguero), 5:154
Sennacherib (King of Assyria, 705-682
  B.C.), 7:642, 9:531
Senne, R. le, 4:24
Sennert, D., 1:834
Sens, Councils of (1140-1528), 1:18, 19,
  3:319, 4:685, 5:849
*Le Sens commun, la philosophie de
  l'être et les formules dogmatiques*
  (Garrigou-Lagrange), 6:102
Sensation, 3:345, **12:906–909**
  Aristotle, 1:682
  certitude, 3:356
  defined, 8:208
  Democritus, 4:644
  Epicureanism, 5:283
  Hume, D., 8:218
  immateriality, 7:346
  Kant, I., 8:219
  knowledge, 4:73, 367
  qualitative change in sensory organ,
    10:17
  Scholastics, 11:804
  Thomism, 8:203–204
  See also Faculties of the Soul
Sense knowledge, **12:909–911**
  Aquinas, 8:24, 208
  certitude, 3:355
  classifying, 8:202
  consciousness, 4:152
  criteriology, 4:367–368
  immortality, 7:350
  Kant, I., 8:121
  love, 8:827–828
  spirit, 13:422
  truth, 14:224
The Sense of Beauty (Santayana), 12:680
The Sense of History (d'Arcy), 4:527
Senses, 3:344–345, 12:*911*, **911–914**
  abstraction, 1:45
  agnosticism, 1:181
  appetite, 1:601–602
  Aristotle, 1:682
  art, 1:748
  cogitative power, 3:822–823
  concupiscence, 4:67
  custody of the, 4:448
  devotion, 4:709
  human act, 7:170

sensibles, 12:914
  supernatural, 13:618–619
  Thomism, 8:208
  yoga, 14:891
Sensible love, 8:825, 827
Sensible pleasure, 8:873, 11:417
Sensible qualities, 11:849
Sensibles, 3:344, 7:346, 8:387,
  12:914–916
Sensism, 1:795, 4:72–73, 322, **12:916**
  See also Empiricism
Sensory receptors, 12:912
Sensory-tonic theory, 10:20
Sensus fidelium (beliefs of the faithful),
  5:40, **12:916–918**
Sentences. See *Book of Sentences* (Peter
  Lombard)
Sentences (Anselm of Laon), 1:498
Sentences (John of Lichtenberg), 14:46
Sentences (Nicholas of Dinkelsbühl),
  10:376
Sentences (*Sententiae*). See *Book of
  Sentences* (Peter Lombard)
Sentences (Thomas of Claxton), 14:46
Sentences and Summae, 4:726, 727,
  12:918–920
Sentences of Sextus, 3:465, **13:52**
Sententiae (St. Isidore of Seville), 7:604
Sententiae ad intellegibilia ducentes
  (Porphyry), 11:520
Sententiarum libri quinique (Peter of
  Poitiers), 11:202
*Die Sentezen des Kardinals humber: Dos
  erste Rechtsbuch der pápstlichen
  Reform* (Michel), 13:39
*Sentiments de quelques théolgiens de
  Holland* (Le Clerc, J.), 8:432
Sentiments of a Church of England Man
  (Swift), 5:966–967
Senyshyn, Ambrose (Bp.), 4:124
Separate Congregationalists, 2:79
Separatists (Puritans). *See* Puritans
Sepcies impressa (impressed species),
  12:753
Seper, Franjo (Card.), 7:528
Sepet, Marius, 4:897–898
Sephirot, 2:833–834
SEPI. *See* Southeast Pastoral Institute
September 11 terrorist attacks (U.S.,
  2001), 1:153, 10:319–320
''September Papacy.'' *See* John Paul I
  (Pope)
Sept-Fonds Abbey. *See* Sept-Fons Abbey
  (Bourbonnais, France)
Sept-Fons Abbey (Bourbonnais, France),
  12:920

Septimius Severus. *See* Severus, Lucius Septimius (Roman Emperor)

Septuagint (LXX), **12:920–924**

agape, 1:169

Alma prophecy, 1:297

biblical Chronicler, 3:565

canonicity, 3:21, 26

Comitoli, Paolo, 4:4

creation account, 4:338–339

Dead Sea Scrolls version, 4:562

devil, 4:704

dogma, 4:810

justification, 8:76

Kings, Book of, 8:175

laity, 8:290

Lamentations, Book of, 8:312

leprosy, 8:510

Letter of Aristeas, 1:666

love for neighbor, 8:831

names of God, 8:3

See also Bible, texts and versions; Old Testament

Sepulcher, Holy. *See* Holy Sepulcher

Sepúlveda, Juan Ginés, 1:70, 8:341

Sequences, **13:1–5**

Adam, 7:249

Adam of Saint-Victor, 1:109

Ave Regina caelorum, 1:931

development, 13:2–4, 3–4

emergence, 13:1–2

Gottschalk of Limburg, 6:370

hymns and tradition, 7:247, 248, 253–254

medieval Latin literature, 9:446

Notker's role in development, 10:455

prosula texts, 13:4

Stabat Mater, 13:467

Victimae paschali laudes, 14:476–477

Seraphic crown. *See* Franciscan crown

Seraphim, **13:5–6,** *6*

Seraphina, St., **13:6**

Seraphina Sforza, Bl., **13:6**

Seraphino, St., **13:6–7**

Serapion of Antioch (Bp.), 1:526, 3:29, 4:797

Serapion of Thmuis, St., 1:273, **13:7,** 41

Serapis (Egyptian deity). *See* Sarapis (Egyptian deity)

Serapis, temple of (Alexandria), 1:268

Serbia and Montenegro, **13:7–11,** *9*

Serbian Orthodox Church, 10:696–700, **696–700,** *697,* 13:8, 10, 11

Bosnia-Herzegovina, 2:547

Croatia, 4:370, 371

founding, 4:196

Macedonian Orthodox Church, 9:15

official favor, 13:226

Yugoslavia, 4:371

Serbs, 4:370–372, 7:214, 216

Serédi, Jusztinian (Abp. of Esztergom), 7:218

Serédi, Jusztinian (Card.), 3:55

Serenelli, Alessandro, 6:363–364

Serenen, Donough, 7:582

Sergeant, John, **13:11–12**

Sergeant, Richard, Bl., 5:229, **13:12**

Sergei of Reshaina, 1:671

Sergius (Bp. of Rome), 3:86

Sergius (Patriarch of Moscow), 12:435, **13:12**

Sergius (Reuchlin), 12:181

Sergius I (Patriarch of Constantinople), **13:13**

Apollinarianism, 1:559

compromise election, 10:913

Monophysitism, 2:748, 749

Monothelitism, 2:821, 4:193, 7:80, 81

Sophronius, St., 13:324

Sergius I (Pope), St., **13:13–14**

Agnus Dei, 1:185, 12:328

Constantinople Council II, 4:192

Dormition of the Virgin, 4:876

Euphemia, St., 5:449

Quinisext Synod, 2:750

Schola Cantorum, 12:746

Sergius II (Patriarch of Constantinople), 2:757, **13:13**

Sergius II (Pope), 4:908–909, 5:28, **13:14**

Sergius III (Pope), **13:15**

Adalgar of Bremen, St., 1:103

Auxilius of Naples, 1:928

Christopher (Antipope), 3:562

Eugenius Vulgarius, 5:447

Leo VI's fourth marriage, 5:24

reordination, 12:128

tetragamy dispute, 2:756, 823

Sergius IV (Pope), 2:757, 4:450, 10:141, **13:15,** *16*

Sergius of Antioch, 7:691

Sergius of Radonezh, St., 12:421, **13:15–16**

Sergius of Resaina, **13:16–17**

Series episcoporum (Gams), 6:86

Serious Call to a Devout and Holy Life (Law), 8:402, 403

Seripando, Girolamo (Card.), **13:17–18**

Augustinianism, 1:875, 879–880, 883, 884, 889

Counter Reformation, 3:611

Laínez refutation, 8:287

School of Cologne, 3:846

Serlio, Sebastiano, 3:672, 674, 701

Serlo of Wilton, 9:458

Serlon of Savigny (Abbot), 12:711

Sermisy, Claude de, **13:18**

Sermo Epinicius (Bradwardine), 14:29

Sermon against Auxentius (St. Ambrose), 3:633

Sermon literature and collections, 11:612–613, 620, 632–635, 634–635

Sermon on the Mount, 1:133, 3:28–29, 228, 7:4, 9:354

Sermon on the Plain, 8:857

See also Sermon on the Mount

Sermones (Gilbert of Holland), 6:215

Sermones (Piosistratus), 9:449

Sermones ad novicios (Á Kempis), 14:13

Sermones Catholicae (Aelfric Grammaticus), 11:632–633

Sermones vulgares (Jacques de Vitry), 7:693

Sermons, **13:18**

See also Homilies; Preaching

Sermons of Jacob of Sarûg (Bedjan), 2:198

Sermons on the Gospels (Maurice of Sully), 9:369

Seroux d'Agincourt, 12:598

Serpentine, alleged magical properties of, 11:646

Serpents (as symbols), **13:18–22**

in the Bible, 11:776

burning and seraphim, 13:6

fertility symbol, 13:21

mythological monster, 13:19–20

natural snake with magical powers, 13:20–21

symbol of life, 13:21–22

Serra, A., 1:30

Serra, Gálvez, 2:862

Serra, Junípero, 2:862, 8:789, *789,* 12:644, 13:22, **22–23**

Serra International, 2:641, **13:23,** 69

Serran (periodical), 13:23

Serrano Frias, Francisco, 3:498, 4:732

Serrat, Raymond (Abbot), 5:751

Serroni, Hyacinthe (Bp. of Albi), 1:229

Sersale, Antonio, 3:795

Sertillanges, Antonin Gilbert, 1:311, 12:777, **13:23–24**

Servandoni, J. N., 3:708

Servant of the Lord, Christ as, 7:807

Servantes du Sacré-Coeur de Jésus, 12:498

Servants for the Poor, Society of the, 5:191

Servants of Charity, 6:549

Servants of Jesus of Charity, 12:659

Servants of Mary, 2:5, 10:223, 12:659, **13:24**

Servants of Mary (OSM). *See* Mantellate Sisters

Servants of Mary, Sisters, **13:24**

Servants of Our Lady Queen of the Clergy, **13:24–25**

Servants of Relief for Incurable Cancer. *See* Congregation of St. Rose of Lima

Servants of the Blessed Sacrament (SSS), **2:436**, 5:572

Servants of the Holy Child Jesus of the Third Order Regular of St. Francis, Congregation of, 5:877

Servants of the Holy Heart of Mary, **7:29–30**

Servants of the Holy Paraclete, 12:677

Servants of the Holy Trinity and the Poor, 3:461

Servants of the Immaculate Heart of Mary, Sisters, 7:*339*

Servants of the Most Sacred Heart of Jesus, 11:63

Servants of the Paraclete, **10:873–874**, 12:678, **13:25**

Servants of the Poor, 4:447

Servants of the Sacred Heart, 14:577

Servetus, Michael, 1:369, 2:889, 3:87, 214, 13:25, **25–26**, 14:303

Service d'Information Pastorale Catholique (SIPECA), 4:14

Servien, François (Bp. of Bayeux), 2:163

Servite Third Order (OSM). *See* Servites

Servites, **13:26–29**

   Austria, 1:912

   discalced order, 4:765

   foundation, organization, growth, 13:26–27

   Lépicier, A., 8:506–507

   as mendicant order, 9:491

   modern renewal, 13:29

   Monte Senario, 13:27

   origins, 3:602

   primitive observance, 13:26–27

   reform movement, 13:27–29

   scholasticism, 12:765

   Servants of Mary, 13:24

   Seven Founders, 13:26

   sorrows of Mary, 13:328

Servitude of Christ, 13:451–452

Servus Dei (martyr of Córdoba), 4:262

Sesame and Lilies (Ruskin), 12:414

Sessorianum, 4:181

Sesto Al Réghena Abbey (Italy), **13:30**

Seston, W., 4:180

Set theory, 4:216–217

Seters, John van, 11:97

Sethians, 6:260

Seton, Elizabeth Ann, St., 2:165, **13:30–35**, *31*

   Boston Archdiocese, 2:553

   canonization, 13:175, 176

   Carroll, John, 3:181

   Cheverus, Jean Louis Lefebvre de, 3:472

   Conference of Mother Seton's Daughters, 13:175–176

   religious habit, 12:100

   Sisters of St. Joseph founding, 2:40

Seton, Robert (Abp.), **13:35–36**

Seton Hall College. *See* Seton Hall University (New Jersey)

Seton Hall University (New Jersey), 9:406, 10:283, 330–331

Settenari sacri (St. Charles of Sezze), 3:435

Settimo Abbey (Italy), **13:36**

Settlement Act of 1701 (England), 5:253

Seux, Raphael, 1:635

Seven (number), 5:7, 12:458, 460–461, 470–471

Seven affirmations of blessedness, 2:178

Seven cities of Cibola, 10:284

Seven Heavens, 6:265–266

Seven last words (of Jesus), **13:36–38**

Seven Last Words (Schütz), 12:792

The Seven Sacraments (van der Wyden), 12:487

Seven Sleepers of Ephesus, 1:785, **13:38**

Seven Sorrows of Mary, Feast of the, 9:158, 13:327–328

The Seven Works of Mercy, 9:506

Seven Years' War (1756-63), 1:155, 3:6, 118

"Seveners" (Muslim sect), 7:624

Seventh Provincial Council of Baltimore (1849), 10:286

Seventh-Day Adventists, 1:135, 548, 12:454, **13:38–39**

Seventy Weeks of Years, **13:39–40**

Seventy-Five Theses (Erastus), 5:317

Seventy-Four Titles, Collection of, 1:494, 3:45, 60, **13:39**

Severian of Gabala, 5:511, **13:40–41**

Severin (Abbot of Monastery of Agaunum), 13:41

Severin (Bp. of Septempeda), 13:41

Severin (Bp. of Treves), 13:41

Severin (protector of Cologne), 5:485, 13:41

Severin, St. (apostle of Noricum), 1:908, 13:41

Severin, SS., **13:41**

Severinus (Pope), 7:81, **13:42**

Severoli, Antonio Gabriele (Card.), **13:42**

Severus (Patriarch of Antioch), 1:525, 5:155, 10:548, **13:43–44**

   Anastasius I (Byzantine Emperor), 1:50, 386, 523

   Anthimus of Trebizond, 1:503

   biblical catenae, 3:259

   Communion antiphon, 4:32

   Council of Chalcedon, 2:793

   creedal statements, 4:354

   Cyril of Alexandria, St., 3:595

   Julian of Halicarnassus, 8:48

   Julianists (Aphthartodocetism), 8:52

   Justin I (Emperor), 13:705

   Leontius of Jerusalem, 8:503

   liturgical history, 8:652

   Sergius of Resaina, 13:16

   studies, 8:429

Severus (Syrian monk), 12:585

Severus, Flavius Valerius (Roman Emperor), 6:57

Severus, Gabriel, 6:456

Severus, Lucius Septimius (Roman Emperor), 1:266, 268, 3:593–594, 797, 12:305, 311–312

   See also Roman persecution era

Severus, Sextus Julius, 2:84

Severus, Sulpiciu. *See* Sulpicius Severus

Severus Alexander (Roman Emperor), 1:752, 3:594, 723, 12:312

Severus ibn Al-Mukaffa' (Bp. of Ashmounein), 4:253, **13:42–43**

Severus of Barcelona (Bp.), 12:585

Severus of Naples (Bp.), 12:585

Severus of Ravenna (Bp.), 12:585

Şevi, Shabbatai, 6:660

Seville, Councils of (619), 4:87, 7:602, 603

Seville Cathedral (Spain), 3:601

Sewal de Bovill, **13:44**

Sex, **13:44–47**

   Christian view, 13:47

   eros and agape, 8:826

   isolation, 13:46–47

Janssens, Louis on conjugal morality, 7:722

John Paul II (Pope) on Church's sexual ethic, 7:1001

lust, 8:871–877

marriage, 13:45–46

sensible vs. rational love, 8:828

serpent as symbol, 13:21

sexual urges, 13:44–45

See also Human sexuality

Sex, in the Bible, 8:871, 13:21, **47–51**

Sexism, **13:51–52**

Sexism and God-Talk (Ruether), 5:677

Sextus, Sentences of. *See Sentences of Sextus*

Sextus Empiricus, 13:203–204

Sexual abuse allegations against clergy. *See* Clergy sex scandals

Sexual assault, 1:491

Sexual desire, 4:66–69, 318–322

Sexual display, 9:758

Sexual morality, 11:514

Sexual orientation, 7:67–70, 71–72

See also Homosexuality

Sexual relations, 4:64–65, 218–222, 266, 13:46

Sexuality, 1:192, 774, 3:442–445, 9:316, 13:47–48

See also Virginity

Seychelles, **13:52–53**, *53*, *54*

Seymour, William J., 1:788

SFCC. *See* Sisters for Christian Community

Sfeir, Nasrallah, 9:*202*

Sfondrati, Celestino (Card.), 13:54

Sfondrati, Francesco (Card.), 3:431, 13:53

Sfondrati, Niccolò. *See* Gregory XIV (Pope)

Sfondrati, Paolo Camille (Card.), 13:53–54

Sfondrati family, **13:53–54**, *55*

Sforza, Ascanio Maria, 13:54

Sforza, Bianca Maria, 13:55

Sforza, Caravaggio, 13:55

Sforza, Caterina, 13:55

Sforza, Francesco (1401-1466), 12:115–116, 117, 13:54

Sforza, Francesco, II (1495-1535), 13:55

Sforza, Galeazzo Maria (Duke of Milan). *See* Milan, Galeazzo Maria Sforza, Duke of

Sforza, Gian Galeazzo, 13:55

Sforza, Ippolita Maria, 13:54

Sforza, Ludovico il Moro, 7:668, 12:736, 13:55, *56*

Sforza, Massimiliano, 13:55

Sforza, Muzio Attendolo (Card.), 13:54

Sforza, Pesaro, 13:55

Sforza, Santafiora, 13:55

Sforza, Segundo, 13:54–55

Sforza family, **13:54–55**

Sgambati, Andreas, **13:55–56**

Sha'are Orah (Gates of Light) (Gikatilla), 6:211

Shabbatai Ṣevi of Smyrna, 7:871

Shabbataiïsm, 2:835, 5:913, 8:9, **13:56–57**

Shabbati (Sabbatai) Sevi (Zevi), 13:56–57

Shaddai, **13:58**

Shadows Cast Before (Resch), 12:137

Shāfiʿite school, 7:623

Shaftesbury, Anthony, 1:447, 2:623

Shahan, Thomas Joseph (Bp.), 3:279, 4:124, 7:22, 10:*167–168*, **13:58–59**

Shahbadine, Gregory Peter. *See* Ignatius Peter VI (Patriarch of Syria)

Shahrastānī, 1:782

Shaizar, 4:402

Shakers, **13:59–60**, *60*

Shakespeare, J. H., 5:928

Shakespeare, William, 1:367, 2:116, **13:60–66**

Shalmaneser V (Assyrian king), 7:641

Shaman and medicine man, 5:154, 8:238, **13:66–67**, *67*

Shamanism, 9:37

Shamanism: Archaic Techniques of Ecstasy (Eliade), 5:154

Shamash (god), 8:393–394

Shame, 13:45, 67–68, **67–68**

Shanahan, John W. (Bp.), 12:541

Shanahan, Joseph (Bp.), 9:734

Shandao, 3:510

Shangqing Sect (Daoism), 4:524

Shanley, John, 5:624, 10:440

Shannon, James (Bp.), 12:575

Shannon v. Frost (1842), 3:658

Shao Yong (Shao Yung), 3:511

The Shape of Things to Come (Wells), 14:361

Shapur (Sassanid king), 1:14

Shapur I (King of Persia), 9:107–108, 11:138

Shapur II (King of Persia), 1:628, 11:138

Shāpūraqān (Mānī), 9:113

Sharastānī (1086-1152), 9:114

Sharbel Makhlouf, St., **13:69**

Sharīʿah. See Islamic law

Sharing the Light of Faith: National Catechetical Directory for Catholics of the United States, 3:236

Sharp, John K., 11:625, 12:263

Shaughnessy, Gerald (Bp. of Seattle, WA), 12:852, **13:69**

Shaw, George Benard, 3:470

Shaw, John William (Abp.), 8:813–814, 10:294–295, 12:642

Shaw, Joseph Coolidge, 14:454

She Who Is (Johnson), 5:679

Shea, George, 10:68

Shea, John Dawson Gilmary, 10:152, **13:69–71**, *70*

Shechem, 1:36, 2:379, 8:523, **13:71–72**

Sheed, Francis Joseph, **13:73**

Sheehan, Luke Francis, **13:73–74**

Sheehan, Michael J. (Abp. of Sante Fe, NM), 10:288, 12:678

Sheehy, M. P., 8:379

Sheen, Fulton J. (Bp.), 5:170, **13:74–75**, *75*

Sheen Charterhouse, 5:243, **13:75**

Sheeran, James B., **13:75–76**

Shehan, Lawrence Joseph (Card.), 2:39, 4:125, **13:76–77**

Sheil, Bernard J. (Bp.), 1:288, 3:478, **13:77**

Shekinah, 2:834, 8:3, **13:77–78**

Shelhot, Ignatius George (Patriarch of Syria), 13:709

Shelley, Edward, Bl., 5:230, 783–784, **13:78**

Shelomoh ben Yishaq. *See* Rashi (Rabbi Shelomoh ben Yishaq) (medieval commentator)

Shema, 2:290

Shen Jihe, St., **13:78**

Shenouda III (Coptic Pope), 4:254, *256*

Shenoute of Atripe, 3:335, **13:78–79**

Sheol, 1:164, 5:337–338, 6:107, 13:37, **79**, *336*

Shepey, John de, **13:79**

Shepherd, Massey, Jr., 4:201, 12:186

Shepherd, W. H., Jr., 6:796

Shepherd of Hermas

    Apostolic Fathers, 1:587, 588

    apostolic succession, 1:591

    biblical canon, 3:21, 22, 26, 31, 32

    bishops, 2:412–413

    Canon Law, 3:37

    catechumenate, 3:250

    Christian way of life, 3:547

    Church history, 3:592

    martyrs and martyrdom, 9:228

    Old Testament, 3:29

Shepherd of Hermas *(continued)*
    sacraments, 12:467
    See also Apostolic Fathers
Shepherd of Hermas (apocalyptic work), **6:785–786**, 11:68
Shepherds, patron saint of, 5:31
Shepherd-Smith, Christopher, 7:794
Sheppard, Henry. *See* Morse, Henry, St.
Sheptyts'kei, Andrii (Ukrainian Metropolitan), 2:747, 5:687, 12:429, **13:79–80**
Sherbert v. Verner (1963), 3:662–663
Sherborn, Robert (Bp. of Chichester), 3:481
Sherborne, Ancient See of (England), 12:616–617
Sherborne Abbey (England), **13:80**, *81*
Sheridan, Terence James, **13:80**
Sherlock, Richard, 3:153
Sherlock, Robert, 7:579
Sherman, Hygrade Provision Company v. (1925), 3:660
Sherman, Thomas Ewing, **13:80–81**
Sherson, Martin, 5:237
Shert, John, Bl., 5:227–228, 799, **13:82**
Sherwin, Ralph, St., 2:611–612, 922, 5:227, **13:82**
Sherwood, Thomas, Bl., 5:227, 12:371, **13:82–83**
Sheshet, Isaac ben, 4:361
Shi shōsetsu, 13:85
Shibata, Mancio de S. Thomas, Bl., 7:733
Shibboleth, **13:83**
Shichiyemon, Bartholomew Kawano, Bl., 7:733
Shichiyemon, Peter, Bl., 7:733
Shiel, Malachy, 7:581
Shield of St. George, 12:547
Shields, Thomas Edward, 3:282, 13:59, **83**
Shields, Vincent, 3:283
Al-Shifa (The Cure) (Avicenna), 1:621
Shī'ites, 1:287, 611–612, 2:873, **13:83–85**
    Al Hussein Mosque, 13:*84*
    Druzes, 4:913
    imām, 7:328
    Isma'ilis, 13:84–85
    Mahdī, Al-, 9:48
    Safavids, 12:526–527
    Shi'a Islam, 13:83–84
    Twelver Shi'a, 13:84
    Zaydis, 13:85
Shikirō, Thomas, Bl., 7:733
Shiloh, Y., 2:380

Shils, Edward, 1:919
Shimabara uprising (Japan, 1637-38), 7:727, 730, 740
Shimazaki, Tōson, **13:85**
Shining Path (guerilla group), 11:166
Shinsuke, Paul, Bl., 7:734
Shinto Rites controversy, 3:515–516
Shintoism, 7:736, **13:85–87**
    ancestor worship, 1:394
    animism, 1:459
    Buddhism, 2:665
    festival, 13:*86*
    Shinto Rites controversy, 3:515–516
Shinyemon, Mark, Bl., 7:733
Ship symbolism, 3:630, 13:667
Shipman, Andrew Jackson, **13:87**
Shirwood, John (Bp. of Durham), **13:87–88**
Shishak I (Egyptian ruler), 7:639, 766
Shishkov, Josaphat, 2:548
Shī'sm, 7:610
    See also Babism; Baha'ism; Ismā'īlīs
Shoah. *See* Holocaust (Shoah)
Shobyōye, Dominic, Bl., 7:734
Shofar, 1:*838*
The Shores of Fisherman (West), 14:686
Short, Patrick (Father), 6:669, 12:497
A Short History of Freethought (Robertson), 5:967
Shoun, John Yoshida, Bl., 7:732
Shoun, Mary, Bl., 7:733
Showbread, **13:88**
Shreveport Diocese (LA), 4:534
Shrine at Sanctuary of Chimayo (New Mexico), 10:*285*
Shrine of Charlemagne (Aachen), 1:2, *2*
Shrines, **13:88–95**
    Austria, 1:913
    Catholic beliefs and devotions, 13:94
    Lourdes, 8:819–820, 13:93
    Marian, 13:90–93
    Mary Mother of the Church: Mary Model of All Christians, 10:728
    Mount of Olives, 10:33–34
    Nicaraguan, 10:353–354
    Oblates of Mary Immaculate and care of Marian, 10:514
    relics of the Passion, 13:89–90
    sacred spaces, 12:500–501
    Saints, 13:93–94
    Stephen, St., 13:511
    Torah, 13:677
    types, 13:88
Shroud of Turin, 13:95–97, **95–97**
    authenticity, 13:96–97

Chevalier, Ulysse, 3:471
    history, 13:95–96
    indications of nails, 10:137
    shrine, 13:90
Shrove Tuesday, **13:97–99**
Shu (Egyptian deity), 4:337
Shulhan 'Arukh (Caro), 3:148, 7:870, 8:9
Shunzhi (Shun-chih) (Emperor of China), 3:496, 12:728
Shuster, George N., **13:99**
Shuwairite Order (Basilian), 1:13
Siam. *See* Thailand
Siberian Orthodox mission, 9:694–695
Sibert of Beka, 3:125, 133, 141, **13:99–100**
Sibyl of Delphi, 13:100
Sibyllina Biscossi, Bl., **13:100**
Sibylline Books, 10:965
Sibylline Emperor of the Last Days, 9:636
Sibylline Oracles, 4:784, **13:100**
    acrostics in, 1:72
    apocrypha, 1:553–554
    Church history, 3:592
    Lactantius, 8:274
    Roman religion, 12:325
    Tiburtine Sibyl, 13:*101*
Sic et Non (Abelard), 3:45, 47, 60, 258, 12:753, 758
Sicardus of Cremona, 1:289, 3:47, 50, 10:627, **13:100–102**
Siccardi laws (Italy), 3:313
Sichar, 13:72
Sichem, William van, 12:764
Sichrowski, Benignus, 1:880
Sicilian Vespers War (1282-1302), 7:664, 666, 13:103–104
Sicily, **13:102–104**
    Adrian IV (Pope), 1:126–127
    Clement IV (Pope), 3:778
    Dusmet, Giuseppe Benedetto, 4:954
    Honorius IV (Pope), 7:86
    Italo-Albanian Church, 7:651
    Monarchia sicula, 12:288
    Roger of Sicily, 12:287–288
Sick, patron of the, 5:921
Sicke Mannes Salve (Becon), 1:733
Sickingen, Franz von, 3:430
Siculo, Lucio Marineo, 12:118
Sidarouss, Fadel, 7:528
Siddur (Jewish prayerbook), 8:8
Sidereus Nuncius (Starry Messenger) (Galileo), 6:60
Sidero, Luigi. *See* Carafa, Vincenzo
Sidetes, Philip, 1:272

Sidgwick, Henry, 2:624, 5:397

Sidney, Algernon, 4:641

Sidon, Council of (394), 1:365

Sidon, Synod of (511), 5:155

Sidonians. *See* Phoenicians

Sidonius Apollinaris, St. (Bp. of Clermont), 3:407, 769, **13:104**

Sidotti, Giovanni, 7:741

Siedenburg, Frederic, **13:104–105**

Siedliska, Franciszka, Bl., 7:24, *24*, 13:*105*, **105**

Siegert, Matthias, 6:166

Siegman, E. F., 5:523

Siena (Italy), **13:105–109**, 199

Siena Cathedral (Italy), 13:*106, 107*, 109

Sierra Conde, Epifanio, Bl., 4:494

Sierra Leone, 1:162, **13:109–110**, *111, 112*

Sierra Uncar, Nicasio (Father), 2:92

Las Siete palabras de la Virgen (Orozco), 10:674

Siete Partidas, 1:155

Siffrin, Peter, **13:110–111**

Sigaud, C., 13:793–794

Sigebert III (King of Austrasia), St., 4:438, 9:79, **13:111**

Sigebert of Gembloux, 1:289, 462, 6:124, 9:451, 12:270, **13:111–112**

Sigehard (Patriarch of Aquileia), 1:608

Siger de Brabant d'aprés ses ouvres inédites (Van Steenberghen), 14:386

Siger of Brabant, **13:112–113**
    Albert the Great, St., 1:225, 935
    Arabian philosophy, 1:623
    double truth theory, 4:882
    Latin Averroism controversy, 1:674, 935, 2:457, 12:761
    mendicant controversy, 2:483
    Thomas Aquinas, St., 14:20
    unity of intellect, 7:512
    University of Paris, 2:483, 3:603

Sigfrid, St., **13:114**

Sigillography, **13:114–115**

Sigiramnus (Abbot), 12:541

Sigismund (Holy Roman Emperor), **13:115–116**
    Constance Council, 4:168–169, *169*, 170
    Council of Basel, 2:133, 134
    Hus, John, 7:228
    Hussites, 3:605, 4:481, 7:231
    John XXIII (Antipope), 7:939
    Western Schism, 2:246, 504, 3:604

Sigismund (King of Burgundy), St., 1:663, 12:567, **13:115**

Sigismund (King of Hungary), 4:413, 538, 7:211

Sigismund, John (King of Transylvania), 2:432

Sigismund II Augustus (King of Poland), 4:309, 312, 11:441

Sigismund III (King of Poland and Sweden), 2:605, 606, 4:314, 5:733, 9:66

Sigler, Gerald J., 4:201

Sign (periodical), 11:818

Sign of the cross. *See* Cross

Signay, Joseph (Abp.), 3:7

Signorelli, Luca, 1:544, 2:375, 12:601, 13:*194*

Signoriello, Nunzio, 12:671, 773

Signs, 4:52, **13:116–117**, 661

Signs of Soul, 10:158

Signs of the times, **13:117–118**

Sigurd (King of Norway), 4:410

Sík, Sándor, 7:218

Sikhism, **13:118–119**, *119*

Silas (Silvanus), **13:119–120**

Silesia (historical European region), 12:693, 14:163

Silesian Catechism (Felbiger), 5:665

Silius Italicus, 12:308

Le Sillon (periodical), 12:667

Sillon Movement, 2:395, 12:667

Siloam Inscription, **13:120**

Silos Abbey (Spain), **13:120–121**

Silva, Atenógenes, **13:121–122**

Silvacane Abbey (France), 1:197, 3:750

Silvanus (Bp. of Emesa), 5:191

Silvanus of Tarsus, 4:471

Silveira, Gonçalo da, Ven., 10:38, **13:122**, 14:926

Silver, thirty pieces, 8:15

Silver and Gold (De reliquiis preciosorum martirum Albini et Rufini) (Garcí of Toledo), 6:93–94

Silverio of St. Teresa, **13:122**

Silverius (Pope), St., 2:224, 4:186, **13:122–123**

Silvester, Bernard. *See* Bernard Silvester

Silvester Guzzolini, St., 2:274, **13:123**

Silvestrelli, Bernard Maria of Jesus, Bl., 10:*932*, **13:124**

Silvestri, Tommaso, 3:418

Silvestrinia, Achille (Card.), 5:*21*

Sim, Cornelius, 2:643

Simeon (Czar of Bulgaria), 2:745–746

Simeon, Canticle of. *See* Nunc Dimittis

Simeon, Marc (Nestorian Patriarch), 3:796

Simeon, prophecy of, 3:14

Simeon V bar Māmā (Chaldean Patriarch), 3:366

Simeon IX (Chaldean Patriarch), 3:367

Simeon XI (Chaldean Patriarch), 3:367

Simeon XII (Chaldean Patriarch), 3:367

Simeon XIII (Chaldean Patriarch), 3:367

Simeon and Levi Killing the Men of Hamor's City, 8:524

Simeon bar Yochai, 2:832

Simeon Barsabae, St. (Bp. of Selecia-Ctesiphon, Mesopotamia), **13:124**

Simeon Denḥā, 3:367

Simeon of Durham, **13:124–156**

Simeon of Polirone, St., 12:643, **13:125**

Simeon of Syracuse, St., **13:125**

Simeon of Thessalonica, 2:827, 828, 5:279

Simeon Stylites, St., 1:*522*, 523

Simeon the Armenian. *See* Simeon of Polirone, St.

Simeoni, Giovanni (Card.), 6:206

Simi, Philippe, 1:635

Similarity, 4:779, **13:125–126**

Simmel, Georg, 6:885, 8:579, 12:731, 13:281

Simmias (philosopher), 9:418–419

Simmons, William J., 8:251

Simon (Syrian physician), 2:82

Simon, Apostle, St., 2:123–124, 7:769, **13:126–127**, *127*

Simon, Jordan, 12:765

Simon, Jules, 5:47

Simon, Richard, **13:127**
    Bible texts, 2:366
    Bossuet, Jacques Bénigne, 2:550
    exegesis, 5:519
    father of biblical criticism, 11:89
    higher criticism, 6:825
    scholasticism, 12:765

Simon, Yves René Marie, 1:918, 8:460, 10:185, 194, **13:127–128**

Simon III Basidi (Chaldean Patriarch), 3:366

Simon Ballachi, Bl., **13:128**

Simon de Ghent, **13:128–129**

Simon de Longpré, Marie Catherine of St. Augustine, Bl., **13:129**

Simon de Montfort, 1:229, 714, 12:233

Simon de Muis, 5:518

Simon Fidati of Cascia, Bl., 1:872, 888, **13:129**

Simon Hinton, **13:129–130**

Simon Islip (Abp. of Canterbury), **13:130**

Simon Langham, **13:130**

Simon Magus, 6:259, **13:130–131**

Simon Mepham (Abp. of Canterbury), **13:131**

Simon Niger, 1:521

Simon of Aulne, Bl., **13:131**

Simon of Bisignano, **13:131–132**

Simon of Brie. *See* Martin IV (Pope)

Simon of Cramaud (Card.), **13:132**

Simon of Saint-Quentin, **13:132–133**

Simon of Southwell, 3:49

Simon of Sudbury (Abp. of Canterbury), 3:72, **13:133**

Simon of Tournai, **13:133**

Simon of Trent (Simeon), **13:133–134**

Simon Stock, St., 13:93, **134**, *135*

Simon the Zealot. *See* Simon, Apostle, St.

Simonetta, Bonifacio, 13:134

Simonetta, Francesco, 13:134

Simonetta, Giacomo, 13:134–135

Simonetta, Giovanni, 13:134

Simonetta, Ludovico, 13:135

Simonetta family, **13:134–135**

Simons, Anna, 2:524

Simons, Menno, 1:368, 369

  See also Mennonites

Simony, 6:471, **13:135–136**

  Alexandre, Noël, 1:267

  Clement III (Antipope), 3:778

  English abolition, 3:70–71

  First Lateran Council, 2:880

  Fourth Lateran Council, 8:354

  Leo I (Byzantine Emperor) prohibition, 8:472

  origins of term, 13:131

  papal prohibition, 10:837

  reordination, 12:128

Simor, János (Card.), **13:136–137**

Simple conversion, 11:769

Simple priors. *See* Obedientiary priors

Simple substances, 13:577

Simple supposition, 13:625

Simplicianus, St., 1:337, 857

Simpliciter (simply), 12:753

Simplicity, virtue of, 2:266, 6:320, **13:137**

Simplicity of God, **13:137–139**

Simplicius (Pope), St., **13:140–141**

  Acacian Schism, 1:49

  Acacius, support of, 2:149

  cardinalate, 3:103

  churches in Rome, 12:355

  Church-State relations, 3:633

  eclecticism, 5:47

Simplicius of Cilicia, 1:670, 676

Simpson, Albert B., 3:530

Simpson, O. von, 3:674

Simpson, Richard, Bl., 1:85, 5:229, **13:141**

Simson, B., 5:615

Simulation, 7:263, **13:141**

Sin

  angels, 1:419–420

  annihilation, 1:471

  Anselm of Canterbury, St., 1:497

  Bonaventure, St., 2:490–491

  compunction, 4:45

  courtesy, 4:318

  deadly (capital), 4:565–567

  death as consequence, 4:573–574

  disorder of moral evil, 14:331

  Divine concurrence, 4:72

  double effect principle, 4:881

  God's permission, 9:772

  hellfire, 6:728

  Hittite conception, 6:894–895

  Jeremiah, 7:755

  Mary, Blessed Virgin, 9:250–251

  mercy, 5:152

  Mesopotamia, ancient, 9:537

  moral doubt, 4:884–885

  moral injury, 7:466

  moral theology, 9:854–855

  penance, 9:861

  presumption, 11:686

  purpose of amendment, 11:840

  pusillanimity, 11:842

  redemption, 11:966–967, 975, 979–982

  reparation, 12:129

  sacrilege, 12:520–521

  spiritual purification, 11:832–833

  suffering as punishment, 13:586

  superstitions, 13:623–624

  tendency of man, 9:87

  See also Contrition; Mortal sin; *specific sins*

Sin (phenomenology of), **13:148–149**

Sin (theology of), **13:149–156**

  analogy, 1:379

  avarice, 1:928

  connection of sins, 13:152–153

  gravity compared, 13:153

  Kierkegaard's subjectivism, 8:167

  lust, 8:871–877, 874–876

  Lutheranism, 8:892–893

  omission and commission, 13:144

  proximate occasions, 13:157

  punishable by death, 13:144

  remote occasions, 13:157

Schoonenberg, Piet, 12:783

  serious and slight, 13:144

  simony, 13:135

  simulation, 13:141

  so-called natural, 8:875

  social sin, 8:545

Sin, against the Holy Spirit, 2:435, 13:158, **158**

Sin, cooperation in, **13:156–157**

Sin, in the Bible, 8:301, 10:664–665, **13:141–148**, 159

Sin, Jaime (Card.), 11:*259*, 260

Sin, occasions of, 8:866, **13:157–158**

Sin offerings, in the Bible, **13:159**

Sinai, Mount (Egypt), **13:159–160**

  See also Horeb, Mount

Sinai peninsula, 9:800–801

Sinaloa Jesuit Mission (Mexico), 9:708

The Sincere Christian (Hay), 3:243

Singapore, **13:160–161**, *162*

Singeisen, Johann Jodokus, 10:65

Singenberger, John, 2:842

Singer, Peter, 1:456

Singh, Sadhu Sunder, 7:405

Singidunum, Martyrs of, **13:161**

Single tax doctrine, 9:397–398

Singulari nos (encyclical, Gregory XVI), 3:619, 6:508, 8:310

Singulari quadam (encyclical, Pius X), 11:389, 14:139

Singularia (Pontanus Romanus), 11:472

Singulars in Ockhamish, 10:535

Sinhala people, 13:465–466

Sinibaldi, Giacomo, 5:435

Sinn Féin, 7:564

Sinner, habitual, 10:74, **13:161–162**

Sinnich, John, 12:246, **13:162–163**

Sino-Japanese War (1937-1945), 3:500

Sinsinawa Dominican Congregation of the Most Holy Rosary, 4:844, 9:390

Sinusiati (schismatic group), 1:560

Sinzig, Pedro, **13:163–164**

Sioux City Diocese (IA), **13:164**

Sioux Falls Diocese (SD), **13:164–165**, 165

Sioux people, 8:280, 12:552, 572

  de Smet, Pierre Jean, 4:692

  Ravoux, Augustin, 11:934

  schools, 13:368

  South Dakota reservations, 11:911

SIPECA (*Service d'Information Pastorale Catholique*), 4:14

Siponto, Syond of (1050), 5:24

Sir Gawain and the Green Knight (poem), 11:51–52

Sirach, Book of, 5:36, **13:166**
　authorship, 1:488
　beatitudes, 2:177
　biblical canon, 3:24, 26
　Dead Sea Scrolls version, 4:562–563
　Elijah, 5:159
　Enoch, 5:265
　generosity to poor, 13:311
　gluttony, 6:251
　justification, 8:77
　law as Divine wisdom, 8:396
　lying as sin, 8:900
　perseverance, 11:133
　slavery, 13:250–251
　sobriety, 13:239
　spirit of God, 13:427
　texts, 2:359
　wisdom personified, 8:760
　See also Wisdom of Ben Sira
Sirach, Canticle of, 3:73
Sirāj (Enlightenment) (Maimonides), 9:52
Sirena, E., 2:844
Siricius (Pope), St., **13:166–167**
　Christmas, 3:553
　clerical celibacy/marriage, 3:325
　decretals as form, 4:599, 600
　Rufinus of Aquileia, 12:404
　virgin birth, 14:534
Siris (Berkeley), 2:298
Sirleto, Guglielmo (Card.), 13:*167*, **167**
Sirmium, Ancient See of (Yugoslavia), 4:475
Sirmium, Synods of, 1:662, 663
Sirmium formula, 8:555, **13:167–168**
Sirmond, Jacques, 4:302, 7:782, **13:168**
Sis, Councils of, 1:706, 3:733
Sisebut (Visigothic king), 9:440
Sisinnius (Pope), **13:168**
Sisinnius I (Patriarch of Constantinople), 2:757, **13:169**
Sisinnius II (Patriarch of Constantinople), 13:13, **169**
Sismonda, Rosalia (d. 1903), 9:141
Sister Disciples of the Divine Master, 6:203
Sister Formation Bulletin, 13:170
Sister Formation Conference, 13:170
Sister Formation Movement, 2:577–578, 10:460, **13:169–170**
Sister Servants of the Sick of St. Camillus, 2:88, 89
''Sister Songs'' (Thompson), 14:58
Sisterhood of the Holy Cross (London), 12:101

SISTER-L (Internet discussion group), 2:578
Sisters, Faithful Companions of Jesus (FCJ), **13:171**
Sisters, Servants of the Immaculate Heart of Mary. *See* Good Shepherd Sisters of Quebec
Sisters Adorers of the Precious Blood (APB), 3:9, **13:171**
Sisters College (Washington, DC), 13:83
Sisters for Christian Community (SFCC), **13:171–172**
Sisters Magdalens, 11:64
Sisters of Bon Secours (CBS), **2:476**
Sisters of Cardinal Sancha, 4:417
Sisters of Charity
　Bedford (OH), 13:180
　Canada, 13:179
　Cincinnati, 13:178
　Colorado, 3:858–859
　founding, 3:744
　of the Immaculate Conception, 13:178, 179
　Ireland, 1:194
　Leavenworth, 13:179–180
　Nazareth, 13:179
　New York, 13:178
　Our Lady of Mercy (OLM), 13:179
　Les Religieuses de Nôtre Dame du Sacré-Coeur, 13:178, 179
　Saint Elizabeth, 13:178–179
　St. Vincent de Paul, 13:178
　Seton Hill, 13:179
　slavery, 1:156
　Soubirous, M., 13:331–332
　Vincentian Sisters of Charity of Pittsburgh, 13:180
Sisters of Charity, Federation of, 8:144, 316, 811, **13:172–180**
Sisters of Charity Federation in the Vincentian and Setonian Tradition, 13:35, 175–176
Sisters of Charity of Lovere, 3:89, 6:189
Sisters of Charity of Montreal. *See* Grey Nuns
Sisters of Charity of Nazareth, 3:180, 4:538, 8:148, 13:35, 401
Sisters of Charity of Our Lady of Mercy (Charleston, SC), 5:223, 13:365
Sisters of Charity of Saint Augustine, **12:537**
Sisters of Charity of St. Elizabeth (Madison, NJ), 9:406
Sisters of Charity of St. Joseph, 3:181
Sisters of Charity of Saint Joseph's, 13:33, 172, 173–175

Sisters of Charity of the Blessed Virgin Mary, 3:765, 8:779
Sisters of Charity of the Hôspital Général de Montréal (Canada), 3:6, 9
Sisters of Charity of the Incarnate Word, **7:369–370**, 8:813, 12:641, 642
Sisters of Charity of the Incarnate Word, Houston, 7:369
Sisters of Charity of the Incarnate Word, San Antonio, 7:369–370
Sisters of Christian Charity, **3:533–534**, 8:812, 9:78
Sisters of Christian Doctrine (Nancy), **3:535**
Sisters of Christian Doctrine, Martyrs of, BB., **13:180–181**
Sisters of Christian Instruction of Saint-Gildas-des-Bois, 4:686
Sisters of Divine Providence, 12:641, 846, **13:181**
Sisters of Divine Providence at Our Lady of the Lake (Texas), 12:641–642
Sisters of Divine Providence of Kentucky, 13:181, **181–182**
Sisters of Divine Providence of Ribeauvillé, 5:307
Sisters of Divine Providence of Texas, **13:182**
Sisters of Immaculate Heart of the Blessed Virgin Mary, **7:339–340**
Sisters of Jesus Crucified. *See* Poor Sisters of Jesus Crucified and the Sorrowful Mother
Sisters of Loretto, 8:113, 148, 316, **786**, 10:249, 288–289
Sisters of Loretto at the Foot of the Cross, 1:156, 691, 3:180
Sisters of Mary of the Presentation, **11:682**
Sisters of Mercy, **13:182–188**
　California, 2:868
　Detroit, 4:698
　founding, 9:391, 12:416–417, 14:650
　Georgia, 1:830
　Nebraska, 10:223
Sisters of Mercy of the Americas, 3:437
Sisters of Mercy of the Holy Cross, 5:773, **7:22**, 12:734–735
Sisters of Notre Dame (SND), 2:394, 10:223, **457–458**
Sisters of Notre Dame de Namur, 2:867–868, 8:838, **10:458–460**
Sisters of Our Lady of Charity of the Good Shepherd, **6:357–358**, 10:722, 11:64, 13:331
Sisters of Our Lady of Christian Doctrine, **3:535**

Sisters of Our Lady of Consolation, 9:764–765

Sisters of Our Lady of Sorrows, 12:127

Sisters of Our Lady of Suffrage (Italy), 5:581

Sisters of Our Lady of the Garden (OLG), **10:724**

Sisters of Our Lady of the Missions (RNDM), **10:724**

Sisters of Perpetual Adoration of the Blessed Sacrament, 13:417

Sisters of Providence, 1:209–210, 3:419, 4:619, **13:188**

Sisters of Providence (Rouen), 12:291

Sisters of Providence of Saint Mary-of-the-Woods, 6:558, **13:188–189**, *189*

Sisters of St. Agnes, 8:504

Sisters of St. Anianus, 1:454

Sisters of St. Anne, 1:209, 210, 2:442, **12:534**

Sisters of St. Casimir, **12:541–542**

Sisters of Saint Catherine, 11:775

Sisters of St. Charles, 3:419

Sisters of St. Dominic of the American Congregation of the Sacred Heart of Jesus, 4:844

Sisters of St. Dorothy of Cemmo, 3:816

Sisters of St. Elizabeth, 1:2, 3:419

Sisters of St. Felix of Cantalice, 5:886

Sisters of St. Francis, 5:886–887

Sisters of St. Francis Congregation of Our Lady of Lourdes, 5:887

Sisters of St. Francis of Assisi, 5:887

Sisters of St. Francis of Calais, 8:278

Sisters of St. Francis of Penance and Christian Charity, 5:887–888

Sisters of St. Francis of Perpetual Adoration, 5:888

Sisters of St. Francis of Philadelphia, 5:888, 890

Sisters of St. Francis of Savannah, Missouri, 5:888

Sisters of St. Francis of the Holy Cross, 5:888–889

Sisters of St. Francis of the Holy Eucharist of Independence, Missouri, 5:889

Sisters of St. Francis of the Holy Family, 5:889

Sisters of St. Francis of the Immaculate Conception, 5:889

Sisters of St. Francis of the Immaculate Heart of Mary, 5:889

Sisters of St. Francis of the Immaculate Virgin Mary Mother of God, 5:889–890

Sisters of St. Francis of the Martyr St. George, 5:890

Sisters of St. Francis of the Mission of the Immaculate Virgin, 5:890

Sisters of St. Francis of the Providence of God, 5:890

Sisters of St. Francis of the Third Order Regular (Williamsville, NY), 5:890

Sisters of St. Francis Regis, 12:31

Sisters of St. John of God (SSJG), 6:35, **12:551**

Sisters of St. John the Baptist, **12:551**

Sisters of St. Joseph (SSJ), 1:830, 2:40, 555, 3:419, **12:554–556**, 572, 589

Sisters of St. Joseph of Carondelet, 8:791

Sisters of St. Joseph of Cluny. *See* St. Joseph Sisters

Sisters of St. Joseph of Orange, 8:793

Sisters of St. Joseph of Peace, 4:445–446

Sisters of St. Joseph of the Third Order of St. Francis, 5:890–891

Sisters of St. Louis, 2:161

Sisters of St. Mary of Namur, **12:565**

Sisters of St. Mary of Oregon, **12:565**

Sisters of St. Paul (Chartres), **12:570**, **573**

Sisters of St. Thomas of Villanova, **12:587**

Sisters of St. Vincent, 3:437

Sisters of St. Vincent de Paul, 1:323, 4:292

Sisters of San Rafael, 2:867

Sisters of Social Service, 7:218

Sisters of the Adoration of the Blessed Sacrament (SABS), **13:189–190**

Sisters of the Agony of Jesus in Gethsemane Ursuline, 8:444

Sisters of the Assumption, **1:797**

Sisters of the Blessed Sacrament, **2:436–437**

Sisters of the Blessed Sacrament for Indians and Colored People, 11:87

Sisters of the Child Jesus (*Soeurs du Saint-Enfant Jésus de Reims*), 12:291

Sisters of the Christian Schools of Mercy, **3:543–544**, 11:554

Sisters of the Congregation de Notre Dame (CND), 2:566–567, **10:458**

Sisters of the Congregation of Mary. *See* Marist Sisters

Sisters of the Congregation of Our Lady (Montréal), 3:4

Sisters of the Cross, 6:558

Sisters of the Divine Compassion, **4:786–787**

Sisters of the Divine Redeemer, **4:787**

Sisters of the Divine Savior, **4:788**, 12:631

Sisters of the Good Shepherd, 2:555, 3:419, 8:817

Sisters of the Good Shepherd of Divine Providence, 8:128–129

Sisters of the Holy Childhood, 14:186

Sisters of the Holy Childhood of Jesus and Mary of Ste. Chrétienne, 12:595

Sisters of the Holy Cross, 8:375, 13:327

Sisters of the Holy Cross and Seven Dolors, 9:893

Sisters of the Holy Family, 2:505, **7:23**, 8:811, 812, 9:381–382, 10:292

Sisters of the Holy Family of Bergamo, 3:350

Sisters of the Holy Family of Nazareth, **7:24**, 13:105

Sisters of the Holy Family of Villefranche, **7:24**

Sisters of the Holy Infant Jesus, **7:30**

Sisters of the Holy Infant Jesus of Providence of Rouen, 2:117

Sisters of the Holy Names, 8:791

Sisters of the Holy Spirit, **7:52**

Sisters of the Holy Spirit and Mary Immaculate, **7:52–53**

Sisters of the Humility of Mary, **7:207**

Sisters of the Immaculate Heart of Mary, 2:868, 872, 12:609

Sisters of the Incarnate Word and the Blessed Sacrament, 3:474

Sisters of the Most Holy Sacrament (MHS), 8:812, 10:293, **13:190**

Sisters of the Most Holy Trinity, **14:208–209**

Sisters of the Most Precious Blood, 11:644

Sisters of the Order of St. Basil the Great (Basilians), **2:144–145**

Sisters of the Poor Child Jesus, 5:708, 8:375, **11:493–494**

Sisters of the Poor of Saint Catherine of Siena, 11:219

Sisters of the Precious Blood, 11:644–645

Sisters of the Presentation (CA), 2:868

Sisters of the Presentation of Mary, **11:683–684**, 12:261–262

Sisters of the Presentation of the Blessed Virgin Mary, **11:684**

Sisters of the Sacred Heart of Jesus, 8:375, 12:737

Sisters of the Sacred Hearts, 1:950, 12:274

Sisters of the Sacred Hearts of Jesus and Mary. *See* Sisters of the Sacred Hearts

Sisters of the Sacred Hearts of Jesus and Mary and Adoration (SS. CC.). *See* Sisters of the Sacred Hearts

Sisters of the Society Devoted to the Sacred Heart, **12:493**

Sisters of the Sorrowful Mother, 12:631

Sisters of the Third Franciscan Order, 5:891

Sisters of the Third Order of St. Francis, 5:891–892

Sisters Servants of Mary, 1:158

Sisters Servants of Mary Immaculate (SSMI), 2:464, 8:246, 813, **9:285**, 10:294

Sisters Servants of the Holy Spirit of Perpetual Adoration, **11:131**

Sisters Servants of the Immaculate Heart of Mary, 1:157, **7:338–339**

Sisters Survey, 8:422–423

Sistine Chapel (Vatican City), 3:606, **13:190–191**, *194*

  Bible cycles, 2:375

  Botticelli fresco, 13:*192*

  Clement XIII (Pope), 3:793

  erection of, 13:197, 14:396

  Ghirlandaio fresco, 13:*193*

  iconography of Apostles in, 1:575

Sistine Chapel (Vatican City), restoration of, **13:191–193**, *195*

Sistine choir (Rome), 1:1, 2:841, 3:523

Sistine edition of the Bible, 14:596

Sitjar, Buenaventura, 2:865

Sittich of Hohenems, Mark (Abp. of Salzburg), 1:912

Sitting liturgical gestures, 8:648

Situation (*Situs*), 1:61, 4:215, 8:742, 10:18, **13:193**

Śiva (Hindu deity), 6:849–850, **13:193–194**

Siviard, St., 12:541

Six livres de la République (Bodin), 12:124

Six Sermons on Temperance (Beecher), 2:199

Six Systems (Indian philosophy), 7:407–410

Sixteen nations, 11:104

Sixteen Revelations of Divine Love (Julian of Norwich), 8:49

Sixth beatitude, 2:172

Sixth Day. *See* Crucifixion

Sixtus I (Pope), St., 13:*194*, **194**

Sixtus II (Pope), St., 2:146, 5:665, **13:194–195**, *196*

Sixtus III (Pope), St., 3:555, 4:364, 601, 8:474, **13:195–196**

Sixtus IV (Pope), **13:197**

  Alexandrine bulls, 1:273

  Angelo Carletti di Chivasso, Bl., 1:413

  appeals to a future council, 1:599

  Carmelites, 3:144

  Clareni, 3:763

  family, 4:631

  Felix of Cantalice, 5:669

  Fruttuaria Abbey, 6:17

  Ghibelline-Guelf conflict, 3:855

  Immaculate Conception, 7:334

  indulgences, 4:556, 7:438

  nepotism by, 10:247, 12:219

  pre-Reformation spiritual hunger, 3:606

  Renaissance humanism, 12:118

  Sisters of the Holy Spirit, 7:52

  Sistine Chapel, 13:190, 191

  Solemnity of All Saints, 1:290

  term limits for Superior Generals, 2:128

  Vatican construction, 14:396

  Vatican Library, 14:420

Sixtus V (Pope), **13:197–199**

  Allen, William, 1:296

  Ambrosians, 1:346

  Apostolic Penitentiary, 11:75–76

  canonization, 3:63, 12:607–608

  capital punishment, 3:87

  cardinalate, 3:105, 106–107

  Carmelites, 1:468

  church architecture, 3:704

  clerical dress, 3:801

  Colonna family, 3:856

  Congregation of Ceremonies, 3:349

  Congregation of Rites, 8:640

  Congregation of Sacred Rites and Ceremonies founder, 12:256

  contraception, 4:221

  Counter Reformation, 3:611

  Curia, 4:438

  ecclesiastical archives, 1:636

  Feuillants, 3:747, 5:707

  Index of Prohibited Books, 7:390

  papacy development, 10:843

  Philip II, 11:248

  Pontificia Facoltà Teological "San Bonaventura," 11:490

  Sistine edition of the Bible, 14:596

  statuary, 2:109

  works of charity, 3:417

Sixtus of Siena, 3:20, **13:199**

Sixty Books (Leo VI), 8:474

Skarga, Piotr, 2:606, 7:782, 12:433, **13:199–200**

Skavronska, Martha. *See* Catherine I (Russian Empress)

Skehan, Patrick W., 1:305–306, 5:520, **13:200**

Skepticism, 6:442, 11:285, **13:200–205**

  absolute, 1:41

  Aristotelianism, 1:668

  atheism, 1:823

  causality, 3:298

  certitude, 3:352

  Charron, Pierre, 3:439

  contingency, 4:214

  criteriology, 4:367

  Cyrenaics, 4:464

  equipollence, 13:203, 204

  Hobbes, Thomas, 9:416

  Huet, Pierre Daniel, 7:148

  Hume, David, 7:200–202

  idealism, 7:296, 297

  knowledge, theories of, 8:214

  liberal arts, 8:537

  Locke's influence, 8:745

  methodical doubt distinguished from, 4:884

  partial, 4:884

  relativism, 12:47

  solipsism, 13:303

  speculative, 4:884

  universal, 4:884

  wisdom, 14:785

Sketches of the Establishment of the Church in New England (Fitton), 5:751

Skiing, 8:868

Skillin, Edward, 4:22–23, **13:205**

Skinner, B. F., 13:784, 14:361

Skinner, Charles R., 11:562

Sky and sky gods, 5:696–697, **13:205–206**

Slade, John, Bl., 2:452, 5:228

Slater, Edward, 1:900

Slaton, Paris Adult Theater v. (1973), 11:519

Slattery, Edward J. (Bp. of Tulsa), 14:235

Slavery

  abolitionism, 1:156, 444, 768, 13:*211*, 214

  Angola, 1:450

  Bahamas, 3:120–121

  Barbados, 3:120

  Brazil, 2:590–591, 596–597

  Catholic Church apology, 3:628

Slavery *(continued)*

Central African Republic, 3:344

child slavery in Benin, 2:282

Claver, St. Peter, 3:417, 770–771

Colombia, 3:847

Cortez letter to Charles V, 13:*209*

defense of, 13:365–366

Dutch Caribbean Islands, 3:116–117

early Church, 1:828

Epistle to Philemon, 11:243

French Caribbean Islands, 3:118

Gregory XVI (Pope), 2:44, 6:510

Hughes, John Joseph, 7:161

hymnology, 7:257–258

inter-island migration, 3:121–122

Jamaica, 3:111

Latin America, 3:417, 770–771

Magyars, 7:209

Malone, Sylvester, 9:81

marriage, 3:117

parasitic, 13:208

religious education for slaves, 12:394

religious orders, 1:156

religious slavery in Ghana, 6:201

Roman Empire, 12:306–307

Sabbath Year, 12:460–461

symbiotic, 13:208

temperance movements, 13:800

Trinidad and Tobago, 3:114, 115

United States

African American Catholics, 1:155–156

Alabama Catholic Church, 1:201

Baltimore Council discussion, 2:45

Baptist division, 2:80

Know-Nothing Party, 8:200

Louisiana, 8:815–816

Massachusetts, 9:307

Mauritius mission, 8:384

McFarland, Francis P., 4:123

Methodist Episcopal Church, South (U.S.), 9:562

Missouri, 9:742

Seychelles, 13:52–53

South Carolina, 13:365

Tennessee, 13:822

Virginia, 14:542

Virgin Islands, 3:119

works of charity, 3:404, 409, 417, 770–771

See also Abolition Movement

Slavery, history of, **13:209–215**

abolition, 8:389, 443, 512, 13:110

Amistad mutiny, 4:116

Christians, 8:520

Congo mission, 4:105

Congo Republic mission, 4:108

Congregationalist mission, 4:116

Constantine I (the Great) (Roman Emperor), 4:182

Cuba, 4:417

evangelizing former slaves, 8:556

historic roots, 13:214–215

Laos, 8:329

Leo XIII (Pope), 8:491

Liberia's creation, 8:551

Slavery, in the Bible, **13:206–207**

legislation, 13:206–207

New Testament, 13:207

Old Testament, 13:207

social principle, 13:250–251

Slavery and the Church, **13:207–209**, 252, 258

Slavic Church, 2:743–744, 3:27

Slavic philology, 13:237

Slavic religion, 4:474–476, **13:215**

Slavic solidarity, 8:249

Slavonic hagiography, 6:614

Slavonic liturgy, 4:370, 475–476

Slavophilism, 8:165, 12:425, **13:216**, 307

Slavorum apostoli (encyclical, John Paul II), 3:627, 7:1003, 9:682, **13:216–217**, 14:107

Slavs (Slavic region), 7:209, 9:694

Sleeba Mar Osthathiose, St., 7:406

Sleep, 3:346–347

Sleep without Anxiety (Dormi secure) (Johannes of Werden), 11:613

Slipyj, Josyf (Card.), **13:217–218**, *218*

Slomšek, Anton Martin, Bl., **13:218–219**

Sloth. *See* Acedia

"Sloth" (Boilly), 13:*150*

Slovak Catholic People's Party, 13:221, 222

Slovakia, **13:219–224**, *221*, *222*

Cyril and Methodius, SS., 1:125

Czech Republic, 4:478

demographic statistics, 13:219

ecclesiastical organization, 13:219, 221, 222, 224

Hutterites, 7:234

map, 13:*220*

See also Czechoslovakia

Slovakian Church (Canada), 3:11

Slovenia, **13:224–228**, *226*

Sloyan, Gerard, 12:97

SMA (Society of African Missions), 10:393, 14:98

Smaldone, Filippo Mariano, Bl., **13:228**

Smalebecker, Johann, 8:564

Small, Albion W., 13:282

Small Catechism (Luther), 4:78

Small Catechism (Moghila), 10:700–701

Smaragdus of Saint-Mihiel, 3:160, 634, 12:568–569, **13:228**

Smart, J. J. C., 9:419

Smart, Roderick Ninian, **13:228–230**

SMB (Bethlehem Mission Immensee). *See* Bethlehem Fathers

Smedt, Charles de, 2:472, **13:230**

Smend, Rudolf, 5:520, 11:96

Smet, Eugénie de, Bl., **13:230**

Smetana, Bedřich, **13:230–231**, *231*

Smith, Adam, 2:285, 4:19, 5:703, 12:33, **13:231–232**, *232*, 14:361

Smith, Al (presidential candidate), 7:542

Smith, Alfred E., 1:693, 10:171, 172, 324

Smith, Alphonse J. (Bp. of Nashville, TN), 13:823

Smith, Bob, 1:242

Smith, E. G., 4:435

Smith, Employment Division v. (1990), 3:663–664

Smith, G. B., 3:22

Smith, Henry Ignatius, **13:232–233**, *233*

Smith, Ian, 14:926

Smith, J. A., 1:679

Smith, James, **13:233**

Smith, John (Cambridge Platonist), 2:908–909

Smith, John Talbot, **13:233–234**

Smith, Joseph, 8:372–375, **13:234**, *235*

Smith, Richard, 4:955, 5:248, **13:234**

Smith, Richard (Bp. of Chalcedon), 2:102, **13:234–235**

Smith, Sydney, 1:438

Smith, W. B., 7:850

Smith, W. Robertson, 10:122

Smith, Wilfrid Cantwell, **13:235–236**

Smith, William Henry, 1:160

Smith, William Robertson, **13:236–237**

Smith Act (U.S., 1940). *See* Alien Registration Act (U.S., 1940)

Smith v. Nelson (1846), 3:658

Smolenskin, Peretz, 6:663

Smotryts'kyi, Meletii, **13:237**

SMR (Society of Mary Reparatrix), **9:290**

Smuggling, **13:237**

Smyrnaeans, Epistle to the (St. Ignatius of Antioch), 1:170

Smyth (Smith), John, 2:78, **13:237–238**

Smyth, Clement (Bp. of Dubuque), 4:922

Snaith, N. H., 2:355, 356

SND (Sisters of Notre Dame), 2:394, 10:223, 457–458

Snettisham, Richard, 12:263

Snow, C. P., 5:88, 13:786

Snow, Peter, Bl., 5:233, **13:238**

The Snowbird Statement (1995), 8:710–711

Snowdon, David A., 12:782

Soane, John, 3:709

Soanen, Jean (Bp. of Senez), 1:600

Soares, Antony, Bl., 1:951

Sobieski, John (King of Poland), 12:422

Sobornost, 5:773, 783, 8:165, 12:437, **13:238**

Sobreviela, Manuel, **13:238–239**

Sobriety, **13:239**

Sobrino, Jon, 4:766, 8:548, 549

So-Called Albright People, 5:468, 469

Social and Cultural Dynamics (Sorokin), 8:212

Social Apostolate, 8:805

Social Catholicism, 8:310, 371

Social Christianity, 2:138, 143

Social classes, 9:237

Social consciousness and concern, 2:80, 6:5

The Social Contract (Rousseau), 12:392, 393

Social contracts, **13:239–241**
  authority, 1:920, 13:239
  Church-State relations, 3:635, 639
  community, 4:38
  covenant theology, 4:328–329
  Hobbes, Thomas, 6:900
  Mayflower Compact, 9:382
  natural law doctrine, 10:183
  social principle, 13:252
  society, 13:278–279
  theory, 13:483

Social ethics, 9:867

Social Gospel, 2:717, 4:117, 8:175, 10:387, **13:241–242**

Social Gospel Movement, 2:80, 5:76–77

Social issues and programs
  California, 2:871–872
  Catholic organizations, 3:622
  Iowa, 7:542
  Ireland, 7:567–569
  John XXIII (Pope), Bl., 3:625
  John Paul II (Pope), 3:342–343
  Vatican Council II, 2:469

See also Charity, works of; Social justice and social justice issues

Social Justice (newspaper), 4:294–295

Social justice and social justice issues, **13:242–244**
  Arrupe, Pedro, 1:726
  Australia, 1:904
  Bolivia, 2:470
  Call to Action Conference, 2:874–876
  Canada, 3:9, 11, 388
  Center Party (Germany), 3:341
  charismatic renewal movement, 3:392
  Chávez, César Estrada, 2:872, 3:460
  Cipitria y Barriola, Bl. Cándida María de Jesús, 3:738–739
  Connecticut, 4:126
  Coughlin, Charles Edward, 4:294–295
  Day, Dorothy, 4:545–546
  Dearden, John Francis, 4:569
  Delgado, José Matías, 4:628
  Dempsey, Timothy, 4:655
  diaconia, 4:718–720
  distributism, 4:782–783
  Hovda, Robert W., 7:141
  Hume, George Basil, 7:203
  Kingdom of God, 8:173–174
  Korea, 8:239, 240
  Lacordaire, J. H., 8:272
  LaFarge, J., 8:277
  Land, P., 8:317–318
  Latin American Church, 4:157–158
  liberation theology, 1:655, 2:598, 3:852, 8:544–546, 546–550
  medieval Church, 8:296
  Methodism, 8:561–562
  Native North Americans, 3:11
  19th-20th century overview, 3:620
  Rerum novarum (encyclical), 5:205–206, 855, 12:136–137
  Rummel, J. F., 8:815
  social effects of technology, 13:787
  social encyclicals, 8:773
  in the state, 13:485
  virtue of justice, 8:67–69
  worker movements, 8:266
  works of charity, 3:420

See also Social issues and programs

Social legislation, 8:161, 13:487

Social lies, 8:901–902

Social Mission Sisters, 7:218

Social Order (periodical), 8:317, 14:252

Social organization, 14:667

Social programs, Church's role in, 2:15, 6:200–201, 622, 11:166–167, 13:400

Social Question, 8:310, 492, 578, 896

Social reform, 8:160, 211, 9:397–398, 583–584, 614, 13:241–242

Social Relations in the Urban Parish (Fichter), 5:709

Social satire, 9:882

Social sciences, 8:725, 13:287, 14:668

Social security in the State, 13:487

Social Service, Sisters of, **13:244**

Social Sin, **13:244–247**, 287

The Social Sources of Denominationalism (Niebuhr), 10:386

Social Statics (Spencer), 13:412

Social structure, 13:487

Social teaching. *See* Social thought, Catholic

Social theology, 5:773

Social thought, Catholic, 8:544–560, **13:246–257**

Social thought, papal, 8:549, **13:257–269**

Social triage, 14:178

Social virtues, 6:423

Social work, 8:156, 807, 13:104–105

Socialism, 5:221–222
  Buchez, Philippe Joseph Benjamin, 2:654
  Catholic social thought, 13:256
  Cathrein, Viktor, 3:294
  overview, 3:619–620
  rejection of Christianity, 5:397
  Rerum novarum (encyclical), 5:205–206, 855, 12:136–137
  solidarism, 13:300–301
  Spain, 13:398–399
  works of charity, 3:420

Socialism: Promise or Menace? (Ryan), 12:445

Socialist humanism, 7:193

Socialization, religious, **13:269–275**

Socialized medicine, 9:407

Socialum scientiarum (motu proprio, John Paul II), 11:475

Socianism, **13:290–291**, *291*

Socianized Minor Church, 13:290–291

Società Editrice Romana, 6:537

Societal harms, 11:547–548

Societas Ancillarum Sanctissimi Sacramenti. See Servants of the Blessed Sacrament

Societas Liturgica, 8:679, 680, **13:275**

Societas Marie. *See* Marianists

Societas Missionarium Domesticorum Americas (Home Missioners of America). *See* Glenmary Home Missioners

Societas Papidum et Papidissarum (Society of the Sons and Daughters of the Pope), 11:636

Societas Rosicruciana in America, 12:382

Societas Rosicruciana in Anglia, 12:382

Société d'Économie Charitable, 9:482–483

Société des Bons Amis, 12:219

Societies of Methodism, 9:558

Society, **13:275–285**

  associations, 1:791

  authority, 1:918–919

  common good, 4:16–22

  communication philosophy, 4:24–25

  Durkheim, Émile, 4:951–952

  evolutionary view, 13:413

  function, 13:276

  functional analysis, 8:461

  integration attempts, 13:283–285

  leisure, 8:460, 461

  Middle Ages, 9:614

  notion of order, 10:629

  organic view, 13:413

  philosophical analysis, 13:275–279

  private ownership, 13:265–266

  psychological models, 13:282

  sociological analysis, 13:279–283

  sociological definition, 13:279–280

  solidarism, 13:300–301

  Spencer, Herbert, 13:413

  spirital and acting totality, 13:407

  state, 13:480–481

  subjectivity of, 13:302

  theological object, 13:287

  types, 13:278

  women, role of, 14:812–819

Society (Church as), **13:285–287**

Society, theology of, 8:35–37, **13:287–288**

Society and Solitude (Emerson), 5:188

Society for Promoting Christian Knowledge (SPCK), 1:446, 9:12, **13:288**

Society for Psychical Research, 11:463

Society for the Propagation of the Faith, 3:622, 5:796, 7:744, 933, 9:294, **11:752–754**

  founding, 4:113, 10:291–292

  Leopoldine Society, 8:504

  Ludwig Mission Society, 8:853

  missionary work in Oceania, 10:528

Pallotti, Vincent, St., 10:809

  reorganization (1817), 10:847

Society for the Propagation of the Gospel (SPG), 5:296, 13:288, **288–289**

Society for the Relief of Poor Widows with Small Children, 13:31

''Society method'' mission and educational support, 2:79–80

Society of African Missions, 5:878, 8:552, 9:175, 13:110

Society of Brothers, 7:235

Society of Catholic College Teachers of Sacred Doctrine, 13:289–290

Society of Catholic Medical Missionaries. *See* Medical Mission Sisters (MMS)

Society of Friends. *See* Quakers (Religious Society of Friends)

Society of Helpers. *See* Helpers of the Holy Souls

Society of Jesus. *See* Jesuits

Society of Mary. *See* Marianists

Society of Mary Auxiliatrix, 13:331

Society of Mary in America, 8:736

Society of Mary of Montfort. *See* Montfort Fathers

Society of Mary Reparatrix (SMR), **9:290**

Society of Missionaries of Africa. *See* Missionaries of Africa

Society of Missionary Priests of St. Paul the Apostle. *See* Paulists

Society of Our Lady of the Way, **10:725**

Society of Pius V, 3:289

Society of Pius X, 3:289, 11:30, 391

Society of Rosicuricians (*Societas Rosicruciana in America*), 12:382

Society of St. Adalbert, 13:221

Society of St. Edmund, 10:50, **12:545**

Society of St. Elizabeth, 3:420

Society of St. Francis de Sales (*Societas Sancti Francisci Salesii*). *See* Salesians

Society of St. John the Evangelist (SSJE). *See* Cowley Fathers

Society of St. Joseph of the Sacred Heart, 1:157

Society of St. Paul for the Apostolate of Communications. *See* Pauline Fathers and Brothers

Society of St. Teresa of Jesus, 8:813, **12:587**

Society of Saint Teresa of Jesus for Christian education (Spain), 10:706

Society of St. Ursula of the Blessed Virgin, **12:587–588**, 14:875

Society of Science (Berlin), 8:456

Society of Sisters, Pierce v. (1925), 3:660

Society of the Atonement, 5:874–875, 14:662

Society of the Divine Savior (SDS), 12:630–631

Society of the Divine Word (SVD), **4:789**, 9:739

  African American Catholics, 1:157, 159

  China, 3:500

  founding, 3:621

  Louisiana, 8:278

Society of the Friends of Reform in Frankfurt, 8:9–10

Society of the Holy Child Jesus, 4:126–127, **7:17–18**

Society of the Holy Family, 1:159

Society of the Immaculate Heart of Mary, 8:556

Society of the Poor Brothers of St. Francis, 1:2

Society of the Priests of St. Sulpice. *See* Sulpicians

Society of the Rose and Cross, 12:382

Society of the Sacred Heart, 4:928, 6:64, **12:493–494**

Society of the Sacred Heart of Jesus, **12:496**

Society of the Sons and Daughters of the Pope (*Societas Papidum et Papidissarum*), 11:636

Society of Ville-Marie, 3:4

Socinianism, 2:894, 3:608, 8:841

Socinius, Faustus, 1:369, 2:432, 13:290, 291, *291*

Socinus, Laelius, 13:290, 291

Sociocultural criticism, 6:795

Socio-economic problems, 8:266

Sociological pessimism, 11:168

Sociological reading approach, 10:307

Sociology

  Bureau, Paul, 2:696

  Comte, Auguste, 4:46–48, 11:543–544

  cults, 4:425

  Durkheim, Émile, 4:951–953

  Kerby, W. J., 8:155–156

  society, 13:279–283

  Spencer, Herbert, 13:412–414

  theology, 13:924–925

Sociology and prayer, **13:924–925**

Sociology of religion. *See* Religion, sociology of

Socrates (Greek philosopher), **13:291–293**, *292*

  Al-Kindī, 8:170

appreciation, 13:293

beauty, 2:184

causality, 3:297, 302

certitude, 3:352

conscience, 4:139

consciousness, 4:152

criteriology, 4:367

Cynics, 4:455

daimonion, 4:497

death, 7:347

democracy, 4:638

disciple as term, 4:768

distinction, 4:780–781

educational philosophy, 5:88

ethics, 5:392–393

final causality, 5:723

free will, 5:929

freedom, 5:937

friendship, 6:6

God, 6:307

idea, 7:292

induction, 7:432

knowledge, 8:213

life, 13:291–292

moral guide, 4:760

providence of God, 11:781

religious veneration, 6:445

substantial change, 13:580

teaching, 13:292–293

trial, 3:630–631

wonder, 14:832

Socrates the Historian, 1:809, 2:148, 797, **13:293**

Soctus, John Duns. *See* Duns Scotus, John

Sod ha-Hashmal (Secret of the Electrum) (Gikatilla), 6:211

Sōdai, Paul Aibara, Bl., 7:734

Sodalities of Our Lady, National Federation of, 3:622, **13:294–295**

Sodalitium Pianum, 7:503, **13:295–296**

Sodalitium Pianum, dissolution of, 2:279

Sodality Movement, 8:779

Sodality of Mary, 5:834

Sodality of Our Lady, 13:294

Sodality of St. Peter Claver for the African Missions. *See* Missionary Sisters of St. Peter Claver

Sodano, Angelo (Card.), 3:*104*, 5:644

Soden, H. von, 7:16

SODEPAX (organization), 8:317, 13:296, **296**

Söderblom, Nathan (Abp.), 8:577–578, **13:296–297**, *297*, 14:841

Sodor and Man, Ancient See of (Isle of Man), **13:297–298**

Sodoth ha-Mitzvoth (Secrets of the Commandments) (Gikatilla), 6:211

Soeharto (Indonesian dictator), 7:431

Soens, Lawrence, 13:164

Soeurs de Saint Paul de Chartres (SPDC), 12:571

Sofer-Schreiber, Rabbi Moses, 7:873

Sofranov, I., 2:684

Soglia Ceroni, Giovanni (Card.), **13:298**

Söhngen, G., 10:98

Soirées de St. Pétersbourg (Maistre), 9:61

Soiron, Catherine, Bl., 4:44

Soiron, Thaddeus, 5:813, 11:624–625

Soiron, Thérèse, Bl., 4:44

Soissons, Councils of (853-1121), 1:21, 3:336, 6:838

Soissons, Synod of (744), 1:244

Soissons Cathedralh (France), 3:695

Soka Gakkai, **13:298**

Sokolski, Joseph (Abp. of Bulgaria), 2:681

Sol Invictus, 4:180, 181

Solana Ruiz, Benito, Bl., 4:494

Solano, Francis, St., 12:616, **13:299**

Solano, Vicente, 5:64

Soldiers of the Cross (Salpointe), 10:287, 12:676

Solemn League and Covenant, 4:329–330

Solemn magisterium, 2:173–174, 13:352–353

Solemnis, St., 3:441

Solemnity of Mary, Mother of God (feast), 9:159

La Solennità (Pius XII), 13:259–260

Soler, Mariano, **13:299**

Soler, Peter, 4:503

Soler, Vicente, 10:29

Soler Pérez, Luis, 5:645

Solesmes Abbey (France), 3:380, 13:121, **299–300**, *300*

Solesmes theory, 6:466–467

Solid Philosophy (Sergeant), 13:12

Solidarism, **13:300–301**

Solidarity, 13:267–268, **301–302**, 485

Solidarity (labor union), 7:997–998, 11:452–454

Solidarność. *See* Solidarity (labor union)

Solignac Abbey (France), 5:157, **13:302–303**

Solikowski, John (Abp. of Lvov, Poland), 2:605

Soliloquies in England (Santayana), 12:680

Soliloquium animae (Á Kempis), 14:13

Solimarius (Gunther of Pairis), 6:584

Solinus (3rd. c. Latin writer), 2:342, 343

Solipsism, 5:107–108, 7:229–230, 297, **13:303**

Solis, Concepción (Mother), 7:372

Solis, Francisco de (Card.), 3:795

Solis, Teresita (Mother), 7:372

Solisius, Antonius, 3:328

Solitaries of Port-Royal, 11:524–525

Solitude, **13:303**

Sollicita ac Provida (apostolic constitution, Benedict XIV), 7:390–391

Sollicitudo ecclesiarum (papal bull, Gregory XVI), 6:509, 510

Sollicitudo omnium ecclesiarum (apostolic constitution, Pius VII), 7:787

Sollicitudo onmium Ecclesarium (*motu proprio*, Paul IV), 8:451

Sollicitudo rei socialis (encyclical, John Paul II), 5:206, 7:1001, 10:616, 11:566–567, **13:303–305**

exploitation and discrimination, 13:258–259

papal social teaching, 13:269

social justice, 13:244

solidarity, 13:301

Solminihac, Alain de (Bp. of Cahors), Bl., **13:305**

Solmization, 6:564

Solomon (King of Israel), 7:*630*, **13:305–306**

Astarte, 1:808

biblical Chronicler, 3:566

David, 4:537

Ecclesiastes, 5:34

reign, 7:639

Temple, 7:765–766, 13:*306*, 809–810

wisdom, 14:788

Solomon (Syrian monk), 2:144

Solomon III (Abbot of Sankt Gallen), 12:669

Solomon Islands, 10:533

Solórzano Pereira, Juan de, 10:978

Solov'ev, Vladimir Sergeevich, 5:773, 12:435, **13:306–307**

Bulgakov, Sergeĭ Nikolaevich, 2:679

doctrine, 4:807

panentheism, 10:821

pantheism, 10:827

Solutiones rationum animae mortalium probantium (Javelli), 7:747

Somalia, **13:307–309**, *309*

Somascan Fathers, 3:418, 610, 782, 5:191, **13:309–310**

Somaschi. *See* Somascan Fathers

El Sombrero de Tres Picos (The Three Cornered Hat) (Falla), 5:612

''Some Contributions of Anthropology to Ethics'' (Beis), 10:194

Some Pages of Franciscan History (Robinson), 12:274

Some Thoughts concerning the Present Revival of Religion in New England (Edwards), 5:97

Somers, Thomas, Bl., 3:198, 5:234, 12:271

Somerville, John, 1:645

Somma morale (Somma Pacifica) (Pacificus of Novara), 10:744

Sommer, Peter, 5:44

Sommervogel, Carlos, 2:9

Sommes de péchés qui se commettent en tous états (Bauny), 2:160

Somoza, Anastasio, 10:351

Son of David, **13:310**

Son of God, 7:808, **13:310–316**
  apotheosis, 1:599
  in the Bible, 5:718, 13:311–315
  Dead Sea Scrolls, 4:564
  Divine missions, 9:735–736, 737
  life, concept of, 8:569–571
  Mark's Gospel, 9:185–186, 186–187
  monarchianism, 9:780
  Origen's theology, 10:657
  Son of David, 13:310
  subordinationism, 13:566
  theology, 13:315

The Son of God (Adam), 1:107

Son of Man, 5:336, 7:808, 833–834, **13:316–318**
  Daniel, Book of, 9:544–545
  Divine judgment, 8:29
  Mark's Gospel, 9:187
  Matthew's Gospel, 9:547

Sonara Jesuit Mission (Mexico), 9:709

Sondergotik architecture, 3:698

Song for a Listener (Feeney), 5:663

The Song of Roland (epic poem), 1:763, 3:422

Song of Songs, 3:25, 13:50–51, **318–319**

Songs of Sion (Ha-Levi), 7:869

La Sonnambula (Bellini), 2:229

Sonnenschein, Karl (Father), 1:915, 5:920

Sonnet, Religious Use of, **13:319–320**

Sonnius, F. (Bp. of Antwerp), 1:539

Sons of Divine Providence (FDP), 10:672, **13:320–321**

Sons of God, 13:311, **321–323**

Sons of Mary Health of the Sick (FMSI), 2:556, **13:323**

Sons of Mary Immaculate, 5:920

Sons of Mary Immaculate of Luçon, 2:158

Sons of Temperance, 13:799

Sons of the Holy Family, 7:23

Sons of the Immaculate Heart of Mary. *See* Claretians

Sons of the Sacred Heart. *See* Servants of Charity

Sons of the Scriptures (Benê Mikrā), 7:868

The Sooner Catholic (newspaper), 10:576

Sophia (regent of Russia), 11:180–181

Sophie (Queen of Bohemia), 7:977

Sophie de Rottembourg (Mother), 3:309–310

Sophism and Sophists, 5:392, 6:442, **13:323–324**
  asceticism, 1:773
  certitude, 3:351
  concept of truth, 14:222
  conscience, 4:139
  defined, 5:612
  dialectics, 4:721, 722
  disciple as term, 4:768
  free will, 5:929
  humanism, 7:195
  knowledge, 8:213
  liberal arts, 8:536
  literary myth, 10:120
  relativism, 12:46
  state, 13:239

Sophist (Plato), 10:417

Sophistici elenchi (Aristotle), 12:263

Sophocles (Greek playwright), 4:148, 10:179

Sophronius (Patriarch of Jerusalem), St., 2:749, **13:324**
  Christology, 3:559
  disciple of John Moschus (Eucratas), 10:6
  Monothelitism, 2:821, 7:80, 81
  Protoevangelium Jacobi, 1:469

Sophronius Eusebius. *See* Jerome, St.

Sopplimenti musicali (Zarlino), 14:910

Sor Abbey. *See* Sora Abbey (Italy)

Sor Mariá del Socos. *See* Mary de Cervellón, St.

Sora Abbey (Italy), 4:832, **13:325**

Sorazu, Ángeles, 13:*325*, **325**

Sorbon, Robert de, **13:326**

Sorbonne (University of Paris), 13:326

Sorbonne Church (Paris), 3:706

Sordi, Domenico, 12:772

Sordi, Serafino, 12:772

Soreth, John, Bl., 2:551, 3:126, 134, 142, **13:326**

Sorin, Edward Frederick (Father), 1:641, 3:477, 7:21–22, 10:461, **13:327**

Sorokin, P. A., 4:427, 431, 8:212, 12:65, 13:283

Sorores Scholarum Christianorum a Misericordia. See Sisters of the Christian Schools of Mercy

Sorribes Teixidó, Alfonso, 2:92

Sorrowful Mother of the Third Order of St. Francis, Sisters of the, 5:891

Sorrows of Mary, **13:327–328**

Sortes Homericae, Vergilianae, Biblicae, **13:328**

Sosnowski, Tomasz Oskar, 4:530

Sossianus Hierocles, 1:562, 4:748

Sotelo, Luis, Bl., 7:734

Soter (Pope), St., 3:403, 4:755, **13:328–329**

Soterichus Panteugenus (Patriarch of Antioch), 2:759, 825

Soteriology, **13:329**
  expiation, 5:565–566
  Gnosticism, 6:258–259
  Manichaeism, 9:110–111
  Paul, St., 10:100–101
  redemption, 9:260, 261–262

Soto, Domingo de, **13:329–330**
  Ambrosius Catharinus, 1:347
  Aristotelianism, 1:677
  impetus, 7:363
  mechanics, 12:816
  natural law, 10:182
  role in second Thomism, 14:49
  scholasticism, 12:766
  vision of God, 4:691

Soto, Pedro de, **13:330–331**
  Alphonsus Liguori, St., 1:311
  catechesis, 3:242
  scholasticism, 12:766

Sōtō School, 14:916

Sottocornola, Xaverian Franco, 7:743

Soubiran, Marie Thérèse de, Bl., **13:331**

Soubirous, Bernadette, St., 3:623, 8:819, 13:94, **331–332**, *332*

Souckar, M., 8:287

Souillac Abbey (France), **13:332**, *333*

Soul, **13:332–335**
  Apostolici regiminis, 1:595

Aristotle, 1:682

Augustine, St., 1:865–866, 876

Bergson, Henri Louis, 2:297

existence of, 12:884

Hinduism, 6:853, 7:410

hominisation, 7:64–65

immortality of, 2:854–855, 13:626

Isaac of Stella, 7:589–590

Jainism, 7:697

Origenism, 10:658

particular judgment of God, 8:37–38

parts, 13:335

Petau, Denis, 11:172–173

Plato, 11:409

Plotinus, 11:422

purgatory, 11:828–829

Scholastics, 11:804

sensitive soul, 13:335

Thomistic metaphysics, 10:908

transmigration, 14:155–158

types, 13:335

vegetative soul, 13:335

Wolff, Christian, 14:808

See also Faculties of the Soul;
Immortality

Soul, human, **13:336–353**

Arab philosophy, 8:171

Epicureanism, 5:284

immateriality, 13:349–350

intellect, 13:113, 335

nature of, 13:349

tranquillity, 8:849

Soul, human, origin of, **13:353–356**

See also Faculties of the Soul

Soul, in the Bible, 8:566, 572,
13:335–336

Soul, William Good (Abp. of Rouen),
2:190

Soul and Body (Evans), 10:308

The Soul of the Apostate (*L'Âme de tout
apostolat*) (Chautard), 3:458

Soul of the Church, 4:336, **13:358–359**

Soul-body relationship, 3:185,
4:578–579, 7:238, **13:356–358**

Soulerin, Jean Mathieu, 2:142, **13:359**

Soulier de satin (Claudel), 3:768

''The Sound Traditions,'' 7:623

Source criticism, 6:794

Source of Knowledge (St. John
Damascene), 7:951–952

Sources chrétiennes collection, 8:839

Les Sources du Pentatueque (Lagrange),
5:520

Sous le soleil de Satan (Bernanos),
2:303

Souterliedekens (Psalter), 11:798

South Africa, 8:228–229, **13:359–362**,
362, 363, 364

South African Catholic Bishops'
Conference (SACBC), 13:361

South African Catholic Magazine, 8:228

South America, patron saints of,
10:974–975

South American College (Rome), 5:573

South Carolina, 3:646, 652, **13:362–367**

*See also specific dioceses and
archdioceses*

South Dakota, 12:568, 13:165, **368–369**

Sioux reservations, 11:911

*See also specific dioceses and
archdioceses*

South Korea. *See* Korea

South West Africa Peoples' Organization
(SWAPO), 10:143–144

Southeast Pastoral Institute (SEPI),
8:290

Southern Baptist Convention, 2:80, 81

The Southern Cross (periodical), 12:709,
710

Southern kingdom, 8:177, 178

Southern Methodist Church (U.S.), 9:562

Southern Parish (Fichter), 5:709

Southerne, William, Bl., 5:235, **13:369**

Southwell, Nathanael (Bacon), **13:369**

Southwell, Robert, St., 5:232, 11:959,
960, **13:369–370**

Southworth, John, St., 1:725, 5:236,
13:94, **370, *371***

Souvenirs d'Assise (Hébert), 6:690–691,
9:753–754

Souvenirs d'un voyage en Terre-Sainte
(Emard), 5:186

Souvigny Abbey (France), **13:370–371**

Souzy, Jean-Baptiste, 12:278

Soveral, André de, Bl., 2:587

Sovereign authority, 9:781–782

Sovereign of the State of Vatican City.
See Pope (title)

Sovereign Reason (Nagel), 10:205

Sovereignty, 8:390, **13:371–372**, 410

See also Church and State; *specific
countries*

Soverign of the State of Vatican City.
See Pope (title)

Soviet Union

anti-Catholicism, 2:212–213

Benedict XV (Pope), 2:250

Church-state relations, 2:745, 3:642

collapse, 1:705, 2:213, 744

Holy See, 3:201

Jews, 7:874

Latvia, 8:375–377

Lenin, 8:467–468

Lithuania, 8:607–608

Pius XI (Pope), 11:394

Sheptyts'kei, Andrii, 13:79–80

Stalin, Joseph, 9:323–324

See also Communism and
Communist bloc; Russia

Soyemon, John, Bl., 7:733

Sozaburō, Cosmas Takeya, Bl., 7:732

Sozaburō, Francisco, Bl., 7:733

Sozaburō, Ines, Bl., 7:733

Sozomen (Greek historian), 2:797,
12:320, **13:372–373**

Confession, 4:77

on the cross, 4:384

Cyril of Jerusalem, 4:471

ecclesiastical historiography, 6:872

Space, 4:217, **13:373–375**

Space, Time, and Deity (Alexander),
1:251

Space, Time and Architecture (Giedion),
3:680

Space-time continuum, 4:217

Spadafora, Dominic, Bl., **13:375**

Spagnoli, John Baptist. *See* Baptist of
Mantua (Spagnoli), Bl.

Spagnuolo, John Baptist. *See* Baptist of
Mantua (Spagnoli), Bl.

Spain, **13:375–401**, *379, 380, 381, 382,
383*

anti-Catholicism, 4:441, 739, 14:566

baroque period, 2:107

Basilians, 2:141

Byzantine Basilians, 2:143

cabala, 2:832

Canon Law, 3:40, 49

Canons Regular of St. Augustine,
3:67

Carmelites, 3:127–128, 129, 135,
143, 144–145

Carthusians, 3:195

catechesis, 3:245

Christmas customs, 3:557

chronicles and annals, 1:465

church architecture, 3:696, 706, 707,
713

Cistercians, 5:751

colonialism, 9:692, 14:691

colonialism, North American, 6:148,
9:571–574, 737–738, 740–741

Confirmation, 4:87, 88

Congregation for the Propagation of
the Faith, 11:750, 751–752

Congregation of the Incarnate Word
and Blessed Sacrament, 7:371

Spain *(continued)*

conquistadores, 4:129–133

Council of Trent, 4:312

Counter Reformation, 3:610, 4:310, 314

creedal statements, 4:356

Crusades, 4:401, 409, 412

de auxiliis controversy, 4:111

demographic statistics, 13:376

disciplinary canons, 5:178

dueling, 4:928

education, 3:49, 12:773

Elvira Council (c. 324), 5:178

freedom of religion, 5:947

Gregory I (Pope), St., 6:481

Gregory XVI (Pope), 6:508

Hapsburg monarchy, 6:640

Honorius I (Pope), 7:79–80

Hugh of Remiremont, 7:155

Jesuits, 3:792, 7:786–787, 11:337–338, 12:220, 399–400

Jews, 2:834, 4:263, 946–947, 7:870, 8:8

Jews and Arabs, 7:868–869

laicism, 8:283

Leander of Seville, St., 8:425–426

liturgy, 8:653, 673–674

Louis XIV (King of France), 8:802–803

Louis of Granada, 8:806–807

map, 13:*378*

Martyrs of Córdoba, 4:261–262

Martyrs of the Diocesan Worker Priests, 12:407–408

Martyrs of the Spanish Civil War, 2:88, 91–92, 6:56

medieval drama, 4:895, 896, 897, 899, 900

medieval literature, 9:439–440, 445–446

missions, 9:109, 12:220, 399–400

music, 8:688–689

Muslim conquest, 2:688

Order of Christ, 4:596

Peace of God Movement, 11:50

Philip II (King of Spain), 11:247–248

Pius XI (Pope), 11:395

preaching, 11:622

Presbyterianism, 11:679

Priscillianism, 11:720

reconquest, 2:858, 3:601

Renaissance, 8:688–689, 12:118–119

Servites, 13:28

Sicily, 13:104

slavery, 13:212–213

Spanish Armada, 1:696–697

spirituality, 13:447

works of charity, 3:408–409, 418

See also Inquisition; Mission in colonial America, Spanish; Mission in postcolonial Latin America; Spanish Civil War (1936-39)

Spalatin, Georg, **13:401**

Spalding, Catherine (Mother), **13:401**

Spalding, Henry H., 2:635

Spalding, John Lancaster (Bp. of Peoria, IL), 5:889, 891, **13:401–403**

apostolic delegation in the United States, 1:584–585

Baltimore Catechism, 2:41

bishop uncle, 13:402

catechesis, 3:244

Catholic University of America, 3:290, 13:402–403

Irish Catholic Colonization Assn. of the U.S., 7:573

The Life of the Most Rev. M. J. Spalding (J.L. Spalding), 13:402

Spalding, Martin John (Abp. of Baltimore), 2:39, 165, 5:758, **13:403–405**

African American Catholics, 1:157

apostolic delegation in the United States, 1:582

as Bp. of Louisville, 8:149, 169, 817, 820, 821

Catholic University of America, 3:290

Corcoran, James Andrew, 4:260

Gibbons, James, 6:204

Second Baltimore Plenary Council (1866), 2:46

Vatican Council I, 2:555

Spangenberg, Augustus Gottlieb (Bp.), **13:406**

Spangenberg, J. von, 5:658

Spangler, David, 10:273

Spanheim, Ezechiel And Friedrich, **13:406–407**

Spanish America, 5:201–203

Spanish Armada, **1:696–697**, 13:199

Spanish art, 2:182, 4:263, 395, 397

Spanish Civil War (1936-39)

anarchism, 1:384–385

Dominicans, 4:854

Franco supporters, 13:205, 395–396

Loyalist firing squad, 13:*382*

martyrs of, 12:407–408

Abad Casasempere, Amalia and Companions, BB., 1:4–5

Almería, 1:298–299

Asensio Barroso, Florentino, 1:781

Blanes Giner, Bl. Marino, 2:432

Carmelite sisters, 3:126

Claretian martyrs, 2:91–92

Colotitlán martyrs, 2:884

Díaz Gandía, Carlos, Bl., 4:732–733

Diez y Bustos de Molina, Vitoria, 4:744

Faubel Cano, Juan Bautista, Bl., 5:644–645

Ferragud Girbés, José Ramón, Bl., 5:690–691

Hospitallers of St. John of God, 7:122–125

Lasallian martyrs, 2:88

martyrs of Turón during, 14:246–248

Ontinyent martyrs, 6:56

Pamplona, Dionisio and Companions, BB., 1:187, 3:12, 101, 108, 200

Ripoll Morata, Felipe, Bl., 12:252–253

Sisters of Christian Doctrine, BB., 13:180–181

Sons of the Holy Family, 7:23

See also Spain

Spanish Congregation of Hermits of St. Jerome. *See* Hieronymites (Los Jerónimos)

Spanish Devotional Image of the Virgin and Child Enthroned, 9:250

Spanish Episcopal Conference (CEE), 13:399–400

Spanish Inquisition. *See* Inquisition

Spanish monarchy, 9:702

Spanish Visigothic Church, 13:376–377

Spanish-American War (1898), 3:482, 4:417–418, 13:81

Spann, Othmar, **13:407**

Sparks, H. F. D., 14:597

Sparrow, Anthony (Bp. of Norwich), 3:153

SPCK (Society for Promoting Christian Knowledge), 1:446, 9:12, **13:288**

Spe, Friedrich, 2:716

Speaking in tongues. *See* Glossolalia

Spearman, C., 5:587

Special Assembly of the Asian Synod of Bishops (1999), 13:*687*

Special General Chapter (1969), 10:460

Special Introduction to the Study of the Old Testament (Gigot), 6:211

Species, **13:407–408**

Aristotle, 1:681

categories of being, 3:256

classification, 13:408

evolution, 5:493–494

God's primacy of being, 13:139

knowledge and love, 8:206

parts signifying, 10:905

Species, as predicable, 11:659–660

Species, doctrine of, 3:185

Species, intentional, 3:823, 8:209–210, 13:126, **408–410**

Species expressa (expressed species), 12:753

Specimina Codd. graec. Vaticani, 5:865

Spectator (periodical), 14:291

Speculative grammar, 6:214

Speculative habits, 6:599

Speculative philosophy, 11:269

Speculum caritatis (St. Aelred), 1:137–138, 9:454

Speculum ecclesiae (Edmund of Abingdon), 5:86

Speculum fidei (William of Saint-Thierry), 14:753

Speculum iudiciale (Duranti the Elder), 3:48, 4:949–950, 10:642

Speculum: Liber de Pater Noster (play), 9:880–881

Speculum maius (Vincent of Beauvais), 5:206, 9:463, 14:522

Speculum Meditantis (Gower), 6:378

Speculum morale (Vincent of Beauvais), 14:522

Speculum regis Edwardii (Mepham), 13:130

Speculum regum (Alvaro Pelayo), 1:327

Speculum—A Journal of Medieval Studies, 9:435

Spedalieri, Nicola, **13:410**

Spee, Friedrich von, **13:410**

Speech, indecent and vulgar, **13:411**

Speed, John, Bl., 5:232, **13:411**

Speer, Robert Elliott, **13:411**

Speiser, E. A., 13:18–19, 83

Spelaiotes. *See* Elias of Reggio, St.

Spellman, Francis Joseph (Card.), 1:*96*, *726*, 5:885, 9:628–629, 10:317–318, *322*, 13:74, **411–412**

Spelman, Henry, 5:702

Speltz, George H. (Bp.), 12:543

Spence, John. *See* Speed, John, Bl.

Spence, Sir Basil, 4:330

Spencer, Herbert, 5:520, **13:412–414**, *413*, 14:227

animism, 1:459

appetite, 1:603

associationism, 1:796

British moralists, 2:624

causality, 3:306

conscience, 4:140

cultural evolution, 4:433

educational philosophy, 5:93

egoism, 5:107

evolutionary theory, 5:397, 440

experience, 5:554

Green, Thomas Hill, 7:299

Howison, George Holmes, 7:301

hylozoism, 7:240

relativism, 12:48

society, 13:281

theory of the Unknowable, 6:312

Spencer, Stanley, 12:602

Spener, Philipp Jakob, 5:910, **13:414**

Arnold, Gottfried, 1:718

Bible study circles, 8:891

biblical theology, 2:383

Böhme, Jakob, 2:462

Carpzov, Johann Benedikt (II), 3:174

doctrine, 4:805

Pietism, 11:330

shift in systematic theology, 8:87

Spengler, Oswald, 3:679, 8:579, **13:414**, *415*

Spenser, Edmund, 1:263, 762, 764

Spenser, William, Bl., 5:231, **13:414–415**

Speraindeo (9th c. Abbot), 11:43–44

Sperandea, St., **13:415**

Le Speranze d'Italia (Balbo), 10:234

Sperber, Julius, 12:382

Sperry, Jacques Hyacinthe, 14:50

Spes (Abbot), 12:673

Spescha, Placia, 4:775

Speusippus (Greek philosopher), 11:412

Speyer, Second Diet of (1529), 3:430

Speyer Cathedral (Germany), 3:691, 6:*175*

Speyr, Adrienne von, 2:34, **13:415–416**

Spezielle Moraltheologie (Schwane), 12:793

Sphinx (Cairo, Egypt), 5:*125*

Sphrantzes, George, 2:801

Spicilegium historicum CSSR, 8:836

Spicilegium Romanum (Mai), 9:50

Spicilegium Sacrum Lovaniense, 8:429

Spicq, C., 5:523

Spiegel, Ferdinand August (Abp. of Cologne), 3:843, 845, **13:416**

Spieghel der Volcomenheit (Henry of Herp), 6:754

Spies, J., 5:650

Spils, James C., 1:210

Spina, B., 1:347

Spina, Guiseppe (Card.), 2:324, 4:61, 62, **13:416–417**

Spinelli (Card.), 3:791

Spinelli, Francesco, Bl., 4:3, **13:417**

Spinola, Carlo, Bl., 7:733

Spínola, Cristóbal Rojas de (Bp. of Winer-Neustadt), **13:417**

Spínola y Maestre, Marcelo (Card. Abp.), Bl., **13:417–418**

Spinoza, Baruch (Benedict), 11:293, 13:*418*, **418–420**

absolute, 1:42

accident, 1:62, 63

Alexander, Samuel, 1:252

Alphonsus Liguori, St., 1:310

anticipating, 8:521

aseity, 1:780

Brunschvicg, Leon, 2:650

Cartesianism, 3:183

causality, 3:306

certitude, 3:352

chance, 3:377

contingency, 4:214

Crescas, Ḥasdai ben Abraham, 4:361

demonstration, 4:654

determinism denies free will, 5:931, 938, 940

eclecticism, 5:47

Enlightenment, 5:255

eternity, 5:381

exemplarism, 5:527

existence, 5:534

freedom of speech, 5:968

good, 6:349

hylozoism, 7:240

identity, 7:302

identity principle, 7:303

immanence, 7:340

infinity, 7:459

modern Jewish philosophy, 7:865

ontological arguments, 10:603

ontological perfection, 11:119

pantheism, 5:395, 10:826–827

quality, 11:849

rationalism, 11:920

reason and faith, 6:286

romantic philosophy, 12:733

scholasticism, 12:768

selfless love, 8:829

soul, 13:346

Spinoza, Baruch (Benedict) *(continued)*
  substance, 13:577
  universals, 14:325
  will and willing, 14:723
Spiration, 8:764, **13:420–421**
Spire, John de, 2:522
Spire, Wendelin de, 2:522
Spirit, **13:421–424**
  Christian concept, 13:421
  good and evil, 13:425
  Hegel, Georg Wilhelm Friedrich,
    9:811
  history-affirming destiny, 8:840
  human soul, 13:349–352, 421–423
  love, 8:827, 828
  objective, 13:423
  transcendental principle, 4:372–374
Spirit, Adversary of the Soul (Klages),
  8:579–580
Spirit, in the Bible, 8:566, **13:424–426**
The Spirit of Catholicism (Adam), 1:107
Spirit of God, 4:266, 8:566–567, 840,
  13:424, **426–428**, 431–432
The Spirit of Mediaeval Philosophy
  (Gilson), 6:228
The Spirit of Solidarity (Tischner), 14:90
The Spirit of the Age (Channing), 14:149
Spiritan Senior Seminary (Ireland),
  8:446
Spiritans (Congregation of the Holy
  Ghost), 1:692
Spiritism, **13:428–429**
Spirit-paraclete, 10:873
Spirits, in Persian religion, 11:143
Spiritual (song form), 7:257–258
Spiritual Alphabet. *See Abecedario
  Espiritual (Spiritual Alphabet)*
  (Frances of Osuna)
The Spiritual Canticle (St. John of the
  Cross), 7:988
Spiritual Combat, **13:429–430**
Spiritual Conferences (Faber), 5:582
Spiritual Conferences (Francis de Sales),
  5:869
Spiritual Consolation (Fisher), 5:749
Spiritual Dialogues (St. Catherine of
  Genoa), 3:271
Spiritual Document (Flete), 5:761
The Spiritual Espousals (Rutherford),
  12:439–441
Spiritual Exercises (St. Ignatius of
  Loyola), 1:72, 5:344, 435, 584,
  10:725, **13:430–433**
  Alphonsus Liguori, St., 1:309, 310
  Anima Christi, 1:455
  approval of, 7:313, 314

authorship, 7:312
Bernini, Giovanni Lorenzo, 2:325
Cenacle Sisters, 4:293
concept of God, 7:307–308
conformity, 4:93–94
conscience, 4:147
direction, 4:762
discernment, 4:766
Huonder, Anton, 7:225
love, 7:309
prayer, 7:308
renewal, 13:431
spiritual man, 7:308
Spiritual freedom, **5:944–945**, 8:828,
  881
A Spiritual Guide (Molinas), 3:614,
  9:773
Spiritual Journal (Leseur), 8:514–515
Spiritual Journal (Loyola), 7:307, 308
Spiritual Journey (Seton), 13:32
Spiritual life, 13:433–434
Spiritual maternity of Mary, Blessed
  Virgin, 9:264–266
Spiritual Paradise (Nicetas Stethatos),
  10:357
Spiritual purification, 4:530, 8:469–470,
  10:106, **11:832–834**, 13:148
Spiritual theology, **13:433–436**, 909–910
  consolations, 4:166–167
  Garrigou-Lagrange, Réginald, 6:102
  history, 6:881
  Kingdom of God, 8:174
  Le Gaudier, A., 8:452
  Louis of Granada, 8:806–807
  lukewarmness, 8:865–866
  Middle Ages, 8:853–854
  Scaramelli, Giovanni Battista, 12:724
  Sertillanges, A., 13:23
Spiritual union, 6:7
Spiritualism, 11:284, **13:436–437**
  anticlericalism, 8:283
  Cousin, Vincent, 4:323
  Malebranche, Nicolas, 9:74–75
  renewal, 9:87
  Thomism, 9:90
Spiritualists (heretical group), 11:572,
  13:437
*La Spiritualité chrétienne (Christian
  Spirituality)* (Pourrat), 11:564
La Spiritualité moderne (Saudreau),
  12:708
Spiritualities of mission, 9:729
Spirituality
  action, 13:442
  death and human activity, 4:578–579

feminist theology, 5:680
integration of spiritualities,
  13:449–450
Malebranche, Nicolas, 9:75
non-Christian, 13:66–67
Spanish, 13:392
the three ways, 14:65–66
See also Direction, spiritual
Spirituality, Christian, 7:158–159,
  13:437–443
  apostolic, 8:298
  Cyril of Alexandria, 4:469
  discernment of spirit, 8:298
  historical nature, 13:439–441
  interpersonal life, 13:438–439
  late Middle Ages, 13:129, 445–446
  Leseur, E., 8:514–515
  mystical phenomena, 10:105–109
  scriptural origins, 13:443
  significance of mysticism, 10:116
  supernatural quality, 13:441–443
Spirituality, Christian, history of,
  8:296–297, **13:443–451**
Spirituality, French school of,
  2:338–339, 13:451, **451–453**
Spirituality, Rhenish, **13:453–454**
Spirituality of the Low Countries,
  13:454–456
Spirituals, **13:456–457**
Spirituals (Franciscan). *See* Franciscan
  Spirituals
Spiritus Paraclitus (encyclical, Benedict
  XV), 2:250, 5:523, **13:457–458**
Spitz, D., 1:667
Spitzer, Robert L., 7:69
SPLA (Sudan People's Liberation
  Army), 13:582–583
Splendor of glorified bodies, 6:689
*The Splendor of Truth. See Veritatis
  splendor* (encyclical, John Paul II)
Splendori Riflessi di Gloria Celeste
  (Balthasar of St. Catherine of Siena),
  2:36
Spohr, Louis (Ludwig), **13:458**, *459*
Spokane people, 3:226
Spondanus, Henri (de Sponde) (Bp.),
  13:458–459
Sponsa Regis (periodical), 12:552
Sponsalia et Matrimonia
  (Schmalzgrueber), 12:741
Sponsors, **13:459**
Spontaneous Generation, 8:573–574,
  13:459–460
Spontaneous worship, Quakers, 6:4
Spontini, Gaspare, **13:460–461**, *461*
Sporer, Patritius, **13:461**

Sportelli, Caesar, Ven., **13:461**

Spring (Undset), 14:295

Spring Hill College (Mobile, AL), 1:*200*, 2:166

Springfield Diocese (MA), **13:462**

Sproll (Bp. of Berlin), 6:186

Sprott, Thomas, Bl., 5:233, **13:462**

Spurgeon, Charles Haddon, **13:462–463**

"Square of opposition," 10:611

Šrámek, John, 4:484

Sri Aurobindo. *See* Ghose, Aurobindo

Sri Lanka, 2:661–662, 13:*463*, **463–467**, *464*

SSCA. *See* Summer School of Catholic Action

SSJG (Sisters of St. John of God), 6:35, **12:551**

Śsṅkhya, 7:407–408

Śsvetāmbaras (Jains), 7:697, 698

Staatslexikon, 5:207

Stabat Mater, 13:328, **467**

Stabat Mater (Rossini), 12:389

Stäblein, Bruno, 1:186, 4:118

Stade, B., 5:519, 520

Staël, Madame de, 3:447

Stafford, Henry, Sir, 2:184

Stafford, J. Francis (Card.), 3:859, 4:670, 13:824

Stafford, John (Abp. of Canterbury), **13:467–468**

Stafford, Peter, 7:581

Stafford, Raymond, 7:581

Stafford, William Cletus (Father), 3:119

Stafford, William Howard, Viscount, 10:495–496

Stagel, Elsbeth (Elbethe), **13:468**

Stager, L. E., 2:379

Stages on Life's Way (Kierkegaard), 8:166

Stahl, Ignaz, 4:670–671

Stählin, O., 3:797

Stained glass, 3:694–695, **13:468–475**

    12th to 13th centuries, 13:472–473

    Canterbury Cathedral, 3:*71*, 73, 13:*469*

    Chartres Cathedral, 3:440, *440*, 13:*471*, 472, 473

    Cistercians, 3:750–751

    evolution, 13:473–475

    fabric, 13:468–470

    flashed glass, 13:469

    luminosity, 13:472

    making cartoons, 13:*470*

Stained Glass (periodical), 8:386

Staley, William, 10:494

Stalin, Joseph, 5:94, 8:607, 9:323–324, 12:427–428, 14:213

Stallings, George, 1:161

Stammel, J. T., 1:117

Stanbrook Abbey (Worcester, England), 13:90, **476**

Standards of conduct. *See* Conduct, human

Standing vs. kneeling, 8:647–648

Standonck, J., 5:847

Stang, William (Bp. of Fall River, MA), 5:611, 9:307, 12:497

Stangassinger, Caspar. *See* Stangassinger, Kaspar, Bl.

Stangassinger, Gaspar. *See* Stangassinger, Kaspar, Bl.

Stangassinger, Kaspar, Bl., **13:476**

Stanhope, Philip Dormer, 7:561

Staniloae, Dumitru, 12:333, **13:476–477**

Stanislaus (Bp. of Cracow), St., 7:236, 13:*477*, **477–478**

Stanislaus, Mary (Mother), 7:34

Staniukynas, Anthony, Rev., 12:541

Stanley, D. M., 5:523

Stanley, Thomas (Earl of Derby). *See* Derby, Thomas Stanley, Earl of

Stantes Pagnino. *See* Pagnini, Santes

Stanyhurst, Richard, **13:478**

Staphylus, Friedrich, **13:478**

Staples, Edward (Bp. of Meath, Ireland), 2:637

Stapleton, Theobald, 7:581

Stapleton, Thomas, **13:479**

Starkie. *See* Whitaker, Thomas, Bl.

Starkie, Thomas. *See* Whitaker, Thomas, Bl.

Starnina, Gerardo, 12:486

Starry Messenger (Sidereus Nuncius) (Galileo), 6:60

Stars, symbols of, 13:668

Stary Sacz Abbey (Poland), 8:172

The State, **13:479–490**

    authority, 1:920

    papal social thought, 13:259

    role of in subsidiarity, 13:567–568

    society, 5:256–257, 950, 13:278

    sovereignty, 13:371–372, 372

    theory, 13:253, 14:570–571

    See also Church and State

The State and the Church (Ryan), 12:445

The State in its Relations with the Church (Gladstone), 6:236

State of grace, **6:410–411**, 11:133–134

The State of the Church and the Legitimate Authority of the Roman Pontiff. . . (Febronius), 5:658

State v. Manuel, 6:106

State v. Will, 6:106

States of the Church, 5:695, **13:490–497**

    Adrian I (Pope), 1:121, 122

    Adrian VI (Pope), 1:129

    Albornoz, Gil Álvarez Carrillo de, 1:232, 233

    Alexander IV (Pope), 1:257

    Alexander VI (Pope), 1:259

    Antonelli, Giacomo, 1:532–533

    Avignon, 1:941–942, 943

    banditry, 13:198

    Benedict XIV (Pope), 2:248

    Bernetti, Tommaso, 2:323

    Boniface IX (Pope), 2:504

    Carbonari, 3:100–101

    Carolingian Dynasty, 3:165, 167, 169, 422, 425, 426

    catechisms, 3:234

    Cavour, Camillo Benso di, 3:314

    Church-State relations, 3:637, 641, 642

    Clement III (Pope), 3:776

    Clement VII (Antipope), 3:783

    Clement VIII (Pope), 3:784

    Clement XII (Pope), 3:790

    Concordat of 1801, 4:63, 138

    Congress of Vienna, 3:618

    Consalvi, Ercole, 4:138–139

    Constantine II (Antipope), 4:178

    Counter Reformation, 3:612

    Döllinger, Johannes, 4:823

    Donation of Constantine establishing, 10:835

    Donation of Pepin (756), 1:121–122, 3:165, 635

    economic reforms, 12:402

    end of temporal power, 11:385–386

    Formosus controversy, 5:814–815

    Frederick II, 7:44

    Gregory XVI (Pope), 6:508

    Italian unification, 3:314

    Julius II (Pope), 1:259, 8:56–57

    Kulturkampf, 8:254, 444

    Lambert of Spoleto's power, 8:305

    Leo XII (Pope), 8:489

    Leo XIII (Pope), 8:490–491

    Napoleon, 3:618

    origins, 3:597–598

    Paul I (Pope), St., 11:18–19, 19–20

    Pius VI (Pope), 11:376

    Pius VII (Pope), 11:379, 381

States of the Church (continued)
  political reforms, 12:388
  reclaimed by Cardinal Albornoz, 14:338
  restoration in Germany, 8:444
  Risorgimento, 12:253–255
  Roman Question, 12:322–323
  San Marino, 12:653
  Sanfedists, 12:666
  Swiss Guards, protection of, 13:642–643
  See also Roman question
Statesman (Plato), 6:335
Statics (science), in the Middle Ages, 12:813
Stational churches, 8:470, **13:497–499**
Stational liturgy, 8:652
Stations of the Cross, 1:327, 4:710, **13:499–501**
Statius, 12:308
Stattler, Benedikt, 12:769, 901
Statuta ecclesiae antiqua (Gennadius of Marseilles), 3:40, 59, **13:501**
Statutory, Oaths (1867-1910), 10:502
Stauffer, Ethelbert, 2:387, 7:850, 851
Staupitz, Johann von, 8:878, 12:730, **13:501–502**
Stave churches, **13:502–503**, *503*
Stavelot Abbey (Belgium), 8:304, 13:111, **503**
  See also Malmédy Abbey (Liège, Belgium)
Stealing. *See* Theft
Stearns, Shubael, 2:79
Stebbins, H. Lyman, **13:503–504**
Steck, Francis Borgia, **13:504–505**
Steck, Henry. *See* Steck, Francis Borgia
Stedingers, 11:572
Steenberghen, F. van, 1:878
Steenhoven, Cornelius, 5:358
Steensen, Nikolaus. *See* Stense, Niels (Bp.), Bl.
Steensen, Nils. *See* Stense, Niels (Bp.), Bl.
Stefan (Bp. of Riazan), 7:53, 12:424, **13:505**
Stefan Dushan (Serbian tsar), 2:788
Stegmüller, F., 1:265
Stehle, Aurelius (ArchAbbot), 12:591
Stehle, Emile (Bp. of Ecuador), 5:66
Steichele, Antonius (Abp. of Munich-Freising), 1:848
Steiger, Mathias (Father), 5:877
Stein, Edith, St., 3:130, 139, 7:*16*, **13:505–506**, *506*

Stein am Rhein Abbey (Schaffhausen, Switzerland), **13:506–507**
Steinberg, Milton, 8:13
Steinbüchel, Theodor, 6:185
Steiner, L., 2:350
Steiner, Rudolf, 1:512, 513, **13:507**
Steinman, J., 8:45
Steinmeyer, Ferdinand. *See* Farmer, Ferdinand (Father)
Steles, **13:507–508**
Stella, Didacus, 11:621
Die Stellung des Menschen im Kosmos (Scheler), 12:731
Stenberg v. Carhart, 1:35
Stengel, E. E., 1:243
Steno, Nils. *See* Stense, Niels (Bp.), Bl.
Stenonis, Nils. *See* Stense, Niels (Bp.), Bl.
Stens, Nils. *See* Stense, Niels (Bp.), Bl.
Stense, Niels (Bp.), Bl., 4:666, **13:508–509**
Stéphan, J., 1:115
Stephan the Great (Prince of Romania), 12:330
Stephanites, 5:400
Stephansdom (Vienna), 3:697
Stephanus Costa, 3:52
Stephen (Bp. of Ephesus), 2:151
Stephen (Byzantine astronomer), 2:808
Stephen (King of England), 9:331, 12:287, **13:512–513**, 864
Stephen, Protomartyr, St., 13:511
Stephen, St., 11:3, **13:509–512**
  Christmas cycle, 3:556
  ecstatic visions, 5:61
  hymns for feast of, 4:700
  liturgical gestures, 8:648
  office, 12:246
  relics, 4:280
Stephen I (King of Hungary), St., 7:209–210, 13:*513*, **513–514**
  Anastasius, St., 1:385
  father of Emeric of Hungary, 5:188
  Gerard of Csanád, St., 6:161–162
  Gisela, St., 6:232–233
  Pilgrim of Passau, 1:909
Stephen I (Pope), St., 3:593, 4:457–459, 5:740, 11:502, **13:514–515**
Stephen II (III) (Pope, 752-757), **13:515–517**
  Byzantine Church, 2:752
  Carolingian Dynasty, 1:121, 478, 3:124, 164, 421, 563, 598
  Donation of Constantine, 4:860–861
Stephen II (Pope, 752), 5:842, 7:656, 11:110, 502, **13:515**

Stephen III (IV) (Pope), 1:103, 121, 4:178, 7:282, **13:517–518**
Stephen IV (V) (Pope), 3:169, **13:518–519**
Stephen V (Armenian Catholicos), 1:702
Stephen V (VI) (Pope), 4:195, 604, 5:814, **13:519–520**
Stephen VI (VII) (Pope), 5:815, 12:346, **13:520**
Stephen VII (VIII) (Pope), **13:520–521**
Stephen VIII (IX) (Pope), **13:521**
Stephen IX (X) (Pope), 2:242, 4:175, 7:199, **13:521–522**
Stephen al-Duwaihi (Aldoensis) (Maronite Patriarch), 1:333
Stephen Bar-Sūdhailē, **13:522**
Stephen Báthory (King of Poland), 2:153, 432, 7:214, 12:425
Stephen Harding, St., 3:746, 748, 749, 751, 12:268, **13:522–523**
  Cistercians founding, 9:792
  influence of, 3:601
  manuscript illumination, 3:750
Stephen Langton, St. (Card.), 1:407, 5:516, 9:40, 459, **13:523–524**
Stephen of Bâgé (Bp. of Autun), 1:926
Stephen of Byzantium, 2:799
Stephen of Châtillon. *See* Stephen of Die (Bp.), St.
Stephen of Die (Bp.), St., **13:524**
Stephen of Fougères, 3:519
Stephen of Gravesend (Bp. of London), 12:233, **13:524–525**
Stephen of Muret, St., **13:525**
Stephen of Narbonne, St., **13:525**
Stephen of Obazine, Bl., 10:503, **13:525–526**
Stephen of Poligny, 1:110
Stephen of Rouen, 2:190
Stephen of Saint-Thibery. *See* Stephen of Narbonne, St.
Stephen of Salagnac, **13:526**
Stephen of Sevan (Armenian Catholicos), 1:453
Stephen of Tournai, 3:47, 4:599
Stephen the Great (Prince of Moldavia), 10:219
Stephen the Younger, St., 2:751, 7:281–282
Stephen Thomas (King of Bosnia), 2:881
Stephens, John, 7:580
Stephens, Thomas, **13:526**
Stephens, Uriah S., 8:192
Stephenson, Vivian, 4:125
Stepinac, Alojzije Viktor (Victor) (Card. of Zagreb), Bl., 3:625, 4:371, 372, 13:*527*, **527–528**

Stepinac, Aloysius Victor. *See* Stepinac, Alojzije Viktor (Victor) (Card. of Zagreb), Bl.

Stepinac, Louis Victor. *See* Stepinac, Alojzije Viktor (Victor) (Card. of Zagreb), Bl.

Sterckx, Engelbert (Abp. of Mechelen), **13:528**

Sterilization, 11:515

Stern, L. W., 14:4

Stern, Robert, 5:203

Sternhold, Thomas, 3:150, 7:256

Sternhold and Hopkins Psalter, 11:798

Stern-Sigismund, 8:13

Sterzinger, Ferdinand, **13:528**

Stettler v. O'Hara (Oregon, 1913), 10:566

Stettner, Joseph (Father), 12:495

Steuart, Robert Henry (Father), **13:528–529**

Steudel, J. C. F., 2:384

Steuernagel, Carl, **13:529**

Stevan Dušan (Emperor of the Serbs and Greeks), 10:697

Stevens, Alfred, 10:4

Stevenson, C. L., 5:397

Stevenson, Joseph, **13:529**

Stevenson, R. L., 14:467

Stevin, S., 1:678

Stevin, Simon, 12:816

Steward, J. H., 4:434

Stewardship, Benedictines on, 2:266

Stewardship of Money, A Manual for Parishes (NCSC), 7:523

Stewardship of Time and Talent, A Parish Manual for Lay Ministries (NCSC), 7:523

Stewart, Dugald, 12:840

Stewart, Henry, Lord Darnley. *See* Darnley, Henry Stewart, Lord

Stewart, James, 12:533

Stewart, John (Duke of Albany), 2:179

Stewart, Lyman, 6:27, 29

Stewart, Milton, 6:27, 29

Stewart Evangelistic Fund, 6:27, 30

Stichometry of Nicephor, 1:558

Stigmata, Feast of the, 5:871

Stigmata and stimatization, **13:530–532**
   Bonaventure, St., 2:490
   definition, 10:108
   Dominicans, 4:847
   Francis of Assisi, St., 5:871
   Lateau, L., 8:346–347
   Lutgardis, 8:877
   modern theologians, 10:266–267
   Neumann, Theresa, 10:266–267

Padre Pio, St., 10:751
   St. Francis Receiving the Stigmata (van Eyck), 13:*531*
   Speyr, Adrienne von, 13:415–416
   See also specific saints and blesseds

Stigmatine Fathers, 2:335, 3:622, **13:529–530**

Stile antico, 1:1, 234, 293, 3:123

Stile moderno, 1:234, 3:123

Stilicho, Flavious (Roman general), 7:87, 12:321

Stilla, Bl., **13:532–533**

Stillingfleet, Edward, 3:830

Stillington, Robert (Bp. of Bath and Wells), 13:533

Stilting, J., 2:472

Stimmen aus Maria Laach (periodical), 12:745

Stinginess, magnificence and, 9:44

Stirling, James Hutchenson, 6:711, 7:299

Stirner, Max, 1:384

Štítný, Thomas, 4:480

Sto Spirito Church (Florence), 3:699

Stobaeus, John, 2:808

Stock, Simon, St., 12:723

Stöcker, Adolf, 7:873

Stöckl, Albert, 12:774

Stöcklein, Joseph, **13:533**

Stoddard, Charles W., 3:291

Stohr, Albert (Bp. of Mainz), **13:533**

Stoicism, 11:288–289, **13:534–539**
   acedia, 1:66
   allegory, 1:292
   ambition, 1:334
   anarchism, 1:384
   anthropocentrism, 1:508
   Apostolic Fathers, 1:588
   Aristides, 1:666
   Aristotelianism, 1:668–669, 671, 672, 673
   ars moriendi, 1:728
   asceticism, 1:773–774
   astral religion, 1:809
   astrology, 1:812
   casuistry, 3:220
   causality, 3:298, 303
   certitude, 3:352
   chastity, 3:444
   Clement of Alexandria, St., 3:798
   conscience, 4:142, 143, 148
   Constantine I (the Great) (Roman Emperor), 4:182
   Coornhert, Dirck Volkertszoon, 4:248
   criteriology, 4:367
   Cynics, 4:455, 456

   determinism and free will, 5:929, 937
   distinction, 4:779
   early Christian theology, 3:591
   educational philosophy, 5:90
   emotion, 5:193
   Epistle of Clement, 3:775
   ethics, 5:393
   experience, 5:554
   explanation of the world and way of salvation, 6:448–449
   fatalism, 5:638
   final causality, 5:724
   God, 6:308
   good, 6:347
   Greek religion, 6:454
   humanism, 7:197
   hylozoism, 7:239
   identity principle, 7:303
   immanence, 7:340
   immortality, 7:348
   judgment, 8:21, 23
   Justin Martyr, St., 8:93–94
   knowledge, 8:214
   liberal arts, 8:537
   logical history, 8:749
   Marcus Aurelius, 3:593
   matter, 9:342
   natural law development under, 10:180
   natural law in political thought, 10:201
   neoplatonism, 10:240
   nominalism, 10:411
   pantheism of, 10:826
   philosophy, 5:283
   philosophy as a school for life, 6:447
   pleasure, 11:418
   procreation, 4:218
   providence of God, 11:781
   slavery, 13:209, 211
   soul, 13:339
   teachers and missionaries, 6:446–447
   works, 13:538
   world soul, 14:843
   Zeno of Citium founder of, 5:197, 554

Stokes, Peter, 12:131

Stokes, Whitley, 2:368

Stoles, 8:633, **13:539**

Stollenwerk, Helena (Sister), Bl., **13:539–540**

Stollenwerk, Maria. *See* Stollenwerk, Helena (Sister), Bl.

Stoltz, Alban, 11:623

Stolz, Anselm, 4:208, 8:433–434, **13:540**

Stone, Barton W., 3:534, 4:117

Stone, James Kent, **13:540**

Stone, John, St., 1:888, 5:226, **13:541**

Stone, William L., 10:170

Stone v. Graham (1980), 3:666

Stones, sacred, 1:615–616, 5:697, 13:*541*, **541–542**

Stones, sacred, in the Bible, **13:542**

The Stones of Venice (Ruskin), 12:414

Stoppani, Antonio, 1:228

Stöppel, J. (Father), 3:117

Storch, Nicholas, 1:368, 10:62

Storchenau, Sigmund von, 12:769–770

Storehouse of Mysteries (Bar-Hebraeus), 2:82

Storer, Franz, **13:542**

Storey, Edward (Bp. of Chichester), 3:481

Storia Abelardo (Tosti), 14:120

Storia del Concilio di Costanza (Tosti), 14:120

Storia del probabalismo e rigorismo (Concina), 4:59

Storia della Lega Lombarda (Tosti), 14:120

Storia di Bonifacio VIII (Tosti), 14:*120*

Storia di Monte Cassino (Tosti), 14:120

Storia di San Benedetto e dei suoi tempi (Schuster), 12:790

Storia d'Italia (Guicciardini), 6:561–562

Storia sociale della Chiesa (Benigni), 2:279–280

La Storicità dei Vangeli (Bea), 2:167

Stork, Abbé, 3:418

Storr, Gottlieb Christian, 2:383

Story, John, Bl., 5:227, **13:543**

Story of a Soul (*Histoire d'une âme*) (Thérèse de Lisieux), 3:139

Story of Christ (Papini), 7:852

A Story of Courage (George and Rose Lathrop), 8:360

The Story of Yesterday (Tolstoi), 14:105

Stoss, Andreas, 3:142

Stowe Missal, 3:331–332, **13:543**

Strabo, Walafrid. *See* Walafrid Strabo

Strachan, John (Anglican Bp. of Toronto, Canada), **13:543**

Stracke, D. A., 1:331

Stradella, Alessandro, **13:543–544**

Stradivari, Antonio, **13:544**, *545*

Straforelli, Nicholas, 1:880

Stragorodsky, Ivan Nikolaeievich. *See* Sergius (Patriarch of Moscow)

Strahl, Daniel, 12:768

Strahov Monastery (Prague), 8:765, **13:544–545**, *546*

Straling, Phillip F. (Bp. of Reno), 12:127

Strambi, Vincenzo Maria, St., 11:622, **13:545**, *547*

Strange, J. F., 2:380

Strangers, social principle, 13:249–250

Stransham, Edward, Bl., 5:229, 966, **13:545**

Stransky, Thomas F., 11:42

Strasbourg, Treaty of (1189), 3:776

Strasbourg Papyrus, 1:273

Strategic Points in the World's Conquest (Mott), 9:697

Strato of Lampsacus, 1:668, 7:239

Strauch, B., 5:665

Strauss, David Friedrich, 5:521, **13:546**

  biographies of Christ, 7:848

  Christology, 10:309

  demythologizing, 4:656

  Hegelianism, 6:709

  historical Jesus, 3:623

  materialism, 9:320–321

  mythical character of the New Testament, 10:124

  supernatural, 1:564–565

  Tübingen School, 14:234

Strauss, Richard, 12:28

Stravinsky, Igor Feodorovich, 10:73, **13:546–547**, *548*

Strawbridge, Robert, 14:308

Streicher, F., 3:16

Streit, Karl, **13:547–548**

Streit, Robert, **13:548**

Streitel, Amalia (Mother Frances of the Cross), 5:891

Strengthening of the Faith (Ḥizzuk Emuna) (Isaac ben Abraham), 7:588

Strepa, James (Abp.), Bl., **13:548**

Strict literary hand style, 10:768, 769

Strigel, Victorinus, 4:416

Strigolniki, 12:433

Stritch, Samuel Alphonsus (Card. of Chicago), 3:479, **13:549–550**, 14:781

Stritch, Thomas, 7:582

Strittmatter, Denis, Rev., 12:591

Strobl, Andreas, **13:550**

Strode, Ralph, 4:913

Stroessner, Alfredo, 7:999

Stromata (St. Clement of Alexandria), 3:798, 799, 4:83, 5:510, 6:256

Strommen, Merton, 13:270

Strong, Charles A., 10:824

Strong, Josiah, 5:467

Strossmayer, Josip Juraj (Bp.), **13:550–551**

Stroup, George, 10:153, 154

Strozzi, Palla, 1:659

Strozzi Palace courtyard (Florence, Italy), 7:*657*

Structural analysis approach, 10:306–307

Structural criticism, 6:794

Structuralism, 8:862, **13:551–553**

La Structure de l'âme et l'expérience mystique (Gardeil), 6:94

The Structure of Science (Nagel), 10:205

Struggl, Marc, 12:765

Strumi Abbey (Italy), 1:407, **13:553**

Stuaropegia (planting of the cross) privilege, 10:946

Stuart, Henry Benedict Maria Clement (Card. of York), **13:553**

Stuart, Janet Erskine, **13:553–554**

Stuart, Mary. *See* Mary Stuart (Queen of Scots)

Studein zur Naturphilosophie der Spätscholastik (Maier), 9:51

Student Volunteer Movement (SVM), **13:554**

  China, 3:500–501

  Latourette, K. S., 8:372

  NCCC-USA, 10:165

  Protestant mission, 9:697

  Wilder, Robert P., 13:554

  world mission, 13:411

Studi e Testi series (1900), 14:421

Studia latinitatis (motu proprio, Paul VI), 11:488

Studia Liturgica, 8:679, 13:275

Studien zum antiken Synkretismus aus Iran und Griechenland (Reitzenstein), 12:40

Studies in Early Church History (Turner), 14:242

Studies in Psychology and Psychiatry, 10:740

Studion Monastery (Constantinople), 7:242, 309, **13:554–555**

  filioque, 2:752, 822

  independence from Church and State, 2:753

  liturgical poetry, 2:803

  Octoechos, 10:548

  Photius, 2:755–756

Studiorum ducem (encyclical, Pius XI), 6:287, 14:23

Studiousness, virtue of, 4:440, 11:941, **13:555**

Studiu. *See* Studion Monastery (Constantinople)

Studium Biblicum Franciscanum, 2:381

''Study Commission on the Role of Women in Church and Society'' (1973), 10:851

668

NEW CATHOLIC ENCYCLOPEDIA

A Study in Medieval Iconography and Its Sources of Inspiration (Mâle), 3:676

A Study of History (Toynbee), 6:886, 8:579

Stufler, J. B., 12:777

Stuhlmueller, Carroll, 4:341, 11:767, **13:555–556**

Stuhlmueller, William Ignatius. *See* Stuhlmueller, Carroll

Stumpe, William, 9:81

Stumpf, Carl, 12:731

Stumpf, S. E., 10:191

Sturm, Jacob, 12:526

Sturmi, St., 2:496, 6:21, **13:556**

Sturzo, Luigi, 2:250, **13:556–557**, 557

Stuttgart Old Testament, 2:356

Stutz, U., 3:42

Styger, P., 1:753

Stylianos of Neocaesarea (Abp.), **13:557**

Stylites, 8:421, **13:557**

Stynthesis against the Latins (Nicetas Stethatos), 10:357

Suárez, Domingo, 12:651

Suárez, Francisco, 7:782, **13:558–561**
    absolutism, 1:44
    act, 1:74
    action and passion, 1:78
    active life, 1:83
    Alamanni, Cosmo, 1:204
    Alphonsus Liguori, St., 1:311
    Ambrosius Catharinus, 1:347
    analogy, 1:373, 378
    Aristotelianism, 1:677, 678
    Arriaga, Rodrigo de, 1:723
    aseity, 1:780
    bilocation, 2:396
    causality, 3:305–306
    Church-State relations, 3:639
    civil authority, 1:921–922
    Coimbra University, 3:828
    concept of time, 14:78
    congruism, 4:120–121
    conservation, 4:161
    continuum, 4:215
    demonology, 4:648
    distinction, 4:780, 781
    Divine concurrence, 4:71
    Divine right of kings, 4:788
    division, 4:793
    epikeia, 5:290
    essence and existence, 5:367
    exemplary causality, 5:528
    free will, 5:938
    friendship with God, 6:11
    grace, 6:391

Henríquez, Enrique, 6:735
    human will, 14:723
    individuation, 7:427
    Joseph, St., 7:1040
    judgment, 8:23
    justification theory, 8:86
    just-war tradition, 14:636–637
    Leibniz influenced, 8:456
    Mariology, 9:171
    natural law, 10:182
    Oath of Allegiance of 1606, 10:500
    person, 11:147
    philosophy of law, 5:395
    potency and act, 11:559
    public order, 11:808
    purgatory, 11:827
    relation, 12:42
    relics, 12:55
    religion as moral virtue, 12:85
    scholasticism, 12:766, 767, 768
    slavery, 13:213
    social contract, 13:240
    speculative theology, 3:613
    subsistence, 13:572–573
    Thomistic philosophy, 12:619
    transcendental properties, 2:186
    transcendentals, 14:150
    transubstantiation, 14:160
    universality of Christianity, 3:293
    will and willing, 14:723
    works, 13:558
    See also Suarezianism

Suárez, Juan (Bp. of Portugal), 1:325, 879

Suarezianism, **13:561–563**

Subalternation, 4:652

Subcinctorium, 10:856

Subconscious, consciousness compared to, 4:153

Subdeacons, 7:36–37, **13:564**

Subdiaconate, 10:639

Subiaco Congregation, 2:256, 273

Subiaco Monastaries (Italy), **13:564–565**

Subida del Alma a Dios (Joseph of Jesus Mary), 2:36

Subjective happiness, 6:637

Subjective idealism, 13:303

Subjective regeneration, 5:322–323

Subjectivism
    criteriology, 4:368
    existence of God, 6:314
    existential ethics, 5:538, 12:3
    idea, 7:295
    Locke, John, 8:744, 746

moral relativism, 12:49–50
    Nietzsche, Friedrich Wilhelm, 10:390

Subjects, **13:565–566**

Sublimis Deus (papal bull, Paul III), 11:22

Submersion, baptism, 2:75

Submission of the Clergy (1531), 4:244

Subordinationism, 3:561, **13:566–567**
    Council of Nicaea I, 14:193
    Dionysius (Pope), St., 4:753, 12:462
    Holy Trinity controversy, 14:203–204
    Novatian (Antipope), 10:465
    Son of God, 4:890
    Tertullian, 3:560
    Trinitarian processions, 11:734

Subsidiarity, 13:268, **567–569**
    common good, 4:19
    Kirk defense, 8:182
    Mater et Magistra (encyclical, John XXIII), 9:317
    Quadragesimo anno (encyclical), 13:259
    solidarism, 13:301
    in the state, 13:485

Subsidiarity, in the Church, **13:569–570**

Subsistence, 11:512–513, 13:138–139, **570–573**, 577
    See also Personality

Subsistence in Christology, **13:573–574**

Substance, **13:574–579**
    absolute, 1:42
    abstraction, 1:47
    accident, 1:59
    being, 2:206
    Boethius, 2:456
    categories of being, 3:256
    causality, 3:308
    Chaucer, Geoffrey, 3:453
    cogitative power, 3:823
    God, 13:419–420
    history, 14:143
    Hume, David, 7:201
    Locke, John, 8:744
    monism, 9:811
    motion of augmentation, 10:18
    naturalism, 10:207
    principle, 5:745
    self and others, 8:830
    soul, 13:334
    Spinoza, 13:419
    See also Essence

Substantial change, **13:579–581**
    accident, 1:64
    Aristotle, 1:682, 9:347–348

Substantial change (*continued*)
  disposition, 4:777
  hylomorphism, 7:238
  soul, 13:354
  See also Motion
Substantial intellectual locutions, 8:747
Substantial perfection, 11:117
Subtlety of glorified bodies, 6:689
Suburbicariis sedibus (*motu proprio*, John XXIII), 3:106, 7:936
Suburra, Conrad de. *See* Anastasius IV (Pope)
Successive intellectual locutions, 8:747
Successor of the Chief of the Apostles. *See* Pope (title)
Succincta sacrorum canonum doctrina, seu compendium iuris ecclesiastici (Schmalzgrueber), 12:741
Succubi, 4:648
Suda, 2:808
Sudan, **13:581–585**, *584*
  Comboni, Daniele, 4:1
  demographic statistics, 13:582
  ecclesiastical organization, 13:584–585
  map, 13:*583*
  missions, 4:1, 2, 13:582, 584
Sudan People's Liberation Army (SPLA), 13:582–583
Sudermann, Daniel, 12:795
Sue, Eugène, 1:519
Suenesn, Leon-Joseph (Card.), 8:824, **13:585**
Suetonius (Roman historian), 3:160, 591, 4:859, 12:308, 350, **13:586**
Suevi, 1:663, 11:533
Suffering, 5:489, **13:586–588**, 766
Suffering Servant, Songs of the, 4:478, **13:588–592**
  in the Eucharist, 5:412
  kenotic theology, 8:143
  Seven Last Words, 13:37
  Son of God, 13:313
  Son of Man, 13:317
The Sufferings of Our Lord Jesus Christ (Thomas of Jesus), 14:35
Sufficient grace, 6:398
Sufficient reason, 5:534, 745, 8:457, 12:784, **13:592–594**
Sūfísm, 7:611–612, **13:594–597**
  alchemy, 1:237
  Algazel, 1:281
  Arabian philosophy, 1:621, 622
  Avicenna, 1:941
Sugar, John, Bl., 5:234, **13:597**

Suger of Saint-Denis, 12:544, **13:597–598**
  architecture, 1:576, 3:695
  chronicle of, 1:463
  iconography of Apostles, 1:576
  light symbolism, 3:674
  stained glass, 13:472–473
Suhard, Emmanuel Célestin (Card.), 9:684, **13:598**
Suhr, Theodore (Bp. of Denmark), 4:667, 668
Sui generis (unique), 12:753
Suicide, 5:457–459, 7:299, **13:598–599**
Suicide (Durkheim), 4:952
Suidbert, St. *See* Swithbert, St.
Suitbert, St. *See* Swithbert, St.
Sukejirō, Peter, St., 7:732
Sukizayemon, Michael Ichinose, Bl., 7:735
Sukkot (Feast of Booths), 2:131, **530–533**, *531*, 4:607, 5:656
Sukuyemon, Leo, Bl., 7:733
Sulaqa, John (Chaldean Patriarch), 1:807, 3:367, 5:19
Süleiman II (Sultan), 8:385
Süleyman I (Ottoman Emperor), 3:430, 431, 8:193, 10:*718*
Sulle fonti delle istituzioni di Giustiniano (Ferrini), 5:696
Sullivan, Francis A., 7:181
Sullivan, George, 1:211
Sullivan, James S. (Bp. of Fargo, ND), 5:625
Sullivan, Joseph V. (Bp. of Baton Rouge, LA), 2:156
Sullivan, Walter F. (Bp. of Richmond, VA), 14:543
Sullivan brothers of Waterloo (IA), 7:542
Sully, Eudes de, 5:436
Sulpician method of catechesis, 3:235
Sulpicians (Society of Saint Sulpice), 8:271, 9:43, 13:33, 173, **599–602**
  art and architecture, 12:601
  Canada, 3:4, 5, 6, 9
  Émery, Jacques André, 5:190
  Fenlon, John F., 5:684
  Frayssinous, Denis, 5:922
  Reilly, Wendell, 12:34–35
  Ribet, Jérôme, 12:221
  Robert, André, 12:262
  St. Mary's Seminary, 2:40
  scholasticism, 12:771
  slavery, 1:156
Sulpiciua of Bourges, SS., **13:603**

Sulpicius I Severus (Bp. of Bourges), 13:603
Sulpicius II (the Pious) (Bp. of Bourges), 13:603
Sulpicius Severus, 1:461, 482, 4:384, 12:606, **13:603–604**
Sulprizio, Nunzio, Bl., 13:*604*, **604**
Sulzer, J. G., 5:263
Sumatra, 3:145, 4:755
Sumer. *See* Babylonia
Sumerian law, 8:392–393
Sumerians, 4:325, 9:527, *527*, 13:205
Summa (Alan of Lille), 3:260
Summa (Alexander of Hales), 5:899
Summa (Hostiensis), 3:48
Summa (Rainier of Sacconi), 3:260
Summa (Simon of Bisignano), 13:132
Summa, as form, 4:605
Summa ad instructionem iuniorum (Simon Hinton), 13:129
Summa Aurea (Trombelli), 14:213
Summa aurea (William of Auxerre), 14:737
Summa casuum conscientiae (Bl. Angelo Carletti di Chivasso), 1:413–414
Summa Confessorum (John of Freiburg), 7:968
Summa contra gentiles (St. Thomas Aquinas), 1:564, 5:390, 693, 727, 12:240, 14:18, 24
Summa de arithmetica, geometrica, proportioni et proportionalita (Pacioli), 10:749
Summa de bono (Philip the Chancellor), 2:184
Summa de casibus conscientiae (Bartholomew of San Concordio), 2:127
Summa de casibus poenitentiae (St. Raymond of Peñafort), 11:936–937
Summa de ecclesia (Torquemada), 5:37
Summa de matrimonio (Vacarius), 14:365
Summa de ordine iudiciario (Richard de Mores), 12:229
Summa de summo bono (Ulric), 14:283
Summa de temporibus (*De concordia temporum*) (Giles of Lessines), 6:219
Summa decretalium questionum, 7:88
Summa decretorum (Rufinus), 12:403
Summa decretorum (Sicardus), 13:101, 102, *102*
Summa divinae philosophiae (Dominic of Flanders), 14:48
Summa Doctrinae Christianae (Canisius), 3:17–18, 233

Summa fratris Alexandri (Alexander of Hales, et al), 2:184–185

Summa logicales (Peter of Spain), 12:762

Summa Monacensis (commentary on Decretum), 3:47

Summa moralis (Antoninus, St.), 9:461

Summa parisiensis (anonymous), 3:47, **13:604–605**

Summa perfectionis (Geber), 1:238

Summa philosophiae (Eustachius a S. Paolo), 12:768

Summa philosophiae (Pseudo-Grosseteste), 6:538–539

Summa philosophica (Nicholas of Strassburg), 10:378

Summa philosophica (Roselli), 12:772

Summa philosophica (Zigliara), 12:773

Summa philosophica D. Thomase ex variis eius libris in ordinem cursus philosophici accomodata (Alamanni), 12:766

Summa philosophica iuxta scholasticorum principia (Russo), 12:777

Summa praedicantium (John of Bromyard), 5:529, 7:965, 11:620

Summa questionum (Richard de Mores), 12:229

Summa sentiarum (Robert of Melun), 5:516

Summa super corpore decretorum (Huguccio), 7:164–165

Summa super Decretis (Huguccio), 12:403

Summa super Sententias Petri Lombardi (Udo), 14:263

Summa theologiae (Aquinas), 1:29, 2:854, 3:396–400, 10:524, 902, 14:*15*

　ambition, 1:334

　appetite, 5:727–728

　common good, 4:18

　communication, 4:24

　Cursus Theologicus, 12:612, 618–619

　dialectics, 4:727

　Dominican theology text, 4:852

　double effect principle, 4:881

　ethics and moral theology, 5:390

　Eucharist, 5:424, 425

　existential metaphysics, 5:540

　freedom of religion, 5:947–949

　happiness, 5:344

　life of Thomas Aquinas, St., 14:18, 19, 22, 24–25

　Mariology, 9:170

　person of the word, 5:789

　Piana edition, 5:352

relics, 12:54–55

Sa, Manoel, 12:449

Salas, Juan de, 12:612

　supplement by Reginald of Peperino, 12:30

　See also Thomas Aquinas, St.

Summa theologiae (Ulric), 14:283

Summa theologiae moralis (Merkelbach), 9:514

Summa theologiae moralis (Noldin), 10:409

Summa theologiae moralis (St. Antoninus), 14:47

Summa theologiae scholastica et moralis in quatuor partes distributa (Herincx), 6:781

Summa theologiae scholasticae (Becanus), 2:191

Summa theologica (Alexander of Hales), 1:265, 4:36

Summa theologica (Roland of Cremona), 12:292, 14:5

Summa theologica (St. Antoninus), 1:537

Summa totius philosophiae (Veneto), 14:435

Summa totius philosophiae e divini Thomae Aquinatis doctrina (Alamanni), 12:766

Summae confessorum, 3:52, 220, 221

Summae dictaminis, as form, 4:757

Summae F. Dñci Sto Segobiensis, Ord. Praed. Magistri (Soto), 13:330

Summarium theologiae moralis (Arregui), 1:722

"Summary Agreement" (1676), 7:481

Summer School of Catholic Action (SSCA), 8:779

Summer solstice, 3:526

Summi Pontificatus (encyclical, Pius XII), 10:191, 956, 11:395, **13:605**

Summi Pontificis electio (motu proprio, John XXIII), 7:936

Summis desiderantes (Innocent VIII), 10:841

Sumner, Charles (Bp. of Llandaff), 5:472

Sumner, William Graham, 13:282

Sun gods, 5:191, 13:*206, 605*

Sun worship, 8:476, **13:605–606**

Sunday, 5:656, **13:606–609**

　Christian week, 8:641–642

　dominical letter denoting, 4:832

　as Lord's Day, 8:781–782

　modern calendars, 8:644

　Paschal mystery, 8:717

　Proper of the Time, 8:721

Sunday, Billy. *See* Sunday, William (Billy) Ashley

Sunday, William (Billy) Ashley, 12:205, **13:609**

Sunday and Holyday Observance, **13:609–612**

Sunday Missal (O'Connell), 10:542

Sunesen, Anders, 4:665

Sunnites, 1:287, 611, 2:873, **13:612–615**

　imām, 7:327

　Mahdī, Al-, 9:48

　Saladin, 12:610

　Somalia, 13:307–309

　See also Shī'ites

Suñol, Gregorio María, **13:615–616**

Suore Bigie, 10:812

Suore Operaie della Sanda Casa di Nazareth, 13:730

Super cathedram (papal bull, Boniface VIII), 4:850

Super librum de causis expositio (St. Thomas Aquinas), 14:27

Super Petri solio (papal bull, Boniface VIII), 2:503

Super universas (papal bull, Urban VIII), 2:12, 10:259

Supererogation, works of, 4:307, **13:616**

Superga Church (Italy), 3:707–708

Superior Diocese (WI), 8:243

Superiori anno (Greogry XVI), 10:358

Supernatural, **13:616–622**

　apologetics, 1:564–565, 7:342–343

　Augustinianism, 1:883

　Bernanos, Georges, 2:304

　Blondel, Maurice, 2:440–441

　certitude, 3:355

　charisms, 3:390

　Church's use of term, 6:394

　contemplation and virtues, 4:204–205

　deliberation, 4:629–630

　destiny, 4:693–695

　doctrine, 4:806–809

　elevation, 8:840

　existence, 5:532

　faith, 5:599

　hope, 7:95–96

　human nature, 10:211

　Ignatian retreat, 13:431

　life, concept of, 8:572

　light of glory, 8:585

　mysteries, 10:84–85

　obediential potency, 10:509

　primitive revelation, 12:193

　religious liberalism, 8:540

　signs, 9:665

Supernatural *(continued)*
  sin, 13:144
  soul of the Church, 13:359
  spirituality, 13:441–443
  Voltaire, 14:579
Supernatural elements in man, 9:90–91
Supernatural existential, 5:828, 10:204,
  13:622–623
Supernatural grace, 6:399
Supernatural habits, 6:600, 603–604
Supernatural knowledge, 8:202–203, 747
Supernatural mysteries, 10:84–85
Supernatural order, 4:573, 693–695,
  8:855, 9:735, 737, 10:212–213,
  13:623
Supernatural perfection, 11:119
Supernatural power, 4:304–305
Supernatural virtues, 14:551–552
Supernaturalness of God, 13:559
Superno Dei mutu (*motu proprio*, John
  XXIII), 7:937
Superstition, 8:848–849, 12:326–327,
  13:623–624, 14:798
Suppiluliuma (Hittite King), 6:897
Supplément au Dictionnaire de la Bible,
  12:262
*The Supplement to Boughainville's
  Voyage* (Diderot), 14:361
Supplementa ad Lexicon Hebraicum
  (Michaelis), 6:697
*Supplementum et castigatio ad scriptores
  Trium Ordinum S. Francisci a
  Waddingo aliisque descriptos*, 12:717
Supplices te rogamus, 5:279
Supposition (logic), 8:750, **13:624–625**
  See also Hypothesis; Theory
Supralapsarians, 1:712, 2:894, 11:650,
  655, 12:132, **13:625–626**
Supremacy, Acts of. *See* Acts of
  Supremacy
Supremacy, Oath of. *See* Oath of
  Supremacy
Supreme good, 6:353, **354–355**
Supreme Pontiff of the Universal
  Church. *See* Pope (title)
Supremi Apostolatus (papal bull,
  Clement XIV), 10:931
Sur la tolérance de l'Église (Schroeder),
  12:787
Sur les délais de la justice divine
  (Maistre), 9:61
Surgery, 13:880
Surin, Jean Joseph, **13:626–627**
Suriname, 4:864–865, **13:627–628**, *628*
Surius, Lawrence, 3:192, 4:302, 6:614,
  13:628–629

Surnaturel: Études historiques (Lubac),
  9:101, 10:193, 11:823
Surplices, 13:*629*, **629**
Survival Till Seventeen (Feeney), 5:663
Susan (Oldmeadow), 10:583
Susanna (biblical heroine), 4:508, 509,
  13:629–631, *630*
Susanna, St., 13:*631*, **631**
Suso, Henry, 13:453, 468, 765
Sutherland, Graham, 4:330–331
Sutras, **13:631–632**
Sutri, Councils of (1046-1059), 1:100,
  13:632
Sutri, Synod of (1059), 3:777
Sutton, Christopher, 3:152
Sutton, David, 7:579
Sutton, John, 7:579
Sutton, Robert, Bl., 5:229, 230, **13:632**
Suwayr, Order of. *See* Basilian Order of
  St. John Baptist
Suzuki, Paul, St., 7:732
SVD (Society of the Divine Word),
  10:529, 14:98
Sverker the Elder (King of Sweden),
  1:327
Sveti Georgi Church (Bulgaria), 2:*682*
Svetlov, Pavel Iakovlevich, 12:435,
  13:632–633
SVM. *See* Student Volunteer Movement
Swabey, M. C., 6:884
Swabia, 12:671
Swabian League, 8:324
Swaggart, Jimmy, 1:789
Swallowell, George, Bl., 2:551, 5:232
Swastika, **13:633**
Swaziland, **13:633–634**, *634*
Sweden, **13:634–638**, *637*
  Anderson, Lars, 1:399
  Botvid, St., 2:562
  Counter Reformation, 4:313, 9:66
  demographic statistics, 13:635–636
  ecclesiastical organization, 4:664
  Gregory XII (Pope), 6:501, 503
  Lutheranism, 8:888–889, 9:45, 12:19
  map, 13:*636*
  patron saint, 5:319–320
  Protestant Reformation, 1:327, 399,
    643, 4:309
  Sigfrid, St., 13:114
Sweden, Church of, 8:884
Swedenborg, Emanuel, 1:835, 2:428,
  3:759, 10:283, **13:638–640**, *639*
Swedenborgian Church (New Jerusalem
  Church), 10:283
Swedish Intervention (1630-35), 14:10

Swedish-French War (1635-48), 14:10
Sweelinck, Jan Pieters, 13:*640*, **640**
Sweeney, James J. (Bp. of Honolulu),
  6:671
Sweeney, Timothy (Archabbot), 12:568
Sweet odors, 10:109
Sweetheart Abbey (Scotland). *See* New
  Abbey (Scotland)
Sweyenheym, Conrad, 2:522
Sweynheyn, Konrad, **13:640**
Swiatek, Kazmierz (Card.), 2:214
Swieten, G. van, 5:658
Swift, Jonathan, 5:966, **13:640–642**, *641*
Swinburne, R., 5:384
Swinderby, William, 8:766
Swint, John Joseph (Abp.), **13:642**,
  14:688
The Swiss and Their Mountains (Lunn),
  8:868
Swiss Brethren, 2:69
Swiss Guards, **13:642–644**, *643*
Swiss League, 13:648
Swiss-American Congregation, 2:255,
  273, 12:568
Swithbert, St., **13:644**
Swithin of Winchester (Bp.), St., **13:645**
Switzerland, 5:773–774, **13:645–651**
  Calvinism, 2:895
  Canons Regular of St. Augustine,
    3:69
  Carthusians, 3:195
  church architecture, 3:712, 8:623
  confessions of faith, 4:79
  demographic statisics, 13:646
  ecclesiastical organization, 13:650
  education, 9:160
  Gregory XVI (Pope), 6:509
  Kulturkampf, 8:255–256
  liturgical movement, 8:674
  map, 13:*647*
  missions, 3:599
  Presbyterianism, 11:678
  Protestant Reformation, 4:309,
    12:19–20
  Reformed churches, 12:23
Sword of Honour (Waugh), 14:663
Sword of the Spirit, 3:131, 5:252,
  13:651
Swordbrothers, 4:414
Syagrius (Bp. of Autun), St., 1:926
Sybil (Queen of Jerusalem), 7:774
Sybils (oracles), 4:784
Sykes, Edmund, Bl., 5:229, **13:651**
Syllabic Chant, 6:466

Syllabus of Errors (Pius IX), 5:855, 951, 10:261, 12:745, **13:651–654**
  Acton, John Emerich Edward Dalberg, 1:85
  Albertario, Davide, 1:228
  Americanism, 1:354
  Bilio, Luigi, 2:393
  Church-State relations, 3:641
  Dupanloup, Félix, 4:942
  freedom of conscience, 4:149
  Kulturkampf, 8:253
  liberalism, 3:619
  Schrader, Klemens, 12:786
  Schwarzenberg, Friedrich Joseph von, 12:794
  society (Church as), 13:286
  sovereignty, 13:371
Sylloge monumentorum ad mysterium conceptionis Immaculatae Virginis Deiparae illustrandum (Ballerini), 2:31
Syllogism, **13:654–655**
  argumentation, 1:658
  Aristotle, 1:681
  art, 1:747
  de Morgan, Augustus, 4:655
  demonstrative, 4:651–654
  division, 4:794
  logic, 8:748, 750, 753
  methodology, 9:564
Syllogisms (Apelles), 5:509
Sylveira, Jorge, 1:236
Sylvester I (Pope), St., 3:164–165, 556, 4:83, 182–183, **13:655–657**
Sylvester II (Pope), **13:657–659**, *658*
  Adso of Montier-en-der, 1:130
  Bobbio Abbey, 2:446
  dialectics, 4:725
  medieval Latin literature works, 9:448
  papal name taken, 10:141
  scholasticism, 12:758
Sylvester III (Antipope), 4:362
Sylvester III (Pope), **13:659**
Sylvester IV (Antipope), **13:659–660**
Sylvester Prierias, 3:52
Sylvestrine Benedictines, **2:274–275**, 13:123
Sylvius, Aeneas. *See* Pius II (Pope)
Sylvius, Francis (du Bois), 2:396, **13:660**
Symbol, 4:349, 351–352, 8:753–754
Symbol formation, theory of, 11:319
Symbol of union, 4:466

Symbolae ad illustrandam historiam ecclesiae orientalis in terris coronae S. Stephani (Nilles), 10:396
Symbolic interactionist perspective, 13:273
Symbolic logic. *See* Logic, symbolic
Symbolic realities, in the Bible, 13:663
Symbolik (Möhler), 6:877
Symbolik und Mythologie der Naturreligion des Altertums (Baur), 14:234
Symbolism
  altars, 1:319, 320
  Amalarius of Metz, 1:329
  analogy, 1:373
  anchors, 1:396
  angels, 1:418
  animals, 1:457–458, 574
  apocalyptic style, 1:546
  Christian anthropology, 3:532
  Church, 3:629–630
  church architecture, 1:576, 3:630, 672–676, 688, 694, 812
  fish, 5:746–747, 746–748
  flowers, 5:784
  Judeo-Christian symbolism, 13:664–665
  learned ignorance method using, 10:374–375
  magic, 9:37–38
  millenarianism, 9:635
  New Age Movement, 10:275
  numerology, 10:243, 477–478
  primitive art, 1:739–741
  ritual studies, 12:259
  temples, 13:806–807
  virgin birth, 14:536
  See also Iconology and iconography; Symbolism, theological
Symbolism, early Christian, 1:753–754, 755, **13:664–669**
Symbolism, the Sacred and the Arts (Eliade), 5:155
Symbolism, theological, 10:628–629, **13:669–671**
Símbolo católico indiano (Oré), 10:643
Symbolon, 4:351–352
Symbols, **13:660–662**
Symbols, revelation in, **13:662–664**
Symeon Logothetes, 2:799
Symeon Metaphrastes, 1:93, 12:606
Symeon the New Theologian (Monk of the Studion), 2:794, 12:436, **13:671–672**
  banished, 13:13
  Byzantine civilization, 2:769

  hesychasm, 2:763, 826
  Michael Psellus, 2:758
Symmachians, 5:31
Symmachus (Pope), St., **13:672–673**
  Acacian Schism, 1:50, 3:595
  Aeonius of Arles, St., 1:140
  altar of Victory, 1:337–338
  cardinalate, 3:104
  Church-State relations, 3:633
  Cosmas and Damian, 4:282
  decretal collections, 4:602
  Dioscorus (Antipope), 4:756
  Easter date controversy, 5:13
  Ennodius, 5:264, 265
  Lawrence (Antipope), 8:404
  papal authority, 12:355
  St. Agnes Basilica, 1:178
  Vatican construction, 14:393, 394
Symmachus, Quintus Aurelius, **13:673–674**
Sympathetic magic, 9:38
Symphoniae sacrae (Schütz), 12:792
Symposium Aristotelicum, 1:679
Sympto-Thermal methods (STM), 10:176
Synagoge (Paulus Euergetinos), 11:45
Synagoge Canonum, 3:38
Synagogues, 4:945–946, 8:780, 12:502, **13:674–675**, 760
Synagogues, ancient, 13:675, **675–678**
Synave, P., 3:26
Synaxarium, 5:466
Synaxary, 12:606, **13:678–679**
Synaxary of Constantinople, 13:679
Syncerae et verae doctrinae de Coena Domini defensio (Ochino), 10:535
Syncretism, 12:67, 68
Syncretistic controversy, 3:174
Synderesis, 4:144, 674, **13:679–681**, 14:225
Synechism, 11:58
Synergism, **13:681–682**
Synesius of Cyrene (Bp. of Ptolemais), 1:268, 829, 2:803–804, 3:323, **13:682–683**
Synnot, Paul, 7:581
Synnot, Richard, 7:581
"The Synod in Exile" (Karlovtsy Synod), 10:683
Synod of Baltimore (1791). *See* Baltimore, Councils of
Synod of Dort, 4:79
Synod of German Reformed Church, 5:468
Synodal Hall (Sens, France), 3:698

Synodal Letter (Basil of Ancyra), 2:139
Synodical Letter (Sophronius), 13:324
Synodicus (Warnerius of Basel), 9:449
Synodos endēmousa, 10:946
Synods (early church), 3:593,
    8:293–294, 845, **13:694–695**
    See also specific synods
Synods of Bishops, 10:852, **13:683–688**
    Canadian positions, 3:9
    collegiality of, 5:39
    common good, 4:21
    communio, 4:30
    denial of papal primacy, 8:463
    ecclesiology of communion, 5:38
    Episcopal conferences, 5:300–301
    establishment of, 5:39
    John Paul II (Pope), 13:*686*
    People of God, 5:37
    social justice, 13:244, 245
Synods of Bishops, assemblies, 8:292,
    318, **13:688–694**
    African Bishops (1994), 13:*692*
    American Bishops (1997), 13:*686*
    Asian Synod of Bishops (1998),
        13:*687*
    European Bishops (1999), 13:*684*
    Lebanese Bishops (1995), 13:*689*
    first ordinary general assembly
        (1967), 14:820
    fifth World Synod of Bishops (1980),
        13:*691*
    sixth ordinary general assembly
        (1983), 13:*688*
    eighth ordinary assembly (1990),
        13:*690*
    ninth ordinary assembly (1994),
        13:*693*
Synoptic Gospels, **13:695–697**
    Andrew, Apostle, St., 1:402, 403
    baptism of the Lord, 14:202
    biblical theology, 2:386
    canonicity, 3:32
    Church, 3:579
    exegetical studies, 5:511, 522
    grace, 6:381
    guilt, 6:571
    Jesus Christ, temptation of,
        13:816–818
    Jesus Christ, trial of, 14:178–181
    John's Gospel, 7:892–893, 904
    messianism, 9:545–547
    miracles, 9:663–664
    parables, 10:871–872
    Peter, Apostle, St., 11:174, 175

redaction criticism scholarship,
    10:303–304
Son of Man, 13:317
suffering servant, songs of the,
    13:591
taxation and moral obligation, 13:768
temptation, 13:816
Thomas, St., 14:11–12
type and antitype, 14:254–255
will of God, 14:724
    See also Luke, Gospel According to;
        Mark, Gospel According; Matthew,
        Gospel According to
Synoptic problem, canonicity, 3:29
Die synoptischen Streitgespräche
    (Albertz), 5:521, 812
Syntagma (Against All Heresies) (St.
    Hippolytus of Rome), 6:859
Syntagma (Blastares), 2:435
Syntagma Canonum Antiochenum, 3:38,
    39, 59, **13:697–698**
La Synthèse thomiste (Garrigou-
    Lagrange), 6:101
Synthesis, 11:948, **13:698**, 899
    See also Analysis and synthesis
Synthetic Philosophy (Spencer), 13:412
Syntogma (St. Justin Martyr), 6:773
Syon Abbey (England), 5:243, **13:698**
Syracuse Cathedral (Italy), 7:*663*
Syria, **13:698–700**, *703*
    church architecture, 3:685
    Church-state relations, 3:631
    Commingling rite, 4:12
    concelebration, 4:50
    Confirmation, 4:85–86
    covenant treaties, 4:325, 326
    creedal statements, 4:352
    cross, 4:380, 384–385
    crucifixion art, 4:392–393
    Crusades, 4:404
    demographic statistics, 13:699
    Laodicea, 8:328
    liturgical history, 8:651–652
    Manichaeism mission, 9:108–109
    map, 13:*700*
    Maronite Church, 9:192–194
    monasticism, 9:789, 801
    Syrian Catholic Church (Eastern
        Catholic), 13:706–710
    Syrian Orthodox Church (Oriental
        Orthodox), 13:705–706
    See also Antioch, Ancient See of;
        Dura-Europos; East Syrian liturgy
Syriac Creed, 2:72

Syriac language and literature,
    13:700–702
    Aristotelianism, 1:671
    biblical catenae, 3:259
    Elias Bar Shināyā, 5:156
    father of literature, 13:16–17
    hymnody, 7:241–242
    text publication, 2:198
Syriac lectionary, 5:5
Syrian Catholic Church (Eastern
    Catholic), 13:706–710, 708–709
Syrian Christianity, 2:744, 3:358–359,
    4:295–296, 731, **13:703–710**
Syrian Church
    ambos, 1:336
    biblical canon, 3:26, 28, 32, 565
    chorbishops, 3:526
    clerical celibacy/marriage, 3:325
    early, 3:593
    lectors, 7:37
    Monophysitism, 1:523
    Passion tradition, 10:924–925
    Solemnity of All Saints, 1:289
    See also Jacobites (Syrian)
Syrian Jacobite Church. *See* Jacobite
    Church
Syrian liturgy, 3:556, 8:713, 11:125,
    13:710–711
    See also East Syrian liturgy
Syrian Orthodox Church, 5:19,
    13:705–706, 708–709
    See also Jacobite Church
Syrian Orthodox Jacobite Church, 7:400
Syrianus (Greek philosopher), 1:670,
    10:241
Syro-Malabar Church, 7:400,
    13:711–715
    Carmelites, 3:130, 146–147, 459
    Catholic Near East Welfare
        Association, 3:286
    Chaldean Catholic Church, 3:369
    clerical celibacy/marriage, 3:324
    religious women, 13:189–190
Syro-Malabar liturgy, 5:3, 13:713,
    715–718
Syro-Malankara Church, 3:286, 7:400,
    13:718–722
Syro-Palestinian archaeology. *See*
    Biblical archaeology
Syropoulos, Sylvester, **13:722–723**
System der christlichen Gewissheit
    (Frank), 5:323
System der christlichen Wahrheit
    (Frank), 5:323
System der Philosophie im Grundriss
    (Hartmann), 6:655

System des tranzendentalen Idealismus (Schelling), 12:732

System of Logic (Hegel), 12:346

System of Logic, Ratiocinative and Inductive: Being a Connected View of the Principles of Evidence and the Methods of Scientific Investigation (Mill), 9:566, 630

System of reason, 12:346

Systema naturae (Linnaeus), 5:260

Systematic theology, 13:903

    Barth, Karl, 2:120

    grace, 6:398

    Kingdom of God, 8:175

    Lipsius, R., 8:597

    liturgical theology, 8:714–715

    personalism, 8:227

    as term, 4:814

    See also Dogmatic theology

Systematic Theology (Hodge), 6:901

Systematic Theology (Tillich), 14:76

Le Système de la nature (Holbach), 9:320

Système de la nature, ou des lois du monde physique et du monde moral (Holbach), 5:261

Système de Philosophie (Régis), 3:185, 9:74

Système de politique positive (Comte), 4:48

Szántó, Arator. *See* Szántó, István

Szántó, István, **13:723**

Szoka, Edmund (Abp. of Detroit), 4:699

T

Ta Duc Thinh, Martin, 14:497

Taaffe, Peter, 7:581

Tābal (ritual cleansing), 2:57

Tabb, John Banister, **13:725**

Tabennisi (Egypt), **13:725–726**

Tabernacle Church of Christ (Columbus, IN), 3:716

Tabernacle Pulpit collection (Spurgeon), 13:463

Tabernacle Society, 8:134

Tabernacles, 1:317, 348, 13:726, **726**

Tabernacles, Feast of, **2:530–533**

Table of the Seven Deadly Sins (Bosch), 4:566

Tables de Chaulnes (Fénelon), 5:683

The Tablet (periodical), 8:842, 10:325, **13:726–727**

Taboo and phenomenology of sin, 13:149

Taborga, Miguel de los Santos (Abp. of Sucre), **13:728**

Taborites, 1:548, 4:481, 7:231, 9:637, **13:728**

Tabouillot, Nicolas, 12:278

Tabourat, Anna (Mother), 7:207

Tabula aurea (Peter of Bergamo), 14:48

Tacci Venturi, Pietro, 7:791, 792

Taché, Alexandre Antonin (Abp. of Saint Boniface, MB), 3:8, 8:280, **13:728–729**, *729*

Tacitus, Cornelius, 5:264, 12:308, **13:729–730**

    Christian (term), 3:529

    Church history, 3:591

    Corvey Abbey, 4:281

    Mount Carmel, 3:125

    Nero, 10:250, 12:350

    Roman persecutions, 3:592

Tacitus, Marcus Claudius (Roman Emperor), 12:313

Tack, Theodore, 1:891

Tadini, Arcángelo, Bl., **13:730**

Tadwinus. *See* Tatwine (Abp. of Canterbury), St.

Tafel der kerstlygken Levens (treatise), 3:241

Tafna churches (Syria), 1:756, 757

Tafoya, Arthur N. (Bp. of Pueblo), 3:859

Taft, Robert F., 2:812, 5:7

Tagle, Luis, 7:528

Tagore, Rabindranath, **13:730–731**, *731*

Taháfut al-Falācifah (Algazel), 1:622

Tahāfut al-Tahāfut (Averroës), 1:622

Taigi, Anna Maria, Bl., **13:731–732**

Taille, Maurice de la, 4:207, 335–336

Tailleferre, Germaine, 11:562

Taine, Hippolyte, 2:478, 7:287, **13:732–733**

Taino people, 3:108

Tait, Archibald (Abp. of Canterbury), 1:444, 447

Taiwan, 12:226, 13:189, 733–735, *734*

Taizé, music of, 2:332, 333, **13:735–736**

Taj Mahal (Agra, India), 7:*619*

Takach, Basil (Bp. of Pittsburgh), 5:20, 11:86

Takeya, Cosmas, St., 7:732

Talamo, S., 12:671

Talavera, Hernando de (Abp. of Talavera), 3:866, 6:823

Talavera y Mendoza, Fernando de (Abp. of Granada), 3:610

Talavero de la Reina (Spain), Martyrs of, 7:122

Talbot, Francis Xavier, **13:736–737**

Talbot, George, 3:119

Talbot, James, **13:737**

Talbot, John, Bl., 5:233, 10:447, **13:737**

Talbot, Matt, **13:737–738**

Talbot, Peter and Richard, 7:582, **13:738**

Talebearing, 4:230, **13:739**

Tales of the Mermaid Tavern (Noyes), 10:471

Talev, Damial (Bp.), 2:684

Talking ass, tale of (Book of Numbers), 2:26

Tall, Ammonius, 13:739

Tall, Dioscorus (Bp.), 13:739

Tall, Eusebius, 13:739

Tall, Euthymius, 13:739

Tall Brothers, **13:739**

Tallaght Abbey (Ireland), 4:423, **13:739–740**

Talley, T., 3:553

Talleyrand-Périgord, Charles Maurice de (Bp. of Autun), 5:971, **13:740–741**, *741*

    Bernier, Étienne Alexandre, 2:324

    Celles-Sur-Belle Monastery, 3:329

    Civil Constitution of the Clergy, 3:753

    Dupanloup, Félix, 4:942

    Pius VII (Pope), 4:62

Tallis, Thomas, **13:741–742**, *742*

Talmud, 5:508, 7:867, **13:742–747**, *743*

    Akiba ben Joseph, 1:199

    Apostles, 1:571

    biblical canon, 3:24

    biblical Chronicler, 3:565

    Bomberg, Daniel, 2:476

    books, 8:7

    Caro, Joseph ben Ephraim, 3:148

    challenged, 8:9

    mishnah, 9:672

    names for God, 13:77–78

    origins, 8:7

    Pharisees, 8:6

    rabbinical statements, 8:7–8

    See also Rabbinic literature

Tam multa (apostolic brief, Pius VII), 11:212

Tamagna, Giuseppe, 12:770

Tamar (biblical figure), 6:126

Tamaron y Romeral, Pedro (Bp. of Durango), **13:747–748**

Tamburini, Michelangelo, **13:748**

Tamburini, Pietro, 14:934

Tamburini, Tommaso, 8:411, **13:748–749**, *749*

Tametsi decree (1563), 3:54, 10:218–219, **13:749–750**, 14:173

Tamhīd of al-Bāquillānī, 8:110

Tamil language, 2:339–340

Tamil people, 13:465–466

The Taming of the Shrew (Shakespeare), 2:116

Tamisier, Marie Marthe Emilia, 5:433

Tammuz, **13:750**

Tanaka, Catherine, Bl., 7:734

Tanaka, John, Bl., 7:734

Tanaka, Maria, Bl., 7:733

Tanaka, Paul, Bl., 7:733

Tānās, Cyril (Patriarch), 1:13

Tanaura, Mary, Bl., 7:733

Tanchelm, 9:636, **13:750**

Tancred (Norman crusader), 4:402, 10:642, 12:229, **13:751**
    Bernard of Parma, St., 2:314
    Canon Law, 2:314, 3:49

Tancred of Lecce, 3:776

Tancredi (Rossini), 12:389

Tanda, Damian Yamichi, Bl., 7:733

Tanda, Michael, Bl., 7:733

Tanjur (Lamaist texts), 8:299

Tannaim (repeaters), 8:2

Tannaitic literature, 13:746

Tanner, Adam, 7:782, **13:751–752**

Tanner, Edmund (Bp. of Cork and Cloyne, Ireland), **13:752**

Tannery, P., 1:678

Tanquerey, Adolphe Alfred, 12:777, **13:752–753**

Tansi, Cyprian Michael Iwene, Bl., **13:753**

Tansi, Michael. *See* Tansi, Cyprian Michael Iwene, Bl.

Tansillo, Luigi, 4:313

Tantric yoga, 14:892

Tantrism, 13:*753*, **753–754**

Tanucci, Bernardo, 1:71, 308, 3:792, 793–794, **13:754–755**

Tanzania, **13:755–756**, *757*

Taoism. *See* Daoism

Tao-Klardjethie monastic movement (8th-10th centuries), 10:689

Taparelli d'Azeglio, Luigi, 5:397, 12:766, 772, 13:242, **756**

Taparelli d'Azeglio, Massimo. *See* Azeglio, Massimo Taparelli d'

Tapia, Gonzalo de, **13:757–758**

Tapis, Estevan, 2:862

Tapper, Ruard, 2:18–19, **13:758**

Tappouni, Ignatius Gabriel (Card.), **13:758–759**

Tara, Synod of (697), 1:110

Tarahumara Alta Jesuit Mission (Mexico), 9:709

Tarahumara Baja Jesuit Mission (Mexico), 9:709

Tarancón (Card.), 13:398

Tarango, Yolanda, 5:677

Tarantella (Belloc), 2:231

Tarascan people, 11:939

Tarasius (Patriarch of Constantinople), St., 2:752–753, 793, 821, 7:282, **13:759**

Tarde, Gabriel, 2:696

Tardini, Domenico, **13:759–760**

Targums, 8:173, 759, **13:760–762**

Tārîḫ Taifat ar-Rūm al-Malakîyat war Rahbānīat alMuḫalliṣīat (History of the Catholic Melkhite Community and of the Salvatorian Order) (Bacha), 2:8

Tarlattini, John Dominic, 10:*931*

Tarphon, Rabbi, **13:762–763**

Tarragon, Jean-Michel de, 5:51

Tarsicius, St., **13:763**

Tartars, 1:768, 4:370

Tartini, Giuseppe, 13:*763*, **763–764**

Tartosa, Spain, 4:827

Taschereau, Elzéar Alexandre (Card.), 3:8, **13:764**

Tassin, R. P., 10:773

Tasso, Torquato, 2:*109*, 111, 4:313, 401

Tate and Brady Psalter, 11:798

Tatham, John, 10:281

Tatian (Syrian Christian writer), **13:764–765**
    biblical canon, 3:30
    Christian philosophy, 3:538
    Church history, 3:593
    dialectics, 4:725
    Diatessaron, 4:731
    Divine judgment, 8:32
    Edessa, 5:82
    immortality, 7:348
    Justin's tradition, 8:95
    procreation, 4:218

Tatwin. *See* Tatwine (Abp. of Canterbury), St.

Tatwine (Abp. of Canterbury), St., **13:765**

Tau sign, as early Christian symbol, 13:667

Tauler, Johannes, 3:605, **13:765–766**
    Albert the Great, St., 1:226
    apophatic theology, 1:568
    Dominican mysticism, 5:789
    Luther, Martin, 8:84
    pantheism, 2:629

Rhenish spirituality, 13:453, 454

Taunton, Ethelred Luke, **13:766–767**

Taurinus, St., 8:323

Taurobolium, 4:450, 10:92, 12:145, **13:767**

Tausen, Hans, **13:767**

Tavares dos Reis, Francisco (Father), 5:10

Tavast, Magnus, 5:732

Taveira, Antonio, 5:8

Taverner, John, 8:689, **13:767–768**

Tax Commission, Walz v. (1970), 3:667

Taxation
    Church property, 3:726
    clergy, 4:243, 244, 253
    Clericis laicos, 2:502, 3:803
    Magna Carta, 9:40
    See also Papal taxation

Taxation and moral obligation, **13:768–769**

Taylor, A. E., 1:678

Taylor, Charles, 8:552–553

Taylor, Deodat, 4:122

Taylor, E. B., 5:520

Taylor, Frances Margaret, 11:494, 13:*769*, **769–770**

Taylor, Harriet, 9:630

Taylor, Hugh, Bl., 2:573, 5:228, **13:770**

Taylor, James Hudson, 3:499

Taylor, Jeremy (Bp. of Down and Connor), 1:733, 3:152, **13:770**

Taylor, Mark C., 4:594

Taylor, Myron Charles, **13:770–771**

Taylor, Nathaniel William, 10:280, **13:771**

Taylor, Thomas, 1:677, 11:416

Taylor, V., 7:850

Taylor, William, **13:771**

Taylorism. *See* New Haven theology

Te Deum (Bach), 2:6

Te Deum (Nicetas of Remesiana), **13:771–773**

Te Deum, in papal ceremony and vesture, 4:891, 7:252, 10:856

Te Lucis Ante Terminum (anonymous), **13:773**

Teach Them (statement of U.S. bishops), 13:774

Teachers, Ministry of, 13:169–170, **773–775**

Teaching Authority of the Church (Magisterium), **13:775–782**

Teaching of the Twelve Apostles. See Didache

Teaching Sisters of the Holy Cross, 5:773

Team ministry (Canon Law), 8:116, 424, **13:782–783**

Tears of blood and bloody sweat (hematidrosis), 10:108

Teatro critico universal sopra los erroes communes (Feijóo y Montenegro), 12:770

Teatro eclesiástico de las ciudades e iglesias catedrales de España: Vida de sus obispos y cosas memorables de sus obispados (González Dávila), 6:343

Teatro mexicano (Vetancurt), 14:465

The Technological Bluff (Ellul), 5:172

Technological societies, 13:784–786

The Technological Society (Ellul), 5:172

The Technological System (Ellul), 5:172

Technology
cultural evolution, 4:433–434
cybernetics, 4:451–453
innovation, as cause of moral complexity, 11:745
medical advances and ethics, 9:430
moral theology, 9:869

Technology, philosophy of, **13:783–786**

Technology, social effects of, **13:786–788**

Techo, Nicolás Del, **13:788**

Teefy, John Read, 2:142

Teens Encounter Christ, in Kansas, 8:116

Tefnut (Egyptian deity), 4:337

Tegern See Abbey (Bavaria), **13:788**

Teilhard de Chardin, Pierre, **13:788–790**, *789*
Angela of Foligno, Bl., 1:412
atheism, 1:825
causality, 3:306–307
community, 4:39
creation doctrine, 4:345, 347
defended by de Lubac, 8:840
end of the world, 5:217
evil, 4:649
final causality, 5:725, 727
humanism, 7:182
influence of, 5:859
mystical vision of, 10:116
opponent of Ruffini, Ernesto, 12:402
original sin, 10:670
panentheism, 10:821, 824
philosophy of technology, 13:786
process theology, 11:731
recapitulation in Christ, 11:953

Tejada, Adalberto, 6:581

Tejero Molina, Ignacio, Bl., 7:123

Tekakwitha, Kateri, Bl., 3:5, 8:383, 10:310, 13:790, **790–791**

Tel Aviv (Israel), 7:*631*

Tel Hazor (Israel), 10:*779*

Tela Ignea Satanae (The Fiery Darts of Satan) (Wagenseil), 7:588

Telecommunications, 8:843

Télémaque (Fénelon), 5:682

Teleological ethics, 4:160, **13:791**

Teleologists, 11:768

Teleology, 2:407–408

Telepathy, 3:759

Telescope, 6:60

Telesio, Bernardino, 1:677, 2:917, 12:122, *123*, 13:345, **791**

Telesphorus (Pope), St., 12:351, **13:792**

Telesphorus of Cosenza, **13:792**

Telesthesia, 3:759

''Tell It Like It Is''—Catechetics from the Black Perspective, 10:158

Tell Keisan (Israel), 2:380

Tellenbach, G., 3:813

Tellenpeck, Paul, 12:33

Telliamed (Maillet), 5:260

Tello, Antonio, **13:792**

Tellus Mater (Roman deity), 5:3, 697

Telmon, Peter, 7:33–34

Temanza, T., 3:675

Tembleque, Francisco de, **13:792–793**

Temperament, 3:387, **13:793–794**

Temperance, virtue of, 3:388, 4:212, 13:239, **794–795**

Temperance Movements, 8:134, 449, **13:795–802**, *798*

Les Tempes Modernes (periodical), 12:697

The Tempest (Shakespeare), 13:64, 66

Tempier, Étienne (Bp. of Paris), **13:802**
Aristotelian physics, 12:811
Latin Averroism controversy, 1:623, 674, 936, 12:761, 14:20–21
Siger of Brabant, 13:112
unity of intellect, 7:511

Tempier, Stephen (Bp. of Paris), 1:51, 4:882

Tempietto, 3:671

Templars, 9:625, *626*, **13:802–805**, 14:489
abolition of, 4:301
Armenia, 1:702
banking, 3:726
chivalry, 3:519
Duranti, William the Younger, 4:950
founding, 5:843
Honorius II (Pope), 7:82

James II, 12:547
Jerusalem, 7:774
Knights of Malta, 8:193
Knights of the Sword, 8:199
Louis VII, 8:799
military order, 4:402
Philip IV, 1:943
Scottish religious orders, 12:833
Spain, 13:3, 88
suppression, 1:194–195, 3:603, 779

The Temple (Herbert), 5:161

Temple, Frederick (Abp. of Canterbury), 1:594

Temple, presentation at. *See* Presentation of the Lord

Temple, William (Abp. of York and Canterbury), 2:622, 12:98, **13:805**

Temple, William, Sir, 13:641

Temple of Jerusalem, 7:*633*, 643–644, 767

Temple of Ramses II (Nubia), 11:*882*

Temple of Solomon (Erlach), 13:*809*

Temple of Zerubbabel (Israel), 13:810

Temples, 5:*120, 122,* 125–126, *126,* 131–132, 9:535–537, **13:805–808**
See also Synagogues, ancient

Temples, in the Bible, 13:306, *306,* **808–811**

Temples and Temple-Service in Ancient Israel (Haran), 14:858

Templum Dei Mysticum (Papczyński), 10:860

Temporal values, theology of, 4:695, **13:811–812**

Temptation, 3:387, 4:68, **13:812–814**

Temptation, in the Bible, **13:814–816**

Temptations of Jesus, 4:717, 8:857, **13:816–818**

Tempting God, **13:818**

Ten Books on Architecture (Vitruvius), 12:308

Ten Commandments, **4:4–9,** *5,* 10:*9,* 13:159–160, *160*
Bible, 4:4–6, 703
catechesis, 3:234, 240, 242, 4:8–9
moral theology, 4:6–8

Ten Decades of Alms (Roemer), 12:283

Ten Thousand Martyrs, Legend of, **13:818–819**

Tencarari, Zoen (Bp. of Avignon), 1:942–943

Tencin, Pierre Guérin de (Card.), **13:819**

Tenebrae, **13:819–820**

Tengström, Sven, 11:97

Teniers, David, 1:539

Tennant, F. R., 2:223

Tennent, Gilbert, 5:969, 11:676

Tennent, William, 6:425

Tennessee, **13:820–824**

See also specific dioceses and archdioceses

Tennyson, Alfred, 1:762

Tenon, M., 7:131

Tenorio, Gonzalo, **13:824–825**

Tents of meeting, 3:466, 4:607, **13:825**

  altars, 1:320

  anointing, 1:477

  ark of the covenant, 1:690

  expiatory sacrifice, 13:159

  Shekinah, 13:77–78

  showbread, 13:88

  Yom Kippur, 1:838

Teoctist Arăpaşu (Romanian Orthodox Church Patriarch), 10:692

Tep Im Sotha, 2:902

Tepehuanes Jesuit Mission (Mexico), 9:709

Tephillah, 2:290

Tepl Monastery (Prague), 7:144, **13:825–826**

Ter Doest Abbey (Lissewege, Belgium), **13:826**

Ter Khatchik I Archaruni (Armenian Catholicos), 1:453

Teresa, M. Angeline (Mother), 3:128

Teresa Benedicta of the Cross, St. *See* Stein, Edith, St.

Teresa Margaret of the Sacred Heart, St., 3:128, **13:826**

Teresa of Avila, St., 2:109, 5:167, **13:826–830**, *827, 828*

  Alphonsus Liguori, St., 1:310

  Álvarez, Baltasar, 1:325

  Angela of Foligno, Bl., 1:412

  Anne of Jesus, Ven., 1:468

  Anne of St. Bartholomew, Bl., 1:468

  Arbiol y Diez, Antonio, 1:629

  Báñez, Domingo, 2:49–50

  Carmelite spirituality, 3:130, 135, 139

  contemplation, 4:204, 205, 206, 209

  Counter Reformation, 3:611

  critical editions, 13:122

  Discalced Carmelites, 3:127, 142–143, 144–145, 611

  as Doctor of the Church, 11:32

  enclosure, 3:126

  Francis of Osuna, 5:872

  gift of tears, 4:45

  Gratian, Jerome, 6:422

  John of the Cross, St., 7:987

  life of, by Ribera, 12:220

  mental prayer, 11:599

  mystical phenomena, 10:106

  mystical prose, 10:118

  prayer of quiet, 11:866

  reform, 4:310, 311, 313

  spiritual direction, 4:762

  spirituality, 13:447

  universal call to holiness, 7:6

  Vita Christi, 8:853

Teresa of Calcutta. *See* Mother Teresa of Calcutta

Teresa of Firenze. *See* Manetti, Teresa Maria della Croce, Bl.

Teresa of Florence. *See* Manetti, Teresa Maria della Croce, Bl.

Teresa of Jesus (Mother). *See* Gerhardinger, Karolina Elizabeth Frances, Bl.

Teresian Institute, 11:564–565, **13:830**

Teresian Sisters, 12:587

Terill, Anthony, **13:830–831**

Terme, Jean Pierre Éteinne, 4:293, 12:31

Termehr, Josephine (Mother Xavier), 5:889

Terminorum musicae diffinitorium (Tinctoris), 14:87

Términos de origen costarricense que se encuentran en documentos de los siglos XVII y XVIII (Thiel), 14:1

Terms (logic), 1:949, 4:609–611, **13:831**

Ternovskey, Peter, 12:434

Terreni, Guido, 3:133

Territorial churches, 6:181

Terrorism, 1:153, 286, 10:319–320

Tertio Millennio Adveniente (apostolic letter, John Paul II), 7:1003, 11:747, 13:692, **832–834**

Tertius (African deacon), 3:403

Tertullian (ecclesiastical writer), 3:186, 11:290, **13:834–838**, *835*

  Acts of the Martyrs, 1:93

  agape, 1:170

  anima naturaliter christiana, 1:455, 489

  Antichrist, 1:516

  Apocalypse iconography, 1:543

  apostolic succession, 1:591

  Arnobius the Elder, 1:717

  astrology, 1:812

  baptism, 2:62–63, 67, 75

  baptism and penance, 12:467

  biblical canon, 3:21, 26, 32

  Britain, 2:620

  burial, 2:699

  Canon Law, 3:37

  capital punishment, 3:85

  catechumenate, 3:250

  Catholic term, 3:274

  causality, 3:303

  Christian persecution, 12:353

  Christology, 3:560

  Church property, 3:723

  Clement I (Pope), St., 3:774

  clerical celibacy/marriage, 3:323

  Confirmation, 4:86

  consubstantiality, 4:198, 7:65

  contraception, 4:220

  corporate character of penance, 7:436

  creedal statements, 4:350, 351

  Cyprian, St., 4:457, 458

  danger of secular paideia to faith, 10:754

  demonology, 4:646

  descent of Christ into hell, 4:684

  dialectics, 4:725

  Divine judgment, 8:32

  docetism, 4:797

  Donatism, 4:863

  Easter Vigil, 5:14–15

  Ebionites, 5:31

  exegetical works, 5:509, 511–512

  exorcism, 5:551

  fish as symbol of Christ, 5:747

  following Christ, 5:788

  founder of theology in the West, 13:904

  Greco-Roman schooling, 6:430

  Holy Trinity, 14:191–192, 203

  immortality, 7:348, 349, 353

  impassibility of God, 7:358

  Latin used, 8:362

  lauds, 8:380

  libelli pacis, 8:531

  liturgical history, 8:652

  Luke's Gospel, 8:859

  martyrs and martyrdom, 4:83, 9:228–229

  military service, 9:626–627

  Montanism, 1:547, 3:186, 5:148, 9:636, 828

  morning and evening prayers, 14:462

  On Prayer, 8:413

  original sin, 5:651

  patristic theology, 10:967

  penance, 4:225

  penitential controversy, 11:72–73

  philosophy, 10:958–959

  preaching, 11:607–608

  presbyters, 11:674

  priesthood, 11:698–699

THEOCRACY

refreshment (*refrigerium*), 12:26

rings, 12:248

Roman persecutions, 3:592

sabellianism, 12:462

soul, 13:342, 354

standing and kneeling, 8:648

theological use of prescription, 11:681

unity of Church, 4:28

works of charity, 3:402, 403

See also Patristic era

Teseida (Boccaccio), 2:448

Tesellated pavements, 10:1–3

Tesser, J. H. M., 3:16

Test Act (England, 1673), 5:248

Test Oaths (England, 1672-1678), 10:501

Testament (St. Clare of Assisi), 5:898

Testament (St. Francis of Assisi), 5:898

Testament, in the Bible, **13:838**

Testamentum Domini, 3:38

Testamentum Nephtali, 3:630

Testem benevolentiae (apostolic letter, Leo XIII), 1:84, 354, 356, 6:779, **13:838–839**

Testera, Jacobo de, **13:839**

Testimonia (Cyprian), 4:457, 13:37, **839**

Testimony in Israel (Teʿûdâ be-Yiśraʾēl) (Levinsohn), 6:663

Tête d'or (Claudel), 3:767–768

Tetens, J. N., 5:263

Tetragamy dispute (Byzantine Church), 1:646, 2:756–757, 786, 823, 4:174, 8:473–474

Tetragrammaton. *See* Yahweh

Tetrapla (Origen), 10:654

Tetrarch, **13:839**

Tetzel, Johann, 1:233, 8:879, 12:16, **13:839–840**

Teʿûdâ be-Yiśraʾēl (Testimony in Israel) (Levinsohn), 6:663

Teutonic Knights, **13:840–844**

castle, 13:*841*

Christian of Prussia, 3:537

Christianity in Russia, 12:419

colonization, 4:414

Conrad of Querfurt, 4:137

Knights of Columbus, 8:190

Knights of Dobrin, 8:192

Knights of the Sword merge, 8:199

Lithuania, 8:604

opposition, 8:341, 342

tyrannicide, 4:171

works of charity, 3:412

See also Knights of the Sword

Tewkesbury Abbey (Gloucestershire, England), 13:*844*, **844–845**

Texas, **13:845–847**

Catholic archives, 1:640

Congregation of Incarnate Word and Blessed Sacrament, 7:371, 372

labor issues, 8:843

Oblate Fathers of Texas, 12:676

Sisters of Charity of the Incarnate Word, 7:369–370

Sisters of Divine Providence at Our Lady of the Lake (Texas), 12:641–642

Sisters of Divine Providence of Texas, 13:182

Spanish mission, 9:716

See also specific dioceses and archdioceses

Texas Monthly v. Bullock (1989), 3:661

The Text of the New Testament (Lake), 8:297

Tezza, Luigi, Bl., **13:848**

Thābit, Zayd ibn, 11:877, 878

Thabit ibn Qurra, 12:810

Thaddeus of Parma, 1:675, 937

Thailand, 2:*657*, 671–672, 8:186, **13:849–851**, *850, 851*

Thailand, Seven Martyrs of, BB., **13:848–849**

Thaïs, St., **13:851–852**

Thales (Greek philosopher), 6:440

astrology, 1:811

atomism, 1:832, 4:958

causality, 3:297

hylozoism, 7:239

matter, 9:339

physical sciences, 12:800–801

Thalhofer, Valentin, **13:852**

Thalia (Banquet) (Arius), 10:347

Thamby, Joseph, 7:406

Thanatology, **13:852–855**

Thanet Abbey (England), 5:324

Thangbrand, 7:275

Thangmar of Hildesheim, 2:328, **13:855–856**

Thanh Thi Le, Inés, 14:497

Thanh Van Dinh, Juan-Baptist, 14:497

Thanksgiving, as an end to prayer, 11:592, 594

Thannabaur, P. J., 12:665

The Thantos Syndrome (Percy), 11:114

Thaumur, Louise, 6:528

Thayer, John, 2:553, **13:856**

Thé, Nicolás, 14:497

Theaetetus (Plato), 12:398

Theandric Acts of Christ, **13:856–857**

Theas, Pierre (Bp.), 11:45

Theater

baroque period, 2:115–116

Crusades theater, 4:401

Jesuits, 4:313

Romans, 4:893

Rousseau, Jean-Jacques, 12:392

See also Drama

Theater of the Absurd, 1:49

Theatine Sisters, 2:282

Theatines, **13:857–858**

Armenia, 1:703

church architecture, 3:703

Diana, Antonino, 4:729

founding, 2:855–856, 3:54, 610, 782, 4:310, 13:857–858

Somascans, 13:310

Theatrum crudelitatum (Verstegan), 14:460

Thebaid (Egypt), 4:686, **13:858**

La Thébaide en Amérique ou Apologie de la vie solitaire et contemplative (Rouquette), 12:391

Theban Legion, 5:438, 12:567, **13:859**

Thébaud, Augustus, **13:859**

Thebes (Egypt), 1:362

Thecla (Mother) (Teresa Merlo), 12:570

Thecla, St., **13:859–860**

Theft, 4:41–43, 5:84, 12:142–144, **13:860–861**

Theft, in the Bible, **13:861**

Theglath-Phalasar I. *See* Tiglath-Pileser I (King of Assyria)

Theiner, Augustin, **13:861–862**

Theisen, Jerome (Father), 12:553

Theism, 1:310, 12:768, **13:862–864**

See also Deism

Thelen, Bonaventure (Brother), 1:275

Thematization, process of, 13:896

Thémines, Bishop de, 11:212

Themistius (Greek rhetorician), 1:277, 670, 676, 833, 2:768, 7:510

Theobald (Abp. of Canterbury), 1:219, 2:125, 5:240, 7:984–985, 12:232, 13:*864*, **864**

Theobald, St., 3:99

Theobald IV of Champagne, 4:411

Theobald of Canossa, 12:643

Theobald of Étampes, 10:729, **13:864–865**

Theobald of Provins, St., **13:865**

Theobald of Vaux-de-Cernay, St., **13:865**

Theocentrism, 1:508, **13:865–866**

Theocracy, 3:631, 13:248, **866–867**

See also Government

NEW CATHOLIC ENCYCLOPEDIA

679

Theoctistos (Byzantine logothete), 4:474

Theoctistus, St., 5:460, 12:509

Theodard of Narbonne (Abp.), St., **13:867**

Theodatus (King of the Ostrogoths), 1:172

Theodemir (Bp.), 12:681, 683

Theoderic (Antipope). *See* Theodoric (Antipope)

Theodicy, 1:496, 780, 8:458, 13:586, **867–869**

See also Natural theology

Theodolinda (Queen of the Lombards), 1:664

Theodora (Byzantine empress, c. 497-548), **13:869–871**, *870*

Agapetus I (Pope), St., 1:172

Anthimus of Trebizond, 1:503

early life, 8:96

Justinian I, 8:101–102

Monophysitism, 1:525, 3:596, 13:123

new patriarchs, 8:97

Procopius of Caesarea, 11:738

Theodora (Byzantine empress, c. 810-862), 2:793, 821, 5:23, 7:309, 11:310, **13:871–872**

Theodora the Elder (d. 926), 1:387, 8:321, 13:869

Theodora the Younger (d. 950), 8:321, 13:869

Theodore (Antipope), **13:872**

Theodore (Bp. of Valais), St., 12:567

Theodore (Mother), 5:878

Theodore I (Pope), 2:749–750, 11:843, 844, **13:872**

Theodore I Lascaris (Byzantine Emperor), 2:760, 787

Theodore II (Pope), 12:346, **13:872–873**

Theodore II Ghesquière (Abbot), 12:533

Theodore II Lascaris (Byzantine Emperor), 1:257, 735, 2:761, 809

Theodore Ascidas (Abp. of Caesarea), 3:596, 4:191, 858, 5:587, 8:97–98, **13:873**

Theodore de Beze, 5:867

Theodore Lector, 2:797, 6:872, 13:91, **873–874**

Theodore of Canterbury, St., 3:70, 598, 5:239, **13:874**

Chad, St., 3:359

ecclesiastical meetings, 4:243

Ermenburga, St., 5:324

Hedda, St., 6:701

Theodore of Celles, 2:609, 4:377

Theodore of Gaza, 1:676, 2:762

Theodore of Mopsuestia (Bp.), 5:4, 5, 83, **13:874–876**

Adrianus, 1:130

apocatastasis, 1:548

baptism of Jesus, 2:72

catechesis, 3:228

catechumenate, 3:251

Christology controversies (patristic era), 1:119, 523, 3:365, 561

condemnation, 4:191, 192, 467

Council of Chalcedon, 3:365

Council of Orléans, 1:895

creedal statements, 4:352, 353–354

Diodore of Tarsus, 4:750, 751

exegetical works, 5:511

Julian of Eclanum, 8:48

Leontius of Byzantium, 8:502

liturgical history, 8:652

Nestorianism doctrine, 10:252–253

Nestorius, 10:14, 254

School of Antioch, 1:524, 527

Song of Songs, 13:318

theology of Christ, 7:814, 816

Three Chapters controversy, 14:63–64

works, 13:875

Theodore of Rhaithu, **13:876**

Theodore of Sykeaon, St., **13:876**

Theodore of Tarsus (Abp. of Canterbury), 1:448, 449, 2:196, 3:408, 5:14

Theodore the Studite, St., 2:794, 13:877, **877–878**

Byzantine chant, 2:742, 743, 803

Byzantine Church, 2:752

Great Lavra Rule, 10:31

hymnology, 7:242

iconoclasm, 2:753, 793, 821, 7:282, 10:915

Leo III (Pope), St., 8:480

Leo V (Byzantine Emperor), 8:473

pentarchy, 2:822

poetry, 2:804–805

Ukraine, 13:79

Theodoret (Bp. of Cyr), **13:878–879**

Adrianus, 1:130

Apollinarianism, 1:560

clerical celibacy/marriage, 3:324

condemnation, 4:191, 192, 860

Council of Chalcedon, 3:365, 561

Council of Orléans, 1:895

Cyril of Alexandria, 2:793

deposition of Nestorius, 4:467

Diatessaron, 4:731

diptychs, 4:759

ecclesiastical historiography, 6:872

editions of works, 13:168

Eutyches, 5:461

excommunication, 5:273

exegetical works, 5:511

Fathers of the Church, 5:640

historiography, 2:797

James, St., 12:681

Nestorianism, 1:391, 527

relics, 12:52

Robber Council of Ephesus, 3:363

School of Antioch, 1:524, 527

studies, 8:429

taking baptismal name practice, 10:139

Three Chapters controversy, 14:64

works, 13:878–879

Theodoric (Antipope), **13:879–880**

Theodoric Borgognoni of Lucca (Bp. of Cervia), **13:880**

Theodoric of Freiberg, 1:226, 675, 12:798, 813, **13:880–881**

Theodoric the Goth, 13:103

Theodoric the Great (King of the Ostrogoths), 3:595, 6:369, 8:92, 404, 453, 11:932, **13:881–882**

Arator, 1:627

Cassiodorus, Flavius Magnus Aurelius, 3:208

Castel Sant'Angelo, 3:212

Catholic establishment, 7:656

churches in Rome, 12:355

Ennodius' sermon in honor of, 5:265

Epiphanius of Pavia, 5:292

sarcophagus of, 12:691

Symmachus (Pope), St., 13:672

Theodoricus Teutonicus de Vriberg. *See* Theodoric of Freiberg

Theodorouych, Josaphat (Mother), 2:145

Theodosius (Monophysite Patriarch of Alexandria), 1:503, 8:97, **13:882**

Theodosius, St., 2:143

Theodosius I (Roman Emperor), 9:*334*, 12:319, 13:*884*, **884**

Ambrose, St., 1:338

Ammianus, Marcellinus, 1:361

Apollinarianism, 1:560

Arianism, 1:663

Church history, 3:594

Constantinople Council I, 4:184, 354

defensor civitatis, 4:609

divination, 4:786

ecclesiastical organization of the empire, 5:17–18

Euphrasia, St., 5:449

First Council of Constantinople, 2:780

Gratian, 6:422–423

Oracle of Delphi, 4:632

relics, 1:314

Theodosius I Boradiotes (Partriarch of Constantinople), **13:883–884**

Theodosius II (Byzantine Emperor), 12:322, **13:882–883**, *883*

Assyrian Church of the East, 1:805

Atticus of Constantinople, St., 1:839

Boniface I (Pope), St., 2:498

Celestine I (Pope), St., 3:317

clerical celibacy/marriage, 3:324

Council of Chalcedon, 3:363

Council of Ephesus, 5:273

Dioscorus (Patriarch of Alexandria), 4:756

Domnus of Antioch, 4:859–860

Nestorius exiled, 10:254

philosophical school of Constantinople, 2:820

Pulcheria, St., 11:815

Sisinnius (Pope), succession of, 13:169

Sozoman, 13:372

works of charity, 3:409

Theodosius of Palestine, St., **13:884–885**

Theodosius the Deacon, collection of, **13:885**

Theodotos Melissenos Cassiteras (Patriarch of Constantinople), 1:504, 2:753

Theodotus (Gnostic writer), **13:885**

Theodotus of Ancyra (Bp.), 1:93, **13:885–886**

Theodotus of Laodicea (Bp.), 5:451

Theodramatik (Balthasar), 2:34–35

Theoduin (Bp.), 1:498

Theodulf (Abp. of Orléans), 5:842, 6:241, 12:539, **13:886**, 14:595

Angers, 1:431

Canon Law, 3:43

Carolingian reform, 3:156, 425

Carolingian Renaissance, 3:159, 160, 425

Clement of Ireland, St., 3:799

hymns, 7:246, 253

Lediradus, 8:458

Libri carolini, 8:557

medieval Latin literature, 9:443, 444

preaching, 11:611

Theōdūs abū Qurra (Melkite Bp. of Harran), **13:886–887**

Theognis of Nicaea, 1:527, 4:181

Theognostus (Byzantine archimandrite), 1:272, **13:887**

Theogonic myths, 10:127

Theogony (Hesiod), 4:283, 5:2

Theoleptus (metropolitan of Philadelphia), **13:888**

Theologal life, 13:438

Theologia Christiana (Abelard), 1:19

Theologia Christiana dogmatico-moralis (Concina), 4:59

Theologia dogmatica catholica (Schwetz), 12:795

Theologia dogmatica et moralis ad usum seminariorum (Bailly), 12:771

Theologia dogmatica et moralis secundum ordinem Catechismi Tridentini (Alexandre), 1:267

Theologia dogmatica orthodoxa (Palmieri), 10:812

Theologia mentis et cordis (Contenson), 4:211

Theologia moralis (Busenbaum), 12:766

Theologia moralis (Lacroix), 8:273

Theologia moralis (Lehmkuhl), 8:455

Theologia moralis (Reiffenstuel), 12:34

Theologia moralis (St. Alphonsus Liguori), 1:310–311, 14:48, 51

Theologia moralis in quinque libros partita (Laymann), 8:419

Theologia moralis super decalogum et sacramentia (Sporer), 13:461

Theologia moralis universa ad mentem S. Alphonsi (Scavini), 12:726

Theologia naturalis (Liber creaturarum) (Raymond of Sabunde), 11:937

Theologia platonica (Ficino), 5:710, 12:121

Theologia scholastica (Tanner), 13:751

Theologia scholastico-dogmatica luxta mentem D. Thomae (Gotti), 14:51

Theologia Thomistica (Xarrié), 12:773

Theologia thomistico-scholastica Salisburgensis (Mezger), 14:51

Theologia Wirceburgensis (Wirceburgenses), 14:776

Theologiae graecorum patrum vindicatae circa universam materiam gratiae libri III (Habert), 6:595

Theologiae Jesuitarum praecipua capita (Chemnitz), 3:463

Theologiae Moralis adv. Laxiores probabilistas pars prior (Baron), 2:104–105

Theologiae Moralis Institutiones (Génicot), 6:135

Theologiae moralis principia, responsa, consilia (Vermeersch), 14:452

Theologiae moralis summa bipartita (Baron), 2:104–105

Theologiae verae christianae apologia (An Apology for the True Christian Divinity: Being an Explanation and Vindication of the People Called Quakers) (Barclay), 2:97, 6:4

Theologians, 11:76, 13:780

See also specific theologians

Theologica eclectica (Taylor, Jeremy), 13:770

Theologica Germanica (treatise, anonymous), **13:888**

Theologica scholastica secundum viam et doctrinam diviger (Mezger), 12:765

Theologicae regulae (Alan of Lille), 1:65

A Theological Anthropology (Balthasar), 9:814

Theological censure, 10:453

Theological College of the Sulpician (Washington, DC), 13:*600*

Theological conclusions, 10:454, **13:888–889**

Theological Gallicanism, 6:75, 77

Theological Investigations (Rahner), 10:667

Theological methods, 13:913

"Theological Oath" (1813), 10:502

Theological Orations (St. Gregory of Nazianzus), 6:515–516

Theological Seminary of Virginia, 5:297

Theological Studies (periodical), 10:68, 433

Theological symbolism, **13:669–671**

Theological terminology, **13:889–891**

Theologically certain notes, 10:454

Theologie der Hoffnung (Moltmann), 13:925

Theologie der Vorzeit (Kleutgen), 12:774

Theologie moralis decalogalis et sacramentalis per modum conferentiarum casibus practicis illustrata (Elbel), 5:143

La Théologie naturelle (Yves de Paris), 14:898

Théologie sacramentaire (Theology of the Sacraments) (Pourrat), 11:564

Theologik (Balthasar), 2:34–35

Die theologische Lehre über die Verträge (Schwane), 12:793

Theologische Quartalschrift (Schanz), 12:729, 14:234

Theologischen Jugendschriften (Hegel), 6:705

Theologisches Literaturblatt (newspaper), 12:181

Theologisches Wörterbuch zum Neuen Testament (Kittel), 8:186, 14:234

Theology, **13:891–902**

  accident, 1:64–65

  adoptionism, 10:252

  Advent, 1:134

  African American Catholics, 1:160, 162

  Anointing of the Sick, 1:480–484

  anthropomorphism, 1:512

  Apostles, 1:572–573

  articles of faith, 1:764

  ascension of Jesus Christ, 1:771–772

  Austrian manual of, 8:188

  Canon Law, 3:49–50

  catechesis, 3:232

  Christian philosophy, 3:540, 541

  concept of transcendental multitude, 10:59

  conscience, 4:141–146

  conservatism and liberalism, 4:163

  death of God, 4:583–586

  deconstructionism, 4:594–595

  definition, 9:849, 870

  demons, 4:646–650

  demonstration, 4:653

  diaconate, 4:552–553

  disposition, 4:778

  Divine revelation, 13:914

  early Church, 5:339–340

  Ecumenical dialogues, 5:78–79

  final causality, 5:727–728

  function, 8:764

  genetic technologies, 7:178

  historical interpretation, 8:177

  human soul, 13:352–353

  humility, 7:205–207

  immortality, 7:352–354

  Jansenist mentality, 7:719

  justification, 8:81–84

  kalām, 8:110

  kerygma, 8:158

  loci theologici, 8:743

  narrative, 10:151–154

  natural law doctrine and contemporary, 10:193–195

  nature, 10:211–213

  obedience, 10:506–508

  omnipotence of God, 10:591–592

  omniscience, 10:596–599

  ontologism, 10:604

  optimism, 10:614

  original justice, 10:663–664

  original sin, 10:665–671

  Parousia, 10:900–902

  religious studies, 13:229

  retrieval and reinterpretation, 8:545

  revelation, 13:892

  science, 9:568–569

  scripture, 13:902–913

  17th-18th century overview, 3:613–615

  sobornost, 8:165

  Spanish hegemony, 13:392

  substance, 13:579

  symbols, 13:663

  traducianism and generationism, 14:140

  transubstantiation, 14:158–160

  wisdom, 8:743, 14:786–787

  See also Angelology; Biblical theology; Christocentrism; Christology; Death, theology of; Dogmatic theology; Person, in theology; Positive theology; Sacramental theology; Theology, speculative; *specific issues*; *specific theologians*

Theology, history of, 8:743, **13:902–918**

Theology, influence of Greek philosophy on, 8:758–764, **13:918–921**

Theology, natural, **13:921–923**

Theology, speculative, 4:813–814, 818–820, 13:894, 898–900, 903–904, 907

  Baader, Franz Xaver von, 2:1

  Benoit, Pierre, 2:285

  Clement of Alexandria, St., 3:799

  mysteries, 10:84–85

  mysticism, 13:908

  Origenism, 10:656, 657–659

  patristic, 10:965–966

  positive theology, 13:900–901

  Thomism, 13:906–907

Theology and prayer, **13:923–924**

Theology and sociology, **13:924–925**

Theology of History (Balthasar), 6:891

Theology of Hope, **13:925–927**

Theology of Liberation, A (Gutiérrez), 10:623, 11:166

Theology of Proclamation (Rahner), 11:892

Theology of Saint Luke, The (Conzelmann), 10:303

Theology of the New Testament (Bultmann, tr. by Grobel), 5:523

Theology of the Sacraments (Théologie sacramentaire) (Pourrat), 11:564

Theonas of Alexandria, St., **13:927**

Theonilla (martyr), 3:770

Theopaschite controversy, 7:262, 8:92, 96

Theopaschite formula, 3:596, 4:191

Theopempt (Metropolitan of Kiev), 14:272

Theophane of Nicaea, 2:828

Theophanes (9th c. monk), 13:928

Theophanes (Byzantine religious), **13:927–928**

Theophanes III (Metropolitan of Nicaea), 2:827, 13:928

Theophanes Continuatus, 2:798

Theophanes Graptos, St., 13:927–928

Theophanes Nonnus, 2:799

Theophanes of Medaia, 13:928

Theophanes Siciliotes, 13:928

Theophanes the Confessor, St., 8:473, **13:929**

Theophania (Eusebius of Caesarea), 5:452

Theophanies, **13:929–930**

Theophano (Byzantine princess), 7:926, 927

Theophanu (Holy Roman empress), 10:714

Theophilanthropy, 5:853, 975, **13:930**

Theophilos of Edessa, 1:172

Theophilus (Benedictine writer), **13:930–931**

Theophilus (Bp. of Caesarea), 2:846–847

Theophilus (Byzantine Emperor), 2:753, 7:282, **13:931–932**

Theophilus (Roswitha of Gandersheim), 12:389

Theophilus of Alexandria (Patriarch), 5:279, 292, **13:932**

  Anastasius I (Pope), St., 1:387

  Arianism, 1:268

  Cyril of Alexandria, 4:465

  Innocent I (Pope), St., 7:468

  John Chrysostom, St., 3:595, 7:946–947

  Moses the Black, St., 10:8

  Origen controversy, 12:404

  Synod of the Oak, 10:491–492

  transmigration of souls, 14:157

  works, 13:932

Theophilus of Antioch (Bp.), St., 2:172, 3:32, 228, 274, 560, **13:932–933**

Theophilus of Corte, St., **13:933**

Theophilus Protospatharios, 2:808

Theophoros, Christ as, 1:391

Theophrastus (Greek philosopher), 1:668, 680, 684

  biology, 2:400

  Boethius, 1:673

logic, 8:748–749

unity of intellect, 7:510

Theophylactus (Abp. of Orchrid, Yugoslavia), **13:934**

Theophylactus (Count of Tusculani), **13:933–934**

Theophylactus (Metropolitan of Bulgaria), 2:824

Theophylactus (Patriarch), 2:458

Theophylactus (Roman politician), 1:387, 8:321, 321–322, 13:15

Theophylactus Simocatta, 2:798

Theorema theologiae angelicae Beneditino-Thomistica (Pley), 12:765

Theoremata metaphysicorum (Martini), 12:768

Theory, 1:949, 8:544, 10:20–21, **13:934**

See also Knowledge, theories of

Theory of Evolution Judged by Reason and Faith, The (Ruffini), 12:402

Theory of Justice, A (Rawl), 10:205

Theory of the unconditioned, 1:183

Theosevia (religion), 6:459

Theosis, 4:237

Theosophy, 1:512, 8:539, 12:660, **13:934–936**

Theotecnus (Bp. of Caesarea), 10:800

Theotocopuli, Domenico. *See* El Greco (painter)

Theotokos, 5:273, 10:13, 252–253, **13:936–937**

Armenia, 1:700

Byzantine theology, 2:766, 823

Cassian, John, 3:206

Celestine I (Pope), St., 3:317

Christology, 3:561

Council of Chalcedon, 3:365

Council of Ephesus, 10:14

Cyril of Alexandria, 1:391, 3:317, 4:465–466

doctrine, 10:252–253

false doctrines regarding, 10:13–14

icons, 7:278, 279, *279*

Lawrence of Brindisi, 8:406

liturgical commenorations, 10:15

mystery, 10:14–15

Nestorianism denial, 10:252–253

Origen, 10:657

title given to Mary, 10:14

See also Christology controversies (patristic era); Mary, Blessed Virgin; Mother of God

Theotokos, a Theological Encyclopedia of the Blessed Virgin Mary, 5:208

Theotonius, St., 12:673, **13:937**

Therapeutae (Egypt), 1:776, **13:937–938**

Thérèse de Lisieux, St., 3:128, 130, 138, 7:207, **13:938–939**

Thérèse Desqueyroux (Mauriac), 5:219

Thérèse of St. Augustin (Mother), 4:44

Thérèse of St. Ignatius, Bl., 4:44

Thérèse of the Child Jesus. *See* Thérèse de Lisieux, St.

Thérèse of the Heart of Mary, Bl., 4:44

Theresia, Bl., **13:939–940**

Therry, John Joseph, 1:900, 13:*940*, **940**

Thervingi. *See* Visigoths

Thesaurus casuum conscientiae (Sayer), 12:716

Thesaurus indicus (Avendaño), 1:932

Thesaurus silviniacensis (Mesgrigny), 13:371

Theses on Feuerbach (Marx), 5:707

Theses theologicae (Lessius), 8:518

Thessalonians, Epistles to the, 5:304–305, **13:940–942**

Antichrist in, 1:515

authorship, 4:704

baptism, 2:60

charisms, 3:578

Church, 3:578–579, 582–583

edification, 5:85

escatological events, 13:40

grace, 6:382

heaven, 6:685

human sexuality, 13:48

Kingdom of God, 8:174

Lord's Prayer, 8:783, 784

Parousia, 5:216, 7:354, 10:895–896, 898

peace, 11:50

Silas (Silvanus), 13:119

sin, 13:145

spirit, 13:425

spirituality, 13:438

Word of God, 13:438

Thessalonica, massacre of (390), 1:338

Thessalonica, Treaty of (1148), 1:126

Thessalonica Basilica, 1:171

Thessalonicensis, 3:40

Thetford Priory (Norwich, England), **13:942**

Theuderic (King of Burgundy), 3:864

Thevarparampil, Augustine (Father), 7:406

Thévenet, Claudine, St., 12:101, **13:942**

Thévenet, Marie Saint-Ignace. *See* Thévenet, Claudine, St.

Thi Dang Le, José, 14:497

Thi Van Truong, Pedro, 14:497

Thibault, Philip, 3:137, 143

Thiel, Bernardo Augusto (Bp. of Costa Rica), 4:289, **14:1**

Thiemann, Ronald, 5:830

Thiemo, Bl., 12:670, **14:1–2**

Thien van Tran, Tomás, 14:497

Thiering, Barbara, 4:563

Thierry, Augustin, 5:703

Thierry de Fribourg. *See* Theodoric of Freiberg

Thierry of Chartres, **14:2–3**

Bernard Silvester, 2:317

Boethius, 2:457

cathedral and episcopal schools, 3:441

Clarenbaud of Arras, 3:761

number symbolism, 3:674

School of Chartres, 12:758

Thierry of Fleury, **14:3**

Thiéry, Armand, 12:776

Thietmar (Bp. of Merseburg), 1:462, 9:451, **14:3**

Thill, Frank A., 3:287

Thils, Gustave, 1:596, 6:890

Thimelby, Gabriel, 5:237

Thin Trong Pham, Luca, 14:497

Things, 1:60, 4:780, **14:4–6**

Thinking with the Church, Rules for (St. Ignatius of Loyola), 14:6

Thiofrid of Echternach, 7:248, **14:6**

Thionville (Diedenhofen), Councils of, 1:248, **14:7**

Third Collection (Lonergan), 8:773–774

Third General Conference of the Latin American Episcopate. *See* Puebla (Mexico) Conference (1979)

Third Isaiah. *See* Trito-Isaiah (anonymous poet-prophet)

Third Messenger (Manichaeism), 9:112

Third Order Carmelite Sisters of Saint Teresa, Manetti, Teresa Maria della Croce, founding, 9:106

Third Order Dominican Sisters, 9:589

Third Order of St. Francis. *See* Franciscans, Third Order Secular

"Third Rome" (Moscow), 10:694–695, 12:423

Third Spiritual Alphabet (Francis of Osuna), 3:135

Third Unitarian Church (Chicago), 3:716

Thirkeld, Richard, Bl., 5:228, **14:7**

Thirlby, Thomas (Bp. of Ely), 5:180

Thirteen Days Devotion, 5:874

Thirteen Principles (Judaism), 8:8

Thirty Years' War (1618-48), 3:612, **14:8**

Altenburg Abbey, 1:321

Thirty Years' War (1618-48) (continued)
  Austria, 1:912
  background and impact, 14:10–11
  Bohemian War (1618-23) of, 4:483, 14:8–9
  Catholic revival, 4:313–314
  Charles I, 3:432
  church architecture, 3:706
  Comenius, John Amos, 4:1, 2
  Corbey Abbey, 4:281
  Danish War (1625-29) of, 14:9–10
  Edict of Restitution, 12:144
  Ferdinand II, 5:688
  Germany, 6:181–182
  Hapsburgs, 6:639
  Swedish Intervention (1630-35), 14:10
  Swedish-French War (1635-48), 14:10
  See also Westphalia, Peace of
Thirty-Nine Articles, 4:80, **14:7–8**
  Anglican orders problem, 1:434
  Anglican protest, 5:188
  Anglican Reformation, 1:443, 3:608, 609
  Anglo-Catholic interpretation of, 5:795
  apocrypha, 3:27
  Augsburg Confession, 1:850
  Donne, John, 4:868
  Episcopal Church (U.S.), 5:298
  Westminster Assembly, 4:79
Thiry, Paul, 3:716
Thmuis (Egypt), **14:11**
Tho, Martin, 14:497
Tholuck, Friedrich A. G., 5:322, 467, 12:726
Thomaeus, Leonicus, 1:676
Thomar (Tomar) Monastery (Portugal), **14:11**
Thomas (17th c. Irish martyr), 7:581
Thomas (17th c. Japanese martyr), 7:734
Thomas (King of Bosnia), 2:459
Thomas, Apostle, St., **14:11–12**
  Afghanistan, 1:153
  India, 7:392, 394
  legendary missionary to China, 3:489
  mystic's knowledge of God, 10:113
  notion of order, 10:628–629
  omniscience and study, 10:599
  shrine, 13:94
  Syro-Malabar Church founding, 13:711
  transcendentals, 14:5
  truth, 14:224–225, 226

Thomas, Bradwardine, **14:29**
Thomas, Evangeline (Sister), 1:639
Thomas, John, 3:527
Thomas, Joseph, 3:350
Thomas, L., 1:170
Thomas, M. M., 7:405
Thomas À Kempis, 5:774, **14:12–13**, *13*
  Amort, Eusebius, 1:363
  Bernard of Clairvaux, 2:311
  Brethren of the Common Life, 2:607
  Canons Regular of St. Augustine, 3:69
  Devotio Moderna, 4:708, 12:767
  mysticism, 3:605
  spiritual direction, 4:762
Thomas I (Bp. of Syro-Malankara Church), 13:718–719
Thomas II of York, **14:39–40**
Thomas Agni, **14:13**
Thomas Aquinas, St., 5:424, 7:*424*, **14:13–22**, *16*
  abortion, 1:29
  Abrabanel, Isaac, 1:36
  absolute, 1:41–42
  abstraction, 1:45, 47, 48, 12:820, 13:579
  academic freedom, 1:51
  accident, 1:60–61, 62, 63, 65
  acedia, 1:67
  act, 1:73–75
  action and passion, 1:77, 78, 79
  action at a distance, 1:80
  active life, 1:83
  Adam, 1:105
  adoration, 12:85
  Adoro Te Devote, 1:120
  aesthetics, 1:142, 145
  agility, 1:176–177
  Albert the Great, St., 1:224, 226
  alchemy, 1:239
  Alexandre, Noël, 1:267
  Alphonsus Liguori, St., 1:311
  ambition, 1:334
  analogy, 1:372, 374–379, 377–379
  analysis and synthesis, 1:381–382
  angelology, 1:414–415, 420, 422
  Anima Christi, 1:455
  Anointing of the Sick, 1:482
  Anselm of Canterbury, St., 1:496
  Antoninus, St., 1:537
  anxiety, 1:540
  apologetics, 1:564
  apophatic theology, 1:568
  Apostles' Creed, 1:577

  Arabian philosophy, 1:622, 623, 672, 674
  aristocracy, 1:667
  Aristotelianism, 1:670, 675
  art, 1:744
  articles of faith, 1:764
  Ascension of Jesus Christ, 1:772
  aseity, 1:779–780
  Assumption of Mary, 1:800
  assumptus homo theology, 1:802
  astrology, 1:813
  Athanasian Creed, 1:815
  atomism, 1:833, 834
  atonement, 1:837
  attributes of being, 14:152
  attrition, 1:842–843
  Augustinianism, 1:878
  avarice, 1:928, 929
  Avicebron, 1:939
  Avicenna, 1:941
  Bartholomew of Lucca, 2:126
  beatific vision, 2:169, 170, 171–172
  beatitudes in Christian life, 2:178–179
  beauty, 2:185
  being, 2:206–209
  Bernard Lombardi, 2:306
  Bernard of Auvergne, 2:306
  Bessarion, Cardinal, 2:341
  biblical canon, 3:26
  biblical catenae, 3:258–259
  biblical hermeneutics, 6:792–793
  biblical inspiration, 7:495–496
  biblical theology, 2:382
  Biel, Gabriel, 2:391
  bilocation, 2:396
  bishops, 2:418
  blasphemy, 2:434
  Boethius, 1:673, 2:457
  Brentano, Franz, 2:604
  Byzantine theology, 2:826, 837
  Canon Law, 3:50
  canonization, 14:22–23
  canonization and vindication, 14:47
  "capital grace" doctrine, 11:986
  capital punishment, 3:87
  Carmelite spirituality, 3:137
  Cassian, John, 3:207
  casuistry, 3:219–220
  catechesis, 3:232, 241
  Catechism of the Council of Trent, 3:239
  Catherine of Siena, St., 3:273

causa finalis or *motivum* of action, 10:27

causality, 3:298–299
    agents, 1:175
    analogy, 1:376
    Divine causality, 3:303, 304
    efficient causality, 1:78
    first cause, 3:308–309
    formal cause, 3:300
    substance, 3:301

certitude, 3:351, 354

chance, 3:376

charisms, 3:391

charity, 1:83, 3:395, 396–400, 8:826

chastity, 3:444, 8:872

choice, 3:520–521

Christian philosophy, 3:540, 541

Church-State relations, 1:675, 3:637

civil authority, 1:921

classification of the sciences, 12:819–820

cogitative power, 3:823, 824

commentary by Rubio, Antonio, 12:399

common good, 4:18

communion of saints, 4:36

compatibility of Casel's doctrine, 10:99

Complutenses, 4:45

concept/conceptualism, 4:51, 52, 53

conformity, 4:93

connatural knowledge, 8:205

conscience, 4:144–145, 148–149

consciousness, 4:152

consent, 4:158–159

consequentialism, 4:159, 160

conservation, 4:161, 162

contemplation, 4:204, 205–206, 207

Contenson, Guillaume de, 4:211

continence, 4:211

contingency, 4:213, 5:504

continuum, 4:215

contradiction, 4:223

contrition-attrition distinction, 4:226, 227–230

contumely vs. derision, 4:677

conversion, 4:240

Corpus Christi feast, 4:272

correctoria, 4:274–278

cosmological argument, 4:285–287

David of Dinant, 4:541

definition, 4:610

degrees of ecstasy, 5:60

democracy, 4:639–640

demonology, 4:648

demonstration, 4:653

descent of Christ into hell, 4:685

devotion, 4:708–709

dialectics, 4:727

distinction, 4:779

Divine concurrence, 4:71–73

Divine indwelling, 7:442, 443

division, 4:793–794

docility, 4:797

dogma as term, 4:811

double effect principle, 4:881

double truth theory, 4:882

doubt, 4:883

dreams, 4:904, 905

drunkenness, 4:911

dualism, 4:915

dulia, 4:932

Durandus of Saint-Pourçain, 4:947

ecclesiastical approval, 14:22–24

empiricism, 5:197

end of the world, 5:216

envy, 5:269

epikeia, 5:290

epistemology, 5:301–304

eschatology, 5:344

essence and existence, 5:361, 364–367, 534–536, 539

eternity, 5:381, 383

ethics, 5:389–390

Eucharist, 1:65, 471, 5:424, 425

eudaemonism, 5:439–440

eutrapelia (recreation), 5:461

exemplarism, 5:525–526

existence of first unmoved mover, 10:21, 24

existential metaphysics, 5:539–540

experience, 5:554, 555

expiation, 5:565

expositions of Aristotle, 14:26

extrinsicism, 5:571

faith, 3:357, 5:597, 598

faith and beliefs, 2:222, 223

Farges, Albert, 5:624

Farrell, Walter, 5:631

Ferrariensis, 5:693

final causality, 5:724, 727–728

final perseverance, 11:133, 134

finite being, 5:730–731

first principles, 5:745

following of Christ, 5:789

freedom and will, 5:929, 935–936, 938

freedom of conscience, 4:148–149

freedom of religion, 5:947–949

friendship, 6:8

friendship with God, 6:11

fruits of the Holy Spirit, 7:46

fundamental option, 6:26

Garrigou-Lagrange, Réginald, 6:102

generation, 5:718

Giles of Rome, 1:888, 6:220–221

glorified body, 6:242–243

good, 6:348–349

good works, 6:358

grace, 3:390, 533, 6:387–389, 393, 402

grace, state of, 6:410

grace and human freedom, 8:772–773

grace and nature, 6:411

habit, 6:598, 599–600

habitual sin, 13:162

happiness, 2:170

hell, 6:727

hellfire, 6:728

Henry II, 5:788

Hervaeus Natalis, 6:659

Holy Orders as sacrament, 7:38

Holy Spirit, baptism in, 7:45

Holy Spirit, gifts of, 7:48

Holy Trinity, 1:86, 14:196–197, 205

hominisation, 7:64

honor, 7:78

hope, 7:92, 94, 95, 101

human knowledge of Christ, 7:819

human will, 14:722

humanism, 7:194, 198

humility, 7:206–207

hylomorphism, 7:238

hymns, 7:249, 253

idea, 7:293–294

idealism, 7:297

identity, 7:303

identity principle, 7:304

ignorance, 7:315

illumination, 7:320

images, veneration of, 7:325–326

imagination, 12:913

immanence, 7:340

immortality, 7:349

immutability of God, 7:355–356, 358–359

impenetrability, 7:362

incest, 7:377–378

incommunicability, 7:379

indifferent acts, 7:420–421

individuation, 7:425–426

indulgences, 7:437

ineffability of God, 7:445–446

Thomas Aquinas, St. (continued)

infinity, 7:458–459

infinity of God, 7:460–461

innatism, 5:743

intellect, 7:507, 508

intellection, 8:204

intellectualism, 7:514

intelligible species, 13:408–409

intention and species, 13:408

intentionality, 7:517–519

intuition, 7:533, 534

involuntarity, 7:539–540

irrationalism, 7:586

jealousy, 7:748

John Baconthorp, 7:940

joy, 7:1059

judgment, 8:24–25

justice of God, 8:72

justification, 9:511–512

justification and merit, 8:83

just-war tradition, 14:636

Kantianism and Maréchal, 8:127

Kant's ideas compared, 8:124

knowledge, 8:200–201

acquisition of, 8:208

intellectual, 12:795–796

principles, 5:744

theories of, 8:216–217

knowledge of Christ, 7:829

knowledge of principles, 12:796

Latin Averroism, 1:670, 933, 935, 936

Latin use, 8:364

Lauda Sion salvatorem, 8:377–379

law, 8:390, 391

lay confession, 8:412

Liber de causis, 8:533

liberal arts, 8:537–538

lifelong learning, 5:95

light of glory, 2:174–175

living God, 8:572

location, 8:742

logical relations, 12:43

love, 8:830

luck, 8:848

lying, 8:900

Maimonides, 1:673

man, concept of, 9:90–91

man, natural end of, 9:98–99

Mariology, 9:170

marriage, 1:151

master-servant relationship, 13:208

mathematics, 9:326

matter, 9:343

medieval Latin literature works, 9:460

merits of ontological argument, 10:602

metaphysics, 5:745, 9:551–552

methodology, 9:565

moderate realism, 11:943

modesty, 9:758–759

monarchy, 9:781

moral circumstances, 3:742

moral theology, 5:394, 9:862

morals, definition of, 9:850

mystery of God, 6:283–284

mystical theology, 13:434

mysticism prose of, 10:118, 822

natural law, 10:179, 181, 184, 185, 186–191, 202

natural theology, 13:921–922

nature, 13:618

necessity, 10:225

necessity of the Incarnation, 7:375–376

nonbeing, 10:417

notion of truth, 14:223, 231

noumena concept, 10:463

ontological perfection, 11:118

ordination, 7:39

origin of life, 8:576, 577

participation, 10:907–910

patristic thought on image of God, 10:962

penance, 11:70

person, 11:146, 147

personality, 11:155

Peter of Bergamo, 11:197

phantasm, 11:225–226

philosophy of nature, 10:209, 11:305

physical evils, 5:489

physical laws, 11:315

physical premotion, 11:669, 670, 671

pietas element of love for fatherland, 10:956

place, 11:401–402

place of God in philosophy, 6:309–310

pleasure, 11:418

Polemiccal works, 14:27

political authority, 13:239–240

possibility, 11:551, 552

potency, 11:556–557

potency and act, 11:558–559

power of generative action, 10:14

prayer, 11:593

preaching, 11:627

predestination, 11:647, 651

predetermination, 11:658, 659

priesthood, 11:701–702

primacy of Christ, 7:836

private property, 13:254

privation, 11:722, 723

professorships, 14:17–18, 19–21

proofs for the existence of God, 6:298–305, 315–317

propassions of Christ, 11:754

prophecy, 11:763

proportionality, 11:767

providence of God, 11:782–783

prudence, 11:789–792

psychology, 11:803, 805–806

pure acts, 11:821

pure nature, 11:823–824

pure spirits, 13:423

purgatory, 11:827

quiddity, 11:864

redemption, 11:985, 988

reflection, 12:1–2

Reginald of Peperino, 12:30

relation, 12:43–44

relics, 12:54–55

rhetoric, 12:212

Romano of Rome, 12:340

Roselli, Salvatore Maria, 12:380–381

sacerdotium et regnum, 11:700

sacramental theology, 12:468–470, 13:671

Sacraments, 1:925

sacrifice, 12:516–517

sanctity, 7:2

scholars of, 8:230

scholastic education, 5:90

scholasticism, 12:767–779

science, 12:795

self, concept of, 12:882

sense knowledge, 4:22, 12:910

senses, 12:912

sensibles, 12:915

sexual relations, 8:872, 873–874, 875

Siger of Brabant, 13:113

similarity, 13:126

Simon, Yves René Marie, 13:128

simony defined, 13:135

simple apprehension, 1:604, 605

sin, mortal and venial, 13:151, 155

social vs. general justice, 13:242

society, 13:276, 277

society (church as), 13:285

soul, 13:334–335, 344, 355

soul-body relationship, 13:357–358

speculative theology, 13:906–907

speculative-practical cognition, 3:825, 826

spiritual discernment, 4:765–766

spiritual life, 13:433, 446

spiritual perfection, 11:120–121

spirituality, 13:453

spontaneous generation, 13:460

state, nature of, 13:253

subsistence, 13:571–572, 574

substance, 13:575–577, 576

substantial change, 13:580–581

supernatural, 13:617

teaching of theology, 13:923–924

temperament, 13:793

temperance, 13:794–795

temptation, 13:812–813

Ten Commandments, 4:8

theft, 13:860

theodicy, 13:868

theological application of music, 10:72

theological mysteries, 10:83

theology of Church, 3:581–582, 586–588

transcendentals, 14:150

transubstantiation doctrine, 14:158–159

Trinitarian processions, 11:734–735

two natures of Christ, 7:818

tyrannicide, 14:256

understanding, 14:293–294

understanding faith, 13:894

unicity thesis, 5:817

union between God and the created intellect, 2:175

unity of intellect, 7:511–512

universals, 14:324

virtue, 14:549

virtue of justice, 8:67

vision of God, 4:690–691

voluntarity, 14:584

war, 4:150

will and willing, 14:722

wisdom, 14:785

words, 14:836

works and English translations, 14:24–28

works of charity, 1:301, 302

See also Neoscholasticism and Neothomism; *Summa theologiae* (Aquinas); Thomism

Thomas Aquinas and Radical Aristotelianism (Van Steenberghen), 14:387

Thomas Association, 5:631

Thomas Bellaci, Bl., **14:29**

Thomas Corsini, Bl., **14:30**

Thomas de S. Jacinto, Bl., 7:734

Thomas del S. Rosario, Bl., 7:733

Thomas Gallus of Vercelli, 2:184, **14:30**

Thomas Hélye, Bl., **14:30–31**

Thomas Jorz, **14:31**

Thomas Magister, 2:773, 810

Thomas Netter of Walden. *See* Netter, Thomas

Thomas of Bayeux, **14:31**, 894

Thomas of Brotherton, 10:421

Thomas of Buckingham, **14:31**

Thomas of Bungey, **14:32**

Thomas of Cantelupe, St., 5:242, **14:32**

Thomas of Cantimpré, 9:462, **14:32–33**

Thomas of Celano, 4:742, 5:737, 871, 898, 8:50, **14:33**

Thomas of Charmes, 12:767

Thomas of Claudiopolis (Bp.), 7:280

Thomas of Claxton, **14:33–34**

Thomas of Cobham, **14:34**

Thomas of Corbridge, **14:34**

Thomas of Eccleston, 5:899, **14:35**

Thomas of Farfa, St., 5:623–624, **14:35**

Thomas of Jesus (De Andrada), 1:889, 3:146, **14:35**

Thomas of Jesus (Díaz Sanchez de Avila), 3:145, 4:206, **14:36**

Thomas of London. *See* Becket, Thomas, St.

Thomas of Marleberge, 5:487

Thomas of Pavia, 12:288, **14:36**

Thomas of Štítné, 7:230

Thomas of Strassburg, 1:875, 879, 883, 888, **14:37**

Thomas of Sutton, 4:275–276, 5:818, **14:37**, 45

Thomas of Todi, 11:619

Thomas of Tolentino, Bl., 10:557, **14:38**

Thomas of Villanova, St., 1:236, 888, **14:38**

Thomas of Wilton, 1:937, **14:39**

Thomas of York, 1:878, 2:185, 10:72, 12:760, **14:39**

Thomas v. Review Board (1981), 3:663

Thomas Waleys, **14:40**

Thomasius, Christian, 3:174, 5:47, 255, 262, 10:183, 14:844

Thomasius, Gottfried, 5:323

Thomassin (Louis d'Eynac), 12:765, **14:40**, *41*

Thomism, **14:40–57**
  16th century renewal, 9:862–863
  19th century revival, 12:394, 671
  abstraction, 1:45–46

accident, 1:60–61, 62

act, 1:73–74

action and passion, 1:77

aesthetics, 1:145–146

Aeterni patris, 1:74, 147, 592, 678–679, 3:624, 12:774

Alamanni, Cosmo, 1:204

Albert the Great, St., 1:226

Alexandre, Noël, 1:268

Álvarez, Diego, 1:326

analogy, 1:372–373, 378–379

apologetics, 1:566

appetite, 1:600–602

Arabian philosophy, 1:672

Aristotelianism, 1:674

aseity, 1:779–780

Augustinianism, 1:883

Bernard of Auvergne, 2:306

Bernard of Trille, 2:317

Billot, Louis, 2:395

Billuart, Charles René, 2:396

Blondel, Maurice, 2:441

Cajetan (Tommaso de Vio), 2:854, 3:588

Capreolus, John, 3:92–93

Carmelites, 3:136, 137, 139, 14:46

Cathrein, Viktor, 3:294

causality, 3:304–305

Chenu, Marie-Dominique, 3:466

Chesterton, Gilbert Keith, 3:470

choice, 3:521

classification of the sciences, 12:821

cogitative power, 3:823, 824

Commer, Ernst, 4:11

communication, 4:24

Complutenses, 4:45

concepts, 4:51

condemnation, 14:44

contrition-attrition distinction, 4:226, 227–230

correctoria, 4:274–278

Council of Trent, 14:23, 49–50

Counter Reformation, 4:311–312

cowardice, 4:332

Crathorn, John, 4:334–335

created actuation by uncreated act, 4:336

creation doctrine, 4:345

Crockaert, Peter, 4:374

Cursus theologicus, 12:618–619

diffusion, 14:47–48

discursive power as term in, 4:775

distinction, 4:779–782

Divine concurrence, 4:71–72

Thomism *(continued)*
    doctrines, 14:41–43
    Dominic of Flanders, 4:831
    Dominican legislation, 14:45
    early controversies (13th century), 12:266, 269
    early Jesuit legislation, 14:49
    Franciscan opposition, 14:44–45
    German School, 14:46
    Gilson, Étienne Henri, 6:227–228
    González y Díaz Tuñón, Ceferino, 6:346
    Humani generis, 7:181
    humanism, 7:194, 198
    hylomorphism, 7:238
    Immaculate Conception, 7:334
    impeccability, 7:360–361
    Jansenism, 1:892, 2:396
    John of the Cross, St., 3:136
    Journet, Charles, 7:1058
    Leo XIII (Pope), 1:147, 592, 678–679, 2:395, 854, 3:624
    Maritain, Jacques, 9:178
    matter and form, 9:351–352
    mechanism, 9:418
    neoscholasticism and neothomism revival, 10:244
    19th-20th century renewal, 3:624
    nominalism, 4:51, 335
    Oxford controversy, 12:230, 266
    Pegis, Anton Charles, 11:56
    Peter of Bergamo, 11:197
    Peter of La Palu, 11:200
    philosophical pluralism, 11:427–428
    Le Point de départ de la métaphysique (Maréchal, Joseph), 9:145–146
    prior to Council of Trent, 14:48–49
    reaction to condemnation, 14:44
    Roselli, Salvatore Maria, 12:380–381
    Schäler, Konstantin von, 12:730
    scholasticism, 12:757–779
    second movement, 14:48–51
    sensation, 12:907
    17th-century commentaries and textbooks, 14:50–51
    soul, 13:344
    speculative theology, 13:906–907
    Suarezianism, 13:561
    Torquemada, Juan de, 3:604
    William of Ockham, 9:862
    See also Neoscholasticism and Neothomism; Scholasticism; Scotism; Thomas Aquinas, St.; Thomism, transcendental

Thomism, transcendental, 6:311, 14:52–57
Le Thomisme devant la philosophie critique (Maréchal), 14:53
Thomistarum Triumphus (Charles of the Assumption), 3:436
Thomistic analysis
    awareness of natural law, 10:190
    connatural knowledge, 8:205
    Divine law vs. natural law, 10:202
    Divine revelation and papal teaching, 10:190–191
    effects of natural law, 10:189–190
    essentials of natural-law doctrine, 10:187–189
    Institute of Philosophy at Leuven, 8:824
    Ledesma, P., 8:443
    Leo XIII (Pope), 8:491, 493
    León, Luis de, 8:497
    Leonine Commission, 8:499–500
    liberal arts, 8:537–538
    Liberatore, M., 8:550
    limbo, 8:590
    limitation, 8:591–592
    natural law, 10:186–187, 187
    order of universe, 14:329–332
    role of theology, 8:774
    Sertillanges, A., 13:23–24
    similarity, 13:126
    sin, constitutive elements of, 13:152
    time, 14:79–82
    unity, 14:317
Thompson, David B. (Bp. of Charleston, SC), 13:367
Thompson, Francis, **14:57–58**
Thompson, James, Bl., 5:228, **14:58**
Thompson, John. *See* Woodcock, John, Bl.
Thompson, Newton, 10:36
Thomson, J. J., 1:836
Thomson, William, Bl., 5:229, **14:58**
Thong Kim Nguyen, Andrew, 14:498
Thoreau, Henry David, 3:755, **14:58–59**, 59, 146, 147–148
Thoresby, John (Abp. of York), 4:8
Thorlák Thórhallsson, St., 7:275, **14:59**
Thorman, Donald Joseph, **14:60**
Thornburgh v. American College of Obstetricians and Gynecologists, 1:33–34
Thorndike, Herbert, 3:152
Thorndike, L., 10:207
Thorne, John, Bl., 5:226
Thorney Abbey (England), 1:22, **14:60**
Thornhill, John, 7:528

Thornton, John, 1:544
Thorpe, Catharine Antoninus (Mother), 4:839
Thorpe, Robert, Bl., 5:231, **14:60–61**
Thou, Nicholas (Bp. of Chartres), **14:61**
Thought (periodical), 10:904
Thoughts, morality of, 6:25, 9:323, 13:153, **14:61–62**
Thoughts on Religious Experience (Alexander), 1:251
Thoughts on the Comets of 1680 (Bayle), 2:164
Thoulouze, Jean de, 12:590
Thouret, Joan Antida, St., **14:63**
Thraseas (Bp. of Eumenia), 1:785
Threat, **14:63**
Three Chapters, **14:63–65**
    African Church, 10:432
    Ambrosian Rite, 1:343
    Aquileia, 1:607
    Assyrian Church of the East, 1:805
    Athala of Bobbio, St., 1:815
    Carthage, 3:187
    Christology, 3:561
    condemnation, 8:97–98
    Constantinople Council II, 4:186, 191–192
    Council of Orléans, 1:895
    Eustace of Luxeuil, St., 5:456
    Facundus of Hermiane, 5:587
    Honorius I (Pope), 7:79
    Istrian schism, 2:499–500
    John III (Pope), 7:920
    Justinian I (Byzantine Emperor), 2:820, 3:596
    Leontius of Byzantium, 8:502
    Liberatus, 8:550
    Mennas (Patriarch of Constantinople), 9:494
    Vigilius (Pope), 14:509–510, 510–511
Three Conversations (Solov'ev), 13:307
Three Deaths (Tolstoi), 14:105
Three Essays on Religion (Mill), 9:632
''Three hypostases'' formula (St. Basil), 2:137
Three identical figures iconography, 14:207
Three Magi Shrine (Cologne), 3:844
The Three men iconography, 14:207
Three Patriarchs, 10:944–945
The Three Ways (spirituality), **14:65–67**
Three-Self Patriotic Movement (TSPM) (China), 3:501, 502, 503
''Three-source model,'' 11:96–97
Threni, 10:45

Throne of grace iconography, 14:208

Through Scylla and Charybdis (Tyrrell), 14:259

Thuan, Peter, 14:498

Thucydides (Greek historian), 10:179–180

Thuet, Charles, 3:235

Thules, John, Bl., 5:235, **14:66–67**

Thumb, Peter, 1:321, 12:669

Thurian, Max, 7:528

Thuribles. *See* Censers

Thurneysen, E., 4:721

Thurstan of York (Abp.), 2:880, 5:832, **14:67**

Thurston, Herbert, 4:717, 5:434, 821, **14:67**

Thurstone, L., 5:587

Thwaites, Reuben Gold, 7:778

Thwing (Thweng), Thomas, Bl., 5:237, **14:68**

Thwing, Edward, Bl., 5:233, **14:67–68**

Thyräus, Hermann, **14:68**

Thyräus, P., 4:718

Tiamat (Babylonian goddess), 4:337, 341

Tian ("Heaven"), 3:513

Tian Gengxin (Tien Ken-Hsin), Thomas, 3:*493*, 500

Tianjin, Treaty of (1858), 3:498

Tianming (Mandate of Heaven), 3:507–508

Tiara, papal, **14:68–69**, *69*, *70*

Tiaras, as ecclesiastical symbol, 6:763

Tibergeau, Jean (Abbot), 12:541

Tiberius (Roman Emperor), 12:301, 310, **14:69–70**, *71*

Tiberius II (Byzantine Emperor), 2:748, 7:916

Tibesar, Antonine, **14:70**

Tibet, **14:71–72**, *73*

   Buddhism, 2:666–668

   Cassiano da Macerata, 3:208

   Lamaism, 8:299

   missions, 1:401–402, 3:208, 14:71–72

Tiburtine Sibyl, 13:*101*

Tichborne, Nicholas, Ven., 5:234

Tichborne, Thomas, Ven., 5:234

Tiedemann, D., 8:126

Tieffentaller, Joseph, **14:72–73**

Tiemann, Walter, 2:524

Tienen, Beatrijs van. *See* Beatrice of Nazareth, Bl.

Tiepolo, Giovanni Battista, 2:114

Tier (Germany), 14:*183*, **183–185**

Tierney, Brian, 1:599, 7:451

Tierney, Michael (Bp. of Hartford), 4:124, 6:653

Tierney, Richard Henry, **14:73–74**

Tiers livre de Pantagruel (Rabelais), 11:885–886

Tiersot, Lazare, 12:278

Tiffany, Louis Comfort, 13:475

Tiglath-Pileser I (King of Assyria), 9:530

Tiglath-Pileser III (King of Assyria), 4:674, 7:641, 9:530–531

Tihen, John Henry (Bp. of Denver), 3:859

Al-Tijāni, Ahmad, 7:613

Tikhon (Patriarch of Moscow), 5:687, 10:682, 695, 13:12, **14:74**

Tillard, Jean-Marie Roger, 3:588, 7:528, **14:74–75**

Tillemont, Louis Sébastien le Nain de, 1:839, 4:471, 14:*75*, **75–76**

Tillich, Paul, 5:468, 14:*76*, **76–77**

   analogy, 1:373, 379

   atheism, 1:825

   conception of God, 4:585

   critical theory, 5:914

   deconstructionism, 4:594

   doctrine development, 4:808

   existentialism, 5:544

   faith, 2:222

   guilt, 6:573

   humanism, 7:197

   justification, 8:90

   origin and development of mythology, 10:128–129

   panentheism, 10:821

Tillman, Frank A., 6:185

Tillmann, Godfrey, 3:192

Tillot, François du, 3:792

Tilmann, K., 3:245

Tilton, Elizabeth, 2:199

Tilton, Theodore, 2:199

Tilton v. Richardson (1971), 3:667

Timaeus (Greek historian), 5:195

Timaeus (Plato), 1:746, 5:524

Timan, Johannes, 6:253

Time, **14:77–82**

   accident, 1:61–62

   ancient period concept, 14:77–78

   Aristotelian-Thomistic analysis, 14:79–82

   in the Bible, 5:215–216, 333

   computus, 4:46

   conservation, 4:162

   contemporary period concept of, 14:79

   continuum, 4:215, 217

   essence of experience, 8:219–220

   existence, 14:81

   irreversibility, 14:82

   medieval period concept, 14:78

   modern period concept, 14:78–79

   motion, 14:79, 80–81

   natural, 14:79–80

   now, 10:470

   perception, 14:81

   prayer, 11:597

   unity, 14:81–82

Time and Free Will (Bergson), 2:296

Time in Canon Law, **14:82–83**

Time in the New Testament, **14:84**

Time in the Old Testament, **14:83**

The Time Machine (Wells), 14:361

Times of Troubles (Russia, 1604-13), 12:423–424

Timidity. *See* Cowardice

Timmers, Matthew, 14:*392*

Timon, John (Bp. of Buffalo, NY), 5:880, 9:741, 10:322, **14:84–85**, *85*, 528

   Bonaventure University, St., 12:540

   San Antonio (TX), 12:640

Timon of Phlius, 11:843

Timoneda, Juan de, 1:925

Timor Lorosae. *See* East Timor

Timotheus I (Assyrian Catholicos), 1:807

Timotheus I (Nestorian patriarch), **14:85**

Timotheus I (Patriarch of Constantinople), **14:85–86**

Timotheus Salofaciakos (Patriarch of Alexandria), 4:252, 253

Timothy (Bp. of Cyprus), 3:366

Timothy, Epistles to, 10:938–940

   beatific vision, 2:169

   Christian law, 8:403

   deacons, 4:550–551

   deposit of faith, 4:675

   faith, 6:382

   general intercessions, 6:128

   Gnosis, 6:254, 255

   grace of man, 9:87

   hatred, 6:666

   homosexuality, 7:66

   intoxicant use, 13:239

   justice of God, 8:72

   kerygma, 8:157

   kindness, 8:171

   Luke's Gospel, 8:855

   magic, 9:39

   merit, 6:383

   Pastoral Epistle, 10:938–940

Timothy, Epistles to (continued)
Paul's successor, 8:596
presbyters, 11:672–673
sin, 13:148
slavery, 13:211
spirit of God, 13:427, 428
Timothy, St., 8:845, **14:86**
Timothy Aelurus (Patriarch of Alexandria), 3:595, 5:155, **14:86–87**
Basiliscus, 2:149
election, 4:252, 253
Proterius, St., 11:775
studies, 8:429
Timothy of Constantinople, 4:356
Timothy "the Cat" (Coptic Patriarch), 1:269
Timpe, George, 12:582
Timur (Tamerlane), 1:807, 2:788, 10:718, **14:87**
Tinbergen, Niko, 2:404
Tinctoris, Johannes, 2:398, **14:87–88**
Tindal, Matthew, 4:617, 5:263
Ting, K. H. (Bp.), 3:504
Tinh Bao Le, Paul, 14:498
Tintern Abbey (England), **14:88**, 89
Tintoretto (Italian painter). See Robusti, Jacobo
Tipler, Frank, 5:351
Tirant lo Blanc (Martorell), 4:401
Tírechán (Bp.), 1:644
Tiridates II (King of Armenia), 1:699, 704, 707, 5:18, **14:88**
Tiron Abbey (France), 2:316, 8:169, **14:88–89**
Tirry, William, 7:582, **14:89–90**
Tischendorf, Konstantin von, 2:366–367, **14:90**
Tischner, Józer Casimir, **14:90**
Tissera, Juan C. (Bp. of Córdoba), 3:759
Tisserant, Eugene (Card.), 11:483
Titans (in Greek religion), 3:574
Titchener, E.B., 1:796
Tit-for-Tat (Liutprand), 9:447
Tithes, 3:411, 726, **14:90–92**, 91
Titian (Italian painter). See Vecelli, Tiziano
Tito, Josip Broz, 4:371, 10:698, 13:527
Titular bishops, 4:304, **14:92–93**
Titular See (partibus infidelium), **14:93**
In Titulum de poenitentia ejusque partibus commentarius, sc. de poenitentia cordis, de confessione, de satisfactione, de jejuniis, de eleemosyna (Medina), 9:465
Titus (Bp. of Bostra), **14:93–94**
Titus (Roman Emperor), 12:304

Titus, Epistle to, 10:938–940, 11:672–673, 909, 951, 967, 13:428
Titus, St., **14:93**
Tixeront, Joseph, **14:94–95**
Tkach, Joseph W., Jr., 14:848
Tkachuk, Dionysius, 2:144
Tlaxcala, Martyrs of, BB., **14:95**
Tlingit people, 1:209
TM (Transcendental meditation), 10:298, **14:144–145**
TM-Siddhi program, 14:144–145
To Live in Christ Jesus, 7:69–70
To Protect the Faith. See Ad tuendam fidem
"To Reach Peace, Teach Peace" (John Paul II, 1979), 10:747
To Teach as Jesus Did (pastoral), 13:774
To Theopompus, On the Passible and Impassible in God (St. Gregory Thaumaturgus), 6:525
To Turn the Tide (Reinert), 12:39
To Young Men, on How They Might Profit from Pagan Literature (Basil of Caesarea), 10:755
Toai, Domingo, 14:498
Toan, Tomás, 14:498
Tobia, Abba (Bp.), 5:404
Tobias, Book of. See Tobit, Book of
Tobin, Fiacre, 7:582
Tobit, Book of, **14:95–97**
Achior, 1:191
canonicity, 3:26
catechumenate, 3:250
Dead Sea Scrolls version, 4:563
demonology, 4:646, 716, 717
deportation, 4:674
Gentiles, 6:140
Raphael (archangel), 11:909, 911
texts, 2:359
Tobit, Canticle of, 3:73
Tocca, William de, 1:120
Tocqueville, Alexis de, 4:641
Todd, Mary Jane (Sister Mary Joseph), 5:880
Todea, Alexandru, 12:339
Toebbe, Augustus Maria (Bp. of Covington), 4:331
Togo, **14:98–99**, 99
La Toison d'Or, the Chronique de l'histoire de France (Fillastre), 5:723
Tokuan, Andrew Murayama, Bl., 7:732
Tokuan, Mary, Bl., 7:733
Tokugawa Iyeysau, 7:729–730, 740
Toland, John, 1:564, 4:617, 5:263, 966

Toledo, Councils of (396-694), **14:99–101**
antisemitism, 7:79–80
Apocalypse iconography, 1:543
Canon Law, 3:40
Carolingian Renaissance, 3:160
chrism, 4:87
Christmas cycle, 3:556
circumincession, 3:742
clerical celibacy/marriage, 3:325
Constantinople Council III, 4:193
creedal statements, 4:356
deacons, 4:551
Eugene II of Toledo, St., 5:445
God the Holy Spirit, 6:293
Isidore of Seville, St., 7:602
Julian of Toledo, 8:50
property, 11:757–758
Visigoths converted, 8:426
Toledo, Fernando Álvarez de (Duke of Alva). See Álvarez de Toledo, Fernando (Duke of Alba)
Toledo, Francisco de (Card.), 1:677, 2:186, 12:765–766, **14:101–102**, 102
Toledo Cathedral (Spain), 3:696
Tolentino, Treaty of (1797), 10:146
Tolerance, 2:164, 4:944, 8:803–804, 11:399, **14:102–103**
Tolerance (Vermeersch), 14:452
Toleration Acts of Connecticut (1784), 3:650
Toleration Acts of Maryland (1639, 1649), 2:886–887, 3:641, 649, **14:103–104**
Toleration Acts of New Hampshire (1819), 3:651
Toletus, Francis (Card.), 1:72, 12:399
Tolkien, J. R. R., **14:104–105**, 105
Tolomeo of Lucca. See Bartholomew of Lucca (Bp. of Torcello)
Tolstoi, Leo Nikolaevich, 1:384, 921, 13:307, **14:105–106**, 106
Tolton, Augustus, 1:158, 7:317
Tom Playfair (Finn), 5:735
Tom Watson's Magazine, 10:171
Tomacelli, Pietro (Card.). See Boniface IX (Pope)
Tomachi, Dominic, Bl., 7:734
Tomachi, John, Bl., 7:734
Tomachi, Michael, Bl., 7:734
Tomachi, Paul, Bl., 7:734
Tomachi, Thomas, Bl., 7:734
Tómas de Jesús (Díaz Sanchez de Avila), 3:136
Tomás de Santa María, **14:106**

Tomášek, František (Card.), 3:200, 4:486, 487, **14:106–107**

Tomasi, Giuseppe Maria Carol, St., 14:*107*, **107–108**

Tomasius, Jakob, 12:768

Tomazin, Ignatius, 12:542

Tomb Effigy of Pope Martin V, 9:*218*

Tomb of Pope VIII (Bernini), 14:*341*

Tombrock, Elizabeth (Mother Immaculata of Jesus), 5:885

"Tome of Leo," 7:817

Tome to Flavian (Leo I), 1:50, 392, 3:561, 595, 5:275, 759

Tomlinson, A. J., 1:789

Tommaseo, Niccolò, 7:673

Tommasi, John Baptist, 8:194

Tommaso da Cori, St., **14:108**

Tommaso di Giovanni di Simone Guidi (Masaccio), 2:374

Tomos pisteos (Tome on Faith) (Gregory II Cyprius), 6:478

Tomus ad Armenios de fide (St. Proclus), 11:737

Tone, Theobald Wolfe, 10:541

Tonga, 10:533–534

Tonge, Israel, 10:493

Tongerloo Abbey (Belgium), **14:108–109**

Tongiorgi, Salvatore, 12:748, **14:109**

Toniolo, Giuseppe, 3:418, 7:673, **14:109**

Tonkin (Vietnam) mission, 12:218–219

Tonneau, J., 13:243

Tönnies, Ferdinand, 1:792, 13:278, 281

Tönnies, Mary (Mother), 11:131

Tonquédee, J. de, 4:25

Tonsure, 3:331, 6:*587*, 7:37, 8:293–294, 14:*110*, **110**

Toohey, Isabel, 13:175

Toolen, Thomas Joseph (Abp.), 1:202, 9:749, **14:110–111**

Tootell, Hugh (Charles Dodd), **14:111**

Topeka (KS), 8:*114*

Topics (Aristotle), 10:610

Topographia Hiberniae (Giraldus Cambrensis), 6:231

Topographical and Anatomical Aspects of the Gothic Cathedral (Fingesten), 3:676

Torah
criticism, 3:33
law, 8:396
lectionaries, 8:434
Nahmanides, 10:136
Pharisees, 8:5
Reform Judaism, 8:10
Shammai and Hillel, 8:5

significance, 8:4
social sin, 13:245

Torah shrines, 13:677

Torcaso v. Watkins (1961), 3:652, 653, 666

Torch (periodical), 13:232

Torchbearers (Noyes), 10:471

Torelli, Ludovica, 14:902

Torello, Bl., **14:111**

Torgau, League of, 3:430, 637

Torgau Articles, 4:78

Toribio Medina, José, 1:723

Torni, Julio, 1:307

Tornielli, Bonaventure, Bl., **14:112**

Toro, Tomás (Bp. of Cartagena), 3:848

Toronto (Canada), 3:8, 9, 8:903–904

Toronto School of Theology, 3:9

Torosowicz, Nicholas (Bp.), 1:706

Torpor vs. will power, 14:726

Torquato Tasso (Goethe), 6:331

Torquemada (Hugo), 5:874

Torquemada, Juan de (Card.), **14:112–113**
Canon Law, 3:51
Caracciolo, Landolf, 3:96
conciliarism, 3:604
ecclesiology, 5:37
eucharistic epiclesis, 5:279
printed books, 2:522
universality of Christianity, 3:293

Torquemada, Juan de (historian), **14:113**

Torquemada, Tomás de, 7:489, 490, **14:113–114**

Torrentius, L. (Bp. of Antwerp), 1:539

Torres, Balthasar de, Bl., 7:734

Torres, Camillo, **14:114**

Torres, Cosme de (Father), 7:737

Torres, Francisco, **14:114–115**

Torres, Fulgentius, 10:289

Torres, Herbert de, 2:850

Torres, Luis de, **14:115**

Torres Acosta, María Soledad, St., 12:659, 13:24, **14:115**

Torres Bollo, Diego de, **14:115**

Torres Lloret, Pascual, Bl., **14:116**

Torres Morales, Genoveva, Bl., **14:116–117**

Torres Saez, Manuel, 2:92

Torrey, C. C., 3:565, 566, 567, 568

Torrigiani, Luigi (Card.), 3:791

Torrijos, Omar, 10:819

Torriti (Italian painter), 2:374

Torró García, Manuel, Bl., **14:117**

Torroja, E., 3:677

Torrubia, José, **14:117–118**

Tortura Torti (Andrewes), 1:408

Torture, **14:118–119**

Torture of St. Hippolyte (Dieric Bouts the Elder), 9:*228*

Tory, Geoffrey, 2:523

Toscanini, Arturo, 14:*119*, **119**

Tosephta, 5:508

Tosi, Paschal, 1:208, 209

Tostado, Alonzo, 3:26, **14:119–120**

Tosti, Luigi, 3:81, 7:673, **14:120**

Tostig (Earl of Northumbria), 6:650

Totalitarian gnosis, 9:110
See also Gnosis

Totalitarianism
aristocracy, 1:667
authority, 1:920
Church-State relations, 3:642
common good, 4:20
government power, 6:377
masses (population), 9:312
Pius XI (Pope), 11:393
Plato, 5:89

Totality, principle of, 11:767

Totemism, 2:443, **14:120–121**

Toth, Alexis, 5:20, **14:121**

Tóth, Tihamér, 7:218

Totila (King of the Ostrogoths), 3:349

Totius latinitatis lexicon (Forcellini), 5:798

Totius rationalis, naturalis, divinae, et moralis philosophiae compendium (Javelli), 7:747

Toto (Duke of Nepi), 4:178

Touceda Fernández, Román, Bl., 7:125

Toulet, Pierre, 1:396

Toulmin, Stephen, 5:398

Toulouse Abbey (France), 3:691

Toulouse Cathedral (France), 3:67

Touraine Reform (1608-15), 7:982–983, 8:495, **14:122–123**

Touré, Ahmed Séku, 6:574

La Tourette Monastery (France), 3:678

Tourism, Jamaica, 3:113

Tournay, Maurice, Bl., **14:111–112**

Tournay, Raymond, 5:50

Tournély, Éléonor François de, 12:493, 496, **14:123**

Tournely, Honoré de, 1:309, 4:121, 12:767, **14:123–124**

Tournon, Charles Thomas Maillard de (Patriarch of Antioch), 3:498, 515, 4:630, 7:411–412, 14:*124*, **124–125**

Tournus Abbey (France), 14:*125*, **125**

Touron, Antoine, **14:125**

Tours, Councils of (567-1163), 1:254, 3:557, 4:89, 11:611–612, **14:121–122**

Tours, François Marie de, 7:411

Tours, Synod of (567), 3:410

Tours Abbey (France), 3:691

Tours Archdiocese (France), **14:125–127**

Toussaint, Pierre, 1:159, 10:545–546, **14:127**

Toussaint Abbey (Angers, France), 1:432

Toustain, C. F., 10:773

Touvier, M., 5:405

Tovini, Giuseppe Antonio, Bl., **14:127–128**

Tower of Babel, 10:129, 11:104, 13:143, **14:128–130**

Toynbee, Arnold Joseph, 1:7, 4:435, 6:882, 8:579

Toyotomi Hideyoshi, 7:726, 728, 728–729, 738–739

Tozo, Michael, Bl., 7:734

Tozzo (Bp. of Augsburg), St., **14:130**

Tra le sollecitudini (motu proprio, Pius X), 4:118, 11:390

Trach, Domingo, 14:498

Tract 18 (Newman), 10:733

Tract 90 (Newman), 10:734, 14:8

Tract on Virginity, 5:82

Tractarian Movement, 10:332–333

Tractarianism, **14:131**
　　Anglo-Catholics, 1:444, 446, 12:25
　　Caroline Divines, 3:153
　　Coleridge, Henry James, 3:830
　　Keble defense, 8:136
　　progressive Anglo-Catholics, 8:182
　　Tract 90, 14:8
　　See also Oxford Movement

Tractationes XVIII theologales variae (Nacchianti), 10:133

Tractatus (John XXI), 7:930

Tractatus (Wittgenstein), 14:804

Tractatus apolgeticus integritatem societatis de Rosea Cruce defendens (Fludd), 12:382

Tractatus canonicus de Matrimonio (Gasparri), 6:103

Tractatus contra perfidos Judaeos de conditionibus veri Messiae, scilicet Christi vel uncti (Peter Nigri), 11:193

Tractatus de anima (John Blund), 7:941, 942

Tractatus de anima (Pseudo-Grosseteste), 6:538

Tractatus de conceptione sanctae Mariae (Eadmer of Canterbury), 5:1

Tractatus de contractibus mercatorum (Nider), 10:386

Tractatus de fide Trinitatis (Abelard), 1:18–19

Tractatus de haeresi, schismate, apostasia, sollicitatione in sacramento paenitentiae, et de potestatae romani pontificis in his delictis puniendis (Santarelli), 12:680

Tractatus de iuribus regni et imperii (Lupold), 8:869

Tractatus de jurisdictione ecclesiae super regnum Sicilae et Apuliae (Bartholomew of Lucca), 2:126

Tractatus de lectione Scripturarum (Neercassel), 10:230

Tractatus de legibus (Suárez), 12:766

Tractatus de Missionibus (Rovenius), 12:395

Tractatus de mysteriis (Hillary), 5:104

Tractatus de non dissolvendo Henrici Regis cum Catherina matrimonio (Powell), 11:574

Tractatus de potestate regia et papali (John of Paris), 3:636

Tractatus de potestate summi pontificis in rebus temporalibus (Bellarmine), 10:500

Tractatus de privilegiis et juribus monasteriorum (Engel), 5:220

Tractatus de proportionibus (Bradwardine), 14:29

Tractatus de regio patronata (Frasso), 10:978

Tractatus de sanctorum. . .cultu (Neercassel), 10:230

Tractatus de Sphaera (John de Sacrobosco), 7:956

Tractatus interius canonicum et civile (Bartolo di Sassoferrato), 3:52

Tractatus mysteriorum (Hilary of Poitiers), 5:512

Tractatus pro clericorum connubio (Ulric of Augsburg), 3:326

Tractatus regliae (Celestino), 13:54

Tractatus theologici (Goudin), 6:372–373

Tractaus theologico-politicus (Spinoza), 5:968

Tracts, 3:499, **14:130–131**

Tracts for the Times (Oxford Movement), 10:733

Tractus de sex dierum operibus (Thierry of Chartres), 14:2

Tracus super Psalmos (St. Hilary of Poitiers), 6:112

Tracy, David, 5:829, 6:791, 11:586, 12:203

Tracy, Robert T. (Bp. of Baton Rouge), 2:156

Trade, 8:64, 163–164

Trade unions. See Labor and trade unions; Labor organizations

Traditi humilitati nostrae (encyclical, Pius VIII), 11:382

Traditio (periodical), 8:257

Traditio Apostolica (Hippolytus of Rome), 3:37–38, 59

Traditio Legis, 1:573–574

Tradition, 1:380

Tradition, in the Bible, 10:337–338, **14:131–133**

Tradition de l'Église sur l'institution des évêques (La Mennais), 8:308, 311

La Tradition et les semipélagiens de la philosophie (Ventura), 14:442

La Tradition et les traditions (Congar), 4:103

Tradition in theology, 13:893, **14:133–138**
　　continuity and progress, 14:136
　　Council of Trent on scripture, 14:134, 136, 169
　　loci theologici, 8:743
　　Lubac, H. de, 8:841
　　Lutheranism, 8:895
　　meaning, 14:134
　　Newman's doctrine, 10:336–338
　　organs, 14:134–136
　　scripture, 14:136–137

The Tradition of Natural Law (Simon), 10:194

Traditional African religions, 3:113, 12:67
　　See also specific countries

Traditional Catholics of America, 3:289

Traditionalism, 3:624, **14:138–140**
　　Bonald, Louis Gabriel Ambroise de, 2:478
　　Bonnetty, Augustin, 2:508
　　Donoso Cortés, Juan, 4:869–870
　　heresy, 6:778–779
　　philosophical romanticism, 12:346
　　religious liberalism, 8:541
　　See also Catholic traditionalism

Traducianism, 1:140, 13:342, 353–354, **14:140**

Tragedy of Nestorius, 10:254

Tragical History of the Life and Death of Doctor Faustus (Marlowe), 5:650

Traicté contre l'erreur viel et renovuelé (Espence), 5:358

Un Traité cathère inédit, 3:260

Traité de la Nature et de la Grâce (Malebranche), 9:74

Traité de la sphère (Oresme), 10:380

Traité de l'action de Dieu sur les créatures (Boursier), 9:74

Traité de l'amour de Dieu (Malebranche), 9:74

Traité de l'amour de Dieu (Regis), 12:31

Traité de l'éloquence chrétienne (Leo of St. John), 8:495

Traité de l'esprit de l'homme (de la Forge), 3:185

Traité de l'homme (Descartes), 3:185

Traité de l'indifference (Yves de Paris), 14:898

Traité de morale (Malebranche), 9:74

Traité des premières (Buffier), 12:771

Traité des sensations (Condillac), 4:73, 5:261

Traité des systèmes (Condillac), 4:73

Traité des vraies et fausses idées (Arnauld), 9:74

Traité du choix et de la méthode des études (Fleury), 5:762

Traité théologique pour l'autorité et l'infaillibilité du pape (Petit-Didier), 11:211

Traitéde l'Education des filles (Fénelon), 5:682

Traités historiques et dogmatiques sur divers points de la discipline de l'Église et de la morale chrétienne (Thomassin), 14:40

Trajan (Marcus Ulpius Traianus) (Roman Emperor), 1:567, 3:592, 4:945, 12:304, 310, **14:140–141**, *141*

Tran van Tuan, Joseph, 14:498

Tranchepain, Marie St. Augustin, Mother, **14:141**

Transactional functionalism theory, 10:20

Transcendence, **14:141–143**
    Augustine, St., 1:881
    causality, 3:303
    God, 6:322, 13:765
    humanism, 7:187
    immanence, 7:340
    magic, 9:36
    Marcel, Gabriel, 9:134
    meaning, 14:14
    religion, 12:59–60
    salvific, 8:301
    thought, Thomism, 4:53

The Transcendence of the Ego (Sartre), 12:697

Transcendent theology, 7:1011

Transcendental (Kantian), 4:154, 368, 8:122, 126, **14:144**

Transcendental meditation (TM), 10:298, **14:144–145**

Transcendental method, **14:145**

Transcendental relations, 12:41

Transcendental Thomism. *See* Thomism, transcendental

Transcendental unity, 14:296

Transcendentalism, 2:627, 639–640, 12:346, 783–785, 13:241, **14:146–147**

Transcendentalism, literary, 5:188, 12:733–734, **14:147–149**

Transcendentals, **14:149–153**
    Balthasar, Hans Urs von, 2:34–35
    beauty, 2:184–186
    being, 2:207
    first principles, 5:745
    good, 2:187, 6:346–354
    knowledge, 13:419
    status, 14:5
    truth, 2:187

Transcultural process of methodology, 9:567–568

Transfiguration, 7:796, *800*, **14:153–155**

The Transfiguration (Raphael), 14:*153*

Transfiguration Basilica (Israel), 2:*147*

Transforming Grace: Christian Tradition and Women's Experience (Carr), 5:677

Transforming Mission (Bosch), 10:623

Transformistic theories, 4:804, 805–806

Transham, Edward. *See* Stransham, Edward, Bl.

The Transient and Permanent in Christianity (Parker), 10:892

Transiturus de hoc mundo ad Patrem (papal bull, Urban IV), 5:463, 12:521

Transitus Mariae, 9:275

Translatio SS. Marcellini et Petri (Einhard), 5:139

Translations
    Arabic language, 4:830
    Bible, 8:362–364
    Bible de Jérusalem (Lyonnet), 8:906
    Catholic and Protestant, 8:175
    Contemporary English Version (CEV), 8:442
    French versions of New Testament, 8:449, 465
    Instruction on Translation of Liturgical Texts (Comme le prévoit), 8:669
    Iraq, 8:170
    liberal arts, 8:537
    liturgy, as term, 8:727
    New American Bible, 13:200
    Sheed, F., 13:73

Transmigration of souls, 5:196, **14:155–158**, 157, 157–158
    See also Metempsychosis

Transubstantiation, **14:158–159**
    accident, 1:65
    Aelfric Grammaticus, 1:136
    Amalricians, 1:330
    annihilation, 1:471
    baroque period emphasis, 2:111
    Council of Trent, 14:159, 171
    doctrine, 5:248
    hylomorphism, 7:238
    John of Paris, 7:979
    theological analysis, 14:159–160
    truth, 13:895–896
    Wyclif, John, 5:243, 14:866
    See also Eucharist

Transylvania, 4:309, 538, 12:332, 338
    Counter Reformation, 7:214
    defense, 7:213
    Hapsburg Empire, 7:216
    Hutterites, 7:234
    Protestant Reformation, 7:213
    religious freedom, 7:214

Traoré, Moussa, 9:77

Trapé, Agostino, 1:889

Trapp, Damasus, 1:889

La Trappe Abbey (France), 3:747, **8:372**
    See also Trappists

Trappistines, 3:745

Trappists, 3:747–748, **14:160–163**
    Chautard, Jean Baptiste, 3:457–458
    China, 3:499
    Congregation of Mariannhill Missionaries, 9:163
    missions, 8:147, 149, 9:163
    reform, 8:372

Tratado de indulgentiis (Oré), 10:643

Tratado de la oracioń y meditación (St. Peter of Alcántara), 11:195

Tratados historicos, Politicos, ethnicos y modernas (Navarrete), 10:215

Tratato degli Angeli Custodi (Trombelli), 14:213

Trattato apologetico (Comitoli), 4:4

Trattato della divinatione naturale cosmologica (Foscarini), 5:825

Trattato delle tre vie della meditazione (St. Charles of Sezze), 3:435

Tratto dei Delitti e delle Pene (Essay on Crimes and Punishments) (Beccaria), 2:191

Traube, Ludwig, 2:263, **14:163**, 448

Les Travaux des Capucins sur l'Ecriture Sainte aux XVII-XVIII siècle (Ubald), 14:261

The Travels of Sir John Mandeville (Odoric of Pordenone), 10:557

Travers, John, Ven., 5:226

Traversari, Ambrogio, 5:768

La Traviata (Verdi), 14:446

Traynor, William J., 1:352

Tre Fontane Abbey (Italy), **14:163**

Treacy, John P. (Bp. of La Crosse, WI), 8:273, 14:782

Treasure of Life (Mānī), 9:113

Treasury (Siq Canyon, Jordan), 7:*1031*

"Treasury of Orthodoxy" (Nicetas Choniates), 10:356

Treatise Concerning Religious Affections (Edwards), 5:97

Treatise of Human Nature (Hume), 7:200–202, 10:203

The Treatise of Perfection of the Sons of God (Rutherford), 12:439

A Treatise on Baptism (Kenrick), 8:144

A Treatise on Confirmation (Kenrick), 8:144

Treatise on Imperial and Pontifical Power (William of Ockham), 5:900

Treatise on Logic (Maimonides), 9:52, 53

Treatise on Moral Conscience (Rosmini-Serbati), 12:384

Treatise on Prayer (Origen), 10:655

Treatise on Purgatory (St. Catherine of Genoa), 3:271

A Treatise on Smallpox and Measles (Greenhill), 12:210

Treatise on the Atonement (Ballou), 14:321

Treatise on the Love of God (St. Francis de Sales), 5:868, 10:516

The Treatise on the Miracles (Thomas of Celano), 14:33

Treatise on the New Testament, That Is, the Holy Mass (Luther), 5:427

Trebnitz Abbey (Silesia), **14:163**

Trebonianus Gallus (Roman Emperor), 12:312

Tréca, Joseph M., 1:209

Trecy, Jeremiah, 10:221, 587, **14:163–164**

Tree and Leaf (Tolkien), 14:105

Tree of Jesse, **14:164**, *165*

Tree of Knowledge, 10:874–875, 13:18–22, **14:164**, **166**

Tree of Life, 10:874, **14:166–167**

Trees, symbols of, 13:666–667

Tregelles, S. P., 2:366

Treger, Konrad, 1:889

Treinen, Sylvester (Bp. of Idaho), 7:291

Trejo y Sanabria, Fernando de (Bp. of Tucumán), 1:649, **14:167–168**, *168*

Tremblaye, Guillaume de la, 2:190

Trendelenburg, Friedrich Adolf, 1:678, 6:711

Trenquelléon, Adèle, 9:160, *161*

Trent, Councils of (1543-63), 1:347, 9:29, **14:168–176**

'Abdīshô IV, 1:14

Adam, 1:105

Agustín, Antonio, 1:189

Alfonso de Castro, 1:278

anathema, 1:390

Anglican orders problem, 1:437

Anointing of the Sick, 1:480, 483

archdeacons, 1:633

architecture, 3:701

Aristotelianism, 1:677

atonement, 1:837

attrition, 1:843

Augsburg Peace, 4:11

Augustinianism, 1:879–880, 884

Augustinians, 1:889

beginning of faith, 5:605

Bérulle, Pierre de, 2:338–339

biblical canon, 3:26, 27, 28, 32, 33, 565

Billick, Eberhard, 2:394

bishops, 2:418, 3:53

Blarer, Jakob Christoph, 2:433

Boonen, Jacques, 2:529

Borromeo, St. Charles, 2:540

Breviary, Roman, 8:661, 730

Bugnini, Annibale, 2:676

Bus, César de, Bl., 2:714

Cabasilas, Nicolas, 2:837

Camaiani, Pietro, 2:896

Canisius, St. Peter, 3:16

Cano, Melchior, 3:19

Canon Law, 3:51, 53–54

capital punishment, 3:87

cardinal legates, 13:17

cardinalate, 3:105

Carmelites, 3:126, 134, 135, 142

Carranza, Bartolomé, 1:347, 3:175

casuistry, 3:219

Catechism of, 4:9

Catholic traditionalism, 3:289

censorship, 3:336

Cesarini, Alessandro, 3:357

charity, 3:397

Charles V (Holy Roman Emperor), 3:430, 431

Christian iconography, 8:621

Church property, 3:727

Church-State relations, 3:638

Clement VIII (Pope), 3:785

clerical celibacy/marriage, 3:327–328

clerical dress, 3:801

commendation, 1:10

Communion, 8:660

communion and sacrifice of the mass, 14:172

Communion on weekdays, 4:37

Compagnia dei servi de' puttini carità, 3:214

composition, 4:302

conciliarism, 3:604

concubinage, 4:64, 65

condemnation of Anabaptists, 2:69

Confirmation, 4:89

contrition-attrition distinction, 4:226–227, 229, 230

conversion, 4:240–241

convocation, 4:301, 14:168–169

copresidents, 8:57–58

deacons, 4:551

death, 4:576

decree on sacred scripture and tradition, 8:463

decrees, 12:684

deliberation on sacraments, 14:170

demonology, 4:649

diocesan synods, 2:41

Divine indwelling, 7:442

dogmatic theology, 4:813, 12:620

Dominican participation, 4:852, 13:330

dueling, 4:929

ecclesiastical archives, 1:636

Epistles of John, 7:897

Espence, Claude Togniel de, 5:358

establishment of seminaries, 14:173

Eucharist, 1:64, 65, 3:610

eucharistic controversy, 5:426, 427–429, 435

ex opere operato, 5:500, 501, 12:469

exemption, 5:530

Faber, Peter, Bl., 5:584

Figliucci, Felix, 5:717

final perseverance, 11:133, 134

Foreiro, Francisco, 5:799

Fransen's studies, 5:918

free will and grace, 5:936

French rejection, 3:612

friendship with God, 6:10

grace, 6:396, 397, 403

Gregorian Chant, 6:467–468

historical signification, 14:174–175

Holy Orders, 7:35, 36

homily, 7:63

hope, 7:93

iconography of saints, 12:601

Index of Prohibited Books, 11:518

indulgences, 7:439

ius divinum of episcopal office, 14:172–173

Jedin, Hubert, 7:750

Jerome's translation, 8:363

judicial vicar office, 8:42

justice through grace of God, 8:75

justification, 3:532, 8:69–70, 84–85, 86, 89

Laínez, D., 8:287

lay confession, 8:412

lectionary systems, 8:437

L'Hôpital, 8:530

lithograph (18th-century), 14:*169*

liturgical books, 8:640–641, 661, 12:258, 328

liturgical inculturation, 7:384–385

liturgical language, 8:667

liturgical laws, 8:670

liturgical reform, 8:437

Louvain, Catholic University of, 8:823

Luther, 8:883

marriage, 1:151–152

marriage law, 13:749–750

merit (virtue), 9:512–513

monastic reform, 2:272

music, 8:588, 700

Nadal's role during, 10:133

original sin, 4:69, 14:170

overview, 3:609–610

patristic studies, 10:962

Paul III (Pope), 3:609, 610, 638, 11:22–23, 14:169–171

penance, 11:71

perseverance, 11:132

Peruvian adoption of regulations, 8:741

Pius IV (Pope), 11:372, 14:171–174

Pole, Reginald, 11:457, 12:9

preaching, 11:614

priesthood, 11:703–704

prohibited books, 7:390

providence of God, 11:784

Pseaume, Nicholas, 11:798–799

purgatory, 4:556, 11:825–826

purpose of amendment, 11:840

redemption, 11:975–976

reform, 4:312

reform peititions and decrees, 14:172–174

reforms proposed, 8:58

religious instruction, 4:803

residence and jurisdiction of bishops, 14:170

retention of medieval baptism rite, 2:65

revelation, 12:191, 194

reviviscence of merit, 12:206

Roman Breviary, 2:610

sacramental grace, 6:407

sacraments, 8:660

sacred images, 12:685

sacred music and art, 2:110, 111–112, 114

saints, Catholic teaching, 12:604

Sander, Nicholas, 12:665

scholastic philosophy, 12:766

School of Cologne, 3:846–847

seminary education, 12:893–895

Seripando, G., 13:135

Servites, 13:28

seven sacraments, 12:470

simony, 13:136, 198

sin, 13:152, 155

Sirleto memoranda, 13:167

Spain, 13:393

Tametsi decree, 3:54, 10:218–219, 13:749–750, 14:173

teachings on Adam, 10:663

Thomas Aquinas, St., 14:23, 49–50

tradition in theology, 14:134, 136, 169

transfer to Bologna and return to Trent, 14:170–171

transubstantiation, 8:660, 14:159, 171

veneration of images, 2:111

veneration of relics, 12:55

vernacular language, 8:660

Vulgate, 14:596

works of charity, 3:415

See also Catechism of the Council of Trent

Tres abhnic annos (Instruction), 8:669

Tres estudios sobre la familia (Franceschi), 5:864

Les Trés riches heures du Duc de Berry, 9:129

Tresham, Thomas (1543-1605), 14:176

Tresham, Thomas (d. 1471), 14:176

Tresham, Thomas (d. 1559), 14:176

Tresham family, **14:176**

Trévern, Le Pappe de (Bp.), 2:161

Trevisa, John, 1:464, **14:177**

Tri Smerti (Tolstoi), 14:105

Triadis thaumaturgae seu divorum Patricii, Columbae, et Brigidae acta (O'Clery), 10:537

Triage, **14:177–178**

Trial of Jesus, 8:858, **14:178–181**, *179*, 180–181

Trianon, Treat of (1920), 7:218

Tribonian (Roman lawyer), 8:100

Tribuanal sacramentale (Marchant), 9:140

Tribunals, ecclesiastical, 8:42–43

Tribunals of the Curia, 4:439

Tribune (Greeley), 14:148

Tribur, Synod of (895), 1:103

Trichet, Marie-Louise of Jesus, Bl., **14:181**

Triclinium, Roman, 8:344

Triclinius, Demetrius, 2:810

Tri-Conference Commission, 8:424

Tridentine Catechism. *See Catechism of the Council of Trent*

Tridentine Index, 7:390

Tridentine liturgy, 3:288–289

Tridentine Mass, 3:289, 4:742, **14:181–182**

Tridentine Profession of faith, 11:740

Tridentini decreti de iustificatione expositio et defensio libris XV distincta (Vega), 14:430

Triduum (space of three days), 4:711, 8:718, **14:182–183**

Triennial Convention, 2:79

Trier, See of (Germany), 8:738, 13:90

Trier, Synod of (1227), 3:240

Triest, Antoine (Bp.), **14:185**

Triest, Peter Joseph, **14:185–186**, *186*

Trieu van Nguyen, Manuel, 14:498

Trifa, Josif, 12:335

Trigault, Nicolas, 3:494, **14:186**

Triglandius (Jacobus Trigland), 3:184

Trilingual colleges, 6:696

Trinh Vu'o'ng (CMR), 4:113–114

Trinidad and Tobago, 3:112, 113–116

Trinitarian controversies, 2:792

See also Arianism

Trinitarian doctrine, 10:960–961, 13:420

Trinitarian formula, baptism, 2:59, 61–62

Trinitarian Monastery (Ireland), 14:*188*

Trinitarian seal (13th century mosaic), 14:*187*

Trinitarian theology, 6:834, 12:45–46, 783, 13:441, 453

Trinitarian-Christological theology, 11:148

Trinitarians, 14:186–188, **186–188**
  Amalricians, 1:330
  Blandrata, Giorgio, 2:432
  Carthage, 3:187
  discalced order, 4:765
  Felix of Valois cofounder of, 5:670
  John of Matha, St., founding, 5:670, 7:974
  Rojas, Simon de, St., 12:291
  Somalia, 13:308
  works of charity, 3:414, 419
Trinitas, a Theological Encyclopedia of the Holy Trinity, 5:208
La Trinité Cathedral (Vendôme, France), 3:697
La Trinité Church (Caen, France), 3:695
The Trinity (El Greco), 14:*206*
Trinity, Feast of the, 14:205
Trinity, Holy, **14:189–201**
  appropriation, 1:606–607
  Arianism, 1:660
  Augustine, St., 1:863–864
  Basil, St., 2:137
  beatific vision, 6:688
  Biddle, John, 2:391
  Billot, Louis, 2:395
  Böhme, Jakob, 2:462
  Bonaventure, St., 2:484–486, 487
  circumincession, 3:741–742
  communio, 4:28
  community, 4:38, 14:199
  Constantinople Council I, 4:190
  Constantinople Council II, 4:191
  consubstantiality, 4:197–198
  contemporary theology, 6:289
  Council of Trent, 8:89
  creeds, 4:349–355
  Divine indwelling, 7:442–444
  dogma, 14:194–197
  evolution of fourth-century dogma, 14:189, 191–194
  Filioque approach to, 14:200
  Gilbert de la Porrée, 6:213–214
  God the Father, 6:292
  God the Holy Spirit, 6:292–293
  Gregory of Nyssa, St., 6:519–520
  immutability of God, 7:356, 359
  indwelling, 9:736
  Joachim of Fiore, 7:876
  Johannine Comma, 7:891–892
  life, concept of, 8:570, 572
  liturgy's relation, 8:169
  Logos, 8:758–764
  mission and missions, 9:685

modalism, 9:750
mystery of mysteries, 10:84
neo-economic trinitarianism, 14:198–199
neo-modalism, 14:197–198
Nicaean Council I (325), 10:966, 14:192–194
notional acts, 1:86
Novatian (Antipope), 10:464–465
"persons" in God approach to, 14:199–200
pneumatology, 14:200–201
process approach, 14:200
Racovian Catechism, 4:80
spiration, 13:420, 420–421
spirituality, 13:438
Suárez, Francisco, 13:558–559
theology in nature, 10:212
Thomas Aquinas, St., 14:196–197
The Trinity (El Greco), 14:*206*
The Trinity of the Old Testament (Rublyov), 14:*190*
Trinity with Christ crucified (panel painting), 14:*205*
Trinity With the Virgin Enthroned (Carenzio), 14:*191*
William of Saint-Thierry, 14:753
Trinity, Holy, controversies on, 13:25, **14:202–205**
Trinity, Holy, devotion to, 13:137, **14:205**
Trinity, Holy, iconography of, **14:205–208**
Trinity, Holy, in the Bible, **14:201–202**
Trinity Church (Boston), 3:670, *700*, 709, 715
Trinity Church (New York), 3:*701*, 709, 715
Trinity College (Dublin), 7:566
Trinity College (Washington, DC), 9:399
Trinity Hospital (Rome), 3:418
The Trinity of the Old Testament icon (Rublyov), 14:*190*
Trinity Western University (BC), 3:11
Trinity with Christ crucified (panel painting), 14:*205*
Trinity With the Virgin Enthroned (Carenzio), 14:*191*
Trinkaus, Charles, 7:193, 12:119
Trionfo della Chiesa ossia istoria delle eresie colle loro confutazioni (St. Alphonsus Liguori), 1:310
Il trionfo della Santa Sede e Della Chiesa (Pius VII), 10:847

Il Trionfo della Santa Sede e della Chiesa contro gli assalti dei novatori combattuti e respinti colle stese loro armi (The Triumph of the Holy See against the Assaults of the Innovators) (Gregory XVI), 6:506–507, 877
Tripartita (St. Ivo of Chartres), 7:680
Tripartite Commentary on Fiefs (Hotman), 5:702
The Triple Way (St. Bonaventure), 2:482, 14:65
Triplici Nodo, Triplex cuneus (James I, King of England), 10:500
Tripoli, as Crusaders' state, 4:402, 403
Trisagion (doxology), **14:209**
Tritheism, 14:204
Trithemius, Johannes (Tritheim), 2:551, 12:119, 293, **14:209**
Tritius, Ferdinand, 3:328
Trito-Isaiah (anonymous poet-prophet), 5:336, 7:595, 597–598
Triumph, Roman, **14:209–210**
"The Triumph of Love" (Pesellino), 3:443
The Triumph of Religion (Fitton), 5:751
Triumph of St. Thomas Aquinas over Averroes (Traini), 7:509
Triumphalism, **14:210**
Triumphis Herculis helvetici (Zwingli), 12:612
The Triumphs of Christ (Flodoard), 12:607
Triumphus Cupidinis (Petrarch), 11:215
Trivium, 3:262
Trivulzio, Agostino (Card.), 14:210–211
Trivulzio, Alessandro, 14:210
Trivulzio, Alessandro Teodoro, 14:211
Trivulzio, Antonio (Card.), 14:210–211
Trivulzio, Carlo, 14:211
Trivulzio, Gian Galeazzo Sforza, 14:210
Trivulzio, Gian Giacomo, 14:210
Trivulzio, Scarmuzza, 14:210–211
Trivulzio, Teodoro (1474-1551), 14:210
Trivulzio, Teodoro (Card., d. 1657), 14:210–211
Trivulzio family, **14:210–211**
Troarn Abbey (France), **14:211**
Trobec, James (Bp.), 12:542
Trochta, Šteán (Card.), 4:486
Troeltsch, Ernst, 7:148, 8:579, 12:860–861, 13:924, **14:211–212**
Troiani, Caterina, Bl., **14:212**
Troilus and Criseyde (Chaucer), 3:453, 454, 457
Les Trois vérités (Charron), 3:439
Trois-Fontaines Abbey (France), 3:758

Trois-Rivières (Canada), 3:4, 6, 7

Troitskaya Laura (Russia), 13:16, **14:212–213**

Trojan Horse in the City of God (Hildebrand), 6:831

Troki (apologist). *See* Isaac ben Abraham

Trokosi (religious slavery, Ghana), 6:201

Trombelli, John Chrysostom, **14:213**

Trombetta, Antonio, 12:764, **14:213**

Tromp, Sebastian, 5:37

Trong Van Tran, Andrew, 14:498

Tronson, Louis, **14:213–214**

Tropes, **14:214–217**

    Aenesidemus, 13:204

    Agnus Dei, 1:*185*, 186

    Agrippa, 13:204

    drama, 4:893–894

    Kyrie eleison, 7:254, 8:260

    medieval Latin literature works, 9:446

    rahmen and textual, 8:260

    Sequence tradition, 7:247

    Sextus Empiricus, 13:204

    vernacular hymnody, 7:254

Trophimus (Bp.), 1:694

Troshani, Nikollë, 1:216

Trosly, Council of (909), 3:326

Troubadors, courtly love and, 4:318–322

"Troubles" of Northern Ireland, 7:569

Il Trovatore (Verdi), 14:446

Troy, John Thomas (Abp. of Dublin), **14:217–218**

Troyennes histoires (Fillastre), 5:723

Troyes, Council of (1107), 10:916

Troyes, Treaty of (1564), 3:266

Truat Van Vu, Peter, 14:498

Truce of God Movement, 3:411, 518, 11:51

    See also Peace of God

Truchsess Von Waldburg, Otto and Gebhard, 1:848, 3:16, 843, 5:173, 8:463, **14:218**

Tructatus de parvulis trahendis ad Christum (Gerson), 3:232, 241

Trudo of Brabant (Trond), St., 3:519, 12:587, **14:218–219**

Trudpert, St., **14:219**

The True Devotion to the Blessed Virgin Mary. See *The Love of the Eternal Wisdom* (Grignion de Montfort)

True Discourse (Celsus), 3:329

True Doctrine of the Sabbath (Bound), 12:454

True Jesus Church, 3:501

True Morality and Its Counterfeits (Hildebrand), 6:831

True Philosopher (iconography), 7:856–857

Trullan Synod (692), 4:186

Trullanum. *See* Constantinople, Councils of

Trullo, Council of. *See* Quinisext Synod

Trung Van Tran, Francisco, 14:498

Trusse, Jean, 2:506

Trusteeism, **14:219–221**

    Blanc, Anthony, 2:430

    Church-State relations, 3:656

    Connolly, John, 4:127

    Conwell, Henry, 4:245

    Dubois, John, 4:918

    Hughes, John Joseph, 7:161

    Massachusetts, 2:554

    Milwaukee (WI), 9:647

    Philadelphia, 11:236–237

    Polish National Catholic Church, 11:458

    Synod of Baltimore, 2:42–43

Truszkowska, Angela Maria, Bl., **14:221–222**

Truszkowska, Sophia Camille. *See* Truszkowska, Angela Maria, Bl.

Truszkowska, Zofia Camille. *See* Truszkowska, Angela Maria, Bl.

Truth, 11:284–285, **14:222–230**

    as a transcendental, 2:187

    absolute, 1:41

    accident, 1:62

    axiomatic system, 1:949

    certitude, 3:351, 5:743

    criteriology, 4:366–368

    deceit, 4:588–589

    detraction, 4:696

    dissimulation, 4:778

    dogmatism, 4:821

    double truth theory, 4:881–883

    doubt and discovery, 4:883

    epistemology, 5:303–304, 14:224–228

    history of notion, 14:222–224

    laws, 8:398–399

    mental reservation, 9:497, 499

    method, 13:419

    monism, 9:811

    moral theology, 9:857

    nilhilist emphasis, 10:395

    oath demanding, 10:497

    ontology, 14:228–230

    praxis, 11:587–588

    property of being, 14:152

    property of knowledge, 8:202

    religious, 9:752

    semantics, 12:890

    skepticism, 13:200–205

    speculative reason, 8:389–390

    speculative-practical cognition, 3:825

    spirit-paraclete as witness of the, 10:873

    theology, 13:894, 895–896

    torture, 14:118–119

    verification of, 14:450

    wonder, 14:833

    See also Dialectics; Doctrine

Truth, Divine, 5:596–597, **14:230–231**

Truth and Method (Gadamer), 6:46, 789–790

Truth Teller (periodical), 10:312, 313

Truthfulness (veracity), 8:25, 899–903, 13:141, **14:231–232**

Trutznachtigal (Spee), 13:410

Trypho the Jew, 2:382

Tryphon (Regent of Syria), 9:11

Tschiderer zu Gleifheim, Johann Neopmuk, Bl., **14:232–233**

Tsofnath Pa'aneah (Revealer of Hidden Things) (Gikatilla), 6:211

Tsūji, Thomas, Bl., 7:734

Tu, Dúc (Emperor of Vietnam), 14:501

Tu Khac Nguyen, Pedro, 14:498

Tu Van Nguyen, Peter, 14:498

Tuam Abbey (Ireland), **14:233**

Tuan, Joseph, 14:498

Tuan Ba Nguyen, Pedro, 14:498

Tübingen School, 2:160–161, 5:827, 12:256, **14:234–235**

Tübingen University (Germany), 5:173, 12:729, **14:233–234**, 234

Tübinger theologische Jahrbücher, 14:234

Tuc, Joseph, 14:498

Tucson Diocese (AZ), 10:288

Tucumán Diocese (Argentina), 1:649

Tudela, Guilhem de, 4:400

Tudeschis, Nicolaus de, 3:51, 8:296, **14:235**

Tudor, Margaret. *See* Margaret Tudor

Tudor, Mary. *See* Mary Tudor (Queen of England)

Tuigg, John (Bp.), 11:85–86, 367

Tuke, William, 7:132

Tully, Thomas, 7:582

Tulsa Diocese (OK), **14:235**

Tumi, Christian Wiyghan (Card.), 2:913

Tungern, Arnold von, 5:306

Tunisia, 3:186–188, 8:389, **14:235–237**, *237, 238*

See also Carthage

Tunlop, Seila, 2:904

Tunstal, Thomas, Bl., 5:235

Tunstall, Cuthbert (Bp. of Durham), **14:237**

Tuoc, Domingo, 14:498

Tuong, Andrew, 14:498

Tuong, Vincent, 14:498

Tupí people, 2:587–588

Turberville, Henry, 3:243

Tureaud, Alexander Pierre, 1:161

Turgenev, Ivan, 10:394

Turgot, Anne Robert, 5:210

Turin, Council of (398), 1:694

Turinaz, Charles (Bp. of Nancy), 1:355

Turkey, **14:238–240**, *241*

　Ecumenical Patriarchate, 4:196–197

　John XXIII (Pope), Bl., 7:934

　Khazars, 8:163–164

　map, 14:*240*

　Ottoman Empire, 4:196, 254, 370, 412, 462–463

　See also Ottoman Turks

Turks. See Ottoman Turks; Seljuk Turks

Turley, Daniel (Bp. of Chulucanas), 1:891

Turmel, Abbé, 9:754

Turmel, Joseph, **14:240–241**

Turner, Antony, Bl., 5:236–237, **14:241**

Turner, Cuthbert Hamilton, **14:241–242**

Turner, Edward, 5:238

Turner, Thomas Wyatt, 1:160, **14:242–245**

Turner, Victor, 12:87, 259–260, **14:245–246**

Turner, William (Bp. of Buffalo, NY), 5:879, **14:246**

Turón, Martyrs of, SS., **14:246–248**

Turpin (Abp. of Reims), 12:36, **14:248–249**

Turre, Ludovicus a, 3:96

Turrettini, Benedict, **14:249**

Turrettini, François, 14:249

Turrettini, Jean Alphonse, 14:249

Turrettini family, **14:249**

Tur-Sinai, N. H., 12:458

Tusculani family, 1:387, 3:854, **14:249–250**

Tutiorism, 4:145, 5:168, 9:879–880, **14:250**

Tuvalu, 10:534

Tuy Le, Pedro, 14:498

The Twelve, 1:572–573, 922–923, 3:24, 4:769–774, **14:250–251**

See also Apostles

Twelve Articles of Memmingen (1525), 11:53, 12:17

The Twelve Patriarchs (Benjamin major) (Richard of Saint-Victor), 12:234–235

Twelve Patriarchs, Testament of the, 1:554–555

Twelver Shi'a (Muslim sect), 13:84

"Twelvers," 7:624

Twenty-four Hours Prayers (Nerses Gratiosus), 10:251

The Two Cities: A Chronicle of Universal History to the Year 1146 (Otto of Freising), 6:888

The Two Cultures (Snow), 13:786

The Two Edged Sword: An Interpretation of the Old Testament (McKenzie), 9:402

Two Hussars (Tolstoi), 14:105

Two Source Hypothesis (Synoptic Gospels), 13:695–696

Two Sources of Morality and Religion (Bergson), 2:296, 12:71

Two Tales of the Occult (Eliade), 5:155

Two Ways, **14:251**

Twomey, Louis J., **14:251–252**

Tyconius, 4:862, 863

Tye, Christopher, **14:252**

Tygodnik Powszechny (weekly), 14:90

Tyler, William Barber (Bp. of Hartford), 4:122, 6:652, 12:214

Tylor, Edward Burnett, Sir, 1:458–459, 4:426, 427, 433, 12:64

Tyndale, William, 2:507, 3:833, **14:252–254**

Tynemouth Priory (England), **14:254**

Type and Antitype, **14:254–255**

Typography, 7:187–188

Typos (Constans II Pogonatus decree, 648), 4:173, **14:255–256**

Tyrannicide, 2:716, 4:171, 7:884, **14:256–257**

Tyranny, 1:920, 4:637, **14:257**

Tyrconnell, Richard Talbot, Duke of. See Talbot, Peter and Richard

Tyre, Council of (335), 1:685, 817, 5:451, 452, 8:53

Tyrie, James, 1:20, **14:258**

Tyrol Passion plays, 10:928

Tyrrell, Anthony, 1:112

Tyrrell, George, 7:790, **14:258–259**

　Bremond, Henri, 2:601

　doctrine, 4:806

　dogma, 9:754

　Hügel, Friedrich von, 7:149

　modernism, 9:756

　Petre, Maude Dominica, 11:218

　religious experience, 5:556

Tzaddik, 6:660–661

Tzadua, Paulos (Card.), 5:401

Tzetzes, John, 2:807, 809

U

Ubaghs, Casimir, 12:771

Ubald, Bl. See Vivald, Bl.

Ubald d'Alençon, **14:261**

Ubald of Gubbio (Bp.), St., **14:261**

'Ubayd-Allāh, Abū 'Imrān Mūsā ibn Maimūn ibn. See Maimonides (Jewish philosopher)

Ubeda, Luis de, 12:674

Über den Ursprung der menschlichen Seelen (Frohschammer), 6:15

Über den Willen in der Natur (Schopenhauer), 12:784

Über die Freiheit der Wissenschaft (Frohschammer), 12:901

Über die Religion (Schleiermacher), 12:739–740

Über die vierfache Wurzel des Satzes vom zureichenden Grunde (Schopenhauer), 12:784

Ubertino da Casale, 1:412, 2:629, 4:136, 5:896, 897, **14:261–262**, *262*

Ubi arcano (encyclical, Pius XI), 11:392

Ubi nos (encyclical, Pius IX), 6:549

Ubi periculum (papal bull, Gregory X), 6:499, 11:499

Ubi primum (encyclical, Benedict XIV), 5:205

Ubi primum (encyclical, Leo XII), 8:489, 10:433, 12:789

Ubiarco Robles, Tranquilino, St., **14:262–263**

Ubiquitarianism, 2:715, **14:263**

Uccelli, Pietro, 12:776

Udairicus, St., 12:607

Udalschalk of Stille, 12:880

UDF (Union of Democratic Forces) (Bulgaria), 10:687

Udo (12th c. theologian), **14:263**

Udovenko, Andrei, 12:430

Ueber das Gedächtnis (Ebbinghaus), 5:27

Ueberlieferung und Bestand der hagiographischen under himiletischen Literatur der griechischen Kirche (Ehrhard), 5:138

Ugalde Irurzun, Felix, Bl., 4:494

Uganda, 8:899, **14:265–266**, *267*

Uganda, Martyrs of, SS., **14:263–264**

Ugarit (Syrian coast), 1:808, 3:2, **14:266–267**, *268*

 Baal, 4:493

 Elohim in texts found at, 5:174

 fertility and vegetation cults, 5:698

 Leviathan, 8:522

 serpent as symbol, 13:19

 sons of God, 13:321

Ugaritic-Canaanite religion, **14:267–271**

Ugliness, **14:271–272**

Ugo (Bp. of Assisi), 1:790

Ugolino of Orvieto, 1:883

Uguzo, St., **14:272**

Uhde, Fritz von, 7:860

Uhl, O., 3:712

UISG (International Union of Superiors General) (Women), **7:529**

Ukon, Justus Takayama, 7:726

Ukraine, **14:272–277**, *274*

 Byzantine Basilians, 2:143, 144

 Mennonite churches, 9:496

 monasticism, 9:803

 pre-Lent period, 13:98

 Sheptyts'kei, Andrii, 13:79–80

 Slipyj, Josyf, 13:217–218

 Smotryts'kyi, Meletii, 13:237

Ukrainian Americans, 2:145, 4:124–125, 7:317

Ukrainian Catholic Church (Eastern Catholic), 1:533–534, 2:606, 747, 5:19, 717, **14:277–281**, *278*

Ukrainian Church (Canada), 3:11

Ukrainian Orthodox Church, 1:533–534, 10:696

Ukrainian Rite Catholics in the U.S., 5:687, 12:787

Ukrainians in West, 13:217–218

Uleurrunus, Michael, 3:52

Ulfilas (Bp.), 3:596, **14:281**

Ulger (Bp. of Angers), 1:432

Ulich, Robert, 5:94

Ullathorne, William Bernard (Abp.), 1:900, 14:*281*, **281–282**

Ullerston, Richard, **14:282**

Ulmanis, Karlis, 8:375

Ulpian, 10:180–181, 13:211

Ulric (Bp. of Imola), 3:326

Ulric, Bl., 6:188–189

Ulric VIII Rosch (Abbot), 12:669

Ulric of Augsburg, St., 3:326, 9:448, 12:671, **14:282**

Ulric of Strassburg, 1:224, 2:185, **14:282–283**

Ulric of Zell, St., 12:668, **14:283**

Ulrich of Sankt Paul (Abbot), 12:670

Ultimate Questions: An Anthology of Modern Russian Religious Thought (Schmemann), 12:742

Ultramontanism, 3:622, 642, 5:252, 853, **14:283–286**

 Acton, John Emerich Edward Dalberg, 1:85

 Assumptionists, 1:801

 Bourget, Ignace, 2:567

 critics, 8:246

 Czechs, 4:484

 de Courcy, Henry, 4:596

 Dupanloup, Félix, 4:942

 Essai sur le principe générateur des constitutions politiques (Maistre), 9:61

 impact on papacy, 10:847

 Lacordaire, J. H., 8:271

 Lemmenais, F., 8:309

 Netherlands support of, 10:261

 Prussia, 8:253

 Rohrbacher, René François, 12:290

Ultrarealism, 4:51

Ulysses (Joyce), 1:292, 11:519

Umayyad 'Umar II, 14:286

Umayyads, 1:611, **14:286–287**

 'Abbāsids, 1:6

 Agapios of Hierapolis, 1:172

 Córdoba, 4:261

 Kalām, 8:109

 Lebanon, 8:426

 Spain, 13:378

 Zaydis, 13:85

Umberg, Johannes B., 4:671

Umbratilem (apostolic constitution, Pius XI), 3:194

Umbrian school, 4:396

Umileniye, 9:272, 274

UN. *See* United Nations

Una Sancta (periodical), 3:625, **14:287**

Una Sancta Movement, 8:892

Unam sanctam (papal bull, Boniface VIII), 1:207, 2:503, 3:603, 636, 4:518, **14:287–288**

Unamuno y Jugo, Miguel de, 5:544, **14:288–289**, *289*

Unbaptized infants, fate of, 2:70

Unbaptized persons, as negative infidels, 7:455

Uncertainty principle, 1:836, 5:102, **14:289–290**

Unconscious, 4:153, 348–349, 592–593

Unda (*Association Catholique Internationale pour la Radio et la Téléision*), **14:290–291**

Unda-USA, 14:290–291

The Undergraduate (periodical), 10:332

Underground Catholic Church (China), 3:502, 505

Underhill, Evelyn, **14:291**

Understanding, 5:744, **14:291–294**

 art, 1:748

 Augustine, St., 1:876

 intentional species, 13:4108–4110

 positive theology, 13:897–898

 soul, 13:350

 speculative theology, 13:898–900

 spirit, 13:422

 theology, 13:893–895, 900–901

 Thomistic concept, 14:293–294

 truth, 14:225

Understanding, gift of, 8:207, **14:295**

Undset, Sigrid, 14:*295*, **295–296**

The Uneasy Conscience of Modern Fundamentalism (Henry), 5:473

Unemployment Appeals Comm'n of Florida, Hobbie v. (1987), 3:663

The Unfortunate Gift of Freedom (Tischner), 14:90

Unicity and plurality of forms, 5:816–819, 12:230–231, 266

Unicity of God, 6:320, **14:296–297**

Unicity of the Church, **14:297–298**

Unification Church, 10:298, **14:299**

Unified field theory, 4:217

Uniformity, 3:293, 11:316, **14:299–300**

Unigenitus (papal bull, Clement XI), 1:57, 3:789, 790, 10:406, 844, 14:124, **301–302**

 Alexandre, Noël, 1:268

 appellants, 1:600

 Du Pin, Louis Ellies, 4:944

 Jansensim, 7:718

Unigentius Dei Filius (papal bull, Clement VI), 5:851, 12:454

L'Union (Ecumenical review), 14:381

Union (Relly), 14:321

Union, prayer of, 4:205, 209

Union économique, 8:805

Union of Brest (1596), 2:212, 11:442

Union of Catholic Workers, 5:691

Union of Democratic Forces (UDF) (Bulgaria), 10:687

Union of Fribourg (1886), 3:420

Union of Horodlo (1413), 7:696

Union of Orthodox Jewish Congregations of America, 8:11

Unión Popular (Mexico), 6:344

Unione Sacra (1916), 7:674

L'Unità cattolica (periodical), 9:152

Unitarian Church (Madison, WI), 3:716

Unitarian Church of Transylvania, 2:431, 432

Unitarian Universalist Association (UUA), **14:302**, 322

Unitarians, **14:302–304**
  Anabaptists, 1:369
  Calvinists, 5:193
  Channing, William Ellery, 3:379
  community churches, 4:39
  Congregationalism, 4:116
  Dávid, Franz, 4:538
  Radical Reformation, 3:608
  social gospel, 13:241

Unitary state of government, 6:377

Unitas association, 3:625

Unitas Fratrum. See Moravian Church

Unitatis redintegratio (Decree on Ecumenism) (Vatican Council II), 3:590, 626, 4:30, 5:70, 75–76, 12:197, 700, 14:416

United Arab Emirates, **14:304–305**, *306*

United Brethren, 2:454, **14:305–306**

United Brethren in Christ, 5:468, 471, 12:261

United Brothers, 7:58

United Catholic Church of Poland, 11:443, 445, 449

United Church Board for World Ministries, 4:116

United Church of Canada, 3:9, 4:82, 9:561

United Church of Christ, 3:719, 4:117–118, 199–200, 5:72, 468, 7:114, **14:306–308**

United Evangelical Action, 10:157

United Kingdom. *See* Britain, early church in; England; Northern Ireland; Scotland; Wales

United Lutheran Church, 8:887

United Methodist Church, 4:199–200, 5:469, 471, 9:561, 14:*308*, **308–309**

United Methodist Church of Great Britain, 8:561

United Methodist Free Churches (England), 9:559–560

United Nations (UN), 3:10, 88, 7:565, 13:99, 177, 14:638

United Nations Declaration of Human Rights, 10:203

United Presbyterian Church in the U.S.A., 11:677

United Presbyterian Church of North America, 11:677

United Seventh Day Brethren, 1:135

United Society of Believers in Christ's Second Appearing. *See* Shakers

United States
  abortion, 1:32–35
  academic freedom, 1:51–54
  Anglican-Episcopalian Religious Orders, 12:103
  anti-Catholicism, 2:44, 197, 10:169–172
  anti-Semitism, 7:874
  apostolic delegation, 1:581–585
  Augustinians, 1:890–891
  Basilian institutions, 2:142
  Benedictine abbeys and priories, 2:254–256
  Benedictine congregations, 2:259–261, 274
  Blenkinsop family, 2:435–436
  Buddhism, 2:673–674
  Byzantine Basilians, 2:144
  Calvinism, 2:895
  Canon Law Society of America, 3:58–59
  capital punishment, 3:88
  Carmelites, 3:127, 128, 129, 129–130, 143, 145–146, 180
  Carroll, John, 3:178–181
  catechesis, 3:243, 244
  catechetical directory, 3:236
  Catholic Charities USA, 3:279–280
  Catholic Daughters of the Americas, 3:281–282
  Catholic schools, 9:161–162
  church architecture, 3:709, 714–718
  church membership, 3:718–721
  Cistercians, 3:748
  civil religion, 3:755–757
  clerical dress, 3:801–802
  confessions of faith, 4:81–82
  congregational singing, 4:118–120
  Constitution, 8:746
  courts and public order, 11:808
  defense of morality, 11:518–520
  deism, 4:617–618
  diocesan consultors, 3:66
  Dominican order, 4:854–855
  Eastern Catholic churches, 2:747
  ecclesiastical archives, 1:636–642
  evangelicalism, 5:473
  feminism, 9:868
  first canonized saint, 13:30–35, *31*
  first native-born sisterhood, 13:173
  first priest ordained, 2:39
  first U.S. cardinal, 2:165
  fraternal organizations, 3:281, 622
  freedom of association, 1:792
  Germanizing influence, 6:227
  Haiti invasion (1994), 6:621–622
  Holy See diplomatic relations, 1:585, 3:627, 659
  hospice movement, 7:117–118
  hymns, 7:256–259, 260–262
  iconography, 7:286
  idealism, 7:301–302
  Immaculate Conception feast, 7:334
  Islam, 3:718, 719–720
  Jesuits, 1:584, 2:41, 3:649, 9:725
  Jewish communities, 8:13
  Judaism, 3:718, 719–721
  laicism, 8:284
  liberalism, 11:391
  limited tithing system, 14:92
  liturgical inculturation, 7:387
  liturgical movement, 8:674
  liturgical music history, 8:696–699
  Loretto Sisters, 8:786, 787
  Lovers of the Holy Cross, 8:835–836
  Mantellate Sisters, 13:24
  Marian shrines, 13:92
  Maronite Church, 9:198–200
  Mennonite churches, 9:496
  Methodist churches, 9:560, 561–562
  Mexico, 9:*579*
  mission. *See specific states*
  nativism, 10:172–173, 173
  origins of literary transcendentalism in, 14:147–148
  Orthodox Church in America, 2:744, 745, 3:717, 10:681–683
  Passionists, 10:933
  Pius X (Pope), St., devotion to, 11:391
  Platonic studies in the Midwest, 11:417
  popular devotions in, 4:710, 711
  Presbyterian churches in, 11:675–677
  Prône in, 11:747
  prostitution in, 11:774
  Puerto Rico, as commonwealth of, 11:814
  Puritans, 3:640, 645, 646–647
  Red Mass celebrated in, 11:961
  Redemptorists in, 11:995–996
  religious discrimination of Catholics, 19th c., 2:44
  religious orders, development, 12:896
  Revolution, 3:176–178, 179, 649–652
  Romanian Catholic Church, 2:748
  Romanian Orthodox Church, 2:745, 10:693
  Russian Byzantine Catholic Church, 2:748

sacramental theology, 12:478–479

See also American Civil War (1861-65); American Revolution (1775-83); Church and State, U.S.; Know-Nothingism; National Conference of Catholic Bishops (NCCB); Nativism; *specific American ethnic groups*; *specific states, dioceses, and archdioceses*

seminary education, 12:895–899

Servants of Mary, Sisters, 13:24

Sisters of Mercy, 13:184

Sisters of Mercy of the Union, 13:185

Sisters of the Order of St. Basil the Great (Basilians), 2:145

social gospel, 13:241–242

social justice issues, 3:620

spoils system, 6:415

Sulpicians, 13:601

taxation and moral obligations, 13:769

technical aspects of preaching, 11:614

temperance movements, 13:796–802

Trappists, 14:162

Trinitarian Order, 14:187–188

Ukrainian Catholics, 2:747, 14:278, 280

Unitarians, 14:303–304

Universalism, 14:321–322

Vatican City, 13:770–771

Xaverian Brothers, 14:876

United States, Arver v. (1918), 3:660

United States, Girouard v. (1946), 3:660

United States, Reynolds v. (1878), 3:655, 661

United States, Roth v. (1957), 11:519

United States, Welsh v. (1970), 3:661

United States Armed Forces, Archdiocese for, **9:628–630**

U.S. Catholic Almanac, 10:67

United States Catholic Conference, 5:203, 300

United States Catholic Historical Society, 6:765, 12:243, 13:70

U.S. Catholic Magazine, 2:40, 10:67, 13:70

United States Catholic Miscellany (newspaper), 2:192, 5:223, 8:904

United States Catholic Mission Association (USCMA), **14:309**

United States Conference of Catholic Bishops (USCCB), 5:300, **14:310–316**

Council of Major Superiors of Women Religious, 4:298

deacons, 4:552, 553–554

Ethical and Religious Directives for Catholic Care Services, 5:459

Holocaust teaching, 7:15

liturgical music, 8:703

women religious, 8:424

United States Temperance Union. *See* American Temperance Union

United States v. Macintosh (1931), 3:660

United States v. Seeger (1965), 3:661

United Student Christian Council, 10:165

United Synagogue of America, 8:10

Unity, **14:316–318**

community churches, 4:39

concelebration, 4:50

concept of unicity, 14:296

Consultation on Church Union, 4:199–200

Cyril of Alexandria, 4:468

Dante Alighieri, 4:521

identity principle, 7:303

Leo XIII (Pope), 12:700

marks of the Church, 9:189–191

multitude opposition, 10:58–59

property of being, 14:152

Unity of Brethren. *See* Bohemian Brethren

Unity of Christians, Secretariat for the Promotion of the, 5:74

Unity of Faith, 3:625, **14:319**

Unity of Philosophical Experience (Gilson), 10:207

Unity of Protestantism, 4:117–118

Unity of the Church, **14:319–320**

branch theory of the Church, 2:582–583

Carolingian Dynasty dissolution, 3:170

Cyprian, St., 4:457–459

Ecumenical councils, 4:303

Ecumenical Movement, 5:74

19th-20th century overview, 3:625

The Unity of the Church (Möhler), 9:763

Unity Temple (Chicago), 3:669, 679, 715

L'Univers (newspaper), 14:465–466

Universa congregatio Vallis Umbrosana, 14:378

Universa Laus (UL), 8:707–708, **14:320–321**

Universae philosophiae studia (Passionei), 10:930

Universal analogy, 2:487–488

Universal call to holiness, 7:5–7

"Universal Call to Holiness" mosaic (Washington, DC), 10:168

Universal/collective eschatology, 5:333, 342

Universal Council (*Consiglio universale*), 10:416

Universal History (Bossuet), 10:673

Universal love, 9:679

Universal prayer. *See* General intercessions

Universal skepticism, 9:821

Universal World Council on Life and Work, 8:577

Universalis ecclesiae (papal bull, Julius II), 10:978

Universalist Church of America, 14:322

Universalistic hedonism. *See* Utilitarianism

Universalists, 1:548, 13:407, **14:321–322**

Universality of Christianity, 1:489, 3:274–275, 292–294

See also Catholicity

Universals, 5:361, 11:769, **14:322–327**

Abelard, Peter, 1:15, 19, 12:758

abstraction, 1:46

Adelard of Bath, 1:113

Aristotle, 1:681

Averroës, 1:933

Boethius, 1:673, 2:456

conceptualism, 4:51, 53

Crathorn, John, 4:335

criteriology, 4:367

division, 4:792–793

history, 14:322–323

knowledge, 13:419

medieval debate, 14:323–325

modern thinkers, 14:325–327

Roscelin of Compiègne, 12:377

sign, 13:117

simple apprehension, 1:605

unity and multiplicity opposition problem, 10:58

Universals controversy, 3:441

Universe, Order of, 10:23, 375, 13:423, **14:328–332**, 329–332

Universi dominici gregis (apostolic constitution, John Paul II), 2:910, 3:58, 106, 107, 4:60, 7:1001–1002

Universitas (hospital guild), 7:128–129

Universitas Catholica Lovaniensis. *See* Louvain, Catholic University of

Université de Moneton (Canada), 3:9

Universities and colleges. *See specific cities and countries*; *specific colleges and universities*

University Gallicanism. *See* Theological Gallicanism

University of Paris, 7:156

University rectors, 11:957

Univocity of being, 4:936

Unknown God (Noyes), 10:471

Unleavened Bread, Feast of, 5:656, 10:933–934, 14:332–333

Unleavened bread, in the Bible, 10:933–934, **14:332–333**

Unni of Hamburg, St., **14:333**

Unpopular Essays against the Aristotelians (Exercitations paradoxicae adversus Aristoteleos) (Gassendi), 6:105

Unterkoefler, Ernest L. (Bp. of Charleston, SC), 13:367

Untersuchunchen zur Menschensohn-Christologie im Johannes Evangelium (Schulz), 5:522

Unto This Last (Ruskin), 12:414

The Unvarying Mean (Confucius), 10:186

Uomini e Religioni (1998), 12:672–673

Upadhyaya, Brahmabandhav, 7:405

Upanishads, 6:840, 842–843, 7:407, **14:334**
  emanationism, 5:180
  pantheism, 10:825
  soul, 13:337–338

Upjohn, Richard, 3:709, 715

Upper Canada, Vicarate Apostolic of, 3:7, 8, 9

Uppsala Cathedral (Sweden), 3:696–697

Uppsala School, 11:93–94

Ur (ancient Mesopotamian city), 8:392, 9:528–529, **14:334**

Urban, Wilbur Marshall, 1:948, 12:70, 14:380

Urban I (Pope), St., 10:481, **14:334–335**, *335*

Urban II (Pope), Bl., **14:335–336**
  Alexandrine bulls, 1:274
  Andrew of Strumi, Bl., 1:407
  Anselm of Canterbury, St., 1:495
  Arras, 1:722
  Bruno of Segni, St., 2:648
  Bruno the Carthusian, St., 2:649
  in *bulla cruciata*, 2:688
  Canon Law, 3:45
  Carthusians, 3:193
  Clement III (Antipope), 3:778
  Cluny Abbey, 7:150
  Crusades, 2:760, 3:518, 4:406, 407, 408, 410
  cursus, 4:444

election, 5:843

Frangipani family, 5:912

Gebhard III of Constance, 6:114

Gelasius II (Pope), 6:123

Geoffrey of Vendôme, 6:142

Hugh of Die, 7:151

Hugh of Remiremont, 7:155

investiture struggle, 7:538

Philip I, 11:244

preaching of the First Crusade, 14:335–336

Urban III (Pope), 4:600–601, **14:336**

Urban IV (Pope), Bl., **14:336–337**
  Bec Abbey reconstruction, 2:190
  Catena aurea commissioned, 14:18–19
  Corpus Christi feast, 1:924, 2:217, 4:272, 8:52
  Crusades, 4:413

Urban V (Pope), Bl., **14:337–338**
  Angers, 1:432
  Avignon papacy, 1:943, 12:357
  bishops, 3:602
  Charles of Blois, Bl., 3:435
  Eastern Schism, 2:763

Urban VI (Pope), 14:*337*, 338–339, *339*
  Adam Easton, 1:107
  Catherine of Siena, St., 3:273
  Clement VII (Antipope), 3:783
  Despenser, Henry, 4:692–693
  election of, 3:604
  French monarchy, 5:846
  Holy Year, 7:57
  Low Countries, 10:258
  Western Schism, 14:691–693
  See also Western Schism (1378-1417)

Urban VII (Pope), 5:670, **14:339–340**

Urban VIII (Pope), **14:340–342**
  approval of Basilian Order of St. Josaphat, 2:143
  Barberini family, 2:94–95
  Basilian scholarships, 2:143
  canonization, 3:63
  cardinalate, 3:105
  catechesis, 3:234
  Clement IX (Pope), 3:786
  comma pianum controversy, 4:4
  Congregation for the Propagation of the Faith, 5:21
  de auxiliis controversy, 4:113
  family, 4:279
  Galileo, 6:61, 62
  grace controversies, 7:715
  hymn corrections, 7:254

Irish Act of Settlement, 1:77

Jansenism, 14:342

monument, 14:*340*

papacy development, 10:843

papal decline, 3:612

Piarists, 7:1043

St. Peter's Basilica, 2:109

Sisters of Loretto, 8:787

slavery, 3:771

tomb, 14:*341*

The Urban Catholic University (Reinert), 12:39

Urbanavicius, Alphonsus Maria, 11:495

Urbanus Averroista, 13:27

Urbs Beata Jerusalem Dicta Pacis Visio, **14:342**

Ur-Correctorium, 4:275

Urdaneta, Andrés de, 1:889, 4:422, **14:342**

Urdanos Aldaz, Tomás, Bl., 7:123

Uribe Velasco, David, St., 6:545, **14:342–343**

Uriel (angel), **14:343**

Urim and Thummim, 4:785, 10:619, **14:343**

Urráburu, Juan José, **14:343–344**

Ursacius of Singidunum (Bp.), 1:662, 663, 8:54, 12:692

Ursicinus of Ravenna (Bp.), St., **14:344**

Ursinus (Antipope), 4:504, **14:344**

Ursinus, Zacharias, 4:79, **14:344–345**

Ursmar (Bp.), St., 5:787, **14:345**

Ursula, St., 5:166, **14:345**, *346, 347*

Ursulina Venerii, Bl., **14:345**

Ursuline Daughters of Mary Immaculate, 1:186

Ursuline Sisters of Mary Immaculate, 9:894

Ursulines, **14:345, 347–350**
  Alaska, 1:210
  among martyrs of Orange, 10:620–621
  Brazil, 2:593
  Canada, 3:4
  Central American martyrdom, 8:132–133
  Cittadini, Bl. Caterina, 3:752
  Counter Reformation, 3:610, 782
  founding, 4:310
  Gray Ursulines, 8:444
  Kentucky, 8:817
  19th-20th century overview, 3:621
  Owensboro Diocese, 10:728
  Sisters of the Agony of Jesus in Gethsemane, 8:444
  slavery, 1:156

Ursulines of Cincinnati, 14:348–349

Ursulines of Cleveland, 14:349

Ursulines of Jesus, 2:158

Ursulines of Kansas City, 14:349

Ursulines of Kentucky, 14:349

Ursulines of Mt. Calvary, 14:349

Ursulines of Quebec, 14:349–350

Ursulines of Tildonk (Beglium), 14:349

Uruguay, 9:496, 13:299, **14:350–352**, *352*

Ury, John, 10:311

L'Usage de la raison de la foi (Regis), 12:31

USCCB. *See* United States Conference of Catholic Bishops (USCCB)

USCMA. *See* United States Catholic Mission Association

Usebtis (little figurines), 9:38

Useful good, 6:353

Usener, Hermann, 1:678, 3:552, 5:285, 10:128

Ushaw College (England), 5:572

Ussher, James, **14:352**

Usuard (9th c. martyrologist), 3:161, 4:262, 5:446, 9:233, 12:548, **14:352–353**

Usury, 3:260, 13:251, 252, **14:353–354**

Ut ampliores et uberiores fructus (apostolic letter, Pius IV), 11:490

Ut in Omnibus Glorificetur Deus (Benedictine motto), **14:355**

Ut Periculosa (apostolic constitution, Boniface VIII), 12:100

Ut Queant Laxis Resonare Fibris (hymn), **14:355**

Ut si quis papa superstite (apostolic constitution, St. Symmachus), 3:104

Ut sit (apostolic constitution, John Paul II), 11:527

Ut unum sint (encyclical, John Paul II), 5:40, 205, 7:1002, 10:853, 12:700, **14:355–356**

Utah, 7:224, **14:356–359**

See also specific dioceses and archdioceses

Uter (Fulcoius of Beauvais), 6:21

Uterque (Fulcoius of Beauvais), 6:21

Uthmān, 14:286

Uthred of Boldon, **14:359**

Utilitarianism, 2:285–286, 624, 13:413, 791

Utility, friendship and, 6:6

Utjesenović, Juraj. *See* Martinuzzi, György (Card.)

Utnapishtim (literary character), 6:223

Utopia (More), 1:667, 7:189–190, 9:*888*, 891–892, 14:360

Utopia and Utopianism, **14:359–362**

Utopian colonies of Ferdinand IV, 12:402

Utraquists, 4:481, **14:362–363**

Bohemian Brethren, 2:460–461

clerical celibacy/marriage, 3:327

Eucharist, 3:605

Hussites, 7:230, 231

Utrecht, Council of (1763), **14:363–364**

Utrecht, Schism of (1723), 3:614, 816, 9:164, 10:260, 579

See also Codde, Pieter (Coddaeus)

Utrecht, Treaty of (1713), 3:788, 7:670

Utrecht, University of (Netherlands), 3:184

Utrecht psalter, 3:154, 9:128

Utriusque sexus (Fourth Lateran Council), 3:231

Utrum forma fiat ex aliquo (Thomas of Sutton), 14:37

Utrum visio creaturae possit naturaliter intendi (Nicholas of Autrecourt), 10:370

Uttara Mīmāṁsā (Hindu philosophy), 6:845–846

Utto, Bl., 9:570, **14:364**

UUA (Unitarian Universalist Association), 14:302, 322

Uvakhshtra (founder of the Medes), 9:428

Uy Van Bui, Domingo, 14:492

Uyarra, Evencio Ricardo, St., 1:298, 299

Uyen Dinh Nguyen, Jose, 14:498–499

Užhorod, Union of (1646), 3:613

Uzon, Jean de, 3:329

V

Vacandard, E., 4:76–77

Vacant, Alfred, **14:365**

Vacante Sede Apostolica (apostolic constitution, Pius X), 11:499

Vacarius (Roman glossator), **14:365**

Vacherot, Étienne, 5:47

Vachon, Alexandre (Abp. of Ottawa), 3:10

Vadstena Abbey (Sweden), 2:618

Vaga, Perino del, 3:484

Vagarshapat, Council of (491), 1:705

Vagnozzi, Egidio, 1:585, **14:365–366**

Vago, P., 3:713

Vahan (Armenian Catholicos), 1:453

Vahanian, Gabriel, 4:586

Vahrām V (King of Persia), 1:700, 805

Vaihinger, Hans, 11:299

Vainglory, 9:42, **14:366**

Vaiśeṣkia (Hindu philosophy), 6:845

Vaishnavism, **14:366**

Vaison, Councils of (529), 11:611

Vajk. *See* Stephen I (King of Hungary), St.

Vajrayāna (Diamond Vehicle), 10:399, **14:366–367**

Vakhtang I Gorgasal (King of Iberia), 6:152

Valadés, Diego, **14:367–368**

Valadier, L., 8:622

Valamo Abbey (Russia), **14:368**

Valbebertus, Bl. *See* Joscio, Bl.

Valcobado Granado, Felipe, Bl., 4:494

Val-de-Grâce Church (France), 3:706

Valdemar the Great (King of Denmark), 1:40

Valdes (Waldo), Peter, 1:231

See also Waldenses

Valdés, Fernando de, (Abp.), 3:176, **14:368**

Valdés, Juan de, 2:856, 3:856, **14:368–369**

Valdes of Lyons, 14:607

Val-des-ecoliers Monastery (France), **14:367**

Valdina, John, 3:328

Valdivia, Luis de, 3:485, **14:369**

Valdivia, Pedro de, 4:132

Valdivielso, José de, 1:925

Valdivieso y Zañartu, Rafael Valentín, (Abp. of Santiago, Chile), 3:486, 5:327, **14:369–370**

Valence, Councils of (374-855), 1:116, 3:518, 4:929, 8:326, 11:783–784, **14:370**

Valencia, Martín de, 12:528, **14:370**

Valenciana Church (Guanajuato, Mexico), 9:*580*

Valenciennes, Martyrs of, 5:973, **14:371**

Valens (Bp. of Mursa), 1:662, 663, 818, 8:54, 12:692

Valens (Roman Emperor), 5:455, 12:318–319, 355, **14:371**

Arianism, 1:51, 522, 663, 3:632

Cyril of Jerusalem, 4:471

Diodore of Tarsus, 4:750

Julian Sabas, St., 8:51

Valentine (Pope), **14:371**

Valentine, Ferdinand, 11:625

Valentine, St., **14:371–372**

Valentini, Pier Francesco, **14:372**

Valentinian I (Roman Emperor), 12:318, 355, **14:373**, 392

Valentinian II (Roman Emperor), 1:338, 6:422, 12:318

Valentinian III (Roman Emperor), 3:363, 6:118, 10:431, 12:365, 13:196, **14:373**

Valentinus (Bp. of Chartres), 3:441

Valentinus (Gnostic philosopher), 10:13, **14:373–374**

   Anicetus (Pope), St., 1:455

   emanationism, 5:181

   fame, 6:260

   Gnosticism, 12:351

   homoousios, 7:65

   procreation, 4:218

Valera, Eamon de, 9:407

Valerian (Bp. of Aquileia), 3:564

Valerian (Roman Emperor), **14:374**

   capture, 12:312

   Paul of Samosata, 5:666

   persecution under, 1:268, 3:103, 223–224, 594, 10:430

Valerio of Bierzo, **14:375**

Valerius, Augustinus, 11:621

Valéry, Waleric. *See* Walarich, St.

Valfré, Sebastian, Bl., **14:375**

Valignano, Alessandro, 7:726, 728, 737, 739, **14:375–376**

   Cerqueira, Luís de, 3:351

   missions, 3:493, 9:4, 12:223

Valla, Giorgio, 1:675

Valla, Joseph, 12:771, 773

Valla, Lorenzo, **14:376–377**

   Aristotelianism, 1:676

   Bessarion, Cardinal, 2:341

   Donation of Constantine, 4:860

   Epicureanism, 5:107, 394, 12:117–118

   Erasmus, 5:314–315

   Hutten, Ulrich von, 7:233

   logic, 8:750

   Renaissance humanism, 7:187, 12:117–118

   Renaissance philosophy, 12:120–121

Vallabha (Hindu teacher), 6:847–848

Valle, Pietro della, 2:360, 3:416

Vallées, Marie de, 2:325, 3:573

Vallgornera, Tomas de, **14:377**

Valliscaulian Order, **14:377–378**

Vallombrosa Abbey (Italy), 5:766, **14:378**

Vallombrosans, **14:378–379**

   Andrew of Strumi, Bl., 1:407

   Canons Regular of St. Augustine, 3:67

   founding, 3:600, 7:957

   Sesto al Réghena Abbey, 13:30

   Settimo Abbey, 13:36

Valls Espí, Crescencia, Bl., 1:4, **14:379**

Valois, Madeline de, 2:179

Valous, G. de, 3:814

Valterius (Bp. of Autun), 1:926

Value, philosophy of, 8:158, 514

Value and culture, theory of, 2:157–158

Value and good, 6:353–354

Value judgment, 1:143–144, 3:824, 8:211, **14:379–380**

Values, 9:875, 10:206–207

Valverde, Vicente de (Bp. of Peru), 3:198, **14:380**

Valverde Téllez, Emeterio (Bp.), **14:380–381**

Vampires, 2:442–443

Van Acken, J., 3:711

Van Bragt, Jan, 7:743

Van Buren, Amilius, 2:607

Van Buren, Paul, 11:890

Van Caloen, Gerard (Bp.), **14:381**

Van de Velde, James O. (Bp.), 3:476–477, 517, 7:685

Van de Ven, Cornelius (Bp. of Alexandria, LA), 1:270

Van de Vyver, Augustine (Bp. of Richmond, VA), **14:383**, *384*, 542–543

Van den Berghe, Pierre, 13:294

Van den Bosch, Anna Maria Tauscher. *See* Mary Teresa of St. Joseph (Mother)

Van Den Broek, Theodore, **14:383**

Van den Eynde, Jan, 3:706

Van der Goes, Hugo, 1:315

Van der Leeuw, G., 3:672

Van Der Schrieck, Louise (Sister), **14:383**

Van der Sterre, J. C., 1:539

Van Der Weyden, Roger, 12:487

Van Dyck, Anthony, 1:539

Van Esche, Nikolaus, 3:16, 192

Van Eyck, Jan, 1:544, 2:374–375

Van Heynoert, Andrew Wouters, 6:364

Van Hilvarenbeek, Adrian, 6:364

Van Hoornaer, John, 6:364

Van Hout, Maria, 3:192

Van Malderen, John. *See* Malderus, John (Bp. of Antwerp)

Van Nice, R. L., 4:188

Van Noort, Gerard, **14:385**

Van Quickenborne, Charles Felix, 4:921, 8:112, 12:562, **14:385–386**

Van Riet, Georges, 12:776

Van Roo, W., 12:475

Van Rossum, Willem Marinus (Card.), **14:386**, *387*

Van seven manieren van Heiligher Minnen (*De divina charitate et septem ejus gradibus*) (Beatrice of Nazareth), 2:181

Van Steenberghen, Fernand, 10:607, 12:776, **14:386–389**

Van van Doan, Peter, 14:499

Van Waeyenbergh, Honoré, 8:824

Van Wely, D., 4:387

Vandals, **14:381–383**

   Arianism, 1:663, 3:186–187, 189

   Desiderius of Cahors, 4:688

   Germany, 6:171

   invasions, 1:284, 3:40, 186–187, 686

   Leo I (Pope), St., 3:595

   rule over Africa (429-534), 10:431–432

Vandame, Charles (Abp. of Chad), 3:361

Vangadizza Abbey (Italy), **14:384**

Vanier, Georges, 3:9

Vanier, Jean, 1:635

Vanini, G. C., 1:677

Vann, Gerald, **14:384–385**

Vanna of Orvieto. *See* Joan of Orvieto, Bl.

Vanne, St. *See* Vitonus (Bp. of Verdun), St.

Vannini, Giuseppina, Bl., 14:*385*, **385**

Vannucci, Pietro. *See* Perugino (Umbrian painter)

Vanuatu, 10:534

Varangians, 10:444–445

Vardan, Mamikonian, St., **14:388–389**

Vardhamāna. *See* Mahāvīra (founder of Jainism)

Varela, Félix (Father), 5:357

Varela, José Isabel Flores, St., 6:545

Vargas, Alonso, 1:879, 888

Vargas, Diego de, 1:687

Vargas, Francisco, 3:145

Vargas, Getúlio, 8:465–466

Variae (Cassiodorus), 9:438

The Varieties of Religious Experience (James), 7:704, 10:115, 12:70

Variety of Religious Experience (James), 1:242

Varin, Joseph, 12:496

Varin d'Ainville, Joseph Désiré, 2:394, 12:493, **14:389**

Varius Avitus Bassianus. *See* Elagabalus (Varius Avitus Bassianus) (Roman Emperor)

Varna, Crusade of (1444), 2:788

Varnhem Abbey (Sweden), 3:750

Varro, Marcus Terentius, 1:673, 3:730, 11:412

Varus, Publius Quinctilius, 12:301

Vas, Caspar, Bl., 7:734

Vasa Gustav (King of Sweden), 5:732

Vasari, Giorgio, 12:111

Vascanelles, Ferraria v. (1860), 3:658

Vasconcelos, Luis Fernandes de, 2:588

Vásquez, Delores (Sister Maria de la Cruz de Cristo Crucificado), 5:879

Vasquez, Pedro, Bl., 7:734

Vásquez de Coronado, Juan, 4:288

Vassalage, Carolingian Dynasty, 3:163, 170, 171, 172

Vassy, Massacre of (1562), 3:266

Västerås, Diet of (1527), 11:218

Vatelot, Jean Baptiste, 3:535

Vatelottes. *See* Sisters of Christian Doctrine (Nancy)

Vatican, **14:389–397**

  art, 1:*598*

  La Civiltà Cattolica, 3:758

  early history, 14:389–394

  Lateran replaced, 8:347

  modern development, 14:396–397

  official representation to U.S., 10:486

  papal residence, 10:366

  Renaissance history, 14:394–396

  Sistine Chapel, 13:190–193

  unofficial diplomatic recognition by U.S., 10:485–486

  See also Holy See; Papacy; Vatican City, State of

Vatican archives, 8:492, 9:500, 10:858–859, 14:*393*, **397–399**, 421

Vatican catalogue (OPAC), 14:422

Vatican City, State of, 12:*350*, 14:*390*, **399–403**

  creation, 2:509, 3:212, 621, 642

  Lateran Pacts, 8:356, 12:323

  map, 14:*400*

  Opening Procession of Vatican Council I (McMahon) in, 14:*402*

  Sistine Chapel, 13:190–193

  United States, 13:770–771

Vatican Council I (1869-70), **14:403–407**

  Aeterni patris, 1:147

  Albertario, Davide, 1:228

  Alemany, Joseph Sadoc, 1:249–250

  Alzog, Johann Baptist, 1:328

  Amat, Thaddeus, 1:332, 8:790

  Baltimore Council (1884), 2:46

  biblical canon, 3:32

  biblical inspiration, 7:494

  Bilio, Luigi, 2:393

Bonnechose, Henri Marie Gaston de, 2:507

  Canon Law, 3:54, 817

  catechesis, 3:234, 244

  Catholic traditionalism, 3:289

  Center Party (Germany), 3:340

  certitude, 3:355, 357

  Church-State relations, 1:914

  composition of, 4:302

  conciliarism, 4:57–58

  Connolly, Thomas Louis, 4:128

  convocation, 4:301

  Corcoran, James Andrew, 4:260

  Cullen, Paul, 4:424

  Czechs, 4:484

  Darboy, Georges, 4:526

  De fide catholica, 8:187

  Dehon, Léon Gustave, 4:613

  Dei Filius (constitution), 5:919

  deposit of faith, 4:675

  dogma as term, 4:811

  dogmatic definition, 4:612

  dogmatic questions, 8:444

  Döllinger, Johannes, 4:824

  Dupanloup, Félix, 4:942–943

  ecclesiastical discipline, 8:264

  Ecumenical councils, 4:305

  Elder, William Henry, 5:144

  evolutionary theory, 5:496

  faith, 5:594, 8:893

  Feehan, Patrick Augustine, 5:663

  fideism, 5:712

  Fitzgerald, Edward, 5:752

  Gasser, Vinzenz Ferrer, 6:106

  God's existence, 6:287

  God's knowledge, 10:593

  Healy, Alexander Sherwood, 1:158

  Hefele, Carl Joseph von, 6:*704*

  hope, 7:95

  immutability of God, 7:356

  Index of Prohibited Books, 7:391

  Ledóchowski, M. H., 8:444

  Lynch, P., 8:904

  magisterium's duty, 14:135

  Manning, Henry Edward, 9:121

  marriage, 1:152

  Melkite Catholic Church, 1:526

  Melkite Greek Church, 9:480

  miracles, 9:659–660, 666–667

  natural theology, 13:921–922

  Opening Procession of Vatican Council I (McMahon), 14:*402*

papal infallibility, 3:621, 4:193, 5:855, 7:448, 449, 450, 12:182, 417

  Acton, John Emerich Edward Dalberg and, 1:85

  Alphonsus Liguori, St., 1:310, 312

  Bilio, Luigi, 2:393

  Bonnechose, Henri Marie Gaston de and, 2:507

  Brentano, Franz and, 2:604

  Canon Law and, 3:54

  Center Party (Germany), 3:340

  Chair of Peter, 3:361

  conciliatory stance, 8:388–389

  de Lugo, J., 8:855

  Fitzgerald, Edward M., 1:692

  Friedrich, Johann, 6:3

  Gallicanism, 3:639

  Germany, 8:253, 255

  Loyson, C., 8:838

  Melchers, Paulus, 3:843

  opposition, 8:146, 149, 160, 13:136

  primacy of jurisdiction, 10:848

  Scheeben defense, 12:730

  Schneemann, Gerhard, 12:745

  Spalding, Martin John, 2:555

  support, 8:269, 904

  teaching authority of the Church, 13:780

  U.S. vote against, 8:613

papal primacy, 1:85, 526, 2:414, 3:621, 11:708–709

primacy of St. Peter, 11:495–496

principle of continuity and progress, 14:136

providence of God, 11:783

reason and revelation, 12:194, 197

redemption, 11:976

refused by Old Catholics, 10:579

Reisach, Karl August von, 12:40

Ryan, Patrick John, 12:447

Schrader, Klemens, 12:786

simplicity of God, 13:137

supernatural destiny, 4:694

teaching authority of the Church, 13:776–777

theological reasoning, 11:949

Thomas Aquinas, St., 14:23

true mysteries defined, 10:83–84

Ultramontanism, 14:285

Williams, John P., 2:555

See also specific documents

Vatican Council II (1962-65),
14:407–418
abortion, 1:28–29
academic freedom, 1:54
adult baptism, 2:65
Agagianian XV, Gregory Peter,
1:169
Agnus Dei, 1:186
Albania, 1:217
altars, 1:318
Alter, Karl J., 3:737
ambos, 1:336
amices, 1:358
Anglican-Catholic dialogue,
1:438–439, 447
Anointing of the Sick, 1:483, 486
apologetics, 1:565–566
apostolic succession, 1:589–590
Apostolicam actuositatem decree of,
10:616
apostolicity, 1:595–596
Argentina, 1:652–653
Arrupe, Pedro, 1:726
asceticism, 1:778
Assumptionists, 1:802
atheism, 1:823–824
Augustinian spirituality, 1:875
Augustinians, 1:888
Australia, 1:905–906, 8:224
Austria, 1:916
Belgium, 2:220–221
Berthier, Jacques, 2:332
Bethlehem Fathers, 2:348
biblical hermeneutics, 6:793
biblical inspiration, 7:496
biblical theology, 2:387–388
bishops, 2:414, 415, 418, 420, 3:626,
7:36
blessings, 2:439–440
Bolivia, 2:469–470
Brazil, 2:598
Brothers of the Christian Schools,
2:631–632, 633, 634
Bulgaria, 2:684
Cameroon, 2:913
Canada, 3:8–9, 10
cantors, 3:73, 75
Cardijn, Joseph, 3:103
Carmelites, 3:130, 146
Carthusians, 3:195
casuistry, 3:221
catafalques, 3:225
catechetical directories, 3:236
catechumenate, 3:252
Catholic Action, 3:277–278

Catholic Theological Union at
Chicago, 3:288
Catholic traditionalism, 3:288–289
Catholic University of America,
3:292
censorship, 3:336
Central Preparatory Commission,
8:447, 13:412
charismatic renewal movement, 3:392
charisms, 3:393
chasubles, 3:446
choirs, 3:522
Christian (term), 3:528
Christian anthropology, 3:532
Christocentrism, 3:558
church architecture, 3:712, 717
Church in New Zealand, 10:327–328
Church-State relations, 1:356–357,
3:642–643, 644
La Civiltà Cattolica, 3:758
clerical celibacy/marriage, 3:328
clerical state, 8:285, 285–286
Code of Canons of the Eastern
Churches, 3:817, 818
commitment to unity of the Church,
14:355
common good, 4:21
communio, 4:27, 29–31
communion of saints, 4:34
Communion outside the liturgy, 4:37
communism, 4:418
concelebration, 4:50
conciliarism, 4:57–58
Confirmation, 4:88
Congar, Yves Marie-Joseph, 4:102,
103
Congo, 4:106
congregational singing, 4:118,
119–120
Consilium from, 4:164–165
*Constitution on the Sacred Liturgy
(Sacrosanctum Concilium)*, 8:611,
12:663
contraception, 1:490
conversion, 4:237, 242
convocation of, 4:301–302
Council of European Bishops'
Conferences, 4:296–297
Daniélou, Jean, 4:516
deacons, 4:552
Dearden, John Francis, 4:568
Declaration on Religious Freedom,
14:103
declarations, 14:417–418

Decree on Church's Missionary
Activity (*Ad gentes*), 5:480, 741,
14:309
Decree on Eastern Catholic Churches
(*Orientalium Ecclesiarum*), 5:20
Decree on Ecumenism (*Unitatis
redintegratio*), 3:590, 626, 4:30,
5:70, 75–76, 12:197, 700, 14:416
Decree on the Bishops' Pastoral
Office in the Church (*Christus
Dominus*), 5:38, 300
decrees, 14:416–417
delegates, 5:252, 665
Dezza, Paolo, 4:713
Diekmann, Godfrey, 4:740
doctrine, 4:808
Dogmatic Constitution on Divine
Revelation (*Dei Verbum*), 10:304,
12:191–192
Dogmatic Constitution on the Church
(*Lumen gentium*), 5:37, 39, 40, 299,
859
Dominican Rite, 4:838
Döpfner, Julius, 4:874
ecclesiastical office, 10:559–560, 561
Ecumenical councils, 4:303, 304, 305
ecumenism, 3:625, 5:74–75
enclosure, 3:806
episcopal collegiality, 3:837
equality for women, 12:550–551
eschatology, 5:346–347
Eucharist outside Mass, 5:432
eucharistic sacrifice, 5:429
evangelical counsels, 4:307
federations of congregations, 13:175
formation, importance of, 8:289
freedom of conscience, 4:149
freedom of inquiry and prohibited
books, 7:390
French participation in, 5:859
Gaudium et spes, 8:358–359, 360
Georgetown University, 6:146
gifts of Holy Spirit, 7:47
grace, 6:394, 400
heresy, 6:779
hierarchy of truths, 4:819, 6:822
historical theology, 6:869–870
holiness as universal, 7:5–7
Holocaust, 7:13
Holy Spirit, 4:857
human rights, 1:456
Hungary, 7:223
hymns and hymnals, 7:259–262
inculturation, 9:678
indifferentism, 7:421
infallibility, 7:448, 449

interest in pacifism and peace issues during, 10:747

Ireland, 7:565–566

Is It the Same Church? (Sheed), 13:73

Jamaica, 3:112

Jesuits, 1:725, 7:793

John XXIII (Pope), Bl., 7:936

John Paul II (Pope) at, 7:994–995

justification dialogues, 8:90–91

just-wars, 14:640–641

Kingdom of God, 8:175

kiss of peace, 8:185

König, Franz, 8:232

Korea, 8:239

laity, 8:288, 290, 291–292, 412

Lateran Pacts (1985), 8:357

Latin American Church, 4:157

lay spirituality, 8:413, 416–417

Léger, P., 8:452

Lent, 8:469

liberation theology, 4:820

liturgical reforms, 12:258

liturgical conference, 8:646

liturgical gestures, 8:650

liturgical inculturation, 7:383, 385, 430

liturgical language, 8:668–669

liturgical movement, 8:676

liturgical music history, 8:699–701

liturgical reform, 8:61–62, 438, 440, 617, 625–626, 628–630, 664–666, 10:43, 564

liturgical vessels, 3:370

liturgy, 8:727

liturgy and sacraments, 12:256, 468, 471, 472

Liturgy of the Hours, 8:731–733

local and universal Church, 5:38

Logos, 8:764

Louisville Archdiocese, 8:818

Louvain, Catholic University of, 8:824

mandatory retirement, 12:642

Marianists, 9:162

Mariology, 9:172, 257

Maryknoll Fathers and Brothers missions, 9:296–297

matrimony, Sacrament of, 9:336

McQuaid, John Charles, 9:407–408

Melkite Catholic Church, 1:526

Melkite Greek Catholic Church, 9:480

Mercy Sisters, 13:185–186

Meyer, Albert Gregory, 3:479, 9:588–589

ministry of reconciliation, 11:955, 956

missiology, 9:677–678

mission, 3:429, 9:684–685

moral education, 9:847

moral theology, 9:866–867

Murray, John, 10:69

Mysterium fidei (''Mystery of the Faith'') on liturgy reform of, 10:77–79

natural-law theory, 10:185

nature of God, 6:287

new morality, 8:868

nonviolence, 14:642–644

Order of Mass, 14:182

Orthodox Church, 1:829

overview, 3:626

papal primacy, 11:709

Passionists, 10:932

Paul VI (Pope), 11:29–30, 33

penance, 11:71–72

Perfectae Caritatis decree of, 10:460, 483

periods, 14:409–415

Philippines, 11:261–262

Pontifical Bible Commission, 11:477–478

Pontifical Commission for the Neo-Vulgate, formation of, 14:598

popular devotions, 4:710

Portugal, 11:539–540

poverty, 11:566

preaching, 11:615–616, 628

Prepatory Commission, 12:258, 396

priesthood, 11:705–706

Pro Mundi Vita (Brussels), 11:726

pronouncements, 14:415–416

prophecy, 11:761

reform of ordination rites, 10:640

reform of viaticum, 14:470–471

religious freedom, 5:946–947, 952–954, 8:232

religious habit, 12:100

religious pluralism, 12:858–859

renewal of religious communities, 13:171, 176, 186

revelation, 12:191, 196–197

Roman Breviary, 2:610

Roman Curia reform, 12:272

Roman Pontifical, 11:474

rural life, 8:586

Sacraments, 12:467, 468, 476, 479–481

sanctoral cycle of the Roman calendar, 12:663

Secretariat for Non-Believers, 12:858

secular institutes, 12:862

sensus fidelium, 12:917

Servite revisions, 13:29

Sisters, Servants of the Immaculate Heart of Mary, 7:339

Sisters for Christian Community founding, 13:171

Slovakia, 13:223

social effects of technology, 13:786

social issues, 2:469

social justice, 13:244

Spain, 13:397

spirituality, 13:448–449

Sri Lanka, 13:465–466

strict constructionist view, 8:250

study of the Fathers, 10:963

Suenens, Leon-Joseph, 13:585

Sunday observance, 13:608, 609

systematic theology, 4:814

teaching, 13:774

teaching authority of the Church, 13:778

team ministry, 13:782

theological and pastoral writing, 10:623–624

theological anthropology, 1:509

theological commission, 8:840

theological reasoning, 11:950

theology of Christ and world religions, 7:840

theology of Church, 3:590

theology of hope, 13:927

theology of society, 13:287

Thomism, 3:466

tolerance theory and practice, 14:103

universality of Christianity, 3:293

vernacular in liturgy, 4:201, 7:523

vision of Church as *Communio*, 10:852

war, 4:151

women, status of, 14:819–820

See also Code of Canon Law (CIC) (1983); *Constitution on the Sacred Liturgy*; *specific documents*

Vatican Library, 5:865, **14:418–422**, *419*

Canon Law, 8:257

catalogue of manuscripts, 13:167

Chigi family, 3:484

Clement XIII (Pope), 3:793

establishment and development, 14:396

new building, 13:198

Vatican Library *(continued)*
    Nicholas V (Pope), 7:185, 10:369
    opened to outside researchers,
        13:197, 14:399
Vatican Library database (ISTC), 14:422
Vatican museums, 14:396–397
Vatican Observatory, 14:*392*, 397
Vatican Palace, 1:261
Vatican press, 9:130
Vatican Registers, 10:859
Vaticana, 3:39
La Vaticane de Paul IV à Paul V
    (Batiffol), 2:*155*
Vaticinium Sibillae Erithreae
    (apocalyptic text), 7:980
Vatier, Antoine (Father), 3:185
Vatke, J. K. Wilhelm, 2:384, 385, 5:519
Vatra Moldoviţa Abbey. *See* Moldoviţa
    Abbey (Moldova)
Vaugeois, Henri, 1:81
Vaughan, Bernard John, **14:422–423**,
    423
Vaughan, Herbert (Card.), 5:879, 880,
    9:632, 10:515, **14:423**
    Dublin Review, 4:917
    Ealing Abbey, 5:2
    Josephites founding, 7:1047
    Westminster Abbey, 5:252
Vaughan, R. A., 10:114
Vaughan, Roger William Bede (Abp. of
    Sydney, Australia), **14:424**
Vaughan, Thomas, 5:238
Vaughan Williams, Ralph, **14:424**, *425*
Vaux, Laurence, 3:233, 243, 5:237
Vaux, R. de, 2:532, 7:764
Vaux-De-Cernay Abbey (France),
    14:425, *426*
Vawter, B., 5:523
Vaz, Amaro, Bl., 1:951
Vaz, Joseph, Bl., 7:406, **14:425–426**
Vázques, Gabriel, 7:782
Vázquez, Donato, 2:468
Vázquez, Francisco Javier, **14:426**
Vázquez, Gabriel, 14:49, 51, **427**
    Alamanni, Cosmo, 1:204
    Aloysius Gonzaga, St., 1:305
    distinction, 4:780
    moral theology, 9:848
    scholasticism, 12:766
    Thomistic philosophy, 12:619
Vazquez, Lucy (Sister), 3:58
Vázquez, Pablo (Bp.), **14:427–428**
Vázquez de Espinosa, Antonio, 3:143,
    14:428
Vázquez de Herrera, Francisco, **14:428**

Veatch, John C., 10:649
Vecchi, Juan, 12:614
Vecchio, Giorgio del, 10:185
Vecelli, Tiziano, 1:37, 2:114, 4:*319*,
    8:345, 13:*142*
Vechel, Leonard, 6:364
Vedānta, 7:408, **14:429**
Vedas, 7:407, 9:125, **14:429**
Vedast of Arras, St., 1:721, 2:904,
    10:255, 12:588, **14:429**
Vedder, Elihu, 5:*637*
Vedic scriptures, 6:840
Vedruna de Mas, Joaquina, St., 3:129,
    14:429–430
Vedulph, St., 1:721
Vega, Andreas de, **14:430**
Vega, Angel, 1:889
Vega, Lope de, 1:925, 2:111, 116
Vegetation cults. *See* Fertility and
    vegetation cults
Il Veggente del secolo XIX (Tosti),
    14:120
Vegius, Mapheus, **14:430**
Vehementer nos (encyclical, Pius X),
    4:63, 11:390
Vehr, Urban J. (Abp. of Denver), 2:348,
    3:859, 4:669–670
Veils, **3:370**, 4:249, *249*, 254, 257,
    8:630–631, 14:546
Veith, Johann Emmanuel, 1:914
Velasco, Catalina, 3:461
Velasco, Pedro de, **14:430–431**
Velázquex Peláez, Juan Bautista, Bl.,
    7:123
Velázquez, Diego Rodríquez de Silva,
    1:739, 2:114, 376, 4:397
Velázquez de Cuéllar, Diego, 4:417
Vélez Saldarriaga, Rafael Gildardo
    (Father), 5:450
Velitchkovsky, Paissy, 9:802, 12:425,
    14:431
Velleity, 4:158
"Velvet Revolution" of 1988
    (Czechoslovakia), 14:107
Venantius (Bp. of Viviers), St.,
    14:431–432
Venantius Fortunatus, 4:380
Venantius of Tours, St., **14:431**
Vénard, Jean Théophane, St., **14:432**,
    499
A Venatione aegrocerotis assertio
    (Emser), 5:200
Vence, Chapelle du Rosaire, 4:324,
    8:623, 627, 636, **14:432–433**
Vendeville, Jean, 1:295, 11:749
Vendôme (Sainte-Trinité) Abbey
    (France), **14:433**

Vendramini, Elisabetta, Bl., **14:433**
Vendville, Jean (Bp.), **14:433–434**
Venegas de la Torre, Marí de Jesús
    Sacramentado, St., **14:434**
Venerabilem, (decretal, Innocent III),
    7:43
Venerable (title), **14:434**
Venerable Bede. *See* Bede, St.
Veneration of Mary, Blessed Virgin,
    9:266, 269
Veneration of the cross, 6:355–356
Venerini, Rose, Bl., 5:722
Venerini Sisters, **14:434**
Venerius (Bp. of Marseilles), 8:435
Venetian choir (St. Marks), 3:523
Venetian Inquisition, 7:491
Veneto, Paolo, 1:675, 937, 8:750,
    14:435
Veneziano, G., 12:679
Venezuela, **14:435–438**, *439*, *440*, *441*
    Augustinian Recollects, 1:324
    Caribbean Sea, 3:116
    Coll y Prat, Narciso, 3:835–836
    demographic statistics, 14:435
    ecclesiastical organization, 14:438
    map, 14:*437*
    missions, 3:94, 9:711, 12:407,
        14:435–436
Vengeance, 1:814, 815, 2:443, 444,
    444–445, 12:140–141, **14:438–439**
Veni creator spiritus (hymn), 9:443,
    14:439–440
Veni Creator Spiritus, a Theological
    Encyclopedia of the Holy Trinity,
    5:208
Veni sancte spiritus (sequence), 9:460,
    14:440–441, **440–441**
Venial sins, 9:903, 11:825, 13:150, 155
Veniaminov, Innokentij (Bp. of
    Kamchtka, 1797-1879), 9:695
Veniaminov, John, 10:682
Venice (Italy), 4:413, 461–462, 13:98
Venice, Treaty of (1177), 1:255, 3:319
Venice, Truce of (1177), 8:767
Venida del mesías en gloria y majestad
    (Lacunza), 8:274
Venizy, Étienne de, 1:265
Ventaja Milan, Diego (James) (Bp. of
    Almería), St., 1:299
Ventura, G., 14:138
Ventura, St. (17th c. Japanese martyr),
    7:732
Ventura di Raulica, Gioacchino, 12:771,
    773, **14:441–443**, *442*
Venturini, K. H. G., 7:847
Venturino of Bergamo, **14:443**

Venus (planet), 6:60

Vera, Jacinto (Bp. of Montevideo), 14:351, **443**

La Vera chiesa di Cristo (Gotti), 6:370

Vera Cruz, Fray Alonso de la, **14:443–444**

Veranus (Bp. of Cavaillon), St., **14:444**

Veranus (Bp. of Venice), St., 5:438

Veráscola, Francisco de, 5:875

Verbal inspiration, 3:174

Verbeke, Gérard, 12:776

Verbi sponsa (instruction, John Paul II), 1:586, 3:806

Verbiest, Ferdinand, 3:497, 7:784

Verbist, Theophile, 7:337, **14:444–445**, *445*

Verbum (periodical), 5:840

Verbum Caro, an Encyclopedia on Jesus, 5:208

Verbum supernum prodiens (hymns), **14:445**

Verdadera informaçam das terras do Preste Joam (Álvares), 1:324, 325, *325*

Verdi, Giuseppe, **14:445–446**, *446*

Verdun, synod of (947), 1:172

Verdun, Treaty of (843), 3:155, 157, 170, 172, 8:481, 795

Verdun-Sur-Meuse Abbey (France), 5:760, **14:447**

Veremundus (Carl Muth), 10:75

Veremundus, St., **14:447**

Vereula Monastery (Spain), 14:*461*

Der Verfall der kirchlichen Kunst (*La Decadence de l'art sacré*) (Cingria), 3:711

Vergara, Francisco de, 1:95–96

Vergel de oració y monte de contemplación (Orozco), 10:674

Vergentis in senium (decretal, Innocent III), 1:231, 7:472, 488

Verger, Rafael, **14:447**

Vergerio, Pier Paolo, 5:90, 12:622, **14:448**

Vergil (Publius Vergilius Maro), 1:167–168, 540, 928, 4:519–520, 12:307, **14:448–449**, *449*

Vergil, Polydore, **14:449–450**

Vergil, St. *See* Virgilius of Salzburg, St.

Vergilian *sortes*. *See* Sortes Homericae, Vergilianae, Biblicae

Vergote, A., 12:475

Verhaegen, Peter J., 12:562, **14:450**

Verheijen, Luc, 1:868, 869

Verification, 1:949, 3:352, 8:756, **14:450–451**

Verification theory of meaning, 3:147

Verigin, Peter Vasilivich, 4:887

Verità della fede (St. Alphonsus Liguori), 1:310

La Véritable décision (Basile of Soissons), 2:140

Veritatis splendor (encyclical, John Paul II), 5:205, 560, 6:26, 7:998, 10:852, **14:451–452**

   casuistry, 3:219, 220, 221

   consequentialism, 4:160

   human capacity to know truth, 7:1002

   moral circumstances, 3:743

   moral relativism, 3:627

   natural law reasoning, 10:185

Verkamp, Gabriel (Archabbot), 12:568

Vermeer, Jan, 2:114

Vermeersch, Arthur, 4:222, 13:242–243, **14:452–453**

Vermes, Geza, 6:866

Vermeylen, Jacques, 11:97

Vermigli, Peter Martyr, 2:653, 7:167, 10:535

Vermont, **14:453–456**

   See also specific dioceses and archdioceses

Vernacular

   catechesis, 3:230–231, 234, 246

   choirs, 3:524

   Council of Trent, 8:660

   Culdees, 4:423

   Cummins, Patrick, 4:437

   early translations, 8:364

   humanism, 7:189–190

   inclusive language use, 8:439–440

   La Salle, John Baptist de, 4:622–623

   lectionaries, 8:439

   Malaysia, 9:71

   New Testament in French, 8:449, 460

   19th-20th century Bible translations, 3:623

   Orthodox missions, 9:694

   Sri Lanka, 13:465–466

   Sunnnites, 13:614

   U.S., 8:675–676

   Vatican Council II, 4:201

   See also Hymnology, vernacular

Vernacular Passion plays, 10:927–928

Vernazza, Battista, 3:271

Vernazza, Ettore, 3:270, 271, 415, 4:787

Verner, Sherbert v. (1963), 3:662–663

Verney, L. A., 12:770

Vernia, Nicoletto, 1:676, 937

Vernice, Mary (Sister), 3:283

Vernier, St. *See* Werner of Oberwesel, St.

Vernoy de Montjournal, Jean-Baptiste Ignace Pierre, 12:278

Verny, St. *See* Werner of Oberwesel, St.

Verona Fathers, 3:622, 4:1, 13:582

Verona illustrata (Maffei, Francesco Scipione), 9:32

Verona-Rome Maffei. *See* Maffei family

Veronese, Paolo, 2:114

Veronica (biblical figure), **14:457**, *458*

Verot, Jean Pierre Augustin Marcellin (Bp. of Savannah), 3:243, 12:709, **14:457–459**, *458*

Verreydt, Felix, 10:220

"Vers del lavador" (Marcabru), 4:400

Verschaffelt, Pierre (Pietro Fiammingo), 3:213

Verses to the Memory of an Unfortunate Lady (Pope), 11:497

Versiglia, Aloisius (Bp.), 12:615

Versiglia, Louis (Bp.), 3:99

Versiglia, Luigi, St., **14:459**

Versperbuch lateinisch und deutsch, 12:785

Verstegan, Richard, **14:460**

Verstegan, Rowlands. *See* Verstegan, Richard

Versuch einer Kritik aller Offenbarung (Fichte), 5:708

Vert, Claude de, 8:647

Vertin, John, **14:460**

Veruela Abbey (Spain), **14:460**

Verum et bonum convertuntur (Truth and good are convertible), 12:756–757

Verum Sapientia (apostolic constitution, John XXIII), 11:488

Verus, Lucius Aurelius (Roman Emperor), 12:304

Verus, Marcus Annius. *See* Marcus Aurelius (Roman Emperor)

Verwyst, Chrysostom Adrian, **14:461**

Very, Jones, 14:148

Verzeri, Girolamo (Bp.), 3:816

Verzeri, Teresa Eustochio, Bl., 12:490, **14:462**

Vesailus, Andreas, 2:402, 12:817

Vespasian (Roman Emperor), 7:1048, 12:301, 304, 311, 351

Vespers, **14:462–463**, *463*

   Custodes Hominum Psallimus Angelos, 4:448

   Iam Sol Recedit Igneus, 7:269

   Iam Toto Subitus Vesper, 7:269

   importance, 8:732

   Liturgy of the Hours, 8:729

   Sacred Heart, Feast of the, 5:201

Vespers *(continued)*
  Scripture reading, 8:733
  Vatican Council II, 8:731
  See also Lucernarium (lighting of the lamps)
Vespucci, Amerigo, 14:*438*
Vestal virgins, 3:322, 14:*464*, **464**
Vestiarian controversy, 3:197
Vestments. *See* Clerical dress
Vetancurt, Agustín de, **14:464–465**
Veterans, Knights of Columbus, 8:19, 190–191
Veteris et Novi Testamenti nova translatio (Pagnini), 10:753
Veterum Patrum Latinorum opuscula (Trombelli), 14:213
Veterum sapientia (apostolic constitution, John XXIII), 7:937, 8:365
Veth, Martin (Abbot), 12:539
Vetus et nova ecclesiae disciplina (Thomassin), 6:876
Vetus Romana, 3:39
Veuillot, Louis François, **14:465–466**
  Dupanloup, Félix, 4:942
  freedom of religion, 5:948
  French Catholic controversy, 5:855
  Napoleon III, 10:150
  Ultramontanism, 10:847
Veuster, Joseph de (Fr. Damien), Bl., 6:670, **14:466–467**, *467*, *468*
Veuthey, Michel, 14:321
Vexilla Regis Prodeunt (hymn), 4:380, 5:823, **14:467–468**
Vexillum, 4:180
Vezzosi, Antonio Francesco, **14:468**
Via Coeli (Heaven's Way), 12:678
Via della salute (St. Alphonsus Liguori), 1:309
Via media, 10:733–734, 851
Via negativa, 10:113
Via regia (Smaragdus), 13:228
Via sancti Oswaldi auctore anonymo (Raine, ed.), 10:708
Viadana, Lodovico da, **14:468**
Viage santo (Ambrosio de Morales), 5:775
Vialar, Émilie de, St., **14:469**
Viance, St. *See* Vincentian, St.
Vianney, Jean Baptiste Marie, St., 3:374, 473, 759, 4:363, 12:31, **14:469–470**
Viard (Guy), Ven., 3:296
Viaticum, 1:482, 486, 5:418, 432, **14:470–471**
Viator of Sologne, St., 8:275
Viatorians, 3:622, 13:74, **14:471**

Vicar Forane, **14:472**
Vicar of Christ, **14:472**
  See also specific popes
Vicari, Hermann von (Abp. of Freiburg im Breisgau), **14:472–473**
Vicariate apostlic, 8:368
Vicariate Apostolic of New Mexico (1850), 10:286–287
Vicariate Apostolic of the Territory East of the Rocky Mountains, 10:221
Vicariate Apostolic of the Two Guineas, 10:383
Vicariate of Nebraska, 10:221
Vicar's Tribunal in Naples (18th c.), 8:*42*
Vice, **14:473–474**
  deadly sins, 4:565–567
  human act, 7:170–171
  iconography, 14:555–557
  natural law, 10:190
  sin compared, 13:150
  Soirées de St. Pétersbourg (Maistre), 9:61
  superstitions of God as, 13:623
  virtues, 9:881, 14:550
Vicelinus (Bp. of Oldenburg), St., **14:474**
Vicente Castillo, Primo Martínez de S, Bl., 7:122
Vichev, Kamen, 2:548
Viciariate Apostolic East of the Rocky Mountains to Missouri, 8:113, 117
Vico, Giambattista, 14:*475*, **475–476**
  atomism, 1:835
  characteristics of music, 10:72–73
  dialectic, 8:539
  philosophical romanticism, 12:345
  philosophy of history, 6:884, 885
Victim, perfect, 4:74
Victimae paschali laudes, 4:894, 13:5, **14:476–477**
Victimas del Corazón Eucarística de Jesús, 12:274
Victor. *See* Victurius (Bp. of Le Mans, France), St.
Victor (3rd c. martyr), 12:590
Victor (Bp. of Tunnuna), **14:482**
Victor (Bp. of Vita), **14:482–483**
Victor, SS., **14:477**
Victor I (Pope), St., 5:13, 11:857, 12:351, **14:477–478**
Victor II (Pope), Bl., 7:199, **14:478**
Victor III (Pope), 1:306, 7:151, **14:478–481**, *479*

Victor IV (Antipope), 1:254, 2:548, 10:916
  Callistus III (Antipope), 2:882
  confusion over numbering of, 11:502
  Elizabeth of Schönau, 5:166
  Frederick I Barbarossa, 5:925
  Gerhoh of Reichersberg, 6:167
  Hugh Bonnevaux, 7:149
Victor IV (Antipope, fl. 1138), **14:480**
Victor IV (Antipope, fl. 1159-1164), **14:480–481**
Victor IV (Count of Sicily), 7:470
Victor Amadeus I (Duke of Savoy). *See* Savoy, Victor Amadeus I, Duke of
Victor Amadeus II (Duke of Savoy). *See* Savoy, Victor Amadeus II, Duke of
Victor Amadeus III (Duke of Savoy). *See* Savoy, Victor Amadeus III, Duke of
Victor Emannuel II (King of Italy), 3:314, **14:481–482**
Victor of Plancy, St., **14:482**
Victor of Tunnuna, 1:461
Victor of Vita, 3:186, 12:606
Victoria (martyr of Córdoba), 4:261
Victoria, Francisco de (Bp. of Tucumán), 1:649
Victoria, Tomás Luis de, 8:688, **14:483–484**
Victoria and Anatolia, SS., **14:484**
Victoria de mundo (Orozco), 10:674
Victoriano Pío, Br., 14:248
Victorine spirituality, **14:484–486**
  charity, 3:395
  Edmund of Abingdon, 5:86
  history, 13:446
  John of the Cross, St., 3:136
  Lull, 8:866
  Thomas (prior), 12:589
Victorinus, Marius, **9:181–182**
Victorinus of Pettau, St., 5:512, 7:48, 12:186, **14:486**
Victorius. *See* Victurius (Bp. of Le Mans, France), St.
Victorius of Aquitaine, 5:13
Victricius (Bp. of Rouen), St., 10:426, 12:582, **14:486**
Victurius (Bp. of Le Mans, France), St., **14:486–487**
Vicuña, Laura, Bl., **14:487**
Vicuná Larraín, Manuel (Abp. of Santiago), 3:12, 486, **14:487**
Vida (St. Teresa of Avila), 2:49
Vida, Marco Girolamo, **14:487–488**
La Vida Breve (Falla), 5:612

Vida de Don Quijote y Sancho (Unamuno y Jugo), 14:288

La Vida de la madre Teresa de Jesús (Ribera), 12:220

La Vida espiritual coronada por la tripe manifestación de Jesucristo (Sorazu), 13:325

Vida maravillosa de la Venerable Virgen Doña Marina de Escobar, 5:353

Vida y Virtudes del V. Hermano Pedro de San José Betancur (Vázquez de Herrera), 14:428

Vidal, Ricardo (Card.), 11:*258*

Vidal, St. Croix (Mother), 12:496

Vidal de Furno. *See* Vital du Four (Card. Bp. of Albano)

Vidal Pastor, María de la Purificación, Bl., 1:4

Vidauretta Labra, Atanasio, 2:92

Vidaurre, Manuel Lorenzo, 1:724

Videla, Jorge Rafael, 1:655

Vidēvdāt (Persian text), 11:142, 143

Vie, Dominic de (Abp. of Auch), 2:190

La Vie de Jesus (Steinmann), 7:391

La Vie de Jésus Christ (Life of Jesus) (Renan), 7:848, 852, 12:126

Vie de la bienheureuse Germaine Cousin, bergére (Veuillot), 14:466

La Vie de l'union à Dieu et les moyens d'y arriver, d'après les grands mîtres de la spiritualité (Saudreau), 12:708

Vie de M. Olier (Nagot), 10:135

Vie de Notre Seigneur Jésus-Christ (Veuillot), 14:465

Vie de S. François (Sabatier), 12:453

Vie de saint Louis (Joinville), 4:401

Vie Diocésaine de Dijon (periodical), 2:98

Vie et grandeurs de la très sainte Vierge Marie (Gibieuf), 6:208

La Vie et le royaoume de Jésus dans les âmes chrétiennes (St. Eudes), 5:441

La Vie et l'esprit de S. Charles Borromée (Touron), 14:125

La Vie inconnue de Jésus Christ (Notovitch), 7:852

La vie intellectuelle (Sertillanges), 13:23

La Vie intérieure simplifyée et ramenée à son fondement (Pollien), 11:462

La Vie littéraire (France), 5:841

La Vie liturgique (Beauduin), 2:183

Vie mondaine et vie chrétienne à la fin du II siécle (Tixeront), 14:95

Vieban, Anthony, **14:487–488**

Vieira, Antônio, 2:115, 591, **14:488–489**

Viel, Placida, Bl., **14:489**

Viel, Victoria Eulalia Jacqueline. *See* Viel, Placida, Bl.

Viel Ferrando, María del Carmen, Bl., 1:4

Viela Ezcurdia, Agustín, 2:92

Vien Dinh Dang, Joseph, 14:499

Vienamese parish (New Orleans), 10:297

Vienna, Congress of (1814), 3:*617*, 618

Vienna, Treaty of (1735), 7:670

Vienna, University of (Austria), 1:913–914, 8:187, 232, 313

Vienna Archdiocese (Austria), 8:188

Vienna Cathedral (Austria), 12:487

Vienna Circle, 3:147, 301, 8:220–221, 755–756

Vienna formula, 8:232

Vienna Itinerary (*De locis sanctis martyrum quae sunt foris civitatem Romae*), 7:676–677

Vienne, Council of (1311-12), **14:489–491**

   Apostolic Penitentiary, 11:76

   beatific vision, 2:169

   Clementinae, 3:46, 48, 50, 780, 800

   collation, 4:707

   condemnation of Olivi's teachings, 14:23

   Duranti, William the Younger, 4:950

   exegesis, 5:517

   Franciscan Spirituals debate, 12:232

   preaching, 11:612, 613

   university curriculum, 12:611

   usury, 14:354

Vieria, Antônio, 3:417, 7:785

Vierne, Louis Victor, **14:491**

Vierzehnheiligen Church (Franconia), 3:671, 675, 707

Les Vies des saints (Baillet), 6:615

Les Vies des saints dont on fait l'office dans le cours de l'année (Giry), 6:232

Vietnam, **14:499–507**, *504*, *505*

   Andrew the Catechist, Bl., 1:407–408

   Buddhism, 2:669–670

   Cao Dai, 3:79–80, *79*

   congregations, 4:113–114

   demographic statistics, 14:500

   ecclesiastical organization, 14:501

   Lovers of the Holy Cross (LHC), 8:834–835

   map, 14:*503*

   missions, 1:407–408, 8:186, 834, 9:700, 12:218–219, 14:500

   Our Lady of La Vang, 8:385–386

Vietnam, Martyrs of, SS., **14:491–499**

Vietnam War (1959-1975), 3:756, 4:151, 8:30, 329, 385–386

Vietnamese Americans, 2:872, 4:114, 8:816

Vietnamese Dominican Sisters of St. Catherine of Siena, 4:834–835

Vietnamese Episcopal Conference, 14:503, 504

A View from the Ridge (West), 14:686

A View of the Evidences of Christianity (Paley), 10:803

Viganò, Egidio, 12:614

Vigerio, Marco (Card. Bp. of Palestrina), **14:507**

Vigil, Francisco de Paula González, 3:102, **14:507–509**, *508*

Vigil, Jose Miguel (Father), 3:857

Vigil for the Deceased, 6:31–32

Vigilantiae (apostolic letter, Leo XIII), 11:476

Vigilantus of Toulouse, 12:51

Vigilius (Bp. of Auxerre), St., **14:511**

Vigilius (Pope), 11:59, **14:509–511**

   Ambrosian Rite, 1:343

   Bragan Rite, 2:579

   Cerbonius, St., 3:349

   Constantinople Council II, 4:191–192

   creedal statements, 4:354

   demonology, 4:649

   diptychs, 4:759

   Eutychius (Patriarch of Constantinople), 5:463

   Facundus of Hermiane condemned, 5:587

   Judicatum, 14:64

   Justinian I (Byzantine Emperor), 3:596, 4:186, 191, 8:97–99

   papal rule, 12:355

   prohibited books, 7:390

   Silverius (Pope), St., 13:123

   Theodore of Mopsuestia, 7:816

   Three Chapters, 4:191, 192, 5:587, 7:656

Vigils, 9:332–333, 11:350

Vignier, Jérôme, **14:511–512**

Vignola, Giacomo. *See* Barozzi, Giacomo

Vignon, Pierre, 3:708

Vigor (Bp. of Bayeux), 2:163

Vigouroux, Fulcran Grégoire, **14:512**

Vikings, 1:149, 279–281, 449, 7:554, 10:444–445, 12:830–832

Vikstrom, John (Abp.), 5:734

Viktring Abbey (Carinthia, Austria), **14:512**

Vilar David, Vicente, Bl., **14:512**

Vilarrasa, Francis Sadoc, 12:646–647, **14:513**

Villa Albani, 3:793

Villa of the Mysteries fresco (Pompeii), 10:*87*, 93–94

Villagómez, Pedro (Bp. of Arequipa), 3:101

Villa-Lobos, Heitor, 14:*513*, **513–514**

Villalobos, Marqués, 3:110

Villalón, Aurelio María, St., 1:298, 299

Villalonga Villalba, Pilar, Bl., 1:4

Villani, Filippo, 12:110

Villani, Giovanni, 1:465, **14:514**

Villanova University (Philadelphia), 1:891, **14:514–515**

Villanueva Igual, Faustino, Bl., 7:124

Villanuevo Larráyoz, Pedro de Alcántara, 7:124

Villarroel, Gaspar de (Bp.), **14:515**

La Ville (Claudel), 3:768

Villehardouin, Geoffroi de, 4:401

Villèle, Joseph de, 8:198

Villeneuve, Jean Marie Rodrigue (Card.), **14:515–516**

Villeneuve-Bargemont, Jean Paul Alban de, **14:516–517**

Villeneuve-les-Avignon Abbey (France), **14:517**

Villenoce, Drogon Hennequin de, 2:323

Villers Abbey (Belgium), 3:436, 750, **14:517**

Villot, Jean (Card.), **14:517–518**

Villula, John de, 2:152

Vilsack, Tom, 7:543

Vimont, Barthélemy, 3:4

Vincennes Diocese (IN), 7:413, 417

Vincent, A., 5:520

Vincent, H., 4:385

Vincent, John Heyl (Bp.), 3:458, 722

Vincent, Louis-Hugues, 5:50, 7:767–768

Vincent, Paul Marie Théodore. *See* Indy, Vincent d'

Vincent, Widmar v. (1981), 3:664

Vincent Castillo, Primo Martínez de S., 7:122

Vincent de Paul, St., 3:417, 5:750, **14:518–520**, *519*

   Bonal, Raymond, 2:478

   Bossuet, Jacques Bénigne, 2:549, 550

   catechesis, 3:235

   Chrysostom of Saint-Lô, John, 3:573

   Church reform in France, 5:850

   Compagnie du Saint-Sacrement, 4:41

   Condren, Charles de, 4:74

   Cottolengo, Giuseppe, 4:292

   Counter Reformation, 1:926, 3:612

   hospitals, 7:139

   The Little Method, 11:621–622

   prisoners, 3:419

   shrine, 13:94

   Sisters of Charity, Federation of, 13:172

   Vincentians founding, 14:525

Vincent de S. José, Bl., 7:733

Vincent Ferrer, St., 8:750, 9:461, **14:520–521**

Vincent Madelgarius, St., 6:233, **14:521–522**

Vincent of Beauvais, 5:206, 529, **14:522–523**

   bestiaries, 2:343

   chronicle of, 1:463, 464

   medieval Latin literature works, 9:463

   Simon's *Historia*, 13:132

Vincent of Lérins, St., 6:*112*, 14:136, **523–524**

   Calixtus, Georg, 2:874

   doctrine, 4:804

   Fathers of the Church, 5:640

   studies, 8:268

   universality of Christianity, 3:275

Vincent of Spain (Bp.), 3:48, 14:524, **524–525**

Vincentian, St., **14:525**

Vincentian Rule, 13:34, 172

Vincentians, 5:651, **14:525–529**

   Algeria, 1:285

   Carthage, 3:188

   Chinese persecution, 14:528

   journalism in China, 8:428–429

   Kulturkampf, 8:254

   missions, 8:18, 809

   19th-20th century overview, 3:621

   slavery, 1:156

   Vincent de Paul, St., founding, 14:518

   See also Lazarists

Vincentino, Nicola, 1:766, **14:475**

Vincenzo Maria of the Order of Preachers. *See* Benedict XIII (Pope)

Vindicationes Societatis Jesus (Pallavicino), 10:806

Vindiciae alfonsianae, 1:311

Vindiciae contra tyrannos, 13:240

Vindiciae pro suprema pontificis potestate contra Febronium (St. Alphonsus Liguori), 1:310

Vindicianus of Cambrai-Arras (Bp.), St., **14:529**

Vine symbolism, 3:629

Vinea electa (apostolic letter, Pius X), 11:485

Vineam Domini (apostolic constitution, Clement XI), 7:718, 10:406

Vineam Domini (papal bull, Clement XI), 3:789, 5:358

Vines, symbols of, 13:666–667

Vinet, Alexandre Rodolphe, **14:529–530**

Vintimille, Charles de (Abp. of Aix), 1:197

Violence, 4:149–151, 159, **14:530–531**, 584

   See also Capital punishment; Force and fear; Force and moral responsibility

Viollet-le-Duc, Eugène Emmanuel, 3:677, 694, 709, 13:472, 474–475

Viracocha (Incan deity), 7:368

Viret, Pierre, **14:531**

Virgil. *See* Vergil (Publius Vergilius Maro)

Virgilius (Abp. of Arles), St., **14:531**

Virgilius of Salzburg, St., 1:529–530, 908, 2:496, 12:413, 671, **14:531–532**

The Virgin and Child (Luca della Robbia), 14:*533*

Virgin and Child with Saints (Titian), 7:667

Virgin birth, 5:162–163, 9:168–169, **14:532–539**

   Christ in Book of Isaiah, 5:192

   Joseph and Mary, 9:241–242, 244

   Mary as chosen vessel, 9:243–244

   See also Immaculate Conception

The Virgin Blacherniotissa, 9:272

The Virgin Chalcopratia, 9:272

The Virgin Hagioritissa, 9:272

Virgin in Majesty (Majestas Mariae), 9:274

Virgin Islands, 3:119–120

Virgin Mary. *See* Mary, Blessed Virgin

Virgin Mary, Feast of the, 3:556

The Virgin Mary in the Kingdom of the Divine Will, 5:865

The Virgin Odigitria (Our Lady Guide of Wayfarers), 9:272

The Virgin of Humility and Saint Jerome translating the Gospel of John (Benedetto di Bindo), 7:*903*

Virgin of Tenderness (Eleousa), 9:272

The Virgin of the Cherries, 9:249

Virgines Subintroductae, 3:326, **14:539–540**

Virginia, 3:641, 645–646, 652, **14:540–544**

   See also specific dioceses and archdioceses

Virginis Proles Opifexque Matris (anonymous), **14:544**

Virginity, **14:544–548**

Basil of Ancyra, 2:139–140

clerical celibacy/marriage, 3:322

common good, 4:18

consecration, 4:156

contemplative life, 4:210

Isidore of Pelusium, St., 7:601

Marian devotion, 1:339

Mary, Blessed Virgin, 1:476, 800, 2:629, 9:255–256, 14:532, 535

New Testament, 4:306–307

penance, 11:66

Pius XII (Pope), encyclical, 12:464

superior asceticism, 8:720

virgins in monasteries, 5:773

See also Chastity; Sex

Virtual prayer, 11:599–600

Virtualiter (virtually), 12:751

Virtue and virtues, **14:548–554**

acquired, 14:550

character, 3:387–388

charisms, 3:390

common good, 4:16–17

connection, 13:152

continence, 4:211–212

devotion, 4:708–709

emotion, 5:195

epikeia (reasonableness), 5:290

eutrapelia, 5:461

friendship, 6:6

fruits of the Holy Spirit, 7:46

gifts of Holy Spirit distinguished from, 7:48–49

human act, 7:170–171

hypocrisy, 7:263

long-suffering, 8:775

Machiavelli, Niccolo, 9:22

Mencius, 9:487

natural law, 10:190

observantia (dulia), 4:932

prayer, 11:595–596

social justice, 13:242–244

Socrates, 13:291–293

tendency of man, 9:87

vice, 14:473

voluntary nature, 13:440

See also Charity; Faith; Fidelity; Hope; Humility; Moral virtue; *specific virtues*

Virtue and virtues, heroic, 9:252–253, **14:554–555**

Virtue and virtues, iconography of, 8:872, **14:555–557**

Virtues and Vices, Last Judgement Portal (in Notre Dame, Paris), 14:*556*

Virtues of St. Martin of Tours (Gregory of Tours), 12:606

Virtus consistit in medio (Virtue is found in the mean), 12:757

Visch, Charles de, **14:557**

Visconti, Teobaldo. *See* Gregory X (Pope), Bl.

Visdelou, Claude de (Bp. of Claudiopolis), **14:557–558**

Visher, Lukas, 5:721

Vishnu (Hindu deity), 6:*306*, 848–849, 14:*558*

Visibility of the Church, **14:558–559**

Visigothic rite. *See* Mozarabic Rite

Visigoths, 6:369, 14:*559*, **559–561**

Albi Archdiocese, 1:229

anointing, 1:478, 485

Arianism, 1:663–664

Church in Gaul, 6:112

conversion of, 3:409, 596

Germany, 6:171–172

Honorius (Roman Emperor), 7:87

Huns, 7:224

invasions, 3:686

Isidore of Seville, St., 7:603

sack of Rome (410), 1:859

Spain, 13:376–377

synodic practice, 4:302

Visintainer, Amabile Lucia, Bl., **14:561**

Visio Baronti monachi Longoretensis (St. Barontus), 2:106

Visio Wettini (Walafrid Strabo), 9:443, 14:606

A Vision (Yeats), 14:885

Visión espiritual de la guerra (Franceschi), 5:864

Vision literature, **14:561–562**

Vision of God. *See* Beatific vision

Vision of St. Anthony (Murillo), 10:66

Vision of Saint Peter Nolasco (Zurbaran), 11:*194*

The Vision of William concerning Piers the Plowman. See Piers Plowman (Langland)

Visiones (Elizabeth of Schönau), 5:166

Visions, **14:562–563**

definition, 10:107

Elizabeth of Schönau, 5:166

Labouré, Catherine, St., 8:267

locutions, 8:747

Luria, I., 8:870

private revelations, 12:200–203

Revelation, Book of, 12:185–186

scapular, 13:134, *135*

shrines honoring apparitions of Mary, 13:92–93

Soubirous, B., 13:331–332

Speyr, Adrienne von, 13:415–416

Visions (Hadewijch), 6:605

Viśiṣṭāvaita (Hindu doctrine), 6:847, 7:409

Visita al SS. Sacramento (St. Alphonsus Liguori), 1:309

Visitandines. *See* Visitation Nuns

Visitatio Sepulchri, 4:894

The Visitation, 14:*565*

Visitation, Feast of the, 9:158, 14:564

Visitation Nuns, 3:621, 4:955, 8:299, **14:563**

Visitation of Holy Mary, Congregation of the, 5:868

Visitation of Mary, 5:162–163, 8:856, **14:564**

Visitation Sisters, Martyrs of, BB., **14:564, 566**

Visits to the Blessed Sacrament (St. Alphonsus Ligouri), 5:435

Visser't Hooft, Willem Adolf, **14:566–567**, 842–843

Vita abbatum, 3:348

Vita abscondita (Cienfuegos), 3:731

Vita Apostolica Movement, 3:131, 134

Vita Basini (Thiofrid of Echternach), 14:6

Vita beatorum abbatum (Bede), 3:348

Vita Bennonis (Emser), 5:200

Vita Carmelitana (periodical), 6:42

Vita Casimiri ex Poloniae (Ferreri), 5:694

Vita Christi (Ludolph of Saxony), 5:788, 9:460–461

Vita communis, 1:322

Vita consecrata (apostolic exhortation, John Paul II), 1:586, 7:1003

Vita Constantini (Lactantius), 4:180, 182

Vita della serra di Dio Angelica Cospari (Scaramelli), 12:724

Vita di Castruccio Castracani (Machiavelli), 9:21

Vita di Messer Francesco Petrarca (Bruni), 12:110

Vita di Suor Maria Crocifissa Satellico (Scaramelli), 12:724

Vita domini nostri Jesu Christi ex quatuor evangeliis (Ludolf), 8:853–854

Vita e culto di S. Giuseppe (Trombelli), 14:213

Vita e Dottrina (St. Catherine of Genoa), 3:271

Vita et epistola beatissimae Egeriae (Valerio of Bierzo), 14:375

Vita Eulogii (Paulus Albarus), 11:44

Vita Florentii (Á Kempis), 14:13

Vita Fulgentii (Ferrandus of Carthage), 5:691

Vita Gerardi Magni (Á Kempis), 14:13

Vita Gregorii Magni (John the Deacon of Rome), 7:1017

Vita Hariolfi (Ermenrich of Passau), 5:173

Vita Jesu Christi e quatuor evangeliis et scriptoribus orthodoxis concinnata (Ludolph of Saxony), 7:845

Vita Julianae, 5:463

Vita Liutwini (Thiofrid of Echternach), 14:6

Vita Mariae Oigniacensis (Jacques de Vitry), 7:693

Vita Martini (Sulpicius Severus), 6:112

Vita Meinwerci, 1:14

Vita Nuova (Dante), 3:310, 4:517, 5:189

Vita nuova (periodical), 10:69

Vita patrum Jurensium, 8:63

Vita s. Anselmi (Eadmer of Canterbury), 5:1

Vita s. Euthymii (Cyril of Scythopolis), 5:461

Vita s. Fari (Hildegar of Meaux), 5:631

Vita s. Francisci Solani (Reiffenstuel), 12:34

Vita s. Irminae (Thiofrid of Echternach), 14:6

Vita s. Maioli (St. Odilo of Cluny), 10:552

Vita s. Martini (Fortunatus), 5:823

Vita s. Medardi, 5:148

Vita s. Oswaldi, 5:96

Vita s. Rochi (Diedo), 12:276

Vita Willibrordi (Thiofrid of Echternach), 14:6

Vitae, 6:873

Vitae et res gestae pontificum Romanorum et S.R.E. cardinalium (Chacon), 6:876

Vitae fratrum (Gerard de Frachet), 14:33

Vitae mysterium (*motu proprio*, John Paul II), 11:475

Vital, Ḥayyim, 2:835

Vital du Four (Card. Bp. of Albano), **14:567–568**

Vital impulse (*élan vital*) theory, 10:824

Vital of Fécamp, 2:322

Vitale, Engel v. (1962), 3:666

Vitalian (general), 1:50

Vitalian (Pope), St., 2:750, **14:568**

Vitalis (Bp. of Antioch), 1:559

Vitalis, St., **14:569**

Vitalis de Furno. *See* Vital du Four (Card. Bp. of Albano)

Vitalis de Thebes, 3:52, 4:273

Vitalis of Salzburg (Bp. of Sankt Peters), St., **14:569**

Vitalis of Savigny, Bl., 12:711, **14:569**

Vitalism, 2:405, 9:419–420, 13:335, 346

La Vitalité chrétienne (Ollé-Laprune), 10:585

Vitelleschi, Mutius, 7:309, **14:569–570**

Vitello (Polish philospher). *See* Witelo (Polish philosopher)

Vitis Mystica (St. Bonaventure), 12:491

Vitonus (Bp. of Verdun), St., **14:570**

Vitoria, Francisco de, 14:49, **570–572**

Aristotelianism, 1:677, 678

Cano, Melchior, 3:19

Forerio, Francisco, 5:799

just-war tradition, 14:636–637

Salazar, Domingo de, 12:613

scholasticism, 12:764, 766

slave trade, 5:395, 13:213

Vitri, Philippe de. *See* Vitry, Philippe de (Bp. of Meaux)

Vitruvian man, 9:86

Vitruvius (Roman writer), 12:308

Vitry, Jacques de, 5:793

Vitry, Philippe de (Bp. of Meaux), 8:685, 10:13, **14:572**

Vittori, Francesco, 9:20

Vittorino da Feltre, 5:90, **14:572–573**

Vittorino de' Rambaldoni. *See* Vittorino da Feltre

Vitus, Modestus and Crescentia, SS., **14:573**

Vitus, St., 3:526, 4:280

Viva, Domenica, **14:573**

Vivald, Bl., **14:574**

Vivaldi, Antonio, 2:114, **14:574**, *575*

Vivaldi, Francis de, 12:542

Vivani, René, 3:802

Viventiolus (Bp. of Lyons), St., **14:574–575**

Vives, Juan Bautista, 5:90, 92, **14:575**

Vives, Juan Luis

Adrian VI (Pope), 1:129

catechesis, 3:232

empiricism, 5:197

quality, 11:851

Renaissance philosophy, 12:124

works of charity, 3:417, 418

Vivian Bible, 3:154

Viviani, René, 8:283

Vix pervenit (encyclical, Benedict XIV), 2:32, 14:354

Vixdum Poloniae (papal bull, Pius XI), 11:448

Vizcardó, Anselmo, 14:576

Vizcardó, Juan Pablo, **14:575–576**

Vizcarro, Francisco, 12:209

Vlachich, Matthias. *See* Flacius Illyricus, Matthias

Vladimir, St., 2:755, 775, 786, 3:689, 12:419, 14:272, **576–577**

Vladimiri, Paul, 11:439

Vlazney, John (Abp. of Portland, OR), 11:531

Vlk, Moloslav (Abp. of Prague), 4:488

Võ Dang Khoa, Pedro, 14:499

Vocabulário da Lingoa de Japam, 12:282

Vocal prayer, 11:600

The Vocation of Man (Fichte), 12:69

Vocations, 7:40, 8:830, 9:336–337, 13:23, 439

La Voce del Popolo (periodical), 13:108, 14:128

La Voce dell'Operaio (weekly), 10:65

Voecht, James de, 2:607

Voegelin, E., 10:630

Voegtle, A., 5:523

Voëtius (Gijsbert Voët), 1:677, 3:184

Vogel, Cyrille, 6:120

Vögelin, M. E., 4:416

Vogels, Heinrich Joseph, 2:367

Vogelsang, Karl von, 1:914

Vogelweide, Walther von der, 4:400

Vogt, Karl, 9:320

Voice (periodical), 12:34–35

The Voice of St. Jude (periodical), 14:60

Voices in the Wilderness (organization), 7:548

Void, 4:217, 9:339, 12:811–812, **14:577**

La Voie qui mène à Dieu (Saudreau), 12:708

Les Voies ordinaires de la vie spirituelle (Farges), 5:624

Voigt, George, 12:112

Voina i mir (Tolstoi), 14:105–106

Volansky, Ivan (Father), 11:86

Volition, 4:158

Volitional acts of will, 14:720

Völker, W., 3:799

Volksliturgie (Parsch), 10:903

Volksverein, 6:185

Vollard, Ambroise, 2:524

Vollert, C., 12:730

Vollständigen Katechesen für die untere Klasse der katholische Volksschule (Mey), 9:586

Vologeses, 5:277

Volpicelli, Caterina, Bl., **14:577–578**

Volta, Carmel, 4:503

Voltaire, 5:210, 255, 261, 14:*578*, **578–580**
  anticlericalism, 1:518
  Berthier, Guillaume François, 2:332
  Catherine the Great, 3:264
  censorship, 3:796
  deism, 4:616, 617
  Divine providence, 5:489
  freedom of religion, 5:947
  laicism, 8:283
  pessimism, 11:169
  philosophy of history, 6:883–884
  Renaissance concept, 12:111
  Utopianism, 14:361

Volterra Maffei. *See* Maffei family

Voluntarism, **14:580–583**
  Aiguani, Michele, 1:194
  Alumbrados, 1:323
  contingency, 4:213
  Duns Scotus, John, 13:907
  Hooker, Richard, 7:91
  justice and law, 8:401
  justification theory, 8:83
  Nietzsche's influence, 10:390
  Richard Rufus of Cornwall, 12:236

Voluntarity, 5:931–932, 7:172–173, **14:583–586**
  See also Choice; Determinism; Human will; Voluntarism

Voluntary suffering, 13:588

Volusenus, Florentius, **14:586–587**

Volusianus (Bp. of Tours), St., **14:587**

Vom alten und neun Gott, Glauben und Lehre (anonymous tract), 14:254

Vom geschichtlichen Werden der Liturgie (Baumstark), 2:160

Von dem gemeinen Vorurtheile der thätigen und wirkenden Hexerei (Sterzinger), 13:528

Von Dobschütz, E., 2:363

Von Harnack, A., 1:20, 3:22, 30

Von Keppler, Paul Wilhelm (Bp.), 11:624

Von Maldeghem, R. J., 2:841–842

Von Papen, Franz, 3:341

Von Rad, Gerhard. *See* Rad, Gerhard von

Von Reimarus zu Wrede (Schweitzer), 5:521

Von Reimarus zu Wreede: Eine Geschichte der Leben-Jesu Forschung (Schweitzer), 5:331

Von Soden, H., 2:367

Vondel, Joost van den, 2:116

Vonier, Anscar, 2:655, 10:99, **14:587**

Voodoo, 6:622, **14:587–588**
  See also Magic; Witchcraft

Vorau Monastery (Austria), **14:588**

Vorgrimler, Herbert, 4:685

"Vorläufige Thesen Zur Reform der Philosophie" (Feuerbach), 6:710

Vorlesungen aus der Pastoraltheologie (Sailer), 11:623

Vorlesungen über die Methode des akademischen Studiums (Schelling), 12:733

Die vornehmsten Wahrheiten der natürlichen Religion (Reimarus), 12:35

Vortex theory, 9:417

Vos, John, 2:607

Vos, Wiebe, 8:679–680, 13:275

Vosmeer, Sasbout, 12:395

Vosté, Jacques Marie, **14:588–589**

Vota per quae vos (papal bull, Clement VII), 5:692

Votive offerings, 8:525, **14:589–590**

Votive offices, 8:611

Votum, **14:590**

Vouet, Simon, 1:416

Vows, in the Bible, **14:590–591**

Vows, religious, 12:88

Vox Clamantis (Gower), 6:378, 9:462

Vox clara ecce intonat (hymn), 5:201

Vox in excelso (papal bull, Clement V), 13:804

Vox populi, 3:62

Voyage du monde de Descartes (Daniel), 3:186

Voyage romances, 2:602, *602*

Vraie et fausse reforme dans l'Église (Congar), 4:102

Les Vrais principes de l'Église gallicane (Frayssinous), 5:922

Vree, Franciscus van, 10:261

Vretanja, Simeon (Bp. of Marča), 4:370

Vriezen, T. C., 2:385, 386

Vulfilaic, St. *See* Wulflaicus, St.

Vulfride, St. *See* Wulphilda, St.

Vulgar speech, 13:411

Vulgate, **14:591–600**
  biblical canon, 3:26, 32
  Clement VIII (Pope), 3:785
  Daniel, Book of, 4:509
  Dead Sea Scrolls, 4:563

Jerome, St., 8:363

Kings, Book of, 8:175

Lamentations, Book of, 8:312

Valla, Lorenzo, 7:187

Vulgate Gospels, 14:591

Vulmar, St. *See* Wulmar, St.

Vulpes, Angelo, 2:581, **14:600**

Vulpius, Christiane, 6:331

Vyshensky, Ivan, **14:600**

W

Wace (Norman poet), 1:760–761

Wach, Joachim, **14:601**

Wachock Abbey (Poland), 3:750

Waco (TX), 4:542–543

Wadding, Luke, 1:110, 5:761, 12:717, 764, 826, **14:601–602**, *602*

Wade, John Francis, 1:115, 7:254

Wade, Roe v. (1973), 1:32, 34, 12:575, 14:315

Wadhams, Edgar Philip (Bp. of Ogdensburg, NY), **14:602–603**

Wærferth (Bp. of Worcester), 1:148

Wagenseil, Johann Christoph, 7:588

Wagner, Liborius, Bl., **14:603**

Wagner, Otto, 3:710, 711

Wagner, Richard, 14:*603*, **603–604**
  Arthurian legends, 1:762
  Brahms, Johannes, 2:580
  Bruckner, Anton, 2:642
  Caecilian Movement, 2:842
  Chopin, Frédéric François, 3:525
  philosophy of music, 10:73
  Reger, Max, 12:28
  works, 14:603–604

Wahhābis, 1:612, 7:613, **14:605**

Die Wahlverwandtschaften (Goethe), 6:332

Der Wahrheitsfreund (periodical), 6:733

Wahrheitsfreund (periodical), 10:558

Waire (Maire), John, Ven., 5:226

Waitangi, Treaty of (1840), 10:325

Waitz, Theodor, 1:678

Wakana shu (Young Herbs) (Shimazaki), 13:85

Wakefield (England), medieval drama of, 4:899

Wakeman, Roger, 5:237

Wala, St., 2:446, 4:280, **14:605**

Walafrid Strabo, 3:26, 7:246, 9:443, 12:32, **14:606**
  Ambrosian Rite, 1:342
  biblical catenae, 3:258
  Carolingian Renaissance, 3:160

Walafrid Strabo (continued)
Córdoba, 4:261
creedal statements, 4:356
''orienting'' the basilica, 2:148
Walarich, St., **14:606**
Walburga of Heidenheim, St.,
14:606–607
Walcaud of Liège (Bp.), 12:549
Walcott, Joe, 11:725
Wald, Florence, 7:117
Waldassen Abbey (Bavaria, Germany),
14:609
Waldeck-Rousseau Law, 8:283
Waldemar I (the Great) (King of
Denmark), 4:665
Waldemar II (King of Denmark), 1:221
Walden: or, Life in the Woods
(Thoreau), 14:59, 147
Walden Two (Skinner), 14:361
Waldenses, **14:607–608**
Albigensians, 1:229, 231, 3:259–260
Angelo Carletti di Chivasso, Bl.,
1:413
Anthony Pavonius, Bl., 1:508
Bernard of Fontcaude, 2:314
Böhm, Hans, 2:461
cabala, 2:831
capital punishment, 3:87
Church property, 3:727
France, 5:845
heresy, 6:774
Humiliati, 7:204
Hungary, 7:211
lay role, 8:295
pacifism, 10:746
papal Antichrist, 1:517
Poverty Movement, 11:572
preaching, 11:612
works of charity, 3:413
Waldetrud, St., 6:233, **14:608–609**
Waldhauser, Konrad, 4:480
Waldipert (Lombard priest), 11:243
Waldreck-Rousseau, Pierre, 5:855
Waldron, John A., **14:609**
Walendorf, J. P. von, 5:658
Wales, **14:609–613**
demographic statistics, 14:610
ecclesiastical organization,
14:610–611, 612
Free Churches, 5:928
literary studies, 5:199
maps, 5:241, 14:611
Marian shrines, 13:92
patron of, 12:543
Presbyterianism, 11:680

religious education, 12:98
See also Ancient sees; England;
England, Scotland, and Wales,
Martyrs of; Northern Ireland;
Scotland
Wałęsa, Lech, 4:490, 11:453, 454, 455
Waleys, John. See John of Wales
Waleys, Thomas, 11:619
Walfrid, St., **14:613**
Walfroy, St. See Wulflaicus, St.
Walgrave, Jan, 7:528
Walīd ibn 'Abd al-Malik, 14:286
Walker, Alice, 5:573, 14:822
Walker, Emery, 2:523
''Walking'' (Thoreau), 14:147
Wall, John, St., 5:237, **14:613–614**
Wall, Richard, 3:792
Wallace, Alfred Russell, 2:403, 4:532,
5:49
Wallace v. Jaffree (1985), 3:666
Wallenstein, Albrecht Eusebius Wenzel
von, 5:688, **14:614**
Walley, Thomas, 2:553, 3:472
Wallingford, William, **14:615**
Wallis, John, 3:418
Wallis, Territory of, 10:534
Wallrath, Clement, 1:275
Walls Are Crumbling: Seven Jewish
Philosophers Discover Christ
(Oesterreicher), 10:559
Walpole, Henry, St., 5:225, 232, 14:615,
615–616
Walram of Naumberg (Bp.), **14:616**
Walsh, Daniel F. (Bp.), 8:346, 10:271,
12:127
Walsh, Edmund Aloysius, 7:791, **14:616**
Walsh, Emmet Michael (Bp. of
Charleston, SC), 13:366–367
Walsh, Francis Augustine, **14:617**
Walsh, James Anthony (Bp. of
Jiangmen), 9:294, 295, 11:688,
12:289, **14:617–618**
Walsh, James Edward (Bp.), 14:391,
618–619
Walsh, John (15th c. Irish martyr), 7:580
Walsh, John (Abp. of Toronto), **14:619**
Walsh, Louis Sebastian (Bp. of Portland,
ME), 9:58, 11:531
Walsh, Mary Rosalia (Sister),
14:619–620
Walsh, Michael P., 2:558
Walsh, Patrick, 14:459
Walsh, Peter, 3:173, 7:560, **14:620**
Walsh, Robert Arsenius (Father), 6:669
Walsh, Thomas Joseph, 10:329–330,
12:104

Walsh, Tomás, 1:653
Walsh, W. H., 6:884
Walsh, Walter (17th c. Irish martyr),
7:582
Walsh, William (Bp. of Meath, Ireland),
7:579, **14:620**
Walsh, William F., 1:210
Walsh, William Joseph (Abp. of
Dublin), 4:375, 7:563, **14:620–621**
Walsingham, Francis, Sir, 12:11
Walsingham, Thomas, 1:464, 3:805,
12:532, **14:622**
Walsingham Monastery (Norfolk,
England), **14:621–622**
Walter, Henry, 14:254
Walter, Hubert (Abp. of Canterbury),
6:231
Walter, Wolman v. (1977), 3:667–668
Walter Burley, 1:223, **14:622–623**, 623
Walter de Gray (Abp. of York), **14:623**
Walter de Stapeldon (Bp. of Exeter),
5:530, **14:623**
Walter Giffard (Abp. of York),
6:325–326, **14:624**
Walter Jorz (Abp. of Armagh), **14:624**
Walter Joyce. See Walter Jorz (Abp. of
Armagh)
Walter Map, 9:456, **14:624**
Walter of Birbeck, Bl., **14:624–625**
Walter of Bruges (Bp. of Poitiers),
14:625
Walter of Cantelupe (Bp. of Worcester),
14:625
Walter of Châtillon, 9:458, **14:625–626**
Walter of Chatton, 1:110, 12:762,
14:626–627
Walter of Coincy, **14:627**
Walter of Hemingburgh, 1:464
Walter of Merton (Bp.), 12:266, 14:627
Walter of Mortagne (Bp. of Laon),
3:761, 9:455, **14:627–628**
Walter of Pontoise, St., **14:628**
Walter of Saint-Victor, 1:19, 4:726,
6:328, 12:589, **14:628–629**
Walter of Skirlaw (Bp. of Durham),
14:629
Walter Reynolds (Abp. of Canterbury),
14:629
Walter the Penniless, 1:275
Walters, Annette (Sister), 2:578
Walters, Henry, 3:715
Waltham Monastery (London, England),
14:629–630
Waltheof, St., **14:630**
Walther, Carl Ferdinand William, 8:886,
14:630–631
Waltman of Antwerp, Bl., **14:631**

Walton, Brian, 3:25

Walton, Clarence, 3:292

Walworth, Clarence Augustus, 2:23, 6:700, 11:40, **14:631**

Walworth, James, Bl., 5:226, 12:279

Walz v. Tax Commission (1970), 3:667

Wandelbert of Prüm, 3:160, 7:246

Wandering Jew, Legend of the, **14:631–632**

Wandregisilus, St. *See* Wandrille, St.

Wandrille, St., 5:793, **14:632**

Wang Erman, Peter, St., **14:632**

Wang Jou-Mei, Joseph. *See* Wang Yumei, Joseph, St.

Wang Li, Mary, St., **14:632–633**

Wang Liangzuo, 3:501

Wang Rui, John, St., **14:633**

Wang Yangming, 3:512, 4:98

Wang Yumei, Joseph, St., **14:633**

Wangtao, 3:516

Waningus, St., **14:633–634**

Wanita Katolik (organization), 7:431

Wapner, S., 10:20

Wappeler, William (Father), 11:81, 235

War, 3:411, 518, 4:410, 881, 13:260, 14:570–571

See also Pacifism; Wars of religion

War, in the Bible, 13:249, **14:634–635**

War, morality of, 4:149–151, 6:540–541, 8:341, **14:635–644**

War, penitential. *See* Crusades

War and Peace (Tolstoi), 14:105–106

War of Reform (Mexico, 1857-1862), 9:578–579

War of Troy, 2:806–807

Warbur, Aby, 7:287, 288

Warcop, Thomas, Bl., 5:233

Ward, Barbara, **14:644–645**

Ward, Bernard (Bp. of Brentwood, England), **14:645**

Ward, Cornelius, **14:645–646**

Ward, Fergal, 7:579

Ward, Henry. *See* Morse, Henry, St.

Ward, Hugh, 3:834, 5:760, **14:646**

Ward, Justine Bayard Cutting, 8:674–675, **14:646–647**

Ward, K., 5:384

Ward, Maisie, 13:73, **14:647**

Ward, Margaret, St., 5:230, 784, **14:647–648**

Ward, Mary, 8:786–787, **14:648**

Ward, Patrick (Mother), 7:207

Ward, Wilfrid Philip, 4:917, **14:648–649**

Ward, William (18th c. missionary), 7:403

Ward, William, Bl. (English martyr), 5:235, **14:649**

Ward, William George, 4:917, 5:251, 14:*649*, **649–650**

Ward method (Gregorian chant), 14:646

Wardâ, George, 5:6

Warde, Mary Frances Xavier (Mother), 3:480, **14:650–651**

Wardlaw, Henry de (Bp.), **14:651**

Warelwast, William (Bp. of Exeter), 5:530

Warfel, Michael W., 1:209

Warfield, Benjamin Breckinridge, 5:473, 6:28, **14:651**

Warham, William (Abp. of Canterbury), 2:130, 198, 3:72, 268, **14:651–652**, *652*

Warin, Bl., 7:289, **14:652**

Warlock, Peter, 3:151–152

Warmund, Bl., **14:652–653**

Warnach, V., 10:98

Warnerius of Basel, 9:449

Waroquier, H. de, 1:545

"Warranted assertion" theory, 7:502

Warren's Well (Jerusalem), 7:763

Wars of religion, 3:612

Ainay Abbey, 1:196

Airvault Monastery, 1:196

Albi Archdiocese, 1:229

Bernay Abbey, 2:323

Beza, Theodore, 2:352

Chaise-Dieu Abbey, 3:362

Cistercians, 3:747, 751

Clement VIII (Pope), 3:784

La Ferté Abbey, 8:279

L'Hôpital, Michel de, 7:167, 8:531

Saint-Savin-sur-Gartempe Abbey, 12:585

See also Huguenots; Thirty Years' War (1618-48)

Wars of Succession, 3:788, 7:670–671

Wars of the Lord (Levi ben Gerson), 7:865, 8:521

"Wars of the Lord" (Naḥmanides), 10:135

Wartenberg, Franz Wilhelm von (Card.), **14:653**

Warwick, John Dudley, Earl of, 12:9

Washing of the feet, 7:55, 8:344, **14:653**

Washington (state), **14:653–657**

See also specific dioceses and archdioceses

Washington, Booker T., 1:160, 14:243

Washington, DC Archdiocese, 2:38, 4:12, 12:418, 13:799, **14:657–659**

Washington, George, 2:553, 3:180, 715

Washington Department of Services for the Blind, Witters v. (1986), 3:668

Washington Temperance Society, 13:799

Washington Theological Union, **14:659**

Wasmann, Erich, **14:659–660**, *660*

The Waste Land (Eliot), 5:160, 14:271

Wastefulness, 9:44

Wastell, John, 3:73

Wasyluk, Onufry, 11:584

Watch Tower (periodical), 12:416

Watch Tower Bible and Tract Society (Columbus, OH), 7:751

Water, 5:697, 7:761–763, 12:476

Water, liturgical use of, **14:660–662**

Water, living, symbolism of, 13:667–668

Water to wine miracle, historical/geographical context, 3:1

Waters, Vincent S. (Bp. of Raleigh, NC), 10:438, 11:900

Waterson, Edward, Bl., 5:232, 8:308, **14:662**

Watkins, O., 4:77

Watkins, Torcaso v. (1961), 3:652, 653, 666

Watkinson, Robert, Bl., 5:234

Watkinson, Thomas, Bl., 5:231, **14:662**

Watson, James D., 2:404, 7:175

Watson, Nicholas. *See* Postgate, Nicholas, Bl.

Watson, Richard, 10:757

Watson, Tom, 1:693

Watson v. Jones (1871), 3:657, 658

Watt, James, 5:260

Watt, W. M., 1:782

Watterson, John A. (Bp. of Columbus), 3:868

Watts, G. F., 10:4

Watts, Isaac, 7:256, 257, 13:456

Wattson, Lewis Thomas. *See* Wattson, Paul James Frances, Rev.

Wattson, Paul James Frances, Rev., 5:874, 883, **14:662**

Wauchop, Robert, 4:887

Waugh, Evelyn, 14:*663*, **663**

Waverly Abbey (Winchester, England), **14:663–664**

Wawryszuk, Michał, 11:584

The Way (Consideraciones espirituales) (Escrivá de Balaguer y Albás), 5:355

Way, William, Bl., 5:230, 784, **14:664**

Way of Perfection (Teresa of Avila), 5:167, 13:829–830

Way of the Cross. *See* Stations of the Cross

The Way of the Lord Jesus (Grisez), 10:185

Wayfarers, intercession of, 7:520
Waynflete, William (Bp.), **14:664**
The Ways of Russian Theology
(Florovsky), 5:782
Ways to Perfect Religion (Fisher), 5:749
Wazo (Bp. of Liège), 1:498, 2:216–217,
14:664–665
WCC. *See* World Council of Churches
"We Care, We Share" program, 7:316
*We Hold These Truths: Reflections on
the American Proposition* (Murray),
10:69
*We Remember: A Reflection on the
Shoah* (1998), 7:14, 10:853
Weakland, Rembert G. (Abp. of
Milwaukee, WI), 9:649, 14:783
Wealth, social principle of, 13:250
Wealth of Nations (Smith), 5:703,
13:231–232
Wearmouth Abbey (Northumbria,
England), 3:348, **14:665**
Weavers, patron of, 12:585
Webb, Benedict Joseph, 3:675, **14:665**
Webb, Francis. *See* Wall, John, St.
Weber, Anselm, **14:665–666**
Weber, Carl Maria von, 14:*666*, **666**
Weber, Jerome, 12:578
Weber, K., 3:712
Weber, Magdalena, 11:644
Weber, Martin, 3:710, 711
Weber, Max, **14:666–668**, *667*
biblical theology, 2:385
Calvinism, 2:895
civil religion, 3:755
legitimate government, 5:703
mysticism, 10:115
society, 13:282
sociology of religion, 12:74
Weber, Urban, 1:117
Webern, Anton Von, 12:746, 14:*668*,
668
Webley, Henry, Bl., 5:230, **14:668**
Webley, Thomas, Ven., 1:278, 5:228
Websites of Church, 4:420
Webster, Augustine, St., 5:225, 12:8,
210, **14:669**
Webster, Daniel, 3:472
Webster v. Reproductive Health Services
(1989), 1:34
Wechs, Thomas, 3:711
Wednesday (Christian week), 8:718
Week, Christian, 8:641–642, 717–718
*A Week on the Concord and Merrimack
Rivers* (Thoreau), 14:59
Weekly Register, 10:313

Weeping Madonna shrine (Syracuse,
Italy), 3:712
Weerden, Jerome, 6:364
Wehrle, Vincent de Paul (Bp. of
Bismarck, ND), 2:423, 10:440,
14:*669*, **669**
Wei wo (egoism), 3:509
Weigel, Gustave, **14:669–670**, 670
Weights and measures, in the Bible,
14:670–671
Weil, Felix, 5:914
Weil, R. W., 7:763
Weil, Simone, 10:116, **14:671**
Weiller, Cajetan von, 12:770
Weimar, Peter, 11:96
Weiner, Norbert, 4:451, *452*
Weingarten Abbey (Wüttemberg,
Germany), **14:672**
Weinzierl, Barbara, 6:166
Weisheipl, James Athanasius (Father),
14:672–673
Weisman, Lee v. (1992), 3:666–667
Weismann, August, 2:403
Weiss, Albert Maria, 12:777, **14:673**
Weiss, Bernhard, 2:367, 5:521, 7:848
Weiss, George, 12:795
Weiss, Johannes, 2:690, 4:265, 5:331,
521, 8:175
Weiss, Liberat (Father), **14:673–674**
Weiss, Paul, 10:608, 11:730
Weiss, R., 12:113
Weissagung und Erfüllung (Hofmann),
5:323
Weissenau Monastery (Germany),
14:674
Weissenburg Abbey (France), **14:674**
Welbourne, Thomas, Bl., 5:234,
14:674–675
Welch, A. C., 3:565–566
Welch, Sidney, **14:675**
Welch, Thomas (Bp. of Arlington, VA),
14:543
Weld, Thomas (Card.), 2:162, 12:569,
14:*675*, **675–676**
A Well Conducted Farm (Edwards),
13:797
Wellesley, Arthur (Duke of Wellington).
See Wellington, Arthur Wellesley,
Duke of
Wellhausen, Julius, **14:676**
biblical theology, 2:384, 385
exegesis, 5:519
Jewish influence on Islam, 7:607
Mount Sinai, 13:159
natural-evolutionism, 8:186
pentateuchal studies, 11:90

works, 14:676
Wellhausen School, 5:519
Wellington, Arthur Wellesley, Duke of,
10:539
Wells, Alice, 14:676
Wells, H. G., 3:470, 14:361
Wells, John de. *See* John of Wales
Wells, Swithun, St., 5:231, 6:138,
14:676
Wells Diocese (England). *See* Bath and
Wells, Ancient See of
Welsh penitentials, 11:74
Welsh v. United States (1970), 3:661
Die Welt als Wille und Vorstellung
(Schopenhauer), 12:784
Weltanschauung (World view), **14:677**
Weltanschauungslehre, 4:746
Welte, Bernard, 5:828
Wemmers, James (Father), 5:404
Wenailus, St., **14:677**
Wenceslaus (Duke of Bohemia), St.,
4:479, 8:851, **14:677–678**, *678*
Wenceslaus IV (King of Bohemia),
2:504, 7:228, 977, **14:678–679**
Wendelin, St., **14:679**
Wends people, 4:414
Weninger, Francis Xavier, 1:583, **14:679**
Wenlock Abbey (Hereford, England),
14:679
Wenrich of Trier, **14:680**
Wentworth, Thomas W., 8:378
Wenzeslaus, Klemens, 5:658
Werburga, St., **14:680**
Werden Abbey (Ruhr, Germany),
14:680–681
Werenfrid, St., **14:681**
Werner, H., 10:20
Werner, Karl, 12:774
Werner, M., 5:331
Werner of Oberwesel, St., **14:681**
Werner of Tegernsee, **14:681–682**
Wernherlied von der Magd, 9:275–276,
277, 278–279
Werr, Antonie, 5:877
Wertheimer, Max, 10:20
Werz, Franz Xavier, 7:790–791
Das Wesen des Christentums
(Feuerbach), 5:707, 6:710
Das Wesen des Christentums (Von
Harnack), 6:648, 8:543
Wesley, Charles, 3:151, 5:472, 7:256,
14:682, 683
Wesley, John, 9:557–559, **14:682–684**,
683
Augsburg Confession, 1:850
carols, 3:151

confessions of faith, 4:81–82

Evangelicalism, 1:444

Holiness churches, 7:7

hymns, 7:256, 257

justification, 8:87

Lawrence of the Resurrection, 3:137

Methodist Church in America, 9:561

preaching, 5:472

scholasticism, 12:768

Wesley, Charles, 14:682

Zinzendorf, Nikolaus, 14:928

Wesleyan Methodist Association, 9:559

Wesleyan Methodist Church (U.S.),
9:561–562

Wessenberg, Ignza Heinrich von,
14:684–685

Wessobrunn Abbey (Germany), 1:321,
14:685

West, Morris L., **14:685–687**, *686*

West Indies. *See* Caribbean; *specific countries*

West Point Military Academy chapel,
3:715

West Virginia, 3:661–662, **14:687–690**

See also specific dioceses and archdioceses

West Virginia Board of Education v. Barnette (1943), 3:661–662

Westcott, Brooke Foss (Bp. of Durham,
England), 2:367, **14:690**

Westcott, William Wynn, 12:382

Westermarck, E., 5:397

Western Catholic Conference (Canada),
3:8

Western indiction. *See* Indiction of Bede

The Western Messenger (1835-40),
14:149

Western Mysticism (Butler), 4:208

Western Sahara, **14:690–691**, *692*

Western Schism (1378-1417),
14:691–694

Acciaioli, Angelo, 1:58

Alexander V (Antipope), 1:258

Antoninus, St., 1:536

Avignon papacy, 1:941, 945

Benedict XIII (Antipope), 2:246

Boniface IX (Pope), 2:504

Brevicoxa, 2:611

Callistus III (Antipope), 2:882

Canon Law, 3:49, 51

capitulations, 3:91

Carmelites, 1:194, 3:141–142

Carthusians, 3:194

Castel Sant'Angelo, 3:213

Catherine of Siena, St., 3:273, 783

Cistercians, 3:751

Clement VII (Antipope), 3:783–784

Clement VIII (Antipope), 3:785

clerical celibacy/marriage, 3:327

conciliarism, 4:53–56, 136, 168–170,
171–172

Crusades, 4:409, 413

Despenser, Henry, 4:692–693

Dominici, John, 4:855

end of, 4:170, 172

England, 5:243, 13:79

France, 5:846

French Revolution, 12:13

Germany, 6:178

Ghibelline-Guelf conflict, 3:855

Gregory XII (Pope), 6:500

John XXIII (Antipope), 7:938

Lollards, 8:766

Low Countries, 10:258

Lucius III (Pope), 8:847

Martin V (Pope), 9:217–218

ordonnances cabochiennes, 10:888

overview, 3:604–605

role of Orsini family, 10:676

Salutati, Coluccio, 12:622

Scottish Church, 12:533, 833

Simon of Cramaud, 13:132

Spain, 13:381

as symptom of unresolved
constitutional conflicts, 10:839

unification under Sigismund, 13:116

University of Paris, 10:888, 13:132

Venerii Ursulina's efforts to end,
14:345

Vincent Ferrer, St., 14:520–521

works of charity, 3:414

See also Constance, Councils of;
Eastern Schism (1054); Pisa,
Councils of (1409-1512)

Western Unitarian Conference (1885),
14:304

Western Wall (Jerusalem), 7:*632*, 8:*4*

Western Watchman (periodical), 11:228

Westminster, Synod of (1138), 1:219

Westminster Abbey (England), 14:*694*,
694

Ampleforth Abbey, 1:365

anointing, 1:479

building of, 5:242

Capitular Hall, 3:698

Edward the Confessor burial site,
5:96

Hume, George Basil (Abp.),
7:202–204

Malvern Abbey, 9:84

Manning, Henry (Abp.), 5:251

Westminster Cathedral (London), 3:709,
5:*248*, 252, 11:*961*, 12:602

Westminster Confession, 4:79,
14:694–695

American Presbyterian Church,
adoption of, 11:675

biblical canon, 3:27

Calvinism, 2:895

Cambridge Platform, 2:907–908

Church-State relations, 3:647

Philadelphia Confession, 4:82

Saybrook Articles, 4:81

Weston, William (Father), 6:99, 100,
14:695–696

Westphal, Joachim, 4:416, 6:253

Westphalia, Peace of (1648), 1:848, 849,
3:612, 639, **14:696**

Wette, W. M. L. de, 1:845

Wettingen Abbey (Germany), 5:30

Wettingen-Mehrerau Abbey
(Switzerland), **14:696–697**

Wettstein, J. J., 2:366

Wexford (Ireland) martyrs, 7:579

Weyden, Roger van der, crucifixion art
of, 4:396

Weyl, H., 4:216

''Whaler's Church'' (Sag Harbor, NY),
3:715

Wharton, Charles, 3:179

Wharton, Christopher, Bl., 5:233, **14:697**

Wharton, Edith, 4:919

What is Education? (Leen), 8:446

What Is to Be Done? (Chernishevsky),
10:395

What We Have Seen and Heard (pastoral
letter), 1:161

Whately, Richard (Anglican Abp. of
Dublin), **14:697**

Whealon, John Francis (Abp. of
Hartford, CT), 4:125, 6:654, 10:276,
14:698

Wheeler, Nicholas. *See* Woodfen,
Nicholas, Bl.

Wheeler, R. E. M., 2:379

Wheeling Jesuit University (WV),
14:690

Wheelwright, John, 3:647

Whelan, Charles Maurice, 10:311,
14:698–699

Whelan, James (Bp. of Nashville, TN),
13:822

Whelan, Richard Vincent (Bp. of
Wheeling, WV), 14:541, 687–688

Whelan, Robert L. (Bp. of Fairbanks,
AK), 1:209

Whethamstede, John (Abbot), 12:532

Which Way Democracy? (Parsons), 10:904

Whichcote, Benjamin, 2:908

Whip. *See* The Discipline

Whitaker, Thomas, Bl., 2:48, 5:236, **14:699**

Whitbread, Thomas, Bl., 5:236, 686, **14:699**

Whitby, Synod of (663-64)
  Cedd, St., 3:316
  Celtic Church, conforming of, 12:830
  Celtic Rite, 3:331
  Cuthbert of Lindisfarne, St., 1:153, 4:449
  Easter date, 1:449
  union of English Church, 3:598, 5:239

Whitby Abbey (Yorkshire, England), 5:153, **14:699–701**, *700*

White, Andrew, 7:786, 12:569, **14:701**

White, Calvin, 3:472

White, Charles Ignatius, 2:40, **14:701–702**

White, Ellen G., 1:135, 4:542, 13:38

White, Eustace, St., 5:231, **14:702**

White, Henry J., 7:581, 14:597

White, James, 13:38

White, Leslie A., 4:433–434, 12:65

White, Lurana Mary (Mother), 5:874, 883

White, Lynn, Jr., 5:52–53

White, Stephen, **14:702**

White, Thomas, 7:574, 12:370, **14:702–703**

White, William (Bp. of Philadelphia), 5:297

White, William J. (Msgr.), 3:279

White Canons. *See* Premonstratensians

White Citizens Councils, 8:252

White Fathers, 8:388
  See also Missionaries of Africa

White Ladies. *See* Order of Magdalens

White magic, 9:37

White martyrdom, 9:229, *229*
  See also Martyrdom

White Penitents, 3:418

"White Sisters." *See* Missionary Sisters of Our Lady of Africa

Whitefield, George, 1:444, 2:454, 5:969, 6:425, 14:*703*, **703–704**

Whitehead, Alfred North, 11:297, 14:*704*, **704–706**
  Alexander, Samuel, 1:252
  Aristotelianism, 1:678
  classes, 13:408
  concept of time, 14:79

  eternity, 5:381
  form, 5:803
  as idealistic naturalist, 12:71
  knowledge, 8:220
  logic and mathematics, 12:415
  notion of order, 10:630
  organicism theory, 10:652
  panentheism, 10:821, 824
  philosophy and science, 11:301
  process philosophy, 11:728–729
  process theology, 11:730–731
  soul, 13:348
  study of religion, 12:65

Whitehead, Charles, 3:393

Whitemore, Nicholas. *See* Postgate, Nicholas, Bl.

Whiterig, John. *See* Monk of Farne

Whitfield, George, 5:757

Whitfield, James (Abp. of Baltimore), 2:43, 4:926, 5:41, **14:706**

Whitford, Richard, **14:706**

Whitgift, John (Abp.), 3:197, 7:91, **14:707**

Whitgift, Thomas. *See* Pormort, Thomas, Bl.

Whithorn Priory (Wigtownshire, Scotland), **14:707**

Whiting, Richard, Bl., 5:226, 6:237, **14:707–708**

Whitman, Walt, 14:*147*, 149

Whitman massacre (Oregon Territory, 1847), 2:431, 635

Whitmore, Nicholas. *See* Postgate, Nicholas, Bl.

Whitney, Eli, 5:261

Whitney, P. J., 12:570

Whole, 4:214–217, 13:551, **14:708–709**

The Whole Booke of Psalmes Faithfully Translated into English Metre. See Bay Psalm Book

The Whole Christ (Mersch), 9:521

Why God Became Man (*Cur Deus Homo*) (St. Anselm of Canterbury), 1:496–497

Why Six Instructions? (Schlarman), 12:739

Whybray, R. N., 11:97

Wiaux, Louis Joseph. *See* Wiaux, Mutien-Marie, St.

Wiaux, Mutien-Marie, St., 2:633, **14:709**

Wibald of Stavelot, 4:281, 9:79

Wiborada, St., **14:710**

Wicca, **14:710**

Wicelius, Georg. *See* Witzel, Georg

Wichita Diocese (KS), 8:113, 115–116, **14:710–711**

Wichmann of Arnstein, Bl., **14:711–712**

WICS (Women in Community Services), 10:164

Widdrington, Roger. *See* Preston, Thomas

Wider das Interim (Flacius Illyricus), 5:754

Wider die räuberischen Rotten der Bauern (Luther), 6:180

Widmar v. Vincent (1981), 3:664

Widmerpool, Robert, Bl., 2:922, 5:230, **14:712**

Wido. *See* Witelo

Widor, Charles Marie, **14:712**, *713*

Widows and widowhood, in the Bible, 13:249–250, **14:712–713**, 828–829

Widows and widowhood, in the early Church, **14:713–714**

Widukind of Corvey, 4:280–281, 9:447, **14:714**

Wied, Hermann von (Abp. of Cologne), 2:394, 653

Die Wiederbelebung des classischen Altertums (Voigt), 12:112

Wiedergeburt der Dichtung aus dem religiösen Erlebnis (Muth), 10:75

Wiegand, William, 2:524

Wiesel, Elie, 7:13

Wigand, Johannes, 6:253

Wigbert of Hersfeld, St., 5:103, **14:714**

Wigger, Winand Michael (Bp. of Newark, NJ), 10:329, **14:714–715**
  Americanism, 1:354
  Corrigan, Patrick, 4:279
  Cusack, Margaret Anna, 4:446
  St. Raphael's Society, 12:582
  Seton, R., 13:35

Wigilia, 11:511

Wigorniensis. See Worcester, Ancient See of

Wijmelenberg, Henricus van den, 4:378

Wikenhauser, A., 3:741, 5:522

Wikterp, St., **14:715**

Wilamowitz-Moellendorff, U. von, 12:58

Wilbald of Stavelot, **14:709–710**

Wilberforce, Arthur. *See* Wilberforce, Bertrand

Wilberforce, Bertrand, **14:715**

Wilberforce, Henry William, **14:716**

Wilberforce, Samuel (Bp.), 5:495

Wilberforce, William, 3:372, **14:716**, *717*

Wilcox, Robert, Bl., 2:722, 922, 5:230, **14:716**

Wild, J., 1:670

Wild Flowers (Rouquette), 12:391

The Wild Orchid (Undset), 14:295

Wilder, Robert P., 13:554

Wilfred, Felix, 7:405, 528

Wilfrid of York, St., **14:716–717**

    Agatho (Pope), St., 1:174

    Ancient See of Chichester, 3:481

    Brithwald of Canterbury, St., 2:622

    Caedwalla, St., 2:843

    Chad, St., 3:359

    Elfleda of Whitby, 5:153

    Ethelreda (Queen of Northumbria), 5:387

    missionary work, 10:255

    Ripon Abbey, 12:253

    Theodore of Tarsus, 1:449

    Whitby debate, 5:239

Wilfrida, St. *See* Wulphilda, St.

Wilgis, St., **14:717–718**

Wilhelm Meister (Goethe), 6:332

Wilhering, Cholo, 14:718

Wilhering, Ulrich, 14:718

Wilhering Abbey (Austria), 14:*718*, **718**

Wiligelmo da Modena, 2:373, **14:718–719**

Wilkes, Edward, 5:237

Will

    absolute, 1:42

    appetite, 1:602

    Avicebron, 1:939

    character, 3:387

    connatural knowledge, 8:205

    existential, 8:167

    habit, 6:599

    human act, 7:170, 173–174

    immortality, 7:350

    intellect, 8:206

    motion, 10:24–25

    Nemesius of Emesa, 10:232

    simple apprehension, 1:605

    spirit, 13:422–423

    See also Free will

Will, State v., 6:106

Will and willing, **14:719–723**

    See also Human will

Will of God, 4:92–94, 213–214, 239–241, 577–578, 582, **14:723–725**

Will power, **14:725–726**

    See also Habit

Will to Believe (James), 12:397

Willaert, Adrian, **14:726**, *727*

Willaik, St., **14:726**

Wille zur Macht (Nietzsche), 14:150

Willebold, Bl., **14:726–727**

Willebrands, Johannes Gerardus Maria (Card.), 1:439, 5:67, 68, 74, 14:320, **727–728**, *728*

Willehad (Bp. of Bremen), St., **14:728–729**

Willging, Joseph Clement (Bp. of Pueblo), 3:859

William (Abp. of Bourges), St., **14:737**

William (Abp. of Tyre), **14:755**

William (Bp. of Tortosa), 3:132

William I (King of Belgium), 11:382

William I (King of England), 14:*729*, **729–730**

    advisors, 8:323

    Alexander II (Pope), 1:253

    Barking Abbey, 2:98

    Battle Abbey, 2:156

    Church in England under, 5:240

    conqueror of English, 10:427

    Domesday Book, 4:825–826, *826*

    Durham See, 4:951

    Ealdred of York, 5:1

    Ely Abbey, 5:179

    Gloucester Abbey, 6:250

    Harold II, 6:650

    Lanfranc, 3:70, 72

    marriage dispensation from Nicholas II (Pope), 2:189

William I (King of Netherlands), 2:218, 8:823, 10:261, 11:384

William I (King of Scotland), 1:256

William I (King of Sicily), 1:126

William II (Emperor of Germany), 3:340

William II of Sicily, 13:103, *103*

William II Rufus (King of England), 1:495, 3:72, 124, 5:240–241, 10:428, **14:730**, *731*

William III (King of England), 3:648, 649, 5:249, 7:560

William IV of Bavaria, **14:730–731**

William IV of Brussels (Abbot), 12:587

William and Mary College (Williamsburg, VA), 5:297

William Arnaud, Bl., **14:731**

William de Gaynesburgh, **14:731–732**

William de Grenefield (Abp. of York), **14:732**

William de Hothum (Abp. of Dublin), 5:818, 12:231, 14:45, **732**

William de la Mare, **14:732–733**

    Augustinianism, 1:878

    Averroism controversy, 12:761–762

    commentaries, Robert of Orford, 12:269

    correctoria, 4:275, 276, 14:44–45

    Richard of Middleton, 12:234

unity thesis, 5:818

William de Melton (Abp. of York), **14:733**

William de Mideltoun. *See* William of Melitona

William de Montibus, **14:733–734**

William de Warenne, 8:527

William Firmatus, St., **14:734**

William Fitzherbert, St., 1:388, 5:444, 832, 6:749, **14:734**

William Gilbert of Colchester, 12:816

William Houghton. *See* William de Hothum (Abp. of Dublin)

William la Zouche (Abp. of York), **14:734–735**

William of Aebelholt, St., **14:735**

William of Alnwick (Bp. of Giovinazzo), 12:232, 762, **14:735**

William of Aquitaine, St., 12:549, **14:736**

William of Auvergne (of Paris), **14:736**

    Anointing of the Sick, 1:482

    attrition, 1:842, 843

    Avicenna, 5:364

    beauty, 2:184

    contrition and attrition, 4:226

    Latin Averroism, 1:623, 674, 934

    preaching, 11:619

    University of Paris, 3:603

William of Auxerre, 1:224, 265, 266, 482, 927, **14:736–737**

William of Champeaux (Bp. of Châlons-sur-Marne), **14:737–738**

    Abelard, Peter, 1:15, 18

    Anselm of Laon, 1:498

    Bernard of Clairvaux, 2:311

    Robert Pullen, 12:270

    Saint-Victor Monastery founded, 12:589, 759

    Victorine spirituality founding, 5:516, 14:484

    works, 14:738

William of Conches, **14:738–740**

    Abelard, Peter, 1:19

    atomism, 1:833

    Bernard Silvester, 2:317

    cathedral and episcopal schools, 2:307, 3:441

    medieval Latin literature works, 9:453

    number symbolism, 3:673

    Platonism, 11:415

    School of Chartres, 12:758

William of Cremona (Bp.), 1:883, **14:740**

William of Drogheda, 3:49, **14:740**

William of Edyndon (Bp. of Winchester), **14:740–741**

William of Garo. *See* William of Ware

William of Guarro. *See* William of Ware

William of Hecham, **14:741**

William of Heytesbury, 12:812, **14:741**

William of Hildernisse, 7:64

William of Hirsau, Bl., 6:114, 12:668, **14:742**

William of Jumièges, 12:270

William of Kilkenny (Bp. of Ely), **14:742**

William of MacClesfeld, 4:275, 276–277, 5:818, 12:269, 14:45–46, **742–743**

William of Maleval, St., **14:743**, 758

William of Malmesbury, **14:743**

    Aldhelm, St., 1:246

    chronicles of, 1:464

    Florence of Worcester, 5:772

    Latin literature, 3:601

    life of Oswald of York, St., 10:708

    Malmesbury Abbey, 9:80–81

William of Melitona (Middleton), **14:743–744**

    Alexander of Hales, 1:265

    Bonaventure, St., 2:479

    Franciscan theological tradition, 5:899

William of Middleton. *See* William of Melitona

William of Militona. *See* William of Melitona

William of Moerbeke (Abp.), **14:744–745**

    Platonism, 11:415

    translations for Aquinas, 14:19

    translations from Aristotle, 1:673, 674, 936, 4:850

William of Mont Lauzun, 3:48, 800

William of Nevers (Count), 3:394

William of Newburgh, 5:269, 12:244, **14:745**

William of Norwich, St., 10:451, **14:745–746**

William of Notingham, **14:746**

William of Notre Dame de l'Olive, St., **14:746**

William of Ockham, **14:746–749**

    accident, 1:62

    Adam Wodham, 1:110

    agnosticism, 1:180

    Albert of Saxony, 1:223

    analogy, 1:372

    Aristotelianism, 1:670

    Augustinianism, 1:879

    Biel, Gabriel, 2:391

    Calvin, John, 2:891

    certitude, 3:352

    concept of time, 14:78

    conceptualism of, 4:53

    conciliarism, 4:55–56, 136

    contingency, 4:213–214

    de Morgan, Augustus, 4:655

    defense of Thomistic teachings, 14:46

    dialectics, 4:727

    Divine causality, 3:305

    Durandus of Saint-Pourçain, 4:948

    empiricism, 5:197

    ethics, 5:394

    exemplarism, 5:526

    fideism, 5:711

    final causality, 5:724

    flight from Avignon, 7:932

    grace, 6:390, 402

    Holcot, Robert, 12:265

    human will, 14:722–723

    intentionality, 7:518

    John XXII (Pope), 3:603

    John Lutterell, 7:961

    justification, 8:83

    knowledge, theories of, 8:217

    Landini, F., 8:322

    Latin Averroism, 1:937

    logical history, 8:750

    Luther, Martin, influence, 8:878

    metaphysics, 9:553

    moral goodness, 6:351

    natural law, 10:182

    nominalist theology, 13:908

    Oxford School (Franciscan), 5:242, 900

    papal absolutism, 9:463

    possibility, 11:551

    Richard of Campsall, 12:232

    skepticism, 13:201–202

    study of motion, 10:18

    universal essences, 5:361

    universals, 14:324–325

    will and willing, 14:722–723

    works, 5:902, 12:541, 14:749

    See also Nominalism; Ockhamism

William of Orange. *See* William III (King of England)

William of Pagula, 3:50, **14:749–750**

William of Peter of Godin, 14:46, **750**

William of Poul. *See* William of Pagula

William of Rievaulx, 5:240

William of Rouen, 8:59

William of Ruisbroek (Ruysbroeck), **14:750**

William of Saint-Amour, 1:224, 2:479, 481, 6:159, 14:16, 20, 750–752

William of Saint-Bénigne of Dijon, St., 3:600, 5:659, 12:548, **14:752**

William of Saint-Brieuc, St., 14:752

William of Saint-Thierry, **14:752–754**

    Abelard, Peter, 1:18, 19

    Carthusian spirituality, 3:190

    dialectics, 4:726

    medieval Latin literature works, 9:453, 453–454

    mysticism, 3:749

William of Sandwich, Chronicle of, **14:754**

William of Savoy (Abbot), 12:528

William of Sherwood (Shyreswood), 12:762, **14:754**

William of Shyreswood. *See* William of Sherwood

William of Toulouse, St., **14:754**

William of Tripoli, **14:754–755**

William of Turbeville (Bp. of Norwich), **14:755**

William of Tyre, 2:29

William of Varro. *See* William of Ware

William of Vaspail (Abbot), 5:659

William of Vaurouillon, 3:96, **14:755–756**

William of Vercelli, St., **14:756**, 757–758

William of Ware, 1:878, 3:96, **14:756–757**

William of Wykeham (Bp.), 5:243, **14:867–868**

William Procurator, 1:465

William Rede (Bp. of Chichester), 3:481

William Rufus. *See* William II Rufus (King of England)

William Tell (Rossini), 12:384

William the Conqueror. *See* William I (King of England)

William the Lion (King of Scotland), 8:848

William Wickwane (Abp. of York), **14:757**

William Wodeford. *See* William Woodford

William Woodford, **14:757**

William Wydford. *See* William Woodford

Williamites, 1:886, 7:86, 14:743, **757–758**

Williams, Daniel Day, 11:731

Williams, J. Kendrick (Bp. of Lexington), 8:529

Williams, John Joseph (Abp. of Boston), 1:158, 2:555, 9:307–308, **14:758–759**

Williams, Leighton, 2:80

Williams, Michael, **14:759**

Williams, Richard, Ven., 5:232

Williams, Roger, 2:79, 3:647, 648, 10:321, 12:214, **14:759–760**

Williams, Samuel Wells, 3:499

Williams, Theodore (Mother), 1:158

Williams, William, **14:760**

Williamson, Richard, 3:289

Willibald of Eichstätt, St., 2:496, 3:599, 14:606, **761**

Willibrord of Utrecht, St., **14:761–762**

   Adalbert the Deacon, St., 1:102

   Antwerp (Belgium), 1:538

   Boniface, St., 2:495

   Charles Martel, 3:163, 434

   influence of, 3:599

   missionary activity, 2:267–268, 4:662, 5:103, 10:255

   pilgrimage to tomb, 5:42

   shrine, 13:94

   successors, 8:430–431

   Wilgis, St., 14:717

Willigis, St., **14:762**

Willis, Geoffrey, 12:328

Willmann, Otto, **14:762–763**

Willson, Robert William (Bp. of Hobart, Tasmania), **14:763**

Will-to-live, 7:298–299

Wilmart, André, 1:120, 5:629, 6:67, 7:250, **14:763–764**

Wilmington Diocese (DE), 2:38, **14:764–765**

Wilpert, Joseph, 1:753, **14:765–766**

Wilson, B. (sociologist), 12:87

Wilson, Bill (A.A. founder), 1:242

Wilson, E. B., 2:403

Wilson, Florence. *See* Volusenus, Florentius

Wilson, Ian, 13:95

Wilson, John, 1:*443*, 12:569

Wilson, R. M. L., 6:263

Wilson, Samuel, 4:839

Wilson, Thomas, 1:676

Wilson, Thomas (Bp. of Sodor and Man), 3:153

Wilson, William A., 3:627

Wilson, Woodrow, 10:171

Wilson v. Pres. Church of John's Island (1846), 3:657

Wilton Abbey (Wiltshire, England), **14:766**

Wiltrude, Bl., **14:766**

Wimborne Abbey (Dorsetshire, England), 4:449, 8:596, **14:766–767**

Wimmer, Boniface, 2:254, 11:83–84, 12:591, 735, **14:767**

Wimmer, Franziska (Mother), 5:888

Wimpina, Konrad Koch, 5:43, 14:*767*, **767–768**

Winchcombe Monastery (England), 8:136

Winchelsea, Robert, 5:242

Winchester, Ancient See of (England), 1:22, 3:481, 4:317, **14:768**

Winchester, Synod of (1308), 4:88

Winchester Troper (manuscript), 8:683

Winckelmann, Johann Joachim, 3:679

Winckler, Hugo, 5:520, 10:820

Windelband, Wilhelm, 5:398, 8:220, 10:237, 238

Windesheim Monastery (Netherlands), 2:608, 3:69, **14:768**, 770

Windesheim school, 14:13

Winds, worship of the, **14:770**

Windsor, David, 8:822

Windsor Forest (Pope), 11:496

Windthorst, Ludwig, 3:340, 8:255, 13:256, **14:770–771**, *771*

Wine, liturgical use of, **14:771–773**

Winebrenner, John, 5:468

Winebrenner v. Colder (1862), 3:658

Wini (Bp. of Winchester, England), 14:768

Winnebago people, 1:163, 4:363, 8:697, 778

Winnebald, St., 2:496, 14:606, 761, **773**

Winning, Thomas Joseph (Card.), 12:839, **14:773**

Winnoc, St., **14:773–774**

Winona Diocese (MN), **14:774–775**

Winram, John, 12:534

Winston, Charles, 13:474

Winstone, Harold E. (Father), **14:775**

Winter solstice, 8:719

Winthir, St., **14:775**

Winthrop, John, 3:647

Winthrop, John, Jr., 4:2–3

Winwaloe, St., **14:775–776**

Winzen, Damasus (Father), 2:256

Wipo (11th c. writer), 9:449

Wirceburgenses, **14:776–777**

Das Wirken des dreieinigen Gottes (Schell), 12:732

Die Wirksamkeit des Bittgebetes (Schmid), 12:743

Wirnt, Bl., **14:777**

Wirt, Caupo. *See* Wirt, Wigand

Wirt, Martin. *See* Wirt, Wigand

Wirt, Wigand, **14:777**

Wirt, William, 10:169

Wirth, Karl Joseph, 6:185

Wisconsin, **14:777–784**

   Catholic education, 5:753

   Dabrowski, Joseph, 4:491

   Englehardt, Zephyrin, 5:221

   immigration, 8:256

   Jesuits, 9:722

   missions, 12:633

   See also specific dioceses and archdioceses

Wisconsin v. Yoder (1972), 3:663

Wisdom, **14:784–788**

   Achamoth, 5:181

   charity, 3:399

   Christian philosophy, 3:538

   docta ignorantia, 4:798

   Lawrence Justinian, St., 8:405

   Logos image, 8:759

   metaphysics, 9:552

   mystical contemplation, 4:206

   speculative habit, 5:745

Wisdom, Book of, **14:792–793**

   beatific vision, 2:169, 171

   canonicity, 3:26

   creation, 4:341–342

   death, 4:573

   eschatology, 5:336

   friendship with God, 6:10

   gates of hell, 6:107

   glory of God (end of creation), 6:245

   God's spirit, 13:426, 427

   Hades, 6:604

   idol worship ridicule, 2:211

   Kingdom of God, 8:172

   lying as sin, 8:900

   manna, 9:118–119

   retribution, 12:178

   serpent as symbol, 13:19, 20

   sin, 13:144

   spirit, 13:425

   wisdom personified, 8:760

   Word of God, 8:759

Wisdom, gifts of, **14:793**

   See also Holy Spirit

Wisdom, in the Bible, **14:788–792**

Wisdom literature, 1:190–191, 5:134

   See also Sapiential books

Wisdom of Ben Sira, 5:36, **14:794–796**

   See also Sirach, Book of

Wise, F., 3:465

Wise, John, 4:115

Wise Blood (O'Connor), 10:547

Wiseman, Nicholas Patrick (Card.), 1:346, 4:916–917, 5:251, 9:120–121, 12:730, **14:796–797**, *797*

Wishart, George, 12:834, **14:797–798**

Wisinska, Rose (Mother Mary Anna), 5:880

Wiśniowetski, Koribut, 12:422

Wissembourg Abbey. *See* Weissenburg Abbey (France)

Die Wissensformen und die Gesellschaft (Scheler), 12:731

Witchcraft, 5:42, 8:419, 777, 13:410, 14:710, **798–801**

Witches Apprehended, Examined and Executed, for notable villanies by them committed both by Land and Water, 14:799

"Witches Bull" (*Summis desiderantes*) (Innocent VIII), 10:841

Witelo (Polish philosopher), **14:801**

Witham Charterhouse (Somerset, England), 7:154, **14:801**

Withburga, St., **14:801–802**

Withers, George, 5:317

Witherspoon, John, **14:802**

Witness, Christian, **14:802–803**

Wito. *See* Witelo (Polish philosopher)

Witt, Franz X., 2:842

Witta, St., **14:803**

Wittenberg (England), 8:878, **14:803–804**

Witters v. Washington Department of Services for the Blind (1986), 3:668

Wittgenstein, Ludwig, **14:804–805**
  analytic philosophy, 5:95, 11:297
  Anscombe, Gertrude Elizabeth Margaret, 1:492
  foundationalism, 5:829
  knowledge, 8:220–221
  logicla atomism, 12:415
  Vienna Circle, 8:756

Wittich, C., 3:184

Wittig, Josef, 12:26

Wittkower, R., 3:674, 700

Wittman, Cornelius, 12:552

Wittmann, George Michael (Bp. of Regensburg), 6:166, 12:780

Witzel, Georg (Wicelius), 2:874, 3:241, **14:805**

Wives, duties of, 11:334

Wives of Catholic Clergy (Fichter), 5:709

Wiwina, St., **14:805–806**

Wizo (Anglo-Saxon writer), 3:13

Władysław II (King of Poland). *See* Jagiełło (King of Poland)

Włocławek, Michał (Bp.), 11:450

Wodeham, Adam de, 10:412, 12:541

Wogan, Nicholas, 7:581

Wogan, William, 7:579

Wojtyła, Karol (Card.). *See* John Paul II (Pope)

Wolcott, Oliver, 3:650

Wolf, Christian. *See* Wolff, Christian

Wolf, Erik, 10:194

Wolf, Friedrich, 11:274

Wolf, Hieronymus, 2:765

Wolf, Innocent (Abbot), 12:539

Wolf, Jones v. (1979), 3:662

Wolf, P. P., 3:796

Wolfaria (utopian state), 5:31

Wolfdietrich of Reitenau (Abp. of Salzburg), 1:912

Wolfe, David, 7:557

Wolff, Christian, **14:806–808**, *807*
  accident, 1:62
  antimonies, 1:520
  Aristotelianism, 1:677
  aseity, 1:780
  Christian philosophy, 3:540
  classification of the sciences, 12:820
  cosmological argument, 4:285
  cosmology, 4:287
  Czechs, 4:483
  eclecticism, 5:47
  Enlightenment, 5:255, 262–263
  existence, 5:534
  law of nature, 10:183
  ontology, 10:606–607
  possibility, 11:551
  rationalism, 11:921
  Reimarus, 12:35
  scholasticism, 12:765, 767, 769
  works, 14:806–807

Wolff, George Dering, **14:808–809**

Wolff, Mary Evaline. *See* Madeleva, Mary (Sister)

Wölffin, Eduard, 2:263

Wölfflin, H., 3:679

Wolfgang of Regensburg (Bp.), St., 5:139, 319, 10:709, 12:668, **14:809**

Wolfhard of Verona, St., **14:809–810**

Wolfhelm, Bl., 2:586, **14:810**

Wolfhilda, St. *See* Wulphilda, St.

Wolfram of Sens, St. *See* Wulfram of Sens, St.

Wolfrat, Anthony, 1:912

Wolhgemuth, Michael, 2:522

Wollstonecraft, Mary, 5:672

Wolman v. Walter (1977), 3:667–668

Wolsey, Thomas (Card.), **14:810–811**, *811*
  Bonner, Edmund, 2:507
  Clerk, John, 3:803
  Cromwell, Thomas, 4:376
  Henry VIII's divorce, 3:268, 782, 5:244, 6:740, 12:7–8
  Saint Albans Abbey, 12:532
  York, Ancient See of, 2:179, 14:894

Wolter, Maurus, 2:259, 350, 8:671, **14:811–812**

Wolter, Placidus, 2:350

Woman Clothed with the Sun, 3:579, **14:821–822**

Woman in the Nineteenth Century (Fuller), 14:148

Womanist theology, **14:822–823**

Woman's Holy War, 13:798

Women, **14:812–819**
  agents of evil, 13:51
  Baptism by immersion, 7:37
  CELAM IV (Santo Domingo), 12:686
  contraception, 4:220
  Cuban religious orders, 4:417
  Daughters of Isabella, 4:533–534
  decorations of laity, 4:596
  disciples, 4:770
  during French Revolution, 4:43–44
  Ecumenical councils, 4:303
  education of, 5:682, 834, 12:291, 587
  election of papal candidates, 8:321
  fable of woman pope, 8:321
  Homines Intelligentiae, 7:64
  hospices for working girls, 8:778
  Hungary, 7:218–219
  hysterectomy, 7:265–266
  Jesuits, 7:313
  Knights of Labor, 8:192
  Knights of the Holy Sepulcher, 8:198
  Latina theology, 8:369–370
  liturgical movement, 8:674–675
  Marian invocations, current, 8:603
  ministers, 8:87, 116, 227, 295, 547, 589
  Montanism, 8:281
  nuns, mirroring roles of noble women, 2:256
  religious orders, 4:210
  roles, 14:821
  same nature as man, 13:249
  same-sex sexual activity, 13:49
  Sanctoral cycle of virgins and holy women, 8:720

status of, 1:153, 2:773–774, 3:409,
4:321

temperance movements, 13:797, 801

theological studies for, 5:676–677

Woman's Holy War, 13:798

work hours, 14:818

*See also specific religious orders;
specific women*

Women, Canon Law on, **14:819–821**

Women, in the Bible, 6:126–127,
13:249, **14:828–832**

See also specific biblical figures

Women, role in the Church

acolytes, 1:68

Adam, 1:104

Anglican ordination, 1:*435*, 439, 441,
447, 7:203

choir participation, 3:522, 8:699, 701

deaconesses, 4:554–555, 7:37

Egeria's *Itinerarium*, 5:104

Hispanic ministry, 5:204

John Paul II (Pope), 1:68, 3:549

Pro Mundi Vita (Brussels), 11:727

reform congregations, 2:257–258

religious orders, 3:622

Sister Formation Movement,
13:169–170

Vatican II petitions, 12:550

See also Ordination of women;
Women and papal teaching

Women and papal teaching, 5:68, 8:699,
701, **14:823–828**

The Women at the Window or the
Duenna (Murillo), 10:66

Women in Community Services (WICS),
10:164

Women in labor (birth), patron of, 5:173

Women in Theological Research,
European Society of (ESWTR),
5:677

Women of Nazareth. *See* Grail (lay
women's group)

Women Worshippers (Herondas), 12:509

Women's rights, 12:550–551

Women's suffrage, 12:550–551

Wonder, 4:883, **14:832–833**

Wood, Annie. *See* Besant, Annie

Wood, James Frederick (Abp. of
Philadelphia), 11:85, 239–240, 240

Woodbridge, Frederick J. E., 10:204

Woodcock, John, Bl., 2:48, 5:236,
14:833

Woodfen, Nicholas, Bl., 5:229,
14:833–834

Woodhead, Abraham, 4:168

Woodhouse, Thomas, Bl., 5:227, **14:834**

Woodruff, Wilford, 8:373

Woodstock Theological Center
(Washington, DC), **14:834–835**

Woodward, W. H., 14:448

Wool industry, 7:204–205

Woollett, J. Sidney, 7:699

Woolman, John, **14:835**

Worcester (England), **14:835–836**

Worcester, Ancient See of (England),
14:835

Worcester, Council of, 4:88

Worcester, William, 1:464

The Word, **14:836–838**

Apollinarianism, 1:559

apologetics, 1:563

Barth, Karl, 2:121

Books of Kings, 8:177

creation, 4:341, 344

Diodore of Tarsus, 4:750–751

dogmatic definition, 4:611–612

Hebrew view, 8:566

Leontius of Byzantium, 8:502

life, concept of, 8:566

Lutheranism, 8:893

Old Testament, 8:759

sacramental theology, 12:468, 475

substantial locutions, 8:747

See also Logos

Word and Object (Quine), 10:608

Word of God, 7:809, 13:314, 438–439

Worde, Wynkyn de, 2:523

Words, **14:836**

Wordsworth, John, 10:774, 14:597

Wordsworth, William, 1:142, 5:188, 189,
13:320

Work

abstinence from, on Sunday,
13:611–612

John Paul II (Pope), 13:263–264

just remuneration, 13:263

leisure related, 8:460, 461

love, 8:830

multiplicity of values, 13:262–263

nobility of, 13:261–262

Work hours of women, 14:818

Work of Prisons, 3:419

Worker education, 9:778

Worker Priests, 5:858, 7:935, 9:684,
11:573, 12:407–408, **14:838–839**

Workers

Belgium, 8:672

Colombian social action program,
8:869–870

France, workers' circles, 8:371

Germany, 8:160–161

industry council plan, 13:259

just remuneration, 13:263

Laborem Exercens, 8:266

Lamennais, F., 8:310

Lie'nart, Achille (Card.), 8:564

Louis of Besse, 8:805

moral theology, 8:455

papal social thought, 13:259, 260,
261

participation in ownership and
management, 8:266

religious liberalism, 8:541

social justice, 8:67–68, 13:244

social principle, 13:250

solidarity, 8:266

subjects, 8:266

Young Christian Worker Movement,
8:416

*The Workers Are Few (Operarii autem
pauci)* (Manna), 9:119–120

Workers' circles (*Oeuvre des cercles
ouvriers*), 5:855

Workers of the Holy House of Nazareth,
13:730

Workhouses, 3:417

Workingman's Party, 2:869

Workplace, spirituality of, 8:418

Works and Days (Hesiod), 14:360

Works of God (biblical expression),
4:342–343, **14:839**

World (Descartes), 4:678, 681

World, in the Bible, **14:839–840**

World Alliance of Reformed Churches,
5:68

The World and the Individual (Royce),
12:397

*The World Chronicle (Chronicorum libri
duo)* (Sulpicius Severus), 1:461

World Chronicle (Theophilos of Edessa),
1:172

World Conference of Faith and Order
(1927), 1:577

World Council of Churches (WCC),
1:586, 10:30, **14:840–843**

American Council of Christian
Churches, 1:351

apostolicity, 1:597

Athenagoras I (Patriarch), 1:829

Brent, Charles Henry, 2:603

Canada, 3:9

confessions of faith, 4:82, 355

Ecumenical Movement, 5:71–75

Faith and Order Commission, 5:40,
67, 606–608

founding, 5:71, 73, 606, 8:578,
12:700, 13:297

World Council of Churches (WCC)
(continued)
John XXIII (Pope), Bl., 7:937
Joint Working Group, 13:296
Knutson, K. S., 8:227
liturgical aspects, 8:168
Lund Conference (1952), 5:72
Lutherans, 8:887, 892
mission, 9:698
signs of the times, 13:117–118
SODEPAX, 13:296
Vatican II, 3:625
Youth Department, 12:742
World Day of Prayer for Peace (1986),
10:853
World Evangelical Fellowship, 1:351,
9:697–698
World Federation of Sodalities,
13:294–295
World Harmony (Kepler), 8:155
World Methodist Council (WMC) (1971-
1986), 5:68
World Missionary Conference (1910),
9:697
World soul, **14:843–845**
Bruno, G., 13:345–346
Cardano's defense of doctrine of,
10:823
causality, 3:302
emanationism, 5:180, 181
hylozoism, 7:239
metaphysics of light, 7:319, 8:583
Plato, 13:338
World Temperance Convention (1846),
13:800
World Trade Center bombings (2001).
See September 11 terrorist attacks
(U.S., 2001)
World Union of Catholic Women's
Organizations (WUCWO), 10:164
World War I (1914-18)
Armenia, 1:706
Austria, 1:915
Catholic War Council, 12:786
Center party (Germany), 3:341
Chaldean Catholic Church, 3:369
Church-State relations, 3:642, 660
French Jesuits, 7:791
Greece, 6:436
Hapsburgs, 6:641
Klan re-emergence, 8:251
Knights of Columbus, 8:190–191
Louvain, Catholic University of,
8:824
Lutheranism, 8:886–887
papal social thought, 13:260

Poland, 12:613
prisoners and displaced persons,
13:297
seminarians, 8:156
U.S. Navy in Virginia, 14:543
Vatican neutrality, 2:249–250
Vatican peace proposal, 2:250
World War II (1939-45)
Aachen (Germany), 1:1
Algeria, 1:285–286
Anscombe, Gertrude Elizabeth
Margaret, 1:493
Apocalypse iconography, 1:545
Bulgaria, 2:681–682
Catholic University of America,
3:291
Cimatti, Bl. Maria Raffaella, 3:734
Cologne (Germany), 3:842, 843
concentration camps, 8:560–561
Coughlin, Charles Edward,
4:294–295
defense of Christian civilization,
8:868
Denmark, 4:667–668
France, Nazi opposition, 8:564
French Indochina, 8:329
Greece, 6:436–437
Hungary, 8:228
Indonesia, 7:429
Ireland, 7:565
Libya, 8:558–559
Lithuania, 8:607
Louvain, Catholic University of,
8:824
Maglione, Luigi, 9:40
Maryknoll Fathers and Brothers,
overseas mission, 9:296
papal social thought, 13:260
rescue of Jews, 8:229
Sapieha, Adam Stefan, 12:688
Slovenia, 13:227
Yugoslavia, 13:10
See also Holocaust (Shoah)
World Woman's Christian Temperance
Union, 13:801
World Youth Days, 7:1001, 10:852,
14:845
World-formation theory, 5:180
World's Christian Fundamentals
Association, 6:27, 30
World's Congress of Religion (1893),
1:355
World's Evangelical Alliance, 5:467
World's Parliament of Religion,
14:845–847
Worldwide Church of God, **14:847–848**

Worldwide Marriage Encounter, **14:848**
Worlock, Derek John Harford (Abp. of
Liverpool), **14:848**
Worms, Concordat of (1122), 3:601,
635, 7:539, 663, 10:257, 12:27,
14:849–850
Worms, Councils of (1540-1557), 2:394,
889, 3:17, **14:850**
Worms, Diet of (1521), 3:430, 482, 781
Worms, Synod of (1076), 3:777
Worms Cathedral (Germany), 3:691
Worrell, J., 2:379
Worringer, W., 3:676
Worship, **14:850–851**, 852–855
Worship (hymnal), 7:261
Worship (periodical), 5:168
Worship (Underhill), 14:291
Worship, in the Bible, **14:855–859**
Worthington, Thomas, **14:859–860**
Wotton, H., 3:675
Woulfe, James, 7:581
Wounds of Our Lord, devotion to,
14:860
Woywod, Stanislas, **14:860**
The Wreck of the Deutschland
(Hopkins), 5:880
Wrede, William, 2:384, 5:521, 6:865
Wren, Christopher, 3:678, 707, 12:577
Wrenn, Lawrence G., 3:59
Wrenno, Roger, Bl., 5:235, **14:860–861**
Wright, C. F., 3:716
Wright, Frank Lloyd, 3:669, 679, 680,
715, 716
Wright, John Joseph (Card.), 5:664,
9:309, 11:88, 367, **14:861–862**
Wright, Peter, Bl., 5:236, **14:862**
Wright, William, **14:862**
The Writings of St. Francis (Robinson),
12:274
Wu, Y. T. *See* Wu Yaozong (Chinese
Church leader)
Wu Anbang, Peter, St., **14:862–863**
Wu Li (Chinese priest), **14:863**
Wu Yaozong (Chinese Church leader),
3:501
WUCWO (World Union of Catholic
Women's Organizations), 10:164
Wuerl, Donald W. (Bp. of Pittsburgh),
11:367–368
Wüger, G., 2:350
Wulfhilda, St. *See* Wulphilda, St.
Wulfila (missionary to Goths), 1:663
Wulflaicus, St., **14:863**
Wulfram of Sens, St., 5:793, **14:863–864**
Wulfstan II (Abp. of York), 14:894

Wulfstan of Worcester, St., 5:772, 7:247, 9:84, **14:864**

Wúllenweber, Theresia von, 4:788

Wulmar, St., **14:864**

Wulphilda, St., **14:865**

Wulphy, St. See Wulflaicus, St.

Wunder des Herren (Fonck), 5:789

Wundt, Wilhelm, 1:796, 7:532, 10:120, 128, 13:793

Würzburg Lectionary, 3:555, 556

WWS. See New Testament of Wordsworth-White-Sparks

Wyatt, Thomas, Sir, 5:163

Wycislo, Aloysius J. (Bp. of Green Bay, WI), 14:783

Wyclif, John, 3:605, **14:865–867**
    Adam Easton, 1:107
    Canterbury Hall warden, 13:130
    Church property, 3:727
    Church-State relations, 3:636
    clerics and laity, 8:281
    Congregationalism, 4:114
    Constance Council, 4:170
    Courtenay, William, 4:170, 317–318
    Crumpe, Henry, 4:398, 400
    Crusade indulgences, 4:693
    Czechs, 4:480
    denial of transubstantiation, 5:243
    determinism and free will, 5:938
    flagellation, 5:755
    Hereford, Nicholas, 6:769
    heresy, 6:774
    Hus and Hussitism, 7:228, 230
    influence of, 14:867
    Jerome of Prague, 7:760
    John Kynyngham, 7:959–960
    leniency, 13:133
    necessity of the Incarnation, 7:376
    papal Antichrist, 1:517
    relics, 12:55
    religious habit, 12:722
    Repington, Philip, 12:131–132
    Richard Fitzralph, influence, 12:230
    Robert Waldby of York, 12:271
    Rygge, Robert, 12:447
    secularization of Church property, 12:871
    Simon of Cramaud, 13:132
    simony attacked, 13:136
    sin, venial, 13:155
    theological censure, 3:337
    William Woodford, 14:757
    works, 8:325, 14:866–867
    See also Lollards

Wyclif Bible, 3:27

Wye, St. See Guido of Anderlecht, St.

Wynfrith. See Boniface, St.

Wynhoven, Peter M. H., 8:814

Wynne, John Joseph, 14:*868*, **868**

Wyoming, **14:868–871**
    See also specific dioceses and archdioceses

Wyszyński, Casimir, Ven., **14:871–872**

Wyszyński, Stefan (Card.), 4:490, 7:996, 11:*28*, *442*, 450, 451, 452, 14:*872*, **872–873**

X

Xainctonge, Anne de, Ven., 12:587, **14:875**

Xanthopulus, Nicephorus Callistus, **14:875–876**

Xarrié, Francisco, 12:773

Xaverian Brothers, 3:622, 12:448, 13:404, **14:876–877**

Xaverian Missionary Fathers, 3:622, 4:94, **14:877**

Xaverian Missionary Sisters of Mary, 14:877

Xavier (Mother), 5:889

Xavier, Francis, St., 14:*877*, **877–879**
    Asian mission, 7:401, 737, 784
    Berse, Gaspar, 2:331
    bilocation, 2:397
    Counter Reformation, 4:312
    Criminali, Antonio, 4:364
    Faber, Peter, 5:583, 584
    inculturation, 3:493
    Indian mission, 9:692
    Malaysian mission, 9:70
    preaching, 11:621

Xavier University of Louisiana (New Orleans), 1:162, 4:906, **14:879–881**, *880*

Xenocrates (Greek philosopher), 11:412

Xenodochium, 3:409, 7:126–127

Xenophanes of Colophon (Greek philosopher), 6:306, 441, 453, 10:825, 13:922

Xenophon (Greek historian), 4:497, 10:180, 12:309, 13:292

Xerxes I (King of Persia), 11:135

Xiberta, B. M., 12:777

Xifré, José, 3:764

Ximenes, Francis (Card.), 7:187

Ximénez de Cisneros, Francisco (Card.), **14:881–882**
    Adrian VI (Pope), 1:129
    Algeria, 1:285
    Angela of Foligno, Bl., 1:412

Bible texts, 2:366

Charles V (Holy Roman Emperor), 3:429

Counter Reformation, 3:610

Hispano-Mozarabic Rite preserved, 10:43

Spanish reform, 13:391, 392

University of Alcalá, 1:236

Ximénez de Rada, Rodrigo (Abp. of Toledo, Spain), 5:751, **14:882**

Ximénez Ximénez, Sofía, Bl., 1:4

Xinxue (School of the Mind), 3:512

Xiximíes Jesuit Mission (Mexico), 9:708–709

Xosrov Anjewac'i, 1:709

Xu Guangqi (Hsü Kuang-ch'i), 3:494, 495

Xuanzang (Chinese translator), 3:510

Xunzi (Confucian philosopher), 4:97

Xuyen Van Nguyen, Domingo, 14:499

XXX Dialoghi (Ochino), 10:535

Y

Yabalāhā III, 3:366

Yabalāhā IV (Chaldean Patriarch), 3:367

Yabhalaha III (Assyrian Catholicos), 1:807, 3:492

Yadin, Y., 2:379

Yago, Bernard (Card.), 7:681

Yago, John, Bl., 7:733

Yahweh, **14:883–884**
    afterlife, 1:164
    confidence, 7:102–103
    conscience, 4:143, 148
    covenant, 4:324, 326–327
    creation, 4:339, 340–345
    curses, 4:442
    David (King of Israel), 9:541
    holiness of man, 7:3
    images, 7:322–323
    importance of prophets, 8:177
    love for His people, 8:831
    magic forbidden, 9:39
    Mary, Blessed Virgin, 9:243–244
    mediator role of Moses, 6:272–273, 10:6–7
    messianism, 9:540, 542, 543
    original meaning, 10:592
    people's sonship, 13:322
    saving action, 10:666–667
    seraphim, 13:5–6
    Shaddai, 13:58
    showbread, 13:88
    simplicity of God, 13:137

Yahweh (continued)
  Spirit of God, 13:426–428
  substitute names, 8:780, 13:77–78
  temples, 13:808–809, 810
  See also God
Yahwist document form, 11:90–91,
  14:884
  biblical myths in accounts, 10:129,
    131
  covenant, 4:326–327
  creation, 4:341
  serpent as symbol, 13:18, 19, 21
Yahwist tradition, 1:2, 36, 2:437
Yahya ibn-'Adi (philosopher), 1:671
Yaiser, Hildebrand, 12:534
Yajur Veda, 6:840
Yakichi, Andrew, Bl., 7:734
Yakichi, Francis, Bl., 7:734
Yakichi, Louis, Bl., 7:734
Yakichi, Lucy, Bl., 7:734
Yale Divinity School (New Haven, CT),
  13:771
Yale University (New Haven, CT),
  4:115, 116, 12:245–246
Yamada, Anthony, Bl., 7:733
Yamada, Clara, Bl., 7:733
Yamada, Dominic, Bl., 7:733
Yamada, Lawrence, Bl., 7:734
Yamada, Michael, Bl., 7:734
Yan Guodong, James, St., **14:884**
Yanez de la Almedina, Fernando, 3:268
Yang Guangxian, 3:496–497
Yang Tingyun (Yang T'ing-yün), 3:494
Yang Zhu, 3:509
Yanyshev, I. L., 12:435
Yaquis Jesuit Mission (Mexico), 9:709
Yaroslav the Wise, 12:419
Yashar, Book of. See Jashar, Book of
Yashts (Persian hymns), 11:142
Yasna (Persian text), 11:142, 143
Yavis, C., 3:672
Yavorksy, Stephan, 12:434
Yaxley, Richard, Bl., 5:231, **14:884**
Yazdgard I (King of Persia), 1:700, 805
Ybarra de Villalonga, Rafaela, Bl.,
  14:885
Yearly Meetings (Quakers), 6:4
Yeats, William Butler, 14:885, **885–886**
Yehiel, Asher ben. See Asher ben Jehiel
Yeldho, Baselius, St., 7:406
Yeltsin, Boris, 2:213, 10:695, 12:429
Yemen, **14:886–888**, 887
Yempo, Simon, Bl., 7:734
Yen Do, Vicente, 14:499

Yermo y Parres, José María de, St.,
  14:888
Yerovi, José María (Bp. of Quito),
  14:888–889
Yeṣirah, Book of, 6:266, 12:450,
  14:889–890
Yesterday and Today (Murray), 10:69
Yevele, Henry, 3:73, 489
Yezdegird era, 5:311
Yezid II (Caliph), 2:751
Yezidi religion, **14:890**
Yijing (Book of Changes), 3:508
Yin-yang, 3:508, 4:522–523
Yishaq, Rabbi Shelomoh ben. See Rashi
  (Rabbi Shelomoh ben Yishaq)
  (medieval commentator)
Yoder, Wisconsin v. (1972), 3:663
Yoga, 6:845, 7:408, 10:116, 11:591,
  13:149, **14:890–893**
  See also Hinduism
Yoga, Immortality and Freedom (Eliade),
  5:154
Yogam, 7:396
Yom Kippur (Day of Atonement),
  1:838–839, 2:443–444, 8:525,
  12:456, 720–721, 13:159
Yongming Yanshou, 3:511
Yongzheng (Emperor of China), 3:498
York (England), medieval drama of,
  4:899, 900
York, Ancient See of (England), 13:297,
  14:893–894
York, Convocation of, 3:240, 4:243–244
York Cathedral (England), 1:544,
  14:893, 893
York Use, **14:894–895**
Yorke, Peter Christopher, 2:869, 12:648,
  14:895–896
Yoshida, Andrew, Bl., 7:732
You Can Change the World (Keller),
  8:137
You'd Better Come Quietly (Feeney),
  5:663
Yougbaré, Dieudonné (Bp. of Koupéla),
  2:704
Young, Arthur, 3:751
Young, Brigham, 14:357, **896**, 897
Young, Josue Moody (Bp. of Erie, PA),
  1:156, 9:56
Young, Nicholas, 7:580
The Young Apostle (Godfrey), 6:325
Young Calvinist Federation of North
  America, 12:25
Young Catholic Workers, 3:536
Young Christian Student (JEC), 5:857
Young Christian Workers, 3:103
Young Hegelian Movement, 6:709–710

Young Herbs (Wakana shu) (Shimazaki),
  13:85
Young Italy, 3:101
Young Men's Christian Association
  (YMCA), 3:501, 10:30, 12:205
Young Women's Christian Association
  (YWCA), 3:501
Your Second Childhood (Feeney), 5:663
Youssif, P., 5:5
Youth, patron of, 5:919
Youth organizations, 3:500–501, 501,
  535–536
The Youth's Companion (Fitton), 5:751
Youville, Marie Marguerite d', St., 3:9,
  6:528, **14:896–897**
Ysambert, Nicolas, 4:121, **14:897**
Ysarnus, St., **14:897–898**
Ytha of Killeedy, St. See Ita of Killeedy,
  St.
Yugoslavia
  Bosnia-Herzegovina, 2:545–547
  Byzantine Basilians in, 2:144
  Carthusians, 3:194
  formation of, 4:371
  Macedonia, 9:14–15
  monasticism, 9:801
  religious freedom, 13:227
  Serb majority, 10:698
  See also Serbia and Montenegro;
    Slovenia
Yuḥanna (Bp. of Mosul), 2:678
Yung-cheng (Emperor of China). See
  Yongzheng (Emperor of China)
Yunqi Zhuhong, 3:511
Yup'ik people, 1:209
Yves Congar award, 4:75
Yves de Paris, **14:898–899**

Z

Zabarella, Francesco, 3:51, 636, 4:55,
  169, 170, **14:901**
Zabarella, Jacopo, 1:382, 676, 834,
  14:901–902
Zaccaria, Anthony Mary, St., 2:103, 104,
  3:610, 782, 5:692, **14:902**
Zaccaria, Francesco Antonio,
  14:902–903
Zachariae, Gotthilf Traugott, 2:383
Zachariae, Johann, **14:903**
Zacharias (Father) (Indian priest), 7:406
Zacharias (father of St. John the
  Baptist). See Zachary (father of St.
  John the Baptist)
Zacharias (Patriarch of Jerusalem),
  14:903

Zacharias (Pope), St. *See* Zachary (Pope), St.

Zachary (father of St. John the Baptist), 1:320, 5:61, 7:1012–1013

Zachary (Pope), St., **14:904**

 antipodes question, 1:529–530

 Canon Law, 3:41

 Carolingian Dynasty, 3:164

 Childeric III, 10:835

 chorbishops, 3:526

 Cologne (Germany), 3:842

 diaconia, 4:720

 Eoban, 5:269

 Fulda Abbey, 6:21

 Gallican rites, 6:70

 Monte Cassino monastery, 2:238

 Pepin III, 11:110

 prohibited books, 7:390

 supplies to Rome, 12:355

Zachary the Rhetor, 2:797, 13:43, **14:904–905**

Zaehner, Robert, 10:116

Zafra, John de, Bl., 1:952

Zago, Marcello, **14:905**

Zagorsk Monastery (Russia). *See* Troitskaya Laura (Russia)

Zagreb (Croatia), bishopric of, 8:275

Zahalka, Magdalene (Mother Hyacinth), 5:886

Zahan, D., 1:740

Zahara, Antoninus, 3:367

Zahm, John Augustine, **14:905–906**

Zahn, Theodor von, 3:21–22, 5:323

Zahorowski, Jerome, 9:812

Zainer, Gunther, 2:355

Zairean Episcopa Confernece, 4:106, 107

Zakkai, David ben, 12:449

Zambia, **14:906–909**, *908*

Zamometič, Andrea (Abp.), **14:909**

Zamora, Alfonso de, **14:909**

Zamoyski, John, 2:605

Zander, L., 12:436

Zanella, Giacomo, 7:673

Zanin, Mario (Abp.), 3:516

Zapata de Cárdenas, Luis (Abp. of Bogotá), 3:246, 848–850, **14:909–910**

Zapata y Sandoval, Juan (Bp. of Guatemala), **14:910**

Zarathustra. *See* Zoroaster (Persian religious leader)

Zarathustra (Persian reformer), 11:144

Zarb, S., 3:21

Zardetti, Otto (Bp.), 12:542

Zarlino, Gioseffo, 1:766, **14:910–911**

Zatvornik, Theophan (Bp.), **14:911**

Zautzes, Stylianus, 5:460

Zaya, Nicholas (Chaldean Patriarch), 3:368–369

Zazen (Zen technique), 14:915

Zdík, Henry (Bp. of Olomouc), 4:479

Zdislava of Lemberk, St., **14:911–912**

Zeal, 2:266–267, **14:912**

The Zeal of Thy House (Sayers), 12:717

Zealots, 8:6, 13:126, **14:912**

Zechariah (Hebrew prophet), 14:912–913

Zechariah, Book of, **14:912–914**

 apocalyptic style, 1:546

 cross, 4:384

 Day of the Lord, 4:548

 eschatology, 5:336

 God's spirit, 13:426

 hope of salvation, 7:106

 kingship, 8:179

 liturgy, 9:63

 Logos image, 8:759

 magic, 9:39

 Malachi, Book of, split from, 9:62–63

 peace, 11:49

 rebuilding of Temple, 4:529

 ritual bathing and purification, as symbol of baptism, 2:57–58

 Son of David, 13:310

 spirit, 13:424

 Sukkot, 2:532

Zechariah, Canticle of. *See* Benedictus

Zedekiah (King of Judah), 7:642–643

Zedekunst dat is Wellevenskunste (Coornhert), 4:248

Zedillo, Ernesto, 9:585–586

Zegada, Escolástico, **14:914–915**

Zeitschrift für Missionswissenshaft, 12:743

Zeitschrift für Psychologie und Physiologie der Sinnesorgane (Leipzig), 5:27

Zeitschrift für Theologie und Kirche, 14:234

Zeitschrift für wissenschaftliche Theologie, 14:234

Zelada, Francesco Saverio, 3:795

Zeller, Eduard, 1:678, 2:385, 570, 14:234

Zen, **14:915–916**

 China, 2:663–664

 Japan, 2:665

 Korea, 2:668

 moral guidance, 4:760

 study of mysticism, 10:115, 116

See also Buddhism

Zengi (*atabeg* of Aleppo and Mosul), 4:404

Zenkovsky, V. V., 12:436

Zeno (Byzantine Emperor), **14:916–917**

 Acacian Schism, 1:49, 50

 anarchism, 1:384

 Armenia, 1:700, 704

 Basiliscus, 2:149

 Chalcedonian orthodoxy, 13:140

 Church-State relations, 2:851, 3:634

 condemnation of, 7:111

 Coptic divisions, 4:253

 creedal statements, 4:354

 Cyprus, 1:502, 523

 Gelasius I (Pope), St., 6:121

 Iberian Church, 6:152

 Monophysitism, 2:748, 3:595, 6:734–735

 Ostrogoth invasion, 12:321

 suicide of, 5:458

 See also Henoticon (Zeno)

Zeno of Citium (Greek philosopher), 5:197, 393, 554, 638, 10:180, 13:*534*

 See also Stoicism

Zeno of Elea (Greek philosopher), 1:393, 2:577, 4:217, 6:441, 10:16–17, **14:917**

Zeno of Verona, St., 11:610, **14:917–918**, *918*

Zenzelinus de Cassanis, 3:48

Zephaniah, Book of, 1:546, 2:5, 178, 4:547, 5:334, **14:918–919**

Zephyrinus (Pope), St., 3:222, **14:919–920**

Zerbolt, Gerard, 2:607

Zerr, Clementine (Mother), 11:644

Zervanism, 1:191–192, **14:920**

Zeus (Greek deity), 6:451, 10:87, 88, 91, 94, 618

Zeus temple ruins (Dodona, Greece), 10:*754*

Zevi, Bruno, 3:672, 679, 680

Zevi, Shabbetai, 5:913

Zhang Banniu, Peter, St., **14:920**

Zhang He, Thérèse, St., **14:921**

Zhang Huailu, St., **14:921**

Zhang Huan, John, St., **14:921**

Zhang Jingguang, St., **14:921–922**

Zhang Rong, Francis, St., **14:922**

Zhang Zai (Chang Tsai), 3:511

Zhang Zhihe, Philip, St., **14:922**

Zhao, John Baptist and Peter, SS., **14:922–923**

Zhao, Mary, Mary, and Rosa, SS., **14:923**

Zhao Quanxin, James, St., **14:923**

Zhenrong, Paul Li (Bp. of Cangzhou, China), 7:793

Zhiyi (Buddhist philsopher), 3:510

Zhou Dunyi (Chou Tun-i), 3:511

Zhou Enlai, 3:501

Zhu Rixin, Peter, St., **14:923**

Zhu Wu, Mary, St., **14:923–924**

Zhu Wurui, John Baptist, St., **14:924**

Zhu Xi (Chu-Hsi), 3:511–512, 4:98

Zhuangzi (Chinese philosopher), 3:510, 4:523, 524, **14:924**

Zia-ul-Haq, General, 10:762

Ziegenbalg, Bartholomew, 7:402–403

Zigabenus, Euthymius, 2:794, 824–825, **14:925**

Ziggiotti, Renato, 12:614

Ziggurats, 9:536, 14:*129*

Zigliara, Tommaso, 12:773, **14:925**

Ziller, T., 10:61

Zimara, Marco Antonio, 1:676, **14:925–926**

Zimbabwe, **14:926–928**, *927*

Zimmer, Patrick, 12:770, **14:928**

Zingarelli, Niccolò Antonio, 2:841

Zinzendorf, Nikolaus Ludwig von, 2:606, 8:87, 9:885, 12:795, 13:406, **14:928**

Zion, **14:929–930**

Zipfel, Paul A. (Bp. of Bismarck, ND), 2:423

Zipporah (wife of Moses), 10:6

Zirc Abbey (Hungary), **14:930**

Zita, St., **14:930–931**

Žižka, John, 7:231, *231*, 11:320, **14:931**

Znamenie, 9:272, 274

Zoa, Jean Baptiste (Abp. of Yaoundé), 2:913

Zoanettus, Franciscus, 3:52

Zobah (Aramaean state), 1:624

Zobor Abbey (Nitra, Slovakia), **14:931**

Zobrest v. Catalina Hills School District (1993), 3:668

Zodiac, christianization of, 13:668

Zoe Karbonopsina, 4:174

Zoe Movement, 6:460

Zoërardus and Benedict, SS., **14:931–932**

Zohar (Cabalistic work), 1:938, 2:832–834, 8:870, **14:932–933**
See also Cabala

Zoïlus of Alexandria, **14:933**

Zola, Giovanni Battista, Bl., 7:734

Zola, Guiseppe, **14:933–934**

Zolli, Eugenio, **14:934**

Zonaras, John, 2:795, 3:46, **14:934**

Zoology, Aristotle on, 12:806

Zorach v. Clauson (1952), 3:666

Zoroaster (Persian religious leader), 9:*34*, 11:144, **14:935**

Zoroastrianism, **11:142–145**
Ahura Mazda and Ahriman, 1:191–192
Amesha Spenta, 1:357
astral religion, 1:810
Avesta, 1:937–938
Church-State relations, 3:631
Fravashi, 5:922
Magi, 9:34
Manichaeism, 9:114–115
optimism of, 10:612–613
prayer, 11:591
See also Persian religions, ancient

Zosimos the Panopolitan, 1:237

Zosimus (Byzantine historian), 2:798, 12:319

Zosimus (Pope), St., **14:935–936**
Arles, 1:694
Boniface I (Pope), St., 2:497, 498
decretals, 4:600
Julian of Eclanum, 8:48
jurisdictional conflicts, Gaul, 6:112
North African Church, 10:431
Pelagianism, 1:860, 3:188, 11:62, 12:621, 14:936

Zoticus (Bp. of Comana), 3:525

Zouaves, Papal, **14:936–937**

Zoungrana, Paul (Abp. of Ouagadougou), 2:704

Zubiria, Jose Antonio Laureano de, 10:286

Zudaire Galdeano, Maria Ines (1900-1936), 14:564, 566

Zugibe, F., 13:97

Zumárraga, Juan de (Abp. of Mexico), 3:246, 247, 415, 9:207–208, **14:937–938**

Zumarraga, Thomas del Espiritu Santo, Bl., 7:733

Zumel, Francisco, 4:111

Zumkeller, A., 1:329

Zuñi people, 1:687

Zuniga, Pedro de, Bl., 7:733

Zuntz, G., 2:366

Zunz, Leopold, 7:873

Zur Johanneischen Tradition (Noack), 5:522

Zuraire, Stephen, Bl., 1:951

Zurbarán, Francisco de, 2:114

Zurlauben, Placidus, 10:65

Zutphen, Geert Zerbolt von, 4:707

Zwart Front (Netherlands), 10:262

Zwettl Abbey (Austria), **14:938–939**

Zwiefalten Abbey (Germany), 5:325, **14:939**

Zwingli, Huldrych, 14:159, **939–941**, *940*
Anabaptists, 1:368
Apostles' Creed, 1:577
Church-State relations, 3:638
confessions of faith, 4:79
Constance jurisdiction, 4:168
Eck, Johann, 5:43
Einsiedeln Abbey, 5:139
Emser, Hieronymus, 5:200
Faber, Johannes, 5:583
Grebel, Conrad, 6:426
heresy, 6:776
Oecolampadius, Johannes, 10:558
predestination, 11:655
Protestant Reformation, 3:608, 12:15, 16, 612
Reformation exegesis, 5:518
sacramentals, 12:481

Zwinglianism, 1:848, 2:689, 12:19–20, **14:941–942**

Zwoty Swietych (Lives of the Saints) (Skarga), 13:200

ISBN 0-7876-4019-0

90000

9 780787 640194